Alameda County
street guide

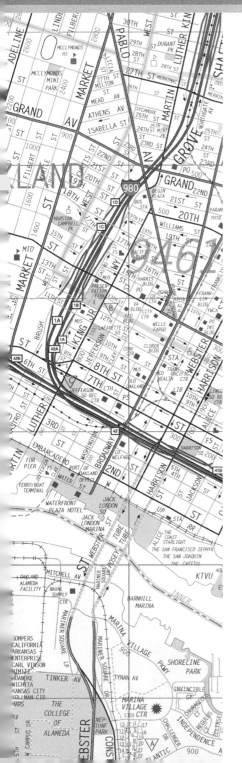

TELL US WHAT YOU THINK
comment card on last page

Contents

Introduction

Using Your Street Guide	A
PageFinder™ Map	B
Legend	D

Maps

Airport Map	E
Downtown Map	F
Freeway Access Map	G
Street Guide Detail Maps	609-794
Vicinity Map	Inside back cover

Lists and Indexes

Cities & Communities Index	795
List of Abbreviations	796
Street Index	797
Points of Interest Index	835
Cross Street Index	843
Comment Card	Last page

Rand McNally Consumer Affairs
P.O. Box 7600
Chicago, IL 60680-9915
randmcnally.com

For comments or suggestions, please call
(800) 777-MAPS (-6277)
or email us at:
consumeraffairs@randmcnally.com

Legend

Freeway	
Interchange/ramp	
Highway	
Primary road	
Secondary road	
Minor road	
Restricted road	
Alley	
Unpaved road	
Tunnel	
Toll road	
High occupancy vehicle lane	
Stacked multiple roadways	
Proposed road	
Proposed freeway	
Freeway under construction	
One-way road	
Two-way road	
Trail, walkway	
Stairs	
Railroad	
Rapid transit	
Rapid transit, underground	

Ferry	
City boundary	
County boundary	
State boundary	
International boundary	
Military base, Indian reservation	
Township, range, rancho	
River, creek, shoreline	
ZIP code boundary, ZIP code	98607
Interstate	5
Interstate (Business)	5
U.S. highway	3
State highways	1 4 8 9
Carpool lane	
Street list marker	A
Street name continuation	
Street name change	
Station (train, bus)	
Building (see List of Abbreviations page)	
Building footprint	
Public elementary school	
Public high school	

Private elementary school	
Private high school	
Fire station	
Library	
Mission	
Winery	
Campground	
Hospital	H
Mountain	
Section corner	
Boat launch	
Gate, locks, barricades	
Lighthouse	
Major shopping center	
Dry lake, beach	
Dam	
Intermittent lake, marsh	
Exit number	29
Golden Gate Transit	
Caltrain Station	
San Mateo Transit	samTrans
Santa Clara Transit	
ACE	

Oakland International Airport (OAK)

Oakland International Airport is located approximately seven miles from Downtown Oakland and 15 miles from Downtown San Francisco, with easy freeway access to parking, flights and baggage. Southwest Airlines' flights depart from Terminal 2. All other airlines, including international flights, depart from Terminal 1. Parking rates in the lots located across from the terminals are $2.00 per 30 minutes, with a maximum of $32 per day in the Hourly Lot; $22 per day in the Daily A & B Lots; and $19 per day in the Economy lot (subject to change). Parking shuttles run every 10–15 minutes. For more information, visit oaklandairport.com.

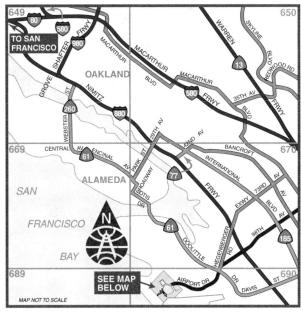

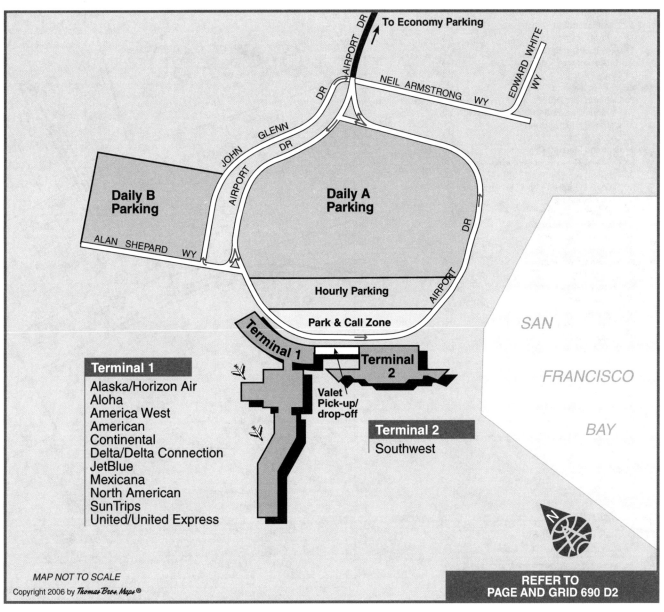

Terminal 1
Alaska/Horizon Air
Aloha
America West
American
Continental
Delta/Delta Connection
JetBlue
Mexicana
North American
SunTrips
United/United Express

Terminal 2
Southwest

Valet Pick-up/drop-off

Daily B Parking

Daily A Parking

Hourly Parking

Park & Call Zone

To Economy Parking

SAN FRANCISCO BAY

REFER TO
PAGE AND GRID 690 D2

Downtown Oakland

Points of Interest

1	Alameda County Health Department	C6
2	Alameda County Welfare Building	C6
3	Alice Arts Center	D5
4	Asian Branch Library	C6
5	Bank of America Building	D4
6	BART Headquarters	D6
7	Broadway Building	C5
8	California Building	D5
9	Chinatown	C6
10	City Center	C5
11	Clorox Building	C5
12	County Administration Building	D6
13	Courthouse	E6
14	Dellums Train Station (Amtrak)	C7
15	Edoff Memorial Bandstand	E4
16	Financial Center Building	D5
17	Franklin Building	D5
18	H J Kaiser Convention Center	E6
19	Jack London Square	C7
20	Kaiser Center	D4
21	Laney College	E7
22	Morgan Building	C5
23	Oakland City Hall	C5
24	Oakland Convention Ctr & Vis Auth	C5
25	Oakland Federal Building	C5
26	Oakland Main Library	D6
27	Oakland Marriott City Center	C5
28	Oakland Museum of California	D6
29	Oakland State Building	C5
30	Oakland Unified School Dist Admin	E6
31	Pacific Building	C4
32	Paramount Theatre	D4
33	Pardee Home Museum	C5
34	Port of Oakland Office	C7
35	Samuel Merritt College	E2
36	Storefront Museum	C5
37	The Ordway	D4
38	Trans Pacific Center	C5
39	Tribune Tower	C5
40	Veterans Building	C5
41	Victorian Row Old Oakland	C6
42	Waterfront Plaza Hotel	B7
43	Wells Fargo Building	C5
44	YMCA	D4
45	YWCA	D5

Map Scale

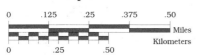

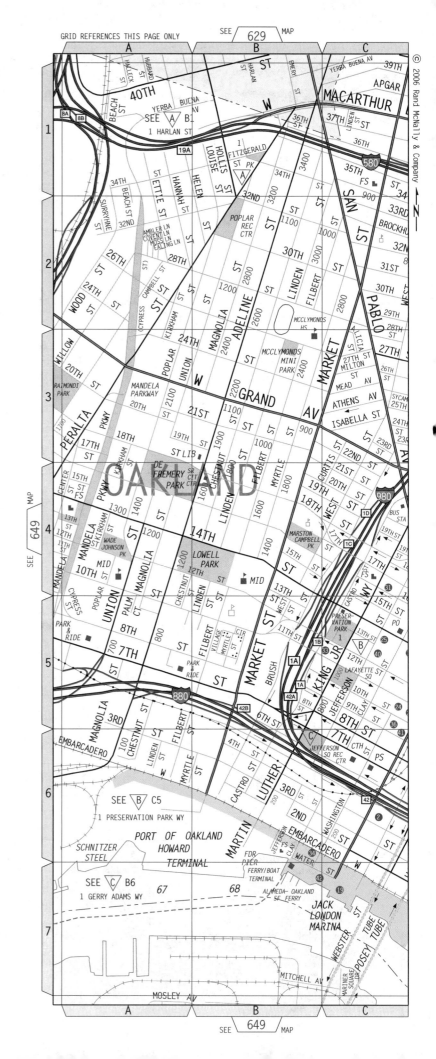

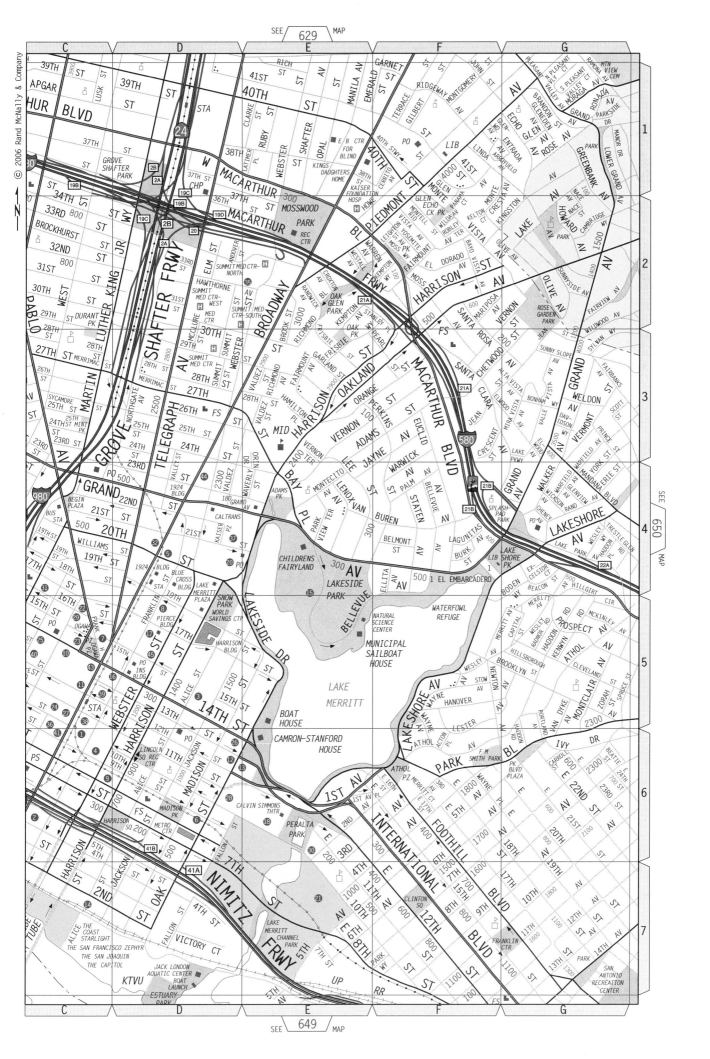

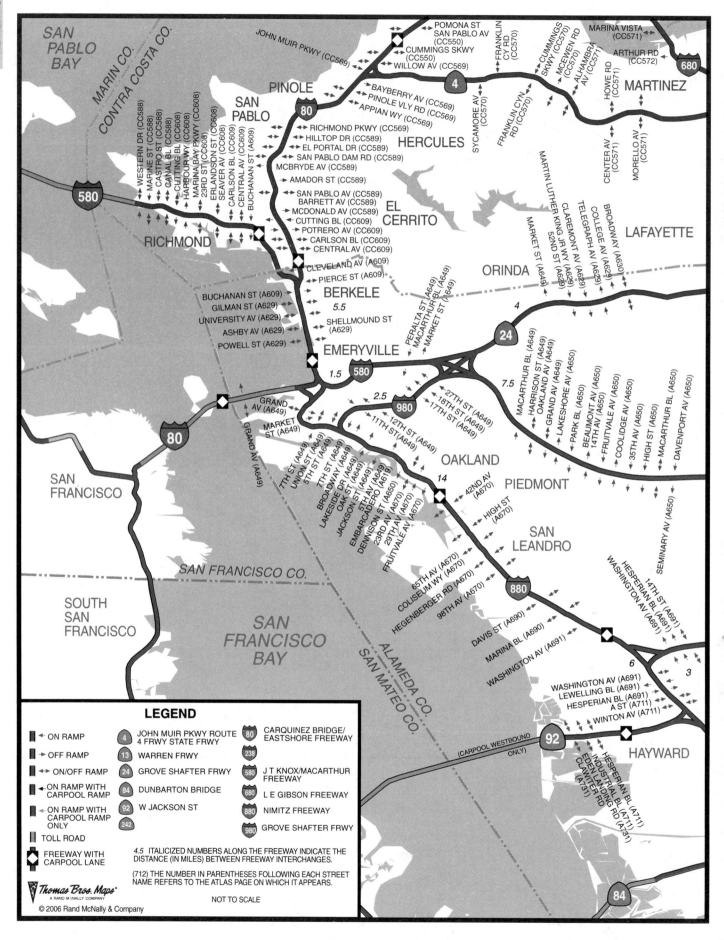

SAN PABLO BAY

MARIN CO.
CONTRA COSTA CO.

JOHN MUIR PKWY (CC569)

POMONA ST
SAN PABLO AV (CC550)
CUMMINGS SKWY (CC550)
WILLOW AV (CC569)

FRANKLIN CY RD (CC570)

CUMMINGS SKWY (CC570)
MCEWEN RD (CC570)
ALHAMBRA AV (CC571)

MARINA VISTA (CC571)
ARTHUR RD (CC572)

680

PINOLE

SAN PABLO

80

4

BAYBERRY AV (CC569)
PINOLE VLY RD (CC569)
APPIAN WY (CC569)

SYCAMORE AV (CC570)
FRANKLIN CYN RD (CC570)

CENTER AV (CC571)
MORELLO AV (CC571)

MARTINEZ

HERCULES

RICHMOND PKWY (CC569)
HILLTOP DR (CC589)
EL PORTAL DR (CC589)
SAN PABLO DAM RD (CC589)
MCBRYDE AV (CC589)
AMADOR ST (CC589)
SAN PABLO AV (CC589)
BARRETT AV (CC589)
MCDONALD AV (CC589)
CUTTING BL (CC609)
POTRERO AV (CC609)
CARLSON BL (CC609)
CENTRAL AV (CC609)

EL CERRITO

MARTIN LUTHER KING JR WY (CC649)

CLAREMONT AV (CC629)
COLLEGE AV (CC629)
52ND ST (CC629)
TELEGRAPH AV (CC629)
BROADWAY (CC630)

LAFAYETTE

580

WESTERN DR (CC588)
MARINE ST (CC588)
CASTRO ST (CC588)
CANAL BL (CC588)
CUTTING BL (CC608)
HARBOUR WY (CC608)
MARINA BAY PKWY (CC608)
23RD ST (CC608)
ERLANDSON ST (CC608)
SEAVER AV (CC608)
CARLSON BL (CC609)
CENTRAL AV (CC609)
BUCHANAN ST (A609)

RICHMOND

CLEVELAND AV (A609)
PIERCE ST (A609)

ORINDA

PERALTA ST (A649)
MACARTHUR BL (A649)
MARKET ST (A649)

BUCHANAN ST (A609)
GILMAN ST (A629)
UNIVERSITY AV (A629)
ASHBY AV (A629)
POWELL ST (A629)

BERKELE

5.5

SHELLMOUND ST (A629)

4

24

7.5

MACARTHUR BL (A649)
HARRISON ST (A649)
OAKLAND AV (A649)
GRAND AV (A649)
LAKESHORE AV (A650)
PARK AV (A650)
BEAUMONT AV (A650)
14TH AV (A650)
FRUITVALE AV (A650)
COOLIDGE AV (A650)
35TH AV (A650)
HIGH ST (A650)
MACARTHUR BL (A650)
DAVENPORT AV (A650)

EMERYVILLE

1.5

580

GRAND AV (A649)

2.5

980

27TH ST (A649)
18TH ST (A649)
17TH ST (A649)
12TH ST (A649)
11TH ST (A649)

80

SAN FRANCISCO

MARKET ST (A649)

GRAND AV (A649)

7TH ST (A649)
UNION ST (A649)
5TH ST (A649)
7TH ST (A649)
BROADWAY (A649)
LAKESIDE DR (A649)
OAK ST (A649)
JACKSON ST (A649)
5TH AV (A650)
EMBARCADERO (A619)
DENNISON ST (A670)
23RD AV (A670)
29TH AV (A670)
FRUITVALE AV (A670)

OAKLAND

14

42ND AV (A670)

HIGH ST (A670)

PIEDMONT

SAN LEANDRO

SEMINARY AV (A650)

147TH ST (A691)

HESPERIAN BL (A691)
WASHINGTON AV (A691)

SAN FRANCISCO CO.

SOUTH SAN FRANCISCO

SAN FRANCISCO BAY

65TH AV (A670)
COLISEUM WY (A670)
HEGENBERGER RD (A670)
98TH AV (A670)

DAVIS ST (A690)
MARINA BL (A690)

WASHINGTON AV (A691)

880

6

3

WASHINGTON AV (A691)
LEWELLING BL (A691)
HESPERIAN BL (A691)
A ST (A711)
WINTON AV (A711)

ALAMEDA CO.
SAN MATEO CO.

(CARPOOL WESTBOUND ONLY)

92

HESPERIAN BL (A711)
INDUSTRIAL BL (A711)
EDEN LANDING RD (A711)
CLAWITER RD (A731)

HAYWARD

84

LEGEND

◄■ ON RAMP
■► OFF RAMP
◄■► ON/OFF RAMP
◄■ ON RAMP WITH CARPOOL RAMP
◄■ ON RAMP WITH CARPOOL RAMP ONLY
▌▌ TOLL ROAD
◆ FREEWAY WITH CARPOOL LANE

4 JOHN MUIR PKWY ROUTE 4 FRWY STATE FRWY
13 WARREN FRWY
24 GROVE SHAFTER FRWY
84 DUNBARTON BRIDGE
92 W JACKSON ST
242

80 CARQUINEZ BRIDGE/ EASTSHORE FREEWAY
238
580 J T KNOX/MACARTHUR FREEWAY
680 L E GIBSON FREEWAY
880 NIMITZ FREEWAY
980 GROVE SHAFTER FRWY

4.5 ITALICIZED NUMBERS ALONG THE FREEWAY INDICATE THE DISTANCE (IN MILES) BETWEEN FREEWAY INTERCHANGES.

(712) THE NUMBER IN PARENTHESES FOLLOWING EACH STREET NAME REFERS TO THE ATLAS PAGE ON WHICH IT APPEARS.

NOT TO SCALE

ALAMEDA/CONTRA COSTA COUNTIES FREEWAY ACCESS MAP

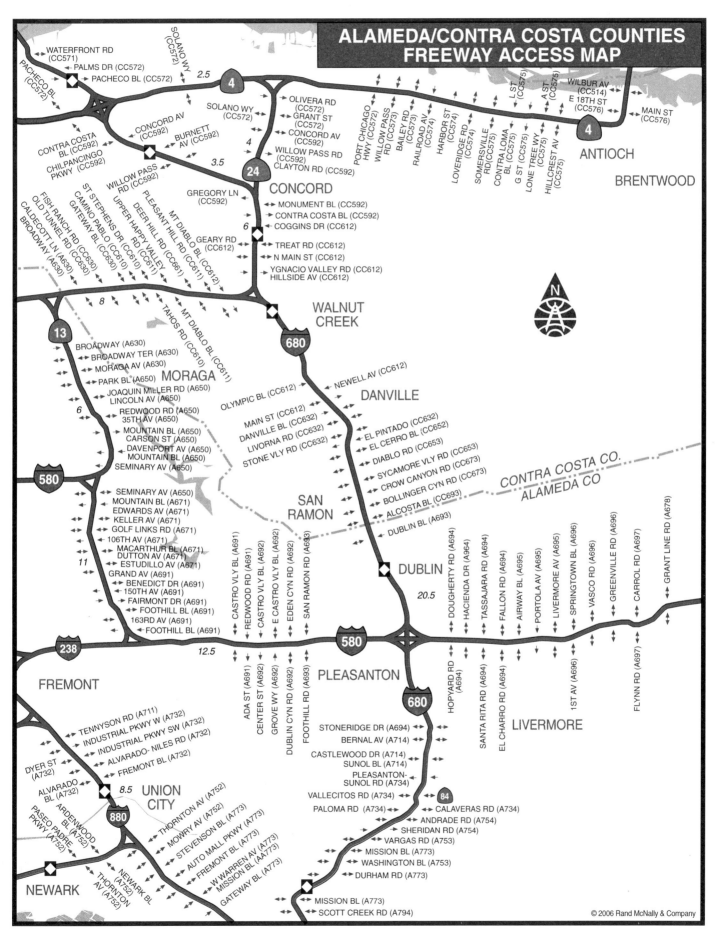

WATERFRONT RD (CC571)
SOLANO WY (CC572)
PALMS DR (CC572)
PACHECO BL (CC572)
PACHECO BL (CC572)
2.5
4
WILBUR AV (CC514)
L ST (CC575)
A ST (CC575)
E 18TH ST (CC576)
MAIN ST (CC576)
OLIVERA RD (CC572)
SOLANO WY (CC572)
GRANT ST (CC572)
CONCORD AV (CC592)
CONCORD AV (CC592)
PORT CHICAGO HWY (CC572)
WILLOW PASS RD (CC573)
BAILEY RD (CC573)
RAILROAD AV (CC574)
HARBOR ST (CC574)
LOVERIDGE RD (CC574)
SOMERSVILLE RD(CC575)
CONTRA LOMA BL (CC575)
G ST (CC575)
LONE TREE WY (CC575)
HILLCREST AV (CC575)
4
ANTIOCH
BRENTWOOD
CONTRA COSTA BL (CC592)
CHILPANCINGO PKWY (CC592)
BURNETT AV (CC592)
CONCORD AV (CC592)
4
3.5
24
WILLOW PASS RD (CC592)
CLAYTON RD (CC592)
GREGORY LN (CC592)
CONCORD
MONUMENT BL (CC592)
CONTRA COSTA BL (CC592)
COGGINS DR (CC612)
6
TREAT RD (CC612)
N MAIN ST (CC612)
YGNACIO VALLEY RD (CC612)
HILLSIDE AV (CC612)
WILLOW PASS RD (CC592)
ST STEPHENS DR (CC630)
CAMINO PABLO (CC630)
GATEWAY BL (CC630)
UPPER HAPPY VALLEY RD (CC610)
DEER HILL RD (CC611)
PLEASANT HILL RD (CC661)
MT DIABLO BL (CC612)
GEARY RD (CC612)
FISH RANCH RD (CC630)
OLD TUNNEL RD (CC630)
CALDECOTT LN (A630)
BROADWAY (A630)
8
TAHOS RD (CC610)
MT DIABLO BL (CC611)
WALNUT CREEK
680
13
BROADWAY (A630)
BROADWAY TER (A630)
MORAGA AV (A630)
PARK BL (A650)
MORAGA
JOAQUIN MILLER RD (A650)
LINCOLN AV (A650)
REDWOOD RD (A650)
35TH AV (A650)
MOUNTAIN BL (A650)
CARSON ST (A650)
DAVENPORT AV (A650)
MOUNTAIN BL (A650)
SEMINARY AV (A650)
6
NEWELL AV (CC612)
OLYMPIC BL (CC612)
MAIN ST (CC612)
DANVILLE BL (CC632)
LIVORNA RD (CC632)
STONE VLY RD (CC632)
DANVILLE
EL PINTADO (CC632)
EL CERRO BL (CC652)
DIABLO RD (CC653)
SYCAMORE VLY RD (CC653)
CROW CANYON RD (CC673)
BOLLINGER CYN RD (CC673)
ALCOSTA BL (CC693)
CONTRA COSTA CO.
ALAMEDA CO
580
SEMINARY AV (A650)
MOUNTAIN BL (A671)
EDWARDS AV (A671)
KELLER AV (A671)
GOLF LINKS RD (A671)
106TH AV (A671)
MACARTHUR BL (A671)
DUTTON AV (A671)
ESTUDILLO AV (A671)
GRAND AV (A691)
BENEDICT DR (A691)
150TH AV (A691)
FAIRMONT DR (A691)
FOOTHILL BL (A691)
163RD AV (A691)
FOOTHILL BL (A691)
11
SAN RAMON
DUBLIN BL (A693)
DOUGHERTY RD (A694)
HACIENDA DR (A964)
TASSAJARA RD (A694)
FALLON RD (A694)
AIRWAY BL (A695)
PORTOLA AV (A695)
LIVERMORE AV (A695)
SPRINGTOWN BL (A696)
VASCO RD (A696)
GREENVILLE RD (A696)
CARROL RD (A697)
GRANT LINE RD (A678)
DUBLIN
20.5
CASTRO VLY BL (A691)
REDWOOD RD (A691)
CASTRO VLY BL (A692)
E CASTRO VLY BL (A692)
EDEN CYN RD (A692)
SAN RAMON RD (A693)
580
238
12.5
FREMONT
ADA ST (A691)
CENTER ST (A692)
GROVE WY (A692)
DUBLIN CYN RD (A692)
FOOTHILL RD (A693)
PLEASANTON
1ST AV (A696)
FLYNN RD (A697)
LIVERMORE
680
SANTA RITA RD (A694)
EL CHARRO RD (A694)
HOPYARD RD (A694)
STONERIDGE DR (A694)
BERNAL AV (A714)
CASTLEWOOD DR (A714)
SUNOL BL (A714)
PLEASANTON-SUNOL RD (A734)
VALLECITOS RD (A734)
PALOMA RD (A734)
84
CALAVERAS RD (A734)
ANDRADE RD (A754)
SHERIDAN RD (A754)
VARGAS RD (A753)
MISSION BL (A773)
WASHINGTON BL (A753)
DURHAM RD (A773)
TENNYSON RD (A711)
INDUSTRIAL PKWY W (A732)
INDUSTRIAL PKWY SW (A732)
INDUSTRIAL PKWY RD (A732)
ALVARADO- NILES RD (A732)
FREMONT BL (A732)
DYER ST (A732)
ALVARADO BL (A732)
ARDENWOOD BL (A752)
PASEO PADRE PKWY (A752)
8.5
UNION CITY
880
THORNTON AV (A752)
MOWRY AV (A752)
STEVENSON BL (A773)
AUTO MALL PKWY (A773)
FREMONT BL (A773)
W WARREN AV (A773)
MISSION BL (AA773)
GATEWAY BL (A773)
NEWARK BL (A752)
THORNTON AV (A752)
NEWARK
MISSION BL (A773)
SCOTT CREEK RD (A794)

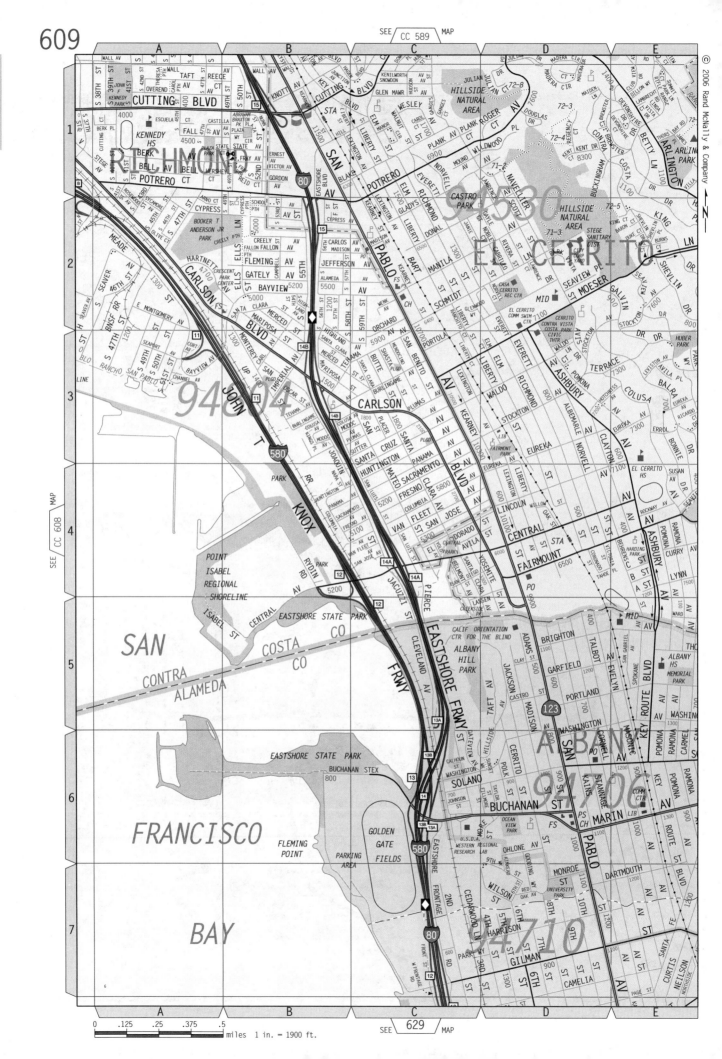

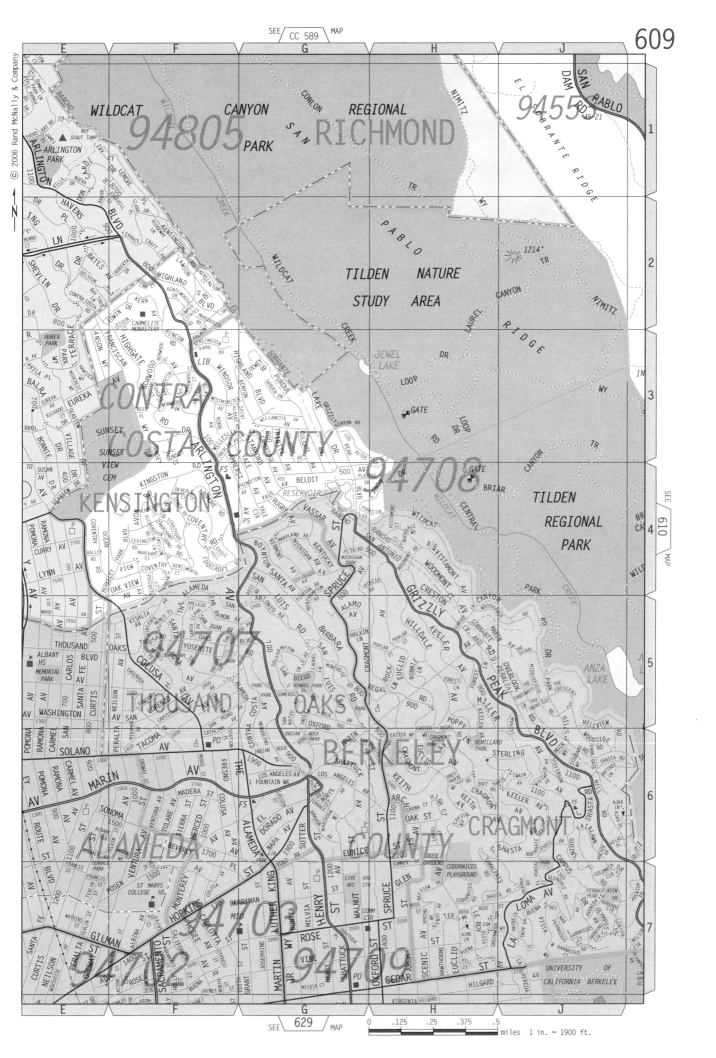

SEE CC 589 MAP

SEE 610 MAP

SEE 629 MAP

0 .125 .25 .375 .5 miles 1 in. = 1900 ft.

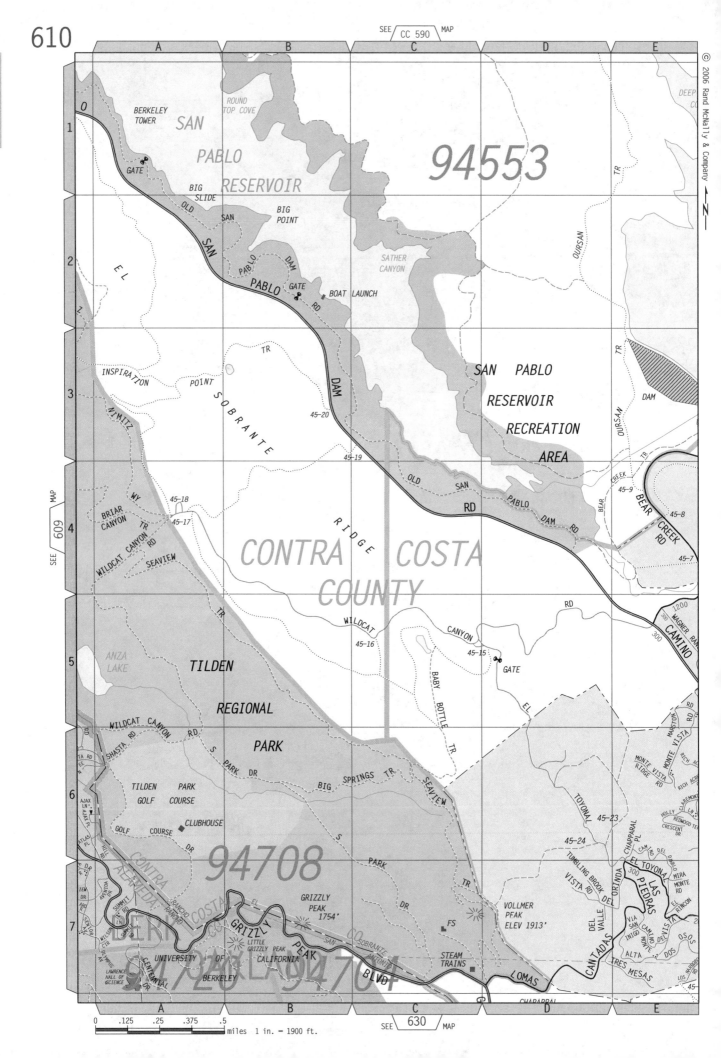

ALAMEDA CO.

© 2006 Rand McNally & Company

SEE CC 590 MAP

A   B   C   D   E

94553

BERKELEY
TOWER
SAN
PABLO
RESERVOIR

ROUND
TOP COVE

GATE

BIG
SLIDE

OLD

SAN

BIG
POINT

SAN

PABLO

PABLO

DAM

GATE

BOAT LAUNCH

SATHER
CANYON

EL

RD

SAN   PABLO

RESERVOIR

RECREATION

AREA

NIMITZ

INSPIRATION

POINT

TR

SOBRANTE

DAM

45-20

45-19

OURSAN

TR

OURSAN

DAM

CREEK

BEAR

45-9

BEAR

SEE 609 MAP

WY

45-18

45-17

BRIAR
CANYON

TR

WILDCAT CANYON   RD

SEAVIEW

OLD   SAN   PABLO   DAM   RD

RIDGE

CONTRA   COSTA

COUNTY

WILDCAT

45-16

CANYON

45-15

GATE

45-8

CREEK
RD

45-7

1200

WAGNER RAN
CAMINO   300
300

TR

ANZA
LAKE

TILDEN

REGIONAL

PARK

WILDCAT   CANYON   RD

SHASTA   RD

TILDEN   PARK
GOLF   COURSE

GOLF   COURSE   DR

CLUBHOUSE

S   PARK   DR

BIG   SPRINGS   TR

S

SEAVIEW

PARK

BABY

BOTTLE

TR

EL

RD

RD

MARSTON

MONTE   VISTA

MONTE   VISTA
RIDGE   RD

RICH   AC

RICH   AC

CLAREMONT

HOLLY

REDWOOD   TER

CRESCENT
DR

94708

AJAX
LN

AJAX PL

ATLAS
PL

CONTRA

ALAMEDA

RANCHO

RANCHO

EL

GRIZZLY
PEAK
1754'

SAN

CO

SOBRANTE

FS

TOYONAL   45-23

45-24

TUMBLING   BROOK   RD

VISTA   RD

CHAPARRAL   PL

CAMINO   DEL   DIABLO

EL   TOYONAL

ORINDA

300

LAS
PIEDRAS

MIRA
MONTE
RD

EL

RINCON

ATLAS
PL

HILL

IEW
DR

SUMMIT
LN

WILSON
CTR   PL
OLYMPUS

CENTURY
DR

AVENIDA
DR

BERKELEY

UNIVERSITY
OF
CALIFORNIA
BERKELEY

LITTLE
GRIZZLY PEAK

GRIZZLY   PEAK

CENTENNIAL   DR

LAWRENCE
HALL OF
SCIENCE

94720   LA   94704

ANTONIO

BLVD

STEAM
TRAINS

VOLLMER
PEAK
ELEV 1913'

LOMAS

CANTADAS

DEL   VALLE

VIA   SAN
INIGO

CAMINO
DEL   DIABLO

VISTA

MONTE

ALTA

TRES   MESAS

DOS

OS OS

LOS   AC

45

CHAPARRAL

A   B   C   D   E

0   .125   .25   .375   .5

miles   1 in. = 1900 ft.

SEE 630 MAP

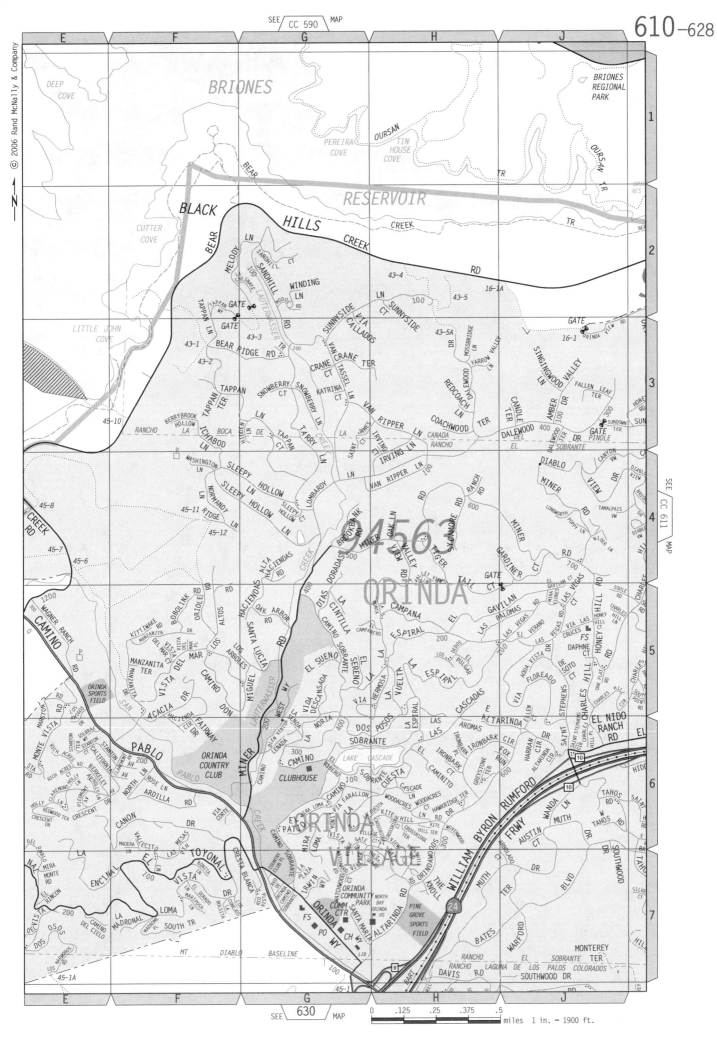

ALAMEDA CO.

© 2006 Rand McNally & Company

SEE CC 590 MAP

SEE CC 611 MAP

BRIONES

DEEP COVE

OURSAN TR

BRIONES REGIONAL PARK

PEREIRA COVE

OURSAN TIN HOUSE COVE

CUTTER COVE

BLACK HILLS

RESERVOIR

CREEK

CREEK

RD

TR

TR

LITTLE JOHN COVE

BEAR

94563

ORINDA

PABLO

ORINDA COUNTRY CLUB

ORINDA SPORTS FIELD

CLUBHOUSE

ORINDA VILLAGE

ORINDA COMMUNITY PARK

COMM CTR

North Bay Orinda HS

PINE GROVE SPORTS FIELD

MONTEREY TER

DAVIS

RANCHO LAGUNA DE LOS PALOS COLORADOS

SOUTHWOOD DR

WILLIAM BYRON RUMFORD FRWY

THE KNOLL

24

BART

SEE 630 MAP

0 .125 .25 .375 .5
miles 1 in. = 1900 ft.

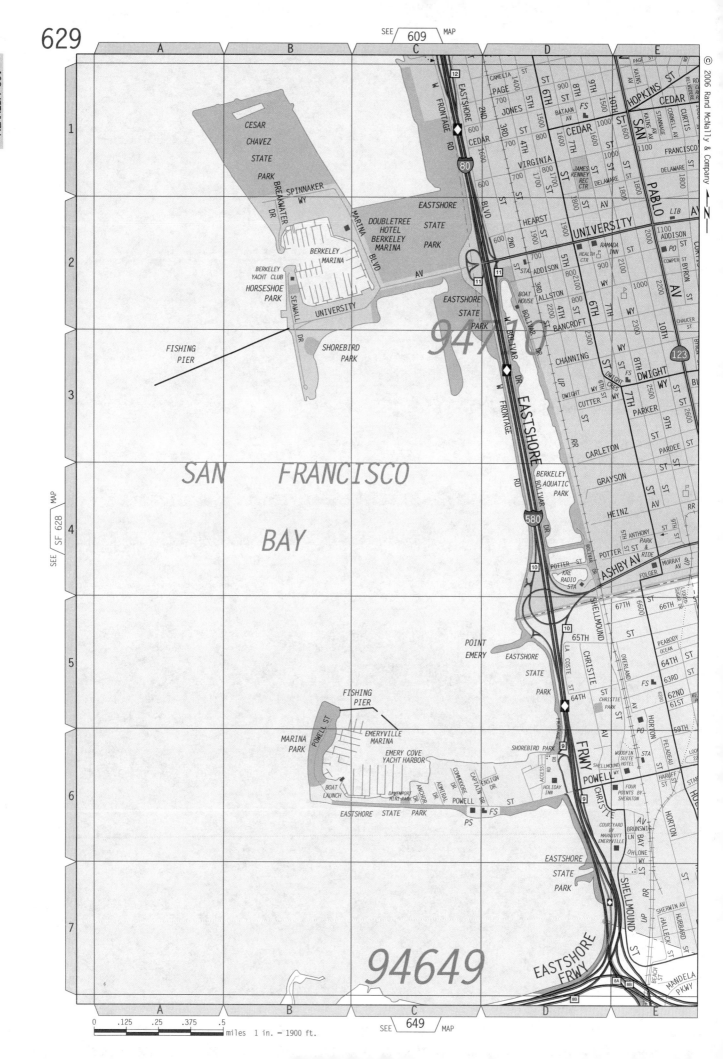

ALAMEDA CO.

SEE 609 MAP

SEE SF 628 MAP

SAN FRANCISCO

BAY

CESAR CHAVEZ STATE PARK

SPINNAKER WY

BREAKWATER DR

MARINA BLVD

DOUBLETREE HOTEL BERKELEY MARINA

EASTSHORE STATE PARK

BERKELEY MARINA

BERKELEY YACHT CLUB

HORSESHOE PARK

SEAWALL DR

UNIVERSITY AV

FISHING PIER

SHOREBIRD PARK

EASTSHORE STATE PARK

94710

EASTSHORE RD

W FRONTAGE RD

BERKELEY AQUATIC PARK

BERKELEY BOLIVAR DR

BOLIVAR DR

POINT EMERY

EASTSHORE STATE PARK

KRE RADIO STA

POTTER ST

ASHBY AV

SHELLMOUND ST

CHRISTIE AV

LA COSTE ST

OVERLAND AV

FISHING PIER

POWELL ST

EMERYVILLE MARINA

MARINA PARK

EMERY COVE YACHT HARBOR

BOAT LAUNCH

DAVENPORT MINI-PARK DR

ANCHOR DR

COMMODORE DR

CAPTAIN DR

ADMIRAL DR

ENSIGN ST

POWELL ST

EASTSHORE STATE PARK

PS

FS

FRWY

POWELL

CHRISTIE

HOLIDAY INN

SHELLMOUND HOTEL

WOODFIN SUITE HOTEL

FOUR POINTS BY SHERATON

SHOREBIRD PARK

COURTYARD BY MARRIOTT EMERYVILLE

EASTSHORE STATE PARK

SHELLMOUND

HORTON ST

BRUNSWICK LN

BAY

OHLONE WY

SHELLMOUND ST

EASTSHORE FRWY

MANDELA PKWY

94649

SEE 649 MAP

0 .125 .25 .375 .5
miles 1 in. = 1900 ft.

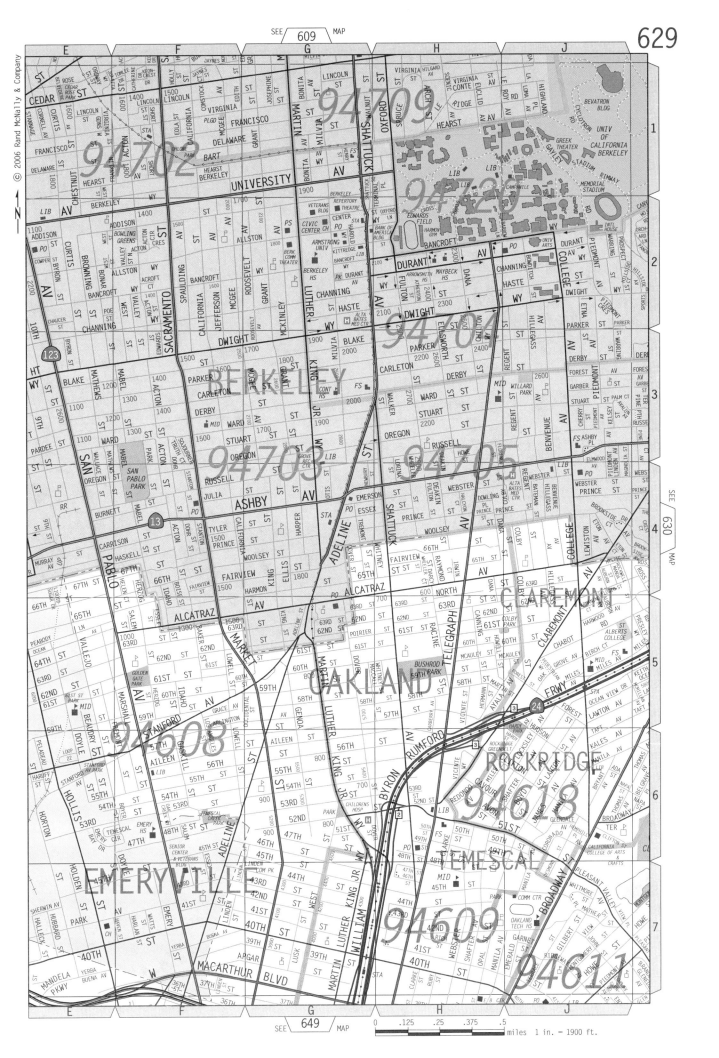

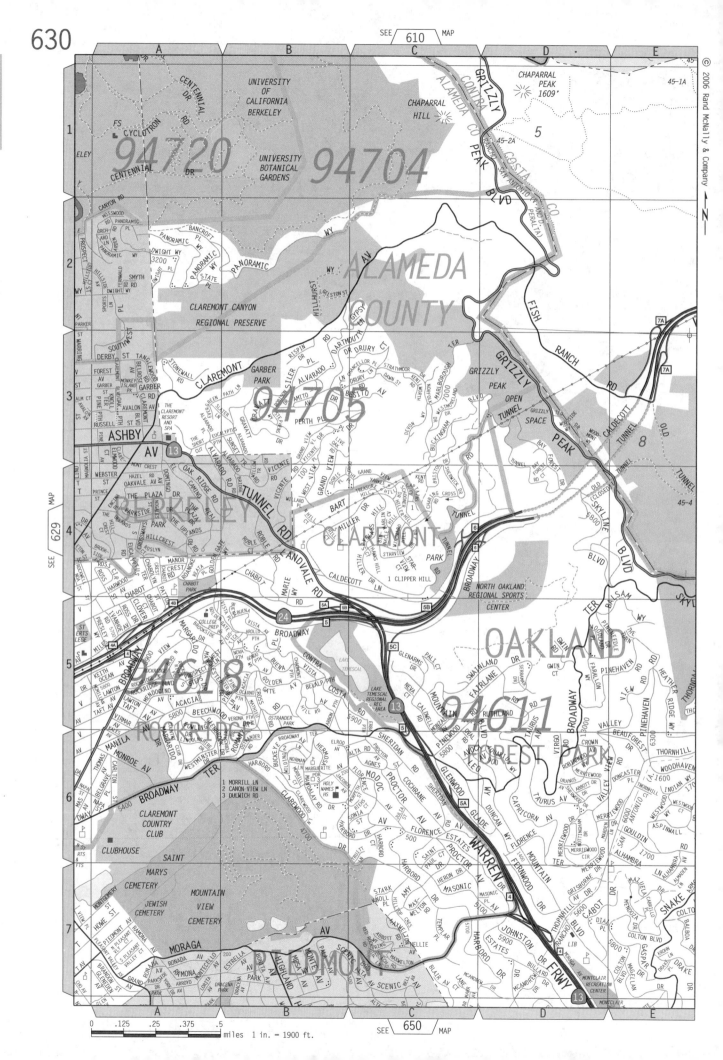

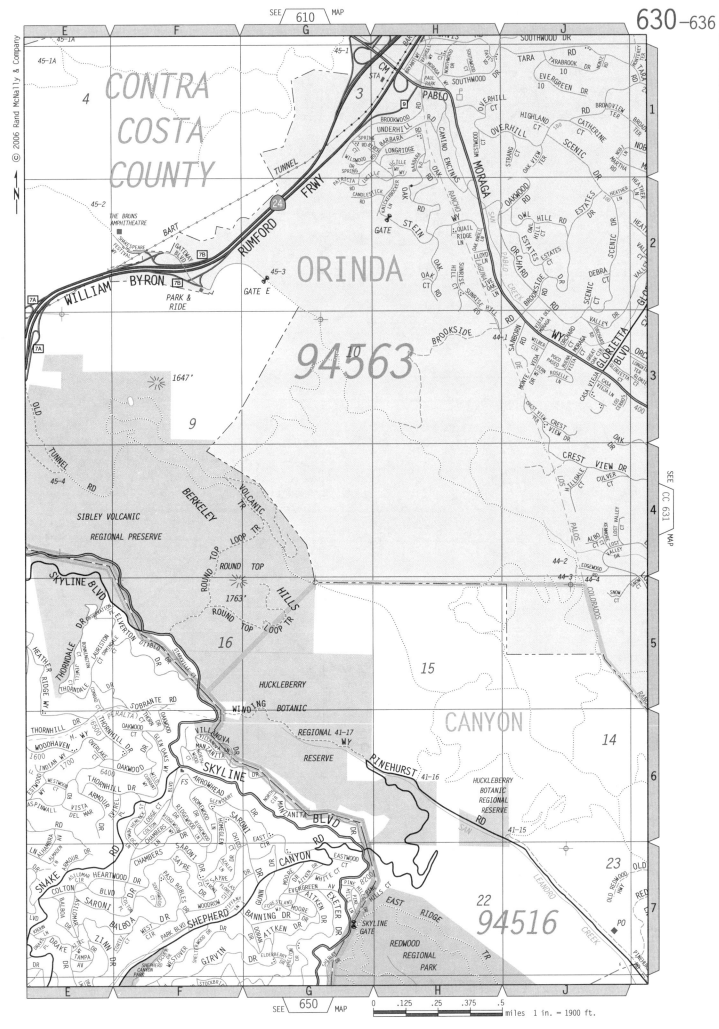

© 2006 Rand McNally & Company

CONTRA
COSTA
COUNTY

ORINDA

94563

SIBLEY VOLCANIC
REGIONAL PRESERVE

BERKELEY

ROUND TOP

1763'

HILLS

ROUND TOP LOOP TR

HUCKLEBERRY

WINDING   BOTANIC

CANYON

REGIONAL 41-17

RESERVE

SKYLINE BLVD

THORNHILL DR

WOODHAVEN

SKYLINE   DR

SKYLINE

CANYON   RD   BLVD

MANZANITA

REDWOOD
REGIONAL
PARK

94516

SNAKE

SHEPHERD

EAST   RIDGE

1647'

9

16

15

14

23

22

10

4

3

2

1

2

3

4

5

6

7

0 .125 .25 .375 .5
miles 1 in. = 1900 ft.

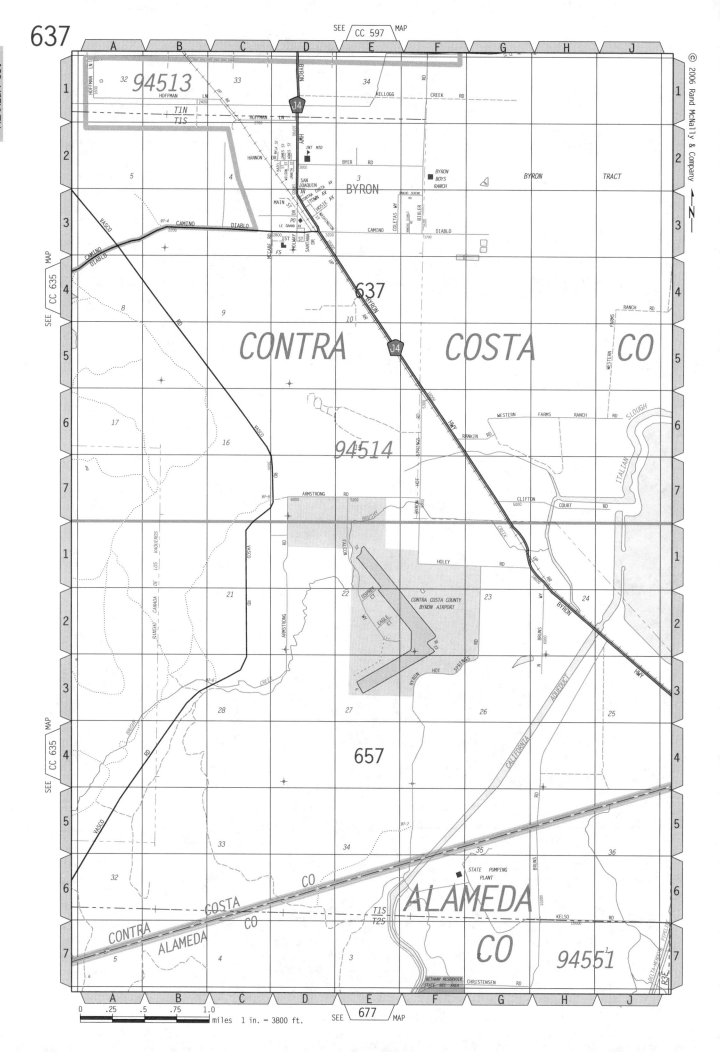

ALAMEDA CO.

© 2006 Rand McNally & Company

94513

94514

94551

657

CONTRA COSTA CO

ALAMEDA CO

BYRON

BYRON BOYS RANCH

BYRON TRACT

CONTRA COSTA COUNTY BYRON AIRPORT

STATE PUMPING PLANT

BETHANY RESERVOIR STATE REC. AREA

SEE CC 635 MAP

SEE CC 635 MAP

0   .25   .5   .75   1.0
miles   1 in. = 3800 ft.

SEE 677 MAP

ALAMEDA CO.

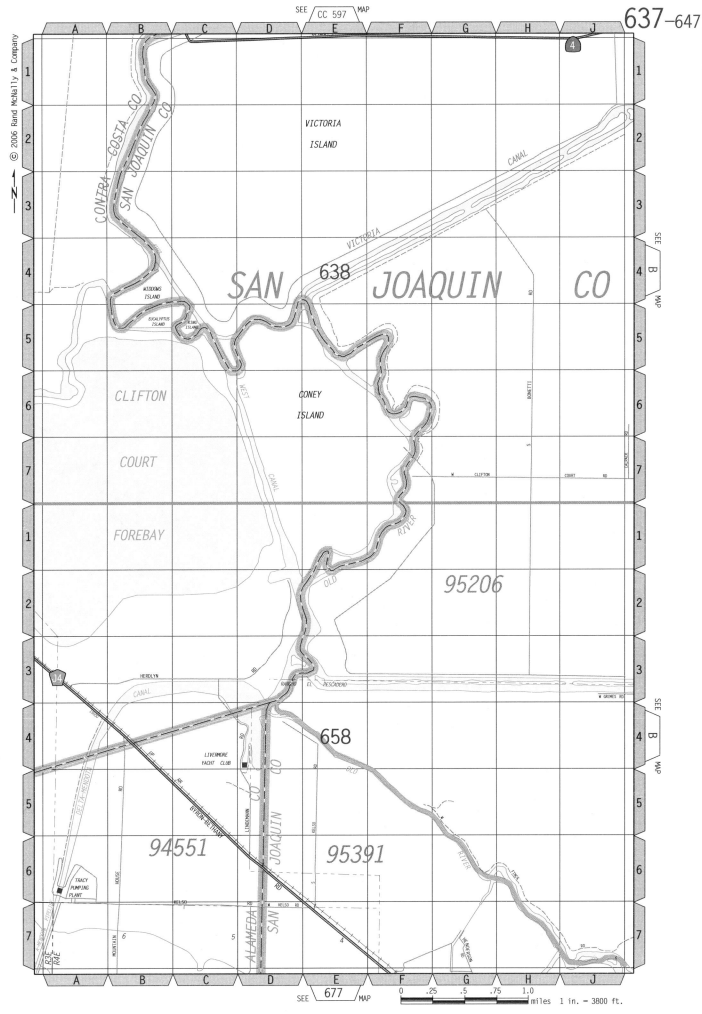

N

A B C D E F G H J

CONTRA COSTA CO.
SAN JOAQUIN CO

VICTORIA ISLAND

CANAL

SAN JOAQUIN CO
638

VICTORIA

WIDDOWS ISLAND

EUCALYPTUS ISLAND
KING ISLAND

BONETTI

CLIFTON

CONEY ISLAND

CALPACK

COURT

WEST

CANAL

S

W CLIFTON COURT RD

FOREBAY

OLD

RIVER

95206

RD

HERDLYN

CANAL

RANCHO EL PESCADERO

W GRIMES RD

658

LIVERMORE YACHT CLUB

SAN JOAQUIN CO

OLD

BYRON-BETHANY

LINDEMANN

KELSO

RIVER

FINCK

94551

95391

HENDERSON RD

DELTA-MENDOTA

RD

HOUSE

TRACY PUMPING PLANT

KELSO

ALAMEDA

SAN JOAQUIN

RD

W KELSO RD

MOUNTAIN 6

5

4

R3E
R4E

A B C D E F G H J

0   .25   .5   .75   1.0
miles   1 in. = 3800 ft.

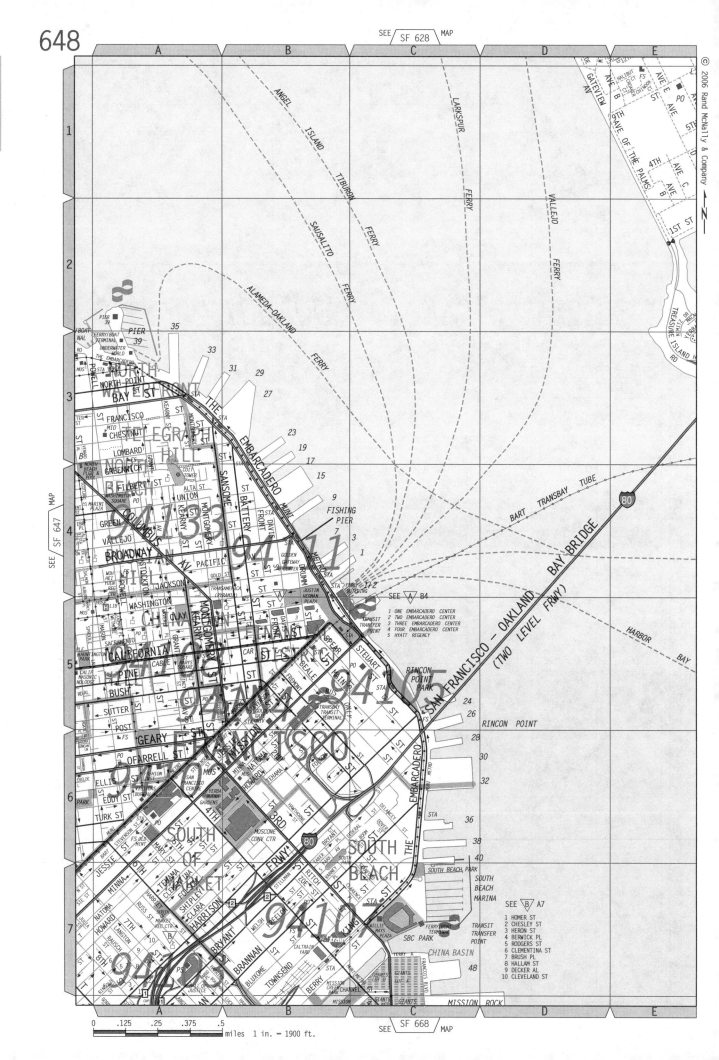

ALAMEDA CO.

SEE SF 628 MAP

© 2006 Rand McNally & Company

SEE SF 647 MAP

SEE A B4

1 ONE EMBARCADERO CENTER
2 TWO EMBARCADERO CENTER
3 THREE EMBARCADERO CENTER
4 FOUR EMBARCADERO CENTER
5 HYATT REGENCY

SEE B A7

1 HOMER ST
2 CHESLEY ST
3 HERON ST
4 BERWICK PL
5 RODGERS ST
6 CLEMENTINA ST
7 BRUSH PL
8 HALLAM ST
9 DECKER AL
10 CLEVELAND ST

0 .125 .25 .375 .5
miles 1 in. = 1900 ft.

SEE SF 668 MAP

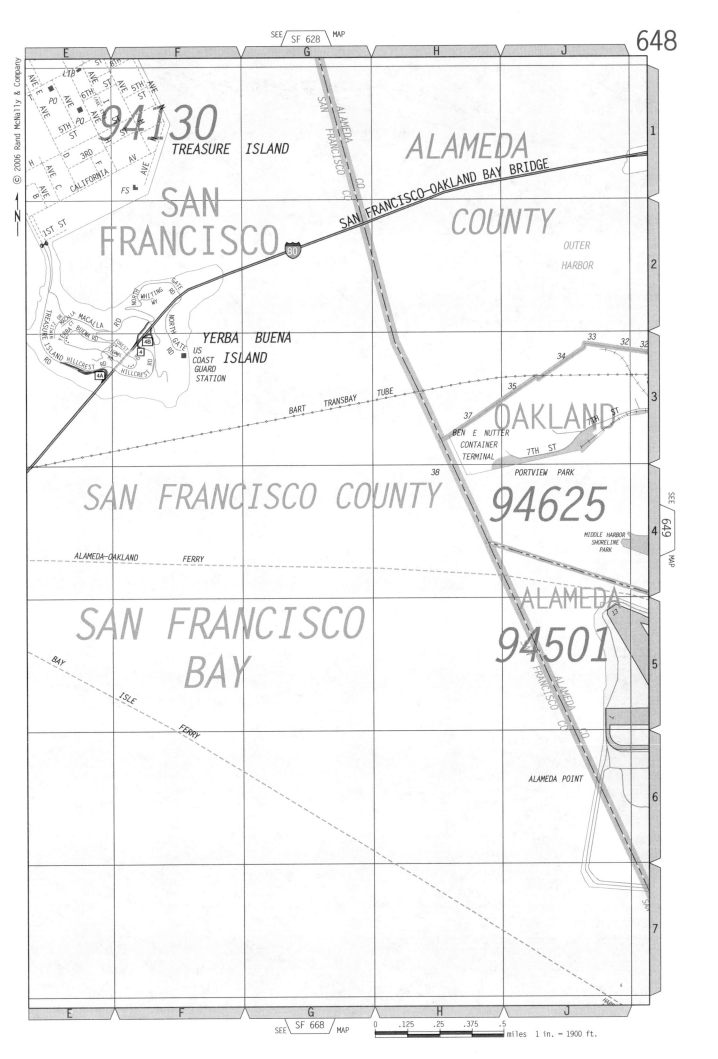

SEE SF 628 MAP

94130

TREASURE ISLAND

ALAMEDA

SAN

FRANCISCO

COUNTY

OUTER HARBOR

SAN FRANCISCO-OAKLAND BAY BRIDGE

80

SAN FRANCISCO CO.

ALAMEDA CO.

NORTH GATE RD

WHITING WY

TREASURE ISLAND RD

MACALLA CT

YERBA BUENA RD

TWIN DR

FOREST RD

SIGNAL RD

HILLCREST RD

MACALLA RD

NORTH GATE RD

4B

4

4A

TREASURE ISLAND HILLCREST RD

HILLCREST

YERBA BUENA ISLAND

US COAST GUARD STATION

33

34

32

32

35

37

BEN E NUTTER CONTAINER TERMINAL

OAKLAND

7TH ST

7TH ST

BART TRANSBAY TUBE

SAN FRANCISCO COUNTY

38

PORTVIEW PARK

94625

MIDDLE HARBOR SHORELINE PARK

ALAMEDA-OAKLAND FERRY

SAN FRANCISCO

BAY

BAY

ISLE

FERRY

ALAMEDA

94501

13

ALAMEDA SAN FRANCISCO CO.

ALAMEDA POINT

SEE 649 MAP

SEE SF 668 MAP

0 .125 .25 .375 .5
miles 1 in. = 1900 ft.

N

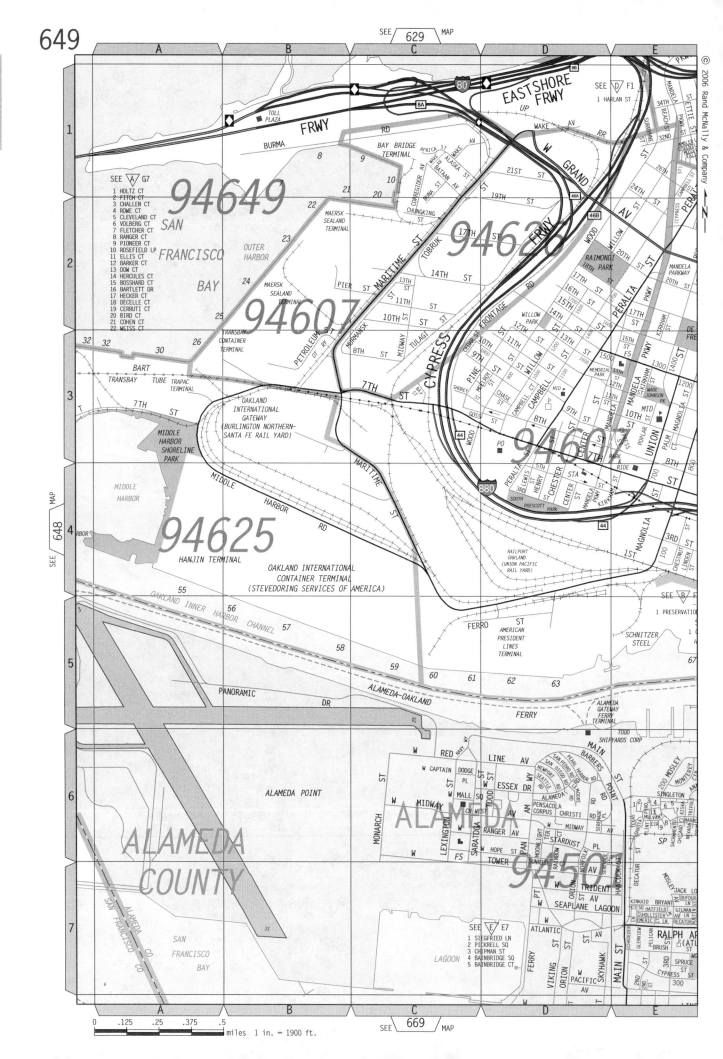

649

ALAMEDA CO.

SEE 629 MAP

© 2006 Rand McNally & Company

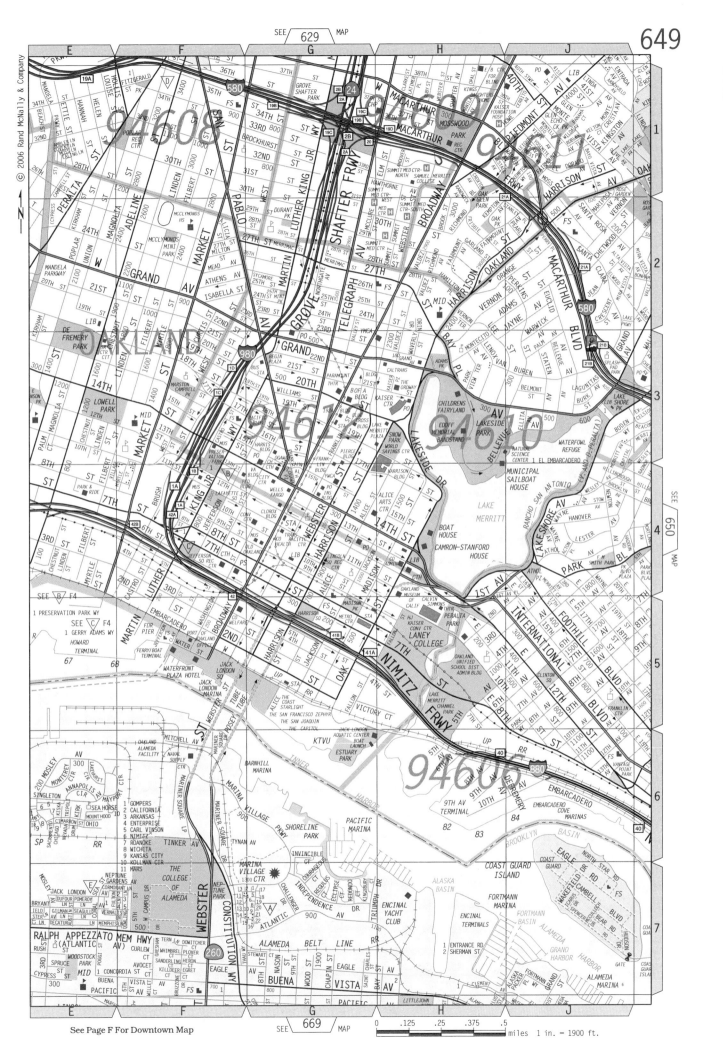

© 2006 Rand McNally & Company

94608

94609

94611

94610

94612

94606

0 .125 .25 .375 .5

miles 1 in. = 1900 ft.

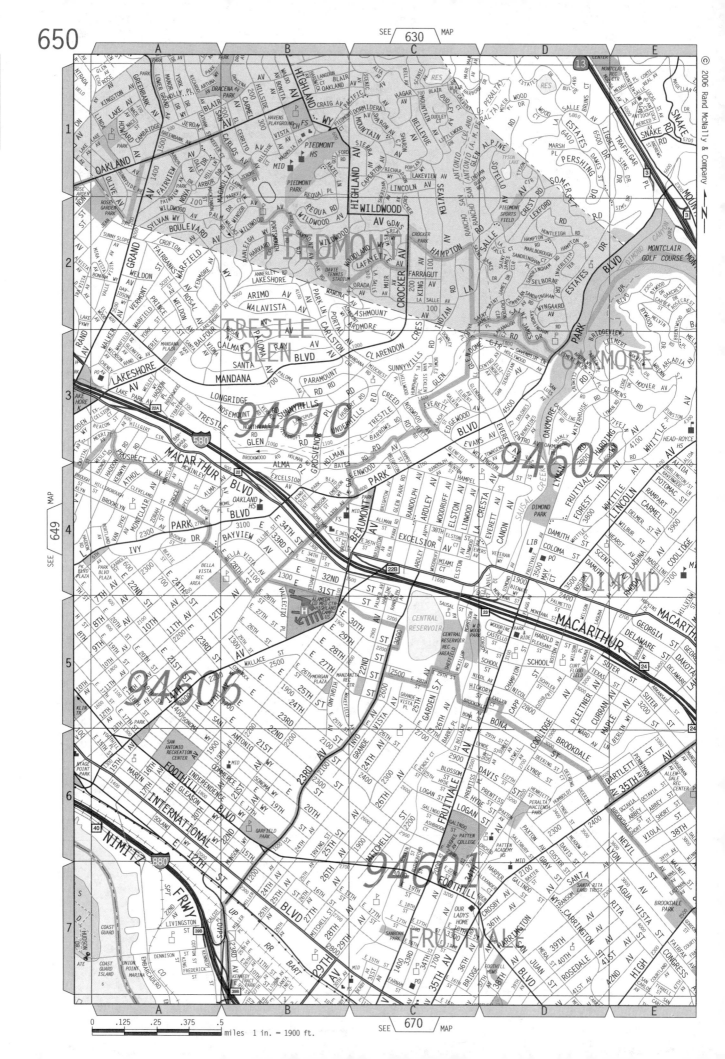

ALAMEDA CO.

© 2006 Rand McNally & Company

SEE 630 MAP

SEE 649 MAP

SEE 670 MAP

PIEDMONT

TRESTLE GLEN

OAKMORE

94610

94602

DIMOND

94606

94601

FRUITVALE

0   .125   .25   .375   .5
miles 1 in. = 1900 ft.

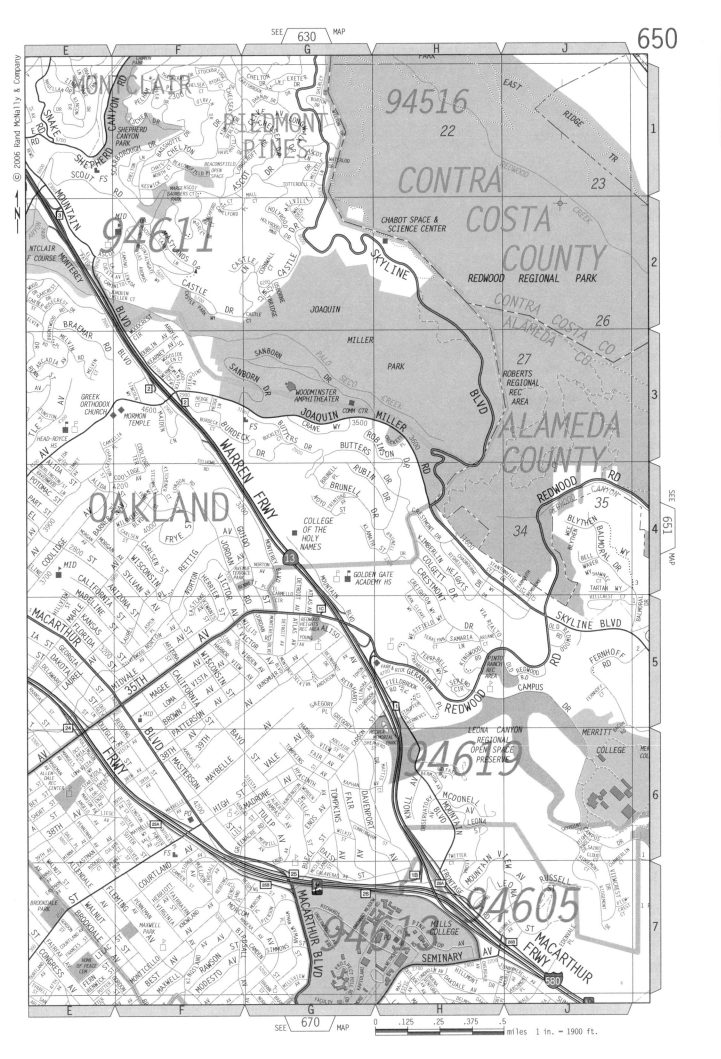

ALAMEDA CO.

94516

CONTRA
COSTA
COUNTY

REDWOOD REGIONAL PARK

CONTRA COSTA CO
ALAMEDA CO

ROBERTS
REGIONAL
REC
AREA

ALAMEDA
COUNTY

94611

CHABOT SPACE &
SCIENCE CENTER

JOAQUIN

MILLER
PARK

WOODMINSTER
AMPHITHEATER

OAKLAND

COLLEGE
OF THE
HOLY
NAMES

GOLDEN GATE
ACADEMY HS

KIMBERLIN
HEIGHTS

REDWOOD RD

SKYLINE BLVD

FERNHOFF
RD

94619

LEONA CANYON
REGIONAL
OPEN SPACE
PRESERVE

MERRITT

COLLEGE

MACARTHUR
FRWY

94605

MILLS
COLLEGE

94613

SEMINARY

MACARTHUR
BLVD

SEE 630 MAP

SEE 670 MAP

SEE 651 MAP

0 .125 .25 .375 .5   miles 1 in. = 1900 ft.

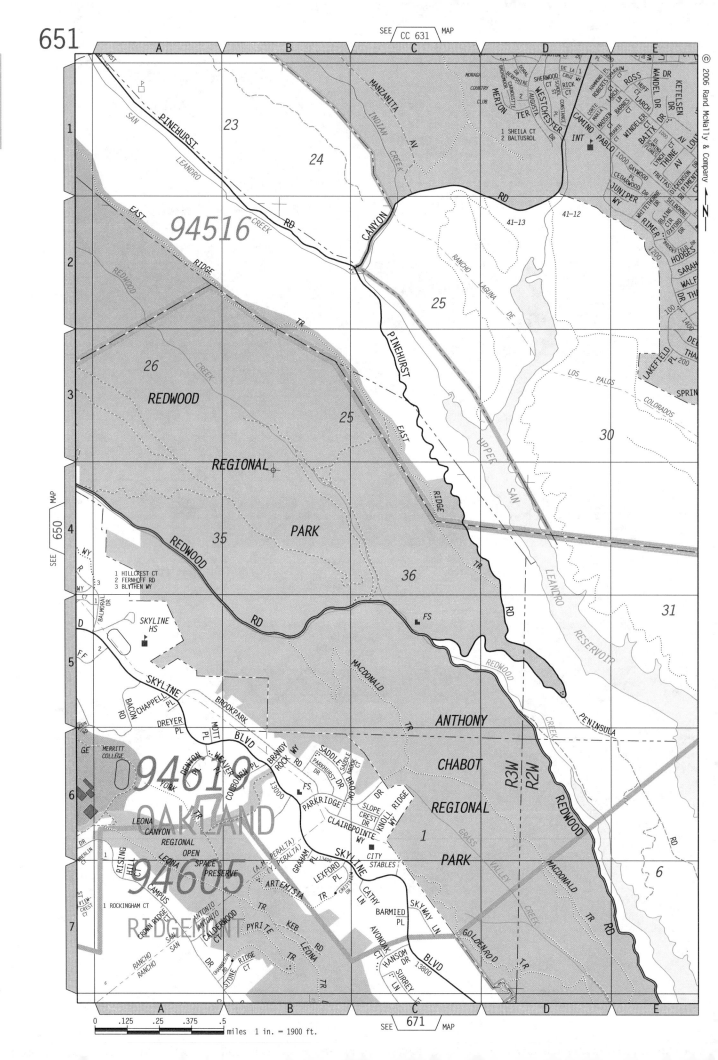

ALAMEDA CO.

SEE CC 631 MAP

94516

REDWOOD

REGIONAL

PARK

94619

OAKLAND

94605

RIDGEMONT

ANTHONY

CHABOT

REGIONAL

PARK

1 HILLCREST CT
2 FERNHOFF RD
3 BLYTHEN WY

1 HELA CT
2 BALTUSROL

1 SHEILA CT
2 BALTUSROL

1 ROCKINGHAM CT

MERRITT
COLLEGE

SKYLINE
HS

LEONA
CANYON
REGIONAL
OPEN
SPACE
PRESERVE

SKYLINE
STABLES

CITY
STABLES

SEE 650 MAP

0 .125 .25 .375 .5
miles 1 in. = 1900 ft.

SEE 671 MAP

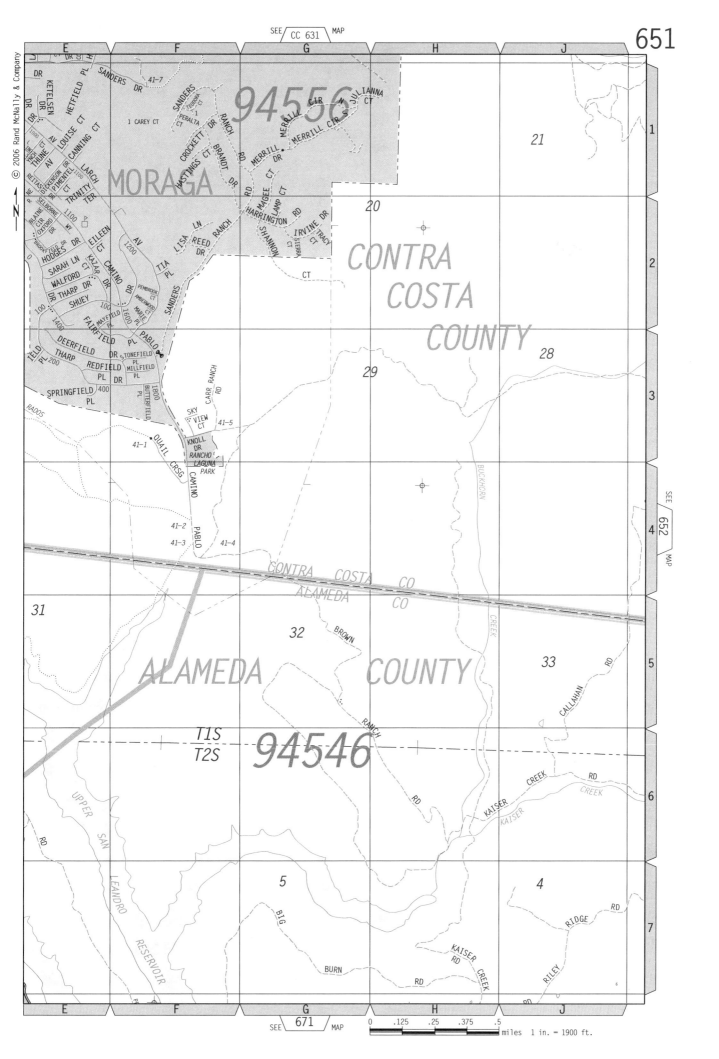

SEE CC 631 MAP

E   F   G   H   J

94556

MORAGA

1 CAREY CT

21

20

CONTRA

COSTA

COUNTY

29   28

SEE 652 MAP

CONTRA COSTA CO
ALAMEDA CO

31

32   BROWN   33

ALAMEDA   COUNTY

T1S
T2S   94546

UPPER SAN

LEANDRO RESERVOIR

5   4

1
2
3
4
5
6
7

E   F   G   H   J

SEE 671 MAP

0   .125   .25   .375   .5

miles 1 in. = 1900 ft.

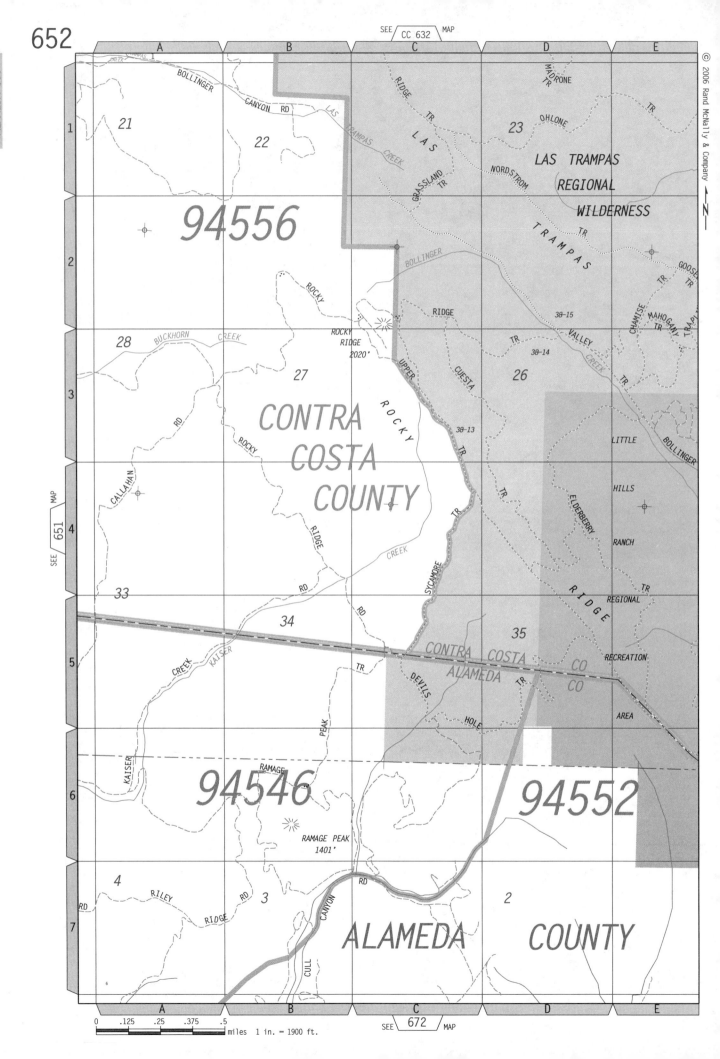

SEE CC 632 MAP

© 2006 Rand McNally & Company

94556

94546

94552

CONTRA COSTA COUNTY

ALAMEDA COUNTY

LAS TRAMPAS REGIONAL WILDERNESS

SEE 651 MAP

SEE 672 MAP

0 .125 .25 .375 .5 miles 1 in. = 1900 ft.

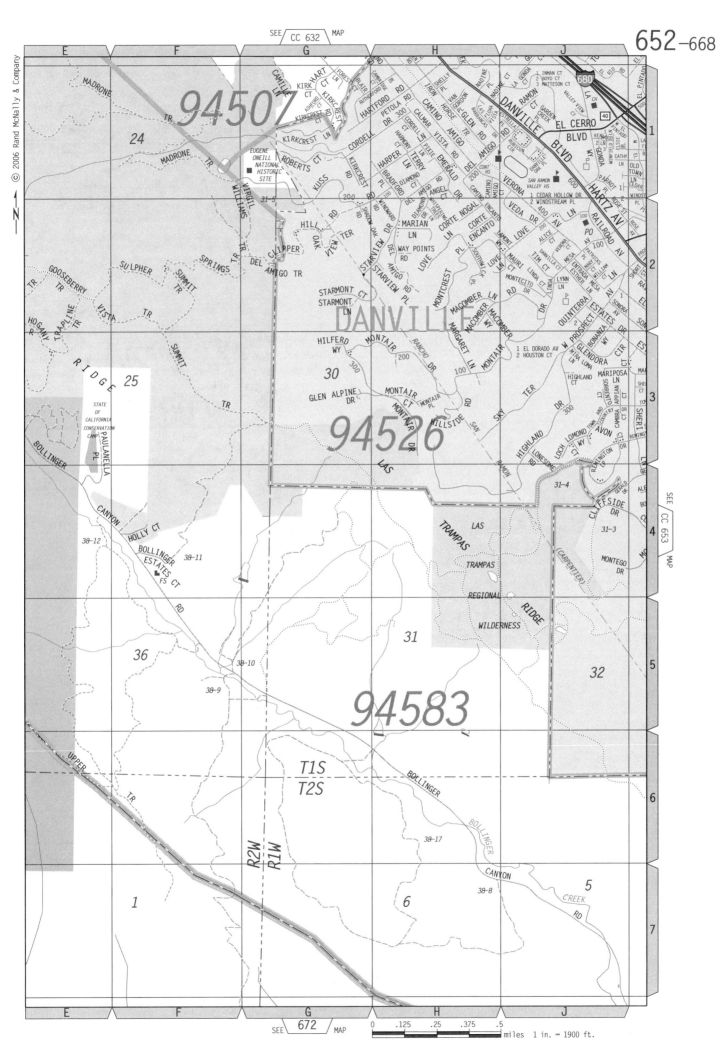

© 2006 Rand McNally & Company

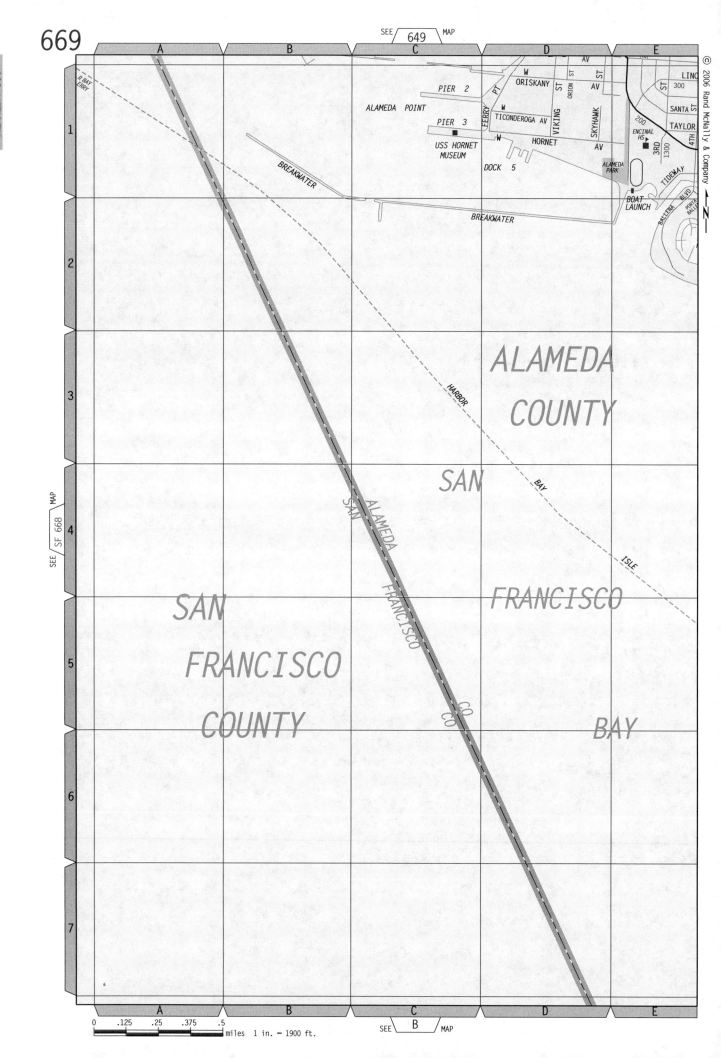

SEE 649 MAP

A B C D E

1

R BAY FERRY

PIER 2

ALAMEDA POINT

PIER 3

USS HORNET MUSEUM

DOCK 5

BREAKWATER

FERRY
PT

W ORISKANY

W TICONDEROGA AV

VIKING ST

ORTON ST

SKYHAWK

W HORNET

AV

ST
AV

ST
AV

LINC
300

SANTA ST

TAYLOR

ENCINAL HS

ALAMEDA PARK

200

3RD
1300

ST

4TH ST

TIDEWAY

BOAT LAUNCH

BALLENA BLVD

PORTA BALLE

N

2

BREAKWATER

SEE SF 668 MAP

3

HARBOR

ALAMEDA COUNTY

SAN

BAY

4

SAN

ALAMEDA

ISLE

FRANCISCO

5

SAN

FRANCISCO

COUNTY

SAN

FRANCISCO

CO

CO

FRANCISCO

BAY

6

7

A B C D E

SEE B MAP

0 .125 .25 .375 .5
miles 1 in. = 1900 ft.

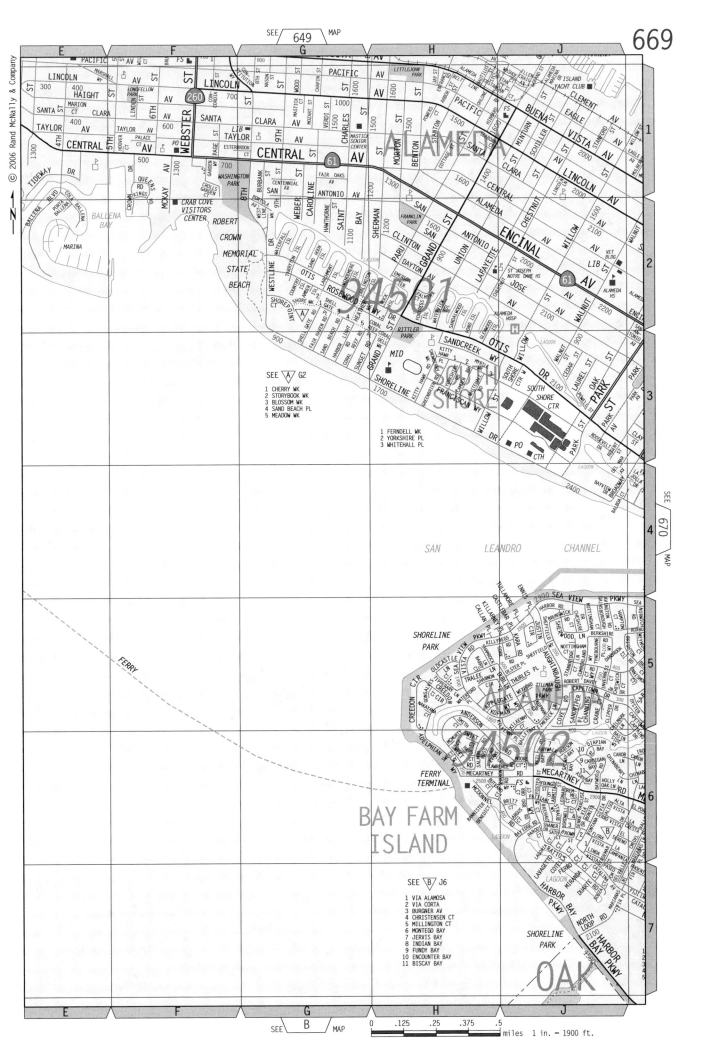

SEE 649 MAP

N

E F G H J

ALAMEDA

94501

PACIFIC AV

LINCOLN AV
300 400 HAIGHT AV
SANTA ST CLARA
400 AV
TAYLOR AV
1300 4TH CENTRAL AV

LINCOLN
WEBSTER ST
700
SANTA CLARA AV
LIB TAYLOR
PO
CENTRAL ST AV

PACIFIC AV

BUENA VISTA AV
CLEMENT AV
EAGLE AV
LINCOLN AV

ALAMEDA
ENCINAL AV
61 AV

1

2

TIDEWAY DR
BALLENA BLVD
COTA BALLENA
PORTA BALLENA
BALLENA BAY
MARINA

CRAB COVE
VISITORS
CENTER
ROBERT
CROWN
MEMORIAL
STATE
BEACH

McKAY AV
QUEENS RD
KINGS
CROWN DR
WASHINGTON PARK
CROLLS GARDEN

8TH ST
BURBANK
PORTOLA
9TH
WEBER
CAROLINE
SAINT
BAY
SHERMAN
1100 1200

CLINTON AV
SAN ANTONIO AV
PARU
DAYTON
GRAND ST
SAN
900
UNION
LAFAYETTE ST
JOSE AV
2100

ANTONIO AV
ALAMEDA AV
CHESTNUT AV
WILLOW AV
1500
WALNUT

VET BLDG
LIB
ALAMEDA HS

2

WESTLINE DR
TARRYTON ISL
SAND HOOK ISL
OTIS
ROSEWOOD
HEATHER
SHOREP CT
SHORE WK
SHELL GATE
FAIR HAVEN RD
SAND BEACH RD
HARBOR RD
CORAL REEF RD
SUNSET RD
900 GRAND ST
1700

SHORELINE DR

MID

RITTLER PARK
SANDCREEK WY
KITTY HAWK
MYRTLE
SOUTH SHORE
SAN FRANCISCAN
WILLOW DR

OTIS DR
SOUTH
SHORE
CTR
WALNUT ST
CEDAR ST
LAUREL ST
OAK
PARK ST

H
ALAMEDA HOSP

3

SEE A G2
1 CHERRY WK
2 STORYBOOK WK
3 BLOSSOM WK
4 SAND BEACH PL
5 MEADOW WK

1 FERNDELL WK
2 YORKSHIRE PL
3 WHITEHALL PL

PO
CTH

ROOSEVELT
PARK

LAGOON

BAYVIEW

SEE 670 MAP

4

SAN LEANDRO CHANNEL

FERRY

SHORELINE
PARK

SEA VIEW PKWY

TULLAMORE
KILLARNEY
CASTLEBAR
CALLAN
HARBOR RD
SHERWOOD LN
BERKSHIRE
NOTTINGHAM

SEA VIEW PKWY
OLDCASTLE CIR
CREEDON CIR
SEA VIEW RD
VISTA RD
TRALEE
TIPPERARY
CREEDON
SHANNON
APPLEGATE
KOFMAN
ANDERSON
SMITH
ADELPHIAN WY
SWIFT

ALAMEDA
94502

MECARTNEY RD

SHORELINE
PARK

5

FERRY
TERMINAL
McDONNELL

BAY FARM
ISLAND

MECARTNEY

LAGOON

HARBOR BAY PKWY
NORTH LOOP

HARBOR BAY PKWY

6

SEE B J6
1 VIA ALAMOSA
2 VIA CORTA
3 BURGNER AV
4 CHRISTENSEN CT
5 MILLINGTON CT
6 MONTEGO BAY
7 JERVIS BAY
8 INDIAN BAY
9 FUNDY BAY
10 ENCOUNTER BAY
11 BISCAY BAY

OAK

7

E F G H J

SEE B MAP

0 .125 .25 .375 .5
miles 1 in. = 1900 ft.

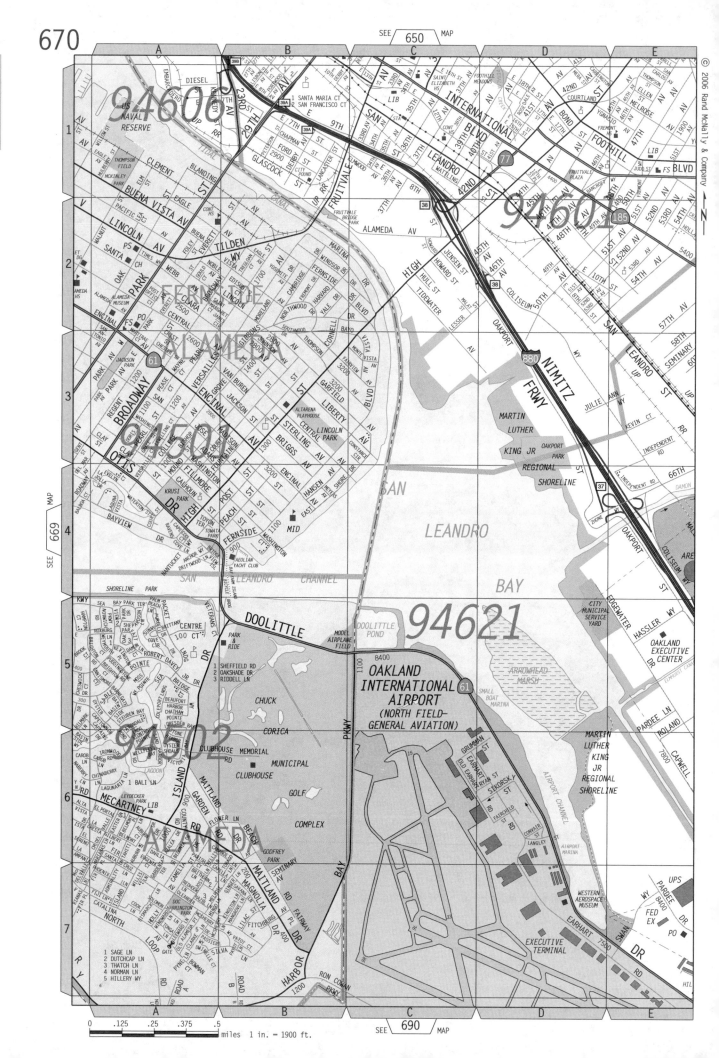

SEE 650 MAP

94606

94601

94501

94621

94502

SEE 669 MAP

SEE 690 MAP

0 .125 .25 .375 .5
miles 1 in. = 1900 ft.

OAKLAND
INTERNATIONAL
AIRPORT
(NORTH FIELD—
GENERAL AVIATION)

ALAMEDA CO.

See Page E For Detail Airport Map

0   .125   .25   .375   .5
miles   1 in. = 1900 ft.

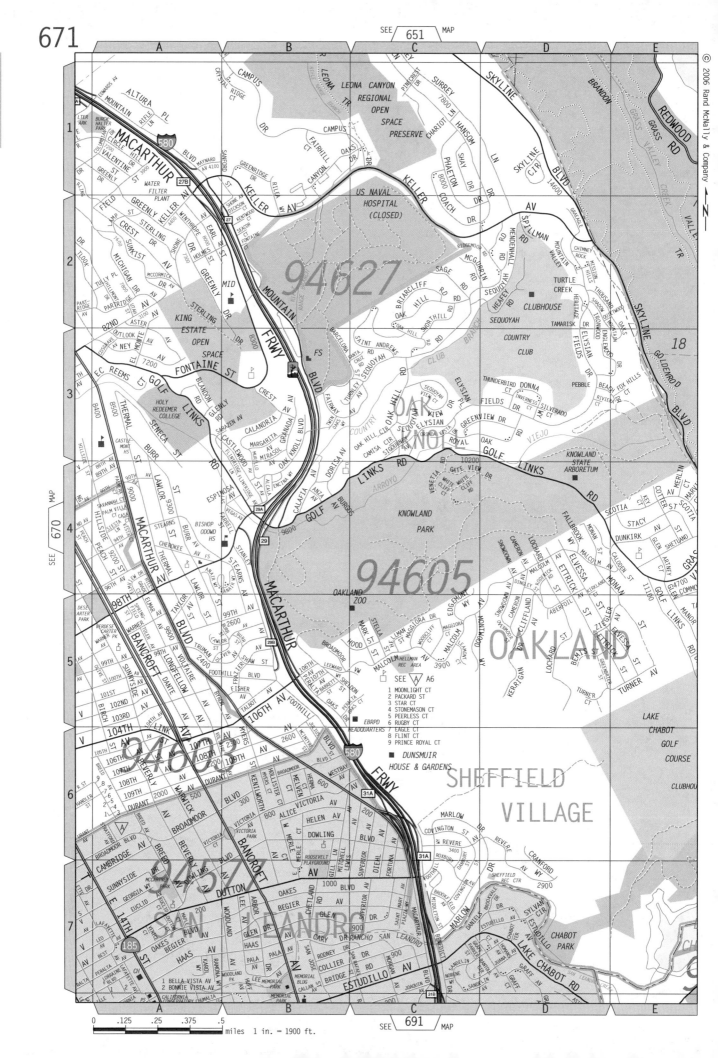

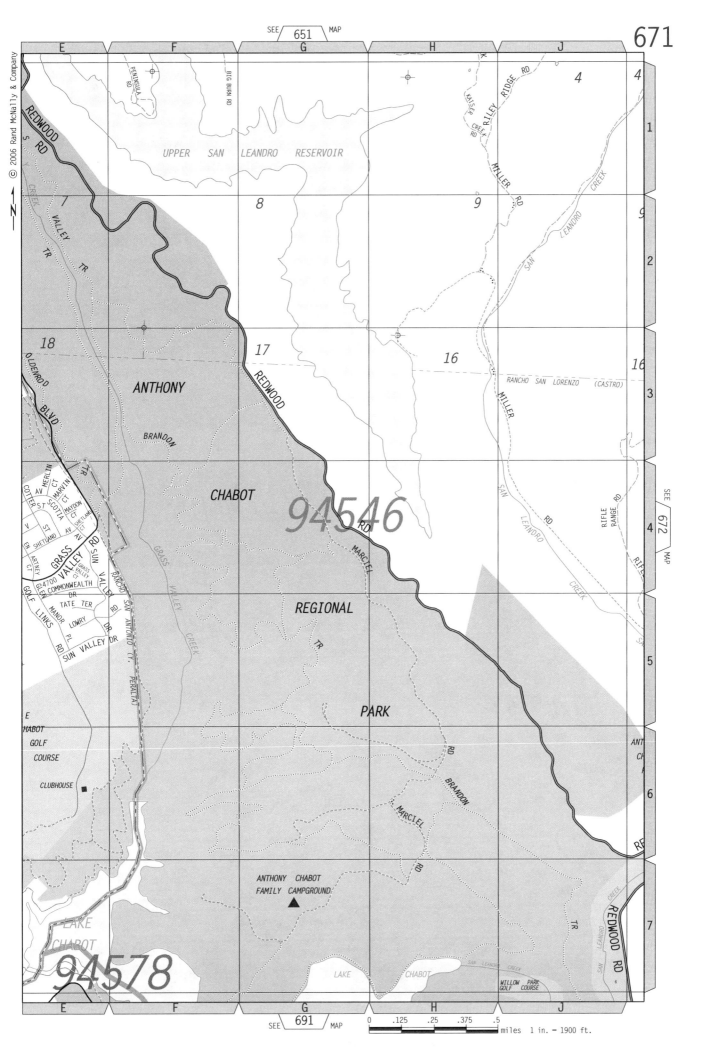

ALAMEDA CO.

SEE 651 MAP

E   F   G   H   J

4

4

1

REDWOOD RD

PENINSULA RD

BIG BURN RD

KAISER CREEK RD

RILEY RIDGE RD

MILLER RD

UPPER SAN LEANDRO RESERVOIR

SAN LEANDRO CREEK

VALLEY TR

8

9

9

2

18

17

16

16

3

ANTHONY

REDWOOD

RANCHO SAN LORENZO (CASTRO)

MILLER RD

BRANDON

CHABOT

94546

SAN LEANDRO RD

RIFLE RANGE RD

SEE 672 MAP

RIFLE

MERLIN CT
MARVIN LT
COTTER ST
SCOTIA ST
MAYDON CT
SHETLAND CT
SHETLAND AV
SHETLAND EN
ARTNEY CT
GRASS VALLEY CT
GLEN 4700 COMMONWEALTH DR
TATE TER
GOLF LINKS RD
MANOR PL
LOWRY DR
SUN VALLEY DR
SUN VALLEY DR
GRASS VALLEY RD

RANCHO SAN ANTONIO (Y. PERALTA)

GRASS VALLEY CREEK

REGIONAL

TR

MARCIEL

4

5

PARK

RD

BRANDON

ANT CH

E

HABOT
GOLF
COURSE

CLUBHOUSE

MARCIEL
RD

6

ANTHONY CHABOT
FAMILY CAMPGROUND

TR

REDWOOD RD

RD

R

7

LAKE
CHABOT

94578

LAKE   CHABOT

SAN LEANDRO CREEK

SAN LEANDRO CREEK

WILLOW PARK
GOLF COURSE

E   F   G   H   J

SEE 691 MAP

0   .125   .25   .375   .5
miles 1 in. = 1900 ft.

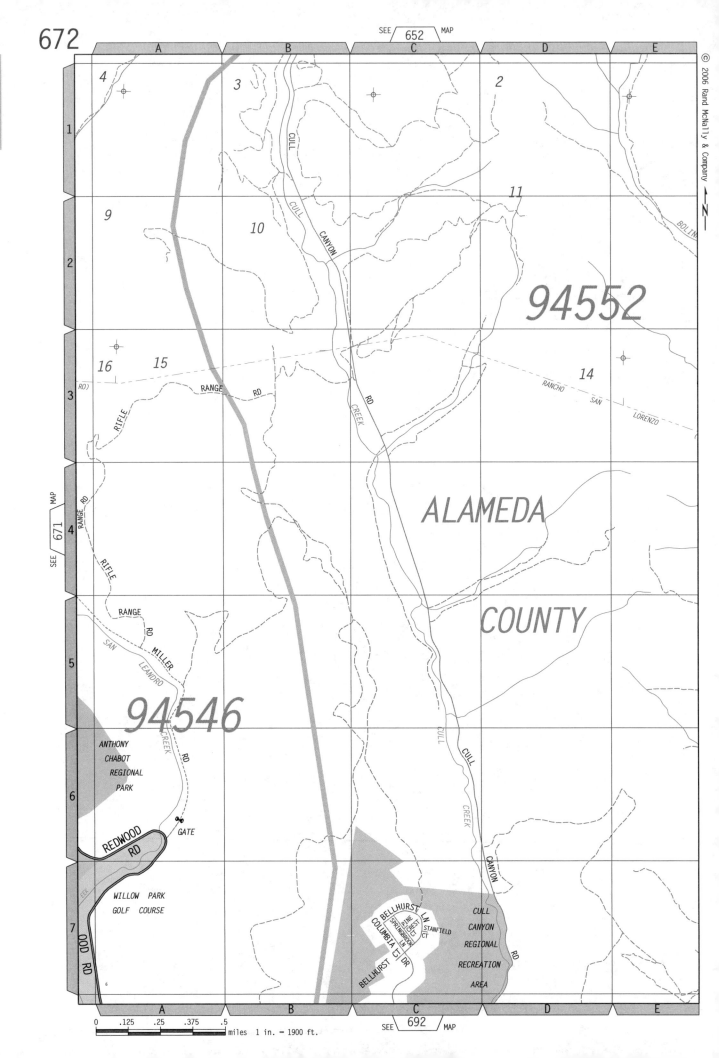

ALAMEDA CO.

—N—

SEE 652 MAP

A · B · C · D · E

4 · 3 · 2

1

9 · 10 · 11

CULL

CULL CANYON

BOLIN

2

94552

16 · 15 · 14

RANGE RD

RIFLE

RD

CREEK

RANCHO SAN LORENZO

3

SEE 671 MAP

RANGE RD

ALAMEDA

RIFLE

4

RANGE RD

SAN

MILLER

LEANDRO

COUNTY

5

94546

ANTHONY
CHABOT
REGIONAL
PARK

CREEK

RD

CULL

CULL

6

REDWOOD RD

GATE

CREEK

CANYON

WILLOW PARK
GOLF COURSE

CULL
CANYON
REGIONAL
RECREATION
AREA

7

OOD RD

BELLHURST LN
SPRINGBROOK LN
PINE CREST CT
STANFIELD CT
COLUMBIA CT DR
BELLHURST CT DR

RD

A · B · C · D · E

0 .125 .25 .375 .5
miles 1 in. = 1900 ft.

SEE 692 MAP

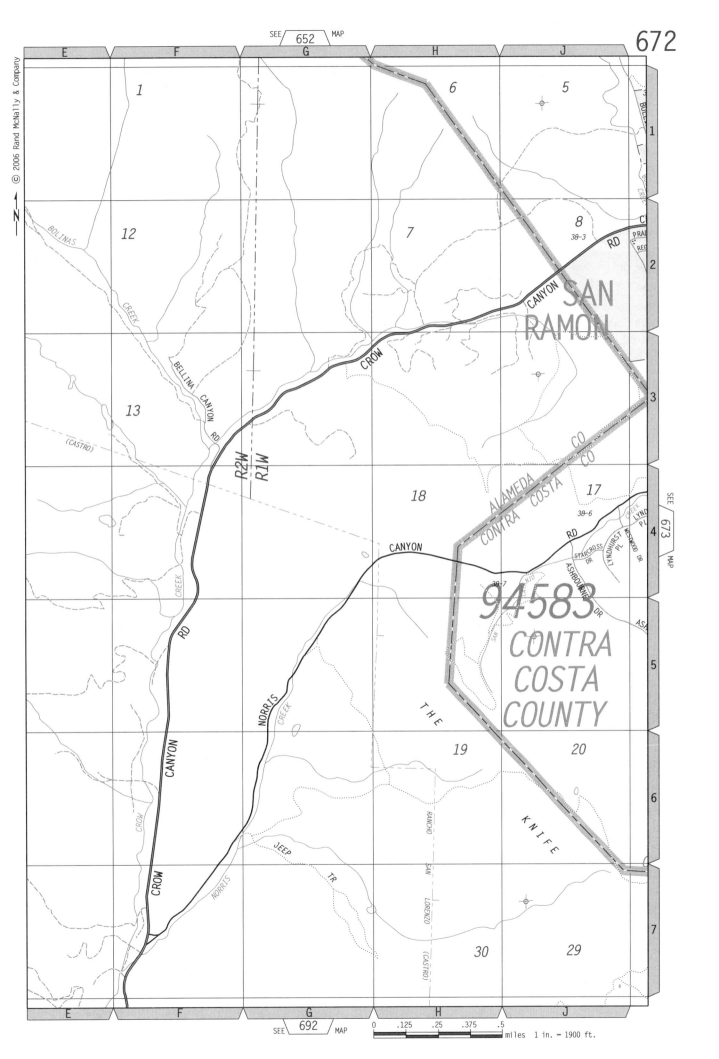

ALAMEDA CO.

© 2006 Rand McNally & Company

SEE 652 MAP

E   F   G   H   J

1

12   7   8
38-3

RD

CANYON SAN
RAMON

CROW

BELLINA CANYON RD

13

(CASTRO)

BOLINAS   CREEK

R2W
R1W

18

CANYON

17
38-6

CO
CO

ALAMEDA
CONTRA COSTA

RD

STARCROSS DR
LYNDHURST PL
WESTWOOD DR
LYND PL
ASHBOURNE DR
ASP

SEE 673 MAP

94583
CONTRA
COSTA
COUNTY

38-7

CREEK

RD

CANYON

CREEK

NORRIS

THE

19   20

KNIFE

JEEP

TR

RANCHO SAN LORENZO (CASTRO)

CROW

NORRIS

30   29

1   2   3   4   5   6   7

E   F   G   H   J

SEE 692 MAP

0 .125 .25 .375 .5
miles 1 in. = 1900 ft.

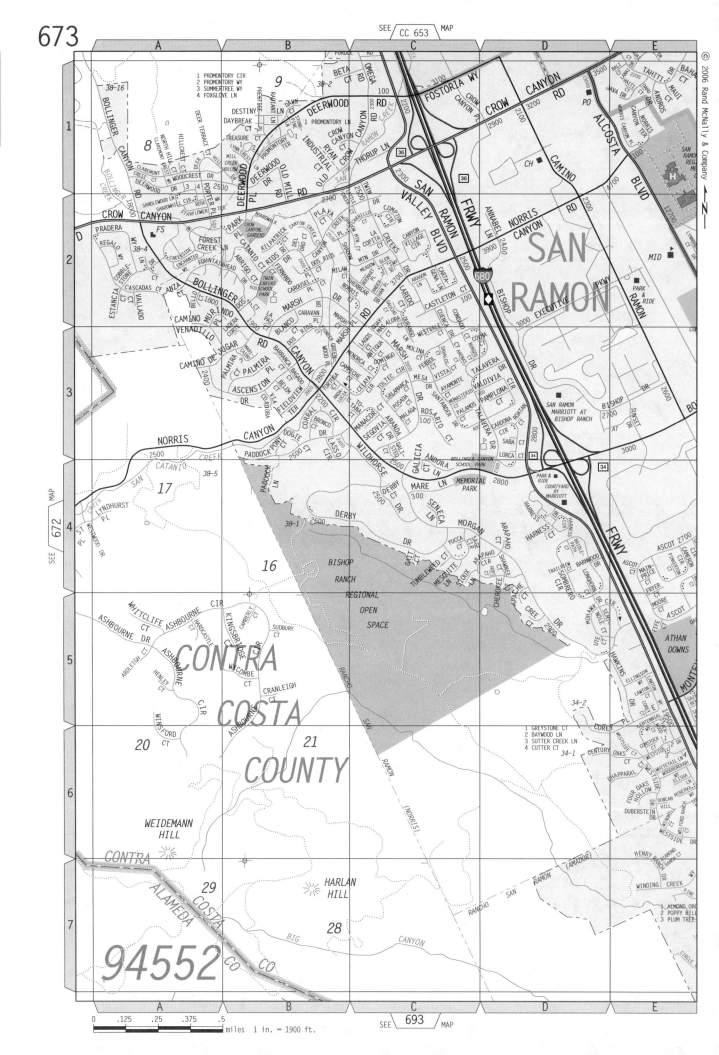

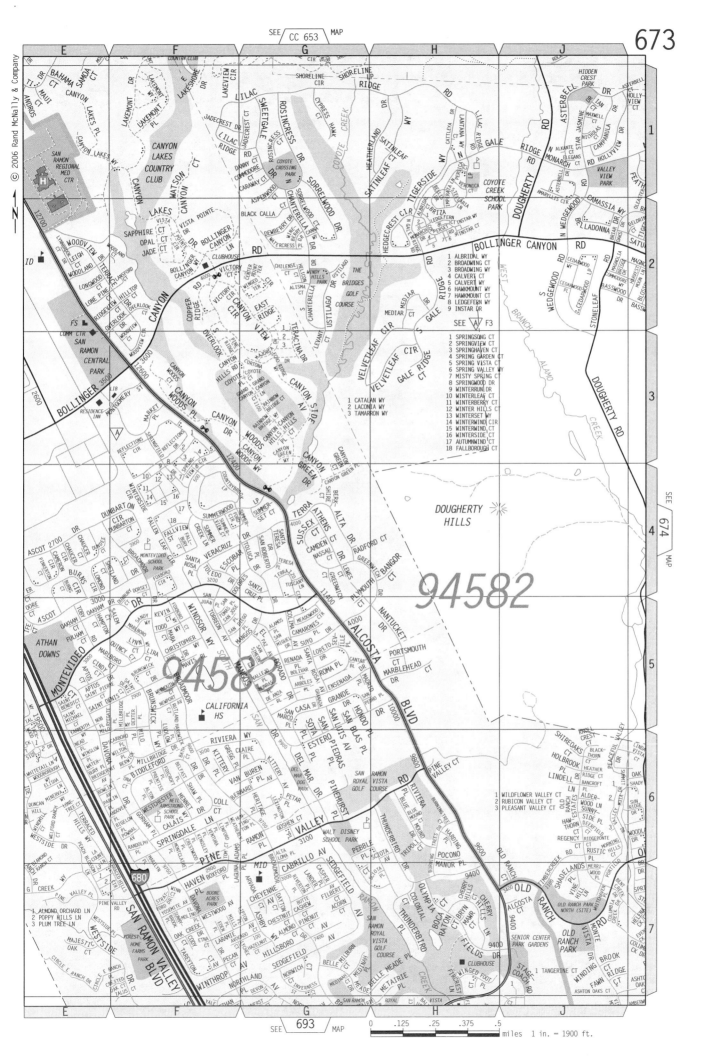

© 2006 Rand McNally & Company

SEE CC 653 MAP

SEE 674 MAP

SEE 693 MAP

94582

94583

DOUGHERTY HILLS

1 ALBRIDAL WY
2 BROADWING CT
3 BROADWING WY
4 CALVERT CT
5 CALVERT WY
6 HAWKMOUNT WY
7 HAWKMOUNT CT
8 LEDGEFERN WY
9 INSTAR DR

SEE A F3

1 SPRINGSONG CT
2 SPRINGVIEW CT
3 SPRINGHAVEN CT
4 SPRING GARDEN CT
5 SPRING VISTA CT
6 SPRING VALLEY WY
7 MISTY SPRING CT
8 SPRINGWOOD DR
9 WINTERRUN DR
10 WINTERLEAF CT
11 WINTERBERRY CT
12 WINTER HILLS CT
13 WINTERSET WY
14 WINTERWIND CIR
15 WINTERWIND
16 WINTERSIDE CT
17 AUTUMNWIND CT
18 FALLBOROUGH CT

1 CATALAN WY
2 LACONIA WY
3 TAMARRON WY

1 WILDFLOWER VALLEY CT
2 RUBICON VALLEY CT
3 PLEASANT VALLEY CT

1 ALMOND ORCHARD LN
2 POPPY HILLS LN
3 PLUM TREE LN

1 TANGERINE CT

miles 1 in. = 1900 ft.
0   .125   .25   .375   .5

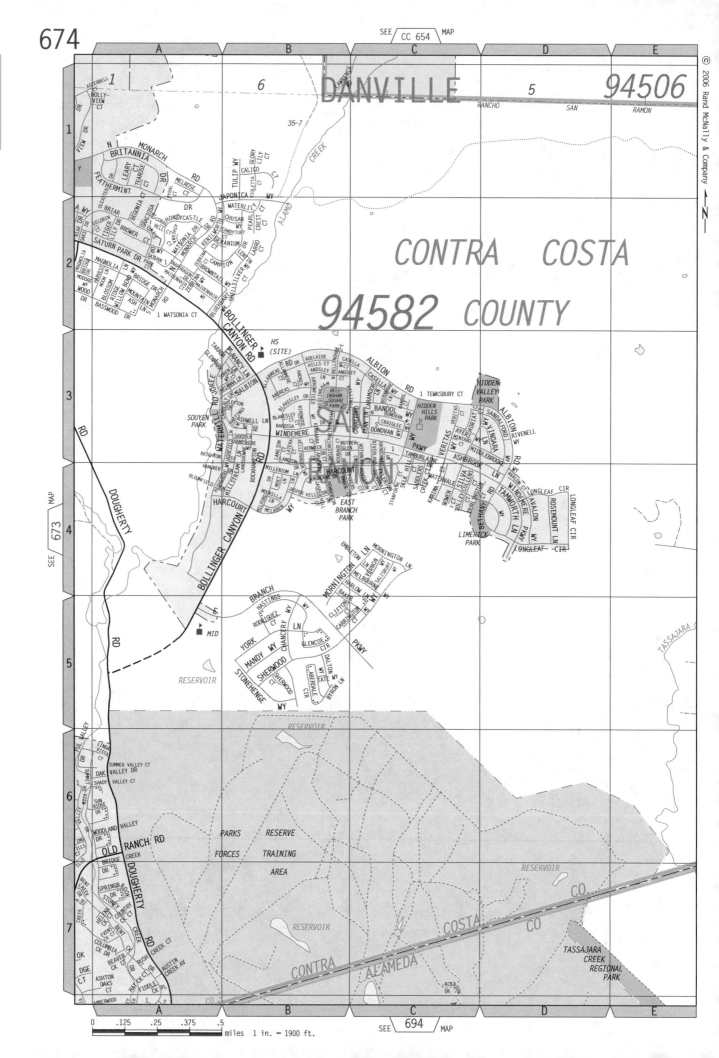

ALAMEDA CO.

© 2006 Rand McNally & Company

SEE CC 654 MAP

DANVILLE

94506

CONTRA COSTA

94582 COUNTY

SAN
RAMON

SEE 673 MAP

SEE 694 MAP

0   .125   .25   .375   .5
miles   1 in. = 1900 ft.

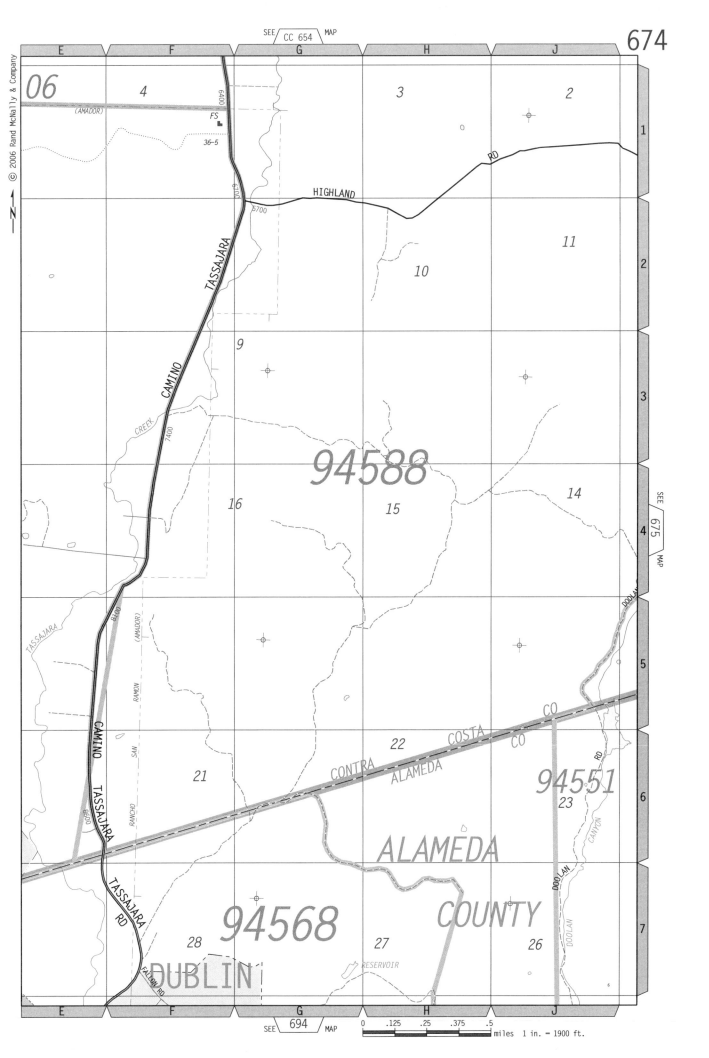

ALAMEDA CO.

SEE CC 654 MAP

E   F   G   H   J

06   4   3   2

(AMADOR)   1

FS

36-5   6400

6100   HIGHLAND   RD

5700   2

TASSAJARA   11

10

CAMINO   9

3

CREEK   7400

94588

SEE 675 MAP

16   15   14   4

8100   5

TASSAJARA   (AMADOR)

RAMON   DOOLAN

CAMINO   SAN   22   COSTA   CO   94551

CONTRA   ALAMEDA   RD   23   6

TASSAJARA   21   CANYON

8600   RANCHO   ALAMEDA   DOOLAN

TASSAJARA   COUNTY

RD   94568   27   26   7

28   DUBLIN   RESERVOIR   DOOLAN

FALLON RD   6

E   F   G   H   J

SEE 694 MAP

0   .125   .25   .375   .5

miles 1 in. = 1900 ft.

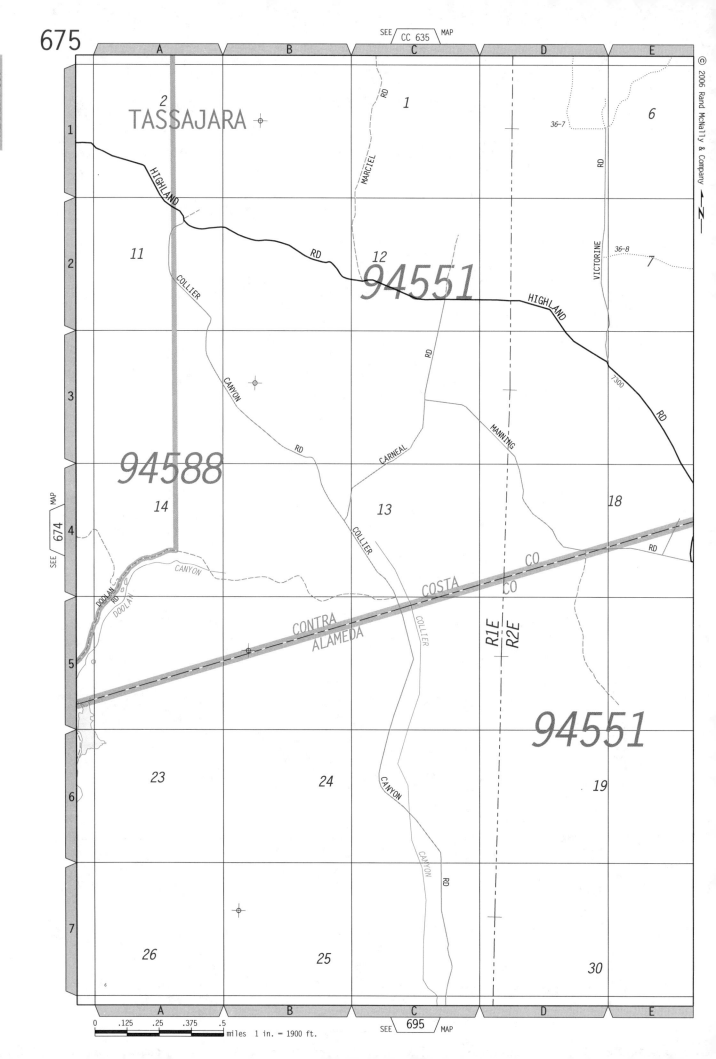

ALAMEDA CO.

—N—

SEE CC 635 MAP

A B C D E

TASSAJARA

2   1   6
          MARCIEL RD   36-7   RD

HIGHLAND

1

11   RD   12   VICTORINE   36-8   7
COLLIER   94551   HIGHLAND

2

CANYON   RD   MANNING   7300   RD

3

94588   CARNEAL

14   RD   13   18
                    COLLIER   CO   RD

4

CANYON   COLLIER   COSTA   CO

DOOLAN RD   CONTRA   COLLIER   R1E | R2E
DOOLAN   ALAMEDA

5   94551

23   24   19
                    CANYON

6   CANYON   RD

7
                                    +

26   25   30

A B C D E

SEE 695 MAP

0 .125 .25 .375 .5
miles 1 in. = 1900 ft.

SEE 674 MAP

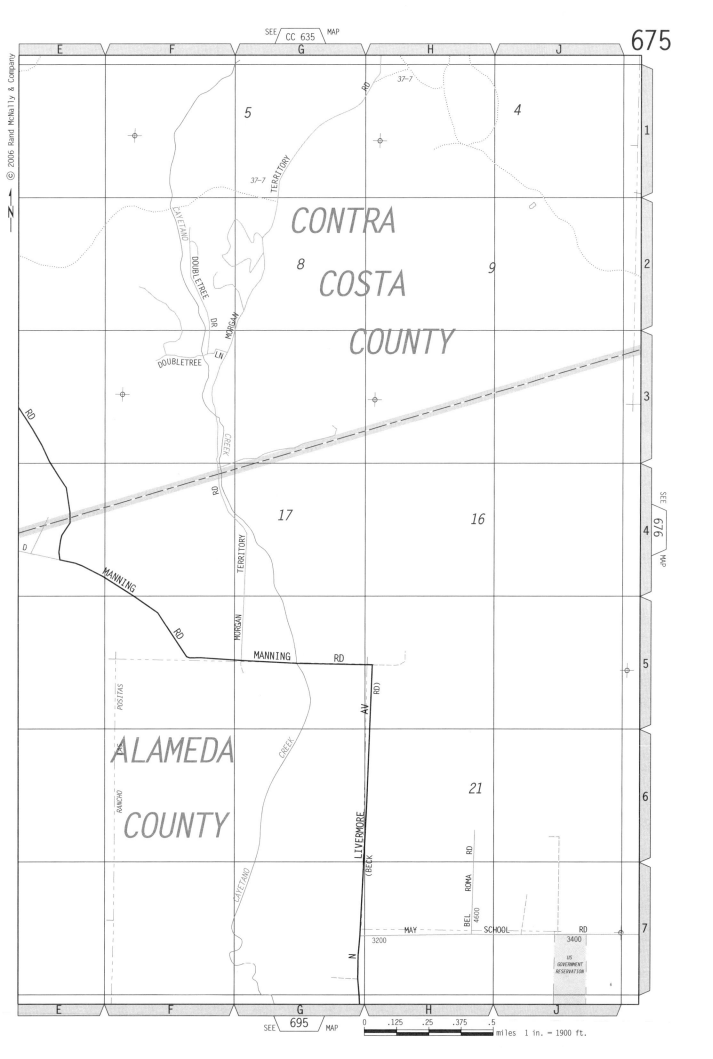

ALAMEDA CO.

SEE CC 635 MAP

E   F   G   H   J

CONTRA

COSTA

COUNTY

ALAMEDA

COUNTY

SEE 676 MAP

US
GOVERNMENT
RESERVATION

SEE 695 MAP

0   .125   .25   .375   .5
miles   1 in. = 1900 ft.

© 2006 Rand McNally & Company

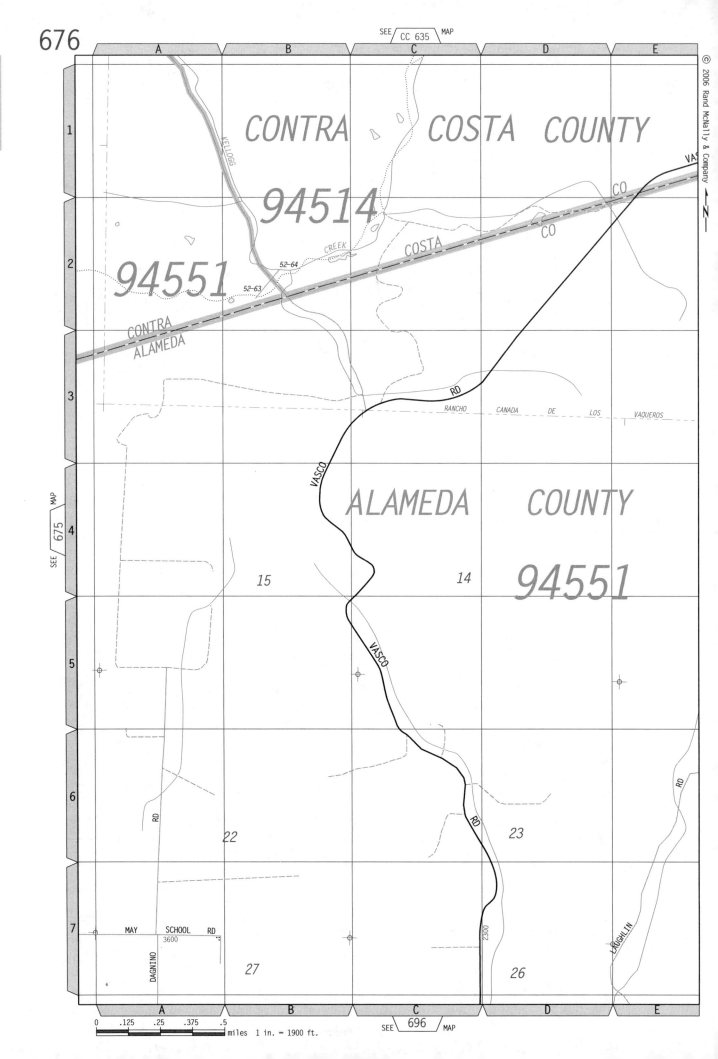

ALAMEDA CO.

© 2006 Rand McNally & Company

SEE CC 635 MAP

A   B   C   D   E

1

CONTRA COSTA COUNTY

94514

KELLOGG

94551

CREEK

52–64

52–63

COSTA

CO

CO

VA

2

CONTRA
ALAMEDA

3

RD

RANCHO CANADA DE LOS VAQUEROS

VASCO

SEE 675 MAP

ALAMEDA COUNTY

4

94551

15

14

VASCO

5

VASCO

22

RD

23

6

RD

2300

7

MAY SCHOOL RD

3600

LAUGHLIN

DAGNINO

27

26

A   B   C   D   E

SEE 696 MAP

0   .125   .25   .375   .5

miles 1 in. = 1900 ft.

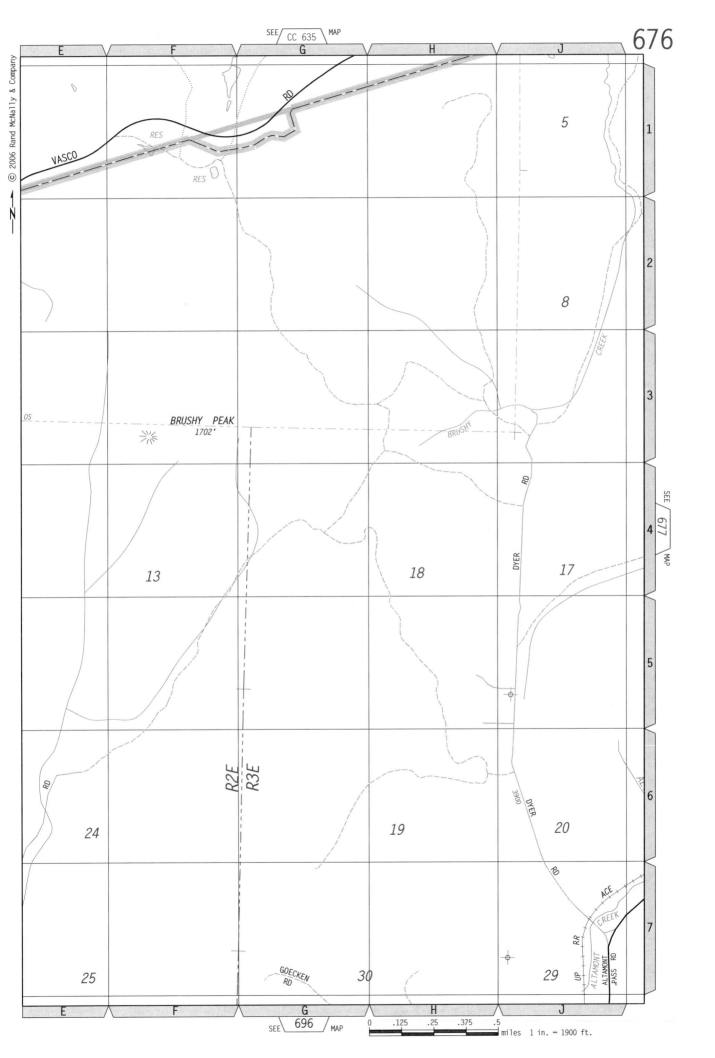

© 2006 Rand McNally & Company

N

SEE / CC 635 \ MAP

E   F   G   H   J

1

VASCO   RD

RES

RES

OS

5

8

2

3

CREEK

BRUSHY PEAK
1702'

BRUSHY

RD

SEE / 677 \ MAP

13

18

DYER

17

4

5

R2E   R3E

RD

24

19

DYER

3900

20

6

RD

ACE

CREEK

RR

7

25

GOECKEN
RD

30

UP

ALTAMONT

ALTAMONT
PASS RD

29

E   F   G   H   J

SEE / 696 \ MAP

0   .125   .25   .375   .5

miles 1 in. = 1900 ft.

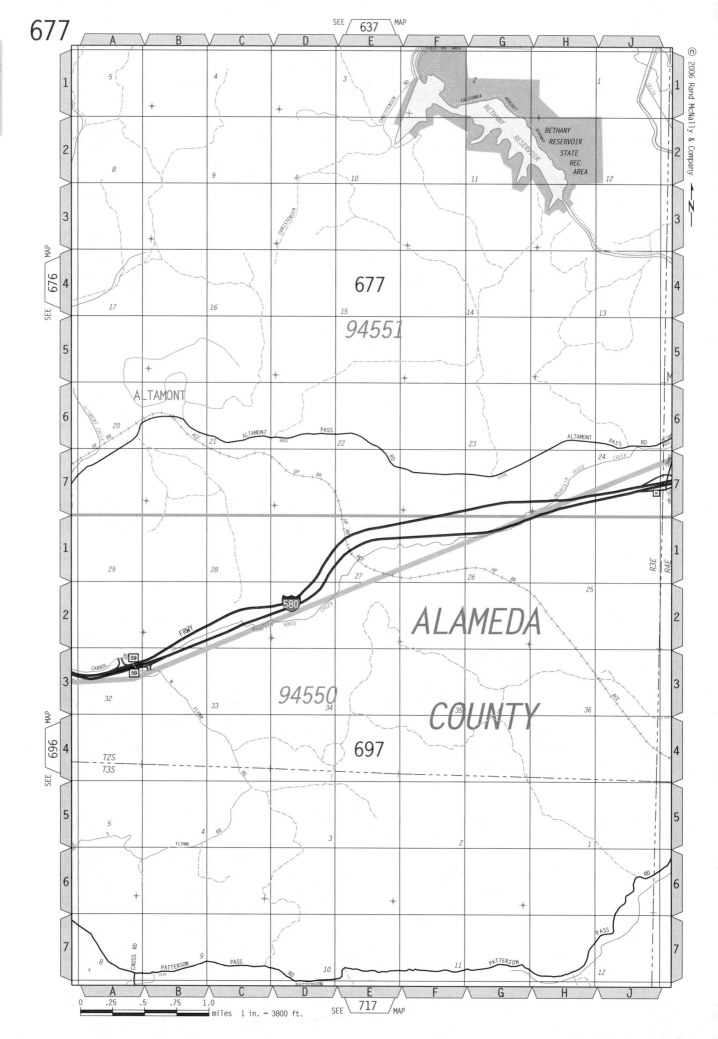

ALAMEDA CO.

SEE 637 MAP

—N—

SEE 676 MAP

STATE REC AREA

BETHANY RESERVOIR

CALIFORNIA

BETHANY RESERVOIR STATE REC AREA

677

94551

ALTAMONT

ALTAMONT PASS

ALTAMONT PASS RD

580 FRWY

ALAMEDA

59

59

CARROL RD

N FLYNN

94550

COUNTY

R3E R4F

697

T2S
T3S

SEE 696 MAP

FLYNN RD

CROSS RD

PATTERSON PASS

PATTERSON RD

PATTERSON PASS

SEE 717 MAP

0 .25 .5 .75 1.0
miles 1 in. = 3800 ft.

ALAMEDA CO.

© 2006 Rand McNally & Company

N

94551

678

BETHANY

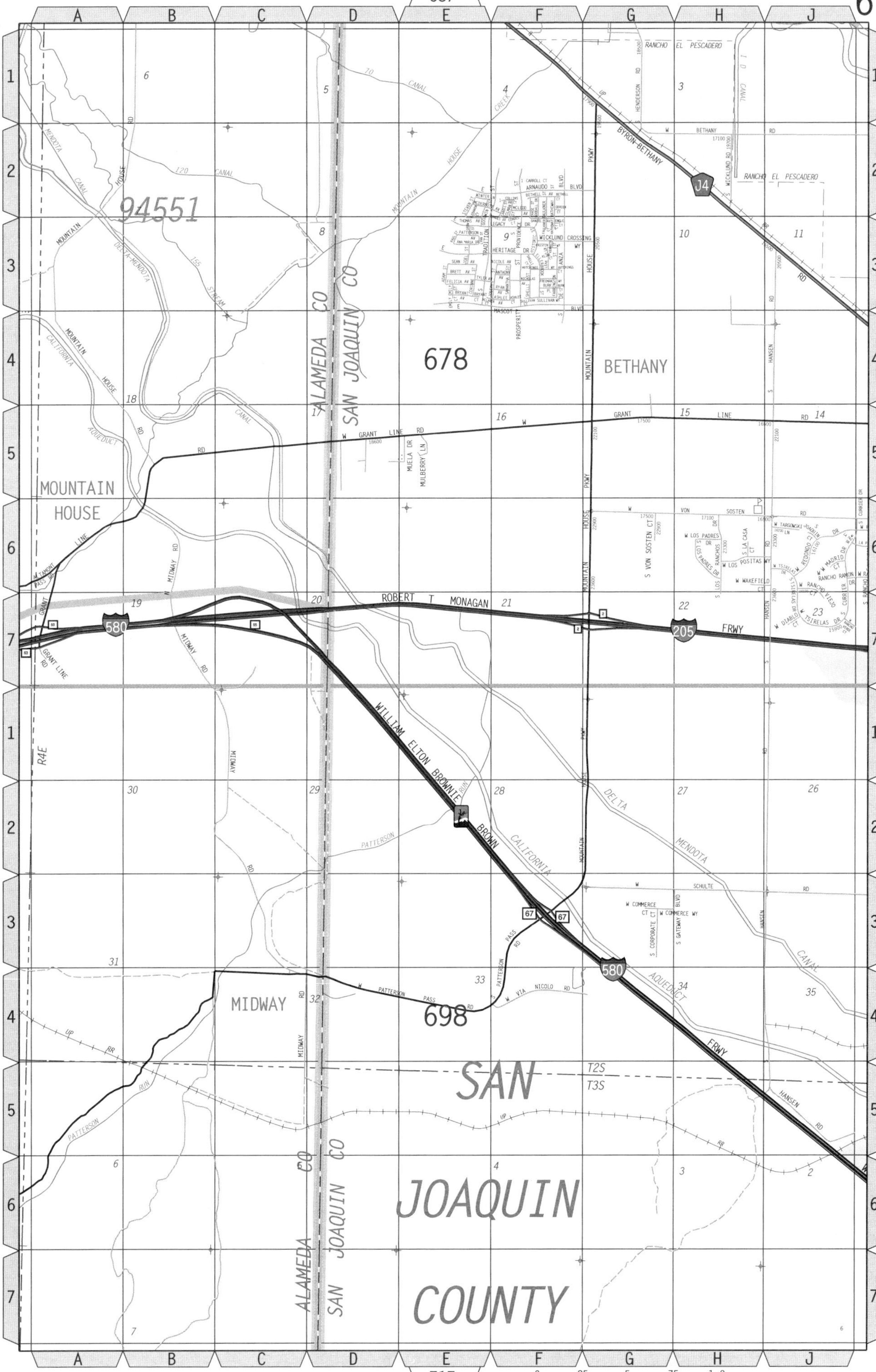

J4

MOUNTAIN HOUSE

RANCHO EL PESCADERO

RANCHO EL PESCADERO

GRANT LINE

ROBERT T MONAGAN FRWY

580

205

WILLIAM ELTON BROWN TE

67

67

580

698

MIDWAY

SAN

JOAQUIN

COUNTY

ALAMEDA CO

SAN JOAQUIN CO

T2S
T3S

0 .25 .5 .75 1.0
miles 1 in. = 3800 ft.

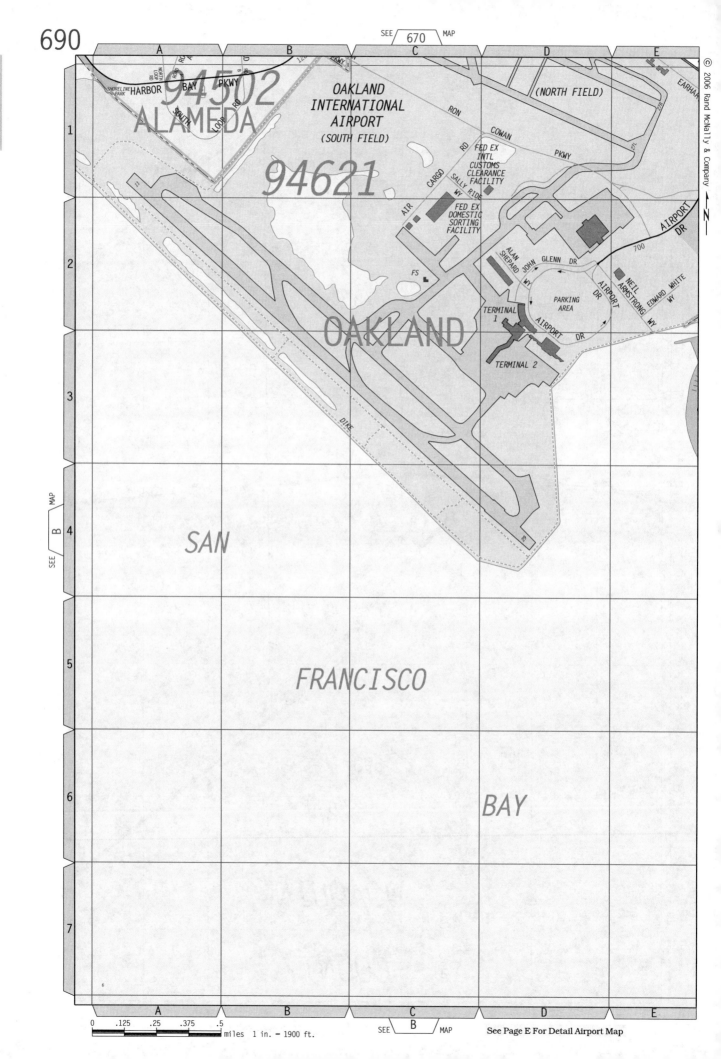

ALAMEDA CO.

SEE 670 MAP

94502
ALAMEDA

OAKLAND
INTERNATIONAL
AIRPORT
(SOUTH FIELD)

(NORTH FIELD)

94621

EARHAR

SHORELINE
PARK

HARBOR BAY PKWY

NORTH LOOP RD

SOUTH LOOP RD

RON

COWAN

FED EX
INTL
CUSTOMS
CLEARANCE
FACILITY

PKWY

CARGO RD

AIR

SALLY RIDE WY

FED EX
DOMESTIC
SORTING
FACILITY

AIRPORT DR

N

700

FS

ALAN SHEPARD WY

JOHN

GLENN DR

DR

NEIL ARMSTRONG WY

EDWARD WHITE WY

OAKLAND

AIRPORT DR

PARKING
AREA

AIRPORT DR

TERMINAL
1

TERMINAL 2

DIKE

SEE B MAP

SAN

FRANCISCO

BAY

0 .125 .25 .375 .5
miles 1 in. = 1900 ft.

SEE B MAP

See Page E For Detail Airport Map

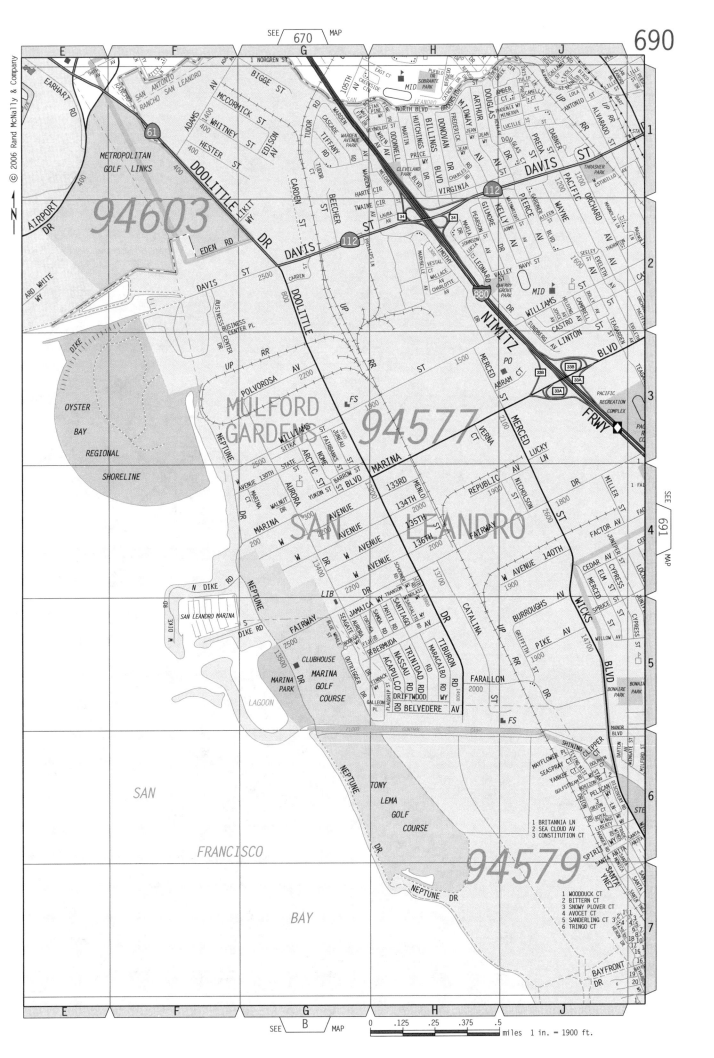

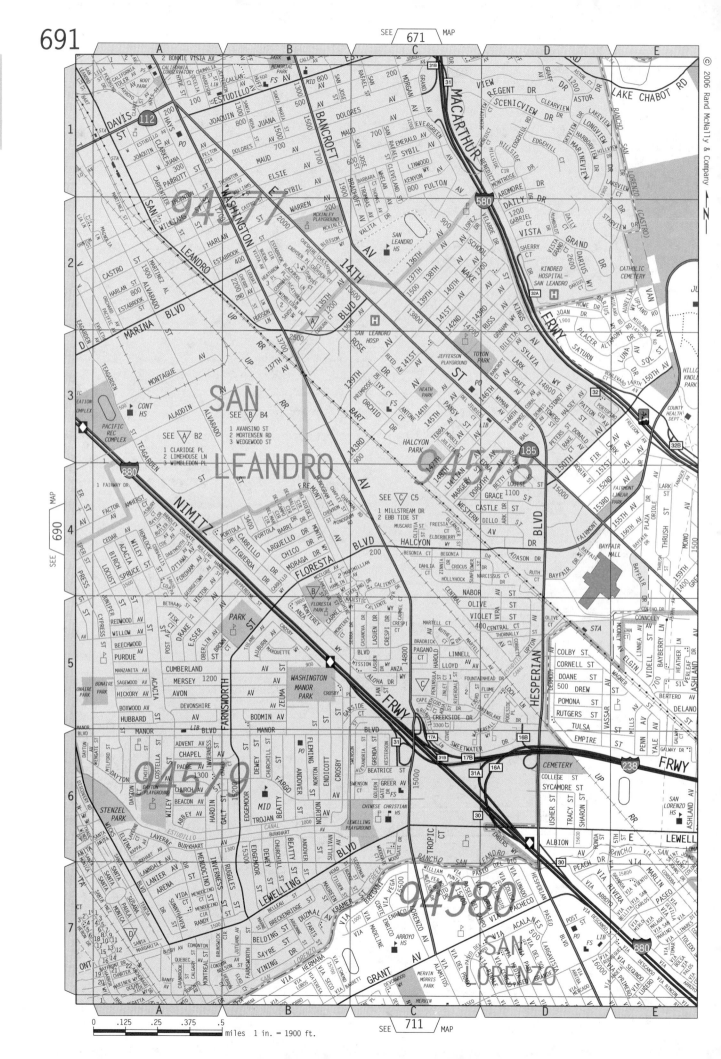

SAN
LEANDRO

94577

94578

94579

94580

SAN
LORENZO

SEE 690 MAP

0   .125   .25   .375   .5
miles   1 in. = 1900 ft.

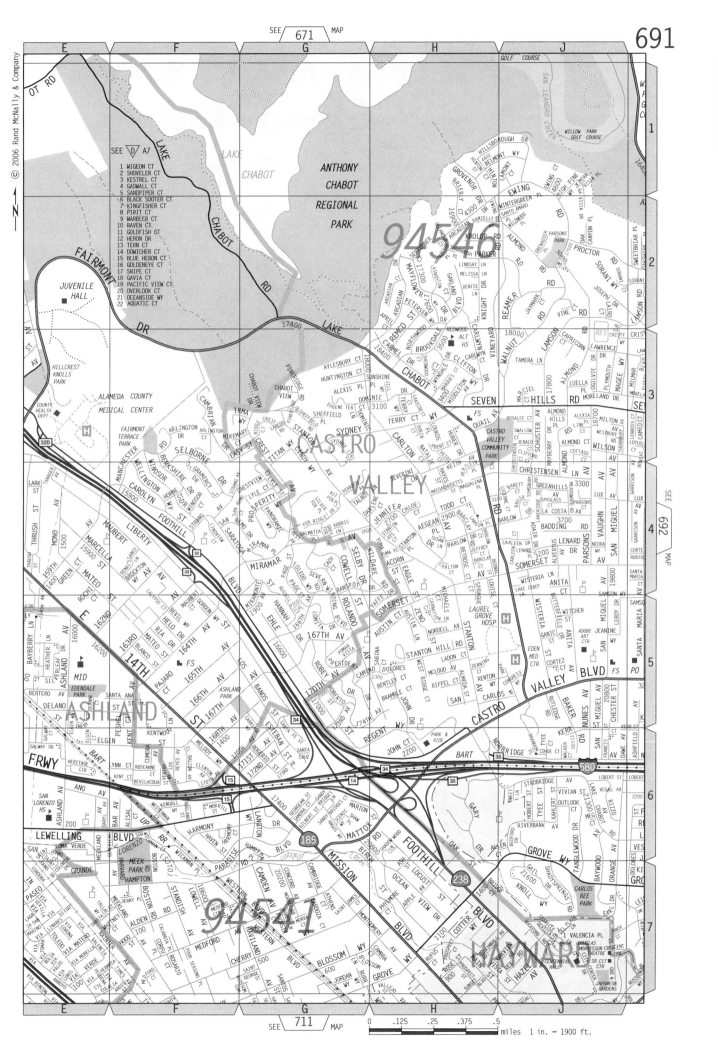

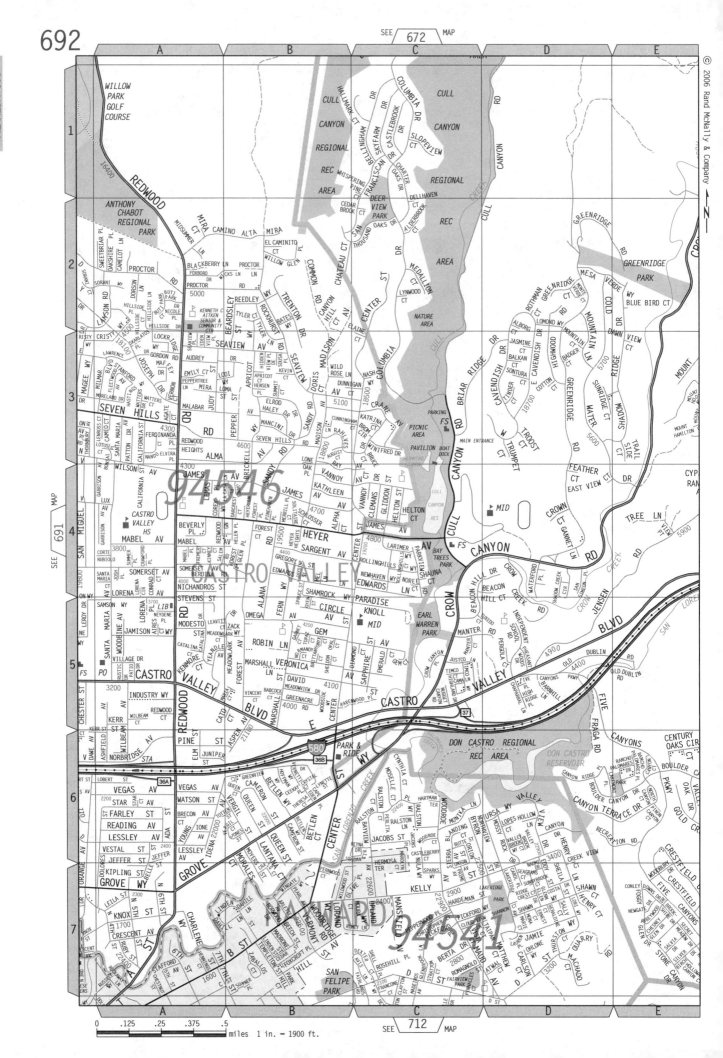

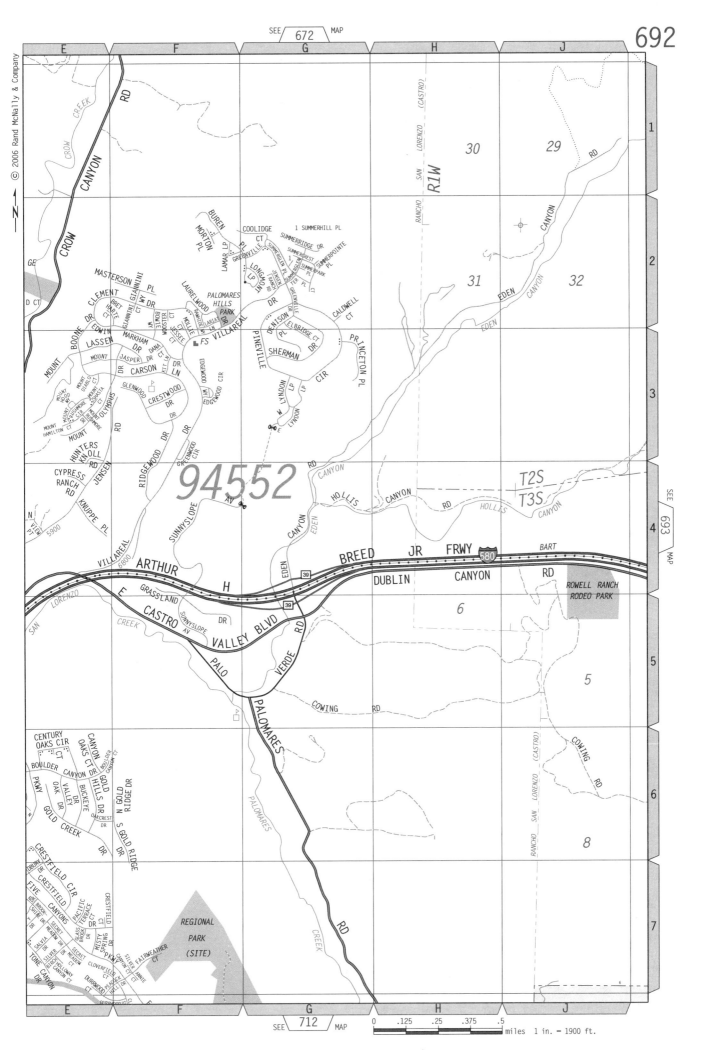

SEE 672 MAP

© 2006 Rand McNally & Company

N

CROW CREEK

CROW CANYON RD

GE

D CT

(CASTRO)

RANCHO SAN LORENZO

R1W

30

29

RD

31

32

EDEN CANYON

EDEN

BUREN

COOLIDGE

1 SUMMERHILL PL

MORTON PL

LAMAR LP

COOLIDGE CT

GREENVILLE PL

SUMMERGLEN PL

SUMMERRIDGE DR

SUMMERCREST

SUMMERPOINTE

LONGMONT LP

JENSEN RANCH RD

SUMMER PARK PL

SUMMER PARK PL

MASTERSON PL

CLEMENT

GIANNINI WY DR

GIANNINI

BRET HARTE CT

LAURELWOOD DR

PALOMARES HILLS PARK

GREENVILLE DR

CALDWELL CT

BOONE DR

EDWIN

BOWIE

WOOSTER CT

JESSEE CT

MILLIE WY

PAMWILLE WY

LABIA LN

FS VILLAREAL DR

DENISON

ELBRIDGE CT

PRINCETON PL

LASSEN

MARKHAM DR

DANA DR

DR

PINEVILLE

SHERMAN DR

SHERMAN CIR

MOUNT

JASPER DR

KIT LN

EDGEWOOD WY

EDGEWOOD CIR

CARSON

DR

MOUNT DIABLO

MOUNT SHASTA

RUSHMORE CT

MOUNT OLYMPUS

GLENWOOD DR

CRESTWOOD DR

CRESTWOOD DR

LYNDON LP

LYNDON LP

LYNDON

W

E

MOUNT SHOW WY

MOUNT RUSHMORE CT

MOUNT BENMORE

MOUNT BENMORE

RIDGEWOOD DR

GREENWOOD CIR

MOUNT HAMILTON CT

MOUNT

RD

HUNTERS KNOLL RD

CANYON

CYPRESS RANCH RD

JENSEN

N VIEW PT

5900

KNUPPE PL

94552

RD

CANYON

HOLLIS CANYON

RD

HOLLIS

CANYON

T2S

T3S

SUNNYSLOPE

EDEN

CANYON

EDEN

SEE 693 MAP

VILLAREAL

6800

ARTHUR

H

GRASSLAND DR

SUNNYSLOPE AV

DR

BREED   JR   FRWY

580

BART

1080

DUBLIN

CANYON

RD

6

39

ROWELL RANCH RODEO PARK

SAN LORENZO

CASTRO

E

VALLEY BLVD

39

VERDE RD

PALO

VERDE

5

5

COWING RD

PALOMARES

CENTURY OAKS CIR

CANYON OAKS CT

BOULDER CT

CANYON OAKS DR

BOULDER CANYON CT

CANYON CT

GOLD HILLS DR

GOLD RIDGE DR

COWING RD

RANCHO SAN LORENZO (CASTRO)

8

BOULDER PKWY

OAK VALLEY DR

BUCKEYE DR

N GOLD RIDGE DR

GOLD CREEK

OAKCREST DR

DR

S GOLD RIDGE DR

CRESTFIELD CIR

DRURY DR

CRESTFIELD

FIVE CANYONS

PACIFIC TERRACE

CRESTFIELD CT

MISTY SPRING

REGIONAL PARK (SITE)

SILVER BROOK

SPRING DR

GLASS MEADOW DR

SECRET SPRING

SALVIA DR

SILVER MEADOW CT

SECRET MEADOW

HOLLOWAY CT

CLOVERFIELD

CANYON CT

SILVER ANNIE

FAIRWEATHER CT

PEACOCK

DELL

TONE CANYON DR

DURGMOOD CT

CANYON CT

BURNWOOD DR

CREEK

RD

PALOMARES

0 .125 .25 .375 .5

miles 1 in. = 1900 ft.

E   F   G   H   J

693

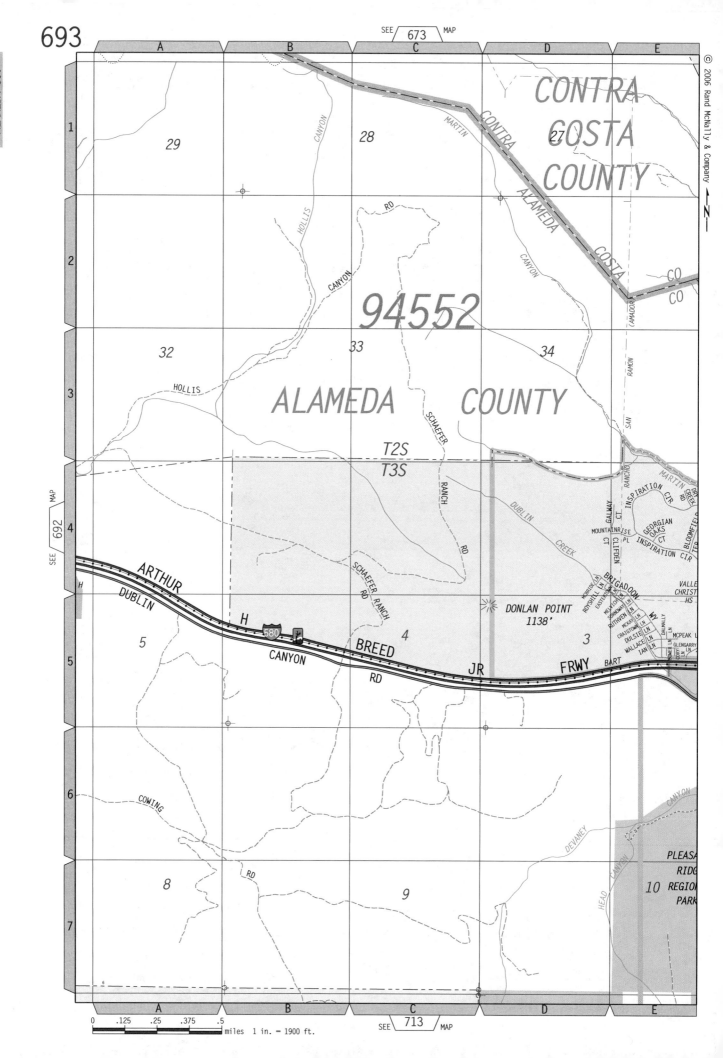

ALAMEDA CO.

SEE 673 MAP

© 2006 Rand McNally & Company

N

CONTRA COSTA COUNTY

CONTRA COSTA
ALAMEDA

CO CO

94552

ALAMEDA COUNTY

29

28

27

32

33

34

HOLLIS

HOLLIS

CANYON

CANYON

RD

MARTIN

CANYON

RAMON

SAN

CO CO

AMADOR

T2S
T3S

SCHAEFER RANCH RD

DUBLIN CREEK

RANCHO

MARTIN

DRY CREEK

GALWAY CT

INSPIRATION CIR

MOUNTAINRISE CT

CLIFDEN PL

GEORGIAN OAKS CT

INSPIRATION CIR

BLOOMFIELD TER

ARTHUR
DUBLIN

H

580

CANYON

BREED

RD

JR

FRWY

BART

SCHAEFER RANCH RD

DONLAN POINT 1138'

5

4

3

BRIGADOON

VALLE CHRIST HS

MCBRIDE LN

ROYSHILL LN

EXTENTION

SORNOWAY LN

RUTHVEN LN

MCKAY LN

CRAIGTOWN LN

DULSIE LN

WALLACE LN

IAN LN

DALMALLY

GLENGARRY LN

MCPEAK LN

SEE 692 MAP

COWING

RD

8

9

10

PLEASA RIDG REGIO PARK

DEVANEY

HEAD CANYON

CANYON

0 .125 .25 .375 .5   miles 1 in. = 1900 ft.

SEE 713 MAP

A   B   C   D   E

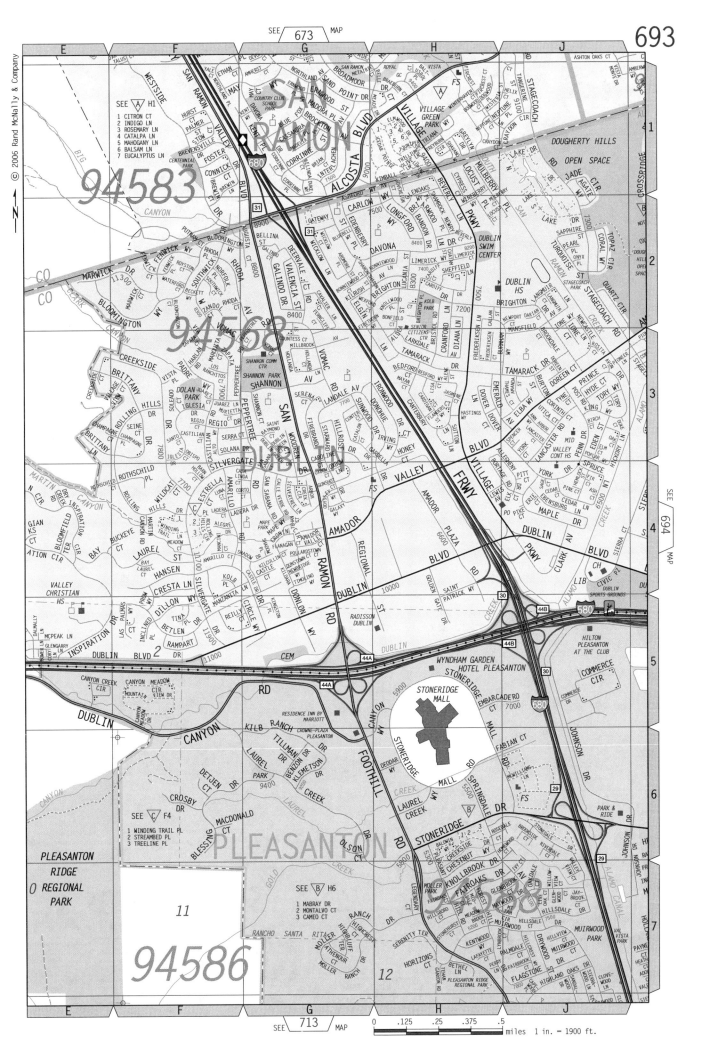

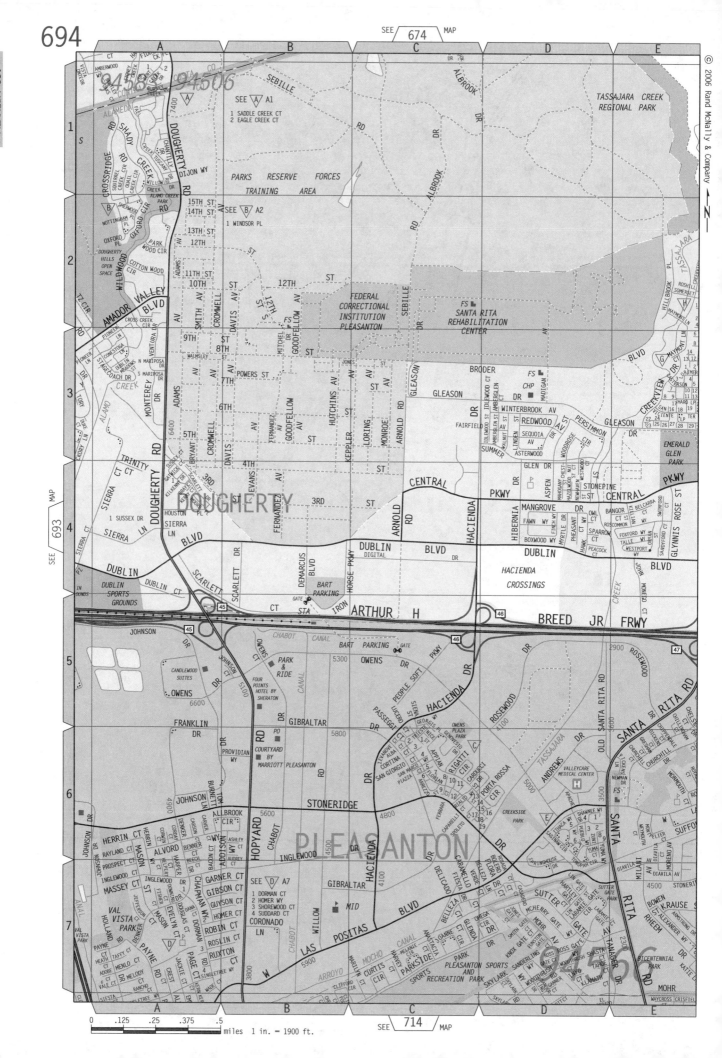

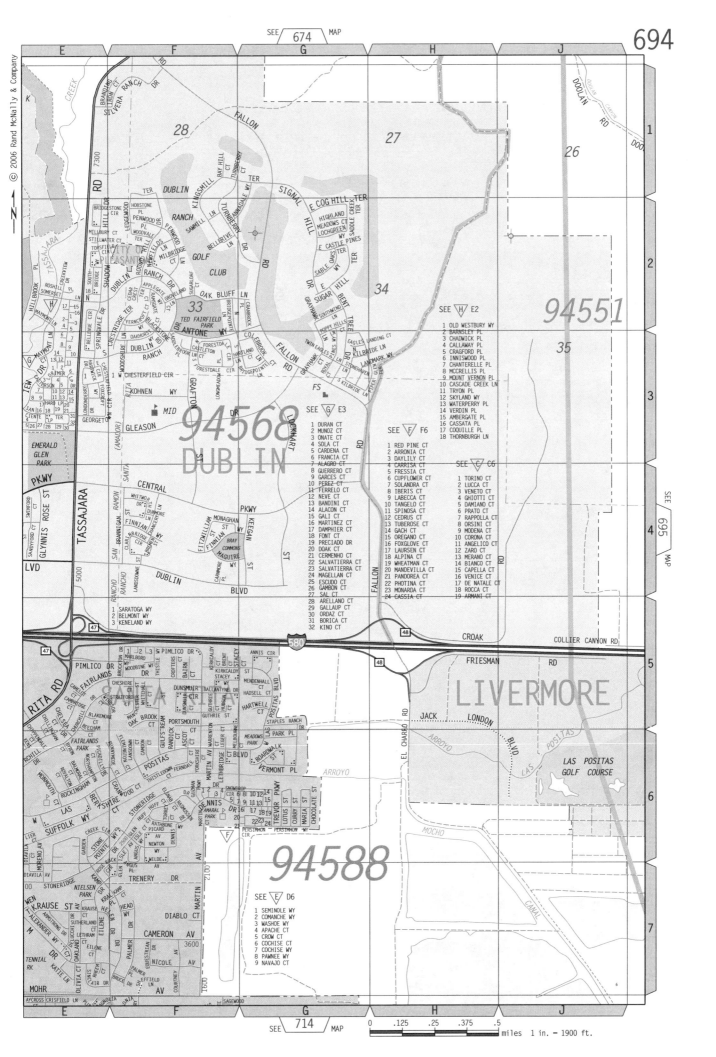

ALAMEDA CO.

94551

94568

DUBLIN

94588

LIVERMORE

SEE H E2
1 OLD WESTBURY WY
2 BARNSLEY PL
3 CHADWICK PL
4 CALLAWAY PL
5 CRAGFORD PL
6 INNISWOOD PL
7 CHANTERELLE PL
8 MCCRELLIS PL
9 MOUNT VERNON PL
10 CASCADE CREEK LN
11 TRYON PL
12 SKYLAND WY
13 WATERPERRY PL
14 VERDIN PL
15 AMBERGATE PL
16 CASSATA PL
17 COQUILLE PL
18 THORNBURGH LN

SEE G E3
1 DURAN CT
2 MUNOZ CT
3 ONATE CT
4 SOLA CT
5 CARDENA CT
6 FRANCIA CT
7 ALAGRO CT
8 GUERRERO CT
9 GARCES CT
10 PEREZ CT
11 FERRELO CT
12 NEVE CT
13 BANDINI CT
14 ALACON CT
15 GALI CT
16 MARTINEZ CT
17 DAMPHIER CT
18 FONT CT
19 PRECIADO DR
20 DOAK CT
21 CERMENHO CT
22 SALVATIERRA CT
23 SALVATIERRA CT
24 MAGELLAN CT
25 ESCUDO CT
26 GAMBON CT
27 SAL CT
28 ARELLANO CT
29 GALLAUP CT
30 ORDAZ CT
31 BORICA CT
32 KINO CT

1 SARATOGA WY
2 BELMONT WY
3 KENELAND WY

SEE F F6
1 RED PINE CT
2 ARRONIA CT
3 DAYLILY CT
4 CARRISA CT
5 FRESSIA CT
6 CUPFLOWER CT
7 SOLANDRA CT
8 IBERIS CT
9 LABECCA CT
10 TANGELO CT
11 SPINOSA CT
12 CEDRUS CT
13 TUBEROSE CT
14 GACH CT
15 OREGANO CT
16 FOXGLOVE CT
17 LAURSEN CT
18 ALPINA CT
19 WHEATMAN CT
20 MANDEVILLA CT
21 PANDOREA CT
22 PHOTINA CT
23 MONARDA CT
24 CASSIA CT

SEE C C6
1 TORINO CT
2 LUCCA CT
3 VENETO CT
4 GHIOTTI CT
5 DAMIANO CT
6 PRATO CT
7 RAPPOLLA CT
8 ORSINI CT
9 MODENA CT
10 CORONA CT
11 ANGELICO CT
12 ZARO CT
13 MERANO CT
14 BIANCO CT
15 CAPELLA CT
16 VENICE CT
17 DE NATALE CT
18 ROCCA CT
19 ARMANI CT

SEE E D6
1 SEMINOLE WY
2 COMANCHE WY
3 WASHOE WY
4 APACHE CT
5 CROW CT
6 COCHISE CT
7 COCHISE WY
8 PAWNEE WY
9 NAVAJO CT

0 .125 .25 .375 .5
miles 1 in. = 1900 ft.

695

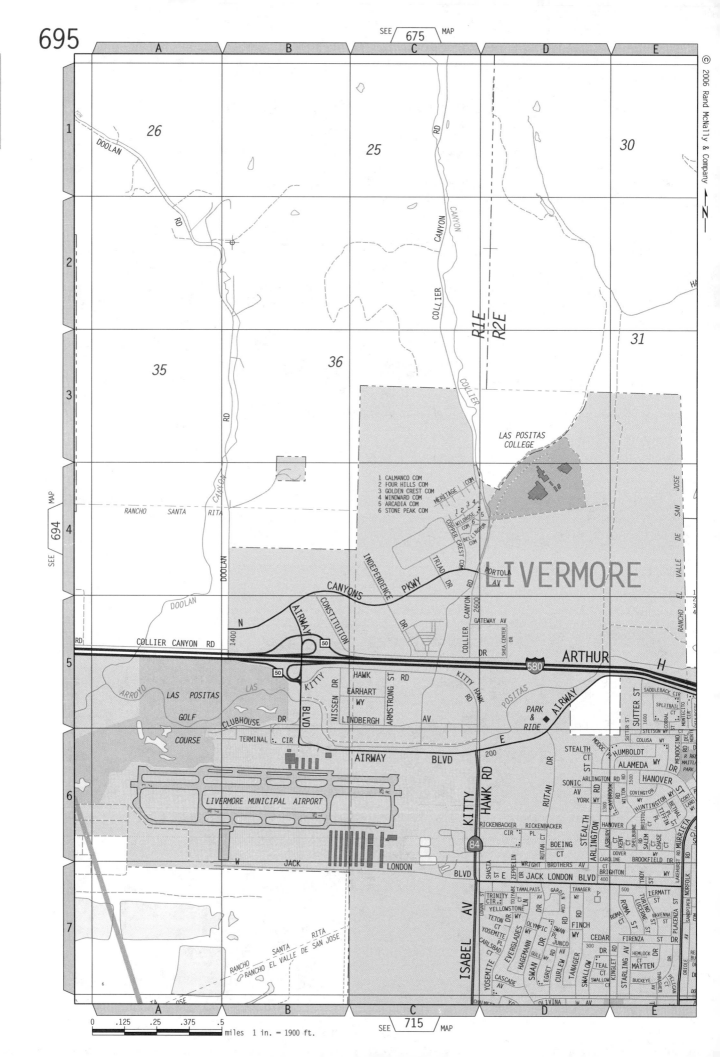

© 2006 Rand McNally & Company

SEE 675 MAP

A   B   C   D   E

1 26   25   30

DOOLAN RD

2

COLLIER CANYON

R1E R2E

31

3 35   36   COLLIER

LAS POSITAS COLLEGE

SEE 694 MAP

RANCHO SANTA RITA

1 CALMANCO COM
2 FOUR HILLS COM
3 GOLDEN CREST COM
4 WINDWARD COM
5 ARCADIA COM
6 STONE PEAK COM

MERITAGE COM
1 2 3 4
WILDROSE COM
6 5
COPPER CREST COM
BELLINGTON COM

PORTOLA AV

LIVERMORE

4 DOOLAN   CANYON   CANYONS   PKWY   INDEPENDENCE   TRIAD DR   COLLIER CANYON 2600   RANCHO EL VALLE DE SAN JOSE
1
2
3
4

CONSTITUTION   DR   GATEWAY AV   SHEA CENTER DR

RD   N   AIRWAY   1400   COLLIER CANYON RD   50   DR

5 RD   COLLIER CANYON RD   50   ARTHUR   I-580   H

ARROYO LAS   KITTY   HAWK   HAWK   KITTY HAWK RD   LAS POSITAS   PARK & RIDE   AIRWAY   SADDLEBACK CIR
LAS POSITAS GOLF   NISSEN DR   EARHART WY   ARMSTRONG ST RD   RD   SPLITRAIL   CT
COURSE   CLUBHOUSE   DR   BLVD   LINDBERGH   AV   RUTAN DR   E   CORRAL ST   MONTECITO ST
TERMINAL CIR   E   200   STEALTH CT   HUMBOLDT   DEL RE
AIRWAY   BLVD   KITTY HAWK RD   STEALTH   ALAMEDA WY   MAITLA PARK
SONIC AV   ARLINGTON RD   HANOVER   MENDOCINO DR
6 LIVERMORE MUNICIPAL AIRPORT   YORK WY   1300   COVINGTON WY   BETHEL ST   LAND CT   R   LAND
ARLINGTON RD   1500   HUNTINGTON WY   TIFFIN ST   MURRIETA
HANOVER   BRISTOL ST   SHELBURNE RD   CHASE WY
RICKENBACKER CIR   RICKENBACKER PL   ASBURY CT   SALEM CT
BOEING CT   RUTAN CT   DOVER   BROOKFIELD WY   LAKEHURST RD   NORFOLK
W   JACK   LONDON   BLVD   84   ZEPPELIN DR   WRIGHT BROTHERS AV   CAROLINE CT   TRBY WY
BRIGHTON   400
SHASTA ST E   JACK LONDON BLVD   ZERMATT CT
7 LOGAN ST   TAMALPAIS   TANAGER   GARDEN RD   500   ROMA ST   TURING ST   PLACENZA
TRINITY CIR   DR   DR   LUCERNE
YELLOWSTONE WY   OLYMPIC DR   WY   RAVENNA ST   AV   SANDPIPER
TETON CT   SWAN PL   FINCH WY   FIRENZA ST   DEL
RANCHO   RANCHO EL VALLE DE SAN JOSE   YOSEMITE   JUNCO   CEDAR   300
SANTA RITA   HAGEMANN   CURLEM AV   STARLING AV   HEMLOCK CT   RE
CARLSBAD   TAMGER   SWALLOW   KINGLET RD   MAYTEN
ISABEL AV   CASCADE AV   SWAN   EGRET   TEAL CT   DR   BUCKEYE   ORIOLE
YOSEMITE CT   GULL WY   SWALLOW AV   THRASHER
CHALMER   OLIVINA   AV

0 .125 .25 .375 .5
miles 1 in. = 1900 ft.

SEE 715 MAP

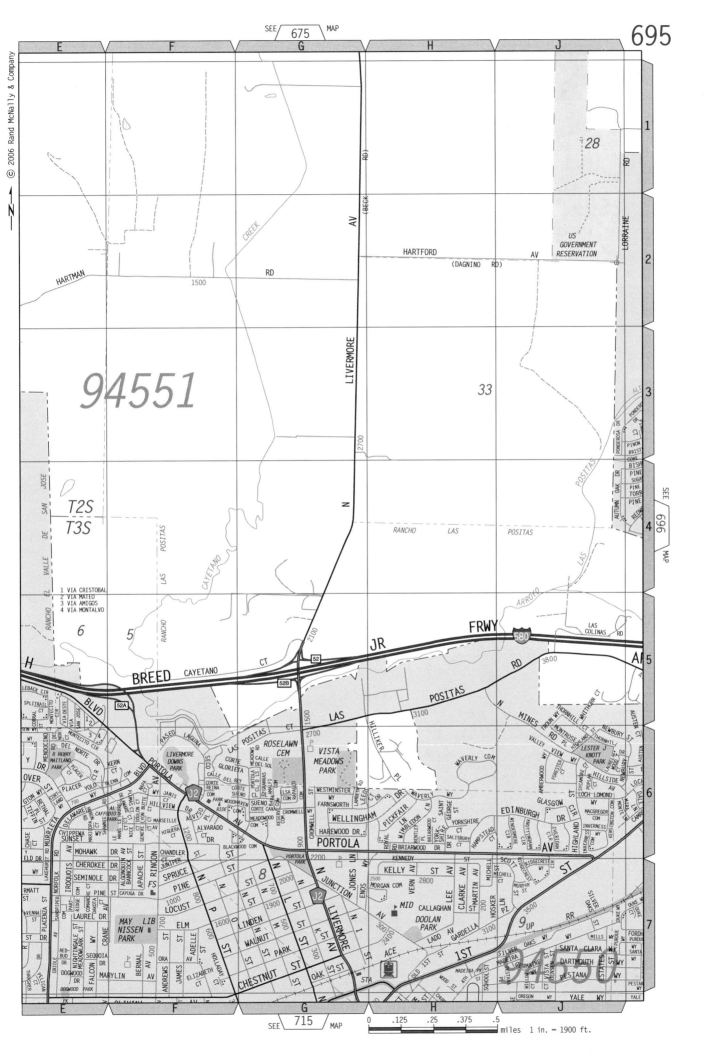

SEE 675 MAP

SEE 696 MAP

SEE 715 MAP

94551

94550

US GOVERNMENT RESERVATION

1 in. = 1900 ft.

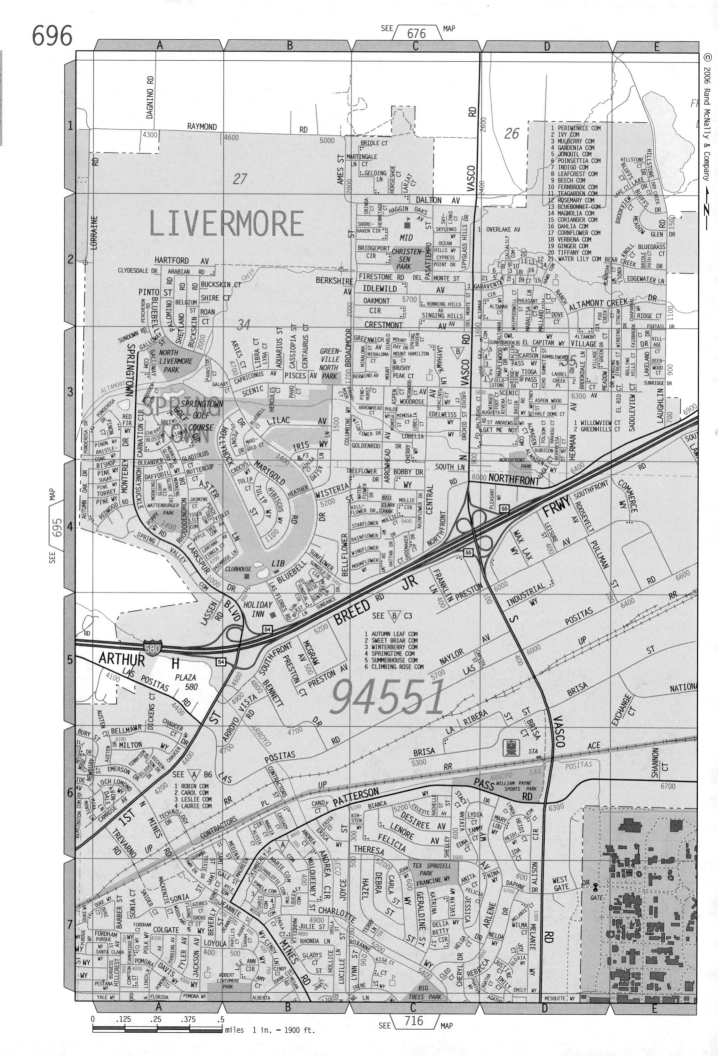

© 2006 Rand McNally & Company

E F R2E | R3E G H J

FRICK
LAKE

25

30

29

1

GOECKEN RD

R3R
R EN
RD ASS
CT
DR
LN
CT
TAIL ILL-GE
CT EER-OOD
CT IDGE
DR
DR
DR
DR

1500 DR

1100

ALTAMONT

ACE

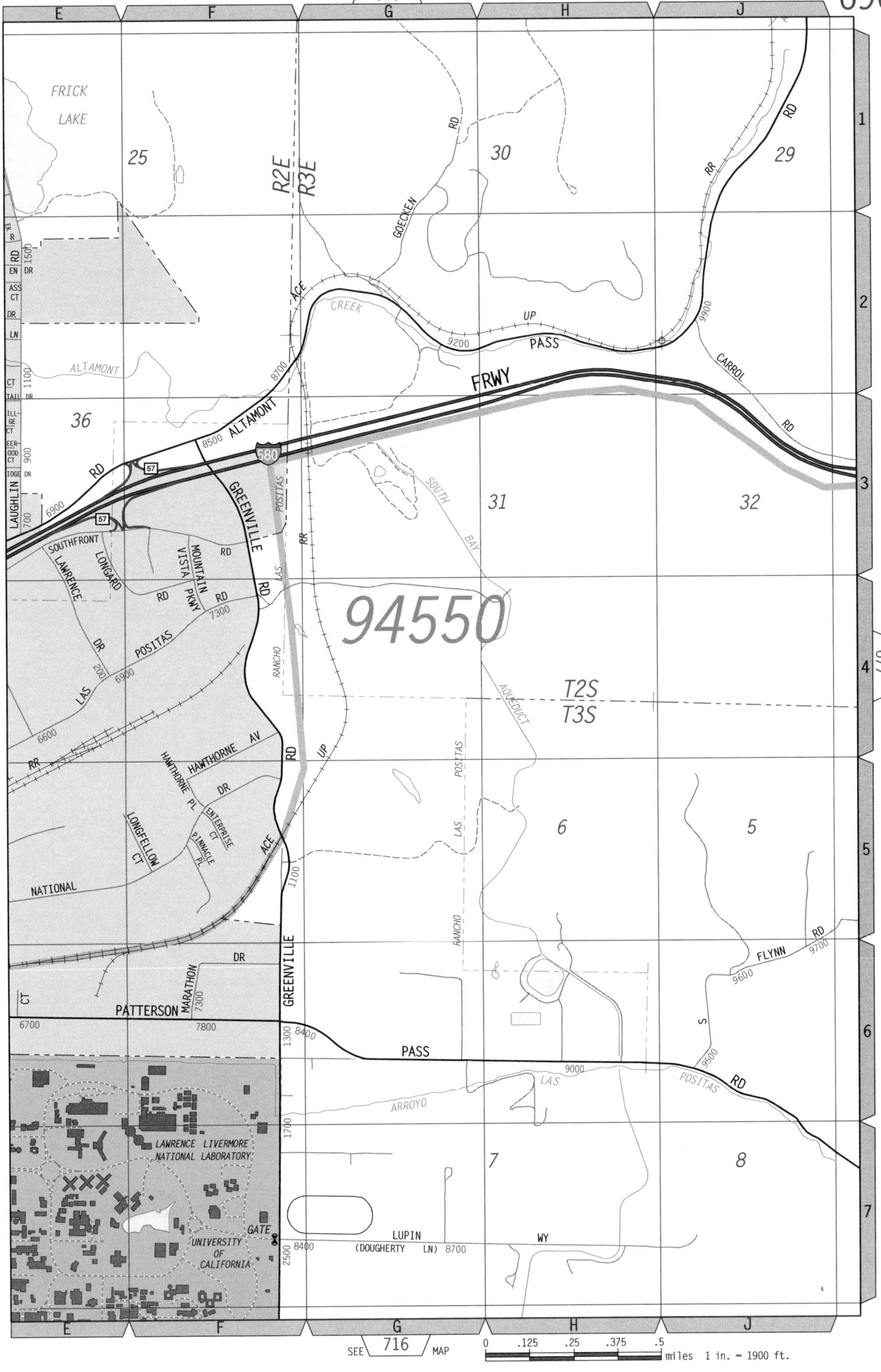

CREEK

9200

UP PASS

9900

CARROL

2

RR

36

ALTAMONT RD

8700

8500 ALTAMONT

57

580

FRWY

RD

3

900

LAUGHLIN RD

6900 700

57

SOUTHFRONT

LAWRENCE LONGARD

POSITAS RD

MOUNTAIN VISTA PKWY

GREENVILLE RD

RD

RD

RD 7300

POSITAS RR

SOUTH BAY

31

32

94550

4

LAS DR

200

6900

LAS

6600

RANCHO RD

UP

HAWTHORNE AV

HAWTHORNE PL

DR

ENTERPRISE CT

PINNACLE PL

LONGFELLOW CT

NATIONAL

1100

ACE

AQUEDUCT

LAS POSITAS

T2S
T3S

6

5

LAS

RANCHO

FLYNN RD

9700

9600

S

9500

RD

6

MARATHON DR

7300

CT

PATTERSON

6700 7800

GREENVILLE RD

1300 8400

PASS

ARROYO

9000

LAS

POSITAS RD

LAWRENCE LIVERMORE
NATIONAL LABORATORY

1700

XXX

7

8

GATE

UNIVERSITY
OF
CALIFORNIA

2500 8400

LUPIN
(DOUGHERTY LN) 8700

WY

7

6

E F G H J

0 .125 .25 .375 .5 miles 1 in. = 1900 ft.

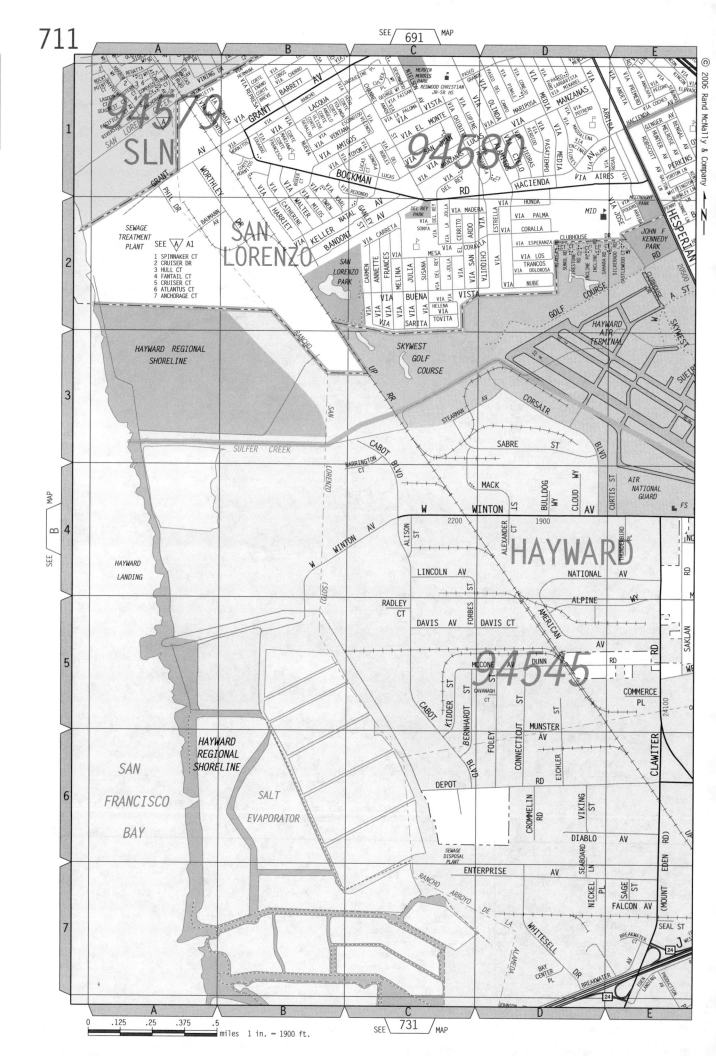

© 2006 Rand McNally & Company

94579
SLN

94580

SAN
LORENZO

SEWAGE
TREATMENT
PLANT

SEE ▽ A1
1 SPINNAKER CT
2 CRUISER DR
3 HULL CT
4 FANTAIL CT
5 CRUISER CT
6 ATLANTUS CT
7 ANCHORAGE CT

SAN
LORENZO
PARK

HAYWARD REGIONAL
SHORELINE

SULFER CREEK

HAYWARD
LANDING

SAN
FRANCISCO
BAY

HAYWARD
REGIONAL
SHORELINE

SALT
EVAPORATOR

SKYWEST
GOLF
COURSE

HAYWARD
AIR
TERMINAL

JOHN F
KENNEDY
PARK

AIR
NATIONAL
GUARD

HAYWARD

94545

SEWAGE
DISPOSAL
PLANT

0 .125 .25 .375 .5 miles   1 in. = 1900 ft.

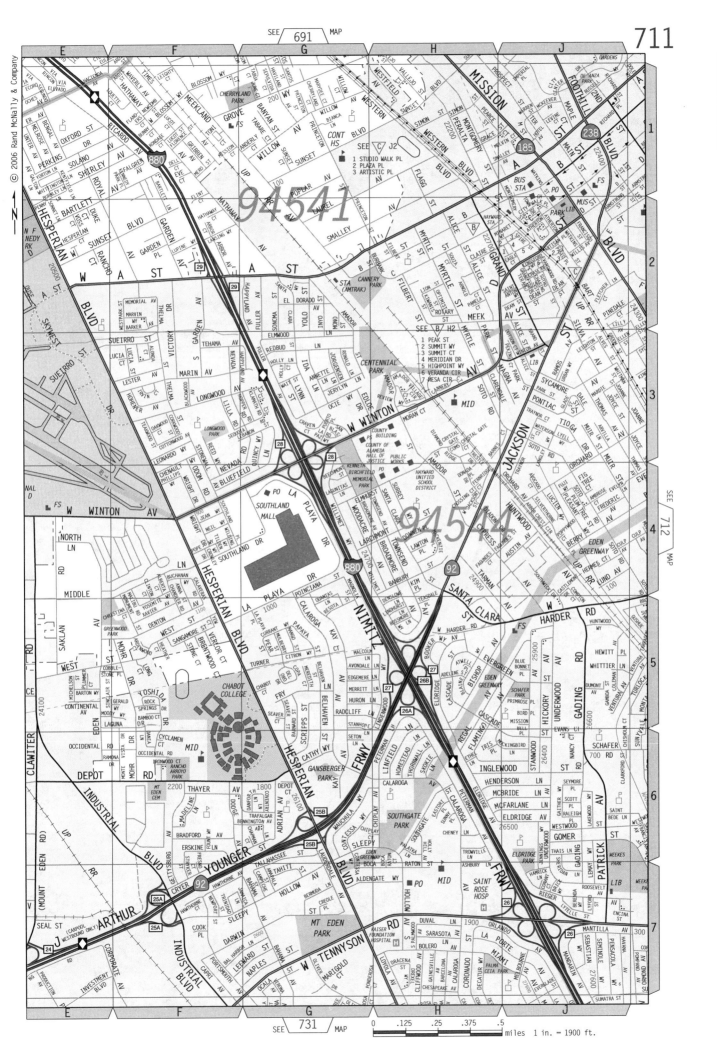

94541

94544

© 2006 Rand McNally & Company

SEE 712 MAP

0 .125 .25 .375 .5
miles 1 in. = 1900 ft.

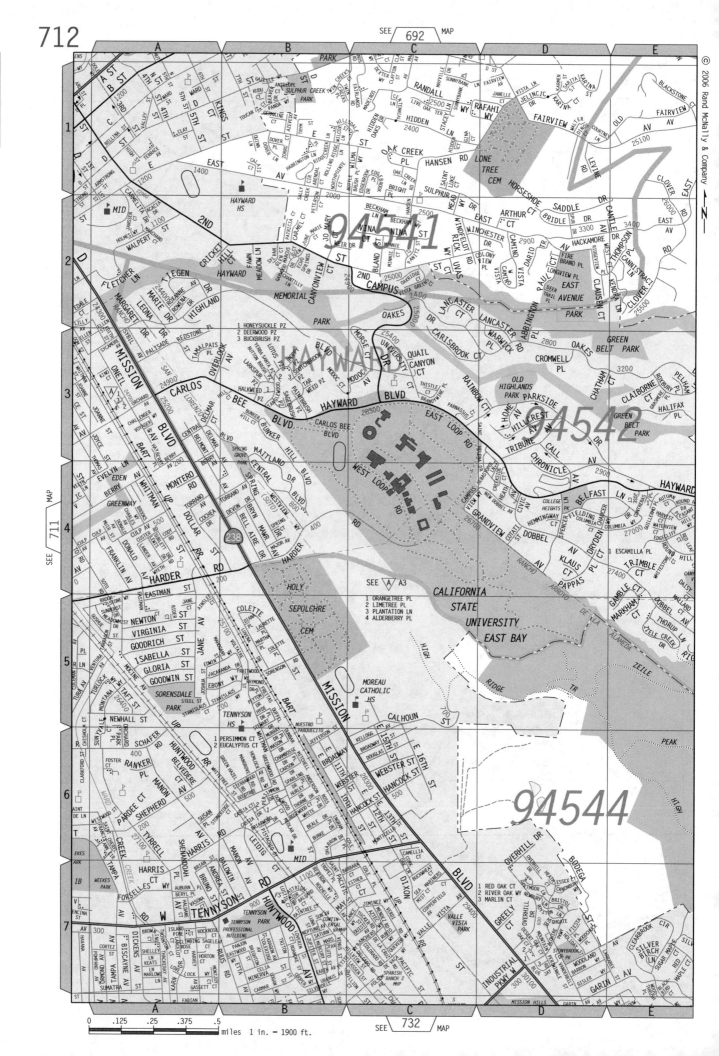

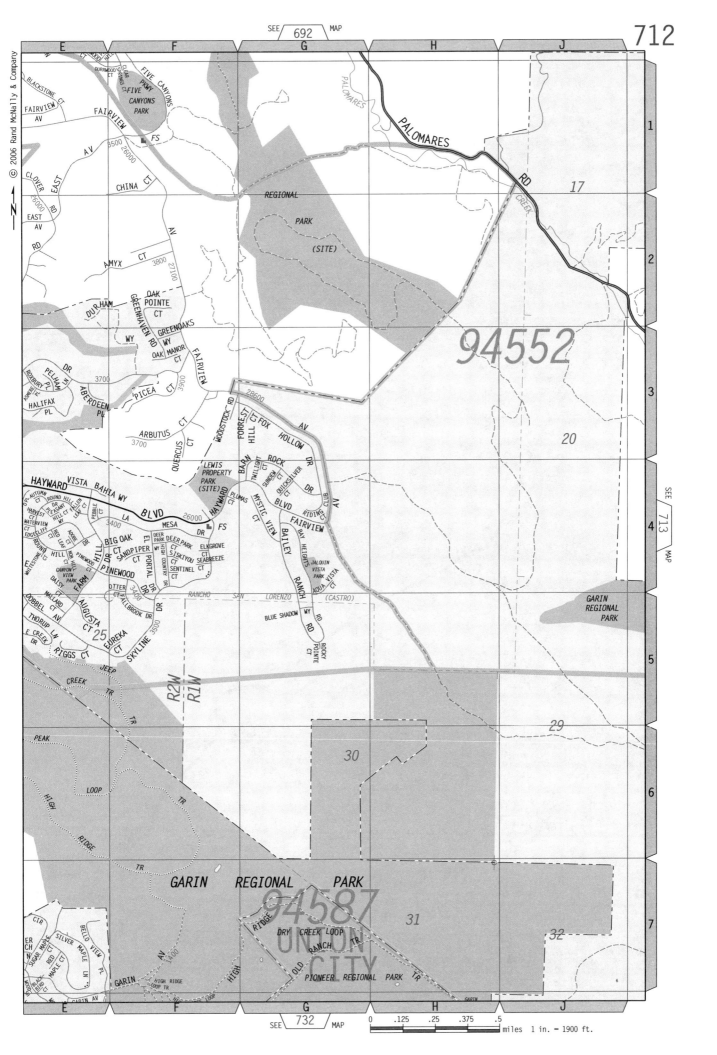

ALAMEDA CO.

© 2006 Rand McNally & Company

SEE 692 MAP

E   F   G   H   J

1

2

3

4

5

6

7

SEE 713 MAP

94552

17

20

PALOMARES RD

CREEK

REGIONAL PARK (SITE)

BLACKSTONE CT
FAIRVIEW AV
FAIRVIEW AV
CLOVER RD
EAST AV
EAST RD
CHINA CT
FIVE CANYONS PARK
FIVE CANYONS PKWY
CLEAR SPRINGS CT
DURRWOOD CT
FS
3500 26000

AMYX CT
3800 27100
DURHAM
GREENHAVEN RD
OAK POINTE CT
GREENOAKS WY
OAK MANOR
FAIRVIEW AV
3700 3900

PELHAM DR
ROXBURY PL
ASHORE PL
HALIFAX PL
ABERDEEN PL
PICEA CT
ARBUTUS CT
QUERCUS CT
3700

WOODSTOCK RD
28600
FORREST HILL CT
FOX HOLLOW AV
BARN
TWILIGHT CT
ROCK
SUNDEW CT
QUICKSILVER DR
RIDING CT
DR
AV

LEWIS PROPERTY PARK (SITE)

HAYWARD VISTA BAHIA WY
BLVD
26000
HAYWARD
PLUMAS CT
MYSTIC VIEW CT
MESA DR
FS

AUTUMN
ROUND HILL
PL
PLEASANT
HARVEST CT
HILL CT
FALLEN LEAF CT
WATERVIEW CT
WY
PEBBLE
EDGECLIFF CT
RED LEAF CT
3400
ADOBE
ROUND HILL
NEB
PINEWOOD
WHITESTONE CT
BIG OAK CT
SANDPIPER
EL PORTAL DR
DEER PARK
DEER PARK CT
HIGH COUNTRY DR
ELKGROVE CT
SISKIYOU CT
SEABREEZE
CANYON VIEW PARK
HILL
PINEWOOD DR
FARM
SENTINEL CT
DAISY CT
OTTER CT
3400
MALLARD CT
FALLBROOK DR
DOBBEL AV
THORUP LN
E CREEK DR
AUGUSTA CT
EUREKA CT
SKYLINE DR
3500
RIGGS CT
25

FAIRVIEW
BAILEY
BAY HEIGHTS CT
RANCH
BLVD
JALQUIN VISTA PARK
AQUA VISTA CT

RANCHO SAN LORENZO (CASTRO)
BLUE SHADOW WY
RD
ROCKY POINTE CT

GARIN REGIONAL PARK

R2W R1W

JEEP TR
CREEK
TR

PEAK
HIGH
LOOP TR
RIDGE TR

29

30

31

32

GARIN REGIONAL PARK

94587 UNION CITY

CIR
ERCH
SUGAR MAPLE
RED
BLACK
MAPLE CT
BELLO VIEW
SILVER MAPLE LN
PL
BLVD
GARIN
GARIN AV
AV
1400
HIGH RIDGE LOOP TR
RIDGE TR
DRY CREEK LOOP
RANCH TR
OLD
HIGH
LOOP
PIONEER REGIONAL PARK
GARIN
TR

0 .125 .25 .375 .5 miles   1 in. = 1900 ft.

SEE 693 MAP

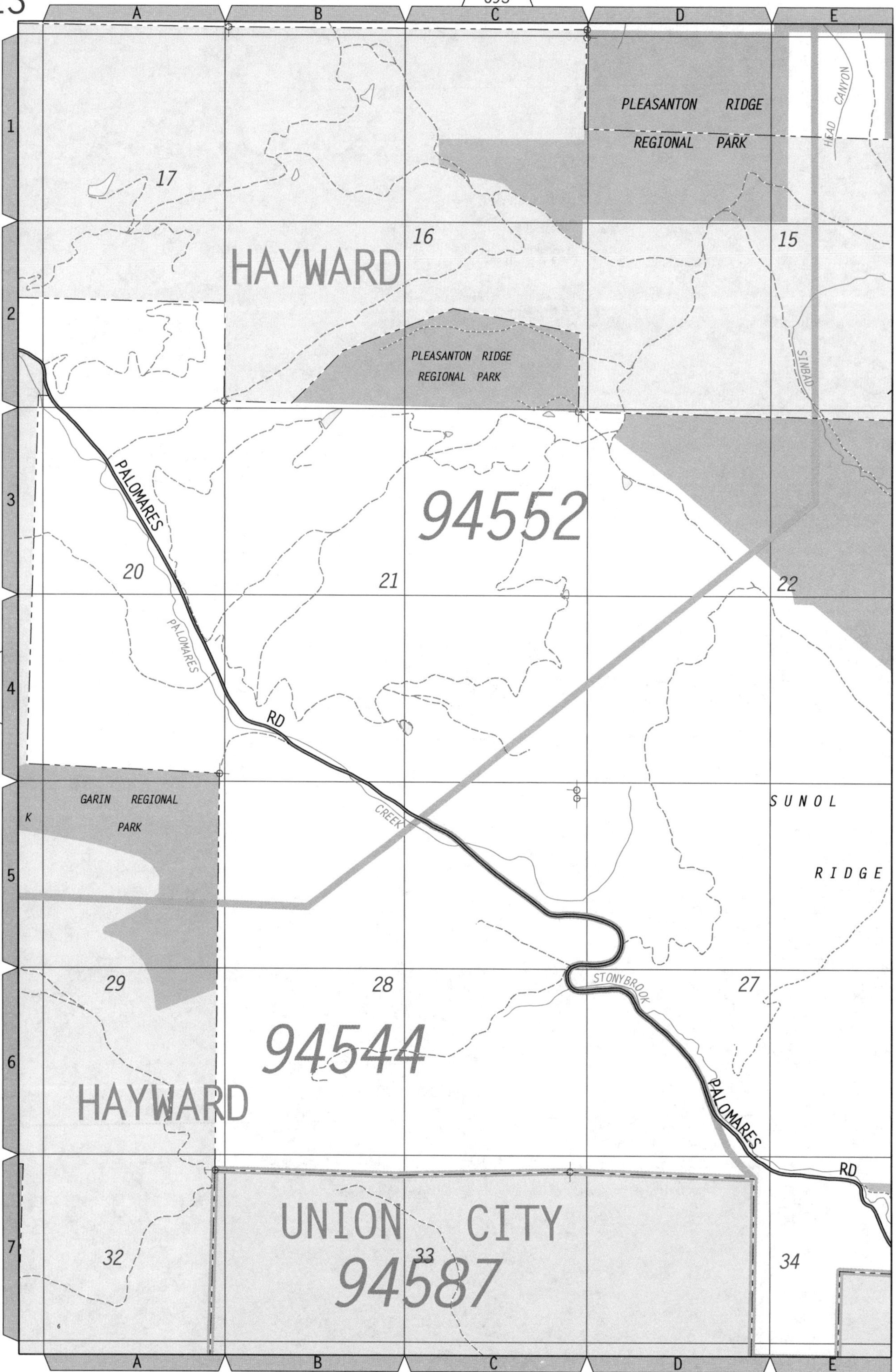

A   B   C   D   E

—N—

1

PLEASANTON RIDGE
REGIONAL PARK

HEAD CANYON

17

16

HAYWARD

15

2

PLEASANTON RIDGE
REGIONAL PARK

SINBAD

PALOMARES

3

94552

20

PALOMARES

21

22

SEE 712 MAP

4

RD

CREEK

GARIN REGIONAL
PARK

SUNOL

RIDGE

K

5

29

28

STONYBROOK

27

6

94544

PALOMARES

HAYWARD

RD

7

UNION CITY
94587

32

33

34

A   B   C   D   E

SEE 733 MAP

0   .125   .25   .375   .5

miles   1 in. = 1900 ft.

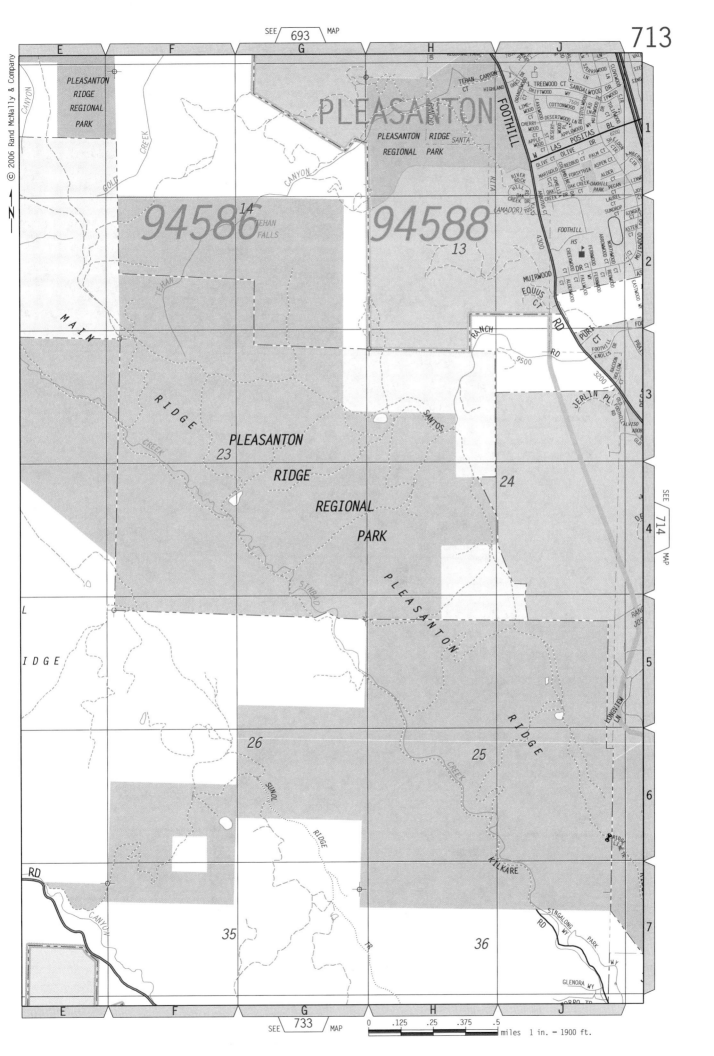

ALAMEDA CO.

SEE 693 MAP

E F G H J

1

PLEASANTON RIDGE REGIONAL PARK

PLEASANTON

PLEASANTON RIDGE Santa
REGIONAL PARK

FOOTHILL

TREEWOOD CT SANDALWOOD CT
TEHAN CANYON
CT
HIGHLAND
OAKS DR
ORANGEWOOD DR
DRIFTWOOD WY
LIME WOOD CT
LAKEWOOD CT
CHERRY WOOD CT
DESERTWOOD WY
COTTONWOOD WY
APPLE WOOD CT
LAS POSITAS BL
6200
W LAS POSITAS OLIVE
OLIVE CT PALM CT
MARIGOLD REDBUD CT
CAMELLIA FORSYTHIA
OAK CREEK OAK CT
ARBUTUS CT OAK CREEK DR
RIVER ROCK
OAK HILL
OAKHILL PARK
ASPEN CT
ALDER
PECAN
LAUREL
SUNDROP
GINGER
LINW
JOS
ASTER CT
MULBERRY CT

94586
14
TEHAN FALLS

94588
13

RITA (AMADOR)

FOOTHILL HS

NORTHWOOD CT
CREEKWOOD
FERNWOOD DR
ARROWOOD CT
REDWOOD
FERNWOOD
EASTWOOD

MUIRWOOD

EQUUS CT

ALDERWOOD
FALLWOOD

2

MAIN

RIDGE

RANCH
9500

PURI
CT
FOOTHILL KNOLLS
MELLOW
PRAI
FO

RD

JERLIN PL
3200
OLD FOOTHILL RD
ALVISO
ADOBE
OLD

3

PLEASANTON
23

SANTOS

24

SEE 714 MAP

JO
DE

4

RIDGE

L

IDGE

PLEASANTON

RANG
JOS

RIDGE

LONGVIEW LN

5

26

25

CREEK

RIDGE LINE TR

6

SUNOL

RIDGE

KILKARE

35

36

SINGALONG WY
PARK
GLENORA WY
CORRO TR
RD
WY

7

E F G H J

SEE 733 MAP

0 .125 .25 .375 .5
miles 1 in. = 1900 ft.

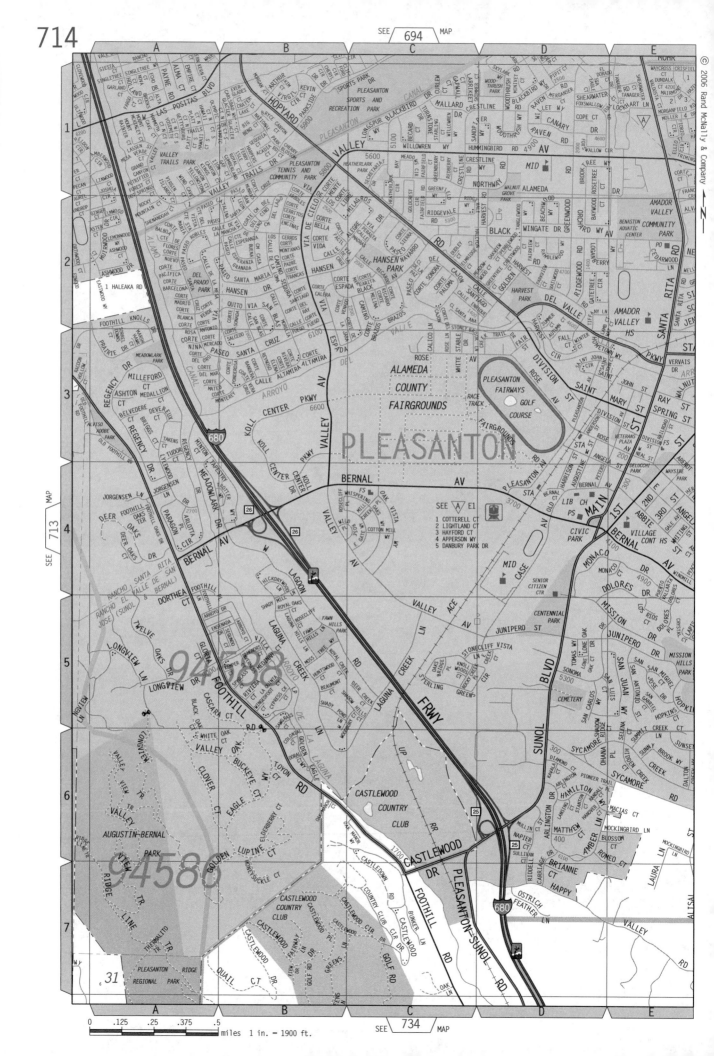

ALAMEDA CO.

PLEASANTON

ALAMEDA COUNTY FAIRGROUNDS

PLEASANTON FAIRWAYS GOLF COURSE

94588

94586

SEE A E1
1 COTTERELL CT
2 LIGHTLAND CT
3 HAYFORD CT
4 APPERSON WY
5 DANBURY PARK DR

0 .125 .25 .375 .5
miles 1 in. = 1900 ft.

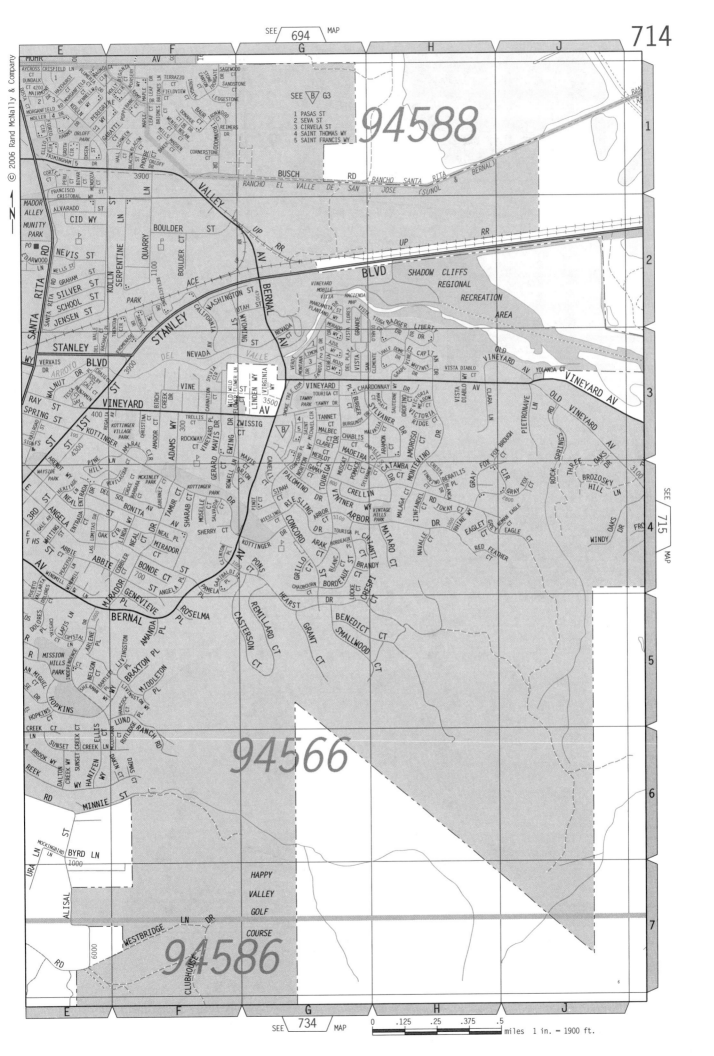

ALAMEDA CO.

94588

SEE B G3

1 PASAS ST
2 SEVA ST
3 CIRVELA ST
4 SAINT THOMAS WY
5 SAINT FRANCIS WY

SHADOW CLIFFS
REGIONAL
RECREATION
AREA

94566

94586

HAPPY
VALLEY
GOLF

COURSE

0 .125 .25 .375 .5
miles 1 in. = 1900 ft.

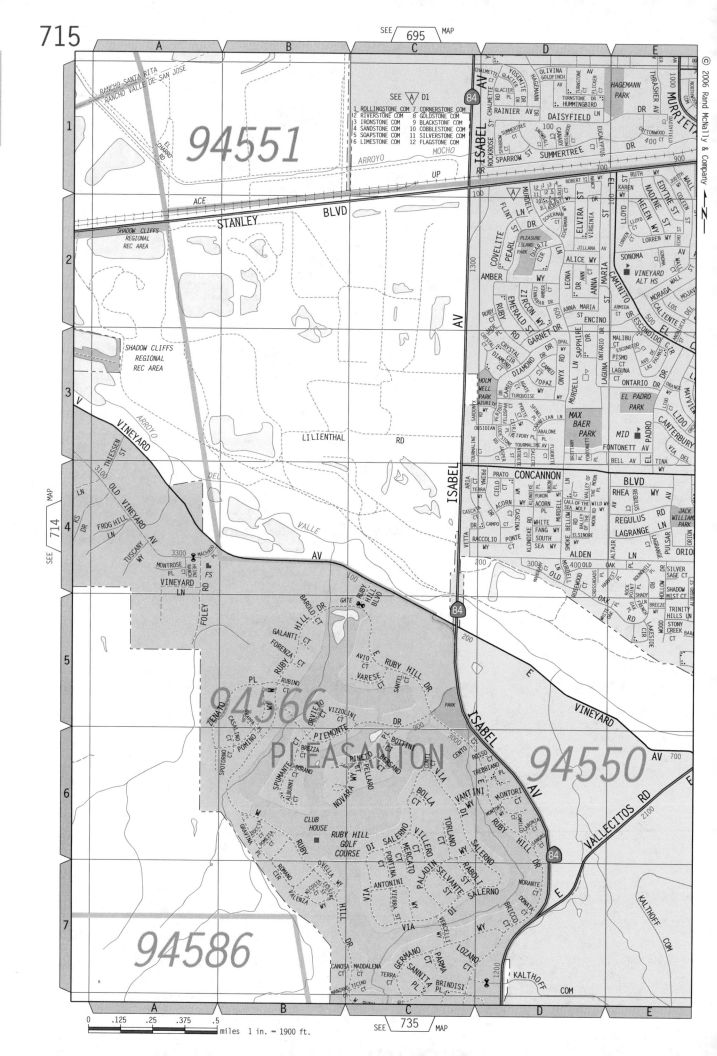

ALAMEDA CO.

© 2006 Rand McNally & Company

94551

94566

PLEASANTON

94550

94586

SEE 695 MAP

SEE 735 MAP

SEE 714 MAP

SEE D1
1 ROLLINGSTONE COM   7 CORNERSTONE COM
2 RIVERSTONE COM   8 GOLDSTONE COM
3 IRONSTONE COM   9 BLACKSTONE COM
4 SANDSTONE COM   10 COBBLESTONE COM
5 SOAPSTONE COM   11 SILVERSTONE COM
6 LIMESTONE COM   12 FLAGSTONE COM

0   .125   .25   .375   .5   miles   1 in. = 1900 ft.

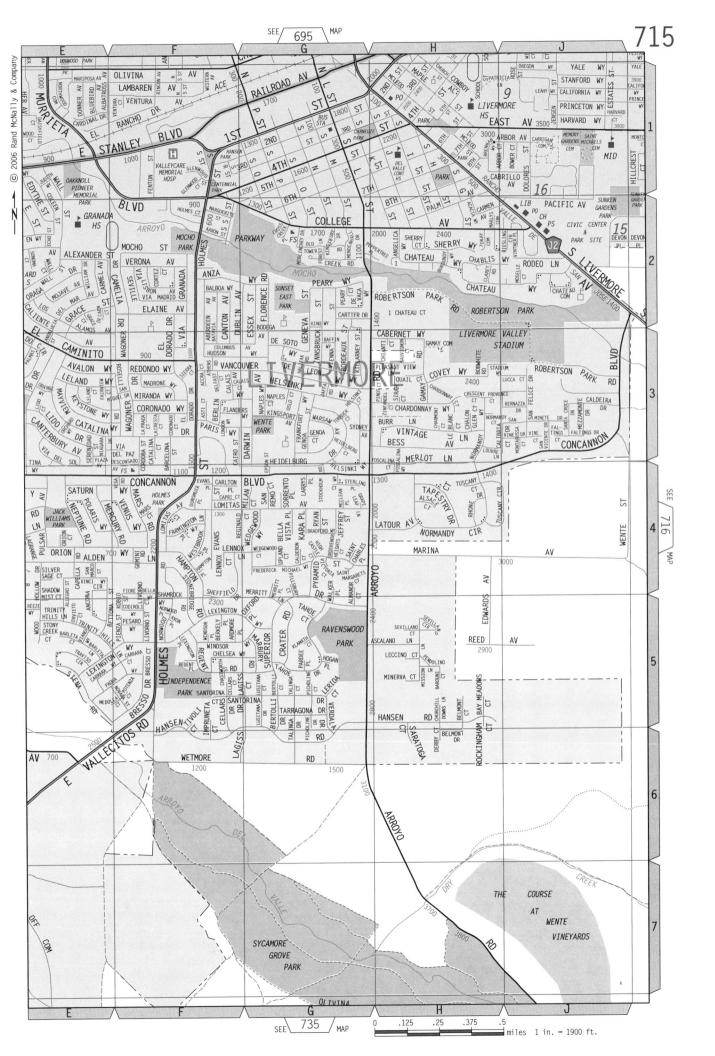

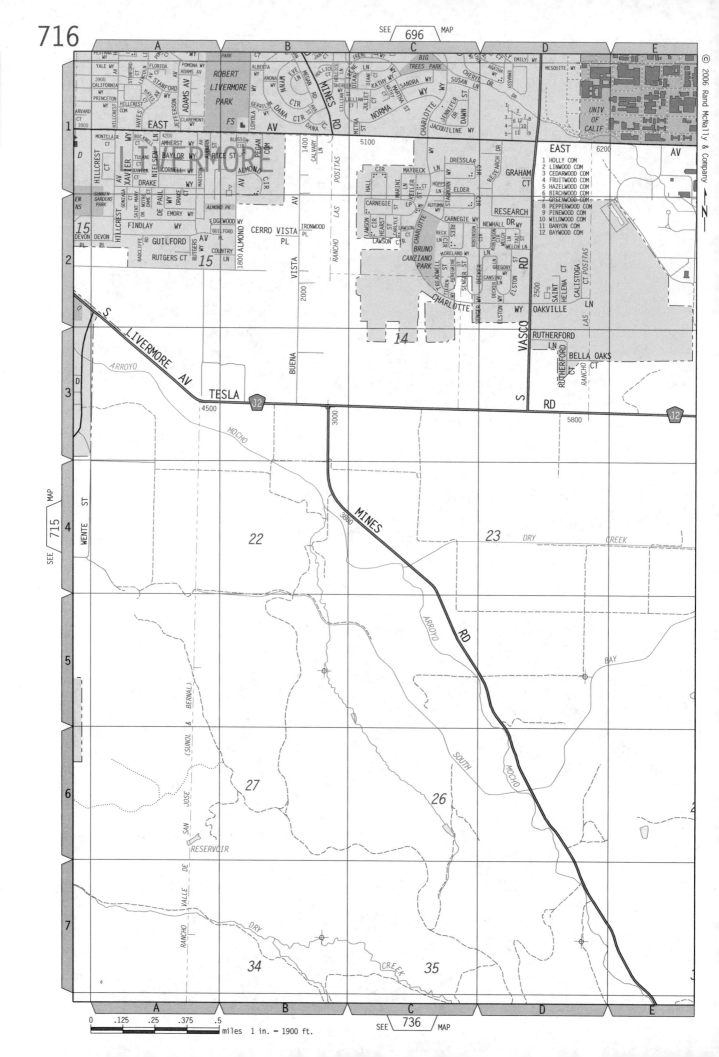

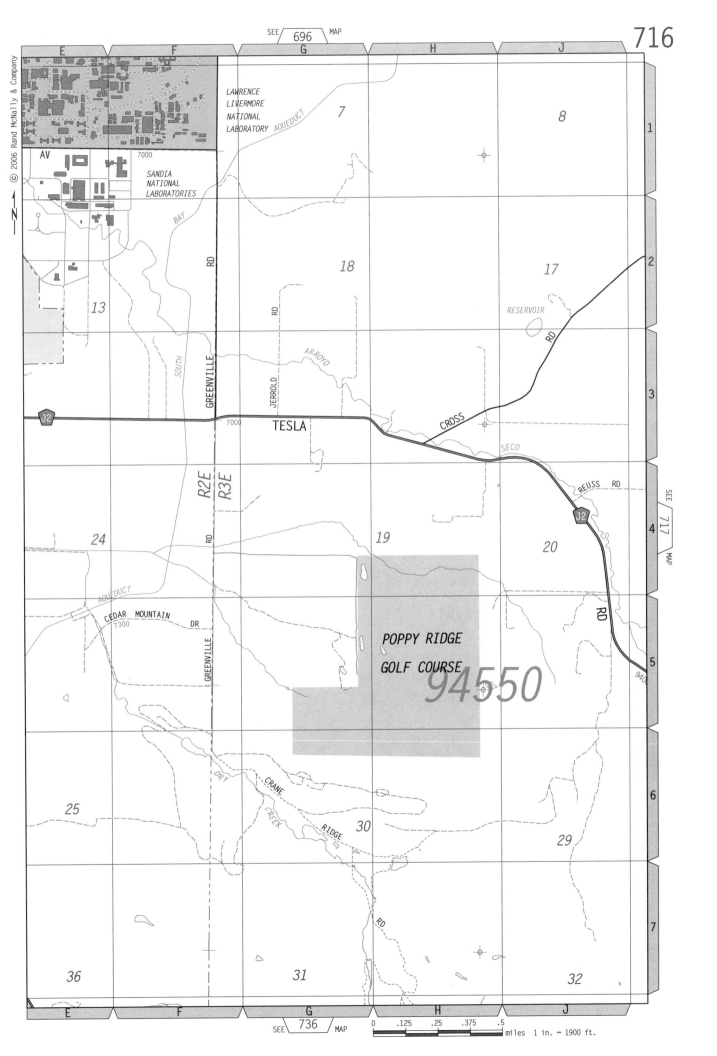

ALAMEDA CO.

SEE 696 MAP

E F G H J

LAWRENCE
LIVERMORE
NATIONAL
LABORATORY

AQUEDUCT

7

8

1

AV

7000

SANDIA
NATIONAL
LABORATORIES

BAY

RD

18

17

2

13

RESERVOIR

RD

ARROYO

3

GREENVILLE

JERROLD

SOUTH

J2

7000

TESLA

CROSS

SECO

REUSS RD

SEE 717 MAP

J2

R2E R3E

24

19

20

4

RD

AQUEDUCT

CEDAR MOUNTAIN

7300

DR

GREENVILLE

RD

POPPY RIDGE

GOLF COURSE

94550

940

5

DRY

CRANE

25

CREEK

RIDGE

30

29

6

RD

7

36

31

32

E F G H J

SEE 736 MAP

0 .125 .25 .375 .5 miles 1 in. = 1900 ft.

ALAMEDA CO.

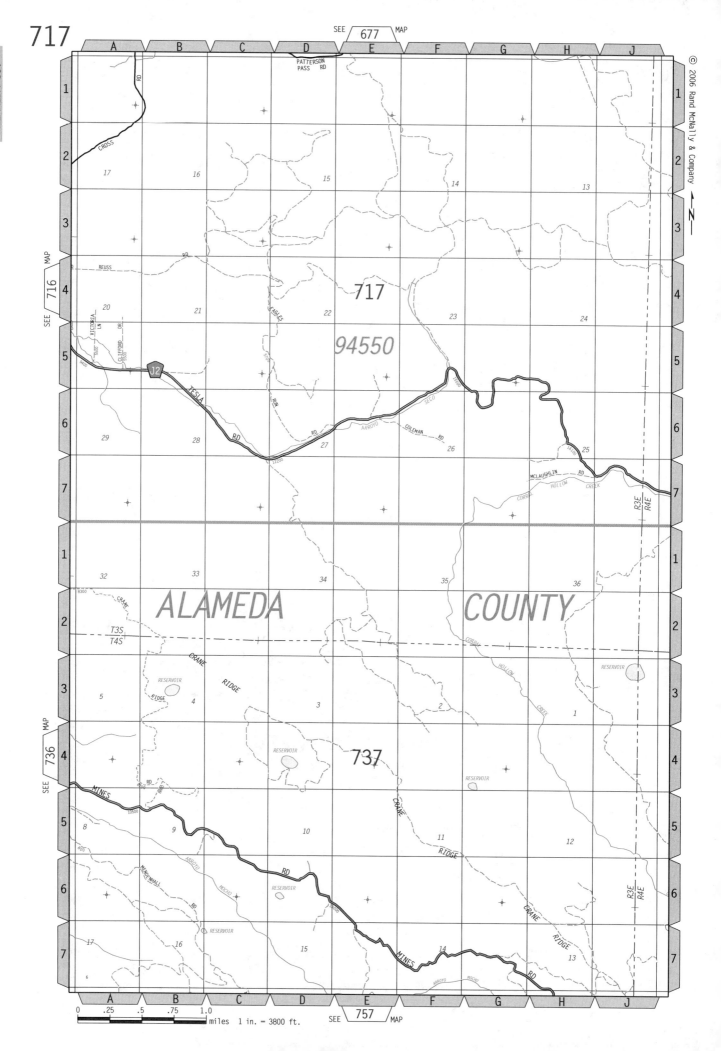

SEE 677 MAP

© 2006 Rand McNally & Company

N

717

94550

ALAMEDA COUNTY

737

SEE 716 MAP

SEE 736 MAP

SEE 757 MAP

0   .25   .5   .75   1.0
miles   1 in. = 3800 ft.

© 2006 Rand McNally & Company

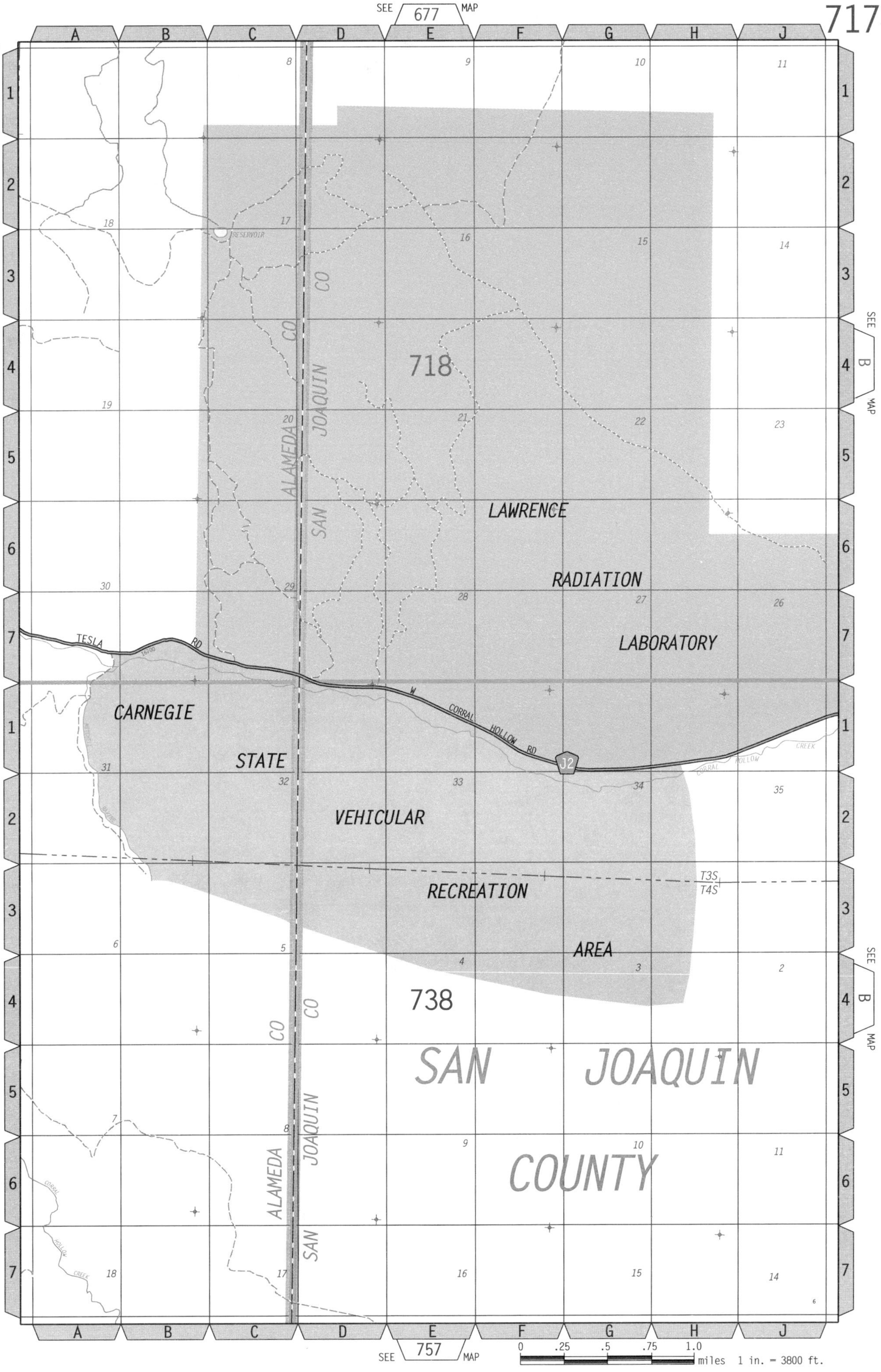

N

A B C D E F G H J

8 9 10 11

RESERVOIR

17 16 15 14

ALAMEDA CO

SAN JOAQUIN CO

718

18 19 20 21 22 23

LAWRENCE

30 29 28 27 26

RADIATION

TESLA RD

LABORATORY

CORRAL HOLLOW RD

CARNEGIE

J2

CORRAL HOLLOW CREEK

31 32 33 34 35

STATE

VEHICULAR

T3S
T4S

RECREATION

6 5 4 3 2

AREA

738

SAN JOAQUIN

ALAMEDA CO

SAN JOAQUIN CO

7 8 9 10 11

COUNTY

CORRAL HOLLOW CREEK

18 17 16 15 14

6

0 .25 .5 .75 1.0
miles 1 in. = 3800 ft.

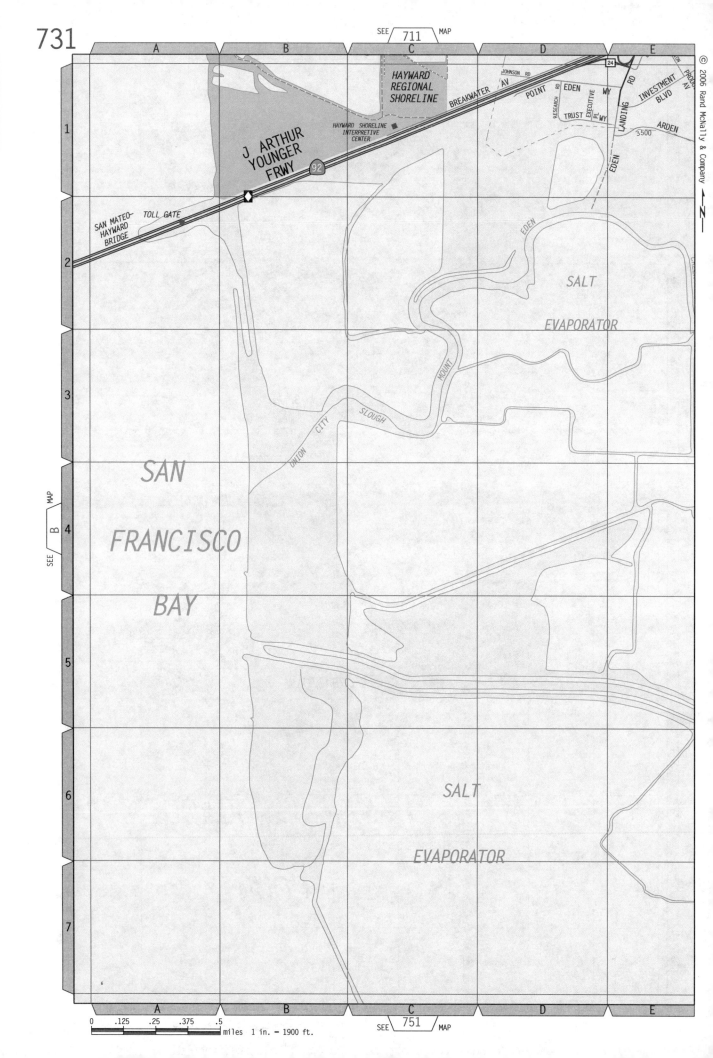

ALAMEDA CO.

HAYWARD
REGIONAL
SHORELINE

BREAKWATER AV

JOHNSON RD

POINT

EDEN

RESEARCH RD

TRUST

EXECUTIVE

PL WY

INVESTMENT
BLVD

LANDING

EDEN

ARDEN

3500

© 2006 Rand McNally & Company

N

J ARTHUR
YOUNGER
FRWY

92

HAYWARD SHORELINE
INTERPRETIVE
CENTER

SAN MATEO-
HAYWARD
BRIDGE

TOLL GATE

EDEN

SALT

EVAPORATOR

MOUNT

SAN

UNION CITY

SLOUGH

FRANCISCO

SEE MAP B

BAY

SALT

EVAPORATOR

0   .125   .25   .375   .5
miles 1 in. = 1900 ft.

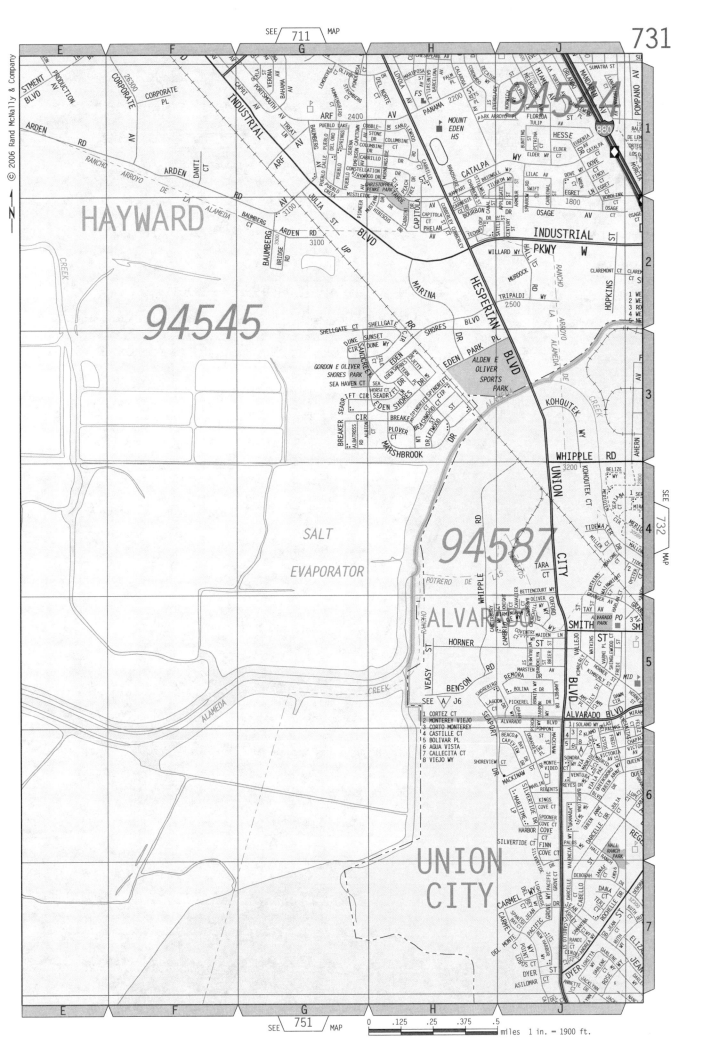

ALAMEDA CO.

© 2006 Rand McNally & Company

SEE 711 MAP

HAYWARD

94545

SALT

EVAPORATOR

94544

94587

ALVARADO

UNION
CITY

UNION
CITY

SEE A J6
1 CORTEZ CT
2 MONTEREY VIEJO
3 CORTO MONTEREY
4 CASTILLE CT
5 BOLIVAR PL
6 AGUA VISTA
7 CALLECITA CT
8 VIEJO WY

SEE 732 MAP

SEE 751 MAP

0 .125 .25 .375 .5 miles 1 in. = 1900 ft.

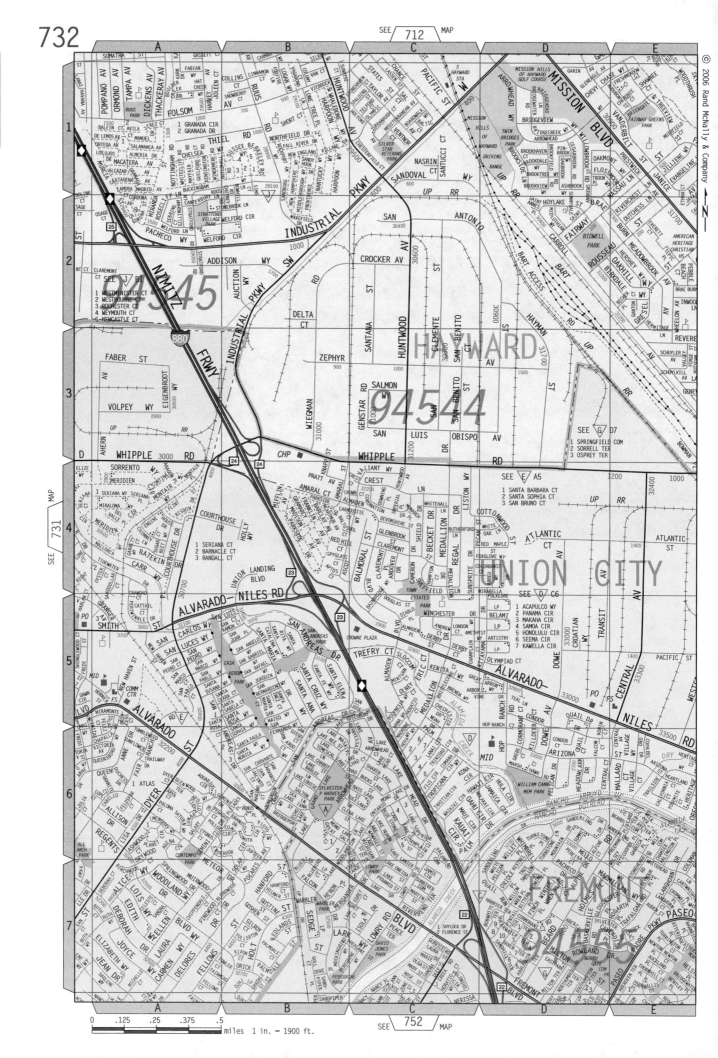

SEE 712 MAP

SEE 731 MAP

SEE 752 MAP

0   .125   .25   .375   .5
miles 1 in. = 1900 ft.

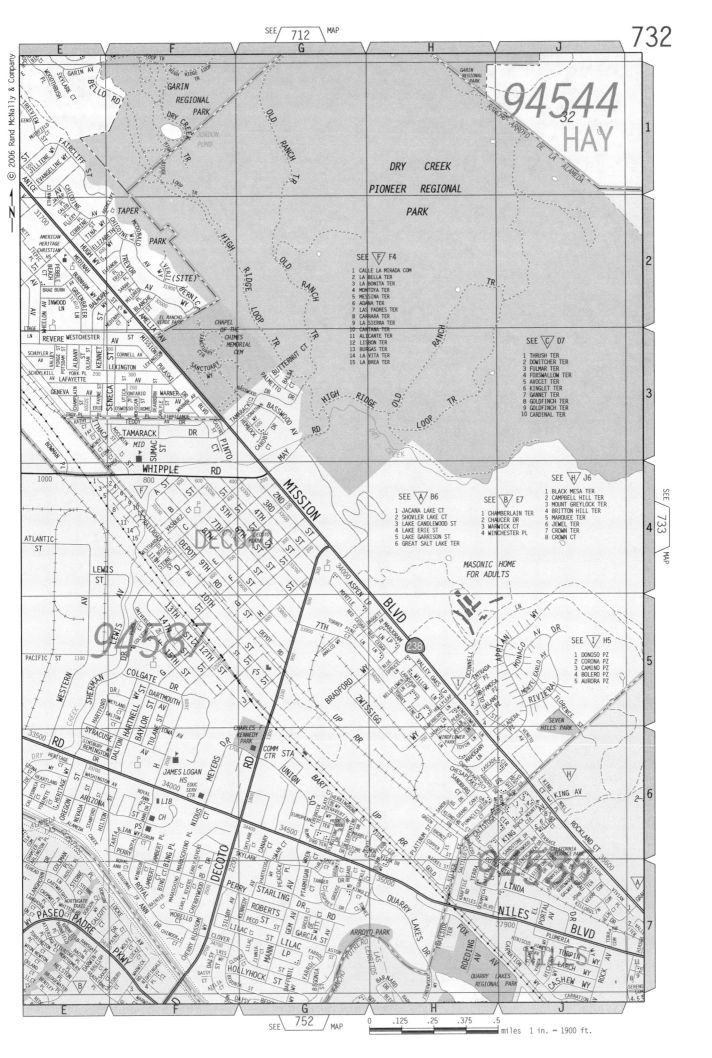

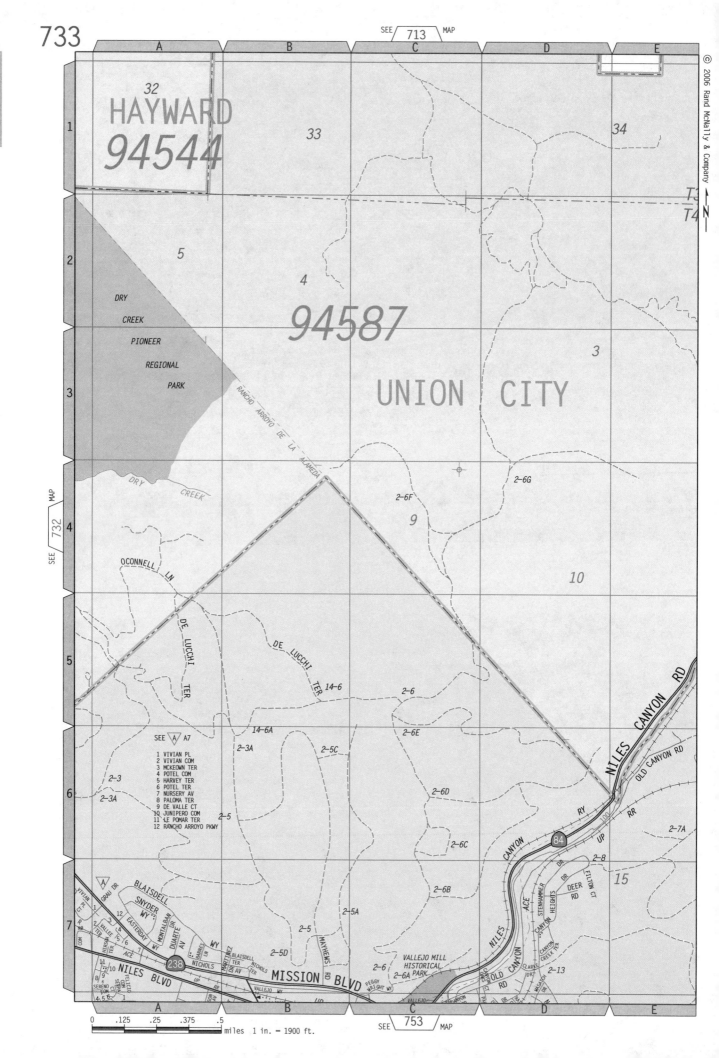

733

ALAMEDA CO.

A   B   C   D   E

1

32
HAYWARD
94544

33

34

© 2006 Rand McNally & Company

—N—

T3
T4

2

5

4

DRY

CREEK

94587

PIONEER

REGIONAL

3

PARK

UNION CITY

RANCHO ARROYO DE LA ALAMEDA

3

DRY   CREEK

2-6G

SEE 732 MAP

4

OCONNELL   LN

2-6F

9

10

DE   LUCCHI   TER

5

DE LUCCHI TER   14-6

2-6

NILES CANYON RD

14-6A

2-6E

SEE A A7
1 VIVIAN PL
2 VIVIAN COM
3 MCKEOWN TER
4 POTEL COM
5 HARVEY TER
6 POTEL TER
7 NURSERY AV
8 PALOMA TER
9 DE VALLE CT
10 JUNIPERO COM
11 LE POMAR TER
12 RANCHO ARROYO PKWY

2-3A

2-5C

OLD CANYON RD

2-3

2-6D

RY   RR

2-3A

2-5

2-7A

6

2-6C

CANYON   UP

84

2-8

15

BLAISDELL

2-6B

DR   DR   FILTON CT

A   GRAU DR   SNYDER   WY

2-5A

ACE   STENHAMMER   DEER
HEIGHTS   RD

VIVIAN PL   EASTERDAY WY   MONTALBAN WY   DUARTE AV

NILES   CANYON

CANYON   CREEK TER

7

VALLEE TER   ACE

2-5   2-5

MARTINEZ DR AV   BLAISDELL TER   NICHOLS

MAYHEWS RD   OLD CANYON RD

DR   CLARKE DR

2-6   2-5D   VALLEJO MILL   HISTORICAL   PARK   MASAGA

11   10   NICHOLS

2-13

9   8

238   NILES   BLVD

FELICIA COM   SERENA   MISSION   BLVD   PEGGY WRIGHT WY   2-6A

SERENO DR   UP   RR   VALLEJO WY   VALLEJO   CANYON

4 5 6   1

0   .125   .25   .375   .5
miles   1 in. = 1900 ft.

SEE 753 MAP

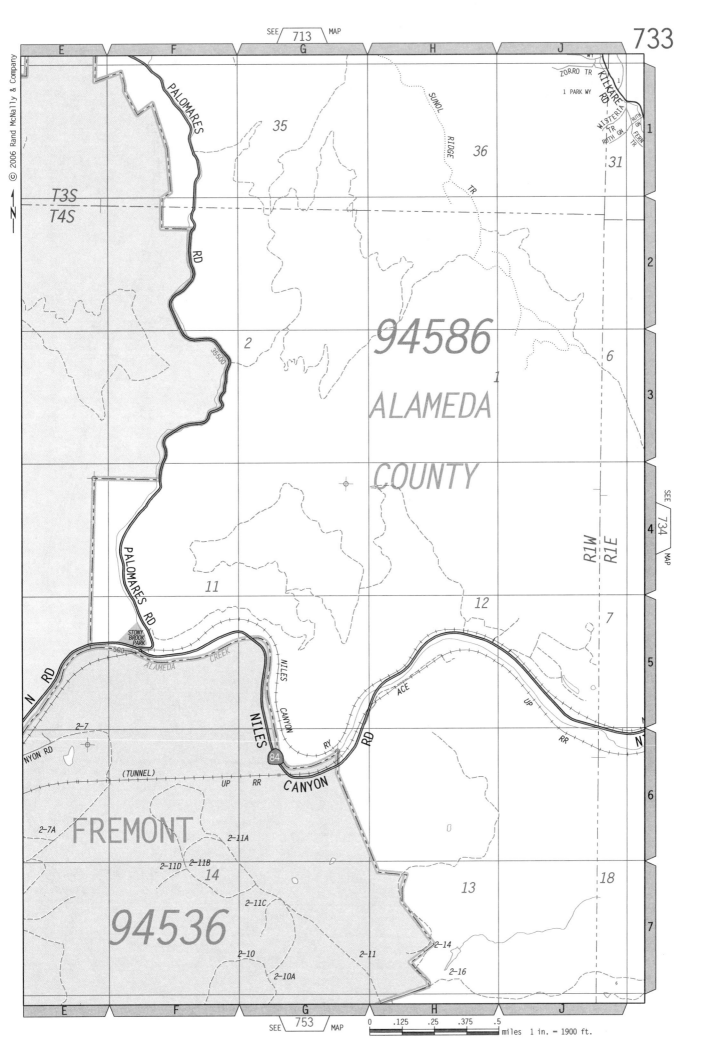

ALAMEDA CO.

SEE 713 MAP

E   F   G   H   J

ZORRO TR

KILKARE RD

1 PARK WY

WISTERIA TR

RUTH GN

RUTH GN

FERN TR

35

SUNOL RIDGE TR

36

31

1

T3S

T4S

N

2

35500

94586

2

1

6

ALAMEDA

COUNTY

SEE 734 MAP

3

4

R1W R1E

PALOMARES

RD

PALOMARES RD

11

12

7

STONY BROOK PARK

590

ALAMEDA CREEK

N RD

NILES CANYON

ACE

UP

RR

5

2-7

NYON RD

NILES

CANYON

RY

RD

N

84

(TUNNEL)   UP   RR   CANYON

6

FREMONT

2-7A

2-11A

2-11D 2-11B

14

13

18

2-11C

94536

2-10

2-11

2-14

2-10A

2-16

6

E   F   G   H   J

SEE 753 MAP

0   .125   .25   .375   .5

miles 1 in. = 1900 ft.

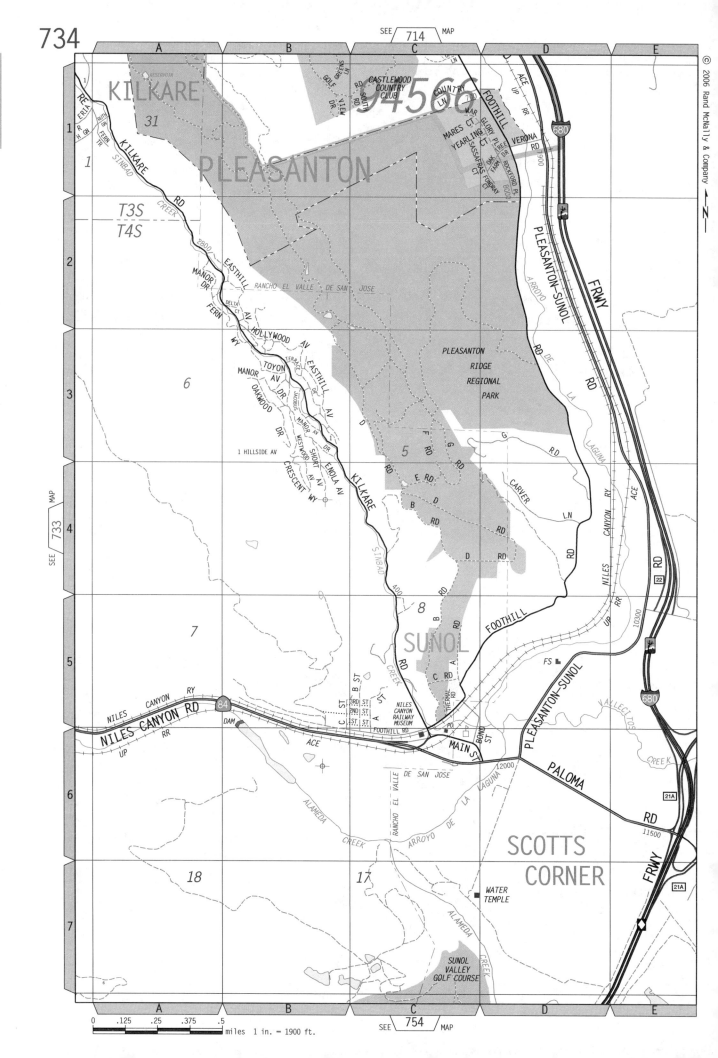

ALAMEDA CO.

—N—

KILKARE

94566

PLEASANTON

CASTLEWOOD COUNTRY CLUB

GOLF VIEW DR

GREENS LN
RD
SOUTH
LN
COUNTRY

ACE
UP
RR

FOOTHILL

680

T3S
T4S

MARES CT
YEARLING
SASSAFRAS
CT
GLORY
CT
WAR
PL
FOX
DR
OAK
FARM
ROCKFORD PL
FAIRWAY

VERONA
RD
900

PLEASANTON-SUNOL FRWY

MANOR DR

EASTHILL
AV

RANCHO EL VALLE DE SAN JOSE

FERN
WY

DELTA
CT

HOLLYWOOD AV

TERRACE
DR

EASTHILL
DR

2800

6

MANOR
DR

TOYON
AV

OAKWOOD
DR

JACOBUS

MANOR AV

PLEASANTON RIDGE REGIONAL PARK

RD DE LA LAGUNA

ARROYO

SEE 733 MAP

1 HILLSIDE AV

WESTWOOD
AV

SHORT
AV

ENOLA AV

CRESCENT WY

5

F
RD

G
RD

G
RD

CARVER

LN

KILKARE

B
RD

E
RD

D
RD

D
RD

RD

SINBAD

400

D
RD

8

RD

B

RD

FOOTHILL

NILES
CANYON
RY

ACE

10300

22

680

7

SUNOL

FS

PLEASANTON-SUNOL

NILES CANYON RY

UP

84

NILES CANYON RD

RR

UP

DAM

ACE

B ST
3RD ST
2ND ST
1ST ST
C ST
A ST

THERMAL
RD

C RD

NILES CANYON RAILWAY MUSEUM

FOOTHILL RD

PD
BOND
ST

MAIN ST

PALOMA

PLEASANTON-SUNOL

VALLECITOS
CREEK

12000

ALAMEDA
CREEK

RANCHO EL VALLE DE SAN JOSE

ARROYO DE LA LAGUNA

SCOTTS
CORNER

RD

11500

21A

21A

FRWY

18

17

WATER TEMPLE

ALAMEDA CREEK

SUNOL VALLEY GOLF COURSE

6

miles 1 in. = 1900 ft.
0   .125   .25   .375   .5

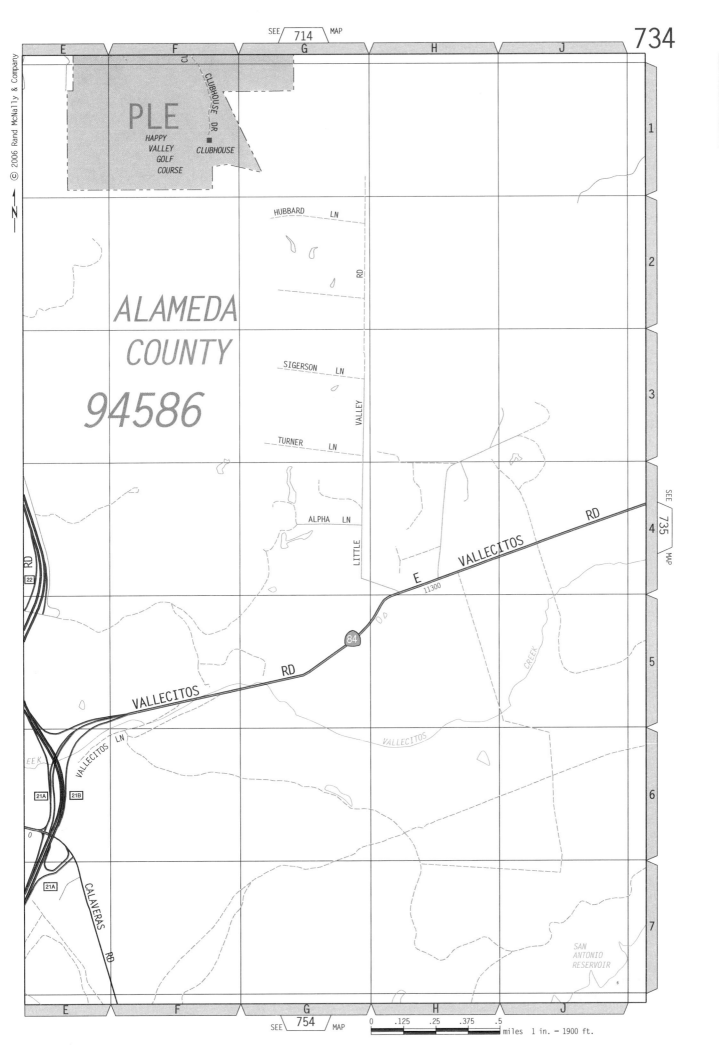

© 2006 Rand McNally & Company

N

E   F   G   H   J

1

PLE

HAPPY
VALLEY
GOLF
COURSE

CLUBHOUSE DR

CLUBHOUSE

HUBBARD   LN

RD

2

ALAMEDA

COUNTY

94586

SIGERSON   LN

VALLEY

3

TURNER   LN

SEE 735 MAP

ALPHA   LN

LITTLE

RD

E   VALLECITOS

4

11300

RD

22

84

CREEK

5

VALLECITOS   RD

VALLECITOS   LN

VALLECITOS

VALLECITOS

EE K

21A   21B

6

0

21A

CALAVERAS

7

SAN
ANTONIO
RESERVOIR

RD

6

E   F   G   H   J

0   .125   .25   .375   .5

miles 1 in. = 1900 ft.

735

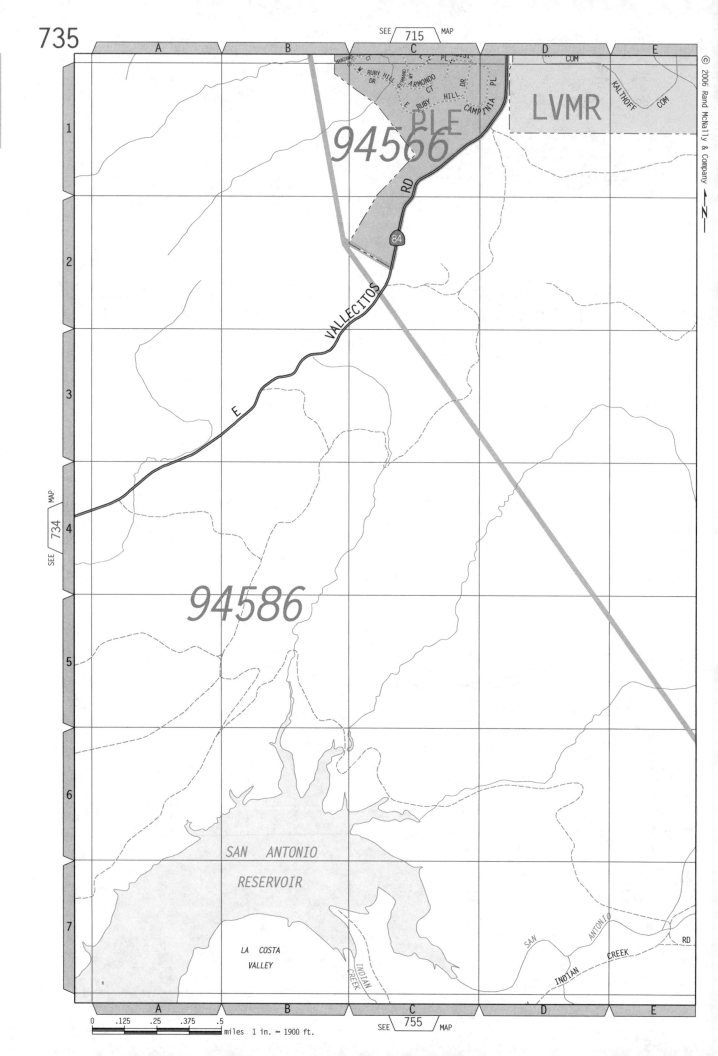

SEE 715 MAP

A   B   C   D   E

LVMR

94566

KALTHOFF COM

MANZANO

RUBY HILL DR

ARMONDO CT

RUBY HILL

CAMPINIA PL

COM

84

VALLECITOS

SEE 734 MAP

94586

SAN ANTONIO

RESERVOIR

LA COSTA
VALLEY

INDIAN CREEK

SAN ANTONIO

CREEK

INDIAN

RD

A   B   C   D   E

SEE 755 MAP

0   .125   .25   .375   .5
miles 1 in. = 1900 ft.

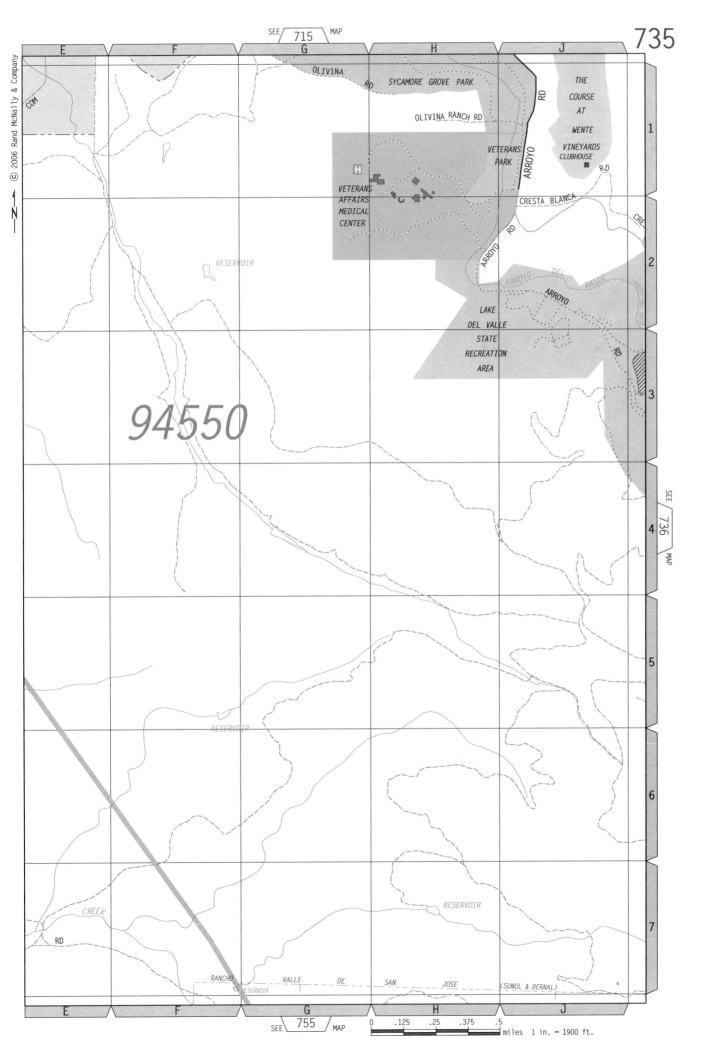

ALAMEDA CO.

SEE 715 MAP

E F G H J

1

OLIVINA

RD SYCAMORE GROVE PARK

OLIVINA RANCH RD

THE
COURSE
AT
WENTE
VINEYARDS
CLUBHOUSE

RD

VETERANS
PARK

RD

ARROYO

H

VETERANS
AFFAIRS
MEDICAL
CENTER

CRESTA BLANCA

RD

CRE

2

RESERVOIR

ARROYO

ARROYO DEL VALLE

ARROYO

LAKE
DEL VALLE
STATE
RECREATION
AREA

RD

3

94550

SEE 736 MAP

4

5

RESERVOIR

6

7

CREEK

RESERVOIR

RD

RANCHO VALLE DE SAN JOSE (SUNOL & BERNAL)

RESERVOIR

E F G H J

SEE 755 MAP

0 .125 .25 .375 .5

miles 1 in. = 1900 ft.

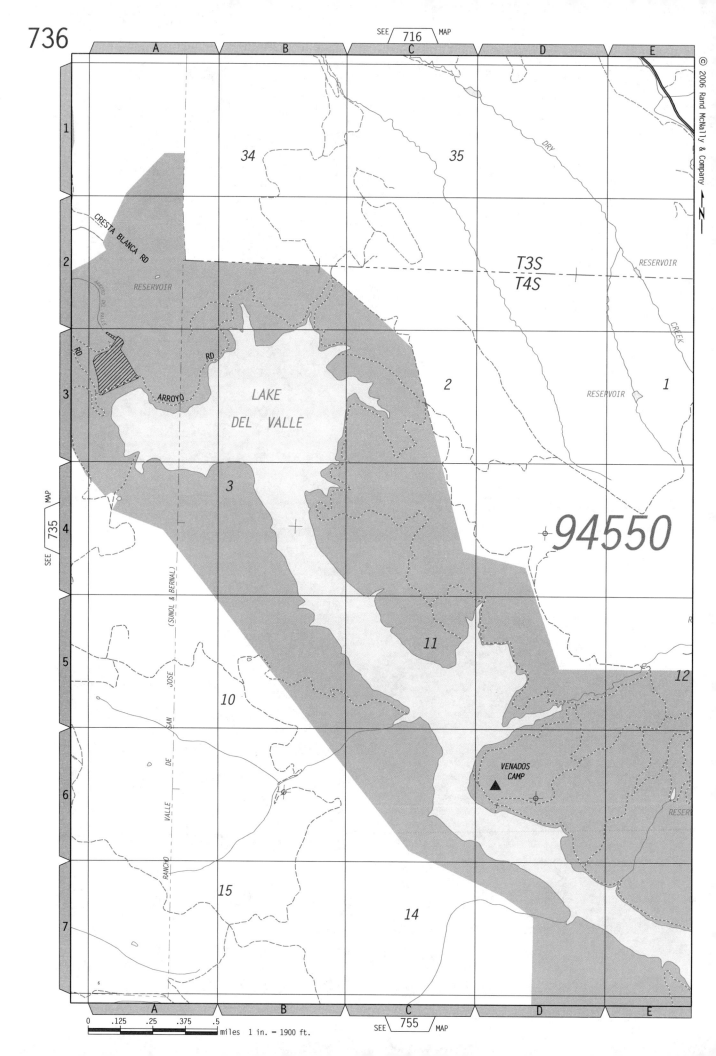

736

A B C D E

SEE 716 MAP

34 35

CRESTA BLANCA RD

RESERVOIR

T3S
T4S

RESERVOIR

RD

ARROYO DEL VALLE

RD

LAKE
DEL VALLE

2

1

RESERVOIR

3

94550

11

SEE 735 MAP

(SUNOL & BERNAL)

12

10

SAN JOSE

VALLE DE

VENADOS
CAMP

RESER

RANCHO

15

14

A B C D E

SEE 755 MAP

0 .125 .25 .375 .5
miles 1 in. = 1900 ft.

© 2006 Rand McNally & Company N

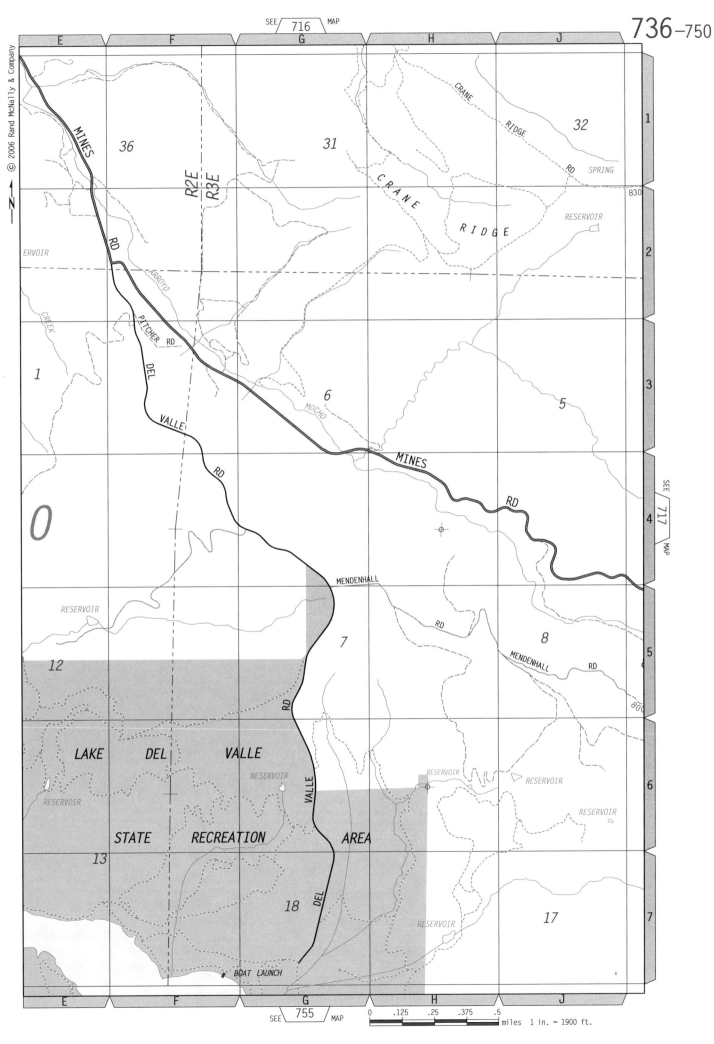

ALAMEDA CO.

E   F   G   H   J

N

1

MINES

36

R2E
R3E

31

CRANE

RIDGE

RD

32

SPRING

2

ERVOIR

CRANE

RIDGE

830

RESERVOIR

ARROYO

CREEK

PITCHER   RD

DEL

1

VALLE

RD

6

MOCHO

5

3

MINES

RD

4

SEE 717 MAP

0

MENDENHALL

7

RD

8

5

MENDENHALL   RD

RESERVOIR

12

800

LAKE   DEL   VALLE

RESERVOIR

VALLE

RESERVOIR

RESERVOIR

6

RESERVOIR

STATE   RECREATION   AREA

RESERVOIR

13

VALLE

DEL

18

17

7

RESERVOIR

E   F   G   H   J

BOAT LAUNCH

0   .125   .25   .375   .5

miles   1 in. = 1900 ft.

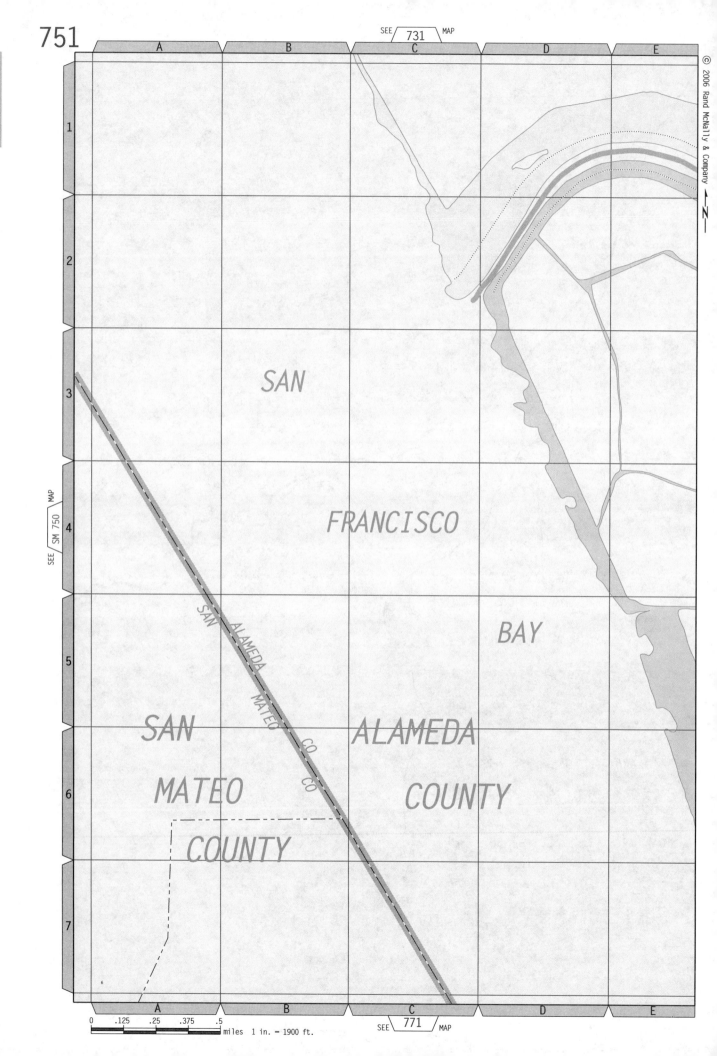

751

© 2006 Rand McNally & Company ⟵N⟶

SEE / SM 750 \ MAP

SAN

FRANCISCO

BAY

SAN

ALAMEDA

MATEO

COUNTY

COUNTY

SAN

ALAMEDA

MATEO

CO

CO

0 .125 .25 .375 .5 miles   1 in. = 1900 ft.

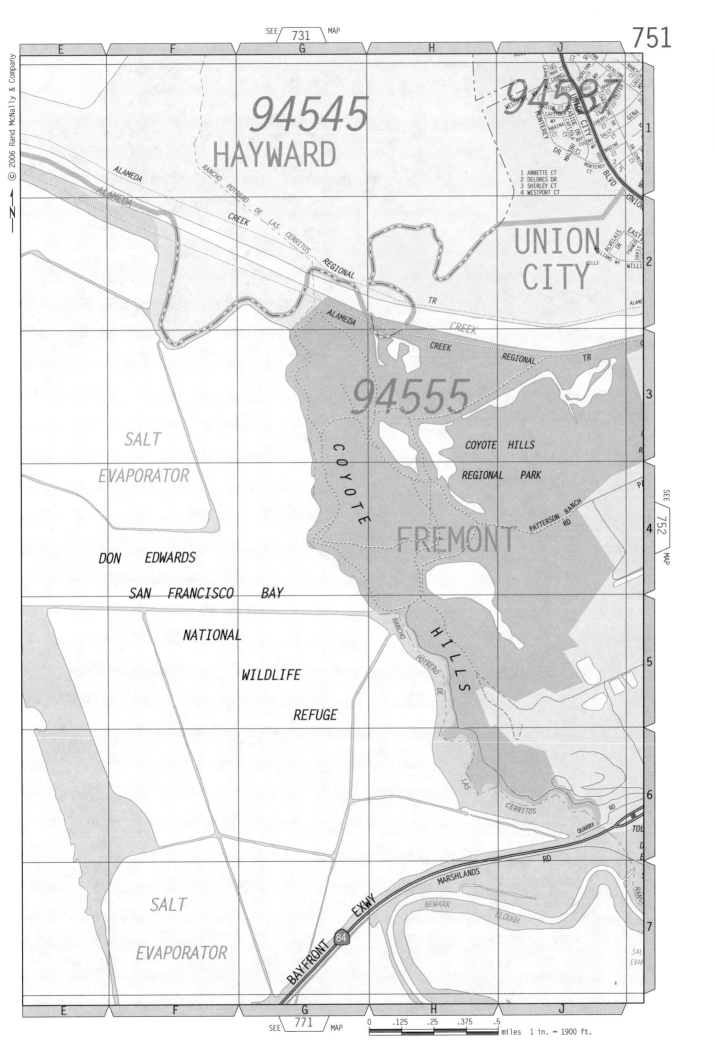

ALAMEDA CO.

E   F   G   H   J

94545

HAYWARD

94537

UNION CITY

1 ANNETTE CT
2 DELORES DR
3 SHIRLEY CT
4 WESTPORT CT

**UNION
CITY**

1

2

ALAMEDA

ALAMEDA

CREEK

RANCHO POTRERO DE LAS CERRITOS REGIONAL

ALAMEDA   CREEK   REGIONAL   TR

TR

CREEK

94555

3

SALT

EVAPORATOR

C O Y O T E

COYOTE HILLS

REGIONAL PARK

SEE
752
MAP

4

FREMONT

PATTERSON RANCH RD

DON   EDWARDS

SAN   FRANCISCO   BAY

NATIONAL

RANCHO

H I L L S

5

WILDLIFE

REFUGE

POTRERO

DE

LAS

6

CERRITOS

QUARRY RD

RD

TOL

SALT

MARSHLANDS

7

EVAPORATOR

NEWARK

SLOUGH

BAYFRONT EXWY

84

E   F   G   H   J

0   .125   .25   .375   .5

miles 1 in. = 1900 ft.

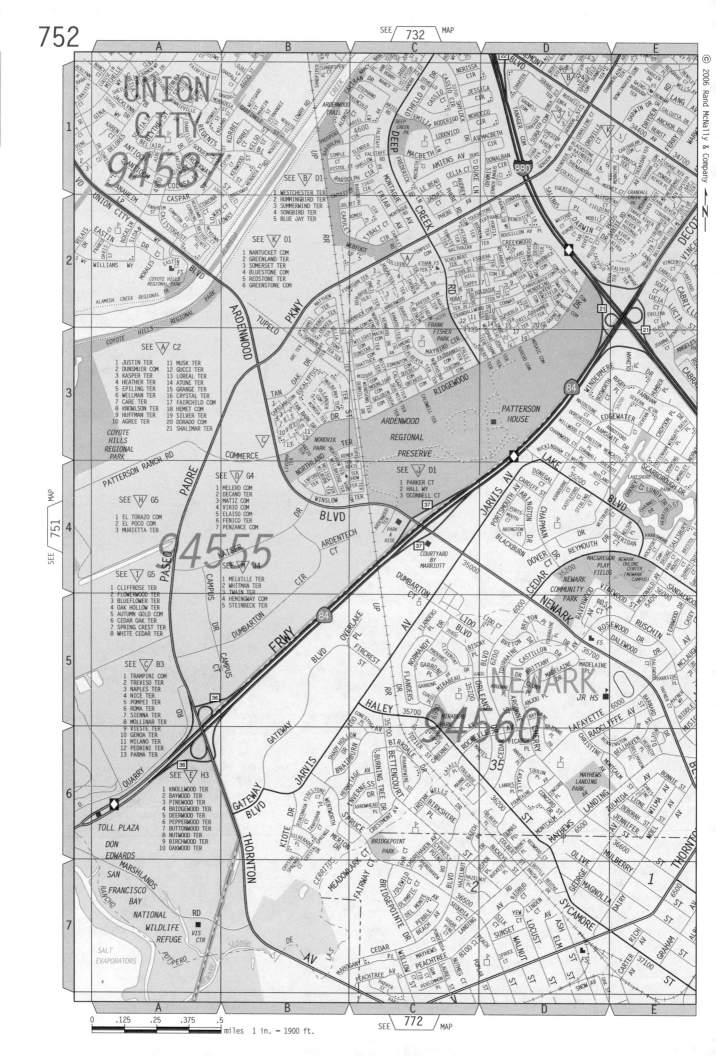

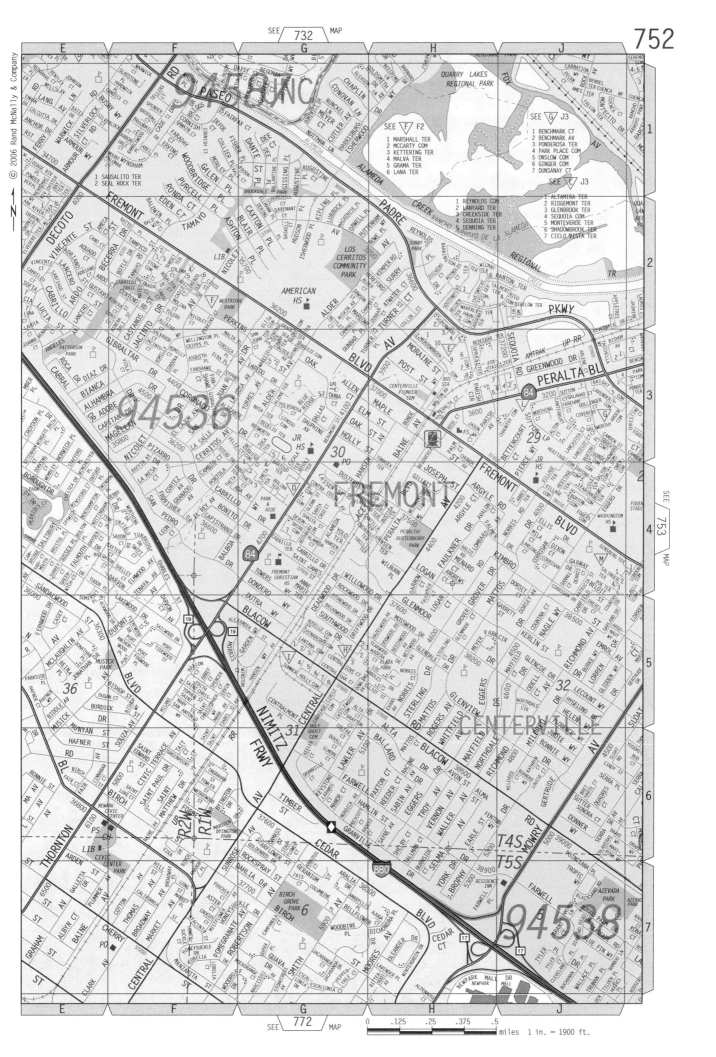

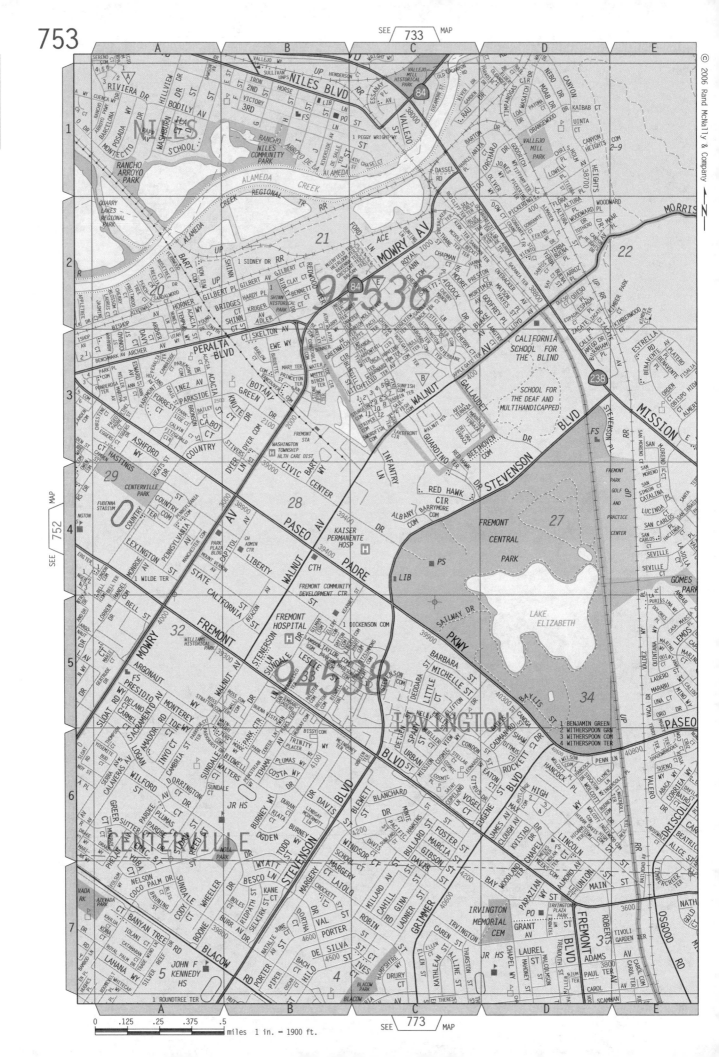

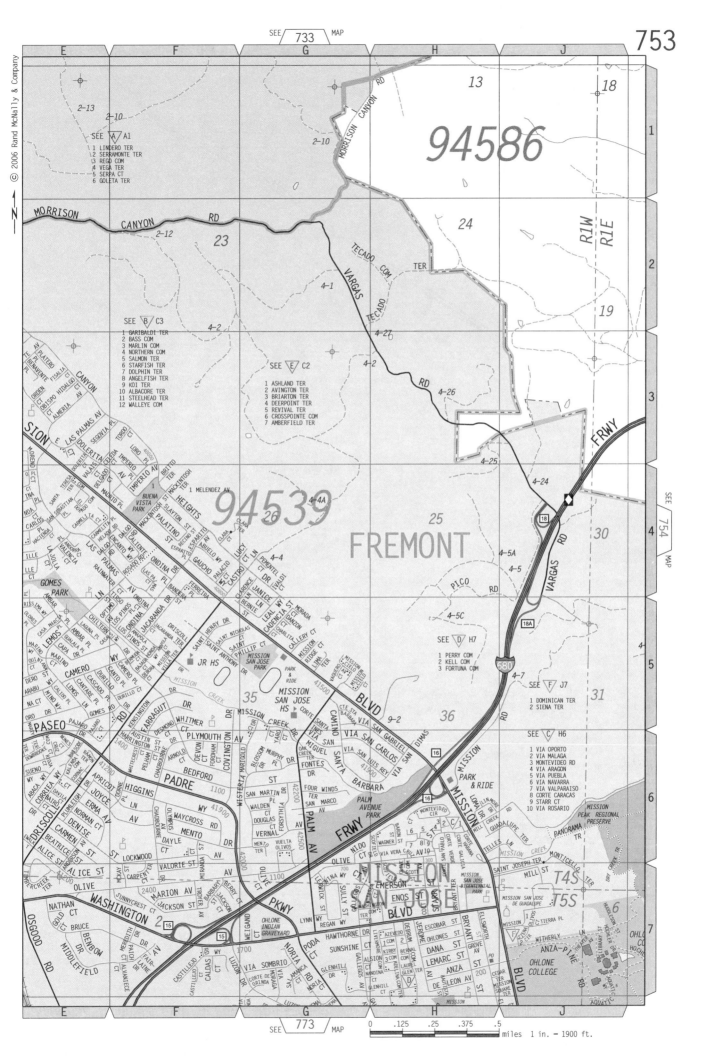

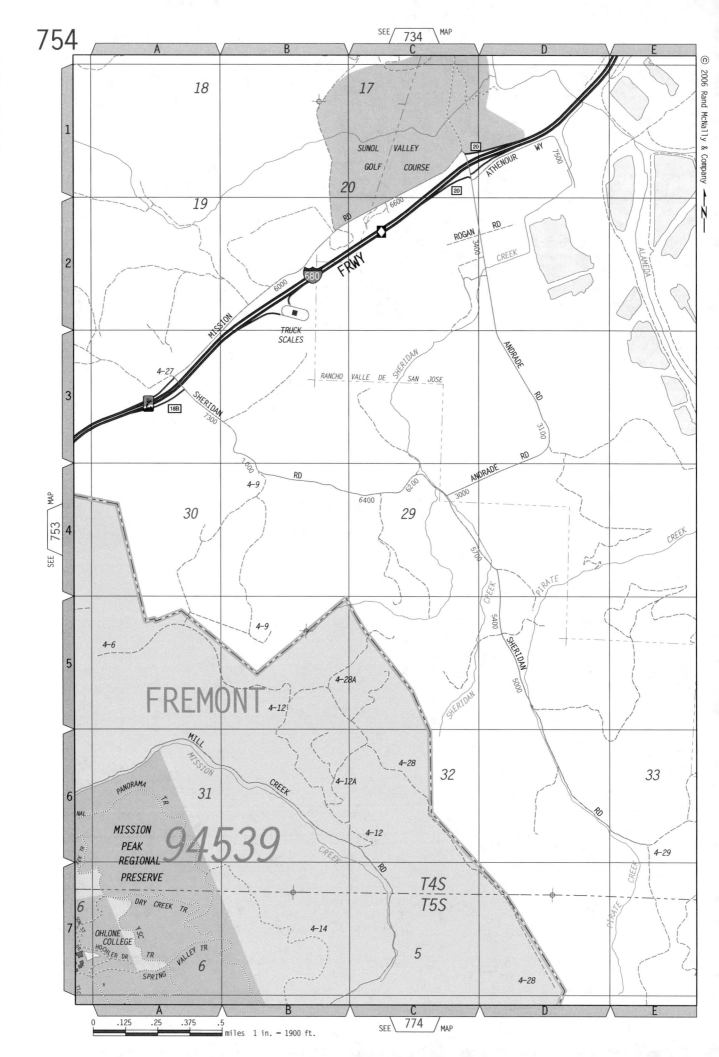

754

—N—

A B C D E

18

17

1

SUNOL VALLEY
GOLF COURSE

ATHENOUR WY

20

7500

19

20

RD

6600

680 FRWY

ROGAN RD

CREEK

3400

2

MISSION

6000

TRUCK
SCALES

ANDRADE RD

3100

4-27

SHERIDAN

RANCHO VALLE DE SHERIDAN SAN JOSE

3

18B

7300

ANDRADE RD

1000

RD

4-9

62.00

3000

30

29

4

6400

5700

CREEK

4-9

5400

PIRATE

4-6

4-28A

SHERIDAN

5000

FREMONT

4-12

SHERIDAN

5

MILL

MISSION

32

33

PANORAMA TR

CREEK

4-28

6

31

4-12A

NAL

94539

4-12

MISSION
PEAK
REGIONAL
PRESERVE

CREEK

RD

T4S
T5S

6

DRY CREEK TR

4-29

6

OHLONE
COLLEGE

4-14

5

HOCHLER DR

VALLEY TR

7

SPRING

6

4-28

A B C D E

0 .125 .25 .375 .5
miles 1 in. = 1900 ft.

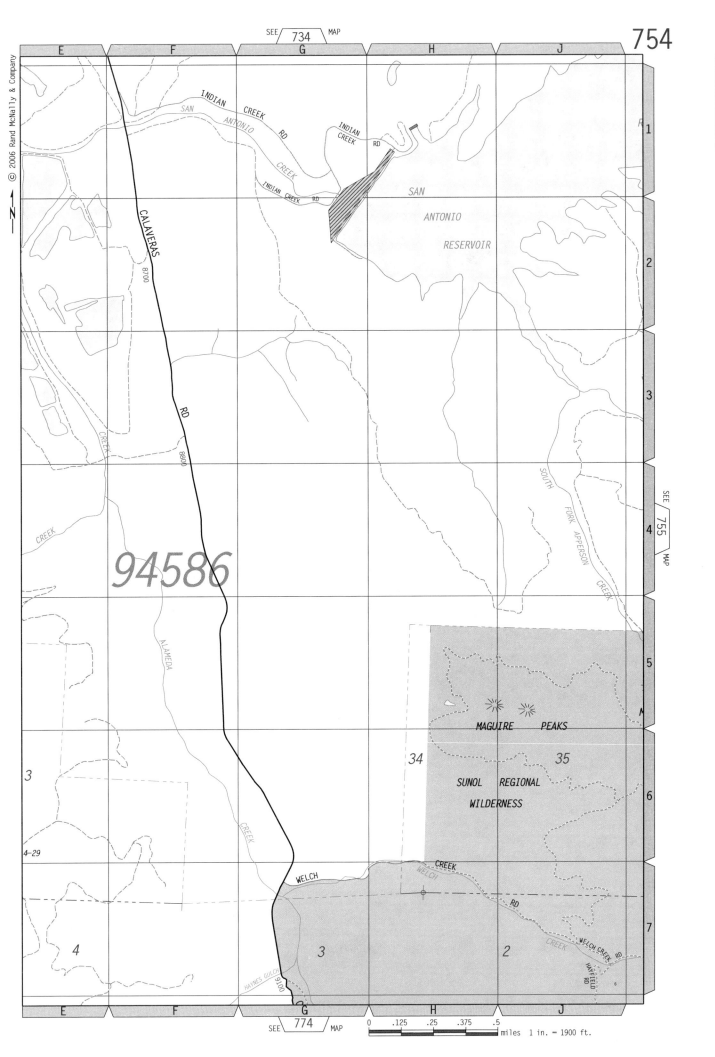

© 2006 Rand McNally & Company

SEE 734 MAP

E F G H J

SEE 755 MAP

1

2

3

4

5

6

7

INDIAN CREEK RD

SAN ANTONIO CREEK

INDIAN CREEK RD

INDIAN CREEK RD

CALAVERAS RD

8700

8800

SAN ANTONIO RESERVOIR

SOUTH FORK APPERSON CREEK

94586

CREEK

ALAMEDA CREEK

CREEK

3

4-29

4

3

WELCH

WELCH CREEK

WELCH CREEK RD

WELCH CREEK RD

HAYFIELD RD

2

34

35

MAGUIRE PEAKS

SUNOL REGIONAL WILDERNESS

HAYNES GULCH

9100

E F G H J

SEE 774 MAP

0 .125 .25 .375 .5 miles 1 in. = 1900 ft.

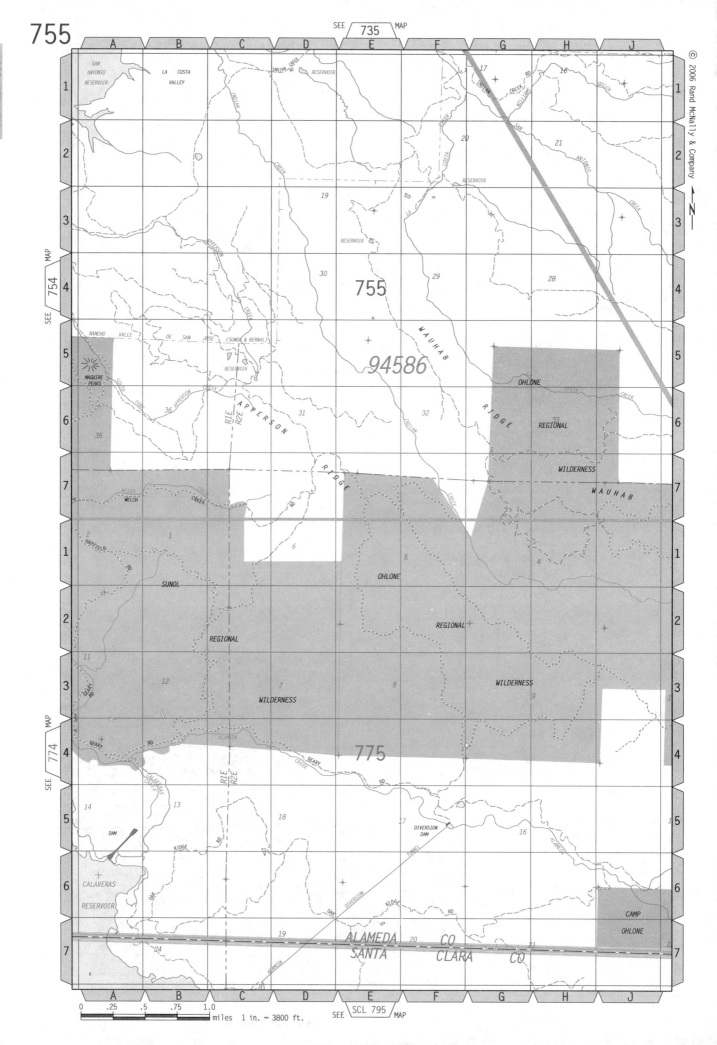

ALAMEDA CO.

© 2006 Rand McNally & Company

—N—

SEE 754 MAP

SEE 774 MAP

755

94586

775

SAN ANTONIO RESERVOIR

LA COSTA VALLEY

INDIAN CREEK RD

RESERVOIR

17

16

INDIAN CREEK

WILLIAMS RD

SAN

GULCH

20

21

ANTONIO

CREEK

19

RESERVOIR

30

29

28

RANCHO VALLE DE SAN JOSE (SUNOL & BERNAL)

RESERVOIR

WAUHAB

MAGUIRE PEAKS

SOUTH FORK

36 APPERSON CREEK

R1E R2E

APPERSON

31

32

INDIAN

RIDGE

OHLONE

COSTA CREEK

REGIONAL

WILDERNESS

35

WELCH CREEK

RIDGE

WAUHAB

WELCH

6

2

HAYFIELD RD

1

6

5

4

SUNOL

OHLONE

REGIONAL

11

12

7

8

REGIONAL

9

GEARY RD

WILDERNESS

WILDERNESS

1

GEARY RD

ALAMEDA

CALAVERAS CREEK

GEARY

CREEK

GEARY RD

R1E R2E

775

14

13

18

17

DIVERSION DAM

16

ALAMEDA

15

DAM

RIDGE RD

RD

TUNNEL

CALAVERAS

OAK

RIDGE

DIVERSION

RD

CAMP

RESERVOIR

19

ALAMEDA CO

20

21

OHLONE

24

OAK

ALAMEDA

SANTA CLARA CO

6

© 2006 Rand McNally & Company

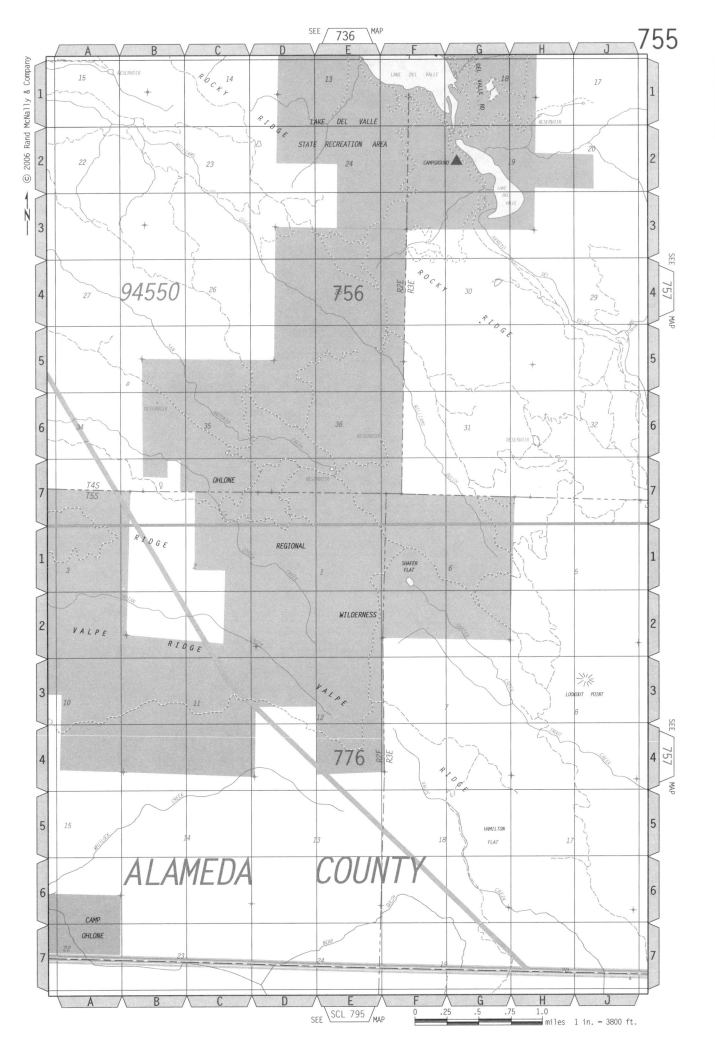

94550

756

776

OHLONE

REGIONAL

WILDERNESS

VALPE   RIDGE

CAMP
OHLONE

ALAMEDA   COUNTY

LAKE DEL VALLE
STATE RECREATION AREA

CAMPGROUND

LOOKOUT   POINT

SHAFER
FLAT

HAMILTON
FLAT

0   .25   .5   .75   1.0
miles   1 in. = 3800 ft.

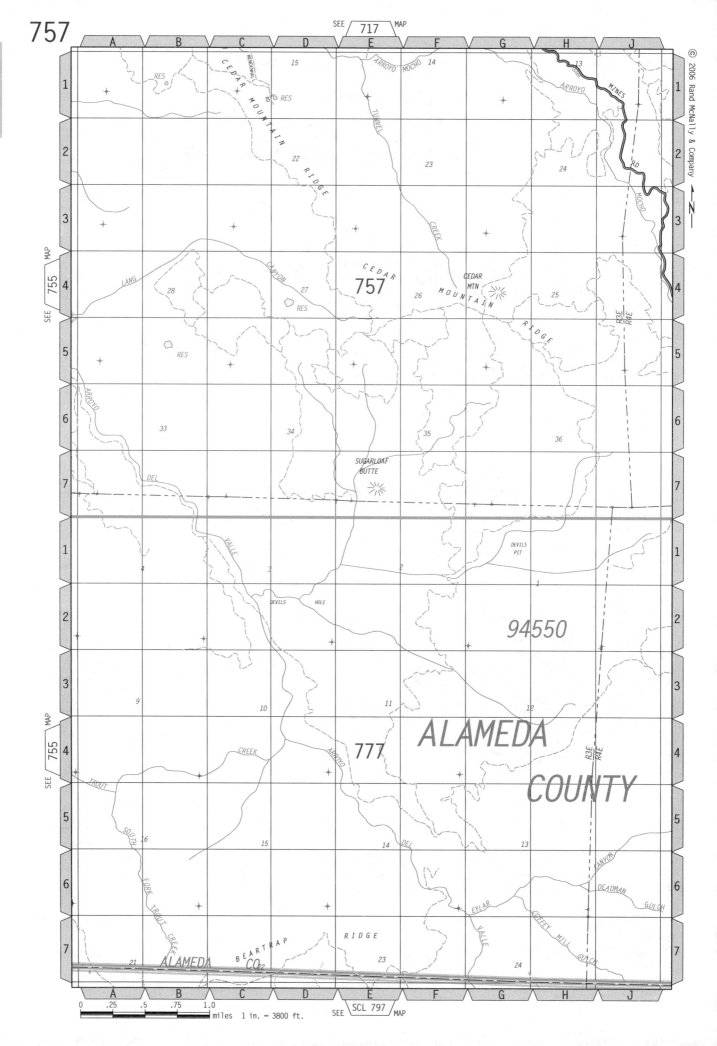

© 2006 Rand McNally & Company

—N—

SEE 755 MAP

CEDAR MOUNTAIN RIDGE

ARROYO MOCHO

TUNNEL

CREEK

15

14

22

23

24

LANG

CANYON

CEDAR
MTN
757

CEDAR
MOUNTAIN
RIDGE

28

27

RES

26

25

RES

ARROYO

33

34

35

36

DEL

SUGARLOAF
BUTTE

R3E
R4E

VALLE

DEVILS
PIT

4

3

2

1

DEVILS   HOLE

94550

9

10

11

12

SEE 755 MAP

CREEK

ARROYO

777

ALAMEDA

COUNTY

R3E
R4E

TROUT

SOUTH
16

15

14   DEL

13

FORK

TROUT CREEK

EYLAR

VALLE

COFFEY MILL GULCH

CANYON

DEADMAN

GULCH

21

BEARTRAP

RIDGE

ALAMEDA   CO   22

23

24

0   .25   .5   .75   1.0

miles 1 in. = 3800 ft.

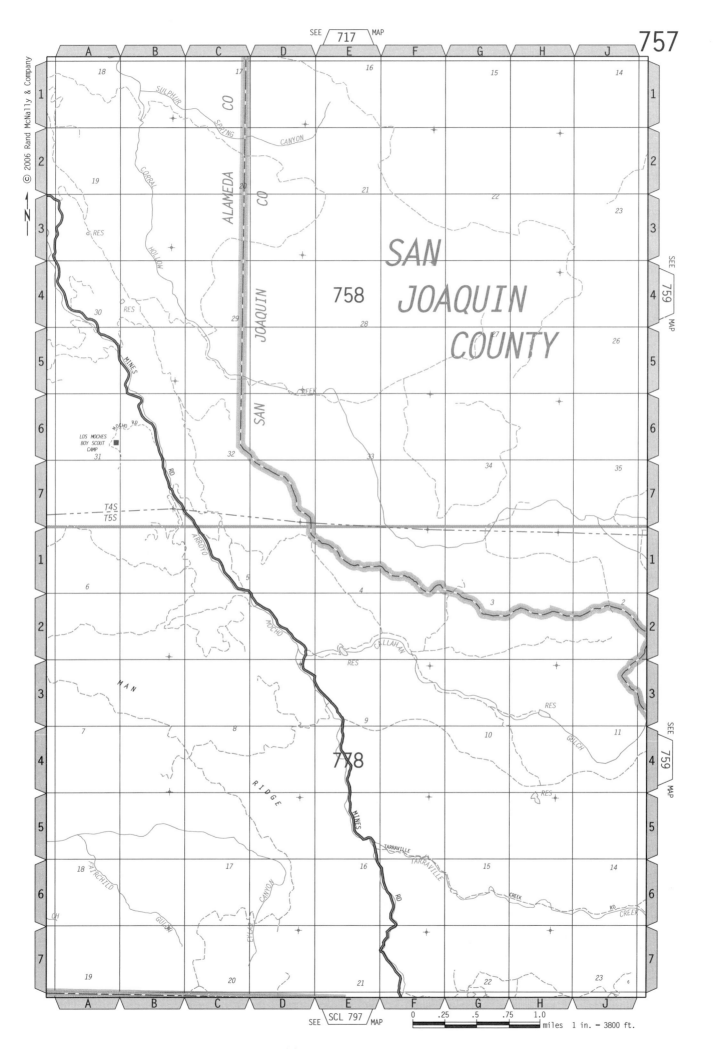

SAN
JOAQUIN
COUNTY

758

778

0 .25 .5 .75 1.0 miles 1 in. = 3800 ft.

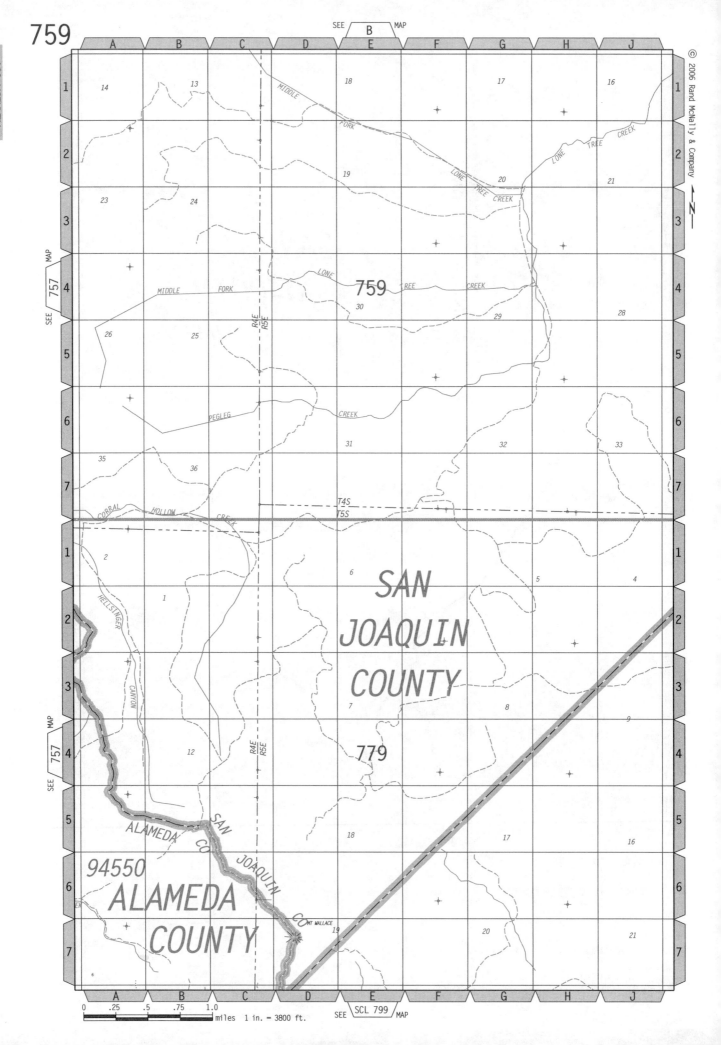

ALAMEDA CO.

© 2006 Rand McNally & Company

N

A   B   C   D   E   F   G   H   J

1   14   13   18   17   16   1

2   2

3   23   24   20   21   3

4   SEE 757 MAP   MIDDLE   FORK   LONE   759   TREE   CREEK   28   4

5   26   25   30   29   5

6   PEGLEG   CREEK   31   32   33   6

7   35   36   7

CORRAL   HOLLOW   CREEK   T4S / T5S

1   2   6   5   4   1

2   HEILSINGER   2

3   1   CANYON   7   8   9   3

4   SEE 757 MAP   12   R4E/R5E   779   4

5   ALAMEDA   CO   18   17   16   5

6   94550   ALAMEDA   SAN   JOAQUIN   CO   MT WALLACE   19   20   21   6

7   COUNTY   6   7

SAN JOAQUIN COUNTY

A   B   C   D   E   F   G   H   J

0   .25   .5   .75   1.0   miles   1 in. = 3800 ft.

SEE SCL 799 MAP

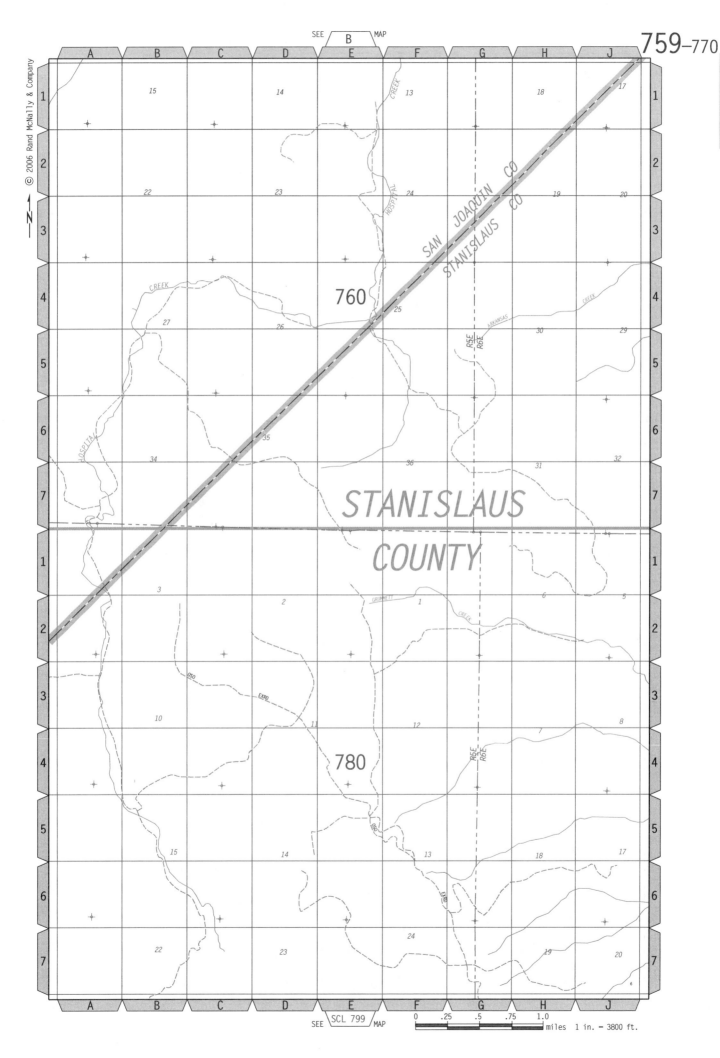

ALAMEDA CO.

SEE B MAP

SEE SCL 799 MAP

0   .25   .5   .75   1.0
miles 1 in. = 3800 ft.

© 2006 Rand McNally & Company

N

760

780

STANISLAUS

COUNTY

SAN JOAQUIN CO

STANISLAUS CO

HOSPITAL CREEK

CREEK

CREEK

HOSPITAL

ARKANSAS

GRUMMETT

CREEK

R5E R6E

R5E R6E

OSO

EXRD

OSO

EXRD

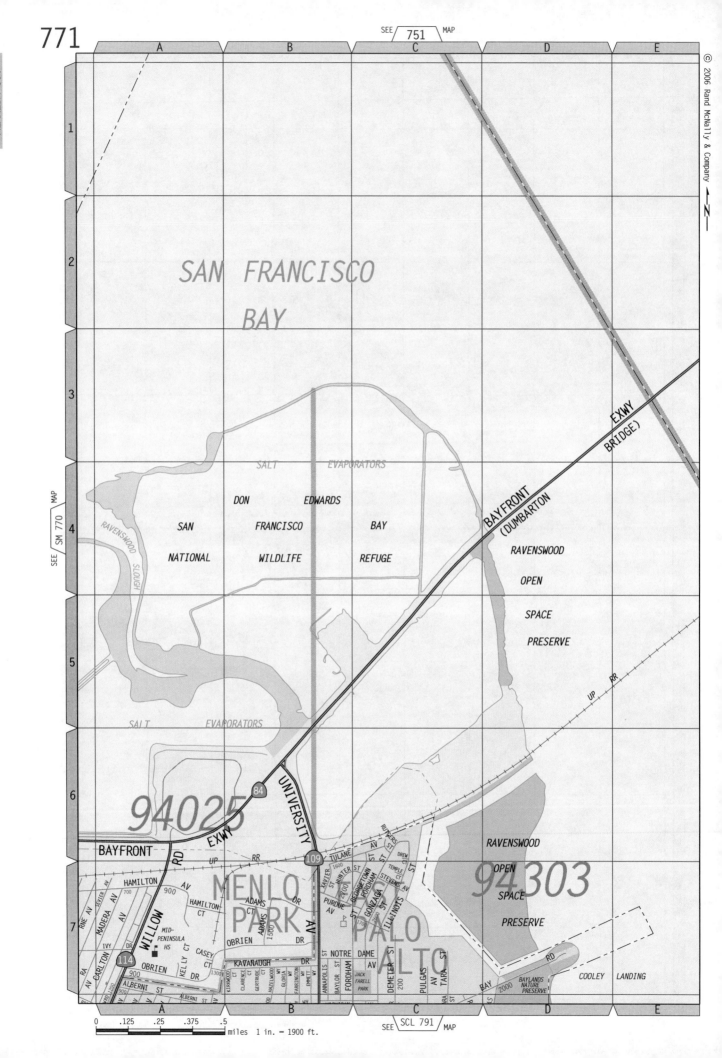

771

ALAMEDA CO.

© 2006 Rand McNally & Company

SEE 751 MAP

A   B   C   D   E

1

2

SAN FRANCISCO

BAY

3

SEE SM 770 MAP

SALT   EVAPORATORS

DON   EDWARDS

SAN   FRANCISCO   BAY

NATIONAL   WILDLIFE   REFUGE

RAVENSWOOD SLOUGH

4

BAYFRONT (DUMBARTON

RAVENSWOOD

OPEN

SPACE

PRESERVE

EXWY BRIDGE)

5

UP RR

SALT   EVAPORATORS

6

94025

84

UNIVERSITY

EXWY

RAVENSWOOD

OPEN

SPACE

PRESERVE

94303

BAYFRONT   RD

UP   RR

109

TULANE

AV

RUTGERS ST

DREW

BAYLOR ST

HUNTER ST

XAVIER ST

TEMPLE CT

STEVENS ST

HAMILTON   AV   700

RHE AV   SEXTER AV

MADERA AV   900

ADAMS CT

GEORGETOWN

FORDHAM

GONZAGA

ILLINOIS

MENLO

PARK   AV

HAMILTON CT

PURDUE AV   1500

WEST

PALO ALTO

7

WILLOW

MID-PENINSULA HS

ALBERNI ST

IVY

DR

CASEY CT

KELLY DR

OBRIEN   DR

KAVANAUGH   DR

KIRKWOOD CT

CLARENCE CT

GERTRUDE

GLORIA WY

HAZELWOOD

FARRINGTON WY

EMMET WY

ANNAPOLIS ST

BAYLOR ST

FORDHAM ST

NOTRE DAME AV

JACK FARELL PARK

DEMETER ST   200

PULGAS   AV

TARA ST

BAY

2000

BAYLANDS NATURE PRESERVE

COOLEY   LANDING

114

OBRIEN

CARLTON   AV

RA AV

900

MB 1200

900

ALBERNI ST

RD

SEE SCL 791 MAP

0   .125   .25   .375   .5
miles 1 in. = 1900 ft.

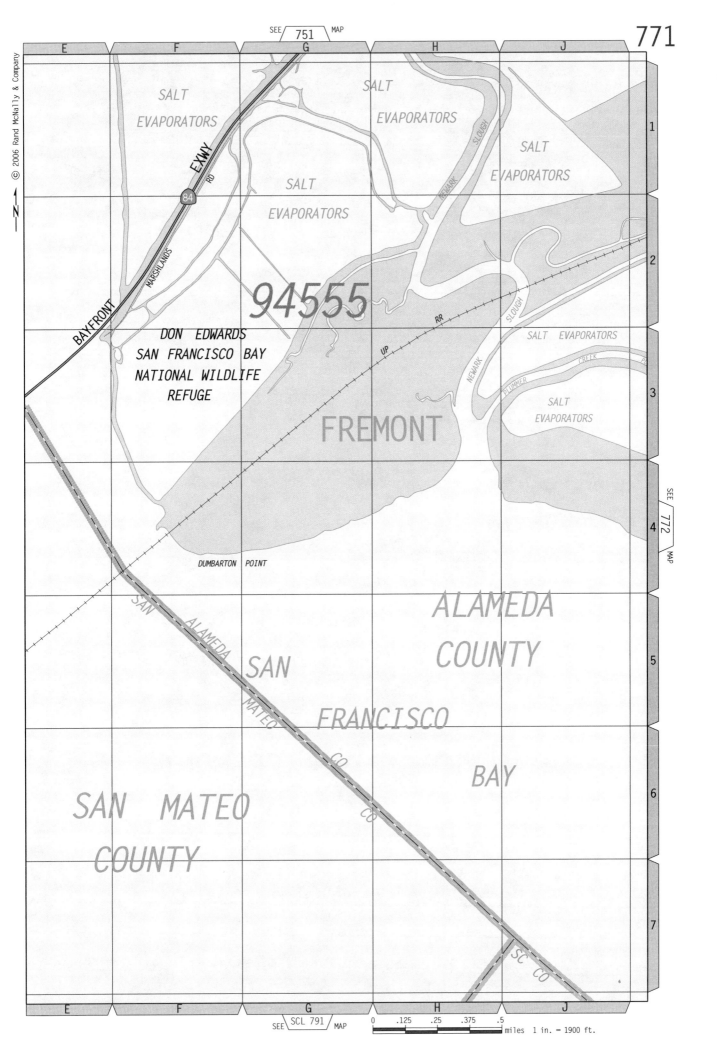

SEE 751 MAP

E   F   G   H   J

1

SALT EVAPORATORS

SALT EVAPORATORS

SALT EVAPORATORS

SALT EVAPORATORS

EXWY

84

RD

NEWARK SLOUGH

2

MARSHLANDS

BAYFRONT

94555

DON EDWARDS
SAN FRANCISCO BAY
NATIONAL WILDLIFE
REFUGE

UP

RR

NEWARK SLOUGH

SALT EVAPORATORS

PLUMMER CREEK

SALT EVAPORATORS

3

FREMONT

SEE 772 MAP

4

DUMBARTON POINT

ALAMEDA

COUNTY

SAN

SAN ALAMEDA

MATEO

CO

CO

SAN

FRANCISCO

5

BAY

SAN MATEO

6

COUNTY

SC CO

7

6

E   F   G   H   J

0   .125   .25   .375   .5

miles 1 in. = 1900 ft.

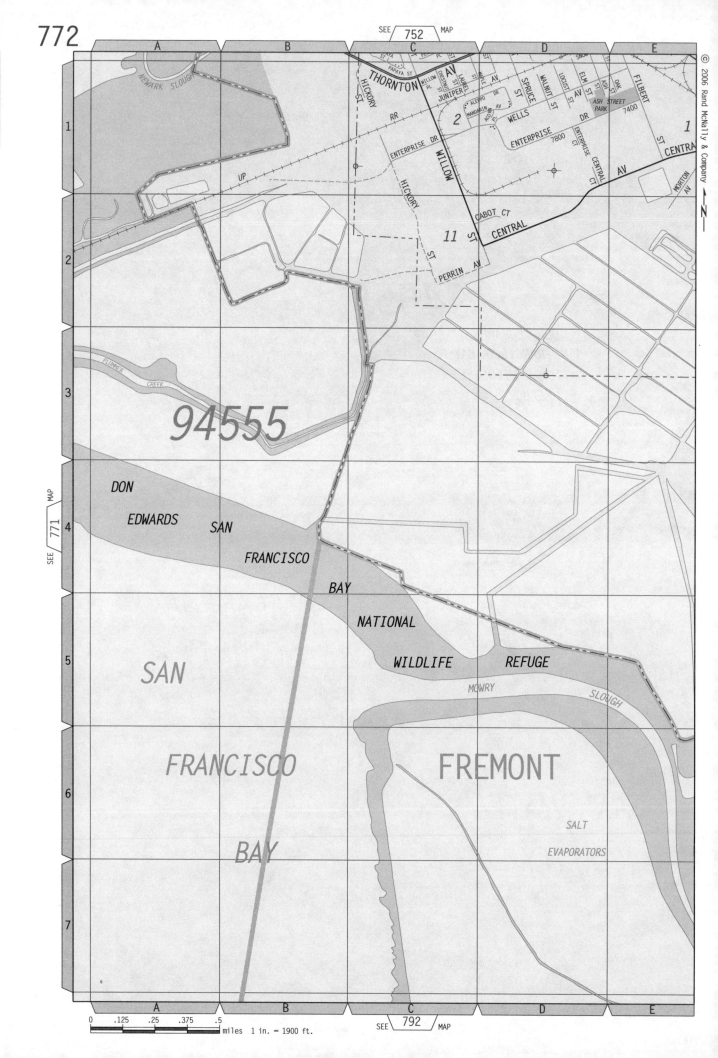

ALAMEDA CO.

SEE 752 MAP

A   B   C   D   E

THORNTON AV
PAPAYA ST
HICKORY ST
WILLOW PL
JUNIPER ST
LAUREL ST
CHESTNUT ST
MAPLE AV
ALEPPO AV
MANDARIN AV
MOTOR AV
2
SPRUCE ST
WALNUT ST
LOCUST ST
ELM ST
ASH ST
OAK ST
FILBERT ST
ASH STREET PARK
7400
WELLS
RR
ENTERPRISE DR
WILLOW ST
ENTERPRISE 7800
ENTERPRISE DR
CENTRAL CT
ENTERPRISE CT
1
CENTRAL AV
CENTRA
MORTON AV

© 2006 Rand McNally & Company

N

UP
CABOT CT
11 ST
CENTRAL
HICKORY ST
PERRIN AV

PLUMMER CREEK

94555

DON
EDWARDS SAN
FRANCISCO
BAY
NATIONAL
WILDLIFE   REFUGE
MOWRY   SLOUGH

SAN

FRANCISCO   FREMONT

BAY

SALT
EVAPORATORS

NEWARK SLOUGH

SEE 771 MAP

1

2

3

4

5

6

7

A   B   C   D   E

0 .125 .25 .375 .5
miles 1 in. = 1900 ft.

SEE 792 MAP

772

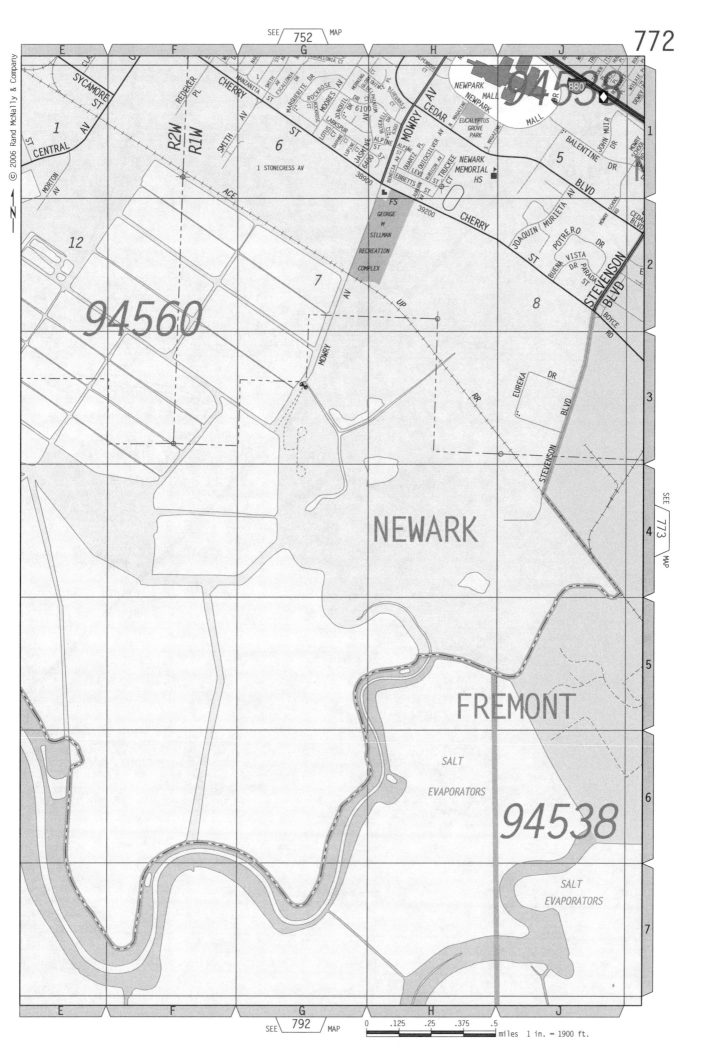

ALAMEDA CO.

© 2006 Rand McNally & Company

SEE 752 MAP

94558

NEWPARK MALL

NEWARK

FREMONT

94560

94538

SALT EVAPORATORS

SALT EVAPORATORS

SEE 773 MAP

SEE 792 MAP

0 .125 .25 .375 .5 miles 1 in. = 1900 ft.

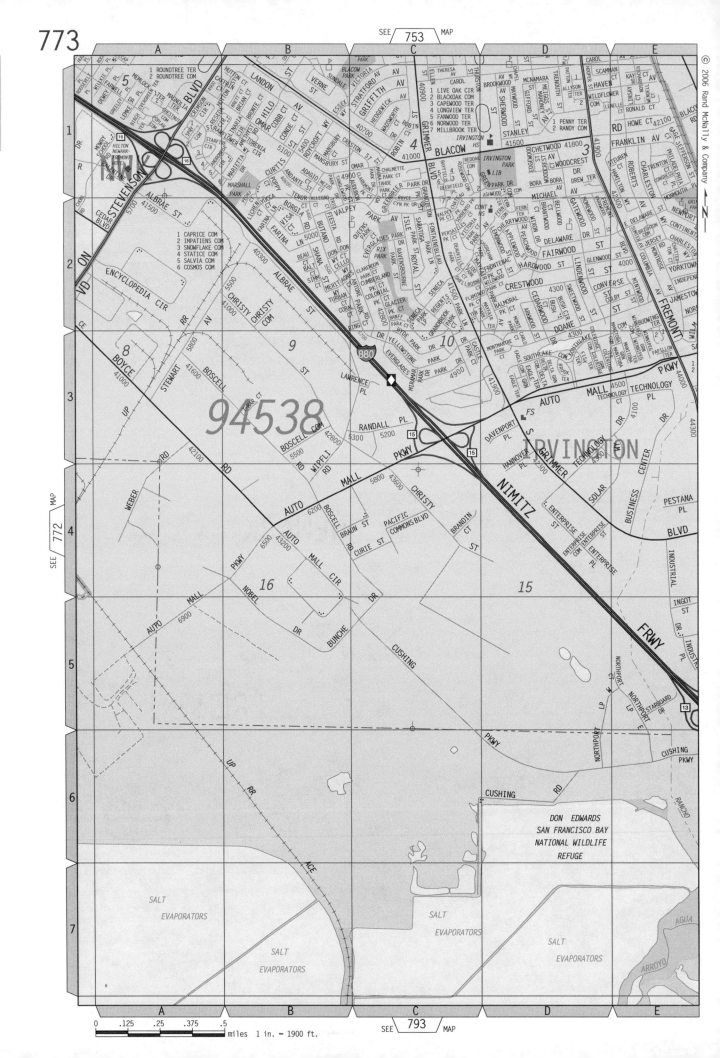

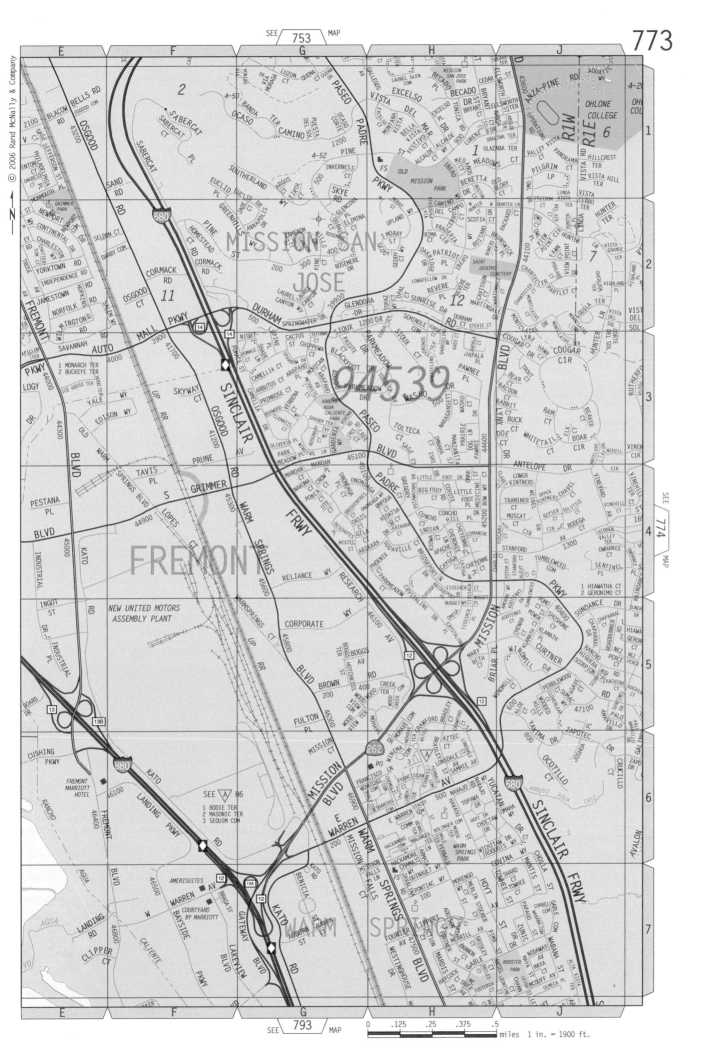

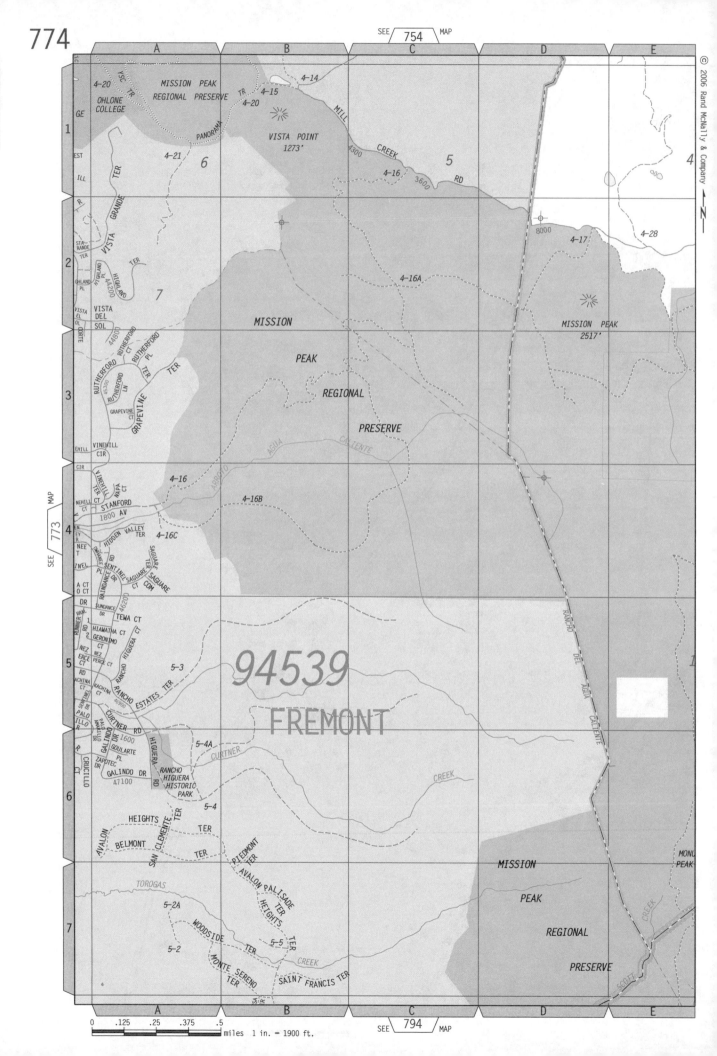

ALAMEDA CO.

© 2006 Rand McNally & Company

SEE 754 MAP

SEE 773 MAP

SEE 794 MAP

OHLONE COLLEGE

MISSION PEAK REGIONAL PRESERVE

4-20
4-21
YSC TR
PANORAMA TR
4-14
4-15
4-20

VISTA POINT 1273'

MILL CREEK RD
4300
3600
4-16

8000
4-17
4-28
4-16A

MISSION

PEAK

REGIONAL

PRESERVE

MISSION PEAK 2517'

VISTA GRANDE TER
HIGHLAND TER
VISTA GRANDE TER
STA GRANDE TER
GHLAND PL
HIGHLAND PL
44200

VISTA DEL SOL
VISTA EL OL CORTE

RUTHERFORD CT
RUTHERFORD PL
RUTHERFORD TER
RUTHERFORD TER
RUTHERFORD
45300
RUTHERFORD LN
GRAPEVINE CT
GRAPEVINE

EHILL
VINEHILL CIR
VINEHILL TER
NEHILL CT
NAPA CT

STANFORD 1800 AV

AGUA CALIENTE
ARROYO

4-16
4-16B

HIDDEN VALLEY TER
4-16C

SENTINEL DR
RATNDANCE PL
OKLAHOMA RD
SAGUARE CT
SAGUARE TER
SAGUARE COM

RANCHO DEL AGUA CALIENTE

SUNDANCE DR
TEWA CT
HIAWATHA CT
GERONIMO CT
NEZ PERCE CT
NEZ PERCE CT
KACHINA CT
RANCHO HIGUERA CT
RANCHO HIGUERA CT
46200
46900

5-3
RANCHO ESTATES TER

94539

FREMONT

RUNNER RD
1
2
NEZ ERCE CT
KACHINA CT
RD
PALO TILLO R
CURTNER RD

GALINDO DR 1600
GOULARTE PL
ZAPOTEC
GALINDO DR
47100
PAUL AMARILLO DR
HIGUERA RD
CRUCILLO CT

5-4A
CURTNER

RANCHO HIGUERA HISTORIC PARK
5-4

CREEK

AVALON HEIGHTS
BELMONT
SAN CLEMENTE TER
TER
TER

PIEDMONT TER
AVALON PALISADE HEIGHTS TER
TER

MISSION

PEAK

REGIONAL

PRESERVE

MISSION PEAK

MONU PEAK

TOROGAS
5-2A
WOODSIDE TER
5-5
5-2
MONTE SERENO TER
SAINT FRANCIS TER
CREEK

SCOTT CREEK

0 .125 .25 .375 .5
miles 1 in. = 1900 ft.

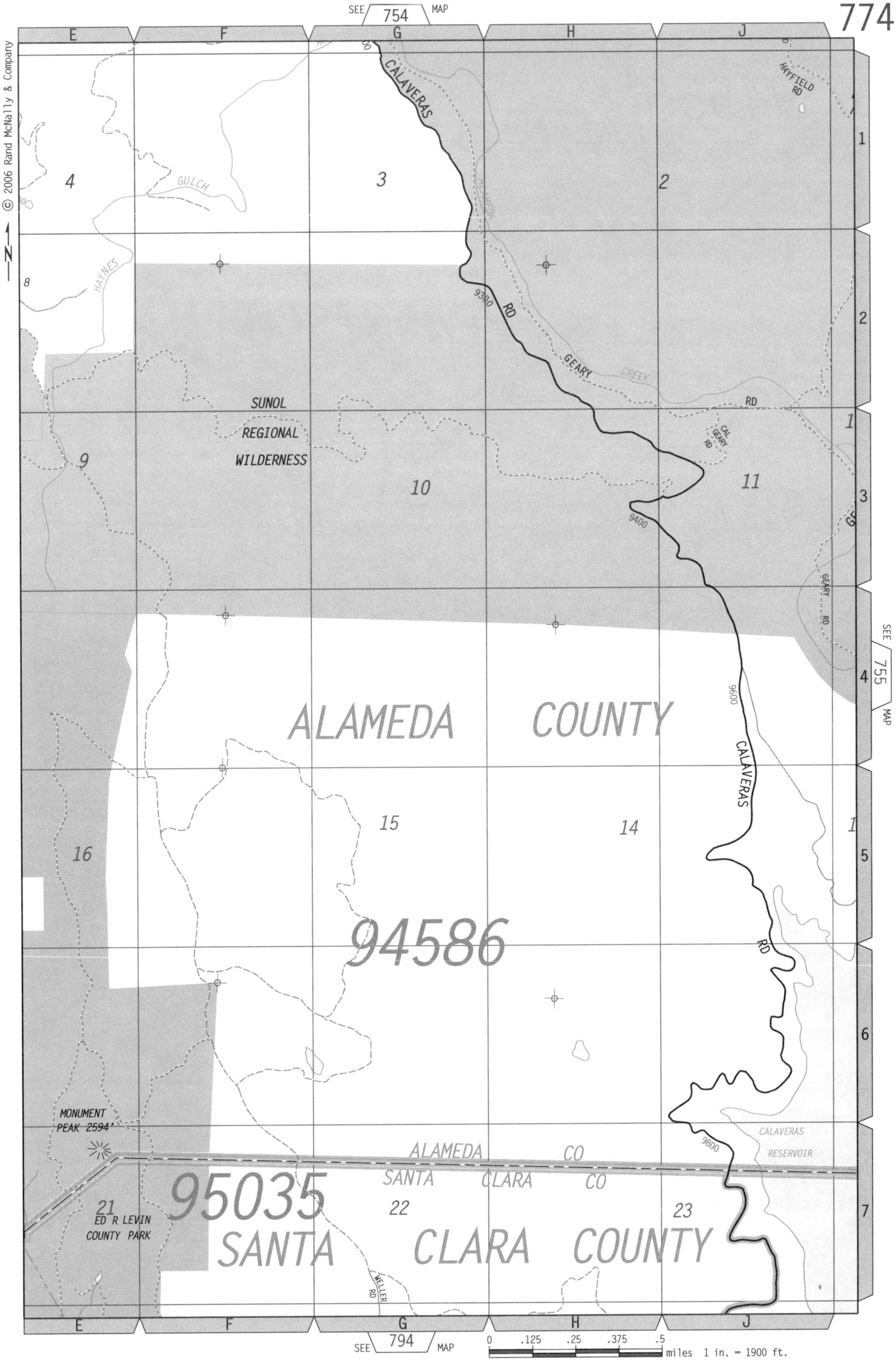

ALAMEDA CO.

SEE 754 MAP

N

CALAVERAS

E F G H J

4

3

2

1

GULCH

HAYFIELD RD

8

HAYNES

9300 RD

GEARY

CREEK

2

SUNOL

REGIONAL

WILDERNESS

9

10

RD

CAL GEARY RD

11

1

GEARY RD

GE

3

9400

SEE 755 MAP

4

ALAMEDA COUNTY

9600

CALAVERAS

15

14

1

16

5

94586

CALAVERAS

RD

6

9800

CALAVERAS RESERVOIR

MONUMENT PEAK 2594'

ALAMEDA CO

SANTA CLARA CO

7

21

ED R LEVIN COUNTY PARK

95035

SANTA

22

23

CLARA COUNTY

NELLER RD

E F G H J

SEE 794 MAP

0 .125 .25 .375 .5 miles 1 in. = 1900 ft.

ALAMEDA CO.

© 2006 Rand McNally & Company

94555

ALAMEDA COUNTY

SAN

DON EDWARDS
SAN FRANCISCO BAY
NATIONAL WILDLIFE
REFUGE

CALAVERAS PT

FRANCISCO

COYOTE   CREEK

SANTA   CLARA   COUNTY

BAY

95002

GUADALUPE   SLOUGH

SEE SCL 791 MAP

SALT

EVAPORATORS

SALT

94089

EVAPORATOR

SHORELINE
AT
MOUNTAIN
VIEW

MOFFETT FEDERAL
AIRFIELD

RD

MTVW

SUNNYVALE

CRITTENDEN LN

94043

AMES
RESEARCH
CENTER

ZOOK

RANCHO POSOLMI

94035

MARRIAGE RD

MOFFETT FIELD
GOLF COURSE

SEE 772 MAP

SEE SCL 812 MAP

0 .125 .25 .375 .5
miles 1 in. = 1900 ft.

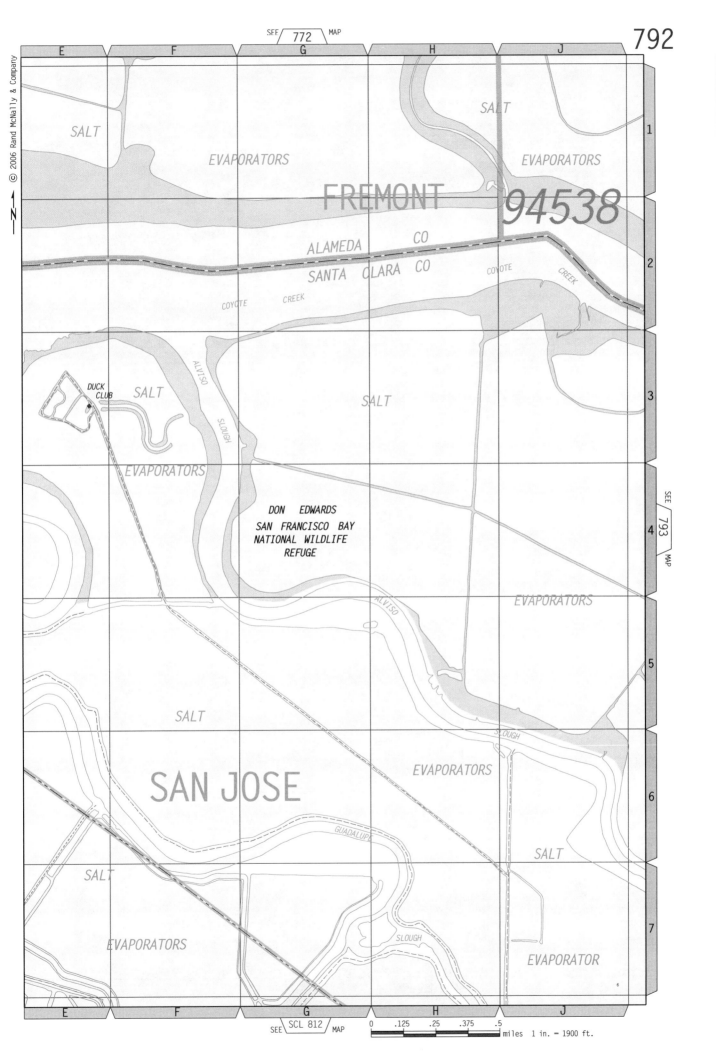

ALAMEDA CO.

SEE 772 MAP

E   F   G   H   J

1

SALT

EVAPORATORS

SALT

EVAPORATORS

FREMONT

94538

ALAMEDA   CO

SANTA   CLARA   CO

2

COYOTE   CREEK

COYOTE

CREEK

DUCK
CLUB

SALT

ALVISO

SLOUGH

SALT

3

EVAPORATORS

SEE 793 MAP

DON   EDWARDS
SAN FRANCISCO BAY
NATIONAL WILDLIFE
REFUGE

4

ALVISO

EVAPORATORS

5

SALT

SLOUGH

SAN JOSE

EVAPORATORS

6

GUADALUPE

SALT

SALT

EVAPORATORS

SLOUGH

EVAPORATOR

7

6

E   F   G   H   J

SEE SCL 812 MAP

0   .125   .25   .375   .5

miles 1 in. = 1900 ft.

ALAMEDA CO.

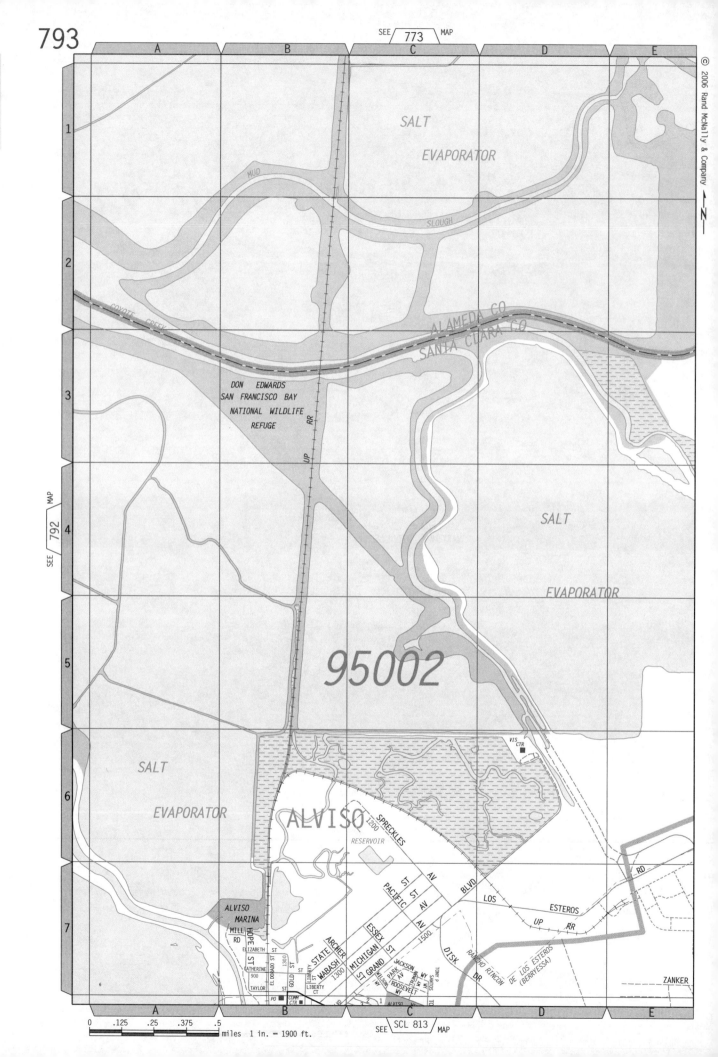

—N—

SEE 773 MAP

SALT

EVAPORATOR

MUD

SLOUGH

COYOTE CREEK

ALAMEDA CO
SANTA CLARA CO

DON EDWARDS
SAN FRANCISCO BAY
NATIONAL WILDLIFE
REFUGE

UP RR

SALT

EVAPORATOR

SEE 792 MAP

95002

VIS CTR

SALT

EVAPORATOR

ALVISO

SPRECKLES

RESERVOIR

RD

LOS

ESTEROS

UP RR

ALVISO
MARINA

MILL
RD

HOPE

ST

Elizabeth ST

CATHERINE ST

900

TAYLOR

EL DORADO ST

1300

GOLD ST

PO

LIBERTY ST

LIBERTY CT

COMM CTR

STATE ST

WABASH

1300

ARCHER ST

MICHIGAN ST

GRAND

ESSEX ST

PACIFIC ST

ST

ST

AV

AV

AV

AV

AV

BLVD

1500

JACKSON

PARK AV

WILSON WY

ROOSEVELT WY

TONY P SANTOS

TRIMBLE WY

TONY P

DISK

DR

RANCHO RINCON

DE LOS ESTEROS
(BERRYESSA)

ZANKER

ALVISO

SPRECKLES

SEE SCL 813 MAP

0 .125 .25 .375 .5
miles 1 in. = 1900 ft.

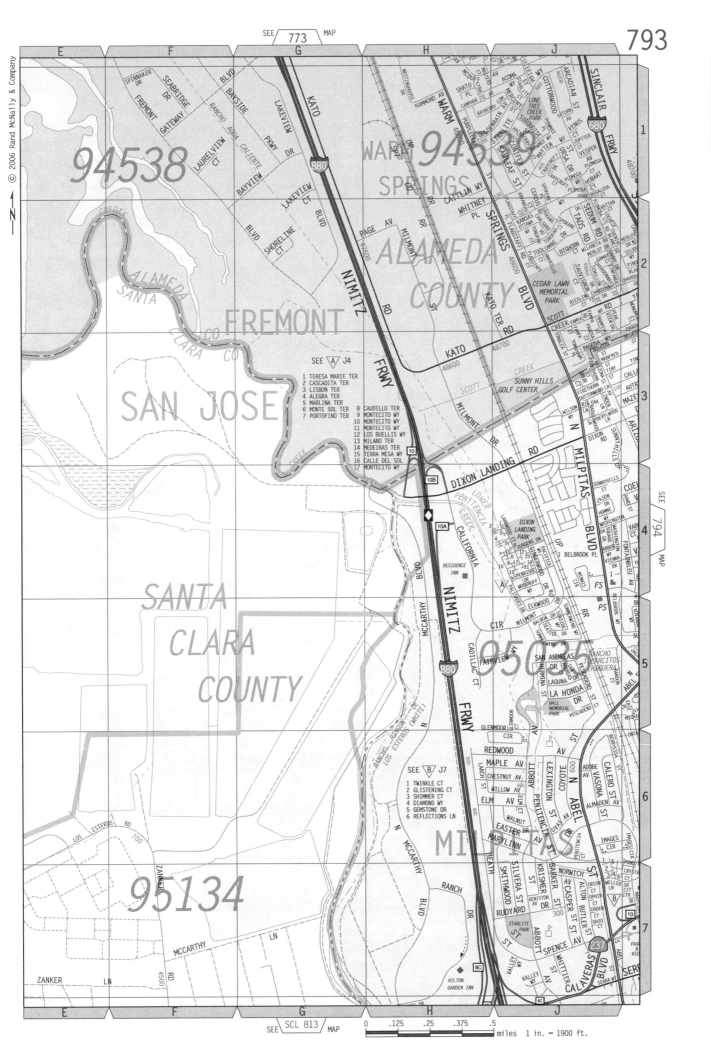

© 2006 Rand McNally & Company

N

E F G H J

94538

SPINNAKER DR
SEABRIDGE DR
FREMONT GATEWAY
BAXSIDE BLVD
RANCHO AGUA CALIENTE
LAKEVIEW PKWY
LAURELVIEW CT
BAYVIEW
LAKEVIEW CT
SHORELINE CT
LAKEVIEW BLVD

KATO

880

NIMITZ FRWY RD

COYOTE

ALAMEDA
SANTA
CLARA
CO
CO

FREMONT

SAN JOSE

CREEK

94539

WARM
SPRINGS

ALAMEDA
COUNTY

WARM SPRINGS BLVD

HAMMOND AV

PAGE AV

MILMONT

KATO TER

SCOTT
CREEK

KATO

MILMONT

48600
48700

DIXON RD

SUNNY HILLS
GOLF CENTER

CEDAR LAWN
MEMORIAL
PARK

SCOTT   CREEK

SEE A J4
1 TERESA MARIE TER
2 CASCADITA TER
3 LISBON TER
4 ALEGRA TER
5 MARLINA TER
6 MONTE SOL TER   8 CAUDILLO TER
7 PORTOFINO TER   9 MONTECITO WY
                 10 MONTECITO WY
                 11 MONTECITO WY
                 12 LOS BUELLIS WY
                 13 MILANO TER
                 14 MEDEIRAS TER
                 15 TERRA MESA WY
                 16 CALLE DEL SOL
                 17 MONTECITO WY

10

10B

DIXON LANDING RD

DIXON LANDING RD

MILPITAS BLVD

10A

DIXON
LANDING
PARK

RESIDENCE
INN

CALIFORNIA

LOWER PENITENCIA CREEK

SANTA
CLARA
COUNTY

SEE 794 MAP

BELBROOK PL

SUNNYHILLS

95035

NIMITZ

MCCARTHY

BLVD

880 FRWY

CIR   MILMONT
FAIRVIEW
CADILLAC CT

SAN ANDREAS

LA HONDA DR

HALL MEMORIAL PARK

GLENMOOR
CIR

RANCHO — DE
LOS ESTEROS (WHITE)

SEE B J7
1 TWINKLE CT
2 GLISTENING CT
3 SHIMMER CT
4 DIAMOND WY
5 GEMSTONE DR
6 REFLECTIONS LN

REDWOOD AV

MAPLE AV

CHESTNUT AV

WILLOW AV

ELM AV

WALNUT

EASTER DR

MARYLINN

LARCH ST
ELM ST

ABBOTT
LEXINGTON
PENITENCIA
UVAS

ADOBE
CALERO ST
VASONA
ALMADEN ST

IMAGES CIR

MILPITAS

HEATH

SMITHWOOD ST
SILVERA ST
RUDYARD ST

KRISMER AV
BARKER

NORWICH
ORION CT
ALTON
CASPER

STARLITE
PARK

SPENCE

BUTLER ST

WHITTIER AV
VALLEY WY

CALAVERAS BLVD
SERRA

237

10

95134

LOS ESTEROS RD

700

ZANKER

MCCARTHY

BLVD

RANCH DR

8C

HILTON
GARDEN INN

9C

ZANKER LN

MCCARTHY RD

4500

LN

PARK & RID

0 .125 .25 .375 .5

miles 1 in. = 1900 ft.

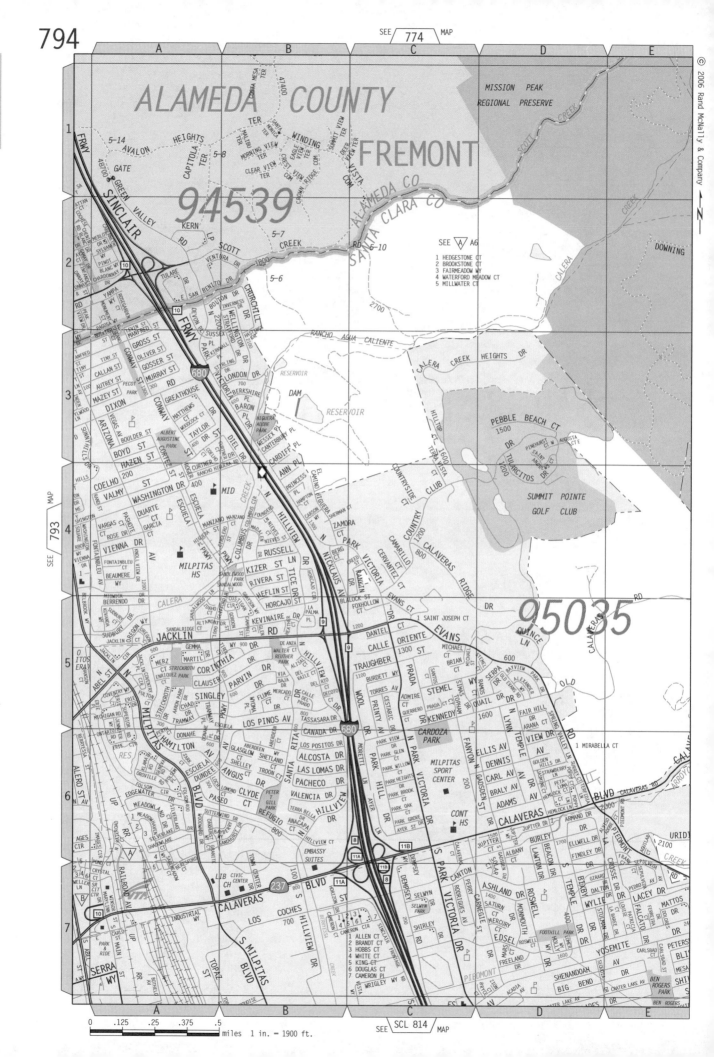

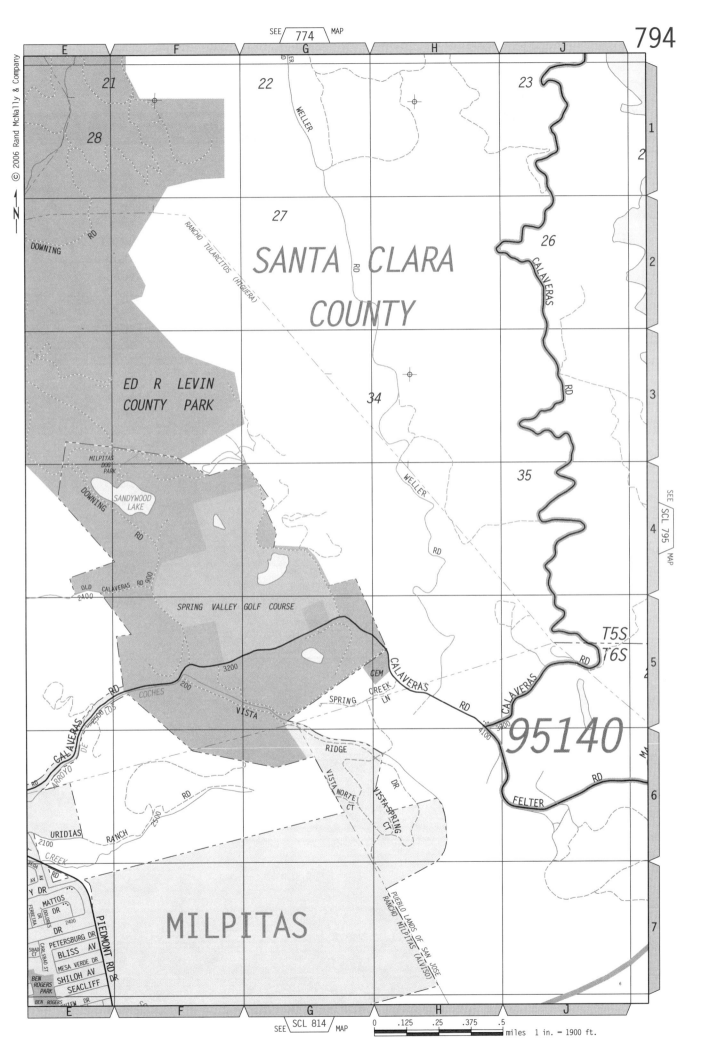

ALAMEDA CO.

© 2006 Rand McNally & Company

—N—

E   F   G   H   J

21   22   23

28

27

RANCHO TULARCITOS (HIGUERA)

SANTA CLARA

COUNTY

DOWNING   RD

WELLER

26

CALAVERAS   RD

ED R LEVIN
COUNTY PARK

MILPITAS
DOG
PARK

34

DOWNING
RD

SANDYWOOD
LAKE

35

WELLER

RD

SEE SCL 795 MAP

OLD CALAVERAS RD 900

2400

SPRING VALLEY GOLF COURSE

CALAVERAS   RD

T5S
T6S

3200

COCHES   200

VISTA

CALAVERAS   CREEK   CEM
SPRING   LN

CALAVERAS

RD

CALAVERAS   RD

95140

GALAVERAS   RD

ARROYO DE   LOS   COCHES

RIDGE

VISTA
NORTE
CT

VISTA-SPRING
CT   DR

3900
4100

FELTER   RD

RD   2500

URIDIAS   RANCH

2100

CREEK

Y DR

MATTOS
DR

PIEDMONT   RD   DR

PETERSBURG DR

BLISS AV

MESA VERDE DR

SHILOH AV

SEACLIFF

BEN ROGERS
PARK

BEN ROGERS   VIEW DR

MILPITAS

PUEBLO LANDS OF SAN JOSE
RANCHO MILPITAS (ALVISO)

6

E   F   G   H   J

0   .125   .25   .375   .5
miles   1 in. = 1900 ft.

Cities and Communities

Community Name	Abbr.	ZIP Code	Map Page	Community Name	Abbr.	ZIP Code	Map Page
* Alameda	ALA	94501	670	Mission San Jose		94539	753
-- Alameda County	AlaC			Montclair		94611	650
* Albany	ALB	94706	609	Mountain House		94550	678
Altamont		94550	677	Mulford Gardens		94577	690
Alvarado		94587	731	* Newark	NWK	94560	752
Ashland		94578	691	Niles		94536	753
Bay Farm Island		94502	669	Oak Knoll		94605	671
* Berkeley	BERK	94710	629	* Oakland	OAK	94601	649
Brookfield Village		94603	670	Oakmore		94602	650
Castro Valley		94546	691	* Piedmont	PDMT	94611	650
Centerville		94536	752	Piedmont Pines		94611	650
Claremont		94705	630	* Pleasanton	PLE	94566	714
Cragmont		94708	609	Ridgemont		94619	651
Dimond		94602	650	Rockridge		94618	630
Dougherty		94566	694	* San Leandro	SLN	94577	671
* Dublin	DBLN	94568	693	San Lorenzo		94580	711
Eastmont		94605	671	Santa Rita		94566	694
Elmhurst		94603	670	Scotts Corner		94586	734
* Emeryville	EMVL	94608	629	Seminary		94619	670
Fernside		94501	670	Sheffield Village		94605	671
Forest Park		94611	630	South Shore		94501	669
* Fremont	FRMT	94536	753	Spring Town		94550	696
Fruitvale		94601	650	Sunol		94586	734
* Hayward	HAY	94541	711	Temescal		94609	629
Irvington		94538	753	Thousand Oaks		94707	609
Kilkare		94586	734	Trestle Glen		94610	650
* Livermore	LVMR	94550	715	* Union City	UNC	94587	732
Melrose		94601	670	Warm Springs		94539	773
Midway		94550	698				

*Indicates incorporated city

List of Abbreviations

PREFIXES AND SUFFIXES					
AL	ALLEY	CTST	COURT STREET	PZ D LA	PLAZA DE LA
ARC	ARCADE	CUR	CURVE	PZ D LAS	PLAZA DE LAS
AV, AVE	AVENUE	CV	COVE	PZWY	PLAZA WAY
AVCT	AVENUE COURT	DE	DE	RAMP	RAMP
AVD	AVENIDA	DIAG	DIAGONAL	RD	ROAD
AVD D LA	AVENIDA DE LA	DR	DRIVE	RDAV	ROAD AVENUE
AVD D LOS	AVENIDA DE LOS	DRAV	DRIVE AVENUE	RDBP	ROAD BYPASS
AVD DE	AVENIDA DE	DRCT	DRIVE COURT	RDCT	ROAD COURT
AVD DE LAS	AVENIDA DE LAS	DRLP	DRIVE LOOP	RDEX	ROAD EXTENSION
AVD DEL	AVENIDA DEL	DVDR	DIVISION DR	RDG	RIDGE
AVDR	AVENUE DRIVE	EXAV	EXTENSION AVENUE	RDSP	ROAD SPUR
AVEX	AVENUE EXTENSION	EXBL	EXTENSION BOULEVARD	RDWY	ROAD WAY
AV OF	AVENUE OF	EXRD	EXTENSION ROAD	RR	RAILROAD
AV OF THE	AVENUE OF THE	EXST	EXTENSION STREET	RUE	RUE
AVPL	AVENUE PLACE	EXT	EXTENSION	RUE D	RUE D
BAY	BAY	EXWY	EXPRESSWAY	RW	ROW
BEND	BEND	FOREST RT	FOREST ROUTE	RY	RAILWAY
BL, BLVD	BOULEVARD	FRWY	FREEWAY	SKWY	SKYWAY
BLCT	BOULEVARD COURT	FRY	FERRY	SQ	SQUARE
BLEX	BOULEVARD EXTENSION	GDNS	GARDENS	ST	STREET
BRCH	BRANCH	GN, GLN	GLEN	STAV	STREET AVENUE
BRDG	BRIDGE	GRN	GREEN	STCT	STREET COURT
BYPS	BYPASS	GRV	GROVE	STDR	STREET DRIVE
BYWY	BYWAY	HTS	HEIGHTS	STEX	STREET EXTENSION
CIDR	CIRCLE DRIVE	HWY	HIGHWAY	STLN	STREET LANE
CIR	CIRCLE	ISL	ISLE	STLP	STREET LOOP
CL	CALLE	JCT	JUNCTION	STOF	STREET OF
CL DE	CALLE DE	LN	LANE	ST OF THE	STREET OF THE
CL DL	CALLE DEL	LNCR	LANE CIRCLE	STOV	STREET OVERPASS
CL D LA	CALLE DE LA	LNDG	LANDING	STPL	STREET PLACE
CL D LAS	CALLE DE LAS	LNDR	LAND DRIVE	STPM	STREET PROMENADE
CL D LOS	CALLE DE LOS	LNLP	LANE LOOP	STWY	STREET WAY
CL EL	CALLE EL	LP	LOOP	STXP	STREET EXPRESSWAY
CLJ	CALLEJON	MNR	MANOR	TER	TERRACE
CL LA	CALLE LA	MT	MOUNT	TFWY	TRAFFICWAY
CL LAS	CALLE LAS	MTWY	MOTORWAY	THWY	THROUGHWAY
CL LOS	CALLE LOS	MWCR	MEWS COURT	TKTR	TRUCK TRAIL
CLTR	CLUSTER	MWLN	MEWS LANE	TPKE	TURNPIKE
CM	CAMINO	NFD	NAT'L FOREST DEV	TRC	TRACE
CM DE	CAMINO DE	NK	NOOK	TRCT	TERRACE COURT
CM DL	CAMINO DEL	OH	OUTER HIGHWAY	TR, TRL	TRAIL
CM D LA	CAMINO DE LA	OVL	OVAL	TRWY	TRAIL WAY
CM D LAS	CAMINO DE LAS	OVLK	OVERLOOK	TTSP	TRUCK TRAIL SPUR
CM D LOS	CAMINO DE LOS	OVPS	OVERPASS	TUN	TUNNEL
CMTO	CAMINITO	PAS	PASEO	UNPS	UNDERPASS
CMTO DEL	CAMINITO DEL	PAS DE	PASEO DE	VIA D	VIA DE
CMTO D LA	CAMINITO DE LA	PAS DE LA	PASEO DE LA	VIA DL	VIA DEL
CMTO D LAS	CAMINITO DE LAS	PAS DE LAS	PASEO DE LAS	VIA D LA	VIA DE LA
CMTO D LOS	CAMINITO DE LOS	PAS DE LOS	PASEO DE LOS	VIA D LAS	VIA DE LAS
CNDR	CENTER DRIVE	PAS DL	PASEO DEL	VIA D LOS	VIA DE LOS
COM	COMMON	PASG	PASSAGE	VIA LA	VIA LA
COMS	COMMONS	PAS LA	PASEO LA	VW	VIEW
CORR	CORRIDOR	PAS LOS	PASEO LOS	VWY	VIEW WAY
CRES	CRESCENT	PASS	PASS	VIS	VISTA
CRLO	CIRCULO	PIKE	PIKE	VIS D	VISTA DE
CRSG	CROSSING	PK	PARK	VIS D L	VISTA DE LA
CST	CIRCLE STREET	PKDR	PARK DRIVE	VIS D LAS	VISTA DE LAS
CSWY	CAUSEWAY	PKWY, PKY	PARKWAY	VIS DEL	VISTA DEL
CT	COURT	PL	PLACE	WK	WALK
CTAV	COURT AVENUE	PLWY	PLACE WAY	WY	WAY
CTE	CORTE	PLZ, PZ	PLAZA	WYCR	WAY CIRCLE
CTE D	CORTE DE	PT	POINT	WYDR	WAY DRIVE
CTE DEL	CORTE DEL	PTAV	POINT AVENUE	WYLN	WAY LANE
CTE D LAS	CORTE DE LAS	PTH	PATH	WYPL	WAY PLACE
CTO	CUT OFF	PZ DE	PLAZA DE		
CTR	CENTER	PZ DEL	PLAZA DEL		

DIRECTIONS	
E	EAST
KPN	KEY PENINSULA NORTH
KPS	KEY PENINSULA SOUTH
N	NORTH
NE	NORTHEAST
NW	NORTHWEST
S	SOUTH
SE	SOUTHEAST
SW	SOUTHWEST
W	WEST

BUILDINGS	
CH	CITY HALL
CHP	CALIFORNIA HIGHWAY PATROL
COMM CTR	COMMUNITY CENTER
CON CTR	CONVENTION CENTER
CONT HS	CONTINUATION HIGH SCHOOL
CTH	COURTHOUSE
FAA	FEDERAL AVIATION ADMIN
FS	FIRE STATION
HOSP	HOSPITAL
HS	HIGH SCHOOL
INT	INTERMEDIATE SCHOOL
JR HS	JUNIOR HIGH SCHOOL
LIB	LIBRARY
MID	MIDDLE SCHOOL
MUS	MUSEUM
PO	POST OFFICE
PS	POLICE STATION
SR CIT CTR	SENIOR CITIZENS CENTER
STA	STATION
THTR	THEATER
VIS BUR	VISITORS BUREAU

OTHER ABBREVIATIONS	
BCH	BEACH
BLDG	BUILDING
CEM	CEMETERY
CK	CREEK
CO	COUNTY
COMM	COMMUNITY
CTR	CENTER
EST	ESTATE
HIST	HISTORIC
HTS	HEIGHTS
LK	LAKE
MDW	MEADOW
MED	MEDICAL
MEM	MEMORIAL
MHP	MOBILE HOME PARK
MT	MOUNT
MTN	MOUNTAIN
NATL	NATIONAL
PKG	PARKING
PLGD	PLAYGROUND
RCH	RANCH
RCHO	RANCHO
REC	RECREATION
RES	RESERVOIR
RIV	RIVER
RR	RAILROAD
SPG	SPRING
STA	SANTA
VLG	VILLAGE
VLY	VALLEY
VW	VIEW

STREET Block City ZIP Pg-Grid

A

A RD
100 AlaC 94586 734-C5
A ST
- HAY 94541 711-J1
100 AlaC 94586 734-C5
100 AlaC 94541 711-G2
600 UNC 94587 732-F4
1200 HAY 94541 712-A1
1200 HAY 94541 692-A7
1300 AlaC 94546 692-A7
7200 ELCR 94530 609-E4
8200 OAK 94621 670-H4
9000 OAK 94603 670-H5
W A ST
- HAY 94541 711-E2
200 AlaC 94541 711-F2
AARON ST
1200 LVMR 94550 715-F2
AARON PARK DR
700 MPS 95035 794-A5
ABACA WY
2300 FRMT 94539 753-E6
ABALONE CT
3500 UNC 94587 731-J4
ABALONE PL
200 LVMR 94550 715-D3
ABBEY AV
1400 SLN 94579 691-A6
ABBEY CT
5000 NWK 94560 752-F5
ABBEY ST
2700 OAK 94619 650-E6
ABBEY TER
4000 FRMT 94536 752-J4
ABBEYWOOD DR
- AlaC 94552 692-E7
ABBIE CT
600 PLE 94566 714-E4
ABBIE ST
100 PLE 94566 714-E4
ABBINGTON PL
25900 HAY 94542 712-D3
ABBOTFORD CT
5000 NWK 94560 752-D3
ABBOTT AV
- MPS 95035 793-J6
ABBOTT DR
- OAK 94611 630-D6
ABBOTT WY
- PDMT 94618 630-C7
ABEL PL
3500 FRMT 94536 752-F1
N ABEL ST
- MPS 95035 793-J6
- MPS 95035 794-A5
S ABEL ST
- MPS 95035 793-J7
ABELOE TER
43700 FRMT 94539 773-J1
ABERCROMBIE PL
33800 FRMT 94555 732-D7
ABERDALE CIR
- CCCo 94582 674-B5
ABERDEEN AV
900 LVMR 94550 715-F3
ABERDEEN CT
600 MPS 95035 794-B6
ABERDEEN PL
26900 HAY 94542 712-E3
ABERDEEN TER
34100 FRMT 94555 732-E7
34100 FRMT 94555 752-E1
ABERDEEN WY
500 MPS 95035 794-B6
ABERFOIL AV
4200 OAK 94605 671-D5
ABINGTON CT
5600 NWK 94560 752-D4
ABINGTON DR
5500 NWK 94560 752-D4
ABRAHAM ST
37800 FRMT 94536 753-A3
ABRAM CT
1600 SLN 94577 690-J3
ABREU WY
2300 UNC 94587 732-D4
ABRIGO CT
600 SRMN 94583 673-B2
ABUELO WY
40800 FRMT 94539 753-F4
ACACIA AV
- BERK 94708 609-G4
5800 OAK 94618 630-A5
ACACIA CT
38200 FRMT 94536 753-A3
ACACIA DR
- ORIN 94563 610-F6
1200 HAY 94541 712-A2
ACACIA ST
1400 SLN 94579 691-A4
38000 FRMT 94536 753-A2
ACACIA WY
900 LVMR 94550 715-H2
ACADIA AV
1200 MPS 95035 794-D7
ACADIA CT
6000 PLE 94588 714-B1
ACALANES DR
10500 OAK 94603 670-H7
ACAPULCO RD
14100 SLN 94577 690-H5
ACAPULCO WY
100 UNC 94587 732-D5
ACCESS RD
- EMVL 94608 629-D6
ACCOLADE DR
- SLN 94577 670-H7
ACCRA CT
1200 LVMR 94550 715-F3
ACOMA WY
200 FRMT 94539 793-J1
ACORN CT
700 SRMN 94583 673-G7
ACORN PL
- LVMR 94550 715-D4
- NWK 94560 772-D1
ACORN ST
2600 AlaC 94546 691-H4
ACORN WY
- LVMR 94550 715-D4
ACROFT CT
1400 BERK 94702 629-F2
ACTION CT
100 FRMT 94539 773-H7
ACTON CIR
- BERK 94702 629-F2
ACTON CRES
1400 BERK 94702 629-F2
ACTON PL
200 OAK 94606 649-J4
ACTON ST
1300 BERK 94706 609-F7
1400 BERK 94702 609-F7
1500 BERK 94702 629-F1
ADA AV
36700 FRMT 94536 752-F4
ADA ST
200 OAK 94618 629-J6
1300 BERK 94702 609-E7
1500 BERK 94702 629-E1
21700 AlaC 94546 692-A6
ADAGIO CT
4900 FRMT 94538 773-B1
ADAIR DR
19600 AlaC 94546 691-J4
ADAM ST
- SJCo 95391 (678-E3 See Page 677)
ADAMS AV
- DBLN 94568 694-A2
700 LVMR 94550 716-A1
1400 MPS 95035 794-D6
1700 SLN 94577 670-F7
1700 SLN 94577 690-F1
3600 FRMT 94538 753-D7
ADAMS CT
1300 MLPK 94025 771-B7
ADAMS DR
1500 MLPK 94025 771-B7
1500 EPA 94303 771-B7
1500 MLPK 94303 771-B7
ADAMS PL
100 SRMN 94583 673-F6
ADAMS ST
200 OAK 94610 649-H2
400 ALB 94706 609-D5
2800 ALA 94501 670-A3
3400 ELCR 94530 609-D5
ADAMS WY
300 PLE 94566 714-F3
ADANA TER
- UNC 94587 732-G2
ADASON DR
900 SLN 94578 691-D4
ADCOCK DR
38600 FRMT 94536 753-C2
ADCOCK PL
38600 FRMT 94536 753-C2
ADDISON CT
200 FRMT 94539 773-H7
ADDISON ST
600 BERK 94710 629-D2
1100 BERK 94702 629-E2
1500 BERK 94703 629-E2
1900 BERK 94704 629-E2
ADDISON WY
1700 HAY 94544 732-A2
4300 PLE 94588 694-B7
ADELAIDE ST
4300 OAK 94619 650-G6
ADELAIDE HILLS CT
- SRMN 94582 674-B3
ADELE CT
- SF 94133 648-A4
ADELINA COM
43300 FRMT 94539 753-H7
ADELINA TER
43500 FRMT 94539 753-H7
43500 FRMT 94539 773-H1
ADELINE ST
100 OAK 94607 649-F2
800 HAY 94544 711-H5
2700 BERK 94703 629-G4
2800 OAK 94608 649-F2
3500 EMVL 94608 629-F6
3500 OAK 94608 629-G5
ADELL CT
3300 OAK 94602 650-D4
ADELLE ST
300 LVMR 94551 695-F7
300 LVMR 94551 715-F1
ADELPHIAN WY
200 ALA 94502 669-H6
ADLER CT
1100 FRMT 94536 753-B2
ADMIRAL DR
- EMVL 94608 629-C6
ADMIRALTY LN
1100 ALA 94502 670-A7
ADMIRE CT
1300 MPS 95035 794-C5
ADOBE AV
100 MPS 95035 793-J6
ADOBE CT
6800 PLE 94588 694-A7
27800 HAY 94542 712-E4
ADOBE DR
35800 FRMT 94536 752-E3
ADRIAN AV
26100 HAY 94545 711-G6
ADRIANO CT
4200 FRMT 94536 752-E2
ADRIANO ST
35100 FRMT 94536 752-E2
ADRIATIC CT
- SRMN 94582 674-C3
ADVENT AV
1300 SLN 94579 691-A6
AEGEAN PL
- AlaC 94546 691-H4
AFRICA ST
- OAK 94607 649-C1
AGATE CT
- LVMR 94550 715-D3
18500 AlaC 94546 692-A3
AGATE TER
34300 FRMT 94555 752-C2
AGATE WY
7900 DBLN 94568 693-J1
AGATHA CT
- LVMR 94550 696-D7
AGATHA WY
- LVMR 94550 696-C7
- LVMR 94550 716-D1
AGAVE CT
46800 FRMT 94539 773-J5
AGENA CIR
4300 UNC 94587 732-A6
AGNES CT
5600 FRMT 94538 773-B2
AGNES LN
20600 AlaC 94541 691-G7
AGNES ST
- CCCo 94514 637-D2
- LVMR 94550 696-A7
- OAK 94618 630-C6
AGREE TER
34600 FRMT 94555 752-A3
AGUA VISTA
4400 UNC 94587 731-H6
AGUA VISTA ST
3900 OAK 94601 650-E7
AGUILA TER
44700 FRMT 94539 773-J2
AGUILAR CT
2100 MPS 95035 794-E6
AHERN AV
9900 UNC 94587 732-A3
AHERN WY
- SF 94103 648-A7
AIKEN CT
34300 FRMT 94555 752-D1
AILEEN ST
500 OAK 94609 629-G6
800 OAK 94608 629-F6
1200 SLN 94577 690-J2
AINSLEE CT
500 HAY 94544 712-A5
AIR CARGO RD
- OAK 94621 690-C2
AIRES CT
3500 AlaC 94546 692-A5
AIRPORT DR
- OAK 94603 670-E7
- OAK 94621 670-F7
100 OAK 94603 690-E2
100 OAK 94621 690-D2
AIRWAY BLVD
100 LVMR 94551 695-B5
E AIRWAY BLVD
200 LVMR 94551 695-D5
700 AlaC 94551 695-D5
AITKEN DR
6500 OAK 94611 630-G7
AJAX PL
- BERK 94708 609-J6
- BERK 94708 610-A6
AJUGA CT
38400 NWK 94560 752-H7
ALACON CT
- DBLN 94568 694-G4
ALADDIN AV
600 SLN 94577 691-A3
ALAGRO CT
- DBLN 94568 694-G4
ALAMEDA AV
1500 ALA 94501 669-H2
2300 ALA 94501 670-A2
3200 OAK 94601 670-C2
5500 RCH 94804 609-B2
5600 ELCR 94530 609-B2
ALAMEDA CT
37000 FRMT 94536 752-G4
ALAMEDA DR
400 LVMR 94551 695-E6
4300 FRMT 94536 752-G4
4700 PLE 94566 714-D1
ALAMEDA RD
- ALA 94501 649-D6
ALAMEDA MARINA DR
- ALA 94501 669-J1
ALAMEDA-OAKLAND FERRY
- ALA - 648-E4
- ALA - 649-A4
- OAK - 649-F5
- SF - 648-B2
ALAMO AV
- BERK 94708 609-G5
ALAMO CT
4400 UNC 94587 731-J6
ALAMO ST
4400 UNC 94587 731-J6
ALAMO TER
5400 FRMT 94555 752-B3
ALAMOS PL
200 SRMN 94583 673-G5
ALANA RD
19500 AlaC 94546 692-B5
ALAN SHEPARD WY
- OAK 94621 690-D2
ALASKA ST
- OAK 94607 649-C1
ALASKA PACKER PL
2000 ALA 94501 649-J7
ALBA CT
4100 PLE 94588 694-C6
ALBACORE TER
- FRMT 94536 753-F3
ALBANY COM
39400 FRMT 94538 753-C4
ALBANY CT
1500 MPS 95035 794-D6
ALBANY ST
31900 HAY 94544 732-E3
ALBANY TER
1500 ALB 94706 609-E6
ALBATROSS AV
100 LVMR 94551 715-E1
300 LVMR 94551 695-F7
ALBATROSS RD
- HAY 94545 731-G3
ALBEMARLE ST
400 ELCR 94530 609-D3
ALBERNI ST
900 EPA 94303 771-A7
ALBERT ST
4300 OAK 94619 650-G6
ALBERT WY
200 LVMR 94550 715-D2
ALBERTA CT
24100 HAY 94545 711-F4
ALBERTA TER
34400 FRMT 94555 752-C3
ALBERTA WY
200 LVMR 94550 716-B1
ALBINA AV
1200 BERK 94706 609-F7
ALBION AV
200 AlaC 94580 691-D6
ALBION CT
- HAY 94545 731-H3
ALBION RD
- CCCo 94582 674-C3
- SRMN 94582 674-B3
ALBO CT
- ORIN 94563 630-J4
ALBORG CT
5400 AlaC 94552 692-D2
ALBRAE ST
40000 FRMT 94538 773-A1
ALBRIDAL CT
- SRMN 94582 673-H2
ALBRIDAL WY
- SRMN 94582 673-H2
ALBROOK DR
- DBLN 94568 674-C7
- DBLN 94568 694-C1
ALBURNI CT
3000 PLE 94566 715-B6
ALBYN CT
6600 NWK 94560 752-E7
ALCALA AV
9500 OAK 94605 671-B4
ALCALDE CT
500 FRMT 94539 773-H1
ALCALDE WY
500 FRMT 94539 773-H1
ALCATRAZ AV
300 BERK 94705 629-G4
300 OAK 94618 629-G4
400 OAK 94609 629-G4
700 BERK 94703 629-G4
1000 BERK 94702 629-F5
1000 OAK 94608 629-F5
ALCAZAR AV
1400 HAY 94544 732-A1
ALCAZAR CT
35800 FRMT 94536 752-F2
ALCOSTA BLVD
8900 SRMN 94583 693-G1
9300 SRMN 94583 673-D1
9400 SRMN 94582 673-G5
ALCOSTA CT
100 SRMN 94583 673-J7
ALCOSTA DR
800 MPS 95035 794-B6
ALDEA ST
8000 DBLN 94568 693-H3
ALDEN LN
200 LVMR 94550 715-D4
200 AlaC 94550 715-D4
ALDEN RD
100 AlaC 94541 691-F7
ALDENGATE WY
2000 HAY 94545 711-G7
ALDER AV
- FRMT 94536 752-G2
ALDER CT
7400 PLE 94588 713-J1
36500 FRMT 94536 752-G2
ALDER ST
7800 OAK 94621 670-H3
ALDER TER
36500 FRMT 94536 752-G3
ALDERBERRY PL
- HAY 94544 712-C5
ALDERBROOK CT
5800 AlaC 94552 692-C2
ALDER CREEK CIR
- SLN 94577 670-J7
- SLN 94577 690-H1
ALDERWOOD CT
4000 PLE 94588 713-J2
ALDERWOOD LN
200 SRMN 94583 673-J6
ALDRICH AL
- SF 94105 648-B6
ALEGRA TER
400 MPS 95035 793-G3
ALEGRE DR
11500 DBLN 94568 693-F4
ALEMA TER
4300 FRMT 94536 752-G3
ALENE ST
7800 DBLN 94568 693-H3
ALEPPO DR
- NWK 94560 772-C1
ALEUT CT
200 FRMT 94539 773-J4
ALEXANDER CT
2000 PLE 94588 694-E7
3400 OAK 94601 650-C7
21000 HAY 94545 711-D4
ALEXANDER ST
700 LVMR 94550 715-E2
37000 FRMT 94536 752-F5
ALEXANDER WY
400 MPS 95035 794-D5
2100 PLE 94588 694-E7
ALEXANDRIA ST
15000 SLN 94579 691-C6
ALEXIA PL
- AlaC 94546 691-J3
ALEXIS PL
- AlaC 94546 691-G3
ALGONQUIN AV
900 LVMR 94551 695-F7
ALHAMBRA AV
5900 OAK 94611 630-E7
ALHAMBRA DR
4500 FRMT 94536 752-E3
ALHAMBRA LN
1700 OAK 94611 630-E6
ALICANTE DR
36300 FRMT 94536 752-F3
ALICANTE TER
- UNC 94587 732-G3
ALICE AV
700 SLN 94577 671-B6
ALICE CT
100 DNVL 94526 652-J2
ALICE ST
- OAK 94607 649-G4
1200 OAK 94612 649-G4
14600 FRMT 94539 753-E6
22500 HAY 94541 711-H2
24100 HAY 94544 711-J3
ALICE WY
300 LVMR 94550 715-D2
4400 UNC 94587 732-A7
ALICIA ST
2700 OAK 94607 649-F2
ALIDA CT
- OAK 94602 650-E3
ALIDA ST
2400 OAK 94602 650-E4
ALISAL CT
800 MPS 95035 794-B5
16800 AlaC 94580 691-F6
ALISAL ST
6000 AlaC 94566 714-E7
6200 AlaC 94586 714-E7
6200 PLE 94566 714-E7
6200 PLE 94586 714-E7
ALISMA CT
- SRMN 94582 673-G2
ALISO AV
3800 OAK 94619 650-G5
ALISON CIR
600 LVMR 94550 696-D7
ALISON ST
22900 HAY 94545 711-C4
ALKANTE CT
- SRMN 94582 673-J1
ALLANMERE CT
- SRMN 94582 674-B3
ALLANMERE DR
- SRMN 94582 674-B3
ALLBROOK CIR
6000 PLE 94588 694-A6
ALLEGHENY CT
34600 FRMT 94555 752-D2
ALLEGHENY DR
6900 DBLN 94568 693-H3
ALLEGRO CT
4800 FRMT 94538 773-B2
ALLEGRO ST
- LVMR 94550 715-E5
ALLEN CT
- MPS 95035 794-C7
1500 AlaC 94546 691-H6
36900 FRMT 94536 752-G3
ALLENDALE AV
3500 OAK 94619 650-E6
ALLINE ST
41100 FRMT 94538 753-C7
41100 FRMT 94538 773-C1
ALLISON DR
32200 UNC 94587 732-A6
ALLMAN ST
1400 OAK 94602 650-C4
ALLSTON WY
700 BERK 94710 629-D2
1100 BERK 94702 629-F2
1400 BERK 94703 629-F2
1800 BERK 94704 629-F2
ALLYSON TER
4000 FRMT 94538 773-D1
ALMA AV
600 OAK 94610 650-A4
4300 AlaC 94546 692-A3
ALMA CT
3900 PLE 94588 714-A1
ALMA PL
900 OAK 94610 650-B4
ALMA ST
38600 FRMT 94536 752-H6
ALMADEN AV
100 MPS 95035 793-J6
100 MPS 95035 794-A6
ALMADEN BLVD
32400 UNC 94587 732-C5
ALMADEN CT
- LVMR 94551 696-D3
ALMADEN LN
5900 OAK 94611 630-E7
ALMADEN PL
2400 UNC 94587 732-C5
38700 FRMT 94536 753-D2
ALMADEN WY
- LVMR 94551 696-D3
ALMANOR CT
2500 LVMR 94550 715-G5
ALMANZA DR
500 OAK 94603 670-H7
ALMEDA ST
20400 AlaC 94546 691-H5
ALMERIA AV
200 FRMT 94539 753-E3
ALMERIA DR
1400 HAY 94544 732-A1
ALMOND AV
1100 LVMR 94550 716-B2
1300 AlaC 94550 716-B2
3700 FRMT 94538 753-D7
ALMOND CIR
4600 LVMR 94550 716-B1
ALMOND CT
300 SRMN 94583 673-G7
3700 AlaC 94546 691-J3
ALMOND RD
4400 AlaC 94546 691-J2
ALMOND HILLS PL
3800 AlaC 94546 691-J3
ALMOND ORCHARD LN
- SRMN 94583 673-E7
ALOE CT
46900 FRMT 94539 773-J5
ALOHA DR
300 SLN 94578 691-C5
ALONDA CT
800 HAY 94541 711-F3
ALONSO CT
4600 FRMT 94555 752-B1
ALORA CT
300 SRMN 94583 673-C2
ALPENROSE CT
- NWK 94560 772-H1
ALPHA CT
19100 AlaC 94546 692-B4
ALPHA LN
1200 AlaC 94586 734-G4
ALPINA CT
2700 PLE 94588 694-H4
ALPINE CT
3100 FRMT 94555 732-D6
ALPINE DR
3100 FRMT 94555 732-D7
ALPINE ST
38900 NWK 94560 772-H1
ALPINE TER
100 OAK 94618 630-B5
ALPINE WY
1900 HAY 94545 711-D5
ALQUIRE PKWY
700 HAY 94544 712-D7
ALSACE CT
- LVMR 94550 715-H4
ALSION CT
700 FRMT 94539 753-G7
ALTA AV
- PDMT 94611 630-C7
- PDMT 94611 650-C1
ALTA CT
4000 PLE 94588 714-A1
37700 FRMT 94536 752-G5
ALTA DR
37800 FRMT 94536 752-H5
ALTA RD
- BERK 94708 609-G4
100 OAK 94618 630-C6
ALTA ST
- SF 94133 648-A4
ALTA HACIENDAS
100 ORIN 94563 610-G4
ALTAIR AV
1800 LVMR 94550 715-E4
ALTA LOMA PL
500 SRMN 94583 673-G6
ALTAMAR CIR
- LVMR 94551 696-D2
ALTAMAR CT
- LVMR 94551 696-D2
ALTAMAR WY
1500 LVMR 94551 696-D3
ALTAMIRA TER
- FRMT 94536 752-J2
ALTAMONT AV
3700 OAK 94605 670-J1
ALTAMONT CIR
1600 LVMR 94551 696-D3
ALTAMONT DR
400 MPS 95035 794-A5
ALTAMONT RD
2000 AlaC 94578 691-D3
ALTAMONT CREEK DR
- LVMR 94551 696-D2
ALTAMONT PASS RD
8500 AlaC 94551 696-F3
8800 AlaC 94551 676-J7
9200 AlaC 94551 677-B6
10700 AlaC 94551 (678-A6 See Page 677)
ALTARINDA CIR
- ORIN 94563 610-J6
E ALTARINDA DR
- ORIN 94563 610-H6
ALTARINDA RD
- ORIN 94563 610-H7
ALTA VISTA
- ORIN 94563 610-E7
3000 ALA 94502 669-J6
3000 ALA 94502 670-A6
ALTA VISTA AV
300 OAK 94610 649-J2
ALTA VISTA TER
- FRMT 94539 773-J7
- FRMT 94539 793-J1
ALTO WY
7700 DBLN 94568 693-F3
ALTON CT
3300 FRMT 94536 752-J3
ALTON PL
- SRMN 94583 673-F6
ALTON ST
- MPS 95035 793-J7
ALTURA PL
400 FRMT 94536 753-D2
7200 OAK 94605 671-A1
ALTURA ST
38700 FRMT 94536 753-D2
ALVANIECE CT
42400 FRMT 94539 753-F7
ALVARADO BLVD
- UNC 94545 731-J5
31500 UNC 94587 731-J5
31800 UNC 94587 732-A5
32100 FRMT 94555 732-A5
ALVARADO CT
1600 LVMR 94551 695-F6
ALVARADO PL
- OAK 94705 630-A3
ALVARADO RD
- BERK 94705 630-A3
- OAK 94705 630-A3
ALVARADO ST
- SLN 94577 670-J7
700 SLN 94577 690-J1
1600 SLN 94577 691-A2
3300 SLN 94578 691-A3
4000 PLE 94566 714-E2
ALVARADO - NILES RD
- FRMT 94536 732-D5
- UNC 94587 732-A5
ALVELAIS DR
- UNC 94555 751-J2
ALVERTUS AV
19600 AlaC 94546 691-J4
ALVES ST
24200 HAY 94544 711-J3
ALVISO PL
1600 LVMR 94551 695-F6
ALVISO ADOBE CT
- MPS 95035 794-D6
ALVORD WY
6100 PLE 94588 694-A6
ALYCE ST
200 FRMT 94555 732-C7
200 FRMT 94555 752-C1
ALYSIA CT
- LVMR 94550 696-B6
AMADOR AV
1100 BERK 94707 609-G6
AMADOR CT
300 PLE 94566 714-F3
AMADOR PL
6000 NWK 94560 752-F7
AMADOR RD
4300 FRMT 94538 753-A6
AMADOR ST
22500 HAY 94541 711-G2
24000 HAY 94544 711-H3
AMADOR PLAZA RD
6800 DBLN 94568 693-H4
AMADOR VALLEY BLVD
6500 DBLN 94568 693-G4
6500 DBLN 94568 694-A2
AMADOR VALLEY CT
8000 DBLN 94568 693-G4
AMADOR VILLAGE CT
- HAY 94544 711-H3
AMALCO WY
700 UNC 94587 732-G5
AMALFI COM
- LVMR 94551 695-G6
AMANDA PL
4700 PLE 94566 714-F5
AMANDA ST
7200 DBLN 94568 693-J3
AMAPALA ST
26600 HAY 94545 711-G7
AMAPOLA CT
41000 FRMT 94539 753-F5
AMAPOLA DR
40800 FRMT 94539 753-F5
AMARAL CIR
400 PLE 94566 714-F3
AMARAL CT
2400 HAY 94587 732-B4
2400 UNC 94587 732-B4
AMARAL ST
31900 HAY 94587 732-B4
31900 UNC 94587 732-B4
AMARILLO CT
11600 DBLN 94568 693-F4
48700 FRMT 94539 793-J2
AMARILLO RD
7300 DBLN 94568 693-F4
AMARYLLIS CIR
- SRMN 94582 673-J1
AMARYLLIS PL
- NWK 94560 752-G7
AMBAR PL
40500 FRMT 94539 753-E4
AMBER CT
500 LVMR 94550 715-D2
1200 SLN 94577 690-J1
AMBER ISL
500 ALA 94501 669-G2
AMBER LN
700 PLE 94566 714-D6
800 AlaC 94566 714-D6
AMBER WY
100 LVMR 94550 715-D2
AMBERFIELD TER
600 FRMT 94536 753-G3
AMBERGATE PL
- DBLN 94568 694-H3
AMBERGLEN CT
- DBLN 94568 694-D3
AMBERGLEN ST
- DBLN 94568 694-D3
AMBER VALLEY DR
100 ORIN 94563 610-J3
AMBERWOOD CIR
4100 PLE 94588 713-J1
4100 PLE 94588 714-A1
AMBERWOOD CT
- MRGA 94556 651-F2
AMBERWOOD DR
5000 FRMT 94555 752-C2
AMBERWOOD WY
- SRMN 94582 693-J1
- SRMN 94582 694-A1
500 LVMR 94551 695-J6
AMBLER LN
- OAK 94608 649-E1
AMBROSE CT
300 HAY 94544 711-J4
AMECA CT
4100 FRMT 94536 752-E2
AMELIA AV
32000 HAY 94544 732-F2
AMELIA ST
8300 OAK 94621 670-G4
AMERICAN AV
2000 HAY 94545 711-D5
AMES ST
2800 LVMR 94551 696-B1
AMES TER
36400 FRMT 94536 752-J1
AMETHYST RD
5200 FRMT 94538 773-B1
AMETHYST WY
- UNC 94587 732-C5
AMHERST AV
100 CCCo 94708 609-F3
AMHERST CT
500 SRMN 94583 673-G7
500 SRMN 94583 693-G1
1200 SLN 94579 691-A4
AMHERST WY
4200 LVMR 94550 716-A1
AMIENS AV
4400 FRMT 94555 752-C1
AMITO AV
1000 OAK 94705 630-B3
AMOROK WY
- FRMT 94539 773-J5
AMOROSO CT
2900 PLE 94566 714-H3
AMUR CT
2000 MPS 95035 793-J3
AMY CT
3800 UNC 94587 731-J5
4600 LVMR 94550 696-B7
AMY DR
5600 OAK 94618 630-C7
AMY PL
3800 UNC 94587 731-J5
AMYX CT
3800 AlaC 94542 712-F2
ANACAPA CT
700 MPS 95035 794-B6
ANAHEIM LP
5000 UNC 94587 752-A1
ANAHEIM ST
5000 UNC 94587 752-A2
ANAIR WY
- OAK 94605 671-A4
ANA MARIA DR
- SJCo 95391 (678-E3 See Page 677)
ANASTACIA CT
3200 PLE 94588 694-C7
ANCHOR DR
- EMVL 94608 629-C6
34600 FRMT 94555 752-E1
ANCHOR WY
300 ALA 94501 670-A4
ANCHORAGE CT
- SLN 94579 711-A2
ANCHORAGE DR
- SLN 94579 691-A7
- SLN 94579 711-A1
ANCONA CIR
- LVMR 94550 715-E5
ANDALUCIA CT
3700 SRMN 94583 673-B3
ANDALUCIA ST
1000 LVMR 94550 715-E3
ANDANTE ST
40600 FRMT 94538 773-B1
ANDERHAN PL
3700 SRMN 94583 673-C2
ANDERLY CT
100 AlaC 94541 711-G1
ANDERSON AV
2600 FRMT 94539 753-E7
4300 OAK 94619 650-G5
ANDERSON PL
27600 HAY 94544 712-B6
ANDERSON RD
100 ALA 94502 669-H5
ANDERSON ST
400 PLE 94566 714-D3
ANDORA LN
300 SRMN 94583 673-C3
ANDORRA CT
40400 FRMT 94539 753-E4
ANDOVER DR
2400 UNC 94587 732-C4
ANDOVER PL
- SRMN 94583 673-F6
ANDOVER ST
3400 OAK 94609 649-H1
15000 SLN 94579 691-B6
ANDRADE RD
3000 AlaC 94586 754-D3
ANDREA CIR
300 LVMR 94550 696-B6
ANDREA CT
4800 LVMR 94550 696-B6
ANDREA ST
27600 HAY 94544 712-A7
ANDREA WY
4700 UNC 94587 731-J7
ANDREAS WY
- SRMN 94582 674-B3
ANDRES CT
- SRMN 94582 674-B3
ANDREW CT
2400 UNC 94587 732-C5
ANDREWS CT
37800 FRMT 94536 752-H4

© 2006 Rand McNally & Company

STREET Block City ZIP Pg-Grid

ANDREWS DR
3600 PLE 94588 694-D6
ANDREWS ST
300 LVMR 94551 695-F7
300 LVMR 94551 715-F1
2100 OAK 94611 650-E1
ANDROMEDA CIR
5400 FRMT 94538 773-A1
ANDROS DR
300 SRMN 94582 673-E1
ANDSLEY LN
- SRMN 94582 674-B3
ANGEL CT
- DNVL 94526 652-H1
ANGELA PL
4000 PLE 94566 714-F4
E ANGELA ST
- PLE 94566 714-E4
W ANGELA ST
- PLE 94566 714-D3
ANGELES AV
4500 FRMT 94536 752-E3
ANGELFISH TER
- FRMT 94536 753-F3
ANGELICA WY
1000 LVMR 94550 715-H2
ANGELICO CT
5100 PLE 94588 694-H4
ANGEL ISLAND TIBURON FERRY
- SF - 648-B1
ANGELO AV
3700 OAK 94619 650-E6
ANGSLEY CT
- SRMN 94582 674-B3
ANGUS CT
34200 FRMT 94555 752-D1
ANGUS DR
400 MPS 95035 794-B6
ANGUS PL
3500 PLE 94588 694-F6
ANGUS WY
- PLE 94588 694-F6
1200 AlaC 94541 691-G6
ANITA AV
19700 AlaC 94546 691-J5
ANITA CT
3200 AlaC 94546 691-J4
5500 LVMR 94550 696-C7
38300 FRMT 94536 753-C1
ANJOU PL
35900 NWK 94560 752-D5
ANN CT
400 LVMR 94550 715-D2
38100 FRMT 94536 753-A3
ANN PL
600 MPS 95035 794-B4
ANN ST
100 FRMT 94555 732-C7
100 FRMT 94555 752-C1
2500 FRMT 94536 753-A3
ANNA ST
24300 HAY 94545 711-F4
ANNABEL LN
- SRMN 94583 673-D2
ANNADALE WY
- DBLN 94568 694-F2
ANNA MARIA ST
100 LVMR 94550 715-D2
ANNAPOLIS CIR
2000 ALA 94501 649-E6
ANNAPOLIS DR
2100 FRMT 94539 773-G2
ANNAPOLIS ST
2500 EPA 94303 771-B7
ANN ARBOR WY
6900 DBLN 94568 693-J3
ANNE MARIE TER
37200 FRMT 94536 752-G4
ANNERLEY RD
1000 OAK 94610 650-B2
1000 PDMT 94610 650-B2
ANNETTE CT
32300 UNC 94587 731-J7
32300 UNC 94587 751-J1
ANNETTE LN
300 HAY 94541 711-G3
ANNIE CT
- AlaC 94552 692-F7
ANNIE ST
- SF 94105 648-A6
- SF 94103 648-A6
ANNIS CIR
3600 PLE 94588 694-G5
ANO AV
200 AlaC 94580 691-E6
ANONA WY
- LVMR 94550 716-B1
ANSEL CT
47700 FRMT 94539 773-H7
ANSON PL
- SF 94108 648-A5
ANSON WY
- CCCo 94707 609-E3
ANTELOPE CT
1700 HAY 94541 712-B1
ANTELOPE DR
- FRMT 94539 773-J3
ANTHONY AV
- SJCo 95391 (678-F3 See Page 677)
ANTHONY ST
- SF 94105 648-B5
800 BERK 94710 629-E4
ANTIGUA CT
400 SRMN 94583 673-C3
ANTIOCH CT
2000 OAK 94611 650-E1
32900 UNC 94587 752-A1
ANTIOCH LP
4900 UNC 94587 752-A1
ANTIOCH ST
4900 UNC 94587 752-A1
6200 OAK 94611 650-E1
ANTONE CT
14300 SLN 94578 691-C3
ANTONE RD
5500 FRMT 94538 773-C2
ANTONE WY
- DBLN 94568 694-F3
ANTONINI WY
3800 PLE 94566 715-C7
ANTONIO ST
700 SLN 94577 690-J1
ANVERS PL
36100 NWK 94560 752-D6
ANZA AV
9700 OAK 94605 671-B4
ANZA CT
100 SRMN 94583 673-A2
ANZA ST
100 FRMT 94539 753-H7
ANZA WY
300 SLN 94578 691-B5
1200 LVMR 94550 715-F2
ANZA-PINE RD
100 FRMT 94539 753-J7
200 FRMT 94539 773-J1
ANZIO TER
34300 FRMT 94555 752-B3
APACHE CT
- PLE 94588 694-G7
- SRMN 94583 673-D5
200 FRMT 94539 773-H4
APACHE DR
- PLE 94588 694-D6
APACHE ST
1000 LVMR 94551 695-F7
APGAR ST
600 OAK 94609 629-F7
800 OAK 94608 629-F7
APOLLO CIR
4200 UNC 94587 732-A6
APPERSON WY
2000 PLE 94566 714-C4
APPIAN CT
- DNVL 94526 652-J3
APPIAN ST
3800 PLE 94588 694-C6
APPIAN WY
100 UNC 94587 732-J5
APPLE AV
1100 AlaC 94541 691-H7
1300 HAY 94541 691-H7
APPLE ST
700 OAK 94603 670-H6
APPLEGATE CT
- DBLN 94568 694-F2
APPLEGATE ST
28200 HAY 94545 731-J2
APPLE GATE TER
39000 FRMT 94536 753-C3
APPLEGATE WY
- DBLN 94568 694-F2
- ALA 94502 669-H5
APPLE TREE COM
4600 LVMR 94551 696-A4
APPLETREE CT
- FRMT 94536 752-J2
APPLEWOOD CT
7900 PLE 94588 713-J1
APPLEWOOD ST
42600 FRMT 94538 773-D2
APPLEWOOD WY
7500 PLE 94588 713-J1
APRICOT CT
- AlaC 94546 692-B3
APRICOT LN
41200 FRMT 94539 753-E6
APRICOT ST
10700 OAK 94603 670-J6
11000 SLN 94577 670-J6
APRICOT WY
17800 AlaC 94546 692-B3
APRIL CT
17700 AlaC 94546 691-H2
APTOS CT
100 SRMN 94583 673-E5
2400 UNC 94587 732-B4
APTOS DR
2800 SRMN 94583 673-E5
AQUA ST
- SLN 94578 691-C5
AQUADO CT
35200 FRMT 94536 752-E2
AQUARIUS CIR
4100 UNC 94587 732-A6
AQUARIUS ST
1700 LVMR 94551 696-B3
AQUARIUS WY
900 OAK 94611 630-D6
AQUATIC CT
- SLN 94579 691-F2
AQUATIC WY
800 FRMT 94539 753-J7
800 FRMT 94539 773-J1
AQUA VISTA
- ORIN 94563 610-J5
AQUA VISTA CT
- HAY 94542 712-G4
ARABIAN RD
4300 LVMR 94551 696-A2
ARAGON AV
28400 HAY 94544 712-B7
ARAGON LN
3800 SRMN 94583 673-C2
ARAGON PL
30200 UNC 94587 732-A4
ARAK CT
1100 PLE 94566 714-G4
ARALIA DR
38200 NWK 94560 752-G7
ARAMON CT
800 PLE 94566 714-H3
ARANA CT
1700 MPS 95035 794-D5
ARANDA DR
2500 SRMN 94583 673-C3
ARAPAHO AV
2000 FRMT 94539 773-G3
ARAPAHO CIR
100 SRMN 94583 673-C4
ARAPAHO CT
- SRMN 94583 673-D4
ARAPAHO PL
44400 FRMT 94539 773-G3
ARBEAU DR
7100 NWK 94560 752-C6
ARBOLADO CT
- ORIN 94563 610-H6
ARBOLES PL
700 SRMN 94583 673-G5
ARBON PTH
- OAK 94618 630-B5
ARBOR AV
3000 LVMR 94550 715-H1
21800 AlaC 94541 711-F2
ARBOR CT
800 LVMR 94550 715-J1
3500 PLE 94566 714-G4
21600 AlaC 94541 711-F2
ARBOR DR
- PDMT 94610 650-A1
600 SLN 94577 671-B7
3400 PLE 94566 714-G4
8600 ELCR 94530 609-E2
ARBOR ST
1700 ALA 94501 669-H1
ARBOR WY
700 MPS 95035 793-J4
ARBOR CREEK CIR
7400 DBLN 94568 693-G4
ARBOR CREST CIR
- HAY 94544 711-J4
ARBORDALE CT
35100 FRMT 94536 752-F1
ARBOR VINE DR
32800 UNC 94587 732-C5
ARBUTUS CT
2000 FRMT 94539 773-G3
3700 AlaC 94542 712-F3
4400 PLE 94588 713-J1
5600 NWK 94560 752-G7
ARC TER
- FRMT 94555 752-B3
ARCADE AV
- BERK 94708 609-J6
ARCADIA AV
4400 OAK 94602 650-E3
ARCADIA COM
- LVMR 94551 695-C4
ARCADIA DR
- HAY 94541 711-J2
ARCADIAN CT
3500 AlaC 94546 691-H2
ARCADIAN DR
3300 AlaC 94546 691-H2
ARCADIAN ST
48200 FRMT 94539 793-J1
ARCH ST
1100 BERK 94708 609-H6
1100 BERK 94707 609-H6
1300 BERK 94709 609-H7
1600 BERK 94709 629-H1
ARCHCLIFF CT
700 HAY 94544 732-E2
ARCHER AV
1900 FRMT 94536 753-A3
ARCHER CT
38000 FRMT 94536 753-A2
ARCHER ST
1300 SJS 95002 793-B7
ARCHMONT PL
3900 OAK 94605 650-J7
ARCTIC ST
1900 SLN 94577 690-G3
ARDEN COM
3000 FRMT 94536 753-A3
3000 FRMT 94536 752-J3
ARDEN PL
4300 OAK 94602 650-D3
ARDEN RD
- BERK 94704 630-A2
3100 HAY 94545 731-E1
ARDEN ST
37000 NWK 94560 752-E6
ARDEN WY
1400 OAK 94602 650-D3
ARDENTECH CT
6000 FRMT 94555 752-B4
ARDENWOOD BLVD
34100 FRMT 94555 752-B2
34100 UNC 94555 752-B2
34100 UNC 94587 752-B2
ARDENWOOD CT
24500 HAY 94545 711-F5
ARDENWOOD TER
5700 FRMT 94555 752-C4
ARDILLA RD
- ORIN 94563 610-F6
ARDIS ST
- AlaC 94541 691-F7
- AlaC 94541 711-F1
- AlaC 94580 691-F7
- AlaC 94580 711-F1
ARDLEIGH CT
- CCCo 94583 673-A5
ARDLEY AV
3500 OAK 94602 650-C4
ARDMORE AV
1000 OAK 94610 650-C2
ARDMORE DR
1200 SLN 94577 691-D1
ARDMORE PL
1400 LVMR 94550 715-F5
8400 DBLN 94568 693-G2
ARDMORE RD
- CCCo 94707 609-F4
ARDMORE ST
8400 DBLN 94568 693-G2
ARDO CT
35300 FRMT 94536 752-E2
ARDO ST
4000 FRMT 94536 752-E2
ARELLANO CT
- DBLN 94568 694-G5
ARENA ST
1500 SLN 94579 691-A7
ARENAS CT
- SRMN 94583 673-C3
ARENDAL CT
24300 AlaC 94541 712-B1
ARENDT WY
100 PLE 94566 714-E3
ARF AV
2300 HAY 94545 731-G1
ARGONAUT CT
4200 FRMT 94536 753-A5
ARGONAUT WY
38700 FRMT 94536 752-J5
38800 FRMT 94536 753-A5
39000 FRMT 94538 753-A5
ARGONNE PL
35800 NWK 94560 752-D5
ARGONNE ST
15400 SLN 94579 691-B7
35800 NWK 94560 752-D5
ARGUELLO DR
700 SLN 94578 691-B4
ARGUS CT
- ALA 94502 669-J6
1800 FRMT 94539 773-G1
ARGYLE CT
4100 FRMT 94536 752-H4
ARGYLE RD
37600 FRMT 94536 752-H4
ARGYLE ST
2700 OAK 94602 650-F2
ARIA CT
- LVMR 94550 715-C4
ARIANE CT
- OAK 94619 650-H5
ARIANNA LN
- SRMN 94582 674-A3
ARIEL AV
4500 FRMT 94555 752-C1
ARIEL RD
33600 FRMT 94555 752-C1
ARIES CT
4700 LVMR 94551 696-B3
ARIKARA CT
700 FRMT 94539 773-H4
ARIKARA DR
700 FRMT 94539 773-G4
ARIMO AV
600 OAK 94610 650-B2
ARIZONA AV
1100 MPS 95035 794-A3
1800 MPS 95035 793-J3
ARIZONA ST
3100 OAK 94602 650-E4
33000 UNC 94587 732-D6
ARK DR
900 SLN 94578 691-D4
ARKANSAS
3000 ALA 94501 649-F6
ARKANSAS CT
48400 FRMT 94539 793-J1
ARKANSAS ST
3200 OAK 94602 650-E5
ARKWOOD ST
43200 FRMT 94538 773-D2
ARLENE CT
37700 FRMT 94536 752-J3
ARLENE PL
4700 PLE 94566 714-E5
ARLENE WY
5400 LVMR 94550 696-D7
ARLETTE AV
22500 HAY 94541 692-B7
ARLEWOOD CT
- SRMN 94582 674-B3
ARLINGTON AV
- BERK 94707 609-F3
- CCCo 94530 609-F3
- CCCo 94707 609-F3
- CCCo 94708 609-F3
800 OAK 94608 629-F5
800 ELCR 94530 609-F3
ARLINGTON BLVD
900 ELCR 94530 609-E1
ARLINGTON CT
- CCCo 94707 609-F3
400 PLE 94566 714-D6
2300 AlaC 94578 691-F3
ARLINGTON DR
2200 AlaC 94578 691-F3
6300 PLE 94566 714-D6
ARLINGTON ISL
600 ALA 94501 669-G2
ARLINGTON LN
- CCCo 94707 609-F3
ARLINGTON PL
2800 FRMT 94555 732-E6
ARLINGTON RD
1000 LVMR 94551 695-D6
ARLMONT DR
- CCCo 94707 609-F3
ARLOTTA PL
2500 PLE 94588 714-A4
ARMAND DR
1700 MPS 95035 794-D6
ARMANI CT
5200 PLE 94588 694-H5
ARMANINO CT
- OAK 94618 629-J5
ARMATA ST
47100 FRMT 94539 773-H6
ARMIDA CT
400 LVMR 94550 715-E2
ARMITAGE ST
2700 ALA 94502 669-J6
ARMONDO CT
- PLE 94566 735-C1
ARMOUR CT
34900 FRMT 94555 752-E1
ARMOUR DR
6600 OAK 94611 630-E6
ARMOUR ST
28200 HAY 94545 731-J2
ARMOUR WY
34800 FRMT 94555 752-E1
ARMSTRONG DR
2100 PLE 94588 694-E7
ARMSTRONG RD
3700 CCCo 94514 (657-D1 See Page 637)
3700 CCCo 94514 637-E7
ARMSTRONG ST
1000 HAY 94541 711-J2
1000 HAY 94541 712-A1
2400 LVMR 94551 695-C5
ARMY ST
1300 SLN 94577 690-J2
E ARNAUDO BLVD
- SJCo 95391 (678-F2 See Page 677)
ARNO CT
4700 RCH 94804 609-A2
ARNOLD CT
1200 FRMT 94539 753-F6
22700 HAY 94541 711-H2
ARNOLD RD
- DBLN 94568 694-C3
AROLLO PTH
- OAK 94618 630-B5
ARREZZO ST
5200 PLE 94588 694-C6
ARRONIA CT
2800 PLE 94588 694-H3
ARROWFIELD WY
- SRMN 94582 674-B3
ARROWHEAD AV
1000 LVMR 94551 696-C4
ARROWHEAD CT
5400 LVMR 94551 696-C3
ARROWHEAD DR
1600 OAK 94611 630-F6
ARROWHEAD PL
7700 NWK 94560 752-C6
ARROWHEAD WY
500 HAY 94544 732-D1
ARROWTAIL TER
1000 FRMT 94536 753-C3
ARROWWOOD CT
3900 PLE 94588 713-J2
ARROYO AV
- PDMT 94611 630-A7
200 SLN 94577 691-A1
ARROYO CT
- UNC 94587 732-J6
2100 PLE 94588 714-B5
ARROYO DR
- UNC 94587 732-H6
8000 PLE 94588 714-A5
ARROYO RD
900 LVMR 94550 715-H5
1100 AlaC 94550 715-H6
3800 AlaC 94550 735-J1
5900 AlaC 94550 736-A3
ARROYO VISTA RD
4700 LVMR 94551 696-B6
ARROYUELO AV
4200 OAK 94611 649-J1
ARROZ PL
200 FRMT 94536 753-D2
ARTHUR AV
700 SLN 94577 690-H1
ARTHUR CT
2900 AlaC 94541 712-D2
ARTHUR DR
5800 PLE 94588 714-B1
ARTHUR ST
6400 OAK 94605 670-H2
7800 OAK 94621 670-H3
ARTHUR H BREED JR FRWY I-580
- AlaC - 691-H6
- AlaC - 692-F4
- AlaC - 693-A4
- AlaC - 694-C5
- AlaC - 695-D5
- AlaC - 696-A5
- DBLN - 693-A4
- DBLN - 694-C5
- LVMR - 694-C5
- LVMR - 695-D5
- LVMR - 696-A5
- PLE - 693-A4
- PLE - 694-C5
ARTISAN PL
- HAY 94541 711-J2
ARTISTIC PL
- HAY 94541 711-G1
ARTISTRY LP
- UNC 94587 732-D5
ARTUNA AV
- PDMT 94611 650-A1
ARVADA CT
100 SRMN 94583 673-G7
ARVILLA LN
24800 HAY 94544 711-J3
ARYA CT
32000 UNC 94587 732-A6
ASBURY CT
400 LVMR 94551 695-D6
1200 SLN 94579 691-A4
ASBY BAY
100 ALA 94502 669-J6
ASCALANO LN
- LVMR 94550 715-G5
ASCENSION DR
2400 SRMN 94583 673-B3
ASCOT CT
- OAK 94611 650-F1
- SRMN 94583 673-E4
3100 PLE 94588 694-F6
ASCOT DR
- OAK 94611 650-F1
2600 SRMN 94583 673-E4
ASCOT LN
- OAK 94611 650-G1
ASCOT PL
- OAK 94611 650-F2
ASCOT WY
2400 UNC 94587 732-B4
ASH CT
6800 DBLN 94568 693-J4
ASH ST
1200 AlaC 94541 691-H7
7800 OAK 94621 670-H3
36700 NWK 94560 752-D7
37100 NWK 94560 772-D1
ASHBOURNE CIR
- CCCo 94583 673-A5
ASHBOURNE CT
5300 NWK 94560 752-D4
ASHBOURNE DR
- CCCo 94583 672-J4
- CCCo 94583 673-A5
ASHBROOK CT
2900 OAK 94601 650-C6
ASHBROOK LN
- SRMN 94582 674-C3
ASHBROOK WY
- HAY 94544 732-D1
ASHBURY AV
- ALB 94706 609-E4
- ELCR 94530 609-D3
ASHBURY LN
1600 HAY 94545 711-H7
ASHBY AV Rt#-13
400 BERK 94710 629-D4
1100 BERK 94702 629-F4
1500 BERK 94703 629-F4
2100 BERK 94705 629-F4
2800 BERK 94705 630-A3
ASHBY PL
2700 BERK 94705 629-J3
ASHBY WY
9600 SRMN 94583 673-G7
ASHFIELD AV
20800 AlaC 94546 692-A6
ASHFIELD LN
- SRMN 94582 674-B3
ASHFORD CT
- CCCo 94507 652-G1
ASHFORD WY
7500 DBLN 94568 693-G2
38100 FRMT 94536 753-A3
ASHLAND AV
16000 AlaC 94580 691-E5
ASHLAND DR
1400 MPS 95035 794-D7
ASHLAND TER
500 FRMT 94536 753-G3
ASHLEE AV
- SJCo 95391 (678-F3 See Page 677)
ASHLEE CT
- SJCo 95391 (678-F3 See Page 677)
ASHLEY CT
4700 UNC 94587 731-J7
6000 PLE 94588 694-B6
ASHLEY WY
32200 UNC 94587 731-J7
ASHMOUNT AV
1000 OAK 94610 650-C2
1200 PDMT 94610 650-C2
ASHMOUNT WY
- OAK 94610 650-B2
ASHTON AV
300 OAK 94603 670-G6
ASHTON CT
7500 PLE 94588 714-A3
ASHTON PL
35700 FRMT 94536 752-F2
ASHTON OAKS CT
- SRMN 94582 673-J7
- SRMN 94582 674-A7
ASHWELL LN
- SRMN 94582 674-B3
ASHWOOD COM
4400 FRMT 94538 773-D1
ASHWOOD CT
4400 UNC 94587 732-A6
7300 PLE 94588 714-A2
ASHWOOD DR
3600 PLE 94588 714-A2
ASILOMAR CIR
- OAK 94611 630-E7
ASILOMAR CT
- UNC 94545 731-J7
ASILOMAR DR
1900 OAK 94611 630-E7
ASIMUTH CIR
4100 UNC 94587 732-B6
ASPEN AV
21100 AlaC 94546 692-B6
ASPEN CT
- LVMR 94551 696-C3
7400 PLE 94588 713-J1
ASPEN LP
- UNC 94587 732-G4
ASPEN PL
4000 OAK 94602 650-F5
7600 NWK 94560 752-D7
ASPEN ST
- DBLN 94568 694-D4
ASPENRIDGE DR
200 MPS 95035 793-J4
ASPENWOOD COM
37100 FRMT 94536 752-H2
ASPENWOOD CT
- SRMN 94582 673-G2
ASPEN WOOD ST
6400 LVMR 94551 696-D3
ASPINWALL RD
6000 OAK 94611 630-E6
ASQUITH PL
36000 FRMT 94536 752-F3
ASTER AV
8300 OAK 94605 671-A2
ASTER CT
7400 PLE 94588 714-A2
37600 NWK 94560 752-F7
ASTER LN
1100 LVMR 94551 696-A4
ASTERBELL CT
- SRMN 94582 673-J1
ASTERBELL DR
- SRMN 94582 673-J1
ASTERWOOD DR
- DBLN 94568 694-D3
ASTI CT
1200 LVMR 94550 715-F3
ASTOR CT
1700 SLN 94577 671-D7
1700 SLN 94577 691-D1
ASTOR DR
1800 SLN 94577 691-D1
ASTOR ST
35100 UNC 94587 732-G7
ASTRIDA DR
- HAY 94544 712-B7
ATHEANA CT
- CCCo 94582 674-A2
ATHENOUR CT
- PLE 94588 693-G7
ATHENOUR WY
7000 AlaC 94586 754-D1
ATHENS AV
800 OAK 94607 649-F2
ATHENS CT
20900 AlaC 94541 691-G7
ATHENS DR
5000 SRMN 94582 673-G4
ATHENS RD
1200 LVMR 94550 715-F3
ATHERTON PL
22600 HAY 94541 711-J2
ATHERTON ST
- BERK 94704 629-H2
8000 OAK 94605 670-J3
22600 HAY 94541 711-J2
ATHOL AV
100 OAK 94606 649-J4
400 OAK 94606 650-A4
600 OAK 94610 650-A4
ATHY CT
38500 FRMT 94536 753-B2
ATHY ST
38500 FRMT 94536 753-B3
ATLANTIC AV
100 ALA 94501 649-E7
W ATLANTIC AV
- ALA 94501 649-D7
ATLANTIC CT
1600 UNC 94587 732-D4
ATLANTIC ST
1100 UNC 94587 732-E4
ATLANTUS AV
2200 SLN 94579 711-A1
ATLANTUS CT
- SLN 94579 711-A2
ATLAS
32200 UNC 94587 732-A6
ATLAS AV
3700 OAK 94619 650-G4
ATLAS PL
- BERK 94708 609-J6
- BERK 94708 610-A6
ATTERIDGE CT
34300 FRMT 94555 732-E7
ATTERIDGE PL
34200 FRMT 94555 732-E7
ATUNE TER
5000 FRMT 94555 752-A3
ATWAL CT
- AlaC 94541 692-D7
ATWATER CT
3400 FRMT 94536 752-H2
ATWELL AV
2800 OAK 94601 650-D6
ATWELL PL
25800 HAY 94544 711-H5
ATWELL RD
1400 ELCR 94530 609-E1
AUBURN AV
- NWK 94560 772-H1
1000 SLN 94579 691-B5
6000 OAK 94618 629-J4
AUBURN CT
800 FRMT 94538 773-G7
1000 ALA 94502 670-A6
AUBURN DR
1000 ALA 94502 670-A6
AUBURN PL
700 HAY 94544 712-A7
AUBURN ST
1000 LVMR 94550 716-A1
1100 FRMT 94538 773-G7
AUCKLAND CT
34300 FRMT 94555 732-E7
AUCKLAND PL
34200 FRMT 94555 732-E7
AUCTION WY
29900 HAY 94544 732-B2
AUDEN CT
34100 FRMT 94555 732-E7
AUDREY CT
6000 PLE 94588 694-B7
34100 FRMT 94555 752-C1
AUDREY DR
4700 AlaC 94546 692-A3
AUDRY ST
- LVMR 94550 696-B7
AUDUBON CT
600 HAY 94544 732-E1
AUDUBON ST
30100 HAY 94544 732-D1
AUDUBON PARK CT
5300 FRMT 94538 773-C1
AUGHINBAUGH WY
100 ALA 94502 669-J5
AUGUST AL
- SF 94133 648-A4
AUGUST CT
5000 AlaC 94546 692-B3
AUGUSTA CT
3400 HAY 94542 712-E5
8700 DBLN 94568 693-G2
AUGUSTA CT E
1500 MPS 95035 794-D3
AUGUSTA DR
800 MRGA 94556 651-D1
AUGUSTA WY
6100 LVMR 94551 696-D3
AUGUSTINE CT
35700 FRMT 94536 752-G1
AUGUSTINE PL
35600 FRMT 94536 752-G1
AUGUSTINE ST
4500 PLE 94566 714-D4
AURELIA WY
14600 AlaC 94578 691-E2
AURORA DR
1500 SLN 94577 690-G4
AURORA PZ
100 UNC 94587 732-J5
AURORA TER
38600 FRMT 94536 753-D2
AUSEON AV
1400 OAK 94621 670-H4
2000 OAK 94605 670-J4
AUSTEN CT
700 LVMR 94551 696-A5
AUSTEN DR
600 LVMR 94551 696-A6
AUSTIN AV
- HAY 94544 711-J4
AUSTIN CT
- ORIN 94563 610-J6
2300 AlaC 94546 691-H5
AUSTIN LN
19600 AlaC 94546 691-H5
AUSTIN ST
- ALA 94501 649-E7
1200 FRMT 94539 753-F6
2000 OAK 94601 650-C7
AUSTIN CREEK AV
- SRMN 94582 674-A7
AUTO MALL CIR
43200 FRMT 94538 773-B4
AUTO MALL PKWY
3800 FRMT 94539 773-E3
4000 FRMT 94538 773-D3
AUTREY ST
100 MPS 95035 793-J3
100 MPS 95035 794-A3
AUTUMN CT
1100 PLE 94566 714-D3
27700 HAY 94542 712-E4
AUTUMN WY
- LVMR 94550 716-C2
AUTUMN GOLD COM
- FRMT 94536 752-A5
AUTUMN LEAF COM
- LVMR 94551 696-C5
AUTUMN OAK DR
1600 LVMR 94551 695-J4
1800 LVMR 94551 696-A4
AUTUMNWIND CT
- SRMN 94583 673-H3
AVA ST
1100 LVMR 94550 716-B1
AVALON AV
2900 BERK 94705 629-J3
2900 BERK 94705 630-A3
AVALON CT
- SRMN 94582 674-D4
4100 FRMT 94536 752-H4
AVALON WY
- SRMN 94582 674-D4
700 LVMR 94550 715-E3
AVALON HEIGHTS TER
- FRMT 94539 774-A6
47400 FRMT 94539 794-A1
AVANSINO ST
3700 SLN 94578 691-B3
AVENAL AV
5700 OAK 94605 670-G2
AVENIDA DR
- BERK 94708 609-J7
100 BERK 94708 610-A7
AVENIDA DE LAS PALMAS
1100 LVMR 94550 715-E3
AVENIDA DE ORINDA
- ORIN 94563 610-G7
W AVENUE 130TH
2500 SLN 94577 690-G4
W AVENUE 133RD
2000 SLN 94577 690-H4
W AVENUE 134TH
2000 SLN 94577 690-H4
W AVENUE 135TH
2000 SLN 94577 690-H4
W AVENUE 136TH
2100 SLN 94577 690-H4
W AVENUE 140TH
2000 SLN 94577 690-J4
AVENUE B
- SF 94130 648-E1
AVENUE C
- SF 94130 648-E1
AVENUE D
- SF 94130 648-E1
AVENUE E
- SF 94130 648-E1
AVENUE EYE
- SF 94130 648-E1
AVENUE F
- SF 94130 648-E1
AVENUE H
- SF 94130 648-E1
AVENUE I
- SF 94130 648-E1
AVENUE M
- SF 94130 648-F1
AVENUE N
- SF 94130 648-F1

STREET	Block	City	ZIP	Pg-Grid
AVENUE OF THE PALMS				
	-	SF	94130	648-E1
AVILA CT				
	-	HAY	94544	732-A1
AVILA PL				
	700	ELCR	94530	609-E3
AVILA ST				
	5800	ELCR	94530	609-C4
AVILA TERRAZA				
	900	FRMT	94536	753-C3
AVINGTON RD				
	100	ALA	94502	669-J5
	100	ALA	94502	670-A5
AVINGTON TER				
	500	FRMT	94536	753-G3
AVIO CT				
	-	PLE	94566	715-C5
AVIS DR				
	900	ELCR	94530	609-D3
AVIS LN				
	23000	AlaC	94541	692-C7
AVIS RD				
	-	BERK	94707	609-G4
AVOCA AV				
	5900	OAK	94611	630-C6
AVOCADO CT				
	-	HAY	94544	711-J4
	100	SRMN	94583	673-F7
AVOCET CT				
	-	ALA	94501	649-F7
	-	SLN	94579	690-J7
AVOCET TER				
	3800	FRMT	94555	732-J3
AVON				
	-	DNVL	94526	652-J3
AVON AV				
	1000	SLN	94579	691-A5
AVON CT				
	7200	DBLN	94568	693-J3
AVON PL				
	2300	LVMR	94550	715-F5
AVON RD				
	-	CCCo	94707	609-F4
AVON ST				
	400	OAK	94618	629-H6
	38500	FRMT	94536	752-H6
AVONDALE LN				
	300	LVMR	94551	696-A6
	1000	HAY	94545	711-G5
AVONDALE LNDG				
	-	ALA	94502	670-A6
AVONOAK CT				
	-	OAK	94605	651-C7
AYALA AV				
	5700	OAK	94609	629-H5
AYAMONTE CT				
	-	SRMN	94583	673-C3
AYER LN				
	1100	MPS	95035	794-C6
AYER ST				
	1200	MPS	95035	794-C6
AYERS WY				
	-	SRMN	94582	674-C3
AYLESBURY CT				
	3100	AlaC	94546	691-G3
AZALEA CT				
	-	HAY	94541	711-D2
	5300	LVMR	94551	696-B4
AZALEA DR				
	1000	ALA	94502	670-A6
AZALEA LN				
	-	OAK	94611	630-F7
AZALEA RD				
	17900	HAY	94541	711-D2
AZELIA CT				
	2900	UNC	94587	732-F7
AZEVEDO AV				
	23900	AlaC	94541	712-B1
AZEVEDO COM				
	600	FRMT	94539	753-H7
AZORES CT				
	-	LVMR	94550	696-A7
AZTEC CT				
	600	FRMT	94539	773-H6
AZTEC RD				
	29000	HAY	94544	712-C7
AZTEC WY				
	-	OAK	94611	630-E7
AZUL WY				
	2200	PLE	94566	714-G3
AZURITE WY				
	-	LVMR	94550	715-D3
B				
B RD				
	100	AlaC	94586	734-C4
B ST				
	100	AlaC	94586	734-C5
	100	HAY	94541	711-G2
	500	UNC	94587	732-F4
	1200	HAY	94541	712-A1
	1400	HAY	94541	692-B7
	7100	ELCR	94530	609-E4
	8000	OAK	94621	670-G4
	9000	OAK	94603	670-H5
BABCOCK CT				
	3700	AlaC	94546	692-B5
BABY BOTTLE TR				
	-	CCCo	94563	610-C5
	-	CCCo	94708	610-C5
BACH CT				
	4700	FRMT	94538	753-B7
BACINADA CT				
	4100	FRMT	94536	752-F2
BACINADA DR				
	4000	FRMT	94536	752-F2
BACON CT				
	4400	PLE	94588	694-A7
BACON PL				
	34400	FRMT	94555	732-E7
BACON RD				
	5300	OAK	94619	650-J6
	5400	OAK	94619	651-A5
BADDING RD				
	3300	AlaC	94546	691-J4
BADGER CT				
	5800	AlaC	94552	692-D3
BADGER DR				
	3000	PLE	94566	714-H2
BADGERWOOD LN				
	1900	MPS	95035	793-J3
BAFFIN AV				
	4700	FRMT	94536	752-F4
BAFFIN WY				
	1200	LVMR	94550	715-G3
BAGADO CT				
	500	SRMN	94583	673-B3
BAGSHOTTE DR				
	5800	OAK	94611	650-F1
BAHAMA AV				
	26700	HAY	94545	711-G7
	27400	HAY	94545	731-G1
BAHAMA COM				
	34600	FRMT	94555	752-E1
BAHAMA CT				
	100	SRMN	94582	673-E1
BAILEY CT				
	2600	FRMT	94536	753-A3
BAILEY RANCH RD				
	-	HAY	94542	712-G4
BAINBRIDGE CT				
	-	ALA	94501	649-C7
BAINBRIDGE SQ				
	-	ALA	94501	649-C7
BAINBRIDGE WY				
	2400	UNC	94587	732-C5
BAINE AV				
	4000	FRMT	94536	752-H3
	6000	NWK	94560	752-F6
BAIRN CT				
	3700	PLE	94588	694-F5
BAIRO CT				
	41000	FRMT	94539	753-E6
BAITX DR				
	-	MRGA	94556	651-E1
BAJADA CT				
	900	FRMT	94539	753-F5
BAKER DR				
	-	PLE	94588	714-F1
BAKER RD				
	20800	AlaC	94546	691-J5
BAKER ST				
	3200	BERK	94702	629-F5
	6100	OAK	94608	629-F5
BAKER WY				
	-	CCCo	94582	674-B4
BAL CT				
	1500	SLN	94578	691-D3
BALANCE ST				
	-	SF	94133	648-B4
BALBOA CT				
	300	ALA	94501	669-J4
	300	ALA	94501	670-A4
BALBOA DR				
	100	MPS	95035	793-J5
	5500	OAK	94611	630-E7
BALBOA WY				
	1200	LVMR	94550	715-F2
	4700	FRMT	94536	752-F4
BALDWIN CT				
	3900	FRMT	94536	752-F2
BALDWIN PL				
	35400	FRMT	94536	752-F2
BALDWIN ST				
	8300	OAK	94621	670-F5
	27800	HAY	94544	712-B7
BALDWIN WY				
	-	PLE	94588	693-H6
BALEIN CT				
	-	HAY	94544	732-A1
BALENTINE DR				
	39600	NWK	94560	773-A1
	39700	NWK	94560	772-J1
BALFOUR AV				
	3600	OAK	94610	650-A3
BAL HARBOR LN				
	2600	HAY	94545	711-F7
BALI CT				
	600	SRMN	94582	673-E1
BALI LN				
	3100	ALA	94502	670-A6
BALKAN CT				
	5400	AlaC	94552	692-D3
BALLANTINE PL				
	35600	FRMT	94536	752-G1
BALLANTYNE DR				
	3500	PLE	94588	694-F5
BALLARD CT				
	-	HAY	94544	712-B7
BALLARD DR				
	37900	FRMT	94536	752-H6
BALLENA BLVD				
	1100	ALA	94501	669-E2
BALLEYBAY				
	-	ALA	94502	669-J6
BALMORAL CT				
	3200	PLE	94588	694-E6
BALMORAL DR				
	5600	OAK	94619	650-J4
	5600	OAK	94619	651-A5
BALMORAL ST				
	2400	UNC	94587	732-C4
BALMORAL WY				
	300	HAY	94544	732-E2
BALMORAL PARK CT				
	4500	FRMT	94538	773-D2
BALRA DR				
	400	ELCR	94530	609-E3
BALSA CT				
	700	UNC	94587	732-G3
BALSAM LN				
	-	SRMN	94583	693-F1
BALSAM TER				
	600	FRMT	94536	753-B2
BALSAM WY				
	6900	OAK	94611	630-E5
BALT CT				
	5500	FRMT	94538	773-B2
BALTHAZAR TER				
	4700	FRMT	94555	752-C2
BALTIC CT				
	29800	HAY	94544	732-C1
BALTUSROL				
	-	MRGA	94556	651-D1
BALTUSROL CT				
	-	LVMR	94551	696-C3
	-	SRMN	94583	693-H1
	2400	UNC	94587	732-B4
BALTUSROL PL				
	100	SRMN	94583	693-H1
BALTUSROL RD				
	-	LVMR	94551	696-C3
BAMBOO CT				
	1900	HAY	94545	711-F5
BAMBOO LN				
	5200	FRMT	94538	752-J7
BANBURY ST				
	400	HAY	94544	711-H4
BANCROFT AV				
	200	SLN	94577	671-B6
	1200	SLN	94577	691-B1
	2200	OAK	94601	670-E1
	5500	OAK	94605	670-H2
	8600	OAK	94603	670-H2
	8800	OAK	94603	671-A5
	12100	SLN	94578	691-B1
BANCROFT CT				
	1500	SLN	94578	691-D3
BANCROFT PL				
	400	OAK	94704	630-A2
	600	SRMN	94582	673-J6
BANCROFT WY				
	600	BERK	94710	629-D3
	1100	BERK	94702	629-E2
	1400	OAK	94601	670-D1
	1500	BERK	94703	629-F2
	2000	BERK	94704	629-G2
	2200	BERK	94720	629-H2
BANDA TER				
	43300	FRMT	94539	773-G1
BANDERA ST				
	40800	FRMT	94539	753-F4
BANDINI CT				
	-	DBLN	94568	694-G4
BANDOL CT				
	-	SRMN	94582	674-C3
BANDOL WY				
	-	SRMN	94582	674-C3
BANDON DR				
	8400	DBLN	94568	693-H2
	8800	SRMN	94583	693-H2
BANDONI AV				
	1500	AlaC	94580	711-B2
BANFF AV				
	2000	SLN	94579	691-A7
BANFF PARK CT				
	5000	FRMT	94538	773-C2
BANGOR CT				
	-	DBLN	94568	694-D4
	-	SRMN	94582	673-H4
BANNAM PL				
	-	SF	94133	648-A4
BANNCOCK ST				
	1000	LVMR	94551	695-F7
BANNING DR				
	6600	OAK	94611	630-G7
BANNISTER CT				
	200	ALA	94502	669-J6
BANNISTER WY				
	-	ALA	94502	669-H6
BANNON CT				
	47600	FRMT	94539	773-H7
BANTRY AV				
	3000	OAK	94605	670-J1
BANYAN ST				
	21500	AlaC	94541	711-G1
BANYAN TREE CT				
	39500	FRMT	94538	753-A7
BANYAN TREE RD				
	39600	FRMT	94538	753-A7
BANYON COM				
	-	LVMR	94550	716-D2
BAR AV				
	16700	AlaC	94580	691-F6
BARBARA CT				
	300	HAY	94544	712-B7
	600	SLN	94577	691-C1
	4200	PLE	94566	714-F4
	4800	UNC	94587	751-J1
BARBARA RD				
	-	ORIN	94563	630-H1
	700	OAK	94610	650-A3
BARBARA ST				
	39900	FRMT	94538	753-C5
BARBARY ST				
	2100	FRMT	94539	753-F7
BARBER ST				
	100	LVMR	94550	696-A7
BARBERS POINT RD				
	-	ALA	94501	649-D6
BARCELONA AV				
	27500	HAY	94545	711-H7
	27600	HAY	94545	731-H1
BARCELONA DR				
	400	FRMT	94536	753-A1
BARCELONA ST				
	1600	LVMR	94550	715-F4
	8900	OAK	94605	671-B3
BARCELONA WY				
	4500	UNC	94587	731-J6
BARCLAY AV				
	-	UNC	94587	732-B4
BARCLAY CT				
	2700	AlaC	94546	691-H4
BARCLAY RD				
	19200	AlaC	94546	691-H4
BARDOLPH CIR				
	33400	FRMT	94555	752-B1
BARDOLPH RD				
	4700	FRMT	94555	752-C1
BARETT CT				
	3100	AlaC	94546	691-J4
BARKER AV				
	700	HAY	94541	711-F2
BARKER CT				
	-	ALA	94501	649-A2
BARKER ST				
	100	MPS	95035	793-J7
BARLETA CT				
	-	LVMR	94550	715-E5
BARLETA LN				
	700	LVMR	94550	715-E5
BARLOW CT				
	1400	FRMT	94536	753-B3
	19500	AlaC	94546	691-H4
BARLOW DR				
	2700	AlaC	94546	691-H4
BARMIED PL				
	-	OAK	94619	651-C7
BARNACLE CT				
	3500	UNC	94587	731-J4
	3500	UNC	94587	732-A4
BARNARD DR				
	35500	FRMT	94536	732-H7
	35500	FRMT	94536	752-H1
BARNARD ST				
	25400	HAY	94545	711-G6
	36300	NWK	94560	752-E5
BARNEGATE BAY				
	-	ALA	94502	670-A5
BARNER AV				
	3900	OAK	94602	650-E4
BARNER PL				
	-	OAK	94602	650-E4
BARNES CT				
	-	MRGA	94556	651-E1
	-	HAY	94544	711-H3
BARNES LN				
	-	FRMT	94536	733-A7
BARNFIELD CT				
	34300	FRMT	94555	732-E7
BARNFIELD PL				
	34200	FRMT	94555	732-E7
BARNHILL LN				
	22100	AlaC	94552	692-D5
BARN HOLLOW CT				
	7700	DBLN	94568	693-F4
BARN ROCK DR				
	28500	HAY	94542	712-G4
BARNSLEY PL				
	-	DBLN	94568	694-H3
BARNWOOD DR				
	800	SRMN	94583	673-D4
BAROLO CT				
	-	PLE	94566	715-B5
BARON CT				
	7700	ELCR	94530	609-E2
BARON PL				
	600	MPS	95035	794-B3
BARON ST				
	42600	FRMT	94539	753-H6
BAROSSA DR				
	-	SRMN	94582	674-B3
BAROUNI CT				
	-	LVMR	94550	715-H5
BARRANCA CT				
	400	SRMN	94583	673-B3
BARRETT ST				
	2900	OAK	94605	671-B5
BARRI DR				
	700	SLN	94578	691-B4
BARRINGTON CT				
	2300	HAY	94545	711-C4
BARRINGTON TER				
	2600	FRMT	94536	752-H2
BARRON WY				
	600	HAY	94544	712-D7
BARRONS WY				
	30800	UNC	94587	731-J5
BARROW LN				
	-	BERK	94720	629-H2
BARROW ST				
	2200	SLN	94577	690-G4
BARROWS RD				
	1300	OAK	94610	650-C3
BARRY CT				
	-	ALA	94502	669-H5
BARRY PL				
	2700	OAK	94601	650-C6
BARRY WY				
	1000	FRMT	94536	753-B3
BARRYMORE COM				
	1900	FRMT	94538	753-C4
BART WY				
	2000	FRMT	94538	753-B4
BART ACCESS RD				
	-	HAY	94544	732-D2
BARTLETT AV				
	300	AlaC	94541	711-E2
BARTLETT DR				
	-	ALA	94501	649-A2
BARTLETT LN				
	20600	AlaC	94541	711-F1
BARTLETT PL				
	1000	PLE	94566	714-E5
BARTLETT ST				
	2300	OAK	94601	650-D6
	2600	OAK	94602	650-D6
BARTOL ST				
	-	SF	94133	648-A4
BARTOLO TER				
	4500	FRMT	94536	752-G4
BARTON DR				
	38300	FRMT	94536	753-C1
BARTON WY				
	1900	HAY	94545	711-E5
BASIN SIDE WY				
	-	ALA	94502	669-J6
	100	ALA	94502	670-A5
BASKERVILLE RD				
	3400	FRMT	94555	732-D7
BASS COM				
	38800	FRMT	94536	753-F3
BASS LAKE ST				
	32800	FRMT	94555	732-C6
BASSWOOD AV				
	33100	UNC	94587	732-G3
BASSWOOD CT				
	33000	UNC	94587	732-F3
BASSWOOD DR				
	-	CCCo	94582	673-J2
	-	CCCo	94582	674-A2
BATAAN AV				
	100	OAK	94607	649-C1
	900	BERK	94710	629-D1
BATAVIA AV				
	1000	LVMR	94550	715-F3
BATEMAN ST				
	3000	BERK	94705	629-J4
BATES AV				
	800	ELCR	94530	609-E2
BATES BLVD				
	-	ORIN	94563	610-H7
BATES DR				
	34700	FRMT	94555	752-E1
BATES RD				
	1200	OAK	94610	650-B4
	1200	OAK	94602	650-B4
BATES WY				
	5100	AlaC	94546	692-B2
BATH CT				
	-	SRMN	94583	673-F6
BATH PL				
	4900	NWK	94560	752-E3
BATTERY ST				
	-	SF	94104	648-B4
	-	SF	94111	648-B4
BAUMANN AV				
	2400	AlaC	94580	711-A2
BAUMBERG AV				
	2700	HAY	94545	731-G1
BAUMBERG CT				
	2700	HAY	94545	731-G2
BAUR CT				
	-	PLE	94588	714-F1
BAUTISTA ST				
	43500	FRMT	94539	753-H7
BAVA COM				
	-	LVMR	94551	695-G6
BAXTER ST				
	2100	OAK	94601	650-D7
BAY PL				
	100	OAK	94612	649-H3
	100	OAK	94610	649-H3
BAY RD				
	1900	EPA	94303	771-C7
BAY ST				
	-	EMVL	94608	629-E6
	-	SF	94111	648-A3
	-	SF	94133	648-A3
	500	OAK	94607	649-C3
	1100	ALA	94501	669-G2
	1700	ALA	94501	649-H7
	4000	FRMT	94538	753-D7
BAYBERRY COM				
	200	FRMT	94539	793-H1
BAYBERRY LN				
	15900	AlaC	94580	691-E5
BAYBERRY WY				
	-	MPS	95035	794-A6
BAY CENTER PL				
	3800	HAY	94545	711-D7
BAY COLONY WY				
	-	UNC	94545	751-J1
BAY EDGE RD				
	-	ALA	94502	669-J6
BAYFAIR DR				
	-	SLN	94578	691-D4
	300	AlaC	94578	691-E4
BAYFAIR WY				
	1200	SLN	94578	691-D4
BAYFIELD PL				
	41900	FRMT	94538	773-C1
BAY FOREST CT				
	-	OAK	94611	630-D4
BAY FOREST DR				
	-	OAK	94611	630-D3
BAYFRONT DR				
	1900	SLN	94579	691-A7
	2000	SLN	94579	690-J7
BAYFRONT EXWY Rt#-84				
	-	FRMT	94555	751-G7
	-	FRMT	94555	771-E3
	-	MLPK	94025	771-A6
	-	MLPK	94303	771-D4
BAY HEIGHTS RD				
	-	HAY	94542	712-G4
BAY HILL CT				
	-	DBLN	94568	694-F1
BAY LAUREL CT				
	-	DBLN	94568	693-F4
BAY LAUREL ST				
	-	DBLN	94568	693-E4
BAYLIS ST				
	2800	FRMT	94538	753-D5
BAYLOR AV				
	1200	SLN	94579	691-A4
BAYLOR ST				
	1700	UNC	94587	732-F6
	2500	EPA	94303	771-B7
BAYLOR WY				
	4200	LVMR	94550	716-A1
BAY MEADOWS CIR				
	2300	PLE	94566	714-C1
BAY MEADOWS CT				
	-	LVMR	94550	715-H5
BAYO ST				
	3800	OAK	94619	650-F6
BAYONNE DR				
	36000	NWK	94560	752-D5
BAYONNE PL				
	36000	NWK	94560	752-D5
BAYO VISTA AV				
	-	OAK	94611	649-J1
	3000	ALA	94501	670-B2
BAY PARK TER				
	-	ALA	94502	670-A5
BAYPOINT AV				
	-	SLN	94579	691-A7
	-	SLN	94579	711-A1
BAYSIDE PKWY				
	47000	FRMT	94538	773-F7
	47000	FRMT	94538	793-F1
BAYSIDE VILLAGE PL				
	-	SF	94107	648-C6
BAY TREE LN				
	700	ELCR	94530	609-E2
BAYTREE LN				
	-	BERK	94708	609-J6
	-	BERK	94708	610-A6
BAYVIEW AV				
	900	OAK	94610	650-B4
	4800	RCH	94804	609-B2
	22400	AlaC	94541	692-C6
	22600	HAY	94541	692-C6
BAYVIEW DR				
	-	FRMT	94538	793-G1
	2600	ALA	94501	669-J4
	2600	ALA	94501	670-A4
BAYVIEW PL				
	1300	BERK	94708	609-H7
BAYVIEW PARK DR				
	400	MPS	95035	794-D5
BAYWALK RD				
	2800	ALA	94502	669-J6
BAYWOOD AV				
	21800	AlaC	94546	691-J7
BAYWOOD COM				
	-	LVMR	94550	716-D2
BAYWOOD CT				
	1700	PLE	94566	714-D2
BAYWOOD LN				
	-	SRMN	94583	673-D6
BAYWOOD RD				
	600	ALA	94502	669-J6
BAYWOOD TER				
	3300	FRMT	94536	752-A6
BEACH RD				
	200	ALA	94502	670-B6
BEACH ST				
	-	SF	94133	648-A3
	1500	OAK	94608	629-E7
	3300	OAK	94608	649-E1
BEACHWOOD ST				
	-	HAY	94545	731-H3
BEACHWOOD WY				
	1700	PLE	94566	714-D2
BEACON AV				
	1400	SLN	94579	691-A6
	3400	FRMT	94538	753-B5
BEACON DR				
	-	MPS	95035	794-D6
BEACON ST				
	500	OAK	94610	649-J3
	500	OAK	94610	650-A3
BEACON BAY DR				
	-	UNC	94545	731-J6
BEACON HILL CT				
	20400	AlaC	94552	692-D4
BEACON HILL DR				
	4700	AlaC	94552	692-C5
BEACONSFIELD PL				
	2600	OAK	94611	650-F1
BEAL AV				
	2600	OAK	94605	670-F1
BEALE DR				
	300	HAY	94544	712-B6
BEALE ST				
	-	SF	94105	648-B5
	400	SF	94107	648-B5
BEAR CT				
	100	FRMT	94539	773-J3
BEAR RD				
	-	ALA	94501	649-J7
BEAR CREEK DR				
	6600	LVMR	94551	696-D2
BEAR CREEK RD				
	1200	ORIN	94563	610-F2
	1200	CCCo	94553	610-E4
	1200	CCCo	94563	610-F2
BEAR CREEK TR				
	-	CCCo	94553	610-G1
	-	CCCo	94563	610-G1
	-	ORIN	94563	610-D4
BEARD COM				
	2800	FRMT	94555	732-E6
BEARD RD				
	2800	FRMT	94555	732-D7
BEARD TER				
	2800	FRMT	94555	732-E6
BEARDSLEY ST				
	17800	AlaC	94546	692-B2
BEAR RIDGE RD				
	-	ORIN	94563	610-F3
BEAR RIDGE TR				
	100	ORIN	94563	610-G3
BEATIE ST				
	700	OAK	94606	650-A4
BEATRICE ST				
	500	SLN	94579	691-C6
	41100	FRMT	94539	753-E6
BEATRON WY				
	28100	HAY	94544	712-B7
BEATTY ST				
	15000	SLN	94579	691-B6
BEAU CT				
	5500	FRMT	94538	773-B2
BEAUDRY ST				
	5500	EMVL	94608	629-E5
BEAUFOREST DR				
	100	OAK	94611	630-E6
BEAUFORT HARBOR				
	-	ALA	94502	670-A5
BEAUMERE WY				
	100	MPS	95035	794-A4
BEAUMONT AV				
	3000	OAK	94606	650-C4
	3100	OAK	94602	650-C4
BEAUMONT CT				
	-	PLE	94588	714-B5
BEAUMONT ST				
	4200	FRMT	94536	752-G3
BEAVER CT				
	800	FRMT	94539	773-J3
BEAVER DR				
	-	HAY	94541	712-B1
BEAVER CREEK CT				
	800	SRMN	94582	674-A7
BECADO DR				
	300	FRMT	94539	773-H1
BECADO PL				
	400	FRMT	94539	773-H1
BECARD CT				
	2100	UNC	94587	732-G7
	2600	PLE	94566	714-C1
BECERRA DR				
	4000	FRMT	94536	752-E2
BECK LN				
	-	LVMR	94550	716-C2
BECK RD				
	400	AlaC	94551	675-H7
	1800	AlaC	94551	695-H2
BECKER PL				
	-	HAY	94544	732-E2
BECKET DR				
	2400	UNC	94587	732-C4
BECKET TER				
	38500	FRMT	94536	753-C2
BECKETT ST				
	-	SF	94133	648-A4
BECKETT WY				
	8600	DBLN	94568	693-F2
BECKHAM LN				
	2100	AlaC	94541	712-C2
BECKHAM WY				
	2100	AlaC	94541	712-C2
BEDELIO TER				
	36500	FRMT	94536	752-G3
BEDFORD CT				
	7400	DBLN	94568	693-H3
BEDFORD DR				
	21400	AlaC	94546	691-J6
	21400	HAY	94546	691-J6
BEDFORD PL				
	-	SF	94133	648-A4
BEDFORD ST				
	700	FRMT	94539	753-F6
BEDFORD WY				
	7300	DBLN	94568	693-H3
BEECH COM				
	2100	LVMR	94551	696-D1
BEECH CT				
	6300	PLE	94588	694-A7
BEECH PL				
	36300	NWK	94560	752-C6
BEECH ST				
	22600	HAY	94541	692-B7
BEECHAM CT				
	3400	PLE	94588	694-E5
BEECHER ST				
	900	SLN	94577	690-G1
BEECHMONT ST				
	500	HAY	94544	711-G4
BEECHWOOD AV				
	1500	SLN	94579	691-A5
	4700	FRMT	94536	752-H5
BEECHWOOD DR				
	-	OAK	94618	630-A5
BEETHOVEN COM				
	-	FRMT	94538	753-C3
BEGIER AV				
	-	SLN	94577	671-A7
BEGONIA CT				
	-	SRMN	94582	674-A2
	400	SLN	94578	691-C4
	1800	PLE	94588	714-F1
BEGONIA DR				
	600	SLN	94578	691-C4
	1000	ALA	94502	670-A6
BEGONIA ST				
	2500	UNC	94587	732-F7
	2500	UNC	94587	752-G1
BEHRENS ST				
	100	ELCR	94530	609-E4
	500	ALB	94706	609-E4
BEL AIR CT				
	-	FRMT	94539	773-J2
BEL AIRE CT				
	32700	UNC	94587	752-A1
BEL AIRE ST				
	32700	UNC	94587	752-A1
BELALP PTH				
	-	OAK	94618	630-B5
BELAMI LP				
	-	UNC	94587	732-D5
BELBROOK PL				
	1200	MPS	95035	793-J4
BELBROOK WY				
	1100	MPS	95035	793-J4
	1100	MPS	95035	794-A4
BELCARRA CT				
	-	DBLN	94568	694-E4
BELDEN ST				
	-	SF	94104	648-A5
BELDEN TER				
	3200	FRMT	94536	752-H2
BELDING ST				
	1400	SLN	94579	691-B7
BELEM CT				
	600	SRMN	94583	673-B3
BEL ESTOS WY				
	4300	UNC	94587	731-J5
BELFAST AV				
	4600	OAK	94619	650-H6
BELFAST CT				
	1300	LVMR	94550	715-F3
BELFAST LN				
	27000	HAY	94542	712-D4
BELFAST PL				
	-	SRMN	94583	673-F6
BELGIUM ST				
	-	LVMR	94551	696-A2
BELGRAVE PL				
	5300	OAK	94618	629-J6
	5300	OAK	94618	630-A6
BELHAVEN ST				
	25000	HAY	94545	711-G5
BELINDA CT				
	-	SRMN	94583	693-G1
BELIZE WY				
	3000	UNC	94587	731-J4
	3000	UNC	94587	732-A4
BELL AV				
	100	PDMT	94611	630-C7
	100	PDMT	94611	650-C1
	400	LVMR	94550	715-E3
	4100	RCH	94804	609-A1
BELL COM				
	4100	FRMT	94536	752-J4
	4100	FRMT	94536	753-A4
BELL CT				
	4500	RCH	94804	609-A1
BELL ST				
	38700	FRMT	94536	753-A5
BELL TER				
	4000	FRMT	94536	753-A4
BELLADONNA DR				
	-	SRMN	94582	673-J2
BELLAIR PL				
	-	SF	94133	648-A3
BELL AIRE DR				
	25800	HAY	94542	712-B4
BELLAIRE PL				
	2700	OAK	94601	650-C6
BELLA OAKS CT				
	-	AlaC	94550	716-D3
	-	LVMR	94550	716-D3
BELLA VISTA				
	600	FRMT	94539	773-H1
BELLA VISTA AV				
	800	SLN	94577	671-A7
	800	SLN	94577	691-A1
	1000	OAK	94610	650-B4
BELLA VISTA PL				
	-	LVMR	94550	715-G4
BELLE ST				
	22000	AlaC	94546	692-A7
BELLEAU ST				
	1000	SLN	94579	691-B7
BELLE MEADE DR				
	9400	SRMN	94583	693-H1
	9500	SRMN	94583	673-G7
BELLE MEADE PL				
	100	SRMN	94583	673-H7
BELLERIVE LN				
	-	DBLN	94568	694-F2
BELLEVIEW DR				
	100	SLN	94577	670-J7
	100	SLN	94577	671-A7
BELLEVUE AV				
	-	PDMT	94611	650-C1
	300	OAK	94610	649-J3
BELLEVUE CIR				
	-	DBLN	94568	694-E3
BELLEZA DR				
	5600	PLE	94588	694-C7
BELLEZA LN				
	5600	PLE	94588	694-C7
BELLFLOWER DR				
	5700	NWK	94560	752-G7
BELLFLOWER LN				
	-	UNC	94587	732-H5
BELLFLOWER ST				
	700	LVMR	94551	696-B4
BELLHAVEN AV				
	6000	NWK	94560	752-E6
BELLHAVEN PL				
	6200	NWK	94560	752-E6
BELLHURST CT				
	6400	AlaC	94552	672-C7
BELLHURST LN				
	6400	AlaC	94552	672-C7
BELLINA ST				
	1200	HAY	94541	712-A1
	8600	DBLN	94568	693-G2
BELLINA CANYON RD				
	-	AlaC	94552	672-F3
BELLINGHAM DR				
	5900	AlaC	94552	692-C1
BELLINGHAM SQ				
	-	SRMN	94582	674-B3
N BELLINGHAM WY				
	-	SRMN	94582	674-B3
S BELLINGHAM WY				
	-	SRMN	94582	674-B3
BELLINGTON COM				
	100	LVMR	94551	695-C4
BELLIS DR				
	-	SRMN	94582	673-H1
BELLMAWR DR				
	4100	LVMR	94551	696-A6
BELLO CT				
	200	SRMN	94583	673-A2
BELLO RD				
	30600	AlaC	94544	732-E1
	30600	HAY	94544	712-E7
	30600	HAY	94544	732-E1
	30600	AlaC	94544	712-E7
BELLO VIEW PL				
	-	HAY	94544	712-E7
BELLS RD				
	2000	FRMT	94539	773-E1
BELL WAVER WY				
	-	OAK	94619	650-J4
BELLWOOD CT				
	42600	FRMT	94538	773-D2
BELMONT AV				
	3200	ELCR	94530	609-C4
	3200	RCH	94804	609-C4
	25100	HAY	94542	712-A3
BELMONT CT				
	-	LVMR	94550	715-H5
BELMONT DR				
	-	LVMR	94550	715-H6
BELMONT PL				
	3200	ALA	94502	670-A6
BELMONT ST				
	300	OAK	94610	649-J3

STREET
Block City ZIP Pg-Grid

BELMONT TER
- FRMT 94539 774-A6
BELMONT WY
3100 ALA 94502 670-A6
3800 PLE 94588 694-F5
4400 AlaC 94546 691-H1
BELOIT AV
400 CCCo 94708 609-G4
BELOIT ST
38600 FRMT 94536 752-J4
BELOVERIA CT
4000 FRMT 94536 752-H4
BEL ROMA RD
4700 AlaC 94551 675-H7
BELROSE AV
2700 BERK 94705 630-A3
BELVEDERE AV
1500 BERK 94702 629-E1
2200 SLN 94577 690-H5
BELVEDERE CT
7500 PLE 94588 714-A3
27000 HAY 94544 712-A6
BELVEDERE ST
5200 OAK 94601 670-F1
BELVEDERE TER
34900 FRMT 94555 752-E2
BEMIS ST
4200 OAK 94605 671-D5
BENAVENTE AV
39400 FRMT 94539 753-E3
BENAVENTE PL
39500 FRMT 94539 753-E3
BENBOW DR
41900 FRMT 94539 753-E7
BENCHMARK AV
2400 FRMT 94536 752-J1
2400 FRMT 94536 753-A3
BENCHMARK CT
37800 FRMT 94536 752-J1
BENDEL TER
36400 FRMT 94536 752-J1
BENECIA AV
6200 NWK 94560 772-H1
BENEDICK CT
4500 FRMT 94555 752-D2
BENEDICK LN
34300 FRMT 94555 752-D2
BENEDICT CT
- ALA 94502 669-H6
1200 SLN 94577 691-C1
1300 PLE 94566 714-G5
BENEDICT DR
1300 SLN 94577 671-C7
1300 SLN 94605 671-C7
1300 OAK 94605 671-C7
1300 SLN 94577 691-C1
BENEVIDES AV
4600 OAK 94602 650-D3
BENGAL AV
18200 AlaC 94541 711-E1
BENICIA ST
47000 FRMT 94538 773-G7
BENJAMIN CT
- PLE 94566 714-E3
BENJAMIN GRN
2900 FRMT 94538 753-D5
BENNER CT
6300 PLE 94588 694-A6
BENNETT CT
1100 FRMT 94536 753-B2
BENNETT DR
4700 LVMR 94551 696-B5
BENNETT PL
4300 OAK 94602 650-F4
BENNINGTON DR
6100 NWK 94560 752-D6
BENNINGTON LN
2200 HAY 94545 711-F6
BENNS TER
47000 FRMT 94539 773-H6
BENSON RD
4300 UNC 94587 731-H5
BENT CREEK DR
2000 SRMN 94582 673-J7
2000 SRMN 94582 674-A7
2100 SRMN 94582 694-A1
BENTLEY CT
2300 AlaC 94546 691-H5
34500 FRMT 94555 752-E1
BENTLEY PL
600 LVMR 94551 695-H6
34400 FRMT 94555 732-E7
34400 FRMT 94555 752-E1
BENTLEY OAKS CT
- SRMN 94582 694-A1
BENTON ST
1200 ALA 94501 669-H1
1400 OAK 94602 650-C4
BENT TREE DR
- DBLN 94568 694-G2
BENVENUE AV
2500 BERK 94704 629-J3
2700 BERK 94705 629-J3
3100 OAK 94618 629-J4
BENZON DR
9200 PLE 94588 693-G6
BERATLIS PL
- PLE 94566 714-H4
BERDINA RD
4000 AlaC 94546 692-A4
BERENDA WY
27400 HAY 94544 711-J7
BERESFORD CT
100 MPS 95035 794-A7
BERET TER
34700 FRMT 94555 752-D3
BERETTA DR
43900 FRMT 94539 773-H1
BERG CT
1100 MPS 95035 794-B4
BERGEDO DR
200 OAK 94603 690-H1
300 OAK 94603 670-H7
BERK AV
500 RCH 94804 609-A1
BERK PL
100 RCH 94804 609-A1
BERKELEY AV
- ORIN 94563 610-E6
BERKELEY COM
38400 FRMT 94536 753-B2
BERKELEY RD
29000 HAY 94544 732-B1
BERKELEY WY
1200 BERK 94702 629-E2
1500 BERK 94703 629-F1
1900 BERK 94704 629-F1
BERKELEY PARK BLVD
200 CCCo 94707 609-E4
BERKELY PL
1300 LVMR 94550 715-F5

BERKSHIRE
- MRGA 94556 651-D1
BERKSHIRE AV
- LVMR 94551 696-B2
BERKSHIRE CT
100 SRMN 94582 673-G4
3100 PLE 94588 694-E6
BERKSHIRE DR
15900 AlaC 94578 691-F3
BERKSHIRE PL
600 MPS 95035 794-B3
BERKSHIRE RD
- ALA 94502 669-J5
BERLIN WY
1300 LVMR 94550 715-F3
3100 OAK 94602 650-E6
BERMUDA AV
2200 SLN 94577 690-H5
4300 OAK 94619 650-H6
BERMUDA CT
900 FRMT 94539 753-F5
BERMUDA LN
2300 HAY 94545 711-G7
BERNAL AV
300 LVMR 94551 695-F7
300 LVMR 94551 715-F1
1000 PLE 94566 714-G2
3400 AlaC 94566 714-G2
7700 PLE 94588 714-A4
BERNAL COM
500 FRMT 94539 753-H7
BERNAL CT
300 PLE 94566 714-D4
BERNAL ST
19600 AlaC 94546 691-H4
BERNARD AV
3000 SRMN 94583 673-F6
BERNEVES CT
- OAK 94619 650-H5
BERNHARDT DR
9800 OAK 94603 670-G7
BERNHARDT ST
23000 HAY 94545 711-C6
BERNICE WY
32000 HAY 94544 732-F2
BERNIE ST
41100 FRMT 94539 753-G5
BERRENDO DR
- MPS 95035 794-A5
BERRY AV
200 HAY 94544 711-J4
300 HAY 94544 712-A4
800 HAY 94542 712-A4
BERRY CT
1800 FRMT 94539 753-F7
BERRY ST
100 SF 94107 648-B7
BERRYBROOK HOLLOW
- ORIN 94563 610-F3
BERRYESSA CT
- LVMR 94551 696-D3
BERRYESSA ST
- LVMR 94551 696-D4
600 MPS 95035 793-J6
600 MPS 95035 794-A6
BERRYMAN ST
1800 BERK 94703 609-F7
1900 BERK 94709 609-F7
BERSANO CT
3000 PLE 94566 715-C6
BERTA DR
2800 AlaC 94541 692-C7
BERTERO AV
15900 AlaC 94580 691-E5
BERTOLLI CT
- LVMR 94550 715-G5
BERTOLLI DR
- LVMR 94550 715-G5
BERWICK PL
- SF 94103 648-D7
100 SRMN 94583 673-F6
BERWIND AV
5500 LVMR 94551 696-C3
BERYL PL
700 HAY 94544 712-A7
BERYLWOOD LN
- MPS 95035 793-J3
BESCO DR
39800 FRMT 94538 753-B7
BESITO AV
1100 OAK 94705 630-B3
BESS AV
2100 LVMR 94550 715-H3
BEST AV
100 SLN 94577 671-A7
200 SLN 94577 670-J7
2400 OAK 94601 670-F1
2600 OAK 94619 650-F7
2600 OAK 94619 670-F1
BETA CT
- SRMN 94583 673-B1
BETHAL PL
600 LVMR 94551 695-E6
BETHANY RD
- SRMN 94582 674-D4
W BETHANY RD
15300 SJCo 95304 (678-H2 See Page 677)
15300 SJCo 95391 (678-G2 See Page 677)
BETHANY ST
14600 SLN 94579 691-A5
BETHEL LN
8000 PLE 94588 693-H7
BETHELL AV
- SJCo 95391 (678-F2 See Page 677)
BETHELL CT
- SJCo 95391 (678-F2 See Page 677)
BETLEN CT
2700 AlaC 94546 692-B6
BETLEN DR
11200 DBLN 94568 693-F5
BETLEN WY
21800 AlaC 94546 692-B6
BETROSE CT
19600 AlaC 94546 691-H4
BETTENCOURT CT
3900 FRMT 94536 752-J3
BETTENCOURT ST
35700 NWK 94560 752-C6
BETTENCOURT WY
4300 UNC 94587 731-J4
BETTONA ST
2300 LVMR 94550 715-E5
BETTY AV
1200 SLN 94578 691-D4
BETTY CIR
5400 LVMR 94550 696-C7
BETTY LN
8400 ELCR 94530 609-E1

BEUTKE DR
36600 NWK 94560 752-D7
BEVERLY AV
100 SLN 94577 671-A6
10500 OAK 94603 671-A6
BEVERLY CT
- CCCo 94707 609-F4
8400 DBLN 94568 693-H2
BEVERLY LN
8400 DBLN 94568 693-H1
BEVERLY PL
1500 ALB 94706 609-F6
1500 BERK 94706 609-F6
1600 BERK 94707 609-F6
4100 AlaC 94546 692-A4
BEVERLY RD
- CCCo 94707 609-F4
BEVERLY ST
400 LVMR 94550 696-A7
BEVIL WY
16300 AlaC 94578 691-F5
BEVILACQUA CT
4200 PLE 94566 714-E4
BEVILACQUA ST
900 AlaC 94580 691-F6
BIANCA DR
4500 FRMT 94536 752-E3
BIANCA LN
- AlaC 94541 711-G1
BIANCA WY
5100 LVMR 94550 696-C6
BIANCO CT
5100 PLE 94588 694-H4
BIDDLE AV
5800 NWK 94560 752-E5
BIDDLEFORD DR
2800 SRMN 94583 673-F6
BIDWELL DR
3900 FRMT 94538 753-B5
BIEHS CT
- OAK 94618 630-C6
BIENATI WY
2100 OAK 94602 650-D4
BIEN VENIDA
- ORIN 94563 610-G6
BIG BASIN RD
1000 LVMR 94551 696-D3
BIG BEND CT
6000 PLE 94588 714-B1
BIG BEND DR
1500 MPS 95035 794-D7
BIG BURN RD
- AlaC 94546 651-G7
- AlaC 94546 671-F1
BIGELOW PL
- SRMN 94583 673-F6
BIGELOW TER
- FRMT 94536 752-J2
BIG FOOT CT
500 FRMT 94539 773-H4
BIGGE ST
9800 OAK 94603 670-F7
9800 SLN 94577 670-F7
10000 SLN 94577 690-G1
BIGHORN CT
48700 FRMT 94539 793-J2
BIG OAK CT
3400 HAY 94542 712-E4
BIG OAK LN
- MPS 95035 793-J3
BIG SPRINGS TR
- CCCo 94708 610-B6
BILLINGS BLVD
600 SLN 94577 690-H1
BILTMORE ST
- SLN 94577 670-J7
- SLN 94577 690-J1
BING CT
2500 UNC 94587 732-F7
BING PL
2400 UNC 94587 732-F7
BINNACLE HILL
- OAK 94618 630-C4
BIRCH
- ORIN 94563 630-G1
BIRCH CT
5800 OAK 94618 629-J5
6700 DBLN 94568 693-J3
BIRCH PL
6000 NWK 94560 752-F7
BIRCH ST
8100 OAK 94621 670-H3
9000 OAK 94603 670-J4
10000 OAK 94603 671-A5
14300 SLN 94579 691-A4
20800 AlaC 94541 691-G6
36700 NWK 94560 752-E6
38700 NWK 94560 772-H1
BIRCH TER
5700 FRMT 94538 773-A1
BIRCH CREEK DR
200 PLE 94566 714-F3
BIRCHWOOD COM
- LVMR 94550 716-D1
BIRCHWOOD CT
4500 UNC 94587 732-A7
BIRCHWOOD TER
3500 FRMT 94536 752-A6
BIRD CT
- ALA 94501 649-A2
BIRD PL
700 HAY 94544 711-J5
BIRDSALL AV
2800 OAK 94619 670-F1
2900 OAK 94619 650-F7
BIRDWOOD CT
- SRMN 94582 674-B3
BIRKDALE DR
7300 NWK 94560 752-C6
BIRKDALE WY
31000 HAY 94544 732-D2
BIRKSHIRE PL
36200 NWK 94560 752-C6
BIRMINGHAM WY
- UNC 94587 731-J5
BISCAY BAY
100 ALA 94502 669-H7
BISCAY PL
35500 NWK 94560 752-C5
BISCAYNE AV
27800 HAY 94544 712-A7
BISHOP AV
400 HAY 94544 711-H5
1900 FRMT 94536 753-A3
2500 FRMT 94536 752-J3
BISHOP CT
37800 FRMT 94536 753-A3
BISHOP DR
2400 SRMN 94583 673-D2
BISHOP ST
1100 ALA 94501 670-A3
36600 NWK 94560 752-E5

BISHOP WY
5500 NWK 94560 752-F5
BISHOP PINE WY
4100 LVMR 94551 695-J4
4100 LVMR 94551 696-A4
BISMARCK LN
1100 ALA 94502 670-A7
BISSY COM
39700 FRMT 94538 753-B6
BITTERN CT
- SLN 94579 690-J7
BITTERN PL
3500 FRMT 94555 732-D7
BITTERROOT AV
5900 NWK 94560 752-H7
BIVAR CT
1600 PLE 94566 714-E1
BIXBY DR
100 MPS 95035 794-D7
BIXCO ST
- SLN 94577 670-J7
- SLN 94577 690-J1
BIXLER RD
3100 CCCo 94514 637-F1
4100 CCCo 94513 637-F1
BLACHFORD CT
- OAK 94611 650-F2
BLACK AV
4300 PLE 94566 714-C2
BLACKBERRY LN
5000 AlaC 94546 692-A2
BLACKBIRD CT
- HAY 94544 712-E7
BLACKBIRD DR
5100 PLE 94566 714-C1
BLACKBIRD WY
2400 PLE 94566 694-D7
2400 PLE 94566 714-D1
BLACKBURN DR
35100 NWK 94560 752-D4
BLACK CALLA CT
- SRMN 94582 673-G2
BLACKFOOT DR
1500 FRMT 94539 773-G3
BLACK MESA TER
- FRMT 94536 732-J4
BLACK MOUNTAIN CIR
- FRMT 94536 732-J6
BLACKOAK COM
4500 FRMT 94538 773-C1
BLACK OAK CT
2100 PLE 94588 714-A5
BLACKOAK CT
1600 LVMR 94551 696-D2
BLACK PINE DR
600 SLN 94577 690-G1
BLACKPOOL LN
2400 SLN 94577 691-B2
BLACKPOOL PL
2200 SLN 94577 691-B2
BLACKSAND RD
5000 FRMT 94538 752-J7
BLACK SOOTER CT
- SLN 94579 691-F2
BLACKSTONE COM
- LVMR 94550 715-C1
BLACKSTONE CT
- AlaC 94542 712-E1
BLACKSTONE RD
- DBLN 94568 694-F2
BLACKSTONE WY
34300 FRMT 94555 752-D1
BLACKTHORN CT
200 SRMN 94582 673-J6
BLACKWOOD AV
22600 HAY 94541 711-F3
BLACKWOOD COM
1700 LVMR 94551 695-F6
BLACKWOOD DR
36400 NWK 94560 752-E4
BLACOW CT
3900 PLE 94566 714-F1
BLACOW RD
37000 FRMT 94536 752-G5
39000 FRMT 94538 752-H6
39400 FRMT 94538 753-A7
40200 FRMT 94538 773-C1
42400 FRMT 94539 773-E1
BLACOW ST
4000 PLE 94566 714-F1
BLAINE CIR
- MRGA 94556 651-E2
BLAINE ST
8500 OAK 94621 670-G5
BLAINE WY
600 HAY 94544 711-H5
BLAIR AV
- PDMT 94611 650-A1
800 OAK 94611 630-C7
800 OAK 94611 650-C1
BLAIR CT
- DNVL 94526 652-G1
BLAIR PL
- OAK 94611 650-C1
- PDMT 94611 650-C1
35700 FRMT 94536 752-G2
BLAISDELL TER
- FRMT 94536 733-B7
BLAISDELL WY
- FRMT 94536 733-A7
BLAKE AV
200 FRMT 94536 753-C3
BLAKE ST
1100 BERK 94702 629-E3
1500 BERK 94703 629-G3
2000 BERK 94704 629-G3
6300 ELCR 94530 609-B1
BLAKEMORE CT
3400 PLE 94588 694-E5
BLAKESLEY CT
- SRMN 94582 674-B3
BLAKESLEY DR
- SRMN 94582 674-B3
BLALOCK ST
1000 MPS 95035 794-B5
BLANC CT
1100 PLE 94566 714-G4
BLANCHARD ST
40100 FRMT 94538 753-C6
BLANCHE ST
400 HAY 94544 732-F2
BLANCO CT
400 SRMN 94583 673-B3
BLANCO ST
16300 AlaC 94578 691-F5
BLAND ST
24800 AlaC 94541 712-C2
BLANDING AV
2300 ALA 94501 670-A1
BLANDING CT
13100 AlaC 94541 692-C6

BLANDON RD
3200 OAK 94605 671-A3
BLENHEIM ST
700 OAK 94603 670-H7
BLESSING DR
9400 PLE 94588 693-F6
BLEWETT ST
4100 FRMT 94538 753-C6
BLISS AV
2100 MPS 95035 794-E7
BLISS CT
39600 FRMT 94538 753-A7
BLONDWOOD CT
4300 UNC 94587 732-A7
BLOOM ST
- SLN 94577 670-J7
BLOOMFIELD LN
- SRMN 94582 674-A4
BLOOMFIELD TER
- DBLN 94568 693-E4
BLOOMINGTON CT
8600 DBLN 94568 693-F2
BLOOMINGTON WY
11400 DBLN 94568 693-E2
BLOSSOM CIR
1200 LVMR 94550 716-B1
BLOSSOM COM
- AlaC 94541 691-F7
- AlaC 94541 711-G1
BLOSSOM CT
600 PLE 94566 714-D6
2800 UNC 94587 752-F1
20600 AlaC 94541 711-F1
BLOSSOM DR
41700 FRMT 94539 753-G6
BLOSSOM LN
800 AlaC 94541 691-G7
BLOSSOM ST
3000 OAK 94601 650-C6
BLOSSOM WK
- ALA 94501 669-G3
BLOSSOM WY
- AlaC 94541 711-F1
300 AlaC 94541 691-G7
500 SLN 94577 691-B2
W BLOSSOM WY
- AlaC 94541 711-F1
BLOSSOM RIDGE LN
- CCCo 94582 674-A2
BLUEBELL CT
1500 LVMR 94551 696-B3
38900 NWK 94560 772-H1
BLUEBELL DR
900 LVMR 94551 696-A2
38800 NWK 94560 772-H1
BLUEBELL WY
7600 DBLN 94568 693-G2
BLUEBIRD AV
100 LVMR 94551 715-E1
BLUE BIRD CT
5800 AlaC 94552 692-E2
BLUEBIRD CT
32800 FRMT 94555 732-B7
BLUEBIRD LP
32800 FRMT 94555 732-B7
BLUEBONNET COM
6300 LVMR 94551 696-D2
BLUE BONNET PL
400 HAY 94544 711-J5
BLUE CORAL TER
- FRMT 94536 753-C2
BLUEFIELD LN
500 HAY 94541 711-F4
BLUE FIN WY
39400 FRMT 94538 752-J7
BLUEFLOWER TER
- FRMT 94536 752-A5
BLUE FOX WY
7400 SRMN 94583 693-G1
BLUEGILL ST
- FRMT 94536 753-B3
BLUEGRASS CT
6900 LVMR 94551 696-E2
38800 NWK 94560 772-H1
BLUEHEART WY
- CCCo 94582 674-A2
BLUE HERON CT
- SLN 94579 691-F2
BLUE JAY DR
500 HAY 94544 712-D7
BLUE JAY TER
- FRMT 94555 752-B2
BLUE MOUND CT
200 SRMN 94583 673-H6
BLUE MOUND DR
9600 SRMN 94583 673-H6
BLUE RIDGE ST
4200 FRMT 94536 752-G3
BLUE SHADOW WY
- HAY 94542 712-G5
BLUE SPRUCE LN
- UNC 94587 732-H5
BLUESTONE COM
34500 FRMT 94555 752-B2
BLUE WHALE ST
- SLN 94577 690-G5
BLUFFS CT
- LVMR 94551 696-E1
BLUFFS DR
- LVMR 94551 696-E1
BLUXOME ST
- SF 94107 648-B7
BLYTHE ST
4800 UNC 94587 752-A1
BLYTHEN WY
- OAK 94619 651-A4
12100 OAK 94619 650-J4
BOAR CIR
100 FRMT 94539 773-J3
BOARDMAN PL
- SF 94103 648-A7
BOARDWALK
- SRMN 94583 673-B2
BOARDWALK ST
3000 PLE 94588 694-G6
BOARDWALK WY
100 HAY 94544 732-C1
BOBBY DR
5500 LVMR 94551 696-C4
BOBBY ST
- FRMT 94555 752-C1
BOB KAUFMAN AL
- SF 94133 648-A4
BOBOLINK CT
1700 HAY 94545 731-J2
BOBOLINK RD
- ORIN 94563 610-F5
BOBWHITE RD
1700 LVMR 94550 715-H3
BOBWHITE TER
3700 FRMT 94555 732-D7

BOCA RATON CT
- SRMN 94583 673-H7
26800 HAY 94545 711-H7
BOCA RATON ST
1800 HAY 94545 711-G7
BOCKMAN RD
600 AlaC 94580 711-B1
BOCMART PL
3700 SRMN 94583 673-C2
BODEGA AV
1500 LVMR 94550 715-G2
BODEGA CT
1600 FRMT 94539 773-J4
BODEGA ST
29200 AlaC 94544 712-D6
29200 HAY 94544 712-D6
BODEGA WY
2500 SLN 94577 690-G5
BODEN WY
500 OAK 94610 649-J3
500 OAK 94610 650-A3
BODIE TER
46900 FRMT 94539 773-F6
BODILY AV
36800 FRMT 94536 753-A1
BODKIN TER
34300 FRMT 94555 752-C2
BODMIN AV
1000 SLN 94579 691-B5
BOEING CT
300 LVMR 94551 695-D6
BOGALUSA CT
600 FRMT 94539 793-J1
BOGGS AV
800 FRMT 94539 773-G5
BOGGS TER
800 FRMT 94539 773-G5
BOISE ST
3200 BERK 94702 629-F4
BOITANO DR
44100 FRMT 94539 773-H2
BOLERO AV
2000 HAY 94545 711-H7
BOLERO CT
3000 PLE 94588 694-D6
BOLERO PZ
100 UNC 94587 732-J5
BOLES CT
4700 FRMT 94538 753-B7
BOLINA DR
4200 UNC 94587 731-J5
BOLINA TER
36900 FRMT 94536 752-G4
BOLINGER COM
400 FRMT 94539 773-H6
BOLINGER TER
300 FRMT 94539 773-H6
BOLIVAR DR
- BERK 94710 629-D2
W BOLIVAR DR
- BERK 94710 629-D2
BOLIVAR PL
800 SRMN 94583 673-G5
4400 UNC 94587 731-H6
BOLLA CT
3200 PLE 94566 715-C6
BOLLINGER CANYON LN
500 SRMN 94582 673-F2
BOLLINGER CANYON RD
- CCCo 94582 673-H2
- CCCo 94582 674-A4
- SRMN 94582 674-A4
1200 CCCo 94556 651-J1
1200 CCCo 94556 652-A1
2700 SRMN 94583 673-A1
3600 SRMN 94582 673-H2
13100 CCCo 94583 673-A1
18400 CCCo 94583 652-E3
18600 CCCo 94583 672-J1
BOLLINGER CANYON WY
600 SRMN 94582 673-F2
BOLLINGER ESTATES CT
300 CCCo 94583 652-F4
BOLTON DR
800 MPS 95035 794-A2
BOLTON PL
5100 NWK 94560 752-E4
BONA ST
2700 OAK 94601 650-C5
BONANZA WY
300 DNVL 94526 652-J3
BONAR ST
2000 BERK 94702 629-E2
BOND ST
4200 OAK 94601 670-D1
12200 AlaC 94586 734-D6
BONDE CT
700 PLE 94566 714-F4
BONDE WY
3700 FRMT 94536 752-H3
S BONETTI RD
10300 SJCo 95206 (638-G3 See Page 637)
BONFIELD CT
7500 DBLN 94568 693-H2
BONHAM WY
400 OAK 94610 649-J2
400 OAK 94610 650-A2
BONIFACIO ST
- SF 94107 648-B6
BONITA AV
- PDMT 94611 630-B7
100 PDMT 94611 650-B1
400 PLE 94566 714-F4
1200 BERK 94709 609-G7
1500 BERK 94709 629-G1
1900 BERK 94704 629-G1
BONITA LN
- ORIN 94563 610-F7
BONITA WY
31200 UNC 94587 731-J5
BONITO DR
36600 FRMT 94536 752-F4
BONNER AV
1000 FRMT 94536 753-B3
1200 FRMT 94538 753-B3
BONNIE DR
400 ELCR 94530 609-E3
BONNIE LN
- BERK 94708 609-H5
BONNIE ST
36500 NWK 94560 752-E6
BONNIE WY
38800 FRMT 94536 752-J6
BONNIE VISTA AV
800 SLN 94577 671-A7
BONNIEWOOD CT
7700 DBLN 94568 693-G2
BONNIEWOOD LN
7500 DBLN 94568 693-H2

BONNINGTON CT
- OAK 94611 630-E5
BONSAI PL
3900 AlaC 94546 692-A4
BOOKER ST
2500 OAK 94606 650-A4
BOOKER WY
25800 HAY 94544 711-H5
BOONE DR
4600 FRMT 94538 753-A7
6100 AlaC 94552 692-E3
BORA BORA AV
4300 FRMT 94538 773-D1
BORDEAUX PL
3400 PLE 94566 714-G4
BORDEAUX ST
1100 LVMR 94550 715-G3
1100 PLE 94566 714-G4
BORDWELL CT
- ALA 94502 669-J6
BORGIA RD
5400 FRMT 94538 773-B2
BORICA CT
- DBLN 94568 694-G5
BOSCELL COM
42000 FRMT 94538 773-B3
BOSCELL RD
42000 FRMT 94538 773-A3
BOSSHARD CT
- ALA 94501 649-A2
BOSTON AV
3100 OAK 94602 650-D4
BOSTON CT
43900 FRMT 94539 773-H1
BOSTON RD
17100 AlaC 94541 691-F7
BOSWELL TER
3700 FRMT 94536 752-J4
BOSWORTH CT
4900 NWK 94560 752-D3
36500 FRMT 94536 752-G3
BOTANY GRN
38400 FRMT 94536 753-B3
BOTHELO AV
- MPS 95035 794-A7
BOTTINI CT
2900 PLE 94566 715-C6
BOTTLE BRUSH CT
36500 NWK 94560 752-D7
BOTTLE BRUSH PL
24300 AlaC 94541 712-C1
BOULDER CT
- PLE 94566 714-F2
BOULDER ST
200 MPS 95035 794-A3
3400 PLE 94566 714-F2
BOULDER CANYON CT
5700 AlaC 94552 692-E6
BOULDER CANYON DR
3800 AlaC 94552 692-D6
BOULDER CREEK DR
1100 HAY 94544 732-A1
BOULEVARD CT
14800 AlaC 94578 691-D3
BOULEVARD WY
400 OAK 94610 650-A2
400 PDMT 94610 650-A2
BOURBON DR
2100 HAY 94545 731-H2
BOWDITCH ST
2300 BERK 94704 629-J2
BOWEN CT
- SRMN 94582 674-C4
BOWEN ST
4400 PLE 94588 694-E7
BOWER CT
800 LVMR 94550 715-J1
BOWER LN
- DBLN 94568 693-E5
BOWERS CT
44100 FRMT 94539 773-H2
BOWHILL RD
- HAY 94544 732-B1
BOWIE COM
34700 FRMT 94555 752-D2
BOWIE WY
6600 AlaC 94552 692-F2
BOWLES PL
- OAK 94610 650-C3
BOWLIN AV
2800 SRMN 94583 673-E6
BOWLING DR
- OAK 94618 630-A5
BOWLING GRN
100 SLN 94577 670-J7
BOWLINGREEN COM
34100 FRMT 94555 752-E1
BOWMAN CT
3500 ALA 94502 670-A7
BOWMAN PL
- HAY 94544 732-E3
BOXER CT
1900 AlaC 94580 711-B1
BOXFORD PL
- SRMN 94583 673-F7
BOXSTEAD COM
3900 FRMT 94555 752-D1
BOXWOOD AV
1400 SLN 94579 691-A5
1600 SLN 94579 690-J5
BOXWOOD CT
- LVMR 94551 696-C3
BOXWOOD WY
- DBLN 94568 694-D4
2000 FRMT 94539 773-G3
BOYCE RD
- FRMT 94538 772-J2
41500 FRMT 94538 773-A3
BOYD AV
5200 OAK 94618 629-J6
BOYD CT
- DNVL 94526 652-J1
BOYD ST
200 MPS 95035 794-A3
BOYER ST
5300 OAK 94608 629-F6
BOYLE DR
4100 FRMT 94536 752-F2
BOYLE ST
- UNC 94587 732-F4
BOYNTON AV
400 BERK 94707 609-G4
400 CCCo 94707 609-G4
BRADFORD AV
2400 HAY 94545 711-F6
BRADFORD PL
500 DNVL 94526 652-H1
BRADFORD WY
- LVMR 94550 715-G4
700 UNC 94587 732-G5
BRADHOFF AV
2000 SLN 94577 691-B1

STREET Block City ZIP Pg-Grid

BRADLEY CT
46500 FRMT 94539 773-H5
BRADLEY ST
14300 SLN 94579 691-A4
46600 FRMT 94539 773-H6
BRADRICK DR
400 SLN 94578 691-C5
BRADSHIRE RD
28200 HAY 94545 731-H1
BRAE BURN AV
30500 HAY 94544 732-D2
BRAEBURN CT
- SRMN 94583 693-H1
BRAEMAR RD
2000 OAK 94602 650-E2
BRAGA ST
- FRMT 94538 773-F7
BRAIDBURN AV
7200 NWK 94560 752-B6
BRALY AV
1500 MPS 95035 794-D6
BRAMBLE CT
2300 AlaC 94546 691-H5
BRANAUGH CT
- HAY 94544 732-C1
E BRANCH PKWY
- CCCo 94582 674-B5
- SRMN 94582 674-B5
BRANDIN CT
5000 FRMT 94538 773-C4
BRANDING IRON CT
- DBLN 94568 694-E1
BRANDON PL
2600 AlaC 94546 691-J6
BRANDON ST
1000 PDMT 94611 630-A7
1000 OAK 94611 630-A7
BRANDT CT
- MPS 95035 794-C7
BRANDT DR
- MRGA 94556 651-F1
BRANDY CT
3400 PLE 94566 714-G4
BRANDY ROCK WY
5000 OAK 94619 651-B6
BRANDYWINE PL
- HAY 94542 712-C3
BRANDYWINE ST
35900 NWK 94560 752-C6
BRANN ST
5400 OAK 94619 650-G7
5400 OAK 94619 670-G1
5500 OAK 94605 670-G1
BRANNAN ST
- SF 94107 648-B7
600 SF 94103 648-B7
BRANNIGAN ST
- DBLN 94568 694-F4
BRANTWOOD CT
42600 FRMT 94538 773-D2
BRAUN ST
- FRMT 94538 773-B4
BRAXTON COM
- FRMT 94538 753-B5
BRAXTON PL
1000 PLE 94566 714-F5
BRAY CT
- DBLN 94568 694-A4
BRAYTON CT
37700 FRMT 94536 752-G5
BREAKER CIR
- HAY 94545 731-G3
BREAKER LN
- HAY 94545 731-H3
BREAKWATER AV
3500 HAY 94545 711-D7
3900 HAY 94545 731-C1
BREAKWATER CT
3400 HAY 94545 711-E7
BREAKWATER DR
- BERK 94710 629-B1
BRECKENRIDGE ST
1000 SLN 94579 691-B7
BRECON CT
2500 AlaC 94546 692-A6
BREED AV
100 SLN 94577 671-A6
10500 OAK 94603 671-A6
BREEZE WY
- LVMR 94550 715-E5
BREHAUT CT
- ALA 94502 669-J6
BREMEN ST
- DBLN 94568 694-F4
BRENDA WY
32600 UNC 94587 732-C5
BRENNAN WY
800 LVMR 94550 715-H1
BRENT CT
3100 AlaC 94546 691-H3
3500 PLE 94588 694-F5
BRENTWOOD CT
24700 HAY 94545 711-F5
BRENTWOOD PL
- OAK 94602 650-E3
BRENTWOOD RD
1800 OAK 94602 650-E3
BRESSO CT
- LVMR 94550 715-F5
BRESSO DR
- LVMR 94550 715-F5
BRET HARTE CT
4700 FRMT 94538 752-J6
6400 AlaC 94552 692-F2
BRET HARTE RD
- BERK 94708 609-H6
BRET HARTE WY
- BERK 94708 609-H6
BRETON DR
35400 NWK 94560 752-D5
BRETON PL
6000 NWK 94560 752-D5
BRETT AV
- SJCo 95391 (678-E3 See Page 677)
BRETT CT
5000 FRMT 94538 773-B1
BREVENSVILLE DR
- SRMN 94583 693-F1
BREWIN CT
- SRMN 94583 693-F1
BREWIN LN
- SRMN 94583 693-F1
BREWSTER CT
1300 ELCR 94530 609-D1
BREWSTER DR
1100 ELCR 94530 609-D1
BREZZA CT
2800 PLE 94566 715-B6
BRIAN CT
- SRMN 94583 693-G1
1400 MPS 95035 794-C5

BRIAN CT
5000 FRMT 94538 773-B1
BRIAN ST
400 HAY 94544 712-A7
BRIANNE CT
300 PLE 94566 714-D7
BRIAR PL
46200 FRMT 94539 773-H5
BRIAR CANYON TR
- CCCo 94553 610-A4
- CCCo 94708 609-H4
- CCCo 94708 610-A4
BRIARCLIFF RD
4300 OAK 94605 671-C2
BRIAR OAKS DR
- SRMN 94582 673-J2
- SRMN 94582 674-A2
BRIAR RIDGE DR
5400 AlaC 94552 692-C3
BRIARTON TER
500 FRMT 94536 753-G3
BRIARWOOD CT
500 LVMR 94551 695-H6
BRIARWOOD DR
100 HAY 94544 712-B6
2500 LVMR 94551 695-H6
37400 FRMT 94536 752-G5
BRIARWOOD LN
8400 DBLN 94568 693-H2
BRICCO CT
800 PLE 94566 715-D7
BRICK WY
27200 HAY 94544 711-J7
BRICKELL WY
18700 AlaC 94546 692-B4
BRIDGE AV
1500 OAK 94601 650-C7
BRIDGE CT
21500 AlaC 94546 691-H7
21500 HAY 94546 691-H7
BRIDGE RD
- BERK 94705 630-B4
700 SLN 94577 671-B7
3200 HAY 94545 731-G2
BRIDGE CREEK DR
700 SRMN 94582 674-A7
BRIDGECREEK WY
- HAY 94544 732-D1
BRIDGEHEAD LN
- HAY 94544 732-D1
BRIDGEPOINTE DR
36300 NWK 94560 752-C7
N BRIDGEPOINTE LN
- DBLN 94568 694-F2
S BRIDGEPOINTE LN
- DBLN 94568 694-G3
BRIDGEPOINTE PL
4900 UNC 94587 752-A2
BRIDGEPORT AV
2800 SRMN 94583 673-E6
BRIDGEPORT CIR
5500 LVMR 94551 696-C2
BRIDGEPORT DR
45500 FRMT 94539 773-H4
BRIDGEPORT PL
45700 FRMT 94539 773-H4
BRIDGEPORT ST
32500 FRMT 94555 732-B6
BRIDGES CT
1400 FRMT 94536 753-A2
BRIDGESTONE CIR
- DBLN 94568 694-E2
BRIDGEVIEW DR
4300 OAK 94602 650-D3
BRIDGE VIEW ISL
3300 ALA 94501 670-A4
BRIDGEVIEW WY
- HAY 94544 732-D1
BRIDGEWATER PL
34400 FRMT 94555 732-E7
BRIDGEWATER RD
- HAY 94544 732-D1
BRIDGEWOOD TER
3400 FRMT 94536 752-A6
BRIDLE CT
3000 LVMR 94551 696-C1
BRIDLE DR
3200 AlaC 94541 712-D2
BRIDLE PATH CT
1600 LVMR 94551 696-E2
BRIDLEPATH CT
- SRMN 94583 673-D4
BRIDWELL WY
2100 HAY 94545 731-H1
BRIER ST
31000 UNC 94587 731-J5
BRIERGATE WY
600 HAY 94544 732-E1
BRIERLY CT
16900 AlaC 94546 691-H1
BRIGADOON WY
- DBLN 94568 693-D4
BRIGGS AV
3200 ALA 94501 670-B3
BRIGGS CT
2700 PLE 94588 714-A3
3200 FRMT 94536 752-F1
BRIGHT COM
37800 FRMT 94536 752-J3
37900 FRMT 94536 753-A3
BRIGHT PL
2100 AlaC 94541 712-C1
BRIGHTON AV
1100 ALB 94706 609-D5
3500 OAK 94602 650-C3
BRIGHTON COM
43000 FRMT 94538 773-E2
BRIGHTON CT
200 ALA 94502 670-A5
7400 DBLN 94568 693-H2
36200 NWK 94560 752-E4
BRIGHTON DR
6800 DBLN 94568 693-H2
BRIGHTON PL
8100 DBLN 94568 693-H2
BRIGHTON RD
- ALA 94502 670-A5
- ALA 94502 669-J5
BRIGHTON ST
- SRMN 94582 674-A3
28400 HAY 94544 712-B7
BRIGHTON WY
400 LVMR 94551 695-D7
BRILES CT
47700 FRMT 94539 773-H7
BRINDISI PL
4200 PLE 94566 715-C7
4200 PLE 94566 735-C1
BRIONES CT
- PLE 94588 714-F1
BRIONES LN
- PLE 94588 714-F1

BRISA CT
- LVMR 94551 696-D5
BRISA ST
5300 LVMR 94551 696-D5
BRISCOE
1900 FRMT 94539 753-E6
BRISTLECONE CT
2200 UNC 94587 732-C5
BRISTLECONE WY
4100 LVMR 94551 695-J3
4100 LVMR 94551 696-A3
BRISTOL BLVD
100 SLN 94577 670-J6
BRISTOL CT
500 LVMR 94551 695-E6
BRISTOL DR
600 HAY 94544 712-D7
6800 OAK 94705 630-C4
BRISTOL PL
5200 NWK 94560 752-E4
BRISTOL RD
7800 DBLN 94568 693-H3
BRISTOLWOOD RD
4300 PLE 94588 713-J1
BRITANNIA DR
- SRMN 94582 674-A1
BRITANNIA LN
2000 SLN 94579 690-J6
BRITHORN LN
3400 ALA 94502 670-A7
BRITT CT
- ALA 94502 669-J6
BRITTANY AV
6000 NWK 94560 752-D5
BRITTANY CT
20100 AlaC 94546 692-B5
BRITTANY DR
- ALA 94502 670-A5
8000 DBLN 94568 693-F3
BRITTANY LN
11100 AlaC 94552 693-E3
11100 DBLN 94568 693-E3
BRITTANY PL
300 LVMR 94550 715-D3
BRITTO TER
- FRMT 94539 753-F4
BRITTON HILL TER
- FRMT 94536 732-J4
BRIZA LP
- SRMN 94582 673-H2
BROADMOOR
- MRGA 94556 651-D1
BROADMOOR BLVD
- SLN 94577 670-J6
- SLN 94577 671-A6
W BROADMOOR BLVD
100 SLN 94577 670-J7
BROADMOOR CT
- SRMN 94583 693-H1
1600 LVMR 94551 696-B3
BROADMOOR DR
9400 SRMN 94583 693-G1
9500 SRMN 94583 673-F4
BROADMOOR ST
1700 LVMR 94551 696-C3
BROADMOOR VW
3000 OAK 94605 671-B5
BROADMORE AV
24200 HAY 94544 711-G4
BROADVIEW TER
- ORIN 94563 630-J1
BROADWAY
- OAK 94607 649-F5
300 ALA 94501 669-J4
300 ALA 94501 670-A2
500 HAY 94544 712-B6
500 SF 94111 648-A4
700 SF 94133 648-A4
1200 OAK 94612 649-H2
2800 OAK 94611 649-H2
3200 OAK 94611 630-C4
4000 OAK 94611 629-J7
4700 OAK 94618 630-A5
5200 OAK 94618 629-J7
BROADWAY Rt#-61
800 ALA 94501 670-A3
BROADWAY AV
6100 NWK 94560 752-F7
BROADWAY PL
6100 NWK 94560 752-F7
BROADWAY ST
500 HAY 94544 712-C6
BROADWAY TER
5200 OAK 94618 629-J6
5300 OAK 94618 630-B6
5400 OAK 94611 630-D5
BROADWING CT
- SRMN 94582 673-H2
BROADWING WY
- SRMN 94582 673-H2
BROCKHURST ST
600 OAK 94609 649-F1
700 OAK 94608 649-F1
BROCKTON AV
9500 SRMN 94583 693-G1
BROCKTON DR
3700 PLE 94588 694-F5
BROCKTON WY
- AlaC 94578 691-F4
BROCKWAY CT
33000 UNC 94587 752-B2
BROCKWAY ST
32900 UNC 94587 752-A1
BRODER BLVD
5300 DBLN 94568 694-C3
BROM CIR
5200 AlaC 94546 692-C3
BROMLEY AV
5900 OAK 94621 670-F2
BRONCO CT
- SRMN 94583 673-B3
BRONSON ST
38300 FRMT 94536 753-A3
BRONTE CT
5000 FRMT 94538 773-B1
BRONZE ST
- UNC 94587 732-H6
BROOK ST
3000 OAK 94611 649-H2
BROOK TER
- FRMT 94538 773-D3
BROOKBANK RD
- ORIN 94563 610-G4
BROOKDALE AV
2700 OAK 94602 650-C5
2700 OAK 94601 650-C5
3500 OAK 94619 650-E6
4800 OAK 94619 670-F1
4800 OAK 94601 670-F1
5500 OAK 94605 670-F1
BROOKDALE BLVD
3300 AlaC 94546 691-H3

BROOKDALE CT
- LVMR 94551 696-D3
7300 DBLN 94568 693-J3
BROOKDALE LN
- LVMR 94551 696-D3
BROOKDALE WY
- HAY 94544 732-D1
BROOKFIELD AV
3000 OAK 94605 671-C7
BROOKFIELD DR
- MRGA 94556 651-E2
500 LVMR 94551 695-E6
BROOKFIELD RD
- HAY 94544 732-D1
BROOKHAVEN CT
- HAY 94544 732-D1
BROOKLYN AV
600 OAK 94606 649-J4
600 OAK 94606 650-A4
BROOKLYN PL
- SF 94108 648-A5
BROOKLYN ST
31100 UNC 94587 731-J5
BROOKMILL CT
3400 FRMT 94536 752-F1
BROOKMILL DR
3400 FRMT 94536 752-F1
BROOKPARK RD
12500 OAK 94619 651-A5
BROOKS CT
4000 PLE 94588 714-A1
BROOKS WY
25400 HAY 94544 712-A4
BROOKSHIRE DR
- AlaC 94552 692-E7
BROOKSIDE AV
- BERK 94705 629-J4
- BERK 94705 630-A4
6100 OAK 94618 630-A5
BROOKSIDE CT
100 BERK 94705 629-J4
5300 PLE 94588 693-J6
BROOKSIDE DR
100 BERK 94705 629-J4
BROOKSIDE LN
- HAY 94544 732-D1
BROOKSIDE RD
- ORIN 94563 630-J2
BROOKSIDE ST
1300 SLN 94577 690-H1
BROOKSTONE CT
- MPS 95035 794-C2
BROOKSTONE WY
- HAY 94544 712-A5
100 HAY 94544 711-J5
BROOKTREE WY
- HAY 94544 732-D1
1800 PLE 94566 714-D1
BROOKVALE CT
35600 FRMT 94536 752-G1
BROOKVALE DR
1100 SLN 94577 671-D7
BROOKVIEW CT
- LVMR 94551 696-E2
BROOKVIEW WY
- HAY 94544 732-D1
BROOKWOOD AV
4300 FRMT 94538 773-D1
BROOKWOOD PL
600 OAK 94610 650-A3
BROOKWOOD RD
- ORIN 94563 630-H1
1000 OAK 94610 650-B3
BROPHY DR
4900 FRMT 94536 752-H7
BROWER CT
- SRMN 94582 674-A2
BROWER WY
- CCCo 94582 674-A2
- SRMN 94582 674-A2
BROWN AV
3600 OAK 94619 650-F5
BROWN CT
1200 SLN 94579 691-A5
BROWN RD
200 FRMT 94539 773-G5
BROWN ST
1100 ALA 94502 669-J6
BROWNING CT
27800 HAY 94544 712-A7
BROWNING ST
2100 BERK 94702 629-E2
BROWN RANCH RD
- AlaC 94546 651-G5
- CCCo 94556 651-G5
BROWNTAIL WY
- CCCo 94582 674-A2
BROZOSKY HILL LN
- PLE 94566 714-J4
- PLE 94566 715-A4
BRUCE CT
5100 AlaC 94546 692-C3
BRUCE DR
2400 FRMT 94539 753-E7
5300 PLE 94588 694-F7
BRUCE ST
3500 OAK 94602 650-B4
BRUNELL DR
3200 OAK 94602 650-G4
BRUNELL PL
- OAK 94602 650-G4
BRUNETTI LN
1500 SLN 94578 691-C5
BRUNING ST
39600 FRMT 94538 753-A7
BRUNO ST
27800 HAY 94544 712-A7
BRUNS CT
5900 OAK 94611 650-D1
BRUNS RD
4900 AlaC 94551 (657-H5 See Page 637)
5500 AlaC 94514 (657-H5 See Page 637)
5500 CCCo 94514 (657-J2 See Page 637)
N BRUNS WY
6000 CCCo 94514 (657-H1 See Page 637)
BRUNSWICK CIR
15400 SLN 94579 691-A7
BRUNSWICK CT
9900 SRMN 94583 673-F5
BRUNSWICK PL
100 FRMT 94539 773-H2
BRUNSWICK RD
100 ALA 94502 669-J5
BRUNSWICK WY
9800 SRMN 94583 673-F5
BRUNSWIG LN
- EMVL 94608 629-E6

BRUSH PL
- SF 94103 648-D7
BRUSH ST
100 ALA 94501 649-E7
200 OAK 94607 649-F4
1200 OAK 94612 649-F4
BRUSHY PEAK CT
5500 LVMR 94551 696-C3
BRUSK CT
19300 AlaC 94546 691-J4
BRUZZONE DR
- ALA 94501 649-F7
BRYANT AL
- SF 94133 648-A4
BRYANT AV
- ALA 94501 649-E7
- DBLN 94568 694-A4
- SJCo 95391 (678-E3 See Page 677)
5300 OAK 94618 629-J6
BRYANT CT
- SJCo 95391 (678-E3 See Page 677)
300 FRMT 94539 773-H1
BRYANT ST
- SF 94105 648-B6
- SF 94107 648-B6
100 SF 94107 648-B6
800 SF 94103 648-A7
43300 FRMT 94539 753-H7
43400 FRMT 94539 773-H1
BRYANT TER
- FRMT 94539 753-H7
BRYANT WY
- ORIN 94563 610-H7
- ORIN 94563 630-H1
BRYCE CT
500 MPS 95035 794-D7
BRYCE CANYON CT
5900 PLE 94588 714-B1
BRYCE CANYON PK DR
4800 FRMT 94538 773-C2
BRYN MAWR AV
25800 HAY 94542 712-B4
BRYN MAWR CT
- SRMN 94583 673-H7
BUCHANAN PL
5400 FRMT 94538 752-J7
BUCHANAN ST
700 ALB 94706 609-D6
800 ALB 94710 609-D6
BUCHANAN STEX
800 ALB 94710 609-B6
BUCHANAN WY
1100 HAY 94545 711-F4
BUCK CT
- FRMT 94539 773-J3
BUCKBOARD COM
38700 FRMT 94536 753-C2
BUCKBRUSH PZ
- HAY 94542 712-B3
BUCKEYE AV
- OAK 94618 630-B6
BUCKEYE CT
- DBLN 94568 693-E4
1900 PLE 94588 714-B6
BUCKEYE DR
500 LVMR 94551 695-E7
25300 AlaC 94552 692-E6
BUCKEYE PL
7500 NWK 94560 752-D7
BUCKEYE ST
36400 NWK 94560 752-D6
BUCKEYE TER
43600 FRMT 94538 773-E3
BUCKINGHAM BLVD
6800 OAK 94705 630-C3
BUCKINGHAM CT
35000 NWK 94560 752-D3
BUCKINGHAM DR
8300 ELCR 94530 609-D1
BUCKINGHAM WY
1300 HAY 94544 732-A1
BUCKLEY CT
- OAK 94602 650-G3
BUCKNELL CT
1000 LVMR 94550 716-A1
BUCKNER TER
5400 FRMT 94555 752-B3
BUCKSKIN CT
4400 LVMR 94551 696-A2
BUCKSKIN RD
2000 LVMR 94551 696-A3
BUCKS LAKE ST
32700 FRMT 94555 732-C6
BUCKWHEAT CT
600 HAY 94544 712-C7
BUD CT
39100 FRMT 94538 753-A6
BUDGE ST
15500 SLN 94579 691-B7
BUDWING TER
4000 FRMT 94538 773-E2
BUELL ST
3700 OAK 94619 650-G7
3700 OAK 94613 650-G7
BUENA AV
1500 BERK 94703 609-F7
BUENA VENTURA AV
6100 OAK 94605 650-H7
6100 OAK 94605 670-H1
BUENA VISTA
- ORIN 94563 630-J3
39500 FRMT 94538 753-B5
BUENA VISTA AV
400 ALA 94501 649-G7
1300 ALA 94501 669-J1
1400 AlaC 94550 716-B3
2100 ALA 94501 670-A1
2100 SLN 94577 691-B2
5600 OAK 94618 630-B5
BUENA VISTA DR
6200 NWK 94560 772-J2
BUENA VISTA PL
- OAK 94618 630-B5
BUENA VISTA WY
2500 BERK 94708 609-H7
BULLARD DR
6000 OAK 94611 630-D7
6100 OAK 94611 650-D1
BULLARD ST
4100 FRMT 94538 753-C6
BULLDOG WY
21500 HAY 94545 711-D4
BULMER ST
31100 UNC 94587 731-J5
BUNA ST
- OAK 94607 649-C2
BUNCHE DR
- FRMT 94538 773-B5
BUNKER LN
- AlaC 94566 714-C7

BUNKER HILL BLVD
25300 HAY 94542 712-B3
BUNKER HILL CT
25300 HAY 94542 712-B3
BUNNY CT
200 AlaC 94541 711-F1
BUNTING LN
38400 FRMT 94536 753-C2
BUNTING ST
28000 HAY 94545 731-J1
BUOY CT
- SLN 94579 711-A1
BURBANK ST
1300 ALA 94501 669-G1
22500 HAY 94541 711-H2
BURCKHALTER AV
3900 OAK 94605 670-J1
BURDECK CT
- OAK 94602 650-F3
BURDECK DR
2900 OAK 94602 650-F3
BURDETT WY
1100 MPS 95035 794-C5
BURDETTE COM
38400 FRMT 94536 753-B3
BURDETTE ST
38300 FRMT 94536 753-B3
BURDICK ST
36600 NWK 94560 752-E5
BUREN PL
3700 AlaC 94552 692-F2
BURGAS TER
- UNC 94587 732-G3
BURGER CT
500 PLE 94566 714-G3
BURGESS ST
200 LVMR 94550 696-A7
BURGNER AV
2800 ALA 94502 669-H7
BURGOS AV
9700 OAK 94605 671-B4
BURGOS CT
- SRMN 94583 673-C3
BURGUNDY DR
3200 PLE 94566 714-G3
BURGUNDY WY
1100 LVMR 94550 715-H2
BURIAT ST
- SLN 94577 670-J7
BURK CT
- SJCo 95391 (678-F3 See Page 677)
BURK PL
- SJCo 95391 (678-F3 See Page 677)
BURK ST
400 OAK 94610 649-J3
BURKE DR
300 HAY 94544 712-B6
BURKE WY
4300 FRMT 94536 752-J5
BURKHART AV
900 SLN 94579 691-A6
BURLEY DR
1600 MPS 95035 794-D6
BURLINGAME AV
5100 RCH 94804 609-B3
BURLINGTON ST
2400 OAK 94602 650-E4
BURLWOOD AV
300 OAK 94603 670-G7
BURMA RD
100 OAK 94607 649-B1
100 OAK 94649 649-B1
BURNBRAE LN
- SRMN 94582 674-C3
BURNETT ST
1200 BERK 94702 629-E4
BURNEY WY
4300 FRMT 94538 753-B6
BURNEY CREEK PL
600 SRMN 94582 694-A1
BURNHAM PL
- FRMT 94539 753-D3
BURNHAM WY
7400 DBLN 94568 693-J3
31300 HAY 94544 732-E2
BURNING TREE CT
400 SRMN 94583 673-H6
BURNING TREE DR
35800 NWK 94560 752-C6
BURNING TREES DR
3200 SRMN 94583 673-H7
BURNLEY LN
600 AlaC 94541 711-E1
BURNS CIR
500 SRMN 94583 673-E4
BURNS CT
- SRMN 94583 673-E4
7800 ELCR 94530 609-E2
BURNSIDE CT
5300 FRMT 94536 752-H7
BURR AV
39800 FRMT 94538 753-A7
BURR LN
2000 LVMR 94550 715-H3
BURR ST
8800 OAK 94605 671-A3
BURR WY
21400 AlaC 94541 691-G7
BURRITT ST
- SF 94108 648-A5
BURROUGHS AV
2000 SLN 94577 690-J5
BURTON COM
3800 FRMT 94536 752-J4
BURTON DR
2800 OAK 94611 650-G1
BURTON ST
7100 DBLN 94568 693-J3
BUSBY AV
2000 SLN 94579 691-A7
BUSBY WY
34800 FRMT 94555 752-E1
BUSCH RD
- PLE 94566 714-G1
3100 AlaC 94588 714-G1
3100 PLE 94588 714-G1
BUSH CIR
4400 FRMT 94538 773-D2
BUSH CT
43200 FRMT 94538 773-D2
BUSH ST
- SF 94111 648-A5
- SF 94104 648-A5
200 SF 94108 648-A5
600 SF 94102 648-A5
BUSINESS CENTER DR
- SLN 94577 690-F2
4000 FRMT 94538 773-E4
BUSINESS CENTER PL
- SLN 94577 690-F2

BUSKIRK ST
100 MPS 95035 793-J3
100 MPS 95035 794-A3
BUTANO PARK DR
5300 FRMT 94538 773-B2
BUTI PARK CT
17600 AlaC 94546 692-A2
BUTI PARK DR
4900 AlaC 94546 692-A2
BUTLER AV
1200 SLN 94579 691-A4
BUTLER ST
- MPS 95035 793-J7
BUTTE AV
3000 SRMN 94583 673-G7
BUTTE CT
1100 LVMR 94551 695-F6
BUTTE ST
1600 RCH 94804 609-C3
2900 AlaC 94541 692-C6
BUTTERCUP CT
1500 LVMR 94551 696-A4
BUTTERFIELD DR
20000 AlaC 94546 691-J5
BUTTERFIELD PL
400 MRGA 94556 651-F3
BUTTERNUT CT
700 UNC 94587 732-G3
BUTTERS DR
2700 OAK 94602 650-G3
BUTTON BRUSH PZ
- HAY 94542 712-B3
BUTTONWOOD TER
3500 FRMT 94536 752-A6
BUXTON COM
38000 FRMT 94536 752-J4
BUXTON PL
38000 FRMT 94536 752-J3
BYER RD
3100 CCCo 94514 637-D2
BYINGTON DR
- NWK 94560 752-F6
BYRD LN
1000 AlaC 94566 714-E6
BYRON AV
10000 OAK 94603 671-A5
BYRON CT
3400 PLE 94588 694-E6
BYRON HWY Rt#-J4
10600 CCCo 94513 637-D1
10600 CCCo 94514 637-D1
17600 CCCo 94514 (657-G1 See Page 637)
19100 CCCo 94514 (658-A3 See Page 637)
BYRON LN
- CCCo 94582 674-B5
BYRON ST
2100 BERK 94702 629-E2
22500 AlaC 94541 692-C6
BYRON-BETHANY RD Rt#-J4
15300 SJCo 95304 (678-G1 See Page 677)
16500 SJCo 95391 (678-F1 See Page 677)
17900 SJCo 95391 (658-D6 See Page 637)
20200 AlaC 94551 (658-B4 See Page 637)
20200 CCCo 94514 (658-B4 See Page 637)
BYRON HOT SPRINGS RD
5500 CCCo 94514 637-F5
5800 CCCo 94514 (657-F1 See Page 637)
BYWOOD DR
1900 OAK 94602 650-E2

C

C RD
12200 AlaC 94586 734-C5
C ST
100 AlaC 94586 734-B5
200 HAY 94541 711-H2
300 UNC 94587 732-F4
1100 HAY 94541 712-A1
1600 HAY 94541 692-A7
7100 ELCR 94530 609-E4
9200 OAK 94603 670-H5
CABELLO CT
4800 UNC 94587 731-J7
CABELLO ST
4500 UNC 94587 731-J7
13500 UNC 94587 732-A6
CABERNET AV
6700 NWK 94560 752-C6
CABERNET CT
4200 PLE 94566 714-F4
CABERNET WY
2000 LVMR 94550 715-H3
48800 FRMT 94539 794-A2
CABONIA CT
- PLE 94566 715-D6
CABOT BLVD
22600 HAY 94545 711-C3
CABOT CT
2600 FRMT 94536 753-A3
8400 NWK 94560 772-C2
CABOT DR
5600 OAK 94611 630-D7
CABRAL DR
35000 FRMT 94536 752-E3
CABRILLO AV
800 LVMR 94550 715-H1
3000 SRMN 94583 673-G7
CABRILLO CT
2300 HAY 94545 731-H1
35000 FRMT 94536 752-E2
CABRILLO DR
2400 HAY 94545 731-G1
35100 FRMT 94536 752-E2
CABRILLO PL
- OAK 94611 630-E7
CABRILLO ST
1200 ELCR 94530 609-D2
CABRILLO TER
37000 FRMT 94536 752-G4
CABRINI DR
28300 HAY 94545 731-H2
CACTUS ST
2200 FRMT 94539 773-G3
CADE DR
3200 FRMT 94536 752-F1
CADELL PL
- SF 94133 648-A4
CADENCIA ST
- FRMT 94539 753-G5
CADILLAC CT
1100 MPS 95035 793-H5

STREET
Block City ZIP Pg-Grid

CADIZ CT
4100 FRMT 94536 752-F2
CADIZ DR
35800 FRMT 94536 752-F2
CADMAN RD
3000 FRMT 94538 753-D6
CADY CT
2400 AlaC 94578 691-G4
CAFFRIN CT
40000 FRMT 94538 773-A1
CAHILL ST
4300 FRMT 94538 753-C7
CAIRO RD
100 OAK 94603 670-F7
100 OAK 94621 670-F7
CAIRO ST
1400 LVMR 94550 715-F4
CAITLIN WY
- FRMT 94539 793-H2
CALABRIA PL
19100 AlaC 94541 691-F7
CALAFIA AV
3500 OAK 94605 671-B4
CALAIS AV
1300 LVMR 94550 715-F3
CALAIS CT
1400 LVMR 94550 715-F3
1700 AlaC 94541 712-B1
CALAIS DR
2800 SRMN 94583 673-F6
CALAIS PL
7100 NWK 94560 752-C6
CALANDRIA
3400 OAK 94605 671-B3
CALAROGA AV
24600 HAY 94545 711-G5
27700 HAY 94545 731-H1
CALAVERAS AV
4500 FRMT 94538 753-A6
4500 FRMT 94538 752-J6
4800 OAK 94619 650-G7
CALAVERAS BLVD
1400 MPS 95035 794-D6
CALAVERAS BLVD Rt#-237
300 MPS 95035 793-J7
500 MPS 95035 794-A7
CALAVERAS CT
- MPS 95035 794-C6
CALAVERAS RD
2000 MPS 95035 794-E6
3100 SCIC 95035 794-H5
4000 SCIC 95140 794-J2
8500 AlaC 94586 734-E7
8500 AlaC 94586 754-F2
9100 AlaC 94586 774-G1
9600 SCIC 95035 774-J4
9600 SCIC 95140 774-J4
24300 HAY 94545 711-F4
CALAVERAS RIDGE DR
800 MPS 95035 794-C4
CALCITE CT
- LVMR 94550 715-D3
CALCOT PL
1000 OAK 94606 650-A7
CALCOTT CT
3000 FRMT 94555 732-E7
CALCUTTA DR
34600 FRMT 94555 752-E1
CALDAS CT
42700 FRMT 94539 753-F7
CALDECOTT LN
100 OAK 94618 630-B4
100 OAK 94611 630-B4
CALDEIRA DR
- LVMR 94550 715-J3
CALDERON CT
- LVMR 94550 715-G4
CALDERWOOD CT
4800 OAK 94605 651-A7
CALDWELL CT
7800 AlaC 94552 692-G2
CALDWELL RD
700 OAK 94611 630-C5
CALDWELL TER
5100 FRMT 94555 752-C3
CALEB PL
500 HAY 94544 732-E2
CALERA CREEK HEIGHTS DR
1600 MPS 95035 794-C3
CALERO ST
800 MPS 95035 793-J6
CALGARY ST
15500 SLN 94579 691-A7
15600 SLN 94579 711-A1
CALGARY TER
34400 FRMT 94555 752-C3
CAL GEARY RD
- AlaC 94586 774-J3
CALHOUN ST
- ALB 94706 609-C6
700 HAY 94544 712-C5
2500 ALA 94501 670-A4
CALHOUN TER
- SF 94133 648-A4
CALI CT
- PLE 94566 714-E3
CALIBAN DR
33400 FRMT 94555 752-B1
CALIBRIA CT
- LVMR 94550 715-J3
CALIBRIA DR
- LVMR 94550 715-J3
CALICO CT
- CCCo 94582 674-B1
CALICO LN
5500 PLE 94566 714-C3
CALIDO PL
40800 FRMT 94539 753-E5
CALIENTE AV
500 LVMR 94550 715-E2
CALIENTE CIR
200 SLN 94578 691-C5
CALIENTE DR
200 SLN 94578 691-C4
CALIENTE WY
40500 FRMT 94539 753-F4
CALIFORNIA
3000 ALA 94501 649-F6
CALIFORNIA AV
- ORIN 94563 610-E6
- PLE 94566 714-F2
- SF 94130 648-E1
- SLN 94577 671-A7
- SLN 94577 691-A1
CALIFORNIA CIR
1200 MPS 95035 793-H4
CALIFORNIA CT
- UNC 94587 732-E6
CALIFORNIA ST
- SF 94111 648-A5
300 SF 94104 648-A5
600 SF 94108 648-A5
1300 BERK 94703 609-F7
1500 BERK 94703 629-F1
2800 OAK 94602 650-E4
3500 OAK 94619 650-F5
6000 OAK 94608 629-F4
18800 AlaC 94546 692-A3
37300 NWK 94560 752-F7
39300 FRMT 94538 753-A5
CALIFORNIA WY
3800 LVMR 94550 715-J1
3900 LVMR 94550 716-A1
CALIFORNIA DELTA HWY Rt#-4
15100 SJCo 95206 (638-H1 See Page 637)
CALISTOGA CIR
400 FRMT 94536 732-H6
CALISTOGA CT
- LVMR 94550 716-D2
CALISTOGA ST
4900 UNC 94587 752-A2
CALL AV
26500 HAY 94542 712-D3
CALLAGHAN ST
3000 LVMR 94551 695-H7
CALLAHAN RD
- AlaC 94546 651-J5
- AlaC 94546 652-A4
- CCCo 94556 652-A4
CALLALILY COM
2100 LVMR 94551 696-D2
CALLAN AV
- SLN 94577 691-B1
500 SLN 94577 671-B7
CALLAN PL
- ALA 94502 669-H5
CALLAN ST
100 MPS 95035 793-J3
100 MPS 95035 794-A3
7700 DBLN 94568 693-H2
CALLAWAY PL
- DBLN 94568 694-H3
CALLAWAY ST
- SLN 94577 670-J7
- SLN 94577 690-J1
CALLE ALEGRE
2600 PLE 94566 714-C2
CALLE ALTAMIRA
6300 PLE 94566 714-B3
CALLE AMIGO DR
- FRMT 94539 753-D3
CALLECITA CT
4400 UNC 94587 731-H6
CALLE DE LA LOMA
2700 PLE 94566 714-B2
CALLE DE LA MANCHA
6500 PLE 94566 714-B2
CALLE DE LA MESA
2900 PLE 94566 714-A2
CALLE DE LA PAZ
1900 PLE 94566 714-C2
CALLE DE LAS GRANVAS
- LVMR 94551 695-G6
CALLE DEL PRADO
600 MPS 95035 794-B5
CALLE DEL REY
- LVMR 94551 695-F6
CALLE DEL SOL
- LVMR 94551 695-G6
1400 MPS 95035 793-H3
CALLE DEL SUENO
- LVMR 94551 695-G6
CALLE ENRIQUE
1400 PLE 94566 714-C2
CALLE ESPERANZA
6400 PLE 94566 714-B2
CALLE FUEGO
6200 PLE 94566 714-B3
CALLE LA MIRADA COM
- UNC 94587 732-G2
CALLE MADRAS
2500 PLE 94566 714-C2
CALLE MORELIA
2600 PLE 94566 714-B2
CALLE ORIENTE
1100 MPS 95035 794-C5
CALLE REYNOSO
2600 PLE 94566 714-B3
CALLE RICARDO
2000 PLE 94566 714-C2
CALLERY CT
- FRMT 94539 753-G5
CALLE SANTA ANA
1500 PLE 94566 714-C2
CALLE SANTIAGO
1500 PLE 94566 714-C2
CALLE VERDE RD
7500 DBLN 94568 693-G4
CALL OF THE WILD CT
- LVMR 94550 715-D4
CALL OF THE WILD WY
- LVMR 94550 715-D4
CALMANCO COM
- LVMR 94551 695-C4
CALMAR AV
600 OAK 94610 650-A3
CALMAR VISTA RD
600 DNVL 94526 652-H1
CALODEN ST
9900 OAK 94605 671-E4
CALVARY LN
1400 AlaC 94550 716-B1
CALVERT CT
- SRMN 94582 673-H2
- OAK 94611 650-C1
- PDMT 94611 650-C1
CALVERT WY
- SRMN 94582 673-H2
CALVIN CT
2800 FRMT 94536 753-A3
CALYPSO COM
34700 FRMT 94555 752-D2
CALYPSO CT
16200 AlaC 94578 691-F4
CALYPSO TER
4200 FRMT 94555 752-E2
CAMA LN
3500 AlaC 94552 692-C5
CAMANOE LN
3400 ALA 94502 670-A6
CAMARILLO CT
1000 MPS 95035 794-C4
CAMARONES PL
3300 SRMN 94583 673-G5
CAMASS CT
5600 NWK 94560 752-G6
CAMASSIA WY
- SRMN 94582 673-J2
CAMBELL BLVD
- ALA 94501 649-J7
- ALA 94501 650-A7
CAMBERLY CT
- CCCo 94583 673-B5
CAMBERLY LN
- SRMN 94582 674-B3
CAMBIO CT
4600 FRMT 94536 752-F4
CAMBRA CT
- DNVL 94526 652-J3
21300 AlaC 94541 691-H7
CAMBRIA ST
4300 FRMT 94538 753-A6
CAMBRIAN AV
- PDMT 94611 650-D2
CAMBRIAN DR
15800 AlaC 94578 691-F3
CAMBRIDGE AV
- SLN 94577 671-A7
200 CCCo 94708 609-G3
20500 AlaC 94541 691-G7
CAMBRIDGE CT
- FRMT 94536 753-A3
- DNVL 94526 652-H1
300 LVMR 94550 696-A7
3600 PLE 94588 694-E5
5300 NWK 94560 752-E4
CAMBRIDGE DR
1700 ALA 94501 670-B2
CAMBRIDGE WY
- PDMT 94611 650-A1
200 LVMR 94550 696-A7
4200 UNC 94587 731-J5
CAMDEN AV
19900 AlaC 94541 691-G7
CAMDEN CT
100 SRMN 94582 673-G4
CAMDEN RD
400 ALA 94501 669-H3
CAMDEN ST
2700 OAK 94605 670-G1
4400 OAK 94619 650-F7
5400 OAK 94619 670-G1
37800 FRMT 94536 752-J3
38000 FRMT 94536 753-A3
CAMDON CT
3100 PLE 94588 694-F6
CAMELFORD CT
- OAK 94611 650-F2
CAMELFORD PL
- OAK 94611 650-F2
CAMELIA DR
900 LVMR 94550 715-F2
1000 ALA 94502 670-A7
CAMELIA ST
600 BERK 94710 629-D1
800 BERK 94710 609-D7
1100 BERK 94702 609-D7
CAMELLIA CT
600 HAY 94544 712-C6
1100 SLN 94577 690-J1
2200 FRMT 94539 773-G3
4300 PLE 94588 713-J1
CAMELLIA DR
44300 FRMT 94539 773-G3
CAMELOT CT
- CCCo 94707 609-F4
3600 PLE 94588 694-E5
CAMELOT LN
17700 AlaC 94546 692-A2
CAMEO CT
- PLE 94588 693-G7
1300 LVMR 94550 715-D3
18800 AlaC 94546 692-A3
CAMEO DR
- LVMR 94550 715-D3
CAMERO PL
40900 FRMT 94539 753-F5
CAMERO WY
900 FRMT 94539 753-E5
CAMERON AV
3600 PLE 94588 694-F7
10700 OAK 94605 671-D4
CAMERON CIR
- MPS 95035 794-B7
300 SRMN 94583 673-E4
CAMERON CT
- MPS 95035 794-B7
CAMERON DR
2400 UNC 94587 732-C4
CAMERON PL
- MPS 95035 794-C7
CAMERON ST
21900 AlaC 94546 692-B6
CAMERON HILLS CT
1800 FRMT 94539 773-G2
CAMERON HILLS DR
43700 FRMT 94539 773-G2
CAMILLE LN
900 CCCo 94507 652-G1
CAMILLIA PL
- OAK 94602 650-E3
CAMILLO CT
- PLE 94566 715-D6
CAMINO PZ
100 UNC 94587 732-J5
CAMINO ALTA MIRA
5000 AlaC 94546 692-B2
CAMINO AMIGO
600 DNVL 94526 652-H1
CAMINO AMIGO CT
100 DNVL 94526 652-H2
CAMINO BRAZOS
2100 PLE 94566 714-C2
CAMINO CASA BUENA
2700 PLE 94566 714-B2
CAMINO DE JUGAR
2400 SRMN 94583 673-B3
2400 CCCo 94583 673-B3
CAMINO DEL CAMPO
600 FRMT 94539 773-H2
CAMINO DEL CIELO
- ORIN 94563 610-E7
CAMINO DEL CINO
3000 PLE 94566 714-B2
CAMINO DEL DIABLO
- ORIN 94563 610-E6
CAMINO DEL LAGO
6200 PLE 94566 714-B2
CAMINO DEL MONTE
- ORIN 94563 610-E7
CAMINO DEL VALLE
1000 ALA 94502 670-A6
1100 ALA 94502 669-J7
CAMINO DIABLO
800 CCCo 94513 637-B3
800 CCCo 94514 637-B3
CAMINO DOLORES
2200 AlaC 94546 691-H5
CAMINO DON MIGUEL
- ORIN 94563 610-F5
CAMINO ENCANTO
100 DNVL 94526 652-H2
CAMINO ENCINAS
- ORIN 94563 630-H1
CAMINO LENADA
- ORIN 94563 610-G6
2600 OAK 94611 650-F2
CAMINO PABLO
- ORIN 94563 630-H1
- ORIN 94563 610-F6
- CCCo 94563 610-F6
1000 MRGA 94556 651-D1
1800 CCCo 94556 651-F4
CAMINO RAMON
2100 SRMN 94583 673-E2
2100 DNVL 94526 673-E2
CAMINO SANTA BARBARA
41900 FRMT 94539 753-G6
CAMINO SEGURA
2600 PLE 94566 714-B2
CAMINO SOBRANTE
- ORIN 94563 610-G5
CAMINO TASSAJARA
5000 CCCo 94506 674-F2
5100 CCCo 94582 674-F2
5100 CCCo 94588 674-E6
5100 CCCo - 674-F2
CAMINO VENADILLO
2700 SRMN 94583 673-A3
CAMINO VISTA
25500 AlaC 94541 712-D2
W CAMINO VISTA
25600 AlaC 94541 712-D2
CAMISA CIR
- OAK 94605 671-C3
CAMPANULA CT
6000 NWK 94560 752-G7
CAMPANULA DR
- SRMN 94582 673-J1
CAMPBELL AV
1800 SLN 94577 690-J2
CAMPBELL CT
800 OAK 94607 649-D3
3600 FRMT 94536 752-G2
CAMPBELL PL
3700 FRMT 94536 752-G3
CAMPBELL ST
700 OAK 94607 649-E1
900 MPS 95035 794-B5
1000 RCH 94804 609-B2
CAMPBELL HILL TER
- FRMT 94536 732-J4
CAMPECHE CT
2600 SRMN 94583 673-B3
CAMPECHE ST
26000 HAY 94545 711-G7
CAMPHOR AV
100 FRMT 94539 793-H1
CAMPINIA PL
4300 PLE 94566 715-C7
4300 PLE 94566 735-C1
CAMPION DR
- CCCo 94582 674-A2
CAMPO CT
- LVMR 94550 715-D4
CAMPTON PL
- SF 94108 648-A5
CAMPUS CT
8200 FRMT 94555 752-A5
CAMPUS DR
1200 BERK 94708 609-J6
8000 FRMT 94555 752-A4
11800 OAK 94619 650-J5
13400 OAK 94605 651-A7
13400 OAK 94619 651-A7
13600 OAK 94605 671-B1
24900 AlaC 94541 712-C2
24900 HAY 94541 712-C2
24900 HAY 94542 712-C2
W CAMPUS DR
- ALA 94501 649-F7
CAMPUS VIEW WY
26800 HAY 94542 712-C4
CAMROSE AV
4000 LVMR 94551 695-J6
4000 LVMR 94551 696-A6
CANADA DR
700 MPS 95035 794-B6
CANAL ST
2200 HAY 94545 731-H2
CANAL TER
34900 FRMT 94555 752-E2
CANARY CT
- LVMR 94551 715-D1
2100 UNC 94587 732-G6
CANARY DR
4600 PLE 94566 714-D1
CANDICE CT
- FRMT 94555 752-E1
CANDLE TER
- ORIN 94563 610-J3
CANDLESTICK RD
- ORIN 94563 630-G2
CANDLEWOOD PL
27900 HAY 94545 731-J1
CANDY CT
4900 LVMR 94550 696-B6
CANDYTUFT CT
- CCCo 94582 674-B2
CANELLI CT
3600 PLE 94566 714-G3
CANFIELD DR
4200 FRMT 94536 752-J5
CANNA WY
- SRMN 94582 673-G2
CANNERY CT
- HAY 94544 711-H3
CANNING CT
- MRGA 94556 651-E1
CANNING ST
5800 OAK 94609 629-H5
CANNISTRACI LN
25700 AlaC 94541 712-E2
CANO CT
35200 FRMT 94536 752-E2
CANOGA ST
40300 FRMT 94538 753-D5
CANON AV
3700 OAK 94602 650-D4
CANON DR
200 ORIN 94563 610-F6
600 CCCo 94708 609-H4
CANONBURY WY
700 HAY 94544 712-D7
CANON VIEW LN
- OAK 94618 630-B6
CANOSA CT
2100 PLE 94566 715-B7
CANSINO LN
- LVMR 94550 716-D2
CANTANA TER
- UNC 94587 732-G3
CANTARE PL
40900 FRMT 94539 753-E5
CANTAS PL
100 SRMN 94583 673-G5
CANTERBURY AV
600 LVMR 94550 715-E3
CANTERBURY CT
- UNC 94587 731-H5
3200 FRMT 94536 752-J3
7600 DBLN 94568 693-H3
CANTERBURY LN
7500 DBLN 94568 693-H3
29500 HAY 94544 732-A2
CANTERBURY PL
600 MPS 95035 794-B3
CANTERBURY ST
37600 FRMT 94536 752-J3
CANTERBURY WY
- UNC 94587 731-J5
CANTILLY TER
- FRMT 94536 752-G4
CANTLE AV
25500 AlaC 94541 712-D2
CANTO PL
40900 FRMT 94539 753-E5
CANTON AV
1100 LVMR 94550 715-F3
CANTON DR
1200 MPS 95035 794-C7
CANVASBACK COM
4700 FRMT 94555 752-D2
CANYON CT
- AlaC 94552 692-E6
CANYON DR
3500 AlaC 94541 692-D6
CANYON RD
- BERK 94704 629-J2
- BERK 94704 630-A2
- BERK 94720 629-J2
- BERK 94720 630-A2
1500 MRGA 94556 651-C2
1500 CCCo 94556 651-C2
1900 CCCo 94516 651-C2
1900 MRGA 94516 651-C2
CANYON VW
- ORIN 94563 610-J4
CANYON WY
7600 PLE 94588 693-H6
CANYON CREEK CIR
7500 PLE 94588 693-E5
CANYON CREEK CT
200 SRMN 94583 673-B2
CANYON CREEK DR
2700 SRMN 94583 673-B2
CANYON CREEK TER
1000 FRMT 94536 733-D7
CANYON GREEN CT
- SRMN 94582 673-G3
CANYON GREEN DR
1000 SRMN 94582 673-G3
CANYON GREEN PL
100 SRMN 94582 673-G4
CANYON GREEN WY
- SRMN 94582 673-G3
CANYON HEIGHTS COM
- FRMT 94536 753-D1
CANYON HEIGHTS DR
38000 FRMT 94536 733-D7
38300 FRMT 94536 753-D1
39200 FRMT 94539 753-E3
CANYON HILL CT
5200 AlaC 94546 692-B2
CANYON HILLS CT
- SRMN 94582 673-G3
CANYON HILLS PL
- SRMN 94582 673-G3
CANYON HILLS RD
1000 SRMN 94582 673-F3
CANYON LAKES DR
2000 SRMN 94582 673-F1
CANYON LAKES PL
200 SRMN 94582 673-E1
CANYON LAKES WY
100 SRMN 94582 673-E1
CANYON MEADOW CIR
- PLE 94588 693-F5
CANYON MEADOW DR
- PLE 94588 693-F5
CANYON OAKS CT
25200 AlaC 94552 692-E6
38100 FRMT 94536 733-D7
38100 FRMT 94536 753-D1
CANYON OAKS DR
400 OAK 94605 671-B1
CANYON RIDGE PL
22600 AlaC 94552 692-D6
N CANYONS PKWY
500 LVMR 94551 695-B4
CANYON SIDE AV
1100 SRMN 94582 673-G3
CANYON TERRACE DR
3700 AlaC 94552 692-D6
CANYON VIEW CIR
100 SRMN 94582 673-F2
CANYONVIEW CT
24800 HAY 94541 712-B2
CANYON VILLAGE CIR
1000 SRMN 94583 673-C2
CANYON WOODS CT
- SRMN 94582 673-F3
CANYON WOODS DR
100 SRMN 94582 673-F3
CANYON WOODS PL
- SRMN 94582 673-F3
CANYON WOODS WY
200 SRMN 94582 673-G3
CAPA DR
40700 FRMT 94539 753-E5
CAPARELLI CT
5200 PLE 94588 694-C6
CAPE COD CT
3200 ALA 94501 670-A4
CAPE COD DR
400 SLN 94578 691-C5
CAPE EDEN PL
22000 AlaC 94546 692-B6
CAPELL ST
500 OAK 94606 650-A4
500 OAK 94610 650-A4
CAPELLA CT
3500 PLE 94588 694-H4
CAPELLA LN
3400 ALA 94502 670-A7
CAPELLA RD
2100 LVMR 94550 715-E4
CAPERTON AV
- PDMT 94611 650-C1
CAPETOWN AV
27900 HAY 94545 731-G1
CAPETOWN DR
100 ALA 94502 669-J5
300 ALA 94502 670-A5
CAPEVIEW DR
- UNC 94545 731-J6
CAPEWOOD PL
7700 PLE 94588 693-J7
7700 PLE 94588 713-J1
CAPEWOOD TER
4500 FRMT 94538 773-C1
CAPISTRANO AV
1500 BERK 94707 609-F5
CAPISTRANO DR
500 OAK 94603 670-H7
36600 FRMT 94536 752-F4
CAPITAL ST
400 OAK 94606 649-J4
400 OAK 94610 649-J4
CAPITAN DR
4600 FRMT 94536 752-E3
CAPITOL AV
3100 FRMT 94538 753-B4
CAPITOL ST
- LVMR 94551 696-C5
CAPITOLA CT
2500 HAY 94545 731-H2
32400 UNC 94545 751-J1
CAPITOLA ST
28200 HAY 94545 731-H2
CAPITOLA TER
- FRMT 94539 794-A1
CAPITOLA WY
5100 UNC 94545 751-J1
CAPP ST
2900 OAK 94602 650-D5
CAPPY TER
4900 FRMT 94555 752-C2
CAPRI AV
27000 HAY 94545 711-F7
27000 HAY 94545 731-F1
CAPRI CT
- LVMR 94550 715-F4
CAPRIANA COM
5900 FRMT 94555 752-B3
CAPRICE COM
5600 FRMT 94538 773-A2
CAPRICONUS AV
4700 LVMR 94551 696-B3
CAPRICORN AV
100 OAK 94611 630-D6
CAPRICORN CT
18400 AlaC 94546 691-J3
CAPTAIN DR
- EMVL 94608 629-C6
W CAPTAIN DODGE PL
- ALA 94501 649-C6
CAPTAINS CV
- OAK 94618 630-C4
- OAK 94705 630-C4
CAPTAINS DR
- ALA 94502 669-J5
- ALA 94502 670-A5
CAPULET CIR
33800 FRMT 94555 752-B2
CAPULET RD
- FRMT 94555 752-C2
CAPWELL DR
7800 OAK 94621 670-E6
CARAMELLO CT
3100 PLE 94588 694-C6
CARAMOOR LN
- SRMN 94582 674-C3
CARAVAN PL
- SRMN 94583 673-B2
CARAWAY CT
- SRMN 94582 673-G1
CARBERRY AV
5600 OAK 94609 629-H5
CARD AL
- SF 94133 648-A4
CARDEN ST
2100 SLN 94577 690-G1
CARDENA CT
- DBLN 94568 694-G3
CARDENAS TER
3100 FRMT 94536 752-H3
CARDIFF CT
8100 DBLN 94568 693-H2
CARDIFF DR
8000 DBLN 94568 693-H2
CARDIFF PL
600 MPS 95035 794-B3
CARDIFF ST
35000 NWK 94560 752-D4
CARDIGAN BAY
100 ALA 94502 669-J6
CARDIGAN CT
7600 DBLN 94568 693-H3
CARDIGAN ST
7600 DBLN 94568 693-H3
CARDINAL DR
700 LVMR 94551 715-E1
CARDINAL ST
28200 HAY 94545 731-J2
CARDINAL TER
3700 FRMT 94555 732-J3
CARDONA CIR
300 SRMN 94583 673-D3
CARDOZA CT
20900 AlaC 94541 691-G7
CARDUCCI DR
- PLE 94588 694-C6
CARE TER
34300 FRMT 94555 752-A3
CAREN ST
4400 FRMT 94538 753-C7
CAREY CT
- MRGA 94556 651-F1
CARIBBEAN COM
4000 FRMT 94555 752-E1
CARISBROOK CT
2500 HAY 94542 712-C3
CARISBROOK DR
2600 OAK 94611 650-F1
CARISBROOK LN
- OAK 94611 650-G1
CARL AV
1600 MPS 95035 794-D6
5300 RCH 94804 609-B3
CARLA ST
600 LVMR 94550 696-C7
CARLEEN CT
19600 AlaC 94546 691-J4
CARLEEN DR
3000 AlaC 94546 691-J4
CARLETON ST
700 BERK 94710 629-D3
1100 BERK 94702 629-F3
1500 BERK 94703 629-F3
1900 BERK 94704 629-H3
CARLISLE CT
- SRMN 94583 673-J7
- SRMN 94583 693-J1
E CARLO ST
- MPS 95035 793-J7
- MPS 95035 794-A7
CARLOS AV
5600 ELCR 94530 609-B2
5600 RCH 94804 609-B2
CARLOS BEE BLVD
24900 HAY 94542 712-A3
CARLOTTA AV
1200 BERK 94707 609-F7
1300 BERK 94703 609-F7
CARLOW WY
7500 DBLN 94568 693-G2
CARLSBAD CT
600 LVMR 94551 695-C7
600 MPS 95035 794-E7
3500 PLE 94588 714-B1
CARLSBAD RD
48500 FRMT 94539 793-J2
CARLSBAD ST
500 MPS 95035 794-E7
CARLSBAD WY
3600 PLE 94588 714-B1
CARLSEN ST
2900 OAK 94602 650-F4
CARLSON BLVD
700 RCH 94804 609-A2
2900 ELCR 94530 609-C3
CARLSON CT
23500 AlaC 94541 692-D7
CARLSTON AV
600 OAK 94610 650-B2
CARLTON AV
800 MLPK 94025 771-A7
17900 AlaC 94546 691-H3
CARLTON CT
19500 AlaC 94546 691-H4
CARLTON PL
1300 LVMR 94550 715-F4
CARLTON ST
5400 OAK 94618 630-A6
CARL VINSON
4000 ALA 94501 649-F6
CARLWYN CT
3700 AlaC 94546 691-H3
CARLWYN DR
18300 AlaC 94546 691-H2
CARLYLE ST
- LVMR 94550 716-C2
32500 HAY 94544 732-F3
CARMAR ST
400 HAY 94544 712-B7
500 HAY 94544 732-B1
CARMEL AV
100 ELCR 94530 609-E6
500 ALB 94706 609-E6
700 LVMR 94550 715-E2
2900 PDMT 94611 650-B1
CARMEL CT
- AlaC 94541 712-B2
- UNC 94545 751-J1
800 SLN 94578 691-C5
39000 FRMT 94538 753-A5
CARMEL DR
17800 AlaC 94546 691-H3
CARMEL ST
2400 OAK 94602 650-E4
CARMEL WY
- UNC 94545 731-J7
- UNC 94545 751-J1
3700 SLN 94578 691-B5
CARMELITA CT
40400 FRMT 94539 753-E4
CARMELITA DR
23900 HAY 94541 712-A1
CARMELITA PL
200 FRMT 94539 753-E4
CARMEN AV
2700 LVMR 94550 715-H2
CARMEN CT
4600 UNC 94587 732-A7
4600 UNC 94587 752-A1
CARMEN ST
41100 FRMT 94539 753-E6
CARMEN WY
4500 UNC 94587 732-A7
4600 UNC 94587 752-A1
CARNATION CIR
1700 LVMR 94551 696-A3
CARNATION CT
200 PLE 94566 714-F3
2600 AlaC 94546 691-H5
CARNATION LN
19700 AlaC 94546 691-H5
CARNATION WY
35600 FRMT 94536 732-J7
36000 FRMT 94536 752-J1
CARNEAL RD
7900 CCCo 94551 675-C4
CARNEGIE CT
2400 HAY 94545 731-H2
CARNEGIE DR
- MPS 95035 794-C7
CARNEGIE LP
- LVMR 94550 716-C2
CARNEGIE WY
- LVMR 94550 716-C2
CARNELIAN LN
1400 LVMR 94550 715-D3
CARNMORE PL
- DBLN 94568 694-F4
CARNOUSTIE
- MRGA 94556 651-D1
CARNOUSTIE CT
2500 UNC 94587 732-B4
CAROB LN
100 ALA 94502 669-J6
100 ALA 94502 670-A6
CAROBE CT
500 UNC 94587 732-G3
CAROL AV
3600 FRMT 94538 753-D7
3600 FRMT 94538 773-C1
CAROL COM
- LVMR 94550 696-A6
41500 FRMT 94538 753-E7
CAROL CT
7000 ELCR 94530 609-C1
CAROL PL
3700 AlaC 94541 692-D7
CAROL PTH
4200 RCH 94804 609-A1
CAROL TER
41600 FRMT 94538 753-E7
CAROLINE CT
1100 LVMR 94551 695-D6
7900 DBLN 94568 693-G3
CAROLINE ST
1200 ALA 94501 669-G2

STREET Block	City	ZIP	Pg-Grid
CAROLL ST			
-	SJCo	95391	(678-F2 See Page 677)
CAROLYN ST			
16000	AlaC	94578	691-F4
CAROUSEL CT			
-	SRMN	94583	673-B2
CAROUSEL PL			
-	SRMN	94583	673-B2
CARPENTER CT			
2300	FRMT	94539	753-F7
CARPENTIER ST			
400	SLN	94577	691-A1
CARR WY			
30600	UNC	94587	732-A4
CARRARA CT			
-	LVMR	94550	715-F5
CARRARA TER			
-	UNC	94587	732-G2
CARRARA WY			
-	LVMR	94550	715-E5
CARRIAGE DR			
6300	PLE	94566	714-D7
CARRIAGE WY			
16800	AlaC	94578	691-G5
CARRIAGE CIRCLE COM			
37600	FRMT	94536	752-G5
CARRIE CT			
4800	UNC	94587	751-J1
CARRIGAN COM			
3600	LVMR	94550	715-J1
CARRILLO CT			
400	SRMN	94583	673-C2
CARRILLO DR			
3400	SLN	94578	691-B4
CARRILLO WY			
900	SLN	94578	691-B4
CARRINGTON CT			
-	CCCo	94582	674-B5
CARRINGTON ST			
3600	OAK	94601	650-D7
4100	OAK	94601	670-D1
CARRINGTON WY			
3600	OAK	94601	650-D7
CARRISA CT			
2800	PLE	94588	694-H4
CARRISON ST			
1100	BERK	94702	629-E4
CARROL RD			
9900	AlaC	94551	696-J2
9900	AlaC	94551	(697-A3 See Page 677)
CARROLL AV			
30400	HAY	94544	732-D2
CARROLL CT			
-	SJCo	95391	(678-F2 See Page 677)
CARROLL ST			
2200	OAK	94606	650-A4
CARR RANCH RD			
-	CCCo	94556	651-F3
CARSON CT			
4600	PLE	94588	694-A6
CARSON DR			
300	HAY	94544	712-B6
CARSON LN			
17000	AlaC	94552	692-F3
CARSON ST			
4000	OAK	94619	650-G6
CARSON WY			
1000	MPS	95035	794-B4
CARSON PASS WY			
6000	LVMR	94551	696-D3
CARTAGENA AV			
1400	HAY	94544	732-A1
CARTAGENA LN			
500	SRMN	94583	673-C2
CARTER AV			
7300	NWK	94560	752-E7
CARTER ST			
1700	OAK	94602	650-E2
CARTIER DR			
1800	LVMR	94550	715-G2
CARTWRIGHT PL			
34100	FRMT	94555	732-E7
CARVER CT			
4500	PLE	94588	694-A6
CARVER LN			
-	AlaC	94586	734-D4
CARY AV			
10100	OAK	94603	670-H7
CARY CT			
-	OAK	94603	670-G6
CARY DR			
600	SLN	94577	671-B7
CASA CT			
-	OAK	94603	671-A4
CASADERO CT			
3000	PLE	94588	694-D7
CASA GRANDE DR			
3200	SRMN	94583	673-G5
CASA GRANDE PL			
-	SRMN	94583	673-G6
CASA LINDA CT			
11700	DBLN	94568	693-F4
CASALINO CT			
-	PLE	94566	715-B5
CASALS WY			
900	FRMT	94539	753-E5
CASA MARCIA PL			
1000	FRMT	94539	753-E5
CASANOVA DR			
800	SLN	94578	691-C5
CASA VIEJA			
-	ORIN	94563	630-J3
CASA VIEJA LN			
100	ORIN	94563	630-J3
CASCADAS CT			
-	SRMN	94583	673-A2
CASCADE AV			
-	LVMR	94551	695-D7
CASCADE LN			
-	ORIN	94563	610-H6
CASCADE RD			
400	SLN	94577	690-G1
CASCADE ST			
25700	HAY	94544	711-H5
CASCADE CREEK LN			
-	DBLN	94568	694-H3
CASCADES CIR			
-	UNC	94587	732-H6
CASCADITA TER			
400	MPS	95035	793-G3
CASCADO PL			
40900	FRMT	94539	753-E5
CASCARA CT			
2100	PLE	94588	714-A5
CASCATA CT			
-	LVMR	94550	715-C4
CASCINA CT			
-	LVMR	94550	715-D4
CASE AV			
5100	PLE	94566	714-D4
CASELLA CT			
-	SRMN	94582	674-B3
CASELLA WY			
-	SRMN	94582	674-C3
CASEY CT			
-	MLPK	94025	771-A7
36200	NWK	94560	752-E5
CASHEW CT			
500	SRMN	94583	673-G7
CASHEW WY			
800	FRMT	94536	732-J7
CASLAND DR			
6200	OAK	94621	670-F2
6200	OAK	94605	670-F2
CASPAR ST			
4900	UNC	94587	752-A2
CASPER PL			
200	SRMN	94583	673-G7
CASPER ST			
-	MPS	95035	793-J7
CASSADY CT			
-	LVMR	94550	696-B6
CASSANDRA PL			
100	SRMN	94583	693-G1
CASSATA PL			
-	DBLN	94568	694-H3
CASSIA CT			
-	HAY	94544	712-B6
3100	PLE	94588	694-H5
CASSIA DR			
-	HAY	94544	712-B6
CASSIO CIR			
33700	FRMT	94555	752-C1
CASSIO CT			
4300	FRMT	94555	752-C1
CASSIOPIA ST			
1800	LVMR	94551	696-B3
CASTANOS ST			
4200	FRMT	94536	752-F3
CASTELLO ST			
2500	OAK	94602	650-D5
CASTERLINE RD			
1700	OAK	94602	650-D3
CASTERSON CT			
4100	PLE	94566	714-F5
CASTERSON DR			
-	DBLN	94568	694-E3
CASTILIAN CT			
11600	DBLN	94568	693-F3
CASTILIAN RD			
7600	DBLN	94568	693-F3
CASTILLA AV			
4700	RCH	94804	609-A1
CASTILLE CT			
4400	UNC	94587	731-H6
CASTILLE LN			
22000	HAY	94541	691-J7
CASTILLEJO CT			
42700	FRMT	94539	753-F7
CASTILLEJO RD			
2100	FRMT	94539	753-F7
CASTILLEJO WY			
2000	FRMT	94539	753-F7
CASTILLON DR			
6100	NWK	94560	752-D5
CASTLE CT			
-	OAK	94611	650-G2
11700	DBLN	94568	693-G4
CASTLE DR			
5600	OAK	94611	650-F2
7200	DBLN	94568	693-G4
CASTLE LN			
-	OAK	94611	650-F2
CASTLE ST			
-	SF	94133	648-A4
900	SLN	94578	691-C4
CASTLEBAR PL			
-	ALA	94502	669-H5
CASTLEBERRY CT			
2700	AlaC	94541	692-C6
CASTLEBROOK DR			
5900	AlaC	94552	692-C1
CASTLEDOWN RD			
-	AlaC	94566	714-C6
CASTLEFORD CT			
5300	NWK	94560	752-D4
CASTLEMONT DR			
100	HAY	94544	711-J4
CASTLE PARK CT			
43300	FRMT	94538	773-C3
CASTLE PARK WY			
-	OAK	94611	650-F2
E CASTLE PINES TER			
-	DBLN	94568	694-G2
CASTLETON CT			
-	DBLN	94568	694-F3
100	SRMN	94583	673-C2
CASTLETON LN			
-	DBLN	94568	694-F3
CASTLEWOOD CIR			
-	AlaC	94566	714-B7
CASTLEWOOD COM			
5000	FRMT	94536	752-G5
CASTLEWOOD CT			
18000	HAY	94541	711-E2
CASTLEWOOD DR			
-	AlaC	94566	734-B1
-	AlaC	94566	714-B7
6800	PLE	94566	714-C7
6800	PLE	94588	714-C7
6800	AlaC	94588	714-C7
CASTLEWOOD PL			
-	AlaC	94566	714-B7
CASTLEWOOD ST			
8900	OAK	94605	671-B3
CASTLEWOOD WY			
18000	HAY	94541	711-E2
CASTRO LN			
-	FRMT	94539	753-F4
CASTRO ST			
-	SLN	94577	691-A2
200	OAK	94607	649-F4
900	ALB	94706	609-D5
900	SLN	94577	690-J3
1100	OAK	94612	649-F3
32700	UNC	94587	732-F3
CASTRO VALLEY BLVD			
1400	AlaC	94541	691-H5
1400	AlaC	94546	691-H5
3100	AlaC	94546	692-A5
E CASTRO VALLEY BLVD			
3900	AlaC	94546	692-C5
4000	AlaC	94552	692-F5
CASWELL AV			
300	OAK	94603	670-G7
CATALAN WY			
300	SRMN	94582	673-G3
CATALINA AV			
1800	BERK	94707	609-F6
3000	ALA	94502	669-J7
3100	ALA	94502	670-A7
CATALINA CT			
1500	LVMR	94550	715-F3
3700	AlaC	94546	692-A5
CATALINA DR			
600	LVMR	94550	715-E3
20000	AlaC	94546	692-A5
CATALINA PL			
40000	FRMT	94539	753-E4
CATALINA ST			
13700	SLN	94577	690-H5
CATALON CT			
7600	DBLN	94568	693-G3
CATALPA CT			
1700	HAY	94545	731-J1
CATALPA LN			
-	SRMN	94583	693-F1
CATALPA WY			
1800	HAY	94545	731-H1
CATAMARAN CT			
39600	FRMT	94538	753-A7
CATANIO CT			
500	SRMN	94583	673-B2
CATAWBA CT			
3100	PLE	94566	714-H4
CATHERINE CT			
100	ORIN	94563	630-J1
CATHERINE DR			
1400	BERK	94702	629-F1
CATHERINE ST			
900	SJS	95002	793-B7
CATHY LN			
-	DNVL	94526	652-J1
-	OAK	94619	651-C7
CATHY WY			
1300	HAY	94545	711-G6
CATO CT			
20900	AlaC	94546	692-A5
CATRON DR			
100	OAK	94603	690-H1
500	OAK	94603	670-H7
CATTAIL CT			
3500	UNC	94587	732-A5
CATTLEYA CT			
-	SRMN	94582	673-H1
CATTLEYA DR			
-	SRMN	94582	673-H1
CAUDILLO TER			
400	MPS	95035	793-H3
CAVALIER CT			
-	UNC	94587	731-J5
8400	DBLN	94568	693-G2
CAVALIER LN			
8200	DBLN	94568	693-G2
CAVANAGH CT			
2700	HAY	94545	711-D5
CAVANAUGH CT			
-	PDMT	94610	650-D3
E CAVENDISH DR			
18500	AlaC	94552	692-D3
W CAVENDISH DR			
18600	AlaC	94552	692-D3
CAVENDISH LN			
-	OAK	94602	650-D3
CAVENDISH PL			
34000	FRMT	94555	732-D7
CAVISSON CT			
44400	FRMT	94539	773-H2
CAVOUR ST			
300	OAK	94618	629-H6
CAXTON PL			
35700	FRMT	94536	752-G2
CAYETANO CT			
-	AlaC	94551	695-F5
CAYUGA CT			
45700	FRMT	94539	773-H4
CAYUGA DR			
900	LVMR	94551	695-F7
CAYUGA PL			
-	FRMT	94539	773-H4
CAYUGA WY			
300	FRMT	94539	773-H4
CECELIA CT			
1000	SLN	94577	671-A7
1000	SLN	94577	691-A1
CEDAR AV			
1300	SLN	94579	691-A4
1500	SLN	94579	690-J4
CEDAR BLVD			
6000	NWK	94560	752-D4
38800	NWK	94560	772-H1
39900	NWK	94560	773-A2
CEDAR CT			
5500	NWK	94560	752-H7
6900	DBLN	94568	693-J4
CEDAR DR			
300	LVMR	94551	695-D7
CEDAR LN			
6800	DBLN	94568	693-J4
CEDAR ST			
-	OAK	94607	649-C3
100	FRMT	94539	773-H1
600	BERK	94710	629-C1
800	ALA	94501	669-J3
1100	BERK	94702	629-E1
1500	BERK	94703	629-E1
1800	HAY	94541	692-B7
1900	BERK	94709	629-E1
2000	BERK	94709	609-H7
2300	BERK	94708	609-H7
CEDAR TER			
-	FRMT	94539	753-H7
CEDAR BROOK CT			
5700	AlaC	94552	692-B2
CEDARBROOK RD			
-	HAY	94544	732-D1
CEDAR CREST TER			
-	DBLN	94568	694-F2
CEDAR HOLLOW DR			
-	DNVL	94526	652-J1
CEDAR MOUNTAIN DR			
7300	AlaC	94550	716-E5
CEDAR OAK TER			
-	FRMT	94536	752-A5
CEDAR POINTE LP			
-	SRMN	94583	693-H1
CEDARWOOD COM			
-	LVMR	94550	716-D1
CEDARWOOD DR			
1100	MRGA	94556	651-E1
43200	FRMT	94538	773-D2
CEDARWOOD LN			
1100	BERK	94710	609-C7
1400	PLE	94566	714-E2
CEDARWOOD LP			
-	CCCo	94582	673-J2
CEDARWOOD PL			
-	CCCo	94582	673-J2
CEDARWOOD WY			
-	CCCo	94582	673-J2
CEDRUS CT			
2800	PLE	94588	694-H4
CEEKAY PL			
2800	AlaC	94546	692-B6
CELAYA CIR			
2600	SRMN	94583	673-C3
CELEDA CT			
100	FRMT	94539	753-E3
CELESTE AV			
5300	LVMR	94550	696-C6
CELESTE CT			
32400	UNC	94587	732-A7
CELIA CT			
4500	FRMT	94555	752-C1
CELIA ST			
200	HAY	94544	712-B7
CELLARS CT			
-	LVMR	94550	715-F5
CELLARS DR			
-	LVMR	94550	715-F5
CELLO WY			
5600	FRMT	94538	773-B2
CENTAURUS CT			
1700	LVMR	94551	696-B3
CENTENNIAL AV			
800	ALA	94501	669-G1
CENTENNIAL DR			
-	BERK	94708	610-A7
-	BERK	94720	610-A7
-	BERK	94720	629-J1
-	BERK	94720	630-A1
-	OAK	94708	610-A7
-	OAK	94720	610-A7
-	OAK	94720	630-A1
CENTENNIAL LN			
-	AlaC	94541	712-C1
CENTENNIAL WY			
2700	SRMN	94583	673-E6
CENTENO RD			
35500	FRMT	94536	752-F2
CENTER ST			
300	OAK	94607	649-D3
1900	BERK	94704	629-G2
18200	AlaC	94546	692-C4
18200	AlaC	94552	692-C2
22400	AlaC	94541	692-B6
22500	HAY	94541	692-B6
CENTER POINT TER			
-	SRMN	94582	673-G2
CENTO CT			
-	PLE	94566	715-C6
CENTRAL AV			
100	ALA	94501	649-E7
100	ALA	94501	669-E1
700	LVMR	94551	696-C4
2100	ALA	94501	670-A2
2600	UNC	94587	732-E5
4000	FRMT	94536	752-G5
4800	RCH	94804	609-D4
5400	NWK	94560	752-F7
5500	ELCR	94530	609-D4
6400	NWK	94560	772-E1
15200	SLN	94578	691-C4
CENTRAL AV Rt#-61			
200	ALA	94501	669-G1
CENTRAL BLVD			
800	HAY	94542	712-A3
CENTRAL CT			
400	SLN	94578	691-D5
2600	UNC	94587	732-D6
37200	NWK	94560	772-D1
CENTRAL PKWY			
6600	DBLN	94568	694-C4
CENTRAL COVE CT			
-	FRMT	94536	752-G5
CENTRALMONT PL			
37400	FRMT	94536	752-G5
CENTRAL OAK CT			
-	FRMT	94536	752-G5
CENTRAL PARK DR			
500	CCCo	94708	609-H4
CENTRE CT			
500	ALA	94502	670-A5
CENTURY PL			
-	SF	94104	648-B5
CENTURY ST			
28400	HAY	94545	731-J2
CENTURY OAKS CIR			
25000	AlaC	94552	692-E6
CENTURY OAKS CT			
2600	SRMN	94583	673-D6
3700	AlaC	94552	692-E6
CERAMICA WY			
-	FRMT	94536	732-H7
CEREUS CT			
48400	FRMT	94539	793-J1
CEREZA DR			
1000	PLE	94566	714-G3
CERMENHO CT			
-	DBLN	94568	694-G4
CERRITO AV			
3800	OAK	94611	649-J1
CERRITO ST			
700	ALB	94706	609-D6
CERRITOS AV			
4500	FRMT	94536	752-F3
CERRO CT			
43900	FRMT	94539	773-H2
CERRO VISTA			
3000	ALA	94502	669-J6
CERRO VISTA PL			
4800	AlaC	94550	716-B2
CERRUTI CT			
-	ALA	94501	649-A2
CERVANTEZ CT			
1000	MPS	95035	794-C4
CESTARIC DR			
500	MPS	95035	794-C5
CHABLIS CT			
-	FRMT	94539	773-J4
3200	PLE	94566	714-G3
CHABLIS WY			
2500	LVMR	94550	715-H2
CHABOLYN TER			
5900	BERK	94618	630-A4
5900	OAK	94618	630-A4
CHABOT CT			
1500	HAY	94545	711-G5
5800	OAK	94618	630-A5
CHABOT DR			
4500	PLE	94588	694-B6
CHABOT RD			
5800	OAK	94618	629-J5
6000	OAK	94618	630-B4
CHABOT TER			
1600	SLN	94577	671-D7
CHABOT VW			
18500	AlaC	94546	691-G3
CHABOT CREST			
5900	OAK	94618	630-A4
6000	BERK	94618	630-A4
CHABOT VIEW DR			
-	AlaC	94578	691-G3
CHAD DR			
300	MPS	95035	794-A5
CHADBOURN CT			
1400	PLE	94566	714-G4
CHADBOURNE DR			
41500	FRMT	94539	753-F6
CHADBOURNE WY			
-	OAK	94619	650-H4
CHADWICK PL			
-	DBLN	94568	694-H3
CHALLEN CT			
-	ALA	94501	649-A2
CHALLENGER DR			
1000	ALA	94501	649-G7
CHALLENGER WY			
800	HAY	94544	712-A3
CHALMETTE CT			
-	LVMR	94551	715-C1
CHALMETTE RD			
200	LVMR	94551	715-D1
CHALMETTE PARK CT			
4800	FRMT	94538	773-C1
CHALON GLEN CT			
1900	LVMR	94550	715-H3
CHAMA WY			
100	FRMT	94539	773-H7
CHAMBERLAIN TER			
34200	FRMT	94555	732-H4
34200	FRMT	94555	752-D1
CHAMBERLIN CT			
4300	OAK	94619	650-J7
CHAMBERS DR			
6800	OAK	94611	630-F7
CHAMBERS LN			
-	OAK	94611	630-F7
CHAMBERS ST			
28300	HAY	94545	731-H1
CHAMBOSSE DR			
300	HAY	94544	712-B6
CHAMIER PL			
2800	FRMT	94555	732-E6
CHAMISE TR			
-	CCCo	94583	652-E3
CHAMPAGNE CT			
11200	DBLN	94568	693-E3
CHAMPAGNE PL			
11300	DBLN	94568	693-F3
CHAMPION ST			
3000	OAK	94602	650-D5
CHAMPLAIN CT			
-	UNC	94587	732-C5
CHAMPLAIN ST			
32100	HAY	94544	732-E3
CHAMPLAIN WY			
-	UNC	94587	732-C5
CHANCE ST			
29200	HAY	94544	732-C1
CHANCELLOR LN			
-	OAK	94705	630-C3
CHANCELLOR PL			
-	OAK	94705	630-C3
CHANCERY LN			
-	DBLN	94568	694-F4
CHANCERY WY			
-	CCCo	94582	674-B5
CHANDLER CT			
1300	LVMR	94551	695-F6
CHANDLER RD			
1100	HAY	94545	711-F4
CHANDLER ST			
-	OAK	94603	670-J6
-	OAK	94603	671-A6
CHANEL TER			
34700	FRMT	94555	752-D3
CHANN CT			
48000	FRMT	94539	773-J7
CHANNEL AV			
5100	RCH	94804	609-A3
CHANNEL DR			
5200	NWK	94560	752-E4
CHANNEL ST			
300	SF	94107	648-B7
15800	AlaC	94580	691-C7
15800	AlaC	94580	711-C1
CHANNING WY			
200	ALA	94502	669-J5
700	BERK	94710	629-D3
1100	BERK	94702	629-E3
1500	BERK	94703	629-G2
1900	BERK	94704	629-G2
CHANTECLER CT			
44500	FRMT	94539	773-J2
CHANTECLER DR			
100	FRMT	94539	773-J2
N CHANTERELLA DR			
-	SRMN	94582	673-G1
S CHANTERELLA DR			
-	SRMN	94582	673-G2
CHANTERELLE PL			
-	DBLN	94568	694-H3
CHANTILLY DR			
7700	DBLN	94568	694-A1
CHANTILLY LN			
1800	HAY	94541	712-B2
CHAPALLA WY			
4200	UNC	94587	732-A6
CHAPARRAL CT			
46400	FRMT	94539	773-J5
CHAPARRAL DR			
46400	FRMT	94539	773-J5
CHAPARRAL LN			
22000	AlaC	94552	692-D5
CHAPARRAL PL			
4100	AlaC	94552	692-D5
CHAPARRAL WY			
1400	LVMR	94551	696-E2
CHAPEL AV			
1200	SLN	94579	691-A6
CHAPEL CT			
15100	SLN	94579	691-B6
CHAPEL WY			
40400	FRMT	94538	753-D7
41100	FRMT	94538	773-D1
CHAPIN ST			
1600	ALA	94501	669-G1
1700	ALA	94501	649-G7
CHAPLET ST			
-	SLN	94578	691-B4
CHAPLIN DR			
35500	FRMT	94536	752-G1
CHAPMAN CT			
26300	HAY	94545	711-G6
38600	FRMT	94536	753-C2
CHAPMAN DR			
5300	NWK	94560	752-D4
CHAPMAN RD			
14300	SLN	94578	691-B4
CHAPMAN ST			
2800	OAK	94601	670-B1
CHAPMAN WY			
4200	PLE	94588	694-A7
CHAPPARAL CT			
2600	SRMN	94583	673-E6
CHAPPARAL PL			
-	ORIN	94563	610-E6
CHAPPELL PL			
5600	OAK	94619	651-A5
CHARDONNAY CT			
1900	LVMR	94550	715-H3
48800	FRMT	94539	793-J2
CHARDONNAY DR			
400	FRMT	94539	793-J2
400	FRMT	94539	794-A2
2900	PLE	94566	714-G3
CHARDONNAY PL			
3100	PLE	94566	714-G3
CHARDONNAY WY			
2200	LVMR	94550	715-H3
CHARING ST			
-	HAY	94541	711-J2
CHARING CROSS RD			
6600	OAK	94618	630-C4
6600	OAK	94705	630-C4
CHARIOT LN			
5200	OAK	94605	671-C1
CHARLENE WY			
22400	AlaC	94546	692-A7
CHARLES AV			
25400	HAY	94544	712-A4
CHARLES RD			
1600	SLN	94577	690-H1
CHARLES ST			
36400	NWK	94560	752-F4
CHARLES HILL CIR			
-	ORIN	94563	610-J5
CHARLES HILL LN			
-	ORIN	94563	610-J5
CHARLES HILL PL			
-	ORIN	94563	610-J6
CHARLES HILL RD			
-	ORIN	94563	610-J5
CHARLESTON ST			
2400	OAK	94602	650-E3
CHARLESTON WY			
42500	FRMT	94538	773-E1
CHARLESTOWN PL			
-	SF	94105	648-B6
CHARLITA CT			
41300	FRMT	94539	753-G5
CHARLOTTE AV			
2000	SLN	94577	690-H2
CHARLOTTE COM			
300	LVMR	94550	696-B7
CHARLOTTE WY			
-	AlaC	94550	716-C2
4700	LVMR	94550	696-B7
5500	LVMR	94550	716-C1
CHARMONT CT			
2000	LVMR	94550	715-H3
CHARMWOOD CT			
35000	NWK	94560	752-D3
CHARTER WY			
-	SLN	94579	691-A7
CHARTER OAKS DR			
5800	AlaC	94552	692-C1
CHARTER SQUARE TER			
34100	FRMT	94555	752-D1
CHASE AV			
-	HAY	94541	711-J2
CHASE CT			
200	FRMT	94536	753-C1
600	LVMR	94551	695-E6
CHASE ST			
-	SJCo	95391	(678-F2 See Page 677)
1700	OAK	94607	649-D3
CHASTWORTH ST			
2500	LVMR	94550	715-F5
CHATAM ST			
8300	DBLN	94568	693-H2
CHATEAU COM			
1300	LVMR	94550	715-J2
CHATEAU CT			
2100	LVMR	94550	715-H2
17600	AlaC	94552	692-B2
CHATEAU WY			
1300	LVMR	94550	715-H2
CHATEAU PARK CT			
4600	FRMT	94538	773-C2
CHATELI CT			
800	PLE	94566	714-G3
CHATHAM CT			
26400	HAY	94542	712-D3
CHATHAM PL			
-	SF	94108	648-A5
CHATHAM RD			
1100	OAK	94610	650-B4
1300	OAK	94602	650-B4
CHATHAM POINTE			
-	ALA	94502	670-A5
CHATSWORTH CT			
-	OAK	94611	650-F1
CHATTERTON CT			
43200	FRMT	94538	773-E2
CHAUCER CIR			
400	SRMN	94583	673-E4
CHAUCER CT			
-	SRMN	94583	673-E4
4300	LVMR	94551	696-A5
CHAUCER DR			
3100	FRMT	94555	732-E7
3500	FRMT	94555	752-E1
CHAUCER ST			
1100	BERK	94702	629-E2
CHAUCER WY			
-	HAY	94542	712-D4
800	LVMR	94551	696-A6
CHAUMONT PTH			
-	OAK	94618	630-B5
CHAUNTRY COM			
37500	FRMT	94536	752-J3
CHAVEL CT			
-	FRMT	94539	773-J4
CHECHESTER DR			
32200	UNC	94587	732-C5
CHELSEA CT			
-	OAK	94611	650-F1
3600	PLE	94588	694-E5
CHELSEA DR			
2400	OAK	94611	650-F1
3500	PLE	94588	694-E6
5000	NWK	94560	752-E4
CHELSEA PL			
-	SF	94108	648-A5
CHELSEA WY			
-	HAY	94544	732-A1
1300	LVMR	94550	715-F5
CHELTON DR			
5600	OAK	94611	650-F1
6500	OAK	94611	630-G7
CHELTON LN			
-	OAK	94611	650-F1
CHEMULT COM			
46800	FRMT	94539	773-H6
CHENAB CT			
400	FRMT	94539	773-J5
CHENAULT WY			
800	HAY	94541	711-F4
CHENEY AV			
400	OAK	94610	650-A3
CHENEY LN			
1600	HAY	94545	711-H6
CHENIN BLANC DR			
48800	FRMT	94539	793-J2
48800	FRMT	94539	794-A2
CHEROKEE AV			
2500	OAK	94605	671-A4
CHEROKEE CT			
-	SRMN	94583	673-D5
600	HAY	94544	732-E1
CHEROKEE DR			
800	LVMR	94551	695-E7
CHEROKEE LN			
45500	FRMT	94539	773-H4
CHERRY CT			
38600	FRMT	94536	753-C3
CHERRY LN			
38500	FRMT	94536	753-C2
CHERRY ST			
-	FRMT	94538	772-H2
2200	SLN	94577	691-B2
2800	BERK	94705	629-J3
6400	NWK	94560	772-F1
9000	OAK	94603	670-J4
36000	NWK	94560	752-D6
CHERRY WK			
-	ALA	94501	669-G3
CHERRY WY			
-	AlaC	94541	691-F7
5700	LVMR	94551	696-C4
CHERRY BLOSSOM CT			
-	FRMT	94536	753-A2
2800	PLE	94588	714-B1
CHERRY BLOSSOM WY			
2600	UNC	94587	732-F7
4300	LVMR	94551	696-A3
CHERRY HILLS CT			
-	SRMN	94583	673-H7
CHERRY HILLS LN			
9400	SRMN	94583	673-H7
CHERRYLAND CT			
21600	AlaC	94541	711-G1
CHERRY MANOR CT			
400	FRMT	94536	753-C2
CHERRYWOOD AV			
100	SLN	94577	670-J7
100	SLN	94577	671-A7
4300	FRMT	94538	773-D2
CHERRYWOOD CT			
7900	PLE	94588	713-J1
CHERRYWOOD DR			
2400	UNC	94587	732-F7
CHERYL CIR			
3200	PLE	94588	714-B1
CHERYL CT			
4800	UNC	94587	751-J1
CHERYL DR			
-	LVMR	94550	716-C1
1300	LVMR	94550	696-C7
CHERYL ANN CIR			
900	HAY	94544	712-A6
CHESAPEAKE AV			
2100	HAY	94545	711-H7
CHESAPEAKE CT			
-	UNC	94587	732-H6
CHESAPEAKE DR			
-	UNC	94587	732-H6
CHESHIRE CT			
-	ALA	94502	669-J5
2400	SLN	94577	691-B2
3800	PLE	94588	694-F5
CHESHIRE PL			
2300	SLN	94577	691-B2
CHESLEY ST			
-	SF	94103	648-D7
CHESNEY GLEN DR			
-	AlaC	94552	692-E7
CHESTER CT			
34300	FRMT	94555	752-D1
CHESTER ST			
300	OAK	94607	649-D4
2500	ALA	94501	670-A3
20800	AlaC	94546	691-J5
E CHESTERFIELD CIR			
-	DBLN	94568	694-E3
W CHESTERFIELD CIR			
-	DBLN	94568	694-F3
CHESTERFIELD CT			
-	HAY	94544	732-C1
CHESTNUT AV			
400	MPS	95035	793-H6
CHESTNUT COM			
5600	FRMT	94538	773-A1
CHESTNUT CT			
-	DBLN	94568	694-D4
200	SRMN	94583	673-G7
CHESTNUT ST			
100	OAK	94607	649-E3
100	SF	94133	648-A3
500	SF	94111	648-A3
800	ALA	94501	669-H2
1500	BERK	94702	629-E2
1800	LVMR	94551	695-G7
2700	OAK	94608	649-E3
22500	HAY	94541	692-A7
22500	HAY	94541	712-A1
37000	NWK	94560	772-C1
CHESTNUT WY			
7600	PLE	94588	693-H7
CHESWICK CT			
200	ALA	94502	669-J5
CHESWYCKE COM			
2900	FRMT	94536	752-H2
CHESWYCKE TER			
2900	FRMT	94536	752-H2
CHETLAND RD			
600	SLN	94577	671-B7
CHETWOOD AV			
4200	FRMT	94538	773-D1
CHETWOOD ST			
600	OAK	94610	649-J2
600	OAK	94610	650-A2
CHEVIOT CT			
35300	NWK	94560	752-D4
CHEVRON ST			
-	SLN	94578	691-B4
CHEVY CHASE WY			
600	HAY	94544	732-D1
CHEYENNE AV			
2900	SRMN	94583	673-G7
CHEYENNE CT			
-	FRMT	94539	773-H4

© 2006 Rand McNally & Company

STREET / Block City ZIP Pg-Grid

CHEYENNE PL
45500 FRMT 94539 773-H4
CHIANTI CT
1200 PLE 94566 714-G4
1400 LVMR 94550 715-H3
CHICAGO
4000 ALA 94501 649-E6
CHICO CT
- OAK 94611 630-F6
CHICO DR
700 SLN 94578 691-B4
CHICOINE AV
31000 HAY 94544 732-E1
CHILD ST
- SF 94133 648-A3
CHILENSE CT
- SRMN 94582 673-G2
CHILLINGHAM CT
3600 PLE 94588 694-E5
CHILMARK LN
- ALA 94502 669-J5
CHILTERN DR
40700 FRMT 94539 753-E5
CHILTON WY
2500 BERK 94704 629-H3
CHIMERA CIR
38500 FRMT 94536 753-C2
CHIMNEY CT
3100 UNC 94587 732-A4
CHIMNEY LN
30600 UNC 94587 732-A4
CHIMNEY ROCK
- OAK 94605 671-D2
CHINA CT
4000 AlaC 94542 712-F1
CHINABERRY COM
- FRMT 94536 752-G5
CHINABERRY LN
100 ALA 94502 669-J6
100 ALA 94502 670-A6
CHINOOK CT
- SF 94130 648-E1
2700 UNC 94587 732-F7
CHIPLAY AV
26500 HAY 94545 711-H6
CHIPLAY CT
2000 HAY 94545 711-G6
CHIPMAN ST
- ALA 94501 649-C7
CHIPPENDALE CT
3500 PLE 94588 694-E5
4400 UNC 94587 732-A7
CHIPPENDALE DR
4300 UNC 94587 732-A7
CHIPPEWA CT
1900 FRMT 94539 773-G3
CHIPPEWA WY
700 LVMR 94551 695-E6
CHISHOLM CT
26500 HAY 94544 711-J6
CHLOE CT
2800 AlaC 94546 691-H4
CHOCOLATE ST
2600 PLE 94588 694-G6
CHOCTAW DR
600 FRMT 94539 773-H6
CHOLLA ST
47400 FRMT 94539 773-J6
CHRIS COM
300 LVMR 94550 696-B7
CHRISHOLM PL
38600 FRMT 94536 753-D1
CHRISTENSEN CT
- ALA 94502 669-H7
19100 AlaC 94546 691-J4
CHRISTENSEN LN
3300 AlaC 94546 691-J4
CHRISTENSEN RD
13600 AlaC 94551 677-F1
13600 AlaC 94551 (657-F7 See Page 637)
CHRISTIE AV
5700 EMVL 94608 629-D5
CHRISTINA CT
300 PLE 94566 714-F3
1400 HAY 94545 711-E5
CHRISTINE CT
3000 FRMT 94536 753-A3
4800 UNC 94587 752-A1
36500 NWK 94560 752-E6
CHRISTINE DR
4800 UNC 94587 751-J1
32500 UNC 94587 752-A1
CHRISTINE ST
36200 NWK 94560 752-D6
CHRISTOPHER CT
- AlaC 94541 692-C7
CHRISTOPHER WY
3100 SRMN 94583 673-F5
CHRISTY COM
41600 FRMT 94538 773-B2
CHRISTY ST
41600 FRMT 94538 773-B2
CHRONICLE AV
2800 HAY 94542 712-D3
CHUMALIA ST
- SLN 94577 691-A1
CHUNGKING ST
100 OAK 94607 649-C2
CHURCH AV
1400 SLN 94579 691-A6
37400 FRMT 94536 752-H3
CHURCH ST
200 LVMR 94550 695-H7
200 LVMR 94550 715-H1
1700 OAK 94605 670-G3
1700 OAK 94621 670-G3
CHURCHILL CT
- UNC 94587 731-J5
3300 FRMT 94536 752-G2
3500 PLE 94588 694-E6
CHURCHILL DR
2000 MPS 95035 794-B2
3900 PLE 94588 694-E5
CHURCHILL ST
15000 SLN 94579 691-B6
CHURCHILL DOWNS LN
- LVMR 94550 715-H5
CHUSAN WY
- CCCo 94582 674-B2
CHUTNEY RD
- HAY 94544 732-B1
CID WY
4000 PLE 94566 714-E2
CIELO CT
- LVMR 94550 715-D4
CIELO VISTA TER
- FRMT 94536 752-J2
CIMARRON ST
4000 ALA 94501 649-E6
CINDEE ST
4700 UNC 94587 731-J7

CINDY CT
300 SRMN 94583 673-E5
4700 LVMR 94550 696-B7
CINDY LN
600 LVMR 94550 696-B7
CINDY WY
18700 AlaC 94546 691-G3
CINNABAR CT
5900 NWK 94560 752-E6
CINNABAR DR
500 LVMR 94550 715-D2
CINNAMON CT
700 HAY 94544 732-B1
CIRCLE AV
4200 AlaC 94546 692-B5
CIRCLE WY
11500 DBLN 94568 693-G5
CIRCLE E RANCH DR
- SRMN 94583 673-E7
CIRCLE E RANCH PL
- SRMN 94583 673-E7
CIRCLE HILL DR
7200 OAK 94605 670-J1
7200 OAK 94605 671-A1
CIROLERO ST
1300 MPS 95035 794-B4
CIRVELA ST
2100 PLE 94566 714-G1
CISCO ST
4100 FRMT 94536 752-F2
CITRINE PL
1500 LVMR 94550 715-D3
CITRON CT
- SRMN 94583 693-F1
CITRON WY
1000 HAY 94545 711-G5
CITRUS DR
40400 FRMT 94538 753-C6
CITY CENTER DR
22200 HAY 94541 691-J7
22200 HAY 94541 711-J1
CITY WALK PL
- HAY 94541 711-J2
CIVIC AV
2500 HAY 94542 712-D4
CIVIC PZ
100 DBLN 94568 693-J4
CIVIC CENTER DR
39000 FRMT 94538 753-B4
CIVIC TERRACE AV
5500 NWK 94560 752-F6
CLAIBORNE CT
26900 HAY 94542 712-E3
CLAIRE PL
600 SRMN 94583 673-F6
CLAIRE ST
500 HAY 94541 711-H2
CLAIREPOINTE WY
13100 OAK 94619 651-B6
CLARA CT
- FRMT 94539 753-F4
- OAK 94603 670-G6
CLARA LN
800 PLE 94566 714-H3
CLARA ST
100 SF 94107 648-A7
300 OAK 94603 670-G7
600 OAK 94621 670-G6
CLAREMONT AV
- ORIN 94563 610-E6
2800 BERK 94705 630-A3
2800 OAK 94705 630-A3
3100 BERK 94705 629-J5
3300 OAK 94618 629-J5
5100 OAK 94609 629-J5
CLAREMONT BLVD
2700 BERK 94705 630-A3
CLAREMONT CT
2200 HAY 94545 731-J2
2200 HAY 94545 732-A2
CLAREMONT PL
2400 UNC 94587 732-C4
CLAREMONT ST
32200 UNC 94587 732-C4
CLAREMONT WY
4300 LVMR 94550 716-A1
CLAREMONT CREST
- BERK 94705 630-A3
CLAREMONT CREST CT
2400 SRMN 94583 673-A1
CLAREMONT CREST WY
- SRMN 94583 673-A1
CLAREMONT PARK CT
4800 FRMT 94538 773-C1
CLARENCE CT
- EPA 94303 771-B7
CLARENCE LN
100 FRMT 94539 753-F5
CLARENCE PL
- SF 94107 648-B7
CLARENDALE ST
24200 HAY 94544 711-H3
CLARENDON CRES
1000 OAK 94610 650-C3
CLARENDON PARK CT
5400 FRMT 94538 773-C2
CLARET CT
600 PLE 94566 714-G3
45500 FRMT 94539 773-J4
CLARET RD
1200 LVMR 94550 715-H2
CLAREWOOD DR
4300 OAK 94618 630-B6
4300 OAK 94611 630-B6
CLAREWOOD LN
- OAK 94618 630-B6
CLARIDGE PL
2200 SLN 94577 691-A3
CLARINBRIDGE CIR
- DBLN 94568 694-F4
CLARK AV
6300 DBLN 94568 693-J4
6600 NWK 94560 752-F7
6600 NWK 94560 772-E1
CLARK PL
900 ELCR 94530 609-F2
CLARKE AV
300 LVMR 94551 695-H7
CLARKE DR
800 FRMT 94536 733-D7
CLARKE LN
1100 ALA 94502 670-A7
CLARKE ST
1100 SLN 94577 691-A1
3900 OAK 94609 629-H6
3900 OAK 94609 649-H1
5100 OAK 94618 629-H6
CLARKFORD ST
26700 HAY 94544 711-J6
CLAUDE LN
- SF 94108 648-A5

CLAUDIA CT
4600 FRMT 94536 752-E3
CLAUSEN CT
25800 AlaC 94541 712-D2
CLAUSER DR
400 MPS 95035 794-A5
CLAWITER RD
22900 AlaC 94545 711-E6
22900 HAY 94545 711-E6
CLAY CT
1100 FRMT 94536 753-B2
CLAY ST
- OAK 94607 649-F4
100 SF 94111 648-A5
700 SF 94108 648-A5
1000 ALB 94706 609-D5
1200 OAK 94612 649-F4
1400 HAY 94541 712-A1
2500 ALA 94501 670-A3
CLAYTON AV
400 ELCR 94530 609-D3
CLAYTON ST
9100 AlaC 94541 692-C7
9100 AlaC 94541 712-C1
CLEARBROOK CIR
29800 HAY 94544 712-E7
CLEAR LAKE ST
32700 FRMT 94555 732-B6
CLEAR SPRINGS CT
- AlaC 94552 692-F7
- AlaC 94552 712-F1
CLEARVIEW DR
1600 SLN 94577 691-D1
CLEAR VIEW TER
- FRMT 94539 794-B1
CLEMANS DR
19000 AlaC 94546 692-C4
CLEMATIS CT
2000 FRMT 94539 773-G3
CLEMENS RD
1700 OAK 94602 650-D3
CLEMENT AV
- ALA 94501 649-H7
1700 ALA 94501 669-J1
2000 ALA 94501 670-A1
CLEMENT DR
18600 AlaC 94552 692-E2
CLEMENTINA ST
- SF 94105 648-A7
300 SF 94103 648-A7
CLEO CT
5400 LVMR 94550 696-C7
CLEREMONT DR
35400 NWK 94560 752-C5
CLEVELAND AV
600 ALB 94710 609-C5
800 ALB 94706 609-C5
CLEVELAND CT
- ALA 94501 649-A2
CLEVELAND PL
5400 FRMT 94538 752-J7
CLEVELAND ST
- SF 94103 648-D7
500 OAK 94606 649-J4
600 OAK 94606 650-A4
1300 SLN 94577 691-C1
CLIFDEN CT
- DBLN 94568 693-E4
CLIFFLAND AV
10900 OAK 94605 671-D5
CLIFFORD CIR
3200 PLE 94588 694-B7
3200 PLE 94588 714-B1
CLIFFORD CT
3500 AlaC 94546 691-J3
CLIFFORD DR
5500 AlaC 94550 717-A4
CLIFFORD LN
600 MPS 95035 794-B5
CLIFFROSE TER
- FRMT 94536 752-A4
CLIFFSIDE DR
300 DNVL 94526 652-J4
CLIFFWOOD AV
27700 HAY 94545 711-H7
27700 HAY 94545 731-H1
CLIFTON CT
- CCCo 94582 674-B5
3300 FRMT 94538 753-C5
CLIFTON ST
- OAK 94618 629-H6
CLIFTON WY
18300 AlaC 94546 691-H3
CLIFTON COURT RD
5000 CCCo 94514 637-G7
W CLIFTON COURT RD
12000 SJCo 95206 (638-F1 See Page 637)
CLIMBING ROSE COM
- LVMR 94551 696-C5
CLIMBING ROSE CT
800 HAY 94544 712-A7
CLINTON AV
1300 ALA 94501 669-H2
16800 AlaC 94578 691-F6
CLINTON CT
24100 HAY 94545 711-F4
CLINTON PL
900 PLE 94566 714-F4
CLIPPER CT
- FRMT 94538 773-E7
2000 SLN 94579 690-J6
CLIPPER DR
- ALA 94502 669-J5
CLIPPER HILL
- OAK 94618 630-C4
CLIPPER HILL RD
100 DNVL 94526 652-G2
300 CCCo 94583 652-G2
CLIVE AV
6200 OAK 94611 650-G1
CLOUD WY
21300 HAY 94545 711-D4
CLOUD VIEW LN
2900 AlaC 94541 692-C7
CLOUGH AV
3700 FRMT 94538 753-D6
CLOVER CT
1900 PLE 94588 714-A6
2900 UNC 94587 732-F7
CLOVER DR
5700 OAK 94618 630-A5
CLOVER RD
25500 AlaC 94542 712-E1
CLOVER ST
34700 UNC 94587 732-F7
CLOVERFIELD CT
- AlaC 94552 692-E7
CLOVERLEAF CT
46800 FRMT 94539 773-J5
CLOVEWOOD LN
4300 PLE 94588 693-J7

CLOVEWOOD LN
4300 PLE 94588 713-J1
CLUBHOUSE DR
- PLE 94586 714-F7
- PLE 94586 734-F1
900 HAY 94541 711-E2
900 LVMR 94551 695-B5
CLUBHOUSE MEMORIAL RD
- ALA 94502 670-A6
CLUB VIEW DR
1300 ELCR 94530 609-E1
CLUNY PL
35800 NWK 94560 752-D5
CLYDE CT
500 MPS 95035 794-B6
CLYDE ST
- SF 94107 648-B7
CLYDESDALE DR
- LVMR 94551 696-A2
CLYMER LN
2500 FRMT 94538 753-D6
COACH DR
8100 OAK 94605 671-C1
COACHWOOD TER
- ORIN 94563 610-H3
COBB CT
5000 FRMT 94538 773-B1
COBBLER CT
4800 PLE 94566 714-F4
COBBLESTONE COM
- LVMR 94550 715-C1
COBBLESTONE CT
- SRMN 94583 673-A2
COBBLESTONE DR
100 SRMN 94583 673-A2
400 FRMT 94536 732-H6
2500 HAY 94545 731-G1
COBBLESTONE LN
- SRMN 94583 673-A2
COBBLESTONE PL
- HAY 94545 711-E5
COBURN CT
800 SLN 94578 691-B3
COCHEA DR
700 HAY 94544 712-A4
COCHISE CT
600 FRMT 94539 793-J2
4600 PLE 94588 694-G7
COCHISE WY
3100 PLE 94588 694-G7
COCHRANE AV
5000 OAK 94618 630-C6
COCO PALM DR
- FRMT 94538 773-A1
4800 FRMT 94538 753-A7
39600 FRMT 94538 752-J7
CODIROLI WY
- LVMR 94550 715-F5
CODMAN PL
- SF 94108 648-A5
CODORNICES RD
- BERK 94708 609-H7
CODY CT
- SRMN 94583 673-F7
4900 FRMT 94538 753-A7
CODY RD
500 HAY 94544 712-A4
COE AV
1200 SLN 94579 691-A4
COELHO CT
400 MPS 95035 794-A3
COELHO DR
15700 AlaC 94578 691-E5
15700 SLN 94578 691-E5
15800 AlaC 94580 691-E5
COELHO ST
100 MPS 95035 794-A4
E COG HILL TER
- DBLN 94568 694-G2
COGNINA CT
4300 FRMT 94536 752-J5
COHEN CT
- ALA 94501 649-A2
COHOE CT
2600 AlaC 94546 691-J6
COIT AV
43000 FRMT 94539 753-H7
COLA BALLENA
400 ALA 94501 669-E1
COLBERT PL
36300 NWK 94560 752-D6
COLBERT ST
36300 NWK 94560 752-D6
COLBOURN PL
5600 OAK 94619 651-B6
COLBY CT
- PLE 94566 714-E3
COLBY ST
400 AlaC 94580 691-D5
400 SLN 94578 691-D5
2900 BERK 94705 629-J4
3100 OAK 94618 629-J4
4100 FRMT 94538 773-D2
5900 OAK 94609 629-J4
COLD WATER DR
5500 AlaC 94552 692-D2
COLE PL
28100 HAY 94544 712-C6
COLE ST
1900 OAK 94601 670-F1
COLEBROOK CT
- DBLN 94568 694-G3
COLEBROOK LN
- DBLN 94568 694-G3
COLEEN ST
200 LVMR 94550 715-E1
COLEMAN AV
26000 HAY 94544 711-J5
COLEMAN PL
2800 FRMT 94555 732-E7
COLEMAN RD
- AlaC 94550 717-E6
COLEPORT LNDG
- ALA 94502 670-A5
COLERIDGE AV
28400 HAY 94544 712-B7
COLERIDGE COM
100 FRMT 94538 773-D2
COLERIDGE GRN
100 FRMT 94538 773-D3
COLERIDGE TER
100 FRMT 94538 773-D3
COLET TER
3600 FRMT 94536 752-J4
COLETAS WY
3700 CCCo 94514 637-E3
COLETTE PL
600 HAY 94544 712-B5
COLETTE ST
26500 HAY 94544 712-B5

COLFAX CT
37700 FRMT 94536 752-G5
COLGATE AV
200 CCCo 94708 609-G3
COLGATE DR
33500 UNC 94587 732-F5
COLGATE ST
14400 SLN 94579 691-A4
COLGATE WY
4100 LVMR 94550 696-A7
COLGETT DR
- OAK 94619 650-H4
COLIMA AV
10100 SRMN 94583 673-G5
COLIMA CT
4100 FRMT 94536 752-F2
COLIN P KELLY JR ST
- SF 94107 648-C6
COLISEUM WY
4200 OAK 94601 670-D2
5900 OAK 94621 670-E4
COLL CT
- SRMN 94583 673-F6
COLLEEN TER
34100 FRMT 94555 752-C2
COLLEGE AV
1000 ALA 94501 670-A3
1200 LVMR 94550 715-G2
2300 BERK 94704 629-J2
2700 BERK 94705 629-J4
3200 OAK 94618 629-J4
COLLEGE CT
1400 UNC 94587 732-F5
COLLEGE ST
100 AlaC 94580 691-D6
COLLIER DR
700 SLN 94577 671-B7
COLLIER PL
35400 FRMT 94536 752-F1
COLLIER CANYON RD
- CCCo 94588 675-A2
1800 AlaC 94551 675-C4
1800 AlaC 94551 695-C2
1800 CCCo 94551 675-C4
1800 AlaC 94551 694-J5
2600 LVMR 94551 695-C5
COLLIN CT
3400 FRMT 94536 752-H2
COLLINS AV
- SJCo 95391 (678-F2 See Page 677)
COLLINS CT
- SJCo 95391 (678-F2 See Page 677)
900 HAY 94544 732-B1
COLLINS DR
8000 OAK 94621 670-F5
COLMA CT
- SRMN 94583 673-C3
COLMAN ST
- SJCo 95391 (678-F2 See Page 677)
COLOMA ST
2100 OAK 94602 650-D4
COLONIAL CT
- SRMN 94583 673-H7
7900 PLE 94588 714-B6
COLONIAL DR
- AlaC 94580 691-E7
COLONIAL PARK CT
5200 FRMT 94538 773-C2
COLONY CT
29000 HAY 94544 712-B7
29000 HAY 94544 732-B1
COLONY VIEW PL
2700 AlaC 94541 712-C2
COLORADO AV
- BERK 94707 609-G4
COLORADO RD
29100 HAY 94544 712-C7
COLORADOS DR
500 OAK 94603 670-H7
COLORBURST CT
- UNC 94587 732-C4
COLTON BLVD
5600 OAK 94611 630-F6
COLTON PL
- OAK 94611 630-F7
COLUMBIA AV
200 CCCo 94708 609-G3
2000 RCH 94804 609-B4
43200 FRMT 94538 773-E2
COLUMBIA CIR
- BERK 94708 609-J7
COLUMBIA CT
27000 HAY 94542 712-D4
COLUMBIA DR
16800 AlaC 94552 672-C7
16800 AlaC 94552 692-C1
COLUMBIA WY
27100 HAY 94542 712-D4
COLUMBIA CREEK DR
500 SRMN 94582 673-J7
500 SRMN 94582 674-A7
COLUMBIAN DR
3300 OAK 94605 670-J1
3700 OAK 94605 671-A1
COLUMBIA SQUARE ST
- SF 94103 648-A7
COLUMBINE CT
2400 HAY 94545 731-H1
COLUMBINE DR
2400 HAY 94545 731-G1
4300 PLE 94588 713-J1
COLUMBINE PL
38100 NWK 94560 752-G7
COLUMBINE WY
1400 LVMR 94551 696-B3
COLUMBUS AV
- SF 94111 648-A4
- SF 94133 648-A4
1200 LVMR 94550 715-F3
COLUMBUS CIR
1300 MPS 95035 794-B4
COLUMBUS DR
1000 MPS 95035 794-B4
COLUSA AV
100 ELCR 94530 609-E3
100 CCCo 94707 609-E3
300 CCCo 94706 609-E3
400 BERK 94707 609-F5
5200 RCH 94804 609-B3
COLUSA ST
4900 UNC 94587 752-A1
COLUSA WY
400 LVMR 94551 695-E6
COLVILLE PL
34400 FRMT 94555 752-D1
COMANCHE CT
- FRMT 94539 773-H4
800 LVMR 94551 695-E7

COMANCHE WY
4400 PLE 94588 694-G7
COMET CIR
4200 UNC 94587 732-B6
COMMERCE CIR
7000 PLE 94588 693-J5
W COMMERCE CT
17400 SJCo 95377 (698-G3 See Page 677)
COMMERCE DR
5700 FRMT 94555 752-B3
7000 PLE 94588 693-J5
COMMERCE PL
2100 HAY 94545 711-E5
COMMERCE WY
400 LVMR 94551 696-E4
1500 OAK 94606 650-A6
W COMMERCE WY
17200 SJCo 95377 (698-H3 See Page 677)
COMMERCIAL ST
400 SF 94111 648-B5
700 SF 94108 648-A5
COMMODORE CT
- SRMN 94582 673-F1
COMMODORE DR
- EMVL 94608 629-C6
COMMODORE WY
- CCCo 94582 673-J2
- CCCo 94582 674-A2
COMMON RD
18000 AlaC 94546 692-B2
COMMONWEALTH DR
4600 OAK 94605 671-E4
COMPASS CV
- SLN 94579 711-A1
COMPTON CIR
100 SRMN 94583 673-C2
COMPTON CT
4000 LVMR 94550 696-A7
25500 HAY 94544 711-J4
33000 UNC 94587 752-A2
COMSTOCK COM
34700 FRMT 94555 752-D2
COMSTOCK CT
1500 BERK 94703 629-F1
2700 SRMN 94583 673-E6
COMSTOCK WY
1500 OAK 94606 650-B5
CONANT CT
27200 HAY 94544 711-J7
CONCANNON BLVD
- LVMR 94550 716-A2
400 LVMR 94550 715-J3
CONCHO CT
45400 FRMT 94539 773-H4
CONCHO DR
- FRMT 94539 773-H4
CONCORD AV
20200 AlaC 94541 691-G7
CONCORD PL
600 PLE 94566 714-G4
36300 NWK 94560 752-D6
CONCORD ST
700 PLE 94566 714-G4
36300 NWK 94560 752-D6
CONCORDIA ST
1600 ALA 94501 669-F1
1700 ALA 94501 649-E7
CONDADO CT
- SRMN 94583 673-C2
CONDE CT
5000 FRMT 94538 773-B1
CONDON ST
40200 FRMT 94538 753-C6
CONDOR CT
2700 UNC 94587 732-D6
CONDOR DR
33100 UNC 94587 732-D5
CONESTOGA LN
6500 DBLN 94568 694-A3
CONESTOGA PL
35600 NWK 94560 752-C5
CONGRESS AV
4500 OAK 94601 650-E7
4800 OAK 94601 670-E1
CONGRESS CT
3600 FRMT 94538 773-E1
CONGRESS WY
20600 AlaC 94546 691-J5
CONIFER ST
48200 FRMT 94539 793-J1
CONLEY DOWNS DR
- AlaC 94542 692-E7
CONLON TR
- CCCo 94708 609-G1
- RCH 94805 609-G1
CONNECTICUT ST
23000 HAY 94545 711-D6
CONNICK CT
- SRMN 94583 693-F1
CONNOLLY AV
15700 AlaC 94578 691-E5
15700 SLN 94578 691-E5
15700 AlaC 94580 691-E5
CONOVAN LN
35600 FRMT 94536 752-G1
CONRAD CT
- OAK 94611 630-E5
19900 AlaC 94546 692-A4
CONRAD ST
38000 FRMT 94536 753-A3
CONSTABLE COM
- FRMT 94536 753-B3
CONSTANCE CIR
3300 ALA 94501 670-C3
CONSTANCE PL
300 MRGA 94556 651-D1
CONSTELLATION DR
2300 HAY 94545 731-G1
CONSTITUTION CT
2000 SLN 94579 690-J6
CONSTITUTION DR
2100 LVMR 94551 695-B5
CONSTITUTION WY
1600 ALA 94501 669-G1
1700 ALA 94501 649-F7
CONTER CT
7700 DBLN 94568 693-G3
CONTESSA WY
26700 HAY 94545 711-G6
CONTI CT
3100 PLE 94566 715-C6
CONTINENTAL AV
2000 HAY 94545 711-E5
CONTINENTAL DR
43000 FRMT 94538 773-E2
CONTRA COSTA AV
700 BERK 94707 609-G6
3100 CCCo 94514 637-D3
4500 FRMT 94536 752-G4

CONTRA COSTA COM
- FRMT 94536 752-G4
CONTRA COSTA DR
900 ELCR 94530 609-D1
CONTRA COSTA PL
- OAK 94618 630-B5
CONTRA COSTA RD
800 ELCR 94530 609-E2
5900 OAK 94618 630-B5
CONTRACTORS PL
- LVMR 94550 696-A6
- LVMR 94551 696-A6
CONTRACTORS ST
- LVMR 94551 696-B6
CONTRERAS PL
3200 HAY 94542 712-E4
CONVAIR ST
1000 OAK 94621 670-D6
CONVERSE ST
4100 FRMT 94538 773-D2
CONWAY ST
1600 MPS 95035 794-A3
CONWAY TER
4900 FRMT 94555 752-D2
COOK LN
3300 ALA 94502 670-A7
COOK PL
2700 HAY 94545 711-F7
COOLIDGE AV
2100 OAK 94601 650-D6
2900 OAK 94602 650-E4
COOLIDGE CT
3700 AlaC 94552 692-G2
COOLIDGE TER
- OAK 94602 650-F3
COOPER AL
- SF 94108 648-A4
COOPER PL
2800 FRMT 94555 732-E6
COOPER WY
28700 HAY 94544 712-B7
COPA DEL ORO DR
2500 UNC 94587 732-E6
24900 HAY 94545 711-G5
COPE CT
4600 PLE 94566 714-D1
COPELAND LN
3800 FRMT 94538 753-C6
COPPA CT
- SLN 94579 691-A4
COPPER ST
- UNC 94587 732-H6
COPPER CREST COM
- LVMR 94551 695-C4
COPPERFIELD AV
300 HAY 94544 712-C7
COPPER RIDGE RD
- SRMN 94582 673-F2
COPPERSET RD
- SRMN 94582 673-H2
COQUILLE PL
- DBLN 94568 694-H3
CORAL AV
1500 SLN 94578 691-D3
CORAL CT
5600 FRMT 94538 773-B2
CORAL RD
9100 OAK 94603 670-F6
CORAL WY
7600 DBLN 94568 693-J2
CORAL BELL CT
- CCCo 94582 674-A2
CORAL DELL WK
- ALA 94501 669-H3
CORALLINE CT
4000 FRMT 94555 752-D1
CORAL REEF PL
1200 ALA 94501 669-H2
CORAL REEF RD
300 ALA 94501 669-G3
CORAL SEA ST
- ALA 94501 649-E7
CORBEL COM
- FRMT 94539 773-J7
CORBETT CT
15200 SLN 94578 691-D5
CORDAY CT
4600 PLE 94588 694-A6
CORDELIA ST
- SF 94133 648-A4
CORDELL CT
700 DNVL 94526 652-H1
CORDELL DR
300 DNVL 94526 652-G1
CORDES AV
- SJCo 95391 (678-F2 See Page 677)
CORDES CT
- SJCo 95391 (678-F3 See Page 677)
CORDOBA AV
1400 HAY 94544 732-A2
CORDOBA ST
1800 LVMR 94550 715-F4
CORDOVA PL
4400 FRMT 94536 752-F3
CORDOVA ST
2400 OAK 94602 650-D5
COREY CT
- SRMN 94583 673-E5
COREY PL E
2600 SRMN 94583 673-D6
COREY WY
19200 AlaC 94546 692-A4
CORFU PL
19000 AlaC 94541 691-F7
CORIANDER COM
1900 LVMR 94551 696-D2
CORINNE ST
- SJCo 95391 (678-E3 See Page 677)
CORINTH CT
7000 DBLN 94568 693-J3
CORINTHIA DR
400 MPS 95035 794-A5
CORK RD
- ALA 94502 669-H5
CORK OAK LN
28600 HAY 94544 712-C6
CORKWOOD ST
22700 HAY 94541 711-F3
CORMACK RD
2500 FRMT 94539 773-F2
CORMORANT CT
2700 UNC 94587 732-D6
CORMORANT LN
- ALA 94501 649-E7
CORMORANT TER
33700 FRMT 94555 732-D7
CORNAC TER
41000 FRMT 94539 753-E6

STREET	Block	City	ZIP	Pg-Grid
CORNELL AV				
	300	HAY	94544	732-F3
	400	ALB	94706	609-D5
	1100	BERK	94706	609-D5
	1200	BERK	94702	609-D5
	1400	BERK	94702	629-E1
CORNELL DR				
	1600	ALA	94501	670-B3
CORNELL ST				
	500	AlaC	94580	691-D5
CORNELL WY				
	4200	LVMR	94550	716-A1
CORNERSTONE COM				
	-	LVMR	94550	715-C1
CORNERSTONE CT				
	-	PLE	94588	714-F1
CORNFLOWER COM				
	1900	LVMR	94551	696-D2
CORNING CT				
	33000	UNC	94587	752-A2
CORNISH CT				
	3300	FRMT	94536	752-F1
CORNISH DR				
	35200	FRMT	94536	752-F1
CORNWALL CT				
	-	OAK	94611	650-G2
CORNWALL PL				
	35200	NWK	94560	752-D3
CORNWALL WY				
	-	SLN	94577	691-B2
CORNWALLIS CT				
	34300	FRMT	94555	732-E7
CORNWALLIS PL				
	34200	FRMT	94555	732-E7
CORONA CT				
	2300	BERK	94708	609-H6
	4900	UNC	94587	752-A2
	5100	PLE	94588	694-H4
CORONA PZ				
	200	UNC	94587	732-J5
CORONADO AV				
	4900	OAK	94618	629-J6
	4900	OAK	94609	629-J6
	5200	OAK	94611	629-J6
CORONADO CT				
	1000	LVMR	94550	715-F3
CORONADO DR				
	4500	FRMT	94536	752-F3
CORONADO LN				
	5900	PLE	94588	694-B7
CORONADO ST				
	300	ELCR	94530	609-D4
	27400	HAY	94545	711-H7
	27500	HAY	94545	731-H1
CORONADO WY				
	900	LVMR	94550	715-F3
CORONATION DR				
	2500	UNC	94587	732-C4
CORPORATE AV				
	26200	HAY	94545	711-E7
	26300	HAY	94545	731-F1
S CORPORATE CT				
	25700	SJCo	95377	(698-G3 See Page 677)
CORPORATE PL				
	3100	HAY	94545	731-F1
CORPORATE WY				
	800	FRMT	94539	773-G5
CORPUS CHRISTI RD				
	100	ALA	94501	649-D6
CORRAL CIR				
	100	SRMN	94583	673-B3
CORRAL ST				
	-	LVMR	94551	695-E5
W CORRAL HOLLOW RD Rt#-J2				
	15000	SJCo	95377	(738-D1 See Page 717)
	19600	SJCo	95377	(718-D7 See Page 717)
CORREGIDOR AV				
	-	OAK	94607	649-C2
CORRIEA CT				
	41000	FRMT	94539	753-E6
CORRIEA WY				
	2300	FRMT	94539	753-E6
CORRIGAN CT				
	38200	FRMT	94536	752-J4
CORRIGAN DR				
	4100	FRMT	94536	752-J4
CORRINE ST				
	400	HAY	94544	732-E2
CORRINNE CT				
	100	SRMN	94583	693-G1
CORRINNE PL				
	7500	SRMN	94583	693-G1
CORRINNE ST				
	7500	SRMN	94583	693-G1
CORSAIR BLVD				
	20300	HAY	94545	711-D3
CORSICA PL				
	36000	FRMT	94536	752-F3
CORT AV				
	5100	RCH	94804	609-A3
CORTE ALTAMIRA				
	6100	PLE	94566	714-B3
CORTE ANGELO				
	15800	AlaC	94580	711-B1
CORTE ANTONIO				
	6900	PLE	94566	714-A3
CORTE ARBOLES				
	5900	PLE	94566	714-B1
CORTE BALBOA				
	7100	PLE	94566	714-A2
CORTE BANDERA				
	2700	PLE	94566	714-B3
CORTE BARCELONA				
	6900	PLE	94566	714-A2
CORTE BELLA				
	2500	PLE	94566	714-B2
CORTE BLANCA				
	7000	PLE	94566	714-A2
CORTE BRAZOS				
	5800	PLE	94566	714-C3
CORTE BREVE				
	1800	AlaC	94580	711-B1
CORTE CALERA				
	6000	PLE	94566	714-B2
CORTE CARACAS				
	42900	FRMT	94539	753-J6
CORTE CAVA				
	-	LVMR	94551	695-G6
CORTE CERRITOS				
	5800	PLE	94566	714-B2
CORTE DE FLORES				
	6800	PLE	94566	714-A2
CORTE DE LA JARA				
	2300	PLE	94566	714-C3
CORTE DEL CAJON				
	5500	PLE	94566	714-C2
CORTE DEL CINO				
	3100	PLE	94566	714-B2
CORTE DEL MAR				
	7000	PLE	94566	714-A3
CORTE DEL ORO				
	7000	PLE	94566	714-A3
CORTE DEL RAY				
	6100	PLE	94566	714-B2
CORTE DEL SOL				
	900	FRMT	94539	773-J3
CORTE DEL VISTA				
	6700	PLE	94566	714-A2
CORTE DE ORINDA				
	1700	FRMT	94539	753-G7
CORTE ELENA				
	2600	PLE	94566	714-B3
CORTE ENANO				
	1800	AlaC	94580	711-B1
CORTE ENCANTO				
	-	DNVL	94526	652-H2
CORTE ENCINAS				
	6000	PLE	94566	714-B2
CORTE ENRICO				
	15500	AlaC	94580	691-C7
CORTE ESPADA				
	5900	PLE	94566	714-B2
CORTE ESPERANZA				
	6300	PLE	94566	714-B2
CORTE EULALIA				
	-	AlaC	94580	691-E7
	-	AlaC	94580	711-E1
CORTE FACIL				
	2500	PLE	94566	714-B2
CORTE FRANCESCA				
	15800	AlaC	94580	711-B1
CORTE FUEGO				
	6200	PLE	94566	714-B2
CORTE GALICIA				
	42900	FRMT	94539	753-H6
CORTE GERALDO				
	15800	AlaC	94580	711-B1
CORTE GLORIETA				
	-	LVMR	94551	695-F6
CORTE HABANA				
	42900	FRMT	94539	753-H6
CORTE HORNITOS				
	2100	AlaC	94580	711-B1
CORTE LIBRE				
	5700	PLE	94566	714-B2
CORTE MADRID				
	6900	PLE	94566	714-A2
CORTE MARGARITA				
	5800	PLE	94566	714-C2
CORTE MARIA				
	-	MRGA	94556	651-D1
CORTE MARIANA				
	15800	AlaC	94580	711-B1
CORTE MATEO				
	6900	PLE	94566	714-A3
CORTE MELINA				
	2200	PLE	94566	714-C2
CORTE MENTE				
	5800	PLE	94566	714-B1
CORTE MERCADO				
	6900	PLE	94566	714-A3
CORTE MONTANAS				
	6000	PLE	94566	714-B2
CORTE MONTEREY				
	6900	PLE	94566	714-A3
CORTE MUNRAS				
	6800	PLE	94566	714-B1
CORTE NINA				
	7000	PLE	94566	714-A3
CORTE NOGAL				
	-	DNVL	94526	652-H2
CORTE NUEVO				
	6800	PLE	94566	714-A2
CORTE PACIFICA				
	6900	PLE	94566	714-A2
CORTE PADRE				
	6100	PLE	94566	714-B2
CORTE PALOMA				
	5400	PLE	94566	714-C2
CORTE PONDEROSA				
	2700	PLE	94566	714-B3
CORTE REAL AV				
	1900	OAK	94611	630-E7
	1900	OAK	94611	650-E1
CORTE REINA COM				
	-	LVMR	94551	695-F6
CORTE RICARDO				
	2100	PLE	94566	714-C2
CORTE RIVERA				
	2500	PLE	94566	714-B3
CORTE ROSA				
	7000	PLE	94566	714-A3
CORTE RUBIOLO				
	3600	AlaC	94546	692-A4
CORTE SALCEDO				
	6800	PLE	94566	714-B3
CORTE SAN BLAS				
	2700	PLE	94566	714-B2
CORTE SAN PABLO				
	200	FRMT	94539	753-H6
CORTE SANTA BARBARA				
	41900	FRMT	94539	753-G5
CORTE SANTA INES				
	41800	FRMT	94539	753-G5
CORTE SANTA MARIA				
	6700	PLE	94566	714-A2
CORTE SANTIAGO				
	6100	PLE	94566	714-B2
CORTE SIERRA				
	5500	PLE	94566	714-C2
CORTE SONADA				
	6800	PLE	94566	714-B2
CORTE SONORA				
	5500	PLE	94566	714-C2
CORTE SUENO				
	-	LVMR	94551	695-F6
CORTE TRANCAS				
	6100	PLE	94566	714-B2
CORTE ULISSE				
	15800	AlaC	94580	711-B1
CORTE VENADO				
	5900	PLE	94566	714-B2
CORTE VERA CRUZ				
	2700	PLE	94566	714-B3
CORTE VERDE				
	6900	PLE	94566	714-A2
	42900	FRMT	94539	753-H6
CORTE VIDA				
	2400	PLE	94566	714-B2
CORTE YOLANDA				
	15800	AlaC	94580	711-B1
CORTEZ AV				
	4700	FRMT	94536	752-F4
CORTEZ CT				
	-	OAK	94611	630-F7
	800	LVMR	94550	715-F2
	1800	PLE	94566	714-E1
	2700	AlaC	94546	691-J5
	4300	UNC	94587	731-H5
CORTEZ ST				
	1100	HAY	94544	712-A7
	1600	MPS	95035	794-A3
CORTINA CT				
	4100	PLE	94588	694-C6
CORTINA WY				
	2800	UNC	94587	732-A4
CORTLAND WY				
	800	LVMR	94551	695-E6
CORTO CT				
	11600	DBLN	94568	693-F4
CORTO MONTEREY				
	4400	UNC	94587	731-H6
CORTONA DR				
	100	SRMN	94582	673-G3
CORUM CT				
	2400	UNC	94587	732-F6
CORVALLIS ST				
	14000	SLN	94579	691-A4
CORWIN CT				
	4700	PLE	94588	694-A6
CORY LN				
	-	DBLN	94568	693-E5
COSGRAVE AV				
	2800	OAK	94605	671-A3
COSMIC CT				
	3700	FRMT	94538	753-C6
COSMIC PL				
	3800	FRMT	94538	753-C6
COSMIC WY				
	3500	FRMT	94538	753-C6
COSMOS COM				
	5500	FRMT	94538	773-A2
COSTA DR				
	3200	AlaC	94541	692-D7
COSTA WY				
	39700	FRMT	94538	753-B6
COSTA MESA TER				
	-	FRMT	94539	794-B1
COSTANOAN CT				
	-	ALA	94501	669-H1
COSTELLA ST				
	15000	SLN	94579	691-A6
COSTIGAN CIR				
	500	MPS	95035	794-B5
COTATI ST				
	2100	HAY	94542	712-D4
COTELLA CT				
	-	ALA	94502	669-J7
COTTAGE CT				
	3700	AlaC	94546	691-J3
COTTAGE ST				
	1400	ALA	94501	669-H1
COTTER ST				
	10700	OAK	94605	671-E4
COTTER WY				
	1200	HAY	94541	691-H7
COTTERELL CT				
	2000	PLE	94566	714-C4
COTTON AV				
	6100	NWK	94560	752-F7
COTTON CT				
	18400	AlaC	94552	692-D3
COTTON ST				
	1000	OAK	94606	650-A7
COTTON MILL WY				
	-	PLE	94566	714-C4
COTTONWOOD AV				
	800	HAY	94541	711-F3
COTTON WOOD CIR				
	6500	DBLN	94568	694-A2
COTTONWOOD CT				
	400	LVMR	94551	715-E1
COTTONWOOD LN				
	7500	PLE	94588	713-J1
COTTONWOOD ST				
	1700	UNC	94587	732-C4
	48200	FRMT	94539	793-J1
COUGAR CIR				
	44900	FRMT	94539	773-J3
COUGAR DR				
	-	FRMT	94539	773-J3
COUNTESS CT				
	7900	DBLN	94568	693-G3
COUNTESS ST				
	8300	DBLN	94568	693-G3
COUNTRY COM				
	38600	FRMT	94536	753-A4
COUNTRY DR				
	2000	FRMT	94536	753-A3
	4100	FRMT	94536	752-J5
COUNTRY ISL				
	500	ALA	94501	669-G2
COUNTRY LN				
	-	LVMR	94550	716-A2
	700	AlaC	94566	734-C1
COUNTRY TER				
	38600	FRMT	94536	753-A4
COUNTRYBROOK LP				
	600	SRMN	94583	673-F4
COUNTRY CLUB CIR				
	-	AlaC	94566	714-C7
COUNTRY CLUB DR				
	1200	MPS	95035	794-C4
	5500	OAK	94618	630-A5
COUNTRY CLUB PL				
	-	ORIN	94563	610-G7
COUNTRY CREEK CT				
	900	SRMN	94582	674-A7
COUNTRYSIDE CT				
	-	MPS	95035	794-C4
COUNTY RD				
	-	ALA	94502	670-A6
COURAGEOUS CT				
	-	ALA	94501	649-G7
COURT ST				
	300	ALA	94501	670-A3
COURTHOUSE DR				
	3100	UNC	94587	732-A4
COURTHOUSE PL				
	3200	UNC	94587	732-A5
COURTLAND AV				
	1900	OAK	94601	670-D1
	2200	OAK	94601	650-E7
	2900	OAK	94619	650-F7
COURTNEY AV				
	1500	PLE	94588	694-F7
COURTNEY LN				
	-	AlaC	94542	712-D1
COVE CT				
	300	SLN	94578	691-C6
COVE RD				
	-	ALA	94502	669-J5
COVELITE LN				
	200	LVMR	94550	715-D2
COVENT LN				
	-	OAK	94608	649-E1
COVENTRY CIR				
	800	MPS	95035	794-A5
COVENTRY CT				
	3300	FRMT	94536	752-J3
	4300	UNC	94587	731-J5
COVENTRY LN				
	26100	HAY	94545	711-G6
COVENTRY RD				
	200	CCCo	94707	609-E4
COVENTRY WY				
	800	MPS	95035	794-A5
	4200	UNC	94587	731-J5
COVEY WY				
	2400	LVMR	94550	715-H3
COVINA WY				
	700	FRMT	94539	773-H7
COVINGTON DR				
	41500	FRMT	94539	753-F6
COVINGTON ST				
	-	OAK	94605	671-C6
COVINGTON WY				
	500	LVMR	94551	695-E6
COWBOY AL				
	400	LVMR	94550	715-H1
COWELL PL				
	-	SF	94111	648-B4
COWELL ST				
	16500	AlaC	94578	691-G4
COWING RD				
	8200	AlaC	94552	692-G5
	8200	AlaC	94552	693-A6
COWPER AV				
	-	CCCo	94707	609-F2
	-	CCCo	94805	609-F2
COWPER ST				
	1100	BERK	94702	629-E2
COYOTE CT				
	-	SRMN	94582	673-G3
COYOTE PL				
	-	SRMN	94582	673-F3
COYOTE RD				
	45300	FRMT	94539	773-H4
COYOTE ST				
	700	MPS	95035	793-J6
CRAFT AV				
	800	ELCR	94530	609-F2
	14600	SLN	94578	691-D3
CRAGFORD PL				
	-	DBLN	94568	694-H3
CRAGMONT AV				
	400	BERK	94708	609-H5
CRAIG AV				
	-	PDMT	94611	650-B1
CRAIG CT				
	-	PLE	94566	714-E3
	2500	AlaC	94546	692-B7
CRAIG ST				
	38200	FRMT	94536	753-A3
CRAIGLEE WY				
	-	SRMN	94582	674-C3
CRAIGTOWN LN				
	-	DBLN	94568	693-E5
CRANBROOK PL				
	-	DBLN	94568	694-G2
CRANBROOK ST				
	15500	SLN	94579	691-A7
	15600	SLN	94579	711-A1
CRANDALLWOOD DR				
	4900	FRMT	94555	752-C2
CRANE AV				
	600	LVMR	94551	695-E7
	5100	AlaC	94546	692-C3
CRANE CT				
	-	ALA	94502	669-J5
	-	ORIN	94563	610-G3
CRANE TER				
	100	ORIN	94563	610-G3
	38700	FRMT	94536	753-D2
CRANE WY				
	3200	OAK	94602	650-G3
CRANEFORD WY				
	-	SRMN	94582	674-C3
CRANE RIDGE RD				
	5400	AlaC	94550	716-G6
	7500	AlaC	94550	736-H1
	8300	AlaC	94550	(737-A2 See Page 717)
CRANFORD LN				
	7800	DBLN	94568	693-H3
CRANFORD WY				
	11700	OAK	94605	671-D6
CRANLEIGH CT				
	-	CCCo	94583	673-B5
CRANWOOD CT				
	3100	PLE	94588	694-F6
CRATER RD				
	2700	LVMR	94550	715-G5
CRATER LAKE AV				
	1500	MPS	95035	794-E7
CRATER LAKE CT				
	6100	PLE	94588	714-B1
CRAVEN CT				
	400	HAY	94541	711-G3
CRAWDAD CT				
	3500	UNC	94587	732-A5
CRAWFORD CT				
	46600	FRMT	94539	773-H5
CRAWFORD PL				
	19500	AlaC	94546	692-A4
CRAWFORD ST				
	46700	FRMT	94539	773-H6
CRAYCROFT CT				
	48400	FRMT	94539	793-J1
CRAYCROFT DR				
	300	FRMT	94539	793-J1
CRAYDON CIR				
	9000	SRMN	94583	693-J1
CRAYDON CT				
	-	SRMN	94583	693-H1
CREE CT				
	-	SRMN	94583	673-D5
	44900	FRMT	94539	773-G3
CREE RD				
	1400	FRMT	94539	773-G3
CREED RD				
	800	OAK	94610	650-C3
CREED ST				
	1000	MPS	95035	794-B4
CREEDON CIR				
	200	ALA	94502	669-H5
E CREEK CT				
	-	PLE	94566	714-D5
CREEK RD				
	1700	LVMR	94550	715-G2
	27100	HAY	94544	712-A6
CREEKSIDE CIR				
	300	OAK	94603	690-G1
CREEKSIDE CT				
	2400	HAY	94542	712-D4
	11200	DBLN	94568	693-E3
CREEKSIDE DR				
	-	PLE	94588	693-H6
	-	SRMN	94583	673-A2
	3000	SLN	94578	691-C5
	7700	DBLN	94568	693-F3
CREEKSIDE TER				
	37100	FRMT	94536	752-H2
CREEK TRAIL DR				
	1200	PLE	94566	714-D3
CREEK VIEW CT				
	3300	AlaC	94541	692-D6
CREEKVIEW DR				
	-	DBLN	94568	694-E2
CREEKWOOD CT				
	3100	PLE	94588	713-J2
CREEKWOOD DR				
	4600	FRMT	94555	752-D2
CREEKWOOD TER				
	34600	FRMT	94555	752-D2
CREELY AV				
	5000	RCH	94804	609-B2
CREELY PTH				
	5000	RCH	94804	609-A2
CREIGHTON WY				
	300	OAK	94619	650-H4
CRELLIN RD				
	800	PLE	94566	714-G4
CREOLE PL				
	26900	HAY	94545	711-G7
CRESCENT AV				
	1400	AlaC	94546	691-J7
	1400	AlaC	94546	692-A7
CRESCENT CT				
	2600	LVMR	94550	715-H3
CRESCENT DR				
	-	ORIN	94563	610-E6
CRESCENT ST				
	400	OAK	94610	649-J2
CRESCENT TER				
	-	FRMT	94536	753-B2
CRESCENT WY				
	900	AlaC	94586	734-B4
CRESPI CT				
	3500	PLE	94566	714-G5
	4000	SLN	94578	691-C5
CRESPI DR				
	800	SLN	94578	691-C5
CREST AV				
	7700	OAK	94605	671-A2
	18100	AlaC	94546	691-G3
	18100	AlaC	94578	691-G3
S CREST AV				
	2500	AlaC	94578	691-G4
	2500	AlaC	94546	691-G4
CREST CT				
	2600	UNC	94587	732-C4
	4000	PLE	94588	694-A7
	4000	PLE	94588	714-A1
CREST LN				
	32200	UNC	94587	732-C4
CREST RD				
	-	PDMT	94611	650-D2
CRESTA LN				
	11400	DBLN	94568	693-F4
CRESTA BLANCA				
	-	ORIN	94563	610-F7
CRESTA BLANCA DR				
	3000	PLE	94566	714-H4
CRESTA BLANCA RD				
	-	AlaC	94550	735-J2
	-	AlaC	94550	736-A2
CRESTED OAK CT				
	-	SRMN	94583	673-E7
CRESTFIELD CIR				
	25500	AlaC	94552	692-E6
CRESTFIELD CT				
	-	AlaC	94552	692-E7
CRESTFIELD DR				
	-	AlaC	94552	692-E7
CRESTLINE RD				
	2000	PLE	94566	714-C1
CRESTLINE WY				
	5200	PLE	94566	714-C1
CRESTMONT AV				
	5500	LVMR	94551	696-C3
	7600	NWK	94560	752-C6
CRESTMONT DR				
	-	OAK	94619	650-H4
	-	OAK	94602	650-H4
CRESTON RD				
	600	BERK	94708	609-H4
CRESTON ST				
	40700	FRMT	94538	773-B1
CRESTRIDGE TER				
	-	DBLN	94568	694-F3
CREST VIEW COM				
	-	FRMT	94539	794-B1
CRESTVIEW CT				
	2400	AlaC	94578	691-G4
CREST VIEW DR				
	100	ORIN	94563	630-J3
CRESTVIEW DR				
	-	OAK	94619	651-B7
CREST VIEW TER				
	100	ORIN	94563	630-J3
CRESTWOOD CT				
	5000	PLE	94566	714-D2
CRESTWOOD DR				
	6400	AlaC	94552	692-F3
CRESTWOOD PL				
	200	SRMN	94583	673-F6
CRESTWOOD ST				
	4000	FRMT	94538	773-D2
CRICKET HILL CT				
	-	HAY	94541	712-A2
CRIMSON CIR				
	5400	FRMT	94538	773-A1
CRIPPS PL				
	36000	FRMT	94536	752-F3
CRISFIELD LN				
	4100	PLE	94566	714-E1
CRIST ST				
	2500	ALA	94501	670-A3
CRISTOBAL WY				
	4000	PLE	94566	714-E1
CRISTY WY				
	4400	AlaC	94546	691-J3
	4400	AlaC	94546	692-A3
CRITTENDEN LN				
	2100	MTVW	94043	792-A7
CRITTENDEN ST				
	5400	OAK	94601	670-E2
CROAK RD				
	3400	DBLN	94568	694-H5
	3400	DBLN	94588	694-H5
CROAKER CT				
	-	SF	94130	648-E1
CROATIAN WY				
	33200	UNC	94587	732-D5
CROCE CT				
	4200	PLE	94566	714-F4
CROCKER AV				
	-	PDMT	94611	650-C1
	100	PDMT	94610	650-C2
	200	OAK	94610	650-C2
	1400	HAY	94544	732-C2
CROCKETT CT				
	4500	FRMT	94538	753-B7
CROCKETT DR				
	-	MRGA	94556	651-F1
CROCKETT PL				
	5100	OAK	94602	650-H3
CROCKETT ST				
	40100	FRMT	94538	753-B7
CROCUS CT				
	37600	NWK	94560	752-F7
CROCUS DR				
	600	SLN	94578	691-C4
CROCUS WY				
	5100	LVMR	94551	696-B4
CROFTERS CT				
	3700	PLE	94588	694-F5
CROFTON AV				
	500	OAK	94610	650-A2
	500	PDMT	94610	650-A2
CROLLS GARDEN CT				
	100	ALA	94501	669-F1
CROMMELIN RD				
	25000	HAY	94545	711-D6
CROMWELL AV				
	-	DBLN	94568	694-A2
CROMWELL PL				
	3000	HAY	94542	712-D3
	34100	FRMT	94555	732-E7
CROMWELL ST				
	900	LVMR	94551	695-G6
CROMWELL WY				
	2200	LVMR	94551	695-G6
CRONIN CIR				
	7200	DBLN	94568	693-G4
CRONIN TER				
	34200	FRMT	94555	752-C2
CROSBY AV				
	2000	OAK	94601	650-D7
CROSBY DR				
	9600	PLE	94588	693-F6
CROSBY PL				
	600	SLN	94579	691-B5
CROSBY ST				
	14700	SLN	94579	691-B5
CROSS RD				
	100	OAK	94618	630-B5
	3000	AlaC	94550	(697-A7 See Page 677)
	3000	AlaC	94550	716-H3
	3000	AlaC	94550	717-A1
CROSS CAMPUS RD				
	-	BERK	94720	629-H2
CROSS CREEK CIR				
	-	DBLN	94568	694-A2
CROSS CREEK PL				
	1500	LVMR	94550	715-G2
CROSSING CT				
	-	HAY	94544	711-H4
CROSSPOINTE COM				
	38400	FRMT	94536	753-G3
CROSSRIDGE CT				
	600	ORIN	94563	610-H6
CROSSRIDGE PL				
	600	ORIN	94563	610-H6
CROSSRIDGE RD				
	7900	DBLN	94568	694-A2
CROSSRIDGE TER				
	-	ORIN	94563	610-H6
CROSSROADS PL				
	-	LVMR	94550	715-D4
S CROSSWAYS				
	-	BERK	94705	630-A4
CROW CT				
	1600	FRMT	94539	773-G4
	4600	PLE	94588	694-G7
CROW CANYON CT				
	-	SRMN	94583	673-B1
CROW CANYON PL				
	2000	SRMN	94583	673-C1
	4400	AlaC	94552	692-C5
CROW CANYON RD				
	2300	SRMN	94583	672-G3
	2300	SRMN	94583	673-D1
	2300	CCCo	94583	672-G3
	2300	CCCo	94583	673-A2
	3400	DNVL	94526	673-D1
	3400	SRMN	94582	673-D1
	4400	AlaC	94552	692-E2
	5700	AlaC	94552	672-G3
CROW CREEK RD				
	19800	AlaC	94552	692-D4
CROWLEY DR				
	24300	HAY	94545	711-F4
CROWN AV				
	6200	OAK	94611	630-D6
CROWN CT				
	-	FRMT	94536	732-J4
	2600	UNC	94587	732-B4
	5200	AlaC	94552	692-D4
CROWN DR				
	1300	ALA	94501	669-F2
CROWN TER				
	-	FRMT	94536	732-J4
CROWN RIDGE COM				
	-	FRMT	94539	794-B2
CROWN RIDGE CT				
	-	OAK	94605	651-A7
CROXTON AV				
	-	OAK	94611	649-H1
CROYDEN CT				
	2400	SLN	94577	691-B2
CROYDEN PL				
	2200	SLN	94577	691-B2
CROYDON CIR				
	-	PDMT	94611	650-D2
CROYDON PL				
	4900	NWK	94560	752-E3
CRUCILLO CT				
	47100	FRMT	94539	773-J6
CRUISER CT				
	-	SLN	94579	711-A2
CRUISER DR				
	-	SLN	94579	711-A2
CRUZ CT				
	40900	FRMT	94539	753-E6
CRYER ST				
	2200	HAY	94545	711-F7
CRYSTAL CIR				
	1100	LVMR	94550	715-D3
CRYSTAL CT				
	-	MPS	95035	793-J7
	-	MPS	95035	794-A7
	600	PLE	94566	714-E5
	1100	LVMR	94550	715-D3
	2800	AlaC	94546	692-B6
CRYSTAL LN				
	700	PLE	94566	714-E5
CRYSTAL TER				
	4900	FRMT	94555	752-A3
CRYSTAL WY				
	-	BERK	94708	609-H6
CRYSTAL GATE COMS				
	-	HAY	94544	711-H3
CRYSTAL GATE CT				
	-	HAY	94544	711-H3
CRYSTALINE DR				
	400	FRMT	94539	773-H4
CRYSTALINE PL				
	500	FRMT	94539	773-H5
CRYSTAL RIDGE CT				
	5000	OAK	94605	671-A1
CRYSTAL SPRINGS CT				
	-	NWK	94560	752-B7
CRYSTAL SPRINGS DR				
	-	NWK	94560	752-B6
CUBBERLEY CT				
	28300	HAY	94545	731-H2
CUBBERLEY ST				
	28300	HAY	94545	731-H2
CUENCA CT				
	-	SRMN	94583	673-C3
	36600	FRMT	94536	752-J1
CUENCA DR				
	2400	SRMN	94583	673-C2
CUENCA WY				
	600	FRMT	94536	752-J1
	600	FRMT	94536	753-A1
CUESTA TR				
	-	CCCo	94583	652-C3
CULL CANYON RD				
	10000	AlaC	94546	652-B7
	10500	AlaC	94552	652-B7
	11000	AlaC	94552	672-B1
	16200	AlaC	94552	692-D2
CULLENS CT				
	-	SRMN	94582	674-C4
CULP AV				
	200	HAY	94544	711-J4
	200	HAY	94544	712-A4
CULVER CT				
	-	ORIN	94563	630-J4
	4100	OAK	94619	650-E6
CULVER PL				
	1400	AlaC	94580	711-C1
CULVER ST				
	4100	OAK	94619	650-F6
CUMANA CIR				
	500	UNC	94587	732-C6
CUMBERLAND AV				
	1000	SLN	94579	691-A5
CUMBERLAND CT				
	200	ALA	94502	669-J5
CUMBERLAND WY				
	100	ALA	94502	669-J5
CUMBERLAND GAP CT				
	3400	PLE	94588	714-B1
CUMBERLAND PARK CT				
	5400	FRMT	94538	773-C2
CUMORA AV				
	16600	AlaC	94580	691-F6
CUNNINGHAM CT				
	5100	AlaC	94546	692-B3
CUNNINGHAM ST				
	4600	OAK	94619	650-G6
CUPFLOWER CT				
	2800	PLE	94588	694-H4
CURIE PL				
	6700	NWK	94560	752-C5
CURIE ST				
	-	FRMT	94538	773-C4
CURLEW CT				
	-	ALA	94501	649-F7
	2700	PLE	94566	714-C1
CURLEW RD				
	500	LVMR	94551	695-D7
CURRAN AV				
	3000	OAK	94602	650-D5
CURRAN WY				
	3400	OAK	94602	650-E5
CURRANT WY				
	900	HAY	94545	711-G5
S CURRIER DR				
	23000	SJCo	95304	(678-J6 See Page 677)
CURRY AV				
	7400	ELCR	94530	609-E4
CURRY ST				
	2600	PLE	94588	694-G6
CURTIS CIR				
	3200	PLE	94588	694-C7
CURTIS ST				
	500	ALB	94706	609-E5
	500	CCCo	94706	609-E5
	1100	BERK	94706	609-E7
	1200	BERK	94702	609-E7
	1200	BERK	94702	629-E1
	2000	OAK	94607	649-F3
	5000	FRMT	94538	773-B1
	21300	HAY	94545	711-E4
CURTNER CT				
	400	MPS	95035	794-A3
CURTNER DR				
	400	MPS	95035	794-A4
CURTNER RD				
	100	FRMT	94539	773-J5
	1100	FRMT	94539	774-A5
CUSHING PKWY				
	4200	FRMT	94538	773-C5
CUSHING RD				
	4700	FRMT	94538	773-D6
CUSTER RD				
	400	HAY	94544	712-A4
CUSTER ST				
	3500	OAK	94601	650-D6
CUSTOM HOUSE PL				
	-	SF	94111	648-B4
CUTHBERT AV				
	3100	OAK	94602	650-D5
CUTLER AV				
	2700	FRMT	94536	752-G1
CUTTER CT				
	-	SRMN	94583	673-D6
CUTTER WY				
	800	BERK	94710	629-D3
CUTTING BLVD				
	3600	RCH	94804	609-A1
	5100	ELCR	94530	609-B1
CUTTING CT				
	900	RCH	94804	609-A1
CYCLAMEN CT				
	1900	HAY	94545	711-F6
CYCLOTRON RD				
	-	BERK	94709	629-J1
	-	BERK	94720	629-J1
	-	BERK	94720	630-A1
	-	OAK	94720	630-A1
CYGNUS CT				
	32300	UNC	94587	732-A6
CYNTHIA CT				
	22100	AlaC	94541	692-C6
CYPRESS AV				
	4500	RCH	94804	609-A2
	5100	ELCR	94530	609-B2
	24800	HAY	94544	711-H4

STREET
Block City ZIP Pg-Grid

CYPRESS CT
8300 DBLN 94568 693-H1
CYPRESS FRWY I-880
- EMVL - 629-D7
- OAK - 629-E7
- OAK - 649-C3
CYPRESS PTH
- RCH 94804 609-B2
CYPRESS ST
- OAK 94608 629-E7
100 ALA 94501 649-E7
600 OAK 94607 649-E2
1400 BERK 94703 609-F7
2800 OAK 94608 649-E2
14300 SLN 94579 690-J4
14400 SLN 94579 691-A5
CYPRESS CREEK CT
7800 PLE 94588 714-B5
CYPRESS HAWK CT
- SRMN 94582 673-G1
CYPRESS POINT DR
5900 LVMR 94551 696-C2
36300 NWK 94560 752-C6
CYPRESS RANCH RD
- AlaC 94552 692-E4
CYPRUS DR
36200 FRMT 94536 752-F3
CYRIL MAGIN ST
- SF 94102 648-A6
CYRIL MAGNIN ST
- SF 94102 648-A6

D

D RD
1000 AlaC 94586 734-C3
D ST
- UNC 94587 732-F4
200 FRMT 94536 753-A1
300 HAY 94541 711-J1
300 HAY 94544 711-J2
1100 HAY 94541 712-A1
1700 AlaC 94541 692-C7
1700 AlaC 94541 712-B1
8200 OAK 94621 670-G4
9000 OAK 94603 670-H5
DABNER ST
- SLN 94577 690-J1
DAFFODIL WY
2600 UNC 94587 752-G1
2600 UNC 94587 732-G7
4300 LVMR 94551 696-A4
DAGGETT AV
400 UNC 94587 732-G5
DAGNINO RD
- AlaC 94551 695-H2
- LVMR 94551 695-H2
3800 AlaC 94551 676-A7
3800 AlaC 94551 696-A1
DAHILL LN
1700 HAY 94541 692-A7
DAHLIA COM
2000 LVMR 94551 696-D2
DAHLIA CT
500 SLN 94578 691-C4
DAHLIA DR
100 ALA 94502 670-A6
37600 NWK 94560 752-F7
DAILY CT
1600 SLN 94577 691-D2
DAILY DR
1200 SLN 94577 691-D2
DAIRY AV
6100 NWK 94560 752-E7
DAISY CT
2900 UNC 94587 732-F7
3300 HAY 94542 712-E4
DAISY LN
1300 LVMR 94551 696-B4
DAISY ST
2900 UNC 94587 732-F7
3800 OAK 94619 650-G6
18900 UNC 94587 752-F1
DAISYFIELD CT
500 LVMR 94551 715-E1
DAISYFIELD DR
- LVMR 94551 715-D1
DAKIN CT
- PLE 94566 714-E6
DAKOTA CT
800 LVMR 94551 695-E7
DAKOTA ST
3000 OAK 94602 650-E5
DALE AV
100 PDMT 94610 650-A1
DALE PL
3800 OAK 94619 650-E6
DALE ST
24600 HAY 94544 711-J3
DALEWOOD CT
36100 NWK 94560 752-E5
DALEWOOD DR
300 ORIN 94563 610-H3
35800 NWK 94560 752-D5
DALEWOOD TER
- ORIN 94563 610-J3
DALGO RD
100 FRMT 94539 753-E4
DALI ST
4200 FRMT 94536 752-F3
DALLAS CT
4200 FRMT 94536 752-G3
DALMALLY LN
- DBLN 94568 693-E5
DALMATIA PL
19000 AlaC 94546 691-G4
DALTON AV
5400 LVMR 94551 696-C2
5800 AlaC 94551 696-C2
DALTON COM
3500 FRMT 94536 752-J4
DALTON CT
33700 UNC 94587 732-E5
DALTON DR
1700 MPS 95035 794-D7
DALTON WY
- CCCo 94582 674-B5
1700 UNC 94587 732-F6
DALTON CREEK WY
5700 PLE 94566 714-E6
DAMIANO CT
5100 PLE 94588 694-H4
DAMON CT
- ALA 94502 670-A5
DAMPHIER CT
- DBLN 94568 694-G4
DAMUTH ST
2000 OAK 94602 650-D4
DANA CIR
700 LVMR 94550 696-B7
700 LVMR 94550 716-B1
DANA CT
4900 LVMR 94550 716-B1
6300 PLE 94588 694-A7
6500 AlaC 94552 692-F3
32200 UNC 94587 731-J7
DANA ST
300 FRMT 94539 753-H7
2300 BERK 94704 629-H2
2700 BERK 94705 629-H4
6300 OAK 94609 629-H4
DANBROOK CT
- ALA 94502 669-J5
- ALA 94502 670-A5
DANBURY ST
- OAK 94605 671-C7
DANBURY PARK DR
1700 PLE 94566 714-C4
DANFORTH LN
26100 HAY 94545 711-G6
DANIA LN
25000 HAY 94545 711-F5
DANIEL AV
- SJCo 95391 (678-F3 See Page 677)
DANIEL CT
1200 MPS 95035 794-C5
DANIELLE WY
4100 AlaC 94546 691-H2
DANIELS DR
1500 SLN 94577 671-C7
DANNY CT
- SRMN 94582 673-F1
DANTE AV
9900 OAK 94603 671-A5
DANTE PL
35500 FRMT 94536 752-G1
DANTI CT
26500 HAY 94545 731-F1
DANVILLA CT
100 DNVL 94526 652-J2
DANVILLE BLVD
600 DNVL 94526 652-H1
DANVILLE ST
32900 UNC 94587 752-A1
DANVILLE OAK PL
- DNVL 94526 652-J1
DANZON CT
41300 FRMT 94539 753-G5
DAPHNE CT
- ORIN 94563 610-J5
6400 NWK 94560 772-G1
DAPHNE DR
5700 LVMR 94550 696-D7
DARBY COM
- FRMT 94539 773-E2
DARCELLE CT
4600 UNC 94587 731-J7
DARCELLE DR
4500 UNC 94587 731-J6
DARCREST CT
19300 AlaC 94546 692-B4
DARCY CT
6400 OAK 94609 629-H4
DARIAN CT
6900 DBLN 94568 693-J2
DARIEN AV
300 OAK 94603 670-G7
DARIO TR
25500 AlaC 94541 712-D2
DARIUS CT
1500 SLN 94577 691-D2
DARIUS WY
2600 SLN 94577 691-D2
14600 AlaC 94578 691-D2
DARLENE CT
2700 AlaC 94546 691-G4
4700 UNC 94587 731-J7
DARLENE WY
32300 UNC 94587 731-J7
32300 UNC 94587 732-A7
32300 UNC 94587 752-A1
DARNBY DR
2700 OAK 94611 650-G1
DARNEL CT
38400 FRMT 94536 752-J4
DARRELL PL
- SF 94133 648-A4
DARROW CT
4500 FRMT 94536 752-H4
DARTMOOR LN
600 HAY 94544 712-D7
DARTMOUTH AV
1200 SLN 94579 691-A4
33700 UNC 94587 732-F5
DARTMOUTH DR
- OAK 94705 630-B3
DARTMOUTH ST
1100 ALB 94706 609-E6
DARTMOUTH WY
3800 LVMR 94550 695-J7
3900 LVMR 94550 696-A7
DARVON AV
36200 NWK 94560 752-F4
DARVON CT
36600 NWK 94560 752-F5
DARWIN AV
1300 LVMR 94550 715-G3
DARWIN DR
3000 FRMT 94555 732-E7
3400 FRMT 94555 752-E1
DARWIN ST
2300 HAY 94545 711-F7
DARYL AV
16700 AlaC 94580 691-E6
DASHELLE HAMMETT ST
- SF 94108 648-A5
DASHWOOD AV
2200 OAK 94605 670-H3
DASSEL RD
- FRMT 94536 753-C1
DATE ST
9100 OAK 94603 670-F6
DAUPHINE AV
36800 FRMT 94536 752-G3
DAVALOS CT
- SRMN 94583 673-C3
DAVENANT CT
3400 FRMT 94536 752-G2
DAVENPORT AV
4400 OAK 94619 650-G6
4800 OAK 94613 650-G6
DAVENPORT PL
4700 FRMT 94538 773-D3
DAVID ST
4100 AlaC 94546 692-B5
DAVIDSON WY
400 OAK 94610 650-A2
DAVILA CT
41000 FRMT 94539 753-E6
DAVIS AV
- DBLN 94568 694-B3
2300 HAY 94545 711-C5
DAVIS CT
2200 HAY 94545 711-D5
40200 FRMT 94538 753-C6
DAVIS RD
- ORIN 94563 610-H7
- ORIN 94563 630-H1
DAVIS ST
- UNC 94555 752-A2
- SF 94111 648-B4
2000 SLN 94577 690-F2
3000 OAK 94601 650-D6
4300 FRMT 94538 753-B6
DAVIS ST Rt#-112
300 SLN 94577 691-A1
700 SLN 94577 690-J1
DAVIS WY
4100 LVMR 94550 696-A7
DAVONA DR
8200 DBLN 94568 693-H2
8800 SRMN 94583 693-G1
9600 SRMN 94583 673-E6
DAVY CT
38000 FRMT 94536 753-A3
DAWE AV
21100 AlaC 94546 691-J6
DAWES ST
6500 OAK 94611 650-D1
DAWN CIR
31200 UNC 94587 731-J5
DAWN CT
1300 SRMN 94583 673-B1
DAWN ST
1200 OAK 94705 630-C3
1600 LVMR 94550 716-C1
DAWN VIEW CT
5700 AlaC 94552 692-D3
DAWSON AV
100 FRMT 94536 733-A7
100 FRMT 94536 753-A1
DAWSON PL
- SF 94108 648-A5
DAWSON ST
36500 FRMT 94536 752-G2
DAYBREAK CT
300 CCCo 94583 673-B1
300 SRMN 94583 673-B1
DAYLE CT
2200 FRMT 94539 753-F6
DAYLILY CT
2800 PLE 94588 694-H3
DAYTON AV
1300 ALA 94501 669-H2
1400 SLN 94579 691-A6
1900 SLN 94579 690-J6
DAYTON COM
- FRMT 94538 773-B5
DAYTON CT
100 SRMN 94583 673-G7
1500 SLN 94579 691-A6
DEADWOOD DR
4600 FRMT 94536 752-G5
DEAKIN ST
2900 BERK 94705 629-H3
3200 OAK 94609 629-H4
DEAN ST
500 HAY 94541 711-J2
DEANNE CT
16200 AlaC 94580 691-E5
S DE ANZA BLVD
- SJCo 95391 (678-F2 See Page 677)
DE ANZA CT
800 MPS 95035 794-B5
DE ANZA PL
3200 SRMN 94583 673-G5
DEARBORN ST
32400 HAY 94544 732-F3
DEAUVILLE PARK CT
42700 FRMT 94538 773-C2
DE BOOM ST
- SF 94107 648-C6
DEBORA CT
900 FRMT 94539 753-F5
DEBORAH CT
4500 UNC 94587 732-A7
DEBORAH DR
32200 UNC 94587 731-J7
32200 UNC 94587 732-A7
DEBORAH ST
36500 NWK 94560 752-E6
DEBRA CT
- ORIN 94563 630-J2
DEBRA ST
500 LVMR 94550 696-C7
DEBRUM COM
43300 FRMT 94539 753-H7
DE CAEN CT
900 LVMR 94550 715-E2
DECANO TER
36600 FRMT 94536 752-B4
DECATUR LN
- ALA 94501 649-E7
DECATUR ST
2100 ALA 94501 649-E7
DECATUR WY
27600 HAY 94545 711-H7
27600 HAY 94545 731-H1
DECELLE CT
- ALA 94501 649-A2
DECKER AL
100 SF 94103 648-D7
DECKER LN
- LVMR 94550 716-D2
DECOTO CT
900 MPS 95035 794-B5
DECOTO RD
100 UNC 94587 732-F7
2700 FRMT 94536 732-F7
2700 FRMT 94536 752-E2
2700 FRMT 94555 732-F7
2700 FRMT 94555 752-E2
DECOY TER
34400 FRMT 94555 752-D2
DEE CT
3100 FRMT 94536 752-G1
DEE PL
35500 FRMT 94536 752-G1
DEEP CREEK RD
4000 FRMT 94555 732-C7
4200 FRMT 94555 752-C1
DEER RD
1100 FRMT 94536 733-D7
DEER CREEK CT
- PLE 94588 714-C5
DEERFIELD CT
- SRMN 94582 673-J6
DEERFIELD DR
200 MRGA 94556 651-E3
DEERFIELD PL
4500 FRMT 94538 773-C1
DEER HILL DR
- SRMN 94583 673-A1
DEERING CT
- OAK 94601 650-D6
DEERING ST
3200 OAK 94601 650-D6
DEER OAKS CT
- PLE 94588 714-A4
DEER OAKS DR
- PLE 94588 714-A4
DEER PARK CT
3500 HAY 94542 712-F4
DEER PARK WY
3500 HAY 94542 712-F4
DEERPOINT TER
500 FRMT 94536 753-G3
DEER TERRACE CT
- SRMN 94583 673-A1
DEER TRAIL PL
25600 AlaC 94541 712-D2
DEERVALE CT
7700 DBLN 94568 693-G2
DEERVALE RD
8300 DBLN 94568 693-G2
DEER VIEW TER
- FRMT 94539 794-B1
DEERWOOD AV
7300 OAK 94605 670-H2
DEERWOOD CT
- LVMR 94551 696-E3
DEERWOOD DR
2400 SRMN 94583 673-A1
DEERWOOD PL
100 SRMN 94583 673-B2
DEERWOOD PZ
- HAY 94542 712-B3
DEERWOOD RD
- DNVL 94526 673-B1
100 SRMN 94583 673-B1
100 CCCo 94583 673-B1
DEERWOOD TER
3400 FRMT 94536 752-A6
DEFOE CT
3200 FRMT 94536 752-F1
DEFREMERY AV
900 OAK 94606 649-H6
DEKKER TER
5400 FRMT 94555 752-B3
DE LA CRUZ RD
29100 HAY 94544 712-C7
DE LA CRUZ WY
1400 MRGA 94556 651-D1
DEL AMIGO RD
- DNVL 94526 652-H1
DEL AMIGO TR
- CCCo 94583 652-G2
DELANCEY ST
500 SF 94107 648-C6
DELANO CT
39100 FRMT 94538 753-A5
DELANO ST
700 AlaC 94580 691-E5
1100 AlaC 94578 691-E5
DELAWARE CT
1300 LVMR 94551 695-F6
DELAWARE DR
4000 FRMT 94538 773-D2
DELAWARE ST
800 BERK 94710 629-D1
1100 BERK 94702 629-E1
1500 BERK 94703 629-F1
1900 BERK 94709 629-F1
2800 OAK 94602 650-E5
E DELAWARE ST
3700 FRMT 94538 773-E2
DELAWARE WY
700 LVMR 94551 695-E6
DEL CAMPO CIR
3400 SLN 94578 691-B4
DELDRIN CT
- SRMN 94582 674-A2
DE LEMOS AV
1500 HAY 94544 732-A1
DE LEON AV
300 FRMT 94539 753-H7
DE LEON WY
1500 LVMR 94550 715-G3
DELGADO CT
- FRMT 94539 753-E4
DELGADO RD
29100 HAY 94544 712-C7
DELIA TER
34100 FRMT 94555 752-B2
DELIA WY
5400 LVMR 94550 696-C7
DELICADO CT
3100 PLE 94588 694-C7
DEL JIUDICE CT
1600 SLN 94578 691-C3
DELL CT
200 AlaC 94541 711-F1
DELLHAVEN CT
17400 AlaC 94552 692-C2
DEL MAR AV
- BERK 94708 609-J7
700 LVMR 94550 715-E2
800 ALA 94501 669-J4
800 ALA 94501 670-A3
DELMAR AV
25000 HAY 94542 712-A3
DEL MAR CIR
3400 SLN 94578 691-B4
DEL MAR CT
- UNC 94545 751-J1
DELMAR CT
25100 HAY 94542 712-A3
DEL MAR DR
9800 SRMN 94583 673-G6
DELMER ST
2400 OAK 94602 650-E4
DELMONT AV
3600 OAK 94605 670-H1
DEL MONTE AV
8000 NWK 94560 752-C7
DEL MONTE CT
- UNC 94545 731-H7
DEL MONTE ST
1900 LVMR 94551 696-C2
DEL MONTE WY
3400 SLN 94578 691-B4
DEL NORTE CT
- BERK 94707 609-G6
1600 LVMR 94551 695-E6
27600 HAY 94545 731-H1
DEL NORTE DR
700 LVMR 94551 695-E6
DEL NORTE ST
2000 BERK 94707 609-G6
DEL ORA TERRAZA
- FRMT 94536 753-C3
DELORES CT
4600 UNC 94587 752-A1
DELORES DR
4300 UNC 94587 732-A7
4600 UNC 94587 752-A1
4800 UNC 94587 751-J1
DEL ORO CT
- SRMN 94583 673-B2
DELPHINIUM CT
38700 NWK 94560 772-G1
DEL PLAYA
1000 PLE 94566 714-G3
DEL REY CT
- UNC 94545 731-J7
DEL RIO CIR
3400 SLN 94578 691-B4
DEL RIO CT
900 MPS 95035 794-B5
DEL SOL AV
300 PLE 94566 714-E4
DELTA COM
- FRMT 94538 773-D3
DELTA CT
1600 HAY 94544 732-B2
1800 AlaC 94586 734-B2
DELTA GRN
- FRMT 94538 773-D3
DELTA PL
- SF 94102 648-A5
DELTA TER
- FRMT 94538 773-D3
DELUCCHI DR
2100 PLE 94588 694-E7
DE LUCCHI TER
600 FRMT 94536 733-A5
600 UNC 94587 732-J5
600 UNC 94587 733-A5
DEL VAILE CT
800 MPS 95035 794-B5
DEL VALLE
- ORIN 94563 610-D7
DEL VALLE CIR
3400 SLN 94578 691-B4
DEL VALLE CT
200 PLE 94566 714-E3
DEL VALLE PKWY
3500 PLE 94566 714-D2
DEL VALLE PL
30500 UNC 94587 732-A4
DEL VALLE RD
6000 AlaC 94550 736-F3
6000 AlaC 94550 (756-G1 See Page 755)
DEMARCUS BLVD
- DBLN 94568 694-B4
DEMETER ST
100 EPA 94303 771-C7
DEMPSEY RD
- MPS 95035 794-C7
DEMPSEY WY
1100 MPS 95035 794-C6
DE NATALE CT
5200 PLE 94588 694-H4
DENHAM DR
35500 FRMT 94555 752-E1
DENISE LN
3800 AlaC 94546 691-H2
DENISE ST
41100 FRMT 94539 753-E6
DENISON PL
7500 AlaC 94552 692-G3
DENKE DR
1000 ALA 94502 669-J6
DENKER DR
4100 PLE 94588 694-A6
DENNING CT
2500 AlaC 94546 691-H5
DENNING TER
37000 FRMT 94536 752-H2
DENNIS AV
1400 MPS 95035 794-D6
1500 SLN 94578 691-D3
DENNIS CT
38400 FRMT 94536 752-J4
DENNIS DR
3200 PLE 94588 694-F6
DENNISON ST
1800 ALA 94501 649-J7
1800 ALA 94501 650-A7
1800 OAK 94606 650-A7
DENSLOWE AV
- OAK 94603 670-G7
DENSLOWE LN
600 HAY 94544 711-H5
DENTON AV
1100 HAY 94545 711-F5
1500 AlaC 94545 711-F5
DENTON PL
5600 OAK 94619 651-A6
DEODAR WY
7700 PLE 94588 693-H6
DEODARA ST
3100 FRMT 94538 753-C5
DEPASSIER WY
3500 ALA 94502 670-A7
DE PAUL WY
1200 LVMR 94550 716-A2
DEPOT CT
1800 HAY 94545 711-G6
DEPOT RD
1800 HAY 94545 711-C6
2200 AlaC 94545 711-C6
33300 UNC 94587 732-F4
DERBY AV
300 OAK 94601 670-B1
1200 OAK 94601 650-C7
DERBY CT
- LVMR 94550 715-H6
- SRMN 94583 673-C4
32400 UNC 94587 732-C5
DERBY DR
2500 SRMN 94583 673-B4
DERBY PL
4900 NWK 94560 752-F4
DERBY ST
- SF 94102 648-A6
1100 BERK 94702 629-F3
1500 BERK 94703 629-F3
1900 BERK 94704 629-H3
2100 BERK 94705 629-H3
2800 BERK 94704 630-A3
2800 BERK 94705 630-A3
32300 UNC 94587 732-C5
DERING PL
35700 FRMT 94536 752-G2
DERMODY AV
15200 AlaC 94580 691-D5
DE SALLE TER
300 FRMT 94536 753-B1
DESCHUTES PL
1400 FRMT 94539 773-G4
DESCONSADO AV
900 LVMR 94550 715-F3
DESERT OAK CT
29600 HAY 94544 712-D7
DESERTWOOD LN
7600 PLE 94588 713-J1
DESERTWOOD PL
4400 PLE 94588 713-J1
DE SILVA CT
40500 FRMT 94538 753-C7
DE SILVA ST
4500 FRMT 94538 753-B7
DESIREE AV
5200 LVMR 94550 696-C6
DESMOND CT
1100 FRMT 94539 753-F6
DESMOND ST
4900 OAK 94618 629-J7
DE SOTO CT
- ORIN 94563 610-J5
DE SOTO WY
1500 LVMR 94550 715-G3
DE SOUSA PL
18000 AlaC 94546 692-B3
DESTINY LN
200 CCCo 94583 673-B1
200 SRMN 94583 673-B1
DETJEN CT
6200 PLE 94588 693-F6
DETJEN ST
3600 FRMT 94538 753-C6
DETROIT AV
4200 OAK 94619 650-G4
DE VACA WY
- HAY 94544 712-C7
1800 LVMR 94550 715-G2
DE VALLE CT
300 FRMT 94536 733-A6
DEVEREUX CT
2800 PLE 94588 714-A3
DEVILS HOLE TR
- AlaC 94546 652-C5
- AlaC 94552 652-C5
- CCCo 94583 652-C5
DEVON CT
400 SRMN 94583 673-G7
41500 FRMT 94539 753-F6
DEVON DR
900 HAY 94542 712-B4
DEVON PL
2100 MPS 95035 794-A2
3900 LVMR 94550 715-J2
3900 LVMR 94550 716-A2
DEVON WY
6900 OAK 94705 630-C3
DEVONSHIRE AV
800 SLN 94579 691-A5
DEVONSHIRE COM
4500 FRMT 94536 752-G4
DEVONSHIRE CT
1300 ELCR 94530 609-E1
DEVONSHIRE DR
1300 ELCR 94530 609-E1
DEVONSHIRE ST
32200 UNC 94587 732-C4
DEVONWOOD WY
15800 AlaC 94580 691-C7
15800 AlaC 94580 711-C1
DEWBERRY DR
- SRMN 94582 673-G2
DEWEY PL
5500 FRMT 94538 773-A1
DEWEY RD
- CCCo 94708 609-G3
DEWEY ST
15000 SLN 94579 691-B6
DE WITT CT
2100 UNC 94587 732-G7
DEXTER CT
2100 AlaC 94541 692-C7
DEXTER PL
200 SRMN 94583 673-F5
DEXTER WY
2200 AlaC 94541 692-C7
6300 AlaC 94541 712-C1
DHILLION CT
- HAY 94544 712-C7
DIABLO AV
3100 HAY 94545 711-D6
DIABLO CT
3600 PLE 94588 694-F7
W DIABLO CT
16300 SJCo 95304 (678-J7 See Page 677)
DIABLO DR
100 CCCo 94563 630-F5
100 OAK 94611 630-F5
DIABLO PL
2400 UNC 94587 732-C5
DIABLO RD
100 DNVL 94526 652-J2
DIABLO VIEW DR
- ORIN 94563 610-J4
DIADON DR
24800 HAY 94544 711-H4
DIAMOND COM
5200 FRMT 94555 752-C3
DIAMOND CT
- DNVL 94526 652-H1
300 PLE 94566 714-D6
1200 LVMR 94550 715-D3
20000 AlaC 94546 692-C5
DIAMOND DR
- DNVL 94526 652-H2
- LVMR 94550 715-D3
DIAMOND WY
200 MPS 95035 793-H6
DIAMOND BAR CT
- SLN 94579 691-A7
- SLN 94579 711-A1
DIAMOND HEAD LN
5200 FRMT 94538 752-J7
DIAMOND RANCH CT
- SRMN 94583 673-E7
DIAMOND RIDGE DR
24500 HAY 94544 711-H3
DIANA COM
5300 FRMT 94555 752-C3
DIANA LN
7900 DBLN 94568 693-H3
DIANA PL
600 HAY 94544 712-B5
DIANE CT
5100 LVMR 94550 716-C1
DIANE LN
5100 LVMR 94550 716-C1
DIAPIAN BAY
100 ALA 94502 669-J6
DIAS DORADAS
- ORIN 94563 610-G5
DIAVILA AV
4200 PLE 94588 694-E7
DIAVILA CT
2800 PLE 94588 694-E6
DIAZ DR
4500 FRMT 94536 752-E3
DIAZ PL
- OAK 94611 630-D7
DICHONDRA PL
5700 NWK 94560 752-H7
DICKENS AV
27700 HAY 94544 712-A7
28000 HAY 94544 732-A1
DICKENS CT
900 LVMR 94551 696-A6
3000 FRMT 94536 752-H2
3500 PLE 94588 694-E6
DICKENSON COM
3400 FRMT 94538 753-C5
DICKENSON DR
- LVMR 94551 696-A6
- MRGA 94556 651-E1
DICKSON CT
4100 OAK 94605 671-B2
DIEGO DR
36400 FRMT 94536 752-F3
DIEHL AV
400 SLN 94577 671-C7
DIEL DR
1500 MPS 95035 794-B3
DIESEL ST
2000 OAK 94606 670-A1
DIGITAL DR
- DBLN 94568 694-C4
DIJON DR
- NWK 94560 752-E6
DIJON WY
6400 DBLN 94568 694-A1
N DIKE RD
- SLN 94577 690-F4
S DIKE RD
- SLN 94577 690-F5
W DIKE RD
- SLN 94577 690-F5
DILETTA AV
1600 SLN 94578 691-D3
DILLO ST
900 SLN 94578 691-D4
DILLON WY
- ELCR 94530 609-E1
11300 DBLN 94568 693-F5
DIMAS CT
- PLE 94566 714-F6
DIMOND AV
3400 OAK 94602 650-D4
DINGLEY ST
4100 OAK 94605 671-D4
DINUBA CT
32700 UNC 94587 752-A1
DINUBA ST
4600 UNC 94587 752-A1
DISCOVERY RD
15100 SLN 94579 690-J6
DISK DR
- SJS 95002 793-C7
- SJS 95134 793-C7
DITMUS CT
40400 FRMT 94538 753-D6
DIVISION ST
300 PLE 94566 714-D3
DIXON CT
38200 FRMT 94536 752-J4
DIXON RD
- MPS 95035 793-J3
100 MPS 95035 794-A3
DIXON ST
28600 HAY 94544 712-C7
29000 HAY 94544 732-D1
DIXON LANDING RD
- FRMT 94538 793-H4
- SJS 95002 793-H4
- MPS 95035 793-H4
1600 MPS 95002 793-H4
DOAK CT
- DBLN 94568 694-G4
DOANE ST
500 AlaC 94580 691-D5
4000 FRMT 94538 773-D3
DOBBEL AV
27100 HAY 94542 712-D4
DOBSON CT
2900 FRMT 94555 732-E7
DOBSON WY
34300 FRMT 94555 732-E7
DOCCIA CT
2200 PLE 94566 715-B6
DODGE AV
25800 HAY 94545 711-F6
DOE CT
100 FRMT 94539 773-J3
DOGIE CT
- SRMN 94583 673-B3
DOGWOOD AV
4600 FRMT 94536 752-H5
DOGWOOD CT
- SRMN 94583 693-H1
200 HAY 94544 712-B6
DOGWOOD DR
700 LVMR 94551 695-E7
DOGWOOD PL
100 SRMN 94583 693-H1
DOHR ST
2700 BERK 94702 629-F3
DOLE WY
22400 HAY 94541 711-J1
22400 HAY 94541 712-A1
DOLERITA AV
100 FRMT 94539 753-E3
DOLERITA CT
- FRMT 94539 753-E4
DOLLAR ST
25600 HAY 94544 712-A4
DOLLINGER CT
3200 FRMT 94536 752-J3
DOLLY AV
1800 SLN 94577 690-J2
DOLORES AV
200 SLN 94577 691-B1
4600 OAK 94602 650-D3
DOLORES CT
4900 PLE 94566 714-E5
DOLORES DR
400 MPS 95035 794-E7
500 PLE 94566 714-E4
3200 SRMN 94583 673-F4
DOLORES PL
500 PLE 94566 714-E5
40500 FRMT 94539 753-E5
DOLORES ST
900 LVMR 94550 715-J1
21500 AlaC 94546 692-A7
DOLPHIN CT
2000 SLN 94579 690-J6
DOLPHIN LN
27700 HAY 94545 731-J1
DOLPHIN TER
1000 FRMT 94536 753-F3

STREET Block	City	ZIP	Pg-Grid
DOMINGO AV			
-	BERK	94705	630-A4
DOMINGO CT			
300	SRMN	94583	673-C3
DOMINIC CT			
2900	AlaC	94546	691-G3
DOMINIC DR			
3100	AlaC	94546	691-G3
DOMINIC LN			
2900	AlaC	94546	691-G3
DOMINICAN TER			
-	FRMT	94539	753-J5
DOMINICI DR			
2700	FRMT	94536	752-G1
DON CT			
5600	FRMT	94538	773-B2
DON WY			
5600	FRMT	94538	773-B2
DONADA PL			
-	HAY	94544	711-H4
DONAHE DR			
300	MPS	95035	794-A6
DONAHE PL			
400	MPS	95035	794-A6
DONAHUE			
-	PLE	94588	714-F1
DONAHUE CT			
-	PLE	94588	714-F1
DONAHUE DR			
-	PLE	94588	714-F1
DONAHUE TER			
34200	FRMT	94555	752-C2
DONAL AV			
6500	ELCR	94530	609-C2
DONALBAN CIR			
4500	FRMT	94555	752-D1
DONALD AV			
14900	SLN	94578	691-D3
25400	HAY	94544	712-A4
DONATA CT			
700	PLE	94566	715-D7
DON CAROL DR			
8600	ELCR	94530	609-E2
DONCASTER PL			
6100	OAK	94611	630-E6
DONDERO WY			
37000	FRMT	94536	752-G4
DONEGAL CT			
35000	NWK	94560	752-D4
DONLON WY			
6700	DBLN	94568	693-G4
DONNA ST			
14800	SLN	94578	691-D3
DONNA WY			
-	OAK	94605	671-D3
DONNER AV			
100	LVMR	94551	715-E1
DONNER WY			
39000	FRMT	94538	752-J6
DONOHUE DR			
7400	DBLN	94568	693-H3
DONOSO PZ			
100	UNC	94587	732-J5
DONOVAN DR			
700	SLN	94577	690-H1
N DONOVAN WY			
-	SRMN	94582	674-C3
S DONOVAN WY			
-	SRMN	94582	674-C3
DOOLAN RD			
5200	AlaC	94551	695-A1
5200	LVMR	94551	695-B4
6100	AlaC	94551	674-J7
6100	AlaC	94551	694-J1
6100	CCCo	94551	674-J7
6100	CCCo	94551	675-A4
6100	CCCo	94588	674-J7
6100	CCCo	94588	675-A4
DOOLITTLE DR			
1200	SLN	94577	690-G2
DOOLITTLE DR Rt#-61			
-	ALA	94502	670-B5
600	SLN	94577	690-F1
600	OAK	94603	690-F1
7900	OAK	94621	670-B5
9400	OAK	94621	690-F1
DORADO COM			
34700	FRMT	94555	752-A3
DORADO DR			
31300	UNC	94545	731-J6
DORAL CT			
7900	PLE	94588	714-B6
DORAL DR			
-	MRGA	94556	651-D1
DORAN DR			
6300	OAK	94611	630-G7
DORCHESTER AV			
-	SLN	94577	670-J7
DORCHESTER CT			
35000	NWK	94560	752-D3
DOREEN CT			
6800	DBLN	94568	693-J3
DOREEN ST			
7200	DBLN	94568	693-J3
DORIC AL			
-	SF	94108	648-A5
DORIS CT			
1000	ALA	94501	670-A3
18500	AlaC	94546	692-B3
DORIS PL			
-	OAK	94705	630-B4
DORISA AV			
3600	OAK	94605	671-B4
DORKING CT			
5000	NWK	94560	752-E4
DORMAN CT			
4300	PLE	94588	694-B7
DORMAN RD			
4000	PLE	94588	694-A7
DORMIDERA AV			
-	PDMT	94611	650-C1
DORNE PL			
2000	FRMT	94539	753-F6
DOROTHY AV			
1200	SLN	94578	691-C4
DOROTHY PL			
-	OAK	94705	630-B3
DORRINGTON CT			
39500	FRMT	94538	753-A6
DORSET CT			
100	SRMN	94583	673-F4
DORSEY AV			
4300	FRMT	94536	752-J5
DORSEY CT			
38200	FRMT	94536	752-J4
DORSON LN			
17500	AlaC	94546	692-A2
DORTHA CT			
40100	FRMT	94538	753-B7
DORTHEA CT			
8000	PLE	94588	714-A5
DOS OSOS			
-	ORIN	94563	610-E7
DOS POSOS			
-	ORIN	94563	610-G6
DOS RIOS CT			
-	SRMN	94583	673-B2
DOS RIOS DR			
2400	SRMN	94583	673-B2
DOS RIOS PL			
-	SRMN	94583	673-B2
DOTSON CT			
24000	HAY	94544	711-J3
DOUBLETREE DR			
12400	CCCo	94551	675-F2
DOUBLETREE LN			
9000	CCCo	94551	675-F3
DOUGHERTY LN			
8400	AlaC	94550	696-G7
DOUGHERTY RD			
-	CCCo	94582	673-J3
-	PLE	94588	694-A4
-	SRMN	94582	673-J3
5800	DBLN	94568	694-A1
7500	CCCo	94582	674-A7
7500	CCCo	94582	694-A1
7500	SRMN	94582	674-A7
7500	SRMN	94582	694-A1
DOUGLAS AV			
400	OAK	94603	670-G7
DOUGLAS CT			
-	MPS	95035	794-C7
900	SLN	94577	690-J1
1600	FRMT	94539	753-G6
4300	PLE	94588	694-A7
DOUGLAS DR			
600	SLN	94577	690-H1
1500	ELCR	94530	609-D1
DOUGLAS ST			
700	HAY	94544	712-C6
2400	UNC	94587	732-C5
DOVE CT			
1700	HAY	94545	731-J1
6400	LVMR	94551	696-D2
DOVE PL			
-	FRMT	94555	732-B7
DOVE WY			
1800	HAY	94545	731-J1
DOVER COM			
38000	FRMT	94536	752-J3
DOVER CT			
7200	DBLN	94568	693-H3
35300	NWK	94560	752-D4
DOVER LN			
7200	DBLN	94568	693-H3
24000	AlaC	94541	712-B1
DOVER PL			
1600	AlaC	94541	712-B1
DOVER ST			
-	SF	94107	648-C6
600	BERK	94703	629-G5
5100	OAK	94609	629-G4
DOVER WY			
400	LVMR	94551	695-E6
DOW CT			
-	ALA	94501	649-A2
38600	FRMT	94536	753-D2
DOW PL			
-	SF	94107	648-B6
DOWE AV			
2700	UNC	94587	732-D5
DOWICHER CT			
-	SLN	94579	691-F2
DOWITCHER CT			
-	ALA	94501	649-F7
DOWITCHER TER			
3600	FRMT	94555	732-J3
DOWLING AV			
4900	FRMT	94536	752-G5
DOWLING BLVD			
200	SLN	94577	671-B6
DOWLING CT			
8000	OAK	94605	670-J3
DOWLING LN			
-	ALA	94501	649-F7
DOWLING PL			
2400	BERK	94705	629-H4
DOWLING ST			
8100	OAK	94605	670-J3
DOWNEN PL			
300	HAY	94544	711-H4
DOWNEY PL			
-	OAK	94610	650-C3
1900	ELCR	94530	609-C1
DOWNIEVILLE ST			
32700	UNC	94587	752-A1
DOWNING CT			
4400	PLE	94588	694-A7
DOWNING PL			
32200	UNC	94587	732-C4
DOWNING RD			
800	MPS	95035	794-E4
1000	SCIC	95035	794-E2
DOYLE ST			
4400	EMVL	94608	629-E6
DRACENA AV			
100	PDMT	94611	630-B7
100	PDMT	94611	650-B1
DRACENA ST			
2200	HAY	94545	711-H7
DRAKE AV			
1200	SLN	94579	691-A5
DRAKE CT			
4200	LVMR	94550	716-A2
DRAKE DR			
1800	OAK	94611	630-E7
1900	OAK	94611	650-E1
DRAKE LN			
-	OAK	94611	650-E1
DRAKE PL			
-	OAK	94611	630-E7
DRAKE WY			
4000	LVMR	94550	716-A1
39300	FRMT	94538	752-J6
39300	FRMT	94538	753-A6
DRESDEN BAY			
200	ALA	94502	670-A5
DRESSLAR CIR			
-	LVMR	94550	716-C1
DREW CT			
2800	EPA	94303	771-C6
DREW ST			
-	SJCo	95391	(678-E3 See Page 677)
500	AlaC	94580	691-D5
500	SLN	94578	691-D5
DREW TER			
4000	FRMT	94538	773-D1
DREXEL CT			
38600	FRMT	94536	752-J5
DREXEL WY			
27500	HAY	94545	711-H7
DREYER PL			
5600	OAK	94619	651-A5
DRIFTWOOD DR			
4700	FRMT	94536	752-G5
DRIFTWOOD LN			
300	ALA	94501	670-A4
DRIFTWOOD ST			
-	HAY	94545	731-H3
DRIFTWOOD WY			
2200	SLN	94577	690-H5
7500	PLE	94588	713-J1
DRISCOLL RD			
100	FRMT	94539	753-E6
DRISCOLL TER			
41000	FRMT	94539	753-F5
DROMANA CT			
-	SRMN	94582	674-C4
DRUM			
4000	ALA	94501	649-E6
DRUMM ST			
-	SF	94111	648-B4
DRURY CT			
1300	OAK	94705	630-C3
4600	FRMT	94538	753-C7
DRURY LN			
-	OAK	94705	630-B3
DRURY RD			
1000	OAK	94705	630-C3
DRY CREEK CT			
-	LVMR	94551	696-E1
DRY CREEK RD			
-	DBLN	94568	693-E4
DRY CREEK TR			
-	AlaC	94544	732-F1
-	UNC	94587	732-F1
DRYDEN CT			
2600	HAY	94542	712-D4
5100	NWK	94560	752-E4
DRYDEN RD			
3600	FRMT	94555	752-E1
DRYWOOD CT			
4400	UNC	94587	732-A7
DRYWOOD ST			
4700	PLE	94588	693-J7
DUARTE AV			
-	FRMT	94536	733-A7
DUARTE CT			
-	ALA	94502	669-J7
-	MRGA	94556	651-E1
200	MPS	95035	794-A4
DUBAL CT			
43800	FRMT	94539	773-G2
DUBERSTEIN DR			
-	SRMN	94583	673-E6
DUBIN CT			
18700	AlaC	94546	691-H3
DUBLIN AV			
900	LVMR	94550	715-G3
5000	OAK	94602	650-F3
DUBLIN BLVD			
6500	DBLN	94568	693-J4
6500	DBLN	94568	694-A4
11000	PLE	94588	693-E5
DUBLIN CT			
6500	DBLN	94568	694-A4
DUBLIN WY			
600	ALA	94502	669-H5
DUBLIN CANYON RD			
6800	AlaC	94552	692-H4
9000	AlaC	94552	693-A5
10600	PLE	94588	693-E5
10700	AlaC	94586	693-E5
10700	AlaC	94588	693-E5
10700	PLE	94586	693-E5
DUBLIN GREEN CT			
7700	DBLN	94568	693-G3
DUBLIN GREEN DR			
11700	DBLN	94568	693-G3
DUBLIN MEADOWS ST			
6900	DBLN	94568	694-A3
N DUBLIN RANCH DR			
-	DBLN	94568	694-F2
S DUBLIN RANCH DR			
-	DBLN	94568	694-F3
DUCHESS DR			
4200	UNC	94587	732-A6
DUDLEY AV			
-	PDMT	94611	650-C1
DUDLEY CT			
-	PDMT	94611	650-C1
5400	PLE	94566	714-C2
DUFFEL PL			
27000	HAY	94544	712-B5
DUFFY TER			
34200	FRMT	94555	752-C2
DUFOUR LN			
-	ALA	94501	649-E7
DUGAN CT			
36600	NWK	94560	752-E5
DUKE CT			
3900	LVMR	94550	696-A7
4400	FRMT	94555	752-C1
6800	DBLN	94568	693-J3
7700	ELCR	94530	609-E2
19600	AlaC	94541	711-E2
DUKE LN			
34100	FRMT	94555	752-C1
DUKE WY			
3900	LVMR	94550	695-J7
3900	LVMR	94550	696-A7
7500	SRMN	94583	693-G1
DULSIE LN			
-	DBLN	94568	693-E5
DULWICH RD			
-	OAK	94618	630-B6
DUMAS PL			
7200	NWK	94560	752-D6
DUMBARTON CIR			
6300	FRMT	94555	752-B5
DUMBARTON CT			
35300	NWK	94560	752-C4
DUMONT AV			
300	HAY	94544	711-J5
DUNBAR CT			
3500	FRMT	94536	752-H2
DUNBAR PL			
3700	FRMT	94536	752-G3
27200	HAY	94544	712-B6
DUNBAR ST			
-	SF	94111	648-A5
DUNBARTON CIR			
3900	SRMN	94583	673-E4
DUNBARTON CT			
-	SRMN	94583	673-F4
DUNCAN WY			
-	OAK	94611	630-D6
DUNCAN HILL			
-	SRMN	94583	673-E6
DUNCOMBE AL			
-	SF	94133	648-A4
DUNDALK CT			
4200	PLE	94566	714-E1
DUNDEE AV			
400	MPS	95035	794-A6
DUNDEE COM			
38000	FRMT	94536	752-J3
DUNDEE CT			
-	SRMN	94583	673-E4
2400	SLN	94577	691-B2
DUNE CIR			
-	HAY	94545	731-G3
DUNHILL DR			
34300	FRMT	94555	752-C3
DUNKIRK AV			
4700	OAK	94605	671-E4
DUNMORE LN			
-	DBLN	94568	694-F4
DUNN RD			
2100	AlaC	94545	711-D5
2100	HAY	94545	711-D5
DUNNES AL			
-	SF	94133	648-A4
DUNNIGAN CT			
5200	AlaC	94546	692-B3
DUNSANAY CT			
3100	FRMT	94536	752-J1
DUNSMUIR AV			
4200	OAK	94619	650-G5
DUNSMUIR CIR			
3600	PLE	94588	694-F5
DUNSMUIR COM			
4900	FRMT	94555	752-A3
DUNSMUIR CT			
3300	PLE	94588	694-F5
DUNSMUIR PL			
1100	LVMR	94550	715-F4
DUNSTOWN CT			
-	DBLN	94568	693-G4
DUPONT AV			
5100	NWK	94560	752-F5
DURAN CT			
-	DBLN	94568	694-G3
39800	FRMT	94538	753-B6
DURANGO LN			
2600	SRMN	94583	673-C2
DURANT AV			
-	SLN	94577	670-J6
-	SLN	94577	671-A6
-	OAK	94603	670-J6
-	OAK	94603	671-A6
900	OAK	94605	671-A6
2000	BERK	94704	629-G2
DURHAM CT			
200	FRMT	94539	773-H2
DURHAM RD			
100	FRMT	94539	773-G2
DURHAM WY			
26500	HAY	94542	712-E2
DURILLO CT			
1000	FRMT	94539	753-F5
DURILLO DR			
40900	FRMT	94539	753-E5
DURLINGTON CT			
-	SRMN	94582	674-C4
DURRWOOD CT			
-	AlaC	94552	692-E7
-	AlaC	94552	712-E1
DUSK TER			
5100	FRMT	94555	752-C3
DUSTERBERRY WY			
37300	FRMT	94536	752-G4
DUTCHCAP LN			
3400	ALA	94502	670-A7
DUTCHESS LN			
300	HAY	94544	732-E2
DUTRA WY			
37000	FRMT	94536	752-G5
DUTTON AV			
-	SLN	94577	671-A7
1500	OAK	94605	671-A7
1500	SLN	94605	671-A7
DUTTON CT			
-	SLN	94577	671-A7
DUTTONWOOD LN			
-	MPS	95035	793-J3
DUVAL LN			
2000	HAY	94545	711-H7
DUVALL CT			
37700	FRMT	94536	752-G6
DUXBURY CT			
200	SRMN	94583	673-F5
DUZMAL AV			
1000	SLN	94579	691-B7
DWIGHT CRES			
800	BERK	94710	629-D3
DWIGHT PL			
500	OAK	94704	630-A2
DWIGHT WY			
700	BERK	94710	629-D3
1100	BERK	94702	629-E3
1500	BERK	94703	629-F3
1800	BERK	94704	629-H2
2800	BERK	94704	630-A2
3200	OAK	94704	630-A2
DWINELLE CT			
-	ALA	94502	670-A7
DYER COM			
2400	FRMT	94536	753-B3
DYER CT			
32200	UNC	94587	732-A6
DYER LN			
2400	FRMT	94536	753-B4
DYER RD			
3300	AlaC	94551	676-J4
DYER ST			
-	UNC	94545	731-J7
2800	UNC	94587	732-A6
4800	UNC	94587	731-J7

E

STREET Block	City	ZIP	Pg-Grid
E RD			
12300	AlaC	94586	734-C4
E ST			
100	FRMT	94536	753-B1
900	HAY	94541	711-J2
1000	HAY	94541	712-A1
1000	UNC	94587	732-F4
1400	AlaC	94541	712-B1
8300	OAK	94621	670-G4
9000	OAK	94603	670-H5
EAGLE AV			
600	ALA	94501	649-F7
1600	ALA	94501	669-J1
2100	ALA	94501	670-A1
EAGLE COM			
-	FRMT	94538	773-D3
EAGLE CT			
-	CCCo	94514	(657-E2 See Page 637)
-	HAY	94541	711-J2
-	LVMR	94551	696-D4
-	OAK	94603	671-C6
EAGLE GRN			
-	FRMT	94538	773-D3
EAGLE RD			
-	ALA	94501	649-J6
-	ALA	94501	650-A7
EAGLE ST			
19500	AlaC	94546	691-H4
EAGLE TER			
-	FRMT	94538	773-D3
EAGLE CREEK CT			
400	SRMN	94582	694-B1
EAGLE HILL			
-	CCCo	94707	609-F4
EAGLES LANDING CT			
-	DBLN	94568	694-G3
EAGLES RUN RD			
5700	AlaC	94550	717-C4
EAGLET CT			
-	PLE	94566	714-H4
EAGLE VIEW TER			
-	FRMT	94539	794-B1
EALING LN			
-	OAK	94608	649-E1
EARHART RD			
7200	OAK	94621	670-C6
9000	OAK	94621	690-E1
EARHART WY			
300	LVMR	94551	695-C5
EARL CT			
7700	ELCR	94530	609-E2
EARL DR			
22000	AlaC	94546	691-J7
EARL ST			
7900	OAK	94605	671-A2
EARLE ST			
5000	FRMT	94536	752-H6
EARLY RIVERS CT			
2500	UNC	94587	732-F7
EARLY RIVERS PL			
2400	UNC	94587	732-F7
EARTH AV			
100	HAY	94544	712-B7
EAST AV			
1400	AlaC	94541	712-A1
1400	HAY	94541	712-A1
2400	LVMR	94550	715-H1
3500	AlaC	94542	712-E1
3900	LVMR	94550	716-A1
4600	AlaC	94550	716-D1
EAST CIR			
-	OAK	94611	630-G6
EAST CT			
-	OAK	94603	670-G7
-	OAK	94603	690-H1
EASTER AV			
400	MPS	95035	793-J6
EASTER LN			
1000	ALA	94502	670-A6
EASTER WY			
-	BERK	94708	609-H6
EASTERDAY WY			
36000	FRMT	94536	733-A7
EASTERTOWN LN			
-	DBLN	94568	693-D5
EASTHILL AV			
1500	AlaC	94586	734-B2
EASTIN CT			
-	UNC	94555	752-A2
EASTIN DR			
-	UNC	94555	751-J2
-	UNC	94555	752-A2
EASTLAKE AV			
4100	OAK	94602	650-F5
EASTLAWN ST			
5800	OAK	94621	670-E2
EAST LOOP RD			
-	HAY	94542	712-C3
EASTMAN AV			
2600	OAK	94619	650-E7
EASTMAN CT			
26000	HAY	94544	712-A4
EASTMAN ST			
200	HAY	94544	712-A5
EASTORI PL			
1600	HAY	94545	711-H6
EASTPARK TER			
34000	FRMT	94555	732-D7
EAST RIDGE			
-	SRMN	94582	673-G2
EASTSHORE BLVD			
1300	BERK	94710	609-B1
1300	BERK	94710	629-C1
1600	ELCR	94530	609-B1
EAST SHORE DR			
1200	ALA	94501	670-B4
EASTSHORE FRWY I-80			
-	ALB	-	609-C5
-	BERK	-	609-C5
-	BERK	-	629-D3
-	ELCR	-	609-C5
-	EMVL	-	629-D3
-	OAK	-	629-D7
-	OAK	-	649-D1
-	RCH	-	609-C5
EASTSHORE FRONTAGE RD			
-	ALB	94710	609-C6
1200	BERK	94710	609-C6
EAST VIEW CT			
5500	AlaC	94552	692-D4
EASTWOOD CT			
-	OAK	94611	630-G7
3800	PLE	94588	714-A2
EASTWOOD WY			
600	HAY	94544	712-B7
3700	PLE	94588	714-A2
EASY ST			
2400	AlaC	94578	691-F3
EATON CT			
40400	FRMT	94538	753-D6
EATON PL			
-	SF	94133	648-A4
EBBETTS ST			
39000	NWK	94560	772-H1
EBB TIDE ST			
14900	SLN	94578	691-C4
EBENSBURG LN			
6500	DBLN	94568	693-J4
EBONY WY			
200	HAY	94544	712-A5
EBRO CT			
35500	FRMT	94536	752-E2
ECHO AV			
-	OAK	94611	629-J7
-	OAK	94611	649-J1
100	OAK	94611	650-A1
900	PDMT	94611	649-J1
900	PDMT	94611	650-A1
ECHO CT			
4200	PLE	94588	714-A1
ECHO LN			
-	PDMT	94618	630-C7
ECHO ST			
500	LVMR	94550	715-E2
ECHO LAKE WY			
3800	FRMT	94555	732-B6
ECHO RIDGE WY			
300	SRMN	94582	673-G3
ECHO SPRINGS DR			
24700	HAY	94541	712-B2
ECHO SUMMIT ST			
1200	LVMR	94551	696-D3
ECKER ST			
-	SF	94105	648-B5
ECLIPSE CT			
-	ALA	94501	649-G7
EC REEMS CT			
2700	OAK	94605	671-A3
EDDY ST			
-	SF	94102	648-A6
23000	AlaC	94541	692-D6
EDELWEISS WY			
5700	LVMR	94551	696-C3
EDEN AV			
23300	HAY	94545	711-E6
23300	AlaC	94545	711-E6
EDEN CT			
35300	FRMT	94536	752-F2
EDEN LN			
3400	OAK	94601	650-C7
EDEN PL			
-	SRMN	94583	673-F7
EDEN RD			
2300	OAK	94603	690-F2
2300	SLN	94577	690-F2
EDEN ST			
6800	DBLN	94568	693-J3
EDENBERRY PL			
8500	DBLN	94568	693-G2
EDENBERRY ST			
8700	DBLN	94568	693-G2
EDEN CANYON RD			
21100	AlaC	94552	692-J2
EDEN LANDING RD			
25900	HAY	94545	711-E7
26000	HAY	94545	731-E1
EDEN PARK PL			
-	HAY	94545	731-H3
EDEN SHORES BLVD			
-	HAY	94545	731-H3
EDEN SHORES CT			
-	HAY	94545	731-H3
EDEN SHORES DR			
-	HAY	94545	731-H3
EDENVALE PL			
3900	OAK	94605	650-J7
3900	OAK	94605	670-J1
EDEN VIEW PL			
17900	AlaC	94546	692-A3
EDES AV			
5800	OAK	94621	670-F5
9000	OAK	94603	670-G6
EDGARDO PL			
-	SF	94133	648-A3
EDGE DR			
4200	OAK	94602	650-E3
EDGEBROOK DR			
24400	AlaC	94541	712-C1
EDGEBROOK PL			
24400	AlaC	94541	712-C1
EDGECLIFF WY			
27900	HAY	94542	712-E4
EDGECROFT RD			
-	CCCo	94707	609-F4
EDGEHILL CT			
1900	SLN	94577	691-D1
8600	ELCR	94530	609-F1
EDGEHILL RD			
1700	SLN	94577	691-D1
EDGEMERE LN			
1000	HAY	94545	711-G5
EDGEMONT WY			
-	OAK	94605	671-C5
EDGEMOOR PL			
3900	OAK	94605	670-J1
EDGEMOOR ST			
14900	SLN	94579	691-B6
EDGERLY ST			
5500	OAK	94621	670-F2
EDGEWATER DR			
-	MPS	95035	794-A6
5200	NWK	94560	752-D3
7100	OAK	94621	670-D4
EDGEWATER LN			
6700	LVMR	94551	696-E2
EDGEWOOD AV			
4300	OAK	94602	650-C3
EDGEWOOD CIR			
20600	AlaC	94552	692-F3
EDGEWOOD RD			
-	ORIN	94563	630-J4
EDGEWOOD ST			
42100	FRMT	94538	773-D1
EDGEWOOD WY			
4400	LVMR	94550	716-A2
6600	AlaC	94552	692-F3
EDINBURGH DR			
3200	LVMR	94551	695-J6
EDISON AV			
2000	SLN	94577	690-G1
EDISON CT			
2600	ALA	94501	670-B2
EDISON WY			
3400	FRMT	94538	773-E3
EDITH ST			
-	SF	94133	648-A4
1400	BERK	94703	609-G7
1500	BERK	94703	629-F1
24300	HAY	94544	712-A3
37000	NWK	94560	752-F5
EDITH WY			
32400	UNC	94587	732-A7
EDLOE DR			
24000	HAY	94541	711-G3
EDMONTON			
1900	SLN	94579	691-A7
EDMONTON COM			
5300	FRMT	94555	752-C3
EDNA CT			
100	UNC	94587	732-E3
5500	LVMR	94550	696-C6
EDNA ST			
14800	SLN	94578	691-C3
EDSEL DR			
1100	MPS	95035	794-D7
EDWARD AV			
38000	FRMT	94536	753-A3
EDWARDS AV			
-	OAK	94605	671-A1
2600	AlaC	94550	715-H5
3900	OAK	94605	670-J1
EDWARDS LN			
4300	AlaC	94546	692-B4
EDWARDS ST			
2300	BERK	94702	629-F3
EDWARD WHITE WY			
-	OAK	94621	690-E2
EDWIN DR			
-	CCCo	94707	609-F2
EDWIN WY			
200	HAY	94544	712-A5
EDWIN MARKHAM DR			
18900	AlaC	94552	692-E2
EDYTHE ST			
100	LVMR	94550	715-E1
EGERTON PL			
34400	FRMT	94555	752-D1
EGGERS COM			
-	FRMT	94536	752-J4
EGGERS CT			
38100	FRMT	94536	753-A3
EGGERS DR			
3000	FRMT	94536	753-A3
3300	FRMT	94536	752-J4
EGRET CT			
-	ALA	94501	649-F7
1700	HAY	94545	731-J1
4000	FRMT	94555	732-C7
EGRET LN			
1800	HAY	94545	731-J1
EGRET RD			
400	LVMR	94551	695-D7
400	LVMR	94551	715-D1
EGRET WY			
33100	FRMT	94555	732-B7
EHLE ST			
16500	AlaC	94578	691-G5
16900	AlaC	94546	691-G5
EICHLER ST			
23100	HAY	94545	711-D6
EIGENBRODT WY			
30000	UNC	94587	732-A3
EILEEN CT			
100	MRGA	94556	651-E2
EILENE CT			
3900	PLE	94588	694-E7
EILENE DR			
2000	PLE	94588	694-E7
ELAINE AV			
800	LVMR	94550	715-F2
ELAINE CT			
5300	AlaC	94546	692-B2
ELAISO COM			
4400	FRMT	94536	752-B4
ELAN LN			
-	SRMN	94582	674-C3
ELBA PL			
36000	FRMT	94536	752-F3
ELBA WY			
7000	DBLN	94568	693-J3
EL BALCON AV			
16700	AlaC	94578	691-F6
ELBERT ST			
1000	OAK	94602	650-C3
ELBRIDGE CT			
20900	AlaC	94552	692-G2
EL CAJON AV			
4500	FRMT	94536	752-F3
EL CAMILLE AV			
5400	OAK	94619	670-F1
EL CAMINITO			
-	ORIN	94563	610-H6
100	LVMR	94550	715-E2
2500	OAK	94611	650-E2
EL CAMINITO CT			
5300	AlaC	94546	692-B2
EL CAMINO FLORES			
-	MRGA	94556	651-E1
EL CAMINO HIGUERA			
1100	MPS	95035	794-B4
1300	SCIC	95035	794-B4
EL CAMINO REAL			
-	BERK	94705	630-A4
EL CAMPANERO			
-	ORIN	94563	610-H5
EL CAPITAN CT			
-	ALA	94501	669-H1
6300	LVMR	94551	696-D3
EL CAPITAN DR			
2800	PLE	94566	714-H3
EL CAPITAN WY			
6400	LVMR	94551	696-D3
EL CARMELLO CIR			
-	OAK	94619	650-G4
EL CENTRO AV			
1000	OAK	94602	650-C3
EL CERRITO AV			
100	PDMT	94611	650-B1
400	PDMT	94610	650-B1
EL CERRO BLVD			
200	DNVL	94526	652-J1
EL CHARRO RD			
-	AlaC	94588	694-H6
-	LVMR	94588	694-H6
600	AlaC	94551	715-A1
600	AlaC	94566	715-A1
ELDER			
-	FRMT	94536	753-D1
ELDER CIR			
-	LVMR	94550	716-C1
ELDER CT			
1800	HAY	94545	731-J1
ELDER WY			
1900	HAY	94545	731-J1
ELDERBERRY CT			
1600	PLE	94588	714-B6
ELDERBERRY DR			
6200	OAK	94611	630-G7
ELDERBERRY LN			
-	UNC	94587	732-H6
ELDERBERRY TR			
-	CCCo	94583	652-D4
ELDERBERRY WY			
600	SLN	94578	691-C4
EL DORADO AV			
100	HAY	94541	711-G2
100	DNVL	94526	652-J3
600	OAK	94611	649-J1
1900	BERK	94707	609-G6
EL DORADO COM			
40100	FRMT	94539	753-E4
EL DORADO CT			
4500	PLE	94566	714-D1
EL DORADO DR			
1100	LVMR	94550	715-F3
10000	SRMN	94583	673-G5
EL DORADO LN			
-	ORIN	94563	610-F7
EL DORADO ST			
1300	SJS	95002	793-B7
5600	ELCR	94530	609-C4
ELDRIDGE AV			
-	OAK	94603	670-G7
25600	HAY	94544	711-H5

STREET
Block City ZIP Pg-Grid

ELDRIDGE CT
- CCCo 94707 609-F4
ELEANOR PL
500 HAY 94544 732-E2
ELEGANS CT
- SRMN 94582 673-J1
EL EMBARCADERO
500 OAK 94610 649-J3
EL GAVILAN
- ORIN 94563 610-H5
EL GAVILAN CT
- ORIN 94563 610-J4
ELGIN CT
- AlaC 94580 691-E6
ELGIN LN
7900 DBLN 94568 693-G2
ELGIN ST
600 AlaC 94578 691-E5
600 AlaC 94580 691-E6
ELGIN WY
800 AlaC 94580 691-E6
ELIM AL
- SF 94105 648-B5
ELIMINA CT
43800 FRMT 94539 773-G2
ELINORA AV
4400 OAK 94619 650-G5
ELIOT DR
- LVMR 94551 696-A6
ELISA COM
4000 FRMT 94536 752-G2
ELISHA LN
- SRMN 94583 673-E6
ELIZABETH CT
300 LVMR 94551 695-F7
ELIZABETH ST
900 SJS 95002 793-B7
5700 OAK 94605 670-F2
5700 OAK 94621 670-F2
ELIZABETH WY
600 HAY 94544 732-E2
32400 UNC 94587 731-J7
32400 UNC 94587 732-A7
ELK CT
7100 DBLN 94568 693-J4
45200 FRMT 94539 773-J3
ELKGROVE CT
3600 HAY 94542 712-F4
ELKHART ST
- SF 94105 648-C6
ELKO CT
15600 SLN 94579 691-B7
ELKWOOD DR
1100 MPS 95035 793-J5
ELLEN CT
- ORIN 94563 610-J6
41100 FRMT 94538 753-C7
ELLEN ST
700 HAY 94544 711-J3
700 HAY 94544 712-A2
4500 OAK 94601 670-E1
41100 FRMT 94538 753-C7
41200 FRMT 94538 773-C1
ELLEN WY
4300 UNC 94587 732-A7
ELLEN CRAIG AV
- ALA 94501 669-J1
ELLERBROOK ST
- SJCo 95391 (678-F3 See Page 677)
ELLERY COM
- FRMT 94538 753-B5
ELLERY PL
500 HAY 94544 732-E2
ELLINGSON WY
2700 SRMN 94583 673-E5
ELLIOT CT
4900 FRMT 94536 752-H5
ELLIOT ST
3200 OAK 94610 650-B4
37700 FRMT 94536 752-G5
ELLIOTT CIR
400 PLE 94566 714-E1
ELLIS AV
1500 MPS 95035 794-D6
ELLIS CT
- ALA 94501 649-A2
- PLE 94566 714-E6
38100 FRMT 94536 752-J4
ELLIS ST
- SF 94102 648-A6
- SF 94108 648-A6
2900 BERK 94703 629-G4
ELLITA AV
400 OAK 94610 649-J3
ELLMANN PL
35700 FRMT 94536 752-G2
ELLS LN
1000 RCH 94804 609-B2
ELLS ST
1100 RCH 94804 609-B2
ELLSWORTH ST
2300 BERK 94704 629-H2
2600 BERK 94705 629-H2
43300 FRMT 94539 773-H1
43300 FRMT 94539 753-H7
ELLSWORTH TER
200 FRMT 94539 773-H1
ELLWELL DR
1700 MPS 95035 794-D6
ELM AV
400 MPS 95035 793-H6
ELM CT
400 MPS 95035 793-J6
1000 ELCR 94530 609-D3
6700 DBLN 94568 693-J3
ELM ST
500 ELCR 94530 609-C1
1000 LVMR 94551 695-F7
1800 ALA 94501 670-A1
3200 OAK 94609 649-H1
14300 SLN 94579 690-J4
21100 AlaC 94546 692-A6
36900 NWK 94560 752-D7
37000 FRMT 94536 752-G3
37100 NWK 94560 772-D1
ELMAR AV
9800 OAK 94603 671-A5
ELMHURST AV
900 OAK 94603 670-H5
S ELMHURST AV
600 OAK 94603 670-G6
ELMHURST ST
400 HAY 94544 711-G4
EL MOLINO PL
100 SRMN 94583 673-F7
EL MONTE AV
2900 OAK 94605 671-A3
ELMORE CT
37700 FRMT 94536 752-G6
ELMRIDGE CT
5300 PLE 94566 714-C2

ELMVIEW DR
9600 OAK 94603 671-A4
ELMWOOD AV
2700 BERK 94705 629-J3
3000 OAK 94601 670-B1
5100 NWK 94560 752-F4
ELMWOOD CIR
7300 PLE 94588 714-A2
ELMWOOD CT
2900 BERK 94705 630-A3
ELMWOOD DR
- SRMN 94583 693-H1
ELMWOOD LN
200 HAY 94541 711-G3
EL NIDO RANCH RD
300 ORIN 94563 610-J6
EL PADRO DR
1200 LVMR 94550 715-E3
EL PASEO
3100 ALA 94502 669-J6
EL PASEO DR
400 OAK 94603 670-H7
EL PATIO
- OAK 94611 650-E2
- ORIN 94563 610-G6
W EL PINTADO
300 DNVL 94526 652-J1
EL POCO COM
4800 FRMT 94536 752-A4
EL PORTAL
3100 ALA 94502 670-A6
EL PORTAL AV
500 FRMT 94536 732-J7
EL PORTAL CT
- BERK 94708 609-J7
EL PORTAL DR
27900 HAY 94542 712-F4
EL PULGAR
- ORIN 94563 610-H5
EL RANCHO DR
700 LVMR 94551 715-E1
EL REY AV
4700 FRMT 94536 752-F4
EL RIBERO
- ORIN 94563 610-G6
EL RINCON
- ORIN 94563 610-E7
EL RIO CT
- LVMR 94551 696-E3
EL RIO RD
400 DNVL 94526 652-J1
ELROD AV
- OAK 94618 630-B6
ELROD DR
4900 AlaC 94546 692-B3
ELSA COM
- LVMR 94551 695-G6
EL SERENO
- ORIN 94563 610-G5
3100 ALA 94502 669-J6
3100 ALA 94502 670-A6
ELSIE AV
200 SLN 94577 691-B1
ELSIE DR
200 DNVL 94526 652-J1
ELSINORE AV
1000 OAK 94602 650-D3
ELSINORE WY
- LVMR 94550 715-D4
ELSNAB CT
2800 PLE 94588 694-F6
ELSTON AV
3700 OAK 94602 650-C4
ELSTON CT
- OAK 94602 650-C4
ELSTON ST
- LVMR 94550 716-D2
ELSTON WY
- LVMR 94550 716-D2
EL SUENO
- ORIN 94563 610-G5
EL SUYO DR
3200 SRMN 94583 673-G5
EL TORAZO COM
4800 FRMT 94536 752-A4
EL TOYONAL
- ORIN 94563 610-E7
300 CCCo 94563 610-D5
EL VERANO
- ORIN 94563 610-J5
EL VERANO ST
9800 OAK 94603 670-G7
ELVERTON DR
6400 OAK 94611 630-F5
6900 CCCo 94563 630-F5
ELVESSA ST
10700 OAK 94605 671-D4
ELVINA DR
1800 SLN 94579 691-A6
ELVIRA PL
4300 AlaC 94546 692-A3
ELVIRA ST
100 LVMR 94550 715-D2
ELWOOD AV
300 OAK 94610 649-J2
400 OAK 94610 650-A2
ELWOOD ST
- SF 94102 648-A6
ELYSIAN PL
- OAK 94605 671-C3
ELYSIAN FIELDS DR
- OAK 94605 671-C3
EMBARCADERO
100 OAK 94606 649-J6
100 OAK 94607 649-J6
1700 OAK 94606 650-A7
1800 OAK 94606 670-A1
39600 FRMT 94538 753-B5
EMBARCADERO W
100 OAK 94607 649-F5
EMBARCADERO CT
7000 PLE 94588 693-H5
EMBASSY DR
- LVMR 94550 696-D7
- LVMR 94550 716-D1
EMBERS WY
1500 AlaC 94580 691-D6
1500 SLN 94579 691-D6
EMBLETON LN
- CCCo 94582 674-B4
EMERALD AV
900 SLN 94577 691-C1
7100 DBLN 94568 693-H3
EMERALD CT
20000 AlaC 94546 692-C5
EMERALD DR
- DNVL 94526 652-H1
EMERALD ST
500 LVMR 94550 715-D2
4100 OAK 94609 629-J7
EMERIC LN
- ALA 94501 649-E7

EMERSON AV
27900 HAY 94545 731-G1
EMERSON CT
700 FRMT 94539 753-G7
EMERSON DR
4000 LVMR 94551 696-A6
EMERSON ST
400 FRMT 94539 753-H7
2000 BERK 94703 629-G4
2100 BERK 94705 629-G4
3600 OAK 94610 650-B4
EMERSON TER
1600 ALA 94501 669-H2
EMERSON WY
3700 OAK 94610 650-B4
EMERY CT
16300 AlaC 94580 691-E5
EMERY LN
- SF 94133 648-A4
EMERY ST
3400 EMVL 94608 629-F7
EMERY BAY DR
- EMVL 94608 629-E6
EMILIA LN
33800 FRMT 94555 752-C1
EMILY CT
- LVMR 94550 696-D7
- SJCo 95391 (678-E3 See Page 677)
4600 AlaC 94546 692-A3
EMILY ST
- SJCo 95391 (678-E3 See Page 677)
EMILY WY
- LVMR 94550 696-D7
EMMA ST
- SF 94108 648-A5
EMMETT WY
2500 EPA 94303 771-B7
EMORY WY
4200 LVMR 94550 716-A2
EMPIRE CT
3900 PLE 94588 694-A7
3900 PLE 94588 714-A1
EMPIRE RD
9200 OAK 94603 670-F7
EMPIRE ST
500 AlaC 94580 691-D6
4600 UNC 94587 752-A1
EMROL AV
38700 FRMT 94536 752-J5
ENCANTO WY
40500 FRMT 94539 753-F4
ENCHANTED WY
- SRMN 94583 673-A2
ENCINA PL
- BERK 94705 630-A4
ENCINA ST
1200 HAY 94544 711-J7
1200 HAY 94544 712-A7
ENCINA WY
3400 OAK 94605 671-B4
ENCINAL AV
2600 ALA 94501 670-A3
ENCINAL AV Rt#-61
1300 ALA 94501 669-J2
2200 ALA 94501 670-A2
ENCINITAS WY
4200 UNC 94587 731-J5
4200 UNC 94587 732-A6
ENCINO DR
300 LVMR 94550 715-D2
ENCOUNTER BAY
200 ALA 94502 669-H7
ENCYCLOPEDIA CIR
40400 FRMT 94538 773-A2
ENDEAVOR WY
32500 UNC 94587 732-A6
ENDICOTT ST
14900 SLN 94579 691-B6
ENEA CT
4000 FRMT 94555 752-D1
ENEA TER
34300 FRMT 94555 752-D1
ENFIELD DR
5000 NWK 94560 752-F4
ENGINE HOUSE DR
30600 UNC 94587 732-A4
ENGLE CT
- SJCo 95391 (678-F3 See Page 677)
ENGLEWOOD DR
10500 OAK 94605 671-D3
ENNIS PL
- ALA 94502 669-J4
ENNISMORE CT
200 ALA 94502 670-A5
ENOLA AV
900 AlaC 94586 734-B4
ENOS AV
3600 OAK 94619 650-G6
ENOS ST
400 FRMT 94539 753-H7
ENOS WY
500 LVMR 94551 695-G7
ENRIQUEZ CT
200 MPS 95035 794-A5
ENSENADA AV
600 BERK 94707 609-F5
ENSENADA DR
3200 SRMN 94583 673-G5
8000 PLE 94588 714-A5
ENSIGN DR
- EMVL 94608 629-D6
ENTERPRISE
3000 ALA 94501 649-F6
ENTERPRISE AV
3300 HAY 94545 711-C7
ENTERPRISE COM
- FRMT 94538 773-D4
ENTERPRISE CT
- LVMR 94551 696-F5
37500 NWK 94560 772-D1
ENTERPRISE DR
7400 NWK 94560 772-C1
ENTERPRISE PL
4400 FRMT 94538 773-D4
ENTERPRISE ST
4300 FRMT 94538 773-D4
ENTERPRISE WY
8400 OAK 94621 670-F5
ENTRADA AV
- OAK 94611 629-J7
- OAK 94611 649-J1
ENTRADA CT
4500 PLE 94566 714-E4
ENTRADA DR
4300 PLE 94566 714-E4
ENTRADA PZ
200 UNC 94587 732-H5
ENTRADA MESA
100 DNVL 94526 652-J2

ENTRANCE RD
1800 ALA 94501 649-H7
1800 ALA 94501 669-H1
EOLA ST
1700 BERK 94703 629-F1
EPILING TER
34300 FRMT 94555 752-A3
EPSON ST
1900 LVMR 94550 715-G4
EQUESTRIAN DR
1700 PLE 94588 694-F7
EQUUS CT
13000 PLE 94588 713-J2
ERBA PTH
- OAK 94618 630-C5
ERIC CT
2100 UNC 94587 732-C5
ERIC ST
39400 FRMT 94538 753-A6
ERICA CT
300 LVMR 94550 696-B6
ERICA PL
500 HAY 94544 732-F2
ERICA WY
300 LVMR 94550 696-B6
ERIE CIR
700 MPS 95035 794-A6
ERIE CT
700 MPS 95035 794-A5
7000 DBLN 94568 693-J4
ERIE DR
300 MPS 95035 794-A5
ERIE PL
100 HAY 94544 732-E3
700 MPS 95035 794-A5
ERIE ST
800 OAK 94610 650-A3
ERLANDSON ST
700 RCH 94804 609-A1
ERMA AV
41200 FRMT 94539 753-E6
ERNEST AV
5200 ELCR 94530 609-B1
5200 RCH 94804 609-B1
ERNEST CT
23200 AlaC 94541 692-D7
ERNWOOD PL
9600 SRMN 94583 693-G1
ERNWOOD ST
9500 SRMN 94583 693-G1
ERROL DR
7400 ELCR 94530 609-E3
ERSKINE LN
2500 HAY 94545 711-F6
ERVIN CT
5200 NWK 94560 752-F5
ERVING CT
35200 FRMT 94536 752-F1
ESCALA TER
4400 FRMT 94536 752-G4
ESCALLONIA CT
6200 NWK 94560 752-G7
ESCALLONIA DR
6200 NWK 94560 752-G7
6300 NWK 94560 772-G1
ESCAMILLA PL
3200 HAY 94542 712-E4
ESCHER DR
5800 OAK 94611 630-F7
5800 OAK 94611 650-F1
ESCOBAR PL
200 SRMN 94583 673-F4
ESCOBAR ST
300 FRMT 94539 753-H7
ESCONDIDO CIR
500 LVMR 94550 715-E2
ESCONDIDO CT
600 LVMR 94550 715-E3
ESCUDO CT
- DBLN 94568 694-G4
ESCUELA CT
4500 RCH 94804 609-A1
ESCUELA PKWY
400 MPS 95035 794-A4
ESCUELA PL
600 MPS 95035 794-A5
ESGUERA TER
4800 FRMT 94555 752-C2
ESPADA CT
- FRMT 94539 753-D2
ESPADA PL
100 FRMT 94539 753-D2
ESPARITO AV
- FRMT 94539 753-F4
ESPARITO PL
- FRMT 94539 753-F4
ESPINOSA AV
3100 OAK 94605 671-A4
ESSANAY AV
- FRMT 94536 753-C1
ESSANAY PL
37700 FRMT 94536 753-C1
ESSER AV
1200 SLN 94579 691-A5
ESSEX CT
700 HAY 94544 712-D7
W ESSEX DR
- ALA 94501 649-D6
ESSEX ST
- SF 94105 648-B6
900 LVMR 94550 715-G3
1400 SJS 95002 793-C7
1900 BERK 94703 629-G4
2100 BERK 94705 629-G4
4300 EMVL 94608 629-F6
6400 OAK 94608 629-F5
ESSEX WY
4800 FRMT 94538 773-B1
ESTABROOK CIR
2100 SLN 94577 691-B2
ESTABROOK ST
- SLN 94577 691-A2
ESTANCIA CT
- SRMN 94583 673-A2
ESTATES CT
- ORIN 94563 630-J2
ESTATES DR
- ORIN 94563 630-J2
- PDMT 94611 650-D2
100 DNVL 94526 652-J2
5300 OAK 94618 630-C6
5800 OAK 94611 630-D7
6100 OAK 94611 650-D1
ESTATES RD
- CCCo 94707 609-F2
ESTATES ST
100 LVMR 94550 695-J7
400 LVMR 94550 715-J1
ESTATES TER
2000 FRMT 94539 774-A5
ESTEBAN ST
16900 AlaC 94541 691-G5

ESTEBAN ST
16900 AlaC 94578 691-G5
ESTEPA DR
10700 OAK 94603 670-H7
10800 OAK 94603 690-H1
ESTERBROOK CT
- ALA 94501 669-F1
ESTERO DR
3300 SRMN 94583 673-G6
ESTHER CT
200 HAY 94544 712-C7
ESTHER LN
100 DNVL 94526 652-J2
ESTRELLA AV
- PDMT 94611 630-B7
ESTRELLA CT
11500 DBLN 94568 693-F4
ESTRELLA PL
- DNVL 94526 652-J1
ESTRELLA RD
100 FRMT 94539 753-E3
ESTUDILLO AV
100 SLN 94577 691-A1
600 SLN 94577 671-B7
1700 SLN 94577 671-D7
W ESTUDILLO AV
200 SLN 94577 691-A1
700 SLN 94577 690-J1
ETHAN CT
300 SRMN 94583 693-F1
500 HAY 94544 732-E2
ETHAN TER
34100 FRMT 94555 752-C2
ETHEL LN
1300 HAY 94544 711-H6
ETHEL ST
2900 FRMT 94536 753-A3
ETNA CT
- SRMN 94583 673-F7
ETNA ST
2500 BERK 94704 629-J2
ETON AV
3100 BERK 94705 629-J4
ETON CT
- BERK 94705 629-J4
ETTA AV
28400 HAY 94544 712-B7
28600 HAY 94544 732-B1
ETTIE ST
3200 OAK 94608 649-E1
ETTRICK ST
10700 OAK 94605 671-D4
EUCALYPTUS CT
- LVMR 94551 715-D1
27600 HAY 94544 712-B6
EUCALYPTUS LN
- SRMN 94583 693-F1
EUCALYPTUS PTH
- OAK 94705 630-A3
EUCALYPTUS RD
- BERK 94705 630-A4
- OAK 94618 630-A4
- OAK 94705 630-A4
EUCALYPTUS TER
34200 FRMT 94555 752-B3
EUCLID AV
- SLN 94577 671-A7
200 OAK 94610 649-J2
500 BERK 94708 609-H5
1600 BERK 94709 609-H7
1600 BERK 94709 629-H1
EUCLID CT
500 SLN 94577 671-A7
EUCLID DR
43500 FRMT 94539 773-F1
EUCLID PL
2300 FRMT 94539 773-F1
EUGENE ST
3500 FRMT 94538 753-C6
EUGENE TER
- AlaC 94546 691-G3
EUGENIA AV
1700 HAY 94545 731-J1
EUGENIA CT
3300 ALA 94502 670-A6
EULL CT
4500 PLE 94566 714-D1
EUNICE ST
2000 BERK 94709 609-G6
2000 BERK 94707 609-G6
2300 BERK 94708 609-G6
EUREKA AV
- CCCo 94707 609-E3
600 ELCR 94530 609-D3
EUREKA CT
3400 HAY 94542 712-E5
EUREKA DR
- NWK 94560 772-J3
EUROPEAN TER
- UNC 94587 732-G6
EUSTICE AV
- OAK 94618 630-B5
EVANGELINE WY
500 HAY 94544 732-E1
EVANS AV
- DBLN 94568 694-B4
4300 OAK 94602 650-C3
4900 FRMT 94536 752-H5
EVANS CT
- ALA 94502 669-H6
900 MPS 95035 794-C4
1000 HAY 94544 711-J6
EVANS PL
1300 LVMR 94550 715-F4
EVANS RD
- MPS 95035 794-C5
- SCIC 95035 794-C5
EVANS ST
1900 LVMR 94550 715-F4
EVANSWOOD RD
- HAY 94541 711-J2
EVE CT
200 AlaC 94541 711-F1
EVE LN
1000 LVMR 94550 716-B1
EVELENA CT
4500 FRMT 94536 752-E2
EVELETH AV
1700 SLN 94577 690-J2
2000 SLN 94577 691-A2
EVELYN AV
400 ALB 94706 609-D5
1100 BERK 94706 609-D5
1300 BERK 94702 609-D5
EVELYN CT
2600 ALA 94501 670-A4
2900 OAK 94602 650-D5
2900 OAK 94601 650-D5
4300 PLE 94588 694-A7
EVELYN LN
400 HAY 94544 711-J4
400 HAY 94544 712-A4

EVELYN WY
5400 LVMR 94550 696-C7
EVENS CREEK CT
700 SRMN 94582 674-A7
EVERETT AV
800 OAK 94602 650-C3
EVERETT CT
31100 HAY 94544 732-E2
EVERETT ST
400 ELCR 94530 609-C1
1400 ALA 94501 670-A2
EVERGLADE ST
1900 HAY 94545 731-J1
1900 HAY 94545 711-J7
EVERGLADES CT
6100 PLE 94588 714-B1
EVERGLADES DR
1700 MPS 95035 794-E7
EVERGLADES LN
400 LVMR 94551 695-D7
EVERGLADES PARK DR
4900 FRMT 94538 773-C2
EVERGREEN AV
800 SLN 94577 691-C1
6600 OAK 94611 630-G7
EVERGREEN DR
- ORIN 94563 630-J1
EVERGREEN ST
25600 HAY 94544 711-H5
EVERGREEN TER
5600 FRMT 94538 773-A1
EVERGREEN PATH LN
- OAK 94705 630-A3
EVERS AV
1700 OAK 94602 650-C4
EVIREL PL
- OAK 94611 630-F6
EWE WY
1300 FRMT 94536 753-B3
EWER PL
- SF 94108 648-A5
EWING CT
4600 AlaC 94546 691-J1
EWING DR
300 PLE 94566 714-F3
EWING RD
4400 AlaC 94546 691-J1
EXCELSIOR AV
1100 OAK 94610 650-B4
1300 OAK 94602 650-C4
EXCELSIOR CT
- OAK 94610 650-A3
EXCELSO CT
700 FRMT 94539 773-H1
EXCELSO DR
43500 FRMT 94539 773-H1
EXCELSO PL
43600 FRMT 94539 773-H1
EXCHANGE CT
500 LVMR 94551 696-E5
EXECUTIVE PKWY
3000 SRMN 94583 673-D2
EXECUTIVE PL
26200 HAY 94545 731-D1
EXETER CT
36200 NWK 94560 752-F4
EXETER DR
6500 OAK 94611 650-G1
6500 OAK 94611 630-G7
EZRA DR
37300 NWK 94560 752-F6

F

F RD
1100 AlaC 94586 734-C3
F ST
100 FRMT 94536 753-B1
100 UNC 94587 732-F4
1500 ELCR 94530 609-B2
9200 OAK 94603 670-H5
FABER ST
2900 UNC 94587 732-A3
FABIAN COM
37800 FRMT 94536 752-J4
FABIAN CT
7000 PLE 94588 693-H6
FABIAN WY
1100 HAY 94544 732-A1
FACTOR AV
1400 SLN 94577 690-J4
1400 SLN 94577 691-A4
FACULTY RD
5200 OAK 94613 670-G1
FAGUNDES CT
200 HAY 94544 711-H4
FAGUNDES ST
- HAY 94544 711-H4
FAIR AV
4200 OAK 94619 650-G6
5800 NWK 94560 752-E6
FAIR CT
36700 NWK 94560 752-E6
FAIR ST
4700 PLE 94566 714-D3
FAIRBAIRN ST
4500 OAK 94619 650-F7
FAIRBANKS AV
400 OAK 94610 650-A2
FAIRBANKS COM
5100 FRMT 94555 752-C3
FAIRBANKS ST
2000 SLN 94577 690-G3
FAIRBROOK CT
- LVMR 94551 696-E3
7700 PLE 94588 693-J7
FAIRCHILD COM
34700 FRMT 94555 752-A3
FAIRCHILD ST
1000 OAK 94621 670-D6
FAIRCLIFF ST
600 HAY 94544 732-E1
FAIRFAX AV
4500 OAK 94601 650-E7
4900 OAK 94601 670-E1
FAIRFAX CT
3100 FRMT 94536 752-F1
FAIRFIELD AV
- DBLN 94568 694-C3
FAIRFIELD CT
2300 PLE 94566 714-C1
FAIRFIELD PL
100 MRGA 94556 651-E2
FAIRFIELD RD
2100 PLE 94566 714-C2
FAIRFIELD ST
32700 UNC 94587 732-A7
32700 UNC 94587 752-A1
FAIRGROUNDS RD
- PLE 94566 714-D3
FAIR HAVEN RD
400 ALA 94501 669-G3

FAIRHILL CT
5100 OAK 94605 671-B1
FAIR HILL DR
1700 MPS 95035 794-D5
FAIRLAINE DR
3700 FRMT 94539 753-F7
FAIRLANDS DR
3600 PLE 94588 694-E5
FAIRLANDS RD
23700 AlaC 94541 692-C7
23700 AlaC 94541 712-C1
FAIRLANE DR
6000 OAK 94611 630-C5
FAIRLAWN DR
- BERK 94708 609-J6
FAIRMEAD ST
32700 UNC 94587 732-A7
FAIRMEADOW WY
200 MPS 95035 794-C2
FAIRMONT DR
1200 SLN 94578 691-D4
1400 AlaC 94578 691-E2
FAIRMOUNT AV
100 OAK 94611 649-J1
500 OAK 94610 649-J1
6000 ELCR 94530 609-D4
FAIR OAKS AV
1000 ALA 94501 669-G1
FAIROAKS CT
7900 PLE 94588 693-H7
FAIROAKS DR
7600 PLE 94588 693-H7
FAIR RANCH RD
4100 UNC 94587 732-A6
FAIRVIEW AV
- PDMT 94610 650-A1
3000 ALA 94501 670-B3
24000 AlaC 94541 712-D1
24800 AlaC 94542 712-E1
26700 HAY 94542 712-G4
27800 HAY 94552 712-F3
FAIRVIEW CT
1300 LVMR 94550 715-E3
1500 PLE 94566 714-D2
FAIRVIEW ST
600 OAK 94609 629-H4
1400 BERK 94702 629-F4
1500 BERK 94703 629-F4
FAIRVIEW WY
300 MPS 95035 793-H5
FAIRWAY AV
3800 OAK 94605 671-B3
FAIRWAY CT
4500 LVMR 94551 696-A3
8100 NWK 94560 752-C7
FAIRWAY DR
- ORIN 94563 610-F6
2500 SLN 94577 690-H4
2500 SLN 94577 691-A4
FAIRWAY LN
- AlaC 94566 714-B7
FAIRWAY PL
400 ALA 94502 670-B7
FAIRWAY ST
- HAY 94544 732-D2
FAIRWEATHER CT
- AlaC 94552 692-F7
FAIRWOOD ST
4000 FRMT 94538 773-D2
FALCATO DR
100 MPS 95035 794-E7
FALCON AV
3000 HAY 94545 711-E7
FALCON CT
2600 UNC 94587 732-D6
FALCON DR
32800 FRMT 94555 732-B7
FALCON WY
- CCCo 94514 637-E7
- CCCo 94514 (657-E1 See Page 637)
400 LVMR 94551 695-E7
400 LVMR 94551 715-E1
FALGREN AV
20100 AlaC 94541 711-F1
FALL AV
4500 RCH 94804 609-A1
FALL CT
4600 PLE 94566 714-D3
FALLBOROUGH CT
- SRMN 94583 673-H3
FALLBROOK DR
27900 HAY 94542 712-F5
FALLBROOK WY
10700 OAK 94605 671-D4
FALLBURY CT
100 SRMN 94583 673-F4
FALL CREEK RD
7900 DBLN 94568 694-A1
FALLEN LEAF CIR
500 SRMN 94583 673-F4
FALLEN LEAF CT
27700 HAY 94542 712-E4
FALLEN LEAF DR
1400 LVMR 94551 696-D3
FALLEN LEAF TER
- ORIN 94563 610-J3
FALLON AV
5000 RCH 94804 609-B2
FALLON PTH
5000 RCH 94804 609-B2
FALLON RD
- AlaC 94568 674-F7
- AlaC 94588 694-H4
- AlaC 94588 694-H4
- DBLN 94568 674-F7
4200 DBLN 94568 694-F1
FALLON ST
100 OAK 94607 649-G5
FALLON TER
36400 FRMT 94536 752-J1
FALL RIVER DR
900 HAY 94544 732-B1
FALLS TER
34500 FRMT 94555 752-C3
FALLVIEW ST
200 SRMN 94583 673-F4
FALLWOOD CT
4000 PLE 94588 713-J2
FALMOUTH PL
5200 NWK 94560 752-E4
FALMOUTH ST
- SF 94107 648-A7
FALSTAFF AV
4600 FRMT 94555 752-C1
FALSTAFF RD
4700 FRMT 94555 752-C1
FALTINGS CT
- LVMR 94550 715-J3
FALTINGS DR
- LVMR 94550 715-J3

STREET Block City ZIP Pg-Grid

FAMOSA PZ
200 UNC 94587 732-H5
FANSHAWE CT
36100 FRMT 94536 752-F3
FANSHAWE ST
36100 FRMT 94536 752-F3
FANTAIL CT
- SLN 94579 711-A2
FANWOOD TER
4600 FRMT 94538 773-C1
FANYON ST
100 MPS 95035 794-C6
FARADAY CT
35200 FRMT 94536 752-F1
FARALLON DR
2000 SLN 94577 690-H5
FARALLON WY
6400 OAK 94611 630-D5
FAREHAM CT
3200 FRMT 94536 752-J3
FARGO AV
600 SLN 94579 691-B6
FARGO CT
4100 PLE 94588 714-A1
FARGO PL
- SF 94103 648-A7
FARINA LN
5100 FRMT 94538 773-B2
FARIS ST
15500 SLN 94579 691-B7
FARLEY ST
2200 AlaC 94546 692-A6
FARM HILL DR
27800 HAY 94542 712-E4
FARMINGTON PL
2100 LVMR 94550 715-F4
FARMINGTON WY
1100 LVMR 94550 715-F4
FARNAM ST
3200 OAK 94601 650-C7
FARNHAM DR
4900 NWK 94560 752-E3
FARNSWORTH DR
2300 LVMR 94551 695-G6
FARNSWORTH ST
14600 SLN 94579 691-B6
14700 SLN 94578 691-B6
FARRAGUT AV
- PDMT 94610 650-C2
FARRAGUT DR
900 FRMT 94539 753-F6
FARRELL ST
9500 OAK 94605 671-A4
FARRELLY DR
100 SLN 94577 670-J7
FARRINGTON ST
- SJCo 95391 (678-F3 See Page 677)
FARRINGTON WY
2500 EPA 94303 771-B7
FARROL AV
2000 UNC 94587 732-G7
FARROL CT
2400 UNC 94587 732-G7
FARWELL DR
37600 FRMT 94536 752-G6
38800 FRMT 94538 752-J7
39100 FRMT 94538 772-J1
39200 FRMT 94538 773-A1
FARWELL PL
5300 FRMT 94536 752-H7
FAULKNER CT
- SJCo 95391 (678-F3 See Page 677)
4500 FRMT 94536 752-H5
FAULKNER DR
4300 FRMT 94536 752-H4
FAULKNER ST
- SJCo 95391 (678-F2 See Page 677)
FAVOR ST
7000 OAK 94621 670-G3
FAWN CT
300 FRMT 94539 773-J2
FAWN DR
- LVMR 94550 696-A7
FAWN WY
- DBLN 94568 694-D4
FAWN HILLS LN
- PLE 94588 714-B5
FAWN MEADOW LN
24600 HAY 94541 712-B2
FAWN RIDGE CT
- SRMN 94582 673-J7
FAY CT
100 UNC 94587 732-E3
FEATHER CT
5500 AlaC 94552 692-D4
FEATHERMINT DR
- CCCo 94582 674-A1
- SRMN 94582 674-A1
FEDERAL ST
- SF 94107 648-C6
FELDSPAR CT
1600 LVMR 94550 715-D3
4300 UNC 94587 732-A6
FELICIA AV
- SJCo 95391 (678-E3 See Page 677)
5100 LVMR 94550 696-C6
FELICIA CT
1000 LVMR 94550 696-C7
FELICIO COM
200 FRMT 94536 733-A7
FELIX TER
34400 FRMT 94555 752-D2
FELIZ CT
36400 FRMT 94536 752-F3
FELLA PL
- SF 94108 648-A5
FELLOWS CT
32700 UNC 94587 732-A7
FELLOWS ST
4300 UNC 94587 732-A7
FELTER RD
4600 SCIC 95035 794-J6
4600 SCIC 95140 794-J6
FENHAM ST
6200 OAK 94621 670-F3
FENICO TER
4400 FRMT 94536 752-B4
FENTON ST
- LVMR 94550 715-F1
FENTON WY
38700 FRMT 94536 752-H6
FENWICK CT
11500 DBLN 94568 693-F2
FENWICK PL
11600 DBLN 94568 693-F2
FENWICK WY
8600 DBLN 94568 693-F2

FERDINANDA PL
4300 AlaC 94546 692-A3
FERINO WY
100 FRMT 94536 753-D2
FERN CIR
42500 FRMT 94538 773-D2
FERN COM
4400 FRMT 94538 773-D2
FERN ST
2400 OAK 94601 650-E7
FERN TER
4300 FRMT 94538 773-D2
FERN TR
2300 AlaC 94586 733-J1
2300 AlaC 94586 734-A1
FERN WY
- ORIN 94563 630-J3
1600 AlaC 94586 734-A2
19600 AlaC 94546 692-B5
FERNALD COM
46800 FRMT 94539 773-H6
FERNALD CT
200 FRMT 94539 773-H7
FERNALD ST
46700 FRMT 94539 773-H6
FERNANDEZ AV
- DBLN 94568 694-B3
FERNANDEZ ST
- UNC 94555 752-B1
FERNANDO CT
400 SRMN 94583 673-B2
FERNBROOK COM
2100 LVMR 94551 696-D1
FERNCLIFF CT
8300 DBLN 94568 693-G2
FERNCROFT CT
- DBLN 94568 694-F2
FERNCROFT WY
- DBLN 94568 694-F2
FERNDALE CT
3000 PLE 94588 694-F6
FERNDELL WK
- ALA 94501 669-H3
FERNHOFF CT
- OAK 94619 650-J5
FERNHOFF RD
5400 OAK 94619 650-J5
5500 OAK 94619 651-A4
FERNRIDGE CT
- HAY 94544 711-H4
FERNSIDE BLVD
900 ALA 94501 670-B2
FERNWALD RD
- BERK 94704 630-A2
FERNWOOD CT
- FRMT 94536 753-A2
2200 AlaC 94541 692-B7
4000 PLE 94588 713-J2
FERNWOOD DR
1400 OAK 94611 630-D6
5400 NWK 94560 752-E5
FERNWOOD WY
3900 PLE 94588 713-J2
FERRARA CT
5200 PLE 94588 694-C6
FERREIRA CT
400 MPS 95035 794-E7
FERREIRA PL
40900 FRMT 94539 753-F4
FERRELO CT
- DBLN 94568 694-G4
FERRO CT
- ALA 94502 669-J7
FERRO DR
- AlaC 94580 691-C7
FERRO ST
- OAK 94607 649-C5
FERROL CT
- SRMN 94583 673-C3
FERRY LN
3500 FRMT 94555 752-E1
FERRY PT
- ALA 94501 649-D7
- ALA 94501 669-D1
FESTIVO CT
500 FRMT 94539 773-H1
FIDDLE CREEK PL
300 SRMN 94582 674-A7
FIELD ST
3500 OAK 94605 671-A2
FIELDBROOK RD
4500 OAK 94619 650-G5
FIELDING CT
34600 FRMT 94555 752-D2
FIELDING DR
27000 HAY 94542 712-D4
FIELDING ST
- SF 94133 648-A3
FIELDSTONE DR
300 FRMT 94536 732-J7
5900 LVMR 94551 696-D3
FIELDVIEW CT
- PLE 94588 714-F1
FIELDVIEW TER
2800 SRMN 94583 673-B3
FIESTA DR
3000 PLE 94588 694-C7
FIESTA PL
600 HAY 94544 712-D7
FIESTA RD
5400 FRMT 94538 773-B2
FIFE CT
- SRMN 94583 673-E5
FIGONE WY
- LVMR 94550 696-A7
FIG TREE CT
300 HAY 94544 711-J4
FIGUEROA DR
800 SLN 94578 691-B4
FIJI CIR
400 UNC 94587 732-C6
FIJI LN
3100 ALA 94502 669-J7
3100 ALA 94502 670-A7
FIJI WY
2200 SLN 94577 690-G5
FILBERT CT
600 SRMN 94583 673-G7
FILBERT ST
100 OAK 94607 649-F3
200 SF 94133 648-A4
2900 OAK 94608 649-F2
22500 HAY 94541 711-H2
37100 NWK 94560 752-E7
37100 NWK 94560 772-E1
FILLMORE ST
900 ALB 94706 609-D6
2800 ALA 94501 670-A4
FILTON CT
1200 FRMT 94536 733-D7
FINBACK WY
- SLN 94577 690-H5

FINCH CT
1700 HAY 94545 731-J1
FINCH PL
3500 FRMT 94555 732-D7
FINCH WY
- DBLN 94568 694-D4
300 LVMR 94551 695-D7
W FINCK RD
18600 SJCo 95206 (658-F5 See Page 637)
FINDLAY WY
4000 LVMR 94550 716-A2
FINDLEY DR
1700 MPS 95035 794-D6
FINN COVE CT
- UNC 94545 731-J6
FINNIAN WY
- DBLN 94568 694-F4
FINNIGAN TER
34100 FRMT 94555 752-B2
FINOVINO CT
900 PLE 94566 714-H4
FIORE BELLA WY
- LVMR 94550 715-F4
FIORIO CIR
1900 PLE 94566 714-E1
FIR AV
1500 AlaC 94578 691-D3
3100 ALA 94502 670-A6
FIR CT
6800 DBLN 94568 693-J4
36800 NWK 94560 752-C7
FIR PL
1100 ALA 94502 670-A7
1100 ALA 94502 669-J7
FIRCREST CT
- SRMN 94583 693-H1
FIRCREST LN
9100 SRMN 94583 693-H1
9400 SRMN 94583 673-H7
FIRCREST ST
35300 NWK 94560 752-C5
FIREBRAND DR
7700 DBLN 94568 693-G3
FIRE BRAND PL
25600 AlaC 94541 712-D2
FIREBRICK TER
- UNC 94587 732-G6
FIRENZA ST
400 LVMR 94551 695-E7
FIRESTONE CT
18000 HAY 94541 711-D2
35900 NWK 94560 752-B6
FIRESTONE RD
5500 LVMR 94551 696-C2
17900 HAY 94541 711-D2
FIRETHORN CT
2000 MPS 95035 793-J3
FIRETHORN ST
- MPS 95035 793-J3
FIRETHORN WY
- DBLN 94568 693-G2
FIRTH CT
1600 FRMT 94539 773-G1
14900 SLN 94578 691-C5
FISALIA CT
200 FRMT 94539 753-E3
FISHER AL
- SF 94133 648-A4
FISHER AV
2600 OAK 94605 671-B5
FISHER CT
4500 PLE 94588 694-A7
FISHER PL
35500 FRMT 94536 752-F1
FISH RANCH RD
- CCCo 94563 630-D2
- OAK 94705 630-D2
FISK CT
14700 SLN 94579 691-A5
FISK TER
100 FRMT 94538 773-D3
FITCH CT
- ALA 94501 649-A2
FITCHBURG AV
500 ALA 94502 670-B7
FITZGERALD CIR
38300 FRMT 94536 753-A3
FITZGERALD ST
1300 OAK 94608 649-F1
FITZPATRICK RD
200 OAK 94603 670-F6
FITZSIMMONS COM
3400 FRMT 94538 753-C5
FITZWILLIAM ST
- DBLN 94568 694-F4
FIVE CANYONS PKWY
- AlaC 94542 712-F1
- AlaC 94552 712-F1
3700 AlaC 94552 692-D5
FJORD ST
14900 SLN 94578 691-C5
FLAGG AV
3300 OAK 94602 650-D5
FLAGG ST
22300 HAY 94541 711-H1
FLAGSHIP ST
14400 SLN 94577 690-H5
FLAGSTAFF CT
48700 FRMT 94539 793-J2
FLAGSTAFF PL
48400 FRMT 94539 793-J2
FLAGSTAFF RD
48500 FRMT 94539 793-J2
FLAGSTONE COM
- LVMR 94550 715-C1
FLAGSTONE DR
- UNC 94587 732-G6
7400 PLE 94588 693-J7
FLAMINGO AV
26100 HAY 94544 711-H6
FLAMINGO LN
5200 FRMT 94538 752-J7
FLAMINGO PARK CT
4600 FRMT 94538 773-C2
FLANAGAN CT
11800 DBLN 94568 693-G4
FLANDERS CT
200 AlaC 94541 711-F1
FLANDERS DR
6400 NWK 94560 752-C5
FLANDERS PL
6400 NWK 94560 752-C5
FLANDERS WY
1300 LVMR 94550 715-F3
7500 DBLN 94568 693-H3
FLEET RD
1100 OAK 94602 650-C3
1100 OAK 94610 650-C3
FLEETWOOD AV
18400 AlaC 94546 692-A3

FLEMING AV
3800 RCH 94804 609-B2
4300 OAK 94619 650-E7
5100 OAK 94619 670-F1
5500 OAK 94605 670-F1
FLEMING ST
15000 SLN 94579 691-B6
FLEMINGTON CT
3200 PLE 94588 694-F6
FLETCHER CT
- ALA 94501 649-A2
700 HAY 94544 711-J2
FLETCHER LN
800 HAY 94544 711-J2
900 HAY 94541 712-A2
900 HAY 94544 712-A2
FLICKER CT
200 LVMR 94551 715-D1
FLIN COM
37200 FRMT 94536 752-J2
FLINT
3000 ALA 94501 649-E6
FLINT CT
- OAK 94603 671-C6
200 AlaC 94541 711-F1
FLINT ST
100 LVMR 94550 715-D2
2900 UNC 94587 732-A4
FLINTRIDGE AV
3200 OAK 94605 671-B4
FLINTRIDGE LN
8900 OAK 94605 671-B3
FLINTWOOD DR
36600 NWK 94560 752-F5
FLORA CT
3000 PLE 94588 694-D7
FLORA PL
400 FRMT 94536 753-D2
FLORA ST
6400 OAK 94605 670-F2
6400 OAK 94621 670-G3
FLORADA AV
- OAK 94610 650-C2
- PDMT 94610 650-C2
FLORA VISTA
- DNVL 94526 652-H1
3000 ALA 94502 669-J6
FLORENCE AV
100 OAK 94618 630-C6
FLORENCE RD
900 LVMR 94550 715-G2
FLORENCE ST
- FRMT 94555 732-C7
- FRMT 94555 752-C1
- AlaC 94541 711-F1
300 UNC 94587 732-J5
300 FRMT 94536 732-J5
2800 BERK 94705 629-H3
FLORENCE TER
5500 OAK 94611 630-D6
FLORENCE WY
38700 FRMT 94536 752-J5
FLORESTA BLVD
500 SLN 94578 691-B4
FLORIAN ST
3500 PLE 94588 694-C6
FLORIDA AV
- BERK 94707 609-G5
FLORIDA CT
4100 LVMR 94550 716-A1
FLORIDA ST
1800 HAY 94545 731-J1
2900 OAK 94602 650-E5
FLORIO ST
6200 OAK 94618 629-J5
6400 OAK 94618 630-A4
FLOSSMOOR WY
30400 HAY 94544 732-D1
FLOWER LN
600 ALA 94502 670-A6
FLOWERWOOD TER
- FRMT 94536 752-A5
FLUME CT
700 SLN 94578 691-D5
700 MPS 95035 794-B5
FLUORITE CT
- LVMR 94550 715-D3
FLYING MIST RD
15100 SLN 94579 690-J6
N FLYNN RD
11700 AlaC 94550 (697-B3 See Page 677)
12000 AlaC 94551 (697-A3 See Page 677)
S FLYNN RD
9500 AlaC 94550 696-J6
9500 AlaC 94550 (697-C5 See Page 677)
FOGGY GLEN DR
- AlaC 94552 692-E7
FOLEY RD
- PLE 94566 715-A5
FOLEY ST
1600 ALA 94501 670-A2
23000 HAY 94545 711-D6
FOLGER AV
- BERK 94710 629-E4
FOLKLORE LP
- UNC 94587 732-D5
FOLSOM AV
100 HAY 94544 732-A1
200 HAY 94544 712-C7
1600 HAY 94544 731-J1
FOLSOM CIR
400 MPS 95035 794-A6
FOLSOM CT
- LVMR 94551 696-D3
400 MPS 95035 794-A6
FOLSOM PL
100 MPS 95035 794-A6
FOLSOM ST
300 SF 94105 648-B6
600 SF 94107 648-B6
600 SF 94103 648-A7
FOLSUM WY
4900 FRMT 94538 753-A7
FONDRAY CT
8200 PLE 94586 734-D1
FONT CT
- DBLN 94568 694-G4
FONTAINBLEU AV
1200 MPS 95035 794-A4
FONTAINBLEU CT
1200 MPS 95035 794-A4
FONTAINE CT
4100 OAK 94605 671-B2
FONTAINE ST
7900 OAK 94605 671-A3
FONTAINEBLEAU PARK LN
42500 FRMT 94538 773-C2

FONTANA DR
1000 ALA 94502 669-J6
FONTES DR
600 FRMT 94539 753-G6
FONTONETT AV
300 LVMR 94550 715-D3
FONTONETT PL
1500 LVMR 94550 715-D3
FOOTHILL BLVD
100 OAK 94606 649-J5
200 OAK 94605 671-A5
200 SLN 94577 671-B5
1100 OAK 94606 650-A6
2300 OAK 94601 650-C7
4000 OAK 94601 670-D1
5500 OAK 94605 670-G1
15000 AlaC 94578 691-F4
17200 AlaC 94546 691-F4
17300 AlaC 94541 691-F4
FOOTHILL BLVD Rt#-238
1000 HAY 94541 711-J1
20400 AlaC 94546 691-H6
20800 AlaC 94541 691-H6
21100 HAY 94541 691-H6
FOOTHILL LN
- PLE 94588 714-A4
FOOTHILL PL
- PLE 94588 714-A4
1400 OAK 94606 650-A6
FOOTHILL RD
1700 PLE 94588 714-A5
3200 AlaC 94588 713-J1
3200 PLE 94588 713-J1
5000 PLE 94588 693-G6
7000 AlaC 94586 734-D5
7600 AlaC 94566 714-C7
7600 AlaC 94586 734-D1
7700 PLE 94566 734-D1
7800 PLE 94586 734-D1
7800 AlaC 94588 714-A5
FOOTHILL WY
- OAK 94605 671-C7
- SLN 94605 671-C7
FOOTHILL KNOLLS DR
7800 PLE 94588 714-A2
7900 PLE 94588 713-J3
FOOTHILL OAKS DR
2700 PLE 94588 714-A4
FOOTHILL OAKS TER
7900 PLE 94588 714-A4
FORBES DR
- NWK 94560 752-F6
FORBES ST
21000 HAY 94545 711-C5
FORD LN
38200 FRMT 94536 753-B2
FORD ST
2800 OAK 94601 670-B1
FORDHAM AV
1200 SLN 94579 691-A4
FORDHAM CT
4000 LVMR 94550 696-A7
41500 FRMT 94539 753-F6
FORDHAM ST
2500 EPA 94303 771-B7
FORDHAM WY
3900 LVMR 94550 695-J7
3900 LVMR 94550 696-A7
FORENZA CT
- PLE 94566 715-B5
FOREST AV
2700 BERK 94705 629-J3
2800 BERK 94705 630-A3
19500 AlaC 94546 692-B5
FOREST CT
4300 AlaC 94546 692-B4
FOREST LN
- BERK 94708 609-H5
800 CCCo 94507 652-G1
900 LVMR 94550 715-G2
FOREST PL
19400 AlaC 94546 692-B4
FOREST RD
- SF 94130 648-F3
FOREST ST
300 OAK 94618 629-J5
FOREST CREEK LN
- SRMN 94583 673-A2
N FORESTDALE CIR
- DBLN 94568 694-F3
S FORESTDALE CIR
- DBLN 94568 694-F3
FORESTER CT
700 LVMR 94551 695-J6
FOREST GLEN PL
4200 AlaC 94546 692-B4
FOREST HILL AV
3800 OAK 94602 650-D4
FOREST HILL COM
4900 FRMT 94555 752-C2
FOREST HILL DR
4900 PLE 94588 693-H7
FORESTLAND WY
6600 OAK 94611 630-G7
FORGET ME NOT COM
- LVMR 94551 696-C3
FORREST CT
2600 FRMT 94536 753-A3
FORREST HILL CT
4100 HAY 94542 712-G3
FORSELLES WY
900 HAY 94542 712-A7
FORSYTHIA CT
7700 PLE 94588 713-J1
FORSYTHIA DR
42200 FRMT 94539 753-G6
FORTMANN WY
1500 ALA 94501 649-J7
FORTNER ST
47500 FRMT 94539 773-H7
FORTRESS ISL
600 ALA 94501 669-H2
FORTUNA AV
400 SLN 94577 671-C7
FORTUNA COM
600 FRMT 94539 753-H5
FORTUNE WY
5900 OAK 94605 670-G2
FOSCALINA CT
- LVMR 94550 715-G3
FOSCALINA WY
- LVMR 94550 715-H4
FOSTER AV
100 OAK 94603 670-G7
FOSTER CT
- OAK 94603 670-G7
600 HAY 94544 712-A6
FOSTER DR
- SRMN 94583 693-F1
FOSTER ST
1000 ALA 94502 669-J6

FOSTER ST
40400 FRMT 94538 753-C6
FOSTORIA WY
3000 SRMN 94583 673-C1
3000 DNVL 94526 673-C1
3000 SRMN 94526 673-C1
FOUNDERS LN
800 MPS 95035 794-B4
FOUNT WY
26100 HAY 94545 711-F6
FOUNTAIN ST
900 ALA 94501 670-A4
FOUNTAIN WK
- BERK 94707 609-G6
FOUNTAINE AV
6500 NWK 94560 752-D6
FOUNTAINHEAD CT
700 SRMN 94583 673-B2
FOUNTAINHEAD DR
600 SLN 94578 691-C5
2500 SRMN 94583 673-A2
FOUR HILLS COM
- LVMR 94551 695-C4
FOURIER AV
100 FRMT 94539 773-H7
FOUR OAKS HOLLOW
- SRMN 94583 673-E6
FOUR SEASONS PL
19100 AlaC 94541 691-F7
FOUR WINDS TER
- FRMT 94539 753-G6
FOWLER CT
32700 UNC 94587 732-A7
FOWLER ST
- NWK 94560 752-F6
FOX AV
- FRMT 94536 732-H7
- FRMT 94536 752-J1
FOX RUN
600 ORIN 94563 610-J6
FOXBORO CIR
10000 SRMN 94583 673-F4
FOXBORO CT
300 SRMN 94583 673-F5
FOXBORO DR
5000 AlaC 94546 692-A2
FOXBORO WY
9900 SRMN 94583 673-F5
FOX BROUGH CT
700 PLE 94566 714-H3
FOX CREEK CT
1400 LVMR 94551 696-D2
FOXCROFT PL
- SRMN 94583 673-F6
1800 HAY 94541 692-B7
FOXCROFT WY
- DBLN 94568 694-E3
FOXFIRE LN
28800 HAY 94544 732-B1
FOXFORD WY
- DBLN 94568 694-E4
FOXGLOVE CT
2700 PLE 94588 694-H4
FOXGLOVE LN
- SRMN 94583 673-A1
FOXGLOVE WY
- UNC 94587 732-C4
FOX HILLS CT
400 OAK 94605 671-E3
FOXHOLLOW CT
1100 MPS 95035 794-C5
FOX HOLLOW DR
28100 HAY 94542 712-G3
FOX RIDGE DR
2400 AlaC 94546 691-G4
FOXSWALLOW CIR
1800 PLE 94566 714-D1
FOXSWALLOW RD
2000 PLE 94566 714-D1
FOXSWALLOW TER
3700 FRMT 94555 732-J3
FOXTAIL DR
- LVMR 94551 696-E2
FOXTAIL TER
3200 FRMT 94536 752-H3
FRAGA RD
3900 AlaC 94552 692-D5
FRANCE RD
4700 FRMT 94555 752-D2
FRANCE WY
34300 FRMT 94555 752-D2
FRANCES ST
2400 OAK 94601 650-E7
FRANCIA CT
- DBLN 94568 694-G3
FRANCINE WY
5300 LVMR 94550 696-C7
FRANCIS CT
3100 AlaC 94546 691-J6
FRANCIS ST
1400 ALB 94706 609-E7
20900 AlaC 94546 691-J6
FRANCISCAN CT
200 FRMT 94539 773-H6
FRANCISCAN WY
- CCCo 94707 609-E3
- ELCR 94530 609-E3
1900 ALA 94501 669-H3
FRANCISCO LN
100 FRMT 94539 773-G6
FRANCISCO ST
100 SF 94133 648-A3
1100 BERK 94702 629-E1
1500 BERK 94703 629-F1
1900 BERK 94709 629-F1
4000 PLE 94566 714-E1
22800 HAY 94541 711-J2
FRANCO CT
- UNC 94555 752-A2
FRANCONE CT
23800 AlaC 94541 692-C7
FRANK CT
2000 MPS 95035 794-E6
FRANKFURT WY
1400 LVMR 94550 715-G3
FRANK H OGAWA PZ
300 OAK 94612 649-G3
FRANKLIN AV
- UNC 94587 732-B4
3700 FRMT 94538 773-E1
25400 HAY 94544 712-A4
FRANKLIN DR
4900 PLE 94588 694-A5
FRANKLIN LN
400 LVMR 94551 696-C4
FRANKLIN ST
- OAK 94607 649-G3
1200 OAK 94612 649-G3
1600 BERK 94702 629-F1
FRAY AV
4900 RCH 94804 609-B1

FRAY PTH
- RCH 94804 609-B1
FRAZIER AV
2600 OAK 94605 671-B5
FREDERIC AV
300 HAY 94544 711-J4
FREDERICK LN
33900 FRMT 94555 752-C1
FREDERICK RD
700 SLN 94577 690-H1
4800 FRMT 94555 752-C2
FREDERICK ST
2100 OAK 94606 650-A7
FREDERICK MICHAEL WY
1500 LVMR 94550 715-G4
FREDERIKSEN CT
7500 DBLN 94568 693-H3
FREDERIKSEN LN
7400 DBLN 94568 693-H3
FREDI ST
31000 UNC 94587 731-J5
FREEDOM AV
15000 AlaC 94578 691-E3
FREEDOM CT
100 FRMT 94539 773-J2
FREELAND DR
1500 MPS 95035 794-D7
FREELON ST
- SF 94107 648-B7
FREEMAN CT
- SF 94108 648-A5
FREEMAN PL
2800 FRMT 94555 732-E6
FREEMAN WY
- SJCo 95391 (678-F3 See Page 677)
FREESIA CT
- FRMT 94536 753-A2
600 SLN 94578 691-C4
FRWY I-80
- OAK - 648-C5
- OAK - 649-C1
- SF - 648-C5
FRWY I-205
- AlaC - (678-B7 See Page 677)
FRWY I-238
- AlaC - 691-D6
- SLN - 691-C5
FRWY I-580
- AlaC - 677-H7
- AlaC - (678-C7 See Page 677)
- AlaC - 691-G6
- AlaC - 696-H2
- AlaC - (697-F1 See Page 677)
FRWY I-680
- AlaC - 714-D7
- AlaC - 734-D1
- AlaC - 753-J3
- AlaC - 754-E1
- DBLN - 693-G2
- DNVL - 652-J1
- DNVL - 673-C1
- FRMT - 753-J4
- FRMT - 773-F1
- PLE - 693-J4
- PLE - 713-J1
- PLE - 714-A1
- SRMN - 673-C1
- SRMN - 693-F1
FRWY I-880
- AlaC - 691-D6
- SLN - 691-D6
FRWY Rt#-84
- FRMT - 751-J6
- FRMT - 752-E2
- NWK - 752-E2
FREITAS DR
- MRGA 94556 651-E1
FREITAS PL
26800 HAY 94544 712-B5
FREMERY CT
19600 AlaC 94546 692-A4
FREMONT AV
800 SLN 94577 691-B4
800 SLN 94578 691-B4
FREMONT BLVD
34000 FRMT 94555 732-D7
34000 FRMT 94555 752-E2
35000 FRMT 94536 752-E2
38300 FRMT 94536 753-A5
38900 FRMT 94538 753-A5
41500 FRMT 94538 773-D2
47000 FRMT 94538 793-F1
FREMONT BLVD Rt#-84
36800 FRMT 94536 752-H3
FREMONT DR
1800 ALA 94501 670-B2
FREMONT ST
- SF 94105 648-B5
5500 OAK 94608 629-E5
FREMONT WY
1700 OAK 94601 670-E1
FRENCH OAK PL
- LVMR 94550 715-E5
FRESHMEADOW CT
700 HAY 94544 732-E1
FRESNO AV
900 BERK 94707 609-F6
5100 RCH 94804 609-B4
FRESNO CT
26300 HAY 94545 711-F6
FRESNO ST
- SF 94133 648-A4
6900 OAK 94605 670-H2
FRESSIA CT
2700 PLE 94588 694-H4
FRIAR AV
4800 FRMT 94555 752-C1
FRIESMAN RD
1600 LVMR 94551 694-H5
1600 LVMR 94588 694-H5
FRISBIE ST
100 OAK 94611 649-H2
FROBISHER DR
36300 FRMT 94536 752-F4
FROG HILL LN
- PLE 94566 715-A4
FRONT ST
- BERK 94710 609-C7
- SF 94111 648-B4
FRONTAGE RD
- OAK 94607 649-D2
- OAK 94626 649-D2
5500 OAK 94605 650-H7
5800 EMVL 94608 629-D5
6500 BERK 94710 629-D5
W FRONTAGE RD
1300 BERK 94710 609-C7

STREET
Block City ZIP Pg-Grid

W FRONTAGE RD
1300 BERK 94710 629-C1
FRONTENAC PARK CT
200 FRMT 94538 773-D2
FRUITVALE AV
400 OAK 94601 670-B2
1200 OAK 94601 650-C6
2900 OAK 94602 650-D4
FRUITWOOD COM
- LVMR 94550 716-D1
FRUITWOOD CT
- FRMT 94536 753-A2
FRUITWOOD WY
500 HAY 94544 712-B5
FRY LN
1300 HAY 94545 711-G5
FRYE ST
2800 OAK 94602 650-F4
FRYER CT
- SRMN 94583 673-E4
FUCHSIA CT
20500 AlaC 94541 691-G7
FUJI WY
- HAY 94544 711-J4
FULHAM CT
100 SRMN 94583 673-E5
FULLER AV
22300 HAY 94541 711-G2
FULLERTON CT
32700 UNC 94587 732-B7
FULLINGTON ST
3300 OAK 94619 650-E6
FULMAR TER
3700 FRMT 94555 732-J3
FULTON AV
700 SLN 94577 691-C1
FULTON CT
700 MPS 95035 794-A5
FULTON LN
- ALA 94501 649-E7
FULTON PL
1000 FRMT 94539 773-G5
FULTON ST
2300 BERK 94704 629-H2
2700 BERK 94705 629-H4
FUNDY BAY
100 ALA 94502 669-H7
FUNSTON PL
2100 OAK 94602 650-E3
FUNSTON GATE CT
4800 PLE 94588 694-D7
4800 PLE 94566 694-D7
FUSCHIA CT
37600 NWK 94560 752-F7
FUSTERIA CT
200 FRMT 94539 773-H7
200 FRMT 94539 793-H1

G

G RD
- AlaC 94586 734-C3
G ST
- UNC 94587 732-F5
100 FRMT 94536 753-B1
8500 OAK 94621 670-G5
8900 OAK 94603 670-H5
S G ST
700 LVMR 94550 715-H1
GABLE COM
47500 FRMT 94539 773-J7
GABLE DR
100 FRMT 94539 773-H7
100 FRMT 94539 793-H1
GABRIEL CT
1200 SLN 94577 691-D2
GABRIELINO TER
- FRMT 94539 773-H3
GABRIELINO WY
- FRMT 94539 773-H3
GACH CT
3100 PLE 94588 694-H4
GADING RD
25800 HAY 94544 711-J5
N GADSDEN DR
- MPS 95035 794-C6
S GADSDEN DR
- MPS 95035 794-D6
GADWALL CT
- SLN 94579 691-F1
GADWELL COM
34300 FRMT 94555 752-D1
GAGE CT
42500 FRMT 94538 773-E1
GAIL DR
21400 AlaC 94546 691-J7
GAINESVILLE AV
27500 HAY 94545 711-H7
27700 HAY 94545 731-H1
GAINSBOROUGH CT
100 ALA 94502 669-J5
GAINSBOROUGH TER
3600 FRMT 94555 752-E1
GAIT CT
- SRMN 94583 673-C4
GAITHER WY
26700 HAY 94544 711-J6
GALAHAD CT
3100 FRMT 94536 752-J3
GALANO PZ
200 UNC 94587 732-H5
GALANTI CT
- PLE 94566 715-B5
GALAXY CT
1800 LVMR 94551 696-A3
GALAXY DR
4100 UNC 94587 732-A6
GALAXY WY
- DBLN 94568 693-G4
GALE AV
4600 PLE 94566 714-E4
GALE ST
4400 LVMR 94550 696-A7
GALEN PL
35400 FRMT 94536 752-F1
GALE RIDGE CT
- SRMN 94582 673-H3
N GALE RIDGE RD
- SRMN 94582 673-H1
S GALE RIDGE RD
- SRMN 94582 673-H2
GALI CT
- DBLN 94568 694-G4
GALICIA CT
- SRMN 94583 673-C4
GALINDO CT
8600 DBLN 94568 693-G2
GALINDO DR
8400 DBLN 94568 693-G2
47100 FRMT 94539 774-A6
GALINDO ST
2900 OAK 94601 650-C6

GALISTEO CT
100 SRMN 94583 673-C3
GALLAGHER LN
200 SF 94103 648-A6
GALLAUDET DR
39300 FRMT 94536 753-C3
39300 FRMT 94538 753-C3
GALLAUP CT
- DBLN 94568 694-G5
GALLEGOS AV
43000 FRMT 94539 753-G7
43500 FRMT 94539 773-H1
GALLEON PL
2500 SLN 94577 690-G5
GALLETTA DR
6300 NWK 94560 752-E7
GALLOWAY COM
2000 LVMR 94551 696-A3
GALLOWAY ST
4100 LVMR 94551 696-A3
GALSWORTHY CT
3300 FRMT 94536 752-J3
GALT ST
15200 SLN 94579 691-B6
GALTON LN
18600 AlaC 94541 711-E1
GALVIN DR
800 ELCR 94530 609-D2
GALVIN ST
1000 OAK 94602 650-C3
GALWAY BAY
200 ALA 94502 669-J6
GALWAY CT
- DBLN 94568 693-D4
16200 AlaC 94580 691-E6
GALWAY DR
700 AlaC 94580 691-E6
GALWAY TER
100 FRMT 94536 732-J7
GAMAY COM
2300 LVMR 94550 715-H3
GAMAY CT
400 FRMT 94539 793-J2
600 PLE 94566 714-G4
GAMAY DR
48800 FRMT 94539 793-J2
48800 FRMT 94539 794-A2
GAMAY RD
1400 LVMR 94550 715-H3
GAMBLE CT
2700 HAY 94542 712-E5
GAMBOA ST
26200 HAY 94544 711-J5
GAMBON CT
- DBLN 94568 694-G4
GANGES CT
7300 ELCR 94530 609-C1
GANGES ST
1700 ELCR 94530 609-C1
GANIC ST
2700 AlaC 94546 691-J5
GANLEY ST
17000 AlaC 94580 711-C2
GANNER CT
4800 PLE 94566 694-D7
GANNET LN
19700 AlaC 94552 692-D4
GANNET TER
33800 FRMT 94555 732-J3
GANNON RD
200 OAK 94603 670-F7
GANNON TER
34100 FRMT 94555 752-B3
GANTON CT
- HAY 94544 732-E2
GAPWALL CT
2600 PLE 94566 714-C1
GAR TER
38900 FRMT 94536 753-C3
GARATTI CT
4100 PLE 94566 714-E1
GARAVENTA RANCH RD
- LVMR 94551 696-C2
GARBER RD
3000 BERK 94705 630-A3
3000 OAK 94705 630-A3
GARBER ST
2700 BERK 94705 629-J3
2800 BERK 94705 630-A3
GARCES CT
- DBLN 94568 694-G4
GARCIA AV
100 SLN 94577 670-J7
GARCIA CT
300 MPS 95035 794-A4
GARCIA ST
35100 UNC 94587 732-G7
GARDELLA DR
7500 DBLN 94568 693-G3
GARDELLA PZ
3000 LVMR 94551 695-H7
GARDEN AV
20400 AlaC 94541 711-F2
S GARDEN AV
22100 HAY 94541 711-F3
GARDEN COM
200 LVMR 94551 695-D7
GARDEN DR
- FRMT 94536 753-C1
- CCCo 94708 609-G3
GARDEN PL
500 AlaC 94541 711-F2
GARDEN RD
- ALA 94502 670-A6
GARDEN ST
2700 OAK 94601 650-C5
GARDEN WY
1300 ALA 94501 669-F1
5000 FRMT 94536 752-G5
GARDEN CREEK CIR
2800 PLE 94588 694-E6
GARDEN CREEK PL
100 DNVL 94526 652-J1
GARDENIA COM
- LVMR 94551 696-D1
GARDENIA PL
3900 OAK 94605 670-J1
GARDENIA TER
1000 ALA 94502 670-A7
GARDENIA WY
44900 FRMT 94539 773-G3
GARDINER CT
- ORIN 94563 610-H4
GARDNER BLVD
1100 SLN 94577 690-J1
GARFIELD AV
1100 ALB 94706 609-D5
3200 ALA 94501 670-B3
7300 OAK 94605 670-H2
GARFINKLE ST
- UNC 94555 752-B1

GARIBALDI PL
4100 PLE 94566 714-F4
GARIBALDI TER
- FRMT 94536 753-F3
GARIN AV
500 HAY 94544 732-D1
600 HAY 94544 712-D7
1300 AlaC 94544 712-F7
GARLAND CT
6800 PLE 94588 714-A1
17500 AlaC 94546 691-H2
GARLAND DR
4200 FRMT 94536 752-J5
GARLAND ST
- OAK 94611 649-H2
GARNER CT
6200 PLE 94588 694-A7
GARNET COM
4700 FRMT 94555 752-D2
GARNET CT
20000 AlaC 94546 692-B5
GARNET DR
100 LVMR 94550 715-D3
GARNET ST
300 OAK 94609 629-J7
300 OAK 94611 629-J7
GARRETT CT
3200 UNC 94587 732-A4
GARRETT ST
38200 FRMT 94536 752-J5
GARRETT WY
30700 UNC 94587 732-A4
GARRICK PL
2800 FRMT 94555 732-E6
GARRISON AV
19100 AlaC 94546 692-A4
GARRONE AV
6500 NWK 94560 752-C5
GARRONE PL
35500 NWK 94560 752-C5
GARSIDE CT
600 SLN 94579 691-B5
GARWAY DR
38400 FRMT 94536 752-J4
GARWOOD GLEN DR
24700 HAY 94541 712-B2
GARY DR
21000 AlaC 94546 691-H6
21000 HAY 94546 691-H6
GASKELL CT
35900 FRMT 94536 752-G2
GASKILL ST
5300 OAK 94608 629-F6
GASPAR DR
1800 OAK 94611 630-E7
GASSETT CT
1100 HAY 94544 712-A7
E GATE WY
- PLE 94566 714-C4
GATELY AV
5000 RCH 94804 609-B2
GATETREE CIR
4500 PLE 94566 714-D2
GATEVIEW AV
- SF 94130 648-D1
700 ALB 94706 609-C6
GATE VIEW DR
- OAK 94605 671-C4
GATEWAY
- DBLN 94568 693-G2
GATEWAY AV
- LVMR 94551 695-C5
GATEWAY BLVD
- NWK 94560 752-B6
- ORIN 94563 630-F2
3400 FRMT 94538 773-G7
3400 FRMT 94538 793-F1
S GATEWAY BLVD
25500 SJCo 95377 (698-H3 See Page 677)
GATEWOOD ST
42100 FRMT 94538 773-D2
GATWICK CT
- DBLN 94568 694-A4
GAUCHO CT
200 SRMN 94583 673-C2
GAUCHO WY
40800 FRMT 94539 753-F4
GAVIA CT
- SLN 94579 691-F2
GAWAIN CT
35200 FRMT 94536 752-F1
GAYLE CT
1300 ELCR 94530 609-D2
GAYLEY RD
- BERK 94720 629-J1
GAYWOOD PL
1400 ALA 94501 670-B3
GAZANIA TER
- FRMT 94536 753-D2
GAZELLE WY
1700 HAY 94541 712-B1
GEARY RD
- AlaC 94586 754-G7
- AlaC 94586 774-H2
- AlaC 94586 (775-A3 See Page 755)
GEARY ST
- SF 94108 648-A6
200 SF 94102 648-A6
GEARY TER
5300 FRMT 94555 752-B3
GEDDY CT
44000 FRMT 94539 773-H2
GEDDY WY
1000 FRMT 94539 773-H2
GELDING LN
2500 LVMR 94551 696-C1
GELSTON PL
700 ELCR 94530 609-E2
GELSTON ST
700 OAK 94705 630-B2
GEM AV
2200 UNC 94587 732-G7
4200 AlaC 94546 692-B5
GEM CT
20000 AlaC 94546 692-C5
GEMINI DR
4100 UNC 94587 732-A6
GEMINI RD
2100 LVMR 94550 715-F4
GEMMA DR
300 MPS 95035 794-A5
GEMSTONE DR
200 MPS 95035 793-H6
300 MPS 95035 794-A7
GENEVA AV
- HAY 94544 732-E3
GENEVA RD
200 MPS 95035 794-A6
GENEVA ST
1000 LVMR 94550 715-G3

GENEVE CT
1300 LVMR 94551 695-F6
GENEVIEVE PL
- AlaC 94541 691-F6
700 PLE 94566 714-F4
GENOA CT
1800 LVMR 94550 715-G3
GENOA PL
- SF 94133 648-A4
GENOA ST
1400 LVMR 94550 715-G3
5100 OAK 94608 629-G5
GENOA TER
6100 FRMT 94555 752-A6
GENOVESIO DR
5600 PLE 94588 694-C6
GENSTAR RD
31000 HAY 94544 732-C3
GENTLE CREEK PL
- DNVL 94526 652-H1
GEORGE AV
6400 NWK 94560 752-D7
GEORGE WY
1500 AlaC 94580 711-C1
GEORGEAN ST
1000 AlaC 94541 691-G6
GEORGETOWN AV
1200 SLN 94579 691-A4
GEORGETOWN CIR
- DBLN 94568 694-E3
GEORGETOWN ST
2700 EPA 94303 771-C7
GEORGIA ST
2900 OAK 94602 650-E5
GEORGIA WY
- SLN 94577 671-A7
GEORGIAN OAKS CT
- DBLN 94568 693-E4
GEORGIS PL
5700 PLE 94588 694-C5
GERALD DR
100 DNVL 94526 652-J4
GERALD WY
1900 HAY 94545 711-F5
GERALDINE CT
23200 AlaC 94541 692-D7
GERALDINE ST
500 LVMR 94550 696-C7
GERANIUM CT
- CCCo 94582 674-A2
GERANIUM PL
4600 OAK 94619 650-H5
GERANIUM ST
38000 NWK 94560 752-G7
GERARD CT
500 PLE 94566 714-F4
GERKE AL
- SF 94133 648-A4
GERMAINE CT
1700 AlaC 94541 712-B1
GERMAINE WY
3500 LVMR 94550 695-J7
GERMANO WY
- PLE 94566 735-C1
1000 PLE 94566 715-C7
GERONIMO CT
1000 FRMT 94539 773-J4
1000 FRMT 94539 774-A5
GERRILYN WY
4600 LVMR 94550 716-B1
GERRY ADAMS WY
700 OAK 94607 649-E5
GERTRUDE CT
- EPA 94303 771-B7
GERTRUDE DR
4500 FRMT 94536 752-J6
16200 FRMT 94536 753-A5
GETTYSBURG AV
25800 HAY 94545 711-F7
GETTYSBURG CT N
3700 PLE 94588 714-A1
GETTYSBURG CT S
3600 PLE 94588 714-A1
GEYSER CT
- FRMT 94539 773-J4
GHIOTTI CT
4000 PLE 94588 694-H4
GHORMLEY AV
100 OAK 94603 670-G7
GIANNINI CT
6600 AlaC 94552 692-F2
GIANNINI WY
6700 AlaC 94552 692-F2
GIBB ST
- SF 94111 648-A4
GIBBONS DR
1400 ALA 94501 670-B3
GIBRALTAR CT
36200 FRMT 94536 752-F3
GIBRALTAR DR
4000 FRMT 94536 752-E3
5500 PLE 94588 694-B5
GIBRALTAR RD
9900 OAK 94603 670-G7
GIBSON CT
6200 PLE 94588 694-A7
GIBSON ST
40400 FRMT 94538 753-C6
GIFFORD ST
41600 FRMT 94538 773-D1
GILA CT
1000 FRMT 94539 773-G4
GILBERT AV
1200 FRMT 94536 753-B2
GILBERT CT
1100 FRMT 94536 753-B2
GILBERT LN
3100 ALA 94502 670-A6
GILBERT PL
1400 FRMT 94536 753-A2
GILBERT ST
- SF 94103 648-A7
1000 AlaC 94541 691-G6
4100 OAK 94611 629-J7
GILL LN
500 SLN 94577 671-B7
GILLETT RD
- FRMT 94536 752-H4
GILLINGHAM LN
28900 HAY 94544 732-A2
GILMAN COM
- FRMT 94538 753-B5
GILMAN LN
- ALA 94501 649-E7
GILMAN ST
600 BERK 94710 609-E7
1000 BERK 94706 609-E7
1000 BERK 94702 609-E7
GILMORE DR
1200 SLN 94577 690-H2
GILROY CT
32700 UNC 94587 732-B7

GINA CT
24400 AlaC 94541 712-C1
GINA ST
4300 FRMT 94538 753-C7
GINA WY
4800 UNC 94587 751-J1
4800 UNC 94587 752-A1
GINGER AV
400 AlaC 94541 711-E1
GINGER COM
- LVMR 94551 696-D2
38100 FRMT 94536 752-J1
GINGER CT
7400 PLE 94588 713-J2
7400 PLE 94588 714-A2
GINGER LN
- ALA 94502 670-B7
GINGERWOOD DR
1100 MPS 95035 793-J4
GINSBERG TER
- FRMT 94536 752-J4
- FRMT 94536 753-A4
GIRARD DR
1700 MPS 95035 794-D7
GIRVIN DR
6100 OAK 94611 650-F1
6300 OAK 94611 630-F7
GISLER WY
600 HAY 94544 712-D7
GISSING PL
35700 FRMT 94536 752-G1
GLACIER CT N
3600 PLE 94588 714-B1
GLACIER CT S
3500 PLE 94588 714-B1
GLACIER DR
100 LVMR 94551 715-D1
1300 MPS 95035 794-D7
GLACIER PL
- LVMR 94551 715-D1
GLACIER PARK CT
5100 FRMT 94538 773-C2
GLADE ST
400 HAY 94544 711-J3
GLADIOLUS CT
1600 LVMR 94551 696-A4
GLADSTONE PL
34500 FRMT 94555 732-E7
34700 FRMT 94555 752-F1
GLADYS AV
6500 ELCR 94530 609-C2
GLADYS CT
4900 LVMR 94550 696-B7
GLASCOCK ST
2900 OAK 94601 670-B1
GLASGLOW CT
400 MPS 95035 794-B6
GLASGOW CIR
3600 LVMR 94551 695-J6
GLASS BROOK DR
- AlaC 94552 692-E7
GLEASON DR
4900 DBLN 94568 694-C3
GLEASON LN
35500 FRMT 94536 752-G1
GLEASON WY
1400 OAK 94606 650-A6
GLEN AV
- OAK 94611 649-J1
100 OAK 94611 630-A7
100 OAK 94611 650-A1
1100 BERK 94708 609-H7
1200 BERK 94709 609-H7
GLEN CT
600 MPS 95035 794-B5
GLEN DR
500 SLN 94577 671-B7
GLEN RD
600 DNVL 94526 652-H1
GLEN ALPINE DR
- DNVL 94526 652-G3
GLEN ALPINE RD
- PDMT 94611 650-C1
100 OAK 94611 650-C1
GLENARMS DR
5900 OAK 94611 630-C5
GLEN ARTNEY CT
10900 OAK 94605 671-E4
GLENBROOK CT
7600 PLE 94588 693-H7
GLENBROOK DR
5700 OAK 94618 630-A5
GLENBROOK LN
23600 AlaC 94541 692-C7
GLENBROOK ST
32200 UNC 94587 732-C4
GLENBROOK TER
- FRMT 94536 752-J2
GLENCOE CIR
- CCCo 94582 674-B5
GLENCOE DR
38600 FRMT 94536 752-J5
GLENCOURT
1000 OAK 94611 630-F6
GLENCOVA PL
43800 FRMT 94539 773-G2
GLENDA CT
3200 PLE 94588 694-C7
GLENDALE AV
300 OAK 94618 629-J6
1300 BERK 94708 609-J7
GLENDALE DR
37900 FRMT 94536 752-H5
GLENDOME CIR
700 OAK 94602 650-C3
GLENDORA AV
1000 OAK 94602 650-C3
GLENDORA CIR
300 DNVL 94526 652-J3
GLENDORA DR
44100 FRMT 94539 773-G2
GLENEAGLE AV
600 HAY 94544 712-E7
600 HAY 94544 732-D1
GLENEDEN AV
- OAK 94611 629-J7
- OAK 94611 630-A7
100 OAK 94611 650-A1
GLENFIELD AV
1300 OAK 94602 650-C3
GLENGARRY LN
- DBLN 94568 693-E5
GLENHILL CT
700 FRMT 94539 753-G7
GLENHILL DR
1000 FRMT 94539 753-G7
GLEN ISLE AV
2500 PLE 94588 694-F7
GLEN ISLE CT
4200 PLE 94588 694-F6
GLENLY RD
3300 OAK 94605 671-A3

GLEN MANOR PL
11100 OAK 94605 671-E4
GLENMARK WY
- SRMN 94582 674-A3
GLEN MAWR AV
6700 ELCR 94530 609-C1
GLENMOOR CIR
400 MPS 95035 793-H5
GLENMOOR CT
500 MPS 95035 793-J5
4500 FRMT 94536 752-H5
GLENMOOR DR
37400 FRMT 94536 752-H5
GLENN COM
1000 LVMR 94551 695-F6
GLENN ST
4500 FRMT 94536 752-G4
GLENN ELLEN DR
23000 AlaC 94541 692-D7
GLEN OAKS WY
6600 OAK 94611 630-F6
GLENOAKS WY
7300 DBLN 94568 693-H2
GLENORA WY
4000 AlaC 94586 713-J7
GLEN PARK RD
3500 OAK 94602 650-C4
GLENVIEW AV
500 OAK 94610 650-A3
GLENVIEW DR
38200 FRMT 94536 752-H5
GLENVIEW ST
- ALA 94501 649-E7
GLENWOOD AV
- OAK 94611 629-J7
GLENWOOD CT
1100 LVMR 94550 715-F1
5000 PLE 94588 693-J7
GLENWOOD DR
20100 AlaC 94552 692-F3
GLENWOOD ISL
600 ALA 94501 669-H3
GLENWOOD ST
1100 LVMR 94550 715-F1
4000 FRMT 94538 773-D2
GLENWOOD TER
- UNC 94587 732-A6
GLENWOOD WY
6500 ELCR 94530 609-C2
GLENWOOD GLADE
100 OAK 94611 630-C6
GLIDDEN WY
4300 FRMT 94536 752-J5
GLIDDON ST
19000 AlaC 94546 692-C4
19100 AlaC 94552 692-C4
GLISTENING CT
- MPS 95035 793-H6
GLORIA CT
2300 PLE 94588 714-A5
GLORIA ST
100 HAY 94544 712-A5
GLORIA WY
- LVMR 94550 696-D7
2500 EPA 94303 771-B7
GLORIETTA BLVD
100 ORIN 94563 630-J3
GLORIETTA CT
- ORIN 94563 630-J3
GLORY COM
- FRMT 94536 752-G3
GLORY LILY CT
- CCCo 94582 674-B1
GLOUCESTER PL
3300 FRMT 94555 732-D7
GLYNNIS ROSE ST
- DBLN 94568 694-E4
GODFREY PL
38800 FRMT 94536 753-D2
GODWIT CT
2100 UNC 94587 732-G7
GOECKEN RD
1000 AlaC 94551 696-G2
4100 AlaC 94551 676-G7
GOLD CT
3200 FRMT 94539 753-E7
GOLD ST
- UNC 94587 732-H7
- SF 94133 648-A4
1300 SJS 95002 793-B7
GOLD CREEK DR
5600 AlaC 94552 692-E6
GOLDCREST CIR
2100 PLE 94566 714-C2
GOLDEN RD
4700 PLE 94566 714-D2
GOLDEN CREST COM
- LVMR 94551 695-C4
GOLDEN EAGLE WY
7800 PLE 94588 714-B6
GOLDENEYE CT
- SLN 94579 691-F2
GOLDEN GATE AV
400 SF 94102 648-A6
5000 OAK 94618 630-B5
GOLDEN GATE DR
6600 DBLN 94568 693-H4
15100 SLN 94579 691-C6
GOLDEN GATE WY
5000 OAK 94618 630-A4
GOLDEN HILLS DR
1700 MPS 95035 794-D6
GOLDENRAIN AV
300 FRMT 94539 793-H1
GOLDENROD DR
5400 LVMR 94551 696-C3
37800 NWK 94560 752-G6
GOLDFINCH AV
200 LVMR 94551 715-D1
GOLDFINCH TER
3700 FRMT 94555 732-J3
GOLDFISH CT
- SLN 94579 691-F2
GOLD HILLS DR
- AlaC 94552 692-E6
N GOLD RIDGE DR
- AlaC 94552 692-F6
S GOLD RIDGE DR
- AlaC 94552 692-F6
GOLDSMITH DR
35600 FRMT 94536 752-G1
GOLDSTONE COM
- LVMR 94550 715-C1
GOLDTREE WY
- HAY 94544 712-B6
GOLETA TER
300 FRMT 94536 753-E1
GOLF DR
4300 LVMR 94551 696-A3
GOLF RD
- AlaC 94566 714-B7
- AlaC 94566 734-B1

GOLF COURSE DR
1200 CCCo 94708 610-A6
1200 OAK 94708 610-A6
3000 BERK 94708 610-A6
GOLF COURSE RD
1000 HAY 94541 711-D2
GOLF LINKS RD
8200 OAK 94605 670-J3
8200 OAK 94605 671-A3
GOLUBIN COM
5400 FRMT 94555 752-C3
GOMER ST
1100 HAY 94544 711-J6
27100 HAY 94544 712-A6
GOMES RD
1400 FRMT 94539 753-E5
GOMPERS
3000 ALA 94501 649-F6
GONDO PTH
- OAK 94618 630-B5
GONSALVES CT
- ALA 94502 669-H5
GONZAGA CT
1200 LVMR 94550 716-A2
GONZAGA ST
2500 EPA 94303 771-C7
GOODALL DR
- SJCo 95391 (678-F2 See Page 677)
GOODFELLOW AV
- DBLN 94568 694-B3
GOODING WY
- ALB 94706 609-D6
- ALB 94710 609-D6
GOODRICH ST
200 HAY 94544 712-A5
GOODRICH WY
38500 FRMT 94536 753-D1
GOODWIN ST
- SJCo 95391 (678-E2 See Page 677)
100 HAY 94544 712-A5
GORDON AV
5200 ELCR 94530 609-B1
5200 RCH 94804 609-B1
GORDON PL
4000 FRMT 94555 752-D1
GORDON RD
4600 AlaC 94546 692-A3
GORDON ST
1000 MPS 95035 794-B5
4000 FRMT 94555 752-D1
4300 OAK 94601 650-E7
GORDON WY
16300 AlaC 94578 691-F5
GORHAM PL
9700 SRMN 94583 673-F6
GOSHEN CT
300 SRMN 94583 673-G6
GOSHEN PL
100 SRMN 94583 673-G6
GOSHEN ST
32700 UNC 94587 732-B7
GOSS ST
1700 OAK 94607 649-C3
GOSSER ST
300 MPS 95035 794-A3
GOULARTE PL
2000 FRMT 94539 774-A6
GOULD CT
1600 ALA 94501 670-A2
GOULD ST
9800 OAK 94603 670-H6
GOULDIN RD
1600 OAK 94611 630-E6
GRACE AV
900 OAK 94608 629-F5
GRACE CT
700 LVMR 94550 715-E2
700 HAY 94541 711-J1
1000 ALA 94501 670-A3
GRACE ST
600 HAY 94541 711-H1
600 LVMR 94550 715-E2
900 SLN 94578 691-D4
GRACE TER
- FRMT 94536 752-G2
GRACIOSA CT
- SRMN 94582 674-A2
GRACKLE CT
2100 UNC 94587 732-G7
GRAEAGLE
- OAK 94605 671-D2
GRAFF AV
1300 SLN 94577 671-C7
1500 SLN 94577 691-D1
GRAFF CT
1600 SLN 94577 671-D7
GRAFFIAN ST
10100 OAK 94603 670-J6
GRAFTON ST
- DBLN 94568 694-F3
GRAHAM AV
6500 NWK 94560 752-E7
GRAHAM CT
5900 LVMR 94550 716-D1
GRAHAM PL
- OAK 94619 651-B7
GRAHAM ST
4000 PLE 94566 714-E2
GRAHAM WY
1600 SLN 94578 691-D3
GRALINA TER
100 FRMT 94539 773-H1
GRAMA TER
4000 FRMT 94536 752-H1
GRAMERCY AV
- UNC 94587 732-B4
GRAMERCY DR
15900 AlaC 94578 691-F4
GRAMERCY PL
300 OAK 94603 670-G7
GRANADA AV
9200 OAK 94605 671-B3
GRANADA CIR
28300 HAY 94544 732-A1
GRANADA DR
100 SRMN 94583 673-G5
28400 HAY 94544 732-A1
GRANADA WY
4600 UNC 94587 731-J6
GRANADO AV
4700 FRMT 94536 752-F4
GRAND AV
- OAK 94612 649-G3
200 OAK 94610 649-J3
1400 SLN 94577 671-C7
1400 SLN 94577 691-C1
1600 OAK 94611 630-A7
1600 PDMT 94611 630-A7
1600 PDMT 94611 650-A2
3000 PDMT 94610 650-A2

STREET
Block City ZIP Pg-Grid

GRAND AV
3200 OAK 94610 650-A2
W GRAND AV
600 OAK 94612 649-F2
800 OAK 94607 649-F2
1900 OAK 94626 649-D1
2100 OAK 94649 649-D1
GRAND BLVD
1200 SJS 95002 793-C7
GRAND ST
300 ALA 94501 669-J1
2000 ALA 94501 649-J7
22500 HAY 94541 711-H2
23000 HAY 94544 711-J3
GRAND TER
- HAY 94541 711-J2
GRANDBROOK PARK CT
43100 FRMT 94538 773-C3
GRAND CANYON CT
- SRMN 94582 673-G3
3900 PLE 94588 714-A1
GRAND CANYON DR
- UNC 94587 732-H6
GRAND CANYON LN
- SRMN 94582 673-G3
GRANDE VISTA AV
2500 OAK 94601 650-C6
GRANDE VISTA PL
2300 OAK 94601 650-C5
GRAND LAKE DR
3000 FRMT 94555 732-B6
GRANDTETON PARK ST
42400 FRMT 94538 773-C1
GRANDVIEW AV
27100 HAY 94542 712-C4
GRAND VIEW DR
1100 OAK 94705 630-B4
1700 OAK 94618 630-C4
GRAND VIEW PL
1000 OAK 94705 630-B3
GRANGE TER
4900 FRMT 94555 752-A3
GRANGER AV
30600 UNC 94587 731-J5
30800 UNC 94587 732-A5
GRANITE CT
- MPS 95035 794-A6
4300 UNC 94587 732-A6
GRANT AV
- SF 94108 648-A5
500 AlaC 94580 691-C7
1000 SF 94133 648-A3
1400 AlaC 94580 711-A1
GRANT CT
4100 PLE 94566 714-G5
5300 FRMT 94538 752-J7
GRANT ST
- FRMT 94538 753-D7
1300 BERK 94703 609-G7
1500 BERK 94703 629-G1
GRANT LINE RD
16100 AlaC 94550 (678-A7
See Page 677)
16400 AlaC 94551 (678-D5
See Page 677)
W GRANT LINE RD
16200 SJCo 95304 (678-G5
See Page 677)
17500 SJCo 95391 (678-G5
See Page 677)
GRANVILLE CT
5300 FRMT 94536 752-G6
GRANVILLE DR
37600 FRMT 94536 752-G6
GRAPE LEAF LN
- LVMR 94550 715-G4
GRAPEVINE CT
45400 FRMT 94539 774-A3
GRAPE VINE DR
500 PLE 94566 714-H3
GRAPEVINE TER
2400 FRMT 94539 774-A3
GRAPPA PL
- PLE 94566 715-B5
GRASMERE PL
26900 HAY 94542 712-E3
GRASSLAND DR
6000 AlaC 94552 692-F4
GRASSLAND TR
- CCCo 94583 652-C2
GRASS VALLEY CT
- OAK 94605 671-E4
GRASS VALLEY RD
4600 OAK 94605 671-E4
GRAU DR
100 FRMT 94536 733-A7
100 FRMT 94536 732-J7
GRAVATT DR
100 OAK 94705 630-B3
GRAVENSTEIN ST
700 OAK 94603 670-H6
GRAVINA PL
3400 PLE 94566 715-B6
GRAY ST
3500 OAK 94601 650-D6
GRAY FOX CIR
800 PLE 94566 714-H4
GRAY FOX CT
1000 PLE 94566 714-J4
GRAYHAWK CT
- DBLN 94568 694-G3
GRAYHAWK LN
- DBLN 94568 694-G2
GRAYSON ST
700 BERK 94710 629-D4
GRAYSON WY
600 MPS 95035 794-B4
GREAT ARBOR WY
2600 UNC 94587 732-C5
GREATHOUSE DR
400 MPS 95035 794-A3
GREAT OAK CIR
- ORIN 94563 630-J3
GREAT SALT LAKE CT
3800 FRMT 94555 732-B6
GREAT SALT LAKE DR
32700 FRMT 94555 732-B6
GREAT SALT LAKE TER
3900 FRMT 94555 732-H4
GREBE CT
33000 UNC 94587 732-D6
GREELEY PL
5500 FRMT 94538 773-A1
GREELY CT
600 HAY 94544 712-D7
GREEN CT
1400 AlaC 94578 691-E4
GREEN ST
- UNC 94587 732-H6
- SF 94111 648-A4
200 SF 94133 648-A4

GREENACRE RD
3600 OAK 94619 650-F6
4100 AlaC 94546 692-B5
GREENBANK AV
- PDMT 94611 650-A1
GREENBERRY CT
2300 PLE 94566 714-C1
GREENBRIER LN
31400 HAY 94544 732-E2
GREENBRIER RD
400 ALA 94501 669-H3
GREENBRIER ST
11300 OAK 94605 671-D5
GREENBRIER PARK DR
42300 FRMT 94538 773-C2
GREENFIELD WY
5400 PLE 94566 714-C1
GREENHAVEN RD
4000 HAY 94542 712-F2
GREEN HAZEL RD
- HAY 94544 712-B6
GREENHILLS AV
3600 AlaC 94546 691-J4
GREENHILLS CT
- LVMR 94551 696-D3
GREENHILLS WY
43400 FRMT 94539 773-F2
GREENLAND TER
4100 FRMT 94555 752-B2
GREENLY DR
7000 OAK 94605 670-J1
7200 OAK 94605 671-A1
GREENOAKS WY
4000 HAY 94542 712-F3
GREENPARK COM
43100 FRMT 94538 773-D1
GREENPARK DR
4400 FRMT 94538 773-D1
GREENPOINT CT
5500 NWK 94560 752-F6
GREENPOINT ST
37100 NWK 94560 752-F6
GREENRIDGE CT
18500 AlaC 94552 692-D2
GREENRIDGE DR
4300 OAK 94605 671-B1
GREENRIDGE RD
5200 AlaC 94552 692-D2
GREENS CT
4400 LVMR 94551 696-A3
GREENS LN
- AlaC 94566 714-B7
- AlaC 94566 734-B1
GREENSTONE COM
34600 FRMT 94555 752-B2
GREENTREE CT
5100 PLE 94566 714-D2
GREEN VALLEY RD
48700 FRMT 94539 794-A1
48900 MPS 95035 794-A1
GREENVIEW CT
21800 AlaC 94546 692-B6
GREENVIEW DR
2700 AlaC 94546 692-B6
10300 OAK 94605 671-C3
GREENVILLE DR
- AlaC 94552 692-G2
GREENVILLE PL
- AlaC 94552 692-F2
GREENVILLE RD
- AlaC 94551 696-F3
- LVMR 94551 696-F3
300 AlaC 94550 696-F6
300 LVMR 94550 696-F6
2900 AlaC 94550 716-F3
GREENWICH AV
5500 LVMR 94551 696-C3
GREENWICH CIR
38700 FRMT 94536 753-B3
GREENWICH CT
100 SRMN 94582 673-G4
5300 NWK 94560 752-E4
GREENWICH DR
4000 SRMN 94582 673-G4
GREENWICH ST
100 SF 94111 648-A4
100 SF 94133 648-A4
GREENWOOD AV
1100 OAK 94602 650-C4
3900 OAK 94610 650-C4
GREENWOOD CIR
21000 AlaC 94552 692-F4
GREENWOOD COM
- LVMR 94550 716-D2
- BERK 94708 609-H7
GREENWOOD DR
3100 FRMT 94536 752-J3
GREENWOOD PL
- SRMN 94583 673-B3
GREENWOOD RD
- HAY 94544 712-B6
1200 PLE 94566 714-D2
GREENWOOD TER
1400 BERK 94708 609-H7
GREER AV
600 SLN 94579 691-C6
GREER CT
2200 UNC 94587 732-G7
4700 FRMT 94538 753-A6
GREGG PL
400 SRMN 94583 673-F6
GREGORY CT
800 FRMT 94539 773-H4
GREGORY PL
- OAK 94619 650-G5
GREGORY ST
4100 OAK 94619 650-G5
4300 AlaC 94546 692-B4
GREGORY WY
- LVMR 94550 716-D2
GRENADIER PL
- AlaC 94546 691-J2
GRENDA ST
15000 SLN 94579 691-C6
GRESEL ST
- HAY 94544 732-E2
GRESHAM CT
3500 PLE 94588 694-E6
GRESHAM DR
- ALA 94501 649-F7
GREY EAGLE CT
- PLE 94566 714-H4
GREY FOX DR
19200 AlaC 94546 691-G4
GREYLYN DR
600 SRMN 94583 693-H1
GREYSTONE CT
- SRMN 94583 673-D6
GREYSTONE TER
- ORIN 94563 610-H6
GRIBBEN AV
20700 AlaC 94541 711-F1

GRIDLEY CT
47600 FRMT 94539 773-H7
GRIFFITH AV
4600 FRMT 94538 773-C1
GRIFFITH ST
14400 SLN 94577 690-J5
GRILLO CT
3700 PLE 94566 714-G4
W GRIMES RD
14600 SJCo 95206 (658-J3
See Page 637)
GRIMMER BLVD
40200 FRMT 94538 753-C7
40900 FRMT 94538 773-C1
S GRIMMER BLVD
43700 FRMT 94538 773-D3
44400 FRMT 94539 773-F4
GRIMMER TER
43000 FRMT 94538 773-C2
GRISBORNE AV
5600 OAK 94611 630-D7
GRIZZLY PEAK BLVD
200 CCCo 94563 610-B7
200 OAK 94704 610-B7
200 CCCo 94708 609-G3
200 CCCo 94708 610-B7
200 OAK 94708 610-B7
500 BERK 94708 609-H4
1300 BERK 94708 610-B7
2900 OAK 94720 610-B7
5000 CCCo 94563 630-C1
5000 OAK 94704 630-C1
5000 OAK 94705 630-D3
5300 OAK 94611 630-D3
GRIZZLY TERRACE DR
700 OAK 94611 630-D3
700 CCCo 94563 630-D3
GROOM ST
700 HAY 94544 711-J3
GROSS ST
300 MPS 95035 794-A3
GROSVENOR PL
700 OAK 94610 650-B4
GROSVENOR HEIGHTS CT
2300 LVMR 94550 715-G4
GROSVENTRES CT
1300 FRMT 94539 773-G4
GROTE PL
- SF 94105 648-B6
GROTH CIR
1400 PLE 94566 714-E1
GROUSE WY
2200 UNC 94587 732-G7
GROVE AV
200 FRMT 94539 753-H7
GROVE CT
- LVMR 94550 696-A7
GROVE ST
1300 ALA 94501 670-A3
GROVE TER
34300 FRMT 94555 752-C2
GROVE WY
100 AlaC 94541 711-F1
500 AlaC 94541 691-H7
600 HAY 94541 691-H7
1400 AlaC 94546 691-J6
2000 AlaC 94546 692-A7
3500 AlaC 94552 692-A7
GROVELAND LN
- DBLN 94568 694-F2
GROVENOR DR
16900 AlaC 94546 691-H1
GROVER CT
4500 FRMT 94536 752-H5
GROVER DR
4300 FRMT 94536 752-H5
GROVE SHAFTER FRWY I-980
- OAK - 649-G2
GROVE SHAFTER FRWY Rt#-24
- OAK - 649-G1
GRUMMAN ST
1000 OAK 94621 670-C6
GRUNION TER
- FRMT 94536 753-C3
GUADALUPE TER
100 FRMT 94539 753-H6
GUALALA PL
40700 FRMT 94539 753-E5
GUARDINO DR
38600 FRMT 94536 753-C3
39000 FRMT 94538 753-C3
GUAVA DR
38000 NWK 94560 752-G7
GUAVA PL
6100 NWK 94560 752-G7
GUAYMAS CT
600 SRMN 94583 673-C3
GUCCI TER
34600 FRMT 94555 752-A3
GUERRERO CT
- DBLN 94568 694-G4
1300 MPS 95035 794-C5
GUIDO ST
3000 OAK 94602 650-F4
GUILDHALL RD
29000 HAY 94544 732-B1
GUILFORD AV
4000 LVMR 94550 716-A2
GUILFORD CT
28900 HAY 94544 732-A1
GUILFORD PL
4400 LVMR 94550 716-A2
GUILFORD RD
- PDMT 94611 650-B1
GUILLERMO PL
3200 HAY 94542 712-E4
GUISO COM
4500 FRMT 94536 752-G3
GULFSTREAM ST
3100 PLE 94588 694-F6
GULFSTREAM WY
2000 SLN 94579 690-J6
GULL CT
33100 FRMT 94555 732-B7
GULL WY
200 LVMR 94551 695-D7
GUM CT
36800 NWK 94560 752-C7
GUNN DR
6600 OAK 94611 630-G7
GUNSHOT CT
7900 DBLN 94568 693-G4
GURDWARA RD
- FRMT 94536 732-J7
GURNARD TER
1000 FRMT 94536 753-C3
GUSHUE ST
26000 HAY 94544 712-A5

GUSTAVO CT
35300 FRMT 94536 752-E2
GUSTINE ST
32700 UNC 94587 732-B7
GUTHRIE CT
3300 PLE 94588 694-F5
GUTHRIE ST
3400 PLE 94588 694-F5
GUY PL
- SF 94105 648-B6
GUYSON CT
6200 PLE 94588 694-A7
GUZMAN PKWY
- PLE 94588 694-F6
GWIN CT
6400 OAK 94611 630-D5
GWIN RD
6400 OAK 94611 630-D5
GYEN ST
19800 AlaC 94546 692-B5
GYPSY LN
- OAK 94705 630-C2

H

H ST
100 FRMT 94536 753-B1
400 UNC 94587 732-G5
S H ST
400 LVMR 94550 715-H1
HAAS AV
100 SLN 94577 671-A7
HACIENDA AV
- AlaC 94541 711-E1
- AlaC 94580 711-D1
HACIENDA CIR
- ORIN 94563 610-F6
HACIENDA CT
40200 FRMT 94539 753-E4
HACIENDA DR
4100 PLE 94588 694-C5
4300 DBLN 94568 694-C4
HACIENDAS RD
- ORIN 94563 610-G5
HACKAMORE COM
100 FRMT 94539 773-H6
HACKAMORE DR
3200 AlaC 94541 712-D2
HACKAMORE LN
100 FRMT 94539 773-H7
HACKBERRY PL
3900 AlaC 94546 691-H2
HACKBERRY ST
48200 FRMT 94539 793-J1
HADDON PL
700 OAK 94610 650-A3
HADDON RD
300 OAK 94606 649-J4
300 OAK 94606 650-A4
600 OAK 94610 650-A4
HADSELL CT
3300 PLE 94588 694-G5
HAFNER CT
36400 NWK 94560 752-E5
HAFNER ST
36400 NWK 94560 752-E6
HAFNER WY
5800 NWK 94560 752-E5
HAGAR AV
100 PDMT 94611 650-C1
HAGEMAN AV
3500 OAK 94619 650-E6
HAGEMANN DR
100 LVMR 94551 715-D1
300 LVMR 94551 695-D7
HAGEN BLVD
6500 ELCR 94530 609-B1
HAGGIN OAKS AV
5500 LVMR 94551 696-C2
HAHN COM
- FRMT 94536 752-H2
HAIGHT AV
100 ALA 94501 649-E7
100 ALA 94501 669-E1
HAITI CT
500 SRMN 94582 673-E1
HALCYON CT
1800 PLE 94566 714-C2
3000 BERK 94705 629-H4
HALCYON DR
700 SLN 94578 691-C4
HALDANE CT
27700 HAY 94544 712-A7
HALE AV
400 OAK 94603 670-G7
HALEAKA RD
3400 PLE 94588 714-A2
HALEY DR
4800 AlaC 94546 692-B3
HALEY ST
35500 NWK 94560 752-C5
HALF DOME CT
6300 LVMR 94551 696-D3
HALF DOME DR
3100 PLE 94566 714-H3
HALIBUT CT
- SF 94130 648-E1
HALIFAX PL
26800 HAY 94542 712-E3
HALIFAX RD
1200 LVMR 94550 715-G3
HALKIN LN
- BERK 94708 609-G5
HALKWEED PZ
24900 HAY 94542 712-B3
HALL CIR
- LVMR 94550 716-C1
HALL CT
4000 PLE 94566 714-F1
HALL RD
28700 HAY 94545 731-J2
HALL WY
34300 FRMT 94555 752-C4
HALLAM ST
- SF 94103 648-D7
HALLECK ST
- SF 94111 648-B5
100 SF 94104 648-B5
4000 EMVL 94608 629-E7
4000 OAK 94608 629-E7
HALLIDAY AV
2300 OAK 94605 670-H2
HALLMARK CT
16800 AlaC 94552 692-B1
HALL RANCH PKWY
32200 UNC 94587 731-J6
HALSEY AV
1500 SLN 94578 691-D3
HAMILTON AV
200 MPS 95035 794-A6
600 MLPK 94025 771-A7

HAMILTON CT
900 MLPK 94025 771-A7
HAMILTON PL
- OAK 94612 649-H2
- OAK 94611 649-H2
HAMILTON ST
6800 OAK 94621 670-F3
HAMILTON WY
400 PLE 94566 714-D6
42800 FRMT 94538 773-E1
HAMLIN ST
38100 FRMT 94536 752-G6
HAMLIN WY
500 SLN 94578 691-B4
HAMLINE AV
3200 OAK 94602 650-C5
HAMMOND AV
- FRMT 94539 793-H1
HAMMOND PL
- MRGA 94556 651-D1
HAMNER TER
- FRMT 94555 752-D2
HAMPEL ST
1100 OAK 94602 650-C3
HAMPSHIRE WY
- SRMN 94582 674-B3
4600 FRMT 94538 753-C7
4600 FRMT 94538 773-C1
HAMPSTEAD CT
3300 LVMR 94551 695-H6
HAMPTON CT
- ALA 94502 669-J5
400 SRMN 94583 673-E5
900 MPS 95035 794-B4
32300 UNC 94587 732-C4
HAMPTON PL
1300 LVMR 94550 715-F4
19000 AlaC 94541 691-G6
HAMPTON RD
- PDMT 94611 650-C2
- PDMT 94610 650-C2
100 AlaC 94541 691-F7
2100 LVMR 94550 715-F4
HAMRICK LN
1400 HAY 94544 711-J7
HANA WY
100 UNC 94587 732-C6
HANCOCK CT
1000 PLE 94566 714-F5
HANCOCK DR
2800 FRMT 94538 753-D6
HANCOCK PL
3100 FRMT 94538 753-D6
HANCOCK ST
- ALA 94501 649-E7
500 HAY 94544 712-C6
HANCOCK WY
700 ELCR 94530 609-E3
HANDEL COM
4000 FRMT 94536 753-A5
HANFORD CT
32700 UNC 94587 732-B7
HANFORD ST
4100 UNC 94587 732-B7
HANIFEN WY
- PLE 94566 714-E6
HANLY RD
3900 OAK 94602 650-D3
HANNA TER
100 FRMT 94536 753-C2
HANNAH DR
16500 AlaC 94578 691-G5
HANNAH ST
3100 OAK 94608 649-E1
HANNON DR
- CCCo 94514 637-D2
HANNOVER PL
4700 FRMT 94538 773-D4
HANOVER AV
200 OAK 94606 649-J4
HANOVER CT
6500 PLE 94566 714-D6
HANOVER DR
- SRMN 94582 674-A4
HANOVER ST
400 LVMR 94551 695-D6
14600 SLN 94579 691-A4
HANSEN AV
1300 ALA 94501 670-B4
4100 FRMT 94536 752-G4
HANSEN CT
37100 FRMT 94536 752-G4
HANSEN DR
5600 PLE 94566 714-B2
7000 DBLN 94568 693-F4
HANSEN RD
- LVMR 94550 715-H5
2200 AlaC 94541 712-C1
25700 SJCo 95377 (698-J5
See Page 677)
S HANSEN RD
20600 SJCo 95304 (678-J3
See Page 677)
23800 SJCo 95377 (678-J7
See Page 677)
24100 SJCo 95377 (698-J1
See Page 677)
HANSOM DR
7500 OAK 94605 651-C7
7600 OAK 94605 671-C1
HANSON CT
900 MPS 95035 793-J5
HAPPYLAND AV
22300 HAY 94541 711-G2
HAPPY VALLEY RD
- AlaC 94566 714-D7
- PLE 94566 714-D7
100 AlaC 94586 714-D7
700 PLE 94586 714-D7
HARBOR RD
600 ALA 94502 669-J5
HARBOR WY
- SLN 94579 691-A7
- SLN 94579 711-A1
HARBOR BAY PKWY
- ALA 94502 670-B7
1100 OAK 94621 670-B7
1100 ALA 94502 670-B7
1400 ALA 94502 690-A1
1400 ALA 94502 690-B1
1500 ALA 94502 669-J7
HARBOR BAY ISLE FERRY
- ALA 94501 669-C3
- SF - 648-E5
- SF - 669-C3
HARBOR COVE CT
- UNC 94545 731-J6
HARBORD CT
- OAK 94618 630-C6
HARBORD DR
4300 OAK 94618 630-B6

HARBORD DR
5900 OAK 94611 630-C7
6000 OAK 94611 650-C1
6100 PDMT 94611 650-C1
HARBOR LIGHT RD
400 ALA 94501 669-G3
HARBOR VIEW AV
3500 OAK 94619 650-F5
HARBORVIEW DR
2100 SLN 94577 691-D1
HARCOURT WY
- CCCo 94582 674-B4
- SRMN 94582 674-A4
HARDCASTLE CT
- CCCo 94583 673-A5
HARDEMAN ST
2900 AlaC 94541 692-C7
HARDER RD
400 HAY 94542 712-B4
800 HAY 94544 712-A4
W HARDER RD
- HAY 94544 711-H5
- HAY 94544 712-A5
HARDIE PL
- SF 94108 648-A5
HARDIN ST
15200 SLN 94579 691-A6
HARDING AV
300 LVMR 94550 696-A7
HARDING CIR
- BERK 94708 609-J7
HARDING PL
300 SRMN 94583 673-H6
HARDING WY
4000 OAK 94602 650-D3
HARDWICK AV
- PDMT 94611 650-B1
HARDWICK PL
200 SRMN 94583 673-F5
34800 FRMT 94555 752-F1
HARDWOOD ST
4200 FRMT 94538 773-D2
HARDY PL
1300 FRMT 94536 753-B2
HARDY ST
400 OAK 94618 629-J6
HAREWOOD DR
2300 LVMR 94551 695-G6
HARLAN CT
30800 UNC 94587 731-J5
HARLAN PL
- SF 94108 648-A5
HARLAN RD
11600 DBLN 94568 693-F3
HARLAN ST
- SLN 94577 691-A2
3400 OAK 94608 649-D1
4000 EMVL 94608 629-F7
HARLEQUIN TER
3700 FRMT 94555 732-D7
HARLON CT
5200 NWK 94560 752-F5
HARLOW LN
- CCCo 94582 674-B4
HARMON AV
5500 OAK 94621 670-F1
HARMON ST
1300 BERK 94702 629-G4
1400 BERK 94703 629-G4
HARMONY CT
- DNVL 94526 652-H1
600 AlaC 94541 691-F6
HARMONY DR
500 AlaC 94541 691-F6
HARMS DR
1800 PLE 94566 714-E1
HARNESS CIR
1000 SRMN 94583 673-D4
HARNESS CT
900 SRMN 94583 673-D4
HARNESS DR
1000 SRMN 94583 673-D4
HARO LP
- DBLN 94568 694-E3
HAROLD AV
14700 SLN 94578 691-C5
HAROLD ST
2400 OAK 94602 650-D5
HAROLD WY
2200 BERK 94704 629-G2
HARPER CT
4500 PLE 94588 694-A6
HARPER LN
300 DNVL 94526 652-H1
HARPER ST
2000 ELCR 94530 609-C1
2900 BERK 94703 629-G4
3400 OAK 94601 650-D7
HARPERS FERRY CT
3300 PLE 94588 714-B1
HARPOON WY
29200 HAY 94544 732-B1
HARRAN CIR
- ORIN 94563 610-J6
HARRIER TER
33600 FRMT 94555 732-D7
HARRIET ST
- SF 94103 648-A7
HARRINGTON AV
1900 OAK 94601 650-D7
HARRINGTON LN
24100 AlaC 94541 712-B1
HARRINGTON PL
24100 AlaC 94541 712-B1
HARRINGTON RD
- MRGA 94556 651-G2
HARRINGTON ST
1300 FRMT 94539 753-F6
HARRIS CT
700 HAY 94544 712-A7
HARRIS PL
- FRMT 94536 753-C1
HARRIS RD
100 HAY 94544 712-A6
HARRISBURG AV
2100 FRMT 94536 752-G1
HARRISON ST
- ALA 94501 649-G5
- OAK 94607 649-G4
- SF 94105 648-A7
600 BERK 94710 609-D7
600 SF 94107 648-A7
1000 SLN 94577 671-A7
1000 SLN 94577 691-A1
1000 SF 94103 648-A7
1100 BERK 94706 609-D7
1200 OAK 94612 649-H2
2400 OAK 94610 649-H2
2700 OAK 94611 649-J2
4800 PLE 94566 714-D4
HART COM
39600 FRMT 94538 753-C5

HART CT
900 CCCo 94507 652-G1
HARTE CIR
2100 SLN 94577 690-G1
HARTFORD AV
- AlaC 94551 695-H2
- LVMR 94551 695-H2
4200 LVMR 94551 696-A2
HARTFORD DR
33500 UNC 94587 732-E5
HARTFORD RD
100 DNVL 94526 652-G1
HARTLAND CT
- DBLN 94568 694-G3
HARTLAND LN
- DBLN 94568 694-F3
HARTLEY GATE CT
2700 PLE 94566 694-D7
HARTMAN RD
1100 AlaC 94551 695-E2
HARTMAN TER
22400 AlaC 94541 692-C6
HARTNELL ST
1700 UNC 94587 732-F6
HARTNETT AV
4700 RCH 94804 609-A2
HARTWELL CT
3300 PLE 94588 694-G5
HARTWICK DR
- DBLN 94568 694-E3
HARTZ AV
100 DNVL 94526 652-J1
HARUFF ST
1400 EMVL 94608 629-E6
HARVARD AV
17100 AlaC 94541 691-F6
HARVARD CIR
- BERK 94708 609-J7
HARVARD CT
3900 LVMR 94550 715-J1
HARVARD DR
1800 ALA 94501 670-B2
HARVARD RD
1000 OAK 94610 650-B2
1000 PDMT 94610 650-B2
HARVARD WY
3800 LVMR 94550 715-J1
HARVEST CIR
1000 PLE 94566 714-D2
HARVEST CT
3200 HAY 94542 712-E4
HARVEST PL
- LVMR 94550 715-D4
HARVEST RD
1100 PLE 94566 714-D2
HARVEST MOON LN
- CCCo 94582 674-A2
HARVEY AV
5400 OAK 94601 670-F1
5500 OAK 94605 670-F1
5500 OAK 94621 670-F1
28000 HAY 94544 712-A7
28300 HAY 94544 732-A1
HARVEY CT
3200 PLE 94588 694-C7
HARVEY TER
- FRMT 94536 733-A6
HARWOOD AV
6000 OAK 94618 629-J5
6100 OAK 94618 630-A4
HASKELL ST
1200 BERK 94702 629-F4
HASSLER WY
- OAK 94621 670-E5
HASTE ST
1900 BERK 94704 629-G2
HASTINGS CT
- MRGA 94556 651-F1
38100 FRMT 94536 753-A3
HASTINGS DR
900 MPS 95035 794-B3
HASTINGS LN
- SRMN 94582 674-B3
HASTINGS ST
38200 FRMT 94536 753-A3
38900 FRMT 94538 753-A3
HASTINGS WY
- CCCo 94582 674-B5
7400 DBLN 94568 693-H3
18400 AlaC 94546 692-A3
HAT CREEK CT
200 SRMN 94582 674-A7
HAT CREEK WY
1100 HAY 94544 732-A1
HATFIELD LN
- ALA 94501 649-E7
HATHAWAY AV
19100 AlaC 94541 711-F1
21200 HAY 94541 711-F2
HATHAWAY CT
200 AlaC 94541 711-F2
HATHEWAY CT
- SJCo 95391 (678-F3
See Page 677)
HATHEWAY ST
- SJCo 95391 (678-F2
See Page 677)
HATTAN DR
700 LVMR 94551 696-C4
HAVANA AV
27600 HAY 94544 711-J7
27800 HAY 94544 731-J1
HAVASU CT
- LVMR 94551 696-D3
HAVASU ST
47000 FRMT 94539 773-H6
HAVEN AV
3600 FRMT 94538 773-D1
HAVEN PL
- SRMN 94583 673-F7
HAVEN ST
4000 EMVL 94608 629-F7
17500 AlaC 94541 691-F6
HAVENS PL
1000 ELCR 94530 609-E2
HAVENSCOURT BLVD
1400 OAK 94621 670-F3
1700 OAK 94605 670-F3
HAVERHILL DR
2600 OAK 94611 650-F1
HAVILAND AV
20000 AlaC 94541 691-G7
21000 AlaC 94541 711-G1
HAWAII CIR
100 UNC 94587 732-C6
HAWAII CT N
3700 PLE 94588 714-A1
HAWAII CT S
3600 PLE 94588 714-A1
HAWK COM
1900 LVMR 94551 696-D2

STREET Block City ZIP Pg-Grid

HAWK CT
300 FRMT 94539 773-J3
HAWK WY
- DBLN 94568 694-D4
HAWKINS DR
12900 SRMN 94583 673-E5
12900 CCCo 94583 673-E5
HAWKINS ST
4100 FRMT 94538 753-C6
HAWKMOUNT CT
- SRMN 94582 673-H2
HAWKMOUNT WY
- SRMN 94582 673-H2
HAWKRIDGE TER
- ORIN 94563 610-H6
HAWKS HILL CT
- OAK 94618 630-C4
HAWLEY ST
6900 OAK 94621 670-F4
HAWTHORN CT
- SRMN 94582 673-J6
HAWTHORNE AV
- LVMR 94551 696-F5
300 OAK 94611 649-G1
300 OAK 94609 649-G1
2600 HAY 94545 711-F7
HAWTHORNE CT
2700 HAY 94545 711-F7
HAWTHORNE DR
700 FRMT 94539 753-G7
HAWTHORNE PL
- LVMR 94551 696-F4
HAWTHORNE ST
- SF 94105 648-B6
- SF 94103 648-B6
100 SF 94107 648-B6
1200 ALA 94501 669-G2
HAWTHORNE TER
1400 BERK 94708 609-H7
HAYBERRY PL
- HAY 94544 712-A3
HAYCOCK CT
100 FRMT 94539 773-H7
HAYES AV
600 LVMR 94550 716-A1
HAYES CT
700 LVMR 94550 716-A1
HAYES ST
5900 OAK 94605 670-F2
5900 OAK 94621 670-F2
19000 AlaC 94546 691-H4
38800 FRMT 94536 753-D2
HAYFIELD RD
- AlaC 94586 754-J7
- AlaC 94586 774-J1
- AlaC 94586 (775-A1 See Page 755)
HAYFORD CT
4200 PLE 94566 714-C4
HAYMAN ST
31400 HAY 94544 732-D2
HAYS CT
- ALA 94502 669-H6
HAYS ST
1100 SLN 94577 691-A1
HAYWARD BLVD
3600 HAY 94542 712-B3
HAZEHURST CT
4100 PLE 94566 714-E1
HAZEL AV
1000 HAY 94541 691-J7
1000 HAY 94541 711-J1
HAZEL LN
- PDMT 94611 650-B1
3400 ALA 94502 670-A7
HAZEL RD
- BERK 94705 630-A4
HAZEL ST
- CCCo 94514 637-D2
500 LVMR 94550 696-C7
HAZELNUT CT
- SRMN 94583 673-G7
HAZELNUT DR
7500 NWK 94560 752-C7
HAZELNUT PL
7700 NWK 94560 752-C7
HAZELWOOD AV
4700 FRMT 94536 752-H5
HAZELWOOD COM
- LVMR 94550 716-D1
HAZELWOOD CT
- OAK 94603 670-G6
HAZELWOOD ST
- DBLN 94568 694-D4
HAZELWOOD WY
2500 EPA 94303 771-B7
HAZEN ST
200 MPS 95035 794-A4
HEAD WY
4200 PLE 94588 694-F7
HEAFEY RD
4500 OAK 94605 671-D2
HEARST AV
600 BERK 94710 629-D2
1100 BERK 94702 629-E1
1500 BERK 94703 629-F1
1900 BERK 94709 629-H1
1900 BERK 94704 629-H1
2200 BERK 94720 629-H1
2400 OAK 94602 650-D4
HEARST DR
900 PLE 94566 714-G5
HEARST ST
- LVMR 94550 716-C2
HEARTLAND CT
- UNC 94587 732-E6
HEARTWOOD DR
6600 OAK 94611 630-E7
HEATH AV
- HAY 94542 712-D4
HEATH CT
700 HAY 94544 712-D7
6800 PLE 94588 694-A7
HEATH ST
- MPS 95035 793-H6
HEATHER CT
800 MPS 95035 794-B5
24600 HAY 94545 711-F5
HEATHER LN
- ORIN 94563 630-J2
900 AlaC 94580 691-E5
1100 LVMR 94551 696-B4
HEATHER TER
34100 FRMT 94555 752-A3
HEATHER WK
- ALA 94501 669-G2
HEATHERLAND DR
- SRMN 94582 673-H1
HEATHERLARK CIR
2400 PLE 94566 714-C2
HEATHER RIDGE CT
400 SRMN 94582 673-J6
HEATHER RIDGE WY
6200 OAK 94611 630-E5
HEATHROW LN
2400 SLN 94577 691-B2
HEATHROW PL
2200 SLN 94577 691-B2
HEATHROW TER
34400 FRMT 94555 752-B3
HEBRIDES CT
5100 NWK 94560 752-E4
HEBRON CT
15600 SLN 94579 691-B7
HECKER CT
- ALA 94501 649-A2
HEDGE CT
2900 OAK 94602 650-F3
HEDGE LN
4900 OAK 94602 650-F3
HEDGECREST CIR
- SRMN 94582 673-H2
HEDGESTONE CT
- MPS 95035 794-C2
HEDGEWICK AV
4600 FRMT 94538 773-C1
HEFLIN ST
700 MPS 95035 794-B4
HEGENBERGER CT
- OAK 94621 670-F6
HEGENBERGER EXWY
900 OAK 94621 670-F4
HEGENBERGER LP
- OAK 94621 670-F7
HEGENBERGER PL
- OAK 94621 670-F7
HEGENBERGER RD
200 OAK 94621 670-F7
500 OAK 94621 690-E1
HEIDELBERG CT
2000 LVMR 94550 715-G3
HEIDELBURG DR
1400 LVMR 94550 715-G4
HEIDI CT
800 LVMR 94550 696-D6
HEIDI ST
18800 AlaC 94546 691-H3
HEIDI WY
5800 LVMR 94550 696-D6
HEINZ AV
800 BERK 94710 629-E4
HEINZ RANCH CT
- PLE 94566 715-A4
HEIRLOOM TER
600 FRMT 94536 753-B2
HELADO RD
200 FRMT 94539 753-E4
HELEN AV
900 SLN 94577 671-B6
HELEN CT
6600 OAK 94608 629-F4
HELEN DR
3500 PLE 94588 694-E7
HELEN PL
- AlaC 94546 692-B4
HELEN ST
2800 OAK 94608 649-E1
HELEN WY
200 LVMR 94550 715-E2
38800 FRMT 94536 752-J5
HELENA CREEK CT
600 SRMN 94582 674-A7
HELGA CT
- LVMR 94550 696-C7
HELICON CT
- SRMN 94582 673-G2
HELIX CT
- SRMN 94583 693-J1
HELLMAN ST
10700 OAK 94605 671-C5
HELM CT
- FRMT 94536 732-J7
HELO DR
16300 AlaC 94578 691-F5
HELPERT CT
4600 PLE 94588 694-A6
HELSINKI CT
1600 LVMR 94550 715-G3
HELSINKI WY
1400 LVMR 94550 715-G3
HELSTON PL
34400 FRMT 94555 732-E7
HELTON CT
5100 AlaC 94546 692-C4
HELTON ST
19000 AlaC 94546 692-C4
HEMET COM
34700 FRMT 94555 752-A3
HEMINGWAY COM
- FRMT 94536 752-B5
- FRMT 94536 753-A4
HEMLOCK CT
- MPS 95035 794-D6
500 LVMR 94551 695-E7
HEMLOCK DR
33100 UNC 94587 732-G3
HEMLOCK LN
- MPS 95035 794-D6
- OAK 94611 630-F6
HEMLOCK RD
- HAY 94544 712-B6
HEMLOCK ST
6500 DBLN 94568 693-J4
7000 OAK 94611 630-F6
14300 SLN 94579 691-A4
HEMMINGWAY CT
26900 HAY 94542 712-D4
HEMPHILL PL
300 OAK 94618 629-J6
HENDERSON CT
- FRMT 94536 753-B1
HENDERSON LN
1200 HAY 94544 711-H6
HENDERSON RD
18500 SJCo 95391 (658-G7 See Page 637)
18500 SJCo 95391 (678-G1 See Page 677)
S HENDERSON RD
18500 SJCo 95391 (678-G1 See Page 677)
HENLEY CT
- CCCo 94583 673-A5
HENNINGS CT
22500 HAY 94541 692-A7
HENRIETTA ST
3400 OAK 94601 650-D6
HENRY CT
23100 AlaC 94541 692-D7
HENRY LN
23000 AlaC 94541 692-D6
HENRY ST
300 OAK 94607 649-D4
1200 BERK 94709 609-G7
1900 BERK 94704 629-G1
HENRY RANCH DR
- SRMN 94583 673-E6
HENSEN PL
18500 AlaC 94546 692-B3
HERCULES CT
- ALA 94501 649-A2
4900 LVMR 94551 696-B3
HERDLYN RD
7500 CCCo 94514 (658-D2 See Page 637)
HEREFORD ST
36500 FRMT 94536 752-G2
HERITAGE
- OAK 94605 671-D2
HERITAGE CIR
- AlaC 94580 691-E6
HERITAGE COM
38000 FRMT 94536 752-J3
HERITAGE CT
- UNC 94587 732-E6
E HERITAGE DR
- SJCo 95391 (678-E3 See Page 677)
HERITAGE LN
200 PLE 94566 714-E4
HERITAGE PL
800 SRMN 94583 673-G6
HERITAGE TER
3700 FRMT 94536 752-J4
HERITAGE WY
- UNC 94587 732-E6
HERMA CT
300 SLN 94577 671-B6
HERMAN AV
800 LVMR 94551 696-D3
HERMANN ST
5700 OAK 94609 629-H5
HERMANOZ CT
1500 SLN 94578 691-D3
HERMES CT
100 HAY 94544 711-J4
HERMINA ST
1000 MPS 95035 793-J5
HERMITAGE AV
7500 NWK 94560 752-B6
HERMITAGE CT
5500 LVMR 94551 696-C2
HERMITAGE LN
- HAY 94544 732-E2
HERMOSA AV
- OAK 94618 630-B6
HERMOSA TER
2500 HAY 94541 692-C7
HERON CT
- ALA 94501 649-F7
HERON DR
- SLN 94579 690-J7
- SLN 94579 691-F2
5800 OAK 94618 630-C7
HERON PL
4000 FRMT 94555 732-B7
HERON ST
- SF 94103 648-D7
HERRIER ST
3300 OAK 94602 650-F4
HERRIN CT
6700 PLE 94588 694-A6
HERRIN WY
4600 PLE 94588 694-A6
HERRINGBONE CT
- UNC 94587 732-G6
HERRINGBONE WY
- UNC 94587 732-G6
HERRIOTT AV
3100 OAK 94619 650-F7
HERSHEY CT
4700 RCH 94804 609-A1
HERSHEY WY
31000 HAY 94544 732-E2
HERTLEIN PL
3200 AlaC 94546 691-H4
HERZOG ST
5900 OAK 94608 629-F4
HESKET RD
9800 OAK 94603 670-G7
HESPERIAN BLVD
14900 SLN 94578 691-D5
15400 AlaC 94580 691-D7
15400 SLN 94579 691-D5
16100 AlaC 94580 711-E2
17200 AlaC 94541 711-E2
18600 HAY 94541 711-E2
24000 HAY 94545 711-F4
24700 AlaC 94545 711-F4
27500 HAY 94545 731-H2
HESPERIAN CT
19800 AlaC 94541 711-E2
HESSE DR
28000 HAY 94545 731-J1
HESTER ST
400 SLN 94577 690-F1
HETFIELD PL
- MRGA 94556 651-E1
HEWITT PL
100 HAY 94544 711-J5
HEYER AV
4100 AlaC 94546 692-B4
4800 AlaC 94552 692-B4
HEYER HTS
4600 AlaC 94546 692-B4
HEYER LN
19200 AlaC 94546 692-B4
HIAWATHA CT
1000 FRMT 94539 773-J4
1000 FRMT 94539 774-A5
HIBBARD ST
1600 ALA 94501 669-H1
HIBERNIA DR
- DBLN 94568 694-D4
HIBISCUS AV
35700 FRMT 94536 732-J7
HIBISCUS DR
2400 HAY 94545 731-H2
HIBISCUS WY
1000 LVMR 94551 696-B4
HICKAM TER
- FRMT 94538 753-D6
HICKORY AV
1600 SLN 94579 691-A5
25900 HAY 94544 711-J5
HICKORY LN
6700 DBLN 94568 693-J4
HICKORY ST
2600 OAK 94602 650-C5
37000 NWK 94560 752-C7
37000 NWK 94560 772-C1
HICKORY WY
800 FRMT 94536 732-J7
HICKORYWOOD LN
- PLE 94588 714-B4
HIDALGO CT
200 FRMT 94539 753-E3
HIDATSA CT
800 FRMT 94539 773-H4
HIDDEN CT
24400 AlaC 94541 712-C1
HIDDEN LN
- ORIN 94563 610-G3
2400 AlaC 94541 712-C1
HIDDEN CREEK CT
5700 PLE 94566 714-E6
HIDDEN OAKS DR
2300 AlaC 94541 712-C1
HIDDEN VALLEY RD
- ORIN 94563 610-J6
HIDDEN VALLEY TER
600 FRMT 94539 773-J4
600 FRMT 94539 774-A4
HIDDEN VIEW PL
18000 AlaC 94546 692-B3
HIGGINS WY
41500 FRMT 94539 753-F6
HIGH COM
3400 FRMT 94538 753-D6
HIGH CT
1100 BERK 94708 609-H6
HIGH ST
300 OAK 94601 670-C2
900 ALA 94501 670-A4
2100 OAK 94601 650-E7
2600 OAK 94619 650-F6
22800 HAY 94541 712-A1
40600 FRMT 94538 753-D6
41000 FRMT 94539 753-D6
HIGHBLUFF TER
- PLE 94588 693-G7
HIGH CASTLE CT
2300 LVMR 94550 715-G4
HIGH COUNTRY DR
27900 HAY 94542 712-F4
HIGHCREST CT
- PLE 94588 693-G7
HIGHGATE CT
- CCCo 94707 609-F3
HIGHGATE DR
29500 HAY 94544 712-D7
HIGHGATE RD
- CCCo 94707 609-F3
- ELCR 94530 609-F3
HIGHGROVE WY
- SRMN 94582 674-A4
HIGH KNOLL DR
4200 OAK 94619 650-J6
HIGHLAND AV
- PDMT 94611 630-B7
100 PDMT 94611 650-C2
2400 OAK 94606 650-B5
5400 RCH 94804 609-B3
HIGHLAND BLVD
- CCCo 94530 609-F2
- CCCo 94707 609-F2
- CCCo 94708 609-F3
900 HAY 94542 712-A2
HIGHLAND CT
- DNVL 94526 652-J3
- ORIN 94563 630-J1
HIGHLAND DR
- AlaC 94552 692-C5
300 DNVL 94526 652-J3
HIGHLAND PL
1700 BERK 94709 629-J1
44100 FRMT 94539 773-J2
44100 FRMT 94539 774-A2
HIGHLAND RD
5600 CCCo 94588 674-G1
5700 CCCo 94551 675-D2
5700 CCCo 94588 675-A1
7300 AlaC 94551 675-D2
HIGHLAND ST
500 LVMR 94551 695-J6
HIGHLAND WY
300 PDMT 94611 650-B1
HIGHLAND MEADOWS CT
- DBLN 94568 694-G2
HIGHLAND OAKS DR
7400 PLE 94588 693-J7
7500 PLE 94588 713-H1
HIGH PINE WY
17000 AlaC 94546 691-J2
HIGHPOINT WY
- HAY 94541 711-H3
HIGH RIDGE PL
4100 AlaC 94552 692-D5
HIGH RIDGE LOOP TR
- AlaC 94544 712-F7
- AlaC 94544 732-F1
- UNC 94587 712-F7
- UNC 94587 732-F2
HIGHWOOD RD
5700 AlaC 94552 692-D3
HIGUERA CT
1200 LVMR 94551 695-F6
HIGUERA PL
1300 MPS 95035 794-A4
HILDASUE TER
4900 FRMT 94555 752-C2
HILDING AV
1800 SLN 94577 690-J2
HILFERD WY
- DNVL 94526 652-G3
HILGARD AV
2300 BERK 94709 609-H7
2300 BERK 94709 629-H1
HILL AV
1800 HAY 94541 692-B7
1800 AlaC 94541 692-B7
HILL CT
- HAY 94542 712-B3
2500 BERK 94708 609-H7
N HILL CT
- OAK 94618 630-B4
S HILL CT
- OAK 94618 630-B4
HILL LN
100 PDMT 94610 650-A1
HILL RD
- BERK 94708 609-J6
100 BERK 94708 610-A6
6100 OAK 94618 630-B5
HILL ST
6300 ELCR 94530 609-B1
37300 NWK 94560 752-F7
HILLBROOK PL
- DBLN 94568 694-E2
HILLCREST AV
200 LVMR 94550 696-A7
400 LVMR 94550 716-A2
2500 HAY 94542 712-D3
HILLCREST COM
4000 LVMR 94550 716-A1
HILLCREST CT
- BERK 94705 630-A4
- OAK 94619 650-J5
- OAK 94619 651-A4
- SRMN 94583 673-A1
1000 LVMR 94550 716-A1
HILLCREST RD
- BERK 94705 629-J4
- BERK 94705 630-A4
- SF 94130 648-E3
100 BERK 94618 630-A4
200 OAK 94618 630-A4
HILLCREST TER
600 FRMT 94539 773-J1
HILLCREST WY
4800 PLE 94588 693-J7
HILLCROFT CIR
900 OAK 94610 650-B3
HILLDALE AV
600 BERK 94708 609-H5
HILLDALE CT
- ORIN 94563 630-J4
HILLEGASS AV
2500 BERK 94704 629-J2
2700 BERK 94705 629-J4
3100 OAK 94618 629-J4
HILLEN DR
5300 OAK 94619 670-F1
HILLER DR
- OAK 94618 630-B4
HILLERY WY
- ALA 94502 670-A7
HILLFLOWER DR
5300 LVMR 94551 696-C4
HILLGIRT CIR
600 OAK 94610 650-A3
HILLGRADE CT
9700 OAK 94603 671-A4
HILLHURST WY
- OAK 94705 630-B2
HILLIKER PL
1300 AlaC 94551 695-H5
2600 LVMR 94551 695-H5
HILLMONT DR
6100 OAK 94605 650-H7
6300 OAK 94605 670-J1
7700 OAK 94605 671-A2
HILLROSE DR
7500 DBLN 94568 693-G3
HILLSBORO AV
7300 SRMN 94583 673-G7
HILLSBORO CT
7900 PLE 94588 693-H7
HILLSBOROUGH DR
4400 AlaC 94546 691-H1
HILLSBOROUGH ST
600 OAK 94606 649-J4
600 OAK 94606 650-A4
HILLSDALE CT
7600 PLE 94588 693-J7
HILLSDALE DR
7300 PLE 94588 693-J7
HILLSDALE ST
1900 AlaC 94541 712-B1
HILLSIDE AV
100 PDMT 94611 630-A2
100 PDMT 94611 650-B1
700 ALB 94706 609-D6
1000 AlaC 94586 734-B3
2400 BERK 94704 629-J2
2400 BERK 94704 630-A2
3700 LVMR 94551 695-J6
3900 LVMR 94551 696-A6
HILLSIDE CIR
2000 SLN 94577 691-D1
HILLSIDE CT
- BERK 94704 629-J2
400 PDMT 94611 650-B1
17600 AlaC 94546 692-A3
35700 FRMT 94536 732-J7
HILLSIDE DR
2000 SLN 94577 691-D1
4600 AlaC 94546 692-A2
HILLSIDE LN
4600 AlaC 94546 692-A2
HILLSIDE PL
4600 AlaC 94546 692-A2
HILLSIDE RD
- DNVL 94526 652-H3
HILLSIDE ST
7300 OAK 94605 670-J2
8800 OAK 94605 671-A4
9000 OAK 94603 671-A4
HILLSTONE CT
- LVMR 94551 696-E1
HILLSTONE DR
- LVMR 94551 696-E1
HILLTOP CRES
5300 OAK 94618 630-C7
HILLTOP CT
- SRMN 94582 673-F2
1500 MPS 95035 794-C3
HILLVIEW CT
900 MPS 95035 794-B6
7400 PLE 94588 693-J7
HILLVIEW DR
100 FRMT 94536 733-A7
100 FRMT 94536 753-A1
1200 LVMR 94551 695-F6
1700 SLN 94577 691-D1
N HILLVIEW DR
100 MPS 95035 794-B4
S HILLVIEW DR
100 MPS 95035 794-B7
HILLVIEW RD
1100 BERK 94708 609-J5
HILLVIEW ST
3700 OAK 94602 650-E5
28900 HAY 94544 712-B7
HILLWOOD PL
- OAK 94610 650-C3
HILMAR ST
32700 UNC 94587 732-B7
HILO ST
4500 FRMT 94538 753-B7
4800 FRMT 94538 773-B1
HILTON ST
2400 UNC 94587 732-E6
5500 OAK 94605 670-F1
HINTON CT
16900 AlaC 94546 691-H1
HINTON ST
16900 AlaC 94546 691-H1
HIRAM DAVIS COM
- FRMT 94538 753-D6
HIRSCH TER
200 FRMT 94536 733-A7
HISTORIC ST
- SJCo 95391 (678-F3 See Page 677)
HOAD ST
900 SLN 94579 691-B7
HOBART CT
600 FRMT 94539 793-J1
HOBBS CT
- MPS 95035 794-C7
HOBERT ST
21200 AlaC 94546 691-J6
HOBSTONE PL
- DBLN 94568 694-F2
HOCHLER DR
- FRMT 94539 753-J7
- FRMT 94539 754-A7
HODGES AL
- SF 94133 648-A4
HODGES DR
100 MRGA 94556 651-E2
HOFFMAN LN
800 CCCo 94513 637-A1
800 CCCo 94514 637-A1
HOFFMAN WY
21800 AlaC 94546 692-B6
HOGAN PL
2700 LVMR 94550 715-G5
HOGAN TER
34200 FRMT 94555 752-C2
HOGARTH PL
3300 FRMT 94555 732-E7
HOHENER AV
800 HAY 94541 711-F3
HOLBROOK PL
300 SRMN 94582 673-J6
HOLDEN ST
4000 EMVL 94608 629-E7
HOLEY RD
- CCCo 94514 (657-F1 See Page 637)
HOLIDAY ST
29600 HAY 94544 712-D7
HOLLADAY CT
300 LVMR 94551 695-F7
HOLLAND AV
38100 FRMT 94536 753-A3
HOLLAND CT
- SF 94103 648-A6
HOLLAND DR
4000 PLE 94588 714-A1
4400 PLE 94588 694-A7
HOLLAND ST
5300 OAK 94601 670-E2
HOLLANDA CT
8000 DBLN 94568 693-G3
HOLLANDA LN
8000 DBLN 94568 693-G3
HOLLICE CT
- LVMR 94550 716-B1
HOLLICE LN
- LVMR 94550 696-B7
- LVMR 94550 716-B1
HOLLIS ST
3000 BERK 94710 629-E6
3000 EMVL 94608 629-E6
3200 OAK 94608 649-E1
3400 OAK 94608 629-E6
HOLLIS CANYON RD
7400 AlaC 94552 692-G4
22900 AlaC 94552 693-A3
HOLLISTER AV
- ALA 94501 649-E7
HOLLISTER CT
200 SLN 94577 671-B6
HOLLOW LN
3200 AlaC 94541 692-D6
HOLLOWAY CANYON CT
- AlaC 94552 692-E7
HOLLY CIR
1600 PLE 94566 714-F1
HOLLY COM
- LVMR 94550 716-D1
HOLLY CT
- CCCo 94583 652-F4
22900 HAY 94541 711-G3
HOLLY LN
100 ORIN 94563 610-E6
400 HAY 94541 711-G3
HOLLY PL
100 PDMT 94611 650-A1
HOLLY ST
1000 ALA 94502 670-A7
1400 BERK 94703 609-F7
1500 BERK 94703 629-F1
7100 OAK 94621 670-G3
9000 OAK 94603 670-J5
37000 FRMT 94536 752-G3
HOLLY WY
- UNC 94587 732-B4
400 MPS 95035 794-D7
HOLLYBURNE AV
1400 MLPK 94025 771-A7
HOLLY HILL AV
26800 HAY 94545 711-H6
HOLLYHOCK DR
500 SLN 94578 691-C4
HOLLYHOCK ST
1000 LVMR 94551 696-B3
34800 UNC 94587 732-F7
35000 UNC 94587 752-G1
HOLLYLEAF LN
- UNC 94587 732-H5
HOLLY OAK LN
100 ALA 94502 669-J6
HOLLYVIEW CT
- SRMN 94582 673-J1
- SRMN 94582 674-A1
HOLLYVIEW DR
- SRMN 94582 673-J1
HOLLYWOOD AV
900 OAK 94602 650-D3
1300 AlaC 94586 734-B3
HOLMAN RD
1100 OAK 94610 650-B3
1300 OAK 94602 650-B3
HOLMES AV
3700 OAK 94605 671-A2
HOLMES CT
1100 LVMR 94550 715-F2
HOLMES PL
3300 FRMT 94555 732-D7
HOLMES ST
400 LVMR 94550 715-F5
HOLMES ST Rt#-84
300 LVMR 94550 715-F2
2900 AlaC 94550 715-F2
HOLMES WY
1000 HAY 94541 712-A2
HOLT ST
4300 UNC 94587 732-B7
HOLTZ CT
- ALA 94501 649-A1
HOLWAY CT
5700 OAK 94621 670-F2
HOLWAY DR
3800 CCCo 94514 637-D3
HOLWAY ST
5500 OAK 94621 670-F2
HOLYOKE AV
- HAY 94544 732-C1
HOLYROOD DR
2900 OAK 94611 650-G2
HOLYROOD MNR
- OAK 94611 650-G2
HOMANS AV
1400 SLN 94577 671-D7
HOME AV
2500 HAY 94542 712-D3
HOME PL E
- OAK 94610 650-A4
HOME PL W
- OAK 94610 650-A4
HOMEGLEN LN
- OAK 94611 630-F6
HOMER CT
6100 PLE 94588 694-A7
HOMER ST
- SF 94103 648-D7
HOMER WY
6200 PLE 94588 694-B7
HOMESTEAD CT
- FRMT 94539 773-F2
HOMESTEAD LN
1300 HAY 94545 711-H6
HOMETOWN WY
1000 PLE 94566 714-D3
HOMEWOOD CT
7500 PLE 94588 693-H6
HOMEWOOD DR
7000 OAK 94611 630-F6
HOMEWOOD ST
42800 FRMT 94538 773-D1
HOMME WY
- MPS 95035 793-J4
HONDA WY
700 FRMT 94539 753-F5
HONDO PL
- SRMN 94583 673-G5
HONEY CT
7500 DBLN 94568 693-H3
HONEYCASTLE DR
- CCCo 94582 674-A2
HONEY HILL CT
- ORIN 94563 610-J5
HONEY HILL RD
- ORIN 94563 610-J5
HONEYSUCKLE CT
1600 PLE 94588 714-B6
6200 NWK 94560 752-F7
HONEYSUCKLE DR
6100 NWK 94560 752-F7
HONEYSUCKLE PZ
- HAY 94542 712-B2
HONEYSUCKLE RD
1400 LVMR 94551 696-A4
HONEYWOOD RD
- ORIN 94563 610-J3
HONKER TER
4800 FRMT 94555 752-D2
HONOLULU CIR
400 UNC 94587 732-D5
HONORS CT
7800 PLE 94588 714-B5
HOOD ST
- AlaC 94541 691-F7
3100 OAK 94605 671-B5
HOOKER AL
- SF 94108 648-A5
HOOPER ST
41500 FRMT 94538 753-D7
41500 FRMT 94538 773-D1
HOOVER AV
1900 OAK 94602 650-E3
HOOVER CT
1400 ALA 94501 669-F1
HOPE ST
1200 SJS 95002 793-B7
W HOPE ST
- ALA 94501 649-D6
HOPI CT
- SRMN 94583 673-D4
HOPI DR
700 FRMT 94539 773-H6
HOPKINS AV
43500 FRMT 94538 773-E2
HOPKINS CT
- BERK 94706 609-F7
5400 PLE 94566 714-E5
HOPKINS PL
2800 OAK 94602 650-E5
HOPKINS ST
1100 BERK 94702 629-E1
1200 BERK 94702 609-F7
1400 BERK 94706 609-F7
1500 BERK 94703 609-F7
1500 BERK 94707 609-F7
28800 HAY 94545 731-J2
HOPKINS WY
800 PLE 94566 714-E5
HOPPER RD
23200 HAY 94541 711-F3
HOPPS LN
- LVMR 94550 716-C1
HOP RANCH CT
33000 UNC 94587 732-D5
HOP RANCH RD
2600 UNC 94587 732-D6
HOPYARD RD
1200 PLE 94566 714-B1
2500 PLE 94588 694-B7
2700 PLE 94588 714-B1
HORAT TER
5000 FRMT 94555 752-C2
HORATIO CT
- UNC 94587 732-C5
4000 FRMT 94555 732-C5
HORATIO WY
4000 FRMT 94555 732-C7
HORCAJO CIR
900 MPS 95035 794-B4
HORCAJO ST
800 MPS 95035 794-B5
HORIZON CT
- SLN 94579 690-J6
HORIZON DR
700 MPS 95035 794-B7
HORIZONS CT
- PLE 94588 693-H7
HORNE ST
2000 AlaC 94578 691-F4
HORNER ST
3700 UNC 94587 731-H5
3700 UNC 94587 732-A5
HORNER WY
1600 FRMT 94536 753-A2
W HORNET AV
- ALA 94501 669-D1

STREET Block	City	ZIP	Pg-Grid
HORSESHOE CT			
2600	LVMR	94551	696-C1
3000	AlaC	94541	712-D1
HORTON CT			
700	HAY	94544	712-A7
HORTON ST			
3800	EMVL	94608	629-E5
3800	OAK	94608	629-E6
HOSIE AV			
3100	CCCo	94514	637-D3
HOSKER LN			
-	LVMR	94551	695-H7
HOTALING ST			
-	SF	94111	648-A4
HOTCHKISS AV			
7200	ELCR	94530	609-D3
HOTCHKISS ST			
45800	FRMT	94539	773-G5
HOTEL AV			
800	HAY	94541	711-J1
HOT SPRINGS CT			
3800	PLE	94588	714-A2
HOUSTON CT			
300	DNVL	94526	652-J3
HOUSTON PL			
6100	DBLN	94568	694-A4
HOWARD AV			
200	PDMT	94611	650-A1
HOWARD COM			
3300	FRMT	94536	752-J3
HOWARD ST			
-	SF	94105	648-B6
600	SF	94103	648-B6
4300	OAK	94601	670-C2
HOWE CT			
3600	FRMT	94538	773-E1
HOWE DR			
1900	AlaC	94578	691-D2
1900	SLN	94577	691-D2
HOWE ST			
2300	BERK	94705	629-H3
3700	OAK	94611	649-J1
4100	OAK	94611	629-J7
4400	OAK	94611	630-A7
HOWELL ST			
5800	OAK	94609	629-H5
HOYA WY			
400	UNC	94587	732-C6
HOYLAKE ST			
30400	HAY	94544	732-D2
HOYT ST			
47400	FRMT	94539	773-H7
HUBBARD AV			
1300	SLN	94579	691-A5
1600	SLN	94579	690-J5
HUBBARD LN			
-	AlaC	94586	734-G2
HUBBARD ST			
4000	EMVL	94608	629-E7
4000	OAK	94608	629-E7
HUBER DR			
18800	AlaC	94546	691-H3
HUBERT RD			
1000	OAK	94610	650-B3
HUDDLESON ST			
-	FRMT	94539	753-J7
HUDSON BAY			
100	ALA	94502	669-J6
HUDSON CT			
3300	PLE	94588	694-F5
HUDSON DR			
-	ALA	94501	649-J7
HUDSON LN			
200	SLN	94577	691-B2
HUDSON PL			
3300	FRMT	94536	752-G2
HUDSON ST			
400	OAK	94618	629-J5
1800	ELCR	94530	609-C1
HUDSON WY			
1200	LVMR	94550	715-F3
HUFF AV			
500	SLN	94577	691-B1
1100	SLN	94577	671-B7
HUFF CT			
-	MRGA	94556	651-E1
3600	PLE	94588	694-F6
HUFF DR			
2700	PLE	94588	694-F6
HUFFMAN TER			
4800	FRMT	94555	752-A3
HUGH WY			
31300	HAY	94544	732-E2
HUGHES AV			
2300	OAK	94601	650-C6
HUGHES PL			
5400	FRMT	94538	752-J7
5400	FRMT	94538	753-A7
5400	FRMT	94538	772-J1
HUGO TER			
-	FRMT	94538	773-E3
HULA CIR			
200	UNC	94587	732-D6
HULBERT AL			
-	SF	94107	648-B7
HULL CT			
-	SLN	94579	711-A2
HULL ST			
4300	OAK	94601	670-C2
HULL TER			
-	FRMT	94536	753-C3
HUMBER PL			
4800	NWK	94560	752-E3
HUMBOLDT AV			
2300	OAK	94601	650-D6
2500	OAK	94602	650-D6
HUMBOLDT DR			
2500	SLN	94577	691-D2
HUMBOLDT WY			
400	LVMR	94551	695-E6
HUMMINGBIRD CT			
27700	HAY	94545	731-G1
HUMMINGBIRD LN			
300	LVMR	94551	715-D1
HUMMINGBIRD RD			
4900	PLE	94566	714-C1
HUMMINGBIRD TER			
-	FRMT	94555	752-B2
HUMPHREY PL			
-	OAK	94610	650-C3
HUNTER AV			
100	OAK	94603	670-G7
18000	AlaC	94541	711-E1
HUNTER CT			
-	OAK	94603	670-G7
W HUNTER CT			
200	FRMT	94539	773-H2
HUNTER LN			
700	FRMT	94539	773-J2
W HUNTER LN			
100	FRMT	94539	773-J2
HUNTER PL			
44200	FRMT	94539	773-J2
HUNTER ST			
2700	EPA	94303	771-B7
HUNTER TER			
44100	FRMT	94539	773-J2
HUNTERS KNOLL RD			
20300	AlaC	94552	692-E3
HUNTINGTON AV			
5100	RCH	94804	609-B4
HUNTINGTON CIR			
38600	FRMT	94536	753-C3
HUNTINGTON COM			
900	FRMT	94536	753-C3
HUNTINGTON CT			
3100	AlaC	94546	691-G3
HUNTINGTON PL			
-	SRMN	94583	673-F6
HUNTINGTON ST			
3800	OAK	94619	650-G6
HUNTINGTON TER			
900	FRMT	94536	753-C3
HUNTINGTON WY			
400	LVMR	94551	695-E6
HUNTLEIGH RD			
-	PDMT	94611	650-D2
HUNTSWOOD CT			
-	PLE	94588	714-B5
HUNTWOOD AV			
2600	UNC	94587	732-C4
24800	HAY	94544	711-J4
25900	HAY	94544	712-A6
28900	HAY	94544	732-B1
31200	HAY	94587	732-C3
HUNTWOOD WY			
-	HAY	94544	711-J5
HURLEY DR			
300	HAY	94544	712-B6
HURON LN			
1100	HAY	94545	711-G5
HURON RD			
-	LVMR	94551	695-E6
HURST AV			
34500	FRMT	94555	752-E1
HURST CT			
-	SRMN	94583	693-F1
HUTCHINGS CT			
-	SJCo	95391	(678-F3 See Page 677)
HUTCHINGS DR			
600	SLN	94577	690-H1
HUTCHINGS WY			
-	SJCo	95391	(678-F3 See Page 677)
HUTCHINS AV			
-	DBLN	94568	694-B3
HUTTON CT			
40000	FRMT	94538	773-B1
HUTTON ST			
5000	FRMT	94538	773-A1
HUXLEY PL			
2800	FRMT	94555	732-E7
HYACINTH AV			
4300	OAK	94619	650-G6
HYACINTH CT			
-	LVMR	94551	696-C3
HYACINTH ST			
37600	NWK	94560	752-F7
HYDE CT			
6700	DBLN	94568	693-J3
HYDE DR			
300	HAY	94544	712-B5
HYDE ST			
1000	SLN	94577	691-A1
3000	OAK	94601	650-C6
HYDE PARK DR			
5000	FRMT	94538	773-C2
HYGELUND DR			
38700	FRMT	94536	752-J5
I			
I ST			
100	FRMT	94536	753-B1
900	UNC	94587	732-F5
N I ST			
200	LVMR	94551	695-G7
S I ST			
300	LVMR	94550	715-H1
IAN CT			
-	SRMN	94582	673-J1
IAN LN			
-	DBLN	94568	693-E5
IAN ST			
1000	SLN	94578	691-C5
IBERIS CT			
2800	PLE	94588	694-H4
IBERO WY			
44100	FRMT	94539	773-H1
ICARUS DR			
-	ALA	94501	649-J7
ICEHOUSE AL			
-	SF	94111	648-B4
ICE HOUSE TER			
-	FRMT	94538	773-E3
ICHABOD LN			
-	ORIN	94563	610-F3
IDA CT			
5800	LVMR	94550	696-D6
IDA LN			
23100	HAY	94541	711-G3
IDAHO CT			
900	MPS	95035	794-A5
IDAHO ST			
3200	BERK	94702	629-F4
3300	OAK	94608	629-F5
IDE CT			
39300	FRMT	94538	753-A5
IDENA AV			
21800	AlaC	94546	692-A6
IDLEWILD AV			
5500	LVMR	94551	696-C2
IDLEWILD CT			
8100	NWK	94560	752-C7
IDLEWOOD CT			
-	DBLN	94568	694-D3
IDLEWOOD ST			
-	DBLN	94568	694-D3
8000	OAK	94605	670-J3
IGLESIA DR			
7900	DBLN	94568	693-F3
ILA CT			
37100	FRMT	94536	753-A1
ILIMA CT			
900	FRMT	94536	732-J7
ILLINOIS ST			
2500	EPA	94303	771-C7
ILS LN			
-	SF	94111	648-A4
IMAGES CIR			
-	MPS	95035	794-A6
-	MPS	95035	793-J6
IMNAHA CT			
44900	FRMT	94539	773-H3
IMPATIENS COM			
5600	FRMT	94538	773-A2
IMPERATA LN			
-	SRMN	94582	673-H2
IMPERIAL AV			
1400	RCH	94804	609-B3
IMPERIAL PL			
1000	HAY	94541	711-J1
32200	UNC	94587	732-C4
IMPERIO AV			
100	FRMT	94539	753-F4
IMPERIO PL			
40300	FRMT	94539	753-F3
IMPRUNETA CT			
-	LVMR	94550	715-F6
INCLINE CT			
1000	HAY	94541	711-D2
INCLINE PL			
18000	HAY	94541	711-D2
INCLINE RD			
18000	HAY	94541	711-D2
INCLINED PL			
7100	DBLN	94568	693-F5
INDEPENDENCE CT			
800	PLE	94566	714-E5
INDEPENDENCE DR			
800	PLE	94566	714-E5
900	ALA	94501	649-G7
2800	LVMR	94551	695-C4
INDEPENDENCE RD			
3500	FRMT	94538	773-E2
INDEPENDENCE WY			
1500	OAK	94606	650-A6
INDEPENDENT RD			
500	OAK	94621	670-E3
INDEPENDENT SCHOOL RD			
21700	AlaC	94552	692-D5
INDIAN BAY			
300	ALA	94502	669-H7
INDIAN RD			
100	PDMT	94610	650-C2
200	OAK	94610	650-C2
INDIAN TR			
-	BERK	94707	609-F5
INDIAN WY			
1700	OAK	94611	630-E6
INDIAN CREEK RD			
3800	AlaC	94550	755-G1
3800	AlaC	94586	755-G1
4000	AlaC	94586	735-D7
11500	AlaC	94586	754-F1
INDIAN GULCH RD			
-	PDMT	94611	650-C1
INDIAN HILL PL			
-	FRMT	94539	773-H4
INDIAN ROCK AV			
800	BERK	94707	609-G5
INDIAN ROCK PTH			
-	BERK	94707	609-G6
INDIAN WELLS DR			
36100	NWK	94560	752-C6
INDIGO COM			
6200	LVMR	94551	696-D1
INDIGO LN			
-	SRMN	94583	693-F1
INDUSTRIAL BLVD			
24700	HAY	94545	711-E6
26700	HAY	94545	731-F1
INDUSTRIAL DR			
44700	FRMT	94538	773-E4
INDUSTRIAL PKWY SW			
29900	HAY	94544	732-B3
29900	HAY	94587	732-B3
29900	UNC	94587	732-B3
INDUSTRIAL PKWY W			
300	HAY	94544	712-D7
300	HAY	94544	732-B2
1900	HAY	94545	732-B2
2200	HAY	94545	731-J2
INDUSTRIAL PL			
45300	FRMT	94538	773-E5
INDUSTRIAL WY			
100	MPS	95035	794-A7
800	OAK	94603	670-G6
6100	LVMR	94551	696-D5
INDUSTRY WY			
3700	AlaC	94546	692-A5
INEZ AV			
37900	FRMT	94536	753-A3
INFANTRY LN			
-	FRMT	94538	753-C3
INGERSOLL PL			
3000	FRMT	94538	753-D6
INGERSOLL TER			
33800	FRMT	94538	753-E6
INGLEWOOD COM			
40800	FRMT	94538	753-D6
INGLEWOOD CT			
6800	PLE	94588	694-A7
INGLEWOOD DR			
5900	PLE	94588	694-A7
INGLEWOOD ST			
1000	HAY	94544	711-H6
INGOT ST			
4000	FRMT	94538	773-E5
INGRAHAM ST			
-	NWK	94560	752-F6
INGRAM PL			
27900	HAY	94544	712-B6
INLET CT			
14900	SLN	94578	691-C5
INMAN CT			
-	DNVL	94526	652-J1
INNISWOOD PL			
-	DBLN	94568	694-H3
INNSBRUCK ST			
1000	LVMR	94550	715-G3
INSPIRATION CIR			
-	DBLN	94568	693-E4
INSPIRATION DR			
-	DBLN	94568	693-E5
INSTAR CT			
-	SRMN	94582	673-H2
INSTAR DR			
-	SRMN	94582	673-H2
INSTAR WY			
-	SRMN	94582	673-H2
INTERLACHEN AV			
7400	SRMN	94583	693-G1
INTERNATIONAL BLVD			
100	OAK	94606	649-J5
1300	OAK	94606	650-A6
2300	OAK	94601	650-A6
3100	OAK	94601	670-C1
INTERNATIONAL BLVD Rt#-185			
3600	OAK	94601	670-C1
5500	OAK	94621	670-H4
9000	OAK	94603	670-H4
INTERNATIONAL BLVD Rt#-185			
10700	SLN	94577	670-H4
INVERLEITH TER			
-	PDMT	94611	650-D2
INVERNESS COM			
3800	LVMR	94551	695-J6
INVERNESS CT			
-	SRMN	94583	673-G7
-	SRMN	94583	693-G1
100	OAK	94605	671-D3
200	ALA	94502	669-J5
1200	FRMT	94539	773-G1
2100	PLE	94588	714-B5
INVERNESS DR			
700	MPS	95035	794-B2
7600	NWK	94560	752-C6
INVERNESS ST			
7400	SRMN	94583	673-G7
15000	SLN	94579	691-A6
INVERNESS WY			
100	ALA	94502	669-J5
300	LVMR	94551	695-J6
INVESTMENT BLVD			
3200	HAY	94545	711-E7
3200	HAY	94545	731-E1
INVINCIBLE CT			
-	ALA	94501	649-G6
INWOOD LN			
300	HAY	94544	732-E2
INYO AV			
2200	OAK	94601	650-C6
INYO CT			
4400	FRMT	94538	753-A6
4600	PLE	94566	694-D7
INYO ST			
22500	HAY	94541	711-G2
IOLANI CT			
39600	FRMT	94538	753-A7
IONE AV			
2600	AlaC	94546	692-A6
IONE CT			
7200	DBLN	94568	693-J2
IONE WY			
6800	DBLN	94568	693-J3
IOWA AV			
33800	UNC	94587	732-F6
IPSWICH CT			
5100	NWK	94560	752-E4
IRENE WY			
5100	LVMR	94550	696-C7
5100	LVMR	94550	716-C1
IRIS CT			
-	SLN	94577	690-J1
38000	NWK	94560	752-G7
IRIS PL			
1100	HAY	94544	711-H6
IRIS ST			
8000	OAK	94605	670-J3
IRIS TER			
4800	FRMT	94555	752-D2
IRIS WY			
5200	LVMR	94551	696-B3
34700	UNC	94587	732-F7
IRMA WY			
2400	AlaC	94546	691-F3
IRONBARK CIR			
600	ORIN	94563	610-H6
IRONBARK CT			
700	ORIN	94563	610-H6
IRONBARK PL			
800	ORIN	94563	610-H6
IRONGATE DR			
-	PLE	94588	694-F7
-	PLE	94588	714-F1
IRONGATE 12			
-	PLE	94588	714-F1
IRON HORSE LN			
37200	FRMT	94536	753-B1
IRON HORSE PKWY			
-	DBLN	94568	694-B5
IRONSTONE COM			
-	LVMR	94550	715-C1
IRONWOOD			
-	OAK	94605	671-D2
IRONWOOD CT			
-	PLE	94588	714-F1
7500	DBLN	94568	693-H3
25200	HAY	94545	711-F6
IRONWOOD DR			
-	PLE	94588	714-F1
7500	DBLN	94568	693-H3
IRONWOOD PL			
4900	AlaC	94550	716-B2
IRONWOOD RD			
200	ALA	94502	670-A6
IROQUOIS AV			
900	LVMR	94551	695-E7
IROQUOIS CT			
900	FRMT	94539	773-J6
IROQUOIS WY			
600	FRMT	94539	773-H6
IRVIN CT			
800	HAY	94541	711-F3
IRVINE DR			
-	MRGA	94556	651-G2
IRVING CT			
-	ORIN	94563	610-H3
IRVING LN			
-	ORIN	94563	610-H4
IRVING ST			
1800	OAK	94601	650-B6
IRVING WY			
8000	DBLN	94568	693-H3
IRVINGTON AV			
4000	FRMT	94538	753-C7
IRWIN CT			
6400	OAK	94609	629-H4
IRWIN WY			
-	ORIN	94563	610-G7
ISABEL AV Rt#-84			
-	PLE	94566	715-C5
1300	LVMR	94550	715-C5
1300	AlaC	94550	715-C4
1300	LVMR	94551	695-C7
1300	LVMR	94551	715-D1
1300	AlaC	94551	715-D1
ISABEL ST			
2500	RCH	94804	609-A5
ISABELLA ST			
100	HAY	94544	712-A5
800	OAK	94607	649-F2
ISHERWOOD PL			
3400	FRMT	94536	752-G2
ISHERWOOD WY			
3100	FRMT	94536	752-G1
3300	FRMT	94536	732-H7
3300	UNC	94587	732-H7
ISHI DR			
45200	FRMT	94539	773-H3
ISLAND DR			
-	ALA	94502	670-A6
ISLAND PINE CT			
800	HAY	94544	712-A7
ISLE CT			
-	HAY	94545	731-H3
ISLE ROYAL CT			
3400	PLE	94588	714-B1
ISLE ROYAL ST			
42500	FRMT	94538	773-C2
ISLETON AV			
100	OAK	94603	670-G7
ISOLA DR			
400	FRMT	94555	732-C7
ITHACA ST			
32200	HAY	94544	732-E3
32300	UNC	94587	732-E3
ITHACA WY			
4600	PLE	94588	694-D6
IVALDI CT			
300	FRMT	94539	753-G4
IVANHOE RD			
5800	OAK	94618	630-A5
IVES CT			
40500	FRMT	94538	753-C7
IVORY PL			
-	LVMR	94550	715-D3
IVY COM			
-	LVMR	94551	696-D1
IVY CT			
1100	ELCR	94530	609-E1
7500	PLE	94588	693-J7
14200	SLN	94578	691-C3
IVY DR			
-	OAK	94610	650-A4
600	MLPK	94025	771-A7
2200	OAK	94606	650-A4
IVY WY			
1900	FRMT	94539	773-G3
J			
J ST			
100	FRMT	94536	753-B1
1000	UNC	94587	732-G5
S J ST			
100	LVMR	94550	715-H1
JACANA LAKE CT			
3800	FRMT	94555	732-H4
JACARANDA CT			
500	FRMT	94539	753-F5
38300	NWK	94560	752-G7
JACARANDA DR			
200	HAY	94544	712-A5
300	FRMT	94539	753-F5
38300	NWK	94560	752-G7
JACINTO CT			
35800	FRMT	94536	752-F3
JACINTO DR			
4000	FRMT	94536	752-F3
JACKIE CT			
4000	PLE	94588	694-A7
JACK KEROUAC AL			
-	SF	94133	648-A4
JACKLIN CIR			
-	MPS	95035	794-A5
JACKLIN CT			
-	MPS	95035	794-A5
JACKLIN PL			
-	MPS	95035	794-A5
JACKLIN RD			
-	MPS	95035	794-A5
JACK LONDON AL			
-	SF	94107	648-B6
JACK LONDON AV			
-	ALA	94501	649-E7
JACK LONDON BLVD			
-	LVMR	94588	694-H5
E JACK LONDON BLVD			
100	LVMR	94551	695-D7
W JACK LONDON BLVD			
100	LVMR	94551	695-B7
JACKLYNN CT			
32300	UNC	94587	731-J7
32300	UNC	94587	751-J1
JACKLYNN DR			
32300	UNC	94587	731-J7
32400	UNC	94587	751-J1
32400	UNC	94587	752-A1
JACKSON AV			
400	LVMR	94550	696-A7
600	LVMR	94550	716-A1
JACKSON CT			
1900	FRMT	94539	753-F7
JACKSON ST			
-	ALB	94710	609-D5
-	SF	94108	648-A4
-	SF	94111	648-A4
-	SF	94133	648-A4
100	OAK	94607	649-G4
500	ALB	94706	609-D5
1200	OAK	94612	649-G4
2100	FRMT	94539	753-F7
2800	ALA	94501	670-B3
JACKSON ST Rt#-92			
-	HAY	94544	711-J4
-	HAY	94541	711-J4
W JACKSON ST			
-	HAY	94544	711-H4
JACKSON WY			
-	SJS	95002	793-C7
JACOBS PL			
2500	AlaC	94541	692-C6
JACOBS ST			
2500	AlaC	94541	692-C6
JACOBUS AV			
1000	AlaC	94586	734-B3
4600	OAK	94618	630-B6
JACQUELINE PL			
1300	AlaC	94580	691-C7
1300	AlaC	94580	711-B1
JACQUILINE WY			
5500	LVMR	94550	716-C1
JACUZZI ST			
3200	RCH	94804	609-C4
JADE CIR			
7800	DBLN	94568	693-J1
JADE CT			
-	SRMN	94582	673-F2
2200	FRMT	94539	773-G2
JADE PL			
600	LVMR	94550	715-D3
JADECREST CT			
-	SRMN	94582	673-G1
JADECREST DR			
-	SRMN	94582	673-F1
JAFFA RD			
1300	LVMR	94550	715-G3
JAMAICA CIR			
200	UNC	94587	732-D6
JAMAICA LN			
26600	HAY	94545	711-F7
JAMAICA TER			
4100	FRMT	94555	752-E1
JAMAICA WY			
2300	SLN	94577	690-G5
JAMES AV			
3700	FRMT	94538	753-D6
4200	AlaC	94546	692-A4
4900	AlaC	94552	692-C4
5200	OAK	94618	629-J6
JAMES PL			
1100	ELCR	94530	609-E1
19200	AlaC	94546	692-B4
JAMES ST			
-	CCCo	94514	637-D2
300	LVMR	94551	695-F7
300	LVMR	94551	715-F1
JAMESTOWN RD			
3500	FRMT	94538	773-E2
JAMI CT			
200	LVMR	94550	696-A7
JAMI ST			
-	LVMR	94550	696-A6
JAMIE CIR			
33200	FRMT	94555	732-C7
JAMIE CT			
-	CCCo	94582	674-B5
JAMIE PL			
-	CCCo	94582	674-B5
JAMIE WY			
3300	AlaC	94541	692-D7
JAMISON WY			
3400	AlaC	94546	692-A5
JAN CT			
800	AlaC	94580	691-E5
JANAE CT			
4500	UNC	94587	731-J7
JANE AV			
26000	HAY	94544	712-A5
JANE CT			
300	HAY	94544	712-A5
JANELLE CT			
3100	AlaC	94541	712-D1
JANET CT			
4900	LVMR	94550	696-B7
JANETH ST			
-	CCCo	94514	637-D2
JANICE AV			
500	HAY	94544	732-E1
JANICE LN			
41200	FRMT	94539	753-G4
JANIE CT			
-	ELCR	94530	609-C2
JANIS CIR			
2600	ALA	94501	670-A2
JANIS CT			
1400	LVMR	94551	695-F6
JANSEN TER			
37400	FRMT	94536	752-H4
JANSSEN CT			
24000	HAY	94541	712-A2
JAPALA CT			
-	FRMT	94539	773-H3
JAPALA PL			
44500	FRMT	94539	773-H3
JAPONICA WY			
-	CCCo	94582	674-B2
JAQUES CT			
4700	FRMT	94555	752-C2
J ARTHUR YOUNGER FRWY Rt#-92			
-	HAY	-	711-E7
-	HAY	-	731-B1
JARVIS AV			
5600	NWK	94560	752-D4
JASMINE AV			
6200	NWK	94560	772-G1
JASMINE CT			
-	FRMT	94536	752-J2
-	FRMT	94536	753-A2
-	UNC	94587	732-H6
100	MPS	95035	794-D6
1400	LVMR	94551	696-A4
5500	AlaC	94552	692-E3
7600	DBLN	94568	693-H3
JASON CT			
-	SF	94133	648-A4
JASON DR			
-	MPS	95035	793-J4
JASON WY			
37300	FRMT	94536	752-H3
JASPER CT			
-	LVMR	94550	715-D3
JASPER PL			
-	SF	94133	648-A4
JASPER HILL CT			
-	SRMN	94582	674-B4
JASPER HILL DR			
-	SRMN	94582	674-B4
JAVA DR			
3400	SRMN	94582	673-D1
JAVALINA RD			
47200	FRMT	94539	773-H7
JAY CT			
-	PLE	94566	714-E3
JAY ST			
1700	ALA	94501	669-H1
JAYAR PL			
500	HAY	94544	732-E2
JAYBROOK CT			
7300	PLE	94588	693-J7
JAYDINE ST			
19500	AlaC	94546	692-B4
JAYHAWK LN			
1300	LVMR	94551	696-C3
JAYMARK CT			
18000	AlaC	94546	691-J2
JAYNE AV			
300	OAK	94610	649-J3
JAYNES ST			
1600	BERK	94703	629-F1
1700	BERK	94703	609-F7
JEAN CT			
4600	UNC	94587	731-J7
JEAN DR			
-	UNC	94545	731-J7
32200	UNC	94587	731-J7
32300	UNC	94587	732-A7
32500	UNC	94587	752-A1
JEAN ST			
400	OAK	94610	649-J2
600	OAK	94610	650-A2
JEAN WY			
900	HAY	94545	711-F4
1300	SLN	94577	690-H1
JEANINE WY			
3300	AlaC	94546	691-J5
JEANNIE CT			
4500	LVMR	94550	696-B7
JEANNIE WY			
300	LVMR	94550	696-A7
JEFFER ST			
2200	AlaC	94546	692-A6
JEFFERSON AV			
600	LVMR	94550	696-A7
JEFFERSON AV			
600	LVMR	94550	716-A1
2000	BERK	94703	629-F3
5600	RCH	94804	609-B2
5700	ELCR	94530	609-B2
JEFFERSON CT			
4600	PLE	94588	694-A7
JEFFERSON ST			
-	OAK	94607	649-F4
500	HAY	94544	712-B6
1100	SLN	94577	691-A1
1200	OAK	94612	649-F4
42600	FRMT	94538	773-E1
JEFFREY CT			
2700	AlaC	94546	691-H4
JEFFREY ST			
-	LVMR	94550	715-G4
JELINCIC DR			
-	AlaC	94541	712-D1
JENKINSON LAKE WY			
3800	FRMT	94555	732-B6
JENNIFER CT			
4800	UNC	94587	751-J1
JENNIFER DR			
1700	LVMR	94550	716-C1
2700	AlaC	94546	691-H4
JENNIFER ST			
36500	NWK	94560	752-E6
JENNIFER WY			
700	MPS	95035	794-A5
JENNINGS WY			
26800	HAY	94544	711-J7
JENSEN RD			
5100	AlaC	94552	692-E4
JENSEN ST			
100	LVMR	94550	695-J7
400	LVMR	94550	715-J1
4200	PLE	94566	714-E2
4300	OAK	94601	670-C2
JENSEN RANCH RD			
6600	AlaC	94552	692-G2
JERALD CT			
3500	AlaC	94546	691-J3
JEREZ CT			
1300	HAY	94544	732-A1
JERLIN PL			
-	PLE	94588	713-J3
JEROME AL			
-	SF	94133	648-A4
JEROME AV			
-	PDMT	94611	650-A1
100	PDMT	94610	650-B1
43300	FRMT	94539	753-H7
JERROLD RD			
3600	AlaC	94550	716-G3
JERRY PL			
17400	AlaC	94541	691-F7
JERSEY RD			
3700	FRMT	94538	773-E2
JERVIS BAY			
100	ALA	94502	669-H7
JERYLYN LN			
200	HAY	94541	711-G3
JESSEE CT			
20000	AlaC	94552	692-F3
JESSEN CT			
-	CCCo	94707	609-F2
JESSICA CIR			
4300	FRMT	94555	752-C1
JESSICA DR			
700	LVMR	94550	696-C7
JESSIE ST			
-	SF	94105	648-B6
100	SF	94103	648-B6
JETTY WY			
-	HAY	94545	731-H3
JEWEL TER			
-	FRMT	94536	732-J4
JEWELL CT			
6800	OAK	94611	630-E5
JIB RD			
17300	SLN	94577	690-H4
JILL WY			
18300	AlaC	94546	691-H3
JILLANA AV			
300	LVMR	94550	715-D2
JILLIENE WY			
500	HAY	94544	732-E1
JIMINEZ WY			
100	HAY	94544	712-C7
JOAN DR			
1900	AlaC	94578	691-D2
JOAN TER			
100	FRMT	94536	732-J7
JOAN WY			
5300	LVMR	94550	696-C7
JOANNA CT			
4600	FRMT	94536	752-E3
JOANNE CIR			
3100	PLE	94588	694-C7
JOANNE ST			
24600	HAY	94544	711-J3
24600	HAY	94544	712-A3
JOAQUIN AV			
100	SLN	94577	691-A1
900	SLN	94577	671-C7
S JOAQUIN CT			
23000	SJCo	95304	(678-J6 See Page 677)
JOAQUIN MILLER CT			
2600	OAK	94611	650-F2
JOAQUIN MILLER RD			
2900	OAK	94602	650-G3
3500	OAK	94619	650-G3
JOAQUIN MURIETA AV			
6000	NWK	94560	772-J2
JOEL ST			
-	SJCo	95391	(678-E3 See Page 677)
JOHN CT			
2200	AlaC	94546	691-H6
JOHN DR			
19900	AlaC	94546	691-H5
JOHN ST			
-	SF	94133	648-A4
100	OAK	94611	629-J7
JOHN GLENN DR			
-	OAK	94621	690-D2
JOHN MAHER ST			
-	SF	94111	648-B4
JOHN MONEGO CT			
-	DBLN	94568	694-E4
JOHN MUIR DR			
5600	NWK	94560	772-J1
JOHNSON AV			
2800	ALA	94501	670-B3
JOHNSON CT			
3500	FRMT	94555	752-E1
5300	PLE	94588	694-A5
JOHNSON DR			
5100	PLE	94588	693-J6
5100	PLE	94588	694-A5

© 2006 Rand McNally & Company

STREET Block City ZIP Pg-Grid

JOHNSON RD
4100 HAY 94545 731-D1
JOHNSON ST
700 ALB 94706 609-C6
1500 SLN 94577 690-H2
JOHNSTON DR
5900 OAK 94611 630-D7
JOHN T KNOX FRWY I-580
- ALB - 609-A3
- RCH - 609-A3
JOICE ST
- SF 94108 648-A5
JOLEEN CT
900 HAY 94544 732-A1
JO MARY CT
24700 AlaC 94541 712-B2
JONATHAN DR
5500 NWK 94560 752-E5
JONATHAN PL
5400 NWK 94560 752-E5
JONATHAN WY
500 UNC 94587 732-G3
JONES AV
300 OAK 94603 670-G7
JONES LN
- LVMR 94551 695-G7
JONES ST
- DBLN 94568 694-B3
600 BERK 94710 629-D1
1100 BERK 94702 629-D1
2600 AlaC 94546 692-B6
JONES WY
38500 FRMT 94536 753-D1
JONES GATE CT
2800 PLE 94566 694-D7
JONQUIL COM
1900 LVMR 94551 696-D1
JONQUIL DR
38700 NWK 94560 772-G1
JORDAN CIR
- AlaC 94541 692-B6
JORDAN RD
2900 OAK 94602 650-F4
3500 OAK 94619 650-G5
JORDAN WY
600 AlaC 94541 691-G7
JOREE LN
- SRMN 94582 674-A3
JORGENSEN LN
7700 PLE 94588 714-A4
23000 HAY 94541 711-G3
JOSE CT
3200 HAY 94542 712-E4
JOSEPH DR
17800 AlaC 94546 691-J2
17800 AlaC 94546 692-A3
JOSEPH ST
- SJCo 95391 (678-F3 See Page 677)
37300 FRMT 94536 752-H4
JOSEPHINE ST
1100 BERK 94707 609-G7
1200 BERK 94703 609-G7
1500 BERK 94703 629-G1
JOSH PL
- AlaC 94546 692-A4
JOSHUA CIR
7300 PLE 94588 714-A1
JOSHUA PL
900 FRMT 94539 773-J6
JOSHUA ST
26500 HAY 94544 712-A5
JOST LN
1000 ALA 94502 670-A7
JOVAN TER
34700 FRMT 94555 752-D3
JOY CT
- LVMR 94550 696-D7
JOYCE AV
1800 SLN 94577 690-J2
41000 FRMT 94539 753-E6
JOYCE ST
200 LVMR 94550 696-B7
24600 HAY 94544 711-J3
24800 HAY 94544 712-A3
JOYCE WY
32400 UNC 94587 732-A7
JUANA AV
100 SLN 94577 691-B1
E JUANA AV
1300 SLN 94577 671-D7
W JUANA AV
100 SLN 94577 691-A1
JUANITA WY
1500 BERK 94702 629-E1
JUAREZ CT
11600 DBLN 94568 693-F3
JUAREZ LN
11700 DBLN 94568 693-F3
JUBILEE LN
- SLN 94577 670-J7
JUDD ST
4900 OAK 94601 670-E1
JUDIE ST
100 FRMT 94555 752-C1
JUDIE WY
38800 FRMT 94536 752-J6
JUDITH WY
- LVMR 94550 715-E1
JUDY ST
18000 AlaC 94546 692-A3
JULIA CT
4400 UNC 94587 731-J6
JULIA ST
- OAK 94618 630-C6
1500 BERK 94703 629-F4
28100 HAY 94545 731-G2
JULIAN CT
1700 ELCR 94530 609-D1
JULIAN DR
1600 ELCR 94530 609-C1
JULIANNA CT
- MRGA 94556 651-G1
JULIE ST
4900 LVMR 94550 696-B7
JULIE ANN WY
600 OAK 94601 670-D3
700 OAK 94621 670-D3
JULIET CIR
33800 FRMT 94555 752-B2
JULIET CT
1300 LVMR 94550 716-C1
JULIETA ST
14600 SLN 94578 691-C3
JULIUS ST
- SF 94133 648-A3
10800 OAK 94605 671-B5
10900 SLN 94577 671-B5
JUNCO AV
200 LVMR 94551 695-D7

JUNCTION AV
200 LVMR 94551 695-G7
1900 ELCR 94530 609-B1
JUNE CT
200 AlaC 94541 711-G1
10400 OAK 94603 670-H7
40000 FRMT 94538 753-B7
JUNE ST
- FRMT 94555 732-C7
- FRMT 94555 752-C1
JUNEAU ST
2000 SLN 94577 690-G3
JUNE MARIE CT
1800 AlaC 94541 712-B2
JUNIPER AV
8000 NWK 94560 772-C1
JUNIPER DR
- SRMN 94583 693-H1
JUNIPER ST
1200 LVMR 94551 695-F7
3500 AlaC 94546 692-A6
14200 SLN 94579 690-J4
14300 SLN 94579 691-A4
JUNIPER WY
- MRGA 94556 651-D1
JUNIPERO COM
200 FRMT 94536 733-A6
JUNIPERO DR
100 PLE 94566 714-D5
JUNIPERO ST
- PLE 94566 714-D5
JUPITER CT
600 FRMT 94539 793-J1
1400 MPS 95035 794-D6
4200 UNC 94587 732-B6
JUPITER DR
1500 MPS 95035 794-D6
JUPITER ST
28600 HAY 94544 712-B7
JUPITER WY
1500 MPS 95035 794-D6
JURGENS DR
200 MPS 95035 793-J4
JUSTCO LN
21000 AlaC 94552 692-C5
JUSTIN CIR
- ALA 94502 669-J5
JUSTIN TER
5000 FRMT 94555 752-A3
JUSTINE CT
- LVMR 94550 696-D7
JUTLAND AV
15400 SLN 94579 691-B7

K

N K ST
100 LVMR 94551 695-G7
100 LVMR 94551 715-G1
S K ST
100 LVMR 94550 715-G1
KACHINA CT
1000 FRMT 94539 773-J5
1000 FRMT 94539 774-A5
KADI CT
44500 FRMT 94539 773-H3
KAHLERT ST
21200 AlaC 94546 691-J6
KAHLUA CT
39500 FRMT 94538 753-A7
KAHN AL
400 OAK 94612 649-G4
KAIBAB CT
800 FRMT 94536 753-D1
KAINS AV
400 ALB 94706 609-D6
1100 BERK 94706 609-D6
1300 BERK 94702 609-D6
1400 BERK 94702 629-E1
KAISER DR
6400 FRMT 94555 752-A4
KAISER PZ
2100 OAK 94612 649-H3
KAISER CREEK RD
- AlaC 94546 651-H6
- AlaC 94546 652-A6
- AlaC 94546 671-H1
- CCCo 94556 652-A6
KALENDA COM
2100 FRMT 94539 753-E6
KALES AV
5400 OAK 94618 629-J6
5400 OAK 94618 630-A5
KALTHOFF COM
- AlaC 94550 715-D7
- LVMR 94550 715-D7
- LVMR 94550 735-E1
KAMP CT
3800 PLE 94588 694-F7
KAMP DR
1700 PLE 94566 714-F1
1700 PLE 94588 714-F1
3500 PLE 94588 694-E7
KANE CT
4600 FRMT 94538 753-B7
KANSAS ST
3000 OAK 94602 650-E5
3500 OAK 94619 650-F6
KANSAS WY
100 FRMT 94539 793-J2
KANSAS CITY
3000 ALA 94501 649-F6
KAPHAN AV
4600 OAK 94619 650-G6
KAPIOLANI RD
3100 OAK 94613 650-G7
3100 OAK 94613 670-G1
KAPLAN LN
- SF 94103 648-B6
KAPPA AV
1700 SLN 94579 691-A6
KARA PL
- LVMR 94550 715-G4
KARA RD
- ALA 94502 669-J5
KAREN CT
32500 UNC 94587 752-A1
KAREN WY
400 LVMR 94550 715-E1
KARINA CT
- AlaC 94541 712-D1
- SRMN 94582 674-C4
KARINA ST
- AlaC 94541 712-D1
KARMEN ST
- AlaC 94541 712-D1
KARN DR
28100 HAY 94544 712-A7
28200 HAY 94544 732-A1
KAROL WY
900 SLN 94577 671-A7

KARRIS LN
19100 AlaC 94546 691-G4
KASPER TER
34100 FRMT 94555 752-A3
KATHLEAN ST
41000 FRMT 94538 753-C7
41100 FRMT 94538 773-C1
KATHLEEN AV
4800 AlaC 94546 692-B4
KATHRYN CT
4800 FRMT 94536 752-J6
KATHY CT
100 UNC 94587 732-E3
1300 LVMR 94550 716-C1
KATHY WY
5100 LVMR 94550 716-C1
KATIE LN
4200 PLE 94588 694-E7
KATO RD
46800 FRMT 94538 773-E4
47600 FRMT 94538 793-G1
48700 FRMT 94539 793-H3
KATO TER
48800 FRMT 94539 793-H2
KATRINA CT
- ORIN 94563 610-G3
5200 AlaC 94546 692-C3
KATRINA ST
700 LVMR 94550 696-C7
KAUAI CIR
300 UNC 94587 732-C6
KAVALA CT
6100 PLE 94566 714-D6
KAVANAUGH DR
1300 EPA 94303 771-B7
1300 MLPK 94025 771-B7
KAWELLA CIR
400 UNC 94587 732-D5
KAY AV
24700 HAY 94545 711-G5
KAY CT
3600 FRMT 94538 773-E1
KAZAR CT
- MRGA 94556 651-E2
KEARNEY AV
5000 OAK 94602 650-F3
KEARNEY ST
400 ELCR 94530 609-B1
3000 FRMT 94538 753-B5
KEARNY ST
- SF 94108 648-A4
300 SF 94104 648-A5
600 SF 94111 648-A5
900 SF 94133 648-A3
KEATS LN
1000 HAY 94544 712-A7
KEATS ST
3100 FRMT 94536 753-A4
KEB RD
- OAK 94605 651-B7
KEEFER CT
- PDMT 94610 650-A1
KEEGAN ST
- DBLN 94568 694-G4
KEELER AV
700 BERK 94708 609-H5
KEELER CT
- LVMR 94550 716-C1
5200 FRMT 94536 752-G6
KEELER ST
- LVMR 94550 716-C2
KEIL BAY
100 ALA 94502 669-J6
KEITH AV
- OAK 94618 629-J5
1000 BERK 94708 609-H6
3000 AlaC 94546 691-H4
5800 OAK 94618 630-A5
KELL COM
500 FRMT 94539 753-H5
KELLER AV
1700 AlaC 94580 711-B2
2900 OAK 94605 671-B1
5900 OAK 94627 671-B1
KELLEYBROOK WY
- SRMN 94582 674-B3
KELLOGG AV
700 HAY 94544 712-C6
KELLOGG CREEK RD
3200 CCCo 94514 637-D1
KELLY AV
1200 SLN 94577 690-H2
KELLY CT
- MLPK 94025 771-A7
KELLY ST
2100 AlaC 94541 692-C7
2100 HAY 94541 692-C7
2500 LVMR 94551 695-H7
40000 FRMT 94538 753-C5
KELSEY ST
2800 BERK 94705 629-J3
KELSO RD
14000 AlaC 94551 (657-G5 See Page 637)
14100 AlaC 94551 (658-A6 See Page 637)
S KELSO RD
17500 SJCo 95391 (658-D4 See Page 637)
W KELSO RD
19500 SJCo 95391 (658-D7 See Page 637)
KELSO ST
4600 UNC 94587 752-B1
KELTON CT
- OAK 94611 649-J1
KEMPER CT
7900 PLE 94588 714-B5
KEMPER RD
3000 FRMT 94536 752-H2
KEMPTON AV
3300 OAK 94611 649-H2
KEMPTON WY
3500 OAK 94610 649-J1
3500 OAK 94611 649-J1
KENDALL WY
600 AlaC 94541 691-F6
KENDRA LN
25800 AlaC 94541 712-D2
25900 AlaC 94542 712-D2
KENELAND WY
3800 PLE 94588 694-F5
KENILWORTH AV
200 SLN 94577 671-B6
6700 ELCR 94530 609-C1
KENILWORTH CT
- CCCo 94707 609-F4
KENILWORTH DR
- CCCo 94707 609-F2
KENILWORTH RD
7000 OAK 94705 630-C3

KENILWORTH WY
- CCCo 94582 674-A2
KENISTON AV
300 MPS 95035 793-J7
KENITA WY
32500 UNC 94587 732-C5
KENMORE AV
500 OAK 94610 650-A2
KENMORE CT
- ORIN 94563 630-J4
3700 AlaC 94546 692-A5
KENNEDY AV
2300 UNC 94587 732-G7
KENNEDY DR
1300 MPS 95035 794-C5
KENNEDY ST
300 OAK 94606 670-A1
500 OAK 94606 650-A7
2600 LVMR 94551 695-H7
KENNEDY PARK PL
- AlaC 94541 711-F1
KENNET ST
31800 HAY 94544 732-E3
KENNETH ST
- SJCo 95391 (678-F3 See Page 677)
KENSINGTON COM
300 LVMR 94551 695-J6
KENSINGTON CT
- CCCo 94707 609-F2
KENSINGTON DR
800 FRMT 94539 753-F5
KENSINGTON RD
- CCCo 94805 609-F2
- ELCR 94530 609-F2
- CCCo 94707 609-F2
KENSINGTON PARK RD
- CCCo 94708 609-F3
KENT AV
16300 AlaC 94578 691-F6
16300 AlaC 94580 691-F6
KENT CT
400 LVMR 94551 695-E6
900 AlaC 94580 691-F6
8300 ELCR 94530 609-D1
KENT DR
8300 ELCR 94530 609-D1
KENT PL
200 SRMN 94583 693-G1
KENT RD
- OAK 94705 630-C4
KENT WY
7500 SRMN 94583 693-G1
KENTFIELD COM
4700 FRMT 94555 752-D2
KENTFIELD LN
18600 AlaC 94541 711-E1
KENTUCKY AV
400 BERK 94707 609-G4
KENTWOOD CT
4100 OAK 94605 671-B2
KENTWOOD LN
1100 AlaC 94578 691-F6
KENTWOOD WY
7900 PLE 94588 693-H7
KENWICK DR
- SRMN 94582 674-B3
KENWOOD DR
34200 FRMT 94555 752-C2
KENWOOD LN
- DNVL 94526 652-J1
KENWOOD ST
4800 UNC 94587 752-B1
KENWYN RD
500 OAK 94606 650-A4
600 OAK 94610 650-A4
KENYON AV
- CCCo 94708 609-F3
800 SLN 94577 691-C1
KEONCREST DR
1400 BERK 94702 629-F1
1500 BERK 94702 609-F7
KEPPLER AV
- DBLN 94568 694-C4
KERANEN CT
- SJCo 95391 (678-E2 See Page 677)
KERLIN ST
38400 FRMT 94536 752-J5
KERN CT
900 LVMR 94551 695-F6
3900 PLE 94588 694-A7
3900 PLE 94588 714-A1
KERN LP
1800 FRMT 94539 794-A2
KERR AV
- CCCo 94707 609-F2
KERR ST
2700 AlaC 94546 691-J6
3100 AlaC 94546 692-A5
KERRIGAN DR
11200 OAK 94605 671-D5
KERRY COM
100 FRMT 94536 732-J7
KERRY CT
- DBLN 94568 694-A4
KERWIN AV
100 OAK 94603 670-G7
KESTERSON
15000 SLN 94579 691-C6
KESTREL CT
- SLN 94579 691-F1
KESTREL PL
3300 FRMT 94555 732-D7
KESWICK CT
- OAK 94611 650-F1
KETELSEN DR
- MRGA 94556 651-E1
KETTERING TER
4000 FRMT 94536 752-H1
KEVIN CT
400 SRMN 94583 673-F5
700 OAK 94621 670-E3
3200 PLE 94588 714-B1
5000 AlaC 94546 692-B3
KEVINAIRE DR
500 MPS 95035 794-B5
KEVINGTON PL
200 ALA 94502 670-A5
KEY BLVD
1800 ELCR 94530 609-B1
KEY CT
- OAK 94605 671-E4
KEYES AL
- SF 94133 648-A4
KEY ROUTE BLVD
500 ALB 94706 609-E6
1100 BERK 94706 609-E6
KEYS PL
2100 HAY 94545 731-H1

KEYSTONE DR
5000 FRMT 94536 752-G6
KEYSTONE WY
800 LVMR 94550 715-E3
KIDDER ST
22900 HAY 94545 711-C5
KILB RANCH DR
- PLE 94588 693-G6
N KILBRIDE LN
- DBLN 94568 694-G3
S KILBRIDE LN
- DBLN 94568 694-G3
KILCULLIN CT
11800 DBLN 94568 693-G4
KILDARA
7200 DBLN 94568 693-G4
KILDARE RD
16500 AlaC 94546 691-G4
16500 AlaC 94578 691-G4
KILKARE RD
- AlaC 94586 734-A1
2600 AlaC 94586 713-H6
2600 AlaC 94586 733-J1
KILKENNY CT
- ALA 94502 669-J5
KILKENNY DR
- DBLN 94568 694-A4
KILKENNY PL
- ALA 94502 669-H5
KILLARNEY PL
- ALA 94502 669-H5
KILLARNEY ST
1100 LVMR 94550 715-G3
KILLDEER CT
- ALA 94501 649-F7
2700 UNC 94587 732-D6
KILLIAN ST
- DBLN 94568 694-E4
KILLORGLIN COM
35800 FRMT 94536 732-J7
KILLYBEGS RD
- ALA 94502 669-H5
KILPATRICK CT
2500 SRMN 94583 673-B2
KILPATRICK DR
100 SRMN 94583 673-B2
KILRUSH AV
7500 DBLN 94568 693-G2
KIM CT
3300 PLE 94588 714-B1
5900 LVMR 94550 696-D6
KIM PL
500 HAY 94544 711-H4
KIMBALL AV
1100 HAY 94541 691-H7
9000 SRMN 94583 693-H1
KIMBER TER
300 FRMT 94539 753-E2
KIMBERLEY CT
- OAK 94611 650-F1
KIMBERLIN HEIGHTS DR
- OAK 94619 650-H4
KIMBERLY COM
4500 LVMR 94550 696-B7
KIMBERLY CT
31200 UNC 94587 731-J5
KIMBERLY ST
3800 UNC 94587 731-J5
KIMBER PARK CT
200 FRMT 94539 753-E2
KIMBERWOOD CT
200 FRMT 94539 753-E2
KIMBRO ST
38000 FRMT 94536 752-H4
KING AV
- PDMT 94611 650-C2
100 FRMT 94536 732-J6
100 PDMT 94610 650-C2
E KING AV
- FRMT 94536 732-J6
KING CT
- MPS 95035 794-C7
1100 ELCR 94530 609-E2
35100 FRMT 94536 732-J6
KING DR
900 ELCR 94530 609-E2
KING ST
- SF 94107 648-B7
800 OAK 94606 650-A7
2900 BERK 94703 629-G4
3400 OAK 94608 629-G5
KING WY
6400 DBLN 94568 693-J3
KINGFISHER CT
- SLN 94579 691-F2
KINGLET CT
34900 UNC 94587 732-G7
KINGLET RD
400 LVMR 94551 695-E7
400 LVMR 94551 715-E1
KINGLET TER
3800 FRMT 94555 732-J3
KINGS CT
14400 SLN 94578 691-D2
22800 HAY 94541 712-A1
KINGS PL
5200 RCH 94804 609-B3
KINGS RD
500 ALA 94501 669-F1
KINGSBRIDGE CT
- CCCo 94583 673-B5
KINGSBURY CT
- ALA 94501 649-G7
KINGSBURY DR
800 LVMR 94550 715-G2
KINGS CANYON CT
3500 PLE 94588 714-A1
KINGS COVE CT
- UNC 94545 731-J6
KINGSFORD WY
- HAY 94541 711-J2
KINGSLAND AV
2400 OAK 94601 670-F1
2500 OAK 94619 670-F1
2700 OAK 94619 650-F7
KINGSLAND PL
- OAK 94619 650-F7
KINGSLEY CIR
5700 OAK 94605 670-G1
KINGSLEY PL
300 SRMN 94583 673-F6
KINGSLEY ST
3600 OAK 94610 650-B4
KINGSMILL TER
- DBLN 94568 694-F2
KINGSPORT AV
1400 LVMR 94550 715-G3
KINGSTON AV
700 OAK 94611 649-J1
700 PDMT 94611 649-J1
700 PDMT 94611 650-A1

KINGSTON LN
1000 ALA 94502 670-B7
KINGSTON PL
7100 DBLN 94568 693-G5
KINGSTON RD
- CCCo 94707 609-F4
KINGSTON WY
17400 AlaC 94546 691-H2
KINGWOOD RD
- OAK 94619 650-H5
KINKAID CT
- ALA 94501 649-E7
KINKAID SQ
- ALA 94501 649-E7
KINKEAD WY
- ALB 94710 609-D6
KINNEY CT
19600 AlaC 94546 692-A4
KINO CT
- DBLN 94568 694-G5
700 HAY 94544 712-A3
KINO WY
1600 LVMR 94550 715-G2
KINVARRA CT
- SRMN 94582 674-B3
KIOTE DR
6800 NWK 94560 752-B6
KIOWA CT
45500 FRMT 94539 773-H4
KIPLING PL
3100 FRMT 94536 752-G2
KIPLING ST
2200 AlaC 94546 692-A7
KIRBY COM
600 FRMT 94539 753-H7
KIRK
4000 ALA 94501 649-E6
KIRK CT
- CCCo 94507 652-G1
KIRK TER
38500 FRMT 94536 753-C2
KIRKCALDY CT
3600 PLE 94588 694-F5
KIRKCALDY ST
3100 PLE 94588 694-F5
KIRKCREST CT
- DNVL 94526 652-G1
- CCCo 94507 652-G1
KIRKCREST LN
900 DNVL 94526 652-G1
KIRKCREST RD
700 DNVL 94526 652-G1
800 CCCo 94507 652-G1
KIRKHAM ST
500 OAK 94607 649-E2
KIRKLAND CT
- OAK 94605 671-D4
KIRKSTONE CT
- SRMN 94582 674-B3
KIRKWALL PL
600 MPS 95035 794-A3
KIRKWOOD CT
- EPA 94303 771-B7
KIRKWOOD DR
2400 HAY 94545 731-G1
KIRSTEN WY
5100 LVMR 94550 696-C6
KISA CT
5200 LVMR 94550 696-C7
KISKA
4000 ALA 94501 649-E6
KIT LN
6700 AlaC 94552 692-F3
KITAYAMA DR
2300 UNC 94587 732-D5
KITCHENER CT
2800 OAK 94602 650-F4
KITE HILL RD
600 ORIN 94563 610-H6
KITE HILL TER
500 ORIN 94563 610-H6
KIT FOX PL
19100 AlaC 94546 691-G4
KITTERY AV
3000 SRMN 94583 673-G6
KITTERY PL
200 SRMN 94583 673-F6
KITTIWAKE RD
- ORIN 94563 610-F5
KITTREDGE ST
2000 BERK 94704 629-G2
KITTY LN
9800 OAK 94603 670-F7
9800 OAK 94603 690-F1
KITTY HAWK PL
1900 ALA 94501 669-H3
KITTY HAWK RD
300 ALA 94501 669-H3
1600 LVMR 94551 695-B5
KITTY HAWK RD Rt#-84
1200 LVMR 94551 695-C6
KIWANIS ST
3300 OAK 94602 650-F5
22800 HAY 94541 711-H2
KIZER ST
800 MPS 95035 794-B4
KLAMATH CT
500 HAY 94541 711-G3
2600 LVMR 94550 715-G5
4600 PLE 94566 694-D7
KLAMATH PL
500 FRMT 94539 773-J5
KLAMATH RD
200 MPS 95035 794-A6
500 HAY 94541 711-G3
KLAMATH ST
3500 OAK 94602 650-G4
46100 FRMT 94539 773-J5
KLAUS CT
27600 HAY 94542 712-D4
KLEMETSON DR
9200 PLE 94588 693-G6
KLINE CT
- SJCo 95391 (678-F3 See Page 677)
KLONDIKE CT
- UNC 94587 732-H6
KLONDIKE DR
- UNC 94587 732-H6
KLONDIKE PL
- LVMR 94550 715-D4
KLONDIKE RD
- LVMR 94550 715-D4
KNAPP ST
31700 HAY 94587 732-B4
KNICKERBOCKER LN
- ORIN 94563 630-H2
KNIGHT CT
- UNC 94587 731-J5
KNIGHT DR
17500 AlaC 94546 691-H2

KNIGHT ST
200 OAK 94603 670-G7
KNOLL AV
4200 OAK 94619 650-H6
KNOLL CT
1700 LVMR 94551 696-E2
KNOLL DR
- CCCo 94556 651-F3
- MRGA 94556 651-F3
KNOLL WY
1600 LVMR 94551 696-E2
21500 AlaC 94546 691-J7
KNOLLBROOK DR
7700 PLE 94588 693-H7
KNOLL CREST CT
- SRMN 94582 673-J6
KNOLL RIDGE WY
- OAK 94619 651-C6
KNOLL VIEW DR
1200 MPS 95035 794-A4
KNOLLWOOD PL
7500 DBLN 94568 693-H2
KNOLLWOOD TER
3500 FRMT 94536 752-A6
KNOLL WOODS CT
- PLE 94566 714-C5
KNOTT AV
6200 ELCR 94530 609-B1
KNOTTINGHAM CIR
300 LVMR 94551 695-J6
KNOWLAND AV
3100 OAK 94619 650-F7
KNOWLSON TER
4900 FRMT 94555 752-A3
KNOX ST
1500 AlaC 94546 691-J7
1500 AlaC 94546 692-A7
KNOX GATE CT
4800 PLE 94588 694-D7
KNUPPE PL
21100 AlaC 94552 692-E4
KNUTE CT
38500 FRMT 94536 753-B3
KOBIO ST
- LVMR 94550 715-F5
KOFMAN CT
- ALA 94502 669-J5
KOFMAN PKWY
1600 ALA 94502 669-H5
KOFORD RD
9800 OAK 94603 670-G7
KOHNEN WY
- DBLN 94568 694-F3
KOHOUTEK CT
29300 UNC 94587 731-J4
KOHOUTEK WY
29300 UNC 94587 731-J3
KOI TER
- FRMT 94536 753-F3
KOKOMA RD
1400 FRMT 94539 773-G3
KOLB PL
7200 DBLN 94568 693-F4
KOLL CENTER DR
- PLE 94566 714-B4
KOLL CENTER PKWY
6900 PLE 94566 714-B3
KOLLMAN CIR
2000 ALA 94501 649-F7
KOLLN ST
700 PLE 94566 714-E1
KONA CIR
100 UNC 94587 732-C6
KONA CT
39500 FRMT 94538 753-A7
KOOTENAI CT
- FRMT 94539 773-J5
KOOTENAI DR
- FRMT 94539 773-J5
KORBEL CT
33000 UNC 94587 752-B1
KORBEL ST
4600 UNC 94587 752-B1
KOTTINGER DR
100 PLE 94566 714-E3
KOVANDA WY
1100 MPS 95035 794-A5
KRAFTILE CT
- FRMT 94536 732-H7
KRAFTILE RD
800 FRMT 94536 732-H7
KRAL PL
3900 PLE 94588 694-E7
KRAMER PL
- SF 94133 648-A4
KRAMER ST
800 SLN 94579 691-B7
KRAUSE AV
6800 OAK 94605 670-H2
KRAUSE CT
4200 PLE 94588 694-E7
KRAUSE ST
4300 PLE 94588 694-E7
KRAUSGRILL PL
- SF 94133 648-A4
KRISMER ST
300 MPS 95035 793-J7
KRISTIN WY
- SJCo 95391 (678-F3 See Page 677)
KROHN LN
- OAK 94611 630-E7
KROLOP RD
4000 AlaC 94546 691-H2
KRUGER AV
1200 FRMT 94536 753-B2
KUDU CT
1700 HAY 94541 712-B1
KUHNLE AV
4000 OAK 94605 650-H7
KUSS RD
100 CCCo 94526 652-G1
100 DNVL 94526 652-G1
KVISTAD DR
3700 FRMT 94538 753-D6
KYLE COM
- LVMR 94550 696-B7

L

L ST
300 FRMT 94536 753-B1
N L ST
- LVMR 94550 715-G1
100 LVMR 94551 695-G7
100 LVMR 94551 715-G1
S L ST
100 LVMR 94550 715-G1
LA BAREE DR
300 MPS 95035 794-E7
LABECCA CT
2700 PLE 94588 694-H4

STREET
Block City ZIP Pg-Grid

LA BELLA TER
- UNC 94587 732-G2
LA BOLSITA
- ORIN 94563 610-F7
LA BONITA TER
- UNC 94587 732-G2
LA BREA TER
- UNC 94587 732-G3
LABRO CT
- CCCo 94582 674-B2
LA CAMPANA
- ORIN 94563 610-H5
LA CAMPANIA
1100 ALA 94502 669-J6
3100 ALA 94502 670-A6
S LA CASA CT
23000 SJCo 95304 (678-H6 See Page 677)
LA CASA LN
- AlaC 94546 692-B4
LACEY AV
6900 OAK 94605 670-H1
LACEY DR
2100 MPS 95035 794-E7
LA CHESNAYE
- ORIN 94563 610-F2
LA CINTILLA
- ORIN 94563 610-G5
LACOCK PL
3300 FRMT 94555 732-E7
LACONIA WY
300 SRMN 94582 673-G3
LA COPITA CT
500 SRMN 94583 673-C2
LA CORONA ST
28800 HAY 94544 732-A2
LA COSA AV
4200 FRMT 94536 752-F3
LA COSTA AV
3600 AlaC 94546 691-J4
LA COSTE ST
6400 EMVL 94608 629-D5
LA COUNT LN
- SRMN 94583 673-E6
LA CRESTA
3100 ALA 94502 669-J6
3100 ALA 94502 670-A6
LA CRESTA AV
3900 OAK 94602 650-D4
LA CRESTA CT
1500 LVMR 94550 715-F3
LA CROSSE DR
- MPS 95035 794-D6
LA CUESTA
- ORIN 94563 610-G6
LA CUESTA AV
2600 OAK 94611 650-E2
LADD AV
2800 LVMR 94551 695-H7
LADERA CT
11500 DBLN 94568 693-F4
LADERA CTE
800 SRMN 94583 673-B3
LADERA DR
7500 DBLN 94568 693-F4
LADERA PZ
200 UNC 94587 732-J6
LADERO ST
40600 FRMT 94539 753-E5
LADNER ST
4300 FRMT 94538 753-C7
LADON CT
2500 AlaC 94546 691-H5
LA ENCINAL
- ORIN 94563 610-E7
LA ESPIRAL
- ORIN 94563 610-G5
LAFAYETTE AV
- HAY 94544 732-E3
- SLN 94577 671-A7
- SLN 94577 691-A1
100 PDMT 94611 650-C2
100 PDMT 94610 650-C2
200 SLN 94577 670-J7
5300 NWK 94560 752-D6
LAFAYETTE CT
7800 PLE 94588 693-H7
LAFAYETTE ST
800 ALA 94501 669-H2
LA FERRERA TER
- SF 94133 648-A3
LAGISS CT
- LVMR 94550 715-G5
LAGISS DR
- LVMR 94550 715-F6
LA GONDA CT
- DNVL 94526 652-J1
LA GONDA WY
400 DNVL 94526 652-J1
LAGOON CT
- SLN 94579 711-A1
- UNC 94587 731-H5
W LAGOON RD
- PLE 94588 714-B4
LAGORIA CT
- ALA 94502 669-J6
LAGOS CT
500 SRMN 94583 673-C3
LAGRANGE CT
2100 LVMR 94550 715-E4
LAGRANGE LN
500 LVMR 94550 715-E4
LAGUNA AV
3400 OAK 94602 650-E4
LAGUNA CT
400 LVMR 94550 715-E3
LAGUNA DR
300 MPS 95035 793-J5
1900 HAY 94545 711-E5
2100 AlaC 94545 711-E5
LAGUNA PL
9700 SRMN 94583 673-F7
40700 FRMT 94539 753-E5
LAGUNA ST
800 LVMR 94550 715-D3
LAGUNA WY
3300 OAK 94602 650-D5
LAGUNA CREEK LN
- PLE 94566 714-C5
- PLE 94588 714-B5
LAGUNA HILLS LN
- PLE 94588 714-B5
LAGUNARIA LN
100 ALA 94502 670-A6
LAGUNA VISTA
300 ALA 94501 670-A4
LAGUNITAS AV
400 OAK 94610 649-J3
LAGUNITAS LN
500 HAY 94544 711-G4
LA HABRA ST
4800 UNC 94587 752-A1

LAHANA WY
39600 FRMT 94538 753-A7
LA HONDA DR
200 MPS 95035 793-J5
LAIOLO RD
40100 FRMT 94538 753-B7
LAIRD AV
6000 OAK 94605 670-H1
LAIRD CT
18000 AlaC 94546 691-J2
LA JOLLA CT
40400 FRMT 94539 753-E4
LA JOLLA DR
2600 ALA 94501 670-A4
LAKE AV
- PDMT 94611 649-J1
- PDMT 94611 650-A1
LAKE BLVD
5300 NWK 94560 752-D3
LAKE CT
- LVMR 94551 696-E2
LAKE DR
- DBLN 94568 693-J2
- LVMR 94551 696-E1
- RCH 94805 609-G3
200 CCCo 94708 609-G3
N LAKE DR
- DBLN 94568 693-J1
S LAKE DR
- DBLN 94568 693-J2
LAKE PKWY
400 OAK 94610 649-J2
400 OAK 94610 650-A2
LAKE ARROWHEAD AV
3200 FRMT 94555 732-B6
LAKE ARROWHEAD CT
3200 FRMT 94555 732-C6
LAKE BARLEE LN
32400 FRMT 94555 732-B6
LAKE BERRYESSA DR
32400 FRMT 94555 732-C5
LAKE BLUE STONE ST
32900 FRMT 94555 732-C6
LAKE CABOT LN
2900 AlaC 94546 691-J4
LAKE CANDLEWOOD ST
32900 FRMT 94555 732-H4
LAKE CHABOT RD
1300 SLN 94577 671-C7
1400 SLN 94577 691-D1
2000 AlaC 94578 671-E7
2000 AlaC 94578 691-D1
7600 AlaC 94546 691-G2
LAKE CHABOT ST
32400 FRMT 94555 732-B6
LAKE CHAD CT
3400 FRMT 94555 732-B6
LAKE CHAD ST
3400 FRMT 94555 732-B6
LAKE CHAMPLAIN CT
33200 FRMT 94555 732-C6
LAKE CHAMPLAIN ST
33100 FRMT 94555 732-C6
LAKECREST CT
18400 AlaC 94546 691-H3
LAKE ERIE ST
32900 FRMT 94555 732-H4
LAKEFIELD PL
200 MRGA 94556 651-E3
LAKEFRONT CIR
38800 FRMT 94536 753-C3
LAKE GARRISON ST
33100 FRMT 94555 732-H4
LAKE HURON ST
32900 FRMT 94555 732-C6
LAKEHURST CIR
2000 ALA 94501 649-E6
LAKEHURST RD
1000 LVMR 94551 695-E7
LAKELAND DR
- LVMR 94551 696-E3
LAKE LANIER PL
33100 FRMT 94555 732-C6
LAKE LOUISE ST
32500 FRMT 94555 732-B6
LAKE MASK PL
32400 FRMT 94555 732-B6
LAKE MEAD CT
3200 FRMT 94555 732-C6
LAKE MEAD DR
3500 FRMT 94555 732-C6
LAKE MICHIGAN ST
32900 FRMT 94555 732-C6
LAKEMONT DR
700 SRMN 94582 673-F1
LAKEMONT PL
700 SRMN 94582 673-F1
22800 AlaC 94552 692-D6
LAKEMONT WY
700 SRMN 94582 673-F1
LAKE ONEIDA ST
33100 FRMT 94555 732-C7
LAKE ONTARIO DR
3400 FRMT 94555 732-C6
LAKE PARK AV
400 OAK 94610 649-J3
400 OAK 94610 650-A3
LAKE PILLSBURY DR
3100 FRMT 94555 732-B6
LAKE PYRAMID ST
33100 FRMT 94555 732-C7
LAKE REE ST
32400 FRMT 94555 732-B6
LAKERIDGE AV
23000 AlaC 94541 692-D7
LAKERIDGE RD
19200 AlaC 94546 691-J4
LAKESHORE AV
600 OAK 94610 650-A2
1300 OAK 94606 649-J4
1300 OAK 94607 649-J4
2200 OAK 94610 649-J4
E LAKESHORE DR
5000 SRMN 94582 673-F1
LAKESIDE CIR
- LVMR 94550 715-E5
LAKESIDE DR
- OAK 94607 649-H3
100 OAK 94612 649-H3
LAKE SUPERIOR CT
33200 FRMT 94555 732-C6
LAKE SUPERIOR PL
33100 FRMT 94555 732-C6
LAKE TAHOE TER
3900 FRMT 94555 732-C7
LAKE TANA ST
32500 FRMT 94555 732-B6
LAKE TEMESCAL LN
32300 FRMT 94555 732-B6
LAKEVIEW AV
- PDMT 94611 650-C1

LAKEVIEW BLVD
47000 FRMT 94538 773-F7
47400 FRMT 94538 793-G1
LAKEVIEW CIR
- SRMN 94582 673-F1
LAKEVIEW CT
- FRMT 94538 793-G2
1800 SLN 94577 691-D1
LAKEVIEW DR
2100 SLN 94577 691-D1
LAKE WAWASEE ST
32900 FRMT 94555 732-C6
LAKEWOOD CT
36600 NWK 94560 752-F5
LAKEWOOD DR
36500 NWK 94560 752-F5
LAKEWOOD ST
4500 PLE 94588 713-J1
LAKEWOOD WY
26800 HAY 94544 711-J6
LAKE WOODLAND COM
3800 FRMT 94555 732-B7
LA LOMA AV
1300 BERK 94708 609-J7
1600 BERK 94709 609-J7
1600 BERK 94709 629-J1
LAM CT
- CCCo 94707 609-F2
- CCCo 94530 609-F2
LA MADRONAL
- ORIN 94563 610-F7
LAMAR LP
3700 AlaC 94552 692-F2
LAMB CT
1000 PLE 94566 714-D3
LAMBAREN AV
800 LVMR 94551 715-F1
LAMBERT CT
2500 UNC 94587 732-F7
LAMBERT PL
2400 UNC 94587 732-F7
LAMBETH RD
900 LVMR 94551 695-G6
LAMBRECHT CT
8600 ELCR 94530 609-E1
LA MESA CT
4700 FRMT 94536 752-F4
LA MESA DR
3400 HAY 94542 712-F4
LAMONT CT
16900 AlaC 94546 691-J1
LAMONT WY
400 DNVL 94526 652-H2
LAMOUREUX ST
3700 SLN 94578 691-B4
LAMP CT
- MRGA 94556 651-G2
LAMP ST
3400 OAK 94605 671-A2
LAMPREY DR
31200 UNC 94587 731-J5
LAMSON RD
17800 AlaC 94546 692-A2
18000 AlaC 94546 691-J3
LANA TER
4000 FRMT 94536 752-H1
LANAI CIR
500 UNC 94587 732-C6
LANAI CT
27800 HAY 94544 731-J1
LANAI DR
3400 SRMN 94582 673-E1
LANCASTER CT
2400 HAY 94542 712-C2
3500 FRMT 94536 752-J3
6900 DBLN 94568 693-J3
LANCASTER RD
2400 HAY 94542 712-D2
6800 DBLN 94568 693-J3
LANCASTER ST
300 OAK 94601 670-B1
LANCE WY
- HAY 94544 712-C7
LANCELOT CT
3500 FRMT 94536 752-J3
27900 HAY 94544 712-A7
LANCERO CT
4400 FRMT 94536 752-E2
LANCERO ST
35100 FRMT 94536 752-E2
LANDALE AV
7500 DBLN 94568 693-G3
LANDER AV
25600 HAY 94544 712-A4
LANDER PL
200 SRMN 94583 673-G7
LANDES PL
36200 NWK 94560 752-D6
LANDING PKWY
46100 FRMT 94538 773-F6
LANDING RD
4000 FRMT 94538 773-E7
LANDMARK WY
- DBLN 94568 694-G3
LANDON AV
40200 FRMT 94538 773-B1
LANDSDOWNE ST
- DBLN 94568 694-F4
LANDSDOWNE WY
- SRMN 94582 674-B4
LANDVALE RD Rt#-13
300 OAK 94618 630-B4
LANE CT
- OAK 94611 630-C7
LANG AV
34600 FRMT 94555 752-E1
LANGDON COM
- FRMT 94538 753-B5
LANGDON CT
- PDMT 94611 650-B1
LANGHORN CT
34100 FRMT 94555 732-E7
LANGHORN DR
2800 FRMT 94555 732-E7
LANGHORNE DR
- SRMN 94582 674-B4
LANGLEY ST
- OAK 94621 670-D6
LANGLEY WY
200 HAY 94544 711-J4
LANGMUIR CT
7500 DBLN 94568 693-J2
LANGMUIR LN
6800 DBLN 94568 693-J2
LANGON PL
19300 AlaC 94546 691-H4
LANGTON CT
- SRMN 94582 674-B3
LANGTON DR
- SRMN 94582 674-B3
LANGTON ST
- SF 94103 648-A7

LANGTON WY
17200 AlaC 94541 691-G6
LANGTRY CT
38900 FRMT 94536 753-D2
LANIER AV
1600 SLN 94579 691-A7
LA NORIA
- ORIN 94563 610-G6
LANSDOWN CT
3100 PLE 94588 694-F6
LANSFORD CT
- SRMN 94582 673-F2
LANSING CT
6500 PLE 94566 714-D6
38100 FRMT 94536 752-J4
LANSING ST
- SF 94105 648-B6
LANSING WY
200 AlaC 94541 711-F2
LANTANA AV
4700 LVMR 94551 696-A4
LANTANA COM
- FRMT 94536 752-G5
LANTANA CT
22100 AlaC 94546 692-B6
LANTANA WY
- SRMN 94582 673-H1
LANYARD TER
37100 FRMT 94536 752-H2
LA PALMA PL
800 MPS 95035 794-B5
LA PAZ AV
10000 SRMN 94583 673-G5
LA PAZ CT
300 SRMN 94583 673-B2
W LA PAZ DR
15700 SJCo 95304 (678-J6 See Page 677)
LA PAZ WY
400 HAY 94541 711-G3
LAPIS LN
4900 PLE 94566 714-E5
LA PLAYA DR
700 HAY 94545 711-G4
LA PLAYA PL
24700 HAY 94545 711-G5
LA PLAZA
- ORIN 94563 610-G7
LA PORTE AV
27400 HAY 94545 711-H7
27700 HAY 94545 731-J1
LA PRADA CT
1500 LVMR 94550 715-F3
LA PRENDA DR
200 OAK 94603 670-H7
LAPU LAPU ST
- SF 94107 648-B6
LA PUNTA
- ORIN 94563 610-H5
LA PURISSIMA PL
1100 FRMT 94539 753-E4
LA PURISSIMA WY
40500 FRMT 94539 753-E5
LA QUINTA CT
7800 PLE 94588 714-B5
LARAMIE AV
2800 SRMN 94583 673-F7
LARAMIE CT
5300 FRMT 94536 752-G6
LARAMIE GATE CIR
2600 PLE 94566 694-D7
LARAMIE GATE CT
4600 PLE 94566 694-D7
LARCH AV
1000 MRGA 94556 651-E1
LARCH LN
- MRGA 94556 651-E1
LARCH ST
500 MPS 95035 793-H6
LARCH WY
36000 FRMT 94536 732-J7
LARCHMONT ISL
500 ALA 94501 669-G2
LARCHMONT ST
300 HAY 94544 711-G4
LAREDO CT
100 SRMN 94583 673-C2
LAREDO DR
36300 FRMT 94536 752-G3
LAREDO RD
18500 AlaC 94546 691-G3
LARIAT CT
2600 LVMR 94551 696-C1
LARIAT LN
6800 AlaC 94552 692-F2
LA RIBERA ST
5600 LVMR 94551 696-C6
LARIMER WY
4800 AlaC 94546 692-C4
LARK CT
4100 FRMT 94555 732-B7
LARK ST
13800 SLN 94578 691-D3
15000 AlaC 94578 691-D3
LARK WY
33100 FRMT 94555 732-B7
LARKDALE AV
7200 DBLN 94568 693-H3
LARKSPUR CT
- UNC 94587 732-H5
LARKSPUR DR
900 LVMR 94551 696-A4
LARKSPUR PZ
- HAY 94542 712-B3
LARKSPUR RD
900 OAK 94610 650-B3
LARKSPUR ST
38600 NWK 94560 772-G1
LARKSPUR FERRY
- SF - 648-C1
LARKWOOD CT
1500 MPS 95035 793-J4
LARMER CT
300 PDMT 94610 650-B1
LARRABEE ST
29800 HAY 94544 712-D7
LARRIKEET CT
2500 PLE 94566 714-C1
LARRY LN
- OAK 94611 650-F2
LARRYS PL
- LVMR 94550 715-G4
LA SALLE AV
- PDMT 94611 650-D1
- PDMT 94610 650-C2
4500 FRMT 94536 752-F3
5600 OAK 94611 650-D1
LA SALLE CT
- PDMT 94611 650-D2
LASALLE DR
36100 NWK 94560 752-D6

LAS AROMAS
- ORIN 94563 610-H6
2600 OAK 94611 650-F2
LAS BARRANCAS DR
600 DNVL 94526 652-H1
LAS CASCADAS
- ORIN 94563 610-H6
LAS COLINAS RD
3600 AlaC 94551 695-J5
LA SENDA
- ORIN 94563 610-G5
LAS FELIZ CT
4200 UNC 94587 732-A5
LAS FLORES CT
- OAK 94611 630-F7
LAS FLORES RD
700 LVMR 94551 696-B4
LA SIERRA TER
- UNC 94587 732-G2
LAS LOMAS DR
700 MPS 95035 794-B6
LAS LOMITAS DR
4500 PLE 94566 714-E4
LAS MESAS PTH
- ORIN 94563 610-F7
LAS PADRES TER
- UNC 94587 732-G2
LAS PALMAS AV
40400 FRMT 94539 753-E4
E LAS PALMAS AV
- FRMT 94539 753-E3
LAS PALMAS CT
100 FRMT 94539 753-F4
11200 DBLN 94568 693-F5
E LAS PALMAS CT
39900 FRMT 94539 753-E3
LAS PALMAS WY
4200 UNC 94587 731-J5
7300 DBLN 94568 693-F5
LAS PALOMAS
- ORIN 94563 610-H5
LAS PIEDRAS
- ORIN 94563 610-E7
W LAS POSITAS BLVD
3100 PLE 94588 694-E6
4300 PLE 94566 694-E6
6300 PLE 94588 714-A1
6900 PLE 94588 713-J1
LAS POSITAS CT
2100 LVMR 94551 695-F6
LAS POSITAS RD
2700 LVMR 94551 695-G5
2700 AlaC 94551 695-G5
2800 AlaC 94551 696-A5
2800 LVMR 94551 696-E4
LASSEN RD
900 LVMR 94551 696-A5
LASSEN ST
1000 BERK 94707 609-G6
5700 ELCR 94530 609-C5
6900 PLE 94588 714-A1
29100 HAY 94544 712-C7
29300 HAY 94544 732-C1
37000 FRMT 94536 752-G4
LASSO CIR
200 SRMN 94583 673-B3
LASUEN DR
800 SLN 94578 691-C5
LAS VEGAS AV
9600 OAK 94605 671-A4
LAS VEGAS CT
- ORIN 94563 610-J5
LAS VEGAS RD
- ORIN 94563 610-J5
LATERA CT
- SRMN 94582 674-B3
LATHAM LN
- BERK 94708 609-J6
LATHAM ST
100 PDMT 94611 650-A1
LATIMER PL
3700 OAK 94609 649-H1
LATOUR AV
- LVMR 94550 715-H4
LAUDERDALE AV
26600 HAY 94545 711-G6
LAUGHLIN RD
700 AlaC 94551 676-E7
700 LVMR 94551 696-E3
700 AlaC 94551 696-E3
LAURA AV
2000 SLN 94577 690-H2
LAURA LN
6200 AlaC 94566 714-E7
LAURA ST
- FRMT 94555 732-C7
LAURA WY
4500 UNC 94587 732-A7
LAUREL AV
100 AlaC 94541 711-G2
300 HAY 94541 711-G2
3200 OAK 94602 650-E5
LAUREL CT
7400 PLE 94588 713-J2
7400 PLE 94588 714-A1
LAUREL DR
700 LVMR 94551 695-E7
LAUREL LN
- BERK 94707 609-F5
LAUREL ST
800 ALA 94501 669-J3
1100 BERK 94708 609-H6
4200 FRMT 94538 753-D7
36800 NWK 94560 752-C7
37000 NWK 94560 772-C1
LAUREL CANYON CT
2000 FRMT 94539 773-G2
LAUREL CANYON TR
- CCCo 94708 609-H3
LAUREL CANYON WY
44000 FRMT 94539 773-G2
LAUREL CREEK DR
5800 PLE 94588 693-G6
LAUREL CREEK PL
- LVMR 94551 696-D3
LAUREL CREEK WY
7600 PLE 94588 693-H6
LAUREL GLEN COM
43400 FRMT 94539 753-H7
43500 FRMT 94539 773-H1
LAUREL GLEN TER
500 FRMT 94539 753-H7
LAURELVIEW CT
- FRMT 94538 793-F1
LAURELWOOD CT
600 LVMR 94551 695-J6
LAURELWOOD DR
19800 AlaC 94552 692-F2
LAUREN PL
23500 AlaC 94541 692-D7
LAURETTE PL
600 HAY 94544 712-B5

LAURIE COM
4600 LVMR 94550 696-A6
LAURISTON CT
8000 OAK 94611 630-E5
LAURSEN CT
2700 PLE 94588 694-H4
LAURUS CT
- FRMT 94536 753-A2
LAVAGETTO CT
- ALA 94502 669-J7
LAVENDER COM
37900 FRMT 94536 752-J3
LAVENDER PL
38600 NWK 94560 752-H7
LAVERDA PTH
3500 OAK 94605 670-J2
LA VEREDA
1500 BERK 94708 609-J7
1600 BERK 94709 609-J7
1600 BERK 94709 629-J1
LA VERNE AV
5500 OAK 94605 670-F1
LAVERNE CT
15200 SLN 94579 691-A6
LAVERNE DR
15200 SLN 94579 691-A6
LA VITA TER
- UNC 94587 732-G3
LA VUELTA
- ORIN 94563 610-H5
LAWLER AV
5000 FRMT 94536 752-G6
LAWLOR ST
8900 OAK 94605 671-A4
LAWNDALE AV
1700 SLN 94579 691-A7
LAWRENCE CT
7300 ELCR 94530 609-D2
LAWRENCE DR
300 LVMR 94551 696-E3
4200 AlaC 94546 691-J3
4300 AlaC 94546 692-A3
LAWRENCE PL
42600 FRMT 94538 773-B3
LAWRENCE RD
- ALA 94502 669-H6
1500 DNVL 94506 674-B1
LAWRENCE ST
1200 ELCR 94530 609-D1
LAWSON CIR
- AlaC 94550 716-C2
- LVMR 94550 716-C2
LAWSON CT
- LVMR 94550 716-C2
LAWSON RD
- CCCo 94707 609-F2
LAWTON AV
4700 OAK 94609 629-J6
5100 OAK 94618 629-J5
5500 OAK 94618 630-A5
LAWTON CT
- SRMN 94583 673-E5
LAWTON DR
- MPS 95035 794-D6
LAWTON PL
400 HAY 94544 711-H4
LAWTON WY
12900 SRMN 94583 673-E5
LEA CT
1600 ALA 94501 670-A2
LEACH ST
4300 OAK 94602 650-C3
LEAFCREST COM
2100 LVMR 94551 696-D1
LEAH LN
- SJCo 95391 (678-F3 See Page 677)
LEAHY WY
3200 LVMR 94550 715-J1
LEAL WY
- FRMT 94539 753-G5
LEAMONT CT
- OAK 94605 671-C5
LEARY CT
- SRMN 94582 674-A1
LEAVITT CT
4000 AlaC 94546 692-A5
LEBANON ST
500 HAY 94541 711-G3
LE BEAU CT
4700 FRMT 94555 752-C1
LE BLANC CT
- LVMR 94550 715-H3
LECCINO CT
- LVMR 94550 715-H5
LE CONTE AV
2300 BERK 94709 629-H1
LECOUNT WY
38700 FRMT 94536 752-J5
LEDGEFERN CT
- SRMN 94582 673-H2
LEDGEFERN WY
- SRMN 94582 673-H2
LEDGESTONE CT
- PLE 94588 714-F1
LEDGEWOOD TER
- DBLN 94568 694-F2
LEE AV
100 LVMR 94551 695-H7
600 SLN 94577 671-B7
LEE ST
200 OAK 94610 649-H2
40900 FRMT 94538 753-D7
LEE ANN CIR
4500 LVMR 94550 696-B7
LEEDS CT
2500 LVMR 94551 695-G6
LEET DR
- OAK 94621 670-E6
LEEWARD LN
1100 ALA 94502 670-A7
LEEWARD ST
2600 HAY 94545 711-F7
LEEWARD WY
3000 OAK 94605 671-B5
E LEGACY DR
- SJCo 95391 (678-E3 See Page 677)
LEGENDARY CT
- PLE 94588 693-H7
LEGER CT
3000 PLE 94588 694-F6
LEGION AV
2300 OAK 94605 670-H3
LE GRAND AV
- CCCo 94514 637-D3
LE HAVRE CT
1300 LVMR 94551 695-F6
LEIDESDORFF ST
- SF 94104 648-B5
200 SF 94111 648-B5

LEIDIG CT
27800 HAY 94544 712-B6
LEIGH CT
- SRMN 94582 673-E2
LEIGH ST
47900 FRMT 94539 773-J7
47900 FRMT 94539 793-J1
LEIGHTON ST
600 HAY 94544 711-J3
3700 OAK 94611 649-J1
LEIGHTY CT
- AlaC 94541 711-F1
LEILA ST
1900 AlaC 94546 692-A7
LEIMERT BLVD
1300 OAK 94602 650-D3
LEIMERT PL
1700 OAK 94602 650-D3
LEISURE ST
400 LVMR 94551 696-D4
LELAND CT
800 LVMR 94550 715-E3
LELAND WY
700 LVMR 94550 715-E3
LE MANS CT
1300 LVMR 94551 695-F6
LEMARC ST
300 FRMT 94539 753-H7
LEMAS PL
19100 AlaC 94546 692-A4
LEMAY WY
27000 HAY 94544 711-J7
LEMKE PL
5500 FRMT 94538 773-A1
LEMONTREE CT
27400 HAY 94545 711-G7
27400 HAY 94545 731-G1
LEMONWOOD ST
42500 FRMT 94538 773-D2
LEMONWOOD WY
7300 PLE 94588 714-A2
LEMOORE RD
100 ALA 94501 649-D6
LEMOS LN
400 FRMT 94539 753-E5
LENARD DR
3200 AlaC 94546 691-J4
LENARD PL
3100 AlaC 94546 691-J4
LENELLE CT
3800 FRMT 94538 773-D1
LENEVE PL
900 ELCR 94530 609-F1
LENNOX CT
- LVMR 94550 715-F4
34200 FRMT 94555 752-D1
LENNOX LN
1300 LVMR 94550 715-F4
LENORE AV
5100 LVMR 94550 696-C6
LENOSO COM
4300 FRMT 94536 752-G3
LENOX AV
200 OAK 94610 649-H3
LENOX RD
- CCCo 94707 609-F4
LENROSS CT
18800 AlaC 94546 692-A3
LENTIN WY
- CCCo 94582 674-B2
LEO AV
200 SLN 94577 670-J7
200 SLN 94577 671-A7
LEO WY
800 OAK 94611 630-C6
LEON CT
4800 FRMT 94536 752-F4
LEONA DR
400 LVMR 94550 715-D2
24500 HAY 94542 712-A2
LEONA ST
5500 OAK 94605 650-H7
5500 OAK 94619 650-H6
LEONARD CT
- ALA 94502 669-J6
LEONARD DR
1300 SLN 94577 690-H2
LEONARDO WY
900 HAY 94541 711-F4
LEONATO WY
4500 FRMT 94555 752-D2
LEONE ST
36500 NWK 94560 752-E6
LEONTINE CT
48000 FRMT 94539 773-J7
48000 FRMT 94539 793-J1
LE POMAR TER
200 FRMT 94536 733-A6
LERIDA CT
- LVMR 94550 715-G5
LE ROY AV
1600 BERK 94709 609-H7
1600 BERK 94709 629-H1
1700 BERK 94708 609-H7
LEROY DR
20000 AlaC 94546 691-J5
LERWICK ST
42600 FRMT 94539 753-G7
LESLIE COM
300 LVMR 94550 696-A6
3400 FRMT 94538 753-C5
LESLIE ST
39600 FRMT 94538 753-B5
LESSER ST
400 OAK 94601 670-C2
LESSINI ST
3500 PLE 94566 715-B7
LESSLEY AV
2100 AlaC 94546 691-J6
2100 AlaC 94546 692-A6
LESTER AV
200 OAK 94606 649-J4
800 HAY 94541 711-F3
LETHBRIDGE CT
2900 PLE 94588 694-F6
LETHRAM CT
4100 PLE 94588 694-E7
LEVANT CT
- SRMN 94582 673-G3
LEVI ST
39000 NWK 94560 772-H1
LEVIN ST
300 MPS 95035 794-A3
LEVINE CT
1000 HAY 94541 711-J1
LEVINE RD
- AlaC 94542 712-D1
LEVISTON AV
7500 ELCR 94530 609-E3
LEWELLING BLVD
400 AlaC 94580 691-B7
500 SLN 94579 691-B7

STREET
Block City ZIP Pg-Grid

E LEWELLING BLVD
100 AlaC 94580 691-E6
400 AlaC 94541 691-E6
LEWELLING CT
1000 ALA 94501 670-A3
LEWES CT
- SRMN 94582 673-G4
LEWIS AV
400 SLN 94577 671-B7
7200 DBLN 94568 693-H4
33200 UNC 94587 732-F5
LEWIS DR
25600 HAY 94544 712-A4
LEWIS ST
300 OAK 94607 649-D4
33100 UNC 94587 732-E4
LEWISTON AV
3100 BERK 94705 629-J4
LEXFORD PL
- OAK 94619 651-B7
LEXFORD RD
- PDMT 94611 650-D2
LEXINGTON AV
100 SLN 94577 670-J7
200 HAY 94544 732-F3
400 ELCR 94530 609-B1
LEXINGTON PL
900 SRMN 94583 673-G6
2400 LVMR 94550 715-F5
LEXINGTON RD
200 CCCo 94707 609-F4
LEXINGTON ST
- ALA 94501 649-C6
700 MPS 95035 793-J6
38600 FRMT 94536 753-A4
LEXINGTON WY
900 LVMR 94550 715-E5
LEYTON DR
- SRMN 94582 674-B3
LIBBY CT
3500 OAK 94619 650-F5
LIBERTY AV
3200 ALA 94501 670-B3
LIBERTY COM
3400 FRMT 94538 753-B5
LIBERTY CT
- ELCR 94530 609-C3
- SJS 95002 793-B7
LIBERTY DR
2900 PLE 94566 714-H3
LIBERTY ST
400 ELCR 94530 609-B1
1600 SJS 95002 793-B7
1800 AlaC 94578 691-F4
39200 FRMT 94538 753-B4
LIBERTY WY
- SLN 94579 690-J6
- SLN 94579 691-A6
LIBRA CT
4800 LVMR 94551 696-B3
LIBRARY ST
- FRMT 94539 753-J7
LICHEN CT
100 FRMT 94538 773-B2
LICK PL
- SF 94108 648-A5
- SF 94104 648-A5
LIDO BLVD
35000 NWK 94560 752-C5
LIDO CT
1400 LVMR 94550 715-E3
6200 NWK 94560 752-D5
LIDO DR
600 LVMR 94550 715-E3
LIDO PARK CT
42800 FRMT 94538 773-C2
LIESE AV
3100 OAK 94619 650-E6
LIGGETT DR
6500 OAK 94611 650-D1
LIGHTHOUSE WY
- UNC 94545 731-J7
LIGHTLAND CT
1900 PLE 94566 714-C4
LIKIT WY
600 SLN 94577 690-G2
LILAC AV
1900 HAY 94545 731-J1
5200 LVMR 94551 696-B3
LILAC CT
34800 UNC 94587 732-G7
LILAC LP
35000 UNC 94587 732-G7
LILAC ST
900 ALA 94502 670-B7
2500 OAK 94601 650-E7
2600 OAK 94619 650-E7
34700 UNC 94587 732-F7
LILAC RIDGE RD
- SRMN 94582 673-F1
LILIENTHAL RD
- AlaC 94566 715-B3
- AlaC 94550 715-B3
- AlaC 94551 715-B3
LILLA RD
23200 HAY 94541 711-F3
LILLE ST
300 SLN 94577 690-J1
300 SLN 94577 691-A1
LILLIAN AV
1200 SLN 94578 691-C4
LILLIAN CT
5100 LVMR 94550 716-B1
LILLIAN ST
1200 LVMR 94550 716-B1
LILLY AV
700 HAY 94544 711-J2
700 HAY 94544 712-A2
LILY ST
3600 OAK 94619 650-F6
31200 UNC 94587 731-J5
LIMA TER
- FRMT 94539 753-G5
LIMEHOUSE LN
2400 SLN 94577 691-A3
LIMERICK CT
7300 DBLN 94568 693-H2
LIMERICK LN
600 ALA 94502 669-J5
LIMERICK WY
7300 DBLN 94568 693-H2
LIMESTONE COM
- LVMR 94550 715-C1
LIMESTONE CT
- UNC 94587 732-G6
LIMESTONE DR
- UNC 94587 732-G6
LIMETA TER
36800 FRMT 94536 752-G4
LIMETREE PL
- HAY 94544 712-C5

LIMEWOOD CT
7900 PLE 94588 713-J1
LIMON ST
2100 PLE 94566 714-G3
LINARIA CIR
40200 FRMT 94538 773-B1
LINCOLN AV
- PDMT 94611 650-C1
300 LVMR 94550 696-A7
300 LVMR 94550 716-A1
400 ALA 94501 669-E1
2100 ALA 94501 670-A2
2300 HAY 94545 711-C4
2400 OAK 94602 650-E4
6400 ELCR 94530 609-D4
LINCOLN CT
3700 FRMT 94538 753-D6
LINCOLN LN
1500 ALA 94501 669-J1
LINCOLN ST
1300 BERK 94702 629-E1
1500 BERK 94703 629-F1
2000 BERK 94709 629-G1
40800 FRMT 94538 753-D6
LINCOLN WY
4900 OAK 94602 650-F3
LINCOLNSHIRE DR
- OAK 94618 630-A6
LINDA AV
- OAK 94611 649-J1
100 PDMT 94611 649-J1
100 PDMT 94611 650-A1
400 PDMT 94610 650-A1
LINDA CT
- DNVL 94526 652-J2
LINDA DR
35500 FRMT 94536 732-J7
LINDA WY
4400 PLE 94566 714-F4
LINDA MESA AV
- DNVL 94526 652-J2
LINDA VISTA
- ORIN 94563 610-G6
3000 ALA 94502 669-J6
LINDA VISTA CT
900 SRMN 94582 674-A6
LINDA VISTA DR
1300 ELCR 94530 609-E1
LINDA VISTA RD
44100 FRMT 94539 773-J2
LINDA VISTA TER
200 FRMT 94539 773-J1
LINDBERGH AV
200 LVMR 94551 695-B5
LINDELL LN
500 SRMN 94582 673-J6
LINDEMANN RD
- CCCo 94514 (658-C3 See Page 637)
6000 AlaC 94551 (658-C4 See Page 637)
LINDEN AV
2900 BERK 94705 629-J4
LINDEN CT
7600 NWK 94560 752-D7
LINDEN LN
1900 MPS 95035 793-J3
LINDEN ST
- DBLN 94568 694-D3
100 OAK 94607 649-E3
1500 ALA 94501 669-F1
1600 LVMR 94551 695-G7
2800 OAK 94608 649-F1
3700 OAK 94608 629-F7
22400 HAY 94541 692-A7
LINDEN WY
300 AlaC 94566 714-G3
LINDENWOOD ST
43100 FRMT 94538 773-D2
LINDENWOOD WY
25100 HAY 94545 711-H5
LINDERO TER
200 FRMT 94536 753-E1
LINDHURST LN
600 HAY 94544 711-H5
LINDSAY LN
3900 AlaC 94546 691-H2
LINDSAY MCDERMOTT LN
39900 FRMT 94538 753-B6
LINDVIEW CT
16200 AlaC 94578 691-F4
LINFIELD LN
1200 HAY 94545 711-H6
LINFORD PL
500 SRMN 94583 673-F6
LINFORD TER
6100 FRMT 94555 752-B4
LIN GATE CT
2600 PLE 94566 694-D7
LIN GATE ST
4500 PLE 94566 694-D7
LINK CT
3800 AlaC 94546 691-J3
LINK ST
2100 OAK 94603 671-A6
LINMORE DR
100 FRMT 94539 753-H6
LINNEA AV
700 AlaC 94580 691-E5
LINNELL AV
400 SLN 94578 691-C5
LINNET AV
4200 OAK 94602 650-E4
LINSAY CT
42000 FRMT 94538 773-E1
LINTON ST
1200 SLN 94577 690-J3
LINWOOD AV
3700 OAK 94602 650-C4
LINWOOD COM
- LVMR 94550 716-D1
LINWOOD CT
7300 PLE 94588 714-A1
LINWOOD WY
1900 SLN 94577 691-C1
LION ST
300 HAY 94541 711-H2
LIPPERT AV
100 FRMT 94539 773-H7
LIPTON PL
100 SRMN 94583 673-F7
LIQUID SUGAR DR
- EMVL 94608 629-E4
LIRA CT
800 SRMN 94583 673-F5
LISA CT
7700 DBLN 94568 693-H3
LISA DR
4300 UNC 94587 732-A6
LISA LN
- MRGA 94556 651-F2

LISBON AV
800 OAK 94601 670-B1
900 LVMR 94550 715-F2
900 OAK 94601 650-B7
LISBON TER
- UNC 94587 732-G3
400 MPS 95035 793-G3
LISTON WY
2400 UNC 94587 732-C4
LITCHFIELD AV
1200 FRMT 94536 753-C3
LITTLE CT
3400 FRMT 94538 753-C5
LITTLE CREEK CT
- SRMN 94583 673-B1
LITTLE FOOT DR
100 FRMT 94539 773-H4
LITTLE FOOT PL
45300 FRMT 94539 773-H4
LITTLE VALLEY RD
6500 AlaC 94586 734-G4
LITTLEWOOD DR
- PDMT 94611 650-C1
LIVE OAK CIR
42100 FRMT 94538 773-C1
LIVE OAK CT
5100 PLE 94588 693-J7
LIVE OAK LN
- ORIN 94563 630-H2
LIVE OAK RD
- OAK 94705 630-B3
LIVE OAK TER
- AlaC 94541 712-C1
N LIVERMORE AV
100 LVMR 94551 695-G3
400 AlaC 94551 675-G6
1700 AlaC 94551 695-G3
N LIVERMORE AV Rt#-J2
100 LVMR 94550 695-G7
100 LVMR 94550 715-G1
100 LVMR 94551 695-G7
S LIVERMORE AV Rt#-J2
- LVMR 94550 715-J2
1400 LVMR 94550 716-A3
1700 AlaC 94550 716-A3
LIVERMORE COM
43200 FRMT 94539 753-H7
LIVINGSTON PL
1000 PLE 94566 714-F5
LIVINGSTON ST
2000 OAK 94606 650-A7
LIVINGSTON WY
600 PLE 94566 714-F5
LIVORNA TER
34300 FRMT 94555 752-B4
LIVORNO CT
- LVMR 94550 715-F5
LIVORNO ST
- LVMR 94550 715-F5
LLOYD AV
100 FRMT 94536 753-D3
400 SLN 94578 691-C5
LLOYD CT
300 LVMR 94550 715-E2
LLOYD LN
- ORIN 94563 630-H2
LLOYD ST
100 LVMR 94550 715-E2
LOA DR
500 FRMT 94536 753-D1
LOBELIA CT
- LVMR 94551 696-C3
37800 NWK 94560 752-F7
LOBELIA DR
37800 NWK 94560 752-F7
LOBELIA WY
5700 LVMR 94551 696-C3
LOBERT ST
2200 AlaC 94546 691-J6
2200 AlaC 94546 692-A6
LOCARNO PTH
100 OAK 94618 630-B5
LOCH LN
4200 SLN 94578 691-D5
LOCHARD ST
10700 OAK 94605 671-D4
LOCHGREEN WY
- DBLN 94568 694-G2
LOCH LOMOND CT
- DNVL 94526 652-J3
400 MPS 95035 794-A6
LOCH LOMOND WY
100 DNVL 94526 652-J3
3900 LVMR 94551 695-J6
3900 LVMR 94551 696-A6
LOCKE AV
34300 FRMT 94555 732-F7
LOCKE CT
- PLE 94566 714-G5
2900 FRMT 94555 732-F7
LOCKHART LN
4600 PLE 94566 714-E1
LOCKHART ST
- DBLN 94568 694-G3
LOCKRIDGE WY
4600 AlaC 94546 692-A3
LOCKSLEY AV
5200 OAK 94618 629-J6
LOCKWOOD AV
1900 FRMT 94539 753-F6
LOCKWOOD CT
41900 FRMT 94539 753-F6
LOCKWOOD ST
6900 OAK 94621 670-G2
LOCUST CT
7000 DBLN 94568 693-H2
LOCUST PL
8100 DBLN 94568 693-H1
LOCUST ST
1000 LVMR 94551 695-F7
7800 OAK 94621 670-G3
14300 SLN 94579 690-J4
14300 SLN 94579 691-A4
20800 AlaC 94541 691-H7
21200 HAY 94541 691-H7
36700 NWK 94560 752-D7
37100 NWK 94560 772-D1
LODESTONE RD
1600 LVMR 94550 715-D3
LODGE CT
- OAK 94611 630-F6
LODI WY
4800 AlaC 94546 692-A3
LODOVICO CT
4500 FRMT 94555 752-C1
LOGAN CT
4500 FRMT 94536 752-H5
LOGAN DR
37600 FRMT 94536 752-H4
38900 FRMT 94538 752-H4

LOGAN DR
38900 FRMT 94538 753-A6
LOGAN ST
800 LVMR 94551 695-D7
2600 OAK 94601 650-C6
LOGAN WY
28800 HAY 94544 712-B7
28800 HAY 94544 732-B1
LOGANBERRY WY
1500 PLE 94566 714-D2
LOIS WY
32400 UNC 94587 732-A7
LOLA ST
- SLN 94577 690-J1
LOMA DR
- FRMT 94539 753-H6
LOMAS CANTADAS
- ORIN 94563 610-D7
100 CCCo 94708 610-D7
100 CCCo 94563 610-D7
LOMA VERDE
100 AlaC 94541 691-E6
100 AlaC 94580 691-E6
LOMA VISTA AV
3400 OAK 94619 650-F5
LOMA VISTA DR
- ORIN 94563 610-F7
LOMA VISTA WY
3300 OAK 94619 650-E6
LOMBARD AV
4100 FRMT 94536 752-H4
LOMBARD ST
- SF 94111 648-A3
- SF 94133 648-A3
LOMBARDY LN
- ORIN 94563 610-G4
LOMER WY
400 MPS 95035 794-D7
LOMITA DR
1900 AlaC 94578 691-G5
LOMITAS AV
1000 LVMR 94550 715-F4
LOMITAS CT
2000 LVMR 94550 715-F4
LOMOND CIR
600 SRMN 94583 673-E4
LOMOND CT
- SRMN 94583 673-F4
LOMOND WY
18400 AlaC 94552 692-D2
LONDON AV
1700 SLN 94579 691-A7
LONDON COM
- FRMT 94536 752-J4
- FRMT 94536 753-A4
LONDON CT
32400 UNC 94587 732-C5
LONDON DR
600 MPS 95035 794-B3
LONDON RD
2800 OAK 94602 650-F4
LONDON WY
1600 LVMR 94550 715-F3
LONDONDERRY DR
- DBLN 94568 694-E3
LONE OAK CT
300 PLE 94566 714-D5
LONE OAK DR
300 PLE 94566 714-D5
LONE OAK PL
4900 AlaC 94546 692-B3
LONE PINE CT
- SRMN 94582 673-E2
LONESOME RD
- DNVL 94526 652-J3
LONE TREE CT
- SRMN 94583 673-E6
LONE TREE PL
29100 HAY 94544 732-B1
LONG CT
- HAY 94545 711-F5
LONG ST
37500 NWK 94560 752-F7
LONGARD RD
- LVMR 94551 696-E3
LONGCROFT DR
6300 OAK 94611 650-F1
LONGFELLOW AV
9900 OAK 94603 671-A5
LONGFELLOW CT
- LVMR 94551 696-F5
LONGFELLOW DR
600 FRMT 94539 773-H2
LONGFORD WY
8400 DBLN 94568 693-H2
LONGHORN CT
- SRMN 94583 673-D4
LONGHORN DR
- SRMN 94583 673-D5
LONGLEAF CIR
- CCCo 94582 674-D4
- SRMN 94582 674-D4
LONGMEADOW PL
- DBLN 94568 694-F3
LONGMONT LP
3700 AlaC 94552 692-G2
LONGRIDGE
- ORIN 94563 630-H1
LONGRIDGE RD
600 OAK 94610 650-A3
LONGSPUR WY
2800 PLE 94566 714-C1
LONGVIEW DR
1800 SLN 94577 691-D1
9000 PLE 94588 714-A5
LONGVIEW LN
9300 PLE 94588 714-A5
9900 PLE 94588 713-J5
LONGVIEW PL
25600 AlaC 94541 712-D2
LONGVIEW TER
4500 FRMT 94538 773-C1
LONGVIEW TR
- PLE 94586 714-A6
- PLE 94588 714-A6
LONGWALK DR
6500 OAK 94611 650-G1
LONGWOOD AV
500 HAY 94541 711-F3
LONGWOOD CT
- SRMN 94582 673-E2
500 HAY 94541 711-G3
LONGWORTH
700 ORIN 94563 610-J4
LONSDALE AV
600 FRMT 94539 773-H6
LONSDALE CT
46800 FRMT 94539 773-H6
LOOP DR
- CCCo 94708 609-H3
LOOP 22
- EMVL 94608 629-E6

LOPES CT
3200 AlaC 94541 692-D6
44900 FRMT 94538 773-F4
LOPEZ DR
1800 SLN 94578 691-C2
LOQUAT LN
2200 SLN 94577 691-B2
LORAN CT
- CCCo 94707 609-F4
LORAND WY
22700 HAY 94541 692-B7
LORCA CT
- SRMN 94583 673-D3
LOREAL TER
34600 FRMT 94555 752-A3
LORENA AV
3500 AlaC 94546 692-A4
LORENA CIR
19900 AlaC 94546 692-A4
LORENA PL
20000 AlaC 94546 692-A5
LORENZO AV
3200 OAK 94619 650-E6
15500 AlaC 94580 691-C7
LORENZO TER
4000 FRMT 94536 752-F2
LORETO DR
3300 SRMN 94583 673-G5
LORETTA WY
4700 UNC 94587 731-J7
LORI WY
23200 AlaC 94541 692-D7
LORIMER LP
- DBLN 94568 694-E3
LORINA ST
2900 BERK 94705 629-H3
LORING AV
- DBLN 94568 694-C3
LORITA AV
- PDMT 94611 630-A7
- PDMT 94611 650-A1
LORO PL
40300 FRMT 94539 753-F3
LORRAINE BLVD
200 SLN 94577 671-A7
200 SLN 94577 690-J1
200 SLN 94577 691-A1
LORRAINE RD
3200 LVMR 94551 695-J1
3200 AlaC 94551 695-J1
LORREN CT
400 LVMR 94550 715-E2
LORREN DR
4200 FRMT 94536 752-J5
4300 FRMT 94536 753-A5
LORREN WY
500 LVMR 94550 715-E2
LOS ALAMOS AV
600 LVMR 94550 715-E2
LOS ALTOS RD
- ORIN 94563 610-F5
200 CCCo 94708 609-G3
LOS AMIGOS DR
- ORIN 94563 610-E5
LOS ANGELES AV
1900 BERK 94707 609-G6
LOS ANGELES ST
5600 OAK 94608 629-F5
LOS ARBOLES
- ORIN 94563 610-F5
LOS ARBOLES DR
37600 FRMT 94536 752-H5
LOS ARBOLES PL
4800 FRMT 94536 752-H5
LOS BANOS ST
16500 AlaC 94578 691-F5
16800 AlaC 94541 691-F5
LOS BUELLIS WY
1400 MPS 95035 793-H3
LOS CERROS
- ORIN 94563 630-J3
LOS COCHES ST
300 MPS 95035 794-B7
LOS CONEJOS
- ORIN 94563 610-F7
LOS DEDOS
- ORIN 94563 610-H5
LOS ESTEROS RD
700 SJS 95002 793-D7
700 SJS 95134 793-E6
LOS NARROBOS RD
- ORIN 94563 610-E7
LOS OJOS DR
1500 HAY 94544 732-A1
S LOS PADRES DR
23000 SJCo 95304 (678-H6 See Page 677)
W LOS PADRES DR
16900 SJCo 95304 (678-H6 See Page 677)
LOS PINOS AV
500 MPS 95035 794-B5
LOS PINOS PL
600 FRMT 94539 753-F5
LOS PINOS ST
600 FRMT 94539 753-F5
W LOS POSITAS WY
16500 SJCo 95304 (678-H6 See Page 677)
LOS POSITOS DR
800 MPS 95035 794-B6
LOS RANCHITOS CT
11600 DBLN 94568 693-F3
S LOS RANCHOS DR
22800 SJCo 95304 (678-H6 See Page 677)
LOS REYES AV
16700 AlaC 94578 691-F6
LOS RIOS CT
400 PLE 94566 714-E5
LOST VALLEY CT
- ORIN 94563 630-J4
LOST VALLEY DR
- ORIN 94563 630-J4
LOTUS CT
3900 AlaC 94546 692-A3
6400 NWK 94560 772-G1
LOTUS PZ
- HAY 94542 712-B3
LOTUS ST
2600 PLE 94588 694-G6
LOUETTE CT
200 AlaC 94541 711-E1
LOUIS CT
200 LVMR 94550 715-D1
LOUISE CT
- MRGA 94556 651-E1
300 MPS 95035 794-E7
4800 FRMT 94536 752-J6
19700 AlaC 94546 691-H4
LOUISE LN
4700 UNC 94587 752-A1

LOUISE ST
1100 SLN 94578 691-D4
3000 OAK 94608 649-E1
LOUISIANA ST
600 OAK 94603 670-G6
LOUKOS PL
18700 AlaC 94546 691-H3
LOUVAINE AV
100 OAK 94603 670-G7
LOUVRE LN
2600 LVMR 94550 715-H3
LOVE LN
100 DNVL 94526 652-H2
LOVE LOCK WY
1000 HAY 94544 712-A7
LOVERIN CT
200 HAY 94544 712-B7
LOWELL AV
18600 AlaC 94541 691-F7
LOWELL PL
400 FRMT 94536 753-D1
LOWELL ST
900 OAK 94608 629-F5
LOWER GRAND AV
1600 PDMT 94611 650-A1
1600 PDMT 94611 630-A7
LOWER VINTNERS CIR
300 FRMT 94539 773-J4
LOWRY CT
4900 UNC 94587 752-A2
LOWRY RD
3500 FRMT 94555 732-C7
4100 FRMT 94555 752-B1
4700 OAK 94605 671-E5
4900 UNC 94555 752-B1
4900 UNC 94587 752-B2
LOYOLA AV
27500 HAY 94545 711-H7
27600 HAY 94545 731-H1
LOYOLA WY
400 LVMR 94550 696-A7
700 LVMR 94550 716-B1
LOZANO CT
1200 PLE 94566 715-C7
LUBBOCK PL
3100 FRMT 94536 752-G2
LUCANIA ST
8300 DBLN 94568 693-H2
LUCAS AV
6500 OAK 94611 650-E1
LUCAS CT
16100 AlaC 94580 711-C1
LUCCA CT
- LVMR 94550 715-J3
4100 PLE 94588 694-H4
LUCERNE CT
3100 AlaC 94546 691-J4
LUCERNE ST
- SF 94103 648-A7
900 LVMR 94551 695-E7
LUCERO CT
4200 PLE 94588 694-C5
LUCIA CT
900 HAY 94541 711-F3
1400 SLN 94577 690-H2
35000 FRMT 94536 752-E2
LUCIA ST
21800 HAY 94541 711-F3
35100 FRMT 94536 752-E2
LUCIEN WY
24900 HAY 94544 711-J4
LUCILLE ST
700 LVMR 94550 696-B7
900 LVMR 94550 716-B1
1000 SLN 94577 690-J1
6600 OAK 94621 670-F3
LUCILLE WY
- ORIN 94563 630-H1
LUCINDA CT
40100 FRMT 94539 753-E4
LUCKY LN
- SLN 94577 690-J3
LUCOT CT
20200 AlaC 94541 711-F1
LUCOT ST
- AlaC 94541 711-F1
LUCY CT
- FRMT 94539 753-F4
LUDLOW PL
200 SRMN 94583 673-F5
LUELLA PL
3900 AlaC 94546 691-J3
LUNA AV
2000 AlaC 94578 691-E3
LUNA CT
11600 DBLN 94568 693-F4
LUNA ST
28600 HAY 94544 712-B7
LUNAR WY
4100 UNC 94587 732-A6
LUND AV
- HAY 94544 711-J4
- HAY 94544 712-A4
LUNDHOLM AV
3600 OAK 94605 650-H7
LUND RANCH RD
1100 PLE 94566 714-F5
LUNDY DR
35600 NWK 94560 752-E4
LUNDY TER
46900 FRMT 94539 773-H6
LUPE CT
32000 UNC 94587 732-A6
LUPIN WY
8400 AlaC 94550 696-G7
LUPINE CT
6400 NWK 94560 772-G1
7600 PLE 94588 714-B6
LUPINE LN
- SRMN 94583 693-H1
LUPINE PL
44200 FRMT 94539 773-G2
LUPINE WY
300 AlaC 94541 711-F2
LURENE DR
100 FRMT 94539 773-H1
LUSITANA CT
- LVMR 94550 715-G5
LUSITANA DR
- LVMR 94550 715-G5
LUSK ST
- SF 94107 648-B7
3800 OAK 94608 629-G7
LUSTIG CT
28200 HAY 94544 712-B7
LUVENA DR
26500 HAY 94544 712-B5
LUX AV
3700 AlaC 94546 691-J4
3800 AlaC 94546 692-A4
LUZON CT
43200 FRMT 94539 773-G1

LUZON DR
42800 FRMT 94539 753-F7
43000 FRMT 94539 773-G1
LYCHEE CT
- SRMN 94583 673-G7
LYDIA CT
5600 LVMR 94550 696-C6
LYELL WY
24600 HAY 94544 711-J3
LYFORD ST
27400 HAY 94544 711-J7
LYLE CT
2400 AlaC 94578 691-G4
LYLE ST
16100 AlaC 94546 691-G4
16100 AlaC 94578 691-G4
LYLEWOOD DR
2700 PLE 94588 714-A3
LYMAN RD
3800 OAK 94602 650-D3
LYNBROOK CT
5000 PLE 94588 693-H7
LYNCH CT
- MRGA 94556 651-E1
LYNDA CT
5800 LVMR 94550 696-D6
LYNDE ST
2800 OAK 94601 650-C6
LYNDHURST PL
- CCCo 94583 672-J4
- CCCo 94583 673-A4
LYNDHURST ST
9800 OAK 94603 670-G6
E LYNDON LP
- AlaC 94552 692-G3
W LYNDON LP
- AlaC 94552 692-G3
LYNETTE ST
3000 AlaC 94546 692-B6
LYNN AV
- MPS 95035 794-D5
7300 ELCR 94530 609-E4
LYNN CT
900 AlaC 94580 691-F6
900 SRMN 94583 673-F5
LYNN LN
300 DNVL 94526 652-J2
LYNN ST
- SJCo 95391 (678-E3 See Page 677)
900 LVMR 94550 696-C7
23200 HAY 94541 711-G3
LYNN WY
900 FRMT 94539 753-G7
LYNNBROOK CT
- SRMN 94582 673-E2
LYNNBROOK DR
300 SRMN 94582 673-E2
LYNN CREST LN
- SRMN 94583 673-B1
LYNWOOD CT
5600 AlaC 94552 692-C2
LYNX CT
100 FRMT 94539 773-J3
LYNX DR
44700 FRMT 94539 773-H3
LYON AV
3500 OAK 94601 650-D6
LYON CT
1300 LVMR 94551 695-F6
LYRA CT
4900 LVMR 94551 696-B3
LYRA ST
48800 FRMT 94539 793-H1
LYTELLE ST
1300 HAY 94544 711-J7

M

M ST
22300 HAY 94541 711-J1
N M ST
200 LVMR 94551 695-G7
S M ST
100 LVMR 94550 715-G1
MAAR AV
400 FRMT 94536 753-D2
MAAR PL
500 FRMT 94536 753-D2
MABEL AV
3900 AlaC 94546 692-A4
MABEL PL
19700 AlaC 94546 692-A4
MABEL ST
2500 BERK 94702 629-F3
MABINI ST
- SF 94107 648-B6
MABRAY DR
- PLE 94588 693-G7
MACALLA CT
- SF 94130 648-E2
MACALLA RD
- SF 94130 648-E2
MACARTHUR BLVD
200 SLN 94577 671-C7
400 OAK 94610 650-A3
400 OAK 94610 649-J2
700 OAK 94605 671-A4
1000 SLN 94605 671-C7
1300 OAK 94602 650-E5
3500 OAK 94619 650-E5
4900 OAK 94613 650-G7
5400 OAK 94605 650-G7
5400 OAK 94605 670-H1
5400 OAK 94619 670-H1
5500 OAK 94613 670-H1
9000 OAK 94603 671-A4
W MACARTHUR BLVD
200 OAK 94611 649-H1
300 OAK 94609 649-H1
1100 EMVL 94608 629-F7
1200 OAK 94608 629-F7
6400 OAK 94609 629-F7
MACARTHUR FRWY I-580
- AlaC - 691-C1
- EMVL - 629-D6
- OAK - 629-D7
- OAK - 649-H1
- OAK - 650-D5
- OAK - 670-J1
- OAK - 671-A1
- SLN - 671-A1
- SLN - 691-C1
MACATERA AV
1400 HAY 94544 732-A1
MACBETH AV
4400 FRMT 94555 752-C1
MACBETH CIR
4400 FRMT 94555 752-D1
MACBETH CT
4600 FRMT 94555 752-C1

STREET
Block City ZIP Pg-Grid

MACCALL ST
5700 OAK 94609 629-G5
MACDONALD CT
9500 PLE 94588 693-F6
MACGREGOR COM
3800 LVMR 94551 695-J6
MACHADO CT
24200 AlaC 94541 692-D7
MACHADO PL
- PLE 94566 715-A4
MACIAS CT
- PLE 94566 714-E6
MACK COM
5200 FRMT 94555 752-C3
MACK ST
20500 HAY 94545 711-D4
MACKENZIE CT
- LVMR 94550 696-A7
MACKENZIE PL
400 HAY 94544 711-H4
3100 FRMT 94536 752-G2
MACKINAW ST
31300 UNC 94545 731-J6
MACKINNON ST
100 PDMT 94610 650-A1
MACKINTOSH ST
100 FRMT 94539 753-F4
MACKINTOSH TER
- FRMT 94539 753-F4
MACMILLAN WY
33800 FRMT 94555 732-D7
MACOMBER LN
- DNVL 94526 652-H2
MACOMBER RD
- DNVL 94526 652-H2
MACOMBER WY
- DNVL 94526 652-H2
MADALEN DR
1200 MPS 95035 794-B4
MADDALENA CT
1800 PLE 94566 715-C7
MADDUX DR
9600 OAK 94603 670-G6
MADEIRA DR
800 PLE 94566 714-G3
MADEIRA WY
3300 LVMR 94550 695-J7
MADEIROS AV
23800 AlaC 94541 692-C7
23800 AlaC 94541 712-C1
MADELAINE DR
6000 NWK 94560 752-D5
MADELAINE PL
6000 NWK 94560 752-D5
MADELIA PL
100 SRMN 94583 693-G1
MADELINE LN
25800 HAY 94545 711-F6
MADELINE ST
2600 OAK 94602 650-E4
MADERA AV
1200 MLPK 94025 771-A7
2700 OAK 94601 670-F1
2700 OAK 94619 670-F1
2800 OAK 94619 650-F7
MADERA CIR
1500 ELCR 94530 609-D1
MADERA CT
1500 ELCR 94530 609-D1
37700 FRMT 94536 752-H5
MADERA DR
1500 ELCR 94530 609-D1
MADERA LN
- ORIN 94563 610-F6
MADERA ST
1700 BERK 94707 609-F6
MADIGAN AV
- DBLN 94568 694-D3
MADISON AV
- UNC 94587 732-B4
1000 LVMR 94550 716-A1
5500 RCH 94804 609-B2
5600 ELCR 94530 609-C2
18200 AlaC 94546 692-B3
MADISON COM
- FRMT 94538 753-B5
MADISON LN
- AlaC 94546 692-B3
MADISON ST
100 OAK 94607 649-G4
100 OAK 94612 649-G4
500 ALB 94706 609-D5
2800 ALA 94501 670-B3
MADORA PL
100 SRMN 94583 693-G1
MADRID AV
1400 HAY 94544 732-A1
MADRID CT
4400 UNC 94587 731-J6
W MADRID CT
15900 SJCo 95304 (678-J6 See Page 677)
MADRID PL
- FRMT 94539 753-E4
- SRMN 94583 673-G5
MADRONE AV
3600 OAK 94619 650-G6
MADRONE PL
- ORIN 94563 610-F7
MADRONE ST
22600 HAY 94541 692-B7
MADRONE TR
- CCCo 94507 652-F1
- CCCo 94526 652-F1
- CCCo 94583 652-D1
MADRONE WY
100 UNC 94587 732-C6
1000 LVMR 94550 715-F3
MADSEN CT
- PLE 94588 714-F1
- MRGA 94556 651-D1
MAFFEY DR
18200 AlaC 94546 692-A3
N MAGAZINE
- NWK 94560 772-H1
S MAGAZINE
- NWK 94560 772-H1
MAGDALENA PL
3200 AlaC 94546 691-H4
MAGEE AV
3600 OAK 94619 650-F5
MAGEE CT
- MRGA 94556 651-G2
MAGEE WY
18300 AlaC 94546 691-J3
MAGELLAN CT
- DBLN 94568 694-G4
MAGELLAN DR
1800 OAK 94611 630-E7
1900 OAK 94611 650-E1
35900 FRMT 94536 752-F3
MAGGIORA CT
- OAK 94605 671-C5
MAGGIORA DR
- OAK 94605 671-C5
MAGNA AV
24100 HAY 94544 711-H3
MAGNOLIA AV
300 PDMT 94611 650-B1
300 PDMT 94610 650-B2
MAGNOLIA CIR
1700 PLE 94566 714-E1
MAGNOLIA COM
6400 LVMR 94551 696-D2
MAGNOLIA CT
900 SLN 94577 690-J2
900 SLN 94577 691-A2
MAGNOLIA DR
300 ALA 94502 670-B7
MAGNOLIA LN
1500 SLN 94577 690-J2
1600 SLN 94577 691-A2
MAGNOLIA ST
600 OAK 94607 649-E2
2900 BERK 94705 629-J4
2900 OAK 94608 649-E2
3400 EMVL 94608 629-J4
3400 OAK 94608 629-J4
24700 HAY 94545 711-G4
36600 NWK 94560 752-D7
MAGNOLIA TER
5500 FRMT 94538 773-A1
MAGNOLIA BRIDGE DR
- CCCo 94582 673-J2
- CCCo 94582 674-A2
MAGUIRE WY
- DBLN 94568 694-F4
MAHOGANY CT
- LVMR 94550 715-D4
MAHOGANY LN
- UNC 94587 732-H6
- SRMN 94583 693-F1
MAHOGANY PL
8500 NWK 94560 752-B7
MAHOGANY ST
- DBLN 94568 694-D4
200 HAY 94544 712-A5
MAHOGANY TR
- CCCo 94583 652-E2
MAHONEY ST
41200 FRMT 94538 753-D7
41200 FRMT 94538 773-D1
MAIDEN LN
- OAK 94602 650-F3
- SF 94108 648-A6
4000 UNC 94587 731-J5
8500 ELCR 94530 609-D1
MAIDENHAIR CT
- CCCo 94582 674-A2
MAIDENHAIR WY
- CCCo 94582 674-A2
MAIDSTONE CT
35000 NWK 94560 752-D3
MAIN ST
- SF 94105 648-B5
1000 PLE 94566 714-D4
1900 ALA 94501 649-D6
3600 CCCo 94514 637-D3
3600 FRMT 94538 753-D7
3600 FRMT 94539 753-D7
12200 AlaC 94586 734-C6
21800 HAY 94541 691-H7
21900 HAY 94541 711-J1
S MAIN ST
- MPS 95035 794-A7
MAINPRICE CT
- SRMN 94583 673-E4
MAIRMONT DR
4200 PLE 94566 714-E1
MAITLAND DR
- ALA 94502 670-A6
25500 HAY 94542 712-B3
MAJESTIC AV
3600 OAK 94605 650-H7
3900 OAK 94605 670-H1
MAJESTIC WY
500 SLN 94578 691-B5
MAJESTIC OAK CT
- SRMN 94583 673-E7
MAJOR AV
900 HAY 94542 712-B4
MAJORCA DR
200 SRMN 94582 673-G3
MAKAHA CIR
400 UNC 94587 732-D5
MAKIN RD
200 OAK 94603 670-F6
MALABAR AV
4500 AlaC 94546 692-A3
MALAGA CT
1000 PLE 94566 714-H4
2500 SRMN 94583 673-C3
MALAT ST
4600 OAK 94601 670-C2
MALBEC CT
500 PLE 94566 714-G3
MALCOLM AV
3100 OAK 94605 671-D4
MALCOLM LN
900 HAY 94545 711-G5
MALCOLMSON ST
41200 FRMT 94538 753-D7
MALDEN AL
- SF 94105 648-B6
MALDON ST
6200 OAK 94621 670-E3
MALE TER
47100 FRMT 94539 773-H6
MALIBU CT
400 LVMR 94550 715-E3
32500 UNC 94545 751-J1
MALIBU RD
24000 HAY 94545 711-F4
MALIBU TER
- FRMT 94539 794-B1
MALL CT
- OAK 94611 650-G1
W MALL SQ
200 ALA 94501 649-C6
MALLARD COM
4600 FRMT 94555 752-D2
MALLARD CT
1700 LVMR 94551 696-D2
2600 UNC 94587 732-E6
3300 HAY 94542 712-E5
MALLARD DR
5300 PLE 94566 714-C1
MALLARD ST
1500 LVMR 94551 696-D3
MALLORCA WY
2900 UNC 94587 731-J4
2900 UNC 94587 732-A4
MALTA CT
- OAK 94603 670-G7
MALTA PL
36000 FRMT 94536 752-F3
MALVA TER
4000 FRMT 94536 752-H1
MALVASIA CT
3100 PLE 94566 714-G3
MALVINA PL
- SF 94108 648-A5
MAMMOTH CAVE CT
3800 PLE 94588 714-A1
MANACOR CT
3700 SRMN 94583 673-C3
MANCHESTER COM
3300 FRMT 94536 753-A4
MANCHESTER DR
5900 OAK 94618 630-A5
MANCHESTER RD
1900 AlaC 94578 691-F4
MANCHESTER ST
3600 PLE 94588 694-F5
MANCINI CT
7400 DBLN 94568 693-F4
MANCINI DR
4800 AlaC 94546 692-B3
MANDALAY RD
- OAK 94618 630-B6
MANDAN CT
1900 FRMT 94539 773-G4
MANDAN PL
1700 FRMT 94539 773-G4
MANDANA BLVD
400 OAK 94610 650-A3
MANDANA CIR
- OAK 94610 650-B3
MANDARIN AV
- NWK 94560 772-C1
27600 HAY 94544 711-J7
27700 HAY 94544 731-J1
MANDELA PKWY
- OAK 94608 629-E7
300 OAK 94607 649-D3
2800 OAK 94608 649-E1
MANDEVILLA CT
3200 PLE 94588 694-H4
MANDY WY
- CCCo 94582 674-B5
MANFRED ST
100 MPS 95035 793-J3
100 MPS 95035 794-A3
MANGELS AV
3500 OAK 94619 650-E6
MANGO ST
24700 HAY 94545 711-G5
MANGOS DR
9900 SRMN 94583 673-F5
MANGROVE DR
- DBLN 94568 694-D4
MANGROVE LN
1000 ALA 94502 670-B7
MANGROVE RD
- HAY 94544 712-B6
MANILA AV
3700 OAK 94609 649-H1
3800 OAK 94609 629-H7
5000 OAK 94618 629-J6
5500 OAK 94618 630-A6
6300 ELCR 94530 609-C2
MANITOBA COM
200 FRMT 94538 773-E2
MANITOBA GRN
200 FRMT 94538 773-E3
MANITOBA TER
100 FRMT 94538 773-E3
MANN AV
2100 UNC 94587 732-G7
MANNING RD
1100 AlaC 94551 675-E4
1100 CCCo 94551 675-D3
MANOA ST
6200 OAK 94618 629-J4
MANON AV
26800 HAY 94544 712-A6
MANOR BLVD
500 SLN 94579 691-A6
1600 SLN 94579 690-J6
MANOR CIR
1700 ELCR 94530 609-C1
MANOR CT
5300 FRMT 94536 752-G6
MANOR DR
- PDMT 94611 630-A7
- PDMT 94611 650-A1
1000 AlaC 94586 734-A2
MANOR WY
1000 ALB 94706 609-F6
MANOR CREST
6700 OAK 94618 630-A4
MANSBURY CT
4900 FRMT 94538 773-B1
MANSBURY ST
4900 FRMT 94538 773-B1
MANSFIELD AV
6800 DBLN 94568 693-J3
22800 AlaC 94541 692-C7
MANTER CT
4600 AlaC 94552 692-C5
MANTER RD
4600 AlaC 94552 692-C5
MANTILLA AV
1200 HAY 94544 711-J7
1200 HAY 94544 712-A7
MANTIS ST
47400 FRMT 94539 773-J6
MANUEL CT
1200 OAK 94603 670-J6
MANUEL DR
1300 HAY 94544 732-A1
MANZANITA AV
- MRGA 94556 651-C1
1500 SLN 94579 691-A5
MANZANITA CT
45000 FRMT 94539 773-H3
MANZANITA DR
100 ORIN 94563 610-F5
1700 OAK 94611 630-F6
2200 CCCo 94516 630-G6
MANZANITA LN
11500 DBLN 94568 693-F5
MANZANITA ST
1400 FRMT 94539 773-H3
2100 PLE 94566 714-G2
37700 NWK 94560 752-F7
38000 NWK 94560 772-F1
MANZANITA TER
- ORIN 94563 610-F5
MANZANO CT
600 MPS 95035 794-B4
2200 PLE 94566 715-C7
MANZANO ST
500 MPS 95035 794-A4
MAPE WY
11700 DBLN 94568 693-G4
MAPLE AV
400 MPS 95035 793-H6
3000 OAK 94602 650-E5
MAPLE CT
600 SLN 94577 671-A7
22400 HAY 94541 711-J1
MAPLE DR
6500 DBLN 94568 693-J4
MAPLE ST
100 LVMR 94550 695-H7
100 LVMR 94550 715-H1
100 LVMR 94551 695-H7
37000 NWK 94560 752-H3
37000 NWK 94560 772-C1
37100 FRMT 94536 752-H3
MAPLE LEAF CT
1400 PLE 94566 714-F1
1400 PLE 94588 714-F1
MAPLE LEAF DR
1400 PLE 94588 714-F1
MAPLEWOOD DR
1400 LVMR 94551 696-D3
MARA CT
200 SRMN 94583 673-F5
MARABU WY
1500 FRMT 94539 753-E5
MARACAIBO RD
14100 SLN 94577 690-H5
MARALISA CT
1600 LVMR 94551 696-D3
MARALISA LN
1700 LVMR 94551 696-D2
MARASCHINO CT
2500 UNC 94587 732-F7
MARASCHINO PL
2400 UNC 94587 732-F7
MARATHON DR
7300 LVMR 94550 696-F6
MARBELLA TERRAZA
39200 FRMT 94536 753-C3
MARBLE CT
- UNC 94587 732-G6
MARBLEHEAD CT
4000 SRMN 94582 673-H5
MARBLEHEAD DR
4000 SRMN 94582 673-H5
MARBURY RD
2400 LVMR 94550 715-G5
MARCELLA CT
4800 LVMR 94550 696-B7
MARCELLA ST
600 LVMR 94550 696-B7
15800 AlaC 94578 691-E4
MARCHAND CT
24000 HAY 94541 712-A2
MARCHANT CT
- CCCo 94707 609-F4
MARCHANT GDNS
- CCCo 94707 609-F4
MARCIA CT
- LVMR 94550 696-B6
MARCIA ST
40400 FRMT 94538 753-C6
MARCIEL CT
18900 AlaC 94546 691-J3
MARCIEL RD
- AlaC 94546 671-G4
2100 CCCo 94551 675-C1
MARCUS CT
1800 HAY 94541 712-B2
MARCUSE ST
1000 ALA 94502 669-J6
MARDEN LN
5900 OAK 94611 630-D6
MARDIE ST
500 HAY 94544 711-J3
MARDIS ST
47600 FRMT 94539 773-H7
MARE LN
300 SRMN 94583 673-C4
MARES CT
400 PLE 94566 734-C1
MARGARET DR
24300 HAY 94542 712-A2
MARGARET LN
- DNVL 94526 652-H2
MARGARIDO DR
5700 OAK 94618 630-A5
MARGARITA AV
3400 OAK 94605 671-B3
MARGE CT
100 UNC 94587 732-F4
MARGERY AV
1200 SLN 94578 691-C4
MARGERY CT
40100 FRMT 94538 753-B7
MARGERY DR
4600 FRMT 94538 753-B7
MARGRAVE PL
- SF 94133 648-A4
MARGUERITA RD
- CCCo 94707 609-F2
MARGUERITE DR
- OAK 94618 630-B6
6100 NWK 94560 772-G1
MARGUERITE ST
1200 LVMR 94550 715-F2
MARIA CT
20600 AlaC 94546 692-A5
MARIA DR
1300 SLN 94577 690-H2
MARIA ST
2600 PLE 94588 694-G6
MARIAN LN
400 DNVL 94526 652-H2
MARIANAS LN
1000 ALA 94502 670-A7
1100 ALA 94502 669-J7
MARICAIBO PL
900 SRMN 94583 673-B3
MARICOPA CT
4200 LVMR 94551 695-E6
MARIE COM
300 LVMR 94550 696-B7
MARIE CT
4200 FRMT 94536 753-A5
MARIE DR
24400 HAY 94542 712-A2
MARIE PL
- MRGA 94556 651-F2
MARIE ST
- FRMT 94555 732-C7
MARIE WY
5900 OAK 94618 630-B4
MARIETTA DR
40000 FRMT 94538 773-B1
MARIGOLD CT
600 FRMT 94539 753-G5
1500 LVMR 94551 696-B3
7800 PLE 94588 713-J1
27300 HAY 94545 711-G7
MARIGOLD DR
41600 FRMT 94539 753-G6
MARIGOLD RD
1000 LVMR 94551 696-B4
MARILYN CT
3200 PLE 94588 694-C7
3200 PLE 94588 714-C1
MARILYN PL
- SRMN 94583 673-F6
MARIN AV
500 HAY 94541 711-F3
1000 ALB 94706 609-E6
1600 ALB 94707 609-G6
1700 BERK 94707 609-G6
2300 BERK 94708 609-H5
MARIN WY
1500 OAK 94606 650-A6
MARINA AV
2200 AlaC 94550 715-H4
2200 LVMR 94550 715-H4
MARINA BLVD
200 SLN 94577 691-A3
1100 SLN 94577 690-G4
2000 BERK 94710 629-B2
MARINA CT
- UNC 94545 751-J1
2000 SLN 94577 690-G4
MARINA DR
- HAY 94545 731-H2
2000 ALA 94501 670-B2
MARINA VILLAGE PKWY
800 ALA 94501 649-F6
MARINER WY
- SLN 94579 691-A7
MARINERS CT
300 HAY 94544 712-C7
MARINER SQUARE DR
2100 ALA 94501 649-F6
MARINER SQUARE LP
2200 ALA 94501 649-F6
MARINEVIEW DR
1800 SLN 94577 691-D1
MARINI LN
- LVMR 94550 716-C2
MARINO CT
40700 FRMT 94539 753-E5
MARINO WY
40600 FRMT 94539 753-E5
MARION AV
2200 FRMT 94539 753-F7
3700 OAK 94619 650-E6
MARION CT
400 ALA 94501 669-E1
MARION ST
20600 AlaC 94541 691-G6
MARIPOSA AV
600 OAK 94610 649-J2
700 LVMR 94551 715-E1
1000 BERK 94707 609-G6
MARIPOSA CT
- DNVL 94526 652-J3
N MARIPOSA DR
6500 DBLN 94568 694-A3
S MARIPOSA DR
6500 DBLN 94568 694-A3
MARIPOSA LN
- ORIN 94563 610-F7
MARIPOSA ST
1300 RCH 94804 609-B2
2300 HAY 94545 731-H1
MARIPOSA WY
39300 FRMT 94538 752-J6
39300 FRMT 94538 753-A6
MARITIME LP
4600 UNC 94545 731-J6
MARITIME ST
- OAK 94607 649-C2
- OAK 94625 649-C3
800 OAK 94626 649-C2
2200 OAK 94649 649-C2
MARJORAM LP
- UNC 94587 732-H5
MARK LN
- SF 94108 648-A5
MARK ST
10600 OAK 94605 671-C5
MARKET AV
6100 NWK 94560 752-F7
MARKET PL
1000 SRMN 94583 673-F3
6100 NWK 94560 752-F7
MARKET ST
- OAK 94607 649-F2
- SF 94105 648-B5
- SF 94111 648-B5
400 SF 94104 648-B5
500 SF 94108 648-B5
600 SF 94103 648-B5
700 SF 94102 648-B5
2800 OAK 94608 649-F1
3300 BERK 94702 629-F5
3300 OAK 94608 629-F5
3300 BERK 94703 629-F5
MARKHAM CT
2600 HAY 94542 712-E5
MARLBORO CT
500 SRMN 94583 673-E5
MARLBORO WY
2900 SRMN 94583 673-F5
3700 PLE 94588 694-F5
MARLBOROUGH CT
- PDMT 94611 650-D2
MARLBOROUGH TER
7000 OAK 94705 630-C3
MARLIN COM
38800 FRMT 94536 753-F3
MARLIN CT
500 HAY 94544 712-D7
31400 UNC 94545 731-J6
MARLIN CV
- OAK 94618 630-C4
MARLINA TER
400 MPS 95035 793-G3
MARLOW DR
100 OAK 94605 671-C6
400 SLN 94605 671-C7
MARLOWE LN
1000 HAY 94544 712-A7
MARLOWE ST
36600 FRMT 94536 752-G2
MARLYS COM
- LVMR 94550 715-H2
MARNE PL
7100 NWK 94560 752-C6
MARNE ST
15400 SLN 94579 691-B7
MAROLYN CT
22700 HAY 94541 692-C6
MARQUEE TER
35500 FRMT 94536 732-J4
MARQUES CT
3400 AlaC 94546 691-H3
MARQUETTE WY
1000 SLN 94579 691-B5
MARQUITA CT
8000 DBLN 94568 693-F3
MARR AV
- OAK 94611 630-C7
- OAK 94611 650-C1
MARRIAGE RD
- SCIC 94035 792-D7
MARS
3000 ALA 94501 649-F7
MARS AV
100 HAY 94544 712-B7
MARS CT
400 MPS 95035 794-D7
900 LVMR 94550 715-F4
MARS RD
1900 LVMR 94550 715-F4
MARSALA CT
600 PLE 94566 714-H3
MARSEILLE AV
900 LVMR 94551 695-F6
MARSH CT
200 SRMN 94583 673-B2
MARSH DR
2500 SRMN 94583 673-B2
MARSH PL
- OAK 94611 650-D1
100 SRMN 94583 673-B3
MARSHALL LN
4000 AlaC 94546 692-B5
MARSHALL ST
5500 OAK 94608 629-F5
20100 AlaC 94546 692-B5
MARSHALL TER
4000 FRMT 94536 752-H1
MARSHALL WY
400 ALA 94501 649-E7
400 ALA 94501 669-E1
MARSHBROOK DR
- HAY 94545 731-H3
MARSH HAWK CT
3300 PLE 94588 714-A3
33000 UNC 94587 732-D6
MARSH HAWK RD
33000 UNC 94587 732-D6
MARSHLANDS RD
9000 FRMT 94555 751-H7
9000 FRMT 94555 752-A7
9000 FRMT 94555 771-F2
9000 NWK 94560 752-A7
MARSTEN AV
4000 UNC 94587 731-J5
MARSTEN DR
- NWK 94560 752-F6
MARSTON RD
- ORIN 94563 610-E6
MARTEL PL
6700 NWK 94560 752-C6
MARTELL AV
14700 SLN 94578 691-C5
MARTELL CT
14700 SLN 94578 691-C5
MARTHA AV
38000 FRMT 94536 753-A3
MARTHA PL
600 HAY 94544 712-B5
MARTHA RD
- ORIN 94563 630-J1
MARTHA ST
1300 LVMR 94550 716-C1
MARTIL WY
300 MPS 95035 794-A5
MARTIN AV
100 LVMR 94551 695-H7
1400 PLE 94588 694-F6
MARTIN BLVD
600 SLN 94577 690-H1
MARTIN CT
2100 PLE 94588 694-F6
MARTIN ST
- UNC 94555 752-B1
600 OAK 94609 629-H5
33300 FRMT 94555 732-C7
MARTIN CANYON RD
7600 DBLN 94568 693-F4
MARTINEZ AL
1900 SLN 94577 691-A2
MARTINEZ CT
- DBLN 94568 694-G4
MARTINEZ DR
- FRMT 94536 733-B7
MARTINEZ ST
1400 SLN 94577 691-A1
MARTINGALE CT
5400 LVMR 94551 696-C1
44400 FRMT 94539 773-J2
MARTINGALE DR
100 FRMT 94539 773-H2
MARTINGALE LN
2800 LVMR 94551 696-B1
MARTIN LUTHER KING JR WY
- OAK 94607 649-F5
600 OAK 94612 649-G2
600 OAK 94609 649-G2
800 OAK 94608 629-G5
800 OAK 94609 629-G5
1000 BERK 94707 609-G7
1200 BERK 94703 609-G7
1200 BERK 94709 609-G7
1500 BERK 94709 629-G1
1500 BERK 94703 629-G1
1900 BERK 94704 629-G1
MARTIRAE CT
2400 ALA 94501 670-A2
MARTY TER
40800 FRMT 94539 753-E5
MARVIN CT
- OAK 94605 671-E4
MARVIN WY
800 HAY 94541 711-F2
MARWICK CT
8800 DBLN 94568 693-F2
MARWICK DR
11200 DBLN 94568 693-E2
MARY CT
- DNVL 94526 652-J2
MARY ST
- FRMT 94555 732-C7
- SF 94103 648-A6
MARY TER
1400 FRMT 94536 753-B3
MARYBELLE AV
1300 SLN 94577 690-H2
MARY BETH CT
46200 FRMT 94539 773-H5
MARYDEE CT
21600 AlaC 94541 711-G1
MARYLAND AV
- BERK 94707 609-G4
MARYLIN AV
700 LVMR 94551 695-E7
MARYLINN DR
- MPS 95035 793-H6
- MPS 95035 794-A7
MARY LOU WY
5700 LVMR 94550 696-D6
E MASCOT BLVD
- SJCo 95391 (678-E3 See Page 677)
MASON CT
6500 PLE 94588 694-A7
MASON DR
300 HAY 94544 712-B6
MASON ST
400 SF 94102 648-A5
1000 SF 94108 648-A5
1500 SF 94133 648-A5
2500 OAK 94605 670-F1
4600 PLE 94588 694-A6
MASONIC AV
500 ALB 94706 609-E5
1100 BERK 94706 609-E5
5100 OAK 94618 630-C7
MASONIC PL
- OAK 94618 630-D7
MASONIC TER
46900 FRMT 94539 773-F6
MASSACHUSETTS ST
2900 AlaC 94546 691-H4
MASSET PL
- SF 94103 648-B6
MASSEY CT
6800 PLE 94588 694-A7
MASTERS CT
47800 FRMT 94539 773-H7
47800 FRMT 94539 793-H1
MASTERSON PL
18700 AlaC 94552 692-E2
MASTERSON ST
4000 OAK 94619 650-F6
MASTICK CT
- ALA 94501 669-G1
MASTLANDS DR
2000 OAK 94611 650-F2
MATARO CT
1100 PLE 94566 714-H4
MATEO CT
4100 FRMT 94536 752-F2
MATEO ST
15800 AlaC 94578 691-E4
MATHER ST
200 OAK 94611 629-J7
MATHEWS ST
2500 BERK 94702 629-E3
MATHIEU AV
6100 OAK 94618 630-B5
MATIZ COM
36700 FRMT 94536 752-B4
MATOZA LN
- SLN 94577 670-J7
MATSON PL
38800 FRMT 94536 753-D2
MATTESON CT
- DNVL 94526 652-J1
MATTHEW CT
400 PLE 94566 714-D6
23500 AlaC 94541 692-D7
MATTHEW TER
5200 FRMT 94555 752-B2
MATTHEWS CT
400 MPS 95035 794-A3
MATTIS CT
4400 OAK 94619 650-H6
MATTOS CT
5000 FRMT 94536 752-H6
MATTOS DR
2300 MPS 95035 794-E7
4000 FRMT 94536 752-H5
MATTOX RD
1000 AlaC 94541 691-G6
MAUBERT AV
15500 AlaC 94578 691-E4
MAUBERT CT
1600 AlaC 94578 691-F5
MAUD AV
200 SLN 94577 691-B1
22900 AlaC 94541 692-C7
23700 AlaC 94541 712-D1
MAUI CIR
200 UNC 94587 732-C6
MAUI CT
200 SRMN 94582 673-E1
MAUNA LOA PARK DR
4800 FRMT 94538 773-C1
MAUREEN CIR
4500 LVMR 94550 696-B7
MAUREEN ST
15400 SLN 94579 691-B7
MAURI CT
- DNVL 94526 652-J2
MAURITANIA AV
5900 OAK 94605 670-H1
MAVIS CT
600 PLE 94566 714-G3
MAVIS DR
200 PLE 94566 714-F3
3100 SRMN 94583 673-F5
MAVIS PL
3100 SRMN 94583 673-F5
MAVIS ST
2400 OAK 94601 670-F1
MAX DR
40500 FRMT 94538 753-D6
MAXIMILLIAN AV
- SLN 94578 691-B4
MAXWELL AV
2500 OAK 94601 670-F1
2600 OAK 94619 650-F7
2600 OAK 94619 670-F1
MAXWELL CT
- SRMN 94582 673-J1
MAXWELTON RD
- PDMT 94618 630-C7
100 OAK 94618 630-C7
MAY CT
- HAY 94544 712-B7
- SRMN 94583 693-G1
3500 OAK 94602 650-D4
MAY RD
100 UNC 94587 732-G3
MAY WY
7500 SRMN 94583 693-F1
MAYA CT
700 FRMT 94539 773-J7
MAYA ST
47700 FRMT 94539 773-J7
MAYAN CT
7800 DBLN 94568 693-H3

STREET	Block	City	ZIP	Pg-Grid
MAYBECK LN				
	-	LVMR	94550	716-C1
MAYBECK TWIN DR				
	-	BERK	94708	609-J7
MAYBELLE AV				
	3400	OAK	94619	650-F6
MAYBELLE WY				
	3300	OAK	94619	650-F6
MAYBERRY DR				
	19000	AlaC	94546	691-J4
MAYBIRD CIR				
	34200	FRMT	94555	752-C3
MAYDON CT				
	-	OAK	94605	671-E4
MAYFAIR RD				
	28900	HAY	94544	732-A1
MAYFAIR PARK AV				
	42700	FRMT	94538	773-C2
MAYFAIR PARK TER				
	43000	FRMT	94538	773-D2
MAYFIELD CT				
	4500	FRMT	94536	752-J5
MAYFIELD DR				
	4600	FRMT	94536	752-H6
MAYFIELD PL				
	-	MRGA	94556	651-E2
MAYFIELD PTH				
	-	OAK	94605	670-J1
MAYFLOWER DR				
	17100	AlaC	94546	691-H2
MAYFLOWER PL				
	2000	SLN	94579	690-J6
MAYHEWS RD				
	-	FRMT	94536	733-B7
MAYHEWS LANDING RD				
	5800	NWK	94560	752-D6
MAYMONT CT				
	-	DBLN	94568	694-E3
MAYMONT LN				
	-	DBLN	94568	694-E2
MAYNARD AV				
	4100	OAK	94605	671-A1
MAYPORT CIR				
	2000	ALA	94501	649-E6
MAY SCHOOL RD				
	3200	AlaC	94551	675-H7
	3200	AlaC	94551	676-A7
MAYTEN DR				
	500	LVMR	94551	695-E7
MAYTEN WY				
	100	FRMT	94539	793-J1
MAYVIEW WY				
	700	LVMR	94550	715-E3
MAYVILLE DR				
	23900	AlaC	94541	692-C7
	23900	AlaC	94541	712-C1
MAYWOOD AV				
	2300	OAK	94605	670-H3
MAYWOOD DR				
	7300	PLE	94588	693-H7
MAYWOOD ST				
	41700	FRMT	94538	773-D1
MAZEY ST				
	100	MPS	95035	793-J3
	100	MPS	95035	794-A3
MAZUELA DR				
	5800	OAK	94611	630-E7
MCANDREW DR				
	5800	OAK	94611	630-D7
	5800	OAK	94611	650-D1
MCARTHUR AV				
	2500	UNC	94587	732-B4
MCAULEY ST				
	400	OAK	94609	629-H5
MCBRIDE LN				
	-	DBLN	94568	693-D5
	1200	HAY	94544	711-H6
MCCABE RD				
	-	CCCo	94514	637-D3
N MCCARTHY BLVD				
	500	MPS	95035	793-H5
	1700	MPS	95002	793-H5
	1900	SJS	95002	793-H5
	1900	FRMT	94538	793-H5
MCCARTHY LN				
	-	SJS	95134	793-F7
MCCARTY COM				
	35600	FRMT	94536	752-H1
MCCLARY AV				
	600	OAK	94621	670-F5
MCCLEAN PL				
	-	LVMR	94550	715-G4
MCCLELLAND ST				
	3700	OAK	94619	650-G7
MCCLURE AV				
	500	SLN	94578	691-B4
MCCLURE ST				
	2900	OAK	94609	649-G2
MCCONE AV				
	2700	HAY	94545	711-C5
MCCORMICK AV				
	8000	OAK	94605	671-A2
MCCORMICK ST				
	400	SLN	94577	690-F1
MCCRELLIS PL				
	-	DBLN	94568	694-H3
MCCULLOCH DR				
	-	ALA	94501	649-J7
MCCUTCHAN CT				
	-	PLE	94566	714-F6
MCDERMOTT AV				
	-	SJCo	95391	(678-E2 See Page 677)
MCDOLE TER				
	38500	FRMT	94536	753-C2
MCDONALD AV				
	5300	NWK	94560	752-E5
MCDONALD WY				
	31500	HAY	94544	732-F2
MCDONELL AV				
	4800	OAK	94619	650-H6
MCDONNEL RD				
	-	ALA	94502	669-H6
MC DUFF AV				
	200	FRMT	94539	773-H7
	200	FRMT	94539	793-H1
MCDUFF AV				
	200	FRMT	94539	793-H1
	400	FRMT	94539	773-J7
MCELROY ST				
	800	OAK	94607	649-D3
MCFARLANE LN				
	1200	HAY	94544	711-H6
MCGEE AV				
	1300	BERK	94703	609-F7
	1500	BERK	94703	629-F1
MCGLINCHEY DR				
	800	LVMR	94550	715-G2
MCGRAW AV				
	500	LVMR	94551	696-B5
MCGURRIN RD				
	8900	OAK	94605	671-C2
MCHENRY GATE WY				
	4700	PLE	94566	694-D7
MCINERNEY TER				
	-	FRMT	94538	753-B6
MCINTYRE ST				
	10800	OAK	94605	671-B6
MCKAY AV				
	1300	ALA	94501	669-F2
MCKAY LN				
	-	DBLN	94568	693-E5
MCKAY ST				
	41900	FRMT	94539	753-F7
MCKEEVER AV				
	1000	HAY	94541	711-J1
MCKEOWN CT				
	33100	UNC	94587	752-A2
MCKEOWN ST				
	33000	UNC	94587	752-A2
MCKEOWN TER				
	36000	FRMT	94536	733-A6
MCKILLUP RD				
	2800	OAK	94602	650-C5
MCKINLEY AV				
	700	OAK	94610	650-A4
	2100	BERK	94703	629-G3
MCKINLEY CT				
	500	SLN	94577	691-B2
MCLAREN CT				
	-	SJCo	95391	(678-E3 See Page 677)
MCLAREN LN				
	-	SRMN	94582	674-B4
MCLAUGHLIN AV				
	5400	NWK	94560	752-E5
MCLAUGHLIN RD				
	18700	AlaC	94550	717-J7
MCLEOD AV				
	-	SJCo	95391	(678-F2 See Page 677)
MCLEOD ST				
	100	LVMR	94550	715-H1
MCLOUD AV				
	2400	AlaC	94546	691-H5
MCMILLAN AV				
	5500	OAK	94618	630-A5
	5600	OAK	94618	629-J5
MCMURTY CT				
	-	ALA	94502	669-H6
MCNAMARA ST				
	4100	FRMT	94538	773-D1
MCPEAK LN				
	-	DBLN	94568	693-E5
MCSHERRY LN				
	3500	ALA	94502	670-A7
MCSHERRY WY				
	3500	ALA	94502	670-A7
MCWILLIAMS LN				
	-	PLE	94588	693-J6
MEAD AV				
	800	OAK	94607	649-F2
MEAD WY				
	24900	AlaC	94541	712-C2
MEADE ST				
	1300	RCH	94804	609-A2
MEADOW CT				
	-	DBLN	94568	693-F4
	-	LVMR	94551	696-D3
MEADOW DR				
	-	LVMR	94551	696-D3
MEADOW ST				
	3500	OAK	94601	650-D6
MEADOW WK				
	-	ALA	94501	669-G3
MEADOWBROOK AV				
	30800	HAY	94544	732-E2
MEADOWBROOK COM				
	36900	FRMT	94536	752-H3
MEADOWBROOK CT				
	7800	PLE	94588	693-H7
MEADOW GLEN DR				
	1800	LVMR	94551	696-E2
	2600	SRMN	94583	673-C2
MEADOW GLEN PL				
	2600	SRMN	94583	673-C2
MEADOW GLEN WY				
	2600	SRMN	94583	673-C2
MEADOWHAVEN WY				
	200	MPS	95035	794-A6
MEADOWLAND DR				
	-	MPS	95035	794-A6
MEADOWLARK CT				
	4000	AlaC	94546	692-A5
	8100	NWK	94560	752-B7
MEADOWLARK DR				
	2300	PLE	94588	714-A4
	2700	UNC	94587	732-D6
	19900	AlaC	94546	692-B5
MEADOWLARK ST				
	400	LVMR	94551	695-E7
	400	LVMR	94551	715-E1
MEADOWMIST DR				
	25800	HAY	94544	712-A5
MEADOWOOD CIR				
	100	SRMN	94583	673-G5
MEADOWOOD COM				
	-	LVMR	94551	695-G6
MEADOWOOD RD				
	19200	AlaC	94546	691-J4
MEADOWS CT				
	-	FRMT	94539	773-H1
MEADOWVIEW DR				
	4000	AlaC	94546	692-B5
MEADOWWOOD CT				
	5200	PLE	94566	714-C2
MECARTNEY RD				
	200	ALA	94502	670-A6
	2500	ALA	94502	669-H6
MEDALLION CT				
	3200	PLE	94588	714-A3
	5700	AlaC	94552	692-C2
MEDALLION DR				
	2100	HAY	94544	732-C4
	2100	HAY	94587	732-C4
	2100	UNC	94587	732-C4
MEDANOS CT				
	400	FRMT	94539	773-H1
MEDAU PL				
	6100	OAK	94611	650-E1
MEDEIRAS TER				
	300	MPS	95035	793-H3
MEDFORD AV				
	100	AlaC	94541	691-F7
	9800	OAK	94603	670-H6
MEDFORD CIR				
	19600	AlaC	94541	691-F7
MEDFORD CT				
	19200	AlaC	94541	691-F7
MEDIAR CT				
	-	SRMN	94582	673-H2
MEDIAR DR				
	-	SRMN	94582	673-H2
MEDICINE BOW CT				
	45300	FRMT	94539	773-H4
MEDICINE BOW WY				
	45300	FRMT	94539	773-H4
MEDINA ST				
	-	LVMR	94550	696-B6
MEDINAH CT				
	-	SRMN	94583	673-G7
	400	HAY	94544	732-F2
	7800	PLE	94588	714-B5
MEDINAH PL				
	100	SRMN	94583	673-G7
MEDINAH ST				
	31300	HAY	94544	732-E2
MEDITERRANEAN AV				
	100	HAY	94544	732-C1
MEDLAR DR				
	27600	HAY	94544	712-B6
MEDOLLA CT				
	-	LVMR	94550	715-E5
MEEK AV				
	300	HAY	94541	711-H2
MEEKLAND AV				
	16600	AlaC	94580	691-E6
	16800	AlaC	94541	691-E6
	19300	AlaC	94541	711-F1
	22400	HAY	94541	711-F1
MEEKS COM				
	3800	FRMT	94538	753-D7
MEEKS TER				
	3800	FRMT	94538	753-D6
MEG CT				
	2000	AlaC	94546	691-J6
MEGAN RD				
	800	LVMR	94550	696-B7
	800	LVMR	94550	716-B1
MEIGGS ST				
	41600	FRMT	94538	773-D1
MEL LN				
	19500	AlaC	94546	692-B4
MELANIE CIR				
	3200	PLE	94588	694-C7
MELANIE CT				
	-	LVMR	94550	696-D7
MELANIE WY				
	-	LVMR	94550	696-D7
MELBOURNE AV				
	27600	HAY	94545	711-J7
	27600	HAY	94545	731-J1
MELBOURNE CT				
	3000	PLE	94588	694-F6
MELBOURNE WY				
	-	CCCo	94582	674-C4
MELCHER ST				
	800	SLN	94577	690-H1
MELDON AV				
	4600	OAK	94619	650-F7
MELENDEZ AV				
	100	FRMT	94539	753-F4
MELERO COM				
	36600	FRMT	94536	752-B4
MELISSA LN				
	3800	AlaC	94546	691-H2
MELISSA TER				
	34500	FRMT	94555	752-B4
MELLO WY				
	33600	FRMT	94555	732-D6
MELODY CT				
	6700	PLE	94588	694-A7
MELODY LN				
	-	ORIN	94563	610-F2
MELODY WY				
	16700	AlaC	94578	691-F6
	17000	AlaC	94541	691-F6
MELROSE AV				
	100	ALA	94502	670-A7
	4400	OAK	94601	670-E1
	18000	AlaC	94541	711-E1
MELROSE CT				
	-	CCCo	94582	674-A1
MELVEN CT				
	300	SLN	94577	671-B6
MELVICH LN				
	-	DBLN	94568	693-D5
MELVILLE DR				
	6200	OAK	94611	650-G2
MELVILLE LN				
	6400	OAK	94611	650-G1
MELVILLE TER				
	-	FRMT	94536	752-B4
MELVIN CT				
	-	OAK	94602	650-E3
	800	HAY	94541	711-H1
MELVIN RD				
	1800	OAK	94602	650-E2
MEMLOCK TER				
	5500	FRMT	94538	773-A1
MEMORIAL AV				
	600	HAY	94541	711-F2
MEMPHIS LN				
	-	ALA	94501	649-E7
MENALTO AV				
	2400	EPA	94303	771-A7
MENARD CT				
	37800	FRMT	94536	752-H4
MENDENHALL CT				
	3500	PLE	94588	694-G5
MENDENHALL DR				
	800	LVMR	94550	715-G2
MENDENHALL RD				
	4700	OAK	94605	671-D2
	10600	AlaC	94550	736-G4
	10600	AlaC	94550	(737-A5 See Page 717)
	10600	AlaC	94550	757-C1
MENDEZ RD				
	29000	HAY	94544	712-C7
MENDOCINO AV				
	800	BERK	94707	609-G5
	5700	OAK	94618	630-A5
MENDOCINO CIR				
	1500	SLN	94579	691-A7
MENDOCINO CT				
	1500	SLN	94579	691-A7
MENDOCINO RD				
	1500	LVMR	94551	695-E6
MENDOCINO ST				
	1600	RCH	94804	609-C3
	15300	SLN	94579	691-A6
MENDOCINO TER				
	4700	FRMT	94555	752-D2
MENDOTA ST				
	4800	UNC	94587	752-B1
MENDOZA CT				
	1500	PLE	94566	714-E1
MENDOZA DR				
	5800	OAK	94611	630-E7
MENLO CT				
	6700	PLE	94588	694-A7
MENLO PL				
	-	BERK	94707	609-F5
MENLO ST				
	13200	SLN	94577	690-H4
MENNET WY				
	9700	SRMN	94583	673-F6
MENORCA CT				
	2600	SRMN	94583	673-B3
MENTO DR				
	1700	FRMT	94539	753-F6
MENTO TER				
	1600	FRMT	94539	753-G6
MERA ST				
	3800	OAK	94601	650-D7
	4000	OAK	94601	670-D1
MERANO CT				
	5100	PLE	94588	694-H4
MERCADO CT				
	600	MPS	95035	794-B5
MERCATO CT				
	3500	PLE	94566	715-C6
MERCED AV				
	6100	OAK	94611	650-E1
MERCED ST				
	1000	BERK	94707	609-F6
	1300	RCH	94804	609-B2
	1800	SLN	94577	690-H3
	14200	SLN	94579	690-J4
MERCHANT ST				
	400	SF	94111	648-B5
MERCURY CT				
	1400	MPS	95035	794-D7
MERCURY RD				
	1900	LVMR	94550	715-E4
MERCURY ST				
	28600	HAY	94544	712-B7
	48000	FRMT	94539	793-J1
MERCURY WY				
	32200	UNC	94587	732-A6
MEREDITH CT				
	25000	HAY	94545	711-G5
MEREDITH DR				
	42000	FRMT	94539	753-F7
MERGANSER CT				
	4800	PLE	94566	714-D1
MERGANSER DR				
	3900	FRMT	94555	732-B7
MERIDIAN DR				
	600	HAY	94541	711-H3
MERIDIEN CIR				
	2900	UNC	94587	732-A4
	30400	UNC	94587	731-J4
MERION DR				
	8000	NWK	94560	752-B6
MERION TER				
	100	MRGA	94556	651-D1
MERIT WY				
	5600	FRMT	94538	773-B2
MERITAGE COM				
	-	LVMR	94551	695-C4
E MERLE CT				
	400	SLN	94577	671-B7
W MERLE CT				
	400	SLN	94577	671-B6
MERLIN CT				
	-	OAK	94605	671-E4
	300	FRMT	94539	773-H7
MERLIN ST				
	-	SF	94107	648-A7
MERLOT CT				
	600	PLE	94566	714-G3
MERLOT DR				
	400	FRMT	94539	793-J2
	600	FRMT	94539	794-A2
MERLOT LN				
	2200	LVMR	94550	715-H3
MERO ST				
	-	AlaC	94541	711-F1
MERRIEWOOD CIR				
	-	OAK	94611	630-D6
MERRIEWOOD DR				
	5500	OAK	94611	630-D6
MERRILL AV				
	100	FRMT	94539	773-H7
	4500	OAK	94619	650-G6
MERRILL CIR N				
	-	MRGA	94556	651-G1
MERRILL CIR S				
	-	MRGA	94556	651-G1
MERRILL DR				
	-	MRGA	94556	651-G1
MERRILL PL				
	19400	AlaC	94546	692-B4
MERRIMAC ST				
	500	OAK	94612	649-G2
	500	OAK	94609	649-G2
MERRIMAC RIVER ST				
	4000	FRMT	94555	752-E1
MERRITT AV				
	400	OAK	94610	649-J4
	400	OAK	94610	650-A3
	500	OAK	94606	649-J4
MERRITT CT				
	-	OAK	94606	649-J4
MERRITT LN				
	1100	HAY	94545	711-G5
	1500	LVMR	94550	715-G4
MERRITT PL				
	2400	LVMR	94550	715-G5
MERRIWOOD PL				
	400	SRMN	94582	673-J7
MERSEY AV				
	1000	SLN	94579	691-A5
MERZ CT				
	200	MPS	95035	794-A5
MESA AV				
	-	PDMT	94611	630-B7
MESA CIR				
	-	HAY	94541	711-H3
MESA VERDE CT				
	3800	PLE	94588	714-A1
MESA VERDE DR				
	2000	MPS	95035	794-E7
MESA VERDE WY				
	18400	AlaC	94552	692-D2
MESA VISTA DR				
	-	SRMN	94583	673-C3
MESQUITE CT				
	44500	FRMT	94539	773-G3
MESQUITE LN				
	-	SRMN	94583	673-C4
MESQUITE WY				
	6000	LVMR	94550	696-D7
	6000	AlaC	94550	696-D7
MESSINA TER				
	-	UNC	94587	732-G2
METAIRIE CT				
	-	SRMN	94583	693-G1
METAIRIE PL				
	100	SRMN	94583	673-H7
	100	SRMN	94583	693-H1
METEOR DR				
	32300	UNC	94587	732-A7
MEYER CT				
	35600	FRMT	94536	752-G1
MEYER PARK CIR				
	-	FRMT	94536	752-H5
MEYERS AV				
	3300	ALA	94501	670-B4
MEYERS DR				
	1600	UNC	94587	732-F6
MEZZAMONTE DR				
	-	LVMR	94550	715-J3
MEZZO CT				
	4800	FRMT	94538	773-B1
MIAMI AV				
	27400	HAY	94545	711-H7
	27600	HAY	94545	731-J1
MIAMI CT				
	1600	OAK	94602	650-C4
MICHAEL AV				
	4000	FRMT	94538	773-D2
MICHAEL CT				
	1400	MPS	95035	794-C5
MICHAEL ST				
	600	MPS	95035	794-C5
MICHAELS CT				
	19700	AlaC	94546	691-H4
MICHELL CT				
	300	LVMR	94551	695-H7
MICHELL ST				
	200	LVMR	94551	695-H7
MICHELLE CT				
	4600	UNC	94587	732-A7
	4600	UNC	94587	752-A1
MICHELLE ST				
	39900	FRMT	94538	753-C5
MICHELLE WY				
	4700	UNC	94587	752-A1
	4800	UNC	94587	751-J1
MICHELSON ST				
	24300	HAY	94545	711-E5
MICHIGAN AV				
	400	BERK	94707	609-G4
	1200	SJS	95002	793-C7
MICHIGAN DR				
	7900	OAK	94605	671-A2
MICHIGAN RD				
	200	MPS	95035	794-A5
MIDCREST RD				
	500	OAK	94610	650-C3
MIDCREST WY				
	700	ELCR	94530	609-E3
MIDDAY COM				
	5400	FRMT	94555	752-C3
MIDDLE LN				
	1500	HAY	94545	711-E4
	1500	AlaC	94545	711-E4
MIDDLEBOROUGH WY				
	29300	HAY	94544	732-B2
MIDDLEBROOKE WY				
	-	SRMN	94582	674-C3
MIDDLEFIELD AV				
	2300	FRMT	94539	753-E7
MIDDLEFIELD RD				
	900	BERK	94708	609-J5
MIDDLE HARBOR RD				
	1200	OAK	94607	649-A4
	3000	OAK	94625	649-A4
MIDDLETON AV				
	3400	AlaC	94546	691-H3
MIDDLETON PL				
	4900	PLE	94566	714-F5
MIDDLETON ST				
	3000	OAK	94605	671-C7
	3100	SLN	94605	671-C7
MIDLAND RD				
	14600	AlaC	94578	691-E2
MIDLOTHIAN WY				
	30400	HAY	94544	732-D2
MIDSUMMER LN				
	-	AlaC	94546	692-A2
MIDVALE AV				
	3400	OAK	94602	650-F5
MIDVALE CT				
	5300	PLE	94588	693-H7
MIDWAY AV				
	700	SLN	94577	690-H1
W MIDWAY AV				
	-	ALA	94501	649-C6
MIDWAY RD				
	500	AlaC	94550	(678-B7 See Page 677)
	16800	AlaC	94550	(698-B1 See Page 677)
N MIDWAY RD				
	400	AlaC	94550	(678-B7 See Page 677)
	400	AlaC	94551	(678-B6 See Page 677)
MIDWAY ST				
	-	SF	94133	648-A3
	300	OAK	94626	649-C3
MIDWICK DR				
	-	MPS	95035	794-A5
MIFFLIN AV				
	-	UNC	94587	732-B4
MIKEMARY CT				
	2400	AlaC	94546	691-F3
MILA CT				
	38100	FRMT	94536	752-J4
MILAN CT				
	1400	LVMR	94550	715-G4
MILANI AV				
	2700	PLE	94588	694-E7
	5300	NWK	94560	752-F5
MILANO TER				
	300	MPS	95035	793-H3
	5900	FRMT	94555	752-A6
MILAW CT				
	-	SRMN	94583	673-B2
MILBRIDGE CT				
	-	DBLN	94568	694-F2
MILBURN CT				
	-	SRMN	94583	673-G7
MILBURN TER				
	34500	FRMT	94555	752-B4
MILDRED CT				
	4900	FRMT	94536	752-J6
MILDRED DR				
	4500	FRMT	94536	752-J6
MILDRED PL				
	500	HAY	94544	732-F2
MILES AV				
	5100	OAK	94618	629-J5
	5600	OAK	94618	630-A5
MILES PL				
	-	SF	94108	648-A5
MILFORD DR				
	-	SRMN	94582	674-B4
MILFORD ST				
	15000	SLN	94579	691-A6
MILL RD				
	-	SJS	95002	793-B7
MILL ST				
	43400	FRMT	94539	753-J7
MILLARD AV				
	4300	FRMT	94538	753-C7
MILLBRIDGE DR				
	2800	SRMN	94583	673-F6
MILLBRIDGE PL				
	2800	SRMN	94583	673-F5
MILLBROOK AV				
	7600	DBLN	94568	693-G3
MILLBROOK TER				
	4600	FRMT	94538	773-C1
MILLBURY CT				
	-	DBLN	94568	694-E2
MILL CREEK PL				
	-	PLE	94566	714-C4
MILL CREEK RD				
	-	FRMT	94539	753-H6
	3600	FRMT	94539	754-A6
	3800	AlaC	94586	774-B1
	3800	FRMT	94539	774-B1
MILLEFORD CT				
	3500	PLE	94588	714-A3
MILLENIUM LN				
	-	SRMN	94582	674-B4
MILLENNIUM TER				
	-	FRMT	94538	753-D7
	-	FRMT	94538	773-D1
MILLER AV				
	900	BERK	94708	609-H5
	1200	OAK	94601	650-B7
MILLER CT				
	-	UNC	94587	731-J4
MILLER PL				
	-	SF	94108	648-A5
	1100	OAK	94601	650-B7
	38000	FRMT	94536	753-A3
MILLER RD				
	7000	AlaC	94546	671-H1
	7000	AlaC	94546	672-A5
MILLER ST				
	2800	SLN	94577	690-J4
MILLFIELD PL				
	400	MRGA	94556	651-F3
MILLINGTON CT				
	-	ALA	94502	669-H7
MILLS AV				
	15900	AlaC	94580	691-E6
MILLS CT				
	-	PLE	94588	714-F1
MILLS PL				
	100	SRMN	94583	673-F7
MILLS WY				
	3800	LVMR	94550	695-J7
MILLSBRAE AV				
	2900	OAK	94605	670-G1
MILLSTREAM DR				
	400	SLN	94578	691-C4
MILLSTREAM LN				
	-	SRMN	94582	674-B4
MILLSVIEW AV				
	3200	OAK	94619	650-G7
MILLWATER CT				
	100	MPS	95035	794-C2
MILLWOOD CT				
	35000	NWK	94560	752-D3
MILMAR BLVD				
	18300	AlaC	94546	692-A3
MILMONT DR				
	-	FRMT	94538	793-H3
	1700	MPS	95035	793-J5
MILMONT ST				
	-	FRMT	94538	793-H2
MILO PL				
	200	SRMN	94583	673-F6
MILO WY				
	2800	SRMN	94583	673-E6
N MILPITAS BLVD				
	100	MPS	95035	794-A5
	1100	MPS	95035	793-J3
S MILPITAS BLVD				
	-	MPS	95035	794-B7
MILTON AV				
	4000	AlaC	94546	691-J3
MILTON ST				
	800	OAK	94607	649-F2
	33900	FRMT	94555	732-D7
	34200	FRMT	94555	752-E1
MILTON TER				
	3700	FRMT	94555	732-D7
	3700	FRMT	94555	752-D1
MILTON WY				
	-	LVMR	94551	696-A6
MILVIA CT				
	1900	BERK	94709	609-G7
MILVIA ST				
	-	BERK	94704	629-G3
	1200	BERK	94709	609-G7
	1500	BERK	94709	629-G1
	2600	BERK	94703	629-G3
MIMOSA CT				
	-	LVMR	94551	696-C3
MIMOSA ST				
	1400	LVMR	94551	696-C3
MIMOSA TER				
	34200	FRMT	94555	752-B3
MINARET WY				
	-	HAY	94541	711-H2
MINER RD				
	-	ORIN	94563	610-G4
MINERVA CT				
	-	LVMR	94550	715-H5
MINERVA ST				
	400	HAY	94544	712-B7
	1000	SLN	94577	690-J1
MINERVA WY				
	-	SRMN	94583	673-E6
MINES RD				
	200	LVMR	94550	696-B7
	200	LVMR	94550	716-B1
	3000	AlaC	94550	716-C4
	5700	AlaC	94550	736-E1
	9900	AlaC	94550	(737-A4 See Page 717)
	15300	AlaC	94550	757-H1
	16500	AlaC	94550	(758-A3 See Page 757)
	20600	AlaC	94550	(778-C1 See Page 757)
N MINES RD				
	100	LVMR	94551	695-J5
	100	LVMR	94551	696-A6
	100	LVMR	94550	696-A6
MINGO LN				
	-	ALA	94502	670-A7
MINIVET CT				
	2400	PLE	94566	714-D1
MINNA AV				
	2600	OAK	94619	650-E6
MINNA ST				
	-	SF	94105	648-B6
	300	SF	94103	648-B6
MINNIE CT				
	24900	AlaC	94541	712-C2
MINNIE ST				
	700	AlaC	94566	714-E6
	700	PLE	94566	714-E6
	2100	AlaC	94541	712-C2
MINNIS CIR				
	-	MPS	95035	793-J4
MINO WY				
	40800	FRMT	94539	753-E5
MINT ST				
	-	SF	94103	648-A6
MINTARO CT				
	-	SRMN	94582	674-C3
MINTON CT				
	2600	PLE	94588	714-A3
MINTURN CT				
	32200	UNC	94587	732-C5
MINTURN ST				
	1500	ALA	94501	669-J1
MINTWOOD ST				
	43200	FRMT	94538	773-E2
MIRA CT				
	15900	AlaC	94546	692-A2
MIRABEAU DR				
	6300	NWK	94560	752-C5
MIRABELLA CT				
	1600	MPS	95035	794-D6
MIRABELLA DR				
	-	UNC	94587	732-C4
MIRADOR CT				
	700	PLE	94566	714-F4
MIRADOR DR				
	4200	PLE	94566	714-E5
MIRA FLORES				
	-	ORIN	94563	610-J5
MIRA LOMA				
	-	ORIN	94563	610-G6
MIRALOMA CT				
	5400	LVMR	94551	696-C3
MIRA LOMA LN				
	-	DNVL	94526	652-J3
MIRA LOMA ST				
	4600	AlaC	94546	692-A3
MIRALOMA ST				
	1700	LVMR	94551	696-C3
MIRALOMA WY				
	2900	UNC	94587	732-A4
	3000	UNC	94587	731-J4
MIRAMAR AV				
	800	BERK	94707	609-F6
	1900	AlaC	94578	691-G4
	2400	AlaC	94546	691-G4
MIRAMAR PL				
	16300	AlaC	94578	691-G4
MIRAMAR PARK DR				
	43300	FRMT	94538	773-C3
MIRAMONTE AV				
	2000	AlaC	94578	691-G5
MIRAMONTE CT				
	1300	BERK	94703	609-F7
MIRA MONTE LN				
	300	LVMR	94551	695-J6
	300	LVMR	94551	696-A6
MIRA MONTE RD				
	-	ORIN	94563	610-E7
MIRAMONTE ST				
	4200	UNC	94587	732-A5
	4200	UNC	94587	731-J5
MIRANDA CT				
	-	ALA	94502	669-J7
MIRANDA ST				
	1300	HAY	94544	732-A2
	41900	FRMT	94539	753-F7
MIRANDA WY				
	900	LVMR	94550	715-F3
MIRASOL AV				
	3400	OAK	94605	671-B3
MIRA VISTA AV				
	500	OAK	94610	649-J2
	500	OAK	94610	650-A2
MIRA VISTA DR				
	4700	AlaC	94546	691-J1
MIRA VISTA PL				
	16900	AlaC	94546	691-J1
MISSION BLVD				
	32100	HAY	94544	732-F3
	42400	FRMT	94539	753-H6
	43500	FRMT	94539	773-H5
	46700	FRMT	94538	773-H5
MISSION BLVD Rt#-185				
	900	HAY	94541	711-H1
	17900	AlaC	94541	691-G6
	21500	HAY	94541	691-G6
MISSION BLVD Rt#-238				
	-	FRMT	94536	732-G4
	-	FRMT	94536	733-B7
	21700	HAY	94541	691-H7
	21700	HAY	94541	711-H1
	23000	HAY	94544	711-J2
	23400	HAY	94544	712-A3
	23600	HAY	94542	712-A3
	29800	HAY	94544	732-D1
	32000	UNC	94587	732-G4
	37500	FRMT	94536	753-E3
	39100	FRMT	94539	753-E3
MISSION BLVD Rt#-262				
	46200	FRMT	94539	773-G6
	46600	FRMT	94538	773-G6
MISSION CT				
	-	AlaC	94541	711-F1
	400	FRMT	94539	773-G6
MISSION DR				
	100	PLE	94566	714-D5
MISSION LN				
	-	LVMR	94550	715-H5
MISSION RD				
	-	FRMT	94539	753-H6
	5700	AlaC	94586	754-A3
MISSION ST				
	-	SF	94105	648-B6
	600	SF	94103	648-B6
MISSION WY				
	3900	SLN	94578	691-C5
MISSION BELL PL				
	800	HAY	94544	711-J5
MISSION CIELO AV				
	41500	FRMT	94539	753-G5
MISSION CIELO CT				
	41600	FRMT	94539	753-G5
MISSION CREEK CT				
	600	FRMT	94539	753-G6
MISSION CREEK DR				
	41600	FRMT	94539	753-G5
MISSION FALLS CT				
	47000	FRMT	94539	773-G6
MISSION FALLS LN				
	100	FRMT	94539	773-G7

STREET Block City ZIP Pg-Grid

MISSION HILLS
- OAK 94605 671-D2
MISSION RIDGE CT
- FRMT 94539 753-G5
MISSION SQUARE TER
- FRMT 94539 753-H7
MISSION TIERRA PL
- FRMT 94539 753-J7
MISSION VIEW DR
3000 FRMT 94538 753-C6
MISSION VILLA TER
- FRMT 94539 753-F5
MISTFLOWER AV
6000 NWK 94560 752-F7
MISTLETOE DR
2400 HAY 94545 731-G1
MISTY TER
- FRMT 94555 752-C3
MISTY SPRING CT
- SRMN 94583 673-H3
MISTY SPRING DR
- AlaC 94552 692-E7
MITCHEL DR
- DBLN 94568 694-B3
MITCHELL AV
- ALA 94501 649-F6
400 SLN 94577 671-B7
MITCHELL PL
27400 HAY 94544 712-B6
MITCHELL ST
1400 OAK 94601 650-C6
MITRA ST
1500 LVMR 94550 716-C1
MIWOK CT
400 FRMT 94539 773-J5
MIXTEC CT
1200 FRMT 94539 773-G4
MOAB DR
38300 FRMT 94536 753-D1
MOBILE CT
34600 FRMT 94555 752-D2
MOCCASIN ST
32700 UNC 94587 732-F3
MOCHO RD
- AlaC 94550 (758-B6 See Page 757)
MOCHO ST
1000 LVMR 94550 715-F2
MOCINE AV
26000 HAY 94544 712-A5
MOCKINGBIRD LN
700 AlaC 94566 714-E6
700 PLE 94566 714-E6
26400 HAY 94544 711-H6
MOCKINGBIRD WY
4200 FRMT 94555 732-B7
MOCKORANGE CT
6200 NWK 94560 752-F7
MODENA CT
5200 PLE 94588 694-H4
MODESTO AV
3000 OAK 94619 650-F7
3000 OAK 94619 670-F1
MODESTO ST
3800 AlaC 94546 692-A5
MODOC AV
400 OAK 94618 630-C6
5300 RCH 94804 609-B3
MODOC CT
1700 HAY 94542 712-B3
MODOC PL
400 LVMR 94551 695-D6
MODOC RD
- ORIN 94563 610-G2
MODOC ST
900 BERK 94707 609-F6
MODOC WY
39600 FRMT 94538 753-B6
MOESER LN
6300 ELCR 94530 609-D2
MOET LN
- SRMN 94582 674-B4
MOHAVE COM
100 FRMT 94539 773-H6
MOHAVE DR
46600 FRMT 94539 773-H5
MOHAVE TER
100 FRMT 94539 773-H6
MOHAWK CIR
2700 SRMN 94583 673-D5
MOHAWK DR
800 LVMR 94551 695-E6
MOHAWK RIVER ST
4100 FRMT 94555 752-E2
MOHICAN CT
1800 FRMT 94539 773-G3
MOHICAN ST
32400 HAY 94544 732-F3
MOHR AV
- AlaC 94588 694-E7
3500 PLE 94588 694-E7
3900 PLE 94566 694-D7
4400 PLE 94566 714-E1
MOHR DR
24400 AlaC 94545 711-F5
24400 HAY 94545 711-F5
MOJAVE AV
600 LVMR 94550 715-E2
MOKELUMNE AV
6400 OAK 94605 670-H1
MOLAKAI CIR
200 UNC 94587 732-C6
MOLINA CT
- SRMN 94583 673-C3
35800 FRMT 94536 752-F2
MOLLER DR
1800 PLE 94566 714-E1
MOLLER RANCH DR
- PLE 94588 693-G7
MOLLIE CIR
5400 LVMR 94551 696-C4
MOLLIE CT
5600 LVMR 94551 696-C4
19900 AlaC 94552 692-F2
MOLLIE TER
- FRMT 94536 753-C2
MOLLINAR TER
6000 FRMT 94555 752-A5
MONACO AV
300 UNC 94587 732-J5
MONACO COM
34700 FRMT 94555 752-D2
MONACO CT
100 PLE 94566 714-D4
MONACO DR
4900 PLE 94566 714-D4
MONADNOCK WY
6000 OAK 94605 670-G1
MONAGHAN ST
- DBLN 94568 694-F4
MONA MARIE CT
23400 AlaC 94541 692-D7
MONAN ST
10900 OAK 94605 671-D4
MONARCH DR
- SRMN 94582 673-H2
MONARCH PL
2500 UNC 94587 732-C4
N MONARCH RD
- CCCo 94582 674-A1
- SRMN 94582 673-J1
- SRMN 94582 674-A1
S MONARCH RD
- CCCo 94582 674-A2
MONARCH ST
- ALA 94501 649-C6
MONARCH TER
43600 FRMT 94538 773-E3
MONARDA CT
2600 PLE 94588 694-H4
MONASTERIO CT
- SRMN 94583 673-C3
MONIKA LN
3200 AlaC 94541 692-C6
MONMOUTH CT
3200 PLE 94588 694-E6
MONMOUTH DR
300 MPS 95035 794-D7
MONMOUTH PL
3500 FRMT 94538 773-E2
MONO AV
1500 AlaC 94578 691-E4
MONO ST
22700 HAY 94541 711-G2
MONOGRAM RD
- SLN 94578 691-B4
MONOGRAM ST
- SLN 94578 691-B4
MONO LAKE DR
32700 FRMT 94555 732-C6
MONO LAKE LN
32700 FRMT 94555 732-B6
MONROE AV
- DBLN 94568 694-C3
3700 FRMT 94536 753-A4
6000 OAK 94618 630-A6
MONROE ST
1000 ALB 94706 609-D7
1000 ALB 94710 609-D7
MONROVIA ST
32900 UNC 94587 752-A1
MONTAGUE AV
500 SLN 94577 691-A3
4800 FRMT 94555 752-C1
MONTAGUE PL
- SF 94133 648-A4
MONTAGUE RD
4800 FRMT 94555 752-C2
MONTAIR CT
- DNVL 94526 652-H3
MONTAIR DR
- DNVL 94526 652-G3
MONTAIR PL
100 DNVL 94526 652-H3
2800 UNC 94587 732-A4
MONTAIR WY
2800 UNC 94587 732-A4
MONTALBAN DR
- FRMT 94536 733-A7
MONTALVO CT
5400 PLE 94588 693-G7
MONTANA DR
1000 PLE 94566 714-G3
MONTANA ST
1700 OAK 94602 650-D4
MONTANA WY
300 HAY 94544 712-A5
MONTANA VISTA
700 FRMT 94539 773-H1
MONTAROSSA CT
- LVMR 94550 715-J3
MONTCALM AV
6200 NWK 94560 752-D6
MONTCLAIR AV
400 OAK 94606 650-A4
600 OAK 94610 650-A4
MONTCLAIR CT
1000 LVMR 94550 716-A1
MONTCLAIRE COM
100 FRMT 94539 773-J2
MONTCLAIRE CT
- FRMT 94539 773-J2
MONTCLAIRE DR
100 FRMT 94539 773-J2
MONTCLAIRE PL
100 SRMN 94583 673-F6
MONTCLAIRE TER
400 FRMT 94539 773-J2
MONTCREST PL
400 DNVL 94526 652-H2
MONTE AV
- PDMT 94611 630-B7
MONTE CT
40300 FRMT 94538 753-C6
MONTE CARLO AV
200 UNC 94587 732-J5
MONTE CARLO PARK CT
4600 FRMT 94538 773-D2
MONTECELLO AV
- PDMT 94611 630-A7
MONTECITO AV
100 OAK 94610 649-H3
MONTECITO CIR
1700 LVMR 94551 695-E5
MONTECITO DR
- DNVL 94526 652-J2
36500 FRMT 94536 752-J1
36700 FRMT 94536 753-A1
MONTECITO WY
300 MPS 95035 793-H4
MONTE CRESTA AV
- OAK 94611 649-J1
MONTEGO BAY
100 ALA 94502 669-H7
MONTEGO DR
200 DNVL 94526 652-J4
MONTELL ST
- OAK 94611 649-J1
MONTEREY AV
1200 BERK 94707 609-F7
1200 BERK 94706 609-F7
MONTEREY BLVD
2300 OAK 94611 650-E2
2300 OAK 94602 650-G4
3400 SLN 94578 691-B5
3500 OAK 94619 650-G5
MONTEREY CIR
2000 ALA 94501 649-E6
MONTEREY CT
- UNC 94545 751-J1
800 SLN 94578 691-B5
MONTEREY DR
1600 LVMR 94551 696-A4
6400 DBLN 94568 694-A3
32500 UNC 94545 751-J1
MONTEREY ST
1300 RCH 94804 609-B3
MONTEREY TER
- ORIN 94563 610-J7
MONTEREY WY
39200 FRMT 94538 753-A5
MONTEREY VIEJO
4400 UNC 94587 731-H5
MONTERO RD
- HAY 94544 712-A4
MONTERRA DR
- UNC 94587 732-H6
MONTE SERENO TER
- FRMT 94539 774-A7
- FRMT 94539 794-B1
MONTE SOL TER
400 MPS 95035 793-G3
MONTE VEDA DR
- ORIN 94563 630-J3
MONTE VERDE CT
6000 AlaC 94552 692-D2
MONTEVERDE TER
- FRMT 94536 752-J2
MONTEVIDEO CIR
- FRMT 94539 753-H6
MONTEVIDEO CT
- SRMN 94583 673-E5
4700 UNC 94587 731-J6
42600 FRMT 94539 753-H6
MONTEVIDEO DR
2900 SRMN 94583 673-E5
MONTEVIDEO RD
- FRMT 94539 753-J6
MONTEVINO DR
700 PLE 94566 714-H4
MONTE VISTA AV
- OAK 94611 649-J1
600 OAK 94610 649-J1
600 OAK 94610 650-A1
3200 ALA 94501 670-C3
MONTE VISTA CIR
- UNC 94587 732-G6
MONTE VISTA DR
24900 AlaC 94545 711-F6
MONTE VISTA RD
- ORIN 94563 610-E6
MONTE VISTA RIDGE RD
200 ORIN 94563 610-E6
MONTGOMERY AV
800 AlaC 94541 691-G7
21500 HAY 94541 691-G7
21500 HAY 94541 711-H1
E MONTGOMERY AV
4900 RCH 94804 609-A2
MONTGOMERY PL
34400 FRMT 94555 732-E7
MONTGOMERY ST
- SF 94108 648-A5
- SF 94104 648-A5
100 SRMN 94583 673-F3
300 SF 94133 648-A4
500 SF 94111 648-A3
4200 OAK 94611 629-J7
4400 OAK 94611 630-A7
22100 HAY 94541 711-H1
MONTICELLO AV
2300 OAK 94601 670-E1
2400 OAK 94601 650-F7
2600 OAK 94619 650-F7
MONTICELLO ST
600 HAY 94544 712-C6
MONTICELLO TER
300 FRMT 94539 753-J6
MONTJOY CT
28100 HAY 94544 712-A7
MONTMARTRE PARK CT
4600 FRMT 94538 773-D3
MONTORI CT
- PLE 94566 715-D6
MONTORI WY
- PLE 94566 715-D6
MONTOYA TER
- UNC 94587 732-G2
MONTPELIER CT
3100 PLE 94588 694-E6
MONTREAL ST
15400 SLN 94579 691-A7
15500 SLN 94579 711-A1
MONTROSE AV
43200 FRMT 94538 773-E2
MONTROSE DR
1200 SLN 94577 691-D1
MONTROSE PL
- PLE 94566 715-A4
3600 LVMR 94551 695-J6
MONTROSE RD
- BERK 94707 609-G5
MONTWOOD WY
- OAK 94605 671-C5
MONUMENT CT
500 FRMT 94539 794-A2
MONUMENT ST
24000 HAY 94545 711-F5
MONZAL AV
5900 OAK 94611 630-C6
MOODY WY
2200 HAY 94545 711-E5
MOONEY AV
700 AlaC 94578 691-E5
700 AlaC 94580 691-E5
MOONEY CT
34600 FRMT 94555 752-D1
MOONFLOWER WY
5300 LVMR 94551 696-C4
MOONLIGHT COM
5400 FRMT 94555 752-C3
MOONLIGHT CT
- OAK 94603 671-C5
MOONLIGHT TER
100 ALA 94501 649-D6
MOORE CT
- ALA 94502 669-J6
- SRMN 94583 673-E5
MOORE DR
6600 OAK 94611 630-G7
38600 FRMT 94536 753-C2
MOORE PL
- DBLN 94568 694-A4
MOORES AV
5600 NWK 94560 752-G7
6000 NWK 94560 772-G1
MOORILLA LN
- SRMN 94582 674-B4
MOORPARK ST
700 OAK 94603 670-H7
MORADA CT
41300 FRMT 94539 753-G5
MORADO WY
2200 PLE 94566 714-G2
MORAGA AV
- PDMT 94611 630-A7
100 OAK 94611 630-A7
900 PDMT 94618 630-D7
5500 OAK 94618 630-D7
6200 OAK 94611 650-D1
MORAGA CT
- ORIN 94563 630-J3
MORAGA DR
500 LVMR 94550 715-E2
700 SLN 94578 691-B4
MORAGA WY
- ORIN 94563 630-H1
MORAINE ST
36900 FRMT 94536 752-H3
MORALES CT
- UNC 94555 752-A2
22200 AlaC 94546 692-B6
MORAN CT
- HAY 94544 711-H3
N MORAY ST
43800 FRMT 94539 773-H2
S MORAY ST
43800 FRMT 94539 773-H2
MORCOM AV
2800 OAK 94619 670-F1
2800 OAK 94619 650-F7
MORCOM PL
- OAK 94619 650-G7
MORE ST
- ALB 94706 609-D6
MORELAND DR
1600 ALA 94501 670-B2
4000 AlaC 94546 691-J3
4200 AlaC 94546 692-A3
MORELAND WY
- LVMR 94550 716-C2
MORELLO CT
2600 UNC 94587 732-F7
MORENGO WY
300 FRMT 94539 773-H7
MORENO AV
2900 PLE 94588 694-E7
MORETTI LN
300 MPS 95035 794-C6
MORGAN AV
1700 SLN 94577 691-C1
1700 SLN 94577 671-C7
2800 OAK 94602 650-E4
MORGAN COM
500 LVMR 94551 695-H7
MORGAN CT
3300 PLE 94588 714-B1
MORGAN DR
2700 SRMN 94583 673-C4
2700 CCCo 94583 673-C4
MORGANFIELD CT
4100 PLE 94566 714-E1
MORGANFIELD RD
4200 PLE 94566 714-E1
MORGAN TERRITORY RD
1100 AlaC 94551 675-G5
1900 CCCo 94551 675-F3
MORKEN ST
6900 OAK 94621 670-G3
MORLEY DR
2800 OAK 94611 650-F2
MORLEY PL
35400 FRMT 94536 752-F1
MORNING GLORY CIR
1300 LVMR 94551 696-A4
MORNING GLORY CT
6000 NWK 94560 752-H7
6000 NWK 94560 772-G1
MORNING GLORY RD
1600 LVMR 94551 696-A3
MORNING HILLS CT
100 SRMN 94582 673-J6
MORNINGSIDE DR
27900 HAY 94545 731-H1
MORNINGTON CT
- CCCo 94582 674-B4
MORNINGTON LN
- CCCo 94582 674-B4
MORNING VIEW TER
- FRMT 94539 794-B1
MORPETH ST
5700 OAK 94618 630-C6
MORRES AV
6400 NWK 94560 772-G1
MORRILL CT
- OAK 94618 630-B6
MORRILL LN
- OAK 94618 630-B6
MORRILL ST
800 AlaC 94541 691-F6
MORRIS AV
6500 ELCR 94530 609-B1
MORRIS CT
14600 SLN 94578 691-C3
MORRIS ST
- SF 94107 648-A7
MORRIS WY
5000 FRMT 94536 752-F5
MORRISON AV
3200 OAK 94602 650-C5
MORRISON CANYON RD
- FRMT 94536 733-H7
100 FRMT 94536 753-E2
100 FRMT 94539 753-G1
1500 AlaC 94586 753-G1
1500 FRMT 94586 753-G1
1500 AlaC 94536 753-G1
MORSE CT
25200 HAY 94542 712-C3
MORSE DR
5500 OAK 94605 670-G1
MORSE TER
47100 FRMT 94539 773-H6
MORTENSEN RD
3700 SLN 94578 691-B3
MORTIMER AV
200 FRMT 94536 753-C2
MORTON AV
7400 NWK 94560 772-E1
MORTON PL
3700 AlaC 94552 692-F2
MORTON ST
1100 ALA 94501 669-H1
MORVA CT
600 AlaC 94541 691-G7
MORVA DR
20500 AlaC 94541 691-G7
MOSAIC COM
34700 FRMT 94555 752-D3
MOSELLE CT
1300 LVMR 94550 715-J2
4000 PLE 94566 714-F4
22100 AlaC 94541 692-C6
MOSLEY AV
- ALA 94501 649-E6
MOSS AV
- OAK 94610 649-J1
100 OAK 94611 649-J1
MOSS LN
- OAK 94608 649-E1
MOSS ST
- SF 94103 648-A7
MOSS WY
100 OAK 94611 649-J1
MOSSBRIDGE LN
- ORIN 94563 610-H3
MOSS POINTE
- ALA 94502 670-A5
MOSS TREE WY
- PLE 94588 714-B5
MOSSWOOD CT
- LVMR 94551 715-D1
MOSSWOOD DR
37600 FRMT 94536 752-H5
MOSSWOOD RD
- BERK 94704 630-A2
MOSSY ROCK DR
22500 AlaC 94541 692-D6
MOTT PL
- OAK 94619 651-A5
MOUND AV
7100 ELCR 94530 609-C1
MOUND ST
900 ALA 94501 670-A4
MOUNTAIN AV
500 PDMT 94611 650-C1
MOUNTAIN BLVD
400 OAK 94611 630-C5
1800 OAK 94611 650-E1
2500 OAK 94602 650-E1
3800 OAK 94619 650-G4
4900 OAK 94605 650-H6
4900 OAK 94613 650-H6
7400 OAK 94605 671-A1
MOUNTAIN CT
5700 AlaC 94552 692-D3
MOUNTAIN DR
3000 FRMT 94555 732-D6
MOUNTAIN LN
18500 AlaC 94552 692-D2
MOUNTAIN ASH LN
- CCCo 94582 674-A2
MOUNTAINGATE WY
2600 OAK 94611 650-F2
MOUNTAIN HOUSE PKWY
19500 SJCo 95304 (678-G1 See Page 677)
19500 SJCo 95391 (678-G1 See Page 677)
23700 SJCo 95377 (678-G7 See Page 677)
23700 SJCo 95377 (698-G1 See Page 677)
MOUNTAIN HOUSE RD
3200 AlaC 94551 (658-B4 See Page 637)
3200 AlaC 94551 (678-B1 See Page 677)
3200 CCCo 94514 (658-B4 See Page 637)
MOUNTAIN OAK CT
29600 HAY 94544 712-D7
MOUNTAINRISE PL
- DBLN 94568 693-D4
MOUNTAIN VALLEY
- OAK 94605 671-D2
MOUNTAIN VIEW AV
4100 OAK 94605 650-H7
MOUNTAIN VIEW DR
- PLE 94588 693-F5
MOUNTAIN VISTA PKWY
- LVMR 94551 696-F3
MOUNT DAY DR
5600 LVMR 94551 696-C3
MOUNT DIABLO CT
6000 AlaC 94552 692-E3
MOUNT DIABLO WY
1700 LVMR 94551 696-C3
MOUNT EDEN RD
25400 HAY 94545 711-E7
MOUNT GREYLOCK TER
- FRMT 94536 732-J4
MOUNT HAMILTON CT
5600 LVMR 94551 696-C3
6000 AlaC 94552 692-E3
MOUNT HOOD
4000 ALA 94501 649-E6
MOUNT HOOD WY
19000 AlaC 94552 692-E3
MOUNT JASPER DR
6000 AlaC 94552 692-F3
MOUNT LASSEN DR
18600 AlaC 94552 692-E3
MOUNT MCKINLEY CT
3900 PLE 94588 714-A1
MOUNT OLYMPUS DR
6000 AlaC 94552 692-E3
MOUNT PALOMAR CT
- FRMT 94536 752-E1
MOUNT RAINIER CT
3900 PLE 94588 714-A1
MOUNT RUSHMORE CIR
6000 AlaC 94552 692-E3
MOUNT SHASTA CT
6100 AlaC 94552 692-E3
MOUNT TAM CIR
5100 PLE 94588 693-J7
MOUNT VERNON AV
39000 FRMT 94538 753-A4
MOUNT VERNON PL
- DBLN 94568 694-H3
MOUNT WHITNEY ST
1100 LVMR 94551 696-D3
MOUNT WHITNEY TER
- FRMT 94536 732-H6
- FRMT 94587 732-H6
- UNC 94587 732-H6
MOURA CT
- HAY 94541 692-C7
MOWRY AV
1100 FRMT 94536 753-A5
1400 FRMT 94538 753-A5
4200 FRMT 94538 752-J6
4200 FRMT 94536 752-J6
5700 NWK 94560 752-J6
5900 NWK 94560 772-H1
MOWRY AV Rt#-84
- FRMT 94536 753-C2
MOWRY SCHOOL RD
5600 NWK 94560 772-J2
5600 NWK 94560 773-A1
MOYER PL
- OAK 94611 650-D1
MOYERS ST
22100 AlaC 94546 692-B6
MOZART ST
1500 ALA 94501 669-G1
MUELA DR
- SJCo 95391 (678-D5 See Page 677)
MUELLER CT
40100 FRMT 94538 753-C6
MUIR AV
- PDMT 94610 650-C2
MUIR ST
24800 HAY 94544 711-J3
25100 HAY 94544 712-A4
MUIR WY
- BERK 94708 609-J6
MUIRFIELD CT
700 HAY 94544 732-E1
MUIRFIELD TER
600 FRMT 94536 753-B2
MUIRWOOD CT
7400 PLE 94588 693-J7
MUIRWOOD DR
3600 PLE 94588 713-J1
3700 PLE 94588 714-A2
4500 PLE 94588 693-H7
32500 UNC 94587 732-A7
MULBERRY COM
- LVMR 94551 696-D1
MULBERRY CT
7000 DBLN 94568 693-H2
MULBERRY LN
- SJCo 95391 (678-E5 See Page 677)
MULBERRY PL
8100 DBLN 94568 693-H1
MULBERRY ST
1800 ALA 94501 670-A1
24700 HAY 94545 711-G5
36500 NWK 94560 752-D6
MULBERRY TER
34300 FRMT 94555 752-B3
MULLIN CT
300 PLE 94566 714-D6
MULQUEENEY COM
4700 LVMR 94550 696-B7
MULQUEENEY ST
200 LVMR 94550 696-B7
MULVANY CIR
- ALA 94501 649-E6
MUNOZ CT
- DBLN 94568 694-G3
MUNRAS PL
3200 SRMN 94583 673-G5
MUNSON WY
1400 OAK 94606 650-B7
MUNSTER AV
3600 HAY 94545 711-D5
MUNYAN ST
36600 NWK 94560 752-E5
MURCIA ST
- HAY 94544 731-J1
28400 HAY 94544 732-A1
MURDELL LN
- LVMR 94550 715-D1
MURDOCK CT
- HAY 94545 731-J2
- OAK 94605 670-G1
MURIETTA CT
11700 DBLN 94568 693-F3
MURIETTA TER
37600 FRMT 94536 752-A4
MURILLO AV
9300 OAK 94605 671-B3
MURINDO PL
300 SRMN 94583 673-A2
MURMANSK ST
1100 OAK 94626 649-B3
MURPHY CT
4800 FRMT 94538 753-A6
MURPHY PL
41700 FRMT 94539 753-G6
MURPHY ST
3500 LVMR 94551 695-J7
MURRAY COM
4000 FRMT 94538 753-B6
MURRAY DR
300 HAY 94544 712-B6
MURRAY ST
300 MPS 95035 794-A3
900 BERK 94710 629-E4
MURRIETA BLVD
1000 LVMR 94550 715-E1
1100 LVMR 94551 715-E1
1100 LVMR 94551 695-E6
MUSCARI ST
- SLN 94578 691-C4
MUSCAT CT
- FRMT 94539 773-J4
3300 PLE 94566 714-G4
MUSICK AV
5500 NWK 94560 752-E6
MUSK TER
34600 FRMT 94555 752-A3
MUSTANG DR
28300 HAY 94545 731-H2
MUTH DR
- ORIN 94563 610-J6
MY WY
- BERK 94708 609-H4
MYERS CT
200 SLN 94577 671-B6
MYERS ST
10600 OAK 94603 671-B6
MYRTLE DR
- DBLN 94568 694-D4
MYRTLE LN
- UNC 94587 732-G4
MYRTLE ST
100 OAK 94607 649-F3
2700 OAK 94608 649-F3
22500 HAY 94541 711-H2
MYRTLE WK
- ALA 94501 669-H3
MYSTIC ST
6300 OAK 94618 629-J4
MYSTIC VIEW CT
- HAY 94542 712-G4

N

N N ST
200 LVMR 94551 695-G7
S N ST
- LVMR 94550 715-G1
NABOR ST
400 SLN 94578 691-C4
NACE AV
- PDMT 94611 650-A1
NACE ST
- PDMT 94611 650-A1
NADINE CT
- DNVL 94526 652-H1
4800 UNC 94587 751-J1
4800 UNC 94587 752-A1
NADINE PL
- DNVL 94526 652-H1
NADINE ST
100 LVMR 94550 715-E1
NAGLE WY
4300 FRMT 94536 752-J5
NAIROBI PL
3800 OAK 94605 650-H7
3800 OAK 94605 670-H1
NAKAYAMA CT
- ALA 94502 669-H5
NAKOMA CT
1800 FRMT 94539 773-G4
NAMPEYO ST
48900 FRMT 94539 793-J2
NANCY CT
1000 HAY 94544 711-J6
32400 UNC 94587 731-J7
32400 UNC 94587 751-J1
32400 UNC 94587 752-A1
NANCY LN
- SRMN 94582 674-B3
NANCY PL
- FRMT 94555 732-C7
- FRMT 94555 752-C1
7200 NWK 94560 752-D6
NANCY ST
- FRMT 94555 752-C1
- LVMR 94550 715-D1
NANDINA CT
700 FRMT 94539 753-G7
NANDO CT
4200 AlaC 94546 692-A3
NANSA CT
43700 FRMT 94539 773-H1
NANTUCKET COM
34500 FRMT 94555 752-B2
NANTUCKET DR
10000 SRMN 94582 673-H5
NANTUCKET WY
300 ALA 94501 670-A4
NANTUCKY WY
29200 HAY 94544 732-B1
NAOMI DR
3200 AlaC 94541 692-D7
NAPA AV
1900 BERK 94707 609-G6
NAPA CT
1100 LVMR 94551 695-F6
1800 FRMT 94539 774-A4
NAPA ST
2100 RCH 94804 609-B4
6000 OAK 94618 629-J6
6000 OAK 94618 630-A6
NAPIER CT
200 PLE 94566 714-D6
NAPIER LN
- SF 94133 648-A4
NAPLES CT
1500 LVMR 94550 715-G3
NAPLES ST
2500 HAY 94545 711-G7
NAPLES TER
6000 FRMT 94555 752-A5
NAPLES WY
1400 LVMR 94550 715-G3
NAPOLEON CT
- SLN 94577 670-H7
NAPOLEON DR
- SLN 94577 670-J7
NARAGANSETT CT
44900 FRMT 94539 773-H3
NARCISSUS AV
6200 NWK 94560 752-G7
6200 NWK 94560 772-G1
NARCISSUS CT
900 SLN 94578 691-C4
NASA TER
36500 FRMT 94536 752-G3
NASH WY
5300 AlaC 94546 692-C3
NASON ST
1700 ALA 94501 649-G7
1700 ALA 94501 669-G1
NASRIN CT
300 HAY 94544 732-C1
NASSAU CT
100 SRMN 94582 673-G4
NASSAU LN
300 HAY 94544 732-D2
NASSAU RD
14300 SLN 94577 690-H5
NATALIE AV
4700 FRMT 94538 753-B7
NATALIE CT
18900 AlaC 94546 691-H3
NATHAN CT
3200 FRMT 94539 753-E7
NATIONAL AV
2200 HAY 94545 711-D4
NATIONAL DR
7500 LVMR 94551 696-E5
NATIONAL PARK RD
3200 PLE 94588 714-B1
NATOMA ST
- SF 94105 648-B6
400 SF 94103 648-A7
NATTRESS WY
400 OAK 94603 670-G7
NAUTILUS ST
1800 ALA 94501 669-H1
NAVAJO CT
- PLE 94588 694-G7
NAVAJO RD
47000 FRMT 94539 773-H6
NAVAJO WY
600 FRMT 94539 773-H6
NAVALLE CT
1100 PLE 94566 714-H4
NAVELLIER ST
1000 ELCR 94530 609-D1
NAVY ST
1300 SLN 94577 690-J2
NAVY WY
3000 ALA 94501 649-C6
NAYLOR AV
5800 LVMR 94551 696-C5
NEAD PL
- SRMN 94583 673-E6
NEAL CT
4400 PLE 94566 714-F4
NEAL PL
700 PLE 94566 714-F4
NEAL ST
- PLE 94566 714-E4
W NEAL ST
100 PLE 94566 714-E3
NEAL TER
3200 FRMT 94538 753-E6
NEBO DR
38300 FRMT 94536 753-D1

STREET Block City ZIP Pg-Grid

NEDRA WY
3500 AlaC 94546 691-J4
NEIL WY
900 HAY 94545 711-F4
NEIL ARMSTRONG WY
11100 OAK 94621 690-E2
NEILSON DR
- AlaC 94580 691-C7
NEILSON ST
500 BERK 94707 609-F5
900 ALB 94706 609-F5
1100 BERK 94706 609-E7
1300 BERK 94702 609-E7
1300 BERK 94702 629-E1
NELDA WY
5600 LVMR 94550 696-D7
NELLIE AV
- PDMT 94618 630-C7
NELSON CT
1000 PLE 94566 714-E5
NELSON PL
5300 NWK 94560 752-E4
NELSON ST
1700 SLN 94579 691-A7
4600 FRMT 94538 753-A7
NEON TER
- FRMT 94536 753-B2
NEPTUNE AV
100 HAY 94544 712-B7
NEPTUNE CT
- SRMN 94583 693-H1
NEPTUNE DR
1600 SLN 94577 690-F3
13800 SLN 94579 690-G6
NEPTUNE PL
100 SRMN 94583 693-H1
NEPTUNE RD
1900 LVMR 94550 715-E4
NEPTUNE GARDENS AV
- ALA 94501 649-E7
NERISSA CIR
4200 FRMT 94555 752-C1
NETTLES CT
3800 FRMT 94536 752-G2
NEVA CT
- OAK 94611 630-C5
NEVADA
4000 ALA 94501 649-E6
NEVADA CT
- PLE 94566 714-G3
NEVADA RD
22500 HAY 94541 711-F3
NEVADA ST
600 OAK 94603 670-G6
2400 UNC 94587 732-E6
3500 PLE 94566 714-F3
NEVE CT
- DBLN 94568 694-G4
NEVIL ST
3600 OAK 94601 650-E6
NEVIS ST
4000 PLE 94566 714-E2
NEWARK BLVD
34800 FRMT 94555 752-D5
34900 NWK 94560 752-D5
NEWBRIDGE WY
11800 DBLN 94568 693-G4
NEWBURY LN
600 HAY 94544 712-D7
NEWBURY ST
600 LVMR 94551 695-J6
600 LVMR 94551 696-A6
2900 BERK 94703 629-G4
NEWCASTLE CT
29000 HAY 94544 732-A2
35300 NWK 94560 752-D3
NEWCASTLE LN
7100 DBLN 94568 693-J2
NEWCOMB ST
- AlaC 94541 711-F1
NEW DOBBEL AV
26600 HAY 94542 712-D4
NEW ENGLAND VILLAGE DR
- HAY 94544 732-B1
NEWFIELDS LN
- DBLN 94568 694-F2
NEWGATE DR
- AlaC 94552 692-E7
NEWHALL ST
- HAY 94544 712-A5
200 HAY 94544 711-J5
NEWHALL WY
- LVMR 94550 716-D2
NEW HAMPSHIRE WY
29200 HAY 94544 732-B2
NEW HARBOR CT
- UNC 94545 731-J7
NEW HARBOR WY
- UNC 94545 731-J7
NEW HAVEN ST
3300 UNC 94587 732-A5
NEWHAVEN ST
- DBLN 94568 694-D4
NEWHAVEN WY
4500 AlaC 94546 692-C4
NEWMAN DR
4400 PLE 94588 694-E6
4400 PLE 94566 694-E6
NEW MONTGOMERY ST
- SF 94105 648-B5
NEWPARK MALL DR
5300 NWK 94560 752-H7
5500 NWK 94560 772-H1
NEWPORT AV
3000 SRMN 94583 673-F5
NEWPORT COM
3400 FRMT 94538 773-E2
NEWPORT CT
7000 DBLN 94568 693-J2
NEWPORT DR
42500 FRMT 94538 773-E2
NEWPORT RD
100 ALA 94501 649-D6
NEWPORT ST
26600 HAY 94545 711-F7
NEWRY PL
8400 DBLN 94568 693-H2
NEWTON AV
- OAK 94606 649-J4
NEWTON CT
34300 FRMT 94555 732-E7
NEWTON PL
34200 FRMT 94555 732-E7
NEWTON ST
100 HAY 94544 712-A5
NEWTON WY
3700 PLE 94588 694-F6
NEY AV
7200 OAK 94605 670-J2
8000 OAK 94605 671-A3

NEYDENE PL
3700 AlaC 94546 692-A5
NEZ PERCE CT
1000 FRMT 94539 773-J5
1000 FRMT 94539 774-A5
NIAGARA DR
1700 LVMR 94550 715-E3
NICE CT
1300 LVMR 94551 695-F6
NICE ST
5600 PLE 94588 694-C6
NICE TER
6000 FRMT 94555 752-A5
NICHANDROS ST
4000 AlaC 94546 692-A4
NICHOLAS AV
- SJCo 95391 (678-F3 See Page 677)
NICHOLAS CT
- SRMN 94582 673-J1
NICHOLS AV
36500 FRMT 94536 733-A7
NICHOLS TER
- FRMT 94536 733-B7
NICHOLSON ST
2500 SLN 94577 690-J4
NICKEL PL
25600 HAY 94545 711-D7
NICKEL ST
- UNC 94587 732-H6
NICKLAUS AV
1000 MPS 95035 794-B4
NICOL AV
2600 OAK 94602 650-C5
NICOL COM
4700 LVMR 94550 696-B7
NICOLE AV
- SJCo 95391 (678-F3 See Page 677)
3600 PLE 94588 694-F7
NICOLE PL
3700 AlaC 94546 692-A2
NICOLET AV
3400 FRMT 94536 752-F2
NICOLET CT
35900 FRMT 94536 752-F2
NICOSIA CT
1900 PLE 94566 715-B7
NIDER LN
700 ORIN 94563 610-J4
NIDO CT
42900 FRMT 94539 753-G6
NIDUS CT
2000 UNC 94587 732-F6
NIELSEN CT
43100 FRMT 94539 753-G7
NIELSEN LN
1000 LVMR 94550 716-A1
NIELSON AV
15800 AlaC 94580 691-C7
15800 AlaC 94580 711-C1
NIEVES CT
1200 MPS 95035 794-B4
NIEVES ST
800 MPS 95035 794-B4
NIGHTINGALE CT
34800 FRMT 94555 732-F7
NIGHTINGALE PL
3000 FRMT 94555 732-F7
NIGHTINGALE ST
500 LVMR 94551 695-E7
NIGHT SHADE LN
2300 FRMT 94539 773-G3
NILAND ST
- UNC 94555 752-A1
4600 UNC 94587 752-A1
NILES BLVD
- FRMT 94536 732-H7
33700 FRMT 94536 733-A7
35500 FRMT 94536 753-B1
NILES CANYON RD
4700 AlaC 94586 733-E6
NILES CANYON RD Rt#-84
100 FRMT 94536 733-G5
100 UNC 94587 733-G5
200 FRMT 94536 753-C1
500 AlaC 94586 733-G5
12000 AlaC 94586 734-A6
NIMITZ
4000 ALA 94501 649-F6
NIMITZ DR
- SF 94130 648-E3
NIMITZ FRWY I-880
- AlaC - 691-D6
- AlaC - 711-G5
- FRMT - 732-A2
- FRMT - 752-G5
- FRMT - 772-J1
- FRMT - 773-D4
- FRMT - 793-G2
- HAY - 711-G5
- HAY - 731-J1
- HAY - 732-A2
- MPS - 793-H4
- NWK - 752-G5
- NWK - 772-J1
- NWK - 773-D4
- OAK - 649-H5
- OAK - 650-A6
- OAK - 670-D3
- OAK - 690-H2
- SLN - 690-H2
- SLN - 691-A3
- UNC - 732-A2
NIMITZ WY
- CCCo 94553 610-A3
- CCCo 94708 609-J2
- CCCo 94708 610-A3
- RCH 94805 609-H1
NINA CT
1900 AlaC 94541 712-C2
NINA ST
2100 AlaC 94541 712-C2
NINA WY
800 FRMT 94539 753-G7
5600 LVMR 94550 696-D7
NISSEN DR
2300 LVMR 94551 695-B5
NOAH DR
32600 UNC 94587 732-C5
NOB PL
- SRMN 94583 673-E5
NOBEL DR
4100 FRMT 94538 773-B4
NOB HILL CIR
- SF 94108 648-A5
NOB HILL CT
28000 HAY 94542 712-E4
NOB HILL PL
- SF 94108 648-A5

NOBI LN
- ORIN 94563 630-J1
NOBLE AV
2500 ALA 94501 670-A2
NOBLE CT
1300 ELCR 94530 609-D2
NOBLES AL
- SF 94133 648-A4
NODAWAY AV
600 FRMT 94539 773-J7
NOEL AV
6200 NWK 94560 752-E6
NOEL PL
- FRMT 94536 732-J6
NOGALES ST
- BERK 94705 630-A4
NOLAN CT
- PLE 94588 714-F1
NOLAN TER
3800 FRMT 94538 753-D7
NOME ST
1800 SLN 94577 690-G3
NONIE RD
- ORIN 94563 630-J1
NORANTE CT
600 PLE 94566 715-D7
NORBRIDGE AV
2600 AlaC 94546 691-H6
3000 AlaC 94546 692-A6
NORDELL AV
2500 AlaC 94546 691-H5
NORDICA AV
5300 FRMT 94536 752-G6
NOREE CT
4700 AlaC 94546 692-C4
NORENE WY
1300 SLN 94577 671-C7
NORFOLK DR
6900 OAK 94705 630-C3
NORFOLK PL
11800 DBLN 94568 693-F2
NORFOLK RD
- ALA 94501 649-D7
900 LVMR 94551 695-E7
3500 FRMT 94538 773-E2
NORGREN ST
9700 OAK 94603 670-G7
NORIA CT
41200 FRMT 94539 753-G7
NORIA RD
42900 FRMT 94539 753-G7
43300 FRMT 94539 773-G1
NORMA WY
5100 LVMR 94550 716-C1
NORMAN CT
41200 FRMT 94539 753-E6
NORMAN LN
- OAK 94618 630-B6
3500 ALA 94502 670-A7
NORMANDIE AV
5300 OAK 94619 650-G7
5300 OAK 94619 670-G1
NORMANDY CIR
- LVMR 94550 715-H4
NORMANDY CT
- LVMR 94550 715-H3
20100 AlaC 94546 692-B5
NORMANDY DR
6300 NWK 94560 752-C5
NORMANDY LN
- ORIN 94563 610-F4
NORMANDY TER
- FRMT 94536 752-G4
NORMANDY WY
1700 LVMR 94550 715-H3
NOROCCO CIR
4500 FRMT 94555 752-C1
NORRIS CT
300 SRMN 94583 673-B2
4700 FRMT 94536 752-H5
NORRIS RD
4000 FRMT 94536 752-J4
NORRIS CANYON PL
100 SRMN 94583 673-E1
NORRIS CANYON RD
2000 CCCo 94583 672-G5
2000 CCCo 94583 673-A3
2000 SRMN 94583 673-D2
8700 AlaC 94552 672-G5
NORRIS CANYON TER
200 SRMN 94583 673-E1
NORTH BLVD
1800 SLN 94577 690-H1
NORTH CIR
- OAK 94611 630-G6
NORTH LN
- ORIN 94563 610-F6
1400 AlaC 94545 711-E4
1400 HAY 94545 711-E4
NORTH MALL
- OAK 94621 670-E4
NORTH ST
400 OAK 94609 629-H4
1500 BERK 94703 609-F7
NORTHAMPTON AV
- BERK 94707 609-G5
NORTHAMPTON CT
3200 PLE 94588 694-E6
5000 NWK 94560 752-E4
NORTH CANYON CT
- AlaC 94552 692-E6
NORTHDALE CIR
38700 FRMT 94536 752-J5
NORTHDALE DR
4500 FRMT 94536 752-H6
NORTHERN COM
38800 FRMT 94536 753-F3
NORTHFIELD DR
900 HAY 94544 732-B1
NORTHFRONT RD
5800 LVMR 94551 696-C4
6800 LVMR 94551 696-D4
NORTHGATE AV
- BERK 94708 609-J6
2200 OAK 94612 649-G2
NORTH GATE RD
- SF 94130 648-F2
NORTH HILL CT
- SRMN 94583 673-A1
NORTHLAND AV
7400 SRMN 94583 693-G1
7400 SRMN 94583 673-G7
NORTHLAND PL
7500 SRMN 94583 673-F7
7500 SRMN 94583 693-F1
NORTHLAND TER
5800 FRMT 94555 752-B4
NORTH LOOP RD
2100 ALA 94502 669-J7
2100 ALA 94502 670-A7
2100 ALA 94502 690-A1

NORTH POINT ST
- SF 94133 648-A3
NORTHPOINTE CT
- AlaC 94541 712-B1
NORTHPORT CT
45100 FRMT 94538 773-E5
NORTHPORT LP E
45600 FRMT 94538 773-E5
NORTHPORT LP W
45300 FRMT 94538 773-D6
NORTHSIDE AV
1300 BERK 94702 609-E7
1300 BERK 94702 629-E1
NORTH STAR RD
- ALA 94501 649-J6
NORTHSTAR TER
34500 FRMT 94555 752-C3
NORTHUMBERLAND TER
3700 FRMT 94555 732-D7
3700 FRMT 94555 752-D1
NORTHVALE RD
800 OAK 94610 650-B3
NORTHVIEW DR
22500 AlaC 94541 692-C6
NORTHWAY RD
5100 PLE 94566 714-C1
NORTHWIND TER
34200 FRMT 94555 752-C2
NORTHWOOD COM
100 LVMR 94551 715-E1
NORTHWOOD CT
- ORIN 94563 630-F6
1700 OAK 94611 630-F6
3800 PLE 94588 713-J2
NORTHWOOD DR
- ORIN 94563 630-H1
- ORIN 94563 610-H7
2900 ALA 94501 670-B2
3400 AlaC 94546 691-H3
NORTON AV
3200 OAK 94602 650-F4
NORTON ST
14900 SLN 94579 691-B6
NORTON WY
3300 PLE 94566 714-G4
NORVELL CT
1100 ELCR 94530 609-D2
NORVELL ST
400 ELCR 94530 609-C1
NORWALK ST
4600 UNC 94587 752-A1
NORWICH AV
200 MPS 95035 793-J7
NORWICH CT
- SRMN 94583 673-G7
NORWICH PL
4900 NWK 94560 752-E3
NORWICH RD
100 ALA 94502 670-A5
NORWICH WY
27800 HAY 94545 731-J1
NORWOOD AV
- CCCo 94707 609-F3
1000 OAK 94602 650-C3
1000 OAK 94610 650-C3
NORWOOD CT
100 CCCo 94707 609-F3
NORWOOD DR
22500 HAY 94541 692-B7
NORWOOD PL
- CCCo 94707 609-F3
1200 LVMR 94550 715-F5
NORWOOD RD
2200 LVMR 94550 715-F5
NORWOOD TER
4600 FRMT 94538 773-C1
NORWOOD VW
- CCCo 94707 609-F3
NOTRE DAME AV
1600 EPA 94303 771-B7
NOTRE DAME CT
1200 LVMR 94550 716-A2
NOTTINGHAM CT
- ALA 94502 669-J5
5000 NWK 94560 752-E4
NOTTINGHAM DR
100 ALA 94502 669-J5
5700 OAK 94611 630-D6
NOTTINGHAM PL
- SF 94133 648-A4
6500 DBLN 94568 694-A2
NOTTINGHAM RD
28900 HAY 94544 732-A1
NOVA CT
4200 PLE 94588 714-A1
NOVA DR
- PDMT 94610 650-A2
NOVA PTH
- OAK 94618 630-B5
NOVA TER
34900 FRMT 94555 752-D2
NOVARA ST
- LVMR 94550 715-F5
NOVARA WY
3200 PLE 94566 715-B6
NOVATO ST
- UNC 94555 752-B1
4600 UNC 94587 752-B1
NOVELDA DR
10900 OAK 94603 670-H7
NOYO ST
3300 OAK 94602 650-G4
NUGGET PL
- FRMT 94539 773-H5
NUGGET WY
- FRMT 94539 773-H5
NUGGET CANYON RD
21900 AlaC 94552 692-C5
NULA WY
22600 AlaC 94541 692-C6
NUNES AV
20800 AlaC 94546 691-J5
NUNES CT
40900 FRMT 94539 753-E6
NUNES LN
- FRMT 94536 753-A2
NUNN ST
5000 RCH 94804 609-B1
NURSERY AV
- FRMT 94536 733-A6
NURSERY WY
1700 PLE 94588 714-F1
NUTMEG CT
36800 NWK 94560 752-C7
NUTTMAN LN
35600 FRMT 94536 752-G1
NUTWOOD TER
3600 FRMT 94536 752-A6
NYLA ST
- CCCo 94514 637-D2
NYLANDER TER
34400 FRMT 94555 752-D2

O

N O ST
300 LVMR 94551 695-F7
S O ST
- LVMR 94550 715-G1
OAHU CIR
200 UNC 94587 732-C6
OAHU CT
400 SRMN 94582 673-E1
OAK CIR
600 PLE 94566 714-E4
OAK CT
200 ORIN 94563 630-H2
6700 DBLN 94568 693-J3
OAK DR
- ORIN 94563 630-J3
OAK LN
- ORIN 94563 610-H4
300 AlaC 94566 714-C7
OAK RD
- ORIN 94563 630-H1
100 PDMT 94610 650-B2
OAK ST
- OAK 94607 649-G5
500 ELCR 94530 609-D4
800 ALA 94501 669-J3
1000 ALA 94501 670-A2
1200 OAK 94612 649-G5
2000 LVMR 94551 695-G7
2300 BERK 94708 609-H6
20800 AlaC 94546 691-H6
20800 HAY 94546 691-H6
20800 AlaC 94541 691-H6
20800 HAY 94541 691-H6
36500 FRMT 94536 752-G3
37100 NWK 94560 752-D7
37100 NWK 94560 772-E1
OAK ARBOR RD
- ORIN 94563 610-G5
OAK BLUFF LN
- DBLN 94568 694-F2
OAK BROOK CT
3700 PLE 94588 694-F5
OAKBROOK RD
- HAY 94544 732-D1
OAK CANYON PL
17400 AlaC 94546 691-J2
OAK CREEK CT
7700 PLE 94588 713-J1
OAK CREEK DR
2800 SRMN 94583 673-F7
7700 PLE 94588 713-J1
OAK CREEK LN
- AlaC 94541 712-C1
OAK CREEK PL
2000 AlaC 94541 712-C1
OAK CREEK TER
- FRMT 94539 753-G6
OAK CREEK WY
- EMVL 94608 629-F6
- OAK 94608 629-F6
OAKCREST DR
- AlaC 94552 692-E6
1900 OAK 94602 650-E2
OAKDALE AV
3800 OAK 94605 670-H1
3900 OAK 94605 650-H7
OAKDALE CT
5100 PLE 94588 693-J7
32800 UNC 94587 752-B1
OAKDALE ST
4500 UNC 94587 732-B7
4500 UNC 94587 752-A1
OAKES BLVD
- SLN 94577 671-A7
OAKES DR
2400 HAY 94542 712-C2
3800 AlaC 94542 712-D3
OAK FLAT RD
- ORIN 94563 610-J5
OAK GROVE AV
5600 OAK 94618 629-J5
OAK GROVE ST
- SF 94107 648-A7
OAKHAM CT
200 SRMN 94583 673-E5
OAKHAM DR
3000 SRMN 94583 673-E5
OAK HILL CIR
- OAK 94605 671-C3
OAK HILL RD
3900 OAK 94605 671-C2
OAKHILL WY
31000 HAY 94544 732-E2
OAK HOLLOW TER
- FRMT 94536 752-A5
OAKHURST CT
- DBLN 94568 694-F2
OAKHURST WY
- DBLN 94568 694-F3
- MPS 95035 794-A6
OAK KNOLL BLVD
3300 OAK 94605 671-B4
OAK KNOLL LN
- ORIN 94563 630-H2
OAK KNOLL PTH
2800 BERK 94705 630-A3
OAK KNOLL TER
2700 BERK 94705 630-A3
OAKLAND AV
100 OAK 94610 649-H2
400 OAK 94611 649-H2
700 OAK 94610 650-A1
700 PDMT 94611 650-A1
700 OAK 94611 650-A1
1000 PDMT 94610 650-A1
1500 PLE 94588 694-E7
OAK MANOR CT
- AlaC 94566 714-B6
4000 HAY 94542 712-F3
OAK MANOR WY
- AlaC 94566 714-B6
OAKMONT AV
- PDMT 94610 650-B2
- PDMT 94611 650-B2
OAKMONT CIR
5500 LVMR 94551 696-C2
OAKMONT WY
30400 HAY 94544 732-D1
OAKMORE PL
1700 OAK 94602 650-D3
OAKMORE RD
3900 OAK 94602 650-D3
OAK PARK DR
100 ALA 94502 670-A5
OAK POINTE CT
4000 HAY 94542 712-F2
OAKPORT ST
4800 OAK 94601 670-D2
4800 OAK 94621 670-E4

OAKRIDGE CT
25000 HAY 94541 712-C2
OAKRIDGE DR
1000 FRMT 94539 773-H2
OAK RIDGE RD
- AlaC 94586 (775-D5 See Page 755)
- SCIC 95140 (775-G7 See Page 755)
- BERK 94705 630-A4
OAKS BRIDGE PL
- PLE 94566 714-C5
OAKSHADE DR
- ALA 94502 670-B5
OAKSHIRE PL
17300 AlaC 94546 692-A2
OAKTREE CT
2700 UNC 94587 752-G1
OAK TREE FARM DR
- PLE 94566 734-D1
- PLE 94586 734-D1
OAKVALE AV
- BERK 94705 630-A4
OAK VALLEY DR
- SRMN 94582 673-J6
- SRMN 94582 674-A6
OAK VIEW AV
1500 CCCo 94706 609-F4
- CCCo 94707 609-F4
OAKVIEW AV
1100 HAY 94541 691-H7
OAKVIEW CT
5100 PLE 94566 714-D2
OAKVIEW DR
1900 OAK 94602 650-E3
OAK VIEW TER
- ORIN 94563 630-J1
100 DNVL 94526 652-G2
OAKVILLE LN
- LVMR 94550 716-D2
OAK VISTA WY
- PLE 94566 714-C4
OAKWOOD CT
- OAK 94611 630-F6
900 HAY 94541 711-F3
OAKWOOD DR
1200 AlaC 94586 734-B3
6400 OAK 94611 630-F6
OAKWOOD RD
- ORIN 94563 630-J2
OAKWOOD TER
3500 FRMT 94536 752-A6
OASIS CT
1100 FRMT 94539 773-G4
OBERLIN AV
600 CCCo 94708 609-F3
1200 SLN 94579 691-A5
OBISPO CT
100 FRMT 94539 753-E3
11500 DBLN 94568 693-F3
OBRIEN CT
- SJCo 95391 (678-F2 See Page 677)
OBRIEN DR
900 MLPK 94025 771-A7
1400 EPA 94303 771-B7
OBRIEN TER
- FRMT 94538 753-C6
OBSERVATION PL
- OAK 94611 630-E5
OBSERVATORY AV
- OAK 94619 650-H6
OBSIDIAN WY
- LVMR 94550 715-C3
OCALA ST
2500 HAY 94545 711-G7
2700 HAY 94545 731-G1
OCASO CTE
43500 FRMT 94539 773-G1
OCASO CAMINO
1000 FRMT 94539 773-F1
OCCIDENTAL RD
2100 HAY 94545 711-F6
2100 AlaC 94545 711-E6
OCCIDENTAL ST
5800 OAK 94608 629-G5
OCEAN AV
1100 OAK 94608 629-E5
1200 EMVL 94608 629-E5
OCEAN BREEZE TER
- FRMT 94536 753-C2
OCEAN HILLS WY
5900 LVMR 94551 696-C2
OCEANSIDE WY
- SLN 94579 691-A7
- SLN 94579 711-A1
OCEAN VIEW AV
300 CCCo 94707 609-E4
OCEAN VIEW DR
5600 OAK 94618 629-J5
5600 OAK 94618 630-A5
20900 AlaC 94541 691-H7
OCIE WY
300 HAY 94541 711-G3
OCONNELL CT
34300 FRMT 94555 752-C4
OCONNELL LN
1100 UNC 94587 733-A4
1100 UNC 94587 732-H5
OCOTILLO CT
46900 FRMT 94539 773-J6
OCTAVIA ST
2700 OAK 94619 650-E6
ODELL CT
4500 FRMT 94536 752-J5
ODOM RD
23300 HAY 94541 711-F4
ODONNELL AV
700 SLN 94577 690-H1
ODYSSEY WY
- DBLN 94568 693-G4
OFARRELL ST
- SF 94108 648-A6
200 SF 94102 648-A6
OGDEN CT
- MPS 95035 793-J7
OGDEN DR
4800 FRMT 94538 753-B6
OGILVIE DR
18300 AlaC 94546 691-J3
OHANA PL
- PLE 94566 714-D6
OHANNESON RD
4900 OAK 94605 651-A7
OHARRON DR
300 HAY 94544 712-B6
OHIO
4000 ALA 94501 649-E6
OHIO CT
100 MPS 95035 793-J7
OHLONE AV
- ALB 94710 609-D6

OHLONE AV
900 ALB 94706 609-D6
OHLONE ST
- ALA 94501 649-H7
- ALA 94501 669-H1
OHLONE TR
- CCCo 94583 652-D1
OHLONE WY
- EMVL 94608 629-E6
3200 AlaC 94541 692-D7
OHLONES ST
300 FRMT 94539 753-H7
OHNA CT
4100 FRMT 94536 752-G3
OJAI LP
4500 UNC 94587 732-B7
4500 UNC 94587 752-B1
OJIBWA CT
2000 FRMT 94539 773-G3
OLAZABA TER
43800 FRMT 94539 773-H1
OLD 1ST ST
2500 LVMR 94550 695-H7
2500 LVMR 94551 695-H7
OLD ALAMEDA PT
1100 ALA 94502 670-A7
OLD BERNAL AV
100 PLE 94566 714-D4
OLD CALAVERAS RD
1900 MPS 95035 794-E4
1900 SCIC 95035 794-D5
OLD CANYON RD
300 FRMT 94536 753-C1
300 FRMT 94536 733-D7
OLDCASTLE LN
100 ALA 94502 669-H5
OLD CHINATOWN LN
- SF 94108 648-A5
OLD CROW CANYON RD
2300 SRMN 94583 673-B1
OLD DUBLIN RD
4700 AlaC 94552 692-D5
OLD EARHART RD
8700 OAK 94621 670-C6
OLD EVANS RD
400 MPS 95035 794-D5
OLD FAIRVIEW AV
- AlaC 94542 712-E1
OLD FOOTHILL RD
3200 PLE 94588 714-A3
3600 PLE 94588 713-J3
OLD GLORY CT
- FRMT 94539 773-H1
OLDHAM PL
35100 NWK 94560 752-E3
OLD MILL RD
- SRMN 94583 673-B1
OLD OAK PL
- LVMR 94550 715-E4
OLD OAK RD
- LVMR 94550 715-D4
OLD RANCH CT
400 SRMN 94582 673-H6
OLD RANCH RD
3400 SRMN 94582 673-J7
3400 SRMN 94583 673-J7
3400 SRMN 94582 674-A6
OLD RANCH TR
- UNC 94587 712-G7
- UNC 94587 732-G1
OLD RANCH ESTATES DR
1500 SRMN 94582 673-J6
OLD REDWOOD HWY
- CCCo 94516 630-J7
OLD REDWOOD RD
5200 OAK 94619 650-J5
OLD SAN PABLO DAM RD
- CCCo 94553 609-J1
- CCCo 94553 610-A2
- CCCo 94563 610-C4
OLD SANTA RITA RD
3500 PLE 94588 694-D6
OLD TOWER RD
1700 LVMR 94550 715-G2
OLD TOWN LN
- DNVL 94526 652-J1
OLD TUNNEL RD
- CCCo 94563 630-E3
2500 OAK 94611 630-D4
OLD VINEYARD AV
1200 PLE 94566 714-J3
1200 PLE 94566 715-A4
OLD WARM SPRINGS BLVD
44000 FRMT 94538 773-E3
OLD WESTBURY WY
- DBLN 94568 694-H2
OLEAN ST
31900 HAY 94544 732-E3
OLEANDER
- FRMT 94536 753-D1
OLEANDER AV
300 ALA 94502 670-A7
OLEANDER COM
5700 FRMT 94555 752-B3
OLEANDER CT
3900 AlaC 94546 691-H2
OLEANDER DR
5700 NWK 94560 752-H7
OLEANDER ST
4200 LVMR 94551 696-A4
14800 SLN 94578 691-C4
OLEASTER DR
- SRMN 94582 674-A2
OLGA ST
- FRMT 94555 732-C7
OLIVE AV
- PDMT 94611 649-J1
- PDMT 94611 650-A1
300 FRMT 94539 753-E7
OLIVE COM
400 FRMT 94539 753-H7
OLIVE CT
500 SLN 94578 691-D5
4600 RCH 94804 609-A2
7800 PLE 94588 713-J1
42400 FRMT 94539 753-G7
OLIVE DR
7700 PLE 94588 713-J1
OLIVE LN
- SRMN 94583 693-H1
OLIVE PL
22700 HAY 94541 692-B7
OLIVE ST
400 SLN 94578 691-C5
7800 OAK 94605 670-H3
7800 OAK 94621 670-H3
9000 OAK 94603 670-J4
9600 OAK 94603 671-A5
36500 NWK 94560 752-D6

STREET Block City ZIP Pg-Grid

OLIVER AV
2500 OAK 94605 671-A5
OLIVER DR
2400 HAY 94545 731-G1
2500 HAY 94545 711-G7
OLIVER ST
300 MPS 95035 794-A3
OLIVER WY
- UNC 94587 731-J5
38500 FRMT 94536 753-D1
OLIVERIA PL
2100 FRMT 94539 773-G3
OLIVIA CT
2000 PLE 94588 694-E7
OLIVIA ST
- SLN 94578 691-C4
OLIVINA AV
200 LVMR 94551 715-D1
1500 LVMR 94551 695-G7
OLIVINA RD
- AlaC 94550 715-G7
- AlaC 94550 735-G1
OLIVINA RANCH RD
- AlaC 94550 735-H1
OLIVOS CT
- FRMT 94539 753-J7
OLNEY CT
32200 UNC 94587 732-C5
OLSEN WY
- UNC 94587 732-H7
OLSON CT
9100 PLE 94588 693-G6
OLYMPIAD CT
- UNC 94587 732-D5
OLYMPIA FIELDS CT
- SRMN 94583 673-H7
OLYMPIA FIELDS DR
9400 SRMN 94583 673-H7
OLYMPIC AV
100 HAY 94544 732-C1
OLYMPIC CT
8000 NWK 94560 752-C7
OLYMPIC CT N
3600 PLE 94588 714-A1
OLYMPIC CT S
3500 PLE 94588 714-A1
OLYMPIC WY
100 LVMR 94551 695-D7
OLYMPUS AV
1400 BERK 94708 609-J7
1500 BERK 94708 610-A7
1500 BERK 94720 610-A7
41700 FRMT 94539 753-F6
OMAHA WY
800 FRMT 94539 773-J6
OMAK ST
45200 FRMT 94539 773-H4
OMAR ST
4800 FRMT 94538 773-B1
OMEGA AV
4100 AlaC 94546 692-B5
OMEGA CIR
3200 PLE 94588 694-D7
OMEGA DR
45900 FRMT 94539 773-H5
OMEGA RD
2100 SRMN 94583 673-C1
ONA CT
- SRMN 94583 673-F6
ONATE CT
- DBLN 94568 694-G3
ONDINA CT
40800 FRMT 94539 753-F5
ONDINA DR
- FRMT 94539 753-F5
ONDINA PL
40700 FRMT 94539 753-F4
ONEIL AV
24500 HAY 94544 712-A3
ONEIL TER
34100 FRMT 94555 752-C2
ONONDAGA CT
1300 FRMT 94539 773-G4
ONONDAGA DR
45100 FRMT 94539 773-G4
ONONDAGA PL
1400 FRMT 94539 773-G4
ONONDAGA WY
1100 FRMT 94539 773-G4
ONSLOW COM
38100 FRMT 94536 752-J1
ONTARIO COM
5300 FRMT 94555 752-C3
ONTARIO DR
300 LVMR 94550 715-D3
ONTARIO PL
200 HAY 94544 732-F3
ONTARIO RD
200 MPS 95035 794-A6
ONYX CT
20000 AlaC 94546 692-B5
ONYX PL
6700 DBLN 94568 693-J2
ONYX RD
1000 LVMR 94550 715-D3
OPAH WY
4300 UNC 94587 731-J5
OPAL CT
- SRMN 94582 673-F2
20000 AlaC 94546 692-B5
44200 FRMT 94539 773-H2
OPAL PL
- SF 94102 648-A6
OPAL ST
3800 OAK 94609 629-H7
3800 OAK 94609 649-H1
OPAL WY
200 LVMR 94550 715-D3
OPERATIONS RD
100 FRMT 94539 773-J1
OPHIR CT
100 MPS 95035 793-J7
OPTIMIST ST
22800 HAY 94541 711-H2
OPTIMO AV
600 FRMT 94539 753-E5
ORA AV
1000 LVMR 94551 695-F7
ORANDA TER
1000 FRMT 94536 753-C3
ORANGE AV
21200 AlaC 94546 691-J7
22100 AlaC 94546 692-A7
ORANGE ST
200 OAK 94610 649-H2
ORANGE WY
600 LVMR 94550 715-E3
ORANGETREE PL
- HAY 94544 712-C5
ORANGEWOOD CT
4700 PLE 94588 713-J1

ORANGEWOOD DR
500 FRMT 94536 753-D1
ORCA TER
1000 FRMT 94536 753-C3
ORCHARD AV
200 HAY 94544 711-J4
500 HAY 94544 712-A3
1200 SLN 94577 690-J1
1700 SLN 94577 691-A2
5900 RCH 94804 609-C3
ORCHARD CT
- ORIN 94563 630-J3
ORCHARD DR
100 FRMT 94536 753-D1
ORCHARD LN
- BERK 94704 630-A2
ORCHARD RD
- ORIN 94563 630-J2
ORCHARD WY
1600 PLE 94566 714-D2
1700 LVMR 94550 715-E3
ORCHARD MEADOW RD
3400 OAK 94613 650-G7
ORCHARD PARK PL
- HAY 94544 712-A6
ORCHID CT
- LVMR 94551 696-C3
ORCHID DR
14200 SLN 94578 691-C3
ORCHID ST
1100 LVMR 94551 696-C3
3300 OAK 94601 650-C6
ORDAZ CT
- DBLN 94568 694-G5
ORDEN CT
100 FRMT 94539 753-E3
ORDWAY ST
900 ALB 94707 609-F6
900 ALB 94706 609-F6
1100 BERK 94706 609-F6
1300 BERK 94702 609-E7
1400 BERK 94702 629-E1
OREGANO CT
2700 PLE 94588 694-H4
OREGON CT
900 MPS 95035 794-A5
OREGON ST
1100 BERK 94702 629-E4
1500 BERK 94703 629-F3
2000 BERK 94705 629-H3
2400 UNC 94587 732-E6
OREGON WY
1000 MPS 95035 794-A5
3500 LVMR 94550 715-J1
ORICK ST
32700 UNC 94587 732-B7
ORIN DR
2400 OAK 94612 649-H2
ORINDA CT
5500 LVMR 94551 696-C2
ORINDA WY
- ORIN 94563 610-G7
ORINDA VIEW RD
- ORIN 94563 610-J3
ORINDA VISTA DR
- OAK 94605 671-C3
ORINDAWOODS DR
100 ORIN 94563 610-H7
ORIOLE AV
400 LVMR 94551 695-E7
400 LVMR 94551 715-E1
1400 AlaC 94578 691-E4
ORIOLE PL
3400 FRMT 94555 732-D7
ORIOLE RD
- ORIN 94563 610-F5
ORION CT
- SLN 94579 690-J6
100 MPS 95035 793-J7
2100 LVMR 94550 715-E4
3800 PLE 94566 714-F4
ORION RD
- SLN 94579 690-J6
ORION ST
- ALA 94501 649-D7
- ALA 94501 669-D1
22600 AlaC 94541 692-C6
ORION WY
600 LVMR 94550 715-E4
W ORISKANY AV
- ALA 94501 669-D1
ORKNEY CT
5100 NWK 94560 752-E4
ORLANDO AV
27400 HAY 94545 711-H7
27700 HAY 94545 731-J1
ORLEANS DR
35400 NWK 94560 752-C5
ORLOFF DR
1200 PLE 94566 714-F1
ORMINDALE CT
- OAK 94611 630-E5
ORMOND AV
27700 HAY 94544 712-A7
27900 HAY 94544 732-A1
ORO DR
1600 FRMT 94539 753-E5
OROFINO CT
600 PLE 94566 714-H3
OROVILLE CT
4000 FRMT 94555 752-D1
OROVILLE RD
400 MPS 95035 794-A6
ORR CT
- ALA 94502 669-J6
ORR RD
- ALA 94502 669-J6
ORRAL ST
7000 OAK 94621 670-G3
ORSINI CT
5100 PLE 94588 694-H4
ORTEGA AV
1500 HAY 94544 732-A1
ORVIETO CT
- LVMR 94550 715-E5
1600 PLE 94566 715-B5
ORWELL PL
3100 FRMT 94536 752-G2
ORYAN ST
- DBLN 94568 694-E4
OSAGE AV
1800 HAY 94545 731-J2
OSAGE CT
1700 HAY 94545 731-J2
1700 HAY 94545 732-A2
OSAGE RIVER CT
34600 FRMT 94555 752-E1
OSAGE RIVER PL
34700 FRMT 94555 752-E1
OSBORNE CT
- OAK 94611 650-G2

OSCAR AL
- SF 94105 648-B6
OSCAR AV
9300 OAK 94603 670-G6
OSCAR CT
4800 FRMT 94538 753-B7
4800 FRMT 94538 773-B1
OSCAR ST
1500 RCH 94804 609-B3
OSGOOD COM
- FRMT 94539 773-E1
OSGOOD CT
3000 FRMT 94539 773-F2
OSGOOD PL
- SF 94133 648-A4
OSGOOD RD
41500 FRMT 94539 753-E7
41500 FRMT 94539 773-E1
OSLO CT
1500 LVMR 94550 715-G3
OSO EXRD
- StCo 95360 (780-B2 See Page 759)
OSPREY CT
- CCCo 94514 (657-E2 See Page 637)
OSPREY DR
2200 UNC 94587 732-G7
OSPREY TER
- FRMT 94555 732-D3
OSTRANDER RD
5900 OAK 94618 630-B6
OSTRICH FEATHER LN
- AlaC 94566 714-D7
OSWOSSO PL
100 HAY 94544 732-F3
OTHELLO DR
4200 FRMT 94555 752-C1
OTHELLO RD
33500 FRMT 94555 752-C1
OTIS DR
900 ALA 94501 669-G2
2500 ALA 94501 670-A3
OTIS DR Rt#-61
- ALA 94502 670-A3
2600 ALA 94501 670-A3
OTIS ST
2900 BERK 94703 629-G4
OTTAWA AV
1200 SLN 94579 691-A4
OTTAWA WY
100 FRMT 94539 793-J2
OTTER CT
3300 HAY 94542 712-E4
OUTLOOK AV
5900 OAK 94605 650-H7
6100 OAK 94605 670-H1
7700 OAK 94605 671-A3
OUTLOOK CT
21300 AlaC 94546 691-J6
OUTRIGGER DR
14400 SLN 94577 690-G5
OVAL RD
- OAK 94611 630-C5
OVELLA WY
3500 PLE 94566 715-B7
OVER ST
3300 OAK 94619 650-E6
OVERACKER AV
38500 FRMT 94536 753-D2
38900 FRMT 94538 753-D2
OVERACKER TER
100 FRMT 94536 753-C2
OVERDALE AV
6100 OAK 94605 650-H7
OVEREND AV
4100 RCH 94804 609-A1
OVERHILL CT
- ORIN 94563 630-H1
OVERHILL DR
600 HAY 94544 712-D6
OVERHILL RD
- ORIN 94563 630-H1
OVERLAKE AV
5900 LVMR 94551 696-D2
OVERLAKE CT
- OAK 94611 630-E6
OVERLAKE PL
6500 NWK 94560 752-B5
OVERLAND AV
6200 EMVL 94608 629-E5
S OVERLOOK
200 SRMN 94582 673-F3
OVERLOOK AV
1100 HAY 94542 712-A3
OVERLOOK CT
- SLN 94579 690-J7
- SLN 94579 691-F2
1100 SRMN 94582 673-F2
OVERLOOK DR
1000 SRMN 94582 673-E2
OVERLOOK RD
900 BERK 94708 609-J5
OVERLOOK TER
44700 FRMT 94539 773-J2
OVERMOOR ST
11000 OAK 94605 671-D5
OWEN COM
3300 FRMT 94536 752-J4
3300 FRMT 94536 753-A3
OWENS CT
5300 PLE 94588 694-B5
OWENS DR
5000 PLE 94588 694-A5
OWHANEE CT
700 FRMT 94539 773-J4
700 FRMT 94539 774-A4
OWL CT
- DBLN 94568 694-D4
100 FRMT 94539 773-J2
OWL DR
44000 FRMT 94539 773-J1
OWL PL
44100 FRMT 94539 773-J2
OWL WY
- LVMR 94551 696-D3
OWL HILL CT
- ORIN 94563 630-J2
OWL HILL RD
- ORIN 94563 630-J2
OXBOW CT
7900 DBLN 94568 693-G4
OXBOW LN
7800 DBLN 94568 693-G4
OXFORD CIR
7400 DBLN 94568 694-A2
OXFORD COM
3600 FRMT 94536 752-J4
OXFORD DR
100 MRGA 94556 651-E2
OXFORD LN
- BERK 94704 629-H2

OXFORD PL
1400 LVMR 94550 715-G5
4900 NWK 94560 752-E4
6500 DBLN 94568 694-A2
OXFORD ST
300 AlaC 94541 711-E1
800 BERK 94707 609-G5
1200 BERK 94709 609-H7
1600 BERK 94709 629-H1
1900 BERK 94720 629-H1
1900 BERK 94704 629-H1
OXFORD WY
- UNC 94587 731-J5
OXSEN ST
1500 PLE 94566 714-E1
OYSTER CT
3500 UNC 94587 732-A4
OYSTER BAY TER
34800 FRMT 94555 752-E1
OYSTER POND RD
- ALA 94502 670-A5
OYSTER SHOALS
- ALA 94502 670-A6
OZARK RIVER WY
34800 FRMT 94555 752-E2

P

N P ST
- LVMR 94550 715-G1
200 LVMR 94551 715-G1
300 LVMR 94551 695-F7
S P ST
200 LVMR 94550 715-G1
PACHECO DR
800 MPS 95035 794-B6
33700 FRMT 94555 732-D7
PACHECO WY
1400 HAY 94544 732-A2
PACIFIC AV
- PDMT 94611 650-B1
100 ALA 94501 649-E7
400 ALA 94501 669-G1
1200 SLN 94577 690-J1
1300 SJS 95002 793-C7
1900 SLN 94577 691-A2
2000 SF 94111 648-A4
2100 ALA 94501 670-A2
2100 SF 94133 648-A4
2900 LVMR 94550 715-J2
W PACIFIC AV
- ALA 94501 649-D7
PACIFIC ST
1100 UNC 94587 732-E5
28200 HAY 94544 712-B7
29400 HAY 94544 732-C1
40200 FRMT 94538 753-C6
PACIFICA CT
- SLN 94579 711-A1
PACIFICA WY
200 MPS 95035 793-J4
PACIFIC COMMONS BLVD
- FRMT 94538 773-C4
PACIFIC GROVE CT
- UNC 94545 731-J7
PACIFIC GROVE WY
- UNC 94545 731-J7
PACIFIC TERRACE CT
- AlaC 94552 692-E7
PACIFIC VIEW CT
- SLN 94579 690-J7
- SLN 94579 691-F2
PACKARD CT
44100 FRMT 94539 773-J2
PACKARD ST
- OAK 94603 671-C5
PACKET LNDG
200 ALA 94502 670-A5
PACU TER
- FRMT 94536 753-C2
PADDOCK DR
2400 SRMN 94583 673-B3
PADDOCK LN
- SRMN 94583 673-B4
PADRE AV
1300 SLN 94579 691-A6
PADRE WY
11600 DBLN 94568 693-F3
PADUA WY
- LVMR 94550 715-E5
PAGANO CT
400 SLN 94578 691-C5
PAGE AV
- FRMT 94538 793-G2
PAGE CT
4000 PLE 94588 694-A7
PAGE ST
700 BERK 94710 629-D1
1100 BERK 94702 629-D1
1100 BERK 94702 609-E7
1400 ALA 94501 669-F1
2500 AlaC 94578 691-G4
PAGODA PL
- SF 94108 648-A5
PAGOSA CT
48900 FRMT 94539 793-J2
PAGOSA WY
- FRMT 94539 793-J3
300 FRMT 94539 794-A2
PAICH CT
2500 FRMT 94539 753-F7
PAINE CT
3000 FRMT 94555 732-F7
PAINTBRUSH PZ
28600 HAY 94542 712-B3
PAIUTE CT
44300 FRMT 94539 773-G3
PAJARO CT
1400 AlaC 94578 691-F5
1600 FRMT 94539 753-E6
PAJARO DR
40900 FRMT 94539 753-E5
PALA AV
- PDMT 94611 630-B7
- PDMT 94611 650-B1
500 SLN 94577 671-B7
PALACE CT
500 ALA 94501 669-F1
PALACIO CT
- FRMT 94539 753-F4
PALADIN WY
1100 PLE 94566 715-C7
PALAMOS CT
- SRMN 94583 673-C3
PALATINO ST
40600 FRMT 94539 753-F4
PALATKA LN
1900 HAY 94545 711-H6
PALI CT
- OAK 94611 630-C5

PALISADE ST
900 HAY 94542 712-A3
PALISADE TER
4000 FRMT 94539 774-B7
PALISADES DR
1100 MPS 95035 793-J4
PALM AV
300 OAK 94610 649-J3
2200 LVMR 94550 715-H2
41700 FRMT 94539 753-G6
PALM CT
- OAK 94607 649-E3
2800 BERK 94705 629-J3
4000 FRMT 94536 752-H3
7400 PLE 94588 713-J1
PALM DR
100 PDMT 94610 650-A2
200 UNC 94587 732-C6
PALM PL
2100 HAY 94545 731-H1
PALM BEACH LN
- ALA 94502 670-A5
PALMDALE CT
7700 PLE 94588 693-J7
32800 UNC 94587 732-B7
PALMDALE ST
4300 UNC 94587 732-B7
PALMER AV
3200 OAK 94602 650-C5
PALMER DR
1800 PLE 94588 694-F7
37800 FRMT 94536 752-H4
PALMER PL
3400 PLE 94588 694-F7
PALMER ST
- SRMN 94583 693-F1
PALMERA CT
- OAK 94603 671-A4
700 ALA 94501 669-H2
PALMETTO DR
33000 UNC 94587 732-G3
PALMETTO ST
2400 OAK 94602 650-D5
PALMIRA CT
700 SRMN 94583 673-B3
PALMIRA PL
2400 SRMN 94583 673-B3
PALM VILLA CT
- OAK 94603 671-A4
PALMWOOD AV
27400 HAY 94545 711-H7
PALO AMARILLO DR
47100 FRMT 94539 773-J5
47100 FRMT 94539 774-A5
PALOMA AV
600 OAK 94610 650-B3
PALOMA CT
32000 UNC 94587 732-A6
PALOMA RD Rt#-84
11500 AlaC 94586 734-D6
PALOMA TER
200 FRMT 94536 733-A6
PALOMARES RD
24400 AlaC 94552 692-G5
24700 AlaC 94552 712-H1
24700 HAY 94542 712-H1
24700 HAY 94552 712-H1
24700 AlaC 94542 712-H1
29300 AlaC 94552 713-A3
29300 HAY 94552 713-A3
32200 AlaC 94586 713-D6
32200 AlaC 94544 713-D6
34000 AlaC 94586 733-F1
35500 UNC 94587 733-F1
PALOMINO COM
33200 FRMT 94555 732-C6
PALOMINO DR
600 PLE 94566 714-G4
PALOMINO RD
2100 LVMR 94551 696-A3
PALOS WY
4700 UNC 94587 731-J6
PALO VERDE RD
6300 AlaC 94552 692-F5
PAMELA COM
4600 LVMR 94550 696-B7
PAMELA CT
400 HAY 94541 711-H2
PAMELA PL
800 PLE 94566 714-F4
PAMPAS AV
4300 OAK 94619 650-G6
PAMPLONA CT
- SRMN 94583 673-D3
PAN AM WY
- ALA 94501 649-D6
PANAMA AV
5100 RCH 94804 609-C3
PANAMA CIR
400 UNC 94587 732-D5
PANAMA CT
4000 OAK 94611 649-J1
PANAMA ST
2000 HAY 94545 731-H1
PANDA WY
1700 HAY 94541 712-B1
PANDOREA CT
3200 PLE 94588 694-H4
PANITZ ST
24900 AlaC 94541 712-C2
PANJON ST
300 HAY 94544 712-B7
PANORAMA CT
- FRMT 94539 773-J1
PANORAMIC DR
- ALA 94501 649-A5
PANORAMIC PL
- BERK 94704 630-A2
PANORAMIC WY
- BERK 94704 629-J2
- BERK 94704 630-A2
300 OAK 94704 630-A2
600 OAK 94705 630-B2
16300 AlaC 94578 691-G4
PANSY ST
14400 SLN 94578 691-C3
PANTON TER
37100 FRMT 94536 752-H2
PAPAGO ST
47500 FRMT 94539 773-J7
PAPAYA ST
24700 HAY 94545 711-G5
36800 NWK 94560 752-C7
36800 NWK 94560 772-C1
PAPAZIAN WY
4000 FRMT 94538 753-D7
PAPILLON TER
4000 FRMT 94538 773-E3
PAPPAS PL
2500 HAY 94542 712-D4
PAR CT
8000 NWK 94560 752-C7

PARADA ST
39900 NWK 94560 772-J2
PARADISE BLVD
500 AlaC 94541 691-F7
PARADISE DR
- FRMT 94536 733-C7
- FRMT 94536 753-D1
PARADISE KNOLL
4400 AlaC 94546 692-C5
PARAGON CIR
2600 PLE 94588 714-A4
PARAMOUNT RD
800 OAK 94610 650-B3
PARDEE AL
- SF 94133 648-A4
PARDEE AV
4500 FRMT 94538 753-A6
PARDEE CT
700 HAY 94544 712-A6
39500 FRMT 94538 753-A6
PARDEE DR
8400 OAK 94621 670-E7
PARDEE LN
7700 OAK 94621 670-E5
PARDEE PL
2800 LVMR 94550 715-G5
PARDEE ST
900 BERK 94710 629-E3
PARFAIT LN
- ALA 94502 670-A5
PARIS WY
1200 LVMR 94550 715-F3
PARISH AV
3600 FRMT 94536 752-H3
PARISH CIR
37300 FRMT 94536 752-H3
PARISH CT
- ALA 94502 670-A6
PARK AV
400 SJS 95002 793-C7
900 ALA 94501 669-J3
1000 ALA 94501 670-A2
1100 EMVL 94608 629-E7
S PARK AV
- SF 94107 648-C6
PARK AV E
1100 ALA 94501 670-A3
PARK AV W
1100 ALA 94501 670-A3
PARK BLVD
- OAK 94611 630-F7
1800 OAK 94606 649-J4
2000 OAK 94606 650-A4
2900 OAK 94610 650-A4
3800 OAK 94602 650-A4
4800 PDMT 94610 650-D3
4900 OAK 94611 650-D3
4900 PDMT 94611 650-D3
S PARK DR
1000 CCCo 94708 610-B6
1500 OAK 94708 610-C7
PARK LN
200 PDMT 94610 650-B2
900 OAK 94610 650-B2
PARK PL
100 SRMN 94583 673-B2
3400 PLE 94588 694-G6
PARK ST
200 SLN 94577 670-J7
300 ALA 94501 669-J3
1100 ALA 94501 670-A2
1600 LVMR 94551 695-G7
2000 OAK 94606 670-A2
2700 BERK 94702 629-F3
24000 HAY 94541 711-H3
24000 HAY 94544 711-J3
PARK WY
- PDMT 94611 630-B7
- PDMT 94611 650-A1
700 BERK 94710 609-C7
800 OAK 94606 649-J5
800 ELCR 94530 609-E3
2600 AlaC 94586 713-J7
2600 AlaC 94586 733-J1
20300 AlaC 94546 691-H5
PARK ARROYO PL
2000 HAY 94545 731-H1
PARK BLVD WY
3700 OAK 94610 650-B4
PARK BROOK CT
1100 MPS 95035 794-C6
PARK CENTER LN
4000 FRMT 94538 753-B6
PARKER AV
2500 OAK 94605 670-J2
PARKER CT
34300 FRMT 94555 752-C4
PARKER RD
17400 AlaC 94546 691-H2
PARKER ST
900 BERK 94710 629-E3
1100 BERK 94702 629-E3
1300 SLN 94577 671-C7
1500 BERK 94703 629-F3
1900 BERK 94704 629-J2
PARK GATE
- BERK 94708 609-J6
PARK GLEN CT
1100 MPS 95035 794-C6
PARK GROVE DR
1100 MPS 95035 794-C6
PARK HEIGHTS DR
1100 MPS 95035 794-C6
PARK HILL CT
22800 HAY 94541 692-B7
PARK HILL DR
- MPS 95035 794-C6
PARK HILLS RD
1000 BERK 94708 609-J5
1100 BERK 94708 610-A6
PARKHURST AL
- SF 94108 648-A5
PARKHURST DR
13000 OAK 94619 651-B6
39400 FRMT 94538 753-A6
PARKHURST TER
4200 FRMT 94538 753-A6
PARKMEADOW CT
45300 FRMT 94539 773-H4
PARKMEADOW DR
44300 FRMT 94539 773-G2
PARK MEADOW PL
2000 FRMT 94539 773-G3
PARKMONT COM
- FRMT 94536 753-A3
PARKMONT DR
37900 FRMT 94536 753-A3
PARK OAK CT
1100 MPS 95035 794-C6
PARK PLACE COM
2800 FRMT 94536 753-A3
2800 FRMT 94536 752-J1

PARKRIDGE DR
5000 OAK 94619 651-B6
PARKSHORE DR
35800 NWK 94560 752-E4
PARKSIDE CT
- LVMR 94551 696-A3
600 CCCo 94708 609-G4
38300 FRMT 94536 753-A3
PARKSIDE DR
- BERK 94705 630-A4
- PDMT 94611 630-A7
2100 FRMT 94536 753-A3
2500 UNC 94587 732-B4
3100 PLE 94588 694-C7
3200 HAY 94542 712-D3
5900 PLE 94588 714-B1
PARKSIDE PL
5700 NWK 94560 752-E5
N PARK VICTORIA DR
- MPS 95035 794-A3
S PARK VICTORIA DR
- MPS 95035 794-C7
PARKVIEW CT
200 PDMT 94610 650-B2
1400 PLE 94566 714-D2
PARK VIEW DR
1100 MPS 95035 794-C6
PARKVIEW RD
4800 AlaC 94546 692-C4
PARK VIEW TER
300 OAK 94610 649-H3
PARK VISTA
7400 ELCR 94530 609-D2
PARK WILLOW CT
1100 MPS 95035 794-C6
PARK WOOD CIR
7300 DBLN 94568 694-A2
PARKWOOD ST
42700 FRMT 94538 773-D1
PARLIN PL
- SRMN 94583 673-E6
PARMA CT
- PLE 94566 715-C7
PARMA TER
34400 FRMT 94555 752-A6
PARNASSUS CT
- HAY 94542 712-C3
E PARNASSUS CT
- BERK 94708 609-J7
W PARNASSUS CT
- BERK 94708 609-J7
PARNASSUS RD
- BERK 94708 609-J7
PARODI CT
- ALA 94502 669-J6
PARROT PL
- DNVL 94526 652-J1
PARROTT ST
- SLN 94577 691-A1
PARSONS AV
18700 AlaC 94546 691-J4
PARSONS CT
3600 AlaC 94546 691-J4
PARTLET CT
44500 FRMT 94539 773-J2
PARTRIDGE AV
2900 OAK 94605 670-J2
2900 OAK 94605 671-A2
PARTRIDGE COM
700 LVMR 94551 695-E7
PARTRIDGE WY
2200 UNC 94587 732-G7
PARU ST
- ALA 94501 649-J7
700 ALA 94501 669-H2
PARVIN DR
700 MPS 95035 794-B5
PASAS ST
2100 PLE 94566 714-G1
PASATIEMPO ST
2100 LVMR 94551 696-C2
PASEO PL
- HAY 94541 711-J2
PASEO CATALINA
6700 PLE 94566 714-A2
PASEO DEL CAJON
1600 PLE 94566 714-C2
PASEO DEL CAMPO
15700 AlaC 94580 691-C7
15900 AlaC 94580 711-D1
PASEO DEL RIO
500 AlaC 94580 691-D7
PASEO GRANADA
3000 PLE 94566 714-B2
PASEO GRANDE
- AlaC 94580 691-D7
- AlaC 94541 691-E7
800 AlaC 94580 711-C1
PASEO LAGUNA SECO
1600 LVMR 94551 695-F6
PASEO LARGAVISTA
15700 AlaC 94580 691-D7
PASEO NAVARRO
5500 PLE 94566 714-C2
PASEO PADRE CT
38100 FRMT 94536 753-A3
PASEO PADRE PKWY
- NWK 94560 752-A4
8900 FRMT 94555 752-A4
30200 FRMT 94555 732-E7
34800 FRMT 94555 752-H2
37900 FRMT 94536 753-B4
38900 FRMT 94538 753-B4
39400 FRMT 94539 753-F6
39700 FRMT 94539 773-G1
PASEO REFUGIO
400 MPS 95035 794-B6
PASEO ROBLES
3100 PLE 94566 714-A2
PASEO SAN LEON
6700 PLE 94566 714-B1
PASEO SANTA CRUZ
6000 PLE 94566 714-A2
PASEO SANTA MARIA
6400 PLE 94566 714-B2
PASHOTE CT
1400 MPS 95035 794-A4
PASO ROBLES DR
6700 OAK 94611 630-F7
PASSEGGI CT
4200 PLE 94588 694-C5
PATIO DR
20600 AlaC 94546 692-A5
PATOMA CT
600 FRMT 94536 753-D1
PATRICIA CT
400 MPS 95035 794-E7
10400 OAK 94603 670-H7
24600 AlaC 94541 712-D2
PATRICIA LN
3100 LVMR 94550 715-H1

© 2006 Rand McNally & Company

STREET
Block City ZIP Pg-Grid

PATRICIA RD
- ORIN 94563 630-G2
PATRICIA ST
4100 FRMT 94536 752-J4
PATRICK AV
26800 HAY 94544 711-J7
PATRICKS PL
- DNVL 94526 652-J2
PATRIOT PL
600 FRMT 94539 773-H2
PATTERSON AV
- SJCo 95391 (678-E3 See Page 677)
3600 OAK 94619 650-F6
PATTERSON PASS RD
6200 LVMR 94550 696-B6
6900 AlaC 94550 696-E6
10100 AlaC 94550 (697-J6 See Page 677)
11800 AlaC 94550 (698-B4 See Page 677)
13200 AlaC 94550 717-D1
S PATTERSON PASS RD
25600 SJCo 95377 (698-F3 See Page 677)
W PATTERSON PASS RD
12900 AlaC 94550 (698-B4 See Page 677)
17700 SJCo 95377 (698-D4 See Page 677)
PATTERSON RANCH RD
6300 FRMT 94555 751-J4
6300 FRMT 94555 752-A4
PATTIANI WY
2700 ALA 94502 669-J6
PATTON AV
14900 SLN 94578 691-D3
PATTON DR
18900 AlaC 94546 692-A3
PATTON ST
5800 OAK 94618 630-A4
PATTON TER
41500 FRMT 94538 773-D1
PAUL CT
25600 AlaC 94541 712-D2
PAUL ST
- SJCo 95391 (678-E3 See Page 677)
PAUL TER
3900 FRMT 94538 753-D7
PAULA CT
4700 LVMR 94550 696-B7
PAULANELLA PL
100 CCCo 94583 652-E3
PAVO CT
5000 LVMR 94551 696-B3
PAWNEE DR
44900 FRMT 94539 773-H3
PAWNEE PL
- FRMT 94539 773-H3
PAWNEE WY
3100 PLE 94588 694-G7
PAXTON AV
3300 OAK 94601 650-D6
PAXTON CT
5200 FRMT 94536 752-H6
PAYNE CT
6800 PLE 94588 694-A7
PAYNE RD
3900 PLE 94588 714-A1
4100 PLE 94588 694-A7
PAYNE ST
32200 HAY 94544 732-E3
PAYOT CT
100 ALA 94502 670-B7
PAYOT LN
- ALA 94502 670-B7
PEABODY LN
1100 OAK 94608 629-E5
1200 EMVL 94608 629-E5
PEACE TER
33300 FRMT 94555 732-C7
PEACEFUL LN
4700 PLE 94566 714-E4
PEACEFUL VALLEY DR
600 SRMN 94582 673-J6
600 SRMN 94582 674-A6
PEACH CT
36700 NWK 94560 752-C7
PEACH DR
200 AlaC 94580 691-D7
PEACH ST
900 ALA 94501 670-B4
9200 OAK 94603 670-J4
9200 OAK 94603 671-A4
PEACH BLOSSOM LN
- SRMN 94583 673-E6
PEACHTREE AV
7700 NWK 94560 752-C7
PEACH TREE COM
1300 LVMR 94551 696-A4
PEACHTREE CT
- FRMT 94536 753-A2
PEACH TREE DR
28200 HAY 94545 731-H1
PEACHWOOD ST
42600 FRMT 94538 773-D2
PEACOCK CT
- DBLN 94568 694-D4
PEACOCK PL
2200 UNC 94587 732-G7
PEACOCK HILL DR
- AlaC 94552 692-E7
- AlaC 94552 712-E1
PEAK ST
- HAY 94541 711-H3
PEAK VIEW DR
48900 FRMT 94539 793-J2
PEAR LN
- UNC 94587 732-H5
PEAR ST
24700 HAY 94545 711-G5
PEARCE ST
22200 HAY 94541 711-H1
PEARL AV
22500 HAY 94541 692-B7
PEARL DR
200 LVMR 94550 715-D2
PEARL PL
6700 DBLN 94568 693-J2
PEARL ST
- OAK 94611 649-J2
100 OAK 94610 649-J2
900 ALA 94501 670-A3
PEARL CREST CT
- CCCo 94582 674-B2
PEARL HARBOR RD
100 ALA 94501 649-D6
PEARMAIN ST
9800 OAK 94603 670-H6
PEARSON AV
1200 SLN 94577 690-H2

PEARY CT
1000 LVMR 94550 715-G2
PEARY WY
1700 LVMR 94550 715-G2
PEASE CT
1200 ALA 94501 670-A3
PEBBLE CT
- SRMN 94583 673-G7
27800 HAY 94542 712-E4
PEBBLE PL
100 SRMN 94583 673-G6
PEBBLE BEACH AV
8100 NWK 94560 752-C7
PEBBLE BEACH CT
1700 MPS 95035 794-D3
31300 HAY 94544 732-E2
PEBBLE BEACH DR
10500 OAK 94605 671-D3
PEBBLEWOOD CT
900 FRMT 94539 773-J5
5000 PLE 94566 714-D2
PECAN CT
- SRMN 94583 673-F7
7400 PLE 94588 713-J1
7400 PLE 94588 714-A1
36100 FRMT 94536 752-J1
PECAN ST
2400 UNC 94587 732-D4
PECO ST
34800 UNC 94587 732-G7
PECOS AV
4100 FRMT 94555 752-D2
PECOS CT
4500 FRMT 94555 752-D2
PEDESTRIAN WY
400 OAK 94618 629-J5
4400 FRMT 94538 753-B6
PEDRINI TER
34300 FRMT 94555 752-A6
PEDRO AV
2100 MPS 95035 794-E7
PEERLESS CT
- OAK 94603 671-C5
PEGAN COM
1300 LVMR 94550 716-B1
PEGASUS CT
32300 UNC 94587 732-A6
PEGGY WRIGHT WY
- FRMT 94536 733-C7
- FRMT 94536 753-C1
PEKING CT
- HAY 94544 711-J3
PELADEAU ST
5700 EMVL 94608 629-E6
PELHAM CT
41400 FRMT 94539 753-F6
PELHAM PL
2200 OAK 94611 650-F1
26800 HAY 94542 712-E3
PELICAN CT
- ALA 94501 649-E7
600 LVMR 94551 695-E7
PELICAN DR
2800 UNC 94587 732-D6
PELICAN WY
2000 SLN 94579 690-J6
PELLARO CT
3100 PLE 94566 715-C6
PELTON CIR
100 SLN 94577 691-A1
PELTON PL
- SF 94133 648-A4
PEMBERTON DR
- SRMN 94582 674-B4
PEMBROKE CT
- OAK 94619 650-J4
PEMBROOK CT
- MRGA 94556 651-F2
PEMENTEL CT
41100 FRMT 94539 753-G4
PENDLETON WY
400 OAK 94621 670-E6
PENDOLINO LN
- LVMR 94550 715-H5
PENINSULA RD
- AlaC 94546 651-D5
- AlaC 94546 671-F1
- AlaC 94619 651-D5
PENINSULA ST
14900 SLN 94578 691-C5
PENITENCIA CT
500 MPS 95035 793-J6
PENITENCIA ST
500 MPS 95035 793-J6
PENN AV
16000 AlaC 94580 691-E6
PENN DR
6800 DBLN 94568 693-J3
PENN LN
40600 FRMT 94538 753-D6
PENNIMAN AV
3400 OAK 94602 650-E6
3500 OAK 94619 650-E6
PENNIMAN CT
4100 OAK 94619 650-E7
PENNSYLVANIA AV
3300 FRMT 94536 753-A4
PENNSYLVANIA COM
3400 FRMT 94536 753-A4
PENNY LN
500 AlaC 94541 711-E2
PENNY TER
4000 FRMT 94538 773-D1
PENSACOLA
100 ALA 94501 649-D6
PENSACOLA WY
27600 HAY 94544 711-J7
27600 HAY 94544 731-J1
PENWOOD LN
- DBLN 94568 694-F2
PENWOOD PL
- DBLN 94568 694-F2
PENZANCE COM
37000 FRMT 94536 752-B4
PEONY CT
100 FRMT 94538 773-B2
PEONY DR
5100 LVMR 94551 696-B3
PEOPLE SOFT PKWY
- PLE 94588 694-C5
PEPPER LN
- UNC 94587 732-H6
PEPPER ST
18200 AlaC 94546 692-B3
PEPPERDINE ST
14700 SLN 94579 691-B4
PEPPERTREE CT
6000 NWK 94560 752-G7
8100 DBLN 94568 693-G3
PEPPERTREE LN
3700 AlaC 94546 692-A3

PEPPERTREE PL
1000 LVMR 94550 715-G2
PEPPERTREE RD
7500 DBLN 94568 693-F3
PEPPERWOOD COM
- LVMR 94550 716-D2
PEPPERWOOD PL
2600 AlaC 94541 692-C7
PEPPERWOOD TER
3400 FRMT 94536 752-A6
PEPYS WY
- FRMT 94536 753-C3
PERALTA AV
- SLN 94577 671-A7
200 SLN 94577 670-J7
400 SLN 94577 690-J1
500 BERK 94707 609-F6
900 ALB 94706 609-F6
1100 BERK 94706 609-E7
1200 BERK 94702 609-E7
PERALTA BLVD
3900 FRMT 94536 752-H4
PERALTA BLVD Rt#-84
1200 FRMT 94536 753-A3
2700 FRMT 94536 752-J3
PERALTA CT
- FRMT 94536 752-H3
- MRGA 94556 651-F1
PERALTA ST
300 OAK 94607 649-E2
2700 OAK 94608 649-E2
3400 EMVL 94608 629-F7
3400 OAK 94608 629-F7
22100 HAY 94541 711-H1
PERALTA TER
2000 FRMT 94536 753-A3
PERALTA OAKS CT
2900 OAK 94605 671-B5
PERALTA OAKS DR
10600 OAK 94605 671-B5
PERCH WY
- UNC 94545 731-J6
PERCHERON RD
2100 LVMR 94551 696-A2
PEREGRINE ST
- AlaC 94550 716-C2
- LVMR 94550 716-C2
PEREGRINE WY
4000 PLE 94566 714-E1
4200 FRMT 94555 732-B7
PEREIRA CT
33600 FRMT 94555 732-D6
PEREZ CT
- DBLN 94568 694-G4
PERGOLA CT
22100 AlaC 94552 692-D5
PERIDOT DR
1500 LVMR 94550 715-D3
PERIWINKLE COM
- LVMR 94551 696-D1
PERIWINKLE DR
30800 UNC 94587 732-A5
PERIWINKLE RD
29600 HAY 94544 712-D7
PERKINS CT
4100 FRMT 94536 752-F3
PERKINS DR
300 AlaC 94541 711-E1
PERKINS ST
100 OAK 94610 649-J2
35900 FRMT 94536 752-F2
PERLITA CT
2600 AlaC 94541 692-C6
PEROLY CT
2600 OAK 94601 650-C6
PERRICH AV
2700 AlaC 94546 691-G4
PERRIN AV
8500 NWK 94560 772-C2
PERRY COM
600 FRMT 94539 753-H5
PERRY LN
7800 PLE 94588 693-H7
PERRY PL
100 OAK 94610 649-J2
PERRY RD
34100 UNC 94587 732-F6
PERRY ST
- SF 94107 648-B6
100 MPS 95035 794-C7
PERSHING DR
- OAK 94611 650-D1
100 SLN 94577 670-J7
800 SLN 94577 671-A7
800 SLN 94577 691-A1
PERSICA CT
- SRMN 94582 673-H1
PERSIMMON CIR
3100 PLE 94588 694-G6
PERSIMMON CT
27600 HAY 94544 712-B6
PERSIMMON DR
27600 HAY 94544 712-B6
PERSIMMON PL
8300 NWK 94560 752-C7
PERSIMMON ST
- DBLN 94568 694-D3
PERSIMMON WY
- PLE 94588 694-G6
PERTH CT
600 MPS 95035 794-A6
PERTH PL
- OAK 94705 630-B3
PERU CT
1700 PLE 94566 714-E1
PESARO WY
- LVMR 94550 715-F5
PESCADERO CT
200 MPS 95035 793-J5
PESCADERO ST
200 MPS 95035 793-J5
PESHEL CT
16400 AlaC 94580 691-F6
PESTANA PL
300 LVMR 94550 695-J7
4000 FRMT 94538 773-E4
PESTANA WY
3300 LVMR 94550 695-J7
3900 LVMR 94550 696-A7
PETALUMA CT
1800 MPS 95035 794-D6
PETAR PL
- SRMN 94583 673-G6
PETARD TER
34200 FRMT 94555 752-C2
PETERMAN AV
26100 HAY 94545 711-H6
PETERMAN LN
25800 HAY 94545 711-H6
PETERS AV
- PLE 94566 714-D4

PETERS ST
1500 SLN 94578 691-D3
PETERSBURG DR
2100 MPS 95035 794-E7
PETERSEN WY
17700 AlaC 94546 691-H2
PETERSON CT
- AlaC 94541 712-B2
PETERSON ST
400 OAK 94601 670-B1
PETITE WY
29100 HAY 94544 712-B7
PETOLA RD
700 DNVL 94526 652-H1
PETRARCH PL
- SF 94104 648-B5
PETRIFIED FOREST CT
3900 PLE 94588 714-A1
PETRINA CT
28000 HAY 94545 731-J1
PETROLEUM ST
- OAK 94607 649-B3
PETUNIA CT
2800 UNC 94587 752-F1
PEUGEOT PL
36400 NWK 94560 752-E6
PEYTON DR
300 HAY 94544 712-B5
PFEIFFER ST
- SF 94133 648-A3
PHAETON DR
7900 OAK 94605 671-C1
PHEASANT CT
- DBLN 94568 694-D4
6400 LVMR 94551 696-D2
PHEASANT ST
33200 FRMT 94555 732-C7
PHEASANT WY
6300 LVMR 94551 696-D2
PHEASANT WOODS DR
21500 AlaC 94552 692-D5
PHEBE AV
4600 FRMT 94555 752-C2
PHEBE RD
- FRMT 94555 752-C1
PHELAN AV
2500 HAY 94545 731-H2
4700 FRMT 94538 753-A7
PHELPS ST
400 OAK 94603 670-F6
PHIL DR
- AlaC 94580 711-A1
PHILADELPHIA PL
42600 FRMT 94538 773-E1
PHILLIPS LN
1900 SLN 94577 690-G2
PHILLIPS WY
900 HAY 94541 711-F4
PHLOX WY
- LVMR 94551 696-C3
PHOEBE CT
3800 PLE 94566 714-F1
PHOENIX CT
800 FRMT 94539 773-H4
PHOENIX LN
3100 ALA 94502 670-A7
PHOENIX WY
1200 SLN 94577 690-H1
PHOTINA CT
2600 PLE 94588 694-H4
PHYLLIS CT
4500 LVMR 94550 696-B7
PHYLMORE CT
1400 AlaC 94541 691-H7
PIAZZA CT
5300 PLE 94588 694-C6
PIAZZA WY
- SLN 94577 671-C7
PICADILLY CT
3200 PLE 94588 694-E6
PICARD AV
3800 PLE 94588 694-F6
PICARDY DR
5800 OAK 94605 670-G1
N PICARDY DR
5500 OAK 94605 670-G1
S PICARDY DR
5500 OAK 94605 670-G1
PICARDY PL
6500 NWK 94560 752-D6
PICEA CT
3900 AlaC 94542 712-F3
PICHOLINE CT
- LVMR 94550 715-G5
PICHOLINE DR
- LVMR 94550 715-G6
PICKENS LN
3400 PLE 94588 694-E6
PICKEREL DR
4200 UNC 94587 731-J5
PICKERING AV
- FRMT 94536 753-D2
W PICKERING AV
- FRMT 94536 753-D2
PICKERING CT
38600 FRMT 94536 753-D1
PICKERING TER
- FRMT 94536 753-D1
PICKFAIR LN
2600 LVMR 94551 695-H6
PICKFORD PL
2700 AlaC 94541 692-C7
PICKFORD WY
2700 AlaC 94541 692-C7
PICKRELL SQ
- ALA 94501 649-C7
PICO PL
2100 AlaC 94578 691-G5
PICO RD
42000 FRMT 94539 753-H4
PIEDMONT AV
- ORIN 94563 610-E6
2300 BERK 94720 629-J2
2300 BERK 94704 629-J2
2700 BERK 94705 629-J3
3300 OAK 94611 649-J1
4100 OAK 94611 629-J7
4300 OAK 94611 630-A7
PIEDMONT CRES
2500 BERK 94704 629-J2
PIEDMONT CT
- PDMT 94611 650-B1
PIEDMONT RD
- MPS 95035 794-E6
200 SCIC 95035 794-E6
PIEDMONT TER
4000 FRMT 94539 774-B7
PIEMONTE DR
- PLE 94566 715-B6
PIENZA ST
- LVMR 94550 715-F5

PIER ST
2300 OAK 94607 649-B2
PIERCE AV
1200 SLN 94577 690-J1
PIERCE ST
500 ALB 94706 609-C4
500 RCH 94804 609-C4
800 ALB 94710 609-C4
PIERCE WY
3900 FRMT 94536 752-J4
PIERPOINT AV
5000 OAK 94602 650-F3
PIERSON ST
3300 OAK 94619 650-G7
PIETRONAVE LN
700 PLE 94566 714-J3
PIKE AV
1900 SLN 94577 690-J5
PIKE COM
38900 FRMT 94536 753-C3
PIKE CT
7100 DBLN 94568 693-J4
PIKE PL
- UNC 94545 731-J6
PILGRIM LP
- FRMT 94539 773-J1
PILLSBURY CT
2600 LVMR 94550 715-G4
PIMA ST
47600 FRMT 94539 773-H7
PIMENTEL CT
- MRGA 94556 651-E1
PIMLICO DR
3500 PLE 94588 694-E5
PINE AV
2900 BERK 94705 630-A3
PINE CT
6900 DBLN 94568 693-J4
43900 FRMT 94539 773-G2
PINE LN
- OAK 94618 630-B5
PINE PTH
- BERK 94705 630-A3
PINE ST
- SF 94111 648-A5
100 FRMT 94539 773-G1
200 SF 94104 648-A5
500 SF 94108 648-A5
700 LVMR 94551 695-E7
700 OAK 94607 649-C3
3400 AlaC 94546 692-A6
PINE CREST CT
6500 AlaC 94552 672-C7
PINECREST DR
5100 OAK 94605 671-C1
PINEDALE CT
800 HAY 94544 711-J2
800 HAY 94544 712-A2
PINEHAVEN PL
19200 AlaC 94546 692-B4
PINEHAVEN RD
6300 OAK 94611 630-D5
PINE HILL LN
400 PLE 94566 714-E4
PINE HILLS CT
- CCCo 94516 630-G7
- OAK 94611 630-G7
PINE HILLS DR
100 OAK 94611 630-G7
PINE HILLS LN
8400 OAK 94611 630-G7
PINEHURST CT
1600 LVMR 94551 696-C3
PINEHURST CT W
1700 MPS 95035 794-D3
PINEHURST PL
800 SRMN 94583 673-G6
PINEHURST RD
- AlaC 94619 651-C3
- CCCo 94516 630-H6
- CCCo 94516 651-A1
- OAK 94611 630-H6
PINEHURST TER
- FRMT 94536 752-G4
PINENEEDLE DR
6500 OAK 94611 630-D5
PINENUT CT
400 SRMN 94583 673-G7
PINE RIDGE
400 SRMN 94582 673-F3
PINERIDGE RD
2700 AlaC 94546 691-G3
PINETO PL
1000 PLE 94566 715-C6
PINE TOP AV
5500 OAK 94613 650-H7
PINE VALLEY CT
3000 SRMN 94582 673-H6
PINE VALLEY PL
- SRMN 94583 673-E7
PINE VALLEY RD
2800 SRMN 94583 673-E7
PINEVILLE CIR
20800 AlaC 94552 692-G3
PINEWOOD COM
- LVMR 94550 716-D2
PINEWOOD CT
3300 HAY 94542 712-E4
4400 UNC 94587 732-A7
PINEWOOD DR
3400 HAY 94542 712-E4
PINEWOOD RD
5800 OAK 94611 630-C6
PINEWOOD TER
3300 FRMT 94536 752-A6
PINKERTON CT
- SRMN 94583 673-E4
PINNACLE PL
- LVMR 94551 696-F5
PINNACLES CT
- UNC 94587 732-H6
23900 AlaC 94541 692-C7
23900 AlaC 94541 712-C1
PINNACLES DR
- UNC 94587 732-H6
PINON CT
2000 LVMR 94551 696-A3
PINON WY
4100 LVMR 94551 695-J3
4100 LVMR 94551 696-A3
PINON CANYON CT
- AlaC 94552 692-E6
PINOT CT
2000 LVMR 94550 715-H3
3800 PLE 94566 714-G4
PINOT BLANC WY
600 FRMT 94539 794-A2
PINRBROOK WY
- HAY 94544 732-D1
PINTAIL TER
3600 FRMT 94555 732-D7

PINTO CT
33100 UNC 94587 732-F3
PINTO ST
- LVMR 94551 696-A2
PIONEER AV
28200 HAY 94545 731-G2
PIONEER CT
- ALA 94501 649-A2
- SRMN 94583 673-B3
PIONEER LN
6500 DBLN 94568 694-A3
6600 DBLN 94568 693-J3
PIONEER TRAIL PL
6100 PLE 94566 714-D6
PIPER ST
4500 FRMT 94538 753-B7
PIPER GLEN TER
- DBLN 94568 694-H3
PIPERS BROOK CT
- SRMN 94582 674-B4
PIPIT CT
- SLN 94579 691-F2
4800 PLE 94566 694-D7
4800 PLE 94566 714-D1
PIPPIN ST
9800 OAK 94603 670-H6
PISA TER
6000 FRMT 94555 752-B3
PISCES AV
5000 LVMR 94551 696-B3
PISMO CT
400 LVMR 94550 715-E3
PISTACHIO CT
27700 HAY 94544 712-B6
PISTOL CT
33600 FRMT 94555 752-B1
PITCHER RD
6000 AlaC 94550 736-F3
PITT CT
7100 DBLN 94568 693-J4
PIXIE LN
600 DNVL 94526 652-H1
PIZARRO DR
36000 FRMT 94536 752-F3
PLACENZA ST
800 LVMR 94551 695-E7
PLACER CIR
1600 LVMR 94551 695-E6
PLACER CT
600 LVMR 94551 695-E6
PLACER DR
1900 AlaC 94578 691-D3
PLACER ST
1900 RCH 94804 609-C3
PLACER WY
39700 FRMT 94538 753-B6
PLANET CIR
4300 UNC 94587 732-A6
PLANK AV
7100 ELCR 94530 609-C1
PLANK CT
7300 ELCR 94530 609-C1
PLANTANO WY
1100 PLE 94566 714-G2
PLANTATION LN
- HAY 94544 712-C5
PLATEAU DR
600 CCCo 94708 609-G4
PLATERO PL
39500 FRMT 94539 753-E3
PLATINUM ST
- UNC 94587 732-H6
PLATINUM TER
34200 FRMT 94555 752-C2
PLATT CT N
3700 PLE 94588 714-A1
PLATT CT S
3600 PLE 94588 714-A1
PLATT RIVER PL
34700 FRMT 94555 752-E2
PLAYA CT
- SRMN 94583 673-B2
PLAZA AV
800 LVMR 94550 715-E3
PLAZA CIR
5000 RCH 94804 609-B1
PLAZA DR
1400 AlaC 94578 691-E4
PLAZA PL
- HAY 94541 711-G1
PLAZA WY
4900 RCH 94804 609-B1
PLEASANT ST
2500 OAK 94602 650-D5
PLEASANT WY
300 SLN 94577 670-J7
700 LVMR 94551 696-D4
24900 HAY 94544 711-J4
PLEASANT HILL CT
27700 HAY 94542 712-E4
PLEASANT HILL RD
5200 PLE 94588 693-H6
PLEASANTON AV
600 PLE 94566 714-D3
PLEASANTON-SUNOL RD
- PLE 94566 714-C7
7900 AlaC 94566 714-C7
7900 AlaC 94566 734-D2
8800 AlaC 94586 734-D2
PLEASANT VALLEY AV
1700 OAK 94611 630-A7
1800 OAK 94611 629-J7
PLEASANT VALLEY CT
- SRMN 94582 673-J6
N PLEASANT VALLEY CT
4500 OAK 94611 630-A7
S PLEASANT VALLEY CT
4500 OAK 94611 630-A7
PLEASANT VIEW LN
2000 AlaC 94550 715-H3
2000 LVMR 94550 715-H3
PLEIADES PL
4100 UNC 94587 732-B6
PLEITNER AV
3000 OAK 94602 650-D5
PLOMOSA CT
600 FRMT 94539 793-J1
PLOMOSA RD
48500 FRMT 94539 793-J2
PLOMOSA WY
- FRMT 94539 793-J1
PLOVER CT
- ALA 94501 649-F7
- HAY 94545 731-H3
PLUMAS AV
5400 RCH 94804 609-B3
PLUMAS CT
1000 LVMR 94551 695-F6
4000 HAY 94542 712-F4
39500 FRMT 94538 753-A6

PLUMAS WY
39700 FRMT 94538 753-B6
PLUMERIA CT
1800 PLE 94566 714-E1
1800 PLE 94588 714-E1
PLUMERIA WY
35800 FRMT 94536 732-J7
PLUMLEIGH DR
2200 FRMT 94539 753-E6
PLUMMER AV
6200 NWK 94560 752-E7
PLUMMER CT
24400 HAY 94545 711-E5
PLUM TREE LN
- SRMN 94583 673-E7
PLUM TREE ST
200 HAY 94544 711-J4
PLUTO ST
28700 HAY 94544 712-B7
PLUTO WY
4100 UNC 94587 732-B6
PLYMOUTH AV
800 FRMT 94539 753-F6
PLYMOUTH CT
- SRMN 94582 673-G5
PLYMOUTH DR
18100 AlaC 94546 691-J3
PLYMOUTH ST
7800 OAK 94621 670-H3
9000 OAK 94603 670-J4
POCONO MANOR PL
400 SRMN 94583 673-H6
POCO PASEO
- ORIN 94563 630-J3
PODA CT
1000 FRMT 94539 753-G7
POE ST
1300 BERK 94702 629-E2
POE TER
- FRMT 94536 752-J4
POGGI ST
1800 ALA 94501 649-E7
POINCIANA PL
39300 FRMT 94538 752-J6
POINCIANA ST
700 HAY 94545 711-G4
POINSETTIA COM
6100 LVMR 94551 696-D1
POINT EDEN WY
3900 HAY 94545 731-D1
POINT LOBOS CT
- UNC 94545 731-J7
POIRIER ST
600 OAK 94609 629-G5
POLARIS AV
4100 UNC 94587 732-B7
POLARIS WY
700 LVMR 94550 715-E4
POLK ST
800 ALB 94706 609-D6
POLK WY
300 LVMR 94550 696-A7
POLLARD PL
- SF 94133 648-A4
POLLARDSTOWN CT
11800 DBLN 94568 693-G4
POLLUX CT
32300 UNC 94587 732-A6
POLONIUS CIR
4000 FRMT 94555 732-C7
POLVOROSA AV
2200 SLN 94577 690-G3
POLVOROSA CT
36500 FRMT 94536 752-G3
POLYNESIA WY
100 UNC 94587 732-C5
POMACE CT
2400 FRMT 94539 773-G3
3200 PLE 94566 714-G4
POMACE ST
44100 FRMT 94539 773-F3
POMAR VISTA
2100 AlaC 94578 691-G5
2300 AlaC 94546 691-G5
POMEGRANATE AV
6100 NWK 94560 752-F7
POMEROY LN
- ALA 94501 649-E7
POMEZIA CT
2100 PLE 94566 715-B6
POMINO WY
- PLE 94566 715-B6
POMO CT
400 FRMT 94539 773-J5
POMONA AV
100 ELCR 94530 609-D3
500 ALB 94706 609-E6
POMONA CT
400 LVMR 94550 696-A7
7300 ELCR 94530 609-D3
POMONA ST
500 AlaC 94580 691-D5
POMONA WY
4000 LVMR 94550 696-A7
4200 LVMR 94550 716-A1
POMPANO AV
27600 HAY 94544 712-A7
27800 HAY 94544 732-A1
POMPEI TER
5900 FRMT 94555 752-A5
POMPONI ST
400 UNC 94545 731-J6
PONCA CT
1700 FRMT 94539 773-G4
POND CT
- MPS 95035 794-A7
POND DR
35600 FRMT 94536 732-J6
POND ISL
600 ALA 94501 669-H3
PONDEROSA CT
27400 HAY 94545 711-G7
27400 HAY 94545 731-G1
36600 NWK 94560 752-C7
PONDEROSA DR
1900 LVMR 94551 695-J3
2000 LVMR 94551 696-A3
PONDEROSA TER
37800 FRMT 94536 752-J1
37900 FRMT 94536 753-A3
PONS CT
4000 PLE 94566 714-G4
PONTE CT
- LVMR 94550 715-D4
PONTIAC ST
100 SLN 94577 670-J6
10400 OAK 94603 670-J6
24400 HAY 94544 711-J3
PONTIAC WY
- FRMT 94539 773-H7
PONTINA CT
3600 PLE 94566 715-C6

STREET
Block City ZIP Pg-Grid

PONY CT
- SRMN 94583 673-B3
POOLSIDE PL
900 SLN 94578 691-D5
POPE WY
900 HAY 94545 711-F4
POPLAR AV
100 AlaC 94541 711-G1
POPLAR COM
5600 FRMT 94538 773-A1
POPLAR CT
600 LVMR 94551 695-J6
POPLAR ST
- BERK 94708 609-H5
1000 OAK 94607 649-E2
2800 OAK 94608 649-E2
37000 NWK 94560 752-C7
37000 NWK 94560 772-D1
POPLAR WY
- PDMT 94611 650-C1
6700 DBLN 94568 693-J3
POPPY CT
100 FRMT 94538 773-B1
100 MPS 95035 794-D6
POPPY LN
- BERK 94708 609-H5
- MPS 95035 794-D6
- ORIN 94563 610-J4
POPPY PZ
- HAY 94542 712-B3
POPPY WY
- LVMR 94551 696-A4
POPPYBANK CT
1500 PLE 94566 714-F1
POPPY HILLS CT
- DBLN 94568 694-G3
POPPY HILLS LN
- DBLN 94568 694-G3
- SRMN 94583 673-E7
POPPYWOOD CT
- HAY 94544 711-J4
PORTA BALLENA
1200 ALA 94501 669-E2
PORTAGE RD
6800 DBLN 94568 693-H4
PORTAL AV
800 OAK 94610 650-B2
PORT ANCHORWOOD PL
36500 NWK 94560 752-F5
PORTA ROSSA CIR
- PLE 94588 694-D6
PORTER PL
200 SRMN 94583 673-A1
PORTER ST
4100 OAK 94619 650-F6
4400 FRMT 94538 753-B7
PORT FOGWOOD PL
36600 NWK 94560 752-F5
PORTIA TER
34300 FRMT 94555 752-D2
PORTICA TER
- FRMT 94536 752-G4
PORTILLO VALLEY DR
5000 SRMN 94582 673-J7
PORTLAND AV
300 OAK 94606 650-A4
1100 ALB 94706 609-D5
1400 BERK 94707 609-D5
PORTOFINO CIR
14900 SLN 94578 691-D3
PORTOFINO TER
400 MPS 95035 793-G3
PORTOLA AV
800 ALA 94501 669-G2
2200 LVMR 94551 695-D4
PORTOLA AV Rt#-J2
1100 LVMR 94551 695-F6
PORTOLA DR
700 SLN 94578 691-A4
4500 FRMT 94536 752-F4
6400 ELCR 94530 609-C3
PORTOLA MEADOWS RD
1100 LVMR 94551 695-G6
PORT SAILWOOD DR
5300 NWK 94560 752-F5
PORTSMOUTH AV
5400 NWK 94560 752-D4
26600 HAY 94545 711-F7
27400 HAY 94545 731-G1
PORTSMOUTH CT
- SRMN 94582 673-H5
3600 PLE 94588 694-F5
5500 NWK 94560 752-D4
PORTSMOUTH RD
- OAK 94610 650-B2
- PDMT 94610 650-B2
PORT TIDEWOOD ST
36600 NWK 94560 752-F5
PORTWOOD AV
800 OAK 94601 670-B1
POSADA CT
100 SRMN 94583 673-C3
POSADA WY
400 FRMT 94536 753-A1
POSEN AV
1400 ALB 94706 609-F7
1500 BERK 94706 609-F7
1600 BERK 94707 609-F7
POST AV
1300 SLN 94579 691-A5
POST RD
5400 OAK 94613 650-H7
6800 DBLN 94568 693-J3
POST ST
- SF 94108 648-A6
- SF 94104 648-A6
- SF 94102 648-A6
400 AlaC 94580 691-D7
900 ALA 94501 670-B4
37000 FRMT 94536 752-H3
POST OFFICE CT
2400 ALA 94501 670-A2
POTAWATAMI DR
45300 FRMT 94539 773-H4
POTEL COM
36100 FRMT 94536 733-A6
POTEL TER
- FRMT 94536 733-A6
POTENZA CT
- LVMR 94550 715-F5
POTOMAC ST
2400 OAK 94602 650-E4
POTOMAC RIVER PL
34700 FRMT 94555 752-E2
POTRERO AV
3900 RCH 94804 609-A1
5100 ELCR 94530 609-C1
POTRERO DR
6100 NWK 94560 772-J2
POTSDAM ST
31800 HAY 94544 732-E3

POTTER ST
400 BERK 94710 629-D4
2400 OAK 94601 650-E7
2400 OAK 94601 670-E1
POULARD CT
44500 FRMT 94539 773-J2
POWDER RIVER PL
34700 FRMT 94555 752-E1
POWELL ST
- SF 94102 648-A4
- SF 94108 648-A4
1100 OAK 94608 629-D6
1200 SF 94133 648-A4
1200 EMVL 94608 629-B6
2200 ALA 94501 669-J3
POWERS CT
- ALA 94501 669-H1
POWERS ST
- DBLN 94568 694-B3
POWNAL AV
2800 SRMN 94583 673-F6
PRADA CT
1300 MPS 95035 794-C5
PRADA DR
400 MPS 95035 794-C5
PRADERA WY
- SRMN 94583 673-A2
PRADERIA CIR
500 FRMT 94539 773-H2
PRAIRIE DR
3300 PLE 94588 714-A3
PRAIRIE DOG LN
100 FRMT 94539 773-H3
PRATO CT
5300 PLE 94588 694-H4
PRATO WY
- LVMR 94550 715-D4
PRATT AV
2400 HAY 94587 732-B4
PRATT PL
- SF 94108 648-A5
PRECIADO DR
- DBLN 94568 694-G4
PREDA ST
400 SLN 94577 690-J1
PRENTISS PL
- SRMN 94583 673-F6
2600 OAK 94601 650-C6
PRENTISS ST
3200 OAK 94601 650-D6
PRESCOTT CT
- SF 94133 648-A4
5300 FRMT 94536 752-G6
PRESERVATION PARK WY
- OAK 94607 649-E5
- OAK 94612 649-E5
PRESIDENT DR
16800 AlaC 94578 691-G5
17000 AlaC 94546 691-G5
PRESIDIO WY
39000 FRMT 94538 753-A5
PRESLEY WY
5800 OAK 94618 630-A5
PRESTIGE PL
900 SRMN 94583 673-B1
PRESTON AV
5000 LVMR 94551 696-B5
PRESTON CT
100 FRMT 94536 753-C2
300 LVMR 94551 696-B5
PRESTON PL
35200 NWK 94560 752-D3
PRESTWICK AV
30400 HAY 94544 732-E1
PRICE RW
- SF 94133 648-A4
PRICE WY
1800 SLN 94577 690-H1
PRIMA DR
- LVMR 94550 715-D4
PRIME AV
22700 AlaC 94541 692-C7
PRIMROSE CT
2000 FRMT 94539 773-G3
PRIMROSE DR
1200 SLN 94578 691-C3
PRIMROSE LN
4800 LVMR 94551 696-A4
PRIMROSE PL
700 HAY 94544 711-J5
PRINCE DR
6900 DBLN 94568 693-J3
PRINCE ST
400 OAK 94610 650-A2
1400 BERK 94702 629-F4
1500 BERK 94703 629-F4
2100 BERK 94705 629-H4
2700 BERK 94705 630-A4
PRINCE ROYAL CT
- OAK 94603 671-C6
PRINCESS CT
4100 UNC 94587 732-A5
PRINCESS PL
600 MPS 95035 794-B4
PRINCETON AV
200 CCCo 94708 609-G4
PRINCETON PL
- AlaC 94552 692-G3
PRINCETON ST
2000 OAK 94601 670-E1
21600 AlaC 94541 711-G1
21900 HAY 94541 711-G1
PRINCETON TER
38300 FRMT 94536 753-B3
PRINCETON WY
3800 LVMR 94550 715-J1
3900 LVMR 94550 716-A1
PRINTY AV
500 MPS 95035 794-C5
PROCTOR AV
4700 OAK 94618 630-C6
PROCTOR LN
3700 AlaC 94546 692-B2
PROCTOR RD
4600 AlaC 94546 691-J2
4600 AlaC 94546 692-A2
PRODUCTION AV
26200 HAY 94545 711-E7
26200 HAY 94545 731-E1
PROMENADE WY
3800 PLE 94566 714-F3
PROMONTORY CIR
- SRMN 94583 673-A1
PROMONTORY LN
100 SRMN 94583 673-B1
PROMONTORY TER
200 SRMN 94583 673-B1
PROMONTORY WY
- SRMN 94583 673-A1
PROSPECT AV
100 DNVL 94526 652-J2

PROSPECT AV
600 OAK 94610 650-A3
600 OAK 94606 650-A3
W PROSPECT AV
200 DNVL 94526 652-J3
PROSPECT CT
6800 PLE 94588 694-A7
21600 HAY 94541 691-H7
PROSPECT RD
- PDMT 94610 650-B2
PROSPECT ST
2300 BERK 94704 629-J2
2300 BERK 94720 629-J2
21600 HAY 94541 691-H7
21800 HAY 94541 711-H1
PROSPECT TER
22300 HAY 94541 711-J1
PROSPECT HILL RD
3100 OAK 94613 650-G7
3100 OAK 94613 670-G1
PROSPECT STEPS
6000 OAK 94618 630-A5
PROSPERITY ST
- SJCo 95391 (678-F3 See Page 677)
PROSPERITY WY
2100 AlaC 94578 691-G4
PROSPERO
4700 FRMT 94555 752-B1
PROVANCE ST
35400 NWK 94560 752-C5
PROVENCE CT
2600 LVMR 94550 715-H3
S PROVIDENCE ST
- SJCo 95391 (678-F2 See Page 677)
PROVIDENCE WY
- HAY 94544 732-B2
PROVIDIAN WY
6000 PLE 94588 694-B6
PROW WY
7200 DBLN 94568 693-F5
PRUNE AV
2000 FRMT 94539 773-F3
PRUNE ST
700 OAK 94603 670-H6
PTARMIGAN CT
2200 UNC 94587 732-G7
PUDDINGSTONE RD
200 ALA 94502 670-A5
PUEBLO DR
10800 OAK 94603 690-H1
PUEBLO TER
34500 FRMT 94555 752-D2
PUEBLO WY
3200 PLE 94588 694-D6
PUEBLO CALLE
27900 HAY 94545 731-G1
PUEBLO CREEK
2600 HAY 94545 731-G1
PUEBLO DEL ORO
27900 HAY 94545 731-G1
PUEBLO LAKE
2600 HAY 94545 731-G1
PUEBLO SERENA
27900 HAY 94545 731-G1
PUEBLO SPRINGS
2700 HAY 94545 731-G1
PUERTO PL
400 HAY 94541 711-G3
PUERTO VALLARTA
500 PLE 94566 714-E4
PUESTA DEL SOL
43500 FRMT 94539 773-G1
PULASKI DR
15400 HAY 94544 732-F3
32800 UNC 94587 732-F3
PULGAS AV
2500 EPA 94303 771-C7
PULLMAN ST
300 LVMR 94551 696-D4
PULSAR AV
1900 LVMR 94550 715-E4
PURCELL DR
- ALA 94502 670-A5
PURCELL PL
35300 FRMT 94536 752-F1
PURDUE AV
100 CCCo 94708 609-G3
1600 EPA 94303 771-B7
PURDUE CT
1400 UNC 94587 732-F5
PURDUE ST
900 SLN 94579 691-A5
PURDUE WY
3900 LVMR 94550 695-J7
3900 LVMR 94550 696-A7
PURI CT
- PLE 94588 713-J3
PURPLELEAF ST
48000 FRMT 94539 793-H1
PUTNAM CT
8700 DBLN 94568 693-F2
PUTTENHAM WY
3100 FRMT 94536 752-G2
PYNE LN
1300 ALA 94502 670-A7
PYRAL CT
- CCCo 94582 674-A1
PYRAMID ST
2200 LVMR 94550 715-G4
PYRITE CT
1500 LVMR 94550 715-D3
PYRO
3000 ALA 94501 649-E6

Q

S Q ST
100 LVMR 94550 715-G1
QUADRES CT
4700 FRMT 94538 752-J6
QUAIL AV
- BERK 94708 609-J6
3500 AlaC 94546 691-H3
QUAIL CRSG
- CCCo 94556 651-F3
QUAIL CT
- AlaC 94566 714-A7
- AlaC 94566 734-B1
1600 LVMR 94550 715-H3
2600 UNC 94587 732-D6
QUAIL DR
1500 MPS 95035 794-D5
33100 UNC 94587 732-D5
QUAIL CANYON CT
2000 HAY 94542 712-C3
QUAIL CREEK CIR
7600 DBLN 94568 694-A1
QUAIL RIDGE LN
100 ORIN 94563 630-H2

QUAIL RUN CT
3600 FRMT 94555 732-D7
QUAIL RUN RD
33400 FRMT 94555 732-D7
QUANTAS LN
800 HAY 94545 711-G5
QUARRY LN
1100 PLE 94566 714-F2
QUARRY RD
- FRMT 94555 751-J6
- FRMT 94555 752-A6
- BERK 94708 609-J7
3400 AlaC 94541 692-D7
QUARRY LAKES DR
3300 UNC 94587 732-H7
QUARTZ CIR
200 LVMR 94550 715-D2
7200 DBLN 94568 693-J2
QUARTZ PL
6200 NWK 94560 772-H1
QUARTZ TER
34200 FRMT 94555 752-C2
QUEBEC AV
1900 SLN 94579 691-A7
QUEBEC COM
5300 FRMT 94555 752-C3
QUEEN CT
21900 AlaC 94546 692-B6
QUEEN ST
22000 AlaC 94546 692-B6
QUEEN ANNE CT
4600 UNC 94587 731-J6
QUEEN ANNE DR
4100 UNC 94587 732-A6
4300 UNC 94587 731-J6
QUEENS RD
500 ALA 94501 669-F1
1200 BERK 94708 609-J6
QUEENSBORO WY
4200 UNC 94587 732-A6
4300 UNC 94587 731-J6
QUEENS PARK CT
42600 FRMT 94538 773-C2
QUEMA CT
1400 FRMT 94539 773-G1
QUEMA DR
1200 FRMT 94539 753-G7
1200 FRMT 94539 773-G1
QUERCUS CT
27900 AlaC 94542 712-F4
QUESO CT
- FRMT 94539 753-D2
QUESO PL
100 FRMT 94539 753-D2
QUEVEDO WY
100 HAY 94544 712-C7
QUICKSILVER AV
6200 NWK 94560 772-H1
QUICKSILVER CT
4400 HAY 94542 712-G4
QUIETWOOD
- OAK 94605 671-D2
QUIGLEY LN
3400 OAK 94602 650-E5
QUIGLEY PL
4200 OAK 94619 650-F6
QUIGLEY ST
3600 OAK 94619 650-E5
QUINAULT WY
100 FRMT 94539 773-H7
QUINCE LN
500 MPS 95035 794-D5
QUINCE PL
38600 NWK 94560 772-H1
QUINCY CT
700 SRMN 94583 673-F5
QUINCY ST
- SF 94108 648-A5
QUINCY WY
600 HAY 94541 711-G4
QUINN LN
24000 AlaC 94541 712-B1
QUINTANA CT
1500 FRMT 94539 753-E5
QUINTANA WY
1100 FRMT 94539 753-E5
QUINTERRA LN
100 DNVL 94526 652-J2
QUIST AV
- HAY 94544 712-C7

R

S R ST
200 LVMR 94550 715-F1
RABBIT CT
- FRMT 94539 773-H3
RABO TER
36600 FRMT 94536 752-F4
RABOLI ST
3700 PLE 94566 715-C7
RACCOLIO WY
- LVMR 94550 715-C4
RACHAEL PL
200 PLE 94566 714-E3
RACHELLE ST
500 LVMR 94550 696-C6
RACINE AV
5100 FRMT 94536 752-H6
RACINE ST
5800 OAK 94609 629-H5
RACOON CT
100 FRMT 94539 773-J3
RACOON HOLLOW CT
7900 PLE 94588 713-J3
RADCLIFF LN
1200 HAY 94545 711-G5
RADCLIFFE AV
6000 NWK 94560 752-D6
RADCLIFFE RD
1600 LVMR 94550 716-A2
RADELE CT
5300 FRMT 94536 752-G6
RADFORD CT
100 SRMN 94582 673-G4
RADIANT LN
900 SRMN 94583 673-B1
RADLEY CT
2400 HAY 94545 711-C5
RADNOR RD
500 OAK 94606 650-A4
RAFAHI WY
3000 AlaC 94541 712-C1
RAGLAND ST
17000 AlaC 94541 691-F6
RAHLVES DR
5000 AlaC 94546 692-B3
RAIL CT
- FRMT 94536 753-D1
RAILROAD AV
- FRMT 94536 753-E7
- DNVL 94526 652-J2

RAILROAD AV
200 MPS 95035 794-A7
1300 LVMR 94550 715-G1
1300 LVMR 94551 715-G1
2100 LVMR 94551 695-H7
2200 LVMR 94550 695-H7
8900 OAK 94603 670-G5
8900 OAK 94621 670-G5
33000 UNC 94587 732-F4
41000 FRMT 94539 753-E7
N RAILROAD CT
200 MPS 95035 794-A6
RAILROAD ST
4300 PLE 94566 714-E3
RAINBOW CT
- HAY 94542 712-C3
- ALA 94501 649-D7
RAINBOW TER
4100 FRMT 94555 752-E1
RAINBOW BRIDGE CT
- SRMN 94582 673-G3
RAINBOW BRIDGE WY
- SRMN 94582 673-G3
RAINDANCE RD
45900 FRMT 94539 774-A5
RAINDEER CT
34400 FRMT 94555 752-D1
RAINDEER RD
3700 FRMT 94555 752-D1
RAINEER CT
- SLN 94577 690-J1
RAINFLOWER DR
5400 LVMR 94551 696-C4
RAINIER AV
- LVMR 94551 715-D1
17500 AlaC 94541 691-E7
17500 AlaC 94580 691-E7
RAINIER CT
2600 UNC 94587 732-F7
RAINTREE CT
- HAY 94544 712-B7
RAINWATER CT
40700 FRMT 94539 753-E4
RAKE CT
1500 SLN 94578 691-D3
RALCO RD
37800 FRMT 94536 752-H4
RALEIGH CT
3100 FRMT 94555 732-E7
RALEIGH PL
1100 HAY 94544 711-J6
RALMAR AV
2400 EPA 94303 771-A7
RALPH APPEZZATO MEMORIAL HWY
100 ALA 94501 649-E7
RALSTON COM
4000 FRMT 94538 753-B5
RALSTON CT
22200 AlaC 94541 692-C6
RALSTON LN
22400 AlaC 94541 692-C6
RALSTON PL
2500 AlaC 94541 692-C6
RALSTON WY
2600 AlaC 94541 692-C6
RAM CT
45100 FRMT 94539 773-J3
RAMAGE PEAK TR
10000 AlaC 94546 652-B6
10000 CCCo 94556 652-B6
RAMBLEWOOD CT
35100 FRMT 94536 752-F1
RAMBLEWOOD PL
- LVMR 94551 696-D3
3500 FRMT 94536 752-F1
RAMBLEWOOD WY
1500 PLE 94566 714-D2
RAMON CT
- DNVL 94526 652-J1
RAMON PL
2000 SRMN 94583 673-G6
RAMON TER
41000 FRMT 94539 753-E6
RAMONA AV
- OAK 94611 630-A7
- PDMT 94611 630-A7
100 ELCR 94530 609-E4
500 ALB 94706 609-E6
RAMONA DR
2400 AlaC 94545 711-E6
RAMONA WY
900 SLN 94577 671-A7
RAMOS AV
400 HAY 94544 711-J3
RAMOS CT
500 MPS 95035 794-D5
RAMPART CT
2400 HAY 94545 731-H1
RAMPART DR
11300 DBLN 94568 693-F5
RAMPART ST
2400 OAK 94602 650-E4
RAMSGATE CT
- DBLN 94568 694-F2
RAMSGATE DR
5100 NWK 94560 752-D3
RAMSGATE PL
34400 FRMT 94555 732-E7
RANCH DR
100 MPS 95035 793-H7
RANCH RD
- ORIN 94563 610-H4
RANCHERO WY
- HAY 94544 712-C7
RANCHITO CT
1000 ELCR 94530 609-C2
RANCHO CT
6700 PLE 94588 694-A7
6700 PLE 94588 714-A1
20300 AlaC 94541 711-E2
RANCHO ARROYO PKWY
400 FRMT 94536 733-A6
400 FRMT 94536 753-A1
500 FRMT 94536 752-J1
RANCHO DIABLO RD
- CCCo 94514 637-F3
RANCHO HIGUERA CT
2000 FRMT 94539 774-A5
RANCHO HIGUERA RD
400 MPS 95035 794-A4
46600 FRMT 94539 774-A5
46600 FRMT 94539 773-J5
RANCHO PALOMARES DR
- AlaC 94552 692-E6
RANCHO PALOMARES PL
22700 AlaC 94552 692-E6
W RANCHO RAMON DR
15500 SJCo 95304 (678-J6 See Page 677)
RANCHO SERENO RD
- CCCo 94514 637-E3

W RANCHO VERDE CT
15800 SJCo 95304 (678-J7 See Page 677)
W RANCHO VIEJO CT
16200 SJCo 95304 (678-J6 See Page 677)
RAND AV
500 OAK 94610 650-A3
RAND ST
1600 MPS 95035 794-A4
RANDALL CT
6400 PLE 94566 714-D6
30900 UNC 94587 732-A4
RANDALL PL
5200 FRMT 94538 773-C3
RANDALL WY
2600 AlaC 94541 712-C1
RANDI CT
4700 UNC 94587 731-J7
RANDICK CT
3100 PLE 94588 694-F6
RANDOLPH AV
3200 OAK 94602 650-C4
RANDOLPH PL
- SRMN 94583 673-F6
RANDWICK AV
- OAK 94611 649-H1
RANDY COM
4000 FRMT 94538 773-D1
RANDY ST
1300 SLN 94579 691-A7
W RANGER AV
- ALA 94501 649-D6
RANGER CT
- ALA 94501 649-A2
RANGER RD
- SLN 94579 690-J6
RANKER PL
400 HAY 94544 712-A6
RANKIN DR
1000 MPS 95035 794-C4
RANLEIGH WY
1100 PDMT 94610 650-B2
RANSOM AV
2100 OAK 94601 650-D7
RANSPOT DR
2300 AlaC 94578 691-G4
RANTOUL CIR
100 SLN 94577 671-D7
RAPALLO COM
- LVMR 94551 695-G6
RAPP AV
37000 FRMT 94536 753-A1
RAPPOLLA CT
5100 PLE 94588 694-H4
RASMUSSEN CT
2600 PLE 94588 694-F6
RATEKIN DR
30600 UNC 94587 732-A4
RATHBONE WY
3400 PLE 94588 694-F6
RATTAN CT
600 FRMT 94539 793-J2
RATTO PL
35400 FRMT 94536 752-F2
RATTO RD
- ALA 94502 669-J6
RAU DR
- FRMT 94536 753-C1
RAUSCH ST
- SF 94103 648-A7
RAVEN CT
- SLN 94579 691-F2
RAVEN RD
2000 PLE 94566 714-D1
RAVEN TER
33800 FRMT 94555 732-D7
RAVENHILL RD
100 ORIN 94563 610-H6
RAVENNA ST
600 LVMR 94551 695-E7
RAVENNA TER
600 FRMT 94536 753-B2
RAVENSBOURNE PARK ST
42600 FRMT 94538 773-C2
RAVENS COVE LN
3200 ALA 94501 670-A4
RAVENWOOD AV
5600 NWK 94560 752-D5
RAVENWOOD LN
2300 OAK 94602 650-E4
RAVENWOOD PL
4100 AlaC 94546 692-B5
RAWHIDE WY
20000 AlaC 94552 692-F2
RAWSON ST
2400 OAK 94601 670-F1
2500 OAK 94619 650-F7
2500 OAK 94619 670-F1
RAY AV
5000 AlaC 94546 692-B4
RAY CT
100 FRMT 94536 753-D2
RAY ST
- PLE 94566 714-E3
RAYLAND CT
6800 PLE 94588 694-A6
RAYMOND DR
300 HAY 94544 712-B5
RAYMOND RD
2800 LVMR 94551 696-A1
4000 AlaC 94551 695-J1
4000 AlaC 94551 696-A1
RAYMOND ST
6400 OAK 94609 629-H4
READING AV
2200 AlaC 94546 692-A6
REAMER RD
18000 AlaC 94546 691-J2
REATA PL
- OAK 94618 630-A4
REBECCA DR
1400 LVMR 94550 696-C7
RECINO ST
100 FRMT 94539 753-F4
RECREATION RD
- AlaC 94552 692-D6
RECTOR COM
4000 FRMT 94538 753-B5
REDBERRY CT
2300 PLE 94566 714-C1
REDBUD CT
7600 NWK 94560 752-D7
7700 PLE 94588 713-J1
REDBUD DR
700 LVMR 94551 695-E7
REDBUD LN
200 HAY 94541 711-G3
RED CEDAR CT
- UNC 94587 732-G5

RED CEDAR LN
- UNC 94587 732-G5
REDCEDAR TER
- FRMT 94536 752-H3
RED CLIFF TER
- FRMT 94536 753-C1
REDCOACH LN
- ORIN 94563 610-H3
REDDING PL
- OAK 94619 650-F7
REDDING ST
3500 OAK 94619 650-F5
REDEKER PL
6500 NWK 94560 752-F7
6500 NWK 94560 772-F1
RED FEATHER CT
- PLE 94566 714-H4
REDFIELD PL
300 MRGA 94556 651-E3
RED FIR WY
4200 LVMR 94551 696-A3
REDGRAVE PL
34400 FRMT 94555 752-E1
RED HAWK CIR
1400 FRMT 94538 753-C4
1400 FRMT 94536 753-C4
RED HAWK TER
1400 FRMT 94538 753-C3
RED HILL CT
2400 UNC 94587 732-B4
REDHOOK LN
3400 AlaC 94502 670-A7
RED LAKE TER
3800 FRMT 94555 732-C6
REDLANDS ST
4300 UNC 94587 732-B7
RED LEAF CT
3200 HAY 94542 712-E4
W RED LINE AV
- ALA 94501 649-C6
RED MAPLE CT
- HAY 94544 712-E7
RED MAPLE ST
1700 UNC 94587 732-D4
RED OAK AV
- ALB 94710 609-D7
REDOAK COM
4400 FRMT 94538 773-C1
RED OAK CT
29600 HAY 94544 712-D7
REDONDO AV
5200 OAK 94618 629-H6
REDONDO CT
- ALA 94501 649-G7
W REDONDO DR
15900 SJCo 95304 (678-J6 See Page 677)
REDONDO WY
900 LVMR 94550 715-F3
RED PINE CT
2800 PLE 94588 694-H3
RED ROCK RD
800 PDMT 94618 630-C7
800 PDMT 94611 630-C7
REDSTONE PL
1000 HAY 94542 712-A3
REDSTONE TER
4100 FRMT 94555 752-B2
REDWING PL
3300 FRMT 94555 732-D7
REDWOOD AV
- DBLN 94568 694-D3
200 MPS 95035 793-H6
1500 SLN 94579 691-A5
REDWOOD CT
3400 AlaC 94546 692-A5
3900 PLE 94588 713-J2
36500 NWK 94560 752-D6
REDWOOD GN
19500 AlaC 94546 692-A4
REDWOOD HTS
4300 AlaC 94546 692-A3
REDWOOD RD
3700 OAK 94619 650-H5
4100 LVMR 94551 696-A4
5700 AlaC 94619 650-J4
6500 AlaC 94619 651-A4
8800 AlaC 94546 651-D6
12700 AlaC 94546 671-E1
15900 AlaC 94546 672-A6
15900 AlaC 94546 692-A1
REDWOOD TER
- ORIN 94563 610-E6
1000 FRMT 94536 753-B2
REECE CT
4600 RCH 94804 609-A1
REED AV
2600 AlaC 94550 715-H5
14000 SLN 94578 691-C3
REED CT
4600 FRMT 94538 753-A6
REED DR
- MRGA 94556 651-F2
REED PL
- CCCo 94707 609-F3
REED WY
23100 HAY 94541 711-F3
REEDER CT
5200 FRMT 94536 752-H6
REEDLEY WY
5200 AlaC 94546 692-B2
REES CIR
- LVMR 94550 716-C2
REFLECTIONS CIR
400 SRMN 94583 673-F3
REFLECTIONS DR
100 SRMN 94583 673-F3
3600 PLE 94566 714-F2
REFLECTIONS LN
- MPS 95035 794-A6
- MPS 95035 793-H6
REGAL AV
25900 HAY 94544 711-H6
REGAL DR
2400 UNC 94587 732-C4
REGAL RD
800 BERK 94708 609-H5
REGALIA AV
800 PLE 94566 714-E3
REGALO WY
- SRMN 94583 673-A2
REGAN WY
800 FRMT 94539 753-G7
REGATTA CT
- SLN 94579 711-A1
REGATTA WY
- SLN 94579 691-A7
- SLN 94579 711-A1
REGENCY CT
900 SRMN 94582 673-J6
1500 ELCR 94530 609-D1

STREET
Block City ZIP Pg-Grid

REGENCY DR
2800 PLE 94588 714-A3
REGENT DR
1400 SLN 94577 691-D1
REGENT PL
1200 LVMR 94550 715-F5
REGENT RD
2400 LVMR 94550 715-F5
REGENT ST
900 ALA 94501 669-J3
900 ALA 94501 670-A3
2500 BERK 94704 629-J3
2700 BERK 94705 629-J3
6400 OAK 94618 629-J4
REGENT WY
7400 AlaC 94546 691-G6
REGENTS BLVD
32200 UNC 94587 731-J6
32200 UNC 94587 732-A6
32500 UNC 94545 731-J6
32700 UNC 94587 752-A1
REGENTS PARK LN
4800 FRMT 94538 773-C2
REGINALD CT
- LVMR 94550 715-F4
REGIO CT
11600 DBLN 94568 693-F3
REGIO DR
11600 DBLN 94568 693-F3
REGIONAL ST
6900 DBLN 94568 693-G4
REGO COM
400 FRMT 94536 753-E1
REGULUS CT
- ALA 94501 649-G7
500 LVMR 94550 715-E4
REGULUS RD
500 LVMR 94550 715-E4
REID CT
5000 RCH 94804 609-B1
REILLY CT
11500 DBLN 94568 693-F5
REIMERS DR
- PLE 94588 714-F1
REINA PL
36400 NWK 94560 752-E5
REINHARDT DR
3900 OAK 94619 650-G5
4800 OAK 94613 650-G5
RELIANCE WY
800 FRMT 94539 773-G4
REMCO ST
3400 AlaC 94546 691-H3
REMER TER
5900 FRMT 94555 752-B3
REMILLARD CT
4100 PLE 94566 714-G5
REMINGTON CT
- DNVL 94526 652-J3
REMINGTON DR
100 DNVL 94526 652-J3
33700 UNC 94587 732-E6
REMINGTON LP
200 DNVL 94526 652-J4
200 CCCo 94583 652-J4
REMMEL CT
- ALA 94502 669-J6
REMORA DR
- UNC 94587 731-J5
RENADA PL
900 SRMN 94583 673-G5
RENAISSANCE LN
- AlaC 94578 691-F4
RENATO CT
4500 FRMT 94536 752-E3
RENNELLWOOD WY
4000 PLE 94566 714-E1
RENTON WY
2600 AlaC 94546 691-H5
RENWICK ST
2400 OAK 94601 650-E7
2600 OAK 94619 650-E7
REPOSO DR
10900 OAK 94603 670-H7
10900 OAK 94603 690-H1
REPUBLIC AV
1900 SLN 94577 690-H4
REQUA PL
- PDMT 94611 650-B1
REQUA RD
100 PDMT 94611 650-B2
RESEARCH AV
46100 FRMT 94539 773-G4
RESEARCH DR
2000 LVMR 94550 716-D1
RESEARCH RD
26200 HAY 94545 731-D1
RESEDA CIR
5200 FRMT 94538 773-A1
RESERVE COM
- LVMR 94551 695-G6
RESOTA ST
700 HAY 94545 711-G5
RETTIG AV
4000 OAK 94602 650-F4
RETTIG PL
4000 OAK 94602 650-F5
REUSS RD
10700 AlaC 94550 716-J4
10700 AlaC 94550 717-C3
REVA AV
200 SLN 94577 690-H1
REVERE AV
- HAY 94544 732-E3
2900 OAK 94605 671-C6
REVERE PL
44200 FRMT 94539 773-H2
REVERE TER
- FRMT 94539 773-H2
REVIEW WY
- HAY 94544 711-H3
REVIVAL TER
500 FRMT 94536 753-G3
REX RD
1100 HAY 94541 691-J7
REYES DR
4500 UNC 94587 731-J6
REYMOUTH DR
35400 NWK 94560 752-D4
REYNA DR
- AlaC 94541 692-C6
REYNOLDS COM
37000 FRMT 94536 752-H2
REYNOLDS CT
3000 FRMT 94536 752-H2
REYNOLDS DR
36600 FRMT 94536 752-H2
REYNOLDS ST
2000 SLN 94577 690-G1
RHEA WY
500 LVMR 94550 715-E4

RHEEM CT
1800 PLE 94588 694-E7
RHEEM DR
1800 PLE 94588 694-E7
RHINE WY
1000 PLE 94566 714-H4
RHODA AV
3400 OAK 94602 650-E4
8300 DBLN 94568 693-F2
RHODA CT
11900 DBLN 94568 693-F2
RHODA PL
8500 DBLN 94568 693-F2
RHODODENDRON CT
1900 LVMR 94551 696-A3
RHODODENDRON DR
1200 LVMR 94551 696-A4
RHONDA LN
- LVMR 94550 696-B7
RHONE DR
- LVMR 94550 715-H4
RIA DR
16300 AlaC 94578 691-F5
RIALTO WY
- PLE 94588 694-C6
RIATA CT
39800 FRMT 94538 753-B6
RIBERA CT
35500 FRMT 94536 752-F2
RIBERA ST
4200 FRMT 94536 752-F3
RICARDO AV
100 PDMT 94611 650-A1
100 PDMT 94611 630-A7
18500 AlaC 94541 711-E1
RICARDO CT
7700 ELCR 94530 609-E3
RICE ST
4400 LVMR 94550 716-A1
RICH AV
7000 NWK 94560 752-E7
RICH ST
400 OAK 94609 629-H7
RICH ACRES CT
- ORIN 94563 610-E6
RICH ACRES RD
- ORIN 94563 610-E6
RICHARD PL
1200 HAY 94541 711-J1
RICHARD ST
1200 HAY 94541 711-J1
RICHARDS RD
4900 OAK 94613 650-G7
RICHARDSON DR
41500 FRMT 94538 753-E7
41500 FRMT 94538 773-E1
RICHARDSON RD
- CCCo 94707 609-F4
RICHARDSON WY
- PDMT 94611 650-C1
RICHMOND AV
2800 OAK 94611 649-H2
4300 FRMT 94536 752-J5
RICHMOND BLVD
3000 OAK 94611 649-H2
RICHMOND ST
400 ELCR 94530 609-C1
RICK CT
- MRGA 94556 651-D1
RICK WY
25300 AlaC 94541 712-C2
RICKENBACKER CIR
100 LVMR 94551 695-C6
RICKENBACKER PL
- LVMR 94551 695-D6
RICO COM
37200 FRMT 94536 752-J2
RIDDELL LN
200 ALA 94502 670-B5
RIDDELL ST
6600 PLE 94566 714-D7
RIDER CT
26000 HAY 94544 712-A5
RIDGE CT
6800 LVMR 94551 696-E2
RIDGE LN
- ORIN 94563 610-F4
RIDGE RD
2400 BERK 94709 629-H1
RIDGE TR
- CCCo 94583 652-C1
RIDGECREEK LN
24100 AlaC 94541 712-B1
RIDGECREST CIR
- LVMR 94551 695-J7
RIDGE CREST CT
- AlaC 94546 691-G3
3200 AlaC 94541 692-D7
RIDGECREST WY
- LVMR 94551 695-J7
RIDGE GATE RD
400 ORIN 94563 610-G7
RIDGE LINE TR
- PLE 94586 713-J6
- PLE 94586 714-A7
RIDGEMONT CT
4200 OAK 94619 650-J6
RIDGEMONT DR
6000 OAK 94619 650-J7
RIDGEMONT TER
- FRMT 94536 752-J2
RIDGEMOOR RD
8900 OAK 94605 671-C2
RIDGEPONTE CT
800 SRMN 94582 673-J6
RIDGESTONE RD
1300 LVMR 94551 696-D3
RIDGESTONE WY
1400 LVMR 94551 696-D3
RIDGEVALE RD
5400 PLE 94566 714-C2
RIDGEVALE WY
5200 PLE 94566 714-C2
RIDGEVIEW CT
- SRMN 94582 673-E2
RIDGEVIEW PL
3300 AlaC 94541 712-D2
RIDGEVIEW TER
600 FRMT 94536 753-C3
RIDGEWAY AV
100 OAK 94611 629-J7
100 OAK 94611 649-J1
RIDGEWAY LN
- ELCR 94530 609-F2
RIDGEWOOD DR
4800 FRMT 94555 752-C3
6300 AlaC 94552 692-F4
6800 OAK 94611 630-F6
RIDGEWOOD LN
- OAK 94611 630-F6
RIDGEWOOD RD
1200 PLE 94566 714-D2

RIDGEWOOD WY
- OAK 94611 630-F6
RIDING CLUB CT
4500 HAY 94542 712-G4
RIDLEY DR
38200 FRMT 94536 753-B2
RIDPATH ST
4600 FRMT 94538 753-B7
RIEGER AV
1200 HAY 94544 711-J7
1200 HAY 94544 712-A7
RIESLING CIR
1100 LVMR 94550 715-J2
RIESLING CT
- FRMT 94539 793-J2
3700 PLE 94566 714-G4
RIESLING DR
900 PLE 94566 714-G4
RIESLING ST
- FRMT 94539 793-J2
RIFFEL CT
2400 AlaC 94546 691-H5
RIFLE LN
4100 OAK 94605 671-A1
RIFLE RANGE RD
- AlaC 94546 671-J4
- AlaC 94546 672-A3
- AlaC 94552 672-A3
1300 ELCR 94530 609-E1
RIGATTI CIR
5000 PLE 94588 694-C6
RIGGS CT
28100 HAY 94542 712-E5
RILEA WY
4300 OAK 94605 671-B1
RILEY RIDGE RD
- AlaC 94546 651-J7
- AlaC 94546 652-A7
- AlaC 94546 671-H1
RIMA CT
1000 FRMT 94539 773-H2
RIMER DR
1100 MRGA 94556 651-E2
RINCON AV
200 LVMR 94551 715-F1
300 LVMR 94551 695-F7
RINCON DR
5900 OAK 94611 650-E1
RINCON RD
- CCCo 94707 609-F3
RINCON ST
100 SF 94107 648-C6
RINCONADA CT
- NWK 94560 752-B6
RING CT
5700 FRMT 94538 773-C2
RINGOLD ST
- SF 94103 648-A7
RIOJA CT
40800 FRMT 94539 753-E6
RIO VISTA
- ORIN 94563 610-G7
RIO VISTA AV
- OAK 94611 649-J1
RIO VISTA ST
21700 HAY 94541 691-H7
RIPON CT
32700 UNC 94587 732-B7
RISDON DR
2900 UNC 94587 732-A4
RISHELL DR
- OAK 94619 650-H4
RISING HILL CT
4600 OAK 94605 651-A7
RISPIN DR
1000 OAK 94705 630-B3
RITCH ST
200 SF 94107 648-B7
RITCHIE ST
2400 OAK 94605 670-J3
RIVENELL WY
- SRMN 94582 674-D3
RIVER DR
- FRMT 94536 753-C1
RIVERA CT
1100 LVMR 94551 696-D3
RIVERA ST
700 MPS 95035 794-B4
1200 ELCR 94530 609-D2
RIVERBANK AV
1800 AlaC 94546 691-J6
1800 HAY 94546 691-J6
RIVERBANK TER
38800 FRMT 94536 753-C3
RIVERBEND TER
3800 FRMT 94555 732-C7
RIVERCREEK DR
200 FRMT 94536 732-J7
RIVERCREST LN
300 HAY 94544 732-E2
RIVERDALE CT
5200 PLE 94588 693-J6
RIVERDALE ST
14900 SLN 94578 691-C5
RIVERLAND CT
- SRMN 94582 674-C3
RIVER OAK WY
600 HAY 94544 712-D7
RIVER ROCK HILL RD
- PLE 94588 713-J1
RIVERSIDE AV
300 FRMT 94536 753-B1
RIVERSIDE CT
- SLN 94579 711-A1
RIVERSTONE COM
- LVMR 94550 715-C1
RIVERTON PL
200 SRMN 94583 673-G7
RIVERWALK DR
- FRMT 94536 752-J3
- FRMT 94536 753-A2
RIVIERA CT
- OAK 94605 671-D3
7900 PLE 94588 714-B5
RIVIERA DR
200 UNC 94587 732-J5
36600 FRMT 94536 753-A1
RIVIERA PL
500 SRMN 94583 673-H6
RIVIERA WY
3000 SRMN 94583 673-F6
RIZAL ST
- SF 94107 648-B6
RIZZO AV
21400 AlaC 94546 691-J6
ROAD A
1400 ALA 94502 670-A7
1400 ALA 94502 690-A1
ROAD B
- ALA 94502 670-B7
- ALA 94502 690-B1

ROADRUNNER RD
46400 FRMT 94539 773-J5
ROAN CT
2100 LVMR 94551 696-A2
ROANOKE
4000 ALA 94501 649-F6
ROANOKE RD
- BERK 94705 630-A4
- OAK 94618 630-A4
ROANOKE ST
28600 HAY 94544 712-B7
ROANOKE WY
38800 FRMT 94536 752-J6
ROATAN CT
- SRMN 94583 673-D3
ROBERT WY
100 LVMR 94550 715-D1
ROBERTA DR
8500 ELCR 94530 609-F2
ROBERT DAVEY JR DR
- ALA 94502 669-J5
2900 ALA 94502 670-A5
ROBERT KIRK LN
- SF 94108 648-A5
ROBERTO ST
17200 AlaC 94546 691-G5
ROBERTS AV
5400 OAK 94619 670-G1
5500 OAK 94605 670-G1
41200 FRMT 94538 753-D7
41500 FRMT 94538 773-E1
ROBERTS CT
- MRGA 94556 651-D1
700 DNVL 94526 652-G1
ROBERTS ST
34800 UNC 94587 732-G7
ROBERTSON AV
5600 NWK 94560 752-F7
ROBERTSON PARK RD
- LVMR 94550 715-H2
ROBERT T MONAGAN FRWY I-205
- AlaC - (678-D7 See Page 677)
- SJCo - (678-D7 See Page 677)
- TRCY - (678-J7 See Page 677)
ROBEY DR
16800 AlaC 94578 691-G5
17000 AlaC 94546 691-G5
ROBIN COM
- LVMR 94550 696-A6
ROBIN CT
2500 UNC 94587 732-D6
4700 FRMT 94538 773-C1
6200 PLE 94588 694-A7
ROBIN LN
4000 AlaC 94546 692-B5
ROBIN ST
15000 AlaC 94578 691-D4
40300 FRMT 94538 753-C7
40500 FRMT 94538 773-C1
ROBINHOOD WY
6200 OAK 94611 630-D6
ROBINSON CIR
- LVMR 94550 716-C2
ROBINSON DR
3100 OAK 94602 650-G3
ROBISON DR
3100 OAK 94705 630-B3
ROBLE CT
- BERK 94705 630-B4
ROBLE RD
- BERK 94705 630-B4
100 OAK 94618 630-B4
ROBLEDO DR
10900 OAK 94603 670-H7
ROBLEY TER
3900 OAK 94611 649-J1
ROBSCOTT AV
17800 AlaC 94541 711-E1
ROCA DR
35300 FRMT 94536 752-E3
ROCCA CT
3500 PLE 94588 694-H4
ROCHDALE WY
- BERK 94708 609-H4
ROCHELLE AV
6400 NWK 94560 752-C6
28200 HAY 94544 712-B7
ROCHELLE DR
4600 UNC 94587 731-J7
ROCHESTER CT
29000 HAY 94544 732-A2
ROCHI CT
16100 AlaC 94578 691-E5
ROCK AV
500 FRMT 94536 732-J7
700 FRMT 94536 752-J1
ROCK ISL
600 ALA 94501 669-H2
ROCK LN
- BERK 94708 609-H5
ROCKAWAY LN
22300 HAY 94541 692-A7
22300 HAY 94541 691-J7
ROCKETT DR
3000 FRMT 94538 753-D6
ROCKFORD PL
8000 PLE 94566 734-D1
8000 PLE 94586 734-D1
ROCKFORD RD
21900 HAY 94541 691-J7
ROCKHAMPTON RD
- SRMN 94582 674-B4
ROCKHURST RD
17600 AlaC 94546 692-B2
ROCKINGHAM CT
- LVMR 94550 715-H6
4600 OAK 94605 651-A7
ROCKINGHAM DR
3900 PLE 94588 694-E6
ROCKLAND AV
35400 FRMT 94536 732-J6
ROCKLIN DR
- UNC 94555 752-A2
4800 UNC 94587 752-A2
ROCK POINT PL
- LVMR 94550 715-E4
ROCKPORT CT
5300 NWK 94560 752-E4
ROCKPORT WY
- HAY 94544 732-B1
ROCKRIDGE BLVD N
6000 OAK 94618 630-A5
ROCKRIDGE BLVD S
6000 OAK 94618 630-A5
ROCKRIDGE PL
- OAK 94618 630-A5
ROCKROSE CT
700 HAY 94544 712-A7

ROCKROSE CT
38500 NWK 94560 772-G1
ROCKROSE DR
6000 NWK 94560 772-G1
ROCKROSE ST
- LVMR 94551 715-D1
ROCKSPRAY ST
37600 NWK 94560 752-G6
ROCK SPRINGS DR
1900 HAY 94545 711-F5
ROCK SPRINGS RD
- PLE 94566 714-J4
ROCKWAY AV
7300 ELCR 94530 609-E4
ROCKWAY CT
900 PLE 94566 714-F3
ROCKWELL ST
6000 OAK 94618 629-J4
ROCKWOOD DR
37400 FRMT 94536 752-G4
ROCKY CREEK PL
- PLE 94566 714-C5
ROCKY MOUNTAIN CT
3700 PLE 94588 714-A2
ROCKY POINT CT
- SLN 94579 711-A1
ROCKY POINTE CT
- HAY 94542 712-G5
ROCKY RIDGE RD
- CCCo 94556 652-B3
ROCKY RIDGE TR
- CCCo 94556 652-B2
- CCCo 94583 652-B2
RODEO LN
2900 LVMR 94550 715-J2
RODERICK RD
4200 OAK 94605 671-D4
RODERIGO
4500 FRMT 94555 752-C1
RODGERS ST
- SF 94103 648-D7
RODNEY COM
3100 FRMT 94538 753-D6
RODNEY DR
700 SLN 94577 671-B7
RODRIGUES AV
100 MPS 95035 794-C7
RODRIGUEZ CT
- CCCo 94582 674-B5
ROEDING AV
1100 FRMT 94536 732-H7
ROGAN RD
12100 AlaC 94586 754-C2
ROGER CT
1600 ELCR 94530 609-D1
ROGER ST
1600 MPS 95035 794-A4
ROGERIO ST
17000 AlaC 94541 691-G6
ROGERS AV
4800 FRMT 94536 752-H6
ROGERS CT
2800 OAK 94619 650-E7
ROJO WY
2200 PLE 94566 714-G3
ROLAND WY
400 OAK 94621 670-E6
ROLANDO AV
16500 AlaC 94578 691-G5
16900 AlaC 94546 691-G5
ROLLING HILLS CIR
7400 DBLN 94568 693-F4
ROLLING HILLS CT
- LVMR 94551 696-E3
ROLLINGHILLS CT
19200 AlaC 94546 692-C4
ROLLING HILLS DR
11100 DBLN 94568 693-F3
ROLLING HILLS PL
11600 DBLN 94568 693-F4
ROLLINGHILLS WY
4700 AlaC 94546 692-C4
ROLLING RIDGE LN
24100 AlaC 94541 712-B1
ROLLINGSTONE COM
- LVMR 94550 715-C1
ROLLINS ST
14600 SLN 94579 691-A4
ROMA CT
500 LVMR 94551 695-E7
ROMA PL
3300 SRMN 94583 673-G5
ROMA ST
800 LVMR 94551 695-E7
ROMA TER
6000 FRMT 94555 752-A5
ROMAGNOLO ST
2800 AlaC 94541 692-C7
ROMAN EAGLE CT
- PLE 94566 714-J4
ROMANO CIR
2300 PLE 94566 715-B7
ROMANY RD
5700 OAK 94618 630-B6
ROME PL
200 HAY 94544 732-F3
ROMEO CT
600 PLE 94566 714-D6
ROMEO PL
4900 FRMT 94555 752-C2
ROMEY LN
2200 HAY 94541 692-B7
ROMILLY CT
35900 FRMT 94536 752-F3
ROMILLY WY
4300 FRMT 94536 752-F3
ROMOLO ST
- SF 94133 648-A4
RONADA AV
- OAK 94611 630-A7
- PDMT 94611 630-A7
RONALD CT
3500 FRMT 94538 773-E1
RONALD LN
23200 HAY 94541 711-G3
RON COWAN PKWY
- ALA 94502 670-B7
- OAK 94621 670-B7
- OAK 94621 690-C1
RONDA CT
35400 FRMT 94536 752-F1
RONDA ST
15600 AlaC 94580 691-D6
RONDALE CT
200 AlaC 94541 711-F1
ROOSEVELT AV
400 LVMR 94551 696-D4
1200 HAY 94544 711-J7
2100 BERK 94703 629-G2
ROOSEVELT DR
2400 ALA 94501 669-J3

ROOSEVELT PL
5400 FRMT 94538 753-A7
5400 FRMT 94538 773-A1
5600 FRMT 94538 772-J1
ROOSEVELT WY
- SJS 95002 793-C7
ROSADA CT
3300 PLE 94588 694-D6
ROSADO RD
200 FRMT 94539 753-F4
ROSAL AV
500 OAK 94610 650-A2
ROSALEE CT
3700 AlaC 94546 691-J3
ROSALITA CT
4100 FRMT 94536 752-F2
ROSARIO CT
100 SRMN 94583 673-C3
19100 AlaC 94541 691-F7
ROSCOMMON WY
- DBLN 94568 694-D4
ROSE AV
200 DNVL 94526 652-J2
200 PLE 94566 714-C3
900 OAK 94611 650-A1
900 PDMT 94611 650-A1
1000 PDMT 94611 630-A7
1000 OAK 94611 630-A7
ROSE CT
3900 FRMT 94536 752-H3
5700 NWK 94560 752-D5
ROSE DR
100 MPS 95035 794-A4
13400 SLN 94577 691-B3
13500 SLN 94578 691-B3
ROSE LN
- ORIN 94563 610-F6
1500 PLE 94566 714-C3
ROSE ST
- FRMT 94555 732-C7
300 DNVL 94526 652-J2
400 LVMR 94550 695-J7
400 LVMR 94550 715-J1
900 HAY 94541 691-H7
1200 BERK 94702 629-E1
1300 BERK 94702 609-F7
1500 BERK 94703 609-F7
1900 BERK 94709 609-G7
2300 BERK 94708 609-H7
ROSE WK
- SRMN 94583 673-A2
2500 BERK 94708 609-H7
ROSE WY
4700 UNC 94587 731-J7
4700 UNC 94587 732-A7
4700 UNC 94587 751-J1
5100 UNC 94545 751-J1
ROSEANNE CT
900 AlaC 94580 691-F6
ROSEBUD CT
2700 UNC 94587 752-G1
ROSECLIFF CT
- PLE 94588 714-B5
ROSECLIFF LN
29000 HAY 94544 732-A2
ROSECLIFF PL
- PLE 94566 714-B4
ROSECREST DR
1800 OAK 94602 650-E2
ROSEDALE AV
1500 OAK 94601 670-D1
1900 OAK 94601 650-D7
ROSEDALE CT
7500 PLE 94588 693-H6
ROSEFIELD LP
- ALA 94501 649-A2
ROSEGARDEN CT
48900 FRMT 94539 794-A2
ROSE GATE COM
- LVMR 94551 696-D3
ROSEGATE TER
38700 FRMT 94536 753-C3
ROSEHILL PL
2200 AlaC 94541 692-C7
ROSELLE COM
37500 FRMT 94536 752-G5
ROSELLE LN
- ORIN 94563 630-J3
ROSELLI DR
1300 LVMR 94550 715-F3
ROSELMA PL
900 PLE 94566 714-F5
ROSEMARY COM
6400 LVMR 94551 696-D2
ROSEMARY CT
1900 FRMT 94539 773-G3
ROSEMARY LN
- SRMN 94583 693-F1
ROSEMERE CT
1500 FRMT 94539 773-G2
ROSEMERE DR
43900 FRMT 94539 773-G2
ROSEMONT AV
- BERK 94708 609-H4
ROSEMOUNT LN
- SRMN 94582 674-D4
ROSEMOUNT RD
600 OAK 94610 650-A3
ROSE ROCK CIR
3700 PLE 94588 694-E7
ROSETREE CT
- FRMT 94536 753-A2
1800 PLE 94566 714-D1
ROSEWALK CT
- FRMT 94539 753-E6
ROSEWOOD AV
4100 RCH 94804 609-A1
ROSEWOOD COM
4500 FRMT 94538 773-C1
ROSEWOOD CT
- LVMR 94550 715-D5
200 HAY 94544 712-B6
300 SLN 94577 670-J7
ROSEWOOD DR
4300 PLE 94588 694-D5
36000 NWK 94560 752-D5
ROSEWOOD WY
1000 ALA 94501 669-G2
ROSHILL PL
- DBLN 94568 694-E2
ROSINCRESS CT
- SRMN 94582 673-G1
ROSINCRESS DR
- SRMN 94582 673-G1
ROSITA CT
7100 DBLN 94568 693-J3
ROSLIN CT
6200 PLE 94588 694-A7
ROSLYN CT
- BERK 94618 630-A4
- BERK 94705 630-A4

ROSOLI TER
4400 FRMT 94536 752-G4
ROSS AL
- SF 94108 648-A4
ROSS CIR
- OAK 94618 630-A4
ROSS COM
39500 FRMT 94538 753-B5
ROSS DR
- MRGA 94556 651-E1
ROSS PL
27700 HAY 94544 712-B6
ROSS RD
- ALA 94502 669-H6
ROSS ST
5800 OAK 94618 630-A4
ROSS TER
4200 FRMT 94538 753-A5
ROSS GATE CT
4700 PLE 94566 694-D7
ROSS GATE WY
4600 PLE 94566 694-D7
ROSSMOOR AV
400 OAK 94603 670-G6
ROSSMOOR CT
- OAK 94603 670-G6
ROSSMORE LN
600 HAY 94544 711-H5
ROSSO CT
- PLE 94566 715-D6
ROSWELL CT
300 MPS 95035 794-D7
ROSWELL DR
100 MPS 95035 794-D7
ROTARY ST
300 HAY 94541 711-H2
ROTHBURY COM
4500 FRMT 94536 752-G4
ROTHBURY CT
- SRMN 94582 674-C3
ROTHMAN CT
5500 AlaC 94552 692-D2
ROTHSCHILD CT
11200 DBLN 94568 693-E4
ROTHSCHILD PL
11400 DBLN 94568 693-F4
ROUBAUD CT
- SRMN 94582 674-B4
ROUND HILL DR
- DBLN 94568 694-F2
3300 HAY 94542 712-E4
ROUNDHILL PL
- LVMR 94550 715-E4
ROUND TOP LOOP TR
- CCCo 94516 630-F5
- CCCo 94563 630-F5
ROUNDTREE COM
5500 FRMT 94538 773-A1
ROUNDTREE TER
5500 FRMT 94538 773-A1
ROUSILLON AV
4600 FRMT 94555 752-D2
ROUSILLON PL
4500 FRMT 94555 752-D2
ROUSSEAU ST
- HAY 94544 732-D2
ROVERTON CT
- SRMN 94582 674-C4
ROWE CT
- ALA 94501 649-A2
ROWE PL
3100 FRMT 94536 752-H2
ROWELL LN
500 PLE 94566 714-F4
ROWENA DR
1100 HAY 94542 712-A2
ROWLAND DR
33800 FRMT 94555 732-D7
ROWLAND ST
- SF 94133 648-A4
ROXANNE AV
1100 HAY 94542 712-A2
ROXANNE CT
5200 LVMR 94550 696-C7
ROXANNE ST
900 LVMR 94550 696-C7
ROXBURG LN
100 ALA 94502 669-J5
100 ALA 94502 670-A5
ROXBURY AV
3000 OAK 94605 671-C6
ROXBURY LN
3600 HAY 94542 712-E3
ROXIE TER
5900 FRMT 94555 752-B4
ROYAL AV
19200 AlaC 94541 711-E1
21400 HAY 94541 711-E1
ROYAL RD
500 LVMR 94551 695-H6
ROYAL ST
900 OAK 94603 670-J7
ROYAL ANN
- UNC 94587 732-F6
ROYAL ANN COM
38500 FRMT 94536 753-C2
ROYAL ANN CT
2500 UNC 94587 732-F7
ROYAL ANN DR
2300 UNC 94587 732-F6
ROYAL ANN ST
10000 OAK 94603 670-H6
ROYAL CREEK CT
- PLE 94588 714-B5
ROYAL OAK RD
10200 OAK 94605 671-C3
ROYAL OAKS CT
- PLE 94588 714-B5
ROYAL PALM DR
4900 FRMT 94538 752-J7
39500 FRMT 94538 753-A7
ROYAL PINES CT
- DBLN 94568 694-G3
ROYAL PINES WY
- DBLN 94568 694-G3
ROYALTON CT
3200 PLE 94588 694-E6
ROYAL WINGS WY
2000 SLN 94579 690-J6
ROYCROFT WY
5100 FRMT 94538 773-B1
ROYSHILL LN
- DBLN 94568 693-D5
ROYSTON CT
8600 DBLN 94568 693-F2
ROYSTON LN
600 HAY 94544 712-D7
RUBICON AV
6200 NWK 94560 772-H1
RUBICON CIR
100 DNVL 94526 652-J1

ALAMEDA CO.

STREET / Block	City	ZIP	Pg-Grid
RUBICON WY			
-	LVMR	94551	696-D3
RUBICON VALLEY CT			
-	SRMN	94582	673-J6
RUBIN DR			
3300	OAK	94602	650-G4
RUBINO CT			
-	PLE	94566	715-B5
RUBIO WY			
100	HAY	94544	712-C7
RUBY CT			
100	LVMR	94550	715-D2
RUBY RD			
500	LVMR	94550	715-D2
RUBY ST			
3700	OAK	94609	649-H1
3900	OAK	94609	629-H7
22400	AlaC	94546	692-A7
RUBY HILL BLVD			
-	PLE	94566	715-C5
E RUBY HILL DR			
3000	PLE	94566	715-C5
4200	PLE	94566	735-C1
W RUBY HILL DR			
-	PLE	94566	735-C1
2800	PLE	94566	715-B5
RUDSDALE ST			
6900	OAK	94621	670-G3
RUDYARD DR			
300	MPS	95035	793-J7
RUFUS CT			
900	AlaC	94541	691-H7
RUGBY AV			
300	BERK	94707	609-G4
300	CCCo	94708	609-G4
RUGBY CT			
-	OAK	94603	671-C5
RUGBY PL			
35100	NWK	94560	752-E3
RUGGLES ST			
15300	SLN	94579	691-B7
RUMFORD TER			
-	UNC	94587	732-G6
RUNCKEL LN			
35600	FRMT	94536	752-G1
RUNNING HILLS AV			
5700	LVMR	94551	696-C2
RUNNYMEDE CT			
3200	PLE	94588	694-E6
RUSCHIN DR			
35700	NWK	94560	752-E5
RUSH CREEK CT			
100	SRMN	94582	674-A7
RUSKIN AV			
3500	FRMT	94536	752-G2
RUSKIN PL			
3700	FRMT	94536	752-G2
RUSS AV			
1600	SLN	94578	691-D2
RUSS ST			
-	SF	94103	648-A7
RUSSELL CT			
16500	AlaC	94578	691-G4
34300	FRMT	94555	752-D1
RUSSELL LN			
700	MPS	95035	794-B4
RUSSELL ST			
-	OAK	94605	650-J7
-	OAK	94619	650-J7
1100	BERK	94702	629-F4
1500	BERK	94703	629-F4
2000	BERK	94705	629-H3
2800	BERK	94705	630-A3
3000	OAK	94705	630-A3
RUSSELL WY			
1100	HAY	94541	711-J1
1300	HAY	94541	691-J7
1300	HAY	94541	692-A7
RUSSET ST			
9800	OAK	94603	670-H7
RUSTIC DR			
20600	AlaC	94546	692-A5
RUSTIC PL			
200	SRMN	94582	673-J6
RUSTICA CIR			
-	FRMT	94536	752-H4
RUSTING AV			
4000	OAK	94605	650-H7
RUTAN CT			
1200	LVMR	94551	695-D6
RUTAN DR			
1400	LVMR	94551	695-D6
RUTGERS CT			
4300	LVMR	94550	716-A2
RUTGERS ST			
500	AlaC	94580	691-D5
1600	EPA	94303	771-C6
RUTGERS WY			
1500	LVMR	94550	716-A2
RUTH AV			
5400	OAK	94601	670-F1
RUTH CT			
400	SLN	94578	691-D4
32300	UNC	94587	732-A7
RUTH GN			
12000	AlaC	94586	733-J1
12000	AlaC	94586	734-A1
RUTH WY			
100	LVMR	94550	715-E1
4600	UNC	94587	731-J7
4600	UNC	94587	732-A7
RUTHELEN CT			
14700	SLN	94578	691-C5
RUTHERFORD CT			
-	AlaC	94550	716-D3
-	LVMR	94550	716-D3
2500	FRMT	94539	774-A3
RUTHERFORD DR			
200	DNVL	94526	652-G1
RUTHERFORD LN			
-	LVMR	94550	716-D3
2000	FRMT	94539	774-A3
32400	UNC	94587	732-C4
RUTHERFORD PL			
2600	FRMT	94539	774-A3
RUTHERFORD ST			
2000	OAK	94601	650-C7
RUTHERFORD TER			
45100	FRMT	94539	774-A3
RUTHERGLEN DR			
-	SRMN	94582	674-B3
RUTHLAND RD			
6100	OAK	94611	630-D5
RUTHVEN LN			
-	DBLN	94568	693-E5
RUTLAND CT			
-	ALA	94502	669-H6
200	SRMN	94583	673-F5
35300	NWK	94560	752-D4
RUTLEDGE COM			
3600	FRMT	94538	753-D6
RUTLEDGE PL			
1000	PLE	94566	714-F6
RUTLEDGE RD			
20700	AlaC	94546	691-J5
RUUS LN			
1300	HAY	94544	732-A1
RUUS RD			
28200	HAY	94544	712-A7
28500	HAY	94544	732-B1
RUXTON CT			
6200	PLE	94588	694-A7
RYAN AV			
-	SJCo	95391	(678-F3 See Page 677)
RYAN ST			
-	LVMR	94550	715-G4
1000	OAK	94621	670-D6
RYAN INDUSTRIAL CT			
100	SRMN	94583	673-B1
RYDAL CT			
-	OAK	94611	650-F1
RYDIN RD			
2700	RCH	94804	609-B4
RYE TER			
33700	FRMT	94555	732-E6
RYEGATE PL			
-	SRMN	94583	673-E5

S

STREET / Block	City	ZIP	Pg-Grid
N S ST			
100	LVMR	94551	715-F1
S S ST			
-	LVMR	94550	715-F1
SABA CT			
-	SRMN	94583	673-D3
SABERCAT CT			
2500	FRMT	94539	773-F1
SABERCAT PL			
43300	FRMT	94539	773-F1
SABERCAT RD			
2500	FRMT	94539	773-F1
SABIN AV			
5100	FRMT	94536	752-H6
SABIN PL			
-	SF	94108	648-A5
SABINA CT			
17000	AlaC	94546	691-H5
SABIO CT			
4100	FRMT	94536	752-F2
SABLE OAKS WY			
-	DBLN	94568	694-G2
SABLE POINTE			
-	ALA	94502	670-A5
SABRE ST			
1600	HAY	94545	711-D3
SACRAMENTO			
4000	ALA	94501	649-E6
SACRAMENTO AV			
4200	FRMT	94538	753-A6
5100	RCH	94804	609-B4
SACRAMENTO ST			
400	SF	94104	648-A5
500	SF	94111	648-A5
700	SF	94108	648-A5
1300	BERK	94703	609-F7
1300	BERK	94702	609-F7
1400	BERK	94703	629-F3
1400	BERK	94702	629-F3
SADDLE DR			
3100	AlaC	94541	712-D2
SADDLEBACK CIR			
500	LVMR	94551	695-E5
SADDLE BACK TER			
500	FRMT	94536	753-C2
SADDLE BROOK CT			
-	OAK	94619	651-B6
SADDLE BROOK DR			
5100	OAK	94619	651-B6
SADDLEBROOK PL			
-	DBLN	94568	694-F3
SADDLE CREEK CT			
500	SRMN	94582	694-B1
SADDLE CREEK TER			
-	DBLN	94568	694-G2
SADDLERS CREEK CT			
-	SRMN	94582	674-C4
SADDLEVIEW CT			
-	LVMR	94551	696-E3
SAGE CIR			
-	SRMN	94583	673-C4
SAGE CT			
1000	FRMT	94539	773-H3
6800	DBLN	94568	693-J4
SAGE LN			
-	ALA	94502	670-A7
SAGE RD			
8900	OAK	94605	671-C2
8900	OAK	94627	671-C2
SAGE ST			
25600	HAY	94545	711-E7
SAGEBRUSH PZ			
-	HAY	94542	712-B3
SAGELEAF CT			
700	HAY	94544	712-A7
SAGEMEADOW CT			
100	MPS	95035	794-A6
SAGEWOOD AV			
1500	SLN	94579	691-A5
SAGEWOOD CT			
-	PLE	94588	714-F1
SAGINAW CIR			
4700	PLE	94588	694-D6
SAGINAW CT			
3100	PLE	94588	694-D6
SAGUARE COM			
1100	FRMT	94539	774-A4
SAGUARE CT			
1100	FRMT	94539	774-A4
SAGUARE TER			
1100	FRMT	94539	774-A4
SAHARA CT			
1000	HAY	94541	711-D2
SAHARA RD			
1000	HAY	94541	711-D2
SAILFISH COM			
38900	FRMT	94536	753-C3
SAILWAY DR			
-	FRMT	94538	753-C5
SAINT ALBANS RD			
100	CCCo	94708	609-G3
SAINT ANDREWS CT			
1800	MPS	95035	794-D3
SAINT ANDREWS RD			
4100	OAK	94605	671-C3
SAINT ANDREWS ST			
-	HAY	94544	732-D2
SAINT ANDREWS WY			
-	LVMR	94551	696-D3
SAINT ANNES PL			
30300	HAY	94544	732-D2
SAINT ANTHONY DR			
41100	FRMT	94539	753-F5
SAINT ANTON WY			
-	HAY	94541	711-J2
SAINT BEDE LN			
800	HAY	94544	711-J6
800	HAY	94544	712-A6
SAINT BENEDICT CT			
-	SRMN	94583	673-E5
SAINT CHARLES PL			
2200	LVMR	94550	715-G4
SAINT CHARLES ST			
1100	ALA	94501	669-G2
1700	ALA	94501	649-G7
SAINT CHRISTOPHER ST			
37000	NWK	94560	752-F5
SAINT CHRISTOPHER WY			
5300	NWK	94560	752-F5
SAINT CLOUD CT			
4300	OAK	94619	650-J6
SAINT DENIS CT			
200	SRMN	94583	673-F5
SAINT DENIS DR			
2800	SRMN	94583	673-E5
SAINT EDWARD ST			
37000	NWK	94560	752-F6
SAINT ELMO DR			
9800	OAK	94603	670-G7
SAINT FRANCIS AV			
27100	HAY	94544	712-A6
SAINT FRANCIS PL			
-	SF	94107	648-B6
SAINT FRANCIS TER			
4400	FRMT	94539	774-B7
SAINT FRANCIS WY			
600	PLE	94566	714-G1
SAINT GEORGE AL			
-	SF	94108	648-A5
SAINT GEORGE ST			
300	AlaC	94541	691-G7
500	LVMR	94551	695-H6
SAINT HELENA CT			
-	LVMR	94550	716-D2
SAINT HELENA DR			
2400	HAY	94542	712-C3
SAINT HENRY DR			
200	FRMT	94539	753-F5
SAINT HILL RD			
-	ORIN	94563	610-J6
SAINT ISABEL AV			
5200	NWK	94560	752-F6
SAINT JAMES AL			
-	SF	94108	648-A4
100	SF	94133	648-A4
SAINT JAMES CIR			
400	PDMT	94611	650-D2
SAINT JAMES CT			
-	ORIN	94563	610-G4
900	AlaC	94541	691-G7
SAINT JAMES DR			
-	PDMT	94611	650-C2
200	PDMT	94610	650-D2
SAINT JAMES PL			
-	PDMT	94610	650-C2
SAINT JAMES ST			
37000	FRMT	94536	752-G4
SAINT JOHN CIR			
600	PLE	94566	714-D3
SAINT JOHN ST			
400	PLE	94566	714-D3
SAINT JOHNS CT			
-	AlaC	94580	691-E6
SAINT JOHNS DR			
15900	AlaC	94580	691-E6
SAINT JOSEPH CT			
1100	MPS	95035	794-C5
SAINT JOSEPH TER			
100	FRMT	94539	753-H7
SAINT LEONARDS WY			
3600	FRMT	94538	753-C6
SAINT LOUIS AL			
-	SF	94108	648-A4
SAINT LUKE CT			
24800	AlaC	94541	712-C1
37000	NWK	94560	752-F6
SAINT MARGARET CT			
2600	ALA	94501	670-A2
SAINT MARGARETS CT			
2200	LVMR	94550	715-G4
SAINT MARK AV			
5300	NWK	94560	752-F6
SAINT MARY AV			
600	SLN	94577	671-C7
SAINT MARY DR			
1200	LVMR	94550	716-A2
SAINT MARY ST			
300	PLE	94566	714-D3
37100	NWK	94560	752-F5
SAINT MATTHEW DR			
5800	NWK	94560	752-F6
SAINT MICHAEL CIR			
700	PLE	94566	714-G3
SAINT MICHAEL CT			
-	SRMN	94583	673-E5
SAINT NICHOLAS CT			
200	FRMT	94539	753-F5
SAINT PATRICK WY			
-	DBLN	94568	693-H4
SAINT PAUL CT			
5800	OAK	94618	630-C6
SAINT PAUL DR			
5700	NWK	94560	752-F6
SAINT PHILLIP CT			
200	FRMT	94539	753-F5
SAINT PIERRE CT			
-	SRMN	94583	673-E5
SAINT RAYMOND CT			
7800	DBLN	94568	693-G3
SAINT STEPHENS CIR			
-	ORIN	94563	610-J6
SAINT STEPHENS DR			
-	ORIN	94563	610-J6
SAINT TENNY PL			
-	SF	94105	648-B6
SAINT THOMAS WY			
500	PLE	94566	714-G1
SAINT TROPEZ PL			
-	HAY	94544	712-B7
SAKLAN RD			
22900	AlaC	94545	711-E5
23300	HAY	94545	711-E5
SAL CT			
-	DBLN	94568	694-G4
29400	HAY	94544	732-C1
SALAMANCA AV			
1400	HAY	94544	732-A1
SALAMANCA CT			
200	SRMN	94583	673-C3
1500	FRMT	94539	753-G7
SALEM CT			
300	SRMN	94583	673-E5
600	LVMR	94551	695-E6
SALEM RD			
19600	AlaC	94546	692-A4
SALEM ST			
4300	EMVL	94608	629-F6
6400	OAK	94608	629-F5
SALEM WY			
43600	FRMT	94538	773-E2
SALINAS PL			
34400	FRMT	94555	752-D1
SALINGER TER			
-	FRMT	94536	752-J4
SALISBURY CT			
3100	FRMT	94555	732-E7
3100	LVMR	94551	695-H6
SALISBURY DR			
5200	NWK	94560	752-E4
SALISBURY ST			
3400	OAK	94601	650-D6
SALISBURY WY			
-	CCCo	94582	674-C4
SALLY CT			
4800	UNC	94587	751-J1
23200	AlaC	94541	692-D7
SALLY CREEK CIR			
1800	AlaC	94541	712-B2
SALLY RIDE WY			
-	OAK	94621	690-C1
SALMON RD			
-	ALA	94502	669-H6
SALMON TER			
38800	FRMT	94536	753-F3
SALMON WY			
31000	HAY	94544	732-C3
SALTILLO PL			
800	FRMT	94536	732-H7
SALTON SEA LN			
32400	FRMT	94555	732-B6
SALVADOR CT			
3900	PLE	94566	714-F4
35800	FRMT	94536	752-F3
SALVATIERRA CT			
-	DBLN	94568	694-G4
SALVIA COM			
5600	FRMT	94538	773-A2
SALVIA DR			
-	AlaC	94552	692-E7
SAMANTHA CT			
32200	UNC	94587	731-J7
SAMANTHA ST			
-	SJCo	95391	(678-F3 See Page 677)
SAMARIA LN			
200	OAK	94619	650-H5
SAMMIE AV			
600	FRMT	94539	773-H6
SAMOA CIR			
400	UNC	94587	732-D5
SAMOA CT			
100	SRMN	94582	673-E1
SAMOA RD			
13800	SLN	94577	690-H5
SAMSON WY			
3400	AlaC	94546	691-J5
3400	AlaC	94546	692-A5
SAN ANDREAS CT			
300	MPS	95035	793-J5
SAN ANDREAS DR			
200	MPS	95035	793-J5
3200	UNC	94587	732-A5
SAN ANGELO WY			
3100	UNC	94587	732-B5
SAN ANTONIO AV			
800	ALA	94501	669-G1
1800	BERK	94707	609-F5
2200	ALA	94501	670-A2
SAN ANTONIO PL			
-	SF	94133	648-A4
SAN ANTONIO ST			
5400	PLE	94566	714-E5
30400	HAY	94544	732-C2
SAN ANTONIO WY			
1600	OAK	94606	650-A5
37000	NWK	94560	752-F5
SAN ARDO CT			
31300	UNC	94587	732-B6
SAN BENITO CT			
30900	HAY	94544	732-C3
E SAN BENITO DR			
1300	FRMT	94539	794-A2
SAN BENITO RD			
900	BERK	94707	609-G6
SAN BENITO ST			
1600	RCH	94804	609-C3
31000	HAY	94544	732-C3
SAN BERNARDINO WY			
3100	UNC	94587	732-B5
SAN BLAS PL			
-	SRMN	94583	673-G5
SAN BLAS RD			
24000	HAY	94541	711-G3
SANBORN DR			
-	OAK	94602	650-F3
-	OAK	94611	650-F3
SANBORN RD			
-	ORIN	94563	630-J3
SANBORN TER			
38500	FRMT	94536	753-C2
SAN BRUNO CT			
31300	UNC	94587	732-D4
SAN CARLOS			
2400	AlaC	94546	691-H5
SAN CARLOS AV			
100	ELCR	94530	609-E6
200	PDMT	94611	650-A1
300	PDMT	94610	650-A1
500	ALB	94706	609-E6
4400	OAK	94601	650-E7
4500	OAK	94601	670-E1
SAN CARLOS CT			
600	FRMT	94539	753-E4
SAN CARLOS PL			
40100	FRMT	94539	753-E4
SAN CARLOS WY			
3200	UNC	94587	732-A5
5600	PLE	94566	714-D5
SAN CARVANTE CT			
31400	UNC	94587	732-B6
SAN CARVANTE WY			
3200	UNC	94587	732-B6
SAN CLEMENTE			
1000	PLE	94566	714-H3
SAN CLEMENTE ST			
30700	HAY	94544	732-C3
SAN CLEMENTE TER			
47400	FRMT	94539	774-A7
SANCTUARY CIR			
-	UNC	94587	732-F3
SANCTUARY WY			
-	UNC	94587	732-F3
SAND RD			
1900	FRMT	94539	773-F1
SANDALFORD WY			
-	SRMN	94582	674-D3
SANDALRIDGE CT			
900	MPS	95035	794-A5
SANDALWOOD CT			
-	FRMT	94536	753-A2
600	MPS	95035	794-A4
SANDALWOOD DR			
4300	PLE	94588	713-J1
4400	PLE	94588	693-J7
SANDALWOOD ISL			
600	ALA	94501	669-H2
SANDALWOOD LN			
900	MPS	95035	794-A5
SANDALWOOD ST			
36000	NWK	94560	752-E4
SAND BEACH PL			
1100	ALA	94501	669-G3
SAND BEACH RD			
300	ALA	94501	669-G3
SANDBURG CT			
-	UNC	94587	732-H6
SANDBURG DR			
-	UNC	94587	732-H6
SANDBURG WY			
29200	HAY	94544	732-B2
SANDCREEK DR			
-	HAY	94545	731-G3
SANDCREEK WY			
1800	ALA	94501	669-H3
SANDDOLLAR CT			
3500	UNC	94587	732-A5
SANDELIN AV			
1200	SLN	94577	671-C7
SANDELIN CT			
1300	SLN	94577	671-D7
SANDERLING CT			
-	ALA	94501	649-F7
-	SLN	94579	690-J7
SANDERLING DR			
2400	PLE	94566	714-D1
2500	PLE	94566	694-D7
2800	FRMT	94555	732-D6
SANDERLING WY			
2600	PLE	94566	694-D7
SANDERS DR			
1000	MRGA	94556	651-E1
SANDERS RANCH RD			
-	MRGA	94556	651-F1
SAND HARBOR			
-	ALA	94502	670-A6
SANDHILL CT			
-	ORIN	94563	610-G2
SANDHILL RD			
-	ORIN	94563	610-G2
SANDHILL TER			
33700	FRMT	94555	732-D7
SAND HOOK ISL			
600	ALA	94501	669-G2
SANDHURST DR			
-	MPS	95035	794-A6
SANDIA DR			
1000	PLE	94566	714-G3
SAN DIEGO CT			
31300	UNC	94587	732-B6
SAN DIEGO PL			
400	SRMN	94583	673-F5
SAN DIEGO RD			
100	ALA	94501	649-D6
700	BERK	94707	609-G5
SAN DIEGO ST			
5600	ELCR	94530	609-C4
SANDLEWOOD DR			
2400	HAY	94545	731-H1
SANDLEWOOD LN			
-	SRMN	94583	673-A2
SANDOVAL WY			
600	HAY	94544	732-C1
SANDPIPER COM			
700	LVMR	94551	695-E7
SANDPIPER CT			
-	SLN	94579	691-F1
3400	HAY	94542	712-F4
4400	FRMT	94555	752-B1
SANDPIPER PL			
-	ALA	94502	669-J5
4400	FRMT	94555	732-B7
4400	FRMT	94555	752-B1
SANDPIPER WY			
2300	PLE	94566	714-C1
SAND POINT DR			
9500	SRMN	94583	693-G1
SANDRA CT			
-	AlaC	94541	691-G6
4500	UNC	94587	732-A7
SANDRA ST			
4000	FRMT	94555	732-C7
4300	FRMT	94555	752-C1
SANDRA WY			
5300	LVMR	94550	716-C1
SANDRINGHAM PL			
-	PDMT	94611	650-D2
SANDRINGHAM RD			
-	PDMT	94611	650-D2
SANDSTONE COM			
-	LVMR	94550	715-C1
SANDSTONE CT			
-	PLE	94588	714-F1
SANDSTONE DR			
200	FRMT	94536	732-J6
SANDY RD			
18600	AlaC	94546	692-B3
SANDY WY			
3000	SRMN	94583	673-F5
SANDY BRIDGES LN			
1200	AlaC	94541	691-G6
SANDYFORD CT			
-	DBLN	94568	694-E4
SANDY HOOK DR			
-	HAY	94544	732-B1
SAN FELICE DR			
-	LVMR	94550	715-J3
SAN FERNANDO AV			
600	BERK	94707	609-F5
SAN FERNANDO WY			
3000	UNC	94587	732-B6
SANFORD ST			
7800	OAK	94605	671-A1
SAN FRANCISCAN DR			
17200	AlaC	94552	692-C2
SAN FRANCISCO CT			
-	OAK	94601	670-B1
SAN FRANCISCO TER			
4000	FRMT	94538	753-B5
SF-OAKLAND BAY BRDG I-80			
-	OAK	-	648-G2
-	OAK	-	649-B1
-	SF	-	648-G2
SAN GABRIEL AV			
600	ALB	94706	609-E5
SAN GABRIEL CT			
400	PLE	94566	714-E5
SAN GABRIEL WY			
3100	UNC	94587	732-B5
SANGAMORE ST			
1200	HAY	94545	711-F5
SAN GIORGIO CT			
4000	PLE	94588	694-C6
SANGRO CT			
-	PLE	94566	715-D6
SAN JACINTO CT			
31400	UNC	94587	732-B6
SAN JOAQUIN AV			
-	CCCo	94514	637-D2
SAN JOAQUIN ST			
1400	RCH	94804	609-B3
SAN JOAQUIN WY			
3100	UNC	94587	732-B5
SAN JOSE AV			
1000	ALA	94501	669-H2
2300	ALA	94501	670-A3
5200	RCH	94804	609-C4
SAN JOSE CT			
31400	UNC	94587	732-C5
SAN JOSE DR			
5400	PLE	94566	714-E5
SAN JOSE PL			
500	SRMN	94583	673-F5
SAN JOSE ST			
900	SLN	94577	671-B7
1200	SLN	94577	691-B1
SAN JUAN AV			
1800	BERK	94707	609-F5
4100	FRMT	94536	752-F3
SAN JUAN CT			
4000	FRMT	94536	752-G3
SAN JUAN PL			
700	SRMN	94583	673-F4
3100	UNC	94587	732-B5
SAN JUAN ST			
3700	OAK	94601	650-D7
SAN JUAN WY			
5400	PLE	94566	714-E5
SAN LEANDRO BLVD			
300	SLN	94577	670-J7
800	SLN	94577	690-J1
900	SLN	94577	691-A2
2500	SLN	94578	691-A2
SAN LEANDRO ST			
3100	OAK	94603	670-F5
3100	SLN	94577	670-F5
3200	OAK	94601	670-C1
5400	OAK	94621	670-F5
SAN LORENZO AV			
1600	BERK	94707	609-F5
SAN LUCES WY			
3200	UNC	94587	732-A5
SAN LUIS AV			
1300	OAK	94602	650-D3
9900	SRMN	94583	673-G5
SAN LUIS CT			
3100	UNC	94587	732-A5
5600	PLE	94566	714-D5
SAN LUIS RD			
500	BERK	94707	609-G4
SAN LUIS ST			
1600	RCH	94804	609-C4
SAN LUIS OBISPO AV			
1100	HAY	94544	732-C3
SAN MARCO AV			
-	FRMT	94539	753-G6
SAN MARCO CT			
3300	UNC	94587	732-A5
SAN MARCO PL			
-	SRMN	94583	673-G5
SAN MARCO ST			
-	LVMR	94550	715-E4
SAN MARCO WY			
-	PLE	94588	694-C6
3200	UNC	94587	732-A5
SAN MARINO CT			
31400	UNC	94587	732-B6
SAN MARTIN PL			
800	FRMT	94539	753-G6
SAN MATEO RD			
-	BERK	94707	609-G5
SAN MATEO ST			
1700	RCH	94804	609-C3
2900	ELCR	94530	609-C3
SAN MATEO WY			
3000	UNC	94587	732-B5
SAN MATEO-HAYWARD BRDG Rt#-92			
-	HAY	-	731-A2
SAN MIGUEL AV			
600	BERK	94707	609-F5
19100	AlaC	94546	691-J4
SAN MIGUEL CT			
500	PLE	94566	714-E5
SAN MIGUEL DR			
100	SRMN	94583	673-G5
800	LVMR	94550	715-F3
SAN MINETE DR			
-	LVMR	94550	715-J3
SAN MORENO CT			
39800	FRMT	94539	753-E3
SAN MORENO PL			
200	FRMT	94539	753-E4
SANNITA PL			
-	PLE	94566	715-C7
-	PLE	94566	735-C1
SAN PABLO AV			
1600	OAK	94612	649-F1
2500	OAK	94607	649-F1
2700	OAK	94608	649-F1
SAN PABLO AV Rt#-123			
500	ALB	94706	609-D6
1000	ALB	94710	609-D6
1100	BERK	94706	609-D6
1100	BERK	94710	609-D6
1300	BERK	94702	609-D6
1400	BERK	94702	629-E1
1400	BERK	94710	629-E1
3000	ELCR	94530	609-B1
3100	OAK	94608	629-E3
3500	OAK	94608	649-F1
3500	EMVL	94608	629-E3
3500	EMVL	94608	649-F1
10200	RCH	94804	609-B1
SAN PABLO CT			
3300	UNC	94587	732-A5
SAN PABLO WY			
3200	UNC	94587	732-A5
SAN PABLO DAM RD			
-	CCCo	94553	609-J1
-	CCCo	94553	610-A2
500	CCCo	94563	610-A2
SAN PEDRO AV			
1800	BERK	94707	609-F5
SAN PEDRO CT			
3300	UNC	94587	732-A5
SAN PEDRO DR			
36000	FRMT	94536	752-F4
SAN PEDRO PL			
-	SRMN	94583	673-G5
SAN PEDRO RD			
100	ALA	94501	649-D6
SAN PEDRO WY			
3200	UNC	94587	732-A5
SAN PIEDRAS PL			
-	SRMN	94583	673-G5
SAN RAFAEL ST			
1000	SLN	94577	671-C7
1300	SLN	94577	691-C1
SAN RAFAEL WY			
3100	UNC	94587	732-B5
SAN RAMON AV			
1800	BERK	94707	609-F5
SAN RAMON CT			
3100	UNC	94587	732-B5
SAN RAMON RD			
7000	DBLN	94568	693-G3
7000	PLE	94588	693-G3
8800	SRMN	94583	693-G3
SAN RAMON VALLEY BLVD			
2100	SRMN	94583	673-C1
20400	SRMN	94583	693-F1
SAN REMO CT			
1500	LVMR	94550	715-G4
2100	AlaC	94578	691-F4
SAN REMO DR			
16200	AlaC	94578	691-F4
SAN ROBERTO PL			
400	SRMN	94583	673-G4
SAN SABANA CT			
7700	DBLN	94568	693-G4
SAN SABANA RD			
7500	DBLN	94568	693-G4
SAN SEBASTIAN			
4600	OAK	94602	650-D3
SAN SEBASTIAN PL			
40200	FRMT	94539	753-E4
SAN SIMEON CT			
39900	FRMT	94539	753-E4
SAN SIMEON PL			
300	SRMN	94583	673-G5
5300	AlaC	94552	692-D4
SANSOME ST			
-	SF	94104	648-A4
400	SF	94111	648-A4
600	SF	94133	648-A4
SANTA ANA ST			
1000	AlaC	94580	691-E5
SANTA ANA WY			
31300	UNC	94587	732-B5
SANTA ANITA			
-	SLN	94579	690-J7
-	SLN	94579	691-A6
SANTA BARBARA CT			
3200	UNC	94587	732-D4
SANTA BARBARA RD			
500	BERK	94707	609-G4
900	BERK	94708	609-G4
SANTA CATALINA WY			
31200	UNC	94587	732-B5
SANTA CLARA AV			
-	OAK	94611	649-J2
-	OAK	94610	649-J2
400	ALA	94501	669-E1
500	BERK	94707	609-F5
1000	ALA	94501	649-J2
1900	RCH	94804	609-C3
2100	ALA	94501	670-A2
2900	ELCR	94530	609-C4
SANTA CLARA CT			
3200	UNC	94587	732-A5
SANTA CLARA ST			
1200	RCH	94804	609-B2
22400	HAY	94541	711-H4
23800	HAY	94544	711-H4
SANTA CLARA WY			
3800	LVMR	94550	695-J7
3900	LVMR	94550	696-A7
22400	HAY	94541	711-G2
SANTA CROCE DR			
-	LVMR	94550	715-J3
SANTA CRUZ			
1700	AlaC	94541	691-G6
SANTA CRUZ AV			
5500	RCH	94804	609-C3
SANTA CRUZ CT			
4500	FRMT	94536	752-G4
SANTA CRUZ LN			
3100	ALA	94502	670-A6
SANTA CRUZ PL			
300	SRMN	94583	673-G4
SANTA CRUZ RD			
4000	OAK	94605	671-B3
SANTA CRUZ WY			
31300	UNC	94587	732-B5
SANTA ELENA WY			
31300	UNC	94587	732-B5
SANTA FE AV			
100	CCCo	94706	609-E5
100	ELCR	94530	609-E5
500	ALB	94706	609-E5
1100	BERK	94706	609-E7
1300	BERK	94702	609-E7
SANTA FE ST			
17000	AlaC	94541	691-G5
SANTA FE WY			
31200	UNC	94587	732-B5
SANTA INES CT			
-	OAK	94601	650-B7
-	OAK	94601	670-B1
SANTA INEZ CT			
3100	UNC	94587	732-B5
SANTA ISABELA CT			
3200	UNC	94587	732-B5
SANTA LUCIA			
-	ORIN	94563	610-G5
SANTA MARGARITA			
-	SLN	94579	691-A7
SANTA MARIA AV			
18800	AlaC	94546	692-A3
SANTA MARIA CT			
-	OAK	94601	670-B1
3600	AlaC	94546	692-A4
SANTA MARIA DR			
31000	UNC	94587	732-B5
SANTA MARIA ST			
1300	SLN	94577	691-B1
SANTA MARIA WY			
-	ORIN	94563	610-G7
SANTA MARTA CT			
3100	UNC	94587	732-B5
SANTA MONICA			
400	SLN	94579	690-J6
400	SLN	94579	691-A7

ALAMEDA COUNTY STREET INDEX

STREET
Block City ZIP Pg-Grid

SANTA MONICA TER
- FRMT 94539 794-B1
SANTA MONICA WY
3200 UNC 94587 732-B6
SANTANA DR
- CCCo 94514 637-D3
SANTANA ST
30800 HAY 94544 732-C3
SANTANDER DR
400 SRMN 94583 673-C3
SANTA PAULA
300 SLN 94579 690-J6
300 SLN 94579 691-A7
SANTA PAULA WY
3200 UNC 94587 732-B6
SANTA RAY AV
500 OAK 94610 650-A3
SANTA RITA DR
300 MPS 95035 794-B6
SANTA RITA RD
1000 PLE 94566 714-E2
2100 PLE 94566 694-E6
2300 PLE 94588 694-E6
SANTA RITA ST
2100 OAK 94601 650-D7
SANTA RITA WY
31200 UNC 94587 732-B5
SANTA ROSA AV
100 OAK 94610 649-J2
500 BERK 94707 609-F5
10000 SRMN 94583 673-G5
SANTA ROSA CT
3200 UNC 94587 732-A5
SANTA ROSA PL
100 SRMN 94583 673-F4
SANTA ROSA ST
1300 SLN 94577 691-B1
SANTA ROSA WY
3200 UNC 94587 732-B5
SANTA SOPHIA CT
3200 UNC 94587 732-D4
SANTA SOPHIA WY
3200 UNC 94587 732-B6
SANTA SUSANA
200 SLN 94579 691-A7
SANTA SUSANA WY
3200 UNC 94587 732-A5
SANTA TERESA
100 SLN 94579 691-A6
SANTA TERESA COM
40100 FRMT 94539 753-E4
SANTA TERESA DR
12200 SRMN 94583 673-G4
SANTA TERESA TER
40100 FRMT 94539 753-E4
SANTA YNEZ
500 SLN 94579 690-J7
500 SLN 94579 691-A7
SANTEE RD
4300 FRMT 94555 752-E2
SANTEL CT
- PLE 94566 715-C5
SANTIAGO RD
13900 SLN 94577 690-H5
SANTIAGO ST
35100 FRMT 94536 752-E2
SANTO CT
11500 DBLN 94568 693-F3
SANTO AMARO PL
- AlaC 94546 691-J2
SAN TOMAS PL
600 SRMN 94583 673-F5
SANTORINA CT
- LVMR 94550 715-F5
SANTORINA DR
- LVMR 94550 715-F5
SANTOS CT
- FRMT 94536 753-D2
600 MPS 95035 794-C5
SANTOS ST
21100 AlaC 94541 691-G7
21100 AlaC 94541 711-G1
SANTOS RANCH RD
9500 AlaC 94586 713-H3
9500 HAY 94586 713-H3
9500 AlaC 94588 713-H3
SANTUCCI CT
20200 HAY 94544 732-C1
SAN VICENTE DR
- LVMR 94550 715-J3
SAN VICIENTE LP
- DBLN 94568 694-E3
SAN VICIENTE TER
- DBLN 94568 694-E3
SAPPHIRE CT
- SRMN 94582 673-F2
SAPPHIRE DR
1000 LVMR 94550 715-D3
SAPPHIRE ST
6700 DBLN 94568 693-J2
19900 AlaC 94546 692-C5
SARAH CT
4600 LVMR 94550 696-B7
SARAH LN
- MRGA 94556 651-E2
SARAH PL
500 HAY 94544 732-F2
SARASOTA LN
2000 HAY 94545 711-H7
SARATOGA AV
1200 EPA 94303 771-A7
SARATOGA CT
- LVMR 94550 715-H5
SARATOGA ST
- ALA 94501 649-C6
2100 AlaC 94578 691-F4
SARATOGA WY
3700 PLE 94588 694-F5
SARATOGA PARK ST
42500 FRMT 94538 773-C2
SARAZEN AV
3300 OAK 94605 671-A3
SARDONYX RD
1600 LVMR 94550 715-C3
SARGENT AV
4400 AlaC 94546 692-B4
SARITA ST
- AlaC 94541 712-D1
SARK CT
400 MPS 95035 794-A6
SARONI CT
- OAK 94611 630-F7
SARONI DR
6600 OAK 94611 630-F6
SASSAFRAS CT
8200 PLE 94566 734-C1
8200 PLE 94586 734-C1
SATELITE ST
28400 HAY 94545 731-J2
SATH CT
- ALA 94502 669-J6

SATINLEAF CT
- SRMN 94582 673-H1
SATINLEAF WY
- SRMN 94582 673-H1
SATURN AV
600 FRMT 94539 793-J1
600 HAY 94544 712-B7
SATURN CT
1400 MPS 95035 794-D7
SATURN DR
14600 AlaC 94578 691-D3
SATURN WY
700 LVMR 94550 715-E4
4200 UNC 94587 732-A6
SATURN PARK CT
- SRMN 94582 674-A2
SATURN PARK DR
- SRMN 94582 673-J2
- SRMN 94582 674-A2
SAUSAL ST
1700 OAK 94602 650-C5
SAUSALITO RD
13800 SLN 94577 690-H5
SAUSALITO TER
34800 FRMT 94555 752-E1
SAUSALITO FERRY
- SF - 648-B2
SAUTERNE WY
900 PLE 94566 714-H3
SAUVIGNON CT
- FRMT 94539 793-J2
1400 LVMR 94550 715-H3
SAVANA LN
3500 ALA 94502 670-B7
SAVANNAH CT
- OAK 94603 671-A4
SAVANNAH RD
3700 FRMT 94538 773-E3
SAVOY LN
- SRMN 94582 674-B3
SAVOY WY
100 SLN 94577 691-B2
SAWGRASS CT
7900 PLE 94588 714-B5
SAWLEAF ST
48200 FRMT 94539 793-J1
SAWMILL LN
- DBLN 94568 694-F2
SAXON CT
3100 FRMT 94555 732-E7
36200 NWK 94560 752-F4
SAYBROOK RD
1300 LVMR 94551 695-E6
SAYRE AV
5300 FRMT 94536 752-H6
SAYRE DR
6900 OAK 94611 630-F7
SAYRE ST
1300 SLN 94579 691-B7
SCAMMAN CT
3800 FRMT 94538 773-D1
SCARBORO PL
100 SRMN 94583 673-F6
SCARBOROUGH DR
5000 NWK 94560 752-E4
5700 OAK 94611 650-F1
SCARLETT CT
5900 DBLN 94568 694-A4
SCARLETT DR
6100 DBLN 94568 694-A4
SCENIC AV
- PDMT 94611 650-C1
100 PDMT 94611 630-B7
1300 BERK 94708 609-H7
1300 LVMR 94551 696-B3
1600 BERK 94709 609-H7
1600 BERK 94709 629-H1
2400 OAK 94602 650-D4
SCENIC CT
- ORIN 94563 630-J2
SCENIC DR
- ORIN 94563 630-J1
SCENIC WY
1100 AlaC 94541 691-G6
SCENICVIEW CT
1700 SLN 94577 691-D1
SCENICVIEW DR
1300 SLN 94577 691-D1
SCHAEFER RANCH RD
26900 DBLN 94552 693-C4
26900 AlaC 94552 693-C3
SCHAFER RD
300 HAY 94544 712-A6
600 HAY 94544 711-J6
SCHELBERT TER
4900 FRMT 94555 752-C2
SCHERMAN CT
100 LVMR 94550 715-D2
SCHERMAN WY
100 LVMR 94550 715-D2
SCHILLER ST
1500 ALA 94501 669-J1
SCHLOSSER CT
4600 AlaC 94546 692-B4
SCHMIDT LN
6300 ELCR 94530 609-C2
SCHOOL AL
100 SF 94133 648-A4
SCHOOL AV
5200 ELCR 94530 609-B2
5200 RCH 94804 609-B2
SCHOOL CT
40100 FRMT 94538 753-B6
SCHOOL PTH
5100 RCH 94804 609-B2
SCHOOL ST
200 FRMT 94536 753-A1
200 LVMR 94550 695-H7
200 LVMR 94550 715-H1
900 SLN 94577 691-C2
1700 MRGA 94556 651-D1
2600 OAK 94602 650-D5
4000 PLE 94566 714-E2
9700 SLN 94578 691-C2
SCHOOL WY
4400 AlaC 94546 691-J2
SCHOONER RD
13700 SLN 94577 690-H4
SCHOONER HILL
- OAK 94618 630-C4
- OAK 94705 630-C4
SCHROEDER LN
- ALA 94501 649-E7
W SCHULTE RD
13500 SJCo 95377 (698-F3 See Page 677)
SCHUSTER AV
19000 AlaC 94546 691-J3
SCHUYLER AV
- HAY 94544 732-E3
SCHUYLKILL AV
- HAY 94544 732-E3

SCHWEEN CT
4000 PLE 94566 714-F1
SCHYLER ST
2900 OAK 94602 650-D5
SCIOTA AV
- SRMN 94583 673-H6
SCIOTA PL
- SRMN 94583 673-H7
SCOFIELD CT
42600 FRMT 94539 753-H7
SCOFIELD DR
42600 FRMT 94539 753-H6
SCORPION PL
900 FRMT 94539 773-J5
SCORPION RD
1000 FRMT 94539 773-J5
SCOTCHBROOK PZ
- HAY 94542 712-B3
SCOTIA AV
4600 OAK 94605 671-D4
SCOTIA CT
200 FRMT 94539 773-H2
SCOTIA ST
4800 UNC 94587 752-A1
SCOTT PL
1100 HAY 94544 711-J6
SCOTT ST
200 LVMR 94551 695-J7
400 FRMT 94539 753-H7
900 OAK 94610 650-A2
1200 ELCR 94530 609-D2
SCOTT CREEK RD
600 FRMT 94539 793-J2
600 FRMT 94539 794-A2
2100 SCIC 95035 794-A2
SCOUT RD
2300 OAK 94611 650-E1
SCOVILLE ST
5500 OAK 94621 670-F2
SCRIPPS ST
25600 HAY 94545 711-G6
SEABOARD LN
25500 HAY 94545 711-D7
SEABORN CT
1600 ALA 94501 669-H1
SEA BREEZE COM
- FRMT 94536 752-G3
SEABREEZE CT
3600 HAY 94542 712-F4
SEA BRIDGE CT
100 ALA 94502 670-A5
SEABRIDGE DR
- FRMT 94538 793-F1
SEA BRIDGE WY
- ALA 94502 670-A5
SEACLIFF DR
2000 MPS 95035 794-E7
SEA CLIFF TER
34800 FRMT 94555 752-E2
SEA CLOUD AV
2000 SLN 94579 690-J6
SEACOR CT
4100 OAK 94605 671-B2
SEACREST CT
- SLN 94579 711-A1
SEA CREST TER
- FRMT 94536 753-C2
SEADRIFT CIR
- HAY 94545 731-G3
SEADRIFT LN
- HAY 94545 731-H3
SEA EAGLE CT
2200 PLE 94566 714-D1
SEAGATE DR
13700 SLN 94577 690-G5
SEAGRAMS CT
2300 AlaC 94541 692-D7
SEAGULL LN
- ALA 94501 649-E7
SEA HAVEN CT
- HAY 94545 731-G3
SEA HORSE
4000 ALA 94501 649-E6
SEA HORSE CT
- HAY 94545 731-H3
SEAL ST
- HAY 94545 711-E7
SEAL ROCK TER
34800 FRMT 94555 752-E1
SEA MIST CT
300 HAY 94544 712-C7
SEA MIST TER
34400 FRMT 94555 752-C3
SEAN AV
- SJCo 95391 (678-E3 See Page 677)
W SEAPLANE LAGOON
- ALA 94501 649-D7
SEAPORT AV
4900 RCH 94804 609-A3
SEAPORT DR
31100 UNC 94587 731-H5
31400 UNC 94545 731-H5
SEASCAPE RD
39400 FRMT 94538 752-J7
SEASIDE CT
5100 UNC 94545 751-J1
SEASIDE DR
100 MPS 95035 793-J5
32400 UNC 94545 751-J1
SEASIDE WY
1100 MPS 95035 793-J5
SEASPRAY CT
2000 SLN 94579 690-J6
SEATTLE RD
100 ALA 94501 649-D6
SEAVER AV
- RCH 94804 609-A2
SEAVER CT
1500 HAY 94545 711-G5
SEAVER ST
25400 HAY 94545 711-G5
SEAVIEW AV
- PDMT 94611 650-C1
100 PDMT 94610 650-C1
4800 AlaC 94546 692-A3
SEAVIEW DR
100 ELCR 94530 609-E2
SEA VIEW PKWY
600 ALA 94502 670-A5
1800 ALA 94502 669-H5
SEAVIEW PL
4800 AlaC 94546 692-A3
7400 ELCR 94530 609-D2
SEAVIEW TR
- CCCo 94708 610-A4
- ORIN 94563 610-C6
SEAWALL DR
- BERK 94710 629-B2
SEA WOLF WY
- LVMR 94550 715-D4

SEBASTIAN WY
27500 HAY 94544 711-J7
SEBASTOPOL LN
2400 HAY 94542 712-D4
SEBILLE RD
- DBLN 94568 694-B1
SEBRING CT
29000 HAY 94544 732-A2
SECRETARIAT DR
2500 PLE 94566 714-C1
SECRET MEADOW CT
- AlaC 94552 692-E7
SECRET MEADOW DR
- AlaC 94552 692-E7
SECURITY PAC PL
- SF 94108 648-A6
SEDGE ST
4100 FRMT 94555 732-B7
SEDGEFIELD AV
7200 SRMN 94583 673-G6
SEDGEFIELD CT
100 SRMN 94583 673-G7
SEDGEMAN ST
15400 SLN 94579 691-C6
SEDUM RD
48600 FRMT 94539 793-J2
SEELEY ST
1200 SLN 94577 690-J2
SEEMA CIR
400 UNC 94587 732-D5
SEGOVIA CT
3700 SRMN 94583 673-C3
SEGOVIA PL
200 FRMT 94539 753-E3
SEGUNDO CT
2200 PLE 94588 714-B5
SEINE CT
11400 DBLN 94568 693-F3
SELBORNE DR
- PDMT 94611 650-D2
15900 AlaC 94578 691-F3
SELBORNE WY
100 MRGA 94556 651-E2
SELBY DR
14500 AlaC 94546 691-G4
14500 AlaC 94578 691-G4
SELDON CT
3000 FRMT 94539 773-E2
SELENA CT
5600 PLE 94566 714-E6
SELKIRK ST
- OAK 94619 650-G5
4600 FRMT 94538 753-B7
SELLERS CT
3500 FRMT 94536 752-F1
SELMA AV
5100 FRMT 94536 752-H7
SELVANTE ST
3700 PLE 94566 715-C7
SELWYN DR
200 MPS 95035 794-C7
SEMILLON DR
48800 FRMT 94539 793-J2
SEMINARY AV
1400 ALA 94502 670-B7
3000 OAK 94605 670-F2
3300 OAK 94613 670-F2
3400 OAK 94605 650-H7
3400 OAK 94613 650-H7
4200 OAK 94621 670-F2
SEMINARY CT
5800 OAK 94605 670-F2
SEMINOLE COM
900 FRMT 94539 773-H2
SEMINOLE CT
- SRMN 94583 673-D5
SEMINOLE DR
800 LVMR 94551 695-E7
SEMINOLE TER
900 FRMT 94539 773-H3
SEMINOLE WY
4400 PLE 94588 694-G7
27600 HAY 94544 711-J7
27600 HAY 94544 731-J1
SENECA LN
- SRMN 94583 673-C4
SENECA ST
8500 OAK 94605 671-A3
32100 HAY 94544 732-F3
SENECA PARK AV
4400 FRMT 94538 773-C2
SENECA PARK LP
4900 FRMT 94538 773-C2
SENGER ST
- AlaC 94550 716-C2
- LVMR 94550 716-C2
SENGER WY
- LVMR 94550 716-D2
SENIOR AV
- BERK 94708 609-J7
- BERK 94708 610-A7
SENTINEL CT
3500 HAY 94542 712-F4
SENTINEL DR
45900 FRMT 94539 774-A4
46900 FRMT 94539 773-J5
SENTINEL PL
45900 FRMT 94539 773-J4
45900 FRMT 94539 774-A4
SEPTEMBER CT
3700 AlaC 94546 691-H2
SEPULVEDA AV
2000 MPS 95035 794-E6
SEPULVEDA CT
200 MPS 95035 794-E7
SEPULVIDA CT
21300 AlaC 94541 711-G1
SEQUIM COM
200 FRMT 94539 773-F6
SEQUOIA AV
- DBLN 94568 694-D3
SEQUOIA COM
- FRMT 94536 752-J2
SEQUOIA CT
500 HAY 94541 711-G3
6000 PLE 94588 714-B1
36600 NWK 94560 752-C7
SEQUOIA DR
500 MPS 95035 794-D7
700 LVMR 94551 695-E7
SEQUOIA RD
500 HAY 94541 711-F3
37200 FRMT 94536 752-J3
SEQUOIA TER
2900 FRMT 94536 752-H2
SEQUOYAH RD
3800 OAK 94605 671-D2
SEQUOYAH VIEW CT
- OAK 94605 671-C3
SEQUOYAH VIEW DR
- OAK 94605 671-C3

SERENA CT
7900 DBLN 94568 693-G3
SERENADE PL
100 ALA 94501 649-D6
SERENIDAD ST
1700 LVMR 94550 715-E3
SERENITY TER
5200 PLE 94588 693-H7
SERENO CIR
- OAK 94619 650-H5
SERENO COM
36400 FRMT 94536 733-A7
36400 FRMT 94536 753-A1
SERIANA CT
3000 UNC 94587 731-J4
3000 UNC 94587 732-A4
SERIANA PL
2900 UNC 94587 732-A4
SERIANA WY
2900 UNC 94587 732-A4
SERPA CT
200 FRMT 94536 753-E1
200 FRMT 94536 733-A7
SERPA DR
1600 MPS 95035 794-D5
SERPENTINE DR
- UNC 94587 732-G6
SERPENTINE LN
1000 PLE 94566 714-F2
SERRA AV
4500 FRMT 94538 753-A6
4600 FRMT 94538 752-J6
SERRA CT
11600 DBLN 94568 693-F3
SERRA DR
800 SLN 94578 691-C5
SERRA PL
39000 FRMT 94538 752-J6
39000 FRMT 94538 753-A6
SERRA WY
100 MPS 95035 793-J7
100 MPS 95035 794-A7
SERRAMAR DR
- OAK 94611 630-D5
SERRAMONTE TER
300 FRMT 94536 753-E1
SERVICE RD
- FRMT 94555 732-C7
SETON LN
1100 HAY 94545 711-G6
SEVA ST
- PLE 94566 714-G1
SEVEN HILLS RD
3400 AlaC 94546 691-H3
4000 AlaC 94546 692-A3
SEVERINI LN
2900 AlaC 94546 691-H4
SEVERN DR
35200 NWK 94560 752-E3
SEVERN PL
4900 NWK 94560 752-E3
SEVERN RD
16400 AlaC 94578 691-G4
SEVIER AV
1300 MLPK 94025 771-A7
SEVILLA RD
22000 HAY 94541 691-J7
SEVILLANO CIR
- LVMR 94550 715-H5
SEVILLANO CT
- LVMR 94550 715-H5
SEVILLE CT
40400 FRMT 94539 753-E4
SEVILLE PL
100 SRMN 94583 673-G5
500 FRMT 94539 753-E4
SEXTUS RD
200 OAK 94603 670-F7
SEYMORE PL
1000 HAY 94544 711-J6
SEYMOUR PL
3000 FRMT 94555 732-E7
SHADDY TER
- FRMT 94539 773-G3
SHADELANDS PL
500 SRMN 94582 673-J7
SHADOW DR
7300 DBLN 94568 693-F4
SHADOW PL
7300 DBLN 94568 693-G4
SHADOWBROOK TER
- FRMT 94536 752-J2
SHADOWBROOKE COM
2200 FRMT 94539 753-E6
SHADOW CREEK CIR
5300 AlaC 94552 692-D5
SHADOWHILL CIR
- SRMN 94583 673-A2
SHADOW HILL DR
- DBLN 94568 694-F2
SHADOW HILLS CT
- PLE 94588 714-B5
SHADOWLAKE CT
200 MPS 95035 794-A6
SHADOW MIST CT
- LVMR 94550 715-E4
SHADOW MOUNTAIN
- OAK 94605 671-D2
SHADOW MOUNTAIN CT
2500 SRMN 94583 673-B2
SHADOW MOUNTAIN DR
2500 SRMN 94583 673-B2
SHADOW MOUNTAIN PL
500 SRMN 94583 673-B2
SHADOW OAK RD
- DNVL 94526 652-G2
SHADOW RIDGE CT
5700 PLE 94566 714-D6
SHADOW RIDGE DR
5600 AlaC 94552 692-E3
SHADOW WOOD LN
- AlaC 94541 691-H6
SHADY LN
- LVMR 94550 715-E4
SHADY CREEK RD
7600 DBLN 94568 694-A1
SHADY HOLLOW DR
7400 NWK 94560 752-B6
SHADY MILL LN
- PLE 94588 714-B5
SHADY POND LN
- PLE 94588 714-B5
SHADYSPRINGS RD
21600 AlaC 94546 691-J7
SHADY VALLEY CT
300 SRMN 94582 673-J6
300 SRMN 94582 674-A6
SHAFTER AV
3700 OAK 94609 649-H1
3800 OAK 94609 629-H7
5100 OAK 94618 629-J6

SHAKESPEARE FESTIVAL WY
- CCCo 94563 630-F2
- ORIN 94563 630-F2
SHALE COM
46800 FRMT 94539 773-G6
SHALIMAR CIR
5000 FRMT 94555 752-D2
SHALIMAR TER
34700 FRMT 94555 752-A3
SHALLOW CT
33700 FRMT 94555 752-C1
SHAMROCK COM
5200 FRMT 94555 752-B2
SHAMROCK LN
- ALA 94502 669-H5
SHAMROCK PL
8600 DBLN 94568 693-H2
SHAMROCK WY
1200 LVMR 94550 715-F4
4200 AlaC 94546 692-B4
SHANA ST
5500 FRMT 94538 773-B2
SHANER DR
2700 ALA 94502 669-J6
SHANIKO COM
- FRMT 94539 773-H6
SHANNON AV
7700 DBLN 94568 693-G3
SHANNON CIR
- ALA 94502 669-H5
SHANNON CT
- MRGA 94556 651-G2
1000 LVMR 94550 696-E6
3200 AlaC 94541 692-D7
7900 DBLN 94568 693-G3
SHARAB CT
4200 PLE 94566 714-F4
SHARD CT
700 FRMT 94539 773-J7
SHARON AV
- PDMT 94611 650-C1
SHARON CT
- PDMT 94611 650-C1
7600 DBLN 94568 693-G2
SHARON RD
- ALA 94502 669-J6
SHARON ST
8300 DBLN 94568 693-G2
15500 AlaC 94580 691-D6
SHASTA
3000 ALA 94501 649-E6
SHASTA CT
4600 PLE 94566 694-D7
SHASTA RD
- CCCo 94708 610-A6
2600 BERK 94708 609-J6
3000 BERK 94708 610-A6
SHASTA ST
- LVMR 94551 695-D7
- AlaC 94541 691-E7
1600 RCH 94804 609-C3
37000 FRMT 94536 752-G4
SHATO PL
100 FRMT 94539 793-H1
SHATTUCK AV
800 BERK 94707 609-G6
1200 BERK 94709 609-G7
1600 BERK 94709 629-G1
1900 BERK 94704 629-G1
2700 BERK 94705 629-H4
2700 BERK 94703 629-H4
4400 OAK 94609 629-H4
5300 FRMT 94555 752-C3
SHATTUCK PL
1400 BERK 94709 609-G7
SHATTUCK SQ
2000 BERK 94704 629-G2
SHAUNA CT
4800 AlaC 94546 692-C4
SHAVANO WY
300 SRMN 94583 693-H1
SHAVER LAKE ST
32600 FRMT 94555 732-C6
SHAW CT
40400 FRMT 94538 753-D6
SHAW PL
- SRMN 94583 673-F6
1100 AlaC 94541 691-G6
SHAW ST
- SF 94105 648-B5
10200 OAK 94605 671-B5
SHAWN CT
3300 AlaC 94541 692-D7
SHAWN WY
3200 AlaC 94541 692-D7
SHAWNA ST
4400 LVMR 94550 696-A7
SHAWNEE CT
- OAK 94619 650-J4
- SRMN 94583 673-D4
700 HAY 94544 732-E1
SHAWNEE PL
300 FRMT 94539 793-J1
SHAWNEE RD
1300 LVMR 94551 695-E6
SHAWNEE WY
300 FRMT 94539 793-J1
4500 PLE 94588 694-D6
SHAY DR
8000 OAK 94605 671-C1
SHEA CENTER DR
- LVMR 94551 695-D5
SHEARWATER CT
4400 PLE 94566 714-E1
SHEARWATER RD
4400 PLE 94566 714-D1
SHEARWATER TER
33600 FRMT 94555 732-D7
SHEFFIELD AV
3000 OAK 94602 650-C5
SHEFFIELD CT
7300 DBLN 94568 693-H2
SHEFFIELD DR
2400 LVMR 94550 715-F4
SHEFFIELD LN
- PLE 94588 694-F7
7200 DBLN 94568 693-H2
32300 UNC 94587 732-C4
SHEFFIELD PL
2700 AlaC 94546 691-G3
SHEFFIELD RD
100 ALA 94502 669-J5
400 ALA 94502 670-B5
18500 AlaC 94546 691-G3
SHEFFIELD WY
- ALA 94502 669-J5
SHEILA CT
200 MRGA 94556 651-D1
32500 UNC 94587 752-A1
SHEILA ST
23100 AlaC 94541 692-D7

SHEILA WY
32500 UNC 94587 752-A1
SHELBURNE RD
1200 LVMR 94551 695-E6
SHELBY CT
5300 FRMT 94536 752-H6
SHELDON CIR
4200 PLE 94588 713-J1
SHELDON CT
20100 AlaC 94546 692-B5
SHELDON ST
10600 OAK 94605 671-B5
SHELL PL
2200 AlaC 94541 692-C7
SHELLBORNE CT
4700 FRMT 94538 773-C2
SHELLEY CT
500 MPS 95035 794-B6
36300 NWK 94560 752-F4
SHELLEY LN
1000 HAY 94544 712-A7
SHELLEY ST
500 LVMR 94550 696-C6
SHELLGATE CIR
- HAY 94545 731-H2
SHELLGATE CT
- HAY 94545 731-G3
SHELL GATE PL
1100 ALA 94501 669-G2
SHELL GATE RD
400 ALA 94501 669-G3
SHELLI CT
- SJCo 95391 (678-F3 See Page 677)
SHELLI ST
- SJCo 95391 (678-F3 See Page 677)
SHELLMOUND ST
4000 EMVL 94608 629-D5
4000 OAK 94608 629-E7
6700 BERK 94710 629-D5
SHELLMOUND WY
5800 EMVL 94608 629-D6
SHELLSILVER CT
- CCCo 94582 674-B2
SHELLY PL
- DNVL 94526 652-H1
SHELTERWOOD DR
6400 OAK 94611 630-F7
SHENANDOAH AV
1500 MPS 95035 794-D7
SHENANDOAH CT
3600 PLE 94588 714-A2
SHENANDOAH PL
600 HAY 94544 712-A6
34400 FRMT 94555 752-D1
SHEPARDSON LN
- ALA 94502 670-A5
SHEPHARD PL
- SF 94108 648-A5
SHEPHERD AV
100 HAY 94544 712-A6
SHEPHERD ST
4400 OAK 94619 650-G6
SHEPHERD CANYON RD
5900 OAK 94611 650-E1
5900 OAK 94611 630-F7
SHERBEAR DR
2700 SRMN 94583 673-B2
SHERIDAN AV
100 PDMT 94611 650-C2
SHERIDAN CIR
400 LVMR 94551 695-J6
SHERIDAN CT
35600 NWK 94560 752-E4
SHERIDAN LN
1300 HAY 94544 711-J6
SHERIDAN RD
- OAK 94618 630-C6
5200 AlaC 94586 754-A3
SHERMAN CT
900 MPS 95035 794-B4
SHERMAN DR
- AlaC 94552 692-G3
1700 UNC 94587 732-E5
SHERMAN ST
- SF 94103 648-A7
1000 ALA 94501 669-H2
1700 ALA 94501 649-H7
SHERMAN WY
900 PLE 94566 714-E5
SHERRY CT
1200 SLN 94577 691-D2
2200 LVMR 94550 715-H2
4000 PLE 94566 714-F4
SHERRY WY
1000 LVMR 94550 715-H2
SHERWICK DR
6800 OAK 94705 630-C4
SHERWIN AV
1400 EMVL 94608 629-E7
SHERWOOD CT
- CCCo 94582 674-B5
- MRGA 94556 651-D1
18300 AlaC 94546 691-H3
SHERWOOD DR
5900 OAK 94611 630-D6
SHERWOOD LN
100 ALA 94502 669-J5
SHERWOOD PL
6400 DBLN 94568 694-A2
SHERWOOD ST
41500 FRMT 94538 773-D1
SHERWOOD WY
- CCCo 94582 674-B5
SHETLAND AV
4700 OAK 94605 671-E4
SHETLAND CT
- OAK 94605 671-E4
- SRMN 94583 673-E4
500 MPS 95035 794-B6
SHETLAND RD
2000 LVMR 94551 696-A3
SHEVLIN DR
800 ELCR 94530 609-E2
SHEVLIN PL
7800 ELCR 94530 609-E2
SHIELD DR
2400 UNC 94587 732-C4
SHILOH AV
2000 MPS 95035 794-E7
SHILOH DR
- UNC 94587 732-J6
SHIMMER CT
- MPS 95035 793-H6
SHINGLEWOOD CT
3800 UNC 94587 731-J5
SHINING STAR LN
15000 SLN 94579 690-J6
SHINN CT
1400 FRMT 94536 753-B2

STREET
Block City ZIP Pg-Grid

SHINN ST
37800 FRMT 94536 753-B2
SHINNING TER
- FRMT 94536 752-G3
SHIPLEY ST
100 SF 94107 648-A7
SHIRE CT
2200 LVMR 94551 696-A2
SHIREOAKS CT
100 SRMN 94582 673-J6
SHIRLEY AV
300 AlaC 94541 711-E1
SHIRLEY CT
4800 UNC 94587 751-J1
4800 UNC 94587 752-A1
SHIRLEY DR
1100 MPS 95035 794-C7
6900 OAK 94611 630-G7
6900 OAK 94611 650-G1
SHIRLEY WY
5000 LVMR 94550 716-B1
SHOEMAKER CT
700 LVMR 94551 696-C4
SHOEMAKER DR
700 LVMR 94551 696-C4
SHONE AV
3600 OAK 94605 671-A2
SHORE DR
- PLE 94566 714-F2
SHORE WK
- ALA 94501 669-G2
SHOREBIRD DR
4400 UNC 94587 731-H5
SHOREHAM PARK CT
42600 FRMT 94538 773-D2
SHOREHAVEN AV
7700 NWK 94560 752-C7
SHOREHAVEN CIR
5500 LVMR 94551 696-C2
SHOREHAVEN PL
36300 NWK 94560 752-C7
SHORELINE CIR
- SRMN 94582 673-G1
SHORELINE CT
- FRMT 94538 793-G2
SHORELINE DR
- SRMN 94582 673-G1
900 ALA 94501 669-H3
SHORELINE LP
- SRMN 94582 673-G1
SHOREPOINT CT
900 ALA 94501 669-G2
SHOREVIEW CT
- UNC 94545 731-H6
SHOREWOOD CT
6300 PLE 94588 694-B7
SHOREY ST
1700 OAK 94607 649-C3
SHORT AV
900 AlaC 94586 734-B3
SHORT CT
400 HAY 94544 732-B1
SHORT ST
1600 BERK 94702 629-F1
2600 OAK 94619 650-E6
SHORTHILL RD
4300 OAK 94605 671-C3
SHOSHONE CT
500 FRMT 94539 773-J5
SHOVELER CT
- SLN 94579 690-J7
- SLN 94579 691-F1
SHOVLER LAKE CT
3800 FRMT 94555 732-H4
SHOW TER
5900 FRMT 94555 752-B4
SHUEY DR
- MRGA 94556 651-E2
SHYLOCK DR
- FRMT 94555 732-C7
7100 FRMT 94555 752-C1
SIDNEY AV
1600 SLN 94578 691-D3
SIDNEY DR
38200 FRMT 94536 753-B2
SIEGFRIED LN
- ALA 94501 649-C7
SIENA CIR
- FRMT 94539 753-J7
SIENA RD
- LVMR 94550 715-E5
SIENA ST
5700 PLE 94588 694-C5
SIENA TER
- FRMT 94539 753-J5
SIENNA TER
6100 FRMT 94555 752-A5
SIERRA AV
- PDMT 94611 650-C1
22600 AlaC 94541 692-C7
SIERRA CT
- MRGA 94556 651-G2
1100 LVMR 94550 715-F3
6200 DBLN 94568 693-J4
6700 DBLN 94568 694-A4
SIERRA LN
6100 DBLN 94568 694-A4
6500 DBLN 94568 693-J4
SIERRA ST
1000 BERK 94707 609-F6
SIERRAWOOD AV
- HAY 94544 712-B6
SIERRAWOOD LN
4400 PLE 94588 693-J7
4400 PLE 94588 713-J1
SIESTA CT
4200 OAK 94619 650-G6
6800 PLE 94588 714-A1
SIESTA LN
- OAK 94603 671-A4
SIGERSON LN
1200 AlaC 94586 734-G3
SIGNAL RD
- SF 94130 648-E3
SIGNAL HILL DR
- DBLN 94568 694-G1
SIGOURNEY AV
9900 OAK 94605 671-C3
SIKORSKY ST
1000 OAK 94621 670-D6
SILER PL
1000 OAK 94705 630-B3
SILK CT
36700 NWK 94560 752-D7
SILK HILL CT
- SRMN 94582 674-C4
SILSBY AV
2400 UNC 94587 732-F7
SILVA AV
600 HAY 94544 711-J2
SILVA CT
43700 FRMT 94539 773-H1

SILVA LN
1000 ALA 94502 670-A7
SILVA WY
- SRMN 94582 674-C4
SILVER ST
- UNC 94587 732-H7
4000 PLE 94566 714-E2
SILVER TER
4800 FRMT 94555 752-A3
SILVERA ST
100 MPS 95035 793-J7
SILVERADO CT
200 OAK 94605 671-D3
900 HAY 94541 711-D2
SILVERADO PL
- NWK 94560 752-B6
SILVERADO RD
900 HAY 94541 711-E2
SILVERA RANCH DR
- DBLN 94568 694-E1
SILVER BIRCH DR
- AlaC 94552 692-E7
SILVER BIRCH LN
- HAY 94544 712-E7
SILVER CANYON CT
- AlaC 94552 692-F7
SILVERDELL WY
400 HAY 94544 712-B7
400 HAY 94544 732-B1
SILVER FOX PL
19100 AlaC 94546 691-G4
SILVERGATE DR
11400 DBLN 94568 693-F4
SILVERLAKE CT
200 MPS 95035 794-A6
SILVERLAKE DR
100 MPS 95035 794-A6
SILVERLEAF DR
16000 AlaC 94580 691-E5
SILVERLOCK CT
34900 FRMT 94555 752-E1
SILVERLOCK RD
3500 FRMT 94555 752-E1
SILVER MAPLE LN
- HAY 94544 712-E7
SILVER OAKS ST
- LVMR 94550 695-J7
SILVER OAKS WY
3500 LVMR 94550 695-J7
SILVER REEF DR
5000 FRMT 94538 753-A7
SILVER SAGE CT
- LVMR 94550 715-E4
SILVERSTONE COM
- LVMR 94550 715-C1
SILVERTHORNE PL
- HAY 94544 711-J4
SILVERTIDE CT
- UNC 94545 731-H6
SILVERTIDE DR
4600 UNC 94545 731-J6
SILVERTREE LN
7600 DBLN 94568 693-G4
SILVERWOOD AV
3700 OAK 94602 650-F5
SIMAS DR
500 MPS 95035 794-C5
SIMM CT
5500 FRMT 94538 773-B2
SIMMONS ST
3300 OAK 94619 650-G7
SIMON ST
500 HAY 94541 711-H1
SIMPLE CT
33600 FRMT 94555 752-B1
SIMS CT
29100 HAY 94544 732-B1
SIMS DR
6700 OAK 94611 650-E1
SIMSBURY RD
19100 AlaC 94546 691-J4
SIMSON ST
6500 OAK 94605 670-H1
SINCLAIR DR
1800 PLE 94588 694-E7
SINCLAIR FRWY I-680
- FRMT - 773-F3
- FRMT - 793-J1
- FRMT - 794-A2
- MPS - 794-A2
SINCLAIR ST
24700 HAY 94545 711-E5
SINCLAIR FRONTAGE RD
200 MPS 95035 794-C7
SINGALONG WY
9900 AlaC 94586 713-J7
SINGING HILLS AV
5700 LVMR 94551 696-C2
SINGINGWOOD LN
- ORIN 94563 610-J3
SINGLETON AV
- ALA 94501 649-E6
SINGLETREE CT
6800 PLE 94588 714-A1
SINGLETREE WY
6300 PLE 94588 694-A7
6400 PLE 94588 714-A1
SINGLEY DR
300 MPS 95035 794-A5
SINSBURY WY
33700 UNC 94587 732-E6
SIOUX CT
1000 FRMT 94539 773-H2
SIOUX DR
1600 FRMT 94539 773-G3
SIOUX LN
- SRMN 94583 673-C4
SIOUX TER
44300 FRMT 94539 773-H3
SIRAH CT
2100 LVMR 94550 715-H3
3600 PLE 94566 714-G4
SISKIYOU CT
3500 HAY 94542 712-F4
SITKA ST
1900 SLN 94577 690-G3
SIWARD DR
34000 FRMT 94555 752-D1
SKARLATOS PL
18000 AlaC 94546 692-A3
SKELTON AV
1300 FRMT 94536 753-B3
SKELTON CT
1500 FRMT 94536 753-B3
SKIMMER CT
2500 PLE 94566 714-C1
SKOKIE LN
1200 HAY 94545 711-H6
SKY TER
- DNVL 94526 652-H3

SKYE RD
43600 FRMT 94539 773-G1
SKYFARM DR
5800 AlaC 94552 692-C1
SKYHAWK ST
- ALA 94501 649-D7
- ALA 94501 669-D1
SKYLAND WY
- DBLN 94568 694-H3
SKYLARK CT
- HAY 94544 732-E1
2100 UNC 94587 732-G6
5000 PLE 94566 694-D7
SKYLARK DR
34600 UNC 94587 732-F6
SKYLARK WY
2400 PLE 94566 694-D7
2400 PLE 94566 714-D1
SKYLINE BLVD
5800 OAK 94611 630-D4
6400 CCCo 94563 630-F6
8600 CCCo 94516 630-F6
8600 OAK 94611 650-G2
10500 AlaC 94619 650-G2
10500 OAK 94602 650-G2
10500 OAK 94619 650-J5
12200 OAK 94619 651-A5
13700 OAK 94605 651-B6
13800 OAK 94605 671-D1
14300 AlaC 94546 671-E2
14300 AlaC 94605 671-D1
SKYLINE CIR
8000 OAK 94605 671-D1
SKYLINE DR
3400 HAY 94542 712-F5
SKYLINKS CT
6100 LVMR 94551 696-C2
SKYLINKS WY
5900 LVMR 94551 696-C2
SKYPOINT CT
4200 OAK 94619 650-J6
SKY VIEW CT
- CCCo 94556 651-F3
SKYVIEW DR
17700 SLN 94577 691-D1
SKYWAY CT
2100 FRMT 94539 773-F3
SKYWAY LN
- OAK 94619 651-C7
SKYWEST DR
19900 HAY 94541 711-E2
SLATE CT
- UNC 94587 732-G6
SLATE DR
- UNC 94587 732-G6
SLATER LN
- OAK 94705 630-A3
SLAYTON ST
40600 FRMT 94539 753-F4
SLEEPY HOLLOW AV
2200 HAY 94545 711-F7
SLEEPY HOLLOW AV S
2000 HAY 94545 711-G6
SLEEPY HOLLOW CT
- ORIN 94563 610-G4
SLEEPY HOLLOW LN
- ORIN 94563 610-F4
SLENDER CT
33600 FRMT 94555 752-C1
SLOAN AL
- SF 94105 648-B5
SLOAN CT
4600 FRMT 94538 753-A6
SLOAN WY
- UNC 94555 752-A2
SLOAT RD
4300 FRMT 94538 753-A5
13700 FRMT 94538 752-J6
SLOCCUM CT
32200 UNC 94587 732-C5
SLOPE CREST DR
13200 OAK 94619 651-C6
SLOPEVIEW CT
6000 AlaC 94552 692-C1
SMALLEY AV
100 AlaC 94541 711-G2
300 HAY 94541 711-H1
SMALLWOOD CT
3700 PLE 94566 714-G5
SMITH AV
- DBLN 94568 694-A3
5700 NWK 94560 752-G7
6200 NWK 94560 772-F1
SMITH CT
- ALA 94502 669-H5
38100 FRMT 94536 753-A2
SMITH ST
3500 UNC 94587 732-A5
3800 UNC 94587 731-J5
SMITH GATE CT
4800 PLE 94588 694-D7
SMITHWOOD ST
- MPS 95035 793-J7
SMOKE BELLOW RD
- LVMR 94550 715-D4
SMOKE TREE COM
3300 PLE 94566 714-G3
SMYTH RD
- BERK 94704 630-A2
SNAKE RD
5500 OAK 94611 650-E1
5900 OAK 94611 630-E7
SNAKE RIVER PL
34700 FRMT 94555 752-E2
SNAPDRAGON DR
- CCCo 94582 674-A2
SNAPPER TER
- FRMT 94536 753-B2
SNELL ST
6900 OAK 94621 670-F4
SNIDER CT
- LVMR 94550 696-A7
SNIPE CT
- SLN 94579 691-F2
SNOW AV
7500 NWK 94560 752-D7
SNOW CT
- ORIN 94563 630-J5
SNOWBALL CT
- LVMR 94551 715-D1
SNOWBERRY CT
- ORIN 94563 610-G3
900 HAY 94544 732-B1
SNOWBERRY LN
- ORIN 94563 610-G3
SNOWBERRY WK
- ALA 94501 669-H3
SNOWDON AV
6700 ELCR 94530 609-C1
SNOWDOWN AV
10700 OAK 94605 671-D4

SNOWDROP CIR
3100 PLE 94588 694-F6
SNOWFLAKE COM
5600 FRMT 94538 773-A2
SNOWY PLOVER CT
- SLN 94579 690-J7
SNYDER WY
- FRMT 94536 733-A7
SOAPSTONE COM
- LVMR 94550 715-C1
SOBRANTE CT
100 FRMT 94536 753-D2
SOBRANTE RD
6500 OAK 94611 630-F5
SOBRANTE ST
38700 FRMT 94536 753-D2
SOCA TER
4400 FRMT 94536 752-G3
SODAVILLE CT
45400 FRMT 94539 773-H4
SOFIA CT
35000 FRMT 94536 752-E2
SOJOURNER TRUTH CT
2700 BERK 94702 629-F3
SOL ST
2100 AlaC 94578 691-E3
SOLA CT
- DBLN 94568 694-G3
SOLANA DR
11600 DBLN 94568 693-F3
SOLANDRA CT
2700 PLE 94588 694-H4
SOLANO AV
300 AlaC 94541 711-E1
700 ALB 94706 609-C6
1500 BERK 94707 609-E6
1600 ALB 94707 609-E6
SOLANO WY
1500 OAK 94606 650-A6
4300 UNC 94587 731-J5
SOLAR CIR
4200 UNC 94587 732-B7
SOLAR CT
- MPS 95035 794-D6
SOLAR WY
4200 FRMT 94538 773-D4
SOLBRAE WY
- ORIN 94563 610-E6
SOLEADO CT
11500 DBLN 94568 693-F3
SOLITAIRE CT
19400 AlaC 94546 692-B4
SOLOMON LN
3300 ALA 94502 670-A7
SOLSTICE CT
- FRMT 94539 773-J4
SOMBRERO CIR
2800 SRMN 94583 673-D4
SOMERSET AV
2100 AlaC 94578 691-H5
2300 AlaC 94546 691-J4
3600 AlaC 94546 692-A4
SOMERSET LN
- DBLN 94568 694-E2
SOMERSET PL
- BERK 94707 609-G5
5200 NWK 94560 752-E5
SOMERSET RD
- OAK 94611 650-D1
- PDMT 94611 650-D1
SOMERSET TER
34500 FRMT 94555 752-B2
SONGBIRD TER
- FRMT 94555 752-B2
SONIA CT
- LVMR 94550 696-A7
SONIA ST
- LVMR 94550 696-A7
- OAK 94618 630-C6
SONIC AV
- LVMR 94551 695-D6
SONNET LN
18800 AlaC 94541 711-E2
SONOMA AV
500 LVMR 94550 715-E2
1400 ALB 94706 609-E6
1600 ALB 94707 609-E6
1700 BERK 94707 609-E6
1700 BERK 94706 609-E6
SONOMA CT
600 LVMR 94550 715-E2
SONOMA DR
5300 PLE 94566 714-D5
SONOMA ST
- SF 94133 648-A4
22300 HAY 94541 711-G2
SONOMA WY
1400 OAK 94606 650-A5
SONORA AV
- DNVL 94526 652-J2
SONORA CT
39000 FRMT 94538 752-J6
SONORA WY
4500 UNC 94587 731-J6
SONTURA CT
5400 AlaC 94552 692-D3
SOQUEL ST
32900 UNC 94587 752-A1
SORA COM
4200 FRMT 94555 752-D1
SORA TER
4200 FRMT 94555 752-D1
SORANI CT
4700 AlaC 94546 691-J2
SORANI WY
4700 AlaC 94546 691-J2
4700 AlaC 94546 692-A2
SORANO CT
2800 PLE 94566 715-B6
SOREN WY
- SRMN 94582 674-A3
SORENSON RD
600 HAY 94544 712-B5
SORNOWAY LN
- DBLN 94568 693-E5
SORREL DOWNS CT
3300 PLE 94588 714-A2
SORRELL TER
- FRMT 94555 732-D3
SORRELWOOD CT
- SRMN 94582 673-G1
SORRELWOOD DR
- SRMN 94582 673-G1
SORRENTO CT
- DNVL 94526 652-J3
SORRENTO PL
1600 LVMR 94550 715-G4
SORRENTO WY
2800 UNC 94587 732-A4
SORRENTO PARK CT
4600 FRMT 94538 773-C2

SOTA PL
- SRMN 94583 673-G5
SOTELLO AV
- PDMT 94611 650-D1
SOTO DR
- AlaC 94580 691-C7
SOTO RD
24100 HAY 94544 712-A4
24100 HAY 94544 711-H3
SOULE RD
- ORIN 94563 610-J5
SOUTH LN
- LVMR 94551 696-C4
SOUTH MALL
- OAK 94621 670-F4
SOUTH RD
- AlaC 94566 734-C1
SOUTH TR
- ORIN 94563 610-F7
SOUTHAMPTON AV
- BERK 94707 609-G5
SOUTHAMPTON LN
700 BERK 94707 609-G5
SOUTHAMPTON TER
3800 FRMT 94555 732-D7
3800 FRMT 94555 752-D1
SOUTHBRIDGE WY
- DBLN 94568 694-E2
SOUTHERLAND WY
43400 FRMT 94539 773-F1
SOUTHFRONT RD
4900 LVMR 94551 696-E3
SOUTHGATE ST
1400 HAY 94545 711-H6
SOUTHLAKE COM
- FRMT 94538 773-D3
SOUTHLAND DR
700 HAY 94545 711-F4
SOUTHLAND PL
24000 HAY 94545 711-F4
SOUTH LOOP RD
1600 ALA 94502 690-A1
SOUTH SEA WY
- LVMR 94550 715-D4
SOUTH SHORE CTR W
500 ALA 94501 669-J3
SOUTHWEST PL
- BERK 94704 630-A3
- BERK 94705 630-A3
SOUTHWICK CT
11800 DBLN 94568 693-F2
SOUTHWICK DR
8500 DBLN 94568 693-F2
8700 SRMN 94583 693-F2
25400 HAY 94544 711-J4
SOUTHWICK PL
400 DNVL 94526 652-H2
SOUTHWIND LN
- DBLN 94568 694-G2
SOUTHWOOD CT
- OAK 94611 630-F7
- ORIN 94563 630-H1
SOUTHWOOD DR
- ORIN 94563 630-H1
- ORIN 94563 610-J6
2900 ALA 94501 670-B2
37400 FRMT 94536 752-G5
SOUTHWYCKE TER
2900 FRMT 94536 752-H2
SOUZA AV
5500 NWK 94560 752-F6
SOUZA CT
- ALA 94502 669-J7
22700 HAY 94541 711-H2
SOVEREIGN CT
8800 DBLN 94568 693-H1
8800 SRMN 94583 693-H1
SPADY ST
40000 FRMT 94538 753-C6
SPALDING ST
- HAY 94544 732-C1
SPANISH BAY CT
- UNC 94545 731-J7
SPARKS WY
2700 AlaC 94541 692-C7
SPARLING DR
300 HAY 94544 712-B6
SPARROW CT
- DBLN 94568 694-D4
- LVMR 94551 715-D1
- MRGA 94556 651-E1
SPARROW DR
2000 FRMT 94539 773-G3
SPARROW RD
28200 HAY 94545 731-J2
SPARROW ST
- LVMR 94551 715-D1
SPAULDING AV
2100 BERK 94703 629-F2
SPEAR ST
- SF 94105 648-B5
SPENCE AV
100 MPS 95035 793-J7
400 FRMT 94536 753-C3
SPENCER CT
5200 NWK 94560 752-F5
6900 DBLN 94568 693-J3
SPENCER LN
2600 HAY 94542 712-D4
SPENCER RD
- ALA 94501 649-J7
SPENCER ST
6900 OAK 94621 670-F3
SPENDER CT
35000 FRMT 94536 752-F1
SPETTI DR
100 FRMT 94536 753-C2
SPILLMAN RD
- OAK 94605 671-D2
SPINDRIFT CIR
- HAY 94545 731-H3
SPINDRIFT CT
- HAY 94545 731-H3
SPINEL PL
1400 LVMR 94550 715-D3
SPINNAKER CT
- SLN 94579 711-A2
SPINNAKER DR
- FRMT 94538 793-F1
SPINNAKER WY
- BERK 94710 629-B1
SPINOSA CT
2700 PLE 94588 694-H4
SPIRE ST
- HAY 94541 711-J2
SPIRIT WY
- SLN 94579 690-J6
SPLITRAIL CT
600 LVMR 94551 695-E5
SPOFFORD LN
- SF 94108 648-A5

SPOKANE AV
600 ALB 94706 609-E5
SPOKANE CT
48400 FRMT 94539 793-J2
SPOKANE PL
48400 FRMT 94539 793-J1
SPOKANE RD
48500 FRMT 94539 793-J2
SPOLETO CT
5200 PLE 94588 694-C6
SPOONBILL COM
34600 FRMT 94555 752-D2
SPOONER COVE CT
4600 UNC 94545 731-J6
SPORTS LN
- BERK 94704 630-A2
SPORTS PARK DR
5000 PLE 94588 714-B1
5000 PLE 94588 694-C7
SPOTORNO CT
- PLE 94566 715-B6
SPRAGUE CT
19700 AlaC 94546 691-H4
SPRECKLES AV
1200 SJS 95002 793-C6
SPRING CT
- ORIN 94563 630-G1
1000 HAY 94542 712-B4
SPRING DR
25500 HAY 94542 712-B4
SPRING PTH
- PDMT 94611 630-C7
- PDMT 94618 630-C7
SPRING RD
- ORIN 94563 630-G1
SPRING ST
- SF 94104 648-A5
100 PLE 94566 714-E3
SPRING WY
1400 BERK 94708 609-H7
SPRINGBROOK DR
800 SRMN 94582 674-A7
SPRINGBROOK LN
16500 AlaC 94552 672-C7
SPRING CREEK LN
3400 SCIC 95035 794-G5
SPRING CREST TER
- FRMT 94536 752-A5
SPRINGDALE AV
5100 PLE 94588 693-H6
SPRINGDALE LN
2800 SRMN 94583 673-F6
SPRINGFIELD COM
- FRMT 94555 752-D1
3900 FRMT 94555 732-D3
SPRINGFIELD DR
- SRMN 94583 673-F3
SPRINGFIELD PL
300 MRGA 94556 651-E3
SPRINGFIELD ST
9800 OAK 94603 671-A5
SPRING GARDEN CT
- SRMN 94583 673-H3
SPRINGHAVEN CT
- SRMN 94583 673-H3
SPRING HAVEN ST
1900 LVMR 94551 696-C3
SPRINGHOUSE DR
- PLE 94588 694-D6
SPRINGLAKE DR
400 SLN 94578 691-C5
SPRINGSONG CT
- SRMN 94583 673-H3
SPRINGSTONE DR
200 FRMT 94536 732-J7
SPRINGTIME COM
- LVMR 94551 696-C5
SPRINGTOWN BLVD
1300 LVMR 94551 696-A3
SPRINGVALE DR
- DBLN 94568 694-E3
SPRING VALLEY COM
1300 LVMR 94551 696-A4
SPRING VALLEY LN
200 MPS 95035 794-D5
SPRING VALLEY WY
100 SRMN 94583 673-H3
SPRINGVIEW CIR
900 SRMN 94583 673-F4
SPRINGVIEW CT
900 SRMN 94583 673-H3
SPRING VISTA CT
- SRMN 94583 673-H3
SPRINGWATER DR
1800 FRMT 94539 773-G2
SPRINGWOOD DR
- SRMN 94583 673-H3
32400 UNC 94587 732-A7
SPRUCE CT
7900 NWK 94560 752-D7
SPRUCE LN
6500 DBLN 94568 693-J4
SPRUCE ST
300 ALA 94501 649-E7
400 BERK 94708 609-G4
400 CCCo 94708 609-G4
400 BERK 94707 609-G4
500 OAK 94606 650-A4
500 OAK 94610 650-A4
1000 LVMR 94551 695-F7
1200 BERK 94709 609-H7
1300 SLN 94579 691-A4
1600 BERK 94709 629-H1
1700 SLN 94579 690-J5
19700 AlaC 94546 692-B5
35800 NWK 94560 752-B6
37000 NWK 94560 772-D1
SPRUCE TER
- FRMT 94536 752-H3
SPRY COM
5600 FRMT 94538 773-A1
SPUMANTE CT
1700 PLE 94566 715-B6
SPUR DR
25500 AlaC 94541 712-D2
SPYGLASS CT
2400 UNC 94587 732-B4
3600 AlaC 94546 691-J4
7900 PLE 94588 714-B5
SPYGLASS HILL
- OAK 94618 630-C4
SPYGLASS HILLS DR
2200 LVMR 94551 696-C2
SQUIRREL CREEK CIR
7700 DBLN 94568 694-A1
STACEY COM
300 FRMT 94539 773-H6
STACEY CT
3500 PLE 94588 694-F5
STACEY LN
24200 AlaC 94541 712-C1

STACEY WY
3400 PLE 94588 694-F5
STACY CT
5500 LVMR 94550 696-C6
STACY ST
4700 OAK 94605 671-E4
STADIUM WY
2700 LVMR 94550 715-H3
STADIUM RIMWAY
- BERK 94704 629-J1
- BERK 94720 629-J1
STAFFORD AV
1500 HAY 94541 692-A7
STAFFORD PL
4900 NWK 94560 752-E4
STAGECOACH DR
6900 DBLN 94568 694-A3
7000 DBLN 94568 693-J3
STAGECOACH RD
7100 DBLN 94568 693-J2
7500 SRMN 94583 673-J7
7500 SRMN 94583 693-J1
STAGHORN WY
- LVMR 94550 716-C2
STANBRIDGE CT
200 ALA 94502 669-J5
STANBRIDGE LN
100 ALA 94502 669-J5
STANDISH AV
18300 AlaC 94541 691-F7
STANFIELD CT
16700 AlaC 94552 672-C7
STANFORD AV
100 CCCo 94708 609-G3
600 FRMT 94539 774-A4
600 FRMT 94539 773-J4
800 BERK 94703 629-F6
800 OAK 94608 629-F6
1200 EMVL 94608 629-E6
4400 AlaC 94546 692-A3
STANFORD CT
- FRMT 94539 773-J4
400 LVMR 94550 716-A1
STANFORD ST
- SF 94107 648-C7
1800 ALA 94501 669-J1
2400 UNC 94587 732-E6
STANFORD WY
3800 LVMR 94550 715-J1
3900 LVMR 94550 716-A1
STANFORTH CT
- SRMN 94582 674-C4
STANHOPE LN
1200 HAY 94545 711-G5
STANISLAUS CT
100 HAY 94544 712-A5
STANISLAUS WY
200 HAY 94544 712-A5
STANLEY AV
4000 FRMT 94538 773-D1
9800 OAK 94605 671-B4
STANLEY BLVD
200 PLE 94566 714-E3
200 AlaC 94566 715-A2
1500 AlaC 94566 714-F3
1500 AlaC 94566 715-A2
E STANLEY BLVD
100 LVMR 94550 715-E1
100 AlaC 94550 715-E1
700 LVMR 94551 715-E1
STANLEY PL
100 OAK 94611 649-J2
STANNAGE AV
400 ALB 94706 609-D6
1100 BERK 94706 609-D6
1300 BERK 94702 609-D6
1400 BERK 94702 629-E1
STANTON AV
- ORIN 94563 610-E6
1600 AlaC 94546 691-G3
STANTON CT
200 ORIN 94563 610-E6
6500 PLE 94566 714-D6
STANTON PL
19300 AlaC 94546 691-H4
STANTON ST
1400 ALA 94501 669-H1
2800 BERK 94702 629-F4
STANTON TER
200 ORIN 94563 610-E6
STANTON HEIGHTS CT
2700 AlaC 94546 691-H4
STANTON HILL RD
2300 AlaC 94546 691-H5
STANTONVILLE CT
- OAK 94619 650-H4
STANTONVILLE DR
200 OAK 94619 650-H4
STANWOOD AV
25800 HAY 94544 711-J6
STAPLES RANCH DR
3000 PLE 94588 694-G5
STAR AV
2200 AlaC 94546 692-A6
3200 OAK 94619 650-E6
STAR CT
- OAK 94603 671-C5
2200 AlaC 94546 692-A6
STARBOARD DR
4300 FRMT 94538 773-E5
STARCROSS DR
- CCCo 94583 672-J4
STARDUST PL
100 ALA 94501 649-D6
STARFIRE CIR
5500 FRMT 94538 773-A1
STARFISH TER
- FRMT 94536 753-F3
STARFLOWER CT
5600 NWK 94560 752-G6
STARFLOWER ST
37600 NWK 94560 752-G6
STARFLOWER TER
- SRMN 94583 673-A2
STARFLOWER WY
5300 LVMR 94551 696-C4
STAR JASMINE DR
- SRMN 94582 673-J1
STARK ST
- SF 94133 648-A4
STARK KNOLL PL
- OAK 94618 630-C7
STARKVILLE CT
6800 CCCo 94563 630-F5
STARLING AV
400 LVMR 94551 695-E7
400 LVMR 94551 715-E1
STARLING CT
2600 PLE 94566 714-C1
STARLING DR
34800 UNC 94587 732-G7

STREET Block City ZIP Pg-Grid

STARLITE CT
48000 FRMT 94539 793-J1
STARLITE WY
- FRMT 94539 773-J7
100 FRMT 94539 793-J1
STARMONT CT
- DNVL 94526 652-G2
STARMONT LN
- DNVL 94526 652-G2
STAR PINE WY
2000 SLN 94577 690-H1
STARR CT
500 FRMT 94539 753-J6
STARR ST
42800 FRMT 94539 753-H6
STARVIEW CT
100 OAK 94618 630-C4
STARVIEW DR
- OAK 94618 630-C4
100 DNVL 94526 652-G2
1700 SLN 94577 691-D2
STARVIEW PL
100 DNVL 94526 652-H2
STARWARD DR
7400 DBLN 94568 693-G3
STATE AV
4900 RCH 94804 609-B1
STATE CT
4800 RCH 94804 609-A1
STATE PL
600 OAK 94704 630-A2
STATE ST
1200 SJS 95002 793-B7
2400 SLN 94577 690-G4
39000 FRMT 94538 753-A4
STATEN AV
300 OAK 94610 649-J3
STATES ST
- HAY 94544 712-C7
29200 HAY 94544 732-C1
STATICE COM
5600 FRMT 94538 773-A2
STATION PL
800 BERK 94707 609-F6
STAUFFER CT
- OAK 94619 650-H5
STAUFFER PL
4600 OAK 94619 650-H5
STEALTH CT
- LVMR 94551 695-D6
STEALTH ST
- LVMR 94551 695-D6
STEARMAN AV
1800 HAY 94545 711-C3
STEARNS AV
2500 OAK 94605 671-A4
STEEL ST
200 HAY 94544 712-A5
STEELE ST
4300 OAK 94619 650-G6
STEELHEAD TER
- FRMT 94536 753-F3
STEGE AV
600 RCH 94804 609-A1
STEIN WY
100 ORIN 94563 630-H2
STEINBECK TER
- FRMT 94536 752-B5
STEINMETZ WY
2800 OAK 94602 650-F4
STELLA ST
10500 OAK 94605 671-C5
STELLAR CT
3600 FRMT 94538 753-C6
STELLARIA LN
- SRMN 94582 673-H1
STEMEL CT
600 MPS 95035 794-D5
STEMEL WY
1300 MPS 95035 794-C5
STENERSON LN
3700 FRMT 94538 753-B5
STENHAMMER DR
37900 FRMT 94536 733-D7
STEPHANO CT
33500 FRMT 94555 752-C1
STEPHENS WY
- OAK 94705 630-B3
STERLING AV
1000 BERK 94708 609-H6
3200 ALA 94501 670-B3
STERLING CT
- LVMR 94550 715-G4
4600 FRMT 94536 752-H5
STERLING DR
500 SLN 94578 691-B4
4800 FRMT 94536 752-H5
7500 OAK 94605 671-A2
7500 OAK 94605 670-J1
STERLING PL
- LVMR 94550 715-G4
STERLING ST
- SF 94107 648-B6
STERLING WY
- LVMR 94550 715-G4
STERLING GREENS CIR
- PLE 94566 714-C5
STERN CT
- SLN 94579 711-A1
STERNE CT
34200 FRMT 94555 732-E7
STERNE PL
2800 FRMT 94555 732-E7
STETSON CT
600 LVMR 94551 695-E6
STETSON WY
500 LVMR 94551 695-E6
STEUART ST
- SF 94105 648-C5
- SF 94111 648-C5
STEUBEN BAY
- ALA 94502 670-A5
STEUBEN CT
3800 FRMT 94538 773-E1
STEVEN ST
- SJCo 95391 (678-E2 See Page 677)
STEVENS AL
- SF 94111 648-B4
STEVENS AV
1700 EPA 94303 771-C7
STEVENS ST
3900 AlaC 94546 692-A5
STEVENSON AV
- BERK 94708 609-J6
STEVENSON BLVD
- FRMT 94539 753-D4
200 FRMT 94538 753-D4
5000 FRMT 94538 773-A2
5700 NWK 94560 773-A2
6100 NWK 94560 772-J2
6100 FRMT 94538 772-J2
STEVENSON COM
3700 FRMT 94538 753-C5
STEVENSON PL
39400 FRMT 94539 753-D3
STEVENSON ST
- SF 94105 648-B5
100 SF 94103 648-A6
STEVIE CT
- FRMT 94539 773-H2
STEWART AV
5500 FRMT 94538 773-A3
STEWART CT
700 ALA 94501 649-G7
STEWART DR
300 HAY 94544 712-B6
STILLMAN ST
- SF 94107 648-B6
STILLWATER COM
38800 FRMT 94536 753-C2
STILLWATER CT
- DBLN 94568 694-E2
STILLWELL DR
2100 HAY 94545 731-H1
STINGRAY TER
- FRMT 94536 753-B2
STIRLING CT
5300 NWK 94560 752-D4
STIRLING DR
600 MPS 95035 794-A3
STIVERS ST
38700 FRMT 94536 753-B3
STOAKES AV
100 SLN 94577 670-J7
100 SLN 94577 671-A7
STOCKBRIDGE DR
2400 OAK 94611 650-F1
STOCKER CT
300 FRMT 94539 773-H7
STOCKHOLM RD
1900 LVMR 94550 715-G4
STOCKTON AV
6300 ELCR 94530 609-E2
STOCKTON ST
- SF 94102 648-A5
- SF 94108 648-A5
1200 SF 94133 648-A4
STOCKTON WY
40700 FRMT 94538 753-D6
STODDARD WY
- BERK 94708 609-J6
STONE CT
24700 HAY 94545 711-F5
STONE ST
- UNC 94587 732-F4
- SF 94108 648-A4
700 OAK 94603 670-H6
STONEBRIDGE DR
200 FRMT 94536 732-J7
STONEBRIDGE RD
2100 LVMR 94550 715-F4
STONEBROOK LN
- HAY 94544 732-A2
STONE CANYON CT
- PLE 94588 714-F1
STONE CANYON DR
- AlaC 94552 692-E7
STONECLIFF VISTA LN
- PLE 94566 714-C5
STONECRESS AV
6200 NWK 94560 752-G7
6200 NWK 94560 772-G1
STONEDALE DR
7200 PLE 94588 693-J6
STONEFIELD PL
400 MRGA 94556 651-F3
STONEFORD AV
300 OAK 94603 670-G7
STONE HARBOR
- ALA 94502 670-A5
STONEHAVEN CT
- HAY 94544 732-B1
STONEHAVEN LN
- DBLN 94568 694-G3
STONEHENGE RD
3000 FRMT 94555 732-E7
STONEHENGE WY
- CCCo 94582 674-B5
STONEHURST CT
7900 PLE 94588 693-H7
STONELEAF RD
- CCCo 94582 673-J2
STONEMASON CT
- OAK 94603 671-C5
STONE PEAK COM
400 LVMR 94551 695-C4
STONEPINE LN
100 SRMN 94583 673-B1
STONEPINE ST
- DBLN 94568 694-D4
STONE PINE TER
- FRMT 94538 753-B3
STONE POINTE WY
3800 PLE 94588 694-E6
STONE RIDGE CT
4900 OAK 94605 651-B7
STONERIDGE CT
- HAY 94544 712-A6
STONERIDGE DR
3500 PLE 94588 694-B6
3800 PLE 94566 694-E7
6700 PLE 94588 693-H6
STONERIDGE MALL RD
5600 PLE 94588 693-H5
STONEWALL AV
23000 HAY 94541 711-F3
STONEWALL RD
100 OAK 94705 630-A3
STONEWOOD DR
37400 FRMT 94536 752-G5
STONEY BROOK LN
100 PLE 94566 714-C2
STONEY CREEK DR
700 SRMN 94582 674-A7
1300 SRMN 94582 694-A1
STONINGTON TER
38600 FRMT 94536 753-C2
STONINGTON POINTE
- ALA 94502 670-A6
STONY CREEK CT
- LVMR 94550 715-E5
STORER AV
3200 OAK 94619 650-F7
STORYBOOK WK
- ALA 94501 669-G3
STOW AV
400 OAK 94606 649-J4
STOW CT
- SRMN 94583 693-F1
STOWE COM
35600 FRMT 94536 752-F2
STRANG AV
2000 AlaC 94578 691-F4
STRANG CT
- ORIN 94563 630-J1
STRATFORD AV
100 SLN 94577 671-A6
4600 FRMT 94538 773-C1
STRATFORD CT
3800 PLE 94588 694-F5
STRATFORD DR
1800 MPS 95035 794-B2
2800 SRMN 94583 673-F7
STRATFORD RD
- CCCo 94707 609-F4
700 OAK 94610 650-A3
29000 HAY 94544 732-A2
STRATHMOOR DR
- OAK 94705 630-C3
STRATTON COM
39400 FRMT 94538 753-A5
STRATTON CT
23600 AlaC 94541 692-C7
STRAUB WY
1100 ALA 94502 669-J6
STRAWBERRY LN
1700 MPS 95035 794-D6
STRAWFLOWER WY
40200 FRMT 94538 773-A1
STREAMBED PL
11500 DBLN 94568 693-F6
STRICKROTH DR
700 MPS 95035 794-A5
STRIPER COM
- FRMT 94536 753-C3
STROBRIDGE AV
1600 AlaC 94546 691-J6
1700 HAY 94546 691-J6
STROMBERG CT
27500 HAY 94545 731-G1
STRYKER ST
26100 HAY 94545 711-F6
STUART ST
1500 BERK 94703 629-F3
2000 BERK 94705 629-H3
3100 OAK 94602 650-B4
STUDIO WALK PL
- HAY 94541 711-G1
STULMAN DR
300 MPS 95035 794-D7
STURGEON COM
- FRMT 94536 753-C3
SUBLETT DR
25600 HAY 94544 712-A4
SUDBURY CT
- CCCo 94583 673-B5
100 MPS 95035 794-A5
SUDBURY DR
- MPS 95035 794-A5
SUDDARD CT
6300 PLE 94588 694-B7
SUEIRRO ST
700 HAY 94541 711-E3
SUENO WY
2300 FRMT 94539 753-E6
SUFFOLK DR
100 SLN 94577 670-J7
SUFFOLK WY
4000 PLE 94588 694-E6
SUGAR BEET WY
3100 UNC 94587 732-A4
SUGARBUSH PL
3900 AlaC 94546 691-H2
E SUGAR HILL TER
- DBLN 94568 694-G2
SUGARLOAF CT
- DBLN 94568 694-F2
SUGAR MAPLE CT
- HAY 94544 712-E7
SUGAR PINE CT
36600 NWK 94560 752-C7
SUGAR PINE WY
4100 LVMR 94551 695-J4
4100 LVMR 94551 696-A4
SULLIVAN AV
15300 SLN 94579 691-B6
SULLIVAN CT
- SJCo 95391 (678-F3 See Page 677)
200 PLE 94566 714-D6
SULLIVAN UNPS
- FRMT 94536 733-B7
- FRMT 94536 753-B1
SULLIVAN WY
- SJCo 95391 (678-F3 See Page 677)
SULLY ST
42600 FRMT 94539 753-G7
SULPHER SPRINGS TR
- CCCo 94583 652-F2
SULPHUR DR
2500 AlaC 94541 712-C1
SUMAC ST
32700 UNC 94587 732-F3
SUMAC WY
900 FRMT 94539 773-J5
SUMATRA ST
1000 HAY 94544 712-A7
1400 HAY 94544 711-J7
1500 HAY 94544 731-J1
SUMMER CT
1200 PLE 94566 714-D2
SUMMER PL
- AlaC 94546 692-A4
SUMMER ST
2200 BERK 94709 609-H7
SUMMER CREEK LN
400 SRMN 94583 673-F4
SUMMERCREST CT
19900 AlaC 94552 692-G2
SUMMERFORD CIR
200 SRMN 94583 673-G4
SUMMER GLEN DR
- DBLN 94568 694-D3
SUMMERGLEN PL
19800 AlaC 94552 692-G2
SUMMERGLEN TER
- AlaC 94552 692-G2
SUMMERHILL PL
- AlaC 94552 692-G2
SUMMER HOLLY COM
- FRMT 94536 752-G5
SUMMERHOUSE COM
- LVMR 94551 696-C5
SUMMERPARK PL
- AlaC 94552 692-G2
SUMMERPOINTE PL
- AlaC 94552 692-G2
SUMMERRIDGE DR
19800 AlaC 94552 692-G2
SUMMERSET CT
100 SRMN 94583 673-G4
SUMMERTREE CT
- LVMR 94551 715-D1
SUMMERTREE DR
- LVMR 94551 715-D1
SUMMERTREE WY
- SRMN 94583 673-A1
SUMMER VALLEY CT
500 SRMN 94582 673-J6
500 SRMN 94582 674-A6
SUMMERVIEW CT
300 SRMN 94583 673-F4
SUMMERWIND DR
100 MPS 95035 793-J5
SUMMERWIND TER
- FRMT 94555 752-B2
SUMMERWIND WY
1100 MPS 95035 793-J5
SUMMERWOOD DR
300 FRMT 94536 732-J7
SUMMERWOOD LP
100 SRMN 94583 673-F4
SUMMIT CT
- HAY 94541 711-H3
18600 AlaC 94546 692-B3
SUMMIT DR
2900 FRMT 94555 732-D6
SUMMIT LN
- BERK 94708 610-A7
SUMMIT RD
1300 BERK 94708 610-A7
SUMMIT ST
2800 OAK 94609 649-H2
SUMMIT TR
- CCCo 94583 652-F2
SUMMIT WY
- HAY 94541 711-H3
SUMMIT CREEK CT
900 PLE 94566 714-E5
SUMMIT CREEK LN
700 PLE 94566 714-E6
SUMMIT PARK CT
8400 ELCR 94530 609-E1
SUMMIT PARK LN
8400 ELCR 94530 609-E1
SUMMIT VIEW DR
3000 SRMN 94582 674-A6
3200 SRMN 94582 673-J6
SUMMIT VIEW TER
- FRMT 94539 794-B1
SUMNER PL
1700 HAY 94541 692-B7
SUMNER ST
- SF 94103 648-A7
SUMTER AV
43100 FRMT 94538 773-E2
SUN AV
100 HAY 94544 712-B7
SUNBURST DR
200 HAY 94544 712-A5
SUNBURST LN
5100 LVMR 94551 696-B5
SUNDALE CT
39500 FRMT 94538 753-A6
SUNDALE DR
39000 FRMT 94538 753-B5
40400 FRMT 94538 773-B1
SUNDANCE DR
900 FRMT 94539 773-J5
1000 FRMT 94539 774-A5
5200 LVMR 94551 696-B5
SUNDBERG AV
1800 SLN 94577 690-J2
SUNDEW CT
4300 HAY 94542 712-G4
SUNDIAL CIR
700 LVMR 94551 696-B4
SUNDOWN RD
4100 LVMR 94551 696-A3
SUNDOWN TER
200 ORIN 94563 610-J3
SUNDROP CT
7400 PLE 94588 713-J2
7400 PLE 94588 714-A2
SUNFISH COM
- FRMT 94536 753-C3
SUNFLOWER CT
4100 UNC 94587 732-A6
5300 LVMR 94551 696-B4
SUNFLOWER ST
1500 SLN 94578 691-C4
SUNGOLD CIR
800 LVMR 94551 696-B4
SUNKIST DR
4000 OAK 94605 671-A2
6900 OAK 94605 670-J1
SUNLAND ST
4200 FRMT 94538 753-C6
SUNNY PL
1600 HAY 94545 711-H6
SUNNYBANK LN
2800 AlaC 94541 712-C1
SUNNYBANK PL
23900 AlaC 94541 712-C1
SUNNYBROOK CT
3200 AlaC 94541 692-D7
SUNNYBROOK PL
100 SRMN 94583 673-F7
SUNNY BROOK WY
700 PLE 94566 714-E6
SUNNYBROOK WY
5900 LVMR 94551 696-D3
SUNNY COVE CIR
- ALA 94502 670-A5
SUNNYCREST CT
2600 FRMT 94539 753-F7
SUNNYDALE CT
- HAY 94544 732-D1
SUNNYHAVEN ST
15300 SLN 94579 691-A7
SUNNYHILLS CT
100 MPS 95035 793-J4
SUNNYHILLS DR
1800 MPS 95035 793-J3
1800 MPS 95035 794-A3
SUNNYHILLS RD
800 OAK 94610 650-B3
SUNNYMERE AV
6200 OAK 94605 650-H7
6400 OAK 94605 670-J1
SUNNYSIDE AV
100 PDMT 94611 649-J1
100 PDMT 94611 650-A1
200 PDMT 94610 650-A1
SUNNYSIDE CT
- ORIN 94563 610-H2
SUNNYSIDE DR
- SLN 94577 671-A7
SUNNYSIDE LN
- ORIN 94563 610-G3
SUNNYSIDE PL
400 SRMN 94582 673-J6
SUNNYSIDE RD
3000 OAK 94613 670-G1
SUNNYSIDE ST
9000 OAK 94603 670-J4
9600 OAK 94603 671-A5
SUNNY SLOPE AV
400 OAK 94610 650-A2
SUNNYSLOPE AV
6000 AlaC 94552 692-F4
SUNNYSLOPE DR
200 FRMT 94536 732-J7
SUNOL BLVD
5300 PLE 94566 714-D6
SUNOL CT
1000 HAY 94541 711-D2
SUNOL RD
17900 HAY 94541 711-D2
SUNRIDGE CT
5600 AlaC 94552 692-D3
SUN RIDGE DR
200 SRMN 94582 673-J6
200 SRMN 94582 674-A6
SUNRIDGE DR
- LVMR 94551 696-E3
SUNRISE CT
- ALA 94501 649-D7
27300 HAY 94544 712-B7
27300 HAY 94544 732-B1
SUNRISE DR
600 FRMT 94539 773-H2
5100 LVMR 94551 696-B4
SUNRISE HILL CT
- ORIN 94563 630-H2
SUNRISE HILL RD
- ORIN 94563 630-H2
SUNRIVER COM
33200 FRMT 94555 732-C7
SUNROSE AV
5700 NWK 94560 752-F7
SUNSET AV
2800 OAK 94601 650-D6
7600 NWK 94560 752-D7
E SUNSET AV
2700 OAK 94601 650-D6
SUNSET BLVD
100 AlaC 94541 711-G1
300 HAY 94541 711-H1
900 HAY 94541 691-H7
W SUNSET BLVD
400 AlaC 94541 711-E2
SUNSET CT
- CCCo 94707 609-F3
21800 AlaC 94541 711-G1
SUNSET DR
- SRMN 94583 673-E3
- CCCo 94707 609-E3
700 LVMR 94551 695-E6
SUNSET LN
- BERK 94708 609-H5
SUNSET RD
300 ALA 94501 669-G3
SUNSET TER
- CCCo 94707 609-F3
4000 FRMT 94536 752-F2
SUNSET TR
- BERK 94705 630-B3
- OAK 94705 630-B3
SUNSET WK
- ALB 94706 609-D6
SUNSET CREEK CT
- PLE 94566 714-E6
SUNSET CREEK LN
800 PLE 94566 714-E6
SUNSET DUNE WY
- HAY 94545 731-H3
SUNSHINE CT
1400 OAK 94621 670-G3
SUNSHINE PL
3100 AlaC 94546 691-G3
SUNSPRITE DR
- UNC 94587 732-C4
SUNSTAR COM
5400 FRMT 94555 752-C3
SUNSTREAM LN
5100 LVMR 94551 696-B5
SUN VALLEY DR
11100 OAK 94605 671-E4
SUNWEST TER
- FRMT 94555 752-D1
SUNWOOD DR
7500 DBLN 94568 693-G3
SUNYVALE CT
26500 HAY 94544 712-A6
SUPERIOR AV
400 SLN 94577 671-C7
SUPERIOR DR
2500 LVMR 94550 715-G5
SUPERIOR RD
600 MPS 95035 794-A5
SURREY CT
100 MPS 95035 794-D6
5300 NWK 94560 752-E4
SURREY LN
7600 OAK 94605 651-C7
7600 OAK 94605 671-C1
SURREY WY
24500 HAY 94544 711-H4
SURRY PL
3000 FRMT 94536 752-H2
SURRYHNE ST
3200 OAK 94607 649-E1
SUSAN AV
7400 ELCR 94530 609-E4
SUSAN LN
2900 AlaC 94546 691-H4
5500 LVMR 94550 716-C1
SUSAN PL
27400 HAY 94544 712-A6
SUSSEX CT
- DBLN 94568 694-A4
100 SRMN 94582 673-G4
SUSSEX DR
- DBLN 94568 694-A4
SUSSEX PL
700 MPS 95035 794-A3
5200 NWK 94560 752-E4
SUSSEX WY
1200 HAY 94544 732-B1
SUTER ST
3000 OAK 94602 650-D5
3500 OAK 94619 650-F6
SUTHERLAND CT
4000 PLE 94588 694-E7
SUTRO ST
22800 HAY 94541 711-J2
SUTTER AV
5500 RCH 94804 609-C3
SUTTER DR
39000 FRMT 94538 752-J6
39300 FRMT 94538 753-A6
SUTTER ST
- SF 94104 648-A5
100 SF 94108 648-A5
200 BERK 94707 609-G6
500 SF 94102 648-A5
1100 BERK 94709 609-G6
1600 LVMR 94551 695-E5
SUTTER CREEK LN
- SRMN 94583 673-D6
SUTTER GATE AV
4400 PLE 94566 694-D7
SUTTERWIND DR
- MPS 95035 794-A6
SUTTON CT
3200 FRMT 94536 752-J3
SUTTON LN
7500 DBLN 94568 693-H3
SUTTON LP
3300 FRMT 94536 752-J3
SWAIN COM
34700 FRMT 94555 752-D2
SWAINLAND RD
6100 OAK 94611 630-C5
SWALLOW CT
400 LVMR 94551 695-D7
3600 AlaC 94546 691-J3
SWALLOW DR
500 LVMR 94551 695-D7
500 LVMR 94551 715-D1
SWAN CT
2100 UNC 94587 732-G6
SWAN DR
200 LVMR 94551 695-D7
SWAN PL
700 LVMR 94551 695-D7
SWAN WY
- OAK 94621 670-E7
SWEET LN
21200 AlaC 94546 691-J6
SWEET RD
100 ALA 94502 669-H6
SWEET WY
- ALA 94502 669-H6
SWEET BRIAR COM
- LVMR 94551 696-C5
SWEETBRIAR PL
17700 AlaC 94546 692-A2
SWEETGALE DR
- SRMN 94582 673-G1
SWEETWATER DR
2400 SLN 94578 691-C6
SWEETWOOD ST
43200 FRMT 94538 773-D2
SWENSON CT
700 SLN 94579 691-B6
SWENSON ST
14900 SLN 94579 691-C6
SWIFT CT
- ALA 94502 669-H6
1900 HAY 94545 731-J1
36300 NWK 94560 752-F4
SWINDON PL
4900 NWK 94560 752-E4
SWINFORD CT
- DBLN 94568 694-E4
SWORDFISH COM
38900 FRMT 94536 753-C3
SYBIL AV
200 SLN 94577 691-B1
24500 HAY 94542 712-A3
SYCAMORE AV
300 HAY 94544 711-J3
700 HAY 94544 712-A3
4300 RCH 94804 609-A2
SYCAMORE CT
600 LVMR 94551 695-J6
SYCAMORE RD
- ORIN 94563 610-H4
300 PLE 94566 714-E6
600 AlaC 94566 714-E6
SYCAMORE ST
100 AlaC 94580 691-D6
200 FRMT 94536 753-C1
200 SLN 94579 691-D6
500 OAK 94612 649-G2
36500 NWK 94560 752-D7
37300 NWK 94560 772-E1
SYCAMORE TR
- AlaC 94546 652-C4
- CCCo 94556 652-C4
- CCCo 94583 652-C4
SYCAMORE CREEK WY
500 PLE 94566 714-D6
SYDNEY AV
1800 LVMR 94550 715-G3
SYDNEY CIR
18700 AlaC 94546 691-G3
SYDNEY WY
2700 AlaC 94546 691-G3
SYLHOWE RD
2800 OAK 94602 650-F3
SYLVAN AV
3000 OAK 94602 650-F4
SYLVAN CIR
1800 SLN 94577 671-D7
SYLVAN WY
- OAK 94610 650-A2
- PDMT 94610 650-A2
SYLVANER CT
3200 PLE 94566 714-G4
SYLVANER DR
600 PLE 94566 714-H3
SYLVANER WY
600 FRMT 94539 794-A2
SYLVAN GLEN CT
24600 HAY 94541 712-B2
SYLVESTER DR
33800 FRMT 94555 732-D7
SYLVIA CIR
100 PLE 94566 714-F3
SYLVIA WY
14600 SLN 94578 691-D3
SYRACUSE AV
33700 UNC 94587 732-E6

T

TABARE CT
- AlaC 94541 711-G1
TABER PL
- SF 94107 648-B7
TABU TER
34600 FRMT 94555 752-D2
TABUA CT
20900 AlaC 94541 691-G7
20900 AlaC 94541 711-G1
TACCHELLA WY
37700 FRMT 94536 752-J3
TACKWOOD CT
- SRMN 94583 673-E5
TACOMA AV
1600 BERK 94707 609-F6
TACOMA COM
5100 FRMT 94555 752-C3
TAFFY CT
6700 PLE 94588 694-A7
TAFT AV
700 ALB 94706 609-D5
4200 RCH 94804 609-A1
5400 OAK 94618 629-J6
5400 OAK 94618 630-A5
TAFT ST
26400 HAY 94544 712-A5
TAHITI DR
2200 SRMN 94582 673-E1
TAHITI LN
1000 ALA 94502 670-A6
TAHITI RD
13800 SLN 94577 690-H5
TAHITI ST
2300 HAY 94545 711-G7
TAHITIAN CIR
300 UNC 94587 732-C6
TAHOE AV
2500 HAY 94545 731-H1
TAHOE CT
1700 LVMR 94550 715-G5
4500 PLE 94566 694-D7
28200 HAY 94545 731-H1
TAHOE DR
2600 LVMR 94550 715-G5
TAHOE PL
6800 ELCR 94530 609-D4
TAHOE PARK CT
4800 FRMT 94538 773-C1
TAHOS RD
300 ORIN 94563 610-J6
W TAHOS RD
400 ORIN 94563 610-J6
TAIPAN CT
23200 AlaC 94541 692-D7
TAIT CT
5500 NWK 94560 752-F6
TAIT ST
- LVMR 94550 716-D2
TAKENS CT
7500 PLE 94588 714-A3
TALAVERA DR
2300 SRMN 94583 673-C3
TALBERT TER
37100 FRMT 94536 752-H2
TALBOT AV
400 ALB 94706 609-D5
1100 BERK 94706 609-D5
1300 BERK 94702 609-D5
2600 OAK 94605 671-B5
TALBOT LN
2700 AlaC 94546 691-G4
TALINGA CT
- LVMR 94550 715-G5
TALINGA DR
- LVMR 94550 715-G6
TALLAC WY
17500 AlaC 94541 691-E7
TALLAHASSEE ST
2200 HAY 94545 711-G7
TALLE WY
- DBLN 94568 694-E4
TALLMAN CT
5300 FRMT 94536 752-H7
TALUS CT
- SRMN 94583 673-F7
- SRMN 94583 693-F1
TAMALPAIS AV
- LVMR 94551 695-D7
TAMALPAIS PL
1100 HAY 94542 712-A3
TAMALPAIS RD
- BERK 94708 609-H6
TAMALPAIS VW
- ORIN 94563 610-J4
TAMARACK DR
100 UNC 94587 732-F3
7000 DBLN 94568 693-H3
TAMARISK DR
10500 OAK 94605 671-D2
TAMARRON WY
300 SRMN 94582 673-G3
TAMAYO ST
4000 FRMT 94536 752-F2
TAMBURLAINE DR
- SRMN 94582 674-C3
TAMERA LN
3700 AlaC 94546 691-J3
TAMMY CT
4800 UNC 94587 751-J1
5600 LVMR 94550 696-C6
TAMPA AV
2000 OAK 94611 630-E7
27100 HAY 94544 712-A7
27900 HAY 94544 732-A1
TAMPICO RD
35300 FRMT 94536 752-F2
TAMUR CT
4200 PLE 94566 714-F4
TAMWORTH LN
- SRMN 94582 674-D4
TANAGER AV
1700 AlaC 94578 691-E4
TANAGER COM
4100 FRMT 94555 752-D1
TANAGER CT
2100 PLE 94566 714-E1
TANAGER DR
2100 PLE 94566 714-E1
2200 PLE 94566 694-D7
TANAGER RD
400 LVMR 94551 695-D7
400 LVMR 94551 715-D1
TANAGER TER
4200 FRMT 94555 752-D1
TANAGER WY
300 LVMR 94551 695-D7
TAN BARK DR
34200 FRMT 94555 752-B3
TANDANG SORA
- SF 94107 648-B6
TANFORAN CT
- NWK 94560 752-B6
TANGELO CT
2800 PLE 94588 694-H4
TANGER CT
34800 UNC 94587 732-G7
TANGERINE CT
200 SRMN 94583 673-J7
200 SRMN 94583 693-J1
TANGERINE ST
9100 SRMN 94583 693-J1
TANGLEWOOD
25400 HAY 94542 712-B3
TANGLEWOOD CT
1600 PLE 94566 714-D2
TANGLEWOOD DR
21400 AlaC 94546 691-J7
TANGLEWOOD RD
- BERK 94705 630-A3

STREET	Block	City	ZIP	Pg-Grid
TANGLEWOOD RD				
	-	OAK	94705	630-A3
TANGLEWOOD WY				
	1700	PLE	94566	714-D2
TANGLEWOOD PARK DR				
	5300	FRMT	94538	773-B1
TANNET CT				
	500	PLE	94566	714-G3
TAN OAK DR				
	5500	FRMT	94555	752-B3
TAOS RD				
	48600	FRMT	94539	793-J2
TAPESTRY CT				
	-	LVMR	94550	715-H4
TAPESTRY DR				
	-	LVMR	94550	715-H4
TAPESTRY WY				
	2500	PLE	94588	714-A3
TAPPAN CT				
	-	ORIN	94563	610-G3
TAPPAN LN				
	-	ORIN	94563	610-F2
TAPPAN TER				
	300	ORIN	94563	610-F3
TAPSCOTT AV				
	1900	ELCR	94530	609-C1
TARA CT				
	30400	UNC	94587	731-J4
TARA RD				
	-	ORIN	94563	630-J1
TARA ST				
	100	EPA	94303	771-C7
TARABROOK DR				
	-	ORIN	94563	630-J1
TARADA LN				
	-	SRMN	94582	674-A3
TAREYTON AV				
	-	SRMN	94583	673-F7
TAREYTON CT				
	-	SRMN	94583	673-F7
W TARGOWSKI LN				
	16300	SJCo	95304	(678-J6 See Page 677)
TARMAN AV				
	24900	HAY	94544	711-H4
TARPON WY				
	31300	UNC	94587	731-J5
TARRAGON ST				
	25900	HAY	94544	712-A5
TARRAGONA DR				
	-	LVMR	94550	715-G5
TARRAVILLE CREEK RD				
	-	AlaC	94550	(778-E5 See Page 757)
TAR RIVER CT				
	34500	FRMT	94555	752-D2
TARRY LN				
	-	ORIN	94563	610-G3
TARRYTON ISL				
	500	ALA	94501	669-G2
TARTAN WY				
	12000	OAK	94619	650-J4
	12100	OAK	94619	651-A4
TARTARIAN ST				
	700	OAK	94603	670-H6
TARTARIAN WY				
	34200	UNC	94587	732-F6
TAR WEED PZ				
	-	HAY	94542	712-B3
TASSAJARA RD				
	-	PLE	94588	694-E4
	5000	DBLN	94568	694-E4
	7200	AlaC	94568	694-E4
	8200	AlaC	94568	674-F7
	8200	DBLN	94568	674-F7
TASSASARA DR				
	800	MPS	95035	794-B5
TATE TER				
	-	OAK	94605	671-E5
TATE WY				
	-	CCCo	94582	674-B5
TAURUS AV				
	-	OAK	94611	630-D6
TAVIS PL				
	3000	FRMT	94538	773-F4
TAWNY DR				
	500	PLE	94566	714-G3
TAWNY TER				
	36500	FRMT	94536	752-G3
TAY AV				
	3900	UNC	94587	731-J5
TAYLOR AV				
	300	ALA	94501	669-E1
	2400	OAK	94605	671-A5
	29200	HAY	94544	732-C1
TAYLOR COM				
	39600	FRMT	94538	753-B5
TAYLOR DR				
	400	MPS	95035	794-A3
TAYLOR ST				
	-	SF	94102	648-A6
	900	SJS	95002	793-B7
	900	ALB	94706	609-D6
T-BAR CT				
	-	FRMT	94538	773-B3
TEAGARDEN COM				
	2100	LVMR	94551	696-D2
TEAGARDEN ST				
	2000	SLN	94577	690-J2
	2200	SLN	94577	691-A3
TEAKWOOD DR				
	37600	FRMT	94536	752-H5
TEAKWOOD ST				
	22600	HAY	94541	711-F3
TEAL COM				
	34600	FRMT	94555	752-D2
TEAL CT				
	500	LVMR	94551	695-D7
TEAL LN				
	2600	UNC	94587	732-D5
TEAROSE CT				
	-	SRMN	94582	674-A1
TEASDALE PL				
	500	HAY	94544	711-H5
TECADO COM				
	40600	FRMT	94539	753-G2
TECADO TER				
	-	FRMT	94539	753-G2
	6400	AlaC	94586	753-G2
TECHNOLOGY CT				
	4000	FRMT	94538	773-D3
TECHNOLOGY DR				
	-	LVMR	94551	696-A6
	2400	HAY	94545	731-H2
	4100	FRMT	94538	773-D4
TECHNOLOGY PL				
	4000	FRMT	94538	773-E3
TEDDY DR				
	100	UNC	94587	732-F3
TEHAMA AV				
	500	HAY	94541	711-F3
	4100	FRMT	94538	753-B6
	5100	RCH	94804	609-B3
TEHAMA ST				
	-	SF	94105	648-B6
	300	SF	94103	648-A7
TEHAN CT				
	-	DBLN	94568	693-G4
TEHAN CANYON CT				
	-	PLE	94588	713-H1
TEHAN CANYON RD				
	-	PLE	94588	693-H7
TELEGRAPH AV				
	1500	OAK	94612	649-G3
	2300	BERK	94704	629-H5
	2700	BERK	94705	629-H5
	2800	OAK	94609	649-G3
	3900	OAK	94609	629-H5
TELEGRAPH PL				
	-	SF	94133	648-A3
TELEGRAPH HILL BLVD				
	-	SF	94133	648-A3
TELFORD CT				
	-	HAY	94544	732-C1
TELLES LN				
	100	FRMT	94539	753-H6
TELVIN ST				
	1000	ALB	94706	609-F6
TEMESCAL CIR				
	-	EMVL	94608	629-E6
TEMPEST COM				
	4800	FRMT	94555	752-C2
TEMPEST TER				
	34200	FRMT	94555	752-C2
TEMPLAR PL				
	-	OAK	94618	630-C7
TEMPLE CT				
	2800	EPA	94303	771-C7
N TEMPLE DR				
	-	MPS	95035	794-D6
S TEMPLE DR				
	-	MPS	95035	794-D7
TEMPLE WY				
	38000	FRMT	94536	753-A2
TEMPLETON ST				
	22600	HAY	94541	692-B7
TENAYA AV				
	5100	NWK	94560	752-F5
TENNYSON DR				
	-	LVMR	94551	696-A6
W TENNYSON RD				
	-	HAY	94544	711-G7
	-	HAY	94544	712-A7
	1600	HAY	94545	711-G7
	2500	HAY	94545	731-F1
TENOR CT				
	4900	FRMT	94538	773-B1
TEODORA CT				
	-	MRGA	94556	651-F1
TEOLA CT				
	-	SLN	94577	670-J7
TEPIC PL				
	31100	HAY	94544	732-E2
TERACINA DR				
	100	SRMN	94582	673-G2
TERALYNN CT				
	-	OAK	94619	650-H5
TERESA PL				
	-	SRMN	94583	673-G4
TERESA MARIE TER				
	1600	MPS	95035	793-G3
TERFIDIA LN				
	-	MPS	95035	794-D6
TERI CT				
	32200	UNC	94587	731-J7
TERMINAL CIR				
	600	LVMR	94551	695-B6
TERMINAL PL				
	2300	BERK	94704	629-H2
TERN CT				
	-	SLN	94579	691-F2
TERN LN				
	-	ALA	94501	649-F7
TERN PL				
	-	HAY	94545	731-H3
TERRA AV				
	1200	SLN	94578	691-C3
TERRA CT				
	-	PLE	94566	715-C7
TERRA WY				
	-	LVMR	94550	715-C4
TERRA ALTA DR				
	4000	SRMN	94582	673-G4
TERRA BELLA DR				
	700	MPS	95035	794-B6
TERRABELLA PL				
	4300	OAK	94619	650-H5
TERRABELLA WY				
	4400	OAK	94619	650-H5
TERRACE AV				
	1200	HAY	94541	712-A1
TERRACE DR				
	1000	AlaC	94586	734-B3
	7300	ELCR	94530	609-F2
	35500	FRMT	94536	732-J6
TERRACE ST				
	1500	ALB	94706	609-E6
	4100	OAK	94611	629-J7
TERRACE WK				
	-	BERK	94707	609-G6
TERRACED HILLS CIR				
	-	SRMN	94583	673-E6
TERRACED HILLS WY				
	-	SRMN	94583	673-E6
TERRA COTTA CIR				
	-	FRMT	94536	732-H7
TERRA MESA WY				
	300	MPS	95035	793-H3
TERRA VISTA CT				
	-	MPS	95035	794-C3
TERRAZZO CIR				
	-	SRMN	94583	673-G4
TERRAZZO CT				
	-	FRMT	94536	732-H6
	-	PLE	94588	714-F1
TERRY CT				
	3100	AlaC	94546	691-H3
TERRY LN				
	600	DNVL	94526	652-H1
	700	LVMR	94550	696-C7
TERRY TER				
	40800	FRMT	94539	753-E6
TERRY WY				
	18400	AlaC	94546	691-H3
TERRY A FRANCOIS BLVD				
	400	SF	94107	648-C7
TESLA RD Rt#-J2				
	4600	AlaC	94550	716-A3
	10100	AlaC	94550	717-A5
	16500	AlaC	94550	(718-A7 See Page 717)
TESSA PL				
	4100	PLE	94566	714-E3
TETON CT				
	800	LVMR	94551	695-D7
TEVIS ST				
	-	OAK	94621	670-E3
TEVLIN ST				
	1100	ALB	94706	609-E7
	1100	BERK	94706	609-E7
TEWA CT				
	1000	FRMT	94539	774-A5
TEWKSBURY CT				
	-	SRMN	94582	674-C3
TEWKSBURY WY				
	-	SRMN	94582	674-C4
TEXAS				
	3000	ALA	94501	649-E6
TEXAS ST				
	3000	OAK	94602	650-D5
THACKERAY AV				
	27800	HAY	94544	712-A7
	28100	HAY	94544	732-A1
THACKERAY DR				
	2300	OAK	94611	650-F1
THAIS LN				
	1300	HAY	94544	711-J6
THAMES CT				
	7200	DBLN	94568	693-J3
THANE ST				
	38500	FRMT	94536	753-C2
THARP DR				
	100	MRGA	94556	651-E2
THATCH LN				
	-	ALA	94502	670-A7
THAU WY				
	1800	ALA	94501	649-F7
THAYER AV				
	2000	HAY	94545	711-F6
THE ALAMEDA				
	500	BERK	94707	609-F5
THEATER AV				
	43200	FRMT	94539	753-J7
THE CRESCENT				
	-	BERK	94708	609-J5
THE CROSSWAYS				
	200	BERK	94708	609-J5
THE EMBARCADERO				
	-	SF	94111	648-A3
	-	SF	94105	648-C6
	600	SF	94107	648-C6
	1300	SF	94133	648-A3
THE GLADE				
	500	ORIN	94563	610-G7
THE KNOLL				
	200	ORIN	94563	610-H7
THELMA ST				
	21800	HAY	94541	711-F2
THE PLAZA DR				
	-	BERK	94705	630-A4
THERESA AV				
	4500	FRMT	94538	753-C7
	4500	FRMT	94538	773-C1
THERESA CT				
	2800	AlaC	94546	692-B6
THERESA PTH				
	-	RCH	94804	609-A1
THERESA WY				
	5100	LVMR	94550	696-C6
THERMAL RD				
	100	AlaC	94586	734-C5
THERMAL ST				
	8500	OAK	94605	671-A3
THERMALITO TR				
	-	PLE	94586	714-A7
THE SHORT CUT				
	-	OAK	94705	630-A3
	-	BERK	94708	609-J5
THE SPIRAL				
	300	BERK	94708	609-J5
THETA CT				
	36700	FRMT	94536	752-G4
THETA ST				
	4500	FRMT	94536	752-F4
THE TURN				
	6800	OAK	94611	630-E5
THE UPLANDS				
	-	BERK	94705	630-A4
THIEL RD				
	1000	HAY	94544	732-A1
THIESSEN ST				
	-	PLE	94566	715-A4
THISTLE CT				
	-	HAY	94542	712-C3
THISTLE WY				
	3700	PLE	94588	694-F5
THISTLEDOWN CT				
	3100	PLE	94588	694-F6
THOITS ST				
	15000	SLN	94579	691-A6
THOMAS AV				
	-	SJCo	95391	(678-E3 See Page 677)
	2000	SLN	94577	691-C1
	5300	OAK	94618	629-J6
	5400	OAK	94618	630-A6
	6100	NWK	94560	752-F7
	24300	HAY	94544	711-J3
	24800	HAY	94544	712-A3
THOMPSON AV				
	3000	ALA	94501	670-B3
THOMPSON CT				
	4500	FRMT	94538	753-A6
THOMPSON PL				
	3400	AlaC	94541	712-E2
THOMPSON ST				
	4500	OAK	94601	670-E1
THORN CT				
	-	OAK	94611	630-F6
THORNALLY ST				
	400	SLN	94578	691-D5
THORNBURGH LN				
	-	DBLN	94568	694-H3
THORNBURY AV				
	18900	AlaC	94546	691-J3
THORNDALE DR				
	6400	OAK	94611	630-E5
THORNE DR				
	300	HAY	94544	712-B6
THORNHILL CT				
	3600	LVMR	94551	695-J5
	6000	OAK	94611	630-E6
	34300	FRMT	94555	732-E7
THORNHILL DR				
	600	LVMR	94551	695-J6
	600	LVMR	94551	696-A6
	5500	OAK	94611	630-E6
THORNHILL PL				
	34200	FRMT	94555	732-E7
THORNTON AV				
	3600	FRMT	94536	752-E7
	5300	NWK	94560	752-B6
	8300	NWK	94560	772-C1
	8900	FRMT	94555	752-B6
THORNTON AV Rt#-84				
	4000	FRMT	94536	752-H3
THORNTON COM				
	4500	FRMT	94536	752-G4
THORNTON CT				
	27900	HAY	94544	712-A7
THORNTON PL				
	-	SLN	94577	691-A2
THORNTON ST				
	-	SLN	94577	691-A1
	900	SLN	94577	690-J2
THORNWALL LN				
	1200	HAY	94545	711-H6
THORS BAY RD				
	8600	ELCR	94530	609-E1
THORUP LN				
	100	SRMN	94583	673-C1
	28000	HAY	94542	712-E5
THOUSAND OAKS				
	-	OAK	94605	671-D2
THOUSAND OAKS BLVD				
	1300	ALB	94706	609-E5
	1500	BERK	94707	609-F5
THOUSAND OAKS DR				
	5700	AlaC	94552	692-C2
THRASHER AV				
	300	LVMR	94551	715-E1
	400	LVMR	94551	695-E7
THRASHER CT				
	2100	UNC	94587	732-G7
THREE OAKS DR				
	-	PLE	94566	714-J4
THRUSH ST				
	1400	AlaC	94578	691-E4
THRUSH TER				
	3600	FRMT	94555	732-J3
THUNDERBIRD CT				
	-	OAK	94605	671-D3
THUNDERBIRD DR				
	9400	SRMN	94583	673-H6
THUNDERBIRD PL				
	9400	SRMN	94583	673-H7
	22300	HAY	94545	711-E4
THUNE AV				
	-	MRGA	94556	651-E1
THURLES PL				
	-	ALA	94502	669-J5
THURSTON CT				
	23300	AlaC	94541	692-D7
THURSTON ST				
	41000	FRMT	94538	753-C7
	41400	FRMT	94538	773-C1
TIA PL				
	-	MRGA	94556	651-F2
TIBURON DR				
	4200	FRMT	94555	752-E2
TIBURON RD				
	14100	SLN	94577	690-H5
TIBURON TER				
	34800	FRMT	94555	752-E2
TICE DR				
	1000	MPS	95035	794-B4
TICINO CT				
	1900	PLE	94566	715-C7
W TICONDEROGA AV				
	-	ALA	94501	669-D1
TIDEWATER AV				
	4400	OAK	94601	670-C2
TIDEWATER DR				
	30700	UNC	94587	731-J4
	30700	UNC	94587	732-A4
TIDEWAY DR				
	300	ALA	94501	669-E1
TIEGEN DR				
	1100	HAY	94542	712-A2
TIERRA ST				
	38700	FRMT	94536	753-D1
TIFFANY COM				
	6500	LVMR	94551	696-D2
TIFFANY LN				
	-	OAK	94611	630-F7
	1100	PLE	94566	714-D2
TIFFANY RD				
	500	SLN	94577	690-G1
TIFFANY TER				
	-	FRMT	94536	753-D1
TIFFIN PL				
	500	LVMR	94551	695-E6
TIFFIN RD				
	1800	OAK	94602	650-E3
TIGER LILY COM				
	-	LVMR	94551	696-A4
TIGER LILY DR				
	-	SRMN	94582	674-A2
TIGERSIDE WY				
	-	SRMN	94582	673-H2
TIGER TAIL CT				
	-	ORIN	94563	610-H4
TILDEN PL				
	5400	FRMT	94538	752-J7
	5500	FRMT	94538	772-J1
TILDEN ST				
	15400	SLN	94579	691-B7
TILDEN WY				
	-	LVMR	94550	716-C2
	2300	ALA	94501	670-A2
	2300	OAK	94601	670-A2
	24300	HAY	94545	711-F4
TILGRIM WY				
	2100	HAY	94545	731-H1
TILLMAN DR				
	6000	PLE	94588	693-G6
TILLMAN PL				
	-	SF	94108	648-A5
TIM CT				
	200	DNVL	94526	652-J2
TIMBER ST				
	37600	NWK	94560	752-G6
TIMBERCREEK RD				
	1100	SRMN	94582	673-J7
TIMBERCREEK TER				
	41400	FRMT	94539	753-E7
TIMCO CT				
	3500	AlaC	94552	692-C5
TIMCO WY				
	21100	AlaC	94552	692-C5
TIMES AV				
	18900	AlaC	94580	691-F7
	19000	AlaC	94541	691-F7
	19000	AlaC	94541	711-F1
TIMES WY				
	2300	ALA	94501	670-A2
TIMOLINO WY				
	-	DBLN	94568	693-G4
TIMOTHY DR				
	1200	SLN	94577	690-H2
TIMPANOGAS CIR				
	38300	FRMT	94536	753-D1
TINA PL				
	7200	DBLN	94568	693-F5
TINA WY				
	500	HAY	94544	732-E2
	600	LVMR	94550	715-E3
TINDER CT				
	5400	AlaC	94552	692-D3
TINKER AV				
	500	ALA	94501	649-F6
TINY ST				
	2000	MPS	95035	793-J3
	2000	MPS	95035	794-A3
TIOGA CT				
	400	PLE	94566	714-H2
TIOGA DR				
	24600	HAY	94544	711-J3
TIOGA PASS CT				
	6300	LVMR	94551	696-D3
TIPPERARY CT				
	-	ALA	94502	669-H5
TIPPERARY LN				
	300	ALA	94502	669-H5
TIPPICANOE AV				
	300	HAY	94544	732-F3
TIPTON CT				
	4800	UNC	94587	752-B1
TIROL CT				
	500	MPS	95035	794-B5
TIRSO ST				
	40700	FRMT	94539	753-F4
TISSIACK CT				
	-	FRMT	94539	773-H4
TISSIACK PL				
	45900	FRMT	94539	773-H5
TISSIACK WY				
	45900	FRMT	94539	773-H5
TITAN WY				
	2500	AlaC	94546	691-G4
TIVOLI CT				
	-	LVMR	94550	715-F5
TIVOLI ST				
	-	SLN	94577	690-J1
TIVOLI GARDEN TER				
	-	FRMT	94538	753-E7
TOBAGO LN				
	1000	ALA	94502	670-B7
TOBRUCK CT				
	1900	LVMR	94550	715-G3
TOBRUK ST				
	100	OAK	94626	649-C2
TOBY RD				
	9900	SRMN	94583	673-E5
TODD CT				
	2900	AlaC	94546	691-H4
TODD ST				
	-	ALA	94501	649-D6
	4500	FRMT	94538	753-B6
TODD WY				
	3100	SRMN	94583	673-F5
TOIYABE CT				
	100	LVMR	94551	695-D7
TOKAY COM				
	1100	LVMR	94550	715-H2
TOKAY CT				
	3100	PLE	94566	714-H4
TOLEDO CT				
	35800	FRMT	94536	752-F2
TOLEDO DR				
	12200	SRMN	94583	673-F4
TOLEDO WY				
	16500	AlaC	94578	691-G4
TOLER AV				
	100	SLN	94577	691-A1
	9800	OAK	94603	671-A5
TOLLEY CT				
	-	SRMN	94582	674-C4
TOLTEC CIR				
	2500	SRMN	94583	673-C3
TOLTECA CT				
	1200	FRMT	94539	773-H3
TOLTECA DR				
	1400	FRMT	94539	773-H3
TOLUCA DR				
	12200	SRMN	94583	673-G4
TOM CT				
	-	SRMN	94583	673-F6
TOMAHAWK PL				
	49000	FRMT	94539	793-J3
TOMAS WY				
	200	PLE	94566	714-D5
TOMASEK TER				
	-	FRMT	94536	752-H3
TOM BURNETT LN				
	4900	PLE	94588	694-A6
TOMLEE DR				
	1300	BERK	94702	629-F1
TOMPKINS AV				
	4100	OAK	94619	650-G6
TONALEA ST				
	48900	FRMT	94539	793-J3
TONGA LN				
	3400	ALA	94502	670-A7
TONI CT				
	-	AlaC	94541	711-F1
TONICA RD				
	43600	FRMT	94539	773-H1
TONOPAH CIR				
	3000	PLE	94588	694-D6
TONOPAH CT				
	3100	PLE	94588	694-D6
	48600	FRMT	94539	793-J2
TONOPAH DR				
	-	FRMT	94539	793-J2
TONY TER				
	34100	FRMT	94555	752-B3
TONY P SANTOS WY				
	-	SJS	95002	793-C7
TOPANGA DR				
	10500	OAK	94603	670-H7
TOPAWA DR				
	600	FRMT	94539	773-H6
TOPAZ CIR				
	7500	DBLN	94568	693-J2
TOPAZ CT				
	20000	AlaC	94546	692-B5
	44200	FRMT	94539	773-H2
TOPAZ ST				
	100	MPS	95035	794-A7
TOPAZ WY				
	100	LVMR	94550	715-D3
	44200	FRMT	94539	773-H2
TOPHAM CT				
	-	MPS	95035	794-C5
TOPSFIELD CIR				
	-	DBLN	94568	694-E2
TORDO CT				
	200	FRMT	94539	753-F3
TORENIA CIR				
	40200	FRMT	94538	773-B1
TORINO CT				
	4100	PLE	94588	694-H4
TORLANO CT				
	3400	PLE	94566	715-C6
TORONTO AV				
	2000	SLN	94579	691-A7
	2000	SLN	94579	711-A1
TORRANO AV				
	700	HAY	94544	712-A4
	900	HAY	94542	712-B4
TORRANO COM				
	300	FRMT	94536	732-J7
TORREON AV				
	9900	SRMN	94583	673-F5
TORRES AV				
	1100	MPS	95035	794-C5
	4200	FRMT	94536	752-G3
TORREY CT				
	2600	PLE	94588	694-F6
TORREY PINE CT				
	-	UNC	94587	732-G5
TORREY PINE LN				
	-	UNC	94587	732-G5
TORREY PINE WY				
	4100	LVMR	94551	695-J4
	4100	LVMR	94551	696-A4
TORRINGTON CT				
	34300	FRMT	94555	732-E7
TORRINGTON PL				
	34200	FRMT	94555	732-E7
TORTOSA CT				
	3700	SRMN	94583	673-B3
TORTUGA RD				
	13800	SLN	94577	690-G5
TORY CT				
	7000	DBLN	94568	693-J3
TORY WY				
	6700	DBLN	94568	693-J3
TOSCA CT				
	-	PLE	94588	713-J2
TOSCANO CT				
	2100	MPS	95035	794-A2
TOTANA CT				
	2600	SRMN	94583	673-C3
TOTEM CT				
	100	FRMT	94539	773-J4
TOTHERO PL				
	400	FRMT	94536	753-D2
TOTTEN ST				
	2600	AlaC	94546	692-A6
TOTTENHAM CT				
	5000	NWK	94560	752-E4
TOTTERDELL ST				
	3000	OAK	94611	650-G1
TOUCAN CT				
	1700	HAY	94541	712-B1
TOUCHSTONE COM				
	4800	FRMT	94555	752-C2
TOUCHSTONE TER				
	4700	FRMT	94555	752-C2
TOULON CT				
	1300	LVMR	94551	695-F6
TOULON PL				
	36200	NWK	94560	752-D6
TOULOUSE ST				
	7000	NWK	94560	752-C6
TOURIGA CT				
	500	PLE	94566	714-G3
TOURIGA DR				
	3200	PLE	94566	714-G4
TOURIGA PL				
	1000	PLE	94566	714-G4
TOURMALINE AV				
	-	LVMR	94550	715-C3
TOURRAINE DR				
	6000	NWK	94560	752-D5
TOURRAINE PL				
	6000	NWK	94560	752-D5
W TOWER AV				
	-	ALA	94501	649-D7
TOWERS ST				
	14800	SLN	94578	691-D3
TOWERS WY				
	37000	FRMT	94536	752-G4
TOWHEE CT				
	700	FRMT	94539	773-J7
	34900	UNC	94587	732-G7
TOWHEE ST				
	47400	FRMT	94539	773-H7
TOWN AV				
	3100	CCCo	94514	637-D3
TOWN DR				
	-	HAY	94541	711-J2
TOWN AND COUNTRY DR				
	100	DNVL	94526	652-J3
TOWN CENTER DR				
	-	MPS	95035	794-B6
TOWNSEND AV				
	4300	OAK	94602	650-D3
	24500	HAY	94544	711-H4
TOWNSEND ST				
	-	SF	94107	648-B7
TOWN SQUARE CT				
	-	OAK	94603	670-J6
TOYON AV				
	1300	AlaC	94586	734-B3
TOYON CT				
	1900	PLE	94588	714-B6
TOYON LN				
	-	UNC	94587	732-H6
TOYON PL				
	4500	OAK	94619	650-G5
TOYON TER				
	3200	ALA	94501	670-A4
TOZIER ST				
	35700	NWK	94560	752-C6
TRACY CT				
	-	MRGA	94556	651-G2
TRACY PL				
	-	SF	94133	648-A4
TRACY ST				
	15500	AlaC	94580	691-D6
TRADE WIND LN				
	5100	FRMT	94538	753-A7
TRADEWINDS RD				
	-	SLN	94579	690-J6
S TRADITION ST				
	-	SJCo	95391	(678-F2 See Page 677)
TRAFALGAR AV				
	2000	HAY	94545	711-G6
TRAFALGAR PL				
	2100	OAK	94611	650-E1
TRAFALGAR RD				
	3100	FRMT	94555	732-E7
TRAIL SIDE CT				
	5500	AlaC	94552	692-E3
TRAILSIDE TER				
	-	FRMT	94536	732-H7
TRAILSIDE WY				
	-	UNC	94587	732-E6
TRAILVIEW CT				
	-	SRMN	94583	673-D4
TRAILWAY DR				
	31800	UNC	94587	732-A6
TRALEE LN				
	300	ALA	94502	669-H5
TRAMINER CT				
	200	FRMT	94539	773-J4
TRAMPINI COM				
	34200	FRMT	94555	752-A5
TRAMWAY DR				
	200	MPS	95035	794-A5
TRAMWAY PL				
	400	MPS	95035	794-A5
TRANSIT AV				
	33000	UNC	94587	732-D5
TRANSOM WY				
	2200	SLN	94577	690-H4
TRAPLINE TR				
	-	CCCo	94583	652-E2
TRASK ST				
	5000	OAK	94601	670-F1
	5600	OAK	94605	670-F1
TRAUGHBER ST				
	1200	MPS	95035	794-C5
TRAVERTINE WY				
	-	UNC	94587	732-G6
TRAVISO CIR				
	-	LVMR	94550	715-E5
TRAYNOR CT				
	24600	HAY	94544	711-J3
TRAYNOR ST				
	-	HAY	94544	711-J4
TREADWELL ST				
	-	LVMR	94550	716-C2
TREASURE CT				
	100	SRMN	94583	673-B1
TREASURE HILL				
	-	OAK	94618	630-C4
TREASURE ISLAND RD				
	-	SF	94130	648-E2
TREASURY PL				
	-	SF	94104	648-B5
TREAT LN				
	27700	HAY	94545	731-G1
TREBBIANO PL				
	-	PLE	94566	715-D6
TREE LN				
	5600	AlaC	94552	692-E4
TREEFLOWER DR				
	5400	LVMR	94551	696-B4
TREELINE PL				
	11500	DBLN	94568	693-F6
TREE SWALLOW PL				
	3300	FRMT	94555	732-D7
TREEVIEW ST				
	30000	HAY	94544	712-E7
	30000	HAY	94544	732-E1
TREEWOOD CT				
	4800	PLE	94588	713-J1
TREFRY CT				
	32100	UNC	94587	732-C5
TREGLOAN CT				
	1700	ALA	94501	670-B2
TRELLIS CT				
	900	PLE	94566	714-F3
TRELLIS LN				
	1000	ALA	94502	670-A7
TRELLIS TER				
	-	FRMT	94536	752-G4
TREMONT ST				
	3000	BERK	94703	629-G4
	3200	OAK	94609	629-G4
TRENERY DR				
	3500	PLE	94588	694-F7
TRENOUTH ST				
	41200	FRMT	94538	753-D7
	41300	FRMT	94538	773-D1
TRENTON CIR				
	100	PLE	94566	714-F3
TRENTON CT				
	3600	FRMT	94538	773-E1
TRENTON DR				
	17600	AlaC	94546	692-B2
TRENTON ST				
	-	SF	94108	648-A5
TRES MESAS				
	-	ORIN	94563	610-E7
TRESTLE DR				
	-	HAY	94544	711-H3
TRESTLE GLEN RD				
	600	OAK	94610	650-A3
	1700	PDMT	94610	650-C3
	1700	OAK	94602	650-C3
	1700	PDMT	94602	650-C3
TREVARNO RD				
	-	LVMR	94550	696-A6
	-	LVMR	94551	696-A6
TREVISO TER				
	5900	FRMT	94555	752-A5
TREVOR AV				
	31500	HAY	94544	732-F2
	32300	UNC	94587	732-F2
TREVOR PKWY				
	2600	PLE	94588	694-G6
TREYBURN CIR				
	500	SRMN	94583	693-H1
TRIAD DR				
	3000	LVMR	94551	695-C4
TRIANA WY				
	100	SRMN	94583	693-H1
TRIBUNE AV				
	2500	HAY	94542	712-D3
W TRIDENT AV				
	-	ALA	94501	649-D7
TRIESTE WY				
	5700	PLE	94588	694-C6
TRILLIUM LN				
	-	SRMN	94583	693-H1
TRIMBLE CT				
	2800	HAY	94542	712-E4
TRIMBOLI WY				
	41000	FRMT	94538	753-D7
TRIMINGHAM DR				
	1400	PLE	94566	714-E1
TRINCULO LN				
	33500	FRMT	94555	752-B1
TRINGO CT				
	-	SLN	94579	690-J7
	-	SLN	94579	691-A7
TRINIDAD AV				
	4800	OAK	94602	650-G4
TRINIDAD CIR				
	500	UNC	94587	732-C6
TRINIDAD RD				
	14300	SLN	94577	690-H5
TRINIDAD ST				
	26700	HAY	94545	711-F7
TRINIDAD TER				
	4100	FRMT	94555	752-E1
TRINITY AV				
	200	CCCo	94708	609-G3
TRINITY CIR				
	-	LVMR	94551	695-D7
TRINITY CT				
	6400	DBLN	94568	694-A3

© 2006 Rand McNally & Company

ALAMEDA CO.

© 2006 Rand McNally & Company

STREET / Block City ZIP	Pg-Grid
TRINITY ST	
- SF 94104	648-A5
- SF 94108	648-A5
TRINITY TER	
- MRGA 94556	651-E2
TRINITY WY	
39500 FRMT 94538	753-B6
TRINITY HILLS LN	
700 LVMR 94550	715-E5
TRINITY PARK DR	
- SJS 95002	793-C7
TRIO CT	
5300 FRMT 94538	773-B2
TRIPALDI WY	
2200 HAY 94545	731-J2
TRIPOLI	
4000 ALA 94501	649-E6
TRIPOLI CT	
100 SRMN 94583	673-H6
TRITON ST	
28400 HAY 94544	712-B7
TRIUMPH DR	
3800 ALA 94501	649-G7
TRIXIE DR	
- LVMR 94550	696-A6
TROJAN AV	
900 SLN 94579	691-B6
TROMBAS AV	
1900 HAY 94577	691-C1
TROON CT	
600 MPS 95035	794-B6
TROON PL	
30500 HAY 94544	732-D1
TROOST CT	
5400 AlaC 94552	692-D3
TROPIC CT	
15300 SLN 94579	691-C6
TROPIC WY	
39200 FRMT 94538	752-J7
TROPICANA WY	
300 UNC 94587	732-C6
TROTTER WY	
7500 PLE 94588	714-B4
TROUN WY	
700 LVMR 94551	695-J6
TROUT CT	
44800 FRMT 94539	773-J3
TROWVILLE LN	
1600 HAY 94545	711-H6
TROY AV	
5100 FRMT 94536	752-H6
TROY PL	
- HAY 94544	732-E3
TROY ST	
- LVMR 94551	695-E7
TROYER AV	
42200 FRMT 94539	753-F7
TRUCKEE CT	
6200 NWK 94560	772-H1
TRUETT ST	
- SF 94108	648-A5
TRUITT LN	
- OAK 94618	630-C6
TRUMAN AV	
2500 OAK 94605	671-A5
TRUMAN PL	
5400 FRMT 94538	752-J7
5500 FRMT 94538	772-J1
TRUMAN WY	
- SJS 95002	793-C7
TRUMPET CT	
4400 AlaC 94552	692-D3
TRUST WY	
3900 HAY 94545	731-D1
TRYM ST	
1800 AlaC 94541	712-B1
TRYON PL	
DBLN 94568	694-H3
S TSIRELAS DR	
23200 SJCo 95304	(678-J6 See Page 677)
W TSIRELAS DR	
15900 SJCo 95304	(678-J6 See Page 677)
TUBEROSE CT	
2700 PLE 94588	694-H4
TUCKER ST	
- HAY 94544	712-C7
- OAK 94603	670-J6
	671-A6
TUDOR CT	
600 SLN 94577	690-G1
7500 PLE 94588	714-A3
TUDOR PL	
36200 NWK 94560	752-E4
TUDOR RD	
400 SLN 94577	690-G1
TULAGI ST	
100 OAK 94626	649-C3
TULANE AV	
1100 SLN 94579	691-B5
1600 EPA 94303	771-B6
TULANE ST	
1600 UNC 94587	732-F6
TULARCITOS DR	
1200 MPS 95035	794-D3
TULARE AV	
900 BERK 94707	609-F6
900 ALB 94707	609-F6
TULARE DR	
48900 FRMT 94539	794-A2
TULE LAKE LN	
32700 HAY 94555	732-B6
TULIP AL	
- SF 94103	648-A7
TULIP AV	
1700 HAY 94545	731-J1
4400 OAK 94619	650-G6
TULIP CT	
- CCCo 94582	674-B1
5100 LVMR 94551	696-B4
TULIP LN	
- SLN 94577	690-J1
TULIP WY	
- CCCo 94582	674-B1
1200 LVMR 94551	696-B4
TULIPWOOD CIR	
7200 PLE 94588	713-J1
TULIPWOOD CT	
4200 PLE 94588	713-J1
TULLAMORE PL	
- ALA 94502	669-H4
TULLY CT	
3000 OAK 94605	671-A2
TULSA ST	
500 AlaC 94580	691-D5
TUMBLEWEED COM	
400 FRMT 94539	773-J4
TUMBLEWEED CT	
- SRMN 94583	673-C4

STREET / Block City ZIP	Pg-Grid
TUMBLEWEED CT	
300 FRMT 94539	773-J5
4100 UNC 94587	732-A6
TUMBLING BROOK RD	
- ORIN 94563	610-D6
TUNBRIDGE DR	
36200 NWK 94560	752-F4
TUNIS RD	
2100 OAK 94603	670-F7
TUNNEL RD	
2100 OAK 94611	630-D3
2100 OAK 94705	630-C4
2100 OAK 94618	630-C4
TUNNEL RD Rt#-13	
- BERK 94705	630-B4
- OAK 94705	630-B4
1100 OAK 94618	630-B4
TUOLUMNE DR	
- FRMT 94539	793-J2
TUPELO ST	
34200 FRMT 94555	752-B2
TUPELO TER	
34400 FRMT 94555	752-C3
TURBAN CT	
5600 FRMT 94538	773-B2
TURINO ST	
800 LVMR 94551	695-E7
TURK ST	
- SF 94102	648-A6
TURK MURPHY LN	
- SF 94133	648-A4
TURLOCK WY	
100 HAY 94544	712-A5
TURNBERRY CT	
- DBLN 94568	694-F1
TURNBERRY DR	
- DBLN 94568	694-F2
TURNER AV	
4300 OAK 94605	671-E5
TURNER CT	
800 HAY 94545	711-G5
1200 AlaC 94545	711-G5
3400 FRMT 94536	752-H3
4300 OAK 94605	671-D5
TURNER LN	
1200 AlaC 94586	734-G3
TURNER PL	
3700 FRMT 94536	752-G3
TURNLEY AV	
3900 OAK 94605	671-B3
TURNSTONE CT	
400 LVMR 94551	715-D1
TURNSTONE DR	
100 LVMR 94551	715-D1
2600 PLE 94566	714-C1
TURNSTONE LN	
3100 FRMT 94555	732-D6
TURNSTONE PL	
33500 FRMT 94555	732-D6
TURPIN WY	
35900 FRMT 94536	732-J7
TURQUOISE DR	
7600 DBLN 94568	693-J2
48200 FRMT 94539	793-J1
TURQUOISE WY	
- LVMR 94550	715-D3
TURTLE CREEK	
- OAK 94605	671-D2
TUSCANY AL	
- SF 94133	648-A3
TUSCANY CIR	
- LVMR 94550	715-J4
TUSCANY CT	
- FRMT 94539	773-J4
- LVMR 94550	715-H4
TUSCANY DR	
7600 DBLN 94568	694-A1
TUSCANY LN	
- SRMN 94583	673-G4
TUSCANY WY	
- PLE 94566	715-A4
TUXEDO COM	
4900 FRMT 94555	752-D3
TUXEDO CT	
20700 AlaC 94552	692-C5
TWAIN AV	
- BERK 94708	609-J6
TWAIN TER	
- FRMT 94536	752-B5
TWAINE CIR	
2100 SLN 94577	690-G2
TWELVE OAKS DR	
- PLE 94588	714-A5
TWILIGHT COM	
5300 FRMT 94555	752-C3
TWILIGHT CT	
4200 HAY 94544	712-G4
TWIN CREEKS CT	
- AlaC 94552	692-C7
- AlaC 94541	712-B1
TWIN CREEKS DR	
2500 SRMN 94583	673-C1
TWIN CREEKS PL	
- AlaC 94541	712-B1
TWIN EAGLES LN	
- DBLN 94568	694-G3
TWINKLE CT	
- MPS 95035	793-H6
TWIN OAKS WY	
3600 OAK 94605	671-B3
TWIN PEAKS TER	
4000 FRMT 94538	753-B5
TWITTER CT	
- OAK 94605	650-H6
TYBALT CT	
33900 FRMT 94555	752-C2
TYEE CT	
21100 AlaC 94546	691-J6
TYEE ST	
21200 AlaC 94546	691-J6
TYLER AV	
- SJCo 95391	(678-E3 See Page 677)
TYLER CT	
5200 AlaC 94546	692-B2
5500 FRMT 94538	752-J7
TYLER LN	
4900 AlaC 94546	692-B2
TYLER PL	
5400 FRMT 94538	752-J7
TYLER ST	
600 OAK 94603	670-G6
1500 BERK 94703	629-F4
TYLERTON CT	
- SRMN 94582	674-C4
TYNAN AV	
- ALA 94501	649-F6
TYNE CT	
6900 DBLN 94568	693-J3
TYNE PL	
5000 NWK 94560	752-E4

STREET / Block City ZIP	Pg-Grid
TYNEBOURNE PL	
100 ALA 94502	669-J5
TYRRELL AV	
26600 HAY 94544	712-A6
TYRRELL ST	
4600 OAK 94601	650-E7
TYSON CIR	
- PDMT 94611	650-D1
TYSON LN	
38500 FRMT 94536	753-C3
U	
UINTA CT	
800 FRMT 94536	753-D1
ULMECA PL	
500 FRMT 94539	773-J7
500 FRMT 94539	793-J1
ULSTER PL	
- ALA 94502	669-J5
UMPQUA CT	
900 FRMT 94539	773-H4
UNA CT	
1800 FRMT 94539	753-E5
UNDERHILL RD	
- ORIN 94563	630-H1
UNDERHILLS RD	
3500 OAK 94610	650-B3
UNDERWOOD AV	
1400 HAY 94544	711-J5
5100 OAK 94613	650-G7
UNION AV	
2900 AlaC 94541	692-C7
UNION SQ	
- UNC 94587	732-G6
UNION ST	
- SF 94111	648-A4
400 SF 94133	648-A4
800 ALA 94501	669-H2
900 OAK 94607	649-E2
2800 OAK 94608	649-E2
3200 FRMT 94538	753-D7
UNION CITY BLVD	
3900 UNC 94587	731-J4
4800 UNC 94587	751-J1
4800 UNC 94587	751-J1
28700 HAY 94545	731-J4
28800 UNC 94545	731-J4
32600 UNC 94555	752-A2
32600 UNC 94555	752-A2
UNION LANDING BLVD	
- UNC 94587	732-B4
UNIVERSITY AV	
- BERK 94710	629-B2
1000 BERK 94702	629-F1
1500 BERK 94703	629-F1
1900 BERK 94704	629-F1
2500 EPA 94303	771-B7
UNIVERSITY AV Rt#-109	
2600 EPA 94303	771-B6
2700 MLPK 94303	771-B6
2800 MLPK 94025	771-B6
UNIVERSITY CT	
25400 HAY 94542	712-C3
UNIVERSITY DR	
33300 UNC 94587	732-F5
UPLAND CT	
2400 LVMR 94550	715-G4
UPLAND RD	
2200 AlaC 94578	691-E2
UPLAND WY	
600 FRMT 94539	773-H2
22800 HAY 94541	692-C7
UPPER TR	
- AlaC 94552	652-E6
- CCCo 94556	652-C3
- CCCo 94583	652-C3
UPPER VINTNERS CIR	
- SRMN 94583	673-J4
UPTON AV	
15200 SLN 94578	691-D5
URANUS AV	
100 OAK 94611	630-D6
100 HAY 94544	712-B7
URANUS DR	
4100 UNC 94587	732-B6
URBAN ST	
40000 FRMT 94538	753-C6
URBAN WY	
400 HAY 94544	711-J3
URIDIAS RANCH RD	
2100 MPS 95035	794-E6
2200 SCIC 95035	794-E6
URSA PL	
48400 FRMT 94539	793-J1
URSA WY	
3200 AlaC 94541	692-D6
URSLA ST	
700 LVMR 94550	696-B7
USHER ST	
15500 AlaC 94580	691-D6
USTILAGO CT	
- SRMN 94582	673-G2
USTILAGO DR	
- SRMN 94582	673-G2
UTAH ST	
3500 PLE 94566	714-G2
8100 OAK 94605	671-A2
UTAH WY	
1900 FRMT 94536	753-A3
UTE CT	
1600 FRMT 94539	773-G4
UTICA CT	
7000 DBLN 94568	693-J3
UTICA ST	
32300 HAY 94544	732-F3
UVAS AV	
200 MPS 95035	793-J6
UVAS CT	
25300 AlaC 94541	712-C2
V	
VACA DR	
40700 FRMT 94539	753-E5
VAGABOND LN	
28900 HAY 94544	712-B7
28900 HAY 94544	732-B1
VAILWOOD CT	
1300 PLE 94566	714-D2
VAL ST	
4500 FRMT 94538	753-B7
VALAIS CT	
- FRMT 94539	753-E4
VALANT PL	
- OAK 94610	650-C2
VALDEZ PL	
1100 FRMT 94539	753-E4

STREET / Block City ZIP	Pg-Grid
VALDEZ ST	
2200 OAK 94612	649-H2
2200 OAK 94611	649-H2
VALDEZ WY	
1200 FRMT 94539	753-E5
VALDIVIA CIR	
100 SRMN 94583	673-C3
VALDOSTA CT	
7500 OAK 94605	671-A1
VALE AV	
3300 OAK 94619	650-F6
VALE CT	
6800 PLE 94588	694-A7
VALENCIA CT	
40400 FRMT 94539	753-E4
VALENCIA DR	
800 MPS 95035	794-B6
VALENCIA PL	
4400 AlaC 94541	691-J7
VALENCIA ST	
8400 DBLN 94568	693-G2
VALENCIA WY	
4700 UNC 94587	731-J7
VALENTINE ST	
3500 OAK 94605	671-A1
VALENZA WY	
3500 PLE 94566	715-B7
VALERO DR	
40800 FRMT 94539	753-E6
VALIANT WY	
2600 UNC 94587	732-C4
VALITA DR	
600 SLN 94577	691-C2
VALLADO CT	
- ORIN 94563	610-F6
VALLECITO LN	
- ORIN 94563	610-F6
VALLECITO PL	
2700 OAK 94606	650-B4
VALLECITOS LN	
- AlaC 94586	734-E6
VALLECITOS RD Rt#-84	
- AlaC 94586	734-F5
E VALLECITOS RD	
- AlaC 94586	734-E6
E VALLECITOS RD Rt#-84	
1200 AlaC 94586	715-D6
1200 LVMR 94550	715-D6
1200 PLE 94566	715-D6
1700 AlaC 94550	735-B3
2900 AlaC 94586	735-B3
11300 AlaC 94586	734-H4
VALLEE TER	
36000 FRMT 94536	733-A7
VALLEJO CT	
600 AlaC 94541	711-H1
VALLEJO PL	
3200 SRMN 94583	673-G5
VALLEJO ST	
- BERK 94707	609-F5
- SF 94111	648-A4
300 SF 94133	648-A4
3900 UNC 94587	731-J5
5500 EMVL 94608	629-E5
5500 OAK 94608	629-E5
21600 AlaC 94541	711-H1
21600 AlaC 94541	711-H1
37800 FRMT 94536	753-C1
VALLEJO WY	
- FRMT 94536	733-B7
VALLEJO FERRY	
- SF	648-D1
VALLE VISTA AV	
200 HAY 94544	712-C7
500 OAK 94610	650-A2
VALLEY AV	
3500 PLE 94566	714-B1
VALLEY DR	
- ORIN 94563	630-J3
VALLEY ST	
1500 CCCo 94707	609-E4
VALLEY ST	
1300 HAY 94541	711-H2
1500 SLN 94577	690-H2
2100 OAK 94612	649-G3
2100 OAK 94601	649-G3
VALLEY ST N	
1200 BERK 94702	629-F2
VALLEY TR	
- CCCo 94583	652-D3
VALLEY WY	
400 MPS 95035	793-J7
VALLEY BROOK CT	
22500 AlaC 94541	692-D6
VALLEY BROOK WY	
3200 AlaC 94541	692-D6
VALLEY FORGE ST	
31700 HAY 94544	732-E3
VALLEY OAK DR	
25100 AlaC 94552	692-E6
VALLEY OAK RD	
2000 PLE 94588	714-A6
VALLEY OAKS LP	
- UNC 94587	732-H5
VALLEY OF THE MOON PL	
13800 SLN 94578	691-D2
VALLEY OF THE MOON RD	
- LVMR 94550	715-D4
VALLEY TRAILS DR	
6900 PLE 94588	714-A1
VALLEY VIEW CT	
7200 PLE 94588	693-J7
VALLEY VIEW DR	
22600 AlaC 94541	692-D6
VALLEY VIEW LN	
- ORIN 94563	610-H4
VALLEY VIEW RD	
- ORIN 94563	610-H4
6000 OAK 94611	630-D5
VALLEY VIEW TR	
- PLE 94586	714-A6
VALLEY VIEW WY	
3700 LVMR 94551	695-J6
VALLEY VISTA CT	
- FRMT 94539	773-J1
VALMY ST	
100 MPS 95035	794-A4
VALORIE ST	
- FRMT 94539	753-F7
VALPEY PARK AV	
4700 FRMT 94538	773-B2
VALPEY PARK CT	
4700 FRMT 94538	773-C2
VAN AV	
14700 AlaC 94578	691-E2

STREET / Block City ZIP	Pg-Grid
VAN CT	
500 HAY 94544	732-B1
VAN BUREN AV	
200 OAK 94610	649-H3
VAN BUREN PL	
500 SRMN 94583	673-F6
VAN BUREN ST	
2800 ALA 94501	670-B3
VAN CLEAVE WY	
- OAK 94619	650-H5
VANCOUVER COM	
38500 FRMT 94536	753-B3
VANCOUVER GRN	
1700 FRMT 94536	753-B3
VANCOUVER WY	
1200 LVMR 94550	715-F3
VANDA WY	
700 FRMT 94536	732-J7
VANDERBILT ST	
29800 HAY 94544	712-D7
29900 HAY 94544	732-E1
VANDEWATER ST	
- AlaC 94541	648-A3
VAN DYKE AV	
400 OAK 94606	650-A4
VANE COM	
34400 FRMT 94555	752-B4
VAN FLEET AV	
5200 RCH 94804	609-C4
VAN GORDON PL	
- DNVL 94526	652-H1
VAN MOURIK ST	
3900 OAK 94605	650-H7
VANNOY AV	
4900 AlaC 94546	692-B4
VANNOY CT	
19000 AlaC 94546	692-C4
VAN RIPPER LN	
- ORIN 94563	610-G3
VAN SICKLEN PL	
- AlaC 94610	650-C3
VAN TASSEL LN	
- ORIN 94563	610-G3
VANTINI WY	
- PLE 94566	715-C6
VAQUERO CT	
- FRMT 94539	753-G5
VARDIN TER	
1000 FRMT 94536	753-C3
VARENNES ST	
- SF 94133	648-A4
VARESE CT	
- PLE 94566	715-C5
VARGAS CT	
100 MPS 95035	794-A4
VARGAS RD	
40400 FRMT 94539	753-G2
41300 AlaC 94539	753-G2
VARNEY PL	
- SF 94107	648-B7
VARNI PL	
31100 UNC 94587	731-J5
VASCO RD	
3600 CCCo 94513	637-A3
3600 CCCo 94514	637-A3
3600 CCCo 94514	(657-C1 See Page 637)
3600 CCCo 94551	676-E1
3600 CCCo 94551	676-E1
3800 AlaC 94551	676-B4
3800 AlaC 94551	696-C1
N VASCO RD	
800 LVMR 94551	696-C3
S VASCO RD	
100 LVMR 94551	696-D5
900 LVMR 94550	696-D5
1700 LVMR 94550	716-D3
2000 AlaC 94550	716-D3
VASHELL WY	
- OAK 94610	649-H2
VASONA CT	
27700 HAY 94544	712-A7
VASONA ST	
600 MPS 95035	793-J6
VASQUEZ CT	
900 UNC 94587	732-F4
VASSAR AV	
300 BERK 94708	609-G4
300 CCCo 94708	609-G4
400 BERK 94707	609-G4
VASSAR PL	
15400 AlaC 94580	691-D5
VAUGHN AV	
18900 AlaC 94546	691-J4
VEASY ST	
31000 UNC 94587	731-H5
VEDA DR	
400 DNVL 94526	652-J2
VEGA RD	
1000 OAK 94610	650-B3
VEGA TER	
400 FRMT 94536	753-E1
VEGAS AV	
1700 MPS 95035	794-A3
VELARDE DR	
2200 AlaC 94546	691-J6
2200 AlaC 94546	692-A6
VELVETLEAF CIR	
- SRMN 94582	673-G3
VENETIA RD	
- OAK 94605	671-C4
VENETO AV	
300 UNC 94587	732-J6
VENETO CT	
- PLE 94588	694-H4
VENETO ST	
34500 UNC 94587	732-H5
VENICE CT	
- SLN 94577	671-A7
VENTNOR CT	
29600 HAY 94544	732-C1
VENTRY WY	
16700 AlaC 94580	691-F6
VENTURA AV	
900 ALB 94707	609-F6
1000 ALB 94706	609-F7
VENTURA CT	
800 LVMR 94551	715-F1
VENTURA DR	
6600 DBLN 94568	694-A3
48900 FRMT 94539	794-A2
VENTURA PL	
400 SRMN 94583	673-F6
VENTURA WY	
4500 UNC 94587	731-J6

STREET / Block City ZIP	Pg-Grid
VENUS CT	
600 FRMT 94539	793-J5
VENUS PL	
4100 UNC 94587	732-B6
VENUS ST	
28500 HAY 94544	712-B7
VENUS WY	
900 LVMR 94550	715-F4
VERA AV	
15200 SLN 94578	691-D5
VERACRUZ PL	
3200 SRMN 94583	673-F4
VERANDA CIR	
700 MPS 95035	794-B5
VERBENA COM	
- LVMR 94551	696-D2
VERBENA CT	
2000 FRMT 94539	773-G3
VERCELLI WY	
- PLE 94566	715-C7
VERDALA DR	
- LVMR 94550	715-G5
VERDE CT	
3200 PLE 94588	694-C7
VERDE DR	
1000 PLE 94566	714-G3
VERDEMAR DR	
1000 ALA 94502	670-A6
1000 ALA 94502	669-J7
VERDI RD	
29000 HAY 94544	712-C7
VERDI ST	
1500 ALA 94501	669-G1
VERDIN PL	
- DBLN 94568	694-H3
VERDITE ST	
- LVMR 94550	715-D3
VERGIL CT	
2600 AlaC 94546	692-B6
VERGIL ST	
21900 AlaC 94546	692-B6
VERIL WY	
31800 HAY 94544	732-F2
VERITAS CT	
- SRMN 94582	674-C3
VERITAS WY	
- SRMN 94582	674-C3
VERLOR CT	
24700 HAY 94545	711-F5
VERMEHR PL	
- SF 94108	648-A5
VERMONT AV	
300 BERK 94707	609-G4
VERMONT CT	
3200 PLE 94588	694-G6
VERMONT ST	
800 OAK 94610	650-A2
22600 AlaC 94541	692-B7
22600 HAY 94541	692-B7
VERN AV	
- SF 94107	648-B7
VERNA CT	
31100 UNC 94587	731-J5
VERNAL AV	
2300 SLN 94577	690-H3
VERNAL CT	
1300 FRMT 94539	753-G6
VERNALIS LN	
- ALA 94501	649-E7
VERNAZZA DR	
- LVMR 94550	715-J3
VERNE ST	
40400 FRMT 94538	773-B1
VERNETTI WY	
21800 AlaC 94546	692-B6
VERNON AV	
5100 FRMT 94536	752-H6
VERNON CT	
18400 AlaC 94546	692-A3
VERNON ST	
- OAK 94610	649-H2
VERNON TER	
100 OAK 94610	649-H2
VERNON WY	
- CCCo 94582	674-C4
VERONA AV	
300 DNVL 94526	652-J1
900 LVMR 94550	715-F2
27400 HAY 94545	711-G7
27400 HAY 94545	731-G1
VERONA CT	
- DNVL 94526	652-J2
VERONA PTH	
15400 AlaC 94618	630-B5
VERONA RD	
- AlaC 94566	734-D1
- AlaC 94566	734-D1
VERONICA AV	
4100 AlaC 94546	692-B5
VERONICA CT	
- SRMN 94582	673-H1
VERRADA RD	
1000 OAK 94610	650-B3
VERSAILLES AV	
900 ALA 94501	670-A3
VERSAILLES PARK CT	
4700 FRMT 94538	773-C2
VERVAIS DR	
4200 PLE 94566	714-E3
VESPER AV	
2200 FRMT 94539	793-J1
VESTAL CT	
2000 SLN 94577	690-H2
VESTAL ST	
2100 AlaC 94541	692-A6
VETERAN WY	
24600 AlaC 94602	650-D4
VETERANS CT	
- ALA 94502	670-A5
VETTA DR	
- LVMR 94550	715-C4
VIA ACALANES	
500 AlaC 94580	691-D7
VIA AIRES	
- SLN 94577	671-A7
VIA ALAMITOS	
15800 AlaC 94580	711-B1
VIA ALAMO	
600 AlaC 94580	711-D1
VIA ALAMOSA	
1100 ALA 94502	669-H7
VIA ALISO	
1000 ALA 94502	669-J7
VIA AMIGOS	
1500 AlaC 94580	711-B1
VIA ANACAPA	
16200 AlaC 94580	691-E7
VIA ANADE	
16000 AlaC 94580	711-C1
VIA ANDETA	
16100 AlaC 94580	691-E7

STREET / Block City ZIP	Pg-Grid
VIA ANDETA	
16100 AlaC 94580	711-E1
VIA ANNETTE	
17200 AlaC 94580	711-C1
VIA ARAGON	
100 FRMT 94539	753-J6
VIA ARRIBA	
16000 AlaC 94580	691-D7
16000 AlaC 94580	711-D1
VIA ARROYO	
15700 AlaC 94580	691-D7
VIA BAJA DR	
700 MPS 95035	794-B5
VIA BARRETT	
1400 AlaC 94580	691-B7
1400 AlaC 94580	711-B1
VIA BELLITA	
200 AlaC 94580	691-E7
VIA BOLSA	
- AlaC 94580	691-E7
VIA BONITA	
2900 ALA 94502	669-J6
VIA BREGANI	
800 AlaC 94580	691-C7
VIA BUENA VISTA	
- AlaC 94580	711-C2
VIA BUFANO	
- SF 94133	648-A4
VIA CALLADOS	
- ORIN 94563	610-G3
VIA CARMEN	
17200 AlaC 94580	711-C2
VIA CARRETA	
1600 AlaC 94580	711-C2
VIA CATHERINE	
16000 AlaC 94580	711-B2
VIA CHIQUITA	
16000 AlaC 94580	711-C1
VIA CHORRO	
1500 AlaC 94580	711-B1
VIA CIELO	
17000 AlaC 94580	711-D1
VIA COCHES	
300 AlaC 94580	711-E1
VIA COLUSA	
15700 AlaC 94580	691-D7
VIA CONEJO	
15800 AlaC 94580	691-D7
VIA CONIL	
100 AlaC 94580	691-E7
VIA CORALLA	
1000 AlaC 94580	711-C2
VIA CORDOBA	
2800 CCCo 94583	673-B3
2800 SRMN 94583	673-B3
15700 AlaC 94580	691-E7
VIA CORONA	
1100 ALA 94502	669-H7
15700 AlaC 94580	691-D7
VIA CORTA	
1100 ALA 94502	669-H7
VIA CRISTOBAL	
1100 LVMR 94551	695-E4
VIA DE CIELO	
5900 PLE 94566	714-B2
VIA DE LA CRUZ	
- PLE 94566	714-B2
VIA DE LOS CERROS	
6000 PLE 94566	714-B2
VIA DE LOS MILAGROS	
2400 PLE 94566	714-B2
VIA DEL PAZ	
900 LVMR 94550	715-F3
VIA DEL PRADO	
15800 AlaC 94580	691-C7
VIA DEL REY	
17000 AlaC 94580	711-C1
VIA DEL ROBLES	
16100 AlaC 94580	711-C1
VIA DEL SALERNO	
1200 PLE 94566	715-C6
VIA DEL SOL	
600 LVMR 94550	715-E3
15800 AlaC 94580	691-D7
15900 AlaC 94580	711-D1
VIA DESCANSO	
300 AlaC 94580	711-D1
VIA DESTE	
1300 LVMR 94551	695-E5
VIA DIEGO	
16000 AlaC 94580	691-E7
VIA DI SALERNO	
1000 PLE 94566	715-C6
VIA DOLOROSA	
17200 AlaC 94580	711-D2
VIA EDUARDO	
17200 AlaC 94580	711-C2
VIA EL CERRITO	
17200 AlaC 94580	711-C2
VIA ELEVADO	
200 AlaC 94580	711-E1
VIA EL MONTE	
17000 AlaC 94580	711-C1
VIA ENCINAS	
17300 AlaC 94580	711-D1
VIA ENRICO	
800 AlaC 94580	691-C7
VIA ESCONDIDO	
1400 AlaC 94580	711-C2
VIA ESMOND	
- AlaC 94580	691-B7
VIA ESPADA	
2200 PLE 94566	714-B3
VIA ESPERANZA	
1100 AlaC 94580	711-D2
VIA ESTRELLA	
1300 AlaC 94580	711-C1
VIA FAISAN	
- ORIN 94563	610-G6
VIA FARALLON	
- ORIN 94563	610-G6
VIA FLOREADO	
- ORIN 94563	610-J5
VIA FLORES	
17000 AlaC 94580	711-D1
VIA FRANCES	
1400 AlaC 94580	711-C2
VIA GRANADA	
750 LVMR 94550	715-F2
15700 AlaC 94580	691-E7
VIA HARRIET	
16000 AlaC 94580	711-B2
VIA HELENA	
1600 AlaC 94580	711-C1
VIA HERMANA	
1300 AlaC 94580	691-B7
1400 AlaC 94580	711-B1
VIA HERMOSA	
16100 AlaC 94580	691-E7
- ORIN 94563	610-H5

STREET
Block City ZIP Pg-Grid

VIA HONDA
900 AlaC 94580 711-D2
VIA HORNITOS
15800 AlaC 94580 711-B1
VIA JOSE
18100 AlaC 94580 711-E2
VIA JULIA
17300 AlaC 94580 711-C2
VIA KARL
16100 AlaC 94580 711-B2
VIA LACQUA
1400 AlaC 94580 711-B1
VIA LA JOLLA
17200 AlaC 94580 711-C2
VIA LA PALOMA
1300 AlaC 94580 711-C1
VIA LA PAZ
4500 UNC 94587 731-J6
VIA LAS CRUCES
- ORIN 94563 610-J5
VIA LINARES
- AlaC 94580 691-E7
VIA LOBOS
1500 AlaC 94580 691-B7
1500 AlaC 94580 711-B1
VIA LOS TRANCOS
1200 AlaC 94580 711-D2
VIA LUCAS
1100 AlaC 94580 711-C1
VIA LUCERO
200 AlaC 94580 691-E7
300 AlaC 94580 711-E1
VIA LUNADO
15700 AlaC 94580 691-D7
VIA LUPINE
16100 AlaC 94580 711-C1
VIA MADELINE
15500 AlaC 94580 691-C7
VIA MADERA
1200 AlaC 94580 711-C2
VIA MADRID
1000 LVMR 94550 715-F2
4400 UNC 94587 731-J6
VIA MAGDALENA
17000 AlaC 94580 711-D1
VIA MALAGA
- FRMT 94539 753-J6
100 AlaC 94580 691-E7
VIA MANZANAS
500 AlaC 94580 711-C1
VIA MARGARITA
17000 AlaC 94580 711-C1
VIA MARGARITA CT
17000 AlaC 94580 711-D1
VIA MARIPOSA
700 AlaC 94580 711-D1
VIA MARLIN
15800 AlaC 94580 691-E7
VIA MATEO
800 LVMR 94551 695-E5
VIA MATERO
- AlaC 94580 691-E7
VIA MEDIA
15800 AlaC 94580 691-D7
16000 AlaC 94580 711-D1
VIA MELINA
17200 AlaC 94580 711-C2
VIA MERCADO
500 AlaC 94580 691-D7
VIA MESA
1400 AlaC 94580 711-C2
VIA MILOS
16100 AlaC 94580 711-B2
VIA MIRABEL
500 AlaC 94580 711-D1
VIA MIRLO
200 AlaC 94580 691-E7
VIA MONTALVO
900 LVMR 94551 695-E5
VIA MORAGA
43000 FRMT 94539 753-G7
43000 FRMT 94539 773-G1
VIA MORELLA
- AlaC 94580 691-E7
VIA MURIETTA
2100 AlaC 94580 711-A1
VIA NATAL
1700 AlaC 94580 711-B2
VIA NAVARRA
42800 FRMT 94539 753-J6
W VIA NICOLO RD
18600 SJCo 95377 (698-G4 See Page 677)
VIANO WY
- LVMR 94550 715-E5
VIA NUBE
1200 AlaC 94580 711-D2
VIA NUEVA
15700 AlaC 94580 711-B1
VIA OLINDA
16000 AlaC 94580 711-D1
VIA OPORTO
42800 FRMT 94539 753-J6
VIA ORINDA
1700 FRMT 94539 753-G7
1700 FRMT 94539 773-G1
VIA OWEN
16100 AlaC 94580 711-B2
VIA PACHECO
500 AlaC 94580 691-D7
VIA PALMA
1000 AlaC 94580 711-D2
VIA PALOS
100 AlaC 94580 691-E7
VIA PARO
15800 AlaC 94580 691-D7
15900 AlaC 94580 711-D1
VIA PASATIEMPO
17000 AlaC 94580 711-D1
VIA PECORO
200 AlaC 94580 711-E1
VIA PEQUENA
18400 AlaC 94580 691-E7
VIA PERALTA
5700 PLE 94566 714-C2
VIA PERDIDO
17000 AlaC 94580 711-D1
VIA PIEDRAS
17000 AlaC 94580 711-D1
VIA PINALE
15800 AlaC 94580 691-D7
16000 AlaC 94580 711-D1
VIA POTRERO
600 AlaC 94580 711-D1
VIA POUDRE
800 AlaC 94580 711-E2
VIA PRADERIA
43900 FRMT 94539 773-H2
VIA PRIMERO
16000 AlaC 94580 691-E7
16400 AlaC 94580 711-E1
VIA PUEBLA
42800 FRMT 94539 753-J6
VIA PUNTA
15700 AlaC 94580 691-C7
VIA QUITO
6800 PLE 94566 714-B2
VIA RANCHO
1500 AlaC 94580 711-B1
VIA REDONDO
1700 AlaC 94580 711-C1
VIA REGIO
15700 AlaC 94580 691-D7
VIA REPRESA
15700 AlaC 94580 711-B1
VIA RIALTO
- OAK 94619 650-H5
VIA RINCON
17400 AlaC 94580 691-E7
17400 AlaC 94580 711-E1
VIA RIVERA
15700 AlaC 94580 691-D7
VIA RODRIGUEZ
300 AlaC 94580 691-D7
VIA ROSARIO
200 FRMT 94539 753-J6
VIA ROSAS
17600 AlaC 94580 711-E1
VIA SAN ARDO
17200 AlaC 94580 711-C2
VIA SAN BLAS
6500 PLE 94566 714-B2
VIA SAN CARLOS
100 AlaC 94580 691-E7
41900 FRMT 94539 753-G6
VIA SAN DIMAS
- FRMT 94539 753-H6
VIA SAN GABRIEL
42000 FRMT 94539 753-H5
VIA SAN INIGO
- ORIN 94563 610-E7
VIA SAN JOSE
1200 LVMR 94551 695-E5
VIA SAN JUAN
1200 AlaC 94580 711-C1
VIA SAN LUIS REY
41900 FRMT 94539 753-G6
VIA SAN MARINO
100 AlaC 94580 691-E7
VIA SAN MIGUEL
41800 FRMT 94539 753-G6
VIA SARITA
1600 AlaC 94580 711-C2
VIA SECO
15700 AlaC 94580 691-B7
15700 AlaC 94580 711-B1
VIA SEGUNDO
16000 AlaC 94580 691-E7
16800 AlaC 94580 711-E1
VIA SEVILLA
16000 AlaC 94580 691-E7
VIA SEVILLE
800 LVMR 94550 715-F2
VIA SOMBRIO
1400 FRMT 94539 753-G7
VIA SONATA
15700 AlaC 94580 711-A1
VIA SONORA
16000 AlaC 94580 711-C1
VIA SONYA
1500 AlaC 94580 711-C2
VIA SORRENTO
15700 AlaC 94580 711-A1
VIA SUSANA
17300 AlaC 94580 711-C2
VIA TOLEDO
15800 AlaC 94580 691-E7
18300 AlaC 94580 711-E1
VIA TOMAR
17000 AlaC 94580 691-E7
VIA TOVITA
1600 AlaC 94580 711-C2
VIA TOYON
1500 AlaC 94580 711-C1
VIA VALENCIA
17000 AlaC 94580 691-E7
VIA VALPARAISO
42900 FRMT 94539 753-J6
VIA VECINOS
16000 AlaC 94580 711-C1
VIA VEGA
15500 AlaC 94580 691-C7
VIA VENTANA
1500 AlaC 94580 711-B1
VIA VERA CRUZ
400 FRMT 94539 753-H6
VIA VERDE
- AlaC 94580 691-E7
VIA VIENTO
100 AlaC 94580 691-E7
VIA VISTA
1100 AlaC 94580 711-C1
VIA WALTER
16000 AlaC 94580 711-B2
VIA ZAPATA
7900 DBLN 94568 693-F3
VICENTE PL
- OAK 94705 630-B3
VICENTE RD
- BERK 94705 630-B4
- OAK 94705 630-B4
VICENTE ST
5500 OAK 94609 629-H5
VICENTE WY
5400 OAK 94609 629-H6
VICKSBURG AV
1900 OAK 94601 670-E1
2300 OAK 94601 650-E7
VICTOR AV
1200 SLN 94579 691-A5
3300 OAK 94602 650-F4
3500 OAK 94619 650-F5
5200 ELCR 94530 609-B1
5200 RCH 94804 609-B1
VICTORIA AV
600 SLN 94577 671-B6
4300 UNC 94587 731-J6
4300 UNC 94587 732-A6
4600 FRMT 94538 753-C7
4600 FRMT 94538 773-C1
VICTORIA BAY
300 ALA 94502 670-A6
VICTORIA CT
500 SLN 94577 671-A6
2300 LVMR 94550 715-G4
VICTORIA LN
5800 AlaC 94550 717-A4
VICTORIA ST
300 ELCR 94530 609-D4
VICTORIA MEADOW CT
2900 PLE 94566 714-H3
VICTORIA PARK CT
4600 FRMT 94538 773-C2
VICTORIA RIDGE CT
2800 PLE 94566 714-H3
VICTORINE RD
2000 CCCo 94551 675-D2
VICTORY CIR
- SRMN 94582 673-F2
VICTORY CT
- SRMN 94582 673-F2
200 OAK 94607 649-G5
VICTORY DR
21900 HAY 94541 711-F3
VICTORY LN
37200 FRMT 94536 753-B1
VIDA CT
1600 SLN 94579 691-A7
VIDA DESCANSADA
- ORIN 94563 610-G5
VIDELL ST
1200 SLN 94579 691-B7
1700 SLN 94579 711-A1
VIEBROCK WY
- HAY 94544 732-B1
VIEJO WY
4400 UNC 94587 731-H6
VIENNA DR
- MPS 95035 793-J4
- MPS 95035 794-A4
VIENNA ST
1000 LVMR 94550 715-G3
VIENTO CT
38800 FRMT 94536 753-D2
VIENTO DR
- FRMT 94536 753-D2
VIERRA ST
3900 PLE 94566 715-C7
VIESTE TER
34300 FRMT 94555 752-A6
VIEW DR
- AlaC 94566 734-B1
- AlaC 94566 714-B7
1200 SLN 94577 691-C1
1700 MPS 95035 794-D6
VIEW PL
4400 OAK 94611 629-J7
VIEW PT
20400 AlaC 94552 692-E4
VIEW ST
4300 OAK 94611 629-J7
VIEWCREST CT
4300 OAK 94619 650-J7
VIEWCREST DR
6100 OAK 94619 650-J7
VIEW POINT CIR
44200 FRMT 94539 773-J2
VIEW POINT CT
300 FRMT 94539 773-J2
VIKING ST
- ALA 94501 649-D7
- ALA 94501 669-D1
25000 HAY 94545 711-D6
VILLA LP
2000 PLE 94588 714-B5
VILLAGE CIR
- OAK 94607 649-E4
VILLAGE COM
38000 FRMT 94536 752-J4
VILLAGE CT
- LVMR 94551 696-E3
2600 UNC 94587 732-E6
VILLAGE DR
- LVMR 94551 696-D3
500 ELCR 94530 609-E3
3300 AlaC 94546 692-A5
VILLAGE PKWY
6800 DBLN 94568 693-H3
8200 SRMN 94583 693-H1
VILLAGE TER
3700 FRMT 94536 752-J4
VILLAGE WY
2500 UNC 94587 732-E6
VILLAGE GATE RD
- ORIN 94563 610-G7
VILLAGE GREEN DR
- LVMR 94551 696-D3
VILLAGE VIEW CT
- ORIN 94563 610-G6
11300 DBLN 94568 693-E3
VILLANOVA DR
- CCCo 94516 630-F6
- OAK 94611 630-F6
VILLANOVA LN
- CCCo 94516 630-F6
- OAK 94611 630-F6
VILLA NUEVA DR
1000 ELCR 94530 609-E1
VILLAREAL DR
6800 AlaC 94552 692-F3
VILLERO CT
3500 PLE 94566 715-C6
VINCENT CT
3800 AlaC 94546 692-B5
VINCENTE AV
400 BERK 94707 609-F5
VINCENTE CT
35000 FRMT 94536 752-E2
VINCENTE ST
4100 FRMT 94536 752-E2
VINCI WY
- LVMR 94550 715-E4
VINDARA LN
- SRMN 94582 674-D3
VINE CT
- AlaC 94546 691-J2
- LVMR 94550 715-J3
VINE DR
- LVMR 94550 715-J3
VINE LN
2500 BERK 94708 609-H7
VINE ST
- BERK 94708 609-G7
200 AlaC 94566 714-F3
1700 BERK 94703 609-G7
1800 BERK 94709 609-G7
3700 PLE 94566 714-F3
VINE TER
- SF 94108 648-A5
VINEHILL CIR
45700 FRMT 94539 773-J3
45700 FRMT 94539 774-A3
VINEHILL CT
1800 FRMT 94539 773-J4
1800 FRMT 94539 774-A4
VINE HILL LN
600 SRMN 94582 673-J7
VINEHILL TER
45700 FRMT 94539 774-A4
VINELAND TER
- FRMT 94536 752-G4
VINEWOOD ST
35700 NWK 94560 752-D4
VINEYARD AV
- AlaC 94566 715-A3
- AlaC 94550 715-A3
- LVMR 94550 715-A3
- PLE 94550 715-A3
- PLE 94566 715-A3
1000 PLE 94566 714-E3
3500 AlaC 94566 714-J3
45200 FRMT 94539 773-J4
E VINEYARD AV
200 AlaC 94550 715-D5
200 LVMR 94550 715-D5
VINEYARD LN
3000 PLE 94566 715-A4
VINEYARD PL
4000 PLE 94566 714-F3
VINEYARD RD
17400 AlaC 94546 691-H3
VINING DR
1200 SLN 94579 691-B7
1700 SLN 94579 711-A1
VINTAGE LN
2000 LVMR 94550 715-H3
VINTAGE TER
36500 FRMT 94536 752-G3
VINTNER PL
- LVMR 94550 715-J2
VINTNER WY
1000 PLE 94566 714-G4
VINTON CT
- SF 94108 648-A5
VIOLA CT
35600 FRMT 94536 752-F3
VIOLA ST
2600 OAK 94619 650-E6
VIOLET AV
4800 LVMR 94551 696-A4
VIOLET ST
400 SLN 94578 691-C5
VIOLETTA CT
- CCCo 94582 674-B1
VIONA AV
600 OAK 94610 650-A3
VIRDEN AV
3700 OAK 94619 650-F5
VIRGIL CIR
3400 PLE 94588 714-B1
VIRGIL WILLIAMS TR
100 CCCo 94526 652-G1
100 CCCo 94583 652-G1
VIRGINIA AV
4300 OAK 94619 650-F7
VIRGINIA DR
300 LVMR 94550 715-D2
VIRGINIA GDNS W
- BERK 94702 629-E1
VIRGINIA ST
100 HAY 94544 712-A5
600 BERK 94710 629-E1
1100 BERK 94702 629-F1
1100 SLN 94577 690-H1
1500 BERK 94703 629-F1
1800 BERK 94709 629-H1
VIRGINIA WY
300 AlaC 94566 714-G3
VIRGIN ISLANDS CT
3600 PLE 94588 714-A1
VIRGO RD
6200 OAK 94611 630-D6
VIRIO COM
4500 FRMT 94536 752-B4
VIRMAR AV
5800 OAK 94618 630-A5
VISA CT
100 FRMT 94538 773-B2
VISALIA AV
1500 ALB 94706 609-F5
1500 BERK 94707 609-F5
VISTA AV
- PDMT 94611 650-B1
VISTA CT
- OAK 94603 671-A4
400 LVMR 94550 695-J7
23200 AlaC 94541 692-C7
VISTA DR
- UNC 94587 732-H6
VISTA LN
- AlaC 94541 712-D1
VISTA PL
11500 DBLN 94568 693-F3
VISTA RD
- ALA 94502 669-H5
VISTA ST
100 LVMR 94550 695-J7
1500 OAK 94602 650-D3
VISTA TR
- CCCo 94583 652-E2
VISTA WY
400 MPS 95035 794-C7
VISTA BAHIA WY
27500 HAY 94542 712-E4
VISTA CERRO TER
600 FRMT 94539 773-J2
VISTA DEL MAR
- OAK 94611 630-E6
- ORIN 94563 610-F5
43400 FRMT 94539 773-H1
VISTA DEL MAR CT
100 ORIN 94563 610-F5
VISTA DEL MAR PL
- ORIN 94563 610-F5
VISTA DEL MORAGA
- ORIN 94563 630-J3
VISTA DEL ORINDA
- ORIN 94563 610-E7
VISTA DEL PLAZA LN
22000 HAY 94541 691-J7
VISTA DEL SOL
44800 FRMT 94539 773-J2
44800 FRMT 94539 774-A2
VISTA DIABLO
1100 PLE 94566 714-H2
VISTA DIABLO CT
2600 PLE 94566 714-H3
VISTA DIABLO WY
2700 PLE 94566 714-H3
VISTA FLORES
1100 PLE 94566 714-G2
VISTA GRAND CT
2600 SLN 94577 691-D2
VISTA GRAND DR
1300 SLN 94577 691-D2
VISTA GRANDE
1000 PLE 94566 714-G3
VISTA GRANDE TER
- FRMT 94539 773-J2
- FRMT 94539 774-A2
VISTA GREENS CT
25000 HAY 94541 712-C2
VISTA HILL TER
600 FRMT 94539 773-J1
VISTAMONT AV
500 BERK 94708 609-H4
VISTAMONT CT
500 BERK 94708 609-H4
VISTA MONTE DR
- SRMN 94582 673-J7
- SRMN 94582 693-J1
VISTA NORTE CT
3500 MPS 95035 794-G6
3500 SCIC 95035 794-G6
VISTA POINTE CIR
1000 SRMN 94582 673-F2
VISTA POINTE DR
800 SRMN 94582 673-F2
VISTA RIDGE DR
200 MPS 95035 794-G6
500 SCIC 95035 794-G6
VISTA SPRING CT
500 MPS 95035 794-H6
VIVIAN COM
100 FRMT 94536 733-A6
VIVIAN DR
600 LVMR 94550 696-C6
VIVIAN PL
35900 FRMT 94536 733-A6
35900 FRMT 94536 732-J7
VIVIAN ST
2000 AlaC 94546 691-J6
VIZZOLINI CT
- PLE 94566 715-B5
VOGEL CT
40400 FRMT 94538 753-C6
VOLBERG CT
- ALA 94501 649-A2
VOLCANIC TR
- CCCo 94563 630-F4
VOLPEY WY
2900 UNC 94587 732-A3
VOLTAIRE AV
9900 OAK 94603 671-A5
VOLTAIRE ST
26500 HAY 94544 712-B5
VOMAC CT
8100 DBLN 94568 693-G3
VOMAC RD
7900 DBLN 94568 693-G3
W VOMAC RD
11800 DBLN 94568 693-F2
VON EUW COM
- FRMT 94536 753-A2
S VON SOSTEN CT
22800 SJCo 95304 (678-G6 See Page 677)
W VON SOSTEN RD
15800 SJCo 95304 (678-G6 See Page 677)
VOSS CT
- AlaC 94541 711-E2
VOYAGER WY
800 HAY 94544 712-A3
VUELTA OLIVOS
1000 FRMT 94539 753-G6

W

WABANA COM
47500 FRMT 94539 773-J7
WABANA ST
47700 FRMT 94539 773-J7
WABASH ST
1200 SJS 95002 793-B7
WABASH RIVER PL
34700 FRMT 94555 752-E2
WADE CT
6200 PLE 94588 694-A7
WADEAN PL
5400 OAK 94601 670-E2
WADSWORTH CT
4700 FRMT 94538 773-C1
WAGNER ST
15400 AlaC 94580 691-E5
42600 FRMT 94539 753-H6
WAGNER RANCH RD
300 ORIN 94563 610-E5
WAGONER DR
700 LVMR 94550 715-F3
WAIKIKI CIR
300 UNC 94587 732-C6
WAINWRIGHT AV
1200 SLN 94577 690-J1
WAINWRIGHT COM
39500 FRMT 94538 753-A6
WAINWRIGHT CT
30700 UNC 94587 731-J4
WAINWRIGHT TER
39100 FRMT 94538 753-A5
WAIT ST
400 HAY 94541 711-G3
WAKE AV
2000 OAK 94607 649-C1
2300 OAK 94626 649-D1
2300 OAK 94649 649-D1
13500 SLN 94577 691-C2
13600 SLN 94578 691-C2
WAKEFIELD AV
2500 OAK 94606 650-B5
W WAKEFIELD CT
16500 SJCo 95304 (678-H6 See Page 677)
WAKEFIELD DR
- ALA 94501 649-J7
1400 HAY 94544 732-B2
WAKEFIELD LP
4100 FRMT 94536 752-G3
WALAVISTA AV
500 OAK 94610 650-B2
WALDECK CT
- OAK 94611 650-G2
WALDEN CT
1600 FRMT 94539 753-G6
WALDO AV
100 PDMT 94611 630-B7
100 PDMT 94611 650-B1
6300 ELCR 94530 609-D3
WALDO LN
7300 ELCR 94530 609-D3
WALFORD DR
100 MRGA 94556 651-E2
WALKER AV
400 OAK 94610 649-J3
700 OAK 94610 650-A3
WALKER CT
21100 AlaC 94546 691-J6
WALKER PL
2500 LVMR 94550 715-G5
WALKER ST
2700 BERK 94705 629-H3
WALL AV
4100 RCH 94804 609-A1
5100 ELCR 94530 609-B1
WALL COM
39600 FRMT 94538 753-B5
WALL CT
400 LVMR 94550 715-E2
WALL ST
100 LVMR 94550 715-E1
2100 ELCR 94530 609-B1
WALLACE AV
2000 SLN 94577 690-H2
WALLACE LN
- DBLN 94568 693-E5
WALLACE PL
5400 FRMT 94538 752-J7
WALLACE RD
100 PDMT 94610 650-B2
WALLACE ST
2400 OAK 94606 650-B5
2700 BERK 94702 629-E3
WALLER AV
5100 FRMT 94536 752-H6
WALLEYE COM
- FRMT 94536 753-F3
WALMSLEY ST
- DBLN 94568 694-A3
WALNUT AV
- FRMT 94536 753-C3
400 FRMT 94538 753-B4
1400 FRMT 94539 753-C3
WALNUT DR
500 MPS 95035 793-J6
2600 SLN 94577 690-G4
4000 PLE 94566 714-E3
WALNUT RD
17600 AlaC 94546 691-J3
WALNUT ST
- DBLN 94568 694-D3
800 ALA 94501 669-J2
1100 BERK 94707 609-G7
1200 BERK 94709 609-G7
1500 ALA 94501 670-A2
1600 LVMR 94551 695-G7
1600 BERK 94709 629-G1
1700 ELCR 94530 609-C1
1900 BERK 94704 629-G1
3900 OAK 94619 650-E7
4900 OAK 94619 670-F1
5500 OAK 94605 670-F1
9000 OAK 94603 670-J4
36800 NWK 94560 752-D7
37200 NWK 94560 772-D1
WALNUT TER
39100 FRMT 94536 753-C3
WALPERT ST
1100 HAY 94541 712-A2
WALTER AV
9200 OAK 94603 670-G6
WALTER DINOS CT
3400 AlaC 94541 712-D1
WALTER LUM PL
- SF 94108 648-A5
WALTERS CT
39500 FRMT 94538 753-A6
WALTON AV
3900 FRMT 94536 752-H3
WANDA LN
- ORIN 94563 610-J6
WANDEL DR
- MRGA 94556 651-E1
WARBLER CT
- SLN 94579 691-F2
WARBLER LP
4200 FRMT 94555 732-B7
WARD AV
7400 ELCR 94530 609-E5
WARD LN
3100 OAK 94602 650-D6
WARD ST
1100 BERK 94702 629-E3
1400 HAY 94541 712-A1
2400 BERK 94705 629-H3
2500 BERK 94703 629-F3
WARDEN AV
400 SLN 94577 690-G1
WARFIELD AV
700 OAK 94610 650-A2
1100 PDMT 94610 650-A2
WARFORD TER
- ORIN 94563 610-J7
WAR GLORY PL
8100 PLE 94566 734-C1
WARM SPRINGS BLVD
45400 FRMT 94539 773-G4
47600 FRMT 94539 793-H1
WARMSPRINGS CT
2000 FRMT 94539 773-F4
WARNER AV
300 HAY 94544 732-F3
1900 OAK 94603 670-J5
1900 OAK 94603 671-A5
WARREN AV
- OAK 94611 649-J1
300 SLN 94577 691-B2
E WARREN AV
100 FRMT 94539 773-G6
200 FRMT 94538 773-G6
W WARREN AV
600 FRMT 94538 773-F7
WARREN FRWY Rt#-13
- OAK - 630-C6
- OAK - 650-F3
WARREN ST
900 HAY 94541 711-J1
E WARREN COMM
100 FRMT 94539 773-H6
WARRENTON CT
3000 PLE 94588 694-F6
WARRING ST
2300 BERK 94704 629-J2
WARSAW AV
1600 LVMR 94550 715-G3
WARWICK AV
100 SLN 94577 671-A6
300 OAK 94610 649-J3
WARWICK CT
34800 FRMT 94555 732-H4
34800 FRMT 94555 752-F1
WARWICK PL
2600 HAY 94542 712-D3
WARWICK RD
3100 FRMT 94555 732-F7
3300 FRMT 94555 752-E1
WASATCH DR
500 FRMT 94536 753-D1
700 FRMT 94536 733-D7
WASHBURN DR
200 FRMT 94536 753-A1
WASHINGTON AV
700 ALB 94710 609-C6
700 ALB 94706 609-E5
1200 SLN 94577 691-A1
1400 BERK 94707 609-E5
13700 SLN 94578 691-A1
14900 SLN 94579 691-A1
15300 AlaC 94580 691-A1
33800 UNC 94587 732-E6
WASHINGTON BLVD
100 FRMT 94539 753-E7
3600 FRMT 94538 753-E7
WASHINGTON COM
3700 FRMT 94539 753-G7
WASHINGTON CT
3300 ALA 94501 670-B4
WASHINGTON DR
- MPS 95035 793-J4
- MPS 95035 794-A4
WASHINGTON LN
- ORIN 94563 610-F4
WASHINGTON ST
- SF 94111 648-A5
100 OAK 94607 649-F5
700 SF 94108 648-A5
2600 ALA 94501 670-A3
3600 PLE 94566 714-F2
3800 CCCo 94514 637-D3
WASHINGTON TER
700 FRMT 94539 753-G7
WASHINGTON SQUARE DR
700 MPS 95035 793-J4
WASHO CT
44900 FRMT 94539 773-H3
WASHO DR
100 FRMT 94539 773-H3
WASHOE CT
- ALA 94501 669-J1
WASHOE PL
- SF 94133 648-A4
WASHOE WY
3100 PLE 94588 694-G7
WAT CT
1000 PLE 94566 714-E3
WATCHWOOD CT
- ORIN 94563 610-G7
WATCHWOOD RD
600 ORIN 94563 610-G7
WATER ST
300 OAK 94607 649-F5
WATERBURY PL
- SRMN 94583 673-E6
WATERCRESS PL
- SRMN 94582 673-G2
WATEREE CT
34500 FRMT 94555 752-D2
WATERFALL ISL
600 ALA 94501 669-G2
WATERFALL WY
2900 SLN 94578 691-C6
WATERFLOWER DR
5800 LVMR 94551 696-C4
WATERFORD CT
8600 DBLN 94568 693-F2
WATERFORD PL
- ALA 94502 669-H5
20100 AlaC 94552 692-D4
WATERFORD MEADOW CT
100 MPS 95035 794-C2
WATERHOUSE RD
3900 OAK 94602 650-D3
WATER LILY COM
- LVMR 94551 696-D2
WATERLILY CT
- CCCo 94582 674-B2
WATERLILY DR
- CCCo 94582 674-B2
WATERLOO DR
- OAK 94611 650-G1
WATERMILL RD
- SRMN 94582 674-B3
WATERPERRY PL
- DBLN 94568 694-H3
WATERSIDE CIR
- FRMT 94538 753-B3
WATERSON CT
24600 HAY 94544 711-J3
WATERTON ST
2800 ALA 94501 670-A4
WATERVALE WY
- SRMN 94582 674-C4
WATERVIEW CT
3200 HAY 94542 712-E4
WATERVIEW ISL
600 ALA 94501 669-H2
WATKINS CT
30600 UNC 94587 731-J4
WATKINS ST
1300 BERK 94706 609-E7
22600 HAY 94541 711-J1
24000 HAY 94544 711-J2
30600 UNC 94587 731-J5
WATSON ST
2500 AlaC 94546 692-A6
WATSON CANYON CT
700 SRMN 94582 673-F2
WATSONIA CT
- CCCo 94582 674-A2
WATSONIA DR
- CCCo 94582 674-A2
WATTERS CT
18400 AlaC 94546 692-A3
WATTERS DR
4300 AlaC 94546 692-A3
WATTLING ST
800 OAK 94601 670-C1
WATTS ST
3600 OAK 94608 629-F7
3600 EMVL 94608 629-F7
WAUCHULA WY
26600 HAY 94545 711-G6
WAUGH PL
3100 FRMT 94536 752-F1
WAVERLY AV
19000 AlaC 94541 711-F1
WAVERLY COM
900 LVMR 94551 695-H6
WAVERLY PL
- SF 94108 648-A5
WAVERLY ST
2300 OAK 94612 649-H3
WAVERLY TER
37100 FRMT 94536 752-H2
WAVERLY WY
2600 LVMR 94551 695-H6
WAWONA AV
800 OAK 94610 650-B2
WAX LAX WY
400 LVMR 94551 696-D4
WAYCROSS CT
4200 PLE 94566 714-E1
WAYCROSS RD
1900 FRMT 94539 753-F6
WAYNE AV
200 OAK 94606 649-J4
200 CCCo 94507 652-G1
1300 SLN 94577 690-J2
WAYNE CT
1300 ALA 94501 670-A3

STREET
Block City ZIP Pg-Grid

WAYNE PL
- SF 94133 648-A4
300 OAK 94606 649-J4
WAY POINTS RD
- DNVL 94526 652-H2
WEATHERLY PL
600 SRMN 94583 673-F6
WEAVER PL
5600 OAK 94619 651-A6
WEBB AV
2400 ALA 94501 670-A2
WEBER RD
6300 FRMT 94538 773-A4
WEBER ST
1200 ALA 94501 669-G2
WEBFOOT LP
34000 FRMT 94555 752-B2
WEBSTER ST
- ALA 94501 649-F5
- OAK 94607 649-G4
500 HAY 94544 712-B6
1200 OAK 94612 649-H2
2300 BERK 94705 629-H4
2700 OAK 94609 649-H1
2700 OAK 94611 649-H1
2800 BERK 94705 630-A4
3800 OAK 94609 629-H7
WEBSTER ST Rt#-260
1400 ALA 94501 669-F1
1700 ALA 94501 649-F7
WEDGEWOOD CT
1500 LVMR 94550 715-G4
N WEDGEWOOD RD
- SRMN 94582 673-J2
S WEDGEWOOD RD
- CCCo 94582 673-J2
WEDGEWOOD ST
- NWK 94560 752-F6
3800 SLN 94578 691-B3
WEDGEWOOD WY
2200 LVMR 94550 715-G4
WEE BLYTHEN
- OAK 94619 650-J4
WEIBEL DR
600 FRMT 94539 773-J4
WEIGAND CT
42700 FRMT 94539 753-G7
WEIR DR
1800 AlaC 94541 712-B2
WEISS CT
- ALA 94501 649-A3
WELCH LN
- LVMR 94550 716-D2
WELCH CREEK RD
3000 AlaC 94586 754-G7
3300 AlaC 94586 755-C5
3700 AlaC 94586 (775-D1 See Page 755)
WELD ST
6900 OAK 94621 670-G2
WELDON AV
400 OAK 94610 650-A2
WELFORD CIR
- HAY 94544 732-A2
WELFORD LN
1800 HAY 94544 732-A2
WELFORD RANCH CT
- SRMN 94583 673-E6
WELK COM
- FRMT 94555 732-E6
WELK TER
33700 FRMT 94555 732-E6
WELLER LN
- MPS 95035 794-A7
- MPS 95035 793-J7
WELLER RD
- SCIC 95035 774-G7
- SCIC 95035 794-G1
WELLESLEY AV
600 CCCo 94708 609-F3
WELLFLEET BAY
- ALA 94502 670-A6
WELLINGHAM DR
2400 LVMR 94551 695-G6
WELLINGTON DR
1800 MPS 95035 794-B2
WELLINGTON PL
35900 FRMT 94536 752-F3
WELLINGTON ST
1000 OAK 94602 650-C3
1000 OAK 94610 650-C3
WELLINGTON WY
15900 AlaC 94578 691-F3
WELLMAN TER
34300 FRMT 94555 752-A3
WELLS AV
7400 NWK 94560 772-D1
34500 FRMT 94555 752-E1
WELLS ST
4000 PLE 94566 714-E2
WELSH ST
- SF 94107 648-B7
WEMBLEY CT
5000 NWK 94560 752-E4
WENATCHEE COM
- FRMT 94539 773-G6
WENDELL CT
42000 FRMT 94538 773-E1
WENDY CT
100 UNC 94587 732-E3
WENGATE ST
15000 SLN 94579 691-A6
WENIG CT
- PLE 94588 714-F1
WENK AV
5900 RCH 94804 609-C2
WENTE ST
2100 AlaC 94550 715-J4
2100 LVMR 94550 715-J4
WENTWORTH AV
5200 OAK 94601 670-E1
WENTWORTH PL
- SF 94108 648-A4
7900 NWK 94560 752-B6
WERNER CT
5000 OAK 94602 650-F3
WESLEY AV
400 OAK 94606 649-J4
500 OAK 94606 650-A3
600 OAK 94610 650-A3
1700 ELCR 94530 609-C1
WESLEY WY
700 OAK 94610 650-A3
WESSEX PL
800 MPS 95035 794-B3
WEST CIR
- OAK 94611 630-F7
WEST CT
10400 OAK 94603 670-G7
25500 AlaC 94541 712-D2
WEST LN
- OAK 94618 630-A5
WEST PL
1000 ALB 94706 609-F7
WEST ST
1100 OAK 94607 649-F3
1200 HAY 94545 711-E5
1400 OAK 94612 649-G2
1500 AlaC 94545 711-E5
2100 BERK 94702 629-E1
2600 OAK 94608 649-G2
2600 OAK 94609 649-G2
3700 OAK 94609 629-G7
3700 OAK 94608 629-G7
WEST WY
- ORIN 94563 610-G5
WESTALL AV
- OAK 94611 649-H1
WESTBAY AV
1100 SLN 94577 671-B6
WESTBOURNE CT
29000 HAY 94544 732-A2
WESTBRIDGE LN
- PLE 94586 714-F7
900 AlaC 94586 714-F7
WESTBROOK LN
2000 LVMR 94550 715-F4
WESTBROOK PL
1200 LVMR 94550 715-F4
WESTBURY CT
5300 NWK 94560 752-D4
WESTBURY RD
3900 AlaC 94546 691-J3
WESTCHESTER
100 MRGA 94556 651-D1
WESTCHESTER DR
2800 SRMN 94583 673-F6
WESTCHESTER ST
300 HAY 94544 732-E3
WESTCHESTER TER
34000 FRMT 94555 752-B1
WESTERMAN CT
16900 AlaC 94541 691-F6
WESTERN AV
100 LVMR 94551 715-F1
14700 SLN 94578 691-C4
33000 UNC 94587 732-E5
WESTERN BLVD
19400 AlaC 94541 691-F7
21000 AlaC 94541 711-G1
21500 HAY 94541 711-H1
WESTERN FARMS RANCH RD
- CCCo 94514 637-J4
- CCCo 94514 (638-A4 See Page 637)
WESTFIELD AV
21600 HAY 94541 691-G7
21600 HAY 94541 711-H1
21600 AlaC 94541 691-G7
WESTFIELD WY
500 OAK 94619 650-H5
WESTGARD ST
- UNC 94555 752-B1
- UNC 94587 732-F4
WEST GATE DR
6000 LVMR 94550 696-D7
6000 AlaC 94550 696-D7
WESTINGHOUSE DR
47500 FRMT 94539 773-H7
47500 FRMT 94539 793-H1
WESTLINE DR
400 ALA 94501 669-G2
WESTLINE WK
600 ALA 94501 669-G2
WEST LOOP RD
- HAY 94542 712-C4
WESTMINISTER CT
29000 HAY 94544 732-A2
WESTMINSTER AV
- CCCo 94708 609-F3
1200 EPA 94303 771-A7
WESTMINSTER CIR
- FRMT 94536 752-H4
WESTMINSTER DR
- OAK 94618 630-A6
WESTMINSTER WY
2300 LVMR 94551 695-G6
WESTMORELAND DR
7000 OAK 94705 630-C3
WESTOVER DR
5900 OAK 94611 650-F1
6200 OAK 94611 630-F7
WESTPARK ST
21600 HAY 94541 711-F2
WESTPORT CT
- UNC 94545 751-J1
WESTPORT WY
- DBLN 94568 694-E4
- UNC 94545 751-J1
WEST RIDGE CT
20100 AlaC 94546 691-H5
WESTSIDE CT
2600 SRMN 94583 673-E6
WESTSIDE DR
- SF 94130 648-D1
2600 SRMN 94583 673-E6
20000 SRMN 94583 693-F1
WESTSIDE PL
- SRMN 94583 673-E7
WESTVALE CT
200 SRMN 94583 673-C3
WEST VIEW DR
1100 OAK 94705 630-B4
WEST VIEW PL
- OAK 94705 630-B3
WESTVIEW WY
25700 HAY 94542 712-B4
WESTWOOD AV
800 AlaC 94586 734-B3
2800 SRMN 94583 673-F7
4600 FRMT 94536 752-H5
WESTWOOD CT
- DBLN 94568 694-D4
- OAK 94611 630-E6
- ORIN 94563 630-H1
WESTWOOD DR
- SRMN 94583 672-J4
WESTWOOD ST
800 HAY 94544 711-J6
800 HAY 94544 712-A6
WESTWOOD WY
- OAK 94611 630-E6
WETMORE RD
1200 AlaC 94550 715-F6
1200 LVMR 94550 715-F6
3000 OAK 94613 650-H7
3000 OAK 94613 670-G1
WETMORE ST
- SF 94108 648-A5
WEXFORD CT
8200 DBLN 94568 693-G2
WEXFORD PL
- ALA 94502 669-J5
WEYBRIDGE CT
- OAK 94611 650-G2
WEYLAND CT
33700 UNC 94587 732-E5
WEYMOUTH CT
100 ALA 94502 670-A5
200 SRMN 94583 673-F5
1200 HAY 94544 732-A2
3100 PLE 94588 694-E6
WHALEBONE WY
29200 HAY 94544 732-B1
WHARF TER
34900 FRMT 94555 752-E2
WHEATMAN CT
2700 PLE 94588 694-H4
WHEELER DR
4500 FRMT 94538 753-A7
WHEELER ST
2900 BERK 94705 629-H3
6500 OAK 94609 629-H4
WHEELON AV
31300 HAY 94544 732-E3
WHELAN AV
1900 SLN 94577 691-C1
WHIMBREL CT
- ALA 94501 649-F7
3400 FRMT 94555 732-D7
WHIMBREL RD
33400 FRMT 94555 732-D6
WHIPPLE RD
200 UNC 94587 731-J3
200 UNC 94587 732-A3
900 HAY 94544 732-A3
1900 HAY 94587 732-C3
WHIPPOORWILL CT
1700 LVMR 94551 696-D2
WHIPPOORWILL ST
1700 LVMR 94551 696-D3
WHISPERING OAKS WY
- PLE 94566 714-B4
WHISPERING PINE CT
5700 AlaC 94552 692-B1
WHISPERING TREES LN
100 DNVL 94526 652-H2
WHITAKER AV
- BERK 94708 609-J6
WHITCLIFE CT
- CCCo 94583 673-A5
WHITE CT
- MPS 95035 794-C7
- OAK 94611 630-G7
WHITE DR
300 HAY 94544 712-B6
WHITE BIRCH TER
- FRMT 94538 753-B3
WHITECAP WY
- FRMT 94538 752-J7
- FRMT 94538 753-A7
- FRMT 94538 773-A1
WHITE CEDAR TER
- FRMT 94536 752-A5
WHITE CLIFF CT
- OAK 94605 671-C4
WHITE CLIFF RD
- OAK 94605 671-C4
WHITECLIFF RD
28900 HAY 94544 732-A1
WHITECREST CT
41300 FRMT 94539 753-F6
WHITE FANG WY
- LVMR 94550 715-D4
WHITE FIR DR
500 SLN 94577 690-G1
WHITEHALL CT
3400 PLE 94588 694-F5
WHITEHALL LN
32300 UNC 94587 732-C4
WHITEHALL PL
2000 ALA 94501 669-H3
WHITEHALL RD
400 ALA 94501 669-H3
WHITEHAVEN PL
800 SRMN 94582 673-J7
WHITEHEAD CT
34200 FRMT 94555 732-E7
WHITEHEAD LN
33700 FRMT 94555 732-E7
WHITE OAK CT
8600 PLE 94588 714-A6
WHITE OAK LN
1700 UNC 94587 732-D4
WHITE OAK PL
- LVMR 94550 715-D5
WHITE PELICAN PL
3400 FRMT 94555 732-D7
WHITESELL DR
25400 HAY 94545 711-D7
WHITE STABLE DR
1400 PLE 94566 714-C3
WHITESTONE CT
28000 HAY 94542 712-E4
WHITETAIL CT
45300 FRMT 94539 773-J3
WHITETAIL LN
- SRMN 94583 673-E6
WHITETHORNE DR
100 MRGA 94556 651-E2
WHITETREE ST
- HAY 94544 712-A6
WHITFIELD AV
4800 FRMT 94536 752-H6
WHITHORN CT
800 LVMR 94551 695-J5
WHITING ST
- SF 94133 648-A3
4600 PLE 94566 714-E4
WHITING WY
- SF 94130 648-F2
WHITMAN ST
24500 HAY 94544 711-J3
24600 HAY 94544 712-A4
WHITMAN TER
39500 FRMT 94538 753-A6
WHITMER CT
1000 FRMT 94539 753-F5
WHITMORE PL
- OAK 94611 629-J7
WHITMORE ST
200 OAK 94611 629-J7
WHITNEY CT
- AlaC 94541 691-E7
WHITNEY DR
2800 PLE 94566 714-H3
WHITNEY PL
- FRMT 94539 793-H2
WHITNEY ST
400 SLN 94577 690-F1
5900 OAK 94609 629-H5
6500 BERK 94703 629-H4
WHITTIER LN
100 HAY 94544 711-J5
100 HAY 94544 712-A5
WHITTIER ST
- MPS 95035 793-J7
WHITTINGTON LN
600 AlaC 94541 711-E1
WHITTLE AV
3800 OAK 94602 650-E3
WHITTLE CT
- OAK 94602 650-D4
WHITWORTH DR
- DBLN 94568 694-F4
WICHITA
3000 ALA 94501 649-F6
WICHITAW DR
700 FRMT 94539 773-H6
WICKLOW CT
8600 DBLN 94568 693-G2
WICKLOW LN
8400 DBLN 94568 693-G2
S WICKLUND RD
19700 SJCo 95391 (678-H2 See Page 677)
WICKLUND CROSSING WY
- SJCo 95391 (678-F3 See Page 677)
WICKMAN CT
- AlaC 94541 691-F6
WICKS BLVD
14200 SLN 94577 690-J5
14400 SLN 94579 690-J5
15000 SLN 94579 691-A6
15600 SLN 94579 711-A1
WICKS LN
- AlaC 94546 692-A2
WICKSON AV
400 OAK 94610 650-A3
WIEGMAN RD
1500 HAY 94544 732-B3
WIGEON CT
- SLN 94579 691-F1
WILANETA AV
400 FRMT 94539 793-J2
WILBEAM AV
20800 AlaC 94546 692-A6
WILBEAM CT
3300 AlaC 94546 692-A5
WILBER CIR
- ORIN 94563 630-J3
WILBUR ST
2300 OAK 94602 650-E4
WILBURN PL
37500 FRMT 94536 752-H4
WILCOX LN
24000 AlaC 94541 712-B1
WILDA AV
3900 OAK 94611 649-J1
WILDCAT CT
11400 DBLN 94568 693-F4
WILDCAT CANYON RD
- CCCo 94553 610-B5
300 CCCo 94563 610-B5
500 BERK 94708 609-G4
500 CCCo 94708 609-H4
800 BERK 94708 610-A6
800 CCCo 94708 610-A4
WILDCAT CREEK RD
- RCH 94805 609-G2
500 CCCo 94708 609-G2
WILD CURRANT WY
7200 OAK 94611 630-F6
WILDE AV
2500 PLE 94588 694-F6
WILDE TER
- FRMT 94536 753-A4
WILDFLOWER COM
3800 FRMT 94538 773-D1
WILD FLOWER CT
200 AlaC 94566 714-F3
200 PLE 94566 714-F3
WILDFLOWER DR
- LVMR 94551 696-C3
WILD FLOWER LN
100 AlaC 94566 714-F3
100 PLE 94566 714-F3
WILDFLOWER VALLEY CT
- SRMN 94582 673-J6
WILDHORSE DR
2400 SRMN 94583 673-C3
WILDING LN
- OAK 94618 630-B6
WILDING WY
24300 HAY 94545 711-F4
WILDROSE COM
200 LVMR 94551 695-C4
WILD ROSE LN
5200 AlaC 94546 692-B3
WILD ROSE PL
- PLE 94566 714-B4
WILDWOOD AV
- OAK 94610 650-A2
- PDMT 94610 650-A2
200 PDMT 94611 650-B2
WILDWOOD COM
- LVMR 94550 716-D2
WILDWOOD DR
- ORIN 94563 630-G1
WILDWOOD GDNS
- PDMT 94611 650-B2
WILDWOOD PL
- ELCR 94530 609-C1
4300 AlaC 94546 691-J2
WILDWOOD RD
1000 DBLN 94568 694-A2
WILDWOOD ST
22600 HAY 94541 692-B7
WILDWOOD PARK CT
4600 FRMT 94538 773-D2
WILEY ST
14300 SLN 94579 691-A4
WILFORD CT
39500 FRMT 94538 753-A6
WILFORD ST
39300 FRMT 94538 753-A6
WILKIE ST
4700 OAK 94619 650-G6
WILLAMETTE AV
200 CCCo 94708 609-G3
WILLARD PL
- OAK 94705 630-B4
WILLARD WY
- HAY 94545 731-H2
WILLBRIDGE TER
34400 FRMT 94555 752-B3
WILLET CT
- ALA 94501 649-F7
WILLET PL
3300 FRMT 94555 732-D6
WILLET WY
2300 PLE 94566 714-D1
WILLIAM CT
- DNVL 94526 652-J2
WILLIAM DR
- AlaC 94580 691-C7
700 LVMR 94550 715-E2
WM BYRON RUMFORD FRWY Rt#-24
- CCCo - 630-E2
- OAK - 629-G7
- OAK - 630-E2
- OAK - 649-G1
- ORIN - 610-H7
- ORIN - 630-E2
WM ELTON BRN BROWN FRWY I-580
- SJCo - (678-D7 See Page 677)
- SJCo - (698-D1 See Page 677)
- TRCY - (698-J5 See Page 677)
WILLIAMS CT
- FRMT 94536 732-J6
WILLIAMS ST
100 SLN 94577 691-B1
600 OAK 94612 649-G3
1000 SLN 94577 690-J2
WILLIAMS WY
- UNC 94555 751-J2
- UNC 94555 752-A2
WILLIMET WY
24100 HAY 94544 711-G4
WILLIS AV
700 HAY 94541 711-J2
WILLIS CT
3500 OAK 94619 650-G5
WILLIS LN
3300 ALA 94502 670-A7
WILLKIE PL
5500 FRMT 94538 773-A1
WILLOW AV
100 AlaC 94541 711-G1
400 MPS 95035 793-J6
1500 SLN 94579 691-A5
1700 SLN 94579 690-J5
WILLOW CT
400 LVMR 94550 695-J7
21600 AlaC 94541 711-G1
WILLOW LN
- UNC 94587 732-H5
100 CCCo 94707 609-F4
WILLOW PL
- NWK 94560 772-C1
WILLOW RD
1200 MLPK 94025 771-A7
4400 PLE 94588 694-B7
WILLOW RD Rt#-114
1200 EPA 94303 771-A7
1200 MLPK 94025 771-A7
WILLOW ST
300 ALA 94501 669-J2
700 OAK 94607 649-E2
1900 ALA 94501 670-A1
6600 ELCR 94530 609-D4
36600 NWK 94560 752-C7
36600 NWK 94560 772-C1
WILLOW TR
- BERK 94705 630-B4
WILLOW BEND WY
- CCCo 94582 674-A2
WILLOWBROOK RD
- HAY 94544 732-D1
WILLOW CREEK DR
6500 DBLN 94568 694-A1
WILLOW GLEN PL
5300 AlaC 94546 692-B2
WILLOWOOD DR
37400 FRMT 94536 752-G4
WILLOWREN WY
2500 PLE 94566 714-C1
WILLOWVIEW CT
- LVMR 94551 696-D3
5100 PLE 94588 693-J7
WILLOW WREN PL
3500 FRMT 94555 732-D7
WILMA AV
6200 NWK 94560 752-E6
WILMA CT
- LVMR 94550 696-D7
WILMA WY
27200 AlaC 94541 712-C1
WILMAC TER
- FRMT 94536 752-H2
WILMINGTON RD
3600 FRMT 94538 773-E3
WILSHIRE BLVD
4100 OAK 94602 650-F4
WILSON AV
3300 OAK 94602 650-D5
3800 AlaC 94546 691-J3
3800 AlaC 94546 692-A4
WILSON CIR
- BERK 94708 610-A7
WILSON COM
2800 FRMT 94538 753-D6
WILSON PL
3300 OAK 94602 650-D5
WILSON ST
- CCCo 94514 637-D2
100 ALB 94710 609-D7
WILSON WY
- SJS 95002 793-C7
- MPS 95035 793-J3
WILTON DR
2800 OAK 94611 650-G1
WILTON PL
100 SRMN 94583 673-F6
WILTON RD
1300 LVMR 94551 695-E6
WIMBLEDON LN
700 LVMR 94551 695-H6
2400 SLN 94577 691-B2
WIMBLEDON PL
2300 SLN 94577 691-A4
WINCHESTER DR
2700 AlaC 94541 712-C2
32300 UNC 94587 732-C5
WINCHESTER PL
4900 NWK 94560 752-E4
34800 FRMT 94555 732-H4
WIND CAVE CT
3500 PLE 94588 714-A1
WINDELER CT
- MRGA 94556 651-E1
WINDEMERE ISL
600 ALA 94501 669-G2
WINDEMERE PKWY
- CCCo 94582 674-B3
- SRMN 94582 674-B3
WINDEMERE RD
28900 HAY 94544 732-A1
WINDERMERE CIR
400 LVMR 94551 695-J6
WINDERMERE DR
35000 NWK 94560 752-D3
WINDFELDT RD
25200 AlaC 94541 712-C2
WINDFLOWER DR
5400 LVMR 94551 696-C4
WINDFLOWER LN
- UNC 94587 732-H5
WINDFLOWER WY
5400 LVMR 94551 696-C4
WINDING BLVD
16600 AlaC 94578 691-G4
WINDING LN
- ORIN 94563 610-G2
44600 FRMT 94539 773-G3
WINDING WY
- CCCo 94516 630-F6
- OAK 94611 630-F6
WINDING BROOK CT
- SRMN 94582 673-J7
WINDING CREEK WY
- SRMN 94583 673-E7
WINDING STREAM CT
- LVMR 94551 696-E3
WINDING STREAM DR
1400 LVMR 94551 696-E3
WINDING TRAIL LN
- DBLN 94568 693-F4
WINDING TRAIL PL
- DBLN 94568 693-F6
WINDING VISTA COM
- FRMT 94539 794-B1
WINDLASS WY
2200 SLN 94577 690-H5
WINDMILL CT
- SRMN 94583 673-E6
600 FRMT 94539 773-J5
WINDMILL DR
46600 FRMT 94539 773-J5
WINDMILL LN
600 PLE 94566 714-E4
WINDMILL WY
100 PLE 94566 714-E4
WINDSONG TER
34300 FRMT 94555 752-C3
WINDSOR AV
- CCCo 94708 609-F3
WINDSOR CT
2000 AlaC 94578 691-F4
2500 UNC 94587 732-F7
3400 PLE 94588 694-E5
40100 FRMT 94538 753-B6
WINDSOR DR
2800 ALA 94501 670-B2
15900 AlaC 94578 691-F3
WINDSOR PL
- SF 94133 648-A4
2400 LVMR 94550 715-F5
7600 DBLN 94568 694-B2
WINDSOR WY
1300 LVMR 94550 715-F5
9900 SRMN 94583 673-F5
WINDSTREAM PL
200 DNVL 94526 652-J2
WINDWARD COM
- LVMR 94551 695-C4
WINDWARD LN
1100 ALA 94502 670-A7
WINDWARD RD
- DNVL 94526 652-H2
WINDWARD HILL
- OAK 94618 630-C4
WINDY OAKS DR
- PLE 94566 714-J4
- PLE 94566 715-A4
WINEBERRY DR
- SRMN 94582 673-G2
WINEBERRY WY
7000 DBLN 94568 693-H2
WINEMA COM
46600 FRMT 94539 773-H6
WINFIELD LN
- DNVL 94526 652-J1
WINGATE DR
4700 PLE 94566 714-D2
WINGATE PL
4900 NWK 94560 752-E3
WINGATE WY
1900 HAY 94541 692-B7
WINGED TER
300 SRMN 94582 673-G2
WINGED FOOT CT
- SRMN 94583 673-H7
7900 LVMR 94551 696-D3
WINGEDFOOT CT
7900 PLE 94588 714-B5
WINGED FOOT PL
100 SRMN 94583 673-H7
WINIFRED DR
5200 AlaC 94546 692-C3
WINN CT
- SRMN 94583 673-F7
28300 HAY 94544 712-B7
WINNIPEG COM
200 FRMT 94538 773-E2
WINNIPEG GRN
300 FRMT 94538 773-E3
WINNIPEG TER
200 FRMT 94538 773-E3
WINSFORD CT
- CCCo 94583 673-A5
5000 NWK 94560 752-E4
WINSLOW PL
- SRMN 94583 673-E6
WINSLOW TER
34500 FRMT 94555 752-B4
WINSOR AV
1000 OAK 94610 650-B2
1000 PDMT 94610 650-B2
WINSOR ST
- MPS 95035 794-A7
WINSTON CT
5100 FRMT 94536 752-G5
WINTER CT
4500 PLE 94566 714-D3
WINTER LN
- SJCo 95391 (678-E2 See Page 677)
WINTER PL
- SF 94133 648-A4
WINTERBERRY COM
- LVMR 94551 696-C5
WINTERBERRY CT
- SRMN 94583 673-H3
WINTERBROOK AV
- DBLN 94568 694-D3
WINTERGREEN DR
5600 NWK 94560 752-H7
WINTERGREEN PL
4400 AlaC 94546 691-J2
WINTERHAVEN CT
- SRMN 94583 693-H1
WINTER HILLS CT
- SRMN 94583 673-H3
WINTERLEAF CT
- SRMN 94583 673-H3
WINTERRUN DR
- SRMN 94583 673-H3
WINTERSET WY
- SRMN 94583 673-H3
WINTERSIDE CIR
700 SRMN 94583 673-F4
WINTERSIDE CT
- SRMN 94583 673-H3
WINTERWIND CIR
300 SRMN 94583 673-H3
WINTERWIND CT
- SRMN 94583 673-H3
WINTER WREN PL
3300 FRMT 94555 732-D7
WINTHROP AV
2800 SRMN 94583 673-F7
WINTHROP ST
- SF 94133 648-A3
WINTHROPE ST
7900 OAK 94605 671-A2
WINTON AV
200 HAY 94544 711-J3
300 HAY 94541 711-J3
W WINTON AV
- HAY 94544 711-G3
100 HAY 94541 711-G3
500 HAY 94545 711-B4
1200 AlaC 94545 711-E4
WIPFLI RD
- FRMT 94538 773-B4
WISCONSIN ST
3000 OAK 94602 650-F4
3500 OAK 94619 650-F5
WISTAR RD
200 OAK 94603 670-F7
WISTARIA WY
- PDMT 94611 650-C2
WISTERIA DR
700 FRMT 94539 753-G6
WISTERIA LN
2900 AlaC 94546 691-J4
WISTERIA ST
6900 SRMN 94583 693-H1
19800 AlaC 94546 691-J5
WISTERIA TR
2300 AlaC 94586 733-J1
2300 AlaC 94586 734-A1
WISTERIA WY
5200 LVMR 94551 696-B4
WITCHER ST
3100 AlaC 94546 691-J5
WITHERLY LN
600 FRMT 94539 753-J7
WITHERSPOON COM
3600 FRMT 94538 753-D6
WITHERSPOON GRN
3500 FRMT 94538 753-D6
WITHERSPOON TER
40600 FRMT 94538 753-D6
WIXON DR
42700 FRMT 94538 773-D2
WOLCOTT COM
3300 FRMT 94538 753-D6
WOLCOTT DR
40600 FRMT 94538 753-D6
WOLCOTT PL
40600 FRMT 94538 753-D6
WOLFE CT
3000 FRMT 94555 732-F7
WOLSEY PL
3000 FRMT 94555 732-E7
WOOD CT
- OAK 94611 650-D1
WOOD DR
5900 OAK 94611 650-D1
WOOD ST
300 LVMR 94550 695-H7
300 LVMR 94550 715-H1
500 OAK 94607 649-D2
1600 ALA 94501 669-G1
1700 ALA 94501 669-G7
3000 OAK 94608 649-D2
3000 OAK 94649 649-D2
WOODACRE AV
24600 HAY 94544 711-G4
WOODACRES CT
- ORIN 94563 610-H6
WOODACRES LN
- ORIN 94563 610-H6
WOODBINE AV
2100 OAK 94602 650-D5
20100 AlaC 94546 692-A5
WOODBINE PL
5800 NWK 94560 752-G7
WOODBINE WY
3600 PLE 94588 694-F5
WOODBOROUGH WY
2700 SRMN 94583 673-E6
WOODBRIDGE PL
35400 FRMT 94536 752-F1
W WOODBURY CT
- PLE 94588 714-B5
WOODBURY DR
- AlaC 94552 692-E7
WOODCHUCK PL
600 HAY 94544 712-D7
WOODCLIFF CT
- OAK 94605 671-C5
WOODCOCK CT
400 MPS 95035 794-A3
WOOD CREEK COM
100 FRMT 94539 773-H5
WOOD CREEK TER
100 FRMT 94539 773-G5
WOODCREST CIR
- OAK 94602 650-F3
WOODCREST CT
42200 FRMT 94538 773-D1
WOODCREST DR
2500 SRMN 94583 673-A1
4000 FRMT 94538 773-D1
WOODDUCK COM
4700 FRMT 94555 752-D2
WOODDUCK CT
4700 SLN 94579 690-J7
4700 SLN 94579 691-A7
WOODED HILLS CT
800 FRMT 94539 773-J5
WOODGATE CT
700 SLN 94579 691-C6
WOODGATE DR
700 SLN 94579 691-C6
WOODGATE PL
700 SLN 94579 691-C6
WOODHAVEN COM
- LVMR 94551 695-F6
WOODHAVEN RD
700 BERK 94708 609-H5

STREET
Block City ZIP Pg-Grid

WOODHAVEN WY
1600 OAK 94611 630-E6
WOOD HOLLOW DR
2400 LVMR 94550 715-E5
WOODHUE TER
34700 FRMT 94555 752-D2
WOODLAND AV
600 HAY 94544 712-D7
600 SLN 94577 671-B7
700 AlaC 94544 712-D7
WOODLAND CT
- LVMR 94550 696-A7
- SRMN 94582 673-E2
WOODLAND DR
900 SRMN 94582 673-E2
32400 UNC 94587 732-A7
WOODLAND PK
300 SLN 94577 671-B7
WOODLAND PL
6600 OAK 94611 630-D5
WOODLAND TER
4000 FRMT 94538 753-D7
WOODLAND WY
- PDMT 94611 650-C2
WOODLAND VALLEY DR
100 SRMN 94582 674-A6
WOODMINSTER LN
5000 OAK 94602 650-F3
WOODMONT AV
500 BERK 94708 609-H4
500 CCCo 94708 609-H4
WOODMONT CT
- BERK 94708 609-H4
WOODMONT WY
- CCCo 94563 630-D3
- OAK 94611 630-D3
WOODREN CT
7700 DBLN 94568 693-G3
WOODRIDGE RD
22600 HAY 94541 692-B7
WOODROE AV
22400 AlaC 94552 692-C6
22400 AlaC 94541 692-C6
WOODROE CT
3000 AlaC 94541 692-C6
WOODROSE CIR
- DBLN 94568 694-D3
WOODROSE WY
5600 LVMR 94551 696-C3
WOODROW DR
7100 OAK 94611 630-F7
WOODRUFF AV
3400 OAK 94602 650-C4
WOODRUFF DR
38000 NWK 94560 752-F7
38000 NWK 94560 772-G1
WOODRUFF WY
200 MPS 95035 793-J4
WOODSHIRE LN
- DBLN 94568 694-F3
WOODSIDE RD
1000 BERK 94708 609-J6
WOODSIDE TER
2700 FRMT 94539 774-A7
WOODSIDE WY
- OAK 94611 630-D3
20600 AlaC 94546 692-B5
WOODSIDE GLEN CT
- OAK 94602 650-F3
WOODSTOCK RD
4000 HAY 94542 712-F3
WOODTHRUSH CT
4700 PLE 94566 694-D7
WOODTHRUSH PL
600 HAY 94544 712-E7
700 HAY 94544 732-E1
WOODTHRUSH RD
4800 PLE 94566 694-D7
5000 PLE 94566 714-D1
WOODTHRUSH WY
2300 PLE 94566 714-D1
WOODVALE TER
- DBLN 94568 694-F2
WOODVIEW CIR
100 SRMN 94582 673-F3
WOOD VIEW COM
46200 FRMT 94539 773-G5
WOODVIEW CT
- SRMN 94582 673-F3
WOOD VIEW TER
500 FRMT 94539 773-G5
WOODVIEW TERRACE DR
100 SRMN 94582 673-E2
WOODWARD DR
- MPS 95035 794-A6
400 FRMT 94536 753-D2
WOODWARD PL
500 FRMT 94536 753-D2
WOOL DR
500 MPS 95035 794-C5
WOOLSEY ST
1500 BERK 94703 629-G4
2100 BERK 94705 629-H4
2200 OAK 94609 629-H4
2400 OAK 94618 629-H4
2800 BERK 94705 630-A4
WOOSTER CT
6600 AlaC 94552 692-F3
WORDEN ST
- SF 94133 648-A3
WORDEN WY
4400 OAK 94619 650-G6
WORTH ST
4000 OAK 94603 670-F6
WORTHING CT
3300 FRMT 94536 752-J3
WORTHING DR
36200 NWK 94560 752-F4
WORTHLEY DR
15600 AlaC 94580 711-A1
WOVENWOOD
400 ORIN 94563 610-H6
WREN CT
2100 UNC 94587 732-G7
28200 HAY 94545 731-J1
WRENN ST
1900 OAK 94602 650-E3
WRIGHT DR
23700 HAY 94541 711-F4
24000 HAY 94545 711-F4
WRIGHT BROTHERS AV
100 LVMR 94551 695-D7
WRIGLEY WY
800 MPS 95035 794-C7
WRIN AV
700 SLN 94577 690-H1
WYATT LN
39800 FRMT 94538 753-B7
WYCOMBE CT
- CCCo 94583 673-B5
WYCOMBE PL
35200 NWK 94560 752-D3
WYETH RD
300 HAY 94544 712-A4
WYLIE DR
1700 MPS 95035 794-D7
WYMAN AV
14600 SLN 94578 691-D3
WYMAN PL
- OAK 94619 650-G7
WYMAN ST
3200 OAK 94619 650-G7
WYNDALE CT
18300 AlaC 94546 691-H3
WYNDALE DR
3400 AlaC 94546 691-H3
WYNDHAM DR
3200 FRMT 94536 752-F1
WYNGAARD AV
- PDMT 94611 650-D2
WYNN CIR
900 LVMR 94550 696-B7
900 LVMR 94550 716-B1
WYOMA PL
500 MPS 95035 794-B5
WYOMING ST
- PLE 94566 714-G2

X

XANADU TER
34200 FRMT 94555 752-C2
XAVIER AV
1300 HAY 94545 711-F5
XAVIER COM
5000 FRMT 94555 752-C2
XAVIER CT
4100 LVMR 94550 716-A1
XAVIER ST
1600 EPA 94303 771-B7
XAVIER WY
1000 LVMR 94550 716-A1

Y

YAFFE DR
2400 AlaC 94578 691-H5
YAKIMA DR
800 FRMT 94539 773-J5
YALE AV
200 CCCo 94708 609-G3
16100 AlaC 94580 691-E6
YALE CIR
- CCCo 94708 609-G4
YALE CT
- SRMN 94583 693-F1
YALE DR
1800 ALA 94501 670-B2
YALE WY
3200 FRMT 94538 773-E3
3800 LVMR 94550 695-J7
3800 LVMR 94550 715-J1
3900 LVMR 94550 716-A1
YAMPA CT
48900 FRMT 94539 793-J2
YAMPA RD
- FRMT 94539 793-J2
YAMPA WY
- FRMT 94539 793-J2
400 FRMT 94539 794-A2
YANKEE CT
2000 SLN 94579 690-J6
YANKEE HILL
- OAK 94618 630-C4
YARMOUTH CT
- OAK 94619 650-J4
5300 NWK 94560 752-E4
YARMOUTH WY
2800 SRMN 94583 673-E6
YARO CT
600 FRMT 94539 753-G6
YARROW VALLEY LN
- ORIN 94563 610-H3
YEANDLE AV
20200 AlaC 94546 692-A5
YEARLING CT
300 PLE 94566 734-C1
YELLOWSTONE CT
3500 PLE 94588 714-A1
YELLOWSTONE WY
- LVMR 94551 695-D7
YELLOWSTONE PARK DR
4800 FRMT 94538 773-C3
YERBA BUENA AV
900 EMVL 94608 629-F7
900 OAK 94608 629-E7
YERBA BUENA PL
200 FRMT 94536 753-D2
YERBA BUENA RD
- SF 94130 648-E3
YERBA BUENA ST
200 FRMT 94536 753-D2
YERBA SANTA PZ
- HAY 94542 712-B3
YEW CT
7700 NWK 94560 752-D7
24600 HAY 94545 711-F5
YGNACIO AV
4300 OAK 94601 670-D1
YOLANDA CT
- PLE 94566 714-J3
YOLO AV
1900 BERK 94707 609-G7
1900 BERK 94709 609-G7
3000 ELCR 94530 609-C4
3000 RCH 94804 609-C4
YOLO ST
22500 HAY 94541 711-G2
YOLO TER
37200 FRMT 94536 752-G4
YOLO WY
700 LVMR 94551 695-E6
YORK AV
100 CCCo 94708 609-F3
YORK CT
7000 DBLN 94568 693-J3
YORK DR
- PDMT 94611 630-A7
- PDMT 94611 650-A1
5300 FRMT 94536 752-H7
6800 DBLN 94568 693-J4
YORK LN
- CCCo 94582 674-B5
YORK PL
100 HAY 94544 732-E3
YORK ST
800 OAK 94610 650-A3
YORK WY
300 LVMR 94551 695-D6
YORKSHIRE CT
500 LVMR 94551 695-H6
2900 PLE 94588 694-F6
YORKSHIRE DR
- OAK 94618 630-B6
500 LVMR 94551 695-H6
YORKSHIRE PL
2000 ALA 94501 669-H3
YORKSHIRE RD
400 ALA 94501 669-H3
YORKSHIRE ST
3800 SLN 94578 691-B4
YORKTOWN RD
3500 FRMT 94538 773-E2
YORTON LN
600 AlaC 94541 711-E1
YOSEMITE AV
- OAK 94611 649-J1
2800 ALA 94501 670-B2
2800 SRMN 94583 673-F7
3100 ELCR 94530 609-C4
YOSEMITE CT
- UNC 94587 732-E6
YOSEMITE CT N
3800 PLE 94588 714-A1
YOSEMITE CT S
3700 PLE 94588 714-A1
YOSEMITE DR
200 LVMR 94551 715-D1
400 LVMR 94551 695-D7
1300 MPS 95035 794-D7
YOSEMITE PL
- LVMR 94551 695-D7
YOSEMITE RD
1800 BERK 94707 609-F5
YOSEMITE WY
1200 HAY 94545 711-F5
39000 FRMT 94538 753-A6
YOSHIDA DR
24900 HAY 94545 711-F5
YOUNG AV
3700 OAK 94619 650-G5
22000 AlaC 94546 692-A6
YOUNG DR
38000 FRMT 94536 753-A2
YOUNG ST
2700 ALA 94502 669-J6
YUBA AV
5300 OAK 94619 670-F1
YUBA CT
39500 FRMT 94538 753-A7
YUCATAN DR
47000 FRMT 94539 773-H6
YUCCA CT
- SRMN 94583 673-C4
100 FRMT 94538 773-B2
YUKON CT
34500 FRMT 94555 752-D2
YUKON PL
- LVMR 94550 715-D4
YUKON ST
2300 SLN 94577 690-G4
YUKON WY
- LVMR 94550 715-D4
YUMA CT
4400 PLE 94588 694-D6
YUMA PL
19400 AlaC 94546 691-H4
YUMA ST
19400 AlaC 94546 691-H4
19400 AlaC 94578 691-H4
YUMA WY
3000 PLE 94588 694-D6
YUROK CT
- FRMT 94539 773-H2

Z

ZABALLOS CT
1800 HAY 94541 692-B7
ZACATE AV
39000 FRMT 94539 753-D2
ZACATE CT
100 FRMT 94539 753-D2
ZACATE PL
- FRMT 94539 753-D3
ZACK WY
3700 AlaC 94546 692-B5
ZAMORA CT
1000 MPS 95035 794-B4
1400 HAY 94544 732-A1
ZANDOL CT
8500 DBLN 94568 693-F2
ZANKER LN
- SJS 95134 793-E7
ZANKER RD
700 SJS 95134 793-F7
ZAPATA CT
11700 DBLN 94568 693-F3
ZAPOTEC DR
46900 FRMT 94539 773-J6
47100 FRMT 94539 774-A6
ZARO CT
5200 PLE 94588 694-H4
ZEBRINA CT
- CCCo 94582 674-A2
ZEBRINA WY
- CCCo 94582 674-A2
ZELMA ST
14800 SLN 94579 691-B5
ZENATO PL
- PLE 94566 715-A6
ZENO PL
- SF 94105 648-B6
ZENO ST
19700 AlaC 94546 691-H5
ZEPHYR AV
900 HAY 94544 732-B3
ZEPPELIN DR
1000 LVMR 94551 695-D7
ZERMATT ST
600 LVMR 94551 695-E7
ZEVANOVE CT
4200 PLE 94588 694-C6
ZHONE WY
1100 OAK 94621 670-D4
ZIEGLER AV
4400 OAK 94605 671-D5
ZIELE CREEK DR
28000 HAY 94542 712-E5
ZINFANDEL CT
1000 PLE 94566 714-H4
2100 LVMR 94550 715-H3
ZINFANDEL ST
- FRMT 94539 793-J2
- FRMT 94539 794-A2
ZINN DR
5900 OAK 94611 630-E7
5900 OAK 94611 650-E1
ZINNIA CT
2800 UNC 94587 732-G7
4700 LVMR 94551 696-A4
ZINNIA DR
15000 SLN 94578 691-C4
ZION CT
1300 MPS 95035 794-D7
ZION CANYON CT
3400 PLE 94588 714-A1
ZIRCON TER
34300 FRMT 94555 752-C2
ZIRCON WY
500 LVMR 94550 715-D2
ZOE ST
- SF 94107 648-B7
ZOOK RD
- SCIC 94035 792-B7
- SUNV 94089 792-B7
ZORAH ST
500 OAK 94606 650-A4
ZORRO CT
24100 AlaC 94541 712-B1
ZORRO TR
12000 AlaC 94586 713-J7
12000 AlaC 94586 733-J1
ZULMIDA AV
6200 NWK 94560 752-D6
ZUNI WY
3100 PLE 94588 694-D6
ZUNIC DR
47500 FRMT 94539 773-J7
ZWISSIG CT
3600 PLE 94566 714-G3
ZWISSIGG WY
34100 UNC 94587 732-G5

#

1ST AV
200 OAK 94606 649-H5
200 OAK 94607 649-H5
1ST ST
- AlaC 94586 734-B5
- CCCo 94514 637-D3
- SF 94105 648-B5
- SF 94130 648-E2
700 OAK 94607 649-E4
1500 LVMR 94551 696-A6
2100 LVMR 94550 715-H1
2200 LVMR 94550 695-H7
2200 LVMR 94551 695-H7
3900 PLE 94566 714-E3
22600 HAY 94541 711-J1
22700 HAY 94541 712-A2
1ST ST Rt#-84
1400 LVMR 94550 715-F1
1ST AV PL
1400 OAK 94606 649-H5
2ND AV
200 SLN 94577 691-B2
1000 OAK 94606 649-H5
2ND ST
- AlaC 94586 734-B5
300 OAK 94607 649-E4
500 SF 94105 648-B6
600 SF 94107 648-B6
1000 ALB 94710 609-C7
1000 BERK 94710 609-C7
1300 BERK 94710 629-C1
1300 LVMR 94550 715-G1
1700 ALA 94501 649-E7
2400 LVMR 94550 695-H7
2500 LVMR 94551 695-H7
4300 PLE 94566 714-E4
22300 HAY 94541 711-J1
22600 HAY 94541 712-A2
24500 AlaC 94541 712-C2
33300 UNC 94587 732-G4
36800 FRMT 94536 753-B1
3RD AV
1100 OAK 94606 649-J4
3RD ST
- AlaC 94586 734-B5
- DBLN 94568 694-A4
- SF 94130 648-E1
- SF 94103 648-A6
300 OAK 94607 649-D4
700 SF 94107 648-B6
1200 BERK 94710 609-C7
1300 ALA 94501 669-E1
1300 BERK 94710 629-D1
1400 LVMR 94550 715-G1
1600 ALA 94501 649-E7
2600 LVMR 94550 695-H7
4500 PLE 94566 714-E4
22500 HAY 94541 712-A1
33200 UNC 94587 732-G4
37200 FRMT 94536 753-B1
N 3RD ST
22200 AlaC 94546 691-J7
22300 HAY 94541 691-J7
4TH AV
1000 OAK 94606 649-H5
4TH ST
- DBLN 94568 694-B4
- OAK 94607 649-F4
- SF 94103 648-A6
- SF 94130 648-E1
300 SF 94107 648-A6
1100 BERK 94710 609-D7
1200 LVMR 94550 715-G1
1200 BERK 94710 629-D1
1300 ALA 94501 669-E1
1600 ALA 94501 649-F7
3000 LVMR 94550 695-H7
22700 HAY 94541 712-A1
33200 UNC 94587 732-G4
38000 FRMT 94536 753-C1
N 4TH ST
1300 HAY 94541 712-A1
22200 AlaC 94546 692-A7
22500 HAY 94541 692-A7
5TH AV
300 OAK 94606 649-H5
2100 OAK 94606 650-A4
5TH ST
- AlaC 94580 691-E6
- DBLN 94568 694-A3
- SF 94130 648-E1
- SF 94103 648-A6
100 OAK 94607 649-D4
300 SF 94107 648-A6
1100 BERK 94710 609-D7
1300 LVMR 94550 715-G1
1300 BERK 94710 629-D1
1400 ALA 94501 669-F1
1600 ALA 94501 649-F7
22500 HAY 94541 692-A7
22700 HAY 94541 712-A1
33100 UNC 94587 732-F4
N 5TH ST
22100 AlaC 94546 692-A7
22600 HAY 94541 692-A7
22600 HAY 94541 712-A1
6TH AV
200 OAK 94606 649-H5
6TH ST
- DBLN 94568 694-A3
- SF 94103 648-A7
- SF 94130 648-E1
300 SF 94107 648-A7
700 OAK 94607 649-F4
1000 ALB 94710 609-D7
1000 BERK 94710 609-D7
1400 ALA 94501 669-F1
1400 BERK 94710 629-D1
1500 LVMR 94550 715-H1
22500 HAY 94541 692-A7
22600 HAY 94541 712-A1
33100 UNC 94587 732-F4
N 6TH ST
22100 AlaC 94546 692-A7
7TH AV
800 OAK 94606 649-J5
1900 OAK 94606 650-A5
7TH ST
- DBLN 94568 694-A3
- SF 94103 648-A7
400 OAK 94606 649-H5
400 OAK 94607 649-D3
1200 BERK 94710 609-D7
1400 BERK 94710 629-D1
2000 LVMR 94550 715-G1
2000 OAK 94626 649-C3
2400 OAK 94625 649-A3
3000 OAK 94625 648-J3
22500 HAY 94541 692-A7
22700 HAY 94541 712-B1
33100 UNC 94587 732-F4
E 7TH ST
2200 OAK 94606 670-B1
2500 OAK 94601 670-B1
8TH AV
200 OAK 94606 649-J5
1800 OAK 94606 650-A5
2700 OAK 94610 650-A5
E 8TH AV
- OAK 94601 670-B1
8TH ST
- OAK 94607 649-D3
- SF 94130 648-F1
200 SF 94103 648-A7
1100 ALB 94706 609-D7
1100 ALB 94710 609-D7
1100 BERK 94710 609-D7
1200 ALA 94501 669-G1
1300 OAK 94626 649-C3
1300 BERK 94710 629-D1
1700 ALA 94501 649-G7
2100 LVMR 94550 715-H1
5700 DBLN 94568 694-A3
33100 UNC 94587 732-F4
E 8TH ST
400 OAK 94606 649-H5
1100 OAK 94606 650-A6
3300 OAK 94601 670-C1
9TH AV
- OAK 94606 649-J5
1700 OAK 94606 650-A5
9TH ST
- DBLN 94568 694-A3
- SF 94130 648-E1
500 OAK 94607 649-C3
900 ALB 94710 609-D6
1100 ALA 94501 669-G1
1100 BERK 94710 609-D7
1400 BERK 94710 629-D1
1700 ALA 94501 649-G7
33100 UNC 94587 732-F4
E 9TH ST
900 OAK 94601 670-B1
2500 OAK 94601 650-B7
10TH AV
500 OAK 94606 649-H6
1700 OAK 94606 650-A5
10TH ST
- DBLN 94568 694-A2
- OAK 94607 649-D3
- OAK 94606 649-H5
1100 ALB 94710 609-D7
1100 BERK 94710 609-D7
1300 BERK 94710 629-D1
1900 OAK 94626 649-C2
33400 UNC 94587 732-F4
E 10TH ST
2500 OAK 94601 650-B7
2800 OAK 94601 670-B1
27500 HAY 94544 712-B6
11TH AV
1000 OAK 94606 649-J6
1500 OAK 94606 650-A5
2800 OAK 94610 650-A5
11TH ST
- DBLN 94568 694-A2
- OAK 94607 649-D3
- OAK 94626 649-C3
33400 UNC 94587 732-F4
E 11TH ST
100 OAK 94606 649-H5
2400 OAK 94601 650-B7
2400 OAK 94606 650-B7
27500 HAY 94544 712-B6
12TH AV
1100 OAK 94606 649-J6
1500 OAK 94606 650-A5
12TH ST
- OAK 94607 649-D2
- OAK 94612 649-F4
1100 DBLN 94568 694-A2
33600 UNC 94587 732-F5
E 12TH ST
- OAK 94607 649-J5
- OAK 94606 649-J5
1300 OAK 94606 650-A6
2200 OAK 94606 650-A6
3000 OAK 94601 670-C1
27500 HAY 94544 712-C6
12TH ST S
- DBLN 94568 694-B2
E 12TH ST PL
4300 OAK 94601 670-D1
13TH AV
1100 OAK 94606 649-J6
1300 OAK 94606 650-A6
2800 OAK 94610 650-B4
3000 OAK 94602 650-B4
13TH ST
- DBLN 94568 694-A2
100 OAK 94612 649-F3
700 OAK 94607 649-D3
1800 OAK 94626 649-C2
33200 UNC 94587 732-F5
E 13TH ST
3000 OAK 94601 650-C7
3000 OAK 94601 670-C1
28300 HAY 94544 712-C6
14TH AV
1200 OAK 94606 650-A5
3100 OAK 94602 650-A5
14TH ST
- DBLN 94568 694-A2
- OAK 94612 649-G4
100 OAK 94606 649-F4
800 OAK 94607 649-D2
1700 OAK 94626 649-C2
33300 UNC 94587 732-F5
E 14TH ST Rt#-185
- OAK 94603 670-J6
- SLN 94577 670-J6
300 SLN 94577 671-A7
900 SLN 94577 691-B2
8400 SLN 94578 691-B2
13500 AlaC 94578 691-F5
15900 AlaC 94580 691-F5
17000 AlaC 94541 691-F5
15TH AV
1200 OAK 94606 650-A6
15TH ST
- DBLN 94568 694-A2
300 OAK 94612 649-F3
700 OAK 94607 649-D2
33600 UNC 94587 732-F5
E 15TH ST
100 OAK 94606 649-H4
1200 OAK 94606 650-A6
2300 OAK 94601 650-C7
3500 OAK 94601 670-C1
5500 OAK 94621 670-E2
27500 HAY 94544 712-C6
16TH AV
1100 OAK 94606 650-A6
16TH ST
500 OAK 94612 649-G3
800 OAK 94607 649-D2
E 16TH ST
100 OAK 94606 649-J4
2300 OAK 94601 650-B7
3600 OAK 94601 670-D1
5500 OAK 94621 670-E2
27600 HAY 94544 712-C6
17TH AV
1200 OAK 94606 650-A5
17TH ST
100 OAK 94612 649-F3
700 OAK 94607 649-D2
1900 OAK 94626 649-C2
E 17TH ST
600 OAK 94606 649-J5
1000 OAK 94606 650-A5
2300 OAK 94601 650-B7
4000 OAK 94601 670-D1
5500 OAK 94621 670-F2
18TH AV
1200 OAK 94606 650-A6
18TH ST
500 OAK 94612 649-G3
800 OAK 94607 649-D2
E 18TH ST
- OAK 94606 649-J5
800 OAK 94606 650-A5
3000 OAK 94601 650-C7
3900 OAK 94601 670-D1
19TH AV
1200 OAK 94606 650-A6
19TH ST
200 OAK 94612 649-F3
800 OAK 94607 649-D2
1200 OAK 94626 649-D2
E 19TH ST
600 OAK 94606 649-J5
700 OAK 94606 650-A5
2300 OAK 94601 650-C7
20TH AV
1200 OAK 94606 650-A6
20TH ST
200 OAK 94612 649-G3
800 OAK 94607 649-E2
E 20TH ST
400 OAK 94606 649-J4
600 OAK 94606 650-A5
2300 OAK 94601 650-B6
21ST AV
1200 OAK 94606 650-B6
21ST ST
200 OAK 94612 649-G3
800 OAK 94607 649-E2
1300 OAK 94626 649-D1
E 21ST ST
400 OAK 94606 649-J4
500 OAK 94606 650-A5
2200 OAK 94601 650-B6
22ND AV
900 OAK 94606 650-C5
3000 OAK 94602 650-C5
22ND ST
300 OAK 94612 649-G3
800 OAK 94607 649-F2
E 22ND ST
500 OAK 94606 650-A4
2200 OAK 94601 650-C7
23RD AV
400 OAK 94606 670-B1
500 OAK 94601 670-B1
600 OAK 94606 650-B6
700 OAK 94601 650-B6
2800 OAK 94602 650-B6
23RD ST
400 OAK 94612 649-F2
E 23RD ST
600 OAK 94606 650-A5
2200 OAK 94601 650-C6
23RD AV OVPS
700 OAK 94606 650-B7
700 OAK 94601 650-B7
24TH AV
1400 OAK 94601 650-B6
24TH ST
300 OAK 94612 649-G2
900 OAK 94607 649-E1
E 24TH ST
700 OAK 94606 650-A4
2300 OAK 94601 650-B5
25TH AV
1000 OAK 94601 650-C5
2800 OAK 94602 650-C5
25TH ST
400 OAK 94612 649-G2
E 25TH ST
1300 OAK 94606 650-B5
2600 OAK 94601 650-C6
26TH AV
900 OAK 94601 650-C6
26TH ST
400 OAK 94612 649-G2
900 OAK 94607 649-E1
E 26TH ST
1300 OAK 94606 650-B5
2300 OAK 94601 650-C6
27TH AV
800 OAK 94601 650-B7
800 OAK 94601 670-B1
27TH ST
300 OAK 94612 649-F2
800 OAK 94607 649-F2
E 27TH ST
1300 OAK 94606 650-B5
2300 OAK 94601 650-C6
28TH AV
1500 OAK 94601 650-B7
28TH ST
200 OAK 94611 649-H2
200 OAK 94612 649-G2
300 OAK 94609 649-G2
800 OAK 94607 649-E1
800 OAK 94608 649-E1
E 28TH ST
800 OAK 94610 650-B4
900 OAK 94606 650-B5
2400 OAK 94602 650-C5
2400 OAK 94601 650-C5
29TH AV
1600 OAK 94601 650-B7
2100 OAK 94601 670-B1
2700 OAK 94606 670-B1
29TH ST
200 OAK 94611 649-G2
300 OAK 94609 649-G2
800 OAK 94608 649-G2
E 29TH ST
1900 OAK 94606 650-B5
2300 OAK 94602 650-C5
2500 OAK 94601 650-C5
30TH AV
1200 OAK 94601 650-B7
30TH ST
400 OAK 94609 649-G2
800 OAK 94608 649-F1
1300 OAK 94611 649-G2
E 30TH ST
1900 OAK 94606 650-B5
2300 OAK 94602 650-B5
31ST AV
1200 OAK 94601 670-C1
1300 OAK 94601 650-C7
31ST ST
500 OAK 94609 649-G1
800 OAK 94608 649-G1
E 31ST ST
1300 OAK 94602 650-B4
1300 OAK 94606 650-B4
32ND ST
600 OAK 94609 649-G1
700 OAK 94608 649-F1
1600 OAK 94607 649-E1
E 32ND ST
1300 OAK 94602 650-B4
33RD AV
800 OAK 94601 670-C1
1500 OAK 94601 650-C7
33RD ST
500 OAK 94609 649-G1
700 OAK 94608 649-G1
E 33RD ST
1000 OAK 94610 650-B4
1300 OAK 94602 650-B4
34TH AV
700 OAK 94601 670-C1
1400 OAK 94601 650-C7
34TH ST
300 OAK 94609 649-G1
300 OAK 94611 649-G1
700 OAK 94608 649-E1
E 34TH ST
1200 OAK 94610 650-B4
1300 OAK 94602 650-B4
35TH AV
800 OAK 94601 670-C1
1400 OAK 94601 650-C7
2500 OAK 94619 650-F5
2600 OAK 94602 650-F5
35TH ST
600 OAK 94609 649-F1
700 OAK 94608 649-F1
36TH AV
700 OAK 94601 670-C1
1400 OAK 94601 650-C7
36TH ST
400 OAK 94609 649-H1
800 OAK 94608 649-F1
1100 OAK 94608 629-F7
2600 OAK 94612 649-F1
E 36TH ST
1300 OAK 94602 650-B4
37TH AV
600 OAK 94601 670-C1
1700 OAK 94601 650-D7
37TH ST
400 OAK 94609 649-G1
700 OAK 94608 649-G1
900 OAK 94608 629-F7
1000 EMVL 94608 629-F7
38TH AV
900 OAK 94601 670-C1
1200 OAK 94601 650-D7
2600 OAK 94619 650-E6
38TH ST
300 OAK 94609 649-H1
300 OAK 94611 649-H1
E 38TH ST
1300 OAK 94602 650-C4
S 38TH ST
400 RCH 94804 609-A1
39TH AV
900 OAK 94601 670-C1
1700 OAK 94601 650-D7
2600 OAK 94619 650-E6
39TH ST
600 OAK 94609 629-G7
800 OAK 94608 629-G7
800 EMVL 94608 629-G7
S 39TH ST
300 RCH 94804 609-A1
40TH AV
900 OAK 94601 670-C1
1800 OAK 94601 650-D7
40TH ST
100 OAK 94611 649-J1
300 OAK 94609 629-H7
300 OAK 94611 629-H7
800 OAK 94608 629-E7
1000 EMVL 94608 629-E7
S 40TH ST
700 RCH 94804 609-A1
40TH STWY
200 OAK 94611 649-J1
41ST AV
1000 OAK 94601 670-D1
1300 OAK 94601 650-D7
41ST ST
- OAK 94611 649-J1
300 OAK 94609 629-H7
500 OAK 94611 629-H7
800 OAK 94608 629-G7

© 2006 Rand McNally & Company

STREET Block City ZIP Pg-Grid

41ST ST
1000 EMVL 94608 629-F7
S 41ST ST
200 RCH 94804 609-A1
42ND AV
900 OAK 94601 670-D1
2000 OAK 94601 650-E7
42ND AV Rt#-77
800 OAK 94601 670-C1
42ND ST
300 OAK 94609 629-H7
300 OAK 94611 629-H7
800 OAK 94608 629-G7
1000 EMVL 94608 629-G7
S 42ND ST
200 RCH 94804 609-A1
43RD ST
300 OAK 94609 629-H7
700 OAK 94608 629-G7
1000 EMVL 94608 629-F7
S 43RD ST
200 RCH 94804 609-A2
44TH AV
1000 OAK 94601 670-D1
44TH ST
300 OAK 94609 629-H7
800 OAK 94608 629-G7
1000 EMVL 94608 629-G7
S 44TH ST
200 RCH 94804 609-A1
45TH AV
700 OAK 94601 670-E1
45TH ST
200 OAK 94611 629-H7
300 OAK 94609 629-H7
800 OAK 94608 629-G6
1000 EMVL 94608 629-F6
S 45TH ST
200 RCH 94804 609-A1
46TH AV
700 OAK 94601 670-D1
46TH ST
500 OAK 94609 629-H7
800 OAK 94608 629-G6
900 EMVL 94608 629-G6
S 46TH ST
200 RCH 94804 609-A2
47TH AV
800 OAK 94601 670-E1
2200 OAK 94601 650-E7
47TH ST
500 OAK 94609 629-H7
700 OAK 94608 629-G6
1000 EMVL 94608 629-F6
S 47TH ST
100 RCH 94804 609-A1
48TH AV
1200 OAK 94601 670-D2
48TH ST
400 OAK 94609 629-H6
1000 EMVL 94608 629-F6
1000 OAK 94608 629-F6
49TH AV
800 OAK 94601 670-D2
49TH ST
300 OAK 94609 629-H6
300 OAK 94611 629-H6
300 OAK 94618 629-H6
S 49TH ST
300 RCH 94804 609-B1
50TH AV
600 OAK 94601 670-D2
50TH ST
300 OAK 94609 629-H6
S 50TH ST
300 RCH 94804 609-B1
51ST AV
800 OAK 94601 670-E1
51ST ST
300 OAK 94611 629-H6
300 OAK 94618 629-H6
300 OAK 94609 629-H6
800 OAK 94608 629-G6
S 51ST ST
1400 RCH 94804 609-A3
52ND AV
800 OAK 94601 670-D2
52ND ST
500 OAK 94609 629-H6
800 OAK 94608 629-G6
S 52ND ST
600 RCH 94804 609-B1
53RD AV
800 OAK 94601 670-D2
53RD ST
500 OAK 94609 629-H6
800 OAK 94608 629-F6
1100 EMVL 94608 629-E6
S 53RD ST
800 ELCR 94530 609-B2
54TH AV
800 OAK 94601 670-E2
54TH ST
500 OAK 94609 629-G6
800 OAK 94608 629-F6
1100 EMVL 94608 629-E6
S 54TH ST
5400 RCH 94804 609-B2
55TH AV
1400 OAK 94601 670-F1
1400 OAK 94621 670-E2
2000 OAK 94605 670-F1
2300 OAK 94619 670-F1
55TH ST
400 OAK 94609 629-G6
800 OAK 94608 629-F6
1200 EMVL 94608 629-E6
S 55TH ST
800 ELCR 94530 609-B2
900 RCH 94804 609-B2
56TH AV
1400 OAK 94621 670-E2
2600 OAK 94605 670-F1
56TH ST
500 OAK 94609 629-G6
800 OAK 94608 629-F6
S 56TH ST
1100 RCH 94804 609-B2
1400 ELCR 94530 609-B2
57TH AV
800 OAK 94621 670-E2
2200 OAK 94605 670-F1
57TH ST
400 OAK 94609 629-H5
800 OAK 94608 629-F6
S 57TH ST
1000 RCH 94804 609-B2
58TH AV
1100 OAK 94621 670-E3
2900 OAK 94605 670-G1
58TH ST
400 OAK 94609 629-G5
800 OAK 94608 629-G5
S 58TH ST
1200 RCH 94804 609-B2
59TH ST
400 OAK 94609 629-H5
800 OAK 94608 629-F5
1200 EMVL 94608 629-E6
S 59TH ST
1200 RCH 94804 609-C3
60TH AV
1100 OAK 94621 670-E3
2400 OAK 94605 670-G1
60TH ST
400 OAK 94609 629-H5
700 OAK 94608 629-F5
1600 OAK 94618 629-H5
61ST AV
1100 OAK 94621 670-F2
2400 OAK 94605 670-G1
61ST ST
300 OAK 94618 629-H5
300 OAK 94609 629-G5
800 OAK 94608 629-F5
1200 EMVL 94608 629-E5
62ND AV
1100 OAK 94621 670-E3
2100 OAK 94605 670-G1
62ND ST
300 OAK 94618 629-J5
400 OAK 94609 629-G5
700 BERK 94703 629-G5
900 OAK 94608 629-F5
1200 EMVL 94608 629-E5
63RD AV
1300 OAK 94621 670-F3
2300 OAK 94605 670-G1
63RD ST
300 OAK 94618 629-J4
400 OAK 94609 629-G5
600 BERK 94703 629-G5
900 OAK 94608 629-F5
1200 EMVL 94608 629-E5
64TH AV
1200 OAK 94621 670-F2
3600 OAK 94605 670-H1
64TH ST
1100 OAK 94608 629-E5
1200 EMVL 94608 629-D5
64TH AV PL
3300 OAK 94605 670-H1
65TH AV
1100 OAK 94621 670-F2
2100 OAK 94605 670-H1
65TH ST
400 OAK 94609 629-H4
1000 BERK 94702 629-E5
1000 OAK 94608 629-E5
1100 EMVL 94608 629-D5
66TH AV
600 OAK 94621 670-F3
2100 OAK 94605 670-H1
66TH ST
400 OAK 94609 629-H4
1000 BERK 94702 629-F4
1000 OAK 94608 629-E4
1100 EMVL 94608 629-E5
67TH AV
1500 OAK 94621 670-F3
1600 OAK 94605 670-G2
67TH ST
1000 BERK 94702 629-F4
1000 OAK 94608 629-E4
1100 EMVL 94608 629-E5
68TH AV
1500 OAK 94621 670-G3
1600 OAK 94605 670-G2
69TH AV
700 OAK 94621 670-G3
1700 OAK 94605 670-H2
70TH AV
800 OAK 94621 670-F3
71ST AV
800 OAK 94621 670-G3
72ND AV
900 OAK 94621 670-G3
3400 OAK 94605 670-J2
73RD AV
700 OAK 94621 670-G3
2100 OAK 94605 670-J2
74TH AV
1400 OAK 94621 670-G3
2500 OAK 94605 670-H2
75TH AV
800 OAK 94621 670-F4
2400 OAK 94605 670-H2
76TH AV
700 OAK 94621 670-G3
2400 OAK 94605 670-H2
77TH AV
700 OAK 94621 670-G3
2300 OAK 94605 670-J2
78TH AV
1100 OAK 94621 670-G3
1800 OAK 94605 670-J2
79TH AV
1100 OAK 94621 670-G3
1800 OAK 94605 670-J3
80TH AV
1200 OAK 94621 670-H3
2000 OAK 94605 670-H3
81ST AV
600 OAK 94621 670-H3
2000 OAK 94605 670-J3
82ND AV
1000 OAK 94621 670-H3
2000 OAK 94605 670-H3
2700 OAK 94605 671-A3
83RD AV
1000 OAK 94621 670-G4
2000 OAK 94605 670-J3
84TH AV
900 OAK 94621 670-G4
1900 OAK 94605 670-J3
85TH AV
500 OAK 94621 670-G4
2000 OAK 94605 670-J3
86TH AV
700 OAK 94621 670-H4
2000 OAK 94605 670-J3
87TH AV
900 OAK 94621 670-H4
2000 OAK 94605 670-J4
88TH AV
900 OAK 94621 670-J4
2000 OAK 94605 670-J4
2400 OAK 94605 671-A4
89TH AV
900 OAK 94621 670-H4
900 OAK 94603 670-G5
2000 OAK 94605 670-J4
2400 OAK 94605 671-A4
90TH AV
900 OAK 94603 670-H4
900 OAK 94621 670-H4
2100 OAK 94605 670-J4
2300 OAK 94603 671-A4
2300 OAK 94605 671-A4
91ST AV
900 OAK 94603 670-G5
92ND AV
800 OAK 94603 670-J4
93RD AV
1200 OAK 94603 670-H5
94TH AV
900 OAK 94603 670-H5
2200 OAK 94603 671-A4
95TH AV
1200 OAK 94603 670-H5
96TH AV
1200 OAK 94603 670-H5
2100 OAK 94603 671-A4
2400 OAK 94605 671-A4
97TH AV
1200 OAK 94603 670-H5
98TH AV
- OAK 94603 670-H6
- OAK 94603 690-E1
- OAK 94621 690-E1
2000 OAK 94603 671-A5
2400 OAK 94605 671-A5
99TH AV
1200 OAK 94603 670-J5
1900 OAK 94603 671-A5
2400 OAK 94605 671-B5
99TH AV CT
9900 OAK 94603 670-J5
100TH AV
700 OAK 94603 670-J5
1900 OAK 94603 671-A5
101ST AV
1100 OAK 94603 670-J5
1700 OAK 94603 671-A5
102ND AV
1100 OAK 94603 670-H6
1700 OAK 94603 671-A5
103RD AV
1100 OAK 94603 670-H6
1800 OAK 94603 671-A5
104TH AV
1100 OAK 94603 670-H6
1700 OAK 94603 671-A6
105TH AV
300 OAK 94603 690-G1
300 OAK 94603 670-H6
400 OAK 94603 671-A6
106TH AV
700 OAK 94603 670-J6
1800 OAK 94603 671-A6
2600 OAK 94605 671-B5
107TH AV
700 OAK 94603 670-H7
1800 OAK 94603 671-A6
2900 OAK 94605 671-B5
108TH AV
1800 OAK 94603 671-A6
2600 OAK 94605 671-A6
109TH AV
1800 OAK 94603 671-A6
2600 OAK 94605 671-B6
135TH AV
1200 SLN 94578 691-B2
1200 SLN 94577 691-B2
136TH AV
1100 SLN 94578 691-B3
1500 SLN 94577 691-C2
137TH AV
700 SLN 94577 691-B3
1500 SLN 94578 691-C2
138TH AV
1400 SLN 94578 691-C2
139TH AV
200 SLN 94578 691-C2
140TH AV
1400 SLN 94578 691-C2
141ST AV
1200 SLN 94578 691-C2
142ND AV
1400 SLN 94578 691-C3
143RD AV
500 SLN 94578 691-C2
144TH AV
1200 SLN 94578 691-C3
145TH AV
1100 SLN 94578 691-C3
146TH AV
1400 SLN 94578 691-D3
147TH AV
1100 SLN 94578 691-C4
148TH AV
1200 SLN 94578 691-D3
149TH AV
1900 AlaC 94578 691-E3
150TH AV
1400 SLN 94578 691-D4
1400 AlaC 94578 691-E3
151ST AV
1400 AlaC 94578 691-D4
152ND AV
1400 AlaC 94578 691-D4
153RD AV
1400 AlaC 94578 691-D4
155TH AV
1400 AlaC 94578 691-E4
156TH AV
1400 AlaC 94578 691-E4
159TH AV
1200 AlaC 94580 691-E5
1200 AlaC 94578 691-E4
162ND AV
1400 AlaC 94578 691-E5
163RD AV
1400 AlaC 94578 691-F5
164TH AV
1400 AlaC 94578 691-F5
165TH AV
1400 AlaC 94578 691-F5
166TH AV
1500 AlaC 94578 691-F5
167TH AV
1300 AlaC 94578 691-F5
168TH AV
1400 AlaC 94578 691-F6
170TH AV
1200 AlaC 94578 691-G5
1200 AlaC 94541 691-G5
1900 AlaC 94546 691-G5
171ST AV
1400 AlaC 94541 691-G6
172ND AV
1400 AlaC 94541 691-G6
173RD AV
1500 AlaC 94541 691-G6
1900 AlaC 94546 691-G6
174TH AV
2200 AlaC 94546 691-G5
I-80 EASTSHORE FRWY
- ALB - 609-C5
- BERK - 609-C5
- BERK - 629-D3
- ELCR - 609-C5
- EMVL - 629-D3
- EMVL - 629-D7
- OAK - 629-D7
- OAK - 649-D1
- RCH - 609-C5
I-80 FRWY
- OAK - 648-C5
- OAK - 649-C1
- SF - 648-C5
I-80 SF-OAKLAND BRDG
- OAK - 648-G2
- OAK - 649-B1
- SF - 648-G2
I-205 ROBERT T MONAGAN FRWY
- AlaC - (678-D7 See Page 677)
- SJCo - (678-D7 See Page 677)
- TRCY - (678-J7 See Page 677)
I-238 FRWY
- AlaC - 691-D6
- SLN - 691-C5
I-580 FRWY
- AlaC - 677-H7
- AlaC - (678-C7 See Page 677)
- AlaC - 691-G6
- AlaC - 696-H2
- AlaC - (697-F1 See Page 677)
I-580 ARTHUR H BREED JR FRWY
- AlaC - 691-H6
- AlaC - 692-F4
- AlaC - 693-A4
- AlaC - 694-C5
- AlaC - 695-D5
- AlaC - 696-A5
- DBLN - 693-A4
- DBLN - 694-C5
- LVMR - 694-C5
- LVMR - 695-D5
- LVMR - 696-A5
- PLE - 693-A4
- PLE - 694-C5
I-580 JOHN T KNOX FRWY
- ALB - 609-A3
- RCH - 609-A3
I-580 MACARTHUR FRWY
- AlaC - 691-C1
- EMVL - 629-D6
- OAK - 629-D7
- OAK - 649-H1
- OAK - 650-D5
- OAK - 670-J1
- OAK - 671-A1
- SLN - 671-A1
- SLN - 691-C1
I-580 WM ELTN BRN BROWN FWY
- SJCo - (678-D7 See Page 677)
- SJCo - (698-D1 See Page 677)
- TRCY - (698-J5 See Page 677)
I-680 FRWY
- AlaC - 714-D7
- AlaC - 734-D1
- AlaC - 753-J3
- AlaC - 754-E1
- DBLN - 693-G2
- DNVL - 652-J1
- DNVL - 673-C1
- FRMT - 753-J4
- FRMT - 773-F1
- PLE - 693-J4
- PLE - 713-J1
- PLE - 714-A1
- SRMN - 673-C1
- SRMN - 693-F1
I-680 SINCLAIR FRWY
- FRMT - 773-F3
- FRMT - 793-J1
- FRMT - 794-A2
- MPS - 794-A2
I-880 CYPRESS FRWY
- EMVL - 629-D7
- OAK - 629-E7
- OAK - 649-C3
I-880 FRWY
- AlaC - 691-D6
- SLN - 691-D6
I-880 NIMITZ FRWY
- AlaC - 691-D6
- AlaC - 711-G5
- FRMT - 732-A2
- FRMT - 752-G5
- FRMT - 772-J1
- FRMT - 773-D4
- FRMT - 793-G2
- HAY - 711-G5
- HAY - 731-J1
- HAY - 732-A2
- MPS - 793-H4
- NWK - 752-G5
- NWK - 772-J1
- NWK - 773-D4
- OAK - 649-H5
- OAK - 650-A6
- OAK - 670-D3
- OAK - 690-H2
- SLN - 690-H2
- SLN - 691-A3
- UNC - 732-A2
I-980 GROVE SHAFTER FRWY
- OAK - 649-G2
Rt#-J2 W CORRAL HOLLOW RD
15000 SJCo 95377 (738-D1 See Page 717)
19600 SJCo 95377 (718-D7 See Page 717)
Rt#-J2 N LIVERMORE AV
100 LVMR 94550 695-G7
100 LVMR 94550 715-G1
100 LVMR 94551 695-G7
Rt#-J2 S LIVERMORE AV
- LVMR 94550 715-J2
1400 LVMR 94550 716-A3
1700 AlaC 94550 716-A3
Rt#-J2 PORTOLA AV
1100 LVMR 94551 695-F6
Rt#-J2 TESLA RD
4600 AlaC 94550 716-A3
10100 AlaC 94550 717-A5
16500 AlaC 94550 (718-A7 See Page 717)
Rt#-J4 BYRON HWY
10600 CCCo 94513 637-D1
10600 CCCo 94514 637-D1
17600 CCCo 94514 (657-G1 See Page 637)
19100 CCCo 94514 (658-A3 See Page 637)
Rt#-J4 BYRON-BETHANY RD
15300 SJCo 95304 (678-G1 See Page 677)
16500 SJCo 95391 (678-F1 See Page 677)
17900 SJCo 95391 (658-D6 See Page 637)
20200 AlaC 94551 (658-B4 See Page 637)
20200 CCCo 94514 (658-B4 See Page 637)
Rt#-4 CALIFORNIA DELTA HWY
15100 SJCo 95206 (638-H1 See Page 637)
Rt#-13 ASHBY AV
400 BERK 94710 629-D4
1100 BERK 94702 629-F4
1500 BERK 94703 629-F4
2100 BERK 94705 629-F4
2800 BERK 94705 630-A3
Rt#-13 LANDVALE RD
300 OAK 94618 630-B4
Rt#-13 TUNNEL RD
- BERK 94705 630-B4
- OAK 94705 630-B4
1100 OAK 94618 630-B4
Rt#-13 WARREN FRWY
- OAK - 630-C6
- OAK - 650-F3
Rt#-24 GROVE SHAFTER FRWY
- OAK - 649-G1
Rt#-24 WM BYRON RUMFORD FRWY
- CCCo - 630-E2
- OAK - 629-G7
- OAK - 630-E2
- OAK - 649-G1
- ORIN - 610-H7
- ORIN - 630-E2
Rt#-61 BROADWAY
800 ALA 94501 670-A3
Rt#-61 CENTRAL AV
200 ALA 94501 669-G1
Rt#-61 DOOLITTLE DR
- ALA 94502 670-B5
600 SLN 94577 690-F1
600 OAK 94603 690-F1
7900 OAK 94621 670-B5
9400 OAK 94621 690-F1
Rt#-61 ENCINAL AV
1300 ALA 94501 669-J2
2200 ALA 94501 670-A2
Rt#-61 OTIS DR
- ALA 94502 670-A3
2600 ALA 94501 670-A3
Rt#-77 42ND AV
800 OAK 94601 670-C1
Rt#-84 1ST ST
1400 LVMR 94550 715-F1
Rt#-84 BAYFRONT EXWY
- FRMT 94555 751-G7
- FRMT 94555 771-E3
- MLPK 94025 771-A6
- MLPK 94303 771-D4
Rt#-84 DUMBARTON BRDG
- FRMT - 771-D4
- MLPK - 771-D4
Rt#-84 FREMONT BLVD
36800 FRMT 94536 752-H3
Rt#-84 FRWY
- FRMT - 751-J6
- FRMT - 752-E2
- NWK - 752-E2
Rt#-84 HOLMES ST
300 LVMR 94550 715-F2
2900 AlaC 94550 715-F2
Rt#-84 ISABEL AV
- PLE 94566 715-C5
1300 LVMR 94550 715-C5
1300 AlaC 94550 715-C4
1300 LVMR 94551 695-C7
1300 LVMR 94551 715-D1
1300 AlaC 94551 715-D1
Rt#-84 KITTY HAWK RD
1200 LVMR 94551 695-C6
Rt#-84 MOWRY AV
- FRMT 94536 753-C2
Rt#-84 NILES CANYON RD
100 FRMT 94536 733-G5
100 UNC 94587 733-G5
200 FRMT 94536 753-C1
500 AlaC 94586 733-G5
12000 AlaC 94586 734-A6
Rt#-84 PALOMA RD
11500 AlaC 94586 734-D6
Rt#-84 PERALTA BLVD
1200 FRMT 94536 753-A3
2700 FRMT 94536 752-J3
Rt#-84 THORNTON AV
4000 FRMT 94536 752-H3
Rt#-84 VALLECITOS RD
11000 AlaC 94586 734-F5
Rt#-84 E VALLECITOS RD
1200 AlaC 94550 715-D6
1200 LVMR 94550 715-D6
1200 PLE 94566 715-D6
1700 PLE 94566 735-B3
1700 AlaC 94550 735-B3
2900 AlaC 94586 735-B3
11300 AlaC 94586 734-H4
Rt#-92 J ARTHUR YOUNGER FRWY
- HAY - 711-E7
- HAY - 731-B1
Rt#-92 JACKSON ST
- HAY 94544 711-J4
- HAY 94541 711-J4
Rt#-92 SAN MATEO-HAYWARD BRDG
- HAY - 731-A2
Rt#-109 UNIVERSITY AV
2600 EPA 94303 771-B6
2700 MLPK 94303 771-B6
2800 MLPK 94025 771-B6
Rt#-112 DAVIS ST
300 SLN 94577 691-A1
700 SLN 94577 690-J1
Rt#-114 WILLOW RD
1200 EPA 94303 771-A7
1200 MLPK 94025 771-A7
Rt#-123 SAN PABLO AV
500 ALB 94706 609-D6
1000 ALB 94710 609-D6
1100 BERK 94706 609-D6
1100 BERK 94710 609-D6
1300 BERK 94702 609-D6
1400 BERK 94702 629-E1
1400 BERK 94710 629-E1
3000 ELCR 94530 609-B1
3100 OAK 94608 629-E3
3500 OAK 94608 649-F1
3500 EMVL 94608 629-E3
3500 EMVL 94608 649-F1
10200 RCH 94804 609-B1
Rt#-185 E 14TH ST
- OAK 94603 670-J6
- SLN 94577 670-J6
300 SLN 94577 671-A7
900 SLN 94577 691-B2
8400 SLN 94578 691-B2
13500 AlaC 94578 691-F5
15900 AlaC 94580 691-F5
17000 AlaC 94541 691-F5
Rt#-185 INTERNATIONAL BLVD
3600 OAK 94601 670-C1
5500 OAK 94621 670-H4
9000 OAK 94603 670-H4
10700 SLN 94577 670-H4
Rt#-185 MISSION BLVD
900 HAY 94541 711-H1
17900 AlaC 94541 691-G6
21500 HAY 94541 691-G6
Rt#-237 CALAVERAS BLVD
300 MPS 95035 793-J7
500 MPS 95035 794-A7
Rt#-238 FOOTHILL BLVD
1000 HAY 94541 711-J1
20400 AlaC 94546 691-H6
20800 AlaC 94541 691-H6
21100 HAY 94541 691-H6
Rt#-238 MISSION BLVD
- FRMT 94536 732-G4
- FRMT 94536 733-B7
21700 HAY 94541 691-H7
21700 HAY 94541 711-H1
23000 HAY 94544 711-J2
23400 HAY 94544 712-A3
23600 HAY 94542 712-A3
29800 HAY 94544 732-D1
32000 UNC 94587 732-G4
37500 FRMT 94536 753-E3
39100 FRMT 94539 753-E3
Rt#-260 WEBSTER ST
1400 ALA 94501 669-F1
1700 ALA 94501 649-F7
Rt#-262 MISSION BLVD
46200 FRMT 94539 773-G6
46600 FRMT 94538 773-G6

AIRPORTS

FEATURE NAME	Address City, ZIP Code	PAGE-GRID
CONTRA COSTA COUNTY BYRON- (SEE PAGE 637)	500 EAGLE CT, CCCo, 94514	657 - F2
HAYWARD AIR TERMINAL	20301 SKYWEST DR, HAY, 94541	711 - D2
LIVERMORE MUNICIPAL	636 TERMINAL CIR, LVMR, 94551	695 - A6
OAKLAND INTL	1 AIRPORT DR, OAK, 94621	690 - B1

BEACHES, HARBORS & WATER REC

FEATURE NAME	Address City, ZIP Code	PAGE-GRID
AEOLIAN YACHT CLUB	FERNSIDE BLVD, ALA, 94501	670 - B4
BARNHILL MARINA	2394 MARINER SQUARE DR, ALA, 94501	649 - G6
BERKELEY MARINA	MARINA BLVD, BERK, 94710	629 - B2
BERKELEY YACHT CLUB	1 SEAWALL DR, BERK, 94710	629 - B2
CROWN, ROBERT MEM ST BCH	620 CENTRAL AV, ALA, 94501	669 - G2
EMBARCADERO COVE MARINAS	EMBARCADERO, OAK, 94606	649 - J6
EMERYVILLE MARINA	POWELL ST, EMVL, 94608	629 - B6
ENCINAL YACHT CLUB	PACIFIC MARINA, ALA, 94501	649 - H7
FORTMANN MARINA	FORTMANN WY & ALASKA PACKER ST, ALA, 94501	649 - H7
ISLAND YACHT CLUB	1853 CLEMENT AV, ALA, 94501	669 - J1
LIVERMORE YACHT CLUB (SEE PAGE 637)	LINDEMANN RD, AlaC, 94551	658 - C4
LONDON, JACK MARINA	54 JACK LONDON SQ, OAK, 94607	649 - F5
PACIFIC MARINA	FOOT OF SHERMAN ST, ALA, 94501	649 - G7
SAN LEANDRO MARINA	S DIKE ST, SLN, 94577	690 - G5
UNION POINT MARINA	EMBARCADERO, OAK, 94606	650 - A7

BUILDINGS

FEATURE NAME	Address City, ZIP Code	PAGE-GRID
FOR DOWNTOWN BUILDINGS SEE PAGE F		-
1 HARRISON ST	1 HARRISON ST, SF, 94105	648 - C5
49 STEVENSON ST	49 STEVENSON ST, SF, 94103	648 - A6
50 FREMONT ST	50 FREMONT ST, SF, 94105	648 - B5
55 HAWTHORNE ST	55 HAWTHORNE ST, SF, 94105	648 - B6
60 SPEAR ST	60 SPEAR ST, SF, 94105	648 - B5
71 STEVENSON ST	71 STEVENSON ST, SF, 94103	648 - A6
75 HAWTHORNE ST PLAZA	75 HAWTHORNE ST PZ, SF, 94105	648 - B6
90 NEW MONTGOMERY	90 NEW MONTGOMERY ST, SF, 94105	648 - B6
100 CALIFORNIA ST	100 CALIFORNIA ST, SF, 94111	648 - B5
100 FIRST PLAZA	100 1ST ST, SF, 94105	648 - B5
100 PINE ST	100 PINE ST, SF, 94111	648 - B5
101 CALIFORNIA ST	101 CALIFORNIA ST, SF, 94111	648 - B5
120 MONTGOMERY ST	120 MONTGOMERY ST, SF, 94104	648 - B5
123 MISSION ST	123 MISSION ST, SF, 94105	648 - B5
160 SPEAR ST	160 SPEAR ST, SF, 94105	648 - B5
180 GRAND AV	180 GRAND AV, OAK, 94612	649 - H3
201 CALIFORNIA ST	201 CALIFORNIA ST, SF, 94111	648 - B5
301 HOWARD ST	301 HOWARD ST, SF, 94105	648 - C5
333 BUSH ST	333 BUSH ST, SF, 94108	648 - A5
333 MARKET ST	333 MARKET ST, SF, 94105	648 - B5
343 SANSOME	343 SANSOME ST, SF, 94104	648 - B5
353 SACRAMENTO ST	353 SACRAMENTO ST, SF, 94104	648 - B5
388 MARKET ST	388 MARKET ST, SF, 94111	648 - B5
425 MARKET ST	425 MARKET ST, SF, 94105	648 - B5
455 MARKET ST	455 MARKET ST, SF, 94105	648 - B5
475 SANSOME ST	475 SANSOME ST, SF, 94111	648 - B5
505 MONTGOMERY ST	505 MONTGOMERY ST, SF, 94111	648 - A5
580 CALIFORNIA ST	580 CALIFORNIA ST, SF, 94104	648 - A5
595 MARKET ST	595 MARKET ST, SF, 94108	648 - A6
601 MONTGOMERY ST	601 MONTGOMERY ST, SF, 94111	648 - A5
605 MARKET ST	605 MARKET ST, SF, 94103	648 - A6
650 CALIFORNIA ST	650 CALIFORNIA ST, SF, 94108	648 - A5
660 MARKET ST	660 MARKET ST, SF, 94108	648 - A6
ABC	900 FRONT ST, SF, 94111	648 - B4
ADAM GRANT	114 SANSOME ST, SF, 94104	648 - B5
AEROFLOT AIRLINES	291 GEARY ST, SF, 94108	648 - A6
AIR FRANCE AIRLINES	360 POST ST, SF, 94102	648 - A5
AMERICAN AIRLINES	51 OFARREL ST, SF, 94108	648 - A6
AMERICAN SAVINGS	MARKET & KEARNY STS, SF, 94108	648 - A6
AT&T	795 FOLSOM ST, SF, 94107	648 - B6
BANKERS INVESTMENT	742 MARKET ST, SF, 94108	648 - A6
BANK OF AMERICA BLDG	1200 BROADWAY, OAK, 94612	649 - G3
BANK OF AMERICA BLDG	1500 PARK ST, ALA, 94501	670 - A2
BANK OF AMERICA BLDG	2129 SHATTUCK AV, BERK, 94704	629 - H2
BANK OF CALIFORNIA COMPUTER CTR	640 BATTERY ST, SF, 94111	648 - B4
BANK OF CANTON	555 MONTGOMERY ST, SF, 94104	648 - A5
BANK OF SAN FRANCISCO	550 MONTGOMERY ST, SF, 94104	648 - A5
BAYSIDE PLAZA	188 THE EMBARCADERO ST, SF, 94105	648 - C6
BEVATRON BLDG	2200 UNIVERSITY AV, BERK, 94720	629 - J1
BLUE CROSS BLDG	1950 FRANKLIN ST, OAK, 94612	649 - G3
BRITISH AIRWAYS	51 OFARRELL ST, SF, 94108	648 - A6
BROOKS BROTHERS	209 POST ST, SF, 94108	648 - A5
CENTRAL TOWER	703 MARKET ST, SF, 94105	648 - B5
CHEVRON	225 BUSH ST, SF, 94108	648 - A5
CHINA AIRLINES	391 STOCKTON ST, SF, 94108	648 - A5
CHRONICLE	5TH ST & MISSION ST, SF, 94103	648 - A6
CITICORP CTR	1 SANSOME ST, SF, 94104	648 - B5
CITY CTR	14TH ST & BROADWAY, OAK, 94612	649 - G4
CLOROX BLDG	1221 BROADWAY, OAK, 94607	649 - G4
COMMERCIAL	833 MARKET ST, SF, 94103	648 - A6
CONTINENTAL AIRLINES	433 CALIFORNIA ST, SF, 94104	648 - B5
CONVENTION PLAZA	201 3RD ST, SF, 94103	648 - B6
DELTA AIRLINES	250 STOCKTON ST, SF, 94108	648 - A6
E B CTR FOR BLIND	3834 OPAL ST, OAK, 94609	649 - H1
ECKER SQUARE	25 ECKER ST, SF, 94105	648 - B5
EIGHT THIRTY MARKET	830 MARKET ST, SF, 94102	648 - A6
EMBARCADERO CTR W	275 BATTERY ST, SF, 94104	648 - B5
EXCHANGE BLOCK	369 PINE ST, SF, 94104	648 - B5
FASHION INSTITUTE	55 STOCKTON ST, SF, 94108	648 - A6
FEDERAL HOME LOAN BANK	600 CALIFORNIA ST, SF, 94108	648 - A5
FEDERAL RESERVE BANK	101 MARKET ST, SF, 94105	648 - B5
FERRY BLDG	EMBARCADERO & WASHINGTON ST, SF, 94111	648 - B4
FIFTEEN CALIFORNIA ST	15 CALIFORNIA ST, SF, 94111	648 - B5
FIFTY HAWTHORNE	50 HAWTHORNE ST, SF, 94103	648 - B6
FILBERT LANDING	201 FILBERT ST, SF, 94133	648 - A4
FINANCIAL CTR BLDG	405 14TH ST, OAK, 94612	649 - G4
FIRST INTERSTATE CTR	BATTERY ST & PINE ST, SF, 94104	648 - B5
FIRST MARKET TOWER	525 MARKET ST, SF, 94108	648 - A5
FIVE FREMONT CTR	5 MISSION ST & FREMONT ST, SF, 94105	648 - B5
FLATIRON	1 SUTTER ST, SF, 94105	648 - B5
FLOOD	870 MARKET ST, SF, 94102	648 - A6
FOLGER	101 HOWARD ST, SF, 94105	648 - C5
FORTY FOUR MONTGOMERY	44 MONTGOMREY ST, SF, 94104	648 - B5
FOUR EMBARCADERO CTR	EMBARCADERO CTR, SF, 94111	648 - C5
FOUR SEVENTEEN MONTGOMERY	417 MONTGOMERY ST, SF, 94104	648 - A5
FRANKLIN BLDG	1624 FRANKLIN ST, OAK, 94612	649 - G4
FREMONT CTR	215 FREMONT ST, SF, 94105	648 - B5
GOLDEN GATE	25 TAYLOR ST, SF, 94102	648 - A6
GOLDEN GATEWAY CTR	460 DAVIS ST, SF, 94111	648 - B4
GREAT WESTERN BANK	425 CALIFORNIA ST, SF, 94104	648 - B5
GUNST, ELKAN	323 GEARY ST, SF, 94102	648 - A6
GUZZARDO	836 MONTGOMERY ST, SF, 94133	648 - A4
HARMON GYMNASIUM	2200 UNIVERSITY AV, BERK, 94720	629 - H2
HARRIS, ELIHU M STATE BLDG	1515 CLAY ST, OAK, 94612	649 - G3
HARRISON BLDG	1800 HARRISON ST, OAK, 94612	649 - H4
HASS	1255 SANSOME ST, SF, 94133	648 - A3
HAYWARD UNIFIED DIST	24411 AMADOR ST, HAY, 94544	711 - H4
HEALTH CTR	850 UNIVERSITY AV, BERK, 94710	629 - D2
HEARST	669 MARKET ST, SF, 94105	648 - B5
HILLS PLAZA 1	345 SPEAR ST, SF, 94105	648 - C5
HILLS PLAZA 2	1 HARRISON ST, SF, 94105	648 - C5
HOBART	582 MARKET ST, SF, 94104	648 - B5
HONG KONG BANK	160 SANSOME ST, SF, 94104	648 - B5
HUMBOLDT BANK	785 MARKET ST, SF, 94103	648 - A6
INDUSTRIAL INDEMNITY	255 CALIFORNIA ST, SF, 94111	648 - B5
INSURANCE BLDG	1404 FRANKLIN ST, OAK, 94612	649 - G4
INSURANCE EXCHANGE	433 CALIFORNIA ST, SF, 94104	648 - A5
INTERNATIONAL	601 CALIFORNIA ST, SF, 94108	648 - A5
INTERNATIONAL HOUSE	2200 UNIVERSITY AV, BERK, 94720	629 - J2
JAPAN AIRLINES	POWELL ST & OFARRELL ST, SF, 94102	648 - A6
KAISER CTR	300 LAKESIDE DR, OAK, 94612	649 - H3
KINGS DAUGHTERS HOME	BROADWAY, OAK, 94611	649 - H1
KOHL	400 MONTGOMERY ST, SF, 94104	648 - A5
KOREAN AIR	251 POST ST, SF, 94108	648 - A5
KOSHLAND	1160 BATTERY ST, SF, 94111	648 - B3
KPIX	855 BATTERY ST, SF, 94111	648 - B4
KRE RADIO STA	POTTER ST & BOLIVAR DR, BERK, 94710	629 - D4
KRESS	939 MARKET ST, SF, 94103	648 - A6
LAKE MERRITT PLAZA	1999 HARRISON AV, OAK, 94612	649 - G3
LEVI STRAUSS	1155 BATTERY ST, SF, 94111	648 - B3
LUFTHANSA	240 STOCKTON ST, SF, 94108	648 - A6
MARATHON PLAZA	303 2ND ST, SF, 94105	648 - B6
MARINE FIREMANS UNION	240 2ND ST, SF, 94105	648 - B6
MARITIME ADMIN	211 MAIN ST, SF, 94105	648 - B5
MARITIME COMMISSION	525 MARKET ST, SF, 94105	648 - B5
MASONIC HOME FOR ADULTS	34400 MISSION BLVD, UNC, 94587	732 - H4
MATHEWS, MERTLE BLDG	4301 E 14TH ST, SLN, 94577	691 - A1
MCMULLEN BLDG	1305 FRANKLIN ST, OAK, 94612	649 - G4
MECHANICS INSTITUTE	57 POST ST, SF, 94108	648 - A5
MEDICO/DENTAL	490 POST ST, SF, 94102	648 - A6
MEMORIAL BLDG	BANCROFT AV & CALLAN AV, SLN, 94577	671 - B7
MERCANTILE CTR	706 MISSION ST, SF, 94103	648 - A6
MERCHANTS EXCHANGE	465 CALIFORNIA ST, SF, 94104	648 - A5
MEXICANA AIRLINES	421 POWELL ST, SF, 94102	648 - A6
MILLS BLDG & TOWER	220 MONTGOMERY ST, SF, 94104	648 - B5
MONADNOCK	685 MARKET ST, SF, 94103	648 - A6
MONTGOMERY WASHINGTON TOWER	655 MONTGOMERY ST, SF, 94111	648 - A4
NATIVE SONS	414 MASON ST, SF, 94102	648 - A6
NEW MONTGOMERY TOWER	33 NEW MONTGOMERY ST, SF, 94105	648 - B6
NINETEEN TWENTY FOUR BLDG	1924 BROADWAY, OAK, 94612	649 - G3
NORTHWEST	433 CALIFORNIA ST, SF, 94104	648 - B5
OAKLAND EXECUTIVE CTR	HASSLER WY, OAK, 94621	670 - E5
OAKLAND UNIFIED DIST ADMIN BLDG	1025 2ND AV, OAK, 94606	649 - H5
OAKLAND WORLD TRADE CTR	EMBARCADERO, OAK, 94607	649 - G5
ONE BUSH ST	1 BUSH ST, SF, 94111	648 - B5
ONE CALIFORNIA ST	1 CALIFORNIA ST, SF, 94111	648 - B5
ONE ELEVEN SUTTER	111 SUTTER ST, SF, 94108	648 - A5
ONE EMBARCADERO CTR	EMBARCADERO CTR, SF, 94111	648 - C5
ONE JACKSON PLACE	633 BATTERY ST, SF, 94111	648 - B4
ONE MARITIME PLAZA	1 MARITIME PZ, SF, 94111	648 - B5
ONE MARKET PLAZA	1 MARKET PZ, SF, 94105	648 - B5
ONE POST BLDG	1 POST ST, SF, 94104	648 - B5
ORDWAY, THE	1 KAISER AVCT, OAK, 94612	649 - H3
PACIFIC BANK	351 CALIFORNIA ST, SF, 94104	648 - B5
PACIFIC BELL	140 NEW MONTGOMERY ST, SF, 94105	648 - B6
PACIFIC BLDG	610 16TH ST, OAK, 94612	649 - G3
PACIFIC CENTRE	22 4TH ST, SF, 94103	648 - A6
PACIFIC COAST STOCK EXCHANGE	301 PINE ST, SF, 94104	648 - B5
PACIFIC GATEWAY	201 MISSION ST, SF, 94105	648 - B5
PACIFIC TELESIS TOWER	1 MONTGOMERY ST, SF, 94108	648 - B5
PARK PLAZA BLDG	3100 MOWRY AV, FRMT, 94538	753 - A4
PHELAN	760 MARKET ST, SF, 94108	648 - A6
PHILIPPINE AIRLINES	447 SUTTER ST, SF, 94108	648 - A5
PIERCE BLDG	385 17TH ST, OAK, 94612	649 - G3
QANTAS AIRWAYS	360 POST ST, SF, 94102	648 - A5
RAY	181 FREMONT ST, SF, 94105	648 - B5
REDWOOD BANK	735 MONTGOMERY ST, SF, 94133	648 - A4
RIALTO	116 NEW MONTGOMERY ST, SF, 94105	648 - B6
RINCON CTR	101 SPEAR ST, SF, 94105	648 - B5
ROBERT DOLLAR	311 CALIFORNIA ST, SF, 94104	648 - B5
ROTHSCHILD	165 POST ST, SF, 94108	648 - A5
RUCKER FULLER	731 SANSOME ST, SF, 94133	648 - B4
RUSS	235 MONTGOMERY ST, SF, 94104	648 - A5
SAILORS UNION OF PACIFIC	450 HARRISON ST, SF, 94105	648 - C6
SANDIA NATL LABORATORIES	EAST AV & GREENVILLE RD, AlaC, 94550	716 - F1
SAN FRANCISCO FEDERAL SAVINGS	POST ST & KEARNY ST, SF, 94108	648 - A5
SEVENTY NINE NEW MONTGOMERY	79 NEW MONTGOMERY ST, SF, 94105	648 - B6
SHAKLEE TERRACES	444 MARKET ST, SF, 94104	648 - B5
SHARON	55 NEW MONTGOMERY ST, SF, 94105	648 - B6
SHELL	100 BUSH ST, SF, 94104	648 - B5
SINGAPORE AIRLINES	476 POST ST, SF, 94102	648 - A6
SIXTY FOUR PINE ST	64 PINE ST, SF, 94111	648 - B5
SOUTHERN PACIFIC	1 MARKET PZ, SF, 94105	648 - B5
SPEAR STREET TERRACE	201 SPEAR ST, SF, 94105	648 - C5
SPEAR STREET TOWER	1 MARKET PZ, SF, 94105	648 - B5

© 2006 Rand McNally & Company

FEATURE NAME	Address City, ZIP Code	PAGE-GRID
STEUART ST TOWER	1 MARKET PZ, SF, 94105	648 - B5
STOCK EXCHANGE TOWER	155 SANSOME ST, SF, 94104	648 - B5
SUMITOMO BANK	320 CALIFORNIA ST, SF, 94104	648 - B5
SUTTER MED DENTAL	450 SUTTER ST, SF, 94108	648 - A5
TACA	870 MARKET ST, SF, 94108	648 - A6
TENNYSON PROFESSIONAL BLDG	781 W TENNYSON RD, HAY, 94544	712 - B7
THREE EMBARCADERO CTR	EMBARCADERO CTR, SF, 94111	648 - C5
TRANSAMERICA	701 MONTGOMERY ST, SF, 94133	648 - A4
TRANSAMERICA (PYRAMID)	600 MONTGOMERY ST, SF, 94111	648 - A4
TRANS PACIFIC CTR	1000 BROADWAY, OAK, 94607	649 - G4
TRANS WORLD AIRLINES	595 MARKET ST, SF, 94104	648 - B5
TWO EMBARCADERO CTR	EMBARCADERO CTR, SF, 94111	648 - C5
TWO RINCON CTR	121 SPEAR ST, SF, 94105	648 - B5
TWO TRANSAMERICA CTR	505 SANSOME ST, SF, 94111	648 - B5
UNION BANK	350 CALIFORNIA ST, SF, 94104	648 - B5
UNITED AIRLINES	124 GEARY ST, SF, 94108	648 - A6
US AIR	433 CALIFORINIA ST, SF, 94104	648 - A5
WELLS FARGO	464 CALIFORNIA ST, SF, 94104	648 - B5
WELLS FARGO BLDG	1345 BROADWAY, OAK, 94612	649 - G4
WORLD SAVINGS CTR	1901 HARRISON ST, OAK, 94612	649 - H3
YERBA BUENA WEST	150 4TH ST, SF, 94103	648 - A6
YMCA	2350 BROADWAY, OAK, 94612	649 - G3
YWCA	1515 WEBSTER ST, OAK, 94612	649 - G4

BUILDINGS - GOVERNMENTAL

FEATURE NAME	Address City, ZIP Code	PAGE-GRID
ALAMEDA COUNTY BLDG	24405 AMADOR ST, HAY, 94544	711 - H3
ALAMEDA COUNTY HEALTH DEPARTMENT	1000 BROADWAY, OAK, 94607	649 - G4
ALAMEDA COUNTY WELFARE BLDG	401 BROADWAY, OAK, 94607	649 - F5
BYRON BOYS RANCH	4491 BIXLER RD, CCCo, 94514	637 - F2
CALTRANS	111 GRAND AV, OAK, 94612	649 - H3
CAMRON-STANFORD HOUSE	1418 LAKESIDE DR, OAK, 94612	649 - H4
CITY CORPORATION YARD	SCHMIDT LN, ELCR, 94530	609 - D2
CITY MUNICIPAL SERVICE YARD	EDGEWATER DR, OAK, 94621	670 - D5
CITY POUND	3065 FORD ST, OAK, 94601	670 - B1
COUNTY ADMIN BLDG	1221 OAK ST, OAK, 94612	649 - H4
COUNTY HEALTH DEPARTMENT	2060 FAIRMONT DR, AlaC, 94578	691 - E3
COUNTY OF ALAMEDA HALL OF JUSTICE	24405 AMADOR ST, HAY, 94544	711 - G3
COURTHOUSE	1225 FALLON ST, OAK, 94612	649 - H4
COURTHOUSE	2233 SHORELINE DR, ALA, 94501	669 - J3
COURTHOUSE	600 WASHINGTON ST, OAK, 94612	649 - G4
COURTHOUSE	7TH ST, OAK, 94607	649 - F4
DUNSMUIR HOUSE & GARDENS	2960 PERALTA OAKS CT, OAK, 94605	671 - C6
EDUCATIONAL SERVICES CTR	ALVARADO-NILES RD & MEYERS DR, UNC, 94587	732 - F6
FEDERAL CORRECTIONAL INST PLEASANTON	8TH ST & GOODFELLOW AV, DBLN, 94568	694 - C2
FREMONT COURTHOUSE	39439 PAS PADRE PKWY, FRMT, 94538	753 - B4
HALL OF JUSTICE	850 BRYANT ST, SF, 94103	648 - A7
JUVENILE HALL	2200 FAIRMONT DR, AlaC, 94578	691 - E2
OAKLAND FEDERAL BLDG	1301 CLAY ST, OAK, 94612	649 - F4
PORT OF OAKLAND OFFICE	530 WATER ST, OAK, 94607	649 - F5
PUBLIC WORKS	399 ELMHURST ST, HAY, 94544	711 - H3
SANTA RITA REHABILITATION CTR	BRODER BLVD, DBLN, 94568	694 - C2
US APPRAISERS BLDG	630 SANSOME ST, SF, 94111	648 - B4
US CUSTOMS HOUSE	555 BATTERY ST, SF, 94111	648 - B5
USDA WESTERN REGL RESEARCH LAB	800 BUCHANAN ST, ALB, 94706	609 - C6
VETERANS BLDG	1301 CLAY ST, OAK, 94612	649 - F4
VETERANS BLDG	2203 CENTRAL AV, ALA, 94501	669 - J2
VETERANS BLDG	CENTER ST, BERK, 94704	629 - G2

CEMETERIES

FEATURE NAME	Address City, ZIP Code	PAGE-GRID
CATHOLIC CEM	STARVIEW DR, AlaC, 94578	691 - E2
CEDAR LAWN MEM PK	48800 WARM SPRINGS BLVD, FRMT, 94539	793 - J2
CENTERVILLE PIONEER CEM	BONDE WY, FRMT, 94536	752 - H3
CHAPEL OF THE CHIMES MEM CEM	32992 MISSION BLVD, UNC, 94587	732 - F2
EVERGREEN CEM	6450 CAMDEN ST, OAK, 94605	670 - H1
HOLY GHOST CEM	CENTRAL AV, FRMT, 94536	752 - G5
HOLY SEPULCHRE CEM	26320 MISSION BLVD, HAY, 94544	712 - B4
HOME OF PEACE CEM	4712 FAIRFAX AV, OAK, 94601	650 - E7
IRVINGTON MEM CEM	41001 CHAPEL WY, FRMT, 94538	753 - C7
JEWISH CEM	4550 PIEDMONT AV, OAK, 94611	630 - A7
LONE TREE CEM	24591 FAIRVIEW AV, AlaC, 94541	712 - C1
MEMORY GARDENS CEM	3873 EAST AV, LVMR, 94550	715 - J1
MOUNTAIN VIEW CEM	5000 PIEDMONT AV, OAK, 94611	630 - A7
MOUNT EDEN CEM	2200 DEPOT RD, HAY, 94545	711 - F6
OHLONE INDIAN GRAVEYARD	1500 WASHINGTON BLVD, FRMT, 94539	753 - G7
ROSELAWN CEM	1240 N LIVERMORE AV, LVMR, 94551	695 - G6
SAINT JOSEPHS CEM	44200 MISSION BLVD, FRMT, 94539	773 - H2
SAINT MARYS CEM	4529 HOWE ST, OAK, 94611	630 - A6
SAINT MICHAELS CEM	EAST AV & DOLORES ST, LVMR, 94550	715 - J1
SUNSET VIEW CEM	101 COLUSA AV, CCCo, 94707	609 - E3

CITY HALLS

FEATURE NAME	Address City, ZIP Code	PAGE-GRID
ALAMEDA	2263 SANTA CLARA AV, ALA, 94501	670 - A2
ALAMEDA WEST	950 W MALL SQ, ALA, 94501	649 - C6
ALBANY	1000 SAN PABLO AV, ALB, 94706	609 - D6
BERKELEY	2180 MILVIA ST, BERK, 94704	629 - G2
DANVILLE	510 LA GONDA WY, DNVL, 94526	652 - J1
DUBLIN	100 CIVIC PZ, DBLN, 94568	693 - J4
EL CERRITO	10890 SAN PABLO AV, ELCR, 94530	609 - C2
EMERYVILLE	1333 PARK AV, EMVL, 94608	629 - E7
FREMONT /ADMIN CTR	39100 LIBERTY ST, FRMT, 94538	753 - B4
HAYWARD	777 B ST, HAY, 94541	711 - J1
LIVERMORE CITY OFFICES	1052 S LIVERMORE AV, LVMR, 94550	715 - J2
MILPITAS	455 CALVAVERAS BLVD, MPS, 95035	794 - B7
NEWARK	37101 NEWARK BLVD, NWK, 94560	752 - F6
OAKLAND	1 FRANK H OGAWA PZ, OAK, 94612	649 - G4
ORINDA	26 ORINDA WY, ORIN, 94563	610 - G7
PIEDMONT	120 VISTA AV, PDMT, 94611	650 - B1
PLEASANTON	200 OLD BERNAL AV, PLE, 94566	714 - D4
SAN LEANDRO	835 E 14TH ST, SLN, 94577	671 - A7
SAN RAMON	2222 CM RAMON, SRMN, 94583	673 - D1
UNION CITY	34009 ALVARADO-NILES RD, UNC, 94587	732 - F6

COLLEGES & UNIVERSITIES

FEATURE NAME	Address City, ZIP Code	PAGE-GRID
ARMSTRONG UNIV	2222 HAROLD WY, BERK, 94704	629 - G2
CALIFORNIA COLLEGE OF ARTS & CRAFTS	BROADWAY & COLLEGE AV, OAK, 94618	629 - J6
CALIFORNIA STATE UNIV EAST BAY	25800 CARLOS BEE BLVD, HAY, 94542	712 - C4
CHABOT COLLEGE	25555 HESPERIAN BLVD, HAY, 94545	711 - F5
COLLEGE OF ALAMEDA, THE	555 ATLANTIC AV, ALA, 94501	649 - F7
COLLEGE OF THE HOLY NAMES	3500 MOUNTAIN BLVD, OAK, 94602	650 - G4
GOLDEN GATE UNIV	536 MISSION ST, SF, 94105	648 - B5
HOLY REDEEMER COLLEGE	GOLF LINKS RD & GLENLY RD, OAK, 94605	671 - A3
LANEY COLLEGE	900 FALLON ST, OAK, 94607	649 - H5
LAS POSITAS COLLEGE	3033 COLLIER CANYON RD, LVMR, 94551	695 - D3
MERRITT COLLEGE	12500 CAMPUS DR, OAK, 94619	650 - J6
MERRITT, SAMUEL COLLEGE	370 HAWTHORNE AV, OAK, 94609	649 - H1
MILLS COLLEGE	5000 MACARTHUR BLVD, OAK, 94613	650 - H7
NEWARK OHLONE CTR - NEWARK CAMPUS	35753 CEDAR BLVD, NWK, 94560	752 - E4
OHLONE COLLEGE	43600 MISSION BLVD, FRMT, 94539	773 - J1
PATTEN COLLEGE	2433 COOLIDGE AV, OAK, 94601	650 - C6
SAINT ALBERTS COLLEGE	5890 BIRCH CT, OAK, 94618	629 - J5
UNIV OF CALIFORNIA BERKELEY	2200 UNIVERSITY AV, BERK, 94720	629 - J1

ENTERTAINMENT & SPORTS

FEATURE NAME	Address City, ZIP Code	PAGE-GRID
ALAMEDA COUNTY FAIRGROUNDS	PLEASANTON AV & ROSE AV, PLE, 94566	714 - C3
CHILDRENS FAIRYLAND	1520 LAKESIDE DR, OAK, 94610	649 - H3
DAVIE TENNIS STADIUM	198 OAK RD, PDMT, 94611	650 - B2
FUDENNA STADIUM	COUNTRY DR & FREMONT BLVD, FRMT, 94536	753 - A4
KAISER, H J CONV CTR	10 10TH ST, OAK, 94607	649 - H5
LONDON, JACK AQUATIC CTR	115 EMBARCADERO, OAK, 94607	649 - G6
MCAFEE COLISEUM	NIMITZ FRWY & HEGENBERGER RD, OAK, 94621	670 - F4
MILPITAS SPORT CTR	N PARK VICTORIA DR & CALAVERAS, MPS, 95035	794 - C6
MOSCONE CONV CTR	747 HOWARD ST, SF, 94103	648 - B6
OAKLAND ALAMEDA COUNTY ARENA	NIMITZ FRWY & HEGENBERGER RD, OAK, 94621	670 - E4
OAKLAND ALAMEDA CO COLISEUM COMPLEX	NIMITZ FRWY & HEGENBERGER RD, OAK, 94621	670 - E4
OAKLAND CONV & VISITORS AUTHORITY	550 10TH ST, OAK, 94607	649 - G4
RACE TRACK	ROSE AV & FAIR ST, PLE, 94566	714 - C3
SBC PARK	KING ST & 3RD ST, SF, 94107	648 - C7
UC BERKELEY MEM STADIUM	2200 UNIVERSITY AV, BERK, 94720	629 - J2

GOLF COURSES

FEATURE NAME	Address City, ZIP Code	PAGE-GRID
BRIDGES GC, THE	9000 S GALE RIDGE, SRMN, 94582	673 - G2
CANYON LAKES CC	640 BOLLINGER CANYON WY, SRMN, 94582	673 - F1
CASTLEWOOD CC	707 CASTLEWOOD DR, AlaC, 94566	714 - B7
CLAREMONT CC	5295 BROADWAY TER, OAK, 94611	630 - A6
CORICA, CHUCK MUNICIPAL GOLF COMPLEX	CLUBHOUSE MEMORIAL RD, ALA, 94502	670 - B6
COURSE AT WENTE VINEYARDS, THE	5050 ARROYO RD, AlaC, 94550	715 - J7
DUBLIN RANCH GC	5900 SIGNAL HILL DR, DBLN, 94568	694 - F1
FREMONT PARK GOLF AND PRACTICE CTR	39751 STEVENSON PL, FRMT, 94539	753 - D4
HAPPY VALLEY GC	8500 CLUBHOUSE DR, PLE, 94586	714 - G7
LAKE CHABOT GC	11450 GOLF LINKS RD, OAK, 94605	671 - E5
LAS POSITAS GC	917 CLUBHOUSE DR, LVMR, 94551	695 - A5
LEMA, TONY GC	13800 NEPTUNE DR, SLN, 94579	690 - H6
MARINA GC	13800 NEPTUNE DR, SLN, 94577	690 - G5
METROPOLITAN GOLF LINKS	10505 DOOLITTLE DR, OAK, 94621	690 - E1
MISSION HILLS OF HAYWARD GC	ARROWHEAD WY & MISSION BLVD, HAY, 94544	712 - D7
MOFFETT FIELD GC	MACON RD & MARRIAGE RD, SCIC, 94035	792 - D7
MONTCLAIR GC	2477 MONTEREY BLVD, OAK, 94602	650 - E2
MORAGA CC	1600 SAINT ANDREWS DR, MRGA, 94556	651 - C1
ORINDA CC	315 CM SOBRANTE, ORIN, 94563	610 - F6
PLEASANTON FAIRWAYS GC	ROSE AV & PLEASANTON AV, PLE, 94566	714 - D3
POPPY RIDGE GC	4280 GREENVILLE RD, AlaC, 94550	716 - H5
RUBY HILL GC	3400 W RUBY HILL DR, PLE, 94566	715 - B6
SAN RAMON ROYAL VISTA GC	9430 FIRCREST LN, SRMN, 94583	673 - G7
SEQUOYAH CC	4550 HEAFEY RD, OAK, 94605	671 - D2
SKYWEST GC	1401 GOLF COURSE RD, HAY, 94541	711 - C3
SPRINGTOWN GC	939 LARKSPUR DR, LVMR, 94551	696 - A3
SPRING VALLEY GC	3441 CALAVERAS RD, MPS, 95035	794 - F5
SUMMIT POINTE GC	1500 COUNTRY CLUB DR, MPS, 95035	794 - D4
SUNNY HILLS GC	49055 WARM SPRINGS BLVD, FRMT, 94539	793 - J3
SUNOL VALLEY GC	6900 MISSION RD, AlaC, 94586	734 - C7
TILDEN PARK GC	GRIZZLY PEAK BLVD & SHASTA RD, CCCo, 94708	610 - A6
WILLOW PARK GC	17007 REDWOOD RD, AlaC, 94546	671 - J7

HOSPITALS

FEATURE NAME	Address City, ZIP Code	PAGE-GRID
ALAMEDA COUNTY MED CTR	15400 FOOTHILL BLVD, AlaC, 94578	691 - E3
ALAMEDA CO MED CTR-HIGHLAND CAMPUS	1411 E 31ST ST, OAK, 94606	650 - B5
ALAMEDA HOSP	2070 CLINTON AV, ALA, 94501	669 - H2
BATES, ALTA MED CTR	2001 DWIGHT WY, BERK, 94704	629 - G2
BATES, ALTA MED CTR	2450 ASHBY AV, BERK, 94705	629 - J4
BATES, ALTA SUMMIT MED CTR	400 29TH ST, OAK, 94609	649 - H2
BATES, ALTA SUMMIT MED CTR-NORTH	350 HAWTHORNE AV, OAK, 94609	649 - H1
BATES, ALTA SUMMIT MED CTR-SOUTH	3100 SUMMIT ST, OAK, 94609	649 - H2
BATES, ALTA SUMMIT MED CTR-WEST	450 30TH ST, OAK, 94609	649 - G2
CHILDRENS HOSP OAKLAND	747 52ND ST, OAK, 94609	629 - G6
CHINESE HOSP	845 JACKSON ST, SF, 94108	648 - A5
EDEN MED CTR	20103 LAKE CHABOT RD, AlaC, 94546	691 - J5
FREMONT HOSP	39001 SUNDALE DR, FRMT, 94538	753 - B5
KAISER FOUNDATION	27400 HESPERIAN BLVD, HAY, 94545	711 - H7
KAISER FNDTN HOSP- EAST BAY CAMPUS	280 W MACARTHUR BLVD, OAK, 94611	649 - H1
KAISER PERMANENTE HOSP	39400 PASEO PADRE PKWY, FRMT, 94538	753 - B4
KINDRED HOSP - SAN LEANDRO	2800 BENEDICT DR, SLN, 94577	691 - D2
LAUREL GROVE HOSP	19933 LAKE CHABOT RD, AlaC, 94546	691 - H5
SAINT ROSE HOSP	27200 CALAROGA AV, HAY, 94545	711 - H7
SAN LEANDRO HOSP	13855 E 14TH ST, SLN, 94578	691 - C3
SAN RAMON REGL MED CTR	6001 NORRIS CANYON RD, SRMN, 94583	673 - E1
VALLEYCARE MED CTR	5555 W LAS POSITAS BLVD, PLE, 94588	694 - D6
VALLEYCARE MEM HOSP	1111 E STANLEY BLVD, LVMR, 94550	715 - F1
VETERANS AFFAIRS MED CTR	4951 ARROYO RD, AlaC, 94550	735 - H2
WASHINGTON TOWNSHIP HLTH CARE DIST	2000 MOWRY AV, FRMT, 94538	753 - B3

HOTELS

FEATURE NAME	Address City, ZIP Code	PAGE-GRID
AMERISUITES	3101 W WARREN AV, FRMT, 94538	773 - F7
ARGENT HOTEL	50 3RD ST, SF, 94103	648 - A6
BEST WESTERN AMERICANIA	121 7TH ST, SF, 94103	648 - A7
CAMPTON PLACE	340 STOCKTON ST, SF, 94108	648 - A5
CANDLEWOOD SUITES	5535 JOHNSON DR, PLE, 94588	694 - A5
CHANCELLOR HOTEL	433 POWELL ST, SF, 94102	648 - A5
CLAREMONT RESORT AND SPA, THE	41 TUNNEL RD, BERK, 94705	630 - A3
CLIFT HOTEL	495 GEARY ST, SF, 94102	648 - A6
COURTYARD BY MARRIOTT	18090 SAN RAMON VALLEY BLVD, SRMN, 94583	673 - D4
COURTYARD BY MARRIOTT	34905 NEWARK BLVD, NWK, 94560	752 - C4
COURTYARD BY MARRIOTT	47000 LAKEVIEW BLVD, FRMT, 94538	773 - F7
COURTYARD BY MARRIOTT EMERYVILLE	5555 SHELLMOUND ST, EMVL, 94608	629 - D6
COURTYARD BY MARRIOTT PLEASANTON	5059 HOPYARD RD, PLE, 94588	694 - B6

FEATURE NAME Address City, ZIP Code	PAGE-GRID
CROWNE PLAZA OAKLAND SOUTH-UNION CITY 32083 ALVARADO-NILES RD, UNC, 94587	732 - C5
CROWNE-PLAZA PLEASANTON 11950 DUBLIN CANYON RD, PLE, 94588	693 - G6
CROWNE PLAZA-UNION SQUARE 480 SUTTER ST, SF, 94108	648 - A5
DONATELLO, THE 501 POST ST, SF, 94102	648 - A6
DOUBLETREE HOTEL BERKELEY MARINA 200 MARINA BLVD, BERK, 94710	629 - C2
EMBASSY SUITES MILPITAS 901 CALAVERAS BLVD, MPS, 95035	794 - B6
FAIRMONT SAN FRANCISCO 950 MASON ST, SF, 94108	648 - A5
FOUR POINTS BY SHERATON 1603 POWELL ST, EMVL, 94608	629 - E6
FOUR POINTS HOTEL BY SHERATON 5115 HOPYARD RD, PLE, 94588	694 - B5
FREMONT MARRIOTT HOTEL 46100 LANDING PKWY, FRMT, 94538	773 - E6
GALLERIA PARK HOTEL 191 SUTTER ST, SF, 94108	648 - A5
GRAND HYATT SAN FRANCISCO 345 STOCKTON ST, SF, 94108	648 - A5
HANDLERY UNION SQUARE, THE 351 GEARY ST, SF, 94102	648 - A6
HILTON GARDEN INN 30 RANCH DR, MPS, 95035	793 - H7
HILTON NEWARK-FREMONT HOTEL 39900 BALENTINE DR, NWK, 94560	773 - A1
HILTON OAKLAND 1 HEGENBERGER RD, OAK, 94621	670 - E7
HILTON PLEASANTON AT THE CLUB 7050 JOHNSON DR, PLE, 94588	693 - J5
HOLIDAY INN 720 LAS FLORES RD, LVMR, 94551	696 - B5
HOLIDAY INN BAY BRIDGE 1800 POWELL ST, EMVL, 94608	629 - D6
HOLIDAY INN-FINANCIAL DIST 750 KEARNY ST, SF, 94111	648 - A5
HOLIDAY INN-OAKLAND 500 HEGENBERGER RD, OAK, 94621	670 - F6
HOPKINS, MARK HOTEL 1 NOB HILL CIR, SF, 94108	648 - A5
HOTEL NIKKO 222 MASON ST, SF, 94102	648 - A6
HOTEL PALOMAR 12 4TH ST, SF, 94103	648 - A6
HYATT REGENCY SAN FRANCISCO 5 EMBARCADERO CTR, SF, 94111	648 - C5
MANDARIN ORIENTAL 222 SANSOME ST, SF, 94104	648 - B5
MARINES MEM CLUB/HOTEL 609 SUTTER ST, SF, 94102	648 - A5
MARRIOTT-SAN FRANCISCO 55 4TH ST, SF, 94103	648 - A6
OAKLAND MARRIOTT 1001 BROADWAY, OAK, 94607	649 - G4
PAN PACIFIC 500 POST ST, SF, 94102	648 - A6
PARK HYATT 333 BATTERY ST, SF, 94104	648 - B5
PARK PLAZA HOTEL 150 HEGENBERGER RD, OAK, 94621	670 - F7
PRESCOTT HOTEL, THE 545 POST ST, SF, 94102	648 - A6
RADISSON DUBLIN 6680 REGIONAL ST, DBLN, 94568	693 - G5
RAMADA INN 920 UNIVERSITY AV, BERK, 94710	629 - D2
RENAISSANCE PARC 55 HOTEL 55 CYRIL MAGNIN ST, SF, 94102	648 - A6
RENAISSANCE STANFORD COURT HOTEL 905 CALIFORNIA ST, SF, 94108	648 - A5
RESIDENCE INN 1501 CALIFORNIA CIR, MPS, 95035	793 - H4
RESIDENCE INN 5400 FARWELL PL, FRMT, 94536	752 - H7
RESIDENCE INN BY MARRIOTT 11900 DUBLIN CANYON RD, PLE, 94588	693 - G5
RITZ CARLTON SAN FRANCISCO 600 STOCKTON ST, SF, 94108	648 - A5
SAN FRANCISCO HILTON AND TOWERS 333 OFARRELL ST, SF, 94102	648 - A6
SAN RAMON MARRIOTT AT BISHOP RANCH 2600 BISHOP DR, SRMN, 94583	673 - D3
SHERATON-PALACE HOTEL 2 NEW MONTGOMERY ST, SF, 94105	648 - B5
SIR FRANCIS DRAKE 450 POWELL ST, SF, 94108	648 - A5
VILLA FLORENCE 225 POWELL ST, SF, 94102	648 - A6
WATERFRONT PLAZA HOTEL 10 WASHINGTON ST, OAK, 94607	649 - F5
WESTIN SAINT FRANCIS 335 POWELL ST, SF, 94102	648 - A6
WOODFIN SUITE HOTEL 5800 SHELLMOUND ST, EMVL, 94608	629 - E6
WEST SAN FRANCISCO HOTEL 181 3RD ST, SF, 94103	648 - B6
WYNDHAM GARDEN HOTEL PLEASANTON 5990 STONERIDGE MALL RD, PLE, 94588	693 - H5

LIBRARIES

FEATURE NAME Address City, ZIP Code	PAGE-GRID
ALAMEDA MAIN 2200 CENTRAL AV, ALA, 94501	669 - J2
ALBANY 1247 MARIN AV, ALB, 94706	609 - E6
ASIAN BRANCH 388 9TH ST, OAK, 94607	649 - G4
BANCROFT UC BERKELEY, BERK, 94720	629 - H1
BAY FARM ISLAND BRANCH 3221 MECARTNEY RD, ALA, 94502	670 - A6
BERKELEY BRANCH LIBRARY CLAREMONT 2940 BENVENUE AV, BERK, 94705	629 - J4
BERKELEY BRANCH LIBRARY NORTH 1170 THE ALAMEDA, BERK, 94707	609 - G6
BERKELEY BRANCH LIBRARY SOUTH 1901 RUSSELL ST, BERK, 94703	629 - G4
BERKELEY BRANCH LIBRARY WEST 1125 UNIVERSITY AV, BERK, 94702	629 - E2
BERKELEY CENTRAL 2090 KITTREDGE ST, BERK, 94704	629 - G2
BROOKFIELD 9255 EDES AV, OAK, 94603	670 - G6
BUSINESS 2400 STEVENSON BLVD, FRMT, 94538	753 - C4
CASTRO VALLEY 20055 REDWOOD RD, AlaC, 94546	692 - A5
CENTERVILLE 3801 NICOLET AV, FRMT, 94536	752 - F2
CHAVEZ, CESAR E 3301 E 12TH ST, OAK, 94601	670 - C1
CHINATOWN 1135 POWELL ST, SF, 94108	648 - A5
CIVIC CENTER 1000 S LIVERMORE AV, LVMR, 94550	715 - J2
DIMOND BRANCH 3565 FRUITVALE AV, OAK, 94602	650 - D4
DOE UC BERKELEY, BERK, 94720	629 - H1
DUBLIN 200 CIVIC PZ, DBLN, 94568	693 - J4
EASTMONT BRANCH EASTMONT MALL-2ND FLOOR, OAK, 94605	670 - H2
EL CERRITO 6510 STOCKTON AV, ELCR, 94530	609 - D3
ELMHURST BRANCH 1427 88TH AV, OAK, 94621	670 - H4
FREMONT MAIN 2400 STEVENSON BLVD, FRMT, 94538	753 - C4
GOLDEN GATE BRANCH 5606 SAN PABLO AV, OAK, 94608	629 - F6
HAYWARD 835 C ST, HAY, 94541	711 - J2
IRVINGTON 41825 GREENPARK DR, FRMT, 94538	773 - D1
KENSINGTON 61 ARLINGTON AV, CCCo, 94708	609 - F3
KING, MARTIN LUTHER JR 6833 E INTERNATIONAL BLVD, OAK, 94621	670 - G3
LAKEVIEW BRANCH 550 EL EMBARCADERO, OAK, 94610	649 - J3
LAW 224 W WINTON AV, HAY, 94544	711 - J3
MANOR BRANCH 1307 MANOR BLVD, SLN, 94579	691 - A6
MELROSE BRANCH 4805 FOOTHILL BLVD, OAK, 94601	670 - E1
MILPITAS COMMUNITY 40 N MILPITAS BLVD, MPS, 95035	794 - A7
MOFFITT UC BERKELEY, BERK, 94720	629 - H1
MONTCLAIR BRANCH 1687 MOUNTAIN BLVD, OAK, 94611	630 - D7
MULFORD MARINA BRANCH 13699 AURORA DR, SLN, 94577	690 - G5
NEWARK 6300 CIVIC TERRACE AV, NWK, 94560	752 - E6
NILES READING CTR 150 I ST, FRMT, 94536	753 - B1
OAKLAND MAIN 125 14TH ST, OAK, 94612	649 - H4
ORINDA 24 ORINDA WY, ORIN, 94563	610 - G7
PIEDMONT AVENUE BRANCH 160 41ST ST, OAK, 94611	649 - J1
PLEASANTON 400 OLD BERNAL AV, PLE, 94566	714 - D4
RINCON BRANCH 725 RINCON AV, LVMR, 94551	695 - F7
ROCKRIDGE BRANCH 5366 COLLEGE AV, OAK, 94618	629 - J6
SAN LEANDRO PUBLIC 300 ESTUDILLO AV, SLN, 94577	691 - A1
SAN LORENZO 395 PAS GRANDE, AlaC, 94580	691 - D7
SAN RAMON 100 MONTGOMERY ST, SRMN, 94583	673 - F3
SOUTH BRANCH 14799 E 14TH ST, SLN, 94578	691 - D3
SPRINGTOWN BRANCH 998 BLUEBELL DR, LVMR, 94551	696 - B4
TEMESCAL BRANCH 5205 TELEGRAPH AV, OAK, 94609	629 - H6
TREASURE ISLAND 9TH ST & AVE I, SF, 94130	648 - E1
UNION CITY 34007 ALVARADO-NILES RD, UNC, 94587	732 - F6
WEEKES, GEORGE BRANCH 27300 PATRICK AV, HAY, 94544	711 - J7
WEST END BRANCH 788 SANTA CLARA AV, ALA, 94501	669 - G1
WEST OAKLAND BRANCH 1801 ADELINE ST, OAK, 94607	649 - E2

MILITARY INSTALLATIONS

FEATURE NAME Address City, ZIP Code	PAGE-GRID
AIR NATIONAL GUARD W WINTON AV, HAY, 94545	711 - E4
AMES RESEARCH CTR R T JONES RD & CLARK RD, MTVW, 94043	792 - B7
COAST GUARD ALAMEDA HARBOR, ALA, 94501	649 - J6
MOFFETT FEDERAL AIRFIELD FAIRCHILD DR & DAILEY RD, SUNV, 94089	792 - B7
PARKS RESERVE FORCES TRAINING AREA DUBLIN BLVD & ARNOLD RD, DBLN, 94568	694 - B1
US COAST GUARD STA SF, 94130	648 - F3
US GOVERNMENT RESERVE HARTFORD AV & LORRAINE RD, AlaC, 94551	695 - J2
US NAVAL RESERVE 2101 CLEMENT AV, ALA, 94501	670 - A1

MUSEUMS

FEATURE NAME Address City, ZIP Code	PAGE-GRID
AFRICAN AMERICAN MUS & LIB 659 14TH ST, OAK, 94612	649 - F3
ALAMEDA MUS 2324 ALAMEDA AV, ALA, 94501	670 - A2
CALIFORNIA HIST SOCIETY MUS 678 MISSION ST, SF, 94103	648 - B6
HAYWARD HIST MUS 22701 MAIN ST, HAY, 94541	711 - J1
NATURAL SCIENCE CTR 553 BELLEVUE AV, OAK, 94610	649 - J3
NILES CANYON RAILWAY MUS 6 KILKARE RD, AlaC, 94586	734 - C5
OAKLAND MUS OF CALIFORNIA 1000 OAK ST, OAK, 94607	649 - H4
PACIFIC HERITAGE MUS 608 COMMERCIAL ST, SF, 94111	648 - A5
PARDEE HOME MUS 672 11TH ST, OAK, 94607	649 - F4
SAN FRANCISCO MUS OF MODERN ART 151 3RD ST, SF, 94103	648 - B6
STOREFRONT MUS 486 9TH ST, OAK, 94607	649 - G4
USS HORNET MUS PIER 3 ALAMEDA POINT, ALA, 94501	669 - C1
WESTERN AEROSPACE MUS 8260 EARNHART RD, OAK, 94621	670 - D7
YERBA BUENA CTR FOR THE ARTS 701 MISSION ST, SF, 94103	648 - B6

OPEN SPACE PRESERVES

FEATURE NAME Address City, ZIP Code	PAGE-GRID
ARDENWOOD REGL PRESERVE ARDENWOOD BLVD & 84 FRWY, FRMT, 94555	752 - C3
BAYLANDS NATURE PRESERVE EMBARCADERO RD, EPA, 94303	771 - D7
BEACONSFIELD OPEN SPACE BEACONSFIELD PL, OAK, 94611	650 - F1
BISHOP RANCH REGL OPEN SPACE MORGAN DR, CCCo, 94583	673 - B4
CLAREMONT CANYON REGL PRESERVE CLAREMONT AV, OAK, 94705	630 - A2
DOUGHERTY HILLS OPEN SPACE AMADOR VLY BL & STAGECOACH RD, DBLN, 94568	693 - J1
EDWARDS, DON SF BAY NATL WLDLF REFUGE HOPE ST & ELIZABETH ST, SJS, 95002	793 - B3
GRIZZLY PEAK OPEN SPACE TUNNEL RD, OAK, 94611	630 - C3
HILLSIDE NATURAL AREA MOESER LN, ELCR, 94530	609 - C1
HUCKLEBERRY BOTANIC REGL RESERVE PINEHURST RD, CCCo, 94516	630 - G5
KING ESTATE OPEN SPACE CREST AV & FONTAINE ST, OAK, 94605	671 - A2
LAS TRAMPAS REGL WILDERNESS BOLLINGER CANYON RD, CCCo, 94583	652 - H4
LEONA CANYON REGL OPEN SPACE PRESERVE CAMPUS DR, OAK, 94605	651 - A6
MISSION PEAK REGL PRESERVE OFF MILL CREEK ROAD, FRMT, 94539	774 - B2
OHLONE REGL WILDERNESS NEAR LAKE DEL VALLE, AlaC, 94550	755 - G5
RAVENSWOOD OPEN SPACE PRESERVE HWY 84 & UNIVERSITY AV, MLPK, 94303	771 - D4
SIBLEY VOLCANIC REGL PRESERVE SKYLINE BLVD, CCCo, 94563	630 - E4
SUNOL REGL WILDERNESS GEARY RD, AlaC, 94586	774 - F2
TILDEN NATURE STUDY AREA CENTRAL PARK DR, CCCo, 94708	609 - G2
UNIVERSITY BOTANICAL GARDENS CENTENNIAL DR, OAK, 94720	630 - B1

PARK & RIDE

FEATURE NAME Address City, ZIP Code	PAGE-GRID
I-680 & MISSION BLVD I-680 & MISSION BLVD, FRMT, 94539	753 - H6
MISSION BLVD MISSION BLVD & CALLERY CT, FRMT, 94539	753 - G5
PARK & RIDE 7295 JOHNSON DR, PLE, 94588	693 - J6
PARK & RIDE 7TH & LINDEN ST, OAK, 94607	649 - E4
PARK & RIDE 7TH ST & UNION ST, OAK, 94607	649 - E3
PARK & RIDE ARDENWOOD BLVD & 84 FRWY, FRMT, 94555	752 - C4
PARK & RIDE BOLLINGER CANYON RD & 680 FRWY, SRMN, 94583	673 - D4
PARK & RIDE CAMINO RAMON & EXECUTIVE PKWY, SRMN, 94583	673 - E2
PARK & RIDE CHABOT DR & OWENS DR, PLE, 94588	694 - B5
PARK & RIDE E AIRWAY BL & RUTAN DR, LVMR, 94551	695 - D5
PARK & RIDE FOLGER AV & 7TH ST, BERK, 94710	629 - E4
PARK & RIDE FOOTHILL BLVD & JOHN DR, AlaC, 94546	691 - H6
PARK & RIDE GATEWAY BLVD & 24 FRWY, ORIN, 94563	630 - F2
PARK & RIDE I-580 & CENTER ST, AlaC, 94546	692 - B6
PARK & RIDE I-580 & FRUITVALE AV, OAK, 94602	650 - D5
PARK & RIDE ISLAND DR & DOOLITTLE DR, ALA, 94502	670 - B5
PARK & RIDE PORTOLA AV & ALVISO PL, LVMR, 94551	695 - F6
PARK & RIDE REDWOOD RD & MOUNTAIN BLVD, OAK, 94619	650 - H5
PARK & RIDE S MAIN ST & CALAVERAS BL, MPS, 95035	794 - A7
THORNTON AV THORNTON AV & CABRILLO DR, FRMT, 94536	752 - G4

PARKS & RECREATION

FEATURE NAME Address City, ZIP Code	PAGE-GRID
25TH ST MINI PK, OAK	649 - G2
61ST ST PK, EMVL	629 - E5
85TH AVENUE MINI PK, OAK	670 - H4
88TH AVENUE MINI PK, OAK	670 - H4
ADAMS PK, OAK	649 - H3
AITKEN, KENNETH C. SR & COMM CTR, AlaC	692 - A2
ALAMEDA PK, ALA	669 - D1
ALAMO CREEK PK, DBLN	694 - A2
ALBANY HILL PK, ALB	609 - C5
ALLENDALE REC CTR, OAK	650 - E6
ALMOND PK, LVMR	716 - A2
ALVARADO PK, UNC	731 - J5
ALVISO PK, SJS	793 - C7
ALVISO ADOBE PK, PLE	713 - J3
AMADOR VALLEY COMM PK, PLE	714 - E2
AMARAL PK, PLE	694 - F6
ANDERSON, BOOKER T JR PK, RCH	609 - A2
ARDENWOOD TRAIL, FRMT	752 - B1
ARLINGTON PK, ELCR	609 - E1
ARMSTRONG, NEIL PK, SRMN	673 - F6
ARROYO PK, UNC	732 - G7
ARROYO AGUA CALIENTE PK, FRMT	773 - G3
ARROYO VIEJO REC AREA, OAK	670 - H3
ASHLAND PK, AlaC	691 - F5
ASH STREET PK, NWK	772 - D1
ATHAN DOWNS, SRMN	673 - E5
ATHOL PLAZA, OAK	649 - J4
AUGUSTIN-BERNAL PK, PLE	713 - J6
AUGUSTINE, ALBERT PK, MPS	794 - A3
AVENUE TERRACE PK, OAK	650 - F4
AZEVADA PK, FRMT	752 - J7
BAER, MAX PK, LVMR	715 - D3
BAY TREES PK, AlaC	692 - C4
BEE, CARLOS PK, AlaC	691 - J7
BEGIN PLAZA, OAK	649 - G3
BELLA VISTA REC AREA, OAK	650 - A4
BELLINGHAM SQUARE PK, SRMN	674 - B3
BENASTON AQUATIC CTR, PLE	714 - E2
BERKELEY AQUATIC PK, BERK	629 - D4
BETHANY RESERVOIR STATE REC AREA, AlaC	677 - H2
BICENTENNIAL PK, PLE	694 - E7
BIDWELL PK, HAY	732 - D2
BIG TREES PK, LVMR	696 - C7
BIRCHFIELD, KENNETH MEM PK, HAY	711 - G4
BIRCH GROVE PK, NWK	752 - G7
BLACOW PK, FRMT	753 - C7
BOEDDEKER PK, SF	648 - A6
BOLLINGER CANYON PK, SRMN	673 - C4
BONAIRE PK, SLN	690 - J5
BOONE ACRES PK, SRMN	673 - F7
BOOSTER PK, FRMT	773 - J7
BOWLING GREENS, BERK	629 - F2
BRAXTON, ABRAHAM PK, RCH	609 - B1
BRAY COMMONS, DBLN	694 - F4
BRIDGEPOINT PK, NWK	752 - C6
BRIONES REGL PK, CCCo	610 - J1
BROOKDALE PK, OAK	650 - E7
BROOKFIELD VILLAGE PK, OAK	670 - F6
BROOKVALE PK, FRMT	752 - G1
BUENA VISTA PK, FRMT	753 - F4
BURCKHALTER PK, OAK	670 - J1
BUSHROD PK, OAK	629 - H5

FEATURE NAME Address City, ZIP Code	PAGE-GRID
BYINGTON PK, NWK	752 - F6
CABRILLO TRAIL, FRMT	752 - F2
CAFFODIO, AL PK, LVMR	695 - E6
CALIFORNIA TERRACE PK, FRMT	732 - J6
CAMPBELL, MARSTON PK, OAK	649 - F3
CAMP OHLONE, AlaC (SEE PAGE 755)	776 - A6
CANNERY PK, HAY	711 - G2
CANN, WILLIAM MEM PK, UNC	732 - D6
CANYON VIEW PK, HAY	712 - E4
CANZIANO, BRUNO PK, LVMR	716 - C2
CARDOZA PK, MPS	794 - C6
CARNEGIE PK, LVMR	715 - G1
CARNEGIE STATE VEHICULAR REC AREA, SJCo- (SEE PAGE 717)	738 - B1
CARNEY, TYRONE PK, OAK	670 - H7
CARTER, VERDESE PK, OAK	670 - J5
CASA CERRITO REC CTR, ELCR	609 - D2
CASA VERDE PK, UNC	732 - B5
CASTRO PK, ELCR	609 - C2
CASTRO VALLEY COMM PK, AlaC	691 - H3
CEDAR ROSE PK, BERK	629 - E1
CENTENNIAL PK, HAY	711 - G3
CENTENNIAL PK, LVMR	715 - F1
CENTENNIAL PK, PLE	714 - D5
CENTENNIAL PK, SRMN	693 - F1
CENTERVILLE PK, FRMT	753 - A4
CENTRAL PK, RCH	609 - C4
CENTRAL RESERVOIR REC AREA, OAK	650 - C5
CERRITO VISTA PK, ELCR	609 - D2
CHABOT, ANTHONY REGL PK, AlaC	671 - F3
CHABOT PK, OAK	671 - D7
CHAVEZ, CESAR STATE PK, BERK	629 - B1
CHERRY GROVE PK, SLN	690 - J2
CHERRYLAND PK, AlaC	711 - F1
CHRISTENSEN PK, LVMR	696 - C2
CHRISTIE PK, EMVL	629 - D5
CIVIC PK, PLE	714 - D4
CIVIC CTR PK, NWK	752 - E6
CLARK, BILL PK, LVMR	696 - C4
CLEVELAND PK, SLN	690 - H1
CLINTON SQUARE, OAK	649 - J5
CODORNICES PLGD, BERK	609 - H7
COLBY PK, OAK	629 - J5
COLISEUM GARDENS, OAK	670 - F3
COLLEGE HEIGHTS PK, HAY	712 - D4
COLUMBIAN GARDENS, OAK	670 - F7
CONCORDIA PK, OAK	670 - G1
CONTEMPO PK, UNC	732 - A6
COUNTRY CLUB PK, SRMN	693 - G1
COYOTE CREEK PK, SRMN	673 - H1
COYOTE CROSSING PK, SRMN	673 - G1
COYOTE HILLS REGL PK, FRMT	751 - H3
CRAGMONT PK, BERK	609 - H6
CRANDALL CREEK PK, FRMT	752 - E1
CREEKSIDE PK, ELCR	609 - C5
CREEKSIDE PK, PLE	694 - D6
CRESCENT PK CTR, RCH	609 - A2
CROCKER PK, PDMT	650 - C2
CULL CANYON REGL REC AREA, AlaC	672 - C7
DAVENPORT MINI PK, EMVL	629 - C6
DAYTON PLGD, SLN	691 - A6
DE ANZA PK, HAY	711 - J1
DECOTO PLAZA, UNC	732 - G4
DEEP CREEK PK, FRMT	752 - C1
DEERVIEW PK, AlaC	692 - C2
DE FREMERY PK, OAK	649 - E3
DEL MAR DOG PK, SRMN	673 - G6
DEL PRADO PK, PLE	714 - A2
DEL REY PK, AlaC	711 - C2
DELUCCHI PK, PLE	714 - E4
DIMOND PK, OAK	650 - D4
DISNEY, WALT PK, SRMN	673 - G6
DIXON LANDING PK, MPS	793 - J4
DOGWOOD PK, LVMR	695 - E7
DOLAN PK, DBLN	693 - F3
DON CASTRO REGL REC AREA, AlaC	692 - C6
DOOLAN PK, LVMR	695 - H7
DRACENA PK, PDMT	630 - A7
DRY CREEK PIONEER REGL PK, UNC	712 - G7
DUBLIN SPORTS GROUNDS, DBLN	693 - J4
DUBLIN SWIM CTR, DBLN	693 - H2
DURANT PK, OAK	649 - G2
EAST AVENUE PK, AlaC	712 - D2
EAST BRANCH PK, SRMN	674 - B4
EASTSHORE STATE PK, ALB	609 - B6
EASTSHORE STATE PK, EMVL	629 - B6
EASTSHORE STATE PK, BERK	629 - C2
EDENDALE PK, AlaC	691 - E5
EDEN GREENWAY, HAY	711 - J4
ELDRIDGE PK, HAY	711 - J6
EL PADRO PK, LVMR	715 - E3
EL RANCHO VERDE PK, HAY	732 - F2
EMERALD GLEN PK, DBLN	694 - E3
ESTUARY PK, OAK	649 - G6
EUCALYPTUS GROVE PK, NWK	772 - H1
FAIRFIELD, TED PK, DBLN	694 - F2
FAIRLANDS PK, PLE	694 - E6
FAIRMONT PK, ELCR	609 - D3
FAIRMONT LINEAR PK, AlaC	691 - E4
FAIRMONT TERRACE PK, AlaC	691 - F3
FAIRVIEW PK, AlaC	692 - C7
FAIRWAY GREENS PK, HAY	732 - E1
FARELL, JACK PK, EPA	771 - C7
FAWN HILLS PK, PLE	714 - B5
FISHER, FRANK PK, FRMT	752 - C3
FIVE CANYONS PK, AlaC	712 - F1
FLOOD, CURT FIELD, OAK	650 - D5
FLORESTA PK, SLN	691 - B5
FOOTHILL PK, MPS	794 - D7
FOOTHILL MEADOWS, OAK	650 - D7
FRANKLIN CTR, OAK	649 - J5
FRANKLIN PK, ALA	669 - H2
FREMONT CENTRAL PK, FRMT	753 - D4
FRUITVALE BRIDGE PK, OAK	670 - B2
FRUITVALE PLAZA, OAK	670 - D1
GANSBERGER PK, HAY	711 - G6
GARBER PK, OAK	630 - B3
GARFIELD PK, OAK	650 - B6
GARIN REGL PK, AlaC	712 - F7
GILL, PETER T PK, MPS	794 - B6
GLEN ECHO CREEK PK, OAK	649 - J1
GODFREY PK, ALA	670 - B6
GOLDEN GATE PK, OAK	629 - F5
GOMES PK, FRMT	753 - E4
GREEN BELT PK, HAY	712 - E3
GREENMAN RECREATIONAL FIELD, OAK	670 - F3
GREENRIDGE PK, AlaC	692 - E2
GREENVILLE NORTH PK, LVMR	696 - B3
GREENWOOD PK, HAY	711 - E5
GRIMMER PK, FRMT	773 - E2
GROVE REC CTR, BERK	629 - G3
GROVE SHAFTER PK, OAK	649 - G1
HAGEMANN PK, LVMR	715 - E1
HALCYON PK, SLN	691 - C3
HALL MEM PK, MPS	793 - J5
HALL RANCH PK, UNC	731 - J6
HANSEN PK, PLE	714 - C2
HANSEN PK, LVMR	715 - F1
HARDING PK, ELCR	609 - E4
HARDY PK, OAK	629 - J5

FEATURE NAME Address City, ZIP Code	PAGE-GRID
HARRINGTON, DOC PK, ALA	670 - A7
HARRISON SQUARE, OAK	649 - G5
HARVEST PK, PLE	714 - D2
HARVEY, SYLVESTER P PK, FRMT	732 - B6
HAVENS PLGD, PDMT	650 - B1
HAYWARD MEM PK, HAY	712 - B2
HAYWARD REGL SHORELINE, HAY	711 - A6
HEATHERLARK PK, PLE	714 - B1
HEATH PK, SLN	691 - C3
HELLMAN REC AREA, OAK	671 - C5
HERMAN, JUSTIN PLAZA, SF	648 - B5
HIDDEN CREST PK, SRMN	673 - J1
HIDDEN HILLS PK, SRMN	674 - C3
HIDDEN VALLEY PK, SRMN	674 - D3
HILLCREST KNOLLS PK, AlaC	691 - E3
HILLSIDE NATURAL AREA, ELCR	609 - D2
HINKEL, J PK, BERK	609 - G5
HOLLY MINI PK, OAK	670 - J5
HOLMES PK, LVMR	715 - F4
HORSESHOE PK, BERK	629 - B2
HUBER PK, ELCR	609 - E3
INDEPENDENCE PK, LVMR	715 - F5
INDIAN ROCK PK, BERK	609 - G6
IRVINGTON PK, FRMT	773 - D1
IRVINGTON PLAZA PK, FRMT	753 - D7
JACKSON PK, ALA	670 - A3
JALQUIN VISTA PK, HAY	712 - G4
JAPANESE GARDENS, HAY	691 - J7
JEFFERSON PLGD, SLN	691 - C3
JEFFERSON SQUARE REC CTR, OAK	649 - F4
JOHNSON, WADE PK, OAK	649 - E3
JONES, DAVID PK, FRMT	732 - C7
KENNEDY, CHARLES F PK, UNC	732 - G6
KENNEDY, JOHN F PK, HAY	711 - E2
KENNEDY, JOHN F PK, RCH	609 - A1
KENNEDY TRACT PK, OAK	650 - B7
KENNEY, JAMES REC CTR, BERK	629 - D1
KING, M L JR REGIONAL SHORELINE, OAK	670 - D3
KNOTT, LESTER J PK, LVMR	695 - J6
KNOWLAND PK, OAK	671 - C4
KOLB PK, DBLN	693 - H2
KOTTINGER PK, PLE	714 - F4
KOTTINGER VILLAGE PK, PLE	714 - F3
KRUSI PK, ALA	670 - A4
LAFAYETTE SQUARE, OAK	649 - F4
LAKE DEL VALLE STATE REC AREA, AlaC	735 - H2
LAKE MERRITT CHANNEL PK, OAK	649 - H5
LAKERIDGE PK, AlaC	692 - C7
LAKESHORE PK, NWK	752 - E4
LAKE SHORE PK, OAK	649 - J3
LAKESIDE PK, OAK	649 - H3
LAKE TEMESCAL REGL REC AREA, OAK	630 - C5
LEVIN, ED R COUNTY PK, SCIC	774 - E7
LEWELLING PLGD, SLN	691 - B6
LEYDECKER PK, ALA	670 - A6
LIMERICK PK, SRMN	674 - C4
LINCOLN PK, ALA	670 - B3
LINCOLN SQUARE REC CTR, OAK	649 - G4
LINDEN COMM PK, OAK	629 - G7
LITTLE HILLS RANCH REGL REC AREA, CCCo	652 - E3
LITTLEJOHN PK, ALA	649 - H7
LIVE OAK REC CTR, BERK	609 - G7
LIVERMORE DOWNS PK, LVMR	695 - F6
LIVERMORE, ROBERT PK, LVMR	716 - A1
LONE TREE CREEK PK, FRMT	793 - J1
LONGFELLOW PK, ALA	669 - F1
LONGWOOD PK, HAY	711 - F3
LOS CERRITOS COMM PK, FRMT	752 - G2
LOWELL PK, OAK	649 - E3
LOWRY PK, FRMT	732 - C7
LYONS FIELD PK, OAK	670 - J5
MACGREGOR PLAY FIELDS, NWK	752 - D4
MADEIRA PK, LVMR	695 - H7
MADISON PK, OAK	649 - G5
MAITLAND, R HENRY PK, LVMR	695 - E6
MANDANA PLAZA, OAK	650 - A3
MANDELA PARKWAY, OAK	649 - E2
MANZANITA REC CTR, OAK	650 - B5
MAPE PK, DBLN	693 - G4
MARINA PK, SLN	690 - G5
MARINA PK, EMVL	629 - B6
MARINI PLAZA, SF	648 - 0
MARSHALL PK, FRMT	773 - B1
MAXWELL PK, OAK	650 - F7
MAYHEWS LANDING PK, NWK	752 - D6
MCCARTNEY PK, SLN	671 - A7
MCCLYMONDS MINI PK, OAK	649 - F2
MCCONAGHY PK, AlaC	711 - E1
MCCREA MEM PK, OAK	650 - G6
MCKINLEY PK, ALA	670 - A1
MCKINLEY PK, PLE	714 - F4
MCKINLEY PLGD, SLN	691 - B2
MEADOWLARK PK, PLE	714 - A3
MEADOWS PK, PLE	694 - G6
MEEK PK, AlaC	691 - F7
MEM PK, ALB	609 - E5
MEM PK, SLN	671 - B7
MEM PK, SRMN	673 - C4
MEM PK, OAK	649 - D3
MICHIGAN PK, BERK	609 - G4
MIDDLE HARBOR SHORELINE PK, OAK	649 - A3
MILL CREEK HOLLOW, SRMN	673 - B1
MILLER, JOAQUIN PK, OAK	650 - G3
MILPITAS DOG PK, MPS	794 - E3
MIRABEAU PK, NWK	752 - C5
MISSION CREEK PK, SF	648 - B7
MISSION HILLS PK, PLE	714 - E5
MISSION SAN JOSE BICENTENNIAL PK, FRMT	753 - H7
MISSION SAN JOSE PK, FRMT	753 - G5
MOCHO PK, LVMR	715 - F2
MODEL AIRPLANE FIELD, ALA	670 - B5
MOLLER PK, PLE	693 - H7
MONKEY ISLAND PK, BERK	630 - A3
MONTCLAIR REC CTR, OAK	630 - D7
MONTEVIDEO PK, SRMN	673 - F4
MORGAN PLAZA, OAK	650 - B5
MORRIS, MERVIN PK, AlaC	711 - C1
MOSSWOOD PK, OAK	649 - H1
MT EDEN PK, HAY	711 - G7
MUIRWOOD PK, PLE	693 - J7
MUSICK PK, NWK	752 - E5
NEPTUNE PK, ALA	649 - F7
NEWARK COMM PK, NWK	752 - D4
NIELSEN PK, PLE	694 - E7
NILES COMM PK, FRMT	753 - B1
NISSEN, MAY PK, LVMR	695 - F7
NOLL PK, FRMT	753 - B6
NORDVIK PK, FRMT	752 - B3
NORTH BEACH PLGD & POOL, SF	648 - A4
NORTHFRONT PK, LVMR	696 - D4
NORTH GATE COMM PK, FRMT	732 - D7
NORTHGATE TRAIL, FRMT	732 - E7
NORTH LIVERMORE PK, LVMR	696 - A3
NORTH OAKLAND REGL SPORTS CTR, OAK	630 - D4
NUESTRO PARQUECITO, HAY	712 - B5
OAK PK, OAK	649 - H2
OAK GLEN PK, OAK	649 - H1
OAKHILL PK, PLE	713 - J1
OAKKNOLL PIONEER MEM PK, LVMR	715 - E1
OAKPORT PK, OAK	670 - D3

FEATURE NAME Address City, ZIP Code	PAGE-GRID
OCEAN VIEW PK, ALB	609 - D6
OFFICER WILKINS PK, OAK	670 - H5
OGAWA PLAZA, OAK	649 - G3
OHLONE PK, BERK	629 - F1
OLD HIGHLANDS PK, HAY	712 - D3
OLD MISSION PK, FRMT	773 - H1
OLD RANCH PK, SRMN	673 - J7
OLIVER, ALDEN E SPORTS PK, HAY	731 - H3
OLIVER, GORDON E SHORES PK, HAY	731 G3
ORINDA COMM PK, ORIN	610 - G7
ORINDA SPORTS FIELD, ORIN	610 - E5
ORLOFF PK, PLE	714 - E1
OSTRANDER PK, OAK	630 - B5
OWENS PLAZA PK, PLE	694 - C5
OYSTER BAY REGL SHORELINE, SLN	690 - E3
PACIFIC RECREATION COMPLEX, SLN	691 - A3
PALMA CEIA PK, HAY	711 - H7
PALM AVENUE PK, FRMT	753 - G6
PALOMARES HILLS PK, AlaC	692 - F2
PARK BOULEVARD PLAZA, OAK	649 - J4
PARKWAY, LVMR	715 - F2
PARSONS PK, AlaC	691 - J2
PATTERSON PK, FRMT	752 - E3
PAUL PK, ORIN	630 - H1
PAYNE, WILLIAM SPORTS PK, LVMR	696 - D6
PECOT PK, MPS	794 - A3
PENKE, CHRISTOPHER PK, HAY	731 - H1
PERALTA PK, OAK	649 - H5
PERALTA/DUSTERBERRY PK, FRMT	752 - H4
PERALTA HACIENDA PK, OAK	650 - D6
PEREGRINE PK, FRMT	732 - B7
PIEDMONT PK, PDMT	650 - B1
PIEDMONT SPORTS FIELD, PDMT	650 - D2
PINE GROVE SPORTS FIELD, ORIN	610 - H7
PINTO RANCH REC AREA, OAK	650 - H5
PIONEER PK, SF	648 - A4
PLAZA PK, RCH	609 - A1
PLAZA PK, FRMT	752 - H5
PLEASANTON RIDGE REGL PK, HAY	713 - F3
PLEASANTON SPORTS AND RECREATION PK, PLE	714 - C1
PLEASANTON TENNIS AND COMM PK, PLE	714 - B1
PLEASURE ISLAND PK, LVMR	715 - D2
PLOMOSA PK, FRMT	793 - J1
POINT ISABEL REGL SHORELINE, RCH	609 - A4
POPLAR REC CTR, OAK	649 - F1
PORTOLA PK, LVMR	695 - G6
PORTSMOUTH SQUARE, SF	648 - A5
PORTVIEW PK, OAK	648 - J4
PRIDE ROCK PK, UNC	732 - G6
QUARRY LAKES REGL PK, FRMT	752 - H1
RAIMONDI PK, OAK	649 - D2
RAINBOW REC CTR, OAK	670 - F2
RANCHO ARROYO PK, HAY	711 - F6
RANCHO ARROYO PK, FRMT	753 - A1
RANCHO HIGUERA HIST PK, FRMT	774 - A6
RANCHO LAGUNA PK, MRGA	651 - F3
RAVENSWOOD PK, LVMR	715 - G5
REDWOOD HEIGHTS REC AREA, OAK	650 - G5
REDWOOD REGL PK, CCCo	650 - H2
REMILLARD PK, BERK	609 - H6
REUTHER, WALTER PK, MPS	794 - B5
RINCON POINT PK, SF	648 - C5
RITTLER PK, ALA	669 - H3
RIX PK, FRMT	773 - C2
ROBERTSON PK, LVMR	715 - H2
ROBERTS REGL REC AREA, AlaC	650 - J3
ROCKRIDGE PK, OAK	630 - A5
ROCKRIDGE GREENBELT, OAK	629 - H6
ROGERS, BEN PK, MPS	794 - E7
ROOSEVELT PLGD, SLN	671 - B6
ROOT PK, SLN	691 - A1
ROSE GARDEN PK, OAK	650 - A2
ROSE GARDENS, BERK	609 - H6
ROWELL RANCH RODEO PK, AlaC	692 - J4
RUUS PK, HAY	732 - A1
SAINT MARYS SQUARE, SF	648 - A5
SAN ANDREAS PK, UNC	732 - B5
SAN ANTONIO REC CTR, OAK	650 - A6
SANBORN PK, OAK	650 - C7
SANDLEWOOD PK, MPS	794 - B4
SAN FELIPE PK, AlaC	692 - B7
SAN LORENZO PK, AlaC	711 - B2
SAN PABLO PK, BERK	629 - F4
SAN PABLO RESERVOIR REC AREA, CCCo	610 - D3
SAN RAMON CENTRAL PK, SRMN	673 - E3
SANTA RITA LAND TRUST, OAK	650 - D7
SAUNDERS, MARGE PK, OAK	650 - F1
SCHAFER PK, HAY	711 - J5
SELWYN PK, MPS	794 - C7
SENIOR CTR PK GARDENS, SRMN	673 - J7
SEVEN HILLS PK, UNC	732 - J5
SHADOW CLIFFS REGL REC AREA, PLE	714 - H2
SHANNON PK, DBLN	693 - G3
SHEFFIELD REC CTR, OAK	671 - D7
SHEPHERD CANYON PK, OAK	650 - F1
SHINN HIST PK, FRMT	753 - B2
SHOREBIRD PK, EMVL	629 - D6
SHOREBIRD PK, BERK	629 - B3
SHORELINE PK, ALA	669 - H5
SHORELINE AT MOUNTAIN VIEW, MTVW	792 - A7
SIEMPRE VERDE PK, SLN	670 - J7
SILLMAN, GEORGE M REC COMPLEX, NWK	772 - H2
SILVER STAR VETERANS PK, HAY	732 - C1
SMITH, F M PK, OAK	649 - J4
SNOW PK, OAK	649 - H3
SOBRANTE PK, OAK	690 - H1
SORENSDALE PK, HAY	712 - A5
SOUTH PK, SF	648 - B6
SOUTH BEACH PK, SF	648 - C7
SOUTHGATE PK, HAY	711 - H6
SOUTH OF MARKET PK, SF	648 - A7
SOUTH PRESCOTT PK, OAK	649 - D4
SOUYEN PK, SRMN	674 - A3
SPLASHPAD PK, OAK	649 - J3
SPRING GROVE PK, HAY	712 - B3
SPRUIELL, TEX PK, LVMR	696 - C7
STAGECOACH PK, DBLN	693 - J2
STANFORD AV PK, EMVL	629 - E6
STARLITE PK, MPS	793 - J7
STENZEL PK, SLN	691 - A6
STONEHURST REC AREA, OAK	670 - H6
STONYBROOK PK, HAY	712 - D7
STONY BROOK PK, AlaC	733 - F5
STRATFORD VILLAGE PK, HAY	732 - A2
STRICKROTH PK, MPS	794 - A5
SULPHUR CREEK PK, AlaC	712 - B1
SUNKEN GARDENS PK, LVMR	715 - J2
SUNSET EAST PK, LVMR	715 - G2
SURRY PK, FRMT	752 - H2
SUTTER GATE PK, PLE	694 - D7
SYCAMORE GROVE PK, AlaC	715 - G7
TASSAFARONGA REC CTR, OAK	670 - G4
TASSAJARA CREEK REGL PK, DBLN	694 - D1
TAWNY PK, PLE	714 - G3
TEMESCAL CREEK PK, EMVL	629 - F6
TENNYSON PK, HAY	712 - B7
TERRACE PK, ALB	609 - E7
TERRACE VIEW PLGD, BERK	609 - J7
THOMPSON FIELD, ALA	670 - A1
THRASHER PK, SLN	690 - J1

FEATURE NAME / Address City, ZIP Code	PAGE-GRID
TILDEN REGL PK, CCCo	609 - J4
TILLMAN PK, ALA	669 - J5
TOWATA PK, ALA	670 - A4
TOWN ESTATES PK, UNC	732 - C4
TOYON PK, SLN	691 - C3
TWIN BRIDGES PK, HAY	732 - D1
TWIN CREEKS PK, SRMN	673 - B2
UNION SQUARE, SF	648 - A6
UNIVERSITY PK, ALB	609 - D7
VALLEJO MILL PK, FRMT	753 - D1
VALLE VISTA PK, HAY	712 - C7
VALLEY TRAILS PK, PLE	714 - A1
VALLEY VIEW PK, SRMN	673 - J1
VAL VISTA PK, PLE	694 - A7
VANTAGE POINT PK, OAK	649 - J6
VETERANS PK, AlaC	735 - H1
VETERANS PLAZA, PLE	714 - E3
VICTORIA PK, SLN	671 - B6
VILLAGE GREEN PK, SRMN	693 - H1
VINTAGE HILLS PK, PLE	714 - H4
VISTA MEADOWS PK, LVMR	695 - G6
WALNUT GROVE PK, PLE	714 - D1
WARBLER PK, FRMT	732 - B7
WARDEN AVENUE PK, SLN	690 - G1
WARM SPRINGS PK, FRMT	773 - H6
WARREN, EARL PK, AlaC	692 - C5
WASHINGTON PK, ALA	669 - F1
WASHINGTON MANOR PK, SLN	691 - B5
WASHINGTON SQUARE, SF	648 - A4
WATTENBURGER PK, LVMR	696 - A4
WAYSIDE PK, PLE	714 - E4
WEEKES PK, HAY	711 - J6
WELL, HOLM PK, LVMR	715 - D3
WENTE PK, LVMR	715 - G3
WESTRIDGE PK, FRMT	752 - F2
WILDCAT CANYON REGL PK, RCH	609 - E1
WILLARD PK, BERK	629 - J3
WILLIAMS, JACK PK, LVMR	715 - E4
WILLOW PK, OAK	649 - D2
WINDFLOWER PK, UNC	732 - H6
WINDY HILLS PK, SRMN	673 - G2
WOH HEI YUEN REC CTR, SF	648 - A4
WOODSTOCK PK, ALA	649 - E7
WOODTHRUSH PK, PLE	714 - D1
WOOD, W D PK, OAK	650 - C5

PERFORMING ARTS

FEATURE NAME	Address City, ZIP Code	PAGE-GRID
ALTARENA PLAYHOUSE	1409 HIGH ST, ALA, 94501	670 - B3
BERKELEY COMM THEATER	1930 ALLSTON WY, BERK, 94703	629 - G2
BERKELEY REPERTORY THEATRE	2025 ADDISON ST, BERK, 94704	629 - G1
BRUNS AMPHITHEATRE, THE	100 GATEWAY BLVD, CCCo, 94563	630 - F2
CALIFORNIA CONSERVATORY	999 E 14TH ST, SLN, 94577	691 - A1
CONTRA COSTA CIVIC THEATRE	951 POMONA AV, ELCR, 94530	609 - D2
CURRAN THEATER	445 GEARY ST, SF, 94102	648 - A6
GEARY THEATRE	415 GEARY ST, SF, 94102	648 - A6
GOLDEN GATE THEATRE	6TH ST & MARKET ST, SF, 94103	648 - A6
MORRISSON, DOUGLAS THEATRE	22331 N 3RD ST, HAY, 94541	691 - J7
PARAMOUNT THEATRE	2025 BROADWAY, OAK, 94612	649 - G3
SIMMONS, CALVIN THEATER	10 10TH ST, OAK, 94607	649 - H5
UC BERKELEY GREEK THEATER	2200 UNIVERSITY AV, BERK, 94720	629 - J1
UNIVERSITY ARTS	BANCROFT WY & BOWDITCH ST, BERK, 94704	629 - J2
WARFIELD THEATRE	982 MARKET ST, SF, 94102	648 - A6
WOODMINSTER AMPHITHEATER	3300 JOAQUIN MILLER RD, OAK, 94611	650 - G3

POINTS OF INTEREST

FEATURE NAME	Address City, ZIP Code	PAGE-GRID
ADOBE ART CTR	ANITA AV, AlaC, 94546	691 - J5
ALICE ARTS CTR	1418 ALICE ST, OAK, 94612	649 - H4
ALVISO MARINA	1195 HOPE ST, SJS, 95002	793 - B7
BOAT HOUSE	BOLIVAR DR, BERK, 94710	629 - D2
CALIF ORIENTATION CTR FOR THE BLIND	400 ADAMS ST, ALB, 94706	609 - C5
CALIFORNIA SCHOOL FOR THE BLIND	WALNUT AV, FRMT, 94538	753 - D3
CARMELITE MONASTERY	JESSEN CT, CCCo, 94707	609 - F2
CENTENNIAL HALL	22292 FOOTHILL BLVD, HAY, 94541	691 - J7
CHABOT SPACE & SCIENCE CTR	10000 SKYLINE BLVD, OAK, 94611	650 - H2
CROW CANYON GARDENS	20 BOARDWALK, SRMN, 94583	673 - B2
DUCK CLUB	SJS, 95002	792 - E3
EDOFF MEM BANDSTAND	BELLEVUE AV, OAK, 94610	649 - H3
EL CERRITO COMM SWIM CTR	7007 MOESER LN, ELCR, 94530	609 - D2
GREEK ORTHODOX CHURCH	4700 LINCOLN AV, OAK, 94602	650 - E3
HAYWARD SHORELINE INTERPRETIVE CTR	4901 BREAKWATER AV, HAY, 94545	731 - B1
KNOWLAND STATE ARBORETUM	GOLF LINKS RD, OAK, 94605	671 - D3
LAWRENCE HALL OF SCIENCE	CENTENNIAL DR, BERK, 94720	610 - A7
LAWRENCE LIVERMORE NATL LABORATORY	7000 EAST AV, AlaC, 94550	696 - F7
LAWRENCE RADIATION LABORATORY- (SEE PAGE 717)	W CORRAL HOLLOW RD, SJCo, 95377	718 - F6
LONDON, JACK MARINA	54 JACK LONDON SQ, OAK, 94607	649 - F5
LOS MOCHES BOY SCOUT CAMP- (SEE PAGE 757)	MOCHO RD, AlaC, 94550	758 - A6
MASTICK SENIOR CTR	1155 SANTA CLARA AV, ALA, 94501	669 - G1
MORMON TEMPLE	4770 LINCOLN AV, OAK, 94602	650 - F3
MUNICIPAL SAILBOAT HOUSE	GRAND AV & BELLEVUE AV, OAK, 94610	649 - J4
OAKLAND ZOO	GOLF LINKS RD, OAK, 94605	671 - B5
OUR LADYS HOME	3499 FOOTHILL BLVD, OAK, 94601	650 - C7
PIER 39	THE EMBARCADERO & PIER 39, SF, 94133	648 - A2
SENIOR CTR & VETERANS BLDG	SALEM ST, EMVL, 94608	629 - F6
STATE OF CALIFORNIA CONSERVATION CAMP	BOLLINGER CANYON RD, CCCo, 94583	652 - E3
STEAM TRAINS	GRIZZLY PEAK BLVD, CCCo, 94708	610 - C7
UNDERWATER WORLD	THE EMBARCADERO AT BEACH ST, SF, 94133	648 - A3
WATER TEMPLE	OFF HWY 84, AlaC, 94586	734 - D7
YERBA BUENA GARDENS	MISSION ST & 3RD ST, SF, 94103	648 - A6

POINTS OF INTEREST - HISTORIC

FEATURE NAME	Address City, ZIP Code	PAGE-GRID
COIT TOWER	TELEGRAPH HILL BLVD, SF, 94133	648 - A4
FOREST HOME FARMS PK	VALLEY BLVD & PINE VALLEY RD, SRMN, 94583	673 - F7
HIGUERA ADOBE PK	N PARK VICTORIA DR & WESSEX PL, MPS, 95035	794 - B3
MISSION SAN JOSE DE GUADALUPE	43300 MISSION BLVD, FRMT, 94539	753 - J7
OLD FEDERAL RESERVE	400 SANSOME ST, SF, 94111	648 - B5
OLD UNITED STATES MINT	88 5TH ST, SF, 94103	648 - A6
ONEILL, EUGENE NATL HIST SITE	1000 KUSS RD, CCCo, 94526	652 - G1
PATTERSON HOUSE	34600 ARDENWOOD BLVD, FRMT, 94555	752 - D3
PRESERVATION PK	1233 PRESERVATION PARK WY, OAK, 94612	649 - F3
VALLEJO MILL HIST PK	MISSION BL & NILES CANYON RD, FRMT, 94536	753 - C1
VICTORIAN ROW OLD OAKLAND	BROADWAY & 9TH ST, OAK, 94607	649 - G4
WILLIAMS HIST PK	39200 FREMONT BLVD, FRMT, 94538	753 - A5

POST OFFICES

FEATURE NAME	Address City, ZIP Code	PAGE-GRID
ALAMEDA	2201 SHORELINE DR, ALA, 94501	669 - J3
ALBANY BRANCH	1191 SOLANO AV, ALB, 94706	609 - D6
ALVARADO STA	3861 SMITH ST, UNC, 94587	731 - J5
BERKELEY MAIN	2000 ALLSTON WY, BERK, 94704	629 - G2
BRADFORD STA	822 C ST, HAY, 94541	711 - J2
BRANNAN STREET STA	460 BRANNAN ST, SF, 94107	648 - B7
BYRON	3852 MAIN ST, CCCo, 94514	637 - D3
CANYON	PINEHURST RD, CCCo, 94516	630 - J7
CASTRO VALLEY BRANCH	20283 SANTA MARIA AV, AlaC, 94546	692 - A5
CHINATOWN	867 STOCKTON ST, SF, 94108	648 - A5
DANVILLE SQUARE STA	43 RAILROAD AV, DNVL, 94526	652 - J2
DIMOND STA	2226 MACARTHUR BLVD, OAK, 94602	650 - D4
DUBLIN	6937 VILLAGE PKWY, DBLN, 94568	693 - J4
EASTMONT	8033 MACARTHUR BLVD, OAK, 94605	670 - J3
EL CERRITO MAIN	11135 SAN PABLO AV, ELCR, 94530	609 - C2
ELMWOOD STA	2705 WEBSTER ST, BERK, 94705	629 - J4
EMERYVILLE	1585 62ND ST, EMVL, 94608	629 - E5
EMPORIUM	835 MARKET ST, SF, 94103	648 - A6
ESTUDILLO STA	1319 WASHINGTON AV, SLN, 94577	691 - A1
FAIRMOUNT STA	6324 FAIRMOUNT AV, ELCR, 94530	609 - D4
FREMONT MAIN	37010 DUSTERBERRY WY, FRMT, 94536	752 - G4
FRUITVILLE STA	1445 34TH AV, OAK, 94601	650 - C7
GRAND LAKE STA	490 LAKE PARK AV, OAK, 94610	650 - A3
HACIENDA STA	4682 CHABOT DR, PLE, 94588	694 - B6
HAYWARD MAIN	24438 SANTA CLARA ST, HAY, 94544	711 - H4
IRVINGTON STA	41041 TRIMBOLI WY, FRMT, 94538	753 - D7
KAISER CTR STA	300 LAKESIDE DR, OAK, 94612	649 - H3
LANDSCAPE STA	1831 SOLANO AV, BERK, 94707	609 - F6
LAUREL STA	3630 HIGH ST, OAK, 94619	650 - F6
LIVERMORE	220 S LIVERMORE AV, LVMR, 94550	715 - H1
MARCUS FOSTER STA	9201 E INTERNATIONAL BLVD, OAK, 94603	670 - H5
MILLS COLLEGE	POST RD, OAK, 94613	650 - H7
MISSION SAN JOSE STA	43456 ELLSWORTH, FRMT, 94539	753 - H7
MOUNT EDEN	2163 ALDENGATE WY, HAY, 94545	711 - H7
NEWARK	6655 CLARK AV, NWK, 94560	752 - F7
NILES	160 J ST, FRMT, 94536	753 - B1
NORTH BEACH	1640 STOCKTON ST, SF, 94133	648 - A4
NORTH BERKELEY STA	1521 SHATTUCK AV, BERK, 94709	609 - G7
NORTH OAKLAND STA	4869 TELEGRAPH AV, OAK, 94609	629 - H6
NUMBER FIFTY SEVEN	170 OFARRELL ST, SF, 94102	648 - A6
OAKLAND CIVIC CTR	201 13TH ST, OAK, 94612	649 - G4
OAKLAND MAIN	1675 7TH ST, OAK, 94607	649 - D3
ORINDA	29 ORINDA WY, ORIN, 94563	610 - G7
PARK CENTRAL STA	1333 PARK AV, ALA, 94501	670 - A2
PARK STA	2900 SACRAMENTO ST, BERK, 94702	629 - F4
PIEDMONT STA	195 41ST ST, OAK, 94611	649 - J1
PLEASANTON	4300 BLACK AV, PLE, 94566	714 - E2
POST OFFICE	1052 S LIVERMORE AV, LVMR, 94550	715 - J2
POST OFFICE	2000 ALCATRAZ AV, BERK, 94703	629 - G5
POST OFFICE	SOUTHLAND DR, HAY, 94545	711 - G4
RINCON CTR	180 STEUART ST, SF, 94105	648 - C5
SAN LEANDRO MAIN	1777 ABRAM CT, SLN, 94577	690 - J3
SAN LORENZO	15888 HESPERIAN BLVD, AlaC, 94580	691 - D7
SAN RAMON	12935 ALCOSTA BLVD, SRMN, 94583	673 - D1
SATHER GATE STA	2515 DURANT AV, BERK, 94704	629 - J2
SOUTH BERKELEY STA	3175 ADELINE ST, BERK, 94703	629 - G4
SOUTH SAN LEANDRO STA	14500 E 14TH ST, SLN, 94578	691 - C3
STATION A	2111 SAN PABLO AV, BERK, 94702	629 - E2
STATION B	1446 FRANKLIN ST, OAK, 94612	649 - G4
STATION D	560 14TH ST, OAK, 94612	649 - G3
STATION E	1954 MOUNTAIN BLVD, OAK, 94611	650 - E1
SUNOL	11925 MAIN ST, AlaC, 94586	734 - C6
SUTTER	150 SUTTER ST, SF, 94108	648 - A5
TREASURE ISLAND	6TH ST & AVE H, SF, 94130	648 - E1
TREASURE ISLAND	9TH ST & AVE F, SF, 94130	648 - E1
UNION CITY MAIN	33170 ALVARADO-NILES RD, UNC, 94587	732 - D5
WARM SPRINGS STA	240 FRANCISCO LN, FRMT, 94539	773 - H6
WASHINGTON MANOR STA	921 MANOR BLVD, SLN, 94579	691 - B6
WEBSTER STA	1415 WEBSTER ST, ALA, 94501	669 - F1
WEST GRAND CARRIER ANNEX	577 W GRAND AV, OAK, 94612	649 - G3

SCHOOLS - PRIVATE ELEMENTARY

FEATURE NAME	Address City, ZIP Code	PAGE-GRID
ACADEMY, THE	2722 BENVENUE AV, BERK, 94705	629 - J3
ACTS CHRISTIAN ACADEMY	6118 INTERNATIONAL BLVD, OAK, 94621	670 - F2
ALL SAINTS	22870 2ND ST, HAY, 94541	712 - A1
AMERICAN HERITAGE CHRISTIAN	425 GRESEL ST, HAY, 94544	732 - E2
ASSUMPTION	1851 136TH AV, SLN, 94578	691 - C2
ATHERTON ACADEMY	8030 ATHERTON ST, OAK, 94605	670 - J3
AURORA	40 DULWICH RD, OAK, 94618	630 - B6
BEACON DAY	2101 LIVINGSTON ST, OAK, 94606	650 - A7
BENTLEY	1 HILLER DR, OAK, 94618	630 - B4
BERKELEY MONTESSORI	1310 UNIVERSITY AV, BERK, 94702	629 - E2
BERKWOOD HEDGE	1809 BANCROFT WY, BERK, 94703	629 - G2
BETHEL CHRISTIAN ACADEMY	36060 FREMONT BLVD, FRMT, 94536	752 - G2
BLACK PINE CIRCLE	2027 7TH ST, BERK, 94710	629 - D2
CALVARY LUTHERAN	17200 VIA MAGDALENA, AlaC, 94580	711 - D1
CAMELOT	2330 POMAR VISTA, AlaC, 94546	691 - G5
CARDEN-WEST	4444 BLACK AV, PLE, 94566	714 - E2
CHALLENGER	35487 DUNBARTON CT, NWK, 94560	752 - C5
CHINESE CHRISTIAN	750 FARGO AV, SLN, 94579	691 - C6
CHRISTIAN COMM	39700 MISSION BLVD, FRMT, 94539	753 - E3
CLARA MOHAMMED	1652 47TH AV, OAK, 94601	670 - D1
COMMUNITY CHRISTIAN	562 LEWELLING BLVD, SLN, 94579	691 - C6
CORPUS CHRISTI	1 ESTATES DR, PDMT, 94611	650 - D3
ECOLE BILINGUE	1009 HEINZ AV, BERK, 94710	629 - E4
FREMONT CHRISTIAN	4760 THORNTON AV, FRMT, 94536	752 - G4
GOLDEN GATE ACADEMY	3800 MOUNTAIN BLVD, OAK, 94619	650 - G4
HEAD-ROYCE	4315 LINCOLN AV, OAK, 94602	650 - E3
HOLY SPIRIT	3930 PARISH AV, FRMT, 94536	752 - H3
LEAS CHRISTIAN	26236 ADRIAN AV, HAY, 94545	711 - G6
MONTESSORI OF FREMONT	155 WASHINGTON BLVD, FRMT, 94539	753 - H7
MONTESSORI OF SAN LEANDRO	16292 FOOTHILL BLVD, AlaC, 94578	691 - F4
NEW HORIZONS	2550 PERALTA BLVD, FRMT, 94536	753 - A3
NORTHERN LIGHT	4500 REDWOOD RD, OAK, 94619	650 - H5
NOTRE DAME VICTORIES	659 PINE ST, SF, 94108	648 - A5
OAKLAND HEBREW DAY	215 RIDGEWAY AV, OAK, 94611	629 - J7
OAKLAND INTERNATIONAL	345 12TH ST, OAK, 94612	649 - G4
OUR LADY OF GRACE	19920 ANITA AV, AlaC, 94546	691 - J4
OUR LADY OF GUADALUPE	40374 FREMONT BLVD, FRMT, 94538	753 - C6
OUR LADY OF THE ROSARY	678 B ST, UNC, 94587	732 - F4
OUR SAVIOR LUTHERAN	1385 S LIVERMORE AV, LVMR, 94550	715 - J2
PACIFIC ACADEMY OF NOMURA	1615 CARLSON BLVD, RCH, 94804	609 - B3
PARK DAY	370 43RD ST, OAK, 94609	629 - H7
PATTEN ACADEMY OF CHRISTIAN ED	2432 COOLIDGE AV, OAK, 94601	650 - D6
PRINCE OF PEACE LUTHERAN	38451 FREMONT BLVD, FRMT, 94536	752 - J4
PROSPECT SIERRA	960 AVIS DR, ELCR, 94530	609 - D2
QUARRY LANE	3750 BOULDER ST, PLE, 94566	714 - F2
RAINBOW BRIDGE CTR	1500 YOSEMITE DR, MPS, 95035	794 - D7
REDWOOD CHRISTIAN-CROSSROADS CAMPUS	20600 JOHN DR, AlaC, 94546	691 - H5

FEATURE NAME	Address City, ZIP Code	PAGE-GRID
REDWOOD CHRISTIAN-REDWOOD CAMPUS	19300 REDWOOD RD, AlaC, 94546	692 - A4
REDWOOD DAY	3245 SHEFFIELD AV, OAK, 94602	650 - C5
SAINT ANTHONY	1500 E 15TH ST, OAK, 94606	650 - A6
SAINT AUGUSTINE	410 ALCATRAZ AV, OAK, 94618	629 - J4
SAINT BARNABAS	1400 6TH ST, ALA, 94501	669 - F1
SAINT BEDES	26910 PATRICK AV, HAY, 94544	711 - J6
SAINT BERNARD	1630 62ND AV, OAK, 94621	670 - F2
SAINT CLEMENT	790 CALHOUN ST, HAY, 94544	712 - C5
SAINT CYRIL	3200 62ND AV, OAK, 94605	670 - G1
SAINT EDWARDS	5788 THORNTON AV, NWK, 94560	752 - F6
SAINT ELIZABETH	1516 33RD AV, OAK, 94601	650 - C7
SAINT FELICITAS	1650 MANOR BLVD, SLN, 94579	691 - A6
SAINT ISIDORE	435 LA GONDA WY, DNVL, 94526	652 - J1
SAINT JARLATH	2634 PLEASANT ST, OAK, 94602	650 - D5
SAINT JEROME	320 SAN CARLOS AV, ELCR, 94530	609 - E4
SAINT JOACHIMS	21250 HESPERIAN BLVD, HAY, 94541	711 - E2
SAINT JOHN	270 E LEWELLING BLVD, AlaC, 94580	691 - E6
SAINT JOHN THE BAPTIST	11156 SAN PABLO AV, ELCR, 94530	609 - C2
SAINT JOSEPH	1910 SAN ANTONIO AV, ALA, 94501	669 - J2
SAINT JOSEPH	43222 MISSION BLVD, FRMT, 94539	753 - J7
SAINT JOSEPH THE WORKER	2125 JEFFERSON AV, BERK, 94703	629 - F2
SAINT LAWRENCE OTOOLE	3695 HIGH ST, OAK, 94619	650 - F6
SAINT LEANDER	451 DAVIS ST, SLN, 94577	691 - A1
SAINT LEO	4238 HOWE ST, OAK, 94611	629 - J7
SAINT LEONARD	3635 ST LEONARDS WY, FRMT, 94538	753 - C6
SAINT MARTIN DE PORRES	675 41ST ST, OAK, 94609	629 - G7
SAINT MICHAELS	372 MAPLE ST, LVMR, 94550	715 - H1
SAINT PASCHAL BAYLON	3710 DORISA AV, OAK, 94605	671 - B4
SAINT PAULS EPISCOPAL	116 MONTECITO AV, OAK, 94610	649 - H3
SAINT PHILIP LUTHERAN	8850 DAVONA DR, DBLN, 94568	693 - G2
SAINT PHILIP NERI	1335 HIGH ST, ALA, 94501	670 - B3
SAINT RAYMOND	11557 SHANNON AV, DBLN, 94568	693 - G3
SAINTS PETER & PAUL	600 FILBERT ST, SF, 94133	648 - A4
SAINT THERESA	4850 CLAREWOOD DR, OAK, 94618	630 - B6
SF CHINESE PARENT COMMUNITY	843 STOCKTON ST, SF, 94108	648 - A5
SCHOOL OF THE MADELEINE	1225 MILVIA ST, BERK, 94709	609 - G7
SHELTONS PRIMARY EDUCATION	3339 MARTIN LUTHER KING JR WY, BERK, 94703	629 - G5
SPRAINGS ACADEMY	89 MORAGA WY, ORIN, 94563	630 - H1
STIVERS ACADEMY	2550 S VASCO RD, LVMR, 94550	716 - D2
UNION CITY CHRISTIAN ACADEMY	33700 ALVARADO-NILES RD, UNC, 94587	732 - F6
VALLEY CHRISTIAN	7508 INSPIRATION DR, DBLN, 94568	693 - E5
VALLEY MONTESSORI	1273 N LIVERMORE AV, LVMR, 94551	695 - G6
WINDRUSH	1800 ELM ST, ELCR, 94530	609 - C1
ZION LUTHERAN	5201 PARK BLVD, PDMT, 94611	650 - D2

SCHOOLS - PRIVATE HIGH

FEATURE NAME	Address City, ZIP Code	PAGE-GRID
AMERICAN HERITAGE CHRISTIAN HS	425 GRESEL ST, HAY, 94544	732 - E2
ARROWSMITH ACADEMY	2300 BANCROFT WY, BERK, 94704	629 - H2
BISHOP ODOWD	9500 STEARNS AV, OAK, 94605	671 - A4
CHINESE CHRISTIAN	750 FARGO AV, SLN, 94579	691 - C6
COLLEGE PREP	6100 BROADWAY, OAK, 94618	630 - A5
FREMONT CHRISTIAN	4760 THORNTON AV, FRMT, 94536	752 - G4
GOLDEN GATE ACADEMY	3800 MOUNTAIN BLVD, OAK, 94619	650 - G4
HEAD-ROYCE	4315 LINCOLN AV, OAK, 94602	650 - E3
HOLY NAMES	4660 HARBORD DR, OAK, 94618	630 - B6
MAYBECK	2362 BANCROFT WY, BERK, 94704	629 - H2
MID-PENINSULA	1340 WILLOW RD, MLPK, 94025	771 - A7
MOREAU CATHOLIC	27170 MISSION BLVD, HAY, 94544	712 - C5
NORTH BAY ORINDA	19 ALTARINDA RD, ORIN, 94563	610 - H7
PATTEN ACADEMY OF CHRISTIAN ED	2432 COOLIDGE AV, OAK, 94601	650 - D6
REDWOOD CHRISTIAN JUNIOR-SENIOR	1000 PAS GRANDE, AlaC, 94580	711 - C1
SAINT ELIZABETH	1530 34TH AV, OAK, 94601	670 - C1
SAINT JOSEPH NOTRE DAME	1011 CHESTNUT ST, ALA, 94501	669 - H2
SAINT MARYS COLLEGE	1294 ALBINA AV, ALB, 94706	609 - F7
VALLEY CHRISTIAN	7506 INSPIRATION DR, DBLN, 94568	693 - E4

SCHOOLS - PRIVATE MIDDLE

FEATURE NAME	Address City, ZIP Code	PAGE-GRID
SAINT MARTIN DE PORRES	1630 10TH ST, OAK, 94607	649 - D3

SCHOOLS - PUBLIC ELEMENTARY

FEATURE NAME	Address City, ZIP Code	PAGE-GRID
ALISAL	1454 SANTA RITA RD, PLE, 94566	714 - E2
ALLENDALE	3670 PENNIMAN AV, OAK, 94619	650 - E6
ALMOND AVENUE	1401 ALMOND AV, LVMR, 94550	716 - B1
ALTAMONT CREEK	6500 GARAVENTA RANCH RD, LVMR, 94551	696 - D2
ALVARADO	31100 FREDI ST, UNC, 94587	732 - A5
ARDENWOOD	33955 EMILIA LN, FRMT, 94555	752 - C1
ARMSTRONG, NEIL A	2849 CALAIS DR, SRMN, 94583	673 - F6
ARROYO MOCHO	1040 FLORENCE RD, LVMR, 94550	715 - G2
ARROYO SECO	5280 IRENE WY, LVMR, 94550	696 - C7
ARTS	5263 BROADWAY TER, OAK, 94618	629 - J6
AZEVADA, JOSEPH	39450 ROYAL PALM DR, FRMT, 94538	752 - J7
BAY	2001 BOCKMAN RD, AlaC, 94580	711 - B1
BAY FARM	200 AUGHINBAUGH WY, ALA, 94502	669 - J5
BEACH	100 LAKE AV, PDMT, 94611	650 - A1
BELLA VISTA	1025 E 28TH ST, OAK, 94606	650 - B4
BERKELEY ARTS MAGNET	1645 MILVIA ST, BERK, 94709	629 - G1
BLACOW, JOHN	40404 SUNDALE DR, FRMT, 94538	753 - B7
BOLLINGER CANYON	2300 TALAVERA DR, SRMN, 94583	673 - D3
BOWMAN	520 JEFFERSON ST, HAY, 94544	712 - B5
BRIER	39201 SUNDALE DR, FRMT, 94538	753 - A6
BROOKFIELD VILLAGE	401 JONES AV, OAK, 94603	670 - G6
BROOKVALE	3400 NICOLET AV, FRMT, 94536	752 - G2
BUNKER, JAMES L	6071 SMITH AV, NWK, 94560	752 - G7
BURBANK	353 B ST, HAY, 94541	711 - H2
BURBANK, LUTHER	3550 64TH AV, OAK, 94605	670 - H1
BURCKHALTER	3994 BURCKHALTER AV, OAK, 94605	670 - J1
BURNETT, WILLIAM	400 FANYON ST, MPS, 95035	794 - C5
CABELLO, REFUGIO M	4500 CABELLO ST, UNC, 94587	732 - A6
CABRILLO	36700 SAN PEDRO DR, FRMT, 94536	752 - F4
CAMINO PABLO	1111 CM PABLO, MRGA, 94556	651 - E2
CANYON	PINEHURST RD, CCCo, 94516	651 - A1
CARMICHAEL, BESSIE	55 SHERMAN ST, SF, 94103	648 - A7
CASTRO	7125 DONAL AV, ELCR, 94530	609 - C2
CASTRO VALLEY	20185 SAN MIGUEL AV, AlaC, 94546	691 - J5
CEIA, PALMA	27679 MELBOURNE AV, HAY, 94545	711 - J7
CHABOT, ANTHONY	6686 CHABOT RD, OAK, 94618	630 - A4
CHABOT	19104 LAKE CHABOT RD, AlaC, 94546	691 - H4
CHADBOURNE, JOSHUA	801 PLYMOUTH AV, FRMT, 94539	753 - F5
CHERRYLAND	585 WILLOW AV, AlaC, 94541	711 - G1
CHINESE EDUCATION CTR	657 MERCHANT ST, SF, 94111	648 - B5
CHIN, JOHN YEHALL	350 BROADWAY ST, SF, 94133	648 - A4
CLEVELAND	745 CLEVELAND ST, OAK, 94606	650 - A4
COLONIAL ACRES	17115 MEEKLAND AV, AlaC, 94541	691 - E7
CORNELL	920 TALBOT AV, ALB, 94706	609 - E6
CORVALLIS	14790 CORVALLIS ST, SLN, 94579	691 - B5
COSTANO	2695 FORDHAM ST, EPA, 94303	771 - B7
COUNTRY CLUB	7534 BLUE FOX WY, SRMN, 94583	693 - G1
COX, E MORRIS	9860 SUNNYSIDE ST, OAK, 94603	671 - A5
COYOTE CREEK	8700 GALE RIDGE RD, SRMN, 94582	673 - H1
CRAGMONT	830 REGAL RD, BERK, 94708	609 - H5
CROCE, LEO R	5650 SCENIC AV, LVMR, 94551	696 - C3
CROCKER HIGHLANDS	525 MIDCREST RD, OAK, 94610	650 - C3
CURTNER	275 REDWOOD AV, MPS, 95035	793 - J6
DAYTON	1500 DAYTON AV, SLN, 94579	691 - A6
DEL REY	1510 VIA SONYA, AlaC, 94580	711 - C2
DISNEY, WALT	3250 PINE VALLEY RD, SRMN, 94583	673 - G6
DONLON	4150 DORMAN RD, PLE, 94588	694 - A7
DOUGHERTY	5301 HIBERNIA DR, DBLN, 94568	694 - D4
DUBLIN	7997 VOMAC RD, DBLN, 94568	693 - G3
DURHAM, J HALEY	40292 LESLIE ST, FRMT, 94538	753 - C5
EARHART, AMELIA	400 PACKET LANDING, ALA, 94502	670 - A5
EAST AVENUE	2424 EAST AV, AlaC, 94541	712 - C2
EASTIN, DELAINE	34901 EASTIN DR, UNC, 94555	752 - A2
EDEN GARDENS	2184 THAYER AV, HAY, 94545	711 - F6
EDEN, LORIN A	27790 PORTSMOUTH AV, HAY, 94545	731 - G1
EDISON	2700 BUENA VISTA AV, ALA, 94501	670 - B2
ELDRIDGE	26825 ELDRIDGE AV, HAY, 94544	711 - J6
EMANUELE, GUY JR	100 DECOTO RD, UNC, 94587	732 - G4
EMERSON	2800 FOREST AV, BERK, 94705	629 - J3
EMERSON	4803 LAWTON AV, OAK, 94609	629 - H7
FAIRLANDS	4151 W LAS POSITAS BLVD, PLE, 94588	694 - E6
FAIRMONT	724 KEARNEY ST, ELCR, 94530	609 - D3
FAIRVIEW	23515 MAUD AV, AlaC, 94541	692 - D7
FOREST PARK	34400 MAYBIRD CIR, FRMT, 94555	752 - C3
FOSTER, MARCUS	2850 WEST ST, OAK, 94609	649 - G2
FRANKLIN	915 FOOTHILL BLVD, OAK, 94606	649 - J5
FRANKLIN	1433 SAN ANTONIO AV, ALA, 94501	669 - H1
FREDERIKSEN	7243 TAMARACK DR, DBLN, 94568	693 - J3
FRUITVALE	3200 BOSTON AV, OAK, 94602	650 - D5
GARFIELD	1640 22ND AV, OAK, 94606	650 - B6
GARFIELD	13050 AURORA DR, SLN, 94577	690 - G4
GARFIELD	420 FILBERT ST, SF, 94133	648 - A4
GLASSBROOK	975 SCHAFER RD, HAY, 94544	711 - J6
GLENMOOR	4620 MATTOS DR, FRMT, 94536	752 - H5
GLENVIEW	4215 LA CRESTA AV, OAK, 94602	650 - D4
GOLDEN GATE	6200 SAN PABLO AV, OAK, 94608	629 - F5
GOMES, JOHN M	555 LEMOS LN, FRMT, 94539	753 - E4
GRAHAM, JAMES A	36270 CHERRY ST, NWK, 94560	752 - D6
GRANT	879 GRANT AV, AlaC, 94580	691 - C7
GRASS VALLEY	4720 DUNKIRK AV, OAK, 94605	671 - E4
GREEN, HARVEY	42875 GATEWOOD ST, FRMT, 94538	773 - D2
GRIMMER, E M	43030 NEWPORT DR, FRMT, 94538	773 - E2
HAIGHT	2025 SANTA CLARA AV, ALA, 94501	669 - J1
HARDER	495 WYETH RD, HAY, 94544	712 - A4
HARDING	7230 FAIRMOUNT AV, ELCR, 94530	609 - E4
HAVENS, FRANK C	1800 OAKLAND AV, PDMT, 94611	650 - B1
HAWTHORNE YEAR-ROUND	1700 28TH AV, OAK, 94601	650 - C7
HEARST	5301 CASE AV, PLE, 94566	714 - D5
HESPERIAN	620 DREW ST, AlaC, 94580	691 - E5
HIDDEN HILLS	12995 HARCOURT WY, SRMN, 94582	674 - C3
HIGHLAND	2021 HIGHLAND BLVD, HAY, 94542	712 - C3
HIGHLAND	8521 A ST, OAK, 94621	670 - H4
HILLCREST	30 MARGUERITE DR, OAK, 94618	630 - B6
HILLSIDE	15980 MARCELLA ST, AlaC, 94578	691 - E4
HILLVIEW CREST	31410 WHEELON AV, HAY, 94544	732 - E2
HIRSCH, O N	41399 CHAPEL WY, FRMT, 94538	753 - D7
HOOVER	890 BROCKHURST ST, OAK, 94608	649 - F1
HOWARD, CHARLES P	8755 FONTAINE ST, OAK, 94605	671 - B3
HUERTA CHARTER LEARNING ACADEMY	1936 COURTLAND AV, OAK, 94601	670 - D1
INDEPENDENT	21201 INDEPENDENT SCHOOL RD, AlaC, 94552	692 - D5
INTERNATIONAL COMMUNITY	2825 INTERNATIONAL BLVD, OAK, 94601	650 - B7
JACKSON AVENUE	554 JACKSON AV, LVMR, 94550	696 - A7
JANSEN RANCH	20001 CARSON LN, AlaC, 94552	692 - F3
JEFFERSON	1400 ADA ST, BERK, 94702	609 - F7
JEFFERSON, THOMAS	14311 LARK ST, SLN, 94578	691 - C3
JEFFERSON YEAR-ROUND	2035 40TH AV, OAK, 94601	650 - D7
KAISER, HENRY J JR	25 S HILL CT, OAK, 94618	630 - B4
KENNEDY, JOHN F	35430 BLACKBURN DR, NWK, 94560	752 - D4
KENSINGTON	90 HIGHLAND BLVD, CCCo, 94708	609 - F3
KING, MARTIN LUTHER JR	960 10TH ST, OAK, 94607	649 - F3
KITAYAMA, TOM	1959 SUNSPRITE DR, UNC, 94587	732 - C5
LA ESCUELITA	1100 3RD AV, OAK, 94606	649 - H5
LAFAYETTE	1700 MARKET ST, OAK, 94607	649 - F3
LAKEVIEW	746 GRAND AV, OAK, 94610	649 - J3
LAMMERSVILLE (SEE PAGE 677)	16555 W VON SOSTEN RD, SJCo, 95304	678 - H6
LAU, GORDON J	950 CLAY ST, SF, 94108	648 - A5
LAUREL	3750 BROWN AV, OAK, 94619	650 - F5
LAZEAR	824 29TH AV, OAK, 94601	670 - B1
LECONTE	2241 RUSSELL ST, BERK, 94705	629 - H3
LEITCH, JAMES	47100 FERNALD ST, FRMT, 94539	773 - H6
LINCOLN	225 11TH ST, OAK, 94607	649 - G4
LINCOLN	36111 BETTENCOURT ST, NWK, 94560	752 - C6
LOCKWOOD	6701 E INTERNATIONAL BLVD, OAK, 94621	670 - F3
LONGFELLOW	3877 LUSK ST, OAK, 94608	629 - G7
LONGFELLOW	500 PACIFIC AV, ALA, 94501	669 - F1
LONGWOOD	850 LONGWOOD AV, HAY, 94541	711 - F3
LUM, DONALD D	1801 SANDCREEK WY, ALA, 94501	669 - H3
LYDIKSEN	7700 HIGHLAND OAKS DR, PLE, 94588	713 - J1
MADERA	8500 MADERA DR, ELCR, 94530	609 - D1
MADISON, JAMES	14751 JUNIPER ST, SLN, 94579	691 - A5
MALCOLM X	1731 PRINCE ST, BERK, 94703	629 - G4

ALAMEDA CO.

FEATURE NAME Address City, ZIP Code	PAGE-GRID
MALONEY, TOM 38700 LOGAN DR, FRMT, 94536	752 - J5
MANN, HORACE 5222 YGNACIO AV, OAK, 94601	670 - E1
MANOR, LORENZO 18250 BENGAL AV, AlaC, 94541	711 - E1
MANZANITA 2409 E 27TH ST, OAK, 94601	650 - C6
MARIN 1001 SANTA FE AV, ALB, 94706	609 - E6
MARKHAM 1570 WARD ST, HAY, 94541	670 - H2
MARKHAM 7220 KRAUSE AV, OAK, 94605	692 - B5
MARSHALL 20111 MARSHALL ST, AlaC, 94546	671 - C5
MARSHALL, JOHN 3400 MALCOLM AV, OAK, 94605	695 - F7
MARYLIN AVENUE 800 MARYLIN AV, LVMR, 94551	752 - G6
MATTOS, JOHN G 37944 FARWELL DR, FRMT, 94536	650 - F7
MAXWELL PARK 4730 FLEMING AV, OAK, 94619	691 - B2
MCKINLEY 2150 E 14TH ST, SLN, 94577	670 - E2
MELROSE 1325 53RD AV, OAK, 94601	715 - F2
MICHELL, JOE 1001 ELAINE AV, LVMR, 94550	752 - F6
MILANI, LOUIS 37490 BIRCH ST, NWK, 94560	773 - C2
MILLARD, STEVEN 5200 VALPEY PARK AV, FRMT, 94538	649 - E6
MILLER, GEORGE P 250 SINGLETON AV, ALA, 94501	650 - E2
MILLER, JOAQUIN 5525 ASCOT DR, OAK, 94611	753 - H7
MISSION SAN JOSE 43545 BRYANT ST, FRMT, 94539	753 - F6
MISSION VALLEY 41700 DENISE ST, FRMT, 94539	694 - F4
MOHR, HENRY P 3300 DENNIS DR, PLE, 94588	670 - J5
MONARCH CHARTER ACADEMY 1445 101ST AV, OAK, 94603	691 - B5
MONROE, JAMES 3750 MONTEREY BLVD, SLN, 94578	652 - J2
MONTAIR 300 QUINTERRA LN, DNVL, 94526	630 - D7
MONTCLAIR 1757 MOUNTAIN BLVD, OAK, 94611	673 - F4
MONTEVIDEO 13000 BROADMOOR DR, SRMN, 94583	711 - J4
MUIR, JOHN 24823 SOTO RD, HAY, 94544	630 - A3
MUIR, JOHN 2955 CLAREMONT AV, BERK, 94705	650 - H5
MUNCK, CARL B 11900 CAMPUS DR, OAK, 94619	693 - H1
MURRAY 8435 DAVONA DR, DBLN, 94568	752 - E5
MUSICK, E L 5735 MUSICK AV, NWK, 94560	693 - G4
NIELSEN 7500 AMARILLO RD, DBLN, 94568	753 - B1
NILES 37141 2ND ST, FRMT, 94536	609 - D6
OCEAN VIEW 1000 JACKSON ST, ALB, 94706	752 - G2
OLIVEIRA 4180 ALDER AV, FRMT, 94536	670 - A4
OTIS, FRANK 3010 FILLMORE ST, ALA, 94501	609 - G6
OXFORD 1130 OXFORD ST, BERK, 94707	669 - E1
PADEN, WILLIAM G 444 CENTRAL AV, ALA, 94501	692 - F5
PALOMARES 6395 PALO VERDE RD, AlaC, 94552	711 - H4
PARK 411 LARCHMONT ST, HAY, 94544	670 - J2
PARKER 7929 NEY AV, OAK, 94605	648 - A4
PARKER, JEAN 840 BROADWAY ST, SF, 94133	753 - B3
PARKMONT 2601 PARKSIDE DR, FRMT, 94536	629 - E2
PARKS, ROSA 920 ALLSTON WY, BERK, 94710	752 - E3
PATTERSON 35521 CABRILLO DR, FRMT, 94536	629 - H5
PERALTA 460 63RD ST, OAK, 94609	629 - J7
PIEDMONT AVENUE 4314 PIEDMONT AV, OAK, 94611	752 - A1
PIONEER 32737 BEL AIRE ST, UNC, 94587	794 - A4
POMEROY, MARSHALL 1505 ESCUELA PKWY, MPS, 95035	695 - G7
PORTOLA, DON GASPAR DE 2451 PORTOLA AV, LVMR, 94551	649 - D3
PRESCOTT 920 CAMPBELL ST, OAK, 94607	692 - A2
PROCTOR 17520 REDWOOD RD, AlaC, 94546	695 - D7
RANCHO LAS POSITAS 401 E JACK LONDON BLVD, LVMR, 94551	794 - C7
RANDALL, ROBERT 1300 EDSEL DR, MPS, 95035	650 - G5
REDWOOD HEIGHTS 4401 39TH AV, OAK, 94619	671 - B6
ROOSEVELT 951 DOWLING BLVD, SLN, 94577	794 - D7
ROSE, ALEXANDER 250 ROSWELL DR, MPS, 95035	732 - A1
RUUS 28027 DICKENS AV, HAY, 94544	732 - B1
RUUS/PEIXOTO 29150 RUUS RD, HAY, 94544	629 - G6
SANTA FE 915 54TH ST, OAK, 94608	711 - J5
SCHAFER PARK 26268 FLAMINGO AV, HAY, 94544	752 - D7
SCHILLING, AUGUST 36901 SPRUCE ST, NWK, 94560	732 - F5
SEARLES 33629 15TH ST, UNC, 94587	650 - D4
SEQUOIA 3730 LINCOLN AV, OAK, 94602	712 - A6
SHEPHERD 27211 TYRRELL AV, HAY, 94544	650 - G7
SHERMAN, ELISABETH 5328 BRANN ST, OAK, 94619	610 - F4
SLEEPY HOLLOW 20 WASHINGTON LN, ORIN, 94563	715 - D3
SMITH, EMMA C 391 ONTARIO DR, LVMR, 94550	752 - C5
SNOW, H A 6580 MIRABEAU DR, NWK, 94560	

FEATURE NAME Address City, ZIP Code	PAGE-GRID
SOBRANTE PARK 470 EL PASEO DR, OAK, 94603	670 - H7
SOUTHGATE 26601 CALAROGA AV, HAY, 94545	711 - H6
SPANGLER, ANTHONY 140 N ABBOTT AV, MPS, 95035	793 - J7
STANTON 2644 SOMERSET AV, AlaC, 94546	691 - H4
STEGE 4949 CYPRESS AV, RCH, 94804	609 - B2
STONEHURST 10315 E ST, OAK, 94603	670 - H6
STROBRIDGE 21400 BEDFORD DR, HAY, 94546	691 - J6
SUNOL GLEN 11601 MAIN ST, AlaC, 94586	734 - C6
SUNSET 1671 FRANKFURT WY, LVMR, 94550	715 - G3
SWETT, JOHN 4551 STEELE ST, OAK, 94619	650 - G6
THORNHILL 5880 THORNHILL DR, OAK, 94611	630 - E7
THOUSAND OAKS 840 COLUSA AV, BERK, 94707	609 - F6
TOLER HEIGHTS 9736 LAWLOR ST, OAK, 94605	671 - A4
TREEVIEW 30565 TREEVIEW ST, HAY, 94544	732 - E1
TWIN CREEKS 2785 MARSH DR, SRMN, 94583	673 - B2
TYRRELL 27000 TYRRELL AV, HAY, 94544	712 - A6
VALLEJO MILL 38569 CANYON HEIGHTS DR, FRMT, 94536	753 - D1
VALLEY VIEW 480 ADAMS WY, PLE, 94566	714 - F3
VANNOY 5100 VANNOY AV, AlaC, 94546	692 - C4
VINTAGE HILLS 1125 CONCORD ST, PLE, 94566	714 - G4
WAGNER RANCH 350 CM PABLO, ORIN, 94563	610 - E5
WALNUT GROVE 1999 HARVEST RD, PLE, 94566	714 - D2
WARM SPRINGS 47370 WARM SPRINGS BLVD, FRMT, 94539	773 - H7
WARWICK 3375 WARWICK RD, FRMT, 94555	752 - E1
WASHINGTON 2300 MARTIN LUTHER KING JR WY, BERK, 94703	629 - G2
WASHINGTON 250 DUTTON AV, SLN, 94577	671 - A7
WASHINGTON 581 61ST ST, OAK, 94609	629 - H5
WASHINGTON 825 TAYLOR AV, ALA, 94501	669 - G1
WEBSTER ACADEMY 8000 BIRCH ST, OAK, 94621	670 - H4
WEIBEL, FRED E 45135 S GRIMMER BLVD, FRMT, 94539	773 - H4
WELLER, JOSEPH 345 BOULDER ST, MPS, 95035	794 - A3
WHITTIER 6328 E 17TH ST, OAK, 94621	670 - F2
WILDWOOD 301 WILDWOOD AV, PDMT, 94611	650 - B2
WILSON, WOODROW 1300 WILLIAMS ST, SLN, 94577	690 - J2
WOODLAND 1025 81ST AV, OAK, 94621	670 - G4
WOODSTOCK 1900 3RD ST, ALA, 94501	649 - E7
YATES, ANNA 1070 41ST ST, EMVL, 94608	629 - F7

SCHOOLS - PUBLIC HIGH

FEATURE NAME Address City, ZIP Code	PAGE-GRID
ALAMEDA 2201 ENCINAL AV, ALA, 94501	669 - J2
ALBANY 603 KEY ROUTE BLVD, ALB, 94706	609 - E5
AMADOR VALLEY 1155 SANTA RITA RD, PLE, 94566	714 - E2
AMERICAN 36300 FREMONT BLVD, FRMT, 94536	752 - G2
ARROYO 15701 LORENZO AV, AlaC, 94580	691 - C7
BERKELEY CONT 1950 CARLETON ST, BERK, 94704	629 - G3
BERKELEY 2223 MARTIN LUTHER KING JR WY, BERK, 94704	629 - G2
BRENKWITZ CONT 22100 PRINCETON ST, HAY, 94541	711 - G1
CALAVERAS HILLS CONT 1331 CALAVERAS BLVD, MPS, 95035	794 - C6
CALIFORNIA 9870 BROADMOOR DR, SRMN, 94583	673 - F5
CASTLEMONT 8601 MACARTHUR BLVD, OAK, 94605	671 - A3
CASTRO VALLEY 19400 SANTA MARIA AV, AlaC, 94546	692 - A4
DEL AMIGO 189 DEL AMIGO RD, DNVL, 94526	652 - H1
DEL VALLE 2253 5TH ST, LVMR, 94550	715 - H1
DEWEY/BAYMART 3709 E 12TH ST, OAK, 94601	670 - C1
DUBLIN 8151 VILLAGE PKWY, DBLN, 94568	693 - J2
EL CERRITO 540 ASHBURY AV, ELCR, 94530	609 - E4
EMERY 1100 47TH ST, EMVL, 94608	629 - F6
ENCINAL 210 CENTRAL AV, ALA, 94501	669 - E1
FOOTHILL 4375 FOOTHILL RD, PLE, 94588	713 - J2
FREMONT 4610 FOOTHILL BLVD, OAK, 94601	670 - D1
GRANADA 400 WALL ST, LVMR, 94550	715 - E2
HAYWARD 1633 EAST AV, HAY, 94541	712 - B2
IRVINGTON 41800 BLACOW RD, FRMT, 94538	773 - C1
ISLAND 2437 EAGLE AV, ALA, 94501	670 - A2
KENNEDY 4300 CUTTING BLVD, RCH, 94804	609 - A1
KENNEDY, JOHN F 39999 BLACOW RD, FRMT, 94538	753 - A7
LINCOLN CONT 2600 TEAGARDEN ST, SLN, 94577	691 - A3
LIVERMORE 600 MAPLE ST, LVMR, 94550	715 - H1
LOGAN, JAMES 1800 H ST, UNC, 94587	732 - F6
MCCLYMONDS 2607 MYRTLE ST, OAK, 94607	649 - F2

FEATURE NAME Address City, ZIP Code	PAGE-GRID
MILPITAS 1285 ESCUELA PKWY, MPS, 95035	794 - A4
MISSION SAN JOSE 41717 PALM AV, FRMT, 94539	753 - G5
MOUNT EDEN 2300 PANAMA ST, HAY, 94545	731 - H1
NEWARK MEM 39375 CEDAR BLVD, NWK, 94560	772 - H1
OAKLAND 1023 MACARTHUR BLVD, OAK, 94610	650 - B4
OAKLAND CHARTER 6038 BRANN ST, OAK, 94605	670 - G1
OAKLAND TECHNICAL 4351 BROADWAY, OAK, 94609	629 - J7
PIEDMONT 800 MAGNOLIA AV, PDMT, 94611	650 - B1
REDWOOD ALTERNATIVE 18400 CLIFTON WY, AlaC, 94546	691 - H3
ROBERTSON CONT 4455 SENECA PARK AV, FRMT, 94538	773 - D2
SAN LEANDRO 2200 BANCROFT AV, SLN, 94577	691 - C2
SAN LORENZO 50 E LEWELLING BLVD, AlaC, 94580	691 - E6
SAN RAMON VALLEY 140 LOVE LN, DNVL, 94526	652 - J1
SKYLINE 12250 SKYLINE BLVD, OAK, 94619	651 - A5
TENNYSON 27035 WHITMAN ST, HAY, 94544	712 - B5
VALLEY CONT 6901 YORK DR, DBLN, 94568	693 - J3
VILLAGE 4645 BERNAL AV, PLE, 94566	714 - E4
VINEYARD ALTERNATIVE 543 SONOMA AV, LVMR, 94550	715 - E2
WASHINGTON 38442 FREMONT BLVD, FRMT, 94536	752 - J4

SCHOOLS - PUBLIC INTERMEDIATE

FEATURE NAME Address City, ZIP Code	PAGE-GRID
MORAGA, JOAQUIN 1010 CM PABLO, MRGA, 94556	651 - D1

SCHOOLS - PUBLIC JUNIOR HIGH

FEATURE NAME Address City, ZIP Code	PAGE-GRID
CENTERVILLE 37720 FREMONT BLVD, FRMT, 94536	752 - J4
HOPKINS, WILLIAM 600 DRISCOLL RD, FRMT, 94539	753 - F5
HORNER, JOHN M 41365 CHAPEL WY, FRMT, 94538	753 - D7
NEWARK 6201 LAFAYETTE AV, NWK, 94560	752 - D5
THORNTON 4357 THORNTON AV, FRMT, 94536	752 - G3
WALTERS, G M 39600 LOGAN DR, FRMT, 94538	753 - A6

SCHOOLS - PUBLIC MIDDLE

FEATURE NAME Address City, ZIP Code	PAGE-GRID
ALBANY 1259 BRIGHTON AV, ALB, 94706	609 - E5
ALVARADO 31604 ALVARADO BLVD, UNC, 94587	732 - A5
AMERICAN INDIAN CHARTER 3637 MAGEE AV, OAK, 94619	650 - F5
BANCROFT 1150 BANCROFT AV, SLN, 94577	691 - B1
BARNARD-WHITE 725 WHIPPLE RD, UNC, 94587	732 - F3
BOHANNON 800 BOCKMAN RD, AlaC, 94580	711 - D2
BREWER, EDNA 3748 13TH AV, OAK, 94602	650 - B4
CANYON 19600 CULL CANYON RD, AlaC, 94552	692 - D4
CARTER, VERDESE 4521 WEBSTER ST, OAK, 94609	629 - H7
CHAVEZ, CESAR 27845 WHITMAN ST, HAY, 94544	712 - B6
CHAVEZ, CESAR 2801 HOP RANCH RD, UNC, 94587	732 - D6
CHIPMAN 401 PACIFIC AV, ALA, 94501	649 - E7
CHRISTENSEN, ANDREW N 5757 HAGGIN OAKS AV, LVMR, 94551	696 - C2
CLAREMONT 5750 COLLEGE AV, OAK, 94618	629 - J5
COLE 1011 UNION ST, OAK, 94607	649 - E3
CREEKSIDE 19722 CENTER ST, AlaC, 94546	692 - C5
EAST AVENUE 3951 EAST AV, LVMR, 94550	715 - J1
EDENDALE 16160 ASHLAND AV, AlaC, 94580	691 - E5
ELMHURST 1800 98TH AV, OAK, 94603	670 - J5
EMERY ACADEMY 1275 61ST ST, EMVL, 94608	629 - E5
EXCELSIOR 14401 BYRON HWY, CCCo, 94514	637 - D2
FALLON, ELEANOR MURRAY 3601 KOHNEN WY, DBLN, 94568	694 - F3
FRANCISCO 2190 POWELL ST, SF, 94133	648 - A3
FRICK 2845 64TH AV, OAK, 94605	670 - G1
HARTE, BRET 1047 E ST, HAY, 94541	712 - A2
HARTE, BRET 3700 COOLIDGE AV, OAK, 94602	650 - E4
HART, THOMAS 4433 WILLOW RD, PLE, 94588	694 - B7
HARVEST PARK 4900 VALLEY AV, PLE, 94566	714 - D1
HAVENCOURT 1390 66TH AV, OAK, 94621	670 - F3
IRON HORSE 12601 ALCOSTA BLVD, SRMN, 94583	673 - E2
JUNCTION AVENUE 298 JUNCTION AV, LVMR, 94551	695 - H7
KING ESTATES 8251 FONTAINE ST, OAK, 94605	671 - B2
KING, MARTIN LUTHER JR 26890 HOLLY HILL AV, HAY, 94545	711 - H7
KING, MARTIN LUTHER JR 1781 ROSE ST, BERK, 94703	609 - G7
LINCOLN 1250 FERNSIDE BLVD, ALA, 94501	670 - B4
LONGFELLOW ARTS & TECHNOLOGY 1500 DERBY ST, BERK, 94703	629 - F3
LOWELL 991 14TH ST, OAK, 94607	649 - F3
MADISON, JAMES 400 CAPISTRANO DR, OAK, 94603	690 - H1
MENDENHALL, WILLIAM 1701 EL PADRO LN, LVMR, 94550	715 - E3

FEATURE NAME Address City, ZIP Code	PAGE-GRID
MONTERA 5555 ASCOT DR, OAK, 94611	650 - F2
MUIR, JOHN 1444 WILLIAMS ST, SLN, 94577	690 - J2
OAKLAND CHARTER ACADEMY 3001 INTERNATIONAL BLVD, OAK, 94601	650 - C7
OCHOA, ANTHONY W 2121 DEPOT RD, HAY, 94545	711 - F6
PIEDMONT 740 MAGNOLIA AV, PDMT, 94611	650 - B1
PINE VALLEY 3000 PINE VALLEY RD, SRMN, 94583	673 - G7
PLEASANTON 5001 CASE AV, PLE, 94566	714 - D4
PORTOLA 1021 NAVELLIER ST, ELCR, 94530	609 - D2
ROOSEVELT 1926 19TH AV, OAK, 94606	650 - B6
RUSSELL, THOMAS 1500 ESCUELA PKWY, MPS, 95035	794 - A4
SIMMONS, CALVIN 2101 35TH AV, OAK, 94601	650 - D7
WASHINGTON MANOR 1170 FARGO AV, SLN, 94579	691 - B6
WELLS 6800 PENN DR, DBLN, 94568	693 - J3
WESTLAKE 2629 HARRISON ST, OAK, 94612	649 - H2
WILLARD 2425 STUART ST, BERK, 94705	629 - H3
WILSON COLLEGE PREP CHARTER ACADEMY 400 105TH AV, OAK, 94603	670 - H7
WINDEMERE RANCH 11611 E BRANCH PKWY, CCCo, 94582	674 - A5
WINTON 119 W WINTON AV, HAY, 94544	711 - H3
WOOD, WILL C 420 GRAND ST, ALA, 94501	669 - H3

SHOPPING - REGIONAL

FEATURE NAME	PAGE-GRID
BAYFAIR MALL E 14TH ST & BAYFAIR DR, SLN, 94578	691 - D4
EASTMONT TOWN CTR 7200 BANCROFT AV, OAK, 94605	670 - H2
HACIENDA CROSSINGS 5000 DUBLIN, DBLN, 94568	694 - D4
NEWPARK MALL MOWRY AV & CEDAR BLVD, NWK, 94560	752 - H7
PLAZA 580 4392 LAS POSITAS RD, LVMR, 94551	696 - A5
SAN FRANCISCO CENTRE 865 MARKET ST, SF, 94103	648 - A6
SOUTHLAND MALL 1 SOUTHLAND MALL, HAY, 94545	711 - G4
SOUTH SHORE CTR 2300 SHORELINE DR, ALA, 94501	669 - J3
STONERIDGE MALL 1 STONERIDGE MALL RD, PLE, 94588	693 - H5

TRANSPORTATION

FEATURE NAME	PAGE-GRID
2ND & KING STA 2ND ST & KING ST, SF, 94107	648 - C7
ACE FREMONT STA 37260 FREMONT BLVD, FRMT, 94536	752 - H3
ACE LIVERMORE STA 2418 RAILROAD AV, LVMR, 94551	695 - G7
ACE PLEASANTON STA 4950 PLEASANTON AV, PLE, 94566	714 - D4
ACE VASCO STA 575 VASCO RD, LVMR, 94551	696 - D6
ALAMEDA GATEWAY FERRY TERMINAL MAIN ST, ALA, 94501	649 - D5
ALAMEDA OAKLAND FERRY TERMINAL WATER ST, OAK, 94607	649 - F5
AMTRAK BERKELEY STA UNIVERSITY AV & 3RD ST, BERK, 94710	629 - D2
AMTRAK DELLUMS STA 245 2ND ST, OAK, 94607	649 - G5
AMTRAK EMERYVILLE STA POWELL ST & HORTON ST, EMVL, 94608	629 - E6
AMTRAK FREMONT STA 37260 FREMONT BLVD, FRMT, 94536	752 - H3
AMTRAK HAYWARD STA 22555 MEEKLAND AV, HAY, 94541	711 - G2
AMTRAK OAKLAND/COLISEUM STA 600 73RD AV, OAK, 94621	670 - F4
BART 12TH STREET STA 1245 BROADWAY, OAK, 94607	649 - G4
BART 19TH STREET STA 1900 BROADWAY, OAK, 94612	649 - G3
BART ASHBY STA 3100 ADELINE ST, BERK, 94703	629 - G4
BART BAYFAIR STA 15242 HESPERIAN BLVD, SLN, 94578	691 - D5
BART BERKELEY STA 2610 SHATTUCK AV, BERK, 94704	629 - G2
BART CASTRO VALLEY STA 3301 NORBRIDGE AV, AlaC, 94546	692 - A6
BART COLISEUM/OAKLAND STA 7200 SAN LEANDRO ST, OAK, 94621	670 - F4
BART DUBLIN/PLEASANTON STA 5801 OWENS DR, PLE, 94588	694 - B5
BART EL CERRITO DEL NORTE STA 6400 CUTTING BLVD, ELCR, 94530	609 - B1
BART EL CERRITO PLAZA STA 6699 FAIRMOUNT AV, ELCR, 94530	609 - D4
BART FREMONT STA 2000 BART WY, FRMT, 94538	753 - B3
BART FRUITVALE STA 3401 E 12TH ST, OAK, 94601	670 - C1
BART HAYWARD STA 699 B ST, HAY, 94541	711 - H2
BART LAKE MERRITT STA 800 MADISON ST, OAK, 94607	649 - G5
BART MACARTHUR STA 555 40TH ST, OAK, 94609	629 - G7
BART/MUNI METRO EMBARCADERO STA 298 MARKET ST, SF, 94105	648 - B5
BART/MUNI METRO MONTGOMERY ST STA 598 MARKET ST, SF, 94105	648 - B5
BART/MUNI METRO POWELL STA POWELL ST & MARKET ST, SF, 94103	648 - A6
BART NORTH BERKELEY STA 1750 SACRAMENTO ST, BERK, 94702	629 - F1
BART ORINDA STA 11 CM PABLO, ORIN, 94563	630 - H1
BART ROCKRIDGE STA 5660 COLLEGE AV, OAK, 94618	629 - J5
BART SAN LEANDRO STA 1401 SAN LEANDRO BLVD, SLN, 94577	691 - A1
BART SOUTH HAYWARD STA 28601 DIXON ST, HAY, 94544	732 - C1
BART UNION CITY STA 10 UNION SQ, UNC, 94587	732 - G6
BART WEST OAKLAND STA 1451 7TH ST, OAK, 94607	649 - D4
BRANNAN STA BRANNAN ST & THE EMBARCADERO, SF, 94107	648 - C6

FEATURE NAME Address City, ZIP Code	PAGE-GRID
CALTRAIN SAN FRANCISCO STA 4TH ST & KING ST, SF, 94107	648 - B7
CHINA BASIN FERRY TERMINAL KING ST & 3RD ST, SF, 94107	648 - C7
FERRY TERMINAL MECARTNEY RD, ALA, 94502	669 - H6
FERRY TERMINAL THE EMBARCADERO & POWELL ST, SF, 94133	648 - A3
FOLSOM STA FOLSOM ST & THE EMBARCADERO, SF, 94105	648 - C5
FREMONT BUS STA 3780 BONDE WY, FRMT, 94536	752 - H3
GREYHOUND BUS STA 2103 SAN PABLO AV, OAK, 94612	649 - G3
GREYHOUND BUS STA 22589 WATKINS ST, HAY, 94541	711 - J1
GREYHOUND BUS TERMINAL 1916 2ND ST, LVMR, 94550	715 - G1
METRO TRANSPORT CTR 101 8TH ST, OAK, 94607	649 - G5
MUNI METRO BEACH ST & STOCKTON ST STA BEACH ST & STOCKTON ST, SF, 94133	648 - A3
MUNI METRO FERRY TERMINAL STA THE EMBARCADERO & MISSION ST, SF, 94111	648 - B4
MUNI METRO STEUART ST STA STEUART ST & MARKET ST, SF, 94111	648 - B5
MUNI METRO THE EMBARCADERO & BAY ST STA THE EMBARCADERO & BAY ST, SF, 94111	648 - A3
MUNI METRO THE EMBRCDERO & BROADWAY STA THE EMBARCADERO & BROADWAY, SF, 94111	648 - B4
MUNI METRO THE EMBRCDERO & CHESTNUT STA THE EMBARCADERO & CHESTNUT ST, SF, 94111	648 - A3
MUNI METRO THE EMBRCDERO & GREEN ST STA THE EMBARCADERO & GREEN ST, SF, 94111	648 - B4
MUNI METRO THE EMBRCDRO & GREENWICH STA THE EMBARCADERO & GREENWICH, SF, 94111	648 - B3
MUNI METRO THE EMBRCDERO & PIER 39 STA THE EMBARCADERO & PIER 39, SF, 94133	648 - A3
MUNI METRO THE EMBRCADERO & WSHNGTN STA THE EMBARCADERO & WASHINGTN ST, SF, 94111	648 - B4
SOUTHERN PACIFIC SAN LEANDRO STA 801 DAVIS ST, SLN, 94577	691 - A1
TRANSBAY TRANSIT TERMINAL 1ST ST & NATOMA ST, SF, 94105	648 - B5
UNION PACIFIC RAILROAD STA 495 ROSE AV, PLE, 94566	714 - D3
UNION PACIFIC STA 1011 W ESTUDILLO AV, SLN, 94577	691 - A1

VISITOR INFORMATION

FEATURE NAME	PAGE-GRID
CRAB COVE VISITORS CTR MCKAY AV, ALA, 94501	669 - F2
SAN FRANCISCO VISITORS BUREAU POWELL ST & MARKET ST, SF, 94102	648 - A6
VISITOR CTR 1751 GRAND BLVD, SJS, 95002	793 - D6
VISITOR CTR 1 MARSHLAND RD, FRMT, 94555	752 - A7

PRIMARY STREET Address	Cross Street	ZIP	CITY Pg-Grid
A			
A ST			**OAK**
	3RD ST	94625	649-B3
	4TH ST	94625	649-B3
	4TH ST	94625	649-B3
	5TH ST	94625	649-B3
8200	82ND AV	94621	670-H4
8300	83RD AV	94621	670-H4
8400	84TH AV	94621	670-H4
8500	85TH AV	94621	670-H4
8600	86TH AV	94621	670-H4
8700	87TH AV	94621	670-H4
8800	88TH AV	94621	670-H4
8900	89TH AV	94621	670-H4
9000	90TH AV	94603	670-H5
9100	91ST AV	94603	670-H5
9770	92ND AV	94603	670-H5
9660	93RD AV	94603	670-H5
9550	94TH AV	94603	670-H5
9430	95TH AV	94603	670-H5
9320	96TH AV	94603	670-H5
9200	97TH AV	94603	670-H5
9320	98TH AV	94603	670-H5
9800	98TH AV	94603	670-H5
9900	MANUEL CT	94603	670-J6
10000	100TH AV	94603	670-J6
ABBEY ST			**OAK**
2800	ALLENDALE AV	94619	650-E6
3000	PENNIMAN AV	94619	650-E6
ABBOTT DR			**OAK**
1	SHERWOOD DR	94611	630-D6
ABBOTT WY			**PDMT**
70	SPRING PTH	94618	630-C7
100	MAXWELTON RD	94618	630-C7
ABERFOIL AV			**OAK**
4350	ELVESSA ST	94605	671-D4
4300	ETTRICK ST	94605	671-D5
4200	LOCHARD ST	94605	671-D5
4300	DINGLEY ST	94605	671-D5
ACACIA AV			**BERK**
1	EUCLID AV	94708	609-G4
100	CRAGMONT AV	94708	609-G4
ACACIA AV			**OAK**
5800	LAWTON AV	94618	630-A5
5800	MANILA AV	94618	630-A5
5800	MARGARIDO DR	94618	630-A5
5840	MARGARIDO DR	94618	630-A5
5900	COUNTRY CLUB DR	94618	630-A5
5980	MANCHESTER DR	94618	630-B5
6000	PINE LN	94618	630-B5
6100	VERONA PTH	94618	630-B5
6180	LOCARNO PTH	94618	630-B5
6180	MATHIEU AV	94618	630-B5
6280	OCEAN VIEW DR	94618	630-B5
6300	CROSS RD	94618	630-B5
6310	GOLDEN GATE AV	94618	630-B5
6400	BUENA VISTA AV	94618	630-B5
ACALANES DR			**OAK**
10500	105TH AV	94603	670-H7
10570	CAPISTRANO DR	94603	670-H7
10800	COLORADOS DR	94603	670-H7
10870	LA PRENDA DR	94603	670-H7
10910	BERGEDO DR	94603	670-H7
11200	CATRON DR	94603	670-H7
ACCESS RD			**EMVL**
	FRONTAGE RD	94608	629-D6
ACROFT CT			**BERK**
1400	ACTON ST	94702	629-F2
ACTON CIR			**BERK**
100	ACTON CRES	94702	629-F2
ACTON CRES			**BERK**
1400	ACTON ST	94702	629-F2
1430	ACTON CIR	94702	629-F2
ACTON PL			**OAK**
200	LESTER AV	94606	649-J4
300	ATHOL AV	94606	649-J4
ACTON ST			**BERK**
1400	GILMAN ST	94702	609-F7
1450	HOPKINS ST	94702	609-F7
1450	HOPKINS ST	94702	609-F7
1470	ADA ST	94702	609-F7
1500	ROSE ST	94702	609-F7
1540	TOMLEE DR	94702	629-F1
1560	KEONCREST DR	94702	629-F1
1590	CEDAR ST	94702	629-F1
1660	LINCOLN ST	94702	629-F1
1690	VIRGINIA ST	94702	629-F1
1740	FRANCISCO ST	94702	629-F1
1800	DELAWARE ST	94702	629-F1
1800	DELAWARE ST	94702	629-F1
1900	HEARST AV	94702	629-F1
1950	BERKELEY WY	94702	629-F2
2000	UNIVERSITY AV	94702	629-F2
2100	ADDISON ST	94702	629-F2
2170	ACTON CRES	94702	629-F2
2200	ALLSTON WY	94702	629-F2
2270	ACROFT CT	94702	629-F2
2300	BANCROFT WY	94702	629-F2
2400	CHANNING WY	94702	629-F3
2500	DWIGHT WY	94702	629-F3
2500	DWIGHT WY	94702	629-F3
2550	BLAKE ST	94702	629-F3
2600	PARKER ST	94702	629-F3
2630	CARLETON ST	94702	629-F3
2670	DERBY ST	94702	629-F3
2700	WARD ST	94702	629-F3
2700	WARD ST	94702	629-F3
2800	OREGON ST	94702	629-F4
2900	RUSSELL ST	94702	629-F4
2900	RUSSELL ST	94702	629-F4
2910	BURNETT ST	94702	629-F4
3000	ASHBY AV	94702	629-F4
3020	CARRISON ST	94702	629-F4
3040	HASKELL ST	94702	629-F4
3100	PRINCE ST	94702	629-F4
3150	67TH ST	94702	629-F4
3200	66TH ST	94702	629-F4
ADA ST			**BERK**
1300	ORDWAY ST	94702	609-E7
1400	ACTON ST	94702	609-F7
1500	SACRAMENTO ST	94703	609-F7
1530	MIRAMONTE CT	94703	609-F7
1560	CALIFORNIA ST	94703	609-F7
1600	MCGEE AV	94703	609-F7
ADA ST			**OAK**
200	BROADWAY	94618	629-J6
300	BRYANT AV	94618	629-J6
ADAMS ST			**ALA**
2800	BISHOP ST	94501	670-A3
2900	MOUND ST	94501	670-A3
3000	COURT ST	94501	670-A3
3100	FOUNTAIN ST	94501	670-B4
3200	HIGH ST	94501	670-B4
3230	POST ST	94501	670-B4
3260	PEACH ST	94501	670-B4
3300	FERNSIDE BLVD	94501	670-B4
ADAMS ST			**ALB**
600	CLAY ST	94706	609-D5
700	CASTRO ST	94706	609-D5
800	WASHINGTON AV	94706	609-D6
900	SOLANO AV	94706	609-D6
1000	BUCHANAN ST	94706	609-D6
ADAMS ST			**OAK**
200	LEE ST	94610	649-H2
300	PERKINS ST	94610	649-J2
400	EUCLID AV	94610	649-J2
500	CHETWOOD ST	94610	649-J2
500	MACARTHUR BLVD	94610	649-J2
ADDISON ST			**BERK**
600	BOLIVAR DR	94804	629-D2
600	W BOLIVAR DR	94804	629-D2
620	2ND ST	94804	629-D2
700	3RD ST	94804	629-D2
720	4TH ST	94804	629-D2
800	5TH ST	94804	629-D2
820	6TH ST	94804	629-D2
900	7TH ST	94804	629-D2
930	8TH ST	94804	629-E2
1000	9TH ST	94804	629-E2
1020	10TH ST	94804	629-E2
1100	SAN PABLO AV	94804	629-E2
1100	SAN PABLO AV	94702	629-E2
1130	BYRON ST	94702	629-E2
1200	CURTIS ST	94702	629-E2
1200	BROWNING ST	94702	629-E2
1250	BONAR ST	94702	629-E2
1300	WEST ST	94702	629-F2
1400	ACTON ST	94702	629-F2
1500	SACRAMENTO ST	94703	629-F2
1520	SPAULDING AV	94703	629-F2
1600	CALIFORNIA ST	94703	629-F2
	JEFFERSON AV	94703	629-F2
1620	JEFFERSON AV	94703	629-F2
1700	MCGEE AV	94703	629-F2
1720	ROOSEVELT AV	94703	629-G2
1800	GRANT ST	94703	629-G2
1820	MCKINLEY AV	94703	629-G2
1900	MARTIN LUTHER KING JR WY	94704	629-G2
2000	MILVIA ST	94704	629-G1
2100	SHATTUCK AV	94704	629-G1
2120	SHATTUCK SQ	94704	629-H1
2150	TERMINAL PL	94704	629-H1
2200	OXFORD ST	94704	629-H1
ADELAIDE ST			**OAK**
4300	HUNTINGTON ST	94619	650-G6
4400	CARSON ST	94619	650-G6
ADELINE ST			**BERK**
2800	SHATTUCK AV	94703	629-H3
2810	WARD ST	94703	629-G3
2830	STUART ST	94703	629-G3
2850	OREGON ST	94703	629-G3
2900	RUSSELL ST	94703	629-G4
3000	ASHBY AV	94703	629-G4
3030	EMERSON ST	94703	629-G4
3060	ESSEX ST	94703	629-G4
3130	WOOLSEY ST	94703	629-G4
3180	MARTIN LUTHER KING JR WY	94703	629-G4
3200	FAIRVIEW ST	94703	629-G4
3250	HARMON ST	94703	629-G4
3300	ALCATRAZ AV	94703	629-G5
3380	MARTIN LUTHER KING JR WY	94703	629-G5
3400	STANFORD AV	94703	629-G5
3500	61ST ST	94703	629-G5
3300	ALCATRAZ AV	94703	629-G5
3350	63RD ST	94703	629-G5
3400	STANFORD AV	94703	629-G5
ADELINE ST			**EMVL**
	W MACARTHUR BLVD	94608	629-F7
	W MACARTHUR BLVD	94608	629-F7
5180	W MACARTHUR BLVD	94608	629-F7
3800	SAN PABLO AV	94608	629-F7
3900	39TH ST	94608	629-F7
3940	YERBA BUENA AV	94608	629-F7
4000	40TH ST	94608	629-F7
4100	41ST ST	94608	629-F7
4200	42ND ST	94608	629-F7
	43RD ST	94608	629-F7
4300	43RD ST	94608	629-F7
4400	44TH ST	94608	629-F6
4500	45TH ST	94608	629-F6
4560	45TH ST	94608	629-F6
4600	46TH ST	94608	629-F6
4700	47TH ST	94608	629-F6
ADELINE ST			**OAK**
200	3RD ST	94607	649-E4
700	7TH ST	94607	649-E4
810	8TH ST	94607	649-E3
1000	10TH ST	94607	649-E3
1200	12TH ST	94607	649-E3
1400	14TH ST	94607	649-E3
1600	16TH ST	94607	649-E3
1800	18TH ST	94607	649-E2
1900	19TH ST	94607	649-E2
2100	21ST ST	94607	649-E2
2200	W GRAND AV	94607	649-F2
2400	24TH ST	94607	649-F2
2600	26TH ST	94607	649-F2
2800	28TH ST	94608	649-F1
3000	30TH ST	94608	649-F1
3200	32ND ST	94608	649-F1
3400	34TH ST	94608	649-F1
3550	35TH ST	94608	649-F1
3600	36TH ST	94608	629-F7
3800	W MACARTHUR BLVD	94608	629-F7
4700	47TH ST	94608	629-F6
5300	53RD ST	94608	629-F6
5340	LOWELL ST	94608	629-F6
5370	53RD ST	94608	629-G6
5400	54TH ST	94608	629-G6
5450	54TH ST	94608	629-G6
5500	55TH ST	94608	629-G6
5530	55TH ST	94608	629-G6
5600	56TH ST	94608	629-G6
3770	AILEEN ST	94608	629-G6
5650	AILEEN ST	94608	629-G6
5690	MARKET ST	94608	629-G6
5700	57TH ST	94608	629-G5
5750	ARLINGTON AV	94608	629-G5
5800	58TH ST	94608	629-G5
5900	59TH ST	94608	629-G5
6000	60TH ST	94608	629-G5
6040	GENOA ST	94608	629-G5
6100	61ST ST	94608	629-G5
ADELL CT			**OAK**
3400	MONTANA ST	94602	650-D4
3400	MACARTHUR BLVD	94602	650-D4
3400	EXCELSIOR AV	94602	650-D4
3460	MONTANA ST	94602	650-D4
ADELPHIAN WY			**ALA**
200	MECARTNEY RD	94502	669-H6
230	SWEET WY	94502	669-H6
300	CREEDON CIR	94502	669-H6
ADMIRAL DR			**EMVL**
1	POWELL ST	94608	629-C6
ADMIRALITY LN			**ALA**
1100	FIR AV	94502	670-A6
1100	TAHITI LN	94502	670-A6
1120	SANTA CRUZ LN	94502	670-A7
1160	PHOENIX LN	94502	670-A7
1200	FIJI LN	94502	670-A7
AFRICA ST			**OAK**
	BURMA RD	94607	649-C1
	CORREGIDOR AV	94607	649-C1
AGNES ST			**OAK**
1	ALTA RD	94618	630-C6
100	PROCTOR AV	94618	630-C6
150	SHERIDAN RD	94618	630-C6
100	COCHRANE AV	94618	630-C6
150	PROCTOR AV	94618	630-C6
AGUA VISTA ST			**OAK**
3800	38TH AV	94601	650-E7
4080	ROSEDALE AV	94601	650-E7
4300	HIGH ST	94601	650-E7
AILEEN ST			**OAK**
500	TELEGRAPH AV	94609	629-H6
530	CARBERRY AV	94609	629-H5
600	SHATTUCK AV	94609	629-H6
700	DOVER ST	94609	629-G6
800	MARTIN LUTHER KING JR WY	94608	629-G6
850	GENOA ST	94608	629-G6
900	MARKET ST	94608	629-G6
910	ADELINE ST	94608	629-G6
910	ADELINE ST	94608	629-G6
950	LOWELL ST	94608	629-F6
1000	LOS ANGELES ST	94608	629-F6
1050	GASKILL ST	94608	629-F6
1100	SAN PABLO AV	94608	629-F6
AIR CARGO RD			**OAK**
	SALLY RIDE WY	94621	690-D1
	AIRPORT DR	94621	690-E2
AIRPORT DR			**OAK**
1	HEGENBERGER RD	94621	670-E7
1	PARDEE DR	94621	670-E7
130	98TH AV	94603	690-F1
240	DOOLITTLE DR	94621	690-E1
360	HEGENBERGER RD	94621	690-E1
470	EARHART RD	94621	690-E1
740	AIR CARGO RD	94621	690-E2
900	JOHN GLENN DR	94621	690-D2
1100	ALAN SHEPARD WY	94621	690-D3
	NEIL ARMSTRONG WY	94621	690-D2
AITKEN DR			**OAK**
6500	DORAN DR	94611	630-G7
6500	WESTOVER DR	94611	630-G7
6560	GIRVIN DR	94611	630-G7
6740	MOORE DR	94611	630-G7
6800	EVERGREEN AV	94611	630-G7
6800	FORESTLAND WY	94611	630-G7
6850	WHITE CT	94611	630-G7
6900	SHEPHERD CANYON RD	94611	630-G7
AJAX PL			**BERK**
1	SUMMIT RD	94708	610-A6
1	ATLAS PL	94708	610-A6
ALAMEDA AV			**ALA**
1500	BENTON ST	94501	669-H1
1500	CENTRAL AV	94501	669-H1
1600	PARU ST	94501	669-H1
1700	GRAND ST	94501	669-H2
1800	UNION ST	94501	669-H2
1900	LAFAYETTE ST	94501	669-J2
2000	CHESTNUT ST	94501	669-J2
2100	WILLOW ST	94501	669-J2
2200	WALNUT ST	94501	669-J2
2300	OAK ST	94501	670-A2
2400	PARK ST	94501	670-A2
ALAMEDA AV			**OAK**
3200	FRUITVALE AV	94601	670-C2
3200	TILDEN WY	94601	670-C2
4100	HOWARD ST	94601	670-C2
4220	E 8TH ST	94601	670-C2
ALAMEDA MARINA DR			**ALA**
	CLEMENT AV	94501	669-J1
ALAMEDA RD			**ALA**
	PAN AM WY	94501	649-D6
	W ESSEX DR	94501	649-D6
	SEATTLE RD	94501	649-D6
80	NEWPORT RD	94501	649-D6
	SAN DIEGO RD	94501	649-D6
	LEMOORE RD	94501	649-D6
180	SAN PEDRO RD	94501	649-D6
200	PEARL HARBOR RD	94501	649-D6
ALAMO AV			**BERK**
1	SPRUCE ST	94708	609-G5
100	HALKIN LN	94708	609-G5
ALAN SHEPARD WY			**OAK**
150	JOHN GLENN DR	94621	690-D2
200	AIRPORT DR	94621	690-D2
ALASKA PACKER PL			**ALA**
	FORTMANN WY	94501	649-J7
ALASKA ST			**OAK**
140	WAKE AV	94607	649-C1
1	WAKE AV	94607	649-C1
	MARITIME ST	94607	649-C1
ALBANY TER			**ALB**
1500	NEILSON ST	94706	609-E6
1600	TELVIN ST	94706	609-E6
ALBERT ST			**OAK**
4300	MADRONE AV	94619	650-G6
4410	HUNTINGTON ST	94619	650-G6
ALBINA AV			**BERK**
1260	HOPKINS CT	94706	609-F7
1400	HOPKINS ST	94706	609-F7
ALCALA AV			**OAK**
9500	OAK KNOLL BLVD	94605	671-B4
9570	CASTLEWOOD ST	94605	671-B4
9600	GOLF LINKS RD	94605	671-B4
ALCATRAZ AV			**BERK**
1000	ESSEX ST	94702	629-F5
1200	IDAHO ST	94702	629-F5
1400	BAKER ST	94702	629-F5
1500	MARKET ST	94703	629-F5
1500	SACRAMENTO ST	94703	629-F5
1600	CALIFORNIA ST	94703	629-G5
	KING ST	94703	629-G5
1700	KING ST	94703	629-G5
1740	ELLIS ST	94703	629-G5
1790	ADELINE ST	94703	629-G5
	ADELINE ST	94703	629-G5
1810	MARTIN LUTHER KING JR WY	94703	629-G5
700	DOVER ST	94703	629-G5
800	SHATTUCK AV	94703	629-G5
2700	COLLEGE AV	94705	629-J4
2750	LEWISTON AV	94705	629-J4
2800	CLAREMONT AV	94705	629-J4
ALCATRAZ AV			**OAK**
2600	COLLEGE AV	94618	629-J4
300	BENVENUE AV	94618	629-J4
340	HILLEGASS AV	94618	629-J4
350	HILLEGASS AV	94618	629-J4
370	REGENT ST	94618	629-J4
390	COLBY ST	94618	629-J4
400	COLBY ST	94609	629-J4
450	DANA ST	94609	629-H4
500	TELEGRAPH AV	94609	629-H4
530	IRWIN CT	94609	629-H4
570	RAYMOND ST	94609	629-H4
600	RACINE ST	94609	629-H4
610	DARCY CT	94609	629-H4
700	SHATTUCK AV	94609	629-H4
1020	ESSEX ST	94608	629-F5
1050	HERZOG ST	94608	629-F5
1070	SALEM ST	94608	629-F5
1100	SAN PABLO AV	94608	629-F5
ALDER ST			**OAK**
7880	78TH AV	94621	670-H3
7900	79TH AV	94621	670-H3
8000	80TH AV	94621	670-H3
ALEXANDER CT			**OAK**
3500	35TH AV	94601	650-D7
ALHAMBRA AV			**OAK**
5900	GOULDIN RD	94611	630-E6
6000	ALHAMBRA LN	94611	630-E6
ALHAMBRA LN			**OAK**
1600	THORNHILL DR	94611	630-E6
1750	ALHAMBRA AV	94611	630-E7
1800	ALMADEN LN	94611	630-E7
ALICE ST			**OAK**
100	EMBARCADERO	94607	649-G5
200	2ND ST	94607	649-G5
400	4TH ST	94607	649-G5
500	5TH ST	94607	649-G5
630	7TH ST	94607	649-G5
780	8TH ST	94607	649-G4
900	9TH ST	94607	649-G4
1000	10TH ST	94607	649-G4
1100	11TH ST	94607	649-G4
1200	12TH ST	94612	649-G4
1300	13TH ST	94612	649-G4
1400	14TH ST	94612	649-G4
1700	17TH ST	94612	649-H4
1900	19TH ST	94612	649-H4
ALICIA ST			**OAK**
2700	27TH ST	94607	649-F2
2800	MARKET ST	94607	649-F2
ALIDA CT			**OAK**
1	ALIDA ST	94602	650-E3
ALIDA ST			**OAK**
2400	LINCOLN AV	94602	650-E3
2470	ALIDA CT	94602	650-E4
2530	LINNET AV	94602	650-E4
2600	LAGUNA AV	94602	650-E4
2600	LAGUNA AV	94602	650-E4
2700	RHODA AV	94602	650-F4
2800	COOLIDGE AV	94602	650-F4
2900	BARNER AV	94602	650-F4
ALISO AV			**OAK**
3800	35TH AV	94619	650-G5
3940	39TH AV	94619	650-G5
4000	ANDERSON AV	94619	650-G5
4110	TOYON PL	94619	650-G5
4160	ELINORA AV	94619	650-G5
4220	FIELDBROOK RD	94619	650-H5
4300	CARSON ST	94619	650-H5
ALLENDALE AV			**OAK**
3500	35TH AV	94619	650-E6
3570	OCTAVIA ST	94619	650-E6
3600	OCTAVIA ST	94619	650-E6
3650	ABBEY ST	94619	650-E6
3680	ABBEY ST	94619	650-E6
3720	SHORT ST	94619	650-E6
3730	SHORT ST	94619	650-E6
	VIOLA ST	94619	650-E6
3760	VIOLA ST	94619	650-E6
3800	38TH AV	94619	650-E6
3900	39TH AV	94619	650-E6
4000	MINNA AV	94619	650-E7
4100	EASTMAN AV	94619	650-E7
4300	HIGH ST	94619	650-E7
4580	LILAC ST	94619	650-F7
4760	RENWICK ST	94619	650-F7
4900	MONTICELLO AV	94619	650-F7
ALLMAN ST			**OAK**
1390	BEAUMONT AV	94602	650-C4
1500	GLEN PARK RD	94602	650-C4
ALLSTON WY			**BERK**
700	3RD ST	94804	629-D2
720	4TH ST	94804	629-D2
800	5TH ST	94804	629-D2
820	6TH ST	94804	629-D2
900	7TH ST	94804	629-D2
920	8TH ST	94804	629-E2
1000	9TH ST	94804	629-E2
1020	10TH ST	94804	629-E2
1100	SAN PABLO AV	94702	629-E2
1130	BYRON ST	94702	629-E2
1200	CURTIS ST	94702	629-E2
1220	BROWNING ST	94702	629-E2
1250	BONAR ST	94702	629-E2
1300	WEST ST	94702	629-E2
1320	VALLEY ST N	94702	629-F2
1400	ACTON ST	94702	629-F2
1500	SACRAMENTO ST	94703	629-F2
1550	SPAULDING AV	94703	629-F2
1600	CALIFORNIA ST	94703	629-F2
1620	JEFFERSON AV	94703	629-F2
1700	MCGEE AV	94703	629-F2
1720	ROOSEVELT AV	94703	629-G2
1800	GRANT ST	94703	629-G2
1830	MCKINLEY AV	94703	629-G2
1900	MARTIN LUTHER KING JR WY	94704	629-G2
2000	MILVIA ST	94704	629-G2
2050	HAROLD WY	94704	629-G2
2100	SHATTUCK AV	94704	629-H2
2200	OXFORD ST	94704	629-H2
ALMA AV			**OAK**
600	PROSPECT AV	94610	650-A4
650	MCKINLEY AV	94610	650-B4
700	MACARTHUR BLVD	94610	650-B4
ALMA PL			**OAK**
800	GROSVENOR PL	94610	650-B4
800	EXCELSIOR AV	94610	650-B4
ALMADEN LN			**OAK**
5900	ALHAMBRA LN	94611	630-E7
ALMANZA DR			**OAK**
450	CAPISTRANO DR	94603	670-H7
700	TOPANGA DR	94603	670-H7
ALPINE TER			**OAK**
110	PINE LN	94618	630-B5
110	LOCARNO PTH	94618	630-B5
200	OCEAN VIEW DR	94618	630-B5
ALTA AV			**PDMT**
1	BLAIR AV	94611	650-C1
	SCENIC AV	94611	630-C7
100	SCENIC AV	94611	630-C7
200	SCENIC AV	94611	630-C7
ALTA RD			**BERK**
1	SPRUCE ST	94708	609-G4
100	CRAGMONT AV	94708	609-G4
ALTA RD			**OAK**
150	PROCTOR AV	94618	630-C6
100	AGNES ST	94618	630-C6
150	FLORENCE AV	94618	630-C6
ALTA VISTA			**ALA**
3000	VIA ALISO	94502	669-J6
3100	VERDEMAR DR	94502	669-J6
ALTA VISTA AV			**OAK**
300	JEAN ST	94610	649-J2
400	MIRA VISTA AV	94610	649-J2

PRIMARY STREET / Address	Cross Street	ZIP	CITY / Pg-Grid
ALTAMONT AV			**OAK**
3900	SUNNYMERE AV	94605	670-J1
3950	HILLMONT DR	94605	670-J1
	MOKELUMNE AV	94605	670-J1
4020	MOKELUMNE AV	94605	670-J1
4100	SIMSON ST	94605	670-J1
ALTURA PL			**OAK**
7500	RIFLE LN	94605	671-A1
ALVARADO PL			**OAK**
100	ALVARADO RD	94705	630-A3
100	EUCALYPTUS PTH	94705	630-A3
ALVARADO RD			**BERK**
100	BRIDGE RD	94705	630-B4
130	WILLOW TR	94705	630-B4
200	VICENTE RD	94705	630-B3
250	WILLOW TR	94705	630-B3
300	EUCALYPTUS PTH	94705	630-B3
ALVARADO RD			**OAK**
1	TUNNEL RD	94705	630-A3
1	THE UPLANDS	94705	630-A3
70	THE SHORT CUT	94705	630-A3
70	EUCALYPTUS PTH	94705	630-A3
70	ALVARADO PL	94705	630-A3
100	BRIDGE RD	94705	630-A3
600	EUCALYPTUS PTH	94705	630-B3
700	SLATER LN	94705	630-B3
800	GRAVATT DR	94705	630-B3
970	ROBISON DR	94705	630-B3
1000	SILER PL	94705	630-B3
1060	AMITO AV	94705	630-B3
1310	GYPSY LN	94705	630-B2
1400	CLAREMONT AV	94705	630-B2
AMADOR AV			**BERK**
1150	MARIPOSA AV	94707	609-G6
1200	SHATTUCK AV	94707	609-G6
AMBER ISL			**ALA**
500	ROSEWOOD WY	94501	669-G2
AMELIA ST			**OAK**
8400	84TH AV	94621	670-G4
8500	85TH AV	94621	670-G4
8500	85TH AV	94621	670-G5
8600	86TH AV	94621	670-G5
AMITO AV			**OAK**
1070	ALVARADO RD	94705	630-B3
1000	DRURY RD	94705	630-B3
1080	GRAVATT DR	94705	630-B3
AMY DR			**OAK**
5600	MAXWELTON RD	94618	630-C7
5700	HARBORD DR	94618	630-C7
5800	MASONIC AV	94618	630-C7
5900	PROCTOR AV	94618	630-C7
ANAIR WY			**OAK**
1	BURR ST	94605	671-A4
100	STEARNS AV	94605	671-B4
ANCHOR DR			**EMVL**
1	POWELL ST	94608	629-C6
ANCHOR WY			**ALA**
300	BRIDGE VIEW ISL	94501	670-A4
ANDERSON AV			**OAK**
4300	REINHARDT DR	94619	650-G5
4400	SELKIRK ST	94619	650-G5
4400	ALISO AV	94619	650-G5
4500	REINHARDT DR	94619	650-G5
ANDERSON RD			**ALA**
100	MOORE CT	94502	669-J6
100	LAWRENCE RD	94502	669-J6
130	EVANS CT	94502	669-H6
160	ROSS RD	94502	669-H6
200	SALMON RD	94502	669-H5
400	SMITH CT	94502	669-H5
400	SWEET RD	94502	669-H5
ANDOVER ST			**OAK**
350	34TH ST	94609	649-H1
ANDREWS ST			**OAK**
2100	SNAKE RD	94611	650-E1
ANGELO AV			**OAK**
3830	38TH AV	94619	650-E6
4000	MINNA AV	94619	650-E6
ANNAPOLIS CIR			**ALA**
2000	SINGLETON AV	94501	649-E6
2100	SINGLETON AV	94501	649-E6
ANNERLEY RD			**OAK**
1000	HARVARD RD	94610	650-B2
1050	PORTSMOUTH RD	94610	650-B2
ANNERLEY RD			**PDMT**
1050	PORTSMOUTH RD	94610	650-B2
1100	HARVARD RD	94610	650-B2
ANTHONY ST			**BERK**
800	5TH ST	94804	629-E4
900	7TH ST	94804	629-E4
1000	9TH ST	94804	629-E4
ANTIOCH CT			**OAK**
2000	MOUNTAIN BLVD	94611	650-E1
2100	ANTIOCH ST	94611	650-E1
ANTIOCH ST			**OAK**
6100	MOUNTAIN BLVD	94611	650-E1
6200	ANTIOCH CT	94611	650-E1
6300	LUCAS AV	94611	650-E1
ANZA AV			**OAK**
9700	CALAFIA AV	94605	671-B4
9800	GOLF LINKS RD	94605	671-B4
APGAR ST			**OAK**
650	MARTIN LUTHER KING JR WY	94609	629-G7
800	WEST ST	94608	629-G7
840	LUSK ST	94608	629-G7
920	MARKET ST	94608	629-F7
1100	W MACARTHUR BLVD	94608	629-F7
APPLE ST			**OAK**
720	GRAVENSTEIN ST	94603	670-H6
800	PEARMAIN ST	94603	670-H6
850	PIPPIN ST	94603	670-H6
900	RUSSET ST	94603	670-H6
APPLEGATE WY			**ALA**
1	KOFMAN PKWY	94502	669-H5
APRICOT ST			**OAK**
10700	107TH AV	94603	670-J6
10800	BLENHEIM ST	94603	670-J7
10900	MOORPARK ST	94603	670-J7
11000	ROYAL ST	94603	670-J7
AQUARIUS WY			**OAK**
900	BROADWAY TER	94611	630-D6
1060	AVOCA AV	94611	630-D6
ARBON PTH			**OAK**
	BROADWAY TER	94618	630-B5
	MANDALAY RD	94618	630-B5
	BUENA VISTA AV	94618	630-B5
	CONTRA COSTA RD	94618	630-B5
ARBOR DR			**PDMT**
1	OAKLAND AV	94610	650-A1
50	FAIRVIEW AV	94610	650-A1
50	FAIRVIEW AV	94610	650-A1
60	FAIRVIEW AV	94610	650-A1
100	NOVA DR	94610	650-A1
100	NOVA DR	94610	650-A1
200	JEROME AV	94610	650-A1
ARBOR ST			**ALA**
1700	PACIFIC AV	94501	669-H1
1800	BUENA VISTA AV	94501	669-H1
ARCADE AV			**BERK**
1	GRIZZLY PEAK BLVD	94708	609-J6
50	FAIRLAWN DR	94708	609-J6
ARCADIA AV			**OAK**
4300	WRENN ST	94602	650-E3
4500	MELVIN RD	94602	650-E3
ARCH ST			**BERK**
1100	SPRUCE ST	94708	609-H6
1100	SPRUCE ST	94707	609-H6
1140	CORONA CT	94708	609-H6
1140	CORONA CT	94707	609-H6
1160	OAK ST	94708	609-H6
1160	OAK ST	94707	609-H6
1200	EUNICE ST	94708	609-H6
1200	EUNICE ST	94707	609-H6
1300	GLEN AV	94708	609-H7
1300	GLEN AV	94709	609-H7
1380	ROSE ST	94708	609-H7
1380	ROSE ST	94709	609-H7
1400	ROSE ST	94708	609-H7
1400	ROSE ST	94709	609-H7
1500	VINE ST	94708	609-H7
1500	VINE ST	94709	609-H7
1600	CEDAR ST	94708	609-H7
1600	CEDAR ST	94709	609-H7
1800	CEDAR ST	94709	609-H7
1700	HILGARD AV	94709	629-H1
1740	VIRGINIA ST	94708	629-H1
1740	VIRGINIA ST	94709	629-H1
1900	HEARST AV	94709	629-H1
1900	LE CONTE AV	94709	629-H1
ARCHMONT PL			**OAK**
3910	SUNNYMERE AV	94605	650-J7
4000	HILLMONT DR	94605	650-J7
ARDEN PL			**OAK**
4300	LEIMERT BLVD	94602	650-D3
4300	OAKMORE RD	94602	650-D3
4330	ARDEN WY	94602	650-D3
ARDEN RD			**BERK**
1	MOSSWOOD RD	94704	630-A2
10	PANORAMIC PL	94704	630-A2
20	ORCHARD LN	94704	630-A2
50	PANORAMIC WY	94704	630-A2
ARDEN WY			**OAK**
1500	ARDEN PL	94602	650-D3
ARDLEY AV			**OAK**
3500	MACARTHUR BLVD	94602	650-C4
3500	23RD AV	94602	650-C4
3600	EXCELSIOR AV	94602	650-C4
3800	E 38TH ST	94602	650-C4
3800	E 38TH ST	94602	650-C4
4100	HAMPEL ST	94602	650-C4
ARDMORE AV			**OAK**
1000	ASHMOUNT AV	94610	650-C2
1100	MANDANA BLVD	94610	650-C2
ARGUS CT			**ALA**
1	MCDONNEL RD	94502	669-J6
ARGYLE ST			**OAK**
2700	KEARNEY AV	94602	650-F3
2800	DUBLIN AV	94602	650-F3
ARIMO AV			**OAK**
600	WALAVISTA AV	94610	650-B2
800	WALAVISTA AV	94610	650-B2
ARIZONA ST			**OAK**
3000	MAPLE AV	94602	650-F5
3200	LAUREL AV	94602	650-F5
3270	ASPEN PL	94602	650-F5
3400	MIDVALE AV	94602	650-F5
3500	35TH AV	94602	650-F5
ARKANSAS			**ALA**
3030	MULVANY CIR	94501	649-E6
3050	ENTERPRISE	94501	649-E6
ARKANSAS ST			**OAK**
3200	MAPLE AV	94602	650-E5
3300	LAUREL AV	94602	650-E5
ARLINGTON AV			**BERK**
500	SANTA BARBARA RD	94707	609-G4
530	SAN LUIS RD	94707	609-F5
600	SAN ANTONIO AV	94707	609-G5
630	SAN FERNANDO AV	94707	609-G5
700	THOUSAND OAKS BLVD	94707	609-G5
800	SOMERSET PL	94707	609-G5
800	YOSEMITE RD	94707	609-G5
850	MENDOCINO AV	94707	609-G6
980	INDIAN ROCK AV	94707	609-G6
1000	FOUNTAIN WK	94707	609-G6
1000	LOS ANGELES AV	94707	609-G6
1000	MARIN AV	94707	609-G6
1000	SUTTER ST	94707	609-G6
1000	DEL NORTE ST	94707	609-G6
ARLINGTON AV			**OAK**
800	MARTIN LUTHER KING JR WY	94608	629-G5
850	GENOA ST	94608	629-G5
900	ADELINE ST	94608	629-G5
910	MARKET ST	94608	629-F5
950	LOWELL ST	94608	629-F5
1000	LOS ANGELES ST	94608	629-F6
1100	GASKILL ST	94608	629-F6
ARLINGTON ISL			**ALA**
600	OTIS DR	94501	669-G2
ARMANINO CT			**OAK**
100	COLLEGE AV	94618	629-J5
ARMITAGE ST			**ALA**
1000	MILLINGTON CT	94502	669-J6
1000	YOUNG ST	94502	669-J6
1100	PATTIANI WY	94502	669-J6
ARMOUR DR			**OAK**
6800	THORNHILL DR	94611	630-E6
6800	SNAKE RD	94611	630-E7
AROLLO PTH			**OAK**
	GOLDEN GATE AV	94618	630-B5
	BUENA VISTA AV	94618	630-B5
ARROWHEAD DR			**OAK**
1600	COLTON BLVD	94611	630-F6
1600	RIDGEWOOD DR	94611	630-F6
1700	HOMEWOOD DR	94611	630-F6
1800	GLENCOURT	94611	630-G6
2100	EAST CIR	94611	630-G6
2400	SHEPHERD CANYON RD	94611	630-G6
ARROYO AV			**PDMT**
60	MONTECELLO AV	94611	630-A7
60	PARK WY	94611	630-A7
30	RICARDO AV	94611	630-A7
	YORK DR	94611	630-A7
	MANOR DR	94611	630-A7
	LOWER GRAND AV	94611	630-A7
	GRAND AV	94611	630-A7
ARROYUELO AV			**OAK**
4200	ENTRADA AV	94611	649-J1
4300	ENTRADA AV	94611	649-J1
ARTHUR ST			**OAK**
6400	64TH AV	94605	670-G2
6500	65TH AV	94605	670-G2
6600	66TH AV	94605	670-G2
6650	HAVENSCOURT BLVD	94605	670-G2
6700	67TH AV	94605	670-G2
6800	68TH AV	94605	670-G2
6860	CHURCH ST	94605	670-G2
6900	69TH AV	94605	670-H2
6830	73RD AV	94605	670-H3
7300	73RD AV	94605	670-H3
7700	DASHWOOD AV	94605	670-H3
7800	78TH AV	94605	670-H3
6900	78TH AV	94605	670-H3
6900	78TH AV	94621	670-H3
7000	79TH AV	94605	670-H3
7000	79TH AV	94621	670-H3
ARTUNA AV			**PDMT**
100	RICARDO AV	94611	650-A1
100	HOLLY PL	94611	650-A1
ASBY BAY			**ALA**
100	BAYWALK RD	94502	669-J6
ASCOT CT			**OAK**
100	ASCOT DR	94611	650-F1
ASCOT DR			**OAK**
5400	MOUNTAIN BLVD	94611	650-E2
5460	LA CUESTA AV	94611	650-E2
5530	CAMINO LENADA	94611	650-F2
5590	MOUNTAINGATE WY	94611	650-F2
5650	ASCOT PL	94611	650-F2
5650	SCOUT RD	94611	650-F2
5700	LARRY LN	94611	650-F2
5800	CHELTON DR	94611	650-F1
5850	MASTLANDS DR	94611	650-F2
6100	MORLEY DR	94611	650-F2
6200	ASCOT CT	94611	650-F1
6280	CAMELFORD PL	94611	650-F1
6280	LONGCROFT DR	94611	650-F1
6320	CAMELFORD PL	94611	650-G1
6400	CHELSEA DR	94611	650-G1
6440	HOLYROOD DR	94611	650-G1
6520	LONGWALK DR	94611	650-G1
6570	MELVILLE DR	94611	650-G1
6650	ASCOT LN	94611	650-G1
6700	SKYLINE BLVD	94611	650-G1
ASCOT LN			**OAK**
1	ASCOT DR	94611	650-G1
ASCOT PL			**OAK**
5590	ASCOT DR	94611	650-F2
5590	SCOUT RD	94611	650-F2
ASH ST			**OAK**
7800	78TH AV	94621	670-H3
7900	79TH AV	94621	670-H3
ASHBROOK CT			**OAK**
3200	FRUITVALE AV	94601	650-C6
ASHBURY AV			**ALB**
1	KEY ROUTE BLVD	94706	609-E5
1	BRIGHTON AV	94706	609-E5
ASHBY AV			**BERK**
900	7TH ST	94804	629-E4
990	9TH ST	94804	629-E4
1200	SAN PABLO AV	94702	629-F4
1300	MABEL ST	94702	629-F4
1400	ACTON ST	94702	629-F4
1420	DOHR ST	94702	629-F4
1440	DOHR ST	94702	629-F4
1460	STANTON ST	94702	629-F4
1470	STANTON ST	94702	629-F4
1500	SACRAMENTO ST	94703	629-F4
1600	CALIFORNIA ST	94703	629-G4
1700	KING ST	94703	629-G4
1750	ELLIS ST	94703	629-G4
1800	HARPER ST	94703	629-G4
1900	MARTIN LUTHER KING JR WY	94703	629-G4
1950	OTIS ST	94703	629-G4
2000	ADELINE ST	94703	629-G4
2070	NEWBERRY ST	94703	629-H4
2100	SHATTUCK AV	94705	629-H4
2140	LORINA ST	94705	629-H4
	WHEELER ST	94705	629-H4
2180	WHEELER ST	94705	629-H4
2230	FULTON ST	94705	629-H4
2270	DEAKIN ST	94705	629-H4
2280	DEAKIN ST	94705	629-H4
2330	ELLSWORTH ST	94705	629-H4
2390	TELEGRAPH AV	94705	629-H4
2460	FLORENCE ST	94705	629-H4
2470	COLBY ST	94705	629-J4
2520	REGENT ST	94705	629-J4
2580	HILLEGASS AV	94705	629-J3
2630	BENVENUE AV	94705	629-J3
2680	COLLEGE AV	94705	629-J3
2720	ASHBY PL	94705	629-J3
2720	ELMWOOD AV	94705	629-J3
2770	ASHBY PL	94705	629-J3
2790	PIEDMONT AV	94705	629-J3
2830	LINDEN AV	94705	629-J3
2860	MAGNOLIA ST	94705	629-J3
2890	PINE AV	94705	630-A3
2930	ELMWOOD CT	94705	630-A3
2960	CLAREMONT CREST	94705	630-A3
3020	CLAREMONT AV	94705	630-A3
3100	DOMINGO AV	94705	630-A3
3100	TUNNEL RD	94705	630-A3
3100	RUSSELL ST	94705	630-A3
ASHBY PL			**BERK**
2700	ASHBY AV	94705	629-J3
2700	ELMWOOD AV	94705	629-J3
2800	ASHBY AV	94705	629-J3
ASHMOUNT AV			**OAK**
1000	PORTAL AV	94610	650-B3
1030	ARDMORE AV	94610	650-B2
1050	ASHMOUNT WY	94610	650-C2
1160	CROCKER AV	94610	650-C2
1160	MANDANA BLVD	94610	650-C2
1200	CLARENDON CRES	94610	650-C2
ASHMOUNT AV			**PDMT**
1200	CLARENDON CRES	94610	650-C2
1300	SEAVIEW AV	94610	650-C2
ASHMOUNT WY			**OAK**
1	ASHMOUNT AV	94610	650-B2
ASHTON AV			**OAK**
300	JONES AV	94603	670-G6
310	CLARA ST	94603	670-G6
400	ROSSMOOR AV	94603	670-G6
500	MADDUX DR	94603	670-G6
ASILOMAR CIR			**OAK**
1	COLTON BLVD	94611	630-E7
1	HEARTWOOD DR	94611	630-E7
100	ASILOMAR DR	94611	630-E7
100	COLTON BLVD	94611	630-E7
ASILOMAR DR			**OAK**
	COLTON BLVD	94611	630-E7
	ASILOMAR CIR	94611	630-E7
1900	SARONI DR	94611	630-E7
1980	BALBOA DR	94611	630-E7
2000	AZTEC WY	94611	630-E7
	ZINN DR	94611	630-E7
2050	TAMPA AV	94611	630-E7
2100	DRAKE DR	94611	630-E7
ASPEN PL			**OAK**
4000	ARIZONA ST	94602	650-F5
ASPINWALL RD			**OAK**
6430	THORNHILL DR	94611	630-E6
6360	WESTWOOD CT	94611	630-E6
6200	VISTA DEL MAR	94611	630-E6
6000	WESTWOOD WY	94611	630-E6
6000	GOULDIN RD	94611	630-E6
6200	GOULDIN RD	94611	630-E6
ASTER AV			**OAK**
8200	82ND AV	94605	671-A2
8400	EL MONTE AV	94605	671-A3
8500	NEY AV	94605	671-A3
ATHENS AV			**OAK**
800	SAN PABLO AV	94607	649-F2
900	MARKET ST	94607	649-F2
ATHERTON ST			**OAK**
8000	80TH AV	94605	670-J3
8100	81ST AV	94605	670-J3
ATHOL AV			**OAK**
100	E 18TH ST	94606	649-J4
160	WAYNE AV	94606	649-J4
180	ACTON PL	94606	649-J4
200	WAYNE PL	94606	649-J4
400	NEWTON AV	94606	649-J4
490	HADDON RD	94606	649-J4
420	PORTLAND AV	94606	650-A4
500	BROOKLYN AV	94606	650-A4
550	CLEVELAND ST	94606	650-A4
600	PROSPECT AV	94610	650-A4
650	MCKINLEY AV	94610	650-A3
700	MACARTHUR BLVD	94610	650-A3
ATLANTIC AV			**ALA**
	W ATLANTIC AV	94501	649-E7
100	MAIN ST	94501	649-E7
110	DECATUR ST	94501	649-E7
300	3RD ST	94501	649-E7
400	COTATI ST	94501	649-E7
420	POGGI ST	94501	649-E7
500	5TH ST	94501	649-F7
550	W CAMPUS DR	94501	649-F7
550	GRESHAM DR	94501	649-F7
600	TERN LN	94501	649-F7
700	WEBSTER ST	94501	649-F7
760	CONSTITUTION WY	94501	649-F7
910	CHALLENGER DR	94501	649-G7
1100	TRIUMPH DR	94501	649-H7
	EAGLE AV	94501	649-H7
	SHERMAN ST	94501	649-H7
W ATLANTIC AV			**ALA**
	FERRY PT	94501	649-D7
	VIKING ST	94501	649-D7
	ORION ST	94501	649-D7
	SKYHAWK ST	94501	649-D7
	ATLANTIC AV	94501	649-E7
ATLAS AV			**OAK**
3700	VICTOR AV	94619	650-G5
3920	MONTEREY BLVD	94619	650-G5
3990	MONTEREY BLVD	94619	650-G5
4110	DETROIT AV	94619	650-G5
4240	YOUNG AV	94619	650-G5
4300	35TH AV	94619	650-G5
4400	35TH AV	94619	650-G5
ATLAS PL			**BERK**
1	HILL RD	94708	610-A6
50	AJAX PL	94708	610-A6
50	SUMMIT RD	94708	610-A6
ATWELL AV			**OAK**
2800	BONA ST	94601	650-D6
2900	LYNDE ST	94601	650-D6
AUBURN AV			**OAK**
6000	HARWOOD AV	94618	629-J5
6200	FLORIO ST	94618	629-J5
6200	FLORIO ST	94618	629-J4
	MYSTIC ST	94618	629-J4
	CLAREMONT AV	94618	629-J4
AUBURN CT			**ALA**
1000	AUBURN DR	94502	670-A6
AUBURN DR			**ALA**
1000	MECARTNEY RD	94502	670-A6
1060	AUBURN CT	94502	670-A6
1100	BELMONT WY	94502	670-A6
AUGHINBAUGH WY			**ALA**
100	SEA VIEW PKWY	94502	669-J5
150	SHEFFIELD WY	94502	669-J5
250	ROBERT DAVEY JR DR	94502	669-J5
250	KOFMAN PKWY	94502	669-J5
270	BAYWALK RD	94502	669-J6
270	MECARTNEY RD	94502	669-J6
280	ORR RD	94502	669-J6
280	PATTIANI WY	94502	669-J6
300	BAY EDGE RD	94502	669-J6
300	RATTO RD	94502	669-J6
AUSEON AV			**OAK**
1400	INTERNATIONAL BLVD	94621	670-H4
1600	HOLLY ST	94621	670-H4
1700	PLYMOUTH ST	94621	670-J4
1800	BIRCH ST	94621	670-J4
2000	OLIVE ST	94621	670-J4
2200	BANCROFT AV	94621	670-J4
2200	BANCROFT AV	94605	670-J3
2300	DOWLING ST	94605	670-J3
AUSTIN ST			**OAK**
	FOOTHILL BLVD	94601	650-C6
	E 22ND ST	94601	650-C6
AVALON AV			**BERK**
2940	OAK KNOLL TER	94705	630-A3
3000	CLAREMONT BLVD	94705	630-A3
3100	CLAREMONT AV	94705	630-A3
AVENAL AV			**OAK**
5700	FOOTHILL BLVD	94605	670-F1
5800	BANCROFT AV	94605	670-F2
5900	SEMINARY AV	94605	670-F2
6000	60TH AV	94605	670-G2
6100	61ST AV	94605	670-G2
6200	62ND AV	94605	670-G2
6230	62ND AV	94605	670-G2
6300	63RD AV	94605	670-G2
6400	64TH AV	94605	670-G2
6500	65TH AV	94605	670-G2
6550	66TH AV	94605	670-G2
6600	HAVENSCOURT BLVD	94605	670-G2
6700	67TH AV	94605	670-G2
6800	68TH AV	94605	670-G2
6900	CHURCH ST	94605	670-G2
AVENIDA DR			**BERK**
1	CAMPUS DR	94708	609-J7
50	OLYMPUS AV	94708	609-J7
1	QUEENS RD	94708	609-J7
90	FAIRLAWN DR	94708	610-A7
200	GRIZZLY PEAK BLVD	94708	610-A7
AVINGTON RD			**ALA**
100	SEA VIEW PKWY	94502	669-J5
200	HAMPTON CT	94502	670-A5
300	NORWICH RD	94502	670-A5
AVIS RD			**BERK**
1	SAN ANTONIO AV	94707	609-G5
100	SAN LUIS RD	94707	609-G5
AVOCA AV			**OAK**
5900	LEO WY	94611	630-C6
6000	MOUNTAIN BLVD	94611	630-C6
6000	AQUARIUS WY	94611	630-D6
6100	MOUNTAIN BLVD	94611	630-D6
AVOCET CT			**ALA**
	GRESHAM DR	94501	649-F7
AVON ST			**OAK**
400	SHAFTER AV	94618	629-H6
500	MILES AV	94618	629-H6
AVONDALE LNDG			**ALA**
1	OYSTER POND RD	94502	670-A5
AVONOAK CT			**OAK**
100	HANSOM DR	94619	651-C7

ALAMEDA CO.
© 2006 Rand McNally & Company

PRIMARY STREET Address	Cross Street	ZIP	CITY Pg-Grid
AVONOAK CT			**OAK**
100	HANSOM DR	94605	651-C7
AYALA AV			**OAK**
5700	57TH ST	94609	629-H5
5740	HERMANN ST	94609	629-H5
5800	MARTIN ST	94609	629-H5
5830	HOWELL ST	94609	629-J5
5900	FOREST ST	94609	629-J5
6000	MCAULEY ST	94609	629-J5
AZALEA DR			**ALA**
1000	MECARTNEY RD	94502	670-A6
1100	DAHLIA DR	94502	670-A6
AZALEA LN			**OAK**
1	SARONI DR	94611	630-F7
AZTEC WY			**OAK**
1	ASILOMAR DR	94611	630-E7
100	DRAKE DR	94611	630-E7
B			
B ST			**OAK**
	3RD ST	94625	649-B3
	4TH ST	94625	649-B3
	5TH ST	94625	649-B3
	15TH ST	94625	649-B3
8000	80TH AV	94621	670-G4
8100	81ST AV	94621	670-G4
8300	83RD AV	94621	670-H4
8400	84TH AV	94621	670-H4
8500	85TH AV	94621	670-H4
8600	86TH AV	94621	670-H4
8700	87TH AV	94621	670-H4
8800	88TH AV	94621	670-H4
8900	89TH AV	94621	670-H5
9000	90TH AV	94603	670-H5
9100	91ST AV	94603	670-H5
9540	92ND AV	94603	670-H5
9460	93RD AV	94603	670-H5
9390	94TH AV	94603	670-H5
9350	95TH AV	94603	670-H5
9320	ELMHURST AV	94603	670-H5
9250	96TH AV	94603	670-H5
9180	97TH AV	94603	670-H5
9800	98TH AV	94603	670-H6
10000	100TH AV	94603	670-H6
BACON RD			**OAK**
5300	SKYLINE BLVD	94619	651-A5
5300	FERNHOFF RD	94619	650-J5
BAGSHOTTE DR			**OAK**
5800	CHELTON DR	94611	650-F1
5820	CHELTON LN	94611	650-F1
5900	SCARBOROUGH DR	94611	650-F1
5980	ESCHER DR	94611	650-F1
5990	WESTOVER DR	94611	650-F1
BAINBRIDGE AV			**ALA**
100	DECATUR ST	94501	649-E7
140	OCEANA CIR	94501	649-E7
190	HOLLISTER CIR	94501	649-E7
220	3RD ST	94501	649-E7
250	VERNALIS CIR	94501	649-E7
300	VERNALIS CIR	94501	649-E7
340	COTATI ST	94501	649-E7
380	SANTA ROSA CIR	94501	649-E7
450	SANTA ROSA CIR	94501	649-F7
500	5TH ST	94501	649-F7
BAKER ST			**BERK**
3200	66TH ST	94702	629-F4
3230	FAIRVIEW ST	94702	629-F4
3260	HARMON ST	94702	629-F5
3300	ALCATRAZ AV	94702	629-F5
BAKER ST			**OAK**
6110	61ST ST	94608	629-F5
6150	61ST ST	94608	629-F5
	62ND ST	94608	629-F5
6200	62ND ST	94608	629-F5
6300	63RD ST	94608	629-F5
6400	ALCATRAZ AV	94608	629-F5
BALBOA CT			**ALA**
300	BAYVIEW DR	94501	669-J4
BALBOA DR			**OAK**
5500	COLTON BLVD	94611	630-E7
5700	ASILOMAR DR	94611	630-E7
5740	CORTEZ CT	94611	630-F7
6000	WEST CIR	94611	630-F7
6100	PASO ROBLES DR	94611	630-F7
BALDWIN ST			**OAK**
8100	85TH AV	94621	670-F5
8180	MCCLARY AV	94621	670-F5
BALFOUR AV			**OAK**
3600	SANTA RAY AV	94610	650-A3
3670	VIONA AV	94610	650-A3
3790	ROSAL AV	94610	650-B2
3910	ROSAL AV	94610	650-B2
3960	PALOMA AV	94610	650-B2
4300	WALAVISTA AV	94610	650-B2
4300	CARLSTON AV	94610	650-B2
BALI LN			**ALA**
	BELMONT PL	94502	670-A6
	EASTER LN	94502	670-A6
BALLENA BLVD			**ALA**
1200	4TH ST	94501	669-E2
1200	COLA BALLENA	94501	669-E2
BALLEYBAY			**ALA**
1	KILKENNY PL	94502	669-J6
BALMORAL DR			**OAK**
5750	BLYTHEN WY	94619	651-A5
5750	TARTAN WY	94619	651-A5
5600	HILLCREST CT	94619	651-A5
5700	TARTAN WY	94619	650-J4
5800	BELL WAVER WY	94619	650-J4
5870	BLYTHEN WY	94619	650-J4
BALSAM WY			**OAK**
6800	BROADWAY TER	94611	630-E5
6800	PINENEEDLE DR	94611	630-E5
BANCROFT AV			**OAK**
4200	42ND AV	94601	670-D1
4340	HIGH ST	94601	670-D1
4380	44TH AV	94601	670-D1
4480	45TH AV	94601	670-D1
4600	46TH AV	94601	670-D1
4700	47TH AV	94601	670-E1
4740	BANCROFT WY	94601	670-E1
4750	BANCROFT WY	94601	670-E1
4800	48TH AV	94601	670-E1
4950	BOND ST	94601	670-E1
4950	FREMONT WY	94601	670-E1
5000	50TH AV	94601	670-E1
5060	51ST AV	94601	670-E1
5100	51ST AV	94601	670-E1
5100	WENTWORTH AV	94601	670-E1
5300	54TH AV	94601	670-E1
5400	FAIRFAX AV	94601	670-F1
5500	COLE ST	94601	670-F1
5540	HARVEY AV	94601	670-F1
5550	55TH AV	94605	670-F1
5600	HILTON ST	94605	670-F1
5610	HILTON ST	94605	670-F1
5690	57TH AV	94605	670-F1
5690	TRASK ST	94605	670-F1
5700	57TH AV	94605	670-F1
5700	TRASK ST	94605	670-F1
5800	AVENAL AV	94605	670-F1
5900	SEMINARY AV	94605	670-G1
	FORTUNE WY	94605	670-G2
6100	60TH AV	94605	670-G2
6200	61ST AV	94605	670-G2
6300	62ND AV	94605	670-G2
6400	63RD AV	94605	670-G2
6400	64TH AV	94605	670-G2
6500	65TH AV	94605	670-G2
6600	66TH AV	94605	670-G2
6640	HAVENSCOURT BLVD	94605	670-H2
6640	HAVENSCOURT BLVD	94605	670-H2
6650	HAVENSCOURT BLVD	94605	670-H2
6700	67TH AV	94605	670-H2
6800	68TH AV	94605	670-H2
6900	CHURCH ST	94605	670-H2
	73RD AV	94605	670-H2
7300	73RD AV	94605	670-H2
	75TH AV	94605	670-H2
7600	76TH AV	94605	670-H2
7700	77TH AV	94605	670-H3
7800	78TH AV	94605	670-H3
7830	PARKER AV	94605	670-H3
7900	79TH AV	94605	670-J3
7920	RITCHIE ST	94605	670-J3
8000	80TH AV	94605	670-J3
8100	81ST AV	94605	670-J3
8200	82ND AV	94605	670-J3
8300	83RD AV	94605	670-J3
8400	84TH AV	94605	670-J3
8500	85TH AV	94605	670-J3
8600	86TH AV	94605	670-J4
8640	AUSEON AV	94605	670-J4
8700	87TH AV	94605	670-J4
8800	88TH AV	94605	670-J4
8900	89TH AV	94605	670-J4
9000	90TH AV	94603	670-J4
9200	92ND AV	94603	670-J4
10470	94TH AV	94603	671-A4
10470	STEARNS AV	94603	671-A4
9600	96TH AV	94603	671-A5
9800	98TH AV	94603	671-A5
9850	WARNER AV	94603	671-A5
9900	99TH AV	94603	671-A5
10000	100TH AV	94603	671-A5
10300	103RD AV	94603	671-A5
10600	106TH AV	94603	671-A6
10600	107TH AV	94603	671-A6
10300	106TH AV	94603	671-A6
10300	LINK ST	94603	671-A6
10200	103RD AV	94603	671-A5
10100	102ND AV	94603	671-A5
10000	101ST AV	94603	671-A5
9900	100TH AV	94603	671-A5
9800	99TH AV	94603	671-A5
9600	98TH AV	94603	671-A5
10470	96TH AV	94603	671-A4
9200	94TH AV	94603	670-J4
9000	92ND AV	94603	670-J4
8900	90TH AV	94603	670-J4
8800	89TH AV	94605	670-J4
8700	88TH AV	94605	670-J4
8640	87TH AV	94605	670-J4
8600	AUSEON AV	94605	670-J4
8500	86TH AV	94605	670-J3
8400	85TH AV	94605	670-J3
8300	84TH AV	94605	670-J3
8200	83RD AV	94605	670-J3
8100	82ND AV	94605	670-J3
8000	81ST AV	94605	670-J3
7920	80TH AV	94605	670-J3
7800	RITCHIE ST	94605	670-H3
7700	78TH AV	94605	670-H3
7600	77TH AV	94605	670-H2
7500	76TH AV	94605	670-H2
7300	75TH AV	94605	670-H2
	73RD AV	94605	670-H2
6900	73RD AV	94605	670-H2
6800	CHURCH ST	94605	670-H2
6700	68TH AV	94605	670-H2
6660	67TH AV	94605	670-H2
10700	107TH AV	94603	671-A6
10800	108TH AV	94603	671-A6
10900	109TH AV	94603	671-A6
11000	DURANT AV	94603	671-A6
BANCROFT PL			**OAK**
600	PANORAMIC WY	94704	630-A2
BANCROFT WY			**BERK**
600	BOLIVAR DR	94804	629-D3
700	3RD ST	94804	629-D3
730	4TH ST	94804	629-D2
800	5TH ST	94804	629-D2
830	6TH ST	94804	629-D2
900	7TH ST	94804	629-E2
930	8TH ST	94804	629-E2
1000	9TH ST	94804	629-E2
1030	10TH ST	94804	629-E2
1100	SAN PABLO AV	94702	629-E2
1120	BYRON ST	94702	629-E2
1200	CURTIS ST	94702	629-E2
1220	BROWNING ST	94702	629-E2
1300	BONAR ST	94702	629-E2
1340	WEST ST	94702	629-F2
1370	VALLEY ST	94702	629-F2
1400	ACTON ST	94702	629-F2
1430	EDWARDS ST	94702	629-F2
1500	SACRAMENTO ST	94703	629-F2
1520	SPAULDING AV	94703	629-F2
1600	CALIFORNIA ST	94703	629-F2
1630	JEFFERSON AV	94703	629-F2
1700	MCGEE AV	94703	629-G2
1730	ROOSEVELT AV	94703	629-G2
1800	GRANT ST	94703	629-G2
1820	MCKINLEY AV	94703	629-G2
1900	MARTIN LUTHER KING JR WY	94703	629-G2
2000	MILVIA ST	94704	629-G2
2120	SHATTUCK AV	94704	629-H2
2210	FULTON ST	94720	629-H2
2210	FULTON ST	94704	629-H2
2210	OXFORD ST	94704	629-H2
2320	ELLSWORTH ST	94720	629-H2
2320	ELLSWORTH ST	94704	629-H2
2440	DANA ST	94720	629-H2
2440	DANA ST	94704	629-H2
2550	TELEGRAPH AV	94720	629-H2
2550	TELEGRAPH AV	94704	629-H2
2590	BARROW LN	94720	629-J2
2590	BARROW LN	94704	629-J2
2660	BOWDITCH ST	94720	629-J2
2660	BOWDITCH ST	94704	629-J2
2780	COLLEGE AV	94720	629-J2
2780	COLLEGE AV	94704	629-J2
2900	PIEDMONT AV	94720	629-J2
2900	PIEDMONT AV	94720	629-J2
2900	GAYLEY RD	94704	629-J2
2800	PIEDMONT AV	94720	629-J2
2800	PIEDMONT AV	94704	629-J2
2830	WARRING ST	94720	629-J2
2830	WARRING ST	94704	629-J2
BANCROFT WY			**OAK**
1400	46TH AV	94601	670-D1
1400	INTERNATIONAL BLVD	94601	670-D1
1580	47TH AV	94601	670-D1
1600	BANCROFT AV	94601	670-D1
1400	INTERNATIONAL BLVD	94601	670-D1
1580	47TH AV	94601	670-D1
1600	BANCROFT AV	94601	670-D1
BANNING DR			**OAK**
6600	SHEPHERD CANYON RD	94611	630-G7
6650	DORAN DR	94611	630-G7
6800	MOORE DR	94611	630-G7
BANNISTER CT			**ALA**
200	BANNISTER WY	94502	669-J6
BANNISTER WY			**ALA**
1	MCDONNEL RD	94502	669-H6
50	RUTLAND CT	94502	669-H6
130	SHARON RD	94502	669-J6
200	BANNISTER CT	94502	669-J6
BANTRY AV			**OAK**
3000	73RD AV	94605	670-J1
3000	MAYFIELD PTH	94605	670-J1
3100	73RD AV	94605	670-J1
BARBARA RD			**OAK**
700	MACARTHUR BLVD	94610	650-A3
700	HILLGIRT CIR	94610	650-A3
BARBERS POINT RD			**ALA**
1	PAN AM WY	94501	649-D6
1	W RED LINE AV	94501	649-D6
30	SAN DIEGO RD	94501	649-D6
60	SAN PEDRO RD	94501	649-D6
90	PEARL HARBOR RD	94501	649-D6
90	PEARL HARBOR RD	94501	649-D6
120	PEARL HARBOR RD	94501	649-E6
150	CORPUS CHRISTI RD	94501	649-E6
150	SERENADE PL	94501	649-E6
BARCELONA ST			**OAK**
8950	SEQUOYAH RD	94605	671-C3
8900	SANTA CRUZ RD	94605	671-B3
BARKER CT			**ALA**
	ROSEFIELD LP	94501	649-F7
BARMIED PL			**OAK**
1	SKYLINE BLVD	94619	651-C7
BARNEGATE BAY			**ALA**
1	SABLE POINTE	94502	670-A5
100	BASIN SIDE WY	94502	670-A5
BARNER AV			**OAK**
3900	MORGAN AV	94602	650-E4
3930	MORGAN AV	94602	650-F4
4140	BARNER PL	94602	650-F4
4200	ALIDA ST	94602	650-F4
BARNER PL			**OAK**
100	BARNER AV	94602	650-F4
BARRETT ST			**OAK**
2900	PERALTA OAKS DR	94605	671-B5
3000	SHELDON ST	94605	671-B5
BARROW LN			**BERK**
	BANCROFT WY	94720	629-H2
BARROWS RD			**OAK**
1300	TRESTLE GLEN RD	94610	650-C3
1500	CREED RD	94610	650-C3
BARRY CT			**ALA**
100	TRALEE LN	94502	669-H5
BARRY PL			**OAK**
2800	E 27TH ST	94601	650-C6
BARTLETT DR			**ALA**
	BIRD CT	94501	649-G7
	ROSEFIELD LP	94501	649-G7
	RANGER CT	94501	649-G7
	CERRUTI CT	94501	649-G7
	VOLBERG CT	94501	649-G7
	DECELLE CT	94501	649-G7
	CLEVELAND CT	94501	649-G7
	ROSEFIELD LP	94501	649-G7
	HECKER CT	94501	649-G7
	MARINA VILLAGE PKWY	94501	649-G7
	ROSEFIELD LP	94501	649-G7
	WEISS CT	94501	649-G7
BARTLETT ST			**OAK**
2300	DAVIS ST	94601	650-D6
2400	LYNDE ST	94601	650-D6
2500	DEERING ST	94601	650-D6
2600	BROOKDALE AV	94602	650-E6
2700	PENNIMAN AV	94602	650-E6
2800	SCHOOL ST	94602	650-E6
BASIN SIDE WY			**ALA**
100	CLIPPER DR	94502	669-J5
30	CHILMARK LN	94502	669-J6
200	CAPTAINS DR	94502	670-A5
220	CAPETOWN DR	94502	670-A5
1	OYSTER POND RD	94502	670-A5
20	BARNEGATE BAY	94502	670-A5
BATAAN AV			**BERK**
900	7TH ST	94804	629-D1
1000	8TH ST	94804	629-D1
BATAAN AV			**OAK**
	MARITIME ST	94607	649-C1
170	WAKE AV	94607	649-C1
200	CORREGIDOR AV	94607	649-C1
BATEMAN ST			**BERK**
3070	PRINCE ST	94705	629-J4
3100	WOOLSEY ST	94705	629-J4
BATES RD			**OAK**
1200	HOLMAN RD	94610	650-C4
1200	HOLMAN RD	94602	650-C4
1400	HOLMAN RD	94610	650-C4
1400	HOLMAN RD	94602	650-C4
BAXTER ST			**OAK**
2100	GALINDO ST	94601	650-D7
BAY EDGE RD			**ALA**
	RATTO RD	94502	669-J6
	AUGHINBAUGH WY	94502	669-J6
BAY FOREST CT			**OAK**
100	BAY FOREST DR	94611	630-D4
BAY FOREST DR			**OAK**
1	OLD TUNNEL RD	94611	630-D4
1	TUNNEL RD	94611	630-D4
20	BAY FOREST CT	94611	630-D3
BAY PARK TER			**ALA**
50	OAK PARK DR	94502	670-A5
150	SHEPARDSON LN	94502	670-A5
BAY PL			**OAK**
200	GRAND AV	94612	649-H3
200	GRAND AV	94610	649-H3
240	MONTECITO AV	94612	649-H3
240	MONTECITO AV	94610	649-H3
280	VERNON ST	94612	649-H3
280	VERNON ST	94610	649-H3
300	27TH ST	94612	649-H3
300	27TH ST	94610	649-H3
300	HARRISON ST	94610	649-H3
BAY ST			**ALA**
1300	SAN ANTONIO AV	94501	669-G1
1400	CENTRAL AV	94501	669-G1
1500	SANTA CLARA AV	94501	669-H1
1600	LINCOLN AV	94501	669-H1
1820	PACIFIC AV	94501	649-H7
1890	BUENA VISTA AV	94501	649-H7
1960	EAGLE AV	94501	649-H7
BAYO ST			**OAK**
3800	PATTERSON AV	94619	650-F5
3920	39TH AV	94619	650-F6
4090	MAYBELLE AV	94619	650-G6
4250	VALE AV	94619	650-G6
4300	HIGH ST	94619	650-G6
BAYO VISTA AV			**ALA**
3000	FAIRVIEW AV	94501	670-B2
3000	NORTHWOOD DR	94501	670-B2
3000	SOUTHWOOD DR	94501	670-B2
3100	CORNELL DR	94501	670-B3
3200	HIGH ST	94501	670-C3
3250	MONTE VISTA AV	94501	670-C3
3300	FAIRVIEW AV	94501	670-C3
BAYO VISTA AV			**OAK**
50	FAIRMOUNT AV	94611	649-J1
100	EL DORADO AV	94611	649-J1
120	HARRISON ST	94611	649-J1
200	OAKLAND AV	94611	649-J1
BAYTREE LN			**BERK**
1	GOLF COURSE DR	94708	609-J6
BAYVIEW AV			**OAK**
900	E 28TH ST	94610	650-B4
1100	ELLIOT ST	94610	650-B4
1130	11TH AV	94610	650-B4
1200	13TH AV	94610	650-B4
1200	E 32ND ST	94610	650-B4
BAYVIEW DR			**ALA**
2600	BROADWAY	94501	669-J4
2600	SHORELINE DR	94501	669-J4
2650	BALBOA CT	94501	669-J4
2700	LAGUNA VISTA	94501	670-A4
2800	LAGUNA VISTA	94501	670-A4
3000	COURT ST	94501	670-A4
800	RAVENS COVE LN	94501	670-A4
900	HIGH ST	94501	670-A4
900	OTIS DR	94501	670-A4
BAYVIEW PL			**BERK**
1300	SCENIC AV	94708	609-H7
1300	ROSE ST	94708	609-H7
1400	EUCLID AV	94708	609-H7
BAYWALK RD			**ALA**
2800	AUGHINBAUGH WY	94502	669-J6
2810	MONTEGO BAY	94502	669-J6
2810	KEIL BAY	94502	669-J6
2830	JERVIS BAY	94502	669-J6
2840	INDIAN BAY	94502	669-J6
2850	HUDSON BAY	94502	669-J6
2870	GALWAY BAY	94502	669-J6
2900	FUNDY BAY	94502	669-J6
2910	ENCOUNTER BAY	94502	669-J6
2920	DIAPIAN BAY	94502	669-J6
2940	CARDIGAN BAY	94502	669-J6
2970	BISCAY BAY	94502	669-J6
2980	ASBY BAY	94502	669-J6
3000	MARCUSE ST	94502	669-J6
3000	MECARTNEY RD	94502	669-J6
BAYWOOD RD			**ALA**
730	HOLLY OAK LN	94502	669-J6
800	FONTANA DR	94502	669-J6
800	MECARTNEY RD	94502	669-J6
BEACH RD			**ALA**
200	FLOWER LN	94502	670-B6
270	MELROSE AV	94502	670-B6
310	SEMINARY AV	94502	670-B7
400	FAIRWAY PL	94502	670-B7
400	FITCHBURG AV	94502	670-B7
BEACH ST			**OAK**
	34TH ST	94608	649-E1
1500	HALLECK ST	94608	629-E7
1570	YERBA BUENA AV	94608	629-E7
BEACHY ST			**OAK**
1000	BOEING ST	94621	670-D7
BEACON ST			**OAK**
500	LAKESHORE AV	94610	649-J3
500	BODEN WY	94610	650-A3
600	BODEN WY	94610	650-A3
700	MACARTHUR BLVD	94610	650-A3
BEACONSFIELD PL			**OAK**
2600	CHATSWORTH CT	94611	650-F1
2600	CHELTON DR	94611	650-F1
2640	KESWICK CT	94611	650-F1
BEAL AV			**OAK**
2650	WALNUT ST	94605	670-G1
BEAR RD			**ALA**
	HUDSON DR	94501	649-J7
	MCCULLOCH DR	94501	649-J7
BEATIE ST			**OAK**
700	7TH AV	94606	650-A4
700	IVY DR	94606	650-A4
800	8TH AV	94606	650-A4
BEAUDRY ST			**EMVL**
5500	55TH ST	94608	629-E6
5700	STANFORD AV	94608	629-E6
5800	POWELL ST	94608	629-E6
5900	59TH ST	94608	629-E5
BEAUFOREST DR			**OAK**
6300	VALLEY VIEW RD	94611	630-E6
6310	THORNHILL DR	94611	630-E6
BEAUFORT HARBOR			**ALA**
1	SEA BRIDGE WY	94502	670-A5
100	COLEPORT LNDG	94502	670-A5
BEAUMONT AV			**OAK**
2770	14TH AV	94606	650-B5
3100	E 31ST ST	94602	650-B4
3200	E 32ND ST	94602	650-B4
3290	E 33RD ST	94602	650-B4
3300	MACARTHUR BLVD	94602	650-B4
3420	MACARTHUR BLVD	94602	650-C4
3420	CHATHAM RD	94602	650-C4
3500	E 36TH ST	94602	650-C4
3600	EXCELSIOR AV	94602	650-C4
3700	ALLMAN ST	94602	650-C4
3800	E 38TH ST	94602	650-C4
3900	PARK BLVD	94602	650-C4
BEECHWOOD DR			**OAK**
1	COUNTRY CLUB DR	94618	630-A5
50	GLENBROOK DR	94618	630-A5
130	YORKSHIRE DR	94618	630-B5
200	ROMANY RD	94618	630-B5
BEGONIA DR			**ALA**
1000	MECARTNEY RD	94502	670-A6
1100	DAHLIA DR	94502	670-A6
BEHRENS ST			**ALB**
100	BRIGHTON AV	94706	609-E5
100	SPOKANE AV	94706	609-E5
BELALP PTH			**OAK**
	GOLDEN GATE AV	94618	630-B5
	BUENA VISTA AV	94618	630-B5
	CONTRA COSTA RD	94618	630-B5
BELFAST AV			**OAK**
4600	MOUNTAIN BLVD	94619	650-H6
4680	BERMUDA AV	94619	650-H6
BELGRAVE PL			**OAK**
5300	BROADWAY TER	94618	630-A6
5400	NAPA ST	94618	630-A6
5500	CARLTON ST	94618	630-A6
BELL AV			**PDMT**
100	BLAIR AV	94611	650-C1
200	SCENIC AV	94611	650-C1

PRIMARY STREET Address	Cross Street	ZIP	CITY Pg-Grid
BELL WAVER WY			**OAK**
1	BALMORAL DR	94619	650-J4
BELLA VISTA AV			**OAK**
1000	E 28TH ST	94610	650-B4
1000	10TH AV	94610	650-B4
1100	11TH AV	94610	650-B4
1200	13TH AV	94610	650-B4
BELLAIRE PL			**OAK**
2730	LYNDE ST	94601	650-C6
2860	BONA ST	94601	650-C5
BELLEVUE AV			**OAK**
300	PALM AV	94610	649-J3
400	VAN BUREN AV	94610	649-J3
450	GRAND AV	94610	649-J3
500	STATEN AV	94610	649-J3
580	ELLITA AV	94610	649-J3
600	PERKINS ST	94610	649-H4
700	GRAND AV	94610	649-H4
BELLEVUE AV			**PDMT**
1	PACIFIC AV	94611	650-C1
100	MOUNTAIN AV	94611	650-C1
BELMONT PL			**ALA**
1000	MECARTNEY RD	94502	670-A6
1030	BALI LN	94502	670-A6
1100	BELMONT WY	94502	670-A6
1100	GILBERT LN	94502	670-A6
BELMONT ST			**OAK**
300	PERKINS ST	94610	649-J3
400	STATEN AV	94610	649-J3
BELMONT WY			**ALA**
3130	BELMONT PL	94502	670-A6
3130	GILBERT LN	94502	670-A6
3160	TAHITI LN	94502	670-A6
3200	AUBURN DR	94502	670-A6
BELROSE AV			**BERK**
2700	CLAREMONT BLVD	94705	630-A3
2700	GARBER ST	94705	630-A3
2800	TANGLEWOOD RD	94705	630-A3
2800	DERBY ST	94705	630-A3
BELVEDERE AV			**BERK**
1500	ROSE ST	94702	629-E1
1600	CEDAR ST	94702	629-E1
1700	VIRGINIA ST	94702	629-E1
BELVEDERE ST			**OAK**
5200	TRASK ST	94601	670-F1
5300	YGNACIO AV	94601	670-F1
5400	FOOTHILL BLVD	94601	670-F1
BEMIS ST			**OAK**
4300	ETTRICK ST	94605	671-D5
4200	GREENBRIER ST	94605	671-D5
BENEDICT CT			**ALA**
1	MCDONNEL RD	94502	669-H6
BENEDICT DR			**OAK**
1300	MARLOW DR	94605	671-C7
BENEDICT DR			**SLN**
1300	MARLOW DR	94605	671-C7
BENEVIDES AV			**OAK**
4600	EL CENTRO AV	94602	650-D3
BENNETT PL			**OAK**
4300	JORDAN RD	94602	650-G4
4390	GUIDO ST	94602	650-G4
4410	GUIDO ST	94602	650-G4
4500	MONTEREY BLVD	94602	650-G4
BENSON ST			**OAK**
1000	EARHART RD	94621	670-D6
1060	LOCKHEED ST	94621	670-D6
BENTON ST			**ALA**
1200	ENCINAL AV	94501	669-H1
1400	ALAMEDA AV	94501	669-H1
1400	CENTRAL AV	94501	669-H1
1500	SANTA CLARA AV	94501	669-H1
1600	LINCOLN AV	94501	669-H1
1700	PACIFIC AV	94501	669-H1
1800	BUENA VISTA AV	94501	669-H1
BENTON ST			**OAK**
1400	RANDOLPH AV	94602	650-C4
1500	WOODRUFF AV	94602	650-C4
BENVENUE AV			**BERK**
2500	DWIGHT WY	94704	629-J2
2600	PARKER ST	94704	629-J3
2700	DERBY ST	94704	629-J3
2700	DERBY ST	94705	629-J3
2800	STUART ST	94705	629-J3
2900	RUSSELL ST	94705	629-J3
2940	ASHBY AV	94705	629-J4
3000	WEBSTER ST	94705	629-J4
3000	WEBSTER ST	94705	629-J4
3100	WOOLSEY ST	94705	629-J4
BENVENUE AV			**OAK**
6400	ALCATRAZ AV	94618	629-J4
6500	WOOLSEY ST	94618	629-J4
BERGEDO DR			**OAK**
200	CATRON DR	94603	690-H1
280	PUEBLO DR	94603	690-H1
400	REPOSO DR	94603	670-H7
500	ESTEPA DR	94603	670-H7
600	NOVELDA DR	94603	670-H7
700	ACALANES DR	94603	670-H7
800	ROBLEDO DR	94603	670-H7
800	EDES AV	94603	670-H7
BERKELEY WY			**BERK**
1200	CHESTNUT ST	94702	629-E2
1400	ACTON ST	94702	629-F1
1500	SACRAMENTO ST	94702	629-F1
1500	SACRAMENTO ST	94703	629-F1
1600	CALIFORNIA ST	94703	629-F1
1700	MCGEE AV	94703	629-G1
1800	GRANT ST	94703	629-G1
1900	MARTIN LUTHER KING JR WY	94704	629-G1
1950	BONITA AV	94704	629-G1
2000	MILVIA ST	94704	629-G1
2050	HENRY ST	94704	629-G1
2100	SHATTUCK AV	94704	629-G1
2100	SHATTUCK AV	94704	629-H1
2160	WALNUT ST	94704	629-H1
2200	OXFORD ST	94704	629-H1
BERKSHIRE RD			**ALA**
50	CUMBERLAND WY	94502	669-J5
1	TYNEBOURNE PL	94502	669-J5
50	INVERNESS WY	94502	669-J5
BERLIN WY			**OAK**
3000	WARD LN	94602	650-E6
3200	SCHOOL ST	94602	650-E6
BERMUDA AV			**OAK**
4300	BELFAST AV	94619	650-H6
4400	MOUNTAIN BLVD	94619	650-H6
BERNEVES CT			**OAK**
1	MOUNTAIN BLVD	94619	650-H5
BERNHARDT DR			**OAK**
9800	SAINT ELMO DR	94603	670-G7
9900	FOSTER AV	94603	670-G7
9920	GHORMLEY AV	94603	670-G7
9950	HUNTER AV	94603	670-G7
9970	ISLETON AV	94603	670-G7
10000	KERWIN AV	94603	670-G7
10030	LOUVAINE AV	94603	670-G7
10060	MALTA CT	94603	670-G7
BERRYMAN ST			**BERK**
1830	JOSEPHINE ST	94703	609-G7
1900	MARTIN LUTHER KING JR WY	94709	609-G7
1950	BONITA AV	94709	609-G7
2000	MILVIA ST	94709	609-G7
2040	HENRY ST	94709	609-G7
2100	SHATTUCK AV	94709	609-G7
BESITO AV			**OAK**
1300	DARTMOUTH DR	94705	630-C3
1300	DRURY RD	94705	630-C3
BEST AV			**OAK**
2400	TRASK ST	94601	670-F1
2600	BROOKDALE AV	94601	670-F1
2600	BROOKDALE AV	94619	670-F1
2600	FLEMING AV	94619	650-F7
2830	FLEMING AV	94619	650-F7
2980	VIRGINIA AV	94619	650-F7
3000	KINGSLAND AV	94619	650-F7
BEVERLY AV			**OAK**
10500	105TH AV	94603	671-A6
10600	106TH AV	94603	671-A6
10700	107TH AV	94603	671-A6
10800	108TH AV	94603	671-A6
10900	109TH AV	94603	671-A6
11000	DURANT AV	94603	671-A6
BEVERLY PL			**BERK**
1500	VENTURA AV	94706	609-F6
1600	MONTEREY AV	94707	609-F7
1700	COLUSA AV	94707	609-F7
1800	HOPKINS ST	94707	609-F7
BIEHS CT			**OAK**
100	HARBORD DR	94618	630-C6
BIGGE AV			**OAK**
10000	98TH AV	94603	670-F7
BINNACLE HILL			**OAK**
1	HILLER DR	94618	630-C4
20	MARLIN CV	94618	630-C4
50	HILLER DR	94618	630-C4
BIRCH CT			**OAK**
5900	COLLEGE AV	94618	629-J5
BIRCH ST			**OAK**
8100	81ST AV	94621	670-H3
8200	82ND AV	94621	670-H3
8300	83RD AV	94621	670-H3
8400	84TH AV	94621	670-J4
8500	85TH AV	94621	670-J4
8600	86TH AV	94621	670-J4
8640	AUSEON AV	94621	670-J4
8700	87TH AV	94621	670-J4
8800	88TH AV	94621	670-J4
8900	89TH AV	94621	670-J4
9000	90TH AV	94621	670-J4
9000	90TH AV	94603	670-J4
9200	92ND AV	94603	670-J4
9400	94TH AV	94603	670-J5
9600	96TH AV	94603	670-J5
9800	98TH AV	94603	670-J5
9870	WARNER AV	94603	670-J5
9900	99TH AV	94603	670-J5
9340	100TH AV	94603	671-A5
10100	101ST AV	94603	671-A5
10200	102ND AV	94603	671-A5
10300	103RD AV	94603	671-A6
10400	104TH AV	94603	671-A6
10500	105TH AV	94603	671-A6
BIRD CT			**ALA**
	BARTLETT DR	94501	649-G7
	ROSEFIELD LP	94501	649-G7
BIRDSALL AV			**OAK**
2800	FLEMING AV	94619	670-F1
2850	YUBA AV	94619	670-F1
2860	YUBA AV	94619	670-F1
2920	ROBERTS AV	94619	670-F1
2960	MORCOM AV	94619	670-F1
2960	MORCOM AV	94619	650-F7
3060	MORCOM AV	94619	650-F7
3100	MADERA AV	94619	650-F7
3140	MODESTO AV	94619	650-F7
3170	RAWSON ST	94619	650-F7
3160	CAMDEN ST	94619	650-F7
3210	MAXWELL AV	94619	650-F7
3250	KINGSLAND AV	94619	650-F7
3300	MONTICELLO AV	94619	650-F7
3330	MORCOM AV	94619	650-F7
3360	KNOWLAND AV	94619	650-F7
3370	MELDON AV	94619	650-F7
3500	REDDING ST	94619	650-F7
BISCAY BAY			**ALA**
100	BAYWALK RD	94502	669-J6
BISHOP ST			**ALA**
1100	WASHINGTON ST	94501	670-A3
1150	ADAMS ST	94501	670-A3
1200	SAN JOSE AV	94501	670-A3
BISMARCK LN			**ALA**
1100	FIR AV	94502	670-A7
1120	WILLIS LN	94502	670-A7
1150	SOLOMON LN	94502	670-A7
1190	COOK LN	94502	670-A7
BLACHFORD CT			**OAK**
1	MORLEY DR	94611	650-F2
BLAINE ST			**OAK**
8500	85TH AV	94621	670-G5
8600	86TH AV	94621	670-G5
BLAIR AV			**OAK**
850	HARBORD DR	94611	630-C7
BLAIR AV			**PDMT**
430	HIGHLAND AV	94611	650-B1
390	WALDO AV	94611	650-B1
380	BONITA AV	94611	650-B1
290	BONITA AV	94611	650-B1
240	HILLSIDE AV	94611	650-B1
200	DRACENA AV	94611	650-B1
130	CARMEL AV	94611	650-B1
50	EL CERRITO AV	94611	650-B1
1	SAN CARLOS AV	94611	650-A1
50	RICARDO AV	94611	650-A1
770	DUDLEY AV	94611	650-C1
770	BLAIR PL	94611	650-C1
750	SCENIC AV	94611	650-C1
750	MOUNTAIN AV	94611	650-C1
700	BELL AV	94611	650-C1
630	ALTA AV	94611	650-C1
620	SCENIC AV	94611	650-C1
530	SCENIC AV	94611	650-B1
500	HARDWICK AV	94611	650-B1
530	HIGHLAND AV	94611	650-B1
830	HARBORD DR	94611	650-C1
800	CALVERT CT	94611	650-C1
830	BLAIR PL	94611	650-C1
BLAIR PL			**PDMT**
20	CALVERT CT	94611	650-C1
1	BLAIR AV	94611	650-C1
20	BLAIR AV	94611	650-C1
20	DUDLEY AV	94611	650-C1
BLAKE ST			**BERK**
1100	SAN PABLO AV	94702	629-E3
1200	MATHEWS ST	94702	629-E3
1300	MABEL ST	94702	629-E3
1400	ACTON ST	94702	629-F3
1500	SACRAMENTO ST	94703	629-F3
1600	CALIFORNIA ST	94703	629-F3
1700	MCGEE AV	94703	629-F3
1800	GRANT ST	94703	629-G3
1900	MARTIN LUTHER KING JR WY	94704	629-G3
2000	MILVIA ST	94704	629-G3
2110	SHATTUCK AV	94704	629-H3
2200	FULTON ST	94704	629-H3
2210	FULTON ST	94704	629-H3
2310	ELLSWORTH ST	94704	629-H3
2410	DANA ST	94704	629-H2
2450	CHILTON WY	94704	629-H2
2500	TELEGRAPH AV	94704	629-H2
BLANDING AV			**ALA**
2300	OAK ST	94501	670-A1
2410	PARK ST	94501	670-A1
2510	EVERETT ST	94501	670-B2
2620	BROADWAY	94501	670-B2
2700	FERNSIDE BLVD	94501	670-B2
2700	TILDEN WY	94501	670-B2
BLANDON RD			**OAK**
3200	GLENLY RD	94605	671-A3
3300	GOLF LINKS RD	94605	671-A3
BLENHEIM ST			**OAK**
800	PEARMAIN ST	94603	670-H7
900	SAN LEANDRO ST	94603	670-H7
1000	APRICOT ST	94603	670-H7
BLOSSOM ST			**OAK**
3200	FRUITVALE AV	94601	650-C6
BLYTHEN WY			**OAK**
12100	WEE BLYTHEN	94619	650-J4
	BALMORAL DR	94619	650-J4
	BALMORAL DR	-	650-J4
	TARTAN WY	-	650-J4
BODEN WY			**OAK**
500	BEACON ST	94610	650-A3
600	BEACON ST	94610	650-A3
600	LAKESHORE AV	94610	649-J3
BOEHMER ST			**OAK**
3600	36TH AV	94601	670-C1
3700	37TH AV	94601	670-C1
BOEING ST			**OAK**
8100	LANGLEY ST	94621	670-D6
8100	WRIGHT ST	94621	670-D7
8150	BEACHY ST	94621	670-D7
8300	COOKE ST	94621	670-D7
BOISE ST			**BERK**
3200	66TH ST	94702	629-F4
3300	HARMON ST	94702	629-F4
BOLIVAR DR			**BERK**
1	ADDISON ST	94804	629-D2
1	W BOLIVAR DR	94804	629-D2
20	BANCROFT WY	94804	629-D3
80	POTTER ST	94804	629-D4
100	ASHBY AV	94804	629-D4
W BOLIVAR DR			**BERK**
20	ADDISON ST	94804	629-D2
20	BOLIVAR DR	94804	629-D2
BONA ST			**OAK**
2800	BELLAIRE PL	94601	650-C5
2900	FRUITVALE AV	94601	650-C5
2900	FRUITVALE AV	94601	650-D5
3100	SUNSET AV	94601	650-D6
3200	ATWELL AV	94601	650-D6
3300	COOLIDGE AV	94601	650-D6
3300	COOLIDGE AV	94601	650-D6
3400	DEERING ST	94601	650-D6
3400	DEERING CT	94601	650-D6
BONAR ST			**BERK**
2000	UNIVERSITY AV	94702	629-E2
2100	ADDISON ST	94702	629-E2
2200	ALLSTON WY	94702	629-E2
2300	BANCROFT WY	94702	629-E2
2320	POE ST	94702	629-E2
2400	CHANNING WY	94702	629-E3
2500	DWIGHT WY	94702	629-E3
BOND ST			**OAK**
4200	42ND AV	94601	670-D1
4400	HIGH ST	94601	670-D1
4510	45TH AV	94601	670-D1
4620	46TH AV	94601	670-E1
4700	47TH AV	94601	670-E1
4800	48TH AV	94601	670-E1
4900	BANCROFT AV	94601	670-E1
4900	FREMONT WY	94601	670-E1
BONHAM WY			**OAK**
400	MIRA VISTA AV	94610	649-J2
400	VALLE VISTA AV	94610	650-A2
450	VALLE VISTA AV	94610	650-A2
500	GRAND AV	94610	650-A2
BONITA AV			**BERK**
1200	YOLO AV	94709	609-G7
1300	BERRYMAN ST	94709	609-G7
1400	ROSE ST	94709	609-G7
1600	VINE ST	94709	609-G7
1600	CEDAR ST	94709	629-G1
1700	VIRGINIA ST	94709	629-G1
1800	DELAWARE ST	94709	629-G1
1900	HEARST AV	94704	629-G1
1920	BERKELEY WY	94704	629-G1
2000	UNIVERSITY AV	94704	629-G1
BONITA AV			**PDMT**
100	BLAIR AV	94611	650-B1
30	PARK WY	94611	630-B7
1	RAMONA AV	94611	630-B7
30	ESTRELLA AV	94611	630-B7
30	MORAGA AV	94611	630-B7
200	BLAIR AV	94611	650-B1
300	OAKLAND AV	94611	650-B1
360	VISTA AV	94611	650-B1
400	MAGNOLIA AV	94611	650-B1
BONNIE LN			**BERK**
1	EUCLID AV	94708	609-H5
1	MARIN AV	94708	609-H5
100	HILLDALE AV	94708	609-H5
BONNINGTON CT			**OAK**
1	THORNDALE DR	94611	630-E5
BOOKER ST			**OAK**
2500	SPRUCE ST	94606	650-A4
2500	7TH AV	94606	650-A4
2600	IVY DR	94606	650-A4
BORDWELL CT			**ALA**
1	CHRISTENSEN CT	94502	669-J6
100	DENKE DR	94502	669-J6
100	LEONARD CT	94502	669-J6
BOSSHARD CT			**ALA**
	ROSEFIELD LP	94501	649-G7
BOSTON AV			**OAK**
3100	SCHOOL ST	94602	650-D5
3250	PLEASANT ST	94602	650-D5
3310	HAROLD ST	94602	650-D5
3360	MONTANA ST	94602	650-D5
3450	PALMETTO ST	94602	650-D5
3500	MACARTHUR BLVD	94602	650-D4
BOULEVARD WY			**OAK**
400	GRAND AV	94610	650-A2
420	SYLVAN WY	94610	650-A2
430	FAIRBANKS AV	94610	650-A2
440	CROFTON AV	94610	650-A2
590	WARFIELD AV	94610	650-A2
610	KENMORE AV	94610	650-B2
700	LAKESHORE AV	94610	650-B2
BOULEVARD WY			**PDMT**
440	CROFTON AV	94610	650-A2
560	CROFTON AV	94610	650-A2
590	WARFIELD AV	94610	650-A2
BOWDITCH ST			**BERK**
2300	BANCROFT WY	94704	629-J2
2320	DURANT AV	94704	629-J2
2400	CHANNING WY	94704	629-J2
2450	HASTE ST	94704	629-J2
2500	DWIGHT WY	94704	629-J2
BOWLES PL			**OAK**
1	SUNNYHILLS RD	94610	650-C3
BOWLING DR			**OAK**
1	COUNTRY CLUB DR	94618	630-A5
100	GLENBROOK DR	94618	630-A5
BOWMAN CT			**ALA**
3550	PYNE LN	94502	670-A7
BOYD AV			**OAK**
5200	CAVOUR ST	94618	629-J6
5300	CLIFTON ST	94618	629-J6
5400	HUDSON ST	94618	629-J6
5500	FOREST ST	94618	629-J6
BOYER ST			**OAK**
5300	53RD ST	94608	629-F6
5400	54TH ST	94608	629-F6
BOYNTON AV			**BERK**
570	COLORADO AV	94707	609-G4
600	FLORIDA AV	94707	609-G4
BRAEMAR RD			**OAK**
2000	BRENTWOOD RD	94602	650-E3
BRANDON ST			**OAK**
	RONADA AV	94611	630-A7
	PARKSIDE DR	94611	630-A7
	GRAND AV	94611	630-A7
1700	ROSE AV	94611	630-A7
1900	PIEDMONT AV	94611	630-A7
BRANDON ST			**PDMT**
	RONADA AV	94611	630-A7
	PARKSIDE DR	94611	630-A7
	GRAND AV	94611	630-A7
	ROSE AV	94611	630-A7
BRANDY ROCK WY			**OAK**
	BROOKPARK RD	94619	651-B6
	SKYLINE BLVD	94619	651-B6
BRANN ST			**OAK**
5300	55TH AV	94619	670-G1
5300	MORCOM AV	94619	650-G7
5500	MORCOM AV	94619	650-G7
5500	55TH AV	94605	670-G1
5600	56TH AV	94605	670-G1
5700	57TH AV	94605	670-G1
5800	58TH AV	94605	670-G1
5840	MILLSBRAE AV	94605	670-G1
5900	SEMINARY AV	94605	670-G1
6000	60TH AV	94605	670-G1
6100	61ST AV	94605	670-G1
6200	62ND AV	94605	670-G1
6400	64TH AV	94605	670-G1
6470	CAMDEN ST	94605	670-H1
6700	FOOTHILL BLVD	94605	670-H1
6700	67TH AV	94605	670-H1
BREAKWATER DR			**BERK**
1	SPINNAKER WY	94804	629-B2
BREED AV			**OAK**
10500	105TH AV	94603	671-A6
10600	106TH AV	94603	671-A6
10700	107TH AV	94603	671-A6
10800	108TH AV	94603	671-A6
10900	109TH AV	94603	671-A6
11000	DURANT AV	94603	671-A6
BREHAUT CT			**ALA**
1	SHANER DR	94502	669-J6
BRENTFORD ST			**OAK**
6700	OLMSTEAD ST	94621	670-F3
6850	OLMSTEAD ST	94621	670-F3
6900	69TH AV	94621	670-F3
BRENTWOOD PL			**OAK**
1820	BRENTWOOD RD	94602	650-E3
1820	MELVIN RD	94602	650-E3
BRENTWOOD RD			**OAK**
1820	BRENTWOOD PL	94602	650-E3
1820	MELVIN RD	94602	650-E3
1830	MELVIN RD	94602	650-E2
1850	BRAEMAR RD	94602	650-E2
1900	ROSECREST DR	94602	650-E2
BRET HARTE RD			**BERK**
1	BRET HARTE WY	94708	609-H6
1	KEITH AV	94708	609-H6
50	CRAGMONT AV	94708	609-H6
50	CRAGMONT AV	94708	609-H6
200	KEELER AV	94708	609-H6
BRET HARTE WY			**BERK**
1	BRET HARTE RD	94708	609-H6
1	KEITH AV	94708	609-H6
100	EUCLID AV	94708	609-H6
BRIARCLIFF RD			**OAK**
4300	OAK HILL RD	94605	671-C2
4500	OAK HILL RD	94605	671-C2
BRIDGE AV			**OAK**
1800	E 16TH ST	94601	650-C7
1900	FOOTHILL BLVD	94601	650-C7
BRIDGE RD			**BERK**
1	ALVARADO RD	94705	630-B4
100	TUNNEL RD	94705	630-B4
BRIDGE VIEW ISL			**ALA**
3320	ANCHOR WY	94501	670-A4
3360	DRIFTWOOD LN	94501	670-A4
BRIDGEVIEW DR			**OAK**
4300	LEIMERT BLVD	94602	650-D3
BRIGGS AV			**ALA**
3200	HIGH ST	94501	670-B3
3300	FERNSIDE BLVD	94501	670-B3
BRIGHTON AV			**ALB**
1100	SAN PABLO AV	94706	609-D5
1120	KAINS AV	94706	609-D5
1140	STANNAGE AV	94706	609-D5
1200	CORNELL AV	94706	609-D5
1210	TALBOT AV	94706	609-D5
1230	EVELYN AV	94706	609-D5
	MASONIC AV	94706	609-E5
1260	SAN GABRIEL AV	94706	609-E5
1280	BEHRENS ST	94706	609-E5
1280	SPOKANE AV	94706	609-E5
1300	ASHBURY AV	94706	609-E5
1300	KEY ROUTE BLVD	94706	609-E5
BRIGHTON AV			**OAK**
3500	MACARTHUR BLVD	94602	650-C4
3700	EXCELSIOR AV	94602	650-C4
3800	E 38TH ST	94602	650-C4
3900	PARK BLVD	94602	650-C4
4000	PARK BLVD	94602	650-C4
4100	GREENWOOD AV	94602	650-C4
BRIGHTON CT			**ALA**
200	BRIGHTON RD	94502	670-A5
200	SHEFFIELD RD	94502	670-A5
BRIGHTON RD			**ALA**
160	BRIGHTON CT	94502	670-A5
160	SHEFFIELD RD	94502	670-A5
70	DANBROOK CT	94502	669-J5
100	ROXBURG LN	94502	669-J5
BRISTOL DR			**OAK**
6800	BUCKINGHAM BLVD	94705	630-C4

PRIMARY STREET Address	Cross Street	ZIP	CITY Pg-Grid
BRISTOL DR			**OAK**
6910	SHERWICK DR	94705	630-C3
7100	BUCKINGHAM BLVD	94705	630-C3
BRITHORN LN			**ALA**
3400	HOLLY ST	94502	670-A7
3500	JOST LN	94502	670-A7
BRITT CT			**ALA**
1	MCDONNEL RD	94502	669-J6
BRITTANY DR			**ALA**
	PACKET LNDG	94502	670-A5
	PURCELL DR	94502	670-A5
BROADMOOR VW			**OAK**
3070	LEEWARD WY	94605	671-C5
3070	MALCOLM AV	94605	671-C5
BROADWAY			**ALA**
300	BAYVIEW DR	94501	669-J4
300	SHORELINE DR	94501	669-J4
900	LA JOLLA DR	94501	670-A4
1000	OTIS DR	94501	670-A3
1100	CALHOUN ST	94501	670-A3
1130	WASHINGTON ST	94501	670-A3
1200	SAN JOSE AV	94501	670-A3
1300	ENCINAL AV	94501	670-A3
1320	CHESTER ST	94501	670-A3
1360	CRIST ST	94501	670-A3
1400	CENTRAL AV	94501	670-A2
1500	SANTA CLARA AV	94501	670-A2
1550	SAINT MARGARET CT	94501	670-A2
1600	LINCOLN AV	94501	670-A2
1650	NOBLE AV	94501	670-B2
1700	BUENA VISTA AV	94501	670-B2
1800	EAGLE AV	94501	670-B2
1800	TILDEN WY	94501	670-B2
1900	CLEMENT AV	94501	670-B2
2000	BLANDING AV	94501	670-B2
BROADWAY			**OAK**
1	WATER ST	94607	649-F5
100	EMBARCADERO W	94607	649-F5
200	2ND ST	94607	649-F5
300	3RD ST	94607	649-F5
400	4TH ST	94607	649-F5
	5TH ST	94607	649-F5
600	6TH ST	94607	649-G4
700	7TH ST	94607	649-G4
800	8TH ST	94607	649-G4
900	9TH ST	94607	649-G4
1000	10TH ST	94607	649-G4
1100	11TH ST	94607	649-G4
1200	12TH ST	94612	649-G4
1290	13TH ST	94612	649-G4
1380	14TH ST	94612	649-G4
1500	TELEGRAPH AV	94612	649-G4
1500	KAHN AL	94612	649-G4
1520	15TH ST	94612	649-G3
1700	17TH ST	94612	649-G3
1830	19TH ST	94612	649-G3
1980	20TH ST	94612	649-G3
2100	21ST ST	94612	649-G3
2200	22ND ST	94612	649-G3
2260	GRAND AV	94612	649-G3
2300	23RD ST	94612	649-G3
2400	24TH ST	94612	649-H2
2550	25TH ST	94612	649-H2
2630	26TH ST	94612	649-H2
2660	WEBSTER ST	94612	649-H2
2710	27TH ST	94612	649-H2
2800	28TH ST	94611	649-H2
2900	29TH ST	94611	649-H2
3000	30TH ST	94611	649-H2
3280	BROOK ST	94611	649-H1
3300	HAWTHORNE AV	94611	649-H1
3310	PIEDMONT AV	94611	649-H1
3400	34TH ST	94611	649-H1
3700	W MACARTHUR BLVD	94611	649-H1
3840	38TH ST	94611	649-H1
3870	38TH ST	94611	649-H1
3970	40TH ST	94611	649-J1
3970	40TH ST	94611	649-J1
3970	40TH WY	94611	649-J1
4100	41ST ST	94611	629-J7
4200	RIDGEWAY AV	94611	629-J7
4220	GARNET ST	94611	629-J7
4300	42ND ST	94611	629-J7
4300	MATHER ST	94611	629-J7
4500	45TH ST	94611	629-J7
4900	49TH ST	94611	629-J7
5000	51ST ST	94611	629-J6
5000	PLEASANT VALLEY AV	94611	629-J6
5200	CORONADO AV	94618	629-J6
5240	COLLEGE AV	94618	629-J6
5280	CLIFTON ST	94618	629-J6
5300	BROADWAY TER	94618	629-J6
5380	NAPA ST	94618	629-J6
5200	ADA ST	94618	629-J6
5600	MANILA AV	94618	630-A6
5600	MONROE AV	94618	630-A6
5660	KALES AV	94618	630-A5
5700	VIRMAR AV	94618	630-A5
5740	TAFT AV	94618	630-A5
5750	TAFT AV	94618	630-A5
5800	LAWTON AV	94618	630-A5
5820	ROCKRIDGE BLVD S	94618	630-A5
5820	LAWTON AV	94618	630-A5
5900	OCEAN VIEW DR	94618	630-A5
6000	KEITH AV	94618	630-A5
	PATTON ST	94618	630-A5
6000	KEITH AV	94618	630-A5
6100	BROOKSIDE AV	94618	630-A5
6150	GOLDEN GATE WY	94618	630-A5
2800	GOLDEN GATE WY	94618	630-B5
BROADWAY TER			**OAK**
5900	CLAREWOOD DR	94618	630-B6
6000	HARBORD DR	94618	630-B6
6250	ARBON PTH	94618	630-B5
6250	MANDALAY RD	94618	630-B5
5200	BROADWAY	94618	629-J6
5250	THOMAS AV	94618	629-J6
5300	BELGRAVE PL	94618	629-J6
5400	CARLTON ST	94618	630-A6
5400	CARLTON ST	94611	630-A6
5500	MONROE AV	94618	630-A6
5500	MONROE AV	94611	630-A6
5590	COUNTRY CLUB DR	94618	630-A6
5590	COUNTRY CLUB DR	94611	630-A6
5590	MARGARIDO DR	94611	630-A6
5810	ROMANY RD	94618	630-A6
5810	ROMANY RD	94611	630-A6
5820	GLENBROOK DR	94618	630-B6
5820	GLENBROOK DR	94611	630-B6
5900	CLAREWOOD DR	94618	630-B6
5920	OSTRANDER RD	94618	630-B6
6040	CROSS RD	94618	630-B5
6190	GOLDEN GATE AV	94618	630-B5
6250	ARBON PTH	94618	630-B6
6250	MANDALAY RD	94618	630-B6
6300	BUENA VISTA AV	94618	630-C6
6390	PROCTOR AV	94618	630-C6
6400	ERBA PTH	94618	630-C5
6400	SHERIDAN RD	94618	630-C5
	PINEWOOD RD	94611	630-C6
6600	GLENWOOD GLADE	94611	630-C6
6800	DUNCAN WY	94611	630-C6
6900	LEO WY	94611	630-D6
6940	MOUNTAIN BLVD	94611	630-D6
6990	AQUARIUS WY	94611	630-D6
7000	CAPRICORN AV	94611	630-D6
8000	SWAINLAND RD	94611	630-D6
9000	TAURUS AV	94611	630-D6
9400	TAURUS AV	94611	630-D6
11000	URANUS AV	94611	630-D6
11900	VIRGO RD	94611	630-D6
12570	MERRIEWOOD DR	94611	630-D6
12610	CROWN AV	94611	630-D5
14000	PINEHAVEN RD	94611	630-D5
16000	GWIN RD	94611	630-D5
17000	PINENEEDLE DR	94611	630-D5
17050	WOODLAND PL	94611	630-D5
18000	BALSAM WY	94611	630-D4
18000	PINENEEDLE DR	94611	630-D4
18100	SKYLINE BLVD	94611	630-D4
BROCKHURST ST			**OAK**
600	MARTIN LUTHER KING JR WY	94609	649-G1
800	WEST ST	94608	649-G1
900	MARKET ST	94608	649-F1
1000	SAN PABLO AV	94608	649-F1
1000	FILBERT ST	94608	649-F1
BROMLEY AV			**OAK**
5900	SEMINARY AV	94621	670-F2
6200	62ND AV	94621	670-F2
6200	62ND AV	94621	670-F2
6300	64TH AV	94621	670-F2
BROOK ST			**OAK**
3000	30TH ST	94611	649-H2
3100	BROADWAY	94611	649-H2
BROOKDALE AV			**OAK**
2800	FRUITVALE AV	94602	650-C5
2800	FRUITVALE AV	94601	650-C5
2800	FRUITVALE AV	94602	650-D5
2900	CAPP ST	94602	650-D5
3000	COOLIDGE AV	94602	650-D6
3400	HUMBOLDT AV	94602	650-D6
3400	HUMBOLDT AV	94601	650-D6
3450	BARTLETT ST	94602	650-D6
3450	BARTLETT ST	94601	650-D6
3500	35TH AV	94602	650-D6
3500	35TH AV	94601	650-D6
3500	35TH AV	94619	650-E6
3500	35TH AV	94601	650-E6
3730	SHORT ST	94619	650-E6
3730	SHORT ST	94601	650-E6
3880	38TH AV	94619	650-E7
3880	38TH AV	94601	650-E7
4070	MINNA AV	94619	650-E7
4070	MINNA AV	94601	650-E7
4160	EASTMAN AV	94619	650-E7
4160	EASTMAN AV	94601	650-E7
4300	HIGH ST	94619	650-E7
4300	HIGH ST	94601	650-E7
4500	FRANCES ST	94619	650-E7
4500	FRANCES ST	94601	650-E7
4600	LILAC ST	94619	650-E7
4600	LILAC ST	94601	650-E7
4700	FERN ST	94619	650-E7
4700	FERN ST	94601	650-E7
4800	RENWICK ST	94619	650-F7
4800	RENWICK ST	94601	650-F7
4800	MONTICELLO AV	94619	650-F7
4800	MONTICELLO AV	94601	650-F7
4910	MONTICELLO AV	94619	650-F7
4910	MONTICELLO AV	94601	650-F7
5300	KINGSLAND AV	94601	670-F1
5170	COLE ST	94601	670-F1
5040	RAWSON ST	94601	670-F1
5040	RAWSON ST	94619	670-F1
5030	MAXWELL AV	94601	670-F1
5030	MAXWELL AV	94619	670-F1
4920	MAXWELL AV	94601	670-F1
4920	MAXWELL AV	94619	670-F1
4910	BEST AV	94601	670-F1
4910	BEST AV	94619	670-F1
4800	BEST AV	94601	670-F1
4800	BEST AV	94619	670-F1
5350	KINGSLAND AV	94619	670-F1
5350	KINGSLAND AV	94601	670-F1
5500	55TH AV	94619	670-F1
5500	55TH AV	94601	670-F1
5500	55TH AV	94605	670-F1
5800	FOOTHILL BLVD	94605	670-F1
BROOKFIELD AV			**OAK**
3040	MARLOW DR	94605	671-C7
3000	COVINGTON ST	94605	671-C7
3050	MIDDLETON ST	94605	671-C7
BROOKLYN AV			**OAK**
600	LAKESHORE AV	94606	649-J4
630	MERRITT AV	94606	649-J4
640	NEWTON AV	94606	649-J4
640	WESLEY AV	94606	649-J4
690	HANOVER AV	94606	649-J4
690	HADDON RD	94606	650-A4
650	HADDON RD	94606	650-A4
700	ATHOL AV	94606	650-A4
750	VAN DYKE AV	94606	650-A4
800	MONTCLAIR AV	94606	650-A4
850	ZORAH ST	94606	650-A4
900	PARK BLVD	94606	650-A4
BROOKPARK RD			**OAK**
12500	SKYLINE BLVD	94619	651-A5
13000	BRANDY ROCK WY	94619	651-B6
13050	SADDLE BROOK DR	94619	651-B6
13100	PARKRIDGE DR	94619	651-B6
BROOKSIDE AV			**BERK**
1	CLAREMONT AV	94705	629-J4
BROOKSIDE AV			**OAK**
6100	BROADWAY	94618	630-A5
6350	EUSTICE AV	94618	630-B5
6350	NOVA PTH	94618	630-B5
6500	OCEAN VIEW DR	94618	630-B5
6500	WEST LN	94618	630-B5
BROOKSIDE CT			**BERK**
100	BROOKSIDE DR	94705	629-J4
BROOKSIDE DR			**BERK**
100	CLAREMONT AV	94705	629-J4
150	BROOKSIDE CT	94705	629-J4
200	CLAREMONT AV	94705	629-J4
BROOKWOOD PL			**OAK**
600	TRESTLE GLEN RD	94610	650-A3
BROOKWOOD RD			**OAK**
1000	TRESTLE GLEN RD	94610	650-B3
1100	TRESTLE GLEN RD	94610	650-B3
BROWN AV			**OAK**
3600	MACARTHUR BLVD	94619	650-F6
3700	KANSAS ST	94619	650-F5
3850	CALIFORNIA ST	94619	650-F5
3990	WISCONSIN ST	94619	650-F5
4100	HARBOR VIEW AV	94619	650-F5
BROWN ST			**ALA**
1150	SHANER DR	94502	669-J6
2800	SATH CT	94502	669-J6
2900	DENKE DR	94502	669-J6
BROWNING ST			**BERK**
2100	ADDISON ST	94702	629-E2
2200	ALLSTON WY	94702	629-E2
2300	BANCROFT WY	94702	629-E2
2400	CHANNING WY	94702	629-E3
2500	DWIGHT WY	94702	629-E3
BRUCE ST			**OAK**
3500	CHATHAM RD	94602	650-B4
3600	E 36TH ST	94602	650-C4
3700	EXCELSIOR AV	94602	650-C4
BRUNELL DR			**OAK**
3200	BUTTERS DR	94602	650-G4
3300	BRUNELL PL	94602	650-G4
3400	TRINIDAD AV	94602	650-G4
3600	ROBINSON DR	94602	650-H4
3700	KLAMATH ST	94602	650-H4
3800	CRESTMONT DR	94602	650-H4
BRUNELL PL			**OAK**
1	BRUNELL DR	94602	650-G4
BRUNS CT			**OAK**
5900	LA SALLE AV	94611	650-D1
BRUNSWICK RD			**ALA**
100	SEA VIEW PKWY	94502	669-J5
160	SHERWOOD LN	94502	669-J5
200	SHEFFIELD RD	94502	669-J5
BRUSH ST			**ALA**
200	2ND ST	94501	649-E7
300	3RD ST	94501	649-E7
BRUSH ST			**OAK**
270	2ND ST	94607	649-F4
360	3RD ST	94607	649-F4
460	4TH ST	94607	649-F4
	5TH ST	94607	649-F4
500	6TH ST	94607	649-F4
700	7TH ST	94607	649-F4
1120	11TH ST	94607	649-F4
1220	12TH ST	94607	649-F3
1310	13TH ST	94612	649-F3
1400	14TH ST	94612	649-F3
1490	15TH ST	94612	649-F3
1590	16TH ST	94612	649-F3
1680	17TH ST	94612	649-F3
1770	18TH ST	94612	649-F3
1880	19TH ST	94612	649-F3
1950	20TH ST	94612	649-F3
2030	21ST ST	94612	649-F3
2120	22ND ST	94612	649-F3
2200	W GRAND AV	94612	649-G2
2260	23RD ST	94612	649-G2
2300	SAN PABLO AV	94612	649-G2
BRUZZONE DR			**ALA**
	DOWITCHER CT	94501	649-F7
	TERN LN	94501	649-F7
	PLOVER CT	94501	649-F7
	WHIMBREL CT	94501	649-F7
	HERON CT	94501	649-F7
	SANDERLING CT	94501	649-F7
	EGRET CT	94501	649-F7
	KILLDEER CT	94501	649-F7
	BUENA VISTA AV	94501	649-F7
BRYANT AV			**OAK**
5300	COLLEGE AV	94618	629-J6
5400	ADA ST	94618	629-J6
5500	MANILA AV	94618	629-J6
BUCHANAN ST			**ALB**
700	CLEVELAND AV	94706	609-C6
770	PIERCE ST	94706	609-C6
870	BUCHANAN STREET EXT	94710	609-C6
	CLEVELAND AV	94706	609-C6
	FILLMORE ST	94706	609-D6
890	TAYLOR ST	94706	609-D6
900	MORE ST	94706	609-D6
910	POLK ST	94706	609-D6
930	CERRITO ST	94706	609-D6
970	JACKSON ST	94706	609-D6
990	MARIN AV	94706	609-D6
1010	MADISON ST	94706	609-D6
1050	ADAMS ST	94706	609-D6
1100	SAN PABLO AV	94706	609-D6
BUCHANAN STREET EXT			**ALB**
870	BUCHANAN ST	94710	609-C6
BUCKEYE AV			**OAK**
1	HARBORD DR	94618	630-B6
10	MORRILL LN	94618	630-B6
70	CANON VIEW LN	94618	630-B6
200	MANDALAY RD	94618	630-B6
BUCKINGHAM BLVD			**OAK**
6800	BRISTOL DR	94705	630-C4
6840	KENT RD	94705	630-C4
6910	NORFOLK DR	94705	630-C3
	BRISTOL DR	94705	630-C3
7300	TUNNEL RD	94705	630-D3
BUCKLEY CT			**OAK**
	BUTTERS DR	94602	650-G3
BUELL ST			**OAK**
3820	TOMPKINS AV	94619	650-G6
3780	DAISY ST	94619	650-G6
3750	STEELE ST	94619	650-G7
3710	CALAVERAS AV	94619	650-G7
3720	MACARTHUR BLVD	94613	650-G7
BUENA AV			**BERK**
1530	HOLLY ST	94703	609-F7
1600	CALIFORNIA ST	94703	609-F7
1700	MCGEE AV	94703	609-F7
1800	CYPRESS ST	94703	609-F7
BUENA VENTURA AV			**OAK**
6100	LUNDHOLM AV	94605	650-H7
6200	LUNDHOLM AV	94605	650-H7
6140	DELMONT AV	94605	670-H1
6320	64TH AV	94605	670-H1
6600	SIMSON ST	94605	670-H1
BUENA VISTA AV			**ALA**
460	POGGI ST	94501	649-E7
500	5TH ST	94501	649-F7
500	GRESHAM DR	94501	649-F7
500	WILLET CT	94501	649-F7
500	BRUZZONE DR	94501	649-F7
700	WEBSTER ST	94501	649-F7
720	CONCORDIA ST	94501	649-F7
750	CONSTITUTION WY	94501	649-G7
800	8TH ST	94501	649-G7
850	NASON ST	94501	649-G7
900	9TH ST	94501	649-G7
950	WOOD ST	94501	649-G7
1000	CHAPIN ST	94501	649-G7
1100	SAINT CHARLES ST	94501	649-G7
1200	BAY ST	94501	649-H7
1300	SHERMAN ST	94501	669-H1
1500	BENTON ST	94501	669-H1
1520	JAY ST	94501	669-H1
1530	ENTRANCE RD	94501	669-H1
1540	ARBOR ST	94501	669-H1
1560	STANTON ST	94501	669-H1
1580	NAUTILUS ST	94501	669-H1
1600	PARU ST	94501	669-J1
1650	HIBBARD ST	94501	669-J1
1700	GRAND ST	94501	669-J1
1750	MINTURN ST	94501	669-J1
1800	UNION ST	94501	669-J1
1850	SCHILLER ST	94501	669-J1
1900	LAFAYETTE ST	94501	669-J1
2000	CHESTNUT ST	94501	669-J1
2050	STANFORD ST	94501	669-J1
2100	WILLOW ST	94501	669-J1
2150	MULBERRY ST	94501	670-A1
2200	WALNUT ST	94501	670-A1
2220	ELM ST	94501	670-A2
2300	OAK ST	94501	670-A2
2400	PARK ST	94501	670-A2
2450	FOLEY ST	94501	670-A2
2500	EVERETT ST	94501	670-A2
2520	TILDEN WY	94501	670-A2
2600	BROADWAY	94501	670-B2
2650	TREGLOAN CT	94501	670-B2
2700	PEARL ST	94501	670-B2
2800	VERSAILLES AV	94501	670-B2
2850	MORELAND DR	94501	670-B2
2900	NORTHWOOD DR	94501	670-B2
BUENA VISTA AV			**OAK**
5700	GOLDEN GATE AV	94618	630-B5
5730	BUENA VISTA PL	94618	630-B5
5800	AROLLO PTH	94618	630-B5
5930	GONDO PTH	94618	630-B5
5940	CONTRA COSTA RD	94618	630-B5
5960	ACACIA AV	94618	630-B5
6000	CHAUMONT PTH	94618	630-B5
6100	BELALP PTH	94618	630-B5
6200	HILL RD	94618	630-B5
6300	ARBON PTH	94618	630-B5
6400	BROADWAY TER	94618	630-B5
BUENA VISTA PL			**OAK**
100	BUENA VISTA AV	94618	630-B5
BUENA VISTA WY			**BERK**
2500	EUCLID AV	94708	609-H7
2600	LE ROY AV	94708	609-H7
2670	GREENWOOD TER	94708	609-H7
2700	LA LOMA AV	94708	609-J7
2720	MAYBECK TWIN DR	94708	609-J7
2900	DEL MAR AV	94708	609-J7
BULLARD DR			**OAK**
6000	ESTATES DR	94611	630-D7
6000	ESTATES DR	94611	630-D7
6140	MCANDREW DR	94611	650-D1
6400	ESTATES DR	94611	650-D1
BURBANK ST			**ALA**
1300	PORTOLA AV	94501	669-G1
1400	CENTRAL AV	94501	669-G1
BURCKHALTER AV			**OAK**
3900	SUNKIST DR	94605	670-J1
3900	HILLMONT DR	94605	670-J1
4000	SUNNYMERE AV	94605	670-J1
BURDECK CT			**OAK**
1	BURDECK DR	94602	650-F3
BURDECK DR			**OAK**
2980	HEDGE LN	94602	650-F3
3060	BURDECK CT	94602	650-G3
3400	BUTTERS DR	94602	650-G3
BURGNER AV			**ALA**
2800	DENKE DR	94502	669-J6
BURGOS AV			**OAK**
9700	DORISA AV	94605	671-B4
9800	GOLF LINKS RD	94605	671-B4
BURK ST			**OAK**
400	LAGUNITAS AV	94610	649-J3
500	EUCLID AV	94610	649-J3
BURLINGTON ST			**OAK**
2400	LINCOLN AV	94602	650-E4
BURLWOOD AV			**OAK**
300	CLARA ST	94603	670-G7
500	MADDUX DR	94603	670-G7
BURMA RD			**OAK**
270	AFRICA ST	94607	649-C1
300	WAKE AV	94607	649-D1
BURNETT ST			**BERK**
1200	SAN PABLO AV	94702	629-E4
1300	MABEL ST	94702	629-F4
1320	PARK ST	94702	629-F4
1400	ACTON ST	94702	629-F4
BURR ST			**OAK**
8700	THERMAL ST	94605	671-A3
8900	LAWLOR ST	94605	671-A4
9400	STEARNS AV	94605	671-A4
9700	CHEROKEE AV	94605	671-A4
9800	98TH AV	94605	671-A4
9810	ANAIR WY	94605	671-A5
9900	99TH AV	94605	671-A5
10000	OLIVER AV	94605	671-B5
10000	OLIVER AV	94605	671-B5
10100	TRUMAN AV	94605	671-B5
BURTON DR			**OAK**
2800	SHIRLEY DR	94611	650-G1
2800	WILTON DR	94611	650-G1
2860	SKYLINE BLVD	94611	650-G1
BUTTERS DR			**OAK**
2700	JOAQUIN MILLER RD	94602	650-G3
2860	BUCKLEY CT	94602	650-G3
2920	BURDECK DR	94602	650-G3
3190	BRUNELL DR	94602	650-G3
3600	ROBINSON DR	94602	650-H4
3700	CRESTMONT DR	94602	650-H4
BYRON ST			**BERK**
2100	ADDISON ST	94702	629-E2
2120	COWPER ST	94702	629-E2
2200	ALLSTON WY	94702	629-E2
2300	BANCROFT WY	94702	629-E2
2400	CHANNING WY	94702	629-E3
2500	DWIGHT WY	94702	629-E3
BYRON ST			**OAK**
10300	MACARTHUR BLVD	94603	671-A5
10380	103RD AV	94603	671-A5
10600	106TH AV	94603	671-A5
BYWOOD DR			**OAK**
1900	WRENN ST	94602	650-E3
2240	MELVIN RD	94602	650-E2
2300	CARTER ST	94602	650-E2
2400	LEIMERT BLVD	94602	650-E2

C

PRIMARY STREET Address	Cross Street	ZIP	CITY Pg-Grid
C ST			**OAK**
9200	92ND AV	94603	670-H5
9500	ELMHURST AV	94603	670-H5
9800	98TH AV	94603	670-H6
10000	100TH AV	94603	670-H6
10000	ROYAL ANN ST	94603	670-H6
CABOT DR			**OAK**
5600	MOUNTAIN BLVD	94611	630-D7
CABRILLO PL			**OAK**
1	MENDOZA DR	94611	630-E7
CAIRO RD			**OAK**
100	HEGENBERGER LP	94603	670-F6
200	EMPIRE RD	94603	670-F7
300	CORAL RD	94603	670-F7
CALAFIA AV			**OAK**
3500	GOLF LINKS RD	94605	671-B4
3570	ANZA AV	94605	671-B4
3600	DORISA AV	94605	671-B4
3700	MOUNTAIN BLVD	94605	671-B4
CALANDRIA			**OAK**
3400	MARGARITA AV	94605	671-B3

Address	Cross Street	ZIP	City / Pg-Grid
CALANDRIA			**OAK**
3400	MURILLO AV	94605	671-B3
3600	CREST AV	94605	671-B3
CALAVERAS AV			**OAK**
4800	DAISY ST	94619	650-G7
4900	TOMPKINS AV	94619	650-G7
	MCCLELLAND ST	94619	650-G7
	BUELL ST	94619	650-G7
CALDECOTT LN			**OAK**
100	HILLER DR	94618	630-B4
170	TUNNEL RD	94618	630-C5
CALDERWOOD CT			**OAK**
4800	CAMPUS DR	94605	651-A7
CALDWELL RD			**OAK**
600	GLENARMS DR	94611	630-C5
600	NEVA CT	94611	630-C5
700	MONZAL AV	94611	630-C6
800	PINEWOOD RD	94611	630-C6
CALHOUN ST			**ALA**
2500	REGENT ST	94501	670-A3
2600	BROADWAY	94501	670-A3
2700	PEARL ST	94501	670-A3
2750	GRACE CT	94501	670-A3
2800	VERSAILLES AV	94501	670-A3
2850	COLLEGE AV	94501	670-A4
2900	MOUND ST	94501	670-A4
3000	COURT ST	94501	670-A4
3200	HIGH ST	94501	670-A4
3230	POST ST	94501	670-A4
3260	PEACH ST	94501	670-B4
CALIFORNIA			**ALA**
3000	GOMPERS	94501	649-E6
CALIFORNIA ST			**BERK**
1300	HOPKINS ST	94703	609-F7
1300	MONTEREY AV	94703	609-F7
1350	ADA ST	94703	609-F7
1400	ROSE ST	94703	609-F7
1400	ROSE ST	94703	609-F7
1450	BUENA AV	94703	609-F7
1500	JAYNES ST	94703	629-F1
1600	CEDAR ST	94703	629-F1
1650	LINCOLN ST	94703	629-F1
1700	VIRGINIA ST	94703	629-F1
1750	FRANCISCO ST	94703	629-F1
1800	DELAWARE ST	94703	629-F1
1900	HEARST AV	94703	629-F1
1950	BERKELEY WY	94703	629-F1
2000	UNIVERSITY AV	94703	629-F2
2100	ADDISON ST	94703	629-F2
2200	ALLSTON WY	94703	629-F2
2300	BANCROFT WY	94703	629-F2
2400	CHANNING WY	94703	629-F2
2500	DWIGHT WY	94703	629-F3
2550	BLAKE ST	94703	629-F3
2600	PARKER ST	94703	629-F3
2650	CARLETON ST	94703	629-F3
2700	DERBY ST	94703	629-F3
2750	WARD ST	94703	629-F3
2800	STUART ST	94703	629-F3
2850	OREGON ST	94703	629-F4
2900	RUSSELL ST	94703	629-F4
2950	JULIA ST	94703	629-F4
3000	ASHBY AV	94703	629-F4
3050	TYLER ST	94703	629-F4
3100	PRINCE ST	94703	629-F4
3150	WOOLSEY ST	94703	629-F4
3200	FAIRVIEW ST	94703	629-F4
3250	HARMON ST	94703	629-G5
3300	ALCATRAZ AV	94703	629-G5
3350	63RD ST	94703	629-G5
3400	62ND ST	94703	629-G5
3450	61ST ST	94703	629-G5
CALIFORNIA ST			**OAK**
3000	MAPLE AV	94602	650-E5
3400	LAUREL AV	94602	650-F5
3300	NORTON AV	94602	650-F5
3300	SILVERWOOD AV	94602	650-F5
3400	MIDVALE AV	94602	650-F5
3500	35TH AV	94602	650-F5
3450	61ST ST	94608	629-G5
3500	MARKET ST	94608	629-G5
3500	35TH AV	94619	650-F5
3600	MAGEE AV	94619	650-F5
3700	LOMA VISTA AV	94619	650-F5
3800	BROWN AV	94619	650-F5
3900	PATTERSON AV	94619	650-F5
4000	38TH AV	94619	650-F5
CALLAN PL			**ALA**
1	SEA VIEW PKWY	94502	669-H5
CALMAR AV			**OAK**
600	MANDANA BLVD	94610	650-A3
630	SANTA RAY AV	94610	650-A3
660	VIONA AV	94610	650-B3
750	PALOMA AV	94610	650-B3
900	CARLSTON AV	94610	650-B3
CALODEN ST			**OAK**
9900	GOLF LINKS RD	94605	671-E4
9900	DUNKIRK AV	94605	671-E4
10720	MALCOLM AV	94605	671-E4
CALVERT CT			**PDMT**
	BLAIR PL	94611	650-C1
	BLAIR AV	94611	650-C1
CAMANOE LN			**ALA**
3400	TRELLIS LN	94502	670-B6
3460	TOBAGO LN	94502	670-B7
3500	MELROSE AV	94502	670-B7
CAMBELL BLVD			**ALA**
	HUDSON DR	94501	649-J7
	MCCULLOCH DR	94501	649-J7
	ICARUS DR	94501	649-J7
	WAKEFIELD DR	94501	649-J7
CAMBRIAN AV			**PDMT**
1	SAINT JAMES DR	94611	650-D2
100	SANDRINGHAM RD	94611	650-D2
CAMBRIDGE DR			**ALA**
1700	NORTHWOOD DR	94501	670-B2
1800	YOSEMITE AV	94501	670-B2
1900	FERNSIDE BLVD	94501	670-B2
2000	WINDSOR DR	94501	670-B2
2100	MARINA DR	94501	670-B2
CAMBRIDGE WY			**PDMT**
1	HOWARD AV	94611	650-A1
90	GRAND AV	94611	650-A1
120	JEROME AV	94611	650-A1
140	MANOR DR	94611	650-A1
160	YORK DR	94611	650-A1
180	LATHAM ST	94611	650-A1
200	RICARDO AV	94611	650-A1
CAMDEN RD			**ALA**
400	FRANCISCAN WY	94501	669-H3
500	MYRTLE WK	94501	669-H3
500	YORKSHIRE PL	94501	669-H3
CAMDEN ST			**OAK**
4400	COURTLAND AV	94619	650-F7
4600	STORER AV	94619	650-F7
5900	MACARTHUR BLVD	94605	670-G1
5900	SEMINARY AV	94605	670-G1
6000	60TH AV	94605	670-G1
6100	61ST AV	94605	670-G1
6200	62ND AV	94605	670-G1
6300	63RD AV	94605	670-G1
6400	64TH AV	94605	670-H1
2900	BRANN ST	94605	670-H2
3000	FOOTHILL BLVD	94605	670-H2
3000	HAVENSCOURT BLVD	94605	670-H2
5430	MILLSVIEW AV	94619	650-G7
5400	MILLSVIEW AV	94619	650-G7
5300	WYMAN ST	94619	650-G7
5200	MORCOM AV	94619	650-G7
5000	MADERA AV	94619	650-G7
5200	BIRDSALL AV	94619	650-G7
5500	55TH AV	94605	670-G1
5500	MACARTHUR BLVD	94605	670-G1
5550	MACARTHUR BLVD	94605	670-G1
CAMELFORD CT			**OAK**
100	CAMELFORD PL	94611	650-F2
CAMELFORD PL			**OAK**
1	ASCOT DR	94611	650-F2
1	LONGCROFT DR	94611	650-F2
30	CAMELFORD CT	94611	650-F2
90	MALL CT	94611	650-F1
100	ASCOT DR	94611	650-F1
CAMELIA DR			**ALA**
1000	MECARTNEY RD	94502	670-A6
1050	DAHLIA DR	94502	670-A6
1100	FIR AV	94502	670-A6
CAMELIA ST			**BERK**
600	2ND ST	94804	629-C1
640	3RD ST	94804	629-D1
680	4TH ST	94804	629-D1
720	5TH ST	94804	629-D1
720	6TH ST	94710	609-D7
900	7TH ST	94710	609-D7
950	8TH ST	94710	609-D7
1000	9TH ST	94710	609-D7
1050	10TH ST	94710	609-D7
1100	SAN PABLO AV	94702	609-E7
1130	KAINS AV	94702	609-E7
1150	STANNAGE AV	94702	609-E7
1170	CORNELL AV	94702	609-E7
1200	SANTA FE AV	94702	609-E7
1200	TALBOT AV	94702	609-E7
CAMERON AV			**OAK**
10800	MALCOLM AV	94605	671-D4
10800	MALCOLM AV	94605	671-D4
10900	DINGLEY ST	94605	671-D5
11100	OVERMOOR ST	94605	671-D5
CAMILLIA PL			**OAK**
1	CHARLESTON ST	94602	650-E3
1	PERKINS RD	94602	650-E3
CAMINO DEL VALLE			**ALA**
1000	MECARTNEY RD	94502	670-A6
1030	EL PORTAL	94502	670-A6
1060	LA CRESTA	94502	670-A6
1100	EL SERENO	94502	670-A6
1130	LA CAMPANIA	94502	669-J7
1160	EL PASEO	94502	669-J7
CAMINO LENADA			**OAK**
2600	ASCOT DR	94611	650-F2
2660	LA CUESTA AV	94611	650-F2
2670	EL CAMINITO	94611	650-F2
CAMISA CIR			**OAK**
1	OAK HILL RD	94605	671-C3
CAMPBELL CT			**OAK**
800	8TH ST	94607	649-D3
1000	10TH ST	94607	649-D3
CAMPBELL ST			**OAK**
800	8TH ST	94607	649-D3
1000	10TH ST	94607	649-D3
1100	11TH ST	94607	649-D3
1200	12TH ST	94607	649-D3
1300	13TH ST	94607	649-D3
1400	14TH ST	94607	649-D3
1500	15TH ST	94607	649-D2
1600	16TH ST	94607	649-D2
1700	17TH ST	94607	649-D2
1800	18TH ST	94607	649-E2
1980	20TH ST	94607	649-E2
2180	W GRAND AV	94607	649-E2
2370	24TH ST	94607	649-E2
2420	MANDELA PKWY	94607	649-E2
2420	MANDELA PKWY	94607	649-E1
2600	26TH ST	94607	649-E1
2800	28TH ST	94607	649-E1
CAMPUS DR			**BERK**
1200	SHASTA RD	94708	609-J6
1240	QUAIL AV	94708	609-J6
1300	GLENDALE AV	94708	609-J7
1420	DEL MAR AV	94708	609-J7
1480	AVENIDA DR	94708	609-J7
1540	PARNASSUS RD	94708	609-J7
CAMPUS DR			**OAK**
11800	REDWOOD RD	94619	650-J5
11800	SERENO CIR	94619	650-J5
13080	SKYPOINT CT	94619	650-J6
13150	HIGH KNOLL DR	94619	650-J6
13500	VIEWCREST DR	94619	651-A6
13350	ROCKINGHAM CT	94605	651-A7
13380	RISING HILL CT	94605	651-A7
13490	CROWN RIDGE CT	94605	651-A7
13600	CALDERWOOD CT	94605	651-A7
13680	OHANNESON RD	94605	651-A7
13680	STONE RIDGE CT	94605	671-B1
13700	CRYSTAL RIDGE CT	94605	671-B1
13820	FAIRHILL CT	94605	671-B1
13870	CANYON OAKS DR	94605	671-C1
13900	KELLER AV	94605	671-C1
W CAMPUS DR			**ALA**
	ATLANTIC AV	94501	649-F7
CANNING ST			**OAK**
5800	58TH ST	94609	629-H5
5900	59TH ST	94609	629-H5
5950	MCAULEY ST	94609	629-H5
6000	60TH ST	94609	629-H5
6100	61ST ST	94609	629-H5
6200	62ND ST	94609	629-H5
6300	63RD ST	94609	629-H5
CANON AV			**OAK**
3700	MACARTHUR BLVD	94602	650-D4
3790	VETERAN WY	94602	650-D4
4100	WELLINGTON ST	94602	650-D4
CANON DR			**BERK**
2300	WILDCAT CANYON RD	94708	609-G4
2300	WOODMONT AV	94708	609-G4
CANON DR			**CCCo**
2300	WILDCAT CANYON RD	94708	609-G4
2300	WOODMONT AV	94708	609-G4
CANON VIEW LN			**OAK**
	WILDING LN	94618	630-B6
	BUCKEYE AV	94618	630-B6
CANYON OAKS DR			**OAK**
	KELLER AV	94605	671-B2
700	CAMPUS DR	94605	671-C1
CANYON RD			**BERK**
	STADIUM RIMWAY	94704	630-A2
	STADIUM RIMWAY	94720	630-A2
CAPE COD CT			**ALA**
	NANTUCKET WY	94501	670-A4
CAPELL ST			**OAK**
500	CLEVELAND ST	94610	650-A4
600	PROSPECT AV	94610	650-A4
650	MCKINLEY AV	94610	650-A4
700	MACARTHUR BLVD	94610	650-A4
CAPELLA LN			**ALA**
3400	TRELLIS LN	94502	670-A7
3420	JOST LN	94502	670-A7
3470	TOBAGO LN	94502	670-B7
3500	MELROSE AV	94502	670-B7
CAPERTON AV			**PDMT**
1	MOUNTAIN AV	94611	650-C1
30	RICHARDSON WY	94611	650-C1
40	SHERIDAN AV	94611	650-C1
50	SHERIDAN AV	94611	650-C1
50	SIERRA AV	94611	650-C1
50	SHERIDAN AV	94611	650-C1
200	HIGHLAND AV	94611	650-C1
CAPETOWN DR			**ALA**
100	COVE RD	94502	669-J5
200	CHANNING WY	94502	669-J5
260	CRANE CT	94502	669-J5
310	CLIPPER DR	94502	670-A5
200	BASIN SIDE WY	94502	670-A5
CAPISTRANO AV			**BERK**
1600	PERALTA AV	94707	609-F6
1640	MIRAMAR AV	94707	609-F6
1700	ENSENADA AV	94707	609-F5
1800	COLUSA AV	94707	609-F5
1850	LAUREL LN	94707	609-F5
1900	THE ALAMEDA	94707	609-F5
1900	THE ALAMEDA	94707	609-F5
2000	CONTRA COSTA AV	94707	609-F5
CAPISTRANO DR			**OAK**
400	ACALANES DR	94603	670-H7
450	EL PASEO DR	94603	670-H7
500	ALMANZA DR	94603	670-H7
700	TOPANGA DR	94603	670-H7
700	EL PASEO DR	94603	670-H7
CAPITAL ST			**OAK**
400	WESLEY AV	94606	649-J4
430	CLEVELAND ST	94610	649-J3
560	MERRITT AV	94610	649-J3
600	MERRITT AV	94610	649-J3
CAPP ST			**OAK**
2900	BROOKDALE AV	94602	650-D5
2960	NICOL AV	94602	650-D5
3040	SCHYLER ST	94602	650-D5
3100	SCHOOL ST	94602	650-D5
CAPRICORN AV			**OAK**
100	BROADWAY TER	94611	630-D6
500	FLORENCE TER	94611	630-D6
W CAPTAIN DODGE PL			**ALA**
	LEXINGTON ST	94501	649-C6
	SARATOGA ST	94501	649-C6
CAPTAIN DR			**EMVL**
1	POWELL ST	94608	629-D6
10	ENSIGN DR	94608	629-C6
CAPTAINS CV			**OAK**
1	CLIPPER HILL	94705	630-C4
50	SCHOONER HILL	94705	630-C4
CAPTAINS DR			**ALA**
1	BASIN SIDE WY	94502	669-J5
100	CHILMARK LN	94502	669-J5
CAPWELL DR			**OAK**
7800	LEET DR	94621	670-E6
7800	PENDLETON WY	94621	670-E6
8400	ROLAND WY	94621	670-E6
CARBERRY AV			**OAK**
5600	56TH ST	94609	629-H6
5650	AILEEN ST	94609	629-H5
5700	57TH ST	94609	629-H5
5800	58TH ST	94609	629-H5
CARDIGAN BAY			**ALA**
100	BAYWALK RD	94502	669-J6
CARISBROOK DR			**OAK**
2700	SKYLINE BLVD	94611	650-G1
	DARNBY DR	94611	650-G1
	CARISBROOK LN	94611	650-G1
	EXETER DR	94611	650-G1
	CHELTON DR	94611	650-F1
	CHELTON DR	94611	650-F1
CARISBROOK LN			**OAK**
	CARISBROOK DR	94611	650-G1
CARL VINSON			**ALA**
4000	MOSLEY AV	94501	649-E6
CARLETON ST			**BERK**
900	7TH ST	94804	629-E3
950	8TH ST	94804	629-E3
1000	9TH ST	94804	629-E3
1050	10TH ST	94804	629-E3
1100	SAN PABLO AV	94804	629-E3
1100	SAN PABLO AV	94702	629-E3
1200	MATHEWS ST	94702	629-E3
1300	MABEL ST	94702	629-F3
1400	ACTON ST	94702	629-F3
1500	SACRAMENTO ST	94703	629-F3
1600	CALIFORNIA ST	94703	629-F3
1700	MCGEE AV	94703	629-G3
1800	GRANT ST	94703	629-G3
1900	MARTIN LUTHER KING JR WY	94704	629-G3
2000	MILVIA ST	94704	629-G3
2100	SHATTUCK AV	94704	629-H3
2210	FULTON ST	94704	629-H3
2310	ELLSWORTH ST	94704	629-H3
2410	DANA ST	94704	629-H3
2470	TELEGRAPH AV	94704	629-H3
CARLOTTA AV			**BERK**
1200	POSEN AV	94707	609-F7
1300	HOPKINS ST	94703	609-F7
1400	ROSE ST	94703	609-F7
CARLSEN ST			**OAK**
2800	WILSHIRE BLVD	94602	650-F4
3000	MAPLE AV	94602	650-F4
3000	MAPLE AV	94602	650-F4
3200	WISCONSIN ST	94602	650-F4
3200	LAUREL AV	94602	650-F4
CARLSTON AV			**OAK**
600	LONGRIDGE RD	94610	650-B3
600	LONGRIDGE RD	94610	650-B3
630	PARAMOUNT RD	94610	650-B3
800	MANDANA BLVD	94610	650-B3
860	SANTA RAY AV	94610	650-B3
910	CALMAR AV	94610	650-B2
1000	WALAVISTA AV	94610	650-B2
1000	BALFOUR AV	94610	650-B2
CARLTON ST			**OAK**
5400	BROADWAY TER	94618	630-A6
5500	BELGRAVE PL	94618	630-A6
5600	MONROE AV	94618	630-A6
CARMEL AV			**ALB**
500	THOUSAND OAKS BLVD	94706	609-E5
660	PORTLAND AV	94706	609-E5
770	WASHINGTON AV	94706	609-E6
900	SOLANO AV	94706	609-E6
900	SOLANO AV	94706	609-E6
1000	MARIN AV	94706	609-E6
CARMEL AV			**PDMT**
200	BLAIR AV	94611	650-B1
300	OAKLAND AV	94611	650-B1
CARMEL ST			**OAK**
2400	LINCOLN AV	94602	650-E4
2600	LAGUNA AV	94602	650-E4
2700	RHODA AV	94602	650-E4
2800	COOLIDGE AV	94602	650-E4
3000	MAPLE AV	94602	650-E4
CAROB LN			**ALA**
100	IRONWOOD RD	94502	670-A6
CAROLINE ST			**ALA**
1300	SAN ANTONIO AV	94501	669-G1
1350	FAIR OAKS AV	94501	669-G1
1400	CENTRAL AV	94501	669-G1
1450	TAYLOR AV	94501	669-G1
1500	SANTA CLARA AV	94501	669-G1
CARRINGTON ST			**OAK**
3700	RANSOM AV	94601	650-D7
3730	38TH AV	94601	650-D7
3760	39TH AV	94601	650-D7
3840	40TH AV	94601	650-D7
3930	ROSEDALE AV	94601	650-D7
4020	41ST AV	94601	650-D7
4080	41ST AV	94601	650-D7
4200	41ST AV	94601	650-D7
4200	42ND AV	94601	670-D1
4300	HIGH ST	94601	670-D1
CARRINGTON WY			**OAK**
3600	HARRINGTON AV	94601	650-D7
4000	RANSOM AV	94601	650-D7
CARRISON ST			**BERK**
1100	SAN PABLO AV	94702	629-F4
1300	MABEL ST	94702	629-F4
1400	ACTON ST	94702	629-F4
CARROLL ST			**OAK**
2200	E 22ND ST	94606	650-A4
2300	IVY DR	94606	650-A4
CARSON ST			**OAK**
4000	TOMPKINS AV	94619	650-G6
4060	FAIR AV	94619	650-G6
4070	FAIR AV	94619	650-G6
4140	HARBOR VIEW AV	94619	650-G6
4190	ADELAIDE ST	94619	650-G6
4220	DAVENPORT AV	94619	650-G6
	REINHARDT DR	94619	650-G6
4300	SHEPHERD ST	94619	650-G6
4480	ELINORA AV	94619	650-H5
4490	ALISO AV	94619	650-H5
	MOUNTAIN BLVD	94619	650-H5
CARTER ST			**OAK**
1700	LEIMERT BLVD	94602	650-E2
1800	BYWOOD DR	94602	650-E2
1850	OAKCREST DR	94602	650-E2
1900	ROSECREST DR	94602	650-E2
CARY AV			**OAK**
600	DOUGLAS AV	94603	670-G7
630	HALE AV	94603	670-H7
700	EDES AV	94603	670-H7
CARY CT			**OAK**
1	98TH AV	94603	670-G6
CASLAND DR			**OAK**
6200	62ND AV	94605	670-F2
6200	62ND AV	94621	670-F2
CASTELLO ST			**OAK**
2500	FRUITVALE AV	94602	650-D5
2600	CORDOVA ST	94602	650-D5
CASTERLINE RD			**OAK**
1700	OAKMORE RD	94602	650-D3
1900	WATERHOUSE RD	94602	650-D3
CASTLE CT			**OAK**
100	CASTLE DR	94611	650-G2
CASTLE DR			**OAK**
5600	MOUNTAINGATE WY	94611	650-F2
5610	MASTLANDS DR	94611	650-F2
5710	CASTLE PARK WY	94611	650-F2
5800	CASTLE PARK WY	94611	650-F2
5920	CASTLE CT	94611	650-F2
6200	CASTLE LN	94611	650-G2
6200	CORNWALL CT	94611	650-G2
6250	WEYBRIDGE CT	94611	650-G2
6300	OSBORNE CT	94611	650-G2
6500	HOLYROOD DR	94611	650-G2
6600	MELVILLE DR	94611	650-G2
CASTLE LN			**OAK**
1	CASTLE DR	94611	650-G2
CASTLE PARK WY			**OAK**
1	CASTLE DR	94611	650-F2
100	CASTLE DR	94611	650-F2
CASTLEBAR PL			**ALA**
1	KARA RD	94502	669-J5
1	SEA VIEW PKWY	94502	669-J5
CASTLEWOOD ST			**OAK**
8900	ALCALA AV	94605	671-B4
9130	OAK KNOLL BLVD	94605	671-B3
9630	SARAZEN AV	94605	671-A3
9630	FLINTRIDGE LN	94605	671-A3
9700	GOLF LINKS RD	94605	671-A3
CASTRO ST			**ALB**
900	JACKSON ST	94706	609-D5
960	MADISON ST	94706	609-D5
1030	ADAMS ST	94706	609-D5
1100	SAN PABLO AV	94706	609-D5
CASTRO ST			**OAK**
200	2ND ST	94607	649-F4
300	3RD ST	94607	649-F4
400	4TH ST	94607	649-F4
	5TH ST	94607	649-F4
600	6TH ST	94607	649-F4
	7TH ST	94607	649-F4
700	8TH ST	94607	649-F4
800	8TH ST	94607	649-F4
870	9TH ST	94607	649-F4
970	10TH ST	94607	649-F4
1070	11TH ST	94607	649-F4
1170	12TH ST	94607	649-F3
1370	14TH ST	94612	649-F3
1460	15TH ST	94612	649-F3
1550	16TH ST	94612	649-F3
1640	17TH ST	94612	649-F3
1740	18TH ST	94612	649-F3
1830	19TH ST	94612	649-G3
1920	20TH ST	94612	649-G3
2100	MARTIN LUTHER KING JR WY	94612	649-G3
2100	SAN PABLO AV	94612	649-G3
CASWELL AV			**OAK**
300	CLARA ST	94603	670-G7
400	DENSLOWE AV	94603	670-G7
500	MADDUX DR	94603	670-G7
CATALINA AV			**ALA**
3000	FONTANA DR	94502	669-J6
3030	VIA ALAMOSA	94502	669-J6
3100	VERDEMAR DR	94502	669-J7
3190	FIR PL	94502	670-A7
3270	FIJI LN	94502	670-A7
3300	ISLAND DR	94502	670-A7
3400	HOLLY ST	94502	670-A7
3460	LEEWARD LN	94502	670-A7
3480	OLD ALAMEDA PT	94502	670-A7
CATALINA AV			**BERK**
1800	COLUSA AV	94707	609-F6
1850	STATION PL	94707	609-F5
1900	THE ALAMEDA	94707	609-F5
CATHERINE DR			**BERK**
1400	KEONCREST DR	94702	629-F1

PRIMARY STREET Address	Cross Street	ZIP	CITY Pg-Grid
CATHERINE DR			**BERK**
1500	KEONCREST DR	94702	629-F1
CATHY LN			**OAK**
1	SKYLINE BLVD	94619	651-C7
CATRON DR			**OAK**
290	BERGEDO DR	94603	690-H1
500	REPOSO DR	94603	690-H1
140	ESTEPA DR	94603	690-H1
600	NOVELDA DR	94603	670-H7
630	ACALANES DR	94603	670-H7
700	ROBLEDO DR	94603	670-H7
CAVANAUGH CT			**PDMT**
1	TRESTLE GLEN RD	94610	650-D3
CAVENDISH LN			**OAK**
1	PARK BLVD	94602	650-D3
CAVOUR ST			**OAK**
300	MANILA AV	94618	629-J6
370	JAMES AV	94618	629-J6
400	LAWTON AV	94618	629-J6
420	BOYD AV	94618	629-J6
450	SHAFTER AV	94618	629-H6
460	LOCKSLEY AV	94618	629-H6
470	MILES AV	94618	629-H6
480	REDONDO AV	94618	629-H6
500	CLAREMONT AV	94618	629-H6
CEDAR ST			**ALA**
900	CLINTON AV	94501	669-J3
CEDAR ST			**BERK**
600	EASTSHORE BLVD	94804	629-C1
650	2ND ST	94804	629-D1
710	3RD ST	94804	629-D1
750	4TH ST	94804	629-D1
800	5TH ST	94804	629-D1
850	6TH ST	94804	629-D1
900	7TH ST	94804	629-D1
950	8TH ST	94804	629-D1
1000	9TH ST	94804	629-D1
1050	10TH ST	94804	629-E1
	HOPKINS ST	94702	629-E1
	SAN PABLO AV	94702	629-E1
1130	KAINS AV	94702	629-E1
1160	STANNAGE AV	94702	629-E1
1200	CORNELL AV	94702	629-E1
1230	CURTIS ST	94702	629-E1
1260	BELVEDERE AV	94702	629-E1
1300	CHESTNUT ST	94702	629-E1
1350	JUANITA WY	94702	629-E1
1370	FRANKLIN ST	94702	629-F1
1400	ACTON ST	94702	629-F1
1500	SACRAMENTO ST	94703	629-F1
1550	HOLLY ST	94703	629-F1
1600	CALIFORNIA ST	94703	629-F1
1640	COMSTOCK CT	94703	629-F1
1700	MCGEE AV	94703	629-F1
1750	EDITH ST	94703	629-G1
1800	GRANT ST	94703	629-G1
1850	JOSEPHINE ST	94703	629-G1
1900	MARTIN LUTHER KING JR WY	94709	629-G1
1950	BONITA AV	94709	629-G1
2030	MILVIA ST	94709	629-G1
2000	HENRY ST	94709	609-G7
2100	SHATTUCK AV	94709	609-G7
2150	WALNUT ST	94709	609-H7
2200	OXFORD ST	94709	609-H7
2250	SPRUCE ST	94709	609-H7
2300	ARCH ST	94708	609-H7
2300	ARCH ST	94709	609-H7
2320	ARCH ST	94708	609-H7
2320	ARCH ST	94709	609-H7
2400	SCENIC AV	94708	609-H7
2400	SCENIC AV	94709	609-H7
2420	SCENIC AV	94708	609-H7
2420	SCENIC AV	94709	609-H7
2450	HAWTHORNE TER	94708	609-H7
2450	HAWTHORNE TER	94709	609-H7
2500	EUCLID AV	94708	609-H7
2500	EUCLID AV	94709	609-H7
2600	LE ROY AV	94708	609-J7
2600	LE ROY AV	94709	609-J7
2700	LA LOMA AV	94708	609-J7
2700	LA LOMA AV	94709	609-J7
2800	LA VEREDA	94708	609-J7
2800	LA VEREDA	94709	609-J7
CEDAR ST			**OAK**
	9TH ST	94607	649-C3
	10TH ST	94607	649-C3
CEDARWOOD LN			**BERK**
1200	HARRISON ST	94710	609-C7
CENTENNIAL AV			**ALA**
900	9TH ST	94501	669-G1
CENTENNIAL DR			**BERK**
	STADIUM RIMWAY	94720	630-A1
CENTENNIAL DR			**OAK**
	GOLF COURSE DR	94708	610-A7
	GRIZZLY PEAK BLVD	94708	610-A7
	CYCLOTRON RD	94720	630-B1
CENTER ST			**BERK**
1900	MARTIN LUTHER KING JR WY	94704	629-G2
2000	MILVIA ST	94704	629-G2
2100	SHATTUCK AV	94704	629-G2
2110	SHATTUCK SQ	94704	629-H2
2200	OXFORD ST	94704	629-H2
CENTER ST			**OAK**
300	3RD ST	94607	649-D4
500	5TH ST	94607	649-D4
700	7TH ST	94607	649-D3
800	8TH ST	94607	649-D3
900	9TH ST	94607	649-D3
1000	10TH ST	94607	649-D3
1100	11TH ST	94607	649-D3
1180	12TH ST	94607	649-D3
1210	12TH ST	94607	649-D3
1270	13TH ST	94607	649-E3
1300	13TH ST	94607	649-E3
1400	14TH ST	94607	649-E3
1500	15TH ST	94607	649-E3
1600	16TH ST	94607	649-E2
	17TH ST	94607	649-E2
1800	17TH ST	94607	649-E2
1900	PERALTA ST	94607	649-E2
CENTRAL AV			**ALA**
	ENCINAL AV	94501	669-H1
	SHERMAN ST	94501	669-H1
160	MAIN ST	94501	649-E7
160	PACIFIC AV	94501	649-E7
200	W ORISKANY AV	94501	669-E1
230	LINCOLN AV	94501	669-E1
	TAYLOR AV	94501	669-E1
300	3RD ST	94501	669-E1
400	4TH ST	94501	669-E1
500	5TH ST	94501	669-F1
520	HOOVER CT	94501	669-F1
550	CROWN DR	94501	669-F1
600	6TH ST	94501	669-F1
650	MCKAY AV	94501	669-F1
700	CROLLS GARDEN CT	94501	669-F1
700	WEBSTER ST	94501	669-F1
720	GARDEN WY	94501	669-F1
750	PAGE ST	94501	669-F1
800	8TH ST	94501	669-G1
850	BURBANK ST	94501	669-G1
900	9TH ST	94501	669-G1
970	WEBER ST	94501	669-G1
1000	CAROLINE ST	94501	669-G1
1100	SAINT CHARLES ST	94501	669-G1
1200	BAY ST	94501	669-H1
1300	SHERMAN ST	94501	669-H1
1400	MORTON ST	94501	669-H1
1500	ALAMEDA AV	94501	669-H1
1500	BENTON ST	94501	669-H1
1550	COTTAGE ST	94501	669-H1
1600	PARU ST	94501	669-H1
1700	GRAND ST	94501	669-H1
1800	UNION ST	94501	669-J2
1900	LAFAYETTE ST	94501	669-J2
2000	CHESTNUT ST	94501	669-J2
2100	WILLOW ST	94501	669-J2
2200	WALNUT ST	94501	669-J2
2300	OAK ST	94501	670-A2
2400	PARK ST	94501	670-A2
2450	PARK AV	94501	670-A2
2460	PARK AV	94501	670-A2
2500	EVERETT ST	94501	670-A2
2520	REGENT ST	94501	670-A2
2600	BROADWAY	94501	670-A3
2700	PEARL ST	94501	670-A3
2800	GIBBONS DR	94501	670-B3
2800	VERSAILLES AV	94501	670-B3
2850	GROVE ST	94501	670-B3
2900	MOUND ST	94501	670-B3
3000	COURT ST	94501	670-B3
3100	FOUNTAIN ST	94501	670-B3
3200	HIGH ST	94501	670-B3
3300	FERNSIDE BLVD	94501	670-B3
3330	HANSEN AV	94501	670-B4
3360	EAST SHORE DR	94501	670-C4
CENTRE CT			**ALA**
100	PACKET LNDG	94502	670-A5
CERRITO AV			**OAK**
3950	40TH WY	94611	649-J1
3800	40TH ST	94611	649-J1
3950	38TH ST	94611	649-J1
CERRITO ST			**ALB**
700	HILLSIDE AV	94706	609-D5
770	WASHINGTON AV	94706	609-D6
880	SOLANO AV	94706	609-D6
1000	BUCHANAN ST	94706	609-D6
CERRO VISTA			**ALA**
3000	FONTANA DR	94502	669-J6
3020	VIA ALISO	94502	669-J6
3100	VERDEMAR DR	94502	669-J6
CERRUTI CT			**ALA**
	BARTLETT DR	94501	649-G7
CESSNA ST			**OAK**
7600	CONVAIR ST	94621	670-D6
7690	STINSON ST	94621	670-D6
CHABOLYN TER			**OAK**
5900	CHABOT RD	94618	630-A4
6010	ROSLYN CT	94618	630-A4
6010	CHABOT CREST	94618	630-A4
CHABOT CREST			**BERK**
5980	MANOR CREST	94618	630-A4
6100	ROSLYN CT	94618	630-A4
6100	CHABOLYN TER	94618	630-A4
CHABOT CREST			**OAK**
5900	CHABOT RD	94618	630-A4
5980	MANOR CREST	94618	630-A4
CHABOT CT			**OAK**
5800	CHABOT RD	94618	630-A5
CHABOT RD			**OAK**
5700	CLAREMONT AV	94618	629-J5
5920	COLLEGE AV	94618	629-J5
6200	PRESLEY WY	94618	630-A5
6290	IVANHOE RD	94618	630-A5
6300	IVANHOE RD	94618	630-A5
6370	ROSS ST	94618	630-A5
6400	ROSS ST	94618	630-A5
6500	CLOVER DR	94618	630-A4
6540	CHABOT CT	94618	630-A4
6580	CHABOLYN TER	94618	630-A4
6600	PATTON ST	94618	630-A4
6630	CHABOT CREST	94618	630-A4
6700	ROANOKE RD	94618	630-A4
6800	REATA PL	94618	630-A4
6900	GOLDEN GATE WY	94618	630-A4
6900	GOLDEN GATE AV	94618	630-A4
6900	GOLDEN GATE AV	94618	630-B4
7200	ROBLE RD	94618	630-B5
7220	MARIE WY	94618	630-B5
CHADBOURNE WY			**OAK**
1	CRESTMONT DR	94619	650-H4
200	KIMBERLIN HEIGHTS DR	94619	650-H4
400	RISHELL DR	94619	650-H4
CHALLEN CT			**ALA**
	ROSEFIELD LP	94501	649-F7
CHALLENGER DR			**ALA**
2000	MARINA VILLAGE PKWY	94501	649-G7
2100	ATLANTIC AV	94501	649-G7
CHAMBERLIN CT			**OAK**
4300	VIEWCREST DR	94619	650-J7
CHAMBERS DR			**OAK**
6960	RIDGEWOOD DR	94611	630-F6
6800	RIDGEWOOD WY	94611	630-F7
6960	COLTON BLVD	94611	630-F7
CHAMBERS LN			**OAK**
50	COLTON BLVD	94611	630-F6
50	HEMLOCK LN	94611	630-F6
100	RIDGEWOOD WY	94611	630-F6
CHAMPION ST			**OAK**
3000	NICOL AV	94602	650-D5
3170	SCHOOL ST	94602	650-D5
3310	PLEASANT ST	94602	650-D5
3350	HAROLD ST	94602	650-D5
3390	MONTANA ST	94602	650-D5
3430	LINCOLN AV	94602	650-D4
3500	MACARTHUR BLVD	94602	650-D4
CHANCELLOR LN			**OAK**
	CHANCELLOR PL	94705	630-C3
	CHANCELLOR PL	94705	630-C3
CHANCELLOR PL			**OAK**
1	STRATHMOOR DR	94705	630-C3
1	DRURY CT	94705	630-C3
1	DRURY RD	94705	630-C3
20	CHANCELLOR LN	94705	630-C3
60	CHANCELLOR LN	94705	630-C3
CHANNING WY			**ALA**
200	SHEFFIELD RD	94502	669-J5
300	ROBERT DAVEY JR DR	94502	669-J5
320	CAPETOWN DR	94502	669-J5
400	SANDPIPER PL	94502	669-J5
450	COVE RD	94502	669-J5
CHANNING WY			**BERK**
750	4TH ST	94804	629-D3
800	5TH ST	94804	629-D3
850	6TH ST	94804	629-D3
900	7TH ST	94804	629-E3
950	8TH ST	94804	629-E3
1000	9TH ST	94804	629-E3
1050	10TH ST	94804	629-E3
1100	SAN PABLO AV	94702	629-E3
1150	BYRON ST	94702	629-E3
1200	CURTIS ST	94702	629-E3
1250	BROWNING ST	94702	629-E3
1300	BONAR ST	94702	629-F2
1340	WEST ST	94702	629-F2
1370	VALLEY ST	94702	629-F2
1400	ACTON ST	94702	629-F2
1450	EDWARDS ST	94702	629-F2
1500	SACRAMENTO ST	94703	629-F2
1550	SPAULDING AV	94703	629-F2
1600	CALIFORNIA ST	94703	629-F2
1650	JEFFERSON AV	94703	629-F2
1700	MCGEE AV	94703	629-G2
1750	ROOSEVELT AV	94703	629-G2
1750	ROOSEVELT AV	94703	629-G2
1800	GRANT ST	94703	629-G2
1850	MCKINLEY AV	94703	629-G2
1900	MARTIN LUTHER KING JR WY	94704	629-G2
2010	MILVIA ST	94704	629-G2
2100	SHATTUCK AV	94704	629-H2
2200	FULTON ST	94704	629-H2
2300	ELLSWORTH ST	94704	629-H2
2400	DANA ST	94704	629-H2
2500	TELEGRAPH AV	94704	629-J2
2600	BOWDITCH ST	94704	629-J2
2700	COLLEGE AV	94704	629-J2
2800	PIEDMONT AV	94704	629-J2
2900	WARRING ST	94704	629-J2
2920	WARRING ST	94704	629-J2
3000	PROSPECT ST	94704	629-J2
CHAPIN ST			**ALA**
1600	LINCOLN AV	94501	669-G1
1700	PACIFIC AV	94501	669-G1
1800	BUENA VISTA AV	94501	649-G7
1910	EAGLE AV	94501	649-G7
CHAPMAN ST			**OAK**
2800	23RD AV	94601	670-B1
2900	PETERSON ST	94601	670-B1
3000	DERBY AV	94601	670-B1
3130	LANCASTER ST	94601	670-B1
3200	FRUITVALE AV	94601	670-B1
CHAPPELL PL			**OAK**
5600	SKYLINE BLVD	94619	651-A5
CHARING CROSS RD			**OAK**
6600	HILLER DR	94618	630-C4
6690	SCHOONER HILL	94705	630-C4
6840	SHERWICK DR	94705	630-C4
7000	TUNNEL RD	94705	630-C4
CHARIOT LN			**OAK**
5200	HANSOM DR	94605	671-C1
5300	SURREY LN	94605	671-C1
CHARLESTON ST			**OAK**
2500	CAMILLIA PL	94602	650-E3
2500	PERKINS RD	94602	650-E3
2600	LAGUNA AV	94602	650-E4
2700	COOLIDGE AV	94602	650-E4
CHASE ST			**OAK**
1700	WILLOW ST	94607	649-D3
1750	WOOD ST	94607	649-D3
1780	MCELROY ST	94607	649-C3
1800	PINE ST	94607	649-C3
CHATHAM POINTE			**ALA**
1	SEA BRIDGE WY	94502	670-A5
CHATHAM RD			**OAK**
1100	PARK BLVD	94610	650-B4
1160	KINGSLEY ST	94610	650-B4
1230	EMERSON ST	94610	650-B4
1300	13TH AV	94602	650-B4
1320	E 36TH ST	94602	650-B4
1380	BRUCE ST	94602	650-B4
1400	BEAUMONT AV	94602	650-B4
1400	MACARTHUR BLVD	94602	650-B4
CHATSWORTH CT			**OAK**
1	BEACONSFIELD PL	94611	650-F1
1	CHELTON DR	94611	650-F1
CHAUCER ST			**BERK**
1100	SAN PABLO AV	94702	629-E2
1200	CURTIS ST	94702	629-E2
CHAUMONT PTH			**OAK**
	GOLDEN GATE AV	94618	630-B5
	BUENA VISTA AV	94618	630-B5
	CONTRA COSTA RD	94618	630-B5
CHELSEA CT			**OAK**
	CHELSEA DR	94611	650-F1
CHELSEA DR			**OAK**
2400	STOCKBRIDGE DR	94611	650-F1
2430	THACKERAY DR	94611	650-F1
2490	CHELSEA CT	94611	650-F1
2600	CHELTON DR	94611	650-F1
2600	KIMBERLEY CT	94611	650-G1
2670	CLIVE AV	94611	650-G1
2740	LONGCROFT DR	94611	650-G1
2900	ASCOT DR	94611	650-G1
CHELTON DR			**OAK**
5600	ASCOT DR	94611	650-F2
5700	SCARBOROUGH DR	94611	650-F1
5740	KESWICK CT	94611	650-F1
5750	CHELTON LN	94611	650-F1
5810	BAGSHOTTE DR	94611	650-F1
5900	BEACONSFIELD PL	94611	650-F1
5900	CHATSWORTH CT	94611	650-F1
5950	GIRVIN DR	94611	650-F1
6100	HAVERHILL DR	94611	650-F1
6200	CHELSEA DR	94611	650-F1
6300	DARNBY DR	94611	650-F1
6400	STOCKBRIDGE DR	94611	650-F1
6500	CARISBROOK DR	94611	650-F1
6500	EXETER DR	94611	630-G7
6500	ELDERBERRY DR	94611	650-G1
6800	CARISBROOK DR	94611	650-G1
CHELTON LN			**OAK**
1	BAGSHOTTE DR	94611	650-F1
100	CHELTON DR	94611	650-F1
CHENEY AV			**OAK**
400	WALKER AV	94610	650-A3
500	RAND AV	94610	650-A3
CHEROKEE AV			**OAK**
2500	THERMAL ST	94605	671-A4
2550	LAWLOR ST	94605	671-A4
2600	BURR ST	94605	671-A4
2700	98TH AV	94605	671-A4
CHERRY ST			**BERK**
2800	STUART ST	94705	629-J3
2900	RUSSELL ST	94705	629-J3
CHERRY ST			**OAK**
9000	90TH AV	94603	670-J4
9200	92ND AV	94603	670-J4
9400	94TH AV	94603	670-J5
9600	96TH AV	94603	670-J5
9800	98TH AV	94603	670-J5
9900	99TH AV	94603	670-J5
10000	100TH AV	94603	670-J5
CHESHIRE CT			**ALA**
1	SHERWOOD LN	94502	669-J5
CHESTER ST			**ALA**
2500	REGENT ST	94501	670-A3
2600	BROADWAY	94501	670-A3
CHESTER ST			**OAK**
300	3RD ST	94607	649-D4
500	5TH ST	94607	649-D4
700	7TH ST	94607	649-D3
800	8TH ST	94607	649-D3
900	9TH ST	94607	649-D3
1200	12TH ST	94607	649-D3
CHESTNUT ST			**ALA**
900	CLINTON AV	94501	669-H2
900	CLINTON AV	94501	669-H2
1000	SAN JOSE AV	94501	669-J2
1100	SAN ANTONIO AV	94501	669-J2
1200	ENCINAL AV	94501	669-J2
1300	ALAMEDA AV	94501	669-J2
1400	CENTRAL AV	94501	669-J2
1500	SANTA CLARA AV	94501	669-J1
1600	LINCOLN AV	94501	669-J1
1700	PACIFIC AV	94501	669-J1
1800	BUENA VISTA AV	94501	669-J1
1900	EAGLE AV	94501	669-J1
2000	CLEMENT AV	94501	669-J1
CHESTNUT ST			**BERK**
1500	ROSE ST	94702	629-E1
1600	CEDAR ST	94702	629-E1
1620	LINCOLN ST	94702	629-E1
1700	VIRGINIA ST	94702	629-E1
1720	FRANCISCO ST	94702	629-E1
1800	DELAWARE ST	94702	629-E1
1900	HEARST AV	94702	629-E1
1950	BERKELEY WY	94702	629-E2
2000	UNIVERSITY AV	94702	629-E2
CHESTNUT ST			**OAK**
270	3RD ST	94607	649-E4
1000	10TH ST	94607	649-E3
1200	12TH ST	94607	649-E3
1400	14TH ST	94607	649-E3
1600	16TH ST	94607	649-E3
1800	18TH ST	94607	649-F3
2100	21ST ST	94607	649-F2
2200	W GRAND AV	94607	649-F2
2400	24TH ST	94607	649-F2
2600	26TH ST	94607	649-F2
2800	28TH ST	94608	649-F1
3000	30TH ST	94608	649-F1
3200	32ND ST	94608	649-F1
3400	34TH ST	94608	649-F1
3600	35TH ST	94608	649-F1
CHESWICK CT			**ALA**
200	SHEFFIELD RD	94502	669-J5
CHETWOOD ST			**OAK**
400	MACARTHUR BLVD	94610	649-J2
400	ADAMS ST	94610	649-J2
500	SANTA CLARA AV	94610	649-J2
600	SANTA ROSA AV	94610	649-J2
CHICAGO			**ALA**
4000	CIMARRON ST	94501	649-E6
4000	KISKA	94501	649-E6
CHICO CT			**OAK**
1	SAYRE DR	94611	630-F7
CHILMARK LN			**ALA**
1	BASIN SIDE WY	94502	669-J5
100	CAPTAINS DR	94502	669-J5
CHILTON WY			**BERK**
2500	BLAKE ST	94704	629-H3
2600	PARKER ST	94704	629-H3
CHIMNEY ROCK			**OAK**
1	ELYSIAN FIELDS DR	94605	671-D2
CHINABERRY LN			**ALA**
100	IRONWOOD RD	94502	670-A6
CHRISTENSEN CT			**ALA**
1	DENKE DR	94502	669-J6
100	BORDWELL CT	94502	669-J6
CHRISTIE AV			**EMVL**
5700	SHELLMOUND ST	94608	629-D6
5800	POWELL ST	94608	629-D6
5850	SHELLMOUND ST	94608	629-D6
6000	59TH ST	94608	629-D5
6300	64TH ST	94608	629-D5
6500	65TH ST	94608	629-D5
CHUNGKING ST			**OAK**
	MARITIME ST	94607	649-C2
	CORREGIDOR AV	94607	649-C2
CHURCH ST			**OAK**
1600	FLORA ST	94605	670-G3
1600	FLORA ST	94621	670-G3
1900	AVENAL AV	94605	670-G2
2300	ARTHUR ST	94605	670-G2
2320	FRESNO ST	94605	670-H2
2350	KRAUSE AV	94605	670-H2
2370	HALLIDAY AV	94605	670-H2
	BANCROFT AV	94605	670-H2
2500	BANCROFT AV	94605	670-H2
2900	68TH AV	94605	670-H2
2900	FOOTHILL BLVD	94605	670-H2
CIMARRON ST			**ALA**
4000	MOSLEY AV	94501	649-E6
4020	ROANOKE	94501	649-E6
4020	SACRAMENTO	94501	649-E6
4040	CHICAGO	94501	649-E6
4040	KISKA	94501	649-E6
4060	NEVADA	94501	649-E6
4060	TRIPOLI	94501	649-E6
4080	DRUM	94501	649-E6
4080	KIRK	94501	649-E6
4100	SEA HORSE	94501	649-E6
4100	MOUNT HOOD	94501	649-E6
CIRCLE HILL DR			**OAK**
7450	GREENLY DR	94605	670-J1
7500	COLUMBIAN DR	94605	671-A1
7600	FIELD ST	94605	671-A1
CLAIREPOINTE WY			**OAK**
13150	SADDLE BROOK DR	94619	651-B6
13300	KNOLL RIDGE WY	94619	651-C6
CLARA CT			**OAK**
1	CLARA ST	94603	670-G6
CLARA ST			**OAK**
300	NORGREN ST	94603	670-G7
300	JONES AV	94603	670-G7
320	CASWELL AV	94603	670-G7
360	BURLWOOD AV	94603	670-G7
400	ASHTON AV	94603	670-G6
520	ROSSMOOR CT	94603	670-G6
560	CLARA CT	94603	670-G6
600	EDES AV	94603	670-G6
600	EDES AV	94621	670-G6
600	EDES AV	94603	670-G6
690	OSCAR AV	94603	670-G6
740	WALTER AV	94603	670-G6
800	RAILROAD AV	94603	670-G6
CLAREMONT AV			**BERK**
2800	TANGLEWOOD RD	94705	630-A3
2870	AVALON AV	94705	630-A3
2930	RUSSELL ST	94705	630-A3
4610	CLAREMONT BLVD	94705	630-A3
3000	ASHBY AV	94705	630-A3
3020	CLAREMONT CREST	94705	630-A3
3040	HAZEL RD	94705	630-A4
3050	WEBSTER ST	94705	630-A4
3070	PRINCE ST	94705	630-A4
3100	THE UPLANDS	94705	630-A4
4000	WOOLSEY ST	94705	629-J4
3100	HILLCREST RD	94705	629-J4
3110	BROOKSIDE DR	94705	629-J4

PRIMARY STREET Address	Cross Street	ZIP	CITY Pg-Grid
CLAREMONT AV			**BERK**
3200	BROOKSIDE DR	94705	629-J4
3210	BROOKSIDE AV	94705	629-J4
3260	ETON CT	94705	629-J4
3260	ETON AV	94705	629-J4
3300	ALCATRAZ AV	94705	629-J4
CLAREMONT AV			**OAK**
6460	GRIZZLY PEAK BLVD	94705	630-C2
6400	GELSTON ST	94705	630-B2
1300	ALVARADO RD	94705	630-B2
1400	RISPIN DR	94705	630-A3
2730	STONEWALL RD	94705	630-A3
2800	TANGLEWOOD RD	94705	630-A3
2870	AVALON AV	94705	630-A3
5100	52ND ST	94609	629-H6
5100	TELEGRAPH AV	94609	629-H6
5200	CLARKE ST	94609	629-H6
5200	CLARKE ST	94618	629-H6
5280	VICENTE WY	94609	629-H6
5280	VICENTE WY	94618	629-H6
5300	CAVOUR ST	94609	629-H6
5300	CAVOUR ST	94618	629-H6
5360	VICENTE WY	94609	629-H6
5360	VICENTE WY	94618	629-H6
5400	CLIFTON ST	94618	629-H6
5520	HUDSON ST	94618	629-J5
	FOREST ST	94618	629-J5
5700	COLBY ST	94618	629-J5
5900	CHABOT RD	94618	629-J5
5990	60TH ST	94618	629-J5
6000	HILLEGASS AV	94618	629-J5
6200	62ND ST	94618	629-J4
6200	COLLEGE AV	94618	629-J4
	MYSTIC ST	94618	629-J4
3300	AUBURN AV	94618	629-J4
3400	ALCATRAZ AV	94618	629-J4
CLAREMONT BLVD			**BERK**
2700	DERBY ST	94705	630-A3
2710	FOREST AV	94705	630-A3
2800	BELROSE AV	94705	630-A3
2800	GARBER ST	94705	630-A3
2880	AVALON AV	94705	630-A3
2940	RUSSELL ST	94705	630-A3
3000	CLAREMONT AV	94705	630-A3
CLAREMONT CREST			**BERK**
1	ASHBY AV	94705	630-A3
100	CLAREMONT AV	94705	630-A3
CLARENDON CRES			**OAK**
900	MANDANA BLVD	94610	650-C3
900	PORTAL AV	94610	650-C3
1100	LONGRIDGE RD	94610	650-C3
1200	ASHMOUNT AV	94610	650-C3
CLAREWOOD DR			**OAK**
4300	BROADWAY TER	94618	630-B6
4300	BROADWAY TER	94611	630-B6
4700	CLAREWOOD LN	94618	630-B6
4700	CLAREWOOD LN	94611	630-B6
5100	TRUITT LN	94618	630-C7
5100	TRUITT LN	94611	630-C7
5200	HARBORD DR	94618	630-C6
CLAREWOOD LN			**OAK**
50	CLAREWOOD DR	94618	630-B6
CLARKE LN			**ALA**
1100	MCSHERRY WY	94502	670-A7
1160	DEPASSIER WY	94502	670-A7
1300	SILVA LN	94502	670-A7
CLARKE ST			**OAK**
3800	38TH ST	94609	649-H1
4000	40TH ST	94609	629-H7
4800	48TH ST	94609	629-H6
4900	49TH ST	94609	629-H6
5000	50TH ST	94609	629-H6
5100	51ST ST	94609	629-H6
5100	51ST ST	94618	629-H6
5150	REDONDO AV	94609	629-H6
5150	REDONDO AV	94618	629-H6
5200	CLAREMONT AV	94609	629-H6
5200	CLAREMONT AV	94618	629-H6
CLAY ST			**ALA**
2500	REGENT ST	94501	670-A3
2700	PEARL ST	94501	670-A4
2800	VERSAILLES AV	94501	670-A4
2900	MOUND ST	94501	670-A4
CLAY ST			**ALB**
1000	MADISON ST	94706	609-D5
1050	ADAMS ST	94706	609-D5
1100	SAN PABLO AV	94706	609-D5
CLAY ST			**OAK**
1	WATER ST	94607	649-F5
100	EMBARCADERO W	94607	649-F5
200	2ND ST	94607	649-F5
300	3RD ST	94607	649-F5
400	4TH ST	94607	649-F5
700	7TH ST	94607	649-F4
800	8TH ST	94607	649-F4
900	9TH ST	94607	649-F4
1000	10TH ST	94607	649-F4
1100	11TH ST	94607	649-F4
1200	12TH ST	94607	649-G4
1400	14TH ST	94612	649-G3
1500	FRANK H OGAWA PZ	94612	649-G3
1600	16TH ST	94612	649-G3
1700	17TH ST	94612	649-G3
1800	SAN PABLO AV	94612	649-G3
CLEMENS RD			**OAK**
1700	LEIMERT BLVD	94602	650-D3
1780	OAKMORE RD	94602	650-D3
1840	LEIMERT PL	94602	650-D3
1880	WATERHOUSE RD	94602	650-E3
1930	LYMAN RD	94602	650-E3
2100	FRUITVALE AV	94602	650-E3
CLEMENT AV			**ALA**
1700	GRAND ST	94501	669-J1
1730	ALAMEDA MARINA DR	94501	669-J1
1750	MINTURN ST	94501	669-J1
1800	UNION ST	94501	669-J1
1850	SCHILLER ST	94501	669-J1
1900	LAFAYETTE ST	94501	669-J1
2000	CHESTNUT ST	94501	669-J1
2050	STANFORD ST	94501	669-J1
2100	WILLOW ST	94501	670-A1
2150	MULBERRY ST	94501	670-A1
2200	WALNUT ST	94501	670-A1
2220	ELM ST	94501	670-A1
2300	OAK ST	94501	670-A1
2400	PARK ST	94501	670-A2
2500	EVERETT ST	94501	670-B2
2600	BROADWAY	94501	670-B2
CLEVELAND AV			**ALB**
800	WASHINGTON AV	94706	609-C6
900	SOLANO AV	94706	609-C6
950	JOHNSON ST	94706	609-C6
980	BUCHANAN ST	94706	609-C6
CLEVELAND CT			**ALA**
	BARTLETT DR	94501	649-G7
CLEVELAND ST			**OAK**
600	CAPITAL ST	94606	649-J4
600	WESLEY AV	94606	649-J4
640	RADNOR RD	94606	650-A4
640	RADNOR RD	94606	650-A4
660	HADDON RD	94606	650-A4
680	KENWYN RD	94606	650-A4
700	ATHOL AV	94606	650-A4
800	MONTCLAIR AV	94606	650-A4
820	ZORAH ST	94606	650-A4
850	SPRUCE ST	94606	650-A4
870	CAPELL ST	94606	650-A4
900	PARK BLVD	94606	650-A4
CLIFFLAND AV			**OAK**
10900	KERRIGAN DR	94605	671-D5
10900	OVERMOOR ST	94605	671-D5
11100	DINGLEY ST	94605	671-D5
CLIFTON ST			**OAK**
300	BROADWAY	94618	629-J6
300	COLLEGE AV	94618	629-J6
320	DESMOND ST	94618	629-J6
350	MANILA AV	94618	629-J6
370	JAMES AV	94618	629-J6
400	LAWTON AV	94618	629-J6
430	BOYD AV	94618	629-J6
450	SHAFTER AV	94618	629-J6
460	LOCKSLEY AV	94618	629-J6
470	MILES AV	94618	629-H6
500	CLAREMONT AV	94618	629-H6
CLINTON AV			**ALA**
1300	SHERMAN ST	94501	669-H2
1600	PARU ST	94501	669-H2
1700	GRAND ST	94501	669-H2
1800	UNION ST	94501	669-H2
1900	LAFAYETTE ST	94501	669-H2
	CHESTNUT ST	94501	669-H2
2000	CHESTNUT ST	94501	669-J2
2100	WILLOW ST	94501	669-J3
2200	WALNUT ST	94501	669-J3
2220	CEDAR ST	94501	669-J3
2260	LAUREL ST	94501	669-J3
2300	OAK ST	94501	669-J3
2400	PARK ST	94501	669-J3
CLIPPER DR			**ALA**
1	CAPETOWN DR	94502	669-J5
100	BASIN SIDE WY	94502	669-J5
CLIPPER HILL			**OAK**
1	SCHOONER HILL	94618	630-C4
30	CAPTAINS CV	94618	630-C4
CLIVE AV			**OAK**
6200	LONGWALK DR	94611	650-G1
6300	CHELSEA DR	94611	650-G1
CLOVER DR			**OAK**
5700	CHABOT RD	94618	630-A5
5900	MILES AV	94618	630-A5
CLUBHOUSE MEMORIAL RD			**ALA**
1	ISLAND DR	94502	670-B6
1	OYSTER SHOALS	94502	670-B6
COACH DR			**OAK**
8000	PHAETON DR	94605	671-C2
8200	HANSOM DR	94605	671-C2
COCHRANE AV			**OAK**
5250	FLORENCE AV	94618	630-C6
4900	SHERIDAN RD	94618	630-C6
5250	AGNES ST	94618	630-C6
CODORNICES RD			**BERK**
1	EUCLID AV	94708	609-H7
COHEN CT			**ALA**
	ROSEFIELD LP	94501	649-G7
COLA BALLENA			**ALA**
400	4TH ST	94501	669-E1
400	BALLENA BLVD	94501	669-E1
450	PORTA BALLENA	94501	669-E2
COLBOURN PL			**OAK**
5600	SKYLINE BLVD	94619	651-B6
COLBY ST			**BERK**
2900	ASHBY AV	94705	629-J4
3000	WEBSTER ST	94705	629-J4
COLBY ST			**OAK**
5900	CLAREMONT AV	94618	629-J5
5970	MCAULEY ST	94609	629-J5
5970	MCAULEY ST	94618	629-J5
6000	60TH ST	94609	629-J5
6000	60TH ST	94618	629-J5
6100	61ST ST	94609	629-J5
6100	61ST ST	94618	629-J5
6140	62ND ST	94609	629-J5
6140	62ND ST	94618	629-J5
6200	62ND ST	94609	629-J5
6200	62ND ST	94618	629-J5
6270	63RD ST	94609	629-J4
6270	63RD ST	94618	629-J4
6300	63RD ST	94609	629-J4
6300	63RD ST	94618	629-J4
6310	NORTH ST	94609	629-J4
6310	NORTH ST	94618	629-J4
6400	ALCATRAZ AV	94609	629-J4
6400	ALCATRAZ AV	94618	629-J4
6400	ALCATRAZ AV	94618	629-J4
6500	WOOLSEY ST	94618	629-J4
COLE ST			**OAK**
2400	TRASK ST	94601	670-F1
2600	BROOKDALE AV	94601	670-F1
2700	KINGSLAND AV	94601	670-F1
5200	TRASK ST	94601	670-F1
5300	YGNACIO AV	94601	670-F1
5360	FOOTHILL BLVD	94601	670-F1
5420	BANCROFT AV	94601	670-F1
5480	PRINCETON ST	94601	670-F1
5500	55TH AV	94601	670-F1
COLEPORT LNDG			**ALA**
50	BEAUFORT HARBOR	94502	670-A5
COLGETT DR			**OAK**
1	CRESTMONT DR	94619	650-H4
COLISEUM WY			**OAK**
6420	NORTH MALL	94621	670-E4
7130	SOUTH MALL	94621	670-F5
7150	SOUTH MALL	94621	670-F4
6400	NORTH MALL	94621	670-E4
6380	66TH AV	94621	670-E4
6240	INDEPENDENT RD	94621	670-E3
6220	INDEPENDENT RD	94621	670-E3
6070	INDEPENDENT RD	94621	670-E3
5900	KEVIN CT	94601	670-E3
5000	JULIE ANN WY	94601	670-D3
4400	50TH AV	94601	670-D2
4300	46TH AV	94601	670-D2
	45TH AV	94601	670-C2
	HIGH ST	94601	670-C2
8100	HEGENBERGER RD	94621	670-F5
8100	EDES AV	94621	670-F5
COLLEGE AV			**ALA**
1000	CALHOUN ST	94501	670-A3
1200	SAN JOSE AV	94501	670-A3
1300	ENCINAL AV	94501	670-A3
COLLEGE AV			**BERK**
2300	BANCROFT WY	94704	629-J2
	DURANT AV	94704	629-J2
2320	DURANT AV	94704	629-J2
2400	CHANNING WY	94704	629-J2
2430	HASTE ST	94704	629-J2
2500	DWIGHT WY	94704	629-J2
2550	PARKER ST	94704	629-J3
2600	PARKER ST	94704	629-J3
2640	DERBY ST	94705	629-J3
2640	DERBY ST	94704	629-J3
2700	DERBY ST	94705	629-J3
2710	FOREST AV	94705	629-J3
2740	GARBER ST	94705	629-J3
2760	STUART ST	94705	629-J3
2800	STUART ST	94705	629-J3
2900	RUSSELL ST	94705	629-J3
2960	ASHBY AV	94705	629-J4
3000	WEBSTER ST	94705	629-J4
3000	WEBSTER ST	94705	629-J4
3030	PRINCE ST	94705	629-J4
3100	WOOLSEY ST	94705	629-J4
3200	ALCATRAZ AV	94705	629-J4
COLLEGE AV			**OAK**
5200	BROADWAY	94618	629-J6
5250	CLIFTON ST	94618	629-J6
5300	BRYANT AV	94618	629-J6
5390	HUDSON ST	94618	629-J6
5400	MANILA AV	94618	629-J6
5430	KALES AV	94618	629-J6
5470	TAFT AV	94618	629-J6
5500	FOREST ST	94618	629-J5
5520	LAWTON AV	94618	629-J5
5590	OCEAN VIEW DR	94618	629-J5
5660	SHAFTER AV	94618	629-J5
	MILES AV	94618	629-J5
5730	MILES AV	94618	629-J5
5740	MILES AV	94618	629-J5
5800	BIRCH CT	94618	629-J5
5820	OAK GROVE AV	94618	629-J5
5930	CHABOT RD	94618	629-J5
6050	HARWOOD AV	94618	629-J5
6120	ARMANINO CT	94618	629-J5
	FLORIO ST	94618	629-J5
6200	62ND ST	94618	629-J4
6200	CLAREMONT AV	94618	629-J4
6300	63RD ST	94618	629-J4
6400	ALCATRAZ AV	94618	629-J4
COLLINS DR			**OAK**
8100	HEGENBERGER RD	94621	670-F5
COLOMA ST			**OAK**
2100	FRUITVALE AV	94602	650-D4
2400	LINCOLN AV	94602	650-D4
COLORADO AV			**BERK**
1	BOYNTON AV	94707	609-G4
40	VERMONT AV	94707	609-G4
100	MICHIGAN AV	94707	609-G4
COLORADOS DR			**OAK**
500	ESTEPA DR	94603	670-H7
700	ACALANES DR	94603	670-H7
COLTON BLVD			**OAK**
5600	MOUNTAIN BLVD	94611	630-E7
5700	MAGELLAN DR	94611	630-E7
5750	GASPAR DR	94611	630-E7
5840	DIAZ PL	94611	630-E7
6000	MENDOZA DR	94611	630-E7
6320	MAZUELA DR	94611	630-E7
6400	SNAKE RD	94611	630-E7
6440	BALBOA DR	94611	630-E7
6510	ASILOMAR DR	94611	630-E7
6510	ASILOMAR CIR	94611	630-E7
6540	ASILOMAR CIR	94611	630-E7
6540	HEARTWOOD DR	94611	630-E7
6650	COLTON PL	94611	630-F7
6700	HEARTWOOD DR	94611	630-F7
6770	CHAMBERS DR	94611	630-F7
6810	CHAMBERS LN	94611	630-F7
6810	HEMLOCK LN	94611	630-F7
6840	HEMLOCK ST	94611	630-F6
6930	RIDGEWOOD WY	94611	630-F6
7000	LODGE CT	94611	630-F6
7070	ARROWHEAD DR	94611	630-F6
7070	RIDGEWOOD DR	94611	630-F6
7400	SNAKE RD	94611	630-F6
COLTON PL			**OAK**
1	COLTON BLVD	94611	630-F7
COLUMBIA CIR			**BERK**
50	FAIRLAWN DR	94708	609-J7
COLUMBIAN DR			**OAK**
3410	CIRCLE HILL DR	94605	671-A1
3540	VALENTINE ST	94605	671-A1
3400	GREENLY DR	94605	670-J1
3300	STERLING DR	94605	670-J1
3400	SUNKIST DR	94605	670-J1
COLUSA AV			**BERK**
500	VISALIA AV	94707	609-F5
570	PERALTA AV	94707	609-F5
600	THOUSAND OAKS BLVD	94707	609-F5
700	VINCENTE AV	94707	609-F5
700	PORTLAND AV	94707	609-F5
750	SAN LORENZO AV	94707	609-F5
800	CAPISTRANO AV	94707	609-F5
830	TACOMA AV	94707	609-F5
850	SAN PEDRO AV	94707	609-F6
870	CATALINA AV	94707	609-F6
900	SOLANO AV	94707	609-F6
900	SOLANO AV	94707	609-F6
980	MARIN AV	94707	609-F6
1020	MADERA ST	94707	609-F6
1080	MONTEREY AV	94707	609-F6
1140	SONOMA AV	94707	609-F6
1180	BEVERLY PL	94707	609-F7
1230	POSEN AV	94707	609-F7
1300	HOPKINS ST	94707	609-F7
COMMERCE WY			**OAK**
1500	16TH AV	94606	650-A6
1600	15TH AV	94606	650-A6
1800	18TH AV	94606	650-A6
1910	19TH AV	94606	650-A6
2010	20TH AV	94606	650-B6
2120	21ST AV	94606	650-B6
2230	22ND AV	94606	650-B6
COMMODORE DR			**EMVL**
1	POWELL ST	94608	629-C6
COMMONWEALTH DR			**OAK**
4600	GLEN MANOR PL	94605	671-E4
4900	SUN VALLEY DR	94605	671-E4
COMSTOCK CT			**BERK**
1500	JAYNES ST	94703	629-F1
1600	CEDAR ST	94703	629-F1
COMSTOCK WY			**OAK**
1500	14TH AV	94606	650-B5
1700	17TH AV	94606	650-B5
CONCORDIA ST			**ALA**
1600	LINCOLN AV	94501	669-F1
1700	PACIFIC AV	94501	669-F1
1800	BUENA VISTA AV	94501	669-F1
CONGRESS AV			**OAK**
4500	HIGH ST	94601	650-E7
4600	COURTLAND AV	94601	650-E7
4700	47TH AV	94601	650-E7
4780	VICKSBURG AV	94601	650-E7
5000	VICKSBURG AV	94601	650-E7
4780	MONTICELLO AV	94601	670-E1
5000	MONTICELLO AV	94601	670-E1
5210	YGNACIO AV	94601	670-E1
5300	FOOTHILL BLVD	94601	670-E1
CONRAD CT			**OAK**
100	SOBRANTE RD	94611	630-E5
CONSTANCE CIR			**ALA**
3300	EAST SHORE DR	94501	670-C3
CONSTITUTION WY			**ALA**
	MITCHELL AV	94501	649-F6
1600	LINCOLN AV	94501	669-G1
1600	8TH ST	94501	669-G1
1700	PACIFIC AV	94501	669-F1
1800	BUENA VISTA AV	94501	649-F7
1900	EAGLE AV	94501	649-F7
2000	ATLANTIC AV	94501	649-F7
2130	MARINA VILLAGE PKWY	94501	649-F7
2200	WEBSTER ST	94501	649-F6
2300	WEBSTER ST	94501	649-F6
2300	MARINER SQUARE LP	94501	649-F6
CONTRA COSTA AV			**BERK**
700	YOSEMITE RD	94707	609-G5
720	CAPISTRANO AV	94707	609-G5
950	SOLANO AV	94707	609-G6
950	SOLANO AV	94707	609-G6
1000	LOS ANGELES AV	94707	609-G6
CONTRA COSTA PL			**OAK**
1	CONTRA COSTA RD	94618	630-B5
CONTRA COSTA RD			**OAK**
5800	BUENA VISTA AV	94618	630-B5
5900	CONTRA COSTA PL	94618	630-B5
6000	CHAUMONT PTH	94618	630-B5
6100	BELALP PTH	94618	630-B5
6200	ARBON PTH	94618	630-B5
6400	ERBA PTH	94618	630-B5
CONVAIR ST			**OAK**
1000	EARHART RD	94621	670-D6
1030	LANGLEY ST	94621	670-D6
1030	LOCKHEED ST	94621	670-D6
1050	LANGLEY ST	94621	670-D6
1070	NORTHRUP ST	94621	670-D6
1090	CESSNA ST	94621	670-D6
1100	DOOLITTLE DR	94621	670-D6
COOK LN			**ALA**
3300	ISLAND DR	94502	670-A7
3400	BISMARCK LN	94502	670-A7
COOKE ST			**OAK**
1000	EARHART RD	94621	670-D7
1060	BOEING ST	94621	670-D7
COOLIDGE AV			**OAK**
2000	FOOTHILL BLVD	94601	650-C7
2200	E 22ND ST	94601	650-C7
2300	E 23RD ST	94601	650-C6
2400	ORCHID ST	94601	650-D6
2460	LOGAN ST	94601	650-D6
2500	HYDE ST	94601	650-D6
2550	PAXTON AV	94601	650-D6
2600	PRENTISS ST	94601	650-D6
2660	DAVIS ST	94601	650-D6
2700	E 27TH ST	94601	650-D6
2780	LYNDE ST	94601	650-D6
2800	LYNDE ST	94601	650-D6
2870	DEERING ST	94601	650-D6
2900	BONA ST	94601	650-D6
2920	BONA ST	94602	650-D6
3000	BROOKDALE AV	94602	650-D5
3080	NICOL AV	94602	650-D5
3020	NICOL AV	94602	650-D5
3230	SCHOOL ST	94602	650-D5
3300	TEXAS ST	94602	650-D5
3300	LAGUNA WY	94602	650-D5
3350	SUTER ST	94602	650-D5
3370	HAROLD ST	94602	650-D5
	MONTANA ST	94602	650-E5
3410	RHODA AV	94602	650-E5
3450	DELAWARE ST	94602	650-E5
3540	GEORGIA ST	94602	650-E5
3540	MACARTHUR BLVD	94602	650-E5
3580	HOPKINS PL	94602	650-E4
3740	MADELINE ST	94602	650-E4
3900	CARMEL ST	94602	650-E4
3980	MORGAN AV	94602	650-E4
4200	ALIDA ST	94602	650-E4
4230	CHARLESTON ST	94602	650-F4
4400	COOLIDGE TER	94602	650-F4
COOLIDGE TER			**OAK**
1	COOLIDGE AV	94602	650-F3
CORAL RD			**OAK**
9200	EMPIRE RD	94603	670-F6
9200	FITZPATRICK RD	94603	670-F6
9300	FITZPATRICK RD	94603	670-F6
9400	MAKIN RD	94603	670-F7
9500	CAIRO RD	94603	670-F7
9600	SEXTUS RD	94603	670-F7
9660	TUNIS RD	94603	670-F7
9700	WISTAR RD	94603	670-F7
9760	GANNON RD	94603	670-F7
9800	EMPIRE RD	94603	670-F7
CORAL REEF PL			**ALA**
1200	CORAL REEF RD	94501	669-H3
1300	SUNSET RD	94501	669-H3
CORAL REEF RD			**ALA**
300	SHORELINE DR	94501	669-G3
500	CORAL REEF PL	94501	669-G3
CORDOVA ST			**OAK**
2400	CASTELLO ST	94602	650-D5
2600	FRUITVALE AV	94602	650-D5
CORK RD			**ALA**
1	KARA RD	94502	669-J5
200	KILLYBEGS RD	94502	669-J5
CORNELL AV			**ALB**
500	BRIGHTON AV	94706	609-D5
600	GARFIELD AV	94706	609-D5
700	PORTLAND AV	94706	609-D5
800	WASHINGTON AV	94706	609-D6
900	SOLANO AV	94706	609-D6
1000	MARIN AV	94706	609-E6
1100	DARTMOUTH ST	94706	609-E6
CORNELL AV			**BERK**
1100	DARTMOUTH ST	94706	609-E7
1300	GILMAN ST	94702	609-E7
1400	CAMELIA ST	94702	609-E7
1460	PAGE ST	94702	609-E7
1460	SANTA FE AV	94702	609-E7
1550	HOPKINS ST	94702	629-E1
1600	CEDAR ST	94702	629-E1
1700	VIRGINIA ST	94702	629-E1
CORNELL DR			**ALA**
1600	THOMPSON AV	94501	670-B3
1650	FAIRVIEW AV	94501	670-B3
1750	BAYO VISTA AV	94501	670-B2
1800	GIBBONS DR	94501	670-B2
1900	FERNSIDE BLVD	94501	670-C2
2000	WINDSOR DR	94501	670-C2
CORNWALL CT			**OAK**
100	CASTLE DR	94611	650-G2
CORONA CT			**BERK**
2300	ARCH ST	94708	609-H6
CORONADO AV			**OAK**
4900	49TH ST	94609	629-J7
4900	49TH ST	94618	629-J7
5100	51ST ST	94618	629-J6
5200	DESMOND ST	94618	629-J6
5260	HEMPHILL PL	94618	629-J6
5260	HEMPHILL PL	94611	629-J6
5300	BROADWAY	94618	629-J6

PRIMARY STREET Address	Cross Street	ZIP	CITY Pg-Grid
CORONADO AV			**OAK**
5300	BROADWAY	94611	629-J6
CORPUS CHRISTI RD			**ALA**
100	PAN AM WY	94501	649-D6
	PENSACOLA	94501	649-D6
150	NORFOLK RD	94501	649-D6
150	BARBERS POINT RD	94501	649-D6
150	SERENADE PL	94501	649-D6
CORREGIDOR AV			**OAK**
1	CHUNGKING ST	94607	649-C1
80	BATAAN AV	94607	649-C1
100	AFRICA ST	94607	649-C1
CORTE REAL AV			**OAK**
2000	MAGELLAN DR	94611	650-E1
CORTEZ CT			**OAK**
100	BALBOA DR	94611	630-F7
COSGRAVE AV			**OAK**
2800	GOLF LINKS RD	94605	671-A3
2900	NEY AV	94605	671-A3
3000	OUTLOOK AV	94605	671-A3
COTATI ST			**ALA**
2000	ATLANTIC AV	94501	649-E7
2100	BAINBRIDGE AV	94501	649-E7
COTELLA CT			**ALA**
1	RATTO RD	94502	669-J6
COTTAGE ST			**ALA**
1400	CENTRAL AV	94501	669-H1
1500	SANTA CLARA AV	94501	669-H1
COTTER ST			**OAK**
10720	SCOTIA AV	94605	671-E4
10800	STACY ST	94605	671-E4
10900	DUNKIRK AV	94605	671-E4
11000	SHETLAND AV	94605	671-E4
COTTON ST			**OAK**
1000	LIVINGSTON ST	94606	650-A7
1100	DENNISON ST	94606	650-A7
COUNTRY CLUB DR			**OAK**
5500	BROADWAY TER	94618	630-A6
5500	MARGARIDO DR	94618	630-A6
5600	WESTMINSTER DR	94618	630-A6
5700	LINCOLNSHIRE DR	94618	630-A5
5760	BOWLING DR	94618	630-A5
5780	BEECHWOOD DR	94618	630-A5
5800	ACACIA AV	94618	630-A5
COUNTRY ISL			**ALA**
500	ROSEWOOD WY	94501	669-G2
COUNTY RD			**ALA**
1	MECARTNEY RD	94502	670-A6
COURAGEOUS CT			**ALA**
1	INDEPENDENCE DR	94501	649-G7
COURT ST			**ALA**
300	BAYVIEW DR	94501	670-A4
400	WATERTON ST	94501	670-A4
1000	OTIS DR	94501	670-A4
1000	CALHOUN ST	94501	670-A4
1050	FILLMORE ST	94501	670-A4
1100	WASHINGTON ST	94501	670-A3
1150	ADAMS ST	94501	670-A3
1200	SAN JOSE AV	94501	670-B3
1250	MADISON ST	94501	670-B3
1300	ENCINAL AV	94501	670-B3
1330	JACKSON ST	94501	670-B3
1360	VAN BUREN ST	94501	670-B3
1400	CENTRAL AV	94501	670-B3
1500	SANTA CLARA AV	94501	670-B3
1550	JOHNSON AV	94501	670-B3
1600	LINCOLN AV	94501	670-B3
COURTLAND AV			**OAK**
1900	FOOTHILL BLVD	94601	670-D1
1900	42ND AV	94601	670-D1
2020	YGNACIO AV	94601	670-D1
2050	HIGH ST	94601	670-D1
2140	MELROSE AV	94601	670-E1
2280	45TH AV	94601	670-E1
2300	THOMPSON ST	94601	670-E1
2300	SAN CARLOS AV	94601	650-E7
2200	SAN CARLOS AV	94601	650-E7
2300	TYRRELL ST	94601	650-E7
2400	CONGRESS AV	94601	650-E7
2500	FAIRFAX AV	94601	650-E7
2900	FLEMING AV	94619	650-F7
2990	PENNIMAN AV	94619	650-F7
3070	VIRGINIA AV	94619	650-F7
3270	CAMDEN ST	94619	650-F7
3500	REDDING ST	94619	650-F7
COVE RD			**ALA**
1	CHANNING WY	94502	669-J5
100	CAPETOWN DR	94502	669-J5
COVINGTON ST			**OAK**
100	MARLOW DR	94605	671-C6
100	FOOTHILL WY	94605	671-C6
200	REVERE AV	94605	671-C6
300	ROXBURY AV	94605	671-C7
400	BROOKFIELD AV	94605	671-C7
COWPER ST			**BERK**
1100	SAN PABLO AV	94702	629-E2
1200	BYRON ST	94702	629-E2
CRAGMONT AV			**BERK**
400	GRIZZLY PEAK BLVD	94708	609-G4
430	ALTA RD	94708	609-G4
530	ACACIA AV	94708	609-H5
700	HALKIN LN	94708	609-H5
730	POPLAR ST	94708	609-H5
800	ROCK LN	94708	609-H5
840	REGAL RD	94708	609-H5
900	MARIN AV	94708	609-H5
960	EASTER WY	94708	609-H6
1000	SANTA BARBARA RD	94708	609-H6
1040	EUCLID AV	94708	609-H6
1040	EUCLID AV	94709	609-H6
1070	REGAL RD	94708	609-H6
1100	BRET HARTE RD	94708	609-H6
1110	BRET HARTE RD	94708	609-H6
1200	SHASTA RD	94708	609-H6
CRAIG AV			**PDMT**
1	HIGHLAND AV	94611	650-B1
100	MOUNTAIN AV	94611	650-B1
CRANE CT			**ALA**
1	CAPETOWN DR	94502	669-J5
CRANE WY			**OAK**
3200	JOAQUIN MILLER RD	94602	650-G3
3500	JOAQUIN MILLER RD	94602	650-G3
CRANFORD WY			**OAK**
11700	REVERE AV	94605	671-D6
CREED RD			**OAK**
800	HOLMAN RD	94610	650-C3
860	BARROWS RD	94610	650-C3
920	TRESTLE GLEN RD	94610	650-C3
CREEDON CIR			**ALA**
210	NAKAYAMA CT	94502	669-H5
250	GONSALVES CT	94502	669-H5
200	ADELPHIAN WY	94502	669-H5
210	NAKAYAMA CT	94502	669-H5
CREEKSIDE CIR			**OAK**
10500	105TH AV	94603	690-G1
CREIGHTON WY			**OAK**
400	WESTFIELD WY	94619	650-H5
300	VAN CLEAVE WY	94619	650-H4
CRESCENT ST			**OAK**
450	SANTA CLARA AV	94610	649-J2
CREST AV			**OAK**
7700	FIELD ST	94605	671-A2
7800	LAMP ST	94605	671-A2
8100	MCCORMICK AV	94605	671-A2
8100	STERLING DR	94605	671-A2
8800	FONTAINE ST	94605	671-B3
9200	CALANDRIA	94605	671-B3
9300	GRANADA AV	94605	671-B3
CREST RD			**PDMT**
80	LA SALLE AV	94611	650-D1
1	SOMERSET RD	94611	650-D2
80	HAMPTON RD	94611	650-D2
CRESTMONT DR			**OAK**
1	SKYLINE BLVD	94619	650-H4
20	CHADBOURNE WY	94619	650-H4
50	RISHELL DR	94619	650-H4
170	BUTTERS DR	94619	650-H4
170	BUTTERS DR	94602	650-H4
250	KIMBERLIN HEIGHTS DR	94619	650-H4
250	KIMBERLIN HEIGHTS DR	94602	650-H4
300	COLGETT DR	94619	650-H4
300	COLGETT DR	94602	650-H4
320	BRUNELL DR	94619	650-H4
520	WESTFIELD WY	94619	650-H5
550	TERALYNN CT	94619	650-H5
640	SAMARIA LN	94619	650-H5
670	KINGWOOD RD	94619	650-H5
700	REDWOOD RD	94619	650-H5
CRESTON RD			**BERK**
600	GRIZZLY PEAK BLVD	94708	609-H4
630	ROSEMONT AV	94708	609-H4
810	SUNSET LN	94708	609-H5
860	MARIN AV	94708	609-H5
880	FOREST LN	94708	609-H5
1020	LATHAM LN	94708	609-J5
1100	GRIZZLY PEAK BLVD	94708	609-J5
CRESTVIEW DR			**OAK**
	LEXFORD PL	94619	651-B7
	RICHMOND RD	94619	651-B7
CRIST ST			**ALA**
2500	REGENT ST	94501	670-A3
2600	BROADWAY	94501	670-A3
CRITTENDEN ST			**OAK**
5400	55TH AV	94601	670-E2
5500	54TH AV	94601	670-E2
CROCKER AV			**OAK**
280	LA SALLE AV	94610	650-C2
300	ASHMOUNT AV	94610	650-C2
300	MANDANA BLVD	94610	650-C2
CROCKER AV			**PDMT**
1	LINCOLN AV	94611	650-C2
50	WILDWOOD AV	94611	650-C2
100	HAMPTON RD	94610	650-C2
100	HAMPTON RD	94611	650-C2
120	WOODLAND WY	94610	650-C2
120	WOODLAND WY	94611	650-C2
180	LAFAYETTE AV	94610	650-C2
200	FARRAGUT AV	94610	650-C2
280	LA SALLE AV	94610	650-C2
CROCKETT PL			**OAK**
5100	JOAQUIN MILLER RD	94602	650-H3
CROFTON AV			**OAK**
450	BOULEVARD WY	94610	650-A2
570	BOULEVARD WY	94610	650-A2
CROLLS GARDEN CT			**ALA**
100	CENTRAL AV	94501	669-F1
100	WEBSTER ST	94501	669-F1
220	GARDEN WY	94501	669-F1
CROSBY AV			**OAK**
1900	FOOTHILL BLVD	94601	650-D7
2100	HARPER ST	94601	650-D7
CROSS CAMPUS RD			**BERK**
	OXFORD ST	94720	629-H2
	OXFORD LN	94720	629-H2
CROSS RD			**OAK**
100	BROADWAY TER	94618	630-B5
200	ROMANY RD	94618	630-B5
230	LOCARNO PTH	94618	630-B5
300	ACACIA AV	94618	630-B5
S CROSSWAYS			**BERK**
60	ROSLYN CT	94705	630-A4
1	HILLCREST RD	94705	630-A4
60	THE UPLANDS	94705	630-A4
CROWN AV			**OAK**
6200	BROADWAY TER	94611	630-D6
6400	MERRIEWOOD DR	94611	630-D6
6400	URANUS AV	94611	630-D6
CROWN DR			**ALA**
1320	KINGS RD	94501	669-F1
1350	QUEENS RD	94501	669-F1
1400	CENTRAL AV	94501	669-F1
CROWN RIDGE CT			**OAK**
	CAMPUS DR	94605	651-A7
CROXTON AV			**OAK**
1	RICHMOND BLVD	94611	649-H1
100	PIEDMONT AV	94611	649-H1
CROYDON CIR			**PDMT**
100	SAINT JAMES DR	94611	650-D2
CRYSTAL RIDGE CT			**OAK**
	CAMPUS DR	94605	671-B1
CRYSTAL WY			**BERK**
1	EUCLID AV	94708	609-H6
CULVER CT			**OAK**
3100	CULVER ST	94619	650-F6
CULVER ST			**OAK**
4100	EASTMAN AV	94619	650-F6
4150	CULVER CT	94619	650-F6
4300	HIGH ST	94619	650-F6
CUMBERLAND CT			**ALA**
200	SHEFFIELD RD	94502	669-J5
200	CUMBERLAND WY	94502	669-J5
CUMBERLAND WY			**ALA**
100	BERKSHIRE RD	94502	669-J5
200	CUMBERLAND CT	94502	669-J5
200	SHEFFIELD RD	94502	669-J5
CUNNINGHAM ST			**OAK**
4600	FAIR AV	94619	650-G6
4700	DAVENPORT AV	94619	650-H6
4800	REINHARDT DR	94619	650-H6
CURLEW CT			**ALA**
	GRESHAM DR	94501	649-F7
CURRAN AV			**OAK**
3050	WARD LN	94602	650-D5
3200	SCHOOL ST	94602	650-D5
3200	SCHOOL ST	94602	650-E5
3250	TEXAS ST	94602	650-E5
3300	SUTER ST	94602	650-E5
CURRAN WY			**OAK**
3400	MONTANA ST	94602	650-E5
3500	DELAWARE ST	94602	650-E5
CURTIS ST			**ALB**
480	VISALIA AV	94706	609-E5
570	THOUSAND OAKS BLVD	94706	609-E5
680	PORTLAND AV	94706	609-E5
780	WASHINGTON AV	94706	609-E6
900	SOLANO AV	94706	609-E6
900	SOLANO AV	94707	609-E6
1000	MARIN AV	94706	609-E6
1050	SONOMA AV	94706	609-E6
1200	FRANCIS ST	94706	609-E6
CURTIS ST			**BERK**
1200	FRANCIS ST	94706	609-E7
1300	GILMAN ST	94702	629-E1
	HOPKINS ST	94702	629-E1
1500	ROSE ST	94702	629-E1
1600	CEDAR ST	94702	629-E1
1700	VIRGINIA ST	94702	629-E1
1720	FRANCISCO ST	94702	629-E1
1800	DELAWARE ST	94702	629-E1
	HEARST AV	94702	629-E1
1900	HEARST AV	94702	629-E2
2000	UNIVERSITY AV	94702	629-E2
2100	ADDISON ST	94702	629-E2
2200	ALLSTON WY	94702	629-E2
2300	BANCROFT WY	94702	629-E2
2330	CHAUCER ST	94702	629-E2
2400	CHANNING WY	94702	629-E3
2500	DWIGHT WY	94702	629-E3
CURTIS ST			**OAK**
2000	20TH ST	94607	649-F3
2100	21ST ST	94607	649-F2
2200	22ND ST	94607	649-F2
2300	W GRAND AV	94607	649-F2
CUSTER ST			**OAK**
3500	35TH AV	94601	650-D6
3600	HARRINGTON AV	94601	650-D6
CUTHBERT AV			**OAK**
3100	NICOL AV	94602	650-D5
3150	SCHYLER ST	94602	650-D5
3200	SCHOOL ST	94602	650-D5
CUTTER WY			**BERK**
800	4TH ST	94804	629-D3
900	7TH ST	94804	629-D3
CYCLOTRON RD			**BERK**
	HEARST AV	94720	629-J1
	HIGHLAND PL	94720	629-J1
CYPRESS ST			**ALA**
200	2ND ST	94501	649-E7
300	3RD ST	94501	649-E7
CYPRESS ST			**BERK**
1460	BUENA AV	94703	609-F7
1500	ROSE ST	94703	609-F7
CYPRESS ST			**OAK**
800	8TH ST	94607	649-E3
970	MANDELA PKWY	94607	649-E3

D

PRIMARY STREET Address	Cross Street	ZIP	CITY Pg-Grid
D ST			**OAK**
9980	82ND AV	94621	670-G4
8300	83RD AV	94621	670-G4
8400	84TH AV	94621	670-G4
8500	85TH AV	94621	670-G4
8600	86TH AV	94621	670-H4
8700	87TH AV	94621	670-H5
8800	88TH AV	94621	670-H5
8900	89TH AV	94621	670-H5
9000	90TH AV	94603	670-H5
9100	91ST AV	94603	670-H5
9200	92ND AV	94621	670-H5
9200	92ND AV	94603	670-H5
9500	ELMHURST AV	94603	670-H5
9800	98TH AV	94603	670-H6
10000	100TH AV	94603	670-H6
DAHLIA DR			**ALA**
100	ISLAND DR	94502	670-A6
110	AZALEA DR	94502	670-A6
130	BEGONIA DR	94502	670-A6
200	CAMELIA DR	94502	670-A6
DAISY ST			**OAK**
5110	REINHARDT DR	94619	650-H7
5000	DAVENPORT AV	94619	650-H7
4900	FAIR AV	94619	650-G7
4800	CALAVERAS AV	94619	650-G7
4700	TOMPKINS AV	94619	650-G7
	MCCLELLAND ST	94619	650-G6
	BUELL ST	94619	650-G6
DAKOTA ST			**OAK**
3000	MAPLE AV	94602	650-E5
3200	LAUREL AV	94602	650-E5
3500	MIDVALE AV	94602	650-E5
3500	QUIGLEY LN	94602	650-E5
DALE AV			**PDMT**
100	FAIRVIEW AV	94610	650-A1
200	NOVA DR	94610	650-A1
DALE PL			**OAK**
3800	38TH AV	94619	650-E6
3900	MINNA AV	94619	650-E6
DAMON CT			**ALA**
1	PARFAIT LN	94502	670-A5
DAMUTH ST			**OAK**
2000	FRUITVALE AV	94602	650-D4
2300	LINCOLN AV	94602	650-D4
2300	LINCOLN AV	94602	650-D4
2600	LAGUNA AV	94602	650-D4
DANA ST			**BERK**
2300	BANCROFT WY	94704	629-H2
2350	DURANT AV	94704	629-H2
2400	CHANNING WY	94704	629-H2
2420	HASTE ST	94704	629-H2
2500	DWIGHT WY	94704	629-H2
2520	BLAKE ST	94704	629-H3
2600	PARKER ST	94704	629-H3
2620	CARLETON ST	94704	629-H3
2700	DERBY ST	94705	629-H3
2800	WARD ST	94705	629-H3
3020	DOWLING PL	94705	629-H4
	PRINCE ST	94705	629-H4
3050	PRINCE ST	94705	629-H4
3100	WOOLSEY ST	94705	629-H4
DANA ST			**OAK**
6300	63RD ST	94609	629-H5
6350	NORTH ST	94609	629-H4
6400	ALCATRAZ AV	94609	629-H4
6500	65TH ST	94609	629-H4
6600	66TH ST	94609	629-H4
6700	WOOLSEY ST	94609	629-H4
DANBROOK CT			**ALA**
1	BRIGHTON RD	94502	670-A5
DANBURY ST			**OAK**
1	REVERE AV	94605	671-C6
100	ROXBURY AV	94605	671-C6
DANTE AV			**OAK**
9900	99TH AV	94603	671-A5
10000	100TH AV	94603	671-A5
10300	103RD AV	94603	671-A5
10600	106TH AV	94603	671-A5
DARCY CT			**OAK**
6400	ALCATRAZ AV	94609	629-H4
DARIEN AV			**OAK**
300	SAINT ELMO DR	94603	670-G7
330	ELDRIDGE AV	94603	670-G7
390	DENSLOWE AV	94603	670-G7
440	ELDRIDGE AV	94603	670-G7
500	GHORMLEY AV	94603	670-G7
DARNBY DR			**OAK**
2860	CARISBROOK DR	94611	650-G1
2700	LONGWALK DR	94611	650-G1
2860	CHELTON DR	94611	650-G1
DARTMOUTH DR			**OAK**
1	DRURY RD	94705	630-B3
1	BESITO AV	94705	630-B3
DARTMOUTH ST			**ALB**
1100	SAN PABLO AV	94706	609-D7
1140	KAINS AV	94706	609-D7
1180	STANNAGE AV	94706	609-E7
1210	CORNELL AV	94706	609-E7
1250	TALBOT AV	94706	609-E7
1280	EVELYN AV	94706	609-E7
1320	MASONIC AV	94706	609-E7
1350	KEY ROUTE BLVD	94706	609-E6
1400	POMONA AV	94706	609-E6
DASHWOOD AV			**OAK**
2200	ARTHUR ST	94605	670-H3
2300	DEERWOOD AV	94605	670-H3
2370	KRAUSE AV	94605	670-H3
DATE ST			**OAK**
9100	PHELPS ST	94603	670-F6
9200	WORTH ST	94603	670-F6
DAVENPORT AV			**OAK**
4400	CARSON ST	94619	650-G6
4540	KAPHAN AV	94619	650-G6
4690	CUNNINGHAM ST	94619	650-H6
4900	DAISY ST	94619	650-H7
	MOUNTAIN BLVD	94613	650-H7
	MOUNTAIN BLVD	94619	650-H7
DAVIDSON WY			**OAK**
	GRAND AV	94610	650-A2
	WALKER AV	94610	650-A2
DAVIS ST			**OAK**
3100	FRUITVALE AV	94601	650-C6
3140	PRENTISS PL	94601	650-D6
3260	COOLIDGE AV	94601	650-D6
3310	34TH AV	94601	650-D6
3400	HUMBOLDT AV	94601	650-D6
3450	BARTLETT ST	94601	650-D6
3500	35TH AV	94601	650-D6
3500	35TH AV	94601	650-D6
3600	HARRINGTON AV	94601	650-D6
DAWES ST			**OAK**
6500	ESTATES DR	94611	650-D1
6500	PERSHING DR	94611	650-D1
6700	ESTATES DR	94611	650-D1
6700	PERSHING DR	94611	650-D1
DAWN ST			**OAK**
	DRURY RD	94705	630-C3
DAYTON AV			**ALA**
1300	SHERMAN ST	94501	669-H2
1600	PARU ST	94501	669-H2
1700	GRAND ST	94501	669-H2
1800	PALMERA CT	94501	669-H2
DE HAVILLAND ST			**OAK**
170	DOOLITTLE DR	94621	670-E7
170	SWAN WY	94621	670-E7
200	EARHART RD	94621	670-E7
DEAKIN ST			**BERK**
2900	RUSSELL ST	94705	629-H3
3000	ASHBY AV	94705	629-H4
3000	ASHBY AV	94705	629-H4
3030	WEBSTER ST	94705	629-H4
3100	PRINCE ST	94705	629-H4
3200	WOOLSEY ST	94705	629-H4
DEAKIN ST			**OAK**
3200	WOOLSEY ST	94609	629-H4
6700	66TH ST	94609	629-H4
DECATUR ST			**ALA**
2110	HOLLISTER CIR	94501	649-E7
	BAINBRIDGE AV	94501	649-E7
	ATLANTIC AV	94501	649-E7
DECELLE CT			**ALA**
	BARTLETT DR	94501	649-G7
DEERING CT			**OAK**
100	DEERING ST	94601	650-D6
100	BONA ST	94601	650-D6
DEERING ST			**OAK**
3200	BONA ST	94601	650-D6
3200	DEERING CT	94601	650-D6
3400	COOLIDGE AV	94601	650-D6
3200	HUMBOLDT AV	94601	650-D6
3350	BARTLETT ST	94601	650-D6
3500	35TH AV	94601	650-D6
DEERWOOD AV			**OAK**
7670	73RD AV	94605	670-H2
7300	73RD AV	94605	670-H3
7500	MAYWOOD AV	94605	670-H3
7600	DASHWOOD AV	94605	670-H3
DEFREMERY AV			**OAK**
900	10TH AV	94606	649-J6
1000	9TH AV	94606	649-J6
DEL MAR AV			**ALA**
1000	OTIS DR	94501	669-J3
DEL MAR AV			**BERK**
1	BUENA VISTA WY	94708	609-J7
70	PARNASSUS RD	94708	609-J7
120	GLENDALE AV	94708	609-J7
200	CAMPUS DR	94708	609-J7
DEL NORTE CT			**BERK**
	DEL NORTE ST	94707	609-G6
DEL NORTE ST			**BERK**
2000	SUTTER ST	94707	609-G6
2010	TERRACE WK	94707	609-G6
2090	DEL NORTE CT	94707	609-G6
2100	FOUNTAIN WK	94707	609-G6
2100	LOS ANGELES AV	94707	609-G6
2100	MARIN AV	94707	609-G6
2100	SUTTER ST	94707	609-G6
2100	ARLINGTON AV	94707	609-G6
DELAWARE ST			**BERK**
800	6TH ST	94804	629-D1
900	7TH ST	94804	629-D1
1000	8TH ST	94804	629-D1
1000	9TH ST	94804	629-E1
1030	10TH ST	94804	629-E1
1100	SAN PABLO AV	94702	629-E1
1200	CURTIS ST	94702	629-E1
1240	CHESTNUT ST	94702	629-E1
1350	FRANKLIN ST	94702	629-F1
	ACTON ST	94702	629-F1
1400	ACTON ST	94702	629-F1
1440	SHORT ST	94702	629-F1
1500	SACRAMENTO ST	94702	629-F1
1600	CALIFORNIA ST	94703	629-F1
1700	MCGEE AV	94703	629-G1
1800	GRANT ST	94703	629-G1
1900	MARTIN LUTHER KING JR WY	94709	629-G1
1920	BONITA AV	94709	629-G1
2000	MILVIA ST	94709	629-G1
2100	SHATTUCK AV	94709	629-G1
2200	WALNUT ST	94709	629-G1
DELAWARE ST			**OAK**
2800	COOLIDGE AV	94602	650-E5
2900	CURRAN WY	94602	650-E5
3000	MAPLE AV	94602	650-E5
3000	MAPLE AV	94602	650-E5
3200	LAUREL AV	94602	650-E5
3500	35TH AV	94602	650-E5
DELMER ST			**OAK**
2400	LINCOLN AV	94602	650-E4
2600	LAGUNA AV	94602	650-E4

PRIMARY STREET Address	Cross Street	ZIP	CITY Pg-Grid
DELMONT AV			**OAK**
3700	BUENA VENTURA AV	94605	670-H1
3770	MOKELUMNE AV	94605	670-H1
3800	OAKDALE AV	94605	670-J1
3900	HILLMONT DR	94605	670-J1
4000	SUNNYMERE AV	94605	670-J1
DENKE DR			**ALA**
1000	LEONARD CT	94502	669-J6
1000	BORDWELL CT	94502	669-J6
1050	MARCUSE ST	94502	669-J6
1100	CHRISTENSEN CT	94502	669-J6
1150	BURGNER AV	94502	669-J6
1200	BROWN ST	94502	669-J6
DENNISON ST			**ALA**
1800	HUDSON DR	94501	649-J7
1800	SPENCER RD	94501	649-J7
1800	EMBARCADERO	94501	650-A7
1890	EMBARCADERO	94501	650-A7
DENNISON ST			**OAK**
1890	EMBARCADERO	94606	650-A7
2000	KING ST	94606	650-A7
2070	COTTON ST	94606	650-A7
2100	KENNEDY ST	94606	650-A7
DENSLOWE AV			**OAK**
1	DARIEN AV	94603	670-G7
70	98TH AV	94603	670-G7
200	CASWELL AV	94603	670-G7
DENTON PL			**OAK**
5600	WEAVER PL	94619	651-A6
DEPASSIER WY			**ALA**
3500	SILVA LN	94502	670-A7
3600	CLARKE LN	94502	670-A7
DERBY AV			**OAK**
400	GLASCOCK ST	94601	670-B1
510	FORD ST	94601	670-B1
610	CHAPMAN ST	94601	670-B1
710	E 7TH ST	94601	670-B1
800	ELMWOOD AV	94601	670-B1
1100	E 10TH ST	94601	670-B1
1200	E 12TH ST	94601	670-B1
1300	INTERNATIONAL BLVD	94601	650-C7
1200	E 13TH ST	94601	650-C7
1300	E 13TH ST	94601	650-C7
1400	INTERNATIONAL BLVD	94601	650-C7
1500	E 15TH ST	94601	650-C7
DERBY ST			**BERK**
1100	SAN PABLO AV	94702	629-E3
1200	MATHEWS ST	94702	629-E3
1300	MABEL ST	94702	629-F3
1400	ACTON ST	94702	629-F3
1500	SACRAMENTO ST	94703	629-F3
1600	CALIFORNIA ST	94703	629-F3
1700	MCGEE AV	94703	629-G3
	GRANT ST	94703	629-G3
1800	GRANT ST	94703	629-G3
1900	MARTIN LUTHER KING JR WY	94704	629-G3
2000	MILVIA ST	94704	629-G3
2100	SHATTUCK AV	94704	629-H3
2100	SHATTUCK AV	94705	629-H3
2110	WALKER ST	94704	629-H3
2110	WALKER ST	94705	629-H3
2200	FULTON ST	94704	629-H3
2200	FULTON ST	94705	629-H3
2300	ELLSWORTH ST	94704	629-H3
2300	ELLSWORTH ST	94705	629-H3
2400	DANA ST	94704	629-H3
2400	DANA ST	94705	629-H3
2420	TELEGRAPH AV	94704	629-H3
2420	TELEGRAPH AV	94705	629-H3
2500	REGENT ST	94704	629-J3
2500	REGENT ST	94705	629-J3
	HILLEGASS AV	94704	629-J3
	HILLEGASS AV	94705	629-J3
2600	HILLEGASS AV	94704	629-J3
2600	HILLEGASS AV	94705	629-J3
	BENVENUE AV	94704	629-J3
	BENVENUE AV	94705	629-J3
2640	BENVENUE AV	94704	629-J3
2640	BENVENUE AV	94705	629-J3
2700	COLLEGE AV	94704	629-J3
2700	COLLEGE AV	94705	629-J3
2700	COLLEGE AV	94704	629-J3
2700	COLLEGE AV	94705	629-J3
2720	ETNA ST	94704	629-J3
2720	ETNA ST	94705	629-J3
	PIEDMONT AV	94704	629-J3
	PIEDMONT AV	94705	629-J3
2800	PIEDMONT AV	94704	629-J3
2800	PIEDMONT AV	94705	629-J3
	WARRING ST	94704	629-J3
	WARRING ST	94705	629-J3
2900	SOUTHWEST PL	94704	630-A3
2900	SOUTHWEST PL	94705	630-A3
2940	CLAREMONT BLVD	94705	630-A3
2960	TANGLEWOOD RD	94705	630-A3
2960	BELROSE AV	94705	630-A3
DESMOND ST			**OAK**
4900	49TH ST	94618	629-J7
5100	51ST ST	94618	629-J6
5200	CORONADO AV	94618	629-J6
5240	HEMPHILL PL	94618	629-J6
5270	GLENDALE AV	94618	629-J6
5300	CLIFTON ST	94618	629-J6
DETROIT AV			**OAK**
4200	35TH AV	94619	650-G5
4300	ATLAS AV	94619	650-G5
4300	35TH AV	94619	650-G4
DEVON WY			**OAK**
7100	NORFOLK DR	94705	630-C3
DIABLO DR			**OAK**
1	SKYLINE BLVD	94611	630-F5
DIAPIAN BAY			**ALA**
100	BAYWALK RD	94502	669-J6
DIAZ PL			**OAK**
1	COLTON BLVD	94611	630-D7
DICKSON CT			**OAK**
4100	MOUNTAIN BLVD	94605	671-B2
DIESEL ST			**OAK**
2200	KENNEDY ST	94606	670-A1
DIMOND AV			**OAK**
3400	MONTANA ST	94602	650-D4
3420	SLOAN ST	94602	650-D4
3500	MACARTHUR BLVD	94602	650-D4
DINGLEY ST			**OAK**
4100	CAMERON AV	94605	671-D4
4140	CLIFFLAND AV	94605	671-D5
4170	RODERICK RD	94605	671-D5
4200	ABERFOIL AV	94605	671-D5
DOHR ST			**BERK**
2700	WARD ST	94702	629-F3
2800	OREGON ST	94702	629-F4
2900	RUSSELL ST	94702	629-F4
2900	RUSSELL ST	94702	629-F4
3000	ASHBY AV	94702	629-F4
3000	ASHBY AV	94702	629-F4
3100	PRINCE ST	94702	629-F4
DOLORES AV			**OAK**
4600	EL CENTRO AV	94602	650-D3
	SAN LUIS AV	94602	650-D3
	PARK BLVD	94602	650-D3

PRIMARY STREET Address	Cross Street	ZIP	CITY Pg-Grid
DOMINGO AV			**BERK**
1	TUNNEL RD	94705	630-A3
1	ASHBY AV	94705	630-A3
1	RUSSELL ST	94705	630-A3
30	EL CAMINO REAL	94705	630-A4
50	HAZEL RD	94705	630-A4
70	OAKVALE AV	94705	630-A4
100	THE PLAZA DR	94705	630-A4
DONCASTER PL			**OAK**
6100	THORNHILL DR	94611	630-E6
DONNA WY			**OAK**
1	ELYSIAN FIELDS DR	94605	671-D3
20	THUNDERBIRD CT	94605	671-D3
100	INVERNESS CT	94605	671-D3
100	SILVERADO CT	94605	671-D3
200	ELYSIAN FIELDS DR	94605	671-D3
DOOLITTLE DR			**ALA**
	HARBOR BAY PKWY	94502	670-B5
	ISLAND DR	94502	670-B5
DOOLITTLE DR			**OAK**
3000	EDEN RD	94603	690-G2
500	AIRPORT DR	94621	690-E1
7280	HEGENBERGER RD	94621	690-E1
7510	DE HAVILLAND ST	94621	670-D7
7510	SWAN WY	94621	670-D7
7770	WRIGHT ST	94621	670-D6
7820	LANGLEY ST	94621	670-D6
7850	CONVAIR ST	94621	670-C5
8500	HARBOR BAY PKWY	94621	670-C5
DOOLITTLE DR			**SLN**
800	EDEN RD	94577	690-G2
DORAN DR			**OAK**
6300	BANNING DR	94611	630-G7
6400	AITKEN DR	94611	630-G7
6400	WESTOVER DR	94611	630-G7
DORIS CT			**ALA**
1000	WASHINGTON ST	94501	670-A3
DORIS PL			**OAK**
1	DOROTHY PL	94705	630-B4
DORISA AV			**OAK**
3600	BURGOS AV	94605	671-B4
3650	CALAFIA AV	94605	671-B4
DORMIDERA AV			**PDMT**
1	MOUNTAIN AV	94611	650-C1
60	SHARON AV	94611	650-C1
100	PACIFIC AV	94611	650-C1
DOROTHY PL			**OAK**
1	GRAND VIEW DR	94705	630-B4
50	DORIS PL	94705	630-B4
DOUGLAS AV			**OAK**
400	KNIGHT ST	94603	670-G7
400	KERWIN AV	94603	670-G7
500	HALE AV	94603	670-G7
560	CARY AV	94603	670-H6
700	EDES AV	94603	670-H6
800	PEARMAIN ST	94603	670-H6
DOVER ST			**BERK**
6250	62ND ST	94703	629-G5
6300	63RD ST	94703	629-G5
6320	63RD ST	94703	629-G5
6400	ALCATRAZ AV	94703	629-G5
DOVER ST			**OAK**
5200	52ND ST	94609	629-H6
5200	52ND ST	94609	629-G6
5300	53RD ST	94609	629-G6
5400	54TH ST	94609	629-G6
5500	55TH ST	94609	629-G6
5600	56TH ST	94609	629-G6
5650	AILEEN ST	94609	629-G5
5700	57TH ST	94609	629-G5
5750	58TH ST	94609	629-G5
5800	58TH ST	94609	629-G5
5830	59TH ST	94609	629-G5
5900	59TH ST	94609	629-G5
6000	60TH ST	94609	629-G5
	61ST ST	94609	629-G5
6100	61ST ST	94609	629-G5
6130	POIRIER ST	94609	629-G5
6200	62ND ST	94609	629-G5
6250	62ND ST	94609	629-G5
	FAIRVIEW ST	94609	629-G4
6550	FAIRVIEW ST	94609	629-G4
DOW CT			**ALA**
	ROSEFIELD LP	94501	649-F7
DOWITCHER CT			**ALA**
	BRUZZONE DR	94501	649-F7
	TERN LN	94501	649-F7
DOWLING CT			**OAK**
8000	80TH AV	94605	670-J3
8100	81ST AV	94605	670-J3
8200	82ND AV	94605	670-J3
DOWLING PL			**BERK**
2400	TELEGRAPH AV	94705	629-H4
2500	DANA ST	94705	629-H4
DOWLING ST			**OAK**
8200	82ND AV	94605	670-J3
8300	83RD AV	94605	670-J3
8690	84TH AV	94605	670-J3
8400	84TH AV	94605	670-J3
8500	85TH AV	94605	670-J3
8600	86TH AV	94605	670-J3
8640	AUSEON AV	94605	670-J3
8700	87TH AV	94605	670-J3
8700	87TH AV	94605	670-J4
8800	88TH AV	94605	670-J4
8900	89TH AV	94605	670-J4
9000	90TH AV	94605	670-J4
DOWNEY PL			**OAK**
1	INDIAN RD	94610	650-C3
1	SUNNYHILLS RD	94610	650-C3
DOYLE ST			**EMVL**
4400	45TH ST	94608	629-F7
4500	47TH ST	94608	629-F7
5500	55TH ST	94608	629-E6
5700	STANFORD AV	94608	629-E6
5800	POWELL ST	94608	629-E6
5900	59TH ST	94608	629-E5
6000	61ST ST	94608	629-E5
6090	62ND ST	94608	629-E5
6230	63RD ST	94608	629-E5
6370	64TH ST	94608	629-E5
6500	OCEAN AV	94608	629-E5
DRACENA AV			**PDMT**
100	BLAIR AV	94611	650-B1
200	PARK WY	94611	650-B1
DRAKE DR			**OAK**
1800	SNAKE RD	94611	630-E7
1810	KROHN LN	94611	630-E7
1830	DRAKE PL	94611	630-E7
1900	AZTEC WY	94611	630-E7
1930	TAMPA AV	94611	630-E7
2010	ASILOMAR DR	94611	650-E1
2000	DRAKE LN	94611	650-E1
2050	ZINN DR	94611	650-E1
2050	ZINN	94611	650-E1
2100	MAGELLAN DR	94611	650-E1
2100	RINCON DR	94611	650-E1
DRAKE LN			**OAK**
	DRAKE DR	94611	650-E1

PRIMARY STREET Address	Cross Street	ZIP	CITY Pg-Grid
DRAKE PL			**OAK**
1	DRAKE DR	94611	630-E7
DRESDEN BAY			**ALA**
300	STONE HARBOR	94502	670-A5
300	VICTORIA BAY	94502	670-A5
DREYER PL			**OAK**
5600	SKYLINE BLVD	94619	651-A5
DRIFTWOOD LN			**ALA**
350	BRIDGE VIEW ISL	94501	670-A4
400	OTIS DR	94501	670-A4
DRUM			**ALA**
4000	CIMARRON ST	94501	649-E6
DRURY CT			**OAK**
100	CHANCELLOR PL	94705	630-C3
100	STRATHMOOR DR	94705	630-C3
100	DRURY RD	94705	630-C3
DRURY LN			**OAK**
1	DRURY RD	94705	630-B3
DRURY RD			**OAK**
1000	AMITO AV	94705	630-B3
1110	DARTMOUTH DR	94705	630-B3
1110	BESITO AV	94705	630-B3
1200	DRURY LN	94705	630-B3
1300	DAWN ST	94705	630-C3
1400	CHANCELLOR PL	94705	630-C3
1400	STRATHMOOR DR	94705	630-C3
1400	DRURY CT	94705	630-C3
DUARTE CT			**ALA**
1	RATTO RD	94502	669-J7
DUBLIN AV			**OAK**
5000	MOUNTAIN BLVD	94602	650-F3
5100	ARGYLE ST	94602	650-F3
DUBLIN WY			**ALA**
600	TRALEE LN	94502	669-H5
630	ULSTER PL	94502	669-J5
650	THURLES PL	94502	669-J5
670	WEXFORD PL	94502	669-J5
700	KOFMAN PKWY	94502	669-J5
700	LIMERICK LN	94502	669-J5
DUDLEY AV			**PDMT**
1	BLAIR AV	94611	650-C1
1	BLAIR PL	94611	650-C1
100	DUDLEY CT	94611	650-C1
130	LITTLEWOOD DR	94611	650-C1
200	MOUNTAIN AV	94611	650-C1
DUDLEY CT			**PDMT**
1	DUDLEY AV	94611	650-C1
DULWICH RD			**OAK**
10	HERMOSA AV	94618	630-B6
10	JACOBUS AV	94618	630-B6
100	HARBORD DR	94618	630-B6
DUNCAN WY			**OAK**
180	FLORENCE TER	94611	630-D6
100	GLENWOOD GLADE	94611	630-D6
1	LEO WY	94611	630-C6
100	BROADWAY TER	94611	630-C6
DUNKIRK AV			**OAK**
4800	COTTER ST	94605	671-E4
4600	GLEN ARTNEY CT	94605	671-E4
4800	CALODEN ST	94605	671-E4
4800	GOLF LINKS RD	94605	671-E4
DUNSMUIR AV			**OAK**
4200	VICTOR AV	94619	650-G5
4240	MONTEREY BLVD	94619	650-G5
4300	SELKIRK ST	94619	650-G5
DURANT AV			**BERK**
2000	MILVIA ST	94704	629-G2
2110	SHATTUCK AV	94704	629-H2
2190	FULTON ST	94704	629-H2
2290	ELLSWORTH ST	94704	629-H2
2390	DANA ST	94704	629-H2
2490	TELEGRAPH AV	94704	629-J2
2590	BOWDITCH ST	94704	629-J2
2700	COLLEGE AV	94704	629-J2
2700	COLLEGE AV	94704	629-J2
2800	PIEDMONT AV	94704	629-J2
DURANT AV			**OAK**
200	E 14TH ST	94603	671-A6
1800	BREED AV	94603	671-A6
2000	BEVERLY AV	94603	671-A6
2100	SUNNYSIDE ST	94603	671-A6
2200	BANCROFT AV	94603	671-A6
2300	VOLTAIRE AV	94603	671-B6
2500	MYERS ST	94603	671-B6
2600	MACARTHUR BLVD	94605	671-B6
2700	MCINTYRE ST	94605	671-B6
2800	JULIUS ST	94605	671-B6
2900	FOOTHILL BLVD	94605	671-B6
DURANT AV			**SLN**
200	E 14TH ST	94577	671-A6
1800	BREED AV	94577	671-A6
2000	BEVERLY AV	94577	671-A6
2100	SUNNYSIDE ST	94577	671-A6
2200	BANCROFT AV	94577	671-A6
2300	VOLTAIRE AV	94577	671-B6
2500	MYERS ST	94577	671-B6
2600	MACARTHUR BLVD	94577	671-B6
2700	MCINTYRE ST	94577	671-B6
2800	JULIUS ST	94577	671-B6
2900	FOOTHILL BLVD	94577	671-B6
DUTCHCAP LN			**ALA**
3400	JOST LN	94502	670-A7
3450	SAGE LN	94502	670-A7
3500	MELROSE AV	94502	670-A7
DUTTON AV			**OAK**
	MACARTHUR BLVD	94605	671-C7
1550	FOOTHILL WY	94605	671-C7
DUTTON AV			**SLN**
	MACARTHUR BLVD	94605	671-C7
1550	FOOTHILL WY	94605	671-C7
DWIGHT CRES			**BERK**
800	6TH ST	94804	629-D3
900	7TH ST	94804	629-D3
900	DWIGHT WY	94804	629-D3
DWIGHT PL			**OAK**
500	DWIGHT WY	94704	630-A2
DWIGHT WY			**BERK**
750	4TH ST	94804	629-D3
800	5TH ST	94804	629-D3
850	6TH ST	94804	629-E3
900	7TH ST	94804	629-E3
900	DWIGHT CRES	94804	629-E3
950	8TH ST	94804	629-E3
1000	9TH ST	94804	629-E3
1050	10TH ST	94804	629-E3
1100	SAN PABLO AV	94702	629-E3
1140	BYRON ST	94702	629-E3
1180	CURTIS ST	94702	629-E3
1200	MATHEWS ST	94702	629-E3
1230	BROWNING ST	94702	629-E3
1270	BONAR ST	94702	629-E3
1290	MABEL ST	94702	629-F3
1330	WEST ST	94702	629-F3
1370	VALLEY ST	94702	629-F3
1400	ACTON ST	94702	629-F3
1400	ACTON ST	94702	629-F3
1450	EDWARDS ST	94702	629-F3
1500	SACRAMENTO ST	94703	629-F3
1540	SPAULDING AV	94703	629-F3
1600	CALIFORNIA ST	94703	629-F3

PRIMARY STREET Address	Cross Street	ZIP	CITY Pg-Grid
1640	JEFFERSON AV	94703	629-F3
	MCGEE AV	94703	629-F3
1700	MCGEE AV	94703	629-G3
1750	ROOSEVELT AV	94703	629-G3
1800	GRANT ST	94703	629-G3
1850	MCKINLEY AV	94703	629-G3
1900	MARTIN LUTHER KING JR WY	94704	629-G3
2050	MILVIA ST	94704	629-G2
2100	SHATTUCK AV	94704	629-H2
2200	FULTON ST	94704	629-H2
2300	ELLSWORTH ST	94704	629-H2
2400	DANA ST	94704	629-H2
2500	TELEGRAPH AV	94704	629-J2
2530	REGENT ST	94704	629-J2
2580	HILLEGASS AV	94704	629-J2
2600	BOWDITCH ST	94704	629-J2
2650	BENVENUE AV	94704	629-J2
2700	COLLEGE AV	94704	629-J2
2750	ETNA ST	94704	629-J2
2800	PIEDMONT AV	94704	629-J2
2820	PIEDMONT CRES	94704	629-J2
2820	PIEDMONT AV	94704	629-J2
	WARRING ST	94704	629-J2
2850	WARRING ST	94704	629-J2
	PROSPECT ST	94704	629-J2
2900	HILLSIDE AV	94704	630-A2
2910	SPORTS LN	94704	630-A2
2930	SOUTHWEST PL	94704	630-A2
2960	FERNWALD RD	94704	630-A2
DWIGHT WY			**OAK**
3200	PANORAMIC WY	94704	630-A2
3500	DWIGHT PL	94704	630-A2
3600	PANORAMIC WY	94704	630-A2
DWINELLE CT			**ALA**
1	SILVA LN	94502	670-A7

E

PRIMARY STREET Address	Cross Street	ZIP	CITY Pg-Grid
E ST			**OAK**
8300	83RD AV	94621	670-G4
8400	84TH AV	94621	670-G4
8500	85TH AV	94621	670-G4
8600	86TH AV	94621	670-G4
8700	87TH AV	94621	670-G5
8780	88TH AV	94621	670-G5
8800	88TH AV	94621	670-G5
8900	89TH AV	94621	670-H5
9000	90TH AV	94603	670-H5
9100	91ST AV	94603	670-H5
9200	92ND AV	94603	670-H5
9200	92ND AV	94603	670-H5
9400	94TH AV	94603	670-H5
9500	ELMHURST AV	94603	670-H5
9800	98TH AV	94603	670-H5
9800	98TH AV	94603	670-H6
10000	100TH AV	94603	670-H6
10100	101ST AV	94603	670-H6
10200	102ND AV	94603	670-H6
10300	103RD AV	94603	670-H6
10400	104TH AV	94603	670-H6
10500	105TH AV	94603	670-H6
10600	106TH AV	94603	670-J6
10700	107TH AV	94603	670-J6
EAGLE AV			**ALA**
630	WEBSTER ST	94501	649-F7
720	CONSTITUTION WY	94501	649-F7
730	THAU WY	94501	649-G7
800	8TH ST	94501	649-G7
900	WOOD ST	94501	649-G7
1000	CHAPIN ST	94501	649-G7
1100	SAINT CHARLES ST	94501	649-G7
1200	BAY ST	94501	649-H7
1300	ATLANTIC AV	94501	649-H7
1300	SHERMAN ST	94501	649-H7
1600	HIBBARD ST	94501	669-J1
	GRAND ST	94501	669-J1
1750	MINTURN ST	94501	669-J1
1800	UNION ST	94501	669-J1
1850	SCHILLER ST	94501	669-J1
1900	LAFAYETTE ST	94501	669-J1
2000	CHESTNUT ST	94501	669-J1
2050	STANFORD ST	94501	669-J1
2100	WILLOW ST	94501	669-J1
2200	MULBERRY ST	94501	669-J1
2300	OAK ST	94501	670-A2
2400	PARK ST	94501	670-A2
2500	EVERETT ST	94501	670-B2
2600	TILDEN WY	94501	670-B2
2600	BROADWAY	94501	670-B2
2600	TILDEN WY	94501	670-B2
2650	TREGLOAN CT	94501	670-B2
2700	PEARL ST	94501	670-B2
EAGLE RD			**ALA**
	HUDSON DR	94501	649-J7
	NORTH STAR RD	94501	649-J7
	WAKEFIELD DR	94501	649-J7
EARHART RD			**OAK**
7200	AIRPORT DR	94621	690-E1
7970	DE HAVILLAND ST	94621	670-D7
8340	COOKE ST	94621	670-D7
8500	WRIGHT ST	94621	670-D7
8660	CONVAIR ST	94621	670-D6
8790	FAIRCHILD ST	94621	670-D6
8890	BENSON ST	94621	670-D6
8960	RYAN ST	94621	670-C6
9120	GRUMMAN ST	94621	670-C6
EARL ST			**OAK**
8000	HOLMES AV	94605	671-A2
7900	SHONE AV	94605	671-A2
8000	KELLER AV	94605	671-A2
EAST CIR			**OAK**
1	ARROWHEAD DR	94611	630-G6
EAST CT			**OAK**
	105TH AV	94603	670-H7
EAST SHORE DR			**ALA**
1300	ENCINAL AV	94501	670-B4
1350	MEYERS AV	94501	670-B4
1400	CENTRAL AV	94501	670-C4
1450	CONSTANCE CIR	94501	670-C3
1500	LIBERTY AV	94501	670-C3
1600	FERNSIDE BLVD	94501	670-C3
1600	GARFIELD AV	94501	670-C3
EASTER LN			**ALA**
1000	MECARTNEY RD	94502	670-A6
1020	BALI LN	94502	670-A6
1100	GILBERT LN	94502	670-A6
EASTER WY			**BERK**
	REGAL RD	94708	609-H6
	EUCLID AV	94708	609-H6
	SPRUCE ST	94708	609-H6
	CRAGMONT AV	94708	609-H6
	EUCLID AV	94708	609-H6
EASTLAKE AV			**OAK**
4180	KIWANIS ST	94602	650-F5
4200	HERRIER ST	94602	650-F5
EASTLAWN ST			**OAK**
5800	58TH AV	94621	670-E2
5900	SEMINARY AV	94621	670-E2
6000	60TH AV	94621	670-F3
6100	61ST AV	94621	670-F3

PRIMARY STREET Address	Cross Street	ZIP	CITY Pg-Grid
EASTLAWN ST			**OAK**
6200	62ND AV	94621	670-F3
6300	63RD AV	94621	670-F3
5800	69TH AV	94621	670-F3
6500	66TH AV	94621	670-F3
6600	65TH AV	94621	670-F3
EASTMAN AV			**OAK**
2600	BROOKDALE AV	94619	650-E7
2700	WALNUT ST	94619	650-E7
2700	ALLENDALE AV	94619	650-E6
2930	PENNIMAN AV	94619	650-E6
3090	CULVER ST	94619	650-F6
3180	SUTER ST	94619	650-F6
3200	SUTER ST	94619	650-F6
EASTSHORE BLVD			**BERK**
1420	GILMAN ST	94710	609-C7
1420	EASTSHORE FRONTAGE RD	94710	609-C7
1560	PAGE ST	94804	629-C1
1610	JONES ST	94804	629-C1
1670	CEDAR ST	94804	629-C1
1750	VIRGINIA ST	94804	629-C2
1900	HEARST AV	94804	629-C2
EASTSHORE FRONTAGE RD			**ALB**
1200	HARRISON ST	94710	609-C6
EASTSHORE FRONTAGE RD			**BERK**
1200	HARRISON ST	94710	609-C7
1300	EASTSHORE BLVD	94710	609-C7
1300	GILMAN ST	94710	609-C7
EASTWOOD CT			**OAK**
100	SHEPHERD CANYON RD	94611	630-G7
EC REEMS CT			**OAK**
2600	MACARTHUR BLVD	94605	671-A3
ECHO AV			**OAK**
1	GLEN AV	94611	649-J1
100	PIEDMONT AV	94611	649-J1
100	ROSE AV	94611	650-A1
150	ROSE AV	94611	650-A1
200	ROSE AV	94611	650-A1
150	LINDA AV	94611	649-J1
ECHO AV			**PDMT**
150	LINDA AV	94611	649-J1
150	ROSE AV	94611	650-A1
200	ROSE AV	94611	650-A1
ECHO LN			**PDMT**
1	MORAGA AV	94618	630-C7
100	MAXWELTON RD	94618	630-C7
ECLIPSE CT			**ALA**
1	INDEPENDENCE DR	94501	649-G7
EDEN LN			**OAK**
	35TH AV	94601	650-D7
EDEN RD			**OAK**
	DOOLITTLE DR	94603	690-F2
EDEN RD			**SLN**
	DOOLITTLE DR	94577	690-F2
EDENVALE PL			**OAK**
3920	SUNNYMERE AV	94605	650-J7
3900	SUNNYMERE AV	94605	650-J7
4000	HILLMONT DR	94605	670-J1
EDES AV			**OAK**
5800	HEGENBERGER RD	94621	670-F5
5800	COLISEUM WY	94621	670-F5
8200	ENTERPRISE WY	94621	670-F5
10320	WORTH ST	94603	670-F6
10320	WORTH ST	94621	670-F6
9000	85TH AV	94621	670-F6
9000	85TH AV	94603	670-F6
9200	PHELPS ST	94621	670-G6
9200	PHELPS ST	94603	670-G6
9360	JONES AV	94621	670-G6
9360	JONES AV	94603	670-G6
9820	CLARA ST	94621	670-G6
9400	CLARA ST	94603	670-G6
9500	S ELMHURST AV	94603	670-G6
9570	MADDUX DR	94603	670-G6
9600	TYLER ST	94603	670-G6
9700	NEVADA ST	94603	670-G6
9800	98TH AV	94603	670-G6
10100	DOUGLAS AV	94603	670-H6
10200	HALE AV	94603	670-H7
10330	CARY AV	94603	670-H7
10500	105TH AV	94603	670-H7
10900	ROBLEDO DR	94603	670-H7
10900	BERGEDO DR	94603	670-H7
EDGE DR			**OAK**
4300	HOOVER AV	94602	650-E3
EDGEMONT WY			**OAK**
100	MALCOLM AV	94605	671-C5
EDGEMOOR PL			**OAK**
3900	HILLMONT DR	94605	670-J1
4000	SUNNYMERE AV	94605	670-J1
EDGERLY ST			**OAK**
5500	55TH AV	94621	670-F2
5700	57TH AV	94621	670-F2
EDGEWATER DR			**OAK**
7300	HASSLER WY	94621	670-E5
7700	PARDEE LN	94621	670-E5
7800	ROLAND WY	94621	670-E6
8300	OAKPORT ST	94621	670-E6
8400	PENDLETON WY	94621	670-F6
8600	HEGENBERGER RD	94621	670-F6
EDGEWOOD AV			**OAK**
4300	WELLINGTON ST	94602	650-C3
4500	EVERETT AV	94602	650-D3
4520	GLENDORA AV	94602	650-D3
4580	EL CENTRO AV	94602	650-D3
4800	HOLLYWOOD AV	94602	650-D3
EDISON CT			**ALA**
2600	PEARL ST	94501	670-B2
EDITH ST			**BERK**
1400	ROSE ST	94703	609-F7
	VINE ST	94703	609-F7
1550	JAYNES ST	94703	609-F7
1600	CEDAR ST	94703	629-F1
1650	LINCOLN ST	94703	629-F1
1700	VIRGINIA ST	94703	629-F1
EDWARD WHITE WY			**OAK**
	NEIL ARMSTRONG WY	94621	690-E2
EDWARDS AV			**OAK**
	MOUNTAIN BLVD	94605	671-A1
3950	SUNNYMERE AV	94605	670-J1
3900	GREENLY DR	94605	670-J1
3950	SUNKIST DR	94605	670-J1
EDWARDS ST			**BERK**
2300	BANCROFT WY	94702	629-F2
2400	CHANNING WY	94702	629-F3
2500	DWIGHT WY	94702	629-F3
EGRET CT			**ALA**
	BRUZZONE DR	94501	649-F7
	KILLDEER CT	94501	649-F7
EL CAMILLE AV			**OAK**
5300	55TH AV	94619	670-F1
5500	KINGSLAND AV	94619	670-F1
EL CAMINITO			**OAK**
2500	MOUNTAIN BLVD	94611	650-E2
2700	CAMINO LENADA	94611	650-E2
EL CAMINO REAL			**BERK**
1	DOMINGO AV	94705	630-A4
150	THE UPLANDS	94705	630-A4
EL CARMELLO CIR			**OAK**
100	MONTEREY BLVD	94619	650-G4
EL CENTRO AV			**OAK**
4700	HOLLYWOOD AV	94602	650-D3
4700	GLENDOME CIR	94602	650-D3
4640	ELSINORE AV	94602	650-D3
4600	GLENDOME CIR	94602	650-C3
1100	GLENDORA AV	94602	650-D3
1160	SAN SEBASTIAN	94602	650-D3
1200	EDGEWOOD AV	94602	650-D3
1300	PARK BLVD	94602	650-D3
1320	DOLORES AV	94602	650-D3
1330	BENEVIDES AV	94602	650-D3
1400	HANLY RD	94602	650-D3
1400	OAKMORE PL	94602	650-D3
EL CERRITO AV			**PDMT**
100	RICARDO AV	94611	650-A1
200	BLAIR AV	94611	650-B1
300	OAKLAND AV	94611	650-B1
400	MAGNOLIA AV	94611	650-B1
400	MAGNOLIA AV	94611	650-B1
400	MAGNOLIA AV	94610	650-B1
470	JEROME AV	94611	650-B1
EL DORADO AV			**BERK**
1900	MARTIN LUTHER KING JR WY	94707	609-G6
1950	LASSEN ST	94707	609-G6
2000	SUTTER ST	94707	609-G6
EL DORADO AV			**OAK**
500	BAYO VISTA AV	94611	649-J1
700	FAIRMOUNT AV	94611	649-J1
EL EMBARCADERO			**OAK**
500	GRAND AV	94610	649-J3
600	LAKESHORE AV	94610	649-J3
500	GRAND AV	94610	649-J3
600	LAKESHORE AV	94610	649-J3
EL MONTE AV			**OAK**
2980	ASTER AV	94605	671-A3
2950	OUTLOOK AV	94605	671-A3
2900	NEY AV	94605	671-A3
2950	GOLF LINKS RD	94605	671-A3
EL PASEO			**ALA**
3100	VERDEMAR DR	94502	669-J7
3100	LA CAMPANIA	94502	669-J7
3200	CAMINO DEL VALLE	94502	669-J7
EL PASEO DR			**OAK**
400	CAPISTRANO DR	94603	670-H7
560	ESTEPA DR	94603	670-H7
590	TOPANGA DR	94603	670-H7
700	TOPANGA DR	94603	670-H7
700	CAPISTRANO DR	94603	670-H7
EL PATIO			**OAK**
1	MOUNTAIN BLVD	94611	650-E2
EL PORTAL			**ALA**
3100	VERDEMAR DR	94502	670-A6
3200	CAMINO DEL VALLE	94502	670-A6
EL PORTAL CT			**BERK**
1	LA LOMA AV	94708	609-J7
EL SERENO			**ALA**
3100	VERDEMAR DR	94502	669-J6
3200	CAMINO DEL VALLE	94502	669-J6
EL VERANO ST			**OAK**
9800	HUNTER AV	94603	670-G7
9860	ISLETON AV	94603	670-G7
9930	KERWIN AV	94603	670-G7
10000	LOUVAINE AV	94603	670-G7
ELBERT ST			**OAK**
1000	EVERETT AV	94602	650-C3
ELDERBERRY DR			**OAK**
6200	CHELTON DR	94611	630-G7
6250	GIRVIN DR	94611	630-G7
ELDRIDGE AV			**OAK**
1	DARIEN AV	94603	670-G7
200	DARIEN AV	94603	670-G7
ELINORA AV			**OAK**
4400	CARSON ST	94619	650-G5
4500	FIELDBROOK RD	94619	650-G5
4600	ALISO AV	94619	650-G5
ELIZABETH ST			**OAK**
5700	57TH AV	94605	670-F2
5700	57TH AV	94621	670-F2
5900	SEMINARY AV	94605	670-F2
5900	SEMINARY AV	94621	670-F2
ELLEN ST			**OAK**
4500	45TH AV	94601	670-E1
4600	47TH AV	94601	670-E1
ELLIOT ST			**OAK**
3200	BAYVIEW AV	94610	650-B4
3300	E 33RD ST	94610	650-B4
3400	E 34TH ST	94610	650-B4
ELLIS CT			**ALA**
	ROSEFIELD LP	94501	649-F7
ELLIS ST			**BERK**
2900	RUSSELL ST	94703	629-G4
3000	ASHBY AV	94703	629-G4
3100	PRINCE ST	94703	629-G4
3150	WOOLSEY ST	94703	629-G4
3200	FAIRVIEW ST	94703	629-G4
3250	HARMON ST	94703	629-G5
3300	ALCATRAZ AV	94703	629-G5
ELLITA AV			**OAK**
400	GRAND AV	94610	649-J3
500	BELLEVUE AV	94610	649-J3
ELLSWORTH ST			**BERK**
2300	BANCROFT WY	94704	629-H2
2350	DURANT AV	94704	629-H2
2400	CHANNING WY	94704	629-H2
2450	HASTE ST	94704	629-H2
2500	DWIGHT WY	94704	629-H2
2550	BLAKE ST	94704	629-H3
2600	PARKER ST	94704	629-H3
2650	CARLETON ST	94704	629-H3
2700	DERBY ST	94705	629-H3
2730	WARD ST	94705	629-H3
2800	STUART ST	94705	629-H3
2820	OREGON ST	94705	629-H3
2900	RUSSELL ST	94705	629-H3
2910	HOWE ST	94705	629-H4
3000	ASHBY AV	94705	629-H4
ELM ST			**ALA**
1800	BUENA VISTA AV	94501	670-A1
1900	CLEMENT AV	94501	670-A1
ELM ST			**OAK**
3100	34TH ST	94609	649-H1
3400	HAWTHORNE AV	94609	649-H1
ELMAR AV			**OAK**
9800	98TH AV	94603	671-A5
9850	WARNER AV	94603	671-A5
9900	99TH AV	94603	671-A5
ELMHURST AV			**OAK**
1000	E ST	94603	670-H5
1100	D ST	94603	670-H5
1150	C ST	94603	670-H5
1200	B ST	94603	670-H5
S ELMHURST AV			**OAK**
600	EDES AV	94603	670-G6
670	OSCAR AV	94603	670-G6
740	WALTER AV	94603	670-G6
800	RAILROAD AV	94603	670-G6
ELMVIEW DR			**OAK**
9700	MACARTHUR BLVD	94603	671-A4
9800	98TH AV	94603	671-A4
ELMWOOD AV			**BERK**
2700	ASHBY AV	94705	629-J4
2750	ASHBY PL	94705	629-J4
2800	PIEDMONT AV	94705	629-J4
ELMWOOD AV			**OAK**
3000	DERBY AV	94601	670-B1
3140	LANCASTER ST	94601	670-B1
3240	FRUITVALE AV	94601	670-C1
3430	34TH AV	94601	670-C1
ELMWOOD CT			**BERK**
2900	ASHBY AV	94705	630-A3
ELROD AV			**OAK**
200	FLORENCE AV	94618	630-B6
ELSINORE AV			**OAK**
1000	EL CENTRO AV	94602	650-D3
1100	SAN SEBASTIAN	94602	650-D3
ELSTON AV			**OAK**
3700	EXCELSIOR AV	94602	650-C4
3750	ELSTON CT	94602	650-C4
3800	E 38TH ST	94602	650-C4
3800	E 38TH ST	94602	650-C4
4100	HAMPEL ST	94602	650-C4
ELSTON CT			**OAK**
50	ELSTON AV	94602	650-C4
ELVERTON DR			**OAK**
6700	SKYLINE BLVD	94611	630-E5
6760	THORNDALE DR	94611	630-F5
6850	ORMINDALE CT	94611	630-F5
7100	SKYLINE BLVD	94611	630-F5
ELVESSA ST			**OAK**
11200	TURNER AV	94605	671-E5
11030	ZIEGLER AV	94605	671-D5
11000	KIRKLAND CT	94605	671-D4
10800	ABERFOIL AV	94605	671-D4
10700	MALCOLM AV	94605	671-D4
ELWOOD AV			**OAK**
300	JEAN ST	94610	649-J2
300	SANTA CLARA AV	94610	649-J2
380	MIRA VISTA AV	94610	649-J2
380	VALLE VISTA AV	94610	650-A2
450	VALLE VISTA AV	94610	650-A2
460	LAKE PKWY	94610	650-A2
500	GRAND AV	94610	650-A2
ELYSIAN FIELDS DR			**OAK**
1	GOLF LINKS RD	94605	671-C3
40	SIGOURNEY AV	94605	671-C3
110	ORINDA VISTA DR	94605	671-C3
130	ELYSIAN PL	94605	671-D3
220	DONNA WY	94605	671-D3
240	ROYAL OAK RD	94605	671-D3
270	DONNA WY	94605	671-D3
390	RIVIERA CT	94605	671-D3
410	PEBBLE BEACH DR	94605	671-D3
430	ENGLEWOOD DR	94605	671-D3
520	TAMARISK DR	94605	671-D2
560	HERITAGE	94605	671-D2
560	IRONWOOD	94605	671-D2
570	SHADOW MOUNTAIN	94605	671-D2
590	THOUSAND OAKS	94605	671-D2
600	TURTLE CREEK	94605	671-D2
630	MISSION HILLS	94605	671-D2
630	MOUNTAIN VALLEY	94605	671-D2
660	CHIMNEY ROCK	94605	671-D2
700	GRAEAGLE	94605	671-D2
700	KELLER AV	94605	671-D2
ELYSIAN PL			**OAK**
1	ELYSIAN FIELDS DR	94605	671-C3
EMBARCADERO			**OAK**
260	EMBARCADERO W	94607	649-G5
140	ALICE ST	94607	649-G5
1	OAK ST	94607	649-G5
300	5TH AV	94606	649-H6
330	5TH AV	94606	649-H6
400	6TH AV	94606	649-H6
600	8TH AV	94606	649-H6
710	9TH AV	94606	649-J6
1000	10TH AV	94606	649-J6
1690	16TH AV	94606	650-A7
1900	LIVINGSTON ST	94606	650-A7
1850	DENNISON ST	94606	650-A7
1930	DENNISON ST	94606	650-A7
1930	E 7TH ST	94606	670-A1
EMBARCADERO W			**OAK**
300	EMBARCADERO	94607	649-G5
360	WEBSTER ST	94607	649-F5
420	FRANKLIN ST	94607	649-F5
490	BROADWAY	94607	649-F5
550	WASHINGTON ST	94607	649-F5
610	CLAY ST	94607	649-F5
680	JEFFERSON ST	94607	649-F5
740	1ST ST	94607	649-F5
740	MARTIN LUTHER KING JR WY	94607	649-F5
EMERALD ST			**OAK**
4100	41ST ST	94609	629-J7
4170	GARNET ST	94609	629-J7
4200	42ND ST	94609	629-J7
EMERSON ST			**BERK**
2000	ADELINE ST	94703	629-G4
2010	TREMONT ST	94703	629-G4
2100	SHATTUCK AV	94705	629-H4
2200	WHEELER ST	94705	629-H4
EMERSON ST			**OAK**
3600	CHATHAM RD	94610	650-B4
3700	EXCELSIOR AV	94610	650-B4
EMERSON TER			**ALA**
	PARU ST	94501	669-H2
EMERSON WY			**OAK**
3700	PARK BLVD	94610	650-B4
3800	PARK BLVD WY	94610	650-B4
EMERY BAY DR			**EMVL**
1	53RD ST	94608	629-E6
60	TEMESCAL CIR	94608	629-F6
90	TEMESCAL CIR	94608	629-F6
100	53RD ST	94608	629-F6
EMERY ST			**EMVL**
	W MACARTHUR BLVD	94608	629-F7
3800	W MACARTHUR BLVD	94608	629-F7
4020	YERBA BUENA AV	94608	629-F7
4240	40TH ST	94608	629-F7
4500	PARK AV	94608	629-F7
4500	45TH ST	94608	629-F7
EMPIRE RD			**OAK**
9200	CORAL RD	94603	670-F6
9200	FITZPATRICK RD	94603	670-F6
9300	MAKIN RD	94603	670-F6
9400	CAIRO RD	94603	670-F7
9500	SEXTUS RD	94603	670-F7
9600	TUNIS RD	94603	670-F7
9700	WISTAR RD	94603	670-F7
9740	GANNON RD	94603	670-F7
9780	CORAL RD	94603	670-F7
9800	98TH AV	94603	670-F7
9820	KOFORD RD	94603	670-F7
9900	KOFORD RD	94603	670-G7
9940	HESKET RD	94603	670-G7
10000	GIBRALTAR RD	94603	670-G7
ENCINA PL			**BERK**
1	THE PLAZA DR	94705	630-A4
1	OAKVALE AV	94705	630-A4
40	PARKSIDE DR	94705	630-A4
100	THE UPLANDS	94705	630-A4
ENCINA WY			**OAK**
3400	OAK KNOLL BLVD	94605	671-B4
3500	OAK KNOLL BLVD	94605	671-B4
ENCINAL AV			**ALA**
1300	SHERMAN ST	94501	669-H1
1300	CENTRAL AV	94501	669-H1
1400	MORTON ST	94501	669-H1
1460	BENTON ST	94501	669-H1
1600	PARU ST	94501	669-H2
1700	GRAND ST	94501	669-H2
1800	UNION ST	94501	669-H2
1900	LAFAYETTE ST	94501	669-J2
2000	CHESTNUT ST	94501	669-J2
2100	WILLOW ST	94501	669-J2
2200	WALNUT ST	94501	669-J2
2300	OAK ST	94501	670-A2
2400	PARK ST	94501	670-A3
2440	PARK AV W	94501	670-A3
2450	PARK AV	94501	670-A3
2460	PARK AV E	94501	670-A3
2500	REGENT ST	94501	670-A3
2600	BROADWAY	94501	670-A3
2650	PEASE AV	94501	670-A3
2650	WAYNE CT	94501	670-A3
2700	PEARL ST	94501	670-A3
2800	VERSAILLES AV	94501	670-A3
	COLLEGE AV	94501	670-A3
2850	GROVE ST	94501	670-A3
2900	MOUND ST	94501	670-B3
3000	COURT ST	94501	670-B3
3100	FOUNTAIN ST	94501	670-B3
3200	HIGH ST	94501	670-B3
3230	POST ST	94501	670-B3
3300	FERNSIDE BLVD	94501	670-B4
3350	HANSEN AV	94501	670-B4
3400	EAST SHORE DR	94501	670-B4
ENCOUNTER BAY			**ALA**
200	BAYWALK RD	94502	669-J6
ENGLEWOOD DR			**OAK**
10700	ELYSIAN FIELDS DR	94605	671-E3
ENNIS PL			**ALA**
1	JUSTIN CIR	94502	669-J5
1	SEA VIEW PKWY	94502	669-J5
ENNISMORE CT			**ALA**
200	SHEFFIELD RD	94502	670-A5
ENOS AV			**OAK**
3600	MACARTHUR BLVD	94619	650-G7
3630	TULIP AV	94619	650-G6
3800	TOMPKINS AV	94619	650-G6
4000	STEELE ST	94619	650-G6
ENSENADA AV			**BERK**
600	PERALTA AV	94707	609-F5
670	PORTLAND AV	94707	609-F5
740	VINCENTE AV	94707	609-F5
780	SAN LORENZO AV	94707	609-F5
810	CAPISTRANO AV	94707	609-F5
850	TACOMA AV	94707	609-F6
920	SOLANO AV	94707	609-F6
1000	MARIN AV	94707	609-F6
ENSIGN DR			**EMVL**
1	CAPTAIN DR	94608	629-D6
ENTERPRISE			**ALA**
3000	ARKANSAS	94501	649-E6
3100	MOSLEY AV	94501	649-E6
ENTERPRISE WY			**OAK**
8400	85TH AV	94621	670-F5
8500	EDES AV	94621	670-F5
ENTRADA AV			**OAK**
100	ARROYUELO AV	94611	649-J1
1	ARROYUELO AV	94611	649-J1
100	PIEDMONT AV	94611	649-J1
ENTRANCE RD			**ALA**
	BUENA VISTA AV	94501	669-H1
EOLA ST			**BERK**
1700	VIRGINIA ST	94703	629-F1
1750	FRANCISCO ST	94703	629-F1
ERBA PTH			**OAK**
	BROADWAY TER	94618	630-C5
	SHERIDAN RD	94618	630-C5
	CONTRA COSTA RD	94618	630-C5
ERIE ST			**OAK**
800	MANDANA BLVD	94610	650-A3
900	PRINCE ST	94610	650-A3
900	PRINCE ST	94610	650-A2
1000	WELDON AV	94610	650-A2
ESCHER DR			**OAK**
5800	SHEPHERD CANYON RD	94611	650-F1
6400	BAGSHOTTE DR	94611	650-F1
ESPINOSA AV			**OAK**
3100	LAS VEGAS AV	94605	671-B4
3100	FARRELL ST	94605	671-B4
3200	GOLF LINKS RD	94605	671-B4
W ESSEX DR			**ALA**
	SARATOGA ST	94501	649-D6
	TODD ST	94501	649-D6
	PAN AM WY	94501	649-D6
	ALAMEDA RD	94501	649-D6
ESSEX ST			**BERK**
1900	ADELINE ST	94703	629-G4
2000	TREMONT ST	94703	629-G4
2100	SHATTUCK AV	94705	629-H4
2200	WHEELER ST	94705	629-H4
ESSEX ST			**EMVL**
4300	43RD ST	94608	629-F7
4500	45TH ST	94608	629-F7
ESSEX ST			**OAK**
6400	ALCATRAZ AV	94608	629-F5
ESTATES DR			**OAK**
5200	FLORENCE AV	94618	630-D7
5200	PROCTOR AV	94618	630-D7
5800	MORAGA AV	94611	630-D7
5840	JOHNSTON DR	94611	630-D7
5990	BULLARD DR	94611	630-D7
5990	BULLARD DR	94611	630-D7
6100	MCANDREW DR	94611	650-D1
6300	BULLARD DR	94611	650-D1
6400	LA SALLE AV	94611	650-D1
6400	LA SALLE AV	94611	650-D1
6500	DAWES ST	94611	650-D1
6500	PERSHING DR	94611	650-D1
6700	PERSHING DR	94611	650-D1
6700	DAWES ST	94611	650-D1
6800	LIGGETT DR	94611	650-E2
6840	SIMS DR	94611	650-E2
6900	SOMERSET RD	94611	650-E2
ESTATES DR			**PDMT**
100	PARK BLVD	94611	650-D2
120	SANDRINGHAM RD	94611	650-D2
150	WYNGAARD AV	94611	650-D2
170	SELBORNE DR	94611	650-D2
180	INVERLEITH TER	94611	650-D2
200	HAMPTON RD	94611	650-D2
300	SOMERSET RD	94611	650-D2
ESTEPA DR			**OAK**
10700	EL PASEO DR	94603	670-H7
10760	COLORADOS DR	94603	670-H7
10840	LA PRENDA DR	94603	670-H7
10920	BERGEDO DR	94603	670-H7
11200	CATRON DR	94603	670-H7

PRIMARY STREET Address	Cross Street	ZIP	CITY Pg-Grid
ESTRELLA AV			**PDMT**
1	MORAGA AV	94611	630-B7
1	BONITA AV	94611	630-B7
100	RAMONA AV	94611	630-B7
ETNA ST			**BERK**
2500	DWIGHT WY	94704	629-J2
2600	PARKER ST	94704	629-J3
2700	DERBY ST	94704	629-J3
ETON AV			**BERK**
3100	WOOLSEY ST	94705	629-J4
3200	CLAREMONT AV	94705	629-J4
3200	ETON CT	94705	629-J4
ETON CT			**BERK**
1	CLAREMONT AV	94705	629-J4
1	ETON AV	94705	629-J4
ETTIE ST			**OAK**
2800	28TH ST	94608	649-E1
2900	32ND ST	94608	649-E1
3350	34TH ST	94608	649-E1
ETTRICK ST			**OAK**
10840	MALCOLM AV	94605	671-D4
11020	ABERFOIL AV	94605	671-D5
11200	ZIEGLER AV	94605	671-D5
11300	BEMIS ST	94605	671-E5
11400	TURNER AV	94605	671-E5
EUCALYPTUS PTH			**OAK**
1	THE SHORT CUT	94705	630-A3
1	ALVARADO RD	94705	630-A3
1	ALVARADO PL	94705	630-A3
30	SUNSET TR	94705	630-B3
100	ALVARADO RD	94705	630-B3
EUCALYPTUS RD			**OAK**
1	HILLCREST RD	94618	630-A4
1	HILLCREST RD	94705	630-A4
200	HILLCREST RD	94618	630-A4
200	HILLCREST RD	94705	630-A4
EUCLID AV			**BERK**
500	GRIZZLY PEAK BLVD	94708	609-H4
590	ACACIA AV	94708	609-H5
800	POPLAR ST	94708	609-H5
810	POPLAR ST	94708	609-H5
900	BONNIE LN	94708	609-H5
900	MARIN AV	94708	609-H5
940	REGAL RD	94708	609-H5
990	EASTER WY	94708	609-H6
1000	EASTER WY	94708	609-H6
1050	CRAGMONT AV	94708	609-H6
1050	CRAGMONT AV	94708	609-H6
1070	KEITH AV	94708	609-H6
1110	BRET HARTE WY	94708	609-H6
1230	CRYSTAL WY	94708	609-H6
1300	EUNICE ST	94708	609-H7
1380	BAYVIEW PL	94708	609-H7
1400	CODORNICES RD	94708	609-H7
1440	HAWTHORNE TER	94708	609-H7
1470	HAWTHORNE TER	94708	609-H7
1500	VINE LN	94708	609-H7
1500	VINE ST	94708	609-H7
1540	BUENA VISTA WY	94708	609-H7
1550	HILL CT	94708	609-H7
1600	CEDAR ST	94709	609-H7
1650	HILGARD AV	94709	609-H7
1700	VIRGINIA ST	94709	629-H1
1750	LE CONTE AV	94709	629-H1
1800	RIDGE RD	94709	629-H1
1900	HEARST AV	94709	629-H1
EUCLID AV			**OAK**
200	ADAMS ST	94610	649-J2
270	JAYNE AV	94610	649-J2
300	WARWICK AV	94610	649-J2
350	PALM AV	94610	649-J3
400	VAN BUREN AV	94610	649-J3
420	LAGUNITAS AV	94610	649-J3
450	BURK ST	94610	649-J3
500	GRAND AV	94610	649-J3
EUGENIA CT			**ALA**
3300	ISLAND DR	94502	670-A6
EUNICE ST			**BERK**
2000	MILVIA ST	94709	609-G7
2040	HENRY ST	94707	609-G6
2040	HENRY ST	94709	609-G6
2040	SUTTER ST	94709	609-G6
2100	SHATTUCK AV	94707	609-G6
2100	SHATTUCK AV	94709	609-G6
2150	WALNUT ST	94707	609-G6
2150	WALNUT ST	94709	609-G6
2200	OXFORD ST	94707	609-H6
2200	OXFORD ST	94709	609-H6
2240	SPRUCE ST	94707	609-H6
2240	SPRUCE ST	94709	609-H6
2300	ARCH ST	94708	609-H6
2300	ARCH ST	94709	609-H6
2370	GLEN AV	94708	609-H6
2440	LAUREL ST	94708	609-H6
2500	EUCLID AV	94708	609-H6
EUSTICE AV			**OAK**
1	BROOKSIDE AV	94618	630-B5
1	NOVA PTH	94618	630-B5
50	GOLDEN GATE AV	94618	630-B5
EVANS AV			**OAK**
4300	WELLINGTON ST	94602	650-C3
4500	EVERETT AV	94602	650-C3
EVANS CT			**ALA**
100	ANDERSON RD	94502	669-H6
EVELYN AV			**ALB**
500	BRIGHTON AV	94706	609-D5
600	GARFIELD AV	94706	609-D5
700	PORTLAND AV	94706	609-E5
800	WASHINGTON AV	94706	609-E6
900	SOLANO AV	94706	609-E6
1000	MARIN AV	94706	609-E6
1100	DARTMOUTH ST	94706	609-E6
EVELYN AV			**BERK**
1100	DARTMOUTH ST	94706	609-E7
1300	GILMAN ST	94702	609-E7
1400	SANTA FE AV	94702	609-E7
EVELYN CT			**ALA**
2600	OTIS DR	94501	670-A4
2600	PEARL ST	94501	670-A4
EVELYN CT			**OAK**
2900	FRUITVALE AV	94602	650-D5
2900	FRUITVALE AV	94601	650-D5
EVERETT AV			**OAK**
800	WELLINGTON ST	94602	650-C3
900	LEACH ST	94602	650-C3
1010	GALVIN ST	94602	650-C3
1120	ELBERT ST	94602	650-C3
1200	EDGEWOOD AV	94602	650-D3
1300	PARK BLVD	94602	650-D3
1300	PARK BLVD	94602	650-D3
1400	EVANS AV	94602	650-D3
1500	LA CRESTA AV	94602	650-D3
1500	TOWNSEND AV	94602	650-D3
4000	VISTA ST	94602	650-D4
4200	WELLINGTON ST	94602	650-D4
4400	HAMPEL ST	94602	650-D4
4500	E 38TH ST	94602	650-D4
EVERETT ST			**ALA**
1400	CENTRAL AV	94501	670-A2
1500	SANTA CLARA AV	94501	670-A2
1550	WEBB AV	94501	670-A2
1600	LINCOLN AV	94501	670-A2
1650	NOBLE AV	94501	670-A2
1670	TILDEN WY	94501	670-A2
1700	BUENA VISTA AV	94501	670-A2
1800	EAGLE AV	94501	670-B2
	CLEMENT AV	94501	670-B2
2000	BLANDING AV	94501	670-B2
EVERGREEN AV			**OAK**
6600	MOORE DR	94611	630-G7
6650	AITKEN DR	94611	630-G7
6650	FORESTLAND WY	94611	630-G7
6720	EXETER DR	94611	630-G7
6800	SKYLINE BLVD	94611	630-G7
EVERGREEN PATH LN			**OAK**
30	SLATER LN	94705	630-A3
EVERS AV			**OAK**
1700	LINWOOD AV	94602	650-D4
1800	E 38TH ST	94602	650-D4
EVIREL PL			**OAK**
1	THORNHILL DR	94611	630-F6
EXCELSIOR AV			**OAK**
1120	PARK BLVD	94610	650-B4
1000	ALMA PL	94610	650-B4
1000	GROSVENOR PL	94610	650-B4
1100	PARK BLVD	94610	650-B4
1160	KINGSLEY ST	94610	650-B4
1230	EMERSON ST	94610	650-B4
1300	13TH AV	94602	650-B4
1370	BRUCE ST	94602	650-C4
1410	BEAUMONT AV	94602	650-C4
1470	BRIGHTON AV	94602	650-C4
1510	GLEN PARK RD	94602	650-C4
1550	RANDOLPH AV	94602	650-C4
1600	ARDLEY AV	94602	650-C4
1640	WOODRUFF AV	94602	650-C4
1690	ELSTON AV	94602	650-C4
1730	LINWOOD AV	94602	650-C4
1800	ADELL CT	94602	650-C4
1800	MACARTHUR BLVD	94602	650-C4
EXCELSIOR CT			**OAK**
1	MACARTHUR BLVD	94610	650-A3
EXETER DR			**OAK**
6700	EVERGREEN AV	94611	630-G7
6500	CHELTON DR	94611	630-G7
	CARISBROOK DR	94611	650-G1
F			
F ST			**OAK**
9200	92ND AV	94603	670-H5
FACULTY RD			**OAK**
5300	KAPIOLANI RD	94613	670-G1
5300	PROSPECT HILL RD	94613	670-G1
FAIR AV			**OAK**
4400	CARSON ST	94619	650-G6
4300	HUNTINGTON ST	94619	650-G6
4500	CARSON ST	94619	650-G6
4560	KAPHAN AV	94619	650-G6
4750	CUNNINGHAM ST	94619	650-G6
4850	WILKIE ST	94619	650-G7
5100	DAISY ST	94619	650-G7
FAIR HAVEN RD			**ALA**
300	SHORELINE DR	94501	669-G3
500	SHELL GATE PL	94501	669-G3
FAIR OAKS AV			**ALA**
1000	CAROLINE ST	94501	669-G1
1100	SAINT CHARLES ST	94501	669-G1
FAIRBAIRN ST			**OAK**
4500	HERRIOTT AV	94619	650-F7
4700	KNOWLAND AV	94619	650-F7
FAIRBANKS AV			**OAK**
400	BOULEVARD WY	94610	650-A2
400	WALKER AV	94610	650-A2
500	VERMONT ST	94610	650-A2
540	SCOTT ST	94610	650-A2
540	WARFIELD AV	94610	650-A2
550	WARFIELD AV	94610	650-A2
600	KENMORE AV	94610	650-A2
FAIRCHILD ST			**OAK**
1000	EARHART RD	94621	670-D6
1060	LOCKHEED ST	94621	670-D6
1100	NORTHRUP ST	94621	670-D6
FAIRFAX AV			**OAK**
4500	HIGH ST	94601	650-E7
4580	COURTLAND AV	94601	650-E7
4650	FRANCES ST	94601	650-E7
4800	FERN ST	94601	650-E7
4800	RENWICK ST	94601	650-E7
4830	RENWICK ST	94601	650-E7
4830	POTTER ST	94601	670-E1
5000	MONTICELLO AV	94601	670-E1
5210	YGNACIO AV	94601	670-E1
5300	FOOTHILL BLVD	94601	670-E1
5330	BANCROFT AV	94601	670-E1
5400	PRINCETON ST	94601	670-E2
5430	WENTWORTH AV	94601	670-E2
5500	55TH AV	94601	670-E2
5500	E 17TH ST	94601	670-E2
FAIRHILL CT			**OAK**
5100	CAMPUS DR	94605	671-B1
FAIRLANE DR			**OAK**
6000	MOUNTAIN BLVD	94611	630-C5
6050	SWAINLAND RD	94611	630-C5
6200	SWAINLAND RD	94611	630-D5
6300	SERRAMAR DR	94611	630-D5
6400	SWAINLAND RD	94611	630-D5
FAIRLAWN DR			**BERK**
1	QUEENS RD	94708	609-J6
130	ARCADE AV	94708	609-J6
170	COLUMBIA CIR	94708	609-J7
240	AVENIDA DR	94708	609-J7
270	HARVARD CIR	94708	609-J7
270	SENIOR AV	94708	609-J7
300	OLYMPUS AV	94708	609-J7
FAIRMOUNT AV			**OAK**
200	GARLAND ST	94611	649-H2
1	29TH ST	94611	649-H2
200	HARRISON ST	94611	649-H2
660	MONTE VISTA AV	94611	649-J1
540	BAYO VISTA AV	94611	649-J1
470	RIO VISTA AV	94611	649-J1
440	YOSEMITE AV	94611	649-J1
410	EL DORADO AV	94611	649-J1
370	MOSS WY	94611	649-J1
370	MOSS AV	94611	649-J1
300	MACARTHUR BLVD	94610	649-J1
300	MACARTHUR BLVD	94611	649-J1
300	SANTA CLARA AV	94611	649-J1
300	W MACARTHUR BLVD	94611	649-J1
370	KEMPTON WY	94610	649-J1
370	KEMPTON WY	94611	649-J1
370	SANTA CLARA AV	94611	649-J1
FAIRVIEW AV			**ALA**
2900	BAYO VISTA AV	94501	670-B3
2900	NORTHWOOD DR	94501	670-B3
2900	SOUTHWOOD DR	94501	670-B3
3100	CORNELL DR	94501	670-B3
3200	HIGH ST	94501	670-C3
3260	BAYO VISTA AV	94501	670-C3
3300	FERNSIDE BLVD	94501	670-C3
FAIRVIEW AV			**PDMT**
1	GRAND AV	94610	650-A2
40	ARBOR DR	94610	650-A1
100	ARBOR DR	94610	650-A1
110	ARBOR DR	94610	650-A1
150	DALE AV	94610	650-A1
200	JEROME AV	94610	650-A1
FAIRVIEW ST			**BERK**
1400	BAKER ST	94702	629-F4
1500	SACRAMENTO ST	94702	629-F4
1500	SACRAMENTO ST	94703	629-F4
1600	CALIFORNIA ST	94703	629-G4
1700	KING ST	94703	629-G4
1800	ELLIS ST	94703	629-G4
1830	HARPER ST	94703	629-G4
1880	ADELINE ST	94703	629-G4
2000	DOVER ST	94703	629-G4
FAIRVIEW ST			**OAK**
600	WHEELER ST	94609	629-H4
700	SHATTUCK AV	94609	629-H4
700	TREMONT ST	94609	629-G4
800	DOVER ST	94609	629-G4
FAIRWAY AV			**OAK**
3900	SEQUOYAH RD	94605	671-B3
4000	TWIN OAKS WY	94605	671-C3
4200	TURNLEY AV	94605	671-C3
FAIRWAY PL			**ALA**
400	FITCHBURG AV	94502	670-B7
400	BEACH RD	94502	670-B7
FALLBROOK WY			**OAK**
10800	MALCOLM AV	94605	671-D4
FALLON AV			**ALA**
	3RD ST	94501	649-E7
	FALLON CIR	94501	649-E7
FALLON CIR			**ALA**
2000	FALLON AV	94501	649-E7
2100	FALLON AV	94501	649-E7
FALLON ST			**OAK**
200	VICTORY CT	94607	649-G5
460	OAK ST	94607	649-G5
500	4TH ST	94607	649-G5
630	7TH ST	94607	649-H5
750	8TH ST	94607	649-H5
870	9TH ST	94607	649-H5
1000	10TH ST	94607	649-H5
FARALLON WY			**OAK**
6600	PINENEEDLE DR	94611	630-D5
FARNAM ST			**OAK**
3200	FRUITVALE AV	94601	650-C7
3300	33RD AV	94601	650-C7
3400	34TH AV	94601	650-C7
FARRAGUT AV			**PDMT**
1	SEAVIEW AV	94610	650-C2
50	KING AV	94610	650-C2
100	CROCKER AV	94610	650-C2
FARRELL ST			**OAK**
9500	98TH AV	94605	671-B4
9700	ESPINOSA AV	94605	671-B4
9700	LAS VEGAS AV	94605	671-B4
FAVOR ST			**OAK**
7000	70TH AV	94621	670-G3
7300	73RD AV	94621	670-G3
FENHAM ST			**OAK**
6200	62ND AV	94621	670-F3
6300	64TH AV	94621	670-F3
6500	65TH AV	94621	670-F3
6600	66TH AV	94621	670-F3
FERN ST			**OAK**
2400	FAIRFAX AV	94601	650-E7
2600	BROOKDALE AV	94601	650-E7
FERNDELL WK			**ALA**
	GREENBRIER RD	94501	669-H3
	KITTY HAWK PL	94501	669-H3
	YORKSHIRE PL	94501	669-H3
	YORKSHIRE RD	94501	669-H3
FERNHOFF CT			**OAK**
1	FERNHOFF RD	94619	650-J5
FERNHOFF RD			**OAK**
5400	BACON RD	94619	650-J5
5470	FERNHOFF CT	94619	650-J5
5700	SKYLINE BLVD	94619	650-J5
FERNSIDE BLVD			**ALA**
900	OTIS DR	94501	670-B4
1080	WASHINGTON CT	94501	670-B4
1100	WASHINGTON ST	94501	670-B4
1150	ADAMS ST	94501	670-B4
1200	SAN JOSE AV	94501	670-B4
1250	MADISON ST	94501	670-B4
1300	ENCINAL AV	94501	670-B4
1340	BRIGGS AV	94501	670-B4
1370	STERLING AV	94501	670-B3
1400	CENTRAL AV	94501	670-B3
1540	LIBERTY AV	94501	670-C3
1600	EAST SHORE DR	94501	670-C3
1600	GARFIELD AV	94501	670-C3
3270	THOMPSON AV	94501	670-C3
3240	FAIRVIEW AV	94501	670-C3
3210	MONTE VISTA AV	94501	670-C3
900	TILDEN WY	94501	670-B2
900	BLANDING AV	94501	670-B2
2700	PEARL ST	94501	670-B2
2800	VERSAILLES AV	94501	670-B2
2850	MORELAND DR	94501	670-B2
2900	CAMBRIDGE DR	94501	670-B2
2950	FREMONT DR	94501	670-B2
3000	HARVARD DR	94501	670-B2
3050	YALE DR	94501	670-B2
3100	CORNELL DR	94501	670-C2
3200	HIGH ST	94501	670-C2
3200	GIBBONS DR	94501	670-C2
	HIGH ST	94501	670-C2
FERNWALD RD			**BERK**
	DWIGHT WY	94704	630-A2
	SMYTH RD	94704	630-A2
FERNWOOD DR			**OAK**
1410	FLORENCE TER	94611	630-D7
1700	MOUNTAIN BLVD	94611	630-D7
FERRO CT			**ALA**
1	RATTO RD	94502	669-J6
FERRO ST			**OAK**
	MIDDLE HARBOR RD	94607	649-D5
FERRY PT			**ALA**
	W HORNET AV	94501	669-D1
	W TICONDEROGA AV	94501	669-D1
	W ORISKANY AV	94501	649-D7
	W ATLANTIC AV	94501	649-D7
	W SEAPLANE LAGOON	94501	649-D7
	W TRIDENT AV	94501	649-D7
	W TOWER AV	94501	649-D7
FIELD ST			**OAK**
3800	CIRCLE HILL DR	94605	671-A1
3700	VALENTINE ST	94605	671-A1
3600	GREENLY DR	94605	671-A1
3500	STERLING DR	94605	671-A2
3600	CREST AV	94605	671-A2
FIELDBROOK RD			**OAK**
4500	ALISO AV	94619	650-G5
4600	ELINORA AV	94619	650-G5
4600	MOUNTAIN BLVD	94619	650-H5
FIJI LN			**ALA**
3100	FIR PL	94502	669-J7
3150	ADMIRALITY LN	94502	670-A7
3200	CATALINA AV	94502	670-A7
FILBERT ST			**OAK**
290	3RD ST	94607	649-E4
700	7TH ST	94607	649-E4
800	8TH ST	94607	649-E4
1000	10TH ST	94607	649-F3
1200	12TH ST	94607	649-F3
1400	14TH ST	94607	649-F3
1600	16TH ST	94607	649-F3
1800	18TH ST	94607	649-F3
2100	21ST ST	94607	649-F2
2200	W GRAND AV	94607	649-F2
2400	24TH ST	94607	649-F2
2600	26TH ST	94607	649-F2
2800	28TH ST	94608	649-F1
3000	30TH ST	94608	649-F1
3200	32ND ST	94608	649-F1
3300	SAN PABLO AV	94608	649-F1
3300	BROCKHURST ST	94608	649-F1
FILLMORE ST			**ALA**
2900	MOUND ST	94501	670-A4
3000	COURT ST	94501	670-A4
3100	FOUNTAIN ST	94501	670-A4
3200	HIGH ST	94501	670-A4
3200	PEACH ST	94501	670-B4
FILLMORE ST			**ALB**
900	SOLANO AV	94706	609-D6
1000	BUCHANAN ST	94706	609-D6
FIR AV			**ALA**
3100	FIR PL	94502	670-A6
3200	ADMIRALITY LN	94502	670-A6
3200	TAHITI LN	94502	670-A6
3300	ISLAND DR	94502	670-A7
3320	WILLIS LN	94502	670-A7
3340	GARDENIA TER	94502	670-A7
3360	BISMARCK LN	94502	670-A7
3370	CAMELIA DR	94502	670-A7
3380	HOLLY ST	94502	670-A7
3380	OLEANDER AV	94502	670-A7
FIR PL			**ALA**
1100	FIR AV	94502	670-A6
1110	SANTA CRUZ LN	94502	670-A6
1150	PHOENIX LN	94502	670-A7
1180	FIJI LN	94502	669-J7
1200	CATALINA AV	94502	669-J7
FISHER AV			**OAK**
2600	MACARTHUR BLVD	94605	671-B5
2650	FRAZIER AV	94605	671-B5
2700	TALBOT AV	94605	671-B5
FITCH CT			**ALA**
	ROSEFIELD LP	94501	649-F7
FITCHBURG AV			**ALA**
500	FAIRWAY PL	94502	670-B7
500	BEACH RD	94502	670-B7
700	MAITLAND DR	94502	670-B7
900	MAGNOLIA DR	94502	670-B7
FITZGERALD ST			**OAK**
1300	PERALTA ST	94608	649-F1
1330	HARLAN ST	94608	649-F1
1330	34TH ST	94608	649-F1
14000	34TH ST	94608	649-F1
14000	HOLLIS ST	94608	649-F1
FITZPATRICK RD			**OAK**
200	CORAL RD	94603	670-F6
200	EMPIRE RD	94603	670-F6
300	CORAL RD	94603	670-F6
FLAGG AV			**OAK**
3350	HAROLD ST	94602	650-D5
3450	MONTANA ST	94602	650-D5
FLEET RD			**OAK**
1100	HOLMAN RD	94610	650-C3
1200	GREENWOOD AV	94610	650-C3
FLEMING AV			**OAK**
4300	HIGH ST	94619	650-E7
4440	COURTLAND AV	94619	650-F7
4800	MONTICELLO AV	94619	650-F7
4850	BEST AV	94619	650-F7
4900	MAXWELL AV	94619	650-F7
5000	KINGSLAND AV	94619	650-F7
5020	RAWSON ST	94619	650-F7
5100	RAWSON ST	94619	650-F7
5100	MODESTO AV	94619	670-F1
5180	MADERA AV	94619	670-F1
5260	MORCOM AV	94619	670-F1
5400	BIRDSALL AV	94619	670-F1
5500	55TH AV	94605	670-F1
5560	MORSE DR	94605	670-F1
5900	SEMINARY AV	94605	670-F1
FLETCHER CT			**ALA**
	ROSEFIELD LP	94501	649-F7
FLINT			**ALA**
3000	MULVANY CIR	94501	649-E6
FLINTRIDGE AV			**OAK**
3200	GOLF LINKS RD	94605	671-B4
FLINTRIDGE LN			**OAK**
9000	CASTLEWOOD ST	94605	671-B3
9000	SARAZEN AV	94605	671-B3
FLORA ST			**OAK**
6400	64TH AV	94605	670-F2
6400	64TH AV	94621	670-F2
6500	65TH AV	94605	670-G2
6500	65TH AV	94621	670-G2
6600	66TH AV	94605	670-G2
6600	66TH AV	94621	670-G2
6650	HAVENSCOURT BLVD	94605	670-G2
6650	HAVENSCOURT BLVD	94621	670-G2
6650	HAVENSCOURT BLVD	94621	670-G3
6700	67TH AV	94621	670-G3
6750	67TH AV	94621	670-G3
6800	68TH AV	94621	670-G3
6830	68TH AV	94621	670-G3
6860	CHURCH ST	94621	670-G3
6900	69TH AV	94621	670-G3
7000	70TH AV	94621	670-G3
FLORA VISTA			**ALA**
3000	FONTANA DR	94502	669-J6
3020	VIA ALAMOSA	94502	669-J6
3100	VERDEMAR DR	94502	669-J6
FLORADA AV			**OAK**
1	PORTAL AV	94610	650-C2
1	WAWONA AV	94610	650-C2
FLORADA AV			**PDMT**
100	LA SALLE AV	94610	650-C2
FLORENCE AV			**OAK**
600	COCHRANE AV	94618	630-C6
590	ESTATES DR	94618	630-C6
590	PROCTOR AV	94618	630-C6
580	MASONIC AV	94618	630-C6
500	PROCTOR AV	94618	630-C6
470	HARBORD DR	94618	630-C6
470	MODOC AV	94618	630-C6
400	JULIA ST	94618	630-C6
310	MODOC AV	94618	630-C6
280	MODOC AV	94618	630-C6
260	MORPETH ST	94618	630-C6
240	HERMOSA AV	94618	630-C6
200	ALTA RD	94618	630-B6

PRIMARY STREET Address	Cross Street	ZIP	CITY Pg-Grid
FLORENCE AV			**OAK**
100	ELROD AV	94618	630-C6
200	PROCTOR AV	94618	630-C6
FLORENCE ST			**BERK**
2830	OREGON ST	94705	629-H3
2900	RUSSELL ST	94705	629-H3
3000	ASHBY AV	94705	629-H3
FLORENCE TER			**OAK**
5500	FERNWOOD DR	94611	630-D6
5520	DUNCAN WY	94611	630-D6
5560	MOUNTAIN BLVD	94611	630-D6
5740	CAPRICORN AV	94611	630-D7
5900	MERRIEWOOD DR	94611	630-D7
FLORIDA AV			**BERK**
40	BOYNTON AV	94707	609-G4
100	SANTA BARBARA RD	94707	609-G4
FLORIDA ST			**OAK**
3000	MAPLE AV	94602	650-E5
3200	LAUREL AV	94602	650-E5
FLORIO ST			**OAK**
6200	COLLEGE AV	94618	629-J4
6290	AUBURN AV	94618	629-J4
6340	AUBURN AV	94618	629-J4
6390	MANOA ST	94618	629-J4
	ROCKWELL ST	94618	630-A4
	ROSS CIR	94618	630-A4
	ROSS ST	94618	630-A4
FLOWER LN			**ALA**
500	BEACH RD	94502	670-B6
700	MAITLAND DR	94502	670-B6
700	MAITLAND DR	94502	670-A6
900	GARDEN RD	94502	670-A6
FOLEY ST			**ALA**
1600	TILDEN WY	94501	670-A2
1700	BUENA VISTA AV	94501	670-A2
FOLGER AV			**BERK**
800	HOLLIS ST	94804	629-E4
900	7TH ST	94804	629-E4
1100	SAN PABLO AV	94804	629-E4
FONTAINE CT			**OAK**
4100	MOUNTAIN BLVD	94605	671-B2
FONTAINE ST			**OAK**
7900	KELLER AV	94605	671-A1
8000	SHONE AV	94605	671-A2
8100	HOLMES AV	94605	671-B2
8800	CREST AV	94605	671-A3
9200	GOLF LINKS RD	94605	671-A3
FONTANA DR			**ALA**
1000	MECARTNEY RD	94502	669-J6
1000	BAYWOOD RD	94502	669-J6
	VIA BONITA	94502	669-J6
1050	CERRO VISTA	94502	669-J6
1100	VIA BONITA	94502	669-J6
1130	VIA CORTA	94502	669-J6
1140	FLORA VISTA	94502	669-J6
1180	VIA CORTA	94502	669-J6
1200	CATALINA AV	94502	669-J6
FOOTHILL BLVD			**OAK**
	MACARTHUR BLVD	94605	671-C6
100	LAKESHORE AV	94606	649-J4
100	1ST AV	94606	649-J4
190	2ND AV	94606	649-J4
300	3RD AV	94606	649-J5
400	4TH AV	94606	649-J5
500	5TH AV	94606	649-J5
600	6TH AV	94606	649-J5
700	7TH AV	94606	649-J5
800	8TH AV	94606	649-J5
900	9TH AV	94606	649-J5
950	E 17TH ST	94606	649-J5
1000	11TH AV	94606	649-J5
2300	23RD AV	94606	650-B6
2300	E 16TH ST	94606	650-B6
1000	12TH AV	94606	650-A5
1100	12TH AV	94606	650-A5
1250	13TH AV	94606	650-A6
1250	FOOTHILL PL	94606	650-A6
1400	14TH AV	94606	650-A6
1450	15TH AV	94606	650-A6
1560	16TH AV	94606	650-A6
1660	17TH AV	94606	650-A6
1770	18TH AV	94606	650-A6
1880	19TH AV	94606	650-A6
1980	20TH AV	94606	650-A6
2090	21ST AV	94606	650-B6
2200	22ND AV	94606	650-B6
2240	MUNSON WY	94606	650-B6
2300	23RD AV	94601	650-B6
2360	MILLER AV	94601	650-B6
2400	24TH AV	94601	650-B6
2410	24TH AV	94601	650-B6
2480	IRVING ST	94601	650-B6
2500	25TH AV	94601	650-B6
2530	25TH AV	94601	650-B6
2600	26TH AV	94601	650-B7
2700	27TH AV	94601	650-C7
2740	MITCHELL ST	94601	650-C7
2750	E 20TH ST	94601	650-C7
2800	28TH AV	94601	650-C7
2900	AUSTIN ST	94601	650-C7
3000	RUTHERFORD ST	94601	650-C7
3200	FRUITVALE AV	94601	650-C7
3280	33RD AV	94601	650-C7
3310	COOLIDGE AV	94601	650-C7
3350	34TH AV	94601	650-C7
3380	34TH AV	94601	650-C7
3480	35TH AV	94601	650-D7
3530	CROSBY AV	94601	650-D7
3590	36TH AV	94601	650-D7
3590	36TH AV	94601	650-D7
3660	BRIDGE AV	94601	650-D7
3690	HARRINGTON AV	94601	650-D7
3700	38TH AV	94601	650-D7
3790	39TH AV	94601	650-D7
3890	40TH AV	94601	650-D7
3900	40TH AV	94601	650-D7
3970	40TH AV	94601	650-D7
3970	ROSEDALE AV	94601	670-D1
4000	ROSEDALE AV	94601	670-D1
4100	41ST AV	94601	670-D1
4190	42ND AV	94601	670-D1
4230	COURTLAND AV	94601	670-D1
4230	42ND AV	94601	670-D1
4400	HIGH ST	94601	670-D1
4500	45TH AV	94601	670-D1
4600	46TH AV	94601	670-E1
4700	47TH AV	94601	670-E1
4800	48TH AV	94601	670-E1
4830	FREMONT WY	94601	670-E1
5000	50TH AV	94601	670-E1
5100	51ST AV	94601	670-E1
5200	VICKSBURG AV	94601	670-E1
5200	54TH AV	94601	670-E1
5250	CONGRESS AV	94601	670-E1
5300	FAIRFAX AV	94601	670-F1
5360	BELVEDERE ST	94601	670-F1
5400	COLE ST	94601	670-F1
5500	55TH AV	94605	670-F1
5500	TRASK ST	94605	670-F1
5600	57TH AV	94605	670-F1
5610	LA VERNE AV	94605	670-F1
5680	BROOKDALE AV	94605	670-F1
5710	AVENAL AV	94605	670-F1
5800	MASON ST	94605	670-F1
5900	SEMINARY AV	94605	670-G1
6000	60TH AV	94605	670-G1
6100	61ST AV	94605	670-G1
6200	62ND AV	94605	670-G1
6300	63RD AV	94605	670-G2
6400	64TH AV	94605	670-G2
6600	CAMDEN ST	94605	670-H2
6600	HAVENSCOURT BLVD	94605	670-H2
6700	67TH AV	94605	670-H2
6700	BRANN ST	94605	670-H2
6750	68TH AV	94605	670-H2
6800	68TH AV	94605	670-H2
6800	CHURCH ST	94605	670-H2
6900	69TH AV	94605	670-H2
7300	73RD AV	94605	670-H2
7300	MACARTHUR BLVD	94605	670-H2
10000	MACARTHUR BLVD	94605	671-B5
10230	FRAZIER AV	94605	671-B5
10500	TALBOT AV	94605	671-B5
10500	STANLEY AV	94605	671-B5
10560	106TH AV	94605	671-B5
10800	108TH AV	94605	671-B5
200	DURANT AV	94605	671-B6
500	MACARTHUR BLVD	94605	671-C6
11800	REVERE AV	94605	671-C6
11900	FOOTHILL WY	94605	671-C6
FOOTHILL BLVD			**SLN**
200	DURANT AV	94577	671-B6
500	MACARTHUR BLVD	94577	671-C6
FOOTHILL PL			**OAK**
1250	13TH AV	94606	650-A6
1250	FOOTHILL BLVD	94606	650-A6
1400	14TH AV	94606	650-A6
1400	GLEASON WY	94606	650-A6
FOOTHILL WY			**OAK**
5900	DUTTON AV	94605	671-C7
5940	FOOTHILL BLVD	94605	671-C7
6030	MIDDLETON ST	94605	671-C7
6110	ROXBURY AV	94605	671-C6
6210	REVERE AV	94605	671-C6
6300	COVINGTON ST	94605	671-C6
6300	MARLOW DR	94605	671-C6
FOOTHILL WY			**SLN**
5900	DUTTON AV	94605	671-C7
5940	FOOTHILL BLVD	94605	671-C7
FORD ST			**OAK**
2800	23RD AV	94601	670-B1
2840	29TH AV	94601	670-B1
2900	PETERSON ST	94601	670-B1
3000	DERBY AV	94601	670-B1
3100	LANCASTER ST	94601	670-B1
FOREST AV			**BERK**
2700	COLLEGE AV	94705	629-J3
2810	PIEDMONT AV	94705	629-J3
3000	CLAREMONT BLVD	94705	629-J3
FOREST HILL AV			**OAK**
3800	WHITTLE AV	94602	650-D4
4100	TIFFIN RD	94602	650-D4
FOREST LN			**BERK**
1	HILLDALE AV	94708	609-H5
100	KEELER AV	94708	609-H5
100	KEELER AV	94708	609-H5
200	GRIZZLY PEAK BLVD	94708	609-H5
200	GRIZZLY PEAK BLVD	94708	609-H5
300	CRESTON RD	94708	609-H5
FOREST ST			**OAK**
	COLLEGE AV	94618	629-J5
400	LAWTON AV	94618	629-J5
430	BOYD AV	94618	629-J5
450	SHAFTER AV	94618	629-J5
	LOCKSLEY AV	94618	629-J5
500	MILES AV	94618	629-J5
530	OAK GROVE AV	94618	629-J5
560	CLAREMONT AV	94618	629-J5
600	AYALA AV	94618	629-J5
FORESTLAND WY			**OAK**
6600	GUNN DR	94611	630-G7
6650	MOORE DR	94611	630-G7
6650	MOORE DR	94611	630-G7
6700	AITKEN DR	94611	630-G7
6700	EVERGREEN AV	94611	630-G7
FORTMANN WY			**ALA**
	GRAND ST	94501	649-J7
	ALASKA PACKER PL	94501	649-J7
FORTRESS ISL			**ALA**
600	OTIS DR	94501	669-H2
FORTUNE WY			**OAK**
5900	63RD AV	94605	670-G2
5990	62ND AV	94605	670-G2
6100	61ST AV	94605	670-G2
6190	60TH AV	94605	670-G2
6200	BANCROFT AV	94605	670-G1
6300	SEMINARY AV	94605	670-G1
FOSTER AV			**OAK**
100	BERNHARDT DR	94603	670-G7
190	FOSTER CT	94603	670-G7
300	SAINT ELMO DR	94603	670-G7
FOSTER CT			**OAK**
1	FOSTER AV	94603	670-G7
FOSTER ST			**ALA**
1020	YOUNG ST	94502	669-J6
1100	PATTIANI WY	94502	669-J6
FOUNTAIN ST			**ALA**
900	OTIS DR	94501	670-A4
1000	FILLMORE ST	94501	670-A4
1100	WASHINGTON ST	94501	670-A4
1150	ADAMS ST	94501	670-B4
1200	SAN JOSE AV	94501	670-B3
1250	MADISON ST	94501	670-B3
1300	ENCINAL AV	94501	670-B3
1330	JACKSON ST	94501	670-B3
1360	VAN BUREN ST	94501	670-B3
1400	CENTRAL AV	94501	670-B3
1500	SANTA CLARA AV	94501	670-B3
1600	LINCOLN AV	94501	670-B3
FOUNTAIN WK			**BERK**
	LOS ANGELES AV	94707	609-G6
	MARIN AV	94707	609-G6
	SUTTER ST	94707	609-G6
	ARLINGTON AV	94707	609-G6
	DEL NORTE ST	94707	609-G6
FOX HILLS CT			**OAK**
500	PEBBLE BEACH DR	94605	671-E3
FRANCES ST			**OAK**
2400	FAIRFAX AV	94601	650-E7
2600	BROOKDALE AV	94601	650-E7
FRANCIS ST			**ALB**
1400	SANTA FE AV	94706	609-E7
1450	CURTIS ST	94706	609-E7
1500	NEILSON ST	94706	609-E7
1500	NEILSON ST	94706	609-E7
1560	TEVLIN ST	94706	609-E7
1600	PERALTA AV	94706	609-E7
FRANCISCAN WY			**ALA**
1900	KITTY HAWK RD	94501	669-H3
1940	GREENBRIER RD	94501	669-H3
1970	YORKSHIRE RD	94501	669-H3
2010	CAMDEN RD	94501	669-H3
2050	WHITEHALL RD	94501	669-H3
2100	WILLOW ST	94501	669-H3
FRANCISCO ST			**BERK**
1100	SAN PABLO AV	94702	629-E1
1200	CURTIS ST	94702	629-E1
1240	CHESTNUT ST	94702	629-E1
1300	FRANKLIN ST	94702	629-F1
1400	ACTON ST	94702	629-F1
1500	SACRAMENTO ST	94703	629-F1
1560	EOLA ST	94703	629-F1
1600	CALIFORNIA ST	94703	629-F1
1700	MCGEE AV	94703	629-G1
1800	GRANT ST	94703	629-G1
1900	MARTIN LUTHER KING JR WY	94709	629-G1
2000	MILVIA ST	94709	629-G1
2100	SHATTUCK AV	94709	629-G1
FRANK H OGAWA PZ			**OAK**
400	14TH ST	94612	649-G4
1480	KAHN AL	94612	649-G3
430	CLAY ST	94612	649-G3
1600	16TH ST	94612	649-G3
1600	SAN PABLO AV	94612	649-G3
1480	KAHN AL	94612	649-G4
FRANKLIN ST			**BERK**
1600	CEDAR ST	94702	629-E1
1700	VIRGINIA ST	94702	629-F1
1730	FRANCISCO ST	94702	629-F1
1800	DELAWARE ST	94702	629-F1
1900	HEARST AV	94702	629-F1
FRANKLIN ST			**OAK**
100	EMBARCADERO W	94607	649-F5
190	2ND ST	94607	649-F5
300	3RD ST	94607	649-F5
400	4TH ST	94607	649-G5
700	7TH ST	94607	649-G4
800	8TH ST	94607	649-G4
900	9TH ST	94607	649-G4
1100	11TH ST	94607	649-G4
1200	12TH ST	94612	649-G4
1300	13TH ST	94612	649-G4
1400	14TH ST	94612	649-G4
1500	15TH ST	94612	649-G4
1700	17TH ST	94612	649-G3
1900	19TH ST	94612	649-G3
2000	20TH ST	94612	649-G3
2100	21ST ST	94612	649-G3
2200	22ND ST	94612	649-G3
FRAZIER AV			**OAK**
2750	STANLEY AV	94605	671-B5
2700	SHAW ST	94605	671-B5
2600	FOOTHILL BLVD	94605	671-B5
2700	FISHER AV	94605	671-B5
FREDERICK ST			**OAK**
2100	KING ST	94606	650-A7
2300	KENNEDY ST	94606	650-A7
FREMONT DR			**ALA**
1800	NORTHWOOD DR	94501	670-B2
1900	FERNSIDE BLVD	94501	670-B2
FREMONT ST			**OAK**
5500	55TH ST	94608	629-F6
5700	STANFORD AV	94608	629-F6
5800	POWELL ST	94608	629-E6
5900	59TH ST	94608	629-E5
6100	61ST ST	94608	629-E5
6200	62ND ST	94608	629-E5
FREMONT WY			**OAK**
1730	FOOTHILL BLVD	94601	670-E1
1700	JUDD ST	94601	670-E1
1730	BANCROFT AV	94601	670-E1
1730	BOND ST	94601	670-E1
FRESNO AV			**BERK**
900	SOLANO AV	94707	609-F6
1020	MARIN AV	94707	609-F6
1090	MONTEREY AV	94707	609-G6
1200	SONOMA AV	94707	609-G6
FRESNO ST			**OAK**
6800	CHURCH ST	94605	670-H2
7300	73RD AV	94605	670-H2
7300	73RD AV	94605	670-H2
7330	73RD AV	94605	670-H3
7500	LEGION AV	94605	670-H3
FRISBIE ST			**OAK**
100	FRISBIE WY	94611	649-H2
200	RICHMOND BLVD	94611	649-H2
200	HARRISON ST	94611	649-H2
300	FRISBIE WY	94611	649-H2
FRISBIE WY			**OAK**
400	STANLEY PL	94611	649-J2
380	PEARL ST	94611	649-H2
340	KEMPTON AV	94611	649-H2
340	FRISBIE ST	94611	649-H2
300	FRISBIE ST	94611	649-H2
340	GARLAND ST	94611	649-H2
FRONT ST			**BERK**
	W FRONTAGE RD	94710	609-C7
FRONTAGE RD			**EMVL**
5970	ACCESS RD	94608	629-D5
6600	W FRONTAGE RD	94608	629-D5
FRONTAGE RD			**OAK**
	14TH ST	94607	649-C3
5500	MOUNTAIN BLVD	94605	650-H7
5780	RUSTING AV	94605	650-H7
5900	MOUNTAIN VIEW AV	94605	650-H7
6000	KUHNLE AV	94605	650-H7
W FRONTAGE RD			**BERK**
1300	FRONT ST	94804	629-C2
2000	UNIVERSITY AV	94804	629-D2
	FRONTAGE RD	94804	629-D5
FRUITVALE AV			**OAK**
400	ALAMEDA AV	94601	670-B1
400	TILDEN WY	94601	670-B1
600	CHAPMAN ST	94601	670-B1
700	E 7TH ST	94601	670-B1
740	ELMWOOD AV	94601	670-B1
760	E 8TH ST	94601	670-B1
800	E 9TH ST	94601	670-C1
1040	E 10TH ST	94601	670-C1
1070	SAN LEANDRO ST	94601	670-C1
1210	E 12TH ST	94601	670-C1
1240	E 12TH ST	94601	670-C1
1330	E 13TH ST	94601	670-C1
1330	INTERNATIONAL BLVD	94601	650-C7
1400	INTERNATIONAL BLVD	94601	650-C7
1440	FARNAM ST	94601	650-C7
1500	E 15TH ST	94601	650-C7
1540	E 16TH ST	94601	650-C7
1600	E 16TH ST	94601	650-C7
1700	E 17TH ST	94601	650-C7
1730	E 17TH ST	94601	650-C7
1800	E 18TH ST	94601	650-C7
1900	E 19TH ST	94601	650-C7
2000	FOOTHILL BLVD	94601	650-C7
2200	E 22ND ST	94601	650-C6
2240	E 23RD ST	94601	650-C6
2250	E 23RD ST	94601	650-C6
2300	ASHBROOK CT	94601	650-C6
2340	GALINDO ST	94601	650-C6
2350	GALINDO ST	94601	650-C6
2400	LOGAN ST	94601	650-C6
2400	LOGAN ST	94601	650-C6
2470	HYDE ST	94601	650-C6
2500	HYDE ST	94601	650-C6
2570	BLOSSOM ST	94601	650-C6
2620	DAVIS ST	94601	650-C6
2700	E 27TH ST	94601	650-C6
2750	LYNDE ST	94601	650-C6
2800	E 29TH ST	94601	650-C5
2840	BONA ST	94601	650-D5
2840	BONA ST	94601	650-D5
2880	BROOKDALE AV	94602	650-D5
2880	BROOKDALE AV	94601	650-D5
2900	BROOKDALE AV	94602	650-D5
2900	BROOKDALE AV	94601	650-D5
2940	EVELYN CT	94602	650-D5
2950	HICKORY ST	94602	650-D5
3040	NICOL AV	94602	650-D5
3000	NICOL AV	94602	650-D5
3100	SCHOOL ST	94602	650-D5
3150	SCHOOL ST	94602	650-D5
3170	CORDOVA ST	94602	650-D5
3200	CASTELLO ST	94602	650-D5
3240	PLEASANT ST	94602	650-D5
3300	WOODBINE AV	94602	650-D5
3340	HAROLD ST	94602	650-D5
3390	MONTANA ST	94602	650-D5
3410	MONTANA ST	94602	650-D5
3430	SLOAN ST	94602	650-D4
3500	MACARTHUR BLVD	94602	650-D4
3620	COLOMA ST	94602	650-D4
3670	DAMUTH ST	94602	650-D4
3730	LYMAN RD	94602	650-D4
3800	WHITTLE AV	94602	650-D4
4030	HARDING WY	94602	650-E3
4130	TIFFIN RD	94602	650-E3
4260	CLEMENS RD	94602	650-E3
4300	FUNSTON PL	94602	650-E3
4400	HOOVER AV	94602	650-E3
4400	WRENN ST	94602	650-E3
FRYE ST			**OAK**
2870	WILSHIRE BLVD	94602	650-F4
2970	LONDON RD	94602	650-F4
3000	MAPLE AV	94602	650-F4
3200	MAPLE AV	94602	650-F4
FULLINGTON ST			**OAK**
	LOMA VISTA WY	94619	650-E6
	OCTAVIA ST	94619	650-E6
	VIOLA ST	94619	650-E6
	OVER ST	94619	650-E6
4000	39TH AV	94619	650-F6
4200	MAYBELLE WY	94619	650-F6
FULTON ST			**BERK**
2200	BANCROFT WY	94704	629-H2
2200	OXFORD ST	94704	629-H2
2260	DURANT AV	94704	629-H2
2320	CHANNING WY	94704	629-H2
2390	HASTE ST	94704	629-H2
2450	DWIGHT WY	94704	629-H3
2500	BLAKE ST	94704	629-H3
2510	BLAKE ST	94704	629-H3
2570	PARKER ST	94704	629-H3
2630	CARLETON ST	94704	629-H3
2700	DERBY ST	94705	629-H3
2730	WARD ST	94705	629-H3
2800	STUART ST	94705	629-H3
2820	OREGON ST	94705	629-H3
2900	RUSSELL ST	94705	629-H3
3000	ASHBY AV	94705	629-H4
3100	PRINCE ST	94705	629-H4
FUNDY BAY			**ALA**
100	BAYWALK RD	94502	669-J6
FUNSTON PL			**OAK**
2100	FRUITVALE AV	94602	650-E3
2200	WHITTLE AV	94602	650-E3
G			
G ST			**OAK**
8500	85TH AV	94621	670-G4
8530	85TH AV	94621	670-G5
8600	86TH AV	94621	670-G5
8620	86TH AV	94621	670-G5
8700	87TH AV	94621	670-G5
8800	88TH AV	94621	670-G5
8900	89TH AV	94603	670-G5
9000	90TH AV	94603	670-G5
9100	91ST AV	94603	670-G5
9200	92ND AV	94603	670-G5
9200	92ND AV	94603	670-H5
GAINSBOROUGH CT			**ALA**
100	SEA VIEW PKWY	94502	669-J5
GALINDO ST			**OAK**
3200	FRUITVALE AV	94601	650-C6
3200	FRUITVALE AV	94601	650-C6
3500	35TH AV	94601	650-D7
3550	BAXTER ST	94601	650-D7
3600	HARRINGTON AV	94601	650-D7
GALVIN ST			**OAK**
1100	EVERETT AV	94602	650-C3
GALWAY BAY			**ALA**
100	BAYWALK RD	94502	669-J6
GANNON RD			**OAK**
200	EMPIRE RD	94603	670-F7
300	CORAL RD	94603	670-F7
GARBER ST			**BERK**
2700	COLLEGE AV	94705	629-J3
2800	PIEDMONT AV	94705	629-J3
2900	OAK KNOLL TER	94705	630-A3
2940	OAK KNOLL TER	94705	630-A3
3000	BELROSE AV	94705	630-A3
3000	CLAREMONT BLVD	94705	630-A3
3100	TANGLEWOOD RD	94705	630-A3
GARDEN RD			**ALA**
1	ISLAND DR	94502	670-A6
140	FLOWER LN	94502	670-A6
200	MECARTNEY RD	94502	670-A6
GARDEN ST			**OAK**
2700	E 27TH ST	94601	650-C5
2860	E 28TH ST	94601	650-C5
GARDEN WY			**ALA**
1300	CROLLS GARDEN CT	94501	669-F1
1400	CENTRAL AV	94501	669-F1
GARDENIA PL			**OAK**
3900	HILLMONT DR	94605	670-J1
4000	SUNNYMERE AV	94605	670-J1
GARDENIA TER			**ALA**
1000	FIR AV	94502	670-A7
GARFIELD AV			**ALA**
3200	HIGH ST	94501	670-B3
3300	FERNSIDE BLVD	94501	670-B3
3300	EAST SHORE DR	94501	670-B3
GARFIELD AV			**ALB**
1100	SAN PABLO AV	94706	609-D5
1140	KAINS AV	94706	609-D5
1170	STANNAGE AV	94706	609-D5
1200	CORNELL AV	94706	609-D5
1230	TALBOT AV	94706	609-D5
1260	EVELYN AV	94706	609-E5
1300	MASONIC AV	94706	609-E5

© 2006 Rand McNally & Company

PRIMARY STREET Address	Cross Street	ZIP	CITY Pg-Grid
GARFIELD AV			**OAK**
	73RD AV	94605	670-H2
7300	73RD AV	94605	670-H2
7400	74TH AV	94605	670-H2
7500	75TH AV	94605	670-H2
7600	76TH AV	94605	670-H2
7700	77TH AV	94605	670-H2
7800	78TH AV	94605	670-J2
7860	PARKER AV	94605	670-J3
7900	79TH AV	94605	670-J3
GARLAND ST			**OAK**
1	HARRISON ST	94611	649-H2
50	FRISBIE WY	94611	649-H2
100	FAIRMOUNT AV	94611	649-H2
GARNET ST			**OAK**
300	BROADWAY	94609	629-J7
400	EMERALD ST	94609	629-J7
GASKILL ST			**OAK**
5300	53RD ST	94608	629-F6
5400	54TH ST	94608	629-F6
5500	55TH ST	94608	629-F6
5600	56TH ST	94608	629-F6
5650	AILEEN ST	94608	629-F6
5700	57TH ST	94608	629-F6
5730	ARLINGTON AV	94608	629-F6
5800	STANFORD AV	94608	629-F6
GASPAR DR			**OAK**
1800	COLTON BLVD	94611	630-E7
2000	SNAKE RD	94611	630-E7
GATE VIEW DR			**OAK**
	WHITE CLIFF RD	94605	671-C4
	VENETIA RD	94605	671-C4
GATEVIEW AV			**ALB**
800	WASHINGTON AV	94706	609-C6
GAYLEY RD			**BERK**
	HEARST AV	94720	629-J1
	LA LOMA AV	94720	629-J1
	STADIUM RIMWAY	94720	629-J1
	PIEDMONT AV	94720	629-J2
	BANCROFT WY	94720	629-J2
GELSTON ST			**OAK**
700	HILLHURST WY	94705	630-B2
800	CLAREMONT AV	94705	630-B2
GENOA ST			**OAK**
5180	52ND ST	94608	629-G6
5270	53RD ST	94608	629-G6
5360	54TH ST	94608	629-G6
5450	55TH ST	94608	629-G6
5540	56TH ST	94608	629-G6
5620	AILEEN ST	94608	629-G6
5690	57TH ST	94608	629-G5
5760	ARLINGTON AV	94608	629-G5
5830	58TH ST	94608	629-G5
5910	59TH ST	94608	629-G5
6000	60TH ST	94608	629-G5
6040	ADELINE ST	94608	629-G5
6100	STANFORD AV	94608	629-G5
GEORGIA ST			**OAK**
2800	COOLIDGE AV	94602	650-E5
2800	MACARTHUR BLVD	94602	650-E5
3000	MAPLE AV	94602	650-E5
3000	MAPLE AV	94602	650-E5
3200	LAUREL AV	94602	650-E5
3400	MIDVALE AV	94602	650-E5
GERANIUM PL			**OAK**
4700	STAUFFER CT	94619	650-H5
4700	STAUFFER PL	94619	650-H5
4900	MOUNTAIN BLVD	94619	650-H5
GHORMLEY AV			**OAK**
100	BERNHARDT DR	94603	670-G7
280	SAINT ELMO DR	94603	670-G7
480	DARIEN AV	94603	670-G7
500	MADDUX DR	94603	670-G7
GIBBONS DR			**ALA**
1400	CENTRAL AV	94501	670-B3
1400	VERSAILLES AV	94501	670-B3
1500	SANTA CLARA AV	94501	670-B3
1550	JOHNSON AV	94501	670-B3
2800	LINCOLN AV	94501	670-B2
2830	NORTHWOOD DR	94501	670-B2
2830	SOUTHWOOD DR	94501	670-B2
3000	NORTHWOOD DR	94501	670-B2
3020	YALE DR	94501	670-B2
3080	CORNELL DR	94501	670-B2
3200	FERNSIDE BLVD	94501	670-B2
3200	HIGH ST	94501	670-B2
GIBRALTAR RD			**OAK**
9900	EMPIRE RD	94603	670-G7
10000	HESKET RD	94603	670-G7
GILBERT LN			**ALA**
3100	EASTER LN	94502	670-A6
3130	BELMONT WY	94502	670-A6
3130	BELMONT PL	94502	670-A6
GILBERT ST			**OAK**
4540	PLEASANT VALLEY AV	94611	629-J7
4470	WHITMORE ST	94611	629-J7
4390	MATHER ST	94611	629-J7
4250	JOHN ST	94611	629-J7
4100	RIDGEWAY AV	94611	629-J7
4020	41ST ST	94611	629-J7
GILMAN ST			**BERK**
600	EASTSHORE BLVD	94710	609-C7
600	EASTSHORE FRONTAGE RD	94710	609-C7
640	2ND ST	94710	609-C7
700	3RD ST	94710	609-D7
750	4TH ST	94710	609-D7
800	5TH ST	94710	609-D7
850	6TH ST	94710	609-D7
900	7TH ST	94710	609-D7
950	8TH ST	94710	609-D7
1000	9TH ST	94710	609-D7
1050	10TH ST	94710	609-D7
1100	SAN PABLO AV	94706	609-E7
1100	SAN PABLO AV	94702	609-E7
1130	KAINS AV	94706	609-E7
1130	KAINS AV	94702	609-E7
1160	STANNAGE AV	94706	609-E7
1160	STANNAGE AV	94702	609-E7
1200	CORNELL AV	94706	609-E7
1200	CORNELL AV	94702	609-E7
1230	TALBOT AV	94706	609-E7
1230	TALBOT AV	94702	609-E7
1250	EVELYN AV	94706	609-E7
1250	EVELYN AV	94702	609-E7
1270	SANTA FE AV	94706	609-E7
1270	SANTA FE AV	94702	609-E7
1300	CURTIS ST	94706	609-E7
1300	CURTIS ST	94702	609-E7
1320	NEILSON ST	94706	609-E7
1320	NEILSON ST	94702	609-E7
1330	NORTHSIDE AV	94706	609-E7
1330	NORTHSIDE AV	94702	609-E7
1340	TEVLIN ST	94706	609-E7
1340	TEVLIN ST	94702	609-E7
1350	PERALTA AV	94706	609-E7
1350	PERALTA AV	94702	609-E7
1370	ORDWAY ST	94706	609-F7
1370	ORDWAY ST	94702	609-F7
1400	ACTON ST	94706	609-F7
1400	ACTON ST	94702	609-F7
1500	HOPKINS ST	94706	609-F7
1500	HOPKINS ST	94702	609-F7
GINGER LN			**ALA**
	MAGNOLIA DR	94502	670-B7
	SAVANA LN	94502	670-B7
GIRVIN DR			**OAK**
5900	CHELTON DR	94611	650-F1
6210	PELHAM PL	94611	650-F1
6240	THACKERAY DR	94611	630-F7
6250	ELDERBERRY DR	94611	630-G7
6300	AITKEN DR	94611	630-G7
GLASCOCK ST			**OAK**
2800	29TH AV	94601	670-B1
2900	PETERSON ST	94601	670-B1
3000	DERBY AV	94601	670-B1
3100	LANCASTER ST	94601	670-B1
GLEASON WY			**OAK**
1400	14TH AV	94606	650-A6
1400	FOOTHILL PL	94606	650-A6
1500	15TH AV	94606	650-A6
1600	16TH AV	94606	650-A6
1700	17TH AV	94606	650-A6
1810	18TH AV	94606	650-A6
1910	19TH AV	94606	650-A6
2010	20TH AV	94606	650-A6
2110	21ST AV	94606	650-B6
2210	22ND AV	94606	650-B6
2300	MUNSON WY	94606	650-B6
GLEN ALPINE RD			**PDMT**
1	HAMPTON RD	94611	650-D2
20	SOTELLO AV	94611	650-D1
30	INDIAN GULCH RD	94611	650-D1
100	SOTELLO AV	94611	650-D1
GLEN ARTNEY CT			**OAK**
11000	GRASS VALLEY RD	94605	671-E4
11000	GLEN MANOR PL	94605	671-E4
10900	SHETLAND AV	94605	671-E4
11000	DUNKIRK AV	94605	671-E4
GLEN AV			**BERK**
1100	OAK ST	94708	609-H6
1200	EUNICE ST	94708	609-H6
1200	EUNICE ST	94709	609-H6
1220	SUMMER ST	94708	609-H7
1220	SUMMER ST	94709	609-H7
2200	ARCH ST	94709	609-H7
2250	SPRUCE ST	94709	609-H7
GLEN AV			**OAK**
80	LINDA AV	94611	649-J1
50	41ST ST	94611	649-J1
1	PANAMA CT	94611	649-J1
50	PIEDMONT AV	94611	649-J1
100	GLENEDEN AV	94611	630-A7
200	ECHO AV	94611	649-J1
GLEN MANOR PL			**OAK**
11200	SUN VALLEY DR	94605	671-E5
11100	COMMONWEALTH DR	94605	671-E4
11200	GLEN ARTNEY CT	94605	671-E4
11200	GRASS VALLEY RD	94605	671-E4
GLEN OAKS WY			**OAK**
6500	OAKWOOD DR	94611	630-F6
6700	WILD CURRANT WY	94611	630-F6
GLEN PARK RD			**OAK**
3500	MACARTHUR BLVD	94602	650-C4
3600	EXCELSIOR AV	94602	650-C4
3700	ALLMAN ST	94602	650-C4
3800	E 38TH ST	94602	650-C4
3800	E 38TH ST	94602	650-C4
4000	HAMPEL ST	94602	650-C4
4000	PARK BLVD	94602	650-C4
GLENARMS DR			**OAK**
5900	CALDWELL RD	94611	630-C5
5900	NEVA CT	94611	630-C5
5950	MOUNTAIN BLVD	94611	630-C5
6010	PALI CT	94611	630-C5
GLENBROOK DR			**OAK**
5500	BROADWAY TER	94618	630-A6
5510	ROMANY RD	94618	630-A6
5600	WESTMINSTER DR	94618	630-A6
5700	BOWLING DR	94618	630-A5
5800	BEECHWOOD DR	94618	630-A5
GLENCOURT			**OAK**
1000	SARONI DR	94611	630-F6
1050	HOMEGLEN LN	94611	630-F6
1200	ARROWHEAD DR	94611	630-F6
GLENDALE AV			**BERK**
1300	CAMPUS DR	94708	609-J7
1380	LA LOMA AV	94708	609-J7
1500	DEL MAR AV	94708	609-J7
GLENDALE AV			**OAK**
300	DESMOND ST	94618	629-J6
400	MANILA AV	94618	629-J6
GLENDOME CIR			**OAK**
700	EL CENTRO AV	94602	650-D3
1000	HOLLYWOOD AV	94602	650-D3
1000	EL CENTRO AV	94602	650-D3
GLENDORA AV			**OAK**
1000	EL CENTRO AV	94602	650-C3
1200	EDGEWOOD AV	94602	650-C3
GLENEDEN AV			**OAK**
1	GLEN AV	94611	630-A7
100	PIEDMONT AV	94611	630-A7
GLENFIELD AV			**OAK**
1300	WOODRUFF AV	94602	650-C3
1500	PARK BLVD	94602	650-C3
GLENLY RD			**OAK**
3300	GOLF LINKS RD	94605	671-A3
3320	BLANDON RD	94605	671-A3
GLENVIEW AV			**OAK**
500	WARFIELD AV	94610	650-A3
600	RAND AV	94610	650-A3
GLENWOOD AV			**OAK**
100	PIEDMONT AV	94611	629-J7
GLENWOOD GLADE			**OAK**
1	DUNCAN WY	94611	630-C6
90	BROADWAY TER	94611	630-C6
GLENWOOD ISL			**ALA**
	OTIS DR	94501	669-H3
GOLDEN GATE AV			**OAK**
	CHABOT RD	94618	630-A4
	GOLDEN GATE WY	94618	630-A4
	CHABOT RD	94618	630-A4
5000	BROADWAY TER	94618	630-B5
5060	ROMANY RD	94618	630-B5
5140	HILL RD	94618	630-B5
5180	BELALP PTH	94618	630-B5
5210	CHAUMONT PTH	94618	630-B5
5380	ACACIA AV	94618	630-B5
5460	GONDO PTH	94618	630-B5
5500	NOVA PTH	94618	630-B5
5580	AROLLO PTH	94618	630-B5
5610	EUSTICE AV	94618	630-B5
5620	BUENA VISTA AV	94618	630-B5
5800	GOLDEN GATE WY	94618	630-B5
GOLDEN GATE WY			**OAK**
5000	CHABOT RD	94618	630-A4
5000	GOLDEN GATE AV	94618	630-A4
5800	GOLDEN GATE AV	94618	630-A5
5830	BROADWAY	94618	630-A5
GOLF COURSE DR			**BERK**
3030	SHASTA RD	94708	610-A6
3100	BAYTREE LN	94708	610-A6
GOLF COURSE DR			**OAK**
1200	CENTENNIAL DR	94708	610-A7
1200	GRIZZLY PEAK BLVD	94708	610-A7
GOLF LINKS RD			**OAK**
8200	82ND AV	94605	670-J3
8400	COSGRAVE AV	94605	671-A3
8500	EL MONTE AV	94605	671-A3
8600	FONTAINE ST	94605	671-A3
8700	BLANDON RD	94605	671-A3
8800	GLENLY RD	94605	671-A3
8900	CASTLEWOOD ST	94605	671-A3
9600	ESPINOSA AV	94605	671-B4
9630	FLINTRIDGE AV	94605	671-B4
9700	ALCALA AV	94605	671-B4
9560	98TH AV	94605	671-B4
9840	MOUNTAIN BLVD	94605	671-B4
9860	CALAFIA AV	94605	671-B4
9780	ANZA AV	94605	671-B4
9880	BURGOS AV	94605	671-C4
9900	SIGOURNEY AV	94605	671-C3
9950	OAK HILL RD	94605	671-C3
10100	ELYSIAN FIELDS DR	94605	671-C3
10200	VENETIA RD	94605	671-D4
10700	SCOTIA AV	94605	671-D4
10900	CALODEN ST	94605	671-E4
10900	DUNKIRK AV	94605	671-E4
11000	SHETLAND AV	94605	671-E4
11100	GRASS VALLEY RD	94605	671-E5
11400	SUN VALLEY DR	94605	671-E6
GOMPERS			**ALA**
3000	MULVANY CIR	94501	649-E6
3020	CALIFORNIA	94501	649-E6
GONDO PTH			**OAK**
	GOLDEN GATE AV	94618	630-B5
	BUENA VISTA AV	94618	630-B5
GONSALVES CT			**ALA**
100	CREEDON CIR	94502	669-H5
GOODING DR			**ALB**
800	RILEY DR	94706	609-D6
800	RILEY DR	94710	609-D6
1000	RILEY DR	94706	609-D6
1000	RILEY DR	94710	609-D6
GORDON ST			**OAK**
4300	HIGH ST	94601	650-E7
4600	RENWICK ST	94601	650-E7
4660	POTTER ST	94601	650-F7
4700	MONTICELLO AV	94601	650-F7
GOSS ST			**OAK**
1700	WILLOW ST	94607	649-D3
1750	WOOD ST	94607	649-C3
1800	PINE ST	94607	649-C3
GOULD CT			**ALA**
1600	LINCOLN AV	94501	670-A2
GOULD ST			**OAK**
9800	98TH AV	94603	670-H6
10000	MEDFORD AV	94603	670-H6
GOULDIN RD			**OAK**
1600	THORNHILL DR	94611	630-E6
1830	ASPINWALL RD	94611	630-E6
1830	ASPINWALL RD	94611	630-E6
1900	ALHAMBRA AV	94611	630-E6
GRACE AV			**OAK**
920	LOWELL ST	94608	629-F5
1000	LOS ANGELES ST	94608	629-F5
GRACE CT			**ALA**
1000	CALHOUN ST	94501	670-A3
GRAEAGLE			**OAK**
1	KELLER AV	94605	671-D2
1	ELYSIAN FIELDS DR	94605	671-D2
GRAFFIAN ST			**OAK**
10100	TOWN SQUARE CT	94603	670-J6
10200	102ND AV	94603	670-J6
10300	103RD AV	94603	670-J6
10400	104TH AV	94603	670-J6
10500	105TH AV	94603	670-J6
10600	106TH AV	94603	670-J6
10700	107TH AV	94603	670-J6
GRAHAM PL			**OAK**
1	SKYLINE BLVD	94619	651-B6
GRAMERCY PL			**OAK**
300	KNIGHT ST	94603	670-G7
300	NATTRESS WY	94603	670-G7
GRANADA AV			**OAK**
9330	CREST AV	94605	671-B3
9430	MARGARITA AV	94605	671-B3
9520	MIRASOL AV	94605	671-B3
9600	OAK KNOLL BLVD	94605	671-B3
GRAND AV			**OAK**
600	MARTIN LUTHER KING JR WY	94612	649-G3
600	W GRAND AV	94612	649-G3
500	NORTHGATE AV	94612	649-G3
460	TELEGRAPH AV	94612	649-G3
430	VALLEY ST	94612	649-G3
390	BROADWAY	94612	649-G3
360	WEBSTER ST	94612	649-H3
300	VALDEZ ST	94612	649-H3
200	HARRISON ST	94612	649-H3
220	HARRISON ST	94612	649-H3
240	BAY PL	94610	649-H3
	BELLEVUE AV	94610	649-H3
250	PARK VIEW TER	94610	649-H3
	LENOX AV	94610	649-H3
300	LEE ST	94610	649-H3
330	PERKINS ST	94610	649-J3
360	ELLITA AV	94610	649-J3
400	STATEN AV	94610	649-J3
450	BELLEVUE AV	94610	649-J3
500	EUCLID AV	94610	649-J3
600	EL EMBARCADERO	94610	649-J3
620	EL EMBARCADERO	94610	649-J3
	MACARTHUR BLVD	94610	649-J3
3110	LAKE PARK AV	94610	649-J3
3200	LAKE PARK AV	94610	649-J3
3290	WALKER AV	94610	649-J3
1650	BRANDON ST	94611	630-A7
1660	RONADA AV	94611	630-A7
1700	MORAGA AV	94611	630-A7
1700	PLEASANT VALLEY AV	94611	630-A7
3290	ELWOOD AV	94610	650-A3
3450	ELWOOD AV	94610	650-A2
3500	MANDANA BLVD	94610	650-A2
3600	DAVIDSON WY	94610	650-A2
3670	BONHAM WY	94610	650-A2
3720	WELDON AV	94610	650-A2
3900	SUNNY SLOPE AV	94610	650-A2
4000	BOULEVARD WY	94610	650-A2
4100	WILDWOOD AV	94610	650-A2
4100	JEAN ST	94610	650-A2
GRAND AV			**PDMT**
1200	WILDWOOD AV	94610	650-A2
1200	JEAN ST	94610	650-A2
1260	FAIRVIEW AV	94610	650-A2
1350	SUNNYSIDE AV	94610	650-A1
1410	LINDA AV	94610	650-A1
1500	OAKLAND AV	94610	650-A1
1540	GREENBANK AV	94611	650-A1
	CAMBRIDGE WY	94611	650-A1
1540	GREENBANK AV	94611	650-A1
1550	LOWER GRAND AV	94611	650-A1
1650	ARROYO AV	94611	630-A7
1650	BRANDON ST	94611	630-A7
W GRAND AV			**OAK**
650	MARTIN LUTHER KING JR WY	94612	649-G3
650	GRAND AV	94612	649-G3
680	SAN PABLO AV	94612	649-G2
700	BRUSH ST	94612	649-F2
800	WEST ST	94607	649-F2
830	CURTIS ST	94607	649-F2
870	ISABELLA ST	94607	649-F2
900	MARKET ST	94607	649-F2
950	MYRTLE ST	94607	649-F2
1000	FILBERT ST	94607	649-F2
1050	LINDEN ST	94607	649-F2
1100	CHESTNUT ST	94607	649-F2
1150	ADELINE ST	94607	649-E2
1200	MAGNOLIA ST	94607	649-E2
1250	UNION ST	94607	649-E2
1350	POPLAR ST	94607	649-E2
1550	MANDELA PKWY	94607	649-E2
1600	MANDELA PKWY	94607	649-E2
1600	PERALTA ST	94607	649-E2
1700	CAMPBELL ST	94607	649-E2
1800	WILLOW ST	94607	649-E2
1910	WOOD ST	94607	649-D2
	FRONTAGE RD	94626	649-D2
	WAKE AV	94626	649-D1
	MARITIME ST	94626	649-D1
GRAND ST			**ALA**
300	SHORELINE DR	94501	669-H3
600	OTIS DR	94501	669-H2
750	PALMERA CT	94501	669-H2
800	DAYTON AV	94501	669-H2
900	CLINTON AV	94501	669-H2
1000	SAN JOSE AV	94501	669-H2
1100	SAN ANTONIO AV	94501	669-H2
1200	ENCINAL AV	94501	669-H2
1300	ALAMEDA AV	94501	669-H1
1400	CENTRAL AV	94501	669-H1
1500	SANTA CLARA AV	94501	669-H1
1550	SEABORN CT	94501	669-H1
1600	LINCOLN AV	94501	669-J1
1700	PACIFIC AV	94501	669-J1
1800	BUENA VISTA AV	94501	669-J1
1900	EAGLE AV	94501	669-J1
2000	CLEMENT AV	94501	669-J1
2050	FORTMANN WY	94501	649-J7
GRAND VIEW DR			**OAK**
1800	PERTH PL	94705	630-B3
1800	GRAND VIEW PL	94705	630-B3
1200	GRAVATT DR	94705	630-C3
1300	LIVE OAK RD	94705	630-B4
1800	DOROTHY PL	94705	630-C4
1870	SCHOONER HILL	94618	630-C4
1870	YANKEE HILL	94618	630-C4
1900	HILLER DR	94618	630-C4
GRAND VIEW PL			**OAK**
1000	VICENTE RD	94705	630-B3
1090	WEST VIEW DR	94705	630-B3
1100	GRAND VIEW DR	94705	630-B3
1100	PERTH PL	94705	630-B3
GRANDE VISTA AV			**OAK**
2400	E 24TH ST	94601	650-C6
2520	E 26TH ST	94601	650-C6
2610	E 27TH ST	94601	650-C5
2650	GRANDE VISTA PL	94601	650-C5
GRANDE VISTA PL			**OAK**
2300	GRANDE VISTA AV	94601	650-C5
GRANT ST			**BERK**
1400	ROSE ST	94703	609-G7
1420	VINE ST	94703	609-G7
1500	CEDAR ST	94703	629-G1
1600	LINCOLN ST	94703	629-G1
1700	VIRGINIA ST	94703	629-G1
1750	FRANCISCO ST	94703	629-G1
1800	DELAWARE ST	94703	629-G1
1900	HEARST AV	94703	629-G1
1950	BERKELEY WY	94703	629-G1
2000	UNIVERSITY AV	94703	629-G2
2100	ADDISON ST	94703	629-G2
2200	ALLSTON WY	94703	629-G2
2300	BANCROFT WY	94703	629-G2
2400	CHANNING WY	94703	629-G2
2500	DWIGHT WY	94703	629-G3
2550	BLAKE ST	94703	629-G3
2600	PARKER ST	94703	629-G3
2650	CARLETON ST	94703	629-G3
2700	DERBY ST	94703	629-G3
2700	DERBY ST	94703	629-G3
2750	WARD ST	94703	629-G3
2800	STUART ST	94703	629-G3
2850	OREGON ST	94703	629-G3
2900	RUSSELL ST	94703	629-G4
GRASS VALLEY CT			**OAK**
	GRASS VALLEY RD	94605	671-E4
GRASS VALLEY RD			**OAK**
4850	GOLF LINKS RD	94605	671-E4
4740	GLEN ARTNEY CT	94605	671-E4
4740	GLEN MANOR PL	94605	671-E4
4660	GRASS VALLEY CT	94605	671-E4
4640	SUN VALLEY DR	94605	671-E4
4600	SCOTIA AV	94605	671-E4
GRAVATT DR			**OAK**
1	ALVARADO RD	94705	630-B3
240	STEPHENS WY	94705	630-B3
390	STEPHENS WY	94705	630-B3
450	AMITO AV	94705	630-B3
700	GRAND VIEW DR	94705	630-B3
GRAVENSTEIN ST			**OAK**
700	APPLE ST	94603	670-H6
810	PEARMAIN ST	94603	670-H6
840	105TH AV	94603	670-H6
850	PIPPIN ST	94603	670-H6
900	105TH AV	94603	670-H6
900	RUSSET ST	94603	670-H6
GRAY ST			**OAK**
3520	35TH AV	94601	650-D7
3600	HARRINGTON AV	94601	650-D7
GRAYSON ST			**BERK**
900	7TH ST	94804	629-E4
930	8TH ST	94804	629-E4
1000	9TH ST	94804	629-E4
1030	10TH ST	94804	629-E3
1100	SAN PABLO AV	94804	629-E3
GREENACRE RD			**OAK**
3600	MACARTHUR BLVD	94619	650-F6
3620	MASTERSON ST	94619	650-G6
3700	MERRILL AV	94619	650-G6
3800	TULIP AV	94619	650-G6
GREENBANK AV			**PDMT**
1	ROSE AV	94611	650-A1
50	KINGSTON AV	94611	650-A1
100	LAKE AV	94611	650-A1
200	GRAND AV	94611	650-A1
200	GRAND AV	94611	650-A1
300	OAKLAND AV	94611	650-A1
GREENBRIER RD			**ALA**
400	FRANCISCAN WY	94501	669-H3
500	FERNDELL WK	94501	669-H3
500	KITTY HAWK PL	94501	669-H3

Address	Cross Street	ZIP	City / Pg-Grid
GREENBRIER ST			**OAK**
11300	BEMIS ST	94605	671-D5
11400	TURNER CT	94605	671-D5
11400	TURNER AV	94605	671-D5
GREENLY DR			**OAK**
7100	EDWARDS AV	94605	670-J1
7200	CIRCLE HILL DR	94605	670-J1
7840	COLUMBIAN DR	94605	671-A1
7700	FIELD ST	94605	671-A2
7800	LAMP ST	94605	671-A2
7900	KELLER AV	94605	671-A2
8000	SHONE AV	94605	671-A2
8100	HOLMES AV	94605	671-A2
8400	STERLING DR	94605	671-A2
GREENRIDGE DR			**OAK**
8000	KELLER AV	94605	671-B1
8180	RILEA WY	94605	671-B1
GREENVIEW DR			**OAK**
10300	ROYAL OAK RD	94605	671-C3
10500	ROYAL OAK RD	94605	671-C3
GREENWOOD AV			**OAK**
3800	PARK BLVD	94602	650-C4
4040	BRIGHTON AV	94602	650-C3
4080	HAMPEL ST	94602	650-C3
4090	HAMPEL ST	94602	650-C3
4180	FLEET RD	94602	650-C3
4200	NORWOOD AV	94602	650-C3
GREENWOOD COM			**BERK**
1	GREENWOOD TER	94708	609-H7
GREENWOOD TER			**BERK**
1400	ROSE ST	94708	609-H7
1470	GREENWOOD COM	94708	609-H7
1500	BUENA VISTA WY	94708	609-H7
GREGORY PL			**OAK**
1	GREGORY ST	94619	650-G5
GREGORY ST			**OAK**
4200	REINHARDT DR	94619	650-G5
4100	GREGORY PL	94619	650-G5
4200	REINHARDT DR	94619	650-G5
GRESHAM DR			**ALA**
	BUENA VISTA AV	94501	649-F7
	WILLET CT	94501	649-F7
	AVOCET CT	94501	649-F7
	CURLEW CT	94501	649-F7
	ATLANTIC AV	94501	649-F7
GRISBORNE AV			**OAK**
5600	THORNHILL DR	94611	630-D7
5800	THORNHILL DR	94611	630-D7
GRIZZLY PEAK BLVD			**BERK**
450	SPRUCE ST	94708	609-G4
450	WOODMONT AV	94708	609-G4
500	CRAGMONT AV	94708	609-H4
570	EUCLID AV	94708	609-H4
600	CRESTON RD	94708	609-H4
650	HILLDALE AV	94708	609-H5
700	KEELER AV	94708	609-H5
800	SUNSET LN	94708	609-H5
870	MARIN AV	94708	609-H5
900	FOREST LN	94708	609-H5
930	FOREST LN	94708	609-H5
1030	LATHAM LN	94708	609-J6
1100	CRESTON RD	94708	609-J6
1130	STEVENSON AV	94708	609-J6
1140	MUIR WY	94708	609-J6
1150	STODDARD WY	94708	609-J6
1190	SHASTA RD	94708	609-J6
1200	SHASTA RD	94708	609-J6
1470	ARCADE AV	94708	609-J6
100	HILL RD	94708	610-A7
110	AVENIDA DR	94708	610-A7
150	SENIOR AV	94708	610-A7
	SUMMIT RD	94708	610-A7
160	SUMMIT RD	94708	610-A7
200	GOLF COURSE DR	94708	610-A7
200	CENTENNIAL DR	94708	610-A7
GRIZZLY PEAK BLVD			**CCCo**
5200	CLAREMONT AV	-	630-D2
GRIZZLY PEAK BLVD			**OAK**
3200	GOLF COURSE DR	94720	610-A7
3200	GOLF COURSE DR	94708	610-A7
3200	CENTENNIAL DR	94708	610-A7
5200	CLAREMONT AV	94705	630-C2
5370	MARLBOROUGH TER	94705	630-D3
5550	GRIZZLY TERRACE DR	94611	630-D3
5660	GRIZZLY TERRACE DR	94611	630-D3
GRIZZLY TERRACE DR			**OAK**
700	GRIZZLY PEAK BLVD	94611	630-D3
740	WOODSIDE WY	94611	630-D3
790	WOODMONT WY	94611	630-D3
800	GRIZZLY PEAK BLVD	94611	630-D3
GROSVENOR PL			**OAK**
700	ALMA PL	94610	650-B4
700	EXCELSIOR AV	94610	650-B4
800	HOLMAN RD	94610	650-B3
880	TRESTLE GLEN RD	94610	650-B3
920	UNDERHILLS RD	94610	650-B3
1040	HUBERT RD	94610	650-B3
1050	SUNNYHILLS RD	94610	650-B3
1100	LONGRIDGE RD	94610	650-B3
GROVE ST			**ALA**
1300	ENCINAL AV	94501	670-A3
1330	JACKSON ST	94501	670-B3
1360	VAN BUREN ST	94501	670-B3
1400	CENTRAL AV	94501	670-B3
1500	SANTA CLARA AV	94501	670-B3
GRUMMAN ST			**OAK**
1000	EARHART RD	94621	670-C6
1040	LOCKHEED ST	94621	670-D6
GUIDO ST			**OAK**
3000	MONTEREY BLVD	94602	650-F4
3250	RETTIG AV	94602	650-F4
3320	NORTON AV	94602	650-G4
3350	NORTON AV	94602	650-G4
3400	BENNETT PL	94602	650-G4
3400	BENNETT PL	94602	650-G5
3500	35TH AV	94602	650-G5
GUILFORD RD			**PDMT**
1	HIGHLAND AV	94611	650-B1
200	HIGHLAND AV	94611	650-B1
GUNN DR			**OAK**
6600	SHEPHERD CANYON RD	94611	630-G7
6800	FORESTLAND WY	94611	630-G7
6800	SHEPHERD CANYON RD	94611	630-G7
6900	SARONI DR	94611	630-G7
GWIN CT			**OAK**
6500	GWIN RD	94611	630-D5
GWIN RD			**OAK**
6400	BROADWAY TER	94611	630-D5
6500	GWIN CT	94611	630-D5
GYPSY LN			**OAK**
1	ALVARADO RD	94705	630-C2
H			
E H ST			**OAK**
	13TH ST	94625	649-C4
	15TH ST	94625	649-C4
HADDON PL			**OAK**
700	TRESTLE GLEN RD	94610	650-A3
HADDON RD			**OAK**
300	PARK BLVD	94606	650-A4
400	PARK BLVD	94606	650-A4
400	ATHOL AV	94606	649-J4
500	BROOKLYN AV	94606	650-A4
550	CLEVELAND ST	94606	650-A4
600	PROSPECT AV	94610	650-A3
700	HILLGIRT CIR	94610	650-A3
HAGAR AV			**PDMT**
170	MOUNTAIN AV	94611	650-C1
100	PACIFIC AV	94611	650-C1
170	PACIFIC AV	94611	650-C1
HAGEMAN AV			**OAK**
3500	35TH AV	94619	650-E6
HAIGHT AV			**ALA**
100	PACIFIC AV	94501	669-E1
200	LINCOLN AV	94501	669-E1
300	3RD ST	94501	669-E1
400	4TH ST	94501	669-E1
500	5TH ST	94501	669-F1
550	LINDEN ST	94501	669-F1
600	6TH ST	94501	669-F1
700	WEBSTER ST	94501	669-F1
800	8TH ST	94501	669-G1
900	9TH ST	94501	669-G1
HALCYON CT			**BERK**
3000	WEBSTER ST	94705	629-H4
3100	PRINCE ST	94705	629-H4
HALE AV			**OAK**
400	DOUGLAS AV	94603	670-G7
440	CARY AV	94603	670-H7
500	EDES AV	94603	670-H7
HALKIN LN			**BERK**
1	SPRUCE ST	94708	609-G5
50	ALAMO AV	94708	609-G5
100	CRAGMONT AV	94708	609-G5
HALLECK ST			**EMVL**
4200	PARK AV	94608	629-E7
4300	SHERWIN AV	94608	629-E7
HALLECK ST			**OAK**
4000	BEACH ST	94608	629-E7
4200	PARK AV	94608	629-E7
HALLIDAY AV			**OAK**
6900	CHURCH ST	94605	670-H2
7300	73RD AV	94605	670-H2
	73RD AV	94605	670-H2
7300	73RD AV	94605	670-H2
7700	77TH AV	94605	670-H2
HAMILTON PL			**OAK**
1	HARRISON ST	94612	649-H2
1	HARRISON ST	94611	649-H2
HAMILTON ST			**OAK**
6900	69TH AV	94621	670-F3
7000	70TH AV	94621	670-F3
7100	71ST AV	94621	670-F3
7200	72ND AV	94621	670-F3
7300	73RD AV	94621	670-G3
	HEGENBERGER EXWY	94621	670-G3
7400	HEGENBERGER EXWY	94621	670-G4
7500	75TH AV	94621	670-G4
7600	76TH AV	94621	670-G4
7700	77TH AV	94621	670-G4
HAMLINE AV			**OAK**
3200	E 32ND ST	94602	650-C4
3200	22ND AV	94602	650-C4
HAMPEL ST			**OAK**
1100	HOLMAN RD	94602	650-C3
1200	GREENWOOD AV	94602	650-C3
1200	GREENWOOD AV	94602	650-C3
1300	PARK BLVD	94602	650-C4
1300	GLEN PARK RD	94602	650-C4
1370	RANDOLPH AV	94602	650-C4
1390	RANDOLPH AV	94602	650-C4
1430	ARDLEY AV	94602	650-C4
1490	WOODRUFF AV	94602	650-C4
1540	ELSTON AV	94602	650-C4
1590	LINWOOD AV	94602	650-C4
1650	LA CRESTA AV	94602	650-D4
1700	EVERETT AV	94602	650-D4
HAMPTON CT			**ALA**
1	AVINGTON RD	94502	669-J5
HAMPTON RD			**PDMT**
1	CROCKER AV	94611	650-C2
1	CROCKER AV	94610	650-C2
60	KING AV	94611	650-C2
60	KING AV	94610	650-C2
100	SEAVIEW AV	94611	650-C2
100	SEAVIEW AV	94610	650-C2
140	INDIAN RD	94611	650-C2
140	INDIAN RD	94610	650-C2
180	SAINT JAMES DR	94611	650-D2
260	GLEN ALPINE RD	94611	650-D2
300	LA SALLE AV	94611	650-D2
330	CREST RD	94611	650-D2
360	LEXFORD RD	94611	650-D2
480	SANDRINGHAM RD	94611	650-D2
520	INVERLEITH TER	94611	650-D2
600	ESTATES DR	94611	650-D2
HANCOCK ST			**ALA**
	W MIDWAY AV	94501	649-E6
	STARDUST PL	94501	649-E6
	SERENADE PL	94501	649-E7
	W TOWER AV	94501	649-E7
	W TRIDENT AV	94501	649-E7
	W SEAPLANE LAGOON	94501	649-E7
HANLY RD			**OAK**
3260	EL CENTRO AV	94602	650-D3
3260	OAKMORE PL	94602	650-D3
4000	WATERHOUSE RD	94602	650-D3
HANNAH ST			**OAK**
2800	PERALTA ST	94608	649-E1
2900	32ND ST	94608	649-E1
3350	34TH ST	94608	649-E1
HANOVER AV			**OAK**
200	LAKESHORE AV	94606	649-J4
220	WAYNE AV	94606	649-J4
240	WAYNE AV	94606	649-J4
280	LESTER AV	94606	649-J4
410	NEWTON AV	94606	649-J4
430	LESTER AV	94606	649-J4
500	BROOKLYN AV	94606	649-J4
HANSEN AV			**ALA**
1300	ENCINAL AV	94501	670-B4
1350	MEYERS AV	94501	670-B4
1400	CENTRAL AV	94501	670-B4
HANSOM DR			**OAK**
7500	SKYLINE BLVD	94619	651-C7
7550	AVONOAK CT	94605	651-C7
7600	SURREY LN	94605	671-C1
7700	PINECREST DR	94605	671-C1
7830	CHARIOT LN	94605	671-C1
7900	PHAETON DR	94605	671-C1
7950	SHAY DR	94605	671-C1
8100	SHAY DR	94605	671-D1
8130	PHAETON DR	94605	671-D2
8200	COACH DR	94605	671-D2
8300	KELLER AV	94605	671-D2
HARBOR BAY PKWY			**ALA**
1100	DOOLITTLE DR	94502	670-C6
1200	MAITLAND DR	94502	670-B7
1280	ROAD B	94502	690-A1
1280	SOUTH LOOP RD	94502	690-A1
	ROAD A	94502	690-A1
1360	SOUTH LOOP RD	94502	690-A1
1360	NORTH LOOP RD	94502	690-A1
1520	NORTH LOOP RD	94502	669-J7
HARBOR BAY PKWY			**OAK**
1100	DOOLITTLE DR	94621	670-C6
1200	MAITLAND DR	94621	670-C6
HARBOR LIGHT RD			**ALA**
300	SHORELINE DR	94501	669-G3
500	SAND BEACH PL	94501	669-G3
HARBOR RD			**ALA**
	SHERWOOD LN	94502	669-J5
HARBOR VIEW AV			**OAK**
3500	35TH AV	94619	650-F5
3600	MAGEE AV	94619	650-F5
3700	LOMA VISTA AV	94619	650-F5
3800	BROWN AV	94619	650-G5
3900	VIRDEN AV	94619	650-G5
3900	PATTERSON AV	94619	650-G5
4200	VALE AV	94619	650-G6
4400	HUNTINGTON ST	94619	650-G6
4500	CARSON ST	94619	650-G6
HARBORD CT			**OAK**
1	HARBORD DR	94618	630-C6
HARBORD DR			**OAK**
4300	BROADWAY TER	94618	630-B6
4400	BUCKEYE AV	94618	630-B6
4510	MORRILL CT	94618	630-B6
4530	MANDALAY RD	94618	630-B6
4600	DULWICH RD	94618	630-B6
4780	MORPETH ST	94618	630-B6
4800	BIEHS CT	94618	630-B6
5120	HARBORD CT	94618	630-C6
5200	MODOC AV	94618	630-C6
5200	FLORENCE AV	94618	630-C6
5200	MODOC AV	94618	630-C6
5300	CLAREWOOD DR	94618	630-C7
5340	HILLTOP CRES	94618	630-C7
5400	AMY DR	94618	630-C7
5440	MAXWELTON RD	94618	630-C7
5500	TEMPLAR PL	94618	630-C7
5600	MORAGA AV	94611	630-D7
5970	MCANDREW DR	94611	630-D7
6020	LANE CT	94611	650-C1
6070	WOOD DR	94611	650-D1
6090	MARR AV	94611	650-C1
6200	BLAIR AV	94611	650-C1
HARDING CIR			**BERK**
1	OLYMPUS AV	94708	609-J7
HARDING WY			**OAK**
4000	FRUITVALE AV	94602	650-E3
4100	TIFFIN RD	94602	650-E3
HARDWICK AV			**PDMT**
50	BLAIR AV	94611	650-B1
1	LANGDON CT	94611	650-B1
50	OAKLAND AV	94611	650-B1
HARDY ST			**OAK**
400	MILES AV	94618	629-J6
HARLAN ST			**EMVL**
4000	40TH ST	94608	629-F7
4100	PARK AV	94608	629-F7
HARLAN ST			**OAK**
3350	FITZGERALD ST	94608	649-F1
3350	34TH ST	94608	649-F1
HARMON AV			**OAK**
5500	55TH AV	94621	670-F2
5700	57TH AV	94621	670-F2
5800	SEMINARY AV	94621	670-F2
5800	SEMINARY AV	94621	670-F2
6200	62ND AV	94621	670-F2
6200	62ND AV	94621	670-F2
6400	64TH AV	94621	670-F2
HARMON ST			**BERK**
1300	IDAHO ST	94702	629-F5
1350	BOISE ST	94702	629-F5
1400	BAKER ST	94702	629-F5
1500	SACRAMENTO ST	94703	629-F5
1600	CALIFORNIA ST	94703	629-G4
1700	KING ST	94703	629-G4
1800	ELLIS ST	94703	629-G4
1800	ADELINE ST	94703	629-G4
1900	65TH ST	94703	629-G4
HAROLD ST			**OAK**
2400	FRUITVALE AV	94602	650-D5
2450	FLAGG AV	94602	650-D5
2490	CHAMPION ST	94602	650-D5
2610	BOSTON AV	94602	650-D5
2680	WILSON PL	94602	650-D5
2740	LAGUNA WY	94602	650-D5
2800	COOLIDGE AV	94602	650-D5
HAROLD WY			**BERK**
2200	ALLSTON WY	94704	629-G2
2300	KITTREDGE ST	94704	629-G2
HARPER ST			**BERK**
2900	RUSSELL ST	94703	629-G4
3000	ASHBY AV	94703	629-G4
3100	PRINCE ST	94703	629-G4
3120	WOOLSEY ST	94703	629-G4
3120	WOOLSEY ST	94703	629-G4
3200	FAIRVIEW ST	94703	629-G4
HARPER ST			**OAK**
3470	35TH AV	94601	650-D7
3540	CROSBY AV	94601	650-D7
3600	36TH AV	94601	650-D7
HARRINGTON AV			**OAK**
1800	FOOTHILL BLVD	94601	650-D7
1880	SAN JUAN ST	94601	650-D7
2140	GALINDO ST	94601	650-D7
2150	CARRINGTON WY	94601	650-D7
2190	SANTA RITA ST	94601	650-D7
2220	GRAY ST	94601	650-D7
2280	CUSTER ST	94601	650-D7
2340	DAVIS ST	94601	650-D7
2400	MEADOW ST	94601	650-D6
2500	LYON AV	94601	650-D6
2570	NEVIL ST	94601	650-E6
HARRISON ST			**ALA**
	MARINER SQUARE DR	94501	649-F6
90	EMBARCADERO W	94501	649-F5
90	EMBARCADERO	94501	649-F5
HARRISON ST			**BERK**
600	EASTSHORE FRONTAGE RD	94710	609-C7
700	2ND ST	94710	609-C7
700	3RD ST	94710	609-C7
710	CEDARWOOD LN	94710	609-C7
750	4TH ST	94710	609-D7
800	5TH ST	94710	609-D7
850	6TH ST	94710	609-D7
900	7TH ST	94710	609-D7
950	8TH ST	94710	609-D7
1000	9TH ST	94710	609-D7
1050	10TH ST	94710	609-D7
1100	SAN PABLO AV	94706	609-D7
1150	KAINS AV	94706	609-E7
1200	STANNAGE AV	94706	609-E7
HARRISON ST			**OAK**
90	EMBARCADERO W	94607	649-G5
90	EMBARCADERO	94607	649-G5
200	2ND ST	94607	649-G5
300	3RD ST	94607	649-G5
400	4TH ST	94607	649-G5
490	5TH ST	94607	649-G5
700	7TH ST	94607	649-G4
800	8TH ST	94607	649-G4
900	9TH ST	94607	649-G4
1000	10TH ST	94607	649-G4
1100	11TH ST	94607	649-G4
1200	12TH ST	94612	649-G4
1300	13TH ST	94612	649-G4
1400	14TH ST	94612	649-G4
1500	15TH ST	94612	649-G4
1800	17TH ST	94612	649-G3
1900	19TH ST	94612	649-H3
2000	20TH ST	94612	649-H3
2100	LAKESIDE DR	94612	649-H3
2120	21ST ST	94612	649-H3
2140	GRAND AV	94612	649-H3
2200	GRAND AV	94612	649-H3
2280	23RD ST	94612	649-H3
2500	24TH ST	94612	649-H3
2500	27TH ST	94612	649-H2
2500	27TH ST	94610	649-H2
2500	BAY PL	94610	649-H2
	HAMILTON PL	94611	649-H2
	HAMILTON PL	94610	649-H2
2830	OAKLAND AV	94611	649-H2
2830	ORANGE ST	94611	649-H2
2860	FAIRMOUNT AV	94611	649-H2
2920	29TH ST	94611	649-H2
3000	GARLAND ST	94611	649-H2
3100	FRISBIE ST	94611	649-J2
3300	PEARL ST	94611	649-J2
3400	STANLEY PL	94611	649-J2
3500	SANTA CLARA AV	94610	649-J2
3520	SANTA CLARA AV	94611	649-J2
3520	SANTA CLARA AV	94610	649-J2
3700	MOSS AV	94611	649-J1
3900	BAYO VISTA AV	94611	649-J1
4000	MONTE VISTA AV	94611	649-J1
HARUFF ST			**EMVL**
1450	PELADEAU ST	94608	629-E6
1500	LANDREGAN ST	94608	629-E6
HARVARD CIR			**BERK**
1	FAIRLAWN DR	94708	609-J7
1	SENIOR AV	94708	609-J7
HARVARD DR			**ALA**
1800	NORTHWOOD DR	94501	670-B2
1900	FERNSIDE BLVD	94501	670-B2
2000	WINDSOR DR	94501	670-B2
2100	MARINA DR	94501	670-B2
HARVARD RD			**OAK**
1000	WINSOR AV	94610	650-B2
1000	LAKESHORE AV	94610	650-B2
1020	ANNERLEY RD	94610	650-B2
1040	RANLEIGH WY	94610	650-B2
HARVARD RD			**PDMT**
1030	RANLEIGH WY	94610	650-B2
1100	PORTSMOUTH RD	94610	650-B2
1120	PROSPECT RD	94610	650-B2
1170	ANNERLEY RD	94610	650-B2
1180	OAKMONT AV	94610	650-B2
1200	LAKESHORE AV	94610	650-B2
HARVEY AV			**OAK**
5500	BANCROFT AV	94601	670-F1
5500	55TH AV	94605	670-F1
5500	55TH AV	94621	670-F1
5700	57TH AV	94605	670-F1
5700	57TH AV	94621	670-F1
HARWOOD AV			**OAK**
6000	COLLEGE AV	94618	629-J5
6150	AUBURN AV	94618	629-J5
6290	ROCKWELL ST	94618	629-J5
	IVANHOE RD	94618	630-A4
	ROSS ST	94618	630-A4
6300	ROSS ST	94618	630-A4
HASKELL ST			**BERK**
1200	SAN PABLO AV	94702	629-F4
1300	MABEL ST	94702	629-F4
1400	ACTON ST	94702	629-F4
HASSLER WY			**OAK**
1	EDGEWATER DR	94621	670-E5
100	OAKPORT ST	94621	670-E5
HASTE ST			**BERK**
1900	MARTIN LUTHER KING JR WY	94704	629-G2
2000	MILVIA ST	94704	629-G2
2110	SHATTUCK AV	94704	629-H2
2190	FULTON ST	94704	629-H2
2290	ELLSWORTH ST	94704	629-H2
2390	DANA ST	94704	629-H2
2490	TELEGRAPH AV	94704	629-J2
2590	BOWDITCH ST	94704	629-J2
2690	COLLEGE AV	94704	629-J2
2800	PIEDMONT AV	94704	629-J2
HAVEN ST			**EMVL**
4000	40TH ST	94608	629-F7
4100	PARK AV	94608	629-F7
HAVENSCOURT BLVD			**OAK**
1400	INTERNATIONAL BLVD	94621	670-G2
1570	FLORA ST	94621	670-G2
1600	FLORA ST	94605	670-G2
2400	AVENAL AV	94605	670-G2
2600	ARTHUR ST	94605	670-G2
2700	BANCROFT AV	94605	670-H2
2800	BANCROFT AV	94605	670-G2
2800	BANCROFT AV	94605	670-H2
2900	FOOTHILL BLVD	94605	670-H2
2900	CAMDEN ST	94605	670-H2
HAVERHILL DR			**OAK**
2600	CHELTON DR	94611	650-F1
2800	LONGCROFT DR	94611	650-F1
HAWKS HILL CT			**OAK**
1	HILLER DR	94618	630-C4
1	SPYGLASS HILL	94618	630-C4
HAWLEY ST			**OAK**
6900	69TH AV	94621	670-F3
7000	70TH AV	94621	670-F4
7100	71ST AV	94621	670-F4
7200	72ND AV	94621	670-F4
7300	73RD AV	94621	670-F4
7400	HEGENBERGER EXWY	94621	670-F4
7400	HEGENBERGER EXWY	94621	670-F4
7500	75TH AV	94621	670-F4
7600	76TH AV	94621	670-F4
7700	77TH AV	94621	670-F4
HAWTHORNE AV			**OAK**
300	BROADWAY	94611	649-H1
300	BROADWAY	94609	649-H1
350	WEBSTER ST	94611	649-H1
350	WEBSTER ST	94609	649-H1
300	WEBSTER ST	94609	649-H1
370	SUMMIT ST	94609	649-H1
440	ELM ST	94609	649-H1
500	TELEGRAPH AV	94609	649-H1
HAWTHORNE ST			**ALA**
1300	SAN ANTONIO AV	94501	669-G2
HAWTHORNE TER			**BERK**
1400	EUCLID AV	94708	609-H7
1500	VINE ST	94708	609-H7

© 2006 Rand McNally & Company

PRIMARY STREET Address	Cross Street	ZIP	CITY Pg-Grid
HAWTHORNE TER			**BERK**
1600	CEDAR ST	94708	609-H7
2500	LE ROY AV	94708	609-H7
2600	EUCLID AV	94708	609-H7
HAYES ST			**OAK**
5900	SEMINARY AV	94621	670-F2
6300	62ND AV	94621	670-F2
6200	62ND AV	94605	670-F2
6400	64TH AV	94605	670-F2
HAYS CT			**ALA**
1	SALMON RD	94502	669-H6
HAZEL LN			**ALA**
3400	JOST LN	94502	670-A7
3450	THATCH LN	94502	670-A7
3500	MELROSE AV	94502	670-A7
HAZEL LN			**PDMT**
1	HIGHLAND AV	94611	650-B1
30	REQUA PL	94611	650-B1
30	REQUA RD	94611	650-B1
HAZEL RD			**BERK**
1	DOMINGO AV	94705	630-A4
100	CLAREMONT AV	94705	630-A4
HAZELWOOD CT			**OAK**
1	MADDUX DR	94603	670-G6
HEAFEY RD			**OAK**
4520	SEQUOYAH RD	94605	671-D2
HEARST AV			**BERK**
600	EASTSHORE BLVD	94804	629-D2
640	2ND ST	94804	629-D2
700	3RD ST	94804	629-D2
730	4TH ST	94804	629-D2
800	5TH ST	94804	629-D2
830	6TH ST	94804	629-D2
900	7TH ST	94804	629-D2
930	8TH ST	94804	629-D2
1000	9TH ST	94804	629-E2
1030	10TH ST	94804	629-E2
1100	SAN PABLO AV	94702	629-E2
1200	CURTIS ST	94702	629-E2
1200	CURTIS ST	94702	629-E1
1260	CHESTNUT ST	94702	629-F1
1350	FRANKLIN ST	94702	629-F1
1400	ACTON ST	94702	629-F1
1430	SHORT ST	94702	629-F1
1500	SACRAMENTO ST	94702	629-F1
1500	SACRAMENTO ST	94703	629-F1
1600	CALIFORNIA ST	94703	629-F1
1700	MCGEE AV	94703	629-G1
1800	GRANT ST	94703	629-G1
1900	MARTIN LUTHER KING JR WY	94709	629-G1
1900	MARTIN LUTHER KING JR WY	94704	629-G1
1960	BONITA AV	94709	629-G1
1960	BONITA AV	94704	629-G1
2020	MILVIA ST	94709	629-G1
2020	MILVIA ST	94704	629-G1
2070	HENRY ST	94709	629-G1
2070	HENRY ST	94704	629-G1
2130	SHATTUCK AV	94709	629-G1
2130	SHATTUCK AV	94704	629-G1
2190	WALNUT ST	94709	629-H1
2190	WALNUT ST	94704	629-H1
2250	OXFORD ST	94709	629-H1
2250	OXFORD ST	94720	629-H1
2290	SPRUCE ST	94709	629-H1
2290	SPRUCE ST	94720	629-H1
2370	LE CONTE AV	94709	629-H1
2370	LE CONTE AV	94720	629-H1
2370	ARCH ST	94720	629-H1
2460	SCENIC AV	94709	629-H1
2460	SCENIC AV	94720	629-H1
2560	EUCLID AV	94709	629-H1
2560	EUCLID AV	94720	629-H1
2660	LE ROY AV	94709	629-J1
2660	LE ROY AV	94720	629-J1
2730	GAYLEY RD	94709	629-J1
2730	GAYLEY RD	94720	629-J1
2730	LA LOMA AV	94720	629-J1
2800	CYCLOTRON RD	94709	629-J1
2800	CYCLOTRON RD	94720	629-J1
2800	HIGHLAND PL	94720	629-J1
HEARST AV			**OAK**
2400	LINCOLN AV	94602	650-E4
2600	LAGUNA AV	94602	650-E4
HEARTWOOD DR			**OAK**
6700	SARONI DR	94611	630-F7
6500	COLTON BLVD	94611	630-E7
6700	ASILOMAR CIR	94611	630-E7
6700	COLTON BLVD	94611	630-E7
HEATHER RIDGE WY			**OAK**
6300	PINEHAVEN RD	94611	630-E5
6300	VALLEY VIEW RD	94611	630-E5
6500	THORNHILL DR	94611	630-E6
HECKER CT			**ALA**
	BARTLETT DR	94501	649-G7
HEDGE CT			**OAK**
2900	HEDGE LN	94602	650-F3
HEDGE LN			**OAK**
4900	BURDECK DR	94602	650-F3
4950	HEDGE CT	94602	650-F3
5000	JOAQUIN MILLER RD	94602	650-F3
HEGENBERGER CT			**OAK**
100	HEGENBERGER LP	94621	670-F6
HEGENBERGER EXWY			**OAK**
1100	73RD AV	94621	670-G3
1100	INTERNATIONAL BLVD	94621	670-G3
950	HAMILTON ST	94621	670-F4
900	HAWLEY ST	94621	670-F4
900	HEGENBERGER RD	94621	670-F4
950	HAWLEY ST	94621	670-F4
1100	HAMILTON ST	94621	670-G3
1400	73RD AV	94621	670-G3
1400	INTERNATIONAL BLVD	94621	670-G3
HEGENBERGER LP			**OAK**
1	HEGENBERGER RD	94621	670-F7
70	CAIRO RD	94621	670-F6
150	HEGENBERGER CT	94621	670-F6
200	HEGENBERGER RD	94621	670-F6
HEGENBERGER PL			**OAK**
1	HEGENBERGER RD	94621	670-F7
HEGENBERGER RD			**OAK**
590	AIRPORT DR	94621	690-E1
50	DOOLITTLE DR	94621	690-E1
100	AIRPORT DR	94621	670-E7
100	PARDEE DR	94621	670-E7
200	HEGENBERGER PL	94621	670-F7
300	LEET DR	94621	670-F7
340	HEGENBERGER LP	94621	670-F6
	EDGEWATER DR	94621	670-F6
280	HEGENBERGER LP	94621	670-F6
560	COLISEUM WY	94621	670-F5
560	EDES AV	94621	670-F5
600	COLLINS DR	94621	670-F5
	SAN LEANDRO ST	94621	670-F4
810	SNELL ST	94621	670-F4
900	HEGENBERGER EXWY	94621	670-F4
HEINZ AV			**BERK**
900	7TH ST	94804	629-E4
920	8TH ST	94804	629-E4
1000	9TH ST	94804	629-E4
1030	10TH ST	94804	629-E4
1100	SAN PABLO AV	94804	629-E4
HELEN CT			**OAK**
6600	66TH ST	94608	629-F4
HELEN ST			**OAK**
2800	PERALTA ST	94608	649-E1
2900	32ND ST	94608	649-E1
3350	34TH ST	94608	649-E1
HELLMAN ST			**OAK**
10800	MALCOLM AV	94605	671-C5
HEMLOCK LN			**OAK**
1	HEMLOCK ST	94611	630-F6
50	CHAMBERS LN	94611	630-F6
50	COLTON BLVD	94611	630-F6
HEMLOCK ST			**OAK**
7000	COLTON BLVD	94611	630-F6
7030	LODGE CT	94611	630-F6
7130	HEMLOCK LN	94611	630-F6
7200	SNAKE RD	94611	630-F6
HEMPHILL PL			**OAK**
300	CORONADO AV	94618	629-J6
400	DESMOND ST	94618	629-J6
HENRIETTA ST			**OAK**
3400	34TH AV	94601	650-D6
HENRY ST			**BERK**
1200	EUNICE ST	94709	609-G7
1200	SUTTER ST	94709	609-G7
1300	BERRYMAN ST	94709	609-G7
1400	ROSE ST	94709	609-G7
1400	SHATTUCK PL	94709	609-G7
1400	ROSE ST	94709	609-G7
1500	VINE ST	94709	609-G7
1600	CEDAR ST	94709	609-G7
1900	HEARST AV	94704	629-G1
2000	BERKELEY WY	94704	629-G1
HENRY ST			**OAK**
300	3RD ST	94607	649-D4
500	5TH ST	94607	649-D3
660	7TH ST	94607	649-D3
800	8TH ST	94607	649-D3
HERCULES CT			**ALA**
	ROSEFIELD LP	94501	649-F7
HERITAGE			**OAK**
	ELYSIAN FIELDS DR	94605	671-D2
	IRONWOOD	94605	671-D2
HERMANN ST			**OAK**
5700	AYALA AV	94609	629-H5
5800	58TH ST	94609	629-H5
5800	MARTIN ST	94609	629-H5
HERMOSA AV			**OAK**
1	MANDALAY RD	94618	630-B6
140	MARGUERITE DR	94618	630-B6
200	DULWICH RD	94618	630-B6
200	JACOBUS AV	94618	630-B6
300	FLORENCE AV	94618	630-B6
HERON CT			**ALA**
	BRUZZONE DR	94501	649-F7
	SANDERLING CT	94501	649-F7
HERON DR			**OAK**
5800	MASONIC AV	94618	630-C7
5900	PROCTOR AV	94618	630-C7
HERRIER ST			**OAK**
3300	NORTON AV	94602	650-F4
3350	EASTLAKE AV	94602	650-F5
3400	MIDVALE AV	94602	650-F5
HERRIOTT AV			**OAK**
3100	VIRGINIA AV	94619	650-F7
3230	FAIRBAIRN ST	94619	650-F7
HERZOG ST			**OAK**
5900	59TH ST	94608	629-F5
6000	60TH ST	94608	629-F5
6100	61ST ST	94608	629-F5
6200	62ND ST	94608	629-F5
6300	63RD ST	94608	629-F5
6400	ALCATRAZ AV	94608	629-F5
6500	65TH ST	94608	629-F5
6600	66TH ST	94608	629-F4
HESKET RD			**OAK**
9900	GIBRALTAR RD	94603	670-G7
10000	EMPIRE RD	94603	670-G7
HIBBARD ST			**ALA**
1600	LINCOLN AV	94501	669-H1
1700	PACIFIC AV	94501	669-J1
	BUENA VISTA AV	94501	669-J1
1900	EAGLE AV	94501	669-J1
HICKORY ST			**OAK**
2700	FRUITVALE AV	94602	650-C5
HIGH CT			**BERK**
1100	OAK ST	94708	609-H6
HIGH KNOLL DR			**OAK**
4200	RIDGEMONT DR	94619	650-J6
4300	CAMPUS DR	94619	650-J6
HIGH ST			**ALA**
900	OTIS DR	94501	670-A4
900	BAYVIEW DR	94501	670-A4
1000	CALHOUN ST	94501	670-A4
1050	FILLMORE ST	94501	670-A4
1100	WASHINGTON ST	94501	670-B4
1150	ADAMS ST	94501	670-B4
1200	SAN JOSE AV	94501	670-B4
1250	MADISON ST	94501	670-B3
1300	ENCINAL AV	94501	670-B3
	JACKSON ST	94501	670-B3
1330	BRIGGS AV	94501	670-B3
	VAN BUREN ST	94501	670-B3
1360	STERLING AV	94501	670-B3
1400	CENTRAL AV	94501	670-B3
1500	SANTA CLARA AV	94501	670-B3
1530	LIBERTY AV	94501	670-B3
1580	GARFIELD AV	94501	670-B3
1600	LINCOLN AV	94501	670-B3
1650	THOMPSON AV	94501	670-B3
1700	FAIRVIEW AV	94501	670-B3
1800	MONTE VISTA AV	94501	670-C3
1900	BAYO VISTA AV	94501	670-C2
2000	FERNSIDE BLVD	94501	670-C2
2000	GIBBONS DR	94501	670-C2
2100	FERNSIDE BLVD	94501	670-C2
2110	MARINA DR	94501	670-C2
HIGH ST			**OAK**
400	TIDEWATER AV	94601	670-C2
430	HULL ST	94601	670-C2
480	HOWARD ST	94601	670-C2
500	HOWARD ST	94601	670-C2
520	JENSEN ST	94601	670-C2
620	COLISEUM WY	94601	670-C2
840	WATTLING ST	94601	670-D2
1010	SAN LEANDRO ST	94601	670-D1
1180	E 12TH ST	94601	670-D1
1260	E 12TH ST PL	94601	670-D1
1380	INTERNATIONAL BLVD	94601	670-D1
1600	BANCROFT AV	94601	670-D1
1690	E 17TH ST	94601	670-D1
1770	BOND ST	94601	670-D1
1900	FOOTHILL BLVD	94601	670-D1
1980	YGNACIO AV	94601	670-D1
2000	COURTLAND AV	94601	670-D1
2030	CARRINGTON ST	94601	670-E1
2090	SAN CARLOS AV	94601	650-E7
2230	SAN CARLOS AV	94601	650-E7
2350	SANTA RITA ST	94601	650-E7
2390	CONGRESS AV	94601	650-E7
2410	AGUA VISTA ST	94601	650-E7
2440	FAIRFAX AV	94601	650-E7
2480	LYON AV	94601	650-E7
2530	GORDON ST	94601	650-E7
2600	BROOKDALE AV	94619	650-E7
2670	WALNUT ST	94619	650-E7
2800	ALLENDALE AV	94619	650-E7
2900	FLEMING AV	94619	650-E7
3000	PENNIMAN AV	94619	650-F7
3030	VIRGINIA AV	94619	650-F7
3100	CULVER ST	94619	650-F7
3200	SUTER ST	94619	650-F6
3400	PORTER ST	94619	650-F6
3440	QUIGLEY PL	94619	650-F6
3480	REDDING ST	94619	650-F6
3600	MACARTHUR BLVD	94619	650-F6
3670	MASTERSON ST	94619	650-F6
3670	MASTERSON ST	94619	650-F6
3720	KANSAS ST	94619	650-F6
3820	PAMPAS AV	94619	650-G6
3820	SIESTA CT	94619	650-G6
3900	BAYO ST	94619	650-G6
3930	STEELE ST	94619	650-G6
4000	HYACINTH AV	94619	650-G6
4100	TOMPKINS AV	94619	650-G6
HIGHLAND AV			**OAK**
2400	E 24TH ST	94606	650-B6
2520	E 25TH ST	94606	650-B5
2530	E 25TH ST	94606	650-B5
2610	E 26TH ST	94606	650-B5
2700	21ST AV	94606	650-B5
2700	E 27TH ST	94606	650-B5
HIGHLAND AV			**PDMT**
390	MAGNOLIA AV	94611	650-B1
1	MORAGA AV	94611	630-B7
100	PARK WY	94611	630-B7
160	PALA AV	94611	650-B1
190	BLAIR AV	94611	650-B1
200	BLAIR AV	94611	650-B1
300	OAKLAND AV	94611	650-B1
340	CRAIG AV	94611	650-B1
370	HIGHLAND WY	94611	650-B1
380	VISTA AV	94611	650-B1
390	MOUNTAIN AV	94611	650-B1
400	PIEDMONT CT	94611	650-B1
600	SIERRA AV	94611	650-C1
620	GUILFORD RD	94611	650-C1
670	GUILFORD RD	94611	650-B1
700	SHERIDAN AV	94611	650-B1
	CAPERTON AV	94611	650-B1
800	HAZEL LN	94611	650-B2
900	WILDWOOD AV	94611	650-B2
HIGHLAND PL			**BERK**
	LE CONTE AV	94709	629-J1
1790	RIDGE RD	94709	629-J1
1900	CYCLOTRON RD	94709	629-J1
1900	HEARST AV	94709	629-J1
HIGHLAND WY			**PDMT**
300	HIGHLAND AV	94611	650-B1
400	MOUNTAIN AV	94611	650-B1
HILGARD AV			**BERK**
2300	ARCH ST	94709	629-H1
2400	SCENIC AV	94709	609-H7
2500	EUCLID AV	94709	609-H7
2570	LE ROY AV	94709	609-J7
2600	LA LOMA AV	94709	609-J7
2700	LA VEREDA	94709	609-J7
HILL CT			**BERK**
2500	EUCLID AV	94708	609-H7
N HILL CT			**OAK**
100	HILLER DR	94618	630-B4
100	S HILL CT	94618	630-B4
S HILL CT			**OAK**
50	HILLER DR	94618	630-B4
50	N HILL CT	94618	630-B4
HILL LN			**PDMT**
100	JEROME AV	94610	650-A1
100	KEEFER CT	94610	650-A1
HILL RD			**BERK**
1	SHASTA RD	94708	609-J6
80	ATLAS PL	94708	609-J6
100	GRIZZLY PEAK BLVD	94708	609-J6
HILL RD			**OAK**
6100	GOLDEN GATE AV	94618	630-B5
6200	BUENA VISTA AV	94618	630-B5
HILLCREST CT			**BERK**
	HILLCREST RD	94705	630-A4
HILLCREST CT			**OAK**
1	BALMORAL DR	94619	650-J5
HILLCREST RD			**BERK**
1	CLAREMONT AV	94705	630-A4
50	EUCALYPTUS RD	94705	630-A4
100	HILLCREST CT	94705	630-A4
120	EUCALYPTUS RD	94705	630-A4
130	S CROSSWAYS	94705	630-A4
200	ROANOKE RD	94705	630-A4
HILLCROFT CIR			**OAK**
900	SUNNYHILLS RD	94610	650-B3
980	LARKSPUR RD	94610	650-B3
1000	SUNNYHILLS RD	94610	650-B3
HILLDALE AV			**BERK**
600	GRIZZLY PEAK BLVD	94708	609-H5
730	POPLAR ST	94708	609-H5
790	BONNIE LN	94708	609-H5
830	MARIN AV	94708	609-H5
860	FOREST LN	94708	609-H5
930	POPPY LN	94708	609-H5
1000	REGAL RD	94708	609-H5
HILLEGASS AV			**BERK**
2500	DWIGHT WY	94704	629-J2
2600	PARKER ST	94704	629-J3
2700	DERBY ST	94704	629-J3
2700	DERBY ST	94705	629-J3
2800	STUART ST	94705	629-J3
2900	RUSSELL ST	94705	629-J3
2940	ASHBY AV	94705	629-J4
3000	WEBSTER ST	94705	629-J4
3100	WOOLSEY ST	94705	629-J4
HILLEGASS AV			**OAK**
6000	CLAREMONT AV	94618	629-J5
6100	61ST ST	94618	629-J5
	62ND ST	94618	629-J5
6200	62ND ST	94618	629-J4
6300	63RD ST	94618	629-J4
6400	ALCATRAZ AV	94618	629-J4
6400	ALCATRAZ AV	94618	629-J4
6500	WOOLSEY ST	94618	629-J4
HILLEN DR			**OAK**
5200	55TH AV	94619	670-F1
5500	MADERA AV	94619	670-F1
HILLER DR			**OAK**
1	CALDECOTT LN	94618	630-B4
60	N HILL CT	94618	630-B4
60	S HILL CT	94618	630-B4
200	SPYGLASS HILL	94618	630-C4
200	TREASURE HILL	94618	630-C4
260	GRAND VIEW DR	94618	630-C4
330	BINNACLE HILL	94618	630-C4
370	WINDWARD HILL	94618	630-C4
400	CHARING CROSS RD	94618	630-C4
430	STARVIEW DR	94618	630-C4
500	WINDWARD HILL	94618	630-C4
530	BINNACLE HILL	94618	630-C4
560	STARVIEW DR	94618	630-C4
600	HAWKS HILL CT	94618	630-C4
600	SPYGLASS HILL	94618	630-C4
700	TUNNEL RD	94618	630-C4
HILLER ST			**OAK**
1000	LOCKHEED ST	94621	670-D6
1060	PIPER ST	94621	670-D6
HILLGIRT CIR			**OAK**
600	MERRITT AV	94610	650-A3
600	PROSPECT AV	94610	650-A3
600	WESLEY AV	94610	650-A3
670	HADDON RD	94610	650-A3
700	KENWYN RD	94610	650-A3
800	BARBARA RD	94610	650-A3
800	MACARTHUR BLVD	94610	650-A3
HILLGRADE CT			**OAK**
9800	98TH AV	94603	671-A4
HILLHURST WY			**OAK**
	GELSTON ST	94705	630-B2
HILLMONT DR			**OAK**
6000	SEMINARY AV	94605	650-H7
6100	OVERDALE AV	94605	650-H7
6230	NAIROBI PL	94605	650-H7
6300	VAN MOURIK AV	94605	650-J7
6420	ARCHMONT PL	94605	650-J7
6500	ARCHMONT PL	94605	650-J7
6400	EDENVALE PL	94605	670-J1
6500	GARDENIA PL	94605	670-J1
6600	DELMONT AV	94605	670-J1
6700	EDGEMOOR PL	94605	670-J1
6800	ALTAMONT AV	94605	670-J1
6830	73RD AV	94605	670-J1
6900	BURCKHALTER AV	94605	670-J1
6900	SUNKIST DR	94605	670-J1
7300	73RD AV	94605	670-J1
7500	75TH AV	94605	670-J2
7710	PARKER AV	94605	670-J2
7980	TULLY PL	94605	671-A2
8100	PARTRIDGE AV	94605	671-A2
HILLSBOROUGH ST			**OAK**
600	WESLEY AV	94606	649-J4
HILLSIDE AV			**ALB**
700	JACKSON ST	94706	609-D5
780	CERRITO ST	94706	609-D5
800	TAFT AV	94706	609-D6
HILLSIDE AV			**BERK**
	PROSPECT ST	94704	629-J2
	HILLSIDE CT	94704	629-J2
2500	DWIGHT WY	94704	630-A2
HILLSIDE AV			**PDMT**
100	PARK WY	94611	630-B7
200	BLAIR AV	94611	650-B1
300	OAKLAND AV	94611	650-B1
360	VISTA AV	94611	650-B1
400	MAGNOLIA AV	94611	650-B1
HILLSIDE CT			**BERK**
1	HILLSIDE AV	94704	629-J2
HILLSIDE CT			**PDMT**
400	MAGNOLIA AV	94611	650-B1
HILLSIDE ST			**OAK**
7500	84TH AV	94605	670-J3
7600	83RD AV	94605	670-J3
	73RD AV	94605	670-H2
8890	73RD AV	94605	670-H2
8770	74TH AV	94605	670-J2
8660	75TH AV	94605	670-J2
8500	76TH AV	94605	670-J2
8400	77TH AV	94605	670-J2
7800	78TH AV	94605	670-J2
7840	PARKER AV	94605	670-J2
7900	79TH AV	94605	670-J3
7920	RITCHIE ST	94605	670-J3
8000	80TH AV	94605	670-J3
8100	81ST AV	94605	670-J3
8200	82ND AV	94605	670-J3
7400	88TH AV	94605	670-J4
7350	88TH AV	94605	671-A4
8900	89TH AV	94605	671-A4
9000	90TH AV	94603	671-A4
9400	STEARNS AV	94603	671-A4
9600	96TH AV	94603	671-A4
HILLTOP CRES			**OAK**
5300	HARBORD DR	94618	630-C7
5350	STARK KNOLL PL	94618	630-C7
5400	MAXWELTON RD	94618	630-C7
HILLVIEW RD			**BERK**
1100	WOODSIDE RD	94708	609-J6
1200	PARK HILLS RD	94708	609-J6
HILLVIEW ST			**OAK**
3600	MADELINE ST	94602	650-E5
HILLWOOD PL			**OAK**
1	SUNNYHILLS RD	94610	650-C3
HILTON ST			**OAK**
5500	55TH AV	94605	670-F1
5600	BANCROFT AV	94605	670-F1
5600	BANCROFT AV	94605	670-F1
5700	57TH AV	94605	670-F2
5900	SEMINARY AV	94605	670-F2
6200	62ND AV	94605	670-F2
6200	62ND AV	94605	670-G2
6300	63RD AV	94605	670-G2
HOLDEN ST			**EMVL**
4000	40TH ST	94608	629-E7
4100	PARK AV	94608	629-E7
4300	45TH ST	94608	629-E7
HOLLAND ST			**OAK**
5300	54TH AV	94601	670-E2
5400	53RD AV	94601	670-E2
5400	55TH AV	94601	670-E2
5500	54TH AV	94601	670-E2
HOLLIS ST			**EMVL**
3800	YERBA BUENA AV	94608	629-E7
4000	40TH ST	94608	629-E7
4200	PARK AV	94608	629-E7
4500	45TH ST	94608	629-E7
5300	53RD ST	94608	629-E6
5570	STANFORD AV	94608	629-E6
5700	POWELL ST	94608	629-E6
5900	59TH ST	94608	629-E5
6100	61ST ST	94608	629-E5
6200	62ND ST	94608	629-E5
6300	63RD ST	94608	629-E5
6400	64TH ST	94608	629-E5
6440	OCEAN AV	94608	629-E5
6500	65TH ST	94608	629-E5
6600	66TH ST	94608	629-E5
6700	67TH ST	94608	629-E4
6800	FOLGER AV	94608	629-E4
HOLLIS ST			**OAK**
3200	PERALTA ST	94608	649-F1
3200	32ND ST	94608	649-F1
3430	34TH ST	94608	649-F1
3430	FITZGERALD ST	94608	649-F1
3670	W MACARTHUR BLVD	94608	629-E7
3800	YERBA BUENA AV	94608	629-E7

PRIMARY STREET Address	Cross Street	ZIP	CITY Pg-Grid
HOLLISTER CIR			**ALA**
2100	DECATUR ST	94501	649-E7
2200	BAINBRIDGE AV	94501	649-E7
HOLLY OAK LN			**ALA**
300	BAYWOOD RD	94502	669-J6
HOLLY PL			**PDMT**
100	LOWER GRAND AV	94611	650-A1
130	MANOR DR	94611	650-A1
160	YORK DR	94611	650-A1
200	RICARDO AV	94611	650-A1
200	ARTUNA AV	94611	650-A1
HOLLY ST			**ALA**
1000	MECARTNEY RD	94502	670-A6
1040	PARISH CT	94502	670-A6
1050	BRITHORN LN	94502	670-A7
1080	REDHOOK LN	94502	670-A7
1100	OLEANDER AV	94502	670-A7
1100	FIR AV	94502	670-A7
1140	SOLOMON LN	94502	670-A7
1150	SOLOMON LN	94502	670-A7
1180	TONGA LN	94502	670-A7
1200	CATALINA AV	94502	670-A7
HOLLY ST			**BERK**
1400	ROSE ST	94703	609-F7
1490	BUENA AV	94703	609-F7
1600	CEDAR ST	94703	609-F7
HOLLY ST			**OAK**
7000	70TH AV	94621	670-G3
7300	73RD AV	94621	670-G3
	73RD AV	94621	670-G3
7300	73RD AV	94621	670-G3
7400	74TH AV	94621	670-H3
7600	76TH AV	94621	670-H3
7700	77TH AV	94621	670-H3
7800	78TH AV	94621	670-H3
7900	79TH AV	94621	670-H3
8000	80TH AV	94621	670-H3
8100	81ST AV	94621	670-H3
8200	82ND AV	94621	670-H4
8300	83RD AV	94621	670-H4
8400	84TH AV	94621	670-H4
8500	85TH AV	94621	670-H4
8600	86TH AV	94621	670-H4
8640	AUSEON AV	94621	670-H4
8700	87TH AV	94621	670-H4
8800	88TH AV	94621	670-H4
8900	89TH AV	94621	670-H4
9000	90TH AV	94621	670-H4
9000	90TH AV	94603	670-H4
9200	92ND AV	94603	670-J5
9400	94TH AV	94603	670-J5
9600	96TH AV	94603	670-J5
9800	98TH AV	94603	670-J5
10000	99TH AV	94603	670-J5
HOLLYWOOD AV			**OAK**
900	EL CENTRO AV	94602	650-D3
900	GLENDOME CIR	94602	650-D3
1000	SAN SEBASTIAN	94602	650-D3
1160	EDGEWOOD AV	94602	650-D3
1300	PARK BLVD	94602	650-D3
HOLMAN RD			**OAK**
1100	TRESTLE GLEN RD	94610	650-B3
1200	GROSVENOR PL	94610	650-B4
1220	BATES RD	94610	650-B3
1360	BATES RD	94610	650-C3
1360	BATES RD	94602	650-C3
1450	HAMPEL ST	94610	650-C3
1550	CREED RD	94610	650-C3
1600	FLEET RD	94610	650-C3
HOLMES AV			**OAK**
3700	GREENLY DR	94605	671-A2
3800	WINTHROPE ST	94605	671-A2
3900	EARL ST	94605	671-A2
4000	FONTAINE ST	94605	671-A2
HOLTZ CT			**ALA**
	ROSEFIELD LP	94501	649-G7
HOLWAY CT			**OAK**
5700	57TH AV	94621	670-F2
HOLWAY ST			**OAK**
5500	55TH AV	94621	670-F2
5700	57TH AV	94621	670-F2
5900	SEMINARY AV	94621	670-F2
6200	62ND AV	94621	670-F2
HOLYROOD DR			**OAK**
2900	ASCOT DR	94611	650-G2
3120	HOLYROOD MNR	94611	650-G2
3200	CASTLE DR	94611	650-G2
HOLYROOD MNR			**OAK**
100	HOLYROOD DR	94611	650-G2
HOME PL E			**OAK**
1	MCKINLEY AV	94610	650-B4
HOME PL W			**OAK**
1	MCKINLEY AV	94610	650-A4
HOMEGLEN LN			**OAK**
1	HOMEWOOD DR	94611	630-F6
100	GLENCOURT	94611	630-F6
HOMEWOOD DR			**OAK**
7000	SARONI DR	94611	630-F7
7030	HOMEGLEN LN	94611	630-F7
7060	RIDGEWOOD DR	94611	630-F6
7300	ARROWHEAD DR	94611	630-F6
HOOD ST			**OAK**
3200	STELLA ST	94605	671-C5
3100	MARK ST	94605	671-C5
HOOVER AV			**OAK**
	LEIMERT BLVD	94602	650-E3
1900	EDGE DR	94602	650-E3
2100	FRUITVALE AV	94602	650-E3
2100	WRENN ST	94602	650-E3
HOOVER CT			**ALA**
1400	CENTRAL AV	94501	669-F1
W HOPE ST			**ALA**
	LEXINGTON ST	94501	649-C6
	SARATOGA ST	94501	649-D6
	PAN AM WY	94501	649-D6
	SUNRISE CT	94501	649-D6
HOPKINS CT			**BERK**
1	ALBINA AV	94706	609-F7
20	HOPKINS ST	94706	609-F7
HOPKINS PL			**OAK**
2800	MACARTHUR BLVD	94602	650-E5
2900	COOLIDGE AV	94602	650-E5
HOPKINS ST			**BERK**
1100	CEDAR ST	94702	629-E1
1100	SAN PABLO AV	94702	629-E1
1130	KAINS AV	94702	629-E1
1170	STANNAGE AV	94702	629-E1
1200	CORNELL AV	94702	629-E1
1210	ROSE ST	94702	629-E1
1220	CURTIS ST	94702	629-E1
1250	NEILSON ST	94702	629-E1
1270	NORTHSIDE AV	94702	629-E1
1300	PERALTA AV	94702	609-E7
1350	ORDWAY ST	94702	609-E7
1400	ACTON ST	94702	609-F7
1420	ACTON ST	94702	609-F7
1440	GILMAN ST	94706	609-F7
1440	GILMAN ST	94702	609-F7
1460	ALBINA AV	94706	609-F7
1460	ALBINA AV	94702	609-F7
1500	SACRAMENTO ST	94706	609-F7
1500	SACRAMENTO ST	94703	609-F7
1530	HOPKINS CT	94706	609-F7
1530	HOPKINS CT	94703	609-F7
1560	CALIFORNIA ST	94707	609-F7
1560	CALIFORNIA ST	94703	609-F7
1560	MONTEREY AV	94703	609-F7
1600	MCGEE AV	94707	609-F7
1600	MCGEE AV	94703	609-F7
1650	CARLOTTA AV	94707	609-F7
1650	CARLOTTA AV	94703	609-F7
1700	COLUSA AV	94707	609-F7
1700	COLUSA AV	94703	609-F7
1800	BEVERLY PL	94707	609-G7
1800	BEVERLY PL	94703	609-G7
1860	JOSEPHINE ST	94707	609-G7
1860	JOSEPHINE ST	94703	609-G7
1870	SONOMA AV	94707	609-G7
1870	SONOMA AV	94703	609-G7
1900	MARTIN LUTHER KING JR WY	94707	609-G6
2000	NAPA AV	94707	609-G6
2100	SUTTER ST	94707	609-G6
W HORNET AV			**ALA**
	FERRY PT	94501	669-D1
	VIKING ST	94501	669-D1
	SKYHAWK ST	94501	669-D1
HORTON ST			**EMVL**
4000	40TH ST	94608	629-E7
4100	PARK AV	94608	629-E7
4400	SHERWIN AV	94608	629-E7
4500	45TH ST	94608	629-E7
5300	53RD ST	94608	629-E6
	LANDREGAN ST	94608	629-E6
	STANFORD AV	94608	629-E6
HORTON ST			**OAK**
3800	YERBA BUENA AV	94608	629-E7
4000	40TH ST	94608	629-E7
HOWARD AV			**PDMT**
200	LAKE AV	94611	650-A1
260	NACE ST	94611	650-A1
320	CAMBRIDGE WY	94611	650-A1
400	OAKLAND AV	94611	650-A1
HOWARD ST			**OAK**
	ALAMEDA AV	94601	670-C2
	HIGH ST	94601	670-C2
4300	HIGH ST	94601	670-C2
HOWE ST			**BERK**
2300	ELLSWORTH ST	94705	629-H3
2400	TELEGRAPH AV	94705	629-H3
HOWE ST			**OAK**
3700	W MACARTHUR BLVD	94611	649-J1
3900	40TH ST	94611	649-J1
4000	40TH WY	94611	649-J1
4100	41ST ST	94611	649-J1
4200	RIDGEWAY AV	94611	629-J7
4300	JOHN ST	94611	629-J7
4400	PLEASANT VALLEY AV	94611	630-A7
HOWELL ST			**OAK**
5800	AYALA AV	94609	629-H5
5900	59TH ST	94609	629-H5
5920	MCAULEY ST	94609	629-H5
5950	MCAULEY ST	94609	629-H5
5980	60TH ST	94609	629-H5
6050	60TH ST	94609	629-H5
HUBBARD ST			**EMVL**
4000	40TH ST	94608	629-E7
4100	PARK AV	94608	629-E7
4300	SHERWIN AV	94608	629-E7
HUBERT RD			**OAK**
1000	GROSVENOR PL	94610	650-B3
1100	SUNNYHILLS RD	94610	650-C3
1200	LONGRIDGE RD	94610	650-C3
1200	PARAMOUNT RD	94610	650-C3
HUDSON BAY			**ALA**
100	BAYWALK RD	94502	669-J6
HUDSON DR			**ALA**
	DENNISON ST	94501	649-J7
	SPENCER RD	94501	649-J7
	BEAR RD	94501	649-J7
	CAMBELL BLVD	94501	649-J7
	EAGLE RD	94501	649-J7
HUDSON ST			**OAK**
	COLLEGE AV	94618	629-J6
300	MANILA AV	94618	629-J6
350	JAMES AV	94618	629-J6
400	LAWTON AV	94618	629-J6
420	BOYD AV	94618	629-J6
450	SHAFTER AV	94618	629-J6
460	LOCKSLEY AV	94618	629-J6
470	MILES AV	94618	629-J5
	CLAREMONT AV	94618	629-J5
HUGHES AV			**OAK**
2300	E 23RD ST	94601	650-C6
HULL ST			**OAK**
4300	HIGH ST	94601	670-C2
HUMBOLDT AV			**OAK**
2300	DAVIS ST	94601	650-D6
2410	LYNDE ST	94601	650-D6
2500	DEERING ST	94601	650-D6
2600	BROOKDALE AV	94602	650-E6
2900	PENNIMAN AV	94602	650-E6
3100	SCHOOL ST	94602	650-E6
HUMPHREY PL			**OAK**
1	TRESTLE GLEN RD	94610	650-C3
HUNTER AV			**OAK**
100	BERNHARDT DR	94603	670-G7
220	EL VERANO ST	94603	670-G7
260	HUNTER CT	94603	670-G7
300	SAINT ELMO DR	94603	670-G7
500	MADDUX DR	94603	670-G7
HUNTER CT			**OAK**
1	HUNTER AV	94603	670-G7
HUNTINGTON ST			**OAK**
3820	ALBERT ST	94619	650-G6
3900	STEELE ST	94619	650-G6
3940	WORDEN WY	94619	650-G6
3960	HYACINTH AV	94619	650-G6
4000	TOMPKINS AV	94619	650-G6
4050	FAIR AV	94619	650-G6
4100	HARBOR VIEW AV	94619	650-G6
4190	ADELAIDE ST	94619	650-G6
HUNTLEIGH RD			**PDMT**
1	LEXFORD RD	94611	650-D2
90	LEXFORD RD	94611	650-D2
HYACINTH AV			**OAK**
4300	HIGH ST	94619	650-G6
4350	MADRONE AV	94619	650-G6
4380	HUNTINGTON ST	94619	650-G6
4500	WORDEN WY	94619	650-G6
HYDE ST			**OAK**
3200	FRUITVALE AV	94601	650-C6
3200	FRUITVALE AV	94601	650-C6
3300	COOLIDGE AV	94601	650-C6

I

PRIMARY STREET Address	Cross Street	ZIP	CITY Pg-Grid
ICARUS DR			**ALA**
	SPENCER RD	94501	649-J7
	CAMBELL BLVD	94501	649-J7
IDAHO ST			**BERK**
3200	66TH ST	94702	629-F4
3230	65TH ST	94702	629-F5
3250	HARMON ST	94702	629-F5
3300	ALCATRAZ AV	94702	629-F5
IDAHO ST			**OAK**
5900	59TH ST	94608	629-F5
6000	60TH ST	94608	629-F5
6100	61ST ST	94608	629-F5
6200	62ND ST	94608	629-F5
6300	63RD ST	94608	629-F5
6400	ALCATRAZ AV	94608	629-F5
IDLEWOOD ST			**OAK**
8000	80TH AV	94605	670-J3
8200	82ND AV	94605	670-J3
INDEPENDENCE DR			**ALA**
900	MARINA VILLAGE PKWY	94501	649-G7
910	INVINCIBLE CT	94501	649-G7
940	COURAGEOUS CT	94501	649-G7
980	REGULUS CT	94501	649-G7
1020	ECLIPSE CT	94501	649-G7
1060	REDONDO CT	94501	649-G7
1100	TRIUMPH DR	94501	649-G7
INDEPENDENCE WY			**OAK**
1500	16TH AV	94606	650-A6
1600	15TH AV	94606	650-A6
1800	18TH AV	94606	650-A6
1900	19TH AV	94606	650-A6
2000	20TH AV	94606	650-B6
2100	21ST AV	94606	650-B6
2200	22ND AV	94606	650-B6
INDEPENDENT RD			**OAK**
500	COLISEUM WY	94621	670-E4
700	COLISEUM WY	94621	670-E4
700	COLISEUM WY	94621	670-E3
INDIAN BAY			**ALA**
100	BAYWALK RD	94502	669-J6
INDIAN GULCH RD			**PDMT**
1	GLEN ALPINE RD	94611	650-C1
INDIAN RD			**PDMT**
100	HAMPTON RD	94610	650-C2
250	LA SALLE AV	94610	650-C2
280	LA SALLE AV	94610	650-C2
400	DOWNEY PL	94610	650-C2
400	SUNNYHILLS RD	94610	650-C2
INDIAN ROCK AV			**BERK**
800	SANTA BARBARA RD	94707	609-G5
850	SAN LUIS RD	94707	609-G5
900	SAN DIEGO RD	94707	609-G5
970	OXFORD ST	94707	609-G6
	SAN MATEO RD	94707	609-G6
	SHATTUCK AV	94707	609-G6
	ARLINGTON AV	94707	609-G6
INDIAN TR			**BERK**
	YOSEMITE RD	94707	609-F5
	SAN FERNANDO AV	94707	609-F5
	THE ALAMEDA	94707	609-F5
	SAN LORENZO AV	94707	609-F5
INDIAN WY			**OAK**
1730	WOODHAVEN WY	94611	630-E6
1700	WESTWOOD WY	94611	630-E6
INDUSTRIAL WY			**OAK**
900	SAN LEANDRO ST	94603	670-G5
INTERNATIONAL BLVD			**OAK**
100	1ST AV	94606	649-H5
100	1ST AV	94606	649-H5
200	2ND AV	94606	649-J5
300	3RD AV	94606	649-J5
400	4TH AV	94606	649-J5
500	5TH AV	94606	649-J5
600	6TH AV	94606	649-J5
700	7TH AV	94606	649-J5
800	8TH AV	94606	649-J5
900	9TH AV	94606	649-J5
1000	10TH AV	94606	649-J5
1100	11TH AV	94606	649-J6
1200	12TH AV	94606	649-J6
1300	13TH AV	94606	649-J6
1300	14TH AV	94606	650-A6
1400	14TH AV	94606	650-A6
1480	15TH AV	94606	650-A6
1570	16TH AV	94606	650-A6
1660	17TH AV	94606	650-A6
1750	18TH AV	94606	650-A6
1850	19TH AV	94606	650-A6
1940	20TH AV	94606	650-A6
2030	21ST AV	94606	650-A6
2120	22ND AV	94606	650-A6
2200	MUNSON WY	94606	650-B7
2300	23RD AV	94601	650-B7
2400	MILLER AV	94601	650-B7
2440	24TH AV	94601	650-B7
2500	25TH AV	94601	650-B7
2510	25TH AV	94601	650-B7
2600	26TH AV	94601	650-B7
2700	27TH AV	94601	650-B7
2760	MITCHELL ST	94601	650-B7
2830	28TH AV	94601	650-B7
2910	29TH AV	94601	650-B7
3010	30TH AV	94601	650-C7
3070	DERBY AV	94601	650-C7
3080	DERBY AV	94601	650-C7
3130	31ST AV	94601	650-C7
3200	FRUITVALE AV	94601	650-C7
3300	FRUITVALE AV	94601	650-C7
3300	33RD AV	94601	670-C1
3370	34TH AV	94601	670-C1
3400	34TH AV	94601	670-C1
3490	35TH AV	94601	670-C1
3570	36TH AV	94601	670-C1
3600	36TH AV	94601	670-C1
3690	37TH AV	94601	670-C1
3790	38TH AV	94601	670-C1
3890	39TH AV	94601	670-C1
3900	39TH AV	94601	670-D1
3990	40TH AV	94601	670-D1
4000	40TH AV	94601	670-D1
4080	41ST AV	94601	670-D1
4130	41ST AV	94601	670-D1
4200	42ND AV	94601	670-D1
4300	HIGH ST	94601	670-D1
4400	44TH AV	94601	670-D1
4500	45TH AV	94601	670-D1
4600	46TH AV	94601	670-D1
4640	46TH AV	94601	670-D1
4640	BANCROFT WY	94601	670-D1
4650	BANCROFT WY	94601	670-D1
4700	47TH AV	94601	670-D1
4730	47TH AV	94601	670-D2
4800	48TH AV	94601	670-D2
4840	48TH AV	94601	670-E2
4900	49TH AV	94601	670-E2
	50TH AV	94601	670-E2
5000	50TH AV	94601	670-E2
	51ST AV	94601	670-E2
5100	51ST AV	94601	670-E2
	52ND AV	94601	670-E2
5200	52ND AV	94601	670-E2
5300	53RD AV	94601	670-E2
5350	54TH AV	94601	670-E2
5400	54TH AV	94601	670-E2
5500	55TH AV	94621	670-E2
5600	56TH AV	94621	670-E2
5700	57TH AV	94621	670-E2
5800	58TH AV	94621	670-F2
5900	SEMINARY AV	94621	670-F2
6000	60TH AV	94621	670-F2
6020	61ST AV	94621	670-F2
6100	61ST AV	94621	670-F2
6200	62ND AV	94621	670-F2
6300	63RD AV	94621	670-F2
6400	64TH AV	94621	670-F3
6420	64TH AV	94621	670-F3
6480	65TH AV	94621	670-F3
6500	65TH AV	94621	670-F3
6550	66TH AV	94621	670-F3
6600	66TH AV	94621	670-F3
6620	HAVENSCOURT BLVD	94621	670-F3
6700	67TH AV	94621	670-F3
6800	68TH AV	94621	670-G3
6900	69TH AV	94621	670-G3
6920	69TH AV	94621	670-G3
7000	70TH AV	94621	670-G3
7030	70TH AV	94621	670-G3
7100	71ST AV	94621	670-G3
7150	71ST AV	94621	670-G3
7200	72ND AV	94621	670-G3
7230	72ND AV	94621	670-G3
7290	73RD AV	94621	670-G3
	73RD AV	94621	670-G3
	HEGENBERGER EXWY	94621	670-G3
7300	73RD AV	94621	670-G3
7300	HEGENBERGER EXWY	94621	670-G3
7400	74TH AV	94621	670-G3
7500	75TH AV	94621	670-G3
7510	SUNSHINE CT	94621	670-G3
7570	76TH AV	94621	670-G3
7600	76TH AV	94621	670-G3
7650	77TH AV	94621	670-G3
7710	77TH AV	94621	670-G3
7800	78TH AV	94621	670-G3
7800	78TH AV	94621	670-G3
7900	79TH AV	94621	670-G3
7920	79TH AV	94621	670-G3
8000	80TH AV	94621	670-H4
8100	81ST AV	94621	670-H4
8200	82ND AV	94621	670-H4
8250	82ND AV	94621	670-H4
8300	83RD AV	94621	670-H4
8340	83RD AV	94621	670-H4
8400	84TH AV	94621	670-H4
8440	84TH AV	94621	670-H4
8500	85TH AV	94621	670-H4
8540	85TH AV	94621	670-H4
8600	86TH AV	94621	670-H4
8630	86TH AV	94621	670-H4
8660	AUSEON AV	94621	670-H4
8710	87TH AV	94621	670-H4
8730	87TH AV	94621	670-H4
8780	88TH AV	94621	670-H4
8800	88TH AV	94621	670-H4
8870	89TH AV	94621	670-H4
8900	89TH AV	94621	670-H4
8960	90TH AV	94621	670-H4
8960	90TH AV	94603	670-H4
9000	90TH AV	94603	670-H4
9090	91ST AV	94603	670-H5
9200	92ND AV	94603	670-H5
9230	92ND AV	94603	670-H5
9280	93RD AV	94603	670-H5
9310	93RD AV	94603	670-H5
9400	94TH AV	94603	670-J5
9500	95TH AV	94603	670-J5
9600	96TH AV	94603	670-J5
9700	97TH AV	94603	670-J5
9800	98TH AV	94603	670-J5
9900	99TH AV	94603	670-J5
9980	100TH AV	94603	670-J5
10000	100TH AV	94603	670-J5
10100	101ST AV	94603	670-J6
10200	102ND AV	94603	670-J6
10230	102ND AV	94603	670-J6
10250	103RD AV	94603	670-J6
10300	103RD AV	94603	670-J6
10330	104TH AV	94603	670-J6
10400	104TH AV	94603	670-J6
10480	105TH AV	94603	670-J6
10500	105TH AV	94603	670-J6
10630	106TH AV	94603	670-J6
10700	107TH AV	94603	670-J6
11000	E 14TH ST	94603	670-J6
INVERLEITH TER			**PDMT**
1	HAMPTON RD	94611	650-D2
100	ESTATES DR	94611	650-D2
INVERNESS CT			**ALA**
200	SHEFFIELD RD	94502	669-J5
200	INVERNESS WY	94502	669-J5
INVERNESS CT			**OAK**
200	DONNA WY	94605	671-D3
200	SILVERADO CT	94605	671-D3
INVERNESS WY			**ALA**
100	BERKSHIRE RD	94502	669-J5
200	INVERNESS CT	94502	669-J5
200	SHEFFIELD RD	94502	669-J5
INVINCIBLE CT			**ALA**
1	INDEPENDENCE DR	94501	649-G7
INYO AV			**OAK**
2260	E 23RD ST	94601	650-B6
2350	E 24TH ST	94601	650-C6
2540	E 26TH ST	94601	650-C5
2700	E 27TH ST	94601	650-C5
IRIS ST			**OAK**
8000	80TH AV	94605	670-J3
8200	82ND AV	94605	670-J3
8300	83RD AV	94605	670-J3
8360	84TH AV	94605	670-J3
IRONWOOD			**OAK**
	ELYSIAN FIELDS DR	94605	671-D2
	HERITAGE	94605	671-D2
IRONWOOD RD			**ALA**
900	MECARTNEY RD	94502	670-A6
900	VERDEMAR DR	94502	670-A6
600	LAGUNARIA LN	94502	670-A6
630	CHINABERRY LN	94502	670-A6
700	CAROB LN	94502	670-A6
IRVING ST			**OAK**
1800	E 20TH ST	94601	650-B6
2000	FOOTHILL BLVD	94601	650-B6
IRWIN CT			**OAK**
6400	ALCATRAZ AV	94609	629-H4
ISABELLA ST			**OAK**
800	W GRAND AV	94607	649-F2
1000	WEST ST	94607	649-F2
ISLAND DR			**ALA**
	DOOLITTLE DR	94502	670-B5
50	VETERANS CT	94502	670-A5
350	ROBERT DAVEY JR DR	94502	670-A5
720	CLUBHOUSE MEMORIAL RD	94502	670-A6
720	OYSTER SHOALS	94502	670-A6
800	MAITLAND DR	94502	670-A6

Address	Cross Street	ZIP	City / Pg-Grid
ISLAND DR			ALA
860	GARDEN RD	94502	670-A6
1000	MECARTNEY RD	94502	670-A6
1050	DAHLIA DR	94502	670-A6
1070	EUGENIA CT	94502	670-A6
1100	FIR AV	94502	670-A7
1110	SANTA CRUZ LN	94502	670-A7
1150	PHOENIX LN	94502	670-A7
1190	COOK LN	94502	670-A7
1200	CATALINA AV	94502	670-A7
ISLETON AV			OAK
100	BERNHARDT DR	94603	670-G7
200	EL VERANO ST	94603	670-G7
IVANHOE RD			OAK
5700	CHABOT RD	94618	630-A5
5900	MILES AV	94618	630-A5
5900	HARWOOD AV	94618	630-A5
6000	CHABOT RD	94618	630-A5
IVY DR			OAK
2200	PARK BLVD	94606	650-A4
2210	5TH AV	94606	650-A4
2300	CARROLL ST	94606	650-A4
2330	E 23RD ST	94606	650-A4
2530	7TH AV	94606	650-A4
2530	BEATIE ST	94606	650-A4
2680	BOOKER ST	94606	650-A4
	8TH AV	94610	650-A4
	8TH AV	94606	650-A4
J			
JACKSON ST			ALA
2800	GROVE ST	94501	670-B3
2900	MOUND ST	94501	670-B3
3000	COURT ST	94501	670-B3
3100	FOUNTAIN ST	94501	670-B3
3200	HIGH ST	94501	670-B3
JACKSON ST			ALB
590	HILLSIDE AV	94706	609-D5
640	CASTRO ST	94706	609-D5
750	WASHINGTON AV	94706	609-D6
860	SOLANO AV	94706	609-D6
1000	BUCHANAN ST	94706	609-D6
1100	8TH ST	94706	609-D6
1100	RILEY DR	94706	609-D6
JACKSON ST			OAK
180	2ND ST	94607	649-G5
390	4TH ST	94607	649-G5
500	5TH ST	94607	649-G5
700	7TH ST	94607	649-G5
800	8TH ST	94607	649-G5
900	9TH ST	94607	649-G4
1000	10TH ST	94607	649-G4
1100	11TH ST	94607	649-G4
1200	12TH ST	94607	649-G4
1300	13TH ST	94612	649-G4
1400	14TH ST	94612	649-H4
1500	15TH ST	94612	649-H4
1700	17TH ST	94612	649-H4
1900	19TH ST	94612	649-H4
2000	LAKESIDE DR	94612	649-H4
JACOBUS AV			OAK
4600	DULWICH RD	94618	630-B6
4600	HERMOSA AV	94618	630-B6
4700	MORPETH ST	94618	630-B6
JAMES AV			OAK
5200	CAVOUR ST	94618	629-J6
5300	CLIFTON ST	94618	629-J6
5400	HUDSON ST	94618	629-J6
JANIS CIR			ALA
2600	PEARL ST	94501	670-A2
JAY ST			ALA
1700	PACIFIC AV	94501	669-H1
1800	BUENA VISTA AV	94501	669-H1
JAYNE AV			OAK
200	LEE ST	94610	649-J2
300	PERKINS ST	94610	649-J2
400	EUCLID AV	94610	649-J2
JAYNES ST			BERK
1600	CALIFORNIA ST	94703	629-F1
1650	COMSTOCK CT	94703	629-F1
1700	MCGEE AV	94703	609-F7
	NORTH ST	94703	609-F7
	EDITH ST	94703	609-F7
JEAN ST			OAK
500	ELWOOD AV	94610	649-J2
500	SANTA CLARA AV	94610	649-J2
550	ALTA VISTA AV	94610	649-J2
600	SANTA ROSA AV	94610	649-J2
600	SUNNY SLOPE AV	94610	650-A2
650	SUNNY SLOPE AV	94610	650-A2
800	GRAND AV	94610	650-A2
800	WILDWOOD AV	94610	650-A2
JEFFERSON AV			BERK
2000	UNIVERSITY AV	94703	629-F2
2100	ADDISON ST	94703	629-F2
2100	ADDISON ST	94703	629-F2
2200	ALLSTON WY	94703	629-F2
2300	BANCROFT WY	94703	629-F2
2400	CHANNING WY	94703	629-F3
2500	DWIGHT WY	94703	629-F3
JEFFERSON ST			OAK
100	EMBARCADERO W	94607	649-F5
300	4TH ST	94607	649-F4
200	3RD ST	94607	649-F5
300	2ND ST	94607	649-F5
	5TH ST	94607	649-F4
600	6TH ST	94607	649-F4
700	7TH ST	94607	649-F4
800	8TH ST	94607	649-F4
900	9TH ST	94607	649-F4
1000	10TH ST	94607	649-F4
1100	11TH ST	94607	649-F4
1200	12TH ST	94612	649-F4
1300	13TH ST	94612	649-F4
1400	14TH ST	94612	649-G3
1500	15TH ST	94612	649-G3
1600	16TH ST	94612	649-G3
1700	17TH ST	94612	649-G3
1800	18TH ST	94612	649-G3
JENSEN ST			OAK
4400	HIGH ST	94601	670-C2
JEROME AV			PDMT
1	CAMBRIDGE WY	94611	650-A1
100	OAKLAND AV	94610	650-A1
150	FAIRVIEW AV	94610	650-A1
230	NOVA DR	94610	650-A1
300	HILL LN	94610	650-B1
300	KEEFER CT	94610	650-B1
350	ARBOR DR	94610	650-B1
400	MAGNOLIA AV	94610	650-B1
400	MAGNOLIA AV	94610	650-B1
500	EL CERRITO AV	94610	650-B1
JERVIS BAY			ALA
100	BAYWALK RD	94502	669-J6
JEWELL CT			OAK
6900	THORNDALE DR	94611	630-E5
JOAQUIN MILLER CT			OAK
	MOUNTAIN BLVD	94611	650-E2
JOAQUIN MILLER RD			OAK
2910	MOUNTAIN BLVD	94602	650-F3
2930	PIERPOINT AV	94602	650-F3
3000	HEDGE LN	94602	650-F3
3100	SANBORN DR	94602	650-G3
3150	BUTTERS DR	94602	650-G3
3300	CRANE WY	94602	650-G3
3500	CRANE WY	94602	650-G3
	ROBINSON DR	94602	650-G3
3550	SANBORN DR	94602	650-H3
3600	CROCKETT PL	94602	650-H4
3800	SKYLINE BLVD	94602	650-H4
JOHN GLENN DR			OAK
	ALAN SHEPARD WY	94621	690-D2
	AIRPORT DR	94621	690-D2
JOHN ST			OAK
100	PIEDMONT AV	94611	629-J7
150	HOWE ST	94611	629-J7
200	MONTGOMERY ST	94611	629-J7
250	VIEW ST	94611	629-J7
300	GILBERT ST	94611	629-J7
JOHNSON AV			ALA
2800	GIBBONS DR	94501	670-B3
2900	MOUND ST	94501	670-B3
3000	COURT ST	94501	670-B3
JOHNSON ST			ALB
700	CLEVELAND AV	94706	609-C6
800	PIERCE ST	94706	609-C6
JOHNSTON DR			OAK
6200	ESTATES DR	94611	630-D7
JONES AV			OAK
400	ASHTON AV	94603	670-G6
600	EDES AV	94603	670-G6
580	CLARA ST	94603	670-G7
580	NORGREN ST	94603	670-G7
JONES ST			BERK
600	EASTSHORE BLVD	94804	629-C1
630	2ND ST	94804	629-D1
700	3RD ST	94804	629-D1
730	4TH ST	94804	629-D1
800	5TH ST	94804	629-D1
850	6TH ST	94804	629-D1
900	7TH ST	94804	629-D1
950	8TH ST	94804	629-D1
1000	9TH ST	94804	629-D1
1040	10TH ST	94804	629-E1
1100	SAN PABLO AV	94702	629-E1
1120	KAINS AV	94702	629-E1
1200	STANNAGE AV	94702	629-E1
JORDAN RD			OAK
2900	LONDON RD	94602	650-F4
3200	RETTIG AV	94602	650-F4
3300	NORTON AV	94602	650-F4
3400	BENNETT PL	94602	650-F5
3500	35TH AV	94602	650-F5
3500	35TH AV	94619	650-G5
3600	MONTEREY BLVD	94619	650-G5
JOSEPHINE ST			BERK
1100	MARTIN LUTHER KING JR WY	94707	609-G6
1100	NAPA AV	94707	609-G6
1170	SONOMA AV	94707	609-G7
1200	HOPKINS ST	94703	609-G7
1300	BERRYMAN ST	94703	609-G7
1400	ROSE ST	94703	609-G7
1500	VINE ST	94703	609-G7
1600	CEDAR ST	94703	629-G1
1700	VIRGINIA ST	94703	629-G1
JOST LN			ALA
1000	CAPELLA LN	94502	670-A7
1020	BRITHORN LN	94502	670-A7
1040	DUTCHCAP LN	94502	670-A7
1070	REDHOOK LN	94502	670-A7
1080	HAZEL LN	94502	670-A7
1100	OLEANDER AV	94502	670-A7
JUANITA WY			BERK
1500	ROSE ST	94702	629-E1
1530	TOMLEE DR	94702	629-E1
1600	CEDAR ST	94702	629-E1
JUDD ST			OAK
4900	50TH AV	94601	670-E1
5000	FREMONT WY	94601	670-E1
JULIA ST			BERK
1500	SACRAMENTO ST	94703	629-F4
1600	CALIFORNIA ST	94703	629-G4
1700	KING ST	94703	629-G4
JULIA ST			OAK
1	FLORENCE AV	94618	630-C6
200	PROCTOR AV	94618	630-C6
JULIE ANN WY			OAK
660	COLISEUM WY	94601	670-E3
JULIUS ST			OAK
10800	108TH AV	94605	671-B6
10950	DURANT AV	94605	671-B6
JUNE CT			OAK
10400	105TH AV	94603	670-H7
JUSTIN CIR			ALA
1	ENNIS PL	94502	669-J5
1	SEA VIEW PKWY	94502	669-J5
K			
KAHN AL			OAK
	FRANK H OGAWA PZ	94612	649-G4
	BROADWAY	94612	649-G4
	TELEGRAPH AV	94612	649-G4
KAINS AV			ALB
500	BRIGHTON AV	94706	609-D5
600	GARFIELD AV	94706	609-D5
700	PORTLAND AV	94706	609-D5
800	WASHINGTON AV	94706	609-D6
900	SOLANO AV	94706	609-D6
1000	MARIN AV	94706	609-D6
1100	DARTMOUTH ST	94706	609-D7
1200	HARRISON ST	94706	609-D7
KAINS AV			BERK
1200	HARRISON ST	94706	609-E7
1300	GILMAN ST	94702	609-E7
1400	CAMELIA ST	94702	609-E7
1470	PAGE ST	94702	629-E1
1540	JONES ST	94702	629-E1
1600	HOPKINS ST	94702	629-E1
1600	CEDAR ST	94702	629-E1
1700	VIRGINIA ST	94702	629-E1
KAISER PZ			OAK
2100	21ST ST	94612	649-H3
2200	22ND ST	94612	649-H3
KALES AV			OAK
5600	MANILA AV	94618	630-A6
5400	BROADWAY	94618	629-J6
5600	COLLEGE AV	94618	629-J6
KANSAS CITY			ALA
3000	MULVANY CIR	94501	649-E6
KANSAS ST			OAK
3000	MAPLE AV	94602	650-E5
3200	LAUREL AV	94602	650-F5
3400	MIDVALE AV	94602	650-F5
3500	35TH AV	94619	650-F5
3600	MAGEE AV	94619	650-F5
3700	LOMA VISTA AV	94619	650-F5
3800	BROWN AV	94619	650-F6
3890	PATTERSON AV	94619	650-F6
3980	38TH AV	94619	650-F6
4100	39TH AV	94619	650-F6
4300	HIGH ST	94619	650-F6
4400	MADRONE AV	94619	650-F6
KAPHAN AV			OAK
4730	MATTIS CT	94619	650-H6
4690	REINHARDT DR	94619	650-G6
4600	DAVENPORT AV	94619	650-G6
4690	FAIR AV	94619	650-G6
KAPIOLANI RD			OAK
3100	PROSPECT HILL RD	94613	670-G1
3100	FACULTY RD	94613	670-G1
3100	RICHARDS RD	94613	650-G7
3320	RICHARDS RD	94613	650-G7
3400	POST RD	94613	650-H7
KARA RD			ALA
1	CASTLEBAR PL	94502	669-J5
1	SEA VIEW PKWY	94502	669-J5
30	KILLYBEGS RD	94502	669-J5
100	CORK RD	94502	669-J5
KEARNEY AV			OAK
5000	MOUNTAIN BLVD	94602	650-F3
5100	ARGYLE ST	94602	650-F3
KEB RD			OAK
	MARGIE LN	94605	651-B7
KEEFER CT			PDMT
1	HILL LN	94610	650-A1
1	JEROME AV	94610	650-A1
KEEL WY			OAK
	13TH ST	94625	649-C4
	14TH ST	94607	649-C5
	15TH ST	94607	649-C5
	MIDDLE HARBOR RD	94607	649-C5
KEELER AV			BERK
700	GRIZZLY PEAK BLVD	94708	609-H5
800	MARIN AV	94708	609-H5
850	FOREST LN	94708	609-H5
900	FOREST LN	94708	609-H5
930	MILLER AV	94708	609-H5
980	POPPY LN	94708	609-H6
1000	STERLING AV	94708	609-H6
1100	BRET HARTE RD	94708	609-J6
1130	TWAIN AV	94708	609-J6
1200	SHASTA RD	94708	609-J6
KEIL BAY			ALA
100	BAYWALK RD	94502	669-J6
KEITH AV			BERK
1000	SPRUCE ST	94708	609-H6
1100	EUCLID AV	94708	609-H6
1150	BRET HARTE RD	94708	609-H6
1150	BRET HARTE WY	94708	609-H6
1300	SHASTA RD	94708	609-H6
KEITH AV			OAK
	MCMILLAN AV	94618	629-J5
	SHAFTER AV	94618	629-J5
5900	PRESLEY WY	94618	630-A5
6000	BROADWAY	94618	630-A5
KELLER AV			OAK
2700	GREENLY DR	94605	671-A2
2800	WINTHROPE ST	94605	671-A2
2900	EARL ST	94605	671-A2
2960	FONTAINE ST	94605	671-A1
4130	MOUNTAIN BLVD	94605	671-A1
4180	SANFORD ST	94605	671-A1
4200	SANFORD ST	94605	671-B1
4220	GREENRIDGE DR	94605	671-B2
4320	RILEA WY	94605	671-B2
4320	RILEA WY	94627	671-B2
7600	CANYON OAKS DR	94605	671-C1
7600	CANYON OAKS DR	94627	671-C1
7770	CAMPUS DR	94605	671-C2
7770	CAMPUS DR	94627	671-C2
8230	HANSOM DR	94605	671-D2
8300	SEQUOYAH RD	94605	671-D2
8320	SURREY LN	94605	671-D2
8340	SPILLMAN RD	94605	671-D2
8460	GRAEAGLE	94605	671-D2
8460	ELYSIAN FIELDS DR	94605	671-D2
8500	SKYLINE BLVD	94605	671-D2
KELSEY ST			BERK
2800	PALM CT	94705	629-J3
2800	STUART ST	94705	629-J3
2900	RUSSELL ST	94705	629-J3
KELTON CT			OAK
1	MONTE CRESTA AV	94611	649-J1
KEMPTON AV			OAK
3200	STANLEY PL	94611	649-H2
3400	FRISBIE WY	94611	649-H2
KEMPTON WY			OAK
3500	SANTA CLARA AV	94611	649-J1
3500	FAIRMOUNT AV	94611	649-J1
3600	W MACARTHUR BLVD	94611	649-J1
KENILWORTH RD			OAK
7100	STRATHMOOR DR	94705	630-C3
KENMORE AV			OAK
500	BOULEVARD WY	94610	650-A2
530	WALAVISTA AV	94610	650-A2
550	FAIRBANKS AV	94610	650-A2
600	LAKESHORE AV	94610	650-A2
KENNEDY ST			OAK
300	23RD AV	94606	670-B1
300	23RD AV	94606	670-B1
410	E 7TH ST	94606	670-A1
430	DIESEL ST	94606	670-A1
540	DENNISON ST	94606	650-A7
460	FREDERICK ST	94606	650-A7
540	FREDERICK ST	94606	650-A7
KENT RD			OAK
	BUCKINGHAM BLVD	94705	630-C4
KENTUCKY AV			BERK
400	VASSAR AV	94707	609-G4
440	MARYLAND AV	94707	609-G4
500	MICHIGAN AV	94707	609-G4
KENTWOOD CT			OAK
4100	MOUNTAIN BLVD	94605	671-B2
KENWYN RD			OAK
500	CLEVELAND ST	94606	650-A4
600	PROSPECT AV	94610	650-A3
650	MCKINLEY AV	94610	650-A3
700	HILLGIRT CIR	94610	650-A3
KEONCREST DR			BERK
1400	ROSE ST	94702	609-F7
1430	CATHERINE DR	94702	629-F1
1500	CATHERINE DR	94702	629-F1
1600	ACTON ST	94702	629-F1
KERRIGAN DR			OAK
11000	CLIFFLAND AV	94605	671-D5
11000	OVERMOOR ST	94605	671-D5
KERWIN AV			OAK
100	BERNHARDT DR	94603	670-G7
200	EL VERANO ST	94603	670-G7
300	DOUGLAS AV	94603	670-G7
300	KNIGHT ST	94603	670-G7
KESWICK CT			OAK
1	BEACONSFIELD PL	94611	650-F1
100	CHELTON DR	94611	650-F1
KEVIN CT			OAK
650	COLISEUM WY	94621	670-E3
KEVINGTON PL			ALA
200	SHEFFIELD RD	94502	670-A5
KEY CT			OAK
1	SCOTIA AV	94605	671-E4
KEY ROUTE BLVD			ALB
500	ASHBURY AV	94706	609-E5
500	BRIGHTON AV	94706	609-E5
550	THOUSAND OAKS BLVD	94706	609-E5
640	PORTLAND AV	94706	609-E5
740	WASHINGTON AV	94706	609-E6
860	SOLANO AV	94706	609-E6
860	SOLANO AV	94706	609-E6
980	MARIN AV	94706	609-E6
1110	DARTMOUTH ST	94706	609-E7
1200	SANTA FE AV	94706	609-E7
KILKENNY CT			ALA
1	KILKENNY PL	94502	669-J5
KILKENNY PL			ALA
1	KOFMAN PKWY	94502	669-J5
60	KILKENNY CT	94502	669-J6
	BALLEYBAY	94502	669-J6
KILLARNEY PL			ALA
1	SEA VIEW PKWY	94502	669-H5
KILLDEER CT			ALA
	BRUZZONE DR	94501	649-F7
	EGRET CT	94501	649-F7
KILLYBEGS RD			ALA
1	KARA RD	94502	669-J5
40	CORK RD	94502	669-H5
KIMBERLEY CT			OAK
1	CHELSEA DR	94611	650-F1
KIMBERLIN HEIGHTS DR			OAK
1	CRESTMONT DR	94619	650-H4
200	RISHELL DR	94619	650-H4
	CHADBOURNE WY	94619	650-H4
	SKYLINE BLVD	94619	650-H4
	STANTONVILLE DR	94619	650-H4
	STANTONVILLE CT	94619	650-H4
KING AV			PDMT
1	LINCOLN AV	94611	650-C2
100	HAMPTON RD	94610	650-C2
200	FARRAGUT AV	94610	650-C2
300	LA SALLE AV	94610	650-C2
KING ST			BERK
2900	RUSSELL ST	94703	629-G4
2950	JULIA ST	94703	629-G4
3000	ASHBY AV	94703	629-G4
3050	TYLER ST	94703	629-G4
3100	PRINCE ST	94703	629-G4
3150	WOOLSEY ST	94703	629-G4
3200	FAIRVIEW ST	94703	629-G4
3250	HARMON ST	94703	629-G5
3300	ALCATRAZ AV	94703	629-G5
3300	ALCATRAZ AV	94703	629-G5
3350	63RD ST	94703	629-G5
3400	62ND ST	94703	629-G5
3500	STANFORD AV	94703	629-G5
KING ST			OAK
800	DENNISON ST	94606	650-A7
1100	FREDERICK ST	94606	650-A7
KINGS RD			ALA
500	CROWN DR	94501	669-F1
550	QUEENS RD	94501	669-F2
KINGSBURY CT			ALA
	TRIUMPH DR	94501	649-G7
KINGSLAND AV			OAK
2400	TRASK ST	94601	670-F1
2490	RUTH AV	94601	670-F1
	MAVIS ST	94601	670-F1
2580	BROOKDALE AV	94601	670-F1
2580	BROOKDALE AV	94619	670-F1
2600	BROOKDALE AV	94619	670-F1
2660	EL CAMILLE AV	94619	670-F1
2680	MADERA AV	94601	670-F1
2680	MADERA AV	94619	670-F1
2680	WALNUT ST	94619	670-F1
2760	COLE ST	94601	670-F1
2760	RAWSON ST	94619	650-F7
2880	RAWSON ST	94619	650-F7
2890	FLEMING AV	94619	650-F7
2930	MAXWELL AV	94619	650-F7
2970	MAXWELL AV	94619	650-F7
3080	BEST AV	94619	650-F7
3200	BIRDSALL AV	94619	650-F7
3300	MADERA AV	94619	650-F7
3400	MORCOM AV	94619	650-F7
3500	REDDING ST	94619	650-G7
KINGSLAND PL			OAK
1	MORCOM AV	94619	650-F7
KINGSLEY CIR			OAK
5700	MASON ST	94605	670-G1
5900	SEMINARY AV	94605	670-G1
KINGSLEY ST			OAK
3600	CHATHAM RD	94610	650-B4
3680	EXCELSIOR AV	94610	650-B4
3700	PARK BLVD WY	94610	650-B4
3700	PARK BLVD	94610	650-B4
KINGSTON AV			OAK
700	MONTE VISTA AV	94611	649-J1
850	MONTE CRESTA AV	94611	649-J1
KINGSTON AV			PDMT
850	GREENBANK AV	94611	650-A1
750	LINDA AV	94611	650-A1
850	LINDA AV	94611	650-A1
850	MONTE CRESTA AV	94611	649-J1
KINGSTON LN			ALA
1000	SAVANA LN	94502	670-B7
1080	NORMAN LN	94502	670-B7
1100	OLEANDER AV	94502	670-B7
KINGWOOD RD			OAK
1	CRESTMONT DR	94619	650-H5
100	REDWOOD RD	94619	650-H5
KIRK			ALA
4000	CIMARRON ST	94501	649-E6
KIRKHAM ST			OAK
620	5TH ST	94607	649-E4
700	7TH ST	94607	649-E4
1220	12TH ST	94607	649-E3
1400	14TH ST	94607	649-E3
1600	16TH ST	94607	649-E2
1800	18TH ST	94607	649-E2
2400	24TH ST	94607	649-E2
2500	26TH ST	94607	649-E1
2600	PERALTA ST	94607	649-E1
KIRKLAND CT			OAK
1	ELVESSA ST	94605	671-D4
KISKA			ALA
4000	CHICAGO	94501	649-E6
4000	CIMARRON ST	94501	649-E6
KITCHENER CT			OAK
2900	WILSHIRE BLVD	94602	650-F4
KITTREDGE ST			BERK
2000	MILVIA ST	94704	629-G2
2060	HAROLD WY	94704	629-G2
2120	SHATTUCK AV	94704	629-H2
2200	OXFORD ST	94704	629-H2
KITTY HAWK PL			ALA
1900	SNOWBERRY WK	94501	669-H3
1900	KITTY HAWK RD	94501	669-H3
2000	FERNDELL WK	94501	669-H3

PRIMARY STREET Address	Cross Street	ZIP	CITY Pg-Grid
KITTY HAWK PL			**ALA**
2000	GREENBRIER RD	94501	669-H3
KITTY HAWK RD			**ALA**
300	SHORELINE DR	94501	669-H3
400	FRANCISCAN WY	94501	669-H3
500	KITTY HAWK PL	94501	669-H3
500	SNOWBERRY WK	94501	669-H3
KITTY LN			**OAK**
9800	98TH AV	94603	690-F1
9900	98TH AV	94603	690-F1
KIWANIS ST			**OAK**
3350	EASTLAKE AV	94602	650-F5
3400	MIDVALE AV	94602	650-F5
KLAMATH ST			**OAK**
3700	BRUNELL DR	94602	650-G4
KNIGHT ST			**OAK**
10300	DOUGLAS AV	94603	670-G7
10300	KERWIN AV	94603	670-G7
10340	GRAMERCY PL	94603	670-H7
10340	NATTRESS WY	94603	670-H7
10400	105TH AV	94603	670-H7
KNOLL AV			**OAK**
4300	MOUNTAIN BLVD	94619	650-H6
KNOLL RIDGE WY			**OAK**
1	CLAIREPOINTE WY	94619	651-C6
60	SLOPE CREST DR	94619	651-C6
KNOWLAND AV			**OAK**
3100	VIRGINIA AV	94619	650-F7
3200	FAIRBAIRN ST	94619	650-F7
3300	BIRDSALL AV	94619	650-F7
KOFMAN CT			**ALA**
1	KOFMAN PKWY	94502	669-J5
KOFMAN PKWY			**ALA**
1600	SEA VIEW PKWY	94502	669-H5
1600	TRALEE LN	94502	669-H5
1630	TIPPERARY LN	94502	669-H5
1660	WATERFORD PL	94502	669-H5
1700	SHANNON CIR	94502	669-H5
1750	APPLEGATE WY	94502	669-H5
1800	KILKENNY PL	94502	669-J5
1900	LIMERICK LN	94502	669-J5
1900	DUBLIN WY	94502	669-J5
1930	KOFMAN CT	94502	669-J5
1970	LIMERICK LN	94502	669-J5
2000	AUGHINBAUGH WY	94502	669-J5
KOFORD RD			**OAK**
9800	EMPIRE RD	94603	670-F7
9900	EMPIRE RD	94603	670-F7
KOLLMAN CIR			**ALA**
2000	MAYPORT CIR	94501	649-E6
KRAUSE AV			**OAK**
6900	CHURCH ST	94605	670-H2
7250	73RD AV	94605	670-H2
7300	73RD AV	94605	670-H2
7400	LEGION AV	94605	670-H2
7500	MAYWOOD AV	94605	670-H3
7630	DASHWOOD AV	94605	670-H3
7660	77TH AV	94605	670-H3
KROHN LN			**OAK**
1	DRAKE DR	94611	630-E7
KUHNLE AV			**OAK**
4000	SEMINARY AV	94605	650-H7
4000	SUNNYMERE AV	94605	650-H7
4060	FRONTAGE RD	94605	650-J7
4170	LEONA ST	94605	650-J7

L

PRIMARY STREET Address	Cross Street	ZIP	CITY Pg-Grid
LA CAMPANIA			**ALA**
	LINDA VISTA	94502	669-J6
	VERDEMAR DR	94502	669-J6
	EL PASEO	94502	669-J6
	VERDEMAR DR	94502	669-J6
3100	VERDEMAR DR	94502	669-J6
3200	CAMINO DEL VALLE	94502	669-J6
LA COSTE ST			**EMVL**
6400	64TH ST	94608	629-D5
6500	65TH ST	94608	629-D5
LA CRESTA			**ALA**
3100	VERDEMAR DR	94502	669-J6
3200	CAMINO DEL VALLE	94502	669-J6
LA CRESTA AV			**OAK**
4100	WELLINGTON ST	94602	650-D4
3800	HAMPEL ST	94602	650-D4
4100	E 38TH ST	94602	650-D4
4300	WELLINGTON ST	94602	650-D3
4400	EVERETT AV	94602	650-D3
4400	TOWNSEND AV	94602	650-D3
LA CUESTA AV			**OAK**
2600	CAMINO LENADA	94611	650-E2
2700	ASCOT DR	94611	650-E2
LA JOLLA DR			**ALA**
2600	BROADWAY	94501	670-A4
LA LOMA AV			**BERK**
1300	GLENDALE AV	94708	609-J7
1330	EL PORTAL CT	94708	609-J7
1370	QUARRY RD	94708	609-J7
1400	ROSE ST	94708	609-J7
1500	BUENA VISTA WY	94708	609-J7
1560	LA VEREDA	94708	609-J7
1600	CEDAR ST	94709	609-J7
1700	HILGARD AV	94709	609-J7
1750	VIRGINIA ST	94709	629-J1
1800	LE CONTE AV	94709	629-J1
1800	LE CONTE AV	94709	629-J1
1850	RIDGE RD	94709	629-J1
1900	GAYLEY RD	94709	629-J1
1900	HEARST AV	94709	629-J1
LA PRENDA DR			**OAK**
500	ACALANES DR	94603	670-H7
700	ESTEPA DR	94603	670-H7
LA SALLE AV			**OAK**
5660	LUCAS AV	94611	650-E1
5730	MOUNTAIN BLVD	94611	650-E1
5820	MOUNTAIN BLVD	94611	650-E1
5820	MORAGA AV	94611	650-E1
5870	TRAFALGAR PL	94611	650-D1
5970	LIGGETT DR	94611	650-D1
5820	BRUNS CT	94611	650-D1
5810	ESTATES DR	94611	650-D1
5800	WOOD DR	94611	650-D1
5480	ESTATES DR	94611	650-D1
5650	TYSON CIR	94611	650-D1
LA SALLE AV			**PDMT**
100	INDIAN RD	94610	650-C2
130	SEAVIEW AV	94610	650-C2
170	KING AV	94610	650-C2
200	CROCKER AV	94610	650-C2
250	MUIR AV	94610	650-C2
300	FLORADA AV	94610	650-C2
400	LAFAYETTE AV	94610	650-C2
400	WOODLAND WY	94610	650-C2
5400	TYSON CIR	94611	650-D1
1	TYSON CIR	94611	650-D1
10	CREST RD	94611	650-D2
20	HAMPTON RD	94611	650-D2
30	LA SALLE CT	94611	650-D2
50	SAINT JAMES DR	94611	650-C2
100	INDIAN RD	94611	650-C2
LA SALLE CT			**PDMT**
	LA SALLE AV	94611	650-D2
LA VEREDA			**BERK**
1500	LA LOMA AV	94708	609-J7
1500	CEDAR ST	94709	609-J7
1600	HILGARD AV	94709	609-J7
1800	VIRGINIA ST	94709	609-J7
LA VERNE AV			**OAK**
5500	FOOTHILL BLVD	94605	670-F1
5700	55TH AV	94605	670-F1
LACEY AV			**OAK**
6900	69TH AV	94605	670-H2
7000	LAVERDA PTH	94605	670-J2
7100	72ND AV	94605	670-J2
7100	NEY AV	94605	670-J2
LAFAYETTE AV			**PDMT**
130	WOODLAND WY	94611	650-C2
130	WOODLAND WY	94610	650-C2
130	LA SALLE AV	94610	650-C2
1	MUIR AV	94611	650-C2
1	MUIR AV	94610	650-C2
130	CROCKER AV	94611	650-C2
130	CROCKER AV	94610	650-C2
LAFAYETTE ST			**ALA**
900	CLINTON AV	94501	669-H2
1000	SAN JOSE AV	94501	669-H2
1100	SAN ANTONIO AV	94501	669-J2
1200	ENCINAL AV	94501	669-J2
1300	ALAMEDA AV	94501	669-J2
1400	CENTRAL AV	94501	669-J2
1500	SANTA CLARA AV	94501	669-J1
1600	LINCOLN AV	94501	669-J1
1700	PACIFIC AV	94501	669-J1
1800	BUENA VISTA AV	94501	669-J1
1900	EAGLE AV	94501	669-J1
2000	CLEMENT AV	94501	669-J1
LAGORIA CT			**ALA**
1	RATTO RD	94502	669-J6
LAGUNA AV			**OAK**
3400	MONTANA ST	94602	650-D5
3500	MACARTHUR BLVD	94602	650-D5
3610	DAMUTH ST	94602	650-E4
3670	SCENIC AV	94602	650-E4
3720	HEARST AV	94602	650-E4
3750	MADELINE ST	94602	650-E4
3790	WILBUR ST	94602	650-E4
3850	DELMER ST	94602	650-E4
3900	CARMEL ST	94602	650-E4
3970	RAMPART ST	94602	650-E4
4030	POTOMAC ST	94602	650-E4
4180	ALIDA ST	94602	650-E4
4210	ALIDA ST	94602	650-E4
4300	CHARLESTON ST	94602	650-E4
LAGUNA VISTA			**ALA**
300	BAYVIEW DR	94501	670-A4
400	BAYVIEW DR	94501	670-A4
LAGUNA WY			**OAK**
3200	HAROLD ST	94602	650-D5
3400	COOLIDGE AV	94602	650-D5
3400	TEXAS ST	94602	650-D5
LAGUNARIA LN			**ALA**
300	IRONWOOD RD	94502	670-A6
LAGUNITAS AV			**OAK**
400	EUCLID AV	94610	649-J3
450	BURK ST	94610	649-J3
LAIRD AV			**OAK**
5900	SEMINARY AV	94605	670-H1
6200	62ND AV	94605	670-H1
6600	68TH AV	94605	670-H1
LAKE AV			**PDMT**
1	GREENBANK AV	94611	650-A1
30	NACE AV	94611	650-A1
60	HOWARD AV	94611	650-A1
100	LINDA AV	94611	650-A1
100	LINDA AV	94611	650-A1
160	LINDA AV	94611	650-A1
160	OLIVE AV	94611	649-J1
100	SUNNYSIDE AV	94611	649-J1
LAKE PARK AV			**OAK**
400	GRAND AV	94610	649-J3
400	GRAND AV	94610	649-J3
410	WALKER AV	94610	649-J3
470	LAKESHORE AV	94610	650-A3
470	RAND AV	94610	650-A3
530	WESLEY WY	94610	650-A3
700	MACARTHUR BLVD	94610	650-A3
LAKE PKWY			**OAK**
	ELWOOD AV	94610	650-A2
	ELWOOD AV	94610	650-A2
	SANTA CLARA AV	94610	649-J2
LAKEHURST CIR			**ALA**
2000	MOSLEY AV	94501	649-E6
2100	MOSLEY AV	94501	649-E6
LAKESHORE AV			**OAK**
1400	1ST AV	94606	649-H4
1400	LAKESIDE DR	94606	649-H4
1640	1ST AV	94606	649-J4
1500	E 15TH ST	94606	649-H4
1690	E 15TH ST	94606	649-J4
1700	FOOTHILL BLVD	94606	649-J4
1700	1ST AV	94606	649-J4
1800	E 18TH ST	94606	649-J4
1800	E 18TH ST	94606	649-J4
1960	HANOVER AV	94606	649-J4
2100	WESLEY AV	94606	649-J4
2120	WAYNE AV	94606	649-J4
2200	BROOKLYN AV	94606	649-J3
2400	BODEN WY	94610	649-J3
2900	EL EMBARCADERO	94610	649-J3
2950	EL EMBARCADERO	94610	649-J3
3090	BEACON ST	94610	649-J3
3090	MACARTHUR BLVD	94610	650-A3
3150	MACARTHUR BLVD	94610	650-A3
3200	LAKE PARK AV	94610	650-A3
3200	RAND AV	94610	650-A3
3420	TRESTLE GLEN RD	94610	650-A3
3460	LONGRIDGE RD	94610	650-A3
3500	MANDANA BLVD	94610	650-A3
3630	SANTA RAY AV	94610	650-A3
3630	PRINCE ST	94610	650-A3
3670	WELDON AV	94610	650-A3
3720	ROSAL AV	94610	650-A2
3780	ROSAL AV	94610	650-A2
3800	KENMORE AV	94610	650-A2
3900	WALAVISTA AV	94610	650-B2
3920	WALAVISTA AV	94610	650-B2
3960	BOULEVARD WY	94610	650-B2
3960	HARVARD RD	94610	650-B2
3960	WINSOR AV	94610	650-B2
4000	BOULEVARD WY	94610	650-B2
4200	HARVARD RD	94610	650-B2
4220	PARK LN	94610	650-B2
4300	WALAVISTA AV	94610	650-B2
LAKESIDE DR			**OAK**
1	1ST AV	94607	649-H5
1	LAKESHORE AV	94607	649-H5
20	14TH ST	94607	649-H5
1200	14TH ST	94612	649-H4
1340	14TH ST	94612	649-H4
1400	OAK ST	94612	649-H4
100	17TH ST	94612	649-H4
160	MADISON ST	94612	649-H4
1800	JACKSON ST	94612	649-H3
1840	20TH ST	94612	649-H3
2100	HARRISON ST	94612	649-H3
LAKEVIEW AV			**PDMT**
50	SEAVIEW AV	94611	650-C1
30	POPLAR WY	94611	650-C1
1	RICHARDSON WY	94611	650-C1
30	SHERIDAN AV	94611	650-C1
LAMP ST			**OAK**
3400	SUNKIST DR	94605	671-A2
3500	CREST AV	94605	671-A2
7700	STERLING DR	94605	671-A2
7900	GREENLY DR	94605	671-A2
LANCASTER ST			**OAK**
380	GLASCOCK ST	94601	670-B1
470	FORD ST	94601	670-B1
550	CHAPMAN ST	94601	670-B1
630	E 7TH ST	94601	670-B1
700	ELMWOOD AV	94601	670-B1
LANDREGAN ST			**EMVL**
	HORTON ST	94608	629-E6
	STANFORD AV	94608	629-E6
5760	HARUFF ST	94608	629-E6
	59TH ST	94608	629-E5
	62ND ST	94608	629-E5
LANDVALE RD			**OAK**
300	TUNNEL RD	94618	630-B4
LANE CT			**OAK**
1	HARBORD DR	94611	630-C7
10	MARR AV	94611	630-C7
LANGDON CT			**PDMT**
100	HARDWICK AV	94611	650-B1
LANGLEY ST			**OAK**
	DOOLITTLE DR	94621	670-D6
	BOEING ST	94621	670-D6
	CONVAIR ST	94621	670-D6
	CONVAIR ST	94621	670-D6
	LOCKHEED ST	94621	670-D6
	BOEING ST	94621	670-D6
LARCHMONT ISL			**ALA**
500	ROSEWOOD WY	94501	669-G2
600	OTIS DR	94501	669-G2
LARKSPUR RD			**OAK**
900	HILLCROFT CIR	94610	650-B3
LARMER CT			**PDMT**
300	MAGNOLIA AV	94610	650-B1
LARRY LN			**OAK**
1	MASTLANDS DR	94611	650-F2
100	ASCOT DR	94611	650-F2
LAS AROMAS			**OAK**
2600	MOUNTAINGATE WY	94611	650-F2
LAS FLORES CT			**OAK**
	WOODROW DR	94611	630-F7
LAS VEGAS AV			**OAK**
9550	ESPINOSA AV	94605	671-B4
9550	FARRELL ST	94605	671-B4
9700	98TH AV	94605	671-B4
LASSEN ST			**BERK**
1000	EL DORADO AV	94707	609-G6
1100	MARIN AV	94707	609-G6
LATHAM LN			**BERK**
1	MILLER AV	94708	609-J5
100	GRIZZLY PEAK BLVD	94708	609-J5
100	CRESTON RD	94708	609-J5
200	OVERLOOK RD	94708	609-J5
LATHAM ST			**PDMT**
100	CAMBRIDGE WY	94611	650-A1
200	OAKLAND AV	94611	650-A1
LATIMER PL			**OAK**
3700	W MACARTHUR BLVD	94609	649-H1
3800	38TH ST	94609	649-H1
LAUREL AV			**OAK**
3200	SCHOOL ST	94602	650-E5
3270	SUTER ST	94602	650-E5
3340	ARKANSAS ST	94602	650-E5
3430	DELAWARE ST	94602	650-E5
3480	DAKOTA ST	94602	650-E5
3520	GEORGIA ST	94602	650-E5
3600	MACARTHUR BLVD	94602	650-E5
3650	FLORIDA ST	94602	650-E5
3700	KANSAS ST	94602	650-E5
3800	MADELINE ST	94602	650-E5
3700	NORTON AV	94602	650-F5
3700	MADELINE ST	94602	650-F5
3800	CALIFORNIA ST	94602	650-F5
3900	ARIZONA ST	94602	650-F5
4070	SYLVAN AV	94602	650-F4
4200	WISCONSIN ST	94602	650-F4
4200	CARLSEN ST	94602	650-F4
LAUREL LN			**BERK**
	SAN DIEGO RD	94707	609-G5
	CAPISTRANO AV	94707	609-F5
	TACOMA AV	94707	609-F5
	SAN PEDRO AV	94707	609-F5
LAUREL ST			**ALA**
800	POWELL ST	94501	669-J3
900	CLINTON AV	94501	669-J3
LAUREL ST			**BERK**
1100	EUNICE ST	94708	609-H6
1200	OAK ST	94708	609-H6
LAURISTON CT			**OAK**
8100	THORNDALE DR	94611	630-E5
LAVAGETTO CT			**ALA**
1	RATTO RD	94502	669-J6
LAVERDA PTH			**OAK**
3400	LACEY AV	94605	670-J2
3600	OUTLOOK AV	94605	670-J2
LAWLOR ST			**OAK**
8900	BURR ST	94605	671-A3
9100	90TH AV	94605	671-A4
9400	STEARNS AV	94605	671-A4
9600	CHEROKEE AV	94605	671-A4
9800	98TH AV	94605	671-A4
9830	TAYLOR AV	94605	671-A5
9900	99TH AV	94605	671-A5
LAWRENCE RD			**ALA**
1	ROSS RD	94502	669-H6
100	SHARON RD	94502	669-J6
200	ANDERSON RD	94502	669-J6
200	MOORE CT	94502	669-J6
LAWTON AV			**OAK**
4500	45TH ST	94609	629-H7
4900	49TH ST	94609	629-J6
5000	50TH ST	94609	629-J6
5100	51ST ST	94618	629-J6
5200	CAVOUR ST	94618	629-J6
5300	CLIFTON ST	94618	629-J6
5400	HUDSON ST	94618	629-J6
5500	FOREST ST	94618	629-J6
5500	COLLEGE AV	94618	629-J5
5800	MCMILLAN AV	94618	630-A5
6000	BROADWAY	94618	630-A5
6000	ROCKRIDGE BLVD S	94618	630-A5
6000	BROADWAY	94618	630-A5
6100	MENDOCINO AV	94618	630-A5
6200	ACACIA AV	94618	630-A5
6200	MANILA AV	94618	630-A5
6200	MARGARIDO DR	94618	630-A5
LE CONTE AV			**BERK**
2300	HEARST AV	94709	629-H1
2300	ARCH ST	94709	629-H1
2440	RIDGE RD	94709	629-H1
2440	SCENIC AV	94709	629-H1
2560	EUCLID AV	94709	629-H1
2670	LE ROY AV	94709	629-J1
2750	LA LOMA AV	94709	629-J1
	LA LOMA AV	94709	629-J1
	HIGHLAND PL	94709	629-J1
LE ROY AV			**BERK**
1400	ROSE ST	94708	609-H7
1400	TAMALPAIS RD	94708	609-H7
1500	HAWTHORNE TER	94708	609-H7
1520	VINE LN	94708	609-H7
1530	BUENA VISTA WY	94708	609-H7
1600	CEDAR ST	94709	609-J7
1700	HILGARD AV	94709	609-J7
1720	VIRGINIA ST	94709	629-H1
1740	LE CONTE AV	94709	629-H1
1770	RIDGE RD	94709	629-J1
1800	HEARST AV	94709	629-J1
LEA CT			**ALA**
1600	LINCOLN AV	94501	670-A2
1700	PACIFIC AV	94501	670-A2
LEACH ST			**OAK**
4300	WELLINGTON ST	94602	650-C3
4400	EVERETT AV	94602	650-C3
LEAMONT CT			**OAK**
1	MALCOLM AV	94605	671-C5
LEE ST			**OAK**
200	VERNON ST	94610	649-H2
250	ADAMS ST	94610	649-H2
260	MONTECITO AV	94610	649-H3
270	JAYNE AV	94610	649-J3
300	VAN BUREN AV	94610	649-J3
500	GRAND AV	94610	649-J3
LEET DR			**OAK**
1	CAPWELL DR	94621	670-E6
1	PENDLETON WY	94621	670-E6
100	HEGENBERGER RD	94621	670-E6
LEEWARD LN			**ALA**
1100	SOLOMON LN	94502	670-A7
1170	TONGA LN	94502	670-A7
1200	CATALINA AV	94502	670-A7
LEEWARD WY			**OAK**
3000	BROADMOOR VW	94605	671-B5
3000	MALCOLM AV	94605	671-B5
	SHELDON ST	94605	671-B5
	106TH AV	94605	671-B5
LEGION AV			**OAK**
2300	FRESNO ST	94605	670-H3
2400	KRAUSE AV	94605	670-H3
LEIGHTON ST			**OAK**
3700	W MACARTHUR BLVD	94611	649-J1
3720	MOSS WY	94611	649-J1
LEIMERT BLVD			**OAK**
1300	PARK BLVD	94602	650-D3
1300	SAINT JAMES DR	94602	650-D3
1440	CLEMENS RD	94602	650-D3
1500	LEIMERT PL	94602	650-D3
1500	OAKMORE RD	94602	650-D3
1500	ARDEN PL	94602	650-D3
1500	OAKMORE RD	94602	650-D3
1570	BRIDGEVIEW DR	94602	650-E3
1640	HOOVER AV	94602	650-E3
1900	OAKVIEW DR	94602	650-E3
1970	WRENN ST	94602	650-E2
2310	CARTER ST	94602	650-E2
2440	BYWOOD DR	94602	650-E2
2500	OAKCREST DR	94602	650-E2
2700	MONTEREY BLVD	94602	650-E2
LEIMERT PL			**OAK**
1700	OAKMORE RD	94602	650-D3
1700	LEIMERT BLVD	94602	650-D3
1800	CLEMENS RD	94602	650-D3
LEMOORE RD			**ALA**
	ALAMEDA RD	94501	649-D6
LENOX AV			**OAK**
200	MONTECITO AV	94610	649-H3
300	VAN BUREN AV	94610	649-H3
500	GRAND AV	94610	649-H3
LEO WY			**OAK**
1000	DUNCAN WY	94611	630-D6
900	BROADWAY TER	94611	630-C6
800	AVOCA AV	94611	630-C6
LEONA ST			**OAK**
5500	TWITTER CT	94605	650-H7
5700	MOUNTAIN BLVD	94605	650-H6
5750	MOUNTAIN VIEW AV	94605	650-H7
5810	RUSTING AV	94605	650-H7
6000	MOUNTAIN VIEW AV	94605	650-J7
6110	KUHNLE AV	94605	650-J7
6380	RUSSELL ST	94605	650-J7
LEONARD CT			**ALA**
1	DENKE DR	94502	669-J6
1	BORDWELL CT	94502	669-J6
LESSER ST			**OAK**
700	TIDEWATER AV	94601	670-C2
730	MALAT ST	94601	670-C2
800	OAKPORT ST	94601	670-C2
LESTER AV			**OAK**
200	HANOVER AV	94606	649-J4
300	ACTON PL	94606	649-J4
400	NEWTON AV	94606	649-J4
400	NEWTON AV	94606	649-J4
500	HANOVER AV	94606	649-J4
LEWELLING CT			**ALA**
1000	WASHINGTON ST	94501	670-A3
LEWIS ST			**OAK**
300	3RD ST	94607	649-D4
520	5TH ST	94607	649-D3
700	7TH ST	94607	649-D3
LEWISTON AV			**BERK**
3100	WOOLSEY ST	94705	629-J4
3200	ALCATRAZ AV	94705	629-J4
LEXFORD PL			**OAK**
1	SKYLINE BLVD	94619	651-B7
20	CRESTVIEW DR	94619	651-B7
LEXFORD RD			**PDMT**
1	HUNTLEIGH RD	94611	650-D2
60	HAMPTON RD	94611	650-D2
200	HUNTLEIGH RD	94611	650-D2
LEXINGTON ST			**ALA**
	W TOWER AV	94501	649-C6
	W HOPE ST	94501	649-C6
	W RANGER AV	94501	649-C6
	W MIDWAY AV	94501	649-C6
	W MALL SQ	94501	649-C6
	W CAPTAIN DODGE PL	94501	649-C6
	NAVY WY	94501	649-C6
	W RED LINE AV	94501	649-C6
LIBBY CT			**OAK**
3500	35TH AV	94619	650-F5
LIBERTY AV			**ALA**
3200	HIGH ST	94501	670-B3
3300	FERNSIDE BLVD	94501	670-C3
3380	EAST SHORE DR	94501	670-C3
LIESE AV			**OAK**
3340	SUTER ST	94619	650-F6

© 2006 Rand McNally & Company

Address	Primary Street / Cross Street	ZIP	City / Pg-Grid
	LIESE AV		**OAK**
3100	MINNA AV	94619	650-E6
3340	38TH AV	94619	650-E6
	LIGGETT DR		**OAK**
6500	LA SALLE AV	94611	650-D1
6650	SIMS DR	94611	650-E1
6800	ESTATES DR	94611	650-E1
	LILAC ST		**ALA**
900	MAGNOLIA DR	94502	670-B7
1000	OLEANDER AV	94502	670-B7
	LILAC ST		**OAK**
2600	BROOKDALE AV	94619	650-E7
2700	WALNUT ST	94619	650-F7
2800	ALLENDALE AV	94619	650-F7
	LILY ST		**OAK**
3650	MASTERSON ST	94619	650-G6
3750	TULIP AV	94619	650-G6
	LIMERICK LN		**ALA**
700	KOFMAN PKWY	94502	669-J5
700	DUBLIN WY	94502	669-J5
800	KOFMAN PKWY	94502	669-J5
	LINCOLN AV		**ALA**
100	CENTRAL AV	94501	669-E1
160	SANTA CLARA AV	94501	669-E1
230	HAIGHT AV	94501	669-E1
300	3RD ST	94501	669-E1
400	4TH ST	94501	669-E1
500	5TH ST	94501	669-F1
500	MARSHALL WY	94501	669-F1
550	LINDEN ST	94501	669-F1
600	6TH ST	94501	669-F1
700	WEBSTER ST	94501	669-F1
720	CONCORDIA ST	94501	669-F1
800	CONSTITUTION WY	94501	669-G1
800	8TH ST	94501	669-G1
900	9TH ST	94501	669-G1
950	WOOD ST	94501	669-G1
960	MASTICK CT	94501	669-G1
980	MOZART ST	94501	669-G1
1000	CHAPIN ST	94501	669-G1
1050	VERDI ST	94501	669-G1
	SAINT CHARLES ST	94501	669-G1
1100	SAINT CHARLES ST	94501	669-G1
1200	BAY ST	94501	669-H1
1300	SHERMAN ST	94501	669-H1
1400	MORTON ST	94501	669-H1
1500	BENTON ST	94501	669-H1
1520	POWERS CT	94501	669-H1
	STANTON ST	94501	669-H1
1540	STANTON ST	94501	669-H1
1600	PARU ST	94501	669-H1
1650	HIBBARD ST	94501	669-H1
1700	GRAND ST	94501	669-J1
1750	MINTURN ST	94501	669-J1
1800	UNION ST	94501	669-J1
1850	SCHILLER ST	94501	669-J1
1900	LAFAYETTE ST	94501	669-J1
	CHESTNUT ST	94501	669-J1
2000	LINCOLN LN	94501	669-J1
2100	WILLOW ST	94501	669-J2
2200	WALNUT ST	94501	670-A2
2280	LEA CT	94501	670-A2
2300	OAK ST	94501	670-A2
2300	TILDEN WY	94501	670-A2
2400	PARK ST	94501	670-A2
2400	TILDEN WY	94501	670-A2
2500	EVERETT ST	94501	670-A2
2520	GOULD CT	94501	670-A2
2600	BROADWAY	94501	670-B2
2700	PEARL ST	94501	670-B2
2800	VERSAILLES AV	94501	670-B2
2830	MORELAND DR	94501	670-B2
2850	GIBBONS DR	94501	670-B3
3000	COURT ST	94501	670-B3
3100	FOUNTAIN ST	94501	670-B3
3200	HIGH ST	94501	670-B3
	LINCOLN AV		**OAK**
3500	CHAMPION ST	94602	650-D5
3520	PALMETTO ST	94602	650-D4
3580	MACARTHUR BLVD	94602	650-D4
3700	COLOMA ST	94602	650-D4
3740	DAMUTH ST	94602	650-D4
3760	DAMUTH ST	94602	650-D4
3790	SCENIC AV	94602	650-D4
3840	HEARST AV	94602	650-D4
3900	WILBUR ST	94602	650-E4
3940	DELMER ST	94602	650-E4
3990	CARMEL ST	94602	650-E4
4020	RAMPART ST	94602	650-E4
4070	POTOMAC ST	94602	650-E4
4100	RAVENWOOD LN	94602	650-E4
4130	BURLINGTON ST	94602	650-E3
4200	ALIDA ST	94602	650-E3
4360	PERKINS RD	94602	650-E3
4680	LINCOLN WY	94602	650-F3
4760	MAIDEN LN	94602	650 F3
4780	MONTEREY BLVD	94602	650-F3
	LINCOLN AV		**PDMT**
1	SHERIDAN AV	94611	650-C1
30	CROCKER AV	94611	650-C1
60	KING AV	94611	650-C1
100	SEAVIEW AV	94611	650-C1
	LINCOLN LN		**ALA**
1500	LINCOLN AV	94501	669-J1
	LINCOLN ST		**BERK**
1300	CHESTNUT ST	94702	629-E1
1400	ACTON ST	94702	629-F1
1480	SHORT ST	94702	629-F1
1500	SACRAMENTO ST	94703	629-F1
1600	CALIFORNIA ST	94703	629-F1
1700	MCGEE AV	94703	629-F1
1730	EDITH ST	94703	629-G1
1800	GRANT ST	94703	629-G1
2000	MILVIA ST	94709	629-G1
2100	SHATTUCK AV	94709	629-G1
	LINCOLN WY		**OAK**
4900	LINCOLN AV	94602	650-F3
5000	MONTEREY BLVD	94602	650-F3
	LINCOLNSHIRE DR		**OAK**
1	COUNTRY CLUB DR	94618	630-A6
100	WESTMINSTER DR	94618	630-A6
	LINDA AV		**OAK**
1	PIEDMONT AV	94611	649-J1
70	GLEN AV	94611	649-J1
100	MONTE CRESTA AV	94611	649-J1
200	ECHO AV	94611	649-J1
	LINDA AV		**PDMT**
200	ECHO AV	94611	649-J1
200	KINGSTON AV	94611	650-A1
210	KINGSTON AV	94611	650-A1
270	LAKE AV	94611	650-A1
280	LAKE AV	94611	650-A1
500	GRAND AV	94611	650-A1
	LINDA VISTA		**ALA**
3000	VIA ALAMOSA	94502	669-J6
3100	LA CAMPANIA	94502	669-J6
3100	VERDEMAR DR	94502	669-J6
	LINDEN AV		**BERK**
2900	ASHBY AV	94705	629-J3
3000	WEBSTER ST	94705	629-J3

Address	Primary Street / Cross Street	ZIP	City / Pg-Grid
	LINDEN ST		**ALA**
1500	SANTA CLARA AV	94501	669-F1
1550	HAIGHT AV	94501	669-F1
1600	LINCOLN AV	94501	669-F1
	LINDEN ST		**OAK**
300	3RD ST	94607	649-E4
1000	10TH ST	94607	649-E3
1200	12TH ST	94607	649-E3
1400	14TH ST	94607	649-F3
1600	16TH ST	94607	649-F3
1800	18TH ST	94607	649-F3
2100	21ST ST	94607	649-F2
2200	W GRAND AV	94607	649-F2
2400	24TH ST	94607	649-F2
2600	26TH ST	94607	649-F2
2700	28TH ST	94608	649-F1
3000	30TH ST	94608	649-F1
3200	32ND ST	94608	649-F1
3400	34TH ST	94608	649-F1
3450	SAN PABLO AV	94608	649-F1
3700	37TH ST	94608	629-F7
3800	W MACARTHUR BLVD	94608	629-F7
4000	40TH ST	94608	629-F7
	41ST ST	94608	629-F7
4100	41ST ST	94608	629-F7
4200	42ND ST	94608	629-F7
4300	43RD ST	94608	629-F7
4400	44TH ST	94608	629-F7
4400	44TH ST	94608	629-F6
4500	45TH ST	94608	629-F6
4500	45TH ST	94608	629-G6
4600	46TH ST	94608	629-G6
	LINK ST		**OAK**
10560	SUNNYSIDE ST	94603	671-A6
10560	104TH AV	94603	671-A6
10490	104TH AV	94603	671-A6
10400	105TH AV	94603	671-A6
10490	106TH AV	94603	671-A6
10490	BANCROFT AV	94603	671-A6
	LINNET AV		**OAK**
4200	ALIDA ST	94602	650-E4
	LINWOOD AV		**OAK**
3700	EXCELSIOR AV	94602	650-C4
3750	EVERS AV	94602	650-C4
3800	E 38TH ST	94602	650-C4
3800	E 38TH ST	94602	650-C4
4100	HAMPEL ST	94602	650-C4
	LISBON AV		**OAK**
920	E 9TH ST	94601	670-B1
1010	E 11TH ST	94601	650-B7
920	E 10TH ST	94601	650-B7
1010	E 10TH ST	94601	650-B7
	LITTLEWOOD DR		**PDMT**
1	DUDLEY AV	94611	650-C1
	LIVE OAK RD		**OAK**
100	GRAND VIEW DR	94705	630-B3
	LIVINGSTON ST		**OAK**
2000	EMBARCADERO	94606	650-A7
2060	22ND AV	94606	650-A7
2280	COTTON ST	94606	650-A7
	LOCARNO PTH		**OAK**
	CROSS RD	94618	630-B5
100	ACACIA AV	94618	630-B5
100	MATHIEU AV	94618	630-B5
110	ALPINE TER	94618	630-B5
110	PINE LN	94618	630-B5
	LOCHARD ST		**OAK**
10870	ABERFOIL AV	94605	671-D5
10800	RODERICK RD	94605	671-D4
10700	MALCOLM AV	94605	671-D4
	LOCKHEED ST		**OAK**
7200	CONVAIR ST	94621	670-D6
7200	LANGLEY ST	94621	670-D6
7460	FAIRCHILD ST	94621	670-D6
7650	BENSON ST	94621	670-D6
7680	SIKORSKY ST	94621	670-D6
7780	RYAN ST	94621	670-D6
7870	HILLER ST	94621	670-D6
8100	GRUMMAN ST	94621	670-D6
	LOCKSLEY AV		**OAK**
5200	CAVOUR ST	94618	629-H6
5300	CLIFTON ST	94618	629-J6
5400	HUDSON ST	94618	629-J6
5500	FOREST ST	94618	629-J6
	LOCKWOOD ST		**OAK**
6900	78TH AV	94621	670-H3
7000	79TH AV	94621	670-H3
6900	69TH AV	94621	670-G2
7300	73RD AV	94621	670-G2
	73RD AV	94621	670-H3
7300	73RD AV	94621	670-H3
7800	78TH AV	94621	670-H3
	LOCUST ST		**OAK**
7800	78TH AV	94621	670-G3
7900	79TH AV	94621	670-G3
	LODGE CT		**OAK**
1	HEMLOCK ST	94611	630-F6
100	COLTON BLVD	94611	630-F6
	LOGAN ST		**OAK**
2600	26TH AV	94601	650-C6
2720	27TH AV	94601	650-C6
3100	FRUITVALE AV	94601	650-C6
3100	FRUITVALE AV	94601	650-C6
3300	COOLIDGE AV	94601	650-C6
	LOMA VISTA AV		**OAK**
3400	QUIGLEY ST	94619	650-F6
3500	REDDING ST	94619	650-F6
3600	MACARTHUR BLVD	94619	650-F6
3600	MACARTHUR BLVD	94619	650-F5
3700	KANSAS ST	94619	650-F5
3800	CALIFORNIA ST	94619	650-F5
4000	WISCONSIN ST	94619	650-F5
4100	HARBOR VIEW AV	94619	650-F5
	LOMA VISTA WY		**OAK**
3300	SUTER ST	94619	650-E6
3400	FULLINGTON ST	94619	650-E6
	LONDON RD		**OAK**
2800	FRYE ST	94602	650-F4
2900	JORDAN RD	94602	650-F4
	LONGCROFT DR		**OAK**
6430	CHELSEA DR	94611	650-G1
6300	HAVERHILL DR	94611	650-F1
6430	ASCOT DR	94611	650-F1
6430	CAMELFORD PL	94611	650-F1
	LONGFELLOW AV		**OAK**
9900	99TH AV	94603	671-A5
10000	100TH AV	94603	671-A5
10300	103RD AV	94603	671-A5
10600	106TH AV	94603	671-A5
	LONGRIDGE RD		**OAK**
600	LAKESHORE AV	94610	650-A3
700	ROSEMOUNT RD	94610	650-B3
790	VERRADA RD	94610	650-B3
930	PALOMA AV	94610	650-B3
930	CARLSTON AV	94610	650-B3
960	CARLSTON AV	94610	650-B3
1000	GROSVENOR PL	94610	650-B3
1120	HUBERT RD	94610	650-C3
1120	PARAMOUNT RD	94610	650-C3
1170	MIDCREST RD	94610	650-C3

Address	Primary Street / Cross Street	ZIP	City / Pg-Grid
1200	CLARENDON CRES	94610	650-C3
	LONGWALK DR		**OAK**
6500	ASCOT DR	94611	650-G1
6720	CLIVE AV	94611	650-G1
6800	DARNBY DR	94611	650-G1
	LORENZO AV		**OAK**
3200	MARION AV	94619	650-E6
3250	SUTER ST	94619	650-E6
	LORINA ST		**BERK**
2900	RUSSELL ST	94705	629-H4
3000	ASHBY AV	94705	629-H4
	LORITA AV		**PDMT**
1	PARK WY	94611	650-A1
	LOS ANGELES AV		**BERK**
1900	THE ALAMEDA	94707	609-G6
1930	CONTRA COSTA AV	94707	609-G6
1980	MENDOCINO AV	94707	609-G6
2000	FOUNTAIN WK	94707	609-G6
2000	MARIN AV	94707	609-G6
2000	SUTTER ST	94707	609-G6
2000	ARLINGTON AV	94707	609-G6
2000	DEL NORTE ST	94707	609-G6
2070	MARIPOSA AV	94707	609-G6
2100	SHATTUCK AV	94707	609-G6
2200	OXFORD ST	94707	609-H6
2300	SPRUCE ST	94707	609-H6
	LOS ANGELES ST		**OAK**
5600	AILEEN ST	94608	629-F6
5660	57TH ST	94608	629-F6
5720	ARLINGTON AV	94608	629-F5
5770	GRACE AV	94608	629-F5
5800	59TH ST	94608	629-F5
5800	STANFORD AV	94608	629-F5
	LOUISE ST		**OAK**
3000	30TH ST	94608	649-E1
3000	POPLAR ST	94608	649-E1
3030	PERALTA ST	94608	649-E1
3150	32ND ST	94608	649-E1
3350	34TH ST	94608	649-E1
	LOUISIANA ST		**OAK**
600	OSCAR AV	94603	670-G6
700	WALTER AV	94603	670-G6
800	RAILROAD AV	94603	670-G6
	LOUVAINE AV		**OAK**
100	BERNHARDT DR	94603	670-G7
200	EL VERANO ST	94603	670-G7
	LOWELL ST		**OAK**
5300	ADELINE ST	94608	629-F6
5320	53RD ST	94608	629-F6
5400	54TH ST	94608	629-F6
5500	55TH ST	94608	629-F6
5600	56TH ST	94608	629-F6
5650	AILEEN ST	94608	629-F6
5700	57TH ST	94608	629-F6
5750	ARLINGTON AV	94608	629-F5
5800	GRACE AV	94608	629-F5
6100	STANFORD AV	94608	629-F5
	LOWER GRAND AV		**PDMT**
1600	GRAND AV	94611	650-A1
1620	HOLLY PL	94611	650-A1
1700	ARROYO AV	94611	650-A1
	LOWRY RD		**OAK**
4820	SUN VALLEY DR	94605	671-E5
	LUCAS AV		**OAK**
6550	MERCED AV	94611	650-E1
6500	ANTIOCH ST	94611	650-E1
6550	LA SALLE AV	94611	650-E1
	LUCILLE ST		**OAK**
6600	69TH AV	94621	670-F3
6900	66TH AV	94621	670-F3
	LUNDHOLM AV		**OAK**
3600	OUTLOOK AV	94605	650-H7
3700	BUENA VENTURA AV	94605	650-H7
3770	OAKDALE AV	94605	650-H7
3800	OAKDALE AV	94605	650-H7
	LUSK ST		**OAK**
3800	APGAR ST	94608	629-G7
3900	39TH ST	94608	629-G7
4000	40TH ST	94608	629-G7
4100	41ST ST	94608	629-G7
4300	42ND ST	94608	629-G7
	LYMAN RD		**OAK**
3730	FRUITVALE AV	94602	650-D4
3800	WATERHOUSE RD	94602	650-D3
4100	TIFFIN RD	94602	650-D3
4100	TIFFIN RD	94602	650-E3
4200	CLEMENS RD	94602	650-E3
	LYNDE ST		**OAK**
2800	BELLAIRE PL	94601	650-C6
2890	FRUITVALE AV	94601	650-D6
3040	E SUNSET AV	94601	650-D6
3100	SUNSET AV	94601	650-D6
3200	ATWELL AV	94601	650-D6
3300	COOLIDGE AV	94601	650-D6
3300	COOLIDGE AV	94601	650-D6
3400	HUMBOLDT AV	94601	650-D6
3450	BARTLETT ST	94601	650-D6
3500	35TH AV	94601	650-D6
	LYNDHURST ST		**OAK**
9800	STONEFORD AV	94603	670-G6
9900	98TH AV	94603	670-G6
	LYON AV		**OAK**
3500	35TH AV	94601	650-D6
3660	HARRINGTON AV	94601	650-E6
3780	RANSOM AV	94601	650-E7
3860	38TH AV	94601	650-E7
4300	HIGH ST	94601	650-E7

M

Address	Primary Street / Cross Street	ZIP	City / Pg-Grid
	MABEL ST		**BERK**
2500	DWIGHT WY	94702	629-F3
2550	BLAKE ST	94702	629-F3
2600	PARKER ST	94702	629-F3
2620	CARLETON ST	94702	629-F3
2700	DERBY ST	94702	629-F3
2720	WARD ST	94702	629-F3
2720	WARD ST	94702	629-F3
2800	OREGON ST	94702	629-F4
2900	RUSSELL ST	94702	629-F4
2900	RUSSELL ST	94702	629-F4
2910	BURNETT ST	94702	629-F4
3000	ASHBY AV	94702	629-F4
3020	CARRISON ST	94702	629-F4
3100	HASKELL ST	94702	629-F4
3120	67TH ST	94702	629-F4
3200	66TH ST	94702	629-F4
	MACARTHUR BLVD		**OAK**
1	FAIRMOUNT AV	94610	649-J1
1	SANTA CLARA AV	94610	649-J1
1	W MACARTHUR BLVD	94610	649-J1
60	SANTA CLARA AV	94610	649-J2
70	HARRISON ST	94610	649-J2
100	OAKLAND AV	94610	649-J2
170	PERRY PL	94610	649-J2
200	VERNON ST	94610	649-J2
230	CHETWOOD ST	94610	649-J2
230	ADAMS ST	94610	649-J2
400	VAN BUREN AV	94610	649-J2
450	GRAND AV	94610	649-J3
450	LAKESHORE AV	94610	650-A3
500	LAKESHORE AV	94610	650-A3
530	EXCELSIOR CT	94610	650-A3
570	BEACON ST	94610	650-A3
590	WESLEY AV	94610	650-A3
760	LAKE PARK AV	94610	650-A3
770	BARBARA RD	94610	650-A3
770	HILLGIRT CIR	94610	650-A3
780	ATHOL AV	94610	650-A3
790	MONTCLAIR AV	94610	650-A3
840	SPRUCE ST	94610	650-A3
900	CAPELL ST	94610	650-B4
1	ALMA AV	94610	650-B4
1300	PARK BLVD	94610	650-B4
740	FOOTHILL BLVD	94605	671-C6
700	FOOTHILL BLVD	94605	671-C6
1000	DUTTON AV	94605	671-C7
1160	PARK BLVD	94610	650-B4
1300	13TH AV	94602	650-B4
1330	STUART ST	94602	650-B4
1350	E 34TH ST	94602	650-B4
1400	BEAUMONT AV	94602	650-B4
1400	BEAUMONT AV	94602	650-C4
1400	CHATHAM RD	94602	650-C4
1470	BRIGHTON AV	94602	650-C4
	14TH AV	94602	650-C4
1500	GLEN PARK RD	94602	650-C4
1560	RANDOLPH AV	94602	650-C4
1610	ARDLEY AV	94602	650-C4
1610	23RD AV	94602	650-C4
1660	WOODRUFF AV	94602	650-C4
1750	SHEFFIELD AV	94602	650-C4
1780	MONTANA ST	94602	650-D4
1860	ADELL CT	94602	650-D4
1860	EXCELSIOR AV	94602	650-D4
1870	E 38TH ST	94602	650-D4
1880	CANON AV	94602	650-D4
1940	DIMOND AV	94602	650-D4
2000	FRUITVALE AV	94602	650-D4
2060	CHAMPION ST	94602	650-D4
2220	MAY CT	94602	650-D4
2400	LINCOLN AV	94602	650-D4
2470	BOSTON AV	94602	650-D4
2540	WILSON AV	94602	650-D5
2600	LAGUNA AV	94602	650-E5
2690	RHODA AV	94602	650-E5
2700	RHODA AV	94602	650-E5
2800	COOLIDGE AV	94602	650-E5
2800	GEORGIA ST	94602	650-E5
2840	HOPKINS PL	94602	650-E5
3000	MAPLE AV	94602	650-E5
3200	LAUREL AV	94602	650-E5
3430	MIDVALE AV	94602	650-F5
3500	35TH AV	94619	650-F5
3600	MAGEE AV	94619	650-F5
3670	LOMA VISTA AV	94619	650-F6
3700	LOMA VISTA AV	94619	650-F6
3800	BROWN AV	94619	650-F6
3900	PATTERSON AV	94619	650-F6
4000	38TH AV	94619	650-F6
4020	38TH AV	94619	650-F6
4100	39TH AV	94619	650-F6
4200	MAYBELLE AV	94619	650-F6
4300	HIGH ST	94619	650-F6
4600	GREENACRE RD	94619	650-G7
4790	ENOS AV	94619	650-G7
4900	BUELL ST	94613	650-G7
4900	BUELL ST	94619	650-G7
5010	PIERSON ST	94613	650-G7
5010	PIERSON ST	94619	650-G7
5020	RICHARDS RD	94613	650-G7
5020	RICHARDS RD	94619	650-G7
5230	SIMMONS ST	94613	650-G7
5230	SIMMONS ST	94619	650-G7
5390	MILLSVIEW AV	94613	650-G7
5390	MILLSVIEW AV	94619	650-G7
5500	CAMDEN ST	94605	670-G1
5500	CAMDEN ST	94619	670-G1
5500	55TH AV	94619	670-G1
5550	CAMDEN ST	94605	670-G1
5550	CAMDEN ST	94613	670-G1
5600	56TH AV	94613	670-G1
5600	56TH AV	94605	670-G1
5700	57TH AV	94613	670-G1
5700	57TH AV	94605	670-G1
5800	58TH AV	94613	670-G1
5800	58TH AV	94605	670-G1
5850	MILLSBRAE AV	94613	670-G1
5850	MILLSBRAE AV	94605	670-G1
3200	CAMDEN ST	94613	670-G1
3200	CAMDEN ST	94605	670-G1
3200	SEMINARY AV	94613	670-G1
5900	SEMINARY AV	94605	670-G1
6000	60TH AV	94605	670-G1
6100	61ST AV	94605	670-H1
6200	62ND AV	94605	670-H1
6300	63RD AV	94605	670-H1
6400	64TH AV	94605	670-H1
6440	64TH AV PL	94605	670-H1
6500	65TH AV	94605	670-H1
6600	66TH AV	94605	670-H1
6800	68TH AV	94605	670-H2
6900	69TH AV	94605	670-H2
7100	72ND AV	94605	670-J2
8600	73RD AV	94605	670-J2
8600	FOOTHILL BLVD	94605	670-J2
7300	73RD AV	94605	670-J2
7400	74TH AV	94605	670-J2
7470	75TH AV	94605	670-J2
7500	75TH AV	94605	670-J2
7600	76TH AV	94605	670-J2
7630	76TH AV	94605	670-J2
7700	77TH AV	94605	670-J2
7800	78TH AV	94605	670-J2
7840	PARKER AV	94605	670-J2
7900	79TH AV	94605	670-J2
7950	RITCHIE ST	94605	670-J2
8000	80TH AV	94605	670-J3
8200	82ND AV	94605	670-J3
8300	83RD AV	94605	670-J3
6780	84TH AV	94605	671-A3
8430	EC REEMS CT	94605	671-A3
8800	88TH AV	94605	671-A3
8900	89TH AV	94605	671-A4
9000	90TH AV	94605	671-A4
9000	90TH AV	94603	671-A4
9400	STEARNS AV	94605	671-A4
9600	96TH AV	94605	671-A4
9600	96TH AV	94603	671-A4
9700	ELMVIEW DR	94605	671-A4
9700	ELMVIEW DR	94603	671-A4
9800	98TH AV	94605	671-A4
9800	98TH AV	94603	671-A4
9850	WARNER AV	94605	671-A5
9850	WARNER AV	94603	671-A5
9870	TAYLOR AV	94605	671-A5
9870	TAYLOR AV	94603	671-A5
9880	99TH AV	94605	671-A5
9880	99TH AV	94603	671-A5
9900	99TH AV	94605	671-A5

PRIMARY STREET Address	Cross Street	ZIP	CITY Pg-Grid
MACARTHUR BLVD			**OAK**
9900	99TH AV	94603	671-A5
9930	TRUMAN AV	94605	671-A5
9930	TRUMAN AV	94603	671-A5
10000	100TH AV	94605	671-A5
10000	100TH AV	94603	671-A5
10180	BYRON ST	94605	671-A5
10180	BYRON ST	94603	671-A5
10200	FOOTHILL BLVD	94605	671-A5
10200	FOOTHILL BLVD	94603	671-A5
10400	FISHER AV	94605	671-B5
10500	TALBOT AV	94605	671-B5
10600	106TH AV	94605	671-B5
10600	106TH AV	94603	671-B5
10640	MYERS ST	94605	671-B5
10640	MYERS ST	94603	671-B5
10700	107TH AV	94605	671-B6
10700	107TH AV	94603	671-B6
10800	108TH AV	94605	671-B6
10800	108TH AV	94603	671-B6
10900	109TH AV	94605	671-B6
10900	109TH AV	94603	671-B6
11000	DURANT AV	94605	671-B6
11000	DURANT AV	94603	671-B6
MACARTHUR BLVD			**SLN**
	FOOTHILL BLVD	94577	671-C6
1000	DUTTON AV	94577	671-C7
W MACARTHUR BLVD			**EMVL**
	APGAR ST	94608	629-F7
	SAN PABLO AV	94608	629-F7
	ADELINE ST	94608	629-F7
	EMERY ST	94608	629-F7
	ADELINE ST	94608	629-F7
	PERALTA ST	94608	629-F7
	WATTS ST	94608	629-F7
W MACARTHUR BLVD			**OAK**
	APGAR ST	94608	629-F7
	LINDEN ST	94608	629-F7
	SAN PABLO AV	94608	629-F7
	EMERY ST	94608	629-F7
	WATTS ST	94608	629-F7
100	FAIRMOUNT AV	94611	649-J1
100	MACARTHUR BLVD	94611	649-J1
100	SANTA CLARA AV	94611	649-J1
130	KEMPTON WY	94611	649-J1
160	RICHMOND BLVD	94611	649-J1
170	LEIGHTON ST	94611	649-J1
210	PIEDMONT AV	94611	649-H1
250	HOWE ST	94611	649-H1
300	BROADWAY	94609	649-H1
330	MANILA AV	94609	649-H1
360	SHAFTER AV	94609	649-H1
390	WEBSTER ST	94609	649-H1
410	RUBY ST	94609	649-H1
440	LATIMER PL	94609	649-H1
500	TELEGRAPH AV	94609	649-H1
580	37TH ST	94609	649-G1
690	MARTIN LUTHER KING JR WY	94609	649-G1
800	WEST ST	94608	629-G7
900	MARKET ST	94608	629-G7
1400	HOLLIS ST	94608	629-F7
MACCALL ST			**OAK**
5700	57TH ST	94609	629-H5
5800	58TH ST	94609	629-G5
5900	59TH ST	94609	629-G5
6000	60TH ST	94609	629-G5
MACKINNON ST			**PDMT**
100	MAGNOLIA AV	94610	650-A2
MADDUX DR			**OAK**
9600	EDES AV	94603	670-G6
9620	HAZELWOOD CT	94603	670-G6
9650	ASHTON AV	94603	670-G6
9670	BURLWOOD AV	94603	670-G6
9700	CASWELL AV	94603	670-G6
9800	98TH AV	94603	670-G6
9800	98TH AV	94603	670-G6
9830	GHORMLEY AV	94603	670-G6
9860	HUNTER AV	94603	670-G7
9900	STONEFORD AV	94603	670-G7
MADELINE ST			**OAK**
2600	LAGUNA AV	94602	650-E4
2700	RHODA AV	94602	650-E4
2800	COOLIDGE AV	94602	650-E4
2930	HILLVIEW ST	94602	650-E5
3000	MAPLE AV	94602	650-E5
3200	LAUREL AV	94602	650-F5
3300	LAUREL AV	94602	650-F5
3300	NORTON AV	94602	650-F5
MADERA AV			**OAK**
2700	WALNUT ST	94601	670-F1
2700	WALNUT ST	94619	670-F1
2700	KINGSLAND AV	94619	670-F1
2750	HILLEN DR	94619	670-F1
2830	FLEMING AV	94619	670-F1
2830	BIRDSALL AV	94619	650-F7
3060	BIRDSALL AV	94619	650-G7
3200	CAMDEN ST	94619	650-G7
3240	SIMMONS ST	94619	650-G7
3370	PIERSON ST	94619	650-G7
3500	KINGSLAND AV	94619	650-G7
MADERA ST			**BERK**
1700	TULARE AV	94707	609-F6
1740	SIERRA ST	94707	609-F6
1780	MERCED ST	94707	609-F6
1800	COLUSA AV	94707	609-F6
MADISON ST			**ALA**
2900	MOUND ST	94501	670-A3
3000	COURT ST	94501	670-B3
3100	FOUNTAIN ST	94501	670-B3
3200	HIGH ST	94501	670-B4
3230	POST ST	94501	670-B4
3260	PEACH ST	94501	670-B4
3300	FERNSIDE BLVD	94501	670-B4
MADISON ST			**ALB**
560	CLAY ST	94706	609-D5
660	CASTRO ST	94706	609-D5
760	WASHINGTON AV	94706	609-D6
870	SOLANO AV	94706	609-D6
1000	BUCHANAN ST	94706	609-D6
MADISON ST			**OAK**
180	2ND ST	94607	649-G5
390	4TH ST	94607	649-G5
500	5TH ST	94607	649-G5
700	7TH ST	94607	649-G5
800	8TH ST	94607	649-G5
900	9TH ST	94607	649-G4
1000	10TH ST	94607	649-G4
1100	11TH ST	94607	649-H4
1200	12TH ST	94607	649-H4
1300	13TH ST	94612	649-H4
1400	14TH ST	94612	649-H4
1500	15TH ST	94612	649-H4
1700	17TH ST	94612	649-H4
1800	19TH ST	94612	649-H4
1900	LAKESIDE DR	94612	649-H4
MADRONE AV			**OAK**
3600	MASTERSON ST	94619	650-F6
3700	KANSAS ST	94619	650-G6
3750	TULIP AV	94619	650-G6
3810	PAMPAS AV	94619	650-G6
3840	ALBERT ST	94619	650-G6
3920	STEELE ST	94619	650-G6
4000	HYACINTH AV	94619	650-G6
MAGEE AV			**OAK**
3600	MACARTHUR BLVD	94619	650-F5
3710	KANSAS ST	94619	650-F5
3860	CALIFORNIA ST	94619	650-F5
4010	WISCONSIN ST	94619	650-F5
4100	HARBOR VIEW AV	94619	650-F5
MAGELLAN DR			**OAK**
1800	COLTON BLVD	94611	630-E7
1950	CORTE REAL AV	94611	630-E7
1990	SNAKE RD	94611	650-E1
2200	RINCON DR	94611	650-E1
2200	DRAKE DR	94611	650-E1
MAGGIORA CT			**OAK**
1	MAGGIORA DR	94605	671-C5
MAGGIORA DR			**OAK**
3000	MALCOLM AV	94605	671-C5
3500	MAGGIORA CT	94605	671-C5
4600	MALCOLM AV	94605	671-C5
MAGNOLIA AV			**PDMT**
100	NOVA DR	94610	650-A2
160	MACKINNON ST	94610	650-A2
300	PARKVIEW CT	94610	650-B1
330	LARMER CT	94610	650-B1
340	JEROME AV	94610	650-B1
350	JEROME AV	94610	650-B1
370	SAN CARLOS AV	94611	650-B1
370	SAN CARLOS AV	94610	650-B1
390	EL CERRITO AV	94611	650-B1
400	EL CERRITO AV	94611	650-B1
600	HILLSIDE CT	94611	650-B1
700	HILLSIDE AV	94611	650-B1
800	BONITA AV	94611	650-B1
1000	HIGHLAND AV	94611	650-B1
MAGNOLIA DR			**ALA**
300	MELROSE AV	94502	670-B7
310	GINGER LN	94502	670-B7
320	MANGROVE LN	94502	670-B7
340	LILAC ST	94502	670-B7
800	FITCHBURG AV	94502	670-B7
1000	OLEANDER AV	94502	670-B7
1050	SILVA LN	94502	670-B7
MAGNOLIA ST			**BERK**
2900	ASHBY AV	94705	629-J3
3000	WEBSTER ST	94705	629-J3
MAGNOLIA ST			**OAK**
700	7TH ST	94607	649-E4
1000	10TH ST	94607	649-E3
1200	12TH ST	94607	649-E3
1400	14TH ST	94607	649-E3
1600	16TH ST	94607	649-E3
2200	W GRAND AV	94607	649-E2
2400	24TH ST	94607	649-F2
2600	26TH ST	94607	649-F2
2800	28TH ST	94608	649-F1
3000	30TH ST	94608	649-F1
3200	32ND ST	94608	649-F1
3400	34TH ST	94608	649-F1
	35TH ST	94608	649-F1
3550	36TH ST	94608	629-F7
3600	PERALTA ST	94608	629-F7
MAIDEN LN			**OAK**
1	LINCOLN AV	94602	650-F3
200	MONTEREY BLVD	94602	650-F3
MAIN ST			**ALA**
1700	CENTRAL AV	94501	649-E7
1700	PACIFIC AV	94501	649-E7
	ATLANTIC AV	94501	649-E7
2420	W MIDWAY AV	94501	649-E6
2600	SINGLETON AV	94501	649-D6
3400	NAVY WY	94501	649-C6
MAITLAND DR			**ALA**
1	ISLAND DR	94502	670-A6
	FLOWER LN	94502	670-B6
100	FLOWER LN	94502	670-B6
	MELROSE AV	94502	670-B6
200	MECARTNEY RD	94502	670-B7
400	FITCHBURG AV	94502	670-B7
500	HARBOR BAY PKWY	94502	670-B7
MAJESTIC AV			**OAK**
5900	OUTLOOK AV	94605	650-H7
6200	OUTLOOK AV	94605	650-H7
6200	62ND AV	94605	670-H1
6400	64TH AV	94605	670-H1
MAKIN RD			**OAK**
200	EMPIRE RD	94603	670-F6
300	CORAL RD	94603	670-F6
MALAT ST			**OAK**
4700	LESSER ST	94601	670-C2
MALCOLM AV			**OAK**
3000	BROADMOOR VW	94605	671-C5
3000	LEEWARD WY	94605	671-C5
3210	MARK ST	94605	671-C5
3300	STELLA ST	94605	671-C5
3400	HELLMAN ST	94605	671-C5
3500	MAGGIORA DR	94605	671-C5
3600	WOODCLIFF CT	94605	671-C5
3620	MAGGIORA DR	94605	671-C5
3700	LEAMONT CT	94605	671-C5
3760	EDGEMONT WY	94605	671-C5
3800	MONTWOOD WY	94605	671-D4
4100	SNOWDOWN AV	94605	671-D4
4190	CAMERON AV	94605	671-D4
4200	CAMERON AV	94605	671-D4
4260	LOCHARD ST	94605	671-D4
4320	ETTRICK ST	94605	671-D4
4400	ELVESSA ST	94605	671-D4
4440	FALLBROOK WY	94605	671-D4
4500	MONAN ST	94605	671-E4
4600	CALODEN ST	94605	671-E4
MALDON ST			**OAK**
6200	62ND AV	94621	670-E3
MALL CT			**OAK**
100	CAMELFORD PL	94611	650-G2
W MALL SQ			**ALA**
	LEXINGTON ST	94501	649-C6
	SARATOGA ST	94501	649-C6
MALTA CT			**OAK**
1	BERNHARDT DR	94603	670-G7
MANCHESTER DR			**OAK**
6000	OCEAN VIEW DR	94618	630-A5
5900	PROSPECT STEPS	94618	630-A5
5900	WEST LN	94618	630-A5
6000	ACACIA AV	94618	630-A5
MANDALAY RD			**OAK**
130	HARBORD DR	94618	630-B6
170	MARGUERITE DR	94618	630-B6
210	NORMAN LN	94618	630-B6
230	WILDING LN	94618	630-B6
260	BUCKEYE AV	94618	630-B6
310	HERMOSA AV	94618	630-B6
400	ARBON PTH	94618	630-B6
400	BROADWAY TER	94618	630-B6
MANDANA BLVD			**OAK**
400	GRAND AV	94610	650-A2
440	WALKER AV	94610	650-A2
450	VERMONT ST	94610	650-A2
480	WARFIELD AV	94610	650-A3
500	WARFIELD AV	94610	650-A3
530	YORK ST	94610	650-A3
550	ERIE ST	94610	650-A3
560	RAND AV	94610	650-A3
600	LAKESHORE AV	94610	650-A3
670	CALMAR AV	94610	650-B3
740	PALOMA AV	94610	650-B3
760	PALOMA AV	94610	650-B3
900	CARLSTON AV	94610	650-B3
920	MANDANA CIR	94610	650-C3
1000	CLARENDON CRES	94610	650-C3
1000	PORTAL AV	94610	650-C3
1100	ARDMORE AV	94610	650-C3
1200	ASHMOUNT AV	94610	650-C3
1200	CROCKER AV	94610	650-C3
MANDANA CIR			**OAK**
1	MANDANA BLVD	94610	650-B3
MANDELA PKWY			**OAK**
500	5TH ST	94607	649-D4
600	7TH ST	94607	649-D4
2800	32ND ST	94607	649-E1
2800	32ND ST	94608	649-E1
2600	28TH ST	94607	649-E1
2570	26TH ST	94607	649-E1
2400	CAMPBELL ST	94607	649-E2
2250	24TH ST	94607	649-E2
2200	PERALTA ST	94607	649-E2
2060	W GRAND AV	94607	649-E2
2000	20TH ST	94607	649-E2
1800	20TH ST	94607	649-E2
1700	18TH ST	94607	649-E2
1600	17TH ST	94607	649-E2
1400	16TH ST	94607	649-E3
1200	14TH ST	94607	649-E3
1000	12TH ST	94607	649-E3
970	10TH ST	94607	649-E3
	CYPRESS ST	94607	649-E3
600	8TH ST	94607	649-D3
600	7TH ST	94607	649-D3
800	8TH ST	94607	649-D3
900	9TH ST	94607	649-E3
1000	10TH ST	94607	649-E3
1100	11TH ST	94607	649-E3
1200	12TH ST	94607	649-E3
1300	13TH ST	94607	649-E3
1400	14TH ST	94607	649-E3
1500	15TH ST	94607	649-E3
1600	16TH ST	94607	649-E2
1700	17TH ST	94607	649-E2
1800	18TH ST	94607	649-E2
2000	20TH ST	94607	649-E2
2050	20TH ST	94607	649-E2
2200	PERALTA ST	94607	649-E2
2200	W GRAND AV	94607	649-E2
2400	24TH ST	94607	649-E2
2450	24TH ST	94607	649-E2
2490	CAMPBELL ST	94607	649-E1
2600	26TH ST	94607	649-E1
2800	28TH ST	94607	649-E1
2800	WILLOW ST	94607	649-E1
2900	32ND ST	94607	649-E1
MANGELS AV			**OAK**
3500	35TH AV	94619	650-E6
MANGROVE LN			**ALA**
1000	MAGNOLIA DR	94502	670-B7
1010	SAVANA LN	94502	670-B7
1100	OLEANDER AV	94502	670-B7
MANILA AV			**OAK**
3700	W MACARTHUR BLVD	94609	649-H1
3800	38TH ST	94609	629-H7
4000	40TH ST	94609	629-H7
4100	41ST ST	94609	629-H7
4200	42ND ST	94609	629-H7
4500	45TH ST	94609	629-J7
4900	49TH ST	94609	629-J7
4900	49TH ST	94609	629-J7
5000	50TH ST	94609	629-J6
5100	51ST ST	94618	629-J6
5200	CAVOUR ST	94618	629-J6
5250	GLENDALE AV	94618	629-J6
5300	CLIFTON ST	94618	629-J6
	HUDSON ST	94618	629-J6
5400	COLLEGE AV	94618	629-J6
5490	BRYANT AV	94618	629-J6
5570	BROADWAY	94618	630-A6
5570	MONROE AV	94618	630-A6
5650	KALES AV	94618	630-A6
5700	MENDOCINO AV	94618	630-A6
5700	VIRMAR AV	94618	630-A6
5740	ACACIA AV	94618	630-A5
5740	LAWTON AV	94618	630-A5
5740	MARGARIDO DR	94618	630-A5
	TAFT AV	94618	630-A5
	MENDOCINO AV	94618	630-A5
MANOA ST			**OAK**
6200	FLORIO ST	94618	629-J4
6300	MYSTIC ST	94618	629-J4
MANOR CREST			**OAK**
6700	CHABOT CREST	94618	630-A4
6800	ROANOKE RD	94618	630-A4
MANOR DR			**PDMT**
60	ARROYO AV	94611	650-A1
100	HOLLY PL	94611	650-A1
200	CAMBRIDGE WY	94611	650-A1
MANOR WY			**ALB**
	PERALTA AV	94706	609-F6
	ORDWAY ST	94706	609-F6
	VENTURA AV	94706	609-F6
MANUEL CT			**OAK**
1200	A ST	94603	670-J6
MANZANITA DR			**OAK**
1700	SKYLINE BLVD	94611	630-F6
1770	NORTHWOOD CT	94611	630-F6
1810	VILLANOVA DR	94611	630-F6
1900	VILLANOVA DR	94611	630-G6
2100	NORTH CIR	94611	630-G6
2500	PINEHURST RD	94611	630-G6
MAPLE AV			**OAK**
3000	NICOL AV	94602	650-D6
3050	WARD LN	94602	650-E5
3200	SCHOOL ST	94602	650-E5
3200	SCHOOL ST	94602	650-E5
3280	TEXAS ST	94602	650-E5
3330	SUTER ST	94602	650-E5
3350	SUTER ST	94602	650-E5
	ARKANSAS ST	94602	650-E5
3430	MONTANA ST	94602	650-E5
3460	DELAWARE ST	94602	650-E5
3480	DELAWARE ST	94602	650-E5
3510	DAKOTA ST	94602	650-E5
3540	GEORGIA ST	94602	650-E5
3560	GEORGIA ST	94602	650-E5
3610	MACARTHUR BLVD	94602	650-E5
3660	FLORIDA ST	94602	650-E5
3710	KANSAS ST	94602	650-E5
3770	MADELINE ST	94602	650-E5
3900	CALIFORNIA ST	94602	650-E4
4000	ARIZONA ST	94602	650-E4
4020	CARMEL ST	94602	650-E4
4050	SYLVAN AV	94602	650-F4
4070	MORGAN AV	94602	650-F4
4100	WISCONSIN ST	94602	650-F4
4130	CARLSEN ST	94602	650-F4
4140	CARLSEN ST	94602	650-F4
4200	FRYE ST	94602	650-F4
4300	FRYE ST	94602	650-F4
MARCUSE ST			**ALA**
1000	MECARTNEY RD	94502	669-J6
1000	BAYWALK RD	94502	669-J6
1050	REMMEL CT	94502	669-J6
1100	DENKE DR	94502	669-J6
MARDEN LN			**OAK**
5900	MERRIEWOOD DR	94611	630-D6
MARGARIDO DR			**OAK**
5600	BROADWAY TER	94618	630-A6
5600	COUNTRY CLUB DR	94618	630-A6
5800	ACACIA AV	94618	630-A6
5800	LAWTON AV	94618	630-A6
5800	MANILA AV	94618	630-A6
5800	ACACIA AV	94618	630-A5
5850	MENDOCINO AV	94618	630-A5
5970	ROCKRIDGE BLVD S	94618	630-A5
5980	PROSPECT STEPS	94618	630-A5
6110	OCEAN VIEW DR	94618	630-A5
MARGARITA AV			**OAK**
3400	GRANADA AV	94605	671-B3
3500	CALANDRIA	94605	671-B3
3500	MURILLO AV	94605	671-B3
MARGIE LN			**OAK**
	OHANNESON RD	94605	651-B7
	RICHMOND RD	94605	651-B7
	KEB RD	94605	651-B7
	RIFLE RANGE RD	94605	651-B7
MARGUERITE DR			**OAK**
1	HERMOSA AV	94618	630-B6
100	MANDALAY RD	94618	630-B6
MARIE WY			**OAK**
5900	CHABOT RD	94618	630-B4
MARIN AV			**ALB**
1000	BUCHANAN ST	94706	609-D6
1100	SAN PABLO AV	94706	609-D6
1130	KAINS AV	94706	609-D6
1160	STANNAGE AV	94706	609-D6
1190	CORNELL AV	94706	609-E6
1220	TALBOT AV	94706	609-E6
1250	EVELYN AV	94706	609-E6
1280	MASONIC AV	94706	609-E6
1300	KEY ROUTE BLVD	94706	609-E6
1340	POMONA AV	94706	609-E6
1370	RAMONA AV	94706	609-E6
1410	CARMEL AV	94706	609-E6
1440	SANTA FE AV	94706	609-E6
1480	CURTIS ST	94706	609-E6
1520	NEILSON ST	94706	609-F6
1550	PERALTA AV	94706	609-F6
1600	ORDWAY ST	94707	609-F6
1600	ORDWAY ST	94706	609-F6
1620	ORDWAY ST	94707	609-F6
1650	VENTURA AV	94707	609-F6
1690	TULARE AV	94707	609-F6
MARIN AV			**BERK**
1690	TULARE AV	94707	609-F6
1730	ENSENADA AV	94707	609-F6
1770	MODOC ST	94707	609-F6
1810	COLUSA AV	94707	609-F6
1870	FRESNO AV	94707	609-G6
1900	MARTIN LUTHER KING JR WY	94707	609-G6
1900	THE ALAMEDA	94707	609-G6
1930	MONTEREY AV	94707	609-G6
1940	LASSEN ST	94707	609-G6
2000	FOUNTAIN WK	94707	609-G6
2000	LOS ANGELES AV	94707	609-G6
2000	SUTTER ST	94707	609-G6
2000	ARLINGTON AV	94707	609-G6
2000	DEL NORTE ST	94707	609-G6
2100	SHATTUCK AV	94707	609-G6
2200	OXFORD ST	94707	609-G6
2250	SAN BENITO RD	94707	609-G6
2300	SANTA BARBARA RD	94707	609-H5
2330	SPRUCE ST	94708	609-H5
2410	CRAGMONT AV	94708	609-H5
2430	REGAL RD	94708	609-H5
2470	BONNIE LN	94708	609-H5
2470	EUCLID AV	94708	609-H5
2530	HILLDALE AV	94708	609-H5
2570	KEELER AV	94708	609-H5
2610	GRIZZLY PEAK BLVD	94708	609-H5
2650	CRESTON RD	94708	609-H5
MARIN WY			**OAK**
1500	15TH AV	94606	650-A6
1600	16TH AV	94606	650-A6
1710	17TH AV	94606	650-A6
1810	18TH AV	94606	650-A6
1910	19TH AV	94606	650-A6
2010	20TH AV	94606	650-A6
2110	21ST AV	94606	650-A6
2210	22ND AV	94606	650-B6
2300	MUNSON WY	94606	650-B6
MARINA BLVD			**BERK**
200	SPINNAKER WY	94804	629-B2
300	UNIVERSITY AV	94804	629-B2
MARINA DR			**ALA**
2800	WINDSOR DR	94501	670-B2
2800	VERSAILLES AV	94501	670-B2
2900	CAMBRIDGE DR	94501	670-B2
3000	HARVARD DR	94501	670-C2
3150	WINDSOR DR	94501	670-C2
3200	HIGH ST	94501	670-C2
MARINA VILLAGE PKWY			**ALA**
800	CONSTITUTION WY	94501	649-F7
810	MARINER SQUARE DR	94501	649-F7
860	BARTLETT DR	94501	649-G7
900	CHALLENGER DR	94501	649-G7
930	INDEPENDENCE DR	94501	649-G6
1360	MARINER SQUARE DR	94501	649-F6
1500	MARINER SQUARE LP	94501	649-F6
MARINER SQUARE DR			**ALA**
2470	MITCHELL AV	94501	649-F6
2300	MARINA VILLAGE PKWY	94501	649-F6
2600	TYNAN AV	94501	649-F6
2800	MARINA VILLAGE PKWY	94501	649-F7
MARINER SQUARE LP			**ALA**
1	TINKER AV	94501	649-F6
100	WEBSTER ST	94501	649-F6
100	CONSTITUTION WY	94501	649-F6
2100	TINKER AV	94501	649-F6
2300	MARINA VILLAGE PKWY	94501	649-F6
MARION AV			**OAK**
3700	STAR AV	94619	650-E6
3800	LORENZO AV	94619	650-E6
3900	38TH AV	94619	650-E6
MARION CT			**ALA**
400	4TH ST	94501	669-E1
MARIPOSA AV			**BERK**
1100	LOS ANGELES AV	94707	609-G6
1150	TERRACE WK	94707	609-G6
1200	AMADOR AV	94707	609-G6
MARIPOSA AV			**OAK**
600	SANTA ROSA AV	94610	649-J1
700	OAKLAND AV	94610	649-J1

PRIMARY STREET Address	Cross Street	ZIP	CITY Pg-Grid
MARITIME ST			**OAK**
	3RD ST	94625	649-B3
620	4TH ST	94625	649-B3
700	7TH ST	94607	649-B3
860	7TH ST EXT	94607	649-B3
860	7TH ST EXT	94626	649-B3
1100	PIER ST	94607	649-C2
1100	PIER ST	94626	649-C2
1500	15TH ST	94607	649-C2
1500	15TH ST	94626	649-C2
1710	CHUNGKING ST	94607	649-C2
1710	CHUNGKING ST	94626	649-C2
1800	BATAAN AV	94607	649-C1
1800	BATAAN AV	94626	649-C1
2000	ALASKA ST	94607	649-D1
2000	ALASKA ST	94626	649-D1
2350	WAKE AV	94649	649-D1
2350	W GRAND AV	94649	649-D1
MARK ST			**OAK**
10700	HOOD ST	94605	671-C5
10800	MALCOLM AV	94605	671-C5
MARKET ST			**BERK**
6350	SACRAMENTO ST	94702	629-F5
6350	SACRAMENTO ST	94703	629-F5
6400	ALCATRAZ AV	94702	629-F5
6400	ALCATRAZ AV	94703	629-F5
6400	SACRAMENTO ST	94703	629-F5
MARKET ST			**OAK**
100	1ST ST	94607	649-E4
300	3RD ST	94607	649-E4
400	4TH ST	94607	649-F4
	5TH ST	94607	649-F4
700	7TH ST	94607	649-F4
800	8TH ST	94607	649-F4
1000	10TH ST	94607	649-F3
1160	12TH ST	94607	649-F3
1250	13TH ST	94607	649-F3
1370	14TH ST	94607	649-F3
1470	15TH ST	94607	649-F3
1560	16TH ST	94607	649-F3
1750	18TH ST	94607	649-F3
1850	19TH ST	94607	649-F3
1920	20TH ST	94607	649-F3
2050	21ST ST	94607	649-F2
2100	21ST ST	94607	649-F2
2130	22ND ST	94607	649-F2
2190	W GRAND AV	94607	649-F2
2260	ATHENS AV	94607	649-F2
2370	MEAD AV	94607	649-F2
2380	24TH ST	94607	649-F2
2480	MILTON ST	94607	649-F2
2590	26TH ST	94607	649-F2
2590	27TH ST	94607	649-F2
2730	ALICIA ST	94607	649-F2
2800	28TH ST	94608	649-F2
2900	SAN PABLO AV	94608	649-F1
2900	30TH ST	94608	649-F1
3100	31ST ST	94608	649-F1
3170	32ND ST	94608	649-F1
3240	BROCKHURST ST	94608	649-F1
3300	33RD ST	94608	649-F1
3390	34TH ST	94608	649-G1
3500	35TH ST	94608	649-G1
3600	36TH ST	94608	649-G1
3400	37TH ST	94608	629-G7
3750	W MACARTHUR BLVD	94608	629-G7
3800	APGAR ST	94608	629-G7
3900	39TH ST	94608	629-G7
4000	40TH ST	94608	629-G7
4100	41ST ST	94608	629-G7
4200	42ND ST	94608	629-G7
4300	43RD ST	94608	629-G7
4400	44TH ST	94608	629-G7
4500	45TH ST	94608	629-G7
4600	46TH ST	94608	629-G6
4700	47TH ST	94608	629-G6
5200	52ND ST	94608	629-G6
5300	53RD ST	94608	629-G6
5400	54TH ST	94608	629-G6
5500	55TH ST	94608	629-G6
5600	56TH ST	94608	629-G6
5650	AILEEN ST	94608	629-G6
5690	ADELINE ST	94608	629-G6
5700	57TH ST	94608	629-G5
5750	ARLINGTON AV	94608	629-G5
5800	58TH ST	94608	629-G5
5900	59TH ST	94608	629-G5
5960	STANFORD AV	94608	629-G5
6000	60TH ST	94608	629-G5
6020	CALIFORNIA ST	94608	629-G5
6100	61ST ST	94608	629-F5
6200	62ND ST	94608	629-F5
6300	63RD ST	94608	629-F5
6350	SACRAMENTO ST	94608	629-F5
MARLBOROUGH CT			**PDMT**
100	SANDRINGHAM RD	94611	650-D2
MARLBOROUGH TER			**OAK**
7000	NORFOLK DR	94705	630-C3
7300	GRIZZLY PEAK BLVD	94705	630-C3
MARLIN CV			**OAK**
30	BINNACLE HILL	94618	630-C4
MARLOW DR			**OAK**
100	COVINGTON ST	94605	671-C6
100	FOOTHILL WY	94605	671-C6
200	REVERE AV	94605	671-D6
300	ROXBURY AV	94605	671-C7
370	BROOKFIELD AV	94605	671-C7
400	MIDDLETON ST	94605	671-C7
500	BENEDICT DR	94605	671-C7
MARLOW DR			**SLN**
400	MIDDLETON ST	94605	671-C7
500	BENEDICT DR	94605	671-C7
MARR AV			**OAK**
1	LANE CT	94611	650-C1
100	HARBORD DR	94611	650-C1
MARS			**ALA**
3000	MULVANY CIR	94501	649-E6
3100	MULVANY CIR	94501	649-E6
MARSH PL			**OAK**
100	PERSHING DR	94611	650-D1
MARSHALL ST			**OAK**
5500	55TH ST	94608	629-F6
5800	POWELL ST	94608	629-F6
5800	STANFORD AV	94608	629-F6
5900	59TH ST	94608	629-F5
6100	61ST ST	94608	629-E5
6200	62ND ST	94608	629-E5
6300	63RD ST	94608	629-E5
6400	64TH ST	94608	629-E5
6450	OCEAN AV	94608	629-E5
6470	PEABODY LN	94608	629-E5
MARSHALL WY			**ALA**
400	PACIFIC AV	94501	649-E7
500	5TH ST	94501	649-E7
500	LINCOLN AV	94501	649-E7
MARTIN LUTHER KING JR WY			**BERK**
	ADELINE ST	94703	629-G5
1000	MARIN AV	94707	609-G6
1000	THE ALAMEDA	94707	609-G6
1100	MONTEREY AV	94707	609-G6
1140	EL DORADO AV	94707	609-G6
1170	JOSEPHINE ST	94707	609-G6
1170	NAPA AV	94707	609-G6
1200	HOPKINS ST	94707	609-G7
1200	HOPKINS ST	94703	609-G7
1220	YOLO AV	94709	609-G7
1220	YOLO AV	94703	609-G7
1300	BERRYMAN ST	94709	609-G7
1300	BERRYMAN ST	94703	609-G7
1400	ROSE ST	94709	609-G7
1400	ROSE ST	94703	609-G7
1300	VINE ST	94709	609-G7
1300	VINE ST	94703	609-G7
1470	CEDAR ST	94709	629-G1
1470	CEDAR ST	94703	629-G1
1650	VIRGINIA ST	94709	629-G1
1650	VIRGINIA ST	94703	629-G1
1740	FRANCISCO ST	94709	629-G1
1740	FRANCISCO ST	94703	629-G1
1820	DELAWARE ST	94709	629-G1
1820	DELAWARE ST	94703	629-G1
1900	HEARST AV	94704	629-G1
1900	HEARST AV	94703	629-G1
1920	BERKELEY WY	94704	629-G1
1920	BERKELEY WY	94703	629-G1
2000	UNIVERSITY AV	94704	629-G1
2000	UNIVERSITY AV	94703	629-G1
2100	ADDISON ST	94704	629-G2
2100	ADDISON ST	94703	629-G2
2150	CENTER ST	94704	629-G2
2150	CENTER ST	94703	629-G2
2200	ALLSTON WY	94704	629-G2
2200	ALLSTON WY	94703	629-G2
2300	BANCROFT WY	94704	629-G2
2300	BANCROFT WY	94703	629-G2
2400	CHANNING WY	94704	629-G2
2400	CHANNING WY	94703	629-G2
2430	HASTE ST	94704	629-G2
2430	HASTE ST	94703	629-G2
2500	DWIGHT WY	94704	629-G3
2500	DWIGHT WY	94703	629-G3
2530	BLAKE ST	94704	629-G3
2530	BLAKE ST	94703	629-G3
2600	PARKER ST	94704	629-G3
2600	PARKER ST	94703	629-G3
2630	CARLETON ST	94704	629-G3
2630	CARLETON ST	94703	629-G3
2700	DERBY ST	94703	629-G3
2800	WARD ST	94703	629-G3
2830	STUART ST	94703	629-G3
2840	STUART ST	94703	629-G3
2850	OREGON ST	94703	629-G3
2860	OREGON ST	94703	629-G3
2900	RUSSELL ST	94703	629-G4
3000	ASHBY AV	94703	629-G4
3100	PRINCE ST	94703	629-G4
3160	WOOLSEY ST	94703	629-G4
	ADELINE ST	94703	629-G4
3300	ALCATRAZ AV	94703	629-G5
3350	63RD ST	94703	629-G5
3400	62ND ST	94703	629-G5
MARTIN LUTHER KING JR WY			**OAK**
100	1ST ST	94607	649-F5
100	EMBARCADERO W	94607	649-F5
200	2ND ST	94607	649-F4
300	3RD ST	94607	649-F4
400	4TH ST	94607	649-F4
	5TH ST	94607	649-F4
	6TH ST	94607	649-F4
700	7TH ST	94607	649-F4
790	8TH ST	94607	649-F4
800	8TH ST	94607	649-F4
900	9TH ST	94607	649-F4
1000	10TH ST	94607	649-F4
1100	11TH ST	94607	649-F4
1200	12TH ST	94612	649-F4
1310	13TH ST	94612	649-F3
1400	14TH ST	94612	649-F3
1500	15TH ST	94612	649-F3
1600	16TH ST	94612	649-F3
1690	17TH ST	94612	649-G3
1760	18TH ST	94612	649-G3
1790	18TH ST	94612	649-G3
1790	19TH ST	94612	649-G3
1840	19TH ST	94612	649-G3
1890	19TH ST	94612	649-G3
2000	20TH ST	94612	649-G3
2130	SAN PABLO AV	94612	649-G3
2130	SAN PABLO AV	94612	649-G3
2130	CASTRO ST	94612	649-G3
2200	22ND ST	94612	649-G3
2300	W GRAND AV	94612	649-G3
2300	GRAND AV	94612	649-G3
	23RD ST	94612	649-G2
2400	23RD ST	94612	649-G2
2460	24TH ST	94612	649-G2
2530	25TH ST	94612	649-G2
2590	SYCAMORE ST	94612	649-G2
2660	26TH ST	94612	649-G2
2730	27TH ST	94612	649-G2
2770	MERRIMAC ST	94609	649-G2
2770	MERRIMAC ST	94612	649-G2
2800	28TH ST	94609	649-G2
2900	29TH ST	94609	649-G2
2940	29TH ST	94609	649-G2
3000	30TH ST	94609	649-G2
3100	31ST ST	94609	649-G1
3200	32ND ST	94609	649-G1
3230	BROCKHURST ST	94609	649-G1
3300	33RD ST	94609	649-G1
3400	34TH ST	94609	649-G1
	35TH ST	94609	649-G1
3540	36TH ST	94609	649-G1
3700	37TH ST	94609	649-G1
3800	W MACARTHUR BLVD	94609	649-G1
3850	APGAR ST	94609	629-G7
3900	39TH ST	94609	629-G7
4000	40TH ST	94609	629-G7
4100	41ST ST	94609	629-G7
4200	42ND ST	94609	629-G7
4300	43RD ST	94609	629-G7
4400	44TH ST	94609	629-G7
4500	45TH ST	94609	629-G7
4600	46TH ST	94609	629-G7
4700	47TH ST	94609	629-G6
4700	47TH ST	94609	629-G6
5000	51ST ST	94608	629-G6
5000	51ST ST	94609	629-G6
5200	52ND ST	94608	629-G6
5200	52ND ST	94609	629-G6
5300	53RD ST	94608	629-G6
5300	53RD ST	94609	629-G6
5300	WEST ST	94609	629-G6
5400	54TH ST	94608	629-G6
5400	54TH ST	94609	629-G6
5500	55TH ST	94608	629-G6
5500	55TH ST	94609	629-G6
5600	56TH ST	94608	629-G6
5600	56TH ST	94609	629-G6
5610	56TH ST	94608	629-G6
5610	56TH ST	94609	629-G6
5700	AILEEN ST	94608	629-G6
5700	AILEEN ST	94609	629-G6
5730	57TH ST	94608	629-G5
5730	57TH ST	94609	629-G5
5770	ARLINGTON AV	94608	629-G5
5770	ARLINGTON AV	94609	629-G5
5800	58TH ST	94608	629-G5
5800	58TH ST	94609	629-G5
5900	59TH ST	94608	629-G5
5900	59TH ST	94609	629-G5
6000	60TH ST	94608	629-G5
6000	60TH ST	94609	629-G5
6100	61ST ST	94608	629-G5
6100	61ST ST	94609	629-G5
MARTIN ST			**OAK**
600	AYALA AV	94609	629-H5
700	58TH ST	94609	629-H5
700	HERMANN ST	94609	629-H5
MARTIRAE CT			**ALA**
2400	PARK AV	94501	670-A3
MARVIN CT			**OAK**
1	SCOTIA AV	94605	671-E4
MARYLAND AV			**BERK**
1	KENTUCKY AV	94707	609-G4
60	MICHIGAN AV	94707	609-G4
100	VERMONT AV	94707	609-G4
MASON ST			**OAK**
2500	FOOTHILL BLVD	94605	670-F1
2600	WALNUT ST	94605	670-G1
2700	KINGSLEY CIR	94605	670-G1
MASONIC AV			**ALB**
500	BRIGHTON AV	94706	609-E5
580	GARFIELD AV	94706	609-E5
660	PORTLAND AV	94706	609-E5
740	WASHINGTON AV	94706	609-E6
900	SOLANO AV	94706	609-E6
1000	MARIN AV	94706	609-E6
1100	DARTMOUTH ST	94706	609-E7
1300	SANTA FE AV	94706	609-E7
MASONIC AV			**OAK**
5100	FLORENCE AV	94618	630-C6
5300	SAINT PAUL CT	94618	630-C7
5400	AMY DR	94618	630-C7
5500	HERON DR	94618	630-C7
5600	MORAGA AV	94618	630-D7
MASONIC PL			**OAK**
100	PROCTOR AV	94618	630-D7
MASTERSON ST			**OAK**
4000	38TH AV	94619	650-F6
4090	39TH AV	94619	650-F6
4190	MAYBELLE AV	94619	650-F6
4300	HIGH ST	94619	650-F6
4300	HIGH ST	94619	650-F6
4360	MADRONE AV	94619	650-F6
4440	LILY ST	94619	650-F6
4500	GREENACRE RD	94619	650-F6
MASTICK CT			**ALA**
1	LINCOLN AV	94501	669-G1
MASTLANDS DR			**OAK**
2100	ASCOT DR	94611	650-F2
2000	LARRY LN	94611	650-F2
2100	CASTLE DR	94611	650-F2
MATHER ST			**OAK**
200	MONTGOMERY ST	94611	629-J7
220	VIEW ST	94611	629-J7
240	GILBERT ST	94611	629-J7
270	TERRACE ST	94611	629-J7
300	42ND ST	94611	629-J7
300	BROADWAY	94611	629-J7
MATHEWS ST			**BERK**
2500	DWIGHT WY	94702	629-E3
2520	BLAKE ST	94702	629-E3
2600	PARKER ST	94702	629-E3
2630	CARLETON ST	94702	629-E3
2700	DERBY ST	94702	629-E3
2720	WARD ST	94702	629-E3
2720	WARD ST	94702	629-E3
2800	OREGON ST	94702	629-E4
2900	RUSSELL ST	94702	629-E4
MATHIEU AV			**OAK**
6100	ROMANY RD	94618	630-B5
6100	OSTRANDER RD	94618	630-B5
6180	VERONA PTH	94618	630-B5
6300	ACACIA AV	94618	630-B5
6300	LOCARNO PTH	94618	630-B5
MATTIS CT			**OAK**
4400	KAPHAN AV	94619	650-H6
MAURITANIA AV			**OAK**
5900	62ND AV	94605	670-H1
6200	SEMINARY AV	94605	670-H1
MAVIS ST			**OAK**
2400	TRASK ST	94601	670-F1
2600	KINGSLAND AV	94601	670-F1
MAXWELL AV			**OAK**
2400	TRASK ST	94601	670-F1
2600	BROOKDALE AV	94601	670-F1
2870	KINGSLAND AV	94619	650-F7
2600	FLEMING AV	94619	650-F7
2870	FLEMING AV	94619	650-F7
2870	BROOKDALE AV	94619	670-F1
2900	KINGSLAND AV	94619	650-F7
3200	BIRDSALL AV	94619	650-F7
MAXWELTON RD			**OAK**
5600	HILLTOP CRES	94618	630-C7
5630	AMY DR	94618	630-C7
5700	HARBORD DR	94618	630-C7
MAXWELTON RD			**PDMT**
1	MORAGA AV	94618	630-C7
50	ECHO LN	94618	630-C7
70	ABBOTT WY	94618	630-C7
100	NELLIE AV	94618	630-C7
200	HILLTOP CRES	94618	630-C7
MAY CT			**OAK**
3500	MACARTHUR BLVD	94602	650-D4
MAYBECK TWIN DR			**BERK**
80	BUENA VISTA WY	94708	609-J7
MAYBELLE AV			**OAK**
3500	REDDING ST	94619	650-F6
3550	MACARTHUR BLVD	94619	650-F6
3600	MASTERSON ST	94619	650-F6
4000	BAYO ST	94619	650-G6
MAYBELLE WY			**OAK**
3330	PORTER ST	94619	650-F6
3300	FULLINGTON ST	94619	650-F6
MAYDON CT			**OAK**
1	SCOTIA AV	94605	671-E4
MAYFIELD PTH			**OAK**
1	73RD AV	94605	670-J1
1	BANTRY AV	94605	670-J1
50	SUNKIST DR	94605	670-J1
MAYNARD AV			**OAK**
4100	MOUNTAIN BLVD	94605	671-A1
4200	SANFORD ST	94605	671-A1
MAYPORT CIR			**ALA**
2000	MOSLEY AV	94501	649-E6
2000	SINGLETON AV	94501	649-E6
2010	KOLLMAN CIR	94501	649-F6
2100	MOSLEY AV	94501	649-E6
MAYWOOD AV			**OAK**
2200	DEERWOOD AV	94605	670-H3
2400	KRAUSE AV	94605	670-H3
MAZUELA DR			**OAK**
5830	COLTON BLVD	94611	630-E7
5900	MENDOZA DR	94611	630-E7
MCANDREW DR			**OAK**
5900	BULLARD DR	94611	630-D7
5800	ESTATES DR	94611	630-D7
5900	HARBORD DR	94611	630-D7
MCAULEY ST			**OAK**
400	COLBY ST	94609	629-J5
420	AYALA AV	94609	629-H5
440	HOWELL ST	94609	629-H5
440	HOWELL ST	94609	629-H5
460	CANNING ST	94609	629-H5
500	TELEGRAPH AV	94609	629-H5
MCCLARY AV			**OAK**
600	BALDWIN ST	94621	670-F5
MCCLELLAND ST			**OAK**
	CALAVERAS AV	94619	650-G7
	DAISY ST	94619	650-G7
MCCLURE ST			**OAK**
2900	30TH ST	94609	649-G2
3000	29TH ST	94609	649-G2
MCCORMICK AV			**OAK**
8000	STERLING DR	94605	671-A2
8000	CREST AV	94605	671-A2
8200	SUNKIST DR	94605	671-A2
MCCULLOCH DR			**ALA**
	SPENCER RD	94501	649-J7
	BEAR RD	94501	649-J7
	CAMBELL BLVD	94501	649-J7
MCDONELL AV			**OAK**
4800	MOUNTAIN BLVD	94619	650-H6
MCDONNEL RD			**ALA**
1	ORR RD	94502	669-J6
100	ARGUS CT	94502	669-J6
200	BRITT CT	94502	669-J6
300	BENEDICT CT	94502	669-H6
400	BANNISTER WY	94502	669-H6
MCELROY ST			**OAK**
850	CHASE ST	94607	649-D3
900	9TH ST	94607	649-D3
MCGEE AV			**BERK**
1300	HOPKINS ST	94703	609-F7
1340	ADA ST	94703	609-F7
1400	ROSE ST	94703	609-F7
1400	ROSE ST	94703	609-F7
1500	BUENA AV	94703	609-F7
1470	VINE ST	94703	609-F7
1500	JAYNES ST	94703	609-F7
1600	CEDAR ST	94703	629-F1
1650	LINCOLN ST	94703	629-F1
1700	VIRGINIA ST	94703	629-F1
1750	FRANCISCO ST	94703	629-F1
1800	DELAWARE ST	94703	629-F1
1900	HEARST AV	94703	629-F1
1950	BERKELEY WY	94703	629-F1
2000	UNIVERSITY AV	94703	629-F2
2100	ADDISON ST	94703	629-F2
2200	ALLSTON WY	94703	629-F2
2300	BANCROFT WY	94703	629-F2
2400	CHANNING WY	94703	629-F2
2500	DWIGHT WY	94703	629-F2
2500	DWIGHT WY	94703	629-G3
2550	BLAKE ST	94703	629-G3
2600	PARKER ST	94703	629-G3
2650	CARLETON ST	94703	629-G3
2700	DERBY ST	94703	629-G3
2750	WARD ST	94703	629-G3
2800	STUART ST	94703	629-G3
2850	OREGON ST	94703	629-G4
2900	RUSSELL ST	94703	629-G4
MCGURRIN RD			**OAK**
8900	SEQUOYAH RD	94605	671-C2
MCINTYRE ST			**OAK**
10900	DURANT AV	94605	671-B6
10800	109TH AV	94605	671-B6
10900	108TH AV	94605	671-B6
MCKAY AV			**ALA**
1300	CENTRAL AV	94501	669-F1
MCKILLUP RD			**OAK**
2550	E 29TH ST	94602	650-C5
MCKINLEY AV			**BERK**
2100	ADDISON ST	94703	629-G2
2200	ALLSTON WY	94703	629-G2
2300	BANCROFT WY	94703	629-G2
2400	CHANNING WY	94703	629-G2
2500	DWIGHT WY	94703	629-G2
MCKINLEY AV			**OAK**
600	KENWYN RD	94610	650-A3
750	ATHOL AV	94610	650-A3
800	MONTCLAIR AV	94610	650-A4
900	SPRUCE ST	94610	650-A4
920	CAPELL ST	94610	650-A4
1000	ALMA AV	94610	650-B4
1100	HOME PL E	94610	650-A4
1130	HOME PL W	94610	650-A4
1200	PARK BLVD	94610	650-A4
1200	8TH AV	94610	650-A4
MCMILLAN AV			**OAK**
5500	LAWTON AV	94618	630-A5
5550	OCEAN VIEW DR	94618	630-A5
5600	KEITH AV	94618	630-A5
5600	SHAFTER AV	94618	630-A5
MCMURTY CT			**ALA**
1	SWEET RD	94502	669-H6
MCSHERRY LN			**ALA**
	MCSHERRY WY	94502	670-B7
	OLEANDER AV	94502	670-B7
MCSHERRY WY			**ALA**
3510	CLARKE LN	94502	670-A7
3540	MCSHERRY LN	94502	670-B7
3600	SILVA LN	94502	670-B7
MEAD AV			**OAK**
800	MARKET ST	94607	649-F2
900	SAN PABLO AV	94607	649-F2
MEADOW ST			**OAK**
3500	35TH AV	94601	650-D6
3600	HARRINGTON AV	94601	650-D6
MECARTNEY RD			**ALA**
2500	ADELPHIAN WY	94502	669-H6
2600	SHARON RD	94502	669-J6
2700	AUGHINBAUGH WY	94502	669-J6
2900	MARCUSE ST	94502	669-J6
2900	BAYWALK RD	94502	669-J6
3000	FONTANA DR	94502	669-J6
3000	BAYWOOD RD	94502	669-J6
3100	VERDEMAR DR	94502	670-A6
3100	IRONWOOD RD	94502	670-A6
	CAMINO DEL VALLE	94502	670-A6
3150	EASTER LN	94502	670-A6
3170	BELMONT PL	94502	670-A6
3200	TAHITI LN	94502	670-A6
3250	AUBURN DR	94502	670-A6
3300	ISLAND DR	94502	670-A6
3320	AZALEA DR	94502	670-A6
3330	COUNTY RD	94502	670-A6
3350	BEGONIA DR	94502	670-A6

ALAMEDA CO.

PRIMARY STREET Address	Cross Street	ZIP	CITY Pg-Grid
MECARTNEY RD			**ALA**
3370	CAMELIA DR	94502	670-A6
3400	HOLLY ST	94502	670-A6
3430	GARDEN RD	94502	670-B6
	MELROSE AV	94502	670-B6
	MAITLAND DR	94502	670-B6
MEDAU PL			**OAK**
6100	MORAGA AV	94611	650-E1
6200	MOUNTAIN BLVD	94611	650-E1
MEDFORD AV			**OAK**
9800	98TH AV	94603	670-H6
10000	GOULD ST	94603	670-H6
MELDON AV			**OAK**
4600	STORER AV	94619	650-F7
4800	BIRDSALL AV	94619	650-F7
MELROSE AV			**ALA**
700	OLEANDER AV	94502	670-A7
730	HAZEL LN	94502	670-A7
800	DUTCHCAP LN	94502	670-B7
900	CAPELLA LN	94502	670-B7
1000	MAGNOLIA DR	94502	670-B7
400	CAMANOE LN	94502	670-B7
420	MECARTNEY RD	94502	670-B6
430	MAITLAND DR	94502	670-B6
500	BEACH RD	94502	670-B6
MELROSE AV			**OAK**
4970	51ST AV	94601	670-E1
4840	50TH AV	94601	670-E1
4700	48TH AV	94601	670-E1
4570	47TH AV	94601	670-E1
4510	46TH AV	94601	670-E1
4440	45TH AV	94601	670-E1
4400	45TH AV	94601	670-E1
4440	COURTLAND AV	94601	670-E1
MELVILLE DR			**OAK**
	SKYLINE BLVD	94611	650-G2
6200	CASTLE DR	94611	650-G2
6240	WALDECK CT	94611	650-G2
6450	TOTTERDELL ST	94611	650-G1
6600	ASCOT DR	94611	650-G1
MELVILLE LN			**OAK**
6400	TOTTERDELL ST	94611	650-G1
6500	SKYLINE BLVD	94611	650-G1
6500	WATERLOO DR	94611	650-G1
MELVIN CT			**OAK**
1	MELVIN RD	94602	650-E3
MELVIN RD			**OAK**
1800	BYWOOD DR	94602	650-E2
1900	ROSECREST DR	94602	650-E3
2000	BRENTWOOD RD	94602	650-E3
2000	BRENTWOOD PL	94602	650-E3
2000	BRENTWOOD RD	94602	650-E3
2100	ARCADIA AV	94602	650-E3
	MELVIN CT	94602	650-E3
MENDENHALL RD			**OAK**
	SEQUOYAH RD	94605	671-D2
MENDOCINO AV			**BERK**
800	ARLINGTON AV	94707	609-G5
1000	LOS ANGELES AV	94707	609-G6
MENDOCINO AV			**OAK**
5700	VIRMAR AV	94618	630-A5
5700	MANILA AV	94618	630-A5
5710	MANILA AV	94618	630-A5
5750	TAFT AV	94618	630-A5
5800	LAWTON AV	94618	630-A5
5900	MARGARIDO DR	94618	630-A5
MENDOZA DR			**OAK**
	MAZUELA DR	94611	630-E7
	CABRILLO PL	94611	630-E7
5830	COLTON BLVD	94611	630-E7
MENLO PL			**BERK**
1	THOUSAND OAKS BLVD	94707	609-F5
50	SANTA ROSA AV	94707	609-F5
100	THE ALAMEDA	94707	609-F5
MERA ST			**OAK**
3800	38TH AV	94601	650-D7
3870	39TH AV	94601	650-D7
3950	40TH AV	94601	650-D7
4020	ROSEDALE AV	94601	650-D7
4100	ROSEDALE AV	94601	650-D7
4100	41ST AV	94601	670-D1
4200	42ND AV	94601	670-D1
MERCED AV			**OAK**
6100	MOUNTAIN BLVD	94611	650-E1
6300	LUCAS AV	94611	650-E1
MERCED ST			**BERK**
1000	SONOMA AV	94707	609-F6
1100	MADERA ST	94707	609-F6
MERLIN CT			**OAK**
1	SCOTIA AV	94605	671-E4
MERRIEWOOD CIR			**OAK**
1	NOTTINGHAM DR	94611	630-D6
100	MERRIEWOOD DR	94611	630-D6
MERRIEWOOD DR			**OAK**
5500	THORNHILL DR	94611	630-E6
5570	MARDEN LN	94611	630-D6
5600	TAURUS AV	94611	630-D6
5700	FLORENCE TER	94611	630-D6
5800	MERRIEWOOD CIR	94611	630-D6
5800	NOTTINGHAM DR	94611	630-D6
5850	NOTTINGHAM DR	94611	630-D6
5870	TAURUS AV	94611	630-D6
5900	TAURUS AV	94611	630-D6
5930	SHERWOOD DR	94611	630-D6
6100	URANUS AV	94611	630-D6
6100	CROWN AV	94611	630-D6
6190	ROBINHOOD WY	94611	630-D6
6300	BROADWAY TER	94611	630-D6
MERRILL AV			**OAK**
4500	TULIP AV	94619	650-G6
4600	GREENACRE RD	94619	650-G6
MERRIMAC ST			**OAK**
	MARTIN LUTHER KING JR WY	94612	649-G2
580	28TH ST	94612	649-G2
700	TELEGRAPH AV	94612	649-G2
MERRITT AV			**OAK**
400	CAPITAL ST	94610	649-J3
410	CAPITAL ST	94610	649-J3
400	HILLGIRT CIR	94610	650-A3
400	PROSPECT AV	94610	650-A3
400	WESLEY AV	94610	650-A3
490	HILLGIRT CIR	94610	650-A3
490	PROSPECT AV	94610	650-A3
490	WESLEY AV	94610	650-A3
600	BROOKLYN AV	94610	649-J3
MERRITT CT			**OAK**
	3RD AV	94606	649-J4
MESA AV			**PDMT**
100	PALA AV	94611	630-B7
1	PARK WY	94611	630-B7
100	MORAGA AV	94611	630-B7
MEYERS AV			**ALA**
3300	HANSEN AV	94501	670-B4
3400	EAST SHORE DR	94501	670-B4
MIAMI CT			**OAK**
1600	WOODRUFF AV	94602	650-C4
MICHIGAN AV			**BERK**
400	MARYLAND AV	94707	609-G4
500	COLORADO AV	94707	609-G4
550	KENTUCKY AV	94707	609-G4
600	SPRUCE ST	94707	609-G4
MICHIGAN DR			**OAK**
7800	PARTRIDGE AV	94605	671-A2
8100	SUNKIST DR	94605	671-A2
MIDCREST RD			**OAK**
500	LONGRIDGE RD	94610	650-C3
600	SUNNYHILLS RD	94610	650-C3
MIDDLE HARBOR RD			**OAK**
1200	ADELINE ST	94607	649-E4
1210	1ST ST	94607	649-E4
1600	FERRO ST	94607	649-C5
1700	KEEL WY	94625	649-C4
1700	KEEL WY	94607	649-C4
	7TH ST EXT	94607	649-B3
	7TH ST	94607	649-B3
MIDDLEFIELD RD			**BERK**
960	THE CROSSWAYS	94708	609-J5
1010	THE SHORT CUT	94708	609-J5
1100	PARK HILLS RD	94708	609-J5
1100	THE CRESCENT	94708	609-J5
MIDDLETON ST			**OAK**
3000	FOOTHILL WY	94605	671-C7
3090	BROOKFIELD AV	94605	671-C7
3200	MARLOW DR	94605	671-C7
MIDDLETON ST			**SLN**
3090	BROOKFIELD AV	94605	671-C7
3200	MARLOW DR	94605	671-C7
MIDVALE AV			**OAK**
3400	QUIGLEY LN	94602	650-E5
3400	DAKOTA ST	94602	650-E5
3460	GEORGIA ST	94602	650-E5
3530	MACARTHUR BLVD	94602	650-F5
3660	KANSAS ST	94602	650-F5
3780	CALIFORNIA ST	94602	650-F5
3890	ARIZONA ST	94602	650-F5
4010	WISCONSIN ST	94602	650-F5
4160	KIWANIS ST	94602	650-F5
4190	HERRIER ST	94602	650-F5
4300	VICTOR AV	94602	650-F5
W MIDWAY AV			**ALA**
	MONARCH ST	94501	649-C6
	LEXINGTON ST	94501	649-C6
	SARATOGA ST	94501	649-D6
	TODD ST	94501	649-D6
	PAN AM WY	94501	649-D6
	MOONLIGHT TER	94501	649-D6
	RAINBOW CT	94501	649-D6
	NORFOLK RD	94501	649-D6
	SERENADE PL	94501	649-E6
	HANCOCK ST	94501	649-E6
	MAIN ST	94501	649-E6
MIDWAY ST			**OAK**
300	8TH ST	94626	649-C3
300	TULAGI ST	94626	649-C3
380	10TH ST	94626	649-C2
420	11TH ST	94626	649-C2
470	14TH ST	94626	649-C2
500	15TH ST	94626	649-C2
MILES AV			**OAK**
	COLLEGE AV	94618	629-J5
5100	51ST ST	94618	629-H6
5150	AVON ST	94618	629-H6
5200	CAVOUR ST	94618	629-H6
5300	CLIFTON ST	94618	629-J6
5370	HARDY ST	94618	629-J6
5400	HUDSON ST	94618	629-J5
5600	FOREST ST	94618	629-J5
	COLLEGE AV	94618	629-J5
	COLLEGE AV	94618	629-J5
5600	PRESLEY WY	94618	630-A5
5700	IVANHOE RD	94618	630-A5
5790	ROSS ST	94618	630-A5
5850	CLOVER DR	94618	630-A5
6000	PATTON ST	94618	630-A5
MILLER AV			**BERK**
900	POPPY LN	94708	609-H5
940	KEELER AV	94708	609-H5
1030	LATHAM LN	94708	609-J6
1120	WHITAKER AV	94708	609-J6
1150	STEVENSON AV	94708	609-J6
1200	SHASTA RD	94708	609-J6
MILLER AV			**OAK**
1100	E 12TH ST	94601	650-B7
1270	INTERNATIONAL BLVD	94601	650-B7
1460	E 15TH ST	94601	650-B7
1620	E 16TH ST	94601	650-B6
1700	FOOTHILL BLVD	94601	650-B6
MILLER PL			**OAK**
1000	E 11TH ST	94601	650-B7
1000	23RD AV OVPS	94601	650-B7
1000	23RD AV	94601	650-B7
1010	E 11TH ST	94601	650-B7
MILLINGTON CT			**ALA**
100	ARMITAGE ST	94502	669-J6
100	YOUNG ST	94502	669-J6
MILLSBRAE AV			**OAK**
2900	ROBERTS AV	94605	670-G1
3000	BRANN ST	94605	670-G1
3100	MACARTHUR BLVD	94605	670-G1
MILLSVIEW AV			**OAK**
3200	CAMDEN ST	94619	650-G7
3300	MACARTHUR BLVD	94619	650-G7
MILTON ST			**OAK**
800	SAN PABLO AV	94607	649-F2
900	MARKET ST	94607	649-F2
MILVIA CT			**BERK**
2000	MILVIA ST	94709	609-G7
MILVIA ST			**BERK**
1200	YOLO AV	94709	609-G6
1220	EUNICE ST	94709	609-G7
1300	BERRYMAN ST	94709	609-G7
1400	ROSE ST	94709	609-G7
1500	VINE ST	94709	609-G7
1680	MILVIA CT	94709	609-G7
1600	CEDAR ST	94709	629-G1
1620	LINCOLN ST	94709	629-G1
1700	VIRGINIA ST	94709	629-G1
1720	FRANCISCO ST	94709	629-G1
1800	DELAWARE ST	94709	629-G1
1900	HEARST AV	94704	629-G1
1920	BERKELEY WY	94704	629-G1
2000	UNIVERSITY AV	94704	629-G1
2000	UNIVERSITY AV	94704	629-G1
2100	ADDISON ST	94704	629-G2
2150	CENTER ST	94704	629-G2
2200	ALLSTON WY	94704	629-G2
2220	KITTREDGE ST	94704	629-G2
2300	BANCROFT WY	94704	629-G2
2350	DURANT AV	94704	629-G2
2400	CHANNING WY	94704	629-G2
2420	HASTE ST	94704	629-G2
2500	DWIGHT WY	94704	629-G3
2520	BLAKE ST	94704	629-G3
2600	PARKER ST	94704	629-G3
2630	CARLETON ST	94704	629-G3
2700	DERBY ST	94703	629-G3
2730	WARD ST	94703	629-G3
2800	STUART ST	94703	629-G3
2820	OREGON ST	94703	629-G3
2900	RUSSELL ST	94703	629-G3
MINGO LN			**ALA**
	OLEANDER AV	94502	670-A7
	NORMAN LN	94502	670-A7
MINNA AV			**OAK**
2600	BROOKDALE AV	94619	650-E7
2700	WALNUT ST	94619	650-E7
2700	ALLENDALE AV	94619	650-E6
2810	DALE PL	94619	650-E6
2930	PENNIMAN AV	94619	650-E6
3030	ANGELO AV	94619	650-E6
3200	LIESE AV	94619	650-E6
MINTURN ST			**ALA**
1600	LINCOLN AV	94501	669-J1
1700	PACIFIC AV	94501	669-J1
1800	BUENA VISTA AV	94501	669-J1
1900	EAGLE AV	94501	669-J1
2000	CLEMENT AV	94501	669-J1
MIRA VISTA AV			**OAK**
500	ELWOOD AV	94610	649-J2
570	BONHAM WY	94610	649-J2
580	ALTA VISTA AV	94610	649-J2
580	VALLE VISTA AV	94610	650-A2
700	VALLE VISTA AV	94610	650-A2
MIRAMAR AV			**BERK**
800	SAN LORENZO AV	94707	609-F6
800	WASHINGTON AV	94707	609-F6
900	CAPISTRANO AV	94707	609-F6
MIRAMONTE CT			**BERK**
1300	ADA ST	94703	609-F7
MIRANDA CT			**ALA**
1	RATTO RD	94502	669-J7
MIRASOL AV			**OAK**
3400	GRANADA AV	94605	671-B3
3600	MURILLO AV	94605	671-B3
MISSION HILLS			**OAK**
1	ELYSIAN FIELDS DR	94605	671-D2
1	MOUNTAIN VALLEY	94605	671-D2
MITCHELL AV			**ALA**
	MARINER SQUARE DR	94501	649-F6
MITCHELL ST			**OAK**
1400	INTERNATIONAL BLVD	94601	650-B7
1600	E 16TH ST	94601	650-B7
1900	FOOTHILL BLVD	94601	650-C7
1910	E 20TH ST	94601	650-C6
2020	E 21ST ST	94601	650-C6
2130	E 22ND ST	94601	650-C6
2200	E 23RD ST	94601	650-C6
MODESTO AV			**OAK**
2800	FLEMING AV	94619	670-F1
2800	BIRDSALL AV	94619	650-F7
3100	BIRDSALL AV	94619	650-F7
MODOC AV			**OAK**
200	FLORENCE AV	94618	630-C6
200	MORPETH ST	94618	630-C6
300	FLORENCE AV	94618	630-C6
400	SONIA ST	94618	630-C6
430	SONIA ST	94618	630-C6
460	HARBORD DR	94618	630-C6
500	FLORENCE AV	94618	630-C6
500	HARBORD DR	94618	630-C6
MODOC ST			**BERK**
900	SOLANO AV	94707	609-F6
1000	MARIN AV	94707	609-F6
MOKELUMNE AV			**OAK**
6400	DELMONT AV	94605	670-H1
6520	SIMSON ST	94605	670-J1
6800	ALTAMONT AV	94605	670-J1
6800	ALTAMONT AV	94605	670-J1
6900	SIMSON ST	94605	670-J1
MONADNOCK WY			**OAK**
5900	64TH AV	94605	670-H1
6030	62ND AV	94605	670-H1
6220	61ST AV	94605	670-H1
6400	SEMINARY AV	94605	670-H1
MONAN ST			**OAK**
11010	MALCOLM AV	94605	671-E4
11130	ZIEGLER AV	94605	671-E5
11300	TURNER AV	94605	671-E5
MONARCH ST			**ALA**
	W TOWER AV	94501	649-C6
	W MIDWAY AV	94501	649-C6
	W RED LINE AV	94501	649-C6
MONROE AV			**OAK**
6000	BROADWAY	94618	630-A6
6000	MANILA AV	94618	630-A6
6020	THOMAS AV	94618	630-A6
6020	CARLTON ST	94618	630-A6
6100	BROADWAY TER	94618	630-A6
MONROE ST			**ALB**
1000	8TH ST	94706	609-D7
1000	8TH ST	94710	609-D7
1050	10TH ST	94706	609-D7
1050	10TH ST	94710	609-D7
1100	SAN PABLO AV	94706	609-D7
1100	SAN PABLO AV	94710	609-D7
MONTANA ST			**OAK**
1800	MACARTHUR BLVD	94602	650-C4
1810	MORRISON AV	94602	650-D4
1850	ADELL CT	94602	650-D4
1870	ADELL CT	94602	650-D4
1910	DIMOND AV	94602	650-D5
2000	FRUITVALE AV	94602	650-D5
2000	FRUITVALE AV	94602	650-D5
2070	FLAGG AV	94602	650-D5
2140	CHAMPION ST	94602	650-D5
2320	BOSTON AV	94602	650-D5
2430	WILSON AV	94602	650-D5
2520	LAGUNA AV	94602	650-D5
	COOLIDGE AV	94602	650-E5
2840	CURRAN WY	94602	650-E5
3000	MAPLE AV	94602	650-E5
MONTCLAIR AV			**OAK**
400	PROSPECT AV	94606	650-A4
470	CLEVELAND ST	94606	650-A4
540	BROOKLYN AV	94606	650-A4
600	PARK BLVD	94606	650-A4
600	PROSPECT AV	94610	650-A4
630	MCKINLEY AV	94610	650-A3
700	MACARTHUR BLVD	94610	650-A3
MONTE AV			**PDMT**
100	PALA AV	94611	630-B7
1	PARK WY	94611	630-B7
100	MORAGA AV	94611	630-B7
MONTE CRESTA AV			**OAK**
1	LINDA AV	94611	649-J1
130	KELTON CT	94611	649-J1
200	KINGSTON AV	94611	649-J1
MONTE VISTA AV			**ALA**
3200	HIGH ST	94501	670-C3
3250	BAYO VISTA AV	94501	670-C3
3300	FERNSIDE BLVD	94501	670-C3
MONTE VISTA AV			**OAK**
1	40TH WY	94611	649-J1
1	PIEDMONT AV	94611	649-J1
200	WILDA AV	94611	649-J1
230	ROBLEY TER	94611	649-J1
260	FAIRMOUNT AV	94611	649-J1
300	KINGSTON AV	94611	649-J1
400	HARRISON ST	94611	649-J1
450	OAKLAND AV	94610	649-J1
500	SANTA ROSA AV	94610	649-J2
500	VERNON ST	94610	649-J2
MONTECELLO AV			**PDMT**
130	MORAGA AV	94611	630-A7
100	RONADA AV	94611	630-A7
1	RAMONA AV	94611	630-A7
100	ARROYO AV	94611	630-A7
100	PARK WY	94611	630-A7
MONTECITO AV			**OAK**
100	BAY PL	94610	649-H3
160	PARK VIEW TER	94610	649-H3
200	LENOX AV	94610	649-H3
300	LEE ST	94610	649-H3
MONTEGO BAY			**ALA**
100	BAYWALK RD	94502	669-J6
MONTELL ST			**OAK**
30	ROBLEY TER	94611	649-J1
90	PIEDMONT AV	94611	649-J1
MONTEREY AV			**BERK**
1000	MARIN AV	94707	609-G6
1850	MARTIN LUTHER KING JR WY	94707	609-G6
1800	FRESNO AV	94707	609-F6
1000	COLUSA AV	94707	609-F6
1100	SONOMA AV	94707	609-F6
1100	SONOMA AV	94706	609-F6
1140	BEVERLY PL	94707	609-F6
1140	BEVERLY PL	94706	609-F6
1170	POSEN AV	94707	609-F7
1170	POSEN AV	94706	609-F7
1200	POSEN AV	94707	609-F7
1200	POSEN AV	94706	609-F7
1300	CALIFORNIA ST	94707	609-F7
1300	CALIFORNIA ST	94706	609-F7
1300	HOPKINS ST	94706	609-F7
MONTEREY BLVD			**OAK**
2300	PARK BLVD	94611	650-E2
2300	TRAFALGAR PL	94611	650-E2
2330	PARK BLVD	94611	650-E2
2690	LEIMERT BLVD	94602	650-F3
2890	LINCOLN WY	94602	650-F3
2970	LINCOLN AV	94602	650-F3
3020	MAIDEN LN	94602	650-F3
3190	SYLHOWE RD	94602	650-F4
3290	GUIDO ST	94602	650-G4
3600	NORTON AV	94619	650-G4
3600	NORTON AV	94602	650-G4
3630	BENNETT PL	94619	650-G4
3630	BENNETT PL	94602	650-G4
3640	EL CARMELLO CIR	94619	650-G5
3640	EL CARMELLO CIR	94602	650-G5
3660	35TH AV	94619	650-G5
3750	JORDAN RD	94619	650-G5
3800	ATLAS AV	94619	650-G5
3800	DUNSMUIR AV	94619	650-G5
3900	ATLAS AV	94619	650-G5
MONTEREY CIR			**ALA**
2000	MOSLEY AV	94501	649-E6
2100	MOSLEY AV	94501	649-E6
MONTGOMERY ST			**OAK**
4100	RIDGEWAY AV	94611	629-J7
4260	JOHN ST	94611	629-J7
	MATHER ST	94611	629-J7
4400	PLEASANT VALLEY AV	94611	629-J7
4420	VIEW PL	94611	629-J7
MONTICELLO AV			**OAK**
2430	TRASK ST	94601	670-E1
2370	FAIRFAX AV	94601	670-E1
2360	CONGRESS AV	94601	670-E1
2300	CONGRESS AV	94601	670-E1
2360	VICKSBURG AV	94601	670-E1
2360	50TH AV	94601	670-E1
2970	BIRDSALL AV	94619	650-F7
2950	VIRGINIA AV	94619	650-F7
2810	VIRGINIA AV	94619	650-F7
2740	FLEMING AV	94619	650-F7
2670	ALLENDALE AV	94619	650-F7
2600	WALNUT ST	94619	650-F7
2540	BROOKDALE AV	94601	650-F7
2460	GORDON ST	94601	650-F7
2540	GORDON ST	94601	650-F7
MONTROSE RD			**BERK**
1	SAN LUIS RD	94707	609-G5
70	SANTA BARBARA RD	94707	609-G5
200	SPRUCE ST	94707	609-G5
MONTWOOD WY			**OAK**
1	MALCOLM AV	94605	671-C5
MONZAL AV			**OAK**
5900	MOUNTAIN BLVD	94611	630-C5
6000	CALDWELL RD	94611	630-C5
MOONLIGHT TER			**ALA**
	W TOWER AV	94501	649-D7
100	SUNRISE CT	94501	649-D6
	STARDUST PL	94501	649-D6
	STARDUST PL	94501	649-D6
	W MIDWAY AV	94501	649-D6
MOORE CT			**ALA**
1	ANDERSON RD	94502	669-J6
1	LAWRENCE RD	94502	669-J6
MOORE DR			**OAK**
6600	AITKEN DR	94611	630-G7
6700	BANNING DR	94611	630-G7
	FORESTLAND WY	94611	630-G7
6760	FORESTLAND WY	94611	630-G7
6800	EVERGREEN AV	94611	630-G7
6900	SHEPHERD CANYON RD	94611	630-G7
MOORPARK ST			**OAK**
800	PEARMAIN ST	94603	670-H7
850	PIPPIN ST	94603	670-H7
900	RUSSET ST	94603	670-H7
900	SAN LEANDRO ST	94603	670-J7
1000	APRICOT ST	94603	670-J7
MORAGA AV			**OAK**
4400	PLEASANT VALLEY AV	94611	630-A7
4400	GRAND AV	94611	630-A7
4500	RAMONA AV	94611	630-A7
4520	RAMONA AV	94611	630-A7
200	MONTECELLO AV	94611	630-B7
350	ESTRELLA AV	94611	630-B7
350	BONITA AV	94611	630-B7
5890	ESTATES DR	94611	630-D7
5870	ESTATES DR	94611	630-D7
5870	ESTATES DR	94618	630-D7
5800	MASONIC AV	94618	630-C7
5800	MASONIC AV	94611	630-C7
5550	HARBORD DR	94618	630-C7
5550	HARBORD DR	94611	630-C7
5600	MAXWELTON RD	94618	630-C7
5600	MAXWELTON RD	94611	630-C7
6100	THORNHILL DR	94611	630-D7
6520	MEDAU PL	94611	650-E1
6600	LA SALLE AV	94611	650-E1
6600	MOUNTAIN BLVD	94611	650-E1
MORAGA AV			**PDMT**
4500	RAMONA AV	94611	630-A7
4510	RAMONA AV	94611	630-A7
200	MONTECELLO AV	94611	630-B7
350	ESTRELLA AV	94611	630-B7
350	BONITA AV	94611	630-B7
400	HIGHLAND AV	94611	630-B7
500	MESA AV	94611	630-B7

PRIMARY STREET Address	Cross Street	ZIP	CITY Pg-Grid
MORAGA AV			**PDMT**
600	MONTE AV	94611	630-B7
700	PALA AV	94611	630-C7
800	SPRING PTH	94618	630-C7
800	SPRING PTH	94611	630-C7
5500	ECHO LN	94618	630-C7
5500	ECHO LN	94611	630-C7
5550	MAXWELTON RD	94618	630-C7
5550	MAXWELTON RD	94611	630-C7
MORCOM AV			**OAK**
2800	FLEMING AV	94619	670-F1
2850	YUBA AV	94619	670-F1
2850	BIRDSALL AV	94619	650-F7
2920	BIRDSALL AV	94619	650-F7
2920	BIRDSALL AV	94619	670-F1
2920	NORMANDIE AV	94619	650-G7
2950	NORMANDIE AV	94619	650-G7
3000	BRANN ST	94619	650-G7
3200	CAMDEN ST	94619	650-G7
3250	SIMMONS ST	94619	650-G7
3300	WYMAN ST	94619	650-G7
3340	PIERSON ST	94619	650-G7
3400	MORCOM PL	94619	650-G7
3450	KINGSLAND AV	94619	650-F7
3500	KINGSLAND PL	94619	650-F7
3600	BIRDSALL AV	94619	650-F7
MORCOM PL			**OAK**
1	MORCOM AV	94619	650-G7
MORE ST			**ALB**
	BUCHANAN ST	94706	609-D6
MORELAND DR			**ALA**
1600	LINCOLN AV	94501	670-B2
1700	BUENA VISTA AV	94501	670-B2
1800	YOSEMITE AV	94501	670-B2
1900	FERNSIDE BLVD	94501	670-B2
MORGAN AV			**OAK**
2800	COOLIDGE AV	94602	650-E4
2880	BARNER AV	94602	650-E4
2900	BARNER AV	94602	650-E4
3000	MAPLE AV	94602	650-E4
MORKEN ST			**OAK**
6900	69TH AV	94621	670-G3
7000	70TH AV	94621	670-G3
MORLEY DR			**OAK**
2800	ASCOT DR	94611	650-F2
2890	BLACHFORD CT	94611	650-F2
MORPETH ST			**OAK**
5700	HARBORD DR	94618	630-B6
5800	JACOBUS AV	94618	630-C6
5900	FLORENCE AV	94618	630-C6
5900	MODOC AV	94618	630-C6
MORRILL CT			**OAK**
1	HARBORD DR	94618	630-B6
MORRILL LN			**OAK**
1	BUCKEYE AV	94618	630-B6
100	WILDING LN	94618	630-B6
MORRISON AV			**OAK**
3200	SHEFFIELD AV	94602	650-C5
3500	MONTANA ST	94602	650-C4
MORSE DR			**OAK**
5500	FLEMING AV	94605	670-G1
5900	SEMINARY AV	94605	670-G1
5900	SEMINARY AV	94605	670-G1
6000	60TH AV	94605	670-G1
6100	61ST AV	94605	670-G1
MORTON ST			**ALA**
1300	SAN ANTONIO AV	94501	669-H1
1300	SAN JOSE AV	94501	669-H1
1350	ENCINAL AV	94501	669-H1
1400	CENTRAL AV	94501	669-H1
1500	SANTA CLARA AV	94501	669-H1
1600	LINCOLN AV	94501	669-H1
1700	PACIFIC AV	94501	669-H1
MOSLEY AV			**ALA**
40	CIMARRON ST	94501	649-E6
90	MULVANY CIR	94501	649-E6
130	NIMITZ	94501	649-E6
140	MULVANY CIR	94501	649-E6
150	ENTERPRISE	94501	649-E6
170	CARL VINSON	94501	649-E6
200	SINGLETON AV	94501	649-E6
250	MONTEREY CIR	94501	649-E6
370	MONTEREY CIR	94501	649-E6
420	LAKEHURST CIR	94501	649-E6
500	MAYPORT CIR	94501	649-E6
550	LAKEHURST CIR	94501	649-E6
600	MAYPORT CIR	94501	649-E6
600	SINGLETON AV	94501	649-E6
MOSS AV			**OAK**
1	VERNON ST	94610	649-J2
70	OAKLAND AV	94610	649-J2
100	HARRISON ST	94611	649-J1
200	FAIRMOUNT AV	94611	649-J1
MOSS POINTE			**ALA**
1	SABLE POINTE	94502	670-A5
MOSS WY			**OAK**
100	LEIGHTON ST	94611	649-J1
200	FAIRMOUNT AV	94611	649-J1
MOSSWOOD RD			**BERK**
1	ORCHARD LN	94704	630-A2
1	PANORAMIC WY	94704	630-A2
20	ARDEN RD	94704	630-A2
MOTT PL			**OAK**
100	SKYLINE BLVD	94619	651-A6
MOUND ST			**ALA**
800	WATERTON ST	94501	670-A4
900	OTIS DR	94501	670-A4
950	CLAY ST	94501	670-A4
1000	CALHOUN ST	94501	670-A4
1050	FILLMORE ST	94501	670-A3
1100	WASHINGTON ST	94501	670-A3
1150	ADAMS ST	94501	670-A3
1200	SAN JOSE AV	94501	670-A3
1250	MADISON ST	94501	670-A3
1300	ENCINAL AV	94501	670-B3
1330	JACKSON ST	94501	670-B3
1360	VAN BUREN ST	94501	670-B3
1400	CENTRAL AV	94501	670-B3
1500	SANTA CLARA AV	94501	670-B3
1600	JOHNSON AV	94501	670-B3
MOUNT HOOD			**ALA**
4100	SEA HORSE	94501	649-E6
4100	CIMARRON ST	94501	649-E6
MOUNTAIN AV			**PDMT**
100	HIGHLAND AV	94611	650-B1
110	HIGHLAND WY	94611	650-B1
160	CRAIG AV	94611	650-B1
170	PACIFIC AV	94611	650-C1
200	DORMIDERA AV	94611	650-C1
300	SHARON AV	94611	650-C1
340	CAPERTON AV	94611	650-C1
460	BELLEVUE AV	94611	650-C1
470	POPLAR WY	94611	650-C1
500	SEAVIEW AV	94611	650-C1
540	DUDLEY AV	94611	650-C1
680	HAGAR AV	94611	650-C1
700	BLAIR AV	94611	650-C1
MOUNTAIN BLVD			**OAK**
550	GLENARMS DR	94611	630-C5
570	FAIRLANE DR	94611	630-C5
690	MONZAL AV	94611	630-C5
800	PINEWOOD RD	94611	630-D5
800	RUTHLAND RD	94611	630-D5
900	AVOCA AV	94611	630-C6
910	AVOCA AV	94611	630-D6
1100	BROADWAY TER	94611	630-D6
1400	FLORENCE TER	94611	630-D7
1610	FERNWOOD DR	94611	630-D7
1640	THORNHILL DR	94611	630-D7
1810	CABOT DR	94611	630-E7
1870	COLTON BLVD	94611	630-E7
1990	MEDAU PL	94611	650-E1
2030	LA SALLE AV	94611	650-E1
2040	ANTIOCH CT	94611	650-E1
2060	ANTIOCH ST	94611	650-E1
2130	LA SALLE AV	94611	650-E1
2130	MORAGA AV	94611	650-E1
2130	MERCED AV	94611	650-E1
2160	SNAKE RD	94611	650-E1
2300	SCOUT RD	94611	650-E1
2320	PARK BLVD	94611	650-E1
2500	ASCOT DR	94611	650-E2
2560	EL PATIO	94611	650-E2
2570	EL CAMINITO	94611	650-E2
2570	EL CAMINITO	94602	650-E2
2610	JOAQUIN MILLER CT	94611	650-F2
2610	JOAQUIN MILLER CT	94602	650-F2
2700	WOODCREST CIR	94602	650-F3
2750	DUBLIN AV	94602	650-F3
2780	KEARNEY AV	94602	650-F3
2850	WERNER CT	94602	650-F3
2880	WOODMINSTER LN	94602	650-F3
2900	JOAQUIN MILLER RD	94602	650-F3
3700	REDWOOD RD	94619	650-G5
4100	REDWOOD RD	94619	650-G5
4120	REDWOOD RD	94619	650-G5
4180	GERANIUM PL	94619	650-H5
4220	FIELDBROOK RD	94619	650-H5
4270	CARSON ST	94619	650-H5
4350	STAUFFER PL	94619	650-H5
4390	BERNEVES CT	94619	650-H6
4560	BELFAST AV	94619	650-H6
4700	KNOLL AV	94619	650-H6
4750	BERMUDA AV	94619	650-H6
4760	MCDONELL AV	94619	650-H6
4780	LEONA ST	94605	650-H6
	TWITTER CT	94605	650-H7
	FRONTAGE RD	94605	650-H7
5470	DAVENPORT AV	94613	650-H7
5470	DAVENPORT AV	94619	650-H7
6900	EDWARDS AV	94605	671-A1
7500	RIFLE LN	94605	671-A1
7890	MAYNARD AV	94605	671-A1
7960	KELLER AV	94605	671-A1
8130	SHONE AV	94605	671-B2
8200	DICKSON CT	94605	671-B2
8260	KENTWOOD CT	94605	671-B2
8320	SEACOR CT	94605	671-B2
8380	FONTAINE CT	94605	671-B2
9320	SEQUOYAH RD	94605	671-B3
9550	CALAFIA AV	94605	671-B4
9700	GOLF LINKS RD	94605	671-B4
MOUNTAIN VALLEY			**OAK**
	ELYSIAN FIELDS DR	94605	671-D2
	MISSION HILLS	94605	671-D2
MOUNTAIN VIEW AV			**OAK**
4200	LEONA ST	94605	650-J7
4100	LEONA ST	94605	650-J7
4200	FRONTAGE RD	94605	650-J7
MOUNTAINGATE WY			**OAK**
2630	CASTLE DR	94611	650-F2
2600	LAS AROMAS	94611	650-F2
2660	ASCOT DR	94611	650-F2
MOYER PL			**OAK**
1	WOOD DR	94611	650-D1
MOZART ST			**ALA**
1500	SANTA CLARA AV	94501	669-G1
1600	LINCOLN AV	94501	669-G1
MUIR AV			**PDMT**
1	LA SALLE AV	94610	650-C2
100	LAFAYETTE AV	94610	650-C2
MUIR WY			**BERK**
60	GRIZZLY PEAK BLVD	94708	609-J6
100	PARK HILLS RD	94708	609-J6
MULBERRY ST			**ALA**
1800	BUENA VISTA AV	94501	670-A1
1900	EAGLE AV	94501	670-A1
2000	CLEMENT AV	94501	670-A1
MULVANY CIR			**ALA**
	MOSLEY AV	94501	649-E6
	MARS	94501	649-E6
	ARKANSAS	94501	649-E6
	PYRO	94501	649-E6
	GOMPERS	94501	649-E6
	TEXAS	94501	649-E6
	SHASTA	94501	649-E6
	PYRO	94501	649-E6
	FLINT	94501	649-E6
	KANSAS CITY	94501	649-E6
	MARS	94501	649-E6
	WICHITA	94501	649-E6
	MOSLEY AV	94501	649-E6
MUNSON WY			**OAK**
1400	INTERNATIONAL BLVD	94606	650-B7
1450	MARIN WY	94606	650-B6
1500	E 15TH ST	94606	650-B6
1540	GLEASON WY	94606	650-B6
1600	FOOTHILL BLVD	94606	650-B6
MURDOCK CT			**OAK**
6000	60TH AV	94605	670-G1
MURILLO AV			**OAK**
9400	OAK KNOLL BLVD	94605	671-B4
9300	MIRASOL AV	94605	671-B3
9400	CALANDRIA	94605	671-B3
9400	MARGARITA AV	94605	671-B3
MURRAY ST			**BERK**
900	7TH ST	94804	629-E4
1100	SAN PABLO AV	94804	629-E4
MY WAY			**BERK**
1	VISTAMONT AV	94708	609-H4
MYERS ST			**OAK**
10900	DURANT AV	94603	671-B6
10800	109TH AV	94603	671-B6
10700	108TH AV	94603	671-B6
10600	107TH AV	94603	671-B6
10700	MACARTHUR BLVD	94603	671-B6
MYRTLE ST			**OAK**
300	3RD ST	94607	649-E4
1400	14TH ST	94607	649-F3
1600	16TH ST	94607	649-F3
1800	18TH ST	94607	649-F3
2100	21ST ST	94607	649-F2
2200	W GRAND AV	94607	649-F2
2400	24TH ST	94607	649-F2
2600	26TH ST	94607	649-F2
2800	28TH ST	94608	649-F1
3000	30TH ST	94608	649-F1
3200	SAN PABLO AV	94608	649-F1
MYRTLE WK			**ALA**
	CAMDEN RD	94501	669-H3
	YORKSHIRE PL	94501	669-H3
	WHITEHALL PL	94501	669-H3
	WHITEHALL RD	94501	669-H3
MYSTIC ST			**OAK**
	CLAREMONT AV	94618	629-J4
6300	AUBURN AV	94618	629-J4
6380	MANOA ST	94618	629-J4
6460	ROCKWELL ST	94618	629-J4
N			
NACE AV			**PDMT**
1	LAKE AV	94611	650-A1
100	NACE ST	94611	650-A1
NACE ST			**PDMT**
1	NACE AV	94611	650-A1
100	HOWARD AV	94611	650-A1
NAIROBI PL			**OAK**
3800	HILLMONT DR	94605	650-H7
3900	HILLMONT DR	94605	650-H7
3900	OAKDALE AV	94605	670-H1
NAKAYAMA CT			**ALA**
100	CREEDON CIR	94502	669-H5
NANTUCKET WY			**ALA**
300	RAVENS COVE LN	94501	670-A4
350	CAPE COD CT	94501	670-A4
NAPA AV			**BERK**
1900	HOPKINS ST	94707	609-G6
1950	JOSEPHINE ST	94707	609-G6
1950	MARTIN LUTHER KING JR WY	94707	609-G6
NAPA ST			**OAK**
6040	BELGRAVE PL	94618	630-A6
6000	THOMAS AV	94618	629-J6
6040	BROADWAY	94618	629-J6
NASON ST			**ALA**
1700	PACIFIC AV	94501	669-G1
1800	BUENA VISTA AV	94501	649-G7
NATTRESS WY			**OAK**
10450	105TH AV	94603	670-H7
10500	GRAMERCY PL	94603	670-H7
10500	KNIGHT ST	94603	670-H7
NAUTILUS ST			**ALA**
	BUENA VISTA AV	94501	669-H1
NAVY WY			**ALA**
	W RED LINE AV	94501	649-C6
	SARATOGA ST	94501	649-C6
	W RED LINE AV	94501	649-C6
	LEXINGTON ST	94501	649-C6
3400	MAIN ST	94501	649-C6
NEIL ARMSTRONG WY			**OAK**
11100	AIRPORT DR	94621	690-E2
11180	EDWARD WHITE WY	94621	690-E2
NEILSON ST			**ALB**
900	SOLANO AV	94706	609-F6
1000	MARIN AV	94706	609-F6
1010	SONOMA AV	94706	609-F6
1010	SONOMA AV	94706	609-E6
1030	ALBANY TER	94706	609-E6
1060	TERRACE ST	94706	609-E6
1090	FRANCIS ST	94706	609-E7
1100	FRANCIS ST	94706	609-E7
1250	WATKINS ST	94706	609-E7
NEILSON ST			**BERK**
500	VISALIA AV	94707	609-F5
600	THOUSAND OAKS BLVD	94707	609-F5
700	PORTLAND AV	94707	609-F5
800	WASHINGTON AV	94707	609-E6
900	SOLANO AV	94707	609-E6
1250	WATKINS ST	94706	609-E7
1300	GILMAN ST	94702	609-E7
1340	NORTHSIDE AV	94702	609-E7
1500	HOPKINS ST	94702	629-E1
NELLIE AV			**PDMT**
100	MAXWELTON RD	94618	630-C7
NEVA CT			**OAK**
100	CALDWELL RD	94611	630-C5
100	GLENARMS DR	94611	630-C5
NEVADA			**ALA**
4000	CIMARRON ST	94501	649-E6
4000	TRIPOLI	94501	649-E6
NEVADA ST			**OAK**
600	EDES AV	94603	670-G6
710	WALTER AV	94603	670-G6
800	RAILROAD AV	94603	670-G6
NEVIL ST			**OAK**
3600	HARRINGTON AV	94601	650-E6
3820	38TH AV	94601	650-E7
NEWBERRY ST			**BERK**
2900	RUSSELL ST	94703	629-G4
3000	ASHBY AV	94703	629-G4
NEWPORT RD			**ALA**
200	ALAMEDA RD	94501	649-D6
100	PAN AM WY	94501	649-D6
NEWTON AV			**OAK**
1	BROOKLYN AV	94606	649-J4
1	WESLEY AV	94606	649-J4
110	STOW AV	94606	649-J4
200	HANOVER AV	94606	649-J4
260	LESTER AV	94606	649-J4
280	LESTER AV	94606	649-J4
370	ATHOL AV	94606	649-J4
500	PARK BLVD	94606	649-J4
NEY AV			**OAK**
7100	72ND AV	94605	670-J2
7100	LACEY AV	94605	670-J2
7400	73RD AV	94605	670-J2
7500	75TH AV	94605	670-J2
7600	76TH AV	94605	670-J2
7910	PARKER AV	94605	670-J2
7940	RITCHIE ST	94605	670-J2
7700	PARTRIDGE AV	94605	670-J3
7620	82ND AV	94605	671-A3
7450	COSGRAVE AV	94605	671-A3
7220	EL MONTE AV	94605	671-A3
7200	ASTER AV	94605	671-A3
NICOL AV			**OAK**
2700	FRUITVALE AV	94602	650-D5
2700	FRUITVALE AV	94602	650-D5
2790	CHAMPION ST	94602	650-D5
2890	CAPP ST	94602	650-D5
2990	CUTHBERT AV	94602	650-D5
3100	COOLIDGE AV	94602	650-D5
3100	COOLIDGE AV	94602	650-D5
3200	PLEITNER AV	94602	650-D6
3340	MAPLE AV	94602	650-D6
NIMITZ			**ALA**
4000	MOSLEY AV	94501	649-E6
4100	ROANOKE	94501	649-E6
NOBLE AV			**ALA**
2500	EVERETT ST	94501	670-A2
2600	BROADWAY	94501	670-A2
NOGALES ST			**BERK**
1	THE PLAZA DR	94705	630-A4
100	PARKSIDE DR	94705	630-A4
NORFOLK DR			**OAK**
6900	BUCKINGHAM BLVD	94705	630-C3
6970	WESTMORELAND DR	94705	630-C3
7000	MARLBOROUGH TER	94705	630-C3
7010	DEVON WY	94705	630-C3
7100	STRATHMOOR DR	94705	630-C3
NORFOLK RD			**ALA**
	ORION ST	94501	649-D7
	W TOWER AV	94501	649-D7
	STARDUST PL	94501	649-D6
110	STARDUST PL	94501	649-D6
	W MIDWAY AV	94501	649-D6
200	CORPUS CHRISTI RD	94501	649-D6
100	PEARL HARBOR RD	94501	649-D6
NORGREN ST			**OAK**
580	CLARA ST	94603	670-G7
580	JONES AV	94603	670-G7
NORMAN LN			**ALA**
3500	MINGO LN	94502	670-B7
3600	KINGSTON LN	94502	670-B7
NORMAN LN			**OAK**
1	MANDALAY RD	94618	630-B6
100	WILDING LN	94618	630-B6
NORMANDIE AV			**OAK**
5300	55TH AV	94619	670-G1
5300	MORCOM AV	94619	650-G7
5500	MORCOM AV	94619	650-G7
NORTH CIR			**OAK**
1	MANZANITA DR	94611	630-G6
NORTH LOOP RD			**ALA**
2100	HARBOR BAY PKWY	94502	670-A7
2300	HARBOR BAY PKWY	94502	670-A7
2300	SOUTH LOOP RD	94502	670-A7
NORTH MALL			**OAK**
1	COLISEUM WY	94621	670-E4
100	COLISEUM WY	94621	670-E4
NORTH ST			**BERK**
	JAYNES ST	94703	609-F7
NORTH ST			**OAK**
400	COLBY ST	94609	629-J4
450	DANA ST	94609	629-J4
500	TELEGRAPH AV	94609	629-H5
600	RACINE ST	94609	629-H5
NORTH STAR RD			**ALA**
	EAGLE RD	94501	649-J7
NORTHAMPTON AV			**BERK**
1	SPRUCE ST	94707	609-G5
100	SANTA BARBARA RD	94707	609-G5
NORTHGATE AV			**BERK**
40	QUAIL AV	94708	609-J6
100	SHASTA RD	94708	609-J6
NORTHGATE AV			**OAK**
2200	GRAND AV	94612	649-G3
2280	23RD ST	94612	649-G2
2380	24TH ST	94612	649-G2
2480	25TH ST	94612	649-G2
2560	SYCAMORE ST	94612	649-G2
2570	36TH ST	94612	649-G2
2700	27TH ST	94612	649-G2
NORTHRUP ST			**OAK**
7600	SIKORSKY ST	94621	670-D6
7640	FAIRCHILD ST	94621	670-D6
7700	CONVAIR ST	94621	670-D6
NORTHSIDE AV			**BERK**
1300	GILMAN ST	94702	609-E7
1360	NEILSON ST	94702	609-E7
1500	HOPKINS ST	94702	629-E1
NORTHVALE RD			**OAK**
800	ROSEMOUNT RD	94610	650-B3
900	SUNNYHILLS RD	94610	650-B3
NORTHWOOD CT			**OAK**
1700	MANZANITA DR	94611	630-F6
NORTHWOOD DR			**ALA**
2900	GIBBONS DR	94501	670-B2
2900	SOUTHWOOD DR	94501	670-B2
2920	BUENA VISTA AV	94501	670-B2
2930	CAMBRIDGE DR	94501	670-B2
2950	FREMONT DR	94501	670-B2
2970	HARVARD DR	94501	670-B2
2980	GIBBONS DR	94501	670-B2
3000	BAYO VISTA AV	94501	670-B2
3000	FAIRVIEW AV	94501	670-B2
3000	SOUTHWOOD DR	94501	670-B2
NORTON AV			**OAK**
3800	CALIFORNIA ST	94602	650-F5
3800	SILVERWOOD AV	94602	650-F5
4000	WISCONSIN ST	94602	650-F5
3900	LAUREL AV	94602	650-F5
3900	MADELINE ST	94602	650-F5
3950	SILVERWOOD AV	94602	650-F5
4000	WISCONSIN ST	94602	650-F5
4200	HERRIER ST	94602	650-F4
4300	JORDAN RD	94602	650-F4
4400	GUIDO ST	94602	650-F4
4400	GUIDO ST	94602	650-G4
4500	MONTEREY BLVD	94602	650-G4
NORWICH RD			**ALA**
100	SEA VIEW PKWY	94502	670-A5
200	AVINGTON RD	94502	670-A5
NORWOOD AV			**OAK**
1000	TRESTLE GLEN RD	94610	650-C3
1200	GREENWOOD AV	94610	650-C3
NOTTINGHAM CT			**ALA**
1	STANBRIDGE LN	94502	669-J5
NOTTINGHAM DR			**ALA**
100	SEA VIEW PKWY	94502	669-J5
200	SHERWOOD LN	94502	669-J5
NOTTINGHAM DR			**OAK**
5700	MERRIEWOOD DR	94611	630-D6
5800	MERRIEWOOD CIR	94611	630-D6
5900	MERRIEWOOD DR	94611	630-D6
NOVA DR			**PDMT**
1	WILDWOOD AV	94610	650-A2
50	WILDWOOD AV	94610	650-A2
60	MAGNOLIA AV	94610	650-A2
	ARBOR DR	94610	650-A1
	ARBOR DR	94610	650-A1
130	DALE AV	94610	650-A1
200	JEROME AV	94610	650-A1
NOVA PTH			**OAK**
	BROOKSIDE AV	94618	630-B5
	EUSTICE AV	94618	630-B5
	GOLDEN GATE AV	94618	630-B5
NOVELDA DR			**OAK**
10900	CATRON DR	94603	670-H7
11200	BERGEDO DR	94603	670-H7
NOYO ST			**OAK**
3400	TRINIDAD AV	94602	650-G4
O			
OAK GROVE AV			**OAK**
5600	COLLEGE AV	94618	629-J5
5680	FOREST ST	94618	629-J5
OAK HILL CIR			**OAK**
1	OAK HILL RD	94605	671-C3
OAK HILL RD			**OAK**
3900	GOLF LINKS RD	94605	671-C3
3920	SIGOURNEY AV	94605	671-C3
3940	CAMISA CIR	94605	671-C3
3970	OAK HILL CIR	94605	671-C3
4000	SEQUOYAH VIEW DR	94605	671-C3
4100	SEQUOYAH VIEW DR	94605	671-C3
4200	SEQUOYAH RD	94605	671-C3
4200	SEQUOYAH RD	94605	671-C3
4260	SHORTHILL RD	94605	671-C3

PRIMARY STREET Address	Cross Street	ZIP	CITY Pg-Grid
OAK HILL RD			**OAK**
4300	SAINT ANDREWS RD	94605	671-C2
4400	BRIARCLIFF RD	94605	671-C2
4500	BRIARCLIFF RD	94605	671-C2
4550	SHORTHILL RD	94605	671-C2
4600	SAGE RD	94605	671-C2
4600	SEQUOYAH RD	94605	671-C2
OAK KNOLL BLVD			**OAK**
3300	CASTLEWOOD ST	94605	671-B4
3330	MURILLO AV	94605	671-B4
3370	ALCALA AV	94605	671-B4
3400	ENCINA WY	94605	671-B4
3430	ENCINA WY	94605	671-B4
3500	GRANADA AV	94605	671-B3
3620	TWIN OAKS WY	94605	671-B3
OAK KNOLL TER			**BERK**
2800	GARBER ST	94705	630-A3
2800	GARBER ST	94705	630-A3
2900	AVALON AV	94705	630-A3
OAK PARK DR			**ALA**
1	BAY PARK TER	94502	670-A5
80	SHEPARDSON LN	94502	670-A5
110	OAKSHADE DR	94502	670-A5
150	PARFAIT LN	94502	670-A5
200	RIDDELL LN	94502	670-A5
OAK RD			**PDMT**
100	OAKMONT AV	94610	650-B2
120	OAKMONT AV	94610	650-B2
180	PARK LN	94610	650-B2
OAK RIDGE RD			**BERK**
1	TUNNEL RD	94705	630-A4
30	THE UPLANDS	94705	630-A4
OAK ST			**ALA**
800	POWELL ST	94501	669-J3
900	CLINTON AV	94501	669-J3
1000	SAN JOSE AV	94501	669-J3
1100	SAN ANTONIO AV	94501	670-A2
1200	ENCINAL AV	94501	670-A2
1300	ALAMEDA AV	94501	670-A2
1400	CENTRAL AV	94501	670-A2
1500	SANTA CLARA AV	94501	670-A2
1550	TIMES WY	94501	670-A2
1600	TILDEN WY	94501	670-A2
1600	LINCOLN AV	94501	670-A2
1700	PACIFIC AV	94501	670-A2
1800	BUENA VISTA AV	94501	670-A2
1900	EAGLE AV	94501	670-A1
	CLEMENT AV	94501	670-A1
2050	BLANDING AV	94501	670-A1
OAK ST			**BERK**
2300	ARCH ST	94708	609-H6
2400	GLEN AV	94708	609-H6
2400	LAUREL ST	94708	609-H6
2500	HIGH CT	94708	609-H6
OAK ST			**OAK**
410	FALLON ST	94607	649-G5
	EMBARCADERO	94607	649-G5
170	2ND ST	94607	649-G5
390	4TH ST	94607	649-G5
500	5TH ST	94607	649-G5
700	7TH ST	94607	649-G5
810	8TH ST	94607	649-H5
900	9TH ST	94607	649-H5
1000	10TH ST	94607	649-H4
1100	11TH ST	94607	649-H4
1200	12TH ST	94612	649-H4
1300	13TH ST	94612	649-H4
1300	12TH ST	94612	649-H4
1400	14TH ST	94612	649-H4
1500	LAKESIDE DR	94612	649-H4
OAKCREST DR			**OAK**
1900	CARTER ST	94602	650-E2
2000	LEIMERT BLVD	94602	650-E2
OAKDALE AV			**OAK**
5900	SEMINARY AV	94605	650-H7
6000	LUNDHOLM AV	94605	650-H7
6000	LUNDHOLM AV	94605	650-H7
6280	LUNDHOLM AV	94605	650-H7
6280	NAIROBI PL	94605	670-H1
6300	DELMONT AV	94605	670-H1
OAKLAND AV			**OAK**
100	HARRISON ST	94611	649-H2
100	HARRISON ST	94610	649-H2
100	ORANGE ST	94610	649-H2
400	PEARL ST	94611	649-J2
400	PEARL ST	94610	649-J2
420	PEARL ST	94611	649-J2
420	PEARL ST	94610	649-J2
	PERRY PL	94610	649-J2
500	SANTA CLARA AV	94610	649-J2
550	MOSS AV	94611	649-J2
550	MOSS AV	94610	649-J2
600	SANTA ROSA AV	94611	649-J2
600	SANTA ROSA AV	94610	649-J2
650	BAYO VISTA AV	94611	649-J1
650	BAYO VISTA AV	94610	649-J1
700	MARIPOSA AV	94611	649-J1
700	MARIPOSA AV	94610	649-J1
750	MONTE VISTA AV	94611	649-J1
750	MONTE VISTA AV	94610	649-J1
750	OLIVE AV	94610	650-A1
750	OLIVE AV	94611	650-A1
850	OLIVE AV	94610	650-A1
850	OLIVE AV	94611	650-A1
OAKLAND AV			**PDMT**
850	OLIVE AV	94611	650-A1
910	SUNNYSIDE AV	94611	650-A1
950	LINDA AV	94611	650-A1
1000	HOWARD AV	94611	650-A1
1000	HOWARD AV	94610	650-A1
1100	GRAND AV	94611	650-A1
1100	GRAND AV	94610	650-A1
1130	ARBOR DR	94611	650-A1
1130	ARBOR DR	94610	650-A1
1200	GREENBANK AV	94611	650-A1
1200	GREENBANK AV	94610	650-A1
1210	JEROME AV	94611	650-A1
1210	JEROME AV	94610	650-A1
1300	LATHAM ST	94611	650-A1
1300	LATHAM ST	94610	650-A1
1400	SAN CARLOS AV	94611	650-B1
1500	EL CERRITO AV	94611	650-B1
1540	CARMEL AV	94611	650-B1
1700	HILLSIDE AV	94611	650-B1
1800	BONITA AV	94611	650-B1
1900	HIGHLAND AV	94611	650-B1
2000	HARDWICK AV	94611	650-B1
2100	SCENIC AV	94611	650-B1
OAKMONT AV			**PDMT**
1	PROSPECT RD	94610	650-B2
120	OAK RD	94610	650-B2
150	OAK RD	94610	650-B2
200	HARVARD RD	94610	650-B2
OAKMORE PL			**OAK**
1700	OAKMORE RD	94602	650-D3
1800	HANLY RD	94602	650-D3
1800	EL CENTRO AV	94602	650-D3
OAKMORE RD			**OAK**
3930	OAKMORE PL	94602	650-D3
4090	CASTERLINE RD	94602	650-D3
4220	CLEMENS RD	94602	650-D3
	LEIMERT PL	94602	650-D3
	LEIMERT BLVD	94602	650-D3
	ARDEN PL	94602	650-D3
	LEIMERT BLVD	94602	650-D3
OAKPORT ST			**OAK**
4400	LESSER ST	94621	670-D3
6600	66TH AV	94621	670-D4
7500	HASSLER WY	94621	670-E4
7800	ROLAND WY	94621	670-F5
8300	EDGEWATER DR	94621	670-F6
OAKSHADE DR			**ALA**
	SEA VIEW PKWY	94502	670-A5
	SHEFFIELD RD	94502	670-A5
	OAK PARK DR	94502	670-A5
OAKVALE AV			**BERK**
10	DOMINGO AV	94705	630-A4
100	ENCINA PL	94705	630-A4
100	THE PLAZA DR	94705	630-A4
OAKVIEW DR			**OAK**
1900	LEIMERT BLVD	94602	650-E3
OAKWOOD CT			**OAK**
1	OAKWOOD DR	94611	630-F6
OAKWOOD DR			**OAK**
6500	THORNHILL DR	94611	630-F6
6600	WILD CURRANT WY	94611	630-F6
6600	OAKWOOD CT	94611	630-F6
6700	GLEN OAKS WY	94611	630-F6
6900	SOBRANTE RD	94611	630-F6
OBSERVATION PL			**OAK**
1	SKYLINE BLVD	94611	630-F5
OCCIDENTAL ST			**OAK**
5900	59TH ST	94608	629-F5
OCEAN AV			**EMVL**
1250	VALLEJO ST	94608	629-E5
1300	DOYLE ST	94608	629-E5
1400	HOLLIS ST	94608	629-E5
OCEAN AV			**OAK**
1100	SAN PABLO AV	94608	629-E5
1140	MARSHALL ST	94608	629-E5
1250	VALLEJO ST	94608	629-E5
OCEAN VIEW DR			**OAK**
5600	COLLEGE AV	94618	629-J5
5800	MCMILLAN AV	94618	630-A5
5900	BROADWAY	94618	630-A5
6100	MARGARIDO DR	94618	630-A5
6130	MANCHESTER DR	94618	630-A5
6150	WEST LN	94618	630-B5
6150	BROOKSIDE AV	94618	630-B5
6170	ALPINE TER	94618	630-B5
6200	ACACIA AV	94618	630-B5
OCEANA CIR			**ALA**
	BAINBRIDGE AV	94501	649-E7
OCTAVIA ST			**OAK**
2800	ALLENDALE AV	94619	650-E6
2800	ALLENDALE AV	94619	650-E6
3000	PENNIMAN AV	94619	650-E6
3300	SUTER ST	94619	650-E6
3400	FULLINGTON ST	94619	650-E6
OHANNESON RD			**OAK**
	MARGIE LN	94605	651-B7
	CAMPUS DR	94605	651-B7
OHIO			**ALA**
4000	SEA HORSE	94501	649-E6
OLD ALAMEDA PT			**ALA**
1100	OLEANDER AV	94502	670-A7
1200	CATALINA AV	94502	670-A7
OLD REDWOOD RD			**OAK**
	REDWOOD RD	94619	650-J5
	REDWOOD RD	94619	650-J5
	REDWOOD RD	94619	650-J5
	REDWOOD RD	94619	650-J5
OLD TUNNEL RD			**OAK**
	BAY FOREST DR	94611	630-D4
	TUNNEL RD	94611	630-D4
	TUNNEL RD	94611	630-D4
2520	SKYLINE BLVD	94611	630-D4
OLDCASTLE LN			**ALA**
100	TIPPERARY LN	94502	669-H5
200	SEA VIEW PKWY	94502	669-H5
OLEANDER AV			**ALA**
3380	HOLLY ST	94502	670-A7
3380	FIR AV	94502	670-A7
3400	JOST LN	94502	670-A7
3440	OLD ALAMEDA PT	94502	670-A7
3470	MELROSE AV	94502	670-A7
3490	MINGO LN	94502	670-A7
3500	MCSHERRY LN	94502	670-B7
3530	KINGSTON LN	94502	670-B7
3600	MANGROVE LN	94502	670-B7
3630	LILAC ST	94502	670-B7
3700	MAGNOLIA DR	94502	670-B7
OLIVE AV			**PDMT**
200	OAKLAND AV	94611	650-A1
200	OAKLAND AV	94611	650-A2
400	SUNNYSIDE AV	94611	650-A2
400	LAKE AV	94611	649-J1
OLIVE ST			**OAK**
7780	78TH AV	94621	670-H3
7780	78TH AV	94605	670-H3
7900	RITCHIE ST	94605	670-H3
7900	RITCHIE ST	94621	670-H3
8000	80TH AV	94621	670-H3
8100	81ST AV	94621	670-J3
8200	82ND AV	94621	670-J3
8200	82ND AV	94621	670-J3
8300	83RD AV	94621	670-J3
8400	84TH AV	94621	670-J3
8500	85TH AV	94621	670-J4
8600	86TH AV	94621	670-J4
8640	AUSEON AV	94621	670-J4
8700	87TH AV	94621	670-J4
8800	88TH AV	94621	670-J4
8900	89TH AV	94621	670-J4
9000	90TH AV	94621	670-J4
9000	90TH AV	94603	670-J4
9200	92ND AV	94603	670-J4
9400	94TH AV	94603	670-J4
9600	96TH AV	94603	670-J5
9190	98TH AV	94603	671-A5
9800	WARNER AV	94603	671-A5
9900	99TH AV	94603	671-A5
10000	100TH AV	94603	671-A5
OLIVER AV			**OAK**
2500	TRUMAN AV	94605	671-B5
2670	BURR ST	94605	671-B5
2700	BURR ST	94605	671-B5
2900	STANLEY AV	94605	671-B5
OLMSTEAD ST			**OAK**
6600	66TH AV	94621	670-F3
6700	BRENTFORD ST	94621	670-F3
6900	BRENTFORD ST	94621	670-F3
OLYMPUS AV			**BERK**
1400	AVENIDA DR	94708	609-J7
1540	HARDING CIR	94708	609-J7
1	FAIRLAWN DR	94708	610-A7
	WILSON CIR	94708	610-A7
OPAL ST			**OAK**
3800	38TH ST	94609	649-H1
4000	40TH ST	94609	629-H7
4100	41ST ST	94609	629-H7
4200	42ND ST	94609	629-H7
ORANGE ST			**OAK**
100	HARRISON ST	94610	649-H2
100	OAKLAND AV	94610	649-H2
300	PERKINS ST	94610	649-J2
400	PEARL ST	94610	649-J2
500	PERRY PL	94610	649-J2
ORCHARD LN			**BERK**
	MOSSWOOD RD	94704	630-A2
	PANORAMIC WY	94704	630-A2
	ARDEN RD	94704	630-A2
ORCHARD MEADOW RD			**OAK**
3480	RICHARDS RD	94613	650-G7
ORCHID ST			**OAK**
3300	COOLIDGE AV	94601	650-D6
3400	34TH AV	94601	650-D6
ORDWAY ST			**ALB**
900	SOLANO AV	94707	609-F6
900	SOLANO AV	94706	609-F6
900	TACOMA AV	94706	609-F6
940	MARIN AV	94707	609-F6
940	MARIN AV	94706	609-F6
940	MARIN AV	94707	609-F6
940	MARIN AV	94706	609-F6
1000	SONOMA AV	94706	609-F6
1050	MANOR WY	94706	609-F7
1100	POSEN AV	94706	609-F7
1300	GILMAN ST	94706	609-F7
ORDWAY ST			**BERK**
1300	GILMAN ST	94702	609-E7
1400	HOPKINS ST	94702	609-E7
1300	ADA ST	94702	609-E7
1400	ROSE ST	94702	609-E7
OREGON ST			**BERK**
1100	SAN PABLO AV	94702	629-E4
1200	WALLACE ST	94702	629-E4
1300	MATHEWS ST	94702	629-F4
1400	MABEL ST	94702	629-F4
1400	PARK ST	94702	629-F4
1420	ACTON ST	94702	629-F4
1450	DOHR ST	94702	629-F4
1470	STANTON ST	94702	629-F4
1500	SACRAMENTO ST	94703	629-F4
1600	CALIFORNIA ST	94703	629-F3
1700	MCGEE AV	94703	629-G3
1800	GRANT ST	94703	629-G3
1900	MARTIN LUTHER KING JR WY	94703	629-G3
1900	MARTIN LUTHER KING JR WY	94703	629-G3
2000	MILVIA ST	94703	629-G3
2040	ADELINE ST	94703	629-G3
2100	SHATTUCK AV	94705	629-H3
2200	FULTON ST	94705	629-H3
2300	ELLSWORTH ST	94705	629-H3
2400	TELEGRAPH AV	94705	629-H3
2440	FLORENCE ST	94705	629-J3
2500	REGENT ST	94705	629-J3
ORIN DR			**OAK**
2400	24TH ST	94612	649-H2
ORINDA VISTA DR			**OAK**
50	ROYAL OAK RD	94605	671-C3
100	ELYSIAN FIELDS DR	94605	671-C3
ORION ST			**ALA**
	W SEAPLANE LAGOON	94501	649-D7
	W TRIDENT AV	94501	649-D7
	NORFOLK RD	94501	649-D7
	W TOWER AV	94501	649-D7
	W ORISKANY AV	94501	649-D7
	W PACIFIC AV	94501	649-D7
	W ATLANTIC AV	94501	649-D7
W ORISKANY AV			**ALA**
	CENTRAL AV	94501	669-E1
	SKYHAWK ST	94501	669-D1
	ORION ST	94501	669-D1
	VIKING ST	94501	669-D1
	FERRY PT	94501	669-D1
ORMINDALE CT			**OAK**
1	ELVERTON DR	94611	630-F5
ORR CT			**ALA**
1	ORR RD	94502	669-J6
ORR RD			**ALA**
	AUGHINBAUGH WY	94502	669-J6
	PATTIANI WY	94502	669-J6
1	ORR CT	94502	669-J6
200	MCDONNEL RD	94502	669-J6
ORRAL ST			**OAK**
7000	70TH AV	94621	670-G3
7100	71ST AV	94621	670-G3
7200	72ND AV	94621	670-G3
7300	73RD AV	94621	670-G3
OSBORNE CT			**OAK**
100	CASTLE DR	94611	650-G2
OSCAR AV			**OAK**
9300	LOUISIANA ST	94603	670-G6
9400	CLARA ST	94603	670-G6
9500	S ELMHURST AV	94603	670-G6
OSTRANDER RD			**OAK**
5800	BROADWAY TER	94618	630-B6
6000	MATHIEU AV	94618	630-B6
6000	ROMANY RD	94618	630-B6
OTIS DR			**ALA**
800	WESTLINE DR	94501	669-G2
820	WATERFALL ISL	94501	669-G2
1000	TARRYTON ISL	94501	669-G2
1050	SAND HOOK ISL	94501	669-G2
1100	LARCHMONT ISL	94501	669-G2
1150	WINDEMERE ISL	94501	669-G2
1200	ARLINGTON ISL	94501	669-H2
1230	ROCK ISL	94501	669-H2
1250	ROSEWOOD WY	94501	669-H2
1700	GRAND ST	94501	669-H2
1760	FORTRESS ISL	94501	669-H2
1820	WATERVIEW ISL	94501	669-H2
1840	SANDCREEK WY	94501	669-H3
1870	SANDALWOOD ISL	94501	669-H3
1920	POND ISL	94501	669-H3
1970	GLENWOOD ISL	94501	669-H3
2050	WILLOW ST	94501	669-J3
2080	WILLOW ST	94501	669-J3
2120	SOUTH SHORE CTR W	94501	669-J3
2400	PARK ST	94501	669-J3
2460	PARK AV	94501	669-J3
2520	REGENT ST	94501	669-J3
2560	DEL MAR AV	94501	670-A3
2600	BROADWAY	94501	670-A4
2700	EVELYN CT	94501	670-A4
2700	PEARL ST	94501	670-A4
2800	VERSAILLES AV	94501	670-A4
2900	MOUND ST	94501	670-A4
3000	COURT ST	94501	670-A4
3100	FOUNTAIN ST	94501	670-A4
3200	HIGH ST	94501	670-A4
3200	BAYVIEW DR	94501	670-A4
3230	POST ST	94501	670-A4
	PEACH ST	94501	670-A4
3260	DRIFTWOOD LN	94501	670-A4
	FERNSIDE BLVD	94501	670-B4
OTIS ST			**BERK**
2900	RUSSELL ST	94703	629-G4
3000	ASHBY AV	94703	629-G4
OUTLOOK AV			**OAK**
5900	SEMINARY AV	94605	650-H7
6000	MAJESTIC AV	94605	650-H7
6100	LUNDHOLM AV	94605	650-H7
6200	LUNDHOLM AV	94605	650-H7
6200	62ND AV	94605	670-H1
6400	64TH AV	94605	670-H1
6480	65TH AV	94605	670-H1
6600	66TH AV	94605	670-H1
6800	68TH AV	94605	670-H1
6900	69TH AV	94605	670-J1
7100	LAVERDA PTH	94605	670-J1
7200	72ND AV	94605	670-J2
7300	73RD AV	94605	670-J2
7480	75TH AV	94605	670-J2
7500	75TH AV	94605	670-J2
7600	76TH AV	94605	670-J2
7800	PARKER AV	94605	670-J2
7700	PARKER AV	94605	670-J2
8000	TULLY PL	94605	671-A2
8100	PARTRIDGE AV	94605	671-A2
8300	EL MONTE AV	94605	671-A3
8200	COSGRAVE AV	94605	671-A3
8300	82ND AV	94605	671-A3
OVAL RD			**OAK**
100	PINEWOOD RD	94611	630-C6
OVER ST			**OAK**
3300	SUTER ST	94619	650-E6
3400	FULLINGTON ST	94619	650-E6
OVERDALE AV			**OAK**
6100	SEMINARY AV	94605	650-H7
6200	HILLMONT DR	94605	650-H7
OVERLAKE CT			**OAK**
1	THORNHILL DR	94611	630-E6
OVERLAND AV			**EMVL**
6200	62ND ST	94608	629-E5
6300	63RD ST	94608	629-E5
6400	64TH ST	94608	629-E5
OVERLOOK RD			**BERK**
930	THE CROSSWAYS	94708	609-J5
950	LATHAM LN	94708	609-J5
1040	PARK HILLS RD	94708	609-J5
OVERMOOR ST			**OAK**
11000	SNOWDOWN AV	94605	671-D5
11050	CAMERON AV	94605	671-D5
11100	CLIFFLAND AV	94605	671-D5
11100	KERRIGAN DR	94605	671-D5
OXFORD LN			**BERK**
100	CROSS CAMPUS RD	94704	629-H2
100	OXFORD ST	94704	629-H2
OXFORD ST			**BERK**
800	INDIAN ROCK AV	94707	609-G6
900	MARIN AV	94707	609-G6
1100	LOS ANGELES AV	94707	609-G6
1200	EUNICE ST	94709	609-H7
1400	ROSE ST	94709	609-H7
1500	VINE ST	94709	609-H7
1600	CEDAR ST	94709	609-H7
1700	VIRGINIA ST	94709	629-H1
1900	HEARST AV	94720	629-H1
1900	HEARST AV	94704	629-H1
1950	BERKELEY WY	94720	629-H1
1950	BERKELEY WY	94704	629-H1
2000	UNIVERSITY AV	94720	629-H1
2000	UNIVERSITY AV	94704	629-H1
2100	ADDISON ST	94720	629-H2
2100	ADDISON ST	94704	629-H2
2120	CENTER ST	94720	629-H2
2120	CENTER ST	94704	629-H2
	CROSS CAMPUS RD	94720	629-H2
	CROSS CAMPUS RD	94704	629-H2
	OXFORD LN	94704	629-H2
	OXFORD LN	94704	629-H2
	ALLSTON WY	94720	629-H2
	ALLSTON WY	94704	629-H2
	KITTREDGE ST	94720	629-H2
	KITTREDGE ST	94704	629-H2
	BANCROFT WY	94720	629-H2
	BANCROFT WY	94704	629-H2
	FULTON ST	94704	629-H2
	FULTON ST	94704	629-H2
OYSTER POND RD			**ALA**
1	ROBERT DAVEY JR DR	94502	670-A5
90	BASIN SIDE WY	94502	670-A5
120	STEUBEN BAY	94502	670-A5
160	AVONDALE LNDG	94502	670-A6
190	STONINGTON POINTE	94502	670-A6
210	WELLFLEET BAY	94502	670-A6
OYSTER SHOALS			**ALA**
1	CLUBHOUSE MEMORIAL RD	94502	670-A6
1	ISLAND DR	94502	670-A6
50	VICTORIA BAY	94502	670-A6

P

PRIMARY STREET Address	Cross Street	ZIP	CITY Pg-Grid
PACIFIC AV			**ALA**
100	CENTRAL AV	94501	649-E7
100	MAIN ST	94501	649-E7
160	2ND ST	94501	649-E7
170	SANTA CLARA AV	94501	649-E7
200	2ND ST	94501	649-E7
250	HAIGHT AV	94501	649-E7
300	3RD ST	94501	649-E7
400	4TH ST	94501	649-E7
420	MARSHALL WY	94501	649-E7
500	5TH ST	94501	669-F1
600	6TH ST	94501	669-F1
700	WEBSTER ST	94501	669-F1
720	CONCORDIA ST	94501	669-F1
750	CONSTITUTION WY	94501	669-G1
800	8TH ST	94501	669-G1
850	NASON ST	94501	669-G1
900	9TH ST	94501	669-G1
950	WOOD ST	94501	669-G1
1000	CHAPIN ST	94501	669-G1
1100	SAINT CHARLES ST	94501	669-G1
1200	BAY ST	94501	669-H1
1300	SHERMAN ST	94501	669-H1
1400	MORTON ST	94501	669-H1
1500	BENTON ST	94501	669-H1
1520	JAY ST	94501	669-H1
1530	ARBOR ST	94501	669-H1
1550	STANTON ST	94501	669-H1
1600	PARU ST	94501	669-H1
1650	HIBBARD ST	94501	669-J1
1700	GRAND ST	94501	669-J1
1750	MINTURN ST	94501	669-J1
1800	UNION ST	94501	669-J1
1850	SCHILLER ST	94501	669-J1
1900	LAFAYETTE ST	94501	669-J1
2000	CHESTNUT ST	94501	669-J1
2100	WILLOW ST	94501	669-J1
2200	WALNUT ST	94501	670-A2
2280	LEA CT	94501	670-A2
2300	OAK ST	94501	670-A2
2400	PARK ST	94501	670-A2
PACIFIC AV			**PDMT**
1	MOUNTAIN AV	94611	650-C1
100	SCENIC AV	94611	650-C1
240	DORMIDERA AV	94611	650-C1

© 2006 Rand McNally & Company

PRIMARY STREET Address	Cross Street	ZIP	CITY Pg-Grid
PACIFIC AV			**PDMT**
290	HAGAR AV	94611	650-C1
390	BELLEVUE AV	94611	650-C1
500	HAGAR AV	94611	650-C1
W PACIFIC AV			**ALA**
	SKYHAWK ST	94501	649-D7
	ORION ST	94501	649-D7
PACKET LNDG			**ALA**
290	BRITTANY DR	94502	670-A5
320	CENTRE CT	94502	670-A5
	ROBERT DAVEY JR DR	94502	670-A5
	SEA BRIDGE WY	94502	670-A5
PAGE ST			**ALA**
1400	CENTRAL AV	94501	669-F1
1450	TAYLOR AV	94501	669-F1
1500	SANTA CLARA AV	94501	669-F1
PAGE ST			**BERK**
700	EASTSHORE BLVD	94804	629-C1
730	2ND ST	94804	629-D1
760	3RD ST	94804	629-D1
790	4TH ST	94804	629-D1
820	5TH ST	94804	629-D1
860	6TH ST	94804	629-D1
890	7TH ST	94804	629-D1
920	8TH ST	94804	629-D1
950	9TH ST	94804	629-D1
980	10TH ST	94804	629-D1
1020	SAN PABLO AV	94702	629-E1
1040	KAINS AV	94702	629-E1
1100	STANNAGE AV	94702	609-E7
1200	CORNELL AV	94702	609-E7
1200	SANTA FE AV	94702	609-E7
PALA AV			**PDMT**
1	HIGHLAND AV	94611	650-B1
100	MESA AV	94611	630-B7
200	MONTE AV	94611	630-B7
400	PARK WY	94611	630-B7
500	MORAGA AV	94611	630-B7
PALACE CT			**ALA**
600	6TH ST	94501	669-F1
PALI CT			**OAK**
40	GLENARMS DR	94611	630-C5
PALM AV			**OAK**
300	PERKINS ST	94610	649-J3
350	STATEN AV	94610	649-J3
380	BELLEVUE AV	94610	649-J3
400	EUCLID AV	94610	649-J3
PALM BEACH LN			**ALA**
	PURCELL DR	94502	670-A5
PALM CT			**BERK**
2800	KELSEY ST	94705	629-J3
2800	STUART ST	94705	629-J3
PALM DR			**PDMT**
100	WILDWOOD AV	94610	650-A2
200	WALLACE RD	94610	650-B2
300	PARKVIEW CT	94610	650-B2
PALMER AV			**OAK**
3200	E 32ND ST	94602	650-C4
3260	E 33RD ST	94602	650-C4
PALMERA CT			**ALA**
1700	GRAND ST	94501	669-H2
1800	DAYTON AV	94501	669-H2
PALMETTO ST			**OAK**
2400	LINCOLN AV	94602	650-D5
2500	BOSTON AV	94602	650-D5
PALOMA AV			**OAK**
600	LONGRIDGE RD	94610	650-B3
800	MANDANA BLVD	94610	650-B3
800	MANDANA BLVD	94610	650-B3
820	SANTA RAY AV	94610	650-B3
840	SANTA RAY AV	94610	650-B3
860	CALMAR AV	94610	650-B3
900	BALFOUR AV	94610	650-B3
PAMPAS AV			**OAK**
4300	HIGH ST	94619	650-G6
4300	SIESTA CT	94619	650-G6
4380	MADRONE AV	94619	650-G6
PAN AM WY			**ALA**
	W TOWER AV	94501	649-D7
	SUNRISE CT	94501	649-D6
	W HOPE ST	94501	649-D6
	STARDUST PL	94501	649-D6
	W RANGER AV	94501	649-D6
	W MIDWAY AV	94501	649-D6
	CORPUS CHRISTI RD	94501	649-D6
	PENSACOLA	94501	649-D6
	ALAMEDA RD	94501	649-D6
	W ESSEX DR	94501	649-D6
	SEATTLE RD	94501	649-D6
	NEWPORT RD	94501	649-D6
	BARBERS POINT RD	94501	649-D6
	W RED LINE AV	94501	649-D6
PANAMA CT			**OAK**
4000	GLEN AV	94611	649-J1
PANORAMIC DR			**ALA**
	W RED LINE AV	94501	649-C5
PANORAMIC PL			**BERK**
	ARDEN RD	94704	630-A2
	PANORAMIC WY	94704	630-A2
	PANORAMIC WY	94704	630-A2
PANORAMIC WY			**BERK**
1	PROSPECT ST	94704	629-J2
1	STADIUM RIMWAY	94704	629-J2
100	MOSSWOOD RD	94704	630-A2
100	ORCHARD LN	94704	630-A2
140	ARDEN RD	94704	630-A2
210	DWIGHT WY	94704	630-A2
300	PANORAMIC PL	94704	630-A2
300	PANORAMIC PL	94704	630-A2
PANORAMIC WY			**OAK**
700	DWIGHT WY	94704	630-A2
800	STATE PL	94704	630-A2
900	BANCROFT PL	94704	630-B2
PARAMOUNT RD			**OAK**
800	CARLSTON AV	94610	650-B3
1000	LONGRIDGE RD	94610	650-B3
1000	HUBERT RD	94610	650-B3
PARDEE DR			**OAK**
8430	SWAN WY	94621	670-E7
8600	AIRPORT DR	94621	670-E7
8600	HEGENBERGER RD	94621	670-E7
PARDEE LN			**OAK**
7700	EDGEWATER DR	94621	670-E5
PARDEE ST			**BERK**
900	7TH ST	94804	629-E3
930	8TH ST	94804	629-E3
1000	9TH ST	94804	629-E3
1030	10TH ST	94804	629-E3
1100	SAN PABLO AV	94804	629-E3
PARFAIT LN			**ALA**
1	OAK PARK DR	94502	670-A5
110	RIDDELL LN	94502	670-A5
150	DAMON CT	94502	670-A5
PARISH CT			**ALA**
1	HOLLY ST	94502	670-A6
PARK AV			**ALA**
800	ROOSEVELT DR	94501	669-J3
900	OTIS DR	94501	669-J3
1100	PARK AV E	94501	669-J3
1100	PARK AV W	94501	669-J3
1300	ENCINAL AV	94501	670-A3
1320	MARTIRAE CT	94501	670-A2
1400	CENTRAL AV	94501	670-A2
1400	CENTRAL AV	94501	670-A2
1450	POST OFFICE CT	94501	670-A2
1500	SANTA CLARA AV	94501	670-A2
PARK AV			**EMVL**
1100	SAN PABLO AV	94608	629-F7
1150	EMERY ST	94608	629-F7
	WATTS ST	94608	629-F7
1200	WATTS ST	94608	629-F7
1250	HARLAN ST	94608	629-F7
1300	HAVEN ST	94608	629-E7
1350	HOLLIS ST	94608	629-E7
1400	HOLDEN ST	94608	629-E7
1450	HORTON ST	94608	629-E7
1500	HUBBARD ST	94608	629-E7
1580	HALLECK ST	94608	629-E7
PARK AV E			**ALA**
1150	PARK AV W	94501	670-A3
1150	PARK AV	94501	670-A3
1200	SAN JOSE AV	94501	670-A3
1300	ENCINAL AV	94501	670-A3
PARK AV W			**ALA**
1150	PARK AV E	94501	670-A3
1150	PARK AV	94501	670-A3
1200	SAN JOSE AV	94501	670-A3
1300	ENCINAL AV	94501	670-A3
PARK BLVD			**OAK**
	PASO ROBLES DR	94611	630-F7
1800	E 18TH ST	94606	649-J4
1800	3RD AV	94606	649-J4
1900	WAYNE PL	94606	649-J4
1960	4TH AV	94606	649-J4
1970	E 20TH ST	94606	649-J4
2000	NEWTON AV	94606	649-J4
2040	E 21ST ST	94606	649-J4
2040	HADDON RD	94606	650-A4
2110	HADDON RD	94606	650-A4
2190	PORTLAND AV	94606	650-A4
2200	IVY DR	94606	650-A4
2250	VAN DYKE AV	94606	650-A4
2370	MONTCLAIR AV	94606	650-A4
2540	BROOKLYN AV	94606	650-A4
2560	SPRUCE ST	94606	650-A4
2700	CLEVELAND ST	94606	650-A4
2800	8TH AV	94610	650-A4
2800	MCKINLEY AV	94610	650-A4
3100	E 28TH ST	94610	650-B4
3400	E 34TH ST	94610	650-B4
3480	MACARTHUR BLVD	94610	650-B4
3490	MACARTHUR BLVD	94610	650-B4
3550	CHATHAM RD	94610	650-B4
3620	EXCELSIOR AV	94610	650-B4
3630	EXCELSIOR AV	94610	650-B4
3700	PARK BLVD WY	94610	650-B4
3700	KINGSLEY ST	94610	650-B4
3750	EMERSON WY	94610	650-B4
3800	13TH AV	94610	650-C4
3800	13TH AV	94602	650-C4
3800	PARK BLVD WY	94602	650-C4
3810	GREENWOOD AV	94602	650-C4
3900	BEAUMONT AV	94602	650-C4
4010	BRIGHTON AV	94602	650-C4
4030	BRIGHTON AV	94602	650-C4
4100	HAMPEL ST	94602	650-C3
4100	GLEN PARK RD	94602	650-C3
4250	GLENFIELD AV	94602	650-C3
4300	WELLINGTON ST	94602	650-C3
4500	EVERETT AV	94602	650-D3
4510	EVERETT AV	94602	650-D3
4600	EL CENTRO AV	94602	650-D3
4700	DOLORES AV	94602	650-D3
4800	HOLLYWOOD AV	94602	650-D3
4830	CAVENDISH LN	94602	650-D3
4860	TRESTLE GLEN RD	94602	650-D3
4880	LEIMERT BLVD	94602	650-D3
4880	SAINT JAMES DR	94602	650-D3
4900	ESTATES DR	94611	650-D2
5250	MONTEREY BLVD	94611	650-E2
5250	TRAFALGAR PL	94611	650-E2
5260	MONTEREY BLVD	94611	650-E1
5300	MOUNTAIN BLVD	94611	650-E1
PARK BLVD			**PDMT**
4860	TRESTLE GLEN RD	94610	650-D3
4880	LEIMERT BLVD	94611	650-D3
4880	SAINT JAMES DR	94611	650-D3
4900	ESTATES DR	94611	650-D2
5250	MONTEREY BLVD	94611	650-D2
5250	TRAFALGAR PL	94611	650-D2
PARK BLVD WY			**OAK**
3700	PARK BLVD	94610	650-B4
3700	KINGSLEY ST	94610	650-B4
3770	EMERSON WY	94610	650-B4
3800	PARK BLVD	94610	650-B4
3800	13TH AV	94610	650-B4
PARK GATE			**BERK**
1	PARK HILLS RD	94708	609-J6
100	SHASTA RD	94708	609-J6
PARK HILLS RD			**BERK**
1000	WILDCAT CANYON RD	94708	609-J5
1030	THE CRESCENT	94708	609-J5
1030	THE SHORT CUT	94708	609-J5
1060	MIDDLEFIELD RD	94708	609-J5
1060	THE CRESCENT	94708	609-J5
1090	OVERLOOK RD	94708	609-J6
1100	MUIR WY	94708	609-J6
1160	PARK GATE	94708	609-J6
1190	WOODSIDE RD	94708	609-J6
	HILLVIEW RD	94708	610-A6
	SHASTA RD	94708	610-A6
PARK LN			**OAK**
900	WALAVISTA AV	94610	650-B2
1060	LAKESHORE AV	94610	650-B2
PARK LN			**PDMT**
1030	OAK RD	94610	650-B2
PARK ST			**ALA**
300	SHORELINE DR	94501	669-J4
900	OTIS DR	94501	669-J3
1100	CLINTON AV	94501	669-J3
1200	SAN JOSE AV	94501	670-A3
1250	SAN ANTONIO AV	94501	670-A3
1300	ENCINAL AV	94501	670-A2
1350	ALAMEDA AV	94501	670-A2
1400	CENTRAL AV	94501	670-A2
1450	POST OFFICE CT	94501	670-A2
1500	SANTA CLARA AV	94501	670-A2
1550	WEBB AV	94501	670-A2
1550	TIMES WY	94501	670-A2
1600	LINCOLN AV	94501	670-A2
1600	TILDEN WY	94501	670-A2
1650	PACIFIC AV	94501	670-A2
1700	BUENA VISTA AV	94501	670-A2
1800	EAGLE AV	94501	670-A2
	CLEMENT AV	94501	670-A2
2000	BLANDING AV	94501	670-A1
PARK ST			**BERK**
2700	WARD ST	94702	629-F3
2800	OREGON ST	94702	629-F4
2900	RUSSELL ST	94702	629-F4
2940	BURNETT ST	94702	629-F4
PARK ST			**OAK**
	23RD AV	94606	670-B1
	29TH AV	94606	670-B1
PARK VIEW TER			**OAK**
200	MONTECITO AV	94610	649-H3
400	GRAND AV	94610	649-H3
PARK WY			**BERK**
700	3RD ST	94710	609-D7
800	4TH ST	94710	609-D7
PARK WY			**OAK**
800	E 8TH ST	94606	649-J5
900	10TH ST	94606	649-J5
PARK WY			**PDMT**
1	ARROYO AV	94611	630-A7
1	MONTECELLO AV	94611	630-A7
50	LORITA AV	94611	650-A1
200	DRACENA AV	94611	630-B7
250	HILLSIDE AV	94611	630-B7
300	BONITA AV	94611	630-B7
350	WALDO AV	94611	630-B7
400	HIGHLAND AV	94611	630-B7
500	MESA AV	94611	630-B7
600	MONTE AV	94611	630-B7
700	PALA AV	94611	630-B7
PARKER AV			**OAK**
2500	BANCROFT AV	94605	670-J3
2600	GARFIELD AV	94605	670-J2
2700	HILLSIDE ST	94605	670-J2
2800	MACARTHUR BLVD	94605	670-J2
2900	NEY AV	94605	670-J2
3000	OUTLOOK AV	94605	670-J2
3060	OUTLOOK AV	94605	670-J2
3100	HILLMONT DR	94605	670-J2
PARKER ST			**BERK**
900	7TH ST	94804	629-E3
940	8TH ST	94804	629-E3
1000	9TH ST	94804	629-E3
1040	10TH ST	94804	629-E3
1100	SAN PABLO AV	94702	629-E3
1200	MATHEWS ST	94702	629-E3
1300	MABEL ST	94702	629-F3
1400	ACTON ST	94702	629-F3
1500	SACRAMENTO ST	94703	629-F3
1600	CALIFORNIA ST	94703	629-F3
1700	MCGEE AV	94703	629-G3
1800	GRANT ST	94703	629-G3
1900	MARTIN LUTHER KING JR WY	94704	629-G3
1990	MILVIA ST	94704	629-G3
2100	SHATTUCK AV	94704	629-H3
2200	FULTON ST	94704	629-H3
2300	ELLSWORTH ST	94704	629-H3
2400	DANA ST	94704	629-H3
2410	CHILTON WY	94704	629-H3
2450	TELEGRAPH AV	94704	629-H3
2500	REGENT ST	94704	629-J3
2600	HILLEGASS AV	94704	629-J3
2630	BENVENUE AV	94704	629-J3
2700	COLLEGE AV	94704	629-J3
1900	WARRING ST	94704	629-J2
2900	WARRING ST	94704	629-J2
2700	COLLEGE AV	94704	629-J3
2730	ETNA ST	94704	629-J3
2800	PIEDMONT AV	94704	629-J2
2900	WARRING ST	94704	629-J2
PARKHURST DR			**OAK**
13000	SADDLE BROOK DR	94619	651-B6
13100	PARKRIDGE DR	94619	651-B6
PARKRIDGE DR			**OAK**
5000	SKYLINE BLVD	94619	651-B6
5050	BROOKPARK RD	94619	651-B6
5070	PARKHURST DR	94619	651-B6
100	SADDLE BROOK DR	94619	651-C6
120	SLOPE CREST DR	94619	651-C6
PARKSIDE DR			**BERK**
1	ENCINA PL	94705	630-A4
100	NOGALES ST	94705	630-A4
160	THE PLAZA DR	94705	630-A4
200	THE PLAZA DR	94705	630-A4
PARKSIDE DR			**PDMT**
100	BRANDON ST	94611	630-A7
PARKVIEW CT			**PDMT**
200	MAGNOLIA AV	94610	650-B1
300	PALM DR	94610	650-B2
400	WINSOR AV	94610	650-B2
E PARNASSUS CT			**BERK**
1	PARNASSUS RD	94708	609-J7
W PARNASSUS CT			**BERK**
1	PARNASSUS RD	94708	609-J7
PARNASSUS RD			**BERK**
1	DEL MAR AV	94708	609-J7
60	E PARNASSUS CT	94708	609-J7
70	W PARNASSUS CT	94708	609-J7
100	CAMPUS DR	94708	609-J7
PARODI CT			**ALA**
1	RATTO RD	94502	669-J6
PARTRIDGE AV			**OAK**
3360	NEY AV	94605	670-J2
3000	OUTLOOK AV	94605	671-A2
3100	HILLMONT DR	94605	671-A2
3150	UTAH ST	94605	671-A2
3200	MICHIGAN DR	94605	671-A2
3400	82ND AV	94605	671-A2
3400	SUNKIST DR	94605	671-A2
PARU ST			**ALA**
700	EMERSON TER	94501	669-H2
800	DAYTON AV	94501	669-H2
900	CLINTON AV	94501	669-H2
1000	SAN JOSE AV	94501	669-H2
1100	SAN ANTONIO AV	94501	669-H2
1200	ENCINAL AV	94501	669-H2
1300	ALAMEDA AV	94501	669-H1
1400	CENTRAL AV	94501	669-H1
1500	SANTA CLARA AV	94501	669-H1
1600	LINCOLN AV	94501	669-H1
1700	PACIFIC AV	94501	669-H1
1800	BUENA VISTA AV	94501	669-H1
PASO ROBLES DR			**OAK**
6700	SARONI DR	94611	630-F7
6800	SOUTHWOOD CT	94611	630-F7
7030	BALBOA DR	94611	630-F7
7050	WOODROW DR	94611	630-F7
7080	PARK BLVD	94611	630-F7
7100	SHEPHERD CANYON RD	94611	630-F7
PATRICIA CT			**OAK**
10400	105TH AV	94603	670-H7
PATTERSON AV			**OAK**
3600	MACARTHUR BLVD	94619	650-F6
3700	KANSAS ST	94619	650-F5
3840	CALIFORNIA ST	94619	650-F5
3890	BAYO ST	94619	650-F5
3980	WISCONSIN ST	94619	650-G5
4100	VIRDEN AV	94619	650-G5
4100	HARBOR VIEW AV	94619	650-G5
PATTIANI WY			**ALA**
2710	AUGHINBAUGH WY	94502	669-J6
2710	ORR RD	94502	669-J6
2730	FOSTER ST	94502	669-J6
2780	STRAUB WY	94502	669-J6
2800	ARMITAGE ST	94502	669-J6
PATTON ST			**OAK**
5800	CHABOT RD	94618	630-A5
	MILES AV	94618	630-A5
	BROADWAY	94618	630-A5
PAXTON AV			**OAK**
3300	34TH AV	94601	650-D6
3400	COOLIDGE AV	94601	650-D6
3500	35TH AV	94601	650-D6
PAYOT CT			**ALA**
100	PAYOT LN	94502	670-B7
PAYOT LN			**ALA**
1	SILVA LN	94502	670-B7
100	PAYOT CT	94502	670-B7
PEABODY LN			**EMVL**
1250	VALLEJO ST	94608	629-E5
1250	VALLEJO ST	94608	629-E5
PEABODY LN			**OAK**
1100	SAN PABLO AV	94608	629-E5
1140	MARSHALL ST	94608	629-E5
1250	VALLEJO ST	94608	629-E5
PEACH ST			**ALA**
900	OTIS DR	94501	670-A4
1000	CALHOUN ST	94501	670-B4
1050	FILLMORE ST	94501	670-B4
1100	WASHINGTON ST	94501	670-B4
1150	ADAMS ST	94501	670-B4
1200	SAN JOSE AV	94501	670-B4
1250	MADISON ST	94501	670-B4
PEACH ST			**OAK**
9390	92ND AV	94603	671-A4
9400	STEARNS AV	94603	671-A4
9600	96TH AV	94603	671-A4
PEARL HARBOR RD			**ALA**
	BARBERS POINT RD	94501	649-D6
100	BARBERS POINT RD	94501	649-D6
	ALAMEDA RD	94501	649-D6
	NORFOLK RD	94501	649-D6
	BARBERS POINT RD	94501	649-D6
PEARL ST			**ALA**
900	EVELYN CT	94501	670-A4
900	OTIS DR	94501	670-A4
950	CLAY ST	94501	670-A3
1000	CALHOUN ST	94501	670-A3
1100	WASHINGTON ST	94501	670-A3
1200	SAN JOSE AV	94501	670-A3
1300	ENCINAL AV	94501	670-A3
1400	CENTRAL AV	94501	670-A3
1500	SANTA CLARA AV	94501	670-A2
1520	JANIS CIR	94501	670-B2
1600	LINCOLN AV	94501	670-B2
1650	EDISON CT	94501	670-B2
1700	BUENA VISTA AV	94501	670-B2
1800	EAGLE AV	94501	670-B2
2000	FERNSIDE BLVD	94501	670-B2
PEARL ST			**OAK**
1	FRISBIE WY	94611	649-J2
100	HARRISON ST	94611	649-J2
150	OAKLAND AV	94611	649-J2
150	OAKLAND AV	94610	649-J2
200	ORANGE ST	94610	649-J2
PEARMAIN ST			**OAK**
9800	98TH AV	94603	670-H6
9900	PRUNE ST	94603	670-H6
10000	100TH AV	94603	670-H6
10100	DOUGLAS AV	94603	670-H6
10200	STONE ST	94603	670-H6
10300	TARTARIAN ST	94603	670-H6
10400	APPLE ST	94603	670-H6
10470	GRAVENSTEIN ST	94603	670-H7
10500	105TH AV	94603	670-H7
10670	106TH AV	94603	670-H7
10700	107TH AV	94603	670-H7
10750	107TH AV	94603	670-H7
10820	BLENHEIM ST	94603	670-H7
10900	MOORPARK ST	94603	670-H7
PEASE AV			**ALA**
1200	ENCINAL AV	94501	670-A3
1200	WAYNE CT	94501	670-A3
PEBBLE BEACH DR			**OAK**
10500	ELYSIAN FIELDS DR	94605	671-D3
10580	FOX HILLS CT	94605	671-E3
PELADEAU ST			**EMVL**
5750	HARUFF ST	94608	629-E6
5800	POWELL ST	94608	629-E6
5900	59TH ST	94608	629-E6
PELHAM PL			**OAK**
2300	WESTOVER DR	94611	650-F1
2400	GIRVIN DR	94611	650-F1
PENDLETON WY			**OAK**
300	EDGEWATER DR	94621	670-E6
500	CAPWELL DR	94621	670-E6
500	LEET DR	94621	670-E6
PENNIMAN AV			**OAK**
3400	HUMBOLDT AV	94602	650-E6
3450	BARTLETT ST	94602	650-E6
3500	35TH AV	94602	650-E6
3500	35TH AV	94619	650-E6
3600	OCTAVIA ST	94619	650-E6
3670	ABBEY ST	94619	650-E6
3730	SHORT ST	94619	650-E6
3800	VIOLA ST	94619	650-E6
3870	38TH AV	94619	650-E6
4010	MINNA AV	94619	650-E6
4100	EASTMAN AV	94619	650-E6
4160	ROGERS CT	94619	650-E6
4180	PENNIMAN CT	94619	650-E7
4300	HIGH ST	94619	650-E7
4400	COURTLAND AV	94619	650-F7
PENNIMAN CT			**OAK**
3000	PENNIMAN AV	94619	650-E6
PENSACOLA			**ALA**
200	PAN AM WY	94501	649-D6
100	CORPUS CHRISTI RD	94501	649-D6
PERALTA AV			**ALB**
900	SOLANO AV	94706	609-F6
1000	MARIN AV	94706	609-F6
1040	SONOMA AV	94706	609-F6
1070	MANOR WY	94706	609-F7
1100	FRANCIS ST	94706	609-E7
1170	POSEN AV	94706	609-E7
PERALTA AV			**BERK**
500	COLUSA AV	94707	609-F5
600	THOUSAND OAKS BLVD	94707	609-F5
650	ENSENADA AV	94707	609-F5
700	PORTLAND AV	94707	609-F5
760	VINCENTE AV	94707	609-F5
800	WASHINGTON AV	94707	609-F6
870	CAPISTRANO AV	94707	609-F6
900	SOLANO AV	94707	609-F6
1170	POSEN AV	94706	609-E7
1300	GILMAN ST	94702	609-E7
1500	HOPKINS ST	94702	609-E7
PERALTA OAKS CT			**OAK**
2900	PERALTA OAKS DR	94605	671-C5
PERALTA OAKS DR			**OAK**
10800	PERALTA OAKS CT	94605	671-B5
10700	BARRETT ST	94605	671-B5
10600	107TH AV	94605	671-B5
10700	106TH AV	94605	671-B5

PRIMARY STREET Address	Cross Street	ZIP	CITY Pg-Grid
PERALTA ST			**EMVL**
3830	MAGNOLIA ST	94608	629-F7
3880	W MACARTHUR BLVD	94608	629-F7
	W MACARTHUR BLVD	94608	629-F7
PERALTA ST			**OAK**
300	3RD ST	94607	649-D4
500	5TH ST	94607	649-D3
800	8TH ST	94607	649-D3
900	9TH ST	94607	649-D3
1000	10TH ST	94607	649-D3
1100	11TH ST	94607	649-D3
1200	12TH ST	94607	649-D3
1300	13TH ST	94607	649-D3
1400	14TH ST	94607	649-D3
1500	15TH ST	94607	649-E3
1610	16TH ST	94607	649-E2
1700	17TH ST	94607	649-E2
1750	CENTER ST	94607	649-E2
1800	18TH ST	94607	649-E2
2000	20TH ST	94607	649-E2
2000	20TH ST	94607	649-E2
2200	MANDELA PKWY	94607	649-E2
2200	W GRAND AV	94607	649-E2
2280	MANDELA PKWY	94607	649-E2
2400	24TH ST	94607	649-E2
2600	26TH ST	94607	649-E1
2700	KIRKHAM ST	94607	649-E1
2800	28TH ST	94608	649-E1
2810	HANNAH ST	94608	649-E1
2930	HELEN ST	94608	649-E1
3000	30TH ST	94608	649-E1
3020	LOUISE ST	94608	649-F1
3160	32ND ST	94608	649-F1
3200	HOLLIS ST	94608	649-F1
3200	32ND ST	94608	649-F1
3400	34TH ST	94608	649-F1
3440	FITZGERALD ST	94608	649-F1
3710	35TH ST	94608	649-F1
3750	WATTS ST	94608	629-F7
3830	MAGNOLIA ST	94608	629-F7
PERKINS RD			**OAK**
2400	LINCOLN AV	94602	650-E3
2500	CAMILLIA PL	94602	650-E3
2500	CHARLESTON ST	94602	650-E3
PERKINS ST			**OAK**
100	ORANGE ST	94610	649-J2
200	VERNON ST	94610	649-J2
250	ADAMS ST	94610	649-J2
280	JAYNE AV	94610	649-J2
300	WARWICK AV	94610	649-J3
360	PALM AV	94610	649-J3
400	VAN BUREN AV	94610	649-J3
420	BELMONT ST	94610	649-J3
460	GRAND AV	94610	649-J3
500	BELLEVUE AV	94610	649-J3
PEROLY CT			**OAK**
100	E 25TH ST	94601	650-C6
PERRY PL			**OAK**
	OAKLAND AV	94610	649-J2
	ORANGE ST	94610	649-J2
	MACARTHUR BLVD	94610	649-J2
PERSHING DR			**OAK**
100	ESTATES DR	94611	650-D1
100	DAWES ST	94611	650-D1
1	MARSH PL	94611	650-D1
100	DAWES ST	94611	650-D1
100	ESTATES DR	94611	650-D1
PERTH PL			**OAK**
1	GRAND VIEW DR	94705	630-B3
1	GRAND VIEW PL	94705	630-B3
PETERSON ST			**OAK**
400	GLASCOCK ST	94601	670-B1
510	FORD ST	94601	670-B1
620	CHAPMAN ST	94601	670-B1
740	E 7TH ST	94601	670-B1
PHAETON DR			**OAK**
7900	HANSOM DR	94605	671-C1
8020	COACH DR	94605	671-C2
8200	HANSOM DR	94605	671-C2
PHELPS ST			**OAK**
400	WORTH ST	94603	670-F6
470	DATE ST	94603	670-F6
500	EDES AV	94603	670-F6
PHOENIX LN			**ALA**
3100	FIR PL	94502	670-A7
3200	ADMIRALITY LN	94502	670-A7
3300	ISLAND DR	94502	670-A7
PICARDY DR			**OAK**
5500	N PICARDY DR	94605	670-G1
5500	S PICARDY DR	94605	670-G1
5800	SEMINARY AV	94605	670-G1
5900	SEMINARY AV	94605	670-G1
6000	60TH AV	94605	670-G1
N PICARDY DR			**OAK**
5500	55TH AV	94605	670-G1
5550	S PICARDY DR	94605	670-G1
5800	PICARDY DR	94605	670-G1
5800	S PICARDY DR	94605	670-G1
S PICARDY DR			**OAK**
5520	N PICARDY DR	94605	670-G1
5830	PICARDY DR	94605	670-G1
5830	N PICARDY DR	94605	670-G1
PIEDMONT AV			**BERK**
	BANCROFT WY	94720	629-J2
	BANCROFT WY	94704	629-J2
	GAYLEY RD	94704	629-J2
	GAYLEY RD	94704	629-J2
2300	BANCROFT WY	94704	629-J2
2320	DURANT AV	94704	629-J2
2400	CHANNING WY	94704	629-J2
2420	HASTE ST	94704	629-J2
2500	DWIGHT WY	94704	629-J2
2500	PIEDMONT CRES	94704	629-J2
2500	DWIGHT WY	94704	629-J2
2600	PARKER ST	94704	629-J3
2700	DERBY ST	94704	629-J3
2700	DERBY ST	94705	629-J3
2720	FOREST AV	94705	629-J3
2740	GARBER ST	94705	629-J3
2800	STUART ST	94705	629-J3
2800	STUART ST	94705	629-J3
2900	RUSSELL ST	94705	629-J3
2900	RUSSELL ST	94705	629-J3
2920	ASHBY AV	94705	629-J3
2950	ELMWOOD AV	94705	629-J4
3000	WEBSTER ST	94705	629-J4
PIEDMONT AV			**OAK**
3300	BROADWAY	94611	649-H1
3370	RANDWICK AV	94611	649-H1
3460	CROXTON AV	94611	649-H1
3590	WESTALL AV	94611	649-H1
3620	WARREN AV	94611	649-H1
3700	W MACARTHUR BLVD	94611	649-J1
3800	YOSEMITE AV	94611	649-J1
3850	RIO VISTA AV	94611	649-J1
3900	MONTELL ST	94611	649-J1
4000	40TH WY	94611	649-J1
4000	MONTE VISTA AV	94611	649-J1
4050	GLEN AV	94611	649-J1
4080	41ST ST	94611	649-J1
4110	41ST ST	94611	649-J1
4160	LINDA AV	94611	649-J1
4200	RIDGEWAY AV	94611	649-J1
4200	ENTRADA AV	94611	629-J7
4230	GLENWOOD AV	94611	629-J7
4280	ECHO AV	94611	629-J7
4300	JOHN ST	94611	629-J7
4490	GLENEDEN AV	94611	629-J7
4300	BRANDON ST	94611	630-A7
4400	PLEASANT VALLEY AV	94611	630-A7
4480	RAMONA AV	94611	630-A7
PIEDMONT CRES			**BERK**
2500	DWIGHT WY	94704	629-J2
2500	PIEDMONT AV	94704	629-J2
2550	WARRING ST	94704	629-J2
PIEDMONT CT			**PDMT**
100	HIGHLAND AV	94611	650-B1
PIER ST			**OAK**
	MARITIME ST	94607	649-C2
PIERCE ST			**ALB**
800	WASHINGTON AV	94706	609-C6
900	SOLANO AV	94706	609-C6
950	JOHNSON ST	94706	609-C6
1000	BUCHANAN ST	94706	609-C6
PIERPOINT AV			**OAK**
5000	JOAQUIN MILLER RD	94602	650-F3
PIERSON ST			**OAK**
3300	MADERA AV	94619	650-G7
3360	MORCOM AV	94619	650-G7
3470	REDDING ST	94619	650-G7
3600	MACARTHUR BLVD	94619	650-G7
PINE AV			**BERK**
2900	RUSSELL ST	94705	630-A3
2920	ASHBY AV	94705	630-A3
3000	WEBSTER ST	94705	630-A3
PINE HILLS CT			**OAK**
1	PINE HILLS DR	94611	630-G7
PINE HILLS DR			**OAK**
1	SKYLINE BLVD	94611	630-G7
40	PINE HILLS LN	94611	630-G7
90	PINE HILLS CT	94611	630-G7
	PINE HILLS LN	94611	630-G7
	SKYLINE BLVD	94611	630-G7
PINE HILLS LN			**OAK**
	PINE HILLS DR	94611	630-G7
	PINE HILLS DR	94611	630-G7
PINE LN			**OAK**
	ALPINE TER	94618	630-B5
	LOCARNO PTH	94618	630-B5
	ACACIA AV	94618	630-B5
PINE ST			**OAK**
590	GOSS ST	94607	649-C3
680	SHOREY ST	94607	649-C3
780	CHASE ST	94607	649-C3
880	9TH ST	94607	649-D3
990	10TH ST	94607	649-D3
1090	11TH ST	94607	649-D2
1200	12TH ST	94607	649-D2
PINE TOP AV			**OAK**
5500	SEMINARY AV	94613	650-H7
5700	POST RD	94613	650-H7
PINECREST DR			**OAK**
5200	HANSOM DR	94605	671-C1
5300	SURREY LN	94605	671-C1
PINEHAVEN RD			**OAK**
6300	THORNHILL DR	94611	630-E6
6300	WOODHAVEN WY	94611	630-E6
6700	HEATHER RIDGE WY	94611	630-E5
6700	VALLEY VIEW RD	94611	630-E5
6900	THE TURN	94611	630-D5
7200	BROADWAY TER	94611	630-D5
PINEHURST RD			**OAK**
	MANZANITA DR	94611	630-G7
	SKYLINE BLVD	94611	630-G7
	SHEPHERD CANYON RD	94611	630-G7
PINENEEDLE DR			**OAK**
6500	BROADWAY TER	94611	630-D5
6530	FARALLON WY	94611	630-E5
6700	BALSAM WY	94611	630-E5
6700	BROADWAY TER	94611	630-E5
PINEWOOD RD			**OAK**
6000	MOUNTAIN BLVD	94611	630-C5
6000	RUTHLAND RD	94611	630-C5
5930	OVAL RD	94611	630-C6
5800	CALDWELL RD	94611	630-C6
5930	BROADWAY TER	94611	630-C6
PIONEER CT			**ALA**
	ROSEFIELD LP	94501	649-G7
PIPER ST			**OAK**
7600	HILLER ST	94621	670-D6
7610	STINSON ST	94621	670-D6
PIPPIN ST			**OAK**
9800	98TH AV	94603	670-H6
9900	PRUNE ST	94603	670-H6
10000	100TH AV	94603	670-H6
10200	STONE ST	94603	670-H6
10400	APPLE ST	94603	670-H6
10500	GRAVENSTEIN ST	94603	670-H7
10700	107TH AV	94603	670-H7
10900	MOORPARK ST	94603	670-H7
PLEASANT ST			**OAK**
2500	WOODBINE AV	94602	650-D5
2600	FRUITVALE AV	94602	650-D5
2700	CHAMPION ST	94602	650-D5
2800	BOSTON AV	94602	650-D5
PLEASANT VALLEY AV			**OAK**
1700	MORAGA AV	94611	630-A7
1700	GRAND AV	94611	630-A7
1800	PIEDMONT AV	94611	630-A7
1800	HOWE ST	94611	629-J7
1850	MONTGOMERY ST	94611	629-J7
2000	GILBERT ST	94611	629-J7
2100	51ST ST	94611	629-J7
2100	BROADWAY	94611	629-J7
N PLEASANT VALLEY CT			**OAK**
4600	S PLEASANT VALLEY CT	94611	630-A7
S PLEASANT VALLEY CT			**OAK**
4400	N PLEASANT VALLEY CT	94611	630-A7
PLEITNER AV			**OAK**
3000	NICOL AV	94602	650-D5
3050	WARD LN	94602	650-D5
	SCHOOL ST	94602	650-D5
3200	SCHOOL ST	94602	650-D5
3250	TEXAS ST	94602	650-D5
3300	SUTER ST	94602	650-D5
PLOVER CT			**ALA**
	BRUZZONE DR	94501	649-F7
	WHIMBREL CT	94501	649-F7
PLYMOUTH ST			**OAK**
7800	78TH AV	94621	670-H3
7900	79TH AV	94621	670-H3
7900	79TH AV	94621	670-H3
8000	80TH AV	94621	670-H3
8100	81ST AV	94621	670-H3
8200	82ND AV	94621	670-H3
8300	83RD AV	94621	670-H4
8400	84TH AV	94621	670-H4
8500	85TH AV	94621	670-H4
8600	86TH AV	94621	670-H4
8640	AUSEON AV	94621	670-H4
8700	87TH AV	94621	670-J4
8800	88TH AV	94621	670-J4
8900	89TH AV	94621	670-J4
9000	90TH AV	94621	670-J4
9000	90TH AV	94603	670-J4
9200	92ND AV	94603	670-J4
9400	94TH AV	94603	670-J5
9600	96TH AV	94603	670-J5
9800	98TH AV	94603	670-J5
9900	99TH AV	94603	670-J5
10000	100TH AV	94603	670-J5
10100	101ST AV	94603	670-J5
10200	102ND AV	94603	670-J6
10300	103RD AV	94603	670-J6
10400	104TH AV	94603	670-J6
POE ST			**BERK**
1300	BONAR ST	94702	629-E2
POGGI ST			**ALA**
400	ATLANTIC AV	94501	649-E7
460	BUENA VISTA AV	94501	649-E7
POIRIER ST			**OAK**
600	SHATTUCK AV	94609	629-G5
700	DOVER ST	94609	629-G5
POLK ST			**ALB**
800	WASHINGTON AV	94706	609-D6
860	SOLANO AV	94706	609-D6
1000	BUCHANAN ST	94706	609-D6
POMONA AV			**ALB**
1	THOUSAND OAKS BLVD	94706	609-E5
700	PORTLAND AV	94706	609-E5
770	WASHINGTON AV	94706	609-E5
780	WASHINGTON AV	94706	609-E6
860	SOLANO AV	94706	609-E6
860	SOLANO AV	94706	609-E6
1000	MARIN AV	94706	609-E6
1150	DARTMOUTH ST	94706	609-E7
1200	SANTA FE AV	94706	609-E7
POND ISL			**ALA**
600	OTIS DR	94501	669-H3
PONTIAC ST			**OAK**
10400	104TH AV	94603	670-J6
10500	105TH AV	94603	670-J6
10600	106TH AV	94603	670-J6
10700	107TH AV	94603	670-J6
POPLAR ST			**BERK**
1	CRAGMONT AV	94708	609-H5
50	ROCK LN	94708	609-H5
100	EUCLID AV	94708	609-H5
100	EUCLID AV	94708	609-H5
200	HILLDALE AV	94708	609-H5
POPLAR ST			**OAK**
1000	10TH ST	94607	649-E3
1190	12TH ST	94607	649-E3
1200	12TH ST	94607	649-E3
1200	UNION ST	94607	649-E3
1410	14TH ST	94607	649-E3
1600	16TH ST	94607	649-E3
1800	18TH ST	94607	649-E2
2030	20TH ST	94607	649-E2
2100	21ST ST	94607	649-E2
2200	W GRAND AV	94607	649-E2
2400	24TH ST	94607	649-E2
2600	26TH ST	94607	649-E1
2800	28TH ST	94608	649-E1
3000	30TH ST	94608	649-E1
3000	LOUISE ST	94608	649-E1
POPLAR WY			**PDMT**
	MOUNTAIN AV	94611	650-C1
	LAKEVIEW AV	94611	650-C1
POPPY LN			**BERK**
1	HILLDALE AV	94708	609-H5
10	MILLER AV	94708	609-H5
100	KEELER AV	94708	609-H5
PORTA BALLENA			**ALA**
1200	COLA BALLENA	94501	669-E2
PORTAL AV			**OAK**
800	CLARENDON CRES	94610	650-B3
800	MANDANA BLVD	94610	650-B3
900	ASHMOUNT AV	94610	650-B2
1200	FLORADA AV	94610	650-B2
1200	WAWONA AV	94610	650-B2
PORTER ST			**OAK**
4170	MAYBELLE WY	94619	650-F6
4230	VALE AV	94619	650-F6
4300	HIGH ST	94619	650-F6
PORTLAND AV			**ALB**
1100	SAN PABLO AV	94706	609-D5
1120	KAINS AV	94706	609-D5
1150	STANNAGE AV	94706	609-D5
1200	CORNELL AV	94706	609-D5
1220	TALBOT AV	94706	609-D5
1240	EVELYN AV	94706	609-E5
1250	MASONIC AV	94706	609-E5
1260	SAN GABRIEL AV	94706	609-E5
1270	SPOKANE AV	94706	609-E5
1300	KEY ROUTE BLVD	94706	609-E5
1310	POMONA AV	94706	609-E5
1330	RAMONA AV	94706	609-E5
1400	CARMEL AV	94706	609-E5
1420	SAN CARLOS AV	94706	609-E5
1450	SANTA FE AV	94706	609-E5
1470	CURTIS ST	94706	609-E5
PORTLAND AV			**BERK**
1470	CURTIS ST	94707	609-E5
1440	NEILSON ST	94707	609-F5
1500	PERALTA AV	94707	609-F5
1700	ENSENADA AV	94707	609-F5
1800	COLUSA AV	94707	609-F5
1800	VINCENTE AV	94707	609-F5
PORTLAND AV			**OAK**
300	PARK BLVD	94606	650-A4
400	ATHOL AV	94606	650-A4
PORTOLA AV			**ALA**
800	8TH ST	94501	669-G2
850	BURBANK ST	94501	669-G2
PORTSMOUTH RD			**PDMT**
1	ANNERLEY RD	94610	650-B2
100	HARVARD RD	94610	650-B2
150	RANLEIGH WY	94610	650-B2
200	WILDWOOD AV	94610	650-B2
PORTWOOD AV			**OAK**
900	E 9TH ST	94601	670-B1
1000	E 10TH ST	94601	670-B1
POSEN AV			**ALB**
1400	PERALTA AV	94706	609-E7
1500	ORDWAY ST	94706	609-F7
1520	VENTURA AV	94706	609-F7
1550	WEST PL	94706	609-F7
POSEN AV			**BERK**
1590	MONTEREY AV	94707	609-F7
1550	WEST PL	94706	609-F7
1590	MONTEREY AV	94707	609-F7
1640	CARLOTTA AV	94707	609-F7
1700	COLUSA AV	94707	609-F7
POST OFFICE CT			**ALA**
2400	PARK ST	94501	670-A2
2500	PARK AV	94501	670-A2
POST RD			**OAK**
5400	KAPIOLANI RD	94613	650-H7
5450	PINE TOP AV	94613	650-H7
5510	WETMORE RD	94613	650-H7
POST ST			**ALA**
900	OTIS DR	94501	670-A4
970	TOYON TER	94501	670-A4
1000	CALHOUN ST	94501	670-B4
1100	WASHINGTON ST	94501	670-B4
1150	ADAMS ST	94501	670-B4
1200	SAN JOSE AV	94501	670-B4
1250	MADISON ST	94501	670-B4
1300	ENCINAL AV	94501	670-B4
POTOMAC ST			**OAK**
2400	LINCOLN AV	94602	650-E4
2600	LAGUNA AV	94602	650-E4
POTTER ST			**BERK**
600	BOLIVAR DR	94804	629-D4
800	5TH ST	94804	629-E4
900	7TH ST	94804	629-E4
1000	9TH ST	94804	629-E4
POTTER ST			**OAK**
2400	GORDON ST	94601	650-E7
2500	GORDON ST	94601	650-E7
2500	FAIRFAX AV	94601	670-E1
POWELL ST			**ALA**
2200	LAUREL ST	94501	669-J3
2250	OAK ST	94501	669-J3
POWELL ST			**EMVL**
1210	VALLEJO ST	94608	629-E6
1270	BEAUDRY ST	94608	629-E6
1330	DOYLE ST	94608	629-E6
1400	HOLLIS ST	94608	629-E6
1450	PELADEAU ST	94608	629-E6
1500	LANDREGAN ST	94608	629-E6
1600	SHELLMOUND ST	94608	629-E6
1700	CHRISTIE AV	94608	629-D6
2200	CAPTAIN DR	94608	629-D6
2300	COMMODORE DR	94608	629-C6
2400	ADMIRAL DR	94608	629-C6
2490	ANCHOR DR	94608	629-B6
POWELL ST			**OAK**
1100	MARSHALL ST	94608	629-F6
1100	STANFORD AV	94608	629-F6
1160	FREMONT ST	94608	629-E6
1210	VALLEJO ST	94608	629-E6
POWERS CT			**ALA**
1	LINCOLN AV	94501	669-H1
PRENTISS PL			**OAK**
3270	PRENTISS ST	94601	650-C6
3300	DAVIS ST	94601	650-C6
PRENTISS ST			**OAK**
3200	COOLIDGE AV	94601	650-D6
3270	PRENTISS PL	94601	650-D6
PRESLEY WY			**OAK**
5700	CHABOT RD	94618	630-A5
5830	MILES AV	94618	630-A5
5900	KEITH AV	94618	630-A5
PRINCE ST			**BERK**
1400	ACTON ST	94702	629-F4
1440	DOHR ST	94702	629-F4
1470	STANTON ST	94702	629-F4
1500	SACRAMENTO ST	94703	629-F4
1600	CALIFORNIA ST	94703	629-G4
1700	KING ST	94703	629-G4
1800	ELLIS ST	94703	629-G4
1820	HARPER ST	94703	629-G4
1900	MARTIN LUTHER KING JR WY	94703	629-G4
2000	TREMONT ST	94703	629-G4
2100	SHATTUCK AV	94705	629-H4
2200	WHEELER ST	94705	629-H4
2220	FULTON ST	94705	629-H4
2300	DEAKIN ST	94705	629-H4
2320	HALCYON CT	94705	629-H4
2400	TELEGRAPH AV	94705	629-H4
2400	TELEGRAPH AV	94705	629-H4
2430	DANA ST	94705	629-H4
2400	DANA ST	94705	629-J4
2500	REGENT ST	94705	629-J4
2600	BATEMAN ST	94705	629-J4
2700	COLLEGE AV	94705	629-J4
2900	CLAREMONT AV	94705	629-J4
PRINCE ST			**OAK**
400	VERMONT ST	94610	650-A2
	WARFIELD AV	94610	650-A2
500	WARFIELD AV	94610	650-A2
530	YORK ST	94610	650-A2
560	ERIE ST	94610	650-A3
560	ERIE ST	94610	650-A3
600	LAKESHORE AV	94610	650-A3
600	SANTA RAY AV	94610	650-A3
PRINCETON ST			**OAK**
5480	55TH AV	94601	670-F1
5400	COLE ST	94601	670-F1
5300	FAIRFAX AV	94601	670-E1
5400	54TH AV	94601	670-E1
PROCTOR AV			**OAK**
4700	BROADWAY TER	94618	630-C6
4720	FLORENCE AV	94618	630-C6
4800	ALTA RD	94618	630-C6
4870	AGNES ST	94618	630-C6
4900	AGNES ST	94618	630-C6
5060	JULIA ST	94618	630-C6
5200	FLORENCE AV	94618	630-C6
5200	ESTATES DR	94618	630-C6
5200	FLORENCE AV	94618	630-C6
5300	SAINT PAUL CT	94618	630-C6
5400	AMY DR	94618	630-C6
5500	HERON DR	94618	630-C7
5600	MASONIC PL	94618	630-C7
PROSPECT AV			**OAK**
610	HILLGIRT CIR	94610	650-A3
610	HILLGIRT CIR	94606	650-A3
610	MERRITT AV	94606	650-A3
610	WESLEY AV	94606	650-A3
650	RADNOR RD	94610	650-A3
650	RADNOR RD	94606	650-A3
670	HADDON RD	94610	650-A3
670	HADDON RD	94606	650-A3
700	KENWYN RD	94610	650-A4
700	KENWYN RD	94606	650-A4
740	ATHOL AV	94610	650-A4
740	ATHOL AV	94606	650-A4
780	MONTCLAIR AV	94610	650-A4
780	MONTCLAIR AV	94606	650-A4
800	MONTCLAIR AV	94610	650-A4
800	MONTCLAIR AV	94606	650-A4
850	SPRUCE ST	94610	650-A4
900	CAPELL ST	94610	650-A4
1000	ALMA AV	94610	650-A4
PROSPECT HILL RD			**OAK**
	KAPIOLANI RD	94613	670-G1
	FACULTY RD	94613	670-G1
5500	SUNNYSIDE RD	94613	670-G1
5530	WETMORE RD	94613	670-G1
PROSPECT RD			**PDMT**
1	WILDWOOD AV	94610	650-B2
50	OAKMONT AV	94610	650-B2
100	HARVARD RD	94610	650-B2
PROSPECT ST			**BERK**
2200	PANORAMIC WY	94704	629-J2
2200	STADIUM RIMWAY	94704	629-J2
2330	CHANNING WY	94704	629-J2

© 2006 Rand McNally & Company

PRIMARY STREET Address	Cross Street	ZIP	CITY Pg-Grid
PROSPECT ST			**BERK**
2380	HILLSIDE AV	94704	629-J2
2500	DWIGHT WY	94704	629-J2
PROSPECT STEPS			**OAK**
6000	MANCHESTER DR	94618	630-A5
6000	WEST LN	94618	630-A5
	MARGARIDO DR	94618	630-A5
	ROCKRIDGE BLVD S	94618	630-A5
PRUNE ST			**OAK**
800	PEARMAIN ST	94603	670-H6
850	PIPPIN ST	94603	670-H6
900	RUSSET ST	94603	670-H6
PUDDINGSTONE RD			**ALA**
200	SHEFFIELD RD	94502	670-A5
270	ROBERT DAVEY JR DR	94502	670-A5
300	SABLE POINTE	94502	670-A5
PUEBLO DR			**OAK**
10800	BERGEDO DR	94603	690-H1
PURCELL DR			**ALA**
1	PALM BEACH LN	94502	670-A5
80	SUNNY COVE CIR	94502	670-A5
90	BRITTANY DR	94502	670-A5
100	SUNNY COVE CIR	94502	670-A5
PYNE LN			**ALA**
1300	SILVA LN	94502	670-A7
1400	BOWMAN CT	94502	670-A7
PYRO			**ALA**
3000	MULVANY CIR	94501	649-E6
3100	MULVANY CIR	94501	649-E6
Q			
QUAIL AV			**BERK**
1	NORTHGATE AV	94708	609-J6
50	CAMPUS DR	94708	609-J6
100	QUEENS RD	94708	609-J6
QUARRY RD			**BERK**
1	LA LOMA AV	94708	609-J7
QUEENS RD			**ALA**
500	CROWN DR	94501	669-F1
600	KINGS RD	94501	669-F1
QUEENS RD			**BERK**
1200	SHASTA RD	94708	609-J6
1200	STERLING AV	94708	609-J6
1270	QUAIL AV	94708	609-J7
1370	FAIRLAWN DR	94708	609-J7
1500	AVENIDA DR	94708	609-J7
QUIETWOOD			**OAK**
	THOUSAND OAKS	94605	671-D2
	SHADOW MOUNTAIN	94605	671-D2
QUIGLEY LN			**OAK**
3400	MIDVALE AV	94602	650-E5
3400	DAKOTA ST	94602	650-E5
3500	35TH AV	94602	650-E5
QUIGLEY PL			**OAK**
4200	HIGH ST	94619	650-F6
QUIGLEY ST			**OAK**
3400	35TH AV	94619	650-E6
3640	LOMA VISTA AV	94619	650-F6
3860	38TH AV	94619	650-F6
3940	39TH AV	94619	650-F6
R			
RACINE ST			**OAK**
5800	58TH ST	94609	629-H5
5800	TELEGRAPH AV	94609	629-H5
5900	59TH ST	94609	629-H5
6000	60TH ST	94609	629-H5
6050	61ST ST	94609	629-H5
6100	61ST ST	94609	629-H5
6150	62ND ST	94609	629-H5
6200	62ND ST	94609	629-H5
6230	63RD ST	94609	629-H5
6300	63RD ST	94609	629-H5
6340	NORTH ST	94609	629-H4
6400	ALCATRAZ AV	94609	629-H4
RADNOR RD			**OAK**
500	PROSPECT AV	94606	650-A4
600	CLEVELAND ST	94606	650-A4
RAILROAD AV			**OAK**
	85TH AV	94621	670-G5
	85TH AV	94603	670-G5
9300	LOUISIANA ST	94603	670-G6
9400	CLARA ST	94603	670-G6
9500	S ELMHURST AV	94603	670-G6
9600	TYLER ST	94603	670-G6
9700	NEVADA ST	94603	670-G6
9800	98TH AV	94603	670-G6
RAINBOW CT			**ALA**
	SUNRISE CT	94501	649-D6
	STARDUST PL	94501	649-D6
150	STARDUST PL	94501	649-D6
100	W MIDWAY AV	94501	649-D6
RAMONA AV			**ALB**
1	THOUSAND OAKS BLVD	94706	609-E5
700	PORTLAND AV	94706	609-E5
770	WASHINGTON AV	94706	609-E6
860	SOLANO AV	94706	609-E6
860	SOLANO AV	94706	609-E6
980	MARIN AV	94706	609-E6
1100	SANTA FE AV	94706	609-E6
RAMONA AV			**OAK**
1	MORAGA AV	94611	630-A7
100	PIEDMONT AV	94611	630-A7
RAMONA AV			**PDMT**
300	BONITA AV	94611	630-B7
200	ESTRELLA AV	94611	630-A7
120	MONTECELLO AV	94611	630-A7
	RONADA AV	94611	630-A7
100	RONADA AV	94611	630-A7
120	MORAGA AV	94611	630-A7
RAMPART ST			**OAK**
2400	LINCOLN AV	94602	650-E4
2600	LAGUNA AV	94602	650-E4
RAND AV			**OAK**
600	LAKE PARK AV	94610	650-A3
600	LAKESHORE AV	94610	650-A3
650	CHENEY AV	94610	650-A3
700	WICKSON AV	94610	650-A3
750	GLENVIEW AV	94610	650-A3
800	MANDANA BLVD	94610	650-A3
RANDOLPH AV			**OAK**
3200	E 32ND ST	94602	650-C4
3400	E 33RD ST	94602	650-C4
3500	MACARTHUR BLVD	94602	650-C4
3600	EXCELSIOR AV	94602	650-C4
3800	E 38TH ST	94602	650-C4
3800	E 38TH ST	94602	650-C4
4100	HAMPEL ST	94602	650-C4
4100	HAMPEL ST	94602	650-C4
4200	BENTON ST	94602	650-C4
RANDWICK AV			**OAK**
1	PIEDMONT AV	94611	649-H2
100	RICHMOND BLVD	94611	649-H2
W RANGER AV			**ALA**
	LEXINGTON ST	94501	649-C6
	SARATOGA ST	94501	649-D6
	PAN AM WY	94501	649-D6
RANGER CT			**ALA**
	BARTLETT DR	94501	649-G7
RANLEIGH WY			**PDMT**
1000	HARVARD RD	94610	650-B2
1200	PORTSMOUTH RD	94610	650-B2
RANSOM AV			**OAK**
2100	CARRINGTON ST	94601	650-D7
2110	CARRINGTON WY	94601	650-D7
2330	SANTA RITA ST	94601	650-D7
2500	LYON AV	94601	650-D7
RATTO RD			**ALA**
1	BAY EDGE RD	94502	669-J6
1	AUGHINBAUGH WY	94502	669-J6
10	PARODI CT	94502	669-J6
20	LAGORIA CT	94502	669-J6
30	LAVAGETTO CT	94502	669-J6
40	COTELLA CT	94502	669-J6
50	FERRO CT	94502	669-J7
60	MIRANDA CT	94502	669-J7
80	DUARTE CT	94502	669-J7
90	SOUZA CT	94502	669-J7
RAVENS COVE LN			**ALA**
3200	BAYVIEW DR	94501	670-A4
3250	NANTUCKET WY	94501	670-A4
RAVENWOOD LN			**OAK**
2300	WHITTLE AV	94602	650-E3
2300	TIFFIN RD	94602	650-E3
2350	WHITTLE AV	94602	650-E3
2400	LINCOLN AV	94602	650-E4
RAWSON ST			**OAK**
2400	TRASK ST	94601	670-F1
2600	BROOKDALE AV	94601	670-F1
2600	BROOKDALE AV	94619	670-F1
2600	KINGSLAND AV	94619	650-F7
2800	KINGSLAND AV	94619	650-F7
2800	BIRDSALL AV	94619	650-F7
3200	FLEMING AV	94619	650-F7
RAYMOND ST			**OAK**
6400	ALCATRAZ AV	94609	629-H4
6600	66TH ST	94609	629-H4
REATA PL			**OAK**
1	CHABOT RD	94618	630-A4
W RED LINE AV			**ALA**
	MONARCH ST	94501	649-C6
	PANORAMIC DR	94501	649-C6
	NAVY WY	94501	649-C6
	LEXINGTON ST	94501	649-C6
	NAVY WY	94501	649-D6
	SARATOGA ST	94501	649-D6
	TODD ST	94501	649-D6
	BARBERS POINT RD	94501	649-D6
	PAN AM WY	94501	649-D6
RED ROCK RD			**PDMT**
800	SPRING PTH	94611	630-C7
800	SPRING PTH	94618	630-C7
REDDING PL			**OAK**
100	REDDING ST	94619	650-F7
REDDING ST			**OAK**
3500	35TH AV	94619	650-F5
3680	LOMA VISTA AV	94619	650-F6
3860	38TH AV	94619	650-F6
3910	39TH AV	94619	650-F6
4120	MAYBELLE AV	94619	650-F6
4660	PIERSON ST	94619	650-G7
4560	KINGSLAND AV	94619	650-F7
4480	REDDING PL	94619	650-F7
4420	BIRDSALL AV	94619	650-F6
4380	STORER AV	94619	650-F6
4300	COURTLAND AV	94619	650-F6
4380	HIGH ST	94619	650-F6
REDHOOK LN			**ALA**
3400	HOLLY ST	94502	670-A7
3500	JOST LN	94502	670-A7
REDONDO AV			**OAK**
5200	CLARKE ST	94618	629-H6
5300	CAVOUR ST	94618	629-H6
REDONDO CT			**ALA**
1	INDEPENDENCE DR	94501	649-G7
REDWOOD RD			**OAK**
3840	MOUNTAIN BLVD	94619	650-G5
4050	MOUNTAIN BLVD	94619	650-H5
4100	MOUNTAIN BLVD	94619	650-H5
4450	TERRABELLA WY	94619	650-H5
4900	CAMPUS DR	94619	650-H5
4900	SERENO CIR	94619	650-H5
5100	KINGWOOD RD	94619	650-H5
5200	CRESTMONT DR	94619	650-H5
5250	VIA RIALTO	94619	650-H5
5260	OLD REDWOOD RD	94619	650-J5
5430	OLD REDWOOD RD	94619	650-J5
5500	OLD REDWOOD RD	94619	650-J5
5550	OLD REDWOOD RD	94619	650-J5
5600	SKYLINE BLVD	94619	650-J5
REGAL RD			**BERK**
800	SPRUCE ST	94708	609-H5
830	CRAGMONT AV	94708	609-H5
900	MARIN AV	94708	609-H5
930	EUCLID AV	94708	609-H5
950	HILLDALE AV	94708	609-H6
960	EASTER WY	94708	609-H6
1000	CRAGMONT AV	94708	609-H6
REGENT ST			**ALA**
850	ROOSEVELT DR	94501	669-J3
900	OTIS DR	94501	669-J3
1000	CLAY ST	94501	670-A3
1100	CALHOUN ST	94501	670-A3
1200	SAN JOSE AV	94501	670-A3
1300	ENCINAL AV	94501	670-A3
1320	CHESTER ST	94501	670-A3
1360	CRIST ST	94501	670-A2
1400	CENTRAL AV	94501	670-A2
REGENT ST			**BERK**
2500	DWIGHT WY	94704	629-J2
2600	PARKER ST	94704	629-J3
2700	DERBY ST	94704	629-J3
2800	STUART ST	94705	629-J3
2850	OREGON ST	94705	629-J3
2900	RUSSELL ST	94705	629-J3
3000	ASHBY AV	94705	629-J4
3080	PRINCE ST	94705	629-J4
3100	WOOLSEY ST	94705	629-J4
REGENT ST			**OAK**
6400	ALCATRAZ AV	94618	629-J4
6500	WOOLSEY ST	94618	629-J4
REGULUS CT			**ALA**
1	INDEPENDENCE DR	94501	649-G7
REINHARDT DR			**OAK**
3900	39TH AV	94619	650-G5
3980	ANDERSON AV	94619	650-G5
3990	ANDERSON AV	94619	650-G5
4050	GREGORY ST	94619	650-G5
4350	GREGORY ST	94619	650-G6
4400	CARSON ST	94619	650-G6
4600	KAPHAN AV	94619	650-H6
4780	CUNNINGHAM ST	94619	650-H6
4880	DAISY ST	94619	650-H7
REMMEL CT			**ALA**
1	MARCUSE ST	94502	669-J6
RENWICK ST			**OAK**
2400	FAIRFAX AV	94601	650-E7
2570	GORDON ST	94601	650-E7
2640	BROOKDALE AV	94619	650-F7
2720	WALNUT ST	94619	650-F7
2800	ALLENDALE AV	94619	650-F7
REPOSO DR			**OAK**
10900	BERGEDO DR	94603	670-H7
11000	CATRON DR	94603	670-H7
REQUA PL			**PDMT**
1	HAZEL LN	94611	650-B1
1	REQUA RD	94611	650-B1
REQUA RD			**PDMT**
100	WILDWOOD AV	94611	650-B2
200	HAZEL LN	94611	650-B2
200	REQUA PL	94611	650-B2
RETTIG AV			**OAK**
4000	WISCONSIN ST	94602	650-F5
4050	RETTIG PL	94602	650-F4
4320	JORDAN RD	94602	650-F4
4400	GUIDO ST	94602	650-F4
RETTIG PL			**OAK**
4000	WISCONSIN ST	94602	650-F5
4200	RETTIG AV	94602	650-F5
REVERE AV			**OAK**
3000	FOOTHILL BLVD	94605	671-C6
3050	FOOTHILL WY	94605	671-C6
3150	DANBURY ST	94605	671-C6
3190	COVINGTON ST	94605	671-C6
3240	MARLOW DR	94605	671-D7
3580	CRANFORD WY	94605	671-D7
RHODA AV			**OAK**
3400	COOLIDGE AV	94602	650-E5
3500	MACARTHUR BLVD	94602	650-E5
3500	MACARTHUR BLVD	94602	650-E4
3740	MADELINE ST	94602	650-E4
3890	CARMEL ST	94602	650-E4
4200	ALIDA ST	94602	650-E4
RICARDO AV			**PDMT**
170	ARROYO AV	94611	650-A1
200	ARTUNA AV	94611	650-A1
200	HOLLY PL	94611	650-A1
220	EL CERRITO AV	94611	650-A1
280	CAMBRIDGE WY	94611	650-A1
300	BLAIR AV	94611	650-A1
RICH ST			**OAK**
400	WEBSTER ST	94609	629-H7
500	42ND ST	94609	629-H7
RICHARDS RD			**OAK**
4900	MACARTHUR BLVD	94613	650-G7
5000	UNDERWOOD AV	94613	650-G7
5460	ORCHARD MEADOW DR	94613	650-G7
5580	KAPIOLANI RD	94613	650-H7
5800	WETMORE RD	94613	650-H7
RICHARDSON WY			**PDMT**
1	CAPERTON AV	94611	650-C1
100	LAKEVIEW AV	94611	650-C1
RICHMOND AV			**OAK**
2800	29TH ST	94611	649-H2
RICHMOND BLVD			**OAK**
3000	30TH ST	94611	649-H2
	FRISBIE ST	94611	649-H2
3360	RANDWICK AV	94611	649-H1
3420	CROXTON AV	94611	649-H1
3600	WESTALL AV	94611	649-H1
3630	WARREN AV	94611	649-J1
3700	W MACARTHUR BLVD	94611	649-J1
RICHMOND RD			**OAK**
	CRESTVIEW DR	94619	651-B7
	MARGIE LN	94605	651-B7
RIDDELL LN			**ALA**
200	OAK PARK DR	94502	670-A5
300	PARFAIT LN	94502	670-A5
RIDGE RD			**BERK**
2400	LE CONTE AV	94709	629-H1
2400	SCENIC AV	94709	629-H1
2500	EUCLID AV	94709	629-H1
2600	LE ROY AV	94709	629-J1
2700	LA LOMA AV	94709	629-J1
2800	HIGHLAND PL	94709	629-J1
RIDGEMONT CT			**OAK**
4200	RIDGEMONT DR	94619	650-J7
RIDGEMONT DR			**OAK**
6140	VIEWCREST DR	94619	650-J7
6100	RIDGEMONT CT	94619	650-J6
6000	HIGH KNOLL DR	94619	650-J6
RIDGEMOOR RD			**OAK**
8900	SEQUOYAH RD	94605	671-D2
RIDGEWAY AV			**OAK**
100	PIEDMONT AV	94611	649-J1
150	HOWE ST	94611	629-J7
200	MONTGOMERY ST	94611	629-J7
250	GILBERT ST	94611	629-J7
270	TERRACE ST	94611	629-J7
300	BROADWAY	94611	629-J7
RIDGEWOOD DR			**OAK**
6800	HOMEWOOD DR	94611	630-F7
6840	RIDGEWOOD LN	94611	630-F6
6900	CHAMBERS DR	94611	630-F6
7000	ARROWHEAD DR	94611	630-F6
7000	COLTON BLVD	94611	630-F6
RIDGEWOOD LN			**OAK**
	RIDGEWOOD DR	94611	630-F6
RIDGEWOOD WY			**OAK**
1	CHAMBERS DR	94611	630-F6
100	CHAMBERS LN	94611	630-F6
200	COLTON BLVD	94611	630-F6
RIFLE LN			**OAK**
4100	MOUNTAIN BLVD	94605	671-A1
4200	ALTURA PL	94605	671-A1
RIFLE RANGE RD			**OAK**
	MARGIE LN	94605	671-B1
RILEA WY			**OAK**
4300	GREENRIDGE DR	94605	671-B1
4350	KELLER AV	94605	671-B1
RILEY DR			**ALB**
700	9TH ST	94710	609-D7
740	GOODING DR	94706	609-D6
880	GOODING DR	94706	609-D6
1000	8TH ST	94706	609-D6
1000	JACKSON ST	94706	609-D6
RINCON DR			**OAK**
5900	MAGELLAN DR	94611	650-E1
5900	DRAKE DR	94611	650-E1
6000	ZINN DR	94611	650-E1
RIO VISTA AV			**OAK**
1	FAIRMOUNT AV	94611	649-J1
100	PIEDMONT AV	94611	649-J1
RISHELL DR			**OAK**
1	CRESTMONT DR	94619	650-H4
200	KIMBERLIN HEIGHTS DR	94619	650-J5
380	CHADBOURNE WY	94619	650-J5
RISING HILL CT			**OAK**
4600	CAMPUS DR	94605	651-A7
RISPIN DR			**OAK**
1000	CLAREMONT AV	94705	630-B3
RITCHIE ST			**OAK**
2850	OLIVE ST	94605	670-J3
2830	BANCROFT AV	94605	670-J3
2500	BANCROFT AV	94605	670-J3
2700	HILLSIDE ST	94605	670-J2
2400	MACARTHUR BLVD	94605	670-J2
2480	NEY AV	94605	670-J2
RIVIERA CT			**OAK**
100	ELYSIAN FIELDS DR	94605	671-D3
ROAD A			**ALA**
	HARBOR BAY PKWY	94502	690-A1
ROAD B			**ALA**
	HARBOR BAY PKWY	94502	670-B7
	SOUTH LOOP RD	94502	670-B7
ROANOKE			**ALA**
4000	CIMARRON ST	94501	649-E6
4000	SACRAMENTO	94501	649-E6
4100	NIMITZ	94501	649-E6
ROANOKE RD			**BERK**
1	THE UPLANDS	94705	630-A4
10	HILLCREST RD	94705	630-A4
60	MANOR CREST	94705	630-A4
ROANOKE RD			**OAK**
60	MANOR CREST	94618	630-A4
100	CHABOT RD	94618	630-A4
ROBERT DAVEY JR DR			**ALA**
	AUGHINBAUGH WY	94502	669-J5
	CHANNING WY	94502	669-J5
2900	OYSTER POND RD	94502	670-A5
3000	PUDDINGSTONE RD	94502	670-A5
3300	PACKET LNDG	94502	670-A5
3400	ISLAND DR	94502	670-A5
ROBERTS AV			**OAK**
5400	55TH AV	94619	670-G1
5500	BIRDSALL AV	94619	670-G1
5500	55TH AV	94605	670-G1
5600	56TH AV	94605	670-G1
5700	57TH AV	94605	670-G1
5800	58TH AV	94605	670-G1
5840	MILLSBRAE AV	94605	670-G1
5900	SEMINARY AV	94605	670-G1
ROBINHOOD WY			**OAK**
6200	MERRIEWOOD DR	94611	630-D6
ROBINSON DR			**OAK**
3100	JOAQUIN MILLER RD	94602	650-H3
3470	BUTTERS DR	94602	650-H4
3530	RUBIN DR	94602	650-H4
3600	BRUNELL DR	94602	650-H4
ROBISON DR			**OAK**
3100	ALVARADO RD	94705	630-B3
ROBLE CT			**BERK**
100	ROBLE RD	94705	630-B4
ROBLE RD			**BERK**
1	TUNNEL RD	94705	630-B4
40	ROBLE CT	94705	630-B4
ROBLE RD			**OAK**
200	CHABOT RD	94618	630-B4
ROBLEDO DR			**OAK**
10900	BERGEDO DR	94603	670-H7
10900	EDES AV	94603	670-H7
11200	CATRON DR	94603	670-H7
ROBLEY TER			**OAK**
1	MONTE VISTA AV	94611	649-J1
30	MONTELL ST	94611	649-J1
ROCHDALE WY			**BERK**
100	VISTAMONT AV	94708	609-H4
ROCK ISL			**ALA**
600	OTIS DR	94501	669-H2
ROCK LN			**BERK**
40	POPLAR ST	94708	609-H5
100	CRAGMONT AV	94708	609-H5
ROCKINGHAM CT			**OAK**
4600	CAMPUS DR	94605	651-A6
ROCKRIDGE BLVD N			**OAK**
6070	ROCKRIDGE BLVD S	94618	630-A5
6100	ROCKRIDGE PL	94618	630-A5
ROCKRIDGE BLVD S			**OAK**
6000	BROADWAY	94618	630-A5
6000	LAWTON AV	94618	630-A5
6070	ROCKRIDGE BLVD N	94618	630-A5
6100	ROCKRIDGE PL	94618	630-A5
6130	PROSPECT STEPS	94618	630-A5
6200	MARGARIDO DR	94618	630-A5
ROCKRIDGE PL			**OAK**
6100	ROCKRIDGE BLVD S	94618	630-A5
6150	ROCKRIDGE BLVD N	94618	630-A5
ROCKWELL ST			**OAK**
6000	HARWOOD AV	94618	629-J4
6200	FLORIO ST	94618	629-J4
6300	MYSTIC ST	94618	629-J4
RODERICK RD			**OAK**
4200	DINGLEY ST	94605	671-D4
4300	LOCHARD ST	94605	671-D4
ROGERS CT			**OAK**
3000	PENNIMAN AV	94619	650-E7
ROLAND WY			**OAK**
400	CAPWELL DR	94621	670-E6
430	EDGEWATER DR	94621	670-E5
500	OAKPORT ST	94621	670-E5
ROMANY RD			**OAK**
5700	BROADWAY TER	94618	630-A6
5710	GLENBROOK DR	94618	630-B6
5870	BEECHWOOD DR	94618	630-B5
5880	MATHIEU AV	94618	630-B5
5880	OSTRANDER RD	94618	630-B5
5940	CROSS RD	94618	630-B5
6100	GOLDEN GATE AV	94618	630-B5
RONADA AV			**OAK**
20	RAMONA AV	94611	630-A7
1	BRANDON ST	94611	630-A7
20	GRAND AV	94611	630-A7
RONADA AV			**PDMT**
20	RAMONA AV	94611	630-A7
100	BRANDON ST	94611	630-A7
100	MONTECELLO AV	94611	630-A7
200	RAMONA AV	94611	630-A7
ROOSEVELT AV			**BERK**
2100	ADDISON ST	94703	629-G2
2200	ALLSTON WY	94703	629-G2
2300	BANCROFT WY	94703	629-G2
2400	CHANNING WY	94703	629-G2
2400	CHANNING WY	94703	629-G2
2500	DWIGHT WY	94703	629-G2
ROOSEVELT DR			**ALA**
2450	PARK AV	94501	669-J3
2500	REGENT ST	94501	669-J3
ROSAL AV			**OAK**
500	WARFIELD AV	94610	650-A2
600	LAKESHORE AV	94610	650-A2
600	LAKESHORE AV	94610	650-A2
700	BALFOUR AV	94610	650-B3
800	BALFOUR AV	94610	650-B3
ROSE AV			**OAK**
900	ECHO AV	94611	650-A1
1100	GREENBANK AV	94611	630-A7
1200	BRANDON ST	94611	630-A7
ROSE AV			**PDMT**
900	ECHO AV	94611	650-A1
1100	GREENBANK AV	94611	630-A7
1200	BRANDON ST	94611	630-A7
ROSE ST			**BERK**
1200	HOPKINS ST	94702	629-E1
1220	CURTIS ST	94702	629-E1
1240	BELVEDERE AV	94702	629-E1
1270	CHESTNUT ST	94702	629-E1
1330	ORDWAY ST	94702	629-E1

Address	Cross Street	ZIP	City / Pg-Grid
ROSE ST			**BERK**
1370	JUANITA WY	94702	629-E1
1400	ACTON ST	94702	609-F7
1460	KEONCREST DR	94702	609-F7
1500	SACRAMENTO ST	94703	609-F7
1550	HOLLY ST	94703	609-F7
1600	CALIFORNIA ST	94703	609-F7
1610	CALIFORNIA ST	94703	609-F7
1680	MCGEE AV	94703	609-F7
1700	MCGEE AV	94703	609-F7
1730	CYPRESS ST	94703	609-F7
1730	CARLOTTA AV	94703	609-F7
1760	EDITH ST	94703	609-F7
1800	GRANT ST	94703	609-G7
1850	JOSEPHINE ST	94703	609-G7
1900	MARTIN LUTHER KING JR WY	94709	609-G7
1950	BONITA AV	94709	609-G7
2000	MILVIA ST	94709	609-G7
2050	HENRY ST	94709	609-G7
2060	SHATTUCK PL	94709	609-G7
2060	HENRY ST	94709	609-G7
2100	SHATTUCK AV	94709	609-G7
2150	WALNUT ST	94709	609-H7
2200	OXFORD ST	94709	609-H7
2250	SPRUCE ST	94709	609-H7
2300	ARCH ST	94709	609-H7
2370	ARCH ST	94708	609-H7
2400	BAYVIEW PL	94708	609-H7
2500	LE ROY AV	94708	609-H7
2500	TAMALPAIS RD	94708	609-H7
2600	GREENWOOD TER	94708	609-J7
2700	LA LOMA AV	94708	609-J7
ROSECREST DR			**OAK**
1800	MELVIN RD	94602	650-E2
1900	CARTER ST	94602	650-E2
	BRENTWOOD RD	94602	650-E2
ROSEDALE AV			**OAK**
1500	E 16TH ST	94601	670-D1
1640	E 17TH ST	94601	670-D1
1700	E 18TH ST	94601	670-D1
1700	E 18TH ST	94601	670-D1
1900	FOOTHILL BLVD	94601	670-D1
1900	FOOTHILL BLVD	94601	670-D1
1900	SAN JUAN ST	94601	650-D7
1960	SAN JUAN ST	94601	650-D7
2010	MERA ST	94601	650-D7
2170	CARRINGTON ST	94601	650-D7
2330	SANTA RITA ST	94601	650-E7
2400	AGUA VISTA ST	94601	650-E7
ROSEFIELD LP			**ALA**
	BARTLETT DR	94501	649-G7
	HOLTZ CT	94501	649-F7
	FITCH CT	94501	649-F7
	CHALLEN CT	94501	649-F7
	ROWE CT	94501	649-F7
	ELLIS CT	94501	649-F7
	FLETCHER CT	94501	649-F7
	BARKER CT	94501	649-F7
	DOW CT	94501	649-F7
	HERCULES CT	94501	649-F7
	BOSSHARD CT	94501	649-G7
	BARTLETT DR	94501	649-G7
	COHEN CT	94501	649-G7
	PIONEER CT	94501	649-G7
	BARTLETT DR	94501	649-G7
	BIRD CT	94501	649-G7
ROSEMONT AV			**BERK**
1	CRESTON RD	94708	609-H4
40	WOODMONT AV	94708	609-H4
100	VISTAMONT AV	94708	609-H4
ROSEMOUNT RD			**OAK**
600	LONGRIDGE RD	94610	650-A3
800	NORTHVALE RD	94610	650-B3
900	VERRADA RD	94610	650-B3
1000	SUNNYHILLS RD	94610	650-B3
ROSEWOOD WY			**ALA**
1000	WESTLINE DR	94501	669-G2
1050	TARRYTON ISL	94501	669-G2
1080	COUNTRY ISL	94501	669-G2
1100	AMBER ISL	94501	669-G2
1130	LARCHMONT ISL	94501	669-G2
1300	OTIS DR	94501	669-H2
ROSLYN CT			**BERK**
1	CHABOLYN TER	94618	630-A4
1	CHABOT CREST	94618	630-A4
100	S CROSSWAYS	94618	630-A4
ROSS CIR			**OAK**
1	ROSS ST	94618	630-A4
200	FLORIO ST	94618	630-A4
200	ROSS ST	94618	630-A4
ROSS RD			**ALA**
1	ANDERSON RD	94502	669-H6
100	LAWRENCE RD	94502	669-H6
ROSS ST			**OAK**
5700	MILES AV	94618	630-A5
5900	CHABOT RD	94618	630-A5
5900	CHABOT RD	94618	630-A5
6000	HARWOOD AV	94618	630-A4
6020	HARWOOD AV	94618	630-A4
6100	ROSS CIR	94618	630-A4
6190	FLORIO ST	94618	630-A4
6190	ROSS CIR	94618	630-A4
ROSSMOOR AV			**OAK**
400	ROSSMOOR CT	94603	670-G6
500	ASHTON AV	94603	670-G6
ROSSMOOR CT			**OAK**
1	CLARA ST	94603	670-G6
60	ROSSMOOR AV	94603	670-G6
ROWE CT			**ALA**
	ROSEFIELD LP	94501	649-F7
ROXBURG LN			**ALA**
50	SHEFFIELD RD	94502	670-A5
50	WEYMOUTH CT	94502	670-A5
70	BRIGHTON RD	94502	670-A5
ROXBURY AV			**OAK**
3100	MARLOW DR	94605	671-C7
3050	COVINGTON ST	94605	671-C7
3000	DANBURY ST	94605	671-C7
3050	FOOTHILL WY	94605	671-C7
ROYAL ANN ST			**OAK**
10000	100TH AV	94603	670-H6
10000	C ST	94603	670-H6
10100	101ST AV	94603	670-H6
10200	102ND AV	94603	670-H6
10300	103RD AV	94603	670-J6
10400	104TH AV	94603	670-J6
10500	105TH AV	94603	670-J6
10600	106TH AV	94603	670-J6
10700	107TH AV	94603	670-J6
ROYAL OAK RD			**OAK**
10500	ELYSIAN FIELDS DR	94605	671-D3
10300	GREENVIEW DR	94605	671-D3
10200	GREENVIEW DR	94605	671-C3
10300	ORINDA VISTA DR	94605	671-C3
ROYAL ST			**OAK**
900	SAN LEANDRO ST	94603	670-J7
1000	APRICOT ST	94603	670-J7
RUBIN DR			**OAK**
3600	ROBINSON DR	94602	650-H4
RUBY ST			**OAK**
3700	W MACARTHUR BLVD	94609	649-H1
3800	38TH ST	94609	649-H1
3800	38TH ST	94609	649-H1
4000	40TH ST	94609	629-H7
RUDSDALE ST			**OAK**
6900	69TH AV	94621	670-G3
7000	70TH AV	94621	670-G3
7100	71ST AV	94621	670-G3
7200	72ND AV	94621	670-G3
7300	73RD AV	94621	670-G3
7500	75TH AV	94621	670-G3
7600	76TH AV	94621	670-G4
7700	77TH AV	94621	670-G4
7800	78TH AV	94621	670-G4
7900	79TH AV	94621	670-G4
7900	79TH AV	94621	670-G4
8000	80TH AV	94621	670-G4
8100	81ST AV	94621	670-G4
8200	82ND AV	94621	670-G4
RUGBY AV			**BERK**
400	VERMONT AV	94707	609-G4
RUSSELL ST			**BERK**
1100	SAN PABLO AV	94702	629-E4
1200	WALLACE ST	94702	629-E4
1250	MATHEWS ST	94702	629-F4
1300	MABEL ST	94702	629-F4
1310	MABEL ST	94702	629-F4
1350	PARK ST	94702	629-F4
1390	ACTON ST	94702	629-F4
1400	ACTON ST	94702	629-F4
1420	DOHR ST	94702	629-F4
1430	DOHR ST	94702	629-F4
1460	STANTON ST	94702	629-F4
1470	STANTON ST	94702	629-F4
1500	SACRAMENTO ST	94703	629-F4
1600	CALIFORNIA ST	94703	629-G4
1700	MCGEE AV	94703	629-G4
1730	KING ST	94703	629-G4
1770	ELLIS ST	94703	629-G4
1800	GRANT ST	94703	629-G4
1830	HARPER ST	94703	629-G4
1900	MARTIN LUTHER KING JR WY	94703	629-G4
1950	OTIS ST	94703	629-G4
2000	MILVIA ST	94703	629-G4
2020	ADELINE ST	94703	629-G3
2060	NEWBERRY ST	94703	629-H3
2100	SHATTUCK AV	94705	629-H3
2140	LORINA ST	94705	629-H3
2180	WHEELER ST	94705	629-H3
2220	FULTON ST	94705	629-H3
2270	DEAKIN ST	94705	629-H3
2310	ELLSWORTH ST	94705	629-H3
2400	TELEGRAPH AV	94705	629-H3
2440	FLORENCE ST	94705	629-J3
2500	REGENT ST	94705	629-J3
2560	HILLEGASS AV	94705	629-J3
2610	BENVENUE AV	94705	629-J3
2660	COLLEGE AV	94705	629-J3
2700	CHERRY ST	94705	629-J3
2740	PIEDMONT AV	94705	629-J3
2760	PIEDMONT AV	94705	629-J3
2790	KELSEY ST	94705	629-J3
2850	PINE AV	94705	630-A3
2980	CLAREMONT BLVD	94705	630-A3
3010	CLAREMONT AV	94705	630-A3
3100	DOMINGO AV	94705	630-A3
3100	TUNNEL RD	94705	630-A3
3100	ASHBY AV	94705	630-A3
RUSSELL ST			**OAK**
	LEONA ST	94605	650-J7
3010	CLAREMONT AV	94705	630-A3
3100	DOMINGO AV	94705	630-A3
3100	TUNNEL RD	94705	630-A3
3100	ASHBY AV	94705	630-A3
RUSSET ST			**OAK**
9800	98TH AV	94603	670-H6
9800	SAN LEANDRO ST	94603	670-H6
9900	PRUNE ST	94603	670-H6
10000	100TH AV	94603	670-H6
10040	SAN LEANDRO ST	94603	670-H6
10200	STONE ST	94603	670-H6
10400	APPLE ST	94603	670-H6
10500	105TH AV	94603	670-H6
10500	GRAVENSTEIN ST	94603	670-H6
10700	107TH AV	94603	670-H7
10900	MOORPARK ST	94603	670-H7
RUSTING AV			**OAK**
4020	LEONA ST	94605	650-H7
4100	FRONTAGE RD	94605	650-H7
RUTH AV			**OAK**
5400	KINGSLAND AV	94601	670-F1
5500	55TH AV	94601	670-F1
RUTHERFORD ST			**OAK**
2000	FOOTHILL BLVD	94601	650-C7
2100	E 22ND ST	94601	650-C7
RUTHLAND RD			**OAK**
	MOUNTAIN BLVD	94611	630-C5
	PINEWOOD RD	94611	630-C5
6250	SWAINLAND RD	94611	630-D5
RUTLAND CT			**ALA**
100	BANNISTER WY	94502	669-H6
RYAN ST			**OAK**
1000	EARHART RD	94621	670-D6
1060	LOCKHEED ST	94621	670-D6
RYDAL CT			**OAK**
100	STOCKBRIDGE DR	94611	650-F1
S			
SABLE POINTE			**ALA**
30	BARNEGATE BAY	94502	670-A5
110	PUDDINGSTONE RD	94502	670-A5
160	MOSS POINTE	94502	670-A5
SACRAMENTO			**ALA**
4000	CIMARRON ST	94501	649-E6
4000	ROANOKE	94501	649-E6
SACRAMENTO ST			**BERK**
1300	HOPKINS ST	94703	609-F7
1300	HOPKINS ST	94702	609-F7
1400	ADA ST	94703	609-F7
1400	ADA ST	94702	609-F7
1410	ROSE ST	94703	609-F7
1410	ROSE ST	94702	609-F7
1600	CEDAR ST	94703	629-F1
1600	CEDAR ST	94702	629-F1
1650	LINCOLN ST	94703	629-F1
1650	LINCOLN ST	94702	629-F1
1700	VIRGINIA ST	94703	629-F1
1700	VIRGINIA ST	94702	629-F1
1750	FRANCISCO ST	94703	629-F1
1750	FRANCISCO ST	94702	629-F1
1800	DELAWARE ST	94703	629-F1
1800	DELAWARE ST	94702	629-F1
1880	HEARST AV	94703	629-F1
1880	HEARST AV	94702	629-F1
1900	HEARST AV	94703	629-F1
1900	HEARST AV	94702	629-F1
1940	BERKELEY WY	94703	629-F1
1940	BERKELEY WY	94702	629-F1
1950	BERKELEY WY	94703	629-F1
1950	BERKELEY WY	94702	629-F1
2000	UNIVERSITY AV	94703	629-F2
2000	UNIVERSITY AV	94702	629-F2
2100	ADDISON ST	94703	629-F2
2100	ADDISON ST	94702	629-F2
2200	ALLSTON WY	94703	629-F2
2200	ALLSTON WY	94702	629-F2
2300	BANCROFT WY	94703	629-F2
2300	BANCROFT WY	94702	629-F2
2400	CHANNING WY	94703	629-F3
2400	CHANNING WY	94702	629-F3
2500	DWIGHT WY	94703	629-F3
2500	DWIGHT WY	94702	629-F3
2550	BLAKE ST	94703	629-F3
2550	BLAKE ST	94702	629-F3
2600	PARKER ST	94703	629-F3
2600	PARKER ST	94702	629-F3
2650	CARLETON ST	94703	629-F3
2650	CARLETON ST	94702	629-F3
2700	DERBY ST	94703	629-F3
2700	DERBY ST	94702	629-F3
2750	WARD ST	94703	629-F3
2750	WARD ST	94702	629-F3
2800	STUART ST	94703	629-F3
2800	STUART ST	94702	629-F3
2850	OREGON ST	94703	629-F4
2850	OREGON ST	94702	629-F4
2900	RUSSELL ST	94703	629-F4
2900	RUSSELL ST	94702	629-F4
2950	JULIA ST	94703	629-F4
2950	JULIA ST	94702	629-F4
3000	ASHBY AV	94703	629-F4
3000	ASHBY AV	94702	629-F4
3050	TYLER ST	94703	629-F4
3050	TYLER ST	94702	629-F4
3100	PRINCE ST	94703	629-F4
3100	PRINCE ST	94702	629-F4
3120	67TH ST	94703	629-F4
3120	67TH ST	94702	629-F4
3150	WOOLSEY ST	94703	629-F4
3150	WOOLSEY ST	94702	629-F4
3160	66TH ST	94703	629-F4
3160	66TH ST	94702	629-F4
	FAIRVIEW ST	94703	629-F4
	FAIRVIEW ST	94702	629-F4
3200	FAIRVIEW ST	94703	629-F4
3200	FAIRVIEW ST	94702	629-F4
3250	HARMON ST	94703	629-F5
3250	HARMON ST	94702	629-F5
3300	ALCATRAZ AV	94703	629-F5
3300	ALCATRAZ AV	94702	629-F5
3300	MARKET ST	94702	629-F5
SACRAMENTO ST			**OAK**
3300	MARKET ST	94608	629-F5
3350	63RD ST	94608	629-F5
3400	62ND ST	94608	629-F5
3450	61ST ST	94608	629-F5
3460	61ST ST	94608	629-F5
3490	60TH ST	94608	629-F5
3500	STANFORD AV	94608	629-F5
SADDLE BROOK CT			**OAK**
100	SADDLE BROOK DR	94619	651-B6
SADDLE BROOK DR			**OAK**
5100	BROOKPARK RD	94619	651-B6
5120	PARKHURST DR	94619	651-B6
5200	SADDLE BROOK CT	94619	651-B6
5260	PARKRIDGE DR	94619	651-B6
5300	CLAIREPOINTE WY	94619	651-B6
SAGE LN			**ALA**
	DUTCHCAP LN	94502	670-A7
SAGE RD			**OAK**
8900	SEQUOYAH RD	94605	671-C2
8900	OAK HILL RD	94605	671-C2
SAINT ANDREWS RD			**OAK**
4100	SEQUOYAH RD	94605	671-C2
4400	OAK HILL RD	94605	671-C2
SAINT CHARLES ST			**ALA**
1300	SAN ANTONIO AV	94501	669-G1
1350	FAIR OAKS AV	94501	669-G1
1400	CENTRAL AV	94501	669-G1
1450	TAYLOR AV	94501	669-G1
1500	SANTA CLARA AV	94501	669-G1
1500	SANTA CLARA AV	94501	669-G1
1600	LINCOLN AV	94501	669-G1
1600	LINCOLN AV	94501	669-G1
1700	PACIFIC AV	94501	669-G1
1800	BUENA VISTA AV	94501	649-G7
1900	EAGLE AV	94501	649-G7
SAINT CLOUD CT			**OAK**
4300	VIEWCREST DR	94619	650-J6
SAINT ELMO DR			**OAK**
9810	BERNHARDT DR	94603	670-G7
9820	DARIEN AV	94603	670-G7
9880	FOSTER AV	94603	670-G7
9920	GHORMLEY AV	94603	670-G7
9950	HUNTER AV	94603	670-G7
9990	STONEFORD AV	94603	670-G7
SAINT JAMES CIR			**PDMT**
500	SAINT JAMES DR	94611	650-D2
SAINT JAMES DR			**PDMT**
350	HAMPTON RD	94611	650-C2
280	LA SALLE AV	94611	650-D2
220	SAINT JAMES CIR	94611	650-D2
170	CAMBRIAN AV	94611	650-D2
150	SAINT JAMES PL	94611	650-D2
150	SAINT JAMES PL	94610	650-D2
1	CROYDON CIR	94611	650-D2
1	CROYDON CIR	94610	650-D2
150	LEIMERT BLVD	94611	650-D2
150	LEIMERT BLVD	94610	650-D2
150	PARK BLVD	94610	650-D2
SAINT JAMES PL			**PDMT**
100	SAINT JAMES DR	94610	650-D2
SAINT MARGARET CT			**ALA**
2600	BROADWAY	94501	670-A2
SAINT PAUL CT			**OAK**
5800	PROCTOR AV	94618	630-C6
5900	MASONIC AV	94618	630-C6
SALEM ST			**EMVL**
4300	43RD ST	94608	629-F7
4400	45TH ST	94608	629-F7
4700	47TH ST	94608	629-F6
4800	48TH ST	94608	629-F6
SALEM ST			**OAK**
6400	ALCATRAZ AV	94608	629-F5
SALISBURY ST			**OAK**
3410	34TH AV	94601	650-D6
3500	35TH AV	94601	650-D6
SALLY RIDE WY			**OAK**
1	AIR CARGO RD	94621	690-C1
SALMON RD			**ALA**
1	ANDERSON RD	94502	669-H6
30	SWIFT CT	94502	669-H6
60	HAYS CT	94502	669-H6
100	SWEET RD	94502	669-H6
SAMARIA LN			**OAK**
1	CRESTMONT DR	94619	650-H5
300	TERALYNN CT	94619	650-H5
SAN ANTONIO AV			**ALA**
900	9TH ST	94501	669-G1
1000	WEBER ST	94501	669-G1
1030	CAROLINE ST	94501	669-G1
1060	HAWTHORNE ST	94501	669-G2
1100	SAINT CHARLES ST	94501	669-G2
1200	BAY ST	94501	669-H2
1300	SHERMAN ST	94501	669-H2
1400	MORTON ST	94501	669-H2
1400	SAN JOSE AV	94501	669-H2
1600	PARU ST	94501	669-H2
1700	GRAND ST	94501	669-H2
1800	UNION ST	94501	669-H2
1900	LAFAYETTE ST	94501	669-J2
2000	CHESTNUT ST	94501	669-J2
2100	WILLOW ST	94501	669-J2
2200	WALNUT ST	94501	669-J2
2300	OAK ST	94501	670-A3
2400	PARK ST	94501	670-A3
SAN ANTONIO AV			**BERK**
1800	SAN RAMON AV	94707	609-F5
1800	THE ALAMEDA	94707	609-F5
1880	ARLINGTON AV	94707	609-G5
1900	AVIS RD	94707	609-G5
2000	SAN LUIS RD	94707	609-G5
SAN ANTONIO WY			**OAK**
1600	16TH AV	94606	650-A5
1700	17TH AV	94606	650-A5
1800	18TH AV	94606	650-B6
1910	19TH AV	94606	650-B6
2010	20TH AV	94606	650-B6
2110	21ST AV	94606	650-B6
2210	22ND AV	94606	650-B6
SAN BENITO RD			**BERK**
900	MARIN AV	94707	609-H6
1000	SPRUCE ST	94707	609-H6
SAN CARLOS AV			**ALB**
560	THOUSAND OAKS BLVD	94706	609-E5
670	PORTLAND AV	94706	609-E5
770	WASHINGTON AV	94706	609-E6
900	SOLANO AV	94706	609-E6
SAN CARLOS AV			**OAK**
4480	47TH AV	94601	670-E1
4400	HIGH ST	94601	650-E7
4480	COURTLAND AV	94601	650-E7
4600	COURTLAND AV	94601	650-E7
SAN CARLOS AV			**PDMT**
200	BLAIR AV	94611	650-A1
300	OAKLAND AV	94611	650-B1
300	OAKLAND AV	94610	650-B1
400	MAGNOLIA AV	94611	650-B1
400	MAGNOLIA AV	94610	650-B1
SAN DIEGO RD			**ALA**
200	ALAMEDA RD	94501	649-D6
100	BARBERS POINT RD	94501	649-D6
SAN DIEGO RD			**BERK**
700	SOUTHAMPTON AV	94707	609-G5
800	LAUREL LN	94707	609-G5
900	INDIAN ROCK AV	94707	609-G5
SAN FERNANDO AV			**BERK**
600	ARLINGTON AV	94707	609-G5
620	SAN RAMON AV	94707	609-F5
650	SAN JUAN AV	94707	609-F5
680	THOUSAND OAKS BLVD	94707	609-F5
700	INDIAN TR	94707	609-F5
700	YOSEMITE RD	94707	609-F5
SAN FRANCISCO CT			**OAK**
	E 10TH ST	94601	670-B1
SAN GABRIEL AV			**ALB**
500	BRIGHTON AV	94706	609-E5
700	PORTLAND AV	94706	609-E5
SAN JOSE AV			**ALA**
1400	MORTON ST	94501	669-H2
1400	SAN ANTONIO AV	94501	669-H2
1600	PARU ST	94501	669-H2
1700	GRAND ST	94501	669-H2
1800	UNION ST	94501	669-H2
1900	LAFAYETTE ST	94501	669-H2
2000	CHESTNUT ST	94501	669-J2
2100	WILLOW ST	94501	669-J2
2200	WALNUT ST	94501	669-J3
2300	OAK ST	94501	669-J3
2400	PARK ST	94501	670-A3
2440	PARK AV W	94501	670-A3
2460	PARK AV E	94501	670-A3
2500	REGENT ST	94501	670-A3
2600	BROADWAY	94501	670-A3
2700	PEARL ST	94501	670-A3
2800	VERSAILLES AV	94501	670-A3
2820	COLLEGE AV	94501	670-A3
2860	BISHOP ST	94501	670-A3
2900	MOUND ST	94501	670-A3
3000	COURT ST	94501	670-B3
3100	FOUNTAIN ST	94501	670-B4
3200	HIGH ST	94501	670-B4
3230	POST ST	94501	670-B4
3260	PEACH ST	94501	670-B4
3300	FERNSIDE BLVD	94501	670-B4
SAN JUAN AV			**BERK**
1800	SANTA CLARA AV	94707	609-F5
1900	SAN FERNANDO AV	94707	609-F5
SAN JUAN ST			**OAK**
3700	HARRINGTON AV	94601	650-D7
3820	38TH AV	94601	650-D7
4010	40TH AV	94601	650-D7
4100	ROSEDALE AV	94601	650-D7
SAN LEANDRO ST			**OAK**
3200	FRUITVALE AV	94601	670-C1
3400	34TH AV	94601	670-C1
3500	35TH AV	94601	670-C1
3600	36TH AV	94601	670-C1
3710	37TH AV	94601	670-C1
3810	38TH AV	94601	670-C1
3910	39TH AV	94601	670-C1
4010	40TH AV	94601	670-C1
4110	41ST AV	94601	670-D1
4130	42ND AV	94601	670-D1
4160	42ND AV	94601	670-D1
4300	HIGH ST	94601	670-D1
4480	44TH AV	94601	670-D2
4650	45TH AV	94601	670-D2
4830	46TH AV	94601	670-D2
5000	47TH AV	94601	670-D2
5100	49TH AV	94601	670-D2
5160	50TH AV	94601	670-D2
5210	51ST AV	94601	670-D2
5260	52ND AV	94601	670-D2
5300	53RD AV	94601	670-D2
5400	54TH AV	94601	670-E3
5900	SEMINARY AV	94621	670-E3
6600	66TH AV	94621	670-F4
6900	69TH AV	94621	670-F4
7500	75TH AV	94621	670-F4
7600	76TH AV	94621	670-F4
7700	77TH AV	94621	670-F4
8500	85TH AV	94621	670-G5
9250	INDUSTRIAL WY	94603	670-G6
9800	98TH AV	94603	670-G6
9800	RUSSET ST	94603	670-G6
9440	RUSSET ST	94603	670-H6

Address	Cross Street	ZIP	Pg-Grid
SAN LEANDRO ST			**OAK**
10500	105TH AV	94603	670-H6
10600	106TH AV	94603	670-H6
10700	107TH AV	94603	670-H7
10800	BLENHEIM ST	94603	670-H7
10900	MOORPARK ST	94603	670-J7
100	ROYAL ST	94603	670-J7
SAN LORENZO AV			**BERK**
1600	MIRAMAR AV	94707	609-F5
1600	WASHINGTON AV	94707	609-F5
1700	ENSENADA AV	94707	609-F5
1800	COLUSA AV	94707	609-F5
1860	SANTA ROSA AV	94707	609-F5
1900	THE ALAMEDA	94707	609-F5
1900	INDIAN TR	94707	609-F5
SAN LUIS AV			**OAK**
1300	DOLORES AV	94602	650-D3
SAN LUIS RD			**BERK**
500	ARLINGTON AV	94707	609-G4
530	AVIS RD	94707	609-G5
650	SAN ANTONIO AV	94707	609-G5
700	SOUTHAMPTON AV	94707	609-G5
700	SOUTHAMPTON AV	94707	609-G5
740	MONTROSE RD	94707	609-G5
900	INDIAN ROCK AV	94707	609-G5
SAN MATEO RD			**BERK**
100	INDIAN ROCK AV	94707	609-G5
SAN MIGUEL AV			**BERK**
600	THOUSAND OAKS BLVD	94707	609-F5
700	SANTA ROSA AV	94707	609-F5
SAN PABLO AV			**ALB**
500	BRIGHTON AV	94706	609-D5
540	CLAY ST	94706	609-D5
600	GARFIELD AV	94706	609-D5
700	CASTRO ST	94706	609-D5
740	PORTLAND AV	94706	609-D5
800	WASHINGTON AV	94706	609-D6
820	WASHINGTON AV	94706	609-D6
900	SOLANO AV	94706	609-D6
970	BUCHANAN ST	94706	609-D6
1000	MARIN AV	94706	609-D6
1070	MONROE ST	94706	609-D7
1070	MONROE ST	94710	609-D7
1100	DARTMOUTH ST	94706	609-D7
1100	DARTMOUTH ST	94710	609-D7
SAN PABLO AV			**BERK**
1100	DARTMOUTH ST	94706	609-D7
1100	DARTMOUTH ST	94710	609-D7
1200	HARRISON ST	94706	609-D7
1200	HARRISON ST	94710	609-D7
1300	GILMAN ST	94702	609-D7
1300	GILMAN ST	94710	609-D7
1360	CAMELIA ST	94702	609-E7
1360	CAMELIA ST	94710	609-E7
1400	PAGE ST	94702	629-E1
1400	PAGE ST	94804	629-E1
1500	JONES ST	94702	629-E1
1500	JONES ST	94804	629-E1
1600	CEDAR ST	94702	629-E1
1600	CEDAR ST	94804	629-E1
1600	HOPKINS ST	94804	629-E1
1700	VIRGINIA ST	94702	629-E1
1700	VIRGINIA ST	94804	629-E1
1750	FRANCISCO ST	94702	629-E1
1750	FRANCISCO ST	94804	629-E1
1800	DELAWARE ST	94702	629-E1
1800	DELAWARE ST	94804	629-E1
1900	HEARST AV	94702	629-E2
1900	HEARST AV	94804	629-E2
2000	UNIVERSITY AV	94702	629-E2
2000	UNIVERSITY AV	94804	629-E2
2070	ADDISON ST	94702	629-E2
2070	ADDISON ST	94804	629-E2
2100	ADDISON ST	94702	629-E2
2100	ADDISON ST	94804	629-E2
2140	COWPER ST	94702	629-E2
2140	COWPER ST	94804	629-E2
2200	ALLSTON WY	94702	629-E2
2200	ALLSTON WY	94804	629-E2
2300	BANCROFT WY	94702	629-E2
2300	BANCROFT WY	94804	629-E2
2350	CHAUCER ST	94702	629-E3
2350	CHAUCER ST	94804	629-E3
2400	CHANNING WY	94702	629-E3
2400	CHANNING WY	94804	629-E3
2500	DWIGHT WY	94702	629-E3
2500	DWIGHT WY	94804	629-E3
2550	BLAKE ST	94702	629-E3
2550	BLAKE ST	94804	629-E3
2600	PARKER ST	94702	629-E3
2600	PARKER ST	94804	629-E3
2660	CARLETON ST	94702	629-E3
2660	CARLETON ST	94804	629-E3
2700	CARLETON ST	94702	629-E3
2700	CARLETON ST	94804	629-E3
2720	DERBY ST	94702	629-E3
2720	DERBY ST	94804	629-E3
2740	PARDEE ST	94702	629-E3
2740	PARDEE ST	94804	629-E3
2760	WARD ST	94702	629-E3
2760	WARD ST	94804	629-E3
2800	GRAYSON ST	94702	629-E4
2800	GRAYSON ST	94804	629-E4
2870	OREGON ST	94702	629-E4
2870	OREGON ST	94804	629-E4
2900	HEINZ AV	94702	629-E4
2900	HEINZ AV	94804	629-E4
2930	RUSSELL ST	94702	629-E4
2930	RUSSELL ST	94804	629-E4
2960	BURNETT ST	94702	629-E4
2960	BURNETT ST	94804	629-E4
3000	ASHBY AV	94702	629-E4
3000	ASHBY AV	94804	629-E4
3040	MURRAY ST	94702	629-E4
3040	MURRAY ST	94804	629-E4
3070	CARRISON ST	94702	629-E4
3070	CARRISON ST	94804	629-E4
3100	FOLGER AV	94702	629-E4
3100	FOLGER AV	94804	629-E4
3150	HASKELL ST	94702	629-E4
3200	67TH ST	94702	629-E4
SAN PABLO AV			**ELCR**
500	BRIGHTON AV	94530	609-D5
SAN PABLO AV			**EMVL**
3700	37TH ST	94608	629-F7
	W MACARTHUR BLVD	94608	629-F7
	W MACARTHUR BLVD	94608	629-F7
3780	W MACARTHUR BLVD	94608	629-F7
3800	ADELINE ST	94608	629-F7
3900	YERBA BUENA AV	94608	629-F7
4000	40TH ST	94608	629-F7
4100	41ST ST	94608	629-F7
4200	PARK AV	94608	629-F7
4300	43RD ST	94608	629-F7
4500	45TH ST	94608	629-F7
4550	45TH ST	94608	629-F6
4700	47TH ST	94608	629-F6
4800	48TH ST	94608	629-F6
5300	53RD ST	94608	629-F6
5320	53RD ST	94608	629-F6
SAN PABLO AV			**OAK**
1600	16TH ST	94612	649-G3
1600	FRANK H OGAWA PZ	94612	649-G3
1700	17TH ST	94612	649-G3
1700	CLAY ST	94612	649-G3
1780	18TH ST	94612	649-G3
1880	19TH ST	94612	649-G3
1960	WILLIAMS ST	94612	649-G3
2030	20TH ST	94612	649-G3
2080	MARTIN LUTHER KING JR WY	94612	649-G3
2120	21ST ST	94612	649-G3
2140	MARTIN LUTHER KING JR WY	94612	649-G3
2140	CASTRO ST	94612	649-G3
2200	W GRAND AV	94612	649-G2
2280	BRUSH ST	94612	649-G2
2300	23RD ST	94612	649-G2
2380	24TH ST	94612	649-G2
2430	WEST ST	94607	649-G2
2430	WEST ST	94612	649-G2
2450	25TH ST	94607	649-G2
2450	25TH ST	94612	649-G2
2480	ATHENS AV	94607	649-G2
2480	ATHENS AV	94612	649-G2
2530	SYCAMORE ST	94607	649-F2
2530	SYCAMORE ST	94612	649-F2
2550	MEAD AV	94607	649-F2
2550	MEAD AV	94612	649-F2
2600	26TH ST	94607	649-F2
2600	26TH ST	94612	649-F2
2620	MILTON ST	94607	649-F2
2620	MILTON ST	94612	649-F2
2670	27TH ST	94607	649-F2
2670	27TH ST	94612	649-F2
2700	27TH ST	94607	649-F2
2700	27TH ST	94608	649-F2
2760	28TH ST	94607	649-F2
2760	28TH ST	94608	649-F2
2800	28TH ST	94608	649-F2
2900	29TH ST	94608	649-F2
3000	MARKET ST	94608	649-F1
3000	30TH ST	94608	649-F1
3030	30TH ST	94608	649-F1
3100	31ST ST	94608	649-F1
3140	MYRTLE ST	94608	649-F1
3170	32ND ST	94608	649-F1
3200	32ND ST	94608	649-F1
3250	BROCKHURST ST	94608	649-F1
3250	FILBERT ST	94608	649-F1
3300	33RD ST	94608	649-F1
3390	34TH ST	94608	649-F1
3400	LINDEN ST	94608	649-F1
3500	35TH ST	94608	649-F1
3600	36TH ST	94608	649-F1
3700	37TH ST	94608	649-F1
5300	53RD ST	94608	629-F6
5320	53RD ST	94608	629-F6
5400	54TH ST	94608	629-F6
5420	54TH ST	94608	629-F6
5500	55TH ST	94608	629-F6
5530	55TH ST	94608	629-F6
5600	56TH ST	94608	629-F6
5640	AILEEN ST	94608	629-F6
5700	57TH ST	94608	629-F6
5750	STANFORD AV	94608	629-F6
5850	59TH ST	94608	629-F5
5900	59TH ST	94608	629-F5
6000	60TH ST	94608	629-F5
6090	61ST ST	94608	629-F5
6100	61ST ST	94608	629-F5
6200	62ND ST	94608	629-F5
6300	63RD ST	94608	629-F5
6340	63RD ST	94608	629-F5
6400	64TH ST	94608	629-F5
6430	ALCATRAZ AV	94608	629-F5
6450	OCEAN AV	94608	629-F5
6470	PEABODY LN	94608	629-F5
6500	65TH ST	94608	629-E5
6600	66TH ST	94608	629-E4
6630	66TH ST	94608	629-E4
6700	67TH ST	94608	629-E4
3150	HASKELL ST	94608	629-E4
3200	67TH ST	94608	629-E4
SAN PEDRO AV			**BERK**
1800	COLUSA AV	94707	609-F5
1850	LAUREL LN	94707	609-F5
1900	THE ALAMEDA	94707	609-F5
SAN PEDRO RD			**ALA**
200	ALAMEDA RD	94501	649-D6
100	BARBERS POINT RD	94501	649-D6
SAN RAMON AV			**BERK**
1800	SAN ANTONIO AV	94707	609-F5
1800	THE ALAMEDA	94707	609-F5
1820	VALLEJO ST	94707	609-F5
1820	SANTA CLARA AV	94707	609-F5
1900	SAN FERNANDO AV	94707	609-F5
SAN SEBASTIAN			**OAK**
4600	EL CENTRO AV	94602	650-D3
4630	ELSINORE AV	94602	650-D3
4700	HOLLYWOOD AV	94602	650-D3
SANBORN DR			**OAK**
	JOAQUIN MILLER RD	94611	650-G3
	JOAQUIN MILLER RD	94611	650-G3
SAND BEACH PL			**ALA**
1100	SAND BEACH RD	94501	669-G2
1200	HARBOR LIGHT RD	94501	669-G2
SAND BEACH RD			**ALA**
300	SHORELINE DR	94501	669-G3
500	SAND BEACH PL	94501	669-G3
SAND HARBOR			**ALA**
50	WELLFLEET BAY	94502	670-A6
SAND HOOK ISL			**ALA**
600	OTIS DR	94501	669-G2
SANDALWOOD ISL			**ALA**
600	OTIS DR	94501	669-H2
SANDCREEK WY			**ALA**
1800	OTIS DR	94501	669-H3
2100	WILLOW ST	94501	669-H3
SANDERLING CT			**ALA**
	BRUZZONE DR	94501	649-F7
	HERON CT	94501	649-F7
SANDPIPER PL			**ALA**
1	CHANNING WY	94502	669-J5
SANDRINGHAM PL			**PDMT**
60	SANDRINGHAM RD	94611	650-D2
SANDRINGHAM RD			**PDMT**
1	HAMPTON RD	94611	650-D2
50	MARLBOROUGH CT	94611	650-D2
70	SANDRINGHAM PL	94611	650-D2
100	SELBORNE DR	94611	650-D2
130	CAMBRIAN AV	94611	650-D2
200	WYNGAARD AV	94611	650-D2
300	ESTATES DR	94611	650-D2
SANFORD ST			**OAK**
7850	MAYNARD AV	94605	671-A1
7900	KELLER AV	94605	671-A1
7900	SHONE AV	94605	671-B2
8000	KELLER AV	94605	671-B2
SANTA BARBARA RD			**BERK**
	CRAGMONT AV	94707	609-H6
	SPRUCE ST	94707	609-H6
500	ARLINGTON AV	94707	609-G4
610	FLORIDA AV	94707	609-G5
660	NORTHAMPTON AV	94707	609-G5
710	SOUTHAMPTON AV	94707	609-G5
780	MONTROSE RD	94707	609-G5
930	INDIAN ROCK AV	94707	609-G6
950	MARIN AV	94707	609-H6
1000	SPRUCE ST	94707	609-H6
SANTA CLARA AV			**ALA**
100	PACIFIC AV	94501	669-E1
200	LINCOLN AV	94501	669-E1
300	3RD ST	94501	669-E1
400	4TH ST	94501	669-E1
500	5TH ST	94501	669-F1
550	LINDEN ST	94501	669-F1
600	6TH ST	94501	669-F1
700	WEBSTER ST	94501	669-F1
750	PAGE ST	94501	669-F1
800	8TH ST	94501	669-G1
900	9TH ST	94501	669-G1
980	MOZART ST	94501	669-G1
1000	CAROLINE ST	94501	669-G1
1050	VERDI ST	94501	669-G1
	SAINT CHARLES ST	94501	669-G1
1100	SAINT CHARLES ST	94501	669-G1
1200	BAY ST	94501	669-H1
1300	SHERMAN ST	94501	669-H1
1400	MORTON ST	94501	669-H1
1500	BENTON ST	94501	669-H1
1540	STANTON ST	94501	669-H1
1570	COTTAGE ST	94501	669-H1
1600	PARU ST	94501	669-H1
1700	GRAND ST	94501	669-H1
1800	UNION ST	94501	669-J1
1850	SCHILLER ST	94501	669-J1
1900	LAFAYETTE ST	94501	669-J1
2000	CHESTNUT ST	94501	669-J2
2100	WILLOW ST	94501	669-J2
2200	WALNUT ST	94501	669-J2
2300	OAK ST	94501	670-A2
2400	PARK ST	94501	670-A2
2450	PARK AV	94501	670-A2
2500	EVERETT ST	94501	670-A2
2600	BROADWAY	94501	670-A2
2700	PEARL ST	94501	670-B3
2800	VERSAILLES AV	94501	670-B3
2830	GIBBONS DR	94501	670-B3
2850	GROVE ST	94501	670-B3
2900	MOUND ST	94501	670-B3
3000	COURT ST	94501	670-B3
3100	FOUNTAIN ST	94501	670-B3
3200	HIGH ST	94501	670-B3
SANTA CLARA AV			**BERK**
500	THOUSAND OAKS BLVD	94707	609-F5
560	SAN JUAN AV	94707	609-F5
600	SAN RAMON AV	94707	609-F5
SANTA CLARA AV			**OAK**
1	KEMPTON WY	94610	649-J1
1	FAIRMOUNT AV	94610	649-J1
100	HARRISON ST	94610	649-J2
1	FAIRMOUNT AV	94611	649-J1
1	FAIRMOUNT AV	94610	649-J1
1	MACARTHUR BLVD	94610	649-J1
1	W MACARTHUR BLVD	94610	649-J1
100	HARRISON ST	94610	649-J2
130	OAKLAND AV	94610	649-J2
200	VERNON ST	94610	649-J2
220	VERNON ST	94610	649-J2
260	CHETWOOD ST	94610	649-J2
300	ELWOOD AV	94610	649-J2
300	JEAN ST	94610	649-J2
360	CRESCENT ST	94610	649-J2
400	LAKE PKWY	94610	649-J3
SANTA CRUZ LN			**ALA**
3100	FIR PL	94502	670-A6
3200	ADMIRALITY LN	94502	670-A7
3300	ISLAND DR	94502	670-A7
SANTA CRUZ RD			**OAK**
4100	BARCELONA ST	94605	671-C3
SANTA FE AV			**ALB**
600	THOUSAND OAKS BLVD	94706	609-E5
700	PORTLAND AV	94706	609-E5
800	WASHINGTON AV	94706	609-E6
840	SOLANO AV	94706	609-E6
1000	MARIN AV	94706	609-E6
1070	RAMONA AV	94706	609-E6
1100	FRANCIS ST	94706	609-E7
1120	POMONA AV	94706	609-E7
1200	KEY ROUTE BLVD	94706	609-E7
SANTA FE AV			**BERK**
1200	KEY ROUTE BLVD	94706	609-E7
1250	MASONIC AV	94706	609-E7
1260	GILMAN ST	94702	609-E7
1300	EVELYN AV	94702	609-E7
1400	CAMELIA ST	94702	609-E7
1400	TALBOT AV	94702	609-E7
1500	CORNELL AV	94702	609-E7
1500	PAGE ST	94702	609-E7
SANTA INES CT			**OAK**
	E 10TH ST	94601	670-B1
SANTA MARIA CT			**OAK**
	E 10TH ST	94601	670-B1
SANTA RAY AV			**OAK**
500	LAKESHORE AV	94610	650-A3
500	PRINCE ST	94610	650-A3
550	BALFOUR AV	94610	650-A3
650	CALMAR AV	94610	650-B3
750	PALOMA AV	94610	650-B3
750	PALOMA AV	94610	650-B3
900	CARLSTON AV	94610	650-B3
SANTA RITA ST			**OAK**
2100	HARRINGTON AV	94601	650-D7
3700	RANSOM AV	94601	650-D7
3800	38TH AV	94601	650-D7
3900	39TH AV	94601	650-E7
4000	40TH AV	94601	650-E7
4030	ROSEDALE AV	94601	650-E7
4100	41ST AV	94601	650-E7
4200	42ND AV	94601	650-E7
4300	HIGH ST	94601	650-E7
SANTA ROSA AV			**BERK**
500	MENLO PL	94707	609-F5
550	THOUSAND OAKS BLVD	94707	609-F5
600	SAN MIGUEL AV	94707	609-F5
700	SAN LORENZO AV	94707	609-F5
SANTA ROSA AV			**OAK**
250	JEAN ST	94610	649-J2
200	CHETWOOD ST	94610	649-J2
170	MONTE VISTA AV	94610	649-J2
170	VERNON ST	94610	649-J2
150	MARIPOSA AV	94610	649-J2
170	OAKLAND AV	94610	649-J2
SANTA ROSA CIR			**ALA**
2100	BAINBRIDGE AV	94501	649-F7
2000	BAINBRIDGE AV	94501	649-E7
2100	BAINBRIDGE AV	94501	649-E7
SARATOGA ST			**ALA**
	W TOWER AV	94501	649-C6
	W HOPE ST	94501	649-C6
	W RANGER AV	94501	649-C6
	W MIDWAY AV	94501	649-C6
	W MALL SQ	94501	649-C6
	W ESSEX DR	94501	649-C6
	W CAPTAIN DODGE PL	94501	649-C6
	W RED LINE AV	94501	649-C6
	NAVY WY	94501	649-C6
SARAZEN AV			**OAK**
3300	CASTLEWOOD ST	94605	671-A3
3300	FLINTRIDGE LN	94605	671-A3
SARONI CT			**OAK**
1	SARONI DR	94611	630-F7
SARONI DR			**OAK**
6500	ASILOMAR DR	94611	630-E7
6750	PASO ROBLES DR	94611	630-F7
6800	HEARTWOOD DR	94611	630-F7
6900	SAYRE DR	94611	630-F7
6980	HOMEWOOD DR	94611	630-F7
7030	SARONI CT	94611	630-F7
7100	AZALEA LN	94611	630-F7
7210	GLENCOURT	94611	630-F6
7300	SAYRE DR	94611	630-G7
7330	GUNN DR	94611	630-G7
7370	WOODROW DR	94611	630-G7
7400	SHEPHERD CANYON RD	94611	630-G7
SATH CT			**ALA**
1	BROWN ST	94502	669-J6
SAUSAL ST			**OAK**
1700	SHEFFIELD AV	94602	650-C5
SAVANA LN			**ALA**
3500	GINGER LN	94502	670-B7
3560	KINGSTON LN	94502	670-B7
3600	MANGROVE LN	94502	670-B7
SAYRE DR			**OAK**
6900	SARONI DR	94611	630-F7
7270	CHICO CT	94611	630-G7
7300	SARONI DR	94611	630-G7
SCARBOROUGH DR			**OAK**
5700	BAGSHOTTE DR	94611	650-F1
5870	CHELTON DR	94611	650-F1
SCENIC AV			**BERK**
1300	BAYVIEW PL	94708	609-H7
1420	SPRING WY	94708	609-H7
1500	VINE ST	94708	609-H7
1600	CEDAR ST	94708	609-H7
1600	CEDAR ST	94709	609-H7
1660	HILGARD AV	94709	609-H7
1710	VIRGINIA ST	94709	629-H1
1800	LE CONTE AV	94709	629-H1
1800	RIDGE RD	94709	629-H1
1900	HEARST AV	94709	629-H1
SCENIC AV			**OAK**
2400	LINCOLN AV	94602	650-E4
2600	LAGUNA AV	94602	650-E4
SCENIC AV			**PDMT**
1	PACIFIC AV	94611	650-C1
30	OAKLAND AV	94611	650-C1
100	BLAIR AV	94611	650-C1
100	BLAIR AV	94611	630-B7
300	ALTA AV	94611	630-C7
400	ALTA AV	94611	630-C7
500	BLAIR AV	94611	650-C1
400	BELL AV	94611	630-C7
500	ALTA AV	94611	630-C7
SCHILLER ST			**ALA**
1500	SANTA CLARA AV	94501	669-J1
1600	LINCOLN AV	94501	669-J1
1700	PACIFIC AV	94501	669-J1
1800	BUENA VISTA AV	94501	669-J1
1900	EAGLE AV	94501	669-J1
2000	CLEMENT AV	94501	669-J1
SCHOOL ST			**OAK**
2700	FRUITVALE AV	94602	650-D5
2700	FRUITVALE AV	94602	650-D5
2780	CHAMPION ST	94602	650-D5
2860	CAPP ST	94602	650-D5
2890	BOSTON AV	94602	650-D5
2940	CUTHBERT AV	94602	650-D5
3000	COOLIDGE AV	94602	650-D5
3100	PLEITNER AV	94602	650-D5
3100	PLEITNER AV	94602	650-D5
3170	CURRAN AV	94602	650-E5
3170	CURRAN AV	94602	650-E5
3220	MAPLE AV	94602	650-E5
3230	MAPLE AV	94602	650-E5
3270	BERLIN WY	94602	650-E5
3320	LAUREL AV	94602	650-E5
3390	HUMBOLDT AV	94602	650-E6
3440	BARTLETT ST	94602	650-E6
3500	35TH AV	94602	650-E6
SCHOONER HILL			**OAK**
1	CHARING CROSS RD	94618	630-C4
60	CLIPPER HILL	94618	630-C4
70	CAPTAINS CV	94618	630-C4
100	GRAND VIEW DR	94618	630-C4
100	YANKEE HILL	94618	630-C4
SCHYLER ST			**OAK**
2900	CAPP ST	94602	650-D5
3000	CUTHBERT AV	94602	650-D5
SCOTIA AV			**OAK**
4600	GOLF LINKS RD	94605	671-E4
4650	STACY ST	94605	671-E4
4750	KEY CT	94605	671-E4
4900	COTTER ST	94605	671-E4
4930	MERLIN CT	94605	671-E4
4940	MARVIN CT	94605	671-E4
4970	MAYDON CT	94605	671-E4
5000	SHETLAND AV	94605	671-E4
5000	SHETLAND CT	94605	671-E4
5100	GRASS VALLEY RD	94605	671-E4
SCOTT ST			**OAK**
900	FAIRBANKS AV	94610	650-A2
1000	WELDON AV	94610	650-A2
SCOUT RD			**OAK**
5600	MOUNTAIN BLVD	94611	650-E1
5700	ASCOT DR	94611	650-E1
5700	ASCOT PL	94611	650-E1
SCOVILLE ST			**OAK**
5500	55TH AV	94621	670-F2
5700	57TH AV	94621	670-F2
SEA BRIDGE CT			**ALA**
100	SEA BRIDGE WY	94502	670-A5
SEA BRIDGE WY			**ALA**
100	PACKET LNDG	94502	670-A5
140	SEA BRIDGE CT	94502	670-A5
200	BEAUFORT HARBOR	94502	670-A5
300	CHATHAM POINTE	94502	670-A5
SEA HORSE			**ALA**
4000	OHIO	94501	649-E6
4020	CIMARRON ST	94501	649-E6
4020	MOUNT HOOD	94501	649-E6
SEA VIEW PKWY			**ALA**
2500	KOFMAN PKWY	94502	669-H5
2500	TRALEE LN	94502	669-H5
2520	OLDCASTLE LN	94502	669-H5
2600	CALLAN PL	94502	669-H5
2620	KILLARNEY PL	94502	669-J5
2640	CASTLEBAR PL	94502	669-J5
2640	KARA RD	94502	669-J5
2660	TULLAMORE PL	94502	669-J5
2680	ENNIS PL	94502	669-J5

ALAMEDA CO.

PRIMARY STREET Address	Cross Street	ZIP	CITY Pg-Grid
SEA VIEW PKWY			**ALA**
2680	JUSTIN CIR	94502	669-J5
2700	AUGHINBAUGH WY	94502	669-J5
2800	BRUNSWICK RD	94502	669-J5
2850	NOTTINGHAM DR	94502	669-J5
2900	GAINSBOROUGH CT	94502	669-J5
2950	AVINGTON RD	94502	669-J5
2970	NORWICH RD	94502	670-A5
3000	OAKSHADE DR	94502	670-A5
3000	SHEFFIELD RD	94502	670-A5
SEABORN CT			**ALA**
1600	GRAND ST	94501	669-H1
SEACOR CT			**OAK**
4200	MOUNTAIN BLVD	94605	671-B2
W SEAPLANE LAGOON			**ALA**
	HANCOCK ST	94501	649-E7
	ORION ST	94501	649-D7
	FERRY PT	94501	649-D7
SEATTLE RD			**ALA**
200	ALAMEDA RD	94501	649-D6
100	PAN AM WY	94501	649-D6
SEAVIEW AV			**PDMT**
1	MOUNTAIN AV	94611	650-C1
20	LAKEVIEW AV	94611	650-C1
20	LINCOLN AV	94611	650-C2
190	HAMPTON RD	94610	650-C2
240	FARRAGUT AV	94610	650-C2
300	LA SALLE AV	94610	650-C2
400	ASHMOUNT AV	94610	650-C2
SEAWALL DR			**BERK**
80	UNIVERSITY AV	94804	629-B2
90	UNIVERSITY AV	94804	629-B3
SELBORNE DR			**PDMT**
1	ESTATES DR	94611	650-D2
100	SANDRINGHAM RD	94611	650-D2
SELKIRK ST			**OAK**
1	39TH AV	94619	650-G5
60	ANDERSON AV	94619	650-G5
100	39TH AV	94619	650-G5
150	DUNSMUIR AV	94619	650-G5
SEMINARY AV			**ALA**
1400	BEACH RD	94502	670-B7
SEMINARY AV			**OAK**
1100	SAN LEANDRO ST	94621	670-E3
1200	TEVIS ST	94621	670-E2
1300	EASTLAWN ST	94621	670-F2
1400	INTERNATIONAL BLVD	94621	670-F2
1600	E 16TH ST	94621	670-F2
1700	E 17TH ST	94621	670-F2
1800	BROMLEY AV	94621	670-F2
1900	HOLWAY ST	94621	670-F2
1070	HARMON AV	94621	670-F2
2000	HARMON AV	94621	670-F2
2150	HAYES ST	94621	670-F2
2150	HAYES ST	94605	670-F2
2200	ELIZABETH ST	94605	670-F2
2240	SEMINARY CT	94605	670-F2
2300	HILTON ST	94605	670-F2
2400	TRASK ST	94605	670-F2
2440	AVENAL AV	94605	670-F2
2500	BANCROFT AV	94605	670-G1
2550	FORTUNE WY	94605	670-G1
2590	FOOTHILL BLVD	94605	670-G1
2600	WALNUT ST	94605	670-G1
2650	KINGSLEY CIR	94605	670-G1
2700	FLEMING AV	94605	670-G1
2730	MORSE DR	94605	670-G1
2800	MORSE DR	94605	670-G1
2820	PICARDY DR	94605	670-G1
2830	PICARDY DR	94605	670-G1
2900	ROBERTS AV	94605	670-G1
3000	BRANN ST	94605	670-G1
3200	CAMDEN ST	94605	670-G1
3200	MACARTHUR BLVD	94605	670-G1
3300	MACARTHUR BLVD	94613	670-G1
3300	MACARTHUR BLVD	94605	670-G1
3330	MONADNOCK WY	94613	670-G1
3330	MONADNOCK WY	94605	670-G1
3400	MAURITANIA AV	94613	670-H1
3400	MAURITANIA AV	94605	670-H1
3050	LAIRD AV	94605	670-H1
3050	LAIRD AV	94613	670-H1
3050	OUTLOOK AV	94605	650-H7
3050	OUTLOOK AV	94613	650-H7
3600	OUTLOOK AV	94613	650-H7
3600	OUTLOOK AV	94605	650-H7
6000	OAKDALE AV	94613	650-H7
6000	OAKDALE AV	94605	650-H7
6060	HILLMONT DR	94613	650-H7
6060	HILLMONT DR	94605	650-H7
6120	PINE TOP AV	94613	650-H7
6120	PINE TOP AV	94605	650-H7
6140	OVERDALE AV	94605	650-H7
6200	KUHNLE AV	94605	650-H7
6200	SUNNYMERE AV	94605	650-H7
SEMINARY CT			**OAK**
5900	SEMINARY AV	94605	670-F2
SENECA ST			**OAK**
8500	THERMAL ST	94605	671-A3
SENIOR AV			**BERK**
1	FAIRLAWN DR	94708	609-J7
1	HARVARD CIR	94708	609-J7
100	GRIZZLY PEAK BLVD	94708	609-J7
SEQUOYAH RD			**OAK**
3800	MOUNTAIN BLVD	94605	671-B3
3830	FAIRWAY AV	94605	671-B3
3940	BARCELONA ST	94605	671-C3
3980	TURNLEY AV	94605	671-C3
4110	SAINT ANDREWS RD	94605	671-C3
4150	OAK HILL RD	94605	671-C3
4170	OAK HILL RD	94605	671-C2
4440	HEAFEY RD	94605	671-C2
4460	SAGE RD	94605	671-C2
4460	OAK HILL RD	94605	671-C2
4520	MCGURRIN RD	94605	671-D2
4610	MENDENHALL RD	94605	671-D2
4680	RIDGEMOOR RD	94605	671-D2
4800	KELLER AV	94605	671-D2
SEQUOYAH VIEW CT			**OAK**
1	SEQUOYAH VIEW DR	94605	671-C3
SEQUOYAH VIEW DR			**OAK**
1	OAK HILL RD	94605	671-C3
40	SEQUOYAH VIEW CT	94605	671-C3
300	OAK HILL RD	94605	671-C3
SERENADE PL			**ALA**
	W MIDWAY AV	94501	649-D6
	CORPUS CHRISTI RD	94501	649-D6
	BARBERS POINT RD	94501	649-D6
	STARDUST PL	94501	649-D6
	HANCOCK ST	94501	649-D6
SERENO CIR			**OAK**
100	CAMPUS DR	94619	650-H5
100	REDWOOD RD	94619	650-H5
SERRAMAR DR			**OAK**
1	FAIRLANE DR	94611	630-D5
SEXTUS RD			**OAK**
200	CORAL RD	94603	670-F7
300	EMPIRE RD	94603	670-F7
SHADOW MOUNTAIN			**OAK**
1	ELYSIAN FIELDS DR	94605	671-D2
100	QUIETWOOD	94605	671-E3
200	THOUSAND OAKS	94605	671-E3
SHAFTER AV			**OAK**
3700	W MACARTHUR BLVD	94609	649-H1
3800	38TH ST	94609	649-H1
4000	40TH ST	94609	629-H7
4100	41ST ST	94609	629-H7
4200	42ND ST	94609	629-H7
4300	43RD ST	94609	629-H7
4400	44TH ST	94609	629-H7
4500	45TH ST	94609	629-H7
4800	48TH ST	94609	629-H7
4900	49TH ST	94609	629-H6
5000	50TH ST	94609	629-H6
5100	51ST ST	94618	629-H6
5150	AVON ST	94618	629-H6
5200	CAVOUR ST	94618	629-J6
5300	CLIFTON ST	94618	629-J6
5400	HUDSON ST	94618	629-J6
5500	FOREST ST	94618	629-J5
5600	COLLEGE AV	94618	629-J5
5760	KEITH AV	94618	629-J5
5760	MCMILLAN AV	94618	629-J5
SHAMROCK LN			**ALA**
1	VISTA RD	94502	669-H5
100	TRALEE LN	94502	669-H5
SHANER DR			**ALA**
2700	BREHAUT CT	94502	669-J6
2750	STRAUB WY	94502	669-J6
2800	BROWN ST	94502	669-J6
SHANNON CIR			**ALA**
50	KOFMAN PKWY	94502	669-H5
SHARON AV			**PDMT**
1	DORMIDERA AV	94611	650-C1
50	SHARON CT	94611	650-C1
100	MOUNTAIN AV	94611	650-C1
SHARON CT			**PDMT**
1	SHARON AV	94611	650-C1
SHARON RD			**ALA**
	LAWRENCE RD	94502	669-J6
	MECARTNEY RD	94502	669-J6
	BANNISTER WY	94502	669-J6
SHASTA			**ALA**
3000	MULVANY CIR	94501	649-E6
SHASTA RD			**BERK**
2600	TAMALPAIS RD	94708	609-J7
2700	TAMALPAIS RD	94708	609-H6
2740	KEITH AV	94708	609-J6
2800	CRAGMONT AV	94708	609-J6
2830	NORTHGATE AV	94708	609-J6
2840	KEELER AV	94708	609-J6
2860	CAMPUS DR	94708	609-J6
2900	STERLING AV	94708	609-J6
2900	QUEENS RD	94708	609-J6
2900	STERLING AV	94708	609-J6
2970	MILLER AV	94708	609-J6
3000	GRIZZLY PEAK BLVD	94708	609-J6
3000	GRIZZLY PEAK BLVD	94708	609-J6
3010	HILL RD	94708	609-J6
	PARK GATE	94708	609-J6
	GOLF COURSE DR	94708	610-A6
	PARK HILLS RD	94708	610-A6
SHATTUCK AV			**BERK**
800	INDIAN ROCK AV	94707	609-G6
880	MARIN AV	94707	609-G6
1000	LOS ANGELES AV	94707	609-G6
1100	WALNUT ST	94707	609-G6
1110	TERRACE WK	94707	609-G6
1160	AMADOR AV	94707	609-G6
1200	EUNICE ST	94709	609-G7
1330	BERRYMAN ST	94709	609-G7
1400	ROSE ST	94709	609-G7
1450	SHATTUCK PL	94709	609-G7
1500	VINE ST	94709	609-G7
1600	CEDAR ST	94709	609-G7
1660	LINCOLN ST	94709	629-G1
1720	VIRGINIA ST	94709	629-G1
1780	FRANCISCO ST	94709	629-G1
1840	DELAWARE ST	94709	629-G1
1900	HEARST AV	94704	629-G1
1950	BERKELEY WY	94704	629-G1
1950	BERKELEY WY	94704	629-G1
2000	UNIVERSITY AV	94704	629-G1
2060	ADDISON ST	94704	629-G2
2110	CENTER ST	94704	629-G2
2130	SHATTUCK SQ	94704	629-G2
2160	ALLSTON WY	94704	629-G2
2210	KITTREDGE ST	94704	629-G2
2270	BANCROFT WY	94704	629-G2
2320	DURANT AV	94704	629-G2
2370	CHANNING WY	94704	629-G2
2420	HASTE ST	94704	629-G2
2470	DWIGHT WY	94704	629-H3
2530	BLAKE ST	94704	629-H3
2580	PARKER ST	94704	629-H3
2630	CARLETON ST	94704	629-H3
2700	DERBY ST	94705	629-H3
2700	DERBY ST	94704	629-H3
2710	ADELINE ST	94705	629-H3
2710	ADELINE ST	94703	629-H3
2730	WARD ST	94705	629-H3
2730	WARD ST	94703	629-H3
2800	STUART ST	94705	629-H3
2800	STUART ST	94703	629-H3
2820	OREGON ST	94705	629-H3
2820	OREGON ST	94703	629-H3
2900	RUSSELL ST	94705	629-H4
2900	RUSSELL ST	94703	629-H4
3000	ASHBY AV	94705	629-H4
3000	ASHBY AV	94703	629-H4
3020	EMERSON ST	94705	629-H4
3020	EMERSON ST	94703	629-H4
3030	ESSEX ST	94705	629-H4
3030	ESSEX ST	94703	629-H4
3100	PRINCE ST	94705	629-H4
3100	PRINCE ST	94703	629-H4
3200	WOOLSEY ST	94705	629-H4
3200	WOOLSEY ST	94703	629-H4
SHATTUCK AV			**OAK**
4500	TELEGRAPH AV	94609	629-H7
4530	45TH ST	94609	629-H7
4600	46TH ST	94609	629-H7
4700	47TH ST	94609	629-H6
4800	48TH ST	94609	629-H6
4900	49TH ST	94609	629-H6
5070	51ST ST	94609	629-H6
5200	52ND ST	94609	629-H6
5300	53RD ST	94609	629-H6
	54TH ST	94609	629-H6
	54TH ST	94609	629-H6
5500	55TH ST	94609	629-H6
5600	56TH ST	94609	629-H6
5650	AILEEN ST	94609	629-H5
5700	57TH ST	94609	629-H5
	58TH ST	94609	629-H5
5800	58TH ST	94609	629-H5
5900	59TH ST	94609	629-H5
6000	60TH ST	94609	629-H5
6050	61ST ST	94609	629-H5
6100	61ST ST	94609	629-H5
6110	POIRIER ST	94609	629-H5
	62ND ST	94609	629-H5
6200	62ND ST	94609	629-H5
	63RD ST	94609	629-H5
6300	63RD ST	94609	629-H5
6400	ALCATRAZ AV	94609	629-H4
6500	65TH ST	94609	629-H4
6530	FAIRVIEW ST	94609	629-H4
6600	66TH ST	94609	629-H4
6700	WOOLSEY ST	94609	629-H4
SHATTUCK PL			**BERK**
1400	ROSE ST	94709	609-G7
1400	HENRY ST	94709	609-G7
1500	SHATTUCK AV	94709	609-G7
SHATTUCK SQ			**BERK**
1	UNIVERSITY AV	94704	629-G1
90	ADDISON ST	94704	629-G2
170	CENTER ST	94704	629-G2
200	SHATTUCK AV	94704	629-G2
SHAW ST			**OAK**
10300	STANLEY AV	94605	671-B5
10200	FRAZIER AV	94605	671-B5
10300	TRUMAN AV	94605	671-B5
SHAWNEE CT			**OAK**
	TARTAN WY	94619	650-J4
SHAY DR			**OAK**
7900	HANSOM DR	94605	671-C1
8100	HANSOM DR	94605	671-C1
SHEFFIELD AV			**OAK**
2900	E 29TH ST	94602	650-C5
3200	MORRISON AV	94602	650-C5
3370	SAUSAL ST	94602	650-C5
3500	MACARTHUR BLVD	94602	650-C4
SHEFFIELD RD			**ALA**
100	BRUNSWICK RD	94502	669-J5
160	SHEFFIELD WY	94502	669-J5
270	STANBRIDGE CT	94502	669-J5
270	STANBRIDGE LN	94502	669-J5
310	CUMBERLAND CT	94502	669-J5
310	CUMBERLAND WY	94502	669-J5
350	CHANNING WY	94502	669-J5
400	INVERNESS CT	94502	669-J5
400	INVERNESS WY	94502	669-J5
450	CHESWICK CT	94502	669-J5
430	ENNISMORE CT	94502	670-A5
500	BRIGHTON CT	94502	670-A5
500	BRIGHTON RD	94502	670-A5
550	PUDDINGSTONE RD	94502	670-A5
560	KEVINGTON PL	94502	670-A5
600	ROXBURG LN	94502	670-A5
700	OAKSHADE DR	94502	670-A5
700	SEA VIEW PKWY	94502	670-A5
SHEFFIELD WY			**ALA**
	AUGHINBAUGH WY	94502	669-J5
	SHEFFIELD RD	94502	669-J5
SHELDON ST			**OAK**
10500	LEEWARD WY	94605	671-B5
10580	107TH AV	94605	671-B5
10730	BARRETT ST	94605	671-B5
SHELL GATE PL			**ALA**
1100	SHELL GATE RD	94501	669-G2
1200	FAIR HAVEN RD	94501	669-G2
SHELL GATE RD			**ALA**
300	SHORELINE DR	94501	669-G3
500	SHELL GATE PL	94501	669-G3
SHELLMOUND ST			**BERK**
6700	67TH ST	94804	629-D4
6800	ASHBY AV	94804	629-D4
SHELLMOUND ST			**EMVL**
5530	CHRISTIE AV	94608	629-E6
5840	CHRISTIE AV	94608	629-D6
6400	64TH ST	94608	629-E5
6500	65TH ST	94608	629-D5
6600	66TH ST	94608	629-D5
6700	67TH ST	94608	629-D5
SHELTERWOOD DR			**OAK**
6400	SHEPHERD CANYON RD	94611	630-F7
6500	WESTOVER DR	94611	630-F7
SHEPARDSON LN			**ALA**
1	OAK PARK DR	94502	670-A5
200	BAY PARK TER	94502	670-A5
SHEPHERD CANYON RD			**OAK**
5700	SNAKE RD	94611	650-E1
	ESCHER DR	94611	630-F7
6420	PASO ROBLES DR	94611	630-F7
6500	SHELTERWOOD DR	94611	630-F7
6600	BANNING DR	94611	630-G7
6630	TIFFANY LN	94611	630-G7
6700	SARONI DR	94611	630-G7
6800	GUNN DR	94611	630-G7
6810	GUNN DR	94611	630-G7
6900	MOORE DR	94611	630-G7
6960	AITKEN DR	94611	630-G7
7000	EASTWOOD CT	94611	630-G7
8000	ARROWHEAD DR	94611	630-G7
8100	SKYLINE BLVD	94611	630-G7
8100	PINEHURST RD	94611	630-G7
SHEPHERD ST			**OAK**
4500	CARSON ST	94619	650-G6
SHERIDAN AV			**PDMT**
100	HIGHLAND AV	94611	650-C1
200	CAPERTON AV	94611	650-C1
200	SIERRA AV	94611	650-C1
200	CAPERTON AV	94611	650-C1
270	LAKEVIEW AV	94611	650-C1
300	LINCOLN AV	94611	650-C2
400	WILDWOOD AV	94611	650-C2
SHERIDAN RD			**OAK**
1	AGNES ST	94618	630-C6
100	BROADWAY TER	94618	630-C6
100	ERBA PTH	94618	630-C6
200	COCHRANE AV	94618	630-C6
SHERMAN ST			**ALA**
1100	DAYTON AV	94501	669-H2
1200	CLINTON AV	94501	669-H2
1300	SAN ANTONIO AV	94501	669-H1
	ENCINAL AV	94501	669-H1
	CENTRAL AV	94501	669-H1
1400	CENTRAL AV	94501	669-H1
1500	SANTA CLARA AV	94501	669-H1
1600	LINCOLN AV	94501	669-H1
1700	PACIFIC AV	94501	669-H1
1800	BUENA VISTA AV	94501	649-H7
1900	ATLANTIC AV	94501	649-H7
1900	EAGLE AV	94501	649-H7
SHERWICK DR			**OAK**
6800	CHARING CROSS RD	94705	630-C4
7000	BRISTOL DR	94705	630-C4
SHERWIN AV			**EMVL**
1400	HORTON ST	94608	629-E7
1500	HUBBARD ST	94608	629-E7
1600	HALLECK ST	94608	629-E7
SHERWOOD DR			**OAK**
5900	MERRIEWOOD DR	94611	630-D6
5940	ABBOTT DR	94611	630-D6
6000	URANUS AV	94611	630-D6
SHERWOOD LN			**ALA**
100	HARBOR RD	94502	669-J5
120	BRUNSWICK RD	94502	669-J5
170	CHESHIRE CT	94502	669-J5
200	NOTTINGHAM DR	94502	669-J5
SHETLAND AV			**OAK**
4880	SCOTIA AV	94605	671-E4
4880	SHETLAND CT	94605	671-E4
4850	STACY ST	94605	671-E4
4800	COTTER ST	94605	671-E4
4700	GLEN ARTNEY CT	94605	671-E4
4800	GOLF LINKS RD	94605	671-E4
SHETLAND CT			**OAK**
100	SCOTIA AV	94605	671-E4
100	SHETLAND AV	94605	671-E4
SHIRLEY DR			**OAK**
	BURTON DR	94611	650-G1
	WILTON DR	94611	650-G1
SHONE AV			**OAK**
3600	STERLING DR	94605	671-A2
3700	GREENLY DR	94605	671-A2
3800	WINTHROPE ST	94605	671-A2
3900	EARL ST	94605	671-A2
4000	FONTAINE ST	94605	671-A2
4100	MOUNTAIN BLVD	94605	671-B2
4200	SANFORD ST	94605	671-B2
SHORELINE DR			**ALA**
900	WESTLINE DR	94501	669-G2
1000	SHELL GATE RD	94501	669-G3
1100	FAIR HAVEN RD	94501	669-G3
1200	SAND BEACH RD	94501	669-G3
1300	HARBOR LIGHT RD	94501	669-G3
1400	CORAL REEF RD	94501	669-G3
1500	SUNSET RD	94501	669-G3
1700	GRAND ST	94501	669-H3
1860	KITTY HAWK RD	94501	669-H3
2070	WILLOW ST	94501	669-H3
2400	PARK ST	94501	669-J4
2600	BAYVIEW DR	94501	669-J4
2600	BROADWAY	94501	669-J4
SHOREPOINT CT			**ALA**
900	WESTLINE DR	94501	669-G2
SHOREY ST			**OAK**
1750	WOOD ST	94607	649-C3
1750	8TH ST	94607	649-C3
1800	PINE ST	94607	649-C3
SHORT ST			**BERK**
1600	LINCOLN ST	94702	629-F1
1700	VIRGINIA ST	94702	629-F1
1800	DELAWARE ST	94702	629-F1
1900	HEARST AV	94702	629-F1
SHORT ST			**OAK**
2600	BROOKDALE AV	94619	650-E6
2800	ALLENDALE AV	94619	650-E6
2800	ALLENDALE AV	94619	650-E6
3000	PENNIMAN AV	94619	650-E6
SHORTHILL RD			**OAK**
4300	OAK HILL RD	94605	671-C2
4500	OAK HILL RD	94605	671-C2
SIERRA AV			**PDMT**
1	HIGHLAND AV	94611	650-C1
100	CAPERTON AV	94611	650-C1
100	SHERIDAN AV	94611	650-C1
SIERRA ST			**BERK**
1000	SONOMA AV	94707	609-F6
1100	MADERA ST	94707	609-F6
SIESTA CT			**OAK**
4300	HIGH ST	94619	650-G6
4300	PAMPAS AV	94619	650-G6
SIGOURNEY AV			**OAK**
10100	ELYSIAN FIELDS DR	94605	671-C3
9900	OAK HILL RD	94605	671-C3
10100	GOLF LINKS RD	94605	671-C3
SIKORSKY ST			**OAK**
1000	LOCKHEED ST	94621	670-D6
1060	NORTHRUP ST	94621	670-D6
SILER PL			**OAK**
1000	ALVARADO RD	94705	630-B3
SILVA LN			**ALA**
1050	MAGNOLIA DR	94502	670-B7
1110	PAYOT LN	94502	670-B7
1150	MCSHERRY WY	94502	670-B7
1200	DEPASSIER WY	94502	670-A7
1230	DWINELLE CT	94502	670-A7
1280	PYNE LN	94502	670-A7
1290	CLARKE LN	94502	670-A7
SILVERADO CT			**OAK**
300	DONNA WY	94605	671-D3
300	INVERNESS CT	94605	671-D3
SILVERWOOD AV			**OAK**
3700	NORTON AV	94602	650-F5
3800	CALIFORNIA ST	94602	650-F5
3800	NORTON AV	94602	650-F5
SIMMONS ST			**OAK**
3480	MACARTHUR BLVD	94619	650-G7
3390	WYMAN ST	94619	650-G7
3300	MORCOM AV	94619	650-G7
3390	MADERA AV	94619	650-G7
SIMS DR			**OAK**
6600	LIGGETT DR	94611	650-E1
6800	ESTATES DR	94611	650-E2
SIMSON ST			**OAK**
6500	MOKELUMNE AV	94605	670-H1
6600	BUENA VENTURA AV	94605	670-H1
6800	ALTAMONT AV	94605	670-J1
6900	MOKELUMNE AV	94605	670-J1
7000	73RD AV	94605	670-J1
SINGLETON AV			**ALA**
1	MAIN ST	94501	649-E6
140	MOSLEY AV	94501	649-E6
230	ANNAPOLIS CIR	94501	649-E6
280	ANNAPOLIS CIR	94501	649-E6
300	MAYPORT CIR	94501	649-E6
300	MOSLEY AV	94501	649-E6
SKYHAWK ST			**ALA**
	W ATLANTIC AV	94501	649-D7
	W PACIFIC AV	94501	649-D7
	W ORISKANY AV	94501	669-D1
	W HORNET AV	94501	669-D1
SKYLINE BLVD			**OAK**
5800	OLD TUNNEL RD	94611	630-D4
6050	BROADWAY TER	94611	630-E4
6300	ELVERTON DR	94611	630-E5
6430	OBSERVATION PL	94611	630-F5
6680	DIABLO DR	94611	630-F5
7100	ELVERTON DR	94611	630-F5
7200	WINDING WY	94611	630-F6
7200	SNAKE RD	94611	630-F6
7400	MANZANITA DR	94611	630-G6
8200	PINEHURST RD	94611	630-G7
8200	SHEPHERD CANYON RD	94611	630-G7
8280	PINE HILLS DR	94611	630-G7
8300	EVERGREEN AV	94611	630-G7
8440	PINE HILLS DR	94611	630-G7
9050	CARISBROOK DR	94611	650-G1
9100	BURTON DR	94611	650-G1
9200	ASCOT DR	94611	650-G1
9210	WILTON DR	94611	650-G1
9300	WATERLOO DR	94611	650-G1
9300	MELVILLE LN	94611	650-G1
9360	TOTTERDELL ST	94611	650-G1
9500	MELVILLE DR	94611	650-G2
11460	JOAQUIN MILLER RD	94619	650-H4
	CRESTMONT DR	94619	650-H4

PRIMARY STREET Address	Cross Street	ZIP	CITY Pg-Grid
SKYLINE BLVD			**OAK**
11790	KIMBERLIN HEIGHTS DR	94619	650-H4
11900	REDWOOD RD	94619	650-J5
12300	FERNHOFF RD	94619	651-A5
12400	BACON RD	94619	651-A5
12500	CHAPPELL PL	94619	651-A5
12530	BROOKPARK RD	94619	651-A5
12600	DREYER PL	94619	651-A6
12700	WEAVER PL	94619	651-A6
12720	MOTT PL	94619	651-B6
12900	COLBOURN PL	94619	651-B6
12950	BRANDY ROCK WY	94619	651-B6
13160	PARKRIDGE DR	94619	651-B6
13400	GRAHAM PL	94619	651-B6
13460	LEXFORD PL	94619	651-C7
13500	CATHY LN	94619	651-C7
13700	SKYWAY LN	94619	651-C7
13720	BARMIED PL	94619	651-C7
13700	HANSOM DR	94619	671-D1
14400	SKYLINE CIR	94619	671-D1
14800	KELLER AV	94605	671-D2
SKYLINE CIR			**OAK**
8000	SKYLINE BLVD	94619	671-D1
SKYPOINT CT			**OAK**
4200	CAMPUS DR	94619	650-J6
SKYWAY LN			**OAK**
1	SKYLINE BLVD	94619	651-C7
SLATER LN			**OAK**
1	ALVARADO RD	94705	630-A3
100	EVERGREEN PATH LN	94705	630-A3
SLOAN ST			**OAK**
2100	DIMOND AV	94602	650-D4
2200	FRUITVALE AV	94602	650-D4
SLOPE CREST DR			**OAK**
13200	KNOLL RIDGE WY	94619	651-C6
13400	PARKRIDGE DR	94619	651-C6
SMITH CT			**ALA**
1	ANDERSON RD	94502	669-H5
1	SWEET RD	94502	669-H5
SMYTH RD			**BERK**
	FERNWALD RD	94704	630-A2
SNAKE RD			**OAK**
5500	MOUNTAIN BLVD	94611	650-E1
5550	ANDREWS ST	94611	650-E1
5650	SHEPHERD CANYON RD	94611	650-E1
5930	MAGELLAN DR	94611	650-E1
6000	ZINN DR	94611	630-E7
6130	GASPAR DR	94611	630-E7
6230	DRAKE DR	94611	630-E7
6400	COLTON BLVD	94611	630-E7
6600	ARMOUR DR	94611	630-F7
7150	THORNHILL DR	94611	630-F6
7200	HEMLOCK ST	94611	630-F6
7380	COLTON BLVD	94611	630-F6
7400	SKYLINE BLVD	94611	630-F6
SNELL ST			**OAK**
6900	69TH AV	94621	670-F4
7000	70TH AV	94621	670-F4
7100	71ST AV	94621	670-F4
7500	75TH AV	94621	670-F4
SNOWBERRY WK			**ALA**
	KITTY HAWK PL	94501	669-H3
	KITTY HAWK RD	94501	669-H3
SNOWDOWN AV			**OAK**
10800	MALCOLM AV	94605	671-D4
10900	OVERMOOR ST	94605	671-D4
SOBRANTE RD			**OAK**
6500	THORNHILL DR	94611	630-E6
6570	CONRAD CT	94611	630-F5
6710	THORNDALE DR	94611	630-E6
6830	THORN CT	94611	630-F5
6960	OAKWOOD DR	94611	630-F5
SOJOURNER TRUTH CT			**BERK**
2700	WARD ST	94702	629-F3
SOLANO AV			**ALB**
700	CLEVELAND AV	94706	609-C6
770	PIERCE ST	94706	609-C6
800	FILLMORE ST	94706	609-D6
840	TAYLOR ST	94706	609-D6
880	POLK ST	94706	609-D6
910	CERRITO ST	94706	609-D6
950	JACKSON ST	94706	609-D6
980	MADISON ST	94706	609-D6
1020	ADAMS ST	94706	609-D6
1060	SAN PABLO AV	94706	609-D6
1100	KAINS AV	94706	609-D6
1140	STANNAGE AV	94706	609-D6
1180	CORNELL AV	94706	609-D6
1210	TALBOT AV	94706	609-E6
1250	EVELYN AV	94706	609-E6
	MASONIC AV	94706	609-E6
	KEY ROUTE BLVD	94706	609-E6
1300	KEY ROUTE BLVD	94706	609-E6
1320	POMONA AV	94706	609-E6
1320	POMONA AV	94706	609-E6
1340	RAMONA AV	94706	609-E6
1340	RAMONA AV	94706	609-E6
1360	CARMEL AV	94706	609-E6
1370	CARMEL AV	94706	609-E6
1380	SAN CARLOS AV	94706	609-E6
1390	SANTA FE AV	94706	609-E6
1420	CURTIS ST	94706	609-E6
1420	CURTIS ST	94706	609-E6
1500	NEILSON ST	94706	609-F6
1540	PERALTA AV	94706	609-F6
1600	ORDWAY ST	94707	609-F6
1600	TACOMA AV	94707	609-F6
1650	VENTURA AV	94707	609-F6
1700	TULARE AV	94707	609-F6
SOLANO AV			**BERK**
	LOS ANGELES AV	94707	609-G6
	MARIN AV	94707	609-G6
	SUTTER ST	94707	609-G6
1420	CURTIS ST	94707	609-E6
1500	NEILSON ST	94707	609-F6
1550	PERALTA AV	94707	609-F6
1600	ORDWAY ST	94707	609-F6
1600	TACOMA AV	94707	609-F6
1650	VENTURA AV	94707	609-F6
1700	TULARE AV	94707	609-F6
1740	ENSENADA AV	94707	609-F6
1780	MODOC ST	94707	609-F6
1800	COLUSA AV	94707	609-F6
1820	COLUSA AV	94707	609-F6
1860	FRESNO AV	94707	609-F6
1900	THE ALAMEDA	94707	609-G6
1950	CONTRA COSTA AV	94707	609-G6
1950	CONTRA COSTA AV	94707	609-G6
	LOS ANGELES AV	94707	609-G6
SOLANO WY			**OAK**
1500	14TH AV	94606	650-A6
1570	15TH AV	94606	650-A6
1670	16TH AV	94606	650-A6
1770	17TH AV	94606	650-A6
1870	18TH AV	94606	650-A6
1960	19TH AV	94606	650-A6
2060	20TH AV	94606	650-A6
2160	21ST AV	94606	650-A6
2260	22ND AV	94606	650-A7
SOLOMON LN			**ALA**
3300	BISMARCK LN	94502	670-A7
3400	HOLLY ST	94502	670-A7
3400	HOLLY ST	94502	670-A7
3420	WINDWARD LN	94502	670-A7
3500	LEEWARD LN	94502	670-A7
SOMERSET PL			**BERK**
1	ARLINGTON AV	94707	609-G5
1	YOSEMITE RD	94707	609-G5
50	SOUTHAMPTON AV	94707	609-G5
SOMERSET RD			**OAK**
400	ESTATES DR	94611	650-E2
SOMERSET RD			**PDMT**
1	ESTATES DR	94611	650-D2
250	CREST RD	94611	650-D2
SONIA ST			**OAK**
1	MODOC AV	94618	630-C6
200	MODOC AV	94618	630-C6
SONOMA AV			**ALB**
1400	CURTIS ST	94706	609-E6
1450	NEILSON ST	94706	609-E6
1470	NEILSON ST	94706	609-F6
1530	PERALTA AV	94706	609-F6
1600	ORDWAY ST	94707	609-F6
1600	ORDWAY ST	94706	609-F6
1630	VENTURA AV	94707	609-F6
1630	VENTURA AV	94706	609-F6
1630	VENTURA AV	94707	609-F6
1630	VENTURA AV	94706	609-F6
1670	TULARE AV	94707	609-F6
1670	TULARE AV	94706	609-F6
SONOMA AV			**BERK**
1670	TULARE AV	94707	609-F6
1670	TULARE AV	94706	609-F6
1700	SIERRA ST	94707	609-F6
1700	SIERRA ST	94706	609-F6
1740	MERCED ST	94707	609-F6
1740	MERCED ST	94706	609-F6
1740	MONTEREY AV	94707	609-F6
1800	COLUSA AV	94707	609-F6
1840	FRESNO AV	94707	609-G7
1890	JOSEPHINE ST	94707	609-G7
1900	HOPKINS ST	94707	609-G7
SONOMA WY			**OAK**
1400	14TH AV	94606	650-A5
1600	16TH AV	94606	650-A5
1700	17TH AV	94606	650-A6
1800	18TH AV	94606	650-A6
2000	20TH AV	94606	650-B6
2120	21ST AV	94606	650-B6
2240	22ND AV	94606	650-B6
SOTELLO AV			**PDMT**
1	GLEN ALPINE RD	94611	650-D1
100	GLEN ALPINE RD	94611	650-D1
SOUTH LOOP RD			**ALA**
1200	HARBOR BAY PKWY	94502	690-A1
1200	NORTH LOOP RD	94502	690-A1
1700	HARBOR BAY PKWY	94502	690-A1
1700	ROAD B	94502	690-A1
SOUTH MALL			**OAK**
1	COLISEUM WY	94621	670-E4
100	COLISEUM WY	94621	670-E4
SOUTH SHORE CTR W			**ALA**
600	OTIS DR	94501	669-J3
SOUTHAMPTON AV			**BERK**
100	SOMERSET PL	94707	609-G5
150	SAN DIEGO RD	94707	609-G5
200	SOUTHAMPTON LN	94707	609-G5
240	SAN LUIS RD	94707	609-G5
250	SAN LUIS RD	94707	609-G5
300	SANTA BARBARA RD	94707	609-G5
SOUTHAMPTON LN			**BERK**
	SOUTHAMPTON AV	94707	609-G5
SOUTHWEST PL			**BERK**
	DWIGHT WY	94705	630-A2
	DERBY ST	94705	630-A2
SOUTHWOOD CT			**OAK**
1	PASO ROBLES DR	94611	630-F7
SOUTHWOOD DR			**ALA**
2900	GIBBONS DR	94501	670-B3
2900	NORTHWOOD DR	94501	670-B3
2950	THOMPSON AV	94501	670-B3
3000	BAYO VISTA AV	94501	670-B3
3000	FAIRVIEW AV	94501	670-B3
3060	NORTHWOOD DR	94501	670-B3
SOUZA CT			**ALA**
1	RATTO RD	94502	669-J7
SPAULDING AV			**BERK**
2100	ADDISON ST	94703	629-F2
2200	ALLSTON WY	94703	629-F2
2300	BANCROFT WY	94703	629-F2
2400	CHANNING WY	94703	629-F3
2500	DWIGHT WY	94703	629-F3
SPENCER RD			**ALA**
	WAKEFIELD DR	94501	649-J7
	ICARUS DR	94501	649-J7
	MCCULLOCH DR	94501	649-J7
	DENNISON ST	94501	649-J7
	HUDSON DR	94501	649-J7
SPENCER ST			**OAK**
6900	69TH AV	94621	670-F3
7000	70TH AV	94621	670-F3
7100	71ST AV	94621	670-F3
7200	72ND AV	94621	670-F4
7300	73RD AV	94621	670-F4
7500	75TH AV	94621	670-F4
7600	76TH AV	94621	670-G4
7700	77TH AV	94621	670-G4
SPILLMAN RD			**OAK**
	KELLER AV	94605	671-D2
SPINNAKER WY			**BERK**
10	BREAKWATER DR	94804	629-B1
300	MARINA BLVD	94804	629-B1
SPOKANE AV			**ALB**
500	BEHRENS ST	94706	609-E5
500	BRIGHTON AV	94706	609-E5
700	PORTLAND AV	94706	609-E5
800	WASHINGTON AV	94706	609-E5
SPORTS LN			**BERK**
	DWIGHT WY	94704	630-A2
SPRING PTH			**PDMT**
	ABBOTT WY	94618	630-C7
	RED ROCK RD	94618	630-C7
	RED ROCK RD	94611	630-C7
	MORAGA AV	94618	630-C7
	MORAGA AV	94611	630-C7
SPRING WY			**BERK**
100	SCENIC AV	94708	609-H7
SPRINGFIELD ST			**OAK**
9900	98TH AV	94603	671-A5
SPRUCE ST			**ALA**
300	3RD ST	94501	649-E7
SPRUCE ST			**BERK**
400	GRIZZLY PEAK BLVD	94708	609-G4
400	WOODMONT AV	94708	609-G4
450	ALTA RD	94708	609-G4
500	VASSAR AV	94708	609-G4
500	VASSAR AV	94707	609-G4
520	MICHIGAN AV	94708	609-G4
520	MICHIGAN AV	94707	609-G4
620	NORTHAMPTON AV	94708	609-G5
620	NORTHAMPTON AV	94707	609-G5
660	ALAMO AV	94708	609-G5
660	ALAMO AV	94707	609-G5
700	HALKIN LN	94708	609-G5
700	HALKIN LN	94707	609-G5
810	MONTROSE RD	94708	609-G5
810	MONTROSE RD	94707	609-G5
840	REGAL RD	94708	609-G5
840	REGAL RD	94707	609-G5
900	MARIN AV	94708	609-H6
900	MARIN AV	94707	609-H6
920	EASTER WY	94708	609-H6
920	EASTER WY	94707	609-H6
950	SANTA BARBARA RD	94707	609-H6
950	SANTA BARBARA RD	94707	609-H6
1000	SAN BENITO RD	94708	609-H6
1000	SAN BENITO RD	94707	609-H6
1030	KEITH AV	94708	609-H6
1030	KEITH AV	94707	609-H6
1100	ARCH ST	94707	609-H6
1120	LOS ANGELES AV	94707	609-H6
1200	EUNICE ST	94709	609-H6
1120	SUMMER ST	94709	609-H7
1300	GLEN AV	94709	609-H7
1400	ROSE ST	94709	609-H7
1500	VINE ST	94709	609-H7
1600	CEDAR ST	94709	609-H7
1640	VIRGINIA ST	94709	629-H1
1700	VIRGINIA ST	94709	629-H1
1900	HEARST AV	94709	629-H1
SPRUCE ST			**CCCo**
400	GRIZZLY PEAK BLVD	94708	609-G4
400	WOODMONT AV	94708	609-G4
SPRUCE ST			**OAK**
2600	BOOKER ST	94606	650-A4
2600	7TH AV	94606	650-A4
400	PARK BLVD	94606	650-A4
600	CLEVELAND ST	94606	650-A4
600	CLEVELAND ST	94610	650-A4
630	PROSPECT AV	94610	650-A4
660	MCKINLEY AV	94610	650-A3
900	MACARTHUR BLVD	94610	650-A3
SPYGLASS HILL			**OAK**
1	HILLER DR	94618	630-C4
1	TREASURE HILL	94618	630-C4
100	HAWKS HILL CT	94618	630-C4
100	HILLER DR	94618	630-C4
STACY ST			**OAK**
4700	SCOTIA AV	94605	671-E4
4900	COTTER ST	94605	671-E4
5000	SHETLAND AV	94605	671-E4
STADIUM RIMWAY			**BERK**
	GAYLEY RD	94720	629-J1
	CENTENNIAL DR	94720	629-J2
	CANYON RD	94704	629-J2
	CANYON RD	94720	629-J2
	PANORAMIC WY	94704	629-J2
	PANORAMIC WY	94720	629-J2
	PROSPECT ST	94720	629-J2
	PROSPECT ST	94720	629-J2
STANBRIDGE CT			**ALA**
260	SHEFFIELD RD	94502	669-J5
260	STANBRIDGE LN	94502	669-J5
STANBRIDGE LN			**ALA**
210	NOTTINGHAM CT	94502	669-J5
260	SHEFFIELD RD	94502	669-J5
260	STANBRIDGE CT	94502	669-J5
STANFORD AV			**BERK**
	ADELINE ST	94703	629-G5
	ADELINE ST	94703	629-G5
800	62ND ST	94703	629-G5
830	KING ST	94703	629-G5
STANFORD AV			**EMVL**
1260	VALLEJO ST	94608	629-E6
1320	BEAUDRY ST	94608	629-E6
1380	DOYLE ST	94608	629-E6
	HOLLIS ST	94608	629-E6
	LANDREGAN ST	94608	629-E6
	HORTON ST	94608	629-E6
STANFORD AV			**OAK**
830	KING ST	94608	629-G5
840	61ST ST	94608	629-G5
840	GENOA ST	94608	629-G5
900	MARKET ST	94608	629-G5
	59TH ST	94608	629-F5
930	60TH ST	94608	629-F5
	SACRAMENTO ST	94608	629-F5
950	LOWELL ST	94608	629-F5
1000	59TH ST	94608	629-F5
1000	LOS ANGELES ST	94608	629-F5
1050	GASKILL ST	94608	629-F6
1100	SAN PABLO AV	94608	629-F6
1140	MARSHALL ST	94608	629-F6
1140	POWELL ST	94608	629-F6
1200	FREMONT ST	94608	629-E6
1260	VALLEJO ST	94608	629-E6
STANFORD ST			**ALA**
1800	BUENA VISTA AV	94501	669-J1
1900	EAGLE AV	94501	669-J1
2000	CLEMENT AV	94501	669-J1
STANLEY AV			**OAK**
9800	98TH AV	94605	671-B4
9900	99TH AV	94605	671-B5
10000	OLIVER AV	94605	671-B5
10100	TRUMAN AV	94605	671-B5
10200	FRAZIER AV	94605	671-B5
10360	SHAW ST	94605	671-B5
10500	FOOTHILL BLVD	94605	671-B5
10500	TALBOT AV	94605	671-B5
STANLEY PL			**OAK**
100	KEMPTON AV	94611	649-J2
200	FRISBIE WY	94611	649-J2
300	HARRISON ST	94611	649-J2
STANNAGE AV			**ALB**
500	BRIGHTON AV	94706	609-D5
600	GARFIELD AV	94706	609-D5
700	PORTLAND AV	94706	609-D5
800	WASHINGTON AV	94706	609-D6
900	SOLANO AV	94706	609-D6
1000	MARIN AV	94706	609-D6
1100	DARTMOUTH ST	94706	609-E7
1200	HARRISON ST	94706	609-E7
STANNAGE AV			**BERK**
1200	HARRISON ST	94706	609-E7
1300	GILMAN ST	94702	609-E7
1400	CAMELIA ST	94702	609-E7
1460	PAGE ST	94702	609-E7
1530	JONES ST	94702	629-E1
1570	HOPKINS ST	94702	629-E1
1600	CEDAR ST	94702	629-E1
1700	VIRGINIA ST	94702	629-E1
STANTON ST			**ALA**
1500	SANTA CLARA AV	94501	669-H1
1600	LINCOLN AV	94501	669-H1
1600	LINCOLN AV	94501	669-H1
1700	PACIFIC AV	94501	669-H1
1800	BUENA VISTA AV	94501	669-H1
STANTON ST			**BERK**
2800	OREGON ST	94702	629-F4
2900	RUSSELL ST	94702	629-F4
2900	RUSSELL ST	94702	629-F4
3000	ASHBY AV	94702	629-F4
3000	ASHBY AV	94702	629-F4
3100	PRINCE ST	94702	629-F4
STANTONVILLE CT			**OAK**
240	STANTONVILLE DR	94619	650-H4
240	KIMBERLIN HEIGHTS DR	94619	650-H4
STANTONVILLE DR			**OAK**
	KIMBERLIN HEIGHTS DR	94619	650-H4
	STANTONVILLE CT	94619	650-H4
	YARMOUTH CT	94619	650-H4
STAR AV			**OAK**
3200	MARION AV	94619	650-E6
3300	SUTER ST	94619	650-E6
STARDUST PL			**ALA**
	PAN AM WY	94501	649-D6
	MOONLIGHT TER	94501	649-D6
	MOONLIGHT TER	94501	649-D6
	RAINBOW CT	94501	649-D6
	NORFOLK RD	94501	649-D6
	SERENADE PL	94501	649-E6
	HANCOCK ST	94501	649-E6
200	NORFOLK RD	94501	649-D6
100	RAINBOW CT	94501	649-D6
STARK KNOLL PL			**OAK**
1	HILLTOP CRES	94618	630-C7
STARVIEW CT			**OAK**
100	STARVIEW DR	94618	630-C4
STARVIEW DR			**OAK**
1	HILLER DR	94618	630-C4
60	STARVIEW CT	94618	630-C4
100	HILLER DR	94618	630-C4
STATE PL			**OAK**
	PANORAMIC WY	94704	630-A2
STATEN AV			**OAK**
300	PALM AV	94610	649-J3
400	VAN BUREN AV	94610	649-J3
430	BELMONT ST	94610	649-J3
450	GRAND AV	94610	649-J3
500	BELLEVUE AV	94610	649-J3
STATION PL			**BERK**
800	CATALINA AV	94707	609-F6
STAUFFER CT			**OAK**
1	GERANIUM PL	94619	650-H5
1	STAUFFER PL	94619	650-H5
STAUFFER PL			**OAK**
4600	MOUNTAIN BLVD	94619	650-H5
4680	GERANIUM PL	94619	650-H5
4680	STAUFFER CT	94619	650-H5
STEARNS AV			**OAK**
1430	94TH AV	94603	671-A4
1430	BANCROFT AV	94603	671-A4
2300	PEACH ST	94603	671-A4
2400	HILLSIDE ST	94603	671-A4
2500	MACARTHUR BLVD	94605	671-A4
2550	THERMAL ST	94605	671-A4
2600	LAWLOR ST	94605	671-A4
9400	BURR ST	94605	671-A4
9600	98TH AV	94605	671-A4
9600	98TH AV	94605	671-B4
9680	ANAIR WY	94605	671-B4
9900	99TH AV	94605	671-B4
STEELE ST			**OAK**
4300	HIGH ST	94619	650-G5
4360	MADRONE AV	94619	650-G6
4420	HUNTINGTON ST	94619	650-G6
4600	ENOS AV	94619	650-G6
4700	BUELL ST	94619	650-G6
STEINMETZ WY			**OAK**
2800	WILSHIRE BLVD	94602	650-F4
STELLA ST			**OAK**
10700	HOOD ST	94605	671-C5
10800	MALCOLM AV	94605	671-C5
STEPHENS WY			**OAK**
1	GRAVATT DR	94705	630-B3
100	GRAVATT DR	94705	630-B3
STERLING AV			**ALA**
3200	HIGH ST	94501	670-B3
3300	FERNSIDE BLVD	94501	670-B3
STERLING AV			**BERK**
1030	KEELER AV	94708	609-J6
1100	TWAIN AV	94708	609-J6
1120	WHITAKER AV	94708	609-J6
1170	SHASTA RD	94708	609-J6
1200	QUEENS RD	94708	609-J6
1200	SHASTA RD	94708	609-J6
STERLING DR			**OAK**
7530	GREENLY DR	94605	671-A2
7730	MCCORMICK AV	94605	671-A2
7730	CREST AV	94605	671-A2
7810	SHONE AV	94605	671-A2
7990	LAMP ST	94605	671-A2
8070	FIELD ST	94605	670-J1
8200	COLUMBIAN DR	94605	670-J1
STEUBEN BAY			**ALA**
1	OYSTER POND RD	94502	670-A5
STEVENSON AV			**BERK**
1	MILLER AV	94708	609-J6
70	GRIZZLY PEAK BLVD	94708	609-J6
STEWART CT			**ALA**
2000	8TH ST	94501	649-G7
STINSON ST			**OAK**
1000	PIPER ST	94621	670-D6
1060	CESSNA ST	94621	670-D6
STOCKBRIDGE DR			**OAK**
2530	CHELTON DR	94611	650-F1
2400	RYDAL CT	94611	650-F1
2500	CHELSEA DR	94611	650-F1
STODDARD WY			**BERK**
1	GRIZZLY PEAK BLVD	94708	609-J6
STONE HARBOR			**ALA**
1	VICTORIA BAY	94502	670-A6
1	DRESDEN BAY	94502	670-A6
STONE RIDGE CT			**OAK**
4900	CAMPUS DR	94605	651-B7
STONE ST			**OAK**
800	PEARMAIN ST	94603	670-H6
850	PIPPIN ST	94603	670-H6
900	RUSSET ST	94603	670-H6
STONEFORD AV			**OAK**
300	SAINT ELMO DR	94603	670-G7
520	MADDUX DR	94603	670-G6
600	LYNDHURST ST	94603	670-G6
STONEWALL RD			**OAK**
1	CLAREMONT AV	94705	630-A3
STONINGTON POINTE			**ALA**
1	OYSTER POND RD	94502	670-A6
STORER AV			**OAK**
3390	REDDING ST	94619	650-F6
3200	MELDON AV	94619	650-F7
3390	CAMDEN ST	94619	650-F7
STOW AV			**OAK**
400	WAYNE AV	94606	649-J4
500	NEWTON AV	94606	649-J4
STRATFORD RD			**OAK**
700	TRESTLE GLEN RD	94610	650-A3
STRATHMOOR DR			**OAK**
1	CHANCELLOR PL	94705	630-C3
1	DRURY CT	94705	630-C3

PRIMARY STREET Address	Cross Street	ZIP	CITY Pg-Grid
STRATHMOOR DR			**OAK**
1	DRURY RD	94705	630-C3
50	KENILWORTH RD	94705	630-C3
200	NORFOLK DR	94705	630-C3
STRAUB WY			**ALA**
1100	PATTIANI WY	94502	669-J6
1200	SHANER DR	94502	669-J6
STUART ST			**BERK**
1500	SACRAMENTO ST	94703	629-F3
1600	CALIFORNIA ST	94703	629-F3
1700	MCGEE AV	94703	629-G3
1800	GRANT ST	94703	629-G3
1900	MARTIN LUTHER KING JR WY	94703	629-G3
1900	MARTIN LUTHER KING JR WY	94703	629-G3
2000	MILVIA ST	94703	629-G3
2050	ADELINE ST	94703	629-G3
2100	SHATTUCK AV	94705	629-H3
2200	FULTON ST	94705	629-H3
2300	ELLSWORTH ST	94705	629-H3
2400	TELEGRAPH AV	94705	629-H3
2500	REGENT ST	94705	629-J3
2600	HILLEGASS AV	94705	629-J3
2630	BENVENUE AV	94705	629-J3
2700	COLLEGE AV	94705	629-J3
2700	COLLEGE AV	94705	629-J3
2720	CHERRY ST	94705	629-J3
2800	PIEDMONT AV	94705	629-J3
2800	PIEDMONT AV	94705	629-J3
2820	KELSEY ST	94705	629-J3
2820	PALM CT	94705	629-J3
STUART ST			**OAK**
3100	E 31ST ST	94602	650-B4
3200	E 32ND ST	94602	650-B4
3300	E 33RD ST	94602	650-B4
3370	E 34TH ST	94602	650-B4
3400	MACARTHUR BLVD	94602	650-B4
SUMMER ST			**BERK**
2200	SPRUCE ST	94709	609-H7
2300	GLEN AV	94709	609-H7
SUMMIT LN			**BERK**
1	SUMMIT RD	94708	610-A7
SUMMIT RD			**BERK**
1300	AJAX PL	94708	610-A6
1300	ATLAS PL	94708	610-A6
1480	SUMMIT LN	94708	610-A7
1500	GRIZZLY PEAK BLVD	94708	610-A7
1500	GRIZZLY PEAK BLVD	94708	610-A7
SUMMIT ST			**OAK**
2800	28TH ST	94609	649-H2
2900	29TH ST	94609	649-H2
2900	29TH ST	94609	649-H2
3000	30TH ST	94609	649-H2
3100	HAWTHORNE AV	94609	649-H2
SUN VALLEY DR			**OAK**
11100	GRASS VALLEY RD	94605	671-E4
11250	COMMONWEALTH DR	94605	671-E5
11350	TATE TER	94605	671-E5
11370	LOWRY RD	94605	671-E5
11560	GLEN MANOR PL	94605	671-E5
11600	GOLF LINKS RD	94605	671-E5
SUNKIST DR			**OAK**
6900	BURCKHALTER AV	94605	670-J1
6900	HILLMONT DR	94605	670-J1
7000	EDWARDS AV	94605	670-J1
7200	MAYFIELD PTH	94605	670-J1
7400	COLUMBIAN DR	94605	670-J2
7800	MICHIGAN DR	94605	671-A2
7860	LAMP ST	94605	671-A2
8060	MCCORMICK AV	94605	671-A2
8200	82ND AV	94605	671-A2
8200	PARTRIDGE AV	94605	671-A2
SUNNY COVE CIR			**ALA**
1	PURCELL DR	94502	670-A5
100	PURCELL DR	94502	670-A5
SUNNY SLOPE AV			**OAK**
400	JEAN ST	94610	650-A2
450	VALLE VISTA AV	94610	650-A2
500	GRAND AV	94610	650-A2
SUNNYHILLS RD			**OAK**
800	TRESTLE GLEN RD	94610	650-B3
850	NORTHVALE RD	94610	650-B3
890	HILLCROFT CIR	94610	650-B3
920	ROSEMOUNT RD	94610	650-B3
990	HILLCROFT CIR	94610	650-B3
1030	GROSVENOR PL	94610	650-C3
1130	HUBERT RD	94610	650-C3
1160	UNDERHILLS RD	94610	650-C3
1170	MIDCREST RD	94610	650-C3
1220	HILLWOOD PL	94610	650-C3
1290	VAN SICKLEN PL	94610	650-C3
1330	BOWLES PL	94610	650-C3
1400	DOWNEY PL	94610	650-C3
1400	INDIAN RD	94610	650-C3
SUNNYMERE AV			**OAK**
6560	EDENVALE PL	94605	650-J7
6640	EDENVALE PL	94605	650-J7
6700	ARCHMONT PL	94605	650-J7
6780	VAN MOURIK AV	94605	650-H7
6900	KUHNLE AV	94605	650-H7
6900	SEMINARY AV	94605	650-H7
6500	GARDENIA PL	94605	670-J1
6600	DELMONT AV	94605	670-J1
6700	EDGEMOOR PL	94605	670-J1
6800	ALTAMONT AV	94605	670-J1
6900	BURCKHALTER AV	94605	670-J1
7000	EDWARDS AV	94605	670-J1
SUNNYSIDE AV			**PDMT**
200	LAKE AV	94611	649-J1
200	OAKLAND AV	94611	650-A1
200	OAKLAND AV	94611	650-A1
240	OLIVE AV	94611	650-A1
300	GRAND AV	94611	650-A1
SUNNYSIDE RD			**OAK**
3000	PROSPECT HILL RD	94613	670-G1
SUNNYSIDE ST			**OAK**
9000	90TH AV	94603	670-J4
9200	92ND AV	94603	670-J4
9400	94TH AV	94603	670-J4
10270	96TH AV	94603	671-A5
9800	98TH AV	94603	671-A5
9860	WARNER AV	94603	671-A5
9900	99TH AV	94603	671-A5
10000	100TH AV	94603	671-A5
10100	101ST AV	94603	671-A5
10200	102ND AV	94603	671-A5
10300	103RD AV	94603	671-A5
10400	LINK ST	94603	671-A6
10400	104TH AV	94603	671-A6
10500	105TH AV	94603	671-A6
10600	106TH AV	94603	671-A6
10700	107TH AV	94603	671-A6
10800	108TH AV	94603	671-A6
10900	109TH AV	94603	671-A6
11000	DURANT AV	94603	671-A6
SUNRISE CT			**ALA**
	PAN AM WY	94501	649-D6
	W HOPE ST	94501	649-D6
	MOONLIGHT TER	94501	649-D6
	RAINBOW CT	94501	649-D6
SUNSET AV			**OAK**
2700	LYNDE ST	94601	650-D6
2800	E 29TH ST	94601	650-D6
2900	BONA ST	94601	650-D6
E SUNSET AV			**OAK**
2600	LYNDE ST	94601	650-D6
2700	E 27TH ST	94601	650-D6
SUNSET LN			**BERK**
1	GRIZZLY PEAK BLVD	94708	609-H5
20	CRESTON RD	94708	609-H5
40	WOODMONT AV	94708	609-H5
80	WOODHAVEN RD	94708	609-H5
100	WILDCAT CANYON RD	94708	609-H5
SUNSET RD			**ALA**
300	SHORELINE DR	94501	669-G3
500	CORAL REEF PL	94501	669-G3
SUNSET TR			**BERK**
1	EUCALYPTUS PTH	94705	630-B3
100	WILLOW TR	94705	630-B3
SUNSHINE CT			**OAK**
1400	INTERNATIONAL BLVD	94621	670-G3
SURREY LN			**OAK**
7600	HANSOM DR	94605	651-C7
7750	PINECREST DR	94605	671-C1
7890	CHARIOT LN	94605	671-D1
8200	KELLER AV	94605	671-D1
SURRYHNE ST			**OAK**
3300	32ND ST	94607	649-E1
SUTER ST			**OAK**
3000	COOLIDGE AV	94602	650-D5
3060	PLEITNER AV	94602	650-E5
3120	CURRAN AV	94602	650-E5
3200	MAPLE AV	94602	650-E5
3200	MAPLE AV	94602	650-E5
3300	LAUREL AV	94602	650-E6
3500	35TH AV	94602	650-E6
3500	35TH AV	94619	650-E6
3600	OCTAVIA ST	94619	650-E6
3680	LOMA VISTA WY	94619	650-E6
3740	VIOLA ST	94619	650-E6
3770	STAR AV	94619	650-E6
3810	OVER ST	94619	650-E6
3840	LORENZO AV	94619	650-E6
3900	38TH AV	94619	650-F6
3950	39TH AV	94619	650-F6
4030	LIESE AV	94619	650-F6
4100	EASTMAN AV	94619	650-F6
4100	EASTMAN AV	94619	650-F6
4300	HIGH ST	94619	650-F6
SUTTER ST			**BERK**
1000	FOUNTAIN WK	94707	609-G6
1000	LOS ANGELES AV	94707	609-G6
1000	MARIN AV	94707	609-G6
1000	ARLINGTON AV	94707	609-G6
1000	DEL NORTE ST	94707	609-G6
1020	SOLANO AV	94707	609-G6
1070	DEL NORTE ST	94707	609-G6
1070	EL DORADO AV	94707	609-G6
1100	HOPKINS ST	94707	609-G5
1170	YOLO AV	94707	609-G6
1170	YOLO AV	94709	609-G6
1200	EUNICE ST	94707	609-G6
1200	EUNICE ST	94709	609-G6
1200	HENRY ST	94709	609-G6
SWAINLAND RD			**OAK**
6100	BROADWAY TER	94611	630-D6
6260	RUTHLAND RD	94611	630-D5
6340	FAIRLANE DR	94611	630-D5
6400	FAIRLANE DR	94611	630-D5
6600	FAIRLANE DR	94611	630-C5
SWAN WY			**OAK**
1	PARDEE DR	94621	670-E7
170	DE HAVILLAND ST	94621	670-E7
170	DOOLITTLE DR	94621	670-E7
SWEET RD			**ALA**
100	SALMON RD	94502	669-H6
200	SWEET WY	94502	669-H6
240	MCMURTY CT	94502	669-H5
400	SMITH CT	94502	669-H5
400	ANDERSON RD	94502	669-H5
SWEET WY			**ALA**
	ADELPHIAN WY	94502	669-H6
	SWEET RD	94502	669-H6
SWIFT CT			**ALA**
1	SALMON RD	94502	669-H6
SYCAMORE ST			**OAK**
500	TELEGRAPH AV	94612	649-G2
600	NORTHGATE AV	94612	649-G2
660	MARTIN LUTHER KING JR WY	94612	649-G2
750	WEST ST	94612	649-G2
800	SAN PABLO AV	94612	649-G2
SYLHOWE RD			**OAK**
2900	MONTEREY BLVD	94602	650-F4
SYLVAN AV			**OAK**
3000	MAPLE AV	94602	650-E4
3200	LAUREL AV	94602	650-F5
SYLVAN WY			**PDMT**
1	WILDWOOD AV	94610	650-A2
100	BOULEVARD WY	94610	650-A2
T			
TACOMA AV			**BERK**
1600	ORDWAY ST	94707	609-F6
1600	SOLANO AV	94707	609-F6
1690	ENSENADA AV	94707	609-F5
1770	COLUSA AV	94707	609-F5
1830	LAUREL LN	94707	609-F5
1900	THE ALAMEDA	94707	609-F5
TAFT AV			**ALB**
800	HILLSIDE AV	94706	609-D5
TAFT AV			**OAK**
5400	COLLEGE AV	94618	629-J5
6000	BROADWAY	94618	629-J5
5700	BROADWAY	94618	630-A5
6000	MENDOCINO AV	94618	630-A5
6060	MANILA AV	94618	630-A5
TAHITI LN			**ALA**
1000	MECARTNEY RD	94502	670-A6
1050	BELMONT WY	94502	670-A6
1100	ADMIRALITY LN	94502	670-A6
1100	FIR AV	94502	670-A6
TALBOT AV			**ALB**
500	BRIGHTON AV	94706	609-D5
600	GARFIELD AV	94706	609-D5
700	PORTLAND AV	94706	609-D5
800	WASHINGTON AV	94706	609-D6
900	SOLANO AV	94706	609-E6
1000	MARIN AV	94706	609-E6
1100	DARTMOUTH ST	94706	609-E6
TALBOT AV			**BERK**
1100	DARTMOUTH ST	94706	609-E7
1300	GILMAN ST	94702	609-E7
1400	SANTA FE AV	94702	609-E7
1400	CAMELIA ST	94702	609-E7
TALBOT AV			**OAK**
2600	FOOTHILL BLVD	94605	671-B5
2600	STANLEY AV	94605	671-B5
2710	FISHER AV	94605	671-B5
2800	MACARTHUR BLVD	94605	671-B5
TAMALPAIS RD			**BERK**
1	LE ROY AV	94708	609-H7
1	ROSE ST	94708	609-H7
10	SHASTA RD	94708	609-H7
200	SHASTA RD	94708	609-H7
TAMARISK DR			**OAK**
10600	ELYSIAN FIELDS DR	94605	671-D2
TAMPA AV			**OAK**
2000	ASILOMAR DR	94611	630-E7
2100	DRAKE DR	94611	630-E7
TANGLEWOOD RD			**BERK**
1	BELROSE AV	94705	630-A3
1	DERBY ST	94705	630-A3
90	GARBER ST	94705	630-A3
TANGLEWOOD RD			**OAK**
90	GARBER ST	94705	630-A3
100	CLAREMONT AV	94705	630-A3
TARRYTON ISL			**ALA**
550	ROSEWOOD WY	94501	669-G2
600	OTIS DR	94501	669-G2
TARTAN WY			**OAK**
12100	SHAWNEE CT	94619	650-J4
12100	BALMORAL DR	94619	650-J4
12200	BALMORAL DR	94619	650-J4
12200	BLYTHEN WY	94619	650-J4
TARTARIAN ST			**OAK**
800	PEARMAIN ST	94603	670-H6
TATE TER			**OAK**
100	SUN VALLEY DR	94605	671-E5
TAURUS AV			**OAK**
1	BROADWAY TER	94611	630-D6
100	MERRIEWOOD DR	94611	630-D6
500	BROADWAY TER	94611	630-D6
5620	MERRIEWOOD DR	94611	630-D6
5600	VALLEY VIEW RD	94611	630-D6
5620	MERRIEWOOD DR	94611	630-D6
TAYLOR AV			**ALA**
	CENTRAL AV	94501	669-E1
300	3RD ST	94501	669-E1
400	4TH ST	94501	669-E1
500	5TH ST	94501	669-E1
500	5TH ST	94501	669-F1
600	6TH ST	94501	669-F1
600	6TH ST	94501	669-F1
700	WEBSTER ST	94501	669-F1
750	PAGE ST	94501	669-F1
800	8TH ST	94501	669-G1
900	9TH ST	94501	669-G1
1000	CAROLINE ST	94501	669-G1
1100	SAINT CHARLES ST	94501	669-G1
TAYLOR AV			**OAK**
2400	MACARTHUR BLVD	94605	671-A5
2500	THERMAL ST	94605	671-A5
2600	LAWLOR ST	94605	671-A5
TAYLOR ST			**ALB**
900	SOLANO AV	94706	609-D6
1000	BUCHANAN ST	94706	609-D6
TELEGRAPH AV			**BERK**
2300	BANCROFT WY	94704	629-H2
2350	DURANT AV	94704	629-H2
2400	CHANNING WY	94704	629-H2
2450	HASTE ST	94704	629-H2
2500	DWIGHT WY	94704	629-H2
2550	BLAKE ST	94704	629-H3
2600	PARKER ST	94704	629-H3
2630	CARLETON ST	94704	629-H3
2700	DERBY ST	94705	629-H3
2730	WARD ST	94705	629-H3
2800	STUART ST	94705	629-H3
2850	OREGON ST	94705	629-H3
2900	RUSSELL ST	94705	629-H3
2910	HOWE ST	94705	629-H3
3000	ASHBY AV	94705	629-H4
3030	WEBSTER ST	94705	629-H4
3040	DOWLING PL	94705	629-H4
	PRINCE ST	94705	629-H4
3100	PRINCE ST	94705	629-H4
3200	WOOLSEY ST	94705	629-H4
TELEGRAPH AV			**OAK**
1500	BROADWAY	94612	649-G4
1500	KAHN AL	94612	649-G4
1610	16TH ST	94612	649-G3
1700	17TH ST	94612	649-G3
1800	18TH ST	94612	649-G3
1830	19TH ST	94612	649-G3
1900	19TH ST	94612	649-G3
1950	WILLIAMS ST	94612	649-G3
2000	20TH ST	94612	649-G3
2080	21ST ST	94612	649-G3
2150	22ND ST	94612	649-G3
2180	22ND ST	94612	649-G3
2230	GRAND AV	94612	649-G3
2300	23RD ST	94612	649-G3
2310	23RD ST	94612	649-G2
2400	24TH ST	94612	649-G2
2440	24TH ST	94612	649-G2
2480	25TH ST	94612	649-G2
2520	25TH ST	94612	649-G2
2560	SYCAMORE ST	94612	649-G2
2590	26TH ST	94612	649-G2
2670	27TH ST	94612	649-G2
2710	MERRIMAC ST	94612	649-G2
2740	28TH ST	94612	649-G2
2740	28TH ST	94609	649-G2
2800	28TH ST	94609	649-G2
2900	29TH ST	94609	649-G2
2910	29TH ST	94609	649-G2
2970	30TH ST	94609	649-G2
3000	30TH ST	94609	649-G2
3040	31ST ST	94609	649-G1
3100	31ST ST	94609	649-G1
3210	HAWTHORNE AV	94609	649-G1
3180	33RD ST	94609	649-G1
3400	34TH ST	94609	649-G1
3600	36TH ST	94609	649-H1
3670	37TH ST	94609	649-H1
3700	37TH ST	94609	649-H1
3750	W MACARTHUR BLVD	94609	649-H1
3820	38TH ST	94609	649-H1
4000	40TH ST	94609	629-H7
4100	41ST ST	94609	629-H7
4200	42ND ST	94609	629-H7
4300	43RD ST	94609	629-H7
4400	44TH ST	94609	629-H7
4450	SHATTUCK AV	94609	629-H7
4500	45TH ST	94609	629-H7
4520	45TH ST	94609	629-H7
4600	46TH ST	94609	629-H7
4700	47TH ST	94609	629-H7
4750	48TH ST	94609	629-H7
4800	48TH ST	94609	629-H6
4870	49TH ST	94609	629-H6
4900	49TH ST	94609	629-H6
4980	50TH ST	94609	629-H6
5100	51ST ST	94609	629-H6
5200	52ND ST	94609	629-H6
5200	CLAREMONT AV	94609	629-H6
5500	55TH ST	94609	629-H6
	AILEEN ST	94609	629-H6
5700	57TH ST	94609	629-H5
5750	58TH ST	94609	629-H5
5750	RACINE ST	94609	629-H5
5800	58TH ST	94609	629-H5
5900	59TH ST	94609	629-H5
5950	MCAULEY ST	94609	629-H5
6000	60TH ST	94609	629-H5
6100	61ST ST	94609	629-H5
6200	62ND ST	94609	629-H5
6300	63RD ST	94609	629-H5
6350	NORTH ST	94609	629-H4
6400	ALCATRAZ AV	94609	629-H4
6500	65TH ST	94609	629-H4
6600	66TH ST	94609	629-H4
6700	WOOLSEY ST	94609	629-H4
TELVIN ST			**ALB**
1300	TERRACE ST	94706	609-E6
1360	ALBANY TER	94706	609-F6
TEMESCAL CIR			**EMVL**
50	EMERY BAY DR	94608	629-E6
150	EMERY BAY DR	94608	629-E6
TEMPLAR PL			**OAK**
100	HARBORD DR	94618	630-C7
TERALYNN CT			**OAK**
1	CRESTMONT DR	94619	650-H5
50	SAMARIA LN	94619	650-H5
TERMINAL PL			**BERK**
2700	ADDISON ST	94704	629-H1
TERN LN			**ALA**
	ATLANTIC AV	94501	649-F7
	BRUZZONE DR	94501	649-F7
	DOWITCHER CT	94501	649-F7
TERRABELLA PL			**OAK**
4300	TERRABELLA WY	94619	650-H5
4500	TERRABELLA WY	94619	650-H5
TERRABELLA WY			**OAK**
4450	REDWOOD RD	94619	650-H5
4200	TERRABELLA PL	94619	650-H5
4450	TERRABELLA PL	94619	650-H5
TERRACE ST			**ALB**
1500	NEILSON ST	94706	609-E6
1600	TELVIN ST	94706	609-E6
TERRACE ST			**OAK**
4200	MATHER ST	94611	629-J7
4100	RIDGEWAY AV	94611	629-J7
4200	41ST ST	94611	629-J7
TERRACE WK			**BERK**
1	DEL NORTE ST	94707	609-G6
50	MARIPOSA AV	94707	609-G6
100	SHATTUCK AV	94707	609-G6
TEVIS ST			**OAK**
5800	58TH AV	94621	670-E3
5900	SEMINARY AV	94621	670-E3
6000	60TH AV	94621	670-E3
6100	61ST AV	94621	670-E3
6200	62ND AV	94621	670-E3
TEVLIN ST			**ALB**
1100	FRANCIS ST	94706	609-E7
TEVLIN ST			**BERK**
1250	WATKINS ST	94706	609-E7
1300	GILMAN ST	94706	609-E7
TEXAS			**ALA**
3000	MULVANY CIR	94501	649-E6
TEXAS ST			**OAK**
3000	COOLIDGE AV	94602	650-D5
3000	LAGUNA WY	94602	650-D5
3070	PLEITNER AV	94602	650-E5
3130	CURRAN AV	94602	650-E5
3200	MAPLE AV	94602	650-E5
THACKERAY DR			**OAK**
2350	CHELSEA DR	94611	650-F1
2300	GIRVIN DR	94611	650-F1
2350	WESTOVER DR	94611	650-F1
THATCH LN			**ALA**
	HAZEL LN	94502	670-A7
THAU WY			**ALA**
1800	EAGLE AV	94501	649-F7
THE ALAMEDA			**BERK**
500	SAN ANTONIO AV	94707	609-F4
500	SAN RAMON AV	94707	609-F4
530	VALLEJO ST	94707	609-F5
560	MENLO PL	94707	609-F5
600	THOUSAND OAKS BLVD	94707	609-F5
620	YOSEMITE RD	94707	609-F5
700	INDIAN TR	94707	609-F5
700	SAN LORENZO AV	94707	609-F5
740	CAPISTRANO AV	94707	609-F5
740	CAPISTRANO AV	94707	609-F5
770	TACOMA AV	94707	609-G5
800	SAN PEDRO AV	94707	609-G5
830	CATALINA AV	94707	609-G6
900	SOLANO AV	94707	609-G6
950	LOS ANGELES AV	94707	609-G6
1000	MARIN AV	94707	609-G6
1000	MARTIN LUTHER KING JR WY	94707	609-G6
THE CRESCENT			**BERK**
	PARK HILLS RD	94708	609-J5
	THE SHORT CUT	94708	609-J5
	WOODSIDE RD	94708	609-J5
	PARK HILLS RD	94708	609-J5
	MIDDLEFIELD RD	94708	609-J5
THE CROSSWAYS			**BERK**
200	OVERLOOK RD	94708	609-J5
300	MIDDLEFIELD RD	94708	609-J5
THE PLAZA DR			**BERK**
1	ENCINA PL	94705	630-A4
1	OAKVALE AV	94705	630-A4
40	NOGALES ST	94705	630-A4
60	DOMINGO AV	94705	630-A4
100	PARKSIDE DR	94705	630-A4
200	PARKSIDE DR	94705	630-A4
THE SHORT CUT			**BERK**
1	PARK HILLS RD	94708	609-J5
1	THE CRESCENT	94708	609-J5
100	MIDDLEFIELD RD	94708	609-J5
THE SHORT CUT			**OAK**
	TUNNEL RD	94705	630-A3
	ALVARADO RD	94705	630-A3
	EUCALYPTUS PTH	94705	630-A3
THE SPIRAL			**BERK**
300	WILDCAT CANYON RD	94708	609-J5
THE TURN			**OAK**
6800	PINEHAVEN RD	94611	630-E5
THE UPLANDS			**BERK**
1	CLAREMONT AV	94705	630-A4
20	ENCINA PL	94705	630-A4
60	S CROSSWAYS	94705	630-A4
150	ROANOKE RD	94705	630-A4
200	EL CAMINO REAL	94705	630-B4
290	OAK RIDGE RD	94705	630-B4
400	ALVARADO RD	94705	630-B4
400	TUNNEL RD	94705	630-B4
THERMAL ST			**OAK**
8500	SENECA ST	94605	671-A3
8800	BURR ST	94605	671-A3
9000	90TH AV	94605	671-A4
9120	90TH AV	94605	671-A4
9400	STEARNS AV	94605	671-A4
9550	CHEROKEE AV	94605	671-A4
9800	98TH AV	94605	671-A4
9850	TAYLOR AV	94605	671-A5

Address	Cross Street	ZIP	City / Pg-Grid
THERMAL ST			**OAK**
9900	99TH AV	94605	671-A5
THOMAS AV			**OAK**
5300	BROADWAY TER	94618	629-J6
5400	NAPA ST	94618	629-J6
5600	MONROE AV	94618	629-J6
THOMPSON AV			**ALA**
2900	SOUTHWOOD DR	94501	670-B3
3100	CORNELL DR	94501	670-B3
3200	HIGH ST	94501	670-B3
3300	FERNSIDE BLVD	94501	670-B3
THOMPSON ST			**OAK**
4500	47TH AV	94601	670-E1
4600	COURTLAND AV	94601	670-E1
THORN CT			**OAK**
1	SOBRANTE RD	94611	630-F6
THORNDALE DR			**OAK**
6400	ELVERTON DR	94611	630-E5
6760	BONNINGTON CT	94611	630-E5
6880	JEWELL CT	94611	630-E5
7160	LAURISTON CT	94611	630-F5
7300	SOBRANTE RD	94611	630-F5
THORNHILL CT			**OAK**
6000	THORNHILL DR	94611	630-E6
THORNHILL DR			**OAK**
5500	MORAGA AV	94611	630-D7
5600	MOUNTAIN BLVD	94611	630-D7
5680	GRISBORNE AV	94611	630-D7
5800	GRISBORNE AV	94611	630-D7
5900	ALHAMBRA LN	94611	630-E6
6000	GOULDIN RD	94611	630-E6
6150	MERRIEWOOD DR	94611	630-E6
6200	THORNHILL CT	94611	630-E6
6300	DONCASTER PL	94611	630-E6
6310	BEAUFOREST DR	94611	630-E6
6320	PINEHAVEN RD	94611	630-E6
6320	WOODHAVEN WY	94611	630-E6
6400	HEATHER RIDGE WY	94611	630-E6
6440	SOBRANTE RD	94611	630-E6
6600	WOODHAVEN WY	94611	630-F6
6700	OVERLAKE CT	94611	630-E6
6800	OAKWOOD DR	94611	630-E6
6900	ASPINWALL RD	94611	630-E6
6950	ARMOUR DR	94611	630-E6
7100	EVIREL PL	94611	630-F6
7160	WILD CURRANT WY	94611	630-F6
7200	SNAKE RD	94611	630-F6
THOUSAND OAKS			**OAK**
1	ELYSIAN FIELDS DR	94605	671-D2
120	QUIETWOOD	94605	671-E3
200	SHADOW MOUNTAIN	94605	671-E3
THOUSAND OAKS BLVD			**ALB**
1300	KEY ROUTE BLVD	94706	609-E5
1330	POMONA AV	94706	609-E5
1350	RAMONA AV	94706	609-E5
1400	CARMEL AV	94706	609-E5
1420	SAN CARLOS AV	94706	609-E5
1450	SANTA FE AV	94706	609-E5
1470	CURTIS ST	94706	609-E5
THOUSAND OAKS BLVD			**BERK**
1470	CURTIS ST	94707	609-E5
1500	NEILSON ST	94707	609-F5
1580	PERALTA AV	94707	609-F5
1600	COLUSA AV	94707	609-F5
1650	VINCENTE AV	94707	609-F5
1670	SAN MIGUEL AV	94707	609-F5
1700	MENLO PL	94707	609-F5
1730	SANTA ROSA AV	94707	609-F5
1760	THE ALAMEDA	94707	609-F5
1800	SANTA CLARA AV	94707	609-F5
1900	SAN FERNANDO AV	94707	609-F5
2000	ARLINGTON AV	94707	609-F5
THUNDERBIRD CT			**OAK**
1	DONNA WY	94605	671-D3
THURLES PL			**ALA**
1	DUBLIN WY	94502	669-J5
W TICONDEROGA AV			**ALA**
	FERRY PT	94501	669-D1
	VIKING ST	94501	669-D1
TIDEWATER AV			**OAK**
4400	LESSER ST	94601	670-C2
4730	HIGH ST	94601	670-C2
TIDEWAY DR			**ALA**
400	4TH ST	94501	669-E1
TIFFANY LN			**OAK**
	SHEPHERD CANYON RD	94611	630-F7
TIFFIN RD			**OAK**
1800	WATERHOUSE RD	94602	650-D3
1890	LYMAN RD	94602	650-D3
1920	LYMAN RD	94602	650-E3
2080	HARDING WY	94602	650-E3
2170	FRUITVALE AV	94602	650-E3
2280	FOREST HILL AV	94602	650-E3
2400	RAVENWOOD LN	94602	650-E3
2400	WHITTLE AV	94602	650-E3
TILDEN WY			**ALA**
2300	OAK ST	94501	670-A2
2300	LINCOLN AV	94501	670-A2
2400	LINCOLN AV	94501	670-A2
2400	PARK ST	94501	670-A2
2450	FOLEY ST	94501	670-A2
2500	EVERETT ST	94501	670-A2
2530	BUENA VISTA AV	94501	670-B2
2510	EAGLE AV	94501	670-B2
2600	BROADWAY	94501	670-B2
2600	EAGLE AV	94501	670-B2
380	FERNSIDE BLVD	94501	670-B2
380	BLANDING AV	94501	670-B2
TILDEN WY			**OAK**
2900	ALAMEDA AV	94601	670-B2
2900	FRUITVALE AV	94601	670-B2
TIMES WY			**ALA**
2300	OAK ST	94501	670-A2
2400	PARK ST	94501	670-A2
2400	WEBB AV	94501	670-A2
TINKER AV			**ALA**
600	MARINER SQUARE LP	94501	649-F6
620	MARINER SQUARE LP	94501	649-F6
700	WEBSTER ST	94501	649-F6
TIPPERARY CT			**ALA**
1	TIPPERARY LN	94502	669-H5
TIPPERARY LN			**ALA**
200	OLDCASTLE LN	94502	669-H5
300	TIPPERARY CT	94502	669-H5
400	KOFMAN PKWY	94502	669-H5
TOBAGO LN			**ALA**
1000	CAMANOE LN	94502	670-B7
1100	CAPELLA LN	94502	670-B7
TOBRUK ST			**OAK**
100	15TH ST	94626	649-C2
140	17TH ST	94626	649-C2
170	19TH ST	94626	649-D1
180	21ST ST	94626	649-D1
TODD ST			**ALA**
	W MIDWAY AV	94501	649-D6
	W ESSEX DR	94501	649-D6
	W RED LINE AV	94501	649-D6
TOLER AV			**OAK**
9850	WARNER AV	94603	671-A5
9900	99TH AV	94603	671-A5
TOMLEE DR			**BERK**
1300	JUANITA WY	94702	629-F1
1400	ACTON ST	94702	629-F1
TOMPKINS AV			**OAK**
4200	VALE AV	94619	650-G6
4290	HIGH ST	94619	650-G6
4400	HUNTINGTON ST	94619	650-G6
4500	CARSON ST	94619	650-G6
4600	ENOS AV	94619	650-G6
4710	BUELL ST	94619	650-G6
4710	WILKIE ST	94619	650-G6
4860	DAISY ST	94619	650-G7
4900	CALAVERAS AV	94619	650-G7
TONGA LN			**ALA**
3300	HOLLY ST	94502	670-A7
3400	WINDWARD LN	94502	670-A7
3500	LEEWARD LN	94502	670-A7
TOPANGA DR			**OAK**
10500	105TH AV	94603	670-H7
10600	CAPISTRANO DR	94603	670-H7
10600	EL PASEO DR	94603	670-H7
10640	ALMANZA DR	94603	670-H7
10700	EL PASEO DR	94603	670-H7
TOTTERDELL ST			**OAK**
3000	SKYLINE BLVD	94611	650-G1
3010	MELVILLE LN	94611	650-G1
3030	MELVILLE DR	94611	650-G1
W TOWER AV			**ALA**
	MONARCH ST	94501	649-C6
	LEXINGTON ST	94501	649-C6
	SARATOGA ST	94501	649-D7
	PAN AM WY	94501	649-D7
	FERRY PT	94501	649-D7
	MOONLIGHT TER	94501	649-D7
	ORION ST	94501	649-D7
	NORFOLK RD	94501	649-D7
	HANCOCK ST	94501	649-D7
TOWN SQUARE CT			**OAK**
10	GRAFFIAN ST	94603	670-J6
TOWNSEND AV			**OAK**
4300	WELLINGTON ST	94602	650-D3
4400	EVERETT AV	94602	650-D3
4400	LA CRESTA AV	94602	650-D3
TOYON PL			**OAK**
4500	ALISO AV	94619	650-G5
TOYON TER			**ALA**
	POST ST	94501	670-A4
TRAFALGAR PL			**OAK**
2000	LA SALLE AV	94611	650-E1
2300	MONTEREY BLVD	94611	650-E2
2300	PARK BLVD	94611	650-E2
TRALEE LN			**ALA**
300	KOFMAN PKWY	94502	669-H5
300	SEA VIEW PKWY	94502	669-H5
320	VISTA RD	94502	669-H5
350	BARRY CT	94502	669-H5
380	SHAMROCK LN	94502	669-H5
400	DUBLIN WY	94502	669-H5
TRASK ST			**OAK**
5000	MONTICELLO AV	94601	670-E1
5100	BEST AV	94601	670-F1
5170	MAXWELL AV	94601	670-F1
5180	BELVEDERE ST	94601	670-F1
5200	RAWSON ST	94601	670-F1
5300	COLE ST	94601	670-F1
5310	COLE ST	94601	670-F1
5330	MAVIS ST	94601	670-F1
5390	KINGSLAND AV	94601	670-F1
5400	YGNACIO AV	94601	670-F1
5500	55TH AV	94605	670-F1
5500	FOOTHILL BLVD	94605	670-F1
5700	BANCROFT AV	94605	670-F1
5700	57TH AV	94605	670-F1
5700	57TH AV	94605	670-F1
5700	BANCROFT AV	94605	670-F1
5900	SEMINARY AV	94605	670-F1
TREASURE HILL			**OAK**
1	HILLER DR	94618	630-C4
1	SPYGLASS HILL	94618	630-C4
TREGLOAN CT			**ALA**
1700	EAGLE AV	94501	670-B2
1800	BUENA VISTA AV	94501	670-B2
TRELLIS LN			**ALA**
1000	CAMANOE LN	94502	670-A6
1100	CAPELLA LN	94502	670-A6
TREMONT ST			**BERK**
3000	EMERSON ST	94703	629-G4
3090	ESSEX ST	94703	629-G4
3190	PRINCE ST	94703	629-G4
3280	WOOLSEY ST	94703	629-G4
TREMONT ST			**OAK**
6500	65TH ST	94609	629-G4
6600	FAIRVIEW ST	94609	629-G4
6700	WOOLSEY ST	94609	629-G4
TRESTLE GLEN RD			**OAK**
600	LAKESHORE AV	94610	650-A3
620	WESLEY WY	94610	650-A3
660	HADDON PL	94610	650-A3
700	BROOKWOOD PL	94610	650-A3
730	STRATFORD RD	94610	650-A3
930	BROOKWOOD RD	94610	650-B3
1020	SUNNYHILLS RD	94610	650-B3
1070	BROOKWOOD RD	94610	650-B3
1100	HOLMAN RD	94610	650-B3
1190	GROSVENOR PL	94610	650-B3
1300	BARROWS RD	94610	650-C3
1420	CREED RD	94610	650-C3
1450	NORWOOD AV	94610	650-C3
1490	HUMPHREY PL	94610	650-C3
1710	VALANT PL	94610	650-C3
TRESTLE GLEN RD			**PDMT**
1710	VALANT PL	94610	650-D3
1710	VALANT PL	94602	650-D3
1800	CAVANAUGH CT	94610	650-D3
1800	CAVANAUGH CT	94602	650-D3
1900	PARK BLVD	94610	650-D3
1900	PARK BLVD	94602	650-D3
W TRIDENT AV			**ALA**
	FERRY PT	94501	649-D7
	ORION ST	94501	649-D7
	HANCOCK ST	94501	649-D7
TRINIDAD AV			**OAK**
4800	BRUNELL DR	94602	650-G4
4900	NOYO ST	94602	650-G4
TRIPOLI			**ALA**
4000	CIMARRON ST	94501	649-E6
4000	NEVADA	94501	649-E6
TRIUMPH DR			**ALA**
3800	ATLANTIC AV	94501	649-G7
3900	INDEPENDENCE DR	94501	649-G7
4000	KINGSBURY CT	94501	649-G7
TRUITT LN			**OAK**
1	CLAREWOOD DR	94618	630-C6
TRUMAN AV			**OAK**
2700	STANLEY AV	94605	671-B5
2630	BURR ST	94605	671-B5
2550	SHAW ST	94605	671-B5
2450	OLIVER AV	94605	671-A5
2550	MACARTHUR BLVD	94605	671-A5
TULAGI ST			**OAK**
260	8TH ST	94626	649-C3
260	MIDWAY ST	94626	649-C3
640	10TH ST	94626	649-C2
830	11TH ST	94626	649-C2
1160	15TH ST	94626	649-D2
1620	17TH ST	94626	649-D2
2100	19TH ST	94626	649-D2
TULARE AV			**ALB**
900	SOLANO AV	94707	609-F6
940	MARIN AV	94707	609-F6
950	MADERA ST	94707	609-F6
1000	SONOMA AV	94707	609-F6
TULARE AV			**BERK**
900	SOLANO AV	94707	609-F6
940	MARIN AV	94707	609-F6
960	MADERA ST	94707	609-F6
1000	SONOMA AV	94707	609-F6
TULIP AV			**OAK**
4400	MADRONE AV	94619	650-G6
4450	LILY ST	94619	650-G6
4510	GREENACRE RD	94619	650-G6
4620	MERRILL AV	94619	650-G6
4700	ENOS AV	94619	650-G6
TULLAMORE PL			**ALA**
1	SEA VIEW PKWY	94502	669-J5
TULLY PL			**OAK**
3000	HILLMONT DR	94605	671-A2
3100	OUTLOOK AV	94605	671-A2
TUNIS RD			**OAK**
200	EMPIRE RD	94603	670-F7
300	CORAL RD	94603	670-F7
TUNNEL RD			**BERK**
1	DOMINGO AV	94705	630-A3
1	ASHBY AV	94705	630-A3
1	RUSSELL ST	94705	630-A3
100	THE SHORT CUT	94705	630-A3
110	OAK RIDGE RD	94705	630-A4
150	ALVARADO RD	94705	630-B4
150	THE UPLANDS	94705	630-B4
170	BRIDGE RD	94705	630-B4
200	ROBLE RD	94705	630-B4
250	VICENTE RD	94705	630-B4
2000	LANDVALE RD	94705	630-B4
TUNNEL RD			**OAK**
1	DOMINGO AV	94705	630-A3
1	ASHBY AV	94705	630-A3
1	RUSSELL ST	94705	630-A3
100	THE SHORT CUT	94705	630-A3
	CALDECOTT LN	94618	630-C4
1800	HILLER DR	94705	630-C4
1800	HILLER DR	94618	630-C4
1870	CHARING CROSS RD	94705	630-C3
1870	CHARING CROSS RD	94618	630-C3
2000	BUCKINGHAM BLVD	94611	630-D3
2500	BAY FOREST DR	94611	630-D4
2500	OLD TUNNEL RD	94611	630-D4
TURNER AV			**OAK**
4400	MONAN ST	94605	671-E5
4350	ELVESSA ST	94605	671-E5
4300	ETTRICK ST	94605	671-E5
4350	TURNER CT	94605	671-E5
4350	GREENBRIER ST	94605	671-E5
TURNER CT			**OAK**
4300	GREENBRIER ST	94605	671-D5
4300	TURNER AV	94605	671-D5
TURNLEY AV			**OAK**
	SEQUOYAH RD	94605	671-C3
	FAIRWAY AV	94605	671-B3
TURTLE CREEK			**OAK**
30	ELYSIAN FIELDS DR	94605	671-D2
TWAIN AV			**BERK**
1	KEELER AV	94708	609-J6
100	STERLING AV	94708	609-J6
TWIN OAKS WY			**OAK**
3800	FAIRWAY AV	94605	671-B3
3860	MOUNTAIN BLVD	94605	671-B3
3900	OAK KNOLL BLVD	94605	671-B3
TWITTER CT			**OAK**
1	LEONA ST	94605	650-H6
100	MOUNTAIN BLVD	94605	650-H6
TYLER ST			**BERK**
1500	SACRAMENTO ST	94703	629-F4
1600	CALIFORNIA ST	94703	629-G4
1700	KING ST	94703	629-G4
TYLER ST			**OAK**
600	EDES AV	94603	670-G6
700	WALTER AV	94603	670-G6
800	RAILROAD AV	94603	670-G6
TYNAN AV			**ALA**
	MARINER SQUARE DR	94501	649-F6
TYNEBOURNE PL			**ALA**
100	BERKSHIRE RD	94502	669-J5
TYRRELL ST			**OAK**
4600	COURTLAND AV	94601	650-E7
4700	47TH AV	94601	650-E7
TYSON CIR			**PDMT**
1	LA SALLE AV	94611	650-D1
100	LA SALLE AV	94611	650-D1
U			
ULSTER PL			**ALA**
1	DUBLIN WY	94502	669-J5
UNDERHILLS RD			**OAK**
900	SUNNYHILLS RD	94610	650-C3
1160	GROSVENOR PL	94610	650-C3
UNDERWOOD AV			**OAK**
5100	RICHARDS RD	94613	650-G7
UNION ST			**ALA**
900	CLINTON AV	94501	669-H2
1000	SAN JOSE AV	94501	669-H2
1100	SAN ANTONIO AV	94501	669-H2
1200	ENCINAL AV	94501	669-H2
1300	ALAMEDA AV	94501	669-H2
1400	CENTRAL AV	94501	669-J1
1500	SANTA CLARA AV	94501	669-J1
1600	LINCOLN AV	94501	669-J1
1700	PACIFIC AV	94501	669-J1
1800	BUENA VISTA AV	94501	669-J1
1900	EAGLE AV	94501	669-J1
2000	CLEMENT AV	94501	669-J1
UNION ST			**OAK**
700	7TH ST	94607	649-E4
800	8TH ST	94607	649-E3
1000	10TH ST	94607	649-E3
1120	POPLAR ST	94607	649-E3
1120	12TH ST	94607	649-E3
1160	12TH ST	94607	649-E3
1330	14TH ST	94607	649-E3
1500	16TH ST	94607	649-E3
1900	19TH ST	94607	649-E2
2030	20TH ST	94607	649-E2
2100	21ST ST	94607	649-E2
2200	W GRAND AV	94607	649-E2
2400	24TH ST	94607	649-E2
2600	26TH ST	94607	649-E1
2800	28TH ST	94608	649-F1
3000	30TH ST	94608	649-F1
3200	32ND ST	94608	649-F1
UNIVERSITY AV			**BERK**
1	SEAWALL DR	94804	629-B2
1	SEAWALL DR	94804	629-B2
290	MARINA BLVD	94804	629-C2
530	W FRONTAGE RD	94804	629-C2
660	2ND ST	94804	629-D2
710	3RD ST	94804	629-D2
760	4TH ST	94804	629-D2
800	5TH ST	94804	629-D2
850	6TH ST	94804	629-D2
890	7TH ST	94804	629-D2
940	8TH ST	94804	629-D2
1000	9TH ST	94804	629-E2
1050	10TH ST	94804	629-E2
1100	SAN PABLO AV	94702	629-E2
1200	CURTIS ST	94702	629-E2
1260	CHESTNUT ST	94702	629-E2
1280	BONAR ST	94702	629-E2
1400	ACTON ST	94702	629-F2
1500	SACRAMENTO ST	94703	629-F2
1600	CALIFORNIA ST	94703	629-F2
1650	JEFFERSON AV	94703	629-F1
1700	MCGEE AV	94703	629-G1
1800	GRANT ST	94703	629-G1
1900	MARTIN LUTHER KING JR WY	94704	629-G1
1950	BONITA AV	94704	629-G1
2000	MILVIA ST	94704	629-G1
2000	MILVIA ST	94704	629-G1
2100	SHATTUCK AV	94704	629-G1
2120	SHATTUCK SQ	94704	629-H1
2160	WALNUT ST	94704	629-H1
2200	OXFORD ST	94704	629-H1
URANUS AV			**OAK**
200	MERRIEWOOD DR	94611	630-D6
200	CROWN AV	94611	630-D6
100	SHERWOOD DR	94611	630-D6
200	BROADWAY TER	94611	630-D6
UTAH ST			**OAK**
8100	82ND AV	94605	671 A2
8200	PARTRIDGE AV	94605	671-A2
V			
VALANT PL			**OAK**
1	TRESTLE GLEN RD	94610	650-C3
VALDEZ ST			**OAK**
2200	GRAND AV	94612	649-H3
2260	23RD ST	94612	649-H3
2410	24TH ST	94612	649-H2
2600	26TH ST	94612	649-H2
2600	26TH ST	94612	649-H2
2700	27TH ST	94612	649-H2
2610	27TH ST	94612	649-H2
2700	28TH ST	94612	649-H2
2800	29TH ST	94611	649-H2
VALE AV			**OAK**
3300	PORTER ST	94619	650-F6
3800	BAYO ST	94619	650-G6
4030	TOMPKINS AV	94619	650-G6
4200	HARBOR VIEW AV	94619	650-G6
VALENTINE ST			**OAK**
7500	FIELD ST	94605	671-A1
7700	COLUMBIAN DR	94605	671-A1
VALLE VISTA AV			**OAK**
400	ELWOOD AV	94610	650-A2
520	BONHAM WY	94610	650-A2
540	MIRA VISTA AV	94610	650-A2
700	SUNNY SLOPE AV	94610	650-A2
VALLECITO PL			**OAK**
2700	14TH AV	94606	650-B5
2710	E 27TH ST	94606	650-B5
2780	E 28TH ST	94606	650-B5
2900	E 31ST ST	94606	650-B5
VALLEJO ST			**BERK**
1	THE ALAMEDA	94707	609-F5
100	SAN RAMON AV	94707	609-F5
VALLEJO ST			**EMVL**
5500	55TH ST	94608	629-E6
5700	STANFORD AV	94608	629-E6
5800	POWELL ST	94608	629-E6
5900	59TH ST	94608	629-E5
6100	61ST ST	94608	629-E5
6200	62ND ST	94608	629-E5
6300	63RD ST	94608	629-E5
6400	64TH ST	94608	629-E5
6430	OCEAN AV	94608	629-E5
6450	PEABODY LN	94608	629-E5
6450	PEABODY LN	94608	629-E5
6500	65TH ST	94608	629-E5
6600	66TH ST	94608	629-E5
VALLEJO ST			**OAK**
5500	55TH ST	94608	629-E6
5700	STANFORD AV	94608	629-E6
5800	POWELL ST	94608	629-E6
5900	59TH ST	94608	629-E5
6100	61ST ST	94608	629-E5
6200	62ND ST	94608	629-E5
6300	63RD ST	94608	629-E5
6400	64TH ST	94608	629-E5
6430	OCEAN AV	94608	629-E5
6450	PEABODY LN	94608	629-E5
VALLEY ST			**BERK**
2300	BANCROFT WY	94702	629-F2
2400	CHANNING WY	94702	629-F3
2500	DWIGHT WY	94702	629-F3
VALLEY ST			**OAK**
2300	24TH ST	94612	649-G2
2250	23RD ST	94612	649-G3
2100	GRAND AV	94612	649-G3
2250	22ND ST	94612	649-G3
VALLEY ST N			**BERK**
2200	ALLSTON WY	94702	629-F2
VALLEY VIEW RD			**OAK**
6000	TAURUS AV	94611	630-E6
6300	BEAUFOREST DR	94611	630-E5
6600	HEATHER RIDGE WY	94611	630-E5
6600	PINEHAVEN RD	94611	630-E5
VAN BUREN AV			**OAK**
200	LENOX AV	94610	649-H3
270	LEE ST	94610	649-J3
320	PERKINS ST	94610	649-J3
420	STATEN AV	94610	649-J3
480	BELLEVUE AV	94610	649-J3
530	EUCLID AV	94610	649-J3
600	MACARTHUR BLVD	94610	649-J3
VAN BUREN ST			**ALA**
2800	VERSAILLES AV	94501	670-B3
2850	GROVE ST	94501	670-B3
2900	MOUND ST	94501	670-B3
3000	COURT ST	94501	670-B3
3100	FOUNTAIN ST	94501	670-B3
3200	HIGH ST	94501	670-B3
VAN CLEAVE WY			**OAK**
1	WESTFIELD WY	94619	650-H5
100	CREIGHTON WY	94619	650-H5
VAN DYKE AV			**OAK**
400	PARK BLVD	94606	650-A4
500	BROOKLYN AV	94606	650-A4
VAN MOURIK AV			**OAK**
3940	SUNNYMERE AV	94605	650-J7

PRIMARY STREET Address	Cross Street	ZIP	CITY Pg-Grid
VAN MOURIK AV			**OAK**
4100	HILLMONT DR	94605	650-J7
VAN SICKLEN PL			**OAK**
1	SUNNYHILLS RD	94610	650-C3
VASSAR AV			**BERK**
350	KENTUCKY AV	94708	609-G4
350	KENTUCKY AV	94707	609-G4
500	SPRUCE ST	94708	609-G4
500	SPRUCE ST	94707	609-G4
VENETIA RD			**OAK**
	GOLF LINKS RD	94605	671-C3
	GATE VIEW DR	94605	671-C4
VENTURA AV			**ALB**
900	SOLANO AV	94707	609-F6
950	MARIN AV	94707	609-F6
1000	SONOMA AV	94707	609-F6
1000	SONOMA AV	94706	609-F6
1030	BEVERLY PL	94706	609-F6
1060	MANOR WY	94706	609-F7
1100	POSEN AV	94706	609-F7
VERDEMAR DR			**ALA**
1000	MECARTNEY RD	94502	670-A6
1000	IRONWOOD RD	94502	670-A6
1020	EL PORTAL	94502	670-A6
1030	ALTA VISTA	94502	670-A6
1060	LA CRESTA	94502	669-J6
1070	CERRO VISTA	94502	669-J6
1100	EL SERENO	94502	669-J6
	FLORA VISTA	94502	669-J6
1130	LA CAMPANIA	94502	669-J6
1180	LA CAMPANIA	94502	669-J6
1180	LINDA VISTA	94502	669-J6
1180	EL PASEO	94502	669-J7
1180	LA CAMPANIA	94502	669-J7
1200	CATALINA AV	94502	669-J7
VERDI ST			**ALA**
1500	SANTA CLARA AV	94501	669-G1
1600	LINCOLN AV	94501	669-G1
VERMONT AV			**BERK**
330	RUGBY AV	94707	609-G4
400	MARYLAND AV	94707	609-G4
500	COLORADO AV	94707	609-G4
VERMONT ST			**OAK**
800	MANDANA BLVD	94610	650-A2
900	PRINCE ST	94610	650-A2
950	WELDON AV	94610	650-A2
1000	FAIRBANKS AV	94610	650-A2
VERNALIS CIR			**ALA**
2100	BAINBRIDGE AV	94501	649-E7
2200	BAINBRIDGE AV	94501	649-E7
VERNON ST			**OAK**
1	BAY PL	94610	649-H3
110	VERNON TER	94610	649-H2
120	LEE ST	94610	649-H2
300	PERKINS ST	94610	649-J2
500	MACARTHUR BLVD	94610	649-J2
500	SANTA CLARA AV	94610	649-J2
500	SANTA CLARA AV	94610	649-J2
550	MOSS AV	94610	649-J2
600	SANTA ROSA AV	94610	649-J2
600	MONTE VISTA AV	94610	649-J2
VERNON TER			**OAK**
100	VERNON ST	94610	649-H2
VERONA PTH			**OAK**
	ACACIA AV	94618	630-B5
	MATHIEU AV	94618	630-B5
VERRADA RD			**OAK**
1000	LONGRIDGE RD	94610	650-B3
1100	ROSEMOUNT RD	94610	650-B3
VERSAILLES AV			**ALA**
920	OTIS DR	94501	670-A4
950	CLAY ST	94501	670-A4
1000	CALHOUN ST	94501	670-A3
1100	WASHINGTON ST	94501	670-A3
1200	SAN JOSE AV	94501	670-A3
1300	ENCINAL AV	94501	670-A3
1380	VAN BUREN ST	94501	670-A3
1400	CENTRAL AV	94501	670-B3
1400	GIBBONS DR	94501	670-B3
1500	SANTA CLARA AV	94501	670-B2
1600	LINCOLN AV	94501	670-B2
1700	BUENA VISTA AV	94501	670-B2
1800	YOSEMITE AV	94501	670-B2
1900	FERNSIDE BLVD	94501	670-B2
2100	MARINA DR	94501	670-B2
2100	WINDSOR DR	94501	670-B2
VETERAN WY			**OAK**
1	CANON AV	94602	650-D4
VETERANS CT			**ALA**
	ISLAND DR	94502	670-A5
VIA ALAMOSA			**ALA**
1100	FLORA VISTA	94502	669-J6
1180	LINDA VISTA	94502	669-J6
1200	CATALINA AV	94502	669-J6
VIA ALISO			**ALA**
1000	ALTA VISTA	94502	669-J6
1100	CERRO VISTA	94502	669-J6
VIA BONITA			**ALA**
1000	FONTANA DR	94502	669-J6
1100	FONTANA DR	94502	669-J6
VIA CORTA			**ALA**
1100	FONTANA DR	94502	669-J6
1200	FONTANA DR	94502	669-J6
VIA RIALTO			**OAK**
	REDWOOD RD	94619	650-H5
VICENTE PL			**OAK**
1	VICENTE RD	94705	630-B3
100	WEST VIEW DR	94705	630-B3
VICENTE RD			**BERK**
1	TUNNEL RD	94705	630-B4
130	VICENTE PL	94705	630-B4
140	GRAND VIEW PL	94705	630-B4
200	ALVARADO RD	94705	630-B4
VICENTE RD			**OAK**
130	VICENTE PL	94705	630-B3
140	GRAND VIEW PL	94705	630-B3
VICENTE ST			**OAK**
5700	57TH ST	94609	629-H5
5800	58TH ST	94609	629-H5
VICENTE WY			**OAK**
5400	CLAREMONT AV	94609	629-H6
5500	55TH ST	94609	629-H6
5600	CLAREMONT AV	94609	629-H6
VICKSBURG AV			**OAK**
1900	FOOTHILL BLVD	94601	670-E1
1900	54TH AV	94601	670-E1
2000	YGNACIO AV	94601	670-E1
2100	51ST AV	94601	670-E1
2200	50TH AV	94601	670-E1
2200	MONTICELLO AV	94601	670-E1
2310	48TH AV	94601	670-E1
2310	CONGRESS AV	94601	650-E7
2400	CONGRESS AV	94601	650-E7
VICTOR AV			**OAK**
3400	MIDVALE AV	94602	650-F5
3500	35TH AV	94602	650-F5
3500	35TH AV	94619	650-F5
3580	VIRDEN AV	94619	650-G5
3700	ATLAS AV	94619	650-G5
3860	DUNSMUIR AV	94619	650-G5
3900	39TH AV	94619	650-G5
VICTORIA BAY			**ALA**
300	STONE HARBOR	94502	670-A6
300	DRESDEN BAY	94502	670-A6
340	OYSTER SHOALS	94502	670-A6
VICTORY CT			**OAK**
1	FALLON ST	94607	649-G5
VIEW PL			**OAK**
	MONTGOMERY ST	94611	629-J7
VIEW ST			**OAK**
4300	MATHER ST	94611	629-J7
4400	JOHN ST	94611	629-J7
VIEWCREST CT			**OAK**
4300	VIEWCREST DR	94619	650-J7
VIEWCREST DR			**OAK**
6100	CAMPUS DR	94619	650-J6
6120	SAINT CLOUD CT	94619	650-J6
6150	CHAMBERLIN CT	94619	650-J7
6250	VIEWCREST CT	94619	650-J7
6300	RIDGEMONT DR	94619	650-J7
VIKING ST			**ALA**
	W HORNET AV	94501	669-D1
	W TICONDEROGA AV	94501	669-D1
	W ORISKANY AV	94501	649-D7
	W ATLANTIC AV	94501	649-D7
VILLANOVA DR			**OAK**
1	VILLANOVA LN	94611	630-F6
50	MANZANITA DR	94611	630-E6
250	MANZANITA DR	94611	630-F6
VILLANOVA LN			**OAK**
1	VILLANOVA DR	94611	630-F6
VINCENTE AV			**BERK**
470	VISALIA AV	94707	609-F5
600	THOUSAND OAKS BLVD	94707	609-F5
760	COLUSA AV	94707	609-F5
760	PORTLAND AV	94707	609-F5
850	ENSENADA AV	94707	609-F5
900	PERALTA AV	94707	609-F5
VINE LN			**BERK**
2500	EUCLID AV	94708	609-H7
2500	VINE ST	94708	609-H7
2600	LE ROY AV	94708	609-H7
VINE ST			**BERK**
1700	MCGEE AV	94703	609-F7
1760	EDITH ST	94703	609-G7
1800	GRANT ST	94703	609-G7
1850	JOSEPHINE ST	94703	609-G7
1900	MARTIN LUTHER KING JR WY	94709	609-G7
1950	BONITA AV	94709	609-G7
2000	MILVIA ST	94709	609-G7
2050	HENRY ST	94709	609-G7
2100	SHATTUCK AV	94709	609-G7
2150	WALNUT ST	94709	609-H7
2200	OXFORD ST	94709	609-H7
2250	SPRUCE ST	94709	609-H7
2300	ARCH ST	94708	609-H7
2350	SCENIC AV	94708	609-H7
2400	HAWTHORNE TER	94708	609-H7
2500	EUCLID AV	94708	609-H7
2500	VINE LN	94708	609-H7
VIOLA ST			**OAK**
2800	ALLENDALE AV	94619	650-E6
2800	ALLENDALE AV	94619	650-E6
3000	PENNIMAN AV	94619	650-E6
3300	SUTER ST	94619	650-E6
3350	FULLINGTON ST	94619	650-E6
VIONA AV			**OAK**
600	BALFOUR AV	94610	650-A3
700	CALMAR AV	94610	650-A3
VIRDEN AV			**OAK**
3600	HARBOR VIEW AV	94619	650-G5
3600	PATTERSON AV	94619	650-G5
3800	VICTOR AV	94619	650-F5
VIRGINIA AV			**OAK**
4300	HIGH ST	94619	650-F7
4420	COURTLAND AV	94619	650-F7
4510	HERRIOTT AV	94619	650-F7
4660	KNOWLAND AV	94619	650-F7
4800	MONTICELLO AV	94619	650-F7
4800	BEST AV	94619	650-F7
4900	MONTICELLO AV	94619	650-F7
VIRGINIA GDNS W			**BERK**
100	VIRGINIA ST	94702	629-E1
VIRGINIA ST			**BERK**
600	EASTSHORE BLVD	94804	629-D1
650	2ND ST	94804	629-D1
700	3RD ST	94804	629-D1
750	4TH ST	94804	629-D1
800	5TH ST	94804	629-D1
850	6TH ST	94804	629-D1
900	7TH ST	94804	629-D1
950	8TH ST	94804	629-D1
1000	9TH ST	94804	629-D1
1050	10TH ST	94804	629-E1
1100	SAN PABLO AV	94702	629-E1
1120	KAINS AV	94702	629-E1
1130	STANNAGE AV	94702	629-E1
1150	CORNELL AV	94702	629-E1
1170	CURTIS ST	94702	629-E1
1180	BELVEDERE AV	94702	629-E1
1200	CHESTNUT ST	94702	629-E1
1300	VIRGINIA GDNS W	94702	629-E1
1340	FRANKLIN ST	94702	629-F1
1400	ACTON ST	94702	629-F1
1460	SHORT ST	94702	629-F1
1500	SACRAMENTO ST	94703	629-F1
1560	EOLA ST	94703	629-F1
1600	CALIFORNIA ST	94703	629-F1
1700	MCGEE AV	94703	629-F1
1750	EDITH ST	94703	629-G1
1800	GRANT ST	94703	629-G1
1850	JOSEPHINE ST	94703	629-G1
1900	MARTIN LUTHER KING JR WY	94709	629-G1
1950	BONITA AV	94709	629-G1
2000	MILVIA ST	94709	629-G1
2100	SHATTUCK AV	94709	629-G1
2130	WALNUT ST	94709	629-H1
2200	OXFORD ST	94709	629-H1
2250	SPRUCE ST	94709	629-H1
2250	ARCH ST	94709	629-H1
2300	SPRUCE ST	94709	629-H1
2300	ARCH ST	94709	629-H1
2400	SCENIC AV	94709	629-H1
2520	EUCLID AV	94709	629-H1
2640	LE ROY AV	94709	629-J1
2750	LA LOMA AV	94709	629-J1
2800	LA VEREDA	94709	629-J1
VIRGO RD			**OAK**
6400	BROADWAY TER	94611	630-D6
VIRMAR AV			**OAK**
5700	MENDOCINO AV	94618	630-A5
5700	MANILA AV	94618	630-A5
5900	BROADWAY	94618	630-A5
VISALIA AV			**BERK**
1500	CURTIS ST	94707	609-F5
1540	NEILSON ST	94707	609-F5
1570	COLUSA AV	94707	609-F5
1700	VINCENTE AV	94707	609-F5
VISTA AV			**PDMT**
100	HIGHLAND AV	94611	650-B1
1	BONITA AV	94611	650-B1
100	HILLSIDE AV	94611	650-B1
VISTA DEL MAR			**OAK**
1	ASPINWALL RD	94611	630-E6
VISTA RD			**ALA**
1	SHAMROCK LN	94502	669-H5
100	TRALEE LN	94502	669-H5
VISTA ST			**OAK**
1500	EVERETT AV	94602	650-D3
1700	WELLINGTON ST	94602	650-D3
VISTAMONT AV			**BERK**
500	WOODMONT AV	94708	609-H4
530	VISTAMONT CT	94708	609-H4
540	ROCHDALE WY	94708	609-H4
570	ROSEMONT AV	94708	609-H4
580	MY WAY	94708	609-H4
700	WOODMONT AV	94708	609-H4
VISTAMONT CT			**BERK**
500	VISTAMONT AV	94708	609-H4
VOLBERG CT			**ALA**
	BARTLETT DR	94501	649-G7
VOLTAIRE AV			**OAK**
9900	99TH AV	94603	671-A5
10080	100TH AV	94603	671-A5
10300	103RD AV	94603	671-A5
10620	106TH AV	94603	671-A6
10710	107TH AV	94603	671-A6
10810	108TH AV	94603	671-A6
10900	109TH AV	94603	671-B6
11000	DURANT AV	94603	671-B6
W			
WADEAN PL			**OAK**
5400	54TH AV	94601	670-E2
5500	55TH AV	94601	670-E2
WAKE AV			**OAK**
2000	BATAAN AV	94607	649-C1
2030	ALASKA ST	94607	649-C1
2030	ALASKA ST	94607	649-C1
2050	BURMA RD	94607	649-C1
2350	MARITIME ST	94649	649-D1
2350	MARITIME ST	94626	649-D1
2350	W GRAND AV	94626	649-D1
WAKEFIELD AV			**OAK**
2500	E 27TH ST	94606	650-B5
2700	23RD AV	94606	650-B5
WAKEFIELD DR			**ALA**
	EAGLE RD	94501	649-J7
	CAMBELL BLVD	94501	649-J7
	SPENCER RD	94501	649-J7
WALAVISTA AV			**OAK**
500	KENMORE AV	94610	650-A2
600	LAKESHORE AV	94610	650-A2
600	LAKESHORE AV	94610	650-B2
640	ARIMO AV	94610	650-B2
810	ARIMO AV	94610	650-B2
850	LAKESHORE AV	94610	650-B2
870	BALFOUR AV	94610	650-B2
870	CARLSTON AV	94610	650-B2
880	PARK LN	94610	650-B2
WALDECK CT			**OAK**
1	MELVILLE DR	94611	650-G2
WALDO AV			**PDMT**
100	BLAIR AV	94611	630-B7
200	PARK WY	94611	630-B7
WALKER AV			**OAK**
750	GRAND AV	94610	649-J3
750	LAKE PARK AV	94610	649-J3
750	CHENEY AV	94610	650-A3
700	CHENEY AV	94610	650-A3
730	WICKSON AV	94610	650-A3
800	MANDANA BLVD	94610	650-A2
850	DAVIDSON WY	94610	650-A2
1000	WELDON AV	94610	650-A2
1100	FAIRBANKS AV	94610	650-A2
WALKER ST			**BERK**
2700	DERBY ST	94705	629-H3
WALLACE RD			**PDMT**
100	WINSOR AV	94610	650-B2
200	PALM DR	94610	650-B2
WALLACE ST			**BERK**
2700	WARD ST	94702	629-E4
2800	OREGON ST	94702	629-E4
2900	RUSSELL ST	94702	629-E4
WALLACE ST			**OAK**
2400	E 24TH ST	94606	650-B5
2510	E 25TH ST	94606	650-B5
2700	19TH AV	94606	650-B5
WALNUT ST			**ALA**
900	CLINTON AV	94501	669-J3
1000	SAN JOSE AV	94501	669-J2
1100	SAN ANTONIO AV	94501	669-J2
1200	ENCINAL AV	94501	669-J2
1300	ALAMEDA AV	94501	669-J2
1400	CENTRAL AV	94501	669-J2
1500	SANTA CLARA AV	94501	669-J2
1600	LINCOLN AV	94501	670-A2
1700	PACIFIC AV	94501	670-A2
1800	BUENA VISTA AV	94501	670-A1
2000	CLEMENT AV	94501	670-A1
WALNUT ST			**BERK**
1100	SHATTUCK AV	94707	609-G6
1200	EUNICE ST	94709	609-G7
1400	ROSE ST	94709	609-G7
1500	VINE ST	94709	609-G7
1600	CEDAR ST	94709	609-G7
1700	VIRGINIA ST	94709	629-H1
1800	DELAWARE ST	94709	629-H1
1900	HEARST AV	94709	629-H1
1920	BERKELEY WY	94704	629-H1
2000	UNIVERSITY AV	94704	629-H1
WALNUT ST			**OAK**
3900	39TH AV	94619	650-E7
4000	MINNA AV	94619	650-E7
4100	EASTMAN AV	94619	650-E7
4300	HIGH ST	94619	650-E7
4600	LILAC ST	94619	650-F7
4800	RENWICK ST	94619	650-F7
4900	MONTICELLO AV	94619	650-F7
5300	MADERA AV	94619	670-F1
5300	KINGSLAND AV	94619	670-F1
5500	55TH AV	94619	670-F1
5500	55TH AV	94605	670-F1
5570	56TH AV	94605	670-F1
5630	57TH AV	94605	670-F1
5680	BEAL AV	94605	670-F1
5750	MASON ST	94605	670-G1
5900	SEMINARY AV	94605	670-G1
9000	90TH AV	94603	670-J4
9200	92ND AV	94603	670-J5
9400	94TH AV	94603	670-J5
9600	96TH AV	94603	670-J5
9800	98TH AV	94603	670-J5
10000	100TH AV	94603	670-J5
10100	101ST AV	94603	670-J5
10200	102ND AV	94603	670-J6
10300	103RD AV	94603	670-J6
10400	104TH AV	94603	670-J6
WALTER AV			**OAK**
9300	LOUISIANA ST	94603	670-G6
9400	CLARA ST	94603	670-G6
9500	S ELMHURST AV	94603	670-G6
9600	TYLER ST	94603	670-G6
9700	NEVADA ST	94603	670-G6
9800	98TH AV	94603	670-G6
WARD LN			**OAK**
3100	CURRAN AV	94602	650-D5
3200	PLEITNER AV	94602	650-D5
3100	MAPLE AV	94602	650-D6
3200	BERLIN WY	94602	650-D6
WARD ST			**BERK**
1100	SAN PABLO AV	94702	629-E3
1160	WALLACE ST	94702	629-E3
1200	MATHEWS ST	94702	629-E3
1210	MATHEWS ST	94702	629-E3
1260	MABEL ST	94702	629-F3
1300	MABEL ST	94702	629-F3
1360	PARK ST	94702	629-F3
1400	ACTON ST	94702	629-F3
1400	ACTON ST	94702	629-F3
1430	DOHR ST	94702	629-F3
1450	SOJOURNER TRUTH CT	94702	629-F3
1500	SACRAMENTO ST	94703	629-F3
1600	CALIFORNIA ST	94703	629-F3
1700	MCGEE AV	94703	629-G3
1800	GRANT ST	94703	629-G3
1900	MARTIN LUTHER KING JR WY	94703	629-G3
2000	MILVIA ST	94703	629-G3
2080	ADELINE ST	94703	629-H3
2100	SHATTUCK AV	94705	629-H3
2200	FULTON ST	94705	629-H3
2300	ELLSWORTH ST	94705	629-H3
2400	DANA ST	94705	629-H3
2500	TELEGRAPH AV	94705	629-H3
WARFIELD AV			**OAK**
700	WICKSON AV	94610	650-A3
750	GLENVIEW AV	94610	650-A3
800	MANDANA BLVD	94610	650-A3
800	MANDANA BLVD	94610	650-A2
900	PRINCE ST	94610	650-A2
900	PRINCE ST	94610	650-A2
950	WELDON AV	94610	650-A2
980	ROSAL AV	94610	650-A2
1000	FAIRBANKS AV	94610	650-A2
1000	FAIRBANKS AV	94610	650-A2
1100	BOULEVARD WY	94610	650-A2
WARFIELD AV			**PDMT**
1100	BOULEVARD WY	94610	650-B2
1200	WILDWOOD AV	94610	650-B2
1200	WINSOR AV	94610	650-B2
WARNER AV			**OAK**
2000	SUNNYSIDE ST	94603	671-A5
2400	OLIVE ST	94603	671-A5
2500	BIRCH ST	94603	671-A5
2200	BANCROFT AV	94603	671-A5
2270	TOLER AV	94603	671-A5
2340	ELMAR AV	94603	671-A5
2400	MACARTHUR BLVD	94603	671-A5
WARREN AV			**OAK**
1	PIEDMONT AV	94611	649-H1
100	RICHMOND BLVD	94611	649-H1
WARRING ST			**BERK**
2300	BANCROFT WY	94704	629-J2
2400	CHANNING WY	94704	629-J2
2400	CHANNING WY	94704	629-J2
2500	DWIGHT WY	94704	629-J2
2500	DWIGHT WY	94704	629-J2
2510	PIEDMONT CRES	94704	629-J2
	PARKER ST	94704	629-J2
	PARKER ST	94704	629-J2
2600	PARKER ST	94704	629-J3
2700	DERBY ST	94704	629-J3
WARWICK AV			**OAK**
300	PERKINS ST	94610	649-J2
400	EUCLID AV	94610	649-J2
WASHINGTON AV			**ALB**
600	CLEVELAND AV	94710	609-C6
600	CLEVELAND AV	94706	609-C6
700	PIERCE ST	94706	609-C6
760	GATEVIEW AV	94706	609-D6
830	POLK ST	94706	609-D6
920	CERRITO ST	94706	609-D6
960	JACKSON ST	94706	609-D6
1000	MADISON ST	94706	609-D6
1050	ADAMS ST	94706	609-D5
1100	SAN PABLO AV	94706	609-D5
1100	SAN PABLO AV	94706	609-D6
1120	KAINS AV	94706	609-D6
1150	STANNAGE AV	94706	609-D5
1200	CORNELL AV	94706	609-D5
1220	TALBOT AV	94706	609-E5
1230	EVELYN AV	94706	609-E5
1250	MASONIC AV	94706	609-E5
1260	SPOKANE AV	94706	609-E5
1270	KEY ROUTE BLVD	94706	609-E5
1300	POMONA AV	94706	609-E5
1300	POMONA AV	94706	609-E5
1320	RAMONA AV	94706	609-E5
1350	CARMEL AV	94706	609-E5
1370	SAN CARLOS AV	94706	609-E5
1400	SANTA FE AV	94706	609-E5
1420	CURTIS ST	94706	609-E5
WASHINGTON AV			**BERK**
1420	CURTIS ST	94707	609-E5
1450	NEILSON ST	94707	609-F5
1470	PERALTA AV	94707	609-F5
1500	MIRAMAR AV	94707	609-F5
1500	SAN LORENZO AV	94707	609-F5
WASHINGTON CT			**ALA**
3300	FERNSIDE BLVD	94501	670-B4
WASHINGTON ST			**ALA**
2600	BROADWAY	94501	670-A3
2650	DORIS CT	94501	670-A3
2700	PEARL ST	94501	670-A3
2750	LEWELLING CT	94501	670-A3
2800	VERSAILLES AV	94501	670-A3
2800	BISHOP ST	94501	670-A3
2900	MOUND ST	94501	670-A3
3000	COURT ST	94501	670-A4
3100	FOUNTAIN ST	94501	670-A4
3200	HIGH ST	94501	670-B4
3230	POST ST	94501	670-B4
3260	PEACH ST	94501	670-B4
3300	FERNSIDE BLVD	94501	670-B4
WASHINGTON ST			**OAK**
100	WATER ST	94607	649-F5
180	EMBARCADERO W	94607	649-F5
250	2ND ST	94607	649-F5
330	3RD ST	94607	649-F5
420	4TH ST	94607	649-F5
	5TH ST	94607	649-F4
600	6TH ST	94607	649-F4
700	7TH ST	94607	649-F4
800	8TH ST	94607	649-F4
900	9TH ST	94607	649-G4
1000	10TH ST	94607	649-G4
WATER ST			**OAK**
400	BROADWAY	94607	649-F5

Address	Cross Street	ZIP	City / Pg-Grid
WATER ST			**OAK**
	WASHINGTON ST	94607	649-F5
	CLAY ST	94607	649-F5
WATERFALL ISL			**ALA**
600	OTIS DR	94501	669-G2
WATERFORD PL			**ALA**
1	KOFMAN PKWY	94502	669-H5
WATERHOUSE RD			**OAK**
3900	LYMAN RD	94602	650-D3
3970	HANLY RD	94602	650-D3
4040	CASTERLINE RD	94602	650-D3
4100	TIFFIN RD	94602	650-D3
4200	CLEMENS RD	94602	650-D3
WATERLOO DR			**OAK**
	SKYLINE BLVD	94611	650-G1
	MELVILLE LN	94611	650-G1
WATERTON ST			**ALA**
2900	MOUND ST	94501	670-A4
3000	COURT ST	94501	670-A4
WATERVIEW ISL			**ALA**
600	OTIS DR	94501	669-H2
WATKINS ST			**BERK**
1300	NEILSON ST	94706	609-E7
1400	TEVLIN ST	94706	609-E7
WATTLING ST			**OAK**
800	HIGH ST	94601	670-D2
900	42ND AV	94601	670-D2
3800	38TH AV	94601	670-C1
3880	39TH AV	94601	670-C1
3950	40TH AV	94601	670-C1
WATTS ST			**EMVL**
4000	40TH ST	94608	629-F7
4100	PARK AV	94608	629-F7
4100	PARK AV	94608	629-F7
4300	45TH ST	94608	629-F7
WATTS ST			**OAK**
	PERALTA ST	94608	629-F7
3650	W MACARTHUR BLVD	94608	629-F7
WAVERLY ST			**OAK**
2300	23RD ST	94612	649-H3
2400	24TH ST	94612	649-H3
WAWONA AV			**OAK**
1000	FLORADA AV	94610	650-B2
1000	PORTAL AV	94610	650-B2
WAYNE AV			**OAK**
200	ATHOL AV	94606	649-J4
300	HANOVER AV	94606	649-J4
300	HANOVER AV	94606	649-J4
440	STOW AV	94606	649-J4
480	WESLEY AV	94606	649-J4
500	LAKESHORE AV	94606	649-J4
WAYNE CT			**ALA**
1300	ENCINAL AV	94501	670-A3
1300	PEASE AV	94501	670-A3
WAYNE PL			**OAK**
300	ATHOL AV	94606	649-J4
360	PARK BLVD	94606	649-J4
400	4TH AV	94606	649-J4
500	5TH AV	94606	649-J5
700	6TH AV	94606	649-J5
WEAVER PL			**OAK**
5670	DENTON PL	94619	651-A6
5700	SKYLINE BLVD	94619	651-A6
WEBB AV			**ALA**
2400	PARK ST	94501	670-A2
2400	TIMES WY	94501	670-A2
2500	EVERETT ST	94501	670-A2
WEBER ST			**ALA**
1300	SAN ANTONIO AV	94501	669-G1
1400	CENTRAL AV	94501	669-G1
WEBSTER ST			**ALA**
1	MITCHELL AV	94501	649-F6
100	EMBARCADERO W	94501	649-F6
1400	CENTRAL AV	94501	669-F1
1400	CROLLS GARDEN CT	94501	669-F1
1450	TAYLOR AV	94501	669-F1
1500	SANTA CLARA AV	94501	669-F1
1550	HAIGHT AV	94501	669-F1
1600	LINCOLN AV	94501	669-F1
1700	PACIFIC AV	94501	669-F1
1800	BUENA VISTA AV	94501	649-F7
1900	EAGLE AV	94501	649-F7
2000	ATLANTIC AV	94501	649-F7
2300	MARINA VILLAGE PKWY	94501	649-F6
	CONSTITUTION WY	94501	649-F6
	MARINER SQUARE LP	94501	649-F6
	TINKER AV	94501	649-F6
2500	MARINA VILLAGE PKWY	94501	649-F6
2530	MARINER SQUARE DR	94501	649-F6
WEBSTER ST			**BERK**
2300	DEAKIN ST	94705	629-H4
2330	HALCYON CT	94705	629-H4
2400	TELEGRAPH AV	94705	629-H4
2460	COLBY ST	94705	629-H4
2560	HILLEGASS AV	94705	629-J4
2620	BENVENUE AV	94705	629-J4
2630	BENVENUE AV	94705	629-J4
2700	COLLEGE AV	94705	629-J4
2700	COLLEGE AV	94705	629-J4
2800	PIEDMONT AV	94705	629-J4
2820	LINDEN AV	94705	629-J4
2830	MAGNOLIA ST	94705	629-J4
2850	PINE AV	94705	630-A4
2900	CLAREMONT AV	94705	630-A4
WEBSTER ST			**OAK**
100	EMBARCADERO W	94607	649-G5
200	2ND ST	94607	649-G5
300	3RD ST	94607	649-G5
400	4TH ST	94607	649-G5
100	EMBARCADERO W	94607	649-F5
200	2ND ST	94607	649-G5
300	3RD ST	94607	649-G5
400	4TH ST	94607	649-G5
700	7TH ST	94607	649-G4
800	8TH ST	94607	649-G4
900	9TH ST	94607	649-G4
1000	10TH ST	94607	649-G4
1100	11TH ST	94607	649-G4
1200	12TH ST	94612	649-G4
1300	13TH ST	94612	649-G4
1400	14TH ST	94612	649-G4
1500	15TH ST	94612	649-G4
1700	17TH ST	94612	649-G3
1900	19TH ST	94612	649-G3
2000	20TH ST	94612	649-G3
2100	21ST ST	94612	649-H3
2180	22ND ST	94612	649-H3
2250	GRAND AV	94612	649-H3
2300	23RD ST	94612	649-H3
2400	24TH ST	94612	649-H2
2610	26TH ST	94612	649-H2
2640	BROADWAY	94612	649-H2
2710	27TH ST	94612	649-H2
2800	28TH ST	94609	649-H2
2800	28TH ST	94611	649-H2
2900	29TH ST	94609	649-H2
2900	29TH ST	94611	649-H2
3000	30TH ST	94609	649-H1
3000	30TH ST	94611	649-H1
3200	HAWTHORNE AV	94609	649-H1
3200	HAWTHORNE AV	94611	649-H1
3300	HAWTHORNE AV	94609	649-H1
	34TH ST	94609	649-H1
3600	36TH ST	94609	649-H1
3700	37TH ST	94609	649-H1
3750	W MACARTHUR BLVD	94609	649-H1
3800	38TH ST	94609	649-H1
4000	40TH ST	94609	629-H7
4100	41ST ST	94609	629-H7
4150	RICH ST	94609	629-H7
4200	42ND ST	94609	629-H7
4300	43RD ST	94609	629-H7
4400	44TH ST	94609	629-H7
4500	45TH ST	94609	629-H7
4800	48TH ST	94609	629-H6
4900	49TH ST	94609	629-H6
5000	50TH ST	94609	629-H6
5100	51ST ST	94609	629-H6
WEE BLYTHEN			**OAK**
1	BLYTHEN WY	94619	650-J4
WEISS CT			**ALA**
	BARTLETT DR	94501	649-G7
WELD ST			**OAK**
6900	69TH AV	94621	670-G2
7000	70TH AV	94621	670-G3
	73RD AV	94621	670-H3
7300	73RD AV	94621	670-H3
7800	78TH AV	94621	670-H3
7800	78TH AV	94621	670-H3
7900	79TH AV	94621	670-H3
WELDON AV			**OAK**
400	GRAND AV	94610	650-A2
450	WALKER AV	94610	650-A2
500	VERMONT ST	94610	650-A2
500	SCOTT ST	94610	650-A2
520	WARFIELD AV	94610	650-A2
540	YORK ST	94610	650-A2
570	ERIE ST	94610	650-A3
600	LAKESHORE AV	94610	650-A3
WELLFLEET BAY			**ALA**
1	OYSTER POND RD	94502	670-A6
100	SAND HARBOR	94502	670-A6
WELLINGTON ST			**OAK**
1000	EVERETT AV	94602	650-C3
1000	EVERETT AV	94610	650-C3
1200	LEACH ST	94602	650-C3
1310	EDGEWOOD AV	94602	650-C3
1340	PARK BLVD	94602	650-C3
1400	EVANS AV	94602	650-C3
1500	TOWNSEND AV	94602	650-D4
1620	LA CRESTA AV	94602	650-D4
1630	LA CRESTA AV	94602	650-D4
1700	EVERETT AV	94602	650-D4
1800	VISTA ST	94602	650-D4
1900	CANON AV	94602	650-D4
WENTWORTH AV			**OAK**
5430	55TH AV	94601	670-F2
5300	FAIRFAX AV	94601	670-E2
5220	54TH AV	94601	670-E1
5200	52ND AV	94601	670-E1
5220	BANCROFT AV	94601	670-E1
5220	51ST AV	94601	670-E1
WERNER CT			**OAK**
5000	MOUNTAIN BLVD	94602	650-F3
5050	WOODMINSTER LN	94602	650-F3
WESLEY AV			**OAK**
400	LAKESHORE AV	94606	649-J4
410	WAYNE AV	94606	649-J4
460	BROOKLYN AV	94606	649-J4
460	NEWTON AV	94606	649-J4
480	HILLSBOROUGH ST	94606	649-J4
500	CAPITAL ST	94606	649-J4
510	CLEVELAND ST	94606	649-J4
600	MACARTHUR BLVD	94610	650-A3
510	HILLGIRT CIR	94606	650-A3
510	MERRITT AV	94606	650-A3
510	PROSPECT AV	94606	650-A3
600	HILLGIRT CIR	94606	650-A3
600	MERRITT AV	94606	650-A3
600	PROSPECT AV	94606	650-A3
WESLEY WY			**OAK**
700	TRESTLE GLEN RD	94610	650-A3
800	LAKE PARK AV	94610	650-A3
WEST CIR			**OAK**
	BALBOA DR	94611	630-F7
WEST CT			**OAK**
10500	105TH AV	94603	670-G7
WEST LN			**OAK**
	OCEAN VIEW DR	94618	630-A5
	BROOKSIDE AV	94618	630-A5
	MANCHESTER DR	94618	630-A5
	PROSPECT STEPS	94618	630-A5
WEST PL			**ALB**
1050	POSEN AV	94706	609-F7
WEST ST			**BERK**
2100	ADDISON ST	94702	629-E2
2200	ALLSTON WY	94702	629-E2
2300	BANCROFT WY	94702	629-F2
2400	CHANNING WY	94702	629-F3
2500	DWIGHT WY	94702	629-F3
WEST ST			**OAK**
1200	12TH ST	94607	649-F3
1300	13TH ST	94607	649-F3
1400	14TH ST	94607	649-F3
1400	14TH ST	94612	649-F3
1510	15TH ST	94607	649-F3
1510	15TH ST	94612	649-F3
1600	16TH ST	94607	649-F3
1600	16TH ST	94612	649-F3
1700	17TH ST	94607	649-F3
1700	17TH ST	94612	649-F3
1760	17TH ST	94607	649-F3
1760	17TH ST	94612	649-F3
1800	18TH ST	94607	649-F3
1800	18TH ST	94612	649-F3
1920	19TH ST	94607	649-F3
1920	19TH ST	94612	649-F3
2000	20TH ST	94607	649-F3
2000	20TH ST	94612	649-F3
2100	21ST ST	94607	649-F3
2100	21ST ST	94612	649-F3
2200	22ND ST	94607	649-F2
2200	22ND ST	94612	649-F2
2300	W GRAND AV	94607	649-F2
2300	W GRAND AV	94612	649-F2
2340	23RD ST	94607	649-F2
2340	23RD ST	94612	649-F2
2450	ISABELLA ST	94607	649-G2
2450	ISABELLA ST	94612	649-G2
2480	SAN PABLO AV	94612	649-G2
2500	25TH ST	94612	649-G2
2570	SYCAMORE ST	94612	649-G2
2630	26TH ST	94612	649-G2
2700	27TH ST	94612	649-G2
2790	28TH ST	94608	649-G2
2790	28TH ST	94609	649-G2
2900	29TH ST	94608	649-G2
2900	29TH ST	94609	649-G2
3000	30TH ST	94608	649-G1
3000	30TH ST	94609	649-G1
3100	31ST ST	94608	649-G1
3100	31ST LN	94609	649-G1
3200	32ND ST	94608	649-G1
3200	32ND ST	94609	649-G1
3250	BROCKHURST ST	94608	649-G1
3250	BROCKHURST ST	94609	649-G1
3300	33RD ST	94608	649-G1
3300	33RD ST	94609	649-G1
3400	34TH ST	94608	649-G1
3400	34TH ST	94609	649-G1
	35TH ST	94608	649-G1
	35TH ST	94609	649-G1
3600	36TH ST	94608	649-G1
3600	36TH ST	94609	649-G1
3700	37TH ST	94609	629-G7
3700	37TH ST	94608	629-G7
3800	W MACARTHUR BLVD	94608	629-G7
3800	W MACARTHUR BLVD	94609	629-G7
3850	APGAR ST	94608	629-G7
3850	APGAR ST	94609	629-G7
3900	39TH ST	94608	629-G7
3900	39TH ST	94609	629-G7
4000	40TH ST	94608	629-G7
4000	40TH ST	94609	629-G7
4100	41ST ST	94608	629-G7
4100	41ST ST	94609	629-G7
4200	42ND ST	94608	629-G7
4200	42ND ST	94609	629-G7
4300	43RD ST	94608	629-G7
4300	43RD ST	94609	629-G7
4400	44TH ST	94608	629-G7
4400	44TH ST	94609	629-G7
4500	45TH ST	94608	629-G7
4500	45TH ST	94609	629-G7
4600	46TH ST	94608	629-G6
4600	46TH ST	94609	629-G6
4700	47TH ST	94608	629-G6
5000	51ST ST	94608	629-G6
5100	52ND ST	94608	629-G6
5200	53RD ST	94608	629-G6
5200	MARTIN LUTHER KING JR WY	94608	629-G6
WEST VIEW DR			**OAK**
1100	GRAND VIEW PL	94705	630-B3
1200	WEST VIEW PL	94705	630-B3
1400	VICENTE PL	94705	630-B4
1500	WILLARD PL	94705	630-B4
WEST VIEW PL			**OAK**
1	WEST VIEW DR	94705	630-B3
WESTALL AV			**OAK**
1	PIEDMONT AV	94611	649-H1
100	RICHMOND BLVD	94611	649-H1
WESTFIELD WY			**OAK**
570	CRESTMONT DR	94619	650-H5
540	CREIGHTON WY	94619	650-H5
500	VAN CLEAVE WY	94619	650-H5
WESTLINE DR			**ALA**
	8TH ST	94501	669-G2
300	SHORELINE DR	94501	669-G2
410	SHOREPOINT CT	94501	669-G2
500	ROSEWOOD WY	94501	669-G2
550	OTIS DR	94501	669-G2
600	8TH ST	94501	669-G2
WESTMINSTER DR			**OAK**
1	COUNTRY CLUB DR	94618	630-A6
70	LINCOLNSHIRE DR	94618	630-A6
100	GLENBROOK DR	94618	630-A6
WESTMORELAND DR			**OAK**
7000	NORFOLK DR	94705	630-C3
WESTOVER DR			**OAK**
	BAGSHOTTE DR	94611	650-F1
5800	PELHAM PL	94611	650-F1
5940	THACKERAY DR	94611	630-F7
6300	SHELTERWOOD DR	94611	630-F7
6500	AITKEN DR	94611	630-F7
6500	DORAN DR	94611	630-F7
WESTWOOD CT			**OAK**
1	WESTWOOD WY	94611	630-E6
100	ASPINWALL RD	94611	630-E6
WESTWOOD WY			**OAK**
6200	INDIAN WY	94611	630-E6
6230	WESTWOOD CT	94611	630-E6
6300	ASPINWALL RD	94611	630-E6
WETMORE RD			**OAK**
3000	PROSPECT HILL RD	94613	670-G1
3500	POST RD	94613	650-H7
3580	RICHARDS RD	94613	650-H7
WEXFORD PL			**ALA**
100	DUBLIN WY	94502	669-J5
WEYBRIDGE CT			**OAK**
100	CASTLE DR	94611	650-G2
WEYMOUTH CT			**ALA**
100	ROXBURG LN	94502	670-A5
WHEELER ST			**BERK**
2900	RUSSELL ST	94705	629-H4
3000	ASHBY AV	94705	629-H4
3000	ASHBY AV	94705	629-H4
3020	EMERSON ST	94705	629-H4
3040	ESSEX ST	94705	629-H4
3100	PRINCE ST	94705	629-H4
3200	WOOLSEY ST	94705	629-H4
WHEELER ST			**OAK**
6500	65TH ST	94609	629-H4
6600	FAIRVIEW ST	94609	629-H4
WHIMBREL CT			**ALA**
	BRUZZONE DR	94501	649-F7
	PLOVER CT	94501	649-F7
WHITAKER AV			**BERK**
70	MILLER AV	94708	609-J6
100	STERLING AV	94708	609-J6
WHITE CLIFF CT			**OAK**
	WHITE CLIFF RD	94605	671-C4
WHITE CLIFF RD			**OAK**
	GATE VIEW DR	94605	671-C4
	WHITE CLIFF CT	94605	671-C4
WHITE CT			**OAK**
1	AITKEN DR	94611	630-G7
WHITEHALL PL			**ALA**
2000	MYRTLE WK	94501	669-H3
2000	WHITEHALL RD	94501	669-H3
2200	WILLOW ST	94501	669-H3
WHITEHALL RD			**ALA**
400	FRANCISCAN WY	94501	669-H3
500	WHITEHALL PL	94501	669-H3
500	MYRTLE WK	94501	669-H3
WHITMORE PL			**OAK**
100	45TH ST	94611	629-J7
100	WHITMORE ST	94611	629-J7
WHITMORE ST			**OAK**
200	GILBERT ST	94611	629-J7
300	45TH ST	94611	629-J7
300	WHITMORE PL	94611	629-J7
WHITNEY ST			**OAK**
5900	59TH ST	94609	629-H5
6000	60TH ST	94609	629-H5
6500	65TH ST	94609	629-H4
6700	WOOLSEY ST	94609	629-H4
WHITTLE AV			**OAK**
3800	FRUITVALE AV	94602	650-D4
3850	FOREST HILL AV	94602	650-D4
1720	WHITTLE CT	94602	650-D4
3950	WILBUR ST	94602	650-E4
4100	RAVENWOOD LN	94602	650-E4
4100	RAVENWOOD LN	94602	650-E3
4100	TIFFIN RD	94602	650-E3
4300	FUNSTON PL	94602	650-E3
WHITTLE CT			**OAK**
1	WHITTLE AV	94602	650-D4
WICHITA			**ALA**
3000	MULVANY CIR	94501	649-E6
WICKSON AV			**OAK**
400	WALKER AV	94610	650-A3
500	WARFIELD AV	94610	650-A3
600	RAND AV	94610	650-A3
WILBUR ST			**OAK**
2300	WHITTLE AV	94602	650-E4
2400	LINCOLN AV	94602	650-E4
2600	LAGUNA AV	94602	650-E4
WILD CURRANT WY			**OAK**
7100	OAKWOOD DR	94611	630-F6
7180	GLEN OAKS WY	94611	630-F6
7300	THORNHILL DR	94611	630-F6
WILDA AV			**OAK**
3900	MONTE VISTA AV	94611	649-J1
WILDCAT CANYON RD			**BERK**
500	CANON DR	94708	609-G4
500	WOODMONT AV	94708	609-G4
600	WOODMONT AV	94708	609-H4
700	SUNSET LN	94708	609-H5
950	THE SPIRAL	94708	609-J5
1000	THE SPIRAL	94708	609-J5
830	PARK HILLS RD	94708	609-J5
WILDCAT CANYON RD			**CCCo**
500	CANON DR	94708	609-G4
500	WOODMONT AV	94708	609-G4
600	WOODMONT AV	94708	609-H4
700	SUNSET LN	94708	609-H5
950	THE SPIRAL	94708	609-J5
1000	THE SPIRAL	94708	609-J5
830	PARK HILLS RD	94708	609-J5
WILDING LN			**OAK**
1	MORRILL LN	94618	630-B6
30	NORMAN LN	94618	630-B6
60	CANON VIEW LN	94618	630-B6
200	MANDALAY RD	94618	630-B6
WILDWOOD AV			**PDMT**
1	GRAND AV	94610	650-A2
1	JEAN ST	94610	650-A2
60	NOVA DR	94610	650-A2
90	SYLVAN WY	94610	650-A2
100	NOVA DR	94610	650-A2
100	SYLVAN WY	94610	650-A2
120	PALM DR	94610	650-A2
200	WINSOR AV	94610	650-A2
200	WINSOR AV	94611	650-B2
200	WARFIELD AV	94610	650-B2
300	PORTSMOUTH RD	94611	650-B2
300	PORTSMOUTH RD	94610	650-B2
320	PROSPECT RD	94611	650-B2
320	REQUA RD	94611	650-B2
400	HIGHLAND AV	94611	650-C2
420	WILDWOOD GDNS	94611	650-C2
450	SHERIDAN AV	94611	650-C2
500	CROCKER AV	94611	650-C2
WILDWOOD GDNS			**PDMT**
10	WILDWOOD AV	94611	650-C2
160	WISTARIA WY	94611	650-C2
200	WOODLAND WY	94611	650-C2
WILKIE ST			**OAK**
4700	TOMPKINS AV	94619	650-G6
4800	FAIR AV	94619	650-G6
WILLARD PL			**OAK**
1	WEST VIEW DR	94705	630-B4
WILLET CT			**ALA**
	BUENA VISTA AV	94501	649-F7
	GRESHAM DR	94501	649-F7
WILLIAMS ST			**OAK**
500	TELEGRAPH AV	94612	649-G3
650	SAN PABLO AV	94612	649-G3
WILLIS CT			**OAK**
3600	35TH AV	94619	650-G5
WILLIS LN			**ALA**
3300	FIR AV	94502	670-A7
3400	BISMARCK LN	94502	670-A7
WILLOW ST			**ALA**
300	SHORELINE DR	94501	669-H3
400	FRANCISCAN WY	94501	669-H3
500	WHITEHALL PL	94501	669-J3
550	SANDCREEK WY	94501	669-J3
600	OTIS DR	94501	669-J3
600	OTIS DR	94501	669-J3
900	CLINTON AV	94501	669-J2
1000	SAN JOSE AV	94501	669-J2
1100	SAN ANTONIO AV	94501	669-J2
1200	ENCINAL AV	94501	669-J2
1300	ALAMEDA AV	94501	669-J2
1400	CENTRAL AV	94501	669-J2
1500	SANTA CLARA AV	94501	669-J2
1600	LINCOLN AV	94501	669-J1
1700	PACIFIC AV	94501	669-J1
1800	BUENA VISTA AV	94501	669-J1
1900	EAGLE AV	94501	669-J1
2000	CLEMENT AV	94501	669-J1
WILLOW ST			**OAK**
770	GOSS ST	94607	649-D3
790	8TH ST	94607	649-D3
840	CHASE ST	94607	649-D3
920	9TH ST	94607	649-D3
1000	10TH ST	94607	649-D3
1100	11TH ST	94607	649-D3
1200	12TH ST	94607	649-D3
1300	13TH ST	94607	649-D3
1400	14TH ST	94607	649-D2
1500	15TH ST	94607	649-D2
1600	16TH ST	94607	649-D2
1700	17TH ST	94607	649-D2
2000	20TH ST	94607	649-E2
2200	W GRAND AV	94607	649-E2
2390	24TH ST	94607	649-E1
2600	26TH ST	94607	649-E1
2700	MANDELA PKWY	94607	649-E1
2700	28TH ST	94607	649-E1
WILLOW TR			**BERK**
	ALVARADO RD	94705	630-B4
	SUNSET TR	94705	630-B4
	ALVARADO RD	94705	630-B4
WILSHIRE BLVD			**OAK**
4100	CARLSEN ST	94602	650-F4
4250	FRYE ST	94602	650-F4
4280	STEINMETZ WY	94602	650-F4
4300	KITCHENER CT	94602	650-F4
WILSON AV			**OAK**
3400	MONTANA ST	94602	650-D5
3500	MACARTHUR BLVD	94602	650-D4
WILSON CIR			**BERK**
70	OLYMPUS AV	94708	610-A7
WILSON PL			**OAK**
3500	HAROLD ST	94602	650-D5
WILSON ST			**ALB**
100	9TH ST	94710	609-D6
400	6TH ST	94710	609-D7

© 2006 Rand McNally & Company

PRIMARY STREET Address	Cross Street	ZIP	CITY Pg-Grid
WILTON DR			**OAK**
6700	SKYLINE BLVD	94611	650-G1
7000	BURTON DR	94611	650-G1
7000	SHIRLEY DR	94611	650-G1
WINDEMERE ISL			**ALA**
600	OTIS DR	94501	669-G2
WINDING WY			**OAK**
	SKYLINE BLVD	94611	630-F6
WINDSOR DR			**ALA**
2800	MARINA DR	94501	670-B2
2800	VERSAILLES AV	94501	670-B2
2900	CAMBRIDGE DR	94501	670-B2
3000	HARVARD DR	94501	670-B2
3100	CORNELL DR	94501	670-C2
3200	MARINA DR	94501	670-C2
WINDWARD HILL			**OAK**
1	HILLER DR	94618	630-C4
100	HILLER DR	94618	630-C4
WINDWARD LN			**ALA**
1120	SOLOMON LN	94502	670-A7
1200	TONGA LN	94502	670-A7
WINSOR AV			**OAK**
1000	HARVARD RD	94610	650-B2
1000	LAKESHORE AV	94610	650-B2
1100	WILDWOOD AV	94610	650-B2
1100	WARFIELD AV	94610	650-B2
WINSOR AV			**PDMT**
1100	WILDWOOD AV	94610	650-B2
1100	WARFIELD AV	94610	650-B2
1100	WILDWOOD AV	94610	650-B2
1110	WALLACE RD	94610	650-B2
1170	PARKVIEW CT	94610	650-B2
WINTHROPE ST			**OAK**
8000	HOLMES AV	94605	671-A2
7900	SHONE AV	94605	671-A2
8000	KELLER AV	94605	671-A2
WISCONSIN ST			**OAK**
3000	MAPLE AV	94602	650-F4
3200	CARLSEN ST	94602	650-F5
3200	LAUREL AV	94602	650-F5
3250	RETTIG PL	94602	650-F5
3290	RETTIG AV	94602	650-F5
3370	NORTON AV	94602	650-F5
3380	NORTON AV	94602	650-F5
3440	MIDVALE AV	94602	650-F5
3500	35TH AV	94619	650-F5
3600	MAGEE AV	94619	650-F5
3700	LOMA VISTA AV	94619	650-F5
3800	BROWN AV	94619	650-F5
3900	PATTERSON AV	94619	650-F5
WISTAR RD			**OAK**
200	EMPIRE RD	94603	670-F7
300	CORAL RD	94603	670-F7
WISTARIA WY			**PDMT**
1	WOODLAND WY	94611	650-C2
200	WILDWOOD GDNS	94611	650-C2
WOOD CT			**OAK**
100	WOOD DR	94611	650-D1
WOOD DR			**OAK**
5900	HARBORD DR	94611	650-D1
6100	MOYER PL	94611	650-D1
6300	WOOD CT	94611	650-D1
6400	LA SALLE AV	94611	650-D1
WOOD ST			**ALA**
1600	LINCOLN AV	94501	669-G1
1700	PACIFIC AV	94501	669-G1
1800	BUENA VISTA AV	94501	649-G7
1900	EAGLE AV	94501	649-G7
WOOD ST			**OAK**
670	GOSS ST	94607	649-D3
700	SHOREY ST	94607	649-D3
700	8TH ST	94607	649-D3
800	CHASE ST	94607	649-D3
900	9TH ST	94607	649-D3
1000	10TH ST	94607	649-D3
1100	11TH ST	94607	649-D3
1200	12TH ST	94607	649-D3
1300	13TH ST	94607	649-D2
1400	14TH ST	94607	649-D2
1500	15TH ST	94607	649-D2
1600	16TH ST	94607	649-D2
1700	17TH ST	94607	649-D2
1800	18TH ST	94607	649-D2
2000	20TH ST	94607	649-E2
2200	W GRAND AV	94607	649-E2
2400	24TH ST	94607	649-E1
3000	32ND ST	94607	649-E1
3400	34TH ST	94649	649-E1
3400	34TH ST	94608	649-E1
WOODBINE AV			**OAK**
2100	FRUITVALE AV	94602	650-D5
2200	PLEASANT ST	94602	650-D5
WOODCLIFF CT			**OAK**
1	MALCOLM AV	94605	671-C5
WOODCREST CIR			**OAK**
1	MOUNTAIN BLVD	94602	650-F3
WOODHAVEN RD			**BERK**
700	SUNSET LN	94708	609-H5
WOODHAVEN WY			**OAK**
1600	PINEHAVEN RD	94611	630-E6
1600	THORNHILL DR	94611	630-E6
1800	INDIAN WY	94611	630-E6
2000	THORNHILL DR	94611	630-E6
WOODLAND PL			**OAK**
6600	BROADWAY TER	94611	630-D5
WOODLAND WY			**PDMT**
30	LAFAYETTE AV	94611	650-C2
30	LA SALLE AV	94611	650-C2
20	WISTARIA WY	94611	650-C2
1	WILDWOOD GDNS	94611	650-C2
20	CROCKER AV	94611	650-C2
WOODMINSTER LN			**OAK**
5000	MOUNTAIN BLVD	94602	650-F3
5100	WERNER CT	94602	650-F3
WOODMONT AV			**BERK**
500	GRIZZLY PEAK BLVD	94708	609-G4
500	SPRUCE ST	94708	609-G4
580	CANON DR	94708	609-G4
580	WILDCAT CANYON RD	94708	609-G4
520	WILDCAT CANYON RD	94708	609-H4
560	VISTAMONT AV	94708	609-H4
580	WOODMONT CT	94708	609-H4
590	WOODMONT CT	94708	609-H4
620	ROSEMONT AV	94708	609-H4
740	VISTAMONT AV	94708	609-H5
770	SUNSET LN	94708	609-H5
WOODMONT AV			**CCCo**
500	GRIZZLY PEAK BLVD	94708	609-G4
500	SPRUCE ST	94708	609-G4
580	CANON DR	94708	609-G4
580	WILDCAT CANYON RD	94708	609-G4
WOODMONT CT			**BERK**
1	WOODMONT AV	94708	609-H4
50	WOODMONT AV	94708	609-H4
WOODMONT WY			**OAK**
1	GRIZZLY TERRACE DR	94611	630-D3
WOODROW DR			**OAK**
7350	SARONI DR	94611	630-F7
7100	LAS FLORES CT	94611	630-F7
7350	PASO ROBLES DR	94611	630-F7

PRIMARY STREET Address	Cross Street	ZIP	CITY Pg-Grid
WOODRUFF AV			**OAK**
3500	MACARTHUR BLVD	94602	650-C4
3550	MIAMI CT	94602	650-C4
3600	EXCELSIOR AV	94602	650-C4
3800	E 38TH ST	94602	650-C4
3800	E 38TH ST	94602	650-C4
4100	HAMPEL ST	94602	650-C4
4150	BENTON ST	94602	650-C4
4200	GLENFIELD AV	94602	650-C4
WOODSIDE RD			**BERK**
1000	THE CRESCENT	94708	609-J5
1060	HILLVIEW RD	94708	609-J6
1200	PARK HILLS RD	94708	609-J6
WOODSIDE WY			**OAK**
1	GRIZZLY TERRACE DR	94611	630-D3
WOOLSEY ST			**BERK**
1500	SACRAMENTO ST	94703	629-F4
1600	CALIFORNIA ST	94703	629-G4
1700	KING ST	94703	629-G4
1800	ELLIS ST	94703	629-G4
1820	HARPER ST	94703	629-G4
1820	HARPER ST	94703	629-G4
1850	MARTIN LUTHER KING JR WY	94703	629-G4
1900	ADELINE ST	94703	629-G4
2000	TREMONT ST	94703	629-G4
2020	WHITNEY ST	94703	629-H4
2100	SHATTUCK AV	94705	629-H4
2200	WHEELER ST	94705	629-H4
2300	DEAKIN ST	94705	629-H4
2340	TELEGRAPH AV	94705	629-H4
2400	DANA ST	94705	629-J4
2430	COLBY ST	94705	629-J4
2500	REGENT ST	94705	629-J4
2510	BATEMAN ST	94705	629-J4
2600	HILLEGASS AV	94705	629-J4
2610	HILLEGASS AV	94705	629-J4
2620	BENVENUE AV	94705	629-J4
2630	BENVENUE AV	94705	629-J4
2700	COLLEGE AV	94705	629-J4
2720	LEWISTON AV	94705	629-J4
2730	ETON AV	94705	629-J4
2900	CLAREMONT AV	94705	629-J4
WOOLSEY ST			**OAK**
2200	WHEELER ST	94609	629-H4
2300	DEAKIN ST	94609	629-H4
2340	TELEGRAPH AV	94609	629-H4
2400	DANA ST	94609	629-J4
2420	COLBY ST	94618	629-J4
2500	REGENT ST	94618	629-J4
2510	BATEMAN ST	94618	629-J4
2600	HILLEGASS AV	94618	629-J4
2600	HILLEGASS AV	94618	629-J4
2620	BENVENUE AV	94618	629-J4
2630	BENVENUE AV	94618	629-J4
2700	COLLEGE AV	94618	629-J4
WORDEN WY			**OAK**
4400	HYACINTH AV	94619	650-G6
4500	HUNTINGTON ST	94619	650-G6
WORTH ST			**OAK**
410	PHELPS ST	94603	670-F6
470	DATE ST	94603	670-F6
500	EDES AV	94603	670-F6
WRENN ST			**OAK**
1900	LEIMERT BLVD	94602	650-E3
1960	BYWOOD DR	94602	650-E3
1980	ARCADIA AV	94602	650-E3
2100	FRUITVALE AV	94602	650-E3
2100	HOOVER AV	94602	650-E3
WRIGHT ST			**OAK**
1000	EARHART RD	94621	670-D7
1090	BOEING ST	94621	670-D6
1100	DOOLITTLE DR	94621	670-D6
WYMAN PL			**OAK**
100	WYMAN ST	94619	650-G7
WYMAN ST			**OAK**
3440	MORCOM AV	94619	650-G7
3350	WYMAN PL	94619	650-G7
3200	SIMMONS ST	94619	650-G7
3350	CAMDEN ST	94619	650-G7
WYNGAARD AV			**PDMT**
1	ESTATES DR	94611	650-D2
100	SANDRINGHAM RD	94611	650-D2
Y			
YALE DR			**ALA**
1800	GIBBONS DR	94501	670-B2
1900	FERNSIDE BLVD	94501	670-B2
YANKEE HILL			**OAK**
80	GRAND VIEW DR	94618	630-C4
80	SCHOONER HILL	94618	630-C4
YARMOUTH CT			**OAK**
	STANTONVILLE DR	94619	650-J4
YERBA BUENA AV			**EMVL**
1050	ADELINE ST	94608	629-F7
	SAN PABLO AV	94608	629-F7
	EMERY ST	94608	629-F7
	HOLLIS ST	94608	629-F7
YERBA BUENA AV			**OAK**
900	40TH ST	94608	629-F7
1050	ADELINE ST	94608	629-F7
1100	HOLLIS ST	94608	629-E7
	HORTON ST	94608	629-E7
	BEACH ST	94608	629-E7
YGNACIO AV			**OAK**
4300	COURTLAND AV	94601	670-D1
4400	HIGH ST	94601	670-D1
4500	45TH AV	94601	670-E1
4600	46TH AV	94601	670-E1
4700	47TH AV	94601	670-E1
5400	TRASK ST	94601	670-F1
5340	COLE ST	94601	670-F1
5280	BELVEDERE ST	94601	670-F1
5210	FAIRFAX AV	94601	670-E1
5150	CONGRESS AV	94601	670-E1
5070	VICKSBURG AV	94601	670-E1
5000	51ST AV	94601	670-E1
4800	50TH AV	94601	670-E1
5000	48TH AV	94601	670-E1
YOLO AV			**BERK**
1900	MARTIN LUTHER KING JR WY	94707	609-G7
1900	MARTIN LUTHER KING JR WY	94709	609-G7
1970	BONITA AV	94707	609-G6
1970	BONITA AV	94709	609-G6
2020	MILVIA ST	94707	609-G6
2020	MILVIA ST	94709	609-G6
2100	SUTTER ST	94707	609-G6
2100	SUTTER ST	94709	609-G6
YORK DR			**PDMT**
60	ARROYO AV	94611	650-A1
100	HOLLY PL	94611	650-A1
200	CAMBRIDGE WY	94611	650-A1
YORK ST			**OAK**
800	MANDANA BLVD	94610	650-A3
900	PRINCE ST	94610	650-A2
1000	WELDON AV	94610	650-A2
YORKSHIRE DR			**OAK**
100	BEECHWOOD DR	94618	630-B6
YORKSHIRE PL			**ALA**
2000	FERNDELL WK	94501	669-H3

PRIMARY STREET Address	Cross Street	ZIP	CITY Pg-Grid
2000	YORKSHIRE RD	94501	669-H3
2100	MYRTLE WK	94501	669-H3
2100	CAMDEN RD	94501	669-H3
YORKSHIRE RD			**ALA**
400	FRANCISCAN WY	94501	669-H3
500	YORKSHIRE PL	94501	669-H3
500	FERNDELL WK	94501	669-H3
YOSEMITE AV			**ALA**
2800	VERSAILLES AV	94501	670-B2
2850	MORELAND DR	94501	670-B2
2900	CAMBRIDGE DR	94501	670-B2
YOSEMITE AV			**OAK**
1	PIEDMONT AV	94611	649-J1
100	FAIRMOUNT AV	94611	649-J1
YOSEMITE RD			**BERK**
1800	THE ALAMEDA	94707	609-F5
1870	INDIAN TR	94707	609-F5
1870	SAN FERNANDO AV	94707	609-F5
1910	CONTRA COSTA AV	94707	609-G5
2000	ARLINGTON AV	94707	609-G5
2000	SOMERSET PL	94707	609-G5
YOUNG AV			**OAK**
3700	ATLAS AV	94619	650-G5
YOUNG ST			**ALA**
2700	FOSTER ST	94502	669-J6
2800	ARMITAGE ST	94502	669-J6
2800	MILLINGTON CT	94502	669-J6
YUBA AV			**OAK**
5300	MORCOM AV	94619	670-F1
5400	BIRDSALL AV	94619	670-F1
5400	BIRDSALL AV	94619	670-F1
5500	55TH AV	94619	670-F1
Z			
ZIEGLER AV			**OAK**
4400	MONAN ST	94605	671-E5
4460	ELVESSA ST	94605	671-D5
4500	ETTRICK ST	94605	671-D5
ZINN			**OAK**
	ZINN DR	94611	630-E7
	DRAKE DR	94611	630-E7
	ZINN DR	94611	630-E7
ZINN DR			**OAK**
5900	SNAKE RD	94611	650-E1
6460	RINCON DR	94611	650-E1
6500	DRAKE DR	94611	650-E1
6500	ZINN	94611	650-E1
6450	ZINN	94611	630-E7
6500	ASILOMAR DR	94611	630-E7
ZORAH ST			**OAK**
500	CLEVELAND ST	94606	650-A4
550	BROOKLYN AV	94606	650-A4
#			
1ST AV			**OAK**
1370	INTERNATIONAL BLVD	94606	649-H5
1300	INTERNATIONAL BLVD	94606	649-H4
1400	1ST AV PL	94606	649-H4
1500	E 15TH ST	94606	649-J4
1550	LAKESHORE AV	94606	649-J4
1560	E 16TH ST	94606	649-J4
1600	FOOTHILL BLVD	94606	649-J4
1600	LAKESHORE AV	94606	649-J4
1300	LAKESHORE AV	94606	649-H5
1300	LAKESIDE DR	94606	649-H5
1400	1ST AV PL	94606	649-H5
	E 12TH ST	94607	649-H5
1300	14TH ST	94606	649-H5
1ST AV PL			**OAK**
1400	1ST AV	94606	649-H4
1500	E 15TH ST	94606	649-H4
1ST ST			**OAK**
740	MARTIN LUTHER KING JR WY	94607	649-F5
740	EMBARCADERO W	94607	649-F5
900	MARKET ST	94607	649-E4
2ND AV			**OAK**
1000	10TH ST	94606	649-H5
1110	E 11TH ST	94606	649-H5
1200	E 12TH ST	94606	649-H5
1220	14TH ST	94606	649-H5
1340	INTERNATIONAL BLVD	94606	649-J5
1450	E 15TH ST	94606	649-J4
1520	E 16TH ST	94606	649-J4
1570	FOOTHILL BLVD	94606	649-J4
1700	E 18TH ST	94606	649-J4
2ND ST			**ALA**
1700	PACIFIC AV	94501	649-E7
1800	CYPRESS ST	94501	649-E7
1900	BRUSH ST	94501	649-E7
1700	PACIFIC AV	94501	649-E7
2ND ST			**BERK**
1200	HARRISON ST	94710	609-C7
1320	GILMAN ST	94710	609-C7
1400	CAMELIA ST	94804	629-C1
1450	PAGE ST	94804	629-C1
1500	JONES ST	94804	629-D1
1600	CEDAR ST	94804	629-D1
1700	VIRGINIA ST	94804	629-D1
1900	HEARST AV	94804	629-D2
2100	ADDISON ST	94804	629-D2
2ND ST			**OAK**
650	MARTIN LUTHER KING JR WY	94607	649-F4
700	CASTRO ST	94607	649-F4
750	BRUSH ST	94607	649-F4
100	OAK ST	94607	649-G5
150	MADISON ST	94607	649-G5
200	JACKSON ST	94607	649-G5
250	ALICE ST	94607	649-G5
	WEBSTER ST	94607	649-G5
370	FRANKLIN ST	94607	649-F5
430	BROADWAY	94607	649-F5
490	WASHINGTON ST	94607	649-F5
550	CLAY ST	94607	649-F5
600	JEFFERSON ST	94607	649-F5
3RD AV			**OAK**
1100	E 11TH ST	94606	649-H5
1250	E 12TH ST	94606	649-J5
1400	INTERNATIONAL BLVD	94606	649-J5
1500	E 15TH ST	94606	649-J5
1600	FOOTHILL BLVD	94606	649-J4
1670	E 17TH ST	94606	649-J4
1710	MERRITT CT	94606	649-J4
1800	E 18TH ST	94606	649-J4
1900	PARK BLVD	94606	649-J4
3RD ST			**ALA**
	CENTRAL AV	94501	669-E1
1400	TAYLOR AV	94501	669-E1
1470	SANTA CLARA AV	94501	669-E1
1550	HAIGHT AV	94501	669-E1
1620	LINCOLN AV	94501	669-E1
1700	PACIFIC AV	94501	649-E7
1770	CYPRESS ST	94501	649-E7
1830	SPRUCE ST	94501	649-E7
1900	BRUSH ST	94501	649-E7
2000	ATLANTIC AV	94501	649-E7
2100	FALLON AV	94501	649-E7
2200	BAINBRIDGE AV	94501	649-E7

PRIMARY STREET Address	Cross Street	ZIP	CITY Pg-Grid
3RD ST			**BERK**
1200	HARRISON ST	94710	609-C7
1240	PARK WY	94710	609-C7
1580	GILMAN ST	94710	609-D7
1400	CAMELIA ST	94804	629-D1
1450	PAGE ST	94804	629-D1
1500	JONES ST	94804	629-D1
1600	CEDAR ST	94804	629-D1
1700	VIRGINIA ST	94804	629-D2
1900	HEARST AV	94804	629-D2
2100	ADDISON ST	94804	629-D2
2200	ALLSTON WY	94804	629-D2
2300	BANCROFT WY	94804	629-D2
3RD ST			**OAK**
1160	B ST	94625	649-B3
1370	A ST	94625	649-B3
1430	MARITIME ST	94625	649-B3
1470	CENTER ST	94607	649-D4
1530	CHESTER ST	94607	649-D4
1580	HENRY ST	94607	649-D4
1640	LEWIS ST	94607	649-D4
1700	PERALTA ST	94607	649-D4
	WEBSTER ST	94607	649-G5
450	FRANKLIN ST	94607	649-F5
510	BROADWAY	94607	649-F5
570	WASHINGTON ST	94607	649-F5
620	CLAY ST	94607	649-F5
680	JEFFERSON ST	94607	649-F4
740	MARTIN LUTHER KING JR WY	94607	649-F4
800	CASTRO ST	94607	649-F4
860	BRUSH ST	94607	649-F4
900	MARKET ST	94607	649-E4
960	MYRTLE ST	94607	649-E4
1010	FILBERT ST	94607	649-E4
1060	LINDEN ST	94607	649-E4
1120	CHESTNUT ST	94607	649-E4
1180	ADELINE ST	94607	649-E4
4TH AV			**OAK**
1000	10TH ST	94606	649-H5
1100	E 11TH ST	94606	649-J5
1200	E 12TH ST	94606	649-J5
1400	INTERNATIONAL BLVD	94606	649-J5
1500	E 15TH ST	94606	649-J5
1600	FOOTHILL BLVD	94606	649-J5
1640	E 17TH ST	94606	649-J5
1700	E 17TH ST	94606	649-J5
1800	E 18TH ST	94606	649-J4
1900	WAYNE PL	94606	649-J4
2000	PARK BLVD	94606	649-J4
4TH ST			**ALA**
1200	COLA BALLENA	94501	669-E1
1200	BALLENA BLVD	94501	669-E1
1300	TIDEWAY DR	94501	669-E1
1400	CENTRAL AV	94501	669-E1
1460	TAYLOR AV	94501	669-E1
1520	SANTA CLARA AV	94501	669-E1
1550	MARION CT	94501	669-E1
1570	HAIGHT AV	94501	669-E1
1630	LINCOLN AV	94501	669-E1
1700	PACIFIC AV	94501	669-E1
4TH ST			**BERK**
1200	HARRISON ST	94710	609-D7
1240	PARK WY	94710	609-D7
1290	GILMAN ST	94710	609-D7
1400	CAMELIA ST	94804	629-D1
1450	PAGE ST	94804	629-D1
1500	JONES ST	94804	629-D1
1600	CEDAR ST	94804	629-D1
1700	VIRGINIA ST	94804	629-D1
1900	HEARST AV	94804	629-D2
2100	ADDISON ST	94804	629-D2
2200	ALLSTON WY	94804	629-D2
2300	BANCROFT WY	94804	629-D3
2400	CHANNING WY	94804	629-D3
2500	DWIGHT WY	94804	629-D3
2540	CUTTER WY	94804	629-D3
4TH ST			**OAK**
	B ST	94625	649-B3
	A ST	94625	649-B3
	A ST	94625	649-B3
100	OAK ST	94607	649-G5
150	MADISON ST	94607	649-G5
200	JACKSON ST	94607	649-G5
300	ALICE ST	94607	649-G5
	WEBSTER ST	94607	649-G5
400	FRANKLIN ST	94607	649-F5
450	BROADWAY	94607	649-F5
500	WASHINGTON ST	94607	649-F5
550	CLAY ST	94607	649-F4
600	JEFFERSON ST	94607	649-F4
650	MARTIN LUTHER KING JR WY	94607	649-F4
700	CASTRO ST	94607	649-F4
750	BRUSH ST	94607	649-F4
800	MARKET ST	94607	649-F4
100	FALLON ST	94607	649-H5
5TH AV			**OAK**
2230	IVY DR	94606	650-A4
2120	E 22ND ST	94606	650-A4
2230	E 22ND ST	94606	650-A4
	EMBARCADERO	94606	649-H6
700	7TH ST	94606	649-H5
810	7TH ST	94606	649-H5
810	E 8TH ST	94606	649-H5
900	E 8TH ST	94606	649-H5
1000	10TH ST	94606	649-H5
1100	E 11TH ST	94606	649-J5
1200	E 12TH ST	94606	649-J5
1400	INTERNATIONAL BLVD	94606	649-J5
1500	E 15TH ST	94606	649-J5
1600	FOOTHILL BLVD	94606	649-J5
1700	E 17TH ST	94606	649-J5
1800	E 18TH ST	94606	649-J5
1910	WAYNE PL	94606	649-J4
2010	E 20TH ST	94606	649-J4
2120	E 21ST ST	94606	649-J4
100	EMBARCADERO	94606	649-H6
5TH ST			**ALA**
	ATLANTIC AV	94501	649-F7
	BAINBRIDGE AV	94501	649-F7
1400	CENTRAL AV	94501	669-F1
1460	TAYLOR AV	94501	669-F1
1470	TAYLOR AV	94501	669-F1
1520	SANTA CLARA AV	94501	669-F1
1570	HAIGHT AV	94501	669-F1
1630	LINCOLN AV	94501	669-F1
1630	MARSHALL WY	94501	669-F1
1700	PACIFIC AV	94501	649-F7
1800	BUENA VISTA AV	94501	649-F7
5TH ST			**BERK**
1200	HARRISON ST	94710	609-D7
1350	GILMAN ST	94710	609-D7
1400	CAMELIA ST	94804	629-D1
1450	PAGE ST	94804	629-D1
1500	JONES ST	94804	629-D1
1600	CEDAR ST	94804	629-D1
1700	VIRGINIA ST	94804	629-D1
1900	HEARST AV	94804	629-D2
2100	ADDISON ST	94804	629-D2
2200	ALLSTON WY	94804	629-D2
2300	BANCROFT WY	94804	629-D3

Address	Cross Street	ZIP	Pg-Grid
5TH ST			**BERK**
2400	CHANNING WY	94804	629-D3
2500	DWIGHT WY	94804	629-D3
2920	ANTHONY ST	94804	629-E4
3000	POTTER ST	94804	629-E4
5TH ST			**OAK**
	B ST	94625	649-B3
	A ST	94625	649-B3
	KIRKHAM ST	94607	649-D4
1400	MANDELA PKWY	94607	649-D4
1450	CENTER ST	94607	649-D4
1500	CHESTER ST	94607	649-D4
1550	HENRY ST	94607	649-D4
1600	LEWIS ST	94607	649-D4
1700	PERALTA ST	94607	649-D4
430	BROADWAY	94607	649-F5
500	WASHINGTON ST	94607	649-F4
630	JEFFERSON ST	94607	649-F4
700	MARTIN LUTHER KING JR WY	94607	649-F4
770	CASTRO ST	94607	649-F4
830	BRUSH ST	94607	649-F4
900	MARKET ST	94607	649-E4
100	OAK ST	94607	649-G5
170	MADISON ST	94607	649-G5
250	JACKSON ST	94607	649-G5
320	ALICE ST	94607	649-G5
400	HARRISON ST	94607	649-G5
6TH AV			**OAK**
1240	WAYNE PL	94606	649-J5
2000	E 20TH ST	94606	650-A5
800	7TH ST	94606	649-H5
900	E 8TH ST	94606	649-H5
1000	10TH ST	94606	649-J5
1100	E 11TH ST	94606	649-J5
1200	E 12TH ST	94606	649-J5
1400	INTERNATIONAL BLVD	94606	649-J5
1500	E 15TH ST	94606	649-J5
1600	FOOTHILL BLVD	94606	649-J5
1700	E 17TH ST	94606	649-J5
1800	E 18TH ST	94606	649-J5
1900	E 19TH ST	94606	649-J5
500	EMBARCADERO	94606	649-H6
6TH ST			**ALA**
1400	CENTRAL AV	94501	669-F1
1450	PALACE CT	94501	669-F1
1460	TAYLOR AV	94501	669-F1
1470	TAYLOR AV	94501	669-F1
1520	SANTA CLARA AV	94501	669-F1
1570	HAIGHT AV	94501	669-F1
1630	LINCOLN AV	94501	669-F1
1700	PACIFIC AV	94501	669-F1
6TH ST			**ALB**
2200	8TH ST	94710	609-D7
1100	WILSON ST	94710	609-D7
6TH ST			**BERK**
1200	HARRISON ST	94710	609-D7
1350	GILMAN ST	94710	609-D7
1450	CAMELIA ST	94804	629-D1
1400	PAGE ST	94804	629-D1
1500	JONES ST	94804	629-D1
1600	CEDAR ST	94804	629-D1
1700	VIRGINIA ST	94804	629-D1
1800	DELAWARE ST	94804	629-D2
1900	HEARST AV	94804	629-D2
2000	UNIVERSITY AV	94804	629-D2
2100	ADDISON ST	94804	629-D2
2200	ALLSTON WY	94804	629-D2
2300	BANCROFT WY	94804	629-D3
2400	CHANNING WY	94804	629-D3
2450	DWIGHT CRES	94804	629-D3
2500	DWIGHT WY	94804	629-D3
6TH ST			**OAK**
450	BROADWAY	94607	649-F4
500	WASHINGTON ST	94607	649-F4
620	JEFFERSON ST	94607	649-F4
680	MARTIN LUTHER KING JR WY	94607	649-F4
740	CASTRO ST	94607	649-F4
800	BRUSH ST	94607	649-F4
7TH AV			**OAK**
2000	E 20TH ST	94606	650-A5
2100	E 21ST ST	94606	650-A4
2200	E 22ND ST	94606	650-A4
2300	E 23RD ST	94606	650-A4
2400	E 24TH ST	94606	650-A4
2500	BEATIE ST	94606	650-A4
2500	IVY DR	94606	650-A4
2600	BOOKER ST	94606	650-A4
2600	SPRUCE ST	94606	650-A4
1900	E 20TH ST	94606	650-A5
2000	E 20TH ST	94606	650-A5
1700	E 17TH ST	94606	649-J5
1800	E 18TH ST	94606	649-J5
1900	E 19TH ST	94606	649-J5
	E 8TH ST	94606	649-J5
1000	10TH ST	94606	649-J5
1100	E 11TH ST	94606	649-J5
1200	E 12TH ST	94606	649-J5
1400	INTERNATIONAL BLVD	94606	649-J5
1500	E 15TH ST	94606	649-J5
1600	FOOTHILL BLVD	94606	649-J5
1700	E 17TH ST	94606	649-J5
7TH ST			**BERK**
1200	HARRISON ST	94710	609-D7
1300	GILMAN ST	94710	609-D7
1400	CAMELIA ST	94710	609-D7
1400	PAGE ST	94804	629-D1
1500	JONES ST	94804	629-D1
1550	BATAAN AV	94804	629-D1
1600	CEDAR ST	94804	629-D1
1700	VIRGINIA ST	94804	629-D1
1800	DELAWARE ST	94804	629-D2
1900	HEARST AV	94804	629-D2
2000	UNIVERSITY AV	94804	629-D2
2100	ADDISON ST	94804	629-D2
2200	ALLSTON WY	94804	629-D2
2300	BANCROFT WY	94804	629-D2
2400	CHANNING WY	94804	629-E3
2500	DWIGHT WY	94804	629-E3
2500	DWIGHT CRES	94804	629-E3
2540	CUTTER WY	94804	629-E3
2600	PARKER ST	94804	629-E3
2700	CARLETON ST	94804	629-E3
2750	PARDEE ST	94804	629-E4
2800	GRAYSON ST	94804	629-E4
2860	HEINZ AV	94804	629-E4
2900	ANTHONY ST	94804	629-E4
2930	POTTER ST	94804	629-E4
2950	ASHBY AV	94804	629-E4
2960	MURRAY ST	94804	629-E4
3000	FOLGER AV	94804	629-E4
7TH ST			**OAK**
2200	7TH ST EXT	94607	649-B3
2200	MIDDLE HARBOR RD	94607	649-B3
	5TH AV	94606	649-H5
	E 8TH ST	94606	649-H5
50	FALLON ST	94607	649-H5
100	OAK ST	94607	649-G5
150	MADISON ST	94607	649-G5
200	JACKSON ST	94607	649-G5
250	ALICE ST	94607	649-G5
300	HARRISON ST	94607	649-G4
350	WEBSTER ST	94607	649-G4
400	FRANKLIN ST	94607	649-G4
450	BROADWAY	94607	649-F4
500	WASHINGTON ST	94607	649-F4
550	CLAY ST	94607	649-F4
600	JEFFERSON ST	94607	649-F4
650	MARTIN LUTHER KING JR WY	94607	649-F4
	CASTRO ST	94607	649-F4
740	8TH ST	94607	649-F4
780	BRUSH ST	94607	649-F4
900	MARKET ST	94607	649-F4
1000	FILBERT ST	94607	649-E4
1200	ADELINE ST	94607	649-E4
1250	MAGNOLIA ST	94607	649-E4
1300	UNION ST	94607	649-E4
1330	KIRKHAM ST	94607	649-E4
1400	MANDELA PKWY	94607	649-D3
1450	CENTER ST	94607	649-D3
1500	CHESTER ST	94607	649-D3
1550	HENRY ST	94607	649-D3
	LEWIS ST	94607	649-D3
1600	PERALTA ST	94607	649-D3
1650	CAMPBELL ST	94607	649-D3
1710	WILLOW ST	94607	649-D3
500	5TH AV	94606	649-H5
600	6TH AV	94606	649-H5
E 7TH ST			**OAK**
2200	EMBARCADERO	94606	670-A1
2500	KENNEDY ST	94606	670-B1
2600	23RD AV	94601	670-B1
2900	PETERSON ST	94601	670-B1
3000	DERBY AV	94601	670-B1
3130	LANCASTER ST	94601	670-B1
3200	FRUITVALE AV	94601	670-B1
7TH ST EXT			**OAK**
700	7TH ST	94607	649-B3
700	MIDDLE HARBOR RD	94607	649-B3
900	MARITIME ST	94607	649-B3
900	MARITIME ST	94626	649-B3
8TH AV			**OAK**
1800	E 19TH ST	94606	650-A5
1900	E 19TH ST	94606	650-A5
2000	E 20TH ST	94606	650-A5
2100	E 21ST ST	94606	650-A5
2210	E 22ND ST	94606	650-A4
2330	E 23RD ST	94606	650-A4
2440	E 24TH ST	94606	650-A4
2520	BEATIE ST	94606	650-A4
2780	IVY DR	94606	650-A4
2780	IVY DR	94610	650-A4
2900	PARK BLVD	94606	650-A4
2900	PARK BLVD	94610	650-A4
2900	MCKINLEY AV	94610	650-A4
800	E 8TH ST	94606	649-J6
1000	10TH ST	94606	649-J5
1100	E 11TH ST	94606	649-J5
1200	E 12TH ST	94606	649-J5
1400	INTERNATIONAL BLVD	94606	649-J5
1500	E 15TH ST	94606	649-J5
1600	FOOTHILL BLVD	94606	649-J5
1700	E 17TH ST	94606	649-J5
1800	E 18TH ST	94606	649-J5
500	EMBARCADERO	94606	649-H6
8TH ST			**ALA**
1700	PACIFIC AV	94501	669-G1
1800	BUENA VISTA AV	94501	669-G7
1850	EAGLE AV	94501	669-G7
1900	STEWART CT	94501	669-G7
1200	WESTLINE DR	94501	669-G2
1220	WESTLINE DR	94501	669-G2
1300	PORTOLA AV	94501	669-G1
1400	CENTRAL AV	94501	669-G1
1450	TAYLOR AV	94501	669-G1
1500	SANTA CLARA AV	94501	669-G1
1550	HAIGHT AV	94501	669-G1
1600	CONSTITUTION WY	94501	669-G1
1600	LINCOLN AV	94501	669-G1
8TH ST			**ALB**
1100	JACKSON ST	94706	609-D7
1100	JACKSON ST	94710	609-D7
1100	RILEY DR	94710	609-D7
1120	MONROE ST	94710	609-D7
1140	9TH ST	94710	609-D7
1140	6TH ST	94710	609-D7
8TH ST			**BERK**
1200	HARRISON ST	94710	609-D7
1300	GILMAN ST	94710	609-D7
1430	CAMELIA ST	94710	609-D7
1400	PAGE ST	94804	629-D1
1500	JONES ST	94804	629-D1
1550	BATAAN AV	94804	629-D1
1600	CEDAR ST	94804	629-D1
1700	VIRGINIA ST	94804	629-D1
1800	DELAWARE ST	94804	629-D2
1900	HEARST AV	94804	629-D2
2000	UNIVERSITY AV	94804	629-D2
2100	ADDISON ST	94804	629-E2
2200	ALLSTON WY	94804	629-E2
2300	BANCROFT WY	94804	629-E3
2400	CHANNING WY	94804	629-E3
2500	DWIGHT WY	94804	629-E3
2600	PARKER ST	94804	629-E3
2700	CARLETON ST	94804	629-E3
2750	PARDEE ST	94804	629-E4
2800	GRAYSON ST	94804	629-E4
2900	HEINZ AV	94804	629-E4
8TH ST			**OAK**
1500	MIDWAY ST	94626	649-B3
1500	TULAGI ST	94626	649-B3
1650	10TH ST	94626	649-C2
	11TH ST	94626	649-C2
	14TH ST	94626	649-C2
900	MARKET ST	94607	649-F4
990	FILBERT ST	94607	649-E4
1200	ADELINE ST	94607	649-E4
1250	UNION ST	94607	649-E3
1400	CYPRESS ST	94607	649-E3
	MANDELA PKWY	94607	649-E3
1400	MANDELA PKWY	94607	649-D3
1450	CENTER ST	94607	649-D3
1500	CHESTER ST	94607	649-D3
1550	HENRY ST	94607	649-D3
1600	PERALTA ST	94607	649-D3
1660	CAMPBELL ST	94607	649-D3
1680	CAMPBELL CT	94607	649-D3
1700	WILLOW ST	94607	649-D3
1750	SHOREY ST	94607	649-D3
1750	WOOD ST	94607	649-D3
700	MARTIN LUTHER KING JR WY	94607	649-F4
	CASTRO ST	94607	649-F4
900	7TH ST	94607	649-F4
50	FALLON ST	94607	649-H5
100	OAK ST	94607	649-G5
150	MADISON ST	94607	649-G5
200	JACKSON ST	94607	649-G5
250	ALICE ST	94607	649-G4
300	HARRISON ST	94607	649-G4
350	WEBSTER ST	94607	649-G4
400	FRANKLIN ST	94607	649-G4
480	BROADWAY	94607	649-G4
500	WASHINGTON ST	94607	649-F4
550	CLAY ST	94607	649-F4
600	JEFFERSON ST	94607	649-F4
700	MARTIN LUTHER KING JR WY	94607	649-F4
800	CASTRO ST	94607	649-F4
E 8TH ST			**OAK**
500	5TH AV	94606	649-H5
500	7TH ST	94606	649-H5
590	5TH AV	94606	649-H5
600	6TH AV	94606	649-H5
700	7TH AV	94606	649-J5
750	PARK WY	94606	649-J6
800	8TH AV	94606	649-J6
900	10TH ST	94606	649-J6
970	10TH AV	94606	649-J6
1100	11TH AV	94606	649-J6
1170	E 11TH ST	94606	649-J6
1200	12TH AV	94606	649-J6
	E 12TH ST	94606	649-J6
	14TH AV	94606	650-A6
	E 12TH ST	94606	650-A6
	14TH AV	94606	650-A6
	E 12TH ST	94606	650-A6
3200	FRUITVALE AV	94601	670-C1
3430	34TH AV	94601	670-C1
3570	36TH AV	94601	670-C1
3680	37TH AV	94601	670-C2
4200	ALAMEDA AV	94601	670-C2
5000	50TH AV	94601	670-D2
5120	51ST AV	94601	670-D2
5250	52ND AV	94601	670-D2
5380	53RD AV	94601	670-D2
5500	54TH AV	94601	670-D2
9TH AV			**OAK**
1710	E 18TH ST	94606	650-A5
1810	E 18TH ST	94606	650-A5
1910	E 19TH ST	94606	650-A5
2010	E 20TH ST	94606	650-A5
2110	E 21ST ST	94606	650-A5
2220	E 22ND ST	94606	650-A5
2330	E 23RD ST	94606	650-A5
2440	E 24TH ST	94606	650-A4
2800	E 28TH ST	94606	650-A4
1000	10TH ST	94606	649-J6
1100	E 11TH ST	94606	649-J5
1200	E 12TH ST	94606	649-J5
1400	INTERNATIONAL BLVD	94606	649-J5
1500	E 15TH ST	94606	649-J5
1600	FOOTHILL BLVD	94606	649-J5
1710	10TH AV	94606	649-J5
1710	E 17TH ST	94606	649-J5
410	DEFREMERY AV	94606	649-H6
500	EMBARCADERO	94606	649-H6
9TH ST			**ALA**
1150	SAN ANTONIO AV	94501	669-G1
1220	CENTENNIAL AV	94501	669-G1
1290	CENTRAL AV	94501	669-G1
1370	TAYLOR AV	94501	669-G1
1440	SANTA CLARA AV	94501	669-G1
1520	HAIGHT AV	94501	669-G1
1590	LINCOLN AV	94501	669-G1
1670	PACIFIC AV	94501	669-G1
1750	BUENA VISTA AV	94501	669-G7
9TH ST			**ALB**
900	WILSON ST	94710	609-D6
930	RILEY DR	94710	609-D7
1000	8TH ST	94710	609-D7
9TH ST			**BERK**
1200	HARRISON ST	94710	609-D7
1300	GILMAN ST	94710	609-D7
1180	CAMELIA ST	94710	609-D7
1400	PAGE ST	94804	629-D1
1500	JONES ST	94804	629-D1
1600	CEDAR ST	94804	629-D1
1700	VIRGINIA ST	94804	629-D1
1800	DELAWARE ST	94804	629-D1
1900	HEARST AV	94804	629-E2
2000	UNIVERSITY AV	94804	629-E2
2100	ADDISON ST	94804	629-E2
2200	ALLSTON WY	94804	629-E2
2300	BANCROFT WY	94804	629-E2
2400	CHANNING WY	94804	629-E3
2500	DWIGHT WY	94804	629-E3
2600	PARKER ST	94804	629-E3
2700	CARLETON ST	94804	629-E3
2750	PARDEE ST	94804	629-E3
2800	GRAYSON ST	94804	629-E4
2860	HEINZ AV	94804	629-E4
2920	ANTHONY ST	94804	629-E4
2950	POTTER ST	94804	629-E4
3000	ASHBY AV	94804	629-E4
9TH ST			**OAK**
1700	WILLOW ST	94607	649-D3
1750	WOOD ST	94607	649-D3
1760	MCELROY ST	94607	649-D3
1800	PINE ST	94607	649-C3
1900	CEDAR ST	94607	649-C3
1400	MANDELA PKWY	94607	649-D3
1460	CENTER ST	94607	649-D3
1520	CHESTER ST	94607	649-D3
1600	PERALTA ST	94607	649-D3
50	FALLON ST	94607	649-H5
100	OAK ST	94607	649-G5
150	MADISON ST	94607	649-G5
200	JACKSON ST	94607	649-G4
250	ALICE ST	94607	649-G4
300	HARRISON ST	94607	649-G4
350	WEBSTER ST	94607	649-G4
400	FRANKLIN ST	94607	649-G4
450	BROADWAY	94607	649-G4
500	WASHINGTON ST	94607	649-F4
550	CLAY ST	94607	649-F4
600	JEFFERSON ST	94607	649-F4
650	MARTIN LUTHER KING JR WY	94607	649-F4
700	CASTRO ST	94607	649-F4
E 9TH ST			**OAK**
2500	23RD AV	94601	650-B7
2550	26TH AV	94601	650-B7
2660	27TH AV	94601	650-B7
2780	27TH AV	94601	650-B7
2780	LISBON AV	94601	670-B1
	PORTWOOD AV	94601	670-B1
3190	FRUITVALE AV	94601	670-C1
3280	33RD AV	94601	670-C1
3380	34TH AV	94601	670-C1
3470	35TH AV	94601	670-C1
3590	36TH AV	94601	670-C1
3700	37TH AV	94601	670-C1
10TH AV			**OAK**
2000	E 20TH ST	94606	650-A5
2110	E 21ST ST	94606	650-A5
2220	E 22ND ST	94606	650-A5
2330	E 23RD ST	94606	650-A5
2440	E 24TH ST	94606	650-A4
2800	BELLA VISTA AV	94606	650-A4
2800	E 28TH ST	94606	650-A4
900	E 18TH ST	94606	650-A5
1800	E 18TH ST	94606	650-A5
1900	E 19TH ST	94606	650-A5
2000	E 20TH ST	94606	650-A5
900	9TH AV	94606	649-J5
900	E 17TH ST	94606	649-J5
1000	E 8TH ST	94606	649-J6
1100	E 11TH ST	94606	649-J6
1200	E 12TH ST	94606	649-J5
1400	INTERNATIONAL BLVD	94606	649-J5
1500	E 15TH ST	94606	649-J5
500	DEFREMERY AV	94606	649-J6
900	EMBARCADERO	94606	649-J6
10TH ST			**ALB**
1100	MONROE ST	94710	609-D7
1200	HARRISON ST	94710	609-D7
10TH ST			**BERK**
1200	HARRISON ST	94710	609-D7
1300	GILMAN ST	94710	609-D7
560	CAMELIA ST	94710	609-D7
1400	PAGE ST	94804	629-D1
1500	JONES ST	94804	629-D1
1600	CEDAR ST	94804	629-E1
1700	VIRGINIA ST	94804	629-E1
1800	DELAWARE ST	94804	629-E1
1900	HEARST AV	94804	629-E2
2000	UNIVERSITY AV	94804	629-E2
2100	ADDISON ST	94804	629-E2
2200	ALLSTON WY	94804	629-E2
2300	BANCROFT WY	94804	629-E2
2400	CHANNING WY	94804	629-E3
2500	DWIGHT WY	94804	629-E3
2600	PARKER ST	94804	629-E3
2700	CARLETON ST	94804	629-E3
2750	PARDEE ST	94804	629-E3
2800	GRAYSON ST	94804	629-E4
2900	HEINZ AV	94804	629-E4
10TH ST			**OAK**
1900	TULAGI ST	94626	649-C2
2060	MIDWAY ST	94626	649-C2
2300	8TH ST	94626	649-C2
1600	PERALTA ST	94607	649-D3
1660	CAMPBELL ST	94607	649-D3
1690	CAMPBELL CT	94607	649-D3
1720	WILLOW ST	94607	649-D3
1780	WOOD ST	94607	649-D3
1840	PINE ST	94607	649-D3
1900	CEDAR ST	94607	649-D3
800	11TH ST	94607	649-F4
900	MARKET ST	94607	649-F3
1000	FILBERT ST	94607	649-E3
1050	LINDEN ST	94607	649-E3
1100	CHESTNUT ST	94607	649-E3
1150	ADELINE ST	94607	649-E3
1200	MAGNOLIA ST	94607	649-E3
1250	UNION ST	94607	649-E3
1300	POPLAR ST	94607	649-E3
	MANDELA PKWY	94607	649-E3
1400	MANDELA PKWY	94607	649-E3
1500	CENTER ST	94607	649-E3
450	BROADWAY	94607	649-G4
500	WASHINGTON ST	94607	649-G4
550	CLAY ST	94607	649-F4
600	JEFFERSON ST	94607	649-F4
650	MARTIN LUTHER KING JR WY	94607	649-F4
700	CASTRO ST	94607	649-F4
300	WEBSTER ST	94607	649-G4
250	HARRISON ST	94607	649-G4
200	ALICE ST	94607	649-G4
150	JACKSON ST	94607	649-G4
100	MADISON ST	94607	649-H4
1	OAK ST	94607	649-H5
1	FALLON ST	94607	649-H5
200	2ND AV	94606	649-H5
400	4TH AV	94606	649-H5
500	5TH AV	94606	649-H5
600	6TH AV	94606	649-J5
700	7TH AV	94606	649-J5
750	PARK WY	94606	649-J5
800	8TH AV	94606	649-J6
900	9TH AV	94606	649-J6
1000	E 8TH ST	94606	649-J6
E 10TH ST			**OAK**
2500	23RD AV	94601	650-B7
2530	25TH AV	94601	650-B7
2600	26TH AV	94601	650-B7
2700	27TH AV	94601	650-B7
2700	LISBON AV	94601	650-B7
2790	LISBON AV	94601	650-B7
2700	SANTA INES CT	94601	670-B1
2790	SANTA MARIA CT	94601	670-B1
2800	PORTWOOD AV	94601	670-B1
2860	SAN FRANCISCO CT	94601	670-B1
2900	29TH AV	94601	670-B1
2900	DERBY AV	94601	670-C1
3200	FRUITVALE AV	94601	670-C1
5000	50TH AV	94601	670-D2
5100	51ST AV	94601	670-D2
5200	52ND AV	94601	670-D2
5300	53RD AV	94601	670-E2
5400	54TH AV	94601	670-E2
11TH AV			**OAK**
1900	E 19TH ST	94606	650-A5
2000	E 20TH ST	94606	650-A5
2100	E 21ST ST	94606	650-A5
2210	E 22ND ST	94606	650-A5
2330	E 23RD ST	94606	650-A5
2440	E 24TH ST	94606	650-A5
2800	E 28TH ST	94610	650-B4
3000	BELLA VISTA AV	94610	650-B4
3200	BAYVIEW AV	94610	650-B4
1600	E 17TH ST	94606	650-A5
1700	E 17TH ST	94606	650-A5
1800	E 18TH ST	94606	650-A5
1900	E 19TH ST	94606	650-A5
1500	FOOTHILL BLVD	94606	649-J5
1400	E 15TH ST	94606	649-J5
1200	INTERNATIONAL BLVD	94606	649-J6
1100	E 12TH ST	94606	649-J6
1000	E 11TH ST	94606	649-J6
1100	E 8TH ST	94606	649-J6
11TH ST			**OAK**
1	TULAGI ST	94626	649-C2
60	MIDWAY ST	94626	649-C2
100	8TH ST	94626	649-C2
1600	PERALTA ST	94607	649-D3
1660	CAMPBELL ST	94607	649-D3
1730	WILLOW ST	94607	649-D3
1800	WOOD ST	94607	649-D3
1860	PINE ST	94607	649-D3
1400	MANDELA PKWY	94607	649-E3
1500	CENTER ST	94607	649-E3
1	12TH ST	94607	649-H4
1	E 12TH ST	94607	649-H4
100	OAK ST	94607	649-H4
150	MADISON ST	94607	649-G4
200	JACKSON ST	94607	649-G4
250	ALICE ST	94607	649-G4
300	HARRISON ST	94607	649-G4
350	WEBSTER ST	94607	649-G4
400	FRANKLIN ST	94607	649-G4
430	BROADWAY	94607	649-G4
580	CLAY ST	94607	649-F4

881 11TH ST

CROSS STREET INDEX - ALA, ALB, BERK, EMVL, OAK & PDMT

E 17TH ST

ALAMEDA CO.

PRIMARY STREET Address	Cross Street	ZIP	CITY Pg-Grid
11TH ST			**OAK**
620	JEFFERSON ST	94607	649-F4
660	MARTIN LUTHER KING JR WY	94607	649-F4
	CASTRO ST	94607	649-F4
730	BRUSH ST	94607	649-F3
800	10TH ST	94607	649-F3
E 11TH ST			**OAK**
100	E 12TH ST	94606	649-H5
220	2ND AV	94606	649-H5
310	3RD AV	94606	649-H5
400	4TH AV	94606	649-H5
500	5TH AV	94606	649-J5
600	6TH AV	94606	649-J5
700	7TH AV	94606	649-J5
800	8TH AV	94606	649-J5
900	9TH AV	94606	649-J6
1000	10TH AV	94606	649-J6
1100	11TH AV	94606	649-J6
1200	E 8TH ST	94606	649-J6
2400	MILLER PL	94601	650-B7
2500	MILLER PL	94601	650-B7
2530	25TH AV	94601	650-B7
2600	26TH AV	94601	650-B7
2700	27TH AV	94601	650-B7
2800	LISBON AV	94601	650-B7
	23RD AV OVPS	94606	650-B7
	23RD AV	94606	650-B7
	23RD AV OVPS	94606	650-B7
12TH AV			**OAK**
2000	E 20TH ST	94606	650-A5
2100	E 21ST ST	94606	650-A5
2210	E 22ND ST	94606	650-A5
2330	E 23RD ST	94606	650-A5
2440	E 24TH ST	94606	650-A5
2800	E 28TH ST	94606	650-A5
1700	E 17TH ST	94606	650-A5
1800	E 18TH ST	94606	650-A5
1900	E 19TH ST	94606	650-A5
2000	E 20TH ST	94606	650-A5
1600	E 17TH ST	94606	650-A5
1500	FOOTHILL BLVD	94606	650-A5
1600	FOOTHILL BLVD	94606	650-A5
1100	E 8TH ST	94606	649-J6
1200	E 12TH ST	94606	649-J6
1400	INTERNATIONAL BLVD	94606	649-J6
1500	E 15TH ST	94606	649-J6
12TH ST			**OAK**
1500	CENTER ST	94607	649-D3
1560	CHESTER ST	94607	649-D3
1600	PERALTA ST	94607	649-D3
1650	CAMPBELL ST	94607	649-D3
1700	WILLOW ST	94607	649-D3
1750	WOOD ST	94607	649-D2
1800	PINE ST	94607	649-D2
1300	POPLAR ST	94607	649-E3
1350	KIRKHAM ST	94607	649-E3
	MANDELA PKWY	94607	649-E3
1400	MANDELA PKWY	94607	649-E3
1500	CENTER ST	94607	649-D3
30	13TH ST	94612	649-H4
30	OAK ST	94612	649-H4
100	OAK ST	94607	649-H4
150	MADISON ST	94607	649-G4
200	JACKSON ST	94607	649-G4
250	ALICE ST	94607	649-G4
300	HARRISON ST	94607	649-G4
350	WEBSTER ST	94607	649-G4
400	FRANKLIN ST	94607	649-G4
460	BROADWAY	94607	649-G4
580	CLAY ST	94607	649-F4
610	JEFFERSON ST	94607	649-F4
650	MARTIN LUTHER KING JR WY	94607	649-F4
690	CASTRO ST	94607	649-F4
700	BRUSH ST	94607	649-F3
790	WEST ST	94607	649-F3
900	MARKET ST	94607	649-F3
1000	FILBERT ST	94607	649-E3
1050	LINDEN ST	94607	649-E3
1100	CHESTNUT ST	94607	649-E3
1150	ADELINE ST	94607	649-E3
1200	MAGNOLIA ST	94607	649-E3
1290	UNION ST	94607	649-E3
1300	POPLAR ST	94607	649-E3
1300	UNION ST	94607	649-E3
1	11TH ST	94607	649-H4
1	E 12TH ST	94607	649-H4
E 12TH ST			**OAK**
1	11TH ST	94607	649-H5
1	12TH ST	94607	649-H5
50	1ST AV	94606	649-H5
130	E 11TH ST	94606	649-H5
200	2ND AV	94606	649-H5
270	14TH ST	94606	649-H5
300	3RD AV	94606	649-H5
400	4TH AV	94606	649-J5
500	5TH AV	94606	649-J5
600	6TH AV	94606	649-J5
700	7TH AV	94606	649-J5
800	8TH AV	94606	649-J5
900	9TH AV	94606	649-J5
1000	10TH AV	94606	649-J6
1100	11TH AV	94606	649-J6
1200	12TH AV	94606	649-J6
1300	13TH AV	94606	649-J6
1300	14TH AV	94606	650-A6
1300	E 8TH ST	94606	650-A6
1400	14TH AV	94606	650-A6
1400	E 8TH ST	94606	650-A6
1500	15TH AV	94606	650-A6
1590	16TH AV	94606	650-A6
1680	17TH AV	94606	650-A6
1770	18TH AV	94606	650-A6
1400	19TH AV	94606	650-A6
1300	13TH AV	94606	649-J6
1400	E 8TH ST	94606	649-J6
1860	19TH AV	94606	650-A6
1950	20TH AV	94606	650-A6
2040	21ST AV	94606	650-A7
2130	22ND AV	94606	650-A7
2130	23RD AV OVPS	94606	650-A7
2300	23RD AV	94601	650-B7
2390	MILLER AV	94601	650-B7
2490	25TH AV	94601	650-B7
2590	26TH AV	94601	650-B7
2900	29TH AV	94601	650-B7
2990	30TH AV	94601	650-B7
3060	30TH AV	94601	650-B7
3060	DERBY AV	94601	670-C1
3130	31ST AV	94601	670-C1
3200	FRUITVALE AV	94601	670-C1
3200	FRUITVALE AV	94601	670-C1
3300	33RD AV	94601	670-C1
3400	34TH AV	94601	670-C1
3500	35TH AV	94601	670-C1
3600	36TH AV	94601	670-C1
3700	37TH AV	94601	670-C1
3800	38TH AV	94601	670-C1
3900	39TH AV	94601	670-C1
4000	40TH AV	94601	670-D1
4100	41ST AV	94601	670-D1
	42ND AV	94601	670-D1
4300	HIGH ST	94601	670-D1
4400	44TH AV	94601	670-D1
4400	E 12TH ST PL	94601	670-D1
4500	45TH AV	94601	670-D2
4600	46TH AV	94601	670-D2
4700	47TH AV	94601	670-D2
4800	48TH AV	94601	670-D2
4900	49TH AV	94601	670-D2
5000	50TH AV	94601	670-D2
5100	51ST AV	94601	670-D2
5200	52ND AV	94601	670-E2
5300	53RD AV	94601	670-E2
5400	54TH AV	94601	670-E2
E 12TH ST PL			**OAK**
4300	HIGH ST	94601	670-D1
4400	44TH AV	94601	670-D1
4400	E 12TH ST	94601	670-D1
13TH AV			**OAK**
1260	E 15TH ST	94606	650-A6
1380	E 15TH ST	94606	650-A6
1500	FOOTHILL BLVD	94606	650-A6
1500	FOOTHILL PL	94606	650-A6
1620	E 17TH ST	94606	650-A5
1740	E 18TH ST	94606	650-A5
1860	E 19TH ST	94606	650-A5
1980	E 20TH ST	94606	650-A5
2100	E 21ST ST	94606	650-A5
2210	E 22ND ST	94606	650-A5
2340	E 23RD ST	94606	650-A5
2400	E 24TH ST	94606	650-B5
2500	E 25TH ST	94606	650-B5
2600	E 26TH ST	94606	650-B5
2700	E 27TH ST	94606	650-B5
2800	E 28TH ST	94610	650-B4
2800	E 28TH ST	94606	650-B4
2870	E 28TH ST	94610	650-B4
2870	E 28TH ST	94606	650-B4
2890	BELLA VISTA AV	94610	650-B4
2890	BELLA VISTA AV	94606	650-B4
3100	E 31ST ST	94610	650-B4
3100	E 31ST ST	94602	650-B4
3200	E 32ND ST	94610	650-B4
3200	E 32ND ST	94602	650-B4
3200	BAYVIEW AV	94602	650-B4
3150	E 33RD ST	94610	650-B4
3150	E 33RD ST	94602	650-B4
3300	E 33RD ST	94610	650-B4
3300	E 33RD ST	94602	650-B4
3400	E 34TH ST	94610	650-B4
3400	E 34TH ST	94602	650-B4
3410	E 34TH ST	94610	650-B4
3410	E 34TH ST	94602	650-B4
3480	MACARTHUR BLVD	94610	650-B4
3480	MACARTHUR BLVD	94602	650-B4
3600	CHATHAM RD	94610	650-B4
3600	CHATHAM RD	94602	650-B4
3700	EXCELSIOR AV	94610	650-B4
3700	EXCELSIOR AV	94602	650-B4
3770	E 38TH ST	94610	650-C4
3770	E 38TH ST	94602	650-C4
3800	PARK BLVD	94610	650-C4
3800	PARK BLVD	94602	650-C4
3800	PARK BLVD WY	94602	650-C4
1200	E 12TH ST	94606	649-J6
1260	INTERNATIONAL BLVD	94606	649-J6
13TH ST			**OAK**
1300	CENTER ST	94607	649-D3
1350	PERALTA ST	94607	649-D3
1400	CAMPBELL ST	94607	649-D3
1450	WILLOW ST	94607	649-D3
1500	WOOD ST	94607	649-D3
1250	MANDELA PKWY	94607	649-E3
1300	CENTER ST	94607	649-E3
1150	BRUSH ST	94607	649-F3
1150	BRUSH ST	94612	649-F3
1190	WEST ST	94607	649-F3
1250	MARKET ST	94607	649-F3
1100	JEFFERSON ST	94612	649-F4
1150	MARTIN LUTHER KING JR WY	94612	649-F4
100	OAK ST	94612	649-H4
100	12TH ST	94612	649-H4
150	MADISON ST	94612	649-H4
200	JACKSON ST	94612	649-G4
250	ALICE ST	94612	649-G4
300	HARRISON ST	94612	649-G4
360	WEBSTER ST	94612	649-G4
430	FRANKLIN ST	94612	649-G4
500	BROADWAY	94612	649-G4
1530	KEEL WY	94625	649-C4
1500	E H ST	94625	649-C4
1530	15TH ST	94625	649-C4
E 13TH ST			**OAK**
3000	DERBY AV	94601	650-C7
3100	DERBY AV	94601	650-C7
3100	31ST AV	94601	670-C1
3200	FRUITVALE AV	94601	670-C1
14TH AV			**OAK**
1200	E 12TH ST	94606	650-A6
1200	E 8TH ST	94606	650-A6
1250	SOLANO WY	94606	650-A6
1300	INTERNATIONAL BLVD	94606	650-A6
1370	E 15TH ST	94606	650-A6
1420	E 15TH ST	94606	650-A6
1470	GLEASON WY	94606	650-A6
1470	FOOTHILL PL	94606	650-A6
1570	FOOTHILL BLVD	94606	650-A6
1630	E 17TH ST	94606	650-A5
1800	E 18TH ST	94606	650-A5
1900	15TH AV	94606	650-A5
1900	E 19TH ST	94606	650-A5
1930	SONOMA WY	94606	650-A5
1970	E 20TH ST	94606	650-A5
2030	E 21ST ST	94606	650-A5
2030	E 21ST ST	94606	650-A5
2070	E 22ND ST	94606	650-A5
2180	E 23RD ST	94606	650-B5
2230	COMSTOCK WY	94606	650-B5
2280	E 24TH ST	94606	650-B5
2380	E 25TH ST	94606	650-B5
2490	E 26TH ST	94606	650-B5
2600	VALLECITO PL	94606	650-B5
2840	19TH AV	94606	650-B5
2920	E 30TH ST	94606	650-B5
2970	BEAUMONT AV	94606	650-B5
3000	E 31ST ST	94602	650-B4
3200	E 32ND ST	94602	650-C4
3320	E 33RD ST	94602	650-C4
3500	MACARTHUR BLVD	94602	650-C4
14TH ST			**OAK**
1800	MIDWAY ST	94626	649-C2
1830	8TH ST	94626	649-C2
1	LAKESIDE DR	94612	649-H4
100	OAK ST	94612	649-H4
150	MADISON ST	94612	649-H4
200	JACKSON ST	94612	649-G4
250	ALICE ST	94612	649-G4
300	HARRISON ST	94612	649-G4
350	WEBSTER ST	94612	649-G4
400	FRANKLIN ST	94612	649-G4
450	BROADWAY	94612	649-G4
500	FRANK H OGAWA PZ	94612	649-G4
550	CLAY ST	94612	649-G4
600	JEFFERSON ST	94612	649-F3
650	MARTIN LUTHER KING JR WY	94612	649-F3
	CASTRO ST	94612	649-F3
700	BRUSH ST	94612	649-F3
770	WEST ST	94607	649-F3
900	MARKET ST	94607	649-F3
950	MYRTLE ST	94607	649-F3
1000	FILBERT ST	94607	649-F3
1050	LINDEN ST	94607	649-E3
1100	CHESTNUT ST	94607	649-E3
1150	ADELINE ST	94607	649-E3
1200	MAGNOLIA ST	94607	649-E3
1250	UNION ST	94607	649-E3
1300	POPLAR ST	94607	649-E3
1340	KIRKHAM ST	94607	649-E3
1400	MANDELA PKWY	94607	649-E3
1410	MANDELA PKWY	94607	649-E3
1460	CENTER ST	94607	649-D3
1600	PERALTA ST	94607	649-D3
1650	CAMPBELL ST	94607	649-D3
1700	WILLOW ST	94607	649-D2
1730	WOOD ST	94607	649-D2
1800	FRONTAGE RD	94607	649-D2
200	E 12TH ST	94606	649-H5
	2ND AV	94606	649-H5
	LAKESIDE DR	94607	649-H4
	LAKESIDE DR	94607	649-H4
	12TH ST	94607	649-H4
	KEEL WY	94625	649-C5
E 14TH ST			**OAK**
1	INTERNATIONAL BLVD	94603	670-J6
120	DURANT AV	94603	670-J6
E 14TH ST			**SLN**
1	INTERNATIONAL BLVD	94577	670-J6
120	DURANT AV	94577	670-J6
15TH AV			**OAK**
1200	E 12TH ST	94606	650-A6
1260	SOLANO WY	94606	650-A6
1330	INTERNATIONAL BLVD	94606	650-A6
1400	MARIN WY	94606	650-A6
1460	E 15TH ST	94606	650-A6
1520	GLEASON WY	94606	650-A6
1590	FOOTHILL BLVD	94606	650-A6
1640	E 17TH ST	94606	650-A6
1660	INDEPENDENCE WY	94606	650-A6
1720	E 17TH ST	94606	650-A5
1720	E 18TH ST	94606	650-A5
1790	COMMERCE WY	94606	650-A5
1860	E 19TH ST	94606	650-A5
1900	14TH AV	94606	650-A5
1900	E 19TH ST	94606	650-A5
15TH ST			**OAK**
1800	TULAGI ST	94626	649-C2
1930	TOBRUK ST	94626	649-C2
1960	MIDWAY ST	94626	649-C2
2000	MARITIME ST	94626	649-C2
1600	PERALTA ST	94607	649-D3
1650	CAMPBELL ST	94607	649-D2
1700	WILLOW ST	94607	649-D2
1800	WOOD ST	94607	649-D2
1400	MANDELA PKWY	94607	649-E3
1500	CENTER ST	94607	649-E3
700	BRUSH ST	94612	649-F3
770	WEST ST	94607	649-F3
900	MARKET ST	94607	649-F3
560	JEFFERSON ST	94612	649-G3
630	MARTIN LUTHER KING JR WY	94612	649-F3
700	CASTRO ST	94612	649-F3
	B ST	94625	649-B3
	13TH ST	94625	649-C4
	E H ST	94607	649-C4
	KEEL WY	94607	649-C4
300	HARRISON ST	94612	649-G4
350	WEBSTER ST	94612	649-G4
400	FRANKLIN ST	94612	649-G4
	BROADWAY	94612	649-G4
150	MADISON ST	94612	649-H4
200	JACKSON ST	94612	649-H4
E 15TH ST			**OAK**
1	LAKESHORE AV	94606	649-J4
60	LAKESHORE AV	94606	649-J4
100	1ST AV	94606	649-J4
150	1ST AV PL	94606	649-J4
200	2ND AV	94606	649-J5
300	3RD AV	94606	649-J5
400	4TH AV	94606	649-J5
500	5TH AV	94606	649-J5
600	6TH AV	94606	649-J5
700	7TH AV	94606	649-J5
800	8TH AV	94606	649-J5
900	9TH AV	94606	649-J5
1000	10TH AV	94606	649-J5
1100	11TH AV	94606	649-J5
1200	12TH AV	94606	649-J6
1300	14TH AV	94606	650-A6
1200	13TH AV	94606	650-A6
1300	13TH AV	94606	650-A6
1400	14TH AV	94606	650-A6
1500	15TH AV	94606	650-A6
1590	16TH AV	94606	650-A6
1680	17TH AV	94606	650-A6
1770	18TH AV	94606	650-A6
1860	19TH AV	94606	650-A6
1950	20TH AV	94606	650-A6
2040	21ST AV	94606	650-A6
2130	22ND AV	94606	650-B6
2200	MUNSON WY	94606	650-B6
2300	23RD AV	94601	650-B7
2380	MILLER AV	94601	650-B7
2420	24TH AV	94601	650-B7
2470	25TH AV	94601	650-B7
2560	26TH AV	94601	650-B7
3000	DERBY AV	94601	650-C7
3100	31ST AV	94601	650-C7
3200	FRUITVALE AV	94601	650-C7
3400	35TH AV	94601	670-C1
4070	41ST AV	94601	670-D1
4100	41ST AV	94601	670-D1
4200	42ND AV	94601	670-D1
5500	55TH AV	94621	670-E2
5700	56TH AV	94621	670-E2
5700	57TH AV	94621	670-F2
16TH AV			**OAK**
	EMBARCADERO	94606	650-A7
1100	E 12TH ST	94606	650-A6
1200	E 12TH ST	94606	650-A6
1270	SOLANO WY	94606	650-A6
1350	INTERNATIONAL BLVD	94606	650-A6
1440	MARIN WY	94606	650-A6
1520	E 15TH ST	94606	650-A6
1580	GLEASON WY	94606	650-A6
1600	FOOTHILL BLVD	94606	650-A6
1650	INDEPENDENCE WY	94606	650-A6
1700	E 17TH ST	94606	650-A6
1740	COMMERCE WY	94606	650-A6
1800	E 19TH ST	94606	650-A5
1900	SONOMA WY	94606	650-A5
2000	E 20TH ST	94606	650-A5
2060	SAN ANTONIO WY	94606	650-A5
2100	E 21ST ST	94606	650-A5
16TH ST			**OAK**
700	BRUSH ST	94612	649-F3
770	WEST ST	94607	649-F3
900	MARKET ST	94607	649-F3
950	MYRTLE ST	94607	649-F3
1000	FILBERT ST	94607	649-F3
1050	LINDEN ST	94607	649-F3
1100	CHESTNUT ST	94607	649-E3
1150	ADELINE ST	94607	649-E3
1200	MAGNOLIA ST	94607	649-E3
1250	UNION ST	94607	649-E3
1300	POPLAR ST	94607	649-E3
1330	KIRKHAM ST	94607	649-E3
	MANDELA PKWY	94607	649-E3
1410	MANDELA PKWY	94607	649-E2
1570	CENTER ST	94607	649-E2
1600	PERALTA ST	94607	649-D2
1650	CAMPBELL ST	94607	649-D2
1700	WILLOW ST	94607	649-D2
1870	WOOD ST	94607	649-D2
500	TELEGRAPH AV	94612	649-G3
540	SAN PABLO AV	94612	649-G3
540	FRANK H OGAWA PZ	94612	649-G3
560	CLAY ST	94612	649-G3
600	JEFFERSON ST	94612	649-G3
650	MARTIN LUTHER KING JR WY	94612	649-F3
700	CASTRO ST	94612	649-F3
E 16TH ST			**OAK**
100	2ND AV	94606	649-J4
200	1ST AV	94606	649-J4
2300	23RD AV	94601	650-B6
2300	FOOTHILL BLVD	94601	650-B6
2380	MILLER AV	94601	650-B7
2430	24TH AV	94601	650-B7
2490	25TH AV	94601	650-B7
2530	25TH AV	94601	650-B7
2590	26TH AV	94601	650-B7
2670	27TH AV	94601	650-B7
2730	MITCHELL ST	94601	650-B7
2800	28TH AV	94601	650-C7
2880	29TH AV	94601	650-C7
3100	FRUITVALE AV	94601	650-C7
3100	FRUITVALE AV	94601	650-C7
3200	33RD AV	94601	650-C7
3200	33RD AV	94601	650-C7
3300	34TH AV	94601	650-C7
3400	35TH AV	94601	650-C7
3520	36TH AV	94601	650-C7
3600	BRIDGE AV	94601	650-C7
3700	BRIDGE AV	94601	650-C7
3700	37TH AV	94601	670-C1
4000	ROSEDALE AV	94601	670-D1
4100	41ST AV	94601	670-D1
4100	41ST AV	94601	670-D1
4200	42ND AV	94601	670-D1
5600	55TH AV	94621	670-E2
5620	56TH AV	94621	670-F2
5700	57TH AV	94621	670-F2
5700	57TH AV	94621	670-F2
5800	SEMINARY AV	94621	670-F2
6000	61ST AV	94621	670-F2
6200	62ND AV	94621	670-F2
6400	64TH AV	94621	670-F2
17TH AV			**OAK**
1900	E 19TH ST	94606	650-A6
1950	SONOMA WY	94606	650-A5
2000	E 20TH ST	94606	650-A5
2060	SAN ANTONIO WY	94606	650-A5
2130	E 21ST ST	94606	650-A5
2270	E 22ND ST	94606	650-B5
2330	E 23RD ST	94606	650-B5
2360	COMSTOCK WY	94606	650-B5
2400	E 24TH ST	94606	650-B5
1200	E 12TH ST	94606	650-A6
1260	SOLANO WY	94606	650-A6
1330	INTERNATIONAL BLVD	94606	650-A6
1400	MARIN WY	94606	650-A6
1470	E 15TH ST	94606	650-A6
1530	GLEASON WY	94606	650-A6
1600	FOOTHILL BLVD	94606	650-A6
17TH ST			**OAK**
1900	TULAGI ST	94626	649-C2
2000	TOBRUK ST	94626	649-C2
1590	CENTER ST	94607	649-E2
1600	PERALTA ST	94607	649-E2
1700	CAMPBELL ST	94607	649-D2
1800	WILLOW ST	94607	649-D2
1900	WOOD ST	94607	649-D2
	MANDELA PKWY	94607	649-E2
1400	MANDELA PKWY	94607	649-E2
1590	CENTER ST	94607	649-E2
710	WEST ST	94612	649-F3
760	WEST ST	94607	649-F3
800	18TH ST	94607	649-F3
100	LAKESIDE DR	94612	649-H4
130	MADISON ST	94612	649-H4
160	JACKSON ST	94612	649-H4
200	ALICE ST	94612	649-H4
300	HARRISON ST	94612	649-G4
330	WEBSTER ST	94612	649-G3
370	FRANKLIN ST	94612	649-G3
400	BROADWAY	94612	649-G3
500	TELEGRAPH AV	94612	649-G3
550	SAN PABLO AV	94612	649-G3
560	CLAY ST	94612	649-G3
600	JEFFERSON ST	94612	649-G3
650	MARTIN LUTHER KING JR WY	94612	649-F3
	CASTRO ST	94612	649-F3
700	BRUSH ST	94612	649-F3
E 17TH ST			**OAK**
300	3RD AV	94606	649-J5
400	4TH AV	94606	649-J5
400	4TH AV	94606	649-J5
500	5TH AV	94606	649-J5
600	6TH AV	94606	649-J5
700	7TH AV	94606	649-J5
700	7TH AV	94606	649-J5
800	8TH AV	94606	649-J5
900	10TH AV	94606	649-J5
900	9TH AV	94606	649-J5
1600	FOOTHILL BLVD	94606	649-J5
1600	11TH AV	94606	650-A5
1100	11TH AV	94606	650-A5
1200	12TH AV	94606	650-A5
1200	12TH AV	94606	650-A5
1300	13TH AV	94606	650-A5
1400	14TH AV	94606	650-A6
1500	15TH AV	94606	650-A6
1500	15TH AV	94606	650-A6
1500	E 18TH ST	94606	650-A6
1600	16TH AV	94606	650-A6
1800	18TH AV	94606	650-A6
1880	19TH AV	94606	650-A6
1960	20TH AV	94606	650-B6
2040	21ST AV	94606	650-B6
2130	22ND AV	94606	650-B6
2300	23RD AV	94601	650-B6

Address	Cross Street	ZIP	CITY Pg-Grid
E 17TH ST			**OAK**
2400	24TH AV	94601	650-B6
2600	27TH AV	94601	650-B7
2800	28TH AV	94601	650-C7
2920	29TH AV	94601	650-C7
3100	FRUITVALE AV	94601	650-C7
3100	FRUITVALE AV	94601	650-C7
3190	33RD AV	94601	650-C7
3200	33RD AV	94601	650-C7
3300	34TH AV	94601	650-C7
3300	34TH AV	94601	650-C7
3400	35TH AV	94601	650-C7
4000	40TH AV	94601	670-D1
4100	ROSEDALE AV	94601	670-D1
4100	41ST AV	94601	670-D1
4200	42ND AV	94601	670-D1
4200	42ND AV	94601	670-D1
4300	HIGH ST	94601	670-D1
5500	55TH AV	94621	670-E2
5500	FAIRFAX AV	94621	670-E2
5700	57TH AV	94621	670-E2
5700	57TH AV	94621	670-F2
5900	SEMINARY AV	94621	670-F2
6050	61ST AV	94621	670-F2
6200	62ND AV	94621	670-F2
6400	64TH AV	94621	670-F2
18TH AV			**OAK**
1200	E 12TH ST	94606	650-A6
1270	SOLANO WY	94606	650-A6
1350	INTERNATIONAL BLVD	94606	650-A6
1440	MARIN WY	94606	650-A6
1520	E 15TH ST	94606	650-A6
1580	GLEASON WY	94606	650-A6
1600	FOOTHILL BLVD	94606	650-A6
1630	INDEPENDENCE WY	94606	650-A6
1700	E 17TH ST	94606	650-A6
1730	COMMERCE WY	94606	650-A6
1800	E 19TH ST	94606	650-A6
1900	SONOMA WY	94606	650-A6
2000	E 20TH ST	94606	650-A6
2050	SAN ANTONIO WY	94606	650-B5
2100	E 21ST ST	94606	650-B5
18TH ST			**OAK**
700	BRUSH ST	94612	649-F3
770	WEST ST	94607	649-F3
820	17TH ST	94607	649-F3
900	MARKET ST	94607	649-F3
950	MYRTLE ST	94607	649-F3
1000	FILBERT ST	94607	649-F3
1050	LINDEN ST	94607	649-F3
1100	CHESTNUT ST	94607	649-E3
1150	ADELINE ST	94607	649-E2
1360	POPLAR ST	94607	649-E2
1430	KIRKHAM ST	94607	649-E2
	MANDELA PKWY	94607	649-E2
1500	MANDELA PKWY	94607	649-E2
1590	PERALTA ST	94607	649-E2
1690	CAMPBELL ST	94607	649-D2
1900	WOOD ST	94607	649-D2
640	MARTIN LUTHER KING JR WY	94612	649-F3
640	19TH ST	94612	649-F3
	CASTRO ST	94612	649-F3
500	TELEGRAPH AV	94612	649-G3
570	SAN PABLO AV	94612	649-G3
600	JEFFERSON ST	94612	649-G3
640	MARTIN LUTHER KING JR WY	94612	649-G3
E 18TH ST			**OAK**
100	LAKESHORE AV	94606	649-J4
1	ATHOL AV	94606	649-J4
140	LAKESHORE AV	94606	649-J4
100	ATHOL AV	94606	649-J4
120	2ND AV	94606	649-J4
300	PARK BLVD	94606	649-J4
300	3RD AV	94606	649-J4
400	4TH AV	94606	649-J4
500	5TH AV	94606	649-J5
600	6TH AV	94606	649-J5
700	7TH AV	94606	649-J5
800	8TH AV	94606	649-J5
800	9TH AV	94606	650-A5
900	9TH AV	94606	650-A5
1000	10TH AV	94606	650-A5
1110	11TH AV	94606	650-A5
1210	12TH AV	94606	650-A5
1310	13TH AV	94606	650-A5
1400	14TH AV	94606	650-A5
1500	15TH AV	94606	650-A5
1500	E 17TH ST	94606	650-A5
3100	FRUITVALE AV	94601	650-C7
3300	34TH AV	94601	650-C7
3400	35TH AV	94601	650-C7
3500	36TH AV	94601	650-C7
3900	39TH AV	94601	670-D1
3960	40TH AV	94601	670-D1
4010	ROSEDALE AV	94601	670-D1
4010	ROSEDALE AV	94601	670-D1
4100	41ST AV	94601	670-D1
4100	41ST AV	94601	670-D1
19TH AV			**OAK**
1200	E 12TH ST	94606	650-A6
1270	SOLANO WY	94606	650-A6
1350	INTERNATIONAL BLVD	94606	650-A6
1430	MARIN WY	94606	650-A6
1510	E 15TH ST	94606	650-A6
1580	GLEASON WY	94606	650-A6
1660	FOOTHILL BLVD	94606	650-A6
1680	INDEPENDENCE WY	94606	650-A6
1700	E 17TH ST	94606	650-A6
1750	COMMERCE WY	94606	650-A6
1800	E 19TH ST	94606	650-B6
2000	E 20TH ST	94606	650-B6
2050	SAN ANTONIO WY	94606	650-B6
2100	E 21ST ST	94606	650-B6
2200	E 22ND ST	94606	650-B5
2300	E 23RD ST	94606	650-B5
2400	E 24TH ST	94606	650-B5
2500	E 25TH ST	94606	650-B5
2600	E 26TH ST	94606	650-B5
2670	WALLACE ST	94606	650-B5
2700	E 27TH ST	94606	650-B5
2800	E 28TH ST	94606	650-B5
2900	E 29TH ST	94606	650-B5
3000	14TH AV	94606	650-B5
19TH ST			**OAK**
1250	TULAGI ST	94626	649-D2
1300	TOBRUK ST	94626	649-D2
1150	ADELINE ST	94607	649-E2
1250	UNION ST	94607	649-E2
700	BRUSH ST	94612	649-F3
770	WEST ST	94607	649-F3
900	MARKET ST	94607	649-F3
650	MARTIN LUTHER KING JR WY	94612	649-G3
700	CASTRO ST	94612	649-G3
500	TELEGRAPH AV	94612	649-G3
600	SAN PABLO AV	94612	649-G3
650	MARTIN LUTHER KING JR WY	94612	649-G3
650	18TH ST	94612	649-G3
650	MARTIN LUTHER KING JR WY	94612	649-G3
100	MADISON ST	94612	649-H4
150	JACKSON ST	94612	649-H4
210	ALICE ST	94612	649-H3
270	HARRISON ST	94612	649-G3
330	WEBSTER ST	94612	649-G3
390	FRANKLIN ST	94612	649-G3
450	BROADWAY	94612	649-G3
500	TELEGRAPH AV	94612	649-G3
E 19TH ST			**OAK**
700	6TH AV	94606	649-J5
800	7TH AV	94606	649-J5
800	8TH AV	94606	650-A5
800	8TH AV	94606	650-A5
900	9TH AV	94606	650-A5
1000	10TH AV	94606	650-A5
1100	11TH AV	94606	650-A5
1100	11TH AV	94606	650-A5
1200	12TH AV	94606	650-A5
1300	13TH AV	94606	650-A5
1400	14TH AV	94606	650-A5
1400	15TH AV	94606	650-A5
1400	15TH AV	94606	650-A5
1600	16TH AV	94606	650-A6
1700	17TH AV	94606	650-A6
1800	18TH AV	94606	650-A6
1900	19TH AV	94606	650-B6
2000	20TH AV	94606	650-B6
2100	21ST AV	94606	650-B6
2200	22ND AV	94606	650-B6
2300	23RD AV	94601	650-B6
2400	24TH AV	94601	650-B6
3100	FRUITVALE AV	94601	650-C7
20TH AV			**OAK**
1200	E 12TH ST	94606	650-A6
1270	SOLANO WY	94606	650-A6
1350	INTERNATIONAL BLVD	94606	650-A6
1430	MARIN WY	94606	650-A6
1510	E 15TH ST	94606	650-A6
1580	GLEASON WY	94606	650-A6
1600	FOOTHILL BLVD	94606	650-A6
1650	INDEPENDENCE WY	94606	650 A6
1700	E 17TH ST	94606	650-B6
1750	COMMERCE WY	94606	650-B6
1800	E 19TH ST	94606	650-B6
1900	SONOMA WY	94606	650-B6
2000	E 20TH ST	94606	650-B6
2050	SAN ANTONIO WY	94606	650-B6
2100	E 21ST ST	94606	650-B6
20TH ST			**OAK**
	MANDELA PKWY	94607	649-E2
1500	MANDELA PKWY	94607	649-E2
1590	PERALTA ST	94607	649-E2
1600	PERALTA ST	94607	649-E2
1660	CAMPBELL ST	94607	649-E2
1730	WILLOW ST	94607	649-D2
1800	WOOD ST	94607	649-D2
1400	UNION ST	94607	649-E2
1430	POPLAR ST	94607	649-E2
	MANDELA PKWY	94607	649-E2
1500	MANDELA PKWY	94607	649-E2
1600	PERALTA ST	94607	649-E2
760	BRUSH ST	94612	649-F3
800	WEST ST	94607	649-F3
850	CURTIS ST	94607	649-F3
1000	MARKET ST	94607	649-F3
200	LAKESIDE DR	94612	649-H3
300	HARRISON ST	94612	649-H3
350	WEBSTER ST	94612	649-G3
400	FRANKLIN ST	94612	649-G3
440	BROADWAY	94612	649-G3
500	TELEGRAPH AV	94612	649-G3
640	SAN PABLO AV	94612	649-G3
650	MARTIN LUTHER KING JR WY	94612	649-G3
700	CASTRO ST	94612	649-G3
E 20TH ST			**OAK**
500	PARK BLVD	94606	649-J4
600	5TH AV	94606	649-J4
650	6TH AV	94606	649-J4
650	7TH AV	94606	650-A5
700	7TH AV	94606	650-A5
700	7TH AV	94606	650-A5
800	8TH AV	94606	650-A5
900	9TH AV	94606	650-A5
1000	10TH AV	94606	650-A5
1000	10TH AV	94606	650-A5
1100	11TH AV	94606	650-A5
1200	12TH AV	94606	650-A5
1200	12TH AV	94606	650-A5
1300	13TH AV	94606	650-A5
1400	14TH AV	94606	650-A5
1500	16TH AV	94606	650-A5
1700	17TH AV	94606	650-A5
1800	18TH AV	94606	650-B6
1900	19TH AV	94606	650-B6
2000	20TH AV	94606	650-B6
2100	21ST AV	94606	650-B6
2200	22ND AV	94606	650-B6
2300	23RD AV	94601	650-B6
2490	24TH AV	94601	650-B6
2590	IRVING ST	94601	650-B6
2650	25TH AV	94601	650-B6
2730	26TH AV	94601	650-C6
2810	27TH AV	94601	650-C6
	MITCHELL ST	94601	650-C7
	FOOTHILL BLVD	94601	650-C7
21ST AV			**OAK**
1200	E 12TH ST	94606	650-A6
1270	SOLANO WY	94606	650-A6
1350	INTERNATIONAL BLVD	94606	650-A6
1430	MARIN WY	94606	650-A6
1510	E 15TH ST	94606	650-A6
1580	GLEASON WY	94606	650-B6
1600	FOOTHILL BLVD	94606	650-B6
1650	INDEPENDENCE WY	94606	650-B6
1700	E 17TH ST	94606	650-B6
1750	COMMERCE WY	94606	650-B6
1800	E 19TH ST	94606	650-B6
1900	SONOMA WY	94606	650-B6
2000	E 20TH ST	94606	650-B6
2050	SAN ANTONIO WY	94606	650-B6
2100	E 21ST ST	94606	650-B6
2200	E 22ND ST	94606	650-B6
2300	E 23RD ST	94606	650-B5
2400	E 24TH ST	94606	650-B5
2500	E 25TH ST	94606	650-B5
2600	E 26TH ST	94606	650-B5
2700	E 27TH ST	94606	650-B5
2700	HIGHLAND AV	94606	650-B5
2800	E 28TH ST	94606	650-B5
2900	E 29TH ST	94606	650-C5
3000	E 30TH ST	94606	650-C5
21ST ST			**OAK**
1400	TOBRUK ST	94626	649-D1
900	MARKET ST	94607	649-F2
950	MYRTLE ST	94607	649-F2
1000	FILBERT ST	94607	649-F2
1050	LINDEN ST	94607	649-F2
1100	CHESTNUT ST	94607	649-F2
1150	ADELINE ST	94607	649-E2
1250	UNION ST	94607	649-E2
1300	POPLAR ST	94607	649-E2
850	MARKET ST	94607	649-F2
800	CURTIS ST	94607	649-F3
750	WEST ST	94612	649-F3
800	BRUSH ST	94612	649-F3
200	HARRISON ST	94612	649-H3
300	KAISER PZ	94612	649-H3
350	WEBSTER ST	94612	649-G3
400	FRANKLIN ST	94612	649-G3
450	BROADWAY	94612	649-G3
500	TELEGRAPH AV	94612	649-G3
700	SAN PABLO AV	94612	649-G3
E 21ST ST			**OAK**
400	PARK BLVD	94606	649-J4
440	5TH AV	94606	649-J4
440	7TH AV	94606	650-A4
630	7TH AV	94606	650-A5
730	8TH AV	94606	650-A5
830	9TH AV	94606	650-A5
920	10TH AV	94606	650-A5
1020	11TH AV	94606	650-A5
1110	12TH AV	94606	650-A5
1300	13TH AV	94606	650-A5
1400	14TH AV	94606	650-A5
1400	14TH AV	94606	650-A5
1500	16TH AV	94606	650-A5
1700	17TH AV	94606	650-A5
1800	18TH AV	94606	650-B5
1900	19TH AV	94606	650-B6
2000	20TH AV	94606	650-B6
2100	21ST AV	94606	650-B6
2200	22ND AV	94606	650-B6
2300	23RD AV	94601	650-B6
2400	24TH AV	94601	650-B6
2500	25TH AV	94601	650-C6
2570	26TH AV	94601	650-C6
2640	27TH AV	94601	650-C6
2710	MITCHELL ST	94601	650-C6
22ND AV			**OAK**
2600	23RD AV	94606	650-C5
2600	E 26TH ST	94606	650-C5
2700	E 27TH ST	94606	650-C5
2800	E 28TH ST	94606	650-C5
2900	E 29TH ST	94606	650-C5
3000	E 30TH ST	94606	650-C5
3100	E 31ST ST	94602	650-C5
3200	E 32ND ST	94602	650-C5
3200	HAMLINE AV	94602	650-C5
1200	E 12TH ST	94606	650-A7
1200	23RD AV OVPS	94606	650-A7
1270	SOLANO WY	94606	650-A7
1350	INTERNATIONAL BLVD	94606	650-A6
1430	MARIN WY	94606	650-B6
1510	E 15TH ST	94606	650-B6
1580	GLEASON WY	94606	650-B6
1600	FOOTHILL BLVD	94606	650-B6
1650	INDEPENDENCE WY	94606	650-B6
1700	E 17TH ST	94606	650-B6
1750	COMMERCE WY	94606	650-B6
1800	E 19TH ST	94606	650-B6
1900	SONOMA WY	94606	650-B6
2000	E 20TH ST	94606	650-B6
2060	SAN ANTONIO WY	94606	650-B6
2100	E 21ST ST	94606	650-B6
900	LIVINGSTON ST	94606	650-A7
22ND ST			**OAK**
750	BRUSH ST	94612	649-F3
800	WEST ST	94607	649-F2
850	CURTIS ST	94607	649-F2
900	MARKET ST	94607	649-F2
300	KAISER PZ	94612	649-H3
350	WEBSTER ST	94612	649-G3
400	FRANKLIN ST	94612	649-G3
410	BROADWAY	94612	649-G3
450	VALLEY ST	94612	649-G3
500	TELEGRAPH AV	94612	649-G3
500	TELEGRAPH AV	94612	649-G3
700	MARTIN LUTHER KING JR WY	94612	649-G3
E 22ND ST			**OAK**
500	5TH AV	94606	650-A4
570	CARROLL ST	94606	650-A4
700	7TH AV	94606	650-A4
800	8TH AV	94606	650-A5
900	9TH AV	94606	650-A5
1000	10TH AV	94606	650-A5
1100	11TH AV	94606	650-A5
1200	12TH AV	94606	650-A5
1300	13TH AV	94606	650-A5
1400	14TH AV	94606	650-A5
1700	17TH AV	94606	650-B5
1890	19TH AV	94606	650-B6
2080	21ST AV	94606	650-B6
2300	23RD AV	94601	650-B6
2400	24TH AV	94601	650-B6
2500	25TH AV	94601	650-C6
2600	26TH AV	94601	650-C6
2700	27TH AV	94601	650-C6
2780	MITCHELL ST	94601	650-C6
2900	AUSTIN ST	94601	650-C6
3000	RUTHERFORD ST	94601	650-C6
3200	FRUITVALE AV	94601	650-C6
3400	COOLIDGE AV	94601	650-C7
23RD AV			**OAK**
1170	E 12TH ST	94606	650-B7
1170	E 12TH ST	94601	650-B7
1290	INTERNATIONAL BLVD	94606	650-B7
1290	INTERNATIONAL BLVD	94601	650-B7
1430	E 15TH ST	94606	650-B7
1430	E 15TH ST	94601	650-B7
1540	E 16TH ST	94606	650-B6
1540	E 16TH ST	94601	650-B6
1540	FOOTHILL BLVD	94601	650-B6
1580	FOOTHILL BLVD	94606	650-B6
1580	FOOTHILL BLVD	94601	650-B6
1680	E 17TH ST	94606	650-B6
1680	E 17TH ST	94601	650-B6
1810	E 19TH ST	94606	650-B6
1810	E 19TH ST	94601	650-B6
1950	E 20TH ST	94606	650-B6
1950	E 20TH ST	94601	650-B6
2100	E 21ST ST	94606	650-B6
2100	E 21ST ST	94601	650-B6
2190	E 22ND ST	94606	650-B6
2190	E 22ND ST	94601	650-B6
2280	E 23RD ST	94606	650-B6
2280	E 23RD ST	94601	650-B6
2380	E 24TH ST	94606	650-B6
2380	E 24TH ST	94601	650-B6
2450	E 25TH ST	94606	650-C6
2450	E 25TH ST	94601	650-C6
2460	WAKEFIELD AV	94606	650-C6
2460	WAKEFIELD AV	94601	650-C6
2550	22ND AV	94606	650-C5
2550	22ND AV	94601	650-C5
2550	E 26TH ST	94601	650-C5
2700	E 27TH ST	94606	650-C5
2700	E 27TH ST	94601	650-C5
2790	E 28TH ST	94606	650-C5
2790	E 28TH ST	94602	650-C5
2890	E 29TH ST	94606	650-C5
2890	E 29TH ST	94602	650-C5
2980	E 30TH ST	94602	650-C5
3100	E 31ST ST	94602	650-C5
3200	E 32ND ST	94602	650-C4
3400	ARDLEY AV	94602	650-C4
3400	MACARTHUR BLVD	94602	650-C4
	23RD AV OVPS	94601	650-B7
	23RD AV OVPS	94606	650-B7
	23RD AV OVPS	94601	650-B7
	23RD AV OVPS	94606	650-B7
	MILLER PL	94606	650-B7
	MILLER PL	94606	650-B7
	23RD AV OVPS	94601	650-B7
	E 11TH ST	94601	650-B7
2400	E 10TH ST	94601	650-B7
2500	E 9TH ST	94601	650-B7
300	29TH AV	94606	670-B1
300	PARK ST	94606	670-B1
390	KENNEDY ST	94606	670-B1
390	KENNEDY ST	94601	670-B1
450	KENNEDY ST	94606	670-B1
450	KENNEDY ST	94601	670-B1
460	FORD ST	94606	670-B1
460	FORD ST	94601	670-B1
560	CHAPMAN ST	94606	670-B1
560	CHAPMAN ST	94601	670-B1
660	E 7TH ST	94606	670-B1
660	E 7TH ST	94601	670-B1
23RD AV OVPS			**OAK**
	22ND AV	94606	650-A7
	E 12TH ST	94606	650-A7
	23RD AV	94606	650-B7
	E 11TH ST	94606	650-B7
	MILLER PL	94601	650-B7
	MILLER PL	94606	650-B7
	23RD AV	94606	650-B7
	23RD AV	94606	650-B7
	23RD AV	94601	650-B7
	23RD AV	94606	650-B7
	E 11TH ST	94606	650-B7
	E 11TH ST	94606	650-B7
23RD ST			**OAK**
600	MARTIN LUTHER KING JR WY	94612	649-G2
800	SAN PABLO AV	94612	649-G2
750	WEST ST	94612	649-F2
800	BRUSH ST	94612	649-F2
500	TELEGRAPH AV	94612	649-G3
620	NORTHGATE AV	94612	649-G2
	MARTIN LUTHER KING JR WY	94612	649-G2
200	HARRISON ST	94612	649-H3
240	WAVERLY ST	94612	649-H3
290	VALDEZ ST	94612	649-H3
340	WEBSTER ST	94612	649-H3
380	BROADWAY	94612	649-G3
440	VALLEY ST	94612	649-G3
500	TELEGRAPH AV	94612	649-G3
E 23RD ST			**OAK**
600	IVY DR	94606	650-A4
700	7TH AV	94606	650-A4
800	8TH AV	94606	650-A4
890	9TH AV	94606	650-A5
990	10TH AV	94606	650-A5
1090	11TH AV	94606	650-A5
1180	12TH AV	94606	650-A5
1280	13TH AV	94606	650-A5
1400	14TH AV	94606	650-A5
1700	17TH AV	94606	650-B5
1890	19TH AV	94606	650-B5
2080	21ST AV	94606	650-B6
2300	23RD AV	94601	650-B6
2340	INYO AV	94601	650-B6
2400	24TH AV	94601	650-C6
2500	25TH AV	94601	650-C6
2600	26TH AV	94601	650-C6
2700	27TH AV	94601	650-C6
2810	MITCHELL ST	94601	650-C6
3200	FRUITVALE AV	94601	650-C6
3200	FRUITVALE AV	94601	650-C6
3300	HUGHES AV	94601	650-C6
3400	COOLIDGE AV	94601	650-C6
24TH AV			**OAK**
2400	E 26TH ST	94601	650-C6
2600	E 24TH ST	94601	650-C6
1660	FOOTHILL BLVD	94601	650-B6
1690	E 17TH ST	94601	650-B6
1810	E 19TH ST	94601	650-B6
1940	E 20TH ST	94601	650-B6
2060	E 21ST ST	94601	650-B6
2180	E 22ND ST	94601	650-B6
2300	E 23RD ST	94601	650-C6
2400	E 24TH ST	94601	650-C6
1400	INTERNATIONAL BLVD	94601	650-B7
1500	E 15TH ST	94601	650-B7
1580	E 16TH ST	94601	650-B7
1660	FOOTHILL BLVD	94601	650-B7
24TH ST			**OAK**
1630	MANDELA PKWY	94607	649-E2
1640	CAMPBELL ST	94607	649-E2
1730	WILLOW ST	94607	649-E1
1800	WOOD ST	94607	649-E1
900	MARKET ST	94607	649-F2
950	MYRTLE ST	94607	649-F2
1000	FILBERT ST	94607	649-F2
1050	LINDEN ST	94607	649-F2
1100	CHESTNUT ST	94607	649-F2
1200	ADELINE ST	94607	649-F2
1300	MAGNOLIA ST	94607	649-E2
1380	UNION ST	94607	649-E2
1450	POPLAR ST	94607	649-E2
1530	KIRKHAM ST	94607	649-E2
1600	PERALTA ST	94607	649-E2
	MANDELA PKWY	94607	649-E2
	MANDELA PKWY	94607	649-E2
600	MARTIN LUTHER KING JR WY	94612	649-G2
800	SAN PABLO AV	94612	649-G2
200	HARRISON ST	94612	649-H3
300	WAVERLY ST	94612	649-H3
310	ORIN DR	94612	649-H2
340	VALDEZ ST	94612	649-H2
370	WEBSTER ST	94612	649-H2
400	BROADWAY	94612	649-G2
460	VALLEY ST	94612	649-G2
500	TELEGRAPH AV	94612	649-G2
500	TELEGRAPH AV	94612	649-G2
550	NORTHGATE AV	94612	649-G2
E 24TH ST			**OAK**
700	7TH AV	94606	650-A4
800	8TH AV	94606	650-A4
900	9TH AV	94606	650-A4
1000	10TH AV	94606	650-A5
1100	11TH AV	94606	650-A5
1200	12TH AV	94606	650-A5
1300	13TH AV	94606	650-B5
1500	14TH AV	94606	650-B5
1540	WALLACE ST	94606	650-B5
1560	17TH AV	94606	650-B5
1900	19TH AV	94606	650-B5
2100	21ST AV	94606	650-B6
2200	HIGHLAND AV	94606	650-B6
2300	23RD AV	94601	650-B6
2340	INYO AV	94601	650-C6
2380	GRANDE VISTA AV	94601	650-C6

ALAMEDA CO.

Address	Cross Street	ZIP	City Pg-Grid
E 24TH ST			**OAK**
2400	24TH AV	94601	650-C6
2440	24TH AV	94601	650-C6
2500	25TH AV	94601	650-C6
2600	26TH AV	94601	650-C6
25TH AV			**OAK**
2700	E 27TH ST	94601	650-C5
2800	E 28TH ST	94601	650-C5
2810	E 28TH ST	94602	650-C5
2810	E 28TH ST	94601	650-C5
2900	E 29TH ST	94601	650-C5
2900	E 29TH ST	94601	650-C5
1800	FOOTHILL BLVD	94601	650-B6
1940	E 20TH ST	94601	650-B6
2040	E 21ST ST	94601	650-C6
2140	E 22ND ST	94601	650-C6
2210	E 23RD ST	94601	650-C6
2320	E 24TH ST	94601	650-C6
2530	E 26TH ST	94601	650-C6
2700	E 27TH ST	94601	650-C6
1600	E 16TH ST	94601	650-B7
1800	FOOTHILL BLVD	94601	650-B7
1400	INTERNATIONAL BLVD	94601	650-B7
1500	E 15TH ST	94601	650-B7
1600	E 16TH ST	94601	650-B7
1200	E 12TH ST	94601	650-B7
1400	INTERNATIONAL BLVD	94601	650-B7
1000	E 10TH ST	94601	650-B7
1080	E 11TH ST	94601	650-B7
25TH ST			
660	MARTIN LUTHER KING JR WY	94612	649-G2
	WEST ST	94612	649-G2
	SAN PABLO AV	94612	649-G2
500	TELEGRAPH AV	94612	649-G2
600	NORTHGATE AV	94612	649-G2
410	TELEGRAPH AV	94612	649-G2
500	BROADWAY	94612	649-G2
E 25TH ST			
1300	13TH AV	94606	650-B5
1500	14TH AV	94606	650-B5
1600	WALLACE ST	94606	650-B5
1900	19TH AV	94606	650-B5
2100	21ST AV	94606	650-B5
2200	HIGHLAND AV	94606	650-B5
2200	HIGHLAND AV	94606	650-B5
2300	23RD AV	94601	650-C6
2600	26TH AV	94601	650-C6
2700	PEROLY CT	94601	650-C6
26TH AV			**OAK**
2700	E 27TH ST	94601	650-C5
2300	E 23RD ST	94601	650-C6
2390	E 24TH ST	94601	650-C6
2460	LOGAN ST	94601	650-C6
2530	E 25TH ST	94601	650-C6
2700	E 27TH ST	94601	650-C6
1760	FOOTHILL BLVD	94601	650-B6
1910	E 20TH ST	94601	650-C6
2050	E 21ST ST	94601	650-C6
2200	E 22ND ST	94601	650-C6
1500	E 15TH ST	94601	650-B7
1600	E 16TH ST	94601	650-B7
1200	E 12TH ST	94601	650-B7
1400	INTERNATIONAL BLVD	94601	650-B7
1000	E 11TH ST	94601	650-B7
900	E 10TH ST	94601	650-B7
1000	E 9TH ST	94601	650-B7
26TH ST			**OAK**
900	MARKET ST	94607	649-F2
900	27TH ST	94607	649-F2
950	MYRTLE ST	94607	649-F2
990	FILBERT ST	94607	649-F2
1050	LINDEN ST	94607	649-F2
1100	CHESTNUT ST	94607	649-F2
1150	ADELINE ST	94607	649-F2
1200	MAGNOLIA ST	94607	649-F2
1250	UNION ST	94607	649-F2
1300	POPLAR ST	94607	649-E2
1350	KIRKHAM ST	94607	649-E2
1400	PERALTA ST	94607	649-E2
1500	CAMPBELL ST	94607	649-E1
	MANDELA PKWY	94607	649-E1
1650	MANDELA PKWY	94607	649-E1
1700	WILLOW ST	94607	649-E1
650	MARTIN LUTHER KING JR WY	94612	649-G2
800	WEST ST	94612	649-G2
900	SAN PABLO AV	94612	649-G2
800	27TH ST	94612	649-H2
820	VALDEZ ST	94612	649-H2
820	VALDEZ ST	94612	649-H2
	WEBSTER ST	94612	649-H2
860	BROADWAY	94612	649-G2
1000	TELEGRAPH AV	94612	649-G2
E 26TH ST			**OAK**
1300	13TH AV	94606	650-B5
1400	14TH AV	94606	650-B5
1900	19TH AV	94606	650-B5
2100	21ST AV	94606	650-B5
2200	HIGHLAND AV	94606	650-B5
2300	22ND AV	94601	650-C5
2300	23RD AV	94601	650-C5
2340	INYO AV	94601	650-C6
2380	GRANDE VISTA AV	94601	650-C6
2440	24TH AV	94601	650-C6
2500	25TH AV	94601	650-C6
27TH AV			**OAK**
1400	INTERNATIONAL BLVD	94601	650-B7
1630	E 16TH ST	94601	650-C6
1700	E 17TH ST	94601	650-C6
1900	FOOTHILL BLVD	94601	650-C6
2000	E 20TH ST	94601	650-C6
2090	E 21ST ST	94601	650-C6
2190	E 22ND ST	94601	650-C6
2270	E 23RD ST	94601	650-C6
2500	LOGAN ST	94601	650-C6
800	E 9TH ST	94601	650-B7
920	E 10TH ST	94601	650-B7
1020	E 10TH ST	94601	650-B7
1120	E 11TH ST	94601	650-B7
27TH ST			**OAK**
850	SAN PABLO AV	94607	649-F2
880	ALICIA ST	94607	649-F2
900	26TH ST	94607	649-F2
900	MARKET ST	94607	649-F2
200	HARRISON ST	94612	649-H3
200	BAY PL	94612	649-H2
290	26TH ST	94612	649-H2
310	VALDEZ ST	94612	649-H2
320	VALDEZ ST	94612	649-H2
360	BROADWAY	94612	649-H2
370	WEBSTER ST	94612	649-H2
500	TELEGRAPH AV	94612	649-G2
	NORTHGATE AV	94612	649-G2
600	36TH ST	94612	649-G2
640	MARTIN LUTHER KING JR WY	94612	649-G2
800	WEST ST	94612	649-G2
850	SAN PABLO AV	94612	649-F2
E 27TH ST			**OAK**
1300	13TH AV	94606	650-B5
1400	VALLECITO PL	94606	650-B5
1900	19TH AV	94606	650-B5
2070	21ST AV	94606	650-B5
2070	HIGHLAND AV	94606	650-B5
2150	WAKEFIELD AV	94606	650-C5
2230	22ND AV	94606	650-C5
2300	23RD AV	94601	650-C7
2330	INYO AV	94601	650-C7
2370	GRANDE VISTA AV	94601	650-C7
2480	25TH AV	94601	650-C5
2500	25TH AV	94601	650-C5
2540	GARDEN ST	94601	650-C5
2600	26TH AV	94601	650-C5
2610	26TH AV	94601	650-C5
2600	BARRY PL	94601	650-C6
3100	FRUITVALE AV	94601	650-C6
3300	E SUNSET AV	94601	650-C6
3300	COOLIDGE AV	94601	650-D6
28TH AV			**OAK**
1400	INTERNATIONAL BLVD	94601	650-B7
1600	E 16TH ST	94601	650-C7
1700	E 17TH ST	94601	650-C7
2100	FOOTHILL BLVD	94601	650-C7
28TH ST			**OAK**
850	SAN PABLO AV	94607	649-F2
850	SAN PABLO AV	94608	649-F2
900	MARKET ST	94607	649-F2
900	MARKET ST	94608	649-F2
940	MYRTLE ST	94607	649-F2
940	MYRTLE ST	94608	649-F2
990	FILBERT ST	94607	649-F2
990	FILBERT ST	94608	649-F2
1050	LINDEN ST	94607	649-F2
1050	LINDEN ST	94608	649-F2
1100	CHESTNUT ST	94607	649-F2
1100	CHESTNUT ST	94608	649-F2
1150	ADELINE ST	94607	649-E1
1150	ADELINE ST	94608	649-E1
1200	MAGNOLIA ST	94607	649-F1
1200	MAGNOLIA ST	94608	649-F1
1250	UNION ST	94607	649-E1
1250	UNION ST	94608	649-E1
1340	POPLAR ST	94607	649-E1
1340	POPLAR ST	94608	649-E1
1410	PERALTA ST	94607	649-E1
1410	PERALTA ST	94608	649-E1
1520	ETTIE ST	94607	649-E1
1520	ETTIE ST	94608	649-E1
1550	CAMPBELL ST	94607	649-E1
1550	CAMPBELL ST	94608	649-E1
1660	MANDELA PKWY	94607	649-E1
1700	MANDELA PKWY	94607	649-E1
1700	WILLOW ST	94607	649-E1
950	SAN PABLO AV	94608	649-G2
900	WEST ST	94608	649-G2
600	MARTIN LUTHER KING JR WY	94609	649-G2
500	TELEGRAPH AV	94612	649-G2
580	TELEGRAPH AV	94609	649-G2
580	MERRIMAC ST	94609	649-G2
580	MERRIMAC ST	94609	649-G2
400	TELEGRAPH AV	94609	649-G2
400	TELEGRAPH AV	94612	649-G2
300	SUMMIT ST	94609	649-H2
300	SUMMIT ST	94612	649-H2
400	WEBSTER ST	94609	649-H2
400	WEBSTER ST	94612	649-H2
280	BROADWAY	94611	649-H2
280	BROADWAY	94612	649-H2
200	VALDEZ ST	94611	649-H2
200	VALDEZ ST	94612	649-H2
E 28TH ST			**OAK**
800	PARK BLVD	94610	650-B4
920	BAYVIEW AV	94610	650-A4
930	9TH AV	94610	650-B4
930	9TH AV	94606	650-B4
1000	BELLA VISTA AV	94610	650-B4
1000	BELLA VISTA AV	94610	650-B4
1000	10TH AV	94606	650-B4
1100	11TH AV	94610	650-B4
1100	11TH AV	94606	650-B4
1200	12TH AV	94610	650-B4
1200	12TH AV	94606	650-B4
1300	13TH AV	94610	650-B4
1300	13TH AV	94606	650-B4
1300	13TH AV	94606	650-B4
1400	VALLECITO PL	94606	650-B5
1900	19TH AV	94606	650-B5
2090	21ST AV	94606	650-C5
2220	22ND AV	94606	650-C5
2300	23RD AV	94606	650-C5
2500	25TH AV	94602	650-C5
2500	25TH AV	94601	650-C5
2600	GARDEN ST	94601	650-C5
29TH AV			**OAK**
1200	E 12TH ST	94601	650-B7
1350	INTERNATIONAL BLVD	94601	650-B7
1580	E 16TH ST	94601	650-C7
1700	E 17TH ST	94601	650-C7
300	23RD AV	94606	650-C7
300	PARK ST	94601	670-B1
400	GLASCOCK ST	94601	670-B1
500	FORD ST	94601	670-B1
740	E 9TH ST	94601	670-B1
800	E 9TH ST	94601	670-B1
830	E 10TH ST	94601	670-B1
29TH ST			**OAK**
650	MARTIN LUTHER KING JR WY	94609	649-G2
800	WEST ST	94608	649-G2
900	SAN PABLO AV	94608	649-G2
500	TELEGRAPH AV	94609	649-G2
700	MARTIN LUTHER KING JR WY	94609	649-G2
200	HARRISON ST	94611	649-H2
250	FAIRMOUNT AV	94611	649-H2
270	RICHMOND AV	94611	649-H2
280	VALDEZ ST	94611	649-H2
300	BROADWAY	94611	649-H2
350	WEBSTER ST	94609	649-H2
370	SUMMIT ST	94609	649-H2
400	SUMMIT ST	94609	649-H2
470	MCCLURE ST	94609	649-H2
500	TELEGRAPH AV	94609	649-G2
E 29TH ST			**OAK**
1900	19TH AV	94606	650-B5
2110	21ST AV	94606	650-C5
2220	22ND AV	94601	650-C5
2500	23RD AV	94602	650-C5
2500	25TH AV	94601	650-C5
2500	25TH AV	94601	650-C5
2560	SHEFFIELD AV	94602	650-C5
2600	MCKILLUP RD	94602	650-D6
2640	FRUITVALE AV	94601	650-D6
3100	SUNSET AV	94601	
30TH AV			**OAK**
1200	E 12TH ST	94601	650-B7
1400	INTERNATIONAL BLVD	94601	650-B7
30TH ST			**OAK**
850	SAN PABLO AV	94608	649-F1
900	MYRTLE ST	94608	649-F1
960	FILBERT ST	94608	649-F1
1030	LINDEN ST	94608	649-F1
1100	CHESTNUT ST	94608	649-F1
1150	ADELINE ST	94608	649-F1
1200	MAGNOLIA ST	94608	649-F1
1250	UNION ST	94608	649-E1
1290	LOUISE ST	94608	649-E1
1290	POPLAR ST	94608	649-E1
1300	PERALTA ST	94608	649-E1
500	TELEGRAPH AV	94609	649-G2
700	MARTIN LUTHER KING JR WY	94609	649-G1
800	WEST ST	94608	649-G1
900	MARKET ST	94608	649-G1
900	SAN PABLO AV	94608	649-G1
200	RICHMOND BLVD	94611	649-H2
250	BROOK ST	94611	649-H2
300	BROADWAY	94611	649-H2
350	WEBSTER ST	94609	649-H2
400	SUMMIT ST	94609	649-H2
450	MCCLURE ST	94609	649-H2
500	TELEGRAPH AV	94609	649-G2
E 30TH ST			**OAK**
1900	14TH AV	94606	650-B5
2150	21ST AV	94606	650-C5
2240	22ND AV	94606	650-C5
2350	23RD AV	94606	650-C5
2350	23RD AV	94602	650-C5
31ST AV			**OAK**
1400	E 15TH ST	94601	650-C7
1300	INTERNATIONAL BLVD	94601	650-C7
1400	INTERNATIONAL BLVD	94601	650-C7
1200	E 12TH ST	94601	670-C1
1300	E 13TH ST	94601	670-C1
31ST ST			**OAK**
650	MARTIN LUTHER KING JR WY	94609	649-G1
800	WEST ST	94608	649-G1
900	MARKET ST	94608	649-F1
1000	SAN PABLO AV	94608	649-F1
500	TELEGRAPH AV	94609	649-G1
600	TELEGRAPH AV	94609	649-G1
E 31ST ST			**OAK**
1300	13TH AV	94602	650-B4
1300	13TH AV	94606	650-B4
1340	VALLECITO PL	94602	650-B4
1340	VALLECITO PL	94606	650-B4
1400	STUART ST	94602	650-B4
1400	STUART ST	94606	650-B4
1550	BEAUMONT AV	94602	650-B5
1550	BEAUMONT AV	94606	650-B5
1550	14TH AV	94602	650-C5
2070	22ND AV	94602	650-C5
2300	23RD AV	94602	650-C5
32ND ST			**OAK**
950	SAN PABLO AV	94608	649-F1
1000	FILBERT ST	94608	649-F1
1050	LINDEN ST	94608	649-F1
1100	CHESTNUT ST	94608	649-F1
1150	ADELINE ST	94608	649-F1
1200	MAGNOLIA ST	94608	649-F1
1250	UNION ST	94608	649-E1
1300	HOLLIS ST	94608	649-F1
1300	PERALTA ST	94608	649-F1
1400	PERALTA ST	94608	649-F1
1450	LOUISE ST	94608	649-E1
1500	HELEN ST	94608	649-E1
1550	HANNAH ST	94608	649-E1
1600	ETTIE ST	94608	649-E1
	MANDELA PKWY	94607	649-E1
1650	MANDELA PKWY	94607	649-E1
1700	WOOD ST	94607	649-E1
1750	SURRYHNE ST	94607	649-E1
650	MARTIN LUTHER KING JR WY	94609	649-G1
800	WEST ST	94608	649-G1
900	MARKET ST	94608	649-F1
950	SAN PABLO AV	94608	649-F1
E 32ND ST			**OAK**
1300	13TH AV	94602	650-B4
1300	BAYVIEW AV	94602	650-B4
1400	STUART ST	94602	650-B4
1500	BEAUMONT AV	94602	650-C4
1520	14TH AV	94602	650-C4
1600	PALMER AV	94602	650-C5
2200	HAMLINE AV	94602	650-C5
2200	22ND AV	94602	650-C5
2250	RANDOLPH AV	94602	650-C5
2300	23RD AV	94602	650-C5
33RD AV			**OAK**
1770	E 17TH ST	94601	650-C7
2000	FOOTHILL BLVD	94601	650-C7
1630	E 16TH ST	94601	650-C7
1770	E 17TH ST	94601	650-C7
1400	FARNAM ST	94601	650-C7
1630	E 16TH ST	94601	650-C7
1200	E 12TH ST	94601	670-C1
1400	INTERNATIONAL BLVD	94601	670-C1
800	E 9TH ST	94601	670-C1
33RD ST			**OAK**
650	MARTIN LUTHER KING JR WY	94609	649-G1
800	WEST ST	94608	649-G1
900	MARKET ST	94608	649-F1
1000	SAN PABLO AV	94608	649-F1
500	34TH ST	94609	649-G1
600	TELEGRAPH AV	94609	649-G1
E 33RD ST			**OAK**
1100	ELLIOT ST	94610	650-B4
1300	13TH AV	94610	650-B4
1300	13TH AV	94602	650-B4
1420	STUART ST	94602	650-B4
1540	BEAUMONT AV	94602	650-B4
1620	14TH AV	94602	650-C4
2000	PALMER AV	94602	650-C4
2300	RANDOLPH AV	94602	650-C4
34TH ST			**OAK**
2000	FOOTHILL BLVD	94601	650-C7
2270	ORCHID ST	94601	650-D6
2420	SALISBURY ST	94601	650-D6
2490	PAXTON AV	94601	650-D6
2620	DAVIS ST	94601	650-D6
2690	HENRIETTA ST	94601	650-D6
1490	FARNAM ST	94601	650-C7
1490	FARNAM ST	94601	650-C7
1600	E 16TH ST	94601	650-C7
1630	E 17TH ST	94601	650-C7
1700	E 17TH ST	94601	650-C7
1800	E 18TH ST	94601	650-C7
2100	FOOTHILL BLVD	94601	650-C7
1400	INTERNATIONAL BLVD	94601	670-C1
1300	INTERNATIONAL BLVD	94601	670-C1
1000	SAN LEANDRO ST	94601	670-C1
800	E 9TH ST	94601	670-C1
700	E 9TH ST	94601	670-C1
600	E 8TH ST	94601	670-C1
34TH AV			**OAK**
1050	LINDEN ST	94608	649-F1
1130	CHESTNUT ST	94608	649-F1
1200	ADELINE ST	94608	649-F1
1280	MAGNOLIA ST	94608	649-F1
1340	PERALTA ST	94608	649-F1
1400	FITZGERALD ST	94608	649-F1
1400	HARLAN ST	94608	649-F1
1400	HOLLIS ST	94608	649-F1
1400	FITZGERALD ST	94608	649-E1
1450	LOUISE ST	94608	649-E1
1500	HELEN ST	94608	649-E1
1550	HANNAH ST	94608	649-E1
1600	ETTIE ST	94608	649-E1
1650	BEACH ST	94608	649-E1
1700	WOOD ST	94608	649-E1
300	BROADWAY	94611	649-H1
300	BROADWAY	94609	649-H1
350	WEBSTER ST	94609	649-H1
440	ANDOVER ST	94609	649-H1
	ELM ST	94609	649-H1
500	TELEGRAPH AV	94609	649-G1
570	33RD ST	94609	649-G1
650	MARTIN LUTHER KING JR WY	94609	649-G1
800	WEST ST	94608	649-G1
900	MARKET ST	94608	649-F1
1000	SAN PABLO AV	94608	649-F1
E 34TH ST			**OAK**
1000	PARK BLVD	94610	650-B4
1100	ELLIOT ST	94610	650-B4
1300	13TH AV	94610	650-B4
1300	13TH AV	94602	650-B4
1380	STUART ST	94602	650-B4
1400	MACARTHUR BLVD	94602	650-B4
35TH AV			**OAK**
1510	E 16TH ST	94601	650-C7
1530	E 16TH ST	94601	650-C7
1600	E 17TH ST	94601	650-C7
1700	E 18TH ST	94601	650-C7
1800	FOOTHILL BLVD	94601	650-D7
1900	EDEN LN	94601	650-D7
1930	ALEXANDER CT	94601	650-D7
2000	HARPER ST	94601	650-D7
2100	GALINDO ST	94601	650-D7
2200	SALISBURY ST	94601	650-D6
2240	GRAY ST	94601	650-D6
2290	PAXTON AV	94601	650-D6
2300	CUSTER ST	94601	650-D6
2340	DAVIS ST	94601	650-D6
2350	DAVIS ST	94601	650-D6
2390	MEADOW ST	94601	650-D6
2420	LYNDE ST	94601	650-D6
2460	LYON AV	94601	650-D6
2510	DEERING ST	94601	650-D6
2560	BROOKDALE AV	94601	650-E6
2560	BROOKDALE AV	94619	650-E6
2600	BROOKDALE AV	94619	650-E6
2600	BROOKDALE AV	94619	650-E6
2700	ALLENDALE AV	94619	650-E6
2700	ALLENDALE AV	94619	650-E6
2840	PENNIMAN AV	94619	650-E6
2840	PENNIMAN AV	94619	650-E6
2950	PENNIMAN AV	94619	650-E6
2950	PENNIMAN AV	94619	650-E6
3070	HAGEMAN AV	94619	650-E6
3070	HAGEMAN AV	94619	650-E6
3120	SCHOOL ST	94619	650-E6
3120	SCHOOL ST	94619	650-E6
3190	MANGELS AV	94619	650-E6
3190	MANGELS AV	94619	650-E6
3220	SUTER ST	94619	650-E6
3220	SUTER ST	94619	650-E6
3250	SUTER ST	94619	650-E6
3250	SUTER ST	94619	650-E6
	DELAWARE ST	94602	650-E5
	DELAWARE ST	94602	650-E5
3400	QUIGLEY ST	94619	650-E5
3420	QUIGLEY LN	94602	650-E5
3420	QUIGLEY LN	94619	650-E5
3450	REDDING ST	94602	650-F5
3450	REDDING ST	94619	650-F5
3600	MACARTHUR BLVD	94619	650-F5
3600	MACARTHUR BLVD	94619	650-F5
3700	KANSAS ST	94602	650-F5
3700	KANSAS ST	94619	650-F5
3810	CALIFORNIA ST	94602	650-F5
3810	CALIFORNIA ST	94619	650-F5
3850	CALIFORNIA ST	94602	650-F5
3850	CALIFORNIA ST	94619	650-F5
3890	ARIZONA ST	94602	650-F5
3890	ARIZONA ST	94619	650-F5
4000	WISCONSIN ST	94602	650-F5
4000	WISCONSIN ST	94619	650-F5
4060	HARBOR VIEW AV	94602	650-F5
4060	HARBOR VIEW AV	94619	650-F5
4120	LIBBY CT	94602	650-F5
4120	LIBBY CT	94619	650-F5
4170	VICTOR AV	94602	650-F5
4170	VICTOR AV	94619	650-F5
4200	VICTOR AV	94602	650-F5
4200	VICTOR AV	94619	650-F5
4230	WILLIS CT	94602	650-G5
4230	WILLIS CT	94619	650-G5
4280	JORDAN RD	94602	650-G5
4280	JORDAN RD	94619	650-G5
3500	JORDAN RD	94602	650-G5
3500	JORDAN RD	94619	650-G5
3540	GUIDO ST	94602	650-G5
3540	GUIDO ST	94619	650-G5
3580	MONTEREY BLVD	94619	650-G5
3620	DETROIT AV	94619	650-G5
3640	DETROIT AV	94619	650-G5
3660	ATLAS AV	94619	650-G5
3680	ATLAS AV	94619	650-G5
3730	ALISO AV	94619	650-G5
1040	SAN LEANDRO ST	94601	670-C1
1310	E 12TH ST	94601	670-C1
1400	INTERNATIONAL BLVD	94601	670-C1
1510	E 15TH ST	94601	670-C1
800	E 9TH ST	94601	670-C1
35TH ST			**OAK**
650	MARTIN LUTHER KING JR WY	94609	649-G1
800	WEST ST	94608	649-G1
900	MARKET ST	94608	649-F1
1000	SAN PABLO AV	94608	649-F1
1050	CHESTNUT ST	94608	649-F1
1100	ADELINE ST	94608	649-F1
1150	MAGNOLIA ST	94608	649-F1
1200	PERALTA ST	94608	649-F1
36TH AV			**OAK**
1900	FOOTHILL BLVD	94601	650-D7
2100	HARPER ST	94601	650-D7
1400	E 16TH ST	94601	650-C7
1620	E 17TH ST	94601	650-D7
1840	E 18TH ST	94601	650-D7
1900	FOOTHILL BLVD	94601	650-D7
1400	INTERNATIONAL BLVD	94601	670-C1
1000	SAN LEANDRO ST	94601	670-C1
1200	E 12TH ST	94601	670-C1
1400	INTERNATIONAL BLVD	94601	670-C1
800	E 9TH ST	94601	670-C1
730	E 8TH ST	94601	670-C1
770	BOEHMER ST	94601	670-C1
36TH ST			**OAK**
650	MARTIN LUTHER KING JR WY	94609	649-G1
800	WEST ST	94608	649-G1
900	MARKET ST	94608	649-F1
1000	SAN PABLO AV	94608	649-F1
1150	ADELINE ST	94608	629-F7

PRIMARY STREET Address	Cross Street	ZIP	CITY Pg-Grid
36TH ST			**OAK**
1190	MAGNOLIA ST	94608	629-F7
400	WEBSTER ST	94609	649-H1
500	TELEGRAPH AV	94609	649-H1
2600	NORTHGATE AV	94612	649-G2
2800	27TH ST	94612	649-G2
E 36TH ST			**OAK**
1300	CHATHAM RD	94602	650-B4
1400	BRUCE ST	94602	650-C4
1420	BEAUMONT AV	94602	650-C4
37TH AV			**OAK**
800	E 9TH ST	94601	670-C1
1090	SAN LEANDRO ST	94601	670-C1
1230	E 12TH ST	94601	670-C1
1400	INTERNATIONAL BLVD	94601	670-C1
1660	E 16TH ST	94601	670-C1
700	BOEHMER ST	94601	670-C1
800	E 8TH ST	94601	670-C1
37TH ST			**EMVL**
1000	LINDEN ST	94608	629-F7
1070	SAN PABLO AV	94608	629-F7
37TH ST			**OAK**
650	MARTIN LUTHER KING JR WY	94609	649-G1
800	WEST ST	94608	649-G1
900	MARKET ST	94608	649-G1
1000	LINDEN ST	94608	649-G1
500	W MACARTHUR BLVD	94609	649-G1
600	TELEGRAPH AV	94609	649-G1
400	WEBSTER ST	94609	649-H1
500	TELEGRAPH AV	94609	649-H1
38TH AV			**OAK**
3600	MACARTHUR BLVD	94619	650-F6
3640	MASTERSON ST	94619	650-F6
3720	KANSAS ST	94619	650-F6
3900	CALIFORNIA ST	94619	650-F6
1400	FOOTHILL BLVD	94601	650-D7
1900	FOOTHILL BLVD	94601	650-D7
1940	SAN JUAN ST	94601	650-D7
2000	MERA ST	94601	650-D7
2100	CARRINGTON ST	94601	650-D7
2300	SANTA RITA ST	94601	650-D7
2400	AGUA VISTA ST	94601	650-E7
2500	LYON AV	94601	650-E7
2530	NEVIL ST	94601	650-E6
2600	BROOKDALE AV	94619	650-E6
2790	ALLENDALE AV	94619	650-E6
2900	DALE PL	94619	650-E6
3010	PENNIMAN AV	94619	650-E6
3100	ANGELO AV	94619	650-E6
3150	LIESE AV	94619	650-E6
3200	MARION AV	94619	650-E6
3290	SUTER ST	94619	650-E6
3400	QUIGLEY ST	94619	650-F6
3500	REDDING ST	94619	650-F6
3600	MACARTHUR BLVD	94619	650-F6
900	WATTLING ST	94601	670-C1
1040	SAN LEANDRO ST	94601	670-C1
1200	E 12TH ST	94601	670-C1
1400	INTERNATIONAL BLVD	94601	670-C1
38TH ST			**OAK**
300	BROADWAY	94609	649-H1
350	MANILA AV	94609	649-H1
360	OPAL ST	94609	649-H1
400	SHAFTER AV	94609	649-H1
420	WEBSTER ST	94609	649-H1
440	RUBY ST	94609	649-H1
450	RUBY ST	94609	649-H1
460	LATIMER PL	94609	649-H1
470	CLARKE ST	94609	649-H1
500	TELEGRAPH AV	94609	649-H1
200	CERRITO AV	94611	649-J1
300	BROADWAY	94611	649-J1
E 38TH ST			**OAK**
1300	13TH AV	94602	650-C4
1400	BEAUMONT AV	94602	650-C4
1460	BRIGHTON AV	94602	650-C4
1510	GLEN PARK RD	94602	650-C4
1530	GLEN PARK RD	94602	650-C4
1570	RANDOLPH AV	94602	650-C4
1590	RANDOLPH AV	94602	650-C4
1640	ARDLEY AV	94602	650-C4
1650	ARDLEY AV	94602	650-C4
1700	WOODRUFF AV	94602	650-C4
1710	WOODRUFF AV	94602	650-C4
1750	ELSTON AV	94602	650-C4
1780	ELSTON AV	94602	650-C4
1800	LINWOOD AV	94602	650-C4
1840	LINWOOD AV	94602	650-C4
1850	LA CRESTA AV	94602	650-D4
1900	EVERETT AV	94602	650-D4
1910	EVERS AV	94602	650-D4
2000	MACARTHUR BLVD	94602	650-D4
39TH AV			**OAK**
3500	MACARTHUR BLVD	94619	650-F6
3550	MASTERSON ST	94619	650-F6
3620	KANSAS ST	94619	650-F6
3840	BAYO ST	94619	650-G5
4050	VICTOR AV	94619	650-G5
4100	SELKIRK ST	94619	650-G5
4200	SELKIRK ST	94619	650-G5
4400	REINHARDT DR	94619	650-G5
4500	ALISO AV	94619	650-G5
3450	QUIGLEY ST	94619	650-F6
3500	REDDING ST	94619	650-F6
3300	SUTER ST	94619	650-F6
3350	FULLINGTON ST	94619	650-F6
2700	WALNUT ST	94619	650-E6
2800	ALLENDALE AV	94619	650-E6
1900	MERA ST	94601	650-D7
2150	CARRINGTON ST	94601	650-D7
2400	SANTA RITA ST	94601	650-D7
1800	FOOTHILL BLVD	94601	650-D7
1900	FOOTHILL BLVD	94601	650-D7
1400	INTERNATIONAL BLVD	94601	670-D1
1800	E 18TH ST	94601	670-D1
900	WATTLING ST	94601	670-C1
1000	SAN LEANDRO ST	94601	670-C1
1200	E 12TH ST	94601	670-C1
1400	INTERNATIONAL BLVD	94601	670-C1
39TH ST			**OAK**
830	LUSK ST	94608	629-G7
900	MARKET ST	94608	629-G7
1100	ADELINE ST	94608	629-G7
650	MARTIN LUTHER KING JR WY	94609	629-G7
800	WEST ST	94609	629-G7
40TH AV			**OAK**
1900	FOOTHILL BLVD	94601	650-D7
1970	SAN JUAN ST	94601	650-D7
2000	MERA ST	94601	650-D7
2200	CARRINGTON ST	94601	650-D7
2400	SANTA RITA ST	94601	650-D7
1750	FOOTHILL BLVD	94601	650-D7
1900	FOOTHILL BLVD	94601	650-D7
1400	INTERNATIONAL BLVD	94601	670-D1
1690	E 17TH ST	94601	670-D1
1750	E 18TH ST	94601	670-D1
900	WATTLING ST	94601	670-C1
1050	SAN LEANDRO ST	94601	670-C1
1200	E 12TH ST	94601	670-D1
1400	INTERNATIONAL BLVD	94601	670-D1
40TH ST			**EMVL**
1000	LINDEN ST	94608	629-F7
1100	ADELINE ST	94608	629-F7
1160	SAN PABLO AV	94608	629-F7
1200	EMERY ST	94608	629-F7
1300	WATTS ST	94608	629-F7
1400	HARLAN ST	94608	629-F7
1420	HAVEN ST	94608	629-E7
1440	HOLLIS ST	94608	629-E7
1460	HOLDEN ST	94608	629-E7
1480	HORTON ST	94608	629-E7
40TH ST			**OAK**
300	BROADWAY	94609	629-J7
300	40TH WY	94609	629-J7
340	MANILA AV	94609	629-H7
360	OPAL ST	94609	629-H7
380	SHAFTER AV	94609	629-H7
400	WEBSTER ST	94609	629-H7
430	RUBY ST	94609	629-H7
460	CLARKE ST	94609	629-H7
500	TELEGRAPH AV	94609	629-H7
650	MARTIN LUTHER KING JR WY	94609	629-G7
800	WEST ST	94608	629-G7
830	LUSK ST	94608	629-G7
900	MARKET ST	94608	629-G7
950	YERBA BUENA AV	94608	629-F7
1000	LINDEN ST	94608	629-F7
1480	HORTON ST	94608	629-E7
1500	HUBBARD ST	94608	629-E7
	BEACH ST	94608	629-E7
	SHELLMOUND ST	94608	629-E7
200	BROADWAY	94611	649-J1
100	CERRITO AV	94611	649-J1
200	HOWE ST	94611	649-J1
40TH WY			**OAK**
100	MONTE VISTA AV	94611	649-J1
100	PIEDMONT AV	94611	649-J1
150	HOWE ST	94611	649-J1
220	CERRITO AV	94611	649-J1
300	40TH ST	94611	649-J1
300	BROADWAY	94611	649-J1
41ST AV			**OAK**
2100	CARRINGTON ST	94601	650-E7
2200	SANTA RITA ST	94601	650-E7
2070	CARRINGTON ST	94601	650-D7
2200	CARRINGTON ST	94601	650-D7
1400	INTERNATIONAL BLVD	94601	670-D1
1490	E 15TH ST	94601	670-D1
1500	E 15TH ST	94601	670-D1
1580	E 16TH ST	94601	670-D1
1590	E 16TH ST	94601	670-D1
1690	E 17TH ST	94601	670-D1
1770	E 18TH ST	94601	670-D1
1780	E 18TH ST	94601	670-D1
1900	FOOTHILL BLVD	94601	670-D1
2070	MERA ST	94601	670-D1
1200	E 12TH ST	94601	670-D1
1400	INTERNATIONAL BLVD	94601	670-D1
1000	SAN LEANDRO ST	94601	670-D1
41ST ST			**EMVL**
1000	LINDEN ST	94608	629-F7
1050	ADELINE ST	94608	629-F7
1100	SAN PABLO AV	94608	629-F7
41ST ST			**OAK**
650	MARTIN LUTHER KING JR WY	94609	629-G7
800	WEST ST	94608	629-G7
830	LUSK ST	94608	629-G7
900	MARKET ST	94608	629-G7
1000	LINDEN ST	94608	629-G7
150	PIEDMONT AV	94611	649-J1
180	HOWE ST	94611	649-J1
250	GILBERT ST	94611	629-J7
280	TERRACE ST	94611	629-J7
300	BROADWAY	94611	629-J7
320	EMERALD ST	94609	629-J7
340	MANILA AV	94609	629-H7
360	OPAL ST	94609	629-H7
380	SHAFTER AV	94609	629-H7
400	WEBSTER ST	94609	629-H7
500	TELEGRAPH AV	94609	629-H7
600	42ND ST	94609	629-H7
1	GLEN AV	94611	649-J1
150	PIEDMONT AV	94611	649-J1
42ND AV			**OAK**
2060	SANTA RITA ST	94601	650-D7
2300	SANTA RITA ST	94601	650-D7
1900	FOOTHILL BLVD	94601	670-D1
2010	MERA ST	94601	670-D1
2060	CARRINGTON ST	94601	670-D1
1390	INTERNATIONAL BLVD	94601	670-D1
1490	E 15TH ST	94601	670-D1
1580	E 16TH ST	94601	670-D1
1610	BANCROFT AV	94601	670-D1
1690	E 17TH ST	94601	670-D1
1710	E 17TH ST	94601	670-D1
1790	BOND ST	94601	670-D1
1900	COURTLAND AV	94601	670-D1
1900	FOOTHILL BLVD	94601	670-D1
900	WATTLING ST	94601	670-D1
1000	SAN LEANDRO ST	94601	670-D1
42ND ST			**EMVL**
1000	LINDEN ST	94608	629-F7
1050	ADELINE ST	94608	629-F7
42ND ST			**OAK**
300	BROADWAY	94611	629-J7
300	MATHER ST	94611	629-J7
330	EMERALD ST	94609	629-J7
350	MANILA AV	94609	629-J7
370	OPAL ST	94609	629-H7
400	SHAFTER AV	94609	629-H7
420	WEBSTER ST	94609	629-H7
480	RICH ST	94609	629-H7
500	TELEGRAPH AV	94609	629-H7
570	41ST ST	94609	629-H7
650	MARTIN LUTHER KING JR WY	94609	629-G7
800	WEST ST	94608	629-G7
830	LUSK ST	94608	629-G7
900	MARKET ST	94608	629-G7
1000	LINDEN ST	94608	629-G7
43RD ST			**EMVL**
1020	ADELINE ST	94608	629-F7
1040	ESSEX ST	94608	629-F7
1060	SALEM ST	94608	629-F7
1100	SAN PABLO AV	94608	629-F7
1000	LINDEN ST	94608	629-F7
1020	ADELINE ST	94608	629-F7
43RD ST			**OAK**
650	MARTIN LUTHER KING JR WY	94609	629-G7
800	WEST ST	94608	629-G7
900	MARKET ST	94608	629-G7
1000	LINDEN ST	94608	629-G7
400	SHAFTER AV	94609	629-H7
420	WEBSTER ST	94609	629-H7
500	TELEGRAPH AV	94609	629-H7
600	44TH ST	94609	629-H7
44TH AV			**OAK**
	SAN LEANDRO ST	94601	670-D2
1180	E 12TH ST	94601	670-D1
1180	E 12TH ST PL	94601	670-D1
1310	INTERNATIONAL BLVD	94601	670-D1
1500	BANCROFT AV	94601	670-D1
44TH ST			**EMVL**
1050	LINDEN ST	94608	629-F7
1100	ADELINE ST	94608	629-F7
44TH ST			**OAK**
600	MARTIN LUTHER KING JR WY	94609	629-G7
800	WEST ST	94608	629-G7
930	MARKET ST	94608	629-G7
1040	LINDEN ST	94608	629-F7
1050	LINDEN ST	94608	629-F7
400	SHAFTER AV	94609	629-H7
430	WEBSTER ST	94609	629-H7
500	TELEGRAPH AV	94609	629-H7
600	43RD ST	94609	629-H7
45TH AV			**OAK**
2000	MELROSE AV	94601	670-E1
2110	ELLEN ST	94601	670-E1
2200	COURTLAND AV	94601	670-E1
1900	YGNACIO AV	94601	670-E1
2000	MELROSE AV	94601	670-E1
	SAN LEANDRO ST	94601	670-D2
1180	E 12TH ST	94601	670-D1
1360	INTERNATIONAL BLVD	94601	670-D1
1550	BANCROFT AV	94601	670-D1
1690	BOND ST	94601	670-D1
1800	FOOTHILL BLVD	94601	670-D1
700	COLISEUM WY	94601	670-D2
45TH ST			**EMVL**
1000	ADELINE ST	94608	629-F6
1040	ESSEX ST	94608	629-F6
1070	SALEM ST	94608	629-F6
1100	SAN PABLO AV	94608	629-F6
960	LINDEN ST	94608	629-F6
1000	ADELINE ST	94608	629-F6
1100	SAN PABLO AV	94608	629-F7
1130	EMERY ST	94608	629-F7
1170	WATTS ST	94608	629-F7
1200	DOYLE ST	94608	629-E7
1300	HOLLIS ST	94608	629-E7
1400	HOLDEN ST	94608	629-E7
1500	HORTON ST	94608	629-E7
45TH ST			**OAK**
500	TELEGRAPH AV	94609	629-H7
500	SHATTUCK AV	94609	629-H7
650	MARTIN LUTHER KING JR WY	94609	629-G7
800	WEST ST	94608	629-G7
890	MARKET ST	94608	629-G6
960	LINDEN ST	94608	629-G6
960	LINDEN ST	94608	629-G6
	WHITMORE PL	94611	629-J7
	WHITMORE ST	94611	629-J7
300	BROADWAY	94609	629-J7
350	MANILA AV	94609	629-J7
380	LAWTON AV	94609	629-H7
400	SHAFTER AV	94609	629-H7
430	WEBSTER ST	94609	629-H7
500	TELEGRAPH AV	94609	629-H7
46TH AV			**OAK**
1900	YGNACIO AV	94601	670-E1
2100	MELROSE AV	94601	670-E1
1400	BANCROFT WY	94601	670-D1
1400	INTERNATIONAL BLVD	94601	670-D1
1600	BANCROFT AV	94601	670-D1
1700	BOND ST	94601	670-D1
1800	FOOTHILL BLVD	94601	670-D1
	SAN LEANDRO ST	94601	670-D2
1160	E 12TH ST	94601	670-D1
1400	INTERNATIONAL BLVD	94601	670-D1
800	COLISEUM WY	94601	670-D2
46TH ST			**EMVL**
950	LINDEN ST	94608	629-F6
1100	ADELINE ST	94608	629-F6
46TH ST			**OAK**
650	MARTIN LUTHER KING JR WY	94609	629-G7
800	WEST ST	94608	629-G6
900	MARKET ST	94608	629-G6
950	LINDEN ST	94608	629-G6
500	TELEGRAPH AV	94609	629-H7
510	SHATTUCK AV	94609	629-H7
600	47TH ST	94609	629-H7
47TH AV			**OAK**
2310	CONGRESS AV	94601	650-E7
2220	TYRRELL ST	94601	650-E7
2310	TYRRELL ST	94601	650-E7
1400	INTERNATIONAL BLVD	94601	670-D1
1570	BANCROFT WY	94601	670-D1
1580	BANCROFT WY	94601	670-D1
1600	BANCROFT AV	94601	670-E1
1700	BOND ST	94601	670-E1
1800	FOOTHILL BLVD	94601	670-E1
2000	YGNACIO AV	94601	670-E1
2100	MELROSE AV	94601	670-E1
2150	ELLEN ST	94601	670-E1
2200	THOMPSON ST	94601	670-E1
2220	SAN CARLOS AV	94601	670-E1
1180	INTERNATIONAL BLVD	94601	670-D1
980	E 12TH ST	94601	670-D2
800	SAN LEANDRO ST	94601	670-D2
47TH ST			**EMVL**
1000	ADELINE ST	94608	629-F6
1080	SALEM ST	94608	629-F6
1100	SAN PABLO AV	94608	629-F6
1300	DOYLE ST	94608	629-F6
47TH ST			**OAK**
650	MARTIN LUTHER KING JR WY	94609	629-G6
650	MARTIN LUTHER KING JR WY	94608	629-G6
800	WEST ST	94608	629-G6
900	MARKET ST	94608	629-G6
500	TELEGRAPH AV	94609	629-H7
530	SHATTUCK AV	94609	629-H7
600	46TH ST	94609	629-H7
48TH AV			**OAK**
1400	INTERNATIONAL BLVD	94601	670-E1
1610	BANCROFT AV	94601	670-E1
1700	BOND ST	94601	670-E1
1730	FOOTHILL BLVD	94601	670-E1
2000	YGNACIO AV	94601	670-E1
2100	MELROSE AV	94601	670-E1
2300	VICKSBURG AV	94601	670-E1
1230	E 12TH ST	94601	670-D2
1400	INTERNATIONAL BLVD	94601	670-D2
48TH ST			**EMVL**
1060	SALEM ST	94608	629-F6
1100	SAN PABLO AV	94608	629-F6
48TH ST			**OAK**
1000	53RD ST	94608	629-F6
500	TELEGRAPH AV	94609	629-H6
530	SHATTUCK AV	94609	629-H6
400	SHAFTER AV	94609	629-H7
430	WEBSTER ST	94609	629-H7
460	CLARKE ST	94609	629-H7
500	TELEGRAPH AV	94609	629-H7
49TH AV			**OAK**
1200	E 12TH ST	94601	670-D2
1400	INTERNATIONAL BLVD	94601	670-D2
930	SAN LEANDRO ST	94601	670-D2
49TH ST			**OAK**
500	TELEGRAPH AV	94609	629-H6
600	SHATTUCK AV	94609	629-H6
300	BROADWAY	94611	629-J7
320	DESMOND ST	94609	629-J7
320	DESMOND ST	94618	629-J7
330	CORONADO AV	94609	629-J7
	MANILA AV	94609	629-J7
340	MANILA AV	94609	629-J7
370	LAWTON AV	94609	629-H6
400	SHAFTER AV	94609	629-H6
430	WEBSTER ST	94609	629-H6
460	CLARKE ST	94609	629-H6
500	TELEGRAPH AV	94609	629-H6
50TH AV			**OAK**
1400	INTERNATIONAL BLVD	94601	670-E1
1700	BANCROFT AV	94601	670-E1
1730	JUDD ST	94601	670-E1
1810	FOOTHILL BLVD	94601	670-E1
1920	YGNACIO AV	94601	670-E1
2000	MELROSE AV	94601	670-E1
2300	VICKSBURG AV	94601	670-E1
2300	MONTICELLO AV	94601	670-E1
730	COLISEUM WY	94601	670-D2
830	E 8TH ST	94601	670-D2
890	SAN LEANDRO ST	94601	670-D2
920	E 10TH ST	94601	670-D2
1100	E 12TH ST	94601	670-D2
1400	INTERNATIONAL BLVD	94601	670-D2
50TH ST			**OAK**
500	TELEGRAPH AV	94609	629-H6
400	WEBSTER ST	94609	629-H6
500	CLARKE ST	94609	629-H6
300	MANILA AV	94609	629-J6
370	LAWTON AV	94609	629-H6
400	SHAFTER AV	94609	629-H6
51ST AV			**OAK**
1800	BANCROFT AV	94601	670-E1
1800	WENTWORTH AV	94601	670-E1
1890	FOOTHILL BLVD	94601	670-E1
2000	YGNACIO AV	94601	670-E1
2020	MELROSE AV	94601	670-E1
2200	VICKSBURG AV	94601	670-E1
1400	BANCROFT AV	94601	670-E2
1800	INTERNATIONAL BLVD	94601	670-E2
960	E 10TH ST	94601	670-D2
1110	E 12TH ST	94601	670-E2
1400	INTERNATIONAL BLVD	94601	670-E2
800	E 8TH ST	94601	670-D2
900	SAN LEANDRO ST	94601	670-D2
51ST ST			**OAK**
300	BROADWAY	94618	629-J7
300	PLEASANT VALLEY AV	94618	629-J7
330	DESMOND ST	94618	629-J6
350	CORONADO AV	94609	629-J6
350	CORONADO AV	94618	629-J6
370	MANILA AV	94609	629-J6
370	MANILA AV	94618	629-J6
400	LAWTON AV	94609	629-J6
400	LAWTON AV	94618	629-J6
430	SHAFTER AV	94609	629-H6
430	SHAFTER AV	94618	629-H6
450	WEBSTER ST	94609	629-H6
450	WEBSTER ST	94618	629-H6
460	MILES AV	94609	629-H6
460	MILES AV	94618	629-H6
470	CLARKE ST	94609	629-H6
500	TELEGRAPH AV	94609	629-H6
600	52ND ST	94609	629-H6
600	SHATTUCK AV	94609	629-H6
800	MARTIN LUTHER KING JR WY	94608	629-G6
800	MARTIN LUTHER KING JR WY	94609	629-G6
900	WEST ST	94608	629-G6
900	WEST ST	94609	629-G6
52ND AV			**OAK**
1400	WENTWORTH AV	94601	670-E2
1700	INTERNATIONAL BLVD	94601	670-E2
980	E 10TH ST	94601	670-D2
1100	E 12TH ST	94601	670-E2
1400	INTERNATIONAL BLVD	94601	670-E2
800	SAN LEANDRO ST	94601	670-D2
900	E 8TH ST	94601	670-D2
52ND ST			**OAK**
500	CLAREMONT AV	94609	629-H6
500	TELEGRAPH AV	94609	629-H6
560	51ST ST	94609	629-H6
600	SHATTUCK AV	94609	629-H6
690	DOVER ST	94609	629-G6
700	DOVER ST	94609	629-G6
800	MARTIN LUTHER KING JR WY	94608	629-G6
820	WEST ST	94608	629-G6
880	GENOA ST	94608	629-G6
950	MARKET ST	94608	629-G6
53RD AV			**OAK**
1500	HOLLAND ST	94601	670-E2
1200	E 12TH ST	94601	670-E2
1400	INTERNATIONAL BLVD	94601	670-E2
1000	E 10TH ST	94601	670-D2
800	E 8TH ST	94601	670-D2
900	SAN LEANDRO ST	94601	670-D2
53RD ST			**EMVL**
1100	SAN PABLO AV	94608	629-F6
1190	BOYER ST	94608	629-F6
1190	EMERY BAY DR	94608	629-E6
1250	EMERY BAY DR	94608	629-E6
1300	HOLLIS ST	94608	629-E6
1500	HORTON ST	94608	629-E6
53RD ST			**OAK**
600	SHATTUCK AV	94609	629-H6
700	DOVER ST	94609	629-G6
800	MARTIN LUTHER KING JR WY	94608	629-G6
800	WEST ST	94608	629-G6
860	GENOA ST	94608	629-G6
900	MARKET ST	94608	629-G6
950	ADELINE ST	94608	629-G6
	ADELINE ST	94608	629-F6
950	LOWELL ST	94608	629-F6
1020	48TH ST	94608	629-F6
1040	GASKILL ST	94608	629-F6
1100	SAN PABLO AV	94608	629-F6
1100	SAN PABLO AV	94608	629-F6
1190	BOYER ST	94608	629-F6
1190	EMERY BAY DR	94608	629-F6
54TH AV			**OAK**
1400	INTERNATIONAL BLVD	94601	670-E2
1450	HOLLAND ST	94601	670-E2
1500	HOLLAND ST	94601	670-E2
1600	CRITTENDEN ST	94601	670-E2
1630	WADEAN PL	94601	670-E1
1700	WENTWORTH AV	94601	670-E1
1700	PRINCETON ST	94601	670-E1
1800	BANCROFT AV	94601	670-E1
1900	FOOTHILL BLVD	94601	670-E1
1900	VICKSBURG AV	94601	670-E1
800	E 8TH ST	94601	670-D2
890	SAN LEANDRO ST	94601	670-D2
1000	E 10TH ST	94601	670-E2
1100	E 12TH ST	94601	670-E2
1400	INTERNATIONAL BLVD	94601	670-E2
54TH ST			**EMVL**
1300	BOYER ST	94608	629-E6
54TH ST			**OAK**
	SHATTUCK AV	94609	629-H6
700	DOVER ST	94609	629-G6

PRIMARY STREET Address	Cross Street	ZIP	CITY Pg-Grid
54TH ST			**OAK**
800	MARTIN LUTHER KING JR WY	94608	629-G6
870	GENOA ST	94608	629-G6
900	MARKET ST	94608	629-G6
930	ADELINE ST	94608	629-G6
	SHATTUCK AV	94609	629-H6
930	ADELINE ST	94608	629-F6
950	LOWELL ST	94608	629-F6
1000	GASKILL ST	94608	629-F6
1100	SAN PABLO AV	94608	629-F6
1100	SAN PABLO AV	94608	629-F6
1300	BOYER ST	94608	629-F6
55TH AV			**OAK**
1400	INTERNATIONAL BLVD	94601	670-E2
1400	INTERNATIONAL BLVD	94621	670-E2
1470	HOLLAND ST	94601	670-E2
1470	HOLLAND ST	94621	670-E2
1500	E 15TH ST	94601	670-E2
1500	E 15TH ST	94621	670-E2
1570	CRITTENDEN ST	94601	670-E2
1570	CRITTENDEN ST	94621	670-E2
1600	E 16TH ST	94601	670-E2
1600	E 16TH ST	94621	670-E2
1670	WADEAN PL	94601	670-E2
1670	WADEAN PL	94621	670-E2
1700	E 17TH ST	94601	670-E2
1700	E 17TH ST	94621	670-E2
1700	FAIRFAX AV	94621	670-E2
1800	SCOVILLE ST	94601	670-F2
1800	SCOVILLE ST	94621	670-F2
1870	WENTWORTH AV	94601	670-F2
1870	WENTWORTH AV	94621	670-F2
1900	EDGERLY ST	94601	670-F2
1900	EDGERLY ST	94621	670-F2
2000	HOLWAY ST	94601	670-F1
2000	HOLWAY ST	94621	670-F1
2010	COLE ST	94601	670-F1
2010	COLE ST	94621	670-F1
2030	PRINCETON ST	94601	670-F1
2030	PRINCETON ST	94621	670-F1
2050	HARMON AV	94601	670-F1
2050	HARMON AV	94621	670-F1
2090	HARVEY AV	94601	670-F1
2090	HARVEY AV	94605	670-F1
2100	BANCROFT AV	94601	670-F1
2100	BANCROFT AV	94605	670-F1
2300	HILTON ST	94601	670-F1
2300	HILTON ST	94605	670-F1
2400	FOOTHILL BLVD	94601	670-F1
2400	FOOTHILL BLVD	94605	670-F1
2400	TRASK ST	94605	670-F1
2450	RUTH AV	94601	670-F1
2450	RUTH AV	94605	670-F1
2470	LA VERNE AV	94601	670-F1
2470	LA VERNE AV	94605	670-F1
2500	BROOKDALE AV	94619	670-F1
2500	BROOKDALE AV	94605	670-F1
2520	BROOKDALE AV	94619	670-F1
2520	BROOKDALE AV	94605	670-F1
2560	EL CAMILLE AV	94619	670-F1
2560	EL CAMILLE AV	94605	670-F1
2600	WALNUT ST	94619	670-F1
2600	WALNUT ST	94605	670-F1
2600	WALNUT ST	94619	670-F1
2600	WALNUT ST	94605	670-F1
2700	HILLEN DR	94619	670-F1
2700	HILLEN DR	94605	670-F1
2800	FLEMING AV	94619	670-F1
2800	FLEMING AV	94605	670-F1
2850	YUBA AV	94619	670-G1
2850	YUBA AV	94605	670-G1
2850	N PICARDY DR	94619	670-G1
2850	N PICARDY DR	94605	670-G1
2900	ROBERTS AV	94619	670-G1
2900	ROBERTS AV	94605	670-G1
2910	ROBERTS AV	94619	670-G1
2910	ROBERTS AV	94605	670-G1
2960	NORMANDIE AV	94619	670-G1
2960	NORMANDIE AV	94605	670-G1
3000	BRANN ST	94619	670-G1
3000	BRANN ST	94605	670-G1
3030	BRANN ST	94619	670-G1
3030	BRANN ST	94605	670-G1
3100	CAMDEN ST	94619	670-G1
3100	CAMDEN ST	94605	670-G1
3100	MACARTHUR BLVD	94605	670-G1
55TH ST			**EMVL**
1230	VALLEJO ST	94608	629-E6
1300	BEAUDRY ST	94608	629-E6
1400	DOYLE ST	94608	629-E6
55TH ST			**OAK**
400	VICENTE WY	94609	629-H6
500	TELEGRAPH AV	94609	629-H6
600	SHATTUCK AV	94609	629-H6
700	DOVER ST	94609	629-G6
800	MARTIN LUTHER KING JR WY	94608	629-G6
850	GENOA ST	94608	629-G6
900	MARKET ST	94608	629-G6
930	ADELINE ST	94608	629-G6
930	ADELINE ST	94608	629-G6
950	LOWELL ST	94608	629-F6
1050	GASKILL ST	94608	629-F6
1100	SAN PABLO AV	94608	629-F6
1100	SAN PABLO AV	94608	629-F6
1150	MARSHALL ST	94608	629-F6
1200	FREMONT ST	94608	629-F6
1250	VALLEJO ST	94608	629-F6
56TH AV			**OAK**
2900	ROBERTS AV	94605	670-G1
3000	BRANN ST	94605	670-G1
3100	MACARTHUR BLVD	94605	670-G1
2600	WALNUT ST	94605	670-F1
1400	INTERNATIONAL BLVD	94621	670-E2
1600	E 15TH ST	94621	670-E2
1700	E 16TH ST	94621	670-E2
56TH ST			**OAK**
530	CARBERRY AV	94609	629-H6
600	SHATTUCK AV	94609	629-H6
700	DOVER ST	94609	629-G6
800	MARTIN LUTHER KING JR WY	94609	629-G6
800	MARTIN LUTHER KING JR WY	94608	629-G6
850	GENOA ST	94608	629-G6
900	MARKET ST	94608	629-G6
910	ADELINE ST	94608	629-G6
950	LOWELL ST	94608	629-F6
1050	GASKILL ST	94608	629-F6
1100	SAN PABLO AV	94608	629-F6
57TH AV			**OAK**
2900	ROBERTS AV	94605	670-G1
3000	BRANN ST	94605	670-G1
3100	MACARTHUR BLVD	94605	670-G1
2650	WALNUT ST	94605	670-F1
2400	BANCROFT AV	94605	670-F1
2400	TRASK ST	94605	670-F1
2500	FOOTHILL BLVD	94605	670-F1
1500	INTERNATIONAL BLVD	94621	670-E2
1500	E 15TH ST	94621	670-F2
1600	E 16TH ST	94621	670-F2
1620	E 16TH ST	94621	670-F2
1660	E 17TH ST	94621	670-F2
1700	E 17TH ST	94621	670-F2
1760	SCOVILLE ST	94621	670-F2
1900	EDGERLY ST	94621	670-F2
1960	HOLWAY CT	94621	670-F2
2000	HOLWAY ST	94621	670-F2
2100	HARMON AV	94621	670-F2
2200	HARVEY AV	94605	670-F2
2200	HARVEY AV	94621	670-F2
2250	ELIZABETH ST	94605	670-F2
2300	HILTON ST	94605	670-F1
2400	BANCROFT AV	94605	670-F1
2400	TRASK ST	94605	670-F1
57TH ST			**OAK**
400	AYALA AV	94609	629-H5
440	VICENTE ST	94609	629-H5
500	TELEGRAPH AV	94609	629-H5
530	CARBERRY AV	94609	629-H5
600	SHATTUCK AV	94609	629-H5
660	MACCALL ST	94609	629-G5
700	DOVER ST	94609	629-G5
800	MARTIN LUTHER KING JR WY	94608	629-G5
850	GENOA ST	94608	629-G6
	ADELINE ST	94608	629-G6
890	MARKET ST	94608	629-F6
950	LOWELL ST	94608	629-F6
990	LOS ANGELES ST	94608	629-F6
1040	GASKILL ST	94608	629-F6
1100	SAN PABLO AV	94608	629-F6
58TH AV			**OAK**
2900	ROBERTS AV	94605	670-G1
3000	BRANN ST	94605	670-G1
3100	MACARTHUR BLVD	94605	670-G1
1200	TEVIS ST	94621	670-E2
1300	EASTLAWN ST	94621	670-E2
1400	INTERNATIONAL BLVD	94621	670-E2
58TH ST			**OAK**
440	HERMANN ST	94609	629-H5
440	MARTIN ST	94609	629-H5
450	CANNING ST	94609	629-H5
480	VICENTE ST	94609	629-H5
500	TELEGRAPH AV	94609	629-H5
500	RACINE ST	94609	629-H5
500	TELEGRAPH AV	94609	629-H5
530	CARBERRY AV	94609	629-H5
600	SHATTUCK AV	94609	629-H5
700	DOVER ST	94609	629-G5
800	MARTIN LUTHER KING JR WY	94608	629-G5
850	GENOA ST	94608	629-G5
900	ADELINE ST	94608	629-G5
950	MARKET ST	94608	629-G5
600	SHATTUCK AV	94609	629-H5
650	MACCALL ST	94609	629-G5
700	DOVER ST	94609	629-G5
59TH ST			**EMVL**
1230	VALLEJO ST	94608	629-E5
1260	BEAUDRY ST	94608	629-E5
1300	DOYLE ST	94608	629-E5
1400	HOLLIS ST	94608	629-E6
1450	PELADEAU ST	94608	629-E6
1500	LANDREGAN ST	94608	629-E6
1700	CHRISTIE AV	94608	629-D6
59TH ST			**OAK**
400	HOWELL ST	94609	629-H5
460	CANNING ST	94609	629-H5
500	TELEGRAPH AV	94609	629-H5
510	RACINE ST	94609	629-H5
600	SHATTUCK AV	94609	629-H5
630	WHITNEY ST	94609	629-H5
650	MACCALL ST	94609	629-G5
700	DOVER ST	94609	629-G5
700	DOVER ST	94609	629-G5
800	MARTIN LUTHER KING JR WY	94608	629-G5
870	GENOA ST	94608	629-G5
900	ADELINE ST	94608	629-G5
960	MARKET ST	94608	629-G5
	OCCIDENTAL ST	94608	629-F5
	STANFORD AV	94608	629-F5
1000	STANFORD AV	94608	629-F5
1000	LOS ANGELES ST	94608	629-F5
1030	IDAHO ST	94608	629-F5
1070	HERZOG ST	94608	629-F5
1100	SAN PABLO AV	94608	629-F5
1100	SAN PABLO AV	94608	629-F5
1150	MARSHALL ST	94608	629-F5
1200	FREMONT ST	94608	629-E5
1230	VALLEJO ST	94608	629-E5
60TH AV			**OAK**
2400	AVENAL AV	94605	670-G2
	FORTUNE WY	94605	670-G2
2500	BANCROFT AV	94605	670-G1
2600	FOOTHILL BLVD	94605	670-G1
2800	MORSE DR	94605	670-G1
2840	PICARDY DR	94605	670-G1
3000	BRANN ST	94605	670-G1
3100	CAMDEN ST	94605	670-G1
3200	MURDOCK CT	94605	670-G1
3300	MACARTHUR BLVD	94605	670-G1
1200	TEVIS ST	94621	670-E3
1300	EASTLAWN ST	94621	670-F2
1400	INTERNATIONAL BLVD	94621	670-F2
60TH ST			**OAK**
350	CLAREMONT AV	94618	629-J5
400	COLBY ST	94609	629-J5
440	HOWELL ST	94609	629-J5
440	HOWELL ST	94609	629-H5
460	CANNING ST	94609	629-H5
500	TELEGRAPH AV	94609	629-H5
600	RACINE ST	94609	629-H5
600	SHATTUCK AV	94609	629-H5
640	WHITNEY ST	94609	629-H5
660	MACCALL ST	94609	629-G5
700	DOVER ST	94609	629-G5
800	MARTIN LUTHER KING JR WY	94608	629-G5
850	GENOA ST	94608	629-G5
850	ADELINE ST	94608	629-G5
900	MARKET ST	94608	629-G5
900	STANFORD AV	94608	629-F5
930	SACRAMENTO ST	94608	629-F5
1050	IDAHO ST	94608	629-F5
1080	HERZOG ST	94608	629-F5
1100	SAN PABLO AV	94608	629-F5
61ST AV			**OAK**
3100	CAMDEN ST	94605	670-G1
3300	MACARTHUR BLVD	94605	670-H1
3400	MONADNOCK WY	94605	670-H1
2400	AVENAL AV	94605	670-G2
2540	FORTUNE WY	94605	670-G2
2600	BANCROFT AV	94605	670-G2
2700	FOOTHILL BLVD	94605	670-G1
2800	MORSE DR	94605	670-G1
3000	BRANN ST	94605	670-G1
1400	INTERNATIONAL BLVD	94621	670-F2
1600	E 16TH ST	94621	670-F2
1700	E 17TH ST	94621	670-F2
1200	TEVIS ST	94621	670-E3
1300	EASTLAWN ST	94621	670-F2
1400	INTERNATIONAL BLVD	94621	670-F2
61ST ST			**EMVL**
1230	VALLEJO ST	94608	629-E5
1300	DOYLE ST	94608	629-E5
1400	HOLLIS ST	94608	629-E5
61ST ST			**OAK**
300	HILLEGASS AV	94618	629-J5
370	COLBY ST	94609	629-J5
460	CANNING ST	94609	629-H5
500	TELEGRAPH AV	94609	629-H5
540	RACINE ST	94609	629-H5
540	RACINE ST	94609	629-H5
600	SHATTUCK AV	94609	629-H5
600	SHATTUCK AV	94609	629-G5
700	DOVER ST	94609	629-G5
700	DOVER ST	94609	629-G5
800	MARTIN LUTHER KING JR WY	94608	629-G5
850	ADELINE ST	94608	629-G5
850	STANFORD AV	94608	629-G5
900	CALIFORNIA ST	94608	629-G5
920	MARKET ST	94608	629-F5
950	SACRAMENTO ST	94608	629-F5
1000	BAKER ST	94608	629-F5
1000	SACRAMENTO ST	94608	629-F5
1020	BAKER ST	94608	629-F5
1050	IDAHO ST	94608	629-F5
1070	HERZOG ST	94608	629-F5
1100	SAN PABLO AV	94608	629-F5
1100	SAN PABLO AV	94608	629-F5
1150	MARSHALL ST	94608	629-E5
1200	FREMONT ST	94608	629-E5
1230	VALLEJO ST	94608	629-E5
62ND AV			**OAK**
2400	AVENAL AV	94605	670-G2
2500	FORTUNE WY	94605	670-G2
2600	BANCROFT AV	94605	670-G2
2700	FOOTHILL BLVD	94605	670-G1
3000	BRANN ST	94605	670-G1
3100	CAMDEN ST	94605	670-H1
3300	MACARTHUR BLVD	94605	670-H1
3340	MONADNOCK WY	94605	670-H1
3400	MAURITANIA AV	94605	670-H1
3500	LAIRD AV	94605	670-H1
2200	MAJESTIC AV	94605	670-H1
2270	OUTLOOK AV	94605	670-H1
1140	MALDON ST	94621	670-E3
1200	TEVIS ST	94621	670-E3
1250	FENHAM ST	94621	670-F3
1300	EASTLAWN ST	94621	670-F3
1400	INTERNATIONAL BLVD	94621	670-F2
1600	E 16TH ST	94621	670-F2
1700	E 17TH ST	94621	670-F2
1900	BROMLEY AV	94621	670-F2
1930	BROMLEY AV	94621	670-F2
1960	HOLWAY ST	94621	670-F2
2080	HARMON AV	94621	670-F2
2100	HARMON AV	94621	670-F2
2200	CASLAND DR	94621	670-F2
2200	CASLAND DR	94605	670-F2
2220	HAYES ST	94621	670-F2
2220	HAYES ST	94605	670-F2
2250	HAYES ST	94605	670-F2
2300	HILTON ST	94605	670-F2
2310	HILTON ST	94605	670-G2
2400	AVENAL AV	94605	670-G2
62ND ST			**BERK**
1800	MARTIN LUTHER KING JR WY	94703	629-G5
1900	DOVER ST	94703	629-G5
900	MARKET ST	94703	629-G5
1600	CALIFORNIA ST	94703	629-G5
1700	KING ST	94703	629-G5
1800	STANFORD AV	94703	629-G5
62ND ST			**EMVL**
1200	VALLEJO ST	94608	629-E5
1300	DOYLE ST	94608	629-E5
1400	HOLLIS ST	94608	629-E5
1530	LANDREGAN ST	94608	629-E5
1600	OVERLAND AV	94608	629-E5
62ND ST			**OAK**
300	CLAREMONT AV	94618	629-J5
300	COLLEGE AV	94618	629-J5
350	HILLEGASS AV	94618	629-J5
350	HILLEGASS AV	94618	629-J5
400	COLBY ST	94618	629-J5
400	COLBY ST	94609	629-H5
460	CANNING ST	94609	629-H5
500	TELEGRAPH AV	94609	629-H5
540	RACINE ST	94609	629-H5
540	RACINE ST	94609	629-H5
600	SHATTUCK AV	94609	629-H5
600	SHATTUCK AV	94609	629-H5
700	DOVER ST	94609	629-G5
930	MARKET ST	94608	629-F5
950	SACRAMENTO ST	94608	629-F5
1000	BAKER ST	94608	629-F5
1000	BAKER ST	94608	629-F5
1050	IDAHO ST	94608	629-F5
1100	HERZOG ST	94608	629-F5
1100	SAN PABLO AV	94608	629-F5
1130	MARSHALL ST	94608	629-E5
1170	FREMONT ST	94608	629-E5
1200	VALLEJO ST	94608	629-E5
63RD AV			**OAK**
3100	CAMDEN ST	94605	670-H1
3300	MACARTHUR BLVD	94605	670-H1
2300	HILTON ST	94605	670-G2
2400	AVENAL AV	94605	670-G2
2550	FORTUNE WY	94605	670-G2
2700	BANCROFT AV	94605	670-G2
2800	FOOTHILL BLVD	94605	670-G2
1300	EASTLAWN ST	94621	670-F3
1400	INTERNATIONAL BLVD	94621	670-F2
63RD ST			**BERK**
1800	MARTIN LUTHER KING JR WY	94703	629-G5
1900	DOVER ST	94703	629-G5
900	MARKET ST	94703	629-G5
1600	CALIFORNIA ST	94703	629-G5
1700	KING ST	94703	629-G5
1800	ADELINE ST	94703	629-G5
63RD ST			**EMVL**
1200	VALLEJO ST	94608	629-E5
1300	DOYLE ST	94608	629-E5
1400	HOLLIS ST	94608	629-E5
1600	OVERLAND AV	94608	629-E5
63RD ST			**OAK**
300	COLLEGE AV	94618	629-J4
350	HILLEGASS AV	94618	629-J4
400	COLBY ST	94618	629-J4
400	COLBY ST	94609	629-J5
440	DANA ST	94609	629-H5
490	CANNING ST	94609	629-H5
500	TELEGRAPH AV	94609	629-H5
540	RACINE ST	94609	629-H5
540	RACINE ST	94609	629-H5
600	SHATTUCK AV	94609	629-H5
600	SHATTUCK AV	94609	629-G5
700	DOVER ST	94609	629-G5
	MARKET ST	94608	629-F5
950	SACRAMENTO ST	94608	629-F5
1000	BAKER ST	94608	629-F5
1030	IDAHO ST	94608	629-F5
1060	HERZOG ST	94608	629-F5
1100	SAN PABLO AV	94608	629-F5
1100	SAN PABLO AV	94608	629-F5
1130	MARSHALL ST	94608	629-E5
1200	VALLEJO ST	94608	629-E5
64TH AV			**OAK**
1500	INTERNATIONAL BLVD	94621	670-F3
1600	E 16TH ST	94621	670-F2
1700	E 17TH ST	94621	670-F2
1900	BROMLEY AV	94621	670-F2
2060	HARMON AV	94621	670-F2
2100	FLORA ST	94605	670-F2
2200	HAYES ST	94605	670-G2
2400	AVENAL AV	94605	670-G2
2600	ARTHUR ST	94605	670-G2
2670	BANCROFT AV	94605	670-G2
2800	FOOTHILL BLVD	94605	670-G2
2900	BRANN ST	94605	670-G1
3100	CAMDEN ST	94605	670-H1
3300	MACARTHUR BLVD	94605	670-H1
3400	MONADNOCK WY	94605	670-H1
3550	MAJESTIC AV	94605	670-H1
3600	OUTLOOK AV	94605	670-H1
3700	BUENA VENTURA AV	94605	670-H1
1100	FENHAM ST	94621	670-F3
1500	INTERNATIONAL BLVD	94621	670-F3
64TH AV PL			**OAK**
3300	MACARTHUR BLVD	94605	670-H1
64TH ST			**EMVL**
1250	VALLEJO ST	94608	629-E5
1300	DOYLE ST	94608	629-E5
1400	HOLLIS ST	94608	629-E5
1590	OVERLAND AV	94608	629-E5
1600	SHELLMOUND ST	94608	629-D5
1700	CHRISTIE AV	94608	629-D5
1800	LA COSTE ST	94608	629-D5
64TH ST			**OAK**
1100	SAN PABLO AV	94608	629-E5
1140	MARSHALL ST	94608	629-E5
1250	VALLEJO ST	94608	629-E5
65TH AV			**OAK**
3300	MACARTHUR BLVD	94605	670-H1
3600	OUTLOOK AV	94605	670-H1
1500	INTERNATIONAL BLVD	94621	670-F2
2100	FLORA ST	94605	670-G2
2400	AVENAL AV	94605	670-G2
2600	ARTHUR ST	94605	670-G2
2700	BANCROFT AV	94605	670-G2
1100	FENHAM ST	94621	670-F3
1300	EASTLAWN ST	94621	670-F3
1500	INTERNATIONAL BLVD	94621	670-F3
65TH ST			**BERK**
1000	IDAHO ST	94702	629-F5
1050	HERZOG ST	94702	629-F5
65TH ST			**EMVL**
1200	VALLEJO ST	94608	629-E5
1400	HOLLIS ST	94608	629-E5
1500	SHELLMOUND ST	94608	629-D5
1600	CHRISTIE AV	94608	629-D5
1700	LA COSTE ST	94608	629-D5
65TH ST			**OAK**
400	DANA ST	94609	629-H4
500	TELEGRAPH AV	94609	629-H4
600	WHEELER ST	94609	629-H4
690	SHATTUCK AV	94609	629-H4
720	WHITNEY ST	94609	629-G4
750	TREMONT ST	94609	629-G4
800	HARMON ST	94609	629-G4
1050	HERZOG ST	94608	629-F5
1100	SAN PABLO AV	94608	629-E5
1200	VALLEJO ST	94608	629-E5
66TH AV			**OAK**
3300	MACARTHUR BLVD	94605	670-H1
3600	OUTLOOK AV	94605	670-H1
1300	INTERNATIONAL BLVD	94621	670-G2
2100	FLORA ST	94605	670-G2
2400	AVENAL AV	94605	670-G2
2600	ARTHUR ST	94605	670-G2
2700	BANCROFT AV	94605	670-G2
600	OAKPORT ST	94621	670-D4
640	COLISEUM WY	94621	670-E3
	SAN LEANDRO ST	94621	670-E3
1000	OLMSTEAD ST	94621	670-F3
1100	FENHAM ST	94621	670-F3
1200	EASTLAWN ST	94621	670-F3
1250	LUCILLE ST	94621	670-F3
1600	INTERNATIONAL BLVD	94621	670-F3
66TH ST			**BERK**
1000	HERZOG ST	94702	629-F4
1200	MABEL ST	94702	629-F4
1270	IDAHO ST	94702	629-F4
1350	BOISE ST	94702	629-F4
1400	ACTON ST	94702	629-F4
1420	BAKER ST	94702	629-F4
1500	SACRAMENTO ST	94702	629-F4
66TH ST			**EMVL**
1200	VALLEJO ST	94608	629-E5
1400	HOLLIS ST	94608	629-E5
	SHELLMOUND ST	94608	629-D5
66TH ST			**OAK**
400	DANA ST	94609	629-H4
500	TELEGRAPH AV	94609	629-H4
550	DEAKIN ST	94609	629-H4
600	RAYMOND ST	94609	629-H4
700	SHATTUCK AV	94609	629-H4
1030	HERZOG ST	94608	629-F4
1070	HELEN CT	94608	629-F4
1100	SAN PABLO AV	94608	629-F4
1100	SAN PABLO AV	94608	629-E5
1200	VALLEJO ST	94608	629-E5
67TH AV			**OAK**
1600	FLORA ST	94605	670-G2
2400	AVENAL AV	94605	670-G2
2600	ARTHUR ST	94605	670-G2
	BANCROFT AV	94605	670-H2
2800	BANCROFT AV	94605	670-H2
2900	FOOTHILL BLVD	94605	670-H2
2900	BRANN ST	94605	670-H2
1400	INTERNATIONAL BLVD	94621	670-G3
1600	FLORA ST	94621	670-G3
67TH ST			**BERK**
1000	SAN PABLO AV	94702	629-F4
1300	MABEL ST	94702	629-F4
1400	ACTON ST	94702	629-F4
1500	SACRAMENTO ST	94702	629-F4
67TH ST			**EMVL**
1400	HOLLIS ST	94608	629-E5
	SHELLMOUND ST	94608	629-D5
67TH ST			**OAK**
1100	SAN PABLO AV	94608	629-E4
68TH AV			**OAK**
2900	FOOTHILL BLVD	94605	670-H2
2900	CHURCH ST	94605	670-H2
3300	MACARTHUR BLVD	94605	670-H1
3470	LAIRD AV	94605	670-H1
3600	OUTLOOK AV	94605	670-H1
1600	FLORA ST	94605	670-G2
2400	AVENAL AV	94605	670-G2
2600	ARTHUR ST	94605	670-H2
	BANCROFT AV	94605	670-H2
2800	BANCROFT AV	94605	670-H2
3000	FOOTHILL BLVD	94605	670-H2
1400	INTERNATIONAL BLVD	94621	670-G3

PRIMARY STREET Address	Cross Street	ZIP	CITY Pg-Grid
68TH AV			**OAK**
1600	FLORA ST	94621	670-G3
69TH AV			**OAK**
3000	FOOTHILL BLVD	94605	670-H2
3300	MACARTHUR BLVD	94605	670-H1
3440	LACEY AV	94605	670-H1
3600	OUTLOOK AV	94605	670-H1
1400	INTERNATIONAL BLVD	94621	670-G3
1600	FLORA ST	94621	670-G3
1700	MORKEN ST	94621	670-G3
2000	WELD ST	94605	670-G2
2000	WELD ST	94621	670-G2
2100	LOCKWOOD ST	94605	670-G2
2200	ARTHUR ST	94605	670-G2
	SAN LEANDRO ST	94621	670-F4
820	SNELL ST	94621	670-F4
870	BRENTFORD ST	94621	670-F3
900	HAWLEY ST	94621	670-F3
1000	SPENCER ST	94621	670-F3
1020	EASTLAWN ST	94621	670-F3
1050	LUCILLE ST	94621	670-F3
1100	HAMILTON ST	94621	670-F3
1300	RUDSDALE ST	94621	670-G3
1400	INTERNATIONAL BLVD	94621	670-G3
70TH AV			**OAK**
1020	INTERNATIONAL BLVD	94621	670-G3
990	FLORA ST	94621	670-G3
940	MORKEN ST	94621	670-G3
890	ORRAL ST	94621	670-G3
840	FAVOR ST	94621	670-G3
800	HOLLY ST	94621	670-G2
840	WELD ST	94621	670-G2
800	SNELL ST	94621	670-F4
900	HAWLEY ST	94621	670-F3
1000	SPENCER ST	94621	670-F3
1100	HAMILTON ST	94621	670-F3
1200	RUDSDALE ST	94621	670-G3
1300	INTERNATIONAL BLVD	94621	670-G3
71ST AV			**OAK**
1400	INTERNATIONAL BLVD	94621	670-G3
980	ORRAL ST	94621	670-G3
800	SNELL ST	94621	670-F4
900	HAWLEY ST	94621	670-F3
1000	SPENCER ST	94621	670-F3
1100	HAMILTON ST	94621	670-G3
1200	RUDSDALE ST	94621	670-G3
1300	INTERNATIONAL BLVD	94621	670-G3
72ND AV			**OAK**
3300	MACARTHUR BLVD	94605	670-J2
3400	NEY AV	94605	670-J2
3400	LACEY AV	94605	670-J2
3500	OUTLOOK AV	94605	670-J2
1400	INTERNATIONAL BLVD	94621	670-G3
1700	ORRAL ST	94621	670-G3
900	HAWLEY ST	94621	670-F4
1000	SPENCER ST	94621	670-F3
1100	HAMILTON ST	94621	670-G3
1200	RUDSDALE ST	94621	670-G3
1300	INTERNATIONAL BLVD	94621	670-G3
73RD AV			**OAK**
1400	INTERNATIONAL BLVD	94621	670-G3
1400	HEGENBERGER EXWY	94621	670-G3
1700	ORRAL ST	94621	670-G3
1800	FAVOR ST	94621	670-G3
1870	HOLLY ST	94621	670-G3
1900	HOLLY ST	94621	670-G3
2000	WELD ST	94621	670-H3
2100	LOCKWOOD ST	94621	670-H3
2110	LOCKWOOD ST	94605	670-H3
2200	ARTHUR ST	94605	670-H2
2230	DEERWOOD AV	94605	670-H2
2300	FRESNO ST	94605	670-H2
2310	FRESNO ST	94605	670-H2
2330	KRAUSE AV	94605	670-H2
3000	HALLIDAY AV	94605	670-H2
2400	HALLIDAY AV	94605	670-H2
	BANCROFT AV	94605	670-H2
2440	BANCROFT AV	94605	670-H2
2600	GARFIELD AV	94605	670-H2
2700	HILLSIDE ST	94605	670-J2
2800	FOOTHILL BLVD	94605	670-J2
2800	MACARTHUR BLVD	94605	670-J2
2900	NEY AV	94605	670-J2
3000	OUTLOOK AV	94605	670-J2
3010	BANTRY AV	94605	670-J1
3100	HILLMONT DR	94605	670-J1
3110	BANTRY AV	94605	670-J1
3110	MAYFIELD PTH	94605	670-J1
3190	SIMSON ST	94605	670-J1
3200	HILLMONT DR	94605	670-J1
1400	INTERNATIONAL BLVD	94621	670-G3
1400	HEGENBERGER EXWY	94621	670-G3
1900	HOLLY ST	94621	670-G3
2000	WELD ST	94621	670-H3
2100	LOCKWOOD ST	94621	670-H3
2200	ARTHUR ST	94605	670-H3
2230	DEERWOOD AV	94605	670-H2
2300	FRESNO ST	94605	670-H2
2330	KRAUSE AV	94605	670-H2
2400	HALLIDAY AV	94605	670-H2
	BANCROFT AV	94605	670-H2
2440	BANCROFT AV	94605	670-H2
2600	GARFIELD AV	94605	670-H2
2700	HILLSIDE ST	94605	670-J2
2800	MACARTHUR BLVD	94605	670-J2
900	HAWLEY ST	94621	670-F4
1000	SPENCER ST	94621	670-F3
1100	HAMILTON ST	94621	670-G3
1200	RUDSDALE ST	94621	670-G3
1300	INTERNATIONAL BLVD	94621	670-G3
74TH AV			**OAK**
2600	GARFIELD AV	94605	670-H2
2700	HILLSIDE ST	94605	670-J2
2800	MACARTHUR BLVD	94605	670-J2
1400	INTERNATIONAL BLVD	94621	670-G3
1900	HOLLY ST	94621	670-G3
75TH AV			**OAK**
3000	OUTLOOK AV	94605	670-J2
3100	HILLMONT DR	94605	670-J2
2800	MACARTHUR BLVD	94605	670-J2
2900	NEY AV	94605	670-J2
3000	OUTLOOK AV	94605	670-J2
	BANCROFT AV	94605	670-H2
2460	BANCROFT AV	94605	670-H2
2600	GARFIELD AV	94605	670-H2
2700	HILLSIDE ST	94605	670-J2
2800	MACARTHUR BLVD	94605	670-J2
	SAN LEANDRO ST	94621	670-F4
850	SNELL ST	94621	670-F4
900	HAWLEY ST	94621	670-F4
1100	SPENCER ST	94621	670-G4
1200	HAMILTON ST	94621	670-G3
1300	RUDSDALE ST	94621	670-G3
1400	INTERNATIONAL BLVD	94621	670-G3
76TH AV			**OAK**
2800	MACARTHUR BLVD	94605	670-J2
2900	NEY AV	94605	670-J2
3000	OUTLOOK AV	94605	670-J2
	BANCROFT AV	94605	670-H2
2500	BANCROFT AV	94605	670-H2
2600	GARFIELD AV	94605	670-J2
2700	HILLSIDE ST	94605	670-J2
2800	MACARTHUR BLVD	94605	670-J2
1400	INTERNATIONAL BLVD	94621	670-G3
1600	HOLLY ST	94621	670-G3
900	HAWLEY ST	94621	670-F4
1000	SPENCER ST	94621	670-G4
1100	HAMILTON ST	94621	670-G4
1200	RUDSDALE ST	94621	670-G3
1400	INTERNATIONAL BLVD	94621	670-G3
800	SAN LEANDRO ST	94621	670-F4
77TH AV			**OAK**
2370	KRAUSE AV	94605	670-H3
2400	HALLIDAY AV	94605	670-H3
	BANCROFT AV	94605	670-H2
2500	BANCROFT AV	94605	670-H2
2600	GARFIELD AV	94605	670-J2
2700	HILLSIDE ST	94605	670-J2
2800	MACARTHUR BLVD	94605	670-J2
1400	INTERNATIONAL BLVD	94621	670-G3
1600	HOLLY ST	94621	670-G3
	SAN LEANDRO ST	94621	670-F4
900	HAWLEY ST	94621	670-F4
1000	SPENCER ST	94621	670-G4
1100	HAMILTON ST	94621	670-G4
1200	RUDSDALE ST	94621	670-G3
1400	INTERNATIONAL BLVD	94621	670-G3
78TH AV			**OAK**
2400	OLIVE ST	94605	670-H3
	BANCROFT AV	94605	670-H3
2500	BANCROFT AV	94605	670-H3
2600	GARFIELD AV	94605	670-J2
2700	HILLSIDE ST	94605	670-J2
2800	MACARTHUR BLVD	94605	670-J2
1400	INTERNATIONAL BLVD	94621	670-G3
1440	LOCUST ST	94621	670-G3
1500	ALDER ST	94621	670-H3
1520	ASH ST	94621	670-H3
1600	HOLLY ST	94621	670 H3
1650	WELD ST	94621	670-H3
1660	WELD ST	94621	670-H3
1700	LOCKWOOD ST	94621	670-H3
1710	LOCKWOOD ST	94621	670-H3
1760	PLYMOUTH ST	94605	670-H3
1760	PLYMOUTH ST	94621	670-H3
1800	ARTHUR ST	94605	670-H3
1800	ARTHUR ST	94621	670-H3
1830	ARTHUR ST	94605	670-H3
1200	RUDSDALE ST	94621	670-G3
1400	INTERNATIONAL BLVD	94621	670-G3
79TH AV			**OAK**
2500	BANCROFT AV	94605	670-J3
2600	GARFIELD AV	94605	670-J3
2700	HILLSIDE ST	94605	670-J2
2900	MACARTHUR BLVD	94605	670-J2
1350	INTERNATIONAL BLVD	94621	670-G3
1400	LOCUST ST	94621	670-H3
1450	ALDER ST	94621	670-H3
1500	ASH ST	94621	670-H3
1550	HOLLY ST	94621	670-H3
1600	WELD ST	94621	670-H3
1650	LOCKWOOD ST	94621	670-H3
1700	PLYMOUTH ST	94621	670-H3
1750	PLYMOUTH ST	94621	670-H3
1800	ARTHUR ST	94605	670-H3
1800	ARTHUR ST	94621	670-H3
1100	RUDSDALE ST	94621	670-G4
1200	RUDSDALE ST	94621	670-G4
1350	INTERNATIONAL BLVD	94621	670-G4
80TH AV			**OAK**
2300	DOWLING CT	94605	670-J3
2400	HILLSIDE ST	94605	670-J3
2450	IRIS ST	94605	670-J3
2500	IDLEWOOD ST	94605	670-J3
2600	MACARTHUR BLVD	94605	670-J3
2200	BANCROFT AV	94605	670-J3
2300	ATHERTON ST	94605	670-J3
2000	OLIVE ST	94605	670-J3
2000	OLIVE ST	94621	670-J3
2200	BANCROFT AV	94605	670-J3
2200	BANCROFT AV	94621	670-J3
1200	RUDSDALE ST	94621	670-G4
1300	B ST	94621	670-G3
1400	INTERNATIONAL BLVD	94621	670-H3
1500	ALDER ST	94621	670-H3
1600	HOLLY ST	94621	670-H3
1700	PLYMOUTH ST	94621	670-H3
81ST AV			**OAK**
2300	DOWLING CT	94605	670-J3
2400	HILLSIDE ST	94605	670-J3
1200	RUDSDALE ST	94621	670-G4
1300	B ST	94621	670-H4
1400	INTERNATIONAL BLVD	94621	670-H4
1600	HOLLY ST	94621	670-H3
1700	PLYMOUTH ST	94621	670-H3
1800	BIRCH ST	94621	670-H3
2000	OLIVE ST	94621	670-J3
	BANCROFT AV	94605	670-J3
2200	BANCROFT AV	94605	670-J3
2300	ATHERTON ST	94605	670-J3
82ND AV			**OAK**
1400	INTERNATIONAL BLVD	94621	670-H4
1600	HOLLY ST	94621	670-H3
1700	PLYMOUTH ST	94621	670-H3
1800	BIRCH ST	94621	670-H3
1990	OLIVE ST	94621	670-J3
2000	OLIVE ST	94621	670-J3
	BANCROFT AV	94605	670-J3
2200	BANCROFT AV	94605	670-J3
2280	DOWLING CT	94605	670-J3
2300	DOWLING ST	94605	670-J3
2400	HILLSIDE ST	94605	670-J3
2450	IRIS ST	94605	670-J3
2500	IDLEWOOD ST	94605	670-J3
2800	MACARTHUR BLVD	94605	670-J3
2680	GOLF LINKS RD	94605	670-J3
2900	NEY AV	94605	671-A3
2930	OUTLOOK AV	94605	671-A3
3050	ASTER AV	94605	671-A2
3150	UTAH ST	94605	671-A2
3500	PARTRIDGE AV	94605	671-A2
3500	SUNKIST DR	94605	671-A2
1050	RUDSDALE ST	94621	670-G4
1100	D ST	94621	670-G4
1230	A ST	94621	670-H4
1400	INTERNATIONAL BLVD	94621	670-H4
83RD AV			**OAK**
2200	MACARTHUR BLVD	94605	670-J3
2290	IRIS ST	94605	670-J3
2200	BANCROFT AV	94605	670-J3
2300	DOWLING ST	94605	670-J3
2400	HILLSIDE ST	94605	670-J3
1400	INTERNATIONAL BLVD	94621	670-H4
1600	HOLLY ST	94621	670-H4
1700	PLYMOUTH ST	94621	670-H3
1800	BIRCH ST	94621	670-J3
2000	OLIVE ST	94621	670-J3
2200	BANCROFT AV	94621	670-J3
1000	E ST	94621	670-G4
1100	D ST	94621	670-G4
1200	B ST	94621	670-H4
1240	A ST	94621	670-H4
1300	A ST	94621	670-H4
1400	INTERNATIONAL BLVD	94621	670-H4
84TH AV			**OAK**
2200	MACARTHUR BLVD	94605	670-J3
2400	IRIS ST	94605	670-J3
2300	DOWLING ST	94605	670-J3
2400	HILLSIDE ST	94605	670-J3
1400	INTERNATIONAL BLVD	94621	670-H4
1600	HOLLY ST	94621	670-H4
1700	PLYMOUTH ST	94621	670-H4
1800	BIRCH ST	94621	670-J3
2000	OLIVE ST	94621	670-J3
	BANCROFT AV	94605	670-J3
2200	BANCROFT AV	94605	670-J3
2300	DOWLING ST	94605	670-J3
800	AMELIA ST	94621	670-G4
1000	E ST	94621	670-G4
1100	D ST	94621	670-G4
1200	B ST	94621	670-H4
1300	A ST	94621	670-H4
1400	INTERNATIONAL BLVD	94621	670-H4
85TH AV			**OAK**
2200	BANCROFT AV	94605	670-J3
2300	DOWLING ST	94605	670-J3
1400	INTERNATIONAL BLVD	94621	670-H4
1600	HOLLY ST	94621	670-H4
1700	PLYMOUTH ST	94621	670-H4
1800	BIRCH ST	94621	670-J4
2000	OLIVE ST	94621	670-J3
2200	BANCROFT AV	94621	670-J3
830	G ST	94621	670-G5
900	G ST	94621	670-G4
1000	E ST	94621	670-G4
1100	D ST	94621	670-H4
1200	B ST	94621	670-H4
1300	A ST	94621	670-H4
1400	INTERNATIONAL BLVD	94621	670-H4
500	EDES AV	94621	670-F6
600	ENTERPRISE WY	94621	670-F5
630	BALDWIN ST	94621	670-F5
630	RAILROAD AV	94621	670-F5
730	SAN LEANDRO ST	94621	670-G5
780	BLAINE ST	94621	670-G5
790	AMELIA ST	94621	670-G5
800	AMELIA ST	94621	670-G5
86TH AV			**OAK**
1400	INTERNATIONAL BLVD	94621	670-H4
1600	HOLLY ST	94621	670-H4
1700	PLYMOUTH ST	94621	670-H4
1800	BIRCH ST	94621	670-J4
2000	OLIVE ST	94621	670-J4
	BANCROFT AV	94605	670-J3
2200	BANCROFT AV	94605	670-J3
2300	DOWLING ST	94605	670-J3
900	G ST	94621	670-G5
1000	E ST	94621	670-G4
1100	D ST	94621	670-H4
1200	B ST	94621	670-H4
1300	A ST	94621	670-H4
1400	INTERNATIONAL BLVD	94621	670-H4
800	BLAINE ST	94621	670-G5
840	AMELIA ST	94621	670-G5
900	G ST	94621	670-G5
87TH AV			**OAK**
2200	BANCROFT AV	94605	670-J4
2270	DOWLING ST	94605	670-J4
2300	DOWLING ST	94605	670-J4
1400	INTERNATIONAL BLVD	94621	670-H4
1600	HOLLY ST	94621	670-H4
1700	PLYMOUTH ST	94621	670-J4
1800	BIRCH ST	94621	670-J4
2000	OLIVE ST	94621	670-J4
2200	BANCROFT AV	94621	670-J4
1000	G ST	94621	670-G5
1000	E ST	94621	670-G5
1100	D ST	94621	670-H4
1200	B ST	94621	670-H4
1300	A ST	94621	670-H4
1400	INTERNATIONAL BLVD	94621	670-H4
88TH AV			**OAK**
2200	MACARTHUR BLVD	94605	671-A3
2300	HILLSIDE ST	94605	671-A3
1400	INTERNATIONAL BLVD	94621	670-H4
1600	HOLLY ST	94621	670-H4
1700	PLYMOUTH ST	94621	670-J4
1800	BIRCH ST	94621	670-J4
2000	OLIVE ST	94621	670-J4
	BANCROFT AV	94605	670-J4
2200	BANCROFT AV	94605	670-J4
2300	DOWLING ST	94605	670-J4
2400	HILLSIDE ST	94605	670-J4
1000	E ST	94621	670-H5
1100	D ST	94621	670-H4
1200	B ST	94621	670-H4
1300	A ST	94621	670-H4
1400	INTERNATIONAL BLVD	94621	670-H4
900	G ST	94621	670-G5
1000	E ST	94621	670-G5
89TH AV			**OAK**
2400	HILLSIDE ST	94605	671-A4
2500	MACARTHUR BLVD	94605	671-A4
2200	BANCROFT AV	94605	670-J4
2300	DOWLING ST	94605	670-J4
1400	INTERNATIONAL BLVD	94621	670-H4
1500	HOLLY ST	94621	670-H4
1700	PLYMOUTH ST	94621	670-J4
1800	BIRCH ST	94621	670-J4
2000	OLIVE ST	94621	670-J4
2200	BANCROFT AV	94621	670-J4
900	G ST	94621	670-G5
1000	E ST	94621	670-H5
1100	D ST	94621	670-H5
1200	B ST	94621	670-H4
1300	A ST	94621	670-H4
1400	INTERNATIONAL BLVD	94621	670-H4
90TH AV			**OAK**
1400	INTERNATIONAL BLVD	94621	670-H4
1400	INTERNATIONAL BLVD	94603	670-H4
1500	HOLLY ST	94621	670-H4
1500	HOLLY ST	94603	670-H4
1520	HOLLY ST	94621	670-H4
1520	HOLLY ST	94603	670-H4
1600	WALNUT ST	94621	670-J4
1600	WALNUT ST	94603	670-J4
1650	PLYMOUTH ST	94621	670-J4
1650	PLYMOUTH ST	94603	670-J4
1700	PLYMOUTH ST	94621	670-J4
1700	PLYMOUTH ST	94603	670-J4
1800	CHERRY ST	94621	670-J4
1800	CHERRY ST	94603	670-J4
1900	BIRCH ST	94621	670-J4
1900	BIRCH ST	94603	670-J4
1910	BIRCH ST	94621	670-J4
1910	BIRCH ST	94603	670-J4
1970	OLIVE ST	94621	670-J4
1970	OLIVE ST	94603	670-J4
2000	OLIVE ST	94621	670-J4
2000	OLIVE ST	94603	670-J4
2100	SUNNYSIDE ST	94621	670-J4
2100	SUNNYSIDE ST	94603	670-J4
	BANCROFT AV	94605	670-J4
	BANCROFT AV	94603	670-J4
2200	BANCROFT AV	94605	670-J4
2200	BANCROFT AV	94603	670-J4
6600	DOWLING ST	94603	671-A4
6600	DOWLING ST	94605	671-A4
2400	HILLSIDE ST	94605	671-A4
2400	HILLSIDE ST	94603	671-A4
	MACARTHUR BLVD	94605	671-A4
2600	THERMAL ST	94605	671-A4
2700	LAWLOR ST	94605	671-A4
	THERMAL ST	94605	671-A4
900	G ST	94621	670-H5
900	G ST	94603	670-H5
1000	E ST	94621	670-H5
1000	E ST	94603	670-H5
1100	D ST	94621	670-H5
1100	D ST	94603	670-H5
1200	B ST	94621	670-H5
1200	B ST	94603	670-H5
1300	A ST	94621	670-H4
1300	A ST	94603	670-H4
1400	INTERNATIONAL BLVD	94621	670-H4
1400	INTERNATIONAL BLVD	94603	670-H4
91ST AV			**OAK**
900	G ST	94603	670-H5
1000	E ST	94603	670-H5
1100	D ST	94603	670-H5
1200	B ST	94603	670-H5
1300	A ST	94603	670-H5
1400	INTERNATIONAL BLVD	94603	670-H5
92ND AV			**OAK**
2200	BANCROFT AV	94603	670-J4
2300	PEACH ST	94603	670-J4
1400	INTERNATIONAL BLVD	94603	670-H5
1500	HOLLY ST	94603	670-J4
1600	WALNUT ST	94603	670-J4
1700	PLYMOUTH ST	94603	670-J4
1800	CHERRY ST	94603	670-J4
1900	BIRCH ST	94603	670-J4
2000	OLIVE ST	94603	670-J4
2100	SUNNYSIDE ST	94603	670-J4
2200	BANCROFT AV	94603	670-J4
900	G ST	94603	670-G5
910	G ST	94603	670-H5
950	F ST	94603	670-H5
1000	E ST	94603	670-H5
1010	E ST	94603	670-H5
1050	D ST	94603	670-H5
1100	D ST	94603	670-H5
1140	C ST	94603	670-H5
1200	B ST	94603	670-H5
1300	A ST	94603	670-H5
1400	INTERNATIONAL BLVD	94603	670-H5
93RD AV			**OAK**
1400	INTERNATIONAL BLVD	94603	670-H5
1200	B ST	94603	670-H5
1300	A ST	94603	670-H5
1400	INTERNATIONAL BLVD	94603	670-H5
94TH AV			**OAK**
1200	B ST	94603	670-H5
1300	A ST	94603	670-H5
1400	INTERNATIONAL BLVD	94603	670-H5
1500	HOLLY ST	94603	670-J5
1600	WALNUT ST	94603	670-J5
1700	PLYMOUTH ST	94603	670-J5
1800	CHERRY ST	94603	670-J4
1900	BIRCH ST	94603	670-J4
2000	OLIVE ST	94603	670-J4
2100	SUNNYSIDE ST	94603	670-J4
	BANCROFT AV	94603	670-J4
	BANCROFT AV	94603	670-J4
	STEARNS AV	94603	670-J4
1000	E ST	94603	670-H5
95TH AV			**OAK**
1200	B ST	94603	670-H5
1300	A ST	94603	670-H5
1400	INTERNATIONAL BLVD	94603	670-H5
96TH AV			**OAK**
1200	B ST	94603	670-H5
1300	A ST	94603	670-J5
1400	INTERNATIONAL BLVD	94603	670-J5
1500	HOLLY ST	94603	670-J5
1600	WALNUT ST	94603	670-J5
1700	PLYMOUTH ST	94603	670-J5
1800	CHERRY ST	94603	670-J5
1900	BIRCH ST	94603	670-J5
2000	OLIVE ST	94603	670-J5
1470	SUNNYSIDE ST	94603	671-A4
2180	BANCROFT AV	94603	671-A4
2200	BANCROFT AV	94603	671-A4
2300	PEACH ST	94603	671-A4
2400	HILLSIDE ST	94605	671-A4
2400	HILLSIDE ST	94603	671-A4
2500	MACARTHUR BLVD	94605	671-A4
2500	MACARTHUR BLVD	94603	671-A4
97TH AV			**OAK**
1200	B ST	94603	670-H5
1300	A ST	94603	670-J5
1400	INTERNATIONAL BLVD	94603	670-J5
98TH AV			**OAK**
100	AIRPORT DR	94603	670-F7
120	KITTY LN	94603	670-F7
130	KITTY LN	94603	670-F7
160	BIGGE AV	94603	670-F7
220	EMPIRE RD	94603	670-F7
400	DENSLOWE AV	94603	670-G7
500	MADDUX DR	94603	670-G6
510	MADDUX DR	94603	670-G6
530	CARY CT	94603	670-G6
560	LYNDHURST ST	94603	670-G6
600	EDES AV	94603	670-G6
700	WALTER AV	94603	670-G6
780	RAILROAD AV	94603	670-G6
840	PEARMAIN ST	94603	670-H6
870	PIPPIN ST	94603	670-H6
	RUSSET ST	94603	670-H6
	SAN LEANDRO ST	94603	670-H6
940	MEDFORD AV	94603	670-H6
960	GOULD ST	94603	670-H6
1000	E ST	94603	670-H6
1030	E ST	94603	670-H6
1100	D ST	94603	670-H5
1150	C ST	94603	670-H5
1200	B ST	94603	670-H5
1250	A ST	94603	670-H5
1300	A ST	94603	670-J5
1400	INTERNATIONAL BLVD	94603	670-J5
1500	HOLLY ST	94603	670-J5
1600	WALNUT ST	94603	670-J5
1700	PLYMOUTH ST	94603	670-J5
1800	CHERRY ST	94603	670-J5
1900	BIRCH ST	94603	670-J5
220	OLIVE ST	94603	671-A5
2100	SUNNYSIDE ST	94603	671-A5
2180	BANCROFT AV	94603	671-A5
2200	BANCROFT AV	94603	671-A5
2300	SPRINGFIELD ST	94603	671-A5

CROSS STREET INDEX - ALA, ALB, BERK, EMVL, OAK & PDMT

Address	Cross Street	ZIP	Pg-Grid
98TH AV			**OAK**
2400	ELMVIEW DR	94603	671-A5
2420	ELMAR AV	94603	671-A4
2470	HILLGRADE CT	94603	671-A4
2500	MACARTHUR BLVD	94605	671-A4
2550	THERMAL ST	94605	671-A4
2600	LAWLOR ST	94605	671-A4
2650	BURR ST	94605	671-A4
2700	CHEROKEE AV	94605	671-A4
2710	STEARNS AV	94605	671-A4
2720	STEARNS AV	94605	671-B4
2800	STANLEY AV	94605	671-B4
2870	FARRELL ST	94605	671-B4
2960	LAS VEGAS AV	94605	671-B4
3000	GOLF LINKS RD	94605	671-B4
99TH AV			**OAK**
2500	MACARTHUR BLVD	94605	671-A5
2550	THERMAL ST	94605	671-A5
2600	LAWLOR ST	94605	671-A5
2650	BURR ST	94605	671-B5
2800	STEARNS AV	94605	671-B5
2900	STANLEY AV	94605	671-B5
2200	BANCROFT AV	94603	671-A5
2240	DANTE AV	94603	671-A5
2270	TOLER AV	94603	671-A5
2300	LONGFELLOW AV	94603	671-A5
2330	ELMAR AV	94603	671-A5
2350	VOLTAIRE AV	94603	671-A5
2400	MACARTHUR BLVD	94603	671-A5
1700	PLYMOUTH ST	94603	670-J5
1800	CHERRY ST	94603	670-J5
1700	BIRCH ST	94603	671-A5
2000	OLIVE ST	94603	671-A5
2100	SUNNYSIDE ST	94603	671-A5
2200	BANCROFT AV	94603	671-A5
1500	HOLLY ST	94603	670-J5
1600	100TH AV	94603	670-J5
1300	99TH AV CT	94603	670-J5
1400	INTERNATIONAL BLVD	94603	670-J5
99TH AV CT			**OAK**
9900	99TH AV	94603	670-J5
100TH AV			**OAK**
1400	INTERNATIONAL BLVD	94603	670-J5
1500	99TH AV	94603	670-J5
1600	WALNUT ST	94603	670-J5
1700	PLYMOUTH ST	94603	670-J5
1800	CHERRY ST	94603	670-J5
1360	BIRCH ST	94603	671-A5
2000	OLIVE ST	94603	671-A5
2100	SUNNYSIDE ST	94603	671-A5
	BANCROFT AV	94603	671-A5
2200	BANCROFT AV	94603	671-A5
2250	DANTE AV	94603	671-A5
2300	LONGFELLOW AV	94603	671-A5
2350	VOLTAIRE AV	94603	671-A5
2400	MACARTHUR BLVD	94603	671-A5
900	E ST	94603	670-H6
1000	D ST	94603	670-H6
1100	ROYAL ANN ST	94603	670-H6
1100	C ST	94603	670-H6
1200	B ST	94603	670-J6
1300	A ST	94603	670-J6
1400	INTERNATIONAL BLVD	94603	670-J6
800	PEARMAIN ST	94603	670-H6
850	PIPPIN ST	94603	670-H6
900	RUSSET ST	94603	670-H6
101ST AV			**OAK**
1400	INTERNATIONAL BLVD	94603	670-J5
1600	WALNUT ST	94603	670-J5
1430	PLYMOUTH ST	94603	670-J5
1900	BIRCH ST	94603	671-A5
2100	SUNNYSIDE ST	94603	671-A5
2200	BANCROFT AV	94603	671-A5
1000	E ST	94603	670-H6
1200	ROYAL ANN ST	94603	670-H6
102ND AV			**OAK**
1400	INTERNATIONAL BLVD	94603	670-J6
1390	WALNUT ST	94603	670-J5
1240	PLYMOUTH ST	94603	671-A5
1900	BIRCH ST	94603	671-A5
2100	SUNNYSIDE ST	94603	671-A5
2200	BANCROFT AV	94603	671-A5
1000	E ST	94603	670-H6
1200	ROYAL ANN ST	94603	670-J6
1300	GRAFFIAN ST	94603	670-J6
1400	INTERNATIONAL BLVD	94603	670-J6
103RD AV			**OAK**
1400	INTERNATIONAL BLVD	94603	670-J6
1910	WALNUT ST	94603	670-J6
1690	PLYMOUTH ST	94603	671-A6
1900	BIRCH ST	94603	671-A5
2100	SUNNYSIDE ST	94603	671-A5
2200	BANCROFT AV	94603	671-A5
2210	BANCROFT AV	94603	671-A5
2250	DANTE AV	94603	671-A5
2300	LONGFELLOW AV	94603	671-A5
2350	VOLTAIRE AV	94603	671-A5
2400	BYRON ST	94603	671-A5
1000	E ST	94603	670-H6
1200	ROYAL ANN ST	94603	670-J6
1300	GRAFFIAN ST	94603	670-J6
1400	INTERNATIONAL BLVD	94603	670-J6
104TH AV			**OAK**
2100	LINK ST	94603	671-A5
1400	INTERNATIONAL BLVD	94603	670-J6
1600	WALNUT ST	94603	670-J6
1350	PLYMOUTH ST	94603	671-A6
1900	BIRCH ST	94603	671-A6
2100	LINK ST	94603	671-A6
2100	SUNNYSIDE ST	94603	671-A6
1000	E ST	94603	670-H6
1200	ROYAL ANN ST	94603	670-J6
1300	GRAFFIAN ST	94603	670-J6
1360	PONTIAC ST	94603	670-J6
1400	INTERNATIONAL BLVD	94603	670-J6
105TH AV			**OAK**
1800	BREED AV	94603	671-A6
1880	BIRCH ST	94603	671-A6
2000	BEVERLY AV	94603	671-A6
2100	SUNNYSIDE ST	94603	671-A6
2200	LINK ST	94603	671-A6
1400	INTERNATIONAL BLVD	94603	670-J6
	RUSSET ST	94603	670-H6
	GRAVENSTEIN ST	94603	670-H6
920	SAN LEANDRO ST	94603	670-H6
1000	E ST	94603	670-J6
1200	ROYAL ANN ST	94603	670-J6
1300	GRAFFIAN ST	94603	670-J6
1360	PONTIAC ST	94603	670-J6
1400	INTERNATIONAL BLVD	94603	670-J6
10030	CREEKSIDE CIR	94603	670-G7
350	EAST CT	94603	670-G7
370	WEST CT	94603	670-G7
380	TOPANGA DR	94603	670-H7
400	KNIGHT ST	94603	670-H7
470	NATTRESS WY	94603	670-H7
540	JUNE CT	94603	670-H7
570	PATRICIA CT	94603	670-H7
600	ACALANES DR	94603	670-H7
700	EDES AV	94603	670-H7

Address	Cross Street	ZIP	Pg-Grid
800	PEARMAIN ST	94603	670-H6
900	GRAVENSTEIN ST	94603	670-H6
106TH AV			**OAK**
1800	BREED AV	94603	671-A6
2000	BEVERLY AV	94603	671-A6
2100	SUNNYSIDE ST	94603	671-A6
	BANCROFT AV	94603	671-A6
	LINK ST	94603	671-A6
2200	BANCROFT AV	94603	671-A6
2230	DANTE AV	94603	671-A6
2270	LONGFELLOW AV	94603	671-A6
2300	VOLTAIRE AV	94603	671-A6
2400	BYRON ST	94603	671-B5
2500	MACARTHUR BLVD	94605	671-B5
2820	FOOTHILL BLVD	94605	671-B5
2920	PERALTA OAKS DR	94605	671-B5
3000	LEEWARD WY	94605	671-B5
900	SAN LEANDRO ST	94603	670-H6
1000	E ST	94603	670-J6
1200	ROYAL ANN ST	94603	670-J6
1300	GRAFFIAN ST	94603	670-J6
1360	PONTIAC ST	94603	670-J6
1400	INTERNATIONAL BLVD	94603	670-J6
800	PEARMAIN ST	94603	670-H7
107TH AV			**OAK**
2900	PERALTA OAKS DR	94605	671-B5
3000	SHELDON ST	94605	671-B5
1800	BREED AV	94603	671-A6
2000	BEVERLY AV	94603	671-A6
2100	SUNNYSIDE ST	94603	671-A6
2200	BANCROFT AV	94603	671-A6
2350	VOLTAIRE AV	94603	671-B6
2500	MYERS ST	94603	671-B6
2600	MACARTHUR BLVD	94603	671-B6
900	SAN LEANDRO ST	94603	670-H6
990	APRICOT ST	94603	670-J6
1000	E ST	94603	670-J6
1200	ROYAL ANN ST	94603	670-J6
1300	GRAFFIAN ST	94603	670-J6
1360	PONTIAC ST	94603	670-J6
1400	INTERNATIONAL BLVD	94603	670-J6
800	PEARMAIN ST	94603	670-H7
850	PIPPIN ST	94603	670-H7
900	RUSSET ST	94603	670-H7
800	PEARMAIN ST	94603	670-H7
108TH AV			**OAK**
1800	BREED AV	94603	671-A6
2000	BEVERLY AV	94603	671-A6
2100	SUNNYSIDE ST	94603	671-A6
2200	BANCROFT AV	94603	671-A6
2350	VOLTAIRE AV	94603	671-B6
2500	MYERS ST	94603	671-B6
2600	MACARTHUR BLVD	94605	671-B5
2700	MCINTYRE ST	94605	671-B5
2800	JULIUS ST	94605	671-B5
2900	FOOTHILL BLVD	94605	671-B5
109TH AV			**OAK**
1800	BREED AV	94603	671-A6
2000	BEVERLY AV	94603	671-A6
2100	SUNNYSIDE ST	94603	671-A6
2200	BANCROFT AV	94603	671-A6
2350	VOLTAIRE AV	94603	671-B6
2500	MYERS ST	94603	671-B6
2600	MACARTHUR BLVD	94605	671-B6
2700	MCINTYRE ST	94605	671-B6

The Thomas Guide®

Thank you for purchasing this Rand McNally Thomas Guide! We value your comments and suggestions.

Please help us serve you better by completing this postage-paid reply card.
This information is for internal use ONLY and will not be distributed or sold to any external third party.

Missing pages? Maybe not... Please refer to the "Using Your Street Guide" page for further explanation.

Thomas Guide Title: Alameda County   ISBN# 0-528-85526-3   Edition: 2006   MKT: SFB

Today's Date: _____   Gender: ☐M ☐F   Age Group: ☐18-24 ☐25-31 ☐32-40 ☐41-50 ☐51-64 ☐65+

1. What type of industry do you work in?
   ☐Real Estate   ☐Trucking   ☐Delivery   ☐Construction   ☐Utilities   ☐Government
   ☐Retail   ☐Sales   ☐Transportation   ☐Landscape   ☐Service & Repair
   ☐Courier   ☐Automotive   ☐Insurance   ☐Medical   ☐Police/Fire/First Response
   ☐Other, please specify: _____

2. What type of job do you have in this industry?_____

3. Where did you purchase this Thomas Guide? (store name & city) _____

4. Why did you purchase this Thomas Guide? _____

5. How often do you purchase an updated Thomas Guide?   ☐Annually   ☐2 yrs.   ☐3-5 yrs.   ☐Other: _____

6. Where do you use it?   ☐Primarily in the car   ☐Primarily in the office   ☐Primarily at home   ☐Other: _____

7. How do you use it?   ☐Exclusively for business   ☐Primarily for business but also for personal or leisure use
   ☐Both work and personal evenly   ☐Primarily for personal use   ☐Exclusively for personal use

8. What do you use your Thomas Guide for?
   ☐Find Addresses   ☐In-route navigation   ☐Planning routes   ☐Other: _____
   Find points of interest: ☐Schools   ☐Parks   ☐Buildings   ☐Shopping Centers   ☐Other:_____

9. How often do you use it?   ☐Daily   ☐Weekly   ☐Monthly   ☐Other: _____

10. Do you use the internet for maps and/or directions?   ☐Yes   ☐No

11. How often do you use the internet for directions?   ☐Daily   ☐Weekly   ☐Monthly   ☐Other:_____

12. Do you use any of the following mapping products in addition to your Thomas Guide?
    ☐Folded paper maps   ☐Folded laminated maps   ☐Wall maps   ☐GPS   ☐PDA   ☐In-car navigation   ☐Phone maps

13. What features, if any, would you like to see added to your Thomas Guide? _____
    _____

14. What features or information do you find most useful in your Rand McNally Thomas Guide? (please specify)
    _____
    _____

15. Please provide any additional comments or suggestions you have. _____
    _____
    _____

We strive to provide you with the most current updated information available if you know of a map correction, please notify us here.

Where is the correction?   Map Page #:_____   Grid #:_____   Index Page #:_____

Nature of the correction: ☐Street name missing   ☐Street name misspelled   ☐Street information incorrect
    ☐Incorrect location for point of interest   ☐Index error   ☐Other: _____

Detail: _____

I would like to receive information about updated editions and special offers from Rand McNally
   ☐via e-mail   E-mail address: _____
   ☐via postal mail
   Your Name: _____   Company (if used for work): _____
   Address: _____   City/State/ZIP: _____

Thank you for your time and help. We are working to serve you better.
This information is for internal use ONLY and will not be distributed or sold to any external third party.

CUT ALONG DOTTED LINE

TG-noCD.06

TAPE SHUT   TAPE SHUT

CUT ALONG DOTTED LINE

2ND FOLD LINE

1ST FOLD LINE

CUT ALONG DOTTED LINE

SGTG.06

The Thomas Guide®

Contra Costa County
street guide

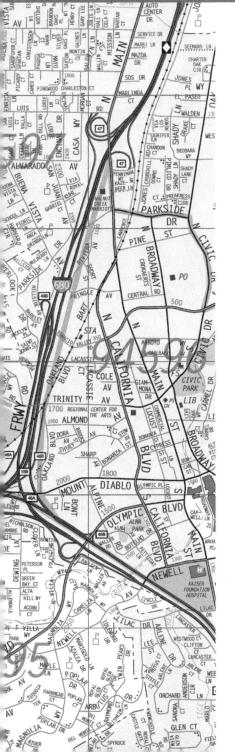

Contents

Introduction

Using Your Street Guide   A
PageFinder™ Map   B
Legend   D

Maps

Airport Map   E
Downtown Map   F
Freeway Access Map   G
Street Guide Detail Maps   549-694
Vicinity Map   Inside back cover

Lists and Indexes

Cities & Communities Index   695
List of Abbreviations   696
Street Index   697
Points of Interest Index   737

Comment Card   Last page

RAND M̱NALLY
Rand McNally Consumer Affairs
P.O. Box 7600
Chicago, IL 60680-9915
randmcnally.com

For comments or suggestions, please call
(800) 777-MAPS (-6277)
or email us at:
consumeraffairs@randmcnally.com

Legend

Freeway	
Interchange/ramp	
Highway	
Primary road	
Secondary road	
Minor road	
Restricted road	
Alley	
Unpaved road	
Tunnel	
Toll road	
High occupancy vehicle lane	
Stacked multiple roadways	
Proposed road	
Proposed freeway	
Freeway under construction	
One-way road	
Two-way road	
Trail, walkway	
Stairs	
Railroad	
Rapid transit	
Rapid transit, underground	

Ferry	
City boundary	
County boundary	
State boundary	
International boundary	
Military base, Indian reservation	
Township, range, rancho	
River, creek, shoreline	
ZIP code boundary, ZIP code	98607
Interstate	5
Interstate (Business)	5
U.S. highway	3
State highways	1 4 8 9
Carpool lane	
Street list marker	
Street name continuation	
Street name change	
Station (train, bus)	
Building (see List of Abbreviations page)	
Building footprint	
Public elementary school	
Public high school	

Private elementary school	
Private high school	
Fire station	
Library	
Mission	
Winery	
Campground	
Hospital	H
Mountain	
Section corner	
Boat launch	
Gate, locks, barricades	
Lighthouse	
Major shopping center	
Dry lake, beach	
Dam	
Intermittent lake, marsh	
Exit number	29
Caltrain Station	Caltrain
Golden Gate Transit	

Oakland International Airport (OAK)

Oakland International Airport is located approximately seven miles from Downtown Oakland and 15 miles from Downtown San Francisco, with easy freeway access to parking, flights and baggage. Southwest Airlines' flights depart from Terminal 2. All other airlines, including international flights, depart from Terminal 1. Parking rates in the lots located across from the terminals are $2.00 per 30 minutes, with a maximum of $32 per day in the Hourly Lot; $22 per day in the Daily A & B Lots; and $19 per day in the Economy lot (subject to change). Parking shuttles run every 10–15 minutes. For more information, visit oaklandairport.com.

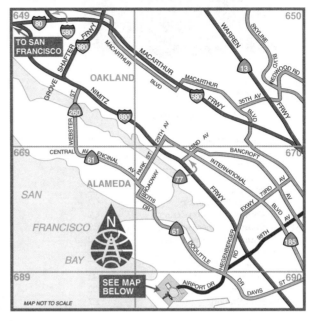

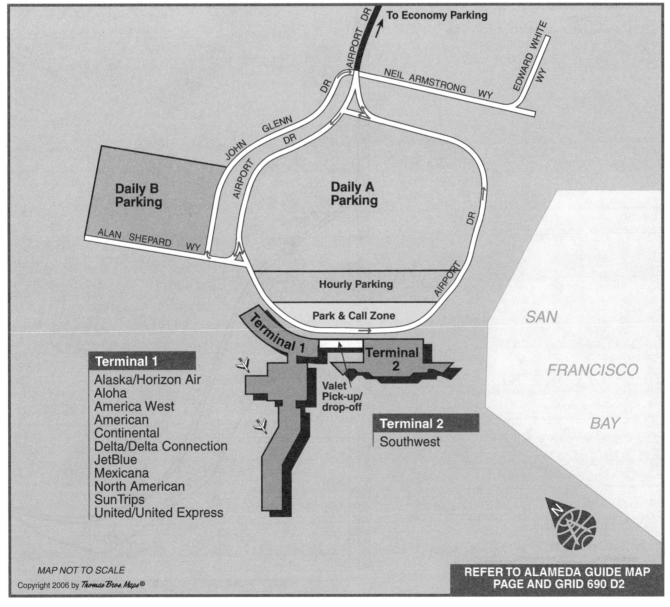

Daily B Parking

Daily A Parking

To Economy Parking

NEIL ARMSTRONG WY

EDWARD WHITE WY

JOHN GLENN DR

AIRPORT DR

ALAN SHEPARD WY

Hourly Parking

Park & Call Zone

Terminal 1

Alaska/Horizon Air
Aloha
America West
American
Continental
Delta/Delta Connection
JetBlue
Mexicana
North American
SunTrips
United/United Express

Valet Pick-up/drop-off

Terminal 2
Southwest

SAN FRANCISCO BAY

MAP NOT TO SCALE
Copyright 2006 by Thomas Bros. Maps®

REFER TO ALAMEDA GUIDE MAP PAGE AND GRID 690 D2

CONTRA COSTA

Downtown Martinez

Points of Interest

1 Amtrak Station — C2
2 Contra Costa Regional Medical Center — C4
3 County Administration Building — C2
4 County Courthouse — C2
5 County Detention Center — C2
6 County Finance Building — C2
7 County Health Building — C2
8 County Library — C2
9 John Muir National Historic Site — C7
10 Martinez City Hall — C3
11 Martinez Museum — C2
12 Muir Station — E7
13 Post Office — C2
14 Superior Courthouse — C2
15 Tourist Bureau — C2
16 Veterans Affairs Medical Center — E6

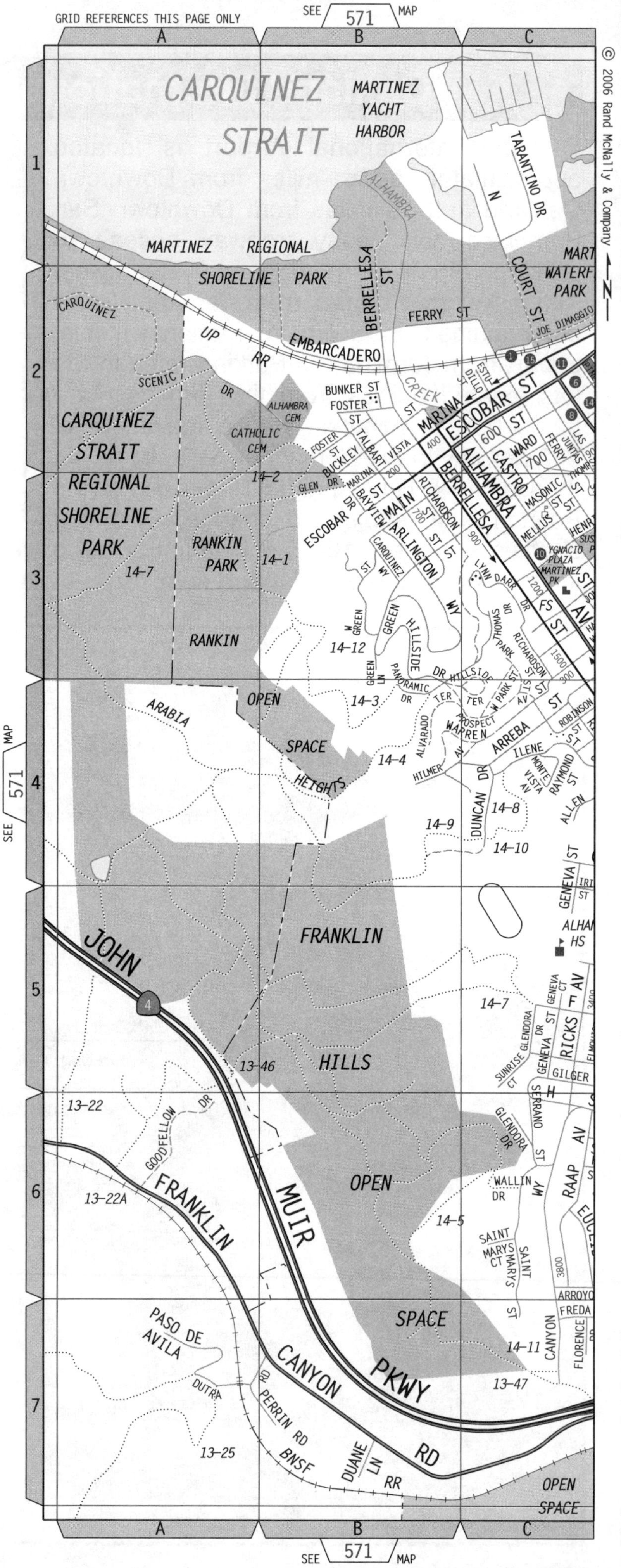

Map Scale

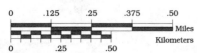

© 2006 Rand McNally & Company

SEE 571 MAP

GRID REFERENCES THIS PAGE ONLY

CARQUINEZ STRAIT

MARTINEZ YACHT HARBOR

MARTINEZ REGIONAL SHORELINE PARK

CARQUINEZ STRAIT REGIONAL SHORELINE PARK

RANKIN PARK

RANKIN

OPEN SPACE HEIGHTS

FRANKLIN HILLS

OPEN SPACE

JOHN MUIR PKWY

FRANKLIN CANYON RD

PASO DE AVILA

OPEN SPACE

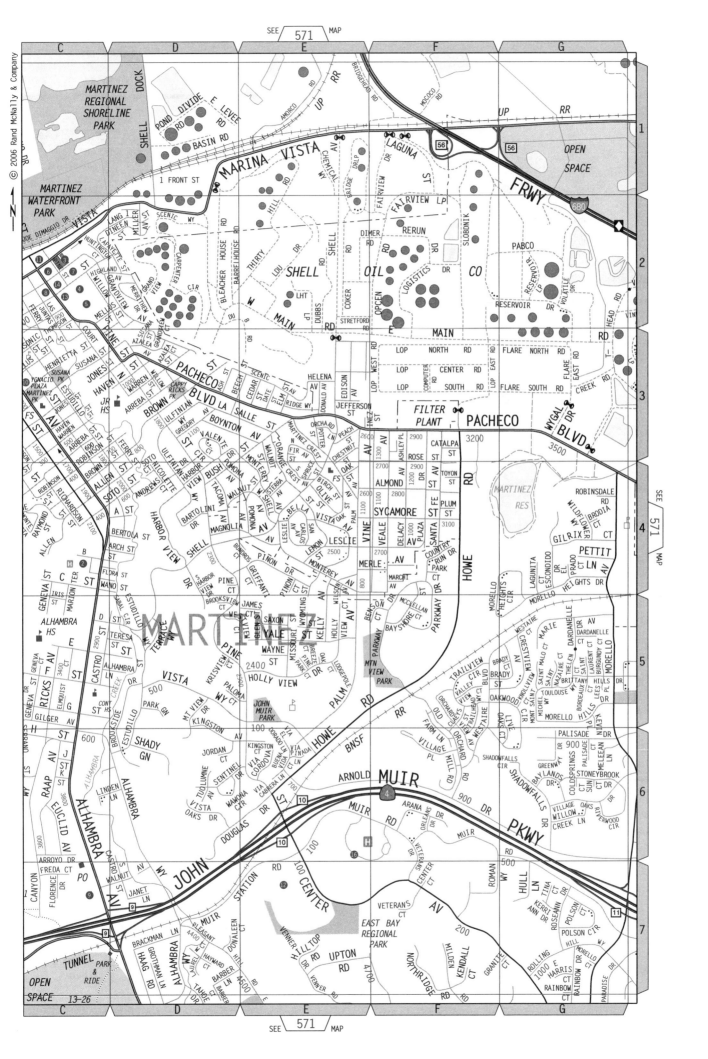

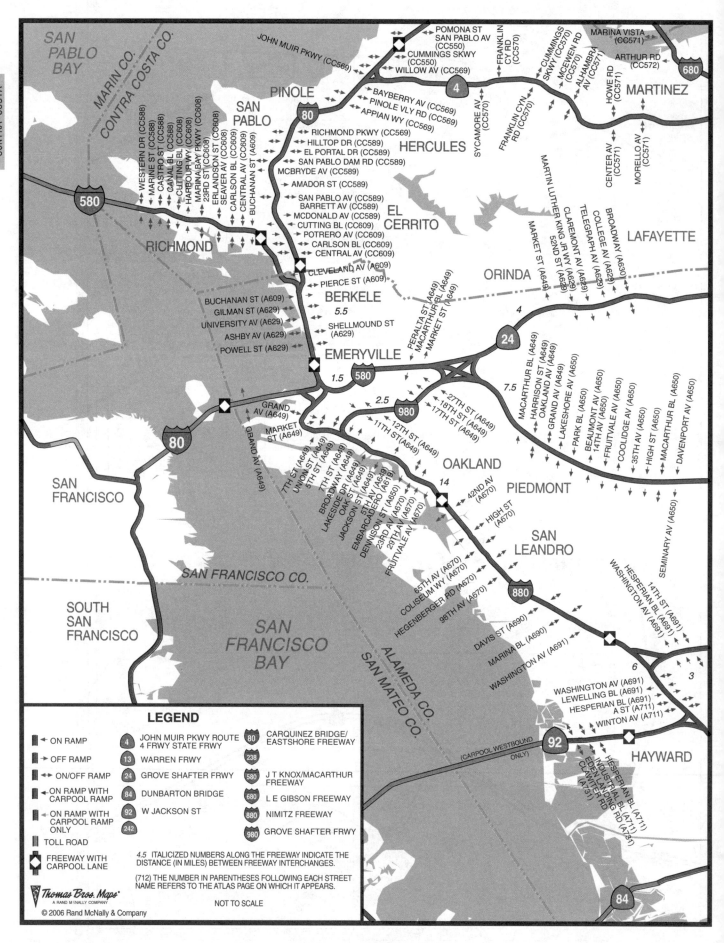

CONTRA COSTA

SAN
PABLO
BAY

MARIN CO.
CONTRA COSTA CO.

JOHN MUIR PKWY (CC569)

POMONA ST
SAN PABLO AV
(CC550)
CUMMINGS SKWY
(CC550)
WILLOW AV (CC569)

FRANKLIN
CY RD (CC570)
CUMMINGS
SKWY (CC570)
MCEWEN RD
(CC570)
ALHAMBRA
AV (CC571)

MARINA VISTA
(CC571)
ARTHUR RD
(CC572)

680

PINOLE

SAN
PABLO

80

BAYBERRY AV (CC569)
PINOLE VLY RD (CC569)
APPIAN WY (CC569)

4

SYCAMORE AV
(CC570)
FRANKLIN CYN
RD (CC570)

MARTINEZ

HOWE RD
(CC571)

CENTER AV
(CC571)

MORELLO AV
(CC571)

RICHMOND PKWY (CC569)
HILLTOP DR (CC589)
EL PORTAL DR (CC589)
SAN PABLO DAM RD (CC589)
MCBRYDE AV (CC589)

HERCULES

WESTERN DR (CC588)
MARINE ST (CC588)
CASTRO ST (CC588)
CANAL BL (CC608)
CUTTING BL (CC608)
HARBOUR WY (CC608)
MARINA BAY PKWY (CC608)
23RD ST (CC608)
ERLANDSON ST (CC608)
SEAVER AV (CC608)
CARLSON BL (CC609)
CENTRAL AV (CC609)
BUCHANAN ST (A609)

AMADOR ST (CC589)

SAN PABLO AV (CC589)
BARRETT AV (CC589)
MCDONALD AV (CC589)
CUTTING BL (CC609)
POTRERO AV (CC609)
CARLSON BL (CC609)
CENTRAL AV (CC609)

EL
CERRITO

LAFAYETTE

580

RICHMOND

CLEVELAND AV (A609)
PIERCE ST (A609)

ORINDA

MARKET ST (A649)
PERALTA ST (A649)
MACARTHUR BL (A649)
MARKET ST (A649)

MARTIN LUTHER KING JR WY (A629)
CLAREMONT AV (A629)
52ND ST (A629)
COLLEGE AV (A629)
TELEGRAPH AV (A629)
BROADWAY (A630)

BUCHANAN ST (A609)
GILMAN ST (A629)
UNIVERSITY AV (A629)
ASHBY AV (A629)
POWELL ST (A629)

BERKELE

5.5

SHELLMOUND ST
(A629)

4

24

7.5

MACARTHUR BL (A649)
HARRISON ST (A649)
OAKLAND AV (A649)
GRAND AV (A649)
LAKESHORE AV (A650)
PARK BL (A650)
BEAUMONT AV (A650)
14TH AV (A650)
FRUITVALE AV (A650)
COOLIDGE AV (A650)
35TH AV (A650)
HIGH ST (A650)
MACARTHUR BL (A650)
DAVENPORT AV (A650)

EMERYVILLE

1.5

580

2.5

980

27TH ST (A649)
18TH ST (A649)
17TH ST (A649)

GRAND
AV (A649)

MARKET
ST (A649)

12TH ST (A649)
11TH ST (A649)

OAKLAND

SAN
FRANCISCO

80

GRAND AV (A649)

7TH ST (A649)
UNION ST (A649)
5TH ST (A649)
7TH ST (A649)
BROADWAY (A649)
LAKESIDE DR (A649)
OAK ST (A649)
JACKSON ST (A649)
5TH AV (A649)
EMBARCADERO (A619)
DENNISON ST (A670)
23RD AV (A670)
29TH AV (A670)
FRUITVALE AV (A670)

14

42ND AV
(A670)

PIEDMONT

HIGH ST
(A670)

SAN
LEANDRO

14TH ST (A691)
SEMINARY AV (A650)
HESPERIAN AV (A691)
WASHINGTON AV (A691)

SAN FRANCISCO CO.

65TH AV (A670)
COLISEUM WY (A670)
HEGENBERGER RD (A670)
98TH AV (A670)

880

SOUTH
SAN
FRANCISCO

DAVIS ST (A690)
MARINA BL (A690)

WASHINGTON AV (A691)

6

3

SAN
FRANCISCO
BAY

ALAMEDA CO.
SAN MATEO CO.

WASHINGTON AV (A691)
LEWELLING BL (A691)
HESPERIAN BL (A691)
A ST (A711)
WINTON AV (A711)

92

(CARPOOL WESTBOUND ONLY)

HAYWARD

HESPERIAN BL (A711)
INDUSTRIAL BL (A711)
EDEN LANDING RD (A731)
CLAWITER RD (A731)

84

LEGEND

→ ON RAMP
→ OFF RAMP
↔ ON/OFF RAMP
→ ON RAMP WITH CARPOOL RAMP
→ ON RAMP WITH CARPOOL RAMP ONLY
TOLL ROAD
◆ FREEWAY WITH CARPOOL LANE

4 JOHN MUIR PKWY ROUTE 4 FRWY STATE FRWY
13 WARREN FRWY
24 GROVE SHAFTER FRWY
84 DUNBARTON BRIDGE
92 W JACKSON ST
242

80 CARQUINEZ BRIDGE/ EASTSHORE FREEWAY
238
580 J T KNOX/MACARTHUR FREEWAY
680 L E GIBSON FREEWAY
880 NIMITZ FREEWAY
980 GROVE SHAFTER FRWY

4.5 ITALICIZED NUMBERS ALONG THE FREEWAY INDICATE THE DISTANCE (IN MILES) BETWEEN FREEWAY INTERCHANGES.

(712) THE NUMBER IN PARENTHESES FOLLOWING EACH STREET NAME REFERS TO THE ATLAS PAGE ON WHICH IT APPEARS.

NOT TO SCALE

Thomas Bros. Maps
A RAND McNALLY COMPANY
© 2006 Rand McNally & Company

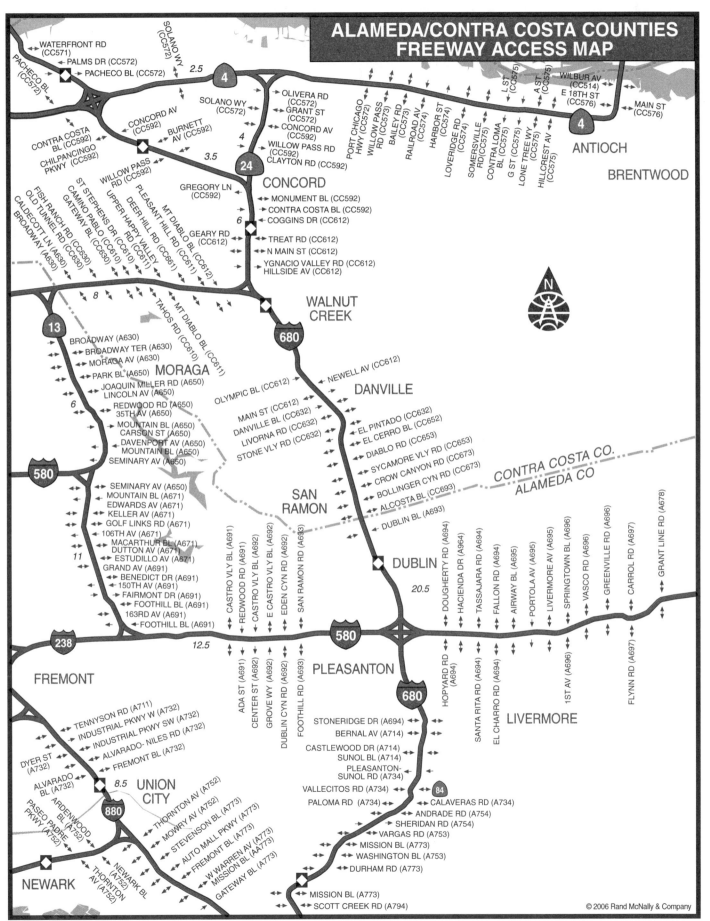

ALAMEDA/CONTRA COSTA COUNTIES FREEWAY ACCESS MAP

WATERFRONT RD (CC571)

SOLANO WY (CC572)

PALMS DR (CC572)

PACHECO BL (CC572)

PACHECO BL (CC572)

4

2.5

OLIVERA RD (CC572)

GRANT ST (CC572)

SOLANO WY (CC572)

CONCORD AV (CC572)

PORT CHICAGO HWY (CC572)

WILLOW PASS RD (CC573)

BAILEY RD (CC573)

RAILROAD AV (CC573)

HARBOR ST (CC574)

LOVERIDGE RD (CC574)

SOMERSVILLE RD(CC575)

CONTRA LOMA BL (CC575)

G ST (CC575)

LONE TREE WY (CC575)

HILLCREST AV (CC575)

L ST (CC575)

A ST (CC575)

WILBUR AV (CC514)

E 18TH ST (CC576)

MAIN ST (CC576)

4

ANTIOCH

BRENTWOOD

CONCORD AV (CC592)

CONTRA COSTA BL (CC592)

CHILPANCINGO PKWY (CC592)

BURNETT AV (CC592)

4

3.5

WILLOW PASS RD (CC592)

CONCORD AV (CC592)

WILLOW PASS RD (CC592)

CLAYTON RD (CC592)

24

6

CONCORD

GREGORY LN (CC592)

MONUMENT BL (CC592)

CONTRA COSTA BL (CC592)

COGGINS DR (CC612)

TREAT RD (CC612)

N MAIN ST (CC612)

YGNACIO VALLEY RD (CC612)

HILLSIDE AV (CC612)

FISH RANCH RD (CC630)

OLD TUNNEL RD (CC630)

CALDECOTT LN (A630)

BROADWAY (A630)

ST STEPHENS DR (CC630)

CAMINO PABLO (CC610)

GATEWAY BL (CC630)

WILLOW PASS RD (CC592)

UPPER HAPPY VALLEY RD (CC611)

DEER HILL RD (CC610)

PLEASANT HILL RD (CC611)

MT DIABLO BL (CC612)

GEARY RD (CC612)

8

13

TAHOS RD (CC610)

MT DIABLO BL (CC611)

WALNUT CREEK

680

BROADWAY (A630)

BROADWAY TER (A630)

MORAGA AV (A630)

PARK BL (A650)

JOAQUIN MILLER RD (A650)

LINCOLN AV (A650)

REDWOOD RD (A650)

35TH AV (A650)

MOUNTAIN BL (A650)

CARSON ST (A650)

DAVENPORT AV (A650)

MOUNTAIN BL (A650)

SEMINARY AV (A650)

MORAGA

6

OLYMPIC BL (CC612)

MAIN ST (CC612)

DANVILLE BL (CC632)

LIVORNA RD (CC632)

STONE VLY RD (CC632)

NEWELL AV (CC612)

DANVILLE

EL PINTADO (CC632)

EL CERRO BL (CC652)

DIABLO RD (CC653)

SYCAMORE VLY RD (CC673)

CROW CANYON RD (CC673)

BOLLINGER CYN RD (CC673)

ALCOSTA BL (CC693)

CONTRA COSTA CO.

ALAMEDA CO

580

SEMINARY AV (A650)

MOUNTAIN BL (A671)

EDWARDS AV (A671)

KELLER AV (A671)

GOLF LINKS RD (A671)

106TH AV (A671)

MACARTHUR BL (A671)

DUTTON AV (A671)

ESTUDILLO AV (A671)

GRAND AV (A691)

BENEDICT DR (A691)

150TH AV (A691)

FAIRMONT DR (A691)

FOOTHILL BL (A691)

163RD AV (A691)

FOOTHILL BL (A691)

11

SAN RAMON

DUBLIN BL (A693)

DUBLIN

20.5

DOUGHERTY RD (A694)

HACIENDA DR (A964)

TASSAJARA RD (A694)

FALLON RD (A694)

AIRWAY BL (A695)

PORTOLA AV (A695)

LIVERMORE AV (A695)

SPRINGTOWN BL (A696)

VASCO RD (A696)

GREENVILLE RD (A696)

CARROL RD (A697)

GRANT LINE RD (A678)

CASTRO VLY BL (A691)

REDWOOD RD (A692)

CASTRO VLY BL (A692)

E CASTRO VLY BL (A692)

EDEN CYN RD (A692)

SAN RAMON RD (A693)

238

12.5

580

680

FREMONT

ADA ST (A691)

CENTER ST (A692)

GROVE WY (A692)

DUBLIN CYN RD (A692)

FOOTHILL RD (A693)

PLEASANTON

HOPYARD RD (A694)

SANTA RITA RD (A694)

EL CHARRO RD (A694)

1ST AV (A696)

FLYNN RD (A697)

LIVERMORE

STONERIDGE DR (A694)

BERNAL AV (A714)

CASTLEWOOD DR (A714)

SUNOL BL (A714)

PLEASANTON-SUNOL RD (A734)

VALLECITOS RD (A734)

PALOMA RD (A734)

84

CALAVERAS RD (A734)

ANDRADE RD (A754)

SHERIDAN RD (A754)

VARGAS RD (A753)

MISSION BL (A773)

WASHINGTON BL (A753)

DURHAM RD (A773)

TENNYSON RD (A711)

INDUSTRIAL PKWY W (A732)

INDUSTRIAL PKWY SW (A732)

INDUSTRIAL PKWY (A732)

ALVARADO- NILES RD (A732)

FREMONT BL (A732)

DYER ST (A732)

ALVARADO BL (A732)

ARDENWOOD BL (A732)

PASEO PADRE PKWY (A752)

880

8.5

UNION CITY

THORNTON AV (A752)

MOWRY AV (A752)

STEVENSON BL (A773)

AUTO MALL PKWY (A773)

FREMONT BL (A773)

W WARREN AV (A773)

MISSION BL (AA773)

GATEWAY BL (A773)

MISSION BL (A773)

SCOTT CREEK RD (A794)

NEWARK BL (A752)

THORNTON AV (A752)

NEWARK

© 2006 Rand McNally & Company

549

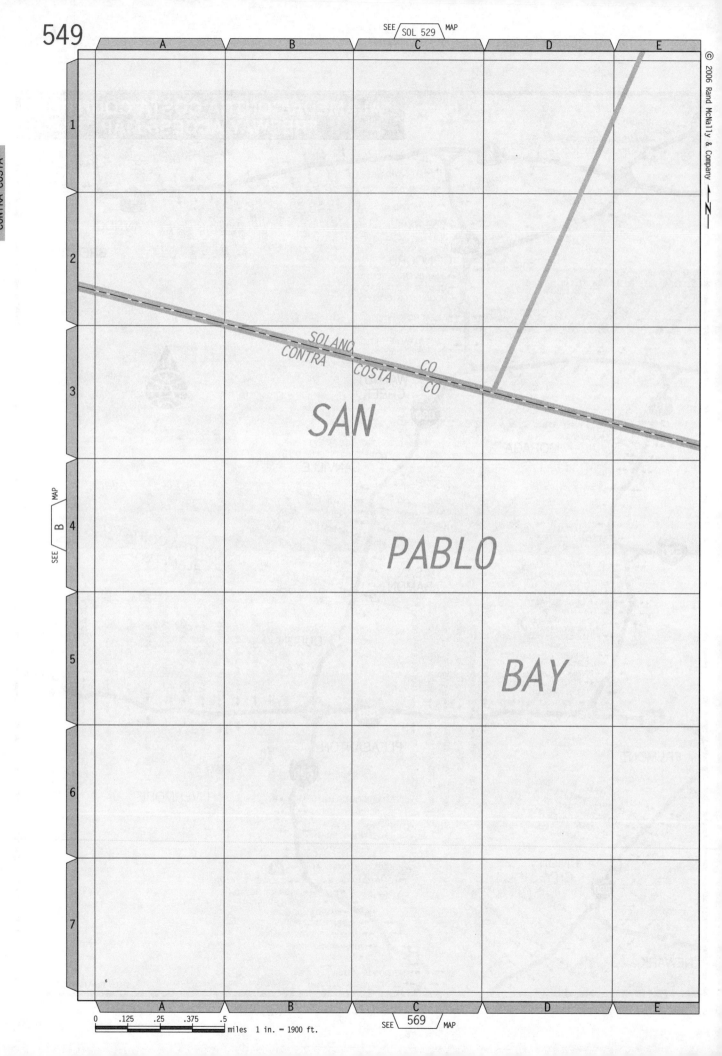

CONTRA COSTA

© 2006 Rand McNally & Company

SEE SOL 529 MAP

SEE B MAP

A B C D E

1

2

3

SOLANO
CONTRA COSTA CO
CO

SAN

4

PABLO

5

BAY

6

7

0 .125 .25 .375 .5 miles 1 in. = 1900 ft.

SEE 569 MAP

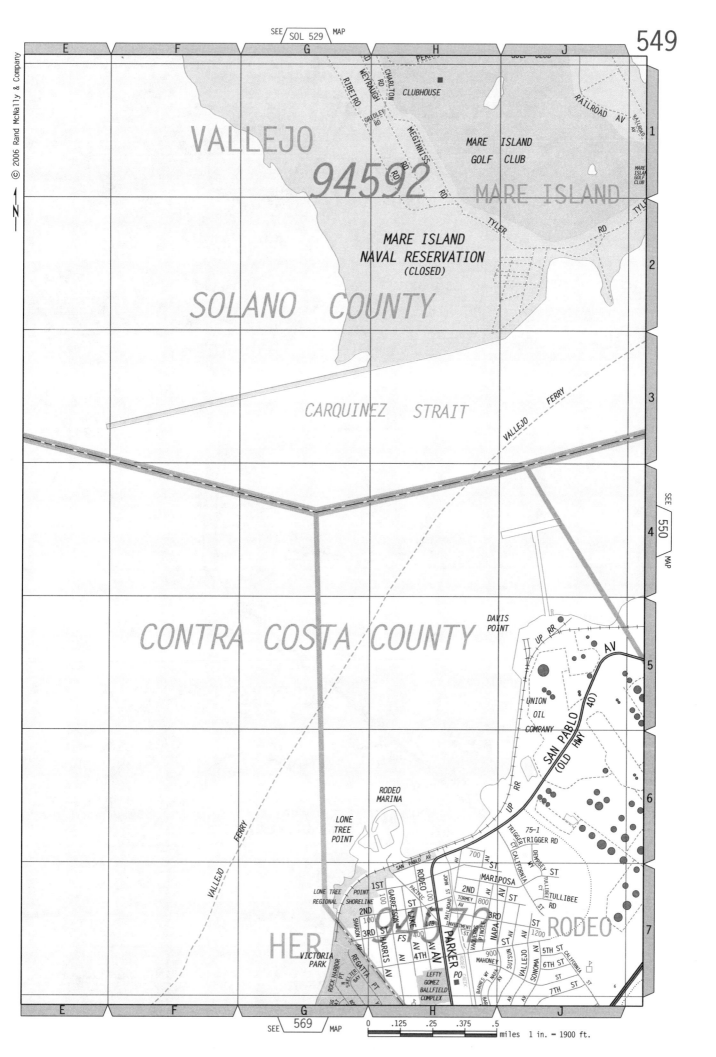

CONTRA COSTA

SEE SOL 529 MAP

E　　F　　G　　H　　J

VALLEJO
94592

CLUBHOUSE

MARE ISLAND
GOLF CLUB

MARE ISLAND

MARE ISLAND
NAVAL RESERVATION
(CLOSED)

SOLANO COUNTY

CARQUINEZ STRAIT

VALLEJO FERRY

SEE 550 MAP

CONTRA COSTA COUNTY

DAVIS POINT

UP RR

AV

UNION OIL COMPANY

SAN PABLO HWY (OLD HWY 40)

UP RR

RODEO MARINA

LONE TREE POINT

75-1

TRIGGER CT TRIGGER RD

CALIFORNIA

DEMPSEY ST

TULLIBEE RD

VALLEJO FERRY

LONE TREE POINT REGIONAL SHORELINE

1ST

2ND

3RD

VICTORIA PARK

SHARON

REGATTA PT

N SHELTER BAY

ROCK HARBOR

SAN PABLO AV

RODEO

PACIFIC

GARRETSON

ST

LANE

JOHN ST

700

ST

MARIPOSA

2ND

TORMEY AV

800

AV

AV

ST

ST

3RD

ST

TULLIBEE

ST

HER

94572

RODEO

PARKER

LIB

FS

400

HARRIS AV

4TH

AV

SHARON

INVESTMENT ST

VAQUEROS

PINOLE

NAPA

3RD

ST

1200

SUTSUN

SONOMA

5TH ST

CALIFORNIA

900

MAHONEY

LEFTY GOMEZ BALLFIELD COMPLEX

PO

BARNES WY

VALLEJO

SONOMA

6TH ST

7TH ST

E　　F　　G　　H　　J

SEE 569 MAP

0 .125 .25 .375 .5
miles   1 in. = 1900 ft.

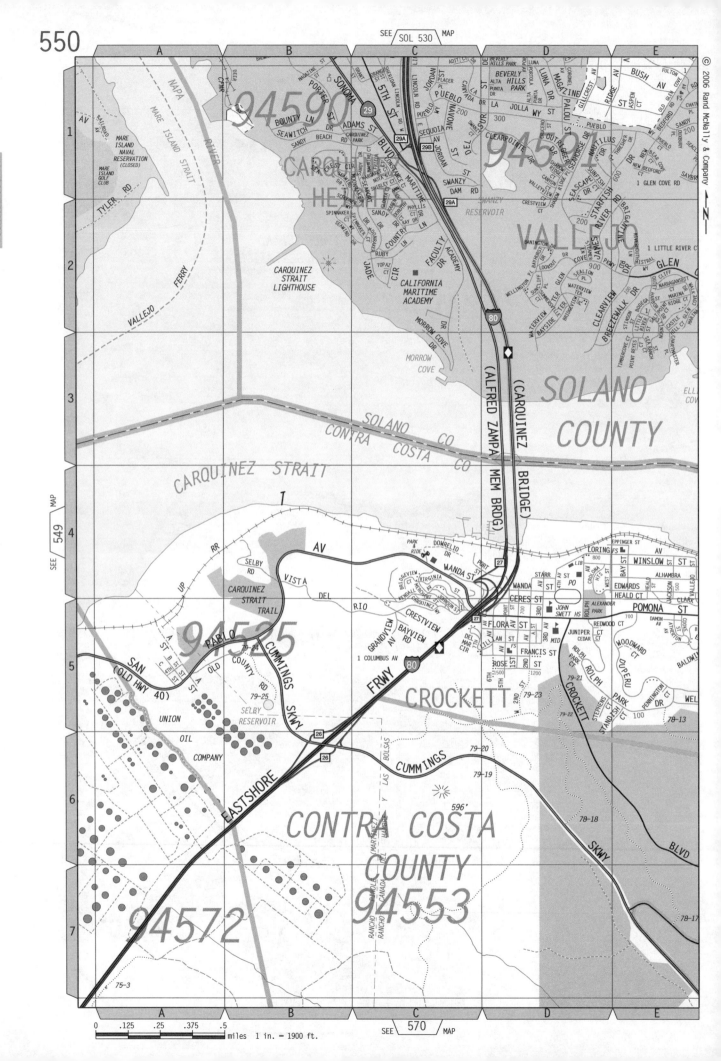

CONTRA COSTA

© 2006 Rand McNally & Company

94590

94591

CARQUINEZ HEIGHTS

VALLEJO

SOLANO COUNTY

SOLANO CO
CONTRA COSTA CO

CARQUINEZ STRAIT

SEE 549 MAP

94525

CROCKETT

CONTRA COSTA COUNTY

94553

94572

MARE ISLAND NAVAL RESERVATION (CLOSED)

MARE ISLAND GOLF CLUB

CALIFORNIA MARITIME ACADEMY

CARQUINEZ STRAIT LIGHTHOUSE

MORROW COVE

(ALFRED ZAMPA MEM BRDG)

(CARQUINEZ BRIDGE)

UNION OIL COMPANY

SELBY RESERVOIR

CARQUINEZ STRAIT TRAIL

596'

0   .125   .25   .375   .5
miles 1 in. = 1900 ft.

SEE 570 MAP

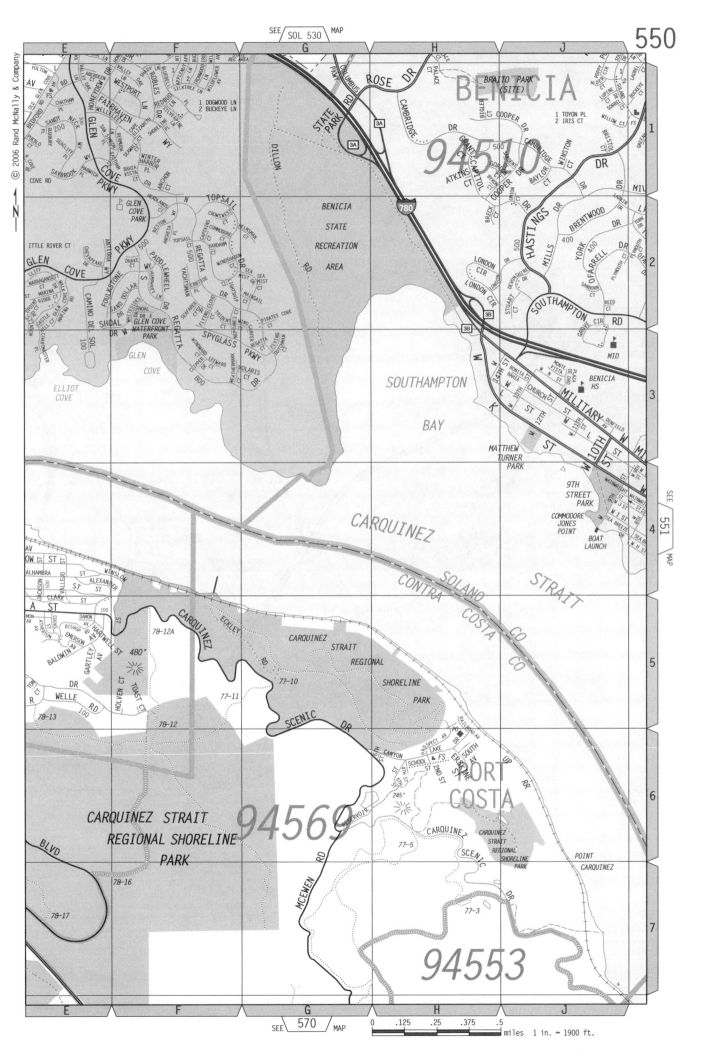

CONTRA COSTA

© 2006 Rand McNally & Company

N

SEE SOL 530 MAP

BENICIA

94510

1 DOGWOOD LN
2 BUCKEYE LN

1 TOYON PL
2 IRIS CT

BENICIA
STATE
RECREATION
AREA

GLEN COVE PARK

GLEN COVE PKWY

LITTLE RIVER CT

GLEN
COVE

ELLIOT
COVE

GLEN COVE WATERFRONT PARK

SPYGLASS

TOPSAIL

SOUTHAMPTON

BAY

MATTHEW TURNER PARK

9TH STREET PARK

COMMODORE JONES POINT

BOAT LAUNCH

BENICIA HS

MID

CARQUINEZ STRAIT

CONTRA COSTA CO

SOLANO CO

ALHAMBRA

WINSLOW

ALEXANDER

CLARK ST

A ST

WELLE RD

CARQUINEZ

ECKLEY RD

SCENIC DR

CARQUINEZ STRAIT REGIONAL SHORELINE PARK

77-10
77-11
78-12A
78-12
78-13
480'
100

CARQUINEZ STRAIT
REGIONAL SHORELINE
PARK

94569

BLVD

78-16

78-17

MCEWEN RD

RESERVOIR

245'

PORT COSTA

SCHOOL FS

CARQUINEZ SCENIC DR

77-5

CARQUINEZ STRAIT REGIONAL SHORELINE PARK

POINT CARQUINEZ

77-3

94553

SEE 551 MAP

SEE 570 MAP

0   .125   .25   .375   .5
miles   1 in. = 1900 ft.

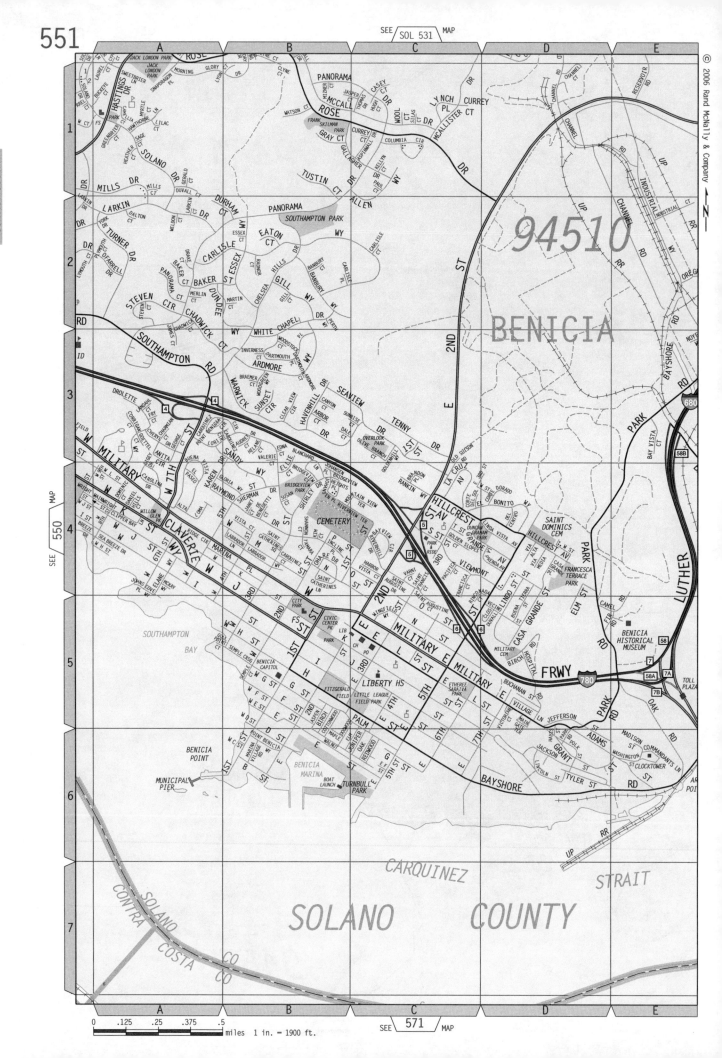

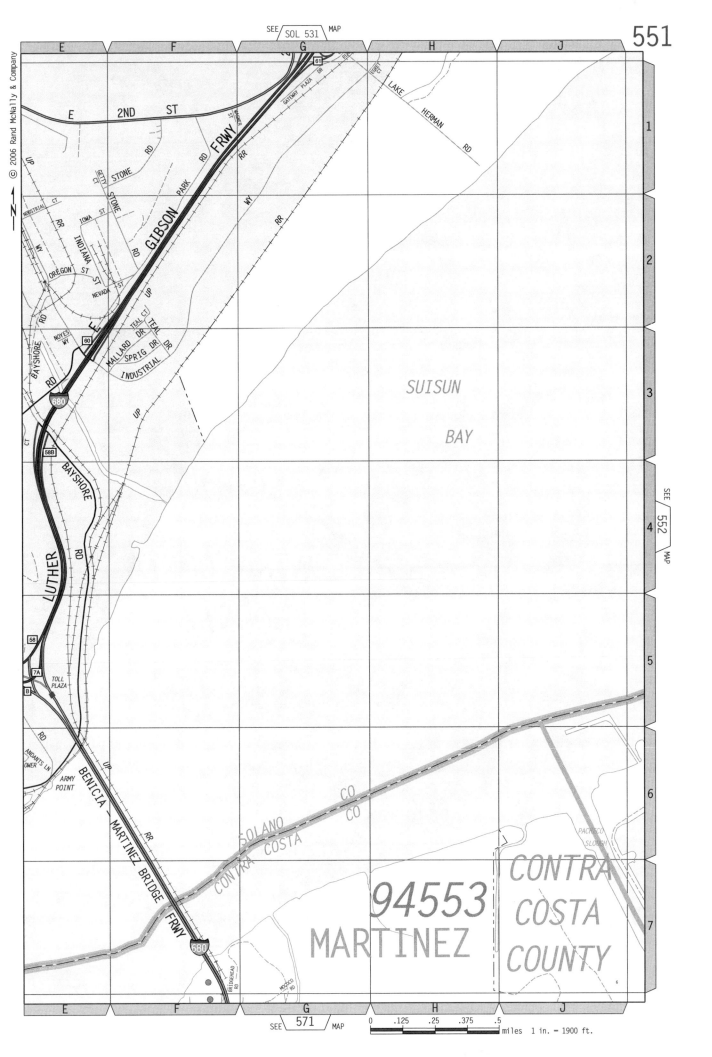

E   F   G   H   J

© 2006 Rand McNally & Company

E   2ND   ST

1

2

SUISUN

3

BAY

SEE 552 MAP

4

5

6

GIBSON FRWY

GATEWAY PLAZA DR

LAKE HERMAN RD

STONE RD

GETTY CT

STONE

IOWA ST

INDIANA ST

OREGON ST

NEVADA ST

INDUSTRIAL CT

RR WY

UP

BAYSHORE RD

NOYES WY

MALLARD DR

TEAL CT

TEAL DR

SPRIG DR

INDUSTRIAL

BAYSHORE

LUTHER RD

TOLL PLAZA

RD

ANDANT'S LN

OWER

ARMY POINT

BENICIA — MARTINEZ BRIDGE FRWY

UP

RR

BRIDGEHEAD RD

MODOCO RD

SOLANO CO

CONTRA COSTA

CO CO

PACHECO SLOUGH

94553
MARTINEZ

CONTRA COSTA COUNTY

0   .125   .25   .375   .5

miles 1 in. = 1900 ft.

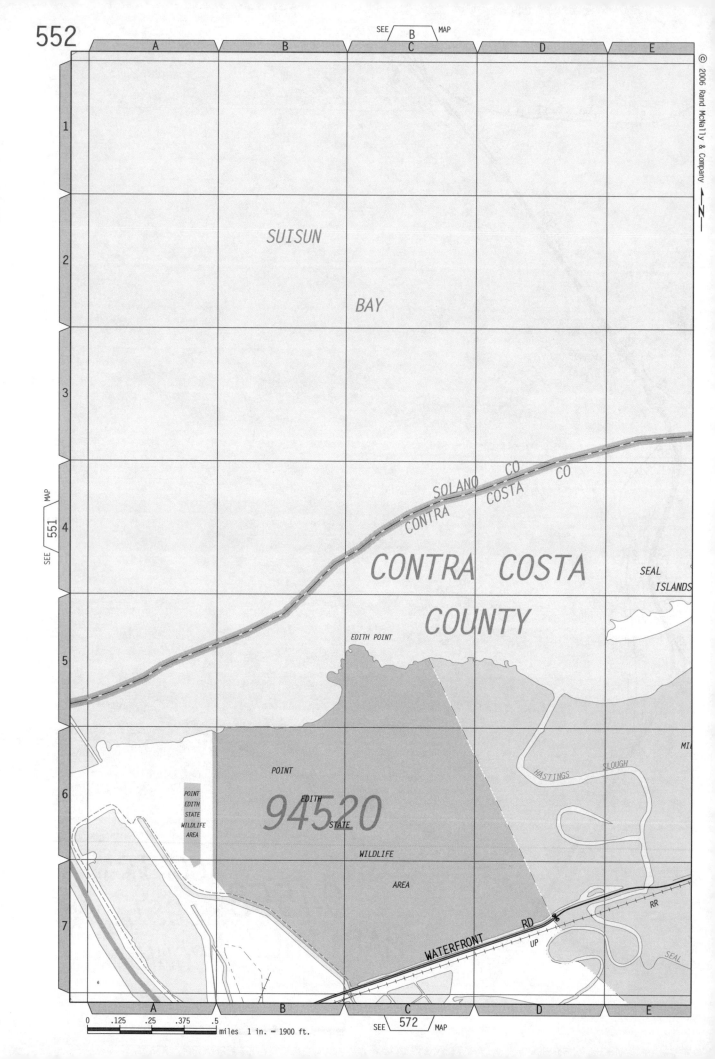

CONTRA COSTA

SEE B MAP

A | B | C | D | E

1

SUISUN

2

BAY

3

SEE 551 MAP

4

SOLANO CO

CONTRA COSTA CO

CONTRA COSTA

COUNTY

SEAL
ISLANDS

EDITH POINT

5

POINT

POINT
EDITH
STATE
WILDLIFE
AREA

EDITH

94520

STATE

HASTINGS SLOUGH

MI

6

WILDLIFE

AREA

SEAL

7

RR

WATERFRONT RD

UP

A | B | C | D | E

SEE 572 MAP

0   .125   .25   .375   .5
miles 1 in. = 1900 ft.

CONTRA COSTA

© 2006 Rand McNally & Company

N

SEE B MAP

E   F   G   H   J

SOLANO COUNTY

RYER ISLAND

1

ROE ISLAND

2

3

SEE 553 MAP

4

AL ISLANDS

SEAL BLUFF LANDING

5

FS

MILITARY

OCEAN

TERMINAL

CONCORD

RR UP

BNSF RR

UP RR

RR

UP RR

RD

WATERFRONT

BNSF RR

RR

UP

MAIN ST

COAST GUARD STATION

PORT CHICAGO HWY

18-3

94565

RR

SEAL CREEK

CANAL

CONTRA COSTA

6

7

E   F   G   H   J

SEE 572 MAP

0   .125   .25   .375   .5
miles 1 in. = 1900 ft.

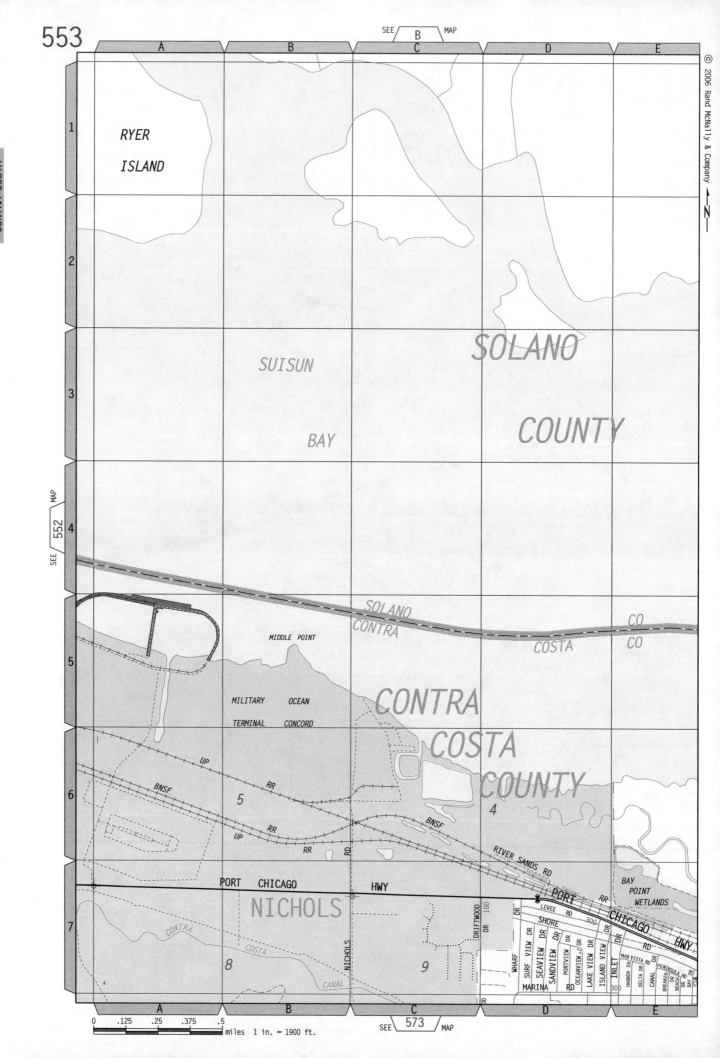

CONTRA COSTA

© 2006 Rand McNally & Company

N

SEE B MAP

A   B   C   D   E

1

RYER

ISLAND

2

SOLANO

SUISUN

COUNTY

3

BAY

SEE MAP 552

4

SOLANO
CONTRA

CO
CO

COSTA

MIDDLE POINT

CONTRA

5

MILITARY   OCEAN

Costa

TERMINAL   CONCORD

COUNTY

UP

BNSF

RR

5

4

6

BNSF

RR

UP

RR

RD

RIVER SANDS RD

BAY
POINT
WETLANDS

PORT CHICAGO HWY

PORT

DRIFTWOOD DR 100

NICHOLS

CHICAGO

LEVEE RD

RR

300

HWY

SHORE DR

RD

CONTRA

NICHOLS

DRIFTWOOD DR

DR

7

COSTA

WHARF DR

SURF VIEW DR

SEAVIEW DR

SANDVIEW DR

PORTVIEW DR

OCEANVIEW DR

LAKE VIEW DR

ISLAND VIEW DR

INLET DR

MAR VISTA RD

DELTA DR

CANAL

PENINSULA RD

BREAKER DR

BEACH DR

BAY DR

8

9

MARINA

RD

300

CANAL

6

A   B   C   D   E

SEE 573 MAP

0   .125   .25   .375   .5

miles 1 in. = 1900 ft.

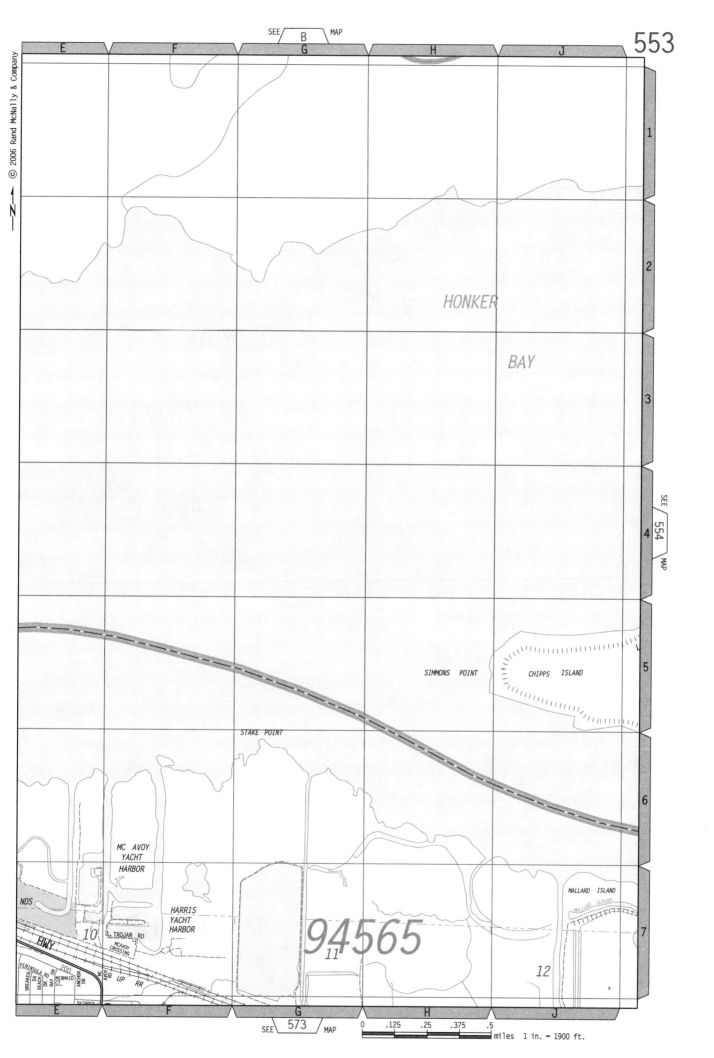

CONTRA COSTA

—N—→

E   F   G   H   J

SEE / B \ MAP

1

2

HONKER

BAY

3

SEE / 554 \ MAP

4

SIMMONS   POINT   CHIPPS   ISLAND

5

STAKE POINT

6

MC AVOY
YACHT
HARBOR

MALLARD   ISLAND

MALLARD SLOUGH

HARRIS
YACHT
HARBOR

NDS

7

94565

10   TROJAN RD
MCAVOY
CROSSING

11

12

HWY

PENINSULA DR
BREAKERS DR
BEACH RD
BAY DR
MERMAID CT.
ANCHOR DR
MC AVOY RD
UP   RR
200

SKIPPER

6

E   F   G   H   J

SEE \ 573 / MAP

0   .125   .25   .375   .5
miles 1 in. = 1900 ft.

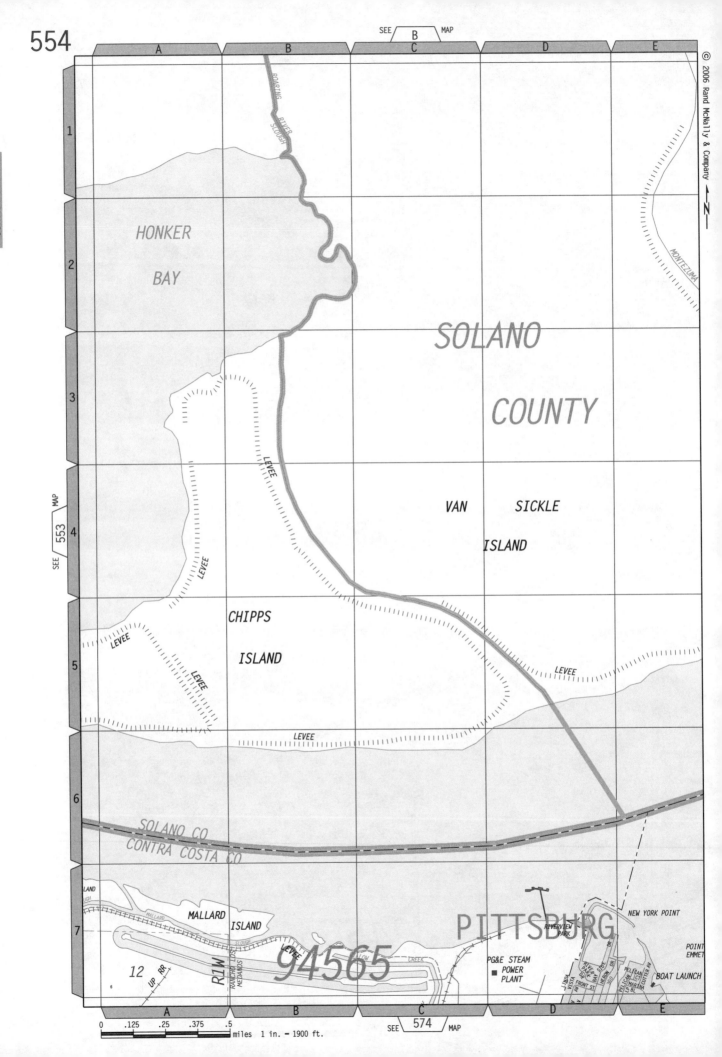

CONTRA COSTA

SEE B MAP

A   B   C   D   E

1

HONKER

BAY

2

SOLANO

COUNTY

MONTEZUMA

3

LEVEE

VAN   SICKLE

ISLAND

SEE 553 MAP

4

LEVEE

LEVEE

CHIPPS

ISLAND

LEVEE

5

LEVEE

LEVEE   LEVEE

6

SOLANO CO

CONTRA COSTA CO

NEW YORK POINT

ISLAND

MALLARD   ISLAND

MALLARD

RANCHO LOS MEDANOS

SLOUGH

PITTSBURG

RIVERVIEW PARK

POINT
EMMET

7

12   UP RR

R1W

LEVEE

94565

CREEK

PG&E STEAM
■ POWER
PLANT

LINDA
VISTA
FRONT ST
3RD
RIVERSIDE DR

BOAT LAUNCH

PELICAN
MARINA
EDITERRA AV

A   B   C   D   E

SEE 574 MAP

0   .125   .25   .375   .5

■ miles 1 in. = 1900 ft.

CONTRA COSTA

SEE B MAP

E F G H J

1

21

22

COLLINSVILLE

STRATTON LN

RD

2

MONTEZUMA

3

SLOUGH

LEVEE

RIVER

SOLANO CO

SACRAMENTO CO

SACRAMENTO

SACRAMENTO

COUNTY

SACRAMENTO CO

CONTRA COSTA CO

SEE SAC 493 MAP

4

SAN

5

JOAQUIN

6

WINTER

LEVEE

ISLAND

RIVER

MIDDLE

LEVEE

CONTRA COSTA

COUNTY

SLOUGH

POINT

BROWNS ISLAND

REGIONAL

SHORELINE

BROWNS ISLAND

POINT

EMMET

7

OAT LAUNCH

E F G H J

SEE 574 MAP

0 .125 .25 .375 .5 miles 1 in. = 1900 ft.

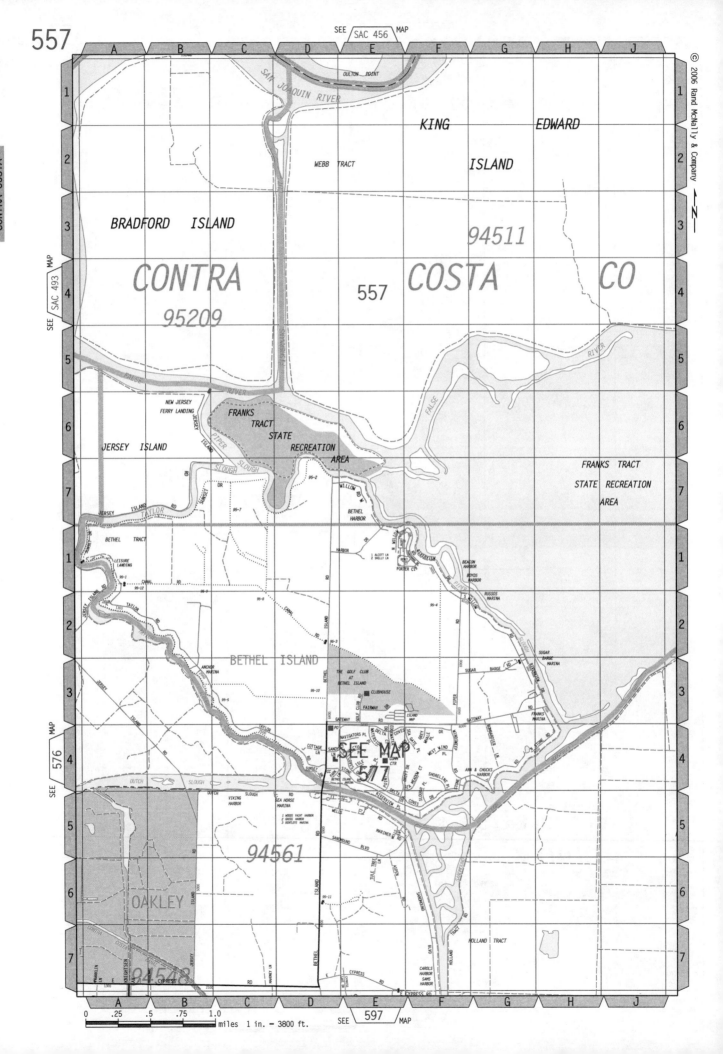

557

CONTRA COSTA

SEE SAC 456 MAP

A B C D E F G H J

OULTON POINT

SAN JOAQUIN RIVER

KING   EDWARD

WEBB TRACT

ISLAND

BRADFORD   ISLAND

94511

CONTRA   COSTA   CO

95209   557

SEE SAC 493 MAP

FALSE   RIVER

RIVER

FALSE

NEW JERSEY
FERRY LANDING

FRANKS
TRACT
STATE
RECREATION
AREA

JERSEY ISLAND

PIPER   SLOUGH

SLOUGH

JERSEY

ISLAND

95-2

WILLOW RD W

FRANKS   TRACT

STATE RECREATION

AREA

DR

SUNSET

TAYLOR   RD

95-7

BETHEL
HARBOR

JERSEY   ISLAND   RD

DR

WILLOW

HARBOR

1 ALCOTT LN
2 SHELLY LN

RIVERVIEW

BERT
PORTER CTR

BEACON
HARBOR

BOYDS
HARBOR

BETHEL   TRACT

LEISURE
LANDING

95-1

CANAL   RD

95-12

95-9

95-8

CANAL

ISLAND
RD

95-4

PIPER   SLOUGH

RUSSOS
MARINA

TAYLOR

JERSEY   ISLAND   RD

RD

RD

95-3

SLOUGH

SUGAR
BARGE
MARINA

BETHEL   ISLAND

ANCHOR
MARINA

THE GOLF CLUB
AT
BETHEL ISLAND

SUGAR   BARGE   RD

JERSEY

95-10

CLUBHOUSE

FAIRWAY

GOLF CLUB RD

ISLAND
MHP

FRANKS
MARINA

95-5

ISLAND

TAYLOR
RD

GATEWAY
RD

GATEWAY

SEE MAP
576

PO

NAVIGATORS PL

COTTAGE
LN

SANDY
LN

DELTA
COVES

SEA GATE PL

COVES

WEST WIND
PL

ANN & CHUCKS
HARBOR

SEE MAP
577

SHORELINE

RIVERVIEW PL

DELTA
COVES

1 MOSES YACHT HARBOR
2 GRISSI HARBOR
3 BENTLEYS MARINA

RD

DUTCH   SLOUGH

VIKING
HARBOR

DUTCH
SLOUGH

SEA HORSE
MARINA

WELLS

MARINER

SANDMOUND   BLVD

94561

ISLAND

95-11

SANDMOUND

TULE TREE LN

ASPEN

HOLLAND   TRACT

OAKLEY

BETHEL

HOLLAND
TRACT
BLVD

CAROLS
HARBOR
SAMS
HARBOR

94548

FRANKLIN

KNIGHTSEN

CYPRESS

CYPRESS

E CYPRESS RD

A B C D E F G H J

0 .25 .5 .75 1.0

miles 1 in. = 3800 ft.

SEE 597 MAP

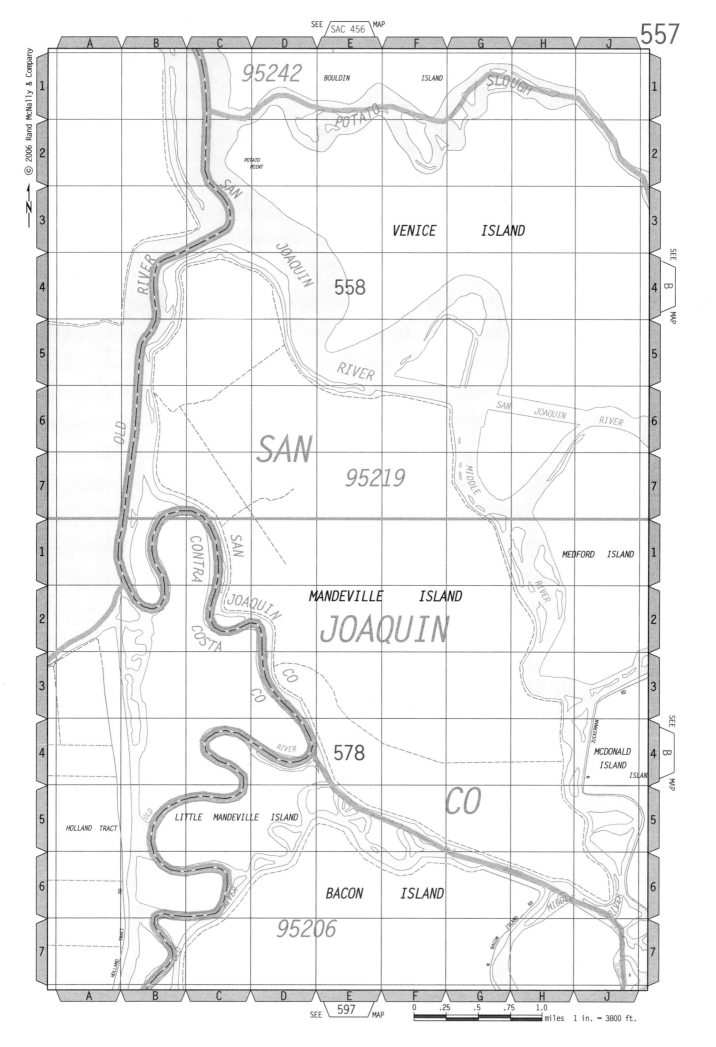

CONTRA COSTA

SEE SAC 456 MAP

95242

BOULDIN   ISLAND

POTATO   SLOUGH

POTATO
POINT

VENICE   ISLAND

SAN

JOAQUIN

558

RIVER

RIVER

SAN   JOAQUIN   RIVER

OLD

SAN

95219

MIDDLE

MEDFORD   ISLAND

CONTRA

COSTA

JOAQUIN

SAN

JOAQUIN

MANDEVILLE   ISLAND

JOAQUIN

CO

CO

RIVER

ZUCKERMAN   RD

SEE B MAP

578

MCDONALD
ISLAND

ISLAN

CO

OLD

HOLLAND   TRACT

OLD

LITTLE   MANDEVILLE   ISLAND

RIVER

RIVER

BACON   ISLAND

95206

BACON   ISLAND   RD

MIDDLE

RIVER

HOLLAND   TRACT   RD

SEE 597 MAP

0 .25 .5 .75 1.0
miles 1 in. = 3800 ft.

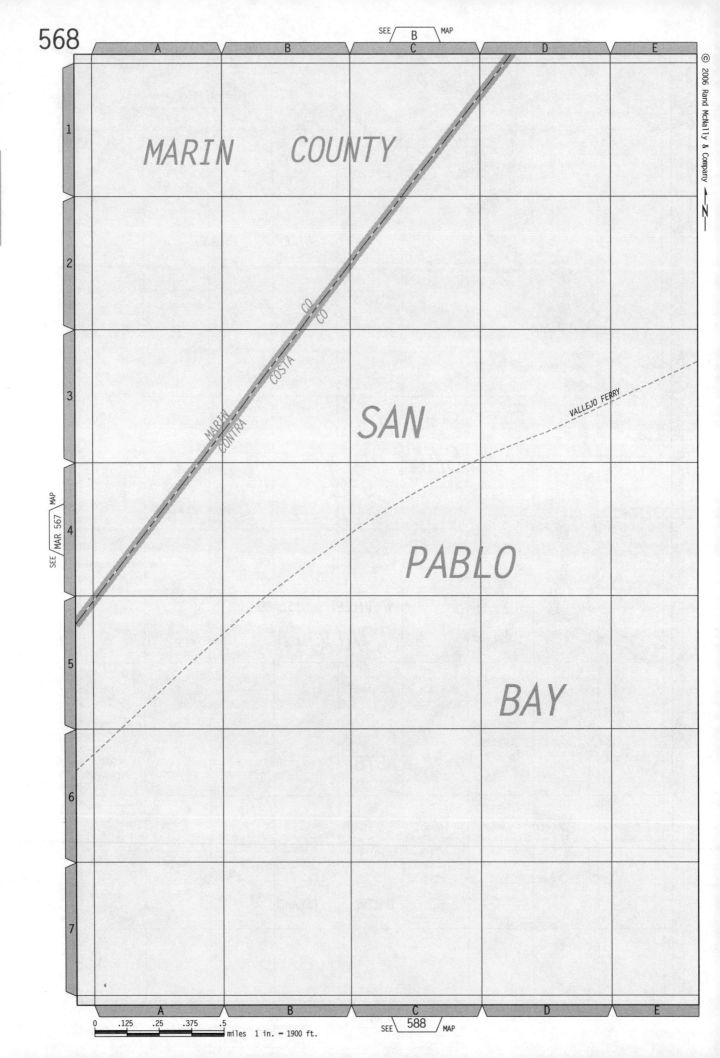

CONTRA COSTA

MARIN COUNTY

CO CO

MARIN
CONTRA
COSTA

SAN

PABLO

BAY

VALLEJO FERRY

SEE B MAP

SEE MAR 567 MAP

SEE 588 MAP

0   .125   .25   .375   .5
miles 1 in. = 1900 ft.

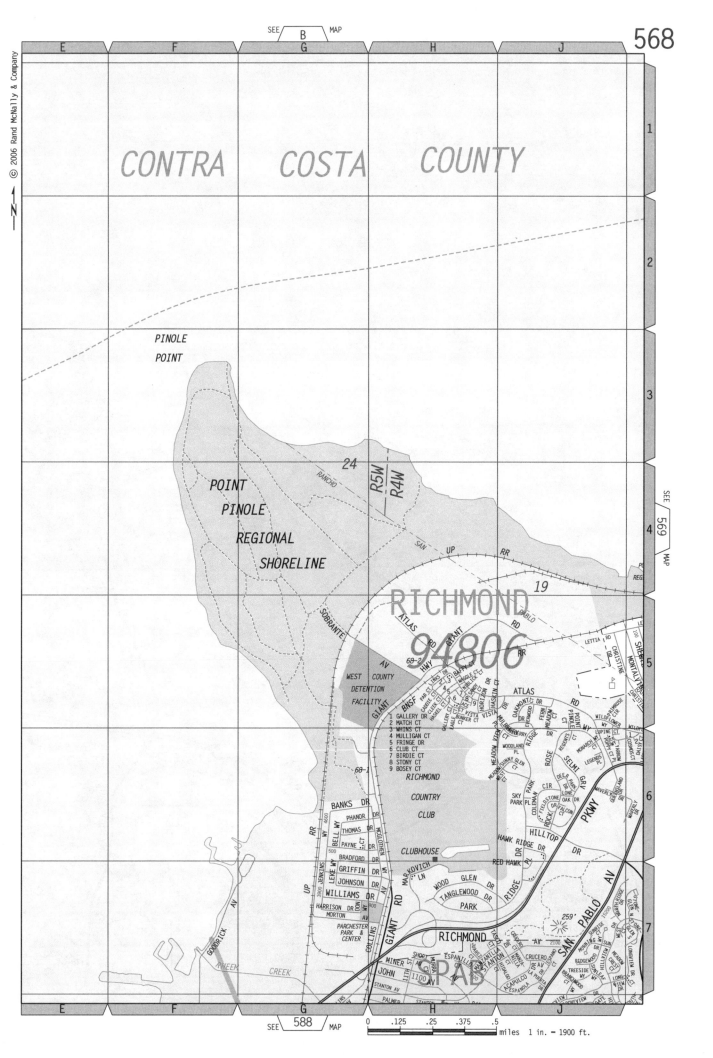

E   F   G   H   J

1

CONTRA   COSTA   COUNTY

2

PINOLE
POINT

3

24
R5W
R4W

RANCHO

POINT
PINOLE
REGIONAL
SHORELINE

SAN   UP   RR

SEE 569 MAP

4

19

SOBRANTE

RICHMOND
94806

ATLAS RD
GIANT
PABLO RD
RR
LETTIA RD

SHERR
MONTALVIN
CHRISTINE

AV
68-2
HWY
DAFFY CT

BNSF
GIANT

PAR CT LINKS DR
CADDIE CT CLERK CT
HASKEL CT
GALLERY DR
EAGLE CT
HASKIN DR
HORIZON DR
BUNKER DR
ACE CT VISTA
EL VISTA VISTA

ATLAS
OAKMONT CT DR
EVERWOOD DR
FERN CT
MEADOW CT

PIONEER CT
POINT WY
LUPINE CT
WILDFLOWER

PRIMROSE CT
WILDF

WEST COUNTY
DETENTION
FACILITY

1 GALLERY DR
2 MATCH CT
3 WHINS CT
4 MULLIGAN CT
5 FRINGE DR
6 CLUB CT
7 BIRDIE CT
8 STONY CT
9 BOSEY CT

MEADOW VIEW CT
WOODLAND PL
SUNNY GLEN CT
MEADOW SUNNY GLEN WEST

REGENTS DR
ROSE DR
MONARCH CT

SELMI GRV
LEGENDS PL

YARROW
COSMOS CT

RICHMOND
COUNTRY
CLUB

68-1

SKY
PARK
COLEMAN PL
FIELDSTONE
ROCK
DEE R
PARK
LONE
OAK
FALCON CT
CT

HAVERLY DR
WAVERLY

6

BANKS DR

PHANOR
THOMAS DR
PAYNE CT
MCCLOTHLIN

BRADFORD DR

HILLTOP
HAWK RIDGE DR
RED HAWK PL

DR

PKWY
DR

RR WY 4600
BELL WY
500

GRIFFIN
JOHNSON DR
WILLIAMS DR

MARKOVICH LN
WOOD GLEN DR
TANGLEWOOD
PARK

RIDGE
DR

SAN PABLO AV

LYNE GLEN WY STONE

JENKINS
LEKE WY
UP 900

CLUBHOUSE

GLEN DR

HARRISON DR
MORTON
DON WY

COLLINS RD
GIANT RD

259

SUNRISE
MORNING WY SUN
RIDGEWOOD WY
SUNLEAF
BRANCHWOOD
VIEW WY CT

LONGVIEW DR
LONG
VIEW DR

7

PARCHESTER
PARK &
CENTER

RICHMOND
SPAB

SAN PABLO AV
2100

GOODRICK AV

MINER AV
SHORT ST
11TH ST
JOHN
1100 AV
STANTON AV

ESPANILLA
MANZANILLA
STANTON
GIMILL
CRUCERO
LA DR A W
LEGRAND
MILL
LA PUERTA
ACAPULCO CT
A ESPANOLA DR

RASPA
GRANDE AV
MTN
HILLVIEW
VIEW
HILLCREST

RHEEM CREEK

PALMER
STANTON

0   .125   .25   .375   .5
miles   1 in. = 1900 ft.

E   F   G   H   J

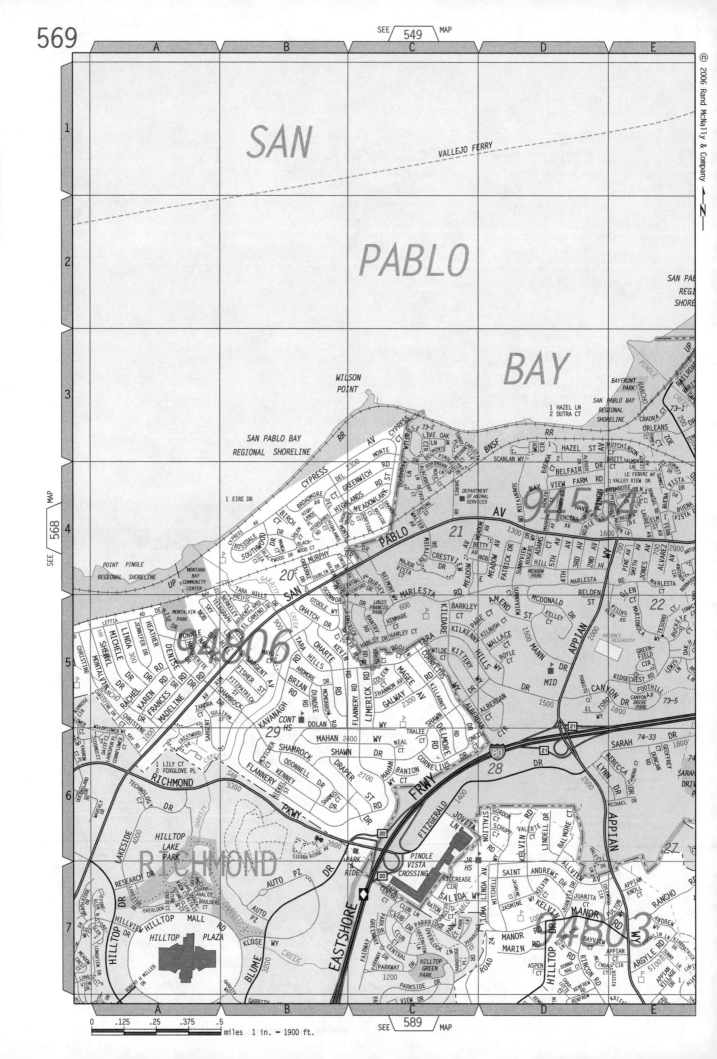

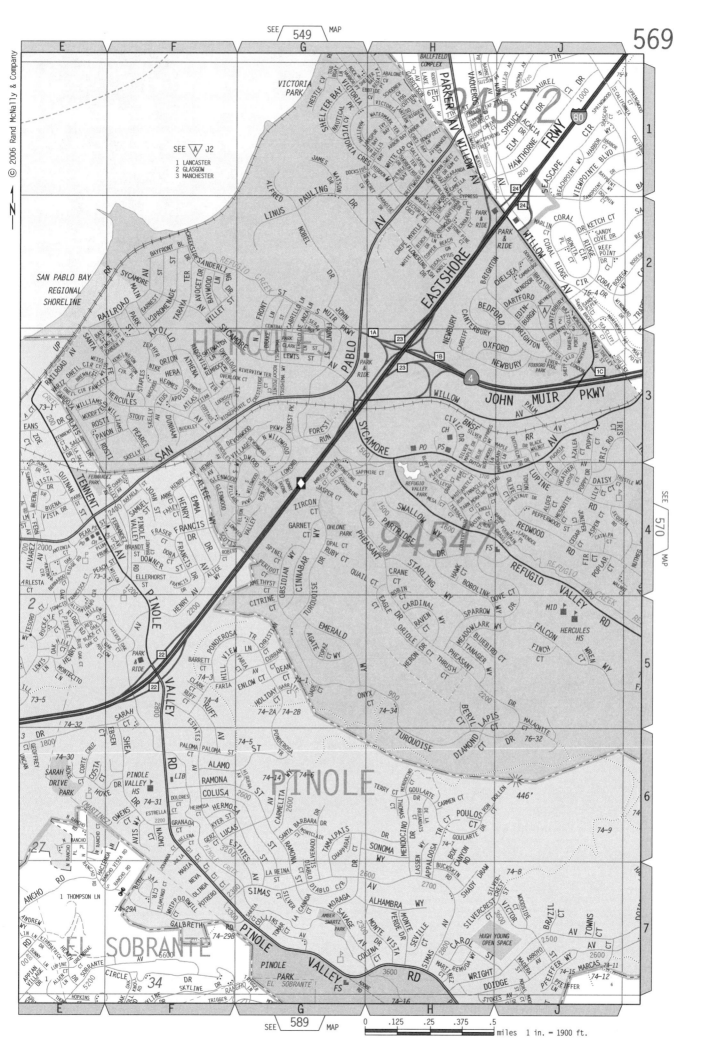

CONTRA COSTA

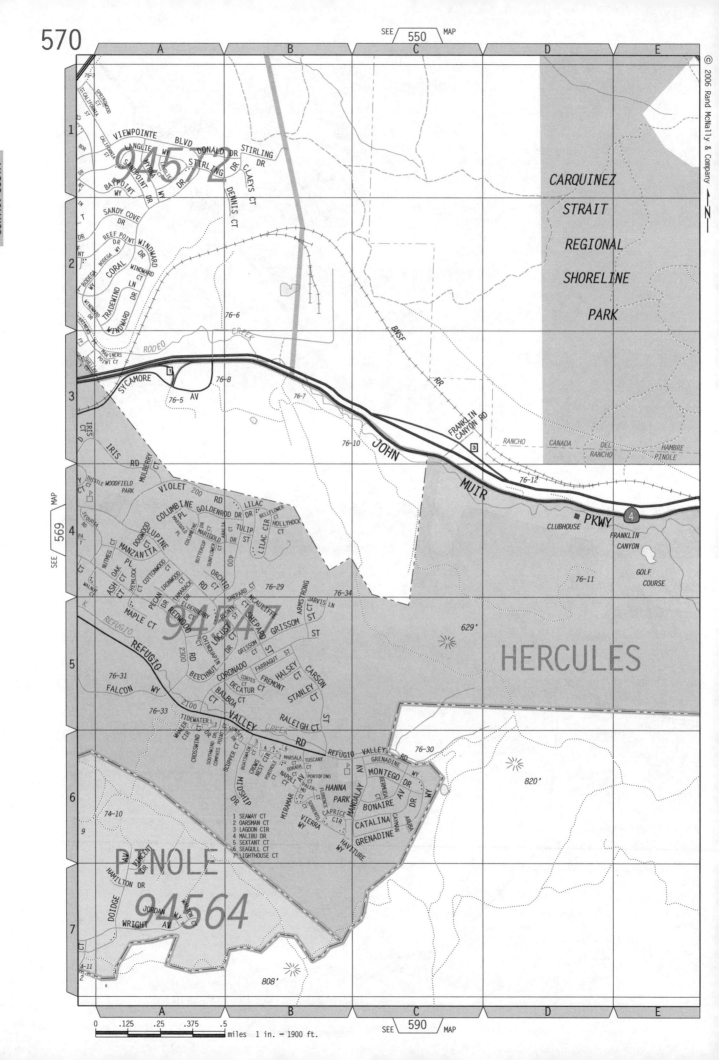

570

© 2006 Rand McNally & Company

CONTRA COSTA

A B C D E

1

VIEWPOINTE BLVD
LANGLIE WY
CALIFORNIA ST
SPRINGWOOD CT
SANDPOINT DR
DONALD DR
STIRLING DR
STIRLING
CLAEYS CT
DENNIS CT
BAYPOINT WY

94572

CARQUINEZ

2

SANDY COVE DR
REEF POINT DR
WINDWARD DR
CORAL
BODEGA WY
WINDWARD CT
TRADEWIND LN
WINDWARD
WINDWARD

STRAIT

REGIONAL

SHORELINE

PARK

CREEK
RODEO
MARINERS POINT CT

3

SYCAMORE AV
76-5
76-8
76-6
76-7
76-10
JOHN
BNSF
RR
FRANKLIN CANYON RD
MUIR
3
76-12
RANCHO CANADA DEL RANCHO
HAMBRE PINOLE

IRIS CT
IRIS RD
MULBERRY
THISTLE CT
WOODFIELD PARK
SEQUOIA CT
VIOLET 200 RD
COLUMBINE PL
GOLDENROD DR
LILAC DR
BELLFLOWER CT
HOLLYHOCK CT
TULIP ST
LILAC CIR

4

PKWY
CLUBHOUSE
FRANKLIN CANYON
GOLF COURSE
76-11

NUTMEG CT
MANZANITA PL
DOGWOOD
LUPINE
MARIGOLD DR
COLUMBINE DR
BUTTERCUP
SUNFLOWER
ORCHID
400
ASH CT
OAK CT
HEMLOCK CT
COTTONWOOD CT
PECAN CT
IRONWOOD
DR
TAMARACK DR
ELDERBERRY
REDWOOD
CHINQUAPIN
LOCUST
SHEPARD CT
MCAULIFFE
SHEPARD
GRISSOM ST
ARMSTRONG
JARVIS LN
76-29
76-34

94547

WALNUT
MAPLE CT
REFUGIO
2300
BEECHNUT
GRISSOM CT
CORONADO
CORTES
FARRAGUT ST
DECATUR CT
FREMONT
HALSEY CT
STANLEY CT
CARSON ST
629'

5

FALCON WY
2100
BALBOA CT
VALLEY
RALEIGH CT
ST
76-31
76-33
HERCULES

6

74-10
9
TIDEWATER 1 2
WHALER CIR
CROSSWINDS
SOUTHWIND
COMPASS POINT
SUNSET
STARLIGHT CT
CROSS NEST CIR
PORTOFILE
MIDSHIP DR
MARSALA CT
DORADA
NAPOLI
TUSCANY CT
PORTOFINO CT
SONGETO
FLORENCE CT
MALER
HALER PV
CAPRICE CIR
HANNA PARK
MANDALAY AV
BERMUDA
MONTEGO WY
BONAIRE
CATALINA
GRENADINE
GRENADINE DR
HAVITURE WY
CAYMAN
ARUBA
VALLEY CREEK RD
REFUGIO VALLEY RD
76-30
820'

MIRAMAR
VIERRA WY

1 SEAWAY CT
2 OARSMAN CT
3 LAGOON CIR
4 MALIBU DR
5 SEXTANT CT
6 SEAGULL CT
7 LIGHTHOUSE CT

PINOLE
94564
HAMILTON DR
DOIDGE
VINCENT DR
JORDAN WY
WRIGHT AV

7

808'
4-11

A B C D E

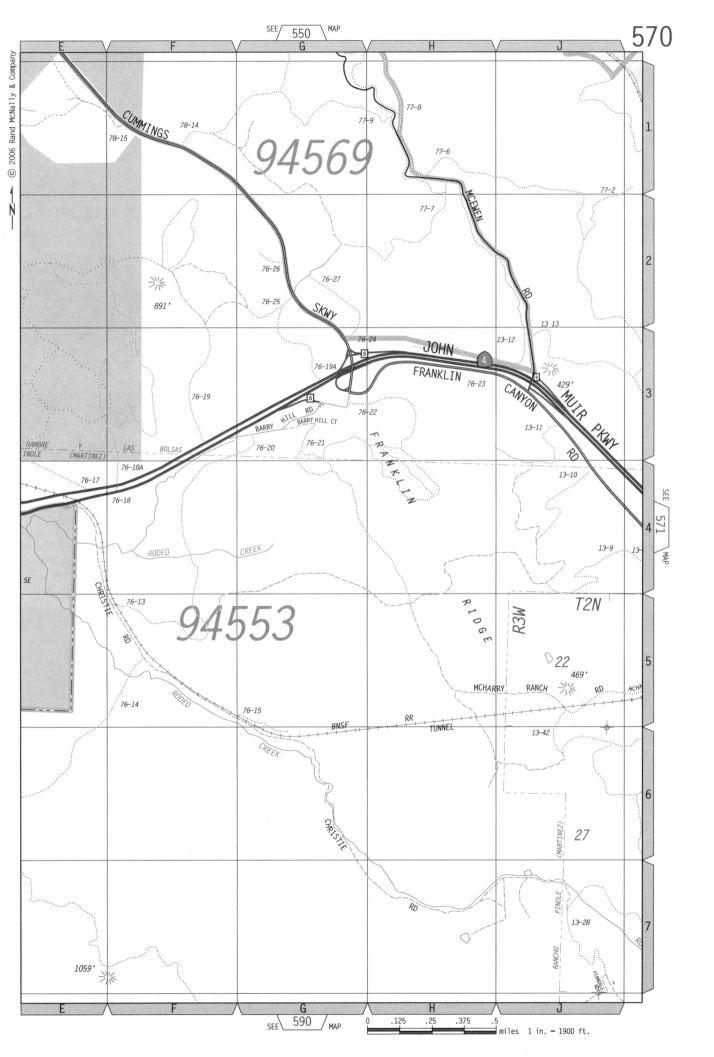

CONTRA COSTA

SEE 550 MAP

E F G H J

CUMMINGS

78–14
78–15

94569

77–8
77–9
77–6
77–7
77–2

MCEWEN RD

76–26
76–27
76–25
891'
SKWY
76–24
76–19A
JOHN
FRANKLIN
13–13
13–12
429'
MUIR PKWY
76–19
76–23
CANYON RD
5
5
BARRY HILL RD
BARRY HILL CT
76–22
76–20
76–21
FRANKLIN
13–11
HAMBRE
INOLE
Y
(MARTINEZ)
LAS BOLSAS
76–18A
13–10
76–17
76–18

SEE 571 MAP

RODEO CREEK
13–9
13
SE
CHRISTIE RD
76–13
94553
RIDGE
R3W
T2N
22
469'
76–14
RODEO
76–15
BNSF RR TUNNEL
MCHARRY RANCH RD
MCHA
13–42
CREEK
CHRISTIE
(MARTINEZ)
27
RD
PINOLE
13–28
1059'
RANCHO
FERNDALE

E F G H J

SEE 590 MAP

0 .125 .25 .375 .5 miles 1 in. = 1900 ft.

1
2
3
4
5
6
7

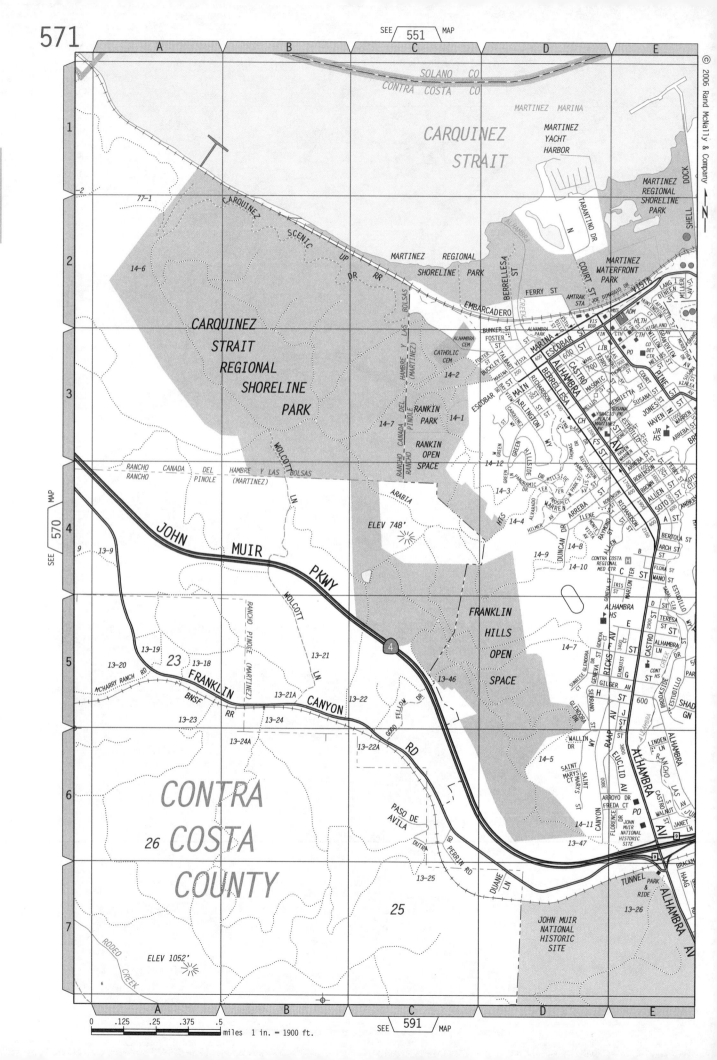

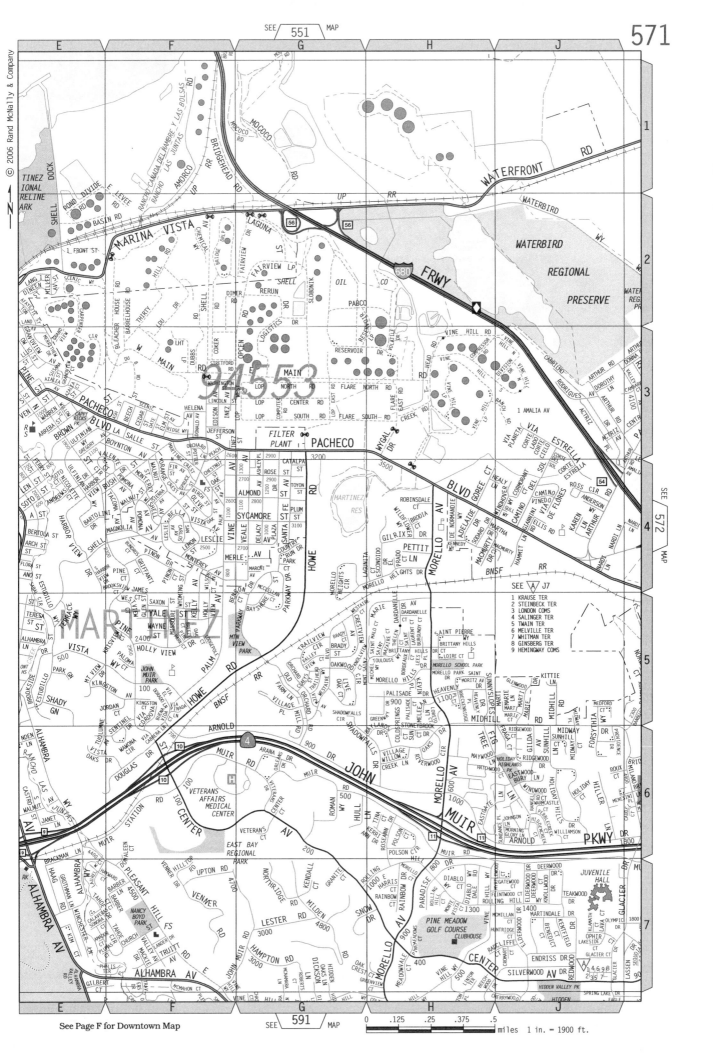

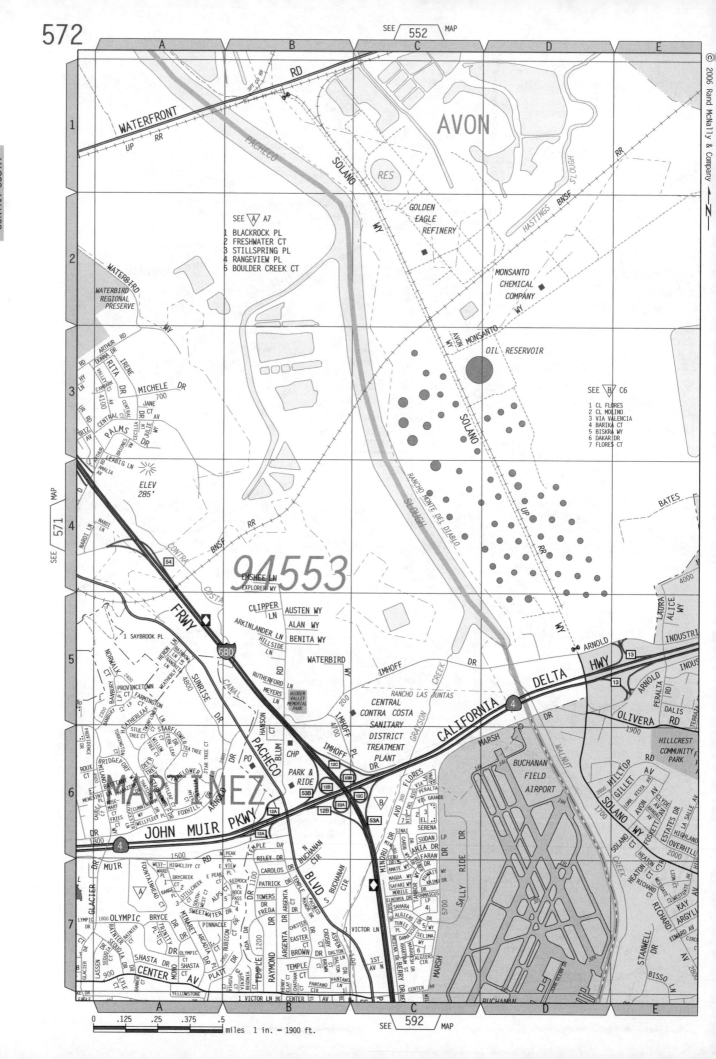

CONTRA COSTA

AVON

WATERFRONT

UP RR

PACHECO

SOLANO WY

RES

GOLDEN
EAGLE
REFINERY

HASTINGS SLOUGH

BNSF RR

SEE A7
1 BLACKROCK PL
2 FRESHWATER CT
3 STILLSPRING PL
4 RANGEVIEW PL
5 BOULDER CREEK CT

WATERBIRD

WATERBIRD
REGIONAL
PRESERVE

MONSANTO
CHEMICAL
COMPANY

MONSANTO WY

OIL RESERVOIR

ARTHUR RD
DONNA DR
RITA DR
IRENE
MICHELE DR 700
JANE CT AV
CENTRAL AV
PALMS DR

SOLANO

SEE C6
1 CL FLORES
2 CL MOLINO
3 VIA VALENCIA
4 BARIKA CT
5 BISKRA WY
6 DAKAR DR
7 FLORES CT

LEABIG LN
AMALIA AV
ELEV
285'

RANCHO MONTE DEL DIABLO SLOUGH

BATES

NARDI LN

RR
BNSF RR
54
CONTRA COSTA

UP RR

4000

94553

EMSHEE LN
EXPLORER WY

LAURA
ALICE WY
INDUSTRI

CLIPPER LN
AUSTEN WY
ARKINLANDER LN   ALAN WY
HILLSIDE LN   BENITA WY
WATERBIRD WY

ARNOLD

DELTA   HWY   13

1 SAYBROOK PL

680

SUNRISE DR

CANAL

RUTHERFORD LN
MEYERS LN

IMHOFF

WATERBIRD WY
IMHOFF DR

GRAYSON CREEK

CALIFORNIA   4

13
ARNOLD
PERALTA RD
ARNOLD
INDUS

NORMALK CT
BARBURY
PROVINCETOWN
FARMINGTON
HEATHERLEAF

HIDDEN
VALLEY
MEMORIAL
PARK

RANCHO LAS JUNTAS

OLIVERA RD
1900

MARSH

BUCHANAN
FIELD
AIRPORT

HILLTOP RD
HILLCREST
COMMUNITY
PARK

PROVIDENCE DR
ROUX CT
BRIDGEPORT
MILANO
TORRINGTON
SILK TREE CT
STARFLOWER CT
DEER TREE
STAR TREE CT
TEA TREE CT

PACHECO
HANSON
BLUM
CHP
PO
PARK &
RIDE

CENTRAL
CONTRA COSTA
SANITARY
DISTRICT
TREATMENT
PLANT DR

FLORES

SOLANO WY
GILLET AV

ESTATES DR
FOSKETTI

MARTINEZ

CAUBE
MENESINI
ROSE-MARY
CUNNINGHAM
FOXHILL
WELLFLEET PL
FRIES

ARNOLD

12A
53B
53A
12B
12C
53B
12C

VIA
VIS GRANDE
EL

HIGHLAND

OVERHILL

JOHN MUIR PKWY
4   1300

N BUCHANAN CIR

MINORU DR
SINAI
CEBU
PERALTA
KUWAIT
FARAN

SALLY RIDE DR

HEATON CT
RICHARD CT
KAY

GLACIER DR
MUIR

PEAK PL
VIEW PL
RILEY DR
CAROLOS DR
PATRICK DR

TEMPLE CIR
N BUCHANAN
BLVD

BUCHANAN CIR

ARIA DR
AMATE WY
MAGDA WY
MOBILE LP
ELMINYA DR
SAHARA

RICHARD

ARGYLL

WEST-HIGHCLIFF CT
WARD PL
DRYCREEK
RANGE
STILLCREEK
SOUTH-WEST CT
SWEETWATER

REDROCK PL
ROCK PASS PL
ALPS CT

ADA

TOWERS DR
PATRICK DR
ARGENTA DR
FREDA

MANOR DR
CHESTER DR
DALTON
CROSBY

ASPEN

VICTOR LN

SUDAN
CAROB WY
DAMASCUS
KAIMU DR
SUEZ DR

ALGIERS
TUNIS
DAMASCUS
HARRISON ST
BERRY DR

SELIMA
6

1ST AV N

STANNELL DR

EDWARD AV
CIRC

OLYMPIC
BRYCE
RAINIER DR
FOUNTAINHEAD
MIMARET DR
PINNACLE
TRINITY DR

OLYMPIC
ARCADIA DR
RUBICON

SHASTA DR
SHASTA CT

RAYMOND DR
ARGENTA DR
TEMPLE

HENRY CLAY
CHATHAM

PANTANO LN
PANTANO CIR

1ST AV

CENTER AV

GLACIER DR
LASSEN DR
SEQUOIA DR
RAINIER DR
SHASTA
900
ONO
CENTER AV
PLATT

LYLE CT
YINDIO
BEGONIA

YELLOWSTONE

MARSH

BUCHANAN

1 VICTOR LN   B CENTER AV

0   .125   .25   .375   .5
miles   1 in. = 1900 ft.

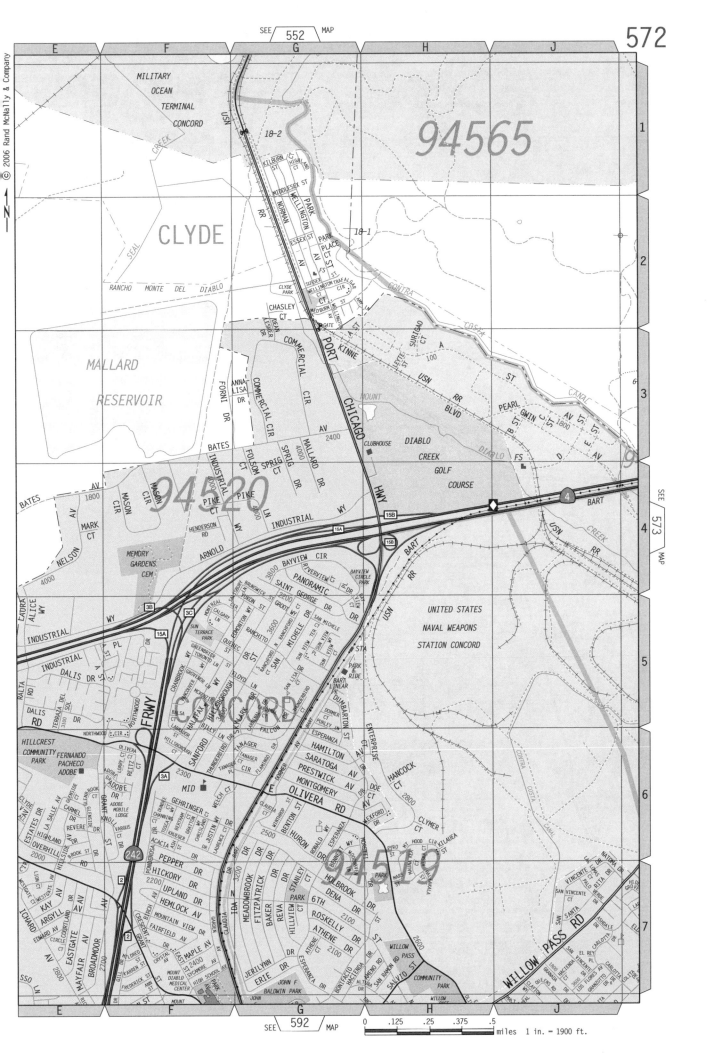

CONTRA COSTA

© 2006 Rand McNally & Company

N

94565

CLYDE

MILITARY
OCEAN
TERMINAL
CONCORD

RANCHO MONTE DEL DIABLO

MALLARD

RESERVOIR

DIABLO
CREEK
GOLF
COURSE

UNITED STATES
NAVAL WEAPONS
STATION CONCORD

94520

CONCORD

HILLCREST
COMMUNITY
PARK
FERNANDO
PACHECO
ADOBE

MEMORY
GARDENS
CEM.

94519

0 .125 .25 .375 .5
miles 1 in. = 1900 ft.

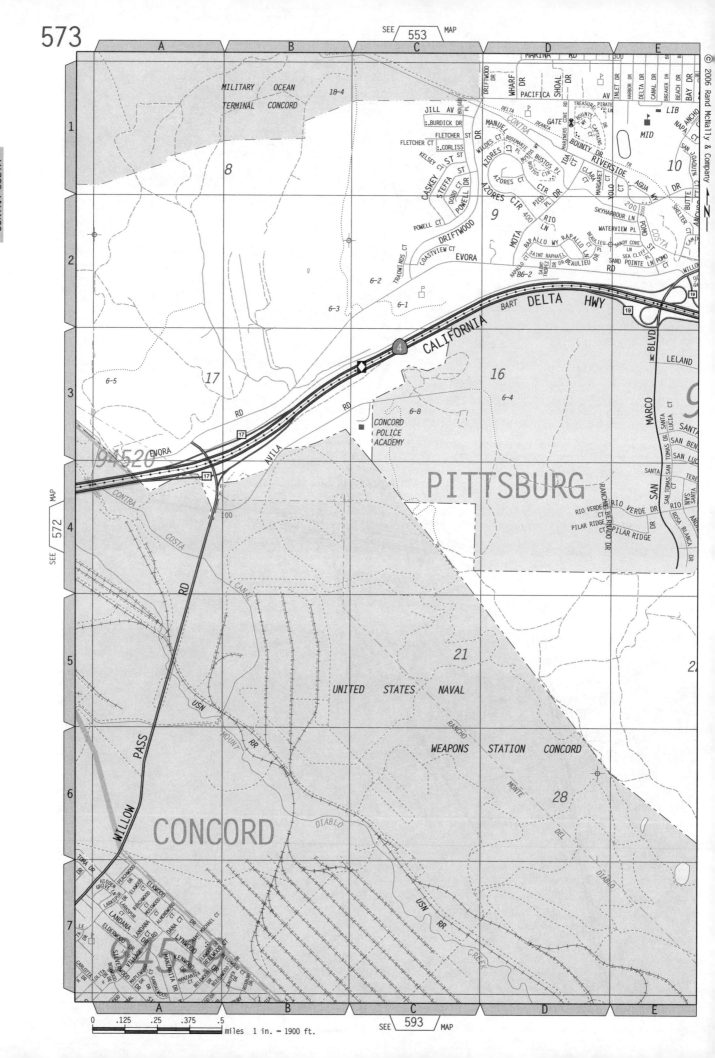

CONTRA COSTA

A   B   C   D   E

SEE 553 MAP

© 2006 Rand McNally & Company

1

MILITARY OCEAN
TERMINAL CONCORD

18-4

MARINA RD

8

JILL AV

BURDICK DR

FLETCHER ST
FLETCHER CT   CORLISS ST
KELSEY CT   STEFFA ST
CASKEY CT   POWELL DR
STEFFA
DODD CT
POWELL CT

DRIFTWOOD DR
WHARF DR
PACIFICA AV
SHOAL DR

DELTA
CONTRA
GATE   DEANZA
MARINERS
BOUNTY   DR
TREASURE
PIRATE
LN

INLET DR
HARBOR DR
DELTA DR
CANAL DR
BREAKER DR
BAY DR

LIB
MID

NAPA DR
SAN ANCHO

10

2

MANUEL
WILDES CT   ROSEMARIE CT   IDA CT
AZORES CT   BUSTOS PL   BUSTOS CIR   CLARA CT
AZORES CIR 400   BUSTOS DR   MARGARET CT   YOLO CT
RIO LN   PICO PL
PICO   PL

9

DRIFTWOOD DR

POWELL CT

WATERVIEW PL
COASTVIEW CT
TRADEWINDS CT
EVORA

MOTA   RAPALLO WY   RAPALLO LN
SAINT RAPHAEL   BEAULIEU
SAINT TROPEZ   DR   BEAULIEU   LN
RAPALLO   DR   DR   PL
86-2

RIVERSIDE DR

SKYHARBOUR LN   200
2000

AGUA WY

SHELTER CT
BUTTE DR

WILLOW

6-2

6-1

SANDY COVE LN
SEA CLIFF LN
SAND POINTE LN

POMO ST

CONTRA COSTA

POMO CT

19

6-3

BART   DELTA   HWY   19

CALIFORNIA

4

LELAND

W   BLVD

3

6-5

17

RD

RD

AVILA

16

6-4

6-8

MARCO

SANTA LUCIA CT
SAN BENI   SANTA
SAN TOMAS   SAN LUC
SANTA

9

94520

EVORA

17

CONCORD
POLICE
ACADEMY

PITTSBURG

SAN   TERE
SANTA

SAN TOMAS DR
SAN TOMAS

RIO VERDE
CT   RIO VERDE DR

RANCHO-BERNADO DR

RIO
ROSA BLANCA DR

4

17

100

CONTRA

COSTA

RD

CANAL

PILAR RIDGE
PILAR RIDGE DR

SEE 572 MAP

5

USN   RR

21

UNITED   STATES   NAVAL

RANCHO

2

6

WILLOW   PASS

MOUNT   DIABLO

RR

WEAPONS   STATION   CONCORD

MONTE

28

DEL

DIABLO

CONCORD

7

TOMA DR

HIDDEN GROVE
PEACHWOOD DR
ELKWOOD DR
ELKWOOD
LARKSPUR CT   ELKWOOD   BEECHWOOD   MOSSWOOD CT
LANDANA   ALMONDWOOD
LANDANA   DANA
ELDERWOOD DR   LYNWOOD DR
KENWOOD CT   SAINT MICHAEL DR
MANZANITA
MAPLEWOOD   MANZANITA CT
BELLWOOD CT   BEECHWOOD DR
LE
CARLOTTA   LOLITA   SLENWOOD   SANDALWOOD DR
DR   BOWING   DR   DENVER DR   RIDGEWOOD
DR

945

DIABLO   CREEK

USN   RR

0 .125 .25 .375 .5
miles 1 in. = 1900 ft.

SEE 593 MAP

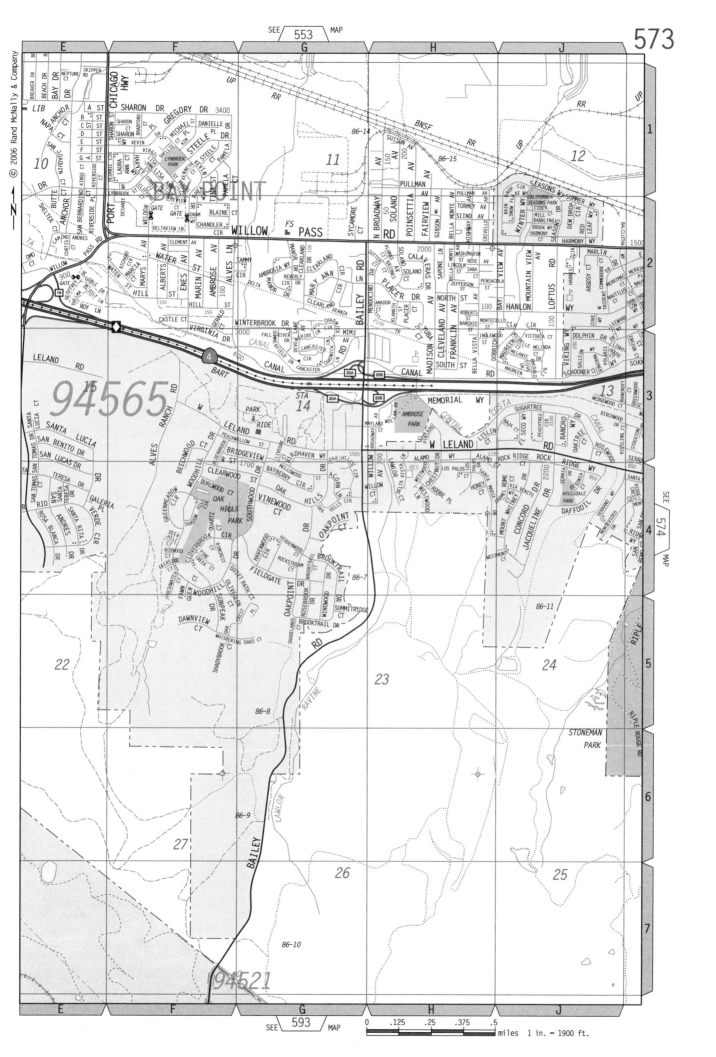

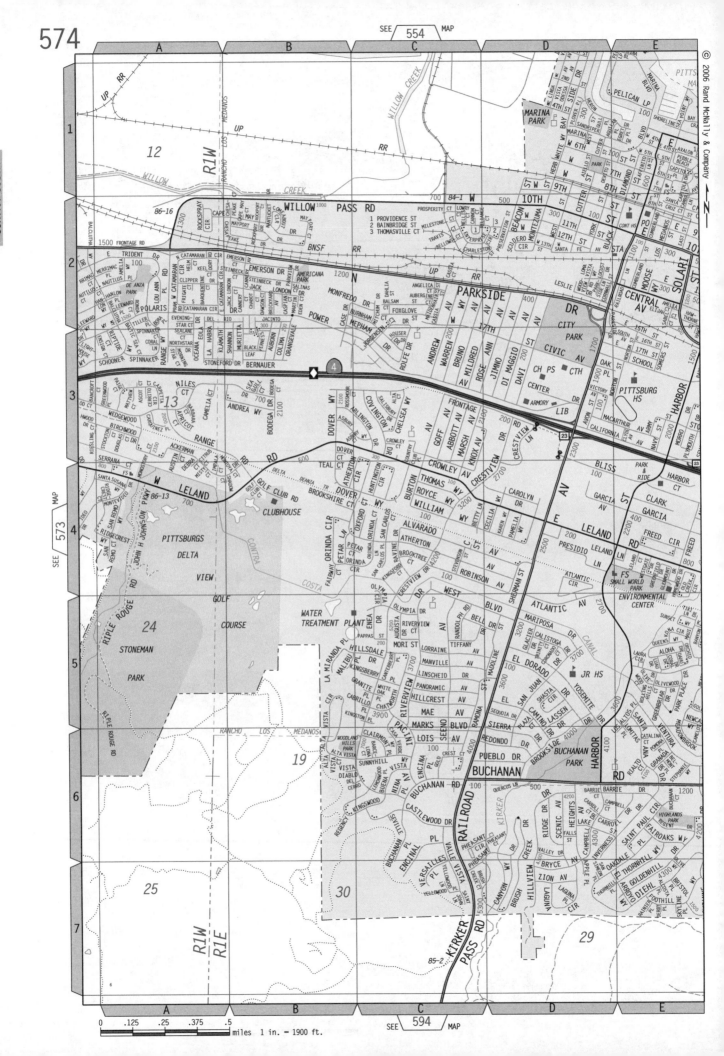

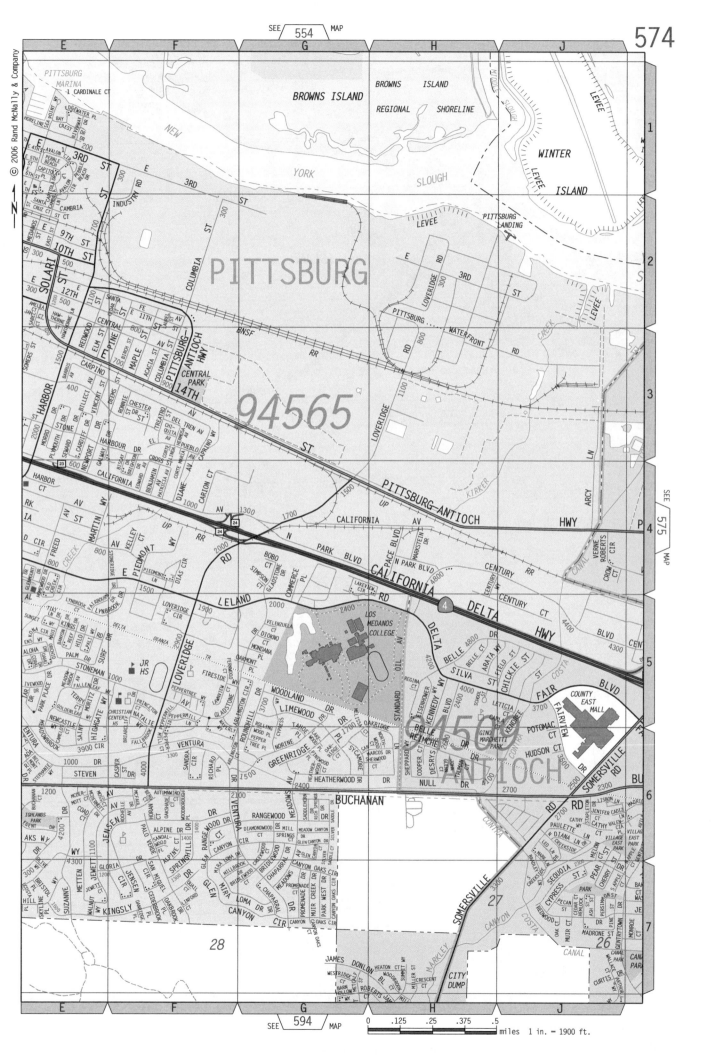

CONTRA COSTA

BROWNS ISLAND

BROWNS ISLAND
REGIONAL SHORELINE

PITTSBURG
MARINA

WINTER
ISLAND

NEW

YORK

SLOUGH

LEVEE

LEVEE

PITTSBURG
LANDING

PITTSBURG

94565

94509
ANTIOCH

LOS
MEDANOS
COLLEGE

COUNTY
EAST
MALL

PITTSBURG-ANTIOCH HWY

CALIFORNIA

DELTA

HWY

BUCHANAN

CITY
DUMP

0 .125 .25 .375 .5 miles   1 in. = 1900 ft.

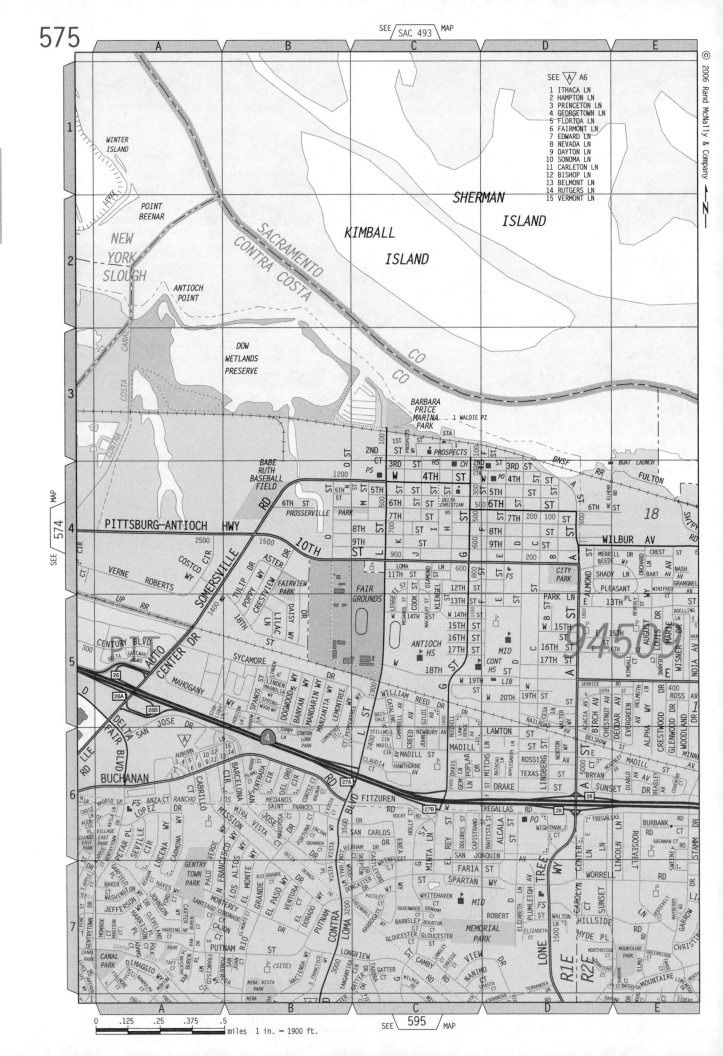

CONTRA COSTA

A   B   C   D   E

SEE A6

1 ITHACA LN
2 HAMPTON LN
3 PRINCETON LN
4 GEORGETOWN LN
5 FLORIDA LN
6 FAIRMONT LN
7 EDWARD LN
8 NEVADA LN
9 DAYTON LN
10 SONOMA LN
11 CARLETON LN
12 BISHOP LN
13 BELMONT LN
14 RUTGERS LN
15 VERMONT LN

WINTER
ISLAND

SHERMAN

ISLAND

POINT
BEENAR

NEW
YORK
SLOUGH

KIMBALL

ISLAND

SACRAMENTO
CONTRA COSTA

ANTIOCH
POINT

CO
CO

DOW
WETLANDS
PRESERVE

BARBARA
PRICE
MARINA
PARK

1 WALDIE PZ

BNSF

BOAT LAUNCH

FULTON

PITTSBURG-ANTIOCH HWY

BABE
RUTH
BASEBALL
FIELD

PROSSERVILLE
PARK

18

WILBUR AV

SEE 574 MAP

COSTCO CIR

VERNE
ROBERTS

SOMERSVILLE RD

CITY
PARK

94501

FAIR
GROUNDS

ANTIOCH
HS

CENTURY BLVD

DELTA
GATEWAY BLVD

26

26A

26B

DELTA
FAIR
BLVD

SAN JOSE DR

BUCHANAN

4

27A

27B

28

FITZUREN
RD

TREGALLAS RD

MEMORIAL
PARK

R1E
R2E

A   B   C   D   E

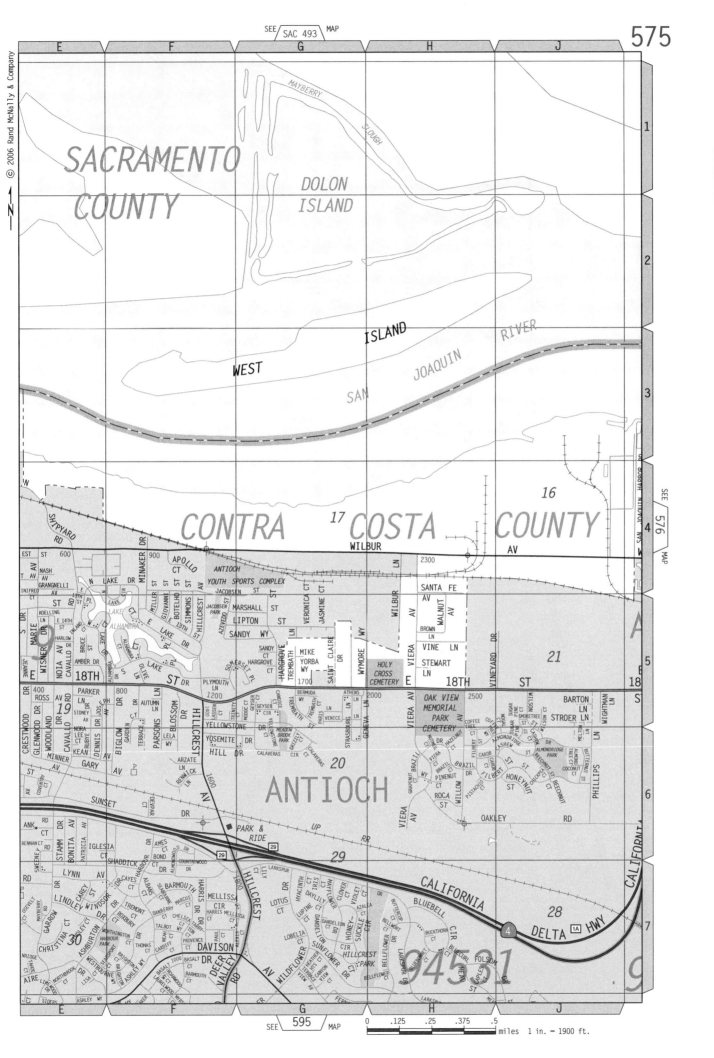

CONTRA COSTA

SEE SAC 493 MAP

SACRAMENTO
COUNTY

DOLON
ISLAND

MAYBERRY SLOUGH

ISLAND

WEST

SAN JOAQUIN RIVER

SEE 576 MAP

CONTRA 17 COSTA COUNTY 16

ANTIOCH

94531

DELTA HWY

SEE 595 MAP

0   .125   .25   .375   .5   miles   1 in. = 1900 ft.

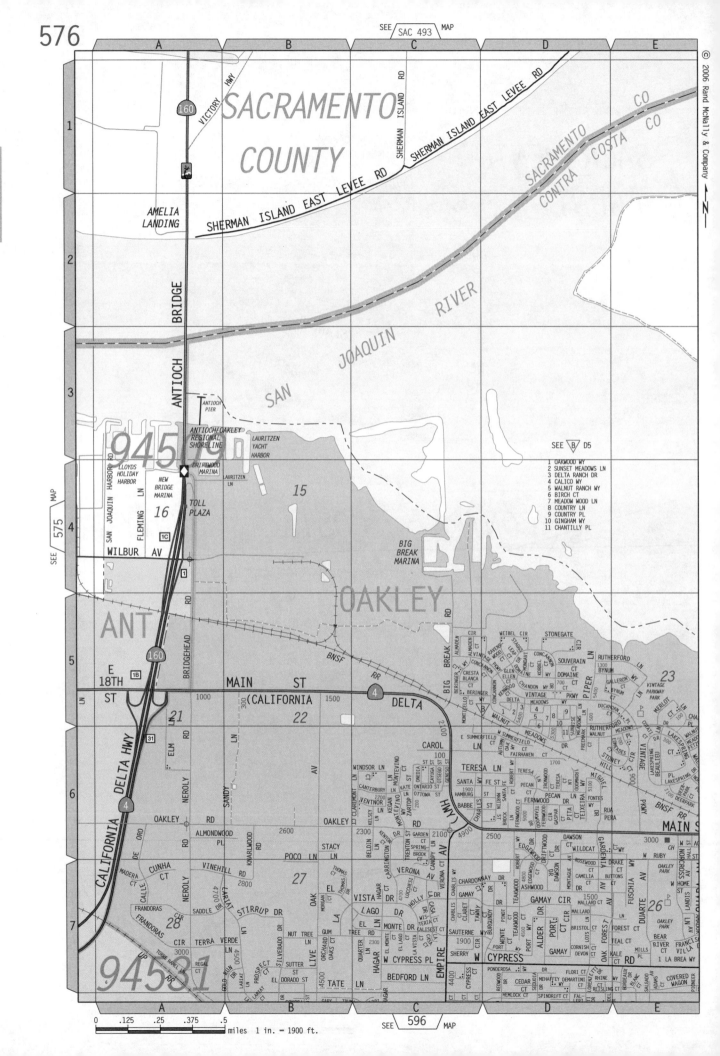

SACRAMENTO
COUNTY

SEE SAC 493 MAP

AMELIA
LANDING

SHERMAN ISLAND EAST LEVEE RD

SHERMAN ISLAND EAST LEVEE RD

VICTORY HWY

160

ANTIOCH BRIDGE

SAN JOAQUIN RIVER

SACRAMENTO CO

CONTRA COSTA CO

N

ANTIOCH PIER

ANTIOCH/OAKLEY
REGIONAL
SHORELINE

LAURITZEN
YACHT
HARBOR

DRIFTWOOD
MARINA

LAURITZEN LN

SEE B D5

1 OAKWOOD WY
2 SUNSET MEADOWS LN
3 DELTA RANCH DR
4 CALICO WY
5 WALNUT RANCH WY
6 BIRCH CT
7 MEADOW WOOD LN
8 COUNTRY LN
9 COUNTRY PL
10 GINGHAM WY
11 CHANTILLY PL

94519

LLOYDS
HOLIDAY
HARBOR

NEW
BRIDGE
MARINA

SAN JOAQUIN HARBOR RD

FLEMING

16

TOLL
PLAZA

15

BIG
BREAK
MARINA

SEE 575 MAP

1C

WILBUR AV

1

OAKLEY

ANT

160

E
18TH
ST

LN
ST

BRIDGEHEAD RD

MAIN ST

BNSF RR

4

DELTA

BIG BREAK RD

23

1B

1000

300

(CALIFORNIA

1500

22

4

WEIBEL CIR

STONEGATE

RUTHERFORD
LN

SOUVERAIN
DOMAINE

VINTAGE
PARKWAY
PARK

1300

BYNUM

CALIFORNIA DELTA HWY

31

21

ELM LN

NEROLY RD

CAROL
LN

100

WALNUT
MEADOWS

PIPER

VINTAGE PKWY

BYNUM

700

GALLERON WY

MERLOT CT

5400

E SUMMERFIELD
W SUMMERFIELD

FAIRHAVEN CT

FREDMARK

RUTHERFORD

MEADOWS

DUCKHORN

100

500

DEERPARK

AUTUMN
SUNRISE

STONEY
HILL

LAKESPRING
900

VINTAGE PKWY

4

SANDY RD

E
18TH

TERESA LN

SANTA
HAMBURG

FE STE

TERESA

1700

PECAN

PECAN CT

IRONWOOD
TERESA

LS
BROCK

MIGUEL

FONTES

FERNWOOD

2100

TEIXEIRA

BNSF RR

MAIN ST

OAKLEY

ALMONDWOOD
PL

KNARLWOOD RD

2600

STACY
LN

POCO LN

27

2300

CLAREMONT LN

WINDSOR LN

CANTERBURY
DR

MONTEVINO WY

KELSEY ST

KEGAN
LN

BELDIN
LN

KENTON
ST

TRENTON ST

2200

KATE ST

OTTOMA ST

CAYUGA ST

GARDEN CT

SPRING-
BROOK

VENTNOR

ZARTOP
RD

ONEIDA
ST

ONTARIO ST

GENESEO ST

SANTA
LN

NILSON

FERNWOOD
CIR

GASPAR

PITA

RUA
PERA

4900

2500

2100

DAWSON
WY

WILDCAT
CT

DAWSON

EDGEWOOD
CT

DRIFTWOOD
DR

3000

NORCROSS RD

DE ORO

MADERA
CT

CUNHA
CT

VINEHILL RD

2800

LARIAT

STIRRUP DR

OAK
EL
LA

THOMAS
CT

MORGAN
CT

VERONA
AV

HOLLY CT

VERONA CT

CHARDONNAY

DR

ROSEWOOD
CT

ROBERT
WY

MO DAWSON WY

CAMELIA
CT

MONTAGUE
DR

4800

EDGEWOOD

GARDEN

DRAKE
WY

BUTTONS
CT

RUBY

OAKLEY
PARK

W HOME

NEROLY RD

OAKLEY RD

SADDLE

4700

NUT TREE
LN

VISTA
LAGO

EL
MONTE
LN

EL
MONTE
DR

WISTERIA
CT

CALISESI CT

CHABLIS WY

CLARET
CT

GAMAY

TAWNY
CT

TEAKWOOD
CT

TEAKWOOD
DR

1500

ASHWOOD

PORT CT

BURGUNDY

GAMAY CIR

MALLARD CT

MALLARD
AV

BRISTOL
CT

FUSCHIA
WY

DUARTE AV

OAKLEY
PARK

LANDIS

28

FRANDORAS
CIR

FRANDORAS
CIR

TERRA VERDE
LN

CALLE

3000

TORRE RAE LN

REGAL
CT

GOLD RUN

PROSPECT
CT

SILVERADO
CT

EL DORADO ST

SUTTER
ST

LIVE
OAK

ORCHARD
OAKS CT

MONTE
TREE RD

GUM
LN

QUARTER
HORSE
LN

HAGAR

CHARLES

HWY

W CYPRESS PL

BEDFORD LN

EMPIRE

4400

SAUTERNE

1900

SHERRY

CORNISH
DEVON

MONTE
WY

PINOT
CT

TEAKWOOD

CLARET
CT

PORT
WY

LOIS
CT

ALDER

CYPRESS

OAK FOREST

TEAL CT

26

BEAR
RIVER

FRANCIS
VILLA

1 LA BREA WY

REDWOOD
CT

PONDEROSA
CT

CEDAR
CT

MEHAFFEY
CT

DEMARTINI
CT

RHINE
CT

RIESLING
CT

FLORI CT

BORDEAUX
DR

ADAMS

COVERED
WAGON

KALE
CT

MILLS
RD

HEMLOCK CT

CYPRESS

SPINDRIFT CT

94531

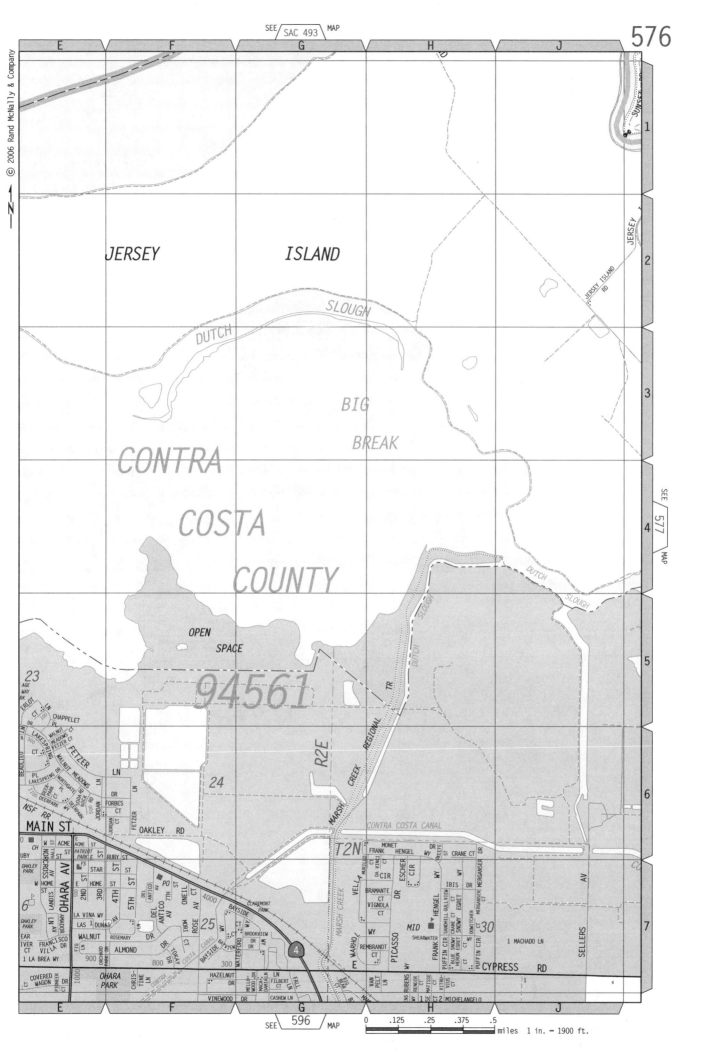

CONTRA COSTA

SEE SAC 493 MAP

E F G H J

1

2

JERSEY ISLAND

3

SLOUGH

DUTCH

BIG

BREAK

CONTRA

COSTA

COUNTY

OPEN SPACE

94561

SEE 577 MAP

DUTCH

SLOUGH

4

5

6

7

MAIN ST

OAKLEY RD

CYPRESS RD

SEE 596 MAP

0 .125 .25 .375 .5

miles 1 in. = 1900 ft.

E F G H J

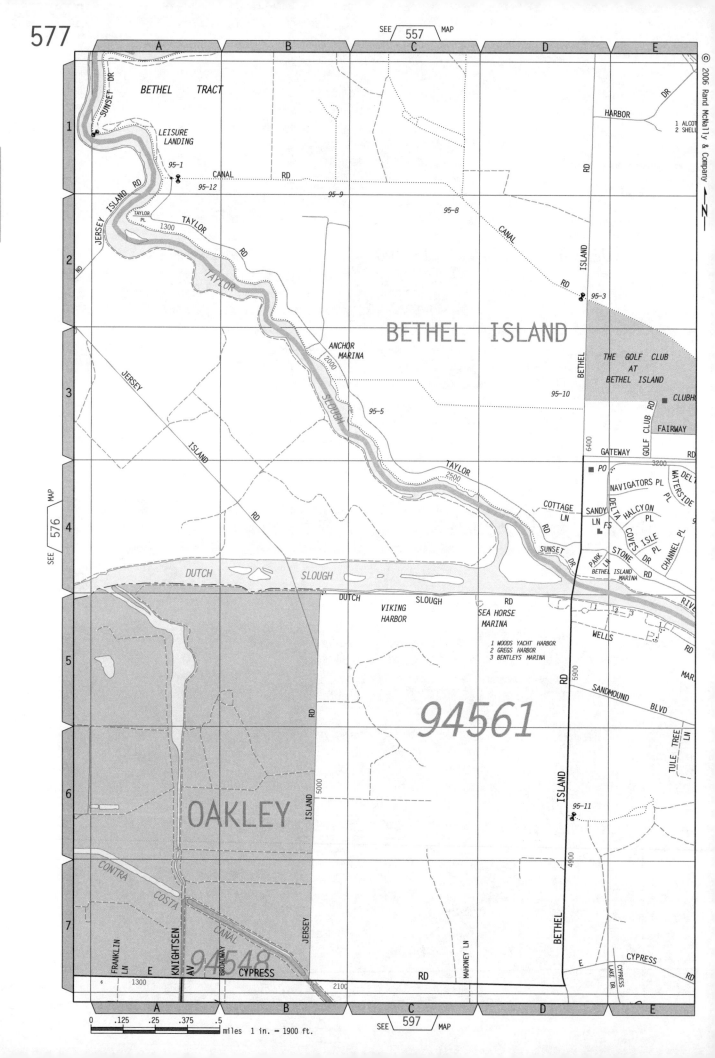

CONTRA COSTA

SEE 557 MAP

© 2006 Rand McNally & Company

1 ALCOT
2 SHELL

BETHEL TRACT

SUNSET DR

LEISURE LANDING

95-1

95-12

CANAL RD

95-9

95-8

HARBOR DR

JERSEY ISLAND RD

TAYLOR PL

TAYLOR RD

1300

TAYLOR

95-3

BETHEL ISLAND

CANAL

ISLAND RD

SEE 576 MAP

JERSEY

ISLAND

RD

SLOUGH

ANCHOR MARINA

2000

95-5

TAYLOR

2500

95-10

THE GOLF CLUB AT BETHEL ISLAND

6400

BETHEL

GOLF CLUB RD

CLUBHO

FAIRWAY RD

GATEWAY

3200

PO

NAVIGATORS PL

DELTA

WATERSIDE PL

DEL

COTTAGE LN

SANDY LN FS

HALCYON PL

COVES

ISLE

STONE PL

CHANNEL PL

SUNSET DR

PARK LN

RD

BETHEL ISLAND MARINA

DUTCH SLOUGH

DUTCH SLOUGH RD

VIKING HARBOR

SEA HORSE MARINA

RD

1 WOODS YACHT HARBOR
2 GREGS HARBOR
3 BENTLEYS MARINA

RIVE

WELLS

MAR

94561

RD

5900

SANDMOUND BLVD

OAKLEY

ISLAND

5000

RD

BETHEL ISLAND RD

4900

95-11

TULE TREE LN

CONTRA

COSTA

CANAL

JERSEY

FRANKLIN LN

KNIGHTSEN AV

BROADWAY

94548

CYPRESS

2100

RD

MAHONEY LN

E

CYPRESS

CYPRESS LAKE DR

RD

0 .125 .25 .375 .5 miles 1 in. = 1900 ft.

SEE 597 MAP

1300

A   B   C   D   E

© 2006 Rand McNally & Company

N

E F G H J

1 ALCOTT LN
2 SHELLY LN

N WILLOW RD
ALCOTT CIR
HAMTHONNE DR
BENET CT
PORTER CIR

RIVERVIEW DR

3900

PIPER DR

S WILLOW RD

4000

95-4

BEACON HARBOR

BOYDS HARBOR

RUSSOS MARINA

SLOUGH

RIVERVIEW DR

FRANKS TRACT

STATE RECREATION

AREA

LUB ND

CLUBHOUSE

FAIRWAY DR

RD

ISLAND MHP

RD

200

DELTA CT
WATERSIDE PL
EDGEWATER PL
COVES
SEA GATE PL
SEAWARD CT
GREY PL
WHALE PL
DR
WINDSWEPT
WEST WIND PL

94511

BOMBARDIER LN

GATEWAY RD

4000

FRANKS MARINA

6900

6600

6900

7000

SUGAR BARGE RD

SUGAR BARGE

SUGAR BARGE MARINA

95-6

COMM CTR

CHANNEL PL
POINT PL
BRIFT DR
SEA MEADOW CT
DELTA
SEA COVES
SLOUGH PL
SHORELINE PL
STONE RD
DR

ANN & CHUCKS HARBOR

N STONE RD

4600

ROOSEVELT

CUT

SEE 557 MAP

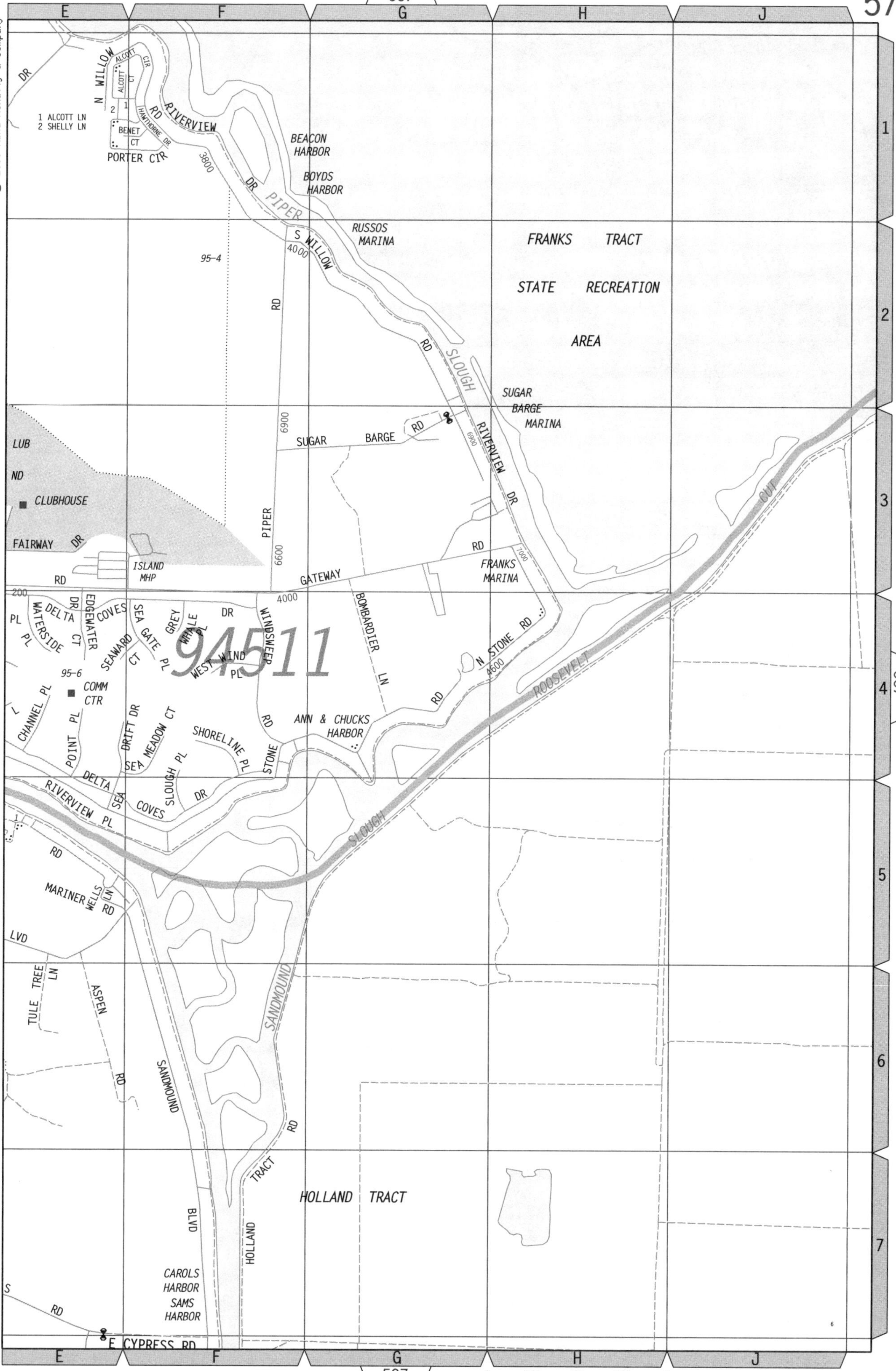

RIVERVIEW PL

RD

MARINER WELLS LN RD

LVD

TULE TREE LN

ASPEN RD

SANDMOUND

SANDMOUND RD

SLOUGH

TRACT RD

HOLLAND TRACT

BLVD

HOLLAND

CAROLS HARBOR

SAMS HARBOR

S RD

E CYPRESS RD

1

2

3

4

5

6

7

E F G H J

0 .125 .25 .375 .5
miles 1 in. = 1900 ft.

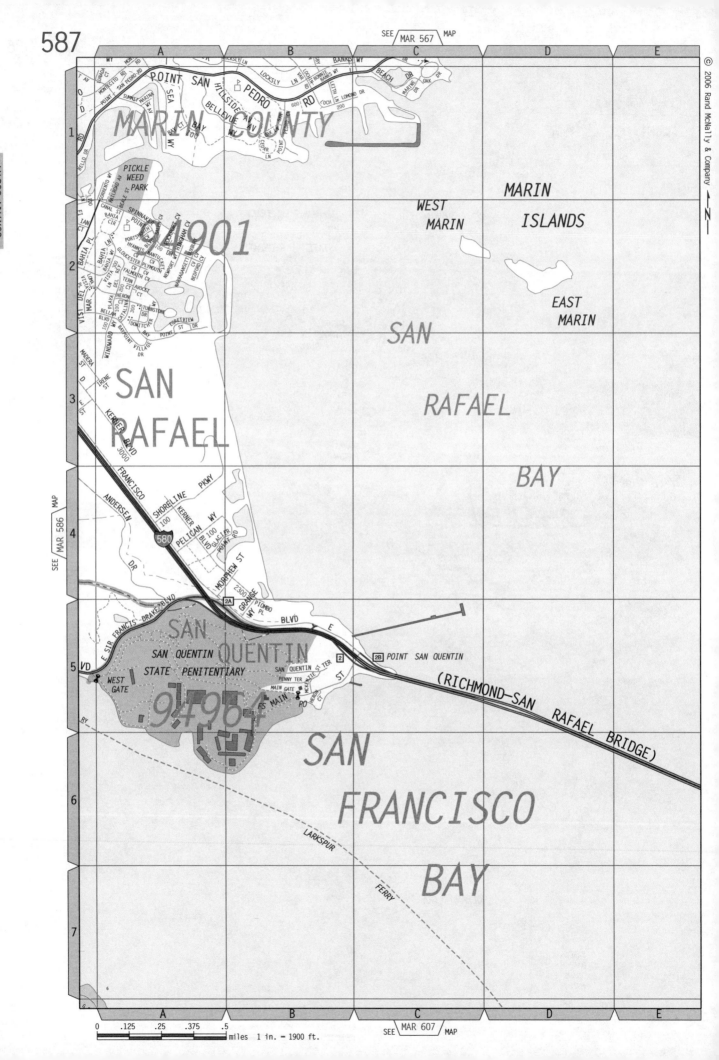

587

SEE MAR 567 MAP

MARIN COUNTY

POINT SAN PEDRO RD

PICKLE WEED PARK

94901

MARIN ISLANDS

WEST MARIN

EAST MARIN

SAN RAFAEL

SAN RAFAEL BAY

SAN QUENTIN

SAN QUENTIN STATE PENITENTIARY

94964

(RICHMOND–SAN RAFAEL BRIDGE)

SAN FRANCISCO BAY

LARKSPUR FERRY

SEE MAR 586 MAP

CONTRA COSTA

© 2006 Rand McNally & Company

0 .125 .25 .375 .5 miles 1 in. = 1900 ft.

SEE MAR 607 MAP

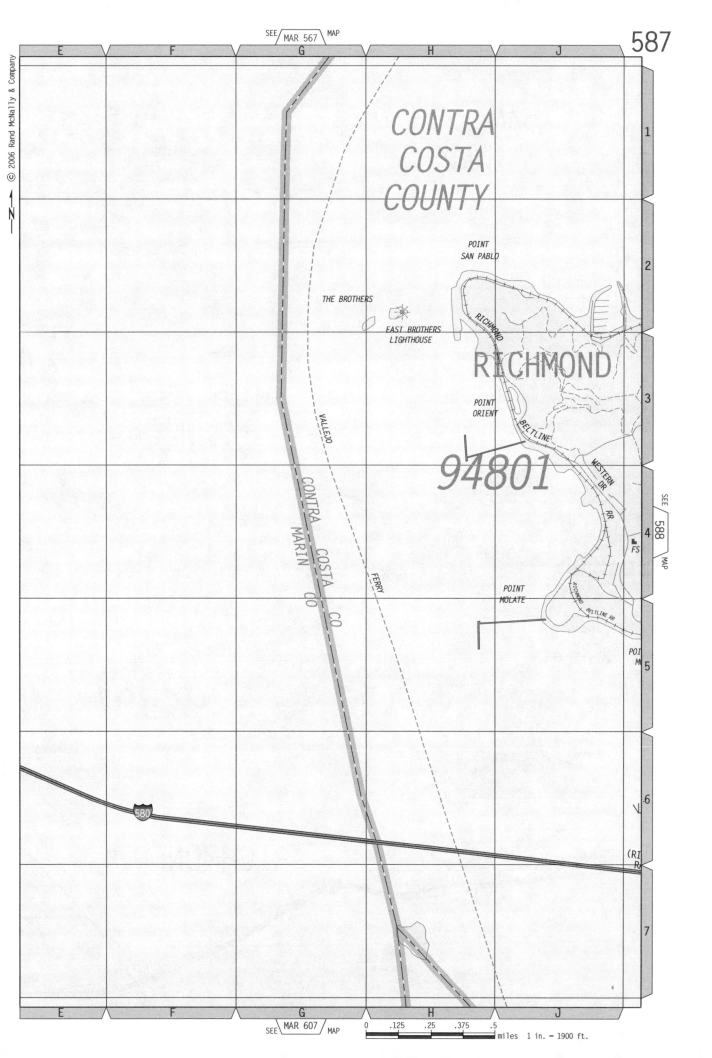

E   F   G   H   J

1

CONTRA
COSTA
COUNTY

POINT
SAN PABLO

2

THE BROTHERS

EAST BROTHERS
LIGHTHOUSE

RICHMOND

RICHMOND

POINT
ORIENT

3

BELTLINE

94801

WESTERN
DR

VALLEJO

RR

SEE / 588 / MAP

4

FS

CONTRA COSTA CO

MARIN CO

FERRY

POINT
MOLATE

RICHMOND

BELTLINE RR

POI
M

5

580

.6

(RI
R

7

E   F   G   H   J

0   .125   .25   .375   .5
miles 1 in. = 1900 ft.

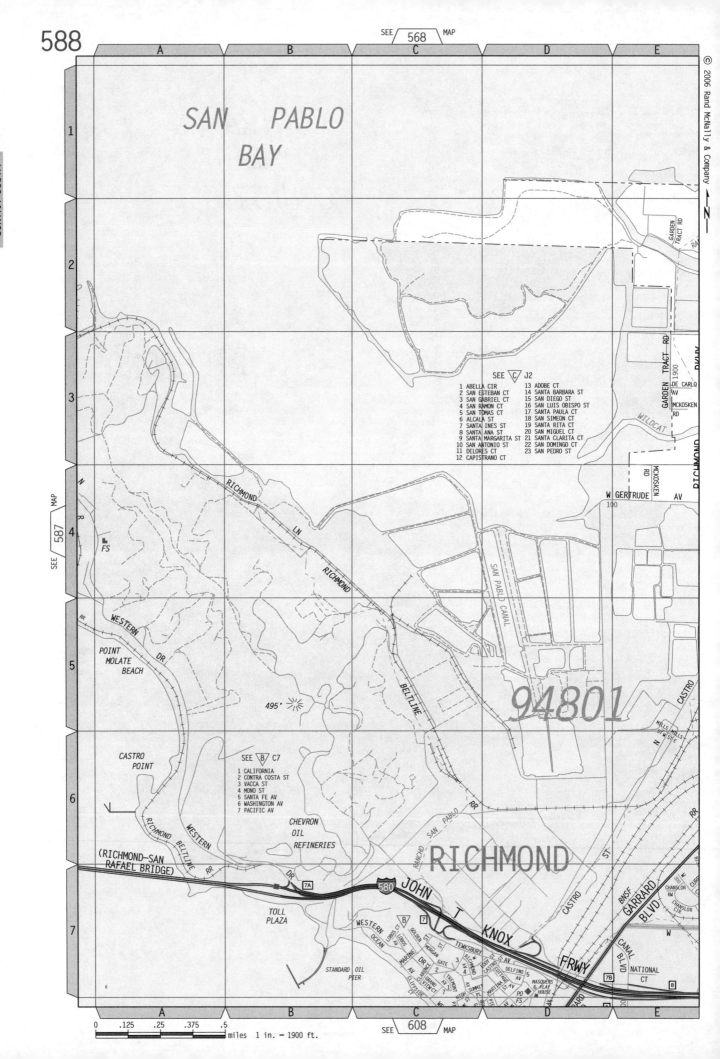

CONTRA COSTA

© 2006 Rand McNally & Company

SEE 568 MAP

SAN PABLO
BAY

SEE C J2

1 ABELLA CIR	13 ADOBE CT
2 SAN ESTEBAN CT	14 SANTA BARBARA ST
3 SAN GABRIEL CT	15 SAN DIEGO ST
4 SAN RAMON CT	16 SAN LUIS OBISPO ST
5 SAN TOMAS CT	17 SANTA PAULA CT
6 ALCALA ST	18 SAN SIMEON CT
7 SANTA INES ST	19 SANTA RITA CT
8 SANTA ANA ST	20 SAN MIGUEL CT
9 SANTA MARGARITA ST	21 SANTA CLARITA CT
10 SAN ANTONIO ST	22 SAN DOMINGO CT
11 DELORES CT	23 SAN PEDRO ST
12 CAPISTRANO CT	

GARDEN TRACT RD

DE CARLO AV
MCKOSKEN RD

RICHMOND

WILDCAT

W GERTRUDE AV
100

MCKOSKEN RD

RICHMOND LN

RICHMOND

SAN PABLO CANAL

SEE 587 MAP

FS

WESTERN DR
POINT MOLATE BEACH

RR

BELTLINE

94801

495'

MILLS MILLS ST W STE

CASTRO POINT

SEE B C7

| 1 CALIFORNIA |
| 2 CONTRA COSTA ST |
| 3 VACCA ST |
| 4 MONO ST |
| 5 SANTA FE AV |
| 6 WASHINGTON AV |
| 7 PACIFIC AV |

CHEVRON OIL REFINERIES

RANCHO SAN PABLO RR

CASTRO ST

RICHMOND

RR

RICHMOND BELTLINE RR

WESTERN

(RICHMOND–SAN RAFAEL BRIDGE)

DR

7A

580

JOHN T KNOX FRWY

BNSF

GARRARD BLVD

CHANSLOR RW
CHANSLOR CIR

TOLL PLAZA

WESTERN
OCEAN

LOBOS CT
LOBOS ST
MARINE DR

GOLDEN GATE
MORGAN ST
RICHMOND
BRAND

TEWKSBURY AV

CADDY ST
CASTRO COTTAGE
DELFINO

7

CANAL BLVD

NATIONAL CT

STANDARD OIL PIER

CLIFTSIDE
BRAND
CLARENCE
AV

TREMONT AV

HIGH
SUMMIT

MARTINA AV
PL
PO
FS

MASQUERS PLAY HOUSE

7B

B

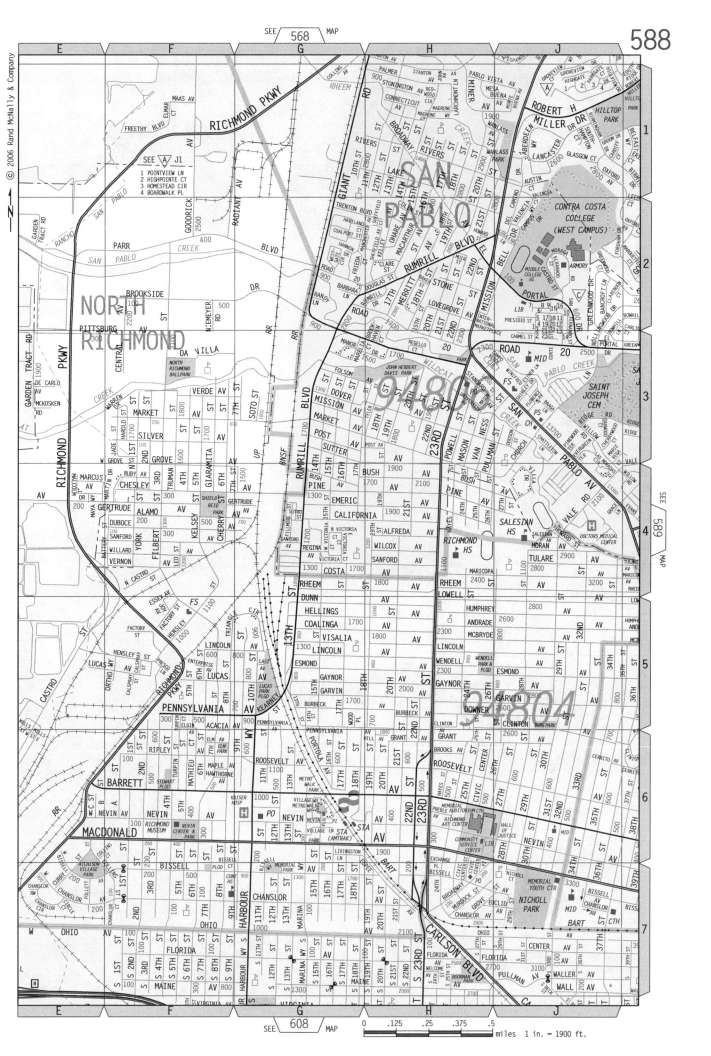

SEE 568 MAP

SEE 589 MAP

SEE 608 MAP

miles   1 in. = 1900 ft.

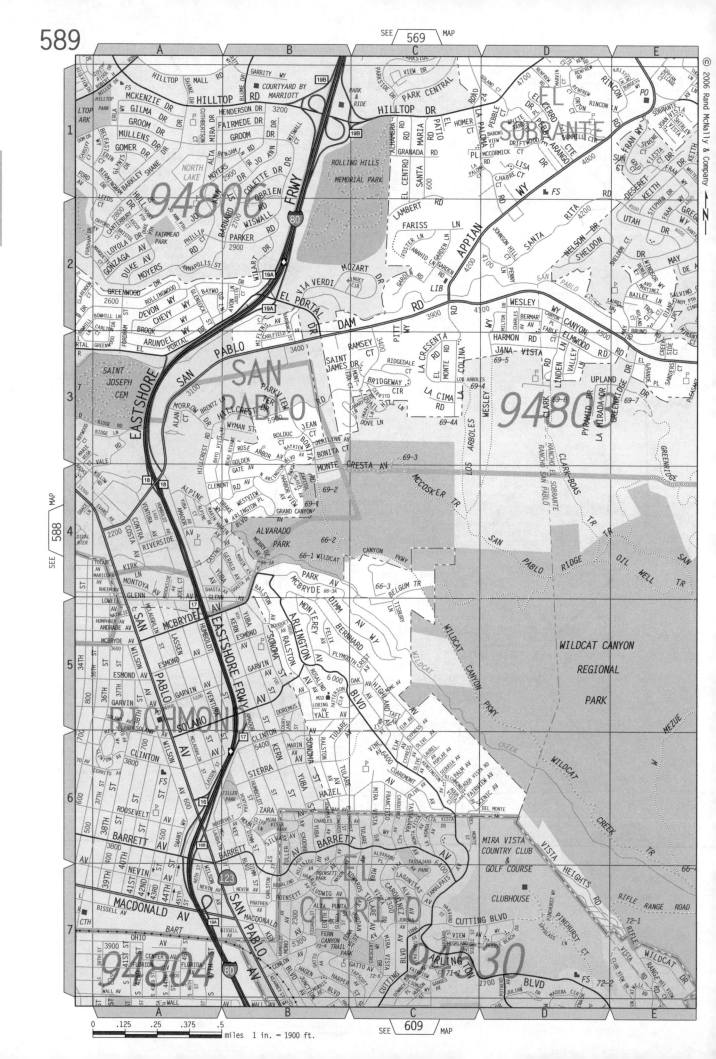

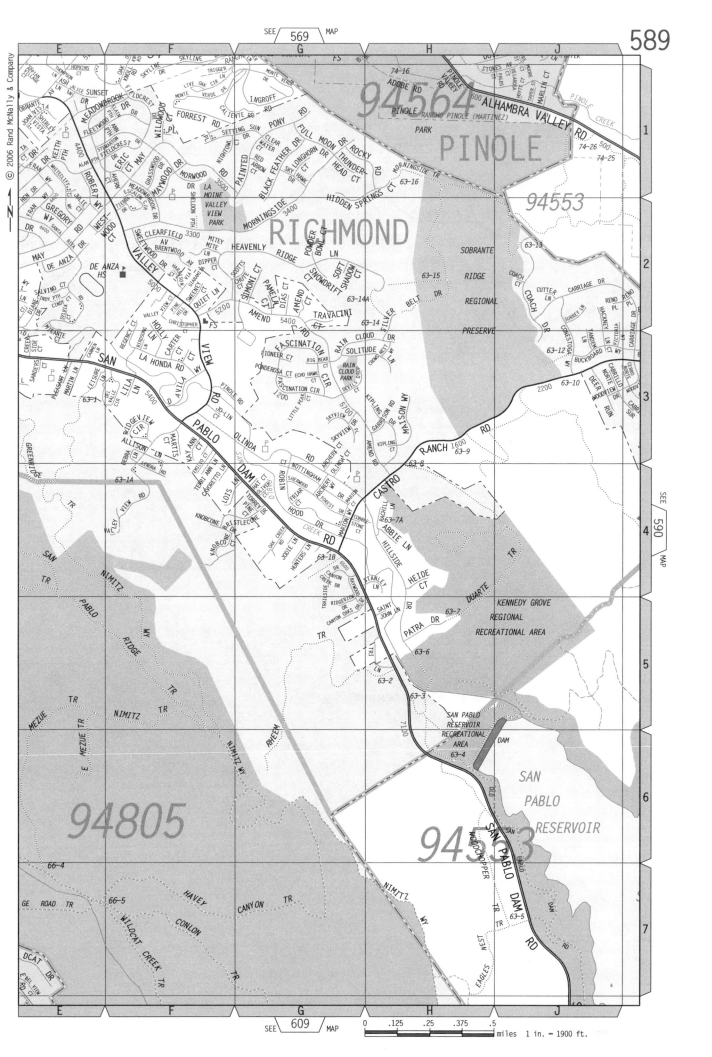

589

CONTRA COSTA

94564

PINOLE

RICHMOND

94553

ALHAMBRA VALLEY RD.

Rancho Pinole (Martinez)

PINOLE CREEK

Sobrante Ridge Regional Preserve

RANCH RD

CASTRO

Kennedy Grove Regional Recreational Area

94805

San Pablo Reservoir Recreational Area

SAN PABLO RESERVOIR

94553

SAN PABLO DAM RD

SEE 590 MAP

0 .125 .25 .375 .5 miles   1 in. = 1900 ft.

590

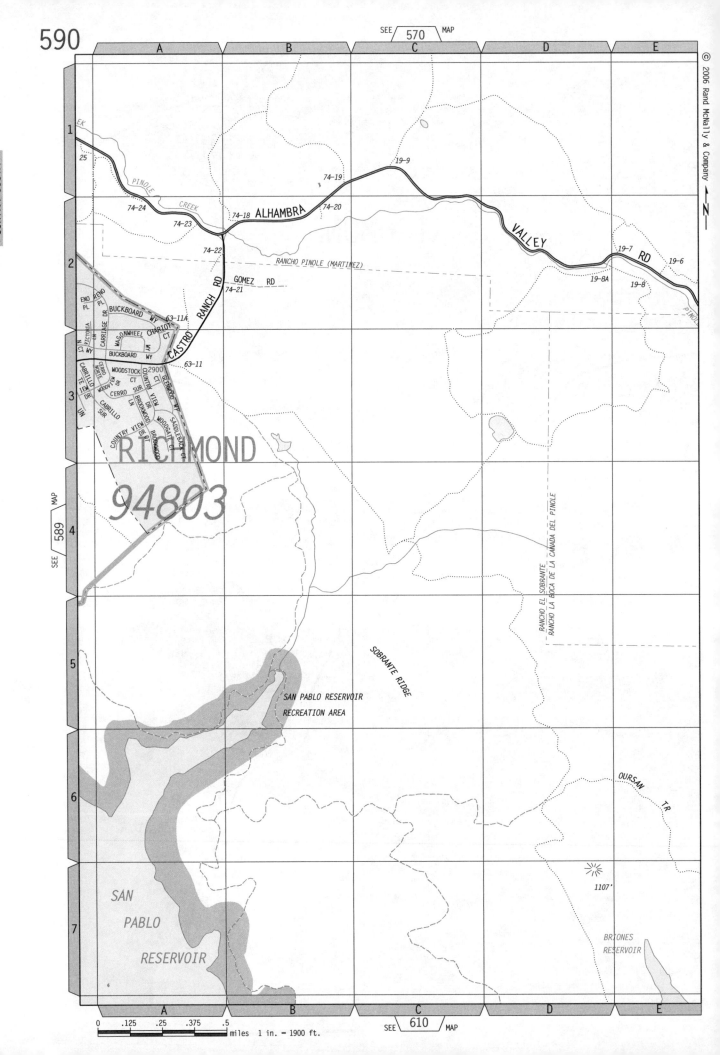

CONTRA COSTA

© 2006 Rand McNally & Company — N —

A B C D E

1

25

PINOLE CREEK

74-24
74-23
74-18 ALHAMBRA
74-20
74-19
19-9

VALLEY RD

19-7
19-6
19-8A
19-8

2

RANCHO PINOLE (MARTINEZ)

74-22
GOMEZ RD
74-21

ENO PL
RENO PL
BUCKBOARD WY
CARRIAGE DR
WAGONWHEEL WY
CHARIOT CT
CASTRO RANCH RD
63-11A

VICTORIA LN
CT WY
BUCKBOARD WY
63-11

WOODSTOCK CT
2900
COUNTRY VIEW DR
GLENWOOD WY
CERRO NORTE
CERRO
MOODY
BRONWOOD LN
SADDLEBACK CT

3

CABRILLO TEE TEM DR
CERRO SUR
CABRILLO SUR
COUNTRY VIEW DR
BRONWOOD DR
WOODGATE CT
BRONWOOD
RICHMOND
94803

RANCHO EL SOBRANTE
RANCHO LA BOCA DE LA CANADA DEL PINOLE

SEE 589 MAP

4

5

SOBRANTE RIDGE

SAN PABLO RESERVOIR
RECREATION AREA

OURSAN TR

6

1107'

SAN PABLO RESERVOIR

7

BRIONES RESERVOIR

A B C D E

0 .125 .25 .375 .5 miles 1 in. = 1900 ft.

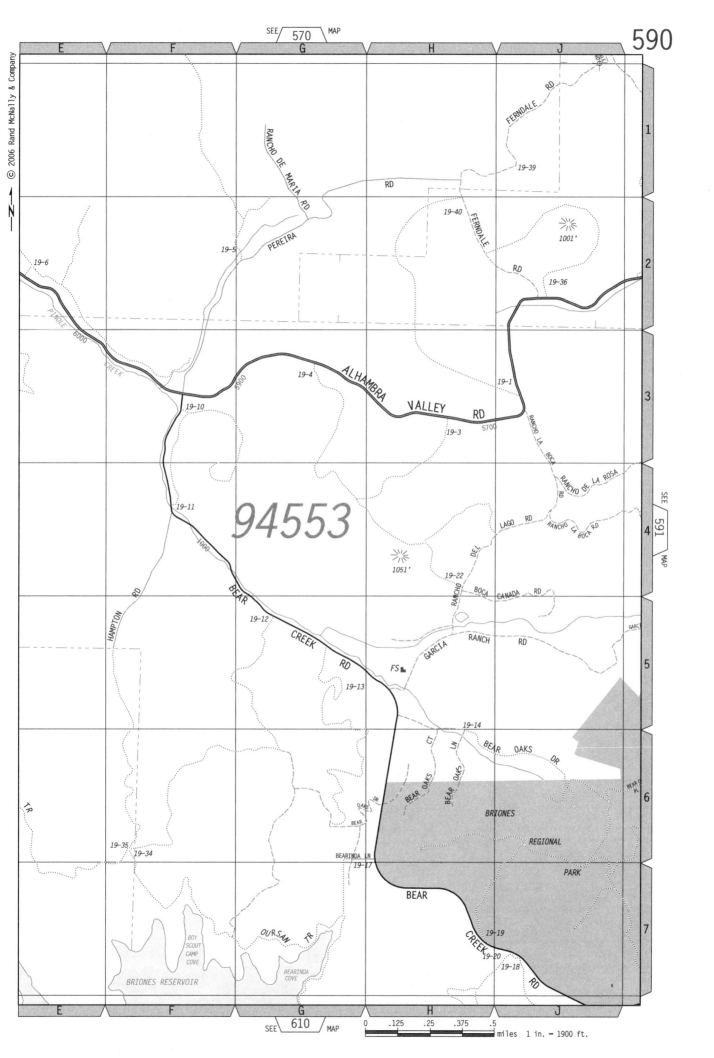

CONTRA COSTA

SEE 570 MAP

E   F   G   H   J

1

FERNDALE RD

RANCHO DE MARIA RD

19-39

RD

19-40

PEREIRA

19-5

FERNDALE

2

19-6

1001'

19-36

PINHOLE 6000 CREEK

RD

ALHAMBRA

5900

19-4

VALLEY

RD

19-10

19-3

5700

3

RANCHO LA BOCA

RANCHO DE LA ROSA

RD

19-1

94553

19-11

DEL

LAGO

RD

RANCHO LA BOCA RD

SEE 591 MAP

4

1000

1051'

19-22

BEAR

RANCHO

BOCA

CANADA

RD

HAMPTON RD

19-12

CREEK

RD

GARCIA

RANCH

RD

GARC

5

FS

19-13

19-14

CT

LN

BEAR   OAKS   DR

BEAR O PL

6

TR

OAKS   DR

BEAR   OAKS

BEAR   OAKS

BRIONES

BEAR

REGIONAL

19-35

19-34

BEARINDA LN

19-17

PARK

BEAR

7

OURSAN   TR

CREEK   19-19

BOY
SCOUT
CAMP
COVE

BEARINDA
COVE

19-20

19-18

RD

BRIONES RESERVOIR

6

E   F   G   H   J

SEE 610 MAP

0   .125   .25   .375   .5

miles 1 in. = 1900 ft.

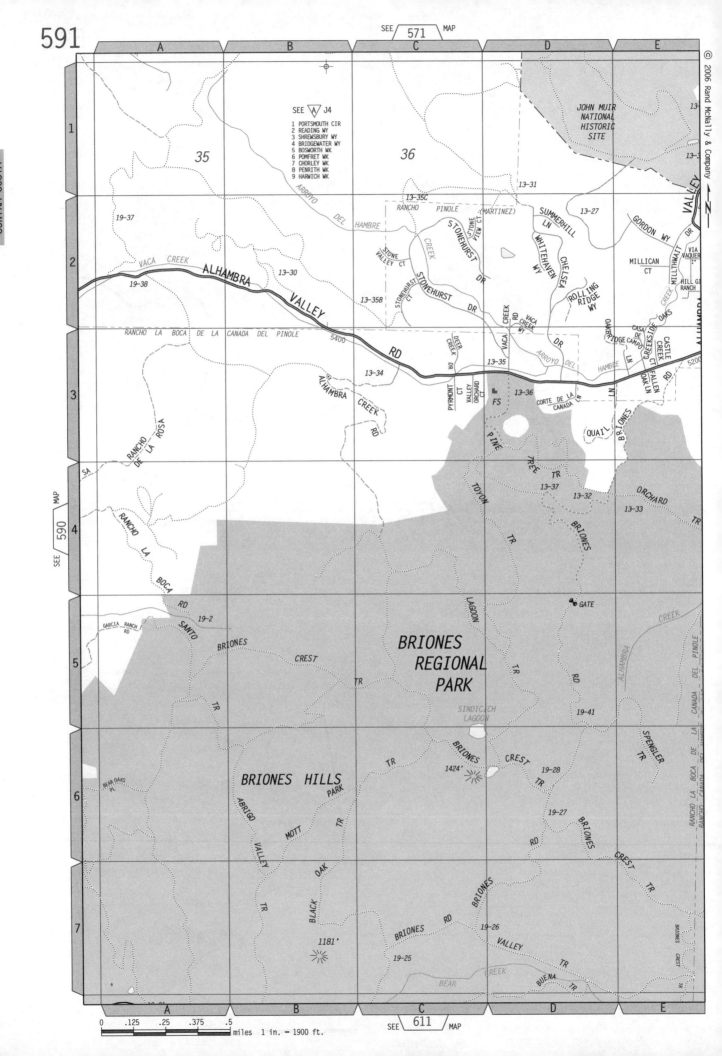

591

CONTRA COSTA

SEE 571 MAP

SEE A J4
1 PORTSMOUTH CIR
2 READING WY
3 SHREWSBURY WY
4 BRIDGEWATER WY
5 BOSWORTH WK
6 POMFRET WK
7 CHORLEY WK
8 PENRITH WK
9 HARWICH WK

35

36

JOHN MUIR
NATIONAL
HISTORIC
SITE

13-31

19-37

13-35C

RANCHO PINOLE (MARTINEZ)

SUMMERHILL LN

13-27

GORDON WY

VACA CREEK

13-30

ALHAMBRA

STONE VALLEY CT

STONEHURST DR

WHITEHAVEN WY

CHELSEA

MILLICAN CT

VIA VAQUERO

19-38

13-35B

VALLEY

STONEHURST CT

STONEHURST DR

ROLLING RIDGE WY

HILL GIRL RANCH

RANCHO LA BOCA DE LA CANADA DEL PINOLE

5400

RD

13-34

DEER CREEK DR

VACA CREEK WY

VACA CREEK RD

ARROYO DEL HAMBRE

OAKBRIDGE CANDO

CASA DE

CREEKSIDE OAKS

CASTLE CREEK

5200

ALHAMBRA CREEK

RD

PYRMONT CT

VALLEY ORCHARD CT

13-35

13-36

FS

CORTE DE LA CANADA

CREEKSIDE CT

FALLEN OAK LN

BRIONES

RANCHO DE LA ROSA

QUAIL

SA

PINE

TREE

TR

13-37

13-32

ORCHARD

RANCHO LA BOCA

TOYON

TR

13-33

TR

SEE 590 MAP

GARCIA RANCH RD

19-2

SANTO

BRIONES

CREST

LAGOON

TR

BRIONES

TR

GATE

BRIONES
REGIONAL
PARK

RD

19-41

ALHAMBRA

CREEK

CREST

TR

SINDICICH
LAGOON

CANADA DEL PINOLE

TR

SPENGLER

TR

BEAR OAKS PL

BRIONES HILLS

PARK

TR

BRIONES

TR

1424'

CREST

19-28

TR

19-27

BRIONES

RD

RANCHO LA BOCA DE LA

ABRIGO

VALLEY

MOTT

TR

BLACK

OAK

TR

BRIONES

RD

BRIONES

CREST

TR

1181'

BRIONES

RD

19-26

VALLEY

BRIONES CREST

19-25

TR

6

BEAR

CREEK

BUENA

TR

SEE 611 MAP

0 .125 .25 .375 .5
miles 1 in. = 1900 ft.

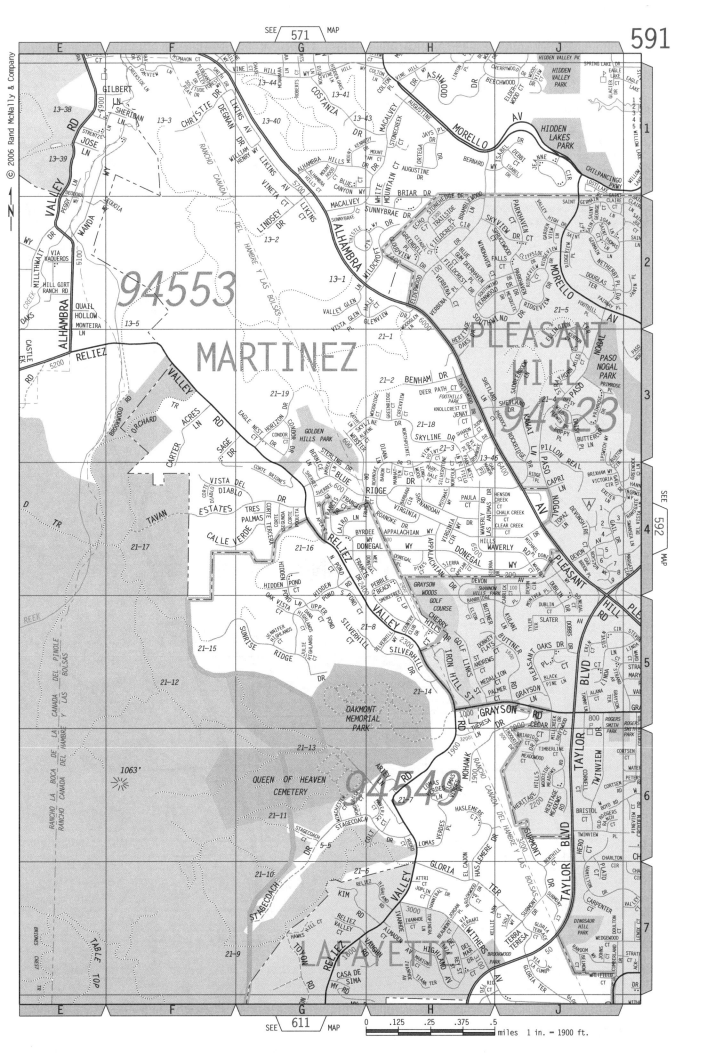

94553

MARTINEZ

PLEASANT HILL

94523

94549

LAFAYETTE

0 .125 .25 .375 .5 miles 1 in. = 1900 ft.

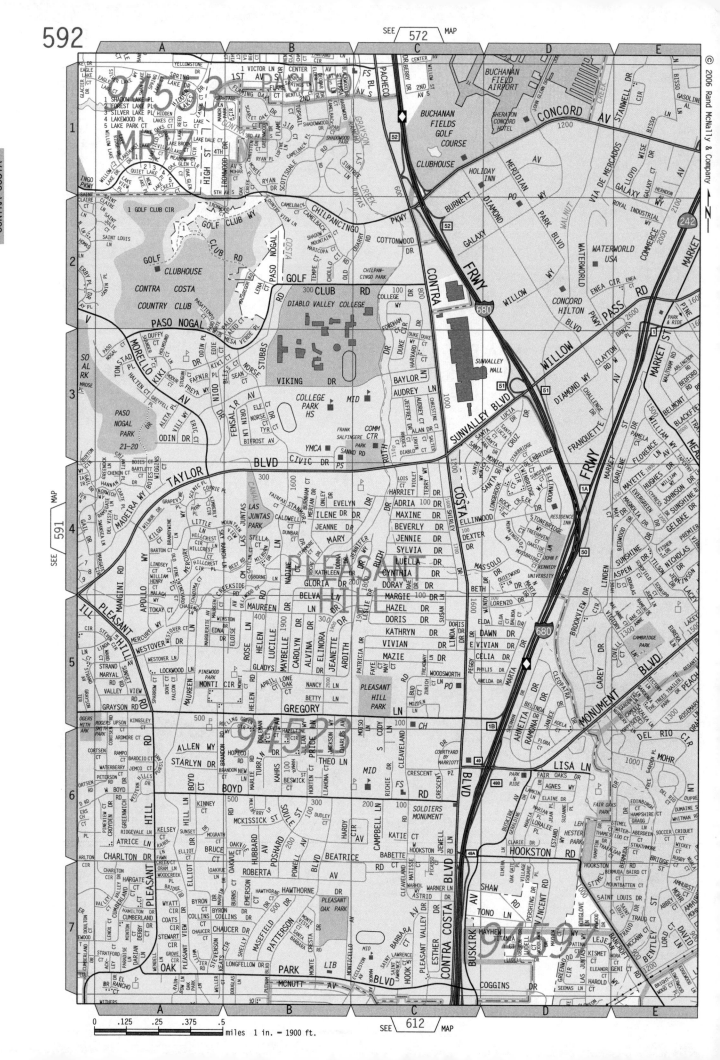

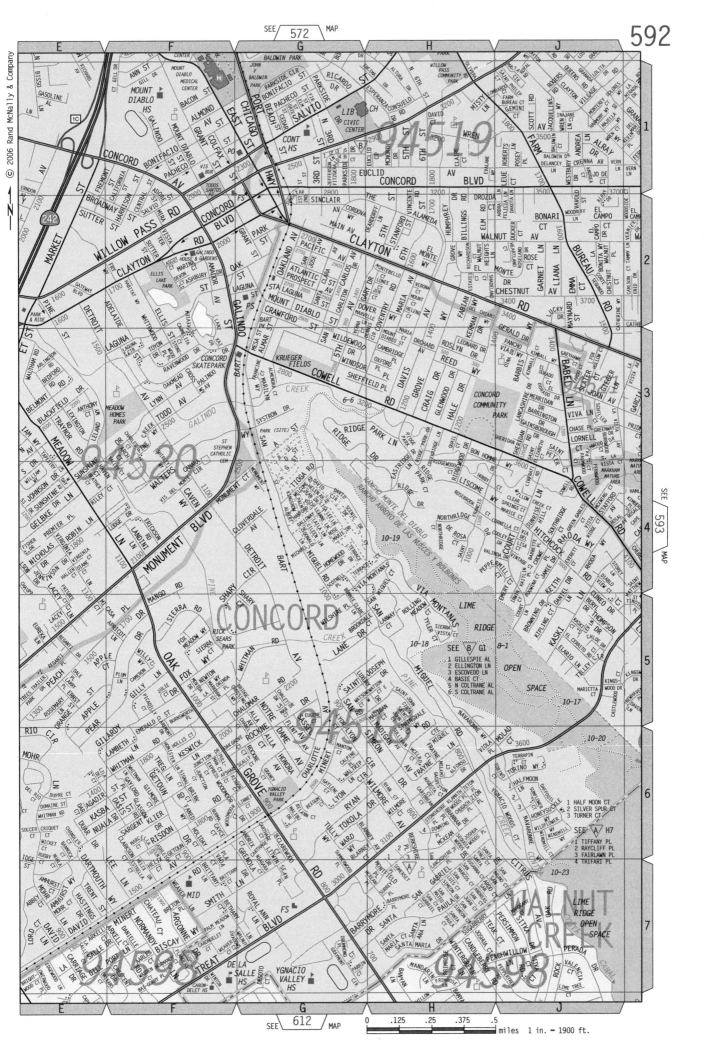

CONTRA COSTA

© 2006 Rand McNally & Company

SEE 572 MAP

SEE 593 MAP

94519

94520

94518

94595

94598

CONCORD

WALNUT CREEK

miles 1 in. = 1900 ft.
0   .125   .25   .375   .5

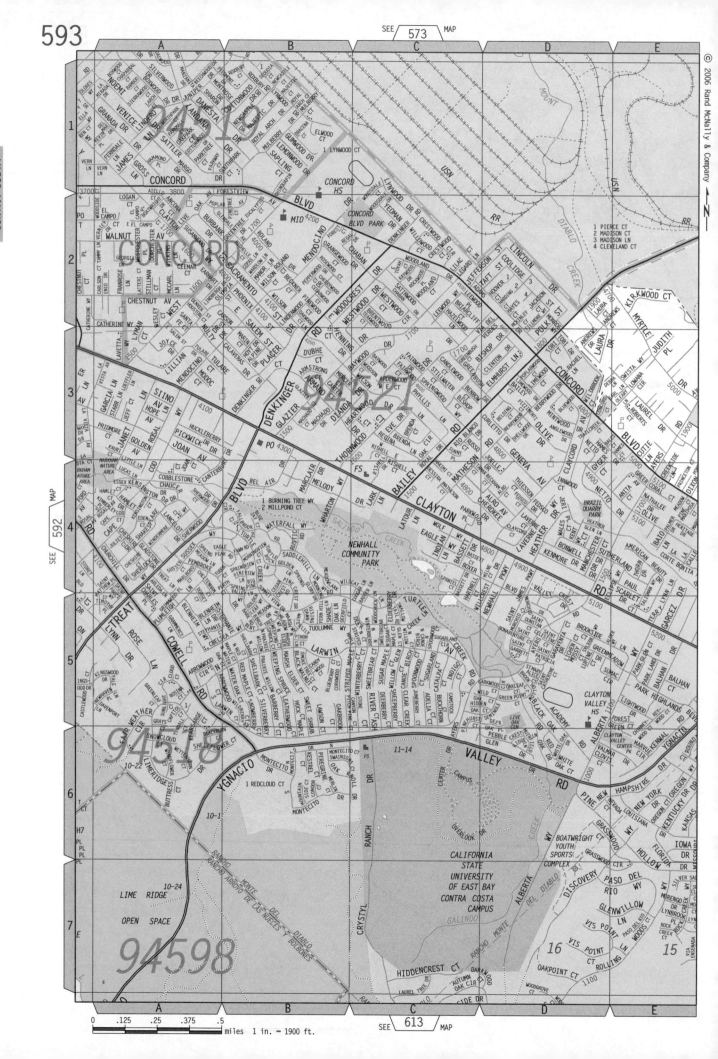

SEE 573 MAP

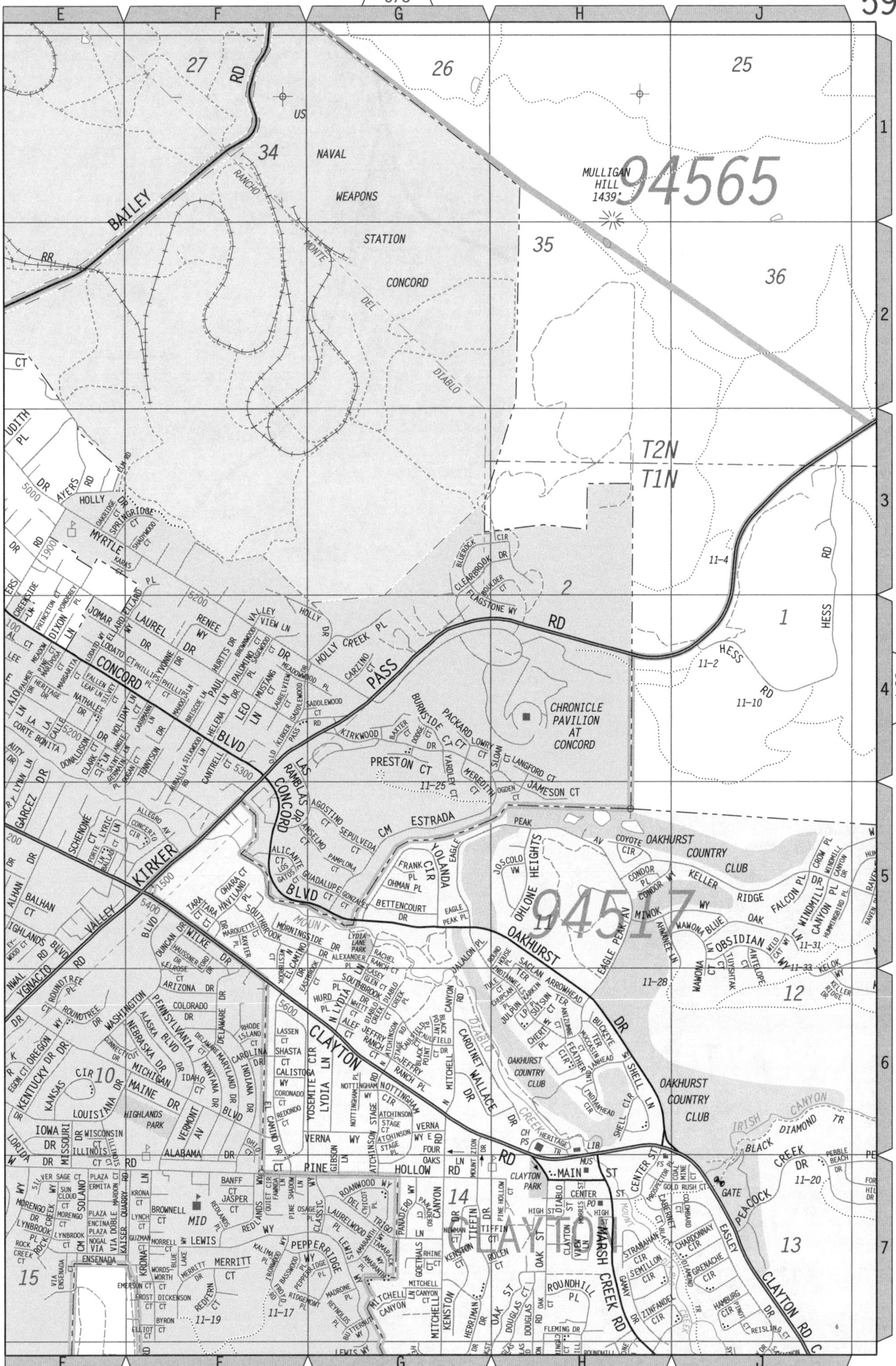

SEE 594 MAP
SEE 613 MAP
0 .125 .25 .375 .5 miles 1 in. = 1900 ft.

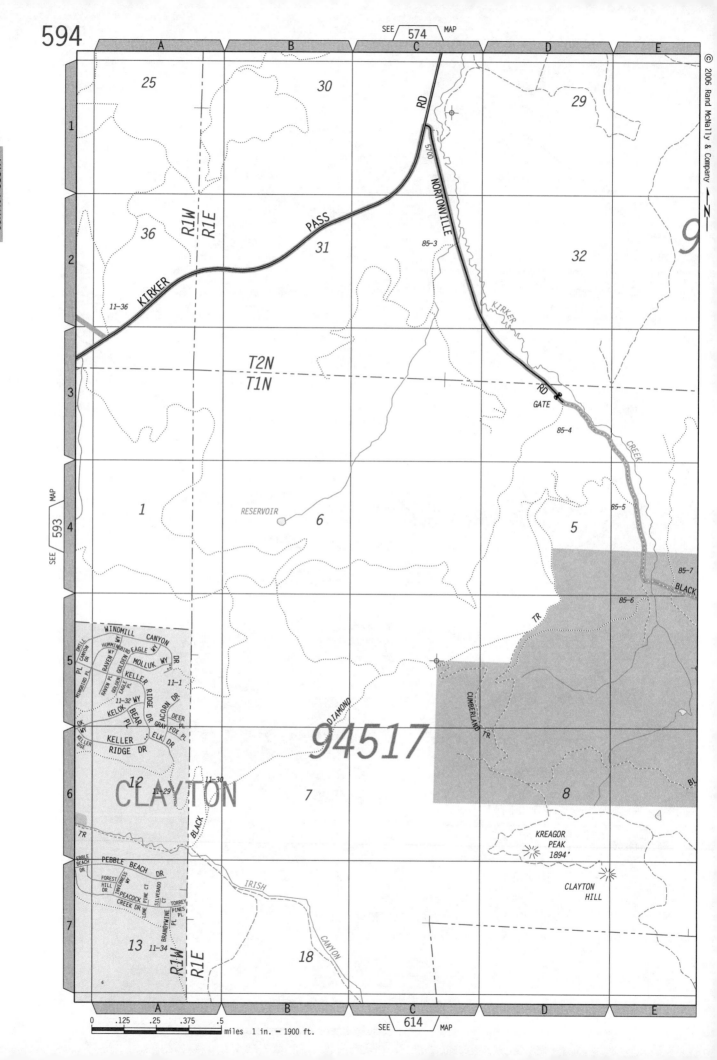

CONTRA COSTA

9

—N—

SEE 574 MAP

A B C D E

25 30 29

1

RD

5700

36 R1W R1E 31 NORTONVILLE 32

2 PASS 85-3

KIRKER KIRKER

11-36

T2N
T1N

RD
3 GATE

85-4

CREEK

MAP

SEE 593

1 RESERVOIR 6 85-5

4 5

85-7

BLACK

85-6

TR

WINDMILL CANYON

5 EAGLE WY MOLLUK WY DR

HUMMINGBIRD WY
RAVEN PL GOLDEN KELLER
RIDGE 11-1
GOLDEN EAGLE PL ACORN DR
11-32 WY GRAY FOX PL CUMBERLAND
KELOK DEER TR
BEAR DR PL
OK WY PL DIAMOND
KELLER ELK DR
KELLER RIDGE DR 94517

6 11-29 11-30

CLAYTON 12 7 8

TR
BLACK KREAGOR
PEAK
7R 1894'
FEBBLE
BEACH PEBBLE BEACH DR CLAYTON
DR FOREST INVERNESS WY IRISH HILL
HILL PEACOCK PINE CT
DR CREEK DR SILVERADO
LONE CT
7 PINES PL
TORREY
BRANDYWINE PL

13 11-34 18
R1W R1E CANYON

6

A B C D E

0 .125 .25 .375 .5
miles 1 in. = 1900 ft.

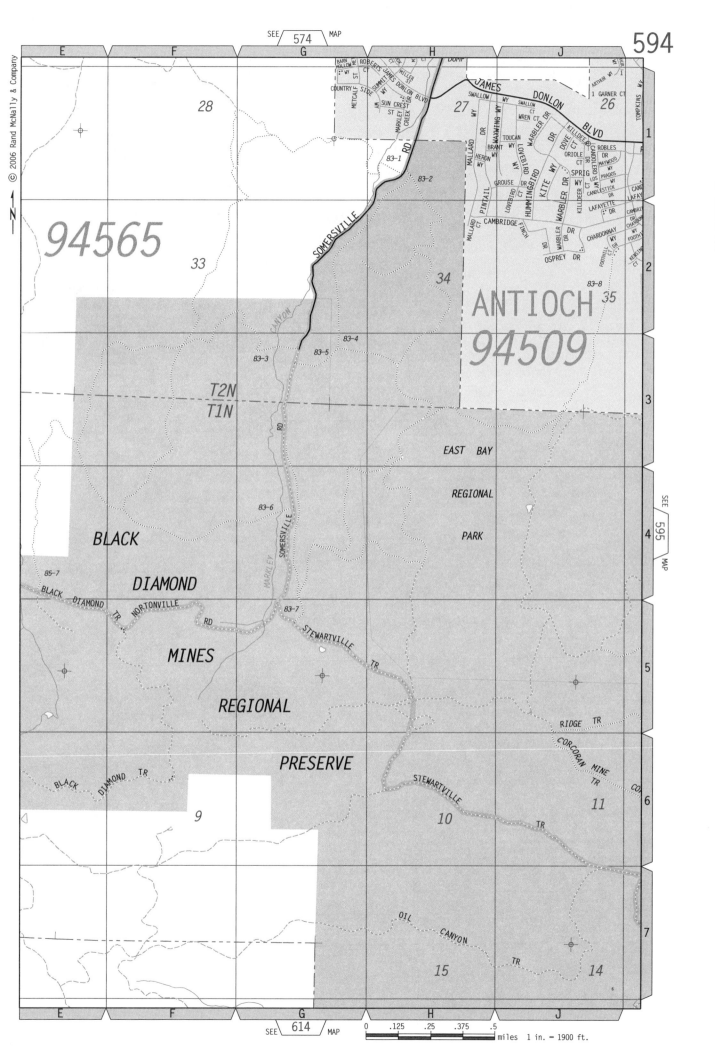

CONTRA COSTA

SEE 574 MAP

E F G H J

28

94565

33

T2N
T1N

SOMERSVILLE

CANYON

RD

83-1
83-2
83-3
83-4
83-5

34

ANTIOCH
94509

JAMES DONLON BLVD

BARN HOLLOW WY
ROBERTS
JAMES DONLON BLVD
MILLER CT
SWALLOW CT
DUMP
COUNTRY SIDE WY
METCALF ST
SUMMIT WY
MARKLEY CREEK DR
SUN CREST ST
27
SWALLOW WY
JAMES
DONLON
SWALLOW WY
WREN CT
26
1 GARNER CT
ARTHUR WY
TOMPKINS WY

MALLARD DR
BRANT WY
HERON WY
TOUCAN WY
WAXWING WY
LOVEBIRD WY
DOVE WY
KITE WY
ORIOLE CT
WARBLER DR
KILLDEER DR
DOVE DR
CANDOLERO DR
ROBLES DR
MAYWOOD WY
LAFAYETTE WY
CAND LAFAY
GROUSE CT
PINTAIL CT
LOVEBIRD CT
HUMMINGBIRD
SPRIG WY
LOS PRADOS WY
CANDLESTICK DR
CAMBRIDGE
FINCH
WARBLER
WARBLER DR
KILLDEER
LAFAYETTE DR
CHARDONNAY WY
CHAMB CAMBRI DR
FOOTH
MALLARD CT
WARBLER CT
DR
WARBLER DR
CHARDONNAY WY
FOOTHILL CT
NEWSING CT
OSPREY DR

2

35
83-8

3

EAST BAY

REGIONAL

PARK

SEE 595 MAP

BLACK

DIAMOND

MINES

REGIONAL

PRESERVE

MARKLEY SOMERSVILLE RD
SOMERSVILLE

83-6

85-7
BLACK DIAMOND TR
NORTONVILLE
RD
83-7
STEWARTVILLE TR

4

BLACK DIAMOND TR

9

5

STEWARTVILLE
TR
RIDGE TR
CORCORAN MINE TR
COR
11
6

10

OIL CANYON
TR
15
14

7

E F G H J

SEE 614 MAP

0 .125 .25 .375 .5
miles 1 in. = 1900 ft.

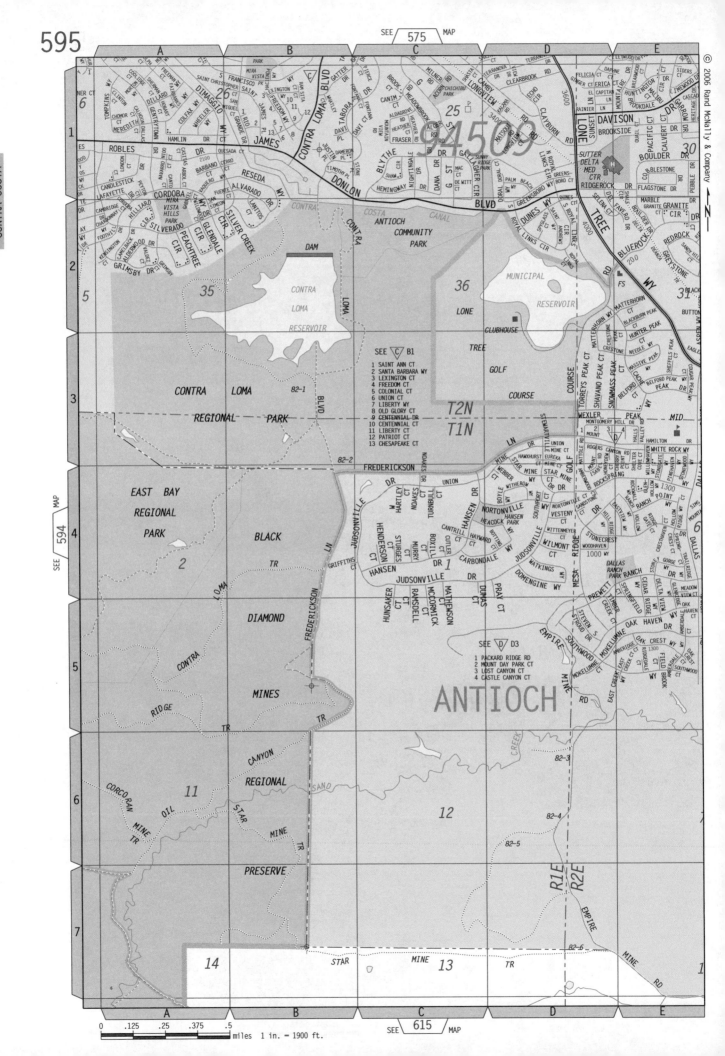

595

CONTRA COSTA

94509

© 2006 Rand McNally & Company

N

SEE 594 MAP

SEE /D/ D3
1 PACKARD RIDGE RD
2 MOUNT DAY PARK CT
3 LOST CANYON CT
4 CASTLE CANYON CT

SEE /C/ B1
1 SAINT ANN CT
2 SANTA BARBARA WY
3 LEXINGTON CT
4 FREEDOM CT
5 COLONIAL CT
6 UNION CT
7 LIBERTY WY
8 OLD GLORY CT
9 CENTENNIAL DR
10 CENTENNIAL CT
11 LIBERTY CT
12 PATRIOT CT
13 CHESAPEAKE CT

ANTIOCH

0 .125 .25 .375 .5
miles 1 in. = 1900 ft.

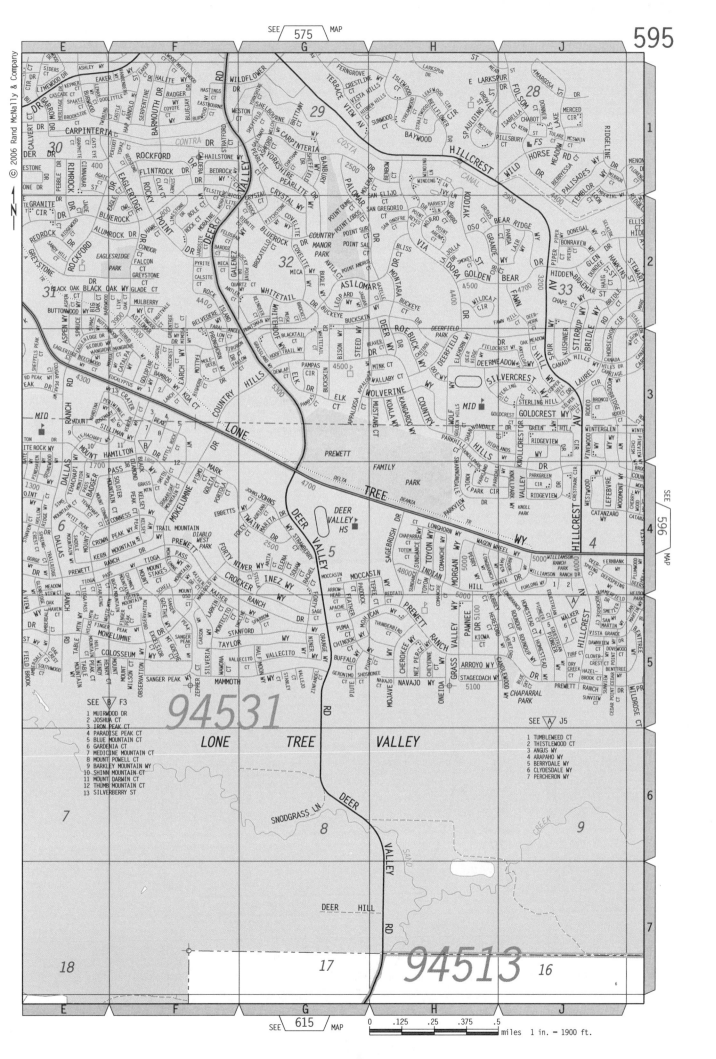

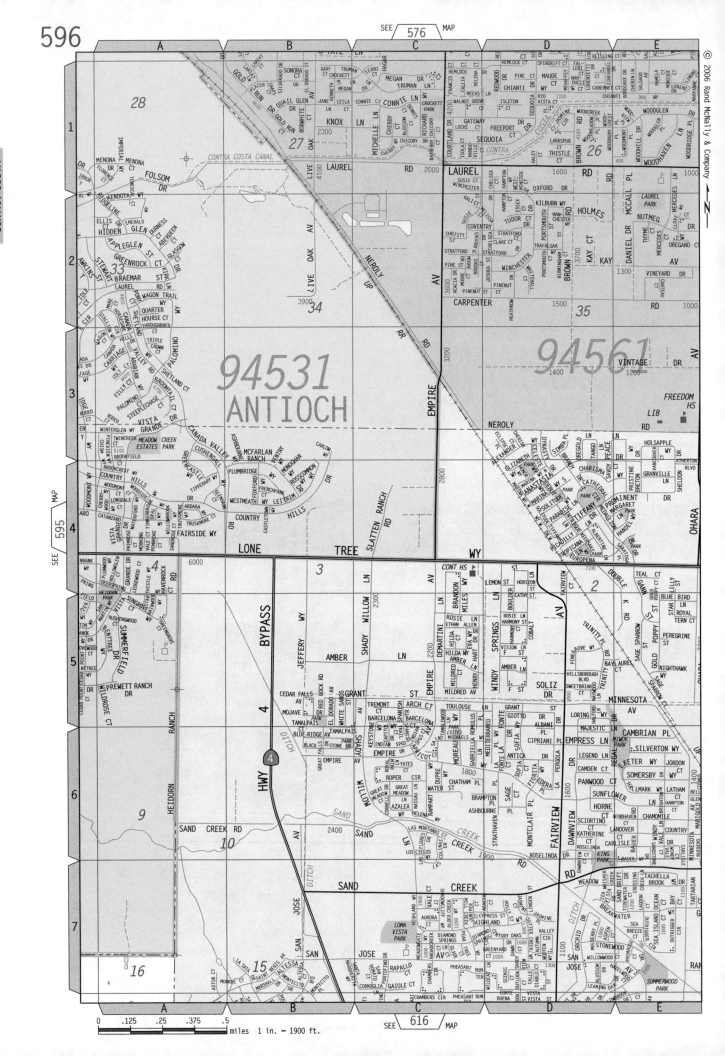

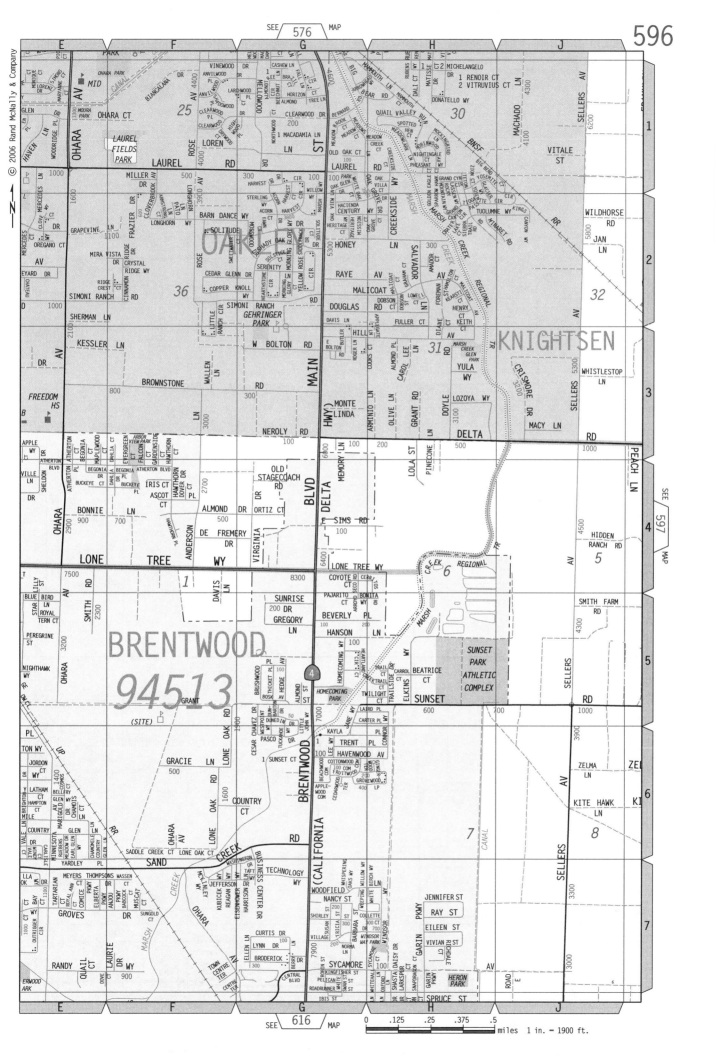

CONTRA COSTA

© 2006 Rand McNally & Company

0   .125   .25   .375   .5
miles   1 in. = 1900 ft.

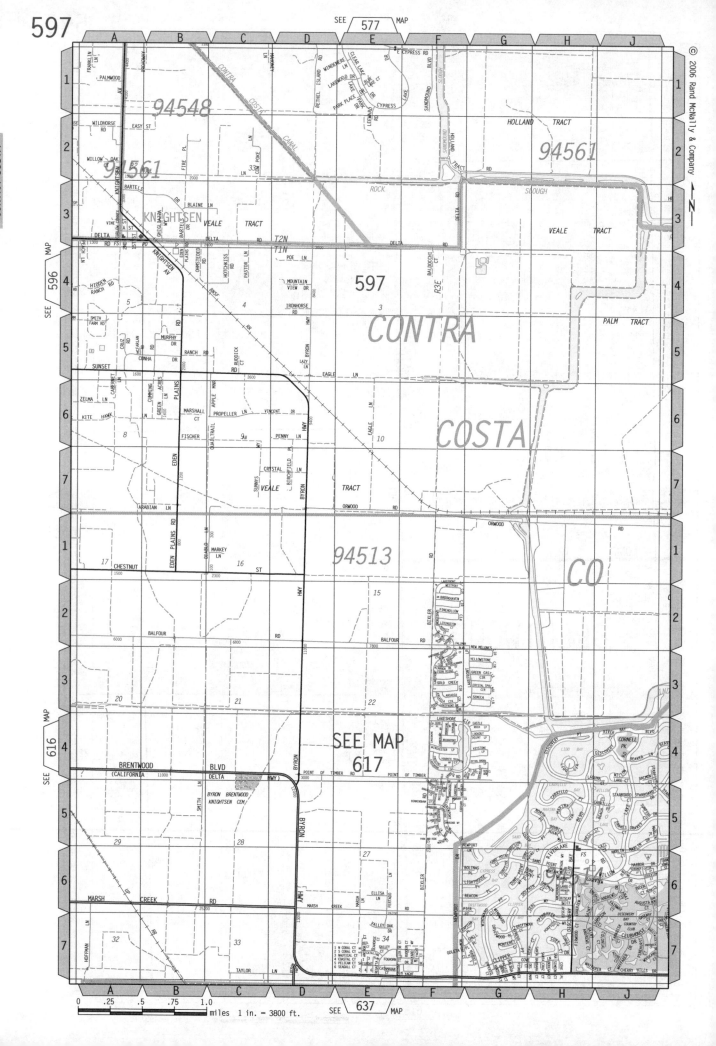

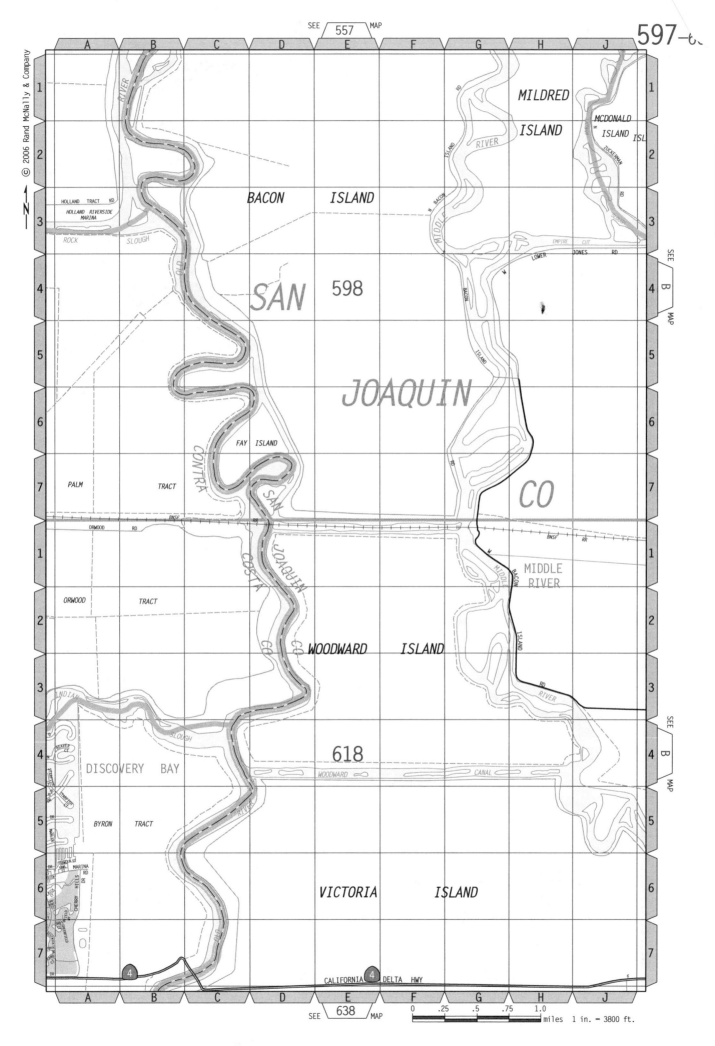

© 2006 Rand McNally & Company

N

MILDRED

ISLAND

RIVER

MCDONALD
ISLAND ISL

ZUCKERMAN

BACON   ISLAND

HOLLAND TRACT RD
HOLLAND RIVERSIDE
MARINA

N BACON

ROCK   SLOUGH

MIDDLE

EMPIRE   CUT

LOWER   JONES   RD

N

OLD

BACON

SAN

598

ISLAND

SEE B MAP

JOAQUIN

RD

CONTRA

FAY ISLAND

SAN

CO

PALM   TRACT

BNSF   RR

ORWOOD   RD

JOAQUIN

COSTA

BNSF   RR

N

MIDDLE

N BACON

MIDDLE

RIVER

ORWOOD   TRACT

CO

ISLAND

CO

WOODWARD   ISLAND

RD

RIVER

INDIAN

SEE B MAP

SLOUGH

618

BEAVER
CT

WOODWARD   CANAL

DISCOVERY BAY

RIVER

BYRON   TRACT

MARINA
RD

CHERRY HILLS DR

VICTORIA   ISLAND

4

CALIFORNIA   4   DELTA HWY

6

0   .25   .5   .75   1.0

miles 1 in. = 3800 ft.

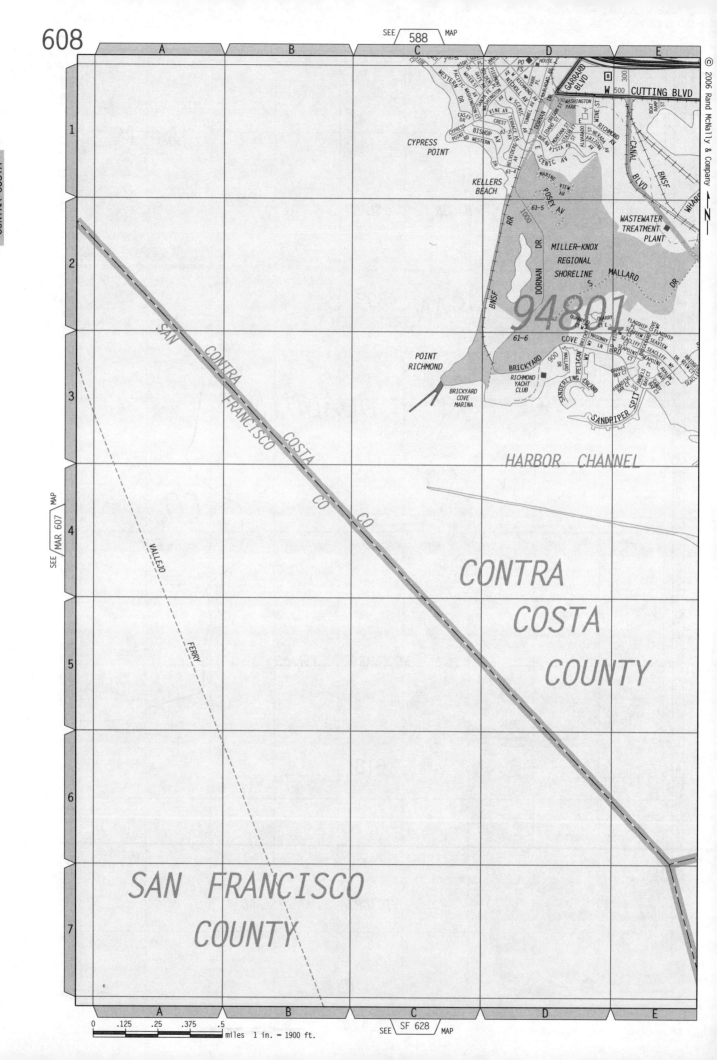

—N—

CUTTING BLVD

CYPRESS POINT

KELLERS BEACH

WASTEWATER TREATMENT PLANT

MILLER-KNOX REGIONAL SHORELINE

MALLARD DR

94801

POINT RICHMOND

BRICKYARD COVE MARINA

RICHMOND YACHT CLUB

BRICKYARD COVE

SANDPIPER SPIT

HARBOR CHANNEL

CONTRA

COSTA

COUNTY

SAN FRANCISCO COUNTY

VALLEJO FERRY

SEE MAR 607 MAP

0 .125 .25 .375 .5
miles 1 in. = 1900 ft.

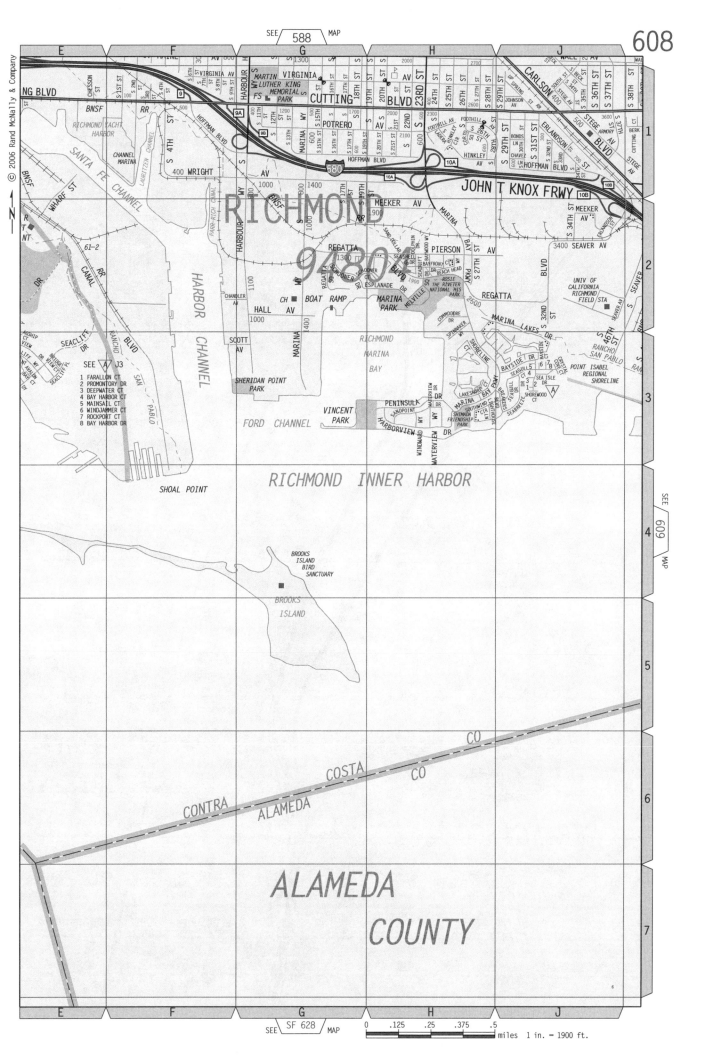

RICHMOND
94804

E   F   G   H   J

SEE 609 MAP

0 .125 .25 .375 .5
miles 1 in. = 1900 ft.

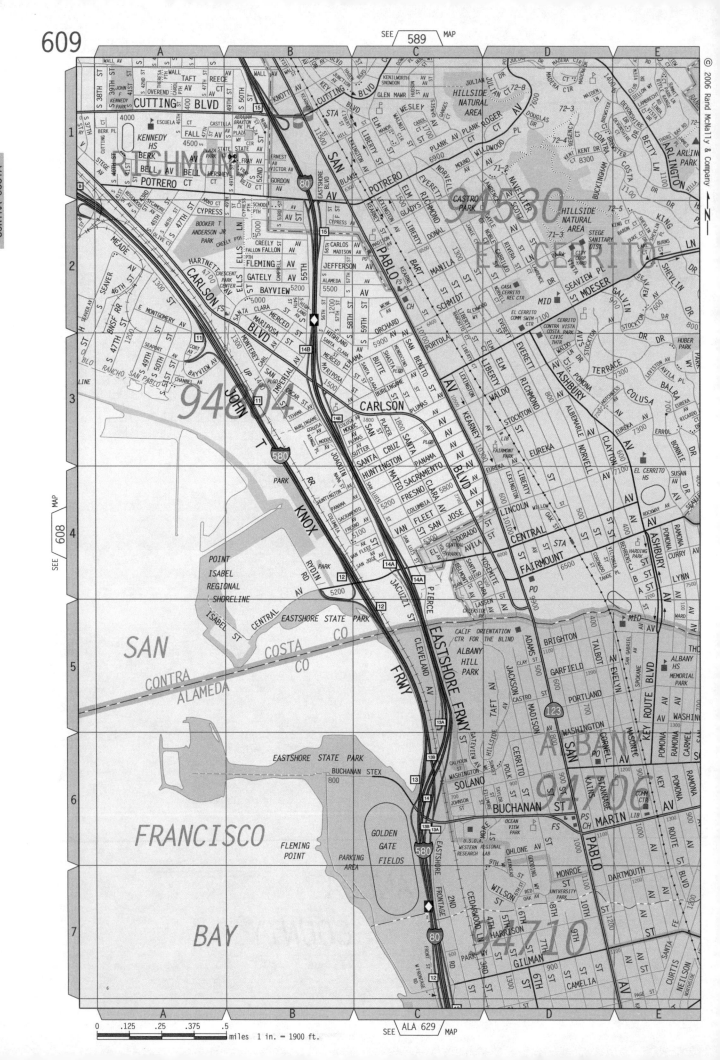

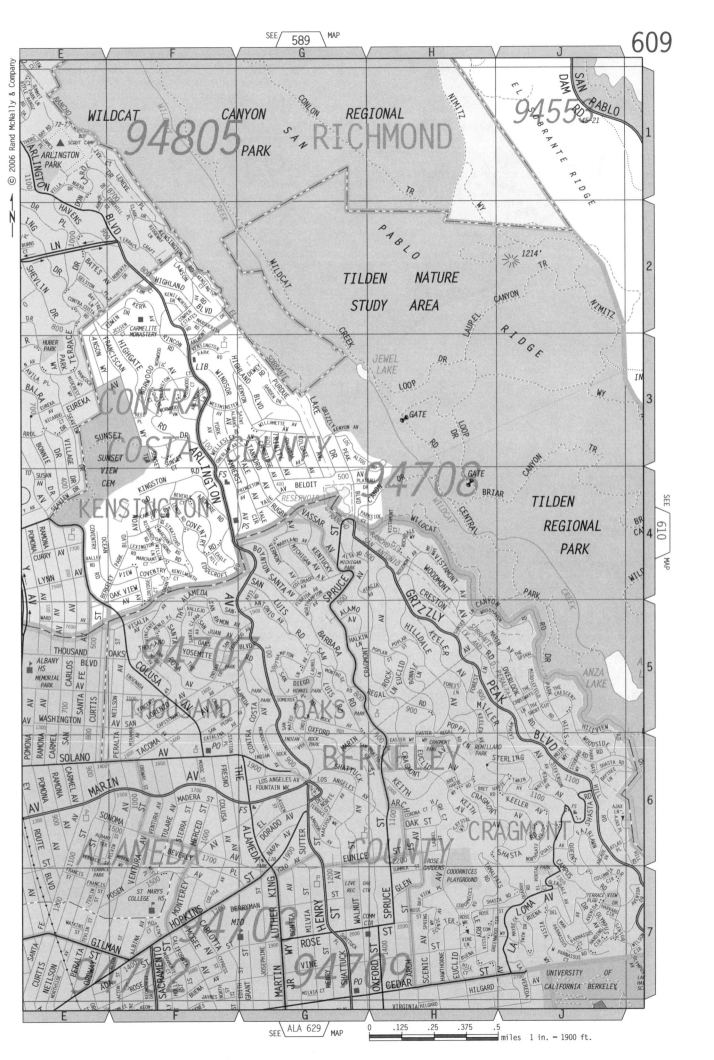

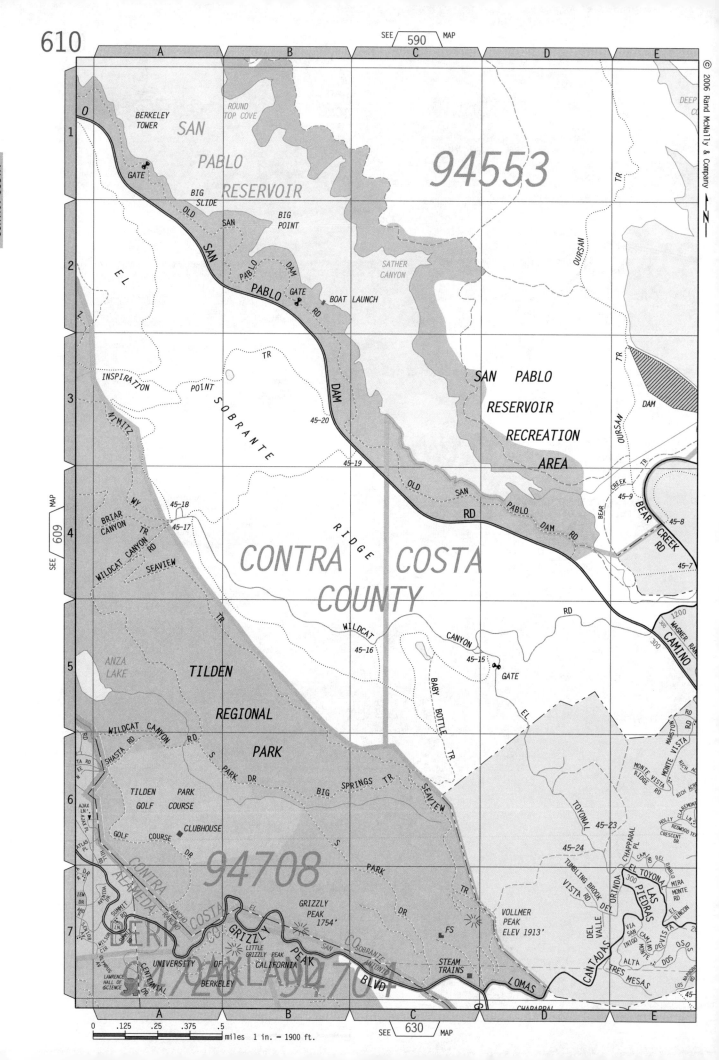

CONTRA COSTA

94553

SAN PABLO RESERVOIR

ROUND TOP COVE

BERKELEY TOWER

GATE

BIG SLIDE

OLD SAN PABLO DAM RD

BIG POINT

SAN

SATHER CANYON

BOAT LAUNCH

GATE

EL

INSPIRATION POINT

NIMITZ

TR

SOBRANTE

DAM

45-20

45-19

SAN PABLO RESERVOIR RECREATION AREA

OURSAN TR

OURSAN DAM

TR

BEAR CREEK TR

45-9

45-8

BEAR CREEK RD

45-7

BRIAR CANYON

WY

45-18

45-17

TR

WILDCAT CANYON RD

SEAVIEW

RIDGE

OLD SAN PABLO DAM RD

CONTRA COSTA COUNTY

WILDCAT

45-16

CANYON RD

45-15

GATE

EL

BABY BOTTLE TR

RD

1200 WAGNER RANCH

300

CAMINO

300

ANZA LAKE

TILDEN REGIONAL PARK

TR

MARSTON RD

MONTE VISTA RD

RICH

MONTE VISTA RIDGE RD

RICH ACRE

WILDCAT CANYON RD

SHASTA RD

S PARK DR

BIG SPRINGS TR

SEAVIEW

TOYONAL

45-23

HOLLY

CLAREMONT

REDWOOD TER

LN

CRESCENT DR

TILDEN PARK GOLF COURSE

CLUBHOUSE

GOLF COURSE DR

S

PARK

DR

TR

45-24

TUMBLING BROOK RD

VISTA DEL

VISTA DEL VALLE

ORINDA

EL TOYONAL

CAMINO DEL DIABLO

CHAPARRAL PL

CAMINO DEL DIABLO

MIRA

ORINDA

300 EL TOYONAL

LAS PIEDRAS

MONTE RD

MIRA MONTE RD

RINCON

94708

CONTRA COSTA CO

ALAMEDA CO

RANCHO RANCHO

EL

GRIZZLY PEAK 1754'

LITTLE GRIZZLY PEAK

SAN ANTONIO

CO SOBRANTE

FS

VOLLMER PEAK ELEV 1913'

VIA SAN INIGO

CAMINO DE VISTA

DOS OSOS

ALTA

TRES MESAS

DEL VALLE

CANTADAS

LOS

MARIPOSA

45

SUMMIT

WILSON CIR

OLYMPUS AV

GRIZZLY PEAK BLVD

UNIVERSITY OF CALIFORNIA BERKELEY

STEAM TRAINS

LOMAS

LAWRENCE HALL OF SCIENCE

CENTENNIAL DR

CHAPARRAL

0 .125 .25 .375 .5 miles 1 in. = 1900 ft.

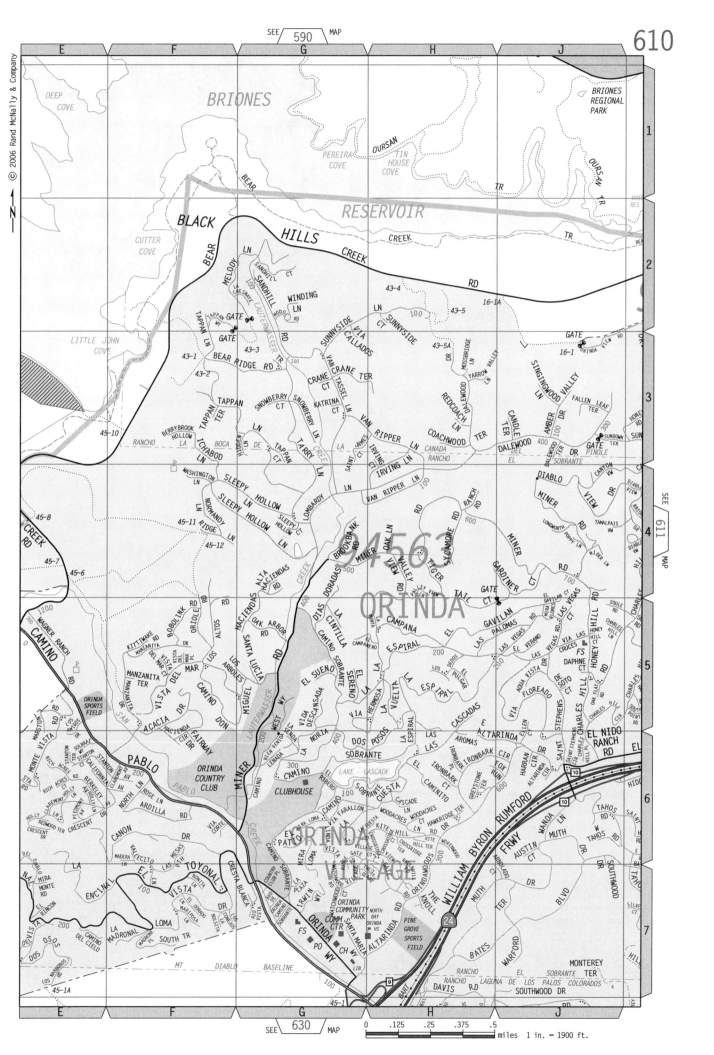

CONTRA COSTA

BRIONES

DEEP COVE

PEREIRA COVE

OURSAN

TIN HOUSE COVE

BRIONES REGIONAL PARK

1

BLACK

HILLS

RESERVOIR

CREEK

LITTLE JOHN COVE

CUTTER COVE

2

BEAR

MELODY LN

SANDHILL CT

WINDING LN

43-4

16-1A

GATE

16-1

ORINDA

3

TAPPAN LN

GATE

43-3

43-1

BEAR RIDGE RD

43-2

SUNNYSIDE

VIA CALLADOS

SUNNYSIDE

43-5A

REDCOACH LN

COACHWOOD TER

SINGINGWOOD VALLEY LN

FALLEN LEAF TER

SUNDOWN TER

TAPPAN TER

SNOWBERRY CT

SNOWBERRY LN

KATRINA CT

CRANE CT

CRANE TER

VAN TASSEL LN

VAN RIPPER LN

CANADA RANCHO

AMBER LN

DALEWOOD 100 DR

CANDLE TER

GATE PINOLE

DALEWOOD 400 DR

DIABLO VIEW DR

HIDDEN LN

TAPPAN CT

ICHABOD LN

BERRYBROOK HOLLOW LA

RANCHO

BOCA

LN DE

LA

TARRY LN

SAINT JAMES CT

IRVING CT

IRVING LN

VAN RIPPER LN

DIABLO VIEW

45-10

WASHINGTON LN

SLEEPY HOLLOW LN

SLEEPY LN

SLEEPY HOLLOW CT

LOMBARDY

RANCH RD

DIABLO MINER RD

LONGWORTH

TAMALPAIS VW

CANYON VW

4

45-8

45-7

45-6

CREEK RD

NORMANDY LN

SLEEPY HOLLOW RIDGE LN

45-11

45-12

ALTA HACIENDAS RD

BROOKBANK RD

DIAS DORADAS

OAK LN

VALLEY VIEW RD

MINER

TIGER TAIL

SYCAMORE RD

600

MINER RD

POPPY LN

ALDER LN

94563

ORINDA

GARDINER CT

700

MAGNER RANCH RD

1200

CAMINO

HACIENDAS RD

OAK ARBOR

SANTA LUCIA RD

LOS ALTOS

LOS ARBOLES

EL SUENO

DIAS CINTILLA

CAMINO SOBRANTE

LA CAMPANA

EL SERENO

ESPIRAL

GATE CT

LAS PALOMAS

EL VERANO

LAS VEGAS

VIA LAS CRUCES

DE SOTO CT

DAPHNE CT

HONEY HILL RD

CHARLES HILL RD

5

KITTIWAKE

BOBOLINK RD

ORIOLE RD

MANZANITA

DEL MAR CT

VISTA DEL MAR PL

DEL MAR

CAMINO DON

MIGUEL

WEST WY

LAUTERWASSER

VIDA DESCANSADA

VIA HERMOSA

LA VUELTA

LA ESPIRAL

LAS CASCADAS

E ALTARINDA

SAINT STEPHENS

DE FLOREADO

AGUA VISTA

CHARLES HILL

OAK FLAT CT

MANZANITA TER

VISTA DR

ACACIA

HACIENDA CIR

FAIRWAY DR

BLEN VENTA

LENADA

LA NORIA

DOS POSOS

VIA FARALLON

SOBRANTE

LAS AROMAS

IRONBARK PL

IRONBARK CT

EL CAMINITO

FOX RUN

GREYSTONE TER

HARRAN CIR

ALTARINDA CIR

SAINT STEPHENS CIR

CHARLES HILL PL

EL NIDO RANCH RD

6

MONTE VISTA

MARSTON RD

STANTON CT

SOLBRAE WY

STANTON AV

CALIFORNIA AV

CLAREMONT AV

ANVIL LN

RICH ACRES RD

BERKELEY AV

PIEDMONT AV

ROSE LN

ARDILLA RD

PABLO

ORINDA COUNTRY CLUB

ORINDA

PABLO

MINER

CAMINO SOBRANTE

300 CAMINO

CLUBHOUSE

LAKE CASCADE

EL RIBERO

S. OBRANTE

CUESTA

WOODACRES LN

WOODACRES

HAMKRIDGE TER

MOVENWOOD

WILLIAM BYRON RUMFORD FRWY

AUSTIN CT

NANDA LN

MUTH DR

TAHOS RD

TAHOS DR

SOUTHWOOD BLVD

10

10

HOLLY

CLAREMONT LN

REDWOOD TER

CRESCENT

CRESCENT DR

CANON DR

VALLECITO

LAS MESAS PTH

MADERA

VIA CORTE

CRESTA BLANCA DR

TOYONAL

MIRA LOMA

EVERGREEN PATIO

VIA PLAZA

IRWIN WY

MIRA VISTA

LA VISTA

KITE HILL

LA CUESTA

CROSSRIDGE TER

KITE TER

HILL TER

THE KNOLL

THE ORINDAWOODS

24

BATES

MUTH DR

WARFORD

SOUTHWOOD DR

7

DEL DIABLO

NA

MIRA MONTE RD

EL RINCON

DE VISTA RD

OSOS

LOS NARBONOS RD

DOS

EL

ENCINAL

LA MADRONAL

EL VISTA DR

LOMA

BONITA LN

EL DORADO LN

MARI POSA

BOLSITA

LOS CONGOS

SOUTH TR

MADRONE PL

CAMINO DEL CIELO

ORINDA VILLAGE

COMM CTR

FS

PO WY

CH

SANTA MARIA

LIB

ORINDA COMMUNITY PARK

NORTH BAY ORINDA HS

ALTARINDA RD

PINE GROVE SPORTS FIELD

9

BART

RANCHO

RANCHO LAGUNA DE LOS PALOS COLORADOS

EL SOBRANTE

MONTEREY TER

SILVER CT

45-1A

MT DIABLO BASELINE

DAVIS

SOUTHWOOD DR

RD

0 .125 .25 .375 .5 miles 1 in. = 1900 ft.

SEE 611 MAP

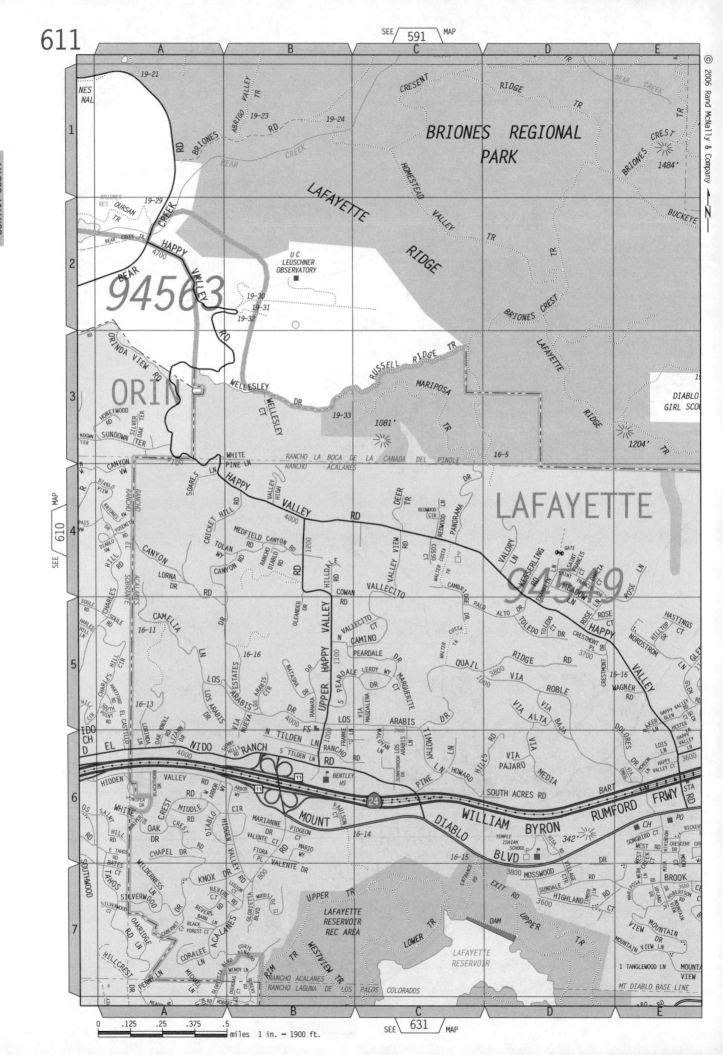

CONTRA COSTA

© 2006 Rand McNally & Company

—N—

BRIONES REGIONAL PARK

94563

ORIN

LAFAYETTE RIDGE

DIABLO GIRL SCO

LAFAYETTE

94549

RANCHO LA BOCA DE LA CANADA DEL PINOLE
RANCHO ACALANES

UPPER HAPPY VALLEY

EL NIDO

MOUNT DIABLO

WILLIAM BYRON RUMFORD FRWY

LAFAYETTE RESERVOIR REC AREA

LAFAYETTE RESERVOIR

RANCHO ACALANES
RANCHO LAGUNA DE LOS PALOS COLORADOS

MT DIABLO BASE LINE

0 .125 .25 .375 .5
miles 1 in. = 1900 ft.

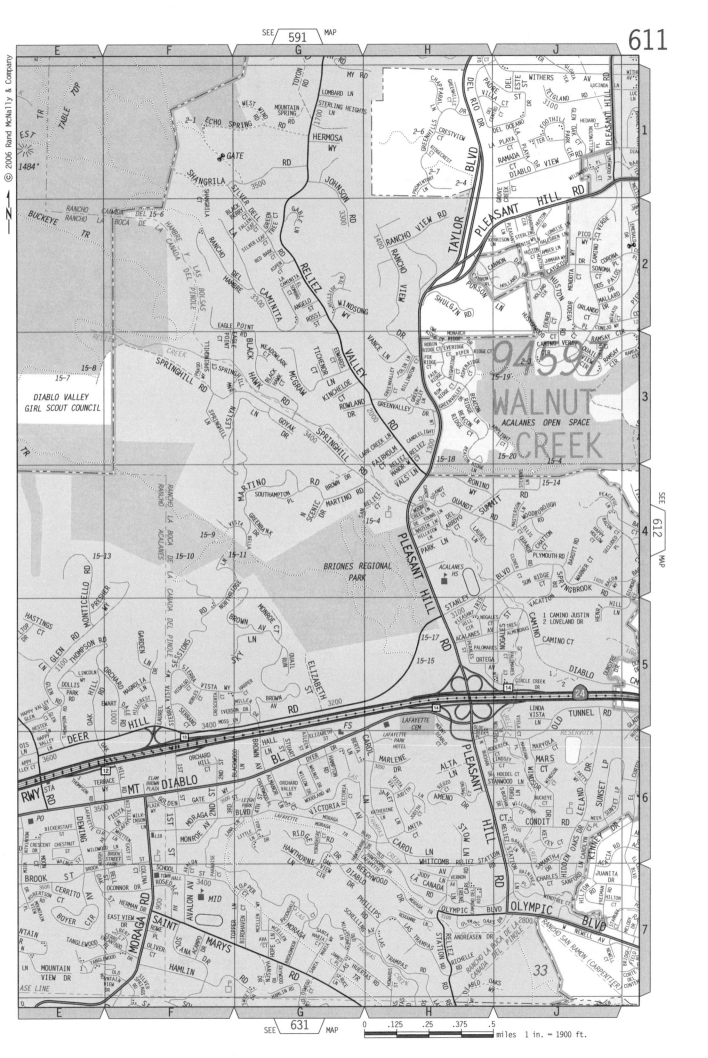

CONTRA COSTA

94595

WALNUT CREEK

ACALANES OPEN SPACE

DIABLO VALLEY
GIRL SCOUT COUNCIL

BRIONES REGIONAL
PARK

LAFAYETTE CEM

Lafayette
Park
Hotel

33

0   .125   .25   .375   .5

miles 1 in. = 1900 ft.

SEE 612 MAP

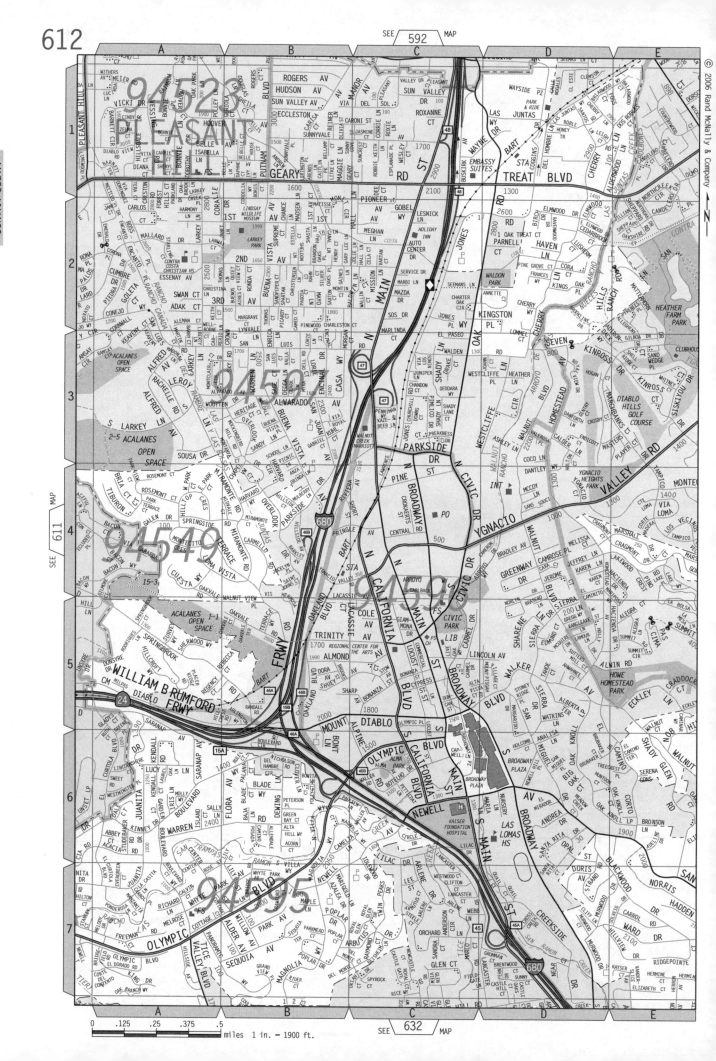

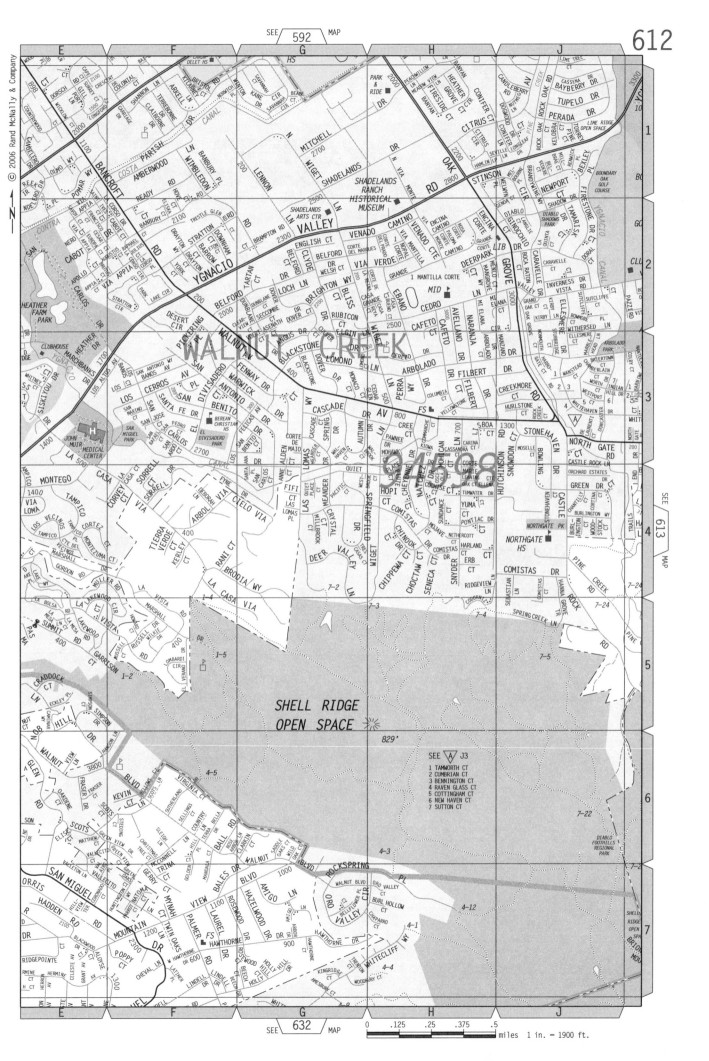

SEE 613 MAP

© 2006 Rand McNally & Company

SHELL RIDGE OPEN SPACE

829'

SEE A J3
1 TAMWORTH CT
2 CUMBRIAN CT
3 BENNINGTON CT
4 RAVEN GLASS CT
5 COTTINGHAM CT
6 NEW HAVEN CT
7 SUTTON CT

0 .125 .25 .375 .5
miles 1 in. = 1900 ft.

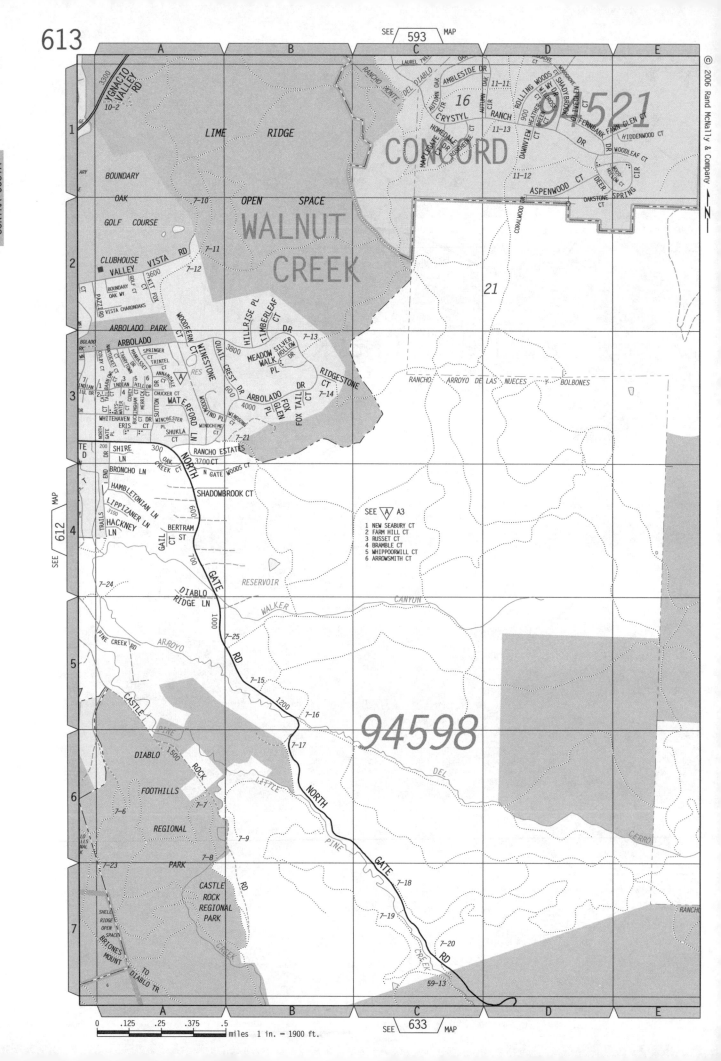

CONTRA COSTA

CONCORD

94521

LIME   RIDGE

BOUNDARY

OAK   OPEN   SPACE

GOLF   COURSE   WALNUT

CLUBHOUSE   CREEK

VALLEY   VISTA   RD

ARBOLADO PARK

ARBOLADO

WATERFORD LN

WHITEHAVEN
ERIS

RANCHO ESTATES

SHIRE
LN

BRONCHO LN

HAMBLETONIAN LN

LIPPIZANER LN

HACKNEY
LN

BERTRAM
ST

GAIL
CT

NORTH   GATE   RD

DIABLO
RIDGE LN

PINE CREEK RD   ARROYO

CASTLE

PINE

DIABLO

FOOTHILLS

REGIONAL

PARK

CASTLE
ROCK
REGIONAL
PARK

SHELL
RIDGE
OPEN
SPACE

BRIONES
MOUNT
TO
DIABLO TR

RESERVOIR

WALKER   CANYON

RANCHO   ARROYO DE LAS   NUECES   Y   BOLBONES

21

94598

NORTH

PINE

GATE   RD

DEL

CERRO

RANCHO

SEE A3
1 NEW SEABURY CT
2 FARM HILL CT
3 RUSSET CT
4 BRAMBLE CT
5 WHIPPOORWILL CT
6 ARROWSMITH CT

SEE 612 MAP

SEE 633 MAP

0   .125   .25   .375   .5

miles 1 in. = 1900 ft.

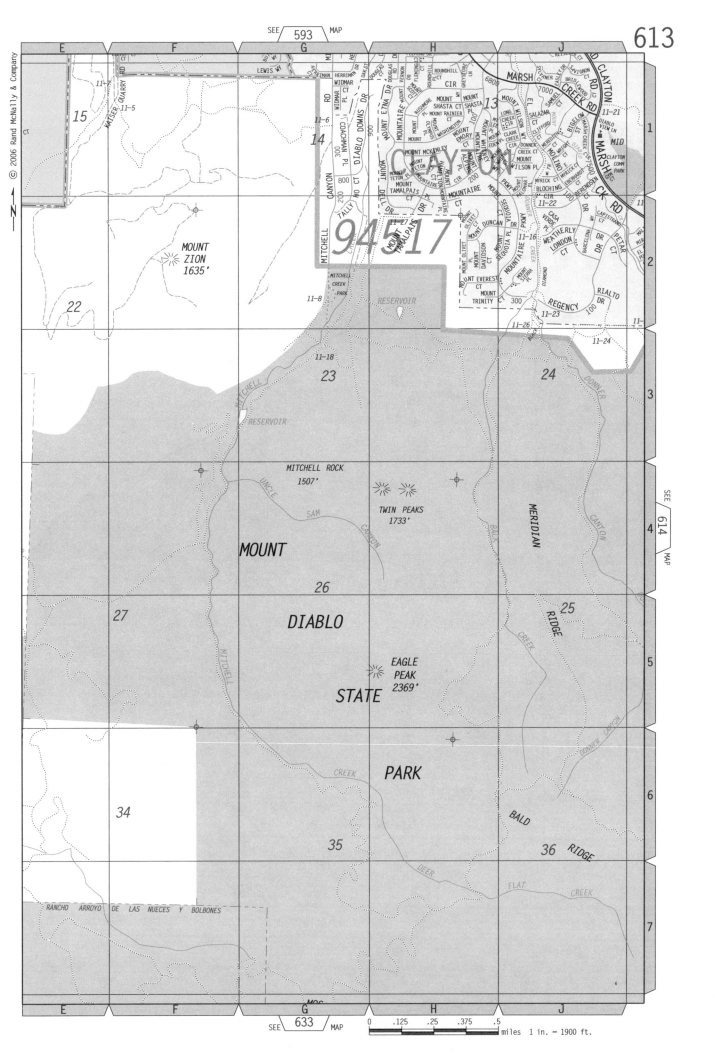

CONTRA COSTA

© 2006 Rand McNally & Company

SEE 593 MAP

E   F   G   H   J

15

14

MOUNT
ZION
1635'

22

11-5
KAISER QUARRY RD

LEWIS WY

WIDMAR RD

DIABLO DOWNS DR

MITCHELL CANYON RD

COACHACHA PL

TALLY HO CT

11-6

11-7

11-8

11-18

CLAYTON

94517

MARSH
CREEK RD
6800
7000

CLAYTON COMM PARK

MARSH CK RD

MID

11-21

DIABLO VIEW LN

MOUNT ETNA DR

MOUNTAIRE

MOUNT RUSHMORE PL

MOUNT WASHINGTON

MOUNT SHASTA CT

MOUNT SHASTA

MOUNT RAINIER CT

MOUNT EMORY

MOUNT MCKINLEY

MOUNT TETON PL

MOUNT TAMALPAIS CT

MOUNT DELL DR

MOUNT TAMALPAIS DR

MOUNT OLIVET PL

MOUNT OLIVET

MOUNT DAVIDSON PL

MOUNT DUNCAN DR

SEQUOIA PL

MOUNTAIRE PKWY

MOUNT EVEREST CT

MOUNT TRINITY

300

13

ROUNDHILL CIR

GREYSTONE

MOUNT WILSON WY

LONG CREEK CIR

CLARK CREEK CT

DONNER CREEK CT

MOUNTAIRE CIR
200

CASA VERDE

WEATHERLY LONDON CT

REGENCY

11-23

11-16

11-26

RIALTO DR

11-24

SALAZAR

BIGELOW

MOLINO

CAPISTRANO CT

PETAR DR

BLOCHING CIR
11-22

WYRICK

BERENDSEN

DONNER

CANYON

BACK CREEK

23

RESERVOIR

RESERVOIR

MITCHELL CANYON

24

DONNER

MITCHELL ROCK
1507'

UNCLE SAM CANYON

TWIN PEAKS
1733'

MERIDIAN

BACK CANYON

MOUNT

26

DIABLO

27

EAGLE
PEAK
2369'

MITCHELL

STATE

25

RIDGE

CREEK

DONNER CANYON

34

PARK

35

CREEK

36

BALD

RIDGE

CREEK

DEER

FLAT CREEK

RANCHO ARROYO DE LAS NUECES Y BOLBONES

SEE 614 MAP

SEE 633 MAP

E   F   G   H   J

1

2

3

4

5

6

7

0   .125   .25   .375   .5
miles   1 in. = 1900 ft.

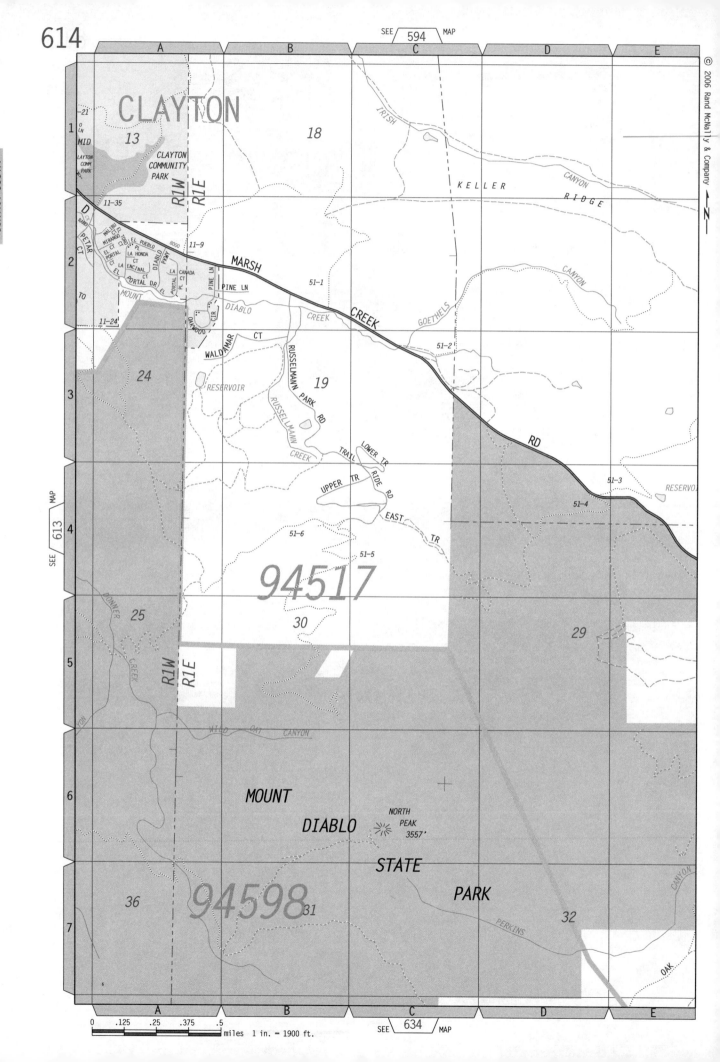

CONTRA COSTA

SEE 594 MAP

A B C D E

CLAYTON

13

18

21

MID

CLAYTON COMM PARK

CLAYTON COMMUNITY PARK

IRISH

KELLER

RIDGE

R1W R1E

1

11-35

D

PETAR CT

RAND

MALIBU CT

MIRANGO CT

EL CT PORTAL

LA PORTAL

EL PUEBLO

LA HONDA CT

EL ENCINAL CT

DIABLO PKWY

EL PORTAL DR

LA CANADA CT

PINE LN

PINE LN

8000

11-9

MARSH

CREEK

CREEK

GOETHELS

CANYON

2

TO

MOUNT

11-24

DIABLO

KNOLLWOOD CIR

WALDAMAR CT

RUSSELMANN PARK RD

RESERVOIR

RUSSELMANN CREEK

TRAIL

LOWER TR

RIDE RD

UPPER TR

EAST TR

51-1

51-2

51-3

51-4

RD

RESERVO

19

3

24

SEE 613 MAP

4

51-6

51-5

94517

5

25

DONNER CREEK

R1W R1E

30

29

WILD OAT CANYON

6

MOUNT

DIABLO

NORTH PEAK 3557'

STATE

PARK

94598

36

31

32

PERKINS

OAK

CANYON

7

A B C D E

SEE 634 MAP

CONTRA COSTA

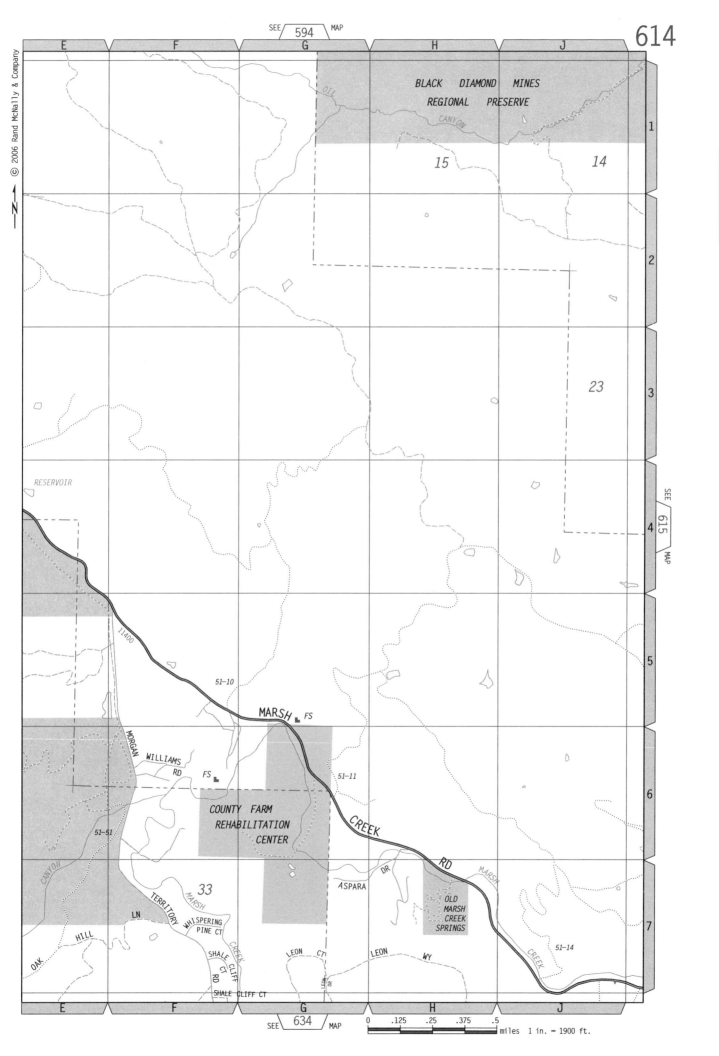

E   F   G   H   J

1

BLACK   DIAMOND   MINES
REGIONAL   PRESERVE

OIL

CANYON

15   14

2

23

3

RESERVOIR

SEE 615 MAP

4

11400

5

51-10

MARSH ▪ FS

MORGAN

WILLIAMS RD

FS ▪

51-11

6

COUNTY FARM
REHABILITATION
CENTER

CREEK

RD

MARSH

51-51

33

CANYON

MARSH

TERRITORY

LN

ASPARA

DR

OLD
MARSH
CREEK
SPRINGS

WHISPERING
PINE CT

OAK

HILL

SHALE CLIFF CT

RD

LEON CT

LEON DR

LEON   WY

CREEK

51-14

7

SHALE CLIFF CT

E   F   G   H   J

0   .125   .25   .375   .5
miles 1 in. = 1900 ft.

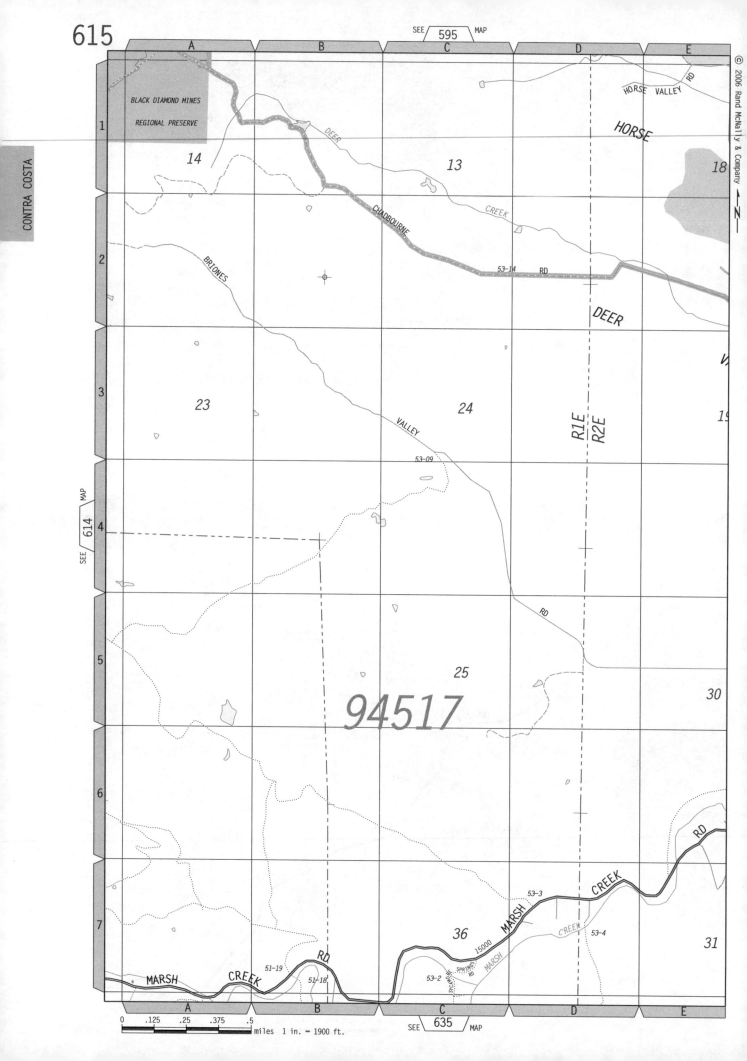

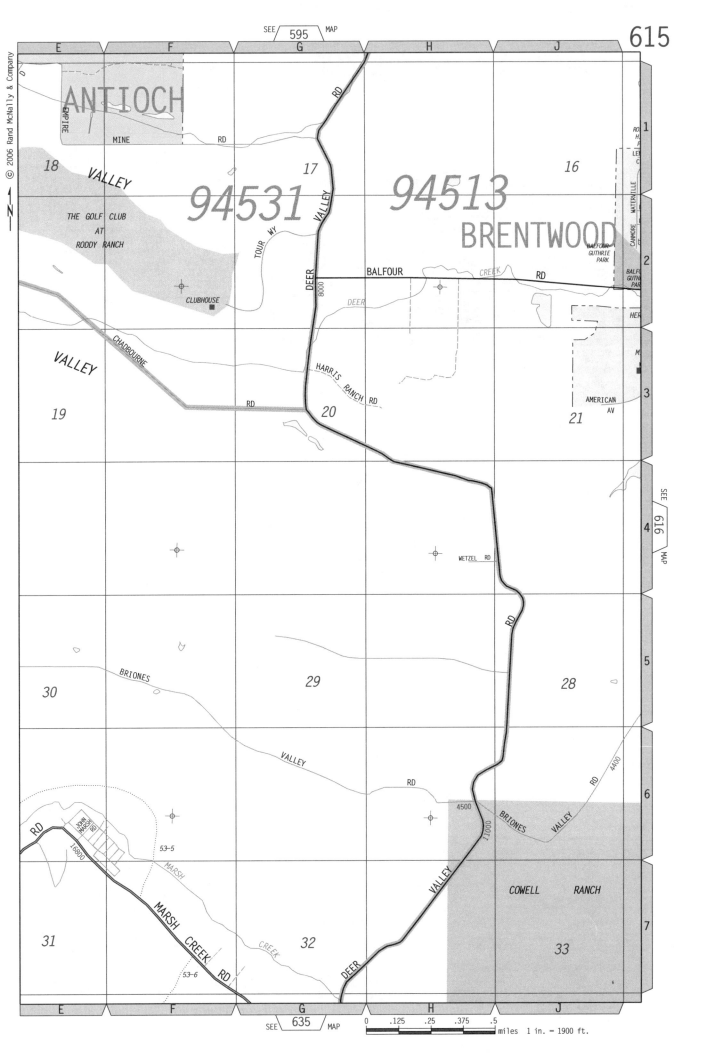

SEE 595 MAP

E F G H J

ANTIOCH

EMPIRE

MINE   RD

18   VALLEY   17   **94513**   16

94531

THE GOLF CLUB
AT
RODDY RANCH

TOUR WY

VALLEY

DEER

8000

BRENTWOOD

BALFOUR   CREEK   RD

BALFOUR
GUTHRIE
PARK

CLUBHOUSE

DEER

CANMORE

WATERVILLE

ROD
H.
P.
LEN
C

BALFO
GUTHA
PAR

HER

1

2

CHADBOURNE

VALLEY

19

RD

HARRIS   RANCH   RD

20

AMERICAN   AV

21

M

3

WETZEL   RD

RD

SEE 616 MAP

4

BRIONES

30   29   28

5

VALLEY

RD

RD   4400

BRIONES   VALLEY

4500

11000

JOHN
MARSH
RD

16800

53-5

MARSH

VALLEY

COWELL   RANCH

6

MARSH   CREEK   RD

53-6

31   CREEK   32   DEER   33

7

E F G H J

SEE 635 MAP

0   .125   .25   .375   .5
miles 1 in. = 1900 ft.

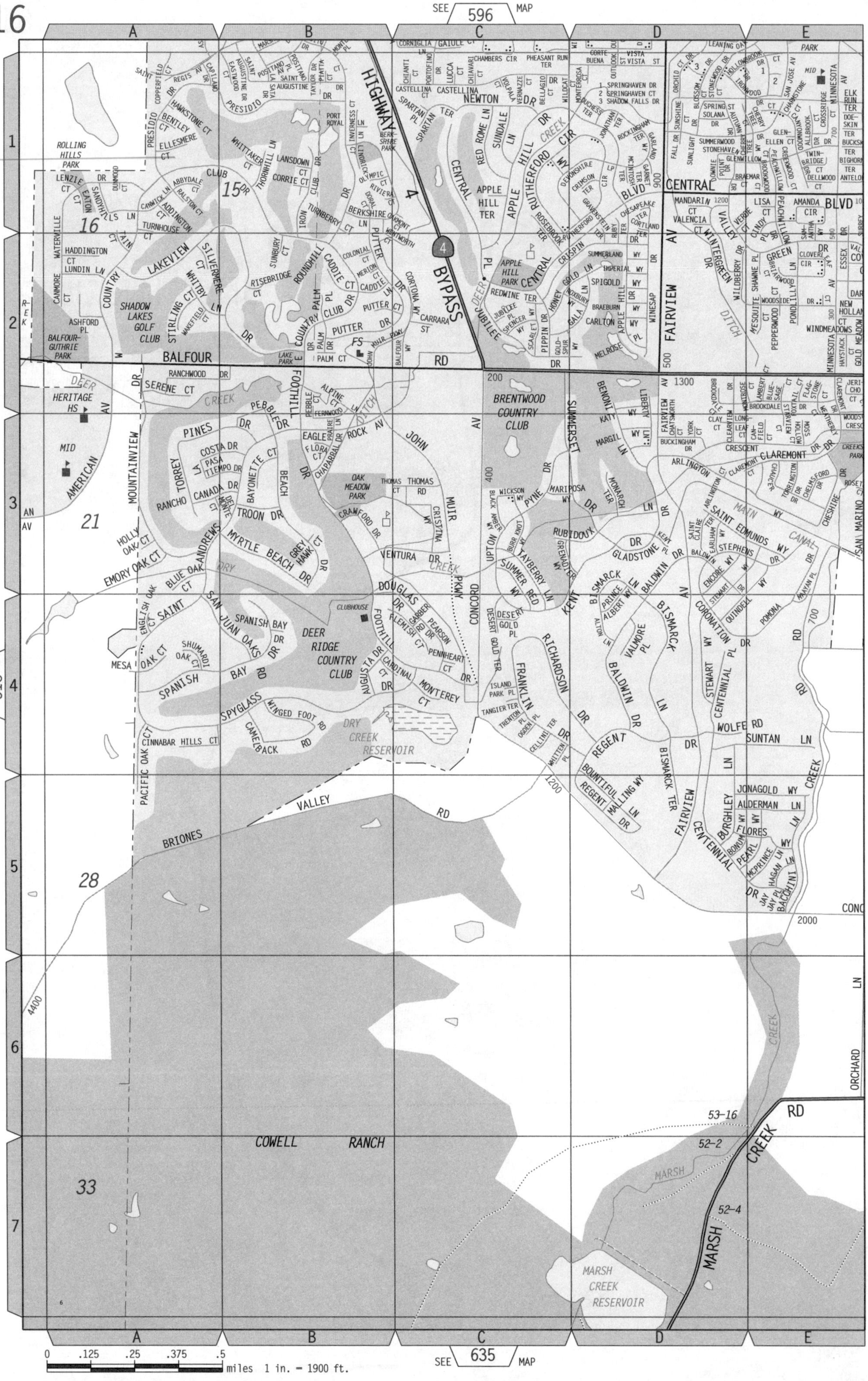

CONTRA COSTA

© 2006 Rand McNally & Company

SEE 596 MAP

A B C D E

1

2

3

4

5

6

7

ROLLING HILLS PARK

BALFOUR-GUTHRIE PARK

SHADOW LAKES GOLF CLUB

LAKEVIEW

BALFOUR

HERITAGE HS

MID AMERICAN

21

DEER CREEK

PINES

TORREY

RANCHO

OAK MEADOW PARK

MYRTLE BEACH

DEER RIDGE COUNTRY CLUB

CLUBHOUSE

SPANISH BAY

SPANISH

SPYGLASS

DRY CREEK RESERVOIR

15

16

HIGHWAY 4 BYPASS

4

NEWTON

APPLE HILL TER

CENTRAL

APPLE HILL PARK

BRENTWOOD COUNTRY CLUB

SUMMERSET

JOHN MUIR PKWY

DEER JUBILEE

200

400

BALDWIN

BISMARCK

CLAREMONT

SAINT EDMUNDS WY

GLADSTONE

MAIN CANAL

RICHARDSON DR

FRANKLIN DR

REGENT

WOLFE RD

SUNTAN LN

FAIRVIEW

CENTENNIAL

BISMARCK TER

CREEK

CENTRAL BLVD

FAIRVIEW AV

VALENCIA

MANDARIN CT

GREEN

WINDMEADOWS

LIBERTY

MINNESOTA

CONCORD 2000

BRIONES

VALLEY RD

28

COWELL RANCH

33

MARSH CREEK

ORCHARD LN

53-16
52-2

MARSH CREEK RD

52-4

MARSH CREEK RESERVOIR

SEE 615 MAP

SEE 635 MAP

A B C D E

0 .125 .25 .375 .5 miles 1 in. = 1900 ft.

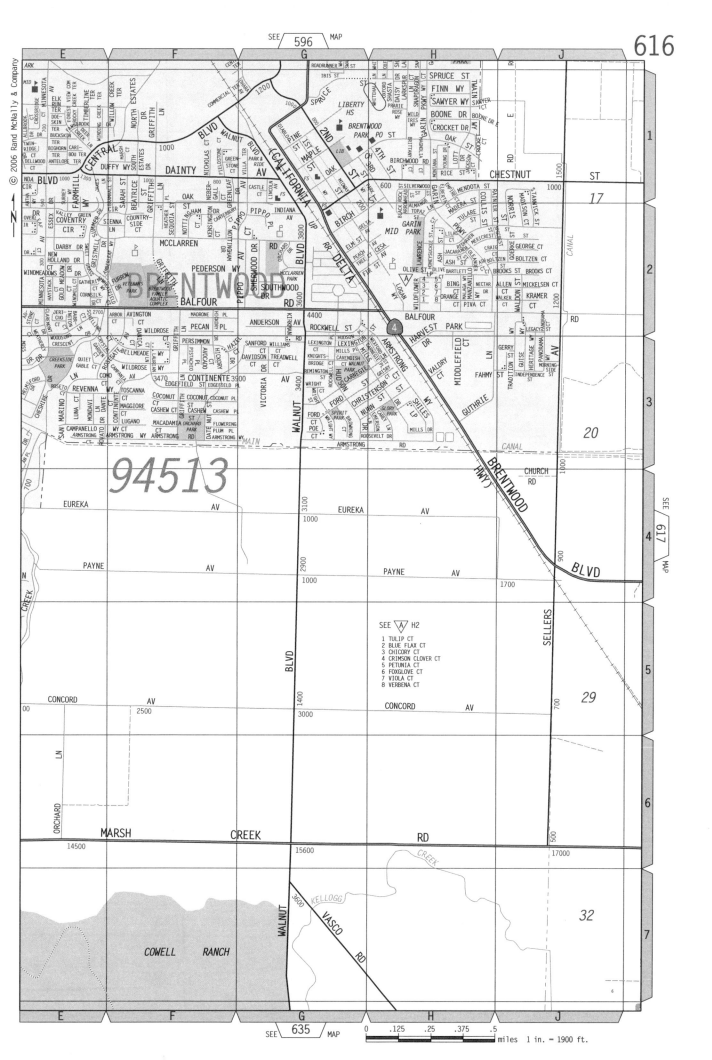

CONTRA COSTA

BRENTWOOD

94513

SEE 617 MAP

SELLERS

SEE 635 MAP

SEE △A H2
1 TULIP CT
2 BLUE FLAX CT
3 CHICORY CT
4 CRIMSON CLOVER CT
5 PETUNIA CT
6 FOXGLOVE CT
7 VIOLA CT
8 VERBENA CT

COWELL RANCH

0 .125 .25 .375 .5
miles 1 in. = 1900 ft.

617

CONTRA COSTA

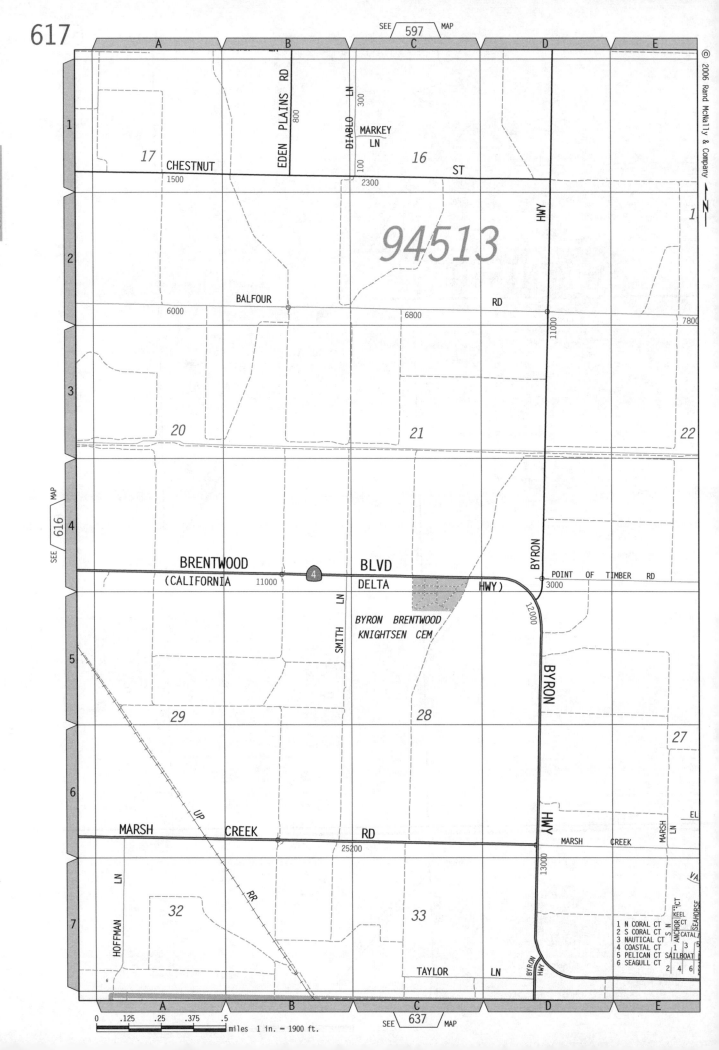

© 2006 Rand McNally & Company

—N—

A   B   C   D   E

1

17

CHESTNUT
1500

EDEN PLAINS RD
800

DIABLO LN
300

MARKEY
LN

100

16   ST
2300

94513

HMY

1

2

BALFOUR
6000

RD
6800

10100

7800

3

20

21

22

SEE 616 MAP

4

BRENTWOOD   BLVD

(CALIFORNIA   11000   4   DELTA   HWY)

POINT   OF   TIMBER   RD
3000

BYRON

12000

BYRON   BRENTWOOD
KNIGHTSEN CEM

SMITH LN

5

29

28

27

BYRON

6

MARSH   CREEK   RD
25200

HWY

MARSH   CREEK

MARSH LN

EL

13000

7

HOFFMAN LN

32

UP

RR

33

TAYLOR   LN

BYRON HWY

1 N CORAL CT
2 S CORAL CT
3 NAUTICAL CT
4 COASTAL CT
5 PELICAN CT
6 SEAGULL CT

ANCHOR CT

KEEL

N

S

CT

CATALZ

SEAHORSE

SAILBOAT

1   3   5
2   4   6

VA

6

A   B   C   D   E

0   .125   .25   .375   .5
miles 1 in. = 1900 ft.

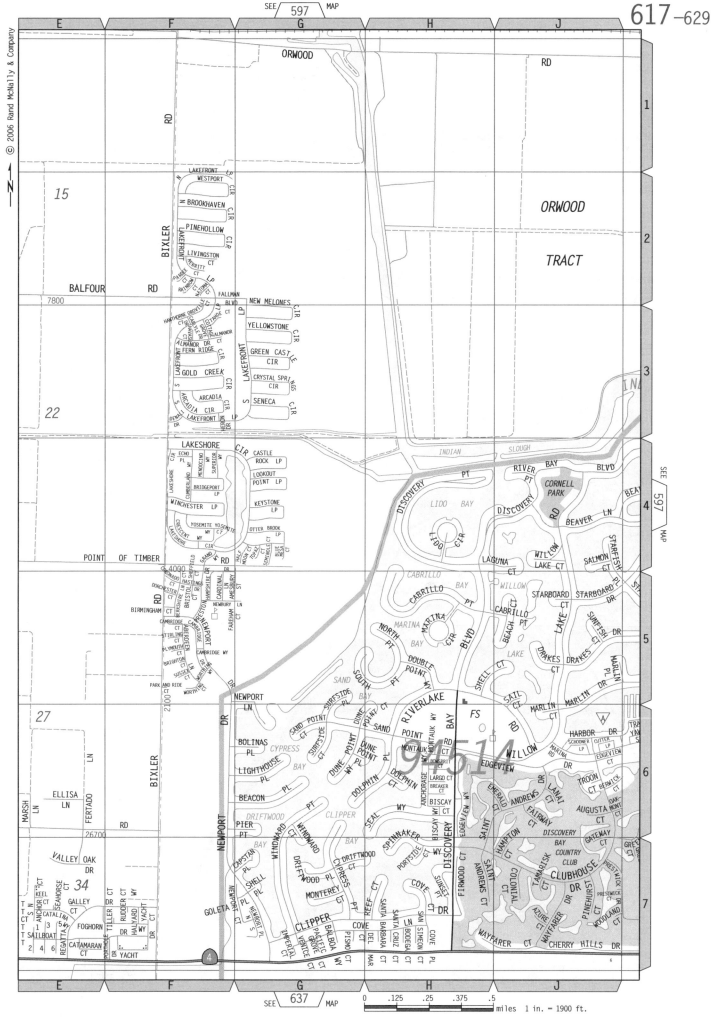

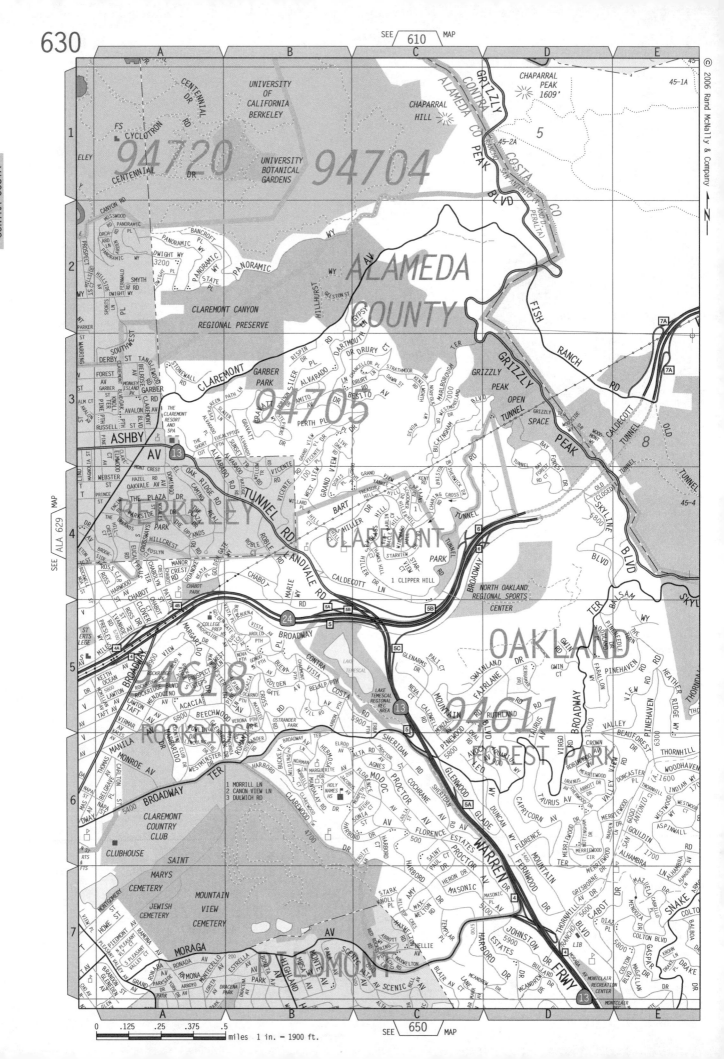

CONTRA COSTA

94720

94704

94705

94618

94611

SEE ALA 629 MAP

0 .125 .25 .375 .5
miles 1 in. = 1900 ft.

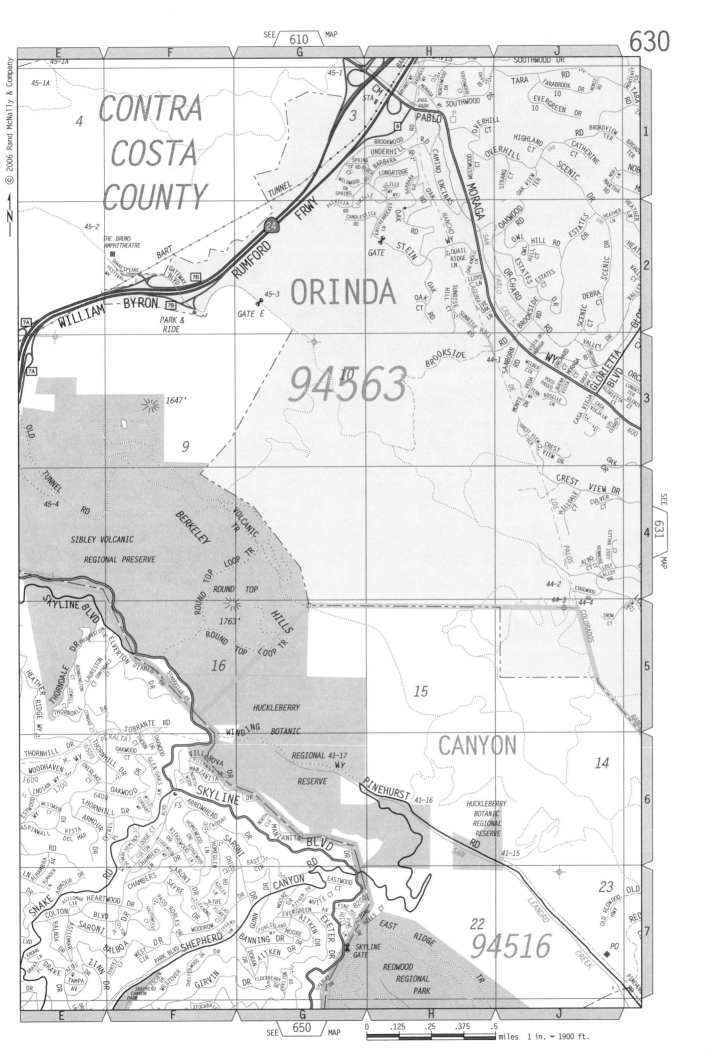

© 2006 Rand McNally & Company

CONTRA
COSTA
COUNTY

ORINDA

94563

SIBLEY VOLCANIC
REGIONAL PRESERVE

BERKELEY

Round Top

HILLS

1763'

HUCKLEBERRY
BOTANIC
REGIONAL
RESERVE

CANYON

HUCKLEBERRY
BOTANIC
REGIONAL
RESERVE

94516

REDWOOD
REGIONAL
PARK

SEE 631 MAP

0 .125 .25 .375 .5
miles 1 in. = 1900 ft.

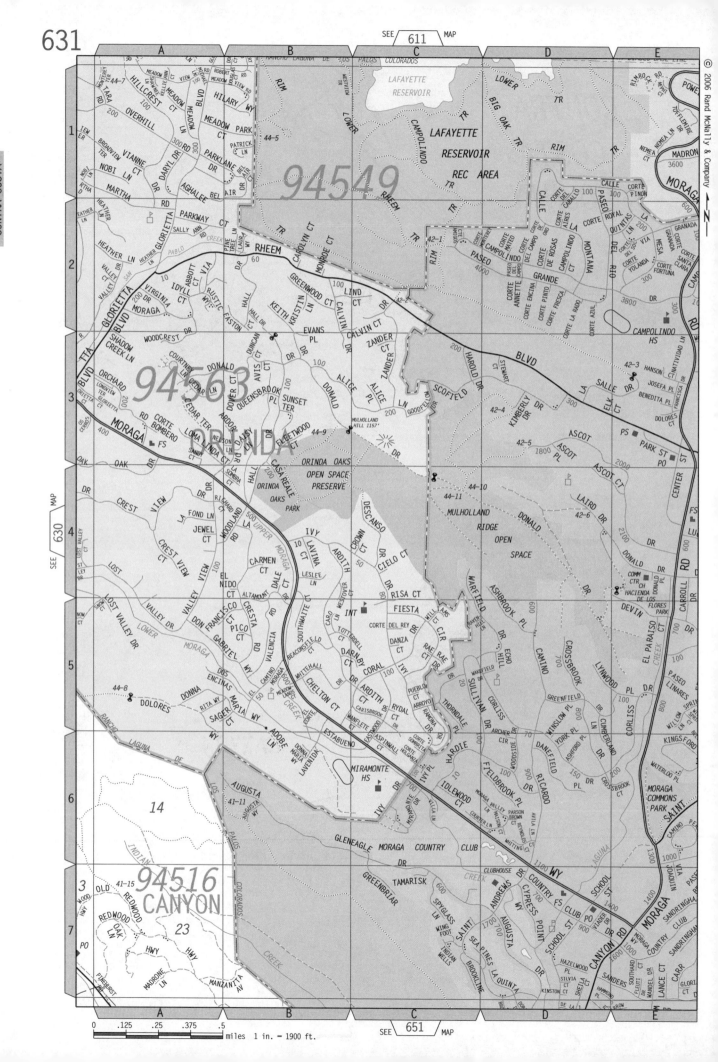

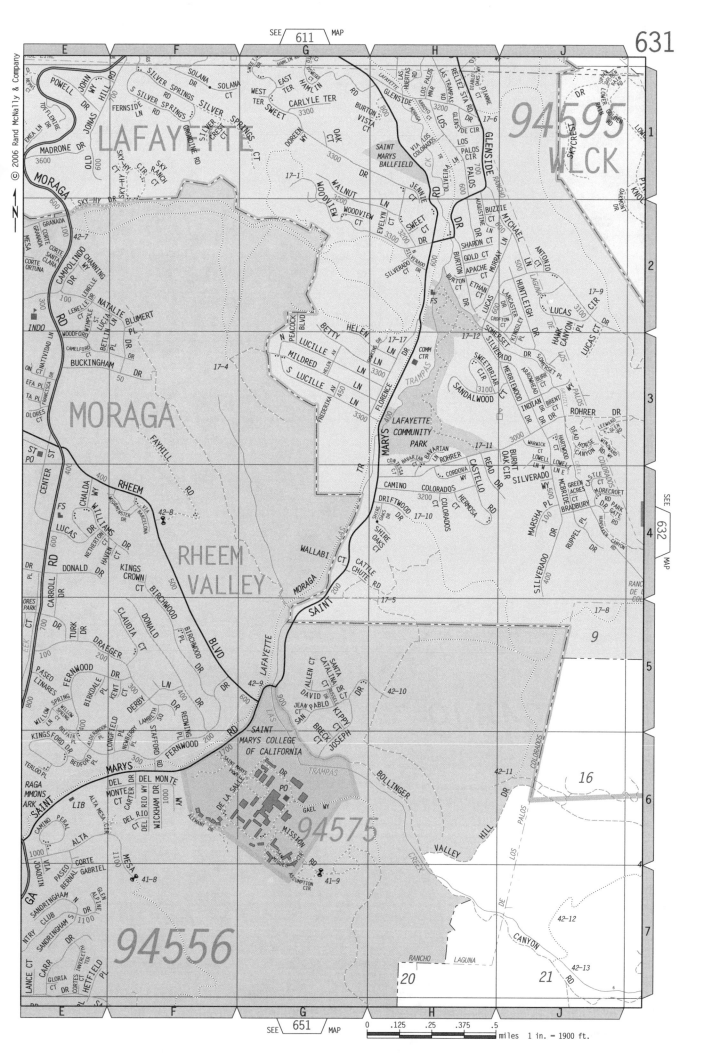

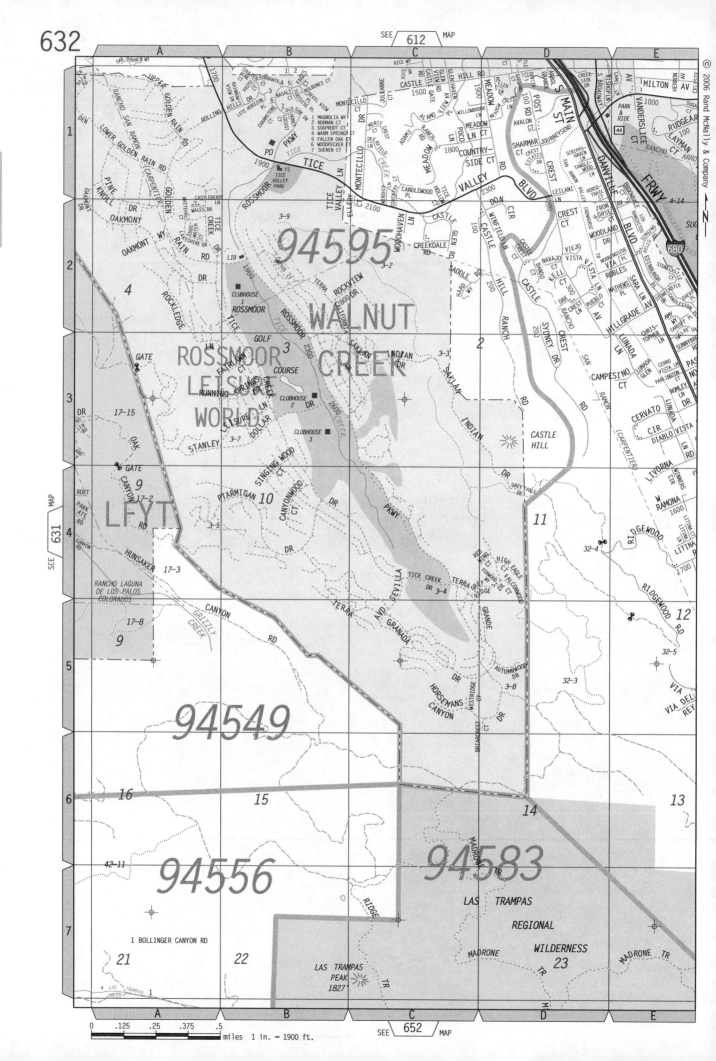

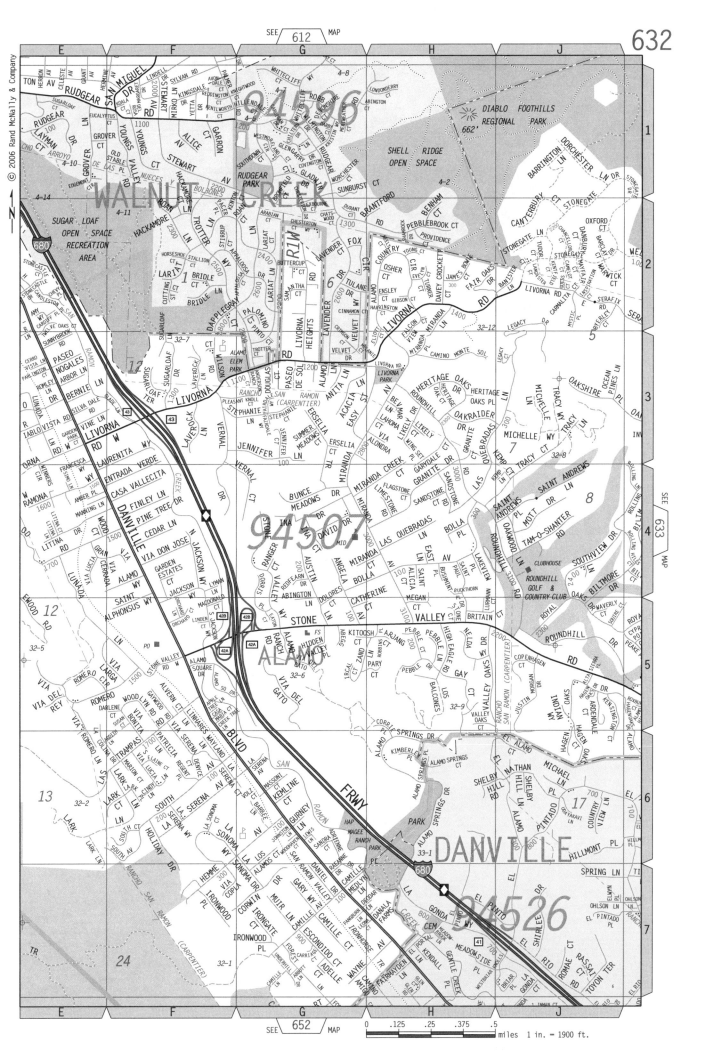

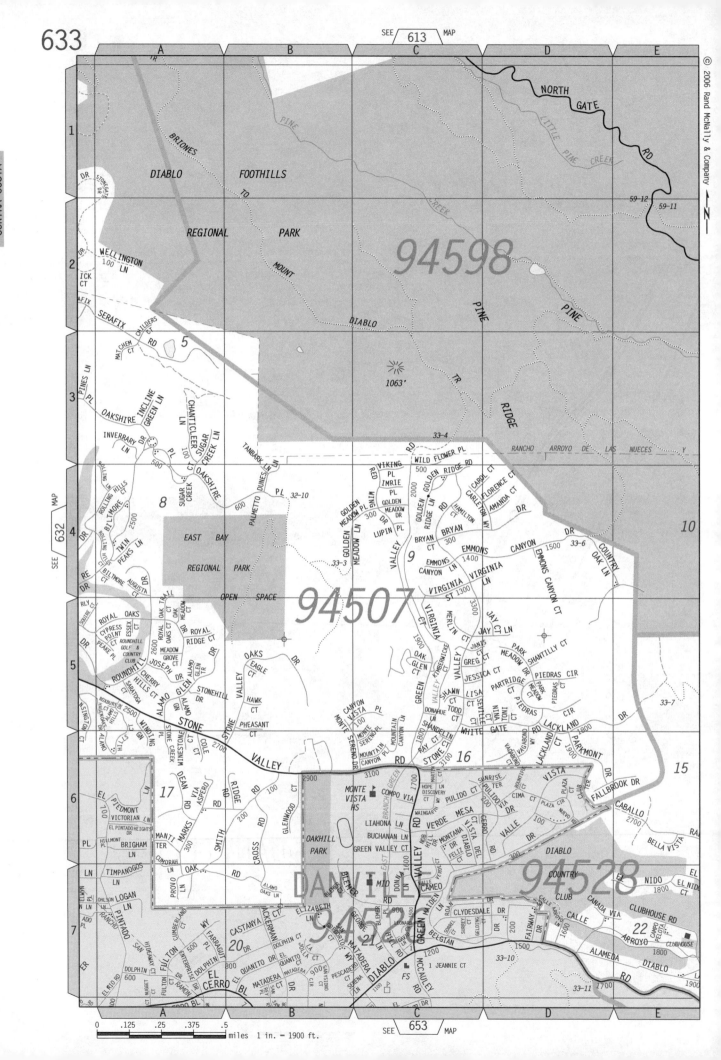

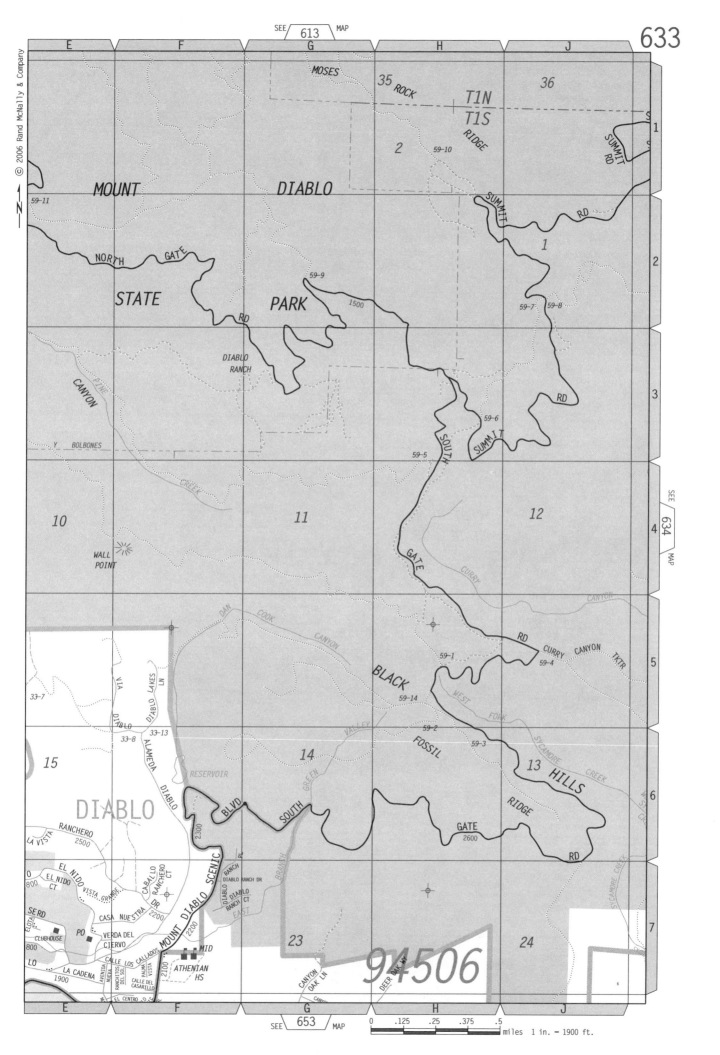

CONTRA COSTA

SEE 613 MAP

E F G H J

© 2006 Rand McNally & Company

N

MOSES

35 ROCK

36

T1N
T1S

RIDGE

2

59-10

MOUNT DIABLO

SUMMIT RD

1

59-11

NORTH GATE

STATE PARK RD

59-9

1500

DIABLO RANCH

59-7   59-8

SUMMIT

SUMMIT RD

59-6

CANYON PINE

Y BOLBONES

CREEK

SOUTH

59-5

10

11

12

SEE 634 MAP

WALL POINT

GATE

CURRY CANYON

DAN COOK CANYON

CANYON

RD

CURRY CANYON TKTR
59-4

BLACK

59-1

59-14

WEST FORK

33-7

VIA

DIABLO

LAKES LN

33-13

33-8

ALAMEDA DIABLO

15

RESERVOIR

VALLEY

59-2

FOSSIL

59-3

SYCAMORE CREEK

13 HILLS

DIABLO

BLVD

2300

SOUTH

GREEN

RIDGE

GATE
2600

RD

RANCHERO
2500

LA VISTA

EL NIDO VISTA GRANDE

CABALLO

RANCHERO CT

CASA NUESTRA

DR   2200

RANCH PL

DIABLO RANCH DR

DIABLO RANCH CT

EAST

BRANCH

W SYCAMORE CREEK

EL NIDO CT

SERD

PO

800

CLUBHOUSE

VERDA DEL CIERVO

800

LA CADENA

LO

1900

ELOTA

AVENIDA NUEVA

RANCHITOS DEL SOL

CALLE LOS CALLADOS

PALMA VISTA

CALLE DEL CASARILLO

EL CENTRO

MOUNT DIABLO SCENIC

2100   2200

MID

ATHENIAN HS

23

CANYON OAK LN

DEER OAK HWY

CANYON

24

94506

SEE 653 MAP

E F G H J

0   .125   .25   .375   .5   miles   1 in. = 1900 ft.

CONTRA COSTA

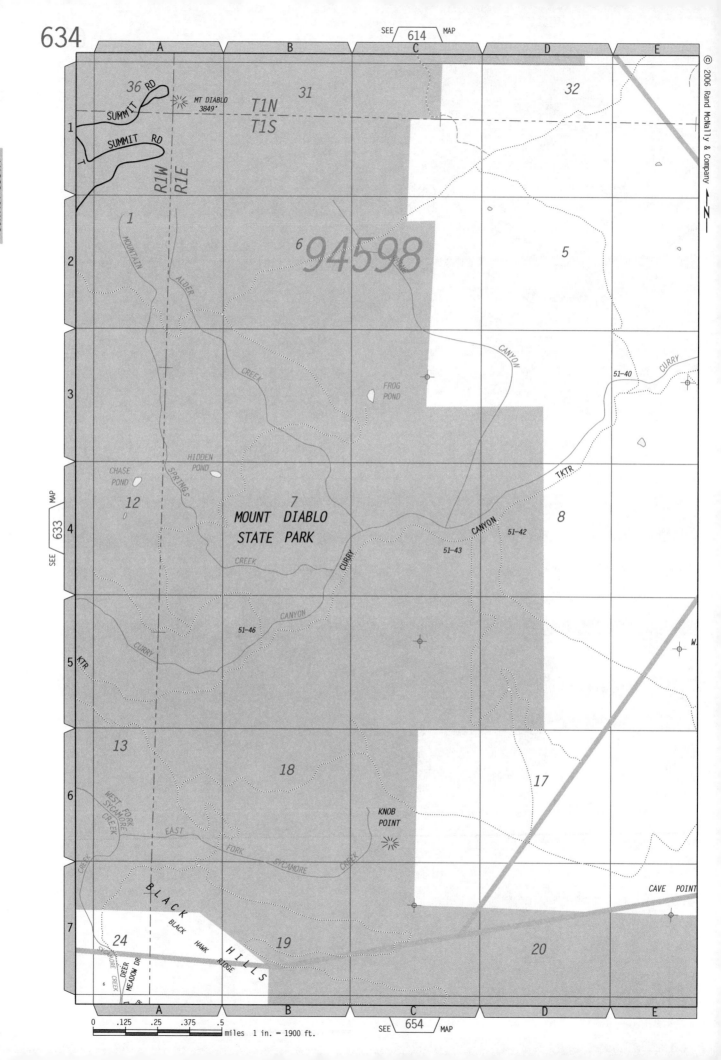

© 2006 Rand McNally & Company ◄—N—►

A   B   C   D   E

36 RD
SUMMIT
MT DIABLO
3849'
T1N
T1S
31
32
SUMMIT RD
T
R1W R1E
1

1
MOUNTAIN
ALDER
6
94598
5

CREEK

CANYON
CURRY
51-40

3
FROG
POND

SEE 633 MAP

HIDDEN
POND
CHASE
POND
TKTR

12
SPRINGS
7
MOUNT DIABLO
STATE PARK
CANYON
CANYON
51-42
8

CREEK
CURRY
51-43

CANYON
51-46
CURRY

5
KTR
W.

13
18
17

WEST FORK
SYCAMORE
CREEK
EAST
KNOB
POINT

6

FORK
SYCAMORE CREEK
CAVE POINT

CREEK
B L A C K
BLACK HAWK RIDGE
H I L L S

24
19
20
7
SYCAMORE
CREEK
DEER MEADOW DR
6

A   B   C   D   E

0 .125 .25 .375 .5 miles 1 in. = 1900 ft.

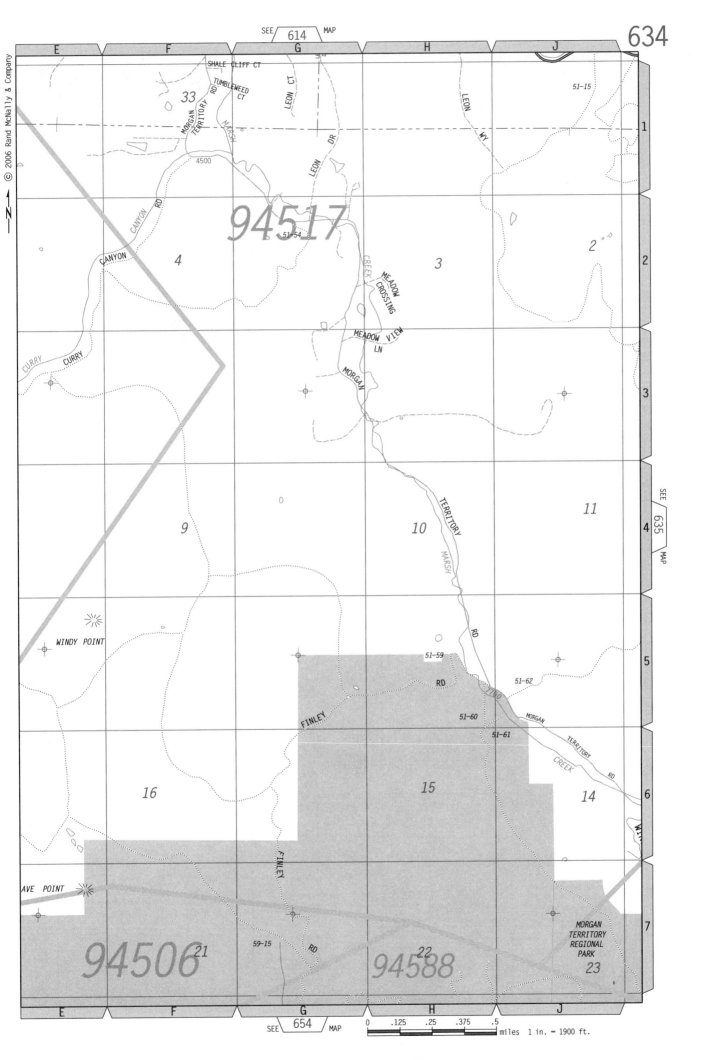

CONTRA COSTA

© 2006 Rand McNally & Company

—N—

SEE 614 MAP

E   F   G   H   J

SHALE CLIFF CT

TUMBLEWEED CT

33

MORGAN TERRITORY RD

MARSH

LEON CT

LEON DR

51-15

1

4500

94517

CANYON RD

CANYON

51-54

4

CREEK

MEADOW CROSSING

3

LEON WY

2

2

CURRY

CURRY

MEADOW VIEW LN

MORGAN

3

9

TERRITORY

10

MARSH

11

SEE 635 MAP

4

WINDY POINT

RD

51-59

51-62

5

RD

FINLEY

51-60

51-61

MORGAN

RD

TERRITORY

RD

6

16

15

CREEK

14

W

AVE POINT

FINLEY

RD

MORGAN TERRITORY REGIONAL PARK

7

94506 21

59-15

RD

94588 22

23

6

E   F   G   H   J

SEE 654 MAP

0   .125   .25   .375   .5   miles   1 in. = 1900 ft.

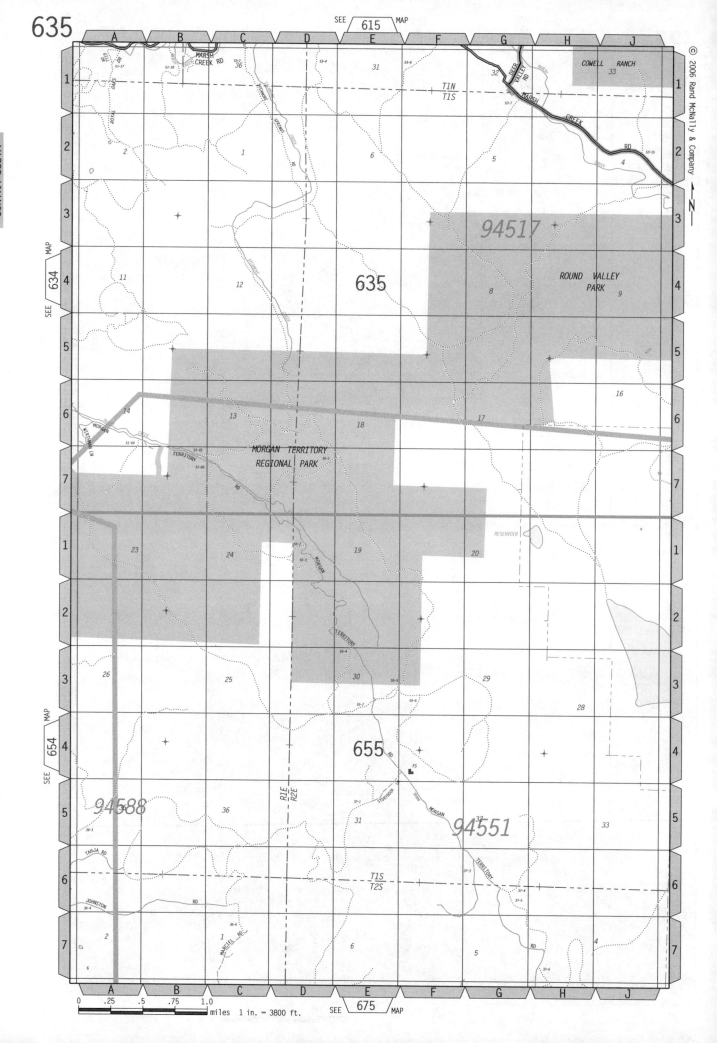

CONTRA COSTA

© 2006 Rand McNally & Company

SEE 634 MAP

SEE 654 MAP

COWELL RANCH

94517

ROUND VALLEY PARK

635

MORGAN TERRITORY REGIONAL PARK

655

94588

94551

MARSH CREEK RD

T1N / T1S

DEER VALLEY RD

RESERVOIR

R1E / R2E

T1S / T2S

0 .25 .5 .75 1.0
miles   1 in. = 3800 ft.

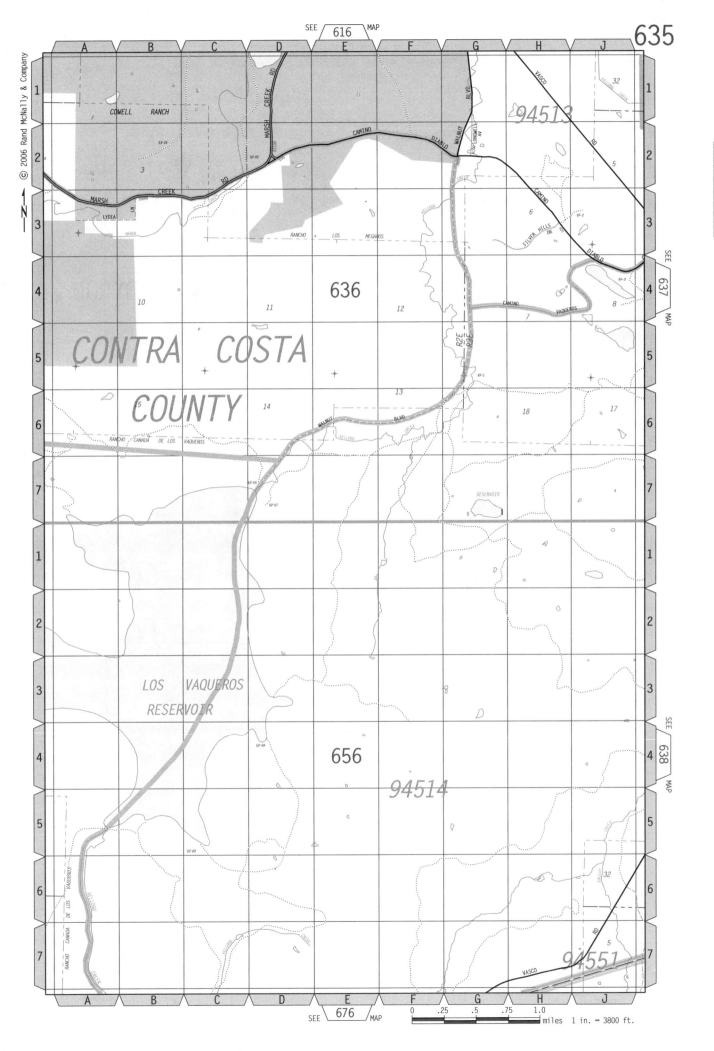

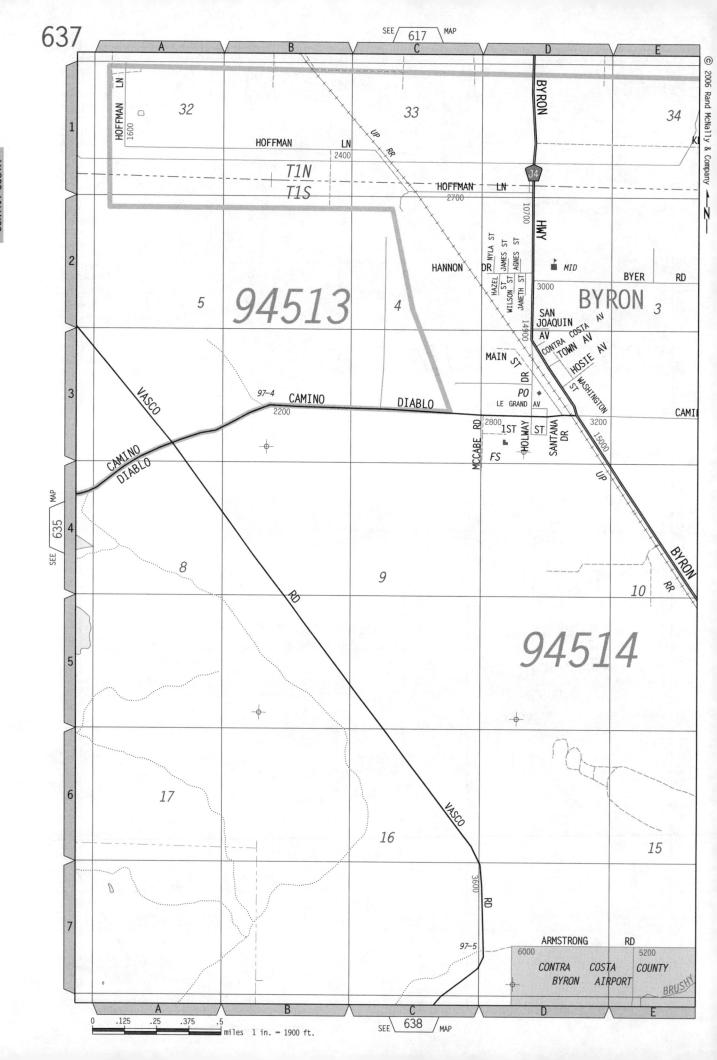

637

CONTRA COSTA

SEE 617 MAP

© 2006 Rand McNally & Company

—N—

A B C D E

1

HOFFMAN LN
1600

32

UP RR

33

BYRON

34

KI

HOFFMAN LN
2400

T1N
T1S

J4

HOFFMAN LN
2700

10700

HWY

2

5

94513

4

HANNON

HAZEL DR
NYLA ST
JAMES ST
WILSON ST
AGNES ST
JANETH ST

MID

3000

BYER RD

BYRON 3

SAN JOAQUIN AV

14060

CONTRA COSTA AV

TOWN AV

HOSIE AV

3

VASCO

97-4

CAMINO
2200

DIABLO

MAIN ST DR

PO

LE GRAND AV

MCCABE RD

2800

1ST

HOLWAY ST

ST

SANTANA DR

3200

15000

WASHINGTON ST

UP

CAMI

4

CAMINO
DIABLO

SEE 635 MAP

8

9

FS

BYRON RR

10

5

94514

6

17

VASCO

16

15

7

RD

3600

97-5

ARMSTRONG RD

6000

CONTRA COSTA
BYRON AIRPORT

5200

COUNTY

BRUSHY

6

A B C D E

SEE 638 MAP

0 .125 .25 .375 .5
miles 1 in. = 1900 ft.

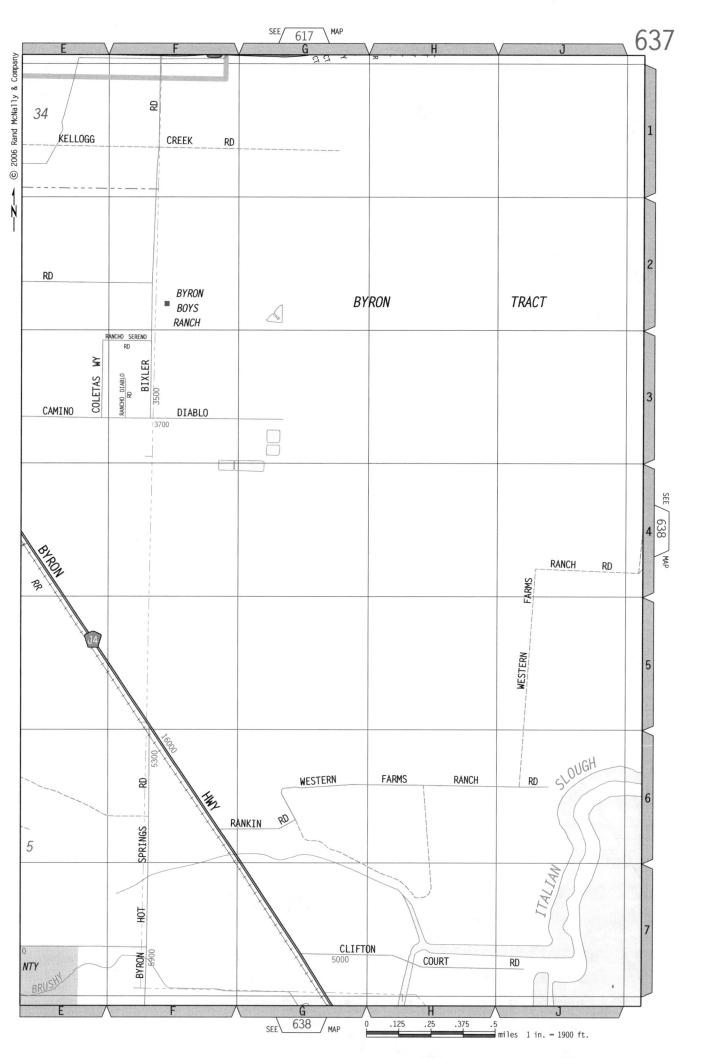

CONTRA COSTA

E   F   G   H   J

© 2006 Rand McNally & Company

34

N

1

KELLOGG   CREEK   RD

RD

2

RD

BYRON
BOYS
RANCH

BYRON   TRACT

RANCHO SERENO
RD

COLETAS WY

RANCHO DIABLO RD

BIXLER

3500

3

CAMINO   DIABLO

3700

SEE 638 MAP

RANCH   RD

4

BYRON

RR

WESTERN   FARMS

J4

5

16000

5300

WESTERN   FARMS   RANCH   RD

SLOUGH

6

HWY

RANKIN   RD

SPRINGS

RD

5

ITALIAN

HOT

7

BYRON

5900

CLIFTON
5000

COURT   RD

NTY

BRUSHY

6

E   F   G   H   J

0   .125   .25   .375   .5
miles   1 in. = 1900 ft.

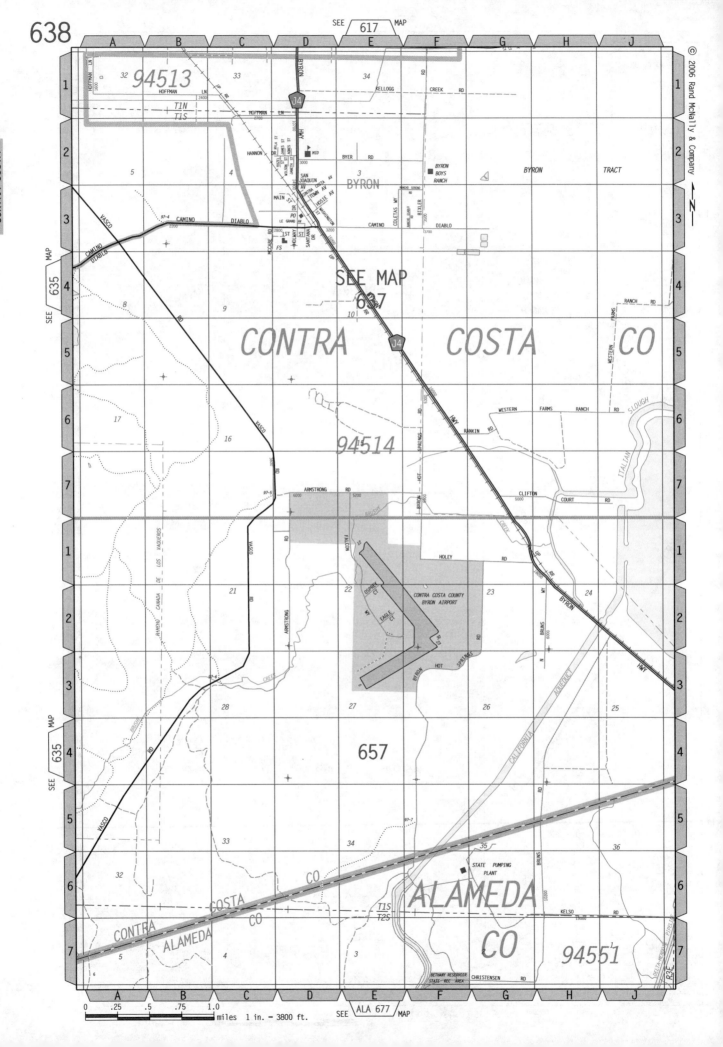

CONTRA COSTA

SEE 617 MAP

© 2006 Rand McNally & Company

94513

BYRON

CONTRA COSTA CO

94514

ALAMEDA CO

94551

657

SEE 635 MAP

SEE 635 MAP

SEE MAP 657

SEE ALA 677 MAP

0 .25 .5 .75 1.0
miles 1 in. - 3800 ft.

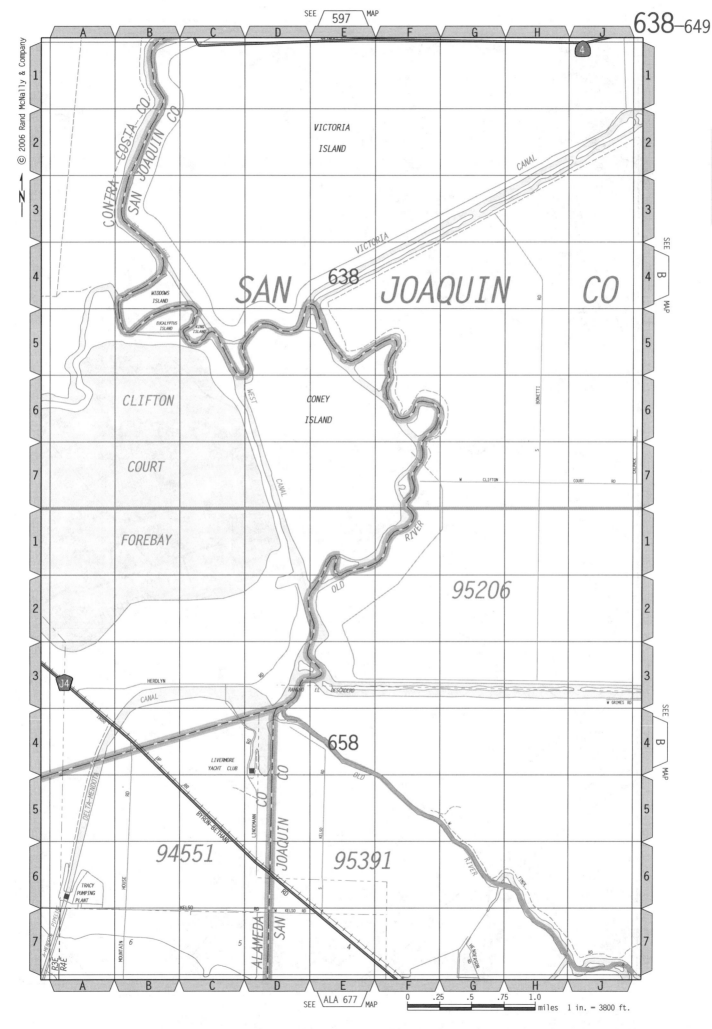

© 2006 Rand McNally & Company

N

CONTRA COSTA CO

SAN JOAQUIN CO

VICTORIA ISLAND

CANAL

VICTORIA

SAN 638 JOAQUIN CO

WIDDOWS ISLAND

EUCALYPTUS ISLAND

KING ISLAND

BONETTI RD

CALPACK RD

SEE B MAP

CLIFTON

COURT

FOREBAY

WEST

CANAL

CONEY ISLAND

W CLIFTON COURT RD

OLD RIVER

95206

HERDLYN

CANAL

RANCHO EL DESCADERO

W GRIMES RD

658

SEE B MAP

LIVERMORE YACHT CLUB

OLD

DELTA-MENDOTA

BYRON-BETHANY RR

LINDEMANN RD

SAN JOAQUIN CO

ALAMEDA CO

KELSO RD

RIVER

FINCK

HENDERSON RD

RD

94551

95391

TRACY PUMPING PLANT

HOUSE RD

MOUNTAIN

6

KELSO RD

5

W KELSO RD

4

R3E R4E

J4

4

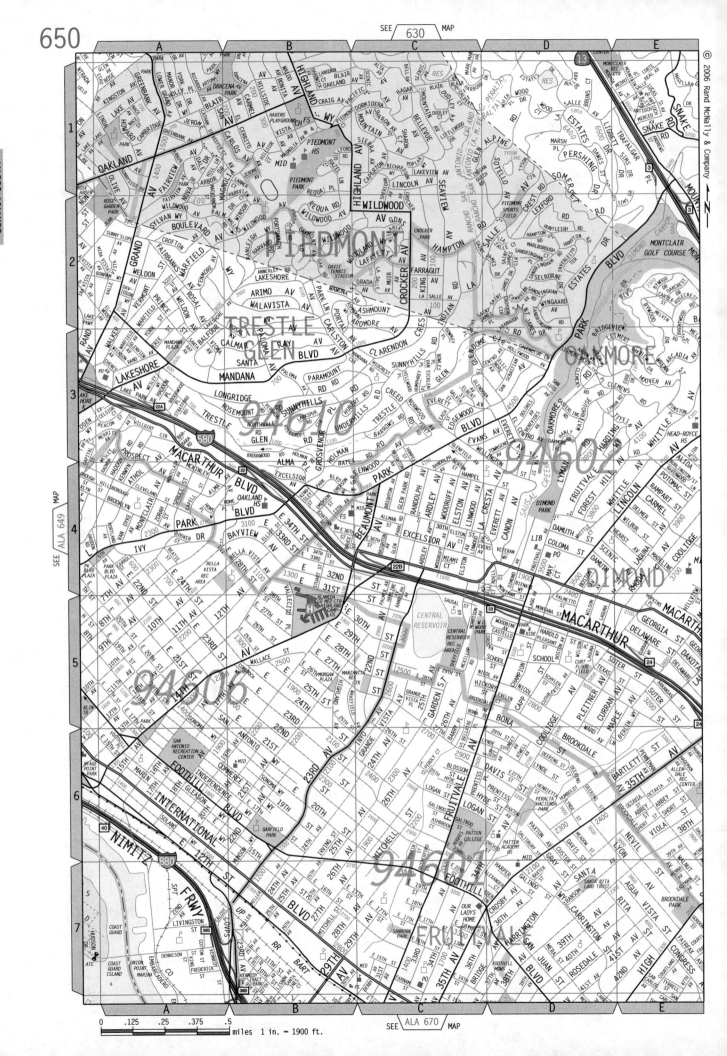

CONTRA COSTA

© 2006 Rand McNally & Company

SEE ALA 649 MAP

0 .125 .25 .375 .5
miles 1 in. = 1900 ft.

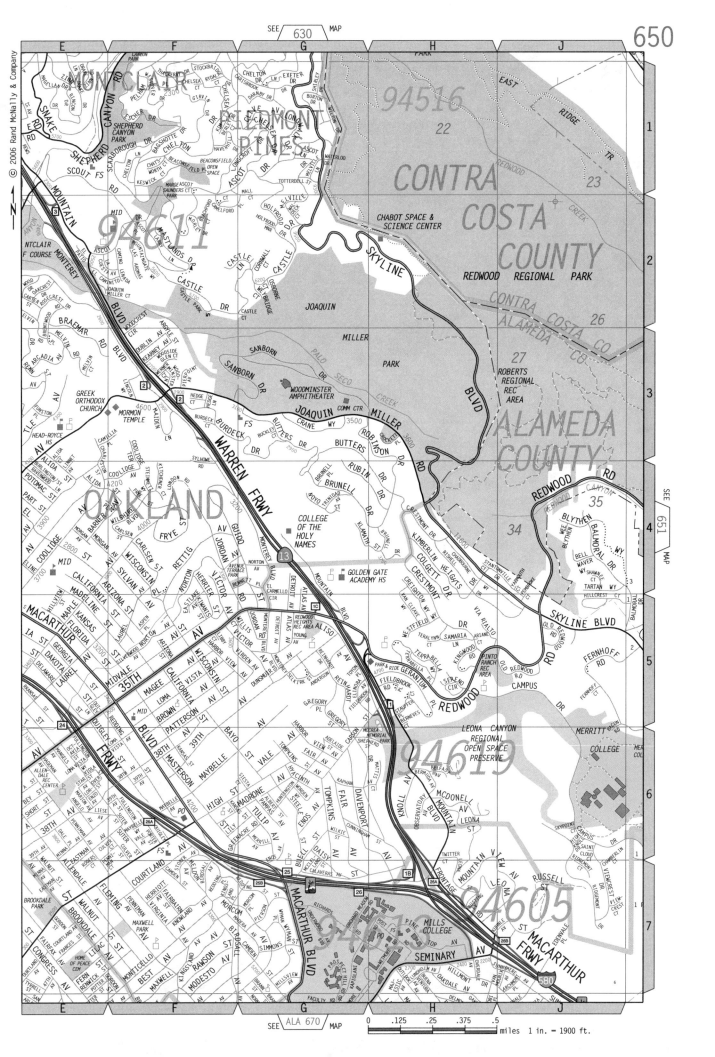

CONTRA COSTA

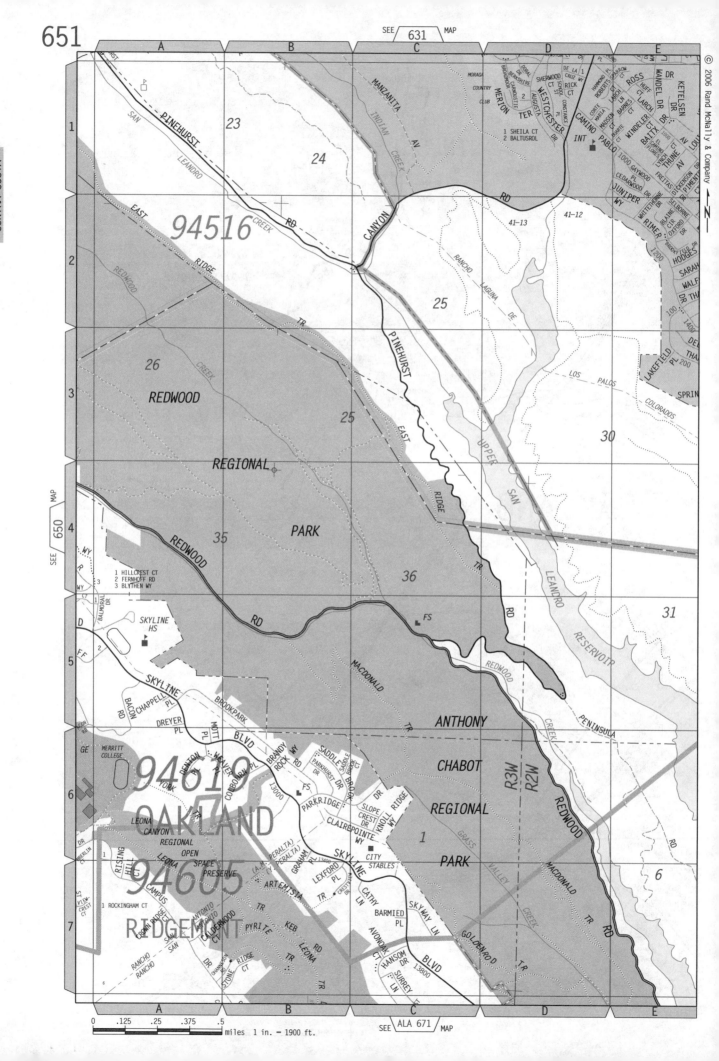

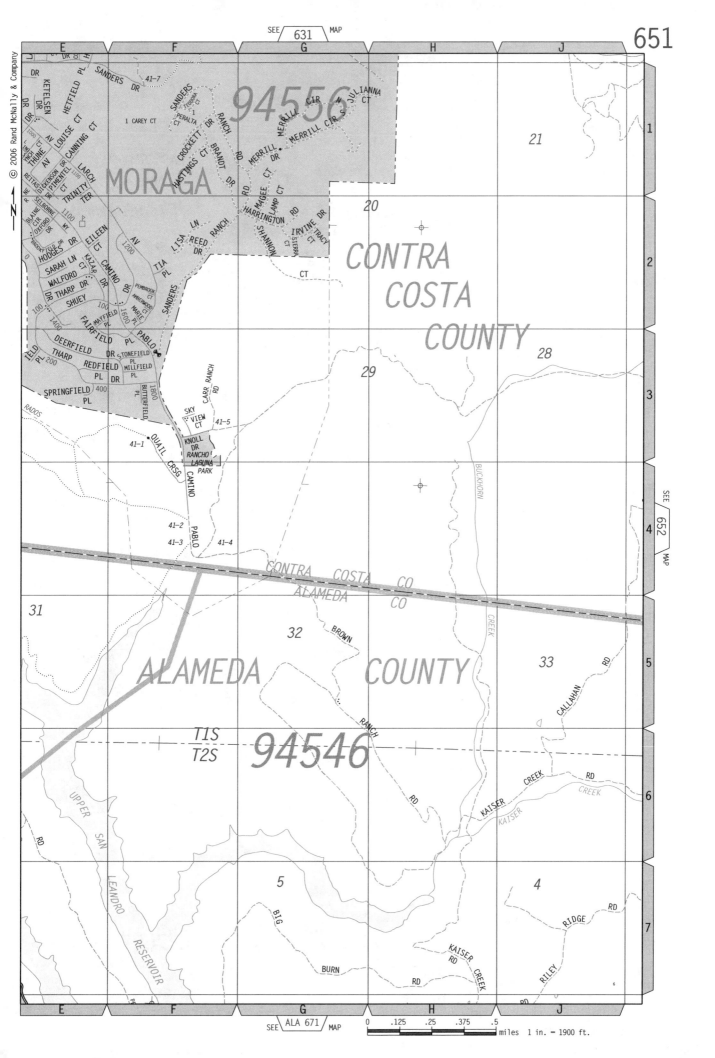

CONTRA COSTA

SEE 631 MAP

E   F   G   H   J

94556

MORAGA

1 CAREY CT

SANDERS DR   41-7

KETTELSEN DR
HETFIELD PL
SANDERS DR
LOUISE CT
CANNING CT
THUNE AV
LARCH
DICKENSON
PIMENTEL CT
TRINITY TER
SELBORNE
BLAINE CIR
OXFORD DR
BROOKFIELD DR
HODGES DR
EILEEN CT
SARAH LN
KAZAR CT
CAMINO
WALFORD DR
THARP DR
SHUEY
MAYFIELD
FAIRFIELD
DEERFIELD
THARP
TIELD PL
REDFIELD PL
SPRINGFIELD PL
STONEFIELD PL
MILLFIELD PL
BUTTERFIELD PL
RADOS

SANDERS
TEODORA CT
PERALTA CT
CROCKETT DR
HASTINGS CT
RANCH RD
BRANDT DR

MERRILL CIR
MERRILL DR
MERRILL CT
MAGEE
LAMP CT
RD
HARRINGTON
LISA LN
REED DR
RANCH
TIA PL
PEMBROOK CT
AMBERWOOD
MARIE PL
SANDERS
PABLO
SHANNON
IRVINE DR
SIERRA DR
TRACY

MERRILL CIR N
JULIANNA CT

CT

CARR RANCH RD
SKY VIEW CT   41-5
KNOLL DR
RANCHO LAGUNA PARK
41-1
QUAIL CRSG
CAMINO
PABLO
41-2
41-3   41-4

CONTRA COSTA
COUNTY

21

20

29

28

BUCKHORN

SEE 652 MAP

CONTRA COSTA CO
ALAMEDA CO

ALAMEDA   COUNTY

31

32   BROWN

33

CALLAHAN RD
CREEK

RANCH

T1S
T2S   94546

UPPER SAN LEANDRO RESERVOIR

RD

RD

KAISER CREEK RD
KAISER
CREEK

5

BIG
BURN

4

RIDGE RD

KAISER RD
RILEY
RD
CREEK
RD

1
2
3
4
5
6
7

E   F   G   H   J

SEE ALA 671 MAP

0   .125   .25   .375   .5

miles 1 in. = 1900 ft.

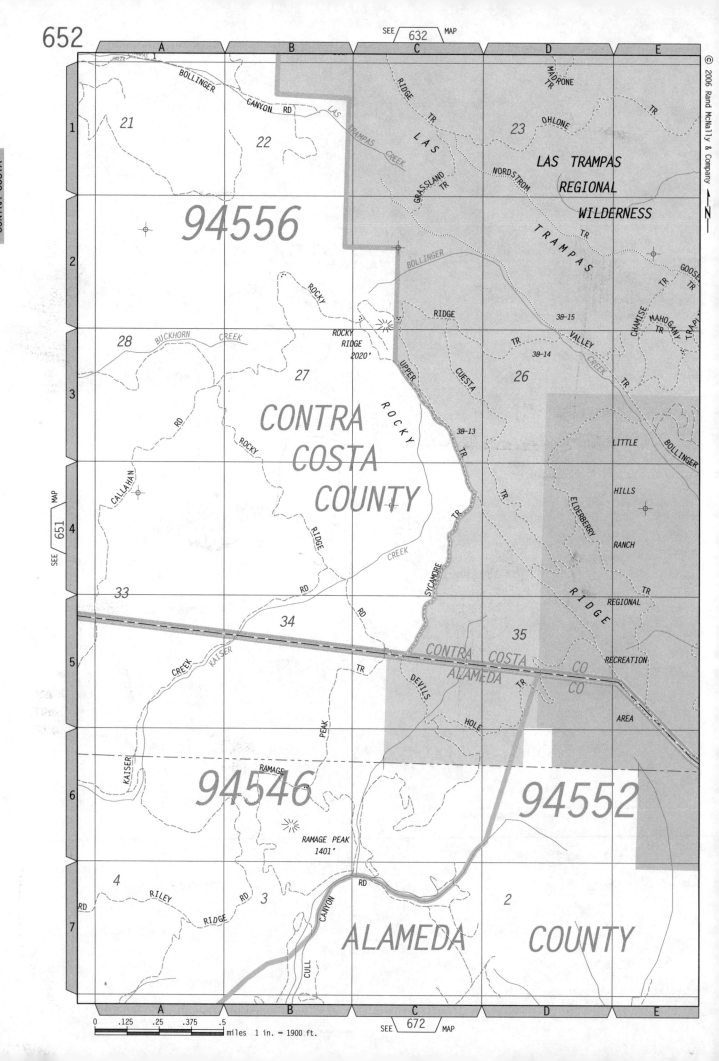

CONTRA COSTA

N

SEE 632 MAP

A   B   C   D   E

BRITT
BOLLINGER
CANYON RD
LAS TRAMPAS CREEK

21

22

94556

LAS
TRAMPAS
REGIONAL
WILDERNESS

RIDGE TR
GRASSLAND TR
NORDSTROM TR
MADRONE TR
OHLONE
TR

1

2

ROCKY

BOLLINGER

TRAMPAS

TR

GOOSE TR
CHAMISE TR
MAHOGANY TR
TRAP

28

BUCKHORN CREEK

27

ROCKY
RIDGE
2020'

UPPER

RIDGE

CUESTA

TR

38-15

38-14

VALLEY CREEK

TR

3

**CONTRA
COSTA
COUNTY**

ROCKY

38-13

TR

26

LITTLE
HILLS
BOLLINGER

CALLAHAN

ROCKY

RD

RIDGE

RD

CREEK

TR

TR

ELDERBERRY

RANCH

TR

4

33

34

SYCAMORE

TR

RD

35

CONTRA COSTA

ALAMEDA

CO

RIDGE

REGIONAL

RECREATION

5

CREEK KAISER

TR

DEVILS

CO

TR

HOLE

AREA

KAISER

RAMAGE

94546

94552

6

RAMAGE PEAK
1401'

4

RILEY

RD

3

CANYON

RD

2

RD

RIDGE

CULL

ALAMEDA   COUNTY

7

SEE 651 MAP

A   B   C   D   E

0   .125   .25   .375   .5
miles 1 in. = 1900 ft.

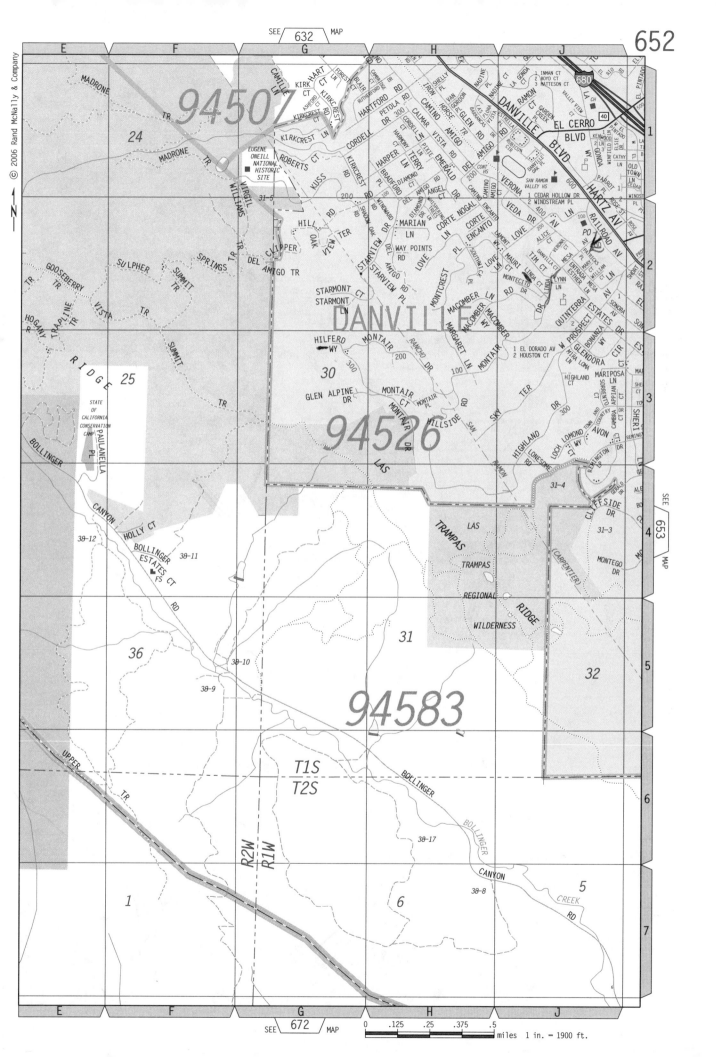

CONTRA COSTA

94507

94526

94583

DANVILLE

DANVILLE BLVD

EL CERRO BLVD

HARTZ AV

RAILROAD AV

24

25

RIDGE

STATE
OF
CALIFORNIA
CONSERVATION
CAMP
PAULANELLA

BOLLINGER
ESTATES

36

30

31

32

LAS TRAMPAS

LAS TRAMPAS

REGIONAL WILDERNESS

RIDGE

(CARPENTER)

T1S
T2S

R2W R1W

BOLLINGER

BOLLINGER

CANYON

CREEK

1

6

5

EUGENE ONEILL NATIONAL HISTORIC SITE

GOOSEBERRY TR

HOGANY R

SULPHER TR

SUMMIT TR

VISTA TR

SPRINGS TR

VIRGIL WILLIAMS TR

MADRONE TR

TRAPLINE TR

SUMMIT TR

SUMMIT TR

DEL AMIGO TR

CLIPPER

HILL OAK VIEW TER

CAMILLE LN

KIRKCREST LN

KIRKCREST LN

KIRKCREST CT

ROBERTS CT

KUSS RD

CORDELL

KIRKCREST RD

SHADOW OAK DR

WINDWARD DR

HARTFORD DR

PETOLA DR

CALMAR

HARMONY LN

CORDELL

BRADFORD CT

HARPER LN

DIAMOND CT

ANGEL

DIAMOND DR

DEL AMIGO

STARVIEW DR

MARIAN LN

STARVIEW RD

WAY POINTS RD

STARMONT CT
STARMONT LN

STARVIEW PL

LOVE

CAMINO AMIGO

CAMINO VISTA RD

PIXIE

EMERALD

DEL AMIGO

CORTE NOGAL

CAMINO ENCANTO

CORTE ENCANTO

LOVE LN

SOUTH LOCK

MONTCREST PL

MACOMBER LN

MACOMBER WY

MACOMBER

MARGARET LN

MONTAIR

HILFERD WY

MONTAIR

RANCHO DR

MONTAIR CT

MONTAIR DR

GLEN ALPINE DR

HILLSIDE

SKY TER

SAN RAMON RD

HIGHLAND DR

LOCH LOMOND WY

LONESOME

REMINGTON LP

AVON

CLIFFSIDE DR

MONTEGO DR

HOLLY CT

FS CT

VERONA

VEDA DR

LOVE

MAURI

LINDA CT

MONTECITO

LYNN LN

QUINTERRA ESTATES

W PROSPECT

GLENDORA

BONANZA WY

HIGHLAND CT

MARIPOSA LN

SORRENTO CT

CAMBRA

COUNTRY

CIR

SHERI LN

SEE 653 MAP

31-5

200

200

300

100

400

500

600

100

200

300

100

300

31-4

31-3

38-12

38-11

38-10

38-9

38-17

38-8

1 CEDAR HOLLOW DR
2 WINDSTREAM PL

1 EL DORADO AV
2 HOUSTON CT

1 INMAN CT
2 BOYD CT
3 MATTESON CT

680

40

PO

CONT HS

SAN RAMON VALLEY HS

OLD TOWN

UPPER TR

0 .125 .25 .375 .5
miles 1 in. = 1900 ft.

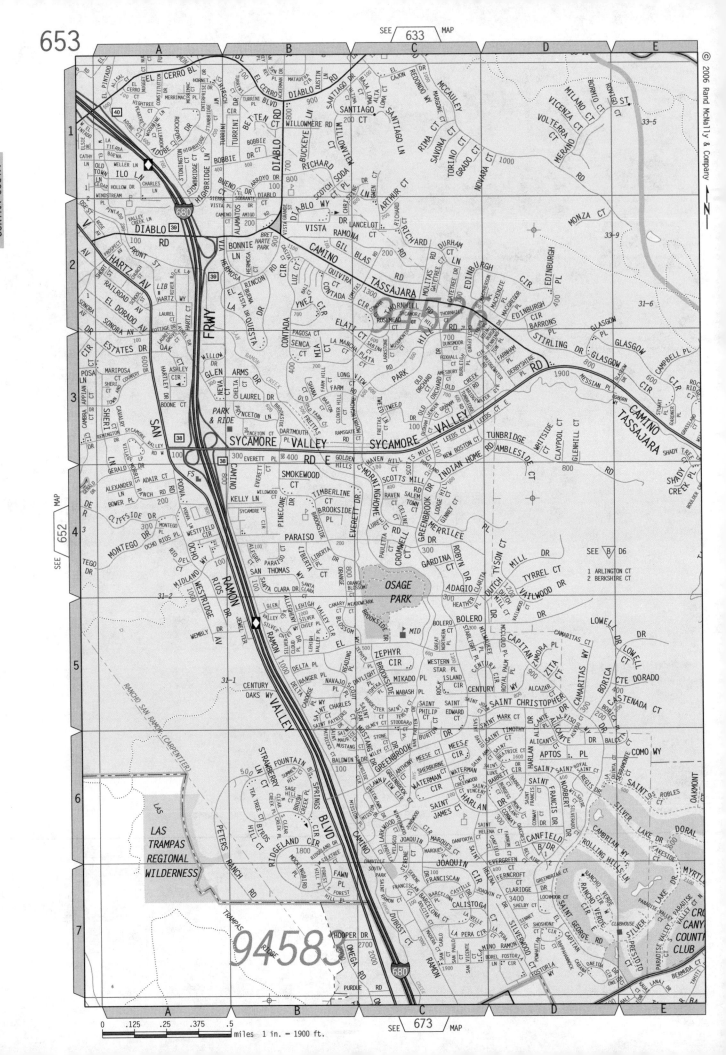

CONTRA COSTA

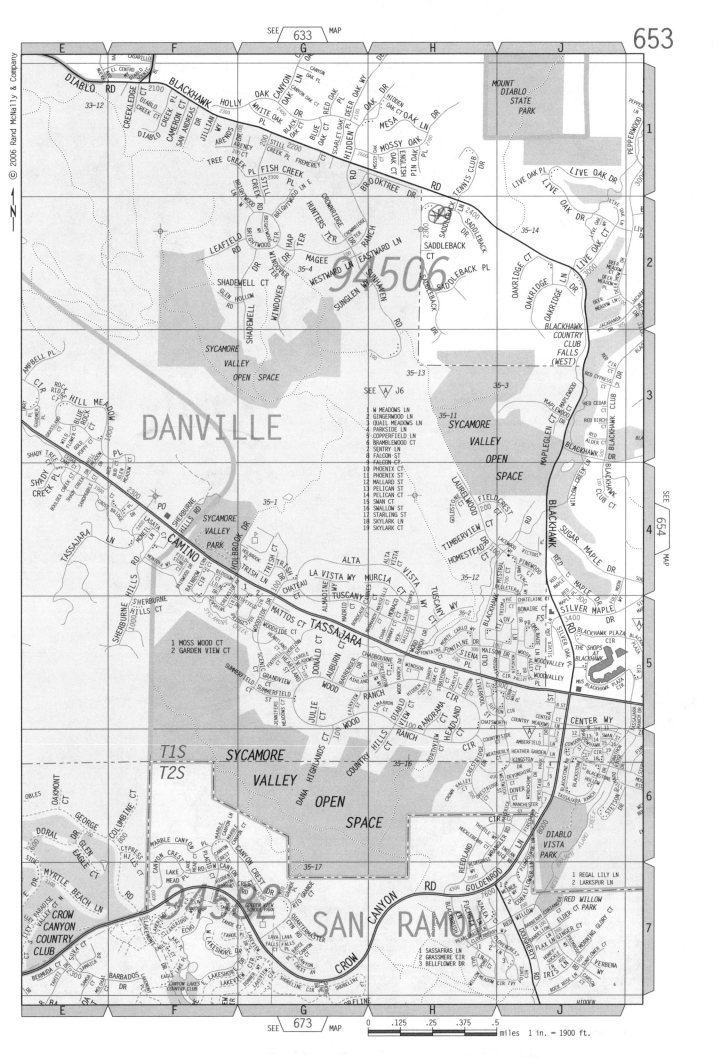

94506

DANVILLE

SAN RAMON

94582

MOUNT DIABLO STATE PARK

BLACKHAWK COUNTRY CLUB FALLS (WEST)

SYCAMORE VALLEY OPEN SPACE

SYCAMORE VALLEY OPEN SPACE

SYCAMORE VALLEY PARK

SYCAMORE VALLEY OPEN SPACE

DIABLO VISTA PARK

RED WILLOW CT PARK

CROW CANYON COUNTRY CLUB

SEE A J6

1 W MEADOWS LN
2 GINGERWOOD LN
3 QUAIL MEADOWS LN
4 PARKSIDE LN
5 COPPERFIELD LN
6 BRAMBLEWOOD CT
7 SENTRY LN
8 FALCON ST
9 FALCON CT
10 PHOENIX CT
11 PHOENIX ST
12 MALLARD ST
13 PELICAN ST
14 PELICAN CT
15 SWAN CT
16 SWALLOW ST
17 STARLING ST
18 SKYLARK LN
19 SKYLARK CT

1 MOSS WOOD CT
2 GARDEN VIEW CT

1 REGAL LILY LN
2 LARKSPUR LN

1 SASSAFRAS LN
2 GRASSMERE CIR
3 BELLFLOWER DR

SEE 654 MAP

0   .125   .25   .375   .5   miles   1 in. = 1900 ft.

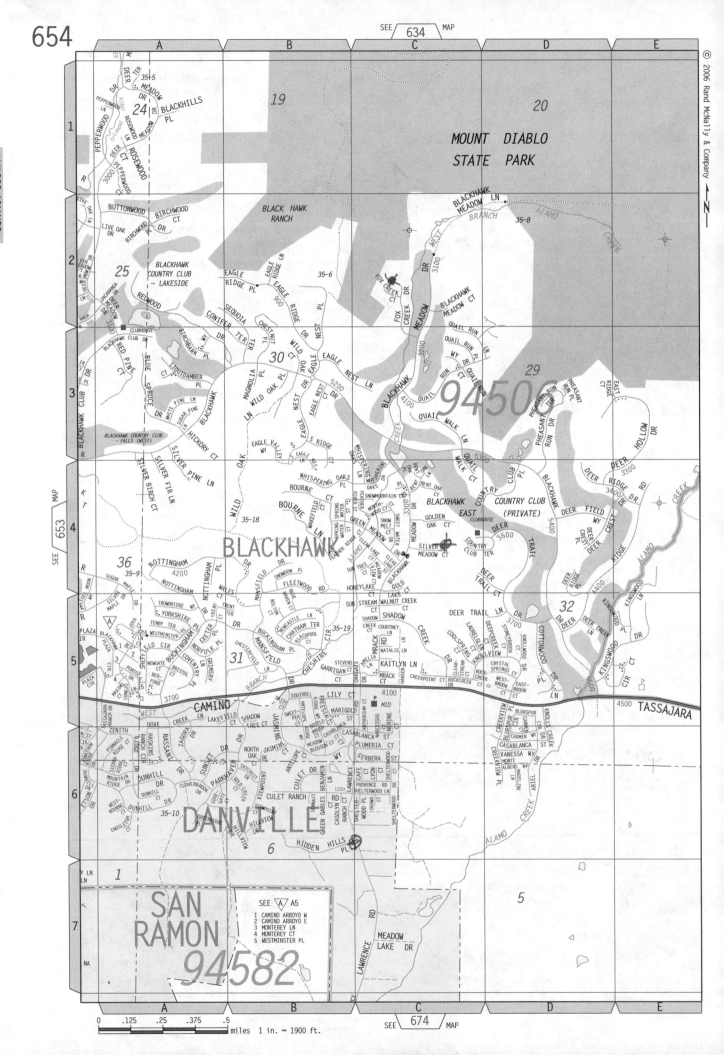

CONTRA COSTA

SEE 634 MAP

© 2006 Rand McNally & Company

N

MOUNT DIABLO
STATE PARK

19

20

24 BLACKHILLS PL
DEER MEADOW DR
35-5
PEPPERWOOD LN
ROSEWOOD MEADOW
SYCAMORE
DEER
PEPPERWOOD CT
3000

BUTTONWOOD
BIRCHWOOD CT
LIVE OAK LA
BIRCHWOOD DR
LIVE OAK DR

BLACK HAWK
RANCH

BLACKHAWK
MEADOW LN
35-8
BRANCH
ALAMO CREEK
3100

25
BLACKHAWK
COUNTRY CLUB
– LAKESIDE
JACARANDA DR
DEER MEADOW
ANDA DR 3100

EAGLE RIDGE PL
EAGLE RIDGE LN
EAGLE RIDGE
900
35-6

FOX CREEK CT
FOX CREEK DR
BLACKHAWK MEADOW DR
BLACKHAWK MEADOW CT
3100
QUAIL RUN WY
QUAIL RUN PL
QUAIL RUN LN

REDWOOD
CLUBHOUSE
RED PINE CT
RED
300
CLUBHOUSE
BLACKHAWK CLUB DR
BIRCHBARK PL
BLUE SPRUCE
LIQUIDAMBER PL
WHITE PINE LN
SUGAR PINE
HICKORY CT
30
CONIFER TER
SEQUOIA
MAGNOLIA PL
WILD OAK CT
CHESTNUT
WILD OAK PL
WILD OAK
EAGLE NEST DR
5200
EAGLE NEST
EAGLE NEST CT
EAGLE NEST LN
BLACKHAWK
4100
QUAIL RUN
QUAIL RUN DR
QUAIL WALK LN
5300
94506
29
PHEASANT RUN TER
PHEASANT RUN PL
PHEASANT RUN DR
EAST RIDGE CT
DEER HOLLOW DR
3300

BLACKHAWK CLUB DR
SILVER PINE LN
SILVER FIR CT
BLACKHAWK COUNTRY CLUB
– FALLS (WEST)
SILVER BIRCH CT
EAGLE VALLEY WY
EAGLE S RIDGE
EAGLE NEST LD
OAK
WILD
WHISPERING OAKS LN
WHISPERING OAKS PL
BOURNE CT
BOURNE
WAKEFIELD
35-18
SPRING WATER
FEATHER RIVER CT
GREEN MEADOW
SNOWMOUNTAIN
NORTHWOOD CT
SNOW MELT
BENT OAK PL
BENT OAK
3300
GOLDEN OAK CT
BLACKHAWK
EAST CLUBHOUSE
COUNTRY CLUB
(PRIVATE)
DEER FIELD WY
DEER CREST PL
DEER CREST DR
DEER RIDGE RD
3400
DEER CREST DR
3300

SEE 653 MAP
NOTTINGHAM PL
NOTTINGHAM
4200
36
35-9
SUGAR MAPLE
SILVER MAPLE
WALES
TRENT
MANSFIELD DR
SNOWDON PL
FLEETWOOD RD
BLUE HAVEN CT
35-19
SHADOW CREEK CT
COURTNEY RD
NATALIE CT
HONEYLAKE
SUN TREE
CLEAR LAKE
SWEET WATER CT
SILVER MEADOW CT
COUNTRY CLUB TER
DEER 3600
DEER TRAIL CT
DEER TRAIL LN
3700
DEER TRAIL
COOLSPRING CT
STONEBROOK
DEEPCREEK
LAUREL GLEN
KNOLLVIEW
CRYSTAL SPRINGS
ROCK CREEK
CLEAR CREEK
WESTBROOK
EAST BROOK PL
KNOLLWOOD DR
COTTONWOOD DR
32
DEER DR
DEER CREEK LN
3700
KINGSWOOD PL
KINGSWOOD CT
KINGSWOOD
4400
ALAMO
CREEK

TROWBRIDGE
YORKSHIRE PL
WESTMINSTER
TENBY TER
EXETER PL
GRIMSBY
A
JOYA
SHEFFIELD CIR
BUCKINGHAM
NORFOLK PL
COVENTRY
31
NEWGATE
PORTO
BRISTOL
BEDFORD
CONWAY
3700
CHESTERFIELD
MANSFIELD DR
CHATHAM TER
BLACKPOOL CT
CHESHIRE CIR
STEVENS CT
GARRIGAN CT
OAKGATE
AMELIA
MRACK CT
MRACK RD
KAITLYN LN
HANSEN
CREEKPOINT CT

PLAZA CIR
BLACKHAWK PLAZA
PLAZA CIR

SQUIRREL LN
LILY CT
FREESIA
ANTELOPE CT
SWEET PEA CT
BOTTLE
MARIGOLD
CASABLANCA
4100
MID
NARCISSUS ST
NERINE ST
ANTHURIUM CT
4500 TASSAJARA
CREEKVIEW BLURSPUR
BLURSPUR PL
CARMEL CT
CARMEN DR
CASABLANCA
VANESSA
MONTE
ALBERS WY
MADELINE
CREEKVIEW PL
KNOLLS CREEK

CAMINO
WEST
DOVE CREEK LN
LAKEFIELD CT
SHADOW TREE CT
JASMINE DR
NORTH JASMINE
ANTELOPE
MEADOW
BLOSSOM CT
PLUMERIA WY
CASABLANCA DR
GERBERA
CAFE CT
LYON CT
PROVENCE CT
SHELTERWOOD LN
SHELTERWOOD

ZENITH
ZAGORA DR
RASSANI DR
HASKINS
SIERRA RIDGE RD
SUNSET DR
PARKHAVEN DR
CULET DR
BENJAMIN LN
LAWRENCE
SHELTER WOOD PL
CASOLYN RANCH RD
LOGAMA CT
SENNACT

PINNACLE RIDGE
MOUNTAIN RIDGE
DUNHILL DR
CLOVERBROOK
EDGE GATE
GOLD CREEK
VIEWPOINT
GREEN GABLES
CULET RANCH RD

PASSARGA RONAN PL
PASSARGA
DUNN
DUNHILL
WESTBOURNE
ENDSLEIGH
35-10
GREENRIDGE
HILLVIEW
DANVILLE
6
HIDDEN HILLS PL

1

SAN RAMON
94582

SEE A5
1 CAMINO ARROYO W
2 CAMINO ARROYO E
3 MONTEREY LN
4 MONTEREY CT
5 WESTMINSTER PL

LAWRENCE RD
MEADOW LAKE DR

5

0 .125 .25 .375 .5 miles 1 in. = 1900 ft.

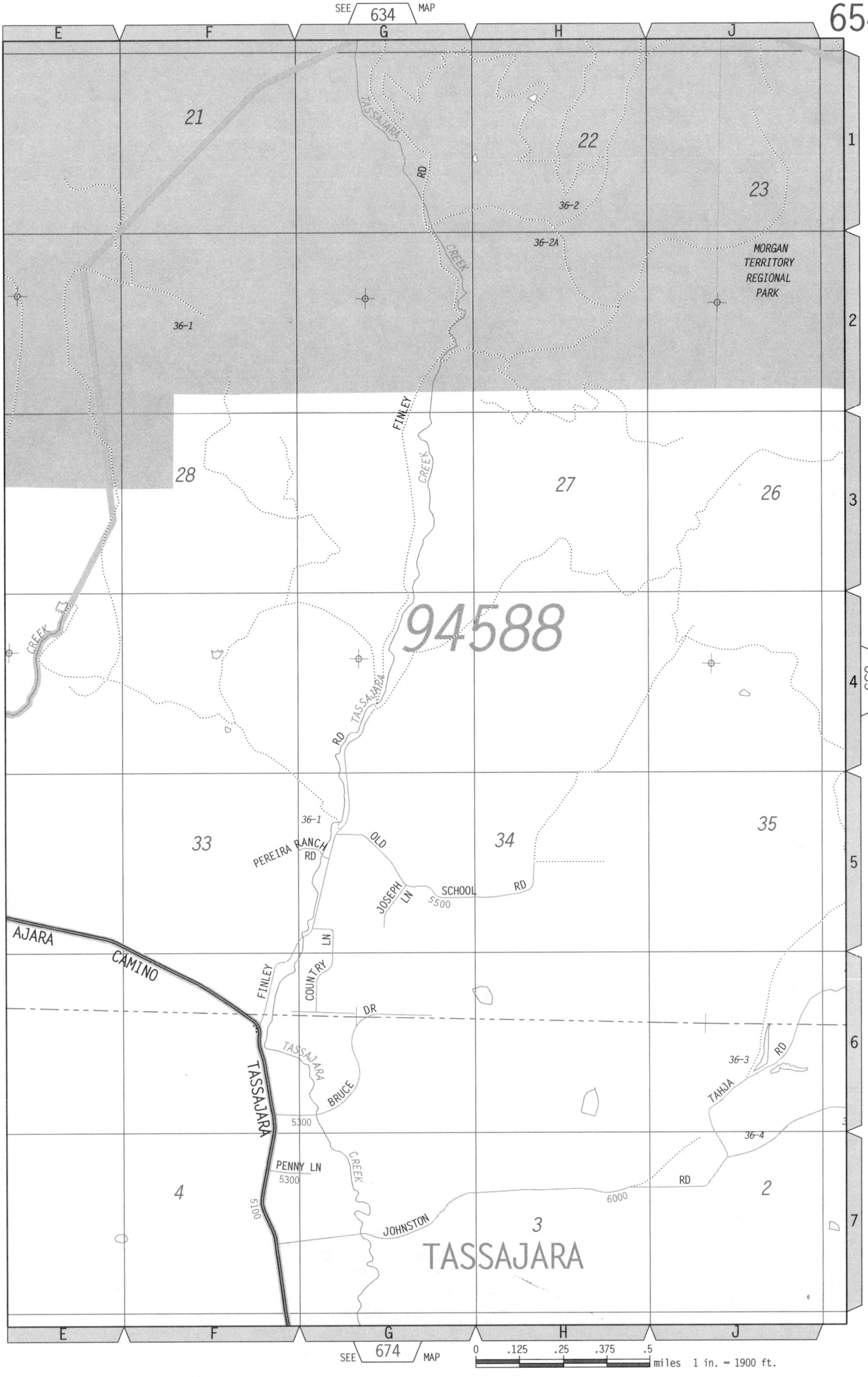

CONTRA COSTA

E   F   G   H   J

21

22

23

TASSAJARA RD

36-2

36-2A

MORGAN
TERRITORY
REGIONAL
PARK

CREEK

36-1

1

2

FINLEY

CREEK

28   27   26

CREEK

3

94588

RD TASSAJARA

4

36-1

33   34   35

PEREIRA RANCH RD

OLD

JOSEPH LN

SCHOOL   RD

5500

5

AJARA

CAMINO

FINLEY

COUNTRY   LN

DR

TASSAJARA

BRUCE

5300

TASSAJARA

36-3   RD

TAHJA

36-4

6

CREEK

PENNY LN
5300

5100

4

JOHNSTON

RD

6000

3

2

7

TASSAJARA

E   F   G   H   J

0   .125   .25   .375   .5
miles 1 in. = 1900 ft.

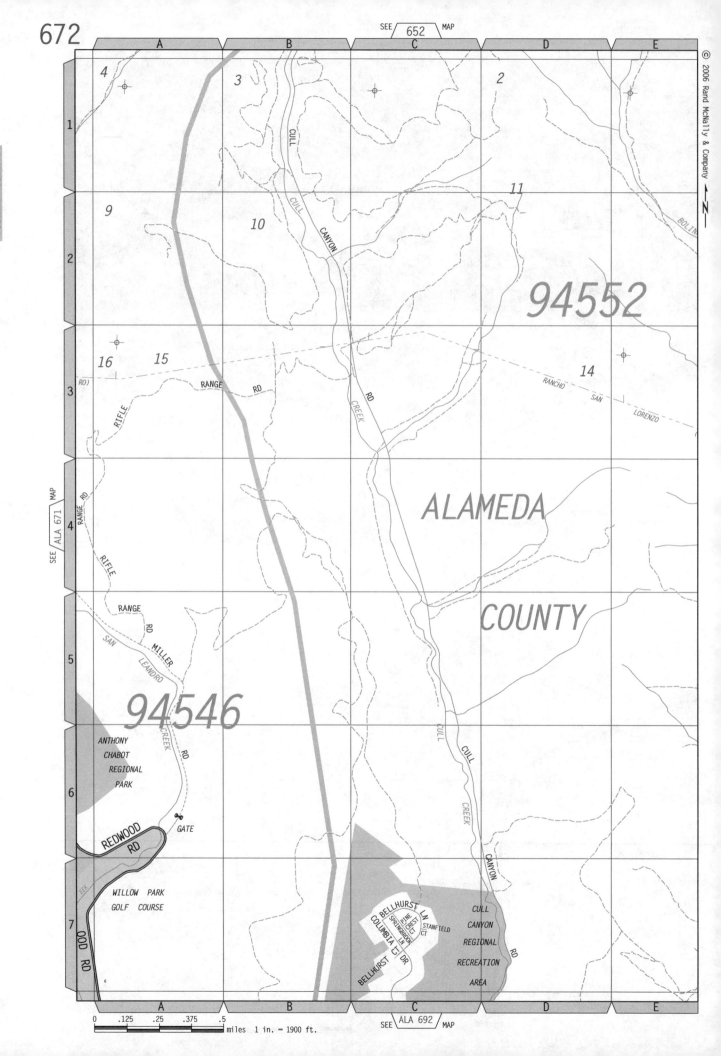

672

CONTRA COSTA

A   B   C   D   E

4   3   2
1
9   10   11

94552
2

16   15   14
3
RIFLE   RANGE   RD   RANCHO   SAN   LORENZO
CREEK
RD)

SEE ALA 671 MAP
RANGE   RD
4
RIFLE
ALAMEDA
RANGE
RD
MILLER
SAN   LEANDRO
5
COUNTY
94546
CREEK   RD
ANTHONY
CHABOT
CULL
REGIONAL
6
PARK
CULL   CREEK
REDWOOD   RD   GATE
CANYON
EEK
WILLOW   PARK
GOLF   COURSE
CULL
BELLHURST LN
CANYON
7
PINE CREST CT
COLUMBIA CT
SPRINGBROOK LN
STANFIELD CT
REGIONAL
OOD   RD
BELLHURST   DR
RECREATION
6
AREA

A   B   C   D   E

0   .125   .25   .375   .5
miles 1 in. = 1900 ft.

N
BOLIN

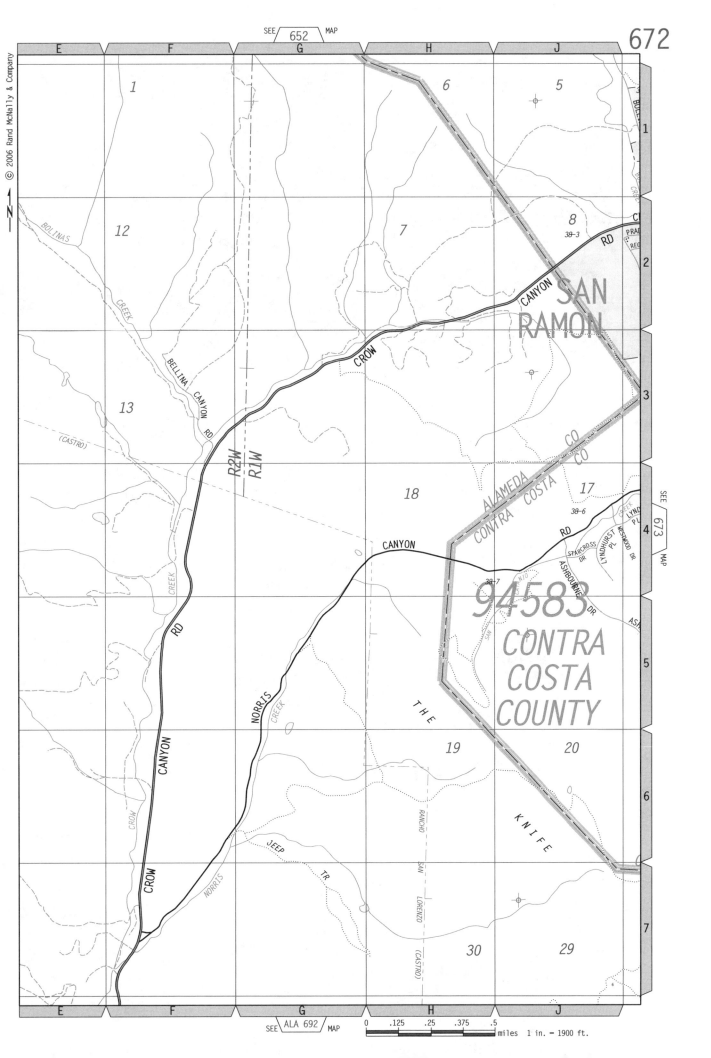

CONTRA COSTA

© 2006 Rand McNally & Company

N

SEE 652 MAP

E F G H J

1

12 7 8
38-3

CANYON SAN
RAMON

CROW

13

BELLINA CANYON RD

(CASTRO)

R2W R1W

ALAMEDA CO
CONTRA COSTA CO

18 17
38-6

RD SPARCROSS DR LYNDHURST PL WESTWOOD DR LYND PL

SEE 673 MAP

CANYON 38-7 ASHBOURNE DR ASH

94583
CONTRA
COSTA
COUNTY

CREEK

RD

NORRIS CREEK

CANYON

THE

19 KNIFE 20

RANCHO SAN LORENZO (CASTRO)

JEEP TR

CROW

NORRIS

30 29

1 2 3 4 5 6 7

E F G H J

SEE ALA 692 MAP

0 .125 .25 .375 .5 miles 1 in. = 1900 ft.

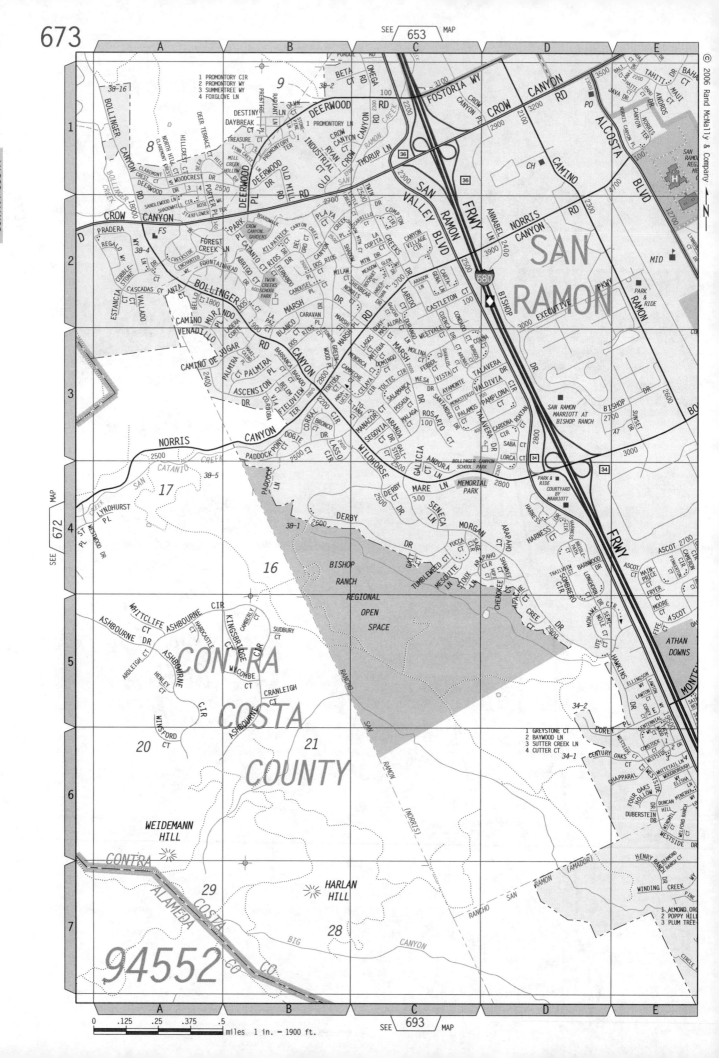

CONTRA COSTA

SEE 653 MAP

SEE 672 MAP

SAN RAMON

CONTRA COSTA COUNTY

94552

SEE 693 MAP

0 .125 .25 .375 .5
miles 1 in. = 1900 ft.

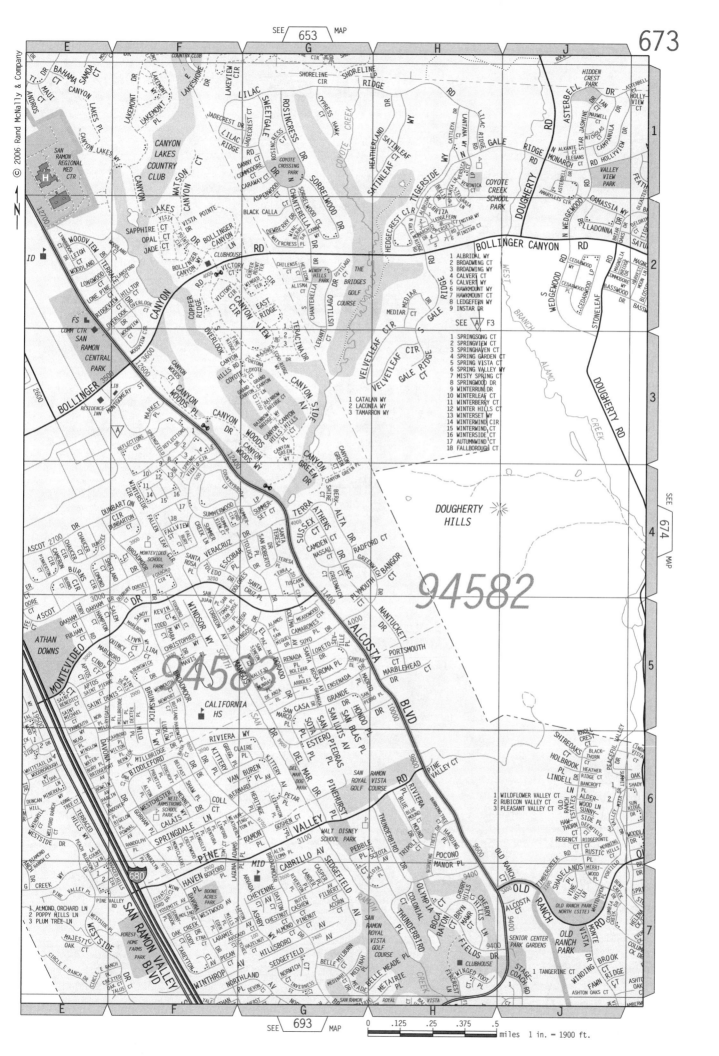

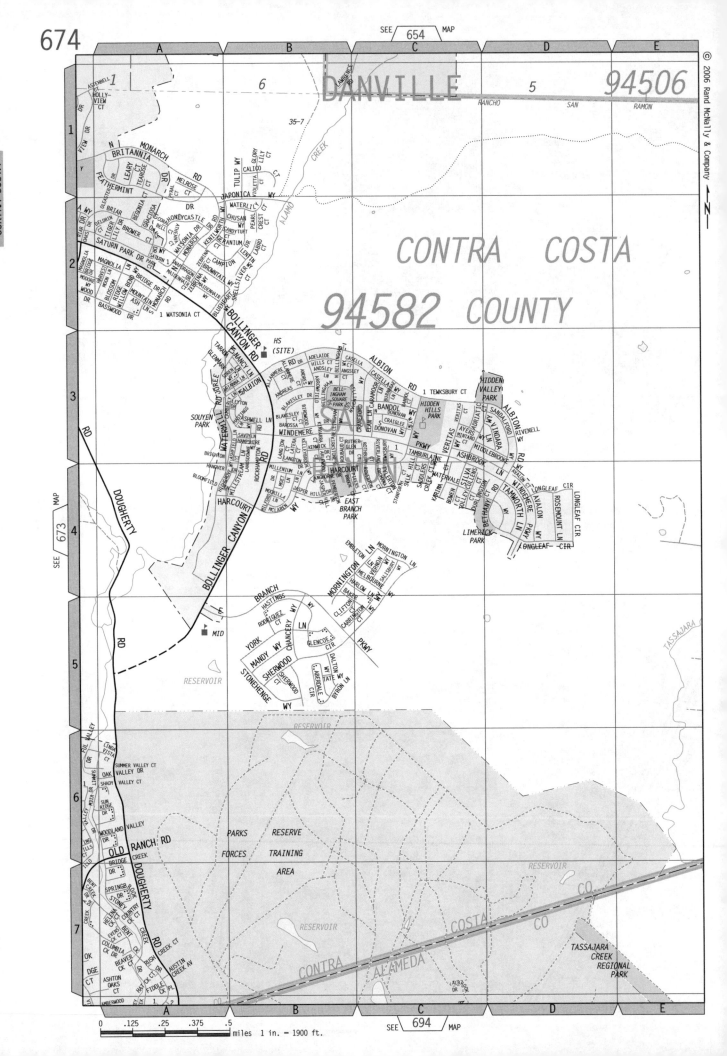

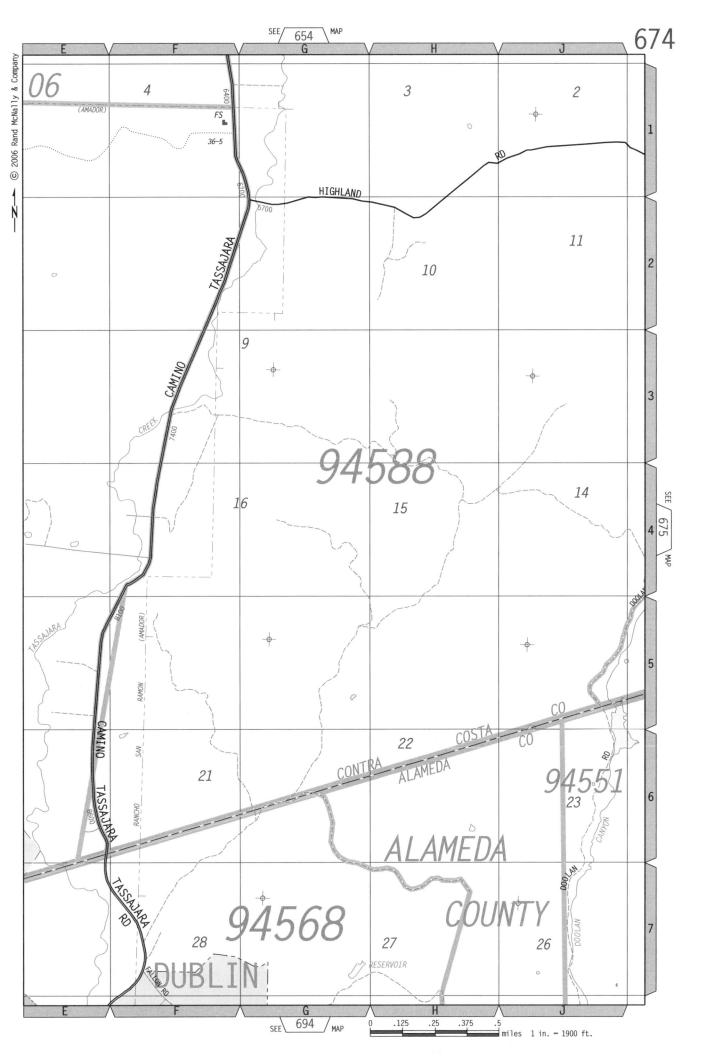

CONTRA COSTA

SEE 654 MAP

| E | F | G | H | J |

06

4

3

2

1

(AMADOR)

FS

6400

6700

36-5

5700

HIGHLAND RD

TASSAJARA

2

10

11

CAMINO

9

3

CREEK

7400

94588

16

15

14

SEE 675 MAP

4

TASSAJARA

(AMADOR)

8100

5

RAMON

SAN

CO

CO

94551

CAMINO

22

COSTA

TASSAJARA

8600

CONTRA

ALAMEDA

21

RANCHO

DOOLAN

23

6

ALAMEDA

DOOLAN RD

CANYON

TASSAJARA RD

94568

COUNTY

DOOLAN

FALLON RD

28

RESERVOIR

27

26

7

DUBLIN

| E | F | G | H | J |

SEE 694 MAP

0 .125 .25 .375 .5

miles 1 in. = 1900 ft.

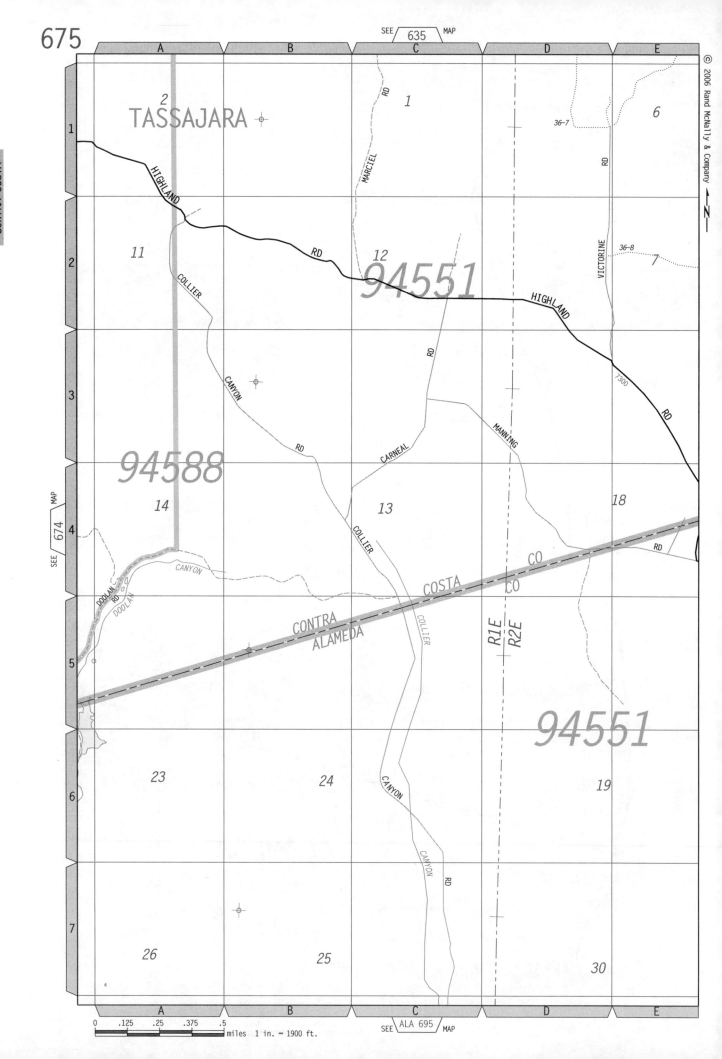

CONTRA COSTA

SEE 635 MAP

A   B   C   D   E

—N—

2

TASSAJARA

1

MARCIEL RD

6

36-7

RD

1

HIGHLAND

11

RD

12

94551

VICTORINE RD

36-8

7

2

COLLIER

HIGHLAND

CANYON

RD

7300 RD

3

RD

CARNEAL

MANNING

94588

14

13

18

COLLIER

RD

CANYON

CO

COLLIER

COSTA

CO

RD

4

CONTRA

ALAMEDA

DOOLAN

DOOLAN RD

R1E R2E

SEE 674 MAP

5

94551

23

24

CANYON

19

6

COLLIER

CANYON RD

26

25

30

7

A   B   C   D   E

SEE ALA 695 MAP

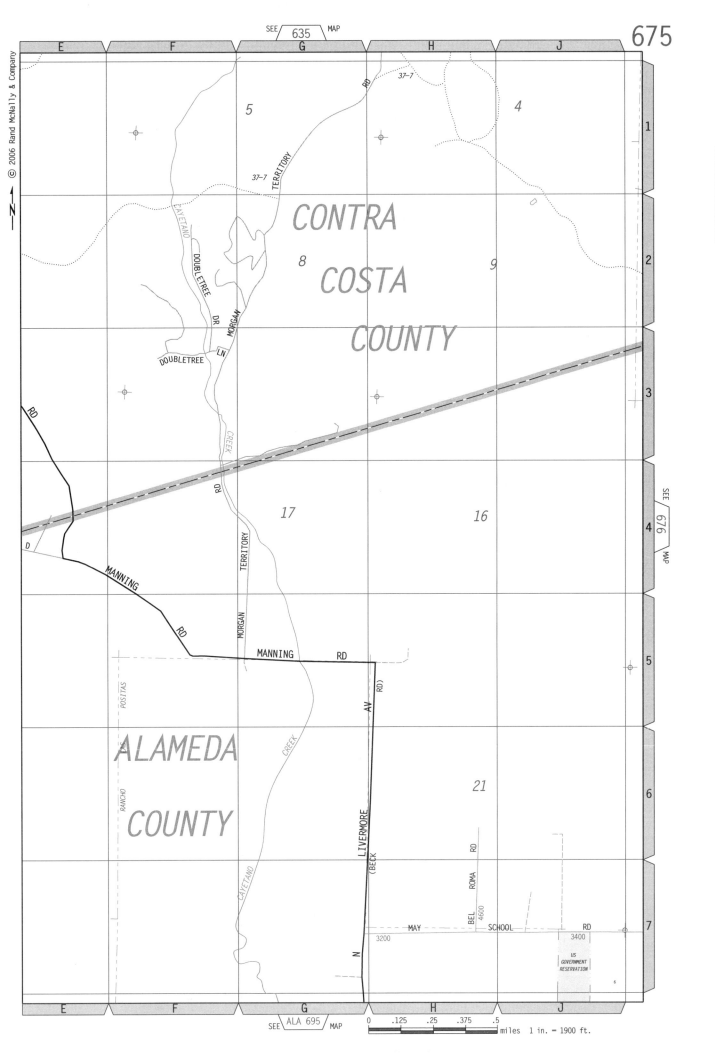

E   F   G   H   J

1

5

4

37-7

RD

37-7

CONTRA

8

COSTA

9

2

COUNTY

SEE 676 MAP

3

CAYETANO

DOUBLETREE

DR

MORGAN

LN

DOUBLETREE

CREEK

RD

17

16

4

TERRITORY

MORGAN

RD

5

MANNING

RD

MANNING   RD

AV

RD)

N

POSITAS

ALAMEDA

LAS

6

RANCHO

CREEK

21

COUNTY

LIVERMORE

(BECK

CAYETANO

MAY

BEL

ROMA

RD

SCHOOL

RD

7

3200

4600

3400

N

US
GOVERNMENT
RESERVATION

6

RD

D

E   F   G   H   J

0   .125   .25   .375   .5
miles   1 in. = 1900 ft.

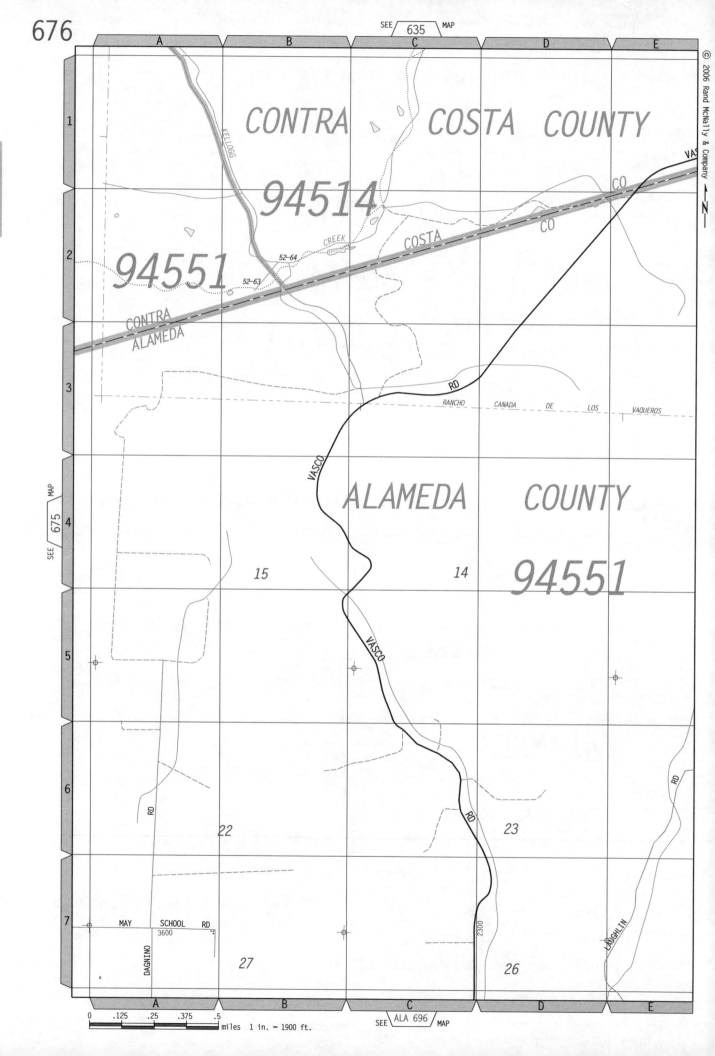

CONTRA COSTA

SEE 635 MAP

A B C D E

1

CONTRA COSTA COUNTY

94514

KELLOGG

94551

CREEK COSTA

52-64

52-63

CO

CO

CO

VA

N

2

CONTRA
ALAMEDA

RD

RANCHO CANADA DE LOS VAQUEROS

3

VASCO

SEE 675 MAP

ALAMEDA COUNTY

94551

15 14

4

VASCO

5

RD

RD

6

22 23

RD

VASCO

RD

2300

LAUGHLIN

7

MAY SCHOOL RD
3600

DAGNINO

27 26

A B C D E

0 .125 .25 .375 .5
miles 1 in. = 1900 ft.

SEE ALA 696 MAP

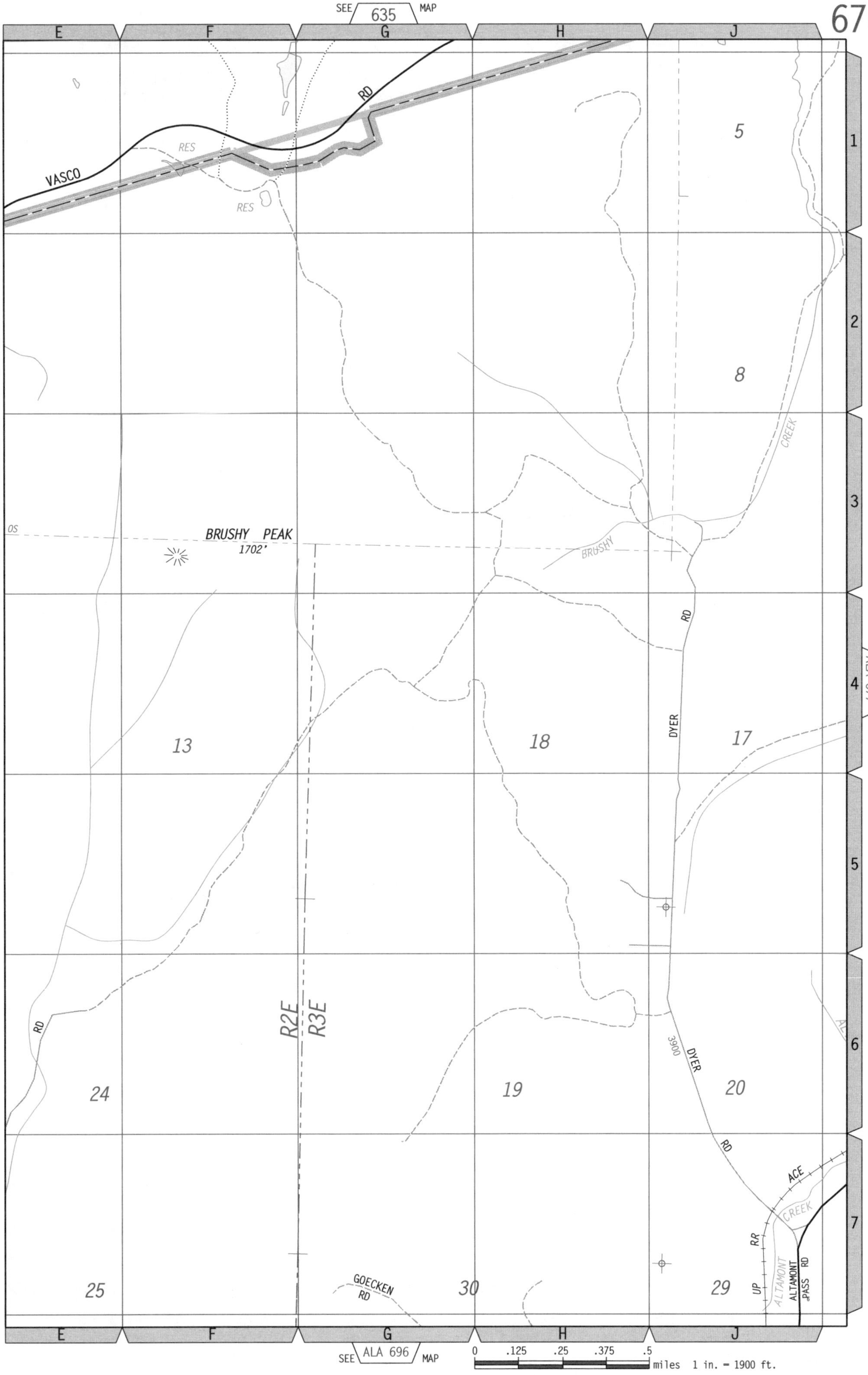

CONTRA COSTA

N

SEE 635 MAP

E F G H J

RD

VASCO

RES

RES

5

1

2

8

CREEK

3

OS

BRUSHY PEAK
1702'

BRUSHY

RD

SEE ALA 677 MAP

4

13

18

DYER

17

5

R2E R3E

RD

6

24

19

3900 DYER

20

RD

ACE

CREEK

RR

7

UP ALTAMONT PASS RD

25

GOECKEN RD

30

29

E F G H J

SEE ALA 696 MAP

0 .125 .25 .375 .5 miles 1 in. = 1900 ft.

693

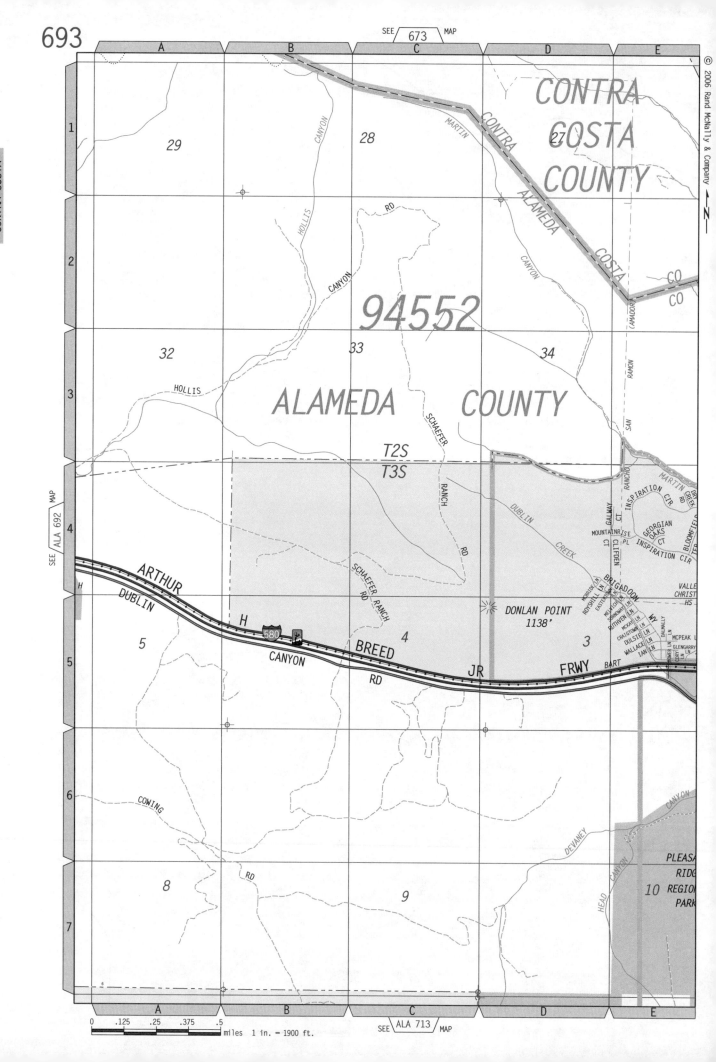

—N—

CONTRA COSTA

SEE 673 MAP

A   B   C   D   E

1

29   28   CONTRA
                    COSTA
                    27   COUNTY

2

94552

32   33   34   CO
                                      CO

3
HOLLIS   ALAMEDA   COUNTY

T2S
T3S

SEE ALA 692 MAP

4

ARTHUR

DUBLIN

5   H
         580   BREED
CANYON   4   DONLAN POINT
         RD   1138'   3
                    JR   FRWY   BART

6
COWING

DEVANEY

PLEASA
RIDG
8   9   10   REGIO
                                 PARK

A   B   C   D   E

0 .125 .25 .375 .5
miles 1 in. = 1900 ft.

SEE ALA 713 MAP

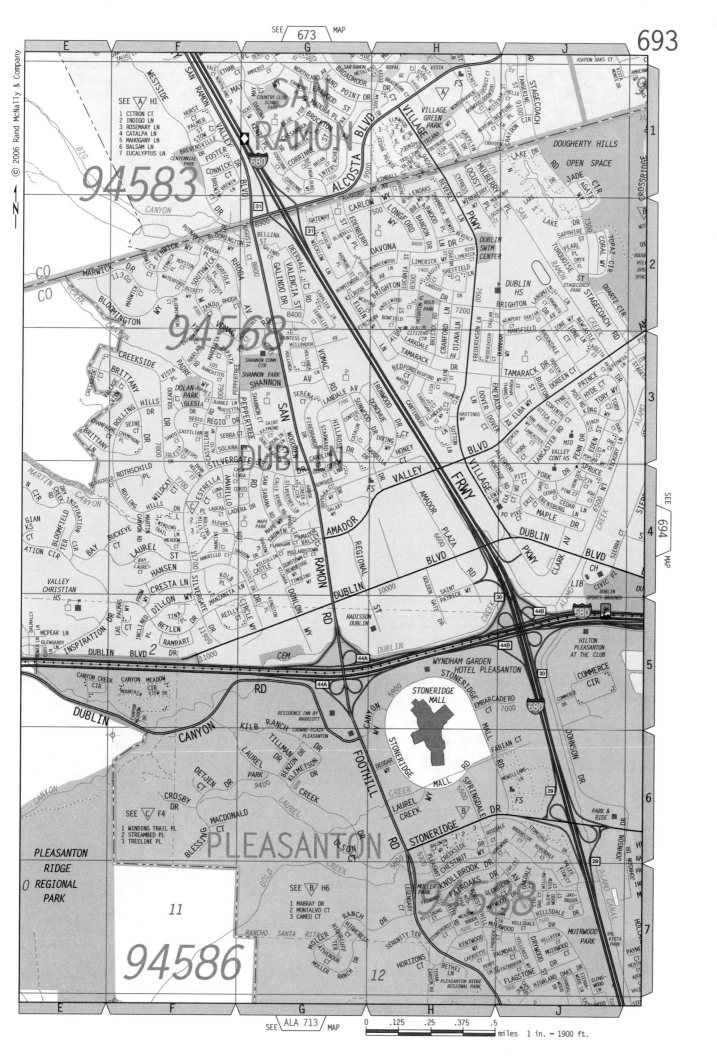

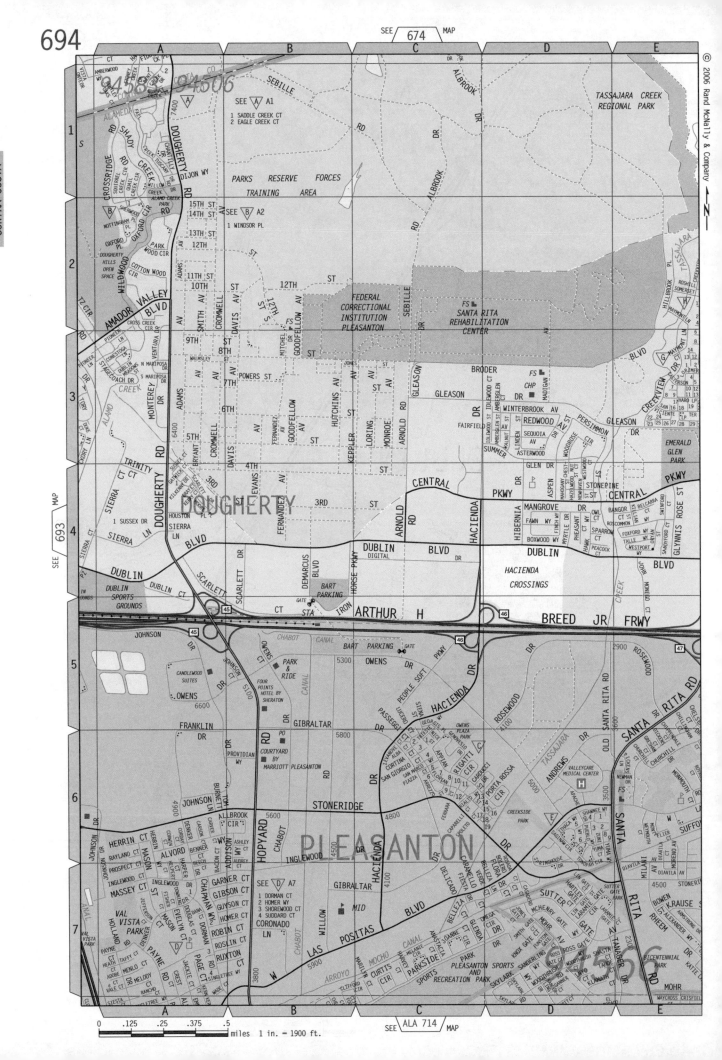

694

CONTRA COSTA

SEE 674 MAP
SEE 693 MAP
SEE ALA 714 MAP

© 2006 Rand McNally & Company

TASSAJARA CREEK REGIONAL PARK

PARKS RESERVE FORCES TRAINING AREA

FEDERAL CORRECTIONAL INSTITUTION PLEASANTON

SANTA RITA REHABILITATION CENTER

EMERALD GLEN PARK

DOUGHERTY

HACIENDA CROSSINGS

ARTHUR H BREED JR FRWY

PLEASANTON

VAL VISTA PARK

PLEASANTON SPORTS AND RECREATION PARK

0 .125 .25 .375 .5 miles 1 in. = 1900 ft.

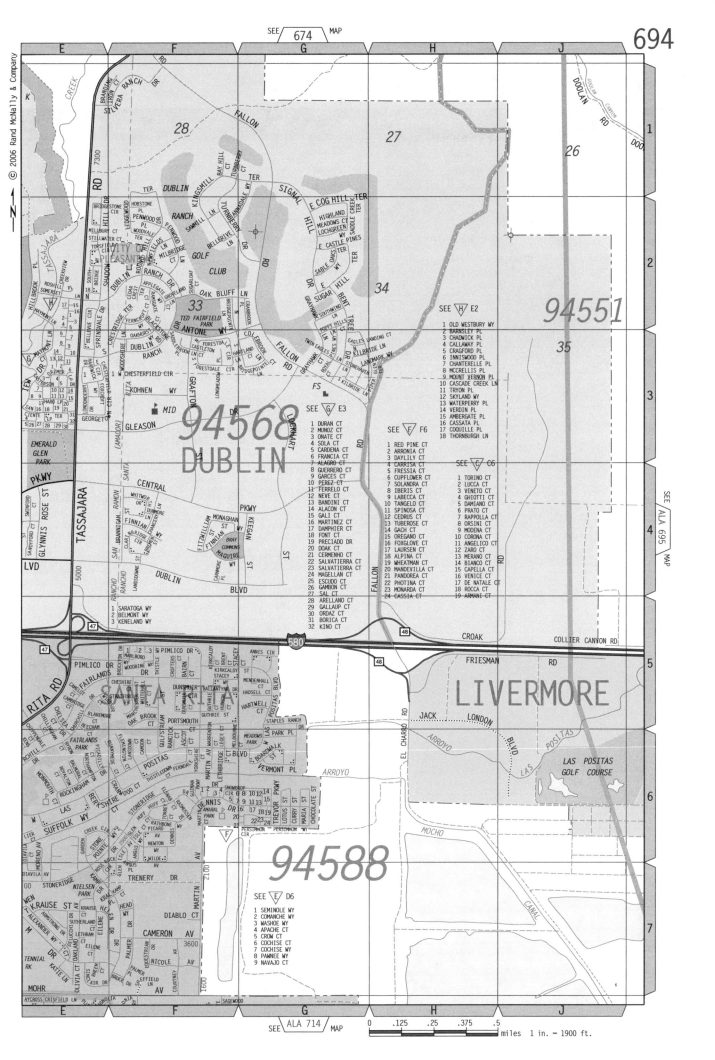

E   F   G   H   J

1

2

94551

3

94568
DUBLIN

4

SEE ALA 695 MAP

94588

5

LIVERMORE

6

7

SEE H E2
1 OLD WESTBURY WY
2 BARNSLEY PL
3 CHADWICK PL
4 CALLAWAY PL
5 CRAGFORD PL
6 INNISWOOD PL
7 CHANTERELLE PL
8 MCCRELLIS PL
9 MOUNT VERNON PL
10 CASCADE CREEK LN
11 TRYON PL
12 SKYLAND WY
13 WATERPERRY PL
14 VERDIN PL
15 AMBERGATE PL
16 CASSATA PL
17 COQUILLE PL
18 THORNBURGH LN

SEE F F6
1 RED PINE CT
2 ARRONIA CT
3 DAYLILY CT
4 CARRISA CT
5 FRESSIA CT
6 CUPFLOWER CT
7 SOLANDRA CT
8 IBERIS CT
9 LABECCA CT
10 TANGELO CT
11 SPINOSA CT
12 CEDRUS CT
13 TUBEROSE CT
14 GACH CT
15 OREGANO CT
16 FOXGLOVE CT
17 LAURSEN CT
18 ALPINA CT
19 WHEATMAN CT
20 MANDEVILLA CT
21 PANDOREA CT
22 PHOTINA CT
23 MONARDA CT
24 CASSIA CT

SEE C C6
1 TORINO CT
2 LUCCA CT
3 VENETO CT
4 GHIOTTI CT
5 DAMIANO CT
6 PRATO CT
7 RAPPOLLA CT
8 ORSINI CT
9 MODENA CT
10 CORONA CT
11 ANGELICO CT
12 ZARO CT
13 MERANO CT
14 BIANCO CT
15 CAPELLA CT
16 VENICE CT
17 DE NATALE CT
18 ROCCA CT
19 ARMANI CT

SEE G E3
1 DURAN CT
2 MUNOZ CT
3 ONATE CT
4 SOLA CT
5 CARDENA CT
6 FRANCIA CT
7 ALAGRO CT
8 GUERRERO CT
9 GARCES CT
10 PEREZ CT
11 FERRELO CT
12 NEVE CT
13 BANDINI CT
14 ALACON CT
15 GALI CT
16 MARTINEZ CT
17 DAMPHIER CT
18 FONT CT
19 PRECIADO DR
20 DOAK CT
21 CERMENHO CT
22 SALVATIERRA CT
23 SALVATIERRA CT
24 MAGELLAN CT
25 ESCUDO CT
26 GAMBON CT
27 SAL CT
28 ARELLANO CT
29 GALLAUP CT
30 ORDAZ CT
31 BORICA CT
32 KINO CT

1 SARATOGA WY
2 BELMONT WY
3 KENELAND WY

SEE E D6
1 SEMINOLE WY
2 COMANCHE WY
3 WASHOE WY
4 APACHE CT
5 CROW CT
6 COCHISE CT
7 COCHISE WY
8 PAWNEE WY
9 NAVAJO CT

0   .125   .25   .375   .5
miles 1 in. = 1900 ft.

Cities and Communities

Community Name	Abbr.	ZIP Code	Map Page	Community Name	Abbr.	ZIP Code	Map Page
Alamo		94507	632	* Lafayette	LFYT	94549	611
* Antioch	ANT	94509	575	* Martinez	MRTZ	94553	571
Avon		94553	572	* Moraga	MRGA	94556	631
Bay Point		94565	573	Nichols		94565	553
Bethel Island		94511	577	North Richmond		94807	588
Blackhawk		94506	654	* Oakley	OAKL	94561	576
* Brentwood	BREN	94513	616	* Orinda	ORIN	94563	610
Byron		94514	637	Orinda Village		94563	610
Canyon		94516	630	Pacheco		94553	592
* Clayton	CLAY	94517	593	* Pinole	PIN	94564	569
Clyde		94520	572	* Pittsburg	PIT	94565	574
* Concord	CNCD	94520	593	* Pleasant Hill	PLHL	94523	592
-- Contra Costa County	CCCO			Port Costa		94569	550
Crockett		94525	550	Rheem Valley		94556	631
* Danville	DNVL	94526	653	* Richmond	RCH	94801	588
Diablo		94528	633	Rodeo		94572	549
Discovery Bay		94514	617	Rossmoor Leisure World		94595	632
* El Cerrito	ELCR	94530	609	* San Pablo	SPAB	94806	588
El Sobrante		94803	569	* San Ramon	SRMN	94583	673
* Hercules	HER	94547	569	Tassajara		94526	655
Kensington		94708	609	* Walnut Creek	WLCK	94595	612
Knightsen		94548	596				

*Indicates incorporated city

List of Abbreviations

CONTRA COSTA

PREFIXES AND SUFFIXES

Abbr	Full	Abbr	Full	Abbr	Full
AL	ALLEY	CTST	COURT STREET	PZ D LA	PLAZA DE LA
ARC	ARCADE	CUR	CURVE	PZ D LAS	PLAZA DE LAS
AV, AVE	AVENUE	CV	COVE	PZWY	PLAZA WAY
AVCT	AVENUE COURT	DE	DE	RAMP	RAMP
AVD	AVENIDA	DIAG	DIAGONAL	RD	ROAD
AVD D LA	AVENIDA DE LA	DR	DRIVE	RDAV	ROAD AVENUE
AVD D LOS	AVENIDA DE LOS	DRAV	DRIVE AVENUE	RDBP	ROAD BYPASS
AVD DE	AVENIDA DE	DRCT	DRIVE COURT	RDCT	ROAD COURT
AVD DE LAS	AVENIDA DE LAS	DRLP	DRIVE LOOP	RDEX	ROAD EXTENSION
AVD DEL	AVENIDA DEL	DVDR	DIVISION DR	RDG	RIDGE
AVDR	AVENUE DRIVE	EXAV	EXTENSION AVENUE	RDSP	ROAD SPUR
AVEX	AVENUE EXTENSION	EXBL	EXTENSION BOULEVARD	RDWY	ROAD WAY
AV OF	AVENUE OF	EXRD	EXTENSION ROAD	RR	RAILROAD
AV OF THE	AVENUE OF THE	EXST	EXTENSION STREET	RUE	RUE
AVPL	AVENUE PLACE	EXT	EXTENSION	RUE D	RUE D
BAY	BAY	EXWY	EXPRESSWAY	RW	ROW
BEND	BEND	FOREST RT	FOREST ROUTE	RY	RAILWAY
BL, BLVD	BOULEVARD	FRWY	FREEWAY	SKWY	SKYWAY
BLCT	BOULEVARD COURT	FRY	FERRY	SQ	SQUARE
BLEX	BOULEVARD EXTENSION	GDNS	GARDENS	ST	STREET
BRCH	BRANCH	GN, GLN	GLEN	STAV	STREET AVENUE
BRDG	BRIDGE	GRN	GREEN	STCT	STREET COURT
BYPS	BYPASS	GRV	GROVE	STDR	STREET DRIVE
BYWY	BYWAY	HTS	HEIGHTS	STEX	STREET EXTENSION
CIDR	CIRCLE DRIVE	HWY	HIGHWAY	STLN	STREET LANE
CIR	CIRCLE	ISL	ISLE	STLP	STREET LOOP
CL	CALLE	JCT	JUNCTION	ST OF	STREET OF
CL DE	CALLE DE	LN	LANE	ST OF THE	STREET OF THE
CL DL	CALLE DEL	LNCR	LANE CIRCLE	STOV	STREET OVERPASS
CL D LA	CALLE DE LA	LNDG	LANDING	STPL	STREET PLACE
CL D LAS	CALLE DE LAS	LNDR	LAND DRIVE	STPM	STREET PROMENADE
CL D LOS	CALLE DE LOS	LNLP	LANE LOOP	STWY	STREET WAY
CL EL	CALLE EL	LP	LOOP	STXP	STREET EXPRESSWAY
CLJ	CALLEJON	MNR	MANOR	TER	TERRACE
CL LA	CALLE LA	MT	MOUNT	TFWY	TRAFFICWAY
CL LAS	CALLE LAS	MTWY	MOTORWAY	THWY	THROUGHWAY
CL LOS	CALLE LOS	MWCR	MEWS COURT	TKTR	TRUCK TRAIL
CLTR	CLUSTER	MWLN	MEWS LANE	TPKE	TURNPIKE
CM	CAMINO	NFD	NAT'L FOREST DEV	TRC	TRACE
CM DE	CAMINO DE	NK	NOOK	TRCT	TERRACE COURT
CM DL	CAMINO DEL	OH	OUTER HIGHWAY	TR, TRL	TRAIL
CM D LA	CAMINO DE LA	OVL	OVAL	TRWY	TRAIL WAY
CM D LAS	CAMINO DE LAS	OVLK	OVERLOOK	TTSP	TRUCK TRAIL SPUR
CM D LOS	CAMINO DE LOS	OVPS	OVERPASS	TUN	TUNNEL
CMTO	CAMINITO	PAS	PASEO	UNPS	UNDERPASS
CMTO DEL	CAMINITO DEL	PAS DE	PASEO DE	VIA D	VIA DE
CMTO D LA	CAMINITO DE LA	PAS DE LA	PASEO DE LA	VIA DL	VIA DEL
CMTO D LAS	CAMINITO DE LAS	PAS DE LAS	PASEO DE LAS	VIA D LA	VIA DE LA
CMTO D LOS	CAMINITO DE LOS	PAS DE LOS	PASEO DE LOS	VIA D LAS	VIA DE LAS
CNDR	CENTER DRIVE	PAS DL	PASEO DEL	VIA D LOS	VIA DE LOS
COM	COMMON	PASG	PASSAGE	VIA LA	VIA LA
COMS	COMMONS	PAS LA	PASEO LA	VW	VIEW
CORR	CORRIDOR	PAS LOS	PASEO LOS	VWY	VIEW WAY
CRES	CRESCENT	PASS	PASS	VIS	VISTA
CRLO	CIRCULO	PIKE	PIKE	VIS D	VISTA DE
CRSG	CROSSING	PK	PARK	VIS D L	VISTA DE LA
CST	CIRCLE STREET	PKDR	PARK DRIVE	VIS D LAS	VISTA DE LAS
CSWY	CAUSEWAY	PKWY, PKY	PARKWAY	VIS DEL	VISTA DEL
CT	COURT	PL	PLACE	WK	WALK
CTAV	COURT AVENUE	PLWY	PLACE WAY	WY	WAY
CTE	CORTE	PLZ, PZ	PLAZA	WYCR	WAY CIRCLE
CTE D	CORTE DE	PT	POINT	WYDR	WAY DRIVE
CTE DEL	CORTE DEL	PTAV	POINT AVENUE	WYLN	WAY LANE
CTE D LAS	CORTE DE LAS	PTH	PATH	WYPL	WAY PLACE
CTO	CUT OFF	PZ DE	PLAZA DE		
CTR	CENTER	PZ DEL	PLAZA DEL		

DIRECTIONS

E	EAST
KPN	KEY PENINSULA NORTH
KPS	KEY PENINSULA SOUTH
N	NORTH
NE	NORTHEAST
NW	NORTHWEST
S	SOUTH
SE	SOUTHEAST
SW	SOUTHWEST
W	WEST

BUILDINGS

CH	CITY HALL
CHP	CALIFORNIA HIGHWAY PATROL
COMM CTR	COMMUNITY CENTER
CON CTR	CONVENTION CENTER
CONT HS	CONTINUATION HIGH SCHOOL
CTH	COURTHOUSE
FAA	FEDERAL AVIATION ADMIN
FS	FIRE STATION
HOSP	HOSPITAL
HS	HIGH SCHOOL
INT	INTERMEDIATE SCHOOL
JR HS	JUNIOR HIGH SCHOOL
LIB	LIBRARY
MID	MIDDLE SCHOOL
MUS	MUSEUM
PO	POST OFFICE
PS	POLICE STATION
SR CIT CTR	SENIOR CITIZENS CENTER
STA	STATION
THTR	THEATER
VIS BUR	VISITORS BUREAU

OTHER ABBREVIATIONS

BCH	BEACH
BLDG	BUILDING
CEM	CEMETERY
CK	CREEK
CO	COUNTY
COMM	COMMUNITY
CTR	CENTER
EST	ESTATE
HIST	HISTORIC
HTS	HEIGHTS
LK	LAKE
MDW	MEADOW
MED	MEDICAL
MEM	MEMORIAL
MHP	MOBILE HOME PARK
MT	MOUNT
MTN	MOUNTAIN
NATL	NATIONAL
PKG	PARKING
PLGD	PLAYGROUND
RCH	RANCH
RCHO	RANCHO
REC	RECREATION
RES	RESERVOIR
RIV	RIVER
RR	RAILROAD
SPG	SPRING
STA	SANTA
VLG	VILLAGE
VLY	VALLEY
VW	VIEW

STREET Block City ZIP Pg-Grid

A

A ST
- CCCo 94565 573-E1
- CNCD 94518 592-G3
- CCCo 94548 597-A3
- CNCD 94520 572-E5
- CNCD 94520 572-F5
- CNCD 94520 572-G3
300 DNVL 94506 653-J5
300 CCCo 94525 550-A5
400 RCH 94801 588-F6
500 MRTZ 94553 571-E4
600 ANT 94509 575-D4
1400 CCCo 94561 597-A3
7200 ELCR 94530 609-E4
AARLES CT
2400 WLCK 94598 592-F7
ABALONE CV
- HER 94547 569-H1
ABBEY CT
- CCCo 94595 612-A6
1400 CNCD 94518 592-E7
ABBEY ST
2700 OAK 94619 650-E6
ABBIE LN
- CCCo 94803 589-H4
ABBOTT AV
2100 PIT 94565 574-C3
ABBOTT CT
- ORIN 94563 631-A2
ABBOTT DR
- OAK 94611 630-D6
ABBOTT LN
- CCCo 94507 632-G7
ABBOTT WY
- PDMT 94618 630-C7
ABBYDALE CT
- BREN 94513 616-A1
ABEGG
- CCCo 94507 632-G5
ABELLA CIR
- SPAB 94806 588-C3
ABERDALE CIR
- CCCo 94582 674-B5
ABERDEEN CT
- ANT 94531 596-A2
100 VAL 94591 550-E1
1300 CNCD 94518 592-E6
ABERDEEN LN
- CCCo 94513 617-F5
ABERDEEN WY
2300 RCH 94806 588-J1
ABIGAIL CIR
- DNVL 94506 653-H5
ABINGTON CT
2100 WLCK 94596 632-G1
ABINGTON LN
- CCCo 94507 632-G5
ABRIGO CT
600 SRMN 94583 673-B2
ACACIA AV
- BERK 94708 609-G4
600 RCH 94801 588-F5
1900 ANT 94509 575-D6
5800 OAK 94618 630-A5
ACACIA CT
- BREN 94513 596-D7
ACACIA DR
- OAKL 94561 596-C2
- ORIN 94563 610-F6
800 CCCo 94572 569-J1
2200 CNCD 94520 572-F6
ACACIA LN
200 CCCo 94507 632-G3
ACACIA RD
2700 CCCo 94595 612-A6
2800 CCCo 94595 611-J7
ACACIA ST
1300 PIT 94565 574-F3
ACADEMY RD
5000 CNCD 94521 593-D5
ACALANES AV
3200 LFYT 94549 611-H5
ACALANES RD
800 LFYT 94549 611-A7
ACAMPO DR
800 LFYT 94549 611-F7
ACAPULCO DR
1700 SPAB 94806 568-J7
ACE CT
- RCH 94806 568-H5
ACKERMAN DR
800 DNVL 94526 653-B1
800 DNVL 94526 633-B7
2100 PIT 94565 574-A3
ACKLEY CT
- PLHL 94523 592-A7
E ACME ST
100 OAKL 94561 576-E6
W ACME ST
100 OAKL 94561 576-E6
ACORN CT
- CCCo 94595 612-B6
200 OAKL 94561 596-G2
700 SRMN 94583 673-G7
ACORN DR
- CLAY 94517 594-A5
3800 OAKL 94561 596-G1
ACORN LN
100 PIT 94565 573-G4
ACORN RD
3100 ANT 94509 595-C1
ACTON ST
1300 BERK 94706 609-F7
1400 BERK 94702 609-F7
ACTRIZ AV
400 CCCo 94553 571-J3
ACTRIZ PL
- CCCo 94553 571-J3
ADA DR
300 CCCo 94553 572-B7
ADA ST
1300 BERK 94702 609-E7
1500 BERK 94703 609-E7
ADAGIO DR
300 DNVL 94526 653-C4
ADAIR CT
- DNVL 94526 653-A4
ADAK CT
- WLCK 94597 612-A2
ADAMS AV
- DBLN 94568 694-A2
ADAMS CT
- OAKL 94561 576-E7
700 PIN 94564 569-D4
3100 ANT 94509 575-A7
ADAMS DR
4500 CNCD 94521 593-C2
ADAMS PL
100 SRMN 94583 673-F6
ADAMS ST
- VAL 94590 550-B1
400 ALB 94706 609-D5
900 BEN 94510 551-D6
3400 ELCR 94530 609-D5
ADAMS RANCH RD
100 CCCo 94595 632-C1
ADDINGTON CT
- BREN 94513 616-A1
ADDISON WY
4300 PLE 94588 694-B7
ADELA CT
100 PLHL 94523 592-D5
ADELAIDE DR
- CCCo 94553 571-H4
ADELAIDE ST
1500 CNCD 94520 592-E2
4300 OAK 94619 650-G6
ADELAIDE HILLS CT
- SRMN 94582 674-B3
ADELIA CT
4400 CNCD 94521 593-C5
ADELINE DR
- CCCo 94596 612-E6
ADELL CT
3300 OAK 94602 650-D4
ADELLE CT
- CCCo 94507 632-G7
ADIRONDACK WY
100 WLCK 94598 612-D2
ADOBE CT
- SPAB 94806 588-D3
- DNVL 94526 653-A1
2700 ANT 94509 575-B6
6800 PLE 94588 694-A7
ADOBE DR
- CNCD 94520 572-F6
600 DNVL 94526 653-A1
ADOBE LN
- ORIN 94563 631-B5
ADOBE PL
1100 PIT 94565 573-H4
ADOBE RD
1200 PIN 94564 569-G7
1200 PIN 94564 589-H1
ADOBE ST
1800 CNCD 94520 592-F1
ADRIA DR
100 PLHL 94523 592-C4
ADRIANA CT
5100 ANT 94531 595-G4
ADRIATIC CT
- SRMN 94582 674-C3
ADRIENNE DR
1000 CCCo 94507 632-G6
AFFINITO LN
600 PIT 94565 574-E1
AFSHAR CT
1900 CNCD 94518 592-F6
AGADIR ST
1600 CNCD 94518 592-E6
AGATE CT
400 ANT 94509 595-E1
AGATE WY
100 HER 94547 569-G5
7900 DBLN 94568 693-J1
AGHALEE
- ORIN 94563 631-A1
AGNES ST
- CCCo 94514 637-D2
- OAK 94618 630-C6
AGNES WY
100 PLHL 94523 592-D6
AGOSTINO CT
5400 CNCD 94521 593-G5
AGUA WY
200 CCCo 94565 573-E1
AGUA VISTA ST
3900 OAK 94601 650-E7
AGUILAR PL
300 PIT 94565 574-D1
AHERN CT
3300 RCH 94803 589-F1
AHNEITA DR
2000 PLHL 94523 592-D6
AHWAHNEE CT
600 WLCK 94596 612-D5
AHWAHNEE LN
300 CLAY 94517 593-H5
AIELLO CT
1700 CNCD 94519 593-A1
AIELLO ST
- PIT 94565 574-D1
AILEEN ST
1000 LFYT 94549 611-G6
AITKEN DR
6500 OAK 94611 630-G7
AJAX PL
- BERK 94708 609-J6
- BERK 94708 610-A6
ALABAMA DR
5500 CNCD 94521 593-F7
ALACON CT
- DBLN 94568 694-G4
ALAGRO CT
- DBLN 94568 694-G4
ALAMATOS DR
100 DNVL 94526 653-B2
ALAMEDA AV
5500 RCH 94804 609-B2
5600 ELCR 94530 609-B2
ALAMEDA DIABLO
1600 CCCo 94528 633-F6
ALAMO AV
- BERK 94708 609-G5
- CCCo 94801 588-F4
200 RCH 94801 588-F4
ALAMO CT
1000 PIT 94565 573-H3
2700 ANT 94509 575-B6
ALAMO GN
- CCCo 94507 633-A5
ALAMO LN
- CCCo 94507 632-G3
- WLCK 94596 632-G3
ALAMO ST
2400 PIN 94564 569-F6
ALAMO WY
1100 PIT 94565 573-H3
1500 CCCo 94507 632-F4
ALAMO COUNTRY CIR
- CCCo 94507 632-H2
ALAMO GLEN DR
2400 CCCo 94507 633-A5
ALAMO GLEN TR
- CCCo 94507 633-A5
ALAMO HILLS CT
100 CCCo 94507 633-A6
ALAMO HILLS DR
100 CCCo 94507 633-A5
ALAMO OAKS LN
- CCCo 94507 633-B7
ALAMO RANCH RD
100 CCCo 94507 632-G5
ALAMOS PL
200 SRMN 94583 673-G5
ALAMO SPRINGS CT
- DNVL 94526 632-H6
ALAMO SPRINGS DR
100 CCCo 94507 632-H6
100 DNVL 94526 632-H6
1100 CCCo 94526 632-H6
ALAMO SPRINGS PL
- CCCo 94507 632-H6
- DNVL 94526 632-H6
ALAMO SQUARE DR
- CCCo 94507 632-F5
ALAMO VIEW PL
200 CCCo 94595 632-C1
ALAN CT
- SPAB 94806 589-A3
ALAN DR
- PLHL 94523 592-C3
ALAN PTH
3400 RCH 94803 589-E1
ALAN WY
- CCCo 94553 572-B5
ALANA CT
800 PLHL 94523 591-J5
ALASKA DR
5500 CNCD 94521 593-F6
ALBA CT
4100 PLE 94588 694-C6
ALBANI PL
- BREN 94513 596-D6
ALBANS CT
1100 ANT 94509 575-F7
ALBANY TER
1500 ALB 94706 609-E6
ALBEMARLE ST
400 ELCR 94530 609-D3
ALBERDAN CIR
1000 PIN 94564 569-C5
ALBERDAN CT
1200 PIN 94564 569-D5
ALBERT
- CNCD 94518 592-G4
ALBERT ST
4300 OAK 94619 650-G6
ALBERTA TER
- WLCK 94596 612-D5
ALBERTA WY
500 CNCD 94521 593-D6
ALBERTINE LN
- BREN 94561 596-D4
ALBERTS AV
- CCCo 94565 573-F2
ALBINA AV
1200 BERK 94706 609-F7
ALBION RD
- CCCo 94582 674-C3
- SRMN 94582 674-B3
ALBO CT
- ORIN 94563 630-J4
ALBRIDAL CT
- SRMN 94582 673-H2
ALBRIDAL WY
- SRMN 94582 673-H2
ALBROOK DR
- DBLN 94568 674-C7
- DBLN 94568 694-C1
ALCALA ST
- SPAB 94806 588-C3
2700 ANT 94509 575-D6
ALCAZAR CT
400 DNVL 94526 653-D5
ALCOSTA BLVD
8900 SRMN 94583 693-G1
9300 SRMN 94583 673-D1
9400 SRMN 94582 673-G5
ALCOSTA CT
100 SRMN 94583 673-J7
ALCOSTA PL
4300 PIT 94565 574-E7
ALCOTT CIR
- CCCo 94511 577-E1
ALCOTT CT
- CCCo 94511 577-E1
ALCOTT LN
- CCCo 94511 577-E1
ALDAGROVE RD
3300 ANT 94509 595-C1
ALDEA ST
8000 DBLN 94568 693-H3
ALDEN CT
- WLCK 94598 612-G3
ALDER AV
- CCCo 94595 612-B7
ALDER CT
100 HER 94547 569-J4
500 BEN 94510 550-J1
ALDER DR
1400 OAKL 94561 576-D7
ALDER WY
1400 CNCD 94521 593-D5
ALDERBROOK PL
200 MRGA 94556 631-E6
ALDERBROOK WY
2200 PIT 94565 573-F4
ALDER CREEK WY
1200 BREN 94513 596-C7
ALDERMAN LN
- BREN 94513 616-D5
ALDERWOOD DR
2400 ANT 94509 595-A2
ALDERWOOD LN
100 CCCo 94597 612-D1
200 SRMN 94582 673-J6
ALDERWOOD RD
- CCCo 94597 612-D1
ALEF CT
- CLAY 94517 593-G6
ALEGRA CT
- WLCK 94598 612-E5
ALEGRA LN
- WLCK 94598 612-E5
ALEGRE CT
- DNVL 94526 653-B4
ALEGRE DR
11500 DBLN 94568 693-F4
ALEMAN CT
- WLCK 94597 612-A2
ALEMANY DR
- MRGA 94556 631-F6
- MRGA 94575 631-F6
ALENE ST
7800 DBLN 94568 693-H3
ALETA PL
500 PLHL 94523 592-A3
ALEXANDER CT
2000 PLE 94588 694-E7
3400 OAK 94601 650-C7
ALEXANDER LN
- DNVL 94526 653-A4
ALEXANDER PL
300 CLAY 94517 593-G5
ALEXANDER ST
100 CCCo 94525 550-E4
ALEXANDER WY
- BREN 94561 596-D4
2100 PLE 94588 694-E7
ALEXIS CT
1500 ANT 94509 575-G7
ALFONSO DR
3200 CNCD 94518 592-H6
ALFRED AV
900 WLCK 94597 612-A3
ALFRED DR
200 PIN 94564 569-D3
ALFREDA AV
1800 SPAB 94806 588-H4
ALFRED NOBEL DR
800 HER 94547 569-G1
ALGER RD
3200 ANT 94509 595-C1
ALGIERS CIR
100 CCCo 94553 572-C7
ALGIERS WY
100 CCCo 94553 572-C7
ALHAMBRA AV
100 MRTZ 94553 591-G2
100 PLHL 94523 591-G2
400 MRTZ 94553 571-D3
5800 CCCo 94553 591-G2
5900 OAK 94611 630-E7
6100 PLHL 94553 591-G2
6100 MRTZ 94553 591-G2
ALHAMBRA CT
- ANT 94509 575-F5
ALHAMBRA DR
1700 ANT 94509 575-F5
ALHAMBRA LN
600 MRTZ 94553 571-E5
1700 OAK 94611 630-E6
ALHAMBRA RD
700 CCCo 94803 589-C1
ALHAMBRA ST
300 CCCo 94525 550-E4
ALHAMBRA WY
500 MRTZ 94553 571-E6
2600 PIN 94564 569-H7
ALHAMBRA CREEK RD
- CCCo 94553 591-B3
ALHAMBRA HILLS CT
5600 MRTZ 94553 591-G1
ALHAMBRA HILLS DR
- MRTZ 94553 591-G1
ALHAMBRA VALLEY RD
- CCCo 94553 591-A2
3900 PIN 94564 589-H1
4900 CCCo 94553 589-H1
4900 CCCo 94564 589-H1
4900 MRTZ 94553 571-E7
4900 MRTZ 94553 591-E3
5200 CCCo 94553 590-B2
ALICANTE CT
200 DNVL 94526 653-D6
1800 CNCD 94521 593-F5
ALICANTE DR
1000 DNVL 94526 653-D5
ALICANTE PL
200 DNVL 94526 653-D6
ALICE AV
2100 WLCK 94596 632-F1
ALICE CT
100 DNVL 94526 652-J2
ALICE LN
100 CCCo 94803 589-E1
100 ORIN 94563 631-B3
ALICE PL
- ORIN 94563 631-C3
ALICE WY
2500 PIN 94564 569-F4
ALIDA CT
- OAK 94602 650-E3
ALIDA ST
2400 OAK 94602 650-E4
ALISAL CT
400 DNVL 94526 653-A1
ALISMA CT
- SRMN 94582 673-G2
ALISO AV
3800 OAK 94619 650-G5
ALKANTE CT
- SRMN 94582 673-J1
ALLA AV
900 CNCD 94518 592-G5
ALLA CT
900 CNCD 94518 592-G6
ALLANMERE CT
- SRMN 94582 674-B3
ALLANMERE DR
- SRMN 94582 674-B3
ALLBROOK CIR
6000 PLE 94588 694-A6
ALLBROOK CT
700 BREN 94513 616-E1
ALLBROOK DR
600 BREN 94513 616-E1
ALLEGHENY DR
500 WLCK 94598 612-E2
1000 DNVL 94526 653-B5
6900 DBLN 94568 693-H3
ALLEGRO AV
1500 CNCD 94521 593-F5
ALLEN CT
100 MRGA 94556 631-G5
800 BREN 94513 616-J2
ALLEN LN
- CCCo 94803 569-E7
ALLEN ST
100 MRTZ 94553 571-E4
ALLEN WY
100 PLHL 94523 592-A6
300 BEN 94510 551-C2
ALLENDALE AV
3500 OAK 94619 650-E6
ALLENDALE CT
- CCCo 94595 612-B6
ALLENSBY LN
- SRFL 94901 587-B1
ALLISON LN
5400 RCH 94803 589-F3
ALLMAN ST
1400 OAK 94602 650-C4
ALLVIEW AV
700 CCCo 94803 569-D7
ALMA AV
600 OAK 94610 650-A4
1300 WLCK 94596 612-C6
ALMA PL
900 OAK 94610 650-B4
ALMADEN CIR
900 OAKL 94561 576-C5
ALMADEN CT
- LFYT 94549 591-H7
100 OAKL 94561 576-C5
ALMADEN LN
5900 OAK 94611 630-E7
ALMADINE WY
100 DNVL 94506 653-G5
ALMANOR CT
- CCCo 94513 617-F3
900 LFYT 94549 611-G6
ALMANOR DR
- CCCo 94513 617-F3
ALMANOR LN
900 LFYT 94549 611-G6
ALMANOR ST
- BREN 94513 616-H2
ALMAR ST
1200 CNCD 94518 592-G3
ALMENDRA CT
1100 CNCD 94518 592-G3
ALMOND AV
1700 WLCK 94596 612-B5
2000 CNCD 94520 592-F1
ALMOND CT
300 SRMN 94583 673-G7
1500 WLCK 94596 612-C5
ALMOND DR
- BREN 94561 596-F4
600 OAKL 94561 576-F7
600 CCCo 94561 596-F4
ALMOND PL
- OAKL 94561 596-H3
ALMOND ST
- BREN 94513 596-G5
900 ANT 94509 575-D4
2600 CCCo 94553 571-G4
ALMOND ORCHARD LN
- SRMN 94583 673-E7
ALMONDRIDGE DR
2700 ANT 94509 575-J6
ALMONDTREE CIR
400 OAKL 94561 596-G1
ALMOND TREE CT
3100 ANT 94509 575-J6
ALMOND TREE LN
200 OAKL 94561 596-G1
ALMONDWOOD CT
3900 CNCD 94519 573-A7
ALMONDWOOD DR
1200 ANT 94509 575-F7
ALMONDWOOD PL
2900 OAKL 94561 576-A6
ALOHA
200 PIT 94565 574-E5
ALORA CT
300 SRMN 94583 673-C2
ALOYSE CT
2300 CCCo 94596 612-E7
ALPHA WY
1800 ANT 94509 575-E6
ALPINA CT
2700 PLE 94588 694-H4
ALPINE CT
- BREN 94513 616-B2
- PIT 94565 574-F7
600 MRTZ 94553 591-G3
1300 SPAB 94806 589-A4
ALPINE DR
1300 PIT 94565 574-F6
1500 CNCD 94521 593-B3
ALPINE RD
1100 WLCK 94596 612-C5
5400 SPAB 94806 589-A4
5700 CCCo 94806 589-A4
ALPINE TER
100 OAK 94618 630-B5
ALPS CT
2200 MRTZ 94553 572-A7
ALRAY DR
1700 CNCD 94519 592-J1
ALRO AV
4800 CNCD 94521 593-D4
ALRO CT
1500 CNCD 94521 593-D4
ALTA AV
- PDMT 94611 630-C7
- PDMT 94611 650-C1
ALTA CT
- PIT 94565 574-C3
ALTA LN
3200 LFYT 94549 611-H6
ALTA RD
- BERK 94708 609-G4
100 OAK 94618 630-C6
ALTA HACIENDAS
100 ORIN 94563 610-G4
ALTA HILL WY
- CCCo 94595 612-B6
ALTA LOMA
- BEN 94510 551-A4
ALTA LOMA CT
- DNVL 94526 653-C1
ALTA LOMA PL
500 SRMN 94583 673-G6
ALTA MESA
1000 MRGA 94556 631-E6
ALTA MESA CIR
100 MRGA 94556 631-E6
ALTA MIRA DR
2900 RCH 94806 589-A1
ALTAMIRANO CIR
1100 PIN 94564 569-E5
ALTAMONT PASS RD
8800 AlaC 94551 676-J7
ALTAMOUNT DR
- ORIN 94563 631-B4
ALTA PUNTA DR
- VAL 94591 550-D1
ALTA PUNTA ST
5600 ELCR 94530 589-B7
ALTARINDA CIR
- ORIN 94563 610-J6
E ALTARINDA DR
- ORIN 94563 610-H6
ALTARINDA RD
- ORIN 94563 610-H7
ALTA SIERRA PL
- CCCo 94507 632-J5
ALTA VISTA
- ORIN 94563 610-E7
300 PIT 94565 574-B6
ALTA VISTA CIR
3900 PIT 94565 574-B6
ALTA VISTA CT
- PIT 94565 574-B6
400 DNVL 94506 653-H4
1100 WLCK 94596 612-C5
ALTA VISTA DR
6400 ELCR 94530 589-C6
ALTA VISTA WY
100 DNVL 94506 653-G4
ALTESSA CT
- BREN 94513 596-B7
ALTESSA DR
- BREN 94513 596-B7
ALTO WY
7700 DBLN 94568 693-F3
ALTON LN
- BREN 94513 616-D4
ALTON PL
- SRMN 94583 673-F6
ALTURA DR
1900 CNCD 94519 572-G7
1900 CNCD 94519 592-H1
ALUMROCK DR
500 ANT 94509 595-E2
ALVA AV
2200 ELCR 94530 589-C7
ALVARADO AV
- PIT 94565 574-C4
1600 WLCK 94597 612-A3
ALVARADO DR
2000 ANT 94509 595-B1
ALVARADO PL
- OAK 94705 630-A3
6100 ELCR 94530 589-C6
ALVARADO RD
- BERK 94705 630-A3
- OAK 94705 630-A3
ALVARADO ST
- SPAB 94806 588-J2
200 RCH 94801 608-D1
ALVARADO TER
100 MRTZ 94553 571-D4
ALVAREZ AV
700 PIN 94564 569-E4
ALVERN CT
100 CCCo 94507 632-F5
ALVES LN
- CCCo 94565 573-F2
ALVES RANCH RD
- CCCo 94565 573-F3
- PIT 94565 573-F3
ALVINA DR
1900 PLHL 94523 592-B5
ALVISO CT
200 DNVL 94526 653-D6
ALVISO WY
200 DNVL 94526 653-D5
ALVORD WY
6100 PLE 94588 694-A6
ALWIN RD
- WLCK 94598 612-D5
AMADOR AV
- OAKL 94561 576-E7
1100 BERK 94707 609-G6
1500 CNCD 94520 592-F2
AMADOR CT
- OAKL 94561 596-H2
- CCCo 94565 573-H2
600 MRTZ 94553 571-E7
AMADOR ST
600 RCH 94805 589-B5
1000 SPAB 94805 589-A4
1000 SPAB 94806 589-A4
AMADOR PLAZA RD
6800 DBLN 94568 693-H4
AMADOR VALLEY BLVD
6500 DBLN 94568 693-G4
6500 DBLN 94568 694-A2
AMADOR VALLEY CT
8000 DBLN 94568 693-G4
AMALIA AV
4100 CCCo 94553 571-J3
4100 CCCo 94553 572-A4
AMANDA CIR
1000 BREN 94513 616-E1
AMANDA CT
- CCCo 94507 633-D4
AMANDA ST
7200 DBLN 94568 693-J3
AMARANTH PL
5700 CNCD 94521 593-G7
AMARANTH WY
1200 CNCD 94521 593-G7
AMARGOSA DR
4200 ANT 94531 595-J1
AMARILLO CT
11600 DBLN 94568 693-F4
AMARILLO RD
7300 DBLN 94568 693-F4
AMARYLLIS CIR
- SRMN 94582 673-J1
AMATE WY
200 CCCo 94553 572-C7
AMBER CT
- HER 94547 569-G4
AMBER DR
500 ANT 94509 575-E5
AMBER LN
- CCCo 94549 611-J2
500 MRTZ 94553 591-G4
2100 BREN 94513 596-B5
AMBER PL
- CCCo 94507 632-E4
AMBERDALE CT
1300 ANT 94531 595-E5
AMBERDALE WY
5400 ANT 94531 595-E5
AMBERFIELD LN
- DNVL 94506 653-J6
AMBERGATE PL
- DBLN 94568 694-H3
AMBERGLEN CT
- DBLN 94568 694-D3
AMBERGLEN ST
- DBLN 94568 694-D3
AMBERIDGE CT
1300 ANT 94531 595-E5
AMBERLEAF WY
200 BREN 94513 616-E2
AMBER VALLEY DR
100 ORIN 94563 610-J3
AMBERWOOD CT
- MRGA 94556 651-F2
4000 ANT 94531 595-D4
AMBERWOOD LN
- WLCK 94598 612-F1
AMBERWOOD WY
- SRMN 94582 693-J1
- SRMN 94582 694-A1
AMBIENCE WY
600 DNVL 94506 653-J4
AMBLESIDE CT
- DNVL 94526 653-D3
AMBLESIDE DR
5200 CNCD 94521 613-C1
AMBROSE AV
- CCCo 94565 573-F2
AMBROSIA WY
- CCCo 94565 573-G2
AMELIA CT
- PIT 94565 574-E2
AMELIA LN
100 CCCo 94506 654-C5
AMELIA WY
- PIT 94565 574-A2
AMEND CT
200 CCCo 94803 589-G2
AMEND RD
5200 CCCo 94803 589-G2
5200 RCH 94803 589-H3
AMEND ST
1000 PIN 94564 569-D5
AMENO CT
1000 LFYT 94549 611-H6
AMENO DR
3200 LFYT 94549 611-H6
AMENO RD
3100 CNCD 94519 572-H7
AMERICAN AV
- BREN 94513 615-J3
- CCCo 94513 615-J3
100 CCCo 94513 616-A3
100 BREN 94513 616-A3
AMERICAN BEAUTY CT
5100 CNCD 94521 593-E4
AMERICAN BEAUTY DR
1500 CNCD 94521 593-E4
AMES CT
1100 ANT 94509 575-F6
AMESBURY CT
- DNVL 94526 653-C3
1900 WLCK 94596 612-G7
1900 WLCK 94596 632-G1
AMESBURY ST
- CCCo 94513 617-F5
AMETHYST CT
100 HER 94547 569-G4
AMHERST AV
100 CCCo 94708 609-F3
AMHERST CT
500 SRMN 94583 673-G7
500 SRMN 94583 693-G1
AMHURST CT
900 CNCD 94518 592-E7
AMHURST WY
1500 CNCD 94518 592-E7
AMIGO LN
- CCCo 94596 612-G7
AMIGO RD
100 DNVL 94526 653-B2
AMITO AV
1000 OAK 94705 630-B3
AMORCO RD
400 MRTZ 94553 571-F1
AMY DR
5600 OAK 94618 630-C7
AMY LN
- CCCo 94520 572-G2
AMY WY
2400 CCCo 94507 632-E2
ANAHID LN
100 CCCo 94803 589-C2
ANALISA LN
- WLCK 94596 612-D6
ANASTACIA CT
3200 PLE 94588 694-C7
ANASTASIA DR
- BREN 94561 596-D4
ANCHETA PL
100 VAL 94591 550-F2
ANCHOR CT
100 VAL 94591 550-F1
100 CCCo 94565 573-E1
N ANCHOR CT
4100 CCCo 94513 617-E7
S ANCHOR CT
4000 CCCo 94513 617-E7
ANCHOR DR
- CCCo 94565 553-E7
- CCCo 94565 573-E2
ANCHORAGE WY
1700 CCCo 94514 617-H6
ANCONA CT
1700 CNCD 94519 593-A2
ANDALUCIA CT
3700 SRMN 94583 673-B3
ANDERHAN PL
3700 SRMN 94583 673-C2
ANDERSEN DR
800 SRFL 94901 587-A4
ANDERSON AV
600 BREN 94513 616-G2
4300 OAK 94619 650-G5
ANDERSON CIR
- WLCK 94595 612-C7
ANDERSON LN
2500 BERK 94561 596-F4
2500 CCCo 94561 596-F4
2800 OAKL 94561 596-F4
ANDERSON WY
100 CCCo 94553 571-J4
ANDERSON RANCH CT
- CCCo 94507 632-G3
ANDORA LN
300 SRMN 94583 673-C3
ANDOVER PL
- SRMN 94583 673-F6
ANDRADE AV
2300 RCH 94804 588-H5
3500 RCH 94804 589-A5
3600 RCH 94805 589-A5
ANDREA CT
1800 CNCD 94519 592-J1
ANDREA DR
100 WLCK 94596 612-D6
ANDREA LN
1800 CNCD 94519 592-J1
ANDREA WY
700 PIT 94565 574-B3
ANDREAS WY
- SRMN 94582 674-B3
ANDREASEN DR
3100 LFYT 94549 611-H7
ANDRES CT
- SRMN 94582 674-B3
ANDREW AV
- PIT 94565 574-C3
ANDREW LN
- WLCK 94597 612-B1
ANDREW WY
600 CCCo 94803 569-E7
ANDREWS CT
1900 CCCo 94521 593-D2
ANDREWS DR
900 MRTZ 94553 571-E4
1800 CNCD 94521 593-D3
3600 PLE 94588 694-D6
ANDREWS ST
2100 OAK 94611 650-E1
ANDRIX CT
800 CNCD 94518 592-G6
ANDROS DR
300 SRMN 94582 673-E1
ANDSLEY LN
- SRMN 94582 674-B3
ANELDA DR
- PLHL 94523 592-C5
ANGEL CT
- DNVL 94526 652-H1
4500 ANT 94509 595-F3
ANGELA AV
100 CCCo 94507 632-G4
ANGELICA CT
- PIT 94565 574-C2
ANGELICA ST
- PIT 94565 574-C2

Street	Block	City ZIP	Pg-Grid
ANGELICO CT	5100	PLE 94588	694-H4
ANGELO AV	3700	OAK 94619	650-E6
ANGELO ST	3300	MRTZ 94553	611-G2
ANGELS BAY CT		RCH 94801	608-E3
ANGIE LN		CNCD 94521	593-E4
ANGLEWOOD DR	4700	CNCD 94521	593-D3
ANGSLEY CT		SRMN 94582	674-B3
ANGUS DR	2100	WLCK 94598	612-G3
ANGUS PL	3500	PLE 94588	694-F6
ANGUS WY	5100	PLE 94588	694-F6
ANITA CIR	700	BEN 94510	551-A3
ANITA CT		ANT 94531	595-G4
	900	LFYT 94549	611-H6
	1700	CNCD 94521	593-E4
ANITA LN		CCCo 94507	632-G3
		WLCK 94596	632-G3
ANIZUMNE CT	700	CLAY 94517	593-H6
ANJOU PKWY	1200	BREN 94513	596-F7
ANN CT	100	VAL 94590	550-C1
ANN PTH		RCH 94803	589-F1
ANN ST	2100	CNCD 94520	572-F7
	2100	CNCD 94520	592-F1
ANNABEL LN		SRMN 94583	673-D2
ANNADALE WY		DBLN 94568	694-F2
ANNALISA DR	2500	CCCo 94520	572-F3
	2500	CNCD 94520	572-F3
ANNANDALE CT	3600	WLCK 94598	613-A3
ANNAPOLIS ST	3200	RCH 94806	589-A2
ANN ARBOR WY	6900	DBLN 94568	693-J3
ANNE CT		WLCK 94598	612-G4
	2600	PIN 94564	569-F4
ANNERLEY RD	1000	OAK 94611	650-B2
	1000	PDMT 94610	650-B2
ANNETTE CT		CCCo 94597	612-D2
ANNIS CIR	3600	PLE 94588	694-G5
ANSELMO CT	5400	CNCD 94521	593-F5
ANSON WY		CCCo 94707	609-E3
ANTELOPE CT		DNVL 94506	654-B6
ANTELOPE TER	800	BREN 94513	616-E1
ANTELOPE WY	4600	ANT 94531	595-J3
ANTELOPE RIDGE WY	400	DNVL 94506	654-B5
ANTHONY CT	100	DNVL 94526	653-C6
	2300	CNCD 94520	592-E3
ANTHURIUM CT		DNVL 94506	654-C6
ANTICA DR		BREN 94513	596-D6
ANTIGUA CT	400	SRMN 94583	673-C3
ANTIGUA WY	100	VAL 94591	550-E2
ANTIOCH CT	2000	OAK 94611	650-E1
ANTIOCH ST	6200	OAK 94611	650-E1
ANTLER CT	2300	ANT 94531	595-F2
ANTONE CT		DBLN 94568	694-F3
ANTONIA CIR	800	PIN 94564	569-E4
ANTONIA CT	700	PIN 94564	569-E4
ANTONIO CT	500	LFYT 94549	631-J2
ANVILWOOD CT	400	OAKL 94561	596-F1
ANVILWOOD PL		OAKL 94561	596-F1
ANZA CT		WLCK 94597	612-B4
	100	SRMN 94583	673-A2
	2700	ANT 94509	575-A6
APACHE CT		PLE 94588	694-G7
		SRMN 94583	673-D5
	3200	LFYT 94549	631-H2
	5000	ANT 94531	595-G5
APACHE DR		PLE 94588	694-D6
APEX CT	2300	MRTZ 94553	591-G4
APOLLO	200	HER 94547	569-H1
APOLLO CT	900	ANT 94509	575-F4
	1800	WLCK 94598	612-E2
APOLLO WY	200	PLHL 94523	592-A5
APPALACHIAN DR	100	MRTZ 94553	591-H4
APPALACHIAN WY		MRTZ 94553	591-H4
	300	MRTZ 94553	591-H4
APPALOOSA CT	2500	WLCK 94596	632-G2
	2800	PIN 94564	569-H6
	4500	ANT 94531	595-G5
APPALOOSA DR	500	WLCK 94596	632-F2
APPALOOSA TR	2600	PIN 94564	569-H7
APPALOOSA WY	4500	ANT 94531	595-G3
APPIA CT	1800	WLCK 94598	612-E2
APPIAN CT		CCCo 94803	569-E7
		DNVL 94526	652-J3
		MRTZ 94553	591-H4
APPIAN ST	3800	PLE 94588	694-C6
APPIAN WY	400	CCCo 94803	589-C2
	600	RCH 94803	589-C2
	700	PIN 94564	569-D5
	900	CCCo 94803	569-E6
APPIAN KNOLL CT	800	CCCo 94803	569-E7
APPIAN VILLAGE CT		CCCo 94803	569-E7
		CCCo 94803	569-E7
		CCCo 94803	589-E1
APPIAN VILLAGE DR		CCCo 94803	569-E7
		CCCo 94803	589-E1
APPLE CT	1000	CNCD 94518	592-E5
APPLE DR	2900	ANT 94509	574-J7
	2900	ANT 94509	575-A6
S APPLE CT		ANT 94509	574-J7
APPLE DR	1300	CNCD 94518	592-E5
APPLE MNR	100	CCCo 94513	597-C5
APPLE PL		PIT 94565	574-D7
APPLEGARTH LN		DBLN 94568	694-F2
APPLEGATE CT		OAKL 94561	596-H2
APPLEGATE LN		DBLN 94568	694-F2
APPLEGATE WY		DBLN 94568	694-F2
APPLEGLEN ST		ANT 94531	596-A2
APPLE HILL DR		BREN 94513	616-C1
APPLE HILL TER	2100	BREN 94513	616-C1
APPLENUT LN	100	VAL 94591	550-F1
APPLE TREE LN		CCCo 94507	632-E6
APPLEWOOD COM		BREN 94513	673-A5
APRICOT CT	2100	PIT 94565	574-A3
APRICOT LN	1000	CNCD 94518	592-F5
APRICOT WY	1900	BREN 94513	596-C6
APRIL CT		PLHL 94523	592-B5
APTOS CT	100	SRMN 94583	673-E5
APTOS DR	2800	SRMN 94583	673-E5
APTOS PL	200	DNVL 94526	653-D6
AQUAMARINE CT		HER 94547	569-G4
AQUARIUS WY	900	OAK 94611	630-D6
AQUA VISTA		ORIN 94563	610-J5
AQUA VISTA CT	6600	CCCo 94805	589-C6
AQUA VISTA RD	1400	CCCo 94805	589-C6
ARABIAN CT		DNVL 94506	653-F1
ARABIAN LN	1600	CCCo 94513	597-B7
ARABIAN WY	4600	ANT 94531	596-A3
ARAGON LN	3800	SRMN 94583	673-C2
ARALIA CT	100	HER 94547	570-B4
ARANA DR		MRTZ 94553	571-G6
ARANDA DR	2500	SRMN 94583	673-C4
ARAPAHO CIR		SRMN 94583	673-C4
ARAPAHO CT		SRMN 94583	673-D4
ARAPAHO WY	2200	ANT 94531	595-J6
ARATA WY	2200	ANT 94509	574-H5
ARBOL CT	2200	ANT 94509	595-A1
ARBOL VIA	300	CCCo 94598	612-F4
ARBOLADO CT		ORIN 94563	610-H6
ARBOLADO DR	3400	WLCK 94598	613-A3
	4200	CCCo 94549	591-H6
ARBOLES PL		SRMN 94583	673-G5
ARBOL GRANDE	1900	WLCK 94595	632-D1
	1900	WLCK 94595	632-D1
ARBON PTH		HER 94547	569-H1
N ARBOR BAY		HER 94547	569-H1
S ARBOR BAY		HER 94547	569-H1
ARBOR CT	300	BEN 94510	551-B3
	700	BEN 94510	551-B3
ARBOR DR		CCCo 94596	612-G7
		PDMT 94610	650-A1
ARBOR LN	1400	CCCo 94507	632-E3
ARBOR WY		LFYT 94549	611-B6
W ARBOR WY		LFYT 94549	611-A6
ARBOR CREEK CIR	7400	DBLN 94568	693-G4
ARBOR SPRINGS LN		CCCo 94553	592-B1
ARBUTUS CT		WLCK 94595	612-C7
ARBUTUS DR	1500	WLCK 94595	612-B7
	1600	CCCo 94595	612-B7
ARCADE AV		BERK 94708	609-J6
ARCADIA AV	4400	OAK 94602	650-E3
ARCADIA CIR		CCCo 94513	617-F3
ARCADIA CT	2200	MRTZ 94553	572-A7
ARCADIA PL	2200	MRTZ 94553	572-A7
ARCH CT		BREN 94513	569-D5
ARCH ST	600	MRTZ 94553	571-E4
	1100	BERK 94708	609-H6
	1100	BERK 94707	609-H6
	1300	BERK 94709	609-H7
ARCHER CIR		MRGA 94556	631-D5
ARCHERY CT		CCCo 94803	589-G4
ARCHERY WY	4000	CCCo 94803	589-G4
ARCHMONT PL	3900	OAK 94605	650-J7
ARCY LN		PIT 94565	574-J4
ARDARA WY		ANT 94531	596-A4
ARDEN PL	4300	OAK 94602	650-D3
ARDEN RD		BERK 94704	630-A2
ARDEN WY	1400	OAK 94602	650-D3
ARDENDALE CT		CCCo 94507	632-J5
ARDENWOOD CT E	1600	CNCD 94521	593-C3
ARDENWOOD CT W	1600	CNCD 94521	593-C3
ARDILLA RD		ORIN 94563	610-F6
ARDITH CT	100	ORIN 94563	631-C5
ARDITH DR	100	ORIN 94563	631-B4
ARDITH LN	100	ORIN 94563	631-B4
ARDLEIGH CT		CCCo 94583	673-A5
ARDLEY AV	3500	OAK 94602	650-C4
ARDMORE AV	1000	OAK 94610	650-C2
	100	BEN 94510	551-B3
ARDMORE DR	2500	CCCo 94806	569-B5
ARDMORE PL	8400	DBLN 94568	693-G2
ARDMORE RD		CCCo 94707	609-F4
ARDMORE ST	8400	DBLN 94568	693-G2
ARDMORE WY	100	BEN 94510	551-B3
ARDOR DR		ORIN 94563	631-A3
ARDRA LN	1700	CNCD 94519	592-J2
ARELLANO CT		DBLN 94568	694-G5
ARENAS CT		SRMN 94583	673-C3
ARENCY CT	200	DNVL 94506	653-F1
ARENDS DR	100	DNVL 94506	653-F1
ARENDS WY		WLCK 94597	612-B1
ARETE CT		HER 94547	569-H4
ARGENTA CT	900	HER 94553	572-B7
ARGENTA DR	900	CCCo 94513	572-B7
ARGONNE DR	1700	CNCD 94518	592-F7
	1700	WLCK 94598	592-F7
ARGOSY CT		PIT 94565	573-J2
ARGYLE RD	5100	CCCo 94803	569-E7
ARGYLE ST	2700	OAK 94602	650-F2
ARGYLL AV	2700	CNCD 94520	572-E7
ARIA DR		CCCo 94553	572-C6
ARIANE CT		OAK 94619	650-H5
ARIANNA LN		SRMN 94582	674-A3
ARIEL DR		CCCo 94506	654-D6
ARIEY LN		CCCo 94549	591-H6
ARIMO AV	600	OAK 94610	650-B2
ARIZONA AV	200	RCH 94801	608-D1
ARIZONA DR	5500	CNCD 94521	593-F6
ARIZONA ST	3100	OAK 94602	650-E4
ARJANG CT		CCCo 94507	632-H5
ARKANSAS ST	3200	OAK 94602	650-E5
ARKELL CT	1900	WLCK 94598	612-E7
ARKELL RD	1000	WLCK 94598	612-F1
	1500	WLCK 94598	592-E7
ARKINLANDER LN	100	CCCo 94553	572-B5
ARLEDA LN	4300	CNCD 94521	593-A4
ARLENE CT		WLCK 94595	612-C7
ARLENE DR	100	WLCK 94595	612-C6
ARLENE LN		WLCK 94595	612-C7
ARLEWOOD CT		SRMN 94582	674-B3
ARLINGTON AV		BERK 94707	609-F3
		BERK 94708	609-F3
		CCCo 94708	609-F3
	800	ELCR 94530	609-F3
ARLINGTON BLVD	900	ELCR 94530	609-E1
	1400	ELCR 94530	589-C7
	2700	CCCo 94805	589-B5
	5500	SPAB 94805	589-B5
N ARLINGTON BLVD	5400	SPAB 94806	589-B4
	5600	CCCo 94806	589-B4
	5600	CCCo 94806	589-B4
ARLINGTON CIR	3700	PIT 94565	574-F5
ARLINGTON CT		CCCo 94707	609-F3
		PIT 94565	574-F6
	300	DNVL 94526	653-D4
	1300	BREN 94513	616-D3
ARLINGTON DR		CCCo 94565	574-B3
ARLINGTON LN		CCCo 94707	609-F3
ARLINGTON RD	2300	CNCD 94520	592-E3
ARLINGTON WY		WLCK 94595	612-B5
	700	MRTZ 94553	571-D3
	1000	BREN 94513	616-D3
ARLMONT DR		CCCo 94707	609-F3
ARMAND DR		OAK 94521	593-B3
ARMANI CT	5200	PLE 94588	694-H5
ARMINIO LN		OAKL 94561	596-H3
ARMOUR DR	6600	OAK 94601	630-E6
ARMSTRONG CT	100	HER 94547	570-B5
	800	BREN 94513	616-E3
	1600	CNCD 94521	593-B3
	3800	OAKL 94561	596-F2
ARMSTRONG RD	900	BREN 94513	616-F3
	1700	PLHL 94523	592-B5
		CCCo 94514	(657-F2)
			See Page 638
	3700	CCCo 94514	637-D7
ARMSTRONG WY	700	BREN 94513	616-E3
ARMY ST	100	PIT 94565	574-E3
ARNO CT	4700	RCH 94804	609-A2
ARNOLD DR	200	MRTZ 94553	571-F6
	1900	MRTZ 94553	572-A6
ARNOLD RD		DBLN 94568	694-C3
ARNOLD INDUSTRIAL PL	1700	CNCD 94520	572-E5
ARNOLD INDUSTRIAL WY	1700	CNCD 94520	572-F5
	1700	CNCD 94520	572-F4
AROLLO PTH		OAK 94618	630-B5
ARREBA ST		MRTZ 94553	571-E3
ARREZZO CT	5200	PLE 94588	694-C6
ARRONIA CT	2800	PLE 94588	694-H3
ARROWFIELD WY		SRMN 94582	674-B3
ARROWHEAD CT	5000	ANT 94531	595-G4
ARROWHEAD DR	500	LFYT 94549	631-J3
	1600	OAK 94601	630-F6
ARROWHEAD ST		BREN 94513	616-H2
ARROWHEAD TER	3100	CLAY 94517	593-H6
ARROWHEAD WY		OAKL 94561	596-G1
ARROWSMITH CT	600	WLCK 94598	613-C4
ARROWWOOD CIR	4300	CNCD 94521	593-A5
ARROWWOOD CT	4400	CNCD 94521	593-A5
ARROYO CT	2500	PIN 94564	569-J7
ARROYO CT	700	LFYT 94549	631-H1
ARROYO DR		MRGA 94556	631-C5
		ORIN 94563	631-C5
	100	DNVL 94526	653-B1
	300	MRTZ 94553	571-D6
ARROYO WY	1200	WLCK 94596	612-C4
	5100	ANT 94531	595-H5
ARROYO SECO RD		BREN 94513	596-G5
ARTHUR CT	200	DNVL 94526	653-C7
ARTHUR RD		CCCo 94553	571-J3
	500	CCCo 94553	572-A3
ARTHUR WY	2300	ANT 94509	574-J7
	2300	ANT 94509	594-J1
ARTHUR H BREED JR FRWY I-580		AlaC	693-A4
		AlaC	694-C5
		DBLN	693-A4
		DBLN	694-C5
		LVMR	694-C5
		PLE	693-A4
		PLE	694-C5
ARTUNA AV		PDMT 94611	650-A1
ARUBA		ANT 94509	595-E3
ARVADA CT	3000	CCCo 94806	589-A3
ARVADA DR	100	SRMN 94583	673-G7
ARZATE LN	2100	ANT 94509	575-F6
ASBURY CT		PIT 94565	574-B3
ASBURY WY		PIT 94565	574-B3
ASCENSION DR	2400	SRMN 94583	673-B3
ASCOT CT		BREN 94513	596-F4
		OAK 94611	650-F1
		SRMN 94583	673-E4
	1800	CNCD 94520	592-F2
	1900	MRGA 94556	631-D3
	2100	PIT 94565	574-A3
	3100	PLE 94588	694-F6
	3300	RCH 94806	589-A2
ASCOT DR		OAK 94611	650-F1
	1900	SRMN 94583	673-E4
	2600	SRMN 94583	673-E4
ASCOT LN		OAK 94611	650-G1
ASCOT PL		BREN 94561	596-F4
		MRGA 94556	631-D3
		OAK 94611	650-F2
ASENATH CT	2100	WLCK 94598	612-G2
ASH CT		BREN 94513	616-H2
		HER 94547	570-A4
	6800	DBLN 94568	693-J4
ASH LN	300	CCCo 94803	589-E1
ASH ST	1400	MRTZ 94553	571-F3
	3000	CNCD 94520	572-F6
	3100	ANT 94509	574-J7
ASHBOURNE CIR		CCCo 94583	673-A5
ASHBOURNE DR		CCCo 94583	672-J4
		CCCo 94583	673-A5
ASHBOURNE PL		BREN 94513	596-C6
ASHBOURNE WY		ANT 94531	596-B3
ASHBROOK CT	2900	OAK 94601	650-C6
ASHBROOK LN		SRMN 94582	674-C3
ASHBROOK PL		MRGA 94556	631-D4
ASHBURTON DR	3000	ANT 94509	575-E7
	3300	ANT 94509	595-E1
ASHBURY AV		ALB 94706	609-E4
		ELCR 94530	609-D3
ASHBURY DR		CNCD 94520	592-F2
ASHBY AV Rt#-13		BERK 94705	630-A3
ASHBY WY		PIT 94565	574-D4
ASHDALE DR	1800	CNCD 94519	572-J7
ASHFIELD LN		SRMN 94582	674-B3
ASHFORD CT		CCCo 94507	652-G1
	2300	ANT 94531	595-G1
ASHFORD PL		BREN 94513	616-A2
		MRGA 94556	631-D6
ASHFORD WY		ANT 94531	596-B3
ASHLAND CT	7500	DBLN 94568	693-G2
ASHLAND AV	1000	DNVL 94506	653-G5
ASHLAND RD		DNVL 94506	653-G5
ASHLEIGH LN		CNCD 94518	592-F6
ASHLEY CIR		DNVL 94526	653-A3
ASHLEY LN		WLCK 94597	612-D3
ASHLEY PL		CCCo 94553	571-G4
	6000	PLE 94588	694-B6
ASHLEY WY		WLCK 94597	612-D3
ASHMOUNT AV		OAK 94610	650-C2
	1200	PDMT 94610	650-C2
ASHMOUNT WY		OAK 94610	650-B2
ASHTON OAKS CT		SRMN 94582	673-J7
ASHWELL LN		SRMN 94582	674-B3
ASHWOOD DR	1400	OAKL 94561	576-D7
	1400	MRTZ 94553	591-H1
ASILOMAR CIR		OAK 94611	630-E7
ASILOMAR DR	1900	OAK 94611	630-E7
	2000	ANT 94509	595-F2
ASPARA DR	3200	CCCo 94517	614-G7
ASPEN		BEN 94510	551-B5
ASPEN CT		ANT 94509	595-E2
		CCCo 94803	569-D7
		LFYT 94549	631-H1
		SolC 94591	550-E1
	100	HER 94547	569-J4
	1100	BREN 94513	596-D7
ASPEN DR	100	CCCo 94553	572-B7
	100	CCCo 94553	572-B7
	1100	CNCD 94520	592-E4
ASPEN RD	3500	OAK 94561	577-E6
ASPEN ST		DBLN 94568	694-D4
ASPENRIDGE CT	1900	WLCK 94597	611-H3
ASPENWOOD CT		SRMN 94582	613-D1
ASPENWOOD DR	5300	CNCD 94521	613-D1
ASPINWALL CT		ORIN 94563	631-C6
ASPINWALL DR		BEN 94510	551-C1
ASPINWALL RD	6000	OAK 94611	630-E6
ASSUMPTION CIR		MRGA 94556	631-G7
ASTER CT	100	HER 94547	569-J4
ASTER DR	1300	ANT 94509	575-B4
ASTERBELL CT	1900	SRMN 94582	673-J1
ASTERBELL DR	1900	SRMN 94582	673-J1
ASTERWOOD DR		DBLN 94568	694-D3
ASTOR CT		BREN 94513	616-A1
ASTRID DR	100	PLHL 94523	592-C7
ATCHINSON STAGE CT		CLAY 94517	593-G6
ATCHINSON STAGE PL		CLAY 94517	593-G6
ATCHINSON STAGE RD		CLAY 94517	593-G7
N ATCHINSON STAGE RD	1400	CLAY 94517	593-G6
ATHEANA CT		CCCo 94582	674-A2
ATHENA	500	HER 94547	569-F3
ATHENE CT	3100	CNCD 94519	572-G7
ATHENE DR	2100	CNCD 94519	572-G7
ATHENOUR CT		PLE 94588	693-G7
ATHENS DR	5000	SRMN 94582	673-G4
ATHENS LN	1800	ANT 94509	575-G5
ATHERTON AV		CCCo 94525	550-E5
		PIT 94565	574-C4
ATHERTON BLVD		BREN 94561	596-E4
ATHERTON CIR		PIT 94565	574-B4
ATHERTON CT		BREN 94561	596-E4
ATHERTON PL		BREN 94561	596-E4
ATHOL AV	400	OAK 94606	650-A4
	600	OAK 94610	650-A4
ATKINS CT	500	BEN 94510	550-H1
ATLANTIC AV	200	PIT 94565	574-D5
ATLANTIC CIR		PIT 94565	574-D4
ATLANTIC ST	2700	CNCD 94518	592-G2
ATLAS	300	HER 94547	569-F3
ATLAS AV	3700	OAK 94619	650-G4
ATLAS PL		BERK 94708	609-J6
		BERK 94708	609-J6
ATLAS RD	5600	RCH 94806	568-H5
ATRICE LN	700	PLHL 94523	592-A6
ATTRI CT		CCCo 94549	591-H7
ATWELL AV	2800	OAK 94601	650-D6
ATWELL RD	1400	ELCR 94530	589-E7
	1400	ELCR 94530	609-E1
AUBERGINE CT		PIT 94565	574-C2
AUBREY CT		ANT 94531	595-H5
AUBURN CT		DNVL 94506	653-G5
AUBURN LN	2500	ANT 94509	575-A6
AUDREY CT	800	PLHL 94523	592-C3
	1700	BEN 94510	551-B3
	6000	PLE 94588	694-B7
AUDREY DR		PLHL 94523	592-C3
AUGUST WY	1200	ANT 94509	575-E5
AUGUSTA CT		CCCo 94507	633-A4
	800	CNCD 94518	592-H6
	5600	CCCo 94514	617-J6
	8700	DBLN 94568	693-G2
AUGUSTA DR		BREN 94513	616-B6
	500	MRGA 94556	631-B6
	800	MRGA 94556	651-D1
	3700	PIT 94565	574-C3
AUGUSTINE DR	100	MRTZ 94553	591-H1
AUGUSTINE LN	600	LFYT 94549	631-H1
AUGUSTUS CT	400	WLCK 94598	612-E2
AURALLIA RD	1700	CNCD 94521	593-F5
AURORA CT	1700	BREN 94513	596-C7
AUSTEN WY		CCCo 94553	572-B5
AUSTIN CT		RCH 94806	588-J1
		ORIN 94563	588-J1
		SPAB 94806	588-J1
AUSTIN LN		CCCo 94507	632-G4
AUSTIN ST	2000	OAK 94601	650-C7
AUSTIN CREEK AV		SRMN 94583	674-A7
AUTO PZ	3200	RCH 94806	569-B7
AUTO CENTER DR		WLCK 94597	612-C2
AUTO CENTER WY		SRMN 94582	612-C2
		CCCo 94520	613-D1
	1700	PIT 94565	575-A5
	1700	PIT 94565	575-A5
AUTUMN DR	700	BREN 94513	616-D1
	700	WLCK 94598	612-G3
AUTUMN LN	800	ANT 94509	575-F5
AUTUMN OAK CIR	900	CNCD 94521	613-C1
AUTUMN OAK WY	1800	OAKL 94561	576-D6
AUTUMN VALLEY CIR	1500	BREN 94513	596-D7
AUTUMNWIND CT		SRMN 94583	673-H3
	1400	PIT 94565	574-F6
AUTUMNWOOD DR		WLCK 94595	632-D5
AVA CT	800	LFYT 94549	611-G7
AVALON AV	800	LFYT 94549	611-F7
	2900	BERK 94705	630-A3
AVALON CIR	200	PIT 94565	574-E1
AVALON CT		SRMN 94582	674-D4
		CCCo 94507	632-D1
	800	LFYT 94549	611-F7
AVALON BAY CT		SRMN 94582	674-D4
AVALON BAY CT		RCH 94801	608-E3
AVELLANO DR	3000	WLCK 94598	612-H2
AVENIDA DR		BERK 94708	609-J7
	100	BERK 94708	610-A7
AVENIDA DE ORINDA		ORIN 94563	610-G7
AVENIDA FLORES	300	CCCo 94553	572-C6
AVENIDA MARTINEZ		CCCo 94803	589-E2
AVENIDA NUEVA	1500	CCCo 94506	653-E1
	1500	CCCo 94528	653-E1
	1500	CCCo 94528	633-E7
AVENIDA SEVILLA		WLCK 94595	632-C5
AVILA CT	4300	ANT 94531	595-G2
AVILA LN		MRGA 94556	575-A6
	900	MRGA 94556	631-D6
AVILA PL	700	ELCR 94530	609-E3
AVILA RD	100	CCCo 94565	573-B4
	100	CNCD 94565	573-B4
	100	PIT 94565	573-B4
	5800	ELCR 94530	609-C4
AVINGTON CT	600	BREN 94513	616-F2
AVIS CT		ORIN 94563	631-B4
AVIS DR	900	ELCR 94530	609-D3
AVIS WY	3100	PIN 94564	569-F6
AVOCA AV	5900	OAK 94611	630-C6
AVOCADO CT		SRMN 94583	673-F7
AVOCADO PL	100	BREN 94513	616-F3
AVOCET CT		SRFL 94901	587-A2
AVOCET DR		HER 94547	569-F2
AVON		DNVL 94526	652-J3
AVON AV	7200	DBLN 94568	693-J3
AVON CT		CCCo 94806	589-B2
AVON LN	3000	CCCo 94806	589-B2
AVON RD		PIT 94565	609-F4
AVON ST	100	PIT 94565	574-D3
AVON WY		CCCo 94520	572-C3
AVONDALE CT	900	WLCK 94596	632-F1
AVONOAK CT	2600	CCCo 94605	651-C7
AYAMONTE CT		SRMN 94583	673-C3
AYERS RD	1300	CNCD 94521	593-E3
	1800	CNCD 94521	593-E3
AYERS WY		SRMN 94582	674-C3
AZALEA AV	1400	MRTZ 94553	571-E3
AZALEA CT	100	HER 94547	569-J3
	1400	MRTZ 94553	571-E3
	2800	ANT 94531	595-G7
AZALEA DR	1900	CCCo 94595	612-B7
AZALEA LN		CNCD 94520	592-E5
		CNCD 94520	592-E5
		SRMN 94582	653-H7
		OAK 94611	630-F7
AZALEA WY		BREN 94513	596-C6
AZEVEDO ST	1200	ANT 94509	575-F5
AZORES CIR	400	CCCo 94565	573-D1
AZORES CT		CCCo 94565	573-D1
AZTEC WY		ANT 94531	595-G2
AZURE CT	5400	CCCo 94514	617-J7

B

Street	Block	City ZIP	Pg-Grid
B ST		CCCo 94565	573-E1
		CCCo 94565	592-G3
		CNCD 94520	572-J3
		DNVL 94526	653-J5
	100	BEN 94510	551-B4
	200	MRTZ 94553	571-E4
	300	ANT 94509	575-D4
	400	RCH 94801	588-E6
	7100	ELCR 94530	609-E4
BABBE ST	1800	OAKL 94561	576-C6
BABBLING BROOK WY	200	PIT 94565	573-J2

CONTRA COSTA

STREET
Block City ZIP Pg-Grid

BABCOCK CT
1200 BREN 94513 596-F7
BABEL LN
1200 CNCD 94518 592-J3
1200 CNCD 94521 592-J3
BABETTE CT
200 PLHL 94523 592-C6
BABY BOTTLE TR
- CCCo 94563 610-C5
- CCCo 94708 610-C5
BACCHINI LN
- BREN 94513 616-E5
BACCHUS
900 HER 94547 569-F3
BACON CT
- LFYT 94549 612-A4
- LFYT 94549 611-J4
4400 PLE 94588 694-A7
BACON RD
5300 OAK 94619 650-J6
5400 OAK 94619 651-A5
BACON ST
2200 CNCD 94520 592-F1
BACON WY
1100 LFYT 94549 611-J4
1100 LFYT 94549 612-A4
N BACON ISLAND RD
- SJCo 95206 (598-G1 See Page 597)
1700 SJCo 95206 (578-G6 See Page 557)
S BACON ISLAND RD
- SJCo 95206 (598-F3 See Page 597)
W BACON ISLAND RD
15200 SJCo 95206 (618-G1 See Page 597)
17700 SJCo 95206 (598-G5 See Page 597)
BADGER LN
1200 CNCD 94521 593-C5
BADGER WY
900 ANT 94509 595-F1
BADGER PASS WY
1800 ANT 94531 595-E4
BAFFY CT
- RCH 94806 568-H5
BAGADO CT
500 SRMN 94583 673-B3
BAGSHOTTE DR
5800 OAK 94611 650-F1
BAHAMA CT
100 SRMN 94582 673-E1
BAHIA CIR
100 SRFL 94901 587-A2
BAHIA LN
200 SRFL 94901 587-A2
BAHIA PL
200 SRFL 94901 587-A2
BAHIA WY
- SRFL 94901 587-A2
BAHIA VISTA CT
100 VAL 94591 550-F1
BAI-GORRY PL
- WLCK 94598 592-F7
- WLCK 94598 612-F1
BAILEY CT
4700 CNCD 94521 593-D3
BAILEY LN
- CCCo 94803 589-E2
BAILEY RD
- CCCo 94565 573-G2
500 PIT 94565 573-G7
800 CNCD 94521 573-G7
800 CNCD 94521 593-C4
800 CNCD 94565 573-G7
800 CNCD 94565 593-E2
1800 CCCo 94521 593-E2
BAINBRIDGE ST
- PIT 94565 574-C2
BAIO LN
1600 CNCD 94521 593-E4
BAIRD CT
1300 CNCD 94518 592-E7
BAIRN CT
3700 PLE 94588 694-F5
BAITX DR
- MRGA 94556 651-E1
BAJA CT
1000 PIT 94565 573-J3
BAJA LN
100 CCCo 94595 612-B6
BAJA LOMA CT
- DNVL 94526 653-C1
BAKER CT
300 BEN 94510 551-A2
2200 ANT 94509 575-A7
BAKER DR
3100 CNCD 94519 572-G7
BAKER LN
3600 LFYT 94549 611-E5
BAKER ST
200 BEN 94510 551-A2
1700 SPAB 94806 588-H2
BAKER WY
- CCCo 94582 674-B4
BALBOA AV
- SRFL 94901 587-A1
BALBOA CT
100 HER 94547 570-A5
1600 PLHL 94523 592-D5
2700 ANT 94509 575-B6
BALBOA DR
5500 OAK 94611 630-E7
BALBOA WY
2400 CCCo 94514 617-G7
BALCETA CT
100 DNVL 94526 653-D6
BALCLUTHA WY
- PIT 94565 573-J2
- PIT 94565 574-A2
BALDOCCHI CT
- CCCo 94513 597-F3
BALDWIN AV
- CCCo 94525 550-E5
BALDWIN CT
- WLCK 94597 612-C2
1800 CNCD 94519 592-J1
BALDWIN DR
- BREN 94513 616-D3
100 DNVL 94526 653-B6
1700 CNCD 94519 592-J1
BALDWIN LN
2600 WLCK 94597 612-C2
BALDWIN WY
- PLE 94588 693-H6
BALES CT
1700 CNCD 94521 593-D3
BALES DR
100 CCCo 94596 612-F7
BALFOUR AV
3600 OAK 94610 650-A3
BALFOUR RD
100 BREN 94513 615-H2

BALFOUR RD
100 BREN 94513 616-F2
100 CCCo 94513 615-H2
100 CCCo 94513 616-F2
4600 CCCo 94513 617-B2
BALFOUR WY
- BREN 94513 616-C2
BALHAN CT
5300 CNCD 94521 593-E5
BALHAN DR
1300 CNCD 94521 593-E5
BALI CT
600 SRMN 94582 673-E1
800 DNVL 94526 653-B2
BALL RD
- CCCo 94596 612-F6
BALLAD CT
1500 CNCD 94521 593-E5
BALLANTYNE DR
3500 PLE 94588 694-F5
BALMORAL CT
3200 PLE 94588 694-E6
BALMORAL DR
5600 OAK 94619 650-J4
5600 OAK 94619 651-A5
BALMORE CT
900 CCCo 94803 569-D6
900 PIN 94564 569-D6
BALRA DR
400 ELCR 94530 609-E3
BALSA CT
2200 CNCD 94520 572-F5
BALSAM CT
- PIT 94565 574-C2
BALSAM LN
- SRMN 94583 693-F1
BALSAM ST
- PIT 94565 574-C2
BALSAM WY
6900 OAK 94611 630-E5
BALTIC SEA CT
300 PIT 94565 574-A2
BALTUSROL
- MRGA 94556 651-D1
BALTUSROL CT
- SRMN 94583 693-H1
BALTUSROL PL
100 SRMN 94583 693-H1
BAMBOO CT
3700 CNCD 94519 593-A1
BAMBOO WY
2100 ANT 94509 595-F3
BANBRIDGE PL
- PLHL 94523 591-H5
BANBURY CT
100 BEN 94510 551-B2
600 WLCK 94598 612-F2
2300 MRTZ 94553 572-A5
BANBURY LP
2300 MRTZ 94553 572-A5
BANBURY PL
2200 WLCK 94598 612-F1
BANBURY RD
2000 WLCK 94598 612-F2
BANBURY WY
- BEN 94510 551-B2
3900 ANT 94531 595-G1
BANCHIO ST
- CCCo 94565 573-H2
BANCROFT CT
1000 WLCK 94598 612-E1
2100 PIT 94565 573-J3
BANCROFT LN
2400 CCCo 94806 588-J2
BANCROFT PL
400 OAK 94704 630-A2
600 SRMN 94582 673-J6
BANCROFT RD
800 WLCK 94597 592-D7
800 CNCD 94518 592-D7
800 WLCK 94598 592-D7
800 WLCK 94598 612-E1
900 CCCo 94523 592-D7
900 WLCK 94523 592-D7
BANDINI CT
- DBLN 94568 694-G4
BANDO CT
100 CCCo 94507 632-D2
BANDOL CT
- SRMN 94582 674-C3
BANDOL WY
- SRMN 94582 674-C3
BANDON DR
8400 DBLN 94568 693-H2
8800 SRMN 94583 693-H2
BANFF CT
5500 CNCD 94521 593-F7
BANGOR CT
- DBLN 94568 694-D4
- SRMN 94582 673-H4
BANINGTON DR
- VAL 94591 550-D2
BANION CT
100 CCCo 94806 569-C6
BANISTER LN
600 CCCo 94507 632-J2
BANKS DR
500 RCH 94806 568-G6
BANNER CT
2100 MRTZ 94553 572-A7
BANNING DR
6600 OAK 94611 630-G7
BANNOCK CT
900 CNCD 94518 592-E6
BANTRY RD
500 PIN 94564 569-C5
BANYAN CIR
500 WLCK 94598 592-H7
500 WLCK 94598 612-H1
BANYAN LN
600 WLCK 94598 592-H7
600 WLCK 94598 612-H1
BANYAN WY
2100 ANT 94509 575-B5
BANYON DR
100 PIT 94565 574-E5
BARBADOS DR
2300 SRMN 94582 653-F7
BARBANO CT
2100 ANT 94509 595-A1
BARBARA CIR
400 MRTZ 94553 591-H4
BARBARA CT
200 PLHL 94523 592-C7
2100 PIT 94565 574-A3
BARBARA LN
1000 SPAB 94806 588-G2
BARBARA RD
- ORIN 94563 630-H1
700 OAK 94610 650-A3
BARBARA ST
1300 BREN 94513 596-G7
BARBEE LN
- CCCo 94507 632-G6

BARBER CT
- MRTZ 94553 571-F7
BARBER LN
- MRTZ 94553 571-F7
BARBERRY CT
4400 CNCD 94521 593-B5
BARBERRY LN
100 SRMN 94582 653-J7
BARBETTE PL
3600 CNCD 94518 592-J4
BARBIS WY
1300 CNCD 94518 592-J3
1400 CNCD 94519 592-J3
BARCELONA CIR
2700 ANT 94509 575-B6
BARCELONA CT
- BREN 94513 596-C5
- DNVL 94526 653-C7
- PIT 94565 574-C6
BARCELONA PL
- DNVL 94526 653-C7
BARCELONA WY
- BREN 94513 596-C5
- CLAY 94517 613-J2
BARCLAY CT
- CCCo 94507 632-J2
BARDOZ CT
- ANT 94531 595-F2
BARIKA CT
- CCCo 94553 572-D3
BARKLEY AV
1900 WLCK 94597 612-B4
BARKLEY CT
900 PIN 94564 569-C5
BARKLEY DR
2900 RCH 94806 589-A1
BARKLEY MOUNTAIN WY
1500 ANT 94531 595-E6
BARKWOOD CT
1000 CNCD 94521 593-C7
2000 ANT 94509 595-E2
BARMIED PL
- OAK 94619 651-C7
BARMOUTH CT
900 ANT 94509 575-F7
BARMOUTH DR
3000 ANT 94509 575-F7
3300 ANT 94509 595-F1
BARN LN
- LFYT 94549 611-A7
BARNARD ST
2600 RCH 94806 589-B2
BARN DANCE WY
- OAKL 94561 596-F2
BARNER AV
3900 OAK 94602 650-E4
BARNER PL
- OAK 94602 650-E4
BARNES CT
- MRGA 94556 651-E1
BARNES WY
500 CCCo 94572 549-H7
500 CCCo 94572 569-H1
BARNETT CIR
1600 PLHL 94523 612-A1
BARNETT TER
1600 PLHL 94523 611-J1
1600 PLHL 94523 612-A1
BARN HOLLOW CT
7700 DBLN 94568 693-F4
BARN HOLLOW WY
- ANT 94565 574-G7
- ANT 94565 594-G1
BARN OWL CT
600 WLCK 94598 613-A3
BARNSLEY CT
900 ANT 94509 575-C7
BARNSLEY PL
- DBLN 94568 694-H3
BARNWOOD DR
800 SRMN 94583 673-D4
BAROCIO CT
- PLHL 94523 592-A6
BARON CT
6500 MRTZ 94553 591-H4
7700 ELCR 94530 609-E2
BARONS VIEW CT
- CCCo 94803 589-D1
BAROSSA DR
- SRMN 94582 674-B3
BAROTT RD
1200 LFYT 94549 611-J4
BARQUENTINE CT
200 PIT 94565 574-A2
BARRANCA CT
400 SRMN 94583 673-B3
BARRANCA ST
4100 CCCo 94803 589-B2
4100 RCH 94803 589-B2
BARRELHOUSE RD
- CCCo 94553 571-F3
BARRENGER DR
1000 DNVL 94506 653-G5
BARRETT AV
- RCH 94801 588-F6
2300 RCH 94804 588-F6
3300 RCH 94805 588-F6
3600 RCH 94805 589-A6
5300 ELCR 94530 589-B6
BARRETT CIR
200 DNVL 94526 653-D6
BARRETT CT
100 DNVL 94526 653-D6
2300 PIN 94564 569-F5
BARRIE CT
- PIT 94565 574-D6
BARRIE DR
- PIT 94565 574-D6
BARRINGTON CT
- BREN 94513 616-E2
BARRINGTON DR
3700 CNCD 94518 592-J3
BARRINGTON LN
200 CCCo 94507 632-J1
BARRONS PL
- DNVL 94526 653-D3
BARROW CT
300 WLCK 94598 612-F2
BARROWS RD
1300 OAK 94610 650-C3
BARRUS AV
1600 PIT 94565 574-E3
BARRY CT
- WLCK 94597 612-A2
BARRY PL
2700 OAK 94601 650-C6
BARRY HILL CT
- CCCo 94553 570-G3
BARRY HILL RD
- CCCo 94553 570-G3
BARRYMORE DR
3000 CNCD 94518 592-G7
BARRYMORE PL
3100 CNCD 94518 592-H7

BART
- CNCD 94520 573-A4
- CNCD 94565 573-A4
BART AV
100 ANT 94509 575-E4
BARTELS DR
1400 CCCo 94548 597-A3
BARTH AV
1500 RCH 94806 589-B4
BARTLETT CT
- PLHL 94523 592-A4
800 BREN 94513 616-H2
BARTLETT ST
2300 OAK 94601 650-D6
2600 OAK 94602 650-D6
BARTOLINI DR
500 MRTZ 94553 571-E4
BARTON CT
- PLHL 94523 592-A4
300 DNVL 94526 653-B3
BARTON LN
3200 ANT 94509 575-J5
BASALT CT
900 ANT 94509 575-F7
1900 WLCK 94595 632-B1
BASALT WY
800 ANT 94509 575-F7
BASIE CT
- CNCD 94519 592-H5
BASIN CT
- HER 94547 569-H4
BASIN RD
- MRTZ 94553 571-E2
BASSETT CT
4800 CNCD 94521 593-C4
BASSETT DR
1400 CNCD 94521 593-C4
BASSWOOD DR
- CCCo 94582 673-J2
- CCCo 94582 674-A2
BASSWOOD PL
1100 CNCD 94521 593-F7
BATACAO LN
300 ANT 94509 575-D6
BATES AV
800 ELCR 94530 609-E2
1800 CCCo 94520 572-F3
1800 CNCD 94520 572-F3
BATES BLVD
- ORIN 94563 610-H7
- ORIN 94563 611-A7
BATES CT
100 ORIN 94563 611-A7
BATES RD
1200 OAK 94610 650-B4
1200 OAK 94602 650-B4
BATH CT
- SRMN 94583 673-F6
BATTERY ST
1200 CCCo 94801 588-F4
BAUER RD
- BREN 94513 596-E6
BAUER WY
- BREN 94513 596-E7
BAUTISTA ST
2700 ANT 94509 575-D6
BAVARIAN CT
500 LFYT 94549 631-H3
BAVARIAN LN
3100 LFYT 94549 631-H3
BAXTER CT
1900 CNCD 94521 593-G4
BAXTER ST
2100 OAK 94601 650-D7
BAY CT
- SRFL 94901 587-A1
1200 BREN 94513 596-E7
BAY DR
- CCCo 94565 553-E7
- CCCo 94565 573-E1
BAY ST
100 HER 94547 569-E3
200 CCCo 94525 550-E4
1600 CCCo 94806 569-A5
BAY WY
- SRFL 94901 587-A1
BAYBERRY CIR
2200 PIT 94565 573-G4
BAYBERRY CT
- OAKL 94561 596-C1
BAYBERRY DR
3400 WLCK 94598 612-J1
BAY CREST DR
200 PIT 94565 574-E1
BAY FOREST CT
- OAK 94611 630-D4
BAY FOREST DR
- OAK 94611 630-D3
BAYFRONT BLVD
- HER 94547 569-F2
BAYFRONT DR
- RCH 94804 608-H2
BAY HARBOR CT
- RCH 94804 608-E3
BAY HARBOR DR
- RCH 94804 608-E3
BAY HILL CT
- DBLN 94568 694-F1
BAYHURST DR
- VAL 94591 550-D2
BAYLANDS DR
200 MRTZ 94553 571-H6
BAY LAUREL CT
- DBLN 94568 693-F4
BAYLAUREL CT
- BREN 94513 596-D5
BAY LAUREL ST
- DBLN 94568 693-E4
BAYLEAF CT
4900 MRTZ 94553 572-A6
BAYLOR CT
500 BEN 94510 550-J1
BAYLOR LN
- PLHL 94523 592-C3
BAYO ST
3800 OAK 94619 650-F6
BAYONETTE CT
- BREN 94513 616-B3
BAYO VISTA AV
1500 CCCo 94806 589-A3
1500 SPAB 94806 589-A3
BAY POINT DR
- SRFL 94901 587-A2
BAYPOINT DR
- SRFL 94901 587-A3
BAYPOINT WY
1000 CCCo 94572 569-J1
1000 CCCo 94572 570-A1
BAYPOINT VILLAGE DR
- SRFL 94901 587-A2
BAYSHORE RD
900 BEN 94510 551-E3
BAYSHORE ST
700 MRTZ 94553 571-G5

BAYSIDE CT
- RCH 94804 608-J3
- CCCo 94806 569-C4
200 OAKL 94561 576-F7
BAY SIDE DR
- PIT 94565 574-D1
- PIT 94565 554-D7
BAYSIDE DR
- RCH 94804 608-J3
BAYSIDE TER
100 VAL 94591 550-D3
BAYSIDE WY
4600 OAKL 94561 576-F7
BAYSWATER CT
700 WLCK 94598 613-A3
BAY TREE LN
700 ELCR 94530 609-E2
BAYTREE LN
- BERK 94708 609-J6
- BERK 94708 610-A6
BAY VIEW AV
- CCCo 94565 573-J2
BAYVIEW AV
900 OAK 94610 650-B4
4800 RCH 94804 609-B2
6100 CCCo 94806 589-B3
BAYVIEW CIR
1600 BEN 94510 551-C4
3700 CNCD 94520 572-G4
BAYVIEW CT
700 CCCo 94803 569-D7
2300 CNCD 94520 572-G5
BAY VIEW DR
100 MRTZ 94553 571-D3
BAYVIEW DR
- MrnC 94901 587-C1
200 OAKL 94561 576-F7
BAYVIEW PL
1300 BERK 94708 609-H7
BAYVIEW RD
- CCCo 94525 550-C5
BAY VIEW FARM RD
1100 PIN 94564 569-D4
BAY VISTA CT
- BEN 94510 551-E3
BAYWOOD CIR
3300 ANT 94531 595-H1
BAYWOOD CT
4200 CNCD 94521 593-C3
BAYWOOD DR
- RCH 94803 589-G4
1600 CNCD 94521 593-C3
BAYWOOD LN
- HER 94547 569-F2
- SRMN 94583 673-D6
3000 CCCo 94806 589-A2
BAYWOOD WY
- RCH 94804 608-H2
BEACH CT
1100 CCCo 94514 617-J5
BEACH DR
- CCCo 94565 553-E7
- CCCo 94565 573-E1
- MrnC 94901 587-C1
BEACH ST
1900 CNCD 94519 592-G1
BEACH HEAD CT
- RCH 94804 608-H2
BEACH HEAD WY
2000 RCH 94804 608-H2
BEACHPOINT WY
900 CCCo 94572 569-J1
BEACHWOOD COM
1800 BREN 94513 596-G6
BEACON PL
4100 CCCo 94514 617-G6
BEACON ST
500 OAK 94610 650-A3
900 PIT 94565 574-D2
BEACON RIDGE CT
1900 WLCK 94597 611-H3
BEACON RIDGE LN
300 WLCK 94597 611-H3
BEACONSFIELD CT
- ORIN 94563 631-B5
BEACONSFIELD PL
2600 OAK 94611 650-F1
BEALE CT
700 WLCK 94598 612-G1
BEALE ST
- SRFL 94901 587-A2
BEAR PL
- CLAY 94517 594-A5
BEAR COVE CT
100 VAL 94591 550-E1
BEAR CREEK RD
1000 CCCo 94553 590-F4
1200 ORIN 94563 610-F2
1200 CCCo 94553 610-E4
1200 CCCo 94553 611-A2
1200 CCCo 94563 610-F2
1200 CCCo 94563 611-A2
1200 CCCo 94549 611-A2
BEAR CREEK TR
- CCCo 94553 610-G1
- CCCo 94553 611-A2
- CCCo 94563 610-G1
- CCCo 94563 611-A2
- ORIN 94563 610-D4
BEARINDA LN
- CCCo 94553 590-G6
BEAR OAKS CT
200 CCCo 94553 590-H6
BEAR OAKS DR
100 CCCo 94553 590-G6
BEAR OAKS LN
300 CCCo 94553 590-H6
BEAR RIDGE RD
- ORIN 94563 610-F3
BEAR RIDGE TR
100 ORIN 94563 610-G3
BEAR RIDGE WY
3300 ANT 94531 595-J2
BEAR RIVER CT
4500 OAKL 94561 576-E7
BEASLEY AV
2300 ANT 94509 575-E6
BEATIE ST
700 OAK 94606 650-A4
BEATRICE CT
- BREN 94513 596-H5
BEATRICE RD
400 PLHL 94523 592-B6
BEATRICE ST
700 BREN 94513 616-F2
BEAUFOREST DR
100 OAK 94611 630-E6
BEAULIEU CT
400 CCCo 94565 573-D2
BEAULIEU DR
1200 CCCo 94565 573-D2
BEAULIEU LN
400 OAKL 94561 576-E6

BEAULIEU PL
- CCCo 94565 573-D2
BEAUMONT AV
3000 OAK 94606 650-C4
3100 OAK 94602 650-C4
BEAUMONT CT
- LFYT 94549 591-H7
BEAU RIVAGE
1500 CCCo 94806 589-B3
BEAVER CT
600 CCCo 94514 617-J4
600 CCCo 94514 (618-A4 See Page 597)
4500 ANT 94531 595-H3
BEAVER LN
700 CCCo 94514 617-J4
5700 CCCo 94514 (618-A4 See Page 597)
BEAVER CREEK CT
800 SRMN 94582 674-A7
BECK RD
400 AlaC 94551 675-H7
S BECK ST
300 RCH 94804 608-J1
300 RCH 94804 588-J7
BECKETT WY
8600 DBLN 94568 693-F2
BECKHAM CT
4800 CNCD 94521 593-D4
BECKNER CT
1600 CNCD 94521 593-B2
BEDFORD
100 HER 94547 569-H2
BEDFORD CT
7400 DBLN 94568 693-H3
BEDFORD CV
- SRFL 94901 587-A2
BEDFORD LN
500 OAKL 94561 576-C7
BEDFORD PL
100 CCCo 94506 654-A5
300 MRGA 94556 631-E6
BEDFORD RD
2300 CNCD 94520 592-E3
BEDFORD WY
7300 DBLN 94568 693-H3
BEDROCK CT
- ANT 94509 595-F1
BEDROCK WY
- ANT 94509 595-F1
BEECH CT
- CCCo 94596 612-G7
6300 PLE 94588 694-A7
BEECH DR
900 CCCo 94596 612-F7
900 CCCo 94596 632-G1
BEECH ST
1300 MRTZ 94553 571-F3
BEECHAM CT
3400 PLE 94588 694-E5
BEECHNUT CT
3000 ANT 94509 575-J6
BEECHNUT DR
100 HER 94547 570-A5
BEECHNUT LN
4300 OAKL 94561 596-G1
BEECHNUT ST
3000 ANT 94509 575-J6
BEECHWOOD CT
- ANT 94509 595-E3
- PIT 94565 573-F4
3900 CNCD 94519 573-B7
BEECHWOOD DR
- OAK 94618 630-A5
1400 MRTZ 94553 571-H7
1400 MRTZ 94553 591-H1
3200 LFYT 94549 611-G7
3800 CNCD 94519 593-A1
3900 CNCD 94519 573-A7
BEECHWOOD WY
- ANT 94509 595-E3
BEEDE WY
- ANT 94509 575-D4
BEEGUM CT
2500 CNCD 94518 592-G6
BEGONIA CT
- BREN 94561 596-E4
- SRMN 94582 674-A2
100 MRTZ 94553 572-B7
100 MRTZ 94553 592-B1
2200 PIT 94565 573-J4
BEGONIA DR
- BREN 94561 596-E4
BEGONIA PL
- BREN 94561 596-F4
BEHRENS ST
100 ELCR 94530 609-E4
500 ALB 94706 609-E4
BEISHEIM LN
- CCCo 94595 612-C7
BEL AIR CT
- ORIN 94563 631-B1
BEL AIR DR
- ORIN 94563 631-A1
1400 CNCD 94521 593-B4
BEL AIRE CT
200 DNVL 94526 653-D6
BELALP PTH
- OAK 94618 630-B5
BELANN CT
800 CNCD 94518 592-G6
BELCARRA CT
- DBLN 94568 694-E4
BELDEN ST
1400 PIN 94564 569-D4
BELDIN LN
4800 OAKL 94561 576-C6
BELDING CT
1700 CNCD 94521 593-D3
BELEM CT
600 SRMN 94583 673-B3
BELFAIR DR
1000 PIN 94564 569-D4
BELFAIR PL
400 MRGA 94556 631-E5
BELFAST AV
4600 OAK 94619 650-H6
BELFAST PL
- SRMN 94583 673-F6
BELFAST WY
3000 RCH 94806 588-J1
3000 RCH 94806 589-A1
BELFORD CT
2200 WLCK 94598 612-G2
4700 ANT 94531 595-E3
BELFORD DR
2000 WLCK 94598 612-F2
BELFORD PEAK WY
4800 ANT 94531 595-E3
BELGIAN DR
100 DNVL 94526 633-C7
BELGRAVE PL
5300 OAK 94618 630-A6

BELGUM TR
5900 CCCo 94805 589-C4
BELINDA CT
- SRMN 94583 693-G1
BELINDA DR
- PLHL 94523 592-D5
BELL AV
100 PDMT 94611 630-C7
100 PDMT 94611 650-C1
4100 RCH 94804 609-A1
BELL CT
4500 RCH 94804 609-A1
BELL DR
- PIT 94565 574-C5
BELL ST
800 LFYT 94549 611-F7
BELL WY
4300 RCH 94806 568-G6
BELLADONNA DR
- SRMN 94582 673-J2
BELLAGIO CT
- BREN 94513 616-C1
BELLAIRE PL
2700 OAK 94601 650-C6
BELLAM BLVD
300 SRFL 94901 587-A2
BELLA MONTE AV
- CCCo 94565 573-H2
BELLAMY CT
1000 WLCK 94597 612-B1
BELLA VISTA
- CCCo 94528 633-E6
BELLA VISTA AV
- CCCo 94565 573-H3
800 CCCo 94553 571-F4
1000 OAK 94610 650-B4
BELLE AV
100 PLHL 94523 612-A1
BELLE CT
- PLHL 94523 612-B1
2200 ANT 94509 574-H5
BELLE DR
3900 ANT 94509 574-H5
BELLE LN
- PLHL 94523 612-B1
BELLE MEADE DR
9400 SRMN 94583 693-H1
9500 SRMN 94583 673-G7
BELLE MEADE PL
100 SRMN 94583 673-H7
BELLERIVE LN
- DBLN 94568 694-F2
BELLETERRE DR
1000 DNVL 94506 653-J4
BELLEVUE AV
- PDMT 94611 650-C1
- SRFL 94901 587-A1
BELLEVUE CIR
- DBLN 94568 694-E3
BELLEZA DR
5600 PLE 94588 694-C7
BELLEZA LN
5600 PLE 94588 694-C7
BELLFLOWER CT
100 HER 94547 570-B4
1600 WLCK 94596 612-G7
2900 ANT 94531 575-G7
BELLFLOWER DR
300 SRMN 94582 653-H7
2800 ANT 94531 575-H7
3200 ANT 94531 595-H1
BELLFLOWER PL
1600 WLCK 94596 612-G7
BELLFRY GLEN WY
- BREN 94513 596-E6
BELLHURST CT
6400 AlaC 94552 672-C7
BELLHURST LN
6400 AlaC 94552 672-C7
BELLINA ST
8600 DBLN 94568 693-G2
BELLINA CANYON RD
- AlaC 94552 672-F3
BELLINGHAM SQ
- SRMN 94582 674-B3
N BELLINGHAM WY
- SRMN 94582 674-B3
S BELLINGHAM WY
- SRMN 94582 674-B3
BELLIS DR
- SRMN 94582 673-H1
BELLMEADE CT
700 BREN 94513 616-E3
BELLMEADE WY
600 BREN 94513 616-F3
BELLO CT
200 SRMN 94583 673-A2
BELLOWS CT
- PIT 94565 574-C2
800 CCCo 94596 612-F6
800 WLCK 94598 612-F6
BELL WAVER WY
- OAK 94619 650-J4
BELLWOOD CT
3900 CNCD 94519 573-A7
BELLWOOD DR
3900 CNCD 94519 573-A7
3900 CNCD 94519 593-A1
BELLWORT CT
2800 ANT 94531 575-H7
BELMONT AV
3200 ELCR 94530 609-C4
3200 RCH 94804 609-C4
BELMONT CT
- PLHL 94523 591-J7
BELMONT LN
2600 ANT 94509 575-D1
BELMONT PL
900 PIT 94565 574-E6
BELMONT RD
1800 CNCD 94520 592-E3
BELMONT WY
900 PIN 94564 569-C4
3800 PLE 94588 694-F5
BELOIT AV
400 CCCo 94708 609-G4
BEL ROMA RD
4700 AlaC 94551 675-H7
BELROSE AV
2700 BERK 94705 630-A3
BELSHAW ST
- ANT 94509 575-D6
BELVA LN
200 PLHL 94523 592-B5
BELVEDERE AV
- RCH 94801 608-D1
BELVEDERE CT
100 WLCK 94598 612-J1
BELVEDERE WY
4400 ANT 94509 595-F2
BEL VIEW CT
8400 ELCR 94530 589-E7
BENBOW CT
4000 ANT 94531 595-H1

STREET Block City ZIP Pg-Grid

BENBOW CT
4600 CNCD 94521 593-C3
BENEDICT CT
100 MRTZ 94553 571-J7
BENEDITA PL
- MRGA 94556 631-E3
BENET CT
- CCCo 94511 577-E1
BENEVIDES AV
4600 OAK 94602 650-D3
BENHAM CT
2300 WLCK 94596 632-H2
BENHAM DR
200 MRTZ 94523 591-H3
200 MRTZ 94553 591-H3
BENICIA-MARTINEZ BRDG I-680
- BEN - 551-E6
- MRTZ - 551-F7
- SolC - 551-E6
BENITA WY
- CCCo 94553 572-B5
BENJAMIN AV
200 PIT 94565 574-F4
BENJAMIN DR
3100 RCH 94806 589-A1
BENJAMIN LN
100 DNVL 94506 654-B6
BEN LOMOND
- HER 94547 569-G4
BENNER CT
6300 PLE 94588 694-A6
BENNETT PL
4300 OAK 94602 650-F4
BENNETT WY
3300 CNCD 94519 572-G7
BENNINGTON CT
3200 WLCK 94598 612-H6
BENONI LN
200 BREN 94513 616-D2
BENSON CT
2600 MRTZ 94553 571-F5
BENT CREEK DR
2000 SRMN 94582 673-J7
2000 SRMN 94582 674-A7
2100 SRMN 94582 694-A1
BENTHILL CT
- CCCo 94549 591-J7
BENTLEY CT
- BREN 94513 616-A1
200 CCCo 94553 592-B1
BENTLEY ST
1200 CNCD 94518 592-E7
BENTLEY OAKS CT
- SRMN 94582 694-A1
BENT OAK CT
- CCCo 94506 654-C4
BENT OAK LN
1400 CCCo 94506 654-C4
BENT OAK PL
400 CCCo 94506 654-C4
BENTON ST
1400 OAK 94602 650-C4
3300 CNCD 94519 572-G6
BENT TREE DR
- DBLN 94568 694-G2
BENT TREE LN
1300 CNCD 94521 593-B5
BENTTREE WY
- ANT 94531 595-J5
- ANT 94531 596-A5
BENZON DR
9200 PLE 94588 693-G6
BERENDSEN CT
900 CLAY 94517 613-J1
BERG CT
1300 PIT 94565 574-F6
BERINGER CT
2000 OAKL 94561 576-C5
BERINGER WY
- OAKL 94561 576-C5
BERK AV
500 RCH 94804 609-A1
BERK PL
100 RCH 94804 609-A1
BERKELEY
100 CCCo 94806 569-B5
BERKELEY AV
- ORIN 94563 610-E6
BERKELEY PARK BLVD
200 CCCo 94707 609-E4
BERKSHIRE
- MRGA 94556 651-D1
BERKSHIRE CT
- CCCo 94513 617-F5
100 SRMN 94582 673-G4
200 DNVL 94526 653-D4
3100 PLE 94588 694-E6
BERKSHIRE LN
- BREN 94513 616-B1
- CCCo 94513 617-F5
BERKSHIRE PL
700 CNCD 94518 592-H6
BERLIN WY
3100 OAK 94602 650-E6
BERMAR AV
4300 CCCo 94803 589-D2
BERMUDA AV
4300 OAK 94619 650-H6
BERMUDA CT
100 HER 94547 570-C6
1200 CNCD 94518 592-D7
3400 SRMN 94582 653-E7
BERMUDA DR
900 CNCD 94518 592-E7
BERMUDA LN
100 VAL 94591 550-F1
BERMUDA WY
1500 ANT 94509 575-G5
BERNARD AV
3000 SRMN 94583 673-F6
BERNARD RD
100 OAKL 94561 596-G1
BERNARD WY
1400 MRTZ 94553 591-H1
BERNARDO CT
900 PIN 94564 569-E4
BERNAUER
100 PIT 94565 574-B3
BERNEVES CT
- OAK 94619 650-H5
BERNHARD AV
5800 CCCo 94805 589-B5
BERNICE LN
500 MRTZ 94553 591-G3
BERNIE LN
1400 CCCo 94507 632-E3
BERRELLESA ST
100 MRTZ 94553 571-D2
BERRY DR
- CCCo 94553 592-C1
100 CCCo 94553 572-C7
BERRY LN
1300 BREN 94513 596-G7
BERRYBROOK HOLLOW
- ORIN 94563 610-F3
BERRYDALE WY
5200 ANT 94531 595-J6
BERRYESSA CT
4300 ANT 94531 595-J1
BERRYMAN ST
1800 BERK 94703 609-F7
1900 BERK 94709 609-F7
BERRYWOOD CT
1700 CNCD 94521 593-D3
BERRYWOOD DR
1700 CNCD 94521 593-D3
BERTA LN
3200 LFYT 94549 611-G6
BERTOLA ST
500 MRTZ 94553 571-E4
BERTRAM CT
3000 CNCD 94520 572-F6
BERTRAM ST
- CCCo 94598 613-A4
BERWICK CT
5600 CCCo 94514 617-J6
5600 CCCo 94514 (618-A6 See Page 597)
BERWICK PL
100 SRMN 94583 673-F6
BERYL CT
700 HER 94547 569-H5
BERYL DR
4100 CNCD 94518 592-J5
BESITO AV
1100 OAK 94705 630-B3
BEST AV
2600 OAK 94619 650-F7
BEST RD
500 PLHL 94523 592-B4
BESTON WY
100 VAL 94591 550-F2
BESWICK CT
- PLHL 94523 592-B6
BETA CT
- SRMN 94583 673-B1
BETH DR
- PLHL 94523 592-C4
BETHANY CT
800 CNCD 94518 592-F7
BETHANY LN
800 CNCD 94518 592-G7
BETHANY RD
- SRMN 94582 674-D4
BETHEL LN
8000 PLE 94588 693-H7
BETHEL ISLAND RD
- CCCo 94511 557-D7
- CCCo 94511 577-D3
- CCCo 94561 597-D1
2700 CCCo 94561 577-D7
BETLEN DR
11200 DBLN 94568 693-F5
BETLIN PL
- MRGA 94556 631-E3
BETTEN CT
- DNVL 94526 653-B1
BETTENCOURT DR
5600 CLAY 94517 593-G5
BETTY AV
800 PIN 94564 569-C4
BETTY LN
200 PLHL 94523 592-B5
3300 LFYT 94549 631-G2
3300 PIT 94565 574-C4
8400 ELCR 94530 609-E1
BEVERLY CIR
- CCCo 94565 573-G2
BEVERLY CT
- CCCo 94707 609-F4
8400 DBLN 94568 693-H2
BEVERLY DR
100 PLHL 94523 592-C4
3000 CCCo 94565 573-G2
BEVERLY LN
8400 DBLN 94568 693-H1
BEVERLY PL
100 BREN 94513 596-G5
1500 ALB 94706 609-F6
1500 BERK 94706 609-F6
1600 BERK 94707 609-F6
BEVERLY RD
- CCCo 94707 609-F4
BEVERLY ST
1200 ANT 94509 575-E5
BEVMAR LN
- CCCo 94507 632-H3
BEXLEY PL
100 WLCK 94598 612-J1
BIANCALANA DR
600 OAKL 94561 596-F1
BIANCO CT
5100 PLE 94588 694-H4
BICKERSTAFF ST
3600 LFYT 94549 611-E6
BIDDLEFORD DR
2800 SRMN 94583 673-F6
BIEHS CT
- OAK 94618 630-C6
BIENATI WY
2100 OAK 94602 650-D4
BIEN VENIDA
- ORIN 94563 610-G6
BIFROST AV
400 PLHL 94523 592-B3
BIG BEAR CT
- OAKL 94561 576-G7
100 RCH 94803 589-G3
BIG BEAR RD
- OAKL 94561 576-G7
- OAKL 94561 596-G1
BIG BEND CT
- OAKL 94561 596-H1
BIG BREAK RD
- OAKL 94561 576-C5
BIG BURN RD
- AlaC 94546 651-G7
BIGELOW PL
- SRMN 94583 673-F6
BIGELOW ST
200 CLAY 94517 613-J1
BIGHORN CT
4500 ANT 94509 595-F3
BIGHORN TER
900 BREN 94513 616-E1
BIGLER CT
500 BEN 94510 550-H1
BIGLOW DR
1800 ANT 94509 575-F6
BIG OAK CT
- WLCK 94596 612-D6
2000 ANT 94509 595-E2
BIG PINE LN
4400 CNCD 94521 593-B4
BIG SPRINGS TR
- CCCo 94708 610-B6
BILLECI AV
1600 PIT 94565 574-E3
BILLINGS RD
1700 CNCD 94519 592-H2
BILLINGTON CT
- LFYT 94549 611-H3
BILLY LN
2200 CNCD 94520 572-F5
BILTMORE CT
200 CCCo 94507 633-A4
BILTMORE DR
300 CCCo 94507 633-A4
1100 CCCo 94507 632-J4
BING CT
800 BREN 94513 616-H2
BINNACLE HILL
- OAK 94618 630-C4
BIRCH
- BEN 94510 551-B5
- ORIN 94563 630-G1
BIRCH AV
1900 ANT 94509 575-D6
2700 CNCD 94520 572-F7
BIRCH CT
- OAKL 94561 576-D4
2100 CCCo 94806 569-B4
6700 DBLN 94568 693-J3
BIRCH DR
- CCCo 94597 612-D2
BIRCH RD
- BEN 94510 551-D5
BIRCH ST
200 BREN 94513 616-G2
1300 PIT 94565 574-F3
2400 CCCo 94553 571-F4
BIRCHBARK PL
100 CCCo 94506 654-A3
BIRCH BARK RD
4300 CNCD 94521 593-B5
BIRCHBARK WY
- CCCo 94506 654-A3
BIRCHFIELD PL
9200 CCCo 94513 597-D6
BIRCHWOOD CT
600 CCCo 94506 654-A2
3900 CNCD 94519 573-A7
BIRCHWOOD DR
200 MRGA 94556 631-F4
800 PIT 94565 574-A3
800 PIT 94565 573-J3
BIRCHWOOD PL
- CCCo 94506 654-A2
- MRGA 94556 631-F5
BIRCHWOOD RD
500 BREN 94513 616-H1
BIRDHAVEN CT
800 LFYT 94549 611-G7
BIRDHAVEN WY
1600 PIT 94565 573-G4
BIRDIE CT
- RCH 94806 568-H6
BIRDSALL AV
2900 OAK 94619 650-F7
BIRDS HILL CT
1700 DNVL 94526 653-B6
BIRDSONG LN
- CCCo 94803 589-F3
BIRDWOOD CT
- SRMN 94582 674-B3
BIRKDALE PL
- MRGA 94556 631-E5
BIRMINGHAM CT
- CCCo 94513 617-F5
- OAKL 94561 596-D2
BIRMINGHAM DR
2900 RCH 94806 589-A1
2900 RCH 94806 588-J1
BIRMINGHAM ST
- OAKL 94561 596-D2
BISCAY CT
2200 CCCo 94514 617-H6
BISCAY DR
2000 PIT 94565 574-F4
BISCAY WY
400 CCCo 94514 617-H6
2500 WLCK 94598 592-F7
BISHOP AV
100 RCH 94801 608-C1
BISHOP CT
4600 CNCD 94521 593-C3
BISHOP DR
1600 CNCD 94521 593-C3
2400 SRMN 94583 673-D2
BISHOP LN
- WLCK 94596 632-D1
2500 ANT 94509 575-D1
BISHOP RD
- CCCo 94525 550-E5
BISHOP PINE LN
- CCCo 94803 569-D7
BISKRA WY
100 CCCo 94553 572-D3
BISMARCK LN
- BREN 94513 616-D4
BISMARCK TER
- BREN 94513 616-D4
BISON WY
4500 ANT 94531 595-G3
BISSELL AV
- RCH 94801 588-F7
2300 RCH 94804 588-H7
3500 RCH 94805 588-J7
3900 RCH 94805 589-A7
W BISSELL AV
100 RCH 94801 588-E6
BISSELL CT
800 RCH 94801 588-F6
BISSELL WY
200 RCH 94801 588-G7
BISSO LN
2300 CNCD 94520 592-E1
2400 CNCD 94520 572-E7
BIXLER RD
- CCCo 94513 597-F7
- CCCo 94513 617-F2
3100 CCCo 94514 637-F3
4100 CCCo 94513 637-F3
BLACHFORD CT
- OAK 94611 650-F2
BLACK AMBER WY
200 BREN 94513 616-C3
BLACK BERRY CT
- LFYT 94549 611-F2
BLACKBERRY LN
400 PIN 94564 569-C4
BLACKBIRD WY
2400 PLE 94566 694-D7
BLACKBRUSH LN
600 SRMN 94582 653-H7
BLACKBURN CT
1100 CNCD 94518 593-A6
BLACKBURN PEAK CT
4700 ANT 94531 595-E2
BLACK CALLA CT
- SRMN 94582 673-G2
BLACK DIAMOND DR
4600 ANT 94531 595-F3
BLACK DIAMOND ST
500 PIT 94565 574-D2
BLACK DIAMOND TR
- CCCo 94517 594-E6
- CCCo 94565 594-E4
- CLAY 94517 593-J6
- CLAY 94517 594-E6
BLACK FEATHER DR
3600 RCH 94803 589-G1
BLACKFIELD DR
2000 CNCD 94520 592-E3
BLACK FOREST CT
- LFYT 94549 611-A7
BLACK HAWK CT
1400 LFYT 94549 611-G3
BLACKHAWK DR
5000 CCCo 94506 653-J3
5000 CCCo 94506 654-A3
5400 CCCo 94588 654-D4
BLACK HAWK RD
3400 LFYT 94549 611-G3
BLACKHAWK RD
2000 CCCo 94506 653-F1
2000 DNVL 94506 653-F1
BLACKHAWK CLUB CT
- CCCo 94506 653-J4
BLACKHAWK CLUB DR
500 CCCo 94506 653-J3
500 CCCo 94506 654-A3
BLACKHAWK MEADOW CT
4200 CCCo 94506 654-C2
BLACKHAWK MEADOW DR
3100 CCCo 94506 654-C3
BLACKHAWK MEADOW PL
4200 CCCo 94506 654-C4
BLACKHAWK PLAZA CIR
4100 CCCo 94506 654-A5
4100 CCCo 94506 653-J5
BLACKHILLS PL
- CCCo 94506 654-A1
BLACK LEAF
300 PIT 94565 574-B3
BLACK OAK CT
- CCCo 94506 653-J3
500 ANT 94509 595-E2
1300 PIN 94564 569-E5
BLACK OAK RD
5000 CNCD 94521 593-D5
BLACK OAK WY
500 ANT 94509 595-E2
BLACK PINE LN
1100 PLHL 94523 591-J5
BLACK POINT CT
600 CLAY 94517 593-G6
BLACK POINT PL
700 CLAY 94517 593-G6
BLACKPOOL CT
100 CCCo 94506 654-B5
BLACKROCK PL
2100 MRTZ 94553 572-B2
BLACK ROCK ST
- BREN 94513 616-H2
BLACKSTONE CT
400 WLCK 94598 612-G3
400 DNVL 94506 653-J6
BLACK STONE DR
- BREN 94513 596-B6
BLACKSTONE DR
100 DNVL 94506 653-J6
1900 WLCK 94598 612-G3
BLACKSTONE RD
- DBLN 94568 694-F2
BLACKSTONE HOLLOW CT
- DNVL 94506 653-J6
BLACKTAIL CT
2500 ANT 94531 595-G3
BLACKTHORN CT
200 SRMN 94582 673-J6
BLACKTHORN DR
- LFYT 94549 611-A6
BLACK WALNUT CT
4400 CNCD 94521 593-B5
BLACK WALNUT PL
- HER 94547 569-J3
BLACKWOOD CT
- CCCo 94806 569-B4
2300 CCCo 94596 612-E7
BLACKWOOD DR
- CCCo 94553 592-B1
2000 CCCo 94806 569-B4
2000 CCCo 94596 612-D6
BLACKWOOD LN
1000 LFYT 94549 611-G6
BLADE CT
- CCCo 94595 612-B6
BLADE WY
- CCCo 94595 612-B6
BLAINE CIR
- MRGA 94556 651-E2
BLAINE CT
- CCCo 94565 573-F2
BLAINE LN
- CCCo 94548 597-B3
BLAIR AV
- PDMT 94611 650-A1
800 OAK 94611 630-C7
800 OAK 94611 650-C1
BLAIR CT
- DNVL 94526 652-G1
BLAIR PL
- OAK 94611 650-C1
- PDMT 94611 650-C1
BLAKE ST
6300 ELCR 94530 609-B1
BLAKEMORE CT
3400 PLE 94588 694-E5
BLAKESLEY CT
- SRMN 94582 674-B3
BLAKESLEY DR
- SRMN 94582 674-B3
BLANC CT
4400 OAKL 94561 576-E7
BLANCHARD LN
300 BEN 94510 551-B3
BLANCO CT
400 SRMN 94583 673-B3
BLARNEY AV
800 CNCD 94518 592-G6
BLARNEY CT
2600 CNCD 94518 592-G6
BLEACHER HOUSE RD
- CCCo 94553 571-F3
- MRTZ 94553 571-F3
BLEMER CT
- DNVL 94526 633-B7
BLEMER PL
- DNVL 94526 633-C7
BLEMER RD
900 DNVL 94526 633-B7
BLENHEIM LN
1200 CNCD 94521 593-A5
BLENHEIM WY
4300 CNCD 94521 593-A5
BLESSING DR
9400 PLE 94588 693-F6
BLISS AV
- PIT 94565 574-D4
BLISS CT
- PLHL 94523 592-B3
200 WLCK 94598 612-G2
2700 ANT 94531 595-H2
BLOCHING CIR
700 CLAY 94517 613-J1
BLOOMFIELD LN
- SRMN 94582 674-A4
BLOOMFIELD TER
- DBLN 94568 693-E4
BLOOMINGTON CT
8600 DBLN 94568 693-F2
BLOOMINGTON WY
11400 DBLN 94568 693-E2
BLOSSOM CT
100 DNVL 94506 653-F4
800 BREN 94513 616-D1
4100 OAKL 94561 596-C1
BLOSSOM DR
800 BREN 94513 596-D7
800 BREN 94513 616-D1
1800 ANT 94509 575-F6
BLOSSOM ST
3000 OAK 94601 650-C6
BLOSSOM RIDGE LN
- CCCo 94582 674-A2
BLUEBELL CIR
2700 ANT 94531 575-H7
BLUEBELL PL
100 VAL 94591 550-F1
BLUEBELL WY
7600 DBLN 94568 693-G2
BLUEBERRY CT
4400 CNCD 94521 593-B5
BLUEBIRD CT
100 HER 94547 569-H5
BLUE BIRD LN
- BREN 94513 596-E5
BLUEBONNET CT
2900 ANT 94531 575-H7
BLUE CANYON CT
100 MRTZ 94553 591-G1
BLUE CANYON WY
100 MRTZ 94553 591-G1
BLUECURL CT
2800 ANT 94531 575-H7
BLUE CYPRESS WY
- HER 94547 569-H3
BLUE FLAX CT
- BREN 94513 616-H5
BLUE FOX WY
7400 SRMN 94583 693-G1
BLUEGRASS WY
600 SRMN 94582 653-H7
BLUE GUM CT
- PLHL 94523 591-H2
BLUE HAVEN CT
- CCCo 94506 654-B4
BLUEHEART WY
- CCCo 94582 674-A2
BLUE HERON CT
- OAKL 94561 576-H7
BLUE JAY CIR
2100 PIN 94564 569-F7
BLUE JAY CT
1200 CNCD 94521 593-B4
BLUEJAY DR
3300 ANT 94509 575-F7
3300 ANT 94509 595-F1
BLUE LAKE CT
- CCCo 94561 597-E1
BLUE LAKE WY
1100 CNCD 94521 593-F7
BLUE MESA CT
- CCCo 94513 617-G4
BLUE MOUND CT
200 SRMN 94583 673-H6
BLUE MOUND DR
9600 SRMN 94583 673-H6
BLUE MOUNTAIN CT
1900 ANT 94531 595-E6
BLUE OAK CT
- BREN 94513 616-A3
1300 PIN 94564 569-E5
2000 CCCo 94506 653-G1
BLUE OAK LN
300 CLAY 94517 593-J5
BLUE RIDGE AV
- BREN 94513 596-B6
BLUE RIDGE DR
100 MRTZ 94553 591-G4
BLUEROCK CIR
2000 CNCD 94521 593-G3
BLUE ROCK CT
- DNVL 94526 653-E3
BLUEROCK CT
300 ANT 94509 595-E2
BLUEROCK DR
- ANT 94531 595-G2
100 ANT 94509 595-E2
BLUESAGE CT
- BREN 94513 616-E2
BLUE SKY CT
5200 ANT 94531 595-J5
BLUE SPRUCE DR
600 CCCo 94506 654-A3
BLUEWOOD CT
1700 CNCD 94521 593-D3
BLUFF CT
- HER 94547 569-H3
BLUM RD
4400 CCCo 94553 572-B6
BLUME DR
3200 RCH 94806 569-B7
3200 RCH 94806 589-B1
3200 CCCo 94806 569-B7
BLUMERT PL
- MRGA 94556 631-F2
BLURSPUR CIR
- CCCo 94506 654-D5
BLYTHE DR
3200 ANT 94509 595-C1
BLYTHEN WY
- OAK 94619 651-A4
12100 OAK 94619 650-J4
BOARDWALK
- SRMN 94583 673-B2
BOARDWALK PL
- RCH 94806 588-F1
BOARDWALK ST
3000 PLE 94588 694-G6
BOAT RAMP ST
- RCH 94804 608-E1
BOATSWAIN CT
300 HER 94547 570-B6
BOATWRIGHT DR
3900 CNCD 94519 593-A2
BOBBIE CT
- DNVL 94526 653-B1
BOBBIE DR
500 DNVL 94526 653-A1
BOBO CT
1400 PIT 94565 574-G4
BOBOLINK RD
- ORIN 94563 610-F5
BOBOLINK WY
100 HER 94547 569-H4
BOBWHITE CT
- OAKL 94561 596-B1
BOCA CANADA RD
1000 CCCo 94553 590-H4
BOCA RATON CT
- SRMN 94583 673-H7
300 WLCK 94598 612-J2
BOCMART PL
3700 SRMN 94583 673-C2
BODEGA CT
1600 WLCK 94597 611-J3
2100 PIT 94565 574-B3
2400 CCCo 94514 617-H7
BODEGA DR
2100 PIT 94565 574-B3
BODEGA PL
1300 WLCK 94597 611-J2
BODEGA ST
300 VAL 94591 550-E2
BODEGA WY
800 CCCo 94572 569-J2
800 CCCo 94572 570-A2
BODEN WY
500 OAK 94610 650-A3
BOIES CT
- PLHL 94523 592-A4
BOIES DR
2900 PLHL 94523 592-A4
BOLBONES CT
1900 WLCK 94595 632-B1
BOLDUC CT
100 CCCo 94806 589-B3
BOLE CT
- ANT 94509 595-F2
BOLERO CT
- DNVL 94526 653-C5
3000 PLE 94588 694-D6
BOLERO DR
300 DNVL 94526 653-C5
BOLGER PL
300 CCCo 94565 573-C1
BOLINAS PL
3900 CCCo 94514 617-G6
BOLIVAR PL
800 SRMN 94583 673-G5
BOLLA AV
- CCCo 94507 632-G4
BOLLA PL
400 CCCo 94507 632-H4
BOLLINGER CANYON LN
500 SRMN 94582 673-F2
BOLLINGER CANYON RD
- CCCo 94582 673-H2
- CCCo 94582 674-A4
- SRMN 94582 674-A4
900 MRGA 94575 631-H6
900 MRGA 94556 631-H6
1100 CCCo 94556 631-H6
1200 CCCo 94556 632-A7
1200 CCCo 94556 651-J1
1200 CCCo 94556 652-A1
2700 SRMN 94583 673-A1
3600 SRMN 94582 673-H2
13100 CCCo 94583 673-A1
18400 CCCo 94583 652-E3
18600 CCCo 94583 672-J1
BOLLINGER CANYON WY
600 SRMN 94582 673-F2
BOLLINGER ESTATES CT
300 CCCo 94583 652-F4
BOLTON CT
- CCCo 94506 654-B5
E BOLTON RD
- OAKL 94561 596-G3
W BOLTON RD
- OAKL 94561 596-G3
BOLTZEN CT
800 BREN 94513 616-J2
BOLTZEN ST
700 BREN 94513 616-H2
BOMBARDIER LN
- CCCo 94511 577-G4
BONA ST
2700 OAK 94601 650-C5
BONAIRE AV
100 HER 94547 570-C6
BONAIRE CT
300 DNVL 94506 653-J5
BONANZA ST
1500 WLCK 94596 612-C5
BONANZA WY
300 DNVL 94526 652-J3
BONARI CT
3500 CNCD 94519 592-J2
BOND CT
1100 ANT 94509 575-F7
BONDS LN
- RCH 94804 608-J1
S BONETTI RD
10300 SJCo 95206 638-G3
BONFIELD CT
7500 DBLN 94568 693-H2
BONHAM WY
400 OAK 94610 650-A2
BON HOMME WY
3600 CNCD 94518 592-H3
BONIFACIO ST
1900 CNCD 94520 592-F1
2600 CNCD 94519 592-G1
3000 CNCD 94519 572-G7
BONITA AV
- PDMT 94611 630-B7
100 PDMT 94611 650-B1
1200 BERK 94709 609-G7
2700 ANT 94509 575-E6
BONITA CT
100 CCCo 94572 569-J2
1200 CCCo 94595 612-B6
6300 RCH 94806 589-B3
BONITA LN
- CCCo 94595 612-B6
- ORIN 94563 610-F7
1200 WLCK 94595 612-B6
BONITA PL
- CCCo 94572 569-J2
BONITA RD
1400 RCH 94806 589-B3
1500 CCCo 94806 589-B3
BONITA WY
200 BREN 94513 596-G5
BONITA BAHIA
1300 BEN 94510 550-J3
BONNIE CT
- PLHL 94523 612-A1
BONNIE DR
- CCCo 94806 569-A5
400 ELCR 94530 609-E3
BONNIE LN
- BERK 94708 609-H5
- PLHL 94523 612-A1
100 DNVL 94526 653-B2
600 BREN 94561 596-E4
BONNIE PL
- PLHL 94523 612-A1
BONNIE BANKS WY
- SRFL 94901 587-B1
BONNIE CLARE LN
900 CNCD 94518 592-G4
BONNIEWOOD CT
7700 DBLN 94568 693-G2
BONNIEWOOD LN
7500 DBLN 94568 693-H2
BONNINGTON CT
- OAK 94611 630-E5
BONNY DOONE
- HER 94547 569-G4
BONRAVEN WY
5000 ANT 94531 595-J2
BONT LN
1100 WLCK 94596 612-B6
BONUM WY
- BREN 94513 616-D5
BONWELL DR
5000 CNCD 94521 593-D4
BOOKER ST
2500 OAK 94606 650-A4
BOONE CT
100 DNVL 94526 653-A3
BOONE DR
- BREN 94513 616-H1
BOONE DR E
- BREN 94513 616-H1
- CCCo 94513 616-H1
BORA PL
- PIT 94565 574-A2
BORDEAUX CT
- DNVL 94506 653-G5
100 MRTZ 94553 571-H5
BORDEAUX DR
4300 OAKL 94561 576-E7
4300 OAKL 94561 596-E1
BOREL LN
2000 DNVL 94526 653-D7
BORICA CT
- DBLN 94568 694-G5
BORICA DR
300 DNVL 94526 653-D5
BORICA PL
200 DNVL 94526 653-D5
BORIS CT
- WLCK 94597 612-B1
BORMIO CT
- DNVL 94526 653-D1
BOSEY CT
- RCH 94806 568-H6
BOSK AV
100 BREN 94513 596-G5
BOSTON AV
3100 OAK 94602 650-D4
BOSWORTH WK
- PLHL 94523 591-B1
BOTELHO DR
1500 WLCK 94596 612-C6
BOTELHO ST
1200 ANT 94509 575-F5
BOTTING CT
- ANT 94531 595-D4
BOTTLEBRUSH CT
- DNVL 94506 654-B6
BOULDER CT
5200 CNCD 94521 593-G3
BOULDER DR
200 ANT 94509 595-E1
BOULDER ST
- BREN 94513 596-D5
BOULDER CREEK CT
- DNVL 94526 653-E4
2200 MRTZ 94553 572-B2
BOULDERS CT
- RCH 94806 569-A7
BOULEVARD CIR
2300 WLCK 94595 612-B6
BOULEVARD CT
- CCCo 94595 612-A7
BOULEVARD WY
400 OAK 94610 650-A2
400 PDMT 94610 650-A2
700 CCCo 94595 612-A6
1100 WLCK 94595 612-A6
1100 WLCK 94597 612-A6
BOUNDARY OAK WY
400 WLCK 94598 613-A2
BOUNTIFUL CT
100 DNVL 94526 633-D6
BOUNTIFUL LN
- BREN 94513 616-D4
BOUNTY DR
600 CCCo 94565 573-D1
BOUNTY LN
- VAL 94590 550-B1
BOUNTY WY
- CCCo 94565 573-D1
BOUQUET AV
5800 CCCo 94805 589-B5
BOURNE CT
- CCCo 94506 654-B4
BOURNE LN
- CCCo 94506 654-B4
BOURTON CT
800 ANT 94509 575-C7
BOUWINA CT
3800 CNCD 94518 592-J5
BOWEN CT
- SRMN 94582 674-C4
BOWEN ST
4400 PLE 94588 694-E7
BOWER LN
- DBLN 94568 693-E5
BOWER PL
- DNVL 94526 653-A4
BOWHILL LN
2700 CCCo 94806 588-J3
2700 CCCo 94806 589-A2
BOWLES PL
- OAK 94610 650-C3
BOWLIN AV
2800 SRMN 94583 673-E6
BOWLING DR
- OAK 94618 630-A5
BOWLING GREEN CT
3100 WLCK 94598 612-J4
BOWLING GREEN DR
2800 WLCK 94598 612-J3

STREET
Block City ZIP Pg-Grid

BOWMORE CT
3300 WLCK 94598 612-J2
BOWSPIRIT LN
- HER 94547 569-H1
BOWSPRIT CT
2000 CCCo 94514 617-H6
BOX CANYON RD
2600 PIN 94564 569-H6
BOXER BLVD
4800 CNCD 94521 593-C4
BOXFORD PL
- SRMN 94583 673-F7
BOXILL CT
- ANT 94531 595-C4
BOXWOOD CT
- PIT 94565 573-F4
3700 CNCD 94519 573-F4
3700 CNCD 94519 593-A1
BOXWOOD DR
1800 CNCD 94519 593-A1
1800 CNCD 94519 573-A7
BOXWOOD LN
- HER 94547 569-H2
BOXWOOD WY
- DBLN 94568 694-D4
BOYD AV
700 RCH 94805 589-A5
BOYD CT
- DNVL 94526 652-J1
- PLHL 94523 592-A6
BOYD RD
- PLHL 94523 592-A6
W BOYD RD
700 PLHL 94523 592-A6
700 PLHL 94523 591-J6
BOYER CIR
3500 LFYT 94549 611-E7
BOYLE CT
1500 PIN 94564 569-D5
BOYLE WY
- ANT 94531 595-D4
BOYNTON AV
400 BERK 94707 609-G4
400 CCCo 94707 609-G4
1900 MRTZ 94553 571-F3
BRACKMAN LN
500 MRTZ 94553 571-E7
BRADBURY DR
500 LFYT 94549 631-J4
BRADENA LN
3100 LFYT 94549 611-J6
BRADFORD DR
500 RCH 94806 568-G6
BRADFORD PL
500 DNVL 94526 652-H1
BRADFORD ST
500 CCCo 94565 573-F1
BRADLEY AV
- WLCK 94596 612-D4
BRADLEY LN
- ANT 94509 574-J6
BRADY CT
600 MRTZ 94553 571-G5
BRADY ST
200 MRTZ 94553 571-G5
BRAEBURN CT
- SRMN 94583 693-H1
BRAEBURN WY
1500 BREN 94513 616-D2
BRAEMAR CT
- BREN 94513 616-D1
BRAEMAR RD
2000 OAK 94602 650-E2
BRAEMAR ST
- ANT 94531 596-A2
4500 ANT 94531 595-J2
BRAEMER CT
100 BEN 94510 551-B3
BRAGA LN
2600 SPAB 94806 588-J3
BRAMANTE CT
- OAKL 94561 576-G7
BRAMBLE CT
700 WLCK 94598 613-C4
BRAMBLEWOOD CT
- DNVL 94506 653-H3
BRAMBLEWOOD LN
100 PLHL 94523 591-H2
BRAMHALL ST
700 BREN 94513 616-F2
BRAMPTON CT
2100 WLCK 94598 612-G2
BRAMPTON PL
- BREN 94513 596-C6
BRAMPTON RD
2200 WLCK 94598 612-G2
E BRANCH PKWY
- CCCo 94582 674-B5
- SRMN 94582 674-B5
BRANCHWOOD CT
2400 RCH 94806 568-J7
BRANDING IRON CT
- DBLN 94568 694-E1
BRANDON CT
- PLHL 94523 592-A6
BRANDON PL
100 BEN 94510 551-C4
BRANDON RD
- PLHL 94523 592-B6
BRANDON ST
1000 PDMT 94611 630-A7
1000 OAK 94611 630-A7
BRANDON MILES WY
- BREN 94513 596-C5
BRANDON OAKS PL
- WLCK 94597 612-B2
BRANDT CT
2500 PIN 94564 569-F4
BRANDT DR
- MRGA 94556 651-F1
BRANDT ST
2500 PIN 94564 569-F4
BRANDY DR
- BREN 94561 596-D3
BRANDY ROCK WY
5000 OAK 94619 651-B6
BRANDYWINE LN
400 PLHL 94523 592-A4
BRANDYWINE PL
- CLAY 94517 594-A7
BRANDYWINE WY
100 WLCK 94598 612-J1
BRANN ST
5400 OAK 94619 650-G7
BRANNAN PL
700 CNCD 94518 592-H6
BRANNIGAN ST
- DBLN 94568 694-F4
BRANT WY
- ANT 94509 594-H1
BRANTFORD
2300 WLCK 94596 632-G2
BRASERO LN
- WLCK 94596 612-D5

BRAY CT
- DBLN 94568 694-A4
BRAZIL CT
200 OAKL 94561 596-G1
2500 ANT 94509 575-H6
3700 PIN 94564 569-J7
BRAZIL DR
2200 ANT 94509 575-H6
BREAKER CT
2100 CCCo 94514 617-H6
BREAKER DR
- CCCo 94565 553-E7
- CCCo 94565 573-E1
BREAKERS BLVD
- RCH 94804 608-J3
BREAKWATER WY
1100 BREN 94513 596-D7
BRECK CT
- MRGA 94556 631-G5
500 BEN 94510 550-H2
BRECKENRIDGE CT
1100 MRTZ 94553 571-H5
BRECKENRIDGE PL
300 MRTZ 94553 571-H5
BREEZEWALK DR
100 VAL 94591 550-D3
BREMEN ST
- DBLN 94568 694-F4
BRENDA CIR
4600 CNCD 94521 593-C3
BRENDA CT
200 PIN 94564 569-D4
1500 CNCD 94521 593-C3
BRENNAN CT
300 ANT 94509 575-E6
BRENNER
100 HER 94547 569-E3
BRENT CT
- LFYT 94549 631-J3
3500 PLE 94588 694-F5
BRENTWOOD AV
3300 RCH 94803 589-F2
BRENTWOOD BLVD
Rt#-4
1400 BREN 94513 596-G6
1500 CCCo 94513 617-A4
3900 BREN 94513 616-H3
6300 BREN 94561 596-G6
7300 CCCo 94513 616-H3
BRENTWOOD CIR
4200 CNCD 94521 593-C2
BRENTWOOD CT
1500 WLCK 94595 612-D7
BRENTWOOD DR
400 BEN 94510 550-J2
BRENTWOOD PL
- OAK 94602 650-E3
BRENTWOOD RD
1800 OAK 94602 650-E3
BRENTZ LN
1700 SPAB 94806 589-A3
BRET HARTE RD
- BERK 94708 609-H6
BRET HARTE WY
- BERK 94708 609-H6
BRETON DR
- BREN 94561 596-E4
BRETON PL
2600 WLCK 94598 592-F7
BRETT CT
1400 PIN 94564 569-D3
BREVENSVILLE DR
- SRMN 94583 693-F1
BREWIN CT
- SRMN 94583 693-F1
BREWIN LN
- SRMN 94583 693-F1
BREWSTER CT
1300 ELCR 94530 609-D1
BREWSTER DR
1100 ELCR 94530 609-D1
BRIA CT
100 CCCo 94597 612-A4
BRIAN CT
- SRMN 94583 693-G1
BRIAN RD
2400 CCCo 94806 569-B5
BRIAR DR
200 MRTZ 94553 591-H1
BRIAR PL
100 DNVL 94526 632-J7
BRIAR CANYON TR
- CCCo 94553 610-A4
- CCCo 94708 609-H4
- CCCo 94708 610-A4
BRIARCLIFF CT
4300 CNCD 94521 593-C2
BRIARCLIFF DR
3700 PIT 94565 574-F6
BRIARCREST CT
6100 WLCK 94595 632-D6
BRIARIDGE CT
200 PLHL 94523 591-J6
BRIAR OAKS DR
- SRMN 94582 673-J2
- SRMN 94582 674-A2
BRIARWOOD CT
- BREN 94513 616-E2
- CCCo 94597 612-E1
3500 ANT 94509 575-E7
3500 ANT 94509 595-E1
BRIARWOOD LN
8400 DBLN 94568 693-H2
BRIARWOOD WY
- CCCo 94597 612-D1
BRICKYARD AV
200 PIT 94565 574-B2
BRICKYARD WY
1200 RCH 94801 608-D3
BRICKYARD COVE RD
300 RCH 94801 608-D3
BRICKYARD COVE WY
- RCH 94801 608-E3
BRIDGE AV
1500 OAK 94601 650-C7
BRIDGE DRLP
- MRTZ 94553 571-F2
BRIDGE RD
- BERK 94705 630-B4
100 PLHL 94523 592-A7
400 CCCo 94595 612-B7
BRIDGE ST
1400 CNCD 94518 592-E6
BRIDGE CREEK DR
700 SRMN 94582 674-A7
BRIDGECROSSING WY
900 CNCD 94518 592-G5
BRIDGEFIELD RD
200 CCCo 94595 612-A7
BRIDGEHEAD RD
- MRTZ 94553 571-F1
- MRTZ 94553 551-F7
5500 OAKL 94561 576-A5
5500 OAKL 94509 576-A5

BRIDGEHEAD RD
5800 ANT 94509 576-A5
N BRIDGEPOINTE LN
- DBLN 94568 694-F2
S BRIDGEPOINTE LN
- DBLN 94568 694-G3
BRIDGEPORT AV
2800 SRMN 94583 673-E6
BRIDGEPORT LP
- CCCo 94513 617-F4
BRIDGEPORT WY
2200 MRTZ 94553 572-A6
BRIDGESIDE CIR
100 DNVL 94506 653-F5
BRIDGESTONE CIR
- DBLN 94568 694-E2
BRIDGE VIEW CT
- RCH 94801 608-E3
BRIDGEVIEW CT
- CCCo 94525 550-C4
300 BEN 94510 551-B4
BRIDGEVIEW DR
4300 OAK 94602 650-D3
BRIDGEVIEW PL
100 VAL 94591 550-D2
BRIDGEVIEW ST
1700 PIT 94565 573-F3
BRIDGEVIEW HEIGHTS PL
1800 BEN 94510 551-B4
BRIDGEWATER CIR
600 DNVL 94526 653-C3
BRIDGEWATER RD
500 DNVL 94526 653-C3
BRIDGEWATER WY
- PLHL 94523 591-B1
BRIDGEWAY CIR
3500 CCCo 94803 589-C3
BRIDLE CT
500 WLCK 94596 632-F2
4800 ANT 94531 595-J2
BRIDLE LN
2600 WLCK 94596 632-F2
BRIDLE WY
4900 ANT 94531 595-J3
BRIDLEPATH CT
- SRMN 94583 673-D4
BRIDLEWOOD CT
- CLAY 94517 613-J1
- PIT 94565 574-G7
BRIDLEWOOD DR
- PIT 94565 574-G6
BRIERTOWN CT
3400 WLCK 94598 612-J3
BRIGADOON WY
- DBLN 94568 693-D4
BRIGANTINE RD
100 VAL 94591 550-E2
BRIGHAM LN
400 DNVL 94526 633-A6
BRIGHTON
100 HER 94547 569-H2
BRIGHTON AV
1100 ALB 94706 609-D5
3500 OAK 94602 650-C3
BRIGHTON CT
- CCCo 94513 617-F5
1000 ANT 94509 575-F7
7400 DBLN 94568 693-H2
BRIGHTON DR
- BREN 94513 596-E6
2000 PIT 94565 574-F4
6800 DBLN 94568 693-H2
BRIGHTON PL
8100 DBLN 94568 693-H2
BRIGHTON ST
- SRMN 94582 674-A3
BRIGHTON WY
2200 WLCK 94598 612-G2
3200 ANT 94509 575-F7
BRIGHTWOOD CIR
- DNVL 94506 653-G2
BRIGHTWOOD CT
1000 WLCK 94598 592-E7
BRIGHTWOOD LN E
100 DNVL 94506 653-G2
BRIGHTWOOD LN W
- DNVL 94506 653-F1
BRIGHTWOOD WY
- DNVL 94506 653-G2
BRINK CT
900 CNCD 94518 592-F6
BRIONES CT
- CCCo 94565 573-H2
BRIONES RD
1000 CCCo 94553 591-E3
1000 CCCo 94553 611-A1
BRIONES VW
- ORIN 94563 611-A4
500 CCCo 94553 572-A3
BRIONES VALLEY RD
4200 BREN 94513 616-A5
4200 CCCo 94513 616-A5
4300 CCCo 94513 615-J6
4300 CCCo 94517 615-F5
BRISCOE LN
1800 CNCD 94521 593-F4
BRISDALE PL
- ANT 94509 575-C5
BRISTLECONE DR
2200 RCH 94803 589-F4
2200 CCCo 94803 589-F4
BRISTOL
100 HER 94547 569-J2
BRISTOL CT
- CCCo 94513 617-F5
- PLHL 94523 591-J6
200 CCCo 94506 654-A5
400 OAKL 94561 576-D7
500 BEN 94510 550-J1
1000 WLCK 94598 612-F1
3100 RCH 94806 589-A2
BRISTOL DR
6800 OAK 94705 630-C4
BRISTOL PL
200 PIT 94565 574-E7
BRISTOL RD
7800 DBLN 94568 693-H3
BRITAIN CT
200 CCCo 94507 632-H5
BRITANNIA DR
- SRMN 94582 674-A1
BRITTANY CT
600 BREN 94513 616-H1
800 CNCD 94518 592-F7
2400 ANT 94531 595-G1
BRITTANY DR
8000 DBLN 94568 693-F3
BRITTANY LN
800 CNCD 94518 592-F7
2200 MRTZ 94553 572-A6
11100 AlaC 94552 693-E3
11100 DBLN 94568 693-E3

BRITTANY HILLS CT
1100 MRTZ 94553 571-H5
BRITTANY HILLS DR
100 MRTZ 94553 571-H5
BRIXHAM WY
100 PLHL 94523 591-J4
BRIZA LP
- SRMN 94582 673-H2
BROADCREEK CT
1000 BREN 94513 596-C7
BROADMOOR
- MRGA 94556 631-D7
- MRGA 94556 651-D1
BROADMOOR AV
2700 CNCD 94520 572-E7
2700 CNCD 94520 592-E1
BROADMOOR CT
- SRMN 94583 693-H1
800 LFYT 94549 611-G7
BROADMOOR DR
9400 SRMN 94583 693-G1
9500 SRMN 94583 673-F4
BROADMORE AV
2100 CCCo 94806 569-B4
BROADVIEW TER
- ORIN 94563 630-J1
- ORIN 94563 631-A1
BROADWAY
- CCCo 94548 577-B7
- CCCo 94548 597-B1
- RCH 94804 588-H7
1300 WLCK 94596 612-C5
3200 OAK 94611 630-C4
4700 OAK 94618 630-A5
N BROADWAY
2000 WLCK 94596 612-C4
S BROADWAY
- CCCo 94596 612-D6
- WLCK 94596 612-D6
- WLCK 94596 632-D1
BROADWAY AV
1000 SPAB 94806 588-H1
N BROADWAY AV
- CCCo 94565 573-H2
S BROADWAY AV
500 CCCo 94565 573-H3
600 PIT 94565 573-H3
BROADWAY PZ
1200 WLCK 94596 612-C6
BROADWAY ST
1500 CNCD 94520 592-E2
BROADWAY TER
5300 OAK 94618 630-B6
5400 OAK 94611 630-D5
BROADWING CT
- SRMN 94582 673-H2
BROADWING WY
- SRMN 94582 673-H2
BROCATELLO CT
- ANT 94531 595-G2
BROCK LN
100 OAKL 94561 576-D6
BROCKET CT
2500 ANT 94531 595-G2
BROCKTON AV
9500 SRMN 94583 693-G1
BROCKTON DR
3700 PLE 94588 694-F5
BRODER BLVD
5300 DBLN 94568 694-C3
BRODERICK DR
- BREN 94513 596-G7
BRODIA CT
- MRTZ 94553 571-H4
BRODIA WY
100 CCCo 94598 612-F4
BROMFIELD CT
2200 WLCK 94596 632-G2
BRONCHO LN
3100 CCCo 94598 613-A4
BRONCO CT
- SRMN 94583 673-B3
5000 ANT 94531 595-J3
BRONSON LN
800 CCCo 94596 612-E6
800 WLCK 94596 612-E6
BROOK CT
500 ANT 94509 595-C1
BROOK ST
2000 CNCD 94520 572-E6
3500 LFYT 94549 611-E7
BROOK WY
2800 CCCo 94806 589-A3
BROOKBANK RD
- ORIN 94563 610-G4
BROOKCREST WY
5000 ANT 94531 595-J4
5000 ANT 94531 596-A4
BROOKDALE AV
- CCCo 94507 632-E2
2700 OAK 94602 650-C5
2700 OAK 94601 650-C5
3500 OAK 94619 650-E6
BROOKDALE CIR
3600 ANT 94509 595-E1
BROOKDALE CT
- CCCo 94507 632-E1
- LFYT 94549 611-G7
1200 BREN 94513 616-D2
2900 CNCD 94518 592-G5
3500 ANT 94509 575-E7
3500 ANT 94509 595-E1
7300 DBLN 94568 693-J3
BROOKDALE DR
1000 BREN 94513 616-E2
BROOKFIELD CT
5100 ANT 94531 596-A3
BROOKFIELD DR
- MRGA 94556 651-E2
BROOKHAVEN CIR
- CCCo 94513 617-F2
BROOKHAVEN CT
2200 SPAB 94806 588-H3
BROOKHAVEN WY
5000 ANT 94531 595-J4
BROOK HOLLOW CT
5000 CNCD 94521 593-D5
BROOKLINE
100 MRGA 94556 631-C7
BROOKLINE DR
- CCCo 94598 612-D2
BROOKLYN AV
600 OAK 94606 650-A4
BROOKPARK RD
12500 OAK 94619 651-A5
BROOKS AV
2300 RCH 94804 588-H6
2600 ELCR 94530 589-B6
BROOKS CT
- OAKL 94561 596-C2
800 BREN 94513 616-J2
BROOKS DR
- OAKL 94561 596-C2

BROOKS ST
700 BREN 94513 616-H2
1500 WLCK 94596 612-B5
BROOKSHIRE CT
- PIT 94565 574-B4
BROOKSIDE AV
- BERK 94705 630-A4
1100 SPAB 94805 589-A4
6100 OAK 94618 630-A5
BROOKSIDE CT
400 ANT 94509 595-E1
5100 CNCD 94521 593-D5
5300 PLE 94588 693-J6
BROOKSIDE DR
100 ANT 94509 595-D1
200 CCCo 94801 588-F2
600 DNVL 94526 653-B3
800 RCH 94801 588-F2
1100 SPAB 94806 588-F2
3200 MRTZ 94553 571-E5
3700 PIT 94565 574-D6
BROOKSIDE LN
5100 CNCD 94521 593-E5
BROOKSIDE PL
100 DNVL 94526 653-B4
BROOKSIDE RD
- ORIN 94563 630-J2
BROOKSVIEW CT
700 MRTZ 94553 571-F4
BROOKTRAIL CT
- PIT 94565 573-G4
BROOKTRAIL DR
- PIT 94565 573-G4
BROOKTREE CT
- PIT 94565 574-C4
BROOKTREE DR
- DNVL 94506 653-G1
BROOKVIEW CIR
1200 CNCD 94520 592-D5
BROOKVIEW DR
300 OAKL 94561 576-G7
1100 CNCD 94520 592-D5
BROOKWOOD CT
- CCCo 94549 591-H7
500 BREN 94513 616-E1
5300 RCH 94803 590-A3
BROOKWOOD DR
3200 CCCo 94549 591-H7
BROOKWOOD LN
5400 RCH 94803 590-A3
BROOKWOOD PL
600 OAK 94610 650-A3
BROOKWOOD RD
- CCCo 94553 591-F3
- ORIN 94563 630-H1
1000 OAK 94610 650-B3
BROOMTAIL CT
4700 ANT 94531 596-A3
BROWER CT
- SRMN 94582 674-A2
BROWER WY
- CCCo 94582 674-A2
- SRMN 94582 674-A2
BROWN AV
1000 LFYT 94549 611-F5
3600 OAK 94619 650-F5
BROWN CT
- CCCo 94553 572-B7
BROWN DR
100 CCCo 94553 572-B7
3300 LFYT 94549 611-G4
BROWN LN
1800 CCCo 94509 575-H5
BROWN RD
3600 OAKL 94561 596-D1
BROWN ST
200 MRTZ 94553 571-E3
BROWNELL CT
- CNCD 94521 593-F7
BROWNING CT
3000 BREN 94513 616-G3
BROWNING DR
4000 CNCD 94518 592-J5
BROWN RANCH RD
- AlaC 94546 651-G5
- CCCo 94556 651-G5
BROWNSTONE RD
300 OAKL 94561 596-F3
BROWNTAIL WY
- CCCo 94582 674-A2
BROWNWOOD CT
1800 CNCD 94521 593-F4
BRUBAKER CT
- WLCK 94596 612-D6
BRUBAKER DR
- WLCK 94596 612-D6
BRUCE CT
- PLHL 94523 592-A6
BRUCE DR
5300 CCCo 94588 654-G6
5300 PLE 94588 694-F7
BRUCE ST
1600 ANT 94509 575-E5
3500 OAK 94602 650-B4
BRUNELL DR
3200 OAK 94602 650-G4
BRUNELL PL
- OAK 94602 650-G4
BRUNO AV
- PIT 94565 574-C3
BRUNO CT
- CCCo 94803 589-E2
BRUNO RD
4700 CCCo 94803 589-E3
BRUNS CT
5900 OAK 94611 650-D1
BRUNS RD
4900 AlaC 94551 (657-H5 See Page 638)
5500 AlaC 94514 (657-H5 See Page 638)
5500 CCCo 94514 (657-J2 See Page 638)
N BRUNS WY
6000 CCCo 94514 (657-H1 See Page 638)
BRUNSWICK CT
9900 SRMN 94583 673-F5
BRUNSWICK ST
2200 CNCD 94520 572-G4
BRUNSWICK WY
9800 SRMN 94583 673-F5
BRUSH CREEK CT
- PIT 94565 574-C7
BRUSH CREEK DR
2000 PIT 94565 574-D7
BRUSH CREEK PL
1600 DNVL 94526 653-B6
BRUSHWOOD PL
100 BREN 94513 596-G5
BRUTUS CT
400 WLCK 94598 612-E2
BRYAN AV
- ANT 94509 575-E6

BRYAN CT
- CCCo 94507 633-C4
BRYAN DR
300 CCCo 94507 633-C4
BRYANT AV
- DBLN 94568 694-A4
BRYANT WY
- ORIN 94563 610-H7
- ORIN 94563 630-H1
BRYCE AV
- PIT 94565 574-D7
BRYCE DR
2100 MRTZ 94553 572-A7
BRYCE CANYON CT
100 SRMN 94582 653-G7
BRYCE CANYON PL
- SRMN 94582 653-G7
BRYN MAWR CT
- SRMN 94583 673-H7
N BUCHAN DR
900 LFYT 94549 611-H6
S BUCHAN DR
900 LFYT 94549 611-J6
N BUCHANAN CIR
400 CCCo 94553 572-B7
S BUCHANAN CIR
- CCCo 94553 572-B7
BUCHANAN CT
4200 PIT 94565 574-E6
BUCHANAN LN
- DNVL 94526 633-C6
BUCHANAN PL
4300 PIT 94565 574-C7
BUCHANAN RD
200 PIT 94565 574-C6
1100 ANT 94509 575-A6
1700 CCCo 94565 574-G6
2100 ANT 94509 574-G6
BUCHANAN ST
700 BEN 94510 551-D5
700 ALB 94706 609-D6
800 ALB 94710 609-D6
BUCHANAN STEX
800 ALB 94710 609-B6
BUCKBOARD WY
4700 RCH 94803 589-J3
4800 RCH 94803 590-A2
BUCKEYE AV
- OAK 94618 630-B6
BUCKEYE CT
- ANT 94531 595-H2
- BREN 94561 596-E4
- DBLN 94568 693-E4
300 LFYT 94549 611-J6
500 BEN 94510 550-J1
500 BEN 94510 551-A1
1500 PIN 94564 569-E5
BUCKEYE LN
- DNVL 94526 653-B1
100 VAL 94591 550-F1
BUCKEYE PL
- BREN 94561 596-F4
BUCKEYE TER
- CLAY 94517 593-H6
BUCKEYE WY
- ANT 94531 595-G2
BUCKINGHAM BLVD
6800 OAK 94705 630-C3
BUCKINGHAM CT
700 WLCK 94598 613-A3
BUCKINGHAM DR
- BREN 94513 616-D3
- MRGA 94556 631-E3
4100 CCCo 94506 654-A5
8300 ELCR 94530 609-D1
BUCKINGHAM PL
800 CCCo 94506 654-B5
BUCKLEY
100 HER 94547 569-F3
BUCKLEY CT
- OAK 94602 650-G3
BUCKLEY ST
100 MRTZ 94553 571-D3
BUCK MOUNTAIN CT
- ANT 94531 595-F4
BUCKSKIN DR
4200 ANT 94531 595-G2
BUCKSKIN RD
2800 PIN 94564 569-H7
BUCKSKIN TER
800 BREN 94513 616-E1
BUCKTHORN CT
2900 ANT 94531 575-H7
4400 CNCD 94521 593-C5
BUCKTHORN PL
- CCCo 94507 632-H4
BUD CT
- PLHL 94523 592-C5
BUELL ST
3700 OAK 94619 650-G7
3700 OAK 94613 650-G7
BUENA AV
1500 BERK 94703 609-F7
BUENA TIERRA ST
1800 BEN 94510 551-D5
BUENA VENTURA AV
6100 OAK 94605 650-H7
BUENA VIDA CT
200 MRTZ 94553 571-F5
BUENA VISTA
- BEN 94510 551-A3
- ORIN 94563 630-J3
- PIT 94565 574-C6
BUENA VISTA AV
- RCH 94801 608-D1
2200 WLCK 94597 612-B2
2300 CCCo 94597 612-B3
5600 OAK 94618 630-B5
BUENA VISTA DR
- DNVL 94526 653-B2
400 PIN 94564 569-E4
BUENA VISTA PL
- OAK 94618 630-B5
700 WLCK 94597 612-B3
BUENA VISTA ST
1400 BREN 94513 616-D1
BUENA VISTA WY
2500 BERK 94708 609-H7
BUENO CT
- DNVL 94526 653-A1
BUENOS AIRES CT
2600 WLCK 94597 612-B2
BUFFALO CT
- ANT 94531 595-G5
BUGLE WY
2600 ANT 94531 595-G2
BULLARD DR
6000 OAK 94611 630-D7
6100 OAK 94611 650-D1
BUNCE MEADOWS DR
- CCCo 94507 632-G4
BUNDROS CT
2300 MRTZ 94553 571-F4

BUNKER CT
- RCH 94806 568-H5
BUNKER ST
200 MRTZ 94553 571-D3
BURBANK CT
300 ANT 94509 575-E6
BURBANK DR
4000 CNCD 94521 593-A2
BURBANK RD
300 ANT 94509 575-E6
BURBECK AV
1300 RCH 94801 588-G5
BURDECK CT
- OAK 94602 650-F3
BURDECK DR
2900 OAK 94602 650-F3
BURDICK DR
500 CCCo 94565 573-C1
BURGESS CT
100 DNVL 94526 653-D6
BURGESS WY
- CCCo 94803 589-E1
BURGHLEY LN
- BREN 94513 616-D5
BURGOS CT
- SRMN 94583 673-C3
BURGUNDY CT
100 MRTZ 94553 571-H5
BURGUNDY DR
4500 OAKL 94561 576-D7
BURLEIGH PL
200 DNVL 94526 653-C3
BURL HOLLOW CT
1800 WLCK 94596 612-H7
BURLINGAME AV
5100 RCH 94804 609-B3
BURLINGTON CT
1000 WLCK 94598 612-J4
BURLINGTON ST
2400 OAK 94602 650-E4
BURLINGTON WY
3000 WLCK 94598 612-J4
BURLWOOD CT
- PIT 94565 573-F4
BURMA RD
1800 CNCD 94518 592-F6
BURNBRAE LN
- SRMN 94582 674-C3
BURNETT AV
1000 CNCD 94520 592-C2
BURNEY CREEK PL
600 SRMN 94582 694-A1
BURNHAM CT
- PLHL 94523 592-B4
BURNHAM DR
1000 PIT 94565 574-B2
BURNHAM WY
7400 DBLN 94568 693-J3
BURNING TREE CT
400 SRMN 94583 673-H6
BURNING TREE WY
- CNCD 94521 593-B4
BURNING TREES DR
3200 SRMN 94583 673-H7
BURNS CIR
500 SRMN 94583 673-E4
BURNS CT
- SRMN 94583 673-E4
100 PLHL 94523 592-B7
7800 ELCR 94530 609-E2
BURNSIDE CT
1900 CNCD 94521 593-G4
BURNSWORTH PL
- CNCD 94518 592-F5
BURNT OAK CIR
- LFYT 94549 631-J3
BURR CT
- LFYT 94549 631-J3
BURR KNOT WY
300 BREN 94513 616-C3
BURRWOOD CT
3800 CNCD 94521 592-J3
BURTON AV
2100 PIT 94565 574-C4
BURTON CT
100 DNVL 94526 653-C6
3200 LFYT 94549 631-H2
BURTON DR
500 LFYT 94549 631-H2
2800 OAK 94611 650-G1
BURTON ST
7100 DBLN 94568 693-J3
BURTON VISTA CT
- LFYT 94549 631-G1
BURWOOD WY
500 ANT 94509 595-E1
BUSH AV
1100 SolC 94591 550-E1
1300 SPAB 94806 588-G4
2300 RCH 94806 588-H4
BUSH ST
900 MRTZ 94553 571-E4
1300 CCCo 94553 571-E4
BUSHMINT PL
- CCCo 94507 632-H4
BUSINESS CENTER DR
- BREN 94513 596-G6
BUSKIRK AV
2300 PLHL 94523 592-D6
2900 CCCo 94597 612-C1
3000 PLHL 94523 612-C1
3200 PLHL 94597 592-C7
3300 CCCo 94523 592-C7
BUSTOS CIR
400 CCCo 94565 573-D1
BUSTOS PL
400 CCCo 94565 573-D1
BUSTOS WY
- CCCo 94565 573-D1
BUTLER
- OAKL 94561 596-G3
BUTTE AV
3000 SRMN 94583 673-G7
BUTTE CT
100 CCCo 94565 573-E2
BUTTE ST
1600 RCH 94804 609-C3
BUTTERCUP CT
- CCCo 94507 632-G2
100 HER 94547 570-A4
2800 ANT 94531 575-H7
BUTTERCUP LN
400 PLHL 94523 591-J3
BUTTERFIELD PL
400 MRGA 94556 651-F3
BUTTERNUT ST
3000 ANT 94509 575-J6
BUTTERNUT WY
1100 CNCD 94521 593-G7
BUTTERS DR
2700 OAK 94602 650-G3
BUTTNER CT
1800 PLHL 94523 591-H5

STREET Block	City	ZIP	Pg-Grid
BUTTNER RD			
1900	PLHL	94523	591-J5
BUTTONS CT			
1400	OAKL	94561	576-D7
BUTTONWOOD CT			
-	ANT	94509	595-E2
BUTTONWOOD DR			
500	CCCo	94506	654-A2
BUTTONWOOD WY			
-	ANT	94509	595-E2
BUTTRESS CT			
4500	CNCD	94518	593-A6
BUXTON CIR			
100	PLHL	94523	591-J4
BUZZIE CT			
600	LFYT	94549	631-H2
BYER RD			
3100	CCCo	94514	637-E2
BYERLEY CT			
-	CCCo	94507	632-J2
BYNUM CT			
600	OAKL	94561	576-E5
BYNUM WY			
1300	OAKL	94561	576-D5
BYRDEE WY			
600	CCCo	94549	591-G4
BYRON CT			
-	CNCD	94521	593-F7
100	PLHL	94523	592-A7
500	BEN	94510	550-H1
3400	PLE	94588	694-E6
BYRON DR			
-	PLHL	94523	592-A7
BYRON HWY			
8100	CCCo	94513	597-D3
9500	CCCo	94513	617-D4
BYRON HWY Rt#-J4			
6800	CCCo	94513	617-D7
10600	CCCo	94513	637-D1
10600	CCCo	94514	637-D1
17600	CCCo	94514	(657-G1 See Page 638)
19100	CCCo	94514	(658-A3 See Page 638)
BYRON HWY Rt#-4			
1900	CCCo	94513	617-D5
BYRON LN			
-	CCCo	94582	674-B5
BYRON-BETHANY RD Rt#-J4			
17900	SJCo	95391	(658-D6 See Page 638)
20200	AlaC	94551	(658-B4 See Page 638)
20200	CCCo	94514	(658-B4 See Page 638)
BYRON HOT SPRINGS RD			
5500	CCCo	94514	637-F7
5800	CCCo	94514	(657-F1 See Page 638)
BYWOOD DR			
1900	OAK	94602	650-E2
C			
C ST			
-	CCCo	94525	550-A5
-	CCCo	94565	573-E1
-	CNCD	94520	572-J3
100	MRTZ	94553	571-E4
300	ANT	94509	575-D4
400	RCH	94801	588-E6
4300	PIT	94565	574-C4
7100	ELCR	94530	609-E4
W C ST			
700	BEN	94510	551-B6
CABALLO RANCHERO CT			
2200	CCCo	94528	633-F7
CABALLO RANCHERO DR			
2200	CCCo	94528	633-E6
CABANA CT			
300	DNVL	94526	653-D7
CABERNET CT			
-	LFYT	94549	611-A7
-	ORIN	94563	611-A7
100	CLAY	94517	593-H7
900	OAKL	94561	596-D1
CABERNET LN			
-	CCCo	94513	597-A5
CABOOSE PL			
200	DNVL	94526	653-B5
CABOT CT			
500	WLCK	94598	612-F2
CABOT DR			
1800	WLCK	94598	612-E2
5600	OAK	94611	630-D7
CABRILHO DR			
4000	CCCo	94553	571-J3
CABRILLO AV			
3000	SRMN	94583	673-G7
CABRILLO CT			
2700	ANT	94509	575-A6
CABRILLO LN			
-	HER	94547	569-G3
CABRILLO PL			
-	OAK	94611	630-E7
300	PIT	94565	574-B5
CABRILLO PT			
1100	CCCo	94514	617-H5
CABRILLO ST			
1200	ELCR	94530	609-D2
CABRILLO NORTE			
5500	RCH	94803	589-J3
CABRILLO SUR			
5500	RCH	94803	589-J3
5500	RCH	94803	590-A3
CACHE PEAK DR			
4700	ANT	94531	595-E3
CACTUS CT			
-	WLCK	94595	632-B2
CADDIE CT			
-	RCH	94806	568-H5
2500	BREN	94513	616-B2
CADDIE LN			
2400	BREN	94513	616-B2
CADIZ LN			
-	ANT	94509	574-J6
-	ANT	94509	575-A6
CAFE CT			
-	DNVL	94506	654-C6
CAFETO CT			
100	WLCK	94598	612-H2
CAFETO DR			
3000	WLCK	94598	612-H2
CAITLIN CT			
-	PLHL	94523	592-B4
CAITLIN PK			
1100	WLCK	94597	612-B1
CAJON CT			
1500	ANT	94509	575-A7
CALAIS DR			
200	PIN	94564	569-E3
2800	SRMN	94583	673-F6
CALAVERAS AV			
4800	OAK	94619	650-G7
CALAVERAS CIR			
1900	ANT	94509	575-G6
CALAVERAS CT			
600	MRTZ	94553	571-E7
1900	ANT	94509	575-G6
CALAVERAS DR			
1900	CCCo	94565	573-H2
4100	CNCD	94521	593-A3
CALCOT PL			
1000	OAK	94606	650-A7
CALDECOTT LN			
100	OAK	94618	630-B4
100	OAK	94611	630-B4
CALDER LN			
1100	WLCK	94598	612-D3
CALDERA WY			
4000	ANT	94509	595-F1
CALDERWOOD CT			
4800	OAK	94605	651-A7
CALDWELL CT			
-	PLHL	94523	592-B4
CALDWELL RD			
700	OAK	94611	630-C5
CALGARY LN			
2100	CNCD	94520	572-F5
CALHOUN CT			
2300	ANT	94509	595-A1
CALHOUN ST			
-	ALB	94706	609-C6
CALICO CT			
-	CCCo	94582	674-B1
CALICO WY			
700	OAKL	94561	576-D4
CALIENTE RD			
8300	CCCo	94803	589-F1
CALIFORNIA			
300	RCH	94801	588-B6
CALIFORNIA AV			
-	ORIN	94563	610-E6
200	PIT	94565	574-D3
1300	SPAB	94806	588-G4
N CALIFORNIA BLVD			
1300	WLCK	94596	612-C4
S CALIFORNIA BLVD			
1100	WLCK	94596	612-C6
CALIFORNIA ST			
100	CCCo	94572	549-J6
700	CCCo	94572	569-J1
800	CCCo	94572	570-A1
1300	BERK	94703	609-F7
2100	CNCD	94520	592-F2
2800	OAK	94602	650-E4
3500	OAK	94619	650-F5
CALIFORNIA DELTA HWY Rt#-4			
-	ANT	94509	574-H4
-	ANT	94509	575-H7
-	ANT	94531	575-H7
-	ANT	94531	576-B5
-	CCCo	94520	572-C6
-	CCCo	94553	572-C6
-	CCCo	94565	573-C3
-	CNCD	94519	572-C6
-	CNCD	94520	572-C6
-	CNCD	94520	573-C3
-	CNCD	94565	572-C6
-	CNCD	94565	573-C3
-	PIT	94565	573-C3
-	PIT	94565	574-H4
600	OAKL	94561	576-B5
900	ANT	94509	576-B5
900	OAKL	94509	576-B5
1400	BREN	94513	596-G7
1500	CCCo	94513	617-A4
3900	BREN	94513	616-G1
4000	OAKL	94561	596-G7
6000	BREN	94561	596-G7
6000	CCCo	94561	596-G7
7200	CCCo	94514	617-A4
7300	CCCo	94513	616-G1
9900	CCCo	94514	(618-B7 See Page 597)
14300	SJCo	95206	(618-J7 See Page 597)
15100	SJCo	95206	638-H1
CALISESI CT			
-	OAKL	94561	576-C7
CALISTOGA CT			
-	DNVL	94526	653-C7
CALISTOGA DR			
200	PIT	94565	574-D5
CALISTOGA WY			
5600	CLAY	94517	593-F6
CALLAHAN RD			
-	AlaC	94546	651-J5
-	AlaC	94546	652-A4
-	CCCo	94556	652-A4
CALLAN ST			
7700	DBLN	94568	693-H2
CALLAWAY PL			
-	DBLN	94568	694-H3
CALLE ARROYO			
1600	CCCo	94528	633-E7
CALLE ARROYO LN			
-	CCCo	94528	633-D7
CALLE DEL CASARILLO			
-	CCCo	94528	633-F7
CALLE DE ORO			
4800	OAKL	94561	576-A6
CALLE DIABLO CT			
-	BREN	94513	596-D7
CALLE ESTE			
-	WLCK	94597	612-D1
CALLE FLORES			
300	CCCo	94553	572-D3
CALLE LA MESA			
100	MRGA	94556	631-E2
CALLE LA MONTANA			
100	MRGA	94556	631-D2
CALLE LOS CALLADOS			
2000	CCCo	94528	633-F7
CALLE MOLINO			
300	CCCo	94553	572-D3
CALLE NOGALES			
100	WLCK	94597	612-D1
CALLE VERDE			
900	MRTZ	94553	591-G4
CALLE VERDE RD			
7500	DBLN	94568	693-G4
CALLIA CT			
200	OAKL	94561	576-C7
200	OAKL	94561	596-C1
CALMAR AV			
600	OAK	94610	650-A3
CALMAR VISTA RD			
600	DNVL	94526	652-H1
CALPINE PL			
2700	CNCD	94518	592-G6
CALSITE CT			
100	ANT	94509	595-F2
CALSPRAY ST			
700	RCH	94801	588-F5
CALVERT CT			
-	SRMN	94582	673-H2
-	OAK	94611	650-C1
-	PDMT	94611	650-C1
300	ANT	94509	595-E1
CALVERT WY			
-	SRMN	94582	673-H2
CALVIN CT			
-	CCCo	94595	612-A7
-	ORIN	94563	631-B3
CALVIN DR			
-	ORIN	94563	631-B2
CAMARA CIR			
2500	CNCD	94520	592-F4
CAMARITAS CT			
100	DNVL	94526	653-D5
CAMARITAS WY			
300	DNVL	94526	653-D5
CAMARONES PL			
3300	SRMN	94583	673-G5
CAMASSIA WY			
-	SRMN	94582	673-J2
CAMBARK CT			
-	CCCo	94553	571-J3
-	CCCo	94553	572-A3
CAMBELL BLVD			
-	ALA	94501	650-A7
CAMBERLY CT			
-	CCCo	94583	673-B5
CAMBERLY LN			
-	SRMN	94582	674-B3
CAMBRA CT			
-	DNVL	94526	652-J3
CAMBRIA CT			
-	PIT	94565	574-E2
CAMBRIA LN			
-	PIT	94565	574-E2
CAMBRIAN AV			
-	PDMT	94611	650-D2
CAMBRIAN PL			
-	BREN	94513	596-E6
CAMBRIAN WY			
500	DNVL	94526	653-D6
CAMBRIDGE			
-	HER	94547	569-J2
CAMBRIDGE AV			
200	CCCo	94708	609-G3
CAMBRIDGE CT			
-	CCCo	94513	617-F5
-	DNVL	94526	652-H1
3600	PLE	94588	694-E5
CAMBRIDGE DR			
-	CCCo	94513	617-F5
500	BEN	94510	550-H1
1100	LFYT	94549	611-C4
2300	ANT	94509	594-H2
2300	ANT	94509	595-A2
CAMBRIDGE PL			
3200	CNCD	94518	592-H3
CAMBRIDGE WY			
-	CCCo	94513	617-F5
-	PDMT	94611	650-A1
CAMBY RD			
2900	ANT	94509	575-C7
3100	ANT	94509	595-C1
CAMDEN CT			
100	SRMN	94582	673-G4
1300	BREN	94513	596-D6
CAMDEN LN			
-	HER	94547	569-E3
CAMDEN ST			
4400	OAK	94619	650-F7
CAMDON CT			
3100	PLE	94588	694-F6
CAMEL LN			
2000	WLCK	94596	612-E7
2000	WLCK	94596	632-E1
CAMEL RD			
2000	BEN	94510	551-D5
CAMELBACK CT			
-	PLHL	94523	592-B2
CAMELBACK DR			
2300	ANT	94509	595-A2
CAMELBACK PL			
900	PLHL	94523	592-B1
CAMELBACK RD			
-	BREN	94513	616-B4
200	PLHL	94523	592-B1
CAMELFORD CT			
-	MRGA	94556	631-E3
-	OAK	94611	650-F2
CAMELFORD PL			
-	OAK	94611	650-F2
CAMELIA CT			
1500	OAKL	94561	576-D7
2100	PIT	94565	574-A3
CAMELIA LN			
100	CCCo	94595	612-B6
200	LFYT	94549	611-A5
CAMELIA ST			
800	BERK	94710	609-D7
1100	BERK	94702	609-D7
CAMELLA CT			
-	CNCD	94518	592-E5
-	HER	94547	569-H1
CAMELLIA CT			
400	BEN	94510	551-A1
CAMELOT CT			
-	CCCo	94707	609-F4
-	CCCo	94507	632-J2
3600	PLE	94588	694-E5
4100	PIT	94565	574-E6
CAMEO CT			
-	PLE	94588	693-G7
-	WLCK	94597	612-B2
CAMEO DR			
100	DNVL	94526	633-C7
CAMERON AV			
3600	PLE	94588	694-F7
CAMERON CIR			
300	SRMN	94583	673-E4
CAMERON CT			
-	DNVL	94506	653-F1
1800	CNCD	94518	592-F5
CAMERON DR			
-	WLCK	94596	612-D4
-	WLCK	94597	612-D4
CAMILLE AV			
100	CCCo	94507	632-G7
CAMILLE CT			
100	CCCo	94507	632-G7
CAMILLE LN			
900	CCCo	94507	632-G7
900	CCCo	94507	652-G1
CAMILLE PL			
-	CCCo	94507	632-G7
900	DNVL	94526	632-G7
CAMILLIA PL			
-	OAK	94602	650-E3
CAMINAR WY			
100	CCCo	94596	612-E5
100	WLCK	94596	612-E5
CAMINO CT			
-	DNVL	94526	653-A2
CAMINO CT			
-	LFYT	94549	611-J5
CAMINO AMIGO			
600	DNVL	94526	652-H1
800	DNVL	94526	632-G7
CAMINO AMIGO CT			
100	DNVL	94526	652-H2
CAMINO ANDRES			
300	CCCo	94565	573-E2
CAMINO ARROYO E			
300	CCCo	94506	654-B7
CAMINO ARROYO W			
400	CCCo	94506	654-B7
CAMINO COLORADOS			
3100	LFYT	94549	631-H4
CAMINO DE JUGAR			
2400	SRMN	94583	673-B3
2400	CCCo	94583	673-B3
CAMINO DEL CIELO			
-	ORIN	94563	610-E7
CAMINO DEL DIABLO			
-	ORIN	94563	610-E6
CAMINO DEL MONTE			
-	ORIN	94563	610-E7
CAMINO DEL RIO			
900	LFYT	94549	611-H7
CAMINO DEL SOL			
-	CCCo	94553	571-J4
100	VAL	94591	550-E3
CAMINO DIABLO			
-	CCCo	94513	(636-E2 See Page 635)
-	CCCo	94517	(636-E2 See Page 635)
800	CCCo	94513	637-C3
800	CCCo	94514	(636-J4 See Page 635)
800	CCCo	94514	637-F3
1200	WLCK	94595	612-A5
1200	WLCK	94597	612-A5
2300	CCCo	94597	612-A5
2500	LFYT	94549	611-J5
2500	LFYT	94549	612-A5
CAMINO DON MIGUEL			
-	ORIN	94563	610-F5
CAMINO ENCANTO			
100	DNVL	94526	652-H2
CAMINO ENCINAS			
-	ORIN	94563	630-H1
CAMINO ESTRADA			
1800	CNCD	94521	593-G5
CAMINO JUSTIN			
-	LFYT	94549	611-J5
CAMINO LAS JUNTAS			
100	PLHL	94523	592-B4
CAMINO LENADA			
-	ORIN	94563	610-G6
2600	OAK	94611	650-F2
CAMINO MONTE SOL			
-	CCCo	94507	632-H3
CAMINO PABLO			
-	ORIN	94563	630-H1
-	ORIN	94563	610-F6
-	CCCo	94563	610-F6
1000	MRGA	94556	651-D1
1800	CCCo	94556	651-F4
CAMINO PERAL			
1300	MRGA	94556	631-E6
CAMINO POSADA			
-	CCCo	94595	612-B6
CAMINO POSADA CT			
-	CCCo	94595	612-B6
CAMINO RAMON			
800	DNVL	94526	653-B5
2100	SRMN	94583	653-D7
2100	SRMN	94583	673-E2
2100	DNVL	94526	673-E2
CAMINO RICARDO			
600	MRGA	94556	631-D6
CAMINO SOBRANTE			
-	ORIN	94563	610-G5
CAMINO SOLANO			
1100	CNCD	94521	593-E7
CAMINO TASSAJARA			
1000	DNVL	94526	653-C2
2500	DNVL	94506	653-G5
3300	CCCo	94506	653-G5
3400	DNVL	94506	654-E5
3400	CCCo	94506	654-E5
4400	CCCo	94588	654-E5
5000	CCCo	94506	674-F2
5100	CCCo	94582	674-F2
5100	CCCo	94588	674-E6
5100	CCCo	-	674-F2
CAMINO VALLECITO			
1100	LFYT	94549	611-C4
CAMINO VAQUEROS			
4300	CCCo	94513	(636-J4 See Page 635)
4300	CCCo	94514	(636-J4 See Page 635)
CAMINO VENADILLO			
2700	SRMN	94583	673-A3
CAMINO VERDE			
1300	WLCK	94597	611-J2
CAMINO VERDE CIR			
1000	WLCK	94597	611-J3
CAMINO VINEDO			
4000	CCCo	94553	571-J4
CAMPANELLO WY			
700	BREN	94513	616-E3
CAMPANIA CT			
600	BREN	94513	616-F3
CAMPANULA DR			
-	SRMN	94582	673-J1
CAMPBELL AV			
100	ANT	94509	575-C6
CAMPBELL CT			
-	PIT	94565	574-D6
CAMPBELL DR			
4200	PIT	94565	574-D6
CAMPBELL LN			
200	PLHL	94523	592-C6
CAMPBELL PL			
-	DNVL	94526	653-E3
CAMPBELL ST			
1000	RCH	94804	609-B2
CAMPECHE CT			
2600	SRMN	94583	673-B3
CAMPESINO CT			
1600	CCCo	94507	632-D3
CAMPION DR			
-	CCCo	94582	674-A2
CAMPOLINDO CT			
-	MRGA	94556	631-D2
CAMPOLINDO DR			
3600	MRGA	94556	631-D2
CAMPO PELOTA			
-	CCCo	94528	633-E7
CAMPO VERDE CIR			
-	SPAB	94806	588-H3
CAMPUS DR			
-	CNCD	94521	593-C6
1200	BERK	94708	609-J6
CAMPUS DR			
2700	SPAB	94806	588-J2
11800	OAK	94619	650-J5
13400	OAK	94605	651-A7
13400	OAK	94619	651-A7
CAMROSE PL			
100	WLCK	94596	612-D4
100	WLCK	94598	612-D4
CAMSTOCK CT			
4400	CNCD	94521	593-C5
CANADA VIA			
100	CCCo	94528	633-D7
CANADA HILLS DR			
5000	ANT	94531	595-J3
5100	ANT	94531	596-A3
CANADA HILLS WY			
5000	ANT	94531	595-J3
CANADA VALLEY RD			
4400	ANT	94531	596-A2
CANAL BLVD			
200	RCH	94804	588-E7
300	RCH	94804	608-E1
300	RCH	94801	608-E1
CANAL DR			
-	CCCo	94565	553-E7
-	CCCo	94565	573-E1
CANAL LN			
-	WLCK	94597	612-B2
CANAL RD			
300	CCCo	94565	573-G3
CANAL ST			
-	SRFL	94901	587-A2
CANARY CT			
-	DNVL	94526	653-B5
CANARY LN			
-	RCH	94803	589-C3
CANDELERO CT			
1600	WLCK	94598	612-E1
CANDELERO DR			
1300	WLCK	94598	612-E1
CANDELERO PL			
100	WLCK	94598	612-E1
CANDICE CT			
1800	ANT	94509	575-G5
CANDLE TER			
-	ORIN	94563	610-J3
CANDLEBERRY RD			
300	WLCK	94598	612-J1
400	WLCK	94598	592-H7
CANDLELIGHT LN			
-	LFYT	94549	611-H3
CANDLESTICK CT			
2300	ANT	94509	595-A1
CANDLESTICK DR			
2300	ANT	94509	595-A1
2400	ANT	94509	594-J1
CANDLESTICK RD			
-	ORIN	94563	630-G2
CANDLESTON PL			
1300	CCCo	94507	632-E2
CANDLEWOOD CT			
4600	CNCD	94521	593-C3
CANDLEWOOD PL			
-	CCCo	94595	632-C1
CANDLEWOOD WY			
5200	ANT	94531	595-H5
CANDOLERO WY			
2400	ANT	94509	594-J1
CANDY CT			
1200	LFYT	94549	611-H4
CANDYTUFT CT			
-	CCCo	94582	674-B2
CANDYWOOD CT			
4500	CNCD	94521	593-B5
CANFIELD CT			
100	BREN	94513	616-E3
200	DNVL	94526	653-D6
CANFIELD DR			
3400	DNVL	94526	653-D6
CANIM CT			
3200	ANT	94509	595-C1
CANIM RD			
3200	ANT	94509	595-C1
CANMORE CT			
-	BREN	94513	616-A2
CANNA WY			
-	SRMN	94582	673-G2
CANNERY AV			
200	PIT	94565	574-B2
CANNERY CT			
200	PIT	94565	574-B2
CANNES CT			
-	DNVL	94506	653-G5
CANNING CT			
-	MRGA	94556	651-E1
CANNON CT			
-	PIT	94565	574-C2
CANNON DR			
1800	WLCK	94597	611-H2
CANNON PL			
1900	WLCK	94597	611-H2
CANOE BIRCH CT			
4400	CNCD	94521	593-C5
N CANOE BIRCH CT			
4300	CNCD	94521	593-C5
CANON AV			
3700	OAK	94602	650-D4
CANON DR			
200	ORIN	94563	610-F6
600	CCCo	94708	609-H4
CANON VIEW LN			
-	OAK	94618	630-B6
CANOPY LN			
4700	OAKL	94561	576-C7
CANTAS PL			
100	SRMN	94583	673-G5
CANTERBERRY PL			
3800	PIT	94565	574-C5
CANTERBURY			
800	HER	94547	569-H2
CANTERBURY CT			
-	BREN	94513	616-F2
300	CCCo	94507	632-J2
7600	DBLN	94568	693-H3
CANTERBURY DR			
1300	CNCD	94521	593-A4
2800	RCH	94806	589-A2
CANTERBURY LN			
2200	OAKL	94561	576-C6
7500	DBLN	94568	693-H3
CANTO CT			
2200	ANT	94509	595-A1
CANTRELL CT			
1700	CNCD	94521	593-F4
CANTRILL CT			
-	ANT	94531	595-C4
CANWICK LN			
-	BREN	94513	616-A1
CANYON CT			
-	VAL	94591	550-D1
300	BEN	94510	551-B3
CANYON DR			
1600	PIN	94564	569-D5
CANYON PL			
-	CCCo	94803	589-D2
CANYON RD			
-	BERK	94704	630-A2
-	BERK	94720	630-A2
1500	MRGA	94556	631-D7
1500	MRGA	94556	651-C2
1500	CCCo	94556	651-C2
1900	CCCo	94516	651-C2
1900	MRGA	94516	651-C2
3900	LFYT	94549	611-A4
4500	CCCo	94803	589-D2
4700	RCH	94803	589-D2
CANYON VW			
-	ORIN	94563	610-J4
-	ORIN	94563	611-A4
CANYON WY			
300	MRTZ	94553	571-D6
3000	PIT	94565	574-D7
7600	PLE	94588	693-H6
CANYON CREEK CIR			
7500	PLE	94588	693-E5
CANYON CREEK CT			
200	SRMN	94583	673-B2
CANYON CREEK DR			
-	RCH	94803	589-G4
2700	SRMN	94583	673-B2
CANYON CREST AV			
2000	SRMN	94582	653-G7
CANYON CREST CT			
-	SRMN	94582	653-F6
CANYON CREST DR			
600	SRMN	94582	653-F6
CANYON CREST RD E			
600	SRMN	94582	653-F7
CANYON CREST RD W			
800	SRMN	94582	653-F7
CANYON GREEN CT			
-	SRMN	94582	673-G3
CANYON GREEN DR			
1000	SRMN	94582	673-G3
CANYON GREEN PL			
100	SRMN	94582	673-G4
CANYON GREEN WY			
-	SRMN	94582	673-G3
CANYON HILLS CT			
-	SRMN	94582	673-G3
CANYON HILLS PL			
-	SRMN	94582	673-G3
CANYON HILLS RD			
1000	SRMN	94582	673-F3
CANYON LAKE DR			
-	CCCo	94569	550-H6
CANYON LAKES DR			
2000	SRMN	94582	673-F1
CANYON LAKES PL			
200	SRMN	94582	673-E1
CANYON LAKES WY			
100	SRMN	94582	673-E1
CANYON MEADOW CIR			
-	PLE	94588	693-F5
CANYON MEADOW DR			
-	PLE	94588	693-F5
CANYON OAK CT			
-	CCCo	94506	653-G1
CANYON OAK LN			
2100	CCCo	94506	653-G1
2100	CCCo	94506	633-G7
CANYON OAK PL			
-	CCCo	94506	653-G1
CANYON OAKS CIR			
-	PIT	94565	574-G7
CANYON OAKS CT			
-	PIT	94565	574-G7
CANYON OAKS DR			
-	RCH	94803	589-G5
CANYON SIDE AV			
1100	SRMN	94582	673-G3
CANYON VIEW CIR			
100	SRMN	94582	673-F2
CANYON VIEW CT			
2900	ANT	94531	575-G7
CANYON VILLAGE CIR			
1000	SRMN	94583	673-C2
CANYON VISTA PL			
100	CCCo	94507	633-B5
CANYONWOOD CT			
-	WLCK	94595	632-B4
600	BREN	94513	616-E1
CANYONWOOD DR			
500	BREN	94513	616-E1
CANYON WOODS CT			
-	SRMN	94582	673-F3
CANYON WOODS DR			
100	SRMN	94582	673-F3
CANYON WOODS PL			
-	SRMN	94582	673-F3
CANYON WOODS WY			
200	SRMN	94582	673-G3
CAPARELLI CT			
5200	PLE	94588	694-C6
CAPE CT			
1700	WLCK	94598	612-E1
CAPE COD CT			
1200	CNCD	94521	593-A4
CAPE COD WY			
1200	CNCD	94521	593-A4
CAPE ELIZABETH CT			
100	VAL	94591	550-F1
CAPELL ST			
500	OAK	94606	650-A4
500	OAK	94610	650-A4
CAPELLA CT			
3500	PLE	94588	694-H4
CAPE MAY CT			
-	PIT	94565	574-B2
CAPE MAY DR			
-	PIT	94565	574-A2
CAPERTON AV			
-	PDMT	94611	650-C1
CAPEWOOD PL			
7700	PLE	94588	693-J7
CAPILANO DR			
-	BREN	94513	616-A1
CAPISTRANO AV			
1500	BERK	94707	609-F5
CAPISTRANO CT			
-	SPAB	94806	588-C3
-	CLAY	94517	613-J2
CAPISTRANO ST			
2700	ANT	94509	575-C6
CAPITOL CT			
4400	CNCD	94518	593-A5
CAPITOL DR			
-	BREN	94513	596-C6
500	BEN	94510	550-H1
CAPITOLA DR			
-	PIT	94565	574-E2
CAPITOLA PL			
-	PIT	94565	574-E1
CAPITOL HILL AV			
1500	RCH	94806	589-B4
1500	CCCo	94806	589-B4
CAPLES CT			
-	ANT	94531	575-H7
CAPP ST			
2900	OAK	94602	650-D5
CAPRI LN			
-	PLHL	94523	591-J4
CAPRICE CIR			
100	HER	94547	570-B6
CAPRICORN AV			
100	OAK	94611	630-D6
CAPRINO WY			
900	PIT	94565	574-F3
CAPSTAN PL			
4000	CCCo	94514	617-G7
CAPTAINS CT			
100	VAL	94591	550-F2
500	CCCo	94565	573-D1
CAPTAINS CV			
-	OAK	94618	630-C4
-	OAK	94705	630-C4
CAPWELL LN			
1300	WLCK	94596	612-C6
CARA CT			
-	WLCK	94596	612-D4
CARAMELLO CT			
3100	PLE	94588	694-C6
CARAMOOR LN			
-	SRMN	94582	674-C3
CARAVAN PL			
-	SRMN	94583	673-B2
CARAVELLE CT			
3200	WLCK	94598	612-J2
CARAVELLE DR			
300	WLCK	94598	612-J2
CARAWAY CT			
-	SRMN	94582	673-G1
CARBONDALE WY			
-	ANT	94531	595-C4
CARDENA CT			
-	DBLN	94568	694-G3
CARDIFF			
100	HER	94547	569-H3
CARDIFF CT			
1100	ANT	94509	575-F7
2700	RCH	94806	588-J1
8100	DBLN	94568	693-H2
CARDIFF DR			
1900	PIT	94565	574-E3
8000	DBLN	94568	693-H2
CARDIFF PL			
1300	CCCo	94507	632-E2
CARDIGAN CT			
1100	WLCK	94596	632-G1
7600	DBLN	94568	693-H3
CARDIGAN DR			
1100	WLCK	94596	632-G1
CARDIGAN ST			
7600	DBLN	94568	693-H3
CARDINAL CT			
-	BREN	94513	616-B4
2400	CNCD	94520	572-G5
CARDINAL DR			
3500	CNCD	94520	572-G5
CARDINAL LN			
-	CCCo	94513	617-F5
CARDINAL WY			
100	HER	94547	569-H5
CARDINALE CT			
-	PIT	94565	574-E1
CARDINET DR			
5900	CLAY	94517	593-G6
CARDONA CIR			
300	SRMN	94583	673-D3
CARDOZA			
100	HER	94547	569-E3
CARDUCCI DR			
-	PLE	94588	694-C6
CAREY CT			
-	MRGA	94556	651-F1
CAREY DR			
1100	CNCD	94520	592-D5
CAREY LN			
3000	BREN	94513	616-H3
CAREY ST			
3000	ANT	94509	575-E7
CARIBBEAN CT			
800	CNCD	94518	592-H6
CARIBOU CT			
4400	ANT	94531	595-H3
CARIBOU TER			
800	BREN	94513	616-E1
CARINA CT			
700	WLCK	94598	612-H3
CARION CT			
-	PIT	94565	574-F4
CARISA CT			
-	WLCK	94597	612-B1
CARISBROOK DR			
-	ORIN	94563	631-C5
2600	OAK	94611	650-F1
CARISBROOK LN			
-	OAK	94611	650-G1
CARL AV			
5300	RCH	94804	609-B3
CARL RD			
800	LFYT	94549	611-H7
CARLA CT			
4000	ANT	94509	574-H5
S CARLBACK AV			
1200	WLCK	94596	612-C4
CARLETON DR			
1300	CNCD	94518	592-G2
CARLETON LN			
2600	ANT	94509	575-D1
CARLETON WY			
500	CCCo	94507	633-C4
CARLFIELD AV			
3500	CCCo	94803	589-B3
CARLISLE CT			
-	BEN	94510	551-C2
-	BREN	94513	596-E6
-	SRMN	94583	673-J7
-	SRMN	94583	693-J1
CARLISLE DR			
-	BREN	94513	596-D6
CARLISLE PL			
100	BEN	94510	551-B2
CARLISLE WY			
-	BEN	94510	551-A2
CARLOS AV			
5600	ELCR	94530	609-B2
5600	RCH	94804	609-B2
CARLOS CT			
-	WLCK	94597	612-A2
CARLOTTA AV			
1200	BERK	94707	609-F7
1300	BERK	94703	609-F7
CARLOTTA CIR			
-	PIN	94564	569-C3
CARLOTTA DR			
1800	CNCD	94519	573-A7
1800	CNCD	94519	572-J7
CARLOW WY			
-	ANT	94531	596-B3

STREET / Block City ZIP Pg-Grid

CARLOW WY
7500 DBLN 94568 693-G2
CARLSEN ST
2900 OAK 94602 650-F4
CARLSON BLVD
- RCH 94801 588-H7
100 RCH 94804 588-H7
300 RCH 94804 608-J1
700 RCH 94804 609-A2
2900 ELCR 94530 609-C3
CARLSON CT
1600 CNCD 94519 593-A2
CARLSTON AV
600 OAK 94610 650-B2
CARLSTON ST
300 RCH 94805 589-B7
CARLTON CT
2700 CCCo 94806 588-J2
2700 CCCo 94806 589-A2
CARLTON ST
5400 OAK 94618 630-A6
CARLTON WY
1500 BREN 94513 616-D2
CARLYLE CT
- DNVL 94506 653-H5
CARLYLE DR
- CCCo 94513 617-F3
CARLYLE TER
3300 LFYT 94549 631-G1
CARMALITA CT
- CCCo 94507 632-J2
CARMEL AV
100 ELCR 94530 609-E6
500 ALB 94706 609-E6
2900 PDMT 94611 650-B1
CARMEL CT
1200 WLCK 94596 612-C5
2200 PIT 94565 573-J4
CARMEL DR
1400 WLCK 94596 612-C5
2000 CNCD 94520 572-E6
CARMEL ST
- SPAB 94806 588-J3
2400 OAK 94602 650-E4
CARMELITA CT
1400 CNCD 94520 592-F2
CARMELITA WY
2500 PIN 94564 569-G6
CARMELLO RD
- CCCo 94597 612-B4
- WLCK 94597 612-B4
CARMEN CT
- CCCo 94506 654-D5
- ORIN 94563 631-B4
2700 PIN 94564 569-H6
CARMEN LN
- CCCo 94803 589-E3
CARMEN WY
- CCCo 94506 654-D6
CARMONA WY
2800 ANT 94509 575-A7
CARNEAL RD
7900 CCCo 94551 675-C4
CARNEGIE LN
4500 BREN 94513 616-G3
CARNEGIE PL
- BREN 94513 616-G3
CARNMORE PL
- DBLN 94568 694-F4
CARNOUSTIE
- MRGA 94556 651-D1
CARO LN
100 ORIN 94563 631-B5
CAROB CT
2700 ANT 94509 575-H6
CAROB ST
2700 ANT 94509 575-H6
CAROB WY
200 CCCo 94553 572-C6
CAROL CT
200 CCCo 94507 633-C4
7000 ELCR 94530 609-C1
CAROL LN
100 OAKL 94561 576-C6
900 LFYT 94549 611-H6
CAROL PTH
4200 RCH 94804 609-A1
CAROL ST
3700 PIN 94564 569-H7
CAROLE MEADOWS CT
100 DNVL 94506 653-G5
CAROLINA DR
- BEN 94510 551-A4
1400 CLAY 94517 593-F6
1400 CNCD 94521 593-F6
CAROLINE CT
7900 DBLN 94568 693-G3
CAROL LEE LN
3300 OAKL 94561 596-H3
CAROLOS DR
100 CCCo 94553 572-B7
CAROLYN CT
- LFYT 94549 611-J6
- ORIN 94563 631-B2
2900 ANT 94509 575-D7
CAROLYN DR
- PIT 94565 574-D4
1900 PLHL 94523 592-B5
CARONDELET CT
2600 CNCD 94518 592-F7
CARONI ST
- WLCK 94597 612-B1
CAROUSEL CT
- SRMN 94583 673-B2
CAROUSEL PL
- SRMN 94583 673-B2
CARPENTER CIR
- CCCo 94553 571-E2
CARPENTER CT
- PLHL 94523 591-J7
CARPENTER RD
1000 OAKL 94561 596-C2
CARPETTA CIR
800 PIT 94565 574-A3
CARPINO AV
500 PIT 94565 574-E3
CARPINTERIA DR
2000 ANT 94509 595-E1
2500 ANT 94531 595-G1
CARQUINEZ AV
1800 CCCo 94805 589-C6
1800 ELCR 94530 589-C7
CARQUINEZ CIR
- BEN 94510 551-A3
CARQUINEZ CT
200 BEN 94510 551-B4
CARQUINEZ PL
2100 PIT 94565 574-A3
CARQUINEZ WY
700 MRTZ 94553 571-D3
1800 CCCo 94525 550-C5
CARQUINEZ SCENIC DR
- CCCo 94553 550-H6
- MRTZ 94553 571-B2

CARQUINEZ SCENIC DR
- CCCo 94569 550-H6
- CCCo 94553 571-B2
100 CCCo 94525 550-F5
CARR DR
- MRGA 94556 631-E7
CARRARA ST
- BREN 94513 616-C2
CARRERIO LN
- WLCK 94597 612-A3
CARRIAGE CT
- CCCo 94507 632-G7
CARRIAGE DR
1300 WLCK 94598 612-F1
1700 WLCK 94598 592-E7
5000 RCH 94803 589-J2
5100 RCH 94803 590-A3
CARRIAGE LN
300 CCCo 94553 592-A1
CARRIAGE WY
5100 ANT 94531 595-J3
5100 ANT 94531 596-A3
CARRICK CT
- PLHL 94523 591-J5
CARRIE CT
- PLHL 94523 612-A1
CARRILLO CT
400 SRMN 94583 673-C2
CARRINGTON CT
- CCCo 94582 674-B5
CARRINGTON DR
4700 OAKL 94561 576-C7
CARRINGTON ST
3600 OAK 94601 650-D7
CARRINGTON WY
3600 OAK 94601 650-D7
CARRISA CT
2800 PLE 94588 694-H4
CARRMANN LN
- CNCD 94521 593-F4
CARROL CT
- BREN 94513 596-H5
CARROL PL
100 CCCo 94595 612-A7
CARROL RD
2100 CCCo 94596 612-E7
CARROLL CT
- PIT 94565 574-D6
CARROLL DR
- PIT 94565 574-D6
600 MRGA 94556 631-E5
CARROLL ST
2200 OAK 94606 650-A4
CARR RANCH RD
- CCCo 94556 651-F3
CARSON CT
- SRMN 94582 653-J7
4600 PLE 94588 694-A6
CARSON ST
100 HER 94547 570-B5
4000 OAK 94619 650-G6
4000 CNCD 94521 593-A2
CARSON WY
- ANT 94531 595-F5
CARTAGENA LN
500 SRMN 94583 673-C2
CARTE PL
- PLHL 94523 592-A4
CARTER CT
- CCCo 94803 589-F3
4200 CNCD 94521 593-B3
CARTER DR
900 MRGA 94556 631-F6
CARTER PL
- BREN 94513 596-G5
CARTER ST
1700 OAK 94602 650-E2
CARTER WY
2900 ANT 94509 575-A7
CARTER ACRES LN
800 MRTZ 94553 591-F4
CARTHAGE CT
800 CNCD 94518 592-G6
CARTHAGE DR
2400 CNCD 94518 592-G6
CARVER CT
4500 PLE 94588 694-A6
CARZINO CT
1900 CNCD 94521 593-G4
CASA WY
2400 WLCK 94597 612-B3
CASABLANCA CT
- DNVL 94506 654-B6
CASABLANCA ST
- CCCo 94506 654-D6
- DNVL 94506 654-B6
CASA BUENO CT
2500 WLCK 94598 612-H2
CASA DE CAMPO
- CCCo 94553 591-E3
CASADERO CT
3000 PLE 94588 694-D7
CASA DE SIMA
- LFYT 94549 591-G7
CASA GRANDE CT
2500 WLCK 94598 612-G2
CASA GRANDE DR
3200 SRMN 94583 673-G5
CASA GRANDE PL
- SRMN 94583 673-G6
2100 BEN 94510 551-D4
CASA GRANDE ST
1800 BEN 94510 551-D5
CASA LINDA CT
11700 DBLN 94568 693-F4
CASA MARIA CT
- CCCo 94507 632-F5
CASA NUESTRA
2000 CCCo 94528 633-E7
CASA REALE
200 ORIN 94563 631-B4
CASA REYA CT
2500 WLCK 94598 612-H2
CASA VALLECITA
1300 CCCo 94507 632-F4
CASA VERDE PL
- CLAY 94517 613-J2
CASA VERDE WY
- PIT 94565 574-C6
CASA VIEJA
- ORIN 94563 630-J3
CASA VIEJA LN
100 ORIN 94563 630-J3
CASCADAS CT
- SRMN 94583 673-A2
CASCADE CT
700 WLCK 94598 612-G3
3700 ANT 94509 595-E1
CASCADE DR
2000 WLCK 94598 612-G3
CASCADE LN
- ORIN 94563 610-H6
CASCADE CREEK LN
- DBLN 94568 694-H3

CASE DR
200 PIT 94565 574-B2
CASELLA CT
- SRMN 94582 674-B3
CASELLA WY
- SRMN 94582 674-C3
CASELTON PL
- LFYT 94549 611-J6
CASEY CT
400 BEN 94510 551-C1
CASEY DR
500 RCH 94801 608-C1
CASEY GLEN CT
- CLAY 94517 593-G6
CASHEW CT
- BREN 94513 616-F3
500 SRMN 94583 673-G7
2900 ANT 94509 575-J6
CASHEW LN
200 OAKL 94561 596-G1
CASHEW PL
- BREN 94513 616-F3
CASHEW ST
- BREN 94513 616-F3
2800 ANT 94509 575-J6
CASINO AV
5600 SPAB 94806 589-A4
CASITA CT
800 DNVL 94526 653-B2
CASITAS CT
2100 ANT 94509 595-A1
CASKEY ST
700 CCCo 94565 573-C2
CASOLYN RANCH CT
1200 DNVL 94506 654-B6
CASPER PL
200 SRMN 94583 673-G7
CASPER ST
4100 PIT 94565 574-F6
CASPIAN CT
- PIT 94565 574-B2
CASSANDRA CT
- WLCK 94598 612-H3
CASSANDRA PL
100 SRMN 94583 693-G1
CASSATA PL
- DBLN 94568 694-H3
CASSENA DR
3400 WLCK 94598 612-J1
CASSIA CT
- PIT 94565 574-C2
3100 PLE 94588 694-H5
CASSIA ST
- PIT 94565 574-C2
CASTANYA CT
400 DNVL 94526 633-B7
CASTELLINA CT
- BREN 94513 616-C1
CASTELLINA DR
- BREN 94513 616-C1
CASTELLO RD
300 LFYT 94549 631-H3
CASTELLO ST
2500 OAK 94602 650-D5
CASTENADA CT
300 DNVL 94526 653-D5
CASTERLINE RD
1700 OAK 94602 650-D3
CASTERSON DR
- DBLN 94568 694-E3
CASTILIAN CT
11600 DBLN 94568 693-F3
CASTILIAN RD
7600 DBLN 94568 693-F3
CASTILLA AV
4700 RCH 94804 609-A1
CASTILLE CT
- DNVL 94526 653-C7
CASTLE CT
- CCCo 94565 573-F2
- OAK 94611 650-G2
100 LFYT 94549 631-J4
600 ANT 94509 595-F1
700 BREN 94513 616-G1
11700 DBLN 94568 693-G4
CASTLE DR
5600 OAK 94611 650-F2
7200 DBLN 94568 693-G4
CASTLE LN
- OAK 94611 650-F2
CASTLEBERRY LN
- WLCK 94595 632-A2
CASTLE CANYON CT
- ANT 94531 595-C5
CASTLE CREEK CT
300 CCCo 94553 591-E3
CASTLE CREST CT
- CCCo 94507 632-D2
CASTLE CREST RD
- CCCo 94507 632-D2
CASTLEFORD CIR
100 DNVL 94526 653-C2
CASTLEFORD DR
2800 ANT 94509 575-C6
CASTLEFORD PL
- DNVL 94526 653-C2
CASTLE GATE RD
1800 WLCK 94595 612-C7
1800 WLCK 94595 632-C1
CASTLE GLEN RD
200 CCCo 94595 632-C2
CASTLE HILL CT
- VAL 94591 550-E2
- WLCK 94595 612-D7
- WLCK 94595 632-D1
CASTLE HILL RD
1500 WLCK 94595 612-D7
1500 WLCK 94595 632-C1
1600 CCCo 94595 632-C1
CASTLE HILL RANCH RD
100 CCCo 94595 632-D2
CASTLE OAKS CT
1800 WLCK 94595 612-D7
1800 WLCK 94595 632-D1
CASTLE PARK WY
- OAK 94611 650-F2
E CASTLE PINES TER
- DBLN 94568 694-G2
CASTLE ROCK CT
- WLCK 94598 612-J3
CASTLE ROCK LN
100 WLCK 94598 612-J3
CASTLE ROCK LP
1000 CCCo 94513 617-G4
CASTLE ROCK RD
- WLCK 94598 612-J4
400 CCCo 94598 612-J4
700 CCCo 94598 613-A5
700 WLCK 94598 613-A5
CASTLETON CT
- DBLN 94568 694-F3
100 SRMN 94583 673-C2

CASTLETON LN
- DBLN 94568 694-F3
CASTLETOWN WY
- ANT 94531 596-B4
CASTLEWOOD CT
4000 CNCD 94518 592-J5
4000 CNCD 94518 593-A5
CASTLEWOOD DR
- PIT 94565 574-C6
CASTRO ST
100 RCH 94801 588-D7
500 MRTZ 94553 571-D3
900 ALB 94706 609-D5
2600 SPAB 94806 588-J2
N CASTRO ST
- CCCo 94801 588-F4
- RCH 94801 588-F4
S CASTRO ST
4100 MRTZ 94553 571-E6
CASTRO RANCH RD
1200 CCCo 94803 589-H4
1400 RCH 94803 589-H4
2500 RCH 94803 590-A3
2900 CCCo 94553 590-A3
CATALAN WY
300 SRMN 94582 673-G3
CATALINA AV
1800 BERK 94707 609-F6
CATALINA BLVD
- SRFL 94901 587-A2
CATALINA CT
800 PIT 94565 574-E6
CATALINA DR
100 HER 94547 570-C6
CATALINA WY
3500 CCCo 94513 617-E7
CATALINE AV
- ANT 94509 575-C5
CATALON CT
7600 DBLN 94568 693-G3
CATALPA CT
100 HER 94547 569-J4
4400 CNCD 94521 593-C5
CATALPA LN
- SRMN 94583 693-F1
CATALPA ST
3100 CCCo 94553 571-G4
CATALPA WY
- ANT 94509 595-F3
E CATAMARAN CIR
200 PIT 94565 574-A2
N CATAMARAN CIR
100 PIT 94565 574-A2
S CATAMARAN CIR
200 PIT 94565 574-A2
W CATAMARAN CIR
100 PIT 94565 574-A2
CATAMARAN CT
- CCCo 94513 617-E7
CATANIO CT
500 SRMN 94583 673-B2
CATANZARO WY
5000 ANT 94531 595-J4
5000 ANT 94531 596-A4
CATHEDRAL CIR
- BREN 94561 596-D4
CATHERINE CT
- CCCo 94507 632-G5
100 ORIN 94563 630-J1
CATHERINE WY
1500 CNCD 94519 592-J3
1500 CNCD 94519 593-A2
CATHY CT
- BREN 94513 596-D5
2500 ANT 94509 574-J6
CATHY LN
- DNVL 94526 652-J1
- DNVL 94526 653-A1
- OAK 94619 651-C7
CATHY WY
2600 ANT 94509 574-J6
CATS EYE CT
- ANT 94509 595-E1
CATTAIL CT
700 WLCK 94598 613-A3
CATTLE CHUTE RD
- LFYT 94549 631-G4
CATTLEYA CT
- SRMN 94582 673-H1
CATTLEYA DR
- SRMN 94582 673-H1
CAUDEL CT
1800 MRTZ 94553 572-A6
CAULFIELD CT
500 CLAY 94517 593-G6
CAVALIER CT
8400 DBLN 94568 693-G2
CAVALIER LN
8200 DBLN 94568 693-G2
CAVALLO RD
1100 ANT 94509 575-E5
CAVALRY CT
- DNVL 94526 653-A3
CAVANAUGH CT
- PDMT 94610 650-D3
CAVEN WY
1100 CNCD 94520 592-F4
CAVENDISH CT
- BREN 94513 616-G3
CAVENDISH LN
- OAK 94602 650-D3
CAVORETTO LN
- CCCo 94803 589-F4
CAYCE CT
900 CNCD 94518 592-F6
CAYES CT
1000 ANT 94509 575-F7
CAYMAN
- HER 94547 570-C6
CAYUCOS DR
1500 WLCK 94597 611-J2
1600 CCCo 94549 611-J2
CAYUGA ST
- OAKL 94561 576-C6
CEBU DR
200 CCCo 94553 572-C6
CECILIA LN
- CCCo 94553 572-A3
CECILIA WY
3200 PIT 94565 574-D4
CEDAR CT
100 HER 94547 569-J4
100 PLHL 94523 591-J5
1000 CCCo 94525 550-D5
1600 OAKL 94561 576-D7
3100 ANT 94509 574-J7
6900 DBLN 94568 693-J4
CEDAR LN
- SRFL 94901 587-B1
- ORIN 94563 631-A1
1300 CCCo 94507 632-F4
6800 DBLN 94568 693-J4
CEDAR ST
1100 PIT 94565 574-F2

CEDAR ST
1400 MRTZ 94553 571-F3
2000 BERK 94709 609-H7
2000 CNCD 94519 592-G1
2300 BERK 94708 609-H7
2300 ELCR 94530 589-B7
CEDAR TER
- ORIN 94563 631-A3
CEDARBROOK CT
- CCCo 94597 612-D2
CEDAR CREST RD
4400 CNCD 94521 593-B4
CEDAR CREST TER
- DBLN 94568 694-F2
CEDAR FALLS AV
- BREN 94513 596-B5
CEDAR GLEN CT
500 WLCK 94598 612-H3
CEDAR GLENN DR
- OAKL 94561 596-F2
CEDAR HOLLOW DR
- DNVL 94526 652-J1
- DNVL 94526 653-A1
CEDAR LANE CT
1000 DNVL 94526 653-E3
CEDAR POINT CT
- ANT 94531 595-J5
CEDAR POINT WY
- ANT 94531 595-J5
CEDAR POINTE LP
- SRMN 94583 693-H1
CEDAR RIDGE WY
5200 ANT 94531 595-E4
CEDARWOOD CT
4200 CNCD 94521 593-B2
CEDARWOOD DR
1100 MRGA 94556 651-E1
CEDARWOOD LN
1100 BERK 94710 609-C7
CEDARWOOD LP
- CCCo 94582 673-J2
CEDARWOOD PL
- CCCo 94582 673-J2
CEDARWOOD TER
1700 BREN 94513 596-G6
CEDARWOOD WY
- CCCo 94582 673-J2
CEDERBROOK PL
- PIT 94565 574-F7
CEDRO LN
2500 WLCK 94598 612-H2
CEDRUS CT
2800 PLE 94588 694-H4
CEEMAR CT
- CNCD 94519 593-A2
CELA CT
- WLCK 94597 612-C2
CELAYA CIR
2600 SRMN 94583 673-C3
CELESTE AV
2000 CCCo 94596 612-E7
2000 CCCo 94596 632-E1
CELESTE WY
- BREN 94561 596-D3
CELIA DR
- PLHL 94523 592-C5
CELINE CT
- DNVL 94526 653-C4
CELLINI TER
- BREN 94513 616-C4
CENTENNIAL CT
3500 ANT 94509 595-C3
CENTENNIAL DR
- BERK 94708 610-A7
- BERK 94720 610-A7
- BERK 94720 630-A1
- BREN 94513 616-D5
- OAK 94708 610-A7
- OAK 94720 610-A7
- OAK 94720 630-A1
3500 ANT 94509 595-C3
CENTENNIAL PL
- BREN 94513 616-D4
CENTENNIAL WY
2700 SRMN 94583 673-E6
CENTER AV
- CCCo 94553 592-B1
100 CCCo 94553 572-C7
300 MRTZ 94553 572-A7
300 MRTZ 94553 592-B1
500 MRTZ 94553 571-F6
2600 RCH 94804 588-J7
3700 RCH 94804 589-A7
CENTER CT
- CCCo 94595 612-A7
900 MRTZ 94553 571-G6
3400 DNVL 94506 653-J5
CENTER DR
- CNCD 94521 593-C6
- PIT 94565 574-D3
CENTER LN
2700 ANT 94509 575-D7
CENTER ST
400 MRGA 94556 631-E4
400 CCCo 94595 612-A6
1000 CLAY 94517 593-H7
CENTER WY
- DNVL 94506 654-A6
3400 DNVL 94506 653-J5
CENTER POINT TER
- SRMN 94582 673-G2
CENTRAL AV
- PIT 94565 574-E2
500 CCCo 94553 571-J3
500 CCCo 94553 572-A3
1900 CCCo 94801 588-F3
4800 RCH 94804 609-D4
5500 ELCR 94530 609-D4
CENTRAL BLVD
900 BREN 94513 616-D1
1200 BREN 94513 596-G7
CENTRAL CT
4000 CCCo 94553 572-A3
CENTRAL PK
- PIN 94564 569-B4
CENTRAL PKWY
6600 DBLN 94568 694-C4
CENTRAL PL
300 BREN 94513 616-C1
CENTRAL RD
1400 WLCK 94596 612-C4
CENTRAL ST
- CNCD 94520 592-F2
- HER 94547 569-G2
CENTRAL PARK DR
500 CCCo 94708 609-H4
CENTRE TER
- BREN 94513 596-F7
- BREN 94513 616-G1
CENTURY BLVD
4400 PIT 94565 574-H4
4600 PIT 94565 575-A5
4800 ANT 94509 574-H4

CENTURY CIR
300 DNVL 94526 653-C5
CENTURY CT
- PIT 94565 574-J5
CENTURY WY
- PIT 94565 574-H5
100 OAKL 94561 596-G2
700 DNVL 94526 653-C5
CENTURY OAKS CT
2600 SRMN 94583 673-D6
CENTURY OAKS DR
1600 BREN 94513 596-D7
CENTURY OAKS WY
- DNVL 94526 653-B5
CERES ST
1200 CCCo 94525 550-D5
CEREZO DR
100 WLCK 94598 612-H3
CERMENHO CT
- DBLN 94568 694-G4
CERRITO AV
3500 RCH 94805 588-J6
3500 RCH 94805 589-A6
CERRITO CT
2100 PIT 94565 574-A3
3600 LFYT 94549 611-E7
CERRITO RD
- CCCo 94803 589-C3
CERRITO ST
700 ALB 94706 609-D6
CERRITOS RD
2400 BREN 94513 596-G4
CERRO CT
- DNVL 94526 633-C6
2000 ANT 94509 595-B1
CERRO ENCANTADO
- LFYT 94549 611-F7
CERRO NORTE
5500 RCH 94803 589-J3
5500 RCH 94803 590-A3
CERRO SUR
5300 RCH 94803 590-A3
CERRO VISTA LN
2500 CCCo 94507 632-E3
CERVATO CIR
1500 CCCo 94507 632-E3
CERVATO DR
1500 CCCo 94507 632-E3
CESA AV
200 BREN 94513 616-H2
CESA LN
- ANT 94509 575-D5
CESAR CT
500 WLCK 94598 612-E2
CESAR CHAVEZ DR
1800 BREN 94513 596-G6
CHABAN DR
4100 CNCD 94521 593-B2
CHABLIS CT
4800 OAKL 94561 576-C7
CHABLIS WY
4900 OAKL 94561 576-C7
CHABOLYN TER
5900 BERK 94618 630-A4
5900 OAK 94618 630-A4
CHABOT CT
200 PIT 94565 574-B2
5800 OAK 94618 630-A5
CHABOT DR
4500 PLE 94588 694-B6
CHABOT RD
6000 OAK 94618 630-B4
CHABOT ST
4100 ANT 94531 595-J1
CHABOT CREST
5900 OAK 94618 630-A4
6000 BERK 94618 630-A4
CHABRE CT
500 CCCo 94803 589-D1
CHADBOURNE CT
2000 DNVL 94506 653-H5
CHADBOURNE DR
- DNVL 94506 653-G5
CHADBOURNE RD
5600 CCCo 94517 615-B2
5600 CCCo 94531 615-B2
CHADBOURNE WY
- OAK 94619 650-H4
CHADIMA CT
- PLHL 94523 592-A5
CHADIMA LN
- PLHL 94523 592-A5
CHADWICK CIR
1000 CCCo 94565 573-G2
CHADWICK CT
200 BEN 94510 551-A2
CHADWICK LN
600 CCCo 94565 573-G3
CHADWICK PL
- DBLN 94568 694-H3
CHALDA WY
400 MRGA 94556 631-E4
CHALET DR
900 CNCD 94518 592-G5
CHALK CREEK CT
100 MRTZ 94553 591-J4
CHALLENGE DR
1600 CNCD 94520 592-D3
CHALOMAR RD
2000 CNCD 94518 592-F5
CHAMBERLAIN CT
3300 WLCK 94598 612-J3
CHAMBERLIN CT
4300 OAK 94619 650-J7
CHAMBERS CIR
1700 BREN 94513 596-C7
1700 BREN 94513 616-C1
CHAMBERS DR
6800 OAK 94611 630-F7
CHAMBERS LN
- OAK 94611 630-F7
CHAMISE TR
- CCCo 94583 652-E3
CHAMOIS CT
- BREN 94513 596-E6
CHAMOMILE LN
1400 BREN 94513 596-E6
CHAMPAGNE CT
11200 DBLN 94568 693-E3
CHAMPAGNE PL
11300 DBLN 94568 693-F3
CHAMPION ST
3000 OAK 94602 650-D5
CHANCE LN
- WLCK 94597 612-B2
CHANCELLOR CT
- CCCo 94507 632-J2
CHANCELLOR LN
- OAK 94705 630-C3
CHANCELLOR PL
- OAK 94705 630-C3
CHANCERY LN
- DBLN 94568 694-F4

CHANCERY WY
- CCCo 94582 674-B5
CHANDLER AV
800 RCH 94804 608-F2
CHANDLER CIR
3400 CCCo 94565 573-F2
CHANDLER CT
900 CNCD 94518 592-E6
CHANDON CT
500 WLCK 94597 612-C3
600 OAKL 94561 576-D5
CHANDON WY
1700 OAKL 94561 576-D5
CHANEL CT
900 CNCD 94518 592-G5
CHANNEL AV
5100 RCH 94804 609-A3
CHANNEL CT
- BEN 94510 551-D1
CHANNEL PL
- CCCo 94511 577-E4
CHANNEL RD
100 BEN 94510 551-D1
CHANNING CT
2200 CNCD 94520 572-F6
CHANNING WY
- MRGA 94556 631-E2
CHANSLOR AV
- RCH 94801 588-G7
100 RCH 94804 588-H7
3500 RCH 94805 588-J7
W CHANSLOR AV
- RCH 94801 588-E7
CHANSLOR CIR
- RCH 94801 588-E7
CHANSLOR CT
- RCH 94801 588-F7
CHANSLOR RW
- RCH 94801 588-E7
N CHANTERELLA DR
- SRMN 94582 673-G1
S CHANTERELLA DR
- SRMN 94582 673-G2
CHANTERELLE PL
- DBLN 94568 694-H3
CHANTICLEER LN
100 CCCo 94507 633-A3
CHANTILLY CT
900 WLCK 94598 612-J4
CHANTILLY DR
7700 DBLN 94568 694-A1
CHANTILLY PL
- OAKL 94561 576-D4
CHAPARRAL CT
3700 CNCD 94519 593-A1
5000 ANT 94531 595-H4
CHAPARRAL DR
- PIT 94565 574-G7
CHAPARRO CT
1800 WLCK 94596 612-H7
CHAPEL DR
- LFYT 94549 611-A6
CHAPEL VW
- WLCK 94597 612-B4
CHAPMAN WY
4200 PLE 94588 694-A7
CHAPPARAL CT
- RCH 94806 569-A7
2600 SRMN 94583 673-E6
2600 PIN 94564 569-G6
CHAPPARAL LN
1700 CCCo 94549 611-H1
CHAPPARAL PL
- ORIN 94563 610-E6
CHAPPARRAL DR
- BREN 94513 616-B3
CHAPPELET PL
- OAKL 94561 576-E5
CHAPPELL PL
5600 OAK 94619 651-A5
CHAPS CT
200 OAKL 94561 596-B1
4900 ANT 94531 595-J2
CHARDONNAY CIR
300 CLAY 94517 593-J7
CHARDONNAY CT
- DNVL 94506 653-H5
4900 OAKL 94561 576-C7
CHARDONNAY DR
1900 OAKL 94561 576-C7
CHARDONNAY WY
2300 ANT 94509 594-J2
2300 ANT 94509 595-A2
CHARING CROSS RD
6600 OAK 94618 630-C4
6600 OAK 94705 630-C4
CHARIOT CT
100 RCH 94803 590-A3
CHARISMA WY
- BREN 94561 596-D4
CHARLES AV
100 PLHL 94523 592-B6
2500 PIN 94564 569-F4
3900 CCCo 94803 589-D2
5700 ELCR 94530 589-B6
CHARLES CT
- LFYT 94549 611-J7
1100 CNCD 94520 592-F3
CHARLES LN
100 DNVL 94526 653-A1
CHARLES WY
5000 OAKL 94561 576-C6
CHARLES HILL CIR
- ORIN 94563 610-J5
- ORIN 94563 611-A5
CHARLES HILL LN
- ORIN 94563 610-J5
CHARLES HILL PL
- ORIN 94563 610-J6
CHARLES HILL RD
- ORIN 94563 610-J5
- ORIN 94563 611-A5
CHARLESTON CT
600 WLCK 94597 612-B2
CHARLESTON ST
- PIT 94565 574-C2
2400 OAK 94602 650-E3
CHARLOTTE AV
2100 CNCD 94518 592-G6
CHARLOTTE CT
- CCCo 94803 569-D7
- CCCo 94803 589-D1
CHARLTON CIR
700 PLHL 94523 591-J6
700 PLHL 94523 592-A7
CHARLTON DR
700 PLHL 94523 592-A6
CHARLTON RD
- VAL 94592 549-H1
CHARMIAN CT
1400 BEN 94510 551-A3
CHARMSTONE CT
700 BREN 94513 616-E1
1900 WLCK 94595 632-B1

STREET
Block City ZIP Pg-Grid

CHARTER OAK CIR
200 WLCK 94597 612-C2
CHARTMASTER PL
300 VAL 94591 550-E3
CHASE CT
- MRTZ 94553 591-G1
CHASE PL
1300 CNCD 94518 592-J3
CHASLEY CT
- CCCo 94520 572-G2
CHATAM ST
8300 DBLN 94568 693-H2
CHATEAU CT
- OAKL 94561 596-E2
- DNVL 94506 653-G4
1900 WLCK 94598 592-F7
CHATELAINE CT
500 DNVL 94506 653-J5
CHATHAM CT
100 CCCo 94553 572-B7
100 CCCo 94553 592-B1
2400 ANT 94531 595-G1
CHATHAM PL
- BREN 94513 596-C6
100 VAL 94591 550-E1
CHATHAM RD
1100 OAK 94610 650-B4
1300 OAK 94602 650-B4
CHATHAM TER
200 CCCo 94506 654-B5
CHATSWOOD CT
1100 WLCK 94596 632-G2
CHATSWORTH CT
- BREN 94513 616-D3
- DNVL 94506 653-H5
- OAK 94611 650-F1
CHATTLETON LN
2800 SPAB 94806 588-J3
CHATTON CT
1200 LFYT 94549 611-J4
CHATTSWOOD DR
6200 MRTZ 94553 591-H3
CHATWORTH
3700 PIT 94565 574-C5
CHAUCER CIR
400 SRMN 94583 673-E4
CHAUCER CT
- SRMN 94583 673-E4
100 PLHL 94523 592-A7
CHAUCER DR
- PLHL 94523 592-A7
300 BREN 94513 616-E3
4100 CNCD 94521 593-A4
CHAUMONT PTH
- OAK 94618 630-B5
CHAVEZ LN
- RCH 94804 608-J1
CHELMSFORD DR
1000 BREN 94513 616-E3
CHELSEA
1400 HER 94547 569-J2
CHELSEA CT
- OAKL 94561 596-D1
- OAK 94611 650-F1
1200 ANT 94509 575-F7
3600 PLE 94588 694-E5
CHELSEA DR
- OAKL 94561 596-D2
2400 OAK 94611 650-F1
3500 PLE 94588 694-E6
5100 CCCo 94553 591-D2
CHELSEA WY
- PIT 94565 574-C3
1200 CNCD 94521 593-A5
CHELSEA HILLS DR
- BEN 94510 551-B2
CHELTA CT
- DNVL 94526 653-B3
CHELTENHAM CT
4300 CNCD 94521 593-A4
CHELTON CT
- ORIN 94563 631-B5
CHELTON DR
5600 OAK 94611 650-F1
6500 OAK 94611 630-G7
CHELTON LN
- OAK 94611 650-F1
CHEMICAL WY
- MRTZ 94553 571-F2
CHENEY AV
400 OAK 94610 650-A3
CHENIN CT
- PLHL 94523 592-A4
CHENIN LN
4300 OAKL 94561 576-E7
4300 OAKL 94561 596-E1
CHERISH CT
- BREN 94561 596-D3
CHEROKEE CT
- SRMN 94583 673-D5
CHEROKEE DR
4800 CNCD 94521 593-C4
CHEROKEE WY
- ANT 94531 595-H5
CHERRY CT
4100 OAKL 94561 596-C1
CHERRY LN
2500 CCCo 94597 612-D1
2500 WLCK 94597 612-D2
CHERRY ST
1300 RCH 94801 588-F4
2900 ANT 94509 574-J7
CHERRY WY
- OAKL 94561 596-C1
- CCCo 94597 612-D2
CHERRY HILLS CT
- CCCo 94549 591-H5
- SRMN 94583 673-H7
2400 CCCo 94507 633-A5
CHERRY HILLS DR
2400 CCCo 94549 591-H5
2400 CCCo 94514 (618-A6 See Page 597)
2600 CCCo 94514 617-J7
CHERRY HILLS LN
9400 SRMN 94583 673-H7
CHERRY POINT CT
- ANT 94531 595-E4
CHERRY TREE CT
700 BREN 94513 616-E1
CHERRY TREE WY
600 BREN 94513 616-E1
CHERRYWOOD CT
2900 SPAB 94806 588-J3
4200 CNCD 94521 593-B2
CHERRYWOOD DR
1500 MRTZ 94553 571-H7
1500 MRTZ 94553 591-H1
CHERRYWOOD WY
4900 ANT 94531 596-A4
CHERT PL
800 CLAY 94517 593-H6
CHERYL DR
700 BEN 94510 551-A3

CHESAPEAKE CT
- PIT 94565 574-B2
3700 ANT 94509 595-C3
CHESAPEAKE DR
- PIT 94565 574-B2
100 VAL 94591 550-E2
CHESAPEAKE TER
500 BREN 94513 616-D1
CHESHIRE CIR
1000 CCCo 94506 654-B5
CHESHIRE CT
1200 CNCD 94521 593-A4
3800 PLE 94588 694-F5
CHESHIRE DR
200 BREN 94513 616-E3
4100 CNCD 94521 593-A4
CHESLEY AV
- CCCo 94801 588-F4
- RCH 94801 588-F4
1200 SPAB 94801 588-F4
1200 SPAB 94806 588-F4
CHESSON ST
- RCH 94804 608-E1
CHESTER CT
- CCCo 94553 572-B7
CHESTER DR
600 PIT 94565 574-F3
E CHESTERFIELD CIR
- DBLN 94568 694-E3
W CHESTERFIELD CIR
- DBLN 94568 694-F3
CHESTERFIELD LN
900 CCCo 94506 654-B5
CHESTERTON CT
1200 WLCK 94596 632-G2
1200 WLCK 94507 632-G2
CHESTERTON DR
1600 WLCK 94507 632-G1
2300 WLCK 94596 632-G1
CHESTERTON WY
1300 WLCK 94507 632-G2
1300 WLCK 94596 632-G2
CHESTNUT AV
1900 ANT 94509 575-D6
3500 CNCD 94519 592-J2
3800 CNCD 94519 593-A2
3900 CNCD 94521 593-A2
CHESTNUT CT
- DBLN 94568 694-D4
200 SRMN 94583 673-G7
1600 CNCD 94519 592-J2
CHESTNUT DR
100 HER 94547 569-J4
2100 PIT 94565 573-H4
CHESTNUT PL
- CCCo 94506 654-B2
CHESTNUT ST
- BREN 94513 616-H1
- CCCo 94513 616-H1
1100 CCCo 94513 617-A1
1300 CCCo 94553 571-F4
3600 LFYT 94549 611-E6
CHESTNUT WY
7600 PLE 94588 693-H7
CHETWOOD ST
600 OAK 94610 650-A2
CHEVAL LN
200 CCCo 94596 612-F7
CHEVY PL
- CCCo 94507 632-E2
CHEVY WY
2900 CCCo 94806 589-A2
CHEYENNE AV
2900 SRMN 94583 673-G7
CHEYENNE CT
- ANT 94531 595-H5
2500 WLCK 94598 612-H4
CHEYENNE DR
700 WLCK 94598 612-H4
CHIANTI CT
- BREN 94513 616-C1
CHIANTI PL
100 PLHL 94523 592-A3
CHIANTI WY
800 OAKL 94561 596-D1
CHIAVARI CT
- BREN 94513 616-C1
CHICKIE ST
2200 ANT 94509 574-J5
CHICKPEA CT
3000 ANT 94509 575-J6
CHICO CT
- OAK 94611 630-F6
CHICORY CT
- BREN 94513 616-H5
4100 OAKL 94561 596-C1
CHICORY DR
2000 OAKL 94561 596-C1
CHICOT PL
1200 CNCD 94521 593-G7
CHILDERS CT
- CCCo 94507 633-A3
CHILENSE CT
- SRMN 94582 673-G2
CHILLINGHAM CT
3600 PLE 94588 694-E5
CHILPANCINGO PKWY
- CCCo 94553 592-B2
- PLHL 94523 592-B2
200 CCCo 94523 592-B2
1900 MRTZ 94553 591-J1
1900 MRTZ 94553 592-B2
CHILTERN DR
1100 WLCK 94596 632-G1
CHIMNEY MOUNTAIN CT
- ANT 94531 595-F4
CHIMNEYWOOD CT
1300 CNCD 94521 593-E6
CHINOOK CT
2500 WLCK 94598 612-H4
5200 ANT 94531 595-G5
CHINOOK DR
2500 WLCK 94598 612-H4
CHINOOK WY
- ANT 94531 595-G5
CHINQUAPIN CT
100 HER 94547 570-A5
1800 CNCD 94519 593-B2
CHIPPENDALE CT
3500 PLE 94588 694-E5
CHIPPEWA CT
1000 WLCK 94598 612-H4
CHIQUITA AV
800 PIT 94565 574-F3
CHISM WY
4800 ANT 94531 596-A3
CHLOE CT
1000 CNCD 94518 592-J5
CHLOE DR
4200 CNCD 94518 592-J5
CHOCOLATE ST
2600 PLE 94588 694-G6
CHOCTAW CT
1000 WLCK 94598 612-H4

CHOLLO CT
100 PLHL 94523 592-B2
CHOMOR CT
2400 ANT 94509 595-A1
CHORLEY WK
- PLHL 94523 591-B1
CHRISLAND CT
3000 CNCD 94520 572-F6
CHRISSE CT
3000 ANT 94509 575-C7
CHRISTEN DR
100 PLHL 94523 592-B1
100 CCCo 94553 592-B1
100 PLHL 94553 592-B1
CHRISTENSEN LN
- WLCK 94597 612-B2
CHRISTENSEN RD
13600 AlaC 94551 (657-F7 See Page 638)
CHRISTENSON CT
- BREN 94513 616-H3
CHRISTENSON ST
4600 BREN 94513 616-G3
CHRISTIAN CT
2400 PIN 94564 569-G5
CHRISTIE DR
100 MRTZ 94553 591-F1
CHRISTIE RD
1000 CCCo 94553 570-E4
1000 HER 94547 570-E4
1000 HER 94553 570-E4
1000 CCCo 94547 570-E4
CHRISTINA CT
400 ANT 94509 575-E7
CHRISTINA LN
- WLCK 94597 612-A2
CHRISTINE CT
- CCCo 94806 569-A5
800 PLHL 94523 592-C3
CHRISTINE DR
100 CCCo 94806 568-J5
100 CCCo 94806 569-A5
600 DNVL 94526 653-B2
CHRISTINE LN
- OAKL 94561 576-F7
CHRISTMAS TREE CT
- CCCo 94596 612-F6
CHRISTOPHER CT
- CCCo 94803 589-F2
CHRISTOPHER LN
- CCCo 94507 632-E2
CHRISTOPHER WY
3100 SRMN 94583 673-F5
CHRISTY ST
- OAKL 94561 596-C2
CHUCKER CT
3600 WLCK 94598 613-A3
CHUGACH PL
3400 CNCD 94518 592-H6
CHUPCAN PL
400 CLAY 94517 593-H6
CHURCH LN
1800 SPAB 94806 588-J3
CHURCH RD
- CCCo 94513 616-J4
CHURCH ST
- DNVL 94526 653-A2
100 MRTZ 94553 571-F7
1100 BEN 94510 550-J3
CHURCHILL CT
3500 PLE 94588 694-E6
CHURCHILL DR
3900 PLE 94588 694-E5
4100 CNCD 94521 593-A4
CHURCHILL DOWNS CT
500 WLCK 94597 612-C3
CHUSAN WY
- CCCo 94582 674-B2
CIDER MILL CT
- PIT 94565 573-J2
CIELO CT
- ORIN 94563 631-C4
CIELO VIA
100 CCCo 94598 612-F4
2900 WLCK 94598 612-F4
CIMARRON CT
100 DNVL 94506 653-H5
CINDY CT
- PLHL 94523 612-A1
300 SRMN 94583 673-E5
2900 RCH 94803 589-E2
CINDY LN
- CCCo 94507 632-F6
CINDY PL
- BREN 94513 616-E2
CINDY PTH
2900 RCH 94803 589-E2
CINNABAR ST
3900 ANT 94509 595-E1
CINNABAR WY
100 HER 94547 569-G4
CINNABAR HILLS CT
- BREN 94513 616-A4
CINNAMON CT
1200 WLCK 94596 632-G2
CINNAMON RIDGE DR
- OAKL 94561 596-F2
CIPRIANI PL
- BREN 94513 596-D6
CIRCLE CT
- RCH 94801 588-E7
2700 CNCD 94520 572-E7
CIRCLE DR
100 CCCo 94595 612-C6
5500 CCCo 94803 569-E7
CIRCLE WY
11500 DBLN 94568 693-G5
CIRCLE CREEK CT
- LFYT 94549 611-J5
CIRCLE CREEK DR
1000 LFYT 94549 611-J5
CIRCLE CREEK LN
1000 LFYT 94549 611-J5
CIRCLE E RANCH DR
- SRMN 94583 673-E7
CIRCLE E RANCH PL
- SRMN 94583 673-E7
CITADEL CT
- PLHL 94523 591-H2
CITRINE CT
100 HER 94547 569-G5
CITRON CT
- SRMN 94583 693-F1
CITRUS AV
700 CNCD 94518 592-J7
2900 WLCK 94598 592-J7
3000 WLCK 94598 612-H1
CITRUS CIR
3000 WLCK 94598 612-H1
CITRUS CT
2100 PIT 94565 574-A3
CIVIC AV
- PIT 94565 574-D3

CIVIC DR
100 HER 94547 569-H3
300 PLHL 94523 592-B3
1100 WLCK 94596 612-C4
1100 WLCK 94597 612-C4
N CIVIC DR
200 WLCK 94596 612-C4
200 WLCK 94597 612-C4
CIVIC PZ
100 DBLN 94568 693-J4
CIVIC CENTER PZ
200 RCH 94804 588-H7
CIVIC CENTER ST
200 RCH 94804 588-H6
CLAEYS CT
1100 CCCo 94572 570-B1
CLAEYS ST
400 MRTZ 94553 571-G5
CLAIBORNE DR
1100 WLCK 94598 612-F1
CLAIRE CT
1800 CNCD 94519 592-H1
CLAIRE PL
600 SRMN 94583 673-F6
CLAIREPOINTE WY
13100 OAK 94619 651-B6
CLAIRMONT PL
- PIT 94565 574-C6
CLARA CT
400 CCCo 94565 573-D1
CLARE CT
- OAKL 94561 596-D2
CLARE ST
2400 SPAB 94806 588-H2
CLAREMONT AV
- ORIN 94563 610-E6
2800 BERK 94705 630-A3
2800 OAK 94705 630-A3
6300 CCCo 94805 589-C6
CLAREMONT BLVD
2700 BERK 94705 630-A3
CLAREMONT CT
1100 BREN 94513 616-D3
5000 OAKL 94561 576-B6
CLAREMONT DR
- BREN 94513 616-E2
1000 CNCD 94518 592-F5
CLAREMONT LN
5100 OAKL 94561 576-C6
CLAREMONT CREST
- BERK 94705 630-A3
CLAREMONT CREST CT
2400 SRMN 94583 673-A1
CLAREMONT CREST WY
- SRMN 94583 673-A1
CLARENCE ST
200 RCH 94801 588-C7
CLARENDON CRES
1000 OAK 94610 650-C3
CLARENDON CT
2700 CCCo 94806 588-J2
CLARET CT
4800 OAKL 94561 576-C7
CLAREWOOD CT
800 CNCD 94518 592-G6
CLAREWOOD DR
4300 OAK 94618 630-B6
4300 OAK 94611 630-B6
CLAREWOOD LN
- OAK 94618 630-B6
CLARIDGE DR
3400 DNVL 94526 653-D7
CLARIE DR
100 PLHL 94523 592-D6
CLARINBRIDGE CIR
- DBLN 94568 694-F4
CLARITA
100 DNVL 94526 653-C4
CLARK AV
6300 DBLN 94568 693-J4
CLARK CT
- CNCD 94521 593-E4
2700 PIN 94564 569-F5
CLARK LN
1600 CNCD 94521 593-E4
2500 WLCK 94597 612-B3
CLARK PL
900 ELCR 94530 609-F2
CLARK RD
3900 RCH 94803 589-D3
3900 CCCo 94803 589-D3
CLARK ST
- HER 94547 569-G3
200 CCCo 94525 550-E5
400 PIT 94565 574-E4
CLARK CREEK CIR
- CLAY 94517 613-J1
CLARKIN CT
300 CCCo 94596 612-G6
CLARKSON CT
900 CNCD 94518 592-F6
CLASSIC WY
1200 CNCD 94521 593-G7
CLAUDIA CT
200 MRGA 94556 631-F5
1000 ANT 94509 575-C6
3300 CNCD 94519 572-G6
CLAUDIA DR
2900 CNCD 94519 572-F7
CLAVERIE WY
500 BEN 94510 551-A4
CLAY CT
900 ANT 94509 595-F1
1200 BREN 94513 616-D3
CLAY ST
100 ALB 94706 609-D5
CLAYBURN RD
3400 ANT 94509 595-D1
CLAYCORD AV
1500 CNCD 94521 593-D4
CLAYCORD CT
5000 CNCD 94521 593-D4
CLAYPOOL CT
- DNVL 94526 653-D3
CLAYTON AV
400 ELCR 94530 609-D3
CLAYTON RD
1500 CNCD 94520 592-F2
2300 CNCD 94519 592-G2
2500 CNCD 94518 592-G2
3600 CNCD 94521 592-G2
3800 CNCD 94519 593-C4
3800 CNCD 94521 593-C4
5400 CLAY 94517 593-F6
6800 CLAY 94517 613-J1
CLAYTON RD W
1500 CNCD 94520 592-D3
CLAYTON WY
1600 CNCD 94519 593-A2
1600 CNCD 94521 593-A2
1800 CNCD 94519 592-J1
1800 CNCD 94519 572-J7
CLAYTON VIEW LN
900 CLAY 94517 593-H7

CLEARBROOK DR
1900 CNCD 94521 593-G3
CLEARBROOK RD
- ANT 94509 595-D1
CLEAR CREEK CT
100 MRTZ 94553 591-H4
4400 CNCD 94521 593-C5
N CLEAR CREEK PL
1600 DNVL 94526 653-B6
S CLEAR CREEK PL
1700 DNVL 94526 653-B6
CLEARFIELD AV
3400 RCH 94803 589-F2
CLEAR LAKE CT
- CCCo 94561 597-E1
- CCCo 94506 654-C4
CLEAR LAKE DR
- CCCo 94561 597-E1
CLEAR LAKE ST
600 CCCo 94506 654-C4
CLEARLAND CIR
2800 CCCo 94565 573-G2
CLEARLAND DR
100 CCCo 94565 573-G2
CLEARPOINTE DR
300 VAL 94591 550-D1
CLEAR SPRINGS CT
3700 CNCD 94518 592-J4
CLEARSTREAM CT
- CCCo 94506 654-C5
CLEAR VIEW CIR
2200 BEN 94510 551-B3
CLEARVIEW CT
2000 WLCK 94598 612-F2
CLEARVIEW DR
- BREN 94513 616-D3
100 VAL 94591 550-D2
CLEAR WATER CT
- RCH 94803 589-G1
CLEARWOOD DR
100 OAKL 94561 596-F1
CLEARWOOD PL
- OAKL 94561 596-F1
CLEARWOOD ST
1700 PIT 94565 573-F4
CLEAVELAND RD
- PLHL 94523 592-C6
CLEEK CT
- RCH 94806 568-H5
CLEMENS RD
1700 OAK 94602 650-D3
CLEMENT AV
- CCCo 94565 573-F2
5700 CCCo 94806 589-A4
CLEMSON CT
- WLCK 94597 612-D1
CLEOPATRA DR
- PLHL 94523 592-D5
CLEVELAND AV
100 CCCo 94565 573-H3
600 ALB 94710 609-C5
800 ALB 94706 609-C5
CLEVELAND CT
1800 CNCD 94521 593-D2
CLEVELAND PL
3000 ANT 94509 575-A7
CLEVELAND ST
600 OAK 94606 650-A4
CLIFDEN CT
- DBLN 94568 693-E4
CLIFF LN
- CCCo 94596 612-D7
500 RCH 94805 589-B6
CLIFFORD CIR
3200 PLE 94588 694-B7
CLIFFORD CT
200 CLAY 94517 613-J1
400 CCCo 94565 573-F1
CLIFFSIDE CT
500 RCH 94801 588-C7
500 RCH 94801 608-C1
CLIFFSIDE DR
300 DNVL 94526 652-J4
300 DNVL 94526 653-A4
800 PLHL 94523 591-J2
CLIFF WALK DR
- VAL 94591 550-E2
CLIFTON CT
- CCCo 94582 674-B5
- WLCK 94595 612-C7
CLIFTON COURT RD
5000 CCCo 94514 637-G7
W CLIFTON COURT RD
12000 SJCo 95206 638-F7
CLINTON AV
2300 RCH 94804 588-H5
3300 RCH 94805 588-J5
3500 RCH 94805 589-A6
5700 CCCo 94805 589-B6
CLINTON CT
2300 ANT 94509 595-A1
CLINTON DR
1700 CNCD 94521 593-D3
CLIPPER DR
100 VAL 94591 550-F3
100 PIT 94565 574-A2
4400 CCCo 94514 617-G7
CLIPPER LN
100 CCCo 94553 572-B5
CLIPPER BAY LN
- BEN 94510 551-A4
CLIPPER HILL
- OAK 94618 630-C4
CLIPPER HILL RD
100 DNVL 94526 652-G2
300 CCCo 94583 652-G2
CLIVE AV
6200 OAK 94611 650-G1
CLOS DUVALL
- BEN 94510 551-D5
CLOUD CT
4300 CNCD 94518 593-A5
CLOUDVIEW DR
1400 PLHL 94523 591-H2
CLOVE CT
- OAKL 94561 596-E2
CLOVE WY
300 OAKL 94561 596-E2
CLOVER CT
1200 LFYT 94549 611-J4
2800 ANT 94531 575-G7
CLOVER DR
5700 OAK 94618 630-A5
CLOVER LN
- CCCo 94595 612-B6
1200 WLCK 94595 612-B6
CLOVERBERRY WY
300 SRMN 94582 653-H7
CLOVERBROOK AV
3800 OAKL 94561 596-F2
CLOVERBROOK CIR
- PIT 94565 573-F4
CLOVERBROOK DR
500 DNVL 94506 654-A6

CLOVERCREST CT
- ANT 94531 595-J5
CLOVERCREST LN
400 SRMN 94582 653-H7
CLOVERDALE AV
2500 CNCD 94518 592-G4
CLOVER HILL CT
100 DNVL 94526 653-B3
CLOVERLEAF CIR
- BREN 94513 616-E2
CLOVEWOOD LN
4300 PLE 94588 693-J7
CLOVIS CT
5200 CNCD 94521 593-D6
CLUB CT
- RCH 94806 568-H6
1200 RCH 94803 569-C7
CLUB DR
1200 RCH 94803 569-C7
CLUB LN
1300 RCH 94803 569-C7
CLUB TER
100 CCCo 94507 633-D6
100 DNVL 94526 633-D6
CLUBHOUSE DR
1400 CCCo 94514 617-J7
CLUBHOUSE RD
1600 CCCo 94528 633-E7
CLUB VIEW DR
1300 ELCR 94530 609-E1
1300 ELCR 94530 589-E7
CLYDE AV
100 PIT 94565 574-E3
1900 CNCD 94520 572-E6
CLYDE DR
100 WLCK 94598 612-G2
CLYDESDALE DR
100 DNVL 94526 633-C7
CLYDESDALE WY
5200 ANT 94531 595-J6
CLYMER CT
2700 CNCD 94519 572-H6
CLYNE CT
500 BEN 94510 551-B1
COACH CT
100 RCH 94803 589-J2
COACH DR
5100 RCH 94803 589-J2
COACHMAN PL
800 CCCo 94517 613-G1
COACHWOOD TER
- ORIN 94563 610-H3
COAD CT
1100 PIT 94565 574-E6
COALINGA AV
1300 RCH 94801 588-G5
COAL MINE CT
- CLAY 94517 593-J7
COALPORT ST
- SPAB 94806 588-G2
COASTAL CT
3900 CCCo 94513 617-E7
COASTVIEW CT
- CCCo 94565 573-C2
COATS CIR
100 PLHL 94523 592-A7
COBALT LN
- BREN 94513 596-D5
COBBLESTONE CT
- SRMN 94583 673-A2
1300 CNCD 94521 593-A4
5800 CCCo 94803 589-G4
COBBLESTONE DR
100 SRMN 94583 673-A2
200 ANT 94509 595-E1
4100 CNCD 94521 593-A4
COBBLESTONE LN
- SRMN 94583 673-A2
COCHISE CT
900 WLCK 94598 612-H4
4600 PLE 94588 694-G7
COCHISE WY
3100 PLE 94588 694-G7
COCHRANE AV
5000 OAK 94618 630-C6
COCO LN
1000 WLCK 94597 612-D3
COCONUT CT
- BREN 94513 616-F3
3000 ANT 94509 575-J6
COCONUT PL
- BREN 94513 616-F3
COCONUT ST
- BREN 94513 616-F3
CODORNICES RD
- BERK 94708 609-H7
CODORNIZ LN
1100 WLCK 94598 612-H5
CODY CT
- SRMN 94583 673-F7
S CODY LN
100 PLHL 94523 592-C6
COFFEE TREE CT
2600 ANT 94509 575-H5
COFFEE TREE WY
2600 ANT 94509 575-H5
COGGINS DR
200 CCCo 94597 592-C7
200 CCCo 94597 612-D1
200 PLHL 94523 592-C7
E COG HILL TER
- DBLN 94568 694-G2
COKER RD
- CCCo 94553 571-F3
- MRTZ 94553 571-F3
COLBOURN PL
5600 OAK 94619 651-B6
COLBY CT
600 WLCK 94598 613-A3
COLDSPRINGS CT
200 MRTZ 94553 571-H6
COLE AV
1600 WLCK 94596 612-C5
COLE CT
- CCCo 94507 633-A6
COLEBROOK CT
- DBLN 94568 694-G3
COLEBROOK LN
- DBLN 94568 694-G3
COLEEN CT
- CCCo 94806 569-C5
COLEMAN CIR
- RCH 94806 568-J6
COLEMAN CT
400 PLHL 94523 592-B6
COLETAS WY
3700 CCCo 94514 637-E3
COLETTE DR
2900 RCH 94806 589-B1
COLFAX ST
1700 CNCD 94519 592-F1
1700 CNCD 94520 592-F1
COLFAX WY
2100 ANT 94509 595-A1

COLGATE AV
200 CCCo 94708 609-G3
COLGETT DR
- OAK 94619 650-H4
COLIMA
200 PIT 94565 574-B3
COLIMA AV
10100 SRMN 94583 673-G5
COLIN ST
1400 SPAB 94806 588-H2
COLINA CT
900 LFYT 94549 611-F7
2400 PIN 94564 569-G7
COLL CT
- SRMN 94583 673-F6
COLLEGE DR
- PLHL 94523 592-C2
COLLEGE LN
2300 SPAB 94806 588-J2
COLLEGE WY
700 PLHL 94523 592-C2
COLLETTE CT
300 BREN 94513 596-G7
COLLIER CANYON RD
- CCCo 94588 675-A2
1800 AlaC 94551 675-C4
1800 CCCo 94551 675-A2
1800 AlaC 94551 694-J5
COLLINS AV
- RCH 94806 588-G1
2300 PIN 94564 569-G7
3400 SPAB 94806 568-H7
3400 RCH 94806 568-H7
COLLINS CT
- RCH 94801 588-E6
100 PLHL 94523 592-A7
COLLINS DR
- PLHL 94523 592-A7
COLLINS ST
100 RCH 94801 588-E6
COLLINSVILLE RD
1100 SolC 94571 554-J1
COLLIS ST
- BREN 94513 616-H1
COLMA CT
- SRMN 94583 673-C3
COLOMA ST
2100 OAK 94602 650-D4
COLOMBARD CT
200 CLAY 94517 593-J7
COLONIAL CT
- BREN 94513 616-B2
- SRMN 94583 673-H7
2200 CCCo 94514 617-J7
2200 WLCK 94598 612-F1
3700 ANT 94509 595-C3
COLORADO AV
- BERK 94707 609-G4
COLORADO DR
5500 CNCD 94521 593-F6
COLORADOS CT
300 LFYT 94549 631-H4
COLOSSEUM WY
- ANT 94531 595-E5
COLT CT
200 CCCo 94549 591-H6
4600 ANT 94531 596-A3
COLTON BLVD
5600 OAK 94611 630-F6
COLTON LN
600 MRTZ 94553 591-H1
COLTON PL
- OAK 94611 630-F7
600 MRTZ 94553 591-H1
N COLTRANE AL
- CNCD 94519 592-H5
S COLTRANE AL
- CNCD 94519 592-H5
COLUMBIA AV
200 CCCo 94708 609-G3
2300 RCH 94804 609-B4
COLUMBIA CIR
- BERK 94708 609-J7
300 BEN 94510 551-C1
COLUMBIA CT
- WLCK 94598 612-H3
COLUMBIA DR
16800 AlaC 94552 672-C7
COLUMBIA ST
1100 PIT 94565 574-F2
COLUMBIA CREEK DR
500 SRMN 94582 673-J7
500 SRMN 94582 674-A7
COLUMBINE CT
800 DNVL 94526 653-F6
COLUMBINE DR
100 HER 94547 570-A4
COLUMBINE PL
100 HER 94547 570-A4
COLUMBUS AV
1800 CCCo 94525 550-C5
COLUMBUS PKWY
- BEN 94510 550-G1
- BEN 94591 550-G1
- SolC 94591 550-G1
COLUSA AV
100 ELCR 94530 609-E3
100 CCCo 94707 609-E3
300 CCCo 94706 609-E3
400 BERK 94707 609-F5
5200 RCH 94804 609-B3
COLUSA ST
2400 PIN 94564 569-F6
COMANCHE CT
5100 ANT 94531 595-H5
COMANCHE WY
4400 PLE 94588 694-G7
5000 ANT 94531 595-H4
COMEABOUT CIR
- PIT 94565 574-B2
COMICE PKWY
1200 BREN 94513 596-E7
COMISTAS CT
- WLCK 94598 612-J4
COMISTAS DR
2000 WLCK 94598 612-H4
COMMANCHE CT
700 WLCK 94598 612-H3
COMMANDANTS LN
- BEN 94510 551-E6
COMMERCE AV
2000 CNCD 94520 592-E2
COMMERCE CIR
7000 PLE 94588 693-J5
COMMERCE DR
7000 PLE 94588 693-J5
COMMERCE PL
2100 PIT 94565 574-G5
COMMERCE WY
1500 OAK 94606 650-A6
COMMERCIAL CIR
5000 CNCD 94520 572-G3
COMMERCIAL LN
1300 WLCK 94596 612-C5

STREET Block City ZIP Pg-Grid

COMMERCIAL TER
- BREN 94513 616-F1
COMMODORE CT
- SRMN 94582 673-F1
- PIT 94565 573-J2
100 VAL 94591 550-F2
COMMODORE DR
100 RCH 94804 608-H2
COMMODORE WY
- CCCo 94582 673-J2
- CCCo 94582 674-A2
COMO CT
700 BREN 94513 616-E3
COMO WY
400 DNVL 94526 653-E6
COMPASS POINT CT
200 HER 94547 570-A6
COMPO VIA
- DNVL 94526 633-C6
COMPRESSOR RD
- CCCo 94553 571-H3
COMPTON CIR
100 SRMN 94583 673-C2
COMPUTER RD
- CCCo 94553 571-G3
COMSTOCK CT
2700 SRMN 94583 673-E6
COMSTOCK WY
1500 OAK 94606 650-B5
CONCANNON CT
- OAKL 94561 576-C5
CONCANNON DR
1700 OAKL 94561 576-D5
CONCERTO CIR
5300 CNCD 94521 593-F5
CONCHA CT
500 DNVL 94526 653-C2
CONCORD AV
200 BREN 94513 616-C4
700 CCCo 94513 616-E5
1000 CCCo 94520 592-D1
1000 CCCo 94553 592-D1
1000 PLHL 94520 592-D1
1000 PLHL 94553 592-D1
1000 CNCD 94520 592-F1
1000 CNCD 94553 592-D1
CONCORD BLVD
1800 CCCo 94521 593-D3
1800 CNCD 94519 592-H1
1800 CNCD 94521 593-D3
1800 CNCD 94520 592-F2
3700 CNCD 94519 593-A1
5400 CLAY 94517 593-F4
CONCORD CT
1800 CNCD 94521 593-D3
CONCORD DR
2200 PIT 94565 573-J4
CONDADO CT
- SRMN 94583 673-C2
CONDIT CT
900 LFYT 94549 611-J6
CONDIT RD
900 LFYT 94549 611-J6
CONDOR CT
- CNCD 94521 593-B6
- DNVL 94506 653-J6
700 MRTZ 94553 591-G3
800 ANT 94509 595-F2
CONDOR DR
700 MRTZ 94553 591-G3
CONDOR PL
- CLAY 94517 593-H5
CONDOR ST
6000 DNVL 94506 653-J6
CONDOR WY
- CLAY 94517 593-H5
CONEJO CT
500 CCCo 94506 654-A5
CONEJO DR
4300 CCCo 94506 654-A5
CONEJO LN
- CCCo 94506 654-A5
CONEJO WY
1100 WLCK 94597 612-A2
1300 WLCK 94597 611-J2
CONESTOGA LN
6500 DBLN 94568 694-A3
CONESTOGA WY
5300 RCH 94803 589-J2
CONGRESS AV
4500 OAK 94601 650-E7
CONIFER CT
300 WLCK 94598 612-H1
CONIFER LN
- WLCK 94598 612-J1
CONIFER TER
200 CCCo 94506 654-A2
CONLON AV
6100 ELCR 94530 589-B7
CONLON TR
- CCCo 94708 609-G1
- RCH 94805 589-F7
- RCH 94805 609-G1
CONNECTICUT AV
1000 SPAB 94806 588-H1
CONNECTICUT DR
5500 CNCD 94521 593-E6
CONNICK CT
- SRMN 94583 693-F1
CONNIE CT
- OAKL 94561 596-C1
- CCCo 94565 573-F1
CONNIE LN
2100 OAKL 94561 596-C1
CONNOR WY
- BREN 94513 596-H6
CONRAD CT
- OAK 94611 630-E5
CONSTANCE DR
- VAL 94590 550-C1
CONSTANCE PL
300 MRGA 94556 651-D1
CONSTITUTION DR
400 DNVL 94526 653-A1
CONSUELO RD
3000 CNCD 94519 592-H1
CONTADA CIR
500 DNVL 94526 653-B2
CONTER CT
7700 DBLN 94568 693-G3
CONTESSA CT
200 LFYT 94549 631-H3
CONTINENTE AV
200 BREN 94513 616-F3
CONTRA COSTA AV
700 BERK 94707 609-G6
1300 SPAB 94806 589-A4
3100 CCCo 94514 637-D3
CONTRA COSTA BLVD
500 PLHL 94523 592-C2
500 PLHL 94520 592-C2
600 CNCD 94520 592-C2
1000 CNCD 94523 592-C2

CONTRA COSTA DR
900 ELCR 94530 609-D1
CONTRA COSTA PL
- OAK 94618 630-B5
CONTRA COSTA RD
800 ELCR 94530 609-E2
5900 OAK 94618 630-B5
CONTRA COSTA ST
200 RCH 94801 588-B6
CONTRA LOMA BLVD
- CCCo 94509 595-B2
2500 ANT 94509 575-B7
3300 ANT 94509 595-B1
CONWAY CT
100 DNVL 94526 653-D6
CONWAY DR
300 DNVL 94526 653-D6
COOK ST
1100 ANT 94509 575-C5
COOKE ST
- CCCo 94525 550-E5
COOKS CT
- OAKL 94561 596-H3
COOL CREEK CT
- CCCo 94572 569-H1
COOLEY DR
3700 CNCD 94518 592-H4
COOLIDGE AV
2100 OAK 94601 650-D6
2900 OAK 94602 650-E4
COOLIDGE CT
2200 ANT 94509 595-A1
COOLIDGE ST
4500 CNCD 94521 593-D2
COOLIDGE TER
- OAK 94602 650-F3
COOLSPRING CT
100 CCCo 94506 654-C5
COOPER CT
2600 ANT 94509 574-H6
COOPER DR
500 BEN 94510 550-H1
COPAS LN
1600 CNCD 94521 593-B2
COPENHAGEN CT
- CCCo 94507 632-J5
COPPER BEACH GN
- HER 94547 569-H2
COPPERFIELD CT
- BREN 94513 616-A1
COPPERFIELD LN
- DNVL 94506 653-H3
COPPER HILL CT
4500 ANT 94531 595-J3
COPPER KNOLL WY
- OAKL 94561 596-F2
COPPER RIDGE RD
- SRMN 94582 673-F2
COPPERSET RD
- SRMN 94582 673-H2
COQUILLE PL
- DBLN 94568 694-H3
CORA CT
- CCCo 94597 612-D2
CORAL CT
5100 CNCD 94521 593-E4
N CORAL CT
- CCCo 94513 617-E7
S CORAL CT
3900 CCCo 94513 617-E7
CORAL DR
- ORIN 94563 631-C5
200 PIT 94565 574-E5
700 CCCo 94572 569-J2
800 CCCo 94572 570-A2
CORAL LN
- PIT 94565 574-A3
CORAL WY
7600 DBLN 94568 693-J2
CORAL BELL CT
- CCCo 94582 674-A2
CORALEE LN
4000 LFYT 94549 611-A7
CORALFLOWER LN
2000 SRMN 94582 653-J7
CORALIE DR
400 WLCK 94597 612-A2
CORAL RIDGE CIR
700 CCCo 94572 569-J2
CORALWOOD DR
- CNCD 94521 613-D2
CORDAY CT
4600 PLE 94588 694-A6
CORDELIA WY
- WLCK 94597 612-B2
CORDELL CT
700 DNVL 94526 652-H1
CORDELL DR
300 DNVL 94526 652-G1
CORDOBA CT
2200 ANT 94509 595-A1
CORDOBA WY
2100 ANT 94509 595-A1
CORDOVA ST
2400 OAK 94602 650-D5
CORDOVA WY
100 CNCD 94519 592-G2
3100 LFYT 94549 631-H4
COREY CT
- SRMN 94583 673-E5
COREY PL E
2600 SRMN 94583 673-D6
CORIANDER CT
- SRMN 94582 653-J7
CORINTH CT
7000 DBLN 94568 693-J3
CORKWOOD CT
4400 CNCD 94521 593-B5
CORLISS DR
- MRGA 94556 631-D5
CORLISS ST
600 CCCo 94565 573-C1
CORMORANT CT
- CCCo 94553 571-J4
CORNELIUS DR
2700 CCCo 94806 569-C5
CORNELL AV
400 ALB 94706 609-D5
1100 BERK 94706 609-D5
1200 BERK 94702 609-D5
CORNELL CT
- PLHL 94523 591-J6
CORNELL DR
- BREN 94513 596-C6
CORNELLA CT
3700 CNCD 94518 592-H4
CORNFLOWER CT
- RCH 94806 569-A6
CORNIGLIA LN
- BREN 94513 596-C7
CORNISH CT
400 OAKL 94561 576-D7
CORNSILK CT
700 BREN 94513 616-E2

CORNWALL CT
- OAK 94611 650-G2
1300 WLCK 94597 612-A3
CORNWALL PL
- DNVL 94506 653-J5
CORNWALL ST
- PIT 94565 574-D2
CORONA CT
2300 BERK 94708 609-H6
5100 PLE 94588 694-H4
CORONA PL
1300 WLCK 94597 612-A2
1300 WLCK 94597 611-J2
CORONADO CT
- CCCo 94513 617-F4
- CCCo 94596 612-E7
- PIT 94565 574-D5
1500 ANT 94509 575-A7
5500 CLAY 94517 593-F6
CORONADO LN
5900 PLE 94588 694-B7
CORONADO ST
- HER 94547 570-A5
300 ELCR 94530 609-D4
CORONATION DR
- BREN 94513 616-D4
CORONEL AV
900 VAL 94591 550-D1
CORRAL CIR
100 SRMN 94583 673-B3
CORRIE CT
- BREN 94513 616-B1
CORRIE LN
1100 WLCK 94597 612-C1
CORRIE PL
300 CCCo 94507 632-H5
800 PLHL 94523 592-A4
CORRIGAN CT
800 BEN 94510 551-A3
CORRINNE CT
100 SRMN 94583 693-G1
CORRINNE PL
7500 SRMN 94583 693-G1
CORRINNE ST
7500 SRMN 94583 693-G1
CORT AV
5100 RCH 94804 609-A3
CORTE ST
- SPAB 94806 588-J3
CORTE AIRES
- MRGA 94556 631-D2
CORTE AMIGOS
- MRGA 94556 631-C2
CORTE ANNETTE
- MRGA 94556 631-D2
CORTE ARANGO
400 CCCo 94803 589-D1
CORTE AZUL
- MRGA 94556 631-D2
CORTE BOMBERO
- ORIN 94563 631-A3
CORTE BRIONES
800 MRTZ 94553 591-G4
CORTE CIELO
- CCCo 94553 571-J3
CORTE CRUZ
1900 PIN 94564 569-E6
CORTE DE LA CANADA LN
- CCCo 94553 591-D3
CORTE DE LA REINA
200 WLCK 94598 612-G2
CORTE DEL CABALLO
- MRGA 94556 631-D2
CORTE DEL CAMPO
- MRGA 94556 631-D2
CORTE DEL CONTENTO
- CCCo 94595 611-J7
- CCCo 94595 612-A7
CORTE DEL MARQUES
2500 WLCK 94598 612-G2
CORTE DEL PRADO
100 WLCK 94598 612-H2
CORTE DEL REY
- ORIN 94563 631-C5
CORTE DEL SOL
- BEN 94510 551-C4
- CCCo 94553 571-J4
- MRGA 94556 631-E2
CORTE DEL VECINOS
1300 WLCK 94598 612-E4
CORTE DE MAIO
2900 WLCK 94598 612-G3
CORTE DE ORO
- MRGA 94556 631-D2
CORTE DE ROSAS
- MRGA 94556 631-D2
CORTE DIABLO
900 MRTZ 94553 591-F4
CORTE DORADO
- BEN 94510 551-D4
400 DNVL 94526 653-E5
CORTE ELLENA
- WLCK 94598 612-H4
CORTE ENCANTO
- DNVL 94526 652-H2
CORTE ENCINA
- MRGA 94556 631-D2
CORTE ESTRELLA
- CCCo 94553 571-J4
CORTE FORTUNA
- MRGA 94556 631-E2
CORTE FRESCA
- MRGA 94556 631-D2
CORTE GABRIEL
300 MRGA 94556 631-E7
CORTE GRANADA
- MRGA 94556 631-E2
CORTE HOLGANZA
- ORIN 94563 631-C6
CORTE LADO
- CCCo 94553 571-J3
CORTE LA RADO
- MRGA 94556 631-D3
CORTE LINDA
100 PIT 94565 574-F3
CORTE LOMA
1300 WLCK 94598 612-E4
CORTE MADERA
1300 WLCK 94598 612-E4
CORTE MARIA
- MRGA 94556 651-D1
100 PIT 94565 574-F4
CORTE MARIE
2700 WLCK 94598 612-H4
CORTE MATEO
- MRGA 94556 631-D2
CORTE MIGUEL
2900 CNCD 94518 592-H6
CORTE MONTEREY
- MRGA 94556 631-D2
CORTE NOGAL
- DNVL 94526 652-H2

CORTE PINON
- MRGA 94556 631-E1
CORTE PINTO
- MRGA 94556 631-D2
CORTE POQUITA
6700 MRTZ 94553 591-G4
CORTE REAL AV
1900 OAK 94611 630-E7
1900 OAK 94611 650-E1
CORTE RINALDO
- LFYT 94549 611-B7
- LFYT 94563 611-B7
CORTE ROYAL
- MRGA 94556 631-D2
CORTES CT
- MRGA 94556 631-E7
100 HER 94547 570-B5
CORTE SANTA CLARA
- MRGA 94556 631-E2
CORTE SEGUNDA
6700 MRTZ 94553 591-G4
CORTE SEGUNDO
3600 CNCD 94519 592-J2
CORTE SOMBRITA
- ORIN 94563 631-C6
CORTE TERCERA
6700 MRTZ 94553 591-G4
CORTE VISTA ST
- BREN 94513 596-D7
CORTE YOLANDA
- MRGA 94556 631-E2
CORTEZ CT
- OAK 94611 630-F7
1400 WLCK 94598 612-E4
2700 ANT 94509 575-B6
CORTINA CT
900 WLCK 94598 612-J4
4100 PLE 94588 694-C6
CORTLAND TER
400 BREN 94513 616-D1
CORTO CT
11600 DBLN 94568 693-F4
CORTO SQ
600 RCH 94804 608-H1
CORTONA DR
100 SRMN 94582 673-G3
CORTONA WY
- BREN 94513 616-C2
CORTSEN CT
- PLHL 94523 591-J6
- PLHL 94523 592-A6
CORTSEN RD
100 PLHL 94523 592-A6
300 PLHL 94523 591-J6
CORVEY CT
1400 WLCK 94598 612-F4
CORWIN CT
4700 PLE 94588 694-A6
CORWIN DR
- CCCo 94507 632-G7
CORY LN
- DBLN 94568 693-E5
COSMOS CT
- BREN 94513 596-E6
- RCH 94806 568-J6
- RCH 94806 569-A6
COSSO CT
- LFYT 94549 611-C4
COSTA AV
1300 SPAB 94806 588-G4
1300 RCH 94801 588-G4
COSTA CT
2000 PIN 94564 569-E6
COSTANZA DR
100 MRTZ 94553 591-G1
COSTCO WY
- ANT 94509 575-A4
COTATI CT
- OAKL 94561 576-E5
COTTAGE AV
- RCH 94801 588-D7
COTTAGE CT
- CCCo 94595 612-A7
COTTAGE DR
- DNVL 94526 653-A3
COTTAGE LN
- HER 94547 569-F3
- CCCo 94595 612-A7
2800 CCCo 94511 577-D4
COTTAGE GROVE DR
- CCCo 94513 617-F3
COTTINGHAM CT
3300 WLCK 94598 612-H6
COTTON ST
1000 OAK 94606 650-A7
COTTONWOOD
- BEN 94510 551-B6
COTTON WOOD CIR
6500 DBLN 94568 694-A2
COTTONWOOD COM
- BREN 94513 596-G6
COTTONWOOD CT
100 HER 94547 570-A4
COTTONWOOD DR
- PLHL 94523 592-C2
3700 CNCD 94519 593-A1
3800 CCCo 94506 654-D5
COTTONWOOD LN
100 CCCo 94506 654-D5
COTTONWOOD PL
100 CCCo 94506 654-D5
COUGAR LN
1200 CNCD 94521 593-C5
COUGAR PEAK WY
4900 ANT 94531 595-E3
COULTER PINE CT
1800 WLCK 94595 632-B1
COUNTESS CT
7900 DBLN 94568 693-G3
COUNTESS ST
8300 DBLN 94568 693-G3
COUNTRY CT
- BREN 94513 596-F6
COUNTRY LN
- OAKL 94561 576-D4
- VAL 94590 550-C2
900 CCCo 94596 612-F6
1000 CCCo 94588 654-G6
COUNTRY PL
- OAKL 94561 576-D4
COUNTRY RUN
- HER 94547 569-H4
COUNTRYBROOK LP
600 SRMN 94583 673-F4
COUNTRY CLUB DR
700 MRGA 94556 631-D7
1000 CCCo 94549 591-H5
5500 OAK 94618 630-A5
E COUNTRY CLUB DR
- BREN 94513 616-B2
W COUNTRY CLUB DR
- BREN 94513 616-B1
COUNTRY CLUB PL
- ORIN 94563 610-G7

COUNTRY CLUB PL
200 PIT 94565 574-C3
3400 CCCo 94506 654-C4
COUNTRY CLUB TER
3400 CCCo 94506 654-C4
COUNTRY CREEK CT
900 SRMN 94582 674-A7
COUNTRY GLEN LN
900 BREN 94513 596-E6
COUNTRY HILLS CT
- DNVL 94506 653-G6
COUNTRY HILLS DR
- ANT 94509 595-F3
4300 ANT 94531 595-H3
5000 ANT 94531 596-A4
COUNTRY MEADOWS LN
200 DNVL 94506 653-J5
COUNTRY OAK LN
- CCCo 94507 633-D4
COUNTRY RUN DR
900 MRTZ 94553 571-G4
COUNTRYSIDE CT
- CCCo 94595 632-C1
- DNVL 94506 653-H6
600 BREN 94513 616-F2
COUNTRY SIDE WY
- ANT 94565 594-G1
COUNTRY VIEW DR
5300 RCH 94803 590-A3
COUNTRY VIEW LN
- DNVL 94526 632-J6
300 PLHL 94523 592-B2
COUNTRYWOOD CT
1600 WLCK 94598 612-E1
COUNTRYWOOD DR
2700 ANT 94509 575-F7
COURT LN
700 CNCD 94518 592-J4
N COURT ST
- MRTZ 94553 571-D2
COURT ST N
500 MRTZ 94553 571-E3
COURTER LN
800 MRGA 94556 631-C6
COURTLAND AV
2200 OAK 94601 650-E7
2900 OAK 94619 650-F7
COURTLAND DR
- OAKL 94561 596-C1
2700 CNCD 94520 572-E7
COURTLAND ST
600 RCH 94805 589-B5
COURTNEY AV
1500 PLE 94588 694-F7
COURTNEY LN
- CCCo 94506 654-C5
200 ORIN 94563 631-A3
COVE CT
2200 CCCo 94514 617-H7
COVE LN
4500 CCCo 94514 617-G7
COVE PL
2400 CCCo 94514 617-H7
COVE WY
- CCCo 94565 573-J2
- PIT 94565 573-J2
500 BEN 94510 551-A4
COVELITE WY
2400 ANT 94531 595-G2
COVENTRY CIR
800 BREN 94513 616-E2
COVENTRY CT
- ANT 94509 575-E6
1900 CCCo 94595 632-C2
COVENTRY DR
- OAKL 94561 596-C2
COVENTRY PL
- HER 94547 569-J3
400 CCCo 94506 654-A5
COVENTRY RD
200 CCCo 94707 609-E4
1200 CNCD 94518 592-H3
COVERED WAGON DR
1000 OAKL 94561 576-E7
COVEY CT
700 WLCK 94598 613-A3
COVINGTON CT
1100 WLCK 94596 632-G1
COVINGTON DR
- PIT 94565 574-C3
COWAN RD
3900 LFYT 94549 611-B4
COWELL RD
1200 CNCD 94521 592-J4
1200 CNCD 94518 592-G3
4000 CNCD 94521 593-A5
4000 CNCD 94518 593-A5
COWING RD
8200 AlaC 94552 693-A6
COWPER AV
- CCCo 94707 609-F2
- CCCo 94805 609-F2
COW POKE LN
- CCCo 94548 597-C2
COYOTE CIR
2000 CLAY 94517 593-H5
COYOTE CT
- SRMN 94582 673-G3
900 ANT 94509 595-F1
8400 BREN 94513 596-G4
COYOTE PL
- SRMN 94582 673-F3
CRABAPPLE CT
- HER 94547 569-H2
CRADDOCK CT
1000 WLCK 94596 612-E5
CRAFT AV
800 ELCR 94530 609-F2
CRAFTSMAN DR
- HER 94547 569-H1
CRAG CT
- HER 94547 569-H4
CRAGFORD PL
- DBLN 94568 694-H3
CRAGMONT AV
400 BERK 94708 609-H5
CRAGMONT CT
- CCCo 94598 612-D4
CRAGMONT DR
100 CCCo 94598 612-E4
CRAIG AV
- PDMT 94611 650-B1
CRAIG CT
700 BREN 94513 616-H2
CRAIG DR
1200 CNCD 94518 592-H3
CRAIGLEE WY
- SRMN 94582 674-C3
CRAIGTOWN LN
- DBLN 94568 693-E5
CRANBROOK PL
- DBLN 94568 694-G2
CRANBROOK WY
3400 CNCD 94520 572-F5

CRANE CT
- OAKL 94561 576-H6
- ORIN 94563 610-G3
100 HER 94547 569-H4
CRANE TER
100 ORIN 94563 610-G3
CRANE WY
3200 OAK 94602 650-G3
CRANEFORD WY
- SRMN 94582 674-C3
CRANFORD LN
7800 DBLN 94568 693-H3
CRANLEIGH CT
- CCCo 94583 673-B5
CRANWOOD CT
3100 PLE 94588 694-F6
CRATER LAKE CT
- OAKL 94561 596-H2
CRATER PEAK WY
1700 ANT 94531 595-F3
CRAWFORD CT
- CCCo 94595 612-B7
CRAWFORD DR
- BREN 94513 616-B3
CRAWFORD ST
2700 CNCD 94518 592-G2
CRAYDON CIR
9000 SRMN 94583 693-J1
CRAYDON CT
- SRMN 94583 693-H1
CREE CT
- SRMN 94583 673-D5
700 WLCK 94598 612-H3
CREED AV
100 ANT 94509 575-C6
CREED RD
800 OAK 94610 650-C3
CREEK RD
- CCCo 94553 571-H3
400 BREN 94513 616-E5
700 CCCo 94513 616-E5
CREEKDALE RD
100 CCCo 94595 632-C2
CREEKLEDGE CT
- DNVL 94506 653-F1
CREEKMORE CT
600 WLCK 94598 612-J3
CREEKPOINT CT
4100 CCCo 94506 654-C5
CREEKRIDGE LN
- CNCD 94518 592-H4
CREEKSIDE AV
1000 DNVL 94506 653-F5
CREEKSIDE CT
100 CCCo 94803 589-E3
4000 OAKL 94561 596-H1
11200 DBLN 94568 693-E3
CREEKSIDE DR
- HER 94547 569-F2
- PLE 94588 693-H6
- SRMN 94583 673-A2
1400 WLCK 94596 612-D7
1400 WLCK 94596 632-D1
7700 DBLN 94568 693-F3
N CREEKSIDE DR
- ANT 94509 574-J6
S CREEKSIDE DR
- ANT 94509 574-J7
CREEKSIDE LN
- MRTZ 94553 571-F7
- MRTZ 94553 591-F1
1800 CNCD 94521 593-E4
CREEKSIDE RD
400 PLHL 94523 592-A4
CREEKSIDE WY
3800 OAKL 94561 596-H2
CREEKSIDE OAKS
- CCCo 94553 591-E3
CREEKTRAIL CT
- BREN 94513 596-G5
CREEK TREE LN
- CCCo 94507 632-F5
CREEKVIEW CT
6300 MRTZ 94553 591-H3
CREEKVIEW DR
- DBLN 94568 694-E2
CREEKVIEW PL
- CCCo 94506 654-D6
CREEKWOOD CT
- PIT 94565 574-G7
- DNVL 94526 653-C6
500 BREN 94513 616-E1
CREEKWOOD PL
900 LFYT 94549 611-G6
CREELY AV
5000 RCH 94804 609-B2
CREELY PTH
5000 RCH 94804 609-A2
CREIGHTON WY
100 DNVL 94506 653-H5
300 OAK 94619 650-H4
CRENNA AV
3600 CNCD 94519 592-J1
CREPE MYRTLE DR
- HER 94547 569-H2
CRESCENT CT
- ANT 94565 574-H7
CRESCENT DR
- PLHL 94523 592-C6
- ORIN 94563 610-E6
700 BREN 94513 616-D3
1600 WLCK 94598 592-F7
1600 WLCK 94598 612-E1
2400 CNCD 94520 572-F7
3600 LFYT 94549 611-E6
CRESCENT PZ
- PLHL 94523 592-C6
CRESCENT WY
- CCCo 94513 617-F4
- ELCR 94530 589-C7
CRESCENTA CT
1100 LFYT 94549 611-F5
CREST AV
- CCCo 94507 632-D1
- RCH 94801 608-D1
1500 CCCo 94805 589-C5
N CREST AV
2200 CCCo 94553 571-F4
S CREST AV
2200 CCCo 94553 571-F4
CREST CT
- CCCo 94507 632-D2
4000 PLE 94588 694-A7
CREST RD
- LFYT 94549 611-A6
- PDMT 94611 650-D2
CREST ST
200 ANT 94509 575-E4
CRESTA LN
11400 DBLN 94568 693-F4
CRESTA BLANCA
- ORIN 94563 610-F7
CRESTA BLANCA CT
- OAKL 94561 576-C5

CRESTED OAK CT
- SRMN 94583 673-E7
CREST ESTATES DR
- CCCo 94507 632-D1
CRESTHAVEN CT
5000 ANT 94531 595-E4
CRESTLINE CT
3100 ANT 94531 595-G1
CRESTMONT DR
- OAK 94619 650-H4
- OAK 94602 650-H4
1100 LFYT 94549 611-D5
CRESTMONT PL
3700 LFYT 94549 611-D5
CRESTON RD
600 BERK 94708 609-H4
2800 WLCK 94597 612-A2
CRESTONE NEEDLE WY
4700 ANT 94531 595-D3
CRESTONE PEAK CT
4700 ANT 94531 595-D3
CRESTPARK CIR
5000 ANT 94531 595-J4
CRESTRIDGE CT
- HER 94547 569-G3
- DNVL 94506 653-H6
CRESTRIDGE DR
100 DNVL 94506 653-H6
CREST RIDGE LN
1100 CNCD 94521 593-D6
CRESTRIDGE TER
- DBLN 94568 694-F3
CRESTVIEW
- CCCo 94525 550-C5
CRESTVIEW AV
200 MRTZ 94553 571-G5
CREST VIEW CT
- ORIN 94563 631-A4
CRESTVIEW CT
- VAL 94591 550-D2
- CCCo 94549 611-H1
CREST VIEW DR
- ORIN 94563 631-A4
100 ORIN 94563 630-J3
CRESTVIEW DR
- OAK 94619 651-B7
700 PIN 94564 569-C4
1200 ANT 94509 575-B5
2100 PIT 94565 574-C4
CRESTVIEW LN
2100 PIT 94565 574-D3
CREST VIEW TER
100 ORIN 94563 630-J3
CRESTWOOD CIR
4400 CNCD 94521 593-C2
CRESTWOOD CT
1800 CNCD 94521 593-C2
CRESTWOOD DR
1800 ANT 94509 575-E6
15800 CCCo 94806 569-A6
CRESTWOOD PL
200 SRMN 94583 673-F6
CRICKET HILL RD
- LFYT 94549 611-A4
CRIMSON CT
1200 WLCK 94596 632-G2
CRIMSON TER
1700 BREN 94513 616-D1
CRIMSON CLOVER CT
- BREN 94513 616-H5
CRIQUET CT
1500 CNCD 94518 592-E6
CRISMORE DR
3100 OAKL 94561 596-J3
CRISPIN DR
1500 BREN 94513 616-C2
CRISTINA WY
- BREN 94513 616-C3
CRIVELLO AV
- CCCo 94565 573-H2
CROAK RD
3400 DBLN 94568 694-H5
3400 DBLN 94588 694-H5
CROCKER AV
- PDMT 94611 650-C1
100 PDMT 94610 650-C2
200 OAK 94610 650-C2
CROCKER WY
2500 ANT 94531 595-F4
CROCKET CT
- BREN 94513 616-H1
CROCKET DR
- BREN 94513 616-H1
CROCKETT BLVD
1300 CCCo 94525 550-D5
1300 CCCo 94553 550-D5
1300 CCCo 94569 550-D5
CROCKETT DR
- MRGA 94556 651-F1
CROCKETT LN
- OAKL 94561 596-B1
CROCKETT PL
5100 OAK 94602 650-H3
CROFTERS CT
3700 PLE 94588 694-F5
CROFTON AV
500 OAK 94610 650-A2
500 PDMT 94610 650-A2
CROFTON CT
600 LFYT 94549 631-H2
CROKAERTS ST
2000 WLCK 94596 612-C4
CROLONA HTS
- CCCo 94525 550-D4
CROMART CT
2000 MRTZ 94553 571-J7
CROMWELL AV
- DBLN 94568 694-A2
CROMWELL CT
- DNVL 94526 653-C4
CRONIN CIR
7200 DBLN 94568 693-G4
CROSBY AV
2000 OAK 94601 650-D7
CROSBY CT
- CCCo 94553 572-B7
- WLCK 94598 612-D3
CROSBY DR
9600 PLE 94588 693-F6
CROSS RD
100 CCCo 94507 633-B6
100 OAK 94618 630-B5
CROSS ST
800 PIT 94565 574-F3
CROSS WY
1300 CNCD 94520 592-F3
CROSS BRIDGE CT
- DNVL 94526 653-F4
CROSS BRIDGE DR
200 DNVL 94526 653-E4
CROSS BRIDGE PL
- DNVL 94526 653-F4
CROSSBROOK CT
800 MRGA 94556 631-D6

STREET
Block City ZIP Pg-Grid

CROSSBROOK DR
700 MRGA 94556 631-D5
CROSS CREEK CIR
- DBLN 94568 694-A2
CROSS CREEK RD
1400 WLCK 94596 612-D7
CROSSING CREEK LN
- BREN 94513 596-E7
CROSSRIDGE CT
600 ORIN 94563 610-H6
600 BREN 94513 616-E1
CROSSRIDGE PL
600 ORIN 94563 610-H6
CROSSRIDGE RD
7900 DBLN 94568 694-A2
CROSSRIDGE TER
- ORIN 94563 610-H6
S CROSSWAYS
- BERK 94705 630-A4
CROSSWIND CT
100 HER 94547 570-A6
CROW CT
- ANT 94509 574-J4
4600 PLE 94588 694-G7
CROW PL
100 CLAY 94517 593-J5
CROW CANYON CT
- SRMN 94583 673-B1
CROW CANYON PL
2000 SRMN 94583 673-C1
CROW CANYON RD
2300 SRMN 94583 672-G3
2300 SRMN 94583 673-D1
2300 CCCo 94583 672-G3
2300 CCCo 94583 673-A2
3400 DNVL 94526 653-G7
3400 DNVL 94526 673-D1
3400 SRMN 94582 653-G7
3400 SRMN 94582 673-D1
5700 AlaC 94552 672-B3
8000 DNVL 94506 653-G7
CROWE PL
1000 CNCD 94518 592-J4
CROWLEY AV
100 PIT 94565 574-C4
CROWLEY CT
- PIT 94565 574-C3
CROWN AV
6200 OAK 94611 630-D6
CROWN CT
- ORIN 94563 631-C4
- WLCK 94597 612-B3
CROWN PEAK WY
- ANT 94531 595-E4
CROWN RIDGE CT
- OAK 94605 651-A7
CROWNRIDGE DR
- DNVL 94506 653-G2
CROWNRIDGE TER
- DNVL 94506 653-G2
CROWN VALLEY CT
- DNVL 94506 653-H6
CROWS NEST CIR
300 HER 94547 570-B6
CROWSNEST CT
100 VAL 94591 550-F2
CROWS NEST WY
1000 RCH 94803 589-H3
CROYDEN DR
200 PLHL 94523 592-A6
CROYDON CIR
- PDMT 94611 650-D2
CRUCERO AV
1900 SPAB 94806 568-J7
CRUCERO CT
- SPAB 94806 568-J7
CRUCERO ST
- VAL 94591 550-D1
CRUZ RD
- CCCo 94513 597-A5
CRYSTAL AV
2600 CNCD 94520 572-F7
CRYSTAL CIR
- HER 94547 569-G4
CRYSTAL CT
- ANT 94531 595-G2
1000 WLCK 94598 612-G4
CRYSTAL LN
2700 CCCo 94513 597-C7
CRYSTAL WY
- ANT 94531 595-G1
- BERK 94708 609-H6
CRYSTAL COVE CT
- RCH 94804 608-J3
CRYSTAL GARDEN CT
700 BREN 94513 616-E3
CRYSTAL RIDGE WY
- OAKL 94561 596-F2
CRYSTAL SPRINGS CIR
- CCCo 94513 617-G3
CRYSTAL SPRINGS CT
600 CCCo 94506 654-D5
CRYSTYL RANCH DR
5100 CNCD 94521 593-C7
5100 CNCD 94521 613-C1
CUADRA CT
2200 PIN 94564 569-E3
CUB CT
- ANT 94531 595-H2
CUENCA CT
- SRMN 94583 673-C3
CUENCA DR
2400 SRMN 94583 673-C2
CUESTA TR
- CCCo 94583 652-C3
CUESTA WY
- CCCo 94597 612-A4
CULET DR
300 DNVL 94506 654-B6
CULET RANCH RD
1200 DNVL 94506 654-B6
CULL CANYON RD
10000 AlaC 94546 652-B7
10500 AlaC 94552 652-B7
11000 AlaC 94552 672-B1
CULLEN CT
1400 WLCK 94597 611-J3
CULLENS CT
- SRMN 94582 674-C4
CULVER CT
- ORIN 94563 630-J4
2200 WLCK 94598 612-G2
4100 OAK 94619 650-E6
CULVER ST
4100 OAK 94619 650-F6
CUMBERLAND CT
- DNVL 94526 633-A7
700 PLHL 94523 592-A7
CUMBERLAND DR
400 PLHL 94523 591-J7
700 PLHL 94523 592-A7
CUMBERLAND LN
- MRGA 94556 631-D5

CUMBERLAND ST
300 PIT 94565 574-E2
CUMBERLAND TR
- CCCo 94517 594-C5
CUMBERLAND WY
- CCCo 94513 617-F4
CUMBRE DR
- WLCK 94597 612-A2
CUMBRIAN CT
3200 WLCK 94598 612-H6
CUMMING RD
1900 CCCo 94513 597-B5
CUMMINGS SKWY
- CCCo 94525 550-B5
300 CCCo 94553 570-F1
300 CCCo 94553 550-C6
300 CCCo 94569 550-C6
300 CCCo 94569 570-F1
CUMORAH LN
- CCCo 94507 633-A6
CUNEO CT
1100 CNCD 94518 592-J5
CUNEO DR
4200 CNCD 94518 592-J5
4200 CNCD 94518 593-A5
CUNHA CT
- OAKL 94561 576-A7
CUNHA DR
- CCCo 94513 597-A5
CUNNINGHAM ST
4600 OAK 94619 650-G6
CUNNINGHAM WY
2000 MRTZ 94553 572-A6
CUPFLOWER CT
2800 PLE 94588 694-H4
CURLETTO DR
1700 CNCD 94521 593-D3
CURLEW CONNEX
3100 CCCo 94561 597-A3
3200 CCCo 94548 597-A3
CURRAN AV
3000 OAK 94602 650-D5
CURRAN CT
2500 PIN 94564 569-G5
CURRAN WY
3400 OAK 94602 650-E5
CURREY CT
- BEN 94510 551-C1
CURRY AV
7400 ELCR 94530 609-E4
CURRY PL
- PIN 94564 569-C3
CURRY ST
100 RCH 94801 588-E7
2600 PLE 94588 694-G6
CURTIS CIR
3200 PLE 94588 694-C7
CURTIS CT
- CCCo 94565 573-E2
CURTIS DR
- ANT 94509 574-J7
- ANT 94509 575-A7
100 BREN 94513 596-G7
CURTIS ST
500 ALB 94706 609-E5
500 CCCo 94706 609-E5
1100 BERK 94706 609-E7
1200 BERK 94702 609-E7
CUSHENDALL WY
- ANT 94531 596-A3
CUSTER ST
3500 OAK 94601 650-D6
CUTHBERT AV
3100 OAK 94602 650-D5
CUTHBERTSON CT
3100 RCH 94806 589-A1
CUTIE LN
1800 CCCo 94521 593-E3
CUTLER CT
- ANT 94531 595-C4
CUTTER AV
900 PIT 94565 554-E7
CUTTER CT
- SRMN 94583 673-D6
CUTTER LN
5200 RCH 94803 589-J2
CUTTER LP
5700 CCCo 94514 617-J6
CUTTER ST
500 PIT 94565 574-D1
CUTTING BLVD
100 RCH 94804 608-G1
2200 ELCR 94530 589-C7
3600 RCH 94804 609-A1
5100 ELCR 94530 609-B1
W CUTTING BLVD
- RCH 94804 608-E1
800 RCH 94801 608-E1
CUTTING CT
- WLCK 94596 632-F2
900 RCH 94804 609-A1
CUTTING ST
2400 WLCK 94596 632-F2
CYCLOTRON RD
- BERK 94720 630-A1
- OAK 94720 630-A1
CYNTHIA DR
- PLHL 94523 592-C4
CYPRESS AV
1600 CCCo 94805 589-C6
2000 CCCo 94806 569-B4
4500 RCH 94804 609-A2
5100 ELCR 94530 609-B2
CYPRESS CT
- HER 94547 569-H2
- CCCo 94806 569-C3
500 BEN 94510 551-A1
1900 OAKL 94561 576-C7
8300 DBLN 94568 693-H1
CYPRESS DR
1200 CNCD 94520 592-E4
W CYPRESS PL
- OAKL 94561 576-C7
CYPRESS PT
2000 CCCo 94514 617-G7
CYPRESS PTH
- RCH 94804 609-B2
E CYPRESS RD
- CCCo 94561 597-F1
100 OAKL 94561 576-H7
1900 OAKL 94561 577-A7
1900 CCCo 94561 576-H7
1900 CCCo 94561 577-E7
2800 OAKL 94548 577-B7
2800 CCCo 94548 577-A7
W CYPRESS RD
100 OAKL 94561 576-D7
CYPRESS ST
- BREN 94513 596-C7
1400 BERK 94703 609-F7
1400 WLCK 94596 612-C5
2300 ANT 94509 574-J7
CYPRESS WY
3700 PIT 94565 574-G6

CYPRESS HAWK CT
- SRMN 94582 673-G1
CYPRESS HILLS CT
200 DNVL 94526 653-F6
CYPRESS LAKE DR
- CCCo 94561 577-E7
- CCCo 94561 597-E1
CYPRESS POINT CT
- CCCo 94507 633-A5
CYPRESS POINT RD
600 RCH 94801 608-C1
CYPRESS POINT WY
100 MRGA 94556 631-D7

D

D ST
- CCCo 94565 573-E1
- CNCD 94518 592-G4
- CNCD 94520 572-J3
100 BEN 94510 551-B6
200 ANT 94509 575-D4
500 MRTZ 94553 571-E5
W D ST
100 BEN 94510 551-B5
DAFFODIL DR
2200 PIT 94565 573-J4
DAFFODIL WY
700 CNCD 94518 592-J6
DAGNINO RD
3800 AlaC 94551 676-A7
DAHLIA CT
- BREN 94561 596-F4
- LFYT 94549 611-D4
DAHLIA DR
- BREN 94561 596-F4
DAHLIA ST
- PIT 94565 574-C2
DAINTY AV
700 BREN 94513 616-F1
DAISY CT
- RCH 94806 569-A6
- DNVL 94506 654-B5
100 HER 94547 569-J4
600 PLHL 94523 591-J3
DAISY LN
- ORIN 94563 631-B3
DAISY PL
500 PLHL 94523 591-J3
DAISY ST
3800 OAK 94619 650-G6
DAISY WY
1500 ANT 94509 575-B5
DAISYFIELD DR
100 DNVL 94506 653-F5
DAKAR DR
100 CCCo 94553 572-D3
DAKOTA LN
1700 CNCD 94519 592-J2
DAKOTA ST
3000 OAK 94602 650-E5
DALE AV
100 PDMT 94610 650-A1
DALE CT
- CCCo 94595 612-A6
- ORIN 94563 631-B4
300 BEN 94510 551-B3
DALE PL
1000 CNCD 94518 592-E5
3800 OAK 94619 650-E6
DALE RD
400 MRTZ 94553 571-H7
DALESSI DR
1700 PIN 94564 569-D6
DALESSI LN
1800 PIN 94564 569-D7
DALEWOOD DR
300 ORIN 94563 610-H3
DALEWOOD TER
- ORIN 94563 610-J3
DALI CT
- OAKL 94561 596-H1
DALIS DR
2000 CNCD 94520 572-E5
DALLAS CT
2300 ANT 94509 595-A1
DALLAS RANCH RD
4600 ANT 94531 595-E4
DALMALLY LN
- DBLN 94568 693-E5
DALTON CT
- CCCo 94553 572-B7
400 BEN 94510 551-A2
DALTON LN
100 CCCo 94553 572-B7
DALTON WY
- CCCo 94582 674-B5
DAMASCUS DR
100 CCCo 94553 572-C7
DAMASCUS LP
100 CCCo 94553 572-C7
DAMERON PL
3500 ANT 94509 595-B1
DAMIANO CT
5100 PLE 94588 694-H4
DAMON AV
- CCCo 94525 550-E5
DAMPHIER CT
- DBLN 94568 694-G4
DAMUTH ST
2000 OAK 94602 650-D4
DANA CT
3900 CNCD 94519 573-A7
6300 PLE 94588 694-A7
DANA DR
3500 ANT 94509 595-C1
DANA HIGHLANDS CT
100 DNVL 94506 653-G6
900 CCCo 94549 591-G5
DANALA FARMS
- CCCo 94507 632-H7
DANBERRY CT
1100 ANT 94509 575-F7
DANBURY CT
- CCCo 94507 632-J2
DANDELION CIR
2800 ANT 94531 575-G7
DANDELION CT
2800 ANT 94531 575-G7
DANDELION LN
200 SRMN 94582 653-J7
DANEFIELD PL
100 MRGA 94556 631-D6
DANESTA DR
1700 CNCD 94519 593-A1
DANFORTH CT
100 DNVL 94526 653-C6
DANFORTH LN
1100 WLCK 94598 612-D3
DANICA CT
100 BREN 94513 616-F2
DANIEL DR
100 CCCo 94507 632-G7
3700 OAKL 94561 596-E2

DANIEL LN
1100 CNCD 94518 592-J5
DANIEL HILLS CT
1100 BEN 94510 551-A4
DANIELLE CT
1800 WLCK 94598 592-F7
DANIELLE PL
3400 CCCo 94565 573-F1
DANNY CT
- SRMN 94582 673-F1
300 PIN 94564 569-D4
DANRIDGE CT
- ANT 94509 575-D7
DANRIDGE PL
- PIT 94565 574-F7
DANTE CT
300 BREN 94513 616-E3
DANTLEY WY
200 WLCK 94598 612-D4
DANVILLA CT
100 DNVL 94526 652-J2
DANVILLE BLVD
600 DNVL 94526 652-H1
700 DNVL 94526 632-F4
800 CCCo 94507 632-F4
2000 WLCK 94507 632-D1
DANVILLE OAK PL
- DNVL 94526 652-J1
DANZA CT
100 ORIN 94563 631-C5
DANZIG PZ
1400 CNCD 94520 592-E3
DAPHNE CT
- ORIN 94563 610-J5
100 PLHL 94523 612-B1
100 ANT 94509 595-D1
DAPPLEGRAY CT
600 WLCK 94596 632-F2
DAPPLEGRAY LN
2100 WLCK 94596 632-F2
DAR CT
900 CNCD 94518 592-E6
DARBY CT
2100 WLCK 94596 632-G1
DARBY DR
900 BREN 94513 616-E2
DARDANELLE CT
100 MRTZ 94553 571-H5
DARDANELLE DR
100 MRTZ 94553 571-H5
DARIAN CT
6900 DBLN 94568 693-J2
DARIAN LN
- PLHL 94523 592-A7
DARLENE CT
- CCCo 94507 632-E5
DARLENE DR
1400 CNCD 94520 592-E4
DARNBY CT
- ORIN 94563 631-B5
DARNBY DR
2700 OAK 94611 650-G1
DARTFORD
100 HER 94547 569-J2
DARTMOUTH DR
- OAK 94705 630-B3
DARTMOUTH PL
- DNVL 94526 653-B3
100 BEN 94510 551-B3
DARTMOUTH ST
1100 ALB 94706 609-E6
DARTMOUTH WY
900 CNCD 94518 592-E7
DARYL DR
- ORIN 94563 631-A1
DATE ST
1400 MRTZ 94553 571-F3
2000 CNCD 94519 592-G1
DATE NUT ST
- BREN 94513 616-F3
DAVALOS CT
- SRMN 94583 673-C3
DAVENPORT
- HER 94547 569-J3
DAVENPORT AV
4400 OAK 94619 650-G6
4800 OAK 94613 650-G6
DAVENPORT LN
- CNCD 94518 592-J5
- CNCD 94518 593-A5
DAVEY CROCKETT CT
200 CCCo 94507 632-H2
DAVI AV
100 PIT 94565 574-D3
DAVI CT
3500 ANT 94509 595-C1
DAVI PL
3500 ANT 94509 595-B1
DAVID AV
1200 CNCD 94518 592-E7
DAVID CIR
100 CNCD 94518 592-G4
DAVID CT
3200 CNCD 94519 592-H1
DAVID DR
- MRGA 94556 631-G5
- CNCD 94518 592-G4
300 CCCo 94507 632-G4
DAVID LN
- DNVL 94526 633-C7
1200 CNCD 94518 592-E7
DAVIDSON CT
100 BREN 94513 616-G3
DAVIDSON WY
400 OAK 94610 650-A2
D AVILA WY
5300 CCCo 94803 589-F3
DA VILLA
500 CCCo 94801 588-F3
DA VINCI CT
- OAKL 94561 576-H7
DAVIS AV
- DBLN 94568 694-B3
1200 CNCD 94518 592-H3
1300 CNCD 94519 592-H3
DAVIS LN
- OAKL 94561 596-G2
2400 ANT 94509 575-C6
7000 CCCo 94513 596-F5
7000 CCCo 94561 596-F5
DAVIS RD
- ORIN 94563 610-H7
- ORIN 94563 630-H1
DAVIS ST
3000 OAK 94601 650-D6
DAVISON DR
- ANT 94509 595-D1
700 ANT 94509 575-F7
DAVONA DR
8200 DBLN 94568 693-H2
8800 SRMN 94583 693-G1
9600 SRMN 94583 673-E6
DAWES ST
6500 OAK 94611 650-D1

DAWKINS DR
500 LFYT 94549 631-H3
DAWN CT
1000 BREN 94513 596-D7
1300 SRMN 94583 673-B1
DAWN DR
- PLHL 94523 592-D5
DAWN ST
1200 OAK 94705 630-C3
DAWNVIEW CT
- ANT 94531 595-J5
- BREN 94513 596-D7
800 CNCD 94521 613-D1
900 PIT 94565 573-F5
DAWNVIEW DR
1500 BREN 94513 596-D6
DAWSON CT
- PIT 94565 574-B2
1600 OAKL 94561 576-D6
DAWSON DR
4800 OAKL 94561 576-D7
W DAY AV
1200 CNCD 94520 592-E4
DAYBREAK CT
300 CCCo 94583 673-B1
300 SRMN 94583 673-B1
DAYLIGHT PL
200 DNVL 94526 653-C5
DAYLILY CT
2800 ANT 94531 575-G7
2800 PLE 94588 694-H3
DAYTON CT
100 SRMN 94583 673-G7
800 CNCD 94518 592-H6
DAYTON LN
2600 ANT 94509 575-D1
DEAD HORSE CANYON RD
200 LFYT 94549 631-J3
DEAN CT
2600 PIN 94564 569-G5
DEAN RD
100 CCCo 94507 633-A6
DEAN LESHER DR
2500 CCCo 94520 572-G2
2500 CNCD 94520 572-G2
DE ANZA DR
2900 RCH 94803 589-E2
DE ANZA LN
- HER 94547 569-G3
DE ANZA PL
3200 SRMN 94583 673-G5
DEARDORFF LN
1600 CNCD 94519 592-H2
DEBBI CT
1500 MRTZ 94553 591-J1
DE BENEDETTI CT
1400 BEN 94510 551-B4
DEBORAH LN
400 CCCo 94598 612-F4
DEBRA CT
- ORIN 94563 630-J2
2100 PIT 94565 574-A4
DEBRA LN
1800 CCCo 94521 593-D3
5300 RCH 94803 589-F3
DEBUT WY
- BREN 94561 596-D4
DE CARLO AV
500 CCCo 94801 588-E3
500 RCH 94801 588-E3
DECATUR CT
100 HER 94547 570-B5
DECCA LN
2500 WLCK 94597 612-B3
DEE CT
- WLCK 94597 612-C1
DEEMS ST
1600 PIT 94565 574-F3
DEEPCREEK CT
300 CCCo 94506 654-D5
DEEPWATER CT
- RCH 94804 608-E3
DEER AV
- SolC 94590 550-B1
700 VAL 94590 550-B1
DEER PL
- CLAY 94517 594-A5
DEER RUN
5400 RCH 94803 589-J3
DEER TR
- LFYT 94549 611-C4
DEER WY
4500 ANT 94531 595-H2
DEERBERRY CT
4400 CNCD 94521 593-C5
DEER CREEK DR
900 CCCo 94553 591-C3
DEER CREEK LN
- CCCo 94506 654-D5
600 BREN 94513 616-E1
4500 CNCD 94521 593-C5
DEER CREST DR
3500 CCCo 94506 654-D4
DEER CREST PL
- CCCo 94506 654-D4
DEERFIELD CT
- SRMN 94582 673-J6
1300 CNCD 94521 593-B5
DEERFIELD DR
200 MRGA 94556 651-E3
4400 ANT 94531 595-H3
DEERFIELD LN
- CCCo 94595 632-C1
DEER FIELD WY
4400 CCCo 94506 654-D4
DEERHAVEN PL
- PLHL 94523 591-H2
DEER HILL
- ANT 94531 595-G7
DEER HILL CT
- PIT 94565 573-F4
DEER HILL DR
- SRMN 94583 673-A1
DEER HILL RD
3200 LFYT 94549 611-E6
DEER HOLLOW DR
3300 CCCo 94506 654-D4
DEERHORN CT
4500 ANT 94531 595-J2
DEERING CT
- OAK 94601 650-D6
DEERING ST
3200 OAK 94601 650-D6
DEER MEADOW CT
- CCCo 94506 653-J2
- CCCo 94506 654-A2
DEER MEADOW DR
2700 CCCo 94506 634-A7
2700 CCCo 94506 654-A1
3000 CCCo 94506 653-J2
DEER MEADOW LN
- CCCo 94506 653-J2

DEER MEADOW PL
- CCCo 94506 653-J2
DEER MEADOW TER
- CCCo 94506 654-A1
DEERMEADOW WY
4400 ANT 94531 595-H3
DEER OAK PL
1000 CNCD 94521 593-D5
DEER OAK WY
2100 CCCo 94506 633-H7
2100 CCCo 94506 653-G1
DEERPARK CT
- OAKL 94561 576-E6
3000 WLCK 94598 612-H2
DEER PARK DR
- RCH 94806 568-J6
DEERPARK DR
2800 WLCK 94598 612-H2
DEERPARK RD
1100 OAKL 94561 576-E6
DEERPARK WY
300 OAKL 94561 576-E6
DEER PATH CT
200 MRTZ 94553 591-H3
DEER RIDGE DR
3400 CCCo 94506 654-D4
DEER RIDGE PL
100 CCCo 94506 654-D4
DEER RIDGE RD
4400 CCCo 94506 654-D5
DEER RIDGE WY
4400 ANT 94531 595-H3
DEER SPRING CIR
700 CNCD 94521 613-D1
DEERSPRING CT
- ANT 94531 595-J4
DEERSPRING WY
- ANT 94531 595-J4
- ANT 94531 596-A4
DEER TERRACE CT
- SRMN 94583 673-A1
DEER TRAIL CT
3700 CCCo 94506 654-D4
DEER TRAIL DR
3600 CCCo 94506 654-D4
DEER TRAIL LN
3800 CCCo 94506 654-C5
DEER TREE CT
2400 MRTZ 94553 572-A6
DEERVALE CT
7700 DBLN 94568 693-G2
DEERVALE RD
8300 DBLN 94568 693-G2
DEER VALLEY LN
2100 WLCK 94598 612-G4
DEER VALLEY RD
- CCCo 94513 595-G6
- CCCo 94531 595-G6
3300 ANT 94509 575-F7
3300 ANT 94531 575-F7
3500 ANT 94509 595-F2
3500 ANT 94531 595-G4
8000 CCCo 94513 615-G2
8000 CCCo 94531 615-G2
9100 CCCo 94517 615-G7
14100 CCCo 94513 635-G1
14100 CCCo 94517 635-G1
DEERWOOD CT
2100 MRTZ 94553 571-J7
DEERWOOD DR
1500 MRTZ 94553 571-J7
2400 SRMN 94583 673-A1
DEERWOOD PL
100 SRMN 94583 673-B2
DEERWOOD RD
- DNVL 94526 673-B1
100 SRMN 94583 673-B1
100 CCCo 94583 673-B1
DE FREMERY DR
100 CCCo 94561 596-F4
DEGNAN DR
5300 MRTZ 94553 591-F1
DE LA BRIANDAIS CT
2700 PIN 94564 569-H6
DE LA CRUZ WY
1400 MRGA 94556 651-D1
DELACY AV
1000 CCCo 94553 571-G4
DEL AMIGO RD
- DNVL 94526 652-H1
DEL AMIGO TR
- CCCo 94583 652-G2
DELANCEY LN
3600 CNCD 94519 592-J1
DEL ANTICO AV
400 OAKL 94561 576-F7
DELAROSA CT
2400 PIN 94564 589-J1
DEL ARROYO CT
1200 LFYT 94549 611-H4
DE LA SALLE DR
- MRGA 94575 631-F6
DE LAURENTI CT
- WLCK 94598 612-J3
DELAWARE CT
5500 CNCD 94521 593-F6
DELAWARE DR
1400 CNCD 94521 593-F6
DELAWARE ST
2800 OAK 94602 650-E5
DEL CAMINO DR
2700 SPAB 94806 588-J2
2900 RCH 94806 588-J2
DEL CENTRO
- BEN 94510 551-D4
DEL CENTRO CT
100 CCCo 94549 611-H1
DEL CERRO
- PIT 94565 574-B6
DEL CHIARO WY
3400 CNCD 94519 592-H2
3400 CNCD 94518 592-H2
DELDRIN CT
- SRMN 94582 674-A2
DEL ESTE ST
1800 CCCo 94549 611-J1
DEL FAVERO DR
4000 ANT 94509 595-D1
DELFINO AV
200 RCH 94801 588-D7
DEL HAMBRE CIR
- WLCK 94595 612-B6
DEL HOMBRE LN
2900 CCCo 94597 612-D1
3000 WLCK 94597 612-D1
DELICADO CT
3100 PLE 94588 694-C7
DELLWOOD CT
- PLHL 94523 592-B5
1000 BREN 94513 616-E1
DEL MAR AV
- BERK 94708 609-J7
DEL MAR CIR
- CCCo 94525 550-C5

DEL MAR CT
2400 CCCo 94514 617-H7
DEL MAR DR
3200 LFYT 94549 591-H7
3500 CNCD 94519 593-A1
9800 SRMN 94583 673-G6
DELMER ST
2400 OAK 94602 650-E4
DEL MONTE AV
6800 CCCo 94805 589-D6
DEL MONTE CT
- BREN 94513 616-B3
1500 MRGA 94556 631-F6
1800 CCCo 94595 612-B7
DEL MONTE DR
100 CCCo 94595 612-C7
100 WLCK 94595 612-C7
300 PIN 94564 569-B4
2100 CCCo 94806 569-B4
DEL MONTE ST
2700 CCCo 94805 589-C6
2700 ELCR 94530 589-C6
DEL MONTE WY
300 PIN 94564 569-C3
1600 MRGA 94556 631-F6
DELMORE RD
2700 CCCo 94806 569-C5
DEL NORTE CT
- BERK 94707 609-G6
DEL NORTE ST
2000 BERK 94707 609-G6
DEL OCEANO DR
3100 CCCo 94549 611-J1
DELORES CT
- SPAB 94806 588-C3
DEL ORO CIR
2700 ANT 94509 575-B6
DEL ORO CT
- SRMN 94583 673-B2
DEL REY CT
- LFYT 94549 591-H7
DEL REY ST
1800 LFYT 94549 591-H7
DEL RIO
- PIT 94565 574-A2
DEL RIO CIR
1400 CNCD 94518 592-E6
DEL RIO CT
- CCCo 94549 591-H7
- CCCo 94549 611-H1
- MRGA 94556 631-F6
1300 CNCD 94518 592-E6
DEL RIO DR
1800 CCCo 94549 611-H1
1800 CCCo 94549 591-J7
DEL RIO WY
1000 MRGA 94556 631-F6
DEL ROSA CT
- CCCo 94596 632-F1
DEL SUR ST
- VAL 94591 550-C1
DELTA AV
200 BREN 94513 616-G2
DELTA DR
- CCCo 94565 553-E7
- CCCo 94565 573-E1
DELTA PL
200 DNVL 94526 653-B5
DELTA RD
- OAKL 94561 596-H3
- CCCo 94561 596-H3
700 CCCo 94513 596-H3
1100 CCCo 94513 597-F2
1100 CCCo 94561 597-F2
1400 CCCo 94548 597-A3
DELTA WY
1100 DNVL 94526 653-B5
DELTA COVES DR
- CCCo 94511 577-E4
DELTA FAIR BLVD
3000 ANT 94509 575-A6
3200 ANT 94509 574-H5
DELTA GATEWAY BLVD
- PIT 94565 575-A5
DELTA MEADOWS WY
1600 OAKL 94561 576-D5
DELTA RANCH DR
5300 OAKL 94561 576-D4
DELTAVIEW LN
1000 CCCo 94565 573-F2
DELTA VIEW WY
5200 ANT 94531 595-E4
DELTA VISTA LN
- PIT 94565 573-H4
DEL TREN AV
800 PIT 94565 574-F3
DEL TRIGO LN
5700 CNCD 94521 593-G7
5700 CLAY 94517 593-G7
DELUCCHI DR
2100 PLE 94588 694-E7
DEL VALLE
- ORIN 94563 610-D7
DEL VALLE CIR
- CCCo 94803 589-F3
DEL VISTA CT
- PLHL 94523 592-A4
DEMARCUS BLVD
- DBLN 94568 694-B4
DEMARTINI CT
- OAKL 94561 576-D7
DEMARTINI LN
- BREN 94513 596-C5
DEMPSEY WY
100 CCCo 94572 549-J6
DENA DR
2100 CNCD 94519 572-G7
DENALI DR
- CCCo 94513 617-F3
DE NATALE CT
5200 PLE 94588 694-H4
DENEB CT
1300 WLCK 94597 611-J2
DENFIELD AV
- BEN 94510 550-J3
DENICIO ST
1200 CCCo 94803 569-C7
DENISE DR
- CCCo 94806 569-A5
DENISE LN
- CCCo 94549 611-J2
DENKER DR
4100 PLE 94588 694-A6
DENKINGER CT
1500 CNCD 94521 593-B3
DENKINGER RD
1500 CNCD 94521 593-C2
DENNIS CIR
1300 CNCD 94518 592-H3
DENNIS CT
200 OAKL 94561 596-C1
1100 CCCo 94572 570-B1
DENNIS DR
2000 ANT 94509 575-E6

STREET Block City ZIP Pg-Grid

DENNIS DR
3200 PLE 94588 694-F6
DENNISON ST
1800 ALA 94501 650-A7
1800 OAK 94606 650-A7
DE NORMANDIE WY
100 CCCo 94553 571-H4
DENTON PL
5600 OAK 94619 651-A6
DENVER ST
4000 CNCD 94521 593-A2
DENYCE CT
- CCCo 94507 632-F6
DEODAR AV
1900 ANT 94509 575-E6
DEODAR DR
100 CCCo 94553 592-B1
DEODAR LN
- CCCo 94507 632-G7
DEODAR WY
7700 PLE 94588 693-H6
DEODARA WY
- WLCK 94597 612-C3
DEODORA WY
100 CCCo 94553 591-E1
DERBY AV
1200 OAK 94601 650-C7
DERBY CT
- SRMN 94583 673-C4
400 PLHL 94523 592-A7
DERBY DR
2500 SRMN 94583 673-B4
DERBY LN
100 MRGA 94556 631-F5
DERBY PL
4300 PIT 94565 574-E7
DERBY ST
2800 BERK 94704 630-A3
2800 BERK 94705 630-A3
DERBYSHIRE PL
600 DNVL 94526 653-D3
DE ROSA CT
3600 CNCD 94518 592-H4
DESANIE CIR
3500 CCCo 94565 573-F1
DESANIE WY
3500 CCCo 94565 573-F2
DESCANSO DR
- ORIN 94563 631-C4
DESERET DR
2900 RCH 94803 589-E2
DESERT CIR
1900 WLCK 94598 612-F2
DESERT GOLD PL
1900 BREN 94513 616-C4
DESERT GOLD TER
400 BREN 94513 616-C4
DE SOTO CT
- ORIN 94563 610-J5
DESOTO CT
800 WLCK 94598 592-G7
DESRYS BLVD
2400 ANT 94509 574-H6
DESSIRA CT
- CNCD 94521 593-C4
DESTINY LN
200 CCCo 94583 673-B1
200 SRMN 94583 673-B1
DETJEN CT
6200 PLE 94588 693-F6
DETROIT AV
900 CNCD 94518 592-G4
1000 CNCD 94520 592-E2
4200 OAK 94619 650-G4
DEVILS DROP CT
700 RCH 94803 589-G3
DEVILS HOLE TR
- AlaC 94546 652-C5
- AlaC 94552 652-C5
- CCCo 94583 652-C5
DEVIL VIEW PL
1900 WLCK 94595 632-B1
DEVIN DR
- MRGA 94556 631-E5
DEVITA CT
2000 WLCK 94595 632-D1
DEVITO ST
- PIT 94565 574-D1
DEVON AV
- PLHL 94523 591-H4
DEVON CIR
- PLHL 94523 591-J4
DEVON CT
400 OAKL 94561 576-D7
400 SRMN 94583 673-G7
1800 CNCD 94520 592-F2
DEVON WY
2900 CCCo 94806 589-A2
6900 OAK 94705 630-C3
DEVONSHIRE CT
- DNVL 94506 653-J6
200 PLHL 94523 591-J4
1300 ELCR 94530 609-E1
2100 WLCK 94596 632-G1
DEVONSHIRE DR
1300 ELCR 94530 609-E1
1700 BEN 94510 550-J2
DEVONSHIRE LN
- CCCo 94565 573-G3
DEVONSHIRE LP
500 BREN 94513 616-C1
DEVONWOOD
500 HER 94547 569-F3
DEVPAR CT
2400 ANT 94509 575-F6
DEWBERRY DR
- SRMN 94582 673-G2
DEW DROP CIR
- PIT 94565 573-J2
DEWEY RD
- CCCo 94708 609-G3
DEWING AV
900 LFYT 94549 611-E6
DEWING LN
1100 WLCK 94595 612-B6
1200 CCCo 94595 612-B6
DE WITT CT
3600 ANT 94509 595-C1
DEWLAP CT
2500 ANT 94531 595-G3
DEXTER DR
- PLHL 94523 592-C4
DEXTER PL
200 SRMN 94583 673-F5
DE YOUNG LN
3200 LFYT 94549 611-H4
DIABLO AV
2300 ANT 94509 575-E6
DIABLO CIR
- LFYT 94549 611-A6
3300 PIN 94564 569-G7
DIABLO CT
- DNVL 94526 653-B2
- PLHL 94523 592-C3
400 MRTZ 94553 571-H7
3200 PIN 94564 569-G7
3600 PLE 94588 694-F7
DIABLO DR
100 CCCo 94563 630-F5
100 OAK 94611 630-F5
900 LFYT 94549 611-G7
DIABLO LN
100 CCCo 94513 617-C1
500 CCCo 94513 597-C7
DIABLO PKWY
- CLAY 94517 614-A2
DIABLO RD
100 DNVL 94526 652-J2
100 DNVL 94526 653-B1
1000 DNVL 94526 633-C7
1400 CCCo 94528 633-C7
1500 DNVL 94506 633-C7
1600 CCCo 94528 653-E1
1600 DNVL 94506 653-E1
1900 CCCo 94506 653-E1
DIABLO ST
1000 CLAY 94517 593-H7
DIABLO WY
- DNVL 94526 653-B2
300 BREN 94513 616-G1
400 MRTZ 94553 571-H7
DIABLO CREEK CT
- DNVL 94506 653-F1
300 CLAY 94517 593-G6
DIABLO CREEK PL
- DNVL 94506 653-F1
400 CLAY 94517 593-G6
DIABLO DOWNS DR
800 CCCo 94517 613-G1
DIABLO LAKES LN
- CCCo 94528 633-F5
DIABLO OAKS WY
- LFYT 94549 611-H7
- LFYT 94549 631-H1
DIABLO RANCH CT
2100 CCCo 94506 633-F7
DIABLO RANCH DR
2100 CCCo 94506 633-F7
DIABLO RANCH PL
2300 CCCo 94506 633-F7
DIABLO RIDGE LN
- CCCo 94598 613-A4
DIABLO SHADOW DR
3000 WLCK 94598 612-J2
DIABLO VIEW CT
- DNVL 94506 653-H5
4200 CNCD 94518 592-J4
DIABLO VIEW DR
- ORIN 94563 610-J4
- ORIN 94563 611-A4
DIABLO VIEW LN
300 CLAY 94517 613-J1
DIABLO VIEW RD
- PLHL 94523 612-A1
3000 PLHL 94523 611-J1
3000 CCCo 94549 611-J1
DIABLO VISTA RD
1500 CCCo 94507 632-E3
DIAMOND BLVD
1900 CNCD 94520 592-C2
DIAMOND CT
- DNVL 94526 652-H1
100 HER 94547 569-H6
DIAMOND DR
- DNVL 94526 652-H2
DIAMOND ST
800 ANT 94509 575-C4
DIAMOND WY
1200 CNCD 94520 592-D3
DIAMOND RANCH CT
- SRMN 94583 673-E7
DIAMOND SPRINGS CT
1700 BREN 94513 596-C7
DIAMOND SPRINGS LN
1700 BREN 94513 596-C7
DIAMONDWOOD CT
- PIT 94565 574-G6
DIANA CT
- PLHL 94523 612-A1
DIANA LN
- ANT 94509 574-J6
6400 MRTZ 94553 591-H3
7900 DBLN 94568 693-H3
DIANDA DR
1500 CNCD 94521 593-B3
DIANE AV
200 PIT 94565 574-F4
DIANE CT
- OAKL 94561 596-H3
1700 CNCD 94520 592-E4
DIANE DR
2400 CCCo 94803 589-E2
2400 RCH 94803 589-E2
DIANNE CT
- LFYT 94549 631-H1
DIAS CIR
100 PIT 94565 574-F4
DIAS CT
- CCCo 94803 589-G2
DIAS DORADAS
- ORIN 94563 610-G5
DIAVILA AV
200 PLE 94588 694-E7
DIAVILA CT
2800 PLE 94588 694-E6
DIAZ PL
- OAK 94611 630-D7
DICKENS CT
3500 PLE 94588 694-E6
DICKENSON CT
- CNCD 94521 593-F7
DICKENSON DR
- MRGA 94556 651-E1
DICKSON LN
- MRTZ 94553 571-G7
- MRTZ 94553 591-G1
DIEHL WY
300 PIT 94565 574-E7
DIGITAL DR
- DBLN 94568 694-C4
DIJON WY
6400 DBLN 94568 694-A1
DILLARD WY
200 ANT 94509 595-A1
DILLON RD
- BEN 94510 550-G1
DILLON WY
- ELCR 94530 609-E1
11300 DBLN 94568 693-F5
DILY LN
- CCCo 94565 573-E2
DI MAGGIO AV
- PIT 94565 574-D3
DIMAGGIO WY
3200 ANT 94509 575-A7
3400 ANT 94509 595-A1
DIMER RD
- CCCo 94553 571-F2
DIMM ST
400 RCH 94805 589-B6
DIMM WY
5900 CCCo 94805 589-B5
DIMOND AV
3400 OAK 94602 650-D4
DINA DR
1400 CNCD 94518 592-J3
DINEEN ST
1400 MRTZ 94553 571-E2
DIOKNO CT
1400 PIT 94565 574-G5
DIORITE CT
- ANT 94531 595-G2
DIPPER CT
- RCH 94803 589-F2
DISCOVERY CT
800 DNVL 94526 633-C6
DISCOVERY PT
4900 CCCo 94514 617-H4
DISCOVERY WY
1000 CNCD 94521 593-D7
DISCOVERY BAY BLVD
- CCCo 94514 617-H7
100 CCCo 94514 (618-A4 See Page 597)
DIVISION DR
- CCCo 94553 571-J3
DIXON LN
1800 CCCo 94521 593-E4
DOAK CT
- DBLN 94568 694-G4
DOBBS DR
- PLHL 94523 591-J5
DOBRICH CIR
700 CCCo 94565 573-H3
DOBSON CT
- OAKL 94561 596-H2
DOBSON ST
- OAKL 94561 596-H2
DOCKSIDE BAY
- HER 94547 569-G1
DODD CT
800 CCCo 94565 573-C2
DODGE CT
5400 CNCD 94521 593-G4
DODSON ST
1900 SPAB 94806 588-J3
DOE CT
2600 CNCD 94519 572-H6
DOE WY
4500 ANT 94531 595-H3
DOESKIN TER
900 BREN 94513 616-E1
DOGIE CT
- SRMN 94583 673-B3
DOGWOOD
- BEN 94510 551-B6
DOGWOOD CT
- SRMN 94583 693-H1
- WLCK 94598 612-J1
100 HER 94547 570-A4
DOGWOOD DR
100 WLCK 94598 612-J1
DOGWOOD LN
100 VAL 94591 550-F1
DOGWOOD PL
100 SRMN 94583 693-H1
DOGWOOD WY
2100 ANT 94509 575-B5
DOHRMANN LN
400 PIN 94564 569-C4
DOIDGE AV
2300 PIN 94564 569-H7
2300 PIN 94564 589-H1
2700 PIN 94564 570-A7
DOLAN WY
2300 CCCo 94806 569-B5
DOLCITA CT
200 DNVL 94526 653-C7
DOLLIS PARK RD
- LFYT 94549 611-E5
DOLORES AV
4600 OAK 94602 650-D3
DOLORES CT
- CCCo 94507 632-G5
- MRGA 94556 631-E3
2300 PIN 94564 569-F6
DOLORES DR
- LFYT 94549 611-E5
3200 SRMN 94583 673-F4
DOLORES ST
2700 ANT 94509 575-C6
DOLORES WY
- ORIN 94563 631-A5
3600 CNCD 94519 592-J1
3600 CNCD 94519 593-A1
DOLPHIN CT
800 DNVL 94526 633-B7
900 CCCo 94572 569-J1
1800 CCCo 94514 617-H6
DOLPHIN DR
- RCH 94804 608-H2
- PIT 94565 573-J3
600 DNVL 94526 633-A7
DOLPHIN PL
1700 CCCo 94514 617-G6
DOMAINE CT
700 OAKL 94561 576-D5
DOMAINE WY
1700 OAKL 94561 576-D5
DOME CT
- HER 94547 569-H4
DOMENGINE WY
- ANT 94531 595-D4
DOMINGO AV
- BERK 94705 630-A4
DOMINGO CT
300 SRMN 94583 673-C3
DOMINIC CT
1100 BEN 94510 551-A4
DON CIR
- CCCo 94595 632-D2
DON WY
3800 RCH 94806 568-G7
DONAHUE LN
- CCCo 94507 633-C5
DONAL AV
6500 ELCR 94530 609-C2
DONALD AV
1400 CCCo 94553 571-F3
DONALD CT
100 DNVL 94506 653-G5
DONALD DR
- ORIN 94563 631-A3
100 MRGA 94556 631-D4
1200 CCCo 94572 570-A1
DONALD LN
- CNCD 94518 592-G4
DONALD PL
- MRGA 94556 631-E4
DONALDSON CT
1600 CNCD 94521 593-E4
DONALEEN CT
100 MRTZ 94553 571-F7
DONATELLO WY
- OAKL 94561 596-H1
DON CAROL DR
8600 ELCR 94530 609-E2
DONCASTER DR
600 WLCK 94598 612-J3
1000 ANT 94509 575-B7
DONCASTER PL
6100 OAK 94611 630-E6
DONEGAL CT
- PLHL 94523 591-J5
DONEGAL PL
- CCCo 94549 591-H4
- MRTZ 94553 591-H4
DONEGAL RD
- PIN 94564 569-E4
DONEGAL WY
- ANT 94531 595-J2
- PLHL 94523 591-J4
100 MRTZ 94553 591-H4
300 CCCo 94549 591-G4
DON GABRIEL WY
- ORIN 94563 631-A5
DONHAM CT
800 ANT 94509 575-C7
DONKEY FLATS CT
- PLHL 94523 591-H5
DONLON WY
6700 DBLN 94568 693-G4
DONNA DR
500 CCCo 94553 571-J3
500 CCCo 94553 572-A3
1800 PLHL 94523 592-B4
DONNA LN
- DNVL 94526 633-C7
DONNA MAE CT
600 CCCo 94803 569-D7
DONNA MARIA WY
- ORIN 94563 631-A5
DONNER CT
4100 ANT 94531 595-J1
DONNER WY
400 SRMN 94582 653-G7
DONNER CREEK CT
- CLAY 94517 613-J1
DONOHUE DR
7400 DBLN 94568 693-H3
N DONOVAN WY
- SRMN 94582 674-C3
S DONOVAN WY
- SRMN 94582 674-C3
DOOLAN RD
6100 AlaC 94551 674-J7
6100 AlaC 94551 694-J1
6100 CCCo 94551 674-J7
6100 CCCo 94551 675-A4
6100 CCCo 94588 674-J7
6100 CCCo 94588 675-A4
DOOLIN CT
- CCCo 94806 569-C5
- PIN 94564 569-C5
DOOLITTLE WY
600 ANT 94509 595-E1
DORA AV
1900 WLCK 94596 612-B5
DORA CT
2500 PIN 94564 569-F4
DORADA CT
200 HER 94547 570-B6
DORAL CT
- BREN 94513 616-B1
- ANT 94509 595-D1
3300 WLCK 94598 612-J2
DORAL DR
- MRGA 94556 631-D7
- MRGA 94556 651-D1
600 DNVL 94526 653-E6
DORAL WY
- ANT 94509 595-D1
DORAN DR
6300 OAK 94611 630-G7
DORAY DR
- PLHL 94523 592-C4
DORCHESTER CT
- CCCo 94513 617-F5
DORCHESTER LN
200 CCCo 94507 632-J1
DORCHESTER PL
1600 CNCD 94519 593-A2
DOREEN CT
6800 DBLN 94568 693-J3
DOREEN ST
7200 DBLN 94568 693-J3
DOREEN WY
600 LFYT 94549 631-G1
DOREMUS AV
5600 CCCo 94805 589-B5
5600 RCH 94805 589-B5
DORIS AV
2000 CCCo 94596 612-D7
2000 WLCK 94596 612-D7
DORIS DR
- PLHL 94523 592-C5
DORIS PL
- OAK 94705 630-B4
DORMAN CT
4300 PLE 94588 694-B7
DORMAN RD
4000 PLE 94588 694-A7
DORMER AV
3400 CNCD 94519 572-G6
DORMER CT
3500 CNCD 94519 572-G5
DORMIDERA AV
- PDMT 94611 650-C1
DORNAN DR
500 RCH 94801 608-D1
DOROTHY CT
- VAL 94590 550-C2
DOROTHY DR
2900 PLHL 94523 612-A1
DOROTHY LN
500 CCCo 94553 571-J3
DOROTHY PL
- OAK 94705 630-B3
DORRIS PL
1200 CCCo 94507 632-G4
DORSCH RD
2000 WLCK 94598 612-E1
DORSET CT
100 SRMN 94583 673-F4
4300 CNCD 94521 593-A4
DORY RD
- PIT 94565 574-A2
DOS ENCINAS
- ORIN 94563 631-A5
DOS OSOS
- ORIN 94563 610-E7
DOS PALOS DR
1400 WLCK 94597 611-J2
1400 WLCK 94597 612-A2
DOS POSOS
- ORIN 94563 610-G6
DOS RIOS CT
- SRMN 94583 673-B2
DOS RIOS DR
2400 SRMN 94583 673-B2
DOS RIOS PL
- SRMN 94583 673-B2
DOS ROBLES CT
- CCCo 94597 612-E1
DOUBLE K RD
- BREN 94513 596-D4
DOUBLE POINT WY
5000 CCCo 94514 617-H5
DOUBLETREE DR
12400 CCCo 94551 675-F2
DOUBLETREE LN
9000 CCCo 94551 675-F3
DOUGHERTY RD
- CCCo 94582 673-J3
- PLE 94588 694-A4
- SRMN 94582 653-J7
- SRMN 94582 673-J3
5800 DBLN 94568 694-A1
7500 CCCo 94582 674-A7
7500 CCCo 94582 694-A1
7500 SRMN 94582 674-A7
7500 SRMN 94582 694-A1
DOUGLAS CT
- ORIN 94563 611-B7
- ORIN 94563 631-B1
900 CLAY 94517 593-H7
900 CLAY 94517 613-H1
1100 CCCo 94507 632-G3
1100 CNCD 94520 592-E4
2100 PIT 94565 574-A3
4300 PLE 94588 694-A7
DOUGLAS DR
- BREN 94513 616-B3
- MRTZ 94553 571-F6
1500 ELCR 94530 609-D1
DOUGLAS LN
200 PLHL 94523 592-B7
200 PLHL 94523 612-B1
DOUGLAS RD
- OAKL 94561 596-G2
500 CLAY 94517 593-H7
500 CLAY 94517 613-H1
DOUGLAS ST
2300 SPAB 94806 588-H2
DOUGLAS TER
1700 PLHL 94523 591-J2
DOULTON CT
400 PLHL 94523 591-J7
DOVE CT
- BREN 94513 596-E7
100 HER 94547 569-H5
500 PLHL 94523 592-A5
3800 ANT 94509 594-J1
DOVE LN
- RCH 94803 589-C3
DOVE CREEK LN
100 DNVL 94506 654-A6
DOVER
600 HER 94547 569-J2
DOVER AV
1300 SPAB 94806 588-G3
DOVER CT
- BREN 94561 596-F4
- DNVL 94506 653-J6
- ORIN 94563 631-B3
- PIT 94565 574-B3
2100 WLCK 94598 612-G2
7200 DBLN 94568 693-H3
DOVER DR
100 WLCK 94598 612-G2
DOVER LN
7200 DBLN 94568 693-H3
DOVER WY
2100 PIT 94565 574-B3
3100 CNCD 94518 592-G2
DOVEWOOD CT
- ANT 94531 595-J5
- ANT 94531 596-A5
DOWITCHER CT
- OAKL 94561 576-H7
DOWITCHER WY
- SRFL 94901 587-A2
DOWNER AV
2300 RCH 94804 588-H5
DOWNER ST
2500 PIN 94564 569-F4
DOWNEY PL
- OAK 94610 650-C3
1900 ELCR 94530 589-C7
1900 ELCR 94530 609-C1
DOWNHAM CT
300 WLCK 94598 612-F2
DOWNIE POINT DR
- BREN 94513 616-D1
DOWNING CT
4400 PLE 94588 694-A7
DOWNING PL
3300 CNCD 94518 592-H6
DOWRELIO DR
1900 CCCo 94525 550-C4
DOYLE RD
3000 OAKL 94561 596-H3
DRACENA AV
100 PDMT 94611 630-B7
100 PDMT 94611 650-B1
DRACENA CT
3900 CNCD 94519 593-B1
DRAEGER DR
100 MRGA 94556 631-E5
DRAKE CT
- WLCK 94597 612-C3
100 VAL 94591 550-F2
300 BEN 94510 551-A2
1400 OAKL 94561 576-E7
DRAKE DR
1800 OAK 94611 630-E7
1900 OAK 94611 650-E1
DRAKE LN
- HER 94547 569-G3
- OAK 94611 650-E1
DRAKE PL
- OAK 94611 630-E7
DRAKE ST
- ANT 94509 575-D6
DRAKE WY
1400 CCCo 94806 589-A4
DRAKES CT
5500 CCCo 94514 617-J5
DRAKES DR
5600 CCCo 94514 617-J5
5800 CCCo 94514 (618-A5 See Page 597)
DRAKES BAY CT
- RCH 94801 608-D3
DRAPER ST
2800 CCCo 94806 569-B6
DRAYTON CT
300 WLCK 94598 612-F2
DRAYTON WY
400 WLCK 94598 612-F2
DREYER PL
5600 OAK 94619 651-A5
DRIFTWOOD CT
- PLHL 94523 591-J6
4400 CCCo 94514 617-G7
4600 CCCo 94803 589-D1
4900 OAKL 94561 576-D7
DRIFTWOOD CV
- HER 94547 569-H1
DRIFTWOOD DR
100 CCCo 94565 553-C7
100 CCCo 94565 573-C1
3200 LFYT 94549 631-H4
DRIFTWOOD PL
4300 CCCo 94514 617-G7
DROLETTE WY
800 BEN 94510 551-A3
DROMANA CT
- SRMN 94582 674-C4
DROZDA CT
- CNCD 94519 592-H2
DRUMMOND PL
700 CNCD 94518 592-G7
DRURY CT
1300 OAK 94705 630-C3
DRURY LN
- OAK 94705 630-B3
DRURY RD
1000 OAK 94705 630-C3
DRY CREEK CT
5200 ANT 94531 595-J5
DRYCREEK CT
2200 MRTZ 94553 572-A7
DRY CREEK RD
- DBLN 94568 693-E4
DRYWOOD CT
- OAKL 94561 596-F1
DRYWOOD ST
4700 PLE 94588 693-J7
DU 8 RD
- CCCo 94553 571-F3
DUANE LN
100 MRTZ 94553 571-D7
DUAR DR
900 CNCD 94518 592-E6
DUARTE AV
4500 OAKL 94561 576-E7
DUARTE CT
- MRGA 94556 651-E1
DUBBS RD
- CCCo 94553 571-F3
DUBERSTEIN DR
- SRMN 94583 673-E6
DUBHE CT
4200 CNCD 94521 593-B3
DUBLIN AV
5000 OAK 94602 650-F3
DUBLIN BLVD
6500 DBLN 94568 693-J4
6500 DBLN 94568 694-A4
11000 PLE 94588 693-E5
DUBLIN CT
- PLHL 94523 591-J5
6500 DBLN 94568 694-A4
DUBLIN DR
- PLHL 94523 591-J4
2000 CCCo 94806 569-B4
DUBLIN CANYON RD
9000 AlaC 94552 693-A5
10600 PLE 94588 693-E5
10700 AlaC 94586 693-E5
10700 AlaC 94588 693-E5
10700 PLE 94586 693-E5
DUBLIN GREEN CT
7700 DBLN 94568 693-G3
DUBLIN GREEN DR
11700 DBLN 94568 693-G3
DUBLIN MEADOWS ST
6900 DBLN 94568 694-A3
N DUBLIN RANCH DR
- DBLN 94568 694-F2
S DUBLIN RANCH DR
- DBLN 94568 694-F3
DUBOCE AV
- CCCo 94801 588-F4
200 RCH 94801 588-F4
DUBOST CT
- DNVL 94526 653-C7
DUCHESS TER
1700 BREN 94513 616-D1
DUCKER CT
1700 CNCD 94519 592-J2
DUCKHORN CT
500 OAKL 94561 576-D5
DUCKHORN PL
500 OAKL 94561 576-E5
DUDLEY AV
- PDMT 94611 650-C1
DUDLEY CT
- PDMT 94611 650-C1
- PLHL 94523 592-B6
DUFFY CT
- PLHL 94523 592-A3
DUFFY WY
1200 BREN 94513 616-E1
DUGAN CT
1600 CNCD 94521 593-F4
DUKE AV
2500 RCH 94806 589-A2
DUKE CIR
700 PLHL 94523 592-C3
DUKE CT
- PLHL 94523 592-C3
6800 DBLN 94568 693-J3
7700 ELCR 94530 609-E2
DUKE PTH
2600 RCH 94806 589-A2
DUKE WY
- PLHL 94523 592-C3
7500 SRMN 94583 693-G1
DULSIE LN
- DBLN 94568 693-E5
DULWICH RD
- OAK 94618 630-B6
DUMAINE ST
1400 CNCD 94518 592-E6
DUMAS CT
- ANT 94531 595-C4
DUMBARTON ST
3500 CCCo 94519 572-G5
DUNBAR CT
- PLHL 94523 592-B4
DUNBARTON CIR
3900 SRMN 94583 673-E4
DUNBARTON CT
- SRMN 94583 673-F4
DUNBARTON DR
1900 BREN 94513 596-G5
DUNBLANE CT
2100 WLCK 94598 612-G2
DUNBLANE DR
100 WLCK 94598 612-G2
DUNCAN CT
- ORIN 94563 631-B3
DUNCAN DR
1400 CNCD 94521 593-F5
1700 MRTZ 94553 571-D4
DUNCAN RD
2500 PIN 94564 569-E6
DUNCAN ST
1700 WLCK 94596 612-C5
DUNCAN WY
- OAK 94611 630-D6
DUNCAN HILL
- SRMN 94583 673-E6
DUNDEE CT
- SRMN 94583 673-E4
3000 CNCD 94520 572-F6
DUNDEE RD
2600 CCCo 94806 569-B5
DUNDEE ST
- ANT 94531 595-J2
DUNDEE WY
200 BEN 94510 551-A2
DUNEDIN DR
- BREN 94513 596-G5
DUNE POINT CT
1600 CCCo 94514 617-G6
DUNE POINT PL
1800 CCCo 94514 617-G6
DUNE POINT WY
1700 CCCo 94514 617-G6
DUNES CT
- ANT 94509 595-D2
DUNES WY
- ANT 94509 595-D2
DUNHAM
100 HER 94547 569-F3
DUNHILL CT
1000 DNVL 94506 654-A6
DUNHILL DR
600 DNVL 94506 653-J6
600 DNVL 94506 654-A6
DUNMOOD CT
- BREN 94513 616-A1
DUNMORE LN
- DBLN 94568 694-F4
DUNN AV
1300 RCH 94801 588-G5
DUNSMOOR CT
- DNVL 94526 653-C3
DUNSMUIR AV
4200 OAK 94619 650-G5
DUNSMUIR CIR
3600 PLE 94588 694-F5
DUNSMUIR CT
3300 PLE 94588 694-F5
DUNSTOWN CT
- DBLN 94568 693-G4
DUNSYRE DR
1100 CCCo 94597 611-J5
1100 LFYT 94549 611-J5
1100 LFYT 94549 612-A5
1100 CCCo 94597 612-A5
DUPERU DR
100 CCCo 94525 550-E5
DUPRE CT
1400 CNCD 94518 592-E6
DUPRE WY
- BREN 94513 596-C6
DURAN CT
- DBLN 94568 694-G3
DURANGO LN
2600 SRMN 94583 673-C2
DURANT CT
1200 WLCK 94596 632-G2
DURHAM CT
300 BEN 94510 551-A2
300 DNVL 94526 653-C2
DURLINGTON CT
- SRMN 94582 674-C4
DURNESS CT
- ANT 94531 596-A2
DURSEY DR
100 PIN 94564 569-C4
DUSTIN LN
- DNVL 94526 653-B1
DUTCH ELM DR
- HER 94547 569-J3
DUTCH MILL CT
- DNVL 94526 653-D4
DUTCH MILL DR
1200 DNVL 94526 653-D4
DUTCH SLOUGH RD
- OAKL 94561 577-B5
1900 CCCo 94561 577-B5
DUTRA CT
200 PIN 94564 569-D3
DUTRA RD
100 MRTZ 94553 571-C6
100 CCCo 94553 571-C6
DUVALL CT
400 BEN 94510 551-A1
DUXBURY CT
200 SRMN 94583 673-F5
DUXBURY CV
- SRFL 94901 587-A2
DUXBURY PL
100 VAL 94591 550-E1
DWIGHT PL
500 OAK 94704 630-A2
DWIGHT WY
2800 BERK 94704 630-A2
3200 OAK 94704 630-A2
DYER DR
1000 LFYT 94549 611-G6
DYER RD
3300 AlaC 94551 676-J4
DYNASTY DR
- BREN 94561 596-D3

E

E ST
- CCCo 94565 573-E1
- CNCD 94520 572-J3
100 BEN 94510 551-B6
100 MRTZ 94553 571-E5
200 ANT 94509 575-D4
W E ST
100 BEN 94510 551-B5
EAGLE CT
- CCCo 94507 633-B5
- CCCo 94514 (657-E2 See Page 638)
- RCH 94806 568-H5
100 HER 94547 569-H5
700 ANT 94509 595-F2
EAGLE LN
100 CCCo 94513 597-D5
EAGLE RD
- ALA 94501 650-A7
EAGLE WY
4800 CNCD 94521 593-C4

STREET Block City ZIP Pg-Grid

EAGLE CREEK CT
400 SRMN 94582 694-B1
EAGLE HILL
- CCCo 94707 609-F4
EAGLE LAKE CT
- SRMN 94582 653-F7
1900 MRTZ 94553 591-J1
1900 MRTZ 94553 592-A1
EAGLE LAKE PL
- SRMN 94582 653-F7
EAGLE NEST CT
400 MRTZ 94553 591-G3
1100 CCCo 94506 654-B3
EAGLE NEST DR
500 MRTZ 94553 591-G3
S EAGLE NEST DR
300 CCCo 94506 654-B3
EAGLE NEST LN
4000 CCCo 94506 654-B3
S EAGLE NEST LN
300 CCCo 94506 654-B3
EAGLE NEST PL
1000 CCCo 94506 654-B3
EAGLE PEAK AV
1800 CLAY 94517 593-G5
EAGLE PEAK PL
- CLAY 94517 593-G5
EAGLE PEAK RD
4300 CNCD 94521 593-A4
EAGLE POINT CT
1400 LFYT 94549 611-F3
EAGLE POINT RD
3500 LFYT 94549 611-F2
EAGLERIDGE CT
- ANT 94509 595-E3
EAGLE RIDGE DR
900 CCCo 94506 654-B2
EAGLERIDGE DR
3700 ANT 94509 595-F1
EAGLE RIDGE LN
- CCCo 94506 654-B2
EAGLE RIDGE PL
900 CCCo 94506 654-B2
EAGLE ROCK DR
- BREN 94513 616-B3
EAGLES LANDING CT
- DBLN 94568 694-G3
EAGLES NEST TR
- CCCo 94553 589-H7
- RCH 94805 589-H7
EAGLE VALLEY WY
400 CCCo 94506 654-B3
EAKER CT
600 ANT 94509 595-F1
EAKER WY
500 ANT 94509 595-E1
EARHART DR
4000 CNCD 94521 593-A2
EARL CT
7700 ELCR 94530 609-E2
EARL LN
1800 CCCo 94521 593-E3
EARL GLEN WY
1400 BREN 94513 596-E6
EARLHAM WY
300 BREN 94513 616-D3
EARNEST ST
- HER 94547 569-F2
EASLEY DR
1100 CLAY 94517 613-J1
1100 CLAY 94517 593-J7
EAST CIR
- OAK 94611 630-G6
EAST LN
100 CCCo 94507 632-H4
EAST ST
800 PIT 94565 574-E2
900 LFYT 94549 611-F6
1600 CNCD 94519 592-F1
1900 CNCD 94520 592-F1
2500 CNCD 94520 572-F7
EAST TER
3300 LFYT 94549 631-G1
EAST TR
1800 CCCo 94517 614-C4
EASTBOURNE CT
1000 ANT 94509 595-F1
EASTBROOK CT
- CLAY 94517 593-F6
800 CCCo 94506 654-D5
EAST CREEK CT
- ANT 94531 595-E5
EAST CREEK WY
- ANT 94531 595-D5
EASTER CT
- CCCo 94553 572-B7
EASTER WY
- BERK 94708 609-H6
EASTERTOWN LN
- DBLN 94568 693-D5
EASTGATE AV
2700 CNCD 94520 572-E7
EASTGATE LN
300 MRTZ 94553 571-H6
EASTHAM CT
100 VAL 94591 550-F1
EASTLAKE AV
4100 OAK 94602 650-F5
EASTMAN AV
2600 OAK 94619 650-E7
EASTON CT
- ORIN 94563 631-A2
EAST RIDGE
- SRMN 94582 673-G2
EAST RIDGE CT
- CCCo 94506 654-E3
EASTRIDGE LN
- CNCD 94518 592-H4
EASTSHORE BLVD
1300 BERK 94710 609-B1
1600 ELCR 94530 609-B1
EASTSHORE FRWY I-80
- ALB - 609-C5
- BERK - 609-C5
- CCCo - 549-J7
- CCCo - 550-B6
- CCCo - 569-H2
- CCCo - 589-A3
- ELCR - 609-C5
- HER - 569-H2
- PIN - 569-B7
- RCH - 569-B7
- RCH - 589-A3
- RCH - 609-C5
- SPAB - 589-A3
EASTSHORE FRONTAGE RD
- ALB 94710 609-C6
1200 BERK 94710 609-C6
EAST VIEW DR
3500 LFYT 94549 611-F7
EASTVIEW WY
4900 ANT 94531 595-D4

EASTWARD LN
- DNVL 94506 653-G2
EASTWOOD CT
- BREN 94513 596-B7
- BREN 94513 616-B1
- OAK 94611 630-G7
EASTWOOD DR
- ORIN 94563 631-C6
EASTWOODBURY LN
1400 MRTZ 94553 571-J6
EASY ST
100 CCCo 94507 632-G3
2800 CCCo 94548 597-B1
EATON CT
- BREN 94513 616-A1
- CCCo 94507 632-G5
200 BEN 94510 551-B2
EBANO DR
200 WLCK 94598 612-H2
EBBETTS WY
5100 ANT 94531 595-F4
EBBTIDE CV
- HER 94547 569-G1
EBBTIDE PL
100 VAL 94591 550-F2
EBENSBURG LN
6500 DBLN 94568 693-J4
EBERHARDT CT
800 CLAY 94517 613-J1
EBSEN CT
1900 PIN 94564 569-F5
ECCLESTON AV
2700 PLHL 94523 592-C7
2700 WLCK 94597 592-C7
2800 WLCK 94597 612-B1
ECHO AV
100 OAK 94611 650-A1
900 PDMT 94611 650-A1
ECHO CIR
- ANT 94509 595-D1
ECHO CT
- PLHL 94523 591-H2
ECHO LN
- PDMT 94618 630-C7
ECHO PL
- CCCo 94513 617-F4
2000 SRMN 94582 653-F7
ECHO HAWK CT
500 RCH 94803 589-G3
ECHO HILL
- MRGA 94556 631-D5
ECHO RIDGE WY
300 SRMN 94582 673-G3
ECHO SPRING RD
3400 LFYT 94549 611-F1
ECKLEY LN
- WLCK 94596 612-E5
- CCCo 94596 612-E5
ECKLEY PL
- WLCK 94596 612-E5
ECKLEY RD
- CCCo 94569 550-F5
ECLIPSE PL
- BREN 94561 596-D3
ECLIPSE WY
1500 CNCD 94521 593-D5
EDDY ST
100 RCH 94801 588-C7
EDEN CT
4100 CNCD 94521 593-A4
EDEN LN
3400 OAK 94601 650-C7
EDEN PL
- SRMN 94583 673-F7
EDEN ST
6800 DBLN 94568 693-J3
EDENBERRY PL
8500 DBLN 94568 693-G2
EDENBERRY ST
8700 DBLN 94568 693-G2
EDEN PLAINS RD
900 CCCo 94513 597-B3
900 CCCo 94513 617-B1
EDENVALE PL
3900 OAK 94605 650-J7
EDERA PL
- BREN 94513 596-D6
EDGE DR
4200 OAK 94602 650-E3
EDGECROFT RD
- CCCo 94707 609-F4
EDGEFIELD PL
- BREN 94513 616-F3
EDGEFIELD ST
- BREN 94513 616-F3
EDGEGATE CT
- DNVL 94506 654-A6
EDGEHILL CT
8600 ELCR 94530 609-F1
EDGEMONT CIR
- WLCK 94596 632-E1
EDGEVIEW CT
- CCCo 94514 617-J6
EDGEVIEW DR
1900 CCCo 94514 617-H6
EDGEVIEW WY
1900 CCCo 94514 617-H6
EDGEWATER CT
- CCCo 94511 577-E4
1200 WLCK 94595 632-A2
EDGEWATER DR
- CCCo 94511 577-E4
EDGEWATER PL
- PIT 94565 574-E1
EDGEWOOD AV
4300 OAK 94602 650-C3
EDGEWOOD CT
4800 OAKL 94561 576-D7
EDGEWOOD DR
1600 OAKL 94561 576-D6
EDGEWOOD LN
1900 WLCK 94598 592-E7
EDGEWOOD RD
- ORIN 94563 630-J4
EDIE CT
- PLHL 94523 592-A3
EDINBURGH
100 HER 94547 569-J2
EDINBURGH CIR
100 DNVL 94526 653-C2
EDINBURGH CT
1300 CNCD 94518 592-E6
EDINBURGH DR
100 DNVL 94526 653-D3
EDINBURGH PL
- CCCo 94507 632-E2
- DNVL 94526 653-D2
EDISON AV
1300 CCCo 94553 571-F3
EDITH ST
1400 BERK 94703 609-G7
2300 ELCR 94530 589-B7
EDMEADES CT
100 OAKL 94561 576-E6

EDMONTON WY
3600 CNCD 94520 572-G5
EDMUND CT
- WLCK 94596 612-D5
EDNA CT
400 BEN 94510 551-B3
EDNA DR
500 PLHL 94523 592-A5
EDNA ST
2300 ELCR 94530 589-B7
EDWARD AV
200 PIT 94565 574-F4
2700 CNCD 94520 572-E7
EDWARD LN
2500 ANT 94509 575-D1
EDWARDS AV
2400 ELCR 94530 589-B6
EDWARDS CT
1400 LFYT 94549 611-G3
EDWARDS ST
200 CCCo 94525 550-E4
EDWARD WERTH DR
- CCCo 94572 569-H1
EDWIN DR
- CCCo 94707 609-F2
EGRET CT
6000 BEN 94510 551-H1
EGRET PL
300 PIT 94565 574-E1
EGRETVIEW ST
- SRFL 94901 587-A2
EILEEN CT
100 MRGA 94556 651-E2
EILEEN LN
100 CNCD 94518 592-G4
EILEEN ST
- BREN 94513 596-H7
EILENE CT
3900 PLE 94588 694-E7
EILENE DR
2000 PLE 94588 694-E7
EIRE DR
16500 CCCo 94806 569-B4
EISENHOWER WY
- BREN 94513 596-G7
4700 ANT 94509 574-H5
EL CTE
- ORIN 94563 631-B5
ELAIN PTH
4500 RCH 94803 589-F1
ELAINE CT
- CCCo 94507 632-F6
ELAINE DR
100 PLHL 94523 592-D6
EL ALAMO
300 DNVL 94526 632-H6
EL ALAMO CT
- DNVL 94526 632-J6
ELAN LN
- SRMN 94582 674-C3
ELANE WY
700 BEN 94510 551-A4
ELARIO LN
4200 CNCD 94518 592-J5
EL ARROYO WY
4300 PIT 94565 574-D7
ELATI CT
300 DNVL 94526 653-B2
ELBA WY
7000 DBLN 94568 693-J3
ELBERT ST
1000 OAK 94602 650-C3
ELBERTA CT
- BREN 94513 616-H1
ELBERTA PKWY
1200 BREN 94513 596-E7
EL BONITO WY
- BEN 94510 551-C4
EL CAJON
- CCCo 94549 591-H7
EL CAJON DR
900 DNVL 94526 633-C7
900 DNVL 94526 653-C1
EL CAMINITO
- ORIN 94563 610-H6
- WLCK 94598 612-D4
2500 OAK 94611 650-E2
EL CAMINO
1700 CCCo 94806 569-B5
EL CAMINO DR
100 PIT 94565 574-D5
1300 CLAY 94517 593-F6
N EL CAMINO DR
1500 CLAY 94517 593-F6
EL CAMINO TER
- CCCo 94596 612-E6
EL CAMINO CORTO
- CCCo 94596 612-D5
- WLCK 94596 612-D5
EL CAMINO FLORES
- MRGA 94556 651-E1
EL CAMINO MORAGA
- ORIN 94563 631-B5
EL CAMINO REAL
- BERK 94705 630-A4
EL CAMPANERO
- ORIN 94563 610-H5
EL CAMPO CT
3600 CNCD 94519 592-J2
3700 CNCD 94519 593-A2
E EL CAMPO CT
3800 CNCD 94519 593-A2
EL CAMPO DR
1600 CNCD 94519 592-J2
EL CAMPO PL
1700 CNCD 94519 593-A2
EL CAPITAN DR
400 DNVL 94526 653-B5
EL CAPITAN LN
100 ANT 94509 595-D1
EL CARMELLO CIR
- OAK 94619 650-G4
EL CASTILLO
- ORIN 94563 611-A5
EL CENTRO
100 CCCo 94528 653-F1
EL CENTRO AV
1000 OAK 94602 650-C3
EL CENTRO RD
600 CCCo 94803 589-C2
EL CERRITO AV
100 PDMT 94611 650-B1
400 PDMT 94610 650-B1
EL CERRITO RD
4200 CNCD 94518 592-J5
EL CERRO BLVD
200 DNVL 94526 652-J1
300 DNVL 94526 653-A1
700 DNVL 94526 633-A7
EL CERRO CT
100 DNVL 94526 653-A1
EL CERRO DR
500 CCCo 94803 589-D1

EL CHARRO RD
- AlaC 94588 694-H6
- LVMR 94588 694-H6
EL CURTOLA BLVD
- CCCo 94597 611-J5
- CCCo 94597 612-A6
1000 CCCo 94595 612-A6
1200 LFYT 94549 612-A6
1200 LFYT 94549 611-J5
ELDA CT
1600 PLHL 94523 592-D5
ELDA DR
- PLHL 94523 592-C5
ELDER CT
200 SRMN 94582 653-J7
ELDER DR
- CCCo 94553 592-B1
ELDERBERRY CT
100 HER 94547 570-A5
ELDERBERRY DR
1300 CNCD 94521 593-C5
6200 OAK 94611 630-G7
ELDERBERRY TR
- CCCo 94583 652-D4
ELDERWOOD CT
1700 MRTZ 94553 591-J1
ELDERWOOD DR
- PLHL 94523 591-H2
400 MRTZ 94553 591-H2
1800 MRTZ 94553 571-J7
1800 CNCD 94519 573-A7
EL DIVISADERO AV
200 WLCK 94598 612-F3
EL DORADO AV
- BREN 94513 596-B5
100 DNVL 94526 652-J3
100 DNVL 94526 653-A2
1900 BERK 94707 609-G6
EL DORADO CT
1400 CNCD 94518 592-J3
EL DORADO DR
100 PIT 94565 574-D5
1300 CNCD 94518 592-J3
10000 SRMN 94583 673-G5
EL DORADO LN
- ORIN 94563 610-F7
EL DORADO RD
100 CCCo 94595 612-A7
EL DORADO ST
- OAKL 94561 576-B7
- OAKL 94561 596-B1
5600 ELCR 94530 609-C4
EL DORADO WY
2900 ANT 94509 575-B7
ELDRIDGE CT
- CCCo 94707 609-F4
ELEANOR CT
400 WLCK 94597 592-D7
ELEGANS CT
- SRMN 94582 673-J1
ELENA CT
- ANT 94531 595-G4
ELF CT
- PLHL 94523 592-B3
EL GAVILAN
- ORIN 94563 610-H5
EL GAVILAN CT
- ORIN 94563 610-J4
ELGIN AV
400 RCH 94801 588-F5
ELGIN LN
2300 WLCK 94598 612-G3
7900 DBLN 94568 693-G2
EL GRANDE PL
4800 CCCo 94803 589-E3
ELIJAH CT
- PIT 94565 574-E2
ELINORA AV
4400 OAK 94619 650-G5
ELINORA DR
1800 PLHL 94523 592-B5
ELIOTT CT
- CCCo 94507 632-H3
ELISE CT
1500 WLCK 94596 612-E6
ELISHA LN
- SRMN 94583 673-E6
ELISKA CT
600 WLCK 94598 612-F2
ELIZABETH CT
300 ANT 94509 575-D7
1300 CCCo 94596 612-E7
ELIZABETH LN
- DNVL 94526 633-B7
3000 ANT 94509 575-D7
ELIZABETH ST
1000 LFYT 94549 611-G5
ELIZABETH WY
- BREN 94561 596-D4
ELK CT
- MRGA 94556 631-D3
4500 ANT 94531 595-G3
7100 DBLN 94568 693-J4
ELK DR
- CLAY 94517 594-A6
4300 ANT 94531 595-G3
ELKHORN WY
4500 ANT 94531 595-H3
ELKINS WY
- BREN 94513 596-H5
ELK RUN TER
900 BREN 94513 616-E1
ELKWOOD CT
3900 CNCD 94519 573-A7
ELKWOOD DR
1800 CNCD 94519 573-A7
EL LAGO CT
4500 OAKL 94561 576-C7
EL LAGO DR
2100 OAKL 94561 576-B7
ELLARD PL
1800 CNCD 94521 593-F4
ELLARD WY
1800 CNCD 94521 593-E4
ELLEN CT
- ORIN 94563 610-J6
ELLEN LN
1300 BREN 94513 596-G7
ELLERHORST ST
2500 PIN 94564 569-F4
2600 ELCR 94530 589-B6
ELLERY CT
- CCCo 94595 632-C2
ELLESMERE CT
- BREN 94513 616-A1
3300 WLCK 94598 612-J3
ELLESMERE DR
400 WLCK 94598 612-J2
ELLIE CT
1700 BEN 94510 551-B4
ELLINGSON WY
2700 SRMN 94583 673-E5
ELLINGTON LN
- CNCD 94519 592-H5

ELLINGTON TER
2000 PLHL 94523 591-J3
ELLINWOOD DR
100 PLHL 94523 592-C4
ELLINWOOD WY
100 PLHL 94523 592-D4
ELLIOT CT
- CNCD 94521 593-F7
- PLHL 94523 592-A6
ELLIOT DR
- PLHL 94523 592-A7
ELLIOT ST
3200 OAK 94610 650-B4
ELLIS CT
- ANT 94531 595-J2
- ANT 94531 596-A2
- LFYT 94549 611-J4
- PLHL 94523 612-B1
ELLIS RD
4000 CCCo 94553 571-J4
ELLIS ST
1500 CNCD 94520 592-F2
ELLISA LN
- CCCo 94513 617-E6
ELLS LN
1000 RCH 94804 609-B2
ELLS ST
1100 RCH 94804 609-B2
ELM
- BEN 94510 551-B6
ELM AV
600 RCH 94801 588-F6
1500 CCCo 94805 589-C5
ELM CT
1000 ELCR 94530 609-D3
6700 DBLN 94568 693-J3
ELM DR
800 CCCo 94572 569-J1
ELM LN
5200 OAKL 94561 576-A6
ELM RD
- CNCD 94521 593-E3
1700 CNCD 94519 592-H2
ELM ST
- BEN 94510 551-D5
300 BREN 94513 616-G2
500 ELCR 94530 609-C1
1300 PIT 94565 574-E3
1400 MRTZ 94553 571-F3
1800 PIN 94564 569-E4
2000 CNCD 94519 592-G1
ELMAR CT
3000 RCH 94801 588-F1
ELMHURST LN
1700 CNCD 94521 593-D3
ELMINYA DR
100 CCCo 94553 572-C7
ELMIRA LN
- PLHL 94523 592-D7
EL MIRADOR
- WLCK 94596 612-D6
ELMO RD
3000 ANT 94509 575-E7
EL MOLINO DR
- CLAY 94517 613-J1
EL MOLINO PL
100 SRMN 94583 673-F7
EL MONTE CT
3000 ANT 94509 575-B7
4500 OAKL 94561 576-C7
EL MONTE DR
2000 OAKL 94561 576-C7
3300 CNCD 94519 592-H2
EL MONTE RD
3900 CCCo 94803 589-C3
EL MONTE WY
100 CNCD 94519 592-H2
2900 ANT 94509 575-B7
ELMQUIST CT
3100 MRTZ 94553 571-E5
ELMWOOD CT
- CCCo 94597 612-D2
2900 BERK 94705 630-A3
ELMWOOD DR
- CCCo 94597 612-D2
- SRMN 94583 693-H1
E ELMWOOD DR
1100 CCCo 94597 612-D2
ELMWOOD RD
4500 CCCo 94803 589-D3
EL NIDO
1600 CCCo 94528 633-E7
EL NIDO CT
- ORIN 94563 631-A4
100 CCCo 94528 633-E7
EL NIDO RANCH RD
300 ORIN 94563 610-J6
3800 LFYT 94549 611-A6
4200 ORIN 94563 611-A6
ELOISE AV
1800 PLHL 94523 592-B5
EL PARAISO CT
- MRGA 94556 631-E5
EL PASEO
- BEN 94510 551-A4
- WLCK 94597 612-C3
EL PASO WY
2900 ANT 94509 575-B7
EL PATIO
- OAK 94611 650-E2
- ORIN 94563 610-G6
700 CCCo 94803 589-C1
EL PINTADO
- PIT 94565 573-H3
400 DNVL 94526 633-A6
400 DNVL 94526 653-A1
600 DNVL 94526 632-J7
W EL PINTADO
200 DNVL 94526 653-A1
300 DNVL 94526 652-J1
EL PINTADO PL
- DNVL 94526 632-J7
- DNVL 94526 633-A7
EL PINTADO HEIGHTS DR
300 DNVL 94526 633-A6
EL PINTO
200 DNVL 94526 632-H7
EL PORTAL
100 DNVL 94526 632-H7
EL PORTAL CT
- BERK 94708 609-J7
- CLAY 94517 614-A2
EL PORTAL DR
- SPAB 94806 588-H2
- CLAY 94517 613-J2
- CLAY 94517 614-A2
- CCCo 94517 614-A2
2700 CCCo 94806 588-J3
2700 CCCo 94806 589-A3
2700 SPAB 94806 589-B2
3100 CCCo 94803 589-B2
3100 RCH 94803 589-B2

EL PORTAL PL
- CLAY 94517 614-A2
- CCCo 94517 614-A2
EL PRADO CT
- MRTZ 94553 571-H4
EL PUEBLO AV
800 PIT 94565 574-F3
EL PUEBLO PL
200 CLAY 94517 614-A2
EL PULGAR
- ORIN 94563 610-H5
EL QUANITO CT
800 DNVL 94526 633-B7
EL QUANITO DR
800 DNVL 94526 633-B7
EL RANCHO CT
- PLHL 94523 592-A7
EL RANCHO DR
- PLHL 94523 592-A7
EL REY PL
1800 CNCD 94519 572-J7
EL REY ST
2700 ANT 94509 575-C7
EL RIBERO
- ORIN 94563 610-G6
EL RINCON
- ORIN 94563 610-E7
EL RINCON RD
900 DNVL 94526 653-B2
EL RIO RD
400 DNVL 94526 632-J7
400 DNVL 94526 633-A7
400 DNVL 94526 652-J1
400 DNVL 94526 653-A1
ELROD AV
- OAK 94618 630-B6
EL SECO WY
2100 PIT 94565 573-J3
EL SERENA
300 CCCo 94553 572-C6
EL SERENO
- ORIN 94563 610-G5
ELSIE DR
200 DNVL 94526 652-J1
200 DNVL 94526 653-A1
ELSINORE AV
1000 OAK 94602 650-D3
ELSNAB CT
2800 PLE 94588 694-F6
EL SOBRANTE DR
200 DNVL 94526 653-B1
EL SOMBRO CT
1500 LFYT 94549 611-G2
ELSTON AV
3700 OAK 94602 650-C4
ELSTON CT
- OAK 94602 650-C4
EL SUENO
- ORIN 94563 610-G5
EL SUYO DR
3200 SRMN 94583 673-G5
ELTON CT
- PLHL 94523 591-H5
EL TORO CT
- CLAY 94517 614-A2
EL TORO WY
1600 PIN 94564 569-D5
EL TOYONAL
- ORIN 94563 610-E7
300 CCCo 94563 610-D5
EL VERANO
- ORIN 94563 610-J5
EL VERANO DR
700 CCCo 94598 612-F5
ELVERTON DR
6400 OAK 94611 630-F5
6900 CCCo 94563 630-F5
ELVIA ST
3200 LFYT 94549 591-H7
ELWOOD AV
400 OAK 94610 650-A2
ELWOOD CT
3900 CNCD 94519 593-B1
ELWYN PL
- DNVL 94526 632-J7
EMBARCADERO
200 MRTZ 94553 571-C2
1700 OAK 94606 650-A7
EMBARCADERO CT
7000 PLE 94588 693-H5
EMBLETON LN
- CCCo 94582 674-B4
EMERALD AV
7100 DBLN 94568 693-H3
EMERALD CT
5300 CCCo 94514 617-H6
EMERALD DR
- DNVL 94526 652-H1
2800 WLCK 94597 612-A2
EMERALD ST
1800 CNCD 94518 592-F6
EMERALD WY
- ANT 94531 596-A2
100 HER 94547 569-G5
EMERALD COVE DR
- CCCo 94565 573-J3
EMERIC AV
1300 SPAB 94806 588-G4
2300 RCH 94806 588-G4
EMERSON AV
- CCCo 94525 550-E5
EMERSON CT
- CNCD 94521 593-E7
- PIT 94565 574-B2
100 PLHL 94523 592-B7
EMERSON DR
- PIT 94565 574-B2
EMERSON LN
3000 BREN 94513 616-H3
EMERSON ST
3600 OAK 94610 650-B4
EMERSON WY
3700 OAK 94610 650-B4
EMERY CT
3700 CNCD 94518 592-J5
EMILIO CT
5400 CCCo 94803 589-F4
EMMA CT
1600 CNCD 94519 592-J2
EMMA DR
2500 PIN 94564 569-F4
EMMONS CANYON CT
- CCCo 94507 633-D4
EMMONS CANYON DR
1400 CCCo 94507 633-C4
EMMONS CANYON LN
100 CCCo 94507 633-C4
EMORY OAK CT
- BREN 94513 616-A3
EMPIRE AV
- OAKL 94561 576-C7
2000 BREN 94513 596-C5
2500 ANT 94531 596-C3
2500 BREN 94561 596-C3

EMPIRE AV
3300 OAKL 94561 596-C3
EMPIRE CT
- BREN 94513 616-H1
3900 PLE 94588 694-A7
EMPIRE MINE RD
- ANT 94531 595-D5
- ANT 94531 615-E1
- CCCo 94531 595-D7
- CCCo 94531 615-E1
EMPRESS LN
1400 BREN 94513 596-D6
EMSHEE LN
- CCCo 94553 572-B4
ENCANTO CT
1700 WLCK 94597 612-A2
ENCANTO PL
1500 WLCK 94597 612-A2
ENCHANTED WY
- SRMN 94583 673-A2
ENCIMA DR
1900 CNCD 94519 592-G1
ENCINA AV
1100 PIN 94564 569-D4
ENCINA CT
1100 ANT 94509 575-B6
ENCINA CTE
200 WLCK 94598 612-H2
ENCINA PL
- BERK 94705 630-A4
- PIT 94565 574-C6
ENCINA CAMINO
2800 WLCK 94598 612-H2
ENCINAL CT
2400 WLCK 94597 612-B2
ENCINAL DR
2400 WLCK 94597 612-B3
ENCINAL PL
100 PIT 94565 574-C7
ENCORE WY
- BREN 94513 616-D3
ENDICOTT CT
300 WLCK 94598 612-D3
ENDRISS DR
1600 MRTZ 94553 571-J7
ENDSLEIGH CT
700 DNVL 94506 654-A6
ENEA CIR
1400 CNCD 94520 592-D2
ENEA CT
1400 CNCD 94520 592-E2
ENEA DR
3700 PIT 94565 574-C5
ENEA WY
2800 ANT 94509 575-C6
ENES AV
- CCCo 94565 573-F2
ENGLISH CT
2200 WLCK 94598 612-G2
ENGLISH OAK CT
- BREN 94513 616-A4
2000 CCCo 94506 653-H1
ENID DR
1600 CNCD 94519 593-A2
ENLOW CT
2600 PIN 94564 569-G5
ENOS AV
3600 OAK 94619 650-G6
ENRICA LN
600 WLCK 94597 612-B3
ENSENADA AV
600 BERK 94707 609-F5
ENSENADA DR
3200 SRMN 94583 673-G5
ENSIGN CT
300 PIT 94565 574-A3
ENSLEY CT
- CCCo 94507 632-H2
ENTERPRISE AV
500 RCH 94801 588-F5
ENTERPRISE CIR
- PIT 94565 574-C2
ENTERPRISE CT
3500 CNCD 94519 572-H6
ENTERPRISE DR
400 DNVL 94526 653-A1
400 DNVL 94526 633-A7
ENTRADA CIR
2700 ANT 94509 575-B6
ENTRADA MESA
100 DNVL 94526 652-J2
ENTRADA VERDE
1400 CCCo 94507 632-E4
ENTRANCE RD
3800 LFYT 94549 611-C7
EOLA
- PIT 94565 574-A3
EPPINGER ST
- CCCo 94525 550-D4
EQUESTRIAN CT
5100 ANT 94531 595-J4
EQUESTRIAN DR
1700 PLE 94588 694-F7
EQUESTRIAN WY
5100 ANT 94531 595-J5
ERB CT
2700 WLCK 94598 612-H4
ERBA PTH
- OAK 94618 630-C5
ERIC CT
- PLHL 94523 592-A3
3400 RCH 94803 589-F1
ERICA CT
100 ANT 94509 595-D1
ERICKSON RD
1100 CNCD 94520 592-F4
ERIE CT
7000 DBLN 94568 693-J4
ERIE DR
2500 CNCD 94519 572-G7
ERIE ST
800 OAK 94610 650-A3
ERIN CT
- PLHL 94523 591-J5
2800 RCH 94806 589-A1
ERIS CT
3500 WLCK 94598 613-A3
ERLA WY
3000 RCH 94806 589-A1
ERLANDSON ST
500 RCH 94804 608-J1
700 RCH 94804 609-A1
ERNEST AV
5200 ELCR 94530 609-B1
5200 RCH 94804 609-B1
ERNST ST
1000 CNCD 94518 592-E5
ERNWOOD PL
9600 SRMN 94583 693-G1
ERNWOOD ST
9500 SRMN 94583 693-G1
ERROL DR
7400 ELCR 94530 609-E3

STREET Block City ZIP Pg-Grid

ERSELIA CT
100 CCCo 94507 632-G3
ERSELIA TR
100 CCCo 94507 632-G3
ERSKINE ST
- CCCo 94569 550-H6
ESCALON CIR
- RCH 94803 589-F1
ESCHER CIR
- OAKL 94561 576-H7
ESCHER DR
5800 OAK 94611 630-F7
5800 OAK 94611 650-F1
ESCOBAR PL
200 SRMN 94583 673-F4
ESCOBAR ST
- MRTZ 94553 571-D3
ESCONDIDO CT
900 CCCo 94507 632-G7
ESCONDIDO DR
100 MRTZ 94553 571-H4
ESCOVEDO LN
- CNCD 94519 592-H5
ESCUDO CT
- DBLN 94568 694-G4
ESCUELA CT
4500 RCH 94804 609-A1
ESMOND AV
1300 RCH 94801 588-G5
2300 RCH 94804 588-J5
3300 RCH 94805 588-J5
3400 RCH 94805 589-A5
ESPANILLO CT
1600 SPAB 94806 568-H7
ESPANO CT
2200 SPAB 94806 568-J7
ESPANOLA DR
1700 SPAB 94806 568-J7
1900 SPAB 94806 588-J1
ESPEE AV
100 RCH 94801 588-G6
ESPERANZA DR
1900 CNCD 94519 592-H1
2900 CNCD 94519 572-G6
ESPLANADE DR
1900 RCH 94804 608-G2
ESPLANADE PL
1000 WLCK 94597 612-C1
ESSENAY AV
2000 WLCK 94597 612-A2
ESSEX AV
1000 RCH 94801 588-F5
ESSEX CT
- OAKL 94561 596-D2
- CCCo 94507 633-A5
200 BEN 94510 551-B2
4000 CNCD 94521 593-A4
ESSEX DR
200 BREN 94513 616-E2
ESSEX ST
100 CCCo 94520 572-G2
ESSEX WY
200 BEN 94510 551-B2
ESTABUENO
- ORIN 94563 631-B5
ESTANCIA CT
- SRMN 94583 673-A2
ESTAND WY
2400 PLHL 94523 592-D6
ESTATES AV
2700 PIN 94564 569-F5
ESTATES CT
- ORIN 94563 630-J2
3300 CNCD 94519 592-H2
ESTATES DR
- DNVL 94526 653-A3
- ORIN 94563 630-J2
- PDMT 94611 650-D2
100 DNVL 94526 652-J2
1100 LFYT 94549 611-B5
2800 CNCD 94520 572-E6
5300 OAK 94618 630-C6
5800 OAK 94611 630-D7
6100 OAK 94611 650-D1
ESTATES RD
- CCCo 94707 609-F2
ESTELLA CT
- WLCK 94597 612-B2
ESTERO DR
3300 SRMN 94583 673-G6
ESTHER DR
1000 PLHL 94523 592-C7
ESTHER LN
- SPAB 94806 588-J3
100 DNVL 94526 652-J2
ESTRELLA AV
- PDMT 94611 630-B7
ESTRELLA CT
- CNCD 94518 592-F7
2300 PIN 94564 569-F6
11500 DBLN 94568 693-F4
ESTRELLA PL
- DNVL 94526 652-J1
ESTUDILLO ST
400 MRTZ 94553 571-D2
ESTUDILLO WY
2900 MRTZ 94553 571-E4
ETHAN CT
- LFYT 94549 631-H2
300 SRMN 94583 693-F1
ETHAN ALLEN DR
- BREN 94513 596-C5
ETNA CT
- SRMN 94583 673-F7
ETON CT
300 WLCK 94598 612-F2
EUCALYPTUS CT
- WLCK 94596 632-E1
1700 CNCD 94521 593-B2
EUCALYPTUS LN
- SRMN 94583 693-F1
EUCALYPTUS PTH
- OAK 94705 630-A3
EUCALYPTUS RD
- BERK 94705 630-A4
- OAK 94618 630-A4
- OAK 94705 630-A4
EUCALYPTUS WY
- ANT 94509 595-F3
EUCALYPTUS KNOLL
- HER 94547 569-H2
EUCLID AV
500 BERK 94708 609-H5
1600 BERK 94709 609-H7
2700 RCH 94804 588-H7
2800 CNCD 94519 592-G1
3900 MRTZ 94553 571-E6
EUCLID CT
1800 CNCD 94519 592-H1
EUGENE CT
2300 CNCD 94518 592-G5
EUNICE ST
2000 BERK 94709 609-G6
2000 BERK 94707 609-G6

EUNICE ST
2300 BERK 94708 609-G6
EUREKA AV
- CCCo 94707 609-E3
100 CCCo 94513 616-E4
600 ELCR 94530 609-D3
EUREKA LN
1100 CNCD 94520 592-E5
EUREKA MINE CT
4900 ANT 94531 595-D3
EUROPA CT
500 WLCK 94598 612-E2
EUROPENA DR
- BREN 94561 596-D4
EUSTICE AV
- OAK 94618 630-B5
EVA WY
- BREN 94513 596-C5
EVALANE WY
1800 CNCD 94519 592-H1
EVANS AV
- DBLN 94568 694-B4
1500 SPAB 94806 589-A4
1500 SPAB 94806 588-J4
4300 OAK 94602 650-C3
EVANS PL
- ORIN 94563 631-B3
EVE DR
1500 CNCD 94521 593-C3
EVELYN AV
400 ALB 94706 609-D5
1100 BERK 94706 609-D5
1300 BERK 94702 609-D5
EVELYN CT
- CCCo 94507 632-H2
600 LFYT 94549 631-H2
2900 OAK 94602 650-D5
2900 OAK 94601 650-D5
4300 PLE 94588 694-A7
EVELYN DR
200 PLHL 94523 592-B4
EVENINGSTAR CT
100 PIT 94565 574-A2
EVENS CREEK CT
700 SRMN 94582 674-A7
EVERETT AV
800 OAK 94602 650-C3
EVERETT CT
- DNVL 94526 653-B4
1100 CNCD 94518 592-J4
EVERETT DR
400 DNVL 94526 653-C4
EVERETT PL
300 DNVL 94526 653-B3
EVERETT ST
400 ELCR 94530 609-C1
EVERGREEN AV
1800 ANT 94509 575-E6
6600 OAK 94611 630-G7
EVERGREEN CT
- BREN 94561 596-F4
- CCCo 94595 612-A7
400 DNVL 94526 653-D7
EVERGREEN DR
- ORIN 94563 630-J1
1300 CNCD 94520 592-E4
EVERGREEN TER
1000 SPAB 94806 588-J3
EVERGREEN PATH LN
- OAK 94705 630-A3
EVERIDGE CT
1900 WLCK 94597 611-H3
EVERS AV
1700 OAK 94602 650-C4
EVERWOOD CT
- RCH 94806 568-J5
EVIREL PL
- OAK 94611 630-F6
EVORA RD
4000 CCCo 94565 573-C2
EWART DALE
- LFYT 94549 611-F5
EXBOURNE CT
2400 WLCK 94596 632-G2
EXCELSIOR AV
1100 OAK 94610 650-B4
1300 OAK 94602 650-C4
EXCELSIOR CT
- ANT 94531 595-F5
- OAK 94610 650-A3
EXCHANGE PL
200 RCH 94804 588-H6
EXECUTIVE PKWY
3000 SRMN 94583 673-D2
EXETER DR
6500 OAK 94611 650-G1
6500 OAK 94611 630-G7
EXETER LN
- PLHL 94523 591-J4
- PLHL 94523 592-A4
EXETER PL
600 CCCo 94506 654-A5
EXETER WY
- BREN 94513 596-E6
EXPLORER WY
- CCCo 94553 572-B4
EXPRESS CT
900 CNCD 94518 592-F6

F

F ST
- BREN 94513 596-D5
- CCCo 94565 573-E1
- MRTZ 94553 571-E5
100 ANT 94509 575-D3
100 BEN 94510 551-B5
1500 ELCR 94530 609-B2
E F ST
- BEN 94510 551-C6
W F ST
100 BEN 94510 551-B5
FABIAN CT
7000 PLE 94588 693-H6
FABIAN WY
100 CNCD 94518 592-H2
100 CNCD 94519 592-H2
FABLE CT
- CCCo 94803 589-D2
FACTORY ST
1000 RCH 94801 588-F5
FACULTY DR
200 VAL 94590 550-C2
FAFNIR PL
- PLHL 94523 592-A3
FAGES CT
1900 WLCK 94595 632-B1
FAHEY CT
2600 PIN 94564 569-F4
FAHMY ST
- BREN 94513 616-H3
FAIR AV
4200 OAK 94619 650-G6

FAIRBAIRN ST
4500 OAK 94619 650-F7
FAIRBANKS AV
400 OAK 94610 650-A2
FAIRBANKS WY
3600 ANT 94509 595-A1
FAIRBOURN DR
2200 PIT 94565 574-E5
FAIRBROOK CT
7700 PLE 94588 693-J7
FAIRDALE WY
- CCCo 94507 632-G3
FAIRFAX AV
4500 OAK 94601 650-E7
FAIRFAX CT
- PLHL 94523 592-B4
FAIRFIELD AV
- DBLN 94568 694-C3
2200 CNCD 94520 572-F7
FAIRFIELD PL
100 MRGA 94556 651-E2
FAIRHAVEN CT
1700 OAKL 94561 576-D6
FAIRHAVEN WY
100 VAL 94591 550-E1
FAIRHOLM CT
3200 LFYT 94549 611-H4
FAIRLANDS DR
3600 PLE 94588 694-E5
FAIRLANE DR
6000 OAK 94611 630-C5
FAIRLAWN CT
- WLCK 94595 632-A3
FAIRLAWN DR
- BERK 94708 609-J6
FAIRLAWN PL
700 CNCD 94518 592-J6
FAIRMAYDEN LN
- DNVL 94526 632-H7
FAIRMEDE DR
3100 RCH 94806 589-A1
FAIRMONT LN
2600 ANT 94509 575-D1
FAIRMOUNT AV
6000 ELCR 94530 609-D4
FAIROAKS CT
7900 PLE 94588 693-H7
FAIR OAKS DR
100 PLHL 94523 592-D6
700 CCCo 94507 632-H2
FAIROAKS DR
7600 PLE 94588 693-H7
FAIROAKS WY
100 PIT 94565 574-E6
FAIR RIDGE CT
1900 WLCK 94597 611-H3
FAIRSIDE CT
- PIT 94565 573-F4
FAIRSIDE WY
5200 ANT 94531 596-A4
FAIRVIEW AV
- BREN 94513 616-D2
- CCCo 94565 573-H2
- PDMT 94610 650-A1
1000 BREN 94513 596-D6
1400 CCCo 94805 589-C6
6900 ELCR 94530 589-C7
FAIRVIEW CT
2200 BREN 94513 596-D4
FAIRVIEW DR
- MRTZ 94553 571-G2
3400 ANT 94509 574-J5
FAIRVIEW LP
- CCCo 94553 571-G2
- MRTZ 94553 571-G2
FAIRVIEW ST
300 DNVL 94506 653-G5
FAIRWAY CT
- PIT 94565 574-B4
5400 CCCo 94514 617-J6
FAIRWAY DR
- CCCo 94511 577-E3
- ORIN 94563 610-F6
200 CCCo 94526 633-D7
200 CNCD 94528 633-D7
200 DNVL 94526 633-D7
1100 RCH 94803 569-C7
FAIRWAY PL
- PLHL 94523 591-J2
- PLHL 94523 592-A2
FAIR WEATHER CIR
1100 CNCD 94518 593-A6
FAIRWOOD CT
4300 CNCD 94521 593-C3
FAIRWOOD DR
- DNVL 94506 653-F4
1600 CNCD 94521 593-C3
FALCON CT
- BREN 94561 596-F4
- RCH 94806 568-J6
- PLHL 94523 592-A5
800 ANT 94509 595-F2
900 DNVL 94506 653-H4
FALCON DR
3500 CNCD 94520 572-G6
FALCON PL
200 CLAY 94517 593-J5
FALCON ST
9000 DNVL 94506 653-H3
FALCON WY
- CCCo 94514 637-E7
- CCCo 94514 (657-E1 See Page 638)
100 HER 94547 569-J5
400 HER 94547 570-A5
FALCON VIEW CT
2700 CCCo 94507 632-H3
FALCONWOOD CT
500 WLCK 94595 632-D4
FALL AV
4500 RCH 94804 609-A1
FALL CIR
300 OAKL 94561 596-G1
FALL DR
600 BREN 94513 616-D1
FALL LN
400 OAKL 94561 596-G1
4400 OAKL 94561 576-G7
FALLBOROUGH CT
- SRMN 94583 673-H3
FALLBROOK CIR
4300 CNCD 94521 593-B4
FALLBROOK CT
3800 PIT 94565 574-F6
4300 CNCD 94521 593-B4
FALLBROOK DR
1800 CCCo 94507 633-D6
FALLBROOK RD
4300 CNCD 94521 593-B4
FALLBURY CT
100 SRMN 94583 673-F4
FALL CREEK RD
7900 DBLN 94568 694-A1

FALLEN LEAF CIR
500 SRMN 94583 673-F4
FALLEN LEAF CT
- CCCo 94572 569-H1
1500 LFYT 94549 611-G2
FALLEN LEAF LN
5200 CNCD 94521 593-E4
FALLEN LEAF TER
- ORIN 94563 610-J3
FALLENLEAF WY
900 PIT 94565 574-E5
FALLEN OAK CT
1900 WLCK 94595 632-B1
FALLEN OAK LN
- CCCo 94553 591-E3
FALLERI CT
- OAKL 94561 596-D1
FALLMAN BLVD
- CCCo 94513 617-F2
FALLON AV
5000 RCH 94804 609-B2
FALLON PTH
5000 RCH 94804 609-B2
FALLON RD
- AlaC 94568 674-F7
- AlaC 94568 694-H4
- AlaC 94588 694-H4
- DBLN 94568 674-F7
4200 DBLN 94568 694-F1
FALLOW CT
4600 ANT 94509 595-F3
FALLOW DR
4500 ANT 94509 595-F3
FALL RIVER DR
- CCCo 94565 573-G3
FALLS CT
700 PLHL 94523 591-H2
FALLS ST
- PIT 94565 574-D6
FALLVIEW ST
200 SRMN 94583 673-F4
FALMOUTH CV
- SRFL 94901 587-A2
FANED WY
900 CNCD 94518 592-F6
FARALLON CT
- RCH 94804 608-E3
4500 ANT 94509 595-F2
FARALLON WY
6400 OAK 94611 630-D5
FARAN DR
200 CCCo 94553 572-C6
FAREHAM CT
- CCCo 94513 617-F5
FARGO CT
1400 CNCD 94521 592-J3
FARIA AV
2400 PIN 94564 569-F5
FARIA CT
2500 PIN 94564 569-G5
FARIA ST
500 ANT 94509 575-C7
FARISS LN
4000 CCCo 94803 589-C2
FARM LN
- MRTZ 94553 571-G5
FARM BUREAU CT
3500 CNCD 94519 592-J1
FARM BUREAU RD
1500 CNCD 94519 592-J1
FARM HILL CT
200 DNVL 94526 653-B3
700 WLCK 94598 612-J3
700 WLCK 94598 613-C4
FARMHILL WY
300 BREN 94513 616-E2
FARMINGTON CT
2400 MRTZ 94553 572-A5
FARNAM ST
3200 OAK 94601 650-C7
FARNHAM PL
500 DNVL 94526 653-D3
FARNUM CT
300 DNVL 94526 653-D6
FARRAGUT AV
- PDMT 94610 650-C2
FARRAGUT PL
500 DNVL 94526 633-A7
FARRAGUT ST
100 HER 94547 570-B5
FASCINATION CIR
1200 RCH 94803 589-G3
FAWCETT
100 HER 94547 569-E3
FAWN CT
- OAKL 94561 596-G2
FAWN PL
- DNVL 94526 653-B7
FAWN RD
4400 CNCD 94521 593-B4
FAWN WY
- DBLN 94568 694-D4
FAWNBROOK DR
800 BREN 94513 616-E1
FAWN CREEK CT
- PLHL 94523 592-A6
FAWNDA LN
- CNCD 94521 593-F7
FAWN GLEN CT
- PIT 94565 573-F5
800 CNCD 94521 613-D1
FAWN HILL CT
4700 ANT 94531 595-H2
FAWN HILL WY
4400 ANT 94531 595-J2
FAWN RIDGE CT
- SRMN 94582 673-J7
FAYE CT
1900 PLHL 94523 592-C5
FAYHILL RD
- MRGA 94556 631-F3
FEATHER CIR
1000 CLAY 94517 593-H6
FEATHER WY
5100 ANT 94531 595-G5
FEATHERMINT DR
- CCCo 94582 674-A1
- SRMN 94582 674-A1
FEATHER RIVER CT
- CCCo 94506 654-B4
FEATHER RIVER ST
800 CCCo 94506 654-C4
FEDSCO CT
4800 CNCD 94521 593-D4
FEDSCO DR
5000 CNCD 94521 593-D4
FELDSPAR CT
- ANT 94531 595-F2
FELICIA CT
- ANT 94509 595-D1
FELICIA LN
1700 CNCD 94519 592-J2
FELIX AV
6000 CCCo 94805 589-B5

FELIZ CT
100 DNVL 94526 633-C6
FELSITE CT
- ANT 94509 595-F1
FELTON
- HER 94547 569-G4
FENSALIR AV
400 PLHL 94523 592-B3
FENWAY CT
- WLCK 94598 612-G3
FENWAY DR
300 WLCK 94598 612-F3
FENWICK CT
11500 DBLN 94568 693-F2
FENWICK PL
11600 DBLN 94568 693-F2
FENWICK WY
8600 DBLN 94568 693-F2
FERN AV
500 PIN 94564 569-E4
FERN CT
- DNVL 94506 653-F4
FERN DR
- WLCK 94595 612-D7
FERN ST
2400 OAK 94601 650-E7
5700 ELCR 94530 589-B7
FERN WY
- ORIN 94563 630-J3
FERNANDEZ AV
- DBLN 94568 694-B3
700 PIN 94564 569-F4
FERNANDO CT
400 SRMN 94583 673-B2
FERNBANK DR
5200 CNCD 94521 613-D1
FERNBANK WY
- ANT 94531 595-J4
- ANT 94531 596-A4
FERNCLIFF CT
8300 DBLN 94568 693-G2
FERNCROFT CT
- DBLN 94568 694-F2
500 DNVL 94526 653-D7
FERNCROFT WY
- DBLN 94568 694-F2
FERNDALE CT
3000 PLE 94588 694-F6
FERNDALE LN
3900 CNCD 94519 593-A1
FERNDALE RD
- CCCo 94553 570-J7
1000 CCCo 94553 590-J1
FERNESS
300 PIT 94565 574-B3
FERNGROVE WY
3000 ANT 94531 575-G7
3000 ANT 94531 595-G1
FERN HILL LN
1300 CNCD 94521 593-B5
FERNHOFF CT
- OAK 94619 650-J5
FERNHOFF RD
5400 OAK 94619 650-J5
5500 OAK 94619 651-A4
FERN LEAF CT
2500 MRTZ 94553 572-A6
FERN MEADOW CT
- RCH 94806 568-J5
FERN RIDGE CIR
- CCCo 94513 617-F3
FERNSIDE LN
700 LFYT 94549 631-F1
FERNWALD RD
- BERK 94704 630-A2
FERNWOOD CIR
5000 OAKL 94561 576-D6
FERNWOOD CT
- PIT 94565 574-F5
3800 CNCD 94518 592-J4
5000 OAKL 94561 576-D6
FERNWOOD DR
100 MRGA 94556 631-E5
200 PLHL 94523 591-H2
1400 OAK 94611 630-D6
1600 OAKL 94561 576-D6
FERNWOOD LN
- BREN 94513 616-B3
FERRARA CT
5200 PLE 94588 694-C6
FERRELO CT
- DBLN 94568 694-G4
FERRELO LN
- HER 94547 569-G3
FERROL CT
- SRMN 94583 673-C3
FERRY ST
300 MRTZ 94553 571-D2
FERTADO LN
1800 CCCo 94513 617-E6
FETZER CT
800 OAKL 94561 576-E6
FETZER LN
1200 OAKL 94561 576-E6
FIDDLE CREEK PL
300 SRMN 94582 674-A7
FIELD ST
2000 ANT 94509 574-J5
FIELD BROOK CT
- ANT 94531 595-E5
FIELDBROOK PL
- MRGA 94556 631-D6
FIELDBROOK RD
4500 OAK 94619 650-G5
FIELDCREST CIR
1400 PLHL 94523 591-H2
FIELDCREST CT
200 DNVL 94506 653-H4
FIELDCREST DR
1500 PLHL 94523 591-H2
4300 CCCo 94803 589-F1
4300 RCH 94803 589-E1
FIELDCREST WY
4500 ANT 94531 595-H3
FIELDGATE DR
1600 PIT 94565 573-G4
FIELDGATE LN
1600 WLCK 94595 612-C7
FIELDSTONE CT
- DNVL 94506 653-F4
800 BREN 94513 616-F1
FIELDSTONE DR
- RCH 94806 568-J6
FIELDVIEW TER
2800 SRMN 94583 673-B3
FIESTA CIR
100 ORIN 94563 631-C5
FIESTA CT
3100 RCH 94803 589-E1
FIESTA DR
3000 PLE 94588 694-C7
FIESTA LN
- LFYT 94549 611-F6

FIFE CT
- SRMN 94583 673-E5
FIFI CT
- CCCo 94598 612-G4
- WLCK 94598 612-G4
FIG LN
4500 OAKL 94561 576-E7
FIG TREE LN
100 MRTZ 94553 571-H6
FILBERT CT
300 OAKL 94561 576-G7
600 WLCK 94598 612-H3
600 SRMN 94583 673-G7
FILBERT DR
2700 WLCK 94598 612-H3
FILBERT ST
1200 RCH 94801 588-F4
2600 ANT 94509 575-H6
FILLMORE CT
2200 ANT 94509 575-A7
FILLMORE ST
900 ALB 94706 609-D6
1300 SPAB 94806 588-G4
FILLMORE WY
1800 CNCD 94521 593-D3
FILLY CT
4600 ANT 94531 596-A3
FINCH CT
100 HER 94547 569-J5
FINCH DR
- ANT 94509 594-J2
FINCH WY
- DBLN 94568 694-D4
W FINCK RD
18600 SJCo 95206 (658-F5 See Page 638)
FINGER PEAK CT
- ANT 94531 595-F5
FINGER PEAK WY
- ANT 94531 595-E5
FINLEY LN
1400 CCCo 94507 632-F4
FINLEY RD
1100 CCCo 94588 654-F6
FINN WY
- BREN 94513 616-H1
FINNIAN WY
- DBLN 94568 694-F4
FIORA PL
4000 LFYT 94549 611-B6
FIORITA WY
- BREN 94513 596-D6
FIR CT
100 HER 94547 569-J4
6800 DBLN 94568 693-J4
FIR RD
- BEN 94510 551-D5
FIR ST
300 BREN 94513 616-G2
2000 CNCD 94519 592-G1
2300 CCCo 94553 571-F4
FIRCREST CT
- SRMN 94583 693-H1
FIRCREST LN
9100 SRMN 94583 693-H1
9400 SRMN 94583 673-H7
FIRE PL
- CCCo 94548 597-B2
FIREBRAND DR
7700 DBLN 94568 693-G3
FIRESIDE CT
500 WLCK 94598 612-H1
FIRESIDE WY
- PIT 94565 574-F5
FIRESTONE CT
200 WLCK 94598 612-J2
FIRESTONE DR
100 WLCK 94598 612-J1
FIRETHORN CT
200 SRMN 94582 653-J6
FIRETHORN WY
- DBLN 94568 693-G2
FIRWOOD CT
2100 CCCo 94514 617-H7
FISCHER AV
2300 CCCo 94513 597-B6
FISH CREEK PL
2300 DNVL 94506 653-G1
FISHER CT
4500 PLE 94588 694-A7
FISHER DR
1600 CNCD 94520 592-E4
FISHER ST
2400 CCCo 94806 569-B5
FISH RANCH RD
- CCCo 94563 630-D2
- OAK 94705 630-D2
FITZGERALD CT
- CNCD 94519 592-G1
FITZGERALD DR
1400 PIN 94564 569-C6
FITZPATRICK DR
3100 CNCD 94519 572-G7
FITZPATRICK ST
2400 CCCo 94806 569-B5
FITZUREN RD
900 ANT 94509 575-C6
FITZWILLIAM ST
- DBLN 94568 694-F4
FLAGG AV
3300 OAK 94602 650-D5
FLAGSHIP CT
- RCH 94801 608-E2
FLAGSHIP PL
- RCH 94801 608-E2
FLAGSTONE CT
- CCCo 94507 632-H4
- BREN 94513 616-E2
FLAGSTONE DR
200 ANT 94509 595-E1
7400 PLE 94588 693-J7
FLAGSTONE WY
2200 CNCD 94521 593-G4
FLAME CT
- CCCo 94553 592-B1
FLAME DR
100 CCCo 94553 592-B1
100 PLHL 94523 592-B1
FLAMINGO CT
2100 PIN 94564 569-F7
FLAMINGO DR
3400 CNCD 94520 572-G6
FLAMING OAK DR
300 PLHL 94523 592-B1
FLANAGAN CT
11800 DBLN 94568 693-G4
FLANDERS CT
1700 WLCK 94598 592-F7
FLANDERS WY
7500 DBLN 94568 693-H3
FLANNERY RD
2700 CCCo 94806 569-C5
FLARE EAST RD
- CCCo 94553 571-H3

FLARE NORTH RD
- CCCo 94553 571-G3
FLARE SOUTH RD
- CCCo 94553 571-G3
FLAX LN
300 SRMN 94582 653-J7
FLEET RD
1100 OAK 94602 650-C3
1100 OAK 94610 650-C3
FLEETWOOD CT
- ORIN 94563 631-B3
FLEETWOOD DR
100 ANT 94509 575-D7
3400 RCH 94803 589-E1
FLEETWOOD RD
4400 CCCo 94506 654-B4
FLEMING AV
3800 RCH 94804 609-B2
4300 OAK 94619 650-E7
FLEMING CT
- CLAY 94517 593-H7
- CLAY 94517 613-H1
FLEMING DR
200 CLAY 94517 593-H7
FLEMING LN
- CCCo 94509 576-A4
FLEMINGTON CT
3200 PLE 94588 694-F6
FLEMISH CT
- BREN 94513 616-C4
FLETCHER CT
- CCCo 94565 573-C1
FLETCHER ST
500 CCCo 94565 573-C1
FLEUTI DR
- MRGA 94556 631-E7
FLINT AV
900 CNCD 94518 592-G5
FLINTROCK DR
900 ANT 94509 595-F1
FLINTWOOD CT
1400 MRTZ 94553 571-H7
FLORA AV
100 CCCo 94595 612-B6
FLORA CT
- BREN 94513 616-B3
- PLHL 94523 592-D6
3000 PLE 94588 694-D7
FLORA ST
500 MRTZ 94553 571-E4
1200 CCCo 94525 550-D5
FLORADA AV
- OAK 94610 650-C2
- PDMT 94610 650-C2
FLORA VISTA
- DNVL 94526 652-H1
FLORENCE AV
- SPAB 94806 588-J3
100 OAK 94618 630-C6
FLORENCE CT
- ANT 94531 596-A1
100 CCCo 94507 633-D4
200 HER 94547 570-B6
FLORENCE DR
400 LFYT 94549 631-H3
4100 MRTZ 94553 571-E6
FLORENCE LN
1800 CNCD 94520 592-E4
FLORENCE TER
5500 OAK 94611 630-D6
FLORES CT
300 CCCo 94553 572-D3
FLORES WY
- BREN 94513 616-D5
FLORI CT
- OAKL 94561 576-D7
FLORIAN ST
3500 PLE 94588 694-C6
FLORIDA AV
- BERK 94707 609-G5
100 RCH 94804 588-F7
3700 RCH 94804 589-A7
FLORIDA DR
5400 CNCD 94521 593-E6
FLORIDA LN
2500 ANT 94509 575-D1
FLORIDA ST
2900 OAK 94602 650-E5
FLORIO ST
6400 OAK 94618 630-A4
FLOWERING ASH DR
- HER 94547 569-H2
FLOWERING PLUM PL
- BREN 94513 616-F3
FLOWERWOOD PL
1100 WLCK 94598 592-E7
1100 WLCK 94598 612-E1
FLOYD LN
2200 CNCD 94520 572-G5
FLYING CLOUD CT
100 VAL 94591 550-F2
FLYING DUTCHMAN CT
100 VAL 94591 550-G3
FOG CUTTER CV
- HER 94547 569-H1
FOGHORN WY
2500 CCCo 94513 617-E7
FOLEY CT
- WLCK 94595 612-B6
5100 ANT 94531 595-G4
FOLIN LN
- LFYT 94549 611-H3
FOLLETT ST
100 RCH 94801 588-E7
FOLSOM AV
1300 SPAB 94806 588-G3
FOLSOM CT
4000 CNCD 94520 572-G3
FOLSOM DR
- ANT 94531 596-A1
3900 ANT 94531 575-H7
3900 ANT 94531 595-J1
FONT CT
- DBLN 94568 694-G4
FONTAINE CT
300 DNVL 94506 653-H5
FONTAINE DR
300 DNVL 94506 653-H5
FONTANA CT
3300 ANT 94509 595-C1
FONTANA PL
3300 ANT 94509 595-B1
FONTES WY
1500 OAKL 94561 576-D6
FOOTHILL AV
1500 PIN 94564 569-E5
2300 RCH 94804 608-H1
FOOTHILL BLVD
1100 OAK 94606 650-A6
2300 OAK 94601 650-C7
FOOTHILL CT
- DNVL 94526 653-G5
2400 ANT 94509 594-J2

STREET
Block City ZIP Pg-Grid

FOOTHILL DR
- BREN 94513 616-B2
2300 ANT 94509 595-A2
2300 ANT 94509 594-J2
FOOTHILL PL
- PLHL 94523 591-J2
1400 OAK 94606 650-A6
FOOTHILL RD
5000 PLE 94588 693-G6
FOOTHILL WY
4200 PIT 94565 574-E7
FOOTHILL PARK CIR
1600 CCCo 94549 611-J1
FOOTHILL PARK TER
- CCCo 94549 611-J1
FORBES CT
- OAKL 94561 576-E6
FORD CT
2800 ANT 94509 575-A7
4500 BREN 94513 616-G3
FORD DR
1400 CNCD 94521 593-F5
FORD LN
3100 LFYT 94549 611-J6
FORD ST
4500 BREN 94513 616-G3
FORDHAM CT
- PLHL 94523 592-C3
FORDHAM DR
2500 RCH 94806 588-J2
2500 RCH 94806 589-A2
FORDHAM ST
2300 SPAB 94806 589-A3
2400 CCCo 94806 589-A3
2400 RCH 94806 589-A3
FOREMAN ST
- OAKL 94561 596-H2
FOREST AV
2800 BERK 94705 630-A3
FOREST CT
1400 OAKL 94561 576-E7
1700 CNCD 94521 593-B2
FOREST LN
- BERK 94708 609-H5
800 CCCo 94507 652-G1
900 CCCo 94507 632-G7
FOREST PK
100 HER 94547 569-G3
FOREST RUN
500 HER 94547 569-G3
FOREST WY
100 MRTZ 94553 591-F1
FOREST CREEK LN
- SRMN 94583 673-A2
N FORESTDALE CIR
- DBLN 94568 694-F3
S FORESTDALE CIR
- DBLN 94568 694-F3
FOREST GREEN CT
5200 CNCD 94521 593-E5
FOREST HILL AV
3800 OAK 94602 650-D4
FOREST HILL DR
- CLAY 94517 593-J7
- CLAY 94517 594-A7
4900 PLE 94588 693-H7
N FOREST HILL PL
1800 DNVL 94526 653-B7
S FOREST HILL PL
1900 DNVL 94526 653-B7
FOREST HILLS CT
- WLCK 94597 612-A2
FOREST LAKE PL
2100 MRTZ 94553 592-A1
FORESTLAND WY
6600 OAK 94611 630-G7
FORESTVIEW AV
4000 CNCD 94521 593-A2
FOREST VIEW COM
700 BREN 94513 616-E1
FORNI DR
5000 CCCo 94520 572-F3
FORREST RD
7600 CCCo 94803 589-F1
FORSYTHIA WY
2100 MRTZ 94553 571-J6
FORTE LN
5300 CNCD 94521 593-E5
FORTUNA CT
2800 ANT 94509 575-B6
FORTY NINER WY
2500 ANT 94531 595-F4
FOSKETT AV
2800 CNCD 94520 572-E6
FOSS CT
- CCCo 94597 612-D1
FOSTER DR
- SRMN 94583 693-F1
FOSTER LN
4100 CCCo 94803 589-C2
FOSTER ST
- MRTZ 94553 571-C3
FOSTER MOUNTAIN CT
- ANT 94531 595-F5
FOSTORIA CIR
200 DNVL 94526 653-D7
FOSTORIA WY
3000 SRMN 94583 673-C1
3000 DNVL 94526 673-C1
3000 SRMN 94526 673-C1
3100 SRMN 94583 653-D7
3100 DNVL 94526 653-D7
FOULKSTONE WY
100 VAL 94591 550-E2
FOUNTAIN WK
- BERK 94707 609-G6
FOUNTAIN GRASS CT
- HER 94547 569-J4
FOUNTAINHEAD CT
- MRTZ 94553 572-A7
700 SRMN 94583 673-B2
FOUNTAINHEAD DR
2500 SRMN 94583 673-A2
FOUNTAIN SPRINGS CIR
1300 DNVL 94526 653-B6
FOUNTAIN SPRINGS DR
1300 DNVL 94526 653-B6
FOUR OAKS LN
5800 CLAY 94517 593-G6
FOUR OAKS HOLLOW
- SRMN 94583 673-E6
FOX CIR
2500 WLCK 94596 632-G2
FOX RUN
600 ORIN 94563 610-J6
FOX WY
2000 CNCD 94518 592-F5
FOXBORO CIR
10000 SRMN 94583 673-F4
FOXBORO CT
300 SRMN 94583 673-F5
FOXBORO WY
9900 SRMN 94583 673-F5

FOX CREEK CT
4000 CCCo 94506 654-C2
FOX CREEK DR
3100 CCCo 94506 654-C2
FOXCROFT PL
- SRMN 94583 673-F6
FOXCROFT WY
- DBLN 94568 694-E3
FOXFORD WY
- ANT 94531 596-B4
- DBLN 94568 694-E4
FOX GLEN PL
800 WLCK 94598 613-B3
FOXGLOVE CT
- BREN 94513 616-H5
- PIT 94565 574-C2
2700 PLE 94588 694-H4
FOXGLOVE LN
- SRMN 94583 673-A1
- CCCo 94523 592-D7
FOXGLOVE PL
- RCH 94806 569-A6
FOXGLOVE ST
- PIT 94565 574-C2
FOXHALL CT
- DNVL 94526 653-C3
FOXHILL DR
2200 MRTZ 94553 572-A6
FOX HOLLOW CT
1400 CNCD 94521 592-J3
FOX MEADOW WY
1000 CNCD 94518 592-F5
FOX RIDGE CT
1900 WLCK 94597 611-H3
FOX TAIL CT
800 WLCK 94598 613-B3
FOXTAIL CT
- BREN 94513 616-E2
FOXWOOD WY
- WLCK 94595 632-D4
FOYE DR
900 LFYT 94549 611-G6
FRAGA CT
400 MRTZ 94553 571-J6
FRAN WY
4100 RCH 94803 589-E1
FRANCES RD
1100 CCCo 94806 569-A5
FRANCES ST
2400 OAK 94601 650-E7
FRANCES WY
- CCCo 94597 612-D2
FRANCESCA WY
- CCCo 94507 632-E4
FRANCIA CT
- DBLN 94568 694-G3
FRANCINE CT
1100 CNCD 94518 592-G3
FRANCIS CT
100 OAKL 94561 576-C7
100 OAKL 94561 596-C1
500 MRTZ 94553 591-G4
FRANCIS DR
500 MRTZ 94553 591-G4
500 CCCo 94549 591-G4
2500 PIN 94564 569-F4
FRANCIS ST
1200 CCCo 94525 550-D5
1400 ALB 94706 609-E7
FRANCISCA CT
1000 PIN 94564 569-E5
1700 BEN 94510 551-C4
FRANCISCA DR
- MRGA 94556 631-E3
FRANCISCAN CT
- DNVL 94526 653-C7
FRANCISCAN DR
1100 DNVL 94526 653-C7
FRANCISCAN WY
- CCCo 94707 609-E3
- ELCR 94530 609-E3
FRANCISCO BLVD E
1100 SRFL 94901 587-A4
FRANCISCO CT
- ORIN 94563 631-A5
600 WLCK 94598 612-E2
S FRANCISCO CT
1600 ANT 94509 575-A7
FRANCISCO WY
2600 CCCo 94805 589-C6
2600 ELCR 94530 589-C6
N FRANCISCO WY
2900 ANT 94509 575-A7
S FRANCISCO WY
3100 ANT 94509 575-A7
3100 ANT 94509 595-B1
FRANCISCO VILLA DR
100 OAKL 94561 576-E7
FRANDORAS CIR
3000 OAKL 94561 576-A7
FRANK PL
5600 CLAY 94517 593-G5
FRANKE LN
3900 LFYT 94549 611-B6
FRANK HENGEL WY
- OAKL 94561 576-H6
FRANKLIN AV
200 CCCo 94565 573-H3
FRANKLIN DR
- BREN 94513 616-C4
4900 PLE 94588 694-A5
FRANKLIN LN
600 CCCo 94803 569-E7
1200 LFYT 94549 611-D5
4300 CCCo 94561 597-A1
4300 CCCo 94561 577-A7
FRANKLIN CANYON RD
1400 MRTZ 94553 571-A5
2000 CCCo 94553 571-A5
2300 CCCo 94553 570-C3
FRANQUETTE AV
1200 CNCD 94520 592-D3
FRANROSE LN
1600 CNCD 94519 593-A2
FRASER CT
- WLCK 94596 612-E6
2500 PIN 94564 569-F4
FRASER DR
- WLCK 94596 612-E6
FRASER RD
3200 ANT 94509 595-C1
FRAY AV
4900 RCH 94804 609-B1
FRAY PTH
- RCH 94804 609-B1
FRAYNE CT
800 CNCD 94518 592-H6
FRAYNE LN
2800 CNCD 94518 592-H6
FRAZIER DR
600 OAKL 94561 596-F2
FREDA CT
300 MRTZ 94553 571-D6

FREDA DR
100 CCCo 94553 572-B7
FREDERICK ST
2100 CNCD 94520 572-F7
2100 OAK 94606 650-A7
FREDERICKSON LN
- ANT 94509 595-C4
- ANT 94531 595-C4
- CCCo 94509 595-B5
FREDERIKA AV
400 LFYT 94549 631-G3
FREDERIKSEN CT
7500 DBLN 94568 693-H3
FREDERIKSEN LN
7400 DBLN 94568 693-H3
FREED AV
2100 PIT 94565 574-E4
FREED CIR
1500 PIT 94565 574-E4
FREEDOM CT
3600 ANT 94509 595-C3
FREEDOM WY
3600 ANT 94509 595-B1
FREEMAN CT
- CCCo 94595 612-A7
2100 ANT 94509 595-A1
FREEMAN RD
3300 CCCo 94595 612-A7
3300 CCCo 94595 611-J7
3400 LFYT 94549 611-J7
FREEMARK CT
- OAKL 94561 576-D6
FREEMARK LN
500 OAKL 94561 576-D6
FREEPORT CT
1700 OAKL 94561 596-D1
FREESIA CT
1000 DNVL 94506 654-B5
FREETHY BLVD
300 RCH 94801 588-F1
FRWY I-80
- CCCo - 550-D3
- SolC - 550-D3
- VAL - 550-C1
FRWY I-580
- MrnC - 587-C5
- RCH - 587-H6
- RCH - 588-A7
- SRFL - 587-A3
FRWY I-680
- BEN - 551-E6
- CCCo - 571-G2
- CCCo - 572-A4
- CCCo - 592-C1
- CCCo - 612-C1
- CCCo - 632-E2
- CNCD - 592-C2
- DBLN - 693-G2
- DNVL - 632-H6
- DNVL - 652-J1
- DNVL - 653-A1
- DNVL - 673-C1
- MRTZ - 551-E6
- MRTZ - 571-F1
- PLE - 693-J4
- PLHL - 592-C1
- PLHL - 612-C1
- SolC - 551-E6
- SRMN - 653-C7
- SRMN - 673-C1
- SRMN - 693-F1
- WLCK - 612-B6
- WLCK - 632-D1
FRWY I-780
- BEN - 550-G1
- BEN - 551-A3
FRWY Rt#-24
- WLCK - 612-B4
FRWY Rt#-160
- ANT - 576-A4
- CCCo - 576-A4
- OAKL - 576-A4
FRWY Rt#-242
- CNCD - 572-F5
- CNCD - 592-F1
- PLHL - 592-D4
FREITAS CT
300 DNVL 94526 653-C3
FREITAS DR
- MRGA 94556 651-E1
FREITAS RD
400 DNVL 94526 653-B3
FREMEREY CT
400 DNVL 94506 653-G1
FREMONT CT
100 HER 94547 570-B5
FREMONT ST
1700 CNCD 94520 592-E1
FRENCHPARK CT
- ANT 94531 596-B4
FRESHWATER CT
- PIT 94565 573-F5
2200 MRTZ 94553 572-B2
FRESNO AV
900 BERK 94707 609-F6
5100 RCH 94804 609-B4
FRESSIA CT
2700 PLE 94588 694-H4
FREYA WY
500 PLHL 94523 592-A3
FRIAR CT
5700 CCCo 94803 589-G4
FRIEDA CT
100 VAL 94590 550-C1
2400 SPAB 94806 588-G2
FRIES CT
2000 MRTZ 94553 572-A6
FRIESMAN RD
1600 LVMR 94551 694-H5
1600 LVMR 94588 694-H5
FRIGATE CT
200 PIT 94565 574-A2
FRINGE DR
- RCH 94806 568-H6
FRISBEE CT
1500 CNCD 94520 592-E4
FRONT ST
- BERK 94710 609-C7
- DNVL 94526 653-A2
400 PIT 94565 554-D7
1400 MRTZ 94553 571-E2
N FRONT ST
- HER 94547 569-G2
S FRONT ST
- HER 94547 569-G2
FRONTAGE RD
- PIT 94565 574-C3
1500 CCCo 94565 574-A2
5500 OAK 94605 650-H7
W FRONTAGE RD
1300 BERK 94710 609-C7
FROST CT
- CNCD 94521 593-F7

FROYD RD
1000 CNCD 94521 593-F7
FRUITVALE AV
1200 OAK 94601 650-C6
2900 OAK 94602 650-D4
FRUITVALE CT
2000 ANT 94509 595-F2
FRUITWOOD COM
- BREN 94513 596-G6
FRUMENTI CT
500 MRTZ 94553 591-H4
FRY CT
1400 BEN 94510 551-A3
FRY WY
- CNCD 94520 592-F2
FRYE ST
2800 OAK 94602 650-F4
FRYER CT
- SRMN 94583 673-E4
FUCHSIA CT
100 HER 94547 569-J3
FUCHSIA LN
- SRMN 94582 653-H7
FUENTE CT
2100 ANT 94509 595-A1
FULHAM CT
100 SRMN 94583 673-E5
FULLER CT
- OAKL 94561 596-H2
FULLINGTON ST
3300 OAK 94619 650-E6
FULL MOON DR
4700 RCH 94803 589-G1
FULL MOON WY
400 CCCo 94506 653-J5
FULTON AV
1100 SolC 94591 550-E1
1300 VAL 94591 550-E1
FULTON CT
400 DNVL 94526 633-A7
FULTON WY
500 DNVL 94526 633-A7
800 CCCo 94803 589-D7
FULTON SHIPYARD RD
200 ANT 94509 575-E4
200 CCCo 94509 575-E4
FUNSTON PL
2100 OAK 94602 650-E3
FUNSTON GATE CT
4800 PLE 94588 694-D7
4800 PLE 94566 694-D7
FURLONG WY
5000 ANT 94531 595-J4
FURROW DR
700 BREN 94513 616-F2
FUSCHIA WY
4800 OAKL 94561 576-E7
FUSHIA CT
100 MRTZ 94553 572-B7
FYNE DR
2800 WLCK 94598 612-F4

G

G ST
- CCCo 94565 573-E1
- CNCD 94518 592-G4
100 ANT 94509 575-C4
100 MRTZ 94553 571-E5
100 BEN 94510 551-B5
3100 ANT 94509 595-C1
W G ST
100 BEN 94510 551-B5
GABLE LN
- LFYT 94549 611-G2
GABRIEL CT
500 WLCK 94597 612-B3
2300 ANT 94509 595-A2
GABRIELLA LN
- BREN 94513 596-C6
GACH CT
3100 PLE 94588 694-H4
GAIL CT
- CCCo 94598 613-A4
GAIL DR
100 PLHL 94523 591-J4
100 PLHL 94523 592-A4
GAINES LN
600 WLCK 94597 612-B2
GAINSBOROUGH DR
3600 CNCD 94518 592-J3
GAIOLE CT
- BREN 94513 596-C7
GAIT CT
- SRMN 94583 673-C4
GALA LN
- BREN 94513 616-D2
GALAXY CT
2200 CNCD 94520 592-E2
GALAXY WY
- DBLN 94568 693-G4
1000 CNCD 94520 592-E1
GALBRETH RD
1900 PIN 94564 569-F7
GALE MEADOW CIR
200 SRMN 94582 653-H7
GALEN DR
100 CCCo 94597 612-A4
GALENEZ WY
- ANT 94531 595-F2
GALERIA PL
- PIT 94565 573-E4
GALE RIDGE CT
- SRMN 94582 673-H3
N GALE RIDGE RD
- SRMN 94582 673-H1
S GALE RIDGE RD
- SRMN 94582 673-H2
GALI CT
- DBLN 94568 694-G4
GALICIA CT
- SRMN 94583 673-C4
GALINDO CT
8600 DBLN 94568 693-G2
GALINDO DR
8400 DBLN 94568 693-G2
GALINDO ST
1300 CNCD 94520 592-F1
1400 CNCD 94518 592-F2
2900 OAK 94601 650-C6
GALISTEO CT
- SRMN 94583 673-C3
GALLAGHER CIR
3600 ANT 94509 595-C1
GALLAGHER DR
300 BEN 94510 551-B1
GALLAUP CT
- DBLN 94568 694-G5
GALLEON WY
- PIT 94565 573-J3
GALLERON CT
- OAKL 94561 576-D5
GALLERY CT
- RCH 94806 568-H6

GALLERY DR
- RCH 94806 568-H5
GALLEY CT
100 CCCo 94513 617-E7
GALLOWAY CT
2400 ANT 94531 595-G1
GALLOWAY DR
- CNCD 94518 592-G4
GALVESTON CT
800 CNCD 94518 592-H6
GALVIN DR
800 ELCR 94530 609-D2
GALVIN ST
1000 OAK 94602 650-C3
GALWAY CT
- DBLN 94568 693-D4
GALWAY DR
1900 PIT 94565 574-E4
GALWAY RD
2200 CCCo 94806 569-C5
GAMAY CIR
1400 OAKL 94561 576-D7
GAMAY DR
1100 CLAY 94517 593-H7
1100 CLAY 94517 613-H1
1700 OAKL 94561 576-C7
GAMBON CT
- DBLN 94568 694-G4
GANGES AV
1900 ELCR 94530 589-C7
GANGES CT
7300 ELCR 94530 609-C1
GANGES ST
1700 ELCR 94530 609-C1
1800 ELCR 94530 589-C7
GANN ST
- BREN 94513 596-E4
GANNER CT
4800 PLE 94566 694-D7
GARAVENTA CT
1400 CNCD 94521 593-D5
GARAVENTA DR
5100 CNCD 94521 593-D5
GARBER RD
- BREN 94513 616-C4
3000 BERK 94705 630-A3
3000 OAK 94705 630-A3
GARBER ST
2800 BERK 94705 630-A3
GARCES CT
- DBLN 94568 694-G4
GARCEZ DR
1500 CNCD 94521 593-E5
GARCIA AV
500 PIT 94565 574-D4
GARCIA LN
1400 CNCD 94521 593-A3
GARCIA RANCH RD
1000 CCCo 94553 590-H5
1200 CCCo 94553 591-A5
GARDELLA DR
7500 DBLN 94568 693-G3
GARDEN AV
2600 CNCD 94520 572-F7
GARDEN CT
- ANT 94509 575-F6
- CCCo 94595 612-A6
2000 OAKL 94561 576-C6
GARDEN DR
- CCCo 94708 609-G3
GARDEN LN
1100 LFYT 94549 611-F5
4100 CCCo 94803 589-C2
GARDEN RD
3900 CCCo 94803 589-C2
GARDEN ST
2700 OAK 94601 650-C5
GARDEN CREEK CIR
2800 PLE 94588 694-E6
GARDEN CREEK PL
100 DNVL 94526 652-J1
GARDEN ESTATES CT
- CCCo 94507 632-F4
GARDENIA AV
4900 OAKL 94561 576-D6
GARDENIA CT
100 MRTZ 94553 572-B7
100 MRTZ 94553 592-B1
800 ANT 94531 595-E6
GARDENIA LN
- CNCD 94520 592-E5
GARDEN PARK CT
- CCCo 94507 632-E3
GARDENSIDE CT
- BREN 94561 596-F4
GARDEN TRACT RD
1900 RCH 94801 588-E3
1900 CCCo 94801 588-E2
GARDEN VIEW CT
- DNVL 94506 653-F5
GARDEN VIEW LN
- PLHL 94523 591-J2
GARDINA CT
1200 DNVL 94526 653-C4
GARDINER CT
- ORIN 94563 610-H4
GARDNER PL
100 DNVL 94526 653-E3
GARFIELD AV
1100 ALB 94706 609-D5
GARFIELD PL
2900 ANT 94509 575-A7
GARIN PKWY
- BREN 94513 596-H7
1200 BREN 94513 616-H1
GARLAND CT
2000 WLCK 94595 632-D1
GARLAND WY
500 BREN 94513 616-D1
GARNER CT
2300 ANT 94509 594-J1
6200 PLE 94588 694-A7
GARNET CT
100 HER 94547 569-G4
GARNET LN
1600 CNCD 94519 592-J2
GARNET TER
500 BREN 94513 616-D1
GARRARD BLVD
- RCH 94801 608-D1
- RCH 94804 608-D1
- RCH 94804 588-E7
- RCH 94801 588-E7
GARRETSON AV
- CCCo 94572 549-H7
400 CCCo 94572 569-H1
400 CCCo 94547 569-H1
GARRIGAN CT
500 CCCo 94506 654-B5
GARRISON CT
400 WLCK 94598 612-E5
GARRISON RD
700 RCH 94803 589-H3

GARRITY CT
2700 PIN 94564 569-G5
GARRITY WY
3100 RCH 94806 589-B1
3100 RCH 94806 569-B7
GARRON CT
- WLCK 94596 632-F1
GARROW DR
2700 ANT 94509 575-E7
3400 ANT 94509 595-E1
GARTLEY AV
- CCCo 94525 550-E5
GARVIN AV
1300 RCH 94801 588-G5
2300 RCH 94804 588-J5
3300 RCH 94805 588-J5
3400 RCH 94805 589-A5
GARY AV
500 ANT 94509 575-E6
GARY CT
- OAKL 94561 596-B1
GARY DR
1400 CNCD 94518 592-H2
GARY WY
- CCCo 94507 632-G7
GARYDALE CT
100 CCCo 94507 632-H4
GARY LEE LN
- WLCK 94597 612-B2
GASOLINE AL
1400 CNCD 94520 592-E1
GASPAR CT
5000 OAKL 94561 576-D6
GASPAR DR
1800 OAK 94611 630-E7
GATELY AV
5000 RCH 94804 609-B2
GATELY DR
- PIN 94564 569-C4
GATETREE CT
100 DNVL 94526 653-C2
GATETREE DR
100 DNVL 94526 653-C2
GATEVIEW AV
700 ALB 94706 609-C6
GATEWAY
- DBLN 94568 693-G2
GATEWAY BLVD
- ORIN 94563 630-F2
1800 CNCD 94520 592-E2
GATEWAY CT
5700 CCCo 94514 617-J7
GATEWAY DR
1600 OAKL 94561 596-C1
GATEWAY RD
4400 CCCo 94511 577-D3
GATEWAY PLAZA DR
- BEN 94510 551-G1
GATEWOOD CT
1400 MRTZ 94553 571-J7
N GATE WOODS CT
- CCCo 94598 613-A4
GATHERING CT
700 BREN 94513 616-E2
GATTER CT
800 ANT 94509 575-C7
GATTER DR
900 ANT 94509 575-C7
900 ANT 94509 595-B1
GATTO AV
6600 ELCR 94530 589-B7
GATWICK CT
- DBLN 94568 694-A4
GAUCHO CT
200 SRMN 94583 673-C2
GAY CT
100 CCCo 94507 632-H5
GAYLE CT
1300 ELCR 94530 609-D2
GAYLENE CT
800 CNCD 94518 592-G6
GAYLORD PL
900 CNCD 94518 592-F6
GAYNOR AV
1300 RCH 94801 588-G5
2300 RCH 94804 588-H5
GAYWOOD PL
- MRGA 94556 651-E1
GAYWOOD RD
- CCCo 94507 632-F5
GAZELLE CT
- ANT 94531 595-H2
GEARY CT
- WLCK 94597 612-B1
GEARY RD
700 WLCK 94597 612-B1
1400 CCCo 94597 612-B1
1800 PLHL 94523 611-J1
1800 PLHL 94523 612-B1
1800 WLCK 94597 611-J1
GEHRINGER DR
2200 CNCD 94520 572-F6
GELBKE LN
1700 CNCD 94520 592-E4
GELDING CT
- DNVL 94526 633-C7
GELSTON PL
700 ELCR 94530 609-E2
GELSTON ST
700 OAK 94705 630-B2
GEM LN
2500 ANT 94509 575-C6
GEMINI CT
3500 CNCD 94519 592-J1
GENESO ST
- OAKL 94561 576-C6
GENEVA AV
4800 CNCD 94521 593-D3
GENEVA CT
3200 MRTZ 94553 571-D5
GENEVA LN
1800 ANT 94509 575-H6
GENEVA ST
2700 MRTZ 94553 571-D5
GENI CT
400 WLCK 94597 592-D7
GENOA CT
100 WLCK 94598 612-J2
GENOVESIO DR
5600 PLE 94588 694-C6
GENTLE CREEK PL
- DNVL 94526 632-H7
- DNVL 94526 652-H1
GENTRY CT
400 WLCK 94598 612-D3
GENTRYTOWN DR
1400 ANT 94509 575-A6
2900 ANT 94509 574-J7
3200 ANT 94509 595-A1
GEOFFREY CT
2500 PIN 94564 569-E6
GEOFFREY DR
- CCCo 94565 573-E2

GEORGE CT
800 BREN 94513 616-J2
1400 BEN 94510 551-A3
GEORGE LN
- DNVL 94526 633-B7
GEORGETOWN CIR
- DBLN 94568 694-E3
GEORGETOWN LN
2500 ANT 94509 575-D1
GEORGIA DR
1600 CNCD 94519 593-A2
GEORGIA ST
2900 OAK 94602 650-E5
GEORGIAN OAKS CT
- DBLN 94568 693-E4
GEORGIS PL
5700 PLE 94588 694-C5
GERALD AV
1200 SPAB 94806 589-B4
GERALD CT
- CCCo 94565 573-F2
400 BEN 94510 551-A1
GERALD DR
100 DNVL 94526 653-A4
100 DNVL 94526 652-J4
3500 CNCD 94519 592-J3
3500 CNCD 94518 592-J3
GERALDINE DR
2300 PLHL 94523 592-D6
GERANIUM CT
- CCCo 94582 674-A2
GERANIUM PL
4600 OAK 94619 650-H5
GERBERA ST
- DNVL 94506 654-C6
GERIOLA CT
- PLHL 94523 612-B1
GERONIMO CT
- ANT 94531 595-G5
GERRY CT
200 CCCo 94596 612-F7
GERRY ST
700 BREN 94513 616-J3
GERTRUDE AV
- CCCo 94801 588-E4
- RCH 94801 588-E4
W GERTRUDE AV
200 CCCo 94801 588-E4
200 RCH 94801 588-E4
GERZ CT
2300 PIN 94564 569-F6
GETOUN CT
1700 CNCD 94518 592-F6
GETOUN DR
900 CNCD 94518 592-F6
GETTY CT
500 BEN 94510 551-E1
GEYSER CIR
1600 ANT 94509 575-G5
GEYSER CT
1800 ANT 94509 575-G5
GHIGLIAZZA WY
- CCCo 94548 597-B3
GHIOTTI CT
4000 PLE 94588 694-H4
GIAMMONA DR
1500 WLCK 94596 612-C5
GIANNINI RD
- CCCo 94553 571-J4
GIANT HWY
2100 RCH 94806 568-H5
GIANT RD
2100 RCH 94806 568-H5
2200 SPAB 94806 588-G2
3200 SPAB 94806 568-H7
GIARAMITA ST
1500 CCCo 94801 588-F4
GIBRALTAR DR
5500 PLE 94588 694-B5
GIBSON AV
- CCCo 94565 573-H2
GIBSON CT
- CCCo 94507 632-H2
6200 PLE 94588 694-A7
GIBSON LN
- CLAY 94517 593-G7
GIEGER LN
1400 CNCD 94521 592-J3
GIGEY DR
- BEN 94510 551-A4
GILARDY DR
1700 CNCD 94518 592-E6
GILBERT CT
100 MRTZ 94553 571-E7
GILBERT LN
100 MRTZ 94553 591-F1
GIL BLAS RD
100 DNVL 94526 653-B2
GILBOA DR
1500 WLCK 94598 612-E3
GILDA AV
400 MRTZ 94553 571-J6
GILGER AV
100 MRTZ 94553 571-D5
GILL CT
100 BEN 94510 551-B2
2600 CNCD 94520 592-F1
GILL DR
2000 CNCD 94520 592-F1
2600 CNCD 94520 572-F7
GILL WY
100 BEN 94510 551-B2
GILLCREST AV
300 SolC 94591 550-D1
300 VAL 94591 550-D1
GILLESPIE AL
- CNCD 94519 592-H5
GILLET AV
2800 CNCD 94520 572-E6
GILL PORT CT
1800 WLCK 94598 612-E1
GILL PORT LN
2000 WLCK 94598 612-E1
2100 WLCK 94598 592-E7
GILLY LN
1800 CNCD 94518 592-F5
GILMA DR
2900 RCH 94806 589-A1
GILMAN ST
600 BERK 94710 609-E7
1000 BERK 94706 609-E7
1000 BERK 94702 609-E7
GILMORE CT
- LFYT 94549 612-A4
900 CNCD 94518 592-F6
GILRIX DR
- MRTZ 94553 571-H4
GINGER CT
- ANT 94509 595-D1
300 SRMN 94582 653-J7
GINGERWOOD LN
400 DNVL 94506 653-H3
GINGERWOOD TER
1800 BREN 94513 596-H6

CONTRA COSTA

STREET Block	City	ZIP	Pg-Grid
GINGHAM WY			
600	OAKL	94561	576-D4
GINNEY CT			
-	DNVL	94526	653-C4
GINOCCHIO CT			
200	WLCK	94598	612-J2
GINSBERG TER			
-	MRTZ	94553	571-J5
GIOTTO DR			
-	BREN	94513	596-D5
GIOVANNI ST			
1200	ANT	94509	575-F5
GIRVIN DR			
6100	OAK	94611	650-F1
6300	OAK	94611	630-F7
GLACIER CT			
1800	MRTZ	94553	571-J7
GLACIER DR			
-	MRTZ	94553	591-J1
-	MRTZ	94553	571-J7
-	MRTZ	94553	572-A7
3700	PIT	94565	574-D5
GLACIER WY			
-	OAKL	94561	596-H1
GLACIER POINT RD			
-	SRFL	94901	587-A4
GLADE CT			
900	ANT	94509	595-F2
1000	BREN	94513	596-C7
GLADE LN			
1200	CCCo	94507	632-E3
GLADSTONE DR			
200	BREN	94513	616-D3
2100	PIT	94565	574-G4
4200	CNCD	94521	593-A4
GLADWIN CT			
2200	WLCK	94596	632-G1
GLADWIN DR			
2200	WLCK	94596	632-G1
GLADYS AV			
6500	ELCR	94530	609-C2
GLADYS CT			
-	LFYT	94549	612-A5
GLADYS DR			
200	PLHL	94523	592-B5
GLASGOW			
-	HER	94547	569-F1
GLASGOW CIR			
100	DNVL	94526	653-D3
GLASGOW CT			
-	ANT	94531	596-A2
2700	RCH	94806	588-J1
GLASGOW DR			
-	DNVL	94526	653-E3
GLASGOW PL			
1000	DNVL	94526	653-D3
GLASGOW RD			
900	CNCD	94518	592-F6
GLAZIER CT			
4200	CNCD	94521	593-B3
GLAZIER DR			
1500	CNCD	94521	593-B3
GLEASON DR			
4900	DBLN	94568	694-C3
GLEASON WY			
1400	OAK	94606	650-A6
GLEN AV			
100	OAK	94611	630-A7
100	OAK	94611	650-A1
1100	BERK	94708	609-H7
1200	BERK	94709	609-H7
GLEN CT			
100	DNVL	94526	632-H7
100	WLCK	94595	612-C7
1600	PIN	94564	569-E5
3600	LFYT	94549	611-E5
GLEN RD			
600	DNVL	94526	652-H1
800	DNVL	94526	632-H7
1000	LFYT	94549	611-E5
GLEN ST			
700	MRTZ	94553	571-F5
GLEN ALPINE			
300	MRGA	94556	631-E7
GLEN ALPINE DR			
-	DNVL	94526	652-G3
GLEN ALPINE RD			
-	PDMT	94611	650-C1
100	OAK	94611	650-C1
GLEN ARMS DR			
300	DNVL	94526	653-A3
GLENARMS DR			
5900	OAK	94611	630-C5
GLENBRIDGE CT			
100	PLHL	94523	592-D4
GLENBROOK CT			
2000	CNCD	94520	572-E6
7600	PLE	94588	693-H7
GLENBROOK DR			
5700	OAK	94618	630-A5
GLEN CANYON CIR			
-	PIT	94565	574-F7
GLEN CANYON CT			
-	PIT	94565	574-G6
GLEN CANYON DR			
-	PIT	94565	574-G6
GLENCOE CIR			
-	CCCo	94582	674-B5
GLENCOURT			
1000	OAK	94611	630-F6
GLEN COVE PKWY			
200	VAL	94591	550-E1
GLEN COVE RD			
100	VAL	94591	550-E1
800	SolC	94591	550-E1
GLEN COVE MARINA RD			
100	VAL	94591	550-E2
GLENDA CT			
3200	PLE	94588	694-C7
GLENDALE AV			
1300	BERK	94708	609-J7
4000	CNCD	94521	593-A2
GLENDALE CIR			
2300	ANT	94509	595-A2
GLENDOME CIR			
700	OAK	94602	650-C3
GLENDORA AV			
1000	OAK	94602	650-C3
GLENDORA CIR			
300	DNVL	94526	652-J3
GLENDORA DR			
100	MRTZ	94553	571-D5
GLENEAGLE			
-	MRGA	94556	631-B6
GLEN EAGLE CT			
700	DNVL	94526	653-E6
GLENEDEN AV			
-	OAK	94611	630-A7
100	OAK	94611	650-A1
GLEN ELLEN CT			
-	OAKL	94561	576-D5
GLENELLEN CT			
1100	BREN	94513	616-E1
GLENFIELD AV			
1300	OAK	94602	650-C3
GLENGARRY DR			
1100	WLCK	94596	632-G1
GLENGARRY LN			
-	DBLN	94568	693-E5
1100	WLCK	94596	632-G1
GLENHANE CT			
-	ANT	94531	596-A4
GLEN HAVEN AV			
1800	WLCK	94595	612-C7
1800	WLCK	94595	632-C1
2100	CCCo	94595	632-C1
GLENHILL CT			
-	DNVL	94526	653-D4
GLEN HOLLOW RD			
-	DNVL	94506	653-F2
GLENHOLLOW WY			
5000	ANT	94531	595-E4
GLEN ISLE AV			
2500	PLE	94588	694-F7
GLEN ISLE CT			
4200	PLE	94588	694-F6
GLENLOCK ST			
2400	CCCo	94806	589-A2
GLENMARK WY			
-	SRMN	94582	674-A3
GLEN MAWR AV			
6700	ELCR	94530	609-C1
GLEN MEADOW CT			
200	DNVL	94526	653-F4
GLENMOUNT DR			
2200	PIT	94565	574-E4
GLENN AV			
1000	SPAB	94805	589-A5
1000	SPAB	94806	589-A5
GLEN OAK CT			
1600	CCCo	94549	611-J1
GLEN OAKS WY			
6600	OAK	94611	630-F6
GLENOAKS WY			
7300	DBLN	94568	693-H2
GLEN PARK RD			
3500	OAK	94602	650-C4
GLENRIDGE WY			
5200	ANT	94531	595-E4
GLENSIDE CIR			
700	LFYT	94549	631-H1
GLENSIDE CT			
2900	CNCD	94520	572-E6
GLENSIDE DR			
500	LFYT	94549	631-H1
2800	CNCD	94520	572-E6
GLEN VALLEY CIR			
-	DNVL	94526	653-B5
GLENVIEW AV			
500	OAK	94610	650-A3
GLENVIEW DR			
100	MRTZ	94553	591-H2
GLEN VIEW RD			
1800	WLCK	94595	612-C7
1800	WLCK	94595	632-C1
GLENWILLOW DR			
1000	BREN	94513	616-D1
GLENWILLOW LN			
1100	CNCD	94521	593-D7
GLENWOOD			
-	HER	94547	569-F4
300	MRTZ	94553	571-J5
GLENWOOD CT			
200	CCCo	94507	633-B6
5000	PLE	94588	693-J7
5400	RCH	94803	590-A3
GLENWOOD DR			
1200	CNCD	94518	592-H3
1900	ANT	94509	575-E6
GLENWOOD WY			
5300	RCH	94803	590-A3
6500	ELCR	94530	609-C2
GLENWOOD GLADE			
100	OAK	94611	630-C6
GLORIA CT			
-	MRGA	94556	631-E7
-	VAL	94590	550-C2
GLORIA DR			
300	PLHL	94523	592-B4
1200	PIT	94565	574-E7
GLORIA ST			
2300	ELCR	94530	589-B7
GLORIA TER			
3000	CCCo	94549	591-H7
3000	CCCo	94549	611-J1
GLORIA WY			
500	BEN	94510	551-A4
GLORIA TERRACE CT			
3100	CCCo	94549	591-J7
GLORIETTA BLVD			
100	ORIN	94563	630-J3
100	ORIN	94563	631-A2
300	LFYT	94549	611-B7
300	ORIN	94563	611-A7
300	LFYT	94563	611-A7
GLORIETTA CT			
-	ORIN	94563	630-J3
-	ORIN	94563	631-A3
GLORY LILY CT			
-	CCCo	94582	674-B1
GLOUCESTER			
-	HER	94547	569-J3
GLOUCESTER CT			
900	ANT	94509	575-C7
GLOUCESTER CV			
-	SRFL	94901	587-A2
GLOUCESTER LN			
2000	MRTZ	94553	572-A6
GLOUCESTER ST			
800	ANT	94509	575-C7
GLYNIS DR			
3000	RCH	94806	589-A1
GLYNNIS ROSE ST			
-	DBLN	94568	694-E4
GOBEL WY			
-	WLCK	94597	612-C2
GOBLE DR			
-	CCCo	94565	573-E2
GOECKEN RD			
4100	AlaC	94551	676-G7
GOERKE ST			
1300	BREN	94513	616-J2
GOETHALS CT			
-	CLAY	94517	593-G7
GOETTEL CT			
800	BEN	94510	551-A3
GOFF AV			
2100	PIT	94565	574-C3
GOLD CT			
3100	RCH	94803	589-E1
3200	LFYT	94549	631-H2
GOLD CREEK CIR			
-	CCCo	94513	617-F3
GOLD CREEK CT			
-	DNVL	94506	654-B6
GOLD CREST CT			
4000	PIT	94565	574-C6
GOLDCREST CT			
4500	ANT	94531	595-H3
GOLDCREST WY			
4600	ANT	94531	595-J3
GOLDEN AV			
4000	CNCD	94521	593-A3
GOLDEN BEAR DR			
4500	ANT	94531	595-H2
GOLDEN EAGLE CT			
-	OAKL	94561	596-H2
GOLDEN EAGLE PL			
6000	CLAY	94517	594-A5
GOLDEN EAGLE WY			
6000	CLAY	94517	594-A5
GOLDEN GATE			
1700	CCCo	94806	569-B5
GOLDEN GATE AV			
200	RCH	94801	608-C1
200	RCH	94801	588-C7
5000	OAK	94618	630-B5
5900	CCCo	94806	589-B4
GOLDEN GATE CT			
100	CCCo	94806	569-B5
GOLDEN GATE DR			
6600	DBLN	94568	693-H4
GOLDEN GATE PK			
-	PIN	94564	569-B4
GOLDEN GATE WY			
3400	LFYT	94549	611-F6
5000	OAK	94618	630-A4
GOLDEN HILL CT			
100	CCCo	94596	612-F6
GOLDENHILL DR			
4200	PIT	94565	574-E7
GOLDEN HILL PL			
100	CCCo	94596	612-F7
GOLDENHILL WY			
2100	BEN	94510	551-C4
GOLDEN HILLS CT			
100	DNVL	94526	653-B3
4500	ANT	94531	595-H3
GOLDEN LEAF WY			
1300	CNCD	94521	593-B5
GOLDENLEAF WY			
900	PIT	94565	574-E5
GOLDEN MEADOW DR			
3000	CCCo	94507	633-C4
GOLDEN MEADOW LN			
-	CCCo	94507	633-B4
GOLDEN MEADOW PL			
300	CCCo	94507	633-B4
GOLDEN OAK CT			
4200	CCCo	94506	654-C4
GOLDEN RAIN RD			
-	WLCK	94595	632-A1
GOLDEN RIDGE LN			
-	CCCo	94507	633-C4
GOLDEN RIDGE RD			
100	CCCo	94507	633-C4
GOLDENROD DR			
100	HER	94547	570-A4
GOLDENROD LN			
2000	SRMN	94582	653-H7
GOLDEN SLOPES CT			
300	BEN	94510	551-C4
GOLDEN SPRINGS LN			
1200	CNCD	94521	593-B4
GOLD LAKE CT			
400	CCCo	94506	654-C4
GOLD MEADOW CT			
-	BREN	94513	616-E2
GOLD MEADOW DR			
-	BREN	94513	616-E2
GOLDPINE CT			
-	ANT	94509	595-F3
GOLDPINE WY			
-	ANT	94509	595-F3
GOLD POPPY CT			
-	BREN	94513	596-E5
-	DNVL	94526	653-E3
GOLD POPPY ST			
-	BREN	94513	596-E5
GOLD RUN CT			
-	OAKL	94561	596-B1
GOLD RUN DR			
4200	OAKL	94561	596-B1
4400	OAKL	94561	576-B7
GOLD RUSH CT			
-	CLAY	94517	593-H7
GOLDSPUR WY			
200	BREN	94513	616-C2
GOLDSTONE CT			
-	DNVL	94506	653-H4
GOLETA CT			
1400	WLCK	94597	612-A2
5100	ANT	94531	595-F4
GOLETA PL			
4000	CCCo	94514	617-F7
GOLF CT			
-	WLCK	94598	613-A2
GOLF CLUB CIR			
800	CCCo	94523	592-A2
800	PLHL	94523	592-A2
GOLF CLUB CT			
-	PIT	94565	574-B4
GOLF CLUB RD			
-	CCCo	94511	577-E3
-	PLHL	94523	592-A2
400	CCCo	94523	592-A2
2200	PIT	94565	574-B4
GOLF CLUB WY			
600	CCCo	94523	592-A2
600	PLHL	94523	592-A2
GOLF COURSE DR			
1200	CCCo	94708	610-A6
1200	OAK	94708	610-A6
3000	BERK	94708	610-A6
GOLF COURSE RD			
4600	ANT	94531	595-D4
4600	ANT	94509	595-D4
GOLF LINKS ST			
200	PLHL	94523	591-H5
GOMER DR			
2900	RCH	94806	589-A1
GOMEZ RD			
-	CCCo	94553	590-B2
GONDO PTH			
-	OAK	94618	630-B5
GONZAGA AV			
2800	RCH	94806	589-A2
GONZALES CT			
5500	CNCD	94521	593-G5
GOODFELLOW AV			
-	DBLN	94568	694-B3
GOOD FELLOW DR			
200	CCCo	94553	571-C6
GOODFELLOW DR			
-	MRGA	94556	631-C3
-	ORIN	94563	631-C3
GOODING WY			
-	ALB	94706	609-D6
-	ALB	94710	609-D6
GOODRICK AV			
2500	RCH	94801	588-F2
GOODRICK AV			
2500	CCCo	94801	588-F2
3000	RCH	94801	568-F7
3000	RCH	94806	568-F7
GORDON AV			
5200	ELCR	94530	609-B1
5200	RCH	94804	609-B1
GORDON CT			
-	CCCo	94803	569-D6
500	BEN	94510	550-H1
GORDON RD			
100	CCCo	94598	612-E4
GORDON ST			
4300	OAK	94601	650-E7
GORDON WY			
100	CCCo	94553	591-E2
GOREE CT			
-	CCCo	94553	571-H4
GORHAM PL			
9700	SRMN	94583	673-F6
GOSHEN CT			
300	SRMN	94583	673-G6
GOSHEN PL			
100	SRMN	94583	673-G6
GOULARTE DR			
2700	PIN	94564	569-H6
GOULDIN RD			
1600	OAK	94611	630-E6
GOYAK DR			
3300	LFYT	94549	611-G3
GRACE LN			
2100	SPAB	94806	588-J4
GRACIE LN			
400	BREN	94513	596-F6
GRACIOSA CT			
-	SRMN	94582	674-A2
GRADO CT			
-	DNVL	94526	653-C1
GRAFTON ST			
-	DBLN	94568	694-F3
GRAGG LN			
1300	CNCD	94518	592-E6
GRAHAM CT			
-	OAKL	94561	596-H2
700	DNVL	94526	653-C3
GRAHAM PL			
-	OAK	94619	651-B7
GRAMMERCY LN			
4300	CNCD	94521	593-A5
GRAN VIA			
-	CCCo	94507	632-E4
GRANADA CT			
1100	ANT	94509	575-B6
2300	PIN	94564	569-F6
GRANADA DR			
100	SRMN	94583	673-G5
1700	CNCD	94519	593-A1
1800	CNCD	94519	592-J1
1800	CNCD	94519	572-J7
4000	PIT	94565	574-E6
GRANADA RD			
4000	CCCo	94803	589-C1
GRAND AV			
1600	OAK	94611	630-A7
1600	PDMT	94611	630-A7
1600	PDMT	94611	650-A2
3000	PDMT	94610	650-A2
3200	OAK	94610	650-A2
GRAND VW			
-	CCCo	94553	571-E3
GRAND WY			
-	CCCo	94513	617-F4
GRAND CANYON AV			
5800	CCCo	94806	589-B4
GRAND CANYON CIR			
-	OAKL	94561	596-H1
GRAND CANYON CT			
-	SRMN	94582	673-G3
GRAND CANYON LN			
-	SRMN	94582	673-G3
GRANDE AV			
-	BEN	94510	551-C4
GRANDE CTE			
2900	WLCK	94598	612-H2
GRANDE CAMINO			
2600	WLCK	94598	612-H2
GRANDE VISTA AV			
2500	OAK	94601	650-C6
GRANDE VISTA PL			
2300	OAK	94601	650-C5
GRAND OAK CT			
400	WLCK	94598	612-J2
GRANDVIEW AV			
-	CCCo	94525	550-C5
700	MRTZ	94553	571-E3
GRAND VIEW CT			
500	RCH	94801	588-C7
GRANDVIEW CT			
-	DNVL	94506	653-G5
1300	MRTZ	94553	571-E3
GRAND VIEW DR			
1100	OAK	94705	630-B4
1700	OAK	94618	630-C4
GRAND VIEW PL			
-	CCCo	94595	612-B7
-	CCCo	94595	632-B1
1000	OAK	94705	630-B3
GRANEY CT			
900	CNCD	94518	592-G6
GRANGE WY			
100	SRFL	94901	587-B5
GRANGNELLI AV			
300	ANT	94509	575-E4
GRANITE CIR			
300	ANT	94509	595-E2
GRANITE CT			
300	ANT	94509	595-E2
900	MRTZ	94553	571-G7
2200	CCCo	94507	632-H3
GRANITE DR			
2100	CCCo	94507	632-H4
GRANITE PL			
300	PIT	94565	574-B5
GRANT AV			
1900	RCH	94801	588-H6
2000	CCCo	94596	612-E7
2000	CCCo	94596	632-E1
2300	RCH	94804	588-H6
GRANT CT			
500	BEN	94510	550-H1
GRANT RD			
3100	OAKL	94561	596-H3
GRANT ST			
100	VAL	94590	550-C1
300	BREN	94513	596-B5
900	BEN	94510	551-D6
1300	BERK	94703	609-G7
1500	CNCD	94520	592-F1
2200	CNCD	94520	572-E6
GRANVILLE LN			
-	BREN	94561	596-E4
GRANZOTTO DR			
3600	CNCD	94519	572-J7
3600	CNCD	94519	592-J1
GRAPENUT CT			
2200	ANT	94509	575-H6
GRAPEVINE LN			
1100	OAKL	94561	596-E2
GRAPEVINE PL			
300	PLHL	94523	592-A4
GRAPHITE CT			
-	ANT	94509	595-E1
GRASSLAND CT			
-	DNVL	94526	653-E3
GRASSLAND TR			
-	CCCo	94583	652-C2
GRASSLAND WY			
2300	ANT	94531	595-G3
GRASSMERE CIR			
100	SRMN	94582	653-H7
GRASS MOUNTAIN CT			
-	ANT	94531	595-F4
GRASS VALLEY WY			
5100	ANT	94531	595-H5
GRASSWOOD CIR			
5300	CNCD	94521	593-D6
GRASSWOOD CT			
5200	CNCD	94521	593-D6
GRASSWOOD DR			
3400	RCH	94803	589-F1
GRATTON WY			
3000	CNCD	94520	572-F6
GRAVATT DR			
100	OAK	94705	630-B3
GRAVENSTEIN TER			
300	BREN	94513	616-D1
GRAY CT			
-	BEN	94510	551-B1
GRAY ST			
3500	OAK	94601	650-D6
GRAY FOX PL			
-	CLAY	94517	594-A5
GRAYHAWK CT			
-	DBLN	94568	694-G3
GRAYHAWK LN			
-	DBLN	94568	694-G2
GRAYMONT CIR			
700	CNCD	94518	592-G7
GRAYMONT CT			
2900	CNCD	94518	592-G7
GRAYS CT			
4400	CNCD	94518	593-A5
GRAYSON LN			
900	PLHL	94523	591-J5
GRAYSON RD			
700	PLHL	94523	592-A5
700	PLHL	94523	591-H5
900	CCCo	94549	591-H5
1000	PLHL	94549	591-H5
GRAYSON TER			
300	PLHL	94523	591-J5
GREAT FALLS DR			
-	BREN	94513	596-B6
GREAT MEADOW CT			
-	BREN	94513	596-C6
GREAT MEADOW LN			
-	BREN	94513	596-C6
GREAT NORTHERN PL			
100	DNVL	94526	653-C5
GREAT OAK CIR			
-	ORIN	94563	630-J3
GREEN LN			
-	MRTZ	94553	571-D4
GREEN ST			
-	MRTZ	94553	571-D3
W GREEN ST			
100	MRTZ	94553	571-D3
GREENACRE RD			
3600	OAK	94619	650-F6
GREEN ACRES CT			
-	LFYT	94549	631-J4
GREEN ACRES LN			
1600	CCCo	94513	597-B5
GREENBANK AV			
-	PDMT	94611	650-A1
GREENBANK DR			
100	LFYT	94549	611-G4
GREEN BAY CT			
-	CCCo	94595	612-B6
GREENBRAE CT			
-	CCCo	94803	569-E7
GREENBRIAR			
100	MRGA	94556	631-C7
GREENBRIAR CT			
400	DNVL	94526	653-D7
GREENBRIAR DR			
3700	PIT	94565	574-E5
GREENBRIER CT			
400	BEN	94510	551-A1
GREENBRIER ST			
2100	CNCD	94520	572-F5
GREENBROOK CT			
100	DNVL	94526	653-C6
GREENBROOK DR			
-	DNVL	94526	653-C4
GREENBUSH CT			
1700	CNCD	94521	593-C3
GREENBUSH DR			
4600	CNCD	94521	593-C3
GREEN CASTLE CIR			
-	CCCo	94513	617-G3
GREENCASTLE WY			
-	ANT	94531	596-A3
GREENDELL PL			
-	PLHL	94523	591-H2
GREENE PL			
-	LFYT	94549	612-A6
GREENFIELD CIR			
1400	PIN	94564	569-E5
GREENFIELD CT			
2000	CCCo	94514	(618-A7 See Page 597)
GREENFIELD DR			
-	MRGA	94556	631-D5
2200	PIT	94565	574-E4
GREENFIELD WY			
5700	CCCo	94514	617-J6
5700	CCCo	94514	(618-A6 See Page 597)
GREEN GABLES CT			
-	CNCD	94518	592-J4
-	DNVL	94506	654-B6
GREENGROVE CT			
-	ANT	94531	596-A5
GREENHALL WY			
3000	ANT	94509	575-C7
GREEN HILL CIR			
4800	ANT	94531	595-J3
GREEN HILL WY			
4800	ANT	94531	595-J3
GREENHILLS CT			
1700	CCCo	94549	611-H1
GREENHILLS DR			
3200	CCCo	94549	611-H1
GREENLAWN DR			
1400	DNVL	94526	653-C6
GREENLEAF CT			
4300	CNCD	94518	593-A5
GREENLEAF DR			
700	BREN	94513	616-F2
GREENMEADOW CIR			
100	PIT	94565	573-F4
GREEN MEADOW DR			
3300	CCCo	94506	654-B4
GREENMEADOW DR			
5100	CNCD	94521	593-D5
GREEN OAKS CT			
-	WLCK	94596	612-F7
GREENOCK LN			
-	PLHL	94523	591-J4
-	PLHL	94523	592-A4
GREEN POINT CT			
1000	CNCD	94521	593-D5
GREENRIDGE CT			
3100	ANT	94509	575-E7
6300	MRTZ	94553	591-H3
GREENRIDGE DR			
1500	PIT	94565	574-G6
2100	RCH	94803	589-E3
2200	CCCo	94803	589-E3
GREENRIDGE PL			
-	DNVL	94506	654-A6
GREENROCK CT			
-	ANT	94531	596-A2
GREENSBORO CT			
-	ANT	94509	595-D1
GREENSBORO WY			
-	ANT	94509	595-D2
GREENSTONE CT			
800	BREN	94513	616-F1
GREEN TREE CT			
-	LFYT	94549	611-G2
GREENTREE CT			
2400	ANT	94509	595-F3
GREENTREE DR			
1600	CNCD	94521	593-B2
GREEN VALLEY CT			
-	DNVL	94526	633-C6
GREENVALLEY CT			
-	LFYT	94549	611-H3
GREENVALLEY DR			
-	WLCK	94597	611-H3
-	LFYT	94549	611-H3
GREENVALLEY LN			
-	LFYT	94549	611-H3
GREEN VALLEY RD			
1500	DNVL	94526	633-C7
1800	CCCo	94507	633-C5
GREEN VIEW CT			
400	CCCo	94596	612-F6
GREENVIEW CT			
1200	MRTZ	94553	571-G7
GREEN VIEW DR			
400	CCCo	94596	612-E6
400	WLCK	94596	612-E6
GREENVIEW LN			
-	RCH	94803	569-C7
GREENWAY DR			
100	WLCK	94596	612-D4
300	MRTZ	94553	571-H5
1200	RCH	94803	569-C7
3800	CNCD	94521	592-J3
GREENWICH CT			
100	SRMN	94582	673-G4
2200	CCCo	94806	569-B4
GREENWICH DR			
100	PLHL	94523	592-A6
4000	SRMN	94582	673-G4
GREENWICH RD			
2200	CCCo	94806	569-B4
GREENWOOD AV			
1100	OAK	94602	650-C4
3900	OAK	94610	650-C4
GREENWOOD CIR			
100	WLCK	94597	592-D7
GREENWOOD COM			
-	BERK	94708	609-H7
GREENWOOD CT			
-	PLHL	94523	592-B1
-	ORIN	94563	631-B2
2400	CCCo	94806	588-J2
GREENWOOD DR			
100	PLHL	94523	592-B1
100	CCCo	94553	592-B1
2300	CCCo	94806	588-J2
2300	CCCo	94806	589-A2
GREENWOOD PL			
-	SRMN	94583	673-B3
2100	PIT	94565	574-A3
GREENWOOD RD			
2700	CCCo	94806	588-J2
GREENWOOD TER			
1400	BERK	94708	609-H7
GREENYARD CT			
1000	BREN	94513	596-D7
GREER AV			
1700	CNCD	94521	593-E4
GREG CT			
-	CCCo	94507	633-C5
GREGG PL			
400	SRMN	94583	673-F6
GREGG WY			
-	WLCK	94596	612-D5
GREGORY AV			
1100	MRTZ	94553	571-E3
GREGORY DR			
3400	CCCo	94565	573-F1
GREGORY LN			
-	PLHL	94523	592-B5
100	BREN	94513	596-G5
GREGORY PL			
-	OAK	94619	650-G5
GREGORY ST			
4100	OAK	94619	650-G5
GREGORY WY			
4500	RCH	94803	589-E2
GRENACHE CIR			
400	CLAY	94517	593-J7
GRENADIER WY			
300	BREN	94513	616-C3
GRENADINE WY			
100	HER	94547	570-C6
GRENOLA DR			
800	CNCD	94518	592-G6
GRESHAM CT			
3500	PLE	94588	694-E6
GREY EAGLE DR			
-	CCCo	94595	632-D4
-	WLCK	94595	632-D4
GREYFELL PL			
-	PLHL	94523	592-A3
GREY HAWK CT			
-	BREN	94513	616-B3
-	RCH	94806	569-A7
GREYHAWK CT			
-	CNCD	94518	592-J3
GREYLYN DR			
600	SRMN	94583	693-H1
GREY RIDGE DR			
-	WLCK	94595	632-C4
GREYSTONE CT			
-	SRMN	94583	673-D6
GREYSTONE CT			
800	ANT	94509	595-F2
GREYSTONE DR			
500	ANT	94509	595-E2
GREYSTONE LN			
1400	CLAY	94517	593-H7
GREYSTONE TER			
-	ORIN	94563	610-H6
GREY WHALE PL			
-	CCCo	94511	577-F4
GRIDLEY RD			
-	VAL	94592	549-G1
GRIFFANTI CT			
2400	MRTZ	94553	571-F4
GRIFFIN DR			
500	RCH	94806	568-G7
GRIFFITH LN			
-	BREN	94513	616-F1
GRIFFITHS CT			
-	ANT	94531	595-B4
W GRIMES RD			
14600	SJCo	95206	(658-J3 See Page 638)
GRIMMWOOD PL			
1200	CNCD	94521	593-A5
GRIMSBY CT			
2300	ANT	94509	595-A2
GRIMSBY DR			
2300	ANT	94509	595-A2
GRIMSBY LN			
500	CCCo	94506	654-A5
GRISBORNE AV			
5600	OAK	94611	630-D7
GRISBY CT			
-	BREN	94513	616-H3
GRISSOM CT			
100	HER	94547	570-B5
GRISSOM ST			
200	HER	94547	570-B5
GRISTMILL DR			
200	BREN	94513	616-E2
GRIZZLY CT			
1900	ANT	94509	575-G6
GRIZZLY PEAK BLVD			
200	CCCo	94563	610-B7
200	OAK	94704	610-B7
200	CCCo	94708	609-G3
200	CCCo	94708	610-B7
200	OAK	94708	610-B7
500	BERK	94708	609-H4
1300	BERK	94708	610-B7
2900	OAK	94720	610-B7
5000	CCCo	94563	630-C1
5000	OAK	94704	630-C1
5000	OAK	94705	630-D3
5300	OAK	94611	630-D3
GRIZZLY TERRACE DR			
700	OAK	94611	630-D3
700	CCCo	94563	630-D3
GRONDINE RD			
700	LFYT	94549	631-F1
GROOM DR			
2700	RCH	94806	588-J1
2700	RCH	94806	589-A1
GROOT WY			
2300	CNCD	94520	572-G5
GROSS LN			
1800	CNCD	94519	593-A1
GROSVENOR PL			
700	OAK	94610	650-B4
GROTHMAN LN			
4500	MRTZ	94553	571-E7
GROUSE DR			
-	ANT	94509	594-H1
GROVE AV			
200	CCCo	94801	588-F3
GROVE CIR			
100	PLHL	94523	592-A7
1200	BEN	94510	550-J3
GROVE CT			
2500	ANT	94509	595-F3
GROVE ST			
-	RCH	94804	588-H7
W GROVE ST			
100	CCCo	94801	588-F3
GROVE WY			
1200	CNCD	94518	592-H3
1400	CNCD	94519	592-H2
GROVE CREEK CT			
-	CCCo	94549	611-J2
GROVELAND LN			
-	DBLN	94568	694-F2
GROVENOR LN			
2100	CNCD	94520	572-F5
GROVER CT			
-	WLCK	94596	632-E1
GROVER LN			
100	WLCK	94596	632-E1
GROVES DR			
600	BREN	94513	596-E7
GROVEVIEW CT			
2400	RCH	94806	588-J1
GROVEVIEW DR			
2500	RCH	94806	568-J7
2500	RCH	94806	588-J1
GROVEWOOD LP			
200	BREN	94513	596-G6
GRUMMAN CT			
-	WLCK	94595	612-D7
GUADALUPE CT			
5500	CNCD	94521	593-F5
GUAYMAS CT			
600	SRMN	94583	673-C3
GUERRERO CT			
-	DBLN	94568	694-G4
GUESS CT			
-	CCCo	94507	632-J2
GUIDO ST			
3000	OAK	94602	650-F4
GUILFORD RD			
-	PDMT	94611	650-B1
GUISE WY			
-	BREN	94513	616-J3
GULFSTREAM ST			
3100	PLE	94588	694-F6
GULL PL			
300	PIT	94565	574-D1
GULL WY			
-	CCCo	94553	571-J4
GULL POINT CT			
300	BEN	94510	551-A5
GULL VIEW CT			
-	OAKL	94561	576-H7
GUM TREE RD			
2300	OAKL	94561	576-B7
GUMWOOD DR			
1700	CNCD	94519	593-B1
GUNN DR			
6600	OAK	94611	630-G7
GUNSHOT CT			
7900	DBLN	94568	693-G4
GURNEY LN			
1100	CCCo	94507	632-G6

STREET	Block	City	ZIP	Pg-Grid
GUTHRIE CT				
	3300	PLE	94588	694-F5
GUTHRIE LN				
	-	BREN	94513	616-H3
GUTHRIE ST				
	3400	PLE	94588	694-F5
GUYSON CT				
	6200	PLE	94588	694-A7
GUZMAN CT				
	-	CNCD	94521	593-F7
GUZMAN PKWY				
	-	PLE	94588	694-F6
GWEN CT				
	600	DNVL	94526	653-C1
GWIN AV				
	-	CNCD	94520	572-J3
GWIN CT				
	6400	OAK	94611	630-D5
GWIN RD				
	6400	OAK	94611	630-D5
GYGER CT				
	1700	CNCD	94521	593-D4
GYM CT				
	-	CLAY	94517	613-J1
GYPSY LN				
	-	OAK	94705	630-C2
H				
H ST				
	-	CNCD	94518	592-G4
	100	BEN	94510	551-B5
	200	MRTZ	94553	571-D5
	300	ANT	94509	575-C4
W H ST				
	100	BEN	94510	551-A4
	700	BEN	94510	550-J4
HAAG RD				
	4400	MRTZ	94553	571-E7
HABITAT WY				
	-	CNCD	94520	592-F2
HACIENDA CIR				
	-	ORIN	94563	610-F6
HACIENDA CT				
	3600	CNCD	94519	572-J7
HACIENDA DR				
	500	OAKL	94561	596-G2
	1000	WLCK	94598	612-D4
	2900	CNCD	94519	572-G7
	2900	CNCD	94519	592-G1
	4100	PLE	94588	694-C5
	4300	DBLN	94568	694-C4
HACIENDA LN				
	-	CCCo	94803	569-E7
HACIENDA WY				
	3300	ANT	94509	575-B7
	3300	ANT	94509	595-B1
HACIENDAS RD				
	-	ORIN	94563	610-G5
HACKAMORE CT				
	2200	WLCK	94596	632-F1
HACKAMORE LN				
	500	WLCK	94596	632-F2
HACKNEY CT				
	5500	RCH	94803	589-J3
HACKNEY LN				
	3100	CCCo	94598	613-A4
	5400	RCH	94803	589-J2
HADDEN RD				
	2100	CCCo	94596	612-E7
HADDINGTON CT				
	-	BREN	94513	616-A2
HADDON PL				
	700	OAK	94610	650-A3
HADDON RD				
	300	OAK	94606	650-A4
	600	OAK	94610	650-A4
HADSELL CT				
	3300	PLE	94588	694-G5
HAGAN LN				
	-	BREN	94513	616-E5
HAGAR AV				
	100	PDMT	94611	650-C1
HAGAR CT				
	4700	OAKL	94561	576-C7
HAGAR LN				
	4400	OAKL	94561	576-C7
	4400	OAKL	94561	596-C1
HAGEMAN AV				
	3500	OAK	94619	650-E6
HAGEN BLVD				
	6400	ELCR	94530	589-B7
	6500	ELCR	94530	609-B1
HAGEN OAKS CT				
	-	CCCo	94507	632-J5
HAGEN OAKS DR				
	-	CCCo	94507	632-J5
	2300	CCCo	94507	633-A5
HAIG CT				
	-	ANT	94531	595-J2
HAILSTONE WY				
	-	ANT	94509	595-F1
HAITI CT				
	500	SRMN	94582	673-E1
HAKIMI CT				
	4700	CNCD	94521	593-C4
HALCYON PL				
	-	CCCo	94511	577-E4
HALE CT				
	100	MRTZ	94553	591-H2
HALE DR				
	1200	CNCD	94518	592-H3
HALEAKALA ST				
	3200	CNCD	94519	572-H7
HALEY CT				
	1900	OAKL	94561	596-D1
HALF MOON CT				
	-	CCCo	94513	617-G4
	3400	CNCD	94518	592-J6
HALFMOON LN				
	3500	CNCD	94518	592-J6
HALF MOON WY				
	-	ANT	94531	595-G5
HALFORD LN				
	-	BREN	94513	596-D5
HALIFAX WY				
	3400	CNCD	94520	572-F6
HALITE WY				
	900	ANT	94509	595-F1
HALKIN LN				
	-	BERK	94708	609-G5
HALL AV				
	1000	RCH	94804	608-G2
HALL DR				
	-	ORIN	94563	631-B2
HALL LN				
	-	WLCK	94597	612-C2
	3400	LFYT	94549	611-G6
HALL ST				
	100	OAKL	94561	576-E6
HALLER CT				
	1600	CNCD	94520	592-E4
HALLGREN LN				
	-	CCCo	94549	611-J2
HALLMARK WY				
	-	BREN	94513	596-E6
HALLS VALLEY RD				
	-	ANT	94531	595-E3
HALSEY CT				
	100	HER	94547	570-B5
HALTEN CT				
	-	PLHL	94523	592-A3
HALYARD WY				
	2400	CCCo	94513	617-F7
HAMAR ST				
	-	PLHL	94523	592-B6
HAMBLETONIAN LN				
	3100	CCCo	94598	613-A4
HAMBURG CIR				
	500	CLAY	94517	593-J7
HAMBURG ST				
	1800	OAKL	94561	576-C6
HAMES CT				
	1700	CNCD	94521	593-E3
HAMES DR				
	4900	CNCD	94521	593-D3
HAMILTON AV				
	2500	CNCD	94519	572-G6
HAMILTON CT				
	-	OAKL	94561	596-H2
	-	CCCo	94507	633-C4
	-	PLHL	94523	592-A7
HAMILTON DR				
	700	PLHL	94523	592-A7
	700	PLHL	94523	591-J7
	2700	PIN	94564	570-A7
HAMLET CT				
	4000	CNCD	94521	593-A4
HAMLET DR				
	4000	CNCD	94521	593-A4
HAMLIN CT				
	2100	ANT	94509	595-A1
HAMLIN DR				
	2100	ANT	94509	595-A1
HAMLIN LP				
	-	WLCK	94598	612-H1
HAMLIN RD				
	3300	LFYT	94549	611-F7
	3300	LFYT	94549	631-G1
HAMLINE AV				
	3200	OAK	94602	650-C5
HAMMIT LN				
	-	CCCo	94553	571-J4
HAMMOND PL				
	-	MRGA	94556	631-D7
	-	MRGA	94556	651-D1
	3600	CNCD	94519	593-A1
HAMPEL ST				
	1100	OAK	94602	650-C3
HAMPSHIRE CT				
	1300	CNCD	94518	592-E6
HAMPSHIRE DR				
	-	CCCo	94513	617-F5
HAMPSHIRE WY				
	-	SRMN	94582	674-B3
HAMPTON CT				
	-	BREN	94513	596-E6
	-	OAKL	94561	596-D2
	400	SRMN	94583	673-E5
	1300	CCCo	94514	617-J7
HAMPTON DR				
	1000	CNCD	94518	592-D6
	1000	PLHL	94523	592-D6
HAMPTON LN				
	2500	ANT	94509	575-D1
HAMPTON PL				
	-	HER	94547	569-F3
HAMPTON RD				
	-	PDMT	94611	650-C2
	-	PDMT	94610	650-C2
	100	CCCo	94553	590-F5
	1000	LFYT	94549	611-G6
	3000	MRTZ	94553	571-G7
HAMPTON WY				
	-	OAKL	94561	596-D1
HANCOCK CT				
	2600	CNCD	94519	572-H6
HANCOCK WY				
	700	ELCR	94530	609-E3
HANDEL WY				
	-	BREN	94561	596-E4
HANFORD AV				
	-	CNCD	94518	592-G4
HANLEY CT				
	500	PIN	94564	569-C5
HANLEY DR				
	400	PIN	94564	569-C5
HANLON PL				
	-	PIT	94565	574-A2
HANLON WY				
	200	CCCo	94565	573-J2
	1700	PIT	94565	573-J2
	1700	PIT	94565	574-A2
HANLY RD				
	3900	OAK	94602	650-D3
HANNA GROVE TR				
	2900	WLCK	94598	612-J4
HANNAN DR				
	2900	PLHL	94523	592-A4
HANNIBAL DR				
	1800	CCCo	94549	591-H7
HANNON DR				
	-	CCCo	94514	637-C2
	1000	SPAB	94806	588-G2
HANOVER DR				
	-	SRMN	94582	674-A4
HANSEN DR				
	-	ANT	94531	595-C4
	3400	LFYT	94549	611-G7
	7000	DBLN	94568	693-F4
HANSEN LN				
	4100	CCCo	94506	654-C5
HANSEN PL				
	1300	PIN	94564	569-D4
HANSOM DR				
	7500	OAK	94605	651-C7
HANSON CT				
	-	MRGA	94556	631-E3
	100	CCCo	94553	572-B6
HANSON LN				
	-	WLCK	94596	612-E6
	100	BREN	94513	596-G5
HAP TER				
	-	DNVL	94506	653-G2
HAP ARNOLD ST				
	700	ANT	94509	595-F1
HAPPY HOLLOW CT				
	200	LFYT	94549	611-J4
HAPPY VALLEY CT				
	900	LFYT	94549	611-E6
HAPPY VALLEY LN				
	3600	LFYT	94549	611-E6
HAPPY VALLEY RD				
	3600	LFYT	94549	611-A4
	4100	ORIN	94563	611-A2
	4400	CCCo	94563	611-A2
	4400	CCCo	94549	611-A2
HAPPY VALLEY GLEN RD				
	1000	LFYT	94549	611-E5
HARBOR CT				
	100	PIT	94565	574-E4
	1000	CCCo	94572	569-J1
HARBOR DR				
	-	CCCo	94565	553-E7
	-	CCCo	94565	573-E1
	3300	CCCo	94511	577-D1
	5800	CCCo	94514	617-J6
	5800	CCCo	94514	(618-A6 See Page 597)
HARBOR ST				
	300	PIT	94565	574-E3
HARBOR WY				
	1000	CCCo	94572	569-J1
HARBORD CT				
	-	OAK	94618	630-C6
HARBORD DR				
	4300	OAK	94618	630-B6
	5900	OAK	94611	630-C7
	6000	OAK	94611	650-C1
	6100	PDMT	94611	650-C1
HARBOR VIEW AV				
	3500	OAK	94619	650-F5
	5900	CCCo	94806	589-B4
	5900	RCH	94806	589-B4
HARBOR VIEW DR				
	1000	MRTZ	94553	571-E4
HARBORVIEW DR				
	-	RCH	94804	608-H3
S HARBOR VIEW DR				
	800	MRTZ	94553	571-E4
HARBOR VISTA CT				
	100	BEN	94510	551-C4
HARBOUR DR				
	2700	ANT	94509	575-F7
HARBOUR WY				
	-	RCH	94801	588-G7
HARBOUR WY S				
	100	RCH	94804	588-G7
	300	RCH	94804	608-G1
HARCOURT WY				
	-	CCCo	94582	674-B4
	-	SRMN	94582	674-A4
HARD WY				
	-	CCCo	94595	632-C2
HARDCASTLE CT				
	-	CCCo	94583	673-A5
HARDESTER CT				
	-	DNVL	94526	653-C5
HARDIE DR				
	-	MRGA	94556	631-C6
HARDING CIR				
	-	BERK	94708	609-J7
HARDING CT				
	1800	ANT	94509	575-A7
	1800	CNCD	94521	593-D2
HARDING PL				
	300	SRMN	94583	673-H6
HARDING WY				
	1700	ANT	94509	575-A7
	4000	OAK	94602	650-D3
HARDWICK AV				
	-	PDMT	94611	650-B1
HARDWICK PL				
	200	SRMN	94583	673-F5
HARDWOOD CT				
	-	PLHL	94523	592-B1
HARDY CIR				
	100	PLHL	94523	592-B6
HARGATE CT				
	-	PLHL	94523	592-A7
HARGROVE CT				
	100	ANT	94509	575-G5
HARGROVE ST				
	1200	ANT	94509	575-G5
HARLAN DR				
	1400	DNVL	94526	653-C6
HARLAN RD				
	11600	DBLN	94568	693-F3
HARLAND CT				
	2700	WLCK	94598	612-H4
HARLOW DR				
	400	ANT	94509	575-E5
HARLOW LN				
	-	CCCo	94582	674-B4
HARMON RD				
	4200	CCCo	94803	589-D3
HARMONY CT				
	-	BREN	94513	596-D5
	-	DNVL	94526	652-H1
	-	PIT	94565	573-J2
HARMONY LN				
	-	WLCK	94597	612-A2
HARMONY ST				
	-	BREN	94513	596-D5
HARMONY WY				
	1500	PIT	94565	573-J2
	3700	CNCD	94519	592-J1
HARNESS CIR				
	1000	SRMN	94583	673-D4
HARNESS CT				
	900	SRMN	94583	673-D4
HARNESS DR				
	1000	SRMN	94583	673-D4
HARO LP				
	-	DBLN	94568	694-E3
HAROLD CT				
	-	WLCK	94597	592-D7
HAROLD DR				
	-	MRGA	94556	631-C3
HAROLD ST				
	1700	CCCo	94801	588-F3
	2400	OAK	94602	650-D5
HARPER CT				
	4500	PLE	94588	694-A6
HARPER LN				
	300	DNVL	94526	652-H1
HARPER ST				
	2000	ELCR	94530	589-B7
	2000	ELCR	94530	609-C1
	3400	OAK	94601	650-D7
HARRAN CIR				
	-	ORIN	94563	610-J6
HARRIET DR				
	-	PLHL	94523	592-C4
HARRINGTON AV				
	1900	OAK	94601	650-D7
HARRINGTON CT				
	-	CCCo	94507	632-H2
HARRINGTON RD				
	-	MRGA	94556	651-G2
HARRIS AV				
	200	CCCo	94572	549-H7
	2400	ELCR	94530	589-B7
HARRIS CIR				
	100	CCCo	94565	573-J2
HARRIS CT				
	1400	ANT	94509	575-F7
E HARRIS CT				
	1100	MRTZ	94553	571-H7
HARRIS DR				
	2800	ANT	94509	575-F7
HARRISON CT				
	-	CCCo	94803	589-F2
	-	RCH	94803	589-F2
HARRISON DR				
	500	RCH	94806	568-G7
HARRISON LN				
	-	BREN	94513	596-G7
HARRISON PL				
	3000	ANT	94509	575-A7
HARRISON ST				
	600	BERK	94710	609-D7
	1100	BERK	94706	609-D7
	1600	CNCD	94520	592-F2
HARRIS RANCH RD				
	-	CCCo	94513	615-G3
HARROGATE CT				
	600	WLCK	94598	612-J3
HARROGATE WY				
	900	ANT	94509	575-C7
HART CT				
	900	CCCo	94507	652-G1
HARTFORD RD				
	-	ORIN	94563	611-A5
	100	DNVL	94526	632-H7
	100	DNVL	94526	652-G1
HARTLAND CT				
	-	DBLN	94568	694-G3
HARTLAND LN				
	-	DBLN	94568	694-F3
W HARTLEY CT				
	-	ANT	94531	595-C4
HARTLEY DR				
	600	DNVL	94526	653-A3
HARTLEY GATE CT				
	2700	PLE	94566	694-D7
HARTNELL CT				
	1400	CNCD	94521	593-C5
HARTNETT AV				
	4700	RCH	94804	609-A2
HARTWELL CT				
	3300	PLE	94588	694-G5
HARTWELL ST				
	-	CCCo	94525	550-E5
HARTWICK DR				
	-	DBLN	94568	694-E3
HARTWOOD CT				
	-	LFYT	94549	631-J3
HARTZ AV				
	100	DNVL	94526	652-J1
	100	DNVL	94526	653-A2
HARTZ CT				
	-	DNVL	94526	653-A2
HARTZ WY				
	400	DNVL	94526	653-A2
HARVARD CIR				
	-	BERK	94708	609-J7
	700	WLCK	94597	612-B3
HARVARD CT				
	-	PLHL	94523	592-C3
HARVARD DR				
	700	PLHL	94523	592-C2
HARVARD RD				
	1000	OAK	94610	650-B2
	1000	PDMT	94610	650-B2
HARVARD ST				
	2200	ELCR	94530	589-C7
HARVARD WY				
	-	CCCo	94597	612-B4
HARVEST CIR				
	3800	OAKL	94561	596-G1
HARVEST CT				
	100	OAKL	94561	596-G2
HARVEST DR				
	-	OAKL	94561	596-G1
HARVEST LN				
	2700	ANT	94531	595-H2
HARVEST MOON LN				
	-	CCCo	94582	674-A2
HARVEST PARK DR				
	400	BREN	94513	616-H3
HARVEY CT				
	3200	PLE	94588	694-C7
HARVEY WY				
	500	CCCo	94565	573-F1
HARWICH PL				
	100	VAL	94591	550-E1
HARWICH WK				
	-	PLHL	94523	591-B1
HARWOOD AV				
	6100	OAK	94618	630-A4
HASKEL CT				
	-	RCH	94806	568-H5
HASKIN CT				
	-	RCH	94806	568-H5
HASKINS RANCH CIR				
	-	DNVL	94506	654-A6
HASLEMERE CT				
	100	CCCo	94549	591-H6
HASLEMERE DR				
	100	CCCo	94549	591-H7
HASTINGS CT				
	-	MRGA	94556	651-F1
	1100	ANT	94509	595-F1
	3600	LFYT	94549	611-E5
HASTINGS DR				
	-	CCCo	94513	617-F5
	100	BEN	94510	551-A1
	200	BEN	94510	550-J2
	900	CNCD	94518	592-E7
HASTINGS LN				
	-	SRMN	94582	674-B3
HASTINGS WY				
	-	CCCo	94582	674-B5
	7400	DBLN	94568	693-H3
HAT CT				
	-	CCCo	94803	589-G4
HATCHWOOD CT				
	1200	MRTZ	94553	571-H6
HAT CREEK CT				
	200	SRMN	94582	674-A7
HAUSSNER DR				
	5400	CNCD	94521	593-F5
HAUTH LN				
	500	WLCK	94597	612-B2
HAVASU CT				
	-	CCCo	94513	617-F3
HAVEN CT				
	-	MRGA	94556	631-E4
	1100	CNCD	94520	592-E4
HAVEN LN				
	-	CCCo	94597	612-D2
HAVEN PL				
	-	SRMN	94583	673-F7
HAVEN ST				
	300	MRTZ	94553	571-E3
HAVEN HILL CT				
	100	DNVL	94526	653-C3
HAVENHILL DR				
	2000	BEN	94510	551-B3
HAVENROCK CT				
	-	ANT	94531	596-A4
HAVENS PL				
	1000	ELCR	94530	609-E2
HAVENWOOD AV				
	200	BREN	94513	596-G6
HAVENWOOD CIR				
	-	PIT	94565	573-G4
HAVERHILL DR				
	2600	OAK	94611	650-F1
HAVEY CANYON TR				
	-	RCH	94805	589-F7
HAVILAND CT				
	1500	CLAY	94517	593-F5
	2500	SPAB	94806	588-G2
HAVILAND PL				
	1500	CLAY	94517	593-F5
HAVITURE WY				
	100	HER	94547	570-B6
HAWK CT				
	-	CCCo	94507	633-B5
	100	HER	94547	569-H4
	800	ANT	94509	595-F2
HAWK WY				
	-	DBLN	94568	694-D4
HAWK CANYON PL				
	-	LFYT	94549	631-J3
HAWKINS DR				
	12900	SRMN	94583	673-E5
	12900	CCCo	94583	673-E5
HAWKINS ST				
	-	ANT	94531	595-J2
HAWKMOUNT CT				
	-	SRMN	94582	673-H2
HAWKMOUNT WY				
	-	SRMN	94582	673-H2
HAWK RIDGE DR				
	-	RCH	94806	568-J6
HAWKRIDGE TER				
	-	ORIN	94563	610-H6
HAWKS HILL CT				
	-	OAK	94618	630-C4
	1800	LFYT	94549	591-G7
HAWKSTONE CT				
	-	BREN	94513	616-A1
HAWTHORN CT				
	-	BREN	94561	596-F4
	-	SRMN	94582	673-J6
HAWTHORN DR				
	-	BREN	94561	596-F4
HAWTHORN PL				
	-	BREN	94561	596-F4
HAWTHORNE AV				
	700	RCH	94801	588-F6
	900	ANT	94509	575-C6
HAWTHORNE CT				
	-	CCCo	94513	617-F3
	-	CCCo	94596	612-G7
	-	PLHL	94523	592-B7
HAWTHORNE DR				
	-	CCCo	94511	577-F1
	-	PLHL	94523	592-B7
	700	CCCo	94572	569-J1
	700	CCCo	94596	612-F7
	900	LFYT	94549	611-G6
W HAWTHORNE DR				
	600	CCCo	94596	612-F7
HAWTHORNE LN				
	-	PIT	94565	574-E3
	400	BEN	94510	551-A1
HAWTHORNE ST				
	400	PIT	94565	574-E2
HAWTHORNE TER				
	1400	BERK	94708	609-H7
HAWXHURST CT				
	4800	ANT	94531	595-D3
HAYES CT				
	1800	CNCD	94521	593-D2
HAYES ST				
	-	BEN	94510	551-D6
	500	RCH	94804	588-H6
	1300	RCH	94806	588-H4
	1600	SPAB	94806	588-H4
HAYES WY				
	2800	ANT	94509	575-A7
HAYSTACK CT				
	-	BREN	94513	616-E2
HAYWARD CT				
	-	ANT	94531	595-C4
W HAYWARD CT				
	-	MRTZ	94553	571-E7
HAZEL AV				
	5600	RCH	94805	589-B6
	5700	CCCo	94805	589-B6
	6400	ELCR	94530	589-B6
HAZEL CT				
	200	BREN	94513	616-F3
HAZEL DR				
	100	PLHL	94523	592-C5
HAZEL LN				
	-	PIN	94564	569-D3
	-	PDMT	94611	650-B1
HAZEL RD				
	-	BERK	94705	630-A4
HAZEL ST				
	-	CCCo	94514	637-D2
	1100	PIN	94564	569-D3
HAZELBROOK CT				
	-	ANT	94531	595-J5
HAZELNUT CT				
	-	SRMN	94583	673-G7
	2400	ANT	94509	575-H6
HAZELNUT DR				
	400	OAKL	94561	576-F7
	400	OAKL	94561	596-F1
HAZELNUT LN				
	300	OAKL	94561	576-G7
HAZELTINE CIR				
	100	PLHL	94523	592-B6
HAZELWOOD CT				
	1200	BREN	94513	596-D7
HAZELWOOD DR				
	700	CCCo	94596	612-G7
HAZELWOOD LN				
	4300	CNCD	94521	593-C2
HAZELWOOD PL				
	100	MRGA	94556	631-D7
HAZELWOOD ST				
	-	DBLN	94568	694-D4
HEACOCK WY				
	-	ANT	94531	595-C4
HEAD WY				
	4200	PLE	94588	694-F7
HEADLAND CT				
	-	DNVL	94506	653-H6
HEADLANDS CT				
	100	VAL	94591	550-F2
HEALD CT				
	600	CCCo	94525	550-E4
HEALD ST				
	500	CCCo	94525	550-E4
HEALY LN				
	-	CCCo	94553	571-H4
HEARST AV				
	2400	OAK	94602	650-D4
HEARTHSTONE CIR				
	-	OAKL	94561	596-G2
HEARTLAND CIR				
	2000	BREN	94513	596-G5
HEARTLAND CT				
	1600	CNCD	94519	592-J2
	2000	BREN	94513	596-G5
HEARTLAND ST				
	-	DNVL	94506	653-G5
HEARTWOOD CT				
	4300	CNCD	94521	593-B3
HEARTWOOD DR				
	1500	CNCD	94521	593-C3
	6600	OAK	94611	630-E7
HEATH CT				
	6800	PLE	94588	694-A7
HEATH DR				
	1900	CCCo	94803	569-E7
HEATHER AV				
	100	HER	94547	569-J4
HEATHER CT				
	-	BEN	94510	551-A1
	1100	CNCD	94520	592-E4
	3400	ANT	94509	595-C1
HEATHER DR				
	-	CCCo	94806	569-A5
	1500	CNCD	94521	593-D4
	1700	WLCK	94598	612-E3
HEATHER LN				
	-	WLCK	94597	612-D3
	-	ORIN	94563	631-A2
	-	ORIN	94563	630-J2
HEATHER PL				
	200	DNVL	94526	653-C5
	500	BREN	94513	616-F2
HEATHER RD				
	3400	ANT	94509	595-C1
HEATHER GARDEN LN				
	-	DNVL	94506	653-J6
HEATHER GLEN LN				
	5000	CNCD	94521	593-D4
HEATHERGREEN CT				
	800	CNCD	94521	613-D1
HEATHER GROVE CT				
	500	WLCK	94598	612-H1
HEATHER HTS CT				
	2800	ANT	94531	575-G7
HEATHERLAND DR				
	-	SRMN	94582	673-H1
HEATHERLEAF LN				
	2400	MRTZ	94553	572-A6
HEATHER RIDGE CT				
	400	SRMN	94582	673-J6
HEATHER RIDGE WY				
	6200	OAK	94611	630-E5
HEATHERWOOD CT				
	-	PIT	94565	574-G6
HEATHERWOOD DR				
	1600	PIT	94565	574-G6
HEATHROW DR				
	-	OAKL	94561	596-D2
HEATON CIR				
	1900	CNCD	94520	572-E6
HEATON CT				
	-	ANT	94565	574-H7
	1900	CNCD	94520	572-E7
HEAVENLY DR				
	1100	MRTZ	94553	571-H5
HEAVENLY PL				
	300	MRTZ	94553	571-H5
HEAVENLY RIDGE LN				
	5100	RCH	94803	589-F2
HEDARO CT				
	3000	CCCo	94549	611-J1
HEDGE AV				
	6800	BREN	94513	596-G5
HEDGE CT				
	2900	OAK	94602	650-F3
HEDGE LN				
	4900	OAK	94602	650-F3
HEDGECREST CIR				
	-	SRMN	94582	673-H2
HEIDE CT				
	2500	CCCo	94803	589-H4
HEIDORN RANCH RD				
	3000	ANT	94531	596-A6
	3000	BREN	94513	596-A6
HEIGHTS AV				
	4200	PIT	94565	574-D6
HELANE CT				
	1700	BEN	94510	551-B3
HELEN AV				
	-	CNCD	94518	592-G4
	400	LFYT	94549	631-G3
HELEN DR				
	3500	PLE	94588	694-E7
HELEN LN				
	3200	LFYT	94549	631-G2
HELEN RD				
	1800	PLHL	94523	592-B5
HELENA AV				
	2300	CCCo	94553	571-F3
HELENA CT				
	300	OAKL	94561	576-C7
	300	OAKL	94561	596-C1
	2300	PIN	94564	569-F6
HELENA DR				
	1800	CNCD	94521	593-F4
HELENA WY				
	-	BREN	94513	596-C6
HELENA CREEK CT				
	600	SRMN	94582	674-A7
HELENE CT				
	3200	CNCD	94518	592-H2
HELICON CT				
	-	SRMN	94582	673-G2
HELIX CT				
	-	SRMN	94583	693-J1
	1700	CNCD	94518	592-F7
HELIX DR				
	900	CNCD	94518	592-F6
HELLINGS AV				
	1300	RCH	94801	588-G5
HELM CT				
	200	PIT	94565	574-A2
HELMSMAN CT				
	100	VAL	94591	550-G2
HELMUTH LN				
	-	ANT	94509	575-E5
HELPERT CT				
	4600	PLE	94588	694-A6
HEMINGWAY COMS				
	-	MRTZ	94553	571-J5
HEMINGWAY DR				
	3200	ANT	94509	595-C1
HEMLEB CT				
	300	PIN	94564	569-D4
HEMLOCK AV				
	2200	CNCD	94520	572-F7
HEMLOCK CT				
	100	HER	94547	570-A4
	1600	OAKL	94561	596-D1
HEMLOCK DR				
	1800	OAKL	94561	596-C1
HEMLOCK LN				
	-	OAK	94611	630-F6
HEMLOCK ST				
	3100	ANT	94509	574-J7
	6500	DBLN	94568	693-J4
	7000	OAK	94611	630-F6
HEMME AV				
	100	CCCo	94507	632-F7
HENDERSON CT				
	-	ANT	94531	595-C4
HENDERSON DR				
	3100	RCH	94806	589-A1
HENDERSON RD				
	-	CNCD	94520	572-F4
	18500	SJCo	95391	(658-G7 See Page 638)
HENLEY CT				
	-	CCCo	94583	673-A5
E HENNING CT				
	4200	CNCD	94521	593-B3
E HENNING DR				
	4200	CNCD	94521	593-B3
HENRIETTA ST				
	400	MRTZ	94553	571-E3
	3400	OAK	94601	650-D6
HENRI HILL LN				
	1600	LFYT	94549	611-J5
	1600	LFYT	94549	612-A5
HENRY AV				
	-	HER	94547	569-F4
	1900	PIN	94564	569-F4
HENRY CT				
	-	OAKL	94561	596-H2
	-	WLCK	94597	612-B2
HENRY ST				
	1200	BERK	94709	609-G7
HENRY CLAY CT				
	100	CCCo	94553	572-B7
	100	CCCo	94553	592-B1
HENRY HART DR				
	-	BREN	94513	596-C5
HENRY RANCH DR				
	-	SRMN	94583	673-E6
HENSLEY ST				
	900	RCH	94801	588-F5
HENSON CREEK CT				
	100	MRTZ	94553	591-J4
HERA				
	100	HER	94547	569-F3
HERB WHITE WY				
	600	PIT	94565	574-D1
HERCULES AV				
	1200	HER	94547	569-F3
HERDLYN RD				
	7500	CCCo	94514	(658-D2 See Page 638)
HEREFORD CT				
	5100	ANT	94531	595-H5
HEREFORD WY				
	5100	ANT	94531	595-J5
HERITAGE CT				
	-	WLCK	94597	612-B3
	100	OAKL	94561	596-G2
HERITAGE DR				
	-	CNCD	94521	593-E4
	3700	ANT	94509	595-E1
HERITAGE PL				
	800	SRMN	94583	673-G6
HERITAGE TR				
	6000	CLAY	94517	593-H6
HERITAGE WY				
	100	BREN	94513	616-J3
	3800	OAKL	94561	596-G2
HERITAGE HILLS DR				
	2200	PLHL	94523	591-J6
HERITAGE MEADOWS RD				
	500	PLHL	94523	591-J6
HERITAGE OAK CT				
	-	CCCo	94507	632-H3
HERITAGE OAKS DR				
	-	PLHL	94523	591-H3
	-	PLHL	94553	591-H3
	2300	CCCo	94507	632-H3
HERITAGE OAKS PL				
	100	CCCo	94507	632-H3
HERITAGE PARK DR				
	100	DNVL	94506	653-J6
HERMAN DR				
	3500	LFYT	94549	611-F7
HERMES				
	700	HER	94547	569-F3
HERMINE AV				
	1300	CCCo	94596	612-E7
	1700	CCCo	94596	632-E1
HERMINE CT				
	1300	CCCo	94596	612-E7
HERMOSA AV				
	-	PIT	94565	574-F3
	-	OAK	94618	630-B6
HERMOSA CT				
	-	DNVL	94526	653-B2
	300	LFYT	94549	631-H4
	2300	PIN	94564	569-F6
HERMOSA ST				
	2400	PIN	94564	569-F6
HERMOSA WY				
	3300	LFYT	94549	611-G1
HERNDON AV				
	1400	CNCD	94520	592-E1
HERO CT				
	-	PLHL	94523	591-J6
HERON CT				
	-	MrnC	94964	587-B5
	-	SRFL	94901	587-A2
HERON DR				
	-	CCCo	94513	617-F3
	100	HER	94547	569-H5
	100	PIT	94565	574-D1
	200	PIT	94565	554-D7
	5800	OAK	94618	630-C7
HERON LN				
	-	CCCo	94553	572-A5
HERON WY				
	-	ANT	94509	594-H1
HERRIER ST				
	3300	OAK	94602	650-F4
HERRIMAN CT				
	-	CLAY	94517	613-G1
HERRIMAN DR				
	5800	CLAY	94517	593-G7
	5800	CLAY	94517	613-G1
HERRIN CT				
	6700	PLE	94588	694-A6
HERRIN WY				
	4600	PLE	94588	694-A6
HERRIOTT AV				
	3100	OAK	94619	650-F7
HERRON AV				
	2000	CCCo	94596	612-E7
	2000	CCCo	94596	632-E1
HERSHEY CT				
	4700	RCH	94804	609-A1
HESS RD				
	2700	CCCo	94517	593-J4

STREET
Block City ZIP Pg-Grid

HESTER LN
3600 LFYT 94549 611-E5
HETFIELD PL
- MRGA 94556 631-E7
- MRGA 94556 651-E1
HIBERNIA DR
- DBLN 94568 694-D4
HICKORY CT
- CCCo 94506 654-A3
100 BREN 94513 616-F3
HICKORY DR
- BREN 94513 616-F2
2200 CNCD 94520 572-F7
HICKORY LN
6700 DBLN 94568 693-J4
HICKORY ST
2600 OAK 94602 650-C5
HICKS MOUNTAIN CT
- ANT 94531 595-E5
HIDALGO CT
- SPAB 94806 568-J7
1100 LFYT 94549 611-F5
HIDDEN CV
- HER 94547 569-H1
HIDDEN LN
- ORIN 94563 610-G3
HIDDEN CANYON CT
- SRMN 94582 653-F7
HIDDENCREEK CT
200 MRTZ 94553 571-J6
HIDDEN CREST CT
- DNVL 94506 653-H5
HIDDENCREST CT
5200 CNCD 94521 593-C7
HIDDEN GLEN DR
- ANT 94531 596-A2
5000 ANT 94531 595-J2
HIDDEN GROVE LN
- CNCD 94519 572-J7
- CNCD 94519 573-A7
HIDDEN HILLS CT
3300 ANT 94531 595-G1
HIDDEN HILLS PL
- DNVL 94506 654-B6
HIDDEN LAKES CT
2200 MRTZ 94553 592-A1
HIDDEN LAKES DR
600 MRTZ 94553 572-A7
600 MRTZ 94553 592-A1
HIDDEN OAK CT
- CCCo 94506 653-H1
1000 CNCD 94521 593-C5
HIDDEN OAK DR
2100 CCCo 94506 653-G1
HIDDEN OAKS DR
- LFYT 94549 611-J7
HIDDEN OAKS LN
- MRTZ 94553 571-G7
- MRTZ 94553 591-G1
HIDDEN POND CT
800 CCCo 94549 591-G4
HIDDEN POND LN
2200 CCCo 94549 591-G4
HIDDEN POND RD
2100 CCCo 94549 591-G4
HIDDEN RANCH RD
- CCCo 94513 596-J4
- CCCo 94513 597-A4
HIDDEN SPRINGS CT
3700 RCH 94803 589-G2
HIDDEN VALLEY PL
- CCCo 94507 632-G5
HIDDEN VALLEY RD
- ORIN 94563 610-J6
- LFYT 94549 611-A6
- ORIN 94563 611-A6
HIDDENWOOD CT
- PIT 94565 573-G4
5300 CNCD 94521 613-E1
HIDEAWAY CT
200 DNVL 94526 633-A7
HIEBER DR
200 CCCo 94553 572-C6
HIGH CT
1100 BERK 94708 609-H6
HIGH ST
100 CCCo 94553 592-A1
100 MRTZ 94553 592-A1
300 PLHL 94523 592-A1
400 RCH 94801 588-C7
400 RCH 94801 608-C1
2100 OAK 94601 650-E7
2600 OAK 94619 650-F6
5900 CLAY 94517 593-H7
HIGHBLUFF TER
- PLE 94588 693-G7
HIGHBRIDGE CT
- DNVL 94526 653-A1
HIGHBRIDGE LN
700 DNVL 94526 653-A2
HIGHCLIFF CT
2200 MRTZ 94553 572-A7
HIGHCREST CT
- PLE 94588 693-G7
HIGH EAGLE CT
500 WLCK 94595 632-D4
HIGH EAGLE RD
- CCCo 94507 632-H5
HIGHGATE CT
- CCCo 94707 609-F3
HIGHGATE DR
2200 RCH 94806 588-J1
HIGHGATE RD
- CCCo 94707 609-F3
- ELCR 94530 609-F3
HIGHGATE WY
3900 PIT 94565 574-E6
HIGHGROVE WY
- SRMN 94582 674-A4
HIGH KNOLL DR
4200 OAK 94619 650-J6
HIGHLAND AV
- PDMT 94611 630-B7
100 PDMT 94611 650-C2
1300 MRTZ 94553 571-E2
1800 LFYT 94549 591-H7
2400 OAK 94606 650-B5
5400 RCH 94804 609-B3
6200 CCCo 94805 589-C5
7200 ELCR 94530 589-C7
HIGHLAND BLVD
- CCCo 94530 609-F2
- CCCo 94707 609-F2
- CCCo 94708 609-F3
HIGHLAND CT
- DNVL 94526 652-J3
- ORIN 94563 630-J1
300 CCCo 94520 572-G1
3700 LFYT 94549 611-D7
HIGHLAND DR
300 DNVL 94526 652-J3
2000 CNCD 94520 572-E6
HIGHLAND RD
3600 LFYT 94549 611-D7
5600 CCCo 94588 674-G1
5700 CCCo 94551 675-D2
5700 CCCo 94588 675-A1
7300 AlaC 94551 675-D2
HIGHLAND WY
300 PDMT 94611 650-B1
1500 BREN 94513 596-C7
HIGHLAND MEADOWS CT
- DBLN 94568 694-G2
HIGHLAND OAKS DR
7400 PLE 94588 693-J7
HIGHLANDS CT
200 CCCo 94806 569-B4
HIGHLANDS PL
200 CCCo 94806 569-B4
HIGHLANDS RD
2100 CCCo 94806 569-B4
HIGHLANDS WY
4800 ANT 94531 595-H3
HIGHPOINTE CT
3200 RCH 94806 588-F1
HIGHRIDGE CT
1900 WLCK 94597 611-H3
HIGH SCHOOL AV
2400 CNCD 94520 572-F7
2400 CNCD 94520 592-F1
HIGHTREE CT
- DNVL 94526 653-A1
HIGHWAY Rt#-160
- CCCo 94509 576-A3
- OAKL 94509 576-A3
18100 SaCo 94571 576-A1
HIGHWAY 4 BYPS Rt#-4
- BREN 94513 596-B5
- BREN 94513 616-C1
HIGHWAY AV
- CCCo 94565 573-H2
HIGHWOOD PL
- OAKL 94561 596-F1
HIGUERA AV
2900 PIN 94564 569-G6
HILARY WY
- ORIN 94563 631-A1
HILDA CT
- BREN 94513 596-C5
HILDA WY
- BREN 94513 596-C5
HILFERD WY
- DNVL 94526 652-G3
HILGARD AV
2300 BERK 94709 609-H7
HILL AV
- OAKL 94561 596-G3
1900 RCH 94801 588-G6
HILL CT
- HER 94547 569-H4
2500 BERK 94708 609-H7
N HILL CT
- OAK 94618 630-B4
S HILL CT
- OAK 94618 630-B4
HILL DR
- ANT 94531 595-E3
1400 ANT 94509 575-F6
HILL LN
- PLHL 94523 592-A6
100 PDMT 94610 650-A1
HILL RD
- BERK 94708 609-J6
100 DNVL 94526 633-C7
100 BERK 94708 610-A6
6100 OAK 94618 630-B5
HILL ST
- CCCo 94565 573-F2
6300 ELCR 94530 609-B1
HILLBROOK PL
- DBLN 94568 694-E2
HILLCREST AV
- BEN 94510 551-C4
- PIT 94565 574-C5
1200 ANT 94509 575-F5
3000 ANT 94531 575-G7
3400 ANT 94531 595-H1
HILLCREST CIR
200 PLHL 94523 592-A4
HILLCREST CT
- BERK 94705 630-A4
- OAK 94619 650-J5
- OAK 94619 651-A4
- SRMN 94583 673-A1
200 PLHL 94523 592-A4
HILLCREST DR
- ORIN 94563 631-A1
100 ORIN 94563 611-A7
1100 LFYT 94549 611-F5
HILLCREST LN
- PLHL 94523 592-A4
HILLCREST PL
200 PLHL 94523 592-A4
HILLCREST RD
- WLCK 94595 612-A5
- BERK 94705 630-A4
100 BERK 94618 630-A4
200 OAK 94618 630-A4
1500 SPAB 94806 589-B3
1500 CCCo 94806 589-B3
3800 CCCo 94803 589-B3
4000 RCH 94803 589-B3
HILLCREST WY
4800 PLE 94588 693-J7
HILLCROFT CIR
900 OAK 94610 650-B3
HILLCROFT WY
- CCCo 94597 612-A5
HILLDALE AV
600 BERK 94708 609-H5
HILLDALE CT
- ORIN 94563 630-J4
HILLDALE RD
1100 LFYT 94549 611-B4
HILLENDALE CT
1000 WLCK 94596 632-F1
HILLER DR
- OAK 94618 630-B4
HILLER LN
5000 MRTZ 94553 571-J6
HILLGIRT CIR
600 OAK 94610 650-A3
HILL GIRT RANCH RD
100 CCCo 94553 591-E2
HILLGRADE AV
1500 CCCo 94507 632-E2
HILLHURST WY
- OAK 94705 630-B2
HILLIARD CIR
2300 ANT 94509 595-A2
HILL MEADOW DR
- DNVL 94526 653-E4
HILL MEADOW PL
1000 DNVL 94526 653-E3
HILLMONT DR
6100 OAK 94605 650-H7
HILLMONT PL
- DNVL 94526 632-J6
- DNVL 94526 633-A6
HILL RIDGE WY
4900 ANT 94531 595-D4
HILLRISE PL
500 WLCK 94598 613-B3
HILLROSE DR
7500 DBLN 94568 693-G3
HILLSBORO AV
7300 SRMN 94583 673-G7
HILLSBORO CT
7900 PLE 94588 693-H7
HILLSBOROUGH BLVD
- BREN 94513 596-D5
HILLSBOROUGH CT
2200 CNCD 94520 572-F6
HILLSBOROUGH DR
3400 CNCD 94520 572-F5
HILLSBOROUGH ST
600 OAK 94606 650-A4
HILLSDALE CT
7600 PLE 94588 693-J7
HILLSDALE DR
300 PIT 94565 574-B5
2900 PLHL 94523 612-A1
7300 PLE 94588 693-J7
HILLSIDE AV
- SRFL 94901 587-A1
100 PDMT 94611 630-A2
100 PDMT 94611 650-B1
700 ALB 94706 609-D6
1600 CCCo 94595 612-A7
2000 WLCK 94597 612-B4
2400 BERK 94704 630-A2
2800 CNCD 94520 572-E7
5400 ELCR 94530 589-B7
HILLSIDE CT
400 PDMT 94611 650-B1
2200 CCCo 94597 612-B4
HILLSIDE DR
1000 MRTZ 94553 571-D3
6100 CCCo 94803 589-H4
HILLSIDE LN
100 CCCo 94553 572-B5
HILLSIDE RD
- ANT 94509 575-D7
- DNVL 94526 652-H3
HILLSIDE TER
- LFYT 94549 611-G2
- MRTZ 94553 571-D4
HILLTOP CRES
- CCCo 94597 612-A4
5300 OAK 94618 630-C7
HILLTOP CT
- SRMN 94582 673-F2
HILLTOP DR
1100 LFYT 94549 611-E5
2800 RCH 94806 568-J6
2800 RCH 94806 569-A7
2900 RCH 94806 589-C1
4100 RCH 94803 589-C1
4100 CCCo 94803 589-C1
4900 CCCo 94803 569-D7
HILLTOP RD
- MRTZ 94553 571-F7
2800 CNCD 94520 572-E6
3100 RCH 94806 589-A1
HILLTOP MALL RD
1000 RCH 94806 569-A7
1400 RCH 94806 589-A1
HILLVIEW CT
- DNVL 94506 654-B6
3100 CNCD 94519 572-G7
7400 PLE 94588 693-J7
HILLVIEW DR
- DNVL 94506 654-B6
2100 CCCo 94596 612-D7
3200 RCH 94806 588-J1
3200 RCH 94806 589-A1
3200 RCH 94806 568-J7
3500 RCH 94806 569-A7
4200 PIT 94565 574-D7
HILL VIEW LN
2400 PIN 94564 569-F5
HILLVIEW LN
1200 LFYT 94549 611-H4
HILLVIEW RD
1100 BERK 94708 609-J5
HILLVIEW ST
3700 OAK 94602 650-E5
HILLVIEW TER
- CCCo 94596 612-E7
HILLWOOD PL
- OAK 94610 650-C3
HILMER AV
200 MRTZ 94553 571-D4
HILO DR
- PIT 94565 574-E5
HILTON CT
- CCCo 94595 611-J7
HILTON RD
700 CCCo 94595 611-J7
HINGHAM CV
- SRFL 94901 587-A2
HINKLEY AV
2500 RCH 94804 608-H1
HINKLEY CIR
- RCH 94804 608-H1
HIRSCH WY
800 DNVL 94526 653-A1
HITCHCOCK RD
3700 CNCD 94518 592-J4
HOBART CT
2200 ANT 94509 595-A1
HOBBY CT
3600 CNCD 94518 592-H4
HOBSTONE PL
- DBLN 94568 694-F2
HOCK MAPLE CT
4400 CNCD 94521 593-B5
HODGES DR
100 MRGA 94556 651-E2
HODUR CT
- PLHL 94523 592-A3
HOEDEL CT
1000 LFYT 94549 611-J6
HOFFMAN BLVD
600 RCH 94804 608-F1
HOFFMAN LN
500 CCCo 94513 617-A7
800 CCCo 94513 637-B1
800 CCCo 94514 637-B1
HOGAN CT
100 WLCK 94598 612-D3
HOKE CT
1800 PIN 94564 569-E6
HOKE DR
2000 PIN 94564 569-E6
HOLBROOK DR
2000 DNVL 94506 653-G4
2100 CNCD 94519 572-G7
HOLBROOK PL
- DNVL 94506 653-G4
300 SRMN 94582 673-J6
HOLCOMB CT
- WLCK 94596 612-D6
HOLEY RD
- CCCo 94514 (657-F1 See Page 638)
HOLIDAY CT
200 MRTZ 94553 571-J6
900 CNCD 94518 592-F6
2700 PIN 94564 569-G5
HOLIDAY DR
- CCCo 94507 632-F6
HOLIDAY LN
- CNCD 94521 593-E4
HOLIDAY HILLS DR
100 MRTZ 94553 571-J6
HOLLAND CIR
1700 WLCK 94597 611-J2
HOLLAND DR
1700 WLCK 94597 611-J2
4400 PLE 94588 694-A7
HOLLANDA CT
8000 DBLN 94568 693-G3
HOLLANDA LN
8000 DBLN 94568 693-G3
HOLLAND TRACT RD
- CCCo 94561 577-F7
7000 CCCo 94561 (578-A3 See Page 557)
7000 CCCo 94561 597-F1
7000 CCCo 94561 (598-A1 See Page 597)
HOLLIS CT
1900 CNCD 94518 592-F6
HOLLIS CANYON RD
22900 AlaC 94552 693-A3
HOLLOWBROOK CT
1100 BREN 94513 616-E1
HOLLOWBROOK DR
800 BREN 94513 616-D1
HOLLOWGLEN CT
- ANT 94531 596-A4
HOLLOW RIDGE CT
5000 ANT 94531 595-E4
HOLLOW RIDGE WY
5000 ANT 94531 595-E4
HOLLY CT
- CCCo 94583 652-F4
1300 ANT 94509 575-C6
HOLLY DR
1900 CCCo 94521 593-E3
1900 CNCD 94521 593-E3
2100 OAKL 94561 576-C7
W HOLLY DR
1000 WLCK 94598 612-D5
HOLLY LN
- CCCo 94803 589-F2
100 ORIN 94563 610-E6
HOLLY PL
100 PDMT 94611 650-A1
HOLLY PTH
3100 RCH 94806 589-A2
HOLLY ST
- BREN 94513 596-D7
- WLCK 94598 612-D5
1400 BERK 94703 609-F7
HOLLY CREEK PL
300 CNCD 94521 593-G4
HOLLY HILL CT
- CCCo 94596 612-G7
HOLLY HILL DR
800 CCCo 94596 612-G7
HOLLYHOCK CT
100 HER 94547 570-B4
HOLLY OAK CT
- BREN 94513 616-A3
HOLLY OAK DR
2300 CCCo 94506 653-F1
HOLLY VIEW CT
2500 MRTZ 94553 571-F5
HOLLYVIEW CT
- SRMN 94582 673-J1
- SRMN 94582 674-A1
HOLLY VIEW DR
2300 MRTZ 94553 571-F5
HOLLYVIEW DR
- SRMN 94582 673-J1
HOLLYWOOD AV
900 OAK 94602 650-D3
HOLMAN RD
1100 OAK 94610 650-B3
1300 OAK 94602 650-B3
HOLMES RD
3700 OAKL 94561 596-D2
HOLMSUND CT
- PLHL 94523 592-A3
HOLSAPPLE WY
- BREN 94561 596-E3
HOLTON CT
200 WLCK 94598 612-D4
HOLVEN CT
- CCCo 94525 550-F5
HOLWAY DR
3800 CCCo 94514 637-D3
HOLYROOD DR
2900 OAK 94611 650-G2
HOLYROOD MNR
- OAK 94611 650-G2
HOME PL E
- OAK 94610 650-A4
HOME PL W
- OAK 94610 650-A4
E HOME ST
200 OAKL 94561 576-E7
W HOME ST
100 OAKL 94561 576-E7
HOMECOMING WY
2000 BREN 94513 596-G5
HOMEDALE DR
5200 CNCD 94521 613-C1
HOMEGLEN LN
- OAK 94611 630-F6
HOMER CT
700 CCCo 94803 589-C1
6100 PLE 94588 694-A7
HOMER WY
6200 PLE 94588 694-B7
HOMESTEAD AV
900 WLCK 94596 612-D4
1000 WLCK 94598 612-D4
1200 CCCo 94598 612-D4
1200 WLCK 94597 612-D3
HOMESTEAD CIR
2300 RCH 94806 588-F1
HOMESTEAD CT
- DNVL 94506 653-H4
5100 ANT 94531 595-J5
HOMESTEAD WY
5100 ANT 94531 595-J5
HOMEWOOD CT
7500 PLE 94588 693-H6
HOMEWOOD DR
100 CNCD 94518 592-G4
2200 PIT 94565 574-E5
7000 OAK 94611 630-F6
HONDO PL
- SRMN 94583 673-G5
HONEY CT
1000 PIT 94565 573-H4
7500 DBLN 94568 693-H3
HONEY LN
200 OAKL 94561 596-G2
HONEY TR
1100 CCCo 94597 612-D1
HONEYCASTLE DR
- CCCo 94582 674-A2
HONEYDEW CT
- ANT 94531 595-D4
HONEYDEW DR
200 VAL 94591 550-E1
HONEY GOLD LN
100 BREN 94513 616-C2
HONEY HILL CT
- ORIN 94563 610-J5
HONEY HILL RD
- ORIN 94563 610-J5
HONEYLAKE CT
500 CCCo 94506 654-B4
HONEY LOCUST CT
1900 WLCK 94595 632-B1
HONEYNUT ST
2900 ANT 94509 575-J6
HONEYSUCKLE CIR
2800 ANT 94531 575-G7
HONEYSUCKLE CT
- BREN 94513 616-H2
2900 ANT 94531 575-G7
HONEYSUCKLE LN
400 SRMN 94582 653-J7
HONEYSUCKLE ST
- BREN 94513 616-H2
HONEYSUCKLE WY
3500 CNCD 94518 592-J6
HONEYWOOD RD
- ORIN 94563 610-J3
- ORIN 94563 611-A3
HONISTER LN
900 CNCD 94518 592-F6
HONOR WY
- BREN 94561 596-D4
HONORA AV
900 CNCD 94518 592-G6
HOOF TRAIL WY
2400 ANT 94531 595-G3
HOOK AV
1000 PLHL 94523 592-C7
HOOKSTON RD
- PLHL 94523 592-D6
1200 CNCD 94518 592-D7
W HOOKSTON RD
- PLHL 94523 592-C6
HOOPER DR
2700 SRMN 94583 653-B7
HOOVER AV
1900 PLHL 94523 612-A1
1900 OAK 94602 650-E3
HOOVER CT
1800 CNCD 94521 593-D2
2100 PLHL 94523 612-A1
HOPE AV
4000 CNCD 94521 593-A3
HOPE LN
100 DNVL 94526 633-C6
800 LFYT 94549 611-G7
HOPECO RD
100 PLHL 94523 592-B6
HOPI CT
- SRMN 94583 673-D4
2500 WLCK 94598 612-H4
HOPKINS CT
- BERK 94706 609-F7
- CCCo 94803 589-E1
HOPKINS PL
2800 OAK 94602 650-E5
HOPKINS ST
1200 BERK 94702 609-F7
1400 BERK 94706 609-F7
1500 BERK 94703 609-F7
1500 BERK 94707 609-F7
HOPYARD RD
2500 PLE 94588 694-B7
HORAN CT
1300 PIT 94565 574-F6
HORIZON CT
200 OAKL 94561 596-G1
1000 DNVL 94506 653-G5
HORIZON DR
- RCH 94806 568-H5
700 MRTZ 94553 591-G3
HORIZON LN
1900 ANT 94509 575-B5
HORIZON ST
- BREN 94513 596-D4
HORIZONS CT
- PLE 94588 693-H7
HORNE CT
1500 BREN 94513 596-D6
HORNET CT
- DNVL 94526 653-A1
HORNET DR
800 DNVL 94526 653-A1
HORSEMANS CANYON DR
5900 WLCK 94595 632-C5
HORSESHOE CIR
4500 ANT 94531 595-J3
4500 ANT 94531 596-A2
HORSESHOE CT
- WLCK 94596 632-F2
HORSETRAIL CT
400 CCCo 94507 632-D1
HORSE VALLEY RD
- CCCo 94531 615-D1
HORTEN CT
- PLHL 94523 592-B6
HOSIE AV
3100 CCCo 94514 637-D3
HOSPITAL RD
1200 BEN 94510 551-D5
HOTCHKISS AV
7200 ELCR 94530 609-D3
HOTCHKISS RD
- CCCo 94513 597-C3
HOUGH AV
900 LFYT 94549 611-E7
HOUSER DR
300 PIT 94565 574-C3
HOUSTON CT
300 DNVL 94526 652-J3
4000 CNCD 94521 593-A2
HOUSTON PL
6100 DBLN 94568 694-A4
HOVE CT
600 WLCK 94598 612-F1
HOWARD AV
200 PDMT 94611 650-A1
HOWARD CT
- CCCo 94598 612-F5
HOWARD ST
2100 SPAB 94806 588-H2
2800 RCH 94804 588-J4
HOWARD HILLS RD
1000 LFYT 94549 611-C6
HOWARDS ST
3300 LFYT 94549 611-H7
HOWE RD
- MRTZ 94553 571-G4
- CCCo 94553 571-G4
HOWE ST
4400 OAK 94611 630-A7
HOYT DR
1500 CNCD 94521 593-B3
HOYTT CT
2300 PIN 94564 589-J1
HUBBARD AV
100 PLHL 94523 592-B7
HUBERT RD
1000 OAK 94610 650-B3
HUCKLEBERRY CT
500 SRMN 94582 653-H6
HUCKLEBERRY DR
4100 CNCD 94521 593-A3
HUDSON AV
3100 WLCK 94597 612-B1
HUDSON CT
3300 PLE 94588 694-F5
3400 ANT 94509 574-J6
HUDSON DR
3000 BREN 94513 616-G3
HUDSON PL
- BREN 94513 616-G3
HUDSON ST
1800 ELCR 94530 609-C1
1900 ELCR 94530 589-C7
HUFF CT
- MRGA 94556 651-E1
3600 PLE 94588 694-F6
HUFF DR
2700 PLE 94588 694-F6
HUGH CT
- BEN 94510 551-C1
HUGHES AV
2300 OAK 94601 650-C6
HUGHES DR
1800 CNCD 94520 592-E4
HULL DR
3000 RCH 94806 589-A2
HULL LN
1300 MRTZ 94553 571-G6
HULL MOUNTAIN CT
- ANT 94531 595-E5
HUMBOLDT AV
1400 SPAB 94806 589-A4
2200 ELCR 94530 589-B7
2200 RCH 94805 589-B7
2300 OAK 94601 650-D6
2500 OAK 94602 650-D6
HUMBOLDT ST
600 RCH 94805 589-A5
1000 SPAB 94805 589-A5
HUMMINGBIRD DR
3800 ANT 94509 594-J2
HUMMINGBIRD PL
4000 CLAY 94517 593-J5
HUMMINGBIRD WY
4000 CLAY 94517 593-J5
4000 CLAY 94517 594-A5
HUMPHREY AV
2300 RCH 94804 588-H5
3400 RCH 94804 589-A5
HUMPHREY DR
1700 CNCD 94519 592-H2
HUMPHREY LN
100 VAL 94591 550-F2
HUMPHREY PL
- OAK 94610 650-C3
HUNSAKER CT
- ANT 94531 595-C5
HUNSAKER CANYON RD
500 CCCo 94549 632-A4
500 LFYT 94549 631-J4
500 LFYT 94549 632-A4
HUNTER PEAK CT
4700 ANT 94531 595-E3
HUNTERS LN
5800 CCCo 94803 589-G4
HUNTERS TER
- DNVL 94506 653-G2
HUNTINGTON AV
5100 RCH 94804 609-B4
HUNTINGTON CIR
- PIT 94565 574-C4
HUNTINGTON CT
700 MRTZ 94553 571-E2
HUNTINGTON DR
200 ANT 94509 595-E1
HUNTINGTON PL
- SRMN 94583 673-F6
HUNTINGTON ST
3800 OAK 94619 650-G6
HUNTINGTON WY
900 WLCK 94596 612-F7
900 CCCo 94596 612-F7
HUNTLEIGH DR
600 LFYT 94549 631-J2
HUNTLEIGH RD
- PDMT 94611 650-D2
HUNTOON CT
- WLCK 94596 612-D6
HUNTRIDGE CT
2000 MRTZ 94553 571-H7
HUNTSMAN WY
2300 ANT 94531 595-G3
HURD PL
100 CLAY 94517 593-G6
HURLSTONE CT
2900 WLCK 94598 612-J3
HURON DR
2100 CNCD 94519 572-G6
HURST CT
- SRMN 94583 693-F1
HURTTS DR
1900 CNCD 94521 593-F4
HUSTON CT
- CCCo 94549 611-J2
HUSTON RD
1300 WLCK 94597 611-J2
1400 CCCo 94549 611-J2
HUSTONWOOD CT
1700 WLCK 94597 611-J2
HUTCHINS AV
- DBLN 94568 694-B3
HUTCHINSON CT
1400 PIN 94564 569-E3
2700 WLCK 94598 612-H4
HUTCHINSON RD
700 WLCK 94598 612-J4
HYACINTH AV
4300 OAK 94619 650-G6
HYACINTH CT
2700 ANT 94531 575-G7
HYANNIS CV
- SRFL 94901 587-A2
HYDE CT
1100 CNCD 94520 592-E4
6700 DBLN 94568 693-J3
HYDE PL
100 ANT 94509 575-D7
HYDE ST
3000 OAK 94601 650-C6

I

I ST
100 BEN 94510 551-B5
100 ANT 94509 575-C4
W I ST
100 BEN 94510 551-A4
800 BEN 94510 550-J4
IAN CT
- SRMN 94582 673-J1
IAN LN
- DBLN 94568 693-E5
IBERIS CT
2800 PLE 94588 694-H4
IBIS DR
- OAKL 94561 576-H7
IBIS ST
- BREN 94513 596-G7
- BREN 94513 616-G1
ICHABOD LN
- ORIN 94563 610-F3
IDA CT
- CCCo 94565 573-D1
IDA DR
3100 CNCD 94519 572-G7
IDAHO CT
1400 CNCD 94521 593-F6
IDAHO ST
- RCH 94801 608-D1
IDLEWOOD CIR
800 CCCo 94803 569-D7
IDLEWOOD CT
- DBLN 94568 694-D3
- MRGA 94556 631-C6
IDLEWOOD DR
- CCCo 94595 612-C6
IDLEWOOD ST
- DBLN 94568 694-D3
IDYLL CT
- ORIN 94563 631-A2
IGLESIA CT
600 ANT 94509 575-E6
IGLESIA DR
7900 DBLN 94568 693-F3
IGNACIO CT
1000 PIN 94564 569-E5
ILENE DR
200 PLHL 94523 592-B4
ILENE ST
300 MRTZ 94553 571-D4
ILLINOIS CT
1200 CNCD 94521 593-E6
ILO LN
300 DNVL 94526 653-A1
IMHOFF DR
4700 CCCo 94553 572-C5
5700 CCCo 94520 572-C5
IMHOFF PL
4700 CCCo 94553 572-B5
IMPALA CT
2100 PIT 94565 574-A4
IMPERATA LN
- SRMN 94582 673-H2
IMPERIAL AV
1400 RCH 94804 609-B3
IMPERIAL CT
- CCCo 94514 617-G7
IMPERIAL WY
- ANT 94531 595-J1
- ANT 94531 596-A1
1500 BREN 94513 616-D2
IMRIE PL
200 CCCo 94507 633-C4
INA CT
- CCCo 94507 632-G4
INA DR
900 CCCo 94507 632-G4
INAJANE CT
3400 CNCD 94519 592-J1
INCLINE CT
- ANT 94531 595-F5
INCLINE PL
100 BEN 94510 551-B4
INCLINED PL
7100 DBLN 94568 693-F5
INCLINE GREEN LN
- CCCo 94507 633-A3
INDEPENDENCE ST
700 BREN 94513 616-J3
INDEPENDENCE WY
1500 OAK 94606 650-A6
INDIAN LN
1400 CNCD 94521 593-C4
INDIAN RD
100 PDMT 94610 650-C2
200 OAK 94610 650-C2
INDIAN TR
- BERK 94707 609-F5
INDIAN WY
- CCCo 94507 632-J5
1700 OAK 94611 630-E6
3100 LFYT 94549 631-J3
INDIANA AV
- BREN 94513 616-G2
INDIANA DR
1300 CNCD 94521 593-F6
INDIANA ST
600 BEN 94510 551-E2
INDIAN GULCH RD
- PDMT 94611 650-C1
INDIANHEAD CIR
2500 CLAY 94517 593-H6
INDIANHEAD WY
2500 CLAY 94517 593-H6
INDIAN HILL DR
3400 WLCK 94598 612-J3
3400 WLCK 94598 613-A3
4800 ANT 94531 595-H4
INDIAN HOME RD
500 DNVL 94526 653-C4
INDIAN RICE RD
3300 SRMN 94582 653-J6
INDIAN ROCK AV
800 BERK 94707 609-G5
INDIAN ROCK PTH
- BERK 94707 609-G6
INDIAN SPRINGS CT
- BREN 94513 596-C6
INDIAN SPRINGS DR
- BREN 94513 596-C6
INDIAN WELLS
- MRGA 94556 631-C7

STREET
Block City ZIP Pg-Grid

INDIANWELLS WY
1600 CLAY 94517 593-H6
INDIGO CT
4400 CNCD 94521 593-C5
INDIGO LN
- SRMN 94583 693-F1
INDUSTRIAL CT
300 BEN 94510 551-E2
INDUSTRIAL WY
- BEN 94510 551-E1
4000 CNCD 94520 572-F3
INDUSTRY RD
600 PIT 94565 574-F2
INEZ AV
- CCCo 94553 571-F3
INEZ ST
1300 CCCo 94553 571-G3
INEZ WY
2500 ANT 94531 595-G4
INGLEWOOD CT
6800 PLE 94588 694-A7
INGLEWOOD DR
5900 PLE 94588 694-A7
INGLEWOOD ST
- CCCo 94565 573-H3
INGROFF RD
7000 CCCo 94803 589-G1
INLAND CT
- ANT 94509 575-E5
INLET DR
- CCCo 94565 553-E7
- CCCo 94565 573-E1
INMAN CT
- DNVL 94526 652-J1
INNISWOOD PL
- DBLN 94568 694-H3
INNWOOD CT
4700 CNCD 94521 593-D4
INSPIRATION CIR
- DBLN 94568 693-E4
INSPIRATION CT
- CCCo 94507 632-J2
INSPIRATION DR
- DBLN 94568 693-E5
INSTAR CT
- SRMN 94582 673-H2
INSTAR DR
- SRMN 94582 673-H2
INSTAR WY
- SRMN 94582 673-H2
INTERLACHEN AV
7400 SRMN 94583 693-G1
INTERNATIONAL BLVD
1300 OAK 94606 650-A6
2300 OAK 94601 650-A6
INTERNATIONAL MARKETPLACE
2400 SPAB 94806 588-H2
INTRIGUE LN
- BREN 94561 596-D4
INVERLEITH TER
- MRGA 94556 631-E7
- PDMT 94611 650-D2
INVERNESS CT
- BREN 94513 616-B1
- SRMN 94583 673-G7
- SRMN 94583 693-G1
100 BEN 94510 551-B3
3200 WLCK 94598 612-J2
INVERNESS DR
3200 WLCK 94598 612-J2
4200 PIT 94565 574-D6
INVERNESS LN
- BREN 94513 616-B1
INVERNESS ST
7400 SRMN 94583 673-G7
INVERNESS WY
- CLAY 94517 594-A7
INVERRARY LN
- CCCo 94507 633-A3
INVESTMENT ST
600 CCCo 94572 549-H7
INYO AV
2200 OAK 94601 650-C6
INYO CT
4600 PLE 94566 694-D7
IONE CT
7200 DBLN 94568 693-J2
IONE WY
6800 DBLN 94568 693-J3
IOWA DR
5400 CNCD 94521 593-E6
IOWA ST
4200 BEN 94510 551-E2
IPSWICH WY
100 PLHL 94523 591-J3
IRCAL CT
- CCCo 94507 632-G5
IRENE DR
4100 CCCo 94553 572-A3
IRENE LN
900 LFYT 94549 611-H7
IRENE ST
200 SRFL 94901 587-A3
IRIS CT
- BREN 94561 596-F4
100 HER 94547 569-J3
500 BEN 94510 550-J1
2700 ANT 94531 575-G7
3200 LFYT 94549 611-H5
IRIS LN
- CCCo 94595 612-A6
500 SRMN 94582 653-J7
IRIS RD
100 HER 94547 569-J4
200 HER 94547 570-A3
IRIS ST
100 MRTZ 94553 571-E4
IRMA AV
6200 ELCR 94530 589-C7
IRONBARK CIR
600 ORIN 94563 610-H6
IRONBARK CT
700 ORIN 94563 610-H6
IRONBARK PL
800 ORIN 94563 610-H6
IRON CLUB DR
- BREN 94513 616-B1
IRONGATE CT
100 CCCo 94507 632-G7
IRONGATE DR
- PLE 94588 694-F7
IRON HILL ST
400 PLHL 94523 591-H5
IRON HORSE CT
300 CCCo 94507 632-D2
IRON HORSE PKWY
- DBLN 94568 694-B5
IRONHORSE RD
- CCCo 94513 597-D4
IRON PEAK CT
1900 ANT 94531 595-E6
IRONWOOD CT
- PLHL 94523 592-A2
100 HER 94547 570-A4
5200 OAKL 94561 576-D6
7500 DBLN 94568 693-H3
IRONWOOD DR
100 CCCo 94553 592-B1
100 PLHL 94523 592-B1
1100 BREN 94513 616-D1
7500 DBLN 94568 693-H3
IRONWOOD LN
100 VAL 94591 550-F1
5200 OAKL 94561 576-D6
IRONWOOD PL
1000 CCCo 94507 632-F7
IRONWOOD WY
1100 CNCD 94521 593-F7
IROQUOIS DR
900 CCCo 94549 591-J6
900 PLHL 94523 591-J6
IRVIN CT
900 PLHL 94523 592-C3
IRVINE DR
- MRGA 94556 651-G2
IRVING CT
- ORIN 94563 610-H3
IRVING LN
- ORIN 94563 610-H4
IRVING ST
1800 OAK 94601 650-B6
IRVING WY
8000 DBLN 94568 693-H3
IRWIN CT
1000 CNCD 94518 592-J5
IRWIN WY
- ORIN 94563 610-G7
ISABEL CT
- PIT 94565 574-E2
ISABEL DR
400 MRTZ 94553 591-J1
ISABEL ST
2500 RCH 94804 609-A5
ISABELLA CT
4100 ANT 94531 595-J1
ISABELLA LN
- PLHL 94523 612-A1
ISLAND CT
- CCCo 94595 612-A6
ISLAND PARK PL
- BREN 94513 616-C4
ISLAND VIEW DR
- CCCo 94565 553-D7
ISLA VISTA LN
- SRFL 94901 587-A2
ISLE PL
- CCCo 94511 577-E4
ISLETON CT
1700 OAKL 94561 596-D1
ISLEWOOD CT
3300 ANT 94531 595-H1
ISOLA CT
- OAKL 94561 596-C1
ISOLA WY
3200 CCCo 94549 591-J7
ITHACA LN
2600 ANT 94509 575-D1
ITHACA WY
4600 PLE 94588 694-D6
IVANHOE AV
1700 LFYT 94549 591-H7
IVANHOE CT
- LFYT 94549 591-H7
IVANHOE RD
5800 OAK 94618 630-A5
IVERSON DR
- LFYT 94549 611-F5
IVY BAY
- HER 94547 569-H1
IVY CT
1100 ELCR 94530 609-E1
7500 PLE 94588 693-J7
IVY DR
- OAK 94610 650-A4
- ORIN 94563 631-B4
- MRGA 94556 631-C6
2200 OAK 94606 650-A4
IVY LN
400 PLHL 94523 612-B1
2700 ANT 94531 595-H1
IVY PL
- MRGA 94556 631-C6
IVY POINTE CIR
500 SRMN 94582 653-J7
IVYWOOD DR
200 CCCo 94523 592-D7

J

J ST
100 BEN 94510 551-B5
200 ANT 94509 575-C4
400 MRTZ 94553 571-E5
W J ST
100 BEN 94510 551-A4
800 BEN 94510 550-J4
JACARANDA CT
- HER 94547 569-H1
JACARANDA DR
300 CCCo 94506 653-J2
300 CCCo 94506 654-A2
JACARANDA ST
- BREN 94513 616-H2
JACINTO
200 PIT 94565 574-B2
JACKIE CT
4000 PLE 94588 694-A7
JACK LONDON BLVD
- LVMR 94588 694-H5
JACK LONDON CT
- PIT 94565 574-B2
JACK LONDON DR
- PIT 94565 574-B2
JACKSON CT
- BREN 94513 616-H1
1800 CNCD 94521 593-D2
JACKSON PL
3100 ANT 94509 575-A7
JACKSON ST
- ALB 94710 609-D5
300 CCCo 94525 550-E5
500 ALB 94706 609-D5
700 BEN 94510 551-D6
JACKSON WY
100 PLHL 94523 592-B6
1400 CCCo 94507 632-F4
N JACKSON WY
- CCCo 94507 632-F4
S JACKSON WY
- CCCo 94507 632-F5
JACOBSEN ST
900 ANT 94509 575-F4
JACOBUS AV
4600 OAK 94618 630-B6
JACQUELINE DR
2100 PIT 94565 573-J4
JACQUELINE WY
1800 CNCD 94519 592-J1
JACUZZI ST
3200 RCH 94804 609-C4
JADE CIR
200 VAL 94590 550-C2
7800 DBLN 94568 693-J1
JADE CT
- SRMN 94582 673-F2
100 HER 94547 569-G5
400 ANT 94509 595-E2
JADE ST
1600 CCCo 94801 588-F3
JADECREST CT
- SRMN 94582 673-G1
JADECREST DR
- SRMN 94582 673-F1
JAGUAR WY
- ANT 94531 595-G2
JAKES LN
700 BREN 94513 616-E1
JALALON PL
- CLAY 94517 593-G6
JAMAICA DR
- SRMN 94582 653-E7
JAMARA WY
3100 CCCo 94549 611-J2
JAMES CT
- WLCK 94597 612-A2
200 BEN 94510 551-A2
2100 MRTZ 94553 571-F4
JAMES LN
1800 CNCD 94519 593-A1
JAMES PL
100 LFYT 94549 611-G7
1100 ELCR 94530 609-E1
JAMES ST
- CCCo 94514 637-D2
JAMES BOWIE CT
300 CCCo 94507 632-H2
JAMES DONLON BLVD
- ANT 94509 594-H1
- ANT 94509 574-G7
- ANT 94565 594-H1
- CCCo 94565 574-G7
1100 ANT 94509 595-B1
1100 ANT 94531 595-B1
JAMESON CT
1900 CNCD 94521 593-H5
JAMES RIVER RD
100 VAL 94591 550-D2
JAMES WATSON DR
100 HER 94547 569-G1
JAMIE CT
- CCCo 94582 674-B5
JAMIE DR
1000 CNCD 94518 592-J4
JAMIE PL
- CCCo 94582 674-B5
JAN LN
- CCCo 94561 596-J2
JANA VISTA
4200 CCCo 94803 589-D3
JANE CT
700 CCCo 94553 572-A3
JANE LN
- OAKL 94561 596-B1
JANE WY
- BREN 94513 596-G5
JANET CT
1400 BEN 94510 551-B4
JANET LN
- WLCK 94597 612-A2
600 MRTZ 94553 571-E6
900 LFYT 94549 611-H6
1300 CNCD 94521 593-A3
JANETH ST
- CCCo 94514 637-D2
JANICE DR
2000 PLHL 94523 592-D5
JANIE CT
- ELCR 94530 609-C2
JANIN PL
- PLHL 94523 591-J2
- PLHL 94523 592-A2
JANIS CT
- CCCo 94507 633-C5
JAPONICA WY
- CCCo 94582 674-B2
JAROSITE CT
4200 ANT 94509 595-F2
JARVIS LN
100 HER 94547 570-B5
JASMINE CIR
1500 OAKL 94561 596-D1
JASMINE CT
- BREN 94513 596-D7
- WLCK 94597 612-C1
- OAKL 94561 596-D7
1000 CCCo 94803 569-D7
1300 ANT 94509 575-G5
4000 DNVL 94506 654-B6
7600 DBLN 94568 693-H3
JASMINE PL
- BREN 94513 596-D7
JASMINE WY
200 DNVL 94506 654-B5
1000 CCCo 94803 569-D7
JASPER CT
- BEN 94510 551-B1
100 HER 94547 569-G4
5500 CNCD 94521 593-F7
JASPER HILL CT
- SRMN 94582 674-B4
JASPER HILL DR
- SRMN 94582 674-B4
JAVA DR
3400 SRMN 94582 673-D1
JAY CT
- CCCo 94507 633-D5
JAY LN
100 CCCo 94507 633-C5
JAYBROOK CT
7300 PLE 94588 693-J7
JAY JAY PL
- BREN 94513 616-E5
JAYNES ST
1700 BERK 94703 609-F7
JAYS PL
1400 MRTZ 94553 591-H1
JEAN CT
- CCCo 94806 589-B3
- MRGA 94556 631-G5
JEAN DR
- CNCD 94518 592-G4
JEAN PL
100 PLHL 94523 592-D6
JEAN ST
600 OAK 94610 650-A2
JEANETTE DR
1900 PLHL 94523 592-B5
JEANNE CIR
1700 MRTZ 94553 591-J1
JEANNE CT
- ANT 94509 575-E5
JEANNE DR
200 PLHL 94523 592-B4
JEANNIE CT
100 DNVL 94526 633-C7
JEFF CT
1400 CNCD 94521 593-A3
JEFFERSON AV
5600 RCH 94804 609-B2
5700 ELCR 94530 609-B2
JEFFERSON CT
4600 PLE 94588 694-A7
JEFFERSON DR
- BREN 94513 596-F7
JEFFERSON LN
- CNCD 94519 592-G1
JEFFERSON ST
- CCCo 94565 573-H2
800 BEN 94510 551-D5
1800 CNCD 94521 593-C2
2500 CCCo 94553 571-F3
JEFFERSON WY
2100 ANT 94509 574-J7
2100 ANT 94509 575-A7
JEFFERY WY
2300 BREN 94513 596-B5
JEFFREY DR
800 PLHL 94523 592-C3
JEFFREY LN
900 WLCK 94598 612-D4
JEFFRY RANCH CT
100 CLAY 94517 593-G6
JEFFRY RANCH PL
200 CLAY 94517 593-G6
JEMCO CT
- PLHL 94523 592-A6
JEN CT
3100 CNCD 94518 592-H2
JENAY CT
200 MRTZ 94553 591-H3
JENIFER CT
2500 ANT 94509 574-J6
JENKINS WY
3800 RCH 94806 568-G7
JENKINSON DR
1600 CNCD 94520 592-E4
JENNIE CT
600 LFYT 94549 631-H1
JENNIE DR
- PLHL 94523 592-C4
JENNIFER CT
100 CCCo 94507 632-G3
JENNIFER DR
100 CCCo 94806 569-A5
JENNIFER LN
- CCCo 94507 632-G3
JENNIFER ST
- BREN 94513 596-H7
JENNIFER WY
200 PLHL 94523 592-C4
JENNIFER HIGHLANDS CT
- CCCo 94549 591-G5
JENNIFERS MEADOWS CT
1000 DNVL 94506 653-G5
JENSEN CIR
900 PIT 94565 574-F7
JENSEN CT
400 DNVL 94526 653-C3
JENSEN DR
1000 PIT 94565 574-F6
JERI PL
5000 CCCo 94521 593-D4
JERICHO CT
- BREN 94513 616-E2
JERILYNN AV
6300 RCH 94803 589-B3
6300 RCH 94806 589-B3
JERILYNN DR
2300 CNCD 94519 572-G7
JEROME AV
- PDMT 94611 650-A1
100 PDMT 94610 650-B1
JEROME CT
100 WLCK 94596 612-D4
JERSEY ISLAND RD
- OAKL 94561 577-B7
100 CCCo 94511 557-B6
5400 CCCo 94561 576-J2
5400 CCCo 94561 577-A2
5800 CCCo 94561 557-A7
JESSEN CT
- CCCo 94707 609-F2
JESSICA CT
- CCCo 94507 633-C5
JEWEL CT
- ORIN 94563 631-A4
JEWEL TER
200 DNVL 94526 653-B5
JEWELL CT
6800 OAK 94611 630-E5
JEWELL LN
2500 PLHL 94523 592-C6
JEWETT AV
900 PIT 94565 574-E7
JEWETT CT
900 PIT 94565 574-E7
JIB CT
- PLHL 94523 592-B1
JILL AV
400 CCCo 94565 573-C1
JILLIAN CT
1200 WLCK 94598 612-E2
JILLIAN WY
- DNVL 94506 653-F1
JIMNO AV
- PIT 94565 574-D3
JOAN AV
3600 CNCD 94521 592-J3
3800 CNCD 94521 593-A3
JOAN CT
1300 CNCD 94521 593-A4
JOANN CT
- WLCK 94597 612-D3
JO ANN DR
2700 RCH 94806 589-B1
JOANNE CIR
3100 PLE 94588 694-C7
JOAN VISTA
300 CCCo 94803 589-E1
JOAQUIN CIR
100 DNVL 94526 653-C7
JOAQUIN CT
- DNVL 94526 653-C7
JOAQUIN DR
100 DNVL 94526 653-C6
JOAQUIN MILLER CT
2600 OAK 94611 650-F2
JOAQUIN MILLER RD
2900 OAK 94602 650-G3
3500 OAK 94619 650-G3
JOCELYN PL
- WLCK 94597 612-B4
JO DE CT
3700 CNCD 94519 592-J1
JODIE LN
- CCCo 94803 589-G4
JOE DIMAGGIO DR
400 MRTZ 94553 571-D2
JOEL CT
1100 SPAB 94805 589-A4
JOELLE DR
1600 CNCD 94521 593-D3
JOHANNA CT
2200 PIN 94564 569-F7
JOHANSEN PL
- BEN 94510 551-B4
JOHN AV
900 SPAB 94806 568-H7
1100 SPAB 94806 588-H1
JOHN ST
- CCCo 94572 549-H7
700 PIN 94564 569-F4
JOHN WY
700 LFYT 94549 631-E1
JOHN GILDI AV
100 ANT 94509 575-C6
JOHN GLENN CT
2600 ANT 94509 574-H6
JOHN GLENN DR
- CCCo 94553 592-D1
- CCCo 94553 572-D7
JOHN H JOHNSON PKWY
2200 PIT 94565 574-A4
JOHN MARSH RD
- CCCo 94517 615-E6
JOHN MONEGO CT
- DBLN 94568 694-E4
JOHN MUIR PKWY
- BREN 94513 616-B2
- HER 94547 569-G2
JOHN MUIR PKWY
Rt#-4
- CCCo 94547 570-C3
- CCCo 94553 570-H3
- CCCo 94553 571-A4
- CCCo 94553 572-A6
- HER 94547 570-C3
- HER 94553 570-C3
- HER 94572 570-C3
- MRTZ 94553 571-G6
- MRTZ 94553 572-A6
1900 CCCo 94572 569-H3
1900 CCCo 94572 570-C3
1900 HER 94547 569-H3
1900 HER 94572 569-H3
JOHN MUIR RD
4700 MRTZ 94553 571-F7
JOHNS CT
- PLHL 94523 591-J7
2300 ANT 94531 595-G4
JOHNS PL
600 BEN 94510 551-A4
JOHNS WY
2400 ANT 94531 595-G4
JOHNSON AV
2900 RCH 94804 608-J1
JOHNSON CT
5300 PLE 94588 694-A5
JOHNSON DR
500 RCH 94806 568-G7
1800 ANT 94509 575-A7
1800 CNCD 94520 592-E4
5100 PLE 94588 693-J6
5100 PLE 94588 694-A5
JOHNSON LN
- MRTZ 94553 571-J6
JOHNSON RD
3300 LFYT 94549 611-G1
JOHNSON ST
700 ALB 94706 609-C6
1900 CCCo 94525 550-C5
JOHNSON HILL CT
- CCCo 94803 589-D2
JOHNSTON DR
5900 OAK 94611 630-D7
JOHNSTON LN
- CCCo 94507 632-G6
JOHNSTON RD
5300 CCCo 94588 654-G7
6300 CCCo 94588 (655-A6 See Page 635)
6400 CCCo 94551 (655-C6 See Page 635)
JOHN T KNOX FRWY
I-580
- ALB - 609-A3
- RCH - 588-C7
- RCH - 608-H1
- RCH - 609-A3
JOLIE LN
- WLCK 94597 612-C2
JO LIN CT
- CCCo 94803 589-F3
JOMAR DR
5100 CNCD 94521 593-E4
JONAGOLD WY
- BREN 94513 616-D5
JONATHAN TER
1600 BREN 94513 616-D1
JONATHON RIDGE DR
400 DNVL 94506 653-J6
400 DNVL 94506 654-A6
JONES AV
700 PIN 94564 569-E4
JONES PL
500 WLCK 94597 612-C2
JONES RD
2400 WLCK 94596 612-C3
2400 WLCK 94597 612-C3
2500 CCCo 94597 612-C2
JONES ST
- DBLN 94568 694-B3
300 MRTZ 94553 571-E3
JONES GATE CT
2800 PLE 94566 694-D7
JOPLIN CT
- CCCo 94549 591-H7
JORDAN AV
5600 ELCR 94530 589-C7
JORDAN CT
- OAKL 94561 576-F6
300 MRTZ 94553 571-E5
JORDAN LN
400 OAKL 94561 576-E6
JORDAN PL
- CCCo 94549 591-H7
JORDAN RD
2900 OAK 94602 650-F4
3500 OAK 94619 650-G5
JORDAN ST
100 VAL 94591 550-C1
JORDAN WY
2800 PIN 94564 570-A7
JORDON LN
- BREN 94513 596-E6
JOREE LN
- SRMN 94582 674-A3
JORGENSEN CT
- PIT 94565 574-C2
JORGENSEN DR
- PIT 94565 574-C3
JOSCOLO VW
100 CLAY 94517 593-H5
JOSE LN
100 CCCo 94553 591-E1
JOSEFA PL
- MRGA 94556 631-E3
JOSEPH AV
1900 ANT 94509 575-E5
JOSEPH DR
1800 MRGA 94556 631-G6
2500 CCCo 94507 633-A5
JOSEPH LN
200 CCCo 94588 654-G5
JOSEPHINE ST
1100 BERK 94707 609-G7
1200 BERK 94703 609-G7
JOSHUA CT
600 WLCK 94598 592-H7
2700 ANT 94509 595-E5
JOSHUA ST
- OAKL 94561 596-D2
JOSHUA WOODS PL
3300 CNCD 94518 592-H6
JOURNEYSEND
100 CCCo 94507 632-D1
JOVITA LN
- CCCo 94803 569-C6
- PIN 94564 569-C6
- PIN 94803 569-C6
JOY AV
- RCH 94801 588-F5
JOYA CT
600 CCCo 94506 654-A5
JOYA LN
4000 CCCo 94506 654-A5
JOYCE DR
4000 CNCD 94521 593-A3
JUANITA CT
900 CCCo 94803 569-D7
JUANITA DR
800 CCCo 94595 611-J7
800 CCCo 94803 569-D7
800 CCCo 94595 612-A6
JUAREZ CT
- SPAB 94806 568-H7
11600 DBLN 94568 693-F3
JUAREZ LN
11700 DBLN 94568 693-F3
JUBILEE DR
1600 BREN 94513 616-C2
JUBILEE PL
- BREN 94513 616-C2
JUDITH CT
3000 CCCo 94806 589-B2
3200 LFYT 94549 611-H6
JUDITH LN
3200 LFYT 94549 611-H6
JUDITH PL
1900 CCCo 94521 593-E3
JUDSONVILLE DR
4900 ANT 94531 595-C4
JUDY CT
100 MRTZ 94553 591-H3
JUDY LN
1100 CNCD 94520 592-E4
3200 LFYT 94549 611-H7
JULIA CT
2300 PIN 94564 569-F7
JULIA ST
- OAK 94618 630-C6
JULIAN CT
1700 ELCR 94530 609-D1
JULIAN DR
1600 ELCR 94530 589-D7
1600 ELCR 94530 609-C1
JULIAN WY
100 PLHL 94523 592-B6
JULIANNA CT
- MRGA 94556 651-G1
JULIANNE CT
- CCCo 94595 632-C1
JULIE CT
200 DNVL 94506 653-G5
1000 CNCD 94518 592-F5
4500 RCH 94803 589-E2
JULIE WY
- CCCo 94553 572-A3
JULIE HIGHLANDS CT
- CCCo 94549 591-G5
JULIET CT
1200 CNCD 94521 593-A4
JULIUS CT
2000 WLCK 94598 612-F2
JULPUN LP
600 CLAY 94517 593-H6
JUNCTION AV
1900 ELCR 94530 609-B1
2000 ELCR 94530 589-B7
JUNCTION CT
900 CNCD 94518 592-F6
JUNCTION DR
1900 CNCD 94518 592-F6
JUNEBERRY CT
4400 CNCD 94521 593-C5
JUNEWOOD CT
- DNVL 94526 653-C6
JUNIPER
- BEN 94510 551-C6
JUNIPER CT
- BREN 94513 596-C7
100 HER 94547 569-J4
900 CCCo 94525 550-D5
JUNIPER DR
- LFYT 94549 611-A6
- SRMN 94583 693-H1
- ORIN 94563 611-A6
3800 CNCD 94519 593-A1
3900 CNCD 94519 573-B7
JUNIPER LN
- WLCK 94597 612-C3
JUNIPER ST
- BREN 94513 596-C7
JUNIPER WY
- MRGA 94556 651-D1
JUSTIN PL
3600 ANT 94509 595-B1
JUSTIN WY
3000 CNCD 94520 572-F6
JUSTIN MORGAN DR
- CCCo 94507 632-J5

K

K ST
100 BEN 94510 551-B5
200 ANT 94509 575-C4
400 MRTZ 94553 571-E5
W K ST
100 BEN 94510 551-A4
800 BEN 94510 550-H3
KAHRS AV
400 PLHL 94523 592-B6
KAIMU DR
200 CCCo 94553 572-C7
KAINS AV
400 ALB 94706 609-D6
1100 BERK 94706 609-D6
1300 BERK 94702 609-D6
KAISER CT
- ANT 94531 595-F4
KAISER WY
- ANT 94531 595-G5
KAISER CREEK RD
- AlaC 94546 651-H6
- AlaC 94546 652-A6
- CCCo 94556 652-A6
KAISER QUARRY RD
- CCCo 94521 613-F1
- CCCo 94598 613-F1
- CNCD 94521 613-F1
- CNCD 94598 613-F1
1100 CNCD 94521 593-F7
1100 CNCD 94598 593-F7
1100 CCCo 94521 593-F7
1100 CCCo 94598 593-F7
KAITLIN PL
1100 CNCD 94518 592-J4
KAITLYN LN
200 CCCo 94506 654-C5
KALAMA RD
- ANT 94509 595-D1
KALE CT
1400 OAKL 94561 576-E7
KALES AV
5400 OAK 94618 630-A5
KALI CT
- OAKL 94561 596-C2
KALIMA PL
1100 CNCD 94521 593-F7
KAMP CT
3800 PLE 94588 694-F7
KAMP DR
3500 PLE 94588 694-E7
KANE CIR
800 WLCK 94598 612-G1
KANGAROO WY
4500 ANT 94531 595-H3
KANSAS CIR
1200 CNCD 94521 593-E6
KANSAS ST
3000 OAK 94602 650-E5
3500 OAK 94619 650-F6
KAPHAN AV
4600 OAK 94619 650-G6
KAPIOLANI RD
3100 OAK 94613 650-G7
KARAS CT
- CNCD 94521 593-E3
KAREN CT
- VAL 94590 550-C2
- WLCK 94598 612-D4
KAREN DR
1400 BEN 94510 551-A4
KAREN LN
- WLCK 94598 612-D4
100 CCCo 94553 571-J4
KAREN RD
1100 CCCo 94806 569-A5
KAREN WY
3300 PIT 94565 574-D4
KARINA CT
- SRMN 94582 674-C4
KARKIN PL
- CLAY 94517 593-H6
KAROL LN
- PLHL 94523 592-A6
KARREN ST
2100 CNCD 94520 572-F7
KASBA ST
1600 CNCD 94518 592-E6
KASKI CT
4100 CNCD 94518 592-J5
KASKI LN
1000 CNCD 94518 592-J5
1100 CNCD 94518 593-A4
KATE LN
- OAKL 94561 576-C6
KATHERINE CT
- BREN 94513 596-D6
KATHERINE LN
1000 LFYT 94549 611-H6
KATHLEEN DR
200 PLHL 94523 592-B4
KATHRYN DR
- PLHL 94523 592-C5
KATHY LN
- MRTZ 94553 591-G3
KATIE CT
- PLHL 94523 592-C6
KATIE LN
4200 PLE 94588 694-E7
KATRINA CT
- ORIN 94563 610-G3
KATY WY
1500 BREN 94513 616-D3
KAUAI CT
300 SRMN 94582 653-E7
KAURI CT
3900 CNCD 94521 593-A3
KAVANAGH RD
2500 CCCo 94806 569-B6
KAWAI LN
- PLHL 94523 591-J3
KAY AV
1400 OAKL 94561 596-D2
2700 CNCD 94520 572-E7
KAY CT
- OAKL 94561 596-D2
KAY DR
- VAL 94590 550-C2
KAY RD
1400 CCCo 94806 569-A6
1400 RCH 94806 569-A6
KAY ANN CT
500 CCCo 94803 589-F3
KAYLA PL
100 BREN 94513 596-G6
KAYSER CT
- CCCo 94596 612-E7
KAYWOOD DR
1700 CNCD 94521 593-C2
KAZAR CT
- MRGA 94556 651-E2
KAZEBEER LN
- WLCK 94597 612-C3
KEAN AV
500 ANT 94509 575-E6
KEARNEY AV
5000 OAK 94602 650-F3

CONTRA COSTA

STREET Block City ZIP Pg-Grid

KEARNEY ST
400 ELCR 94530 609-B1
1000 RCH 94801 588-G5
2100 ELCR 94530 589-B7
KEARSARGE CT
4300 CNCD 94518 593-A6
KEARSTI CT
- OAKL 94561 596-H2
KEATS CIR
200 PLHL 94523 592-B7
KEAVENY CT
- WLCK 94597 612-A3
KEB RD
- OAK 94605 651-B7
KEEFER CT
- PDMT 94610 650-A1
KEEGAN ST
- DBLN 94568 694-G4
KEEL CT
- CCCo 94513 617-E7
100 PIT 94565 574-A2
KEELER AV
700 BERK 94708 609-H5
KEEPSAKE WY
- BREN 94561 596-D4
KEGAN LN
5100 OAKL 94561 576-C6
KEITH AV
1000 BERK 94708 609-H6
5800 OAK 94618 630-A5
KEITH CT
- OAKL 94561 596-H2
600 WLCK 94597 612-A2
KEITH DR
- ORIN 94563 631-B2
1100 CNCD 94518 592-J5
3000 RCH 94803 589-E1
KEITH PTH
- RCH 94803 589-E1
KELL CT
100 CCCo 94507 632-D2
KELLER RIDGE DR
4700 CLAY 94517 593-J5
4800 CLAY 94517 594-A5
KELLEY AV
2500 SPAB 94806 588-H2
KELLEY CT
900 LFYT 94549 611-J6
1200 PIN 94564 569-D5
2100 PIT 94565 574-F4
KELLEYBROOK WY
- SRMN 94582 674-B3
KELLIE ANN CT
- CCCo 94549 591-H7
- ORIN 94563 631-A1
KELLOGG CREEK RD
3200 CCCo 94514 637-E1
KELLY AV
600 MRTZ 94553 571-F5
700 CCCo 94553 571-F5
KELLY LN
100 DNVL 94526 653-B4
KELLYN CT
300 BEN 94510 551-C1
KELOBRA CT
100 WLCK 94598 612-J1
KELOK WY
- CLAY 94517 593-J6
- CLAY 94517 594-A5
KELROSE CT
5500 CNCD 94521 593-F5
KELSEY CT
- CCCo 94565 573-C1
- PLHL 94523 592-A6
KELSEY LN
5000 OAKL 94561 576-C6
KELSEY ST
1200 RCH 94801 588-F4
KELSEY PEAK CT
- ANT 94531 595-F4
KELSEY PEAK WY
- ANT 94531 595-F4
KELSO RD
14000 AlaC 94551 (657-G5 See Page 638)
14100 AlaC 94551 (658-A6 See Page 638)
S KELSO RD
17500 SJCo 95391 (658-D4 See Page 638)
W KELSO RD
19500 SJCo 95391 (658-D7 See Page 638)
KELVIN CT
900 CCCo 94803 569-D7
KELVIN RD
700 CCCo 94803 569-D6
KEMLINE CT
- CCCo 94507 632-G6
KEMP CT
- CCCo 94507 632-H3
KEMP LN
- CCCo 94507 632-J4
KENDALL AV
- CCCo 94525 550-C5
KENDALL CT
1200 CCCo 94595 612-A6
4800 MRTZ 94553 571-G7
KENDALL LN
- DNVL 94526 632-H7
KENDALL RD
100 CCCo 94595 612-A6
KENDREE ST
2000 ANT 94509 574-J6
KENELAND WY
3800 PLE 94588 694-F5
KENILWORTH AV
6700 ELCR 94530 609-C1
KENILWORTH CT
- CCCo 94707 609-F4
900 WLCK 94596 632-F1
KENILWORTH DR
- CCCo 94707 609-F2
KENILWORTH RD
7000 OAK 94705 630-C3
KENILWORTH WY
- CCCo 94582 674-A2
KENMARE CT
500 PIN 94564 569-C5
KENMORE AV
500 OAK 94610 650-A2
KENMORE CT
- ORIN 94563 630-J4
KENMORE DR
5000 CNCD 94521 593-D4
KENNEDY ST
500 OAK 94606 650-A7
KENNEDY WY
2400 ANT 94509 574-H5
3800 CCCo 94553 571-H4
KENNETH CT
- CCCo 94565 573-F1
KENNETH LN
- OAKL 94561 596-B1

KENNEY DR
2500 CCCo 94806 569-B6
KENSINGTON AV
6300 CCCo 94805 589-C6
KENSINGTON CIR
- HER 94547 569-F3
KENSINGTON CT
- BREN 94513 616-F2
- CCCo 94507 632-J5
- CCCo 94707 609-F2
2400 ANT 94509 595-A2
4100 CNCD 94521 593-A4
KENSINGTON DR
4000 CNCD 94521 593-A4
KENSINGTON RD
- CCCo 94805 609-F2
- ELCR 94530 609-F2
- CCCo 94707 609-F2
KENSINGTON PARK RD
- CCCo 94708 609-F3
KENSTON CT
- CLAY 94517 593-G7
KENSTON DR
900 CLAY 94517 593-G7
KENT CT
- MRGA 94556 631-F5
8300 ELCR 94530 609-D1
KENT DR
1600 BREN 94513 616-C4
8300 ELCR 94530 609-D1
KENT PL
- BREN 94513 616-D3
200 SRMN 94583 693-G1
KENT RD
- OAK 94705 630-C4
KENT WY
1500 CNCD 94521 593-D4
7500 SRMN 94583 693-G1
KENTFIELD CT
- CCCo 94507 632-J2
100 MRTZ 94553 571-J7
KENTON CT
700 PLHL 94523 591-J3
2100 OAKL 94561 576-C6
2200 WLCK 94596 632-F2
KENTUCKY AV
400 BERK 94707 609-G4
KENTUCKY DR
1200 CNCD 94521 593-E6
KENTWOOD WY
7900 PLE 94588 693-H7
KENWAL RD
1000 CNCD 94521 593-E6
KENWICK DR
- SRMN 94582 674-B3
KENWOOD CT
- OAKL 94561 576-D5
KENWOOD DR
1800 CNCD 94519 573-A7
KENWOOD LN
- DNVL 94526 652-J1
KENWYN RD
500 OAK 94606 650-A4
600 OAK 94610 650-A4
KENYON AV
- CCCo 94708 609-F3
KEONCREST DR
1500 BERK 94702 609-F7
KEPNER CT
500 ANT 94509 595-E1
KEPPLER AV
- DBLN 94568 694-C4
KERLEY CT
- CCCo 94598 612-F4
KERMAN DR
100 CNCD 94518 592-H3
KERN CT
3900 PLE 94588 694-A7
KERN ST
600 RCH 94805 589-B5
2700 ELCR 94530 589-B6
4100 ANT 94531 595-J1
KERNER BLVD
2300 SRFL 94901 587-A3
KERN MOUNTAIN WY
- ANT 94531 595-E4
KERR AV
- CCCo 94707 609-F2
KERRI ANN DR
1000 MRTZ 94553 571-H6
KERRISON LN
- CCCo 94549 611-H2
KERRY CT
- DBLN 94568 694-A4
- CCCo 94806 569-C5
KESSERLING RD
3800 LFYT 94549 611-D4
KESSLER LN
- OAKL 94561 596-E3
KESTREL CT
- CNCD 94521 593-B6
KESWICK CT
- OAK 94611 650-F1
KESWICK LN
1900 CNCD 94518 592-F6
KETCH CT
800 CCCo 94572 569-J2
KETCH DR
800 CCCo 94572 569-J2
KETELSEN DR
- MRGA 94556 651-E1
KETTLE ROCK CT
1900 ANT 94531 595-F3
KEVIN CT
- PLHL 94523 592-B6
- WLCK 94596 612-F6
400 SRMN 94583 673-F5
KEVIN DR
- CCCo 94565 573-F1
KEVIN PL
100 MRTZ 94553 571-H5
3500 CNCD 94519 592-J1
3500 CNCD 94519 593-A1
KEVIN RD
2500 CCCo 94806 569-B5
KEY BLVD
600 RCH 94805 589-B6
1800 ELCR 94530 609-B1
1900 ELCR 94530 589-B7
KEY ROUTE BLVD
500 ALB 94706 609-E6
1100 BERK 94706 609-E6
KEYSTONE LP
- CCCo 94513 617-G4
KEYSTONE WY
- BREN 94513 596-C6
KEYWOOD CT
1300 CNCD 94521 593-E5
KHARTOUM ST
100 CCCo 94553 572-C7
KIKI CT
400 PLHL 94523 592-A3
KIKI DR
500 PLHL 94523 592-A3

KILARNEY LN
1100 WLCK 94598 612-F1
KILAUEA ST
3300 CNCD 94519 572-H6
KILB RANCH DR
- PLE 94588 693-G6
N KILBRIDE LN
- DBLN 94568 694-G3
S KILBRIDE LN
- DBLN 94568 694-G3
KILBURN CT
500 CCCo 94520 572-G1
KILBURN ST
100 CCCo 94520 572-G1
KILBURN WY
- OAKL 94561 596-D2
KILCREASE CIR
1200 CCCo 94803 569-C7
KILCULLIN CT
11800 DBLN 94568 693-G4
KILDARA
7200 DBLN 94568 693-G4
KILDARE WY
1100 PIN 94564 569-C5
KILGO CT
- PLHL 94523 592-A4
KILKENNY DR
- DBLN 94568 694-A4
KILKENNY WY
900 PIN 94564 569-C5
KILLARNEY RD
2600 CCCo 94806 569-C5
KILLDEER CT
3900 ANT 94509 594-J2
KILLDEER DR
3700 ANT 94509 594-J1
KILLIAN ST
- DBLN 94568 694-E4
KILPATRICK CT
2500 SRMN 94583 673-B2
KILPATRICK DR
100 SRMN 94583 673-B2
KILRUSH AV
7500 DBLN 94568 693-G2
KILRUSH CT
1300 PIN 94564 569-D5
KIM CT
- BEN 94510 551-B4
- MRTZ 94553 571-E7
KIM RD
3300 LFYT 94549 591-G7
KIM ST
400 CCCo 94565 573-F1
KIMBALL AV
9000 SRMN 94583 693-H1
KIMBALL CT
- ANT 94509 575-E5
1400 CNCD 94518 592-J3
KIMBALL WY
3400 CNCD 94518 592-J3
KIMBERLEY CT
- OAK 94611 650-F1
KIMBERLEY PL
- CCCo 94507 632-H6
- DNVL 94526 632-H6
4000 CNCD 94521 592-J4
4000 CNCD 94521 593-A4
KIMBERLIN HEIGHTS DR
- OAK 94619 650-H4
KIMBERLY CIR
300 PLHL 94523 592-A4
KIMBERLY DR
- MRGA 94556 631-D3
KIMBERWICKE CT
300 CCCo 94507 633-C5
KINCHELOE CT
3300 LFYT 94549 611-G3
KING AV
- PDMT 94611 650-C2
100 PDMT 94610 650-C2
KING CT
1100 ELCR 94530 609-E2
KING DR
200 CCCo 94595 612-A7
900 ELCR 94530 609-E2
KING ST
800 OAK 94606 650-A7
KING WY
6400 DBLN 94568 693-J3
KINGFISHER ST
- BREN 94513 596-G7
KINGRIDGE CT
1900 WLCK 94596 612-G7
KINGS CT
- CCCo 94565 573-E1
KINGS PL
5200 RCH 94804 609-B3
KINGS RD
800 PIT 94565 574-E5
KINGSBERRY PL
200 PIT 94565 574-B5
KINGSBRIDGE CT
- CCCo 94583 673-B5
KINGS CANYON WY
- OAKL 94561 596-J2
KINGS CROWN CT
- MRGA 94556 631-F4
KINGSDALE DR
100 CCCo 94596 632-F1
100 WLCK 94596 632-F1
KINGSFORD CT
- PIT 94565 574-C4
KINGSFORD DR
400 MRGA 94556 631-E6
KINGSLAND AV
2700 OAK 94619 650-F7
KINGSLAND PL
- OAK 94619 650-F7
KINGSLEY CT
100 PLHL 94523 592-A5
KINGSLEY PL
300 SRMN 94583 673-F6
3100 LFYT 94549 631-J3
KINGSLEY ST
3600 OAK 94610 650-B4
KINGSLY DR
1500 PIT 94565 574-E7
KINGSMILL TER
- DBLN 94568 694-F2
KINGS OAK PL
- CCCo 94597 612-D2
KINGSROW
- CNCD 94518 592-G4
KINGSTON AV
300 MRTZ 94553 571-E5
700 PDMT 94611 650-A1
KINGSTON CT
200 MRTZ 94553 571-F5
KINGSTON DR
400 DNVL 94506 653-J6
KINGSTON PL
- CCCo 94597 612-D2
- PIT 94565 574-B5

KINGSTON PL
7100 DBLN 94568 693-G5
KINGSTON RD
- CCCo 94707 609-F4
KINGSTON WY
200 WLCK 94597 612-C2
KINGSWOOD
- PIT 94565 574-C6
KINGSWOOD CIR
100 CCCo 94588 654-E5
KINGSWOOD CT
200 CCCo 94588 654-E5
KINGSWOOD DR
4300 CNCD 94518 592-J5
4300 CNCD 94518 593-A5
4500 CCCo 94588 654-D5
KINGSWOOD LN
300 CCCo 94588 654-E5
KINGSWOOD PL
500 CCCo 94588 654-D5
KINGWOOD RD
- OAK 94619 650-H5
KINKEAD WY
- ALB 94710 609-D6
KINNE BLVD
- CNCD 94520 572-G3
KINNEY CT
- PLHL 94523 592-A6
KINNEY DR
2600 CCCo 94595 612-A6
2700 LFYT 94549 612-A6
2800 CCCo 94595 611-J6
KINO CT
- DBLN 94568 694-G5
KINROSS CT
1400 WLCK 94598 612-E3
KINROSS DR
100 SRFL 94901 587-B1
500 WLCK 94598 612-D3
KINSTON CT
- MRGA 94556 631-D7
KINVARRA CT
- SRMN 94582 674-B3
KIOWA CT
2600 WLCK 94598 612-H3
5100 ANT 94531 595-H5
KIPLING CT
700 RCH 94803 589-H3
1000 CNCD 94518 592-J5
KIPLING DR
5800 RCH 94803 589-H3
KIPPY CT
- MRGA 94556 631-G5
KIRBY CT
400 WLCK 94598 612-J2
KIRBY LN
3100 WLCK 94598 612-J2
KIRK CT
- CCCo 94507 652-G1
KIRK LN
- ANT 94531 596-A2
5100 SPAB 94806 589-A4
5100 SPAB 94805 589-A4
KIRKCALDY CT
3600 PLE 94588 694-F5
KIRKCALDY ST
3100 PLE 94588 694-F5
KIRKCREST CT
- DNVL 94526 652-G1
- CCCo 94507 652-G1
KIRKCREST LN
900 DNVL 94526 652-G1
KIRKCREST RD
700 DNVL 94526 652-G1
800 CCCo 94507 652-G1
KIRKER PASS RD
1500 CNCD 94521 593-F5
1500 CLAY 94517 593-F5
2100 CCCo 94517 593-F5
2100 CCCo 94521 593-F5
2900 CCCo 94517 594-A2
3100 CCCo 94565 594-A2
4900 CCCo 94565 574-C7
KIRKMAN RD
- BREN 94513 616-G2
KIRKPATRICK DR
- CCCo 94803 569-E7
KIRKSTONE CT
- SRMN 94582 674-B3
KIRKWOOD CT
- CCCo 94521 593-E2
KIRKWOOD DR
5400 CNCD 94521 593-G4
KISKA CT
3300 CNCD 94519 572-H7
KISMET CT
500 WLCK 94597 592-D7
KISTER CIR
500 CCCo 94803 569-E7
KITCHENER CT
2800 OAK 94602 650-F4
KITE WY
3900 ANT 94509 594-J1
KITE HAWK LN
- CCCo 94513 596-J6
- CCCo 94513 597-B6
KITE HILL RD
600 ORIN 94563 610-H6
KITE HILL TER
500 ORIN 94563 610-H6
KIT FOX CT
400 WLCK 94598 613-A2
KITOOSH CT
- CCCo 94507 632-G5
KITTERY AV
3000 SRMN 94583 673-G6
KITTERY PL
200 SRMN 94583 673-F6
KITTERY WY
900 PIN 94564 569-C5
KITTIE LN
1500 CCCo 94553 571-J5
KITTIWAKE RD
- ORIN 94563 610-F5
KIWANIS ST
3300 OAK 94602 650-F5
KLAMATH
100 PIT 94565 574-A3
KLAMATH CT
300 MRTZ 94553 571-J7
4600 PLE 94566 694-D7
KLAMATH ST
100 CCCo 94565 573-H2
3500 OAK 94602 650-G4
KLAMATH WOODS PL
3400 CNCD 94518 592-H6
KLEMETSON DR
9200 PLE 94588 693-G6
KLENGEL ST
1100 ANT 94509 575-C5
KLIER DR
1700 CNCD 94518 592-F6
KLOSE WY
3100 RCH 94806 569-B7

KNARLWOOD RD
4700 OAKL 94561 576-B7
KNICKERBOCKER LN
- ORIN 94563 630-H2
KNIGHTSBRIDGE CT
- BREN 94513 616-G3
KNIGHTSEN AV
3000 CCCo 94513 597-B3
3100 CCCo 94548 597-A1
3300 CCCo 94561 597-A1
4200 CCCo 94561 577-A7
KNIGHTWOOD CT
1000 WLCK 94596 632-F1
KNOBCONE CT
2200 RCH 94803 589-F4
KNOBCONE DR
5600 RCH 94803 589-F4
KNOLL AV
4200 OAK 94619 650-H6
KNOLL CT
- HER 94547 569-H4
KNOLL DR
- CCCo 94556 651-F3
- MRGA 94556 651-F3
2900 CNCD 94520 572-F6
KNOLLBROOK DR
7700 PLE 94588 693-H7
KNOLL CREST CT
- SRMN 94582 673-J6
KNOLLCREST CT
200 MRTZ 94553 591-H3
4800 ANT 94531 595-J3
KNOLLCREST DR
4800 ANT 94531 595-J4
KNOLLPARK CIR
4500 ANT 94531 595-H4
KNOLLPARK CT
4600 ANT 94531 595-H3
KNOLLPARK WY
4800 ANT 94531 595-J4
KNOLL RIDGE WY
- OAK 94619 651-C6
KNOLLS CREEK DR
- CCCo 94506 654-D5
KNOLLVIEW CT
- MRTZ 94553 571-G5
KNOLLVIEW DR
4200 CCCo 94506 654-C5
KNOLLWOOD CT
500 CCCo 94506 654-D5
KNOLLWOOD DR
2100 MRTZ 94553 571-J7
KNOLLWOOD PL
7500 DBLN 94568 693-H2
KNOTT AV
6200 ELCR 94530 609-B1
KNOWLAND AV
3100 OAK 94619 650-F7
KNOX AV
2100 PIT 94565 574-C4
KNOX DR
- LFYT 94549 611-A7
KNOX LN
2300 OAKL 94561 596-B1
KNOX GATE CT
4800 PLE 94588 694-D7
KOA CT
2200 ANT 94509 595-F3
KOALA CT
- CCCo 94596 632-F1
KOALA WY
4500 ANT 94531 595-H3
KOCH
- CNCD 94518 592-G4
KODIAK ST
3100 ANT 94531 595-H2
KOHNEN WY
- DBLN 94568 694-F3
KOLB PL
7200 DBLN 94568 693-F4
KONA CIR
100 PIT 94565 574-E5
KORBEL CT
- OAKL 94561 576-D5
KRAL PL
3900 PLE 94588 694-E7
KRAMER CT
800 BREN 94513 616-J2
KRAUSE CT
4200 PLE 94588 694-E7
KRAUSE ST
4300 PLE 94588 694-E7
KRAUSE TER
- MRTZ 94553 571-J5
KRISTEN LN
100 CCCo 94803 589-E1
KRISTIN LN
- ORIN 94563 631-B2
KRISTIN WY
1200 WLCK 94596 632-G1
KRISVIEW CT
700 MRTZ 94553 571-F5
KROHN LN
- OAK 94611 630-E7
KRONA CT
- CNCD 94521 593-F7
KRONA LN
1100 CNCD 94521 593-F7
KRUEGER DR
2200 CNCD 94520 572-F6
KUBICEK WY
- BREN 94513 596-F7
KUHL CT
- WLCK 94597 612-B3
KUHNLE AV
4000 OAK 94605 650-H7
KULANI LN
- PLHL 94523 591-J5
KUSHNER WY
4900 ANT 94531 595-J3
KUSS RD
100 CCCo 94526 652-G1
100 DNVL 94526 652-G1
KUWAIT WY
200 CCCo 94553 572-C7
KYER ST
2400 PIN 94564 569-F6

L

L ST
100 ANT 94509 575-C4
1100 CCCo 94509 575-C4
E L ST
200 BEN 94510 551-C5
W L ST
800 BEN 94510 551-A4
900 BEN 94510 550-J3
LABECCA CT
2700 PLE 94588 694-H4
LA BOLSA RD
- WLCK 94598 612-E5
LA BOLSITA
- ORIN 94563 610-F7

LA BONITA WY
1600 CNCD 94519 592-J2
LABRADOR LN
400 BEN 94510 551-B4
LABRADOR ST
2200 CNCD 94520 572-F5
LABRADOR WY
300 BEN 94510 551-B4
LA BREA WY
200 OAKL 94561 576-E7
LABRO CT
- CCCo 94582 674-B2
LA CADENA
1900 CCCo 94528 633-E7
LA CALLE
1700 CNCD 94521 593-E4
LA CAMINITA
1500 LFYT 94549 611-F2
LA CAMPANA
- ORIN 94563 610-H5
LA CANADA CT
- CLAY 94517 614-A2
2400 PIN 94564 569-G7
LA CANADA RD
3200 LFYT 94549 611-H7
LA CANYADA DR
800 VAL 94591 550-C1
LA CASA CT
1500 WLCK 94598 612-F4
4500 OAKL 94561 576-C7
LA CASA DR
4600 OAKL 94561 576-C7
LA CASA VIA
- WLCK 94598 612-E3
200 CCCo 94598 612-F4
LA CASITA LN
- CCCo 94595 612-A7
LACASSIE AV
1500 WLCK 94596 612-B4
LACASSIE CT
- WLCK 94596 612-B5
LACEWOOD WY
- DNVL 94506 653-H4
LACEY CT
1100 CNCD 94520 592-E5
LACEY LN
1100 CNCD 94520 592-E4
LA CHESNAYE
- ORIN 94563 610-F2
LA CIMA RD
3900 CCCo 94803 589-C3
LA CINTILLA
- ORIN 94563 610-G5
LACKLAND CT
100 CCCo 94507 633-D6
LACKLAND DR
1800 CCCo 94507 633-D5
LA COLINA DR
100 CCCo 94507 632-E5
LA COLINA RD
3800 CCCo 94803 589-C3
LACONIA WY
300 SRMN 94582 673-G3
LA COPITA CT
500 SRMN 94583 673-C2
LA CORSO CIR
- WLCK 94598 612-F2
LA CORSO CT
1900 WLCK 94598 612-E2
LA CORSO DR
500 WLCK 94598 612-E1
LA CORSO PL
2000 WLCK 94598 612-F2
LA CORTE BONITA
5100 CNCD 94521 593-E4
LA COSTA DR
- BREN 94513 616-A3
LA COUNT LN
- SRMN 94583 673-E6
LA CRESENTA RD
3900 CCCo 94803 589-C3
LA CRESTA AV
3900 OAK 94602 650-D4
LA CRESTA RD
- ORIN 94563 631-B4
LA CRUZ AV
- BEN 94510 551-C4
LA CUESTA
- ORIN 94563 610-G6
LA CUESTA AV
2600 OAK 94611 650-E2
S LADERA
800 RCH 94804 608-H1
LADERA CT
11500 DBLN 94568 693-F4
LADERA CTE
800 SRMN 94583 673-B3
LADERA DR
100 VAL 94591 550-D1
7500 DBLN 94568 693-F4
LA ENCINAL
- ORIN 94563 610-E7
LA ENCINAL CT
100 CLAY 94517 614-A2
LA ESPIRAL
- ORIN 94563 610-G5
LAFAYETTE AV
100 PDMT 94611 650-C2
100 PDMT 94610 650-C2
LAFAYETTE CIR
- LFYT 94549 611-E6
LAFAYETTE CT
7800 PLE 94588 693-H7
LAFAYETTE DR
2200 ANT 94509 595-A1
2300 ANT 94509 594-J2
LAFAYETTE ST
600 MRTZ 94553 571-E2
LA FOND LN
- ORIN 94563 631-A4
LA FONTE CT
- BREN 94513 596-D6
LA FONTE DR
- BREN 94513 596-D6
LA GONDA CT
- DNVL 94526 632-J7
- DNVL 94526 652-J1
LA GONDA WY
400 DNVL 94526 652-J1
500 DNVL 94526 632-H7
LAGOON CIR
300 HER 94547 570-B6
LAGOON CT
1200 BREN 94513 596-E7
LAGOS CT
500 SRMN 94583 673-C3
LAGUNA AV
3400 OAK 94602 650-E4
LAGUNA CIR
- PIT 94565 574-D7
2000 CNCD 94520 592-F3
LAGUNA CT
5200 CCCo 94514 617-H4

LAGUNA PL
- PIT 94565 574-D7
9700 SRMN 94583 673-F7
LAGUNA ST
1600 CNCD 94520 592-F2
2200 MRTZ 94553 571-G2
2700 CNCD 94518 592-G2
LAGUNA WY
3300 OAK 94602 650-D5
LAGUNITA CT
- MRTZ 94553 571-H4
LAGUNITAS AV
6200 ELCR 94530 589-C7
LA HABRA
- PIT 94565 574-A3
LAHOMA CT
- CCCo 94507 632-H3
LA HONDA AV
2600 ELCR 94530 589-C6
LA HONDA CT
- CCCo 94803 589-F3
- CLAY 94517 614-A2
LA HONDA RD
5000 CCCo 94803 589-F3
LAILA LN
- CNCD 94518 592-G4
LAIR WY
- ANT 94531 595-J2
LAIRD DR
- MRGA 94556 631-D4
LAIRD LN
600 CCCo 94549 591-G4
LAIRD PL
- BREN 94513 596-G5
LA JOLLA CT
- DNVL 94526 633-B7
LA JOLLA DR
2800 ANT 94531 595-H2
LA JOLLA ST
400 VAL 94591 550-D1
LAKE AV
- PDMT 94611 650-A1
100 CCCo 94572 549-H7
500 CCCo 94572 569-H1
N LAKE CIR
- ANT 94509 575-F5
LAKE CT
300 MRTZ 94553 592-A1
E LAKE CT
- ANT 94509 575-F5
S LAKE CT
- ANT 94509 575-F5
W LAKE CT
- ANT 94509 575-F5
LAKE DR
- DBLN 94568 693-J2
- RCH 94805 609-G3
200 CCCo 94708 609-G3
E LAKE DR
- ANT 94509 575-F5
N LAKE DR
- DBLN 94568 693-J1
- ANT 94509 575-F4
S LAKE DR
- DBLN 94568 693-J2
- ANT 94509 575-F5
W LAKE DR
- ANT 94509 575-E5
LAKE PKWY
400 OAK 94610 650-A2
LAKE PL
- WLCK 94598 612-E4
E LAKE PL
- ANT 94509 575-F5
S LAKE PL
- ANT 94509 575-F5
W LAKE PL
100 ANT 94509 575-E5
LAKE ST
- PIT 94565 574-D6
1000 SPAB 94806 588-H1
LAKE WY
- WLCK 94598 612-E4
- CCCo 94598 612-E4
LAKE BROOK CT
300 MRTZ 94553 592-A1
LAKE CREST CT
2200 MRTZ 94553 592-A1
LAKE DALE CT
300 MRTZ 94553 592-A1
LAKEFIELD CT
- DNVL 94506 654-A5
LAKEFIELD PL
200 MRGA 94556 651-E3
2200 MRTZ 94553 592-A1
N LAKEFRONT LP
- CCCo 94513 617-F2
S LAKEFRONT LP
- CCCo 94513 617-F3
LAKE HERMAN RD
- BEN 94510 551-H1
- SolC 94510 551-H1
LAKEHURST DR
300 MRTZ 94553 592-A1
LAKE MEAD CT
- SRMN 94582 653-F7
LAKE MEAD PL
700 SRMN 94582 653-F7
LAKE MEADOW CIR
2300 MRTZ 94553 592-A1
LAKE MEADOW CT
300 MRTZ 94553 592-A1
LAKEMONT DR
700 SRMN 94582 673-F1
3100 SRMN 94582 653-F7
LAKEMONT PL
700 SRMN 94582 653-F7
700 SRMN 94582 673-F1
LAKEMONT WY
700 SRMN 94582 673-F1
LAKE OAKS CT
2200 MRTZ 94553 592-A1
LAKE PARK AV
400 OAK 94610 650-A3
LAKE PARK CT
2300 MRTZ 94553 592-A1
LAKE PARK DR
- CCCo 94561 597-E1
LAKE REED CT
300 MRTZ 94553 592-A1
LAKERIDGE CT
- SRMN 94582 653-F7
LAKE RIDGE DR
2200 MRTZ 94553 592-A1
LAKERIDGE LN
100 SRMN 94582 653-F7
LAKERIDGE PL
1000 SRMN 94582 653-F7
LAKERIDGE WY
200 SRMN 94582 653-F7
LAKESHIRE DR
1900 WLCK 94595 632-A2
LAKESHORE AV
600 OAK 94610 650-A2

CONTRA COSTA COUNTY STREET INDEX

STREET	Block	City	ZIP	Pg-Grid
LAKESHORE CIR	-	CCCo	94513	617-F4
LAKESHORE CT	100	RCH	94804	608-H3
E LAKESHORE DR	4000	SRMN	94582	653-F7
	5000	SRMN	94582	673-F1
W LAKESHORE DR	4000	SRMN	94582	653-F7
LAKESIDE CT	300	MRTZ	94553	571-J7
	700	DNVL	94526	653-E6
LAKESIDE DR	3800	RCH	94806	569-A6
LAKESPRING CT	-	OAKL	94561	576-E6
LAKESPRING DR	5300	OAKL	94561	576-E6
LAKESPRING PL	300	OAKL	94561	576-E6
LAKEVIEW AV	-	PDMT	94611	650-C1
LAKEVIEW CIR	-	SRMN	94582	673-F1
	1100	PIT	94565	574-G4
	6000	SRMN	94582	653-F7
LAKE VIEW CT	-	RCH	94806	569-A7
LAKEVIEW CT	-	CCCo	94561	597-E1
LAKE VIEW DR	-	CCCo	94565	553-D7
LAKEVIEW DR	-	BREN	94513	616-A2
	5000	SRMN	94582	653-G7
LAKE VIEW PL	1900	MRTZ	94553	592-A1
LAKEVIEW PL	300	CCCo	94507	632-H4
	1400	CNCD	94520	592-F3
LAKE VILLA CT	2200	MRTZ	94553	592-A1
LAKEWOOD CIR	400	WLCK	94598	612-E5
LAKEWOOD DR	-	CCCo	94561	597-E1
LAKEWOOD PL	1600	PIT	94565	574-G6
	2200	MRTZ	94553	592-A1
LAKEWOOD RD	-	WLCK	94598	612-D4
	100	CCCo	94598	612-D4
LA LOMA AV	1300	BERK	94708	609-J7
	1600	BERK	94709	609-J7
LAM CT	-	CCCo	94707	609-F2
	-	CCCo	94530	609-F2
LA MADRONAL	-	ORIN	94563	610-F7
LA MANCHA CT	500	DNVL	94526	653-B3
LA MAR CT	2200	CNCD	94518	592-G5
LA MAR DR	2200	CNCD	94518	592-G5
LAMBERT CT	-	BREN	94513	616-E2
LAMBERT RD	4000	CCCo	94803	589-C2
LAMBETH LN	1700	CNCD	94518	592-F6
LAMBETH SQ	-	MRGA	94556	631-F5
LAMBRECHT CT	8600	ELCR	94530	609-E1
LA MESA CT	-	WLCK	94598	612-E5
LA MESA LN	-	WLCK	94598	612-E5
LA MIRADA DR	2100	RCH	94803	589-D3
	3600	CNCD	94519	592-J1
	3600	CNCD	94519	593-A1
LA MIRANDA PL	3800	PIT	94565	574-B5
LAMKIN LN	-	PLHL	94523	592-D6
LAMONT WY	400	DNVL	94526	652-H2
LAMOUR LN	-	WLCK	94598	612-D5
LAMP CT	-	MRGA	94556	651-G2
LAMPLIGHT CT	1800	WLCK	94597	611-H3
LANA LN	3400	LFYT	94549	611-F6
LANAI CT	5500	CCCo	94514	617-J6
LANAI DR	3400	SRMN	94582	673-E1
	3400	SRMN	94582	653-E7
LANCASHIRE DR	1200	CNCD	94518	592-J3
LANCASHIRE PL	3300	CNCD	94518	592-H7
LANCASTER	-	HER	94547	569-F1
LANCASTER CIR	-	CCCo	94565	573-G3
LANCASTER CT	-	WLCK	94595	612-C7
	-	CCCo	94507	632-J2
	6900	DBLN	94568	693-J3
LANCASTER DR	600	LFYT	94549	631-J2
	2200	SPAB	94806	588-H1
	2300	RCH	94806	588-J1
LANCASTER LN	200	CCCo	94565	573-G3
LANCASTER RD	100	WLCK	94595	612-C6
	100	WLCK	94595	632-D1
	6800	DBLN	94568	693-J3
LANCE CT	-	MRTZ	94553	592-A1
	-	MRGA	94556	631-E7
LANCELOT CT	800	DNVL	94526	653-B2
LANCELOT DR	4200	CNCD	94521	593-A4
LANDAHL CT	1400	BEN	94510	551-A3
LANDALE AV	7500	DBLN	94568	693-G3
LANDANA CT	3800	CNCD	94519	573-A7
LANDANA DR	-	CNCD	94519	572-J7
	1700	CNCD	94519	593-A1
	1800	CNCD	94519	573-A7
LANDER DR	-	MRTZ	94553	571-F7
LANDER PL	200	SRMN	94583	673-G7
LANDINI LN	1100	CNCD	94520	592-F4
LANDIS AV	300	OAKL	94561	576-E7
LANDMARK WY	-	DBLN	94568	694-G3
LANDOVER CT	-	BREN	94513	596-D6
LANDSDOWNE ST	-	DBLN	94568	694-F4
LANDSDOWNE WY	-	SRMN	94582	674-B4
LANDVALE RD Rt#-13	300	OAK	94618	630-B4
LANE AV	200	CCCo	94565	573-G3
LANE CT	-	OAK	94611	630-C7
LANE DR	2900	CNCD	94518	592-G5
LANG ST	1400	MRTZ	94553	571-E2
LANGDON CT	-	PDMT	94611	650-B1
LANGFORD CT	5500	CNCD	94521	593-H4
LANGHORNE DR	-	SRMN	94582	674-B4
LANGLEY CT	3000	ANT	94509	575-C7
LANGLIE CT	200	WLCK	94598	612-J2
	1100	CCCo	94572	570-A1
LANGLIE WY	1000	CCCo	94572	570-A1
LANGMUIR CT	7500	DBLN	94568	693-J2
LANGMUIR LN	6800	DBLN	94568	693-J2
LANGTON CT	-	SRMN	94582	674-B3
LANGTON DR	-	SRMN	94582	674-B3
LANI KAI DR	1300	CNCD	94520	592-F2
LANITOS CT	2000	ANT	94509	595-B2
LA NORIA	-	ORIN	94563	610-G6
LANSDOWN CT	-	BREN	94513	616-B1
	3100	PLE	94588	694-F6
LANSFORD CT	-	SRMN	94582	673-F2
LANTANA WY	-	SRMN	94582	673-H1
LANTERN BAY	-	HER	94547	569-H1
LANWAY CT	1900	WLCK	94597	612-A2
	3000	CNCD	94518	592-H5
LA ORINDA PL	2000	CNCD	94518	592-F5
LA PALOMA CT	-	CCCo	94803	589-C1
LA PALOMA PL	-	CCCo	94803	589-C1
LA PALOMA RD	400	CCCo	94803	589-C1
LA PAZ AV	10000	SRMN	94583	673-G5
LA PAZ CT	300	SRMN	94583	673-B2
LA PERA CIR	200	DNVL	94526	653-C7
LA PERA CT	-	DNVL	94526	653-D7
LA PERGOLA DR	-	BREN	94513	596-D6
LAPIS CT	100	HER	94547	569-H5
LA PLAYA CT	3100	CCCo	94549	611-J1
LA PLAYA DR	1700	CCCo	94549	611-J1
LA PLAZA	-	ORIN	94563	610-G7
LA PRENDA AV	-	BEN	94510	551-D4
LA PUERTA DR	100	SPAB	94806	568-J7
LA PUNTA	-	ORIN	94563	610-H5
LA QUESTA DR	100	DNVL	94526	653-B2
LA QUINTA	100	MRGA	94556	631-D7
LA QUINTA CT	200	WLCK	94598	612-J2
	400	DNVL	94526	653-D6
LARAMIE AV	2800	SRMN	94583	673-F7
LARAMIE GATE CIR	2600	PLE	94566	694-D7
LARAMIE GATE CT	4600	PLE	94566	694-D7
LARCH AV	1000	MRGA	94556	631-D7
	1000	MRGA	94556	651-E1
LARCH CT	2700	ANT	94509	595-F3
	3700	CNCD	94519	593-A1
LARCH LN	-	MRGA	94556	651-E1
LARCH WY	2500	ANT	94509	595-F3
LARCHMONT LN	1100	SPAB	94806	588-H1
LARCHWOOD CT	-	OAKL	94561	596-G1
LARCHWOOD PL	-	OAKL	94561	596-F1
LAREDO CT	100	SRMN	94583	673-C2
LA REINA ST	2400	PIN	94564	569-G7
LARGO CT	2000	CCCo	94514	617-H6
LARIAT CT	-	WLCK	94596	632-G2
	100	OAKL	94561	596-B1
LARIAT LN	2100	WLCK	94596	632-F2
	4400	OAKL	94561	596-B1
	4400	OAKL	94561	576-A7
LARK CT	100	CCCo	94507	632-F6
LARK LN	200	CCCo	94507	632-E6
	1400	CNCD	94521	593-C4
LARK PL	-	CCCo	94507	632-F6
LARK CREEK LN	-	LFYT	94549	611-G3
LARKDALE AV	7200	DBLN	94568	693-H3
LARKEY LN	2500	WLCK	94597	612-A2
S LARKEY LN	2200	WLCK	94597	612-A3
LARKEY CREEK PL	-	WLCK	94597	612-A1
LARKIN CT	-	ANT	94531	595-F5
	300	BEN	94510	551-A2
LARKIN DR	300	BEN	94510	551-A2
	400	BEN	94510	550-J2
LARKSPUR BAY	-	HER	94547	569-G1
LARKSPUR CT	-	BREN	94513	596-H7
	-	BREN	94513	616-H1
	1500	OAKL	94561	596-D1
	1800	CNCD	94519	573-A7
LARKSPUR DR	2700	ANT	94531	575-H7
	3000	ANT	94531	595-H1
	3800	CNCD	94519	572-J7
	3800	CNCD	94519	573-A7
E LARKSPUR DR	3900	ANT	94531	595-H1
LARKSPUR LN	-	BREN	94513	616-H1
	2100	SRMN	94582	653-J7
LARKSPUR PL	-	RCH	94806	569-A6
LARKSPUR RD	900	OAK	94610	650-B3
LARKSPUR FERRY	-	CMAD	-	587-B6
	-	MrnC	-	587-B6
	-	TBRN	-	587-B6
LARKSTONE CT	-	DNVL	94526	653-C3
LARKWOOD CIR	100	DNVL	94526	653-C6
LARKWOOD CT	1000	CNCD	94521	593-D5
LARMER CT	300	PDMT	94610	650-B1
LARRY LN	-	OAK	94611	650-F2
LARRY PL	1000	CNCD	94518	592-E5
N LARWIN AV	-	CNCD	94518	593-B5
	100	CNCD	94521	593-B5
S LARWIN AV	4300	CNCD	94521	593-A5
LA SALLE AV	-	PDMT	94611	650-D1
	-	PDMT	94610	650-C2
	2800	CNCD	94520	572-E6
	5600	OAK	94611	650-D1
LA SALLE CT	-	PDMT	94611	650-D2
	300	PIN	94564	569-E3
	1900	WLCK	94598	592-E7
LA SALLE DR	-	MRGA	94556	631-D3
	2100	WLCK	94598	592-E7
	2300	PIN	94564	569-E3
LA SALLE ST	1600	MRTZ	94553	571-F3
LAS ANIMAS DR	6600	MRTZ	94553	591-H4
LAS AROMAS	-	ORIN	94563	610-H6
	2600	OAK	94611	650-F2
LASATA CT	100	DNVL	94526	653-F4
LA SATA DR	-	BREN	94513	596-B7
	-	BREN	94513	616-B1
LAS BARRANCAS DR	600	DNVL	94526	652-H1
LAS CASCADAS	-	ORIN	94563	610-H6
LAS COLINAS DR	-	BREN	94513	596-C7
LAS DUNAS AV	100	OAKL	94561	576-E7
LA SENDA	-	ORIN	94563	610-G5
LA SERENA AV	-	CCCo	94507	632-F6
LA SERENA CT	-	CCCo	94507	632-F6
LA SERENA WY	-	CCCo	94507	632-F6
LAS FLORES CT	-	OAK	94611	630-F7
LAS FLORES DR	-	BREN	94513	596-C7
LAS HUERTAS RD	3300	LFYT	94549	611-G7
	3300	LFYT	94549	631-H1
LAS JUNTAS ST	600	MRTZ	94553	571-E3
LAS JUNTAS WY	-	WLCK	94523	592-D7
	-	WLCK	94597	592-D7
	100	WLCK	94597	612-D1
	1200	CCCo	94597	612-D1
LAS LOMAS CT	2000	CNCD	94519	572-J6
LAS LOMAS PL	300	CCCo	94598	612-G4
	300	WLCK	94598	612-G4
LAS LOMAS WY	-	WLCK	94598	612-G4
	500	CCCo	94598	612-G4
LAS MESAS PTH	-	ORIN	94563	610-F7
LAS MONTANAS CT	-	BREN	94513	596-C6
LAS MORADAS CIR	-	SPAB	94806	588-J3
LA SOMBRA CT	-	ORIN	94563	631-B4
LA SONOMA CT	-	CCCo	94507	632-F6
LA SONOMA DR	-	CCCo	94507	632-G6
LA SONOMA WY	100	CCCo	94507	632-F6
LAS PALMAS CT	11200	DBLN	94568	693-F5
LAS PALMAS WY	7300	DBLN	94568	693-F5
LAS PALOMAS	-	ORIN	94563	610-H5
LAS PIEDRAS	-	ORIN	94563	610-E7
W LAS POSITAS BLVD	3100	PLE	94588	694-E6
	4300	PLE	94566	694-E6
LAS QUEBRADAS LN	-	CCCo	94507	632-H4
LAS RAMBLAS DR	1800	CNCD	94521	593-F4
LASSEN CT	1800	ANT	94509	575-F5
	5600	CLAY	94517	593-F6
LASSEN DR	400	MRTZ	94553	572-A7
	3800	PIT	94565	574-D5
LASSEN ST	600	RCH	94805	589-A5
	1000	BERK	94707	609-G6
	1000	SPAB	94805	589-A5
	5700	ELCR	94530	609-C5
LASSEN WY	-	OAKL	94561	596-H1
	2600	PIN	94564	569-H7
LASSO CIR	200	SRMN	94583	673-B3
LAST AV	100	RCH	94801	588-G5
LAS TRAMPAS RD	-	LFYT	94549	631-H1
	700	LFYT	94549	611-H7
	1500	CCCo	94507	632-E6
LAS VEGAS CT	-	ORIN	94563	610-J5
LAS VEGAS RD	-	ORIN	94563	610-J5
LATE HORIZON PL	1800	WLCK	94595	632-B1
LATERA CT	-	SRMN	94582	674-B3
LATHAM CT	-	BREN	94513	596-E6
LATHAM LN	-	BERK	94708	609-J6
LATHAM ST	100	PDMT	94611	650-A1
LA TIERRA BUENA	300	DNVL	94526	653-A1
LATIMER PL	-	CCCo	94596	612-F7
LATOUR LN	1400	CNCD	94521	593-C4
LATTERI CT	1600	CNCD	94519	593-A2
LAUGHLIN RD	700	AlaC	94551	676-E7
LAURA CIR	-	PIT	94565	574-E5
LAURA CT	1900	CCCo	94521	593-D2
LAURA DR	4700	CCCo	94521	593-D3
LAURA WY	100	ORIN	94563	631-B2
LAURA ALICE WY	1000	CNCD	94520	572-E5
LAURA ANN CT	500	CCCo	94565	573-F1
LAUREL AV	400	PIN	94564	569-E4
	1500	CCCo	94805	589-C6
	3200	OAK	94602	650-E5
LAUREL CT	-	DNVL	94526	653-A2
	-	MRTZ	94553	571-E7
	500	BEN	94510	551-A1
	800	CCCo	94572	569-J1
LAUREL DR	-	DNVL	94526	653-A2
	700	CCCo	94596	612-F7
	1000	LFYT	94549	611-F5
	4900	CCCo	94521	593-E3
	5100	CNCD	94521	593-F4
LAUREL LN	-	BERK	94707	609-F5
	-	CCCo	94803	589-D2
	-	RCH	94803	589-D2
	1200	LFYT	94549	611-H4
LAUREL RD	-	ANT	94531	595-J3
	-	ANT	94531	596-A2
	100	OAKL	94561	596-B1
LAUREL ST	1100	BERK	94708	609-H6
	1100	PIT	94565	574-F2
LAUREL CANYON TR	-	CCCo	94708	609-H3
LAUREL CREEK DR	5800	PLE	94588	693-G6
LAUREL CREEK WY	7600	PLE	94588	693-H6
LAURELGLEN CT	200	CCCo	94506	654-C5
LAUREL GROVE CT	-	DNVL	94526	653-A3
LAUREL OAK LN	1200	CCCo	94595	612-A6
LAUREL TREE DR	1000	CNCD	94521	593-C7
	1000	CNCD	94521	613-C1
LAURELVIEW CT	1800	CNCD	94521	593-F4
LAURELWOOD CT	800	ANT	94509	575-F7
	800	ANT	94509	595-F1
LAURELWOOD DR	-	HER	94547	569-H2
	100	DNVL	94506	653-H4
LAURELWOOD PL	5700	CNCD	94521	593-G7
LAURENCE CT	3000	CNCD	94520	572-F6
LAURENITA WY	1400	CCCo	94507	632-E4
LAURIAN CT	100	BREN	94513	616-F3
LAURIAN LN	100	BREN	94513	616-F3
LAURIE DR	-	BREN	94513	596-F7
LAURISTON CT	8000	OAK	94611	630-E5
LAURITZEN LN	-	OAKL	94561	576-A4
LAURSEN CT	2700	PLE	94588	694-H4
LAVA CT	300	MRTZ	94553	571-J7
LAVA FALLS CT	-	SRMN	94582	653-G7
LAVA FALLS PL	-	SRMN	94582	653-G7
LA VELLE CT	-	DNVL	94526	653-C7
LAVENDER CT	2400	WLCK	94596	632-G2
LAVENDER DR	2400	WLCK	94596	632-G3
LAVENDER PL	-	HER	94547	569-J4
LAVENIDA	-	ORIN	94563	631-B6
LA VEREDA	1500	BERK	94708	609-J7
	1600	BERK	94709	609-J7
LAVERNE CT	1500	CNCD	94521	593-D4
LAVERNE WY	1500	CNCD	94521	593-D4
LAVEROCK LN	1200	CCCo	94507	632-F3
LAVETTA WY	1500	CNCD	94519	593-A3
	1500	CNCD	94521	593-A3
LA VINA	300	CCCo	94553	572-C6
LAVINA CT	-	ORIN	94563	631-B4
LA VINA WY	200	OAKL	94561	576-E7
LA VISTA AV	1200	CNCD	94521	592-J3
	1200	CNCD	94521	593-A3
LA VISTA CT	-	CNCD	94521	592-J3
	-	WLCK	94598	612-E5
	4500	OAKL	94561	576-C7
LA VISTA DR	4600	OAKL	94561	576-B7
LA VISTA RD	300	WLCK	94598	612-E5
	400	CCCo	94598	612-F4
LA VISTA WY	-	DNVL	94506	653-G4
LA VUELTA	-	ORIN	94563	610-H5
LAWLOR CT	-	PIT	94565	573-H3
LAWNVIEW CIR	100	DNVL	94526	653-C6
LAWNVIEW CT	-	PIT	94565	574-F5
LAWRENCE AV	-	ANT	94509	575-C6
LAWRENCE CT	7300	ELCR	94530	609-D2
LAWRENCE LN	-	BREN	94513	616-H2
LAWRENCE RD	1000	DNVL	94506	654-B6
	1500	DNVL	94506	674-B1
LAWRENCE ST	1200	ELCR	94530	609-D1
LAWRENCE WY	2000	WLCK	94596	612-C4
	2300	WLCK	94597	612-C4
LAWSON CT	4400	CNCD	94521	593-B5
LAWSON RD	-	CCCo	94707	609-F2
LAWTON AV	5500	OAK	94618	630-A5
LAWTON CT	-	SRMN	94583	673-E5
LAWTON ST	200	ANT	94509	575-D6
LAWTON WY	12900	SRMN	94583	673-E5
LAYMAN CT	-	WLCK	94596	632-E1
LAZY LN	-	CCCo	94513	597-D5
LDU DR	-	CCCo	94553	571-F3
	-	MRTZ	94553	571-F3
LEA CT	200	CCCo	94806	569-B4
LEABIG LN	-	CCCo	94553	572-A4
LEACH ST	4300	OAK	94602	650-C3
LEAFIELD RD	100	DNVL	94506	653-F2
LEAFWOOD CIR	3500	ANT	94531	595-H1
LEANING OAK CT	2700	WLCK	94598	612-H4
LEANING OAK DR	1200	BREN	94513	596-D7
LEANNE LN	100	CNCD	94518	592-G4
LEARY CT	-	SRMN	94582	674-A1
LEATHERWOOD CT	4400	CNCD	94521	593-B5
LEDGEFERN CT	-	SRMN	94582	673-H2
LEDGEFERN WY	-	SRMN	94582	673-H2
LEDGEWOOD CT	-	ANT	94531	596-A4
LEDGEWOOD TER	-	DBLN	94568	694-F2
LEE LN	900	CNCD	94518	592-F7
LEE ST	-	WLCK	94595	612-C7
LEE WY	-	BREN	94513	596-G6
LEEDS CT	2800	RCH	94806	589-A2
LEEDS CT E	-	DNVL	94526	653-C3
LEEDS CT W	-	DNVL	94526	653-C3
LEES PL	100	MRTZ	94553	571-H5
LEEWARD CT	100	VAL	94591	550-F3
LEEWARD PL	100	PIT	94565	574-A2
LEEWARD RD	-	CCCo	94561	597-E1
LEEWARD WY	-	PIT	94565	573-J2
	-	PIT	94565	574-A2
LEEWARD GLEN RD	-	LFYT	94549	631-J3
	-	LFYT	94549	632-A3
LEEWOOD PL	4300	CNCD	94521	593-C2
LEEWOOD WY	1700	CNCD	94521	593-C2
LE FEBVRE WY	1700	PIN	94564	569-E4
LEFEBVRE WY	4800	ANT	94531	595-J4
LEGACY CT	-	CCCo	94507	632-J3
LEGACY DR	-	CCCo	94507	632-J2
LEGACY ST	800	BREN	94513	616-J2
LEGARO LN	1700	CNCD	94521	593-C2
LEGEND LN	1400	BREN	94513	596-D6
LEGENDARY CT	-	PLE	94588	693-H7
LEGENDS PL	-	RCH	94806	568-J6
LEGER CT	3000	PLE	94588	694-F6
LEGGETT ST	1100	ANT	94509	575-C5
LEGION CT	4000	LFYT	94549	611-B7
LE GRAND AV	-	CCCo	94514	637-D3
LEHIGH VALLEY CIR	1000	DNVL	94526	653-B5
LEHIGH VALLEY PL	1000	DNVL	94526	653-B5
LEIGH CT	-	SRMN	94582	673-E2
	1200	CCCo	94597	612-D1
LEILA CT	-	OAKL	94561	596-B1
LEILANI LN	-	CCCo	94507	632-D1
LEIMERT BLVD	1300	OAK	94602	650-D3
LEIMERT PL	1700	OAK	94602	650-D3
LEISURE LN	-	WLCK	94595	632-B3
	-	CCCo	94803	589-E3
LEITH LN	-	SRFL	94901	587-B1
LEITRIM WY	-	ANT	94531	596-B4
LEJEAN WY	400	WLCK	94597	592-D7
LEKE WY	3900	RCH	94806	568-G7
LELA WY	900	ANT	94509	575-F6
LELAND DR	900	LFYT	94549	611-J6
LELAND LN	100	PIT	94565	574-D4
LELAND RD	2200	PIT	94565	574-E4
E LELAND RD	300	PIT	94565	574-D4
W LELAND RD	-	PIT	94565	574-A4
	800	PIT	94565	573-E3
	1400	CCCo	94565	573-F3
LELAND WY	2000	CNCD	94520	592-E3
LEMAY CT	500	ANT	94509	595-E1
LEMAY WY	500	ANT	94509	595-E1
LEMON ST	-	BREN	94513	596-D4
	900	CCCo	94553	571-F4
LEMONTREE CT	2400	ANT	94509	575-B6
LEMONTREE WY	2100	ANT	94509	575-B5
LEMONWOOD DR	1700	CNCD	94519	593-B1
LEMONWOOD PL	-	PIT	94565	574-C6
LENA CT	100	CCCo	94523	592-B2
LENELLE CT	-	MRGA	94556	631-E2
LENELLE DR	3700	MRGA	94556	631-E2
LENEVE PL	900	ELCR	94530	609-F1
LENNON LN	100	WLCK	94598	612-G1
LENORA RD	5300	RCH	94803	589-F4
LENOX CT	400	PLHL	94523	592-A7
LENOX RD	-	CCCo	94707	609-F4
LENTIN WY	-	CCCo	94582	674-B2
LENZIE CT	-	BREN	94513	616-A1
LEO LN	-	ANT	94509	574-J6
	1800	CNCD	94521	593-F4
LEO ST	1200	RCH	94801	588-F4
LEO WY	800	OAK	94611	630-C6
LEON CT	400	CCCo	94517	614-G7
	400	CCCo	94517	634-G1
LEON DR	400	CCCo	94517	614-G7
	4100	CCCo	94517	634-G1
LEON WY	-	CCCo	94517	614-H7
	-	CCCo	94517	634-H1
LEONA CT	100	CCCo	94507	632-G7
LEONA ST	5500	OAK	94605	650-H7
	5500	OAK	94619	650-H6
LEONARD CT	-	DNVL	94526	633-C7
LEONARD DR	100	CCCo	94518	592-H3
LEOPARD WY	-	ANT	94531	595-G2
LE ROY AV	1600	BERK	94709	609-H7
	1700	BERK	94709	609-H7
LEROY AV	300	PIN	94564	569-E4
LEROY LN	800	WLCK	94597	612-A3
LEROY WY	3900	LFYT	94549	611-C5
LESLEE LN	100	ORIN	94563	631-B4
LESLIE AV	2300	CCCo	94553	571-F4
LESLIE DR	-	PIT	94565	574-D2
	1800	PLHL	94523	592-C5
LESLYN LN	-	LFYT	94549	611-F3
LESNICK LN	1400	WLCK	94597	612-C2
LESTER RD	3000	MRTZ	94553	571-G7
LETHBRIDGE CT	2900	PLE	94588	694-F6
LETHRAM CT	4100	PLE	94588	694-E7
LETICIA CT	4000	ANT	94509	574-H5
LETTIA RD	1000	CCCo	94806	568-J5
	1000	CCCo	94806	569-A5
LEUE CT	-	CNCD	94519	592-J1
LEV LN	4100	CNCD	94518	592-J5
LEVANT CT	-	SRMN	94582	673-G3
LEVEE RD	300	CCCo	94565	553-D7
E LEVEE RD	-	MRTZ	94553	571-F2
LEVISTON AV	7500	ELCR	94530	609-E3
LEWES CT	-	SRMN	94582	673-G4
LEWIS AV	7200	DBLN	94568	693-H4
LEWIS LN	-	CCCo	94507	632-G6
	1300	PIN	94564	569-E5
LEWIS ST	-	HER	94547	569-G3
LEWIS WY	5500	CNCD	94521	593-F7
	5700	CNCD	94521	613-G1
LEXFORD PL	-	OAK	94619	651-B7
LEXFORD RD	-	PDMT	94611	650-D2
LEXINGTON AV	400	ELCR	94530	609-B1
LEXINGTON CT	-	BREN	94513	616-G3
	3600	ANT	94509	595-C3
LEXINGTON PL	-	WLCK	94597	612-B1
	900	SRMN	94583	673-G6
LEXINGTON RD	200	CCCo	94707	609-F4
	1300	CNCD	94520	592-E3
LEXINGTON ST	-	BREN	94513	616-G3
LEXINGTON WY	3400	ANT	94509	595-B1
LEYTE ST	-	CNCD	94520	572-H3
LEYTON DR	-	SRMN	94582	674-B3
LHT LP	-	CCCo	94553	571-F3
LIAHONA CT	-	PLHL	94523	592-B6
LIAHONA LN	1600	DNVL	94526	633-C6
LIANA LN	1600	CNCD	94519	592-J2
LIBBY CT	3500	OAK	94619	650-F5
LIBERATI RD	1100	CNCD	94518	592-J4
LIBERTA CT	-	DNVL	94526	653-B4
LIBERTA PL	-	DNVL	94526	653-B4
LIBERTY CT	-	ELCR	94530	609-C3
	3500	ANT	94509	595-C3
LIBERTY LN	-	BREN	94513	616-D2
	-	WLCK	94597	612-A2
LIBERTY ST	400	ELCR	94530	609-B1
LIBERTY WY	3500	ANT	94509	595-C3
LICHEN CT	1300	CNCD	94521	593-D5
LIDO CIR	900	CCCo	94514	617-H4
LIESE AV	3100	OAK	94619	650-E6
LIGGETT DR	6500	OAK	94611	650-D1
LIGHTHOUSE CT	300	HER	94547	570-B6
	300	PIT	94565	573-J3
LIGHTHOUSE LN	-	RCH	94804	608-H3
LIGHTHOUSE PL	3900	CCCo	94514	617-G6
LIGHTSHIP CT	100	VAL	94591	550-F2
LIGHTWOOD DR	5300	CNCD	94521	593-E5
LIKELY CT	200	CCCo	94507	632-H3
LIKELY DR	200	CCCo	94507	632-H3
LIKINS AV	5300	MRTZ	94553	591-F1
LIKINS CT	5500	MRTZ	94553	591-G2
LILA LN	-	CCCo	94803	589-F3
LILAC CIR	100	HER	94547	570-B4
LILAC CT	-	BREN	94513	616-H2
	400	BEN	94510	551-A1
	1800	CNCD	94521	593-C2
LILAC DR	100	DNVL	94506	653-F4
	100	HER	94547	570-B4
	1500	WLCK	94595	612-C6
	1500	WLCK	94596	612-C6
	1700	CCCo	94595	612-C6
LILAC LN	1600	ANT	94509	575-B5
LILAC ST	2500	OAK	94601	650-E7
	2600	OAK	94619	650-E7
LILAC RIDGE RD	-	SRMN	94582	673-F1
LILA DEL CT	1000	CNCD	94518	592-E6
LILLIAN DR	4000	CNCD	94521	593-A3
LILLIAN ST	1200	CCCo	94525	550-D5
LILY CT	-	DNVL	94506	654-B5
	-	RCH	94806	569-A6
	-	CCCo	94595	612-B6
	100	HER	94547	569-J4
	2700	ANT	94531	575-G7

STREET Block City ZIP Pg-Grid

LILY ST
- CCCo 94595 612-B7
3600 OAK 94619 650-F6
LIMERICK CT
7300 DBLN 94568 693-H2
LIMERICK RD
400 PIN 94564 569-C5
2600 CCCo 94806 569-C5
LIMERICK WY
7300 DBLN 94568 693-H2
LIMERIDGE DR
1100 CCCo 94518 593-A6
LIMESTONE DR
4100 ANT 94509 595-F2
LIMESTONE RD
2900 CCCo 94507 632-H4
LIME TREE CT
3400 WLCK 94598 592-J7
LIMEWOOD CT
1700 CNCD 94521 593-D3
LIMEWOOD DR
400 ANT 94509 575-E7
400 ANT 94509 595-E1
4700 CNCD 94521 593-D3
LIMEWOOD PL
- PLHL 94523 611-J1
1500 PIT 94565 574-G5
LINCOLN AV
- PDMT 94611 650-C1
600 RCH 94801 588-F5
700 BREN 94513 616-G1
1100 WLCK 94596 612-C5
2300 RCH 94804 588-H5
2400 OAK 94602 650-E4
6400 ELCR 94530 609-D4
LINCOLN DR
4500 CNCD 94521 593-D2
LINCOLN LN
2700 ANT 94509 575-E7
LINCOLN PK
- PIN 94564 569-B4
LINCOLN RD E
200 VAL 94591 550-C1
LINCOLN RD W
- VAL 94590 550-C1
LINCOLN ST
- BEN 94510 551-D6
- CCCo 94553 571-F3
- CCCo 94565 573-H2
LINCOLN WY
3600 LFYT 94549 611-E5
4900 OAK 94602 650-F3
LINCOLNSHIRE CT
- LFYT 94549 612-A6
LINCOLNSHIRE DR
- OAK 94618 630-A6
LIND CT
- ORIN 94563 631-B2
LINDA AV
100 PDMT 94611 650-A1
400 PDMT 94610 650-A1
LINDA CT
- DNVL 94526 652-J2
- PLHL 94523 591-J5
LINDA DR
100 CCCo 94806 569-A5
1700 PLHL 94523 592-C5
LINDA LN
100 PLHL 94523 592-A5
200 PLHL 94523 591-J5
LINDA MESA AV
- DNVL 94526 652-J2
100 DNVL 94526 653-A2
LINDA VISTA
- ORIN 94563 610-G6
LINDA VISTA AV
- BEN 94510 551-D4
100 PIT 94565 554-D7
100 PIT 94565 574-D1
LINDA VISTA CT
900 SRMN 94582 674-A6
LINDA VISTA DR
1300 ELCR 94530 609-E1
LINDA VISTA LN
3100 LFYT 94549 611-J5
LINDBERG ST
2100 ANT 94509 575-D6
LINDBERGH DR
1600 CNCD 94521 593-A2
LINDELL DR
1000 CCCo 94803 569-D6
1100 CCCo 94596 612-F7
1200 CCCo 94596 632-F1
LINDELL LN
500 SRMN 94582 673-J6
LINDEMANN RD
- CCCo 94514 (658-C3 See Page 638)
6000 AlaC 94551 (658-C4 See Page 638)
LINDEN CT
- CCCo 94507 632-F5
LINDEN DR
1100 CNCD 94520 592-D4
LINDEN LN
600 MRTZ 94553 571-E6
3800 CCCo 94803 589-D3
LINDEN PL
1700 ANT 94509 575-B5
LINDEN ST
- BREN 94513 596-D7
- DBLN 94568 694-D3
LINDEN WY
1700 ANT 94509 575-B5
LINDENWOOD DR
1600 CNCD 94521 593-B2
LINDERO DR
3600 CNCD 94519 593-A1
LINDLEY CT
3100 ANT 94509 575-E7
LINDLEY DR
400 ANT 94509 575-E7
LINDO ST
1700 BEN 94510 551-D5
LINDRICK CT
- BREN 94513 616-B1
LINDSEY CT
- PLHL 94523 592-A4
1000 LFYT 94549 611-J6
LINDSEY DR
100 MRTZ 94553 591-G2
LINFORD CT
- PIT 94565 574-F7
LINFORD PL
500 SRMN 94583 673-F6
LIN GATE CT
2600 PLE 94566 694-D7
LIN GATE ST
4500 PLE 94566 694-D7
LINHARES LN
100 CCCo 94507 632-F5
LINKS DR
- RCH 94806 568-H5
LINNET AV
4200 OAK 94602 650-E4
LINNET CT
1900 CNCD 94518 592-G6
LINSCHEID DR
- PIT 94565 574-C5
LINTON PL
1400 MRTZ 94553 591-H1
LINTON TER
1400 MRTZ 94553 571-H7
1400 MRTZ 94553 591-H1
LINUS PAULING DR
200 HER 94547 569-G2
LINWOOD AV
3700 OAK 94602 650-C4
LION CT
2900 CNCD 94520 572-E7
LIPPIZANER LN
3100 CCCo 94598 613-A4
LIPTON PL
100 SRMN 94583 673-F7
LIPTON ST
1500 ANT 94509 575-G5
1700 CCCo 94509 575-G5
LIQUIDAMBER CT
- CCCo 94506 654-A3
LIQUIDAMBER PL
700 CCCo 94506 654-A3
LIRA CT
800 SRMN 94583 673-F5
LISA CT
- BREN 94513 616-E1
- CCCo 94507 633-C5
500 CCCo 94803 589-D1
3100 ANT 94509 575-E7
7700 DBLN 94568 693-H3
LISA LN
- MRGA 94556 651-F2
2200 PLHL 94523 592-D6
LISA ANN CT
500 CCCo 94565 573-F1
LISA ANN ST
400 CCCo 94565 573-F1
LISA LEE LN
100 CNCD 94518 592-G4
LISBOA CT
700 WLCK 94598 612-H3
LISBON AV
900 OAK 94601 650-B7
LISBON LN
- ANT 94509 574-J6
LISCOME WY
3500 CNCD 94518 592-H4
LISLIN CT
1000 PIT 94565 573-H3
LITINA CT
1600 CCCo 94507 632-E4
LITINA DR
1500 CCCo 94507 632-E4
LITINA LN
- CCCo 94507 632-E4
LITKE LN
- WLCK 94597 612-B1
LITTLE LN
600 PLHL 94523 592-A4
3400 LFYT 94549 611-G6
4000 CNCD 94521 593-A3
LITTLE CREEK CT
- SRMN 94583 673-B1
LITTLE JOHN WY
1800 BREN 94513 596-G6
LITTLE PEAK CT
400 RCH 94803 589-G3
LITTLE RANCH CIR
- OAKL 94561 596-F2
LITTLE RIVER CT
100 VAL 94591 550-E2
LITTLE RIVER ST
500 VAL 94591 550-E2
LITTLEWOOD DR
- PDMT 94611 650-C1
LITWIN DR
800 CNCD 94518 592-G6
LIVE OAK AV
1700 CNCD 94521 593-A2
3900 ANT 94531 596-B2
3900 OAKL 94561 596-B1
4300 OAKL 94561 576-B7
LIVE OAK CIR
- CCCo 94803 569-G7
- CCCo 94803 589-F1
LIVE OAK CT
300 MRTZ 94553 571-G5
2000 ANT 94509 595-F2
3000 CCCo 94506 653-J2
5100 PLE 94588 693-J7
LIVEOAK CT
- PIT 94565 573-G3
LIVE OAK DR
200 CCCo 94506 653-J1
200 CCCo 94506 654-A2
LIVE OAK LN
- ORIN 94563 630-H2
- CCCo 94506 653-J2
700 PIN 94564 569-C3
LIVE OAK PL
- CCCo 94506 653-J1
LIVE OAK RD
- OAK 94705 630-B3
LIVE OAK WY
- CCCo 94506 653-J2
1600 WLCK 94596 612-C5
N LIVERMORE AV
400 AlaC 94551 675-G6
LIVERPOOL
- HER 94547 569-J3
LIVERPOOL ST
100 DNVL 94506 653-H5
LIVINGSTON CT
- CCCo 94513 617-F2
LIVINGSTON LN
1600 RCH 94801 588-G6
LIVINGSTON ST
2000 OAK 94606 650-A7
LIVORNA RD
100 CCCo 94507 632-F3
900 WLCK 94596 632-H3
LIVORNA RD E
400 CCCo 94507 632-J2
LIVORNA RD W
1200 CCCo 94507 632-E3
LIVORNA HEIGHTS RD
200 CCCo 94507 632-G3
LIZANN DR
1000 LFYT 94549 611-A6
LLOYD LN
- ORIN 94563 630-H2
LLOYD WISE DR
- CNCD 94520 592-E1
LOBELIA CT
2700 ANT 94531 575-G7
LOBOS AV
700 RCH 94801 588-C7
LOBOS CT
200 RCH 94801 588-C7
LOCARNO PTH
100 OAK 94618 630-B5
LOCH LN
2200 WLCK 94598 612-G2
LOCHGREEN WY
- DBLN 94568 694-G2
LOCHINVAR RD
- SRFL 94901 587-B1
LOCH LOMOND CT
- DNVL 94526 652-J3
LOCH LOMOND DR
- SRFL 94901 587-B1
LOCH LOMOND WY
100 DNVL 94526 652-J3
LOCHMOOR CT
600 DNVL 94526 653-D7
LOCKE CT
1800 OAKL 94561 596-C1
LOCKHART ST
- DBLN 94568 694-G3
LOCKSLY LN
- SRFL 94901 587-B1
LOCKWOOD LN
100 PLHL 94523 592-A5
LOCUST CT
100 HER 94547 570-A5
7000 DBLN 94568 693-H2
LOCUST DR
- PIT 94565 574-D2
LOCUST PL
8100 DBLN 94568 693-H1
LOCUST ST
1100 WLCK 94596 612-C5
LODATO CT
5100 CNCD 94521 593-E4
LODATO WY
1800 CNCD 94521 593-E4
LODGE CT
- OAK 94611 630-F6
LODGE DR
- CNCD 94520 592-F4
LODGE HILL CT
- DNVL 94526 653-C4
LODGEPOLE CT
300 MRTZ 94553 571-F5
LOEFFLER LN
1400 CNCD 94521 593-A3
LOFTUS RD
- CCCo 94565 573-J2
LOGAN CT
3800 CNCD 94519 593-A2
LOGAN LN
600 DNVL 94526 633-A7
LOGAN ST
2600 OAK 94601 650-C6
LOGAN WY
- BREN 94513 616-H2
LOGISTICS DR
- CCCo 94553 571-G3
LOIRE CT
100 MRTZ 94553 571-H5
LOIS AV
- PIT 94565 574-C6
LOIS CT
100 PLHL 94523 592-C4
LOIS LN
- LFYT 94549 611-E6
600 CCCo 94803 589-F4
600 OAKL 94561 576-D7
LOLA ST
- CCCo 94561 596-H4
LOLITA DR
3600 CNCD 94519 572-J7
3600 CNCD 94519 573-A7
3600 CNCD 94519 592-J1
LOMA LN
700 ANT 94509 575-C4
LOMA LINDA AV
900 CCCo 94803 569-D7
LOMA LINDA CT
- ORIN 94563 631-A3
LOMAS CANTADAS
- ORIN 94563 610-D7
100 CCCo 94708 610-D7
100 CCCo 94563 610-D7
LOMAS VERDES LN
- CCCo 94549 591-H6
LOMAS VERDES PL
- CCCo 94549 591-H6
LOMAS VERDES WY
- CCCo 94549 591-H6
LOMA VISTA
- CCCo 94597 612-A4
LOMA VISTA AV
2800 CNCD 94520 572-E6
3400 OAK 94619 650-F5
LOMA VISTA DR
- ORIN 94563 610-F7
LOMA VISTA WY
- PIT 94565 574-D2
3300 OAK 94619 650-E6
LOMBARD LN
- LFYT 94549 611-G1
LOMBARDI CIR
200 CCCo 94598 612-F5
LOMBARDO CT
3400 CNCD 94519 592-H1
LOMBARDY LN
- ORIN 94563 610-G4
LOMITAS PL
600 PIT 94565 574-E6
LOMITAS RD
- DNVL 94526 653-B2
LOMMEL CT
- CCCo 94597 612-D3
LOMOND CIR
600 SRMN 94583 673-E4
LOMOND CT
- SRMN 94583 673-F4
2300 WLCK 94598 612-G3
LOMOND LN
2200 WLCK 94598 612-G3
LOMPICO
- HER 94547 569-F4
LONDON
- HER 94547 569-J3
LONDON CIR
1400 BEN 94510 550-H2
LONDON COMS
- MRTZ 94553 571-J5
LONDON CT
- CLAY 94517 613-J2
2300 ANT 94509 595-A1
LONDON DR
500 BEN 94510 550-H2
LONDON RD
2800 OAK 94602 650-F4
LONDONDERRY CT
2100 WLCK 94596 632-H1
LONDONDERRY DR
- DBLN 94568 694-E3
LONEE CT
3100 CNCD 94518 592-H2
LONE OAK CT
- PLHL 94523 592-B5
400 BREN 94513 596-F6
LONE OAK DR
- RCH 94806 568-J6
LONE OAK RD
1700 BREN 94513 596-F6
LONE PINE CT
- CLAY 94517 594-A7
- SRMN 94582 673-E2
LONESOME RD
- DNVL 94526 652-J3
LONE TREE CT
- SRMN 94583 673-E6
LONE TREE WY
1800 ANT 94509 575-D7
1800 ANT 94509 595-D1
4100 ANT 94531 595-D1
5700 ANT 94531 596-B4
5800 BREN 94513 596-B4
6700 BREN 94561 596-E4
8000 CCCo 94561 596-G4
8000 CCCo 94513 596-E4
LONGBRANCH CT
- ANT 94531 595-J4
LONGBRANCH WY
5000 ANT 94531 595-H4
LONGBROOK WY
100 PLHL 94523 592-D4
LONG CREEK CIR
- CLAY 94517 613-J1
LONGCROFT DR
6300 OAK 94611 650-F1
LONGDALE CT
5100 ANT 94531 596-A4
LONGFELLOW DR
100 PLHL 94523 592-B7
LONGFIELD PL
100 MRGA 94556 631-F6
LONGFORD CT
1500 WLCK 94598 612-E1
LONGFORD WY
8400 DBLN 94568 693-H2
LONGHORN CT
- SRMN 94583 673-D4
3700 RCH 94803 589-G1
5000 ANT 94531 595-H4
LONGHORN DR
- SRMN 94583 673-D5
LONGHORN LN
3800 OAKL 94561 596-F1
LONGHORN WY
600 OAKL 94561 596-F2
5000 ANT 94531 595-H4
LONGLEAF CIR
- CCCo 94582 674-D4
- SRMN 94582 674-D4
LONGLEAF CT
1200 BREN 94513 616-D3
LONGLEAF DR
100 WLCK 94598 612-J1
LONGMEADOW PL
- DBLN 94568 694-F3
LONGRIDGE
- ORIN 94563 630-H1
LONGRIDGE RD
600 OAK 94610 650-A3
LONG VIEW CT
- DNVL 94526 653-B3
LONGVIEW CT
200 ANT 94509 595-D1
3300 RCH 94806 569-A7
LONGVIEW DR
2600 RCH 94806 568-J7
2600 RCH 94806 569-A7
LONGVIEW RD
2700 ANT 94509 575-B7
3000 ANT 94509 595-C1
LONGVIEW TER
200 ORIN 94563 631-A3
LONGWALK DR
6500 OAK 94611 650-G1
LONGWELL AV
4100 CCCo 94513 (636-G1 See Page 635)
LONGWOOD CT
- SRMN 94582 673-E2
6500 MRTZ 94553 591-H4
LONGWORTH
700 ORIN 94563 610-J4
LOOKOUT CT
- HER 94547 569-F3
LOOKOUT DR
- VAL 94591 550-D2
LOOKOUT POINT LP
- CCCo 94513 617-G4
LOON CT
- ANT 94531 595-J1
LOOP DR
- CCCo 94708 609-H3
LOP CENTER RD
- CCCo 94553 571-G3
LOP EAST RD
- CCCo 94553 571-G3
LOPES CT
500 PIN 94564 569-E4
LOPES LN
500 PIN 94564 569-E4
LOPEZ DR
1900 ANT 94509 575-A6
LOP NORTH RD
- CCCo 94553 571-G3
LOP SOUTH RD
- CCCo 94553 571-G3
LOP WEST RD
- CCCo 94553 571-G3
LORALEE PL
100 PLHL 94523 592-D6
LORAN CT
- CCCo 94707 609-F4
LORCA CT
- SRMN 94583 673-D3
LORD CT
600 CNCD 94518 592-E7
LOREN LN
100 OAKL 94561 596-F1
LORENZ DR
300 OAKL 94561 596-E1
LORENZETTI DR
4300 OAKL 94561 596-D1
4300 OAKL 94561 576-D7
LORENZO AV
3200 OAK 94619 650-E6
LORENZO DR
100 PLHL 94523 592-D5
LORETO CT
- MRTZ 94553 571-H5
LORETO DR
3300 SRMN 94583 673-G5
LORI DR
300 BEN 94510 551-A3
LORIE CT
100 WLCK 94597 612-B3
LORIE LN
- WLCK 94597 612-B3
LORIMER LP
- DBLN 94568 694-E3
LORINDA LN
1000 LFYT 94549 611-A5
LORING AV
- DBLN 94568 694-C3
400 CCCo 94525 550-D4
5800 CCCo 94805 589-B5
LORING WY
- BREN 94513 596-D5
LORITA AV
- PDMT 94611 630-A7
- PDMT 94611 650-A1
LORNA DR
4100 LFYT 94549 611-A4
LORNELL CT
3800 CNCD 94518 592-J3
LORRAINE AV
- PIT 94565 574-C5
LORRY CT
3400 CNCD 94520 572-F6
LOS ALAMOS CT
- CCCo 94507 632-G6
LOS ALTOS AV
100 WLCK 94598 612-E3
LOS ALTOS PL
3800 PIT 94565 574-E6
LOS ALTOS RD
- ORIN 94563 610-F5
200 CCCo 94708 609-G3
LOS ALTOS WY
2900 ANT 94509 575-B7
LOS AMIGOS DR
- ORIN 94563 610-E5
LOS ANGELES AV
1900 BERK 94707 609-G6
LOS ARABIS CIR
- LFYT 94549 611-B5
LOS ARABIS DR
3800 LFYT 94549 611-A5
LOS ARABIS LN
1000 LFYT 94549 611-C6
LOS ARBOLES
- ORIN 94563 610-F5
3800 CCCo 94803 589-C3
LOS BALCONES
100 CCCo 94507 632-H5
LOS BANOS AV
100 WLCK 94598 612-F3
LOS BANOS CT
- WLCK 94598 612-F3
LOS CERROS
- ORIN 94563 630-J3
LOS CERROS AV
- WLCK 94598 612-F3
LOS CERROS PL
- WLCK 94598 612-F3
LOS CIELOS WY
- BREN 94513 596-C6
LOS CONEJOS
- ORIN 94563 610-F7
LOS DEDOS
- ORIN 94563 610-H5
LOS FELICAS AV
200 WLCK 94598 612-F3
LOS FLORES AV
3600 CNCD 94519 572-J7
LOS GATOS CT
5400 CNCD 94521 593-F5
LOS MEDANOS ST
800 PIT 94565 574-E2
LOS NARROBOS RD
- ORIN 94563 610-E7
LOS PALOS CIR
3200 LFYT 94549 631-H1
LOS PALOS CT
1100 PIT 94565 573-H4
LOS PALOS DR
- PIT 94565 573-H4
600 LFYT 94549 631-H1
LOS PALOS MNR
700 LFYT 94549 631-H1
LOS PRADOS WY
2400 ANT 94509 594-J1
2400 ANT 94509 595-A1
LOS RANCHITOS
- CCCo 94507 632-E2
LOS RANCHITOS CT
11600 DBLN 94568 693-F3
LOS ROBLES CT
600 DNVL 94526 653-E6
LOST CANYON CT
- ANT 94531 595-C5
LOST LAKE PL
1900 MRTZ 94553 591-J1
LOST VALLEY CT
- ORIN 94563 630-J4
LOST VALLEY DR
- ORIN 94563 631-A4
- ORIN 94563 630-J4
LOS VECINOS
1400 WLCK 94598 612-E4
LOTT DR
- BREN 94513 616-H1
LOTUS CT
100 HER 94547 569-J4
2700 ANT 94531 575-G7
LOTUS ST
2600 PLE 94588 694-G6
LOU ANN PL
- PIT 94565 574-A2
LOUIS DR
1300 ANT 94509 575-E5
LOUISE CT
- MRGA 94556 651-E1
LOUISIANA DR
1300 CNCD 94521 593-E6
LOVE LN
100 DNVL 94526 652-H2
LOVEBIRD CT
- ANT 94509 594-J2
LOVEBIRD WY
- ANT 94509 594-J1
LOVEGROVE AV
1900 SPAB 94806 588-H2
LOVELAND DR
100 LFYT 94549 611-J5
LOVELL CT
1100 CNCD 94520 592-E5
LOVERIDGE CIR
500 PIT 94565 574-F5
LOVERIDGE RD
200 PIT 94565 574-H2
LOWANA CIR
1800 CCCo 94521 593-E3
LOWELL AV
2300 RCH 94804 588-H5
3400 RCH 94804 589-A5
3500 SPAB 94805 589-A5
LOWELL CT
- OAKL 94561 596-H2
200 DNVL 94526 653-E5
LOWELL DR
100 DNVL 94526 653-D5
LOWELL LN E
200 LFYT 94549 631-J3
LOWELL LN W
300 LFYT 94549 631-J3
LOWER TR
1500 CCCo 94517 614-C3
LOWER GOLDEN RAIN RD
2400 WLCK 94595 632-A1
2700 WLCK 94595 631-J1
LOWER GRAND AV
1600 PDMT 94611 650-A1
1600 PDMT 94611 630-A7
W LOWER JONES RD
15700 SJCo 95206 (598-J3 See Page 597)
LOWRY CT
- PIT 94565 574-C2
5500 CNCD 94521 593-G4
LOYOLA DR
2800 RCH 94806 589-A2
LOZOYA WY
- OAKL 94561 596-H3
LUAU DR
200 PIT 94565 574-E5
LUCANIA ST
8300 DBLN 94568 693-H2
LUCAS AV
400 RCH 94801 588-E5
2400 PIN 94564 569-F6
6500 OAK 94611 650-E1
LUCAS CIR
3100 LFYT 94549 631-J2
LUCAS CT
- LFYT 94549 631-J3
LUCAS DR
- MRGA 94556 631-E4
600 LFYT 94549 631-H2
LUCAS LN
4000 CNCD 94521 593-A4
LUCCA CT
- BREN 94513 616-C1
4100 PLE 94588 694-H4
LUCCHESI CT
4700 OAKL 94561 576-C7
LUCENA WY
2700 ANT 94509 575-A7
LUCERO CT
4200 PLE 94588 694-C5
LUCIA LN
- MRGA 94556 631-E2
LUCILLE LN
1700 PLHL 94523 592-B5
N LUCILLE LN
3300 LFYT 94549 631-G3
S LUCILLE LN
3200 LFYT 94549 631-G3
LUCILLE WY
- ORIN 94563 630-H1
LUCINDA LN
200 PLHL 94523 611-J1
200 PLHL 94523 612-A1
LUCKY DR
1500 CNCD 94519 592-J2
LUCY LN
2500 CCCo 94595 612-A6
LUDELL CT
3000 CCCo 94597 592-D7
LUDELL DR
100 CCCo 94597 592-D7
LUDLOW PL
200 SRMN 94583 673-F5
LUDWIG AV
5500 ELCR 94530 589-B7
LUELLA DR
- PLHL 94523 592-C4
LUGANO CT
600 BREN 94513 616-F3
LUNA CT
300 BREN 94513 616-E3
11600 DBLN 94568 693-F4
LUNA DR
100 VAL 94591 550-D1
LUNADA CT
- MrnC 94901 587-A1
LUNADA GN
- CCCo 94507 632-E3
LUNADA LN
2400 CCCo 94507 632-E3
LUNDHOLM AV
3600 OAK 94605 650-H7
LUNDIN LN
- BREN 94513 616-A2
LUPIN PL
- CCCo 94507 633-C4
LUPINE CT
- RCH 94806 568-J6
- CCCo 94803 569-E7
500 BEN 94510 550-J1
1300 CNCD 94521 593-D5
2800 ANT 94531 575-G7
LUPINE LN
- SRMN 94583 693-H1
100 PLHL 94523 592-B1
LUPINE RD
1800 HER 94547 569-J4
1900 HER 94547 570-A4
LUREE CT
- DNVL 94526 653-C4
LURMANN CT
- CCCo 94507 632-H5
LUSHERM CT
- CCCo 94597 612-D2
LUTHER E GIBSON FRWY I-680
- BEN - 551-E5
LUXURY DR
800 CNCD 94518 592-G5
LUZ CT
800 DNVL 94526 653-B2
LYCHEE CT
- SRMN 94583 673-G7
LYDIA LN
400 CCCo 94513 (636-B3 See Page 635)
400 CCCo 94517 (636-B3 See Page 635)
1300 CLAY 94517 593-G6
N LYDIA LN
1300 CLAY 94517 593-G6
LYLE CT
2000 MRTZ 94553 572-A7
LYMAN CT
1500 CNCD 94521 593-A3
LYMAN LN
- CCCo 94507 632-F4
LYMAN RD
3800 OAK 94602 650-D3
LYNBROOK CT
2200 PIT 94565 574-E5
5000 PLE 94588 693-H7
5500 CNCD 94521 593-E7
LYNBROOK DR
2200 PIT 94565 574-E5
LYNBROOK PL
5400 CNCD 94521 593-E7
LYNBROOK ST
- CCCo 94565 573-F1
LYNCH CT
- CNCD 94521 593-F7
- MRGA 94556 651-E1
LYNCH PL
- BEN 94510 551-C1
LYNDE ST
2800 OAK 94601 650-C6
LYNDHURST PL
- CCCo 94583 672-J4
- CCCo 94583 673-A4
LYNN AV
400 ANT 94509 575-E7
2500 CNCD 94520 592-F3
7300 ELCR 94530 609-E4
LYNN CT
900 SRMN 94583 673-F5
LYNN DR
100 BREN 94513 596-G7
1800 CNCD 94518 593-A5
2500 PIN 94564 569-D6
LYNN LN
300 DNVL 94526 652-J2
LYNNBROOK CT
- SRMN 94582 673-E2
LYNNBROOK DR
300 SRMN 94582 673-E2
LYNN CREST LN
- SRMN 94583 673-B1
LYNN DARR DR
100 MRTZ 94553 571-D3
LYNVALE LN
1800 WLCK 94597 612-B3
LYNWOOD CT
4000 CNCD 94519 593-B1
LYNWOOD DR
1600 CNCD 94521 593-C1
1700 CNCD 94519 593-B1
1700 CNCD 94519 573-A7
LYNWOOD PL
- MRGA 94556 631-D5
LYNWOOD WY
2000 ANT 94509 595-F2
LYON AV
3500 OAK 94601 650-D6
LYON CIR
2600 CNCD 94518 592-G6
LYON CT
200 DNVL 94506 654-C6
500 BEN 94510 551-A1
900 CNCD 94518 592-G5
LYRIC LN
1500 CNCD 94521 593-E5

M

M ST
400 ANT 94509 575-C4
W M ST
200 BEN 94510 551-B4
MAAS AV
500 RCH 94801 588-F1
MAAYAN PL
- BREN 94513 616-E4
MABRAY DR
- PLE 94588 693-G7
MAC CT
3500 ANT 94509 595-C1
MACADAMIA CT
- BREN 94513 616-F3
MACADAMIA LN
4400 OAKL 94561 576-G7
4400 OAKL 94561 596-G1
MACALVEY DR
- MRTZ 94553 591-H1
MACARTHUR AV
100 PIT 94565 574-D3
2500 SPAB 94806 588-H2
MACARTHUR BLVD
400 OAK 94610 650-A3
1300 OAK 94602 650-E5
3500 OAK 94619 650-E5
4900 OAK 94613 650-G7
5400 OAK 94605 650-G7
MACARTHUR FRWY I-580
- OAK - 650-D5
MACAULAY ST
1100 ANT 94509 575-C5
MACDONALD AV
300 RCH 94801 588-E6
2700 RCH 94804 588-E6
3600 RCH 94805 588-E6
3900 RCH 94805 589-A7
5300 ELCR 94530 589-B7
MACDONALD CT
- CCCo 94507 632-F5
9500 PLE 94588 693-F6
MACGREGOR PL
- DNVL 94526 653-D2
MACGREGOR RD
200 CCCo 94523 592-B2
200 PLHL 94523 592-B2
MACHADO CT
1500 CNCD 94521 593-B3
MACHADO DR
4200 CNCD 94521 593-B3
MACHADO LN
4200 OAKL 94561 576-J7
4200 OAKL 94561 596-J1
MACKENZIE PL
- DNVL 94526 653-D2
MACKIE DR
- MRTZ 94553 571-F7
MACKINNON ST
100 PDMT 94610 650-A1
MACMURTY CT
3800 CCCo 94553 571-J4
MACMURTY DR
100 CCCo 94553 571-H4
MACOMBER LN
- DNVL 94526 652-H2
MACOMBER RD
- DNVL 94526 652-H2
MACOMBER WY
- DNVL 94526 652-H2
MACPHERSON PL
- DNVL 94526 653-C2
MACY LN
- OAKL 94561 596-J3
MADEIRA WY
2800 PLHL 94523 591-J4
2800 PLHL 94523 592-A4
MADELIA PL
100 SRMN 94583 693-G1

STREET Block City ZIP Pg-Grid

MADELINE LN
- CCCo 94506 654-D6
MADELINE RD
900 CCCo 94806 569-A5
MADELINE ST
2600 OAK 94602 650-E4
MADERA AV
2800 OAK 94619 650-F7
MADERA CIR
1500 ELCR 94530 589-D7
1500 ELCR 94530 609-D1
MADERA CT
- DNVL 94526 653-C7
- OAKL 94561 576-A7
1500 ELCR 94530 609-D1
MADERA DR
1500 ELCR 94530 609-D1
8500 ELCR 94530 589-D7
MADERA LN
- ORIN 94563 610-F6
MADERA ST
- BREN 94513 616-H2
- SRFL 94901 587-A3
1700 BERK 94707 609-F6
3800 PIN 94564 569-J7
MADIGAN AV
- DBLN 94568 694-D3
800 CNCD 94518 592-H5
MADIGAN CT
800 CNCD 94518 592-H5
MADILL CIR
- ANT 94509 575-C6
MADILL CT
- ANT 94509 575-D6
MADILL ST
- ANT 94509 575-C6
E MADILL ST
- ANT 94509 575-E6
MADISON AV
- CCCo 94565 573-H3
5500 RCH 94804 609-B2
5600 ELCR 94530 609-C2
MADISON CT
1400 BREN 94513 616-J1
1800 CNCD 94521 593-D2
3000 ANT 94509 575-A7
MADISON LN
1800 CNCD 94521 593-D2
MADISON ST
- BEN 94510 551-E6
500 ALB 94706 609-D5
MADOLINE ST
- PIT 94565 574-D5
MADONNA LN
500 WLCK 94597 612-A3
MADORA PL
100 SRMN 94583 693-G1
MADRID CT
- DNVL 94506 653-G5
MADRID LN
- ANT 94509 575-A6
MADRID PL
- SRMN 94583 673-G5
MADRONE AV
600 PIN 94564 569-D4
3600 OAK 94619 650-G6
MADRONE CT
1300 SPAB 94806 588-H1
MADRONE DR
3600 LFYT 94549 631-E1
MADRONE LN
- CCCo 94516 631-A7
MADRONE PL
- ORIN 94563 610-F7
200 BREN 94513 616-F2
5700 CNCD 94521 593-G7
MADRONE ST
3200 ANT 94509 574-J7
MADRONE TR
- CCCo 94507 652-F1
- CCCo 94526 652-F1
- CCCo 94583 632-C6
- CCCo 94583 652-D1
MADRONE WY
1400 SPAB 94806 588-H1
MADSEN CT
- MRGA 94556 651-D1
MADSEN LN
- WLCK 94597 612-B2
MAE AV
- PIT 94565 574-C5
MAGAZINE ST
500 VAL 94590 550-B1
1500 VAL 94591 550-D1
1500 SolC 94591 550-D1
MAGDA WY
200 CCCo 94553 572-C7
MAGEE AV
2600 CCCo 94806 569-C5
3600 OAK 94619 650-F5
MAGEE CT
- MRGA 94556 651-G2
MAGEE RANCH RD
100 DNVL 94506 653-G2
MAGELLAN CT
- DBLN 94568 694-G4
MAGELLAN DR
1800 OAK 94611 630-E7
1900 OAK 94611 650-E1
MAGGIE LN
- WLCK 94597 612-B1
MAGGIORE CT
500 BREN 94513 616-F3
MAGNOLIA AV
300 PDMT 94611 650-B1
300 PDMT 94610 650-B2
800 CCCo 94553 571-F4
MAGNOLIA CT
- CCCo 94595 612-B6
600 BREN 94513 616-H1
MAGNOLIA DR
1200 CNCD 94520 592-E4
MAGNOLIA LN
1000 LFYT 94549 611-F5
MAGNOLIA PL
- CCCo 94506 654-B3
MAGNOLIA WY
1700 ANT 94509 575-B5
1700 CCCo 94595 612-B6
2100 CCCo 94595 632-B1
MAGNOLIA BRIDGE DR
- CCCo 94582 673-J2
- CCCo 94582 674-A2
MAGUIRE WY
- DBLN 94568 694-F4
MAHAN WY
2300 CCCo 94806 569-B6
MAHOGANY CT
3600 WLCK 94598 592-J7
MAHOGANY LN
- HER 94547 569-J4
- SRMN 94583 693-F1
MAHOGANY ST
- DBLN 94568 694-D4
MAHOGANY TR
- CCCo 94583 652-E2
MAHOGANY WY
1700 ANT 94509 575-A5
MAHONEY LN
- CCCo 94561 577-C7
- CCCo 94561 597-C1
MAHONEY ST
900 CCCo 94572 549-H7
MAHOO LN
1800 CNCD 94521 593-F4
MAHUA WY
- ANT 94509 595-F3
MAIDEN LN
- OAK 94602 650-F3
100 DNVL 94526 633-C7
500 PIN 94564 569-E4
8500 ELCR 94530 609-D1
MAIDEN LN E
- PIN 94564 569-E4
MAIDENHAIR CT
- CCCo 94582 674-A2
MAIDENHAIR ST
- PIT 94565 574-C2
MAIDENHAIR WY
- CCCo 94582 674-A2
MAIN AV
2800 CNCD 94519 592-G2
E MAIN RD
- CCCo 94553 571-G3
W MAIN RD
- CCCo 94553 571-F3
MAIN ST
- CCCo 94520 552-H7
- CCCo 94565 552-H7
- HER 94547 569-F2
- SRFL 94901 587-B5
- SRFL 94964 587-B5
- MRTZ 94553 571-D3
- MrnC 94964 587-B5
3600 CCCo 94514 637-D3
6000 CLAY 94517 593-H7
MAIN ST Rt#-4
600 OAKL 94561 576-B5
900 ANT 94509 576-B5
900 OAKL 94509 576-B5
4000 OAKL 94561 596-G3
6000 BREN 94561 596-G3
6000 CCCo 94561 596-G3
N MAIN ST
1300 WLCK 94596 612-C5
2200 WLCK 94597 612-C2
3100 PLHL 94523 592-C7
3100 PLHL 94523 612-C2
S MAIN ST
1100 WLCK 94596 612-C6
1700 WLCK 94595 612-C6
1900 WLCK 94507 632-D1
1900 WLCK 94595 632-D1
1900 CCCo 94507 632-D1
1900 CCCo 94595 632-D1
MAINE AV
100 RCH 94804 588-F7
MAINE DR
5500 CNCD 94521 593-F6
MAIN GATE TER
700 BEN 94510 551-D5
MAINPRICE CT
- SRMN 94583 673-E4
MAINSAIL CT
- RCH 94804 608-E3
100 VAL 94591 550-G2
MAISON CT
- MRGA 94556 631-D6
MAISON DR
100 DNVL 94506 653-H5
MAISON WY
800 RCH 94803 589-H3
MAJELLA WY
1800 CNCD 94519 592-J1
MAJESTIC AV
3600 OAK 94605 650-H7
MAJESTIC CT
4000 CNCD 94519 593-B1
MAJESTIC DR
3900 CNCD 94519 593-B1
MAJESTIC LN
- BREN 94513 596-D6
MAJESTIC OAK CT
- SRMN 94583 673-E7
MAJORCA DR
200 SRMN 94582 673-G3
MAJOR VISTA CT
600 PIN 94564 569-C4
MALACHITE CT
100 HER 94547 569-J5
MALAGA CT
2500 SRMN 94583 673-C3
MALAGA WY
400 PLHL 94523 592-A4
1200 BREN 94513 616-H2
MALCOLM DR
200 CCCo 94801 588-E4
MALIBU CT
- CLAY 94517 614-A2
200 ANT 94509 595-E1
MALIBU DR
300 HER 94547 570-B6
800 CNCD 94518 592-G6
MALIBU PL
3800 PIT 94565 574-B5
MALICOAT AV
100 OAKL 94561 596-G2
MALICOAT CT
- OAKL 94561 596-H2
MALL CT
- OAK 94611 650-G1
MALLARD CT
- ANT 94509 594-H2
4800 OAKL 94561 576-D7
MALLARD DR
- BEN 94510 551-F3
2000 WLCK 94597 612-A2
2400 WLCK 94597 611-J2
4000 CNCD 94520 572-G3
S MALLARD DR
1300 RCH 94801 608-D2
1300 RCH 94804 608-D2
MALLARD LN
1400 OAKL 94561 576-D7
MALLARD ST
1200 DNVL 94506 653-H4
MALLARD WY
- ANT 94509 594-H1
MALLING WY
- BREN 94513 616-D5
MALOYAN LN
- LFYT 94549 611-C5
MALTA CIR
- CNCD 94519 592-J1
MAMMOTH WY
- ANT 94531 595-F5
MAMMOUTH CT
- OAKL 94561 596-H1
MAMMOUTH LN
- OAKL 94561 576-G7
- OAKL 94561 596-G1
MANACOR CT
3700 SRMN 94583 673-C3
MANCHESTER
- HER 94547 569-F1
MANCHESTER AV
2400 SPAB 94806 588-G2
MANCHESTER CT
1500 CNCD 94521 593-D4
MANCHESTER DR
1500 CNCD 94521 593-D4
5900 OAK 94618 630-A5
MANCHESTER ST
200 DNVL 94506 653-J6
3600 PLE 94588 694-F5
MANCHESTER WY
- OAKL 94561 596-D2
MANCINI CT
7400 DBLN 94568 693-F4
MANDALA CT
100 CCCo 94596 612-F7
MANDALAY AV
100 HER 94547 570-C6
MANDALAY RD
- OAK 94618 630-B6
MANDANA BLVD
400 OAK 94610 650-A3
MANDANA CIR
- OAK 94610 650-B3
MANDARIN CT
1300 BREN 94513 616-D1
MANDARIN LN
600 WLCK 94598 592-H7
MANDARIN WY
2100 ANT 94509 575-B5
MANDERLY RD
- SRFL 94901 587-B1
MANDEVILLA CT
3200 PLE 94588 694-H4
MANDEVILLE CT
- OAKL 94561 596-C1
MANDY WY
- CCCo 94582 674-B5
MANGELS AV
3500 OAK 94619 650-E6
MANGINI RD
- PLHL 94523 592-A5
MANGO RD
2000 CNCD 94518 592-F5
MANGOS DR
9900 SRMN 94583 673-F5
MANGROVE CT
- ANT 94509 595-F3
MANGROVE DR
- DBLN 94568 694-D4
MANGROVE WY
- ANT 94509 595-E3
300 WLCK 94598 612-H2
MANHASSET DR
600 WLCK 94598 613-A3
MANHATTEN CT
6500 MRTZ 94553 591-H4
MANILA AV
5500 OAK 94618 630-A6
6300 ELCR 94530 609-C2
MANN DR
1500 PIN 94564 569-D5
MANNING LN
1500 CCCo 94507 632-E4
MANNING RD
1100 AlaC 94551 675-E4
1100 CCCo 94551 675-D3
MANOA CT
- CCCo 94806 569-B4
MANOR AV
3100 PLHL 94523 592-C7
3100 WLCK 94597 592-C7
3100 WLCK 94597 612-C1
MANOR CIR
1700 ELCR 94530 609-C1
MANOR DR
- PDMT 94611 630-A7
- PDMT 94611 650-A1
- CCCo 94565 573-G2
1300 SPAB 94806 588-G3
MANOR LN
1600 CNCD 94521 593-B2
MANOR RD
700 CCCo 94803 569-D7
MANOR WY
1000 ALB 94706 609-F6
MANOR CREST
6700 OAK 94618 630-A4
MANOR PARK CIR
100 CCCo 94553 592-A1
MANSFIELD AV
6800 DBLN 94568 693-J3
MANSFIELD DR
4300 CCCo 94506 654-B5
MANTI TER
- CCCo 94507 633-A6
MANTILLA CTE
2600 WLCK 94598 612-H2
MANTON CT
800 CNCD 94518 592-G6
MANUEL CT
200 CCCo 94565 573-D1
MANVILLE AV
- PIT 94565 574-C5
MANZANA PL
1000 LFYT 94549 611-J6
MANZANILLA CT
- SPAB 94806 568-J7
MANZANILLA DR
1700 SPAB 94806 568-H7
MANZANILLO WY
1200 BREN 94513 616-H2
MANZANITA AV
- CCCo 94516 631-A7
- MRGA 94556 631-A7
- MRGA 94556 651-C1
MANZANITA CT
- RCH 94806 569-A7
- CCCo 94595 612-A7
3900 CNCD 94519 573-A7
MANZANITA DR
100 ORIN 94563 610-F5
1700 OAK 94611 630-F6
1800 CNCD 94519 593-A1
1800 CNCD 94519 573-A7
2200 CCCo 94516 630-G6
MANZANITA LN
11500 DBLN 94568 693-F5
MANZANITA PL
100 HER 94547 570-A4
MANZANITA TER
- ORIN 94563 610-F5
MANZANITA WY
2100 ANT 94509 575-B6
MANZANO DR
3000 WLCK 94598 612-J3
MAPE WY
11700 DBLN 94568 693-G4
MAPLE
- BEN 94510 551-B6
MAPLE AV
700 RCH 94801 588-F6
2400 CNCD 94520 572-F7
3000 OAK 94602 650-E5
MAPLE CT
100 HER 94547 570-A5
MAPLE DR
6500 DBLN 94568 693-J4
MAPLE LN
- CCCo 94595 612-B7
MAPLE ST
- BREN 94513 616-G1
1100 PIT 94565 574-F3
MAPLEGATE CT
900 CNCD 94521 613-C1
MAPLEGLEN CT
- DNVL 94506 653-J3
MAPLEWOOD CT
- BREN 94561 596-E4
- DNVL 94506 653-J3
3800 CNCD 94519 573-A7
MAPLEWOOD DR
- DNVL 94506 653-J3
3800 CNCD 94519 573-A7
MARA CT
200 SRMN 94583 673-F5
MARAKESH DR
100 CCCo 94553 572-C7
MARAZZANI DR
2000 MRTZ 94553 572-A6
MARBI LN
- WLCK 94597 612-C2
MARBLE DR
200 ANT 94509 595-E2
MARBLE CANYON CT
400 SRMN 94582 653-F6
MARBLE CANYON LN
500 SRMN 94582 653-F6
MARBLE CANYON PL
3100 SRMN 94582 653-F6
MARBLEHEAD CT
4000 SRMN 94582 673-H5
MARBLEHEAD DR
4000 SRMN 94582 673-H5
MARBLEHEAD LN
500 WLCK 94598 612-J3
MARCAS CT
3900 PIN 94564 569-J7
3900 CCCo 94553 569-J7
MARCELLA CT
900 CNCD 94518 592-F6
MARCHANT CT
- CCCo 94707 609-F4
MARCHANT GDNS
- CCCo 94707 609-F4
MARCHBANKS CT
100 WLCK 94598 612-E3
MARCHBANKS DR
1400 WLCK 94598 612-D3
MARCHI AV
2800 MRTZ 94553 571-G4
2800 CCCo 94553 571-G4
MARCIA CT
- CCCo 94565 573-F2
MARCIA DR
2300 PLHL 94523 592-D6
MARCIEL RD
2100 CCCo 94551 (655-C7 See Page 635)
2100 CCCo 94551 675-C1
MARCLAIR DR
1400 CNCD 94521 593-B4
MARCUS AV
- CCCo 94801 588-E4
MARCUS CT
1200 ANT 94509 575-F7
MARDEN LN
5900 OAK 94611 630-D6
MARDON CT
1100 CNCD 94521 593-E7
MARE CT
4400 ANT 94531 596-A2
MARE LN
300 SRMN 94583 673-C4
MARELIA CT
1400 SPAB 94806 588-G3
MARGARET CT
100 VAL 94590 550-C1
300 CCCo 94565 573-D1
MARGARET DR
- CCCo 94596 632-F1
MARGARET LN
- BREN 94561 596-E4
- DNVL 94526 652-H2
MARGARIDO DR
100 WLCK 94596 612-D5
5700 OAK 94618 630-A5
MARGARITA CT
1700 CNCD 94521 593-E4
MARGARITA DR
- MrnC 94901 587-A1
MARGATE CIR
- PLHL 94523 592-A4
MARGIE LN
100 PLHL 94523 592-C5
MARGIL WY
1500 BREN 94513 616-D3
MARGO DR
1700 CNCD 94519 593-A1
MARGONE CT
- DNVL 94526 653-C1
MARGRAVE CT
- WLCK 94597 612-B2
MARGUERITA RD
- CCCo 94707 609-F2
MARGUERITE AV
1900 PLHL 94523 592-A5
MARGUERITE CT
1000 LFYT 94549 611-C5
MARGUERITE DR
- CCCo 94806 569-A5
- OAK 94618 630-B6
MARIA AV
1300 CNCD 94518 592-H2
MARIA CT
2300 PIN 94564 569-F7
MARIA LN
1400 WLCK 94596 612-D6
MARIA ST
2600 PLE 94588 694-G6
MARIAN LN
400 DNVL 94526 652-H2
MARIAN PL
100 PLHL 94523 592-D6
MARIANNE DR
4000 LFYT 94549 611-B6
MARICAIBO PL
900 SRMN 94583 673-B3
MARICE CT
3700 CNCD 94518 592-J4
MARICOPA AV
2300 RCH 94804 588-H4
2300 RCH 94806 588-H4
3500 RCH 94804 589-A4
3500 SPAB 94805 589-A4
MARICOPA CT
100 PLHL 94523 592-B2
MARIE AV
800 MRTZ 94553 571-H5
900 ANT 94509 575-E5
MARIE PL
- MRGA 94556 651-F2
MARIE WY
5900 OAK 94618 630-B4
MARIETTA CT
- CNCD 94518 592-J5
MARIE VEGA CT
- SPAB 94806 588-J3
- SPAB 94806 589-A3
MARIGOLD CT
- DNVL 94506 654-B5
MARIGOLD DR
- BREN 94513 596-E6
100 HER 94547 570-A4
MARIGOLD LN
- CCCo 94595 612-B7
MARIGOLD PL
100 HER 94547 570-A4
MARIGOLD ST
- DNVL 94506 654-B5
MARIGOLD WY
- ANT 94531 595-F5
MARILYN CT
3200 PLE 94588 694-C7
MARILYN PL
- SRMN 94583 673-F6
MARILYN WY
1100 CNCD 94518 592-G3
MARIN AV
- CCCo 94565 573-F2
1000 ALB 94706 609-E6
1200 SPAB 94806 589-A3
1200 SPAB 94805 589-B4
1600 ALB 94707 609-G6
1700 BERK 94707 609-G6
2300 BERK 94708 609-H5
5600 RCH 94805 589-B6
MARIN CT
4100 CNCD 94521 593-B3
MARIN RD
800 CCCo 94803 569-D7
MARIN WY
1500 OAK 94606 650-A6
MARINA BLVD
- PIT 94565 574-D1
- PIT 94565 554-E7
MARINA CIR
1200 CCCo 94514 617-H5
MARINA CT
1800 CNCD 94520 592-F2
MARINA PL
300 BEN 94510 551-A4
MARINA RD
300 CCCo 94565 553-D7
5800 CCCo 94514 617-J6
5800 CCCo 94514 (618-A6 See Page 597)
MARINA WY
- RCH 94801 588-G7
- SRFL 94901 587-A1
MARINA WY N
- BREN 94561 596-D4
MARINA WY S
- BREN 94561 596-D4
100 RCH 94804 588-G7
400 RCH 94804 608-G1
MARINA WY W
- BREN 94561 596-D4
MARINA BAY PKWY
500 RCH 94804 608-H2
MARINA LAKES DR
- RCH 94804 608-H2
MARINA RIDGE CT
- VAL 94591 550-E2
MARINA VILLAGE RD
200 BEN 94510 551-B6
MARINA VISTA
100 MRTZ 94553 571-F2
MARINE DR
- MrnC 94901 587-C1
MARINE ST
200 RCH 94801 588-C7
MARINER CT
- PIT 94565 573-J3
MARINER RD
- CCCo 94561 577-E5
MARINERS PT
800 CCCo 94572 569-J2
800 CCCo 94572 570-A3
MARINERS COVE RD
- CCCo 94565 573-D1
MARINERS POINT CT
800 CCCo 94572 570-A3
MARINE VIEW AV
- RCH 94801 608-D1
MARIO WY
4000 LFYT 94549 611-B6
MARION AV
3700 OAK 94619 650-E6
MARION CT
1900 LFYT 94549 591-H7
4000 CCCo 94803 589-G4
MARION TER
2700 MRTZ 94553 571-E5
MARION WY
3900 CCCo 94803 589-G4
MARIONOLA WY
1100 PIN 94564 569-E5
MARIPOSA AV
1000 BERK 94707 609-G6
MARIPOSA CT
- DNVL 94526 652-J3
- DNVL 94526 653-A3
1700 CNCD 94521 593-E4
2800 ANT 94509 575-B6
MARIPOSA DR
100 PIT 94565 574-D5
N MARIPOSA DR
6500 DBLN 94568 694-A3
S MARIPOSA DR
6500 DBLN 94568 694-A3
MARIPOSA LN
- ORIN 94563 610-F7
MARIPOSA RD
800 LFYT 94549 611-E7
MARIPOSA ST
700 CCCo 94572 549-H7
1300 RCH 94804 609-B2
MARIPOSA WY
- WLCK 94598 612-D4
1800 BREN 94513 616-C3
MARITA DR
5100 ANT 94531 595-G4
MARITIME TER
- HER 94547 569-G1
MARITIME ACADEMY DR
100 VAL 94590 550-C1
MARK CT
- CNCD 94520 572-E4
MARK LN
- ANT 94509 574-J6
MARKET AV
- CCCo 94801 588-F3
900 RCH 94806 588-G3
1100 SPAB 94806 588-G3
MARKET PL
1000 SRMN 94583 673-F3
MARKET ST
1400 CNCD 94520 592-E2
MARKEY LN
100 CCCo 94513 617-C1
MARKHAM ST
900 CNCD 94518 592-F5
MARKLEY CREEK DR
- ANT 94565 594-H1
MARKOVICH LN
- RCH 94806 568-H7
MARKS BLVD
- PIT 94565 574-C6
MARKS RD
100 CCCo 94507 633-A6
MARKSTEIN DR
- PIT 94565 574-H4
MARK TWAIN DR
2100 ANT 94531 595-F4
MARLBORO CT
500 SRMN 94583 673-E5
1200 CNCD 94521 593-A4
MARLBORO WY
2900 SRMN 94583 673-F5
3700 PLE 94588 694-F5
MARLBOROUGH CT
- PDMT 94611 650-D2
MARLBOROUGH TER
7000 OAK 94705 630-C3
MARLEE RD
- PLHL 94523 592-B6
MARLENE DR
3200 LFYT 94549 611-H6
MARLESTA CT
1800 PIN 94564 569-E4
MARLESTA RD
500 PIN 94564 569-C5
MARLIN CT
200 CCCo 94572 569-J2
2300 PIN 94564 589-J1
5500 CCCo 94514 617-J6
MARLIN CV
- OAK 94618 630-C4
MARLIN DR
- PIT 94565 573-J2
5600 CCCo 94514 617-J6
5600 CCCo 94514 (618-A5 See Page 597)
MARLIN PL
1400 CCCo 94514 617-J5
1400 CCCo 94514 (618-A5 See Page 597)
MARLINDA CT
- WLCK 94597 612-C3
MARLO CT
- WLCK 94595 612-C7
MARQUES CT
- DNVL 94526 653-C6
MARQUES PL
- DNVL 94526 653-C6
MARQUETTE CT
- CLAY 94517 593-F5
2600 RCH 94806 589-A2
MARQUITA CT
8000 DBLN 94568 693-F3
MARR AV
- OAK 94611 630-C7
- OAK 94611 650-C1
MARS CT
3100 LFYT 94549 611-J6
MARS ST
- CNCD 94519 572-H7
MARSALA CT
100 HER 94547 570-B6
MARSEILLE CT
- DNVL 94506 653-H5
MARSH AV
2100 PIT 94565 574-C3
MARSH CT
200 SRMN 94583 673-B2
800 BREN 94513 616-F1
MARSH DR
2500 SRMN 94583 673-B2
4900 CCCo 94520 572-C6
4900 CNCD 94520 572-C6
5000 CCCo 94553 572-C6
MARSH LN
2700 CCCo 94513 617-E6
MARSH PL
- OAK 94611 650-D1
100 SRMN 94583 673-B3
MARSH WY
3800 OAKL 94561 596-G2
MARSHA PL
100 LFYT 94549 631-J4
MARSHALL CT
- CCCo 94598 612-E4
2200 CCCo 94513 597-B6
MARSHALL DR
- BREN 94513 596-B7
200 CCCo 94598 612-E4
300 WLCK 94598 612-E4
MARSHALL ST
1500 ANT 94509 575-G5
MARSH CREEK CIR
7200 CLAY 94517 613-J1
MARSH CREEK RD
300 CLAY 94517 613-J1
1400 CLAY 94517 593-H7
7600 CLAY 94517 614-B2
7600 CCCo 94517 614-B2
13200 CCCo 94517 634-J1
13500 CCCo 94517 615-A7
13600 CCCo 94517 635-A1
17900 CCCo 94513 635-G1
19000 CCCo 94513 (636-D1 See Page 635)
19000 CCCo 94517 (636-D2 See Page 635)
21700 CCCo 94513 616-E6
24400 CCCo 94513 617-A6
MARSH ELDER CT
4400 CNCD 94521 593-B5
N MARSH ELDER CT
4300 CNCD 94521 593-B5
MARSH MEADOW WY
4500 CNCD 94521 593-B5
MARSTON RD
- ORIN 94563 610-E6
MARTA DR
1900 PLHL 94523 592-D5
N MARTA DR
1500 PLHL 94523 592-D4
MARTHA DR
3800 CCCo 94553 571-H4
MARTHA RD
- ORIN 94563 630-J1
- ORIN 94563 631-A1
MARTI MARIE CT
200 MRTZ 94553 571-J5
MARTI MARIE DR
300 MRTZ 94553 571-J5
MARTI MARIE LN
300 MRTZ 94553 571-J5
MARTIN AV
1400 PLE 94588 694-F6
MARTIN CT
- DNVL 94526 633-C6
- WLCK 94597 612-A3
200 BEN 94510 551-B2
2100 PLE 94588 694-F6
MARTIN DR
- RCH 94801 588-F4
200 CCCo 94801 588-F4
MARTIN LN
- CCCo 94803 589-E3
- RCH 94803 589-E3
MARTIN ST
5000 OAKL 94561 576-D6
MARTIN WY
2100 PIT 94565 574-E4
MARTINA ST
100 RCH 94801 588-D7
200 RCH 94801 608-D1
MARTIN CANYON RD
7600 DBLN 94568 693-F4
MARTINDALE DR
1500 MRTZ 94553 571-J7
MARTIN EDEN CT
- PIT 94565 574-B2
MARTINEZ AV
2300 CCCo 94553 571-F3
MARTINEZ CT
- DBLN 94568 694-G4
2300 PIN 94564 569-H7
MARTIN LUTHER KING JR WY
1000 BERK 94707 609-G7
1200 BERK 94703 609-G7
1200 BERK 94709 609-G7
MARTINO RD
1000 LFYT 94549 611-G4
MARTIS CT
5400 CCCo 94803 589-F3
MARVELLE LN
3100 CNCD 94518 592-G2
MARVIN CT
- CCCo 94803 589-D1
MARVIN DR
100 PLHL 94523 592-A7
MAR VISTA RD
200 CCCo 94565 553-E7
MARVUE CIR
5200 CNCD 94521 593-E6
MARWICK CT
8800 DBLN 94568 693-F2
MARWICK DR
11200 DBLN 94568 693-E2
MARY CT
- DNVL 94526 652-J2
MARY DR
1600 PLHL 94523 592-B4
MARY LN
- RCH 94803 589-C3
MARYAL RD
300 PLHL 94523 591-J5
300 PLHL 94523 592-A5
MARY ANN LN
2900 CCCo 94565 573-G2
MARYANNE CT
- OAKL 94561 596-E1
MARYLAND AV
- BERK 94707 609-G4
MARYLAND DR
1300 CNCD 94521 593-F6
MARYOLA CT
3100 LFYT 94549 611-J6
MARYS AV
- CCCo 94565 573-F2
MASEFIELD DR
500 PLHL 94523 592-B7
MASON CIR
100 CNCD 94520 572-F4
MASON CT
6500 PLE 94588 694-A7
MASON ST
1800 SPAB 94806 588-H3
4600 PLE 94588 694-A6
MASONIC AV
500 ALB 94706 609-E5
1100 BERK 94706 609-E5
5100 OAK 94618 630-C7
MASONIC PL
- OAK 94618 630-D7
MASONIC ST
400 MRTZ 94553 571-D3
MASONRY LN
500 RCH 94801 608-D3
MASSEY CT
6800 PLE 94588 694-A7
MASSIVE PEAK WY
4800 ANT 94531 595-E3
MASSOLO DR
- PLHL 94523 592-C4
MASSONI CT
- CCCo 94507 632-G6
MASTERS CT
100 WLCK 94598 612-D3
MASTERSON LN
1300 LFYT 94549 611-J4
MASTERSON ST
4000 OAK 94619 650-F6
MASTLANDS DR
2000 OAK 94611 650-F2
MATADERA CIR
800 DNVL 94526 633-B7
800 DNVL 94526 653-B1
MATADERA CT
300 DNVL 94526 633-B7
MATADERA WY
900 DNVL 94526 633-B7
MATCH CT
- RCH 94806 568-H5
MATCHEM CT
- CCCo 94507 633-A3
MATHESON CT
- CNCD 94521 593-C4
MATHESON RD
1500 CNCD 94521 593-C4
MATHEWS PL
- CCCo 94507 632-D2
MATHEWSON CT
- ANT 94531 595-C4

STREET / Block City ZIP Pg-Grid

MATHIEU AV
6100 OAK 94618 630-B5
MATHIEU CT
500 RCH 94801 588-F6
MATISSE CT
- OAKL 94561 576-H7
- OAKL 94561 596-H1
- PLHL 94523 592-C7
500 WLCK 94597 612-B2
MATISSE DR
- OAKL 94561 596-H1
MATSQUI RD
200 ANT 94509 595-D1
MATTERHORN CT
4700 ANT 94531 595-E2
MATTERHORN DR
500 WLCK 94598 612-E2
MATTERHORN WY
4700 ANT 94531 595-D3
MATTESON CT
- DNVL 94526 652-J1
MATTHEW CT
900 WLCK 94596 612-E6
2100 PIT 94565 574-A3
MATTIS CT
4400 OAK 94619 650-H6
MATTOLE RD
- ANT 94531 595-D4
MATTOS CT
100 DNVL 94506 653-G5
MAUDE CT
300 OAKL 94561 596-D1
MAUI CT
200 SRMN 94582 673-E1
MAUI DR
100 PIT 94565 574-E5
MAUNA KEA CT
3300 CNCD 94519 572-H7
MAUREEN CIR
100 CCCo 94565 573-J3
MAUREEN CT
- PLHL 94523 592-A5
MAUREEN LN
300 PLHL 94523 592-A5
MAURI CT
- DNVL 94526 652-J2
MAURINE CT
100 VAL 94590 550-C1
MAVERICK CT
- SRMN 94582 653-J6
300 CCCo 94549 591-H6
MAVIS DR
3100 SRMN 94583 673-F5
MAVIS PL
3100 SRMN 94583 673-F5
MAXIMO CT
- CCCo 94506 654-A5
MAXINE DR
100 PLHL 94523 592-C4
MAXWELL AV
2600 OAK 94619 650-F7
MAXWELL CT
- SRMN 94582 673-J1
MAXWELTON RD
- PDMT 94618 630-C7
100 OAK 94618 630-C7
MAY CT
- SRMN 94583 693-G1
1300 CNCD 94520 592-E4
1900 PLHL 94523 592-C5
3500 OAK 94602 650-D4
MAY RD
2400 CCCo 94803 589-E2
2400 RCH 94803 589-F1
MAY WY
7500 SRMN 94583 693-F1
MAYA WY
- RCH 94801 588-E4
200 CCCo 94801 588-E4
MAYAN CT
7800 DBLN 94568 693-H3
MAYBECK LN
- HER 94547 569-H2
MAYBECK TWIN DR
- BERK 94708 609-J7
MAYBELLE AV
3400 OAK 94619 650-F6
MAYBELLE DR
1800 PLHL 94523 592-B5
MAYBELLE WY
3300 OAK 94619 650-F6
MAYBERRY RD
2900 ANT 94509 575-E7
MAYETTE AV
1600 CNCD 94520 592-E4
MAYFAIR AV
2600 CNCD 94520 572-E7
2600 CNCD 94520 592-E1
MAYFAIR CT
- CCCo 94507 632-J2
MAYFIELD PL
- MRGA 94556 651-E2
MAYFLOWER DR
2700 ANT 94531 575-G7
MAYHEW CT
- CCCo 94523 592-D7
- CCCo 94597 592-D7
MAYHEW WY
- CCCo 94523 592-C7
- PLHL 94523 592-C7
200 WLCK 94523 592-C7
MAYLARD ST
- CCCo 94565 573-G3
MAYMONT CT
- DBLN 94568 694-E3
MAYMONT LN
- DBLN 94568 694-E2
MAYNARD ST
1500 CNCD 94519 592-J3
MAYO CT
2400 CCCo 94806 569-B5
MAYO LN
- WLCK 94597 612-B2
MAYPORT CT
- PIT 94565 574-B2
MAYPORT DR
- PIT 94565 574-B2
MAY SCHOOL RD
3200 AlaC 94551 675-H7
3200 AlaC 94551 676-A7
MAYWOOD DR
3400 RCH 94803 589-F1
7300 PLE 94588 693-H7
MAYWOOD LN
- BREN 94513 596-D5
1200 MRTZ 94553 571-H6
MAYWOOD WY
2400 ANT 94509 594-J1
MAZDA DR
1400 WLCK 94597 612-C2
MAZIE DR
- PLHL 94523 592-C5
MAZUELA DR
5800 OAK 94611 630-E7

MCALLISTER DR
- BEN 94510 551-C1
MCANDREW DR
5800 OAK 94611 630-D7
5800 OAK 94611 650-D1
MCAULIFFE CT
100 HER 94547 570-B5
MCAVOY CRSG
100 CCCo 94565 553-F7
MC AVOY RD
700 CCCo 94565 553-E7
MCBRIDE DR
400 LFYT 94549 631-J4
MCBRIDE LN
- DBLN 94568 693-D5
MCBRYDE AV
2300 RCH 94804 588-H5
3200 RCH 94805 588-H5
3300 RCH 94804 589-A5
3300 RCH 94805 589-A5
5400 SPAB 94805 589-B4
5600 CCCo 94805 589-B4
5700 RCH 94806 589-B4
MCCABE RD
- CCCo 94514 637-C4
MCCALL DR
- BEN 94510 551-B1
MCCALL PL
- OAKL 94561 596-E2
MCCANN CT
1200 CNCD 94518 592-E7
MCCARL LN
1600 CNCD 94519 593-A2
MCCAULEY RD
900 DNVL 94526 653-C1
1000 DNVL 94526 633-C7
MCCLARREN CT
- BREN 94513 616-G2
MCCLARREN RD
600 BREN 94513 616-F2
MCCLELLAN CT
2800 MRTZ 94553 571-G4
MCCLELLAND ST
3700 OAK 94619 650-G7
MCCLOUD PL
300 DNVL 94526 653-D5
MCCLURE CT
4200 ANT 94531 595-H1
MCCONNELL LN
- CCCo 94596 612-F7
MCCORMICK CT
- ANT 94531 595-C4
MCCORMICK RD
- CCCo 94803 589-D1
MCCOY LN
2400 WLCK 94597 612-D4
MCCRELLIS PL
- DBLN 94568 694-H3
MCDERMOTT CT
4200 PIT 94565 574-E6
MCDERMOTT DR
4200 PIT 94565 574-E6
MCDONALD DR
1100 PIN 94564 569-D5
MCDONELL AV
4800 OAK 94619 650-H6
MC ELHENY RD
200 ANT 94509 575-D4
MCELLEN CT
3400 LFYT 94549 611-G7
MCELLEN WY
800 LFYT 94549 611-G7
MCELROY CT
800 CNCD 94518 592-H6
MCEWEN RD
- CCCo 94569 550-G7
- CCCo 94569 570-H1
2400 CCCo 94553 570-H1
MCEWING CT
1200 CNCD 94521 592-J4
MCFARLAN RD
1900 CCCo 94513 597-A5
MCFARLAN RANCH DR
- ANT 94531 596-B3
MCFAUL DR
4200 PIT 94565 574-F6
MCGEE AV
1300 BERK 94703 609-F7
MCGINLEY AV
2300 ANT 94509 575-D6
MCGLOTHEN WY
3900 RCH 94806 568-H6
MCGRATH CT
500 PLHL 94523 592-A6
MCGRAW LN
3300 LFYT 94549 611-G3
MCGUIRE DR
- WLCK 94596 612-D5
MCHARRY RANCH RD
300 CCCo 94553 570-H5
MCHENRY GATE WY
4700 PLE 94566 694-D7
MCINTOSH TER
500 BREN 94513 616-D1
MCKAY LN
- DBLN 94568 693-E5
MCKAY WY
- BEN 94510 551-A4
MCKEAN DR
3100 CNCD 94518 592-H6
MCKEAN PL
700 CNCD 94518 592-G7
MCKENZIE DR
2900 RCH 94806 589-A1
MCKENZIE ST
- MrnC 94964 587-B5
MCKENZIE WY
2200 CNCD 94520 572-F5
MCKILLUP RD
2800 OAK 94602 650-C5
MCKINLEY AV
700 OAK 94610 650-A4
MCKINLEY CT
1800 CNCD 94521 593-D2
MCKINLEY WY
- BREN 94513 596-F7
MCKISSICK ST
- PLHL 94523 592-B6
MCKOSKEN RD
- RCH 94801 588-E3
1400 CCCo 94801 588-E3
MCLAREN LN
- SRMN 94582 674-B4
MCLAUGHLIN ST
400 RCH 94805 589-A6
1000 SPAB 94805 589-A5
MCMAHON CT
200 MRTZ 94553 571-F7
MCMILLAN AV
5500 OAK 94618 630-A5
MCMILLAN CT
2000 MRTZ 94553 571-J7
MCMORROW RD
2600 CCCo 94806 569-B5

MCNAMARA LN
- MRTZ 94553 571-G7
- MRTZ 94553 591-G1
MCNEIL LN
- DNVL 94526 653-F4
MCNEIL PL
800 PLHL 94523 592-B1
MCNORTH DR
1800 CNCD 94519 592-H1
MCNUTT AV
3100 WLCK 94597 592-B7
MCPEAK LN
- DBLN 94568 693-E5
MCPRINCE LN
- BREN 94513 616-E5
MCSWAIN CT
4200 ANT 94531 595-J1
MCVICKER CT
2500 CCCo 94806 569-B6
MCWILLIAMS LN
- PLE 94588 693-J6
MEAD ST
- ANT 94531 575-H7
- ANT 94531 595-H1
MEADE ST
1300 RCH 94804 609-A2
5100 RCH 94804 608-J2
MEADOW AV
700 PIN 94564 569-C4
E MEADOW AV
800 PIN 94564 569-D4
MEADOW CRSG
400 CCCo 94517 634-H2
MEADOW CT
- DBLN 94568 693-F4
- CCCo 94595 632-C1
- ORIN 94563 631-A1
100 OAKL 94561 596-G1
MEADOW GN
1300 CNCD 94521 593-B5
MEADOW LN
100 ORIN 94563 631-A1
1100 CNCD 94520 592-E3
1700 CCCo 94595 632-C1
3700 LFYT 94549 611-D4
MEADOW RD
1900 CCCo 94595 632-D1
MEADOW ST
3500 OAK 94601 650-D6
MEADOW BLOSSOM CT
- DNVL 94506 654-B6
MEADOWBROOK AV
3700 PIT 94565 574-E5
MEADOWBROOK CIR
3800 PIT 94565 574-E5
MEADOW BROOK CT
100 OAKL 94561 596-G1
MEADOWBROOK CT
7800 PLE 94588 693-H7
MEADOW BROOK DR
- BREN 94513 596-D7
MEADOWBROOK DR
3100 CNCD 94519 572-G7
4500 RCH 94803 589-E1
MEADOWBROOK LN
- DNVL 94526 632-H7
MEADOWBROOK RD
3200 ANT 94509 595-C1
MEADOW CANYON DR
- PIT 94565 574-G6
MEADOW CREEK CT
100 OAKL 94561 596-H1
800 WLCK 94596 612-D6
MEADOW CREST CT
2600 RCH 94806 568-J7
MEADOW CREST LN
- CCCo 94595 632-D1
MEADOWGATE WY
1000 BREN 94513 596-C7
MEADOW GLEN DR
2600 SRMN 94583 673-C2
MEADOW GLEN PL
2600 SRMN 94583 673-C2
MEADOW GLEN WY
2600 SRMN 94583 673-C2
MEADOW GROVE CT
- CCCo 94507 633-A5
MEADOW LAKE DR
- DNVL 94506 654-C7
MEADOW LAKE ST
4100 ANT 94531 595-J1
4100 ANT 94531 575-J7
MEADOWLANDS CT
- ORIN 94563 631-B5
MEADOWLARK CT
- DNVL 94526 653-B5
1400 LFYT 94549 611-G3
MEADOWLARK LN
2000 OAKL 94561 596-H1
MEADOWLARK ST
2200 CCCo 94806 569-C4
MEADOWLARK WY
100 HER 94547 569-H5
1200 CNCD 94521 593-B4
MEADOWOOD CIR
100 SRMN 94583 673-G5
MEADOWOOD CT
300 PLHL 94523 591-J6
MEADOW PARK CT
- ORIN 94563 631-A1
MEADOW PINE CT
1700 CNCD 94521 593-E4
MEADOWS AV
4000 PIT 94565 574-G6
MEADOWS LN
4000 OAKL 94561 596-G1
W MEADOWS LN
300 DNVL 94506 653-H3
MEADOWSIDE PL
200 DNVL 94526 632-H7
MEADOWVALE CT
900 MRTZ 94553 571-H7
MEADOW VIEW CT
- CCCo 94506 654-C4
5200 ANT 94531 595-E4
MEADOW VIEW DR
- RCH 94806 568-H6
MEADOW VIEW LN
400 CCCo 94517 634-G3
3100 WLCK 94598 612-H1
MEADOW VIEW RD
- ORIN 94563 611-A7
- ORIN 94563 631-A1
MEADOW WALK PL
- WLCK 94598 613-B3
MEADOW WEST CT
- RCH 94806 568-H6
MEADOW WOOD LN
5300 OAKL 94561 576-D4
MEADOWWOOD PL
5300 CNCD 94521 593-F4
MEANDER CT
800 WLCK 94598 612-G3

MEANDER DR
800 WLCK 94598 612-G4
MEDALLION CT
- PLHL 94523 591-H5
MEDALLION DR
- BREN 94561 596-D4
MEDANOS ST
1100 ANT 94509 575-C5
MEDAU PL
6100 OAK 94611 650-E1
MEDBURN ST
100 CCCo 94520 572-G2
MEDFIELD RD
1200 LFYT 94549 611-B4
MEDFORD CT
4000 MRTZ 94553 571-J5
MEDIAR CT
- SRMN 94582 673-H2
MEDIAR DR
- SRMN 94582 673-H2
MEDICINE MOUNTAIN CT
1900 ANT 94531 595-E6
MEDINA DR
100 CCCo 94553 572-C7
MEDINAH CT
- SRMN 94583 673-G7
MEDINAH PL
100 SRMN 94583 673-G7
MEDITERRANEO PL
- BREN 94513 596-D6
MEDITERRANEO WY
- BREN 94513 596-D6
MEDLYN LN
- CCCo 94507 632-G7
MEEHAN CT
- PIN 94564 569-C3
MEEK PL
- LFYT 94549 611-J6
MEEKER AV
1900 RCH 94804 608-H2
MEEKS LN
- OAKL 94561 596-C1
MEESE CIR
- DNVL 94526 653-C6
MEESE CT
100 DNVL 94526 653-C6
MEGAN CT
- OAKL 94561 596-C1
100 CCCo 94507 632-H5
MEGAN DR
2100 OAKL 94561 596-B1
MEGHAN LN
300 WLCK 94597 612-C2
MEGINNISS RD
- VAL 94592 549-H1
MEHAFFEY WY
4200 OAKL 94561 576-D7
4200 OAKL 94561 596-D1
MEIER RD
- PLHL 94523 612-A1
MELANIE CIR
3200 PLE 94588 694-C7
MELANIE CT
2800 WLCK 94596 632-G3
MELANIE DR
300 CCCo 94565 573-J3
MELBOURNE CT
3000 PLE 94588 694-F6
MELBOURNE PL
3100 WLCK 94598 612-J1
MELBOURNE WY
- CCCo 94582 674-C4
MELDON AV
4600 OAK 94619 650-F7
MELEEAN LN
- MRTZ 94553 571-H5
MELILLO DR
2800 WLCK 94597 612-A1
MELINDA CT
400 CCCo 94565 573-J3
500 CCCo 94803 569-D7
MELISSA CT
- OAKL 94561 596-C2
- PIT 94565 574-G5
1000 WLCK 94598 612-D4
MELLISSA CIR
1400 ANT 94509 575-F7
MELLISSA CT
1500 ANT 94509 575-F7
MELLOWOOD DR
3900 OAKL 94561 596-G1
4000 OAKL 94561 576-G7
MELLOWOOD ST
1600 PIT 94565 573-G4
MELLUS ST
400 MRTZ 94553 571-D3
MELODY CT
6700 PLE 94588 694-A7
MELODY DR
1400 CNCD 94521 593-B4
3500 CCCo 94595 612-A7
MELODY LN
- ORIN 94563 610-F2
MELON CT
2900 ANT 94509 574-J6
MELROSE CT
- CCCo 94582 674-A1
- CCCo 94595 612-A7
MELROSE PL
- BREN 94513 616-D2
MELTON LN
1900 ANT 94509 575-J6
MELVICH LN
- DBLN 94568 693-D5
MELVILLE DR
6200 OAK 94611 650-G2
MELVILLE LN
6400 OAK 94611 650-G1
MELVILLE SQ
1200 RCH 94804 608-H2
MELVILLE TER
- MRTZ 94553 571-J5
MELVIN CT
- OAK 94602 650-E3
MELVIN RD
1800 OAK 94602 650-E2
MEMORIAL WY
100 CCCo 94565 573-H3
100 PIT 94565 573-H3
MEMORY LN
400 CCCo 94561 596-G4
MENDENHALL CT
3500 PLE 94588 694-G5
MENDOCINO AV
800 BERK 94707 609-G5
5700 OAK 94618 630-A5
MENDOCINO CT
2700 PIN 94564 569-H6
MENDOCINO DR
1500 CNCD 94521 593-B2
2000 CCCo 94565 573-H2
2600 PIN 94564 569-H6

MENDOCINO ST
1600 RCH 94804 609-C3
MENDOCINO WY
- CCCo 94513 617-F4
MENDOTA CT
1600 WLCK 94597 611-J2
MENDOTA ST
- BREN 94513 616-H1
MENDOTA WY
- ANT 94531 596-A2
1700 WLCK 94597 611-J2
MENDOZA DR
5800 OAK 94611 630-E7
MENESINI PL
- MRTZ 94553 571-J6
- MRTZ 94553 572-A6
MENLO CT
300 WLCK 94598 612-H2
6700 PLE 94588 694-A7
MENLO PL
- BERK 94707 609-F5
MENNET WY
9700 SRMN 94583 673-F6
MENONA CT
- ANT 94531 596-A1
MENONA DR
- ANT 94531 595-J1
- ANT 94531 596-A1
MENORCA CT
2600 SRMN 94583 673-B3
MEPHAM DR
1000 PIT 94565 574-B2
MERA ST
3800 OAK 94601 650-D7
MERANO CT
5100 PLE 94588 694-H4
MERANO ST
100 DNVL 94526 653-D1
MERCED AV
6100 OAK 94611 650-E1
MERCED CIR
4200 ANT 94531 595-J1
MERCED ST
1000 BERK 94707 609-F6
1300 RCH 94804 609-B2
MERCEDES CT
200 OAKL 94561 596-E2
MERCEDES LN
- OAKL 94561 596-E2
MERCER CT
4200 CNCD 94521 593-B3
MERCHANT ST
1800 CCCo 94525 550-C4
MERCURY CT
- PLHL 94523 592-A4
MERCURY WY
100 PLHL 94523 592-A4
MEREDITH CT
300 CLAY 94517 613-J1
1900 CNCD 94521 593-G4
MEREDITH WY
2100 ANT 94509 595-A1
MERGANSER CT
- OAKL 94561 576-H7
MERGANSER DR
- OAKL 94561 576-H7
MERIAN DR
1600 PLHL 94523 592-B4
MERICREST ST
- BREN 94513 616-H2
MERIDIAN PARK BLVD
2000 CNCD 94520 592-D1
2300 CCCo 94553 592-D1
MERION CT
- BREN 94513 616-B2
MERION TER
100 MRGA 94556 651-D1
MERIWEATHER CT
2100 WLCK 94596 632-G1
MERLE AV
800 CCCo 94553 571-F4
MERLIN CT
- CNCD 94521 593-B6
200 BEN 94510 551-A2
1100 CCCo 94507 633-C5
MERLOT CT
- OAKL 94561 576-E5
MERLOT LN
200 OAKL 94561 576-E5
MERMAID CT
- CCCo 94565 553-E7
MERRICK CT
700 WLCK 94598 613-A3
MERRIDAN DR
3600 CNCD 94518 592-J3
MERRIEWOOD CIR
- OAK 94611 630-D6
MERRIEWOOD DR
500 LFYT 94549 631-J3
5500 OAK 94611 630-D6
MERRILEE PL
300 DNVL 94526 653-C4
MERRILL AV
4500 OAK 94619 650-G6
MERRILL CIR N
- MRGA 94556 651-G1
MERRILL CIR S
- MRGA 94556 651-G1
MERRILL DR
- MRGA 94556 651-G1
100 ANT 94509 575-D4
MERRIMAC CT
- DNVL 94526 653-A1
- PIT 94565 573-J2
- PIT 94565 574-A2
MERRIMAC PL
- PIT 94565 574-A2
700 DNVL 94526 653-A1
MERRITHEW DR
1100 MRTZ 94553 571-E3
MERRITT AV
400 OAK 94610 650-A3
2400 SPAB 94806 588-H2
MERRITT CT
- CCCo 94513 617-F2
5500 CNCD 94521 593-F7
MERRITT DR
5500 CNCD 94521 593-F7
MERRIWOOD PL
400 SRMN 94582 673-J7
MESA AV
- PDMT 94611 630-B7
MESA CT
100 HER 94547 569-H4
MESA ST
1200 CNCD 94518 592-G3
MESA WY
600 RCH 94805 589-A6
MESA BUENA AV
1800 SPAB 94806 588-H1
MESA OAK CT
- BREN 94513 616-A4
- CCCo 94513 616-A4

MESA OAK LN
- CCCo 94506 653-H1
MESA RIDGE DR
4100 ANT 94531 595-D4
MESA VERDE PL
500 PLHL 94523 592-A3
MESA VISTA DR
- SRMN 94583 673-C3
MESQUITE CT
100 BREN 94513 616-E2
100 HER 94547 569-J4
MESQUITE DR
- PLHL 94523 591-J2
MESQUITE LN
- SRMN 94583 673-C4
MESSIAN PL
500 DNVL 94526 653-D3
METAIRIE CT
- SRMN 94583 693-G1
METAIRIE PL
100 SRMN 94583 673-H7
100 SRMN 94583 693-H1
METCALF ST
- ANT 94565 574-G7
- ANT 94565 594-G1
METRO WALK WY
- RCH 94801 588-G6
METTEN AV
1000 PIT 94565 574-E7
MEYERS CT
900 BREN 94513 596-E7
MEYERS LN
100 CCCo 94553 572-B5
MIA CT
600 DNVL 94526 653-B3
MIAMI CT
1600 OAK 94602 650-C4
MICA CT
- ANT 94531 595-F2
MICA WY
- ANT 94531 595-G2
MI CASA CT
1000 CNCD 94520 592-E5
MICHAEL
- CNCD 94518 592-G4
MICHAEL DR
1600 PIN 94564 569-E6
MICHAEL LN
- ORIN 94563 611-A7
- ORIN 94563 631-A1
500 LFYT 94549 631-J2
700 DNVL 94526 632-J6
MICHAEL PL
200 MRTZ 94553 591-J4
3400 CCCo 94565 573-F1
MICHELANGELO DR
- OAKL 94561 596-H1
MICHELE DR
100 CCCo 94806 569-A5
600 CCCo 94553 572-A3
MICHELLE CT
500 CCCo 94565 573-J3
4000 CNCD 94521 593-B2
MICHELLE LN
- CCCo 94507 632-J3
2300 OAKL 94561 596-C1
MICHELLE WY
300 CCCo 94507 632-J3
MICHIGAN AV
400 BERK 94707 609-G4
MICHIGAN BLVD
5400 CNCD 94521 593-F6
5500 CLAY 94517 593-F6
MICKELSEN CT
800 BREN 94513 616-J2
MIDCREST RD
500 OAK 94610 650-C3
MIDCREST WY
700 ELCR 94530 609-E3
MIDDLE RD
- LFYT 94549 611-A6
MIDDLEBROOKE WY
- SRMN 94582 674-C3
MIDDLEFIELD CT
- BREN 94513 616-H3
MIDDLEFIELD RD
900 BERK 94708 609-J5
MIDDLESEX ST
200 CCCo 94520 572-G1
MIDHILL RD
- MRTZ 94553 571-H5
100 CCCo 94553 571-J5
MIDLAND WY
100 DNVL 94526 653-A4
MIDSHIP DR
100 HER 94547 570-B6
MIDVALE AV
3400 OAK 94602 650-F5
MIDVALE CT
- CCCo 94597 612-B4
5300 PLE 94588 693-H7
MIDWAY
500 BREN 94513 616-G1
MIDWAY CT
500 MRTZ 94553 571-J6
MIDWAY DR
100 MRTZ 94553 571-J6
MIDWAY PL
400 MRTZ 94553 571-J5
MI ELANA CIR
2800 WLCK 94598 612-H2
MI ELANA CT
- WLCK 94598 612-H2
MIFLIN AV
3500 CCCo 94803 589-B3
MIFLIN CT
4100 CCCo 94803 589-B2
MIGUEL DR
5000 OAKL 94561 576-D6
MIKADO PL
500 DNVL 94526 653-C5
MIKE YORBA WY
- CCCo 94509 575-G5
MILANI AV
2700 PLE 94588 694-E7
MILANO CT
- DNVL 94526 653-D1
MILANO WY
100 MRTZ 94553 572-A6
4800 MRTZ 94553 571-J6
MILAW CT
- SRMN 94583 673-B2
MILBRIDGE CT
- DBLN 94568 694-F2
MILBURN CT
- SRMN 94583 673-G7
MILBURN DR
1700 PLHL 94523 592-B4
MILDEN RD
4800 MRTZ 94553 571-G7
MILDRED AV
- BREN 94513 596-C5
- PIT 94565 574-C3

MILDRED CT
- BREN 94513 596-C5
MILDRED LN
3300 LFYT 94549 631-G3
MILDRED ST
2100 CNCD 94520 572-F7
MILES AV
5600 OAK 94618 630-A5
MILES CT
600 PLHL 94523 591-J3
MILESTONE CT
- PIT 94565 574-C2
MILFORD DR
- SRMN 94582 674-B4
MILITARY E
100 BEN 94510 551-C5
MILITARY W
100 BEN 94510 551-A3
900 BEN 94510 550-J3
MILL RD
300 MRTZ 94553 571-G5
MILLBRAE CT
100 WLCK 94598 612-J1
MILLBRIDGE DR
2800 SRMN 94583 673-F6
MILLBRIDGE PL
2800 SRMN 94583 673-F5
MILLBROOK AV
7600 DBLN 94568 693-G3
MILLBROOK CT
- DNVL 94526 653-A1
1000 WLCK 94598 612-G4
MILLBROOK DR
- PIT 94565 574-F7
MILLBURY CT
- DBLN 94568 694-E2
MILLCREEK DR
2200 PLHL 94523 591-J6
MILL CREEK WY
1000 BREN 94513 596-C7
MILLENIUM LN
- SRMN 94582 674-B4
MILLER AV
200 MRTZ 94553 571-E2
900 BERK 94708 609-H5
1200 OAK 94601 650-B7
MILLER DR
- LFYT 94549 611-G5
600 OAKL 94561 596-F1
MILLER LN
1900 WLCK 94595 632-D1
1900 CCCo 94595 632-D1
MILLER PL
1100 OAK 94601 650-B7
MILLER RD
7000 AlaC 94546 672-A5
MILLER ST
- ANT 94565 574-H7
- ANT 94565 594-H1
1200 ANT 94509 575-F5
MILLFIELD PL
400 MRGA 94556 651-F3
MILLICAN CT
- CCCo 94553 591-E2
MILLPOND CT
1200 CNCD 94521 593-B4
MILLS CT
400 BEN 94510 551-A1
MILLS DR
400 BEN 94510 550-J2
400 BEN 94510 551-A1
3000 BREN 94513 616-G3
MILLS PL
- BREN 94513 616-G3
100 SRMN 94583 673-F7
1100 OAKL 94561 576-E7
MILLS ST E
- RCH 94801 588-E6
MILLS ST W
- RCH 94801 588-E5
MILL SPRINGS CT
- PIT 94565 574-G6
MILLSTREAM LN
- SRMN 94582 674-B4
MILLSVIEW AV
3200 OAK 94619 650-G7
MILLTHWAIT DR
- CCCo 94553 591-E2
MILNE CT
1400 CNCD 94521 593-D4
MILNER RD
3100 ANT 94509 575-C7
3100 ANT 94509 595-C1
MILO PL
200 SRMN 94583 673-F6
MILO WY
2800 SRMN 94583 673-E6
MILPAS
- CCCo 94597 612-A5
MILTON AV
1300 CCCo 94596 632-E1
1300 WLCK 94596 632-E1
MILTON DR
3800 CCCo 94803 589-D2
MILVIA CT
1900 BERK 94709 609-G7
MILVIA ST
1200 BERK 94709 609-G7
MILWAUKEE PL
200 DNVL 94526 653-C5
MIMOSA CT
2400 ANT 94509 595-F3
MIMOSA WY
2400 ANT 94509 595-F3
MIMS AV
- CCCo 94565 573-G3
MINAKER DR
900 ANT 94509 575-F4
MINARET DR
2200 MRTZ 94553 572-A7
MINARET RD
- OAKL 94561 596-H2
MINER AV
900 SPAB 94806 568-H7
1400 SPAB 94806 588-H1
MINER RD
- ORIN 94563 610-G4
MINERT RD
500 WLCK 94598 592-F7
500 CNCD 94518 592-G6
MINERVA WY
- SRMN 94583 673-E6
MINK CT
4300 ANT 94531 595-H3
MINNA AV
2600 OAK 94619 650-E6
MINNER AV
300 ANT 94509 575-E6
MINNESOTA AV
- BREN 94513 616-E1
700 BREN 94513 596-D5
MINORU DR
200 CCCo 94553 572-C7

STREET
Block City ZIP Pg-Grid

MINORU WY
200 CCCo 94553 572-C6
MINTA LN
2700 ANT 94509 575-C7
MINTARO CT
- SRMN 94582 674-C3
MINTON CT
400 PLHL 94523 592-A7
MINTWOOD DR
1700 CNCD 94521 593-D3
MINUET CIR
4000 RCH 94803 589-C2
MIRA FLORES
- ORIN 94563 610-J5
MIRA LOMA
- ORIN 94563 610-G6
MIRA LOMA DR
- PIT 94565 574-F7
MIRA LOMA LN
- DNVL 94526 652-J3
MIRAMAR AV
- HER 94547 570-B6
800 BERK 94707 609-F6
MIRAMONTE CT
- CCCo 94597 612-B4
1300 BERK 94703 609-F7
MIRAMONTE DR
- MRGA 94556 631-C6
MIRA MONTE RD
- ORIN 94563 610-E7
MIRAMONTE RD
- CCCo 94597 612-A4
MIRANDA AV
2600 CCCo 94507 632-G4
MIRANDA CT
- CCCo 94507 632-G4
MIRANDA LN
300 CCCo 94507 632-H3
MIRANDA PL
200 CCCo 94507 632-H3
MIRANDA CREEK CT
100 CCCo 94507 632-G4
MIRANGO CT
- CLAY 94517 614-A2
MIRANTE CT
2900 RCH 94803 589-E2
MIRA VISTA AV
500 OAK 94610 650-A2
MIRA VISTA CT
1300 ANT 94509 575-B6
MIRA VISTA DR
- OAKL 94561 596-E2
2000 ELCR 94530 589-C7
2600 CCCo 94805 589-C6
MIRA VISTA TER
1800 CNCD 94520 592-F2
MIRKO LN
- CCCo 94596 632-F1
MIRROR CT
- ANT 94531 595-J1
MISSION AV
1300 SPAB 94806 588-G3
MISSION CT
3800 OAKL 94561 596-G2
MISSION DR
1000 ANT 94509 575-A6
1500 DNVL 94526 653-C6
MISSION LN
- WLCK 94597 612-C2
MISSION PL
500 DNVL 94526 653-B6
MISSION RD
- MRGA 94556 631-G6
- MRGA 94575 631-G6
MISSION BELL DR
2400 SPAB 94806 588-H2
MISSION SPRINGS
- HER 94547 569-G4
MISSOURI DR
1200 CNCD 94521 593-E7
MISSOURI ST
400 MRTZ 94553 571-F5
MISTRAL CT
700 DNVL 94506 653-J4
MISTRAL WY
200 VAL 94591 550-E2
MISTY CT
2100 PIT 94565 574-A4
MISTY LN
3400 CNCD 94519 592-H1
MISTY SPRING CT
- SRMN 94583 673-H3
MITCHEL DR
- DBLN 94568 694-B3
MITCHELL DR
2600 WLCK 94598 612-G1
MITCHELL ST
1400 OAK 94601 650-C6
MITCHELL WY
900 CCCo 94803 569-D7
MITCHELL CANYON CT
5800 CLAY 94517 593-G7
MITCHELL CANYON LN
800 CLAY 94517 593-G7
MITCHELL CANYON RD
- CCCo 94598 613-G2
- CCCo 94517 613-G2
500 CLAY 94517 613-G2
700 CLAY 94517 593-G7
N MITCHELL CANYON RD
1400 CLAY 94517 593-G6
MITCHS LN
2400 ANT 94509 575-D6
MITCHUM DR
200 PIT 94565 574-C2
MITEY MITE LN
100 RCH 94803 589-F2
MIWOK WY
3000 CLAY 94517 593-H5
MIZNER CT
400 BEN 94510 551-B1
MOBILE DR
100 CCCo 94553 572-C7
MOCCASIN CT
1100 CLAY 94517 593-H6
5000 ANT 94531 595-G4
MOCCASIN WY
5000 ANT 94531 595-G4
MOCKINGBIRD LN
400 OAKL 94561 596-H1
MOCKINGBIRD PL
1800 DNVL 94526 653-B6
MOCKINGBIRD HILL RD
2500 WLCK 94597 612-B3
MOCOCO RD
- MRTZ 94553 571-F1
100 MRTZ 94553 551-G7
MODENA CT
5200 PLE 94588 694-H4
MODESTO AV
3000 OAK 94619 650-F7
MODOC AV
400 OAK 94618 630-C6
5300 RCH 94804 609-B3
MODOC CT
1800 ANT 94509 575-G5
4100 CNCD 94521 593-A3
MODOC RD
- ORIN 94563 610-G2
MODOC ST
900 BERK 94707 609-F6
MOESER LN
6300 ELCR 94530 609-D2
MOET LN
- SRMN 94582 674-B4
MOHAR CT
300 PLHL 94523 592-B1
MOHAWK CIR
2700 SRMN 94583 673-D5
MOHAWK CT
2500 WLCK 94598 612-H3
MOHAWK DR
900 CCCo 94549 591-H6
900 PLHL 94523 591-H6
MOHICAN CT
800 WLCK 94598 612-H4
MOHICAN WY
5200 ANT 94531 595-G5
MOHR AV
- AlaC 94588 694-E7
3500 PLE 94588 694-E7
3900 PLE 94566 694-D7
MOHR CT
300 CNCD 94518 592-E7
MOHR LN
900 CNCD 94518 592-E6
1000 CNCD 94520 592-E6
MOISO LN
100 PLHL 94523 592-C6
MOJAVE CT
900 WLCK 94598 612-H4
MOJAVE DR
- BREN 94513 596-B5
MOJAVE WY
- ANT 94531 595-H5
MOKELUMNE CT
- ANT 94531 595-D5
MOKELUMNE DR
1300 ANT 94531 595-F4
MOLAD CT
1000 CNCD 94518 592-J6
MOLERA CT
4100 ANT 94531 595-G1
MOLINA CT
- SRMN 94583 673-C3
MOLITAS RD
100 DNVL 94526 653-C2
MOLLER RANCH DR
- PLE 94588 693-G7
MOLLUK WY
7000 CLAY 94517 594-A5
MOLLY WY
- CCCo 94595 612-A6
MOLOKAI CT
- SRMN 94582 653-E7
MONACO CT
- DNVL 94506 653-H5
600 WLCK 94598 612-G3
MONAGHAN ST
- DBLN 94568 694-F4
MONARCH CT
- RCH 94806 568-J6
MONARCH DR
- SRMN 94582 673-H2
N MONARCH RD
- CCCo 94582 674-A1
- SRMN 94582 673-J1
- SRMN 94582 674-A1
S MONARCH RD
- CCCo 94582 674-A2
MONARCH TER
200 BREN 94513 616-D3
MONARCH WY
- RCH 94806 568-J6
MONARCH RIDGE DR
500 WLCK 94597 611-H3
MONARDA CT
2600 PLE 94588 694-H4
MONASTERIO CT
- SRMN 94583 673-C3
MONDANA PL
1400 PIT 94565 574-G5
MONDAVI CT
- OAKL 94561 576-D5
MONDAVI LN
300 BREN 94513 616-E3
MONET CIR
900 WLCK 94597 612-B2
MONET DR
- OAKL 94561 576-H6
MONFREDO DR
1000 PIT 94565 574-B2
MONIQUE CT
- OAKL 94561 596-E1
MONITOR PASS WY
5100 ANT 94531 595-E4
MONIVEA PL
- PLHL 94523 591-J5
MONMOUTH CT
500 WLCK 94598 612-J3
3200 PLE 94588 694-E6
MONO AV
2200 ELCR 94530 589-B7
MONO DR
1900 MRTZ 94553 572-A7
MONO ST
200 RCH 94801 588-B6
MONOGHAN WY
- ANT 94531 596-B4
MONOSTORY CT
2100 PIT 94565 574-A4
MONROE AV
- DBLN 94568 694-C3
3400 LFYT 94549 611-F6
6000 OAK 94618 630-A6
MONROE CT
- BREN 94513 596-A7
- ORIN 94563 631-B2
3000 ANT 94509 575-A7
3400 LFYT 94549 611-G5
MONROE ST
1000 ALB 94706 609-D7
1000 ALB 94710 609-D7
MONROE WY
- CNCD 94521 593-D2
MONSANTO WY
1700 CCCo 94520 572-C3
MONSON LN
- LFYT 94549 611-E6
MONTAGUE AV
4800 OAKL 94561 576-D7
MONTAIR CT
- DNVL 94526 652-H3
MONTAIR DR
- DNVL 94526 652-G3
MONTAIR PL
100 DNVL 94526 652-H3
MONTALVIN DR
- CCCo 94806 569-A5
400 CCCo 94806 568-J5
MONTALVO CT
5400 PLE 94588 693-G7
MONTANA DR
100 DNVL 94526 633-C6
1300 CNCD 94521 593-F6
MONTANA ST
- BREN 94513 616-H1
- RCH 94801 608-D1
1700 OAK 94602 650-D4
MONTANYA CT
100 WLCK 94597 612-A3
MONTARA DR
4400 ANT 94531 595-H2
MONTAUK CT
2000 CCCo 94514 617-H6
MONTAUK WY
2000 CCCo 94514 617-H6
MONTA VISTA AV
2600 ELCR 94530 589-C6
MONT BLANC CT
100 DNVL 94526 653-D6
MONTCLAIR AV
400 OAK 94606 650-A4
600 OAK 94610 650-A4
MONTCLAIR CIR
2000 WLCK 94597 612-A3
MONTCLAIR CT
1900 WLCK 94597 612-A3
2500 PIN 94564 569-G6
MONTCLAIR DR
1900 WLCK 94597 612-A3
MONTCLAIR PL
- BREN 94513 596-D6
MONTCLAIRE PL
100 SRMN 94583 673-F6
MONTCREST PL
400 DNVL 94526 652-H2
MONTE AV
- PDMT 94611 630-B7
MONTE ALBERS WY
- CCCo 94506 654-D6
MONTEBELLO CT
3000 CNCD 94518 592-H2
MONTE BUENA AV
3200 SPAB 94806 588-J1
MONTE CARLO WY
100 DNVL 94506 653-H5
MONTECELLO AV
- PDMT 94611 630-A7
MONTECELLO ST
- CCCo 94565 573-H2
MONTECILLO CT
300 CCCo 94595 632-B1
MONTECILLO DR
200 CCCo 94595 632-C1
300 WLCK 94595 632-C1
MONTECITO CRES
100 CCCo 94597 612-A4
MONTECITO CT
- ANT 94531 595-F5
- BREN 94513 616-B1
N MONTECITO CT
- CNCD 94521 593-B6
MONTECITO DR
- BREN 94513 596-B7
- BREN 94513 616-B1
- CNCD 94521 593-B6
- DNVL 94526 652-J2
N MONTECITO DR
- CNCD 94521 593-B6
S MONTECITO DR
- CNCD 94521 593-B6
MONTECITO LN
1300 PIN 94564 569-E5
MONTECITO PL
- BREN 94513 616-B1
MONTECITO RD
100 MrnC 94901 587-A1
MONTE CREST CT
- CCCo 94595 632-C1
MONTE CRESTA AV
- RCH 94803 589-B4
- RCH 94805 589-B4
6300 RCH 94806 589-B4
MONTE CRESTA DR
- PLHL 94523 592-B7
- WLCK 94597 592-B7
MONTEGO
1200 WLCK 94598 612-E4
MONTEGO DR
100 HER 94547 570-C6
200 DNVL 94526 653-A4
200 DNVL 94526 652-J4
MONTEGO PL
- DNVL 94526 653-A4
MONTEIRA LN
500 CCCo 94553 591-E2
MONTE LINDA
- OAKL 94561 596-G3
MONTERA CT
3700 CCCo 94803 589-C3
MONTEREY AV
1200 BERK 94707 609-F7
1200 BERK 94706 609-F7
2100 MRTZ 94553 571-F4
2200 CCCo 94553 571-F4
5900 CCCo 94805 589-B5
MONTEREY BLVD
2300 OAK 94611 650-E2
2300 OAK 94602 650-G4
3500 OAK 94619 650-G5
MONTEREY CT
- BREN 94513 616-C4
- CCCo 94506 654-B7
3500 CNCD 94519 592-J1
4300 CCCo 94514 617-G7
MONTEREY DR
2500 PIN 94564 569-G7
1000 ANT 94509 575-A7
6400 DBLN 94568 694-A3
MONTEREY LN
100 CCCo 94506 654-B7
MONTEREY ST
1300 RCH 94804 609-B3
MONTEREY TER
- ORIN 94563 610-J7
- ORIN 94563 611-A7
- ORIN 94563 631-A1
MONTERROSA CT
- BREN 94513 616-D1
MONTE SERENO DR
1800 CCCo 94507 633-B5
MONTE SERENO PL
100 CCCo 94507 633-C6
MONTE VEDA DR
- ORIN 94563 630-J3
MONTE VERDE DR
2300 PIN 94564 569-H7
5700 CCCo 94803 589-F1
MONTEVIDEO CT
- SRMN 94583 673-E5
MONTEVIDEO DR
2100 PIT 94565 574-A4
2200 PIT 94565 573-J4
2900 SRMN 94583 673-E5
MONTEVINO CT
- OAKL 94561 576-C6
MONTEVINO WY
- OAKL 94561 576-C6
MONTE VISTA
1200 BEN 94510 550-J3
MONTE VISTA AV
600 OAK 94610 650-A1
1200 MRTZ 94553 571-D4
MONTE VISTA CT
- PLHL 94523 592-B7
1200 MRTZ 94553 571-H7
MONTE VISTA DR
2300 PIN 94564 569-H7
MONTE VISTA RD
- ORIN 94563 610-E6
MONTE VISTA RIDGE RD
200 ORIN 94563 610-E6
MONTEZUMA CT
600 WLCK 94598 612-E4
MONTEZUMA ST
900 PIT 94565 574-D2
MONTFIELD PL
700 CNCD 94518 592-H7
MONTGOMERY AV
2500 CNCD 94519 572-G6
E MONTGOMERY AV
4900 RCH 94804 609-A2
MONTGOMERY ST
100 SRMN 94583 673-F3
4400 OAK 94611 630-A7
MONTGOMERY HILL DR
- ANT 94531 595-D3
MONTI CIR
400 PLHL 94523 592-A5
MONTI CT
400 PLHL 94523 592-B5
MONTICELLO AV
100 PLHL 94523 592-C7
2400 OAK 94601 650-F7
2600 OAK 94619 650-F7
MONTICELLO CT
1800 OAKL 94561 576-C5
MONTICELLO RD
1100 LFYT 94549 611-E5
MONTIN CT
1600 WLCK 94597 612-B2
MONTOYA AV
5000 SPAB 94805 589-A4
MONTOYA CT
2100 PIT 94565 574-A3
MONTOYA WY
- DNVL 94506 653-F4
- DNVL 94526 653-F4
MONTPELIER CT
3100 PLE 94588 694-E6
MONTREAL CIR
3600 CNCD 94520 572-F5
MONTROSE CT
- BREN 94513 616-E2
MONTROSE DR
1700 CNCD 94519 593-A1
MONTROSE RD
- BERK 94707 609-G5
MONT SAINT MICHEL WY
100 MRTZ 94553 571-H5
MONUMENT BLVD
1200 CNCD 94520 592-F4
2000 PLHL 94523 592-D5
MONUMENT CT
2600 CNCD 94520 592-F4
MONUMENT WY
2500 CNCD 94518 592-G4
2500 CNCD 94520 592-G4
MONZA CT
- DNVL 94526 653-D2
MONZAL AV
5900 OAK 94611 630-C6
MOON CT
900 LFYT 94549 611-E6
MOONRAKER CT
100 VAL 94590 550-C2
MOONRAKER DR
300 VAL 94590 550-C1
MOONSTONE CT
- HER 94547 569-G4
MOORE CT
- OAKL 94561 596-C2
- SRMN 94583 673-E5
2400 PIN 94564 569-J7
2400 PIN 94564 589-J1
MOORE DR
- OAKL 94561 596-C2
6600 OAK 94611 630-G7
MOORE PL
- DBLN 94568 694-A4
MOORE ST
2400 PIN 94564 569-J7
MOORILLA LN
- SRMN 94582 674-B4
MOOSE WY
1200 PIT 94565 574-E2
MORAGA AV
- PDMT 94611 630-A7
100 OAK 94611 630-A7
900 PDMT 94618 630-D7
5500 OAK 94618 630-D7
6200 OAK 94611 650-D1
MORAGA BLVD
3300 LFYT 94549 611-F6
MORAGA CT
- ORIN 94563 630-J3
MORAGA DR
2500 PIN 94564 569-G7
MORAGA RD
100 MRGA 94556 631-E7
600 LFYT 94549 631-E1
700 LFYT 94549 611-F7
2600 SPAB 94806 588-J2
MORAGA VIA
- ORIN 94563 631-A2
MORAGA WY
- ORIN 94563 630-H1
400 ORIN 94563 631-A3
700 MRGA 94556 631-E7
MORAGA VALLEY LN
- MRGA 94556 631-C6
MORAINE CT
- HER 94547 569-H4
4000 ANT 94509 595-F2
MORAINE WY
4000 ANT 94509 595-F2
MORAN AV
2800 RCH 94804 588-J4
MORCOM AV
2800 OAK 94619 650-F7
MORCOM PL
- OAK 94619 650-G7
MORE ST
- ALB 94706 609-D6
MOREAU WY
- BREN 94513 596-C6
MORECROFT RD
500 LFYT 94549 631-J4
MORELLO AV
- MRTZ 94553 571-H4
100 CCCo 94553 571-H4
100 PLHL 94523 591-J2
600 MRTZ 94553 591-H1
1700 PLHL 94523 592-A3
MORELLO CT
- MRTZ 94553 571-H7
MORELLO HEIGHTS CIR
2500 MRTZ 94553 571-G4
MORELLO HEIGHTS DR
- MRTZ 94553 571-H4
MORELLO HILLS DR
900 MRTZ 94553 571-H5
MORELLO PARK DR
1100 MRTZ 94553 571-H5
MORENGO CT
5500 CNCD 94521 593-E7
MORENGO DR
5400 CNCD 94521 593-E7
MORENO AV
2900 PLE 94588 694-E7
MORETTI DR
3200 CNCD 94519 572-G6
MORGAN
600 RCH 94801 588-C7
MORGAN AV
2800 OAK 94602 650-E4
MORGAN CT
1500 WLCK 94597 612-B3
4700 OAKL 94561 576-B7
MORGAN DR
2700 SRMN 94583 673-C4
2700 CCCo 94583 673-C4
MORGAN WY
5000 ANT 94531 595-H4
MORGAN TERRITORY RD
1100 AlaC 94551 675-G5
1900 CCCo 94551 675-F3
2400 CCCo 94517 614-F6
3800 CCCo 94517 634-F1
5100 CCCo 94517 635-A6
5100 CCCo 94551 635-A6
9500 CCCo 94551 (655-D1 See Page 635)
MORI CT
- OAKL 94561 576-F7
MORI ST
200 PIT 94565 574-C5
MORLEY DR
2800 OAK 94611 650-F2
MORNING GLORY CT
- OAKL 94561 596-G2
500 SRMN 94582 653-J7
MORNING GLORY DR
500 BEN 94510 551-A1
1200 CNCD 94521 593-B4
MORNING GLORY LN
- MRTZ 94553 571-J6
MORNING GLORY WY
- OAKL 94561 596-G2
MORNING HILLS CT
100 SRMN 94582 673-J6
MORNINGHOME RD
500 DNVL 94526 653-C3
MORNINGSIDE DR
3300 RCH 94803 589-G2
5500 CLAY 94517 593-F5
MORNINGSIDE PL
- CCCo 94507 632-D2
MORNINGSIDE ST
900 BREN 94513 616-J3
MORNINGSIDE WY
800 PLHL 94523 592-D4
MORNING STAR CT
300 PIT 94565 574-A3
MORNING SUN DR
2500 RCH 94806 568-J7
MORNINGTON CT
- CCCo 94582 674-B4
MORNINGTON LN
- CCCo 94582 674-B4
MORNING VALE CT
3900 ANT 94531 596-A4
MORNINGVIEW CT
1300 CNCD 94521 593-B4
MORPETH ST
5700 OAK 94618 630-C6
MORPHEW ST
100 SRFL 94901 587-A4
MORRELL CT
1100 CNCD 94521 593-F7
MORRILL CT
- OAK 94618 630-B6
MORRILL LN
- OAK 94618 630-B6
MORRIS AV
6500 ELCR 94530 589-B7
6500 ELCR 94530 609-B1
MORRIS ST
900 CLAY 94517 593-H7
MORRISON AV
3200 OAK 94602 650-C5
MORRIS RANCH RD
200 DNVL 94526 653-A4
MORRO CT
2900 ANT 94531 595-H2
MORRO DR
1900 PIT 94565 574-E3
2800 ANT 94531 595-H2
MORROW DR
5300 SPAB 94806 589-A3
MORROW COVE DR
- VAL 94590 550-C2
MORTON AV
800 RCH 94806 568-G7
MORTON WY
2100 ANT 94509 595-A1
2100 ANT 94509 575-A7
MORWOOD DR
4700 RCH 94803 589-F1
MOSELLE CT
2800 WLCK 94598 612-J3
MOSS CT
1200 PIT 94565 574-E6
MOSS LN
- LFYT 94549 611-F5
MOSSBRIDGE CT
900 PLHL 94523 592-D4
MOSSBRIDGE LN
- ORIN 94563 610-H3
MOSS HOLLOW CT
100 BREN 94513 616-E3
MOSS WOOD CT
- DNVL 94506 653-F5
MOSSWOOD CT
3900 CNCD 94519 573-A7
MOSSWOOD DR
- OAKL 94561 596-G2
3600 LFYT 94549 611-D7
MOSSWOOD RD
- BERK 94704 630-A2
MOSSY CT
1300 CNCD 94521 593-D5
MOSSY OAK CT
- CCCo 94506 653-H1
MOSSY OAK DR
2600 CCCo 94506 653-H1
MOTA DR
500 CCCo 94565 573-D2
MOTT DR
- CCCo 94507 632-J4
MOTT PL
- OAK 94619 651-A5
MOUND AV
7100 ELCR 94530 609-C1
MOUNT CT
1400 CNCD 94518 592-H2
MOUNT ST
400 RCH 94805 589-B6
MOUNTAIN AV
500 PDMT 94611 650-C1
MOUNTAIN BLVD
400 OAK 94611 630-C5
1800 OAK 94611 650-E1
2500 OAK 94602 650-E1
3800 OAK 94619 650-G4
4900 OAK 94605 650-H6
4900 OAK 94613 650-H6
MOUNTAIN ASH LN
- CCCo 94582 674-A2
MOUNTAIN CANYON LN
100 CCCo 94507 633-C6
MOUNTAIN CANYON PL
100 CCCo 94507 633-C6
MOUNTAINGATE WY
2600 OAK 94611 650-F2
MOUNTAIN HOUSE RD
3200 AlaC 94551 (658-B4 See Page 638)
3200 CCCo 94514 (658-B4 See Page 638)
MOUNTAIN RIDGE DR
300 DNVL 94506 654-A6
300 DNVL 94506 653-J6
MOUNTAINRISE PL
- DBLN 94568 693-D4
MOUNTAIN SIDE CT
- CNCD 94521 593-B6
MOUNTAIN SPRING RD
3400 LFYT 94549 611-G1
MOUNTAIN VALLEY PL
- DNVL 94506 653-J5
MOUNTAIN VIEW AV
- CCCo 94565 573-J2
4100 OAK 94605 650-H7
MOUNTAIN VIEW BLVD
1000 CCCo 94596 612-F7
MOUNTAIN VIEW CT
500 PLHL 94523 592-B4
MOUNTAIN VIEW DR
- BREN 94513 616-A2
- CCCo 94513 616-A2
- PLE 94588 693-F5
800 LFYT 94549 611-E6
2200 CNCD 94520 572-F7
2700 CCCo 94513 597-D4
MOUNTAIN VIEW LN
- LFYT 94549 611-D7
MOUNTAIN VIEW PL
- LFYT 94549 611-E7
MOUNTAIN VIEW RD
3400 ANT 94509 595-C1
MOUNTAIN VIEW TER
- BEN 94510 551-B4
MOUNTAIRE CIR
200 CLAY 94517 613-H1
MOUNTAIRE CT
100 CLAY 94517 613-H2
MOUNTAIRE DR
3100 ANT 94509 575-E7
3500 ANT 94509 595-E1
MOUNTAIRE PKWY
100 CLAY 94517 613-H1
MOUNTAIRE PL
- CLAY 94517 613-H1
MOUNT ALPINE PL
- CLAY 94517 613-H1
MOUNTBATTEN CT
1200 CNCD 94518 592-D7
MOUNT CONNESS CT
- ANT 94531 595-E4
MOUNT CONNESS WY
- ANT 94531 595-F4
MOUNT DARWIN CT
1800 ANT 94531 595-E6
MOUNT DAVIDSON CT
500 CLAY 94517 613-H2
MOUNT DAY PARK CT
- ANT 94531 595-C5
MOUNT DELL DR
500 CLAY 94517 613-H1
MOUNT DIABLO BLVD
1200 WLCK 94596 612-C5
2000 WLCK 94597 612-C5
2200 WLCK 94595 612-C5
3200 LFYT 94549 611-C6
MOUNT DIABLO CT
3200 LFYT 94549 611-H6
MOUNT DIABLO ST
1400 CNCD 94520 592-F1
2500 CNCD 94518 592-G2
MOUNT DIABLO SCENIC BLVD
2000 CCCo 94506 653-F1
2000 CCCo 94528 653-F1
2000 CCCo 94506 633-F7
2000 CCCo 94528 633-F7
2300 CCCo 94528 633-F7
MOUNT DUNCAN DR
600 CLAY 94517 613-H2
MOUNT EDEN PL
- CLAY 94517 613-H1
MOUNT EMORY CT
- CLAY 94517 613-H1
MOUNT ETNA DR
100 CLAY 94517 613-H1
MOUNT EVEREST CT
100 CLAY 94517 613-H2
MOUNT GOETHE CT
- ANT 94531 595-F5
MOUNT GOETHE WY
- ANT 94531 595-F5
MOUNT HAMILTON CT
- CLAY 94517 613-H1
MOUNT HAMILTON DR
1500 ANT 94531 595-E3
MOUNT HENRY CT
- ANT 94531 595-E5
MOUNT HOOD CIR
2700 CNCD 94519 572-H6
MOUNT HOOD CT
5600 MRTZ 94553 591-G1
MOUNT ISABEL RD
- ANT 94531 595-D4
MOUNT KENNEDY DR
100 MRTZ 94553 591-G1
MOUNT LEE PL
- CLAY 94517 613-H1
MOUNT MCKINLEY CT
- CLAY 94517 613-H1
MOUNT OLIVET CT
600 CLAY 94517 613-H2
MOUNT OLIVET PL
500 CLAY 94517 613-H2
MOUNT OLYMPUS PL
- CLAY 94517 613-H1
MOUNT OSO CT
- ANT 94531 595-F5
MOUNT PALOMAR PL
300 CLAY 94517 613-J2
MOUNT PISGAH RD
1300 WLCK 94596 612-D5
MOUNT POWELL CT
1900 ANT 94531 595-E6
MOUNT RAINIER CT
- CLAY 94517 613-H1
MOUNT RUSHMORE PL
- CLAY 94517 613-H1
MOUNT SCOTT CT
- CLAY 94517 613-H1
MOUNT SEQUOIA CT
400 CLAY 94517 613-J2
MOUNT SEQUOIA PL
300 CLAY 94517 613-J2
MOUNT SHASTA CT
100 CLAY 94517 613-H1
MOUNT SHASTA PL
100 CLAY 94517 613-H1
MOUNT SIERRA PL
300 CLAY 94517 613-J2
MOUNT SILLIMAN WY
1600 ANT 94531 595-E3
MOUNT STAKES CT
- ANT 94531 595-F4
MOUNT TAM CIR
5100 PLE 94588 693-J7
MOUNT TAM CT
100 MRTZ 94553 591-H1
MOUNT TAMALPAIS CT
- CLAY 94517 613-H1
MOUNT TAMALPAIS DR
400 CLAY 94517 613-H2
MOUNT TAMALPAIS PL
- CLAY 94517 613-H2
MOUNT TETON CT
- CLAY 94517 613-H1
MOUNT TETON PL
- CLAY 94517 613-H1
MOUNT TRINITY CT
100 CLAY 94517 613-H2
MOUNT VERNON DR
100 CLAY 94517 593-H7
100 CLAY 94517 613-H1
MOUNT VERNON PL
- DBLN 94568 694-H3
MOUNT VIEW DR
400 MRTZ 94553 571-E5
MOUNT WASHINGTON WY
300 CLAY 94517 613-H1
MOUNT WHITNEY CT
- CLAY 94517 613-J1
MOUNT WHITNEY DR
2200 PIT 94565 573-J4
MOUNT WHITNEY WY
- CLAY 94517 613-H1
MOUNT WILSON CT
- ANT 94531 595-F5
MOUNT WILSON PL
200 CLAY 94517 613-J1
MOUNT WILSON WY
- CLAY 94517 613-J1
MOUNT ZION DR
5800 CLAY 94517 593-G6
MOVIDA DR
1000 CNCD 94518 592-F5
MOYER PL
- OAK 94611 650-D1
MOYERS RD
2500 RCH 94806 589-A1
MOZART DR
4000 RCH 94803 589-B2
MOZDEN LN
- PLHL 94523 592-C5
MRACK CT
- CCCo 94506 654-C5
MRACK RD
100 CCCo 94506 654-C5
MUIR AV
- PDMT 94610 650-C2
MUIR CT
3200 ANT 94509 574-J7
MUIR LN
100 CCCo 94507 632-G7
MUIR RD
- MRTZ 94553 571-F6
1500 MRTZ 94553 572-A7
2400 CCCo 94553 572-A7
MUIR ST
2000 SPAB 94806 588-H2
MUIR WY
- BERK 94708 609-J6
MUIR CREEK DR
- PIT 94565 574-G7
MUIRFIELD LN
5100 CNCD 94521 593-D6
MUIR STATION RD
100 MRTZ 94553 571-E6
MUIRWOOD CT
7400 PLE 94588 693-J7
MUIRWOOD DR
- ANT 94509 595-E5
4500 PLE 94588 693-H7
MULBERRY CT
- RCH 94806 568-J6
100 HER 94547 570-A4
900 ANT 94509 595-F2
4000 CNCD 94519 593-B1
7000 DBLN 94568 693-H2
MULBERRY DR
3800 CNCD 94519 593-B1
MULBERRY LN
- CCCo 94597 612-B4
- WLCK 94597 612-B4
MULBERRY PL
- RCH 94806 568-J5
1100 BREN 94513 596-D7
8100 DBLN 94568 693-H1
MULBERRY WY
900 ANT 94509 595-F2
MULEDEER CT
4500 ANT 94509 595-F3

STREET Block	City	ZIP	Pg-Grid
MULLBERRY LP			
100	PLHL	94523	592-B6
MULLENS DR			
2900	RCH	94806	589-A1
MULLER RD			
300	WLCK	94598	612-E4
MULLIGAN CT			
-	RCH	94806	568-H6
MUNOZ CT			
-	DBLN	94568	694-G3
MUNRAS PL			
3200	SRMN	94583	673-G5
MUNSON WY			
1400	OAK	94606	650-B7
MURCHIO CT			
1400	CNCD	94521	593-D5
MURCHIO DR			
4900	CNCD	94521	593-D5
MURCIA CT			
200	DNVL	94506	653-G4
MURDOCK ST			
-	RCH	94804	588-H7
MURIETTA			
-	PIT	94565	574-B3
MURIETTA CT			
11700	DBLN	94568	693-F3
MURILLO CT			
-	OAKL	94561	576-G7
MURINDO PL			
300	SRMN	94583	673-A2
MURPHY DR			
-	CCCo	94513	597-B5
2000	CCCo	94806	569-B4
MURRA CT			
3400	SPAB	94806	568-H7
MURRAY LN			
600	LFYT	94549	631-H2
MURRY CT			
-	ANT	94531	595-C4
MURWOOD CT			
100	CCCo	94596	612-D7
MURWOOD DR			
1400	CCCo	94596	612-D7
MUSCAT CT			
1300	BREN	94513	596-F7
MUSK CT			
2400	ANT	94531	595-G2
MUSTANG CT			
-	DNVL	94526	653-B6
1800	CNCD	94521	593-F4
4500	ANT	94531	595-H3
MUSTANG DR			
1100	DNVL	94526	653-C5
MUTH DR			
-	ORIN	94563	610-J6
MY RD			
-	LFYT	94549	591-G7
-	LFYT	94549	611-G1
MY WY			
-	BERK	94708	609-H4
MYNAH CT			
-	CCCo	94596	612-F7
MYRA DELL RD			
2500	WLCK	94597	612-B3
E MYRICK CT			
500	CLAY	94517	613-J1
W MYRICK CT			
600	CLAY	94517	613-J1
MYRNA WY			
1100	CCCo	94572	570-A1
MYRTLE CT			
400	BEN	94510	551-A1
MYRTLE DR			
-	DBLN	94568	694-D4
4700	CCCo	94521	593-E2
5000	CNCD	94521	593-E3
MYRTLE BEACH DR			
-	BREN	94513	616-B3
MYRTLE BEACH LN			
2100	DNVL	94526	653-E7
MYRTLEWOOD CT			
900	ANT	94509	595-F1
1400	MRTZ	94553	571-J7
MYSTIC PL			
-	CCCo	94507	632-J2
N			
N ST			
100	BEN	94510	551-B4
400	ANT	94509	575-B4
W N ST			
1200	BEN	94510	550-J3
NACE AV			
-	PDMT	94611	650-A1
NACE ST			
-	PDMT	94611	650-A1
NADINE CT			
-	DNVL	94526	652-H1
1800	PLHL	94523	592-B4
NADINE PL			
-	DNVL	94526	652-H1
NAIROBI PL			
3800	OAK	94605	650-H7
NANCY DR			
-	CCCo	94806	569-A5
NANCY LN			
-	SRMN	94582	674-B3
200	PLHL	94523	592-B5
NANCY ST			
200	BREN	94513	596-G7
NANDINA WY			
1700	ANT	94531	595-E3
NANIMO CT			
100	ANT	94509	575-C7
NANTUCKET CT			
600	WLCK	94598	613-A3
NANTUCKET CV			
100	SRFL	94901	587-A2
NANTUCKET DR			
-	PIT	94565	574-B2
10000	SRMN	94582	673-H5
NAOMI CT			
3100	PIN	94564	569-F6
NAPA AV			
100	CCCo	94572	549-H7
600	CCCo	94572	569-H1
1900	BERK	94707	609-G6
NAPA CT			
-	CCCo	94565	573-E1
NAPA ST			
2100	RCH	94804	609-B4
6000	OAK	94618	630-A6
NAPOLI CT			
200	HER	94547	570-B6
NARANJA DR			
3000	WLCK	94598	612-H2
NARCISSUS CT			
-	DNVL	94506	654-C6
NARDI LN			
100	CCCo	94553	571-J4
200	CCCo	94553	572-A4
NARDUCCI CT			
-	OAKL	94561	596-D1
NARRAGANSETT CT			
-	VAL	94591	550-E2
NARRAGANSETT CV			
-	SRFL	94901	587-A2
NASH AV			
300	ANT	94509	575-E4
NASON AV			
2500	ELCR	94530	589-B7
NASSAU CT			
100	SRMN	94582	673-G4
NASSAU LN			
-	BREN	94513	596-C6
NATALIE CT			
3600	RCH	94805	589-A5
NATALIE DR			
100	MRGA	94556	631-E2
NATALIE LN			
400	CCCo	94506	654-C5
NATALIE WY			
1200	PIT	94565	574-F5
NATASHA DR			
4000	LFYT	94549	611-B5
NATCHEZ CT			
900	WLCK	94598	612-H4
NATCHEZ DR			
900	WLCK	94598	612-H4
NATHALEE DR			
5100	CNCD	94521	593-E4
NATHAN PL			
-	DNVL	94526	632-J6
NATIONAL CT			
700	RCH	94804	588-E7
NATIVIDAD LN			
-	MRGA	94556	631-E3
NATOMA CT			
-	CCCo	94513	617-F2
900	WLCK	94596	612-F7
NATOMA DR			
1900	CNCD	94519	572-J6
1900	CNCD	94519	573-A7
NAUSIN LN			
3200	LFYT	94549	611-H4
NAUTICAL CT			
4000	CCCo	94513	617-E7
NAUTICAL CV			
-	HER	94547	569-G1
NAUTILUS CT			
-	PIT	94565	573-J2
-	PIT	94565	574-A2
NAUTILUS DR			
100	VAL	94591	550-D1
NAUTILUS PL			
-	PIT	94565	574-A2
NAVAJO CT			
-	ANT	94531	595-H5
-	PLE	94588	694-G7
-	CCCo	94507	632-D2
NAVAJO PL			
500	DNVL	94526	653-B5
NAVAJO WY			
-	ANT	94531	595-H5
NAVARONNE WY			
700	CNCD	94518	592-H5
NAVARRO CT			
2100	ANT	94509	595-A1
NAVELLIER ST			
1000	ELCR	94530	609-D1
NAVIGATORS PL			
-	CCCo	94511	577-E4
NAVONE ST			
100	VAL	94591	550-C1
NAVY ST			
100	PIT	94565	574-E3
NEAD PL			
-	SRMN	94583	673-E6
NEAH CT			
1100	ANT	94509	575-F7
NEAL CT			
-	CCCo	94806	569-C6
NEAR CT			
100	WLCK	94596	612-D7
NEBERGALL CT			
700	BREN	94513	616-F1
NEBRASKA DR			
5500	CNCD	94521	593-F6
NECTAR DR			
800	BREN	94513	616-H2
NEELY CT			
-	CCCo	94507	632-H2
NEILSON ST			
500	BERK	94707	609-F5
900	ALB	94706	609-F5
1100	BERK	94706	609-E7
1300	BERK	94702	609-E7
NELDA WY			
2100	CCCo	94507	632-H5
NELLIE AV			
-	PDMT	94618	630-C7
NELLIS CT			
-	PIT	94565	574-C2
NELSON AV			
4000	CNCD	94520	572-E4
NELSON DR			
4300	RCH	94803	589-D2
NELSON LN			
-	ORIN	94563	631-A3
NEMEA CT			
-	LFYT	94549	631-E1
NEMEA LN			
700	LFYT	94549	631-E1
NEPHI CT			
-	LFYT	94549	631-E1
NEPTUNE CT			
-	CCCo	94565	573-E1
-	SRMN	94583	693-H1
NEPTUNE PL			
100	SRMN	94583	693-H1
NEPTUNES CT			
100	VAL	94591	550-F3
NERINE CT			
-	DNVL	94506	654-C6
NERO CT			
1900	WLCK	94598	612-E2
NEROLY RD			
4100	BREN	94561	596-C2
4100	OAKL	94561	596-C2
4300	OAKL	94561	576-A6
5200	CCCo	94561	596-G3
NETHERBY DR			
200	PLHL	94523	591-J2
NETHERBY PL			
200	PLHL	94523	591-J2
NETHERCOTT CT			
2600	WLCK	94598	612-H4
NETHERTON CT			
-	MRGA	94556	631-E4
NETTO CT			
1700	CNCD	94521	593-D3
NETTO DR			
4900	CNCD	94521	593-D4
NEVA CT			
-	DNVL	94526	653-A3
-	OAK	94611	630-C5
2300	PIN	94564	569-F7
NEVADA AV			
200	RCH	94801	608-D1
NEVADA CT			
5400	CNCD	94521	593-D6
NEVADA LN			
2600	ANT	94509	575-D1
NEVADA ST			
600	BEN	94510	551-E2
NEVE CT			
-	DBLN	94568	694-G4
NEVIL ST			
3600	OAK	94601	650-E6
NEVIN AV			
100	RCH	94801	588-F6
2300	RCH	94804	588-J6
3300	RCH	94805	588-J6
3700	RCH	94805	589-A7
W NEVIN AV			
-	RCH	94801	588-E6
NEVIN PZ			
-	RCH	94801	588-G6
NEW LN			
100	PLHL	94523	592-B6
NEW BEDFORD CT			
700	VAL	94591	550-E1
NEW BEDFORD RD			
200	VAL	94591	550-E1
NEWBERRY PL			
-	MRGA	94556	631-F6
NEW BOSTON CT			
-	DNVL	94526	653-C3
NEWBRIDGE WY			
11800	DBLN	94568	693-G4
NEWBURY			
100	HER	94547	569-H3
NEWBURY AV			
600	ANT	94509	575-C6
NEWBURY LN			
-	CCCo	94513	617-F5
NEWCASTLE CT			
1800	WLCK	94595	612-C7
4000	CNCD	94519	593-B1
NEWCASTLE LN			
300	CCCo	94506	654-B5
7100	DBLN	94568	693-J2
NEWCASTLE RD			
3900	CNCD	94519	593-B1
NEWCASTLE WY			
900	PIT	94565	574-E5
NEWELL AV			
1200	WLCK	94596	612-C6
1600	WLCK	94595	612-C6
1600	CCCo	94595	612-B7
W NEWELL AV			
2700	CCCo	94595	611-J7
NEWELL CT			
-	CCCo	94595	611-J7
NEWELL HILL PL			
1200	WLCK	94596	612-D6
NEWFIELDS LN			
-	DBLN	94568	694-F2
NEWGATE CT			
300	CCCo	94506	654-A5
NEWHALL PKWY			
1400	CNCD	94521	593-D5
NEW HAMPSHIRE DR			
1200	CNCD	94521	593-D6
NEW HAVEN CT			
600	WLCK	94598	612-H6
NEWHAVEN PL			
-	CNCD	94518	593-A5
NEWHAVEN ST			
-	DBLN	94568	694-D4
NEW HOLLAND CT			
900	BREN	94513	616-E2
NEW HOLLAND DR			
800	BREN	94513	616-E2
NEW LAKE PL			
2300	MRTZ	94553	592-A1
NEWMAN CT			
-	CLAY	94517	593-G7
NEWMAN DR			
4400	PLE	94588	694-E6
4400	PLE	94566	694-E6
NEW MELONES CIR			
-	CCCo	94513	617-G2
NEWPORT AV			
3000	SRMN	94583	673-F5
NEWPORT CT			
2100	CCCo	94514	617-F7
3200	WLCK	94598	612-J1
7000	DBLN	94568	693-J2
NEWPORT DR			
-	CCCo	94513	617-F5
1900	PIT	94565	574-E4
2100	CCCo	94514	617-F7
NEWPORT LN			
2400	CCCo	94514	617-F5
NEWPORT PL N			
4000	CCCo	94514	617-G7
NEWPORT PL S			
2300	CCCo	94514	617-G7
NEWPORT WY			
-	SRFL	94901	587-A2
NEWRY PL			
8400	DBLN	94568	693-H2
NEW SEABURY CT			
600	WLCK	94598	613-C4
NEWTON DR			
900	BREN	94513	616-C1
NEWTON WY			
2000	CNCD	94518	592-F5
3700	PLE	94588	694-F6
NEW YORK DR			
1200	CNCD	94521	593-E6
NEZ PERCE WY			
-	ANT	94531	595-H5
NIAGARA CT			
800	CNCD	94518	592-G6
NIBLICK CT			
-	RCH	94806	568-H5
NICCOLITE CT			
-	ANT	94509	595-F2
NICE ST			
5600	PLE	94588	694-C6
NICHOLAS CT			
-	SRMN	94582	673-J1
800	BREN	94513	616-F1
NICHOLAS DR			
1400	CNCD	94520	592-E4
NICHOLL AV			
-	RCH	94801	608-D1
200	RCH	94801	588-D7
NICHOLL CT			
2800	RCH	94804	588-J7
NICHOLS RD			
500	CCCo	94565	553-B7
NICHOLSON RD			
100	WLCK	94595	612-B6
NICKEL ST			
2600	CCCo	94806	569-B6
NICOL AV			
2600	OAK	94602	650-C5
NICOLE AV			
3600	PLE	94588	694-F7
NICOLETTE CT			
1900	MRTZ	94553	571-E4
NIDER LN			
700	ORIN	94563	610-J4
NIDO CT			
2200	ANT	94509	595-A1
NIEMEYER RD			
-	CCCo	94801	588-F3
NIGHTHAWK WY			
-	BREN	94513	596-E5
NIGHTINGALE CT			
-	OAKL	94561	596-H1
NIGHTINGALE DR			
3500	ANT	94509	595-C1
NIGHTOWL CT			
-	RCH	94803	589-F1
NIKE			
600	HER	94547	569-F3
NILES CT			
700	PIT	94565	574-A3
NIMITZ FRWY I-880			
-	OAK	-	650-A6
NIMITZ WY			
-	CCCo	94553	589-H7
-	CCCo	94553	610-A3
-	CCCo	94708	609-J2
-	CCCo	94708	610-A3
-	RCH	94805	589-F6
-	RCH	94805	609-H1
NINA CT			
-	CCCo	94507	633-D5
NINA PL			
-	PIT	94565	574-C6
NOAKES CT			
-	ANT	94531	595-C4
NOAKES DR			
-	ANT	94531	595-C3
NOB PL			
-	SRMN	94583	673-E5
NOB HILL			
-	CCCo	94806	569-A5
NOB HILL AV			
800	PIN	94564	569-C4
NOB HILL DR			
-	DNVL	94526	633-C6
200	WLCK	94596	612-E6
200	CCCo	94596	612-E6
NOBI LN			
-	ORIN	94563	630-J1
-	ORIN	94563	631-A1
NOBLE CT			
1300	ELCR	94530	609-D2
NOEMI DR			
1800	CNCD	94519	593-A1
1800	CNCD	94519	592-J1
NOGAL CT			
2800	ANT	94509	575-J5
NOGALES CT			
3200	LFYT	94549	611-H5
NOGALES ST			
-	BERK	94705	630-A4
1100	LFYT	94549	611-J5
NOIA AV			
1400	ANT	94509	575-E5
NOME AV			
1600	CCCo	94805	589-C5
NONIE RD			
-	ORIN	94563	630-J1
NOPAL CTE			
100	WLCK	94598	612-H2
NORA CT			
400	WLCK	94597	592-E7
NORA LEE CT			
-	ANT	94509	575-E6
NORCROSS LN			
100	OAKL	94561	576-E6
NORDSTROM LN			
3600	LFYT	94549	611-E5
NORFOLK CT			
6500	MRTZ	94553	591-H4
NORFOLK DR			
6900	OAK	94705	630-C3
NORFOLK PL			
500	CCCo	94506	654-A5
11800	DBLN	94568	693-F2
NORINE DR			
1500	PIT	94565	574-G6
NORLYN DR			
100	WLCK	94596	612-D5
NORMA LN			
-	BREN	94513	596-G7
NORMAN AV			
100	CCCo	94520	572-G2
NORMAN CT			
-	CCCo	94595	632-B1
NORMAN LN			
-	OAK	94618	630-B6
NORMANDIE AV			
5300	OAK	94619	650-G7
NORMANDY CT			
-	DNVL	94506	653-H5
2500	WLCK	94598	592-F7
NORMANDY LN			
-	ORIN	94563	610-F4
-	WLCK	94598	592-F7
NORRIS CT			
300	SRMN	94583	673-B2
NORRIS RD			
2000	CCCo	94596	612-E7
NORRIS ST			
1400	BREN	94513	616-J1
NORRIS CANYON PL			
100	SRMN	94583	673-E1
NORRIS CANYON RD			
2000	CCCo	94583	672-G5
2000	CCCo	94583	673-A3
2000	SRMN	94583	673-D2
8700	AlaC	94552	672-G5
NORRIS CANYON TER			
200	SRMN	94583	673-E1
NORSE CT			
-	PLHL	94523	592-B3
NORSE DR			
1900	PLHL	94523	592-B3
NORTH CIR			
-	OAK	94611	630-G6
NORTH LN			
-	ORIN	94563	610-F6
NORTH PT			
4800	CCCo	94514	617-H5
NORTH ST			
-	CCCo	94565	573-H2
1500	BERK	94703	609-F7
NORTHAMPTON AV			
-	BERK	94707	609-G5
NORTHAMPTON CT			
3200	PLE	94588	694-E6
NORTHBROOK CT			
500	ANT	94509	575-E7
NORTHCREEK CIR			
100	WLCK	94598	612-E1
NORTHCREEK PL			
100	WLCK	94598	612-E2
NORTH ESTATES DR			
900	BREN	94513	616-F1
NORTHGATE AV			
-	BERK	94708	609-J6
NORTH GATE PL			
700	WLCK	94598	613-A3
NORTHGATE PL			
200	OAKL	94561	576-E6
NORTH GATE RD			
-	WLCK	94598	612-J3
100	WLCK	94598	613-A3
100	CCCo	94598	613-A3
600	CCCo	94598	633-D1
NORTH HILL CT			
-	SRMN	94583	673-A1
NORTHLAND AV			
7400	SRMN	94583	693-G1
7400	SRMN	94583	673-G7
NORTHLAND PL			
7500	SRMN	94583	673-F7
7500	SRMN	94583	693-F1
NORTH OAK CT			
-	DNVL	94506	654-B6
NORTHOAK DR			
1000	WLCK	94598	612-E2
NORTHPARK CT			
3700	CNCD	94519	593-A1
NORTHPOINTE CT			
6400	MRTZ	94553	591-H3
NORTHRIDGE CT			
-	ANT	94509	575-D7
1100	CNCD	94518	592-H4
NORTH RIDGE DR			
3700	RCH	94806	568-J7
3800	RCH	94806	569-A7
NORTHRIDGE DR			
3600	CNCD	94518	592-H4
NORTHRIDGE LN			
-	LFYT	94549	611-F5
NORTHRIDGE RD			
4800	MRTZ	94553	571-G7
NORTHSIDE AV			
1300	BERK	94702	609-E7
NORTHSTAR DR			
100	PIT	94565	574-A3
NORTHVALE RD			
800	OAK	94610	650-B3
NORTHVIEW CT			
-	DNVL	94506	653-H6
NORTHWOOD CIR			
2100	CNCD	94520	572-E6
NORTHWOOD CT			
-	CCCo	94506	654-C4
-	ORIN	94563	630-F6
-	PIT	94565	574-H6
1700	OAK	94611	630-F6
4200	OAKL	94561	596-G1
NORTHWOOD DR			
-	ORIN	94563	630-H1
-	ORIN	94563	610-H7
3200	CNCD	94520	572-F5
NORTON AV			
3200	OAK	94602	650-F4
NORTON ST			
1500	PIT	94565	574-E3
NORTON WY			
2200	ANT	94509	575-D6
NORTONVILLE CT			
-	ANT	94531	595-D4
NORTONVILLE RD			
-	CCCo	94509	594-F5
5700	CCCo	94517	594-C1
5700	CCCo	94565	594-F5
NORTONVILLE WY			
-	ANT	94531	595-D4
NORVELL CT			
1100	ELCR	94530	609-D2
NORVELL ST			
400	ELCR	94530	609-C1
NORWALK CT			
2500	MRTZ	94553	572-A5
NORWICH CT			
-	SRMN	94583	673-G7
NORWICH PL			
1000	WLCK	94598	612-F1
NORWICH WY			
-	PLHL	94523	592-A4
NORWOOD AV			
-	CCCo	94707	609-F3
1000	OAK	94602	650-C3
1000	OAK	94610	650-C3
NORWOOD CT			
100	CCCo	94707	609-F3
NORWOOD PL			
-	CCCo	94707	609-F3
NORWOOD VW			
-	CCCo	94707	609-F3
NOTA CT			
100	VAL	94590	550-C1
NOTRE DAME AV			
900	CNCD	94518	592-G5
NOTTINGHAM CIR			
-	CLAY	94517	593-G6
NOTTINGHAM CT			
-	BREN	94513	616-F2
5600	CCCo	94803	589-G4
NOTTINGHAM DR			
500	BREN	94513	616-F2
4200	CCCo	94506	654-A4
5700	OAK	94611	630-D6
5700	CCCo	94803	589-G4
NOTTINGHAM PL			
-	CLAY	94517	593-G6
200	CCCo	94506	654-A5
6500	DBLN	94568	694-A2
NOTTINGHAM WY			
-	CLAY	94517	593-G6
NOVA DR			
-	PDMT	94610	650-A2
NOVA PTH			
-	OAK	94618	630-B5
NOVARA CT			
-	DNVL	94526	653-C1
NOVATO CT			
1400	WLCK	94597	611-J2
NOYES WY			
-	BEN	94510	551-E3
NOYO ST			
3300	OAK	94602	650-G4
NUALA CT			
900	CNCD	94518	592-E6
NUALA ST			
1500	CNCD	94518	592-E6
NUEVO RD			
100	DNVL	94526	633-D6
NUGGET CT			
500	DNVL	94526	633-A7
500	DNVL	94526	653-A1
NULL DR			
4100	ANT	94509	574-H6
NULTY DR			
4000	CNCD	94521	593-A2
NUNN ST			
4600	BREN	94513	616-G3
5000	RCH	94804	609-B1
NURSERY LN			
-	CNCD	94518	592-E5
-	CNCD	94520	592-E5
1400	WLCK	94596	612-D6
NUTMEG CT			
100	HER	94547	570-A4
2300	ANT	94509	575-H6
NUTMEG DR			
1000	OAKL	94561	596-E2
NUTMEG LN			
3300	WLCK	94598	612-J1
NUT TREE LN			
100	OAKL	94561	576-B7
NYLA ST			
-	CCCo	94514	637-D2
O			
O ST			
100	ANT	94509	575-B4
100	BEN	94510	551-C4
OAHU CT			
400	SRMN	94582	673-E1
OAHU DR			
200	PIT	94565	574-E5
OAK			
-	BEN	94510	551-C6
OAK AV			
-	CCCo	94805	589-C5
OAK CT			
-	DNVL	94526	653-A3
100	CLAY	94517	593-H7
100	HER	94547	570-A4
200	ORIN	94563	630-H2
3200	ANT	94509	574-J7
3300	LFYT	94549	631-G1
6700	DBLN	94568	693-J3
OAK DR			
-	ORIN	94563	630-J3
-	ORIN	94563	631-A4
-	MrnC	94901	587-C1
OAK LN			
-	CCCo	94516	631-A7
-	SRFL	94901	587-B1
-	ORIN	94563	610-H4
OAK PL			
100	PIT	94565	574-D3
OAK RD			
-	BEN	94510	551-E5
-	ORIN	94563	630-H1
100	CCCo	94507	633-A7
100	CCCo	94597	612-C3
100	PDMT	94610	650-B2
2500	WLCK	94597	612-C3
OAK ST			
-	CCCo	94513	616-H1
-	BREN	94513	616-F1
500	ELCR	94530	609-D4
800	LFYT	94549	611-E7
900	CLAY	94517	593-H7
900	CLAY	94517	613-G1
1000	CCCo	94553	571-F4
2100	CNCD	94520	592-F2
2300	BERK	94708	609-H6
OAK ARBOR RD			
-	ORIN	94563	610-G5
OAK BLUFF LN			
-	DBLN	94568	694-F2
OAK BRANCH WY			
-	CCCo	94595	612-A7
OAK BREEZE CT			
400	MRTZ	94553	571-F5
OAKBRIDGE LN			
100	CCCo	94553	591-D2
OAK BROOK CT			
3700	PLE	94588	694-F5
OAKBROOK CT			
4400	CNCD	94521	593-B5
OAKBROOK LN			
900	WLCK	94597	612-A1
OAK BROOK PL			
-	PLHL	94523	591-J4
OAKBROOK PL			
-	PIT	94565	574-F7
OAK CANYON RD			
-	CCCo	94549	632-A3
-	WLCK	94595	632-A3
2700	LFYT	94549	632-A3
OAK CREEK CT			
100	PLHL	94523	592-B1
3600	CCCo	94598	613-A3
OAK CREEK DR			
2800	SRMN	94583	673-F7
OAK CREEK RD			
-	CCCo	94803	589-G4
OAK CREST CT			
1200	MRTZ	94553	571-G7
1300	ANT	94531	595-E5
OAKCREST CT			
100	DNVL	94526	653-D6
OAKCREST DR			
1900	OAK	94602	650-E2
OAK CREST LN			
-	CCCo	94507	632-D2
OAK CREST PL			
300	PIT	94565	573-F5
OAK CREST WY			
1300	ANT	94531	595-E5
OAKDALE AV			
3900	OAK	94605	650-H7
OAKDALE CT			
5100	PLE	94588	693-J7
OAKDALE PL			
4200	PIT	94565	574-D7
OAKDENE CT			
-	WLCK	94596	612-E6
OAK FLAT RD			
-	ORIN	94563	610-J5
OAK FOREST AV			
4500	OAKL	94561	576-D7
OAKGATE DR			
100	CCCo	94506	654-C5
OAK GATE PL			
-	PLHL	94523	592-D7
OAK GLEN CIR			
2300	MRTZ	94553	592-A1
OAK GLEN CT			
-	CCCo	94507	633-C5
300	MRTZ	94553	592-A1
OAK GLEN DR			
300	OAKL	94561	596-G1
OAK GROVE CT			
2000	CNCD	94518	592-F6
3800	OAKL	94561	596-H2
OAK GROVE DR			
3900	OAKL	94561	596-G1
OAK GROVE RD			
700	CNCD	94518	592-F5
700	WLCK	94598	592-F5
700	WLCK	94598	612-H1
1000	CNCD	94520	592-F5
OAKHAM CT			
200	SRMN	94583	673-E5
OAKHAM DR			
3000	SRMN	94583	673-E5
OAK HAVEN CT			
1400	ANT	94531	595-E5
OAK HAVEN WY			
1200	ANT	94531	595-E5
OAK HILL CT			
1200	PIN	94564	569-E5
OAK HILL LN			
3500	CCCo	94517	614-E7
OAK HILL RD			
900	LFYT	94549	611-E6
OAK HILLS CIR			
2100	PIT	94565	573-G3
OAK HILLS DR			
2200	PIT	94565	573-G4
OAK HOLLOW CT			
1400	PIN	94564	569-E5
OAKHURST CT			
-	DBLN	94568	694-F2
OAKHURST DR			
5600	CLAY	94517	593-H5
OAKHURST WY			
-	DBLN	94568	694-F3
OAK KNOLL CT			
-	WLCK	94596	612-E6
OAK KNOLL DR			
-	CNCD	94521	593-B6
OAK KNOLL LN			
-	ORIN	94563	630-H2
OAK KNOLL LP			
-	WLCK	94596	612-D6
OAK KNOLL PTH			
2800	BERK	94705	630-A3
OAK KNOLL RD			
1000	LFYT	94549	611-A6
5600	CCCo	94803	569-F7
5600	CCCo	94803	589-F1
OAK KNOLL TER			
2700	BERK	94705	630-A3
OAKLAND AV			
700	OAK	94610	650-A1
700	PDMT	94611	650-A1
700	OAK	94611	650-A1
1000	PDMT	94610	650-A1
1300	CNCD	94518	592-G2
1500	CNCD	94519	592-G2
2200	PLE	94588	694-E7
OAKLAND BLVD			
1300	WLCK	94596	612-B5
1700	WLCK	94597	612-B5
OAKLAND CT			
-	WLCK	94596	612-B5
-	WLCK	94597	612-B5
OAKLEAF CT			
1000	CNCD	94521	593-D5
OAKLEY RD			
2000	OAKL	94561	576-A6
2200	ANT	94509	575-H6
2900	ANT	94509	576-A6
OAK MANOR PZ			
6500	MRTZ	94553	591-H4
OAKMEAD DR			
1700	CNCD	94520	592-F3
OAK MEADOW CT			
-	CCCo	94507	633-A5
4600	ANT	94531	595-J3
OAKMONT AV			
-	PDMT	94610	650-B2
-	PDMT	94611	650-B2
OAKMONT CT			
-	BREN	94513	616-B1
-	CCCo	94806	569-C4
700	DNVL	94526	653-E6
5600	CCCo	94514	617-J6
OAKMONT DR			
-	RCH	94806	568-J5
1100	WLCK	94595	631-J1
1100	WLCK	94595	632-A2
OAKMONT PL			
1400	PIT	94565	574-G5
OAKMONT WY			
2000	WLCK	94595	632-A2
OAKMORE PL			
1700	OAK	94602	650-D3
OAKMORE RD			
3900	OAK	94602	650-D3
OAK PARK BLVD			
1400	PLHL	94523	592-A7
OAKPARK CT			
3700	CNCD	94519	593-A1
OAK PARK LN			
100	PLHL	94523	592-A7
100	PLHL	94523	612-A1
OAKPOINT CT			
-	PIT	94565	573-G4
5300	CNCD	94521	593-D7
OAKPOINT DR			
-	PIT	94565	573-G5
OAKRAIDER DR			
3000	CCCo	94507	632-H3
OAKRIDGE CT			
-	CCCo	94506	653-J2
-	PIT	94565	574-G6
1900	CNCD	94521	593-E3
OAKRIDGE DR			
100	CCCo	94506	653-J2
OAKRIDGE LN			
-	ORIN	94563	611-A7
-	CCCo	94506	653-J2
1800	PIT	94565	574-G5
OAK RIDGE RD			
-	BERK	94705	630-A4
700	PIN	94564	569-E4
OAK ROYAL DR			
1500	CNCD	94521	593-C3
OAKSHADE CT			
1400	PIT	94565	574-F6
OAKSHIRE CT			
1200	WLCK	94598	612-E2
OAKSHIRE PL			
400	CCCo	94507	632-J3
500	CCCo	94507	633-A3
OAKSIDE CT			
900	PLHL	94523	592-D4
OAKSTONE CT			
5300	CNCD	94521	613-D2
OAK TRAIL CT			
-	CCCo	94507	633-A5
OAK TREAT CT			
-	CCCo	94597	612-D2
OAKTREE CT			
900	PIT	94565	573-J3
OAKVALE AV			
-	BERK	94705	630-A4
OAKVALE CT			
-	WLCK	94597	612-B5
OAKVALE RD			
-	WLCK	94596	612-B5
500	CCCo	94597	612-A4
2100	WLCK	94597	612-B5

STREET
Block City ZIP Pg-Grid

OAKVALE TER
500 WLCK 94597 612-B5
OAK VALLEY DR
- SRMN 94582 673-J6
- SRMN 94582 674-A6
OAK VIEW AV
1500 CCCo 94706 609-F4
1600 CCCo 94707 609-F4
OAK VIEW CIR
900 LFYT 94549 611-G6
OAKVIEW DR
1900 OAK 94602 650-E3
OAK VIEW LN
2900 OAKL 94561 596-G2
OAKVIEW LN
- MRTZ 94553 591-F1
OAK VIEW TER
- ORIN 94563 630-J1
100 DNVL 94526 652-G2
OAK VILLA CT
- OAKL 94561 596-H1
OAK VISTA CT
900 CCCo 94549 591-G5
OAKVUE CT
- PLHL 94523 592-B6
OAKVUE LN
300 PLHL 94523 592-A7
OAKVUE RD
- PLHL 94523 592-B7
OAKWOOD CIR
200 MRTZ 94553 571-G5
1100 CLAY 94517 614-A2
OAKWOOD CT
- SPAB 94806 588-J3
- OAK 94611 630-F6
4200 CNCD 94521 593-B2
OAKWOOD DR
6400 OAK 94611 630-F6
OAKWOOD LN
3100 CCCo 94507 632-J4
OAKWOOD RD
- ORIN 94563 630-J2
OAKWOOD WY
800 OAKL 94561 576-D4
OARSMAN CT
100 HER 94547 570-B6
OASIS DR
900 CNCD 94518 592-F6
OBERLIN AV
600 CCCo 94708 609-F3
OBERON DR
3000 CCCo 94597 592-D7
3000 CCCo 94523 592-D7
OBISPO CT
11500 DBLN 94568 693-F3
OBRIEN RD
3000 RCH 94806 589-B2
OBSERVATION PL
- OAK 94611 630-E5
OBSERVATION WY
- ANT 94531 595-F5
OBSERVATORY AV
- OAK 94619 650-H6
OBSIDIAN WY
100 HER 94547 569-G4
400 CLAY 94517 593-J5
OCEAN AV
500 RCH 94801 588-C7
OCEAN CT
1200 BREN 94513 596-E7
OCEANA DR
300 PIT 94565 574-A3
OCEAN PINES LN
- CCCo 94507 632-J3
OCEAN VIEW AV
300 CCCo 94707 609-E4
OCEAN VIEW DR
5600 OAK 94618 630-A5
OCEANVIEW DR
- CCCo 94565 553-D7
OCHO RIOS DR
900 DNVL 94526 653-A4
OCHO RIOS PL
- DNVL 94526 653-A4
OCONNOR DR
400 PIN 94564 569-B4
2400 CCCo 94806 569-B4
3500 LFYT 94549 611-F7
OCTAVIA ST
2700 OAK 94619 650-E6
ODESSA AV
100 PIT 94565 554-D7
100 PIT 94565 574-D1
ODIN DR
400 PLHL 94523 592-A3
ODIN PL
300 PLHL 94523 592-A3
ODONNELL DR
2600 CCCo 94806 569-B6
ODYSSEY WY
- DBLN 94568 693-G4
OFARRELL DR
400 BEN 94510 551-A2
700 BEN 94510 550-J2
OGAWA CT
- DNVL 94506 654-C6
OGDEN CT
5500 CNCD 94521 593-H5
OGDEN PL
- BREN 94513 616-C4
OHANNESON RD
4900 OAK 94605 651-A7
OHARA AV
100 OAKL 94561 576-E7
400 BREN 94513 596-E5
900 OAKL 94561 596-E1
2700 BREN 94561 596-E4
4500 BREN 94513 616-G1
OHARA CT
800 OAKL 94561 596-E1
1500 CLAY 94517 593-F5
OHARE AV
2600 SPAB 94806 588-H2
OHARE DR
1400 BEN 94510 551-B4
OHARTE RD
2500 CCCo 94806 569-B5
OHATCH DR
2400 CCCo 94806 569-B5
OHIO AV
100 RCH 94801 588-F7
100 RCH 94804 588-H7
3700 RCH 94804 589-A7
W OHIO AV
300 RCH 94804 588-E7
300 RCH 94801 588-E7
OHIO CT
5500 CNCD 94521 593-F6
OHLONE AV
- ALB 94710 609-D6
900 ALB 94706 609-D6
OHLONE HTS
1800 CLAY 94517 593-H5
OHLONE TR
- CCCo 94583 652-D1
OHLSON LN
- DNVL 94526 632-J7
- DNVL 94526 633-A7
OHMAN PL
5600 CLAY 94517 593-G5
OHMSTEDED RD
- CCCo 94513 597-B3
OIL CANYON TR
- CCCo 94517 594-H7
OKEEFE ST
- OAKL 94561 576-H6
OLD BLACKHAWK RD
3500 DNVL 94506 653-H5
OLD COUNTY RD
- CCCo 94525 550-A5
OLD CREEK CIR
2200 PIT 94565 574-E4
OLD CREEK RD
700 DNVL 94526 653-C3
OLD CROW CANYON RD
2300 SRMN 94583 673-B1
OLDE CREEK PL
- LFYT 94549 611-H5
OLD FARM CT
500 DNVL 94526 653-B3
OLD FARM RD
400 DNVL 94526 653-B3
OLD GLEN COVE RD
1300 SolC 94591 550-E1
1300 VAL 94591 550-E1
OLD GLORY CT
3600 ANT 94509 595-C3
OLDHAM CT
300 DNVL 94526 653-C3
OLD HAWTHORNE DR
900 LFYT 94549 611-H6
OLD HWY 40
12700 CCCo 94525 550-A5
12700 CCCo 94572 549-J6
12700 CCCo 94572 550-A5
OLD JONAS HILL RD
700 LFYT 94549 611-F7
700 LFYT 94549 631-E1
OLD KILN WY
1100 RCH 94801 608-D3
OLD KIRKER PASS RD
1800 CNCD 94521 593-F4
OLD MILL RD
- SRMN 94583 673-B1
OLD MILLSTONE LN
- LFYT 94549 611-G7
OLD MOUNTAIN VIEW DR
3500 LFYT 94549 611-F7
OLD OAK CT
100 OAKL 94561 596-G1
OLD OAK DR
1900 WLCK 94595 632-B1
OLD ORCHARD CT
400 DNVL 94526 653-C3
OLD ORCHARD DR
500 DNVL 94526 653-C3
OLD ORCHARD RD
- MRTZ 94553 571-G5
OLD QUARRY RD
600 PLHL 94523 592-B2
OLD RANCH CT
400 SRMN 94582 673-H6
OLD RANCH RD
3400 SRMN 94582 673-J7
3400 SRMN 94583 673-J7
3400 SRMN 94582 674-A6
OLD RANCH ESTATES DR
1500 SRMN 94582 673-J6
OLD REDWOOD HWY
- CCCo 94516 630-J7
- CCCo 94516 631-A7
OLD REDWOOD RD
5200 OAK 94619 650-J5
OLD RODGERS RANCH CT
- PLHL 94523 591-J6
OLD SAN PABLO DAM RD
- CCCo 94553 589-H6
- CCCo 94553 609-J1
- CCCo 94553 610-A2
- CCCo 94563 610-C4
OLD SANTA RITA RD
3500 PLE 94588 694-D6
OLD SCHOOL RD
5200 CCCo 94588 654-G5
OLD STABLE PL
- WLCK 94596 632-F1
OLD STAGECOACH RD
- CCCo 94561 596-G4
- BREN 94561 596-G4
OLD SUISUN RD
2200 BEN 94510 551-C3
OLD TOWN LN
- DNVL 94526 652-J1
- DNVL 94526 653-A1
OLD TUNNEL RD
- CCCo 94563 630-E3
2500 OAK 94611 630-D4
3100 LFYT 94549 611-J5
3200 LFYT 94549 612-A5
3200 CCCo 94595 611-J5
3200 CCCo 94595 612-A5
OLD VINE CT
100 PLHL 94523 592-A4
OLD WESTBURY WY
- DBLN 94568 694-H2
OLEANDER DR
1100 LFYT 94549 611-B5
OLEANDER ST
- BREN 94513 616-H2
OLEARY LN
1800 CCCo 94521 593-E3
OLEASTER DR
- SRMN 94582 674-A2
OLINDA CT
- CCCo 94803 589-G4
2300 PIN 94564 569-F7
OLINDA RD
5500 CCCo 94803 589-G3
5800 RCH 94803 589-G3
OLIVE AV
- PDMT 94611 650-A1
1400 CCCo 94805 589-C6
OLIVE CT
- BREN 94513 616-H2
100 HER 94547 569-J4
4600 RCH 94804 609-A2
OLIVE DR
4700 CNCD 94521 593-D3
OLIVE LN
- SRMN 94583 693-H1
1700 ANT 94509 575-F5
3100 OAKL 94561 596-H3
OLIVE ST
- BREN 94513 616-H2
2400 CCCo 94553 571-F4
OLIVE WY
- PIT 94565 574-E7
OLIVE BRANCH CT
200 BEN 94510 551-C3
OLIVEGLEN CT
- PIT 94565 573-F4
800 CNCD 94521 613-D1
OLIVEIRA LN
- LFYT 94549 631-H1
OLIVER CT
- CCCo 94803 589-G4
400 PIN 94564 569-C4
3500 LFYT 94549 611-F7
OLIVERA CT
2100 CNCD 94520 572-F6
OLIVERA RD
- CNCD 94519 572-E5
1900 CNCD 94520 572-E5
E OLIVERA RD
2500 CNCD 94519 572-G6
2700 CNCD 94519 592-H1
OLIVEWOOD CT
700 PIT 94565 574-E5
OLIVEWOOD DR
700 PIT 94565 574-E5
OLIVIA CT
2000 PLE 94588 694-E7
OLIVIA ST
- WLCK 94597 612-B1
OLMO WY
1800 WLCK 94598 612-E1
OLNEY CT
- DNVL 94526 653-C5
OLSON CT
9100 PLE 94588 693-G6
OLYMPIA CIR
3600 PIT 94565 574-C4
OLYMPIA DR
200 PIT 94565 574-C5
OLYMPIA ST
1600 CNCD 94521 593-A2
OLYMPIA FIELDS CT
- SRMN 94583 673-H7
OLYMPIA FIELDS DR
9400 SRMN 94583 673-H7
OLYMPIC BLVD
- CCCo 94595 612-A7
1500 WLCK 94596 612-C6
1900 WLCK 94595 612-C6
2600 CCCo 94595 611-J7
2600 LFYT 94549 611-H7
OLYMPIC CT
- BREN 94513 616-B1
2200 MRTZ 94553 572-A7
OLYMPIC DR
1800 MRTZ 94553 571-J7
1800 MRTZ 94553 572-A7
OLYMPIC PL
- WLCK 94596 612-C5
OLYMPIC OAKS DR
3100 LFYT 94549 611-H7
OLYMPUS
400 HER 94547 569-F3
OLYMPUS AV
1400 BERK 94708 609-J7
1500 BERK 94708 610-A7
1500 BERK 94720 610-A7
OMEGA CIR
3200 PLE 94588 694-D7
OMEGA RD
2000 SRMN 94583 653-B7
2100 SRMN 94583 673-C1
ONA CT
- SRMN 94583 673-F6
ONATE CT
- DBLN 94568 694-G3
ONEDIA ST
- OAKL 94561 576-C6
ONEIDA CIR
2100 DNVL 94526 653-D7
ONEIDA CT
400 DNVL 94526 653-D7
ONEIDA WY
- ANT 94531 595-H5
ONEIL CIR
100 HER 94547 569-E3
ONEIL CT
- CCCo 94806 569-C6
- OAKL 94561 576-F7
ONLEY DR
1600 PLHL 94523 592-B4
ONTARIO ST
100 OAKL 94561 576-C6
ONYX CT
100 HER 94547 569-G5
ONYX PL
6700 DBLN 94568 693-J2
OPAL CT
- SRMN 94582 673-F2
100 HER 94547 569-G4
OPAL ST
1900 CCCo 94596 612-D6
1900 WLCK 94596 612-D6
OPAL WY
4900 ANT 94531 596-A4
OPCEN RD
- CCCo 94553 571-G3
- MRTZ 94553 571-G3
OPHIR CT
300 MRTZ 94553 571-J7
ORAM LN
- PLHL 94523 592-A7
ORAM WY
- CCCo 94565 573-F2
ORANGE CT
800 BREN 94513 616-H2
ORANGE ST
200 VAL 94590 550-C1
1000 CNCD 94518 592-E5
2100 CCCo 94553 571-F4
2100 MRTZ 94553 571-F4
ORANGE WY
2600 ANT 94531 595-G5
ORANGE BLOSSOM CT
- DNVL 94526 653-B4
ORANGE BLOSSOM WY
800 DNVL 94526 653-B4
ORANGEVALE
200 PIT 94565 574-B3
ORANGEWOOD CT
4200 CNCD 94521 593-B2
ORCHARD AV
3300 CNCD 94518 592-H3
5900 RCH 94804 609-C3
ORCHARD CT
- CCCo 94507 632-F5
- ORIN 94563 630-J3
ORCHARD DR
200 BREN 94513 616-G2
ORCHARD LN
- BERK 94704 630-A2
ORCHARD LN
- CCCo 94507 632-F5
900 ANT 94509 575-E4
1500 WLCK 94595 612-C7
1800 CCCo 94513 616-E6
2400 CCCo 94553 571-F3
ORCHARD RD
- ORIN 94563 630-J2
200 ORIN 94563 631-A3
1000 LFYT 94549 611-E5
ORCHARD ESTATES DR
- WLCK 94598 612-J4
ORCHARD HILL CT
3400 LFYT 94549 611-F6
ORCHARD MEADOW RD
3400 OAK 94613 650-G7
ORCHARD OAKS CT
- OAKL 94561 576-B7
ORCHARD PARK DR
4400 OAKL 94561 576-E7
ORCHARD VALLEY LN
3300 LFYT 94549 611-G6
ORCHARD VIEW AV
300 MRTZ 94553 571-G5
ORCHID CT
100 HER 94547 570-A4
800 BREN 94513 616-D1
ORCHID DR
200 PIT 94565 574-E5
900 BREN 94513 596-D7
900 BREN 94513 616-D1
ORCHID ST
3300 OAK 94601 650-C6
ORDAZ CT
- DBLN 94568 694-G5
ORDWAY ST
900 ALB 94707 609-F6
900 ALB 94706 609-F6
1100 BERK 94706 609-F6
1300 BERK 94702 609-E7
OREGANO CT
- OAKL 94561 596-E2
2700 PLE 94588 694-H4
OREGANO WY
200 OAKL 94561 596-E2
OREGOLD LN
- BREN 94561 596-D3
OREGON CT
1200 CNCD 94521 593-E6
OREGON DR
1300 CNCD 94521 593-E6
OREGON ST
- RCH 94801 608-D1
3900 BEN 94510 551-E2
ORIN LN
2100 PLHL 94523 592-B3
ORINDA CIR
- PIT 94565 574-B4
ORINDA CT
- PIT 94565 574-C4
ORINDA LN
- PIT 94565 574-C4
700 WLCK 94597 612-B4
ORINDA WY
- ORIN 94563 610-G7
ORINDA VIEW RD
- ORIN 94563 610-J3
- ORIN 94563 611-A3
ORINDAWOODS DR
100 ORIN 94563 610-H7
ORIOLE CT
100 HER 94547 569-H5
3800 ANT 94509 594-J1
ORIOLE RD
- ORIN 94563 610-F5
ORION
800 HER 94547 569-F3
ORION CT
- CCCo 94803 589-D1
ORLANDO CT
1500 WLCK 94597 611-J2
ORLEANS CT
1700 WLCK 94598 592-E7
1700 WLCK 94598 612-F1
ORLEANS DR
100 MRTZ 94553 571-G6
2200 PIN 94564 569-E3
ORMINDALE CT
- OAK 94611 630-E5
OROURKE DR
100 CCCo 94806 569-B4
ORO VALLEY CIR
1700 WLCK 94596 612-G7
ORO VALLEY CT
1800 WLCK 94596 612-H7
OROVILLE CT
- CCCo 94513 617-F3
OROVILLE ST
3500 ANT 94531 595-H1
ORSINI CT
5100 PLE 94588 694-H4
ORTEGA AV
3200 LFYT 94549 611-H5
ORTEGA DR
1500 MRTZ 94553 591-H1
ORTHO WY
700 RCH 94801 588-F5
ORTIZ CT
- CCCo 94561 596-G4
ORWOOD RD
3500 CCCo 94513 597-D7
4400 CCCo 94513 617-G1
5700 CCCo 94513 (618-B1 See Page 597)
ORYAN ST
- DBLN 94568 694-E4
OSAGE PL
5700 CNCD 94521 593-F7
OSBORN WY
- DNVL 94526 653-D3
OSBORNE CT
- OAK 94611 650-G2
OSBORNE LN
500 PLHL 94523 592-B4
OSCAR ST
1500 RCH 94804 609-B3
OSCEOLA CT
900 WLCK 94598 612-H4
OSHER CT
- CCCo 94507 632-H2
OSO GRANDE WY
- ANT 94531 595-H2
OSPREY CT
- CCCo 94514 (657-E2 See Page 638)
OSPREY DR
- ANT 94509 594-J2
OSTRANDER RD
5900 OAK 94618 630-B6
OSWEGO CT
- LFYT 94549 611-G7
- LFYT 94549 631-G1
OTOOLE WY
2400 CCCo 94806 569-B5
OTSEGO ST
- OAKL 94561 576-C6
OTTER BROOK LP
- CCCo 94513 617-G4
OTTAWA ST
- OAKL 94561 576-C6
OUTLOOK AV
5900 OAK 94605 650-H7
OUTLOOK CT
800 BREN 94513 596-D7
OUTLOOK ST
800 BREN 94513 596-D7
800 BREN 94513 616-D1
OUTRIGGER CIR
700 BREN 94513 596-E7
OUTRIGGER DR
100 VAL 94591 550-D1
OVAL RD
- OAK 94611 630-C5
OVER ST
3300 OAK 94619 650-E6
OVERDALE AV
6100 OAK 94605 650-H7
OVEREND AV
4100 RCH 94804 609-A1
OVERHILL CT
- ORIN 94563 630-H1
OVERHILL RD
- ORIN 94563 630-H1
100 ORIN 94563 631-A1
1800 CNCD 94520 572-E6
OVERLAKE CT
- OAK 94611 630-E6
S OVERLOOK
200 SRMN 94582 673-F3
OVERLOOK CT
- HER 94547 569-F3
- WLCK 94597 612-B4
1100 SRMN 94582 673-F2
OVERLOOK DR
- CNCD 94521 593-C6
1000 SRMN 94582 673-E2
2100 WLCK 94597 612-B3
2300 CCCo 94597 612-B4
OVERLOOK LN
- RCH 94803 569-C7
OVERLOOK RD
900 BERK 94708 609-J5
OVERLOOK TER
- HER 94547 569-F3
OVERLOOK WY
3800 RCH 94806 569-A7
OWENS CT
2100 PIN 94564 569-F6
5300 PLE 94588 694-B5
OWENS DR
5000 PLE 94588 694-A5
OWL CT
- DBLN 94568 694-D4
700 ANT 94509 595-F2
OWL HILL CT
- ORIN 94563 630-J2
OWL HILL RD
- ORIN 94563 630-J2
OWL RIDGE CT
1900 WLCK 94597 611-H2
OXBOW CT
7900 DBLN 94568 693-G4
OXBOW LN
7800 DBLN 94568 693-G4
OXFORD
100 HER 94547 569-H3
OXFORD AV
2700 RCH 94806 588-J1
2800 RCH 94806 589-A2
OXFORD CIR
7400 DBLN 94568 694-A2
OXFORD CT
- PIT 94565 574-C4
100 CCCo 94507 632-J2
OXFORD DR
- OAKL 94561 596-D1
100 MRGA 94556 651-E2
OXFORD LN
- BREN 94513 596-H7
- BREN 94513 616-H1
OXFORD PL
3200 CNCD 94518 592-H3
6500 DBLN 94568 694-A2
OXFORD ST
800 BERK 94707 609-G5
1200 BERK 94709 609-H7

P

P ST
- BEN 94510 551-B4
PABCO
- CCCo 94553 571-G2
PABLO VISTA AV
1700 SPAB 94806 588-H1
PACE BLVD
- PIT 94565 574-H4
PACER PL
- WLCK 94596 632-F2
PACHECO BLVD
1100 MRTZ 94553 571-E3
2300 CCCo 94553 571-G3
4500 CCCo 94553 572-B6
4700 MRTZ 94553 572-B6
5700 CCCo 94553 592-C1
PACHECO ST
1900 CNCD 94520 592-F1
2700 CNCD 94519 592-G1
PACHECO MANOR DR
5300 CCCo 94553 572-B7
PACIFIC AV
- PDMT 94611 650-B1
- CCCo 94572 549-H7
300 RCH 94801 608-C1
400 RCH 94801 588-B6
2700 CNCD 94518 592-G2
PACIFIC CT
200 ANT 94509 595-E1
900 WLCK 94598 612-G4
PACIFIC DR
- CCCo 94806 569-B5
PACIFICA AV
- CCCo 94565 573-D1
PACIFICA CT
1800 BEN 94510 551-C4
PACIFIC GROVE CT
- CCCo 94514 617-G7
PACIFIC OAK CT
- BREN 94513 616-A5
PACINI AV
200 PIT 94565 574-C6
PACKARD CT
1900 CNCD 94521 593-G4
PACKARD RIDGE RD
- ANT 94531 595-C5
PADDLEWHEEL DR
100 VAL 94591 550-F2
PADDOCK CT
- PLHL 94523 591-J3
5100 ANT 94531 595-G4
PADDOCK DR
2400 SRMN 94583 673-B3
PADDOCK LN
- SRMN 94583 673-B4
PADILLA CT
- DNVL 94526 653-C6
PADRE ST
3100 CCCo 94549 611-H1
PADRE WY
11600 DBLN 94568 693-F3
PAGE CT
1200 PIN 94564 569-C5
4000 PLE 94588 694-A7
PAGE ST
1100 BERK 94702 609-E7
PAGOSA CT
700 WLCK 94597 612-B2
700 DNVL 94526 653-B3
PAIGE CT
2100 PIT 94565 574-A3
PAINTED PONY RD
3700 RCH 94803 589-G1
PAISLEY CT
900 ANT 94509 575-C7
PAJARITO CT
100 BREN 94513 596-G5
PALA AV
- PDMT 94611 630-B7
- PDMT 94611 650-B1
PALACE CT
900 BEN 94510 550-H1
PALAMOS CT
- SRMN 94583 673-C3
PALANA CT
- CCCo 94595 612-B6
PALERMO CT
100 HER 94547 570-B6
PALI CT
- OAK 94611 630-C5
PALI WY
- PIT 94565 574-E5
PALINDO AV
- CNCD 94520 592-F3
PALISADE CT
1000 MRTZ 94553 571-H5
PALISADE DR
800 MRTZ 94553 571-H5
PALISADES WY
4400 ANT 94531 595-J1
PALM
- BEN 94510 551-C5
- CNCD 94518 592-G4
PALM AV
- HER 94547 569-J3
400 MRTZ 94553 571-F5
700 CCCo 94553 571-F4
1400 CCCo 94805 589-C6
PALM CT
2400 BREN 94513 616-B2
PALM DR
- PIT 94565 574-E5
- BREN 94513 616-B2
100 PDMT 94610 650-A2
PALM PL
100 BREN 94513 616-B2
PALMA VISTA
- CCCo 94528 633-F7
PALM BEACH WY
- ANT 94509 595-D1
PALMDALE CT
7700 PLE 94588 693-J7
PALMER AV
900 SPAB 94806 588-H1
3200 OAK 94602 650-C5
PALMER CT
- PLHL 94523 591-H5
PALMER DR
- CNCD 94521 593-E4
1800 PLE 94588 694-F7
PALMER PL
3400 PLE 94588 694-F7
PALMER RD
700 CCCo 94596 612-F7
800 CCCo 94596 632-F1
900 WLCK 94596 632-F1
PALMER ST
- SRMN 94583 693-F1
PALMETTO ST
2400 OAK 94602 650-D5
PALMETTO DUNES LN
- CCCo 94507 633-B4
PALMIRA CT
700 SRMN 94583 673-B3
PALMIRA PL
2400 SRMN 94583 673-B3
PALM MEADOW LN
2000 CNCD 94518 592-F7
PALMS DR
500 CCCo 94553 572-A3
PALMWOOD
- CCCo 94561 597-A1
PALMWOOD CT
3800 CNCD 94521 592-J3
PALMWOOD DR
3800 CNCD 94521 592-J3
3800 CNCD 94518 592-J3
PALO ALTO CT
- PLHL 94523 592-B2
PALO ALTO DR
3800 LFYT 94549 611-C5
PALOMA AV
600 OAK 94610 650-B3
PALOMA CT
300 MRTZ 94553 571-F5
2300 PIN 94564 569-F6
PALOMA CTE
- WLCK 94598 612-H2
PALOMA ST
2400 PIN 94564 569-F6
PALOMAR DR
4000 ANT 94531 595-G1
PALOMARES CT
1100 LFYT 94549 611-J5
PALOMARES ST
3100 LFYT 94549 611-H5
PALOMINO CT
700 WLCK 94596 632-G2
4600 ANT 94531 596-A3
PALOMINO PL
1800 CNCD 94521 593-F4
PALOMINO WY
4700 ANT 94531 596-A3
PALOS CT
2400 PIN 94564 589-J1
PALOU ST
800 VAL 94591 550-D1
PALO VERDE DR
1900 CNCD 94519 572-J7
4200 PIT 94565 574-F6
PALO VERDE WY
2900 ANT 94509 575-A7
PAMELA CT
- OAKL 94561 596-E1
- CCCo 94565 573-F1
200 CCCo 94803 589-G2
200 RCH 94803 589-G2
1500 CNCD 94520 592-E3
PAMELA DR
400 CCCo 94565 573-F1
PAMELIA WY
3300 PIT 94565 574-D4
PAMPAS AV
4300 OAK 94619 650-G6
PAMPAS CIR
4400 ANT 94531 595-G3
PAMPAS CT
4400 ANT 94531 595-G3
PAMPLONA CT
- SRMN 94583 673-D3
5500 CNCD 94521 593-G5
PANADERO CT
1000 CLAY 94517 593-G7
PANADERO WY
1000 CLAY 94517 593-G7
PANAMA AV
5100 RCH 94804 609-C3
PANCHO VILLA WY
3500 CNCD 94518 592-J3
PANDA CT
- ANT 94531 595-J2
PANDOREA CT
3200 PLE 94588 694-H4
PANGBURN LN
100 CCCo 94507 632-G7
PANORAMA CT
- BREN 94513 616-J2
- DNVL 94506 653-H5
300 BEN 94510 551-A2
PANORAMA DR
200 BEN 94510 551-B1
1200 LFYT 94549 611-C4
PANORAMA WY
100 BREN 94513 616-J3
PANORAMIC AV
- PIT 94565 574-C5
PANORAMIC DR
1100 MRTZ 94553 571-D4
2200 CNCD 94520 572-G4
PANORAMIC PL
- BERK 94704 630-A2
PANORAMIC WY
- BERK 94704 630-A2
- CCCo 94595 612-A7
300 OAK 94704 630-A2
600 OAK 94705 630-B2
PANTANO CIR
300 CCCo 94553 572-B7
PANTANO LN
200 CCCo 94553 572-B7
PANWOOD CT
- BREN 94513 596-D6
PAPPAS ST
200 PIT 94565 574-C5
PAR CT
- RCH 94806 568-H5
PARADISE CT
800 LFYT 94549 611-F7
PARADISE DR
- HER 94547 569-H2
1100 MRTZ 94553 571-H7
PARADISE LN
- BREN 94561 596-D4
- PLHL 94523 592-A7
PARADISE BAY CT
- RCH 94801 608-E3
PARADISE PEAK CT
1900 ANT 94531 595-E6
PARADISE VALLEY CT
600 DNVL 94526 653-E7
PARADISE VALLEY CT N
700 DNVL 94526 653-E7
PARADISE VALLEY CT S
600 DNVL 94526 653-E7
PARAISO CT
- DNVL 94526 653-B4
PARAISO DR
100 DNVL 94526 653-B4
PARAMOUNT RD
800 OAK 94610 650-B3
PARDEE CT
- CCCo 94513 617-F2
PARIS LN
1800 ANT 94509 575-G5
PARISH DR
2200 WLCK 94598 612-F1
PARK AV
100 CCCo 94595 612-B7
2500 CNCD 94520 572-F7
2500 CNCD 94520 592-F1
5800 CCCo 94805 589-B4
5800 RCH 94805 589-B4
PARK BLVD
- OAK 94611 630-F7
2000 OAK 94606 650-A4
2900 OAK 94610 650-A4
3800 OAK 94602 650-D3
4800 PDMT 94610 650-D3
4900 OAK 94611 650-D3
4900 PDMT 94611 650-D3
N PARK BLVD
- PIT 94565 574-G4
PARK CT
1100 RCH 94803 569-C7
2900 MRTZ 94553 571-G4
E PARK CT
- CCCo 94597 612-A4
W PARK CT
- CCCo 94597 612-A4
S PARK DR
1000 CCCo 94708 610-B6
1500 OAK 94708 610-C7
PARK GN
700 MRTZ 94553 571-E5
PARK LN
- CCCo 94511 577-D4
- ANT 94509 575-D5
100 RCH 94803 569-C7
200 PDMT 94610 650-B2
900 OAK 94610 650-B2
3200 LFYT 94549 611-H4
PARK PL
100 RCH 94801 588-D7
100 RCH 94801 608-D1
100 SRMN 94583 673-B2
1000 PLHL 94523 592-A4
3400 PLE 94588 694-G6
PARK RD
700 BEN 94510 551-F1
PARK ST
- HER 94547 569-F2
100 CCCo 94520 572-G2
400 MRGA 94556 631-E3
1900 MRTZ 94553 571-D4

STREET Block City ZIP Pg-Grid

PARK ST
2200 CNCD 94518 592-G2
2200 CNCD 94519 592-G2
2200 CNCD 94520 592-G2
2200 PIN 94564 569-E4
W PARK ST
2900 MRTZ 94553 571-D4
PARK WY
- PDMT 94611 630-B7
- PDMT 94611 650-A1
500 BREN 94513 616-G1
700 BERK 94710 609-C7
800 ELCR 94530 609-E3
PARK AND RIDE CT
- CCCo 94513 617-F5
PARK BLVD WY
3700 OAK 94610 650-B4
PARK CENTRAL
800 RCH 94803 589-C1
800 RCH 94803 569-C7
PARK CENTRAL CT
800 RCH 94803 569-C7
PARKDALE PZ
6500 MRTZ 94553 591-H4
PARKDALE WY
- ANT 94531 595-H4
PARKER AV
- CCCo 94572 549-H7
400 CCCo 94572 569-H1
PARKER LN
500 ANT 94509 575-E5
PARKER RD
2800 RCH 94806 589-B2
PARK GATE
- BERK 94708 609-J6
PARKGATE CT
2200 RCH 94806 568-J7
2200 RCH 94806 588-J1
PARK GATE RD
- LFYT 94549 631-J4
PARK GLEN CT
700 CNCD 94521 593-E5
PARKGREEN CIR
4900 ANT 94531 595-J4
PARKHAVEN CT
600 PLHL 94523 591-J2
PARKHAVEN DR
100 CCCo 94506 654-A6
100 DNVL 94506 654-A6
1400 PLHL 94523 591-J2
PARK HIGHLANDS BLVD
5200 CNCD 94521 593-E5
PARKHILL CT
4500 ANT 94531 595-H3
PARK HILL RD
500 DNVL 94526 653-C3
PARK HILLS RD
1000 BERK 94708 609-J5
1100 BERK 94708 610-A6
PARKHURST DR
13000 OAK 94619 651-B6
PARK LAKE CIR
200 WLCK 94598 612-F2
PARKLAND CT
4700 ANT 94531 595-H4
PARK LAND DR
1400 CNCD 94521 593-E5
PARKLAND DR
- WLCK 94597 612-A2
PARKLANE DR
- ORIN 94563 631-A1
PARK LANE PZ
300 MRTZ 94553 591-H3
PARKMALL CT
3700 CNCD 94519 593-A1
PARKMEAD CT
100 CCCo 94595 612-B7
PARK MEADOW CT
- CCCo 94507 633-D5
PARK MEADOW DR
1900 CCCo 94507 633-D5
PARKMONT DR
1900 CCCo 94507 633-D6
PARK PLACE CT
- CCCo 94520 572-G2
PARK PLACE DR
- CCCo 94561 597-E1
3700 PIT 94565 574-E5
PARKRIDGE CT
- RCH 94803 569-C7
PARK RIDGE DR
- RCH 94806 568-J6
PARKRIDGE DR
1100 RCH 94803 569-C7
5000 OAK 94619 651-B6
PARKRIDGE PL
- RCH 94803 569-C7
PARKSIDE CIR
2700 CNCD 94519 592-G1
PARKSIDE CT
600 CCCo 94708 609-G4
PARKSIDE DR
- BERK 94705 630-A4
- PDMT 94611 630-A7
- PIT 94565 574-D2
1000 RCH 94803 569-C7
1000 RCH 94803 589-C1
1200 WLCK 94596 612-C3
1400 WLCK 94597 612-C3
1800 CNCD 94519 592-G1
1800 CCCo 94597 612-B4
3100 PLE 94588 694-C7
N PARKSIDE DR
100 PIT 94565 574-C2
PARKSIDE LN
- DNVL 94506 653-H3
- PIT 94565 574-D2
PARK TERRACE CT
- CCCo 94597 612-A4
PARKTREE CT
3700 CNCD 94519 593-A1
PARK VIEW CT
- CCCo 94597 612-A3
PARKVIEW CT
- ANT 94531 595-H4
200 PDMT 94610 650-B2
PARKVIEW DR
- PIT 94565 574-B2
PARKVIEW TERRACE DR
- SPAB 94806 589-B3
PARK VISTA
7400 ELCR 94530 609-D2
PARKWAY CT
- ORIN 94563 631-A2
1200 RCH 94803 569-C7
3700 CNCD 94519 593-A1
PARKWAY DR
700 MRTZ 94553 571-G5
1200 RCH 94803 569-C7
PARK WEST DR
- PIT 94565 574-G7
PARK WOOD CIR
7300 DBLN 94568 694-A2

PARKWOOD PL
1500 CNCD 94521 593-C4
PARLIN PL
- SRMN 94583 673-E6
PARLINGTON CT
- CCCo 94507 632-E3
E PARNASSUS CT
- BERK 94708 609-J7
W PARNASSUS CT
- BERK 94708 609-J7
PARNASSUS RD
- BERK 94708 609-J7
PARNELL CT
- WLCK 94597 612-D2
PARR BLVD
- SPAB 94806 588-F2
- CCCo 94801 588-F2
400 RCH 94801 588-F2
PARRIN CT
2900 CNCD 94518 592-G7
PARROT CT
- WLCK 94596 612-F7
PARROT PL
- DNVL 94526 652-J1
PARSON BROWN CT
- MRGA 94556 631-D6
PARSONS LN
1800 ANT 94509 575-F6
PARTRIDGE CT
- CCCo 94507 633-D5
PARTRIDGE DR
1400 HER 94547 569-H4
PARY CT
- CCCo 94507 632-H5
PASATIEMPO CT
400 PLHL 94523 592-A2
PASA TIEMPO DR
- BREN 94513 616-A3
PASCO DR
- BREN 94513 596-G6
PASEO BERNAL
200 MRGA 94556 631-E7
PASEO CIMA
- WLCK 94598 612-E5
PASEO DEL CAMPO
400 MRGA 94556 631-D2
PASEO DEL RIO
100 MRGA 94556 631-D2
PASEO DE SOL
- CCCo 94507 632-G3
PASEO GRANDE
3800 MRGA 94556 631-D2
PASEO LINARES
- MRGA 94556 631-E5
PASEO NOGALES
1400 CCCo 94507 632-E3
PASO DE AVILA
100 CCCo 94553 571-C6
PASO DEL RIO CT
5400 CNCD 94521 593-E7
PASO DEL RIO WY
5300 CNCD 94521 593-D7
PASO NOGAL
100 CCCo 94523 592-B2
100 PLHL 94523 591-J3
100 PLHL 94523 592-A2
600 MRTZ 94553 591-J3
PASO NOGAL CT
- PLHL 94523 591-J3
- PLHL 94523 592-A3
PASO NORTE DR
- PLHL 94523 592-A3
PASO ROBLES DR
6700 OAK 94611 630-F7
PASSEGGI CT
4200 PLE 94588 694-C5
PASTO CT
1800 WLCK 94595 632-B1
PASTOR LN
- CCCo 94513 597-C3
PATINA CT
- WLCK 94597 592-D7
PATO LN
3800 OAKL 94561 596-F2
PATRA DR
2500 CCCo 94803 589-H5
PATRICIA AV
200 PIT 94565 574-F4
2700 ANT 94509 575-E6
PATRICIA DR
1900 PLHL 94523 592-C5
PATRICIA LN
100 CCCo 94507 632-F6
PATRICIA RD
- ORIN 94563 630-G2
PATRICK DR
200 CCCo 94553 572-B7
800 PIN 94564 569-D4
PATRICK LN
- ORIN 94563 631-B1
PATRICKS PL
- DNVL 94526 652-J2
PATRIOT CT
3500 ANT 94509 595-C3
PATTERSON AV
3600 OAK 94619 650-F6
PATTERSON BLVD
100 PLHL 94523 592-B7
PATTERSON CIR
6200 CCCo 94805 589-B5
PATTON ST
5800 OAK 94618 630-A4
PATTY WY
3100 LFYT 94549 611-J6
PAUL CT
300 BEN 94510 551-C1
1500 ANT 94509 575-F7
PAUL LN
1800 CNCD 94521 593-F4
PAULA CT
200 MRTZ 94553 591-H4
PAULANELLA PL
100 CCCo 94583 652-E3
PAULETTA CT
- DNVL 94526 653-C4
PAULETTE LN
100 ANT 94509 574-J6
PAUL SCARLET DR
5100 CNCD 94521 593-E4
PAULSEN LN
100 CCCo 94595 612-B6
100 WLCK 94595 612-B6
PAULSON CT
900 LFYT 94549 611-B6
PAVON
100 HER 94547 569-E3
PAWNEE DR
2500 WLCK 94598 612-H3
5100 ANT 94531 595-H5
PAWNEE WY
3100 PLE 94588 694-G7
PAXTON AV
3300 OAK 94601 650-D6

PAYNE AV
1900 CCCo 94513 616-E4
PAYNE CT
800 RCH 94806 568-G6
6800 PLE 94588 694-A7
PAYNE DR
500 RCH 94806 568-G6
PAYNE RD
4100 PLE 94588 694-A7
PAZZI RD
400 WLCK 94598 612-J2
400 WLCK 94598 613-A2
PEACE LN
- BREN 94561 596-D3
PEACEFUL LN
100 LFYT 94549 611-J4
PEACEFUL VALLEY DR
600 SRMN 94582 673-J6
600 SRMN 94582 674-A6
PEACH LN
- CCCo 94513 597-A3
PEACH PL
1200 CNCD 94518 592-E5
1700 CNCD 94520 592-E5
PEACH ST
1300 CCCo 94553 571-F3
2100 PIN 94564 569-E4
PEACH BLOSSOM LN
- SRMN 94583 673-E6
PEACHTREE CIR
2100 PIT 94565 573-J3
2300 ANT 94509 595-A2
PEACH TREE CT
300 BREN 94513 616-G2
PEACHWILLOW CT
600 BREN 94513 616-E1
PEACHWILLOW DR
700 BREN 94513 616-E1
PEACHWILLOW LN
3000 WLCK 94598 612-H1
3100 WLCK 94598 592-H7
PEACHWILLOW ST
1700 PIT 94565 573-F3
PEACHWOOD DR
3900 CNCD 94519 573-A7
PEACOCK BLVD
400 LFYT 94549 631-G3
400 LFYT 94556 631-G3
PEACOCK CT
- DBLN 94568 694-D4
PEACOCK CREEK DR
1000 CLAY 94517 593-J7
1000 CLAY 94517 594-A7
PEAK CT
- HER 94547 569-H4
E PEAK CT
2300 MRTZ 94553 572-A7
N PEAK PL
2100 MRTZ 94553 572-B6
PEAKE PL
100 CCCo 94507 633-A5
100 CCCo 94507 632-J5
PEAR DR
1200 CNCD 94518 592-E6
PEAR ST
2100 PIN 94564 569-E4
2900 ANT 94509 574-J7
PEARCE
- HER 94547 569-F3
N PEARDALE DR
3900 LFYT 94549 611-C5
S PEARDALE DR
3900 LFYT 94549 611-B5
PEARL AV
1800 CNCD 94520 572-J3
1800 CCCo 94565 572-J3
1800 CNCD 94565 572-J3
PEARL PL
6700 DBLN 94568 693-J2
PEARL WY
- BREN 94513 616-D5
PEARL CREST CT
- CCCo 94582 674-B2
PEARLGRASS CT
- SRMN 94582 653-H7
PEARLGRASS LN
- SRMN 94582 653-H7
PEARLITE CT
- ANT 94531 595-G1
PEARLITE WY
- ANT 94531 595-G1
PEARSON DR
- BREN 94513 616-C4
PEAR TREE CT
1000 BREN 94513 596-C7
PEARTREE CT
- DNVL 94526 653-A1
PEBBLE BAY
- HER 94547 569-H1
PEBBLE CT
- BREN 94513 616-B2
- SRMN 94583 673-G7
200 CCCo 94507 632-H5
700 CCCo 94803 589-D1
PEBBLE DR
400 CCCo 94803 589-D1
2000 CCCo 94507 632-H5
3900 ANT 94509 595-E1
PEBBLE LN
100 CCCo 94507 632-H5
PEBBLE PL
100 SRMN 94583 673-G6
PEBBLE BEACH CT
7300 ELCR 94530 589-D7
PEBBLE BEACH DR
- BREN 94513 616-B2
- CLAY 94517 593-J7
- CLAY 94517 594-A7
200 PIT 94565 574-E1
7300 ELCR 94530 589-D7
PEBBLE BEACH LP
5200 ANT 94531 595-J6
PEBBLE BEACH PL
200 PIT 94565 574-E1
2400 CCCo 94549 591-H6
PEBBLE BEACH WY
7300 ELCR 94530 589-D7
PEBBLEBROOK CT
1500 WLCK 94596 632-H2
PEBBLECREEK CT
200 MRTZ 94553 571-J6
PEBBLE GLEN DR
5200 CNCD 94521 593-D6
PECAN CT
- SRMN 94583 673-F7
1700 OAKL 94561 576-D6
PECAN DR
100 HER 94547 570-A5
PECAN LN
1600 OAKL 94561 576-D6
PECAN PL
200 BREN 94513 616-F2
PECAN ST
2400 ANT 94509 574-J7
PEDERSON WY
1000 BREN 94513 616-F2

PEGGY DR
1900 PLHL 94523 592-C5
PEGGY LN
- CCCo 94553 591-E2
PELHAM PL
2200 OAK 94611 650-F1
PELICAN CT
- PIT 94565 554-E7
700 DNVL 94506 653-H4
4000 CCCo 94513 617-E7
PELICAN LP
100 PIT 94565 554-E7
100 PIT 94565 574-E1
PELICAN ST
- BREN 94513 596-G7
7100 DNVL 94506 653-H4
PELICAN WY
- SRFL 94901 587-A4
1300 RCH 94801 608-D3
PEMBERTON DR
- SRMN 94582 674-B4
PEMBROKE CT
- OAK 94619 650-J4
3900 ANT 94531 596-A4
PEMBROKE DR
4300 CNCD 94521 593-A4
PEMBROOK CT
- MRGA 94556 651-F2
PENINSULA DR
- RCH 94804 608-H3
PENINSULA RD
- AlaC 94546 651-D5
- AlaC 94619 651-D5
100 CCCo 94565 553-E7
PENN DR
6800 DBLN 94568 693-J3
PENNHEART CT
- BREN 94513 616-C4
PENNIMAN AV
3400 OAK 94602 650-E6
3500 OAK 94619 650-E6
PENNIMAN CT
4100 OAK 94619 650-E7
PENNIMAN WY
- WLCK 94597 612-C3
PENNINGTON CT
- CCCo 94525 550-E5
PENNINGTON PL
400 DNVL 94526 653-D3
PENNSYLVANIA AV
300 RCH 94801 588-F5
PENNSYLVANIA BLVD
1300 CNCD 94521 593-F6
PENNY LN
- ORIN 94563 611-A7
2600 CCCo 94513 597-D6
4100 CCCo 94803 589-D2
5300 CCCo 94588 654-F7
PENNY TER
- MmC 94964 587-B5
PENRITH WK
- PLHL 94523 591-B1
PENSACOLA ST
- CCCo 94565 573-H2
PENWOOD LN
- DBLN 94568 694-F2
PENWOOD PL
- DBLN 94568 694-F2
PEOPLE SOFT PKWY
- PLE 94588 694-C5
PEPPER DR
2300 CNCD 94520 572-F6
PEPPERMILL CIR
3000 PIT 94565 574-F6
PEPPERMILL CT
- PIT 94565 574-F6
1000 CNCD 94518 592-H4
PEPPERMILL LN
100 PIT 94565 574-F5
PEPPERRIDGE PL
5700 CNCD 94521 593-F7
PEPPERRIDGE WY
5700 CNCD 94521 593-F7
PEPPERTREE CT
2400 ANT 94509 575-B6
8100 DBLN 94568 693-G3
PEPPER TREE PL
1500 PIT 94565 574-G6
PEPPERTREE RD
300 WLCK 94598 592-J7
300 WLCK 94598 612-J1
7500 DBLN 94568 693-F3
PEPPERTREE WY
200 PIT 94565 574-F5
2100 ANT 94509 575-B6
PEPPERWOOD CT
100 BREN 94513 616-E2
100 CCCo 94506 654-A1
1600 CNCD 94521 593-B2
PEPPERWOOD DR
800 CCCo 94506 654-A1
PEPPERWOOD LN
- CCCo 94506 654-A1
PEPPERWOOD ST
100 HER 94547 569-J4
PERADA DR
3300 WLCK 94598 612-J1
3600 WLCK 94598 592-J7
PERALES ST
1100 LFYT 94549 611-H5
PERALTA AV
500 BERK 94707 609-F6
900 ALB 94706 609-F6
1100 BERK 94706 609-E7
1200 BERK 94702 609-E7
PERALTA CT
- MRGA 94556 651-F1
PERALTA RD
1000 CNCD 94520 572-E5
PERCHERON WY
5200 ANT 94531 595-J6
PEREGRINE CT
- CNCD 94521 593-B6
PEREGRINE ST
- BREN 94513 596-E5
PEREIRA RD
1000 CCCo 94553 590-G2
PEREIRA RANCH RD
- CCCo 94588 654-F5
PEREZ CT
- DBLN 94568 694-G4
PERIDOT CT
- ANT 94509 595-F1
100 HER 94547 569-G4
PERIWINKLE WY
1700 ANT 94531 595-E3
PEROLY CT
2600 OAK 94601 650-C6
PERRA WY
3100 WLCK 94598 612-H3
PERRIN RD
600 MRTZ 94553 571-C6
PERRY DR
- VAL 94592 549-H1

PERRY LN
7800 PLE 94588 693-H7
PERRY WY
5000 ANT 94531 595-H4
PERSHING DR
- OAK 94611 650-D1
500 CCCo 94523 592-D7
500 PLHL 94523 592-D7
PERSICA CT
- SRMN 94582 673-H1
PERSIMMON CIR
3100 PLE 94588 694-G6
PERSIMMON CT
- WLCK 94598 592-J7
PERSIMMON DR
200 BREN 94513 616-F3
PERSIMMON RD
300 WLCK 94598 592-J7
PERSIMMON ST
- DBLN 94568 694-D3
3100 ANT 94509 574-J7
PERSIMMON WY
- PLE 94588 694-G6
PERTH CT
1300 CNCD 94521 593-A4
5000 ANT 94531 595-J2
PERTH PL
- OAK 94705 630-B3
PERTH WY
- BEN 94510 551-B2
PESCADERO CT
- DNVL 94526 633-B7
PETAR CT
- CLAY 94517 613-J2
- PIT 94565 574-B4
PETAR LN
- PIT 94565 574-B4
PETAR PL
- SRMN 94583 673-G6
2800 ANT 94509 575-A6
PETERSON PL
- CCCo 94595 612-B6
PETERSON RD
- PLHL 94523 592-A6
PETERS RANCH RD
1600 DNVL 94526 653-A6
PETIT PEAK CT
- ANT 94531 595-E4
PETOLA RD
700 DNVL 94526 652-H1
PETTICOAT LN
- WLCK 94596 612-C6
PETTIT LN
- MRTZ 94553 571-H4
PETUNIA CT
- BREN 94513 616-H5
PEYTON CT
2200 ANT 94509 595-A1
PFEIFFER LN
2500 PIN 94564 569-J7
PFEIFFER WY
2500 PIN 94564 569-J7
PHANOR DR
500 RCH 94806 568-G6
PHEASANT CIR
100 PIT 94565 574-C6
PHEASANT CT
- CCCo 94507 633-B5
- DBLN 94568 694-D4
- PIT 94565 574-D6
PHEASANT DR
1000 PIT 94565 574-C7
1600 HER 94547 569-G4
PHEASANT WY
100 OAKL 94561 596-H1
PHEASANT RUN DR
300 CCCo 94506 654-D3
PHEASANT RUN PL
- CCCo 94506 654-D3
PHEASANT RUN TER
- CCCo 94506 654-D3
1800 BREN 94513 596-C7
1800 BREN 94513 616-C1
PHILLIP CT
100 RCH 94806 589-A2
PHILLIPS CT
5200 CNCD 94521 593-F4
PHILLIPS LN
1800 ANT 94509 575-J6
PHILLIPS PL
5200 CNCD 94521 593-F4
PHILLIPS RD
3200 LFYT 94549 611-G7
PHOENIX CT
100 DNVL 94506 653-H4
PHOENIX ST
1000 DNVL 94506 653-H4
4000 CNCD 94521 593-B2
PHOTINA CT
2600 PLE 94588 694-H4
PHYLIS DR
- PLHL 94523 592-C5
PHYLIS PL
4800 MRTZ 94553 571-F7
PHYLIS TER
4800 MRTZ 94553 571-E7
PHYLLIS CT
100 VAL 94590 550-C2
PHYLLIS LN
4600 CNCD 94521 593-C3
PIATTA CT
- BREN 94513 616-B1
PIAZZA CT
5300 PLE 94588 694-C6
PICADILLY CT
1000 CNCD 94518 592-F5
3200 PLE 94588 694-E6
PICADILLY LN
- BREN 94561 596-D4
PICARD AV
3800 PLE 94588 694-F6
PICARDY CT
- WLCK 94597 612-B2
PICASSO CT
- PLHL 94523 592-C7
PICASSO DR
- OAKL 94561 576-H7
PICKENS LN
3400 PLE 94588 694-E6
PICKERING PL
100 WLCK 94598 612-F3
PICKWICK DR
4100 CNCD 94521 593-A3
PICNIC LN
700 WLCK 94597 612-B3
PICO CT
- ORIN 94563 631-B5
1400 WLCK 94597 611-J2
PICO PL
100 CCCo 94565 573-D2
PICO WY
1500 WLCK 94597 611-J2
PIDGEON CT
- LFYT 94549 611-B6

PIEDMONT AV
- ORIN 94563 610-E6
4300 OAK 94611 630-A7
PIEDMONT CT
- PDMT 94611 650-B1
PIEDMONT DR
1700 CNCD 94519 593-A1
PIEDMONT LN
- DNVL 94526 633-A6
100 PIT 94565 574-F4
PIEDMONT PL
200 RCH 94801 608-D1
PIEDMONT WY
2100 PIT 94565 574-F4
PIEDRA DR
1400 WLCK 94597 612-A2
PIEDRAS CIR
1800 CCCo 94507 633-D5
PIEDRAS CT
100 CCCo 94507 633-D5
PIER PT
4000 CCCo 94514 617-G6
PIERCE CT
1800 CNCD 94521 593-D2
3200 ANT 94509 575-C7
3200 ANT 94509 595-C1
PIERCE ST
500 ALB 94706 609-C4
500 RCH 94804 609-C4
800 ALB 94710 609-C4
PIERPOINT AV
5000 OAK 94602 650-F3
PIERSON AV
1400 RCH 94804 608-H2
PIERSON ST
3300 OAK 94619 650-G7
PIKE CT
2200 CNCD 94520 572-F4
7100 DBLN 94568 693-J4
PIKE LN
4000 CNCD 94520 572-G4
PIKES CT
300 MRTZ 94553 591-H4
PILAR RIDGE CT
- PIT 94565 573-D4
PILAR RIDGE DR
- PIT 94565 573-E4
PILLON REAL
- PLHL 94523 591-J3
PILLSBURY CT
4000 ANT 94531 595-J1
PIMENTEL CT
- MRGA 94556 651-E1
PIMLICO CT
500 WLCK 94597 612-C3
PIMLICO DR
200 WLCK 94597 612-C3
400 WLCK 94596 612-C3
3500 PLE 94588 694-E5
PINE AV
700 PIN 94564 569-E4
1300 SPAB 94806 588-G4
2300 RCH 94806 588-H4
2900 BERK 94705 630-A3
PINE CT
700 MRTZ 94553 571-F4
1600 OAKL 94561 596-D1
6900 DBLN 94568 693-J4
PINE LN
- OAK 94618 630-B5
1000 CLAY 94517 614-A2
1000 LFYT 94549 611-C6
1100 CCCo 94517 614-A2
PINE PTH
- BERK 94705 630-A3
PINE ST
- OAKL 94561 596-C2
- BREN 94513 616-G1
500 MRTZ 94553 571-E2
1100 VAL 94590 550-C1
1100 PIT 94565 574-F3
1200 WLCK 94596 612-C4
1600 CNCD 94520 592-E2
2200 CCCo 94553 571-E3
3100 ANT 94509 574-J7
PINECONE DR
400 DNVL 94526 653-B4
PINECONE LN
2900 CCCo 94561 596-H4
PINE CREEK CT
- PIT 94565 573-F4
PINE CREEK RD
100 CCCo 94598 612-J4
100 CCCo 94598 613-A5
PINE CREEK WY
1200 CNCD 94520 592-F3
PINE CREST CT
6500 AlaC 94552 672-C7
PINECREST CT
2500 ANT 94509 595-F3
PINE CREST DR
1200 CNCD 94521 593-B4
PINE GROVE CT
- CCCo 94597 612-D2
PINEGROVE WY
- BREN 94513 596-D5
PINEHAVEN RD
6300 OAK 94611 630-D5
PINEHAVEN WY
4900 ANT 94531 595-E4
PINE HILL DR
- CCCo 94803 589-F2
PINE HILLS CT
- CCCo 94516 630-G7
- OAK 94611 630-G7
PINE HILLS DR
100 OAK 94611 630-G7
PINE HILLS LN
8400 OAK 94611 630-G7
PINEHOLLOW CIR
- CCCo 94513 617-F2
PINE HOLLOW CT
1000 CLAY 94517 593-H7
PINE HOLLOW RD
5200 CNCD 94521 593-D6
5500 CLAY 94517 593-F7
PINEHURST CT
1000 CNCD 94521 593-C6
2100 ELCR 94530 589-D7
2400 CCCo 94514 617-J7
PINEHURST PL
800 SRMN 94583 673-G6
PINEHURST RD
- AlaC 94619 651-C3
- CCCo 94516 630-H6
- CCCo 94516 631-A7
- CCCo 94516 651-A1
- OAK 94611 630-H6
PINEHURST WY
2200 ELCR 94530 589-D7
PINE KNOLL DR
2000 WLCK 94595 632-A1
PINEMEADOWS CT
1000 MRTZ 94553 571-H7

PINENEEDLE DR
6500 OAK 94611 630-D5
PINENUT CT
- OAKL 94561 596-D2
400 SRMN 94583 673-G7
2200 ANT 94509 575-H6
PINENUT ST
- OAKL 94561 596-C2
PINENUT WY
2200 ANT 94509 575-H6
PINE PARK CT
400 MRTZ 94553 571-F5
PINE RIDGE
400 SRMN 94582 673-F3
PINE SHADOW LN
1200 CNCD 94521 593-F7
PINE TOP AV
5500 OAK 94613 650-H7
PINETREE CT
1700 CNCD 94521 593-B2
PINE TREE DR
1400 CCCo 94507 632-F4
PINE TREE LN
- ORIN 94563 631-B2
PINE TREE TR
- CCCo 94553 591-D3
PINE VALLEY CT
3000 SRMN 94582 673-H6
PINE VALLEY PL
- SRMN 94583 673-E7
PINE VALLEY RD
2800 SRMN 94583 673-E7
PINEVIEW CT
- PLHL 94523 592-A6
PINEVIEW LN
1300 CNCD 94521 593-B4
PINEVIEW WY
4800 ANT 94531 596-A3
PINEWOOD CT
- WLCK 94597 612-B2
600 DNVL 94506 653-J4
4200 CNCD 94521 593-B2
PINEWOOD PL
1500 PIT 94565 574-G6
PINEWOOD RD
5800 OAK 94611 630-C6
PINEWOOD TER
1000 SPAB 94806 588-J3
PINKERTON CT
- SRMN 94583 673-E4
PINNACLE CT
- HER 94547 569-H4
PINNACLE DR
2300 MRTZ 94553 572-A7
PINNACLE RIDGE CT
100 DNVL 94506 654-A6
PIN OAK PL
2000 CCCo 94506 653-H1
PINO CREST
- WLCK 94598 612-E4
PINOLE AV
100 CCCo 94572 549-H7
PINOLE RD
5300 CCCo 94803 589-F3
PINOLE ST
100 HER 94547 569-E3
PINOLE SHORES DR
600 PIN 94564 569-C3
PINOLE VALLEY RD
700 PIN 94564 569-F4
3800 PIN 94564 589-H1
PINON AV
100 PIN 94564 569-D4
PINON CT
2400 MRTZ 94553 571-F4
4400 CNCD 94521 593-B5
PINON DR
800 MRTZ 94553 571-F4
PINOT CT
600 CLAY 94517 593-J7
4600 OAKL 94561 576-D7
PINTAIL DR
- ANT 94509 594-H2
PINTO CT
900 WLCK 94596 632-G2
PIOMBO PL
- SRFL 94901 587-B5
PIONEER AV
100 WLCK 94597 612-C2
PIONEER CT
- OAKL 94561 576-E7
- SRMN 94583 673-B3
200 RCH 94803 589-G3
5100 ANT 94531 595-J5
PIONEER LN
6500 DBLN 94568 694-A3
6600 DBLN 94568 693-J3
PIONEER WY
5100 ANT 94531 595-J5
PIPER CT
4400 ANT 94531 595-J2
PIPER LN
5400 OAKL 94561 576-D5
PIPER RD
6900 CCCo 94511 577-F3
PIPER WY
4400 ANT 94531 595-J2
PIPER GLEN TER
- DBLN 94568 694-H3
PIPER RIDGE CT
1900 WLCK 94597 611-H3
PIPERS BROOK CT
- SRMN 94582 674-B4
PIPIT CT
4800 PLE 94566 694-D7
PIPPIN DR
200 BREN 94513 616-C2
PIPPO AV
100 BREN 94513 616-G2
PIPPO PL
400 BREN 94513 616-G2
PIRATE LN
800 CCCo 94565 573-D1
PIRATES COVE CT
100 VAL 94591 550-G2
PISMO CT
2400 CCCo 94514 617-G7
5100 ANT 94531 595-F4
PISTACHIO CT
2800 ANT 94509 575-H6
PISTACHIO PL
100 BREN 94513 616-F3
PITA CT
5000 OAKL 94561 576-D6
PITCH PINE CT
4400 CNCD 94521 593-B5
PITCHSTONE WY
- ANT 94531 595-G2
PITT CT
7100 DBLN 94568 693-J4
PITT WY
- CCCo 94803 589-C3
PITTSBURG AV
300 CCCo 94801 588-E3

STREET	Block	City	ZIP	Pg-Grid
PITTSBURG-ANTIOCH HWY				
	1600	ANT	94509	575-A4
	1600	ANT	94509	574-H4
	1600	PIT	94565	574-F3
PITTSBURG WATERFRONT RD				
	300	PIT	94565	574-H2
PIUTE CT				
	-	ANT	94531	595-G5
	900	WLCK	94598	612-H4
PIUTE WY				
	-	ANT	94531	595-G5
PIVA CT				
	200	BREN	94513	616-H2
PIXIE LN				
	600	DNVL	94526	652-H1
PIZZIMENTI CT				
	4700	CNCD	94521	593-D3
PLACER CT				
	-	CCCo	94565	573-H2
PLACER DR				
	1500	CNCD	94521	593-B3
	2200	CCCo	94565	573-H2
	4300	OAKL	94561	596-B1
PLACER PL				
	100	VAL	94591	550-C1
PLACER ST				
	1900	RCH	94804	609-C3
PLACER RIDGE RD				
	900	CCCo	94597	612-A5
PLACID CT				
	-	SRMN	94582	653-F6
PLANK AV				
	7100	ELCR	94530	609-C1
PLANK CT				
	7300	ELCR	94530	609-C1
PLATA CT				
	400	DNVL	94526	653-C3
PLATEAU CT				
	-	HER	94547	569-H4
PLATEAU DR				
	600	CCCo	94708	609-G4
PLATO CT				
	-	PLHL	94523	591-J7
PLATT DR				
	2300	MRTZ	94553	572-A7
PLA VADA CT				
	800	CNCD	94518	592-F6
PLAYA CT				
	-	HER	94547	569-H4
	-	SRMN	94583	673-B2
PLAYA DEL REY				
	100	SRFL	94901	587-A2
PLAYER CT				
	100	WLCK	94598	612-E3
PLAZA CIR				
	100	DNVL	94526	633-D6
	5000	RCH	94804	609-B1
PLAZA CT				
	-	PIT	94565	574-D6
	100	DNVL	94526	633-D6
PLAZA DR				
	1000	CCCo	94553	571-G4
PLAZA WY				
	3500	LFYT	94549	611-F6
	4900	RCH	94804	609-B1
PLAZA DE ORO				
	1400	BEN	94510	550-J3
PLAZA ENCINA				
	5500	CNCD	94521	593-E7
PLAZA ERMITA				
	5500	CNCD	94521	593-E7
PLAZA NOGAL				
	5500	CNCD	94521	593-E7
PLEASANT CT				
	-	WLCK	94597	612-C1
PLEASANT LN				
	100	RCH	94803	589-E3
	1500	CCCo	94549	611-J2
PLEASANT PL				
	100	ANT	94509	575-D4
PLEASANT ST				
	2500	OAK	94602	650-D5
PLEASANT HILL CIR				
	1100	LFYT	94549	611-H5
PLEASANT HILL RD				
	200	LFYT	94549	611-H4
	1300	CCCo	94549	611-J1
	1300	WLCK	94597	611-J1
	1500	PLHL	94523	611-J1
	1700	PLHL	94523	591-J4
	1700	CCCo	94549	591-J4
	1800	PLHL	94523	592-A5
	5200	PLE	94588	693-H6
PLEASANT HILL RD E				
	4400	MRTZ	94553	571-F7
PLEASANT KNOLL CT				
	-	CCCo	94507	632-F3
PLEASANT OAKS CT				
	200	PLHL	94523	591-J5
PLEASANT OAKS DR				
	800	PLHL	94523	591-J5
PLEASANT OAKS PL				
	-	PLHL	94523	591-J5
PLEASANT VALLEY AV				
	1700	OAK	94611	630-A7
PLEASANT VALLEY CT				
	-	SRMN	94582	673-J6
N PLEASANT VALLEY CT				
	4500	OAK	94611	630-A7
S PLEASANT VALLEY CT				
	4500	OAK	94611	630-A7
PLEASANT VALLEY DR				
	-	WLCK	94597	612-C1
	1000	PLHL	94523	592-C7
	1000	PLHL	94523	612-C1
	5100	MRTZ	94553	591-F1
PLEASANT VIEW DR				
	100	PLHL	94523	592-A7
PLEITNER AV				
	3000	OAK	94602	650-D5
PLOVER PL				
	300	PIT	94565	574-D1
PLUM LN				
	1000	CNCD	94518	592-F5
PLUM ST				
	2100	PIN	94564	569-E4
	3100	CCCo	94553	571-G4
PLUMAS AV				
	5400	RCH	94804	609-B3
PLUMAS CT				
	-	CCCo	94565	573-H2
	600	MRTZ	94553	571-E7
PLUMBRIDGE WY				
	-	ANT	94531	596-B4
PLUMERIA CT				
	-	DNVL	94506	654-C6
PLUMLEIGH AV				
	2800	ANT	94509	575-D7
PLUMLEIGH LN				
	1200	CNCD	94521	593-A5
PLUMPOINTE LN				
	2000	SRMN	94582	653-J7
PLUM TREE LN				
	-	SRMN	94583	673-E7
PLUMWOOD WY				
	-	ANT	94531	596-A4
PLYMOUTH AV				
	6100	CCCo	94805	589-B5
PLYMOUTH CT				
	-	CCCo	94513	617-F5
	-	SRMN	94582	673-G5
	400	BEN	94510	550-J2
	400	BEN	94510	551-A2
PLYMOUTH CV				
	100	SRFL	94901	587-A2
PLYMOUTH DR				
	1900	PIT	94565	574-E3
PLYMOUTH LN				
	1400	ANT	94509	575-F5
PLYMOUTH RD				
	3100	LFYT	94549	611-J4
POCO LN				
	-	CCCo	94595	632-C1
	-	OAKL	94561	576-B6
POCONO MANOR PL				
	400	SRMN	94583	673-H6
POCO PASEO				
	-	ORIN	94563	630-J3
PODVA LN				
	900	DNVL	94526	653-A4
PODVA RD				
	800	DNVL	94526	653-A4
POE CT				
	4500	BREN	94513	616-G3
POE LN				
	2800	CCCo	94513	597-D4
POINSETT AV				
	5300	ELCR	94530	589-B7
	5300	RCH	94805	589-B7
POINSETTIA AV				
	-	CCCo	94565	573-H2
POINT PL				
	-	CCCo	94511	577-E4
POINT ANDRUS CT				
	2600	ANT	94531	595-G2
POINT ARENA CT				
	2800	ANT	94531	595-H2
POINT BENICIA CIR				
	-	BEN	94510	551-A3
POINT BENICIA WY				
	100	BEN	94510	551-B6
POINT DUME CT				
	2600	ANT	94531	595-G2
POINT LOBOS CT				
	2600	ANT	94531	595-G2
POINT OF TIMBER RD				
	1400	CCCo	94513	617-D4
POINT PINOLE CT				
	-	RCH	94806	568-J5
POINT REYES CT				
	900	VAL	94591	550-E3
	2800	ANT	94531	595-H2
POINT SAL CT				
	2600	ANT	94531	595-G2
POINT SAN PEDRO CV				
	-	SRFL	94901	587-B1
POINT SAN PEDRO RD				
	100	SRFL	94901	587-A1
	100	MrnC	94901	587-A1
POINT SUR CT				
	2600	ANT	94531	595-G2
POINTVIEW LN				
	-	RCH	94806	588-F1
POLARIS CT				
	100	VAL	94591	550-G3
POLARIS DR				
	-	PIT	94565	574-A2
	100	PIT	94565	573-J3
POLK CT				
	3100	ANT	94509	575-A7
POLK ST				
	800	ALB	94706	609-D6
	900	BEN	94510	551-D6
	1800	CNCD	94521	593-D3
POLLARDSTOWN CT				
	11800	DBLN	94568	693-G4
POLLEY LN				
	100	PLHL	94523	612-A1
POLSON CIR				
	1100	MRTZ	94553	571-H6
POLSON CT				
	1100	MRTZ	94553	571-H6
POMAR WY				
	1700	WLCK	94598	612-E2
POMFRET WK				
	-	PLHL	94523	591-B1
POMO CT				
	-	CCCo	94565	573-E2
POMO ST				
	2000	CCCo	94565	573-E2
POMONA AV				
	100	ELCR	94530	609-D3
	500	ALB	94706	609-E6
	2100	MRTZ	94553	571-F4
	2200	CCCo	94553	571-F4
POMONA CT				
	7300	ELCR	94530	609-D3
POMONA DR				
	-	BREN	94513	616-E4
POMONA PL				
	4000	PIT	94565	574-E6
POMONA ST				
	-	CCCo	94525	550-E5
N POND CT				
	2300	CCCo	94549	591-G4
S POND CT				
	2400	CCCo	94549	591-G5
POND DIVIDE RD				
	-	MRTZ	94553	571-E2
PONDEREY PL				
	-	CCCo	94521	593-E4
PONDEROSA CT				
	300	RCH	94803	589-G3
	400	CCCo	94549	591-G6
PONDEROSA DR				
	1600	OAKL	94561	576-D7
	2800	CNCD	94520	572-F7
PONDEROSA LN				
	100	CCCo	94595	612-A7
PONDEROSA TR				
	3300	PIN	94564	569-F5
PONDEROSA WY				
	1700	OAKL	94561	576-D7
	3100	ANT	94509	575-A7
PONDLILLY LN				
	100	BREN	94513	616-E2
PONTIAC CT				
	1000	WLCK	94598	612-H4
PONTIAC DR				
	2700	WLCK	94598	612-H4
PONY CT				
	-	ANT	94531	596-A2
	-	SRMN	94583	673-B3
POPLAR AV				
	1500	CCCo	94805	589-C6
	4000	CNCD	94521	593-A2
POPLAR CT				
	-	CCCo	94595	612-B7
	100	HER	94547	569-J4
POPLAR DR				
	1600	CCCo	94595	612-B7
	2400	ANT	94509	575-C6
POPLAR ST				
	-	BERK	94708	609-J6
POPLAR WY				
	-	PDMT	94611	650-C1
	6700	DBLN	94568	693-J3
POPLARWOOD CT				
	1700	CNCD	94521	593-D3
POPPY CIR				
	500	BEN	94510	550-J1
POPPY CT				
	-	RCH	94806	568-J6
	100	CCCo	94596	612-F7
	100	HER	94547	569-J3
POPPY DR				
	100	HER	94547	569-J4
POPPY LN				
	-	BERK	94708	609-H5
	-	ORIN	94563	610-J4
POPPY PL				
	700	PLHL	94523	591-J3
POPPY WY				
	-	RCH	94806	568-J6
	1200	ANT	94509	575-B5
POPPY HILLS CT				
	-	DBLN	94568	694-G3
POPPY HILLS LN				
	-	DBLN	94568	694-G3
	-	SRMN	94583	673-E7
POPPY SEED CT				
	-	CNCD	94518	592-E6
POQUITO CT				
	1500	PIN	94564	569-D5
PORT CT				
	1400	OAKL	94561	576-D7
PORT ST				
	600	CCCo	94525	550-C4
PORT WY				
	1500	OAKL	94561	576-D7
PORTAGE RD				
	6800	DBLN	94568	693-H4
PORTAL AV				
	800	OAK	94610	650-B2
PORTA ROSSA CIR				
	-	PLE	94588	694-D6
PORT CHICAGO HWY				
	200	CCCo	94565	573-F2
	300	CCCo	94565	553-A7
	500	CCCo	94565	552-H7
	800	CCCo	94520	552-H7
	800	CCCo	94520	572-G3
	800	CCCo	94565	572-G3
	1600	CNCD	94519	592-G1
	2000	CNCD	94520	592-G1
	2400	CNCD	94519	572-G3
	2400	CNCD	94520	572-G3
PORTER CIR				
	-	CCCo	94511	577-E1
PORTER PL				
	200	SRMN	94583	673-A1
PORTER ST				
	100	VAL	94590	550-B1
	4100	OAK	94619	650-F6
PORTHOLE CT				
	300	HER	94547	570-B6
PORTHOLE DR				
	-	CCCo	94513	617-F7
PORTILLO VALLEY DR				
	5000	SRMN	94582	673-J7
PORTLAND AV				
	300	OAK	94606	650-A4
	1100	ALB	94706	609-D5
	1400	BERK	94707	609-D5
PORTLAND CT				
	-	DNVL	94526	653-C4
PORTOFINO CT				
	100	HER	94547	570-B6
PORTOFINO DR				
	-	BREN	94513	596-C7
	-	BREN	94513	616-C1
PORTOLA AV				
	-	VAL	94591	550-D1
	500	RCH	94801	588-G6
PORTOLA CT				
	-	CCCo	94506	654-A5
	5100	ANT	94531	595-F4
PORTOLA DR				
	200	CCCo	94506	654-A5
	6400	ELCR	94530	609-C3
PORT ROYAL LN				
	-	BREN	94513	616-B1
PORTSIDE CT				
	2100	CCCo	94514	617-H7
PORTSMOUTH CIR				
	-	PLHL	94523	591-B1
PORTSMOUTH CT				
	-	OAKL	94561	596-D2
	-	SRMN	94582	673-H5
	3600	PLE	94588	694-F5
PORTSMOUTH CV				
	-	SRFL	94901	587-A2
PORTSMOUTH RD				
	-	OAK	94610	650-B2
	-	PDMT	94610	650-B2
PORTSMOUTH ST				
	-	OAKL	94561	596-D2
PORTVIEW DR				
	-	CCCo	94565	553-D7
POSADA CT				
	100	SRMN	94583	673-C3
POSEN AV				
	1400	ALB	94706	609-F7
	1500	BERK	94706	609-F7
	1600	BERK	94707	609-F7
POSEY AV				
	-	RCH	94801	608-D1
POSEY PL				
	1800	CNCD	94519	592-J1
POSHARD ST				
	700	PLHL	94523	592-B7
POSITANO AV				
	-	BREN	94513	596-B7
	-	BREN	94513	616-B1
POSITANO PL				
	-	BREN	94513	616-B1
POST AV				
	1300	SPAB	94806	588-G3
POST RD				
	100	CCCo	94507	632-D1
	5400	OAK	94613	650-H7
	6800	DBLN	94568	693-J3
POTOMAC CT				
	-	ANT	94509	574-J6
POTOMAC ST				
	2400	OAK	94602	650-E4
POTOMAC WY				
	300	MRTZ	94553	591-H4
POTRERO AV				
	1100	RCH	94804	608-G1
	3900	RCH	94804	609-A1
	5100	ELCR	94530	609-C1
	7700	ELCR	94530	589-D7
POTRERO CT				
	2300	PIN	94564	569-F7
POTTER ST				
	1300	CCCo	94553	571-F3
	2400	OAK	94601	650-E7
POULOS CT				
	2800	PIN	94564	569-H6
POWDER BOWL CT				
	-	RCH	94803	589-G2
POWELL AV				
	200	PLHL	94523	592-B7
POWELL CT				
	500	CCCo	94565	573-C2
POWELL DR				
	300	CCCo	94565	573-C2
	3500	LFYT	94549	631-E1
POWELL ST				
	1800	SPAB	94806	588-H3
POWER AV				
	100	PIT	94565	574-B2
POWERS ST				
	-	DBLN	94568	694-B3
POWHATTAN CT				
	200	DNVL	94526	653-D7
POWNAL AV				
	2800	SRMN	94583	673-F6
PRADERA WY				
	-	SRMN	94583	673-A2
PRADO WY				
	-	LFYT	94549	611-F3
PRAIRIE LN				
	-	BREN	94513	616-B3
PRAIRIE WILLOW CT				
	4400	CNCD	94521	593-B5
N PRAIRIE WILLOW CT				
	4300	CNCD	94521	593-B5
PRAM RD				
	-	PIT	94565	574-A2
PRARIE WY				
	5000	ANT	94531	595-H4
PRARIE ROSE WY				
	-	BREN	94513	616-H1
PRATHER AV				
	5100	RCH	94805	589-B7
PRATO CT				
	5300	PLE	94588	694-H4
PRAY CT				
	-	ANT	94531	595-D4
PREAKNESS CT				
	300	WLCK	94597	612-C3
PREAKNESS DR				
	300	WLCK	94597	612-C3
PREBLE AV				
	2300	RCH	94804	588-H6
PRECIADO DR				
	-	DBLN	94568	694-G4
PREMIER PL				
	1700	CNCD	94520	592-E4
PRENTISS PL				
	-	SRMN	94583	673-F6
	2600	OAK	94601	650-C6
PRENTISS ST				
	3200	OAK	94601	650-D6
PRESCO LN				
	1000	RCH	94801	588-F5
PRESERVATION ST				
	-	PIT	94565	574-D2
PRESHER WY				
	1100	LFYT	94549	611-E5
PRESIDIO CT				
	2100	DNVL	94526	653-E7
PRESIDIO DR				
	-	BREN	94513	616-B1
PRESIDIO LN				
	500	PIT	94565	574-D4
PRESIDIO ST				
	-	SPAB	94806	588-J2
PRESLEY WY				
	5800	OAK	94618	630-A5
PRESTIGE PL				
	900	SRMN	94583	673-B1
PRESTON CT				
	5400	CNCD	94521	593-G4
PRESTON DR				
	-	CCCo	94513	617-F5
PRESTWICK AV				
	2500	CNCD	94519	572-G6
PRESTWICK CT				
	5700	CCCo	94514	617-J7
	5700	CCCo	94514	(618-A7 See Page 597)
PRESTWICK DR				
	2100	CCCo	94514	(618-A7 See Page 597)
	2200	CCCo	94514	617-J7
PREWETT RANCH DR				
	-	ANT	94531	596-A5
	1100	ANT	94531	595-E4
PRICE LN				
	-	PLHL	94523	592-B6
PRIDMORE CT				
	3900	CNCD	94521	592-J3
	3900	CNCD	94521	593-A3
PRIMROSE CIR				
	-	RCH	94806	568-J5
	-	RCH	94806	569-A6
PRIMROSE CT				
	-	WLCK	94598	592-H7
	1100	BREN	94513	596-E7
	3900	ANT	94531	596-A4
PRIMROSE DR				
	300	PLHL	94523	591-J3
PRIMROSE LN				
	1600	PIN	94564	569-E4
	3200	WLCK	94598	592-H7
PRIMROSE PL				
	200	PLHL	94523	591-J3
PRIMROSE TER				
	600	PIN	94564	569-E4
PRIMROSE WY				
	-	SRMN	94582	653-J7
PRINCE DR				
	6900	DBLN	94568	693-J3
PRINCE ST				
	400	OAK	94610	650-A2
	2700	BERK	94705	630-A4
PRINCE ALBERT WY				
	-	BREN	94513	616-D4
PRINCETON AV				
	200	CCCo	94708	609-G4
PRINCETON CT				
	-	CCCo	94521	593-E4
	-	DNVL	94526	653-B3
	1200	PIT	94565	574-F5
PRINCETON LN				
	300	DNVL	94526	653-B3
	2600	ANT	94509	575-D1
PRINGLE AV				
	100	WLCK	94596	612-B4
	100	WLCK	94597	612-B4
PRISTINE WY				
	-	BREN	94561	596-E4
PROCTOR AV				
	4700	OAK	94618	630-C6
PROMENADE CT				
	-	PIT	94565	574-G7
PROMENADE DR				
	-	PIT	94565	574-G7
PROMENADE LN				
	200	DNVL	94506	653-J5
PROMENADE ST				
	-	HER	94547	569-F2
PROMINENT DR				
	-	BREN	94561	596-D4
PROMINTORY LN				
	3200	CCCo	94549	611-H1
PROMONTORY CIR				
	-	SRMN	94583	673-A1
PROMONTORY DR				
	-	RCH	94804	608-E3
PROMONTORY LN				
	100	SRMN	94583	673-B1
PROMONTORY TER				
	200	SRMN	94583	673-B1
PROMONTORY WY				
	-	SRMN	94583	673-A1
PRONGHORN CT				
	4400	ANT	94509	595-F3
PRONGHORN WY				
	4400	ANT	94509	595-F3
PROPELLER LN				
	-	CCCo	94513	597-C6
PROSPECT AV				
	-	CCCo	94569	550-H6
	100	DNVL	94526	653-A2
	100	DNVL	94526	652-J2
	600	OAK	94610	650-A3
	600	OAK	94606	650-A3
	1500	MRTZ	94553	571-D4
	2700	CNCD	94518	592-G2
W PROSPECT AV				
	200	DNVL	94526	652-J3
PROSPECT CT				
	-	OAKL	94561	576-B7
	6800	PLE	94588	694-A7
PROSPECT RD				
	-	PDMT	94610	650-B2
PROSPECT HILL RD				
	3100	OAK	94613	650-G7
PROSPECTOR PL				
	-	CLAY	94517	593-H7
PROSPECTS WY				
	100	ANT	94509	575-C3
PROSPECT STEPS				
	6000	OAK	94618	630-A5
PROSPERITY CT				
	-	PIT	94565	574-C2
PROVENCE CT				
	1300	ANT	94509	575-F7
PROVENCE RD				
	100	DNVL	94506	654-C6
PROVIDENCE CT				
	2400	WLCK	94596	632-H2
PROVIDENCE DR				
	4000	MRTZ	94553	571-J6
PROVIDENCE ST				
	-	PIT	94565	574-C2
PROVIDIAN WY				
	6000	PLE	94588	694-B6
PROVINCETOWN CT				
	2400	MRTZ	94553	572-A5
PROVO LN				
	-	CCCo	94507	633-A7
PROW WY				
	7200	DBLN	94568	693-F5
PRUNE ST				
	2100	PIN	94564	569-E4
PTARMIGAN DR				
	-	WLCK	94595	632-B4
PUEBLO CT				
	-	CCCo	94507	632-D2
	-	ORIN	94563	631-C5
	1000	VAL	94591	550-E1
PUEBLO DR				
	200	PIT	94565	574-C6
PUEBLO WY				
	-	VAL	94591	550-C1
	3200	PLE	94588	694-D6
PUFFIN CIR				
	-	OAKL	94561	576-H7
PULIDO CT				
	-	DNVL	94526	633-C6
PULIDO RD				
	100	DNVL	94526	633-D6
PULLMAN AV				
	-	CCCo	94565	573-H1
	-	PIT	94565	573-H1
	2800	RCH	94804	588-J7
PULLMAN CT				
	900	CNCD	94518	592-F6
PULLMAN ST				
	1800	SPAB	94806	588-H4
PUMA CT				
	5200	ANT	94531	595-G5
PURDUE AV				
	100	CCCo	94708	609-G3
PURDUE RD				
	2700	SRMN	94583	653-B7
PURLEY LN				
	3500	CNCD	94519	572-G5
PURSLANE				
	100	PLHL	94523	592-A6
PURSON LN				
	1400	CCCo	94549	611-H2
	1400	WLCK	94597	611-H2
PUTNAM BLVD				
	2900	PLHL	94523	612-B1
	2900	WLCK	94597	612-B1
	3100	PLHL	94523	592-B7
	3100	WLCK	94597	592-B7
PUTNAM CT				
	8700	DBLN	94568	693-F2
PUTNAM ST				
	200	ANT	94509	575-A7
	2200	ANT	94509	574-J7
PUTTER CT				
	1100	BREN	94513	616-B2
PUTTER DR				
	100	BREN	94513	616-B1
PYRAL CT				
	-	CCCo	94582	674-A1
PYRAMID DR				
	2100	RCH	94803	589-D3
PYRENEES PL				
	1500	WLCK	94598	612-E2
PYRITE CT				
	100	ANT	94509	595-F2
PYRMONT CT				
	-	CCCo	94553	591-C3
PYRO ST				
	-	CNCD	94519	572-H6
Q				
QUAIL AV				
	-	BERK	94708	609-J6
QUAIL CRSG				
	-	CCCo	94556	651-F3
QUAIL CT				
	-	BREN	94513	596-E7
	-	PIT	94565	574-F7
	-	WLCK	94596	612-D7
	100	HER	94547	569-G4
	200	ANT	94509	595-E1
	1100	CNCD	94518	592-H3
QUAIL LN				
	-	CCCo	94553	591-D3
QUAIL RUN				
	-	LFYT	94549	611-G5
QUAIL CREEK CIR				
	7600	DBLN	94568	694-A1
QUAIL CREST DR				
	700	WLCK	94598	613-A3
QUAIL GLEN DR				
	-	OAKL	94561	596-B1
QUAIL HILL LN				
	-	CCCo	94803	589-C3
	-	RCH	94803	589-C3
QUAIL HOLLOW				
	-	CCCo	94553	591-E2
QUAIL MEADOWS LN				
	400	DNVL	94506	653-H3
QUAIL RIDGE LN				
	100	ORIN	94563	630-H2
QUAIL RIDGE RD				
	3800	LFYT	94549	611-C5
QUAIL RUN CT				
	4300	CCCo	94506	654-C3
QUAIL RUN DR				
	4100	CCCo	94506	654-C3
QUAIL RUN LN				
	4200	CCCo	94506	654-C3
QUAIL RUN PL				
	4200	CCCo	94506	654-C3
QUAIL RUN WY				
	4200	CCCo	94506	654-C3
QUAILTRAIL				
	1100	CCCo	94513	597-C6
QUAIL VALLEY RUN				
	1000	OAKL	94561	596-H1
QUAIL VIEW CIR				
	1400	WLCK	94597	611-J3
QUAIL WALK CT				
	3400	CCCo	94506	654-C3
QUAIL WALK LN				
	3300	CCCo	94506	654-C3
QUANDT CT				
	1200	LFYT	94549	611-H4
QUANDT RD				
	1200	LFYT	94549	611-H4
QUARRY CT E				
	1200	RCH	94801	608-D2
QUARRY CT W				
	1300	RCH	94801	608-D2
QUARRY RD				
	-	BERK	94708	609-J7
QUARTER LN				
	4500	OAKL	94561	576-C7
QUARTER HOURSE CT				
	-	ANT	94531	596-A2
QUARTERMASTER CYN RD				
	1000	SRMN	94582	653-G7
QUARTZ CIR				
	7200	DBLN	94568	693-J2
QUARTZ CT				
	-	ANT	94531	595-G2
	-	PIT	94565	573-F4
QUARTZ WY				
	-	ANT	94531	595-F2
QUEBEC ST				
	2200	CNCD	94520	572-F5
QUEENS RD				
	1200	BERK	94708	609-J6
	1800	CNCD	94519	592-J1
	1900	CNCD	94519	572-J7
QUEENS WY				
	200	PIT	94565	574-E5
QUEENSBROOK PL				
	-	ORIN	94563	631-B3
QUEENSLAND DR				
	-	RCH	94806	568-J6
QUERCUS LN				
	-	PIT	94565	574-D6
QUESADA CT				
	2000	ANT	94509	595-A1
QUIET CIR				
	1200	CNCD	94521	593-F7
QUIET LN				
	-	CCCo	94803	589-F2
QUIET GABLE CT				
	700	BREN	94513	616-E3
QUIET HARBOR DR				
	100	VAL	94591	550-E2
QUIET LAKE PL				
	2100	MRTZ	94553	592-A1
QUIET PATH CT				
	-	PIT	94565	573-F4
QUIET PLACE CT				
	900	WLCK	94598	612-G4
QUIET PLACE DR				
	2000	WLCK	94598	612-G4
QUIET VIEW CT				
	-	WLCK	94597	612-B2
QUIETWOOD LN				
	-	PLHL	94523	592-D4
QUIGLEY LN				
	3400	OAK	94602	650-E5
QUIGLEY PL				
	4200	OAK	94619	650-F6
QUIGLEY ST				
	3600	OAK	94619	650-E5
QUINAN ST				
	200	PIN	94564	569-E4
QUINCY CT				
	700	SRMN	94583	673-F5
QUINDELL WY				
	-	BREN	94513	616-D4
QUINTAS LN				
	100	MRGA	94556	631-E2
QUINTERRA LN				
	100	DNVL	94526	652-J2
QUIVIRA CT				
	500	DNVL	94526	653-B2
R				
RAAP AV				
	3700	MRTZ	94553	571-E6
RACHEL CT				
	2500	ANT	94531	595-G4
RACHEL LN				
	-	CNCD	94521	593-D3
RACHEL RD				
	1000	CCCo	94806	569-A5
RACHELLE RD				
	1000	WLCK	94597	612-A3
RACHEL RANCH CT				
	-	CLAY	94517	593-G5
RACHILL LN				
	-	CCCo	94803	589-H4
RADCLIFFE CT				
	2000	MRTZ	94553	571-H7
RADFORD CT				
	100	SRMN	94582	673-G4
RADIANT AV				
	2500	CCCo	94801	588-G2
	2500	RCH	94801	588-G2
RADIANT LN				
	900	SRMN	94583	673-B1
RADNOR CT				
	200	BEN	94510	551-B2
RADNOR RD				
	500	OAK	94606	650-A4
RAE CT				
	-	ORIN	94563	631-C5
RAE DR				
	-	ORIN	94563	631-C5
	-	PLHL	94523	592-C4
RAE ANNE CT				
	1100	CNCD	94520	592-D5
RAE ANNE DR				
	1300	CNCD	94520	592-E5
RAEANNE DR				
	100	CCCo	94507	632-G7
RAFAELA ST				
	2500	PIN	94564	569-F4
RAHARA DR				
	1000	LFYT	94549	611-B5
RAHN CT				
	-	WLCK	94597	612-B2
RAILROAD AV				
	-	VAL	94592	549-J1
	-	VAL	94592	550-A1
	-	DNVL	94526	652-J2
	-	HER	94547	569-E2
	-	PIN	94564	569-E3
	-	SRFL	94901	587-A2
	-	CCCo	94569	550-H5
	-	CCCo	94572	549-H7
	-	RCH	94801	588-D7
	-	RCH	94801	608-D1
	100	ANT	94509	575-D5
	100	DNVL	94526	653-A2
	300	PIT	94565	574-C6
RAILROAD LN				
	100	PIT	94565	574-E2
RAINBOW CIR				
	-	DNVL	94506	653-F4
RAINBOW CT				
	-	CCCo	94513	617-F2
	1100	MRTZ	94553	571-H7
RAINBOW DR				
	1100	MRTZ	94553	571-H7
RAINBOW LN				
	-	CCCo	94553	572-A5
	200	PLHL	94523	592-A7
	200	PLHL	94523	612-A1
RAINBOW BRIDGE CT				
	-	SRMN	94582	673-G3
RAINBOW BRIDGE WY				
	-	SRMN	94582	673-G3
RAINBOW VIEW DR				
	1800	WLCK	94595	632-B1
RAIN CLOUD DR				
	5000	RCH	94803	589-G3
RAIN DROP CIR				
	2100	PIT	94565	573-J2
RAINIER CT				
	1900	MRTZ	94553	572-A7
RAINIER DR				
	1900	MRTZ	94553	572-A7
RAINIER LN				
	100	ANT	94509	595-D1
RAINIER PL				
	4300	PIT	94565	574-E7
RAINIER ST				
	-	BREN	94513	616-H1
RAINTREE PL				
	900	LFYT	94549	611-J7
RAINWOOD WY				
	-	ANT	94531	596-A5
RALEIGH CT				
	100	HER	94547	570-B5
RALSTON AV				
	1700	CCCo	94805	589-B4
	5800	RCH	94805	589-B5
RALSTON CT				
	-	BREN	94513	616-A1
RAM CT				
	-	ANT	94509	595-B1
RAMADA CT				
	3100	CCCo	94549	611-J1
RAMAGE PEAK TR				
	10000	AlaC	94546	652-B6
	10000	CCCo	94556	652-B6
RAMER CT				
	1100	CNCD	94520	592-E5
RAMEY CT				
	200	PIN	94564	569-E3
RAMON CT				
	-	DNVL	94526	652-J1
RAMON PL				
	2000	SRMN	94583	673-G6
RAMONA AV				
	-	OAK	94611	630-A7
	-	PDMT	94611	630-A7
	100	ELCR	94530	609-E4
	500	ALB	94706	609-E6
RAMONA DR				
	-	ORIN	94563	631-C5
	2000	PLHL	94523	592-D6
RAMONA RD				
	-	DNVL	94526	653-B2
RAMONA ST				
	-	PIT	94565	574-C6
	2300	PIN	94564	569-F6
W RAMONA WY				
	1500	CCCo	94507	632-E4
RAMPART DR				
	11300	DBLN	94568	693-F5
RAMPART ST				
	2400	OAK	94602	650-E4
RAMPART WY				
	-	BREN	94513	596-C6
RAMPO CT				
	-	PLHL	94523	592-A6
RAMSAY CIR				
	1300	WLCK	94597	611-J3
	1300	WLCK	94597	612-A3
RAMSDELL CT				
	-	ANT	94531	595-C4
RAMSEY CT				
	3700	CCCo	94803	589-C3
RAMSGATE CT				
	-	DBLN	94568	694-F2
	-	DNVL	94526	653-B3
RAMSGATE LN				
	-	PLHL	94523	592-A4

STREET
Block City ZIP Pg-Grid

RANCH RD
- CCCo 94513 597-B5
- CCCo 94553 571-J3
- ORIN 94563 610-H4
N RANCHFORD CT
3600 CNCD 94520 572-G5
S RANCHFORD CT
3600 CNCD 94520 572-G5
RANCH HOLLOW WY
4900 ANT 94531 595-E4
RANCHITA LN
- CCCo 94553 572-A5
RANCHITO CT
1000 ELCR 94530 609-C2
RANCHITO DR
2200 CNCD 94520 572-G5
RANCHITOS DEL SOL
- CCCo 94528 633-F7
RANCHO CT
6700 PLE 94588 694-A7
N RANCHO CT
- PIN 94803 569-E6
N RANCHO PL
- CCCo 94803 569-E6
- PIN 94803 569-E7
RANCHO RD
1900 CCCo 94803 569-E7
1900 PIN 94564 569-E7
3900 LFYT 94549 611-B6
N RANCHO RD
800 CCCo 94803 569-E7
800 PIN 94803 569-E6
1000 PIN 94564 569-E6
S RANCHO RD
2400 CCCo 94803 569-F7
RANCHO WY
2100 PIT 94565 573-J3
RANCHO BERNADO DR
- PIT 94565 573-D4
RANCHO CANADA DR
- BREN 94513 616-A3
RANCHO DE LA ROSA
1400 CCCo 94553 590-J4
1400 CCCo 94553 591-A3
RANCHO DEL HAMBRE
1500 LFYT 94549 611-F2
RANCHO DEL LAGO RD
2400 CCCo 94553 590-H5
RANCHO DE MARIA RD
- CCCo 94553 590-G1
RANCHO DIABLO RD
- CCCo 94514 637-F3
- LFYT 94549 611-B4
RANCHO ESTATES CT
3700 CCCo 94598 613-A3
RANCHO LA BOCA RD
700 CCCo 94553 590-J3
1300 CCCo 94553 591-A4
RANCHO SERENO RD
- CCCo 94514 637-E3
RANCHO VERDE CIR E
1900 DNVL 94526 653-D7
RANCHO VERDE CIR W
1900 DNVL 94526 653-D7
RANCHO VIEW DR
1400 LFYT 94549 611-H2
RANCHO VIEW RD
1500 LFYT 94549 611-H2
RANCHO VISTA RD
- CCCo 94803 569-F7
RANCH POINT WY
1100 ANT 94531 595-E4
RANCHWOOD DR
- BREN 94513 616-A2
RAND AV
500 OAK 94610 650-A3
RANDALL AV
1900 CNCD 94520 572-E6
RANDALL RD
- WLCK 94597 612-B5
RANDICK CT
3100 PLE 94588 694-F6
RANDOLPH AV
3200 OAK 94602 650-C4
RANDOLPH CT
2100 ANT 94509 575-A7
2100 ANT 94509 595-A1
RANDOLPH PL
- SRMN 94583 673-F6
RANDOLPH RD
- PIT 94565 574-C5
RANDOM WY
100 PLHL 94523 591-J7
RANDY LN
900 SPAB 94806 588-G2
RANDY WY
900 BREN 94513 596-E7
RANGE CT
- HER 94547 569-H4
RANGE PL
2100 MRTZ 94553 572-A7
RANGE RD
- PIT 94565 574-A3
RANGEL RD
400 MRTZ 94553 571-J6
RANGER CT
- CCCo 94507 632-G4
RANGER PL
300 DNVL 94526 653-B5
RANGEVIEW PL
2100 MRTZ 94553 572-B2
RANGEWOOD CT
- PIT 94565 574-F6
RANGEWOOD DR
- PIT 94565 574-F6
RANI CT
- CCCo 94598 612-F4
RANKIN WY
100 BEN 94510 551-C4
RANLEIGH WY
1100 PDMT 94610 650-B2
RANSOM AV
2100 OAK 94601 650-D7
RAPALLO CT
- BREN 94513 596-C7
- CCCo 94565 573-D2
RAPALLO LN
300 CCCo 94565 573-D2
RAPALLO WY
2000 CCCo 94565 573-D2
RAPHAEL CT
2000 WLCK 94598 612-F2
RAPPAHANNOCK CT
300 DNVL 94526 653-D7
RAPPOLLA CT
5100 PLE 94588 694-H4
RASMUSSEN CT
2600 PLE 94588 694-F6
RASSAI CT
100 DNVL 94526 632-J7
RASSANI DR
100 DNVL 94506 654-A6
RATHBONE WY
3400 PLE 94588 694-F6

RATON CT
1200 CCCo 94803 569-C7
RAVEN CT
100 DNVL 94526 653-C4
100 HER 94547 569-H5
RAVEN PL
5000 CLAY 94517 594-A5
RAVEN WY
5000 CLAY 94517 594-A5
RAVEN GLASS CT
3200 WLCK 94598 612-H6
RAVENHILL LN
- MRGA 94556 631-C5
RAVENHILL RD
100 ORIN 94563 610-H6
RAVENSWOOD CT
- OAKL 94561 576-D5
RAVENWOOD CT
900 ANT 94509 575-C7
RAVENWOOD DR
- CCCo 94597 612-D2
1700 CNCD 94520 592-F3
RAVENWOOD LN
2300 OAK 94602 650-E4
RAVINE DR
100 PIT 94565 574-C4
RAWSON ST
2500 OAK 94619 650-F7
RAY AV
5800 CCCo 94805 589-B6
5800 ELCR 94530 589-B6
RAY CT
- CCCo 94507 633-C6
RAY ST
- BREN 94513 596-H7
RAYCLIFF PL
700 CNCD 94518 592-J6
RAYE AV
100 OAKL 94561 596-G2
RAYLAND CT
6800 PLE 94588 694-A6
RAYMOND CT
- CCCo 94595 612-C7
RAYMOND DR
200 BEN 94510 551-A4
1100 CCCo 94553 572-B7
1200 CCCo 94553 592-B1
RAYMOND ST
1100 MRTZ 94553 571-D4
READ DR
300 LFYT 94549 631-H3
READING PL
600 DNVL 94526 653-B5
READING WY
- PLHL 94523 591-B1
READY CT
- WLCK 94598 612-F2
READY RD
- WLCK 94598 612-F2
REAGAN CT
2800 ANT 94509 575-A7
REAGAN WY
- BREN 94513 596-F7
REATA PL
- OAK 94618 630-A4
REBECCA CT
- CCCo 94597 612-A5
REBECCA DR
2500 PIN 94564 569-E6
RED ALDER CT
- CCCo 94506 653-J3
RED ARROW CT
- RCH 94803 589-G1
RED BARK CT
- LFYT 94549 611-G2
RED BIRCH CT
- CCCo 94506 653-J3
RED BUD CT
- DNVL 94526 653-F4
REDBUD LN
100 VAL 94591 550-F1
REDBUD WY
- ANT 94509 595-E3
RED CEDAR CT
- CCCo 94506 653-J3
REDCLOUD CT
4300 CNCD 94518 593-B6
REDCOACH LN
- ORIN 94563 610-H3
RED CYPRESS CT
- CCCo 94506 653-J3
RED CYPRESS PL
- CCCo 94506 653-J3
REDDING PL
- OAK 94619 650-F7
REDDING ST
3500 OAK 94619 650-F5
REDDINGTON CT
900 WLCK 94596 632-F1
REDFEARN DR
- CCCo 94507 632-G4
REDFERN CT
1100 CNCD 94521 593-F7
REDFIELD PL
300 MRGA 94556 651-E3
RED FIR CT
- CCCo 94506 653-J3
REDHAVEN ST
800 BREN 94513 616-H2
RED HAWK PL
- RCH 94806 568-H7
REDLANDS PL
1200 CNCD 94521 593-F7
REDLANDS WY
1200 CNCD 94521 593-F7
RED LEAF WY
1100 PIT 94565 573-J2
RED MAPLE CT
- CCCo 94506 653-J4
4400 CNCD 94521 593-B5
N RED MAPLE CT
4300 CNCD 94521 593-B5
RED MAPLE DR
300 CCCo 94506 653-J4
RED MAPLE PL
- CCCo 94506 653-J5
RED OAK AV
- ALB 94710 609-D7
RED OAK CT
1300 PIN 94564 569-E5
RED OAK DR
1000 CNCD 94521 593-D6
RED OAK PL
2100 CCCo 94506 653-G1
REDONDO CT
5500 CLAY 94517 593-F6
REDONDO DR
100 PIT 94565 574-C6
REDONDO WY
100 DNVL 94526 653-C1
RED PINE CT
- CCCo 94506 654-A3
2800 PLE 94588 694-H3

REDROCK DR
300 ANT 94509 595-E2
REDROCK PL
2100 MRTZ 94553 572-B7
RED ROCK RD
- BREN 94513 596-B5
800 PDMT 94618 630-C7
800 PDMT 94611 630-C7
RED ROME LN
500 BREN 94513 616-C1
REDSTONE CT
3900 ANT 94509 595-F1
REDTAIL CT
5100 ANT 94531 595-H5
RED WILLOW RD
100 SRMN 94582 653-J7
REDWINE TER
1700 BREN 94513 616-C2
RED WING CT
600 WLCK 94595 632-C4
RED WING DR
400 CCCo 94507 633-C4
REDWING PL
- MRGA 94556 631-F5
REDWOOD
- BEN 94510 551-C6
REDWOOD AV
- DBLN 94568 694-D3
REDWOOD CIR
- LFYT 94549 611-C4
1300 SPAB 94806 588-H1
REDWOOD CT
800 CCCo 94525 550-D5
REDWOOD DR
800 CCCo 94506 654-A2
1200 CNCD 94520 592-E4
1800 MRTZ 94553 571-J7
2300 ANT 94509 574-J7
4300 OAKL 94561 576-D7
4300 OAKL 94561 596-D1
REDWOOD HWY
- CCCo 94516 631-A7
REDWOOD LN
1200 LFYT 94549 611-C4
REDWOOD RD
1600 HER 94547 569-J4
1900 HER 94547 570-A5
3700 OAK 94619 650-H5
5700 AlaC 94619 650-J4
6500 AlaC 94619 651-A4
8800 AlaC 94546 651-D6
12700 AlaC 94546 672-A6
REDWOOD ST
1100 PIT 94565 574-E3
REDWOOD TER
- ORIN 94563 610-E6
REECE CT
4600 RCH 94804 609-A1
REED CT
400 BEN 94510 550-J2
REED DR
- MRGA 94556 651-F2
REED PL
- CCCo 94707 609-F3
REED WY
3100 CNCD 94518 592-H3
REEDLAND CIR
4000 SRMN 94582 653-H7
REEF CT
2200 CCCo 94514 617-H7
REEF DR
- PIT 94565 574-E5
REEF POINT CT
700 CCCo 94572 569-J2
REEF POINT DR
800 CCCo 94572 569-J2
800 CCCo 94572 570-A2
REFLECTIONS CIR
400 SRMN 94583 673-F3
REFLECTIONS DR
100 SRMN 94583 673-F3
REFUGIO VALLEY RD
1300 HER 94547 569-J4
1700 HER 94547 570-A5
REGAL CT
4300 OAKL 94561 576-A7
REGAL DR
1400 BREN 94513 596-E6
1700 CNCD 94521 593-B2
REGAL RD
800 BERK 94708 609-H5
REGAL LILY LN
2100 SRMN 94582 653-J7
REGALO WY
- SRMN 94583 673-A2
REGANTI DR
1000 CNCD 94520 592-E5
1000 CNCD 94518 592-E5
REGANTI PL
1400 CNCD 94520 592-E5
1400 CNCD 94518 592-E5
REGATTA BLVD
1100 RCH 94804 608-G2
REGATTA CT
- VAL 94591 550-G3
REGATTA DR
3900 CCCo 94513 617-E7
N REGATTA DR
100 VAL 94591 550-F2
S REGATTA DR
100 VAL 94591 550-F2
REGATTA PT
- HER 94547 549-G7
- HER 94547 569-H1
REGATTA SQ
1000 RCH 94804 608-G2
REGELLO CT
1900 SPAB 94806 588-H3
REGENCY
100 PIT 94565 574-B6
REGENCY CT
200 CCCo 94803 589-F3
800 CCCo 94597 612-A5
900 SRMN 94582 673-J6
1500 ELCR 94530 609-D1
REGENCY DR
- CLAY 94517 613-J2
- CLAY 94517 614-A2
REGENT DR
- BREN 94513 616-D4
100 PIT 94565 574-E6
REGENT PL
100 CCCo 94507 632-F6
REGENTS CT
- RCH 94806 568-J6
REGINA AV
1300 SPAB 94806 588-G4
REGINA CT
4600 ANT 94509 574-H5
REGINA LN
4600 CNCD 94521 593-C3
REGIO CT
1000 LFYT 94549 611-H6
11600 DBLN 94568 693-F3

REGIO DR
11600 DBLN 94568 693-F3
REGIONAL ST
6900 DBLN 94568 693-G4
REID CT
5000 RCH 94804 609-B1
REILLY CT
11500 DBLN 94568 693-F5
REIMCHE DR
4100 ANT 94509 574-H6
REINDEER CT
2300 ANT 94531 595-G2
REINER LN
1100 WLCK 94597 612-B1
REINHARDT DR
3900 OAK 94619 650-G5
4800 OAK 94613 650-G5
REISLING CT
- OAKL 94561 576-D7
700 CLAY 94517 593-J7
REITZ CT
3400 CNCD 94520 572-F6
RELIANCE CT
- PIT 94565 574-D2
RELIEZ CT
3200 LFYT 94549 611-H3
RELIEZ MNR W
- LFYT 94549 611-H4
RELIEZ HIGHLAND RD
3300 LFYT 94549 591-G7
RELIEZ STATION LN
900 LFYT 94549 611-J6
RELIEZ STATION RD
700 LFYT 94549 631-H1
700 LFYT 94549 611-H7
RELIEZ VALLEY CT
- LFYT 94549 591-G7
RELIEZ VALLEY RD
1300 LFYT 94549 611-G2
1500 LFYT 94549 591-G7
1700 LFYT 94549 591-G7
1800 CCCo 94549 591-G4
2100 PLHL 94523 591-G4
2100 PLHL 94549 591-G4
2100 CCCo 94523 591-G4
2200 MRTZ 94553 591-E3
2300 CCCo 94553 591-E3
REMBRANDT CT
- OAKL 94561 576-G7
REMINGTON CT
- DNVL 94526 652-J3
REMINGTON DR
100 DNVL 94526 653-A3
100 DNVL 94526 652-J3
REMINGTON LP
200 DNVL 94526 652-J4
200 CCCo 94583 652-J4
REMINGTON ST
- BREN 94513 616-G3
REMUDA WY
3600 PIN 94564 569-H7
RENADA PL
900 SRMN 94583 673-G5
RENEE CT
100 RCH 94803 589-E2
100 CCCo 94803 589-E2
RENEE WY
- CNCD 94521 593-F4
RENFREW CT
100 CCCo 94803 589-D1
RENFREW RD
600 CCCo 94803 569-D7
600 CCCo 94803 589-D1
RENO PL
4800 RCH 94803 589-J2
4800 RCH 94803 590-A2
RENOIR CT
- OAKL 94561 576-H7
- OAKL 94561 596-H1
RENWICK LN
2100 ANT 94509 575-F6
RENWICK PL
100 WLCK 94598 612-J1
RENWICK ST
2400 OAK 94601 650-E7
2600 OAK 94619 650-E7
REQUA PL
- PDMT 94611 650-B1
REQUA RD
100 PDMT 94611 650-B2
RERUN DR
- CCCo 94553 571-G2
RESEARCH DR
3000 RCH 94806 569-A7
RESEDA WY
2000 ANT 94509 595-B1
RESERVOIR DR
- CCCo 94553 571-G3
RESERVOIR LP
- CCCo 94553 571-G3
RESERVOIR RD
- BEN 94510 551-E1
RESERVOIR ST
- CCCo 94569 550-G6
RESNIK ST
- HER 94547 570-B5
RETTIG AV
4000 OAK 94602 650-F4
RETTIG PL
4000 OAK 94602 650-F5
REVA DR
3100 CNCD 94519 572-G7
REVENNA WY
700 BREN 94513 616-E3
REVERE CT
- LFYT 94549 611-A7
REVERE DR
2000 CNCD 94520 572-E6
REVERE RD
- LFYT 94549 611-A7
REYNOLDS CT
- MRGA 94556 631-D6
REYNOLDS PL
5700 CNCD 94521 593-G7
RHEA CT
- CCCo 94565 573-F2
RHEEM AV
1300 RCH 94801 588-G4
2200 RCH 94804 588-H4
3400 RCH 94804 589-A4
3500 SPAB 94805 589-A4
RHEEM BLVD
- ORIN 94563 631-B2
200 MRGA 94556 631-F4
RHEEM CT
1800 PLE 94588 694-E7
RHEEM DR
1800 PLE 94588 694-E7
RHINE CT
- CLAY 94517 593-G7
- OAKL 94561 576-D7
RHINE WY
900 OAKL 94561 576-D7
RHODA AV
3400 OAK 94602 650-E4

RHODA AV
8300 DBLN 94568 693-F2
RHODA CT
11900 DBLN 94568 693-F2
RHODA PL
8500 DBLN 94568 693-F2
RHODA WY
4000 CCCo 94518 592-J4
RHODE ISLAND CT
1400 CNCD 94521 593-F6
RHODES CT
900 PLHL 94523 592-C3
RIALTO CT
4100 PIT 94565 574-E6
RIALTO DR
- CLAY 94517 613-J2
RIALTO WY
- PLE 94588 694-C6
RIBEIRO RD
- VAL 94592 549-G1
RICARDO AV
100 PDMT 94611 650-A1
100 PDMT 94611 630-A7
RICARDO CT
7700 ELCR 94530 609-E3
RICARDO DR
2000 CNCD 94519 592-G1
RICE ST
- BREN 94513 616-H1
RICE WY
1800 WLCK 94595 612-C7
1800 WLCK 94595 632-C1
RICH ACRES CT
- ORIN 94563 610-E6
RICH ACRES RD
- ORIN 94563 610-E6
RICHARD AV
2600 CNCD 94520 592-E1
2600 CNCD 94520 572-E7
RICHARD CIR
- CCCo 94565 573-F2
RICHARD CT
- ORIN 94563 631-A4
300 DNVL 94526 653-C2
2800 CNCD 94520 572-E7
RICHARD LN
100 CCCo 94595 612-A7
800 DNVL 94526 653-B1
RICHARD PL
4100 PIT 94565 574-F6
RICHARD WY
4100 OAKL 94561 596-C1
RICHARDS RD
4900 OAK 94613 650-G7
RICHARDSON CT
1600 CNCD 94519 592-H2
RICHARDSON DR
- BREN 94513 616-C4
RICHARDSON RD
- CCCo 94707 609-F4
RICHARDSON ST
200 MRTZ 94553 571-D3
RICHARDSON WY
- PDMT 94611 650-C1
RICHDALE CT
- BREN 94513 596-H7
RICHELLE RD
- LFYT 94549 611-H7
RICHIE DR
- PLHL 94523 592-C6
RICHMOND AV
6600 CCCo 94805 589-C6
E RICHMOND AV
- RCH 94801 608-D1
W RICHMOND AV
- RCH 94801 608-D1
- RCH 94801 588-C7
RICHMOND LN
- RCH 94801 588-B4
RICHMOND PKWY
- RCH 94806 588-F1
1200 RCH 94801 588-F1
1500 CCCo 94801 588-E4
3000 RCH 94806 568-H7
3100 RCH 94806 569-A6
3500 CCCo 94806 569-A6
3600 PIN 94564 569-A6
RICHMOND ST
400 ELCR 94530 609-C1
RICHMOND-SAN RAFAEL BRDG I-580
- MrnC 587-C5
- RCH 587-C5
- RCH 588-A7
- SRFL 587-C5
RICH SPRINGS DR
- PIT 94565 574-G6
RICK CT
- MRGA 94556 651-D1
RICKS AV
3100 MRTZ 94553 571-E5
RIDER CT
- CCCo 94595 612-B7
RIDGE AV
400 SolC 94591 550-D1
RIDGE CIR
- BEN 94510 551-A4
S RIDGE CT
200 CCCo 94506 654-B3
RIDGE DR
800 CNCD 94518 592-G3
4200 PIT 94565 574-D6
RIDGE LN
- ORIN 94563 610-F4
- SPAB 94806 589-A3
RIDGE PL
- PLHL 94523 591-J4
RIDGE RD
100 CCCo 94507 633-B6
1000 SPAB 94806 588-J3
2600 SPAB 94806 589-A3
3300 LFYT 94549 611-G6
RIDGE TR
- CCCo 94509 594-J5
- CCCo 94556 632-C7
- CCCo 94583 632-C7
- CCCo 94583 652-C1
RIDGE WY
2200 CCCo 94553 571-F3
2200 MRTZ 94553 571-F3
RIDGE CREST CT
- OAKL 94561 596-E2
RIDGECREST CT
- CCCo 94549 611-H1
2200 PIT 94565 574-A4
RIDGECREST RD
1200 PIN 94564 569-E5
RIDGECREST WY
2200 PIT 94565 573-J4
2200 PIT 94565 574-A4
RIDGEDALE CT
- ANT 94531 595-E5
- CCCo 94803 589-C3

RIDGEGATE CT
5000 ANT 94531 595-E4
RIDGE GATE RD
400 ORIN 94563 610-G7
RIDGELAND CIR
1800 DNVL 94526 653-B7
RIDGELAND DR
- DNVL 94526 653-B6
RIDGELINE DR
- ANT 94531 595-J1
- ANT 94531 596-A2
RIDGEMONT CT
4200 OAK 94619 650-J6
RIDGEMONT DR
6000 OAK 94619 650-J7
RIDGEMONT PL
1100 CNCD 94521 593-F7
RIDGE PARK CT
900 CNCD 94518 592-H4
RIDGE PARK DR
900 CNCD 94518 592-H3
RIDGE PARK LN
900 CNCD 94518 592-G3
RIDGEPOINTE CT
- HER 94547 569-F3
2200 CCCo 94596 612-E7
RIDGEPONTE CT
800 SRMN 94582 673-J6
RIDGEROCK DR
100 ANT 94509 595-D1
RIDGESTONE CT
300 WLCK 94598 613-B3
RIDGEVALE LN
200 PLHL 94523 592-A6
RIDGEVIEW CIR
5300 CCCo 94803 589-F3
RIDGEVIEW CT
- SRMN 94582 673-E2
400 PLHL 94523 591-J2
RIDGEVIEW DR
- RCH 94803 589-G5
300 PLHL 94523 591-J2
4800 ANT 94531 595-J3
RIDGEVIEW LN
2700 WLCK 94598 612-H4
RIDGEVIEW PL
200 PLHL 94523 591-J2
RIDGEVIEW TER
- HER 94547 569-F3
RIDGEWAY LN
- ELCR 94530 609-F2
RIDGEWOOD CT
400 ANT 94509 595-E2
1300 MRTZ 94553 571-J6
3500 CNCD 94518 592-H4
RIDGEWOOD DR
400 MRTZ 94553 571-J6
1100 CNCD 94518 592-H4
6800 OAK 94611 630-F6
RIDGEWOOD LN
- OAK 94611 630-F6
RIDGEWOOD RD
1500 CCCo 94507 632-E4
RIDGEWOOD WY
- OAK 94611 630-F6
3300 RCH 94806 568-J7
RIESLING CT
2100 PIT 94565 573-J3
2100 PIT 94565 574-A3
RIFLE RANGE RD
- AlaC 94546 672-A3
- AlaC 94552 672-A3
1300 ELCR 94530 609-E1
1300 ELCR 94530 589-E7
1400 RCH 94805 589-E7
RIFLE RANGE ROAD TR
- RCH 94805 589-E7
RIGATTI CIR
5000 PLE 94588 694-C6
RILEY CT
2000 CNCD 94520 592-E4
RILEY DR
200 CCCo 94553 572-B7
RILEY RIDGE RD
- AlaC 94546 651-J7
- AlaC 94546 652-A7
RIM RD
2600 CCCo 94806 569-A5
RIMA CT
- DNVL 94526 653-C1
RIMCREST CT
- PIT 94565 573-F4
RIMER DR
1100 MRGA 94556 651-E2
RIM RIDGE CT
1900 WLCK 94597 611-H3
RIMROCK DR
3900 ANT 94509 595-E1
RIMROCK LN
- HER 94547 569-F3
RIMROCK RD
- LFYT 94549 631-E1
RINCON DR
5900 OAK 94611 650-E1
RINCON LN
400 CCCo 94803 589-D1
RINCON RD
- CCCo 94707 609-F3
400 CCCo 94803 589-D1
500 CCCo 94803 569-D7
RINCONADA CT
400 BEN 94510 551-C5
RIO LN
4300 CCCo 94565 573-D2
RIO BLANCO DR
1600 CNCD 94521 593-C3
RIO DEL CT
- DNVL 94526 653-A4
RIO GRANDE CT
200 SRMN 94582 653-G7
2400 ANT 94509 575-B7
RIO GRANDE DR
2800 ANT 94509 575-B7
3300 ANT 94509 595-B1
RIO GRANDE PL
300 SRMN 94582 653-G7
RIO VERDE CIR
- PIT 94565 573-E4
RIO VERDE CT
- PIT 94565 573-D4
RIO VERDE DR
- PIT 94565 573-E4
RIO VISTA
- ORIN 94563 610-G7
RIO VISTA CT
1600 OAKL 94561 596-D1
RIO VISTA PL
4200 OAKL 94561 596-D1
RIPLE ROUGE RD
- PIT 94565 573-J5
- PIT 94565 574-A5
RIPLEY AV
- RCH 94801 588-F6

RIPTIDE CT
300 PIT 94565 574-A3
RISA CT
- ORIN 94563 631-C4
RISA RD
900 LFYT 94549 611-D6
RISDON CT
900 CNCD 94518 592-F6
RISDON RD
1600 CNCD 94518 592-F6
RISEBRIDGE CT
- BREN 94513 616-B2
E RISHELL CT
4600 CNCD 94521 593-C4
W RISHELL CT
4600 CNCD 94521 593-C3
RISHELL DR
- OAK 94619 650-H4
1500 CNCD 94521 593-C4
RISING DAWN LN
1300 CNCD 94521 593-B5
RISING GLEN RD
1100 PIN 94564 569-E5
RISING HILL CT
4600 OAK 94605 651-A7
RISPIN DR
1000 OAK 94705 630-B3
RITA DR
4100 CCCo 94553 572-A3
RITA WY
- ORIN 94563 631-A5
RIVENELL WY
- SRMN 94582 674-D3
RIVER PT
5300 CCCo 94514 617-J4
RIVERA ST
1200 ELCR 94530 609-D2
RIVER ASH CT
4400 CNCD 94521 593-C5
RIVERDALE CT
5200 PLE 94588 693-J6
RIVERHILL DR
- BEN 94510 551-C4
RIVERLAKE RD
1500 CCCo 94514 617-H6
RIVERLAND CT
- SRMN 94582 674-C3
RIVERMOUTH LN
100 VAL 94591 550-E2
RIVER PARK DR
- PIT 94565 554-D7
RIVER ROCK LN
1000 DNVL 94526 653-A2
RIVERS ST
1000 SPAB 94806 588-H1
RIVER SANDS RD
- CCCo 94565 553-D6
RIVERSIDE AV
5200 SPAB 94806 589-A4
RIVERSIDE CT
- CCCo 94565 573-E1
RIVERSIDE DR
100 CCCo 94565 573-D1
RIVERSIDE PL
100 CCCo 94565 573-E2
RIVERTON PL
200 SRMN 94583 673-G7
RIVERVIEW CT
3600 PIT 94565 574-C5
3800 CNCD 94520 572-G4
RIVERVIEW DR
- CCCo 94511 557-D7
- CCCo 94511 577-F1
- PIT 94565 574-C5
2200 CNCD 94520 572-G4
RIVERVIEW PL
- CCCo 94511 577-E5
3800 CNCD 94520 572-G4
RIVERVIEW TER
- BEN 94510 551-B4
- HER 94547 569-G3
RIVERWAY DR
100 PIT 94565 574-E1
RIVERWOOD CIR
200 MRTZ 94553 571-H6
RIVIERA AV
1500 WLCK 94596 612-B4
1700 WLCK 94597 612-B4
RIVIERA CT
- BREN 94513 616-B1
RIVIERA PL
500 SRMN 94583 673-H6
RIVIERA WY
3000 SRMN 94583 673-F6
ROAD 20
900 SPAB 94806 588-G2
ROAD 24
900 CCCo 94803 569-D7
900 CCCo 94803 589-D1
900 RCH 94803 569-D7
900 RCH 94803 589-D1
ROAD E
- CCCo 94513 596-J7
- CCCo 94513 616-J1
ROADRUNNER ST
- BREN 94513 596-G7
ROAN CT
- WLCK 94596 632-G2
ROAN DR
100 DNVL 94526 633-C7
ROAN LN
2200 WLCK 94596 632-F2
ROANOKE DR
400 MRTZ 94553 591-H3
ROANOKE RD
- BERK 94705 630-A4
- OAK 94618 630-A4
ROANWOOD CT
800 ANT 94509 575-F7
ROANWOOD WY
1200 CNCD 94521 593-G7
ROATAN CT
- SRMN 94583 673-D3
ROBB RD
2000 WLCK 94596 632-G1
ROBBIE KEITH LN
1600 WLCK 94597 612-C1
ROBBINS PL
- CCCo 94507 632-H5
ROBERT CT
2800 PIN 94564 569-F4
ROBERT RD
- ORIN 94563 631-A1
- LFYT 94549 611-B7
- ORIN 94563 611-B7
ROBERT ST
200 ANT 94509 575-D7
ROBERT WY
4500 RCH 94803 589-E1
5100 OAKL 94561 576-D6
ROBERTA AV
- PLHL 94523 592-B7
ROBERTA DR
8500 ELCR 94530 609-F2

STREET
Block City ZIP Pg-Grid

ROBERT H MILLER DR
2800 RCH 94806 588-J1
2800 RCH 94806 589-A1
2800 RCH 94806 569-A7
ROBERTS CT
- ANT 94565 574-G7
- ANT 94565 594-H1
- MRGA 94556 651-D1
700 DNVL 94526 652-G1
800 MRTZ 94553 571-G7
800 MRTZ 94553 591-G1
1800 CCCo 94521 593-E3
ROBERTS LN
3400 CNCD 94519 592-J1
ROBERTS ST
- CCCo 94565 573-H2
ROBERTSON RD
3600 LFYT 94549 611-E7
ROBIN CT
100 HER 94547 569-H4
6200 PLE 94588 694-A7
ROBIN LN
1800 CNCD 94520 592-E4
ROBIN ST
- BREN 94513 596-G7
ROBIN HOOD DR
5700 CCCo 94803 589-G4
ROBINHOOD WY
6200 OAK 94611 630-D6
ROBIN RIDGE CT
1900 WLCK 94597 611-H3
ROBINSDALE CT
- MRTZ 94553 571-H4
ROBINSON AV
- PIT 94565 574-C4
ROBINSON DR
3100 OAK 94602 650-G3
ROBINSON ST
100 MRTZ 94553 571-D4
ROBINWOOD AV
200 OAKL 94561 596-H1
ROBISON DR
3100 OAK 94705 630-B3
ROBLE AV
400 PIN 94564 569-D4
ROBLE CT
- BERK 94705 630-B4
ROBLE RD
- BERK 94705 630-B4
100 CCCo 94597 612-D1
100 OAK 94618 630-B4
ROBLES CT
1100 LFYT 94549 611-F5
ROBLES DR
300 VAL 94591 550-F1
2100 ANT 94509 595-A1
2300 ANT 94509 594-J1
ROBYN DR
1200 DNVL 94526 653-C4
ROCA ST
2400 ANT 94509 575-H6
ROCCA CT
3500 PLE 94588 694-H4
ROCHDALE WY
- BERK 94708 609-H4
ROCHE DR
1700 PLHL 94523 592-B4
ROCHELLE AV
- PIT 94565 574-F6
ROCK CT
900 ANT 94509 595-F2
ROCK LN
- BERK 94708 609-H5
ROCK CREEK CT
600 WLCK 94598 612-J3
5400 CNCD 94521 593-E7
ROCKCREEK CT
4100 CCCo 94506 654-C5
ROCKCREEK DR
4100 CCCo 94506 654-C5
ROCK CREEK PL
700 PLHL 94523 592-D4
ROCK CREEK WY
300 PLHL 94523 592-D4
1100 CNCD 94521 593-E7
ROCKFORD DR
3800 ANT 94509 595-F1
ROCKHAMPTON RD
- SRMN 94582 674-B4
ROCK HARBOR PT
- HER 94547 549-G7
- HER 94547 569-G1
ROCKINGHAM CT
4600 OAK 94605 651-A7
ROCKINGHAM DR
3900 PLE 94588 694-E6
ROCKINGHAM TER
1600 BREN 94513 616-D1
ROCK ISLAND CIR
600 DNVL 94526 653-C5
ROCK ISLAND DR
4200 ANT 94509 595-F2
ROCKLEDGE LN
- WLCK 94595 632-A2
ROCKNE CT
900 CNCD 94518 592-G6
ROCKNE DR
2000 CNCD 94518 592-G6
ROCK OAK CT
100 WLCK 94598 612-J1
ROCK OAK RD
200 WLCK 94598 612-J1
400 WLCK 94598 592-J7
ROCK PASS PL
2100 MRTZ 94553 572-B7
ROCKPORT CT
- PIT 94565 574-B2
- RCH 94804 608-E3
- DNVL 94526 653-A1
ROCKPORT CV
- SRFL 94901 587-A2
ROCKPORT DR
- PIT 94565 574-B2
ROCKRIDGE BLVD N
6000 OAK 94618 630-A5
ROCKRIDGE BLVD S
6000 OAK 94618 630-A5
ROCK RIDGE CT
- DNVL 94526 653-E3
1000 PIT 94565 573-J3
ROCKRIDGE DR
2800 PLHL 94523 591-J3
ROCKRIDGE PL
- OAK 94618 630-A5
ROCK RIDGE WY
900 PIT 94565 573-J3
ROCKROSE CT
- ANT 94531 595-J5
ROCK ROSE LN
600 SRMN 94582 653-J7
ROCK ROSE WY
- RCH 94806 568-J6
ROCKSPRAY CIR
- PIT 94565 574-A2
ROCKSPRING PL
1600 WLCK 94596 612-G7
1600 WLCK 94598 612-G7
ROCKSPRING WY
900 ANT 94531 595-D4
ROCKSTREAM CT
- PIT 94565 573-G4
ROCKVIEW DR
800 WLCK 94595 632-B2
ROCKWALL WY
5000 ANT 94531 595-E4
ROCKWAY AV
7300 ELCR 94530 609-E4
ROCKWELL PL
- BREN 94513 616-G3
ROCKWELL ST
- BREN 94513 616-G2
ROCKWOOD PL
1700 CNCD 94521 593-C2
ROCKY RD
800 ANT 94509 575-C6
4900 RCH 94803 589-G1
ROCKY CREEK TER
600 BREN 94513 616-E1
ROCKY MOUNTAIN WY
- OAKL 94561 596-H1
ROCKY POINT DR
- ANT 94531 595-F2
3900 ANT 94509 595-F1
ROCKY POINTE CT
- HER 94547 569-G3
ROCKY RIDGE RD
- CCCo 94556 652-B3
ROCKY RIDGE TR
- CCCo 94556 652-B2
- CCCo 94583 652-B2
RODEO AV
- CCCo 94572 549-H7
500 CCCo 94572 569-H1
RODEO CIR
5000 ANT 94531 595-J3
RODEO CT
100 CCCo 94549 591-H6
5100 ANT 94531 595-J3
5100 ANT 94531 596-A3
RODERICK CT
1000 LFYT 94549 611-H6
RODRIGUES AV
400 CCCo 94553 571-J3
RODRIGUES LN
- CCCo 94597 612-A5
RODRIGUEZ CT
- CCCo 94582 674-B5
ROEBUCK WY
4500 ANT 94531 595-H3
ROELLING LN
300 ANT 94509 575-E5
ROGER CT
1600 ELCR 94530 609-D1
ROGER LN
- OAKL 94561 596-G3
ROGERS AV
3100 WLCK 94597 612-B1
ROGERS CT
- PLHL 94523 612-B1
2800 OAK 94619 650-E7
ROGERS RD
3400 CNCD 94519 592-J1
ROGERS WY
800 PIN 94564 569-D4
ROGERS CANYON RD
- ANT 94531 595-D3
ROHRER DR
2700 LFYT 94549 631-H3
2700 LFYT 94549 632-A3
ROLAND CT
- CCCo 94803 589-E2
4000 CNCD 94521 593-B2
ROLAND DR
4000 CNCD 94521 593-B2
ROLANDO AV
200 BREN 94513 616-H2
ROLEN CT
- CLAY 94517 593-H7
ROLFE DR
200 PIT 94565 574-C3
ROLLING LN
400 CCCo 94507 633-A3
ROLLING GREEN CIR
- PLHL 94523 592-B5
ROLLING GREEN WY
- PLHL 94523 592-A5
ROLLING HILL CT
1200 MRTZ 94553 571-H7
ROLLING HILL WY
1000 MRTZ 94553 571-G7
ROLLING HILLS CIR
7400 DBLN 94568 693-F4
ROLLING HILLS CT
2500 CCCo 94507 632-J4
2500 CCCo 94507 633-A4
3700 PIT 94565 574-E5
ROLLING HILLS DR
1900 WLCK 94595 632-A1
3700 PIT 94565 574-E5
11100 DBLN 94568 693-F3
ROLLING HILLS LN
500 DNVL 94526 653-D6
ROLLING HILLS PL
11600 DBLN 94568 693-F4
ROLLING MEADOW CT
3300 CNCD 94518 592-H5
ROLLING RIDGE WY
100 CCCo 94553 591-D2
ROLLINGWOOD DR
2600 CCCo 94806 588-J3
2600 SPAB 94806 588-J3
2700 CCCo 94806 589-A2
ROLLING WOOD PL
1500 PIT 94565 574-G5
ROLLING WOODS WY
900 CNCD 94521 613-D1
1000 CNCD 94521 593-D7
ROLPH AV
300 CCCo 94525 550-D5
ROLPH PARK CT
- CCCo 94525 550-D5
ROLPH PARK DR
- CCCo 94525 550-D5
ROMA PL
3300 SRMN 94583 673-G5
ROMAE CT
300 DNVL 94526 632-J7
ROMAN WY
1300 MRTZ 94553 571-G6
ROMANY RD
5700 OAK 94618 630-B6
ROME CT
2200 PIT 94565 573-J4
ROMERO CIR
100 CCCo 94507 632-E5
ROMLEY LN
1500 CCCo 94507 632-E3
ROMULUS PL
- BREN 94513 596-C6
RONADA AV
- OAK 94611 630-A7
- PDMT 94611 630-A7
RONALD WY
3300 CNCD 94519 572-G6
RONDA CT
- WLCK 94597 612-B2
200 PIT 94565 574-A2
RONINO WY
3200 LFYT 94549 611-H4
RONNIE ST
1600 PIT 94565 574-F3
ROOSEVELT AV
900 RCH 94801 588-G6
2300 RCH 94804 588-H6
3300 RCH 94805 588-H6
3600 RCH 94805 589-A6
ROOSEVELT CT
2700 ANT 94509 575-E7
ROOSEVELT DR
4600 BREN 94513 616-G3
ROOSEVELT LN
2700 ANT 94509 575-E7
ROPER CIR
- BREN 94513 596-C6
ROSA CTE
200 WLCK 94598 612-H2
ROSA BLANCA DR
- PIT 94565 573-E4
ROSADA CT
3300 PLE 94588 694-D6
ROSAL AV
500 OAK 94610 650-A2
S ROSAL AV
1200 CNCD 94521 592-J4
1200 CNCD 94521 593-A4
ROSAL LN
1300 CNCD 94521 593-A3
ROSALIND AV
5300 ELCR 94530 589-B5
5300 RCH 94805 589-B7
6100 CCCo 94805 589-B5
ROSARIO CT
100 SRMN 94583 673-C3
ROSCOMMON WY
- DBLN 94568 694-D4
ROSE AV
- CCCo 94565 573-H2
200 DNVL 94526 652-J2
200 DNVL 94526 653-A2
900 OAK 94611 650-A1
900 PDMT 94611 650-A1
1000 PDMT 94611 630-A7
1000 OAK 94611 630-A7
3900 OAKL 94561 596-F1
4400 OAKL 94561 576-F7
ROSE CT
400 PIN 94564 569-C4
3400 CNCD 94519 592-J2
3700 LFYT 94549 611-D5
ROSE DR
- BEN 94510 551-B1
900 BEN 94510 550-G1
ROSE LN
- ORIN 94563 610-F6
1200 LFYT 94549 611-D5
1900 PLHL 94523 592-B5
4300 CNCD 94518 593-A5
ROSE ST
100 CCCo 94595 612-A7
300 DNVL 94526 652-J2
1200 CCCo 94525 550-D5
1300 BERK 94702 609-F7
1500 BERK 94703 609-F7
1900 BERK 94709 609-G7
2300 BERK 94708 609-H7
2600 CCCo 94553 571-G4
ROSE WK
- SRMN 94583 673-A2
2500 BERK 94708 609-H7
ROSE ANN AV
- PIT 94565 574-C3
ROSEANN DR
1200 MRTZ 94553 571-H6
ROSE ARBOR AV
6100 CCCo 94806 589-B3
ROSE ARBOR LN
- CCCo 94596 612-F6
ROSEBROOK CT
3600 CNCD 94518 592-H4
ROSEBROOK DR
- PIT 94565 573-G5
ROSEBROOK TER
400 BREN 94513 616-C1
ROSECREST DR
1800 OAK 94602 650-E2
ROSEDALE AV
800 LFYT 94549 611-F7
1900 OAK 94601 650-D7
ROSEDALE CT
7500 PLE 94588 693-H6
ROSEDALE DR
2000 CCCo 94806 569-B4
ROSEGATE AV
- BREN 94513 616-E3
ROSEHEDGE CT
900 CNCD 94521 613-C1
ROSELAND DR
1600 CNCD 94519 592-J2
ROSELINDA CT
- BREN 94513 596-D6
ROSELINDA DR
- BREN 94513 596-D6
ROSELLE LN
- ORIN 94563 630-J3
ROSE MARIE DR
100 CNCD 94518 592-G4
ROSEMARIE PL
300 CCCo 94565 573-D1
ROSEMARY CT
1700 ANT 94531 595-E3
2000 MRTZ 94553 572-A6
ROSEMARY LN
- SRMN 94583 693-F1
900 OAKL 94561 576-F7
1300 CNCD 94518 592-E5
ROSEMEAD CT
- DNVL 94526 653-C2
ROSEMONT AV
- BERK 94708 609-H4
ROSEMONT CT
100 CCCo 94597 612-A4
ROSEMOUNT LN
- SRMN 94582 674-D4
ROSEMOUNT RD
600 OAK 94610 650-A3
ROSE ROCK CIR
3700 PLE 94588 694-E7
ROSETO CT
900 BREN 94513 616-E3
ROSEWOOD AV
4100 RCH 94804 609-A1
ROSEWOOD CT
- CCCo 94506 654-A1
800 CCCo 94596 612-G7
900 PIT 94565 573-J3
1500 OAKL 94561 576-D7
4200 CNCD 94521 593-B2
ROSEWOOD DR
700 CCCo 94596 612-F7
4200 CNCD 94521 593-B2
4300 PLE 94588 694-D5
ROSEWOOD LN
- HER 94547 569-H4
- CCCo 94506 654-A1
ROSHILL PL
- DBLN 94568 694-E2
ROSIE LN
- BREN 94513 596-C5
ROSINA CT
4300 CNCD 94518 593-A5
ROSINCRESS CT
- SRMN 94582 673-G1
ROSINCRESS DR
- SRMN 94582 673-G1
ROSITA CT
7100 DBLN 94568 693-J3
ROSKELLY DR
2100 CNCD 94519 572-G7
ROSLIN CT
6200 PLE 94588 694-A7
ROSLYN CT
- BERK 94618 630-A4
- BERK 94705 630-A4
ROSLYN DR
100 CNCD 94518 592-H3
900 CNCD 94519 592-H3
ROSS AV
300 ANT 94509 575-E5
ROSS CIR
- OAK 94618 630-A4
100 CCCo 94553 571-J4
ROSS DR
- MRGA 94556 651-E1
ROSS PL
2600 WLCK 94597 612-A2
ROSS ST
5800 OAK 94618 630-A4
ROSSCOMMON WY
- ANT 94531 596-B4
ROSS GATE CT
4700 PLE 94566 694-D7
ROSS GATE WY
4600 PLE 94566 694-D7
ROSSI AV
- ANT 94509 575-D6
ROSSI ST
3300 LFYT 94549 611-G2
ROSSMOOR CT
- PIT 94565 574-B3
ROSSMOOR PKWY
1200 WLCK 94595 632-B2
ROSTI
100 HER 94547 569-E3
ROTHBURY CT
- SRMN 94582 674-C3
ROTHERHAM DR
900 ANT 94509 575-B6
ROTHSCHILD CT
11200 DBLN 94568 693-E4
ROTHSCHILD PL
11400 DBLN 94568 693-F4
ROUBAUD CT
- SRMN 94582 674-B4
ROUNDHILL CT
300 CLAY 94517 613-H1
ROUND HILL DR
- DBLN 94568 694-F2
ROUNDHILL DR
- BREN 94513 616-B2
2300 CCCo 94507 632-J5
2300 CCCo 94507 633-A5
3700 PIT 94565 574-G6
ROUNDHILL PL
200 CLAY 94517 593-H7
300 CLAY 94517 613-H1
ROUNDHILL RD
- CCCo 94507 632-H3
ROUND HOUSE PL
200 CLAY 94517 593-G5
ROUND TOP LOOP TR
- CCCo 94516 630-F5
- CCCo 94563 630-F5
ROUNDTREE CT
5400 CNCD 94521 593-E6
ROUNDTREE DR
5400 CNCD 94521 593-E6
ROUNDTREE PL
5400 CNCD 94521 593-E6
ROUNDTREE WY
5400 CNCD 94521 593-E6
ROUNDUP CT
5100 ANT 94531 595-J5
ROUNDUP WY
5100 ANT 94531 595-J5
ROUSE CT
100 PLHL 94523 612-B1
ROUX CT
1800 MRTZ 94553 571-J6
1800 MRTZ 94553 572-A6
ROVATO DR
- BREN 94513 616-E3
ROVERTON CT
- SRMN 94582 674-C4
ROVIGO CT
- DNVL 94526 653-D1
ROWE PL
3500 LFYT 94549 611-F7
ROWLAND DR
3300 LFYT 94549 611-G3
ROXANNE CT
100 WLCK 94597 612-C1
ROXANNE LN
- LFYT 94549 611-H7
ROXBURY CT
- CCCo 94507 633-A5
100 CCCo 94507 632-J5
ROXBURY DR
1700 CNCD 94519 593-B1
1700 CNCD 94519 573-B7
ROXBURY WY
1600 BREN 94513 616-C2
ROXIE LN
1100 WLCK 94597 612-C1
ROY LN
- CCCo 94565 573-E2
ROYAL CT
1800 WLCK 94595 612-C7
ROYAL RD
3400 CNCD 94519 572-J7
3400 CNCD 94519 592-J1
ROYAL ANN CT
1200 BREN 94513 596-E7
ROYAL ANN LN
800 CNCD 94518 592-G7
ROYAL ARCH CT
4000 CNCD 94519 593-B1
ROYAL ARCH DR
3900 CNCD 94519 593-B1
ROYAL GLEN CT
- CCCo 94595 612-C7
ROYAL GLEN DR
- CCCo 94595 612-C7
ROYAL INDUSTRIAL WY
1400 CNCD 94520 592-E2
N ROYAL LINKS CIR
- ANT 94509 595-D1
S ROYAL LINKS CIR
4000 ANT 94509 595-D2
ROYAL LINKS CT
4000 ANT 94509 595-D2
ROYAL OAKS CT
- CCCo 94507 633-A5
ROYAL OAKS DR
2300 CCCo 94507 632-J5
2300 CCCo 94507 633-A5
ROYAL PALM LN
- BREN 94513 596-C6
ROYAL PALM PL
200 DNVL 94526 653-D5
ROYAL PINES CT
- DBLN 94568 694-G3
ROYAL PINES WY
- DBLN 94568 694-G3
ROYAL RIDGE CT
- CCCo 94507 633-A5
ROYAL SAINT CT
200 DNVL 94526 653-D6
ROYAL TERN CT
- BREN 94513 596-E5
ROYALTON CT
3200 PLE 94588 694-E6
ROYAL VIEW DR
1500 WLCK 94598 612-D3
ROYCE WY
200 PIT 94565 574-C4
ROYSHILL LN
- DBLN 94568 693-D5
ROYSTON CT
8600 DBLN 94568 693-F2
ROYSTON WK
- PLHL 94523 591-J4
RUA PERA
1500 OAKL 94561 576-D6
RUBENS WY
- OAKL 94561 576-H7
- OAKL 94561 596-H1
RUBICON CIR
100 DNVL 94526 652-J1
RUBICON CT
100 MRTZ 94553 572-B7
2300 WLCK 94598 612-G2
RUBICON VALLEY CT
- SRMN 94582 673-J6
RUBIDOUX LN
1500 BREN 94513 616-C3
RUBIN DR
3300 OAK 94602 650-G4
RUBY AV
100 CCCo 94801 588-F4
100 RCH 94801 588-F4
RUBY CT
100 HER 94547 569-G4
RUBY LN
- VAL 94590 550-C2
E RUBY ST
100 OAKL 94561 576-F6
W RUBY ST
100 OAKL 94561 576-E6
RUBY TER
300 BREN 94513 616-D2
RUBYE DR
1900 ANT 94509 575-E6
RUDDER CT
- CCCo 94513 617-F7
RUDDICK CT
- CCCo 94513 597-C5
RUDGEAR DR
- WLCK 94596 632-E1
RUDGEAR RD
1000 WLCK 94596 632-G1
1100 CCCo 94596 632-G1
RUDGEAR ST
- WLCK 94507 632-E1
- WLCK 94596 632-E1
RUEBENS MEADOW DR
1400 BREN 94513 596-E6
RUFF AV
2700 PIN 94564 569-F5
RUFF CT
2700 PIN 94564 569-F5
RUGBY AV
300 BERK 94707 609-G4
300 CCCo 94708 609-G4
RUGBY CT
1500 CNCD 94518 592-E6
RULE CT
100 CCCo 94595 612-B6
RUMRILL BLVD
1100 SPAB 94806 588-H2
1400 SPAB 94801 588-G4
RUMRILL DR
2300 SPAB 94806 588-G2
RUNNING SPRINGS DR
- WLCK 94595 632-A3
RUNNYMEDE CT
3200 PLE 94588 694-E6
RUPPEL PL
- LFYT 94549 631-J4
RUSH CREEK CT
100 SRMN 94582 674-A7
RUSHINGWOOD CT
- ANT 94531 596-A5
RUSSELL CT
- CCCo 94598 612-F5
RUSSELL DR
- ANT 94509 575-C6
100 CCCo 94598 612-F5
1900 MRGA 94556 631-G5
RUSSELL ST
- OAK 94605 650-J7
- OAK 94619 650-J7
2800 BERK 94705 630-A3
3000 OAK 94705 630-A3
RUSSELMANN PARK RD
1100 CCCo 94517 614-B3
RUSSET CT
600 WLCK 94598 613-C4
RUSSO CT
4700 CNCD 94521 593-C3
RUSTIC PL
200 SRMN 94582 673-J6
RUSTIC RD
4300 CNCD 94521 593-B4
RUSTIC WY
- ORIN 94563 631-A2
RUSTING AV
4000 OAK 94605 650-H7
RUTGERS LN
2600 ANT 94509 575-D1
RUTH CT
- LFYT 94549 612-A6
RUTH DR
700 PLHL 94523 592-C3
RUTHERFORD CIR
500 BREN 94513 616-C1
RUTHERFORD DR
200 DNVL 94526 652-G1
RUTHERFORD LN
- CCCo 94553 572-B5
1300 OAKL 94561 576-D5
RUTHERFORD ST
2000 OAK 94601 650-C7
RUTHERFORD WY
1800 BREN 94513 616-C1
RUTHERGLEN DR
- SRMN 94582 674-B3
RUTHLAND RD
6100 OAK 94611 630-D5
RUTHVEN LN
- DBLN 94568 693-E5
RUTLAND CT
200 SRMN 94583 673-F5
RUXTON CT
6200 PLE 94588 694-A7
RYAN CT
800 CNCD 94518 592-H6
RYAN DR
100 PLHL 94523 592-B1
RYAN PL
800 PLHL 94523 592-B1
RYAN RD
2500 CNCD 94518 592-G6
RYAN INDUSTRIAL CT
100 SRMN 94583 673-B1
RYDAL CT
- OAK 94611 650-F1
- ORIN 94563 631-C5
RYDIN RD
2700 RCH 94804 609-B4
RYEGATE PL
- SRMN 94583 673-E5

S

S ST
200 BEN 94510 551-C4
SABA CT
- SRMN 94583 673-D3
SABAL CIR
2800 MRTZ 94553 571-E4
SABINA CT
200 DNVL 94526 653-C3
SABLE OAKS WY
- DBLN 94568 694-G2
SACLAN TER
300 CLAY 94517 593-H5
SACRAMENTO AV
5100 RCH 94804 609-B4
SACRAMENTO ST
1300 BERK 94703 609-F7
1300 BERK 94702 609-F7
4000 CNCD 94521 593-B2
SADDLE DR
2900 OAKL 94561 576-A7
SADDLE RD
- CCCo 94595 632-C2
SADDLEBACK CT
- CCCo 94506 653-H2
5300 RCH 94803 590-A3
SADDLEBACK DR
- OAKL 94561 596-G2
2300 CCCo 94506 653-H2
2300 DNVL 94506 653-H2
SADDLEBACK LN
- CCCo 94506 653-H2
SADDLEBACK PL
- CCCo 94506 653-H2
SADDLE BROOK CT
- OAK 94619 651-B6
SADDLE BROOK DR
5100 OAK 94619 651-B6
SADDLEBROOK LN
400 PLHL 94523 591-J3
SADDLEBROOK PL
- DBLN 94568 694-F3
SADDLE CREEK CT
400 BREN 94513 596-F6
500 SRMN 94582 694-B1
SADDLE CREEK TER
- DBLN 94568 694-G2
SADDLEHILL LN
1200 CNCD 94521 593-B4
SADDLEHORN DR
- PIT 94565 574-G6
SADDLE MOUNTAIN WY
- ANT 94531 595-E4
SADDLE OAKS CT
100 CCCo 94596 612-G6
SADDLERS CREEK CT
- SRMN 94582 674-C4
SADDLEWOOD CT
5300 CNCD 94521 593-F4
SADDLEWOOD DR
1800 CNCD 94521 593-F4
SAFARI WY
200 CCCo 94553 572-C7
SAGE CIR
- SRMN 94583 673-C4
SAGE CT
- BREN 94513 596-D6
- WLCK 94597 612-B3
400 BEN 94510 551-A1
2600 ANT 94531 595-G5
6800 DBLN 94568 693-J4
SAGE DR
800 MRTZ 94553 591-F3
SAGEBRUSH DR
3900 ANT 94531 595-H4
SAGE HILL CT
- DNVL 94526 653-B6
SAGER CT
- ORIN 94563 631-A5
SAGE SPARROW CT
- BREN 94513 596-E5
SAGE SPARROW ST
- BREN 94513 596-E5
SAGEWOOD CT
1800 CNCD 94521 593-F4
SAGINAW CIR
4700 PLE 94588 694-D6
SAGINAW CT
3100 PLE 94588 694-D6
SAHARA DR
100 CCCo 94553 572-C7
SAIL CT
1400 CCCo 94514 617-J5
SAILBOAT DR
3500 CCCo 94513 617-E7
SAINT ALBANS RD
100 CCCo 94708 609-G3
SAINT ALICIA CT
100 CCCo 94507 632-H4
SAINT ALPHONSUS WY
1500 CCCo 94507 632-F5
SAINT ANDREWS CT
- PLHL 94523 591-H5
2100 CCCo 94514 617-H7
SAINT ANDREWS DR
- BREN 94513 616-A4
900 CCCo 94803 569-D7
1000 CCCo 94514 617-H6
1600 MRGA 94556 631-C7
SAINT ANDREWS LN
- CCCo 94507 632-J4
SAINT ANDREWS PL
- CCCo 94507 632-J4
SAINT ANDREWS WY
4000 ANT 94509 595-D2
SAINT ANN CT
- DNVL 94526 653-C6
3200 ANT 94509 595-C3
SAINT AUGUSTINE CT
300 BEN 94510 551-C4
SAINT AUGUSTINE DR
- BREN 94513 596-B7
- BREN 94513 616-B1
200 BEN 94510 551-C4
SAINT BEATRICE CT
- DNVL 94526 653-D6
SAINT BENEDICT CT
- SRMN 94583 673-E5
SAINT BONAVENTURE CT
5000 CNCD 94521 593-D5
SAINT CATHERINE CT
1300 CNCD 94521 593-D5
SAINT CATHERINES LN
- BEN 94510 551-B4
SAINT CATHERINES SQ
300 BEN 94510 551-B4
SAINT CELESTINE CT
5000 CNCD 94521 593-D5
SAINT CHARLES CT
- DNVL 94526 653-B5
SAINT CHARLES PL
4300 CNCD 94521 593-A4
SAINT CHRISTOPHER CT
3100 ANT 94509 595-A1
SAINT CHRISTOPHER DR
200 DNVL 94526 653-D5
SAINT CLAIRE CT
- PLHL 94523 591-J2
SAINT CLAIRE DR
1200 ANT 94509 575-G5
1200 CCCo 94509 575-G5
SAINT CLAIRE LN
- PLHL 94523 591-J2
- PLHL 94523 592-A2
SAINT CLAIRE TER
300 BREN 94513 616-D3
SAINT CLOUD CT
4300 OAK 94619 650-J6
SAINT DAVID DR
1600 DNVL 94526 653-C5
SAINT DENIS CT
200 SRMN 94583 673-F5
SAINT DENIS DR
2800 SRMN 94583 673-E5
SAINT DUNSTAN CT
5000 CNCD 94521 593-D5
SAINT EDMUNDS WY
1200 BREN 94513 616-D3
SAINT EDWARD CT
100 DNVL 94526 653-C5
SAINT ELIZABETH CT
1200 CNCD 94518 592-J4
SAINT FRANCES DR
900 ANT 94509 575-B6
SAINT FRANCIS CT
- BEN 94510 551-C4
- LFYT 94549 611-D4
100 DNVL 94526 653-D6
SAINT FRANCIS DR
400 DNVL 94526 653-D6
1000 CNCD 94518 592-H4
3700 LFYT 94549 611-D4
SAINT GARRETT CT
5000 CNCD 94521 593-D5
SAINT GEORGE CT
- PLHL 94523 591-J2
SAINT GEORGE DR
2200 CNCD 94520 572-G4
SAINT GEORGE RD
500 DNVL 94526 653-E6
SAINT GERMAIN CT
- PLHL 94523 591-J2
SAINT GERMAIN LN
- PLHL 94523 591-J2
100 PLHL 94523 592-A2
SAINT GERMAIN PL
1600 CNCD 94521 593-E4
SAINT HELENA CT
100 DNVL 94526 653-C6
SAINT HELENA DR
1500 DNVL 94526 653-C6
SAINT HILL RD
- ORIN 94563 610-J6
- ORIN 94563 611-A6
SAINT IVES CT
600 WLCK 94598 612-E1
SAINT JAMES CIR
400 PDMT 94611 650-D2
SAINT JAMES CT
- ORIN 94563 610-G4
100 DNVL 94526 653-C6
SAINT JAMES DR
- PDMT 94611 650-C2
200 PDMT 94610 650-D2
3900 CCCo 94803 589-B3
SAINT JAMES PKWY
1400 CNCD 94521 593-D5
SAINT JAMES PL
- PDMT 94610 650-C2
3200 ANT 94509 595-B1
SAINT JEAN CT
100 DNVL 94526 653-C5
SAINT JOAN CT
- DNVL 94526 653-C5
SAINT JOAN LN
100 PLHL 94523 591-J2
SAINT JOHN CIR
800 CNCD 94518 592-H5
SAINT JOHN CT
800 CNCD 94518 592-H5
SAINT JOHN LN
4400 PIT 94565 574-C7
6300 CCCo 94803 589-H5
SAINT JOHNS CT
- WLCK 94597 612-B4
SAINT JOSEPH DR
2800 CNCD 94518 592-G5

STREET
Block City ZIP Pg-Grid

SAINT JULIE CT
- PLHL 94523 592-A2
SAINT LAURENT CT
100 MRTZ 94553 571-H5
SAINT LAWRENCE CT
- PLHL 94523 592-C7
SAINT LAWRENCE WY
1600 PLHL 94523 592-C7
SAINT LOUIS CT
900 CNCD 94518 592-E7
SAINT LOUIS DR
1200 CNCD 94518 592-D7
SAINT LOUIS LN
- PLHL 94523 591-J2
- PLHL 94523 592-A2
SAINT LUKE CT
- DNVL 94526 653-C6
SAINT MALO CT
100 MRTZ 94553 571-H5
SAINT MARK CT
- DNVL 94526 653-C5
SAINT MARY ALICE CT
5000 CNCD 94521 593-D5
SAINT MARYS CT
100 MRTZ 94553 571-D6
SAINT MARYS PKWY
- MRGA 94575 631-F6
SAINT MARYS RD
200 LFYT 94549 631-G5
200 MRGA 94556 631-E6
1600 MRGA 94575 631-G5
3300 LFYT 94549 611-F7
SAINT MARYS ST
100 MRTZ 94553 571-D6
SAINT MATTHEW PL
1100 CNCD 94518 593-A4
SAINT MAURICE CT
- DNVL 94526 653-B6
SAINT MICHAEL CT
- SRMN 94583 673-E5
3900 CNCD 94519 573-A7
SAINT MICHAELS CT
- BREN 94513 596-C6
SAINT MICHAELS WY
- BREN 94513 596-C6
SAINT MORITZ AV
1200 MRTZ 94553 571-H5
SAINT MORITZ DR
3700 PIT 94565 574-E6
SAINT NAZAIRE CT
100 MRTZ 94553 571-H5
SAINT NORBERT DR
300 DNVL 94526 653-D6
SAINT PATRICIA CT
5000 CNCD 94521 593-D5
SAINT PATRICK WY
- DBLN 94568 693-H4
SAINT PATRICKS CT
- DNVL 94526 653-B6
SAINT PATRICKS DR
100 DNVL 94526 653-B5
SAINT PAUL CIR
4200 PIT 94565 574-E6
SAINT PAUL CT
5800 OAK 94618 630-C6
SAINT PAUL DR
200 CCCo 94507 632-H4
SAINT PAUL WY
4200 CNCD 94518 593-A4
SAINT PETER CT
3700 CNCD 94518 592-J3
SAINT PHILIP CT
100 DNVL 94526 653-C5
1800 CNCD 94519 592-J1
SAINT PIERRE CT
- SRMN 94583 673-E5
SAINT PIERRE WY
100 MRTZ 94553 571-H5
SAINT RAMON CT
- DNVL 94526 653-C7
SAINT RAPHAEL DR
1000 CCCo 94565 573-D2
SAINT RAYMOND CT
7800 DBLN 94568 693-G3
SAINT REGIS AV
- BREN 94513 596-B7
- BREN 94513 616-A1
SAINT REGIS DR
400 DNVL 94526 653-D6
SAINT STEPHENS CIR
- ORIN 94563 610-J6
SAINT STEPHENS DR
- ORIN 94563 610-J6
SAINT TERESA CT
- DNVL 94526 653-C5
SAINT THOMAS CT
- PLHL 94523 591-J2
SAINT THOMAS LN
- PLHL 94523 591-J2
SAINT TIMOTHY CT
- DNVL 94526 653-D6
SAINT TIMOTHY PL
1100 CNCD 94518 592-J5
1100 CNCD 94518 593-A5
SAINT TROPEZ CT
- DNVL 94506 653-H5
SAINT TROPEZ DR
4100 CCCo 94565 573-D2
SAINT VINCENT CT
100 DNVL 94526 653-C6
SAKLAN INDIAN DR
1600 WLCK 94595 632-C3
SAL CT
- DBLN 94568 694-G4
SALAMANCA CT
200 SRMN 94583 673-C3
SALAZAR CT
100 CLAY 94517 613-J1
SALEM CT
- CCCo 94806 569-B4
300 SRMN 94583 673-E5
SALEM CV
- SRFL 94901 587-A2
E SALEM ST
3900 CNCD 94521 593-B2
SALEM TOWN CT
- DNVL 94526 653-C4
SALESIAN AV
2800 RCH 94804 588-J4
SALGADO AV
4200 OAKL 94561 576-E7
4200 OAKL 94561 596-E1
SALIDA WY
1100 CCCo 94803 569-C7
SALINAS CT
- PIT 94565 574-B2
SALINGER TER
- MRTZ 94553 571-J5
SALISBURY DR
- PIT 94565 574-C3
SALISBURY LN
3700 CNCD 94520 572-F5
SALISBURY ST
3400 OAK 94601 650-D6
SALISBURY WY
- CCCo 94582 674-C4
SALLY LN
- CCCo 94595 612-A6
SALLY ANN RD
- ORIN 94563 631-A2
SALLY RIDE DR
500 CCCo 94553 572-C7
SALMON CT
5700 CCCo 94514 617-J4
SALMON LN
- PIN 94564 569-E4
SALTER CT
900 PLHL 94523 592-C3
SALT POINT CT
200 VAL 94591 550-E2
SALT SPRAY TER
- HER 94547 569-H1
SALVADOR LN
- OAKL 94561 596-H2
SALVATIERRA CT
- DBLN 94568 694-G4
SALVINO CT
2900 RCH 94803 589-E2
SALVIO ST
1800 CNCD 94520 592-F2
2500 CNCD 94519 592-G1
3100 CNCD 94519 572-H7
SAMANTHA CT
100 CCCo 94507 632-G2
SAMANTHA DR
- LFYT 94549 611-J7
SAMANTHA WY
700 BREN 94513 616-E2
SAMARIA LN
200 OAK 94619 650-H5
SAMOA CT
100 SRMN 94582 653-E7
100 SRMN 94582 673-E1
SAMUEL CT
100 CLAY 94517 613-J1
SAMUEL ST
2600 PIN 94564 569-F4
SAN ANDREAS CT
700 CNCD 94518 592-H7
SAN ANDREAS DR
- DNVL 94506 653-F1
SAN ANDRES DR
- PIT 94565 573-E4
SAN ANTONIO AV
1800 BERK 94707 609-F5
SAN ANTONIO CT
- WLCK 94598 612-F3
SAN ANTONIO DR
2600 WLCK 94598 612-F3
SAN ANTONIO ST
- SPAB 94806 588-C3
SAN ANTONIO WY
200 WLCK 94598 612-F3
1600 OAK 94606 650-A5
SAN ARDO CT
- WLCK 94598 612-F3
700 CNCD 94518 592-H7
SAN BENITO CT
- WLCK 94598 612-G3
SAN BENITO DR
- PIT 94565 573-E3
2600 WLCK 94598 612-F3
SAN BENITO RD
900 BERK 94707 609-G6
SAN BENITO ST
1600 RCH 94804 609-C3
SAN BERNARDINO CT
100 CCCo 94565 573-E2
SAN BLAS PL
- SRMN 94583 673-G5
SANBORN CT
400 BEN 94510 550-J2
SANBORN DR
- OAK 94602 650-F3
- OAK 94611 650-F3
SANBORN RD
- ORIN 94563 630-J3
SAN BRUNO CT
700 CNCD 94518 592-J7
SAN CARLO CT
- DNVL 94526 653-C7
SAN CARLOS AV
100 ELCR 94530 609-E6
200 PDMT 94611 650-A1
300 PDMT 94610 650-A1
500 ALB 94706 609-E6
1200 CNCD 94518 592-G3
2300 CCCo 94553 571-F4
4400 OAK 94601 650-E7
SAN CARLOS CT
- PIT 94565 574-C4
- WLCK 94598 612-G4
SAN CARLOS DR
900 ANT 94509 575-B6
2500 WLCK 94598 612-F3
N SAN CARLOS DR
300 WLCK 94598 612-E2
900 CCCo 94598 612-E2
SAN CARLOS PL
- PIT 94565 574-C4
SANDALFORD WY
- SRMN 94582 674-D3
SANDALWOOD CT
3000 LFYT 94549 631-H3
SANDALWOOD DR
1800 CNCD 94519 573-A7
1800 CNCD 94519 593-A1
4400 PLE 94588 693-J7
SANDALWOOD PL
- PIT 94565 574-F6
SAND CREEK RD
- BREN 94513 596-A6
SAND DOLLAR DR
- RCH 94804 608-H2
100 VAL 94591 550-E2
SAND DRIFT DR
- BREN 94513 596-E7
SANDERLING DR
- HER 94547 569-F2
2500 PLE 94566 694-D7
SANDERLING WY
2600 PLE 94566 694-D7
SANDERLING ISLAND
1200 RCH 94801 608-D3
SANDERS CT
100 CCCo 94803 589-E3
SANDERS DR
1000 MRGA 94556 631-D7
1000 MRGA 94556 651-E1
SANDERS RANCH RD
- MRGA 94556 651-F1
SANDHILL CT
- ORIN 94563 610-G2
SANDHILL RD
- ORIN 94563 610-G2
SANDHILL CRANE CT
- OAKL 94561 576-H7
SAN DIEGO PL
400 SRMN 94583 673-F5
SAN DIEGO RD
700 BERK 94707 609-G5
SAN DIEGO ST
- SPAB 94806 588-D3
5600 ELCR 94530 609-C4
SANDLEWOOD LN
- SRMN 94583 673-A2
SANDMOUND BLVD
- CCCo 94561 597-F1
3600 CCCo 94561 577-D5
SAN DOMINGO CT
- SPAB 94806 588-D3
SAN DONATO CT
- BREN 94513 596-C7
SANDPEBBLE CT
- DNVL 94526 653-E4
SANDPIPER CT
100 CCCo 94572 569-J2
2600 WLCK 94597 612-B2
SANDPIPER DR
100 PIT 94565 574-D1
SANDPIPER SPIT
1400 RCH 94801 608-D3
SAND POINT CT
2300 CCCo 94514 617-G6
SAND POINT DR
9500 SRMN 94583 693-G1
SANDPOINT DR
- RCH 94804 608-H3
900 CCCo 94572 569-J2
1000 CCCo 94572 570-A1
SAND POINT RD
600 CCCo 94514 617-H6
SAND POINTE LN
100 CCCo 94565 573-D2
SANDRA CIR
4000 PIT 94565 574-F6
SANDRA CT
- WLCK 94595 612-C7
- CCCo 94507 632-G6
1600 PIN 94564 569-E6
SANDRINGHAM N
100 MRGA 94556 631-E7
SANDRINGHAM S
100 MRGA 94556 631-E7
SANDRINGHAM PL
- PDMT 94611 650-D2
SANDRINGHAM RD
- PDMT 94611 650-D2
SANDROSE CT
3900 ANT 94531 596-A4
SANDSTONE CT
1000 ANT 94531 595-D4
3000 CCCo 94507 632-H4
SANDSTONE DR
- BREN 94513 596-E6
SANDSTONE RD
- CCCo 94507 632-H4
SANDVIEW DR
- CCCo 94565 553-D7
SAND WEDGE PL
100 WLCK 94598 612-E3
SANDY CT
- ORIN 94563 631-A3
- RCH 94806 568-H5
1500 ANT 94509 575-G5
SANDY DR
- VAL 94590 550-C1
SANDY LN
- CCCo 94511 577-D4
- WLCK 94597 612-B3
5000 OAKL 94561 576-B6
SANDY WY
400 BEN 94510 551-B3
1500 ANT 94509 575-F5
3000 SRMN 94583 673-F5
SANDY BAY CT
- RCH 94801 608-E3
SANDY BEACH RD
- VAL 94590 550-B1
SANDY BROOK CT
700 CCCo 94572 569-J2
SANDY COVE DR
800 CCCo 94572 569-J2
800 CCCo 94572 570-A2
SANDY COVE LN
200 CCCo 94565 573-E2
SANDYFORD CT
- DBLN 94568 694-E4
SANDY HILL CT
400 ANT 94509 595-E2
SANDYHILLS LN
- BREN 94513 616-A1
SANDY NECK WY
100 VAL 94591 550-E1
SAN ELIJO CT
2700 ANT 94531 595-H2
SAN ESTEBAN CT
- SPAB 94806 588-C3
SAN FERNANDO AV
600 BERK 94707 609-F5
SAN FERNANDO ST
- SPAB 94806 588-J2
SANFORD AV
- CCCo 94801 588-F4
100 RCH 94801 588-F4
1100 SPAB 94806 588-G4
SANFORD CT
100 BREN 94513 616-G3
SANFORD LN
- LFYT 94549 611-J7
SANFORD ST
3400 CNCD 94520 572-F6
SAN GABRIEL AV
600 ALB 94706 609-E5
SAN GABRIEL CT
- SPAB 94806 588-C3
700 CNCD 94518 592-H7
SAN GABRIEL DR
3100 CNCD 94518 592-H7
SANGER PEAK CT
- ANT 94531 595-F5
SANGER PEAK WY
- ANT 94531 595-F5
SAN GIORGIO CT
4000 PLE 94566 694-C6
SAN GREGORIO CT
- DNVL 94526 633-B7
2700 ANT 94531 595-H2
SAN GREGORIO DR
2700 ANT 94531 595-H2
SAN JOAQUIN AV
- CCCo 94514 637-D2
200 ANT 94509 575-C6
SAN JOAQUIN CT
100 CCCo 94565 573-E1
SAN JOAQUIN ST
1400 RCH 94804 609-B3
SAN JOAQUIN HARBOR RD
- CCCo 94509 576-A4
SAN JOSE AV
800 BREN 94513 596-B7
800 BREN 94513 616-E1
1300 CNCD 94518 592-G2
5200 RCH 94804 609-C4
SAN JOSE CT
- WLCK 94598 612-F3
SAN JOSE DR
1100 ANT 94509 575-A6
SAN JOSE PL
500 SRMN 94583 673-F5
SAN JUAN AV
1800 BERK 94707 609-F5
2300 WLCK 94597 612-B3
SAN JUAN CT
700 CNCD 94518 592-H7
3100 ANT 94509 575-B7
SAN JUAN DR
3700 PIT 94565 574-D5
SAN JUAN PL
700 SRMN 94583 673-F4
SAN JUAN ST
3700 OAK 94601 650-D7
SAN JUAN OAKS RD
- BREN 94513 616-A4
SANKO RD
200 PLHL 94523 592-B3
SAN LISA CT
3600 CNCD 94520 572-G5
SAN LORENZO AV
1600 BERK 94707 609-F5
SAN LUCAS DR
- PIT 94565 573-E3
SAN LUIS AV
1300 OAK 94602 650-D3
9900 SRMN 94583 673-G5
SAN LUIS CT
- WLCK 94597 612-B3
700 CNCD 94518 592-H7
SAN LUIS RD
500 BERK 94707 609-G4
1500 WLCK 94597 612-A2
SAN LUIS ST
1600 RCH 94804 609-C4
SAN LUIS OBISPO ST
- SPAB 94806 588-D3
SAN MARCO BLVD
- PIT 94565 573-E4
700 CCCo 94565 573-E4
SAN MARCO PL
- SRMN 94583 673-G5
SAN MARCO WY
- PLE 94588 694-C6
SAN MARCOS CT
700 CNCD 94518 592-H7
SAN MARCOS DR
- PIT 94565 574-G6
SAN MARINO CT
- WLCK 94598 612-F3
SAN MARINO LN
300 BREN 94513 616-E3
SAN MARTIN WY
- ANT 94531 595-J5
- ANT 94531 596-A5
SAN MATEO CT
700 CNCD 94518 592-H7
SAN MATEO RD
- BERK 94707 609-G5
SAN MATEO ST
1700 RCH 94804 609-C3
2900 ELCR 94530 609-C3
SAN MICHELE CT
2300 CNCD 94520 572-G5
SAN MICHELE DR
3600 CNCD 94520 572-G5
SAN MIGUEL AV
600 BERK 94707 609-F5
SAN MIGUEL CIR
- MRGA 94575 631-G6
4300 PIT 94565 574-F7
SAN MIGUEL CT
- SPAB 94806 588-D3
900 CNCD 94518 592-H5
3100 ANT 94509 595-B1
SAN MIGUEL DR
100 SRMN 94583 673-G5
1600 WLCK 94596 612-D5
2000 CCCo 94596 612-E7
2400 CCCo 94596 632-F1
SAN MIGUEL PL
1800 WLCK 94596 612-D6
SAN MIGUEL RD
- CNCD 94518 592-G3
SAN ONOFRE CT
2700 ANT 94531 595-H2
SAN PABLO AV
400 CCCo 94572 549-J6
500 PIN 94564 569-F4
800 CCCo 94525 550-A5
2600 HER 94547 569-F4
4700 CCCo 94572 569-F4
12700 RCH 94805 589-A5
12700 CCCo 94572 550-A5
12900 SPAB 94805 589-A5
13000 SPAB 94806 589-A5
13300 SPAB 94806 588-J3
14800 RCH 94806 588-J3
15000 RCH 94806 568-J7
15000 SPAB 94806 568-J7
15500 RCH 94806 569-B5
15600 CCCo 94806 569-B5
16400 PIN 94806 569-B5
16600 CCCo 94564 569-B5
SAN PABLO AV Rt#-123
500 ALB 94706 609-D6
1000 ALB 94710 609-D6
1100 BERK 94706 609-D6
1100 BERK 94710 609-D6
1300 BERK 94702 609-D6
3000 ELCR 94530 609-B1
10200 RCH 94804 609-B1
11800 ELCR 94530 589-B7
11900 RCH 94805 589-B7
SAN PABLO CT
- MRGA 94556 631-G5
SAN PABLO DAM RD
- CCCo 94553 609-J1
- CCCo 94553 610-A2
500 CCCo 94563 610-A2
2200 SPAB 94806 589-A3
2900 SPAB 94803 589-A3
3000 CCCo 94803 589-E3
3500 RCH 94803 589-A3
7100 CCCo 94553 589-H6
SAN PAULO CT
- DNVL 94526 653-C7
SAN PEDRO AV
1800 BERK 94707 609-F5
SAN PEDRO CT
- WLCK 94598 612-F3
SAN PEDRO PL
- SRMN 94583 673-G5
SAN PEDRO ST
- SPAB 94806 588-D3
SAN PIEDRAS PL
- SRMN 94583 673-G5
SAN QUENTIN TER
- MnC 94964 587-B5
SAN RAFAEL CT
- WLCK 94598 612-F3
SAN RAMON AV
1800 BERK 94707 609-F5
SAN RAMON CT
- SPAB 94806 588-C3
SAN RAMON RD
3100 CNCD 94519 572-H7
7000 DBLN 94568 693-G3
7000 PLE 94588 693-G3
8800 SRMN 94583 693-G3
SAN RAMON VALLEY BLVD
200 DNVL 94526 653-A3
1500 SRMN 94583 653-A3
2100 SRMN 94583 673-C1
20400 SRMN 94583 693-F1
SAN RELIEZ CT
1300 LFYT 94549 611-G4
SAN REMO CT
2200 PIT 94565 574-A4
SAN REMO WY
2200 PIT 94565 574-A4
SAN REY PL
200 DNVL 94526 653-A3
200 DNVL 94526 653-B1
SAN ROBERTO PL
400 SRMN 94583 673-G4
SAN SABANA CT
7700 DBLN 94568 693-G4
SAN SABANA RD
7500 DBLN 94568 693-G4
SAN SEBASTIAN
4600 OAK 94602 650-D3
SAN SIMEON CT
- SPAB 94806 588-D3
700 CNCD 94518 592-H7
2100 ANT 94509 595-A2
2400 CCCo 94514 617-H7
SAN SIMEON DR
700 CNCD 94518 592-G5
SAN SIMEON PL
- PIT 94565 574-D7
100 VAL 94591 550-E1
300 SRMN 94583 673-G5
SANS SOUCI
1000 WLCK 94597 612-D4
SANTA ANA DR
- PLHL 94523 592-D3
700 PIT 94565 574-E5
SANTA ANA LN
700 CNCD 94518 592-H7
SANTA ANA PL
- WLCK 94598 612-G4
SANTA ANA ST
- SPAB 94806 588-C3
SANTA BARBARA CT
2400 CCCo 94514 617-H7
SANTA BARBARA DR
2500 PIN 94564 569-G6
SANTA BARBARA RD
- PLHL 94523 592-B7
500 BERK 94707 609-G4
900 BERK 94708 609-G4
SANTA BARBARA ST
- SPAB 94806 588-D3
SANTA BARBARA WY
3200 ANT 94509 595-C3
SANTA CATALINA CT
100 MRGA 94556 631-G5
SANTA CLARA AV
500 BERK 94707 609-F5
1300 CNCD 94518 592-G2
1900 RCH 94804 609-C3
2900 ELCR 94530 609-C4
SANTA CLARA CT
100 DNVL 94526 653-B4
SANTA CLARA DR
100 DNVL 94526 653-B4
SANTA CLARA ST
1200 RCH 94804 609-B2
SANTA CLARITA CT
- SPAB 94806 588-D3
SANTA CRUZ AV
5500 RCH 94804 609-C3
SANTA CRUZ CT
- PIT 94565 574-E2
2400 CCCo 94514 617-H7
SANTA CRUZ DR
800 PLHL 94523 592-D4
SANTA CRUZ PL
300 SRMN 94583 673-G4
SANTA FE AV
- RCH 94801 588-B6
100 CCCo 94806 609-E5
100 ELCR 94530 609-E5
200 RCH 94801 608-C1
500 ALB 94706 609-E5
1000 CCCo 94553 571-G4
1000 MRTZ 94553 571-G4
1100 BERK 94706 609-E7
1200 HER 94547 569-E3
1300 BERK 94702 609-E7
1800 CCCo 94509 575-H4
E SANTA FE AV
400 PIT 94565 574-E2
W SANTA FE AV
- PIT 94565 574-D2
SANTA FE CT
800 OAKL 94561 576-D6
4000 CNCD 94521 593-A2
SANTA FE DR
200 WLCK 94598 612-F3
SANTA FE ST
1800 OAKL 94561 576-C6
SANTA INES CT
- OAK 94601 650-B7
SANTA INES ST
- SPAB 94806 588-C3
SANTA LUCIA
- ORIN 94563 610-G5
SANTA LUCIA CT
- PIT 94565 573-E3
- PLHL 94523 592-D3
SANTA LUCIA DR
- PIT 94565 573-E3
800 PLHL 94523 592-C3
SANTA MARGARITA ST
- SPAB 94806 588-C3
SANTA MARGHERITA WY
- BREN 94513 596-B7
SANTA MARIA CT
3000 CNCD 94518 592-H7
3300 LFYT 94549 611-G7
SANTA MARIA DR
2200 PIT 94565 573-H4
3000 CNCD 94518 592-H7
SANTA MARIA RD
600 CCCo 94803 589-C1
SANTA MARIA WY
- ORIN 94563 610-G7
800 LFYT 94549 611-G7
SANTA MONICA CT
1000 PLHL 94523 592-C4
SANTA MONICA DR
- PLHL 94523 592-C3
SANTANA DR
- CCCo 94514 637-D3
SANTANDER DR
400 SRMN 94583 673-C3
SANTA PAULA CT
- SPAB 94806 588-D3
700 CNCD 94518 592-H7
SANTA PAULA DR
3000 CNCD 94518 592-H7
SANTA RAY AV
500 OAK 94610 650-A3
SANTA RITA CT
- SPAB 94806 588-D3
- WLCK 94596 612-D7
SANTA RITA DR
- PIT 94565 573-E4
- WLCK 94596 612-D6
3700 CNCD 94519 572-J7
SANTA RITA RD
2100 PLE 94566 694-E6
2300 PLE 94588 694-E6
4100 CCCo 94803 589-D2
4200 RCH 94803 589-E2
SANTA RITA ST
2100 OAK 94601 650-D7
SANTA ROSA AV
500 BERK 94707 609-F5
10000 SRMN 94583 673-G5
SANTA ROSA PL
100 SRMN 94583 673-F4
SANTA SUSANA WY
800 PIT 94565 573-J4
800 PIT 94565 574-A4
SANTA SUSANNA CT
700 CNCD 94518 592-H6
SANTA TERESA DR
- PIT 94565 573-E4
12200 SRMN 94583 673-G4
SANTA YNEZ CT
700 CNCD 94518 592-H6
SAN THOMAS WY
100 DNVL 94526 653-B4
SANTIAGO CT
200 DNVL 94526 653-B1
1600 ANT 94509 575-A7
SANTIAGO DR
100 DNVL 94526 653-B1
SANTIAGO LN
200 DNVL 94526 653-C1
SANTO CT
11500 DBLN 94568 693-F3
SAN TOMAS CT
- PIT 94565 573-E4
- SPAB 94806 588-C3
SAN TOMAS DR
- PIT 94565 573-E4
SAN TOMAS PL
600 SRMN 94583 673-F5
SANTOS LN
2900 CCCo 94597 612-D1
SAN VICENTE CT
- DNVL 94526 653-C7
SAN VICIENTE LP
- DBLN 94568 694-E3
SAN VICIENTE TER
- DBLN 94568 694-E3
SAN VINCENTE CT
1900 CNCD 94519 572-J7
SAN VINCENTE DR
1800 CNCD 94519 572-J7
SAN YSIDRO CT
- DNVL 94526 633-B7
SAPLING CT
1700 CNCD 94519 593-B1
SAPONE LN
- CCCo 94565 573-H2
SAPPHIRE CT
- HER 94547 569-G4
- SRMN 94582 673-F2
SAPPHIRE ST
6700 DBLN 94568 693-J2
SARA CT
- CCCo 94565 573-H2
SARA LN
- CCCo 94507 632-E2
SARAH CT
2100 PIN 94564 569-F5
SARAH DR
1600 PIN 94564 569-E6
SARAH LN
- MRGA 94556 651-E2
SARAH ST
500 BREN 94513 616-F2
SARANAP AV
100 CCCo 94595 612-A5
100 WLCK 94595 612-A5
300 LFYT 94549 612-A5
SARATOGA AV
2500 CNCD 94519 572-G6
SARATOGA CT
- CCCo 94507 633-A5
SARATOGA PL
- BREN 94561 596-E4
SARATOGA WY
3700 PLE 94588 694-F5
SARGENT AV
2700 CCCo 94806 569-B5
SARGENT CT
500 BEN 94510 550-J1
SARGENT RD
1600 CNCD 94518 592-F6
SARITA CT
2300 PIN 94564 569-G7
SARONI CT
- OAK 94611 630-F7
SARONI DR
6600 OAK 94611 630-F6
SASSAFRAS LN
- SRMN 94582 653-H7
SASSEL AV
900 CNCD 94518 592-G5
SATINLEAF CT
- SRMN 94582 673-H1
SATINLEAF WY
- SRMN 94582 673-H1
SATINWOOD DR
4200 CNCD 94521 593-C2
SATTLER DR
1700 CNCD 94519 593-A1
SATURN PARK CT
- SRMN 94582 674-A2
SATURN PARK DR
- SRMN 94582 673-J2
- SRMN 94582 674-A2
SAUSAL ST
1700 OAK 94602 650-C5
SAUTERNE WY
1800 OAKL 94561 576-C7
SAVAGE AV
3300 PIN 94564 569-G7
SAVANNAH CIR
700 WLCK 94598 612-G1
800 WLCK 94598 592-G7
SAVANNAH CT
900 WLCK 94598 592-G7
900 WLCK 94598 612-G1
SAVIGNON CT
800 CLAY 94517 613-J1
SAVONA CT
- DNVL 94526 653-C1
SAVOY CT
- BREN 94561 596-D4
600 WLCK 94598 612-E2
SAVOY LN
- SRMN 94582 674-B3
SAWMILL LN
- DBLN 94568 694-F2
SAWYER CT
- BREN 94513 616-H1
- CCCo 94513 616-H1
SAWYER WY
- BREN 94513 616-H1
SAXON ST
2200 MRTZ 94553 571-F5
SAXTON CT
- WLCK 94597 612-B2
SAYBROOK PL
2400 MRTZ 94553 572-A5
SAYBROOK WY
100 VAL 94591 550-E1
SAYRE DR
6900 OAK 94611 630-F7
SCALLY CT
2000 CNCD 94518 592-G6
SCANLAN WY
900 PIN 94564 569-D3
SCARBORO PL
100 SRMN 94583 673-F6
SCARBOROUGH DR
5700 OAK 94611 650-F1
SCARLET WY
200 BREN 94513 616-C2
SCARLET OAK CT
300 PLHL 94523 592-B1
SCARLET OAK PL
2000 CCCo 94506 653-G1
SCARLETT CT
5900 DBLN 94568 694-A4
SCARLETT DR
6100 DBLN 94568 694-A4
SCENIC AV
- PDMT 94611 650-C1
100 PDMT 94611 630-B7
1300 BERK 94708 609-H7
1400 CCCo 94805 589-C6
1600 BERK 94709 609-H7
1900 MRTZ 94553 571-F3
2300 CCCo 94553 571-F3
2400 OAK 94602 650-D4
4200 PIT 94565 574-D6
E SCENIC AV
- RCH 94801 608-D1
W SCENIC AV
- RCH 94801 608-D1
SCENIC CT
- BREN 94513 596-D7
- DNVL 94506 653-G5
- ORIN 94563 630-J2
100 CNCD 94518 592-G4
SCENIC DR
- ORIN 94563 630-J1
100 CNCD 94518 592-G4
N SCENIC DR
1200 LFYT 94549 611-G4
SCENIC PL
900 PLHL 94523 592-A4
SCENIC ST
2200 ELCR 94530 589-C7
SCENIC WY
- CCCo 94553 571-E2
- MRTZ 94553 571-E2
SCHAEFER RANCH RD
26900 DBLN 94552 693-C4
26900 AlaC 94552 693-C3
SCHAUPP CT
1100 CNCD 94520 592-E4
SCHELLING AV
800 LFYT 94549 611-G7
SCHELL MOUNTAIN WY
- ANT 94531 595-F4
SCHENONE CT
1500 CNCD 94521 593-E5
SCHILLER CT
1300 CNCD 94521 592-J3
SCHILLING CT
- BREN 94513 616-E2
SCHMIDT LN
6300 ELCR 94530 609-C2
SCHOFIELD CT
1100 CNCD 94520 592-E4
SCHOOL AV
5200 ELCR 94530 609-B2
5200 RCH 94804 609-B2
SCHOOL LN
100 WLCK 94597 612-B3
SCHOOL PTH
5100 RCH 94804 609-B2
SCHOOL ST
- CCCo 94569 550-H6
- PIT 94565 574-E3
100 DNVL 94526 653-A2
1000 MRGA 94556 631-D7
1700 MRGA 94556 651-D1
2400 ANT 94509 574-H5
2600 OAK 94602 650-D5
3400 LFYT 94549 611-F7
SCHOONER CT
- RCH 94804 608-G2
SCHOONER CV
- HER 94547 569-H1
SCHOONER DR
- RCH 94804 608-G2
SCHOONER LP
5600 CCCo 94514 617-J6
SCHOONER WY
100 VAL 94590 550-B1
100 CCCo 94565 573-J3
100 PIT 94565 573-J3
200 PIT 94565 574-A3
SCHOONER HILL
- OAK 94618 630-C4
- OAK 94705 630-C4
SCHUPP CT
1100 CCCo 94803 569-D6
SCHYLER ST
2900 OAK 94602 650-D5
SCIORTINO CT
- BREN 94513 596-D6

CONTRA COSTA

© 2006 Rand McNally & Company

STREET
Block City ZIP Pg-Grid

SCIOTA AV
- SRMN 94583 673-H6
SCIOTA PL
- SRMN 94583 673-H7
SCOFIELD DR
200 MRGA 94556 631-C3
SCOTCH CT
200 DNVL 94526 653-B2
SCOTNELL PL
900 CNCD 94518 592-G4
SCOTS CT
- WLCK 94596 612-E6
SCOTS LN
900 CCCo 94596 612-F6
1000 WLCK 94596 612-E6
SCOTT AV
800 RCH 94804 608-F3
SCOTT RD
1800 CNCD 94519 592-J1
SCOTT ST
900 OAK 94610 650-A2
1200 ELCR 94530 609-D2
SCOTTS CHUTE CT
100 RCH 94803 589-G2
SCOTTSDALE RD
200 PLHL 94523 592-B1
SCOTTS MILL CT
200 DNVL 94526 653-C4
SCOTTS MILL RD
400 DNVL 94526 653-C4
SCOTTS VALLEY
100 HER 94547 569-F4
SCOUT PL
400 DNVL 94526 653-B5
SCOUT RD
2300 OAK 94611 650-E1
SCRIPPSHAVEN LN
2000 CCCo 94507 632-D1
SCUDERO CIR
- PIT 94565 574-D2
SCUPPER CT
200 HER 94547 570-B6
SEA WY
- SRFL 94901 587-A1
SEABOURNE CT
1100 ANT 94509 575-F7
SEA BREEZE CT
1100 BREN 94513 596-E7
SEA BREEZE DR
800 BEN 94510 550-J4
800 BEN 94510 551-A4
SEABREEZE DR
- RCH 94804 608-J3
SEA CLIFF CT
700 CCCo 94572 569-J2
SEACLIFF CT
- RCH 94801 608-E3
SEACLIFF DR
1000 RCH 94804 608-E3
1100 RCH 94801 608-E3
SEA CLIFF PL
- CCCo 94565 573-E2
SEACLIFF PL
- RCH 94801 608-E3
100 VAL 94591 550-E1
SEACLIFF WY
- RCH 94801 608-E3
SEA CREST CIR
200 VAL 94590 550-B1
SEA DRIFT DR
- CCCo 94511 577-E5
SEADRIFT DR
- RCH 94804 608-H2
SEAFARER CT
100 VAL 94591 550-F2
SEA GATE PL
- CCCo 94511 577-F4
SEA GULL CT
2100 PIT 94565 574-B3
SEAGULL CT
- RCH 94804 608-J3
400 HER 94547 570-B6
3900 CCCo 94513 617-E7
SEAGULL DR
- RCH 94804 608-J3
SEAHORSE CT
- CCCo 94513 617-E7
SEAHORSE DR
100 VAL 94591 550-D1
SEA ISLAND CT
1100 BREN 94513 596-E7
SEA ISLE DR
- RCH 94804 608-J3
SEAL WY
1700 CCCo 94514 617-H6
SEALANE CT
100 PIT 94565 574-A3
SEALION PL
- VAL 94591 550-D2
SEA MEADOW CT
- CCCo 94511 577-F4
SEA MIST CT
200 VAL 94591 550-G2
SEA MIST DR
100 VAL 94591 550-G2
SEAN CT
- PLHL 94523 592-B3
SEAN PL
800 CNCD 94518 592-G7
SEA PINES
- MRGA 94556 631-C7
SEAPOINT CT
- RCH 94801 608-E3
SEAPOINT PL
- RCH 94801 608-E3
SEA POINT WY
- PIT 94565 574-E1
SEAPORT AV
4900 RCH 94804 609-A3
SEAPORT DR
100 VAL 94590 550-C1
SEA RANCH CT
600 VAL 94591 550-E3
SEARSPORT CT
1000 ANT 94509 575-E7
SEASCAPE CIR
900 CCCo 94572 569-J1
SEASCAPE CT
1000 CCCo 94572 569-J1
SEASCAPE DR
100 VAL 94591 550-D1
SEA SHELL DR
1400 RCH 94804 608-H2
SEASONS DR
1100 PIT 94565 573-J2
SEASONS WY
1900 PIT 94565 573-J1
SEAVER AV
- RCH 94804 609-A2
1300 RCH 94804 608-J2
SEAVIEW AV
- PDMT 94611 650-C1
100 PDMT 94610 650-C1
SEAVIEW CT
- RCH 94801 608-E2
SEAVIEW DR
- RCH 94801 608-E3
- CCCo 94565 553-D7
100 BEN 94510 551-B3
100 ELCR 94530 609-E2
SEAVIEW PL
7400 ELCR 94530 609-D2
SEAVIEW TR
- CCCo 94708 610-A4
- ORIN 94563 610-C6
SEA VISTA DR
1200 BREN 94513 596-D7
SEAWALL CT
100 VAL 94591 550-F1
SEAWARD CT
- CCCo 94511 577-E4
SEAWAY CT
100 HER 94547 570-B6
SEAWIND DR
- VAL 94590 550-B1
SEAWITCH DR
200 VAL 94590 550-B1
SEBASTIAN LN
1100 WLCK 94598 612-J5
SEBILLE RD
- DBLN 94568 694-B1
SECCOMBE CT
2100 WLCK 94598 612-G2
SECLUDED PL
100 LFYT 94549 611-J4
100 LFYT 94549 612-A4
SECRET CV
- HER 94547 569-G1
SEDGEFIELD AV
7200 SRMN 94583 673-G6
SEDGEFIELD CT
100 SRMN 94583 673-G7
SEEMANS LN
- WLCK 94597 612-C2
SEEMAS LN
- WLCK 94597 592-D7
SEENO AV
- PIT 94565 574-C6
SEGOVIA CT
3700 SRMN 94583 673-C3
SEINE CT
11400 DBLN 94568 693-F3
SELBORNE DR
- PDMT 94611 650-D2
SELBORNE WY
100 MRGA 94556 651-E2
SELBY RD
- CCCo 94525 550-B4
SELENA CT
- ANT 94509 595-D2
SELIMA WY
- CCCo 94553 572-C7
SELKIRK CT
5200 ANT 94531 595-J2
SELKIRK ST
- OAK 94619 650-G5
SELLERS AV
1100 CCCo 94513 616-J5
1500 BREN 94513 616-J5
2700 CCCo 94513 596-J5
5100 OAKL 94561 596-J1
5100 CCCo 94561 596-J1
6300 OAKL 94561 576-J7
6300 CCCo 94561 576-J7
SELLINGS CT
- CCCo 94596 612-F6
SELMI GRV
- RCH 94806 568-J6
SEMILLON CIR
300 CLAY 94517 593-H7
SEMINARY AV
3400 OAK 94605 650-H7
3400 OAK 94613 650-H7
SEMINOLE CIR
5000 CNCD 94521 593-D5
SEMINOLE CT
- CCCo 94513 617-G4
- SRMN 94583 673-D5
SEMINOLE WY
4400 PLE 94588 694-G7
SEMPLE CRSG
200 BEN 94510 551-B5
SEMPLE CT
600 BEN 94510 551-B5
SENCA CT
700 DNVL 94526 653-B3
SENECA CIR
- CCCo 94513 617-G3
SENECA CT
1000 WLCK 94598 612-H4
SENECA LN
- SRMN 94583 673-C4
SENIOR AV
- BERK 94708 609-J7
- BERK 94708 610-A7
SENNA CT
- DNVL 94506 654-B6
SENTINEL DR
3400 MRTZ 94553 571-F6
SENTRY LN
- DNVL 94506 653-H3
SEPULVEDA CT
5500 CNCD 94521 593-G5
SEQUOIA AV
- DBLN 94568 694-D3
- CCCo 94595 612-B7
100 VAL 94591 550-C1
1400 CCCo 94805 589-C6
SEQUOIA CT
1900 MRTZ 94553 572-A7
4000 CNCD 94519 593-B1
SEQUOIA DR
100 PIT 94565 574-D5
1900 MRTZ 94553 571-J7
1900 MRTZ 94553 572-A7
2300 ANT 94509 574-J7
2300 ANT 94509 575-A7
4100 OAKL 94561 596-C1
4300 OAKL 94561 576-D7
SEQUOIA RD
100 HER 94547 569-J4
100 HER 94547 570-A4
SEQUOIA ST
500 BREN 94513 616-F2
SEQUOIA TER
- CCCo 94595 612-B7
300 CCCo 94506 654-A2
SEQUOIA WY
- CCCo 94553 591-F2
- MRTZ 94553 591-F2
SEQUOIA WOODS PL
700 CNCD 94518 592-H6
SERAFIX RD
400 CCCo 94507 632-J2
400 CCCo 94507 633-A2
SERENA CT
7900 DBLN 94568 693-G3
SERENA GDNS
- CCCo 94596 612-E6
SERENA LN
- DNVL 94526 633-B7
- DNVL 94526 653-C1
SERENE CT
- BREN 94513 616-A2
- CCCo 94513 616-A2
- DNVL 94526 653-C7
3100 RCH 94803 589-E1
SERENE PL
- DNVL 94526 653-C7
SERENITY LN
- OAKL 94561 596-G2
SERENITY TER
5200 PLE 94588 693-H7
SERENO CIR
- OAK 94619 650-H5
SERPENTINE DR
3300 ANT 94509 575-F7
3300 ANT 94509 595-F1
SERRA CT
11600 DBLN 94568 693-F3
SERRA LN
- HER 94547 569-G2
SERRAMAR DR
- OAK 94611 630-D5
SERRAMONTE CT
600 DNVL 94526 653-E6
SERRANA CT
800 PIT 94565 574-A3
800 PIT 94565 573-J3
SERRANO CT
1000 LFYT 94549 611-F5
SERRANO ST
700 MRTZ 94553 571-D5
SERRANO WY
2200 PIT 94565 573-J4
SERVICE DR
1400 WLCK 94597 612-C2
SERVICE RD
- ANT 94509 575-D5
SESSIONS RD
- LFYT 94549 611-F5
SETTING SUN DR
4600 RCH 94803 589-F1
SETTING SUN PL
- CCCo 94803 589-F1
- RCH 94803 589-F1
SEVEN HILLS RANCH RD
700 CCCo 94598 612-D3
700 WLCK 94598 612-D3
900 WLCK 94597 612-D3
900 CCCo 94597 612-D3
SEVILLE
- PIT 94565 574-C6
SEVILLE CIR
2800 ANT 94509 575-A6
SEVILLE CT
- CCCo 94507 633-C5
2400 PIN 94564 569-H7
SEVILLE LN
- WLCK 94598 612-H1
SEVILLE PL
100 SRMN 94583 673-G5
SEWARD DR
1900 PIT 94565 574-E3
SEXTANT CT
300 HER 94547 570-B6
SHADDICK DR
400 ANT 94509 575-F7
SHADELAND CT
3300 CNCD 94519 592-H2
SHADELANDS CT
- PIT 94565 573-G5
SHADELANDS DR
2500 WLCK 94598 612-G1
SHADELANDS PL
500 SRMN 94582 673-J7
SHADE OAK LN
1300 CNCD 94521 593-B5
SHADEWELL CT
- DNVL 94506 653-F2
SHADEWELL DR
100 DNVL 94506 653-G3
SHADOW CT
2100 PIT 94565 574-B4
SHADOW DR
7300 DBLN 94568 693-F4
SHADOW LN
1700 ANT 94509 575-B6
SHADOW PL
7300 DBLN 94568 693-G4
SHADOWBROOK CT
- CCCo 94598 613-A4
SHADOWCLIFF CT
1200 BREN 94513 596-C7
SHADOWCLIFF WY
1200 BREN 94513 596-C7
SHADOW CREEK CT
100 CCCo 94506 654-C5
SHADOW CREEK DR
3400 CCCo 94506 654-C5
SHADOW CREEK LN
- ORIN 94563 631-A3
SHADOWFALLS CIR
4900 MRTZ 94553 571-G5
SHADOW FALLS DR
1400 BREN 94513 616-D1
SHADOWFALLS DR
4800 MRTZ 94553 571-G6
SHADOWHAWK CIR
- DNVL 94506 653-J6
SHADOW HILL CIR
- PIT 94565 573-F4
SHADOWHILL CIR
- SRMN 94583 673-A2
SHADOW HILL DR
- DBLN 94568 694-F2
SHADOW LAKE PL
2100 MRTZ 94553 592-A1
SHADOW MOUNTAIN CT
100 PLHL 94523 592-B2
2500 SRMN 94583 673-B2
SHADOW MOUNTAIN DR
2500 SRMN 94583 673-B2
SHADOW MOUNTAIN PL
500 SRMN 94583 673-B2
SHADOW OAK RD
- DNVL 94526 652-G2
SHADOWOOD PL
- OAKL 94561 596-F1
SHADOW RIDGE CT
- VAL 94591 550-D1
SHADOW RIDGE PL
- VAL 94591 550-D2
SHADOW TREE CT
- DNVL 94506 654-B5
SHADOWWOOD DR
100 PLHL 94523 592-B1
SHADY GN
700 MRTZ 94553 571-E5
SHADY LN
- WLCK 94597 612-C3
100 ANT 94509 575-D4
100 VAL 94591 550-F1
SHADYBROOK CT
100 PIT 94565 573-F5
SHADYBROOK DR
800 CNCD 94521 613-D1
SHADY CREEK DR
- DNVL 94526 653-E4
SHADY CREEK PL
1000 DNVL 94526 653-E4
SHADY CREEK RD
7600 DBLN 94568 694-A1
SHADY DRAW
2600 PIN 94564 569-H7
SHADY GLEN RD
100 CCCo 94596 612-E6
100 WLCK 94596 612-E6
SHADY LANE CT
- WLCK 94597 612-C3
SHADY OAK CT
- DNVL 94506 653-H5
SHADY OAK DR
- OAKL 94561 596-G2
SHADY TREE CT
100 DNVL 94526 653-E3
SHADY VALLEY CT
300 SRMN 94582 673-J6
300 SRMN 94582 674-A6
SHADY VIEW ST
- BREN 94513 596-D7
SHADY WILLOW LN
2300 BREN 94513 596-C5
SHADYWOOD CT
1900 CNCD 94521 593-F3
SHAHAN CT
100 ANT 94509 575-E7
SHAKESPEARE DR
1200 CNCD 94521 593-A4
SHAKESPEARE FESTIVAL WY
- CCCo 94563 630-F2
- ORIN 94563 630-F2
SHALE CIR
- ANT 94509 595-E1
SHALE CLIFF CT
100 CCCo 94517 614-F7
200 CCCo 94517 634-F1
SHAMROCK DR
2400 CCCo 94806 569-A5
2400 WLCK 94596 632-H2
SHAMROCK PL
8600 DBLN 94568 693-H2
SHAMUS CT
2600 CCCo 94806 569-B6
SHANA CT
400 DNVL 94526 653-B3
SHANDELIN CT
- CCCo 94507 633-C5
SHANE DR
2800 RCH 94806 589-A1
SHANGRILA CT
1600 LFYT 94549 611-F1
SHANGRILA RD
3400 LFYT 94549 611-F1
3500 CCCo 94553 611-F1
SHANNON
100 PIT 94565 574-B3
SHANNON AV
2300 CCCo 94806 569-C5
7700 DBLN 94568 693-G3
SHANNON CT
- MRGA 94556 651-G2
1500 BEN 94510 551-B4
7900 DBLN 94568 693-G3
SHANNON LN
2200 WLCK 94598 612-F1
SHANNONDALE CT
4800 ANT 94531 595-J3
SHANNONDALE DR
4400 ANT 94531 595-H3
SHANTILLY CT
200 CCCo 94507 633-D5
SHARENE LN
100 WLCK 94596 612-D5
SHARMAR CT
- CCCo 94507 632-D1
SHARON AV
- PDMT 94611 650-C1
200 CCCo 94572 549-G7
SHARON CIR
1500 CCCo 94549 611-J2
SHARON CT
- PDMT 94611 650-C1
200 MRTZ 94553 591-H3
3200 LFYT 94549 631-H2
3500 CCCo 94565 573-F1
7600 DBLN 94568 693-G2
SHARON DR
- CCCo 94565 573-F1
1700 CNCD 94519 593-A1
SHARON PL
- CCCo 94565 573-F1
SHARON ST
- CCCo 94565 573-F1
8300 DBLN 94568 693-G2
SHARON WY
- CCCo 94565 573-F1
SHARP AV
1800 WLCK 94596 612-B5
SHARY CIR
1000 CNCD 94518 592-F5
SHARY CT
1000 CNCD 94518 592-G4
SHASTA AV
1200 SPAB 94806 589-A4
SHASTA CIR
3800 PIT 94565 574-D5
SHASTA CT
- SRMN 94582 653-F7
100 ANT 94509 575-D7
100 ANT 94509 595-C1
2200 MRTZ 94553 572-A7
4600 PLE 94566 694-D7
5600 CLAY 94517 593-F6
SHASTA DR
2100 MRTZ 94553 572-A7
SHASTA LN
- WLCK 94597 612-B2
SHASTA RD
- CCCo 94708 610-A6
2600 BERK 94708 609-J6
3000 BERK 94708 610-A6
SHASTA ST
1600 RCH 94804 609-C3
SHASTA DAISY DR
- BREN 94513 596-H7
- BREN 94513 616-H1
SHATTUCK AV
800 BERK 94707 609-G6
1200 BERK 94709 609-G7
SHATTUCK PL
1400 BERK 94709 609-G7
SHAVANO WY
300 SRMN 94583 693-H1
SHAVANO PEAK CT
4800 ANT 94531 595-D3
SHAW CIR
3500 ANT 94509 595-C1
SHAW PL
- SRMN 94583 673-F6
SHAW RD
300 CCCo 94523 592-C7
300 PLHL 94523 592-C7
SHAWN CT
- CCCo 94507 633-C5
SHAWN DR
1200 PIN 94564 569-C5
1200 CCCo 94806 569-C5
SHAWNE PL
- BREN 94513 616-E2
SHAWNEE CT
- OAK 94619 650-J4
- SRMN 94583 673-D4
SHAWNEE LN
- ORIN 94563 631-A1
SHAWNEE WY
4500 PLE 94588 694-D6
SHEA DR
1900 PIN 94564 569-F6
SHEARWATER WY
- OAKL 94561 576-H7
SHEEPBERRY CT
4400 CNCD 94521 593-C5
SHEFFELS PEAK CT
4800 ANT 94531 595-E3
SHEFFIELD
100 HER 94547 569-J3
SHEFFIELD AV
- SPAB 94806 588-H2
3000 OAK 94602 650-C5
SHEFFIELD CIR
3800 CCCo 94506 654-A5
SHEFFIELD CT
- CCCo 94513 617-F5
- SPAB 94806 588-H2
4000 ANT 94531 595-G1
7300 DBLN 94568 693-H2
SHEFFIELD DR
4000 ANT 94531 595-G1
SHEFFIELD LN
- PLE 94588 694-F7
7200 DBLN 94568 693-H2
SHEFFIELD PL
3100 CNCD 94518 592-G3
SHEILA CT
- PLHL 94523 612-B1
200 MRGA 94556 631-D7
200 MRGA 94556 651-D1
SHELBOURNE WY
2300 ANT 94531 595-G1
SHELBY CT
600 DNVL 94526 653-D7
SHELBY HILL LN
- DNVL 94526 632-J6
SHELBY HILL RD
400 DNVL 94526 632-H6
SHELDON CT
- WLCK 94597 612-B2
2700 RCH 94803 589-E2
SHELDON DR
- BREN 94561 596-E4
2500 RCH 94803 589-D2
SHELDON LN
- WLCK 94597 612-B2
SHELDON PTH
2700 RCH 94803 589-F1
SHELL AV
700 MRTZ 94553 571-E4
800 CCCo 94553 571-F2
W SHELL AV
2200 CCCo 94553 571-F4
2200 MRTZ 94553 571-F4
SHELL CIR
1200 CLAY 94517 593-H6
SHELL CT
1300 CCCo 94514 617-H5
SHELL LN
1300 CLAY 94517 593-H6
SHELL PL
- CCCo 94514 617-G7
SHELLBARK CT
4400 CNCD 94521 593-B5
N SHELLBARK CT
4300 CNCD 94521 593-B5
SHELL DOCK
700 MRTZ 94553 571-E2
SHELLEY CT
700 CCCo 94572 569-J3
700 CCCo 94572 570-A3
SHELLEY ST
800 HER 94547 569-J3
800 CCCo 94572 569-J3
800 CCCo 94572 570-A3
800 HER 94572 569-J3
SHELLFLOWER CT
4400 CNCD 94518 593-A6
SHELLIE CT
100 CCCo 94565 573-F1
SHELL RIDGE CT
100 WLCK 94598 612-E3
SHELLSILVER CT
- CCCo 94582 674-B2
SHELLWOOD DR
1700 CNCD 94521 593-D3
SHELLY DR
500 PLHL 94523 592-B7
SHELLY LN
- CCCo 94511 577-E1
SHELLY PL
- DNVL 94526 652-H1
SHELTER BAY
- HER 94547 569-G1
N SHELTER BAY
- HER 94547 549-G7
- HER 94547 569-G1
SHELTER CT
- CCCo 94565 573-E2
SHELTER COVE CT
- ANT 94531 595-E4
SHELTERWOOD CT
300 DNVL 94506 654-C6
SHELTERWOOD DR
- DNVL 94506 654-C6
6400 OAK 94611 630-F7
SHELTERWOOD LN
100 DNVL 94506 654-C6
SHELTERWOOD PL
- DNVL 94506 654-C6
SHENANDOAH DR
200 MRTZ 94553 591-H4
SHEPARD CT
100 HER 94547 570-B5
SHEPARD ST
100 HER 94547 570-B5
SHEPHERD ST
4400 OAK 94619 650-G6
SHEPHERD CANYON RD
5900 OAK 94611 650-E1
5900 OAK 94611 630-F7
SHEPPARD CT
1200 WLCK 94598 612-E2
SHEPPARD RD
1000 WLCK 94598 612-E2
SHEPPARD WY
2600 ANT 94509 574-H6
SHERBEAR DR
2700 SRMN 94583 673-B2
SHERBURNE CT
100 DNVL 94526 653-C6
SHERBURNE HILLS CT
- DNVL 94526 653-F5
SHERBURNE HILLS RD
- DNVL 94526 653-F4
SHERI CT
- DNVL 94526 653-A3
SHERI LN
600 DNVL 94526 653-A3
SHERIDAN AV
100 PDMT 94611 650-C2
SHERIDAN CT
3600 CNCD 94518 592-J3
SHERIDAN LN
100 CCCo 94553 591-F1
100 MRTZ 94553 591-F1
SHERIDAN RD
- OAK 94618 630-C6
1200 CNCD 94518 592-J3
SHERIDAN ST
1000 VAL 94590 550-C1
SHERLOCK WY
1200 CNCD 94521 593-A4
SHERMAN CT
2200 ANT 94509 595-A1
SHERMAN DR
1400 BEN 94510 551-B4
2000 PLHL 94523 592-D6
SHERMAN LN
800 OAKL 94561 596-E2
SHERMAN ST
2900 PIT 94565 574-D5
SHERMAN ISLAND RD
19500 SaCo 94571 576-C1
SHERMAN ISLAND EAST LEVEE RD
20000 SaCo 94571 576-C1
SHERREE CT
600 MRTZ 94553 591-G4
SHERREE DR
500 MRTZ 94553 591-G4
SHERRY CIR
1900 OAKL 94561 576-C7
SHERWICK DR
6800 OAK 94705 630-C4
SHERWOOD CT
- CCCo 94582 674-B5
- MRGA 94556 651-D1
- PIT 94565 574-G6
4200 CNCD 94521 593-A4
SHERWOOD DR
200 BREN 94513 616-G2
1200 CNCD 94521 593-A4
5900 OAK 94611 630-D6
SHERWOOD PL
6400 DBLN 94568 694-A2
SHERWOOD WY
- CCCo 94582 674-B5
- CCCo 94597 612-A5
SHERWOOD FOREST DR
5700 CCCo 94803 589-G4
SHERYL CT
- PLHL 94523 612-A1
SHERYL DR
100 CCCo 94806 569-A5
SHETLAND CT
- ANT 94531 596-A3
- SRMN 94583 673-E4
SHETLAND DR
3000 PLHL 94523 591-J3
SHETLAND LN
- PLHL 94523 591-H3
SHETLAND WY
- ANT 94531 596-A2
SHEVLIN DR
800 ELCR 94530 609-E2
SHEVLIN PL
7800 ELCR 94530 609-E2
SHILES LP
3000 BREN 94513 616-H3
SHINN MOUNTAIN CT
5000 ANT 94531 595-E6
SHIPWATCH LN
- HER 94547 569-F3
SHIRE LN
3100 CCCo 94598 613-A3
SHIRE OAKS CT
300 LFYT 94549 631-H4
SHIREOAKS CT
100 SRMN 94582 673-J6
SHIRE OAKS DR
300 LFYT 94549 631-H4
SHIRLEE DR
400 DNVL 94526 632-J7
SHIRLEY CT
100 VAL 94590 550-C1
SHIRLEY DR
100 SPAB 94806 588-J3
1500 PLHL 94523 592-C4
1600 BEN 94510 551-B4
6900 OAK 94611 630-G7
6900 OAK 94611 650-G1
SHIRLEY ST
200 BREN 94513 596-G7
SHIRLEY WY
1200 CNCD 94520 592-F3
SHIRLEY VISTA
300 CCCo 94803 589-E1
SHOAL DR
- CCCo 94565 573-D1
- CCCo 94565 553-D7
SHOAL DR E
- VAL 94591 550-F2
SHOAL DR W
- VAL 94591 550-E2
SHORE RD
- CCCo 94565 553-D7
SHOREBIRD DR
- HER 94547 569-H1
SHORE HAVEN CT
100 CCCo 94806 569-B4
SHORELINE CIR
- SRMN 94582 653-G7
- SRMN 94582 673-G1
SHORELINE CT
- RCH 94804 608-H3
SHORELINE DR
- SRMN 94582 653-G7
- SRMN 94582 673-G1
100 PIT 94565 574-E1
SHORELINE LP
- SRMN 94582 653-G7
SHORELINE LP
- SRMN 94582 673-G1
SHORELINE PKWY
100 SRFL 94901 587-A4
SHORELINE PL
- CCCo 94511 577-F4
100 VAL 94591 550-F1
SHOREVIEW CT
1000 CCCo 94565 573-F1
SHOREWOOD CT
- RCH 94804 608-J3
6300 PLE 94588 694-B7
SHORT AV
1100 SPAB 94806 568-H7
SHORT ST
100 DNVL 94526 653-A2
2100 WLCK 94596 612-B4
2600 OAK 94619 650-E6
SHOSHONE CIR
2100 DNVL 94526 653-D7
SHOSHONE CT
100 DNVL 94526 653-D7
SHOSHONEE CT
- ANT 94531 595-G5
SHREWSBURY WY
- PLHL 94523 591-B1
- PLHL 94523 592-A4
SHUEY AV
1500 WLCK 94596 612-B5
SHUEY DR
- MRGA 94556 651-E2
SHUKLA CT
3600 WLCK 94598 613-A3
SHULGIN RD
1400 CCCo 94549 611-H2
SHUMARDI OAK CT
- BREN 94513 616-A4
SIBERT CT
800 LFYT 94549 611-F7
SIDERS CT
3500 ANT 94509 595-E1
SIDNEY AV
500 ANT 94509 575-E5
SIENA PL
100 DNVL 94506 653-H5
SIENA ST
5700 PLE 94588 694-C5
SIENNA LN
700 BREN 94513 616-E2
SIERRA AV
- PDMT 94611 650-C1
1000 CCCo 94553 571-F4
5200 RCH 94805 589-B6
5700 CCCo 94805 589-B6
SIERRA CT
- MRGA 94556 651-G2
200 MRTZ 94553 591-H4
2200 CNCD 94518 592-F5
6200 DBLN 94568 693-J4
6700 DBLN 94568 694-A4
SIERRA DR
- WLCK 94596 612-D5
100 PIT 94565 574-D5
200 MRTZ 94553 591-H4
SIERRA LN
- WLCK 94596 612-D5
6100 DBLN 94568 694-A4
6500 DBLN 94568 693-J4
SIERRA RD
2000 CNCD 94518 592-F5
SIERRA ST
1000 BERK 94707 609-F6
SIERRA RIDGE AV
- RCH 94806 569-B6
SIERRA RIDGE CT
- DNVL 94506 654-A6
SIERRA TRAIL RD
- OAKL 94561 596-H2
SIERRA VISTA CT
- LFYT 94549 611-G5
3300 CNCD 94518 592-H5
SIERRA VISTA PL
- DNVL 94526 653-A2
SIERRA VISTA WY
1000 LFYT 94549 611-F5
SIERRAWOOD CT
3700 CNCD 94519 593-A1
SIERRAWOOD LN
4400 PLE 94588 693-J7
SIESTA CT
4200 OAK 94619 650-G6
SIGNAL CT
900 CNCD 94518 592-F6
SIGNAL HILL DR
- DBLN 94568 694-G1
SIINO AV
- CCCo 94565 573-H2
- PIT 94565 573-H2
4000 CNCD 94521 593-A3
W SIINO AV
- CCCo 94565 573-H2
SILAS CT
- BEN 94510 551-C1
SILER PL
1000 OAK 94705 630-B3
SILK HILL CT
- SRMN 94582 674-C4
SILK TREE CT
2400 MRTZ 94553 572-A6
SILKTREE CT
- DNVL 94526 653-B7
SILKTREE LN
100 VAL 94591 550-F1
SILKWOOD LN
1700 CNCD 94521 593-F4
SILVA AV
5200 ELCR 94530 589-B6
5200 RCH 94805 589-B6
SILVA ST
4200 ANT 94509 574-H5
SILVA WY
- SRMN 94582 674-C4
SILVA DALE RD
1400 CCCo 94507 632-E3
SILVER AV
- CCCo 94801 588-F3
SILVER CT
3300 PIN 94564 569-G7
SILVERADO CT
- CLAY 94517 594-A7
300 DNVL 94526 653-D6
3200 LFYT 94549 631-H2
SILVERADO DR
400 LFYT 94549 631-H3
2100 ANT 94509 595-A2
2600 PIN 94564 569-G7
2700 OAKL 94561 576-B7
4300 OAKL 94561 596-B1
N SILVERADO DR
600 LFYT 94549 631-H2
SILVERADO WY
100 LFYT 94549 631-J4
SILVERA RANCH DR
- DBLN 94568 694-E1

STREET
Block City ZIP Pg-Grid

SILVER BELT DR
1100 RCH 94803 589-H2
SILVERBERRY CT
4400 CNCD 94521 593-B5
SILVERBERRY ST
1700 ANT 94531 595-E6
SILVER BIRCH CT
- CCCo 94506 654-A4
SILVER CHIEF PL
400 DNVL 94526 653-B5
SILVER CHIEF WY
400 DNVL 94526 653-B5
SILVER CLOUD PL
100 DNVL 94526 653-B5
SILVER CREEK CIR
2300 ANT 94509 595-B2
SILVER CREST CT
- LFYT 94549 631-F1
SILVERCREST CT
2500 PIN 94564 569-H7
4600 ANT 94531 595-J3
SILVERCREST ST
2500 PIN 94564 569-H7
SILVERCREST WY
4500 ANT 94531 595-H3
SILVER DELL RD
1500 LFYT 94549 611-F1
SILVER FIR LN
- CCCo 94506 654-A3
SILVERGATE DR
11400 DBLN 94568 693-F4
SILVER HILL CT
4800 ANT 94531 595-J3
SILVERHILL CT
1100 CCCo 94549 591-G5
SILVERHILL DR
1000 CCCo 94523 591-H5
1000 CCCo 94549 591-H5
SILVERHILL WY
- CCCo 94549 591-H5
SILVER HILLS DR
- CCCo 94513 (636-G3 See Page 635)
SILVER HOLLOW DR
400 WLCK 94598 613-B3
SILVERIA WY
- ANT 94531 595-F5
SILVER LAKE DR
400 DNVL 94526 653-D6
SILVER LAKE PL
2200 MRTZ 94553 592-A1
SILVER LAKE WY
2000 MRTZ 94553 592-A1
SILVER LEAF CT
- LFYT 94549 611-G2
SILVER MAPLE DR
- HER 94547 569-H3
3400 CCCo 94506 653-J5
3400 CCCo 94506 654-A5
SILVER MEADOW CT
4200 CCCo 94506 654-C4
SILVERMERE CT
- BREN 94513 616-A2
SILVER OAK CT
1400 PIN 94564 569-F5
SILVER OAK LN
500 CCCo 94506 653-J5
SILVER OAK PL
3600 CCCo 94506 653-J5
SILVER OAK TER
100 ORIN 94563 611-A3
SILVER OAKS PL
- WLCK 94597 612-B2
SILVER PINE LN
- CCCo 94506 654-A3
SILVERPINE LN
100 VAL 94591 550-F1
SILVER SADDLE CT
- PIT 94565 574-G7
SILVER SADDLE DR
- PIT 94565 574-G6
SILVER SAGE CT
5400 CNCD 94521 593-E7
SILVER SPRINGS CT
3300 LFYT 94549 631-F1
SILVER SPRINGS RD
3500 LFYT 94549 631-F1
3500 LFYT 94549 611-F7
S SILVER SPRINGS RD
3400 LFYT 94549 631-F1
SILVER SPUR CT
3400 CNCD 94518 592-J6
SILVERSTONE CT
6500 MRTZ 94553 591-H4
SILVERTON WY
- BREN 94513 596-E6
SILVERTREE LN
7600 DBLN 94568 693-G4
SILVERWOOD AV
3700 OAK 94602 650-F5
SILVERWOOD CT
- ORIN 94563 611-A7
1200 DNVL 94526 653-D7
SILVERWOOD DR
- LFYT 94549 611-A7
100 ORIN 94563 611-A7
1500 MRTZ 94553 571-J7
1800 CNCD 94519 573-A7
1800 CNCD 94519 593-A1
SILVERWOOD ST
- BREN 94513 616-H1
SILVEY CT
1700 CNCD 94521 593-E4
SILVIA CT
- MRGA 94556 631-D7
SIMAS AV
2200 PIN 94564 569-G7
SIMBA PL
- BREN 94561 596-D3
SIMMONS ST
1200 ANT 94509 575-F5
3300 OAK 94619 650-G7
SIMO LN
- CCCo 94507 632-E4
SIMONI CT
5100 CCCo 94803 589-G2
5100 RCH 94803 589-G2
SIMONI RANCH RD
- OAKL 94561 596-E2
SIMONS CT
- OAKL 94561 596-E1
SIMPSON CT
- WLCK 94596 612-E5
1400 PIT 94565 574-G4
SIMPSON DR
- CCCo 94596 612-E5
- WLCK 94596 612-E5
SIMS DR
6700 OAK 94611 650-E1
E SIMS RD
100 BREN 94561 596-G4
100 CCCo 94561 596-G4
SIMS MOUNTAIN CT
5100 ANT 94531 595-E4

STREET
Block City ZIP Pg-Grid

SINAI DR
200 CCCo 94553 572-C6
SINCLAIR AV
2600 CNCD 94519 592-G2
SINCLAIR DR
1800 PLE 94588 694-E7
SINGING HILLS RD
- CCCo 94507 632-E2
SINGING WOOD CT
- WLCK 94595 632-B4
SINGINGWOOD LN
- ORIN 94563 610-J3
SINGLETREE WY
6300 PLE 94588 694-A7
SINNET CT
700 DNVL 94526 653-D7
SIOUX LN
- SRMN 94583 673-C4
E SIR FRANCIS DRAKE BLVD
- SRFL 94901 587-A5
- SRFL 94964 587-A5
400 MrnC 94964 587-A5
400 MrnC 94904 587-A5
SISKIYOU CT
200 WLCK 94598 612-E3
SISKIYOU DR
1500 WLCK 94598 612-E3
SITA CT
- ANT 94509 595-B1
SITKA CT
500 WLCK 94598 592-J7
SITKA DR
600 WLCK 94598 592-J7
SKANDER CT
- PLHL 94523 592-A3
SKANDER LN
300 PLHL 94523 592-A3
SKELLY AV
100 HER 94547 569-F3
SKIPPER RD
- CCCo 94565 573-E1
SKIPTON CT
2800 ANT 94509 575-C6
SKY LN
3400 LFYT 94549 611-F5
SKY RD
2400 WLCK 94597 612-B3
SKY TER
- DNVL 94526 652-H3
SKYCREST DR
1100 WLCK 94595 631-J1
1400 DNVL 94506 654-B6
SKYHARBOUR LN
400 CCCo 94565 573-D2
SKY HAWK DR
4800 RCH 94803 589-G1
SKY-HY CIR
600 LFYT 94549 631-F2
600 MRGA 94556 631-F2
SKY-HY CT
600 LFYT 94549 631-F1
SKY-HY DR
500 MRGA 94556 631-E2
500 LFYT 94549 631-E2
SKYLAND WY
- DBLN 94568 694-H3
SKYLARK CT
400 DNVL 94506 653-H4
5000 PLE 94566 694-D7
SKYLARK DR
3500 CNCD 94520 572-G6
SKYLARK LN
4000 DNVL 94506 653-H4
SKYLARK WY
2400 PLE 94566 694-D7
SKY LINE
- CCCo 94806 569-A5
SKYLINE BLVD
5800 OAK 94611 630-D4
6400 CCCo 94563 630-F6
8600 CCCo 94516 630-F6
8600 OAK 94611 650-G2
10500 AlaC 94619 650-G2
10500 OAK 94602 650-G2
10500 OAK 94619 650-J5
12200 OAK 94619 651-A5
13700 OAK 94605 651-B6
SKYLINE DR
600 MRTZ 94553 591-G3
5800 CCCo 94803 569-F7
5900 CCCo 94803 589-F1
SKYLINE PL
4300 PIT 94565 574-E7
SKY PARK PL
- RCH 94806 568-J6
SKYPOINT CT
4200 OAK 94619 650-J6
SKY RANCH CT
600 LFYT 94549 631-F1
SKY RANCH DR
- CCCo 94551 (655-F6 See Page 635)
SKY RANCH LN
- PLHL 94523 592-A4
SKY VIEW CT
- CCCo 94556 651-F3
SKYVIEW CT
500 PLHL 94523 591-J2
SKYVIEW DR
- RCH 94803 589-G3
300 PLHL 94523 591-H2
SKYVIEW PL
5700 RCH 94803 589-G3
SKYWAY LN
- OAK 94619 651-C7
SKYWOOD RD
800 LFYT 94549 611-G7
SLATER AV
700 PLHL 94523 591-J5
700 PLHL 94523 592-A5
SLATER CT
1400 CNCD 94521 592-J3
SLATER LN
- OAK 94705 630-A3
SLATTEN RANCH RD
- ANT 94531 596-C4
SLEEPY HOLLOW CT
- ORIN 94563 610-G4
SLEEPY HOLLOW LN
- ORIN 94563 610-F4
SLEIGH LN
- CCCo 94596 612-F6
SLOAN CT
5500 CNCD 94521 593-H4
SLOBDNIK
- CCCo 94553 571-G2
SLOPE CREST DR
13200 OAK 94619 651-C6
SLOUGH PL
- CCCo 94511 577-F5
SMETZER WY
- ANT 94531 595-J5

STREET
Block City ZIP Pg-Grid

SMITH AV
- DBLN 94568 694-A3
700 PIN 94564 569-E4
SMITH DR
5100 MRTZ 94553 591-F1
SMITH LN
- CCCo 94513 617-B5
2000 CNCD 94518 592-F7
SMITH RD
100 CCCo 94507 633-A6
2300 BREN 94513 596-E5
SMITH FARM RD
- CCCo 94513 596-J5
- CCCo 94513 597-A5
SMITH GATE CT
4800 PLE 94588 694-D7
SMITH PEAK CT
2000 ANT 94531 595-F4
SMOKE TREE CT
4400 CNCD 94521 593-B5
SMOKETREE CT
- CCCo 94549 591-H5
SMOKETREE ST
2700 ANT 94509 575-J5
SMOKEWOOD CT
- DNVL 94526 653-B4
SMOKEY CT
3300 ANT 94531 595-H2
SMYTH RD
- BERK 94704 630-A2
SNAKE RD
5500 OAK 94611 650-E1
5900 OAK 94611 630-E7
SNAPDRAGON CT
- BREN 94513 596-H7
- BREN 94513 616-H1
SNAPDRAGON DR
- CCCo 94582 674-A2
SNAPDRAGON PL
600 BEN 94510 551-A1
SNAPDRAGON WY
- BREN 94513 616-H1
SNODGRASS LN
- ANT 94531 595-G6
SNOW CT
- ORIN 94563 630-J5
- ORIN 94563 631-A5
SNOW DR
900 MRTZ 94553 571-G7
SNOWBERRY CT
- ORIN 94563 610-G3
4400 CNCD 94521 593-B5
SNOWBERRY LN
- ORIN 94563 610-G3
SNOWCLOUD CT
4300 CNCD 94518 593-A6
SNOWDON AV
6700 ELCR 94530 609-C1
SNOWDON CT
700 WLCK 94598 612-J4
SNOWDON PL
400 CCCo 94506 654-B4
SNOWDRIFT CT
- RCH 94803 589-G2
SNOWDROP CIR
3100 PLE 94588 694-F6
SNOW FLAKE WY
300 PIT 94565 573-J2
SNOWMASS PEAK CT
4800 ANT 94531 595-D3
SNOW MELT CT
2600 PIN 94564 569-H6
SNOWMOUNTAIN CT
- CCCo 94506 654-C4
SNOWY EGRET CT
- OAKL 94561 576-H7
SNOWY EGRET WY
- OAKL 94561 576-H7
SNYDER CT
2600 WLCK 94598 612-H4
SNYDER LN
700 WLCK 94598 612-H4
SOAPROOT CT
1800 WLCK 94595 632-B1
SOARES LN
4100 LFYT 94549 611-A4
SOBRANTE AV
- RCH 94806 568-G5
5200 CCCo 94803 589-E1
5200 CCCo 94803 569-E7
SOBRANTE CT
1800 WLCK 94595 632-B1
SOBRANTE RD
6500 OAK 94611 630-F5
SOCCER CT
1400 CNCD 94518 592-E6
SODA PL
100 DNVL 94526 653-B1
SODARO DR
- CCCo 94553 571-H4
SODA ROCK RD
500 OAKL 94561 576-E6
SOFIA CT
- BREN 94513 596-D6
SOFIA WY
- BREN 94513 596-D6
SOFT SHADOW CT
- RCH 94803 589-G2
SOLA CT
- DBLN 94568 694-G3
SOLANA CT
3400 LFYT 94549 631-F1
SOLANA DR
700 LFYT 94549 631-F1
800 LFYT 94549 611-F7
1400 BREN 94513 616-D1
11600 DBLN 94568 693-F3
SOLANDRA CT
2700 PLE 94588 694-H4
SOLANO AV
- CCCo 94565 573-H2
700 ALB 94706 609-C6
1500 BERK 94707 609-E6
1600 ALB 94707 609-E6
3500 RCH 94805 589-A5
5700 CCCo 94805 589-A5
SOLANO CT
- CCCo 94565 573-H2
800 CCCo 94803 589-D1
1900 CNCD 94520 572-E6
SOLANO DR
400 BEN 94510 551-A1
500 BEN 94510 550-J1
SOLANO WY
- CCCo 94520 572-B1
1400 CNCD 94520 572-D6
1500 OAK 94606 650-A6
SOLARI ST
1000 PIT 94565 574-E2
SOLBRAE WY
- ORIN 94563 610-E6
SOLDIER MOUNTAIN CT
- ANT 94531 595-F4

STREET
Block City ZIP Pg-Grid

SOLEADO CT
11500 DBLN 94568 693-F3
SOLITUDE CT
- OAKL 94561 596-G2
SOLITUDE DR
- OAKL 94561 596-F2
SOLITUDE LN
1500 RCH 94803 589-G3
SOLITUDE WY
- BREN 94561 596-D4
SOLITUDE WY W
- BREN 94561 596-D4
SOLITUDE PEAK DR
- MRTZ 94553 591-F1
SOLIZ DR
6700 BREN 94513 596-D5
SOLSTICE CT
- OAKL 94561 596-G2
SOLVEIG DR
2000 CCCo 94596 612-E7
SOMBRERO CIR
2800 SRMN 94583 673-D4
SOMERS ST
1500 PIT 94565 574-E3
SOMERSBY WY
- BREN 94513 596-E6
SOMERSET DR
3100 LFYT 94549 631-H2
SOMERSET LN
- DBLN 94568 694-E2
SOMERSET PL
- BERK 94707 609-G5
700 CNCD 94518 592-H7
1600 ANT 94509 575-F5
3100 LFYT 94549 631-J3
SOMERSET RD
- OAK 94611 650-D1
- PDMT 94611 650-D1
SOMERSVILLE RD
- ANT 94565 594-G2
1100 ANT 94509 575-A5
1600 ANT 94509 574-J6
3000 ANT 94509 594-G2
3000 ANT 94565 574-H7
3000 CCCo 94565 574-H7
4500 CCCo 94509 594-G2
4500 CCCo 94565 594-G2
SONGBIRD CT
- LFYT 94549 611-E6
SONIA ST
- OAK 94618 630-C6
SONOMA AV
400 CCCo 94572 549-J7
600 CCCo 94572 569-J1
1400 ALB 94706 609-E6
1600 ALB 94707 609-E6
1700 BERK 94707 609-E6
1700 BERK 94706 609-E6
2600 ELCR 94530 589-B6
2600 RCH 94530 589-B6
SONOMA BLVD Rt#-29
1000 VAL 94590 550-B1
SONOMA CT
1400 WLCK 94597 611-J2
SONOMA LN
2500 ANT 94509 575-D1
SONOMA ST
600 RCH 94805 589-B5
SONOMA WY
1400 OAK 94606 650-A5
2600 PIN 94564 569-H6
SONORA AV
- DNVL 94526 653-A2
- DNVL 94526 652-J2
SONORA CT
- OAKL 94561 596-B1
600 MRTZ 94553 571-E7
SOREN WY
- SRMN 94582 674-A3
SORNOWAY LN
- DBLN 94568 693-E5
SORREL CT
- DNVL 94526 633-C7
500 BEN 94510 550-J1
SORRELL CT
1500 WLCK 94598 612-F4
SORRELL DR
1600 WLCK 94598 612-F4
SORRELWOOD CT
- SRMN 94582 673-G1
SORRELWOOD DR
- SRMN 94582 673-G1
SORRENTO CT
- DNVL 94526 652-J3
200 HER 94547 570-B6
SORRENTO WY
- SRFL 94901 587-A1
SOS DR
1400 WLCK 94597 612-C2
SOTA PL
- SRMN 94583 673-G5
SOTELLO AV
- PDMT 94611 650-D1
SOTO CT
800 MRTZ 94553 571-E4
SOTO ST
300 MRTZ 94553 571-E4
1800 CCCo 94801 588-G3
SOULE AV
100 PLHL 94523 592-B6
SOULE RD
- ORIN 94563 610-J5
- ORIN 94563 611-A5
SOUSA DR
900 WLCK 94597 612-A3
SOUTH AV
- PIT 94565 574-E3
- CCCo 94569 550-H6
100 CCCo 94507 632-F6
SOUTH CT
100 CCCo 94507 632-F6
SOUTH PT
4900 CCCo 94514 617-G5
SOUTH ST
- CCCo 94565 573-H3
300 RCH 94804 588-J7
300 RCH 94804 608-J1
SOUTH TR
- ORIN 94563 610-F7
SOUTH ACRES RD
1000 LFYT 94549 611-D6
SOUTHAMPTON AV
- BERK 94707 609-G5
SOUTHAMPTON LN
700 BERK 94707 609-G5
SOUTHAMPTON PL
- LFYT 94549 611-G4
SOUTHAMPTON RD
700 BEN 94510 551-A3
1000 BEN 94510 550-J2
SOUTHARD CT
- MRGA 94556 631-E7
SOUTHBRIDGE WY
- DBLN 94568 694-E2

STREET
Block City ZIP Pg-Grid

SOUTHBROOK DR
5500 CLAY 94517 593-F5
SOUTHBROOK PL
200 CLAY 94517 593-G6
SOUTHDOWN CT
1000 WLCK 94596 632-G1
SOUTH ESTATES DR
800 BREN 94513 616-F1
SOUTH GATE RD
2200 CCCo 94598 633-H3
2400 CCCo 94506 633-G6
SOUTHHAMPTON CT
3100 RCH 94806 588-J1
SOUTHPARK CT
1700 CNCD 94519 593-B1
SOUTH POINT RD
- ORIN 94563 611-A5
SOUTHPORT CT
- ANT 94531 595-D4
SOUTHRIDGE CT
1100 CNCD 94518 592-J4
SOUTHRIDGE DR
3200 RCH 94806 588-J1
3200 RCH 94806 589-A1
3300 RCH 94806 568-J7
SOUTHVIEW DR
2400 CCCo 94507 632-J4
SOUTHVIEW LN
100 CCCo 94507 632-J4
SOUTHWAITE CT
- ORIN 94563 631-B5
SOUTHWEST CT
2200 MRTZ 94553 572-A7
SOUTHWEST PL
- BERK 94704 630-A3
- BERK 94705 630-A3
SOUTHWICK CT
11800 DBLN 94568 693-F2
SOUTHWICK DR
8500 DBLN 94568 693-F2
8700 SRMN 94583 693-F2
SOUTHWICK PL
400 DNVL 94526 652-H2
SOUTHWIND CIR
- RCH 94804 608-H3
SOUTHWIND DR
- HER 94547 570-A6
- PLHL 94523 591-H2
SOUTHWIND LN
- DBLN 94568 694-G2
SOUTHWOOD CT
- ANT 94531 595-E5
- OAK 94611 630-F7
- ORIN 94563 630-H1
SOUTHWOOD DR
- ORIN 94563 630-H1
- ORIN 94563 610-J6
600 BREN 94513 616-E2
2000 CCCo 94806 569-B4
2200 PIT 94565 573-G4
SOUTHWOOD WY
- ANT 94531 595-D5
SOUVERAIN CT
800 OAKL 94561 576-D5
SOVEREIGN CT
8800 DBLN 94568 693-H1
8800 SRMN 94583 693-H1
SPAATZ CT
500 ANT 94509 595-E1
SPANIEL CT
4800 CNCD 94521 593-C4
SPANISH TR
- BREN 94513 596-C5
SPANISH BAY DR
- BREN 94513 616-A4
SPANISH TRAIL CT
- BREN 94513 596-C5
SPANOS ST
2100 ANT 94509 575-B5
SPAR CT
- PLHL 94523 592-B1
SPARROW CT
- ANT 94531 595-G5
- DBLN 94568 694-D4
- MRGA 94556 651-E1
- PLHL 94523 592-A5
SPARROW DR
200 HER 94547 569-H5
SPARROW HAWK CT
- OAKL 94561 596-H2
SPARTAN CT
- WLCK 94597 612-B2
SPARTAN PL
300 BREN 94513 616-C1
SPARTAN TER
2200 BREN 94513 616-C1
SPARTAN WY
- ANT 94531 575-C7
SPAULDING ST
4100 ANT 94531 595-H1
SPENCER CT
2500 CCCo 94806 569-B5
6900 DBLN 94568 693-J3
SPENCER PL
2500 CCCo 94806 569-B5
SPENCER WY
1700 BREN 94513 616-C2
SPIGOLD WY
1500 BREN 94513 616-D2
SPINDRIFT CT
200 OAKL 94561 596-D1
SPINEL CT
100 HER 94547 569-G4
SPINNAKER CT
- PIT 94565 574-A3
100 VAL 94590 550-B2
SPINNAKER CV
- HER 94547 569-H1
SPINNAKER WY
100 PIT 94565 574-A3
100 VAL 94590 550-C2
2500 RCH 94804 608-H3
4600 CCCo 94514 617-H7
SPINNAKER POINT DR
- SRFL 94901 587-A2
SPINOSA CT
2700 PLE 94588 694-H4
SPOKANE AV
600 ALB 94706 609-E5
SPOLETO CT
5200 PLE 94588 694-C6
SPOONWOOD CT
4400 CNCD 94521 593-C5
N SPOONWOOD CT
4300 CNCD 94521 593-C5
SPORTS LN
- BERK 94704 630-A2
SPORTS PARK DR
5000 PLE 94588 694-C7
SPOTTED HEN CT
- OAKL 94561 596-H1
SPRIG CT
2400 CNCD 94520 572-G4

STREET
Block City ZIP Pg-Grid

SPRIG DR
3800 BEN 94510 551-F3
4000 CNCD 94520 572-G3
SPRIG WY
3900 ANT 94509 594-J1
SPRING CT
- ORIN 94563 630-G1
SPRING DR
800 WLCK 94598 612-G3
SPRING LN
- DNVL 94526 632-J7
- DNVL 94526 633-A7
SPRING PTH
- PDMT 94611 630-C7
- PDMT 94618 630-C7
SPRING RD
- ORIN 94563 630-G1
SPRING ST
- PIN 94564 569-C4
400 RCH 94804 608-J1
1400 BREN 94513 616-D1
SPRING WY
1400 BERK 94708 609-H7
SPRINGBROOK CT
- CCCo 94597 612-A5
2000 OAKL 94561 576-C6
SPRINGBROOK DR
800 SRMN 94582 674-A7
SPRINGBROOK LN
16500 AlaC 94552 672-C7
SPRINGBROOK RD
1200 CCCo 94597 612-A5
1200 WLCK 94595 612-A5
1200 WLCK 94597 612-A5
1500 LFYT 94549 612-A3
1600 LFYT 94549 611-J4
SPRING CREEK LN
2800 WLCK 94598 612-J5
SPRINGCREST CT
5100 ANT 94531 595-E4
SPRINGCREST ST
- BREN 94513 616-H2
SPRINGDALE AV
5100 PLE 94588 693-H6
SPRINGDALE LN
2800 SRMN 94583 673-F6
SPRINGER CT
3600 WLCK 94598 613-A3
SPRINGFIELD CT
1100 ANT 94531 595-E4
SPRINGFIELD DR
- SRMN 94583 673-F5
900 WLCK 94598 612-G4
SPRINGFIELD PL
300 MRGA 94556 651-E3
SPRING GARDEN CT
- SRMN 94583 673-H3
SPRINGHAVEN CT
- SRMN 94583 673-H3
1100 BREN 94513 616-D1
SPRINGHAVEN DR
700 BREN 94513 616-D1
900 BREN 94513 596-E7
SPRINGHILL CT
3400 LFYT 94549 611-F3
SPRINGHILL DR
1300 PIT 94565 574-F7
SPRINGHILL LN
- LFYT 94549 611-F3
SPRINGHILL MNR
- LFYT 94549 611-F3
SPRINGHILL RD
3200 LFYT 94549 611-F3
SPRINGHOUSE DR
- PLE 94588 694-D6
SPRING LAKE CT
1900 MRTZ 94553 592-A1
SPRING LAKE DR
1900 MRTZ 94553 591-J1
1900 MRTZ 94553 592-A1
SPRING MEADOW LN
1300 CNCD 94521 593-A4
SPRINGRIDGE CT
1900 CNCD 94521 593-E3
SPRINGSIDE RD
100 CCCo 94597 612-A4
SPRINGSONG CT
- SRMN 94583 673-H3
SPRINGVALE CT
2800 CNCD 94518 592-H6
SPRINGVALE DR
- DBLN 94568 694-E3
SPRINGVALE WY
2900 CNCD 94518 592-H6
SPRING VALLEY WY
100 SRMN 94583 673-E3
4500 CNCD 94521 593-B4
SPRINGVIEW CIR
900 SRMN 94583 673-F4
SPRINGVIEW CT
900 SRMN 94583 673-H3
1300 CNCD 94521 593-B4
SPRING VISTA CT
- SRMN 94583 673-H3
SPRING WATER CT
- CCCo 94506 654-B4
SPRING WATER ST
900 CCCo 94506 654-B4
SPRINGWOOD CT
900 CCCo 94572 569-J1
900 CCCo 94572 570-A1
SPRINGWOOD DR
- SRMN 94583 673-H3
SPRINGWOOD ST
- CCCo 94572 569-J1
SPRINGWOOD WY
1700 ANT 94509 575-B5
4600 CNCD 94521 593-C3
SPRUCE CT
800 CCCo 94572 569-J1
SPRUCE LN
- LFYT 94549 611-G7
6500 DBLN 94568 693-J4
SPRUCE ST
- BREN 94513 616-G1
400 BERK 94708 609-G4
400 CCCo 94708 609-G4
400 BERK 94707 609-G4
500 OAK 94606 650-A4
500 OAK 94610 650-A4
1200 BERK 94709 609-H7
1200 CCCo 94553 571-F4
SPRUCE WY
2000 ANT 94509 595-E3
SPRUCEWOOD CT
400 PLHL 94523 591-H2
SPUR WY
4900 ANT 94531 595-J3
SPYGLASS CT
4100 ANT 94509 595-D2
SPYGLASS DR
- BREN 94513 616-B4
SPYGLASS LN
1700 MRGA 94556 631-C7

STREET
Block City ZIP Pg-Grid

SPYGLASS LN
2200 ELCR 94530 589-D7
SPYGLASS PKWY
100 VAL 94591 550-F3
SPYGLASS HILL
- OAK 94618 630-C4
SPYROCK CT
100 WLCK 94595 612-C7
SQUARE RIGGER CV
- HER 94547 569-H1
SQUAW CT
2500 ANT 94531 595-G4
SQUIRE CT
- CCCo 94507 632-J5
- CCCo 94507 633-A5
SQUIRREL CREEK CIR
7700 DBLN 94568 694-A1
SQUIRREL RIDGE WY
300 DNVL 94506 654-B5
STACEY CT
3500 PLE 94588 694-F5
STACEY WY
3400 PLE 94588 694-F5
STACY LN
- OAKL 94561 576-B6
STAFFORD AV
1200 CNCD 94521 592-J4
1200 CNCD 94521 593-A4
STAFFORD RD
- MRGA 94556 631-F5
STAGECOACH CT
600 CCCo 94549 591-G6
STAGECOACH DR
3300 CCCo 94549 591-G6
6900 DBLN 94568 693-A3
7000 DBLN 94568 693-J3
STAGECOACH RD
7100 DBLN 94568 693-J2
7500 SRMN 94583 673-J7
7500 SRMN 94583 693-J1
STAGECOACH WY
5200 ANT 94531 595-H5
STAGGS LEAP CT
- OAKL 94561 576-D5
STAIRLEY ST
- RCH 94801 608-D1
STALLION CT
- WLCK 94596 632-F2
STALLION RD
1100 CCCo 94803 569-D6
1100 PIN 94564 569-D6
STALLION WY
4500 ANT 94531 596-A2
STAMM DR
2700 ANT 94509 575-E6
STANBRIDGE CT
200 DNVL 94526 653-A1
STANDARD AV
2300 SPAB 94806 588-H3
STANDARD OIL AV
- ANT 94509 574-H5
- PIT 94565 574-H5
STANDISH CT
- CCCo 94525 550-D5
STANFIELD CT
16700 AlaC 94552 672-C7
STANFORD AV
100 CCCo 94708 609-G3
STANFORD CT
1500 CNCD 94519 592-H2
STANFORD WY
2500 ANT 94531 595-F5
STANFORTH CT
- SRMN 94582 674-C4
STANLEY BLVD
3100 LFYT 94549 611-H5
STANLEY CT
- ANT 94531 595-G5
- CCCo 94595 611-J7
- CCCo 94595 612-A7
100 HER 94547 570-B5
3200 CNCD 94519 572-G7
STANLEY LN
600 CCCo 94803 589-G4
STANLEY DOLLAR DR
- WLCK 94595 632-A3
STANMORE CT
- PLHL 94523 592-B4
STANMORE DR
1600 PLHL 94523 592-B4
STANNAGE AV
400 ALB 94706 609-D6
1100 BERK 94706 609-D6
1300 BERK 94702 609-D6
STANTON AV
- ORIN 94563 610-E6
900 SPAB 94806 568-H7
900 SPAB 94806 588-H1
STANTON CT
- DNVL 94506 653-H5
200 ORIN 94563 610-E6
STANTON TER
200 ORIN 94563 610-E6
STANTONVILLE CT
- OAK 94619 650-H4
STANTONVILLE DR
200 OAK 94619 650-H4
STANWELL CIR
2300 CNCD 94520 592-E1
STANWELL DR
2300 CNCD 94520 592-E1
2400 CNCD 94520 572-E7
STANWICK ST
1400 BREN 94513 616-J1
STANWOOD LN
3100 LFYT 94549 611-H6
STAPLES
100 HER 94547 569-F3
STAPLES RANCH DR
3000 PLE 94588 694-G5
STAPLETON DR
2700 ANT 94509 574-J6
STAR AV
3200 OAK 94619 650-E6
STAR ST
100 OAKL 94561 576-E7
STARBOARD CT
5500 CCCo 94514 617-J5
STARBOARD DR
5600 CCCo 94514 617-J5
5600 CCCo 94514 (618-A4 See Page 597)
STARBRIDGE CT
400 PLHL 94523 592-D3
STARCROSS DR
- CCCo 94583 672-J4
STARFISH CT
5800 CCCo 94514 (618-A5 See Page 597)
STARFISH DR
300 VAL 94591 550-D2
STARFISH PL
5500 CCCo 94514 617-J4

© 2006 Rand McNally & Company

STREET
Block City ZIP Pg-Grid

STARFISH PL
5500 CCCo 94514 (618-A5 See Page 597)
STARFLOWER DR
4700 MRTZ 94553 572-A6
STARFLOWER TER
- SRMN 94583 673-A2
STAR JASMINE DR
- SRMN 94582 673-J1
STAR KING CT
- ANT 94531 595-E4
STARK KNOLL PL
- CCCo 94618 630-C7
STARKVILLE CT
6800 CCCo 94563 630-F5
STARLIGHT LN
2400 ANT 94509 575-A5
STARLIGHT PL
100 DNVL 94526 653-C5
STAR LILLY ST
- BREN 94513 596-E4
STARLING CT
- WLCK 94597 612-A2
STARLING ST
5000 DNVL 94506 653-H4
STARLING WY
100 HER 94547 569-H4
STARLYN DR
100 PLHL 94523 592-A6
STAR MINE CT
4900 ANT 94531 595-D4
STAR MINE WY
5000 ANT 94531 595-D3
STARMONT CT
- DNVL 94526 652-G2
STARMONT LN
- DNVL 94526 652-G2
STARR LN
1400 CNCD 94521 593-A3
STARR ST
1100 CCCo 94525 550-D4
STAR THISTLE WY
- ANT 94531 596-A5
STAR TREE CT
2600 MRTZ 94553 572-A6
STARVIEW CT
100 BREN 94513 616-E2
100 OAK 94618 630-C4
STARVIEW DR
- OAK 94618 630-C4
100 DNVL 94526 652-G2
STARVIEW PL
100 DNVL 94526 652-H2
STARWARD DR
7400 DBLN 94568 693-G3
STATE AV
4900 RCH 94804 609-B1
STATE CT
4800 RCH 94804 609-A1
STATE PL
600 OAK 94704 630-A2
STATE PARK RD
- BEN 94510 550-G1
STATION PL
800 BERK 94707 609-F6
STAUFFER CT
- OAK 94619 650-H5
STAUFFER PL
4600 OAK 94619 650-H5
STEAMER LN
100 VAL 94591 550-D2
STEDING CT
- CCCo 94596 612-F6
STEED WY
4500 ANT 94531 595-G3
STEELE CT
- WLCK 94595 612-C7
- CCCo 94565 573-F1
STEELE DR
3300 CCCo 94565 573-F1
STEELE ST
4300 OAK 94619 650-G6
STEEPLECHASE CT
4700 ANT 94531 596-A3
STEFFA ST
700 CCCo 94565 573-C1
STEGE AV
400 RCH 94804 608-J1
600 RCH 94804 609-A1
STEIN WY
100 ORIN 94563 630-H2
STEINBECK CT
- PIT 94565 574-A2
STEINBECK DR
- PIT 94565 574-B2
STEINBECK TER
- MRTZ 94553 571-J5
STEINMETZ WY
2800 OAK 94602 650-F4
STELLA CT
- ANT 94531 595-G4
- PLHL 94523 592-B4
STELLARIA LN
- SRMN 94582 673-H1
STEPHANIE CT
- CCCo 94507 632-G3
4300 CNCD 94521 593-A5
STEPHANIE DR
4300 CNCD 94521 593-A5
STEPHANIE LN
- CCCo 94507 632-F3
STEPHANIE WY
4100 PIT 94565 574-E6
STEPHEN DR
2800 RCH 94803 589-E2
STEPHENS CT
- CCCo 94525 550-D5
STEPHENS DR
- BREN 94513 616-D3
STEPHENS WY
- OAK 94705 630-B3
STERLING AV
1000 BERK 94708 609-H6
STERLING CT
4700 ANT 94531 595-J3
STERLING DR
600 MRTZ 94553 591-G3
STERLING WY
- CCCo 94549 611-J2
200 OAKL 94561 596-G2
STERLING HEIGHTS LN
- LFYT 94549 611-G1
STERLING HILL DR
4700 ANT 94531 595-J3
STETSON DR
- DNVL 94506 653-J6
- DNVL 94506 654-A6
STEVEN CIR
200 PLHL 94523 591-J5
200 PLHL 94523 592-A5
300 BEN 94510 551-A2
STEVEN CT
300 BEN 94510 551-A2
STEVEN DR
1000 PIT 94565 574-E6
STEVENS CT
- CCCo 94506 654-B5
STEVENS LN
- LFYT 94549 611-J4
STEVENSON AV
- BERK 94708 609-J6
STEVENSON DR
- PLHL 94523 592-A7
STEVENSON ST
2900 PIT 94565 574-C4
STEVEN S STROUD DR
- ANT 94531 595-D5
STEWART AV
2000 CCCo 94596 632-F1
2100 WLCK 94596 632-F1
STEWART CIR
100 PLHL 94523 592-A7
STEWART CT
- MRGA 94556 631-D3
STEWART LN
1800 CCCo 94509 575-H5
STEWART ST
- ANT 94531 595-J2
- ANT 94531 596-A2
STEWART WY
- BREN 94513 616-D4
STEWARTON DR
3400 RCH 94803 589-E1
STEWARTVILLE DR
4800 ANT 94531 595-D3
STEWARTVILLE TR
- CCCo 94509 594-G5
- CCCo 94509 595-A7
- CCCo 94517 594-G5
- CCCo 94517 595-A7
STILLCREEK CT
2200 MRTZ 94553 572-A7
STILL CREEK PL
1300 DNVL 94506 653-G1
STILL CREEK RD
200 DNVL 94506 653-G1
STILLMAN CT
1600 CNCD 94519 593-A2
STILLSPRING PL
2100 MRTZ 94553 572-B2
STILLWATER CT
- DBLN 94568 694-E2
4600 CNCD 94521 593-C3
STILLWELL CIR
- ANT 94509 575-C6
STIMEL CT
1200 CNCD 94518 592-E6
STIMEL DR
900 CNCD 94518 592-D7
STINSON CIR
3000 WLCK 94598 612-H1
STINSON ST
300 VAL 94591 550-E2
STIRLING CT
- BREN 94513 616-A2
- CCCo 94513 617-F5
STIRLING DR
- DNVL 94526 653-D3
1100 CCCo 94572 570-A1
1200 CCCo 94553 570-B1
STIRRUP CT
2400 WLCK 94596 632-F2
STIRRUP DR
2800 OAKL 94561 576-B7
STIRRUP WY
4900 ANT 94531 595-J3
STOCKBRIDGE DR
2400 OAK 94611 650-F1
STOCKTON AV
6300 ELCR 94530 609-E2
STOCKTON CT
2100 PIT 94565 574-A3
STODDARD CT
- DNVL 94526 653-C5
STODDARD PL
- DNVL 94526 653-C6
STODDARD WY
- BERK 94708 609-J6
STOKES AV
2400 PIN 94564 569-H7
2400 PIN 94564 589-H1
STONE CT
- DNVL 94526 653-C6
2100 CCCo 94507 632-H5
STONE PL
3500 ANT 94509 595-C1
STONE RD
- CCCo 94511 577-E4
400 BEN 94510 551-F1
N STONE RD
- CCCo 94511 577-H4
STONE ST
1900 SPAB 94806 588-H2
STONEBRIDGE CT
500 PLHL 94523 592-D4
STONEBRIDGE WY
300 PLHL 94523 592-D4
STONE CANYON CT
4400 CNCD 94521 593-C5
STONECASTLE CT
- CCCo 94507 632-E2
STONECASTLE DR
- CCCo 94507 632-E2
STONE CLIFF CT
- RCH 94806 569-A7
STONECREEK CT
100 MRTZ 94553 591-H1
STONE CREEK PL
- CCCo 94507 633-A5
STONE CREST CT
- RCH 94806 569-A7
STONECREST DR
1000 ANT 94531 595-D4
STONEDALE DR
7200 PLE 94588 693-J6
STONEFIELD PL
400 MRGA 94556 651-F3
STONEFORD DR
100 PIT 94565 574-A3
STONEGATE CIR
800 OAKL 94561 576-D5
STONEGATE CT
- CCCo 94507 632-J2
STONEGATE DR
2600 CCCo 94507 632-J2
2600 CCCo 94507 633-A1
STONEGATE LN
3100 CCCo 94507 632-J2
STONEGATE WY
4900 ANT 94531 595-E4
STONEGLEN N
3700 RCH 94806 569-A7
STONEGLEN S
3600 RCH 94806 568-J7
3600 RCH 94806 569-A7
STONE HARBOUR DR
600 PIT 94565 574-E3
STONEHAVEN CT
900 WLCK 94598 612-J4
STONEHAVEN DR
- BREN 94513 616-D1
600 WLCK 94598 612-J3
STONEHAVEN LN
- DBLN 94568 694-G3
STONEHEDGE DR
1300 PLHL 94523 591-H2
STONEHEDGE PL
3300 CNCD 94518 592-H6
STONEHENGE WY
- CCCo 94582 674-B5
STONEHILL DR
- CCCo 94507 633-A5
STONEHURST CT
100 CCCo 94553 591-C2
7900 PLE 94588 693-H7
STONEHURST DR
11500 DBLN 94568 693-F6
2000 CCCo 94553 591-C2
STONELEAF RD
- CCCo 94582 673-J2
STONEMAN AV
700 PIT 94565 574-E5
STONE PINE CT
- HER 94547 569-H2
STONEPINE LN
100 SRMN 94583 673-B1
STONEPINE ST
- DBLN 94568 694-D4
STONE POINTE WY
3800 PLE 94588 694-E6
STONE RIDGE CT
4900 OAK 94605 651-B7
STONERIDGE DR
2200 PIT 94565 574-F4
3500 PLE 94588 694-B6
3800 PLE 94566 694-E7
6700 PLE 94588 693-H6
STONERIDGE MALL RD
5600 PLE 94588 693-H5
STONE VALLEY CT
200 CCCo 94553 591-C2
STONE VALLEY RD
700 CCCo 94507 632-G5
2400 CCCo 94507 633-A5
3100 CCCo 94526 633-C6
3100 DNVL 94526 633-C6
STONE VALLEY RD W
3100 CCCo 94507 632-F5
STONE VALLEY WY
200 CCCo 94507 632-G4
STONE VALLEY OAKS DR
- CCCo 94507 633-B6
STONE VIEW CT
300 CCCo 94553 591-C2
STONEWALL RD
100 OAK 94705 630-A3
STONEWOOD CT
800 BREN 94513 616-D1
STONEWOOD DR
800 BREN 94513 596-D7
800 BREN 94513 616-D1
STONEWOOD PL
1400 CNCD 94520 592-F3
STONEWOOD WY
4900 ANT 94531 595-E4
STONEY CT
900 ANT 94509 595-F1
STONEYBROOK CT
400 CCCo 94506 654-D5
STONEYBROOK DR
1000 MRTZ 94553 571-H6
STONEY CREEK DR
700 SRMN 94582 674-A7
1300 SRMN 94582 694-A1
STONEY GORGE WY
1200 ANT 94531 595-E4
STONEY HILL CIR
200 OAKL 94561 576-D6
STONEY HILL CT
- OAKL 94561 576-E6
STONEY HILL PL
- OAKL 94561 576-E6
STONEY RIDGE PL
100 WLCK 94596 612-D5
STONINGTON AV
1000 SPAB 94806 588-H1
STONINGTON CT
- DNVL 94526 653-A1
STONY CT
- RCH 94806 568-H6
STORER AV
3200 OAK 94619 650-F7
STOREY LN
4100 CNCD 94518 592-J4
4100 CNCD 94518 593-A4
STORYBOOK LN
- CCCo 94551 (655-F4 See Page 635)
STOUT
100 HER 94547 569-F3
STOW AV
1700 WLCK 94596 612-C5
STOW CT
- SRMN 94583 693-F1
STOW LN
900 LFYT 94549 611-H6
STOWBRIDGE CT
- DNVL 94526 653-A1
STRAITWOOD CT
3500 ANT 94531 595-H1
STRANAHAN CIR
200 CLAY 94517 593-H7
STRAND AV
200 PLHL 94523 592-A5
300 PLHL 94523 591-J5
STRAND CT
100 PLHL 94523 591-J5
STRAND RD
2000 CCCo 94596 612-D7
STRANG CT
- ORIN 94563 630-J1
STRASBOURG LN
1800 ANT 94509 575-G6
STRATFORD CT
- OAKL 94561 596-D2
- DNVL 94506 653-H5
- PLHL 94523 591-J7
- PLHL 94523 592-A7
2100 ANT 94509 595-F1
3800 PLE 94588 694-F5
STRATFORD DR
- OAKL 94561 596-D2
2800 SRMN 94583 673-F7
STRATFORD PL
- OAKL 94561 596-C2
STRATFORD RD
- CCCo 94707 609-F4
700 OAK 94610 650-A3
STRATHAVEN PL
- BREN 94513 596-D6
STRATHMOOR DR
- OAK 94705 630-C3
STRATHMORE CT
1300 CNCD 94518 592-E6
STRATTON CIR
1900 WLCK 94598 612-F2
STRATTON LN
- SolC 94571 554-J1
STRATTON RD
2000 WLCK 94598 612-F2
STRAWBERRY CT
1300 DNVL 94526 653-B6
2600 ANT 94531 595-G4
STRAWBERRY LN
1300 DNVL 94526 653-B6
STRAYHORN RD
1900 PLHL 94523 591-J3
STREAMBED PL
11500 DBLN 94568 693-F6
STREAMWOOD CT
3300 ANT 94531 595-H1
STRENTZEL LN
100 CCCo 94553 591-E1
STRETFORD RD
- CCCo 94553 571-F3
STRIPED MAPLE CT
4400 CNCD 94521 593-B5
N STRIPED MAPLE CT
4300 CNCD 94521 593-C5
STROER LN
1800 ANT 94509 575-J5
STUART CT
1700 BEN 94510 550-J2
STUART PL
- DNVL 94526 653-E3
STUART ST
1000 LFYT 94549 611-G6
3100 OAK 94602 650-B4
STUBBS RD
- PLHL 94523 592-B3
STUDEBAKER RD
1100 CCCo 94595 612-A6
STUGUN CT
- PLHL 94523 592-A3
STURBRIDGE CT
500 WLCK 94598 612-J3
STURGES CT
- ANT 94531 595-C4
SUDAN LP
200 CCCo 94553 572-C6
SUDBURY CT
- CCCo 94583 673-B5
SUDDARD CT
6300 PLE 94588 694-B7
SUENEN CT
1900 WLCK 94595 632-B1
SUEZ DR
100 CCCo 94553 572-C7
SUFFOLK WY
4000 PLE 94588 694-E6
SUGAR BARGE RD
- CCCo 94511 577-F3
SUGARBERRY LN
3100 WLCK 94598 592-H7
SUGAR CREEK CT
100 CCCo 94507 633-A4
SUGAR CREEK LN
100 CCCo 94507 633-A3
E SUGAR HILL TER
- DBLN 94568 694-G2
SUGARLAND CIR
4600 CNCD 94521 593-C5
SUGARLAND CT
4400 CNCD 94521 593-C5
SUGARLOAF CT
- DBLN 94568 694-F2
- WLCK 94596 632-E1
SUGARLOAF DR
- CCCo 94507 632-F3
SUGARLOAF LN
- CCCo 94507 632-F3
SUGARLOAF TER
- CCCo 94507 632-F3
SUGARLOAF MOUNTAIN CT
1900 ANT 94531 595-F4
SUGAR MAPLE CT
4400 CNCD 94521 593-C5
N SUGAR MAPLE CT
4300 CNCD 94521 593-C5
SUGAR MAPLE DR
4000 CCCo 94506 653-J4
4000 CCCo 94506 654-A4
SUGAR PINE CT
1900 ANT 94509 575-J5
SUGAR PINE LN
- CCCo 94506 654-A3
SUGAR PINE ST
2000 ANT 94509 575-J6
SUGARTREE DR
2100 PIT 94565 573-J3
SUISUN AV
- CCCo 94565 573-H1
200 CCCo 94572 549-J7
500 CCCo 94572 569-H1
SUISUN CT
500 CLAY 94517 593-H6
SULLIVAN AV
800 CNCD 94518 592-H6
SULLIVAN DR
- MRGA 94556 631-C5
SULLIVAN ST
2400 CCCo 94806 569-A5
SULPHER SPRINGS TR
- CCCo 94583 652-F2
SUMAC CIR
1300 CNCD 94521 593-D5
SUMAC WY
- ANT 94509 595-E3
SUMMER CIR
700 BREN 94513 616-E2
SUMMER ST
2200 BERK 94709 609-H7
SUMMER WY
1100 PIT 94565 573-J2
SUMMER BREEZE CT
- CCCo 94572 569-H1
SUMMER CREEK LN
400 SRMN 94583 673-F4
SUMMERFIELD CT
- DNVL 94506 653-F5
E SUMMERFIELD CT
1900 OAKL 94561 576-C6
W SUMMERFIELD CT
1800 OAKL 94561 576-D6
SUMMERFIELD DR
- ANT 94531 595-J4
- ANT 94531 596-A5
200 CCCo 94565 573-G3
SUMMERFIELD ST
100 DNVL 94506 653-G5
SUMMERFORD CIR
200 SRMN 94583 673-G4
SUMMER GLEN DR
- DBLN 94568 694-D3
SUMMER HILL CT
- DNVL 94526 653-B6
SUMMERHILL LN
- CCCo 94553 591-D2
SUMMERLAND WY
1500 BREN 94513 616-D2
SUMMER MEADOWS CT
- CCCo 94507 632-G3
SUMMER RED WY
400 BREN 94513 616-C3
SUMMERSET CT
100 SRMN 94583 673-G4
SUMMERSET DR
- BREN 94513 616-C2
SUMMERSIDE CIR
100 DNVL 94526 653-B6
SUMMERSVILLE CT
- VAL 94591 550-D2
SUMMERTREE WY
- SRMN 94583 673-A1
SUMMER VALLEY CT
500 SRMN 94582 673-J6
500 SRMN 94582 674-A6
SUMMERVIEW CT
300 SRMN 94583 673-F4
SUMMERWOOD DR
500 BREN 94513 616-D1
SUMMERWOOD LP
100 SRMN 94583 673-F4
SUMMERWOOD PL
100 CNCD 94518 592-G6
SUMMIT AV
- SRFL 94901 587-A1
100 MrnC 94901 587-A1
SUMMIT CIR
- WLCK 94598 612-E5
SUMMIT CT
300 PIN 94564 569-E4
SUMMIT DR
300 PIN 94564 569-E4
SUMMIT LN
- BERK 94708 610-A7
SUMMIT PL
300 RCH 94801 588-C7
SUMMIT RD
- CCCo 94598 633-J1
- CCCo 94598 634-A1
100 WLCK 94598 612-E5
1200 LFYT 94549 611-H4
1300 BERK 94708 610-A7
SUMMIT TR
- CCCo 94583 652-F2
SUMMIT WY
- ANT 94565 574-H7
- ANT 94565 594-H1
SUMMIT PARK CT
8400 ELCR 94530 609-E1
SUMMIT PARK LN
8400 ELCR 94530 589-E7
8400 ELCR 94530 609-E1
SUMMITRIDGE CT
- PIT 94565 573-G5
SUMMIT VIEW DR
1200 CNCD 94521 593-B4
3000 SRMN 94582 674-A6
3200 SRMN 94582 673-J6
SUN CT
- MRTZ 94553 571-H6
3000 RCH 94803 589-E1
SUNBURST CT
1200 WLCK 94596 632-G1
SUNBURY CT
- BREN 94513 616-B2
SUNCLIFF PL
- VAL 94591 550-D2
SUN CLOUD CT
5500 CNCD 94521 593-E7
SUNCREST CT
1600 WLCK 94597 612-C1
SUN CREST ST
- ANT 94565 594-H1
SUNDALE LN
500 BREN 94513 616-C1
SUNDALE RD
3600 LFYT 94549 611-D7
SUNDANCE CT
2600 WLCK 94598 612-H4
5100 ANT 94531 595-H4
SUNDANCE PL
- MRTZ 94553 571-J6
SUNDANCE WY
5000 ANT 94531 595-H4
SUNDOWN TER
200 ORIN 94563 610-J3
200 ORIN 94563 611-A3
SUNFISH CT
100 VAL 94591 550-D1
5600 CCCo 94514 617-J5
SUNFLOWER CT
100 HER 94547 570-A4
600 SRMN 94583 653-J7
700 CNCD 94518 592-J6
SUNFLOWER DR
2800 ANT 94531 575-G7
3100 ANT 94531 595-H1
SUNFLOWER LN
1300 BREN 94513 596-D6
SUNGLEN WY
- DNVL 94506 653-G2
SUNGOLD CT
500 BREN 94513 596-F7
SUNGROVE CT
- ANT 94531 596-A5
SUNGROVE WY
- ANT 94531 596-A5
SUNHAVEN RD
100 DNVL 94506 653-H2
SUNHILL CIR
- CCCo 94803 589-D1
SUNHILL CT
400 MRTZ 94553 571-J6
SUNHILL LN
400 MRTZ 94553 571-J6
SUNLEAF WY
3400 RCH 94806 568-J7
SUNLIGHT CIR
1100 CNCD 94518 593-A5
SUNLIGHT CT
4400 CNCD 94518 593-A5
SUNLIGHT DR
700 BREN 94513 616-D1
SUNNY CT
1500 WLCK 94595 612-D7
SUNNY LN
500 CCCo 94803 569-E7
1700 ANT 94509 575-B6
SUNNY PL
4700 CNCD 94521 593-C3
SUNNYBRAE CT
100 MRTZ 94553 591-G2
SUNNYBRAE DR
100 MRTZ 94553 591-G2
SUNNYBROOK DR
900 LFYT 94549 611-C6
SUNNYBROOK PL
100 SRMN 94583 673-F7
SUNNYBROOK RD
1400 CCCo 94507 632-E3
SUNNY COVE ST
- WLCK 94597 612-B1
SUNNY GLEN CT
- RCH 94806 568-J6
SUNNYHILL WY
- PIT 94565 574-C6
SUNNY HILLS RD
900 LFYT 94549 611-A6
SUNNYHILLS RD
800 OAK 94610 650-B3
SUNNYMERE AV
6200 OAK 94605 650-H7
SUNNYS WY
- CCCo 94513 597-C6
SUNNYSIDE AV
100 PDMT 94611 650-A1
200 PDMT 94610 650-A1
SUNNYSIDE CT
- ORIN 94563 610-H2
SUNNYSIDE LN
- ORIN 94563 610-G3
SUNNYSIDE PL
400 SRMN 94582 673-J6
SUNNY SLOPE AV
400 OAK 94610 650-A2
SUNNYSLOPES DR
200 MRTZ 94553 571-H5
SUNNYVALE AV
1500 WLCK 94597 612-B1
SUNNYVALE PL
- WLCK 94597 612-B1
SUNNYVIEW CT
1100 PIN 94564 569-D4
SUNNYVIEW DR
1000 PIN 94564 569-D4
SUNPEAK DR
- PIT 94565 573-F4
SUN RIDGE CT
3100 LFYT 94549 611-J4
SUN RIDGE DR
200 SRMN 94582 673-J6
200 SRMN 94582 674-A6
SUNRISE CT
300 BEN 94510 551-B3
3500 MRTZ 94553 571-D5
3600 RCH 94806 568-J7
SUNRISE DR
100 BREN 94513 596-G5
4800 MRTZ 94553 572-A5
SUNRISE LN
- CCCo 94549 611-J2
SUNRISE TER
- DNVL 94526 633-C6
SUNRISE HILL
1100 CNCD 94518 592-J4
SUNRISE HILL CT
- ORIN 94563 630-H2
SUNRISE HILL RD
- ORIN 94563 630-H2
SUNRISE MEADOWS LN
5300 OAKL 94561 576-D6
SUNRISE RIDGE DR
1000 CCCo 94549 591-G5
SUNSET AV
2300 CNCD 94519 592-G2
2800 OAK 94601 650-D6
E SUNSET AV
2700 OAK 94601 650-D6
SUNSET CIR
100 BEN 94510 551-B3
SUNSET CT
- CCCo 94707 609-F3
- DNVL 94506 654-A6
100 BREN 94513 596-G6
SUNSET DR
- CCCo 94511 577-D4
- SRMN 94583 673-E3
- ANT 94509 575-D6
- CCCo 94707 609-E3
- PLHL 94523 592-A6
200 HER 94547 570-B6
300 DNVL 94506 654-A6
5200 CCCo 94803 589-E1
5200 RCH 94803 589-E1
SUNSET LN
- BERK 94708 609-H5
2700 ANT 94509 575-D7
3300 ANT 94509 595-D1
SUNSET LP
1100 CCCo 94549 611-J6
1100 CCCo 94595 611-J6
1100 LFYT 94549 611-J6
1200 LFYT 94549 612-A6
SUNSET PT
2200 CCCo 94514 617-H7
SUNSET RD
300 PLHL 94523 592-A5
400 BREN 94513 596-H5
700 CCCo 94513 596-H5
1100 CCCo 94513 597-A5
SUNSET TER
- ORIN 94563 631-B3
- CCCo 94707 609-F3
SUNSET TR
- BERK 94705 630-B3
- OAK 94705 630-B3
SUNSET WK
- ALB 94706 609-D6
SUNSET WY
100 PIT 94565 574-E5
SUNSET MEADOWS LN
5400 OAKL 94561 576-D4
SUNSHINE CIR
1000 DNVL 94506 653-F4
SUNSHINE CT
700 BREN 94513 616-D1
SUNSHINE DR
1300 CNCD 94520 592-E4
SUNSPRING CT
200 PLHL 94523 592-D4
SUN STREAM CT
300 CCCo 94506 654-B5
SUNTAN LN
- BREN 94513 616-D4
SUN TREE CT
600 CCCo 94506 654-B4
SUNTREE LN
100 PLHL 94523 592-B1
SUN VALLEY AV
3100 WLCK 94597 612-B1
SUNVALLEY BLVD
1000 CNCD 94523 592-C3
1000 CNCD 94520 592-C3
1000 PLHL 94523 592-C3
SUN VALLEY DR
- WLCK 94597 612-C1
SUN VIEW CT
3600 CNCD 94520 572-G5
SUNVIEW CT
- ANT 94531 595-J5
SUN VIEW PL
2400 CNCD 94520 572-G5
SUN VIEW TER
2400 CNCD 94520 572-G5
SUN VIEW WY
3600 CNCD 94520 572-G5
SUNVIEW WY
- ANT 94531 595-J5
SUNWOOD CT
3300 ANT 94531 595-H1
SUNWOOD DR
7500 DBLN 94568 693-G3
SUPERIOR WY
- CCCo 94513 617-F4
SUPREME CT
- WLCK 94597 612-B2
SURF DR
- PIT 94565 574-E5
SURFSIDE CT
- CCCo 94806 569-C4
1700 CCCo 94514 617-G6
SURFSIDE PL
1800 CCCo 94514 617-G6
SURF VIEW DR
- CCCo 94565 553-D7
SURIGAO CT
- CNCD 94520 572-H3
SURMONT CT
- CCCo 94549 591-J7
SURMONT DR
- CCCo 94549 591-J7
3200 PLHL 94523 591-J6
SURREY CT
- DNVL 94526 633-C7
1600 WLCK 94598 612-E1
SURREY LN
4700 RCH 94803 589-J2
7600 OAK 94605 651-C7
SURREY PL
3100 CNCD 94518 592-H7
SURREY WY
300 BREN 94513 616-E2
SURVEY WY
- CCCo 94597 612-A5
SUSAN AV
7400 ELCR 94530 609-E4
SUSAN CT
- CCCo 94507 632-F5
1600 BEN 94510 551-B4
SUSAN LN
1800 PLHL 94523 592-C5
SUSAN ST
1400 BREN 94513 596-G7
SUSANA ST
400 MRTZ 94553 571-E3
SUSANWOOD DR
4000 CNCD 94521 593-A2
SUSIE CT
- OAKL 94561 596-C1
SUSIE ST
- OAKL 94561 596-C2
SUSSEX CT
- CCCo 94513 617-F5
- DBLN 94568 694-A4
100 SRMN 94582 673-G4
1200 CNCD 94521 593-A4
SUSSEX DR
- DBLN 94568 694-A4
SUSSEX ST
100 CCCo 94520 572-G2
SUSSEX WY
1300 CNCD 94521 593-A4
SUTCLIFFE CT
3400 WLCK 94598 612-J2
SUTCLIFFE PL
400 WLCK 94598 612-J2
SUTER ST
3000 OAK 94602 650-D5
3500 OAK 94619 650-F6
SUTHERLAND CT
1500 CNCD 94521 593-D4
4000 PLE 94588 694-E7
SUTHERLAND DR
100 CCCo 94596 612-F6
100 WLCK 94598 612-F6
5000 CNCD 94521 593-D4
SUTRO ST
1200 SPAB 94806 588-G4
SUTTER AV
1300 SPAB 94806 588-G3
5500 RCH 94804 609-C3
SUTTER CT
- CCCo 94565 573-H2
SUTTER ST
- OAKL 94561 576-B7
200 BERK 94707 609-G6
1100 BERK 94709 609-G6
1500 CNCD 94520 592-E2
SUTTER CREEK LN
- SRMN 94583 673-D6
SUTTER CREEK WY
1000 BREN 94513 596-D7
SUTTER GATE AV
4400 PLE 94566 694-D7
SUTTERS MILL CT
- WLCK 94596 612-D5
SUTTON CIR
100 DNVL 94506 653-H5
SUTTON CT
- DNVL 94506 653-H5
600 WLCK 94598 612-H6
SUTTON DR
600 WLCK 94598 613-A3
SUTTON LN
7500 DBLN 94568 693-H3
SUVA CT
- SRMN 94582 653-E7
SUZANNE DR
4100 PIT 94565 574-E7
4700 CCCo 94565 574-E7
SUZANNE PL
100 PLHL 94523 592-D6
SWAINLAND RD
6100 OAK 94611 630-C5
SWAINSONS CT
- CNCD 94521 593-B6
SWALLOW CT
- ANT 94509 594-J1
SWALLOW ST
3000 DNVL 94506 653-H4
SWALLOW WY
- ANT 94509 594-H1
1600 HER 94547 569-H4
SWALLOW TAIL RD
1300 CNCD 94521 593-C5
SWAN CT
- WLCK 94597 612-A2
200 DNVL 94506 653-H4
SWAN ST
2000 DNVL 94506 653-J6
SWAN LAKE CT
2100 MRTZ 94553 592-A1

STREET Block City ZIP Pg-Grid

SWANS WY
500 RCH 94805 589-A6
SWANSEA LN
- PLHL 94523 592-A4
- PLHL 94523 591-J4
SWANZY CT
100 VAL 94591 550-C1
SWANZY DAM RD
- VAL 94591 550-C1
SWEENEY CT
- CCCo 94803 589-F2
SWEENEY RD
300 ANT 94509 575-E7
SWEET CT
600 LFYT 94549 631-H2
SWEET DR
3200 LFYT 94549 631-G1
3300 LFYT 94549 611-G7
SWEET RD
- LFYT 94549 612-A6
SWEETBRIAR CIR
3100 LFYT 94549 631-H3
SWEETBRIAR CT
- BREN 94513 596-D5
4400 CNCD 94521 593-C5
N SWEETBRIAR CT
4300 CNCD 94521 593-C5
SWEETBRIER LN
500 BEN 94510 551-A1
SWEETGALE DR
- SRMN 94582 673-G1
SWEET GRASS DR
- BREN 94513 616-E2
SWEET GUM CT
- HER 94547 569-H1
SWEETPEA CT
- DNVL 94506 654-B5
SWEET SHRUB CT
4400 CNCD 94521 593-B5
SWEET WATER CT
- CCCo 94506 654-C4
SWEETWATER CT
- OAKL 94561 596-F2
SWEET WATER DR
700 CCCo 94506 654-C4
SWEETWATER DR
2200 MRTZ 94553 572-A7
SWEETWOOD DR
4900 RCH 94803 589-F2
SWINFORD CT
- DBLN 94568 694-E4
SWISTA WY
1800 CCCo 94521 593-E3
SYCAMORE AV
- CCCo 94547 570-A3
- CCCo 94572 570-A3
- HER 94547 570-A3
100 BREN 94513 596-G7
200 CCCo 94513 596-G7
1500 HER 94547 569-F2
2400 CNCD 94520 572-F7
4300 RCH 94804 609-A2
SYCAMORE CIR
300 DNVL 94526 653-B4
SYCAMORE CT
- CCCo 94565 573-G2
1000 BREN 94513 596-H7
SYCAMORE DR
1100 ANT 94509 575-B5
1700 PIT 94565 574-G6
SYCAMORE RD
- ORIN 94563 610-H4
SYCAMORE ST
2600 CCCo 94553 571-G4
SYCAMORE TR
- AlaC 94546 652-C4
- CCCo 94556 652-C4
- CCCo 94583 652-C4
SYCAMORE HILL CT
300 DNVL 94526 653-C2
SYCAMORE VALLEY RD
600 DNVL 94526 653-C3
SYCAMORE VALLEY RD E
100 DNVL 94526 653-B3
SYCAMORE VALLEY RD W
100 DNVL 94526 653-A3
SYDNEY DR
200 CCCo 94507 632-D2
SYLHOWE RD
2800 OAK 94602 650-F3
SYLVAN AV
3000 OAK 94602 650-F4
SYLVAN RD
100 CCCo 94596 632-F1
SYLVAN WY
- CNCD 94521 593-D5
- OAK 94610 650-A2
- PDMT 94610 650-A2
SYLVANER CT
900 CLAY 94517 613-J1
SYLVIA CT
3000 RCH 94803 589-E2
SYLVIA DR
1900 PLHL 94523 592-C4
SYSTRON DR
2700 CNCD 94518 592-G3

T

T ST
300 BEN 94510 551-C4
TABLE MOUNTAIN WY
- ANT 94531 595-E5
TABORA DR
3100 ANT 94509 575-C7
3200 ANT 94509 595-B1
TACHELLA WY
- BREN 94513 596-E7
TACKWOOD CT
- SRMN 94583 673-E5
TACOMA AV
1600 BERK 94707 609-F6
2100 MRTZ 94553 571-F4
2200 CCCo 94553 571-F4
TAFFY CT
6700 PLE 94588 694-A7
TAFT AV
700 ALB 94706 609-D5
4200 RCH 94804 609-A1
5400 OAK 94618 630-A5
6200 CCCo 94805 589-C5
TAFT CT
1700 ANT 94509 575-A7
TAFT ST
1800 CNCD 94521 593-D2
TAFT WY
- BREN 94513 596-G7
TAHITI DR
2200 SRMN 94582 653-E7
2200 SRMN 94582 673-E1
TAHJA RD
6300 CCCo 94588 654-J6

TAHJA RD
6500 CCCo 94551 (655-A6 See Page 635)
6500 CCCo 94588 (655-A6 See Page 635)
TAHOE CIR
4700 MRTZ 94553 571-F7
TAHOE CT
- CCCo 94513 617-F3
- WLCK 94596 612-D5
- SRMN 94582 653-F7
3300 ANT 94509 575-E7
4500 PLE 94566 694-D7
TAHOE DR
600 MRTZ 94553 571-E7
TAHOE PL
- PIT 94565 574-G6
3000 SRMN 94582 653-F7
6800 ELCR 94530 609-D4
TAHOS RD
300 ORIN 94563 610-J6
400 ORIN 94563 611-A7
E TAHOS RD
- ORIN 94563 611-A6
W TAHOS RD
400 ORIN 94563 610-J6
TAIN CT
- BREN 94513 616-A2
TALAVERA DR
2300 SRMN 94583 673-C3
TALBART ST
200 MRTZ 94553 571-D3
TALBOT AV
400 ALB 94706 609-D5
1100 BERK 94706 609-D5
1300 BERK 94702 609-D5
TALBOT WY
3100 ANT 94509 575-F7
TALISMAN WY
1500 CNCD 94521 593-E5
TALLE WY
- DBLN 94568 694-E4
TALLEY WY
- HER 94547 569-F2
TALLY HO CT
700 CCCo 94517 613-G2
TALUS CT
- SRMN 94583 673-F7
- SRMN 94583 693-F1
TAMALPAIS AV
- BREN 94513 596-C5
2000 ELCR 94530 589-C7
TAMALPAIS CT
- BREN 94513 596-B6
7000 ELCR 94530 589-C7
TAMALPAIS DR
2600 PIN 94564 569-G6
TAMALPAIS RD
- BERK 94708 609-H6
TAMALPAIS VW
- ORIN 94563 610-J4
- ORIN 94563 611-A4
TAMAR CT
1600 CNCD 94521 593-C4
TAMARA CT
1400 BEN 94510 551-B4
TAMARACK DR
- HER 94547 570-A5
7000 DBLN 94568 693-H3
TAMARACK WY
5700 CLAY 94517 593-G7
5700 CNCD 94521 593-G7
TAMARISK
- MRGA 94556 631-C7
TAMARISK CT
200 WLCK 94598 612-J2
2200 CCCo 94514 617-J7
TAMARISK DR
200 WLCK 94598 612-J2
TAMARRON WY
300 SRMN 94582 673-G3
TAMBURLAINE DR
- SRMN 94582 674-C3
TAMMY CIR
100 CCCo 94565 573-F2
TAMMY LN
800 PLHL 94523 591-J5
1600 CNCD 94519 593-A2
TAM-O-SHANTER RD
- CCCo 94507 632-J4
TAMPA AV
2000 OAK 94611 630-E7
TAMPICO
100 WLCK 94598 612-E4
TAMPICO PL
1400 WLCK 94598 612-E4
TAMWORTH CT
3200 WLCK 94598 612-H6
TAMWORTH LN
- SRMN 94582 674-D4
TANAGER CIR
2400 CNCD 94520 572-G6
TANAGER CT
2400 CNCD 94520 572-G6
TANAGER DR
2200 PLE 94566 694-D7
TANAGER PL
2400 CNCD 94520 572-F6
TANAGER WY
100 HER 94547 569-H5
TANBARK LN
- CCCo 94507 633-B3
TANBOR WY
- CCCo 94553 572-C7
TANDEM LN
5400 RCH 94803 589-J3
TANGANYIKA CIR
200 ANT 94509 575-B7
TANGELO CT
2800 PLE 94588 694-H4
TANGERINE CT
200 SRMN 94583 673-J7
200 SRMN 94583 693-J1
TANGERINE ST
9100 SRMN 94583 693-J1
TANGIER TER
- BREN 94513 616-C4
TANGLEWOOD DR
- RCH 94806 568-H7
700 LFYT 94549 611-E7
TANGLEWOOD LN
- BREN 94513 596-C6
- LFYT 94549 611-E7
2000 CCCo 94507 632-D1
TANGLEWOOD PL
- LFYT 94549 611-E7
TANGLEWOOD RD
- BERK 94705 630-A3
- OAK 94705 630-A3
TANGO LN
- BREN 94561 596-D3
TAPER ST
2300 PIN 94564 589-J1

TAPESTRY LN
- CNCD 94520 592-E3
TAPPAN CT
- ORIN 94563 610-G3
TAPPAN LN
- ORIN 94563 610-F2
TAPPAN TER
300 ORIN 94563 610-F3
TAPSCOTT AV
1900 ELCR 94530 609-C1
2000 ELCR 94530 589-C7
TARA CT
1500 CLAY 94517 593-F5
TARA DR
5400 CLAY 94517 593-F5
TARA RD
- ORIN 94563 630-J1
- ORIN 94563 631-A1
TARABROOK DR
- ORIN 94563 630-J1
TARADA LN
- SRMN 94582 674-A3
TARA HILLS DR
500 CCCo 94806 569-B4
1200 PIN 94564 569-C5
2700 CCCo 94564 569-C5
2700 PIN 94806 569-C5
TARANTINO DR
- MRTZ 94553 571-D2
TARAYA TER
- HER 94547 569-F2
TAREYTON AV
- SRMN 94583 673-F7
TAREYTON CT
- SRMN 94583 673-F7
TARN CT
- HER 94547 569-H4
TARRY LN
- ORIN 94563 610-G3
TARRYTON CT
1300 ANT 94509 575-F7
TARRYTOWN CT
600 WLCK 94598 613-A3
TARTAN CT
100 WLCK 94598 612-G2
TARTAN WY
12000 OAK 94619 650-J4
12100 OAK 94619 651-A4
TARTARIAN CT
1200 BREN 94513 596-E7
TASCO CT
- SPAB 94806 568-H7
TASSAJARA AV
2500 ELCR 94530 589-C6
2600 CCCo 94805 589-C6
TASSAJARA LN
2400 DNVL 94526 653-E4
TASSAJARA RD
- PLE 94588 694-E4
5000 DBLN 94568 694-E4
7200 AlaC 94568 694-E4
8200 AlaC 94568 674-F7
8200 DBLN 94568 674-F7
TASSAJARA RANCH DR
- DNVL 94506 653-J6
- DNVL 94506 654-A6
TATE LN
400 OAKL 94561 576-B7
TATE WY
- CCCo 94582 674-B5
TAURUS AV
- OAK 94611 630-D6
TAVAN ESTATES DR
800 MRTZ 94553 591-F4
800 CCCo 94553 591-F4
TAWNY CT
4800 OAKL 94561 576-C7
TAYBERRY LN
400 BREN 94513 616-C3
TAYLOR BLVD
- PLHL 94523 592-A4
200 PLHL 94523 591-J6
1400 CCCo 94549 611-H2
1400 LFYT 94549 611-H2
1800 CCCo 94549 591-J7
1800 LFYT 94549 591-J7
TAYLOR DR
- BREN 94513 596-B7
- BREN 94513 616-B1
TAYLOR LN
2600 CCCo 94513 617-C7
TAYLOR PL
1200 CCCo 94511 577-A2
TAYLOR RD
1200 CCCo 94511 577-A2
TAYLOR ST
900 ALB 94706 609-D6
TAYLOR WY
- ANT 94531 595-F5
TEAK CT
600 WLCK 94598 592-H7
TEAKWOOD CT
4200 CNCD 94521 593-C2
4500 OAKL 94561 576-D7
TEAKWOOD DR
1700 MRTZ 94553 571-J7
4700 OAKL 94561 576-D6
TEAL CT
- BREN 94513 596-E4
- PIT 94565 574-B4
1400 OAKL 94561 576-D7
3900 BEN 94510 551-F3
TEAL DR
800 BEN 94510 551-F2
TEAROSE CT
- SRMN 94582 674-A1
TEA TREE CT
- DNVL 94526 653-B6
2500 MRTZ 94553 572-A6
TECHNOLOGY CT
2900 RCH 94806 569-A6
TECHNOLOGY WY
- BREN 94513 596-G7
TEHACHAPI CT
5100 ANT 94531 595-E4
TEHACHAPI WY
5000 ANT 94531 595-E3
TEHAMA AV
5100 RCH 94804 609-B3
TEHAN CT
- DBLN 94568 693-G4
TEHAN CANYON RD
- PLE 94588 693-H7
TEIGLAND RD
3100 CCCo 94549 611-J1
TEIXEIRA WY
5000 OAKL 94561 576-D6
TELEGRAPH HILL
- CCCo 94806 569-A5
TELVIN ST
1000 ALB 94706 609-F6
TEMBLOR WY
4300 ANT 94531 595-J2

TEMESCAL CT
- ANT 94531 596-A1
TEMPE CT
600 PLHL 94523 592-B2
TEMPLAR PL
- OAK 94618 630-C7
TEMPLE CT
- CCCo 94553 572-B7
TEMPLE DR
900 CCCo 94553 572-B6
TENBY TER
100 CCCo 94506 654-A5
TENNENT AV
100 PIN 94564 569-E4
TENNENT CT
2300 PIN 94564 569-E3
TENNIS CLUB DR
- CCCo 94506 653-H1
TENNY DR
100 BEN 94510 551-C3
TENNYSON DR
1700 CNCD 94521 593-F4
TEODORA CT
- MRGA 94556 651-F1
TEPEE CT
5100 ANT 94531 595-H4
TERA CT
900 WLCK 94597 612-A1
TERACINA DR
100 SRMN 94582 673-G2
TERALYNN CT
- OAK 94619 650-H5
TERESA CT
5200 OAKL 94561 576-D6
TERESA LN
1900 OAKL 94561 576-C6
TERESA PL
- SRMN 94583 673-G4
TERESA ST
600 MRTZ 94553 571-E5
TERN CT
- SRFL 94901 587-A2
TERRA LN
- CCCo 94553 592-B1
TERRA ALTA DR
4000 SRMN 94582 673-G4
TERRA BELLA DR
- CCCo 94596 612-F6
TERRABELLA PL
4300 OAK 94619 650-H5
TERRABELLA WY
4400 OAK 94619 650-H5
TERRA CALIFORNIA DR
800 WLCK 94595 632-B2
TERRACE AV
- RCH 94801 608-D1
TERRACE CT
- CNCD 94518 592-H4
100 HER 94547 569-H4
TERRACE DR
- CNCD 94518 592-G4
1900 ANT 94509 575-F6
7300 ELCR 94530 609-F2
TERRACE RD
- CCCo 94597 612-A4
- WLCK 94597 612-A4
TERRACE ST
1500 ALB 94706 609-E6
TERRACE WK
- BERK 94707 609-G6
TERRACE WY
1600 WLCK 94597 612-B5
3000 MRTZ 94553 571-E5
3500 LFYT 94549 611-E6
TERRACED HILLS CIR
- SRMN 94583 673-E6
TERRACED HILLS WY
- SRMN 94583 673-E6
TERRACE VIEW AV
2800 ANT 94531 575-G7
3000 ANT 94531 595-G1
TERRA GRANADA DR
- WLCK 94595 632-B5
TERRA GRANDE
- WLCK 94595 632-C4
TERRANOVA DR
- ANT 94509 575-D7
- ANT 94509 595-D1
TERRAPIN CT
700 CNCD 94518 592-J6
TERRA TERESA
- CCCo 94549 591-J7
TERRA VERDE LN
2900 OAKL 94561 576-A7
TERRAZA DEL SOL
3100 CNCD 94520 572-E5
TERRAZZO CIR
- SRMN 94583 673-G4
TERREBONNE DR
1100 WLCK 94598 612-F1
TERRI CT
- OAKL 94561 596-C1
TERRI ANN LN
- CCCo 94803 589-F4
TERRY CT
900 PIT 94565 574-E5
2700 PIN 94564 569-H6
TERRY LN
600 DNVL 94526 652-H1
TERRY WY
1500 PLHL 94523 592-C4
TERRY LYNN LN
1500 CNCD 94521 593-E5
TESORO CT
1800 PIN 94564 569-E5
TETON PL
3400 CNCD 94518 592-H6
TETON RD
- OAKL 94561 596-H1
TEVLIN ST
1100 ALB 94706 609-E7
1100 BERK 94706 609-E7
TEWKSBURY AV
1300 ALB 94706 609-E5
1500 BERK 94707 609-F5
TEWKSBURY CT
- SRMN 94582 674-C3
TEWKSBURY WY
- SRMN 94582 674-C4
TEXAS ST
- ANT 94509 575-D6
3000 OAK 94602 650-D5
THACKERAY DR
2300 OAK 94611 650-F1
THAMES CT
7200 DBLN 94568 693-J3
THAMES DR
1200 CNCD 94518 592-D6
THARP DR
100 MRGA 94556 651-E2
THATCHER DR
4900 MRTZ 94553 572-A6
T- HEAD RD
- CCCo 94553 571-H3

THE ALAMEDA
500 BERK 94707 609-F5
2800 CNCD 94519 592-G2
THE CRESCENT
- BERK 94708 609-J5
THE CROSSWAYS
200 BERK 94708 609-J5
THE GLADE
500 ORIN 94563 610-G7
THE KNOLL
200 ORIN 94563 610-H7
THELEN CT
100 MRTZ 94553 571-H5
THELMA DR
- CCCo 94565 573-E2
THEO LN
100 PLHL 94523 592-B6
THE PLAZA DR
- BERK 94705 630-A4
THERESA LN
3200 CCCo 94549 591-H6
THERESA PTH
- RCH 94804 609-A1
THE SHORT CUT
- OAK 94705 630-A3
- BERK 94708 609-J5
THE SPIRAL
300 BERK 94708 609-J5
THE TREES TRAILER PARK DR
- CNCD 94518 592-E5
- CNCD 94520 592-E5
THE TURN
6800 OAK 94611 630-E5
THE UPLANDS
- BERK 94705 630-A4
THICKET PL
6900 BREN 94513 596-G5
THIESSEN CT
4800 CNCD 94521 593-D4
THIRTY HILL RD
- CCCo 94553 571-F2
- MRTZ 94553 571-F2
THISTLE CIR
200 MRTZ 94553 591-G2
THISTLE CT
100 HER 94547 569-J4
1500 OAKL 94561 596-D1
THISTLE WY
- SRMN 94582 653-H6
100 MRTZ 94553 591-H2
3700 PLE 94588 694-F5
THISTLEDOWN CT
3100 PLE 94588 694-F6
THISTLEWOOD CT
5100 ANT 94531 595-J6
THOMAS AV
5400 OAK 94618 630-A6
THOMAS CT
- BREN 94513 616-B3
700 WLCK 94597 612-B2
1000 ANT 94509 575-F7
2100 OAKL 94561 576-B7
2700 PIN 94564 569-H6
THOMAS DR
- BEN 94510 551-C1
600 RCH 94806 568-G6
1200 MRTZ 94553 571-D3
4700 OAKL 94561 576-B7
THOMAS LN
700 WLCK 94597 612-A2
THOMAS RD
- BREN 94513 616-C3
THOMAS WY
100 PIT 94565 574-C4
THOMASVILLE CT
- PIT 94565 574-C2
THOMPSON DR
4100 CNCD 94518 592-J5
THOMPSON LN
2000 CCCo 94803 569-E7
2000 CCCo 94803 589-E1
THOMPSON RD
1000 LFYT 94549 611-E5
S THOMPSON RD
900 LFYT 94549 611-E6
THOMPSON ST
900 MRTZ 94553 571-E3
THOMPSONS DR
700 BREN 94513 596-E7
THORN CT
- OAK 94611 630-F6
THORN DR
1500 CNCD 94521 593-E4
THORNBURGH LN
- DBLN 94568 694-H3
THORNDALE DR
6400 OAK 94611 630-E5
THORNDALE PL
- MRGA 94556 631-C5
THORNHILL CT
- DNVL 94526 653-C2
6000 OAK 94611 630-E6
THORNHILL DR
5500 OAK 94611 630-E6
THORNHILL LN
- BREN 94513 616-B1
THORNHILL PL
4300 PIT 94565 574-D7
THORNHILL RD
600 DNVL 94526 653-C2
THORNHILL WY
4200 PIT 94565 574-E7
THORNWOOD CT
4300 CNCD 94521 593-C3
THORNWOOD DR
1500 CNCD 94521 593-B4
THORS BAY RD
8600 ELCR 94530 609-E1
THORUP LN
100 SRMN 94583 673-C1
THOUSAND OAKS BLVD
1300 ALB 94706 609-E5
1500 BERK 94707 609-F5
THRESHER DR
100 VAL 94591 550-E1
THROUGHBRED CT
- ANT 94531 596-A3
THRUSH CT
100 HER 94547 569-H5
THUMB MOUNTAIN CT
2000 ANT 94531 595-E6
THUNDERBIRD CT
- ANT 94531 595-H5
3600 CNCD 94520 572-G5
THUNDERBIRD DR
3400 CNCD 94520 572-F6
9400 SRMN 94583 673-H6
THUNDERBIRD PL
9400 SRMN 94583 673-H7
THUNDERHEAD CT
4900 RCH 94803 589-G1
THUNE AV
- MRGA 94556 651-E1

THYME CT
- OAKL 94561 596-E2
TIA PL
- MRGA 94556 651-F2
TIANA TER
1800 LFYT 94549 591-H7
TIBURON CT
- CCCo 94597 612-A4
4500 ANT 94509 595-F3
TICE CREEK DR
- WLCK 94595 632-A2
TICE HOLLOW CT
2200 CCCo 94595 632-C1
TICE VALLEY BLVD
1600 CCCo 94595 612-A7
1600 WLCK 94595 612-A7
1600 WLCK 94595 632-B1
1600 CCCo 94595 632-B1
2400 CCCo 94507 632-B1
TICE VALLEY LN
- WLCK 94595 632-B2
- CCCo 94595 632-B2
TICHENOR CT
1400 LFYT 94549 611-G3
TIDEWATER CT
1200 BREN 94513 596-E7
TIDEWATER DR
100 HER 94547 570-A5
TIERRA DR
- RCH 94803 589-F2
TIERRA VERDE CT
- CCCo 94598 612-F4
TIFFANY DR
- BREN 94561 596-D4
- PIT 94565 574-C5
TIFFANY DR W
- BREN 94561 596-D4
TIFFANY LN
- OAK 94611 630-F7
TIFFANY PL
700 CNCD 94518 592-J6
TIFFIN CT
- CLAY 94517 593-G7
TIFFIN DR
900 CLAY 94517 593-G7
TIFFIN RD
1800 OAK 94602 650-E3
TIGER LILY DR
- SRMN 94582 674-A2
TIGERSIDE WY
- SRMN 94582 673-H2
TIGER TAIL CT
- ORIN 94563 610-H4
TIKI LN
100 PIT 94565 574-E5
N TILDEN LN
4000 LFYT 94549 611-B6
S TILDEN LN
3900 LFYT 94549 611-B6
TILLER CT
- CCCo 94513 617-F7
TILLER PL
- PIT 94565 574-A2
TILLEY CIR
1000 CNCD 94518 592-J5
TILLMAN DR
6000 PLE 94588 693-G6
TILSON DR
1100 CNCD 94520 592-E4
TIM CT
200 DNVL 94526 652-J2
TIMBER LN
- LFYT 94549 611-D7
TIMBERBROOK WY
4800 ANT 94531 596-A4
TIMBERCOVE CT
800 VAL 94591 550-E3
TIMBER CREEK CT
- ANT 94531 595-D4
TIMBERCREEK RD
1100 SRMN 94582 673-J7
TIMBERLEAF CT
500 WLCK 94598 613-B3
TIMBERLINE CT
100 DNVL 94526 653-B4
400 PLHL 94523 591-J6
TIMBERLINE TER
600 BREN 94513 616-E1
TIMBERVIEW CT
- DNVL 94506 653-H4
TIMOLINO WY
- DBLN 94568 693-G4
TIMOTHY LN
1000 LFYT 94549 611-C6
TIMOTHY PL
3600 ANT 94509 595-B1
TIMPANOGOS LN
600 DNVL 94526 633-A7
TINA CT
1300 MRTZ 94553 571-H6
TINA PL
7200 DBLN 94568 693-F5
TINA ST
- CCCo 94565 573-F2
TIOGA PASS
- OAKL 94561 596-H2
TIOGA RD
3100 CNCD 94518 592-G4
TIOGA PASS CT
- ANT 94531 595-E4
TIOGA PASS WY
- ANT 94531 595-E4
TIPPERARY WY
- ANT 94531 596-A4
TISBURY LN
- CCCo 94805 589-C5
TITAN WY
- HER 94547 569-F3
TITANIA CT
100 CCCo 94597 592-D7
TIVOLI LN
100 DNVL 94506 653-J5
TOAST CT
- CCCo 94525 550-F5
TOBI CT
1800 CNCD 94521 593-D3
TOBI DR
4700 CNCD 94521 593-D3
TOBY RD
9900 SRMN 94583 673-E5
TODD AV
2500 CNCD 94520 592-F3
TODD CT
- CCCo 94507 633-C5
TODD WY
3100 SRMN 94583 673-F5
TOFFLEMIRE DR
- LFYT 94549 631-E1
TOKAY CT
- PLHL 94523 592-A5
TOKAY DR
4500 OAKL 94561 576-F7
TOKOLA DR
2600 CNCD 94518 592-G6

TOLAN WY
- LFYT 94549 611-A4
TOLEDO CT
- LFYT 94549 611-D5
TOLEDO DR
- LFYT 94549 611-D5
12200 SRMN 94583 673-F4
TOLLEY CT
- SRMN 94582 674-C4
TOLTEC CIR
2500 SRMN 94583 673-C3
TOLUCA DR
12200 SRMN 94583 673-G4
TOM CT
- SRMN 94583 673-F6
TOMAR CT
2400 PIN 94564 569-G7
TOM BURNETT LN
4900 PLE 94588 694-A6
TOMPKINS AV
4100 OAK 94619 650-G6
TOMPKINS WY
2300 ANT 94509 595-A1
TONI CT
- CCCo 94507 633-D5
TONO LN
200 CCCo 94523 592-D7
TONOPAH CIR
3000 PLE 94588 694-D6
TONOPAH CT
3100 PLE 94588 694-D6
TONSTAD PL
700 PLHL 94523 592-A3
TOPAZ CIR
7500 DBLN 94568 693-J2
TOPAZ CT
- ANT 94509 595-F1
- CCCo 94513 617-G4
100 HER 94547 569-G5
900 VAL 94590 550-C2
TOPAZ LN
- PLHL 94523 591-J4
TOPAZ ST
- BREN 94513 616-H2
TOPEKA PL
300 DNVL 94526 653-C5
TOPINERA LN
- LFYT 94549 591-H7
TOPPER CT
- LFYT 94549 611-G7
TOPPER LN
800 LFYT 94549 611-G7
TOPSAIL CT
- PLHL 94523 592-B1
100 VAL 94591 550-F2
TOPSAIL DR
300 VAL 94591 550-F2
TOPSFIELD CIR
- DBLN 94568 694-E2
TORINO CT
- DNVL 94526 653-C1
3400 CNCD 94518 592-H6
4100 PLE 94588 694-H4
TORINO WY
3500 CNCD 94518 592-J6
TORMEY AV
- CCCo 94565 573-H2
- PIT 94565 573-H2
700 CCCo 94572 549-H7
TORONTO LN
2100 CNCD 94520 572-F5
TORREON AV
9900 SRMN 94583 673-F5
TORRE RAMEL LN
3000 OAKL 94561 576-A7
TORREY CT
2600 PLE 94588 694-F6
TORREY PINE CT
100 WLCK 94598 612-J1
5600 RCH 94803 589-G4
TORREY PINES DR
- BREN 94513 616-A3
TORREY PINES PL
- CLAY 94517 594-A7
TORREYS PEAK CT
4700 ANT 94531 595-D3
TORRINGTON CT
2100 MRTZ 94553 572-A6
TORRINGTON DR
300 BREN 94513 616-E3
TORTOISE PL
1900 WLCK 94595 632-B1
TORTOSA CT
3700 SRMN 94583 673-B3
TORY CT
7000 DBLN 94568 693-J3
TORY WY
6700 DBLN 94568 693-J3
TOSCA WY
3000 CNCD 94520 572-F6
TOSCANNA CT
500 BREN 94513 616-F3
TOTANA CT
2600 SRMN 94583 673-C3
TOTEM CT
5000 ANT 94531 595-H4
TOTTERDELL CT
- ORIN 94563 631-B5
TOTTERDELL ST
3000 OAK 94611 650-G1
TOUCAN WY
- ANT 94509 594-J1
TOULOUSE LN
- BREN 94513 596-C5
TOULOUSE WY
900 MRTZ 94553 571-H5
TOUR WY
- CCCo 94531 615-G2
TOWERS DR
200 CCCo 94553 572-B7
TOWN AV
3100 CCCo 94514 637-D3
TOWN AND COUNTRY DR
- DNVL 94526 653-A3
100 DNVL 94526 652-J3
TOWN CENTRE TER
300 BREN 94513 596-F7
TOWNS CT
3700 PIN 94564 569-J7
TOWNSEND AV
4300 OAK 94602 650-D3
E TOYAH CT
4200 CNCD 94521 593-C2
TOYON CT
100 HER 94547 569-J4
5100 ANT 94531 595-H4
TOYON DR
1400 CNCD 94520 592-F3
TOYON PL
500 BEN 94510 550-J1
4500 OAK 94619 650-G5
TOYON RD
1700 LFYT 94549 611-G1
1800 LFYT 94549 591-G7

STREET	Block	City	ZIP	Pg-Grid
TOYON ST				
	3100	CCCo	94553	571-G4
TOYON TER				
	-	DNVL	94526	632-J7
TOYON WY				
	5000	ANT	94531	595-H4
TRACY CT				
	-	CCCo	94507	632-J4
	-	MRGA	94556	651-G2
TRACY LN				
	-	CCCo	94507	632-J3
TRACY WY				
	300	CCCo	94507	632-J3
TRADEWIND LN				
	800	CCCo	94572	570-A2
TRADITION WY				
	-	BREN	94513	616-J3
TRADWINDS CT				
	-	CCCo	94565	573-C2
TRAFALGAR CIR				
	2600	CCCo	94520	572-G2
TRAFALGAR CT				
	1200	CNCD	94518	592-D6
	2600	CCCo	94520	572-G2
TRAFALGAR PL				
	2100	OAK	94611	650-E1
TRAFALGAR WY				
	-	OAKL	94561	596-D2
TRAIL CT				
	-	BREN	94513	596-H5
TRAILCREEK CT				
	1700	CNCD	94521	593-D3
TRAILHEAD WY				
	-	MRTZ	94553	571-G5
TRAIL MOUNTAIN WY				
	-	ANT	94531	595-F4
TRAIL RIDE RD				
	1400	CCCo	94517	614-B3
TRAILRIDGE CT				
	5000	ANT	94531	595-E4
TRAILRIDGE WY				
	5000	ANT	94531	595-E4
TRAILS END DR				
	800	CCCo	94598	613-A4
	800	WLCK	94598	613-A4
TRAILSIDE DR				
	-	BREN	94513	596-H5
	-	RCH	94803	589-G5
TRAILSIDE PL				
	-	PLHL	94523	591-H2
TRAILVIEW CIR				
	300	MRTZ	94553	571-G5
TRAILVIEW CT				
	-	SRMN	94583	673-D4
TRALEE CT				
	-	CCCo	94806	569-C6
TRAPLINE TR				
	-	CCCo	94583	652-E2
TRAUD CT				
	1300	CNCD	94518	592-E7
TRAUD DR				
	1200	CNCD	94518	592-E7
TRAVALINI CT				
	100	CCCo	94803	589-G2
TRAVERS DR				
	-	MRTZ	94553	571-F7
	-	MRTZ	94553	591-F1
TRAVIS CT				
	-	PIT	94565	574-C2
TRAWLER ST				
	1500	CCCo	94514	(618-A6 See Page 597)
TRAYNOR RD				
	1300	CNCD	94520	592-E3
TREADWAY LN				
	1900	PLHL	94523	592-C5
TREADWELL CT				
	100	BREN	94513	616-G3
TREASURE CT				
	100	SRMN	94583	673-B1
TREASURE DR				
	700	CCCo	94565	573-D1
TREASURE HILL				
	-	OAK	94618	630-C4
TREAT BLVD				
	1300	CCCo	94597	612-D1
	1500	WLCK	94598	612-D1
	2400	CNCD	94518	592-F7
	2400	WLCK	94598	592-F7
	4000	CNCD	94518	593-A5
	4100	CNCD	94521	593-A5
TREAT LN				
	4300	CNCD	94521	593-A4
TREATRO ST				
	900	PIT	94565	574-F3
TREE CREEK PL				
	2300	DNVL	94506	653-F1
TREECREST PL				
	-	WLCK	94596	612-D6
TREE GARDEN PL				
	-	CNCD	94518	592-E6
TREEHAVEN CT				
	800	PLHL	94523	592-D4
TREELINE PL				
	11500	DBLN	94568	693-F6
TREESIDE WY				
	2500	RCH	94806	568-J7
	2500	RCH	94806	588-J1
TREG LN				
	900	CNCD	94518	592-F6
E TREGALLAS RD				
	-	ANT	94509	575-D6
W TREGALLAS RD				
	300	ANT	94509	575-D6
TRELLIS BAY				
	-	HER	94547	569-H1
TREMBATH CT				
	1700	ANT	94509	575-G5
TREMBATH LN				
	1300	ANT	94509	575-G5
	1400	CCCo	94509	575-G5
TREMBATH ST				
	1800	ANT	94509	575-G5
TREMONT AV				
	500	RCH	94801	588-C7
TREMONT CT				
	-	BREN	94513	596-C5
	800	ANT	94509	575-F7
TRENERY DR				
	3500	PLE	94588	694-F7
TRENT CT				
	700	CCCo	94506	654-A5
TRENT PL				
	-	BREN	94513	596-G6
TRENT ST				
	900	CNCD	94518	592-E7
TRENT TER				
	700	CCCo	94506	654-A5
TRENTON BLVD				
	900	SPAB	94806	588-G2
TRENTON CT				
	1900	WLCK	94596	612-G7
TRENTON PL				
	-	BREN	94513	616-C4
TRENTON ST				
	4800	OAKL	94561	576-C6
TRES ALMENDRAS				
	3100	LFYT	94549	611-J5
TRES CASAS CT				
	1000	WLCK	94598	612-G4
TRES MESAS				
	-	ORIN	94563	610-E7
TRES PALMAS				
	900	MRTZ	94553	591-G4
TRESTLE CV				
	-	HER	94547	569-G1
TRESTLE GLEN CT				
	300	WLCK	94598	612-F2
TRESTLE GLEN RD				
	600	OAK	94610	650-A3
	1700	PDMT	94610	650-C3
	1700	OAK	94602	650-C3
	1700	PDMT	94602	650-C3
	2000	WLCK	94598	612-F2
TREVOR PKWY				
	2600	PLE	94588	694-G6
TREYBURN CIR				
	500	SRMN	94583	693-H1
TRI LN				
	6300	CCCo	94803	589-H5
	6300	RCH	94803	589-H5
TRIANA WY				
	100	SRMN	94583	693-H1
TRIANGLE CIR				
	900	RCH	94801	588-F5
TRICIA ST				
	1400	BREN	94513	596-G7
TRIDENT CT				
	100	VAL	94591	550-F2
E TRIDENT DR				
	-	PIT	94565	573-J2
	-	PIT	94565	574-A2
W TRIDENT DR				
	-	PIT	94565	573-J2
TRIESTE WY				
	5700	PLE	94588	694-C6
TRIFARI PL				
	3200	CNCD	94518	592-J7
TRIGGER CT				
	1200	CCCo	94572	549-J6
TRIGGER LN				
	-	CCCo	94803	569-G7
	-	CCCo	94803	589-F1
TRIGGER RD				
	1200	CCCo	94572	549-J6
TRILLIUM LN				
	-	SRMN	94583	693-H1
TRINA CT				
	-	CCCo	94596	612-F7
TRINIDAD AV				
	4800	OAK	94602	650-G4
TRINITY AV				
	200	CCCo	94708	609-G3
	1700	WLCK	94596	612-B5
TRINITY CT				
	-	PIT	94565	574-D5
	1800	ANT	94509	575-F5
	2100	MRTZ	94553	572-A7
	6400	DBLN	94568	694-A3
TRINITY DR				
	-	BREN	94513	596-D5
TRINITY PL				
	-	BREN	94513	596-D5
	2100	MRTZ	94553	572-A7
TRINITY TER				
	-	MRGA	94556	651-E2
TRINTEL CT				
	3600	WLCK	94598	613-A3
TRIOMPHE CT				
	400	DNVL	94506	653-J5
TRIPLE CROWN CT				
	-	ANT	94531	596-A3
TRIPOLI CT				
	100	SRMN	94583	673-H6
TRISH CT				
	-	DNVL	94506	653-G4
TRISH DR				
	-	DNVL	94506	653-G4
TRISH LN				
	-	DNVL	94506	653-G4
TROJAN RD				
	100	CCCo	94565	553-F7
TROON CT				
	5600	CCCo	94514	617-J6
TROON DR				
	-	BREN	94513	616-B3
TROPICANA LN				
	-	BREN	94561	596-D4
TROTTER CT				
	800	WLCK	94596	632-G3
TROTTER WY				
	2200	WLCK	94596	632-F2
TROWBRIDGE WY				
	1100	CCCo	94506	654-A5
TROY CT				
	300	CCCo	94803	589-E2
TRUCKMORE CT				
	-	ANT	94531	596-A4
TRUITT AV				
	-	MRTZ	94553	571-F7
TRUITT LN				
	-	OAK	94618	630-C6
TRUMAN CT				
	2600	ANT	94509	574-H6
TRUMAN LN				
	2000	OAKL	94561	596-B1
TRUMAN ST				
	1500	CCCo	94801	588-F4
TRUSKMORE WY				
	-	ANT	94531	596-A4
TRYON PL				
	-	DBLN	94568	694-H3
TSUSHIMA ST				
	-	HER	94547	569-G3
TSUSHIMA WY				
	-	HER	94547	569-G3
TUBEROSE CT				
	2700	PLE	94588	694-H4
TUCKAHOE WY				
	1800	BREN	94513	596-G6
TUDOR CT				
	-	OAKL	94561	596-D2
	-	CCCo	94507	632-J2
	1300	CNCD	94521	593-A4
TUG BOAT LN				
	-	HER	94547	569-G1
TULANE DR				
	1200	WLCK	94596	632-G2
TULARE AV				
	900	BERK	94707	609-F6
	900	ALB	94707	609-F6
	1700	CCCo	94805	589-B6
	2300	ELCR	94530	589-B6
	2800	RCH	94804	588-J4
	3400	RCH	94804	589-A4
	3400	SPAB	94806	589-A4
TULARE CT				
	4100	ANT	94531	595-J1
	4100	CNCD	94521	593-A3
TULARE DR				
	4000	CNCD	94521	593-A3
TULARE ST				
	-	BREN	94513	616-H2
TULE CT				
	-	CLAY	94517	593-G6
TULE LN				
	1400	CCCo	94548	597-A2
TULE TREE LN				
	5300	CCCo	94561	577-E6
TULIP AV				
	4400	OAK	94619	650-G6
TULIP CT				
	-	BREN	94513	616-H5
	-	CCCo	94582	674-B1
TULIP DR				
	1200	ANT	94509	575-B5
TULIP ST				
	100	HER	94547	570-B4
TULIP WY				
	-	CCCo	94582	674-B1
TULLER AV				
	2600	ELCR	94530	589-B6
TULLIBEE CT				
	1200	CCCo	94572	549-J7
TULLIBEE RD				
	1200	CCCo	94572	549-J7
TULLY WY				
	800	CNCD	94518	592-G6
TUMBLEWEED CT				
	-	SRMN	94583	673-C4
	200	CCCo	94517	634-F1
	5100	ANT	94531	595-J6
TUMBLING BROOK RD				
	-	ORIN	94563	610-D6
TUMWATER CT				
	900	WLCK	94598	612-H4
TUMWATER DR				
	2700	WLCK	94598	612-H4
TUNBRIDGE RD				
	600	DNVL	94526	653-C3
TUNIS PL				
	-	CCCo	94553	572-C7
TUNNEL AV				
	200	RCH	94801	608-D1
TUNNEL RD				
	2100	OAK	94611	630-D3
	2100	OAK	94705	630-C4
	2100	OAK	94618	630-C4
TUNNEL RD Rt#-13				
	-	BERK	94705	630-B4
	-	OAK	94705	630-B4
	1100	OAK	94618	630-B4
TUOLUMNE AV				
	200	MRTZ	94553	571-E6
TUOLUMNE WY				
	-	OAKL	94561	596-H2
	4500	CNCD	94521	593-B5
TUPELO DR				
	3400	WLCK	94598	612-J1
TURF CT				
	5200	ANT	94531	595-J5
TURK DR				
	-	MRGA	94556	631-E5
TURNBERRY CT				
	-	BREN	94513	616-B1
	-	DBLN	94568	694-F1
TURNBERRY DR				
	-	DBLN	94568	694-F2
TURNBULL CT				
	-	ANT	94531	595-C4
TURNER CT				
	-	CCCo	94507	632-H2
	3400	CNCD	94518	592-J6
TURNER DR				
	400	BEN	94510	551-A2
TURNHOUSE CT				
	-	BREN	94513	616-A1
TURNSTONE DR				
	-	SRFL	94901	587-A2
TURPIN CT				
	600	RCH	94801	588-F5
TURPIN ST				
	500	RCH	94801	588-F6
TURQUOISE DR				
	-	HER	94547	569-G5
TURQUOISE ST				
	7600	DBLN	94568	693-J2
TURRIN DR				
	400	PLHL	94523	592-B6
TURRINI CIR				
	-	DNVL	94526	653-B1
TURRINI CT				
	100	DNVL	94526	653-B1
TURRINI DR				
	700	DNVL	94526	653-B1
TURRINI PL				
	800	DNVL	94526	653-B1
TURTLE CREEK RD				
	4200	CNCD	94521	593-B4
TURTLE ROCK LN				
	1100	CNCD	94521	593-B4
TUSCANY CT				
	100	HER	94547	570-B6
	300	DNVL	94506	653-H4
TUSCANY DR				
	7600	DBLN	94568	694-A1
TUSCANY LN				
	-	SRMN	94583	673-G4
TUSCANY WY				
	-	DNVL	94506	653-G5
TUSTIN CT				
	100	BEN	94510	551-B1
TUYSHTAK CT				
	-	CLAY	94517	593-J5
TWAIN AV				
	-	BERK	94708	609-J6
TWAIN TER				
	-	MRTZ	94553	571-J5
TWAIN WY				
	-	BREN	94513	616-H1
TWEED DR				
	100	DNVL	94526	653-C3
TWEED LN				
	-	DNVL	94526	653-C3
TWELVE OAKS CT				
	1400	CCCo	94507	632-E3
TWILIGHT CT				
	-	BREN	94513	596-G5
TWINBRIDGE CIR				
	300	PLHL	94523	592-D4
TWINBRIDGE CT				
	-	PLHL	94523	592-D4
	500	BREN	94513	616-E1
TWINCREEK CT				
	5100	ANT	94531	596-A3
TWIN CREEKS DR				
	2500	SRMN	94583	673-C1
TWIN EAGLES LN				
	-	DBLN	94568	694-G3
TWINFLOWER CT				
	2400	MRTZ	94553	572-A6
TWINING CT				
	600	ANT	94509	595-E1
TWIN OAKS LN				
	400	CCCo	94596	612-F7
TWIN PEAKS DR				
	-	CCCo	94595	612-C7
TWIN PEAKS LN				
	300	CCCo	94507	633-A4
TWINVIEW DR				
	200	PLHL	94523	591-J6
TWINVIEW PL				
	700	PLHL	94523	591-J6
	700	PLHL	94523	592-A6
TWITTER CT				
	-	OAK	94605	650-H6
TYBURN PL				
	300	DNVL	94526	653-C3
TYLER CT				
	900	CNCD	94518	592-H5
	2200	ANT	94509	575-A7
TYLER RD				
	-	VAL	94592	549-H2
	-	VAL	94592	550-A2
TYLER ST				
	-	BEN	94510	551-D6
	1800	SPAB	94806	588-H3
TYLER TER				
	800	PLHL	94523	591-J5
TYLERTON CT				
	-	SRMN	94582	674-C4
TYNDALL CT				
	4400	CNCD	94518	593-A6
TYNE CT				
	6900	DBLN	94568	693-J3
TYR CT				
	-	PLHL	94523	592-B3
TYRREL CT				
	-	DNVL	94526	653-D4
TYRRELL ST				
	4600	OAK	94601	650-E7
TYSON CIR				
	-	PDMT	94611	650-D1
TYSON CT				
	-	DNVL	94526	653-D4
U				
UDAYAKAVI LN				
	-	DNVL	94526	632-J6
UKIAH CT				
	100	WLCK	94595	612-C7
ULFINIAN WY				
	600	MRTZ	94553	571-E3
ULTIMA CT				
	-	DNVL	94526	653-B1
UNDERHILL DR				
	900	CCCo	94507	632-G7
UNDERHILL RD				
	-	ORIN	94563	630-H1
UNDERHILLS RD				
	900	OAK	94610	650-B3
UNDERWOOD AV				
	5100	OAK	94613	650-G7
UNION CT				
	500	BEN	94510	550-J2
	3700	ANT	94509	595-C3
UNION MINE CT				
	4900	ANT	94531	595-D3
UNION MINE DR				
	4800	ANT	94531	595-C4
UNIVERSITY AV				
	2400	SPAB	94806	588-H3
UPLAND DR				
	800	LFYT	94549	611-E7
	2200	CNCD	94520	572-F7
	4600	RCH	94803	589-D3
UPPER TR				
	-	AlaC	94552	652-E6
	-	CCCo	94556	652-C3
	-	CCCo	94583	652-C3
	1700	CCCo	94517	614-B4
UPPER GOLDEN RAIN RD				
	1800	WLCK	94595	632-A1
	2800	WLCK	94595	631-J1
UPPER HAPPY VALLEY RD				
	1000	LFYT	94549	611-B5
UPPER POND CT				
	2400	CCCo	94549	591-G5
UPSON CT				
	-	PLHL	94523	592-A5
UPTON RD				
	2900	MRTZ	94553	571-F7
UPTON PYNE DR				
	200	BREN	94513	616-C3
URANUS AV				
	100	OAK	94611	630-D6
URSUS CT				
	-	ANT	94531	595-H2
USTILAGO CT				
	-	SRMN	94582	673-G2
USTILAGO DR				
	-	SRMN	94582	673-G2
UTAH DR				
	4400	RCH	94803	589-E2
UTE CT				
	-	SRMN	94583	673-D5
UTICA CT				
	7000	DBLN	94568	693-J3
V				
VACA CREEK RD				
	100	CCCo	94553	591-D3
VACA CREEK WY				
	100	CCCo	94553	591-D2
VACATION DR				
	1100	LFYT	94549	611-J5
VACCA ST				
	100	RCH	94801	588-B6
VAGABOND CT				
	200	CCCo	94507	633-D6
VAGABOND WY				
	100	CCCo	94507	633-D6
VAILWOOD CT				
	-	DNVL	94526	653-D5
VAILWOOD DR				
	1200	DNVL	94526	653-D5
VAL AIRE PL				
	900	WLCK	94596	612-E7
VALANT PL				
	-	OAK	94610	650-C2
	-	PDMT	94610	650-C2
VALDEZ CT				
	2400	ANT	94509	595-A2
VALDIVIA CIR				
	100	SRMN	94583	673-C3
VALDRY CT				
	-	BREN	94513	616-H3
VALE AV				
	3300	OAK	94619	650-F6
VALE CT				
	1200	BREN	94513	596-C7
	6800	PLE	94588	694-A7
VALE RD				
	2000	RCH	94804	588-J4
	2000	SPAB	94806	588-J4
	2300	SPAB	94806	589-A4
VALENCIA CT				
	1300	BREN	94513	616-D1
	2800	SPAB	94806	588-J1
	3400	WLCK	94598	592-J7
VALENCIA PL				
	2800	ANT	94509	574-J6
	2800	ANT	94509	575-A6
VALENCIA RD				
	-	ORIN	94563	631-B5
VALENCIA ST				
	8400	DBLN	94568	693-G2
VALENCIA WY				
	2800	SPAB	94806	588-J2
VALENTE CIR				
	2100	MRTZ	94553	571-E3
VALENTE CT				
	2100	MRTZ	94553	571-E4
	4000	LFYT	94549	611-B6
VALENTE DR				
	4000	LFYT	94549	611-B7
VALERIE CT				
	900	CCCo	94803	569-D6
	1700	BEN	94510	551-B3
VALEROSA PL				
	1000	WLCK	94597	612-D3
VALINDA DR				
	3700	CNCD	94518	592-H4
VALLA CT				
	-	WLCK	94597	612-B3
VALLADO CT				
	-	SRMN	94583	673-A2
VALLECITO CT				
	-	ANT	94531	595-F5
	-	WLCK	94596	612-E6
	1100	LFYT	94549	611-B5
VALLECITO LN				
	-	CCCo	94596	612-E7
	-	ORIN	94563	610-F6
	-	WLCK	94596	612-E7
VALLECITO PL				
	2700	OAK	94606	650-B4
VALLECITO WY				
	2600	ANT	94531	595-G5
VALLEJO AV				
	200	CCCo	94572	549-J7
	500	CCCo	94572	569-J1
VALLEJO CT				
	-	ANT	94531	595-G5
VALLEJO PL				
	3200	SRMN	94583	673-G5
VALLEJO ST				
	-	BERK	94707	609-F5
	300	CCCo	94525	550-E4
VALLEJO FERRY				
	-	CCCo	-	549-J3
	-	CCCo	-	587-G3
	-	HER	-	549-F7
	-	HER	-	569-C1
	-	PIN	-	568-D3
	-	PIN	-	569-C1
	-	RCH	-	568-D3
	-	RCH	-	587-G3
	-	SF	-	608-A4
	-	VAL	-	549-J3
	-	VAL	-	550-A2
VALLETON LN				
	200	CCCo	94596	612-E6
	200	WLCK	94596	612-E6
VALLE VERDE CT				
	100	DNVL	94526	633-C7
VALLE VISTA				
	100	DNVL	94526	633-D6
	4400	PIT	94565	574-C6
VALLE VISTA AV				
	500	OAK	94610	650-A2
VALLEY AV				
	-	MRTZ	94553	571-F7
	600	PIN	94564	569-E4
	4100	CCCo	94553	571-F7
	4100	CCCo	94553	572-A3
VALLEY CT				
	-	ORIN	94563	631-A2
	-	PLHL	94523	592-A7
	1100	CNCD	94520	592-F3
VALLEY DR				
	-	ORIN	94563	630-J3
	-	ORIN	94563	631-A2
	-	PIT	94565	574-D6
	200	PLHL	94523	592-A7
VALLEY LN				
	3800	CCCo	94803	589-D3
VALLEY RD				
	1500	CCCo	94707	609-E4
VALLEY RUN				
	100	HER	94547	569-H4
VALLEY TR				
	-	CCCo	94583	652-D3
VALLEY WY				
	4800	ANT	94531	595-J4
VALLEY CREEK LN				
	200	DNVL	94526	653-A2
VALLEY CREST DR				
	5000	CNCD	94521	593-D4
VALLEY GLEN LN				
	100	MRTZ	94553	591-G2
VALLEY GREEN DR				
	500	BREN	94513	616-D1
VALLEY HIGH				
	-	LFYT	94549	611-B4
VALLEY HIGH DR				
	300	PLHL	94523	591-J2
VALLEY HILL DR				
	100	CCCo	94549	631-H6
	100	CCCo	94556	631-H6
	100	MRGA	94556	631-H6
VALLEY OAK DR				
	3500	CCCo	94505	617-E7
VALLEY OAK LN				
	100	VAL	94591	550-E1
VALLEY OAK PZ				
	200	MRTZ	94553	591-H3
VALLEY OAKS CT				
	-	CCCo	94507	632-H5
VALLEY OAKS DR				
	100	CCCo	94507	632-H5
VALLEY ORCHARD CT				
	4900	CCCo	94553	591-C3
VALLEY VIEW CT				
	-	CCCo	94803	589-F2
	-	DNVL	94526	652-J1
	500	MRTZ	94553	571-G5
	7200	PLE	94588	693-J7
VALLEYVIEW CT				
	-	VAL	94591	550-D1
VALLEY VIEW DR				
	-	ORIN	94563	631-A5
	1900	PIN	94564	569-E4
VALLEY VIEW LN				
	-	ORIN	94563	610-H4
	1900	CNCD	94521	593-F4
VALLEY VIEW RD				
	-	ORIN	94563	610-H4
	300	PLHL	94523	592-A5
	3900	LFYT	94549	611-C4
	4200	CCCo	94803	589-F2
	4300	RCH	94803	589-F2
	5500	RCH	94805	589-F4
	6000	OAK	94611	630-D5
VALLEY VISTA CT				
	400	WLCK	94598	612-J2
VALLEY VISTA RD				
	3000	WLCK	94598	612-J2
	3500	WLCK	94598	613-A2
VALMAR DR				
	5200	CNCD	94521	593-D6
VALMORE PL				
	-	BREN	94513	616-D4
VALORY LN				
	3800	LFYT	94549	611-D4
VALS LN				
	3200	LFYT	94549	611-H4
VAN BUREN CT				
	3000	ANT	94509	575-A7
VAN BUREN DR				
	3000	ANT	94509	575-A7
VAN BUREN PL				
	500	SRMN	94583	673-F6
	3100	ANT	94509	575-A7
VANCE LN				
	-	LFYT	94549	611-H3
VANCLEAVE LN				
	1000	WLCK	94598	612-D5
	1000	WLCK	94596	612-D5
VAN CLEAVE WY				
	-	OAK	94619	650-H5
VANCOUVER CT				
	-	BREN	94561	596-E4
VANCOUVER WY				
	3500	CNCD	94520	572-F5
VANDENBERG WY				
	-	ANT	94509	595-F1
VANDERSLICE AV				
	2000	CCCo	94596	612-E7
	2000	CCCo	94596	632-E1
	2000	WLCK	94596	632-E1
	2000	WLCK	94596	612-E7
VANDERSLICE CT				
	2100	WLCK	94596	632-E1
VAN DYKE AV				
	400	OAK	94606	650-A4
VANESSA WY				
	-	CCCo	94506	654-D6
VAN FLEET AV				
	5200	RCH	94804	609-C4
VAN GORDON PL				
	-	DNVL	94526	652-H1
VAN MOURIK AV				
	3900	OAK	94605	650-H7
VAN NESS ST				
	1800	SPAB	94806	588-H3
VAN PATTEN DR				
	1300	DNVL	94526	653-C6
VAN PELT LN				
	-	OAKL	94561	576-H7
VAN RIPPER LN				
	-	ORIN	94563	610-G3
VAN SICKLEN PL				
	-	OAK	94610	650-C3
VAN TASSEL LN				
	-	ORIN	94563	610-G3
VAQUERO WY				
	2100	ANT	94509	595-A1
VAQUEROS AV				
	-	CCCo	94572	549-H7
	400	CCCo	94572	569-H1
VARGUS CT				
	2600	CNCD	94520	572-F6
VARIZ				
	100	HER	94547	569-E3
VARNI CT				
	1600	BEN	94510	551-C4
VARTAN CT				
	-	WLCK	94597	612-C2
VASCO RD				
	3600	CCCo	94513	616-G7
	3600	CCCo	94513	(636-H1 See Page 635)
	3600	CCCo	94513	637-A3
	3600	CCCo	94514	637-C6
	3600	CCCo	94514	(657-C1 See Page 638)
	3600	CCCo	94514	(656-J6 See Page 635)
	3600	CCCo	94514	676-E1
	3600	CCCo	94551	676-E1
	3800	AlaC	94551	676-B4
VASHELL WY				
	-	ORIN	94563	610-H7
	-	ORIN	94563	630-H1
VASSAR AV				
	300	BERK	94708	609-G4
	300	CCCo	94708	609-G4
	400	BERK	94707	609-G4
VAUGHN RD				
	3300	LFYT	94549	591-G7
VAVOLD ST				
	1700	CNCD	94519	592-J2
VEALE AV				
	800	CCCo	94553	571-G4
	800	MRTZ	94553	571-G4
VECINO ST				
	500	BEN	94510	551-D5
VEDA DR				
	400	DNVL	94526	652-J2
VELASCO CT				
	-	DNVL	94526	653-C6
VELENZUELA CT				
	1400	PIT	94565	574-G5
VELLA CIR				
	-	OAKL	94561	576-G7
VELVET DR				
	2900	WLCK	94596	632-G3
VELVET WY				
	2600	WLCK	94596	632-G3
VELVETLEAF CIR				
	-	SRMN	94582	673-G3
VENADO CTE				
	100	WLCK	94598	612-H2
VENADO CAMINO				
	2500	WLCK	94598	612-G2
VENDOR CT				
	1800	ANT	94531	595-F3
VENDOR WY				
	1800	ANT	94531	595-F3
VENETO CT				
	-	PLE	94588	694-H4
VENICE CT				
	-	CCCo	94514	617-G7
	5100	PLE	94588	694-H4
VENICE DR				
	1800	CNCD	94519	593-A1
VENICE LN				
	1800	ANT	94509	575-G5
VENNER DR				
	4700	MRTZ	94553	571-F7
VENNER RD				
	4800	MRTZ	94553	571-F7
VENTNOR LN				
	2200	OAKL	94561	576-C6
VENTRY WY				
	-	ANT	94531	596-B4
VENTURA AV				
	900	ALB	94707	609-F6
	1000	ALB	94706	609-F7
	1500	SPAB	94806	589-A4
VENTURA CT				
	2900	ANT	94509	575-B7
VENTURA DR				
	-	BREN	94513	616-B3
	-	CCCo	94565	574-F6
	600	PIT	94565	574-E5
	6600	DBLN	94568	694-A3
VENTURA PL				
	400	SRMN	94583	673-F6
VENTURA ST				
	600	RCH	94805	589-A5
	1000	SPAB	94805	589-A5
VERACRUZ DR				
	3200	SRMN	94583	673-F4
VERBENA CT				
	-	BREN	94513	616-H5
	400	PLHL	94523	591-H2
VERBENA PL				
	-	PLHL	94523	591-H2
VERBENA WY				
	-	SRMN	94582	653-J7
VERDA DEL CIERVO				
	100	CCCo	94528	633-E7
VERDE AV				
	200	CCCo	94801	588-F3
VERDE CT				
	1200	BREN	94513	616-D1
	3200	PLE	94588	694-C7
VERDE MESA DR				
	100	DNVL	94526	633-C6
VERDIN PL				
	-	DBLN	94568	694-H3
VERITAS CT				
	-	SRMN	94582	674-C3
VERITAS WY				
	-	SRMN	94582	674-C3
VERMONT AV				
	300	BERK	94707	609-G4
	1300	CNCD	94521	593-F6
VERMONT LN				
	1800	ANT	94509	575-D2
VERMONT PL				
	3200	PLE	94588	694-G6
VERMONT ST				
	800	OAK	94610	650-A2
VERN LN				
	3400	CNCD	94519	592-J1
	3400	CNCD	94519	593-A1
VERNA CT				
	1300	CNCD	94518	592-G3
VERNA WY				
	5700	CLAY	94517	593-G6
VERNA WY E				
	5800	CLAY	94517	593-G6
VERNAL CT				
	-	CCCo	94507	632-F4
VERNAL DR				
	100	CCCo	94507	632-F3
VERNAZZE CT				
	-	BREN	94513	616-C1
VERNE ROBERTS CIR				
	1300	ANT	94509	575-A4
	1600	ANT	94509	574-J4
VERNIER DR				
	1700	CNCD	94519	593-A2
VERNON AV				
	100	CCCo	94801	588-F4
	200	RCH	94801	588-F4
	3200	LFYT	94549	611-H7
VERNON WY				
	-	CCCo	94582	674-C4
VERONA AV				
	300	DNVL	94526	652-J1
	2000	OAKL	94561	576-C7
VERONA CT				
	-	DNVL	94526	652-J2
	2000	OAKL	94561	576-C7
	3200	CNCD	94518	592-H2
VERONA PTH				
	-	OAK	94618	630-B5
VERONICA CT				
	-	SRMN	94582	673-H1
	1300	ANT	94509	575-G5
VERRADA RD				
	1000	OAK	94610	650-B3
VERSAILLES CT				
	-	DNVL	94506	653-H5
VERSAILLES PL				
	100	PIT	94565	574-C7
VESSING RD				
	2900	PLHL	94523	612-A1
VESTENY CT				
	-	ANT	94531	595-D4
VETERAN WY				
	-	OAK	94602	650-D4
VETERANS CT				
	1000	MRTZ	94553	571-G6
VETERANS DR				
	900	MRTZ	94553	571-G6
VIA ALONDRA				
	-	CCCo	94507	632-H3
VIA ALTA				
	1000	LFYT	94549	611-D5
	2100	BEN	94510	551-D4
VIA APPIA				
	500	WLCK	94598	612-E2
VIA ASPERO				
	-	CCCo	94507	633-A6
VIA BAJA				
	1000	LFYT	94549	611-D5
VIA BARCELONA				
	-	MRGA	94556	631-F4
VIA BONITA				
	100	CCCo	94507	632-F5
VIA CABRERA LN				
	100	MRTZ	94553	571-F6
VIA CALLADOS				
	-	ORIN	94563	610-G3
VIA CERRADA				
	-	CCCo	94507	632-E4
VIA CIMA CT				
	100	DNVL	94526	633-D6
VIA COPLA				
	100	CCCo	94507	632-F7
VIA CORDOBA				
	2800	CCCo	94583	673-B3
	2800	SRMN	94583	673-B3
VIA CORDOVA				
	300	MRTZ	94553	571-F6

STREET
Block City ZIP Pg-Grid

VIA CORTE
- ORIN 94563 610-F6
VIA DE FLORES
4000 CCCo 94553 571-J4
VIA DEL GATO
1000 CCCo 94507 632-G5
VIA DEL LISA CT
3700 CNCD 94518 592-J4
VIA DEL REY
400 CCCo 94507 632-E5
VIA DEL SOL
- PLHL 94523 592-C7
- PLHL 94523 612-C1
- WLCK 94597 612-C1
VIA DEL VERDES
1700 CNCD 94521 593-D3
VIA DE MERCADOS
2000 CNCD 94520 592-D2
VIADER DR
1000 MRGA 94556 631-D7
VIA DIABLO
- CCCo 94528 633-F5
VIA DOBLE
1100 CNCD 94521 593-E7
VIA DOMINGUEZ
2800 WLCK 94597 612-A1
VIA DON JOSE
1400 CCCo 94507 632-F4
VIA DORA DR
4300 ANT 94531 595-H2
VIA EL DORADO LN
200 MRTZ 94553 571-F5
VIA ENSENADA
5500 CNCD 94521 593-E7
VIA ENSENADA CT
1100 CNCD 94521 593-E7
VIA ESTRELLA
3900 CCCo 94553 571-J3
VIA FARALLON
- ORIN 94563 610-G6
VIA FERRARI
1800 CCCo 94549 591-H7
VIA FLOREADO
- ORIN 94563 610-J5
VIA GABARDA
1200 LFYT 94549 612-A4
VIA GIARAMITA
- CCCo 94803 589-F2
VIA GRANADA
3700 MRGA 94556 631-E2
3700 LFYT 94549 631-E2
VIA HERMOSA
- ORIN 94563 610-H5
700 DNVL 94526 653-A2
VIA JOAQUIN
100 MRGA 94556 631-E6
VIA LA CUMBRE
- CCCo 94549 591-J7
VIA LARGA
3100 CCCo 94507 632-E5
VIA LAS CRUCES
- ORIN 94563 610-J5
VIA LOMA
1400 WLCK 94598 612-E4
VIA LOS COLORADOS
3500 LFYT 94549 631-H1
VIA LOS NINOS
- WLCK 94597 612-C3
VIA LUCIA
100 CCCo 94507 632-E4
S VIA LUCIA
100 CCCo 94507 632-F6
S VIA LUCIA LN
- CCCo 94507 632-F6
VIA MAGDALENA
- LFYT 94549 611-C5
VIA MANTILLA
100 WLCK 94598 612-H2
VIA MEDIA
1000 LFYT 94549 611-D6
2100 BEN 94510 551-D4
VIA MONTANAS
900 CNCD 94518 592-H4
VIA MONTE
100 WLCK 94598 612-H2
N VIA MONTE
- WLCK 94598 612-H1
VIANNE CT
- ORIN 94563 631-A1
VIA NUEVA
- LFYT 94549 611-B6
VIA ONEG
- LFYT 94549 611-E6
VIA PAJARO
1100 LFYT 94549 611-D6
VIA PERALTA
300 CCCo 94553 572-C6
VIA PINADA LN
200 MRTZ 94553 571-F5
VIA PLANETA
200 CCCo 94553 571-J3
VIA RIALTO
- OAK 94619 650-H5
VIA ROBLE
900 LFYT 94549 611-D5
VIA ROBLES
- CCCo 94507 632-D2
VIA ROMERO
400 CCCo 94507 632-E5
VIA ROMERO LN
1600 CCCo 94507 632-E6
VIA ROYAL
400 WLCK 94597 612-B3
VIA SAN INIGO
- ORIN 94563 610-E7
VIA SERENA
100 CCCo 94507 632-F6
VIA VALENCIA
300 CCCo 94553 572-D3
VIA VAQUEROS
100 CCCo 94553 591-E2
VIA VENITO WY
1000 PIT 94565 573-J4
VIA VERDE
2500 WLCK 94598 612-H2
VIA VERDI
3700 RCH 94803 589-B2
VIA ZAPATA
7900 DBLN 94568 693-F3
VICENTE PL
- OAK 94705 630-B3
VICENTE RD
- BERK 94705 630-B4
- OAK 94705 630-B4
VICENZA CT
- DNVL 94526 653-D1
VICKI DR
1800 PLHL 94523 612-A1
VICKSBURG AV
2300 OAK 94601 650-E7
VICTOR AV
3300 OAK 94602 650-F4
3500 OAK 94619 650-F5
5200 ELCR 94530 609-B1

VICTOR AV
5200 RCH 94804 609-B1
VICTOR LN
- CCCo 94553 572-C7
- CCCo 94553 592-B1
VICTOR ST
3600 PIN 94564 569-J7
VICTORIA AV
3300 LFYT 94549 611-G6
VICTORIA CIR
- PLHL 94523 591-J4
VICTORIA CRES E
- HER 94547 569-H2
VICTORIA CRES W
- HER 94547 569-G1
VICTORIA CT
600 CCCo 94565 573-J3
900 LFYT 94549 611-G6
E VICTORIA CT
1200 SPAB 94806 588-G4
N VICTORIA CT
1400 SPAB 94806 588-G4
S VICTORIA CT
1400 SPAB 94806 588-G4
W VICTORIA CT
1200 SPAB 94806 588-G4
VICTORIA DR
- BREN 94513 616-G3
VICTORIA LN
5400 RCH 94803 589-J3
VICTORIA PK
- HER 94547 569-G1
VICTORIA PL
100 DNVL 94506 653-J4
VICTORIA ST
300 ELCR 94530 609-D4
VICTORIAN CT
- BEN 94510 551-D5
VICTORIAN LN
300 DNVL 94526 633-A6
VICTORINE RD
2000 CCCo 94551 675-D2
VICTORY AV
100 PIT 94565 574-D3
VICTORY CIR
- SRMN 94582 673-F2
VICTORY CT
- SRMN 94582 673-F2
VICTORY HWY
19200 SaCo 94571 576-A1
VICTORY LN
1100 CNCD 94518 592-E5
1100 CNCD 94520 592-D5
VIDA DESCANSADA
- ORIN 94563 610-G5
VIEJO VISTA
- CCCo 94507 632-D2
VIELA CT
1000 LFYT 94549 611-J5
VIERA AV
1400 CCCo 94509 575-H5
2100 ANT 94509 575-H6
VIERA CT
2100 ANT 94509 575-H6
VIERRA WY
100 HER 94547 570-B6
VIEW DR
900 RCH 94803 589-C1
900 RCH 94803 569-C7
3000 ANT 94509 575-C7
3000 ANT 94509 595-D1
7100 ELCR 94530 589-C7
VIEW LN
- CCCo 94596 612-E6
E VIEW PL
2100 MRTZ 94553 572-B7
VIEWCREST CT
4300 OAK 94619 650-J7
VIEWCREST DR
6100 OAK 94619 650-J7
VIEWMONT ST
300 BEN 94510 551-C4
VIEWPOINT CT
- DNVL 94506 654-B6
6400 MRTZ 94553 591-H3
VIEWPOINT DR
200 DNVL 94506 654-B6
VIEWPOINTE BLVD
600 CCCo 94572 569-J2
1000 CCCo 94572 570-A1
VIGNOLA CT
- OAKL 94561 576-H7
VIKING DR
- PLHL 94523 592-B3
VIKING PL
200 CCCo 94507 633-C4
VIKING WY
- PIT 94565 573-J3
VILI WY
500 PLHL 94523 592-A3
VILLA CT
100 CCCo 94549 611-H1
VILLA DR
- SPAB 94806 588-J4
VILLA LN
800 MRGA 94556 631-C6
VILLA TER
900 BREN 94513 616-G1
N VILLA WY
900 CCCo 94595 612-B6
S VILLA WY
1900 CCCo 94595 612-B7
VILLAGE CT
100 WLCK 94596 612-D5
VILLAGE CTR
- LFYT 94549 611-D6
VILLAGE DR
100 BREN 94513 596-G7
500 ELCR 94530 609-E3
VILLAGE LN
- BEN 94510 551-D5
- RCH 94801 588-G6
VILLAGE LP
200 DNVL 94526 653-A3
VILLAGE PKWY
- HER 94547 569-F3
6800 DBLN 94568 693-H4
8200 SRMN 94583 693-H1
VILLAGE PL
200 MRTZ 94553 571-G5
VILLAGE RD
3500 CNCD 94519 592-J1
3600 CNCD 94519 573-A7
3600 CNCD 94519 593-A1
VILLAGE WK
- RCH 94801 588-G6
VILLAGE WY
- RCH 94801 588-G6
VILLAGE GATE RD
- ORIN 94563 610-G7
VILLAGE OAKS DR
900 MRTZ 94553 571-H6
VILLAGE SQUARE PL
- PLHL 94523 592-D7

VILLAGE VIEW CT
- ORIN 94563 610-G6
11300 DBLN 94568 693-E3
VILLANOVA DR
- CCCo 94516 630-F6
- OAK 94611 630-F6
VILLANOVA LN
- CCCo 94516 630-F6
- OAK 94611 630-F6
VILLA NUEVA DR
1000 ELCR 94530 609-E1
VINCENT DR
- CCCo 94513 597-C5
2800 PIN 94564 570-A7
VINCENT RD
3100 PLHL 94523 592-D7
VINCENT ST
1600 PIT 94565 574-E3
VINCENTE AV
400 BERK 94707 609-F5
VINCENTE RD
1700 CNCD 94519 592-H2
VINDARA LN
- SRMN 94582 674-D3
VINE
- CCCo 94561 597-A3
VINE AV
- CCCo 94805 589-C6
- RCH 94801 608-D1
800 CCCo 94553 571-F4
VINE LN
1400 CCCo 94507 632-E3
1900 CCCo 94509 575-H5
2500 BERK 94708 609-H7
VINE ST
- BERK 94708 609-G7
1700 BERK 94703 609-G7
1800 BERK 94709 609-G7
VINE HILL N
200 MRTZ 94553 591-G2
VINE HILL S
- CCCo 94553 571-J3
300 CCCo 94553 572-C6
VINE HILL LN
600 SRMN 94582 673-J7
VINE HILL LP
- CCCo 94553 571-H3
VINE HILL RD
- CCCo 94553 571-H3
VINEHILL RD
2800 OAKL 94561 576-A7
VINE HILL WY
400 MRTZ 94553 571-F7
500 MRTZ 94553 591-F1
VINETA CT
5600 MRTZ 94553 591-G1
VINEWOOD CT
- PIT 94565 573-G4
VINEWOOD DR
400 OAKL 94561 596-F1
VINEWOOD WY
4800 ANT 94531 595-J3
VINEYARD CT
100 PLHL 94523 592-A4
VINEYARD DR
- OAKL 94561 596-E2
1600 ANT 94509 575-J5
VINTAGE CT
3800 CNCD 94518 592-J4
VINTAGE DR
1200 OAKL 94561 596-E3
VINTAGE PKWY
800 OAKL 94561 576-C5
VIOLA CT
- BREN 94513 616-H5
VIOLA PL
- CNCD 94518 592-H6
VIOLA ST
2600 OAK 94619 650-E6
VIOLET CT
2800 ANT 94531 575-G7
VIOLET RD
100 HER 94547 570-A4
VIOLET WY
1500 PLHL 94523 592-C4
VIOLETTA CT
- CCCo 94582 674-B1
VIONA AV
600 OAK 94610 650-A3
VIRDEN AV
3700 OAK 94619 650-F5
VIRGIL CT
- CCCo 94565 573-F1
VIRGIL ST
400 CCCo 94565 573-F1
VIRGIL WILLIAMS TR
100 CCCo 94526 652-G1
100 CCCo 94583 652-G1
VIRGINIA AV
500 RCH 94804 608-F1
4300 OAK 94619 650-F7
VIRGINIA CIR
200 MRTZ 94553 591-H4
VIRGINIA CT
- CCCo 94596 612-F6
100 CCCo 94507 633-C5
1100 CNCD 94520 592-E4
VIRGINIA DR
- ORIN 94563 631-A2
- CCCo 94565 573-F3
2500 CCCo 94561 596-G4
VIRGINIA LN
100 CCCo 94507 633-C4
1100 CNCD 94520 592-E4
VIRGINIA ST
200 CCCo 94525 550-C4
100 CCCo 94507 633-C4
VIRGINIA WY
400 MRTZ 94553 591-H4
VIRGINIA HILLS DR
100 MRTZ 94553 591-H4
VIRGO RD
6200 OAK 94611 630-D6
VIRMAR AV
5800 OAK 94618 630-A5
VISALIA AV
1300 RCH 94801 588-G5
1500 ALB 94706 609-F5
1500 BERK 94707 609-F5
VISION LN
- BREN 94513 596-D5
VISTA AV
- PDMT 94611 650-B1
VISTA CT
- RCH 94806 568-H5
400 BEN 94510 551-B4
S VISTA CT
2700 ANT 94509 575-B6
VISTA DR
- RCH 94806 568-H5
- DNVL 94526 653-B2
VISTA LN
- CCCo 94507 632-D2
VISTA PL
2900 ANT 94509 575-B7

VISTA PL
11500 DBLN 94568 693-F3
VISTA RD
1400 ELCR 94530 589-E7
VISTA ST
1500 OAK 94602 650-D3
VISTA TR
- CCCo 94583 652-E2
VISTA WY
100 MRTZ 94553 571-E5
2800 ANT 94509 575-B6
VISTA BELLA
1000 LFYT 94549 611-G4
VISTA CHARONOAKS
3600 WLCK 94598 613-A2
VISTA DEL DIABLO
100 DNVL 94526 633-C6
800 MRTZ 94553 591-F4
VISTA DEL MAR
- OAK 94611 630-E6
- ORIN 94563 610-F5
200 SRFL 94901 587-A2
VISTA DEL MAR CT
100 ORIN 94563 610-F5
VISTA DEL MAR PL
- ORIN 94563 610-F5
VISTA DEL MONTE
2400 CNCD 94520 592-F4
VISTA DEL MORAGA
- ORIN 94563 630-J3
VISTA DEL ORINDA
- ORIN 94563 610-E7
VISTA DEL RIO
300 CCCo 94553 572-C6
1800 CCCo 94525 550-B5
VISTA DIABLO
3900 PIT 94565 574-B6
VISTA GLEN PL
200 MRTZ 94553 591-G2
VISTA GRANDE
- CCCo 94528 633-E7
300 CCCo 94553 572-C6
VISTA GRANDE DR
- ANT 94531 595-J5
4700 ANT 94531 596-A3
VISTA GRANDE ST
2200 DNVL 94526 653-B2
VISTA HEIGHTS RD
600 RCH 94805 589-D7
VISTA HERMOSA
- WLCK 94597 612-B4
VISTA HILLS CT
3200 ANT 94531 595-H1
VISTAMONT AV
500 BERK 94708 609-H4
VISTAMONT CT
500 BERK 94708 609-H4
VISTA MONTE DR
- SRMN 94582 673-J7
- SRMN 94582 693-J1
VISTA OAKS DR
3400 MRTZ 94553 571-E6
VISTA POINT CT
5300 CNCD 94521 593-D7
VISTA POINT LN
1100 CNCD 94521 593-D7
VISTA POINTE CIR
1000 SRMN 94582 673-F2
VISTA POINTE DR
800 SRMN 94582 673-F2
VISTA RIDGE CT
- CNCD 94518 592-J4
VISTA VIA
- LFYT 94549 611-H6
VITA CT
- PLHL 94523 612-A1
VITALE ST
1200 OAKL 94561 596-J1
VITRUVIUS CT
- OAKL 94561 576-H7
- OAKL 94561 596-H1
VIVA LN
1300 CNCD 94518 592-J3
VIVIAN DR
- PLHL 94523 592-C5
E VIVIAN DR
- PLHL 94523 592-C5
VIVIAN ST
- BREN 94513 596-H7
VOERT CT
2000 WLCK 94598 612-G3
VOLATILE DR
- CCCo 94553 571-H3
VOLCANIC TR
- CCCo 94563 630-F4
VOLPALA CT
- BREN 94513 616-C1
VOLTERRA CT
- DNVL 94526 653-D1
VOLZ CT
100 CCCo 94507 632-G6
VOMAC CT
8100 DBLN 94568 693-G3
VOMAC RD
7900 DBLN 94568 693-G3
W VOMAC RD
11800 DBLN 94568 693-F2
VON DOLLEN CT
2900 PIN 94564 569-H6

W

W ST
- BEN 94510 551-D4
WABASH PL
400 DNVL 94526 653-C5
WADE CT
6200 PLE 94588 694-A7
WADI RUN
100 HER 94547 569-H4
WAGGLE CT
- RCH 94806 568-H5
WAGNER RD
- LFYT 94549 611-E5
WAGNER ST
- BEN 94510 551-F1
WAGNER RANCH RD
300 ORIN 94563 610-E5
WAGON CT
4500 ANT 94531 595-J3
4500 ANT 94531 596-A3
WAGON TRAIL WY
- ANT 94531 596-A2
WAGON WHEEL WY
5000 ANT 94531 595-H4
WAGONWHEEL WY
4900 RCH 94803 590-A3
WAINFLEET CT
900 ANT 94509 575-C7
WAINGARTH WY
800 DNVL 94526 633-C6
WAINWRIGHT ST
800 BEN 94510 550-J4
800 BEN 94510 551-A4

WAKEFIELD AV
2500 OAK 94606 650-B5
WAKEFIELD CT
- BREN 94513 616-A2
- CCCo 94506 654-B4
WAKEFIELD DR
- MRGA 94556 631-C5
WALAVISTA AV
500 OAK 94610 650-B2
WALBROOK CT
800 WLCK 94598 612-H3
WALDALE CT
- WLCK 94597 612-B3
WALDAMAR CT
1100 CCCo 94517 614-A3
WALDECK CT
- OAK 94611 650-G2
WALDEN RD
1200 WLCK 94597 612-C3
1200 CCCo 94597 612-C3
WALDIE PZ
100 ANT 94509 575-C3
WALDO AV
100 PDMT 94611 630-B7
100 PDMT 94611 650-B1
6300 ELCR 94530 609-D3
WALDO LN
7300 ELCR 94530 609-D3
WALDON ST
100 BREN 94513 616-J2
WALES CT
100 CCCo 94506 654-A4
1500 CNCD 94521 593-D4
WALES DR
- WLCK 94595 632-A2
WALFORD DR
100 MRGA 94556 651-E2
WALHAVEN CT
700 WLCK 94598 612-G3
WALKER AV
700 OAK 94610 650-A3
1000 WLCK 94596 612-D5
WALKER CT
700 BREN 94513 616-J2
5200 ANT 94531 595-J5
WALL AV
3300 RCH 94804 588-J7
3700 RCH 94804 589-A7
4100 RCH 94804 609-A1
5100 ELCR 94530 609-B1
WALL ST
2100 ELCR 94530 589-B7
2100 ELCR 94530 609-B1
WALLABI CT
- LFYT 94549 631-G4
WALLABY CT
4300 ANT 94531 595-H3
WALLACE CT
1400 PIN 94564 569-D5
2300 ANT 94509 574-J7
WALLACE DR
5900 CLAY 94517 593-G6
WALLACE LN
- DBLN 94568 693-E5
WALLACE RD
100 PDMT 94610 650-B2
WALLACE ST
2400 OAK 94606 650-B5
WALLEN LN
- OAKL 94561 596-F3
WALLER AV
100 CCCo 94595 612-C6
100 WLCK 94595 612-C6
3300 RCH 94804 588-J7
3800 RCH 94804 589-A7
WALLER RD
- WLCK 94596 612-C6
WALLIN CT
2600 WLCK 94597 612-C2
WALMSLEY ST
- DBLN 94568 694-A3
WALNUT
- BEN 94510 551-B6
WALNUT AV
500 MRTZ 94553 571-E6
1400 WLCK 94598 612-F3
1500 CCCo 94509 575-H5
3300 CNCD 94519 592-H2
3700 CNCD 94519 593-A2
WALNUT BLVD
1100 CCCo 94513 616-G7
2100 WLCK 94597 612-D3
2100 WLCK 94598 612-D3
2500 WLCK 94596 612-D4
3000 BREN 94513 616-F1
3000 CCCo 94596 612-E6
3600 CCCo 94513 (636-G1 See Page 635)
3600 CCCo 94514 (636-G4 See Page 635)
3600 CCCo 94517 (636-G2 See Page 635)
7700 CCCo 94551 (636-D7 See Page 635)
WALNUT CT
- CCCo 94596 612-E5
100 HER 94547 569-J4
100 HER 94547 570-A4
WALNUT DR
600 OAKL 94561 576-E7
1000 LFYT 94549 611-G6
WALNUT LN
3200 LFYT 94549 631-G1
WALNUT PL
1600 CNCD 94519 592-J2
WALNUT ST
- DBLN 94568 694-D3
900 MRTZ 94553 571-F4
900 CCCo 94553 571-F4
1100 BERK 94707 609-G7
1200 BERK 94709 609-G7
1700 ELCR 94530 609-C1
3600 LFYT 94549 611-E6
3900 OAK 94619 650-E7
WALNUT WY
4300 PIT 94565 574-E7
WALNUT CREEK CT
200 CCCo 94506 654-C5
WALNUT GROVE CT
1800 OAKL 94561 596-C1
WALNUT HEIGHTS LN
1600 CNCD 94519 592-H2
WALNUT MEADOWS CT
100 OAKL 94561 576-E6
WALNUT MEADOWS DR
1200 OAKL 94561 576-D5
WALNUT RANCH WY
700 OAKL 94561 576-D4
WALNUT SHADOWS CT
2000 CNCD 94518 592-F7
WALNUT VIEW PL
500 CCCo 94597 612-B5
500 WLCK 94597 612-B5

WALTER AV
600 PIN 94564 569-C4
WALTER WY
- ANT 94509 575-D5
WALTER COSTA TR
1000 LFYT 94549 611-C4
WALTERS WY
- CNCD 94518 592-F4
2300 CNCD 94520 592-F4
WALTHAM RD
1500 CNCD 94520 592-E3
WALTON CT
2900 PIN 94564 570-A7
WALTON LN
1200 ANT 94509 575-D7
WALTRIP LN
2600 CNCD 94518 592-G6
WANDA LN
- ORIN 94563 610-J6
WANDA ST
1100 CCCo 94525 550-C4
WANDA WY
- CCCo 94553 591-E2
WANDEL DR
- MRGA 94556 651-E1
- MRGA 94556 631-E7
WANFLETE CT
- ORIN 94563 631-B5
WANLASS AV
1900 SPAB 94806 588-H1
WANO ST
500 MRTZ 94553 571-E4
WANSTEAD CT
3200 WLCK 94598 612-J3
WARBLER DR
3800 ANT 94509 594-J1
WARD AV
7400 ELCR 94530 609-E5
WARD CT
- PLHL 94523 592-A5
WARD DR
2100 CCCo 94596 612-E7
WARD LN
3100 OAK 94602 650-D6
WARD ST
200 MRTZ 94553 571-D3
WARD WY
2600 CNCD 94518 592-G6
WARDLOW LN
1600 CNCD 94521 593-B2
WARFIELD AV
700 OAK 94610 650-A2
1100 PDMT 94610 650-A2
WARFIELD DR
- MRGA 94556 631-C4
WARFORD TER
- ORIN 94563 610-J7
WARHOL WY
- OAKL 94561 576-G7
- PLHL 94523 592-C7
WARMCASTLE CT
300 MRTZ 94553 571-J6
WARM SPRINGS CT
1900 WLCK 94595 632-B1
WARNER CT
1200 LFYT 94549 611-J4
WARNER LN
2700 PLHL 94523 592-C7
WARREN DR
1800 CCCo 94801 588-F3
WARREN FRWY Rt#-13
- OAK - 630-C6
- OAK - 650-F3
300 OAK - 630-C6
WARREN LN
2400 WLCK 94597 612-B3
WARREN RD
2300 CCCo 94595 612-A6
WARREN ST
- MRTZ 94553 571-E3
WARREN WY
- PIT 94565 574-C3
WARRENTON CT
3000 PLE 94588 694-F6
WARWICK CT
- LFYT 94549 631-J3
100 CCCo 94507 632-J2
WARWICK DR
100 WLCK 94598 612-F3
100 BEN 94510 551-B3
WASDEN CT
2400 WLCK 94598 592-F7
WASHINGTON AV
- RCH 94801 588-B6
100 RCH 94801 608-D1
700 ALB 94710 609-C6
700 ALB 94706 609-C6
1400 BERK 94707 609-E5
WASHINGTON BLVD
1300 CNCD 94521 593-E6
WASHINGTON CT
200 RCH 94801 608-C1
WASHINGTON DR
- BREN 94513 596-F7
WASHINGTON LN
- ORIN 94563 610-F4
WASHINGTON ST
- BEN 94510 551-E6
- CCCo 94553 571-F3
- CCCo 94565 573-H2
3800 CCCo 94514 637-D3
WASHINGTON WY
2200 ANT 94509 574-J7
2200 ANT 94509 575-A7
WASHOE WY
3100 PLE 94588 694-G7
WASSEN CT
600 BREN 94513 596-F7
WATCHWOOD CT
- ORIN 94563 610-G7
WATCHWOOD RD
600 ORIN 94563 610-G7
WATER ST
- BREN 94513 596-C6
- CCCo 94565 573-E2
200 RCH 94801 608-C1
WATERBERRY CT
- PLHL 94523 591-J6
- PLHL 94523 592-A6
WATERBIRD WY
2400 CCCo 94553 571-J2
2400 CCCo 94553 572-A2
WATERBURY PL
- SRMN 94583 673-E6
WATERCRESS PL
- SRMN 94582 673-G2
WATERFALL WY
1200 CNCD 94521 593-B4
WATERFORD CT
400 OAKL 94561 576-G7
8600 DBLN 94568 693-F2
WATERFORD LN
3700 WLCK 94598 613-A3

WATERFORD PL
100 PIN 94564 569-B5
WATERFORD WY
4500 OAKL 94561 576-G7
4900 ANT 94531 596-A4
WATERFRONT RD
- CCCo 94553 571-H1
- MRTZ 94553 571-H1
1100 CCCo 94553 572-A1
1500 CCCo 94520 572-A1
1700 CCCo 94520 552-C7
WATERHOUSE RD
3900 OAK 94602 650-D3
WATERLILY CT
- CCCo 94582 674-B2
WATERLILY DR
- CCCo 94582 674-B2
WATERLILY WY
1300 CNCD 94521 593-B5
WATERLOO CT
1200 CNCD 94518 592-E6
WATERLOO DR
- OAK 94611 650-G1
WATERLOO PL
- MRGA 94556 631-E6
WATERMAN CIR
100 DNVL 94526 653-C6
WATERMAN CT
200 DNVL 94526 653-C6
WATERMARK TER
- HER 94547 569-H1
WATERMILL RD
- SRMN 94582 674-B3
WATER OAK CT
4400 CNCD 94521 593-B5
N WATER OAK CT
4300 CNCD 94521 593-B5
WATERPERRY PL
- DBLN 94568 694-H3
WATERSIDE PL
- CCCo 94511 577-E4
WATERVALE WY
- SRMN 94582 674-C4
WATERVIEW DR
- RCH 94804 608-H3
WATERVIEW PL
300 CCCo 94565 573-D2
WATERVIEW TER
100 VAL 94591 550-D2
WATERVIEW WY
- RCH 94804 608-H3
WATERVILLE DR
- BREN 94513 616-A2
WATERWORLD PKWY
1500 CCCo 94520 592-D2
WATKINGS WY
- ANT 94531 595-D4
WATKINS LN
- WLCK 94596 612-D5
WATKINS ST
1300 BERK 94706 609-E7
WATSON CT
- BEN 94510 551-B1
WATSON CT E
2900 CNCD 94518 592-H5
WATSON CT W
2800 CNCD 94518 592-G5
WATSON CANYON CT
700 SRMN 94582 673-F2
WATSONIA CT
- CCCo 94582 674-A2
WATSONIA DR
- CCCo 94582 674-A2
WAVERLY CIR
- HER 94547 569-H1
WAVERLY CT
- CCCo 94507 632-J5
100 MRTZ 94553 591-J4
WAVERLY DR
- RCH 94806 568-J6
- RCH 94806 569-A6
WAVERLY RD
6500 MRTZ 94553 591-H4
WAVERLY WY
1400 PIT 94565 574-F5
WAWONA AV
800 OAK 94610 650-B2
WAWONA CIR
100 MRTZ 94553 571-F6
WAWONA CT
- ANT 94531 595-F5
400 CLAY 94517 593-J6
WAWONA LN
400 CLAY 94517 593-J5
WAXWING WY
- ANT 94509 594-J1
WAYFARER CT
2500 CCCo 94514 617-H7
WAYFARER DR
2300 CCCo 94514 617-J7
WAYLAND LN
100 CCCo 94507 632-F6
WAYNE AV
100 CCCo 94507 632-G7
200 CCCo 94507 652-G1
WAYNE DR
100 CCCo 94597 612-C1
WAYNE ST
2300 MRTZ 94553 571-F5
WAY POINTS RD
- DNVL 94526 652-H2
WAYSIDE PZ
3100 CCCo 94597 612-D1
WEATHERLY CT
- DNVL 94506 653-H6
100 BREN 94513 616-E2
WEATHERLY DR
- CLAY 94517 613-J2
WEATHERLY LN
- CCCo 94553 572-A5
WEATHERLY PL
600 SRMN 94583 673-F6
WEATHERMARK CT
100 VAL 94591 550-F3
WEAVER CT
2000 CNCD 94518 592-F7
WEAVER LN
800 CNCD 94518 592-F7
800 WLCK 94598 592-F7
WEAVER PL
5600 OAK 94619 651-A6
WEBB LN
900 LFYT 94549 611-E7
1500 WLCK 94595 612-C7
WEBBER CT
5000 ANT 94531 595-D4
WEBSTER DR
500 MRTZ 94553 591-G3
WEBSTER ST
2800 BERK 94705 630-A4
WEDGEWOOD CT
800 PLHL 94523 591-J7
800 PIT 94565 573-J3

STREET / Block City ZIP Pg-Grid

WEDGEWOOD DR
700 PIT 94565 574-A3
800 PIT 94565 573-J3
N WEDGEWOOD RD
- SRMN 94582 673-J2
S WEDGEWOOD RD
- CCCo 94582 673-J2
WEE BLYTHEN
- OAK 94619 650-J4
WEE DONEGAL
600 CCCo 94549 591-H4
WEEPING SPRUCE CT
4400 CNCD 94521 593-B5
N WEEPING SPRUCE CT
4300 CNCD 94521 593-B5
WEEPING WILLOW WY
- BREN 94513 596-G7
WEIBEL CIR
900 OAKL 94561 576-D5
WEINER WY
2100 SRMN 94582 653-J7
WEISS
100 HER 94547 569-E3
WEISS CT
100 HER 94547 569-E3
WELCH CT
- CNCD 94520 572-F6
WELCH WY
3900 ANT 94531 595-G1
WELCOME AV
- CNCD 94518 592-G4
2300 RCH 94804 588-H7
WELDON AV
400 OAK 94610 650-A2
WELDON CT
300 BEN 94510 551-A2
WELDON ST
1000 CCCo 94565 573-F2
WELFORD RANCH CT
- SRMN 94583 673-E6
WELLBORNE CT
900 WLCK 94597 612-A2
WELLE RD
- CCCo 94525 550-E5
WELLER CT
- PLHL 94523 592-A7
- PLHL 94523 612-A1
WELLER LN
- DNVL 94526 653-A1
WELLESLEY AV
600 CCCo 94708 609-F3
WELLESLEY CT
- LFYT 94549 611-B3
WELLESLEY DR
- CCCo 94549 611-B3
- CCCo 94553 611-B3
- LFYT 94549 611-B3
WELLFLEET DR
100 VAL 94591 550-E1
WELLFLEET PL
- MRTZ 94553 572-A6
WELLINGTON AV
100 CCCo 94520 572-G1
WELLINGTON CT
2600 CCCo 94520 572-G2
WELLINGTON LN
100 CCCo 94507 632-J2
100 CCCo 94507 633-A2
WELLINGTON PL
- VAL 94591 550-D2
4000 CCCo 94549 611-J1
WELLINGTON ST
1000 OAK 94602 650-C3
1000 OAK 94610 650-C3
WELLS LN
- CCCo 94561 577-E5
WELLS RD
3600 CCCo 94561 577-D5
WELSH CT
2300 WLCK 94598 612-G2
WELWYN PL
3000 WLCK 94598 612-J1
WEMBLY DR
100 DNVL 94526 653-A5
WENDELL AV
2300 RCH 94804 588-H5
WENDELL LN
1900 PLHL 94523 592-A7
WENDY DR
1500 PLHL 94523 592-D5
WENDY LN
- LFYT 94563 611-B7
WENK AV
5900 RCH 94804 609-C2
WENTE CT
4600 OAKL 94561 576-D7
WENTWORTH CT
- BREN 94513 616-B1
WERNER CT
5000 OAK 94602 650-F3
WESLEY AV
500 OAK 94606 650-A3
600 OAK 94610 650-A3
1700 ELCR 94530 609-C1
WESLEY CT
1000 WLCK 94597 612-C1
1500 CNCD 94521 593-A2
WESLEY WY
700 OAK 94610 650-A3
3800 CCCo 94803 589-D2
WEST BLVD
- PIT 94565 574-C4
WEST CIR
- OAK 94611 630-F7
WEST CT
3600 RCH 94806 568-J7
3600 RCH 94806 569-A7
WEST LN
- OAK 94618 630-A5
WEST PL
1000 ALB 94706 609-F7
WEST RD
3600 LFYT 94549 611-E6
WEST ST
- CCCo 94525 550-D4
300 PIT 94565 574-D1
1500 CNCD 94521 593-A2
1600 CNCD 94519 593-A2
WEST TER
3300 LFYT 94549 631-G1
WEST WY
- ORIN 94563 610-G5
WESTAIRE BLVD
400 MRTZ 94553 571-G5
WESTAIRE CT
300 MRTZ 94553 571-G5
WESTBOURNE CT
- DNVL 94506 654-A6
WESTBOURNE DR
3100 ANT 94509 575-E7
WESTBRIAR KNOLLS
100 DNVL 94526 632-H7
WESTBROOK CT
- CLAY 94517 593-F5

WESTBROOK CT
700 CCCo 94506 654-D5
2300 WLCK 94598 612-G4
WESTBURY DR
1800 CNCD 94519 592-J1
WESTCHESTER
100 MRGA 94556 651-D1
WESTCHESTER DR
2800 SRMN 94583 673-F6
WESTCHESTER PL
1600 CNCD 94519 593-A2
WESTCLIFFE CIR
300 WLCK 94597 612-D3
WESTCLIFFE LN
2200 WLCK 94597 612-C3
WESTCLIFFE PL
400 WLCK 94597 612-C3
WEST CREEK CT
- LFYT 94549 611-E6
WESTERN DR
- RCH 94801 587-J3
- RCH 94801 588-A5
- RCH 94801 608-C1
WESTERN FARMS RANCH RD
- CCCo 94514 637-J5
- CCCo 94514 638-A4
WESTERN HILLS DR
200 PLHL 94523 592-A6
WESTERN STAR PL
600 DNVL 94526 653-C5
WESTFIELD CIR
100 DNVL 94526 653-A4
WESTFIELD CT
6500 MRTZ 94553 591-H4
WESTFIELD WY
500 OAK 94619 650-H5
WESTGATE AV
2700 CNCD 94520 572-E7
WESTGATE CIR
100 SPAB 94806 588-G2
WESTGATE CT
2700 CNCD 94520 572-E7
WESTGATE DR
2200 PIT 94565 574-E4
WESTMEATH WY
- ANT 94531 596-B4
WESTMINSTER AV
- CCCo 94708 609-F3
WESTMINSTER CT
- OAKL 94561 596-D1
WESTMINSTER DR
- OAK 94618 630-A6
WESTMINSTER PL
- LFYT 94549 612-A6
4000 CCCo 94506 654-A5
WESTMONT CT
1000 PIT 94565 573-H4
WESTMORELAND CIR
1100 WLCK 94596 632-G1
WESTMORELAND CT
2200 WLCK 94596 632-G1
WESTMORELAND DR
7000 OAK 94705 630-C3
WESTON CT
2300 ANT 94531 595-F1
WESTOVER CT
- ORIN 94563 631-B5
- PLHL 94523 592-A5
WESTOVER DR
1900 PLHL 94523 592-A5
5900 OAK 94611 650-F1
6200 OAK 94611 630-F7
WESTOVER LN
500 PLHL 94523 592-A5
WESTPOINT WY
1900 BREN 94513 596-G6
WESTPORT CIR
- CCCo 94513 617-F2
WESTPORT CT
3300 WLCK 94598 612-J3
WESTPORT LN
100 VAL 94591 550-F1
WESTPORT WY
- DBLN 94568 694-E4
WESTRIDGE AV
1000 DNVL 94526 653-A4
WESTRIDGE CT
- ANT 94565 574-G7
6100 WLCK 94595 632-C5
WESTSIDE CT
2600 SRMN 94583 673-E6
WESTSIDE DR
2600 SRMN 94583 673-E6
20000 SRMN 94583 693-F1
WESTSIDE PL
- SRMN 94583 673-E7
WESTVALE CT
200 SRMN 94583 673-C3
WESTVIEW CT
800 MRTZ 94553 571-F5
WEST VIEW DR
1100 OAK 94705 630-B4
WEST VIEW PL
- OAK 94705 630-B3
WESTVIEW PL
5700 CCCo 94806 589-B4
WESTWARD LN
- DNVL 94506 653-G2
WESTWARD PL
2100 MRTZ 94553 572-A7
WESTWICH ST
100 DNVL 94506 653-J6
WEST WIND PL
- CCCo 94511 577-F4
WEST WIND RD
- LFYT 94549 611-G1
WESTWOOD AV
2800 SRMN 94583 673-F7
WESTWOOD CT
- DBLN 94568 694-D4
- OAK 94611 630-E6
- ORIN 94563 630-H1
1500 WLCK 94595 612-C7
2200 PIT 94565 573-H4
4200 CNCD 94521 593-C2
4700 RCH 94803 589-E2
WESTWOOD DR
- CCCo 94583 672-J4
1600 CNCD 94521 593-B2
WESTWOOD LN
2200 PIT 94565 573-H4
WESTWOOD WY
- OAK 94611 630-E6
4900 ANT 94531 595-J4
WETMORE RD
3000 OAK 94613 650-H7
WETTERHORN CT
4400 CNCD 94518 593-A6
WETZEL RD
- CCCo 94513 615-H4
- CCCo 94517 615-H4
WEXFORD CT
8200 DBLN 94568 693-G2

WEXFORD DR
2700 CNCD 94519 572-H6
WEXFORD ST
- BREN 94513 616-H3
WEXLER PEAK WY
4700 ANT 94531 595-D3
WEYBRIDGE CT
- OAK 94611 650-G2
WEYMOUTH
300 HER 94547 569-J2
WEYMOUTH CT
200 SRMN 94583 673-F5
3100 PLE 94588 694-E6
WEYRAUGH RD
- VAL 94592 549-G1
WHALER CIR
100 HER 94547 570-A6
WHARF DR
- CCCo 94565 553-D7
- CCCo 94565 573-D1
WHARF ST
800 RCH 94804 608-E2
WHARTON WY
1400 CNCD 94521 593-B4
WHATLEY CT
3200 ANT 94509 595-B1
WHEATFIELD CT
100 BREN 94513 616-E2
WHEATFIELD WY
200 BREN 94513 616-E2
WHEATMAN CT
2700 PLE 94588 694-H4
WHEELER WY
2100 ANT 94509 595-A1
WHINS CT
- RCH 94806 568-H6
WHIPPOORWILL CT
600 WLCK 94598 613-C4
2100 PIN 94564 569-F7
WHISPER CREEK CT
- BREN 94513 596-D7
WHISPERING OAKS CT
- PIT 94565 573-F5
WHISPERING OAKS DR
1200 CCCo 94506 654-C4
WHISPERING OAKS LN
4100 CCCo 94506 654-C3
WHISPERING OAKS PL
1200 CCCo 94506 654-B4
WHISPERING OAKS WY
- BREN 94513 596-G7
WHISPERING PINE CT
1100 CCCo 94517 614-F7
WHISPERING TREES CT
- CCCo 94572 569-H1
WHISPERING TREES LN
100 DNVL 94526 652-H2
WHISTLESTOP LN
- CCCo 94561 596-J3
- CCCo 94561 597-A2
WHITAKER AV
- BERK 94708 609-J6
WHITBY LN
- BREN 94513 616-A2
WHITCLIFE CT
- CCCo 94583 673-A5
WHITCOMB AV
900 LFYT 94549 611-H7
WHITE CT
- OAK 94611 630-G7
WHITE BIRCH DR
- HER 94547 569-H2
WHITE BIRCH WY
- BREN 94513 596-H7
WHITE CAP CV
- HER 94547 569-H1
WHITE CHAPEL DR
100 BEN 94510 551-B3
WHITECLIFF CT
1900 WLCK 94596 632-G1
3100 RCH 94803 589-E1
WHITECLIFF WY
1200 WLCK 94596 632-G1
1300 WLCK 94596 612-H7
4400 RCH 94803 589-E1
WHITE GATE RD
1000 CCCo 94507 633-C6
WHITEHALL CT
- OAKL 94561 596-D2
1200 WLCK 94595 632-A2
3400 PLE 94588 694-F5
WHITEHALL DR
- ORIN 94563 631-B5
WHITEHALL LN
- BREN 94513 596-H7
- BREN 94513 616-H1
WHITEHAVEN CT
700 WLCK 94598 613-A3
800 ANT 94509 575-C7
WHITEHAVEN DR
3200 WLCK 94598 612-J3
3300 WLCK 94598 613-A3
WHITEHAVEN PL
800 SRMN 94582 673-J7
WHITEHAVEN WY
200 CCCo 94553 591-D2
WHITEHOOF WY
4300 ANT 94531 595-G2
WHITE MOUNTAIN CT
- ANT 94531 595-E5
5600 MRTZ 94553 591-H2
WHITE OAK CT
400 OAKL 94561 596-G1
5100 CNCD 94521 593-D6
WHITE OAK DR
- LFYT 94549 611-A6
- ORIN 94563 611-A6
1000 CNCD 94521 593-D6
WHITE OAK PL
200 PIT 94565 574-C5
2400 CCCo 94506 653-G1
WHITE PINE LN
- LFYT 94549 611-B3
- CCCo 94506 654-A3
WHITE ROCK WY
1300 ANT 94531 595-E3
WHITE SANDS CT
4600 CCCo 94803 589-D1
WHITE SANDS PL
4700 CCCo 94803 589-D1
WHITE SANDS ST
- BREN 94513 596-B5
WHITESIDES DR
- VAL 94591 550-F2
WHITE SWAN ST
- BREN 94513 596-G7
- BREN 94513 616-G1
WHITETAIL CT
2600 ANT 94531 595-G3
WHITETAIL DR
2300 ANT 94531 595-G2
WHITETAIL LN
- SRMN 94583 673-E6

WHITETHORNE DR
100 MRGA 94556 651-E2
WHITEWOOD PL
1400 CNCD 94520 592-F2
WHITFIELD CT
- CCCo 94549 591-J7
- PLHL 94523 591-J7
WHITING CT
- MRGA 94556 631-D6
WHITMAN LN
900 CNCD 94518 592-F6
WHITMAN RD
1400 CNCD 94518 592-G5
WHITMAN TER
- MRTZ 94553 571-J5
WHITNEY CT
200 WLCK 94598 612-E3
WHITSIDE CT
- DNVL 94526 653-D3
WHITT CT
- CLAY 94517 593-G6
WHITTAKER CT
- BREN 94513 616-B1
WHITTEN LN
- LFYT 94549 611-F6
WHITTEN PL
- BREN 94513 616-C4
WHITTIER RD
100 PLHL 94523 592-A7
WHITTLE AV
3800 OAK 94602 650-E3
WHITTLE CT
- OAK 94602 650-D4
WHITWORTH DR
- DBLN 94568 694-F4
WHYTE PARK AV
2000 CCCo 94595 612-A7
WICKET CT
1500 CNCD 94518 592-E6
WICKHAM DR
1000 MRGA 94556 631-F6
WICKLOW CT
1500 WLCK 94598 612-E1
8600 DBLN 94568 693-G2
WICKLOW LN
8400 DBLN 94568 693-G2
WICKSON AV
400 OAK 94610 650-A3
WICKSON WY
200 BREN 94513 616-C3
WIDMAR CT
- CLAY 94517 613-G1
WIDMAR PL
100 CLAY 94517 613-G1
WIGET LN
100 WLCK 94598 612-H2
N WIGET LN
100 WLCK 94598 612-G1
WIGGINS CT
100 PLHL 94523 592-A4
WIGHTMAN CT
- ANT 94509 575-D6
WIGHTMAN LN
- ANT 94509 575-J5
WILART DR
2600 CCCo 94806 589-B2
2600 RCH 94806 589-B2
WILBER CIR
- ORIN 94563 630-J3
WILBUR AV
- ANT 94509 575-D4
600 CCCo 94509 575-G4
3300 ANT 94509 576-A4
3300 CCCo 94509 576-A4
WILBUR DR
400 PLHL 94523 592-A4
WILBUR LN
1400 ANT 94509 575-H5
1400 CCCo 94509 575-H5
WILBUR ST
2300 OAK 94602 650-E4
WILCOX AV
1800 SPAB 94806 588-H4
WILDBERRY CT
4400 CNCD 94521 593-B5
WILDBERRY DR
200 BREN 94513 616-D2
WILDBROOK CT
1800 CNCD 94521 593-D3
WILDCAT CIR
4500 ANT 94531 595-H2
WILDCAT CT
- BREN 94513 616-C1
1400 OAKL 94561 576-E6
11400 DBLN 94568 693-F4
WILDCAT DR
8400 ELCR 94530 589-E7
WILDCAT LN
800 BREN 94513 596-D7
800 BREN 94513 616-D1
4500 CNCD 94521 593-B4
WILD CAT WY
- CLAY 94517 593-J5
WILDCAT WY
1400 OAKL 94561 576-D6
WILDCAT CANYON PKWY
- CCCo 94805 589-C5
- RCH 94805 589-C5
WILDCAT CANYON RD
- CCCo 94553 610-B5
300 CCCo 94563 610-B5
500 BERK 94708 609-G4
500 CCCo 94708 609-H4
800 BERK 94708 610-A6
800 CCCo 94708 610-A4
WILDCAT CREEK RD
- RCH 94805 589-F7
- RCH 94805 609-G2
500 CCCo 94708 609-G2
WILDCAT CREEK TR
- RCH 94805 589-D6
WILDCROFT DR
100 MRTZ 94553 591-H2
WILD CURRANT WY
7200 OAK 94611 630-F6
WILDE AV
2500 PLE 94588 694-F6
WILDE CT
800 PIN 94564 569-C5
WILDERNESS LN
100 LFYT 94549 611-A7
WILDES CT
100 CCCo 94565 573-C1
WILDEWOOD DR
3000 CNCD 94518 592-G3
WILDFLOWER AV
100 VAL 94591 550-F1
WILD FLOWER CT
- DNVL 94526 653-E3
WILDFLOWER DR
- PLHL 94523 591-J3
2100 ANT 94509 595-F1
2200 ANT 94531 595-F1
2600 ANT 94531 575-G7

WILDFLOWER LP
- BREN 94513 616-H2
WILD FLOWER PL
500 CCCo 94507 633-C3
WILDFLOWER WY
- RCH 94806 568-J5
- RCH 94806 569-A5
200 MRTZ 94553 571-H4
3500 CNCD 94518 592-J6
WILDFLOWER VALLEY CT
- SRMN 94582 673-J6
WILDHORSE DR
2400 SRMN 94583 673-C3
WILD HORSE RD
- ANT 94531 595-J1
WILDHORSE RD
- CCCo 94561 596-J2
- CCCo 94561 597-A2
WILDING LN
- OAK 94618 630-B6
WILD IRIS WY
- BREN 94513 616-H1
WILD OAK CT
- CCCo 94596 612-G6
- CCCo 94506 654-B3
1000 CNCD 94521 593-C5
WILD OAK LN
- CCCo 94506 654-B4
WILD OAK PL
- CCCo 94506 654-B3
WILDROSE CIR
300 PIN 94564 569-C3
WILDROSE CT
- ANT 94531 596-A5
100 BREN 94513 616-F2
5200 CNCD 94521 613-D1
WILDROSE WY
600 BREN 94513 616-F3
N WILDWOOD
300 HER 94547 569-G3
S WILDWOOD
100 HER 94547 569-G4
WILDWOOD AV
- OAK 94610 650-A2
- PDMT 94610 650-A2
200 PDMT 94611 650-B2
WILDWOOD CT
- DNVL 94526 653-B4
- PLHL 94523 611-J1
2300 ANT 94509 595-A2
4600 RCH 94803 589-F1
WILDWOOD DR
- ORIN 94563 630-G1
WILDWOOD GDNS
- PDMT 94611 650-B2
WILDWOOD LN
3500 LFYT 94549 611-E6
WILDWOOD PL
- ELCR 94530 609-C1
- PLHL 94523 611-J1
4600 RCH 94803 589-F1
WILDWOOD RD
1000 DBLN 94568 694-A2
WILEY CT
- DNVL 94526 653-C6
WILKE DR
5400 CNCD 94521 593-F5
WILKIE DR
100 CCCo 94598 612-F5
WILKIE ST
4700 OAK 94619 650-G6
WILKINS LN
1600 CNCD 94519 593-A2
WILKINSON LN
3500 LFYT 94549 611-F6
WILLAMETTE AV
200 CCCo 94708 609-G3
WILLARD AV
- CCCo 94801 588-F4
200 RCH 94801 588-F4
WILLARD PL
- OAK 94705 630-B4
WILLCREST DR
1400 CNCD 94521 593-C5
WILLET ST
- HER 94547 569-F2
WILLIAM CT
- DNVL 94526 652-J2
WILLIAM WY
- PIT 94565 574-C4
1300 CNCD 94520 592-E3
WILLIAM B RUMFORD FRWY Rt#-24
- CCCo - 611-C6
- CCCo - 612-A5
- CCCo - 630-E2
- LFYT - 611-C6
- OAK - 630-E2
- ORIN - 610-H7
- ORIN - 611-C6
- ORIN - 630-E2
- WLCK - 612-A5
WILLIAM HENRY CT
- PLHL 94523 592-A4
WILLIAM HENRY WY
200 MRTZ 94553 591-F1
WILLIAM REED DR
200 ANT 94509 575-C5
WILLIAMS
1100 HER 94547 569-E3
WILLIAMS CT
- ORIN 94563 631-C5
100 BREN 94513 616-G3
WILLIAMS DR
- MRGA 94556 631-E4
500 RCH 94806 568-G7
WILLIAMS RD
- CCCo 94517 614-F6
WILLIAMSON CT
1700 MRTZ 94553 571-J6
WILLIAMSON RANCH DR
5300 ANT 94531 595-J4
WILLIS CT
3500 OAK 94619 650-G5
WILLOUGHBY CT
300 LFYT 94549 611-J6
WILLOW AV
- HER 94547 569-H3
- CCCo 94595 612-B7
700 PIT 94565 573-H4
800 CCCo 94547 569-J2
800 CCCo 94572 569-H1
2100 ANT 94509 575-H6
WILLOW CT
- PIT 94565 573-H4
500 BEN 94510 550-J1
500 BEN 94510 551-A1
WILLOW DR
- DNVL 94526 653-A3
1000 LFYT 94549 611-G6
WILLOW LN
100 CCCo 94707 609-F4

WILLOW RD
300 SPAB 94806 588-J3
300 SPAB 94806 589-A4
4400 PLE 94588 694-B7
N WILLOW RD
3600 CCCo 94511 577-E1
S WILLOW RD
4000 CCCo 94511 577-F2
WILLOW RD W
- CCCo 94511 557-D7
WILLOW ST
100 CCCo 94553 572-C7
100 CCCo 94553 592-C1
1000 MRTZ 94553 571-E3
1100 PIN 94564 569-F4
6600 ELCR 94530 609-D4
WILLOW TR
- BERK 94705 630-B4
WILLOW WY
600 OAKL 94561 596-G1
1300 CNCD 94520 592-D2
WILLOW BEND WY
- CCCo 94582 674-A2
WILLOWBROOK LN
- CCCo 94595 632-C1
WILLOWBROOK WY
4900 ANT 94531 596-A4
WILLOW CREEK CT
3700 CNCD 94518 592-J4
WILLOW CREEK DR
6500 DBLN 94568 694-A1
WILLOW CREEK LN
100 CCCo 94506 653-J4
300 MRTZ 94553 571-H6
WILLOW CREEK TER
600 BREN 94513 616-F1
WILLOW GLEN CT
4400 CNCD 94521 593-C5
N WILLOW GLEN CT
4300 CNCD 94521 593-C5
WILLOWHAVEN WY
4900 ANT 94531 595-E4
WILLOW LAKE CT
2100 MRTZ 94553 592-A1
5300 CCCo 94514 617-J4
WILLOW LAKE DR
200 MRTZ 94553 592-A1
WILLOW LAKE RD
900 CCCo 94514 617-J6
WILLOWMERE RD
- DNVL 94526 653-B1
WILLOW OAK CT
1200 PIN 94564 569-E5
1300 CCCo 94561 597-A2
WILLOWOOD CT
4400 CNCD 94521 593-C2
WILLOW PASS RD
700 CCCo 94565 574-B2
700 PIT 94565 574-B2
700 CCCo 94565 573-E2
1200 CNCD 94520 592-E2
1500 PIT 94565 573-F2
1800 CNCD 94519 592-E2
3400 CNCD 94519 572-J7
3800 CNCD 94519 573-A6
3900 CNCD 94565 573-A6
WILLOW POND CT
800 SRMN 94582 653-H7
WILLOW SPRING CT
- MRGA 94556 631-E5
WILLOW SPRING LN
- MRGA 94556 631-E5
WILLOW TREE CT
2400 MRTZ 94553 572-A6
WILLOWVIEW CT
- DNVL 94526 653-B1
5100 PLE 94588 693-J7
WILLOWWOOD CT
4400 BREN 94513 596-D7
WILLY WY
1000 CNCD 94518 592-F5
WILMINGTON DR
2100 WLCK 94596 632-G1
WILMONT CT
- ANT 94531 595-D4
WILMORE AV
800 CNCD 94518 592-G6
WILMORE CT
2700 CNCD 94518 592-H6
WILSHIRE BLVD
4100 OAK 94602 650-F4
WILSHIRE CT
100 DNVL 94526 653-D6
WILSHIRE PL
2900 CNCD 94518 592-G5
WILSON AV
300 RCH 94805 589-A5
700 CCCo 94553 571-F4
700 MRTZ 94553 571-F4
3300 OAK 94602 650-D5
WILSON CIR
- BERK 94708 610-A7
WILSON CT
- ANT 94509 575-J6
- CCCo 94507 632-F3
1600 CNCD 94521 593-B2
WILSON LN
3900 CNCD 94521 593-B2
WILSON PL
3300 OAK 94602 650-D5
WILSON RD
- CCCo 94507 632-F3
WILSON ST
- CCCo 94514 637-D2
100 ALB 94710 609-D7
2100 ANT 94509 575-J5
WILSON WY
6900 ELCR 94530 589-C7
WILTON DR
2800 OAK 94611 650-G1
WILTON PL
100 SRMN 94583 673-F6
WIMBLEDON RD
200 WLCK 94598 612-F1
WIMPOLE ST
- MRGA 94556 631-E3
WINCHESTER CT
600 CCCo 94549 591-G6
WINCHESTER DR
- OAKL 94561 596-C1
WINCHESTER LN
4600 MRTZ 94553 571-E7
WINCHESTER LP
- CCCo 94513 617-F4
WINCHESTER PL
3600 WLCK 94598 613-A3
WINDCHIME CT
700 WLCK 94598 613-A3
WINDCHIME DR
300 DNVL 94506 653-J6
WINDELER CT
- MRGA 94556 651-E1
WINDEMERE LN
- CCCo 94561 597-E1

WINDEMERE PKWY
- CCCo 94582 674-B3
- SRMN 94582 674-B3
WINDERMERE CT
4200 CNCD 94521 593-A4
WINDERMERE WY
1200 CNCD 94521 593-A4
WINDFLOWER CT
4400 CNCD 94518 593-A6
WINDHAVEN CT
- BREN 94513 596-E6
- PLHL 94523 591-H2
WINDHOVER WY
- CCCo 94553 571-J4
WINDING GN
- CCCo 94507 633-A5
WINDING LN
- ORIN 94563 610-G2
2700 ANT 94531 595-H1
WINDING WY
- CCCo 94516 630-F6
- OAK 94611 630-F6
WINDING BROOK CT
- SRMN 94582 673-J7
WINDING CREEK TER
600 BREN 94513 616-E1
WINDING CREEK WY
- SRMN 94583 673-E7
WINDING TRAIL LN
- DBLN 94568 693-F4
WINDING TRAIL PL
- DBLN 94568 693-F6
WINDJAMMER CT
- RCH 94804 608-E3
WINDMEADOWS DR
800 BREN 94513 616-E2
WINDMILL CT
- SRMN 94583 673-E6
- BREN 94513 616-E2
700 CNCD 94518 592-J6
WINDMILL WY
3500 CNCD 94518 592-J6
WINDMILL CANYON DR
3000 CLAY 94517 593-J5
3000 CLAY 94517 594-A5
WINDMILL CANYON PL
300 CLAY 94517 593-J5
WINDOVER DR
100 DNVL 94506 653-G2
WINDOVER TER
- DNVL 94506 653-G2
WINDSHADOW CT
100 VAL 94591 550-F2
WINDSONG CT
800 WLCK 94598 613-B3
WINDSONG WY
3300 LFYT 94549 611-G2
WINDSOR
600 HER 94547 569-J2
WINDSOR AV
- CCCo 94708 609-F3
WINDSOR CT
- DNVL 94506 653-H5
500 OAKL 94561 576-C6
3100 LFYT 94549 611-J6
3400 PLE 94588 694-E5
WINDSOR DR
1000 LFYT 94549 611-J6
2700 ANT 94509 575-E7
WINDSOR LN
2200 OAKL 94561 576-C6
WINDSOR PL
3100 CNCD 94518 592-G3
7600 DBLN 94568 694-B2
WINDSOR WY
1300 BREN 94513 596-H7
4600 RCH 94803 589-E2
9900 SRMN 94583 673-F5
WINDSTREAM PL
200 DNVL 94526 652-J2
200 DNVL 94526 653-A1
WINDSURFER CT
100 VAL 94591 550-G2
WINDSWEEP RD
- CCCo 94511 577-F4
WINDTREE CT
2900 LFYT 94549 611-J7
WINDWARD CT
100 VAL 94591 550-F3
700 CCCo 94572 570-A2
1900 CCCo 94514 617-G6
WINDWARD DR
700 CCCo 94572 570-A2
700 CCCo 94572 569-J2
WINDWARD PT
2000 CCCo 94514 617-G7
WINDWARD RD
- DNVL 94526 652-H2
WINDWARD WY
- RCH 94804 608-H3
- LFYT 94549 631-J3
100 SRFL 94901 587-A3
WINDWARD HILL
- OAK 94618 630-C4
WINDWOOD CT
1400 MRTZ 94553 571-J6
WINDWOOD DR
- PIT 94565 573-G5
WINDY PEAK CT
- ANT 94531 595-E5
WINDY SPRINGS LN
- BREN 94513 596-D5
WINDY VALE CT
- BREN 94513 596-E6
WINDY VALE LN
- BREN 94513 596-E6
WINE ST
500 RCH 94801 608-D1
WINEBERRY DR
- SRMN 94582 673-G2
WINEBERRY WY
7000 DBLN 94568 693-H2
WINESAP DR
- BREN 94513 616-D2
WINESTONE CT
100 CCCo 94507 633-A6
300 WLCK 94598 613-A3
WINFIELD LN
- DNVL 94526 652-J1
- CCCo 94595 632-D2
WINGED TER
300 SRMN 94582 673-G2
WINGED FOOT CT
- SRMN 94583 673-H7
WINGED FOOT PL
100 SRMN 94583 673-H7
WINGED FOOT RD
- BREN 94513 616-B4
WINGFIELD WY
- BEN 94510 551-C5
WING FOOT
- MRGA 94556 631-C7
WING SET PL
200 CCCo 94507 632-H3

STREET
Block City ZIP Pg-Grid

WINIFRED CT
- ANT 94509 575-E4
WINIFRED WY
100 SPAB 94806 588-J3
WINN CT
- SRMN 94583 673-F7
WINNERS CIR
2700 CCCo 94507 632-E4
WINSFORD CT
- CCCo 94583 673-A5
WINSHIP LN
- CCCo 94595 632-C2
WINSLOW PL
- MRGA 94556 631-D6
- SRMN 94583 673-E6
WINSLOW ST
100 CCCo 94525 550-E4
WINSOR AV
1000 OAK 94610 650-B2
1000 PDMT 94610 650-B2
WINSTON CT
500 BEN 94510 550-J1
WINSTON DR
500 PLHL 94523 592-A5
WINTER WY
1100 PIT 94565 573-J2
WINTERBERRY CT
- SRMN 94583 673-H3
4400 CNCD 94521 593-C5
N WINTERBERRY CT
4300 CNCD 94521 593-C5
WINTERBROOK AV
- DBLN 94568 694-D3
WINTERBROOK DR
3000 CCCo 94565 573-F2
WINTERGLEN WY
5000 ANT 94531 595-J3
5000 ANT 94531 596-A3
WINTERGREEN DR
300 BREN 94513 616-D2
WINTERGREEN LN
600 WLCK 94598 592-H7
WINTER HARBOR PL
100 VAL 94591 550-F1
WINTERHAVEN CT
- SRMN 94583 693-H1
WINTER HILLS CT
- SRMN 94583 673-H3
WINTERLEAF CT
- SRMN 94583 673-H3
WINTERRUN DR
- SRMN 94583 673-H3
WINTERSET WY
- SRMN 94583 673-H3
WINTERSIDE CIR
700 SRMN 94583 673-F4
WINTERSIDE CT
- SRMN 94583 673-H3
WINTERWIND CIR
300 SRMN 94583 673-H3
WINTERWIND CT
- SRMN 94583 673-H3
WINTERWOOD CT
- DNVL 94526 653-C6
WINTHROP AV
2800 SRMN 94583 673-F7
WINTHROP ST
3300 CNCD 94519 572-G6
WINTON DR
1000 WLCK 94598 612-F1
1100 CNCD 94518 592-F7
1100 CNCD 94518 612-F1
WIRTHMAN LN
- CCCo 94517 635-A6
WISCONSIN CT
5500 CNCD 94521 593-E6
WISCONSIN ST
3000 OAK 94602 650-F4
3500 OAK 94619 650-F5
WISNER DR
1300 ANT 94509 575-E5
WISTARIA WY
- PDMT 94611 650-C2
WISTERIA CT
- OAKL 94561 576-C7
WISTERIA ST
6900 SRMN 94583 693-H1
WISWALL CT
3100 RCH 94806 589-B1
WISWALL DR
2700 RCH 94806 589-B2
WITHEROW WY
- ANT 94531 595-D4
WITHERS AV
100 PLHL 94523 611-J1
100 PLHL 94523 612-A1
3000 CCCo 94549 611-J1
3100 CCCo 94549 591-H7
3200 LFYT 94549 591-H7
WITHERSED LN
3300 WLCK 94598 612-J3
WITTENMEYER CT
- ANT 94531 595-D4
WITTENMYER CT
4900 MRTZ 94553 572-A6
WOLCOTT LN
200 CCCo 94553 571-B3
WOLF WY
4400 ANT 94531 595-H3
4800 CNCD 94521 593-C4
WOLFE RD
- BREN 94513 616-D4
WOLLAM AV
400 CCCo 94565 573-H3
WOLVERINE WY
4300 ANT 94531 595-H3
WOOD CT
- CCCo 94507 632-E4
- OAK 94611 650-D1
WOOD DR
5900 OAK 94611 650-D1
WOOD PL
- RCH 94801 588-G5
WOODACRES CT
- ORIN 94563 610-H6
WOODACRES LN
- ORIN 94563 610-H6
WOODBINE AV
2100 OAK 94602 650-D5
WOODBINE LN
400 DNVL 94526 653-A1
WOODBINE WY
3600 PLE 94588 694-F5
WOODBOROUGH PL
4200 PIT 94565 574-F6
WOODBOROUGH RD
1200 LFYT 94549 611-J4
WOODBOROUGH WY
2700 SRMN 94583 673-E6
WOODBRIDGE WY
4600 ANT 94531 595-J3
WOODBROOK CT
- ANT 94565 574-H7
- ANT 94565 594-H1

STREET
Block City ZIP Pg-Grid

WOODBURY CT
1900 WLCK 94596 612-G7
WOODBURY PL
600 OAKL 94561 596-D1
WOODCHUCK LN
1300 CNCD 94521 593-C5
WOODCREEK PL
- PLHL 94523 592-A7
1300 OAKL 94561 596-D1
WOODCREST CIR
- OAK 94602 650-F3
WOODCREST DR
- ORIN 94563 631-A3
1600 CNCD 94521 593-B2
2500 SRMN 94583 673-A1
WOODCREST PL
300 OAKL 94561 596-D1
WOODED CREEK LN
3200 LFYT 94549 611-H4
WOODFERN CT
500 WLCK 94598 613-A2
WOODFIELD
100 HER 94547 569-E3
WOODFIELD LN
- BREN 94513 596-G7
WOODFORD DR
- MRGA 94556 631-E3
WOODGATE CT
5300 RCH 94803 590-A3
WOOD GLEN DR
- RCH 94806 568-H7
WOODGLEN DR
1000 OAKL 94561 596-E1
WOODGLEN LN
100 MRTZ 94553 591-H2
WOODGLEN PL
200 OAKL 94561 596-E1
WOODGREEN WY
100 BEN 94510 551-B3
WOODGROVE CT
5300 CNCD 94521 593-D7
5300 CNCD 94521 613-D1
WOODHALL WY
2800 ANT 94509 575-B7
WOODHAVEN CT
- CCCo 94507 632-G6
WOODHAVEN LN
- CCCo 94595 632-C2
3300 CNCD 94519 572-G6
4000 OAKL 94561 596-E1
WOODHAVEN RD
700 BERK 94708 609-H5
WOODHAVEN WY
1000 ANT 94531 595-D4
1600 OAK 94611 630-E6
WOODHILL DR
2200 PIT 94565 573-F4
4000 OAKL 94561 596-E1
WOODHOLLOW CT
5300 CNCD 94521 613-E1
WOODLAND CT
- SRMN 94582 673-E2
1700 CNCD 94521 593-C2
5700 CCCo 94514 617-J7
5700 CCCo 94514 (618-A7
See Page 597)
WOODLAND DR
- CCCo 94507 632-D2
900 SRMN 94582 673-E2
1500 PIT 94565 574-G5
1800 ANT 94509 575-E6
4100 CNCD 94521 593-C2
WOODLAND PL
- RCH 94806 568-J6
6600 OAK 94611 630-D5
WOODLAND RD
- ORIN 94563 631-B4
WOODLAND WY
- PDMT 94611 650-C2
3300 LFYT 94549 611-G6
WOODLAND VALLEY DR
100 SRMN 94582 674-A6
WOODLAWN DR
3000 CCCo 94523 592-D7
3000 CCCo 94597 592-D7
WOODLEAF CT
5300 CNCD 94521 613-E1
WOODLYN RD
100 CCCo 94507 632-F5
WOODMEADOW PL
700 OAKL 94561 596-D1
WOODMINSTER DR
400 MRGA 94556 631-F4
WOODMINSTER LN
5000 OAK 94602 650-F3
WOODMONT AV
500 BERK 94708 609-H4
500 CCCo 94708 609-H4
WOODMONT CT
- BERK 94708 609-H4
- DNVL 94526 653-C3
5100 ANT 94531 596-A4
WOODMONT PL
400 OAKL 94561 596-E1
WOODMONT WY
- ANT 94531 595-J4
- CCCo 94563 630-D3
- OAK 94611 630-D3
5100 ANT 94531 596-A4
WOODMOOR CT
1900 CNCD 94518 592-F6
WOODMOOR DR
900 CNCD 94518 592-F6
WOODPECKER CT
1900 WLCK 94595 632-B1
WOOD RANCH CIR
- DNVL 94506 653-G5
WOOD RANCH DR
- DNVL 94506 653-H5
WOODREN CT
7700 DBLN 94568 693-G3
WOODRIDGE CT
6300 MRTZ 94553 591-H3
WOODRIDGE PL
100 OAKL 94561 596-E1
WOODROSE CIR
- DBLN 94568 694-D3
WOODROW DR
7100 OAK 94611 630-F7
WOODRUFF AV
3400 OAK 94602 650-C4
WOODRUFF LN
3600 CNCD 94519 592-J2
WOODSDALE CT
1800 CNCD 94521 593-C2
WOODSDALE DR
1800 CNCD 94521 593-C2
WOODSHIRE LN
- DBLN 94568 694-F3
WOODSIDE CT
- DNVL 94506 653-G5
200 BREN 94513 616-E2
1700 CNCD 94519 593-A2
2600 PIN 94564 569-J7

STREET
Block City ZIP Pg-Grid

WOODSIDE CT
4000 LFYT 94549 611-B7
5200 ANT 94531 596-A4
WOODSIDE DR
- DNVL 94506 653-G5
- MRGA 94556 631-D6
1000 BREN 94513 616-E2
WOODSIDE RD
1000 BERK 94708 609-J6
WOODSIDE WY
- OAK 94611 630-D3
5200 ANT 94531 596-A4
WOODSIDE GLEN CT
- OAK 94602 650-F3
WOODSIDE MEADOWS RD
3000 PLHL 94523 591-J6
WOODSON CT
4200 CNCD 94521 593-C3
WOODSONG LN
700 BREN 94513 616-E3
WOODSTOCK CT
100 BEN 94510 551-B3
100 RCH 94803 590-A3
1000 WLCK 94598 612-J4
WOODSWORTH LN
- PLHL 94523 592-C5
WOODTHRUSH CT
4700 PLE 94566 694-D7
WOODTHRUSH RD
4800 PLE 94566 694-D7
WOODVALE TER
- DBLN 94568 694-F2
WOODVALLEY CT
100 DNVL 94506 653-J5
WOODVALLEY DR
- DNVL 94506 653-J5
WOODVALLEY PL
200 DNVL 94506 653-J5
WOODVIEW CIR
100 SRMN 94582 673-F3
WOODVIEW CT
- SRMN 94582 673-F3
100 MRTZ 94553 591-J1
3300 LFYT 94549 631-G2
WOODVIEW DR
3200 LFYT 94549 631-G1
5500 RCH 94803 589-J3
5500 RCH 94803 590-A3
WOODVIEW PL
300 OAKL 94561 596-E1
WOODVIEW RD
- PIT 94565 574-D2
WOODVIEW TERRACE DR
100 SRMN 94582 673-E2
WOODWARD CT
- CCCo 94525 550-E5
WOODWIND PL
700 WLCK 94598 613-A3
WOOL CT
- BEN 94510 551-C1
WOOLSEY ST
2800 BERK 94705 630-A4
WOOTEN WY
1000 BREN 94513 596-D7
WOOTTEN DR
100 WLCK 94597 612-A3
WORCESTER
- HER 94547 569-J2
WORCHESTER CT
1200 WLCK 94596 632-G1
WORDEN WY
4400 OAK 94619 650-G6
WORDSWORTH CT
- CNCD 94521 593-F7
WORRELL RD
- ANT 94509 575-D7
WORTH CT
3300 WLCK 94598 612-J3
WORTHING
100 HER 94547 569-J3
WORTHING CT
- CCCo 94513 617-F5
WORTHING WY
- CCCo 94513 617-F5
WORTHINGTON CT
1000 ANT 94509 575-E7
WOVENWOOD
400 ORIN 94563 610-H6
WOY CIR
100 PIN 94564 569-D3
WRANGLER RD
3000 SRMN 94582 653-H6
WREN AV
3200 CNCD 94519 592-H1
WREN CT
- ANT 94509 594-J1
- CNCD 94519 592-J1
100 HER 94547 569-J5
WREN LN
1800 CNCD 94519 592-J1
WRENN ST
1900 OAK 94602 650-E3
WRIGHT AV
400 RCH 94804 608-F1
2300 PIN 94564 569-H7
2700 PIN 94564 570-A7
WRIGHT CT
- BREN 94513 616-G3
400 CLAY 94517 613-J1
WRIGHT ST
- BREN 94513 616-G3
WRIGHT WY
3000 BREN 94513 616-G3
WYATT CIR
100 PLHL 94523 592-A7
WYCOMBE CT
- CCCo 94583 673-B5
WYGAL DR
- CCCo 94553 571-H3
WYMAN PL
- OAK 94619 650-G7
WYMAN ST
3200 OAK 94619 650-G7
5800 SPAB 94806 589-B3
WYMORE WY
1200 ANT 94509 575-G5
1200 CCCo 94509 575-G5
WYNGAARD AV
- PDMT 94611 650-D2
WYOMING ST
700 MRTZ 94553 571-F5

X

XAVIER PL
- CLAY 94517 593-F5

Y

YACHT CT
- CCCo 94513 617-F7
YACHT DR
3500 CCCo 94513 617-F7

STREET
Block City ZIP Pg-Grid

YACHTSMAN DR
100 VAL 94591 550-F2
YALE AV
200 CCCo 94708 609-G3
5700 CCCo 94805 589-B5
5700 RCH 94805 589-B5
YALE CIR
- CCCo 94708 609-G4
YALE CT
- SRMN 94583 693-F1
YALE LN
4300 CNCD 94518 593-A5
YALE ST
2200 MRTZ 94553 571-F5
YANKEE HILL
- OAK 94618 630-C4
YARDARM CT
100 VAL 94591 550-F2
YARDLEY CT
1900 CNCD 94521 593-G4
YARDLEY PL
700 BREN 94513 596-E7
YARMOUTH CT
- OAK 94619 650-J4
YARMOUTH WY
2800 SRMN 94583 673-E6
YARROW PL
- RCH 94806 568-J6
YARROW VALLEY LN
- ORIN 94563 610-H3
YATES CT
- BREN 94513 596-C6
YAWL ST
5800 CCCo 94514 (618-A6
See Page 597)
YELLOWOOD LN
4300 PIT 94565 574-C7
YELLOWOOD PL
100 PIT 94565 574-C7
YELLOW ROSE CIR
- OAKL 94561 596-G2
YELLOWSTONE CIR
- CCCo 94513 617-G3
YELLOWSTONE CT
- WLCK 94598 612-H3
1900 ANT 94509 575-G5
YELLOWSTONE DR
1400 ANT 94509 575-F5
2200 MRTZ 94553 572-A7
2200 MRTZ 94553 592-A1
YEOMAN DR
1600 CNCD 94521 593-C2
YETTA DR
- CCCo 94596 632-F1
YGNACIO CT
100 WLCK 94598 612-D4
YGNACIO VALLEY RD
100 WLCK 94597 612-B4
100 WLCK 94596 612-B4
900 WLCK 94598 612-F2
2800 WLCK 94598 613-A1
3300 WLCK 94598 593-B6
4200 CNCD 94521 593-B6
4200 CNCD 94518 593-B6
YGNACIO WOODS CT
700 CNCD 94518 592-H6
YNEZ CIR
700 DNVL 94526 653-B2
YOLANDA CIR
1800 CLAY 94517 593-G5
YOLO AV
1900 BERK 94707 609-G7
1900 BERK 94709 609-G7
3000 ELCR 94530 609-C4
3000 RCH 94804 609-C4
YOLO CT
- CCCo 94565 573-E1
YORK AV
100 CCCo 94708 609-F3
YORK CT
- BREN 94513 616-D3
300 WLCK 94598 612-F2
7000 DBLN 94568 693-J3
YORK DR
- PDMT 94611 630-A7
- PDMT 94611 650-A1
400 BEN 94510 550-J2
400 BEN 94510 551-A2
6800 DBLN 94568 693-J4
YORK LN
- CCCo 94582 674-B5
YORK PL
- MRGA 94556 631-D6
YORK ST
600 PIT 94565 574-D2
800 OAK 94610 650-A3
1200 CCCo 94801 588-F4
1200 RCH 94801 588-F4
YORKSHIRE CT
900 LFYT 94549 611-F6
2900 PLE 94588 694-F6
YORKSHIRE DR
- OAK 94618 630-B6
2300 ANT 94531 595-G1
YORKSHIRE PL
1000 CCCo 94506 654-A5
YOSEMITE AV
2800 SRMN 94583 673-F7
3100 ELCR 94530 609-C4
YOSEMITE CIR
- OAKL 94561 596-H1
1300 CLAY 94517 593-G6
YOSEMITE CT
- CCCo 94513 617-F4
5500 CLAY 94517 593-F7
YOSEMITE DR
100 PIT 94565 574-D5
1400 ANT 94509 575-F6
YOSEMITE RD
- ORIN 94563 611-A4
1800 BERK 94707 609-F5
YOSEMITE WY
- CCCo 94513 617-F4
YOUNG AV
3700 OAK 94619 650-G5
YOUNG CT
- CCCo 94507 632-H2
YOUNG DR
- BREN 94513 616-H1
YOUNGS CT
2100 WLCK 94596 632-F1
YOUNGS VALLEY RD
1200 WLCK 94596 632-F1
YUBA AV
1200 SPAB 94806 589-A4
2500 ELCR 94530 589-B6
YUBA CT
- CCCo 94565 573-H2
YUBA ST
600 RCH 94805 589-B5
1100 SPAB 94806 589-B5
2600 ELCR 94530 589-B5
5500 SPAB 94805 589-B5

STREET
Block City ZIP Pg-Grid

YUCCA CT
- SRMN 94583 673-C4
YUKON ST
2200 CNCD 94520 572-G5
YULA WY
- OAKL 94561 596-H3
YUMA CT
2700 WLCK 94598 612-H4
4400 PLE 94588 694-D6
YUMA WY
3000 PLE 94588 694-D6
YVONNE CT
1700 CNCD 94521 593-F4
YVONNE DR
1800 CNCD 94521 593-F4

Z

ZAGORA DR
300 DNVL 94506 654-A6
ZAMORA PL
300 DNVL 94526 653-D5
ZAND LN
- CCCo 94507 632-G5
ZANDER CT
- ORIN 94563 631-C3
ZANDER DR
- ORIN 94563 631-C3
ZANDOL CT
8500 DBLN 94568 693-F2
ZANDRA CT
100 CCCo 94806 569-A5
ZAPATA CT
11700 DBLN 94568 693-F3
ZARA AV
5300 ELCR 94530 589-B6
5300 RCH 94805 589-B6
ZARO CT
5200 PLE 94588 694-H4
ZARTOP ST
100 OAKL 94561 576-C6
ZEBRINA CT
- CCCo 94582 674-A2
ZEBRINA WY
- CCCo 94582 674-A2
ZELMA CT
- PLHL 94523 612-A1
ZELMA LN
- CCCo 94513 596-J6
- CCCo 94513 597-A6
ZENITH RIDGE DR
500 DNVL 94506 654-A6
ZENNIA DR
2200 PIT 94565 573-J4
ZEPHER CT
- ANT 94531 595-F5
ZEPHYR
100 HER 94547 569-F3
ZEPHYR CIR
500 DNVL 94526 653-C5
ZEPHYR PL
100 DNVL 94526 653-C5
ZEUS
- HER 94547 569-F3
ZEVANOVE CT
4200 PLE 94588 694-C6
ZINFANDEL CIR
400 CLAY 94517 593-H7
400 CLAY 94517 613-H1
ZINFANDEL CT
- ANT 94531 595-G5
- OAKL 94561 596-D1
ZINFANDEL DR
4300 OAKL 94561 596-D1
4300 OAKL 94561 576-D7
ZINN DR
5900 OAK 94611 630-E7
5900 OAK 94611 650-E1
ZINN ST
1600 CCCo 94805 589-C5
ZION AV
- PIT 94565 574-D7
ZION CT
- OAKL 94561 596-H1
ZION PL
3400 CNCD 94518 592-H6
ZIRCON CT
100 HER 94547 569-G4
ZITA CT
500 DNVL 94526 653-D5
ZOE CT
200 PIN 94564 569-E3
ZORAH ST
500 OAK 94606 650-A4
N ZUCKERMAN RD
- SJCo 95219 (578-J3
See Page 557)
- SJCo 95219 (598-J1
See Page 597)
ZUNI WY
3100 PLE 94588 694-D6
ZURICH CT
- PLHL 94523 592-C5

#

1ST AV
500 CCCo 94525 550-D5
1500 WLCK 94597 612-B2
1ST AV N
- CCCo 94553 572-C7
1ST AV S
100 CCCo 94553 592-B1
300 PLHL 94523 592-B1
1ST ST
- CCCo 94514 637-D3
- CCCo 94572 549-H7
- RCH 94801 588-F6
100 BEN 94510 551-C3
200 BREN 94513 616-G1
700 ANT 94509 575-C3
800 LFYT 94549 611-F6
1700 CNCD 94519 592-G2
3100 CCCo 94548 597-A3
N 1ST ST
1500 CCCo 94801 588-F3
S 1ST ST
- RCH 94804 588-F7
400 RCH 94804 608-F1
1ST AV CT
- WLCK 94597 612-B2
2ND AV
500 CCCo 94525 550-D5
700 PIN 94564 569-D4
1500 WLCK 94597 612-B2
2ND AV S
100 CCCo 94553 592-B1
200 PLHL 94523 592-B1
2ND CT
1100 ANT 94509 575-C3
2ND ST
- CCCo 94569 550-H6
- RCH 94801 588-F6
100 CCCo 94572 549-G7

STREET
Block City ZIP Pg-Grid

2ND ST
100 OAKL 94561 576-E7
300 ANT 94509 575-C4
500 BREN 94513 616-G1
900 LFYT 94549 611-F6
1000 ALB 94710 609-C7
1000 BERK 94710 609-C7
1500 CCCo 94801 588-F3
1700 CNCD 94519 592-G2
3000 CCCo 94548 597-A3
E 2ND ST
200 BEN 94510 551-F1
S 2ND ST
100 RCH 94804 588-F7
300 RCH 94804 608-F1
W 2ND ST
400 PIT 94565 574-D1
700 BEN 94510 551-B5
3RD AV
400 CCCo 94525 550-D5
700 PIN 94564 569-D4
1500 WLCK 94597 612-A2
3RD AV S
300 PLHL 94523 592-B1
300 CCCo 94553 592-B1
3RD ST
- DBLN 94568 694-A4
- CCCo 94572 549-G7
- HER 94547 549-J7
- RCH 94801 588-F7
200 OAKL 94561 576-E7
200 ANT 94509 575-C4
400 BREN 94513 616-G1
900 LFYT 94549 611-F6
1200 BERK 94710 609-C7
1500 CCCo 94801 588-F4
1600 CNCD 94519 592-G1
1800 BEN 94510 551-C4
E 3RD ST
- PIT 94565 574-E1
800 BEN 94510 551-C4
N 3RD ST
1900 CNCD 94519 592-G1
S 3RD ST
100 RCH 94804 588-F7
300 RCH 94804 608-F1
W 3RD ST
700 BEN 94510 551-B5
4TH AV
700 PIN 94564 569-D4
1000 CCCo 94525 550-D4
4TH AV S
300 PLHL 94523 592-A1
300 CCCo 94553 592-A1
4TH ST
- CCCo 94525 550-A5
- CCCo 94569 550-H6
- DBLN 94568 694-A4
- RCH 94801 588-F6
100 CCCo 94572 549-H7
200 OAKL 94561 576-F7
500 BREN 94513 616-H1
900 LFYT 94549 611-G6
1100 BERK 94710 609-D7
1500 CCCo 94801 588-F4
E 4TH ST
100 PIT 94565 574-E1
800 BEN 94510 551-C5
S 4TH ST
200 RCH 94804 588-F7
300 RCH 94804 608-F1
W 4TH ST
- PIT 94565 574-D1
100 ANT 94509 575-C4
300 BEN 94510 551-B4
5TH AV
700 PIN 94564 569-D4
800 CCCo 94525 550-D5
1200 CNCD 94518 592-G3
2100 OAK 94606 650-A4
5TH AV S
300 CCCo 94553 592-A1
5TH ST
- CCCo 94569 550-H6
- DBLN 94568 694-A3
200 ANT 94509 575-B4
200 RCH 94801 588-F5
400 OAKL 94561 576-F7
1000 VAL 94590 550-C1
1100 BERK 94710 609-D7
1300 CCCo 94572 549-J7
1500 CCCo 94801 588-F4
1500 CNCD 94519 592-H1
E 5TH ST
- PIT 94565 574-E1
600 BEN 94510 551-C5
S 5TH ST
100 RCH 94804 588-F7
300 RCH 94804 608-F1
W 5TH ST
- PIT 94565 574-E1
900 BEN 94510 551-A4
6TH AV
700 CCCo 94525 550-D5
6TH ST
- DBLN 94568 694-A3
- ANT 94509 575-B4
- CCCo 94569 550-H6
200 RCH 94801 588-F5
300 CCCo 94572 569-H1
1000 ALB 94710 609-D7
1000 BERK 94710 609-D7
1300 CCCo 94572 549-J7
1500 CCCo 94801 588-F4
1600 CNCD 94519 592-H1
E 6TH ST
100 PIT 94565 574-E1
700 BEN 94510 551-C6
N 6TH ST
1900 CNCD 94519 592-H1
1900 CNCD 94519 572-G7
S 6TH ST
200 RCH 94804 588-F7
300 RCH 94804 608-F1
W 6TH ST
- PIT 94565 574-D1
800 BEN 94510 551-A4
7TH AV
800 CCCo 94525 550-C5
1900 OAK 94606 650-A5
7TH ST
- DBLN 94568 694-A3
- ANT 94509 575-C4
- RCH 94801 588-F6
400 OAKL 94561 576-F7
500 CCCo 94572 569-H1
600 CCCo 94547 569-H1
1200 BERK 94710 609-D7
1300 CCCo 94572 549-J7
1500 CCCo 94801 588-G3
E 7TH ST
100 PIT 94565 574-E1
900 BEN 94510 551-C6

STREET
Block City ZIP Pg-Grid

S 7TH ST
100 RCH 94804 588-F7
300 RCH 94804 608-F1
W 7TH ST
- PIT 94565 574-D1
1200 BEN 94510 551-A4
8TH AV
1800 OAK 94606 650-A5
2700 OAK 94610 650-A5
8TH ST
- ANT 94509 575-C4
- RCH 94801 588-F5
1100 ALB 94706 609-D7
1100 ALB 94710 609-D7
1100 BERK 94710 609-D7
5700 DBLN 94568 694-A3
E 8TH ST
100 PIT 94565 574-E2
1100 OAK 94606 650-A6
S 8TH ST
100 RCH 94804 588-F7
300 RCH 94804 608-F1
W 8TH ST
- PIT 94565 574-D1
700 BEN 94510 550-J4
700 BEN 94510 551-A4
9TH AV
1700 OAK 94606 650-A5
9TH ST
- DBLN 94568 694-A3
- RCH 94801 588-G6
200 ANT 94509 575-C4
900 ALB 94710 609-D6
1100 BERK 94710 609-D7
E 9TH ST
200 PIT 94565 574-E2
2500 OAK 94601 650-B7
S 9TH ST
100 RCH 94804 588-F7
300 RCH 94804 608-F1
W 9TH ST
- PIT 94565 574-D1
800 BEN 94510 550-J4
1100 BEN 94510 551-A4
10TH AV
1700 OAK 94606 650-A5
10TH ST
- DBLN 94568 694-A2
- ANT 94509 575-B4
700 RCH 94801 588-G5
1100 ALB 94710 609-D7
1100 BERK 94710 609-D7
1100 CCCo 94509 575-B4
2700 SPAB 94806 588-G1
E 10TH ST
100 PIT 94565 574-E2
2500 OAK 94601 650-B7
W 10TH ST
- PIT 94565 574-D2
1000 BEN 94510 550-J3
11TH AV
1500 OAK 94606 650-A5
2800 OAK 94610 650-A5
11TH ST
- DBLN 94568 694-A2
- RCH 94801 588-G6
400 ANT 94509 575-C4
2700 SPAB 94806 588-H1
3300 SPAB 94806 568-H7
E 11TH ST
700 PIT 94565 574-F2
2400 OAK 94601 650-B7
2400 OAK 94606 650-B7
S 11TH ST
100 RCH 94804 588-G7
500 RCH 94804 608-G1
W 11TH ST
- PIT 94565 574-D2
1100 BEN 94510 550-J3
12TH AV
1500 OAK 94606 650-A5
12TH ST
- RCH 94801 588-G6
400 ANT 94509 575-C4
1100 DBLN 94568 694-A2
2700 SPAB 94806 588-H1
E 12TH ST
300 PIT 94565 574-E2
1300 OAK 94606 650-A6
2200 OAK 94601 650-A6
S 12TH ST
100 RCH 94804 588-G7
300 RCH 94804 608-G1
W 12TH ST
100 PIT 94565 574-D2
1000 BEN 94510 550-J3
12TH ST S
- DBLN 94568 694-B2
13TH AV
1300 OAK 94606 650-A6
2800 OAK 94610 650-B4
3000 OAK 94602 650-B4
13TH ST
- DBLN 94568 694-A2
- RCH 94801 588-G5
300 ANT 94509 575-C5
2700 SPAB 94806 588-H1
E 13TH ST
- ANT 94509 575-D5
3000 OAK 94601 650-C7
S 13TH ST
200 RCH 94804 588-G7
300 RCH 94804 608-G1
W 13TH ST
- PIT 94565 574-D2
1100 BEN 94510 550-J3
14TH AV
1200 OAK 94606 650-A5
3100 OAK 94602 650-A5
14TH ST
- DBLN 94568 694-A2
500 RCH 94801 588-G5
1600 SPAB 94806 588-H1
E 14TH ST
400 PIT 94565 574-F3
400 ANT 94509 575-E5
W 14TH ST
500 ANT 94509 575-C5
1200 BEN 94510 550-H3
15TH AV
1200 OAK 94606 650-A6
15TH ST
- DBLN 94568 694-A2
- RCH 94801 588-G5
500 ANT 94509 575-C5
1100 SPAB 94806 588-H2
E 15TH ST
- ANT 94509 575-D5
100 PIT 94565 574-E3
1200 OAK 94606 650-A6
2300 OAK 94601 650-C7
S 15TH ST
200 RCH 94804 588-G7
300 RCH 94804 608-G1

STREET	Block	City	ZIP	Pg-Grid
W 15TH ST				
	-	ANT	94509	575-D5
16TH AV				
	1100	OAK	94606	650-A6
16TH ST				
	-	ANT	94509	575-C5
	-	RCH	94801	588-G6
	1600	SPAB	94806	588-H2
E 16TH ST				
	-	ANT	94509	575-D5
	200	PIT	94565	574-E3
	2300	OAK	94601	650-B7
S 16TH ST				
	100	RCH	94804	588-G7
	300	RCH	94804	608-G1
17TH AV				
	1200	OAK	94606	650-A5
17TH ST				
	-	ANT	94509	575-C5
	-	RCH	94801	588-G5
	1100	SPAB	94806	588-H1
E 17TH ST				
	100	PIT	94565	574-E3
	1000	OAK	94606	650-A5
	2300	OAK	94601	650-B7
S 17TH ST				
	100	RCH	94804	608-G1
	100	RCH	94804	588-G7
W 17TH ST				
	200	PIT	94565	574-C3
18TH AV				
	1200	OAK	94606	650-A6
18TH ST				
	-	RCH	94801	588-H5
	1100	SPAB	94806	588-H1
E 18TH ST				
	-	ANT	94509	575-E5
	800	OAK	94606	650-A5
	1400	CCCo	94509	575-H5
	3000	OAK	94601	650-C7
	3200	ANT	94509	576-A5
S 18TH ST				
	100	RCH	94804	588-G7
	300	RCH	94804	608-G1
W 18TH ST				
	-	ANT	94509	575-B5
19TH AV				
	1200	OAK	94606	650-A6
19TH ST				
	-	RCH	94801	588-H6
	1300	SPAB	94806	588-H2
E 19TH ST				
	-	ANT	94509	575-D5
	700	OAK	94606	650-A5
	2300	OAK	94601	650-C7
S 19TH ST				
	100	RCH	94804	588-H7
	300	RCH	94804	608-G1
W 19TH ST				
	100	ANT	94509	575-C5
20TH AV				
	1200	OAK	94606	650-A6
20TH ST				
	-	RCH	94801	588-H5
	1100	SPAB	94806	588-H1
E 20TH ST				
	600	OAK	94606	650-A5
	2300	OAK	94601	650-B6
S 20TH ST				
	100	RCH	94804	588-H7
	300	RCH	94804	608-H1
W 20TH ST				
	-	ANT	94509	575-D5
21ST AV				
	1200	OAK	94606	650-B6
21ST ST				
	-	RCH	94801	588-H6
	1300	SPAB	94806	588-H2
E 21ST ST				
	500	OAK	94606	650-A5
	2200	OAK	94601	650-B6
S 21ST ST				
	100	RCH	94804	588-H7
	400	RCH	94804	608-H1
22ND AV				
	900	OAK	94606	650-C5
	3000	OAK	94602	650-C5
22ND ST				
	100	RCH	94801	588-H6
	1800	SPAB	94806	588-H2
E 22ND ST				
	500	OAK	94606	650-A4
	2200	OAK	94601	650-C7
S 22ND ST				
	100	RCH	94804	588-H7
	200	RCH	94804	608-H1
23RD AV				
	700	OAK	94606	650-B6
	700	OAK	94601	650-B6
	2800	OAK	94602	650-B6
23RD ST				
	100	RCH	94804	588-H3
	100	RCH	94801	588-H6
	1100	SPAB	94806	588-H3
	1100	RCH	94806	588-H3
E 23RD ST				
	600	OAK	94606	650-A5
	2200	OAK	94601	650-C6
S 23RD ST				
	100	RCH	94804	588-H7
	300	RCH	94804	608-H1
23RD AV OVPS				
	700	OAK	94606	650-B7
	700	OAK	94601	650-B7
24TH AV				
	1400	OAK	94601	650-B6
24TH ST				
	600	RCH	94804	588-H5
	1300	RCH	94806	588-H4
	1600	SPAB	94806	588-H4
E 24TH ST				
	700	OAK	94606	650-A4
	2300	OAK	94601	650-B5
S 24TH ST				
	300	RCH	94804	588-H7
	300	RCH	94804	608-H1
25TH AV				
	1000	OAK	94601	650-C5
	2800	OAK	94602	650-C5
25TH ST				
	100	RCH	94804	588-H6
	1300	RCH	94806	588-H4
	1600	SPAB	94806	588-H4
E 25TH ST				
	1300	OAK	94606	650-B5
	2600	OAK	94601	650-C6
S 25TH ST				
	200	RCH	94804	588-H7
	300	RCH	94804	608-H1
26TH AV				
	900	OAK	94601	650-C6
26TH ST				
	500	RCH	94804	588-H5
	1300	RCH	94806	588-H4
	1600	SPAB	94806	588-H4
E 26TH ST				
	1300	OAK	94606	650-B5
	2300	OAK	94601	650-C6
S 26TH ST				
	300	RCH	94804	588-H7
	300	RCH	94804	608-H1
27TH AV				
	800	OAK	94601	650-B7
27TH ST				
	300	RCH	94804	588-J6
	1500	RCH	94806	588-J4
E 27TH ST				
	1300	OAK	94606	650-B5
	2300	OAK	94601	650-C6
S 27TH ST				
	100	RCH	94804	588-H7
	300	RCH	94804	608-H1
28TH AV				
	1500	OAK	94601	650-B7
28TH ST				
	200	RCH	94804	588-J5
E 28TH ST				
	800	OAK	94610	650-B4
	900	OAK	94606	650-B5
	2400	OAK	94602	650-C5
	2400	OAK	94601	650-C5
S 28TH ST				
	300	RCH	94804	588-H7
	300	RCH	94804	608-H1
29TH AV				
	1600	OAK	94601	650-B7
29TH ST				
	-	RCH	94804	588-J5
E 29TH ST				
	1900	OAK	94606	650-B5
	2300	OAK	94602	650-C5
	2500	OAK	94601	650-C5
S 29TH ST				
	100	RCH	94804	588-J7
	300	RCH	94804	608-J1
30TH AV				
	1200	OAK	94601	650-B7
30TH ST				
	300	RCH	94804	588-J6
E 30TH ST				
	1900	OAK	94606	650-B5
	2300	OAK	94602	650-B5
S 30TH ST				
	500	RCH	94804	608-J1
31ST AV				
	1300	OAK	94601	650-C7
31ST ST				
	300	RCH	94804	588-J6
E 31ST ST				
	1300	OAK	94602	650-B4
	1300	OAK	94606	650-B4
S 31ST ST				
	100	RCH	94804	588-J7
	500	RCH	94804	608-J1
32ND ST				
	300	RCH	94804	588-J5
E 32ND ST				
	1300	OAK	94602	650-B4
S 32ND ST				
	600	RCH	94804	608-J1
33RD AV				
	1500	OAK	94601	650-C7
33RD ST				
	-	RCH	94804	588-J6
	-	RCH	94805	588-J6
E 33RD ST				
	1000	OAK	94610	650-B4
	1300	OAK	94602	650-B4
S 33RD ST				
	100	RCH	94804	588-J7
	500	RCH	94804	608-J1
34TH AV				
	1400	OAK	94601	650-C7
34TH ST				
	300	RCH	94805	588-J5
	1000	RCH	94804	588-J5
E 34TH ST				
	1200	OAK	94610	650-B4
	1300	OAK	94602	650-B4
S 34TH ST				
	300	RCH	94804	608-J1
35TH AV				
	1400	OAK	94601	650-C7
	2500	OAK	94619	650-F5
	2600	OAK	94602	650-F5
35TH ST				
	100	RCH	94805	588-J6
	700	RCH	94805	589-A5
S 35TH ST				
	100	RCH	94804	588-J7
	300	RCH	94804	608-J1
36TH AV				
	1400	OAK	94601	650-C7
36TH ST				
	300	RCH	94805	588-J7
	600	RCH	94805	589-A5
	1000	RCH	94804	589-A5
E 36TH ST				
	1300	OAK	94602	650-B4
S 36TH ST				
	300	RCH	94804	588-J7
	300	RCH	94804	608-J1
37TH AV				
	1700	OAK	94601	650-D7
37TH ST				
	-	RCH	94805	588-J7
	400	RCH	94805	589-A5
S 37TH ST				
	100	RCH	94804	588-J7
	300	RCH	94804	608-J1
38TH AV				
	1200	OAK	94601	650-D7
	2600	OAK	94619	650-E6
38TH ST				
	300	RCH	94805	589-A5
E 38TH ST				
	1300	OAK	94602	650-C4
S 38TH ST				
	400	RCH	94804	589-A7
	400	RCH	94804	609-A1
39TH AV				
	1700	OAK	94601	650-D7
	2600	OAK	94619	650-E6
39TH ST				
	300	RCH	94805	589-A7
S 39TH ST				
	100	RCH	94804	589-A7
	300	RCH	94804	609-A1
40TH AV				
	1800	OAK	94601	650-D7
40TH ST				
	300	RCH	94805	589-A7
S 40TH ST				
	700	RCH	94804	609-A1
41ST AV				
	2000	OAK	94601	650-D7
41ST ST				
	300	RCH	94805	589-A7
S 41ST ST				
	100	RCH	94804	589-A7
	200	RCH	94804	609-A1
42ND AV				
	2000	OAK	94601	650-E7
42ND ST				
	300	RCH	94805	589-A7
S 42ND ST				
	100	RCH	94804	589-A7
	200	RCH	94804	609-A1
43RD ST				
	300	RCH	94805	589-A7
S 43RD ST				
	200	RCH	94804	589-A7
	200	RCH	94804	609-A2
44TH ST				
	300	RCH	94805	589-A7
S 44TH ST				
	200	RCH	94804	589-A7
	200	RCH	94804	609-A1
45TH ST				
	300	RCH	94805	589-A7
S 45TH ST				
	-	RCH	94804	589-A7
	200	RCH	94804	609-A1
46TH ST				
	400	RCH	94805	589-A7
S 46TH ST				
	200	RCH	94804	589-A7
	200	RCH	94804	609-A2
	1300	RCH	94804	608-J3
47TH AV				
	2200	OAK	94601	650-E7
S 47TH ST				
	-	RCH	94804	589-A7
	100	RCH	94804	609-A1
S 49TH ST				
	300	RCH	94804	609-B1
S 50TH ST				
	300	RCH	94804	609-B1
S 51ST ST				
	1400	RCH	94804	609-A3
S 52ND ST				
	600	RCH	94804	609-B1
S 53RD ST				
	800	ELCR	94530	609-B2
S 54TH ST				
	5400	RCH	94804	609-B2
S 55TH ST				
	800	ELCR	94530	609-B2
	900	RCH	94804	609-B2
S 56TH ST				
	1100	RCH	94804	609-B2
	1400	ELCR	94530	609-B2
S 57TH ST				
	1000	RCH	94804	609-B2
S 58TH ST				
	1200	RCH	94804	609-B2
S 59TH ST				
	1200	RCH	94804	609-C3
I-80 EASTSHORE FRWY				
	-	ALB	-	609-C5
	-	BERK	-	609-C5
	-	CCCo	-	549-J7
	-	CCCo	-	550-B6
	-	CCCo	-	569-H2
	-	CCCo	-	589-A3
	-	ELCR	-	609-C5
	-	HER	-	569-H2
	-	PIN	-	569-B7
	-	RCH	-	569-B7
	-	RCH	-	589-A3
	-	RCH	-	609-C5
	-	SPAB	-	589-A3
I-80 FRWY				
	-	CCCo	-	550-D3
	-	SolC	-	550-D3
	-	VAL	-	550-C1
I-580 ARTHUR H BREED JR FRWY				
	-	AlaC	-	693-A4
	-	AlaC	-	694-C5
	-	DBLN	-	693-A4
	-	DBLN	-	694-C5
	-	LVMR	-	694-C5
	-	PLE	-	693-A4
	-	PLE	-	694-C5
I-580 FRWY				
	-	MrnC	-	587-C5
	-	RCH	-	587-H6
	-	RCH	-	588-A7
	-	SRFL	-	587-A3
I-580 JOHN T KNOX FRWY				
	-	ALB	-	609-A3
	-	RCH	-	588-C7
	-	RCH	-	608-H1
	-	RCH	-	609-A3
I-580 MACARTHUR FRWY				
	-	OAK	-	650-D5
I-580 RICHMND-SAN RAFAEL BRDG				
	-	MrnC	-	587-C5
	-	RCH	-	587-C5
	-	RCH	-	588-A7
	-	SRFL	-	587-C5
I-680 BENICIA -MARTINEZ BRDG				
	-	BEN	-	551-E6
	-	MRTZ	-	551-F7
	-	SolC	-	551-E6
I-680 FRWY				
	-	BEN	-	551-E6
	-	CCCo	-	571-G2
	-	CCCo	-	572-A4
	-	CCCo	-	592-C1
	-	CCCo	-	612-C1
	-	CCCo	-	632-E2
	-	CNCD	-	592-C2
	-	DBLN	-	693-G2
	-	DNVL	-	632-H6
	-	DNVL	-	652-J1
	-	DNVL	-	653-A1
	-	DNVL	-	673-C1
	-	MRTZ	-	551-E6
	-	MRTZ	-	571-F1
	-	PLE	-	693-J4
	-	PLHL	-	592-C1
	-	PLHL	-	612-C1
	-	SolC	-	551-E6
	-	SRMN	-	653-C7
	-	SRMN	-	673-C1
	-	SRMN	-	693-F1
	-	WLCK	-	612-B6
	-	WLCK	-	632-D1
I-680 LUTHER E GIBSON FRWY				
	-	BEN	-	551-E5
I-780 FRWY				
	-	BEN	-	550-G1
	-	BEN	-	551-A3
I-880 NIMITZ FRWY				
	-	OAK	-	650-A6
Rt#-J4 BYRON HWY				
	6800	CCCo	94513	617-D7
	10600	CCCo	94513	637-D1
	10600	CCCo	94514	637-D1
	17600	CCCo	94514	(657-G1 See Page 638)
	19100	CCCo	94514	(658-A3 See Page 638)
Rt#-J4 BYRON-BETHANY RD				
	17900	SJCo	95391	(658-D6 See Page 638)
	20200	AlaC	94551	(658-B4 See Page 638)
	20200	CCCo	94514	(658-B4 See Page 638)
Rt#-4 BRENTWOOD BLVD				
	1400	BREN	94513	596-G6
	1500	CCCo	94513	617-A4
	3900	BREN	94513	616-H3
	6300	BREN	94561	596-G6
	7300	CCCo	94513	616-H3
Rt#-4 BYRON HWY				
	1900	CCCo	94513	617-D5
Rt#-4 CALIFORNIA DELTA HWY				
	-	ANT	94509	574-H4
	-	ANT	94509	575-H7
	-	ANT	94531	575-H7
	-	ANT	94531	576-B5
	-	CCCo	94520	572-C6
	-	CCCo	94553	572-C6
	-	CCCo	94565	573-C3
	-	CNCD	94519	572-C6
	-	CNCD	94520	572-C6
	-	CNCD	94520	573-C3
	-	CNCD	94565	572-C6
	-	CNCD	94565	573-C3
	-	PIT	94565	573-C3
	-	PIT	94565	574-H4
	600	OAKL	94561	576-B5
	900	ANT	94509	576-B5
	900	OAKL	94509	576-B5
	1400	BREN	94513	596-G7
	1500	CCCo	94513	617-A4
	3900	BREN	94513	616-G1
	4000	OAKL	94561	596-G7
	6000	BREN	94561	596-G7
	6000	CCCo	94561	596-G7
	7200	CCCo	94514	617-A4
	7300	CCCo	94513	616-G1
	9900	CCCo	94514	(618-B7 See Page 597)
	14300	SJCo	95206	(618-J7 See Page 597)
	15100	SJCo	95206	638-H1
Rt#-4 HIGHWAY 4 BYPS				
	-	BREN	94513	596-B5
	-	BREN	94513	616-C1
Rt#-4 JOHN MUIR PKWY				
	-	CCCo	94547	570-C3
	-	CCCo	94553	570-H3
	-	CCCo	94553	571-A4
	-	CCCo	94553	572-A6
	-	HER	94547	570-C3
	-	HER	94553	570-C3
	-	HER	94572	570-C3
	-	MRTZ	94553	571-G6
	-	MRTZ	94553	572-A6
	1900	CCCo	94572	569-H3
	1900	CCCo	94572	570-C3
	1900	HER	94547	569-H3
	1900	HER	94572	569-H3
Rt#-4 MAIN ST				
	600	OAKL	94561	576-B5
	900	ANT	94509	576-B5
	900	OAKL	94509	576-B5
	4000	OAKL	94561	596-G3
	6000	BREN	94561	596-G3
	6000	CCCo	94561	596-G3
Rt#-13 ASHBY AV				
	2800	BERK	94705	630-A3
Rt#-13 LANDVALE RD				
	300	OAK	94618	630-B4
Rt#-13 TUNNEL RD				
	-	BERK	94705	630-B4
	-	OAK	94705	630-B4
	1100	OAK	94618	630-B4
Rt#-13 WARREN FRWY				
	-	OAK	-	630-C6
	-	OAK	-	650-F3
Rt#-24 FRWY				
	-	WLCK	-	612-B4
Rt#-24 WILLIAM B RUMFORD FRWY				
	-	CCCo	-	611-C6
	-	CCCo	-	612-A5
	-	CCCo	-	630-E2
	-	LFYT	-	611-C6
	-	OAK	-	630-E2
	-	ORIN	-	610-H7
	-	ORIN	-	611-C6
	-	ORIN	-	630-E2
	-	WLCK	-	612-A5
Rt#-29 SONOMA BLVD				
	1000	VAL	94590	550-B1
Rt#-123 SAN PABLO AV				
	500	ALB	94706	609-D6
	1000	ALB	94710	609-D6
	1100	BERK	94706	609-D6
	1100	BERK	94710	609-D6
	1300	BERK	94702	609-D6
	3000	ELCR	94530	609-B1
	10200	RCH	94804	609-B1
	11800	ELCR	94530	589-B7
	11900	RCH	94805	589-B7
Rt#-160 FRWY				
	-	ANT	-	576-A4
	-	CCCo	-	576-A4
	-	OAKL	-	576-A4
Rt#-160 HIGHWAY				
	-	CCCo	94509	576-A3
	-	OAKL	94509	576-A3
	18100	SaCo	94571	576-A1
Rt#-242 FRWY				
	-	CNCD	-	572-F5
	-	CNCD	-	592-F1
	-	PLHL	-	592-D4

CONTRA COSTA

FEATURE NAME Address City, ZIP Code	PAGE-GRID
AIRPORTS	
BUCHANAN FIELD	572 - D6
550 SALLY RIDE DR, CCCo, 94553	
CONTRA COSTA COUNTY BYRON	637 - D7
500 EAGLE CT, CCCo, 94514	
BEACHES, HARBORS & WATER REC	
ANCHOR MARINA	577 - B3
1970 TAYLOR RD, CCCo, 94511	
ANN & CHUCKS HARBOR	577 - F4
4230 STONE RD, CCCo, 94511	
BEACON HARBOR	577 - F1
3861 WILLOW RD, CCCo, 94511	
BENTLEYS MARINA	577 - E5
DUTCH SLOUGH RD, CCCo, 94561	
BETHEL HARBOR	557 - E7
HARBOR RD, CCCo, 94511	
BETHEL ISLAND MARINA	577 - D4
440 RIVERVIEW PL, CCCo, 94511	
BIG BREAK MARINA	576 - C4
BIG BREAK RD, OAKL, 94561	
BOYDS HARBOR	577 - G1
WILLOW RD, CCCo, 94511	
BROWNS ISLAND REGL SHORELINE	574 - H1
BROWNS ISLAND, PIT, 94565	
CAROLS HARBOR	577 - F7
4850 SANDMOUND BLVD, CCCo, 94561	
DRIFTWOOD MARINA	576 - A4
BRIDGEHEAD RD, OAKL, 94561	
FRANKS MARINA	577 - G3
7050 RIVERVIEW DR, CCCo, 94511	
GREGS HARBOR	577 - E5
DUTCH SLOUGH RD, CCCo, 94561	
HARRIS YACHT HARBOR	553 - F7
MC AVOY RD, CCCo, 94565	
HOLLAND RIVERSIDE MARINA-	598 - A3
(SEE PAGE 597)	
HOLLAND TRACT RD, CCCo, 94561	
KELLERS BEACH	608 - C1
DORNAN DR, RCH, 94801	
LAURITZEN YACHT HARBOR	576 - B3
115 LAURITZEN LN, OAKL, 94561	
LEISURE LANDING	577 - A1
END OF TAYLOR RD, CCCo, 94511	
LIVERMORE YACHT CLUB (SEE PAGE 638)	658 - C4
LINDEMANN RD, AlaC, 94551	
LLOYDS HOLIDAY HARBOR	576 - A4
415 FLEMING LN, CCCo, 94509	
MARTINEZ YACHT HARBOR	571 - D1
TARANTINO DR, MRTZ, 94553	
MC AVOY YACHT HARBOR	553 - F6
780 PORT CHICAGO RD, CCCo, 94565	
NEW BRIDGE MARINA	576 - A4
6325 BRIDGEHEAD RD, CCCo, 94509	
POINT MOLATE BEACH	588 - A5
WESTERN DR, RCH, 94801	
RODEO MARINA	549 - H6
FOOT OF PACIFIC AV, CCCo, 94572	
RUSSOS MARINA	577 - G2
3995 WILLOW RD, CCCo, 94511	
SAMS HARBOR	577 - F7
4776 SANDMOUND BLVD, CCCo, 94561	
SEA HORSE MARINA	577 - D5
2738 DUTCH SLOUGH RD, CCCo, 94561	
SUGAR BARGE MARINA	577 - H2
SUGAR BARGE RD, CCCo, 94511	
UNION POINT MARINA	650 - A7
EMBARCADERO, OAK, 94606	
VIKING HARBOR	577 - C5
DUTCH SLOUGH RD, CCCo, 94561	
WOODS YACHT HARBOR	577 - E5
3307 WELLS RD, CCCo, 94561	
BUILDINGS	
FOR DOWNTOWN BUILDINGS SEE PAGE F	-
DUBLIN SENIOR CITIZENS CTR	693 - H2
7437 LARKDALE AV, DBLN, 94568	
ENVIRONMENTAL CTR	574 - E5
2581 HARBOR ST, PIT, 94565	
GOLDEN EAGLE REFINERY	572 - C2
SOLANO WY, CCCo, 94520	
MONSANTO CHEMICAL COMPANY	572 - D2
1778 MONSANTO WY, CCCo, 94520	
MOUNT DIABLO FAMILY BRANCH YMCA	592 - B3
350 CIVIC DR, PLHL, 94523	
PG&E STEAM POWER PLANT	554 - D7
10TH ST, CCCo, 94565	
RICHMOND YACHT CLUB	608 - D3
351 BRICKYARD COVE RD, RCH, 94801	
UNIV OF CALIFORNIA RICHMOND FIELD	608 - J2
1301 S 46TH ST, RCH, 94804	
BUILDINGS - GOVERNMENTAL	
BRAY, AF COURTHOUSE	571 - E3
1020 WARD ST, MRTZ, 94553	
BYRON BOYS RANCH	637 - F2
4491 BIXLER RD, CCCo, 94514	
CENTRAL CONTRA COSTA SANITARY DIST	572 - C5
5019 IMHOFF DR, CCCo, 94553	
CONCORD POLICE ACADEMY	573 - C3
5060 AVILA RD, CCCo, 94565	
CONTRA COSTA CO ADMIN BUILDING	571 - E2
651 PINE ST, MRTZ, 94553	
CONTRA COSTA CO FINANCE BLDG	571 - E2
COURT ST & MAIN ST, MRTZ, 94553	
CONTRA COSTA CO HEALTH DEPARTMENT	571 - E3
1111 WARD ST, MRTZ, 94553	
CONTRA COSTA CO MUNICIPAL COURTHOUSE	574 - D3
45 CIVIC AV, PIT, 94565	
CONTRA COSTA CO MUNICIPAL COURTHOUSE	588 - J7
100 37TH ST, RCH, 94805	
COUNTY COURTHOUSE	571 - E3
725 COURT ST, MRTZ, 94553	
COUNTY DETENTION CTR	571 - E3
1000 WARD ST, MRTZ, 94553	
DEPARTMENT OF ANIMAL SERVICES	569 - C4
651 PINOLE SHORES DR, PIN, 94564	
FEDERAL CORRECTIONAL INST PLEASANTON	694 - C2
8TH ST & GOODFELLOW AV, DBLN, 94568	
HALL OF JUSTICE	588 - J6
2600 BARRETT AV, RCH, 94804	
JUVENILE HALL	571 - J7
202 GLACIER DR, MRTZ, 94553	
SAN QUENTIN STATE PENITENTIARY	587 - A5
MAIN ST, MrnC, 94964	
SANTA RITA REHABILITATION CTR	694 - C2
BRODER BLVD, DBLN, 94568	
USDA WESTERN REGL RESEARCH LAB	609 - C6
800 BUCHANAN ST, ALB, 94706	
WEST COUNTY DETENTION FACILITY	568 - G5
5555 GIANT HWY, RCH, 94806	

FEATURE NAME Address City, ZIP Code	PAGE-GRID
CEMETERIES	
ALHAMBRA CEM	571 - C3
CARQUINEZ SCENIC DR, MRTZ, 94553	
BYRON BRENTWOOD KNIGHTSEN CEM	617 - C5
11545 BRENTWOOD BLVD, CCCo, 94513	
CATHOLIC CEM	571 - C3
CARQUINEZ SCENIC DR, MRTZ, 94553	
HIDDEN VALLEY MEMORIAL PARK	572 - B5
BLUM RD & IMHOFF DR, CCCo, 94553	
HOLY CROSS CEM	575 - H5
2200 E 18TH ST, CCCo, 94509	
HOME OF PEACE CEM	650 - E7
4712 FAIRFAX AV, OAK, 94601	
JEWISH CEM	630 - A7
4550 PIEDMONT AV, OAK, 94611	
LAFAYETTE CEM	611 - H5
3285 MOUNT DIABLO BLVD, LFYT, 94549	
LIVE OAK CEM	593 - D5
DEER OAK PL, CNCD, 94521	
MEMORY GARDENS CEM	572 - F4
2011 ARNOLD INDUSTRIAL WY, CNCD, 94520	
MILITARY CEM	551 - D5
BIRCH RD, BEN, 94510	
MOUNTAIN VIEW CEM	630 - A7
5000 PIEDMONT AV, OAK, 94611	
OAKMONT MEMORIAL PARK	591 - G5
2099 RELIEZ VALLEY RD, CCCo, 94549	
OAK VIEW MEMORIAL PARK CEM	575 - H5
2500 E 18TH ST, ANT, 94509	
QUEEN OF HEAVEN CEM	591 - G6
1965 RELIEZ VALLEY RD, CCCo, 94549	
ROLLING HILLS MEMORIAL PARK	589 - B1
4100 HILLTOP DR, RCH, 94803	
SAINT DOMINICS CEM	551 - D4
5TH ST & HILLCREST AV, BEN, 94510	
SAINT JOSEPH CEM	588 - J3
2560 CHURCH LN, SPAB, 94806	
SAINT MARYS CEM	630 - A6
4529 HOWE ST, OAK, 94611	
SAINT STEPHEN CATHOLIC CEM	592 - G3
MONUMENT BL & MONUMENT CT, CNCD, 94520	
SUNSET VIEW CEM	609 - E3
101 COLUSA AV, CCCo, 94707	
CITY HALLS	
ALBANY	609 - D6
1000 SAN PABLO AV, ALB, 94706	
ANTIOCH	575 - C4
3RD ST & H ST, ANT, 94509	
BENICIA	551 - C5
250 E L ST, BEN, 94510	
BRENTWOOD	616 - G1
708 3RD ST, BREN, 94513	
CLAYTON	593 - H6
6000 HERITAGE TR, CLAY, 94517	
CONCORD	592 - G1
1950 PARKSIDE DR, CNCD, 94519	
DANVILLE	652 - J1
510 LA GONDA WY, DNVL, 94526	
DUBLIN	693 - J4
100 CIVIC PZ, DBLN, 94568	
EL CERRITO	609 - C2
10890 SAN PABLO AV, ELCR, 94530	
HERCULES	569 - H3
111 CIVIC DR, HER, 94547	
LAFAYETTE	611 - E6
3675 MOUNT DIABLO BLVD, LFYT, 94549	
MARTINEZ	571 - D3
525 HENRIETTA ST, MRTZ, 94553	
MORAGA TOWN HALL	631 - E4
2100 DONALD DR, MRGA, 94556	
OAKLEY	576 - E6
3633 MAIN ST, OAKL, 94561	
ORINDA	610 - G7
26 ORINDA WY, ORIN, 94563	
PIEDMONT	650 - B1
120 VISTA AV, PDMT, 94611	
PINOLE	569 - E4
2131 PEAR ST, PIN, 94564	
PITTSBURG	574 - D3
65 CIVIC AV, PIT, 94565	
PLEASANT HILL	592 - C5
100 GREGORY LN, PLHL, 94523	
RICHMOND	588 - H6
2600 BARRETT AV, RCH, 94804	
SAN PABLO	588 - J3
SAN PABLO AV, SPAB, 94806	
SAN RAMON	673 - D1
2222 CM RAMON, SRMN, 94583	
WALNUT CREEK	612 - C5
1666 N MAIN ST, WLCK, 94596	
COLLEGES & UNIVERSITIES	
CALIFORNIA MARITIME ACADEMY	550 - C2
200 MARITIME ACADEMY DR, VAL, 94590	
CALIFORNIA STATE UNIV OF EAST BAY	593 - C6
4700 YGNACIO VALLEY RD, CNCD, 94521	
COLLEGE OF THE HOLY NAMES	650 - G4
3500 MOUNTAIN BLVD, OAK, 94602	
CONTRA COSTA COLLEGE (WEST CAMPUS)	589 - A2
2600 MISSION BELL DR, RCH, 94806	
DIABLO VALLEY COLLEGE	592 - B2
321 GOLF CLUB RD, PLHL, 94523	
KENNEDY, JOHN F UNIVERSITY	592 - D4
100 ELLINWOOD WY, PLHL, 94523	
LOS MEDANOS COLLEGE	574 - G5
2700 E LELAND RD, PIT, 94565	
MERRITT COLLEGE	650 - J6
12500 CAMPUS DR, OAK, 94619	
MILLS COLLEGE	650 - H7
5000 MACARTHUR BLVD, OAK, 94613	
PATTEN COLLEGE	650 - C6
2433 COOLIDGE AV, OAK, 94601	
SAINT ALBERTS COLLEGE	630 - A5
5890 BIRCH CT, OAK, 94618	
SAINT MARYS COLLEGE OF CALIFORNIA	631 - G6
1928 SAINT MARYS RD, MRGA, 94575	
UNIVERSITY OF CALIFORNIA BERKELEY	630 - B1
2200 UNIVERSITY AV, BERK, 94720	
ENTERTAINMENT & SPORTS	
CONCORD SKATEPARK	592 - F3
MONUMENT BLVD & COWELL RD, CNCD, 94518	
CONTRA COSTA FAIR GROUNDS	575 - B5
1201 10TH ST, CCCo, 94509	
FIRE TRAILS	
1-1	612 - A5
OAKVALE CT, WLCK, 94597	
1-2	612 - F5
461 SUMMIT RD, WLCK, 94598	
1-4	612 - F5
630 LA CASA VIA, WLCK, 94598	

FEATURE NAME Address City, ZIP Code	PAGE-GRID
1-5	612 - F5
MARSHAL DR, WLCK, 94598	
2-1	611 - F1
3550 ECHO SPRING RD, LFYT, 94549	
2-3	611 - J3
1070 CM VERDE CIR, WLCK, 94597	
2-4	611 - H1
1645 GREEN HILLS DR, CCCo, 94549	
2-5	612 - A3
LARKEY LN, WLCK, 94597	
2-6	611 - H1
3238 GREEN HILLS DR, CCCo, 94549	
2-7	611 - H1
TAYLOR BLVD, CCCo, 94549	
3-2	632 - C2
ROCKVIEW DR, WLCK, 94595	
3-3	632 - C3
SAKLAN INDIAN DR, WLCK, 94595	
3-4	632 - C4
ROSSMOOR PKWY, WLCK, 94595	
3-5	632 - A4
PTARMIGAN DR, WLCK, 94595	
3-7	632 - B3
STANLEY DOLLAR DR, WLCK, 94595	
3-8	632 - D5
HORSEMANS CANYON DR, WLCK, 94595	
3-9	632 - B2
CACTUS CT, WLCK, 94595	
4-1	612 - H7
WHITECLIFF WY, WLCK, 94596	
4-2	632 - H1
BENHAM CT, WLCK, 94596	
4-3	612 - H6
1880 ROCKSPRING PL, WLCK, 94598	
4-4	612 - H7
WOODBURY CT, WLCK, 94596	
4-5	612 - F6
SUTHERLAND DR, WLCK, 94598	
4-6	632 - G1
RUDGEAR RD, WLCK, 94596	
4-7	632 - G1
WHITECLIFF WY, WLCK, 94596	
4-8	632 - G1
2086 ROBB RD, WLCK, 94596	
4-10	632 - E1
60 LYMAN CT, WLCK, 94596	
4-11	632 - F2
YOUNGS VALLEY RD, WLCK, 94596	
4-12	612 - H7
ROCKSPRING PL, WLCK, 94596	
4-14	632 - E2
I-680 NORTHBOUND, WLCK, 94507	
5-5	591 - G6
STAGECOACH DR, CCCo, 94549	
6-1	573 - C2
4491 EVORA RD, CCCo, 94565	
6-2	573 - C2
4700 EVORA RD, CCCo, 94565	
6-3	573 - B2
4690 EVORA RD, CCCo, 94565	
6-4	573 - D3
AVILA RD, PIT, 94565	
6-5	573 - A3
EVORA RD, CCCo, 94565	
6-6	592 - G3
COWELL RD, CNCD, 94518	
6-8	573 - C3
AVILA RD, PIT, 94565	
7-2	612 - G4
LAS LOMAS WY, WLCK, 94598	
7-3	612 - H5
DEER VALLEY LN, WLCK, 94598	
7-4	612 - H5
CODORNIZ LN, WLCK, 94598	
7-5	612 - J5
HANNA GROVE TR, WLCK, 94598	
7-6	613 - A6
1000 CASTLE ROCK RD, CCCo, 94598	
7-7	613 - A6
1600 CASTLE ROCK RD, CCCo, 94598	
7-8	613 - A6
1600 CASTLE ROCK RD, CCCo, 94598	
7-9	613 - B6
1600 CASTLE ROCK RD, CCCo, 94598	
7-10	613 - A2
VALLEY VISTA RD, WLCK, 94598	
7-11	613 - A2
VALLEY VISTA RD, WLCK, 94598	
7-12	613 - A2
VALLEY VISTA RD, WLCK, 94598	
7-13	613 - B3
ARBOLADO DR, WLCK, 94598	
7-14	613 - B3
RIDGESTONE CT, WLCK, 94598	
7-15	613 - B5
NORTH GATE RD, CCCo, 94598	
7-16	613 - B5
NORTH GATE RD, CCCo, 94598	
7-17	613 - B6
NORTH GATE RD, CCCo, 94598	
7-18	613 - C7
NORTH GATE RD, CCCo, 94598	
7-19	613 - C7
NORTH GATE RD, CCCo, 94598	
7-20	613 - C7
NORTH GATE RD, CCCo, 94598	
7-21	613 - B3
NORTH GATE RD, CCCo, 94598	
7-22	612 - J6
DIABLO FOOTHILLS REG PK, WLCK, 94598	
7-23	613 - A7
DIABLO FOOTHILLS REG PK, CCCo, 94598	
7-24	612 - J5
PINECREEK RD, CCCo, 94598	
7-24	613 - A4
PINE CREEK RD, CCCo, 94598	
7-25	613 - B5
NORTH GATE RD, CCCo, 94598	
8-1	592 - J5
COURT LN, CNCD, 94518	
10-1	593 - A6
YGNACIO VALLEY RD, CNCD, 94521	
10-2	613 - A1
YGNACIO VALLEY RD, WLCK, 94598	
10-17	592 - J5
LIME RIDGE, CNCD, 94518	
10-18	592 - H5
VIA MONTANAS, CNCD, 94518	
10-19	592 - H4
VIA MONTANAS, CNCD, 94518	
10-20	592 - J6
CENTER LIME RIDGE, CNCD, 94518	
10-22	593 - A6
FAIR WEATHER CIR, CNCD, 94518	
10-23	592 - J7
NAVARONNE WY, WLCK, 94598	
10-24	593 - A7
YGNACIO VALLEY RD, WLCK, 94598	
11-1	594 - A5
WINDMILL CANYON DR, CLAY, 94517	

FEATURE NAME — Address City, ZIP Code	PAGE-GRID	FEATURE NAME — Address City, ZIP Code	PAGE-GRID	FEATURE NAME — Address City, ZIP Code	PAGE-GRID
11-2 — HESS RD, CCCo, 94517	593 - J4	13-41 — COSTANZA DR, MRTZ, 94553	591 - G1	19-10 — BEAR CREEK RD, CCCo, 94553	590 - F3
11-4 — KIRKER PASS RD, CCCo, 94521	593 - J3	13-42 — MCHARRY RANCH RD, CCCo, 94553	570 - J6	19-11 — BEAR CREEK RD, CCCo, 94553	590 - F4
11-5 — KAISER QUARRY RD, CCCo, 94598	613 - F1	13-43 — MOUNT KENNEDY DR, MRTZ, 94553	591 - G1	19-12 — 1190 BEAR CREEK RD, CCCo, 94553	590 - G5
11-6 — 555 MITCHELL CANYON RD, CCCo, 94517	613 - G1	13-44 — 720 VINE HILL WY, MRTZ, 94553	591 - G1	19-13 — 1220 BEAR CREEK RD, CCCo, 94553	590 - G5
11-7 — KAISER QUARRY RD, CCCo, 94598	613 - E1	13-46 — ROANOKE DR, MRTZ, 94553	571 - C5	19-14 — BEAR OAKS LN, CCCo, 94553	590 - H5
11-8 — MITCHELL CANYON RD, CCCo, 94598	613 - G2	13-46 — ROANOKE DR, MRTZ, 94553	591 - H3	19-17 — BEARINDA LN, CCCo, 94553	590 - G7
11-9 — 8125 MARSH CREEK RD, CCCo, 94517	614 - A2	13-47 — CANYON WY, MRTZ, 94553	571 - D6	19-18 — BEAR CREEK RD, CCCo, 94553	590 - J7
11-10 — HESS RD, CCCo, 94517	593 - J4	14-1 — BUCKLEY ST, MRTZ, 94553	571 - C3	19-19 — BEAR CREEK RD, CCCo, 94553	590 - H7
11-11 — PINE HOLLOW RD, CNCD, 94521	613 - D1	14-2 — BUCKLEY ST, MRTZ, 94553	571 - C3	19-20 — BEAR CREEK RD, CCCo, 94553	590 - H7
11-12 — PINE HOLLOW RD, CNCD, 94521	613 - D1	14-3 — 1158 PANORAMIC DR, MRTZ, 94553	571 - D4	19-21 — BEAR CREEK RD, CCCo, 94553	611 - A1
11-13 — PINE HOLLOW RD, CNCD, 94521	613 - D1	14-4 — ARABIA HTS, MRTZ, 94553	571 - D4	19-22 — RANCHO DEL LAGO RD, CCCo, 94553	590 - H4
11-14 — YGNACIO VALLEY RD, CNCD, 94521	593 - C6	14-5 — WALLIN DR, MRTZ, 94553	571 - D6	19-23 — ABRIGO VLY TR, CCCo, 94553	611 - B1
11-16 — 247 MONTAIRE PKWY, CLAY, 94517	613 - J2	14-6 — CARQUINEZ SCENIC DR, CCCo, 94553	571 - A2	19-24 — HOMESTEAD VLY TR, CCCo, 94553	611 - B1
11-17 — IRONWOOD WY, CNCD, 94521	593 - F7	14-7 — F ST, CCCo, 94553	571 - C3	19-25 — BLACK OAK TR, CCCo, 94553	591 - C7
11-18 — MITCHELL CANYON RD, CCCo, 94598	613 - G3	14-8 — 1711 DUNCAN DR, MRTZ, 94553	571 - D4	19-26 — VALLEY TR, CCCo, 94553	591 - C7
11-19 — MERRITT DR, CNCD, 94521	593 - F7	14-9 — DUNCAN DR, MRTZ, 94553	571 - D4	19-27 — BRIONES CREST TR, CCCo, 94553	591 - D6
11-20 — PEACOCK CREEK DR, CLAY, 94517	593 - J7	14-10 — DUNCAN DR, MRTZ, 94553	571 - D4	19-28 — BRIONES RD, CCCo, 94553	591 - D6
11-21 — CLAYTON RD, CLAY, 94517	613 - J1	14-11 — CANYON WY, MRTZ, 94553	571 - D6	19-29 — BEAR CREEK RD, CCCo, 94553	611 - A2
11-22 — 747 BLOCHING CIR, CLAY, 94517	613 - J2	14-12 — GREEN ST, MRTZ, 94553	571 - D4	19-30 — 4935 HAPPY VALLEY RD, CCCo, 94549	611 - B2
11-23 — 157 REGENCY DR, CLAY, 94517	613 - J2	15-3 — BACON WY, WLCK, 94597	612 - A4	19-31 — 4927 HAPPY VALLEY RD, CCCo, 94549	611 - B2
11-24 — RIALTO DR (END), CCCo, 94517	614 - A2	15-4 — 1329 SAN RELIEZ CT, LFYT, 94549	611 - H4	19-32 — 4927 HAPPY VALLEY RD, CCCo, 94549	611 - B2
11-24 — RIALTO DR, CCCo, 94517	613 - J3	15-6 — 3475 RANCHO DEL HOMBRE, LFYT, 94549	611 - F2	19-33 — RUSSEL RDG TR, LFYT, 94549	611 - B3
11-25 — 1908 KIRKWOOD DR, CNCD, 94521	593 - G5	15-7 — SPRINGHILL RD, CCCo, 94553	611 - E3	19-34 — HAMPTON RD, CCCo, 94553	590 - F6
11-26 — REGENCY DR, CCCo, 94517	613 - J2	15-8 — SPRINGHILL RD, CCCo, 94553	611 - E3	19-35 — HAMPTON RD, CCCo, 94553	590 - F6
11-27 — MOUNT TAMALPAIS DR, CCCo, 94517	613 - H2	15-9 — VIS BELLA, LFYT, 94549	611 - F4	19-36 — 5799 ALHAMBRA VALLEY RD, CCCo, 94553	590 - J2
11-28 — AHWANEE CT, CLAY, 94517	593 - H6	15-10 — LAFAYETTE RDG TR, LFYT, 94549	611 - F4	19-37 — 5700 ALHAMBRA VALLEY RD, CCCo, 94553	591 - A2
11-29 — ELK DR, CLAY, 94517	594 - A6	15-11 — SESSIONS RD, LFYT, 94549	611 - F4	19-38 — ALHAMBRA VALLEY RD, CCCo, 94553	591 - A2
11-30 — BLACK DIAMOND TR, CCCo, 94517	594 - A6	15-13 — 1219 MONTICELLO RD, LFYT, 94549	611 - E4	19-39 — 1090 FERNDALE RD, CCCo, 94553	590 - J1
11-31 — BLUE OAK LN, CLAY, 94517	593 - J5	15-14 — SUMMIT RD, LFYT, 94549	611 - J4	19-40 — 1090 FERNDALE RD, CCCo, 94553	590 - H2
11-32 — KELOK WY, CLAY, 94517	594 - A5	15-15 — DEER HILL RD, LFYT, 94549	611 - H5	19-41 — BRIONES RD, CCCo, 94553	591 - D5
11-33 — KELOK WY, CLAY, 94517	593 - J6	15-16 — CRESTMONT DR, LFYT, 94549	611 - D5	21-1 — 6170 ALHAMBRA AV, MRTZ, 94553	591 - H3
11-34 — BRANDYWINE PL, CLAY, 94517	594 - A7	15-17 — DEER HILL RD, LFYT, 94549	611 - H5	21-2 — BENHAM DR, MRTZ, 94553	591 - H3
11-35 — MARSH CREEK RD, CLAY, 94517	614 - A2	15-18 — RELIEZ VALLEY RD, WLCK, 94597	611 - H3	21-3 — VIEWPOINT CT, MRTZ, 94553	591 - H3
11-36 — KIRKER PASS RD, CCCo, 94565	594 - A2	15-19 — MONARCH RIDGE DR, WLCK, 94597	611 - J3	21-4 — PASO NOGAL, PLHL, 94523	591 - J3
13-1 — 5550 ALHAMBRA AV, MRTZ, 94553	591 - G2	15-20 — LAMPLIGHT CT, WLCK, 94597	611 - J3	21-5 — ELLINGTON TER, PLHL, 94523	591 - J2
13-2 — LINDSEY DR, MRTZ, 94553	591 - G2	16-1 — ORINDA VIEW RD, ORIN, 94563	610 - J3	21-6 — RELIEZ VALLEY RD, CCCo, 94549	591 - G7
13-3 — CHRISTIE DR, MRTZ, 94553	591 - F1	16-1A — BEAR CREEK RD, ORIN, 94563	610 - H2	21-7 — STAGE COACH DR, CCCo, 94549	591 - H6
13-5 — 2635 RELIEZ VALLEY RD, CCCo, 94553	591 - F2	16-5 — PANORAMA DR, LFYT, 94549	611 - D3	21-8 — SILVERHILL CT, CCCo, 94549	591 - G5
13-9 — FRANKLIN CANYON RD, CCCo, 94553	570 - J4	16-11 — 120 CAMELIA LN, LFYT, 94549	611 - A5	21-9 — STAGE COACH DR, CCCo, 94553	591 - F7
13-10 — FRANKLIN CANYON RD, CCCo, 94553	570 - J4	16-13 — LORINDA LN, LFYT, 94549	611 - A5	21-10 — BRIONES PK, CCCo, 94553	591 - G7
13-11 — FRANKLIN CANYON RD, CCCo, 94553	570 - J3	16-14 — MT DIABLO BLVD, LFYT, 94549	611 - C6	21-11 — BRIONES PK, CCCo, 94553	591 - G6
13-12 — MCEWEN RD, CCCo, 94569	570 - J3	16-15 — LAFAYETTE RESERVOIR, LFYT, 94549	611 - C6	21-12 — 1965 RELIEZ VALLEY RD, CCCo, 94553	591 - F5
13-13 — MCEWEN RD, CCCo, 94553	570 - J2	16-16 — 1182 ESTATES DR, LFYT, 94549	611 - B5	21-13 — RELIEZ VALLEY RD, CCCo, 94553	591 - G6
13-18 — FRANKLIN CANYON RD, CCCo, 94553	571 - A5	17-1 — WOODVIEW DR, LFYT, 94549	631 - G1	21-14 — 2099 RELIEZ VALLEY RD, CCCo, 94549	591 - H5
13-19 — FRANKLIN CANYON RD, CCCo, 94553	571 - A5	17-2 — MORECROFT RD, LFYT, 94549	632 - A4	21-15 — SUNRISE RIDGE DR, CCCo, 94549	591 - F5
13-20 — MCHARRY RANCH RD, CCCo, 94553	571 - A5	17-3 — HUNSAKER CANYON RD, CCCo, 94549	632 - A4	21-16 — RELIEZ VALLEY RD, CCCo, 94549	591 - G4
13-21 — WOLCOTT LN, CCCo, 94553	571 - B5	17-4 — MILDRED LN, MRGA, 94556	631 - F3	21-17 — TAVAN ESTATES DR, CCCo, 94553	591 - F4
13-21A — WOLCOTT LN, CCCo, 94553	571 - B5	17-5 — CATTLE CHUTE RD, LFYT, 94549	631 - H5	21-18 — SKYLINE DR, MRTZ, 94553	591 - H3
13-22 — 2560 FRANKLIN CANYON RD, CCCo, 94553	571 - C5	17-6 — 788 RELIEZ STATION RD, LFYT, 94549	631 - H1	21-19 — HORIZON DR, MRTZ, 94553	591 - G3
13-22A — 2480 FRANKLIN CANYON RD, CCCo, 94553	571 - C6	17-8 — HUNSAKER CANYON RD, LFYT, 94549	631 - J5	21-20 — BOIES DR, PLHL, 94523	592 - A3
13-23 — FRANKLIN CANYON RD, CCCo, 94553	571 - A5	17-9 — 3160 LUCAS DR, LFYT, 94549	631 - J2	31-1 — 1411 SAN RAMON VALLEY BLVD, DNVL, 94526	653 - A5
13-24 — 2785 FRANKLIN CANYON RD, CCCo, 94553	571 - B5	17-10 — DRIFTWOOD DR, LFYT, 94549	631 - H4	31-2 — MIDLAND WY, DNVL, 94526	653 - A5
13-24A — FRANKLIN CANYON RD, CCCo, 94553	571 - B6	17-11 — ROHRER DR, LFYT, 94549	631 - H3	31-3 — CLIFFSIDE DR, DNVL, 94526	652 - J4
13-25 — DUTRA RD, CCCo, 94553	571 - C7	17-12 — 595 SILVERADO DR, LFYT, 94549	631 - H3	31-4 — NEXT TO 246 REMINGTON LP, CCCo, 94583	652 - J4
13-26 — FRANKLIN CANYON RD, MRTZ, 94553	571 - C7	17-15 — OAK CANYON RD, LFYT, 94549	632 - A3	31-5 — KUSS RD, CCCo, 94526	652 - G2
13-27 — 148 GORDON WY, CCCo, 94553	591 - D2	17-17 — DAWKINS DR, LFYT, 94549	631 - H3	31-6 — CAMPBELL PL, DNVL, 94526	653 - E2
13-28 — 1200 CHRISTIE RD, CCCo, 94553	570 - J7	18-1 — MEDBURN ST, CCCo, 94565	572 - G2	32-1 — CAMILLE AV, CCCo, 94507	632 - F7
13-30 — 5530 ALHAMBRA VALLEY RD, CCCo, 94553	591 - B2	18-2 — NORMAN AV, CCCo, 94565	572 - G1	32-2 — LAS TRAMPAS RD, CCCo, 94507	632 - E6
13-31 — CHELESA DR, CCCo, 94553	591 - D1	18-3 — NICHOLS RD, CCCo, 94565	552 - J7	32-3 — 2130 LAS TRAMPAS RD, CCCo, 94507	632 - D5
13-32 — 1150 BRIONES RD, CCCo, 94553	591 - D4	18-4 — NICHOLS RD, CCCo, 94565	573 - B1	32-4 — RIDGEWOOD RD, CCCo, 94507	632 - D4
13-33 — 1150 BRIONES RD, CCCo, 94553	591 - E4	19-1 — ALHAMBRA VALLEY RD, CCCo, 94553	590 - J3	32-5 — 2600 RIDGEWOOD RD, CCCo, 94507	632 - E5
13-34 — 5433 ALHAMBRA VALLEY RD, CCCo, 94553	591 - C3	19-2 — 5895 ALHAMBRA VALLEY RD, CCCo, 94553	591 - A5	32-6 — ALAMO RANCH RD, CCCo, 94507	632 - G5
13-35 — VACA CREEK RD, CCCo, 94553	591 - D3	19-3 — 6001 ALHAMBRA VALLEY RD, CCCo, 94553	590 - H3	32-7 — SUGARLOAF DR, CCCo, 94507	632 - F3
13-35B — 2000 STONEHURST CT, CCCo, 94553	591 - C2	19-4 — ALHAMBRA VALLEY RD, CCCo, 94553	590 - G3	32-8 — TRACY CT, CCCo, 94507	632 - J3
13-35C — 1055 STONEHURST DR, CCCo, 94553	591 - C2	19-5 — PEREIRA RD, CCCo, 94553	590 - F2	32-9 — HIGH EAGLE RD, CCCo, 94507	632 - H5
13-36 — 5355 ALHAMBRA VALLEY RD, CCCo, 94553	591 - D3	19-6 — ALHAMBRA VALLEY RD, CCCo, 94553	590 - E2	32-10 — OAKSHIRE PL, CCCo, 94507	633 - B4
13-37 — BRIONES RD, CCCo, 94553	591 - D4	19-7 — ALHAMBRA VALLEY RD, CCCo, 94553	590 - E2	32-11 — LIVORNA RD, CCCo, 94507	632 - H2
13-38 — 4950 ALHAMBRA VALLEY RD, MRTZ, 94553	591 - E1	19-8 — ALHAMBRA VALLEY RD, CCCo, 94553	590 - E2	33-1 — ALAMO SPRINGS DR, DNVL, 94526	632 - H6
13-39 — 5026 ALHAMBRA VALLEY RD, MRTZ, 94553	591 - E1	19-8A — ALHAMBRA VALLEY RD, CCCo, 94553	590 - D2	33-3 — GOLDEN MEADOW LN, CCCo, 94507	633 - B4
13-40 — ALHAMBRA AV, MRTZ, 94553	591 - G1	19-9 — ALHAMBRA VALLEY RD, CCCo, 94553	590 - C1	33-4 — GREEN VALLEY RD, CCCo, 94507	633 - C3

CONTRA COSTA

FEATURE NAME Address City, ZIP Code	PAGE-GRID
33-5 MERANO ST, DNVL, 94526	653 - E1
33-6 EMMONS CYN DR & COUNTRY OAK LN, CCCo, 94507	633 - D4
33-7 LACKLAND DR, CCCo, 94528	633 - E5
33-8 VIA DIABLO, CCCo, 94528	633 - F6
33-9 MCCAULEY RD, DNVL, 94526	653 - D2
33-10 DIABLO RD W/O FAIRWAY DR, DNVL, 94526	633 - D7
33-11 DIABLO RD E/O ALAMEDA DIABLO, DNVL, 94526	633 - D7
33-12 DIABLO RD AT AVD NUEVA, DNVL, 94506	653 - E1
33-13 2406 DIABLO LAKES LN, CCCo, 94528	633 - F6
34-1 19251 CENTURY OAKS CT BLVD, CCCo, 94583	673 - D6
34-2 2731 COREY PL, CCCo, 94583	673 - D5
35-1 HOLBROOK DR, DNVL, 94506	653 - G4
35-2 END OF TUSCANY WY, DNVL, 94506	653 - H5
35-3 MAPLEWOOD DR, DNVL, 94506	653 - J3
35-4 WINDOVER DR, DNVL, 94506	653 - G2
35-5 PEPPERWOOD DR, CCCo, 94506	654 - A1
35-6 EAGLE NEST PL, CCCo, 94506	654 - B2
35-7 LAWRENCE RD, CCCo, 94582	674 - B1
35-8 BLACKHAWK MEADOW LN, CCCo, 94506	654 - D2
35-9 NOTTINGHAM DR, CCCo, 94506	654 - A4
35-10 CLOVERBROOK DR AT RASSANI DR, DNVL, 94506	654 - A6
35-11 LAURELWOOD DR AFTER GOLDSTONE, DNVL, 94506	653 - H3
35-12 WEST OF LAURELWOOD DR, DNVL, 94506	653 - H4
35-13 SUNHAVEN RD, DNVL, 94506	653 - H3
35-14 BLACKHAWK RD, CCCo, 94506	653 - J2
35-16 NORTHVIEW CT, DNVL, 94506	653 - H6
35-17 RIO GRANDE PL, SRMN, 94582	653 - G7
35-18 WILD OAK LN, CCCo, 94506	654 - B4
35-19 NEAR 1076 CHESHIRE CIR, CCCo, 94506	654 - B5
36-1 FINLEY RD, CCCo, 94588	654 - F2
36-2 FINLEY RD, CCCo, 94588	654 - H1
36-2A FINLEY RD, CCCo, 94588	654 - H2
36-3 JOHNSTON RD, CCCo, 94588	654 - J6
36-4 7191 JOHNSTON RD, CCCo, 94588	654 - J7
36-5 TASSAJARA RD, CCCo, 94582	674 - F1
36-6 (SEE PAGE 635) MARCIEL RD, CCCo, 94551	655 - C7
36-7 2000 VICTORINE RD, CCCo, 94551	675 - D1
36-8 1059 VICTORINE RD, CCCo, 94551	675 - E2
37-1 (SEE PAGE 635) END OF STORYBOOK LN, CCCo, 94551	655 - E5
37-3 (SEE PAGE 635) MORGAN TERRITORY RD, CCCo, 94551	655 - G6
37-4 (SEE PAGE 635) MORGAN TERRITORY RD, CCCo, 94551	655 - G6
37-5 (SEE PAGE 635) 11625 MORGAN TERRITORY RD, CCCo, 94551	655 - G6
37-6 (SEE PAGE 635) MORGAN TERRITORY RD, CCCo, 94551	655 - H7
37-7 12601 MORGAN TERRITORY RD, CCCo, 94551	675 - G1
37-7 MORGAN TERRITORY RD, CCCo, 94551	675 - H1
38-1 2622 DERBY DR, SRMN, 94583	673 - B4
38-2 DEERWOOD RD, CCCo, 94583	673 - B1
38-3 CROW CYN RD N SIDE 500 E/O CO, CCCo, 94583	672 - J2
38-4 1500 BOLLINGER CYN RD DRIVEWAY, SRMN, 94583	673 - A2
38-5 DRIVEWAY E/O SIDE 2805 NORRIS, CCCo, 94583	673 - A4
38-6 DRIVEWY W/O 2462 NORRIS CYN RD, CCCo, 94583	672 - J4
38-7 2303 REAR OF 2302 NRRIS CYN RD, CCCo, 94583	672 - H4
38-8 18722 BOLLINGER CANYON RD, CCCo, 94583	652 - H7
38-9 18311 BOLLINGER CYN RD, CCCo, 94583	652 - F5
38-10 18320 BOLLINGER CYN RD, CCCo, 94583	652 - F5
38-11 END OF BOLLINGER EST CT, CCCo, 94583	652 - F4
38-12 18181 BOLLINGER CYN RD, CCCo, 94583	652 - E4
38-13 EBRPD GATE N/O 18013 BOLLINGER, CCCo, 94583	652 - C3
38-14 BOLLINGER CYN RD, CCCo, 94583	652 - D3
38-15 BOLLINGER CYN RD, CCCo, 94583	652 - D2
38-16 18869 BOLLINGER CANYON RD, CCCo, 94583	673 - A1
38-17 18475 BOLLINGER CANYON RD, CCCo, 94583	652 - H6
41-1 QUAIL CRSG, CCCo, 94556	651 - F3
41-2 CM PABLO, CCCo, 94556	651 - F4
41-3 CM PABLO, CCCo, 94556	651 - F4
41-4 CM PABLO, CCCo, 94556	651 - F4
41-5 KNOLL DR, CCCo, 94556	651 - F3
41-7 SANDERS DR, MRGA, 94556	651 - F1
41-8 ALTA MESA, MRGA, 94556	631 - F7
41-9 SAINT MARYS COLLEGE, MRGA, 94556	631 - G7
41-11 AUGUSTA DR, MRGA, 94556	631 - B6
41-12 CANYON RD, CCCo, 94556	651 - D2
41-13 CANYON RD, CCCo, 94556	651 - D2
41-15 OLD REDWOOD HWY, CCCo, 94516	631 - A7
41-16 PINEHURST RD, CCCo, 94516	630 - H6
41-17 WINDING WY, CCCo, 94516	630 - G6
42-1 PAS GRANDE, MRGA, 94556	631 - C2
42-2 RHEEM BL N/O ZANDER, ORIN, 94563	631 - C2
42-3 LA SALLE DR, MRGA, 94556	631 - E3
42-4 KIMBERLY DR, MRGA, 94556	631 - D3
42-5 ASCOT DR, MRGA, 94556	631 - D3
42-6 LAIRD DR, MRGA, 94556	631 - D4
42-7 MORAGA RD, MRGA, 94556	631 - E2
42-8 RHEEM BLVD, MRGA, 94556	631 - F4
42-9 ST MARYS RD N/O BOLLINGER, MRGA, 94556	631 - G5
42-10 JOSEPH DR, MRGA, 94556	631 - H5
42-11 BOLLINGER CYN RD, CCCo, 94556	632 - A7
42-11 VALLEY HILL DR, MRGA, 94556	631 - J6
42-12 BOLLINGER CANYON RD, CCCo, 94556	631 - J7
42-13 BOLLINGER CANYON RD, CCCo, 94556	631 - J7
43-1 TAPPAN LN, ORIN, 94563	610 - F3
43-2 TAPPAN LN, ORIN, 94563	610 - F3
43-3 END OF MELODY LN, ORIN, 94563	610 - G3
43-4 BEAR CREEK RD, ORIN, 94563	610 - H2
43-5 END OF SUNNYSIDE LN, ORIN, 94563	610 - H2
43-5A END OF DALEWOOD DR, ORIN, 94563	610 - H3
44-1 BROOKSIDE RD, ORIN, 94563	630 - H3
44-2 END OF EDGEWOOD RD, ORIN, 94563	630 - J4
44-3 END OF EDGEWOOD RD, ORIN, 94563	630 - J5
44-4 END OF EDGEWOOD RD, ORIN, 94563	630 - J5
44-5 END OF MEADOW PARK CT, LFYT, 94549	631 - B1
44-7 HILLCREST DR, ORIN, 94563	631 - A1
44-8 DOLORES WY, ORIN, 94563	631 - A5
44-9 DONALD DR, ORIN, 94563	631 - B3
44-10 ALICE LN, MRGA, 94556	631 - C4
44-11 DONALD DR, MRGA, 94556	631 - C4
45-1 CM PABLO, CCCo, 94563	630 - G1
45-1A END OF LOS NARROBOS, CCCo, 94563	610 - E7
45-2 NORTH END GATEWAY BLVD, CCCo, 94563	630 - E2
45-2A GRIZZLY PARK BLVD, CCCo, 94563	630 - D1
45-3 SOUTH END GATEWAY BLVD, ORIN, 94563	630 - G2
45-4 OLD TUNNEL RD, CCCo, 94563	630 - E4
45-6 BEAR CREEK RD, ORIN, 94563	610 - E4
45-7 BEAR CREEK RD, ORIN, 94563	610 - E4
45-8 BEAR CREEK RD, ORIN, 94563	610 - E4
45-9 BEAR CREEK RD, CCCo, 94553	610 - E4
45-10 BEAR CREEK RD E/O DAM, CCCo, 94563	610 - E3
45-11 RIDGE LN, ORIN, 94563	610 - F4
45-12 RIDGE LN, ORIN, 94563	610 - F4
45-15 WILDCAT CANYON RD, CCCo, 94563	610 - C5
45-16 WILDCAT CANYON RD, CCCo, 94553	610 - C5
45-17 WILDCAT CANYON RD, CCCo, 94553	610 - A4
45-18 WILDCAT CANYON RD, CCCo, 94553	610 - A4
45-19 SAN PABLO DAM RD, CCCo, 94553	610 - B3
45-20 END OF INSPIRATION POINT TR, CCCo, 94553	610 - B3
45-21 SAN PABLO DAM RD, CCCo, 94553	609 - J1
45-23 EL TOYONAL, ORIN, 94563	610 - D6
45-24 EL TOYONAL, ORIN, 94563	610 - D6
51-1 8861 MARSH CREEK RD, CCCo, 94517	614 - B2
51-2 8990 MARSH CREEK RD, CCCo, 94517	614 - C3
51-3 10025 MARSH CREEK RD, CCCo, 94517	614 - E4
51-4 10025 MARSH CREEK RD, CCCo, 94517	614 - D4
51-5 RUSSELMAN RD 1.3 MILES SOUTH, CCCo, 94517	614 - C4
51-6 RUSSELMAN RD 1.3 MILES SOUTH, CCCo, 94517	614 - B4
51-10 11501 MARSH CREEK RD, CCCo, 94517	614 - F5
51-11 MARSH CREEK RD 1.2 MILES EAST, CCCo, 94517	614 - G6
51-14 13265 MARSH CREEK RD, CCCo, 94517	614 - J7
51-15 13580 MARSH CREEK RD, CCCo, 94517	634 - J1
51-17 13600 MARSH CK RD AT GILL DR, CCCo, 94517	635 - A1
51-18 MARSH CR 3.5 MI E MORGAN TER, CCCo, 94517	635 - B1
51-19 MARSH CREEK RD, CCCo, 94517	615 - B7
51-40 CURRY CANYON RD APPROX 2 MILES, CCCo, 94598	634 - E3
51-42 CURRY CANYON RD, CCCo, 94598	634 - D4
51-43 CURRY CANYON RD, CCCo, 94598	634 - C4
51-46 CURRY CANYON RD, CCCo, 94598	634 - B5
51-51 3107 MORGAN TERRITORY RD, CCCo, 94517	614 - E6
51-54 4825 MORGAN TERRITORY RD, CCCo, 94517	634 - G2
51-59 7000 MORGAN TERRITORY RD, CCCo, 94517	634 - H5
51-60 7000 MORGAN TERRITORY RD, CCCo, 94517	634 - H5
51-61 7000 MORGAN TERRITORY RD, CCCo, 94517	634 - J6
51-62 7000 MORGAN TERRITORY RD, CCCo, 94517	634 - J5
51-64 MORGAN TER 6.3 MI S MARSH CK, CCCo, 94551	635 - A6
51-65 MORGAN TER 6.6 MI S MARSH CK, CCCo, 94551	635 - B7
51-66 MORGAN TER 6.8 MI S MARSH CK, CCCo, 94551	635 - B7
52-1 (SEE PAGE 635) MARSH CK RD 3.1 MI E DEER VLY, CCCo, 94513	636 - C2
52-2 MARSH CK 1 MI E CAMINO DIABLO, CCCo, 94513	616 - D7
52-4 MARSH CK 1.5 MI E CAM DIABLO, CCCo, 94513	616 - D7
52-55 (SEE PAGE 635) VASCO RD 3.7 MI S CM DIABLO, CCCo, 94551	636 - D7
52-57 (SEE PAGE 635) VASCO RD 4.8 MI S CM DIABLO, CCCo, 94514	636 - D7
52-59 (SEE PAGE 635) VASCO RD 5.1 MI S CM DIABLO, CCCo, 94514	656 - D4
52-60 (SEE PAGE 635) VASCO RD 5.9 MI S CM DIABLO, CCCo, 94514	656 - C5
52-63 CONTRA COSTA COUNTY ALAMEDA CO, CCCo, 94551	676 - B2
52-64 CONTRA COSTA COUNTY ALAMEDA CO, CCCo, 94514	676 - B2
53-2 15320 MARSH CREEK RD, CCCo, 94517	635 - C1
53-3 MARSH CREEK RD, CCCo, 94517	615 - D7
53-4 15900 MARSH CREEK RD, CCCo, 94517	635 - D1
53-4 MARSH CREEL RD, CCCo, 94517	615 - D7
53-5 MARSH CREEK RD, CCCo, 94517	615 - F6
53-6 MARSH CK 6.3 MI E MORGAN TER, CCCo, 94517	635 - F1
53-6 MARSH CREEK RD, CCCo, 94517	615 - F7
53-7 MARSH CK .1 MI E DEER VALLEY, CCCo, 94517	635 - G1
53-9 BRIONES VALLEY RD, CCCo, 94517	615 - C3
53-14 CHADBOURNE RD, CCCo, 94531	615 - C2
53-15 MARSH CK 1.6 MI E DEER VALLEY, CCCo, 94513	635 - J2
53-16 (SEE PAGE 635) MARSH CK RD 2.2 MI E DEER VLY, CCCo, 94513	636 - B2
53-16 MARSH CR RD 2.2 MI E DEER VAL, CCCo, 94513	616 - D6
55-1 MORGAN TERRITORY RD, CCCo, 94551	635 - D7
55-2 (SEE PAGE 635) MORGAN TER 7.9 MI S MARSH CK, CCCo, 94551	655 - D1
55-3 (SEE PAGE 635) MORGAN TER 7.9 MI S MARSH CK, CCCo, 94551	655 - D1
55-4 (SEE PAGE 635) MORGAN TER 9.1 MI S MARSH CK, CCCo, 94551	655 - E3
55-5 (SEE PAGE 635) 9401 MORGAN TERRITORY RD, CCCo, 94551	655 - E3
55-6 (SEE PAGE 635) 9401 MORGAN TERRITORY RD, CCCo, 94551	655 - F3
55-7 (SEE PAGE 635) 9600 MORGAN TERRITORY RD, CCCo, 94551	655 - E3
59-1 SOUTH GATE RD AT ROCK CITY, CCCo, 94598	633 - H5
59-2 SOUTH GATE RD AT ROCK CITY, CCCo, 94598	633 - H6
59-3 SOUTH GATE RD AT ROCK CITY, CCCo, 94598	633 - H6
59-4 SOUTH GATE RD AT ROCK CITY, CCCo, 94598	633 - J5
59-5 SOUTH GATE RD AT ROCK CITY, CCCo, 94598	633 - H3
59-6 SUMMIT RD, CCCo, 94598	633 - H3
59-7 SUMMIT RD, CCCo, 94598	633 - J2
59-8 SUMMIT RD, CCCo, 94598	633 - J2
59-9 NORTH GATE RD, CCCo, 94598	633 - G2
59-10 SUMMIT RD AT JUNIPER, CCCo, 94598	633 - H1
59-11 NORTH GATE RD, CCCo, 94598	633 - E2
59-12 NORTH GATE RD, CCCo, 94598	633 - E2
59-13 NORTH GATE RD, CCCo, 94598	613 - C7
59-14 SOUTH GATE RD AT ROCK CITY, CCCo, 94598	633 - H5
59-15 1 MI FROM END OF FINLEY RD, CCCo, 94506	634 - G7
61-2 CANAL BLVD, RCH, 94804	608 - E2
61-3 TOP OF CREST, RCH, 94801	608 - D1
61-4 END OF WESTERN DR, RCH, 94801	608 - D1
61-5 DORNAN AND POSEY, RCH, 94801	608 - D2
61-6 SOUTH END OF DORNAN, RCH, 94801	608 - D3
63-1 LEISURE LN, CCCo, 94803	589 - E3
63-1A END OF VALLEY VIEW RD, RCH, 94803	589 - F4
63-1B SAN PABLO DAM RD AT CASTRO, RCH, 94803	589 - G4
63-2 TRI LN, RCH, 94803	589 - H5
63-3 EAST SIDE OF SAN PABLO DAM RD, RCH, 94803	589 - H5
63-4 SAN PABLO DAM RD, CCCo, 94553	589 - H6
63-5 SAN PABLO DAM RD, CCCo, 94553	589 - J7

FEATURE NAME Address City, ZIP Code	PAGE-GRID
63-6 HILLSIDE DR, CCCo, 94803	589 - H5
63-7 PATRA DR, CCCo, 94803	589 - H5
63-7A RACHILL LN, CCCo, 94803	589 - H4
63-8 CASTRO RANCH RD, RCH, 94803	589 - H4
63-9 CASTRO RANCH RD, CCCo, 94803	589 - H3
63-10 CASTRO RANCH RD, CCCo, 94803	589 - J3
63-11 SOUTH SIDE OF CASTRO RANCH RD, CCCo, 94553	590 - A3
63-11A NORTH SIDE OF CASTRO RANCH RD, CCCo, 94553	590 - A2
63-12 SOUTH END OF CONESTOGA WY, RCH, 94803	589 - J3
63-13 COACH DR, RCH, 94803	589 - J2
63-14 WEST SIDE OF SILVER BELT DR, RCH, 94803	589 - H2
63-14A E/O HEAVENLY RIDGE LN, RCH, 94803	589 - G2
63-15 5435 HEAVENLY RIDGE LN, RCH, 94803	589 - H2
63-16 3832 HIDDEN SPRING CT, RCH, 94803	589 - H1
66-1 WILD CAT CANYON PKWY, RCH, 94805	589 - B4
66-1A MCBRIDE & ALVERADO PK ENTRANCE, RCH, 94805	589 - B4
66-2 NORTH SIDE OF WILDCAT CANYON, RCH, 94805	589 - B4
66-3 W/O WILDCAT CANYON, CCCo, 94805	589 - C4
66-3A END OF PARK AV, CCCo, 94805	589 - B4
66-4 E/O WILDCAT CANYON PKWY, RCH, 94805	589 - E7
66-5 WILDCAT CANYON AT HAVEY CANYON, RCH, 94805	589 - F7
68-1 GIANT HWY, RCH, 94806	568 - G6
68-2 GIANT HWY & SOBRANTE AV, RCH, 94806	568 - H5
69-1 CAPITAL HILL, RCH, 94806	589 - B4
69-2 BONITA RD, RCH, 94806	589 - B4
69-3 MONTE CRESTA AV, RCH, 94803	589 - C3
69-4 LA CRESCENTA RD, RCH, 94803	589 - C3
69-4A END OF LA COLINA RD, RCH, 94803	589 - C3
69-5 WESLEY WY, RCH, 94803	589 - D3
69-6 CLARK RD, RCH, 94803	589 - D3
69-7 UPLAND DR, RCH, 94803	589 - E3
71-1 TAMALPAIS CT, ELCR, 94530	589 - C7
71-2 1450 NAVALLIER ST, ELCR, 94530	609 - D1
71-3 7500 SCHMIDT LN, ELCR, 94530	609 - D2
71-4 CONLON AV, ELCR, 94530	589 - B7
72-1 RIFLE RANGE RD, RCH, 94805	589 - E7
72-2 1400 ARLINGTON BL TO PINEHURST, ELCR, 94530	589 - D7
72-3 770 POTRERO AV, ELCR, 94530	609 - D1
72-4 8300 KENT DR, ELCR, 94530	609 - D1
72-5 KING CT, ELCR, 94530	609 - D2
72-6 GATTO AV AT MIRA VISTA, ELCR, 94530	589 - C7
72-7 END OF JAMES PL, ELCR, 94530	609 - E1
72-8 7700 POTRERO AV, ELCR, 94530	609 - D1
73-1 END OF TENNENT AV, PIN, 94564	569 - E3
73-2 END PINOLE SHORES DR, PIN, 94564	569 - C3
73-3 END OF PEACH ST OFF TENNENT AV, PIN, 94564	569 - E4
73-5 END CANYON DR, PIN, 94564	569 - E5
74-1 END OF GARRITY CT, PIN, 94564	569 - G5
74-2A NEXT TO 3300 PONDEROSA TR, PIN, 94564	569 - G5
74-2B NEXT TO 3309 PONDEROSA TR, PIN, 94564	569 - G5
74-3 2457 FARIA, PIN, 94564	569 - F5
74-4 2458 FARIA, PIN, 94564	569 - F5
74-5 END OF PALOMA ST, PIN, 94564	569 - G6
74-6 END OF CARMELITA WY, PIN, 94564	569 - G6
74-7 END OF APPALOOSA TR, PIN, 94564	569 - H6
74-8 END OF SILVERCREST, PIN, 94564	569 - J7
74-9 END OF HAMILTON, PIN, 94564	569 - J6
74-10 END OF DOIDGE, PIN, 94564	570 - A6
74-11 4005 MARCUS, PIN, 94564	569 - J7
74-12 4030 MARCUS, CCCo, 94553	569 - J7
74-14 END LUCAS AV, PIN, 94564	569 - G6
74-15 PFEIFFER WY, PIN, 94564	569 - J7
74-16 END OF ADOBE RD, PIN, 94564	589 - H1
74-18 ALHAMBRA VALLEY RD, CCCo, 94553	590 - B2
74-19 ALHAMBRA VALLEY RD, CCCo, 94553	590 - B1
74-20 ALHAMBRA VALLEY RD, CCCo, 94553	590 - B2
74-21 GOMEZ RD, CCCo, 94553	590 - B2
74-22 AT Y ON CASTRO RANCH RD, CCCo, 94553	590 - A2
74-23 ALHAMBRA VALLEY RD, CCCo, 94553	590 - A2
74-24 ALHAMBRA VALLEY RD, CCCo, 94553	590 - A2

FEATURE NAME Address City, ZIP Code	PAGE-GRID
74-25 AT MOHRING RANCH BARN, CCCo, 94553	589 - J1
74-26 AT MOHRING RANCH BARN, CCCo, 94553	589 - J1
74-29A END OF GALBRETH, CCCo, 94803	569 - F7
74-29B GALBRETH ON LEFT, PIN, 94564	569 - F7
74-30 END OF HOKE CT, PIN, 94564	569 - E6
74-31 ACROSS FROM 2079 SHEA DR, PIN, 94564	569 - F6
74-32 1980 SARAH DR, PIN, 94564	569 - E5
74-33 END OF DUNCAN, PIN, 94564	569 - E6
74-34 TURQUOISE DR NEAR ONYX CT, HER, 94547	569 - H5
75-1 13 PARKER AV, CCCo, 94572	549 - J6
75-3 END OF SPRINGWOOD CT, CCCo, 94572	550 - A7
76-4 VIEWPOINTE BLVD, CCCo, 94572	569 - J2
76-5 RTE 4 & SYCAMORE AV, CCCo, 94547	570 - A3
76-6 RODEO CREEK, CCCo, 94572	570 - B2
76-7 HWY 4, CCCo, 94547	570 - B3
76-8 SYCAMORE AV, CCCo, 94547	570 - A3
76-10 HWY 4 AT FERNANDEZ RANCH, CCCo, 94547	570 - B3
76-11 HWY 4 AT GOLF COURSE, HER, 94547	570 - D4
76-12 HWY 4 AT GOLF COURSE, CCCo, 94553	570 - D4
76-13 CHRISTIE RD, CCCo, 94553	570 - F5
76-14 CHRISTIE RD, CCCo, 94553	570 - F5
76-15 CHRISTIE RD, CCCo, 94553	570 - G5
76-17 HWY 4 WEST OF CUMMINGS, CCCo, 94553	570 - E4
76-18 HWY 4 EAST OF CHRISTIE RD, CCCo, 94553	570 - F4
76-18A HWY 4 EAST OF CHRISTIE RD, CCCo, 94553	570 - F4
76-19 HWY 4, CCCo, 94553	570 - F3
76-19A HWY 4 W OF CUMMINGS, CCCo, 94553	570 - G3
76-20 BARRY HILL RD, CCCo, 94553	570 - G3
76-21 BARRY HILL CT, CCCo, 94553	570 - G3
76-22 CUMMINGS SKWY, CCCo, 94553	570 - G3
76-23 FRANKLIN CANYON RD, CCCo, 94553	570 - H3
76-24 CUMMINGS SKYWAY, CCCo, 94569	570 - G3
76-25 CUMMINGS SKWY, CCCo, 94553	570 - G2
76-26 CUMMINGS SKWY, CCCo, 94553	570 - G2
76-27 CUMMINGS SKWY, CCCo, 94569	570 - G2
76-29 241 SHEPARD CT, HER, 94547	570 - B4
76-30 END OF REFUGIO VALLEY RD, CCCo, 94553	570 - C6
76-31 521 FALCON WY, HER, 94547	570 - A5
76-32 END OF PHEASANT, HER, 94547	569 - J6
76-33 FALCON WY & REFUGIO VALLEY RD, HER, 94547	570 - A5
76-34 341 GRISSOM ST, HER, 94547	570 - B4
77-1 CARQUINEZ SCENIC DR, CCCo, 94553	571 - A2
77-2 CARQUINEZ SCENIC DR, CCCo, 94553	570 - J1
77-3 CARQUINEZ SCENIC DR, CCCo, 94553	550 - H7
77-5 CARQUINEZ SCENIC DR, CCCo, 94569	550 - H6
77-6 MCEWEN RD, CCCo, 94553	570 - H1
77-7 MCEWEN RD, CCCo, 94569	570 - H2
77-8 MCEWEN RD, CCCo, 94553	570 - H1
77-9 MCEWEN RD, CCCo, 94569	570 - G1
77-10 CARQUINEZ SCENIC DR, CCCo, 94569	550 - G5
77-11 CARQUINEZ SCENIC DR, CCCo, 94569	550 - F5
78-12 DUPURU DR, CCCo, 94525	550 - F5
78-12A CARQUINEZ SCENIC DR, CCCo, 94525	550 - F5
78-13 ROLPH PARK DR, CCCo, 94525	550 - E5
78-14 CUMMINGS SKWY, CCCo, 94569	570 - F1
78-15 CUMMINGS SKWY, CCCo, 94553	570 - F1
78-16 CROCKETT BLVD, CCCo, 94553	550 - F7
78-17 CROCKETT BLVD, CCCo, 94553	550 - E7
78-18 CUMMINGS SKWY, CCCo, 94553	550 - D6
79-19 CUMMINGS SKWY, CCCo, 94553	550 - C6
79-20 CUMMINGS SKWY, CCCo, 94553	550 - C6
79-21 CROCKETT BLVD, CCCo, 94525	550 - D5
79-22 CROCKETT BLVD, CCCo, 94525	550 - D5
79-23 2ND AND ROSE ST, CCCo, 94525	550 - D5
79-24 OLD COUNTY RD, CCCo, 94525	550 - B5
79-25 OLD COUNTY RD, CCCo, 94525	550 - B5
82-1 CONTRA LOMA BLVD, ANT, 94509	595 - B3
82-2 CONTRA LOMA BLVD, ANT, 94509	595 - B3
82-3 EMPIRE MINE RD, ANT, 94531	595 - D6
82-4 EMPIRE MINE RD, ANT, 94531	595 - D6

FEATURE NAME Address City, ZIP Code	PAGE-GRID
82-5 EMPIRE MINE RD, ANT, 94531	595 - D6
82-6 EMPIRE MINE RD, CCCo, 94531	595 - D7
83-1 SOMERSVILLE RD, CCCo, 94565	594 - H1
83-2 SOMERSVILLE RD, CCCo, 94509	594 - H1
83-3 SOMERSVILLE RD, CCCo, 94565	594 - G3
83-4 SOMERSVILLE RD, CCCo, 94509	594 - G3
83-5 SOMERSVILLE RD, CCCo, 94509	594 - G3
83-6 SOMERSVILLE RD, CCCo, 94565	594 - G4
83-7 STEWARTVILLE TR, CCCo, 94509	594 - G5
83-8 FOOTHILL CT, ANT, 94509	594 - J2
84-1 W 10TH ST, PIT, 94565	574 - C2
85-2 KIRKER PASS RD, CCCo, 94565	574 - C7
85-3 NORTONVILLE RD, CCCo, 94517	594 - C2
85-4 NORTONVILLE SOMERSVILLE RD, CCCo, 94517	594 - D3
85-5 NORTONVILLE SOMERSVILLE RD, CCCo, 94517	594 - E4
85-6 NORTONVILLE SOMERSVILLE RD, CCCo, 94517	594 - E5
85-7 BLACK DIAMOND TR, CCCo, 94565	594 - E4
86-2 EVORA RD, CCCo, 94565	573 - D2
86-7 BAILEY RD, CCCo, 94565	573 - G4
86-8 BAILEY RD, PIT, 94565	573 - G5
86-9 BAILEY RD, PIT, 94565	573 - G6
86-10 BAILEY RD, CCCo, 94565	573 - G7
86-11 JACQUELINE DR, PIT, 94565	573 - J5
86-13 W LELAND RD, PIT, 94565	574 - A4
86-14 N BROADWAY AV, CCCo, 94565	573 - G1
86-15 POINSETTIA AV, CCCo, 94565	573 - H1
86-16 WILLOW PASS RD, CCCo, 94565	574 - A2
95-1 CANAL RD, CCCo, 94511	577 - A1
95-2 BETHEL ISLAND RD, CCCo, 94511	557 - D7
95-3 CANAL RD, CCCo, 94511	577 - D2
95-4 S OF WILLOW RD W OF PIPER RD, CCCo, 94511	577 - F2
95-5 BETHEL ISLAND RD AT TAYLOR RD, CCCo, 94511	577 - C3
95-6 END OF RANCH LN, CCCo, 94511	577 - E4
95-7 MID CANAL RD SOUTH OF SNSET DR, CCCo, 94511	557 - C7
95-8 CANAL RD, CCCo, 94511	577 - C2
95-9 N OFF OF CANAL RD, CCCo, 94511	577 - B2
95-10 BETHEL ISLE RD N OF GATEWAY RD, CCCo, 94511	577 - D3
95-11 BETHEL ISLE RD S OF SANDMOUND, CCCo, 94561	577 - D6
95-12 CANAL RD, CCCo, 94511	577 - A1
97-1 (SEE PAGE 635) 5000 VASCO RD, CCCo, 94514	636 - G5
97-2 (SEE PAGE 635) 545 CM DIABLO, CCCo, 94513	636 - J3
97-3 (SEE PAGE 635) 1390 CM DIABLO, CCCo, 94514	636 - J4
97-4 2000 CM DIABLO, CCCo, 94513	637 - B3
97-5 6000 ARMSTRONG RD, CCCo, 94514	637 - C7
97-6 (SEE PAGE 638) END OF ARMSTRONG AT VASCO RD, CCCo, 94514	657 - C3
97-7 (SEE PAGE 638) END OF BYRON HOT SPRINGS RD, CCCo, 94514	657 - F5

GOLF COURSES

FEATURE NAME Address City, ZIP Code	PAGE-GRID
BLACKHAWK CC EAST (PRIVATE) 599 BLACKHAWK CLUB DR, CCCo, 94506	654 - C4
BLACKHAWK CC - FALLS (WEST) 599 BLACKHAWK CLUB DR, CCCo, 94506	654 - A3
BLACKHAWK CC - LAKESIDE 599 BLACKHAWK CLUB DR, CCCo, 94506	654 - A2
BOUNDARY OAK GC 3800 VALLEY VISTA RD, WLCK, 94598	613 - A1
BRENTWOOD CC 1740 BALFOUR RD, BREN, 94513	616 - C2
BRIDGES GC, THE 9000 S GALE RIDGE, SRMN, 94582	673 - G2
BUCHANAN FIELDS GC 1091 CONCORD AV, CCCo, 94553	592 - C1
CANYON LAKES CC 640 BOLLINGER CANYON WY, SRMN, 94582	673 - F1
CLAREMONT CC 5295 BROADWAY TER, OAK, 94611	630 - A6
CONTRA COSTA CC 801 GOLF CLUB RD, PLHL, 94523	592 - A2
CROW CANYON CC 711 SILVER LAKE DR, DNVL, 94526	653 - E7
DEER RIDGE CC 801 FOOTHILL DR, BREN, 94513	616 - B4
DIABLO CC 1700 CLUBHOUSE RD, CCCo, 94528	633 - D6
DIABLO CREEK GC 4050 PORT CHICAGO HWY, CNCD, 94520	572 - H3
DIABLO HILLS GC 1551 MARCHBANKS DR, WLCK, 94598	612 - E3
DISCOVERY BAY CC 1475 CLUBHOUSE DR, CCCo, 94514	617 - J6
DUBLIN RANCH GC 5900 SIGNAL HILL DR, DBLN, 94568	694 - F1
FRANKLIN CANYON GC HWY 4 PKWY, HER, 94547	570 - E4
GOLF COURSE AT BETHEL ISLAND, THE 3303 GATEWAY RD, CCCo, 94511	577 - D3
GOLF COURSE AT RODDY RANCH, THE 1 TOUR WY, CCCo, 94531	615 - E2
GRAYSON WOODS GC 400 IRON HILL, PLHL, 94523	591 - H4
LAS POSITAS GC 917 CLUBHOUSE DR, LVMR, 94588	694 - J6

CONTRA COSTA

FEATURE NAME Address City, ZIP Code	PAGE-GRID
LONE TREE GC	595 - C2
4800 GOLF COURSE RD, ANT, 94531	
MARE ISLAND GC	549 - H1
1800 CLUB DR, VAL, 94592	
MIRA VISTA CC & GC	589 - D6
7901 CUTTING BLVD, ELCR, 94530	
MONTCLAIR GC	650 - E2
2477 MONTEREY BLVD, OAK, 94602	
MORAGA CC	631 - C6
1600 SAINT ANDREWS DR, MRGA, 94556	
OAKHURST CC	593 - H6
1001 PEACOCK CREEK DR, CLAY, 94517	
ORINDA CC	610 - F6
315 CM SOBRANTE, ORIN, 94563	
PINE MEADOW GC	571 - H7
451 VINE HILL WY, MRTZ, 94553	
PITTSBURGS DELTA VIEW GC	574 - A4
2242 GOLF CLUB RD, PIT, 94565	
RICHMOND CC	568 - H6
3900 GIANT RD, RCH, 94806	
ROSSMOOR GC	632 - B2
1010 STANLEY DOLLAR DR, WLCK, 94595	
ROUNDHILL GOLF & CC	632 - J4
3169 ROUNDHILL DR, CCCo, 94507	
ROUNDHILL GOLF & CC	633 - A5
3169 ROUNDHILL DR, CCCo, 94507	
SAN RAMON ROYAL VISTA GC	673 - G7
9430 FIRCREST LN, SRMN, 94583	
SHADOW LAKES GC	616 - A2
401 W COUNTRY CLUB DR, BREN, 94513	
TILDEN PARK GC	610 - A6
GRIZZLY PEAK BLVD & SHASTA RD, CCCo, 94708	
WILLOW PARK GC	672 - A7
17007 REDWOOD RD, AlaC, 94546	

HOSPITALS

ALAMEDA CO MED CTR- HIGHLAND CAMPUS	650 - B5
1411 E 31ST ST, OAK, 94606	
CONTRA COSTA REGL MED CTR	571 - D4
2500 ALHAMBRA AV, MRTZ, 94553	
DOCTORS MED CTR SAN PABLO CAMPUS	588 - J4
2000 VALE RD, SPAB, 94806	
KAISER FOUNDATION HOSP	612 - C6
1425 S MAIN ST, WLCK, 94596	
KAISER FOUNDATION HOSP	588 - F6
901 NEVIN AV, RCH, 94801	
MOUNT DIABLO MED CTR	592 - F1
2540 EAST ST, CNCD, 94520	
MUIR, JOHN MED CTR	612 - E3
1601 YGNACIO VALLEY RD, WLCK, 94598	
SAN RAMON REGL MED CTR	673 - E1
6001 NORRIS CANYON RD, SRMN, 94583	
SUTTER DELTA MED CTR	595 - D1
3901 LONE TREE WY, ANT, 94509	
VALLEYCARE MED CTR	694 - D6
5555 W LAS POSITAS BLVD, PLE, 94588	
VETERANS AFFAIRS MED CTR	571 - F6
150 MUIR RD, MRTZ, 94553	

HOTELS

BEST WESTERN HERITAGE INN	551 - C4
1955 E 2ND ST, BEN, 94510	
CANDLEWOOD SUITES	694 - A5
5535 JOHNSON DR, PLE, 94588	
CLAREMONT RESORT AND SPA, THE	630 - A3
41 TUNNEL RD, BERK, 94705	
CONCORD HILTON	592 - D2
1970 DIAMOND BLVD, CNCD, 94520	
COURTYARD BY MARRIOTT	673 - D4
18090 SAN RAMON VALLEY BLVD, SRMN, 94583	
COURTYARD BY MARRIOTT	589 - B1
3150 GARRITY WY, RCH, 94806	
COURTYARD BY MARRIOTT - PLEASANT HILL	592 - C6
2250 CONTRA COSTA BLVD, PLHL, 94523	
COURTYARD BY MARRIOTT PLEASANTON	694 - B6
5059 HOPYARD RD, PLE, 94588	
CROWNE-PLAZA PLEASANTON	693 - G6
11950 DUBLIN CANYON RD, PLE, 94588	
EMBASSY SUITES-WALNUT CREEK	612 - C1
1345 TREAT BLVD, WLCK, 94597	
FOUR POINTS HOTEL BY SHERATON	694 - B5
5115 HOPYARD RD, PLE, 94588	
HILTON PLEASANTON AT THE CLUB	693 - J5
7050 JOHNSON DR, PLE, 94588	
HOLIDAY INN CONCORD	592 - C1
1050 BURNETT AV, CNCD, 94520	
HOLIDAY INN OF WALNUT CREEK	612 - C2
2730 N MAIN ST, WLCK, 94597	
LAFAYETTE PARK HOTEL	611 - H6
3287 MOUNT DIABLO BLVD, LFYT, 94549	
RADISSON DUBLIN	693 - G5
6680 REGIONAL ST, DBLN, 94568	
RESIDENCE INN BY MARRIOTT	693 - G5
11900 DUBLIN CANYON RD, PLE, 94588	
RESIDENCE INN BY MARRIOTT	592 - D4
700 ELLINWOOD WY, PLHL, 94523	
SAN RAMON MARRIOTT AT BISHOP RANCH	673 - D3
2600 BISHOP DR, SRMN, 94583	
SHERATON CONCORD HOTEL	592 - D1
45 JOHN GLENN DR, CCCo, 94553	
WALNUT CREEK MARRIOTT	612 - C3
2355 N MAIN ST, WLCK, 94596	
WYNDHAM GARDEN HOTEL PLEASANTON	693 - H5
5990 STONERIDGE MALL RD, PLE, 94588	

LIBRARIES

ALBANY	609 - E6
1247 MARIN AV, ALB, 94706	
ANTIOCH	575 - D5
501 W 18TH ST, ANT, 94509	
BAY POINT	573 - E1
205 PACIFICA AV, CCCo, 94565	
BENICIA	551 - C5
150 E L ST, BEN, 94510	
BERKELEY BRANCH LIBRARY NORTH	609 - G6
1170 THE ALAMEDA, BERK, 94707	
BRENTWOOD	616 - G1
751 3RD ST, BREN, 94513	
CLAYTON	593 - H6
6125 CLAYTON RD, CLAY, 94517	
CONCORD	592 - G1
2900 SALVIO ST, CNCD, 94519	
CROCKETT	550 - D4
991 LORING AV, CCCo, 94525	
DANVILLE	653 - A2
400 FRONT ST, DNVL, 94526	
DIMOND BRANCH	650 - D4
3565 FRUITVALE AV, OAK, 94602	
DUBLIN	693 - J4
200 CIVIC PZ, DBLN, 94568	
EL CERRITO	609 - D3
6510 STOCKTON AV, ELCR, 94530	
EL SOBRANTE	589 - C2
4191 APPIAN WY, CCCo, 94803	
KENSINGTON	609 - F3
61 ARLINGTON AV, CCCo, 94708	

FEATURE NAME Address City, ZIP Code	PAGE-GRID
LAFAYETTE	611 - F6
952 MORAGA RD, LFYT, 94549	
MARTINEZ	571 - E3
740 COURT ST, MRTZ, 94553	
MONTCLAIR BRANCH	630 - D7
1687 MOUNTAIN BLVD, OAK, 94611	
MORAGA	631 - E6
1500 SAINT MARYS RD, MRGA, 94556	
OAKLEY	596 - E3
1050 NEROLY RD, OAKL, 94561	
ORINDA	610 - G7
24 ORINDA WY, ORIN, 94563	
PINOLE	569 - F6
2935 PINOLE VALLEY RD, PIN, 94564	
PITTSBURG	574 - D3
80 POWER AV, PIT, 94565	
PLEASANT HILL CENTRAL	592 - B7
1750 OAK PARK BLVD, PLHL, 94523	
RICHMOND MAIN	588 - H6
325 CIVIC CENTER PZ, RCH, 94804	
RODEO	549 - H7
220 PACIFIC AV, CCCo, 94572	
ROSSMOOR LEISURE WORLD	632 - B2
1001 GOLDEN RAIN RD, WLCK, 94595	
SAN PABLO	588 - J2
2300 EL PORTAL DR, SPAB, 94806	
SAN RAMON	673 - F3
100 MONTGOMERY ST, SRMN, 94583	
WALNUT CREEK	612 - C5
1644 N BROADWAY, WLCK, 94596	
YGNACIO VALLEY	612 - J2
2661 OAK GROVE RD, WLCK, 94598	

MILITARY INSTALLATIONS

COAST GUARD	650 - A7
ALAMEDA HARBOR, ALA, 94501	
COAST GUARD STA	552 - H6
MAIN ST & PORT CHICAGO HWY, CCCo, 94565	
MARE ISLAND NAVAL RESV (CLOSED)	549 - H2
MARE ISLAND, VAL, 94592	
MILITARY OCEAN TERMINAL CONCORD	553 - B5
WILLOW PASS RD, CCCo, 94565	
NATL GUARD ARMORY	608 - J1
624 CARLSON BLVD, RCH, 94804	
NATL GUARD ARMORY	588 - J2
ALVARADO ST, SPAB, 94806	
NATL GUARD ARMORY	574 - D3
POWER AV & DAVI AV, PIT, 94565	
PARKS RESERVE FORCES TRAINING AREA	674 - B6
DUBLIN BLVD & ARNOLD RD, CCCo, 94582	
US GOVERNMENT RESV	675 - J7
HARTFORD AV & LORRAINE RD, AlaC, 94551	
US NAVAL WEAPONS STA PORT CHICAGO	553 - C6
WILLOW PASS RD, CCCo, 94565	
US NAVAL WEAPONS STA CONCORD	573 - F7
WILLOW PASS RD, CNCD, 94521	

MUSEUMS

BENICIA HIST MUS	551 - E5
2060 CAMEL RD, BEN, 94510	
BLACKHAWK AUTOMOTIVE MUS	653 - J5
3700 BLACKHAWK PLAZA CIR, CCCo, 94506	
CLAYTON HIST SOCIETY MUS	593 - H7
6101 MAIN ST, CLAY, 94517	
LINDSAY WILDLIFE MUS	612 - B2
1931 1ST AV, WLCK, 94597	
MARTINEZ MUS	571 - D2
1005 ESCOBAR ST, MRTZ, 94553	
RICHMOND MUS	588 - F6
400 NEVIN AV, RCH, 94801	
SHADELANDS RANCH HIST MUS	612 - G1
2660 YGNACIO VALLEY RD, WLCK, 94598	

OPEN SPACE PRESERVES

ACALANES OPEN SPACE	612 - A5
FWY 680, WLCK, 94597	
BAY POINT WETLANDS	553 - E7
PORT CHICAGO HWY, CCCo, 94565	
BEACONSFIELD OPEN SPACE	650 - F1
BEACONSFIELD PL, OAK, 94611	
BISHOP RANCH REGL OPEN SPACE	673 - B4
MORGAN DR, CCCo, 94583	
BLACK DIAMOND MINES REGL PRESERVE	594 - E4
FREDERICKSON LN, CCCo, 94517	
CARQUINEZ STRAIT TRAIL	550 - B4
SAN PABLO AV, CCCo, 94525	
CLAREMONT CANYON REGL PRESERVE	630 - A2
CLAREMONT AV, CCCo, 94705	
DOUGHERTY HILLS OPEN SPACE	693 - J1
AMADOR VLY BL & STAGECOACH RD, DBLN, 94568	
DOW WETLANDS PRESERVE	575 - B3
PITTSBURG-ANTIOCH HWY, ANT, 94509	
EAST BAY REGL PARK OPEN SPACE	633 - A4
OFF OAKSHIRE PL, CCCo, 94507	
FRANKLIN HILLS OPEN SPACE	571 - C5
JOHN MUIR PKWY, MRTZ, 94553	
GRIZZLY PEAK OPEN SPACE	630 - C3
TUNNEL RD, OAK, 94611	
HILLSIDE NATURAL AREA	609 - C1
MOESER LN, ELCR, 94530	
HUCKLEBERRY BOTANIC REGL RESERVE	630 - G5
PINEHURST RD, CCCo, 94516	
LAS TRAMPAS REGL WILDERNESS	652 - D1
BOLLINGER CANYON RD, CCCo, 94583	
LEONA CANYON REGL OPEN SPACE PRESERVE	651 - A6
CAMPUS DR, OAK, 94605	
LIME RIDGE OPEN SPACE	593 - A7
YGNACIO VALLEY RD, WLCK, 94598	
LONE TREE POINT REGL SHORELINE	549 - G7
PACIFIC AV & SAN PABLO AV, CCCo, 94572	
MULHOLLAND RIDGE OPEN SPACE	631 - C4
MORAGA WY & MORAGA RD, MRGA, 94556	
OPEN SPACE	576 - F5
MARSH CREEK REGIONAL TR, CCCo, 94561	
ORINDA OAKS OPEN SPACE PRESERVE	631 - B3
HALL DR & FLEETWOOD CT, ORIN, 94563	
POINT PINOLE REGL SHORELINE	568 - F4
GIANT HWY & SOBRANTE AV, RCH, 94806	
RANKIN OPEN SPACE	571 - C3
PANORAMIC DR, MRTZ, 94553	
SAN PABLO BAY REGL SHORELINE	569 - B3
SAN PABLO BAY, CCCo, 94806	
SHELL RIDGE OPEN SPACE	613 - A6
MARSHALL DR, CCCo, 94598	
SIBLEY VOLCANIC REGL PRESERVE	630 - E4
SKYLINE BLVD, CCCo, 94563	
SOBRANTE RIDGE REGL PRESERVE	589 - H2
CASTRO RANCH RD, RCH, 94803	
SYCAMORE VALLEY OPEN SPACE	653 - J3
BLACKHAWK RD, DNVL, 94506	
TILDEN NATURE STUDY AREA	609 - G2
CENTRAL PARK DR, CCCo, 94708	
UNIVERSITY BOTANICAL GARDENS	630 - B1
CENTENNIAL DR, OAK, 94720	
WATERBIRD REGL PRESERVE	571 - J2
WATERFRONT RD & WATERBIRD WY, CCCo, 94553	

FEATURE NAME Address City, ZIP Code	PAGE-GRID
YOUNG, HUGH OPEN SPACE	569 - J7
WRIGHT AV, PIN, 94564	

PARK & RIDE

PARK & RIDE	632 - E1
680 FRWY & RUDGEAR RD, WLCK, 94596	
PARK & RIDE	693 - J6
7295 JOHNSON DR, PLE, 94588	
PARK & RIDE	571 - E7
ALHAMBRA AV & FRANKLIN CANYON, MRTZ, 94553	
PARK & RIDE	574 - E4
BLISS AV & HARBOR ST, PIT, 94565	
PARK & RIDE	673 - D4
BOLLINGER CANYON RD & 680 FRWY, SRMN, 94583	
PARK & RIDE	673 - E2
CAMINO RAMON & EXECUTIVE PKWY, SRMN, 94583	
PARK & RIDE	694 - B5
CHABOT DR & OWENS DR, PLE, 94588	
PARK & RIDE	612 - D1
COGGINS DR & LAS JUNTAS WY, CCCo, 94597	
PARK & RIDE	630 - F2
GATEWAY BLVD & 24 FRWY, ORIN, 94563	
PARK & RIDE	575 - G6
HILLCREST AV & 4 FRWY, ANT, 94509	
PARK & RIDE	589 - C1
HILLTOP DR & EASTSHORE FRWY, RCH, 94803	
PARK & RIDE	650 - D5
I-580 & FRUITVALE AV, OAK, 94602	
PARK & RIDE	551 - C4
I-780 & S ST, BEN, 94510	
PARK & RIDE	612 - H1
MITCHELL DR & OAK GROVE RD, WLCK, 94598	
PARK & RIDE	592 - D6
MONUMENT BLVD & 680 FRWY, PLHL, 94523	
PARK & RIDE	572 - B6
PACHECO BLVD & 4 FRWY, CCCo, 94553	
PARK & RIDE	569 - F5
PINOLE VLY RD & EASTSHORE FRWY, PIN, 94564	
PARK & RIDE	572 - G5
PORT CHICAGO HWY AT BART STA, CNCD, 94519	
PARK & RIDE	650 - H5
REDWOOD RD & MOUNTAIN BLVD, OAK, 94619	
PARK & RIDE	569 - C7
RICHMOND PKWY & EASTSHORE FRWY, CCCo, 94806	
PARK & RIDE	569 - G3
SAN PABLO AV & JOHN MUIR PKWY, HER, 94547	
PARK & RIDE	550 - C4
SAN PABLO AV & WANDA ST, CCCo, 94525	
PARK & RIDE	653 - A3
SYCAMORE VALLEY RD & 680 FRWY, DNVL, 94526	
PARK & RIDE	616 - G1
WALNUT BLVD & DAINTY AV, BREN, 94513	
PARK & RIDE	569 - H2
WILLOW AV & EASTSHORE FRWY, HER, 94547	
PARK & RIDE	592 - E2
WILLOW PASS RD & 242 FRWY, CNCD, 94520	
PARK & RIDE	573 - G3
W LELAND RD & SOUTHWOOD DR, PIT, 94565	

PARKS & RECREATION

9TH STREET PK, BEN	550 - J4
ALAMO CREEK PK, DBLN	694 - A2
ALAMO ELEMENTARY PK, CCCo	632 - F3
ALBANY HILL PK, ALB	609 - C5
ALEXANDER PK, CCCo	550 - D5
ALHAMBRA PK, MRTZ	571 - D3
ALLENDALE REC CTR, OAK	650 - E6
ALMA PK, WLCK	612 - C6
ALMONDRIDGE PK, ANT	575 - J6
ALVARADO PK, RCH	589 - B4
AMARAL PK, PLE	694 - F6
AMBROSE PK, CCCo	573 - H3
AMERICANA PK, PIT	574 - B2
ANDERSON, BOOKER T JR PK, RCH	609 - A2
ANTIOCH COMM PK, ANT	595 - C2
ANTIOCH/OAKLEY REGL SHORELINE, OAKL	576 - A3
ANTIOCH YOUTH SPORTS COMPLEX, ANT	575 - F4
APPLE HILL PK, BREN	616 - C2
ARBOLADO PK, WLCK	613 - A6
ARBOR VIEW PK, BREN	596 - F3
ARLINGTON PK, ELCR	609 - E1
ARMSTRONG, NEIL PK, SRMN	673 - F6
ATCHISON VILLAGE PK, RCH	588 - E7
ATHAN DOWNS, SRMN	673 - E5
AVENUE TERRACE PK, OAK	650 - F4
BALDWIN, JOHN F PK, CNCD	592 - G1
BALFOUR-GUTHRIE PK, BREN	615 - J2
BART LINEAR PK, CNCD	572 - G5
BART PK, CNCD	592 - G2
BAYFRONT PK, PIN	569 - E3
BAYVIEW CIRCLE PK, CNCD	572 - G2
BELLA VISTA REC AREA, OAK	650 - A4
BELLINGHAM SQUARE PK, SRMN	674 - B3
BENICIA STATE REC AREA, BEN	550 - G2
BERKSHIRE PK, BREN	616 - B1
BETHANY RESERVOIR STATE REC AREA, AlaC-	657 - F7
(SEE PAGE 638)	
BEVERLY HILLS PK, VAL	550 - D1
BICENTENNIAL PK, PLE	694 - E7
BOATWRIGHT YOUTH SPORTS COMPLEX, CNCD	593 - D6
BOLLINGER CANYON PK, SRMN	673 - C4
BOONE ACRES PK, SRMN	673 - F7
BOORMAN PK, RCH	588 - H7
BOYD, NANCY PK, MRTZ	571 - F7
BRAXTON, ABRAHAM PK, RCH	609 - B1
BRAY COMMONS, DBLN	694 - F4
BRAZIL QUARRY PK, CNCD	593 - D4
BRENTWOOD FAMILY AQUATIC COMPLEX, BREN	616 - F2
BRENTWOOD PK, BREN	616 - G1
BRIDGEVIEW PK, BEN	551 - B4
BRIONES REGL PK, CCCo	591 - D3
BROOKDALE PK, OAK	650 - E7
BROOK STREET PK, LFYT	611 - F6
BROOKWOOD PK, CCCo	591 - H7
BROWN, ELAM PLAZA, LFYT	611 - F6
BUCHANAN PK, PIT	574 - D6
BURG PK, RCH	588 - J5
CALIFORNIA SEASONS PK, PIT	573 - J2
CAMBRIDGE PK, CNCD	592 - G2
CANAL PK, ANT	574 - J7
CANYON DRIVE PK, PIN	569 - C7
CANYON TRAIL PK, ELCR	589 - B7
CARQUINEZ PK, VAL	550 - J4
CARQUINEZ STRAIT REGL SHORELINE PK, CCCo	571 - A3
CASA CERRITO REC CTR, ELCR	609 - D2
CASTLE ROCK REGL PK, CCCo	613 - A7
CASTRO PK, ELCR	609 - C4
CENTENNIAL PK, SRMN	693 - F1
CENTRAL PK, RCH	609 - C4
CENTRAL PK, PIT	574 - F3
CENTRAL RESERVOIR REC AREA, OAK	650 - F5
CERRITO VISTA PK, ELCR	609 - D2
CHABOT, ANTHONY REGL PK, AlaC	672 - A6
CHABOT PK, OAK	630 - A4
CHAPARRAL PK, ANT	595 - A4
CHICHIBU PK, ANT	595 - C1
CHILPANCINGO PK, PLHL	592 - C1
CITY PK, ANT	575 - D4

FEATURE NAME Address City, ZIP Code	PAGE-GRID
CITY PK, BEN	551 - B5
CITY PK, PIT	574 - D3
CIVIC CTR PK, BEN	551 - B5
CIVIC PK, WLCK	612 - C5
CLAREMONT PK, OAKL	576 - G7
CLAYTON PK, CLAY	593 - H7
CLAYTON COMM PK, CLAY	613 - J1
CLAYTON VALLEY CTR PK, CNCD	593 - D6
CLYDE PK, CCCo	572 - G2
CODORNICES PLGD, BERK	609 - H7
CONCORD BLVD PK, CNCD	593 - B2
CONCORD COMM PK, CNCD	592 - H3
CONTRA LOMA PK, ANT	575 - B6
CONTRA LOMA REGL PK, ANT	595 - A3
CORNELL PK, CCCo	617 - J4
COUNTRY CLUB PK, SRMN	693 - G1
COUNTRY MANOR PK, ANT	595 - G2
COWELL RANCH, CCCo	615 - J7
COYOTE CREEK PK, SRMN	673 - H1
COYOTE CROSSING PK, SRMN	673 - G1
CRAGMONT PK, BERK	609 - H6
CREEKSIDE PK, BREN	616 - E3
CREEKSIDE PK, ELCR	609 - C5
CREEKSIDE PK, PLE	694 - D6
CRESCENT PK CTR, RCH	609 - A2
CROCKER PK, PDMT	650 - C2
CROCKETT PK, OAKL	596 - C1
CULL CANYON REGL REC AREA, AlaC	672 - C7
DALLAS RANCH PK, ANT	595 - D4
DANVILLE SOUTH PK, DNVL	653 - C7
DAVIS, JOHN HERBERT PK, SPAB	588 - H3
DE ANZA PK, PIT	574 - A2
DEERFIELD PK, ANT	595 - H3
DEL MAR DOG PK, SRMN	673 - G6
DIABLO FOOTHILLS REGL PK, CCCo	612 - J6
DIABLO SHADOWS PK, WLCK	612 - J2
DIABLO VISTA PK, DNVL	653 - J6
DIABLO WEST PK, ANT	595 - F4
DIMOND PK, OAK	650 - D4
DINOSAUR HILL PK, PLHL	591 - J7
DISNEY, WALT PK, SRMN	673 - G6
DOLAN PK, DBLN	693 - F3
DRACENA PK, PDMT	630 - A7
DUBLIN SPORTS GROUNDS, DBLN	693 - J4
DUBLIN SWIM CTR, DBLN	693 - H2
EAGLESRIDGE PK, ANT	595 - E2
EAST BAY REGL PK, MRTZ	571 - F6
EAST BAY REGL PK, CCCo	594 - H3
EAST BRANCH PK, SRMN	674 - B4
EASTSHORE STATE PK, ALB	609 - B6
EL DIVISADERO PK, WLCK	612 - F3
ELLIS LAKE PK, CNCD	592 - F2
ELM PK, RCH	588 - F6
EMERALD GLEN PK, DBLN	694 - E3
FAIRFIELD, TED PK, DBLN	694 - F2
FAIRLANDS PK, PLE	694 - E6
FAIRMEAD PK, RCH	589 - A2
FAIRMONT PK, ELCR	609 - D3
FAIR OAKS PK, PLHL	592 - D6
FAIRVIEW PK, ANT	575 - B4
FERNANDEZ PK, PIN	569 - E4
FITZGERALD FIELD, BEN	551 - B5
FLOOD, CURT FIELD, OAK	650 - D5
FOOTHILL MEADOWS, OAK	650 - D7
FOOTHILLS PK, MRTZ	591 - H3
FOXBORO PK, HER	569 - J3
FRANCESCA TERRACE PK, BEN	551 - D4
FRANCIS, LOUIS PK, PIN	569 - C5
FRANKS TRACT STATE REC AREA, CCCo	557 - C6
GARBER PK, OAK	630 - B3
GARFIELD PK, OAK	650 - B6
GARIN PK, BREN	616 - H2
GEHRINGER PK, OAKL	596 - G2
GENTRY TOWN PK, ANT	575 - A7
GLEN COVE PK, VAL	550 - F2
GLEN COVE WATERFRONT PK, VAL	550 - F2
GLORY PK, BREN	616 - H3
GOLDEN HILLS PK, MRTZ	591 - G3
GOLDEN VIEW PK, SRMN	653 - G7
GOMEZ, LEFTY BALLFIELD COMPLEX, CCCo	549 - H7
GRAHAM, DUNCAN PK, BEN	551 - C4
HACIENDA DE LOS FLORES PK, MRGA	631 - E4
HANNA PK, HER	570 - B6
HANSEN PK, ANT	595 - D4
HARBOUR PK, ANT	575 - E7
HARDING PK, ELCR	609 - E4
HARTE, BRET PK, DNVL	653 - B2
HAVENS PLGD, PDMT	650 - B1
HEATHER FARM PK, WLCK	612 - E2
HEIDORN PK, ANT	595 - J5
HERON PK, BREN	596 - H7
HESTER, LEH PK, CNCD	592 - D6
HIDDEN CREST PK, SRMN	673 - J1
HIDDEN HILLS PK, SRMN	674 - C3
HIDDEN LAKES PK, MRTZ	591 - J1
HIDDEN VALLEY PK, SRMN	674 - D3
HIDDEN VALLEY PK, MRTZ	571 - J7
HIGHLANDS PK, CNCD	593 - F6
HIGHLANDS PK, PIT	574 - E6
HILLCREST COMM PK, CNCD	572 - E6
HILLCREST PK, ANT	575 - G7
HILLSDALE PK, PIT	573 - J4
HILLSIDE NATURAL AREA, ELCR	609 - D2
HILLTOP GREEN PK, RCH	569 - C7
HILLTOP LAKE PK, RCH	569 - A6
HILLTOP PK, RCH	588 - J1
HINKEL, J PK, BERK	609 - G5
HOLIDAY HIGHLANDS PK, MRTZ	571 - J6
HOMECOMING PK, BREN	596 - G5
HOWE HOMESTEAD PK, WLCK	612 - E5
HUBER PK, ELCR	609 - E3
INDIAN ROCK PK, BERK	609 - G6
JACOBSEN PK, ANT	575 - F5
KENNEDY GROVE REGL REC AREA, CCCo	589 - J5
KENNEDY, JOHN F PK, RCH	589 - A7
KENNEDY TRACT PK, OAK	650 - B7
KING, MARTIN LUTHER MEM PK, RCH	608 - G1
KING PK, BREN	596 - D6
KNOLL PK, ANT	595 - J4
KOLB PK, DBLN	693 - H2
KRUEGER FIELDS, CNCD	592 - G3
LAFAYETTE COMM PK, LFYT	631 - H3
LAFAYETTE RESERVOIR REC AREA, LFYT	611 - B7
LAKE PK, BREN	616 - B2
LAKE SHORE PK, OAK	650 - A3
LAKE TEMESCAL REGL REC AREA, OAK	630 - C5
LA MOINE VALLEY VIEW PK, RCH	589 - F1
LARKEY PK, WLCK	612 - B2
LAS JUNTAS PK, PLHL	592 - B4
LAUREL FIELDS PK, OAKL	596 - F1
LAUREL PK, OAKL	596 - E2
LEIGH PK, LFYT	611 - G6
LIMERICK PK, SRMN	674 - C4
LITTLE HILLS RANCH REGL REC AREA, CCCo	652 - E3
LITTLE LEAGUE FIELD PK, BEN	551 - C5
LIVE OAK REC CTR, BERK	609 - G7
LIVORNA PK, CCCo	632 - H3
LOMA VISTA PK, BREN	596 - C7
LONDON, JACK PK, BEN	551 - A1
LUCAS PARK PLGD, RCH	588 - G5

FEATURE NAME Address City, ZIP Code	PAGE-GRID
LYDIA LANE PK, CLAY	593 - G5
LYNBROOK PK, CCCo	573 - F1
MAGEE, HAP RANCH PK, DNVL	632 - G6
MANDANA PLAZA, OAK	650 - A3
MANZANITA REC CTR, OAK	650 - B5
MAPE PK, DBLN	693 - G4
MARCHETTI, GINO PK, ANT	574 - H6
MARINA PK, RCH	608 - H2
MARINA PK, PIT	574 - D1
MARKHAM NATURE AREA, CNCD	592 - J4
MARSH CREEK GLEN PK, OAKL	596 - H3
MARTINEZ REGL SHORELINE PK, MRTZ	571 - E1
MARTINEZ WATERFRONT PK, MRTZ	571 - E2
MAXWELL PK, OAK	650 - F7
MCCLARREN PK, BREN	616 - G2
MCCREA MEM PK, OAK	650 - G6
MEADOW BROOK PK, ANT	575 - G6
MEADOW CREEK ESTATES PK, ANT	596 - A3
MEADOW HOMES PK, CNCD	592 - F3
MEADOW PK, PIN	569 - D4
MEADOWS PK, PLE	694 - G6
MEMORIAL PK, ALB	609 - E5
MEMORIAL PK, SRMN	673 - C4
MEMORIAL PK, ANT	575 - C7
MEMORIAL PK, RCH	588 - G7
METRO WALK PK, RCH	588 - G6
MICHIGAN PK, BERK	609 - G4
MILL CREEK HOLLOW, SRMN	673 - B1
MILLER, JOAQUIN PK, OAK	650 - G3
MILLER-KNOX REGL SHORELINE, RCH	608 - D2
MIRA VISTA HILLS PK, ANT	595 - A2
MIRA VISTA PK, RCH	589 - B6
MIRA VISTA PK, ANT	595 - B1
MITCHELL CREEK PK, CCCo	613 - G2
MIWOK PK, BREN	596 - E6
MOLLER PK, PLE	693 - H7
MONKEY ISLAND PK, BERK	630 - A3
MONTALVIN PK, CCCo	569 - A5
MONTARA BAY COMM CTR, CCCo	569 - A4
MONTCLAIR REC CTR, OAK	630 - D7
MONTEVIDEO PK, SRMN	673 - F4
MORAGA COMMONS PK, MRGA	631 - E6
MORELLO PK, MRTZ	571 - H5
MORGAN PLAZA, OAK	650 - B5
MORGAN TERRITORY REGL PK, CCCo	634 - J7
MOUNTAIN VIEW PK, MRTZ	571 - G5
MOUNTAIRE PK, ANT	575 - E7
MOUNT DIABLO STATE PK, CCCo	654 - C1
MOURA PK, OAKL	596 - E1
MUIR, JOHN PK, MRTZ	571 - F5
MUIRWOOD PK, PLE	693 - J7
NEVIN CTR & PK, RCH	588 - F6
NEWHALL COMM PK, CNCD	593 - C4
NICHOLL PK, RCH	588 - J7
NIELSEN PK, PLE	694 - E7
NORTHGATE PK, WLCK	612 - J4
NORTH OAKLAND REGL SPORTS CTR, OAK	630 - D4
NORTH RICHMOND BALLPARK, CCCo	588 - F3
OAKHILL PK, DNVL	633 - B6
OAK HILLS PARK & TRAILS, PIT	573 - F4
OAKLEY PK, OAKL	576 - E7
OAK MEADOW PK, BREN	616 - B3
OCEAN VIEW PK, ALB	609 - D6
OHARA PK, OAKL	576 - E7
OHLONE PK, HER	569 - G4
OLD RANCH PK, SRMN	673 - J7
ORCHARD PK, BREN	616 - F3
ORINDA COMM PK, ORIN	610 - G7
ORINDA OAKS PK, ORIN	631 - B4
ORINDA SPORTS FIELD, ORIN	610 - E5
OSAGE PK, DNVL	653 - C4
OSTRANDER PK, OAK	630 - B5
OVERLOOK PK, BEN	551 - C3
OWENS PLAZA PK, PLE	694 - C5
PARCHESTER PARK & CTR, RCH	568 - G7
PARK BOULEVARD PLAZA, OAK	650 - A4
PASO NOGAL PK, PLHL	591 - J3
PATRIOT PK, OAKL	576 - E6
PAUL PK, ORIN	630 - H1
PERALTA HACIENDA PK, OAK	650 - D6
PICKLE WEED PK, SRFL	587 - A1
PIEDMONT PK, PDMT	650 - B1
PIEDMONT SPORTS FIELD, PDMT	650 - D2
PINE GROVE SPORTS FIELD, ORIN	610 - H7
PINEWOOD PK, PLHL	592 - A5
PINOLE PK, PIN	569 - G7
PINTO RANCH REC AREA, OAK	650 - H5
PLAZA PK, RCH	609 - A1
PLEASANT HILL PK, PLHL	592 - C5
PLEASANT OAK PK, PLHL	592 - B7
PLEASANTON RIDGE REGL PK, AlaC	693 - E6
PLEASANTON RIDGE REGL PK, PLE	693 - H7
PLEASANTON SPORTS AND RECREATION PK, PLE	694 - C7
POINSETT PK, ELCR	589 - B7
POINT EDITH STATE WILDLIFE AREA, CCCo	552 - B6
POINT ISABEL REGL SHORELINE, RCH	608 - J3
PREWETT FAMILY PK, ANT	595 - G3
PRICE, BARBARA MARINA PK, ANT	575 - C3
PROSSERVILLE PK, ANT	575 - B4
RAIN CLOUD PK, RCH	589 - G3
RANCHO LAGUNA PK, MRGA	651 - F3
RANKIN PK, MRTZ	571 - C3
RED WILLOW PK, SRMN	653 - J7
REDWOOD HEIGHTS REC AREA, OAK	650 - G5
REDWOOD REGL PK, CCCo	651 - A3
REFUGIO VALLEY PK, HER	569 - H4
REMILLARD PK, BERK	609 - H6
RICKS, CAPPY PK, MRTZ	571 - E3
RIVERVIEW PK, PIT	554 - D7
ROBERTS REGL REC AREA, AlaC	650 - J3
ROCKRIDGE PK, OAK	630 - A5
ROLLING HILLS PK, BREN	616 - A1
ROSE GARDEN PK, OAK	650 - A2
ROSE GARDENS, BERK	609 - H6
ROSIE THE RIVETER NATL HIST PK, RCH	608 - H2
ROUND VALLEY PK, CCCo	635 - H4
RUDGEAR PK, WLCK	632 - G1
RUTH, BABE BASEBALL FIELD, ANT	575 - B4
SAINT MARYS BALLFIELD, LFYT	631 - H1
SALFINGERE, FRANK PK, PLHL	592 - B3
SAN ANTONIO REC CTR, OAK	650 - A6
SANBORN PK, OAK	650 - C7
SAN MIGUEL PK, WLCK	612 - F3
SAN PABLO RESERVOIR REC AREA, CCCo	589 - H5
SAN RAMON CENTRAL PK, SRMN	673 - E3
SANTA RITA LAND TRUST, OAK	650 - D7
SARAH DRIVE PK, PIN	569 - E6
SARAIVA, ETHEREE PK, BEN	551 - C5
SAUNDERS, MARGE PK, OAK	650 - F1
SEARS, RICK PK, CNCD	592 - F5
SENIOR CENTER PK GARDENS, SRMN	673 - J7
SHADOWOOD PK, PLHL	592 - B1
SHANNON HILLS PK, PLHL	591 - H4
SHANNON PK, DBLN	693 - G3
SHEPHERD CANYON PK, OAK	630 - F7
SHERIDAN POINT PK, RCH	608 - G3
SHIELD REID PK, RCH	588 - F4
SHIMADA FRIENDSHIP PK, RCH	608 - H3
SKILMAN, FRANK PK, BEN	551 - B1
SMALL WORLD PK, PIT	574 - D4

FEATURE NAME Address City, ZIP Code	PAGE-GRID
SMITH, ROGERS PK, PLHL	591 - J5
SOUTHAMPTON PK, BEN	551 - B2
SOUYEN PK, SRMN	674 - A3
SPIRIT PK, BREN	616 - G3
SPLASHPAD PK, OAK	650 - A3
STAGECOACH PK, DBLN	693 - J2
STEWART PLGD, RCH	588 - F6
STONEMAN PK, PIT	573 - J6
SUGAR LOAF OPEN SPACE REC AREA, WLCK	632 - E2
SUMMERWOOD PK, BREN	596 - E7
SUNNY RIDGE PK, ANT	595 - C1
SUNSET PARK ATHLETIC COMPLEX, BREN	596 - H5
SUN TERRACE PK, CNCD	572 - F5
SUSANA PK, MRTZ	571 - E3
SUTTER GATE PK, PLE	694 - D7
SWARTZ, AMBER PK, PIN	569 - G7
SYCAMORE VALLEY PK, DNVL	653 - F4
TASSAJARA CREEK REGL PK, DBLN	674 - D7
TASSAJARA PK, ELCR	589 - C6
TERRACE PK, ALB	609 - E7
TERRACE VIEW PLGD, BERK	609 - J7
TICE VALLEY PK, WLCK	632 - B1
TILDEN REGL PK, CCCo	609 - J4
TILLER PK, RCH	589 - B6
TODOS SANTOS PLAZA, CNCD	592 - F1
TURNBULL PK, BEN	551 - B6
TURNER, MATTHEW PK, BEN	550 - J3
TWIN CREEKS PK, SRMN	673 - B2
UNIVERSITY PK, ALB	609 - D7
VALLEY VIEW PK, SRMN	673 - J1
VAL VISTA PK, PLE	693 - J7
VETERANS PK, BREN	616 - F2
VICTORIA PK, HER	549 - G7
VILLAGE EAST PK, ANT	574 - J6
VILLAGE GREEN PK, SRMN	693 - H1
VINCENT PK, RCH	608 - G3
VINTAGE PARKWAY PARK, OAKL	576 - E5
WALDON PK, WLCK	612 - D2
WALNUT PK, BREN	616 - G3
WANLASS PK, SPAB	588 - H1
WASHINGTON PK, RCH	608 - D1
WENDELL PARK & PLGD, RCH	588 - H5
WILDCAT CANYON REGL PK, RCH	589 - D5
WILLIAMSON RANCH PK, ANT	595 - J4
WILLOW GLEN PK, BEN	551 - A4
WILLOW PASS COMM PK, CNCD	572 - H7
WINDSOR WAY PK, BREN	596 - G7
WINDY HILLS PK, SRMN	673 - G2
WOODFIELD PK, HER	570 - A4
WOODLAND HILLS PK, PIT	574 - B6
WOOD, W D PK, OAK	650 - C5
YGNACIO HEIGHTS PK, WLCK	612 - D4
YGNACIO PLAZA MARTINEZ PK, MRTZ	571 - D3
YGNACIO VALLEY PK, CNCD	592 - G6

PERFORMING ARTS

FEATURE NAME Address City, ZIP Code	PAGE-GRID
BRUNS AMPHITHEATRE, THE 100 GATEWAY BLVD, CCCo, 94563	630 - F2
CHRONICLE PAVILION AT CONCORD 2000 KIRKER PASS RD, CNCD, 94521	593 - H4
CONTRA COSTA CIVIC THEATRE 951 POMONA AV, ELCR, 94530	609 - D2
LESHER, DEAN REGL CTR FOR THE AR 1601 CIVIC DR, WLCK, 94596	612 - C5
MASQUERS PLAYHOUSE 105 PARK PL, RCH, 94801	588 - D7
MEMORIAL AUDITORIUM BARRETT AV & 25TH ST, RCH, 94804	588 - H6
RICHMOND ART CTR 2540 BARRETT AV, RCH, 94804	588 - H6
SHADELANDS ARTS CTR 111 N WIGET LN, WLCK, 94598	612 - G2
TOWN HALL MORAGA RD, LFYT, 94549	611 - F7
WOODMINSTER AMPHITHEATER 3300 JOAQUIN MILLER RD, OAK, 94611	650 - G3

POINTS OF INTEREST

FEATURE NAME Address City, ZIP Code	PAGE-GRID
BROOKS ISLAND BIRD SANCTUARY BROOKS ISLAND, RCH, 94804	608 - G4
CALIF ORIENTATION CTR FOR THE BLIND 400 ADAMS ST, ALB, 94706	609 - C5
CARMELITE MONASTERY JESSEN CT, CCCo, 94707	609 - F2
CARQUINEZ STRAIT LIGHTHOUSE SEAWIND DR, VAL, 94590	550 - B2
CHABOT SPACE & SCIENCE CTR 10000 SKYLINE BLVD, OAK, 94611	650 - H2
CLOCKTOWER 1189 WASHINGTON ST, BEN, 94510	551 - E6
CROW CANYON GARDENS 20 BOARDWALK, SRMN, 94583	673 - B2
DAVIE TENNIS STADIUM 198 OAK RD, PDMT, 94611	650 - B2
DIABLO VALLEY GIRL SCOUT COUNCIL SPRINGHILL RD, CCCo, 94553	611 - E3
EAST BROTHERS LIGHTHOUSE POINT SAN PABLO, RCH, 94801	587 - H3
EL CERRITO COMM SWIM CTR 7007 MOESER LN, ELCR, 94530	609 - D2
GREEK ORTHODOX CHURCH 4700 LINCOLN AV, OAK, 94602	650 - E3
LAWRENCE HALL OF SCIENCE CENTENNIAL DR, BERK, 94720	610 - A7
MORMON TEMPLE 4770 LINCOLN AV, OAK, 94602	650 - F3
OLD MARSH CREEK SPRINGS 12510 MARSH CREEK RD, CCCo, 94517	614 - H7
OUR LADYS HOME 3499 FOOTHILL BLVD, OAK, 94601	650 - C7
STATE OF CALIFORNIA CONSERVATION CAMP BOLLINGER CANYON RD, CCCo, 94583	652 - E3
STEAM TRAINS GRIZZLY PEAK BLVD, CCCo, 94708	610 - C7
U C LEUSCHNER OBSERVATORY 4927 HAPPY VALLEY RD, CCCo, 94553	611 - B2
WATERWORLD USA 1950 WATERWORLD PKWY, CNCD, 94520	592 - D2

POINTS OF INTEREST - HISTORIC

FEATURE NAME Address City, ZIP Code	PAGE-GRID
BENICIA CAPITOL S H PARK 1ST ST & H ST, BEN, 94510	551 - B5
FOREST HOME FARMS PARK VALLEY BLVD & PINE VALLEY RD, SRMN, 94583	673 - F7
GALINDO HOUSE & GARDENS CLAYTON RD & AMADOR AV, CNCD, 94520	592 - F2
MUIR, JOHN NATL HIST SITE 4202 ALHAMBRA AV, MRTZ, 94553	571 - E6
ONEILL, EUGENE NATL HIST SITE 1000 KUSS RD, CCCo, 94526	652 - G1
PACHECO, FERNANDO ADOBE 3119 GRANT ST, CNCD, 94520	572 - E6
SOLDIERS MONUMENT BOYD RD & N MAIN ST, PLHL, 94523	592 - C6

POST OFFICES

FEATURE NAME	Address City, ZIP Code	PAGE-GRID
ALAMO	160 ALAMO PZ, CCCo, 94507	632 - F5
ALBANY BRANCH	1191 SOLANO AV, ALB, 94706	609 - D6
ANTIOCH	2730 W TREGALLAS RD, ANT, 94509	575 - D6
BETHEL ISLAND	6270 BETHEL ISLAND RD, CCCo, 94511	577 - D4
BRENTWOOD	18 OAK ST, BREN, 94513	616 - H1
BYRON	3852 MAIN ST, CCCo, 94514	637 - D3
CANYON	PINEHURST RD, CCCo, 94516	630 - J7
CASA CORREO STA	4494 TREAT BLVD, CNCD, 94521	593 - B3
CLAYTON	6150 CENTER ST, CLAY, 94517	593 - H7
CONCORD MAIN	2121 MERIDIAN PARK BLVD, CNCD, 94520	592 - D2
COUNTRY CLUB STA	1545 SCHOOL ST, MRGA, 94556	631 - D7
COURT STA	815 COURT ST, MRTZ, 94553	571 - E3
CROCKETT	420 ROLPH AV, CCCo, 94525	550 - D4
DANVILLE MAIN	2605 CM TASSAJARA, DNVL, 94526	653 - F4
DANVILLE SQUARE STA	43 RAILROAD AV, DNVL, 94526	652 - J2
DIABLO	1701 EL NIDO, CCCo, 94528	633 - E7
DIMOND STA	2226 MACARTHUR BLVD, OAK, 94602	650 - D4
DOLLAR RANCH STA	1221 ROSSMOOR PKWY, WLCK, 94595	632 - B1
DUBLIN	6937 VILLAGE PKWY, DBLN, 94568	693 - J4
EL CERRITO MAIN	11135 SAN PABLO AV, ELCR, 94530	609 - C2
EL SOBRANTE BRANCH	535 APPIAN WY, CCCo, 94803	589 - E1
FAIRMOUNT STA	6324 FAIRMOUNT AV, ELCR, 94530	609 - D4
FRUITVILLE STA	1445 34TH AV, OAK, 94601	650 - C7
GRAND LAKE STA	490 LAKE PARK AV, OAK, 94610	650 - A3
HACIENDA STA	4682 CHABOT DR, PLE, 94588	694 - B6
HERCULES	1611 SYCAMORE AV, HER, 94547	569 - H3
KNIGHTSEN	3019 KNIGHTSEN AV, CCCo, 94548	597 - A3
LAFAYETTE	3641 MT DIABLO BLVD, LFYT, 94549	611 - E6
LANDSCAPE STA	1831 SOLANO AV, BERK, 94707	609 - F6
LAUREL STA	3630 HIGH ST, OAK, 94619	650 - F6
MARTINEZ MAIN	4100 ALHAMBRA AV, MRTZ, 94553	571 - E6
MILLS COLLEGE	POST RD, OAK, 94613	650 - H7
MIRA VISTA STA	12651 SAN PABLO AV, RCH, 94805	589 - A5
MORAGA MAIN	460 CENTER ST, MRGA, 94556	631 - E3
NORTH BERKELEY STA	1521 SHATTUCK AV, BERK, 94709	609 - G7
OAKLEY	400 DEL ANTICO AV, OAKL, 94561	576 - F7
ORINDA	29 ORINDA WY, ORIN, 94563	610 - G7
PACHECO STA	4980 PACHECO BLVD, CCCo, 94553	572 - B6
PINOLE	2101 PEAR ST, PIN, 94564	569 - E4
PITTSBURG	835 RAILROAD AV, PIT, 94565	574 - E2
PLEASANT HILL	1945 CONTRA COSTA BLVD, PLHL, 94523	592 - C5
POINT RICHMOND STA	104 WASHINGTON AV, RCH, 94801	588 - D7
PORT COSTA	3 CANYON LAKE RD, CCCo, 94569	550 - H6
RICHMOND MAIN	1025 NEVIN AV, RCH, 94801	588 - G6
RODEO	499 PARKER AV, CCCo, 94572	549 - H7
SAINT MARYS COLLEGE STA	1928 SAINT MARYS RD, MRGA, 94575	631 - G6
SAN PABLO BRANCH	2080 23RD ST, SPAB, 94806	588 - H3
SAN QUENTIN	1 MAIN ST, MrnC, 94964	587 - B5
SAN RAMON	12935 ALCOSTA BLVD, SRMN, 94583	673 - D1
STATION A	200 BROADWAY, RCH, 94804	588 - H7
STATION E	1954 MOUNTAIN BLVD, OAK, 94611	650 - E1
TODOS SANTOS STA	2043 EAST ST, CNCD, 94520	592 - G1
WALNUT CREEK MAIN	2070 N BROADWAY, WLCK, 94596	612 - C4

SCHOOLS - PRIVATE ELEMENTARY

FEATURE NAME	Address City, ZIP Code	PAGE-GRID
AURORA	40 DULWICH RD, OAK, 94618	630 - B6
BEACON DAY	2101 LIVINGSTON ST, OAK, 94606	650 - A7
BENTLEY	1 HILLER DR, OAK, 94618	630 - B4
BETHEL CHRISTIAN ACADEMY	431 RINCON LN, CCCo, 94803	589 - D1
BIANCHI	COWELL RD, CNCD, 94521	593 - A5
CALVARY CHRISTIAN ACADEMY	4892 SAN PABLO DAM RD, CCCo, 94803	589 - E3
CALVARY TEMPLE CHRISTIAN	4725 EVORA RD, CCCo, 94565	573 - C2
CANTERBURY	3120 SHANE DR, RCH, 94806	589 - A1
CHRISTIAN CENTER	1210 STONEMAN AV, PIT, 94565	574 - F5
CHRIST THE KING	195 BRANDON RD, PLHL, 94523	592 - A5
CONTRA COSTA CHRISTIAN	2721 LARKEY LN, WLCK, 94597	612 - A2
CORPUS CHRISTI	1 ESTATES DR, PDMT, 94611	650 - D3
DORRIS-EATON	1847 NEWELL AV, CCCo, 94595	612 - C7
EAST BAY WALDORF	3800 CLARK RD, RCH, 94803	589 - D3
EL SOBRANTE CHRISTIAN	5100 ARGYLE RD, CCCo, 94803	569 - E7
FIRST LUTHERAN	4002 CONCORD BLVD, CNCD, 94521	593 - A2
GATEWAY CHRISTIAN	657 MCCLAREN RD, BREN, 94513	616 - G2
GOLDEN GATE ACADEMY	3800 MOUNTAIN BLVD, OAK, 94619	650 - G4
HEAD-ROYCE	4315 LINCOLN AV, OAK, 94602	650 - E3
HERITAGE BAPTIST ACADEMY	5200 HEIDORN RANCH RD, ANT, 94531	596 - A5
HILLTOP CHRISTIAN	320 WORRELL RD, ANT, 94509	575 - E7
HOLY ROSARY	25 E 15TH ST, ANT, 94509	575 - D5
KINGS VALLEY CHRISTIAN	4255 CLAYTON RD, CNCD, 94521	593 - A3
NEW VISTAS CHRISTIAN	68 MORELLO AV, MRTZ, 94553	571 - H4
NORTHERN LIGHT	4500 REDWOOD RD, OAK, 94619	650 - H5
PACIFIC ACADEMY OF NOMURA	1615 CARLSON BLVD, RCH, 94804	609 - B3
PALMER FOR BOYS & GIRLS	2740 JONES RD, CCCo, 94597	612 - C2
PATTEN ACADEMY OF CHRISTIAN EDUCATION	2432 COOLIDGE AV, OAK, 94601	650 - D6
PLEASANT HILL CHRISTIAN	796 GRAYSON RD, PLHL, 94523	591 - J6
PROSPECT	2060 TAPSCOTT AV, ELCR, 94530	589 - B7
PROSPECT SIERRA	960 AVIS DR, ELCR, 94530	609 - D2
QUEEN OF ALL SAINTS	2391 GRANT ST, CNCD, 94520	592 - F1
REDWOOD DAY	3245 SHEFFIELD AV, OAK, 94602	650 - C5
SAINT AGNES	3886 CHESTNUT AV, CNCD, 94519	593 - A2
SAINT ANTHONY	1500 E 15TH ST, OAK, 94606	650 - A6
SAINT CATHERINE OF SIENA	604 MELLUS ST, MRTZ, 94553	571 - D3
SAINT CORNELIUS	201 28TH ST, RCH, 94804	588 - J7
SAINT DAVIDS	871 SONOMA ST, RCH, 94805	589 - B5
SAINT DOMINICS CATHOLIC	935 5TH ST, BEN, 94510	551 - C5
SAINT ELIZABETH	1516 33RD AV, OAK, 94601	650 - C7
SAINT FRANCIS OF ASSISI	866 OAK GROVE RD, CNCD, 94518	592 - G6
SAINT ISIDORE	435 LA GONDA WY, DNVL, 94526	652 - J1
SAINT JARLATH	2634 PLEASANT ST, OAK, 94602	650 - D5
SAINT JEROME	320 SAN CARLOS AV, ELCR, 94530	609 - E4
SAINT JOHN THE BAPTIST	11156 SAN PABLO AV, ELCR, 94530	609 - C2
SAINT JOSEPH	1961 PLUM ST, PIN, 94564	569 - E4
SAINT LAWRENCE OTOOLE	3695 HIGH ST, OAK, 94619	650 - F6
SAINT MARYS	1158 BONT LN, WLCK, 94596	612 - B6
SAINT PATRICKS	907 7TH ST, CCCo, 94572	569 - J1
SAINT PAUL	1825 CHURCH LN, SPAB, 94806	588 - J3
SAINT PERPETUA	3445 HAMLIN RD, LFYT, 94549	611 - F7
SAINT PETER MARTYR	425 W 4TH ST, PIT, 94565	574 - D1
SAINT PHILIP LUTHERAN	8850 DAVONA DR, DBLN, 94568	693 - G2
SAINT RAYMOND	11557 SHANNON AV, DBLN, 94568	693 - G3
SAINT THERESA	4850 CLAREWOOD DR, OAK, 94618	630 - B6
SAKLAN VALLEY	1678 SCHOOL ST, MRGA, 94556	631 - D7
SAN RAMON VALLEY CHRISTIAN ACADEMY	220 W EL PINTADO, DNVL, 94526	653 - A2
SCHOOL OF THE MADELEINE	1225 MILVIA ST, BERK, 94709	609 - G7
SEVEN HILLS	975 N SAN CARLOS DR, CCCo, 94598	612 - D2
SHERWOOD FOREST CHRISTIAN	5570 OLINDA RD, CCCo, 94803	589 - G3
SPRAINGS ACADEMY	89 MORAGA WY, ORIN, 94563	630 - H1
TABERNACLE BAPTIST	4380 CONCORD BLVD, CNCD, 94521	593 - C2
TEHIYAH DAY	2603 TASSAJARA AV, ELCR, 94530	589 - C6
TEMPLE ISAIAH	3800 MOUNT DIABLO BLVD, LFYT, 94549	611 - D6
VALLEY CHRISTIAN	7508 INSPIRATION DR, DBLN, 94568	693 - E5
VISTA CHRISTIAN	2354 ANDRADE AV, RCH, 94804	588 - H5
WALNUT CREEK CHRISTIAN ACADEMY	2336 BUENA VISTA AV, WLCK, 94597	612 - B4
WHITE PONY & MEHER	999 LELAND DR, LFYT, 94549	611 - J6
WINDRUSH	1800 ELM ST, ELCR, 94530	609 - C1
YGNACIO VALLEY CHRISTIAN	4977 CONCORD BLVD, CCCo, 94521	593 - E3
ZION LUTHERAN	5201 PARK BLVD, PDMT, 94611	650 - D2

SCHOOLS - PRIVATE HIGH

FEATURE NAME	Address City, ZIP Code	PAGE-GRID
ATHENIAN	2100 MOUNT DIABLO SCENIC BLVD, CCCo, 94506	633 - F7
BENTLEY	1000 UPPER HAPPY VALLEY RD, LFYT, 94549	611 - B6
BEREAN CHRISTIAN	245 EL DIVISADERO AV, WLCK, 94598	612 - F3
CARONDELET	1133 WINTON DR, CNCD, 94518	592 - F7
CHRISTIAN CENTER	1210 STONEMAN AV, PIT, 94565	574 - F5
COLLEGE PREP	6100 BROADWAY, OAK, 94618	630 - A5
CONTRA COSTA CHRISTIAN	2721 LARKEY LN, WLCK, 94597	612 - A2
DE LA SALLE	1130 WINTON DR, CNCD, 94518	592 - F7
DELTA CHRISTIAN	625 W 4TH ST, ANT, 94509	575 - C4
GOLDEN GATE ACADEMY	3800 MOUNTAIN BLVD, OAK, 94619	650 - G4
HEAD-ROYCE	4315 LINCOLN AV, OAK, 94602	650 - E3
HOLY NAMES	4660 HARBORD DR, OAK, 94618	630 - B6
NORTH BAY ORINDA	19 ALTARINDA RD, ORIN, 94563	610 - H7
PATTEN ACADEMY OF CHRISTIAN EDUCATION	2432 COOLIDGE AV, OAK, 94601	650 - D6
SAINT MARYS COLLEGE	1294 ALBINA AV, ALB, 94706	609 - F7
SALESIAN	2851 SALESIAN AV, RCH, 94806	588 - J4
TEMPLE ISAIAH	3800 MOUNT DIABLO BLVD, LFYT, 94549	611 - D6
VALLEY CHRISTIAN	7506 INSPIRATION DR, DBLN, 94568	693 - E4

SCHOOLS - PRIVATE MIDDLE

FEATURE NAME	Address City, ZIP Code	PAGE-GRID
ATHENIAN	2100 MOUNT DIABLO SCENIC BLVD, CCCo, 94506	633 - F7

SCHOOLS - PUBLIC ELEMENTARY

FEATURE NAME	Address City, ZIP Code	PAGE-GRID
ALAMO	100 WILSON RD, CCCo, 94507	632 - F3
ALLENDALE	3670 PENNIMAN AV, OAK, 94619	650 - E6
ARMSTRONG, NEIL A	2849 CALAIS DR, SRMN, 94583	673 - F6
AYERS	5120 MYRTLE DR, CNCD, 94521	593 - E3
BAHIA VISTA	125 BAHIA WY, SRFL, 94901	587 - A2
BALDWIN, JOHN	741 BROOKSIDE DR, DNVL, 94526	653 - B4
BANCROFT	2200 PARRISH DR, WLCK, 94598	612 - F1
BAYVIEW	3001 16TH ST, SPAB, 94806	588 - H1
BEACH	100 LAKE AV, PDMT, 94611	650 - A1
BEL AIR	663 CANAL RD, CCCo, 94565	573 - H3
BELLA VISTA	1025 E 28TH ST, OAK, 94606	650 - B4
BELSHAW	2801 ROOSEVELT LN, ANT, 94509	575 - E6
BIDWELL	800 GARY AV, ANT, 94509	575 - F6
BOLLINGER CANYON	2300 TALAVERA DR, SRMN, 94583	673 - D3
BRENTWOOD	200 GRIFFITH LN, BREN, 94513	616 - F2
BUENA VISTA	2355 SAN JUAN AV, WLCK, 94597	612 - B3
BURTON VALLEY	561 MERRIEWOOD DR, LFYT, 94549	631 - J3
CAMBRIDGE	1135 LACEY LN, CNCD, 94520	592 - E5
CAMINO PABLO	1111 CM PABLO, MRGA, 94556	651 - E2
CANYON	PINEHURST RD, CCCo, 94516	651 - A1
CASTRO	7125 DONAL AV, ELCR, 94530	609 - C2
CHABOT, ANTHONY	6686 CHABOT RD, OAK, 94618	630 - A4
CHAVEZ, CESAR	960 17TH ST, RCH, 94801	588 - G5
CLEVELAND	745 CLEVELAND ST, OAK, 94606	650 - A4
COLLINS	1224 PINOLE VALLEY RD, PIN, 94564	569 - F5
CORNELL	920 TALBOT AV, ALB, 94706	609 - E6
CORONADO	2001 VIRGINIA AV, RCH, 94804	608 - H1
COUNTRY CLUB	7534 BLUE FOX WY, SRMN, 94583	693 - G1
COYOTE CREEK	8700 GALE RIDGE RD, SRMN, 94582	673 - H1
CRAGMONT	830 REGAL RD, BERK, 94708	609 - H5
CROCKER HIGHLANDS	525 MIDCREST RD, OAK, 94610	650 - C3
DEL REY	25 EL CAMINO MORAGA, ORIN, 94563	631 - B5
DIABLO VISTA	4791 PREWETT RANCH DR, ANT, 94531	595 - H5
DISCOVERY BAY	1700 WILLOW LAKE RD, CCCo, 94514	617 - H6
DISNEY, WALT	3250 PINE VALLEY RD, SRMN, 94583	673 - G6
DONLON	4150 DORMAN RD, PLE, 94588	694 - A7
DOUGHERTY	5301 HIBERNIA DR, DBLN, 94568	694 - D4
DOVER	1871 21ST ST, SPAB, 94806	588 - H3
DOWNER, EDWARD M	1777 SANFORD AV, SPAB, 94806	588 - G4
DUBLIN	7997 VOMAC RD, DBLN, 94568	693 - G3
ELLERHORST	3501 PINOLE VALLEY RD, PIN, 94564	569 - G7
EL MONTE	1400 DINA DR, CNCD, 94518	592 - J3
EL SOBRANTE	1060 MANOR RD, CCCo, 94803	569 - D7
FAIRLANDS	4151 W LAS POSITAS BLVD, PLE, 94588	694 - E6
FAIRMONT	724 KEARNEY ST, ELCR, 94530	609 - D3
FAIR OAKS	2400 LISA LN, PLHL, 94523	592 - D6
FARMAR, MARY	901 MILITARY W, BEN, 94510	551 - A3
FOOTHILL	1200 JENSEN DR, PIT, 94565	574 - F6
FORD	2711 MARICOPA AV, RCH, 94804	588 - J4
FREDERIKSEN	7243 TAMARACK DR, DBLN, 94568	693 - J3
FREMONT	1413 F ST, ANT, 94509	575 - D5
FRUITVALE	3200 BOSTON AV, OAK, 94602	650 - D5
GARFIELD	1640 22ND AV, OAK, 94606	650 - B6
GARIN	250A 1ST ST, BREN, 94513	616 - H2
GEHRINGER	5491 MAIN ST, OAKL, 94561	596 - G3
GLEN COVE	501 GLEN COVE PKWY, VAL, 94591	550 - F2
GLENVIEW	4215 LA CRESTA AV, OAK, 94602	650 - D4
GLORIETTA	15 MARTHA RD, ORIN, 94563	631 - A2
GOLDEN VIEW	5025 CANYON CREST DR, SRMN, 94582	653 - G7

CONTRA COSTA

FEATURE NAME Address City, ZIP Code	PAGE-GRID
GRANT 2400 DOWNER AV, RCH, 94804	588 - H5
GREENBROOK 1475 HARLAN DR, DNVL, 94526	653 - C6
GREEN VALLEY 1001 DIABLO RD, DNVL, 94526	633 - C7
GREGORY GARDENS 200 HARRIET DR, PLHL, 94523	592 - C4
HANNA RANCH 2482 REFUGIO VALLEY RD, HER, 94547	570 - B6
HAPPY VALLEY 3855 HAPPY VALLEY RD, LFYT, 94549	611 - C4
HARDING 7230 FAIRMOUNT AV, ELCR, 94530	609 - E4
HAVENS, FRANK C 1800 OAKLAND AV, PDMT, 94611	650 - B1
HAWTHORNE YEAR-ROUND 1700 28TH AV, OAK, 94601	650 - C7
HEIGHTS 163 WEST BLVD, PIT, 94565	574 - C5
HENDERSON, JOE 650 HASTINGS DR, BEN, 94510	551 - A1
HIDDEN HILLS 12995 HARCOURT WY, SRMN, 94582	674 - C3
HIDDEN VALLEY 500 GLACIER DR, MRTZ, 94553	591 - J1
HIGHLAND 2829 MOYERS RD, RCH, 94806	589 - A2
HIGHLANDS 1326 PENNSYLVANIA BLVD, CNCD, 94521	593 - F6
HIGHLANDS 4141 HARBOR ST, PIT, 94565	574 - D6
HILLCREST 30 MARGUERITE DR, OAK, 94618	630 - B6
HILLCREST 601 CALIFORNIA ST, CCCo, 94572	549 - J7
HOLBROOK 3333 RONALD WY, CNCD, 94519	572 - G6
INDIAN VALLEY 551 MARSHALL DR, WLCK, 94598	612 - F5
INTERNATIONAL COMMUNITY 2825 INTERNATIONAL BLVD, OAK, 94601	650 - B7
JEFFERSON 1400 ADA ST, BERK, 94702	609 - F7
JEFFERSON YEAR-ROUND 2035 40TH AV, OAK, 94601	650 - D7
KAISER, HENRY J JR 25 S HILL CT, OAK, 94618	630 - B4
KENSINGTON 90 HIGHLAND BLVD, CCCo, 94708	609 - F3
KIMBALL 1310 AUGUST WY, ANT, 94509	575 - E5
KING 234 S 39TH ST, RCH, 94804	589 - A7
KNIGHTSEN 1923 DELTA RD, CCCo, 94513	597 - B4
KREY, PAUL R 190 CRAWFORD DR, BREN, 94513	616 - B3
LAFAYETTE 950 MORAGA RD, LFYT, 94549	611 - F6
LAKE 2700 11TH ST, SPAB, 94806	588 - G1
LAS JUNTAS 4105 PACHECO BLVD, CCCo, 94553	571 - J4
LAUREL 1141 LAUREL RD, OAKL, 94561	596 - E1
LAUREL 3750 BROWN AV, OAK, 94619	650 - F5
LEARNER-CENTERED CHARTER 1201 10TH ST, ANT, 94509	575 - C4
LINCOLN 29 6TH ST, RCH, 94801	588 - F7
LOMA VISTA 2110 SAN JOSE AV, BREN, 94513	596 - C7
LONDON, JACK 4550 COUNTRY HILLS DR, ANT, 94531	595 - G3
LOS MEDANOS 610 CROWLEY AV, PIT, 94565	574 - C3
LOS PERALES 22 WAKEFIELD DR, MRGA, 94556	631 - D5
LUPINE HILLS 1919 LUPINE RD, HER, 94547	569 - J4
MADERA 8500 MADERA DR, ELCR, 94530	609 - D1
MANZANITA 2409 E 27TH ST, OAK, 94601	650 - C6
MARIN 1001 SANTA FE AV, ALB, 94706	609 - E6
MARSH 2304 G ST, ANT, 94509	575 - C6
MAXWELL PARK 4730 FLEMING AV, OAK, 94619	650 - F7
MEADOW HOMES 1371 DETROIT AV, CNCD, 94520	592 - F3
MILLER, JOAQUIN 5525 ASCOT DR, OAK, 94611	650 - E2
MILLS 401 E K ST, BEN, 94510	551 - C5
MIRA VISTA 6397 HAZEL AV, CCCo, 94805	589 - C6
MISSION 1711 MISSION DR, ANT, 94509	575 - A6
MNO GRANT 4325 SPAULDING ST, ANT, 94531	595 - H1
MOHR, HENRY P 3300 DENNIS DR, PLE, 94588	652 - J2
MONTAIR 300 QUINTERRA LN, DNVL, 94526	568 - J5
MONTALVIN MANOR 300 CHRISTINE DR, CCCo, 94806	630 - D7
MONTCLAIR 1757 MOUNTAIN BLVD, OAK, 94611	572 - J7
MONTE GARDENS 3841 LARKSPUR DR, CNCD, 94519	673 - F4
MONTEVIDEO 13000 BROADMOOR DR, SRMN, 94583	571 - H5
MORELLO PARK 1200 MORELLO PARK DR, MRTZ, 94553	593 - C3
MOUNTAIN VIEW 1705 THORNWOOD DR, CNCD, 94521	593 - H7
MOUNT DIABLO 5880 MOUNT ZION DR, CLAY, 94517	571 - F5
MUIR, JOHN 205 VISTA WY, MRTZ, 94553	630 - A3
MUIR, JOHN 2955 CLAREMONT AV, BERK, 94705	595 - E2
MUIR, JOHN 615 GREYSTONE DR, ANT, 94509	650 - H5
MUNCK, CARL B 11900 CAMPUS DR, OAK, 94619	589 - E1
MURPHY 4350 VALLEY VIEW RD, RCH, 94803	693 - H2
MURRAY 8435 DAVONA DR, DBLN, 94568	612 - D7
MURWOOD 2050 VANDERSLICE AV, CCCo, 94596	693 - G4
NIELSEN 7500 AMARILLO RD, DBLN, 94568	616 - C2
NUNN, RON 1755 CENTRAL BLVD, BREN, 94513	

FEATURE NAME Address City, ZIP Code	PAGE-GRID
NYSTROM 230 HARBOUR WY S, RCH, 94804	588 - G7
OAKLEY 501 NORCROSS LN, OAKL, 94561	576 - E7
OCEAN VIEW 1000 JACKSON ST, ALB, 94706	609 - D6
OHLONE 1616 PHEASANT DR, HER, 94547	569 - G4
OLINDA 5855 OLINDA RD, RCH, 94803	589 - G4
OXFORD 1130 OXFORD ST, BERK, 94707	609 - G6
PARKMEAD 1920 MAGNOLIA WY, CCCo, 94595	612 - B7
PARKSIDE 985 W 17TH ST, PIT, 94565	574 - C3
PATTERSON, GRACE 1080 PORTER ST, VAL, 94590	550 - B1
PERES 719 5TH ST, RCH, 94801	588 - F5
PLEASANT HILL 2097 OAK PARK BLVD, PLHL, 94523	592 - A7
RANCHO ROMERO 180 HEMME AV, CCCo, 94507	632 - G6
REDWOOD HEIGHTS 4401 39TH AV, OAK, 94619	650 - G5
RHEEM, DONALD L 90 LAIRD DR, MRGA, 94556	631 - D4
RIO VISTA 611 PACIFICA AV, CCCo, 94565	573 - D1
RIVERSIDE 1300 AMADOR ST, SPAB, 94806	589 - A4
RODEO HILLS 545 GARRETSON AV, CCCo, 94572	569 - H1
SAN PEDRO 498 POINT SAN PEDRO RD, SRFL, 94901	587 - B1
SEAVIEW 2000 SOUTHWOOD DR, CCCo, 94806	569 - B4
SEMPLE, ROBERT 2015 E 3RD ST, BEN, 94510	551 - C4
SEQUOIA 277 BOYD RD, PLHL, 94523	592 - C6
SEQUOIA 3730 LINCOLN AV, OAK, 94602	650 - D4
SHANNON 685 MARLESTA RD, PIN, 94564	569 - C5
SHELDON 2601 MAY RD, RCH, 94803	589 - E2
SHERMAN, ELISABETH 5328 BRANN ST, OAK, 94619	650 - G7
SHORE ACRES 351 MARINA RD, CCCo, 94565	573 - D1
SILVERWOOD 1649 CLAYCORD AV, CNCD, 94521	593 - D3
SLEEPY HOLLOW 20 WASHINGTON LN, ORIN, 94563	610 - F4
SPRINGHILL 3301 SPRINGHILL RD, LFYT, 94549	611 - H4
STEGE 4949 CYPRESS AV, RCH, 94804	609 - B2
STEWART 2040 HOKE DR, PIN, 94564	569 - E6
STONEMAN 2929 LOVERIDGE RD, PIT, 94565	574 - F5
STRANDWOOD 416 GLADYS DR, PLHL, 94523	592 - B5
SUN TERRACE 2448 FLOYD LN, CNCD, 94520	572 - G5
SUTTER 3410 LONGVIEW RD, ANT, 94509	595 - C1
SWETT, JOHN 4551 STEELE ST, OAK, 94619	650 - G6
SWETT, JOHN 4955 ALHAMBRA VALLEY RD, MRTZ, 94553	591 - E1
SYCAMORE VALLEY 2200 HOLBROOK DR, DNVL, 94506	653 - G4
TARA HILLS 2300 DOLAN WY, CCCo, 94806	569 - C5
TASSAJARA HILLS 4675 CM TASSAJARA, CCCo, 94588	654 - E5
THORNHILL 5880 THORNHILL DR, OAK, 94611	630 - E7
THOUSAND OAKS 840 COLUSA AV, BERK, 94707	609 - F6
TIMBER POINT 40 NEWBURY LN, CCCo, 94513	617 - F5
TURNER 4207 DELTA FAIR BLVD, ANT, 94509	574 - H5
TWIN CREEKS 2785 MARSH DR, SRMN, 94583	673 - B2
VALHALLA 530 KIKI DR, PLHL, 94523	592 - A3
VALLE VERDE 3275 PEACHWILLOW LN, WLCK, 94598	592 - H7
VALLEY VIEW 3416 MAYWOOD DR, RCH, 94803	589 - F1
VERDE 2000 GIARAMITA ST, CCCo, 94801	588 - F3
VINTAGE PARKWAY 1000 VINTAGE PKWY, OAKL, 94561	576 - E5
VISTA GRANDE 667 DIABLO RD, DNVL, 94526	653 - B1
WAGNER RANCH 350 CM PABLO, ORIN, 94563	610 - E5
WALNUT ACRES 180 CEREZO DR, WLCK, 94598	612 - H3
WALNUT HEIGHTS 4064 WALNUT BLVD, WLCK, 94598	612 - F6
WASHINGTON 565 WINE ST, RCH, 94801	608 - D1
WESTWOOD 1748 WEST ST, CNCD, 94521	593 - B2
WILDWOOD 301 WILDWOOD AV, PDMT, 94611	650 - B2
WILLOW COVE 1880 HANLON WY, PIT, 94565	573 - J2
WILSON 629 42ND ST, RCH, 94805	589 - A6
WOODSIDE 761 SAN SIMEON DR, CNCD, 94518	592 - H7
WREN AVENUE 3339 WREN AV, CNCD, 94519	592 - H1
YGNACIO VALLEY 2217 CHALOMAR RD, CNCD, 94518	592 - G5

SCHOOLS - PUBLIC HIGH

FEATURE NAME Address City, ZIP Code	PAGE-GRID
ACALANES 1200 PLEASANT HILL RD, LFYT, 94549	611 - H4
ALBANY 603 KEY ROUTE BLVD, ALB, 94706	609 - E5
ALHAMBRA 150 E ST, MRTZ, 94553	571 - D5
ANTIOCH 700 W 18TH ST, ANT, 94509	575 - C5
BENICIA 1101 MILITARY W, BEN, 94510	550 - J3
CALIFORNIA 9870 BROADMOOR DR, SRMN, 94583	673 - F5

FEATURE NAME Address City, ZIP Code	PAGE-GRID
CAMPOLINDO 300 MORAGA RD, MRGA, 94556	631 - E2
CLAYTON VALLEY 1101 ALBERTA WY, CNCD, 94521	593 - D5
COLLEGE PARK 201 VIKING DR, PLHL, 94523	592 - B3
CONCORD 4200 CONCORD BLVD, CNCD, 94521	593 - B1
DE ANZA 5000 VALLEY VIEW RD, RCH, 94803	589 - E2
DEER VALLEY 4700 LONE TREE WY, ANT, 94531	595 - G4
DEL AMIGO 189 DEL AMIGO RD, DNVL, 94526	652 - H1
DUBLIN 8151 VILLAGE PKWY, DBLN, 94568	693 - J2
EL CERRITO 540 ASHBURY AV, ELCR, 94530	609 - E4
FREEDOM 1050 NEROLY RD, OAKL, 94561	596 - E3
GOMPERS, SAMUEL 157 9TH ST, RCH, 94801	588 - F7
HERCULES 1900 REFUGIO VALLEY RD, HER, 94547	569 - J5
KENNEDY 4300 CUTTING BLVD, RCH, 94804	609 - A1
LA PALOMA 6651 LONE TREE WY, BREN, 94513	596 - C4
LAS LOMAS 1460 S MAIN ST, WLCK, 94596	612 - D6
LIBERTY 350 K ST, BEN, 94510	551 - C5
LIBERTY 850 2ND ST, BREN, 94513	616 - G1
LIVE OAK 1708 F ST, ANT, 94509	575 - C5
MARTINEZ CONT 600 F ST, MRTZ, 94553	571 - E5
MIDDLE COLLEGE 2600 MISSION BELL DR, SPAB, 94806	588 - J2
MIRAMONTE 750 MORAGA WY, ORIN, 94563	631 - C6
MONTE VISTA 3131 STONE VALLEY RD, DNVL, 94526	633 - B6
MOUNT DIABLO 2450 GRANT ST, CNCD, 94520	592 - F1
NORTH CAMPUS 2465 DOLAN WY, CCCo, 94806	569 - B5
NORTHGATE 425 CASTLE ROCK RD, WLCK, 94598	612 - J4
OAKLAND 1023 MACARTHUR BLVD, OAK, 94610	650 - B4
OLYMPIC 2730 SALVIO ST, CNCD, 94519	592 - G1
PIEDMONT 800 MAGNOLIA AV, PDMT, 94611	650 - B1
PINOLE VALLEY 2900 PINOLE VALLEY RD, PIN, 94564	569 - F6
PITTSBURG 250 SCHOOL ST, PIT, 94565	574 - E3
PROSPECTS 820 W 2ND ST, ANT, 94509	575 - C3
RICHMOND 1250 23RD ST, RCH, 94804	588 - H4
RIVERSIDE 809 BLACK DIAMOND ST, PIT, 94565	574 - E2
SAN RAMON VALLEY 140 LOVE LN, DNVL, 94526	652 - J1
SKYLINE 12250 SKYLINE BLVD, OAK, 94619	651 - A5
SWETT, JOHN 1098 POMONA ST, CCCo, 94525	550 - D5
VALLEY CONT 6901 YORK DR, DBLN, 94568	693 - J3
YGNACIO VALLEY 755 OAK GROVE RD, CNCD, 94518	592 - G7

SCHOOLS - PUBLIC INTERMEDIATE

FEATURE NAME Address City, ZIP Code	PAGE-GRID
MORAGA, JOAQUIN 1010 CM PABLO, MRGA, 94556	651 - D1
ORINDA 80 IVY DR, ORIN, 94563	631 - C5
WALNUT CREEK 2425 WALNUT BLVD, WLCK, 94597	612 - D4

SCHOOLS - PUBLIC JUNIOR HIGH

FEATURE NAME Address City, ZIP Code	PAGE-GRID
CENTRAL 1201 STONEMAN AV, PIT, 94565	574 - F5
CRESPI 1121 ALLVIEW AV, CCCo, 94803	569 - D6
HILLVIEW 333 YOSEMITE DR, PIT, 94565	574 - D5
MARTINEZ 1600 COURT ST, MRTZ, 94553	571 - E3

SCHOOLS - PUBLIC MIDDLE

FEATURE NAME Address City, ZIP Code	PAGE-GRID
ADAMS 5000 PATTERSON CIR, CCCo, 94805	589 - B5
ALBANY 1259 BRIGHTON AV, ALB, 94706	609 - E5
AMERICAN AVENUE 401 AMERICAN AV, BREN, 94513	616 - A3
AMERICAN INDIAN CHARTER 3637 MAGEE AV, OAK, 94619	650 - F5
ANTIOCH 1500 D ST, ANT, 94509	575 - D5
BENICIA 1100 SOUTHAMPTON RD, BEN, 94510	550 - J3
BLACK DIAMOND 4730 STERLING HILL DR, ANT, 94531	595 - H3
BREWER, EDNA 3748 13TH AV, OAK, 94602	650 - B4
BRISTOW, WILLIAM B 855 MINNESOTA AV, BREN, 94513	616 - E1
CARQUINEZ 1099 POMONA ST, CCCo, 94525	550 - D5
DALLAS RANCH 1401 MOUNT HAMILTON DR, ANT, 94531	595 - E3
DEJEAN, LOVONYA 3400 MACDONALD AV, RCH, 94805	588 - J7
DELTA VISTA 4901 FRANK HENGEL WY, OAKL, 94561	576 - H7
DIABLO VIEW 300 DIABLO VIEW LN, CLAY, 94517	613 - J1
DIABLO VISTA 4100 CM TASSAJARA, DNVL, 94506	654 - C5
EL DORADO 1750 WEST ST, CNCD, 94521	593 - B2
EXCELSIOR 14401 BYRON HWY, CCCo, 94514	637 - D2
FALLON, ELEANOR MURRAY 3601 KOHNEN WY, DBLN, 94568	694 - F3
FOOTHILL 2775 CEDRO LN, WLCK, 94598	612 - H2
GLENBROOK 2351 OLIVERA RD, CNCD, 94520	572 - F6

CONTRA COSTA

FEATURE NAME Address City, ZIP Code	PAGE-GRID
HART, THOMAS 4433 WILLOW RD, PLE, 94588	694 - B7
HARTE, BRET 3700 COOLIDGE AV, OAK, 94602	650 - E4
HELMS 2500 RD 20, SPAB, 94806	588 - J3
HERCULES 1900 REFUGIO VALLEY RD, HER, 94547	569 - J5
HILL, EDNA 140 BIRCH ST, BREN, 94513	616 - H2
IRON HORSE 12601 ALCOSTA BLVD, SRMN, 94583	673 - E2
KING, MARTIN LUTHER 1781 ROSE ST, BERK, 94703	609 - G7
LOS CERROS 968 BLEMER RD, DNVL, 94526	633 - C7
MANZANITA CHARTER 3200 BARRETT AV, RCH, 94804	588 - J6
MONTERA 5555 ASCOT DR, OAK, 94611	650 - F2
OAK GROVE 2050 MINERT RD, CNCD, 94518	592 - F7
OAKLAND CHARTER ACADEMY 3001 INTERNATIONAL BLVD, OAK, 94601	650 - C7
OHARA PARK 1100 OHARA AV, OAKL, 94561	596 - E1
PARK 1 SPARTAN WY, ANT, 94509	575 - C7
PIEDMONT 740 MAGNOLIA AV, PDMT, 94611	650 - B1
PINE HOLLOW 5522 PINE HOLLOW RD, CNCD, 94521	593 - F7
PINE VALLEY 3000 PINE VALLEY RD, SRMN, 94583	673 - G7
PINOLE 1575 MANN DR, PIN, 94564	569 - D5
PLEASANT HILL 3100 OAK PARK BLVD, PLHL, 94523	592 - C7
PORTOLA 1021 NAVELLIER ST, ELCR, 94530	609 - D2
RIVERVIEW 205 PACIFICA AV, CCCo, 94565	573 - E1
ROOSEVELT 1926 19TH AV, OAK, 94606	650 - B6
SEQUOIA 265 BOYD RD, PLHL, 94523	592 - C6
SIMMONS, CALVIN 2101 35TH AV, OAK, 94601	650 - D7
STANLEY, M H 3455 SCHOOL ST, LFYT, 94549	611 - F7
STONE VALLEY 3001 MIRANDA AV, CCCo, 94507	632 - G4
VALLEY VIEW 181 VIKING DR, PLHL, 94523	592 - C3
WELLS 6800 PENN DR, DBLN, 94568	693 - J3
WINDEMERE RANCH 11611 E BRANCH PKWY, CCCo, 94582	674 - A5
WOOD, CHARLOTTE 600 EL CAPITAN DR, DNVL, 94526	653 - C5

SHOPPING - REGIONAL

FEATURE NAME Address City, ZIP Code	PAGE-GRID
BROADWAY PLAZA 1275 BROADWAY PZ, WLCK, 94596	612 - D6
COUNTY EAST MALL 2556 SOMERSVILLE RD, ANT, 94509	574 - J5
HACIENDA CROSSINGS 5000 DUBLIN, DBLN, 94568	694 - D4
HILLTOP PLAZA 2200 HILLTOP MALL RD, RCH, 94806	569 - A7
PINOLE VISTA CROSSING FITZGERALD, PIN, 94564	569 - C6
SHOPS AT BLACKHAWK, THE 3480 BLACKHAWK PLAZA CIR, CCCo, 94506	653 - J5
STONERIDGE MALL 1 STONERIDGE MALL RD, PLE, 94588	693 - H5
SUNVALLEY MALL CONTRA COSTA BL & SUNVALLEY BL, CNCD, 94520	592 - C3

TRANSPORTATION

FEATURE NAME Address City, ZIP Code	PAGE-GRID
AMTRAK MARTINEZ STA 401 FERRY ST, MRTZ, 94553	571 - D2
AMTRAK RICHMOND STA MACDONALD AV & 16TH ST, RCH, 94801	588 - G6
BART CONCORD STA 1451 OAKLAND AV, CNCD, 94518	592 - G2
BART DUBLIN/PLEASANTON STA 5801 OWENS DR, PLE, 94588	694 - B5
BART EL CERRITO DEL NORTE STA 6400 CUTTING BLVD, ELCR, 94530	609 - B1
BART EL CERRITO PLAZA STA 6699 FAIRMOUNT AV, ELCR, 94530	609 - D4
BART LAFAYETTE STA 3601 DEER HILL RD, LFYT, 94549	611 - E6
BART NORTH CONCORD MARTINEZ STA 3700 PORT CHICAGO HWY, CNCD, 94519	572 - G5
BART ORINDA STA 11 CM PABLO, ORIN, 94563	630 - H1
BART PITTSBURG/BAY POINT STA 1600 LELAND RD, CCCo, 94565	573 - G3
BART PLEASANT HILL STA 1365 TREAT BLVD, CCCo, 94597	612 - D1
BART RICHMOND STA 1700 NEVIN AV, RCH, 94801	588 - G6
BART WALNUT CREEK STA 200 YGNACIO VALLEY RD, WLCK, 94596	612 - B4
BNSF STA 1ST ST & I ST, ANT, 94509	575 - C3
BNSF STA RAILROAD AV & W SANTA FE AV, PIT, 94565	574 - E2

The Thomas Guide®

Thank you for purchasing this Rand McNally Thomas Guide! We value your comments and suggestions.

Please help us serve you better by completing this postage-paid reply card.
This information is for internal use ONLY and will not be distributed or sold to any external third party.

Missing pages? Maybe not... Please refer to the "Using Your Street Guide" page for further explanation.

Thomas Guide Title: Contra Costa County   ISBN# 0-528-85527-1   Edition: 2006   MKT: SFB

Today's Date: _____   Gender: ☐M ☐F   Age Group: ☐18-24 ☐25-31 ☐32-40 ☐41-50 ☐51-64 ☐65+

1. What type of industry do you work in?
   ☐Real Estate   ☐Trucking   ☐Delivery   ☐Construction   ☐Utilities   ☐Government
   ☐Retail   ☐Sales   ☐Transportation ☐Landscape   ☐Service & Repair
   ☐Courier   ☐Automotive   ☐Insurance   ☐Medical   ☐Police/Fire/First Response
   ☐Other, please specify: _____

2. What type of job do you have in this industry?_____

3. Where did you purchase this Thomas Guide? (store name & city) _____

4. Why did you purchase this Thomas Guide? _____

5. How often do you purchase an updated Thomas Guide? ☐Annually ☐2 yrs. ☐3-5 yrs. ☐Other: _____

6. Where do you use it? ☐Primarily in the car ☐Primarily in the office ☐Primarily at home ☐Other: _____

7. How do you use it? ☐Exclusively for business ☐Primarily for business but also for personal or leisure use
   ☐Both work and personal evenly ☐Primarily for personal use ☐Exclusively for personal use

8. What do you use your Thomas Guide for?
   ☐Find Addresses ☐In-route navigation ☐Planning routes ☐Other: _____
   Find points of interest: ☐Schools ☐Parks ☐Buildings ☐Shopping Centers ☐Other:_____

9. How often do you use it? ☐Daily ☐Weekly ☐Monthly ☐Other: _____

10. Do you use the internet for maps and/or directions? ☐Yes ☐No

11. How often do you use the internet for directions? ☐Daily ☐Weekly ☐Monthly ☐Other:_____

12. Do you use any of the following mapping products in addition to your Thomas Guide?
    ☐Folded paper maps ☐Folded laminated maps ☐Wall maps ☐GPS ☐PDA ☐In-car navigation ☐Phone maps

13. What features, if any, would you like to see added to your Thomas Guide? _____
    _____

14. What features or information do you find most useful in your Rand McNally Thomas Guide? (please specify)
    _____
    _____

15. Please provide any additional comments or suggestions you have. _____
    _____
    _____

We strive to provide you with the most current updated information available if you know of a map correction, please notify us here.

Where is the correction?   Map Page #:_____   Grid #:_____   Index Page #:_____

Nature of the correction: ☐Street name missing   ☐Street name misspelled   ☐Street information incorrect
   ☐Incorrect location for point of interest ☐Index error ☐Other: _____

Detail: _____

I would like to receive information about updated editions and special offers from Rand McNally
   ☐via e-mail   E-mail address: _____
   ☐via postal mail
   Your Name: _____   Company (if used for work): _____
   Address:_____   City/State/ZIP: _____

Thank you for your time and help. We are working to serve you better.
This information is for internal use ONLY and will not be distributed or sold to any external third party.

TG-noCD.06

CUT ALONG DOTTED LINE

RAND MᶜNALLY

The most trusted name on the map.

You'll never need to ask for directions again with these Rand McNally products!

- EasyFinder® Laminated Maps
- Folded Maps
- Street Guides
- Wall Maps
- CustomView Wall Maps
- Road Atlases
- Motor Carriers' Road Atlases